Literature

AN INTRODUCTION TO READING AND WRITING

Seventh Edition

Edgar V. Roberts

Lehman College
The City University of New York

Henry E. Jacobs

PEARSON

Prentice
Hall

Upper Saddle River, New Jersey 07458

Library of Congress Cataloging-in-Publication Data

ROBERTS, EDGAR V.
    Literature: an introduction to reading and writing / Edgar V. Roberts, Henry E. Jacobs.—
7th ed.
      p. cm.
    Includes indexes.
    ISBN 0-13-048584-5
    1. Literature. 2. Exposition (Rhetoric) 3. Literature—Collections. 4. College readers.
    5. Report writing. I. Jacobs, Henry E. II. Title.

PN45.R575 2004
808'.0668—dc21

2003048664

Editor in Chief: Leah Jewell
Editorial Assistant: Jennifer Migueis
Director, Production and Manufacturing:
  Barbara Kittle
Production Editor: Joan E. Foley
Copyeditor: Kathryn Graehl
Text Permissions Specialist: Mary Dalton-Hoffman
Production Assistant: Marlene Gassler
Assistant Manufacturing Manager:
  Mary Ann Gloriande
Prepress and Manufacturing Buyer: Brian Mackey
Director, Marketing: Beth Mejia
Senior Marketing Manager: Rachel Falk
Marketing Assistant: Adam Laitman

Media Production Manager: Lynn Pearlman
Media Project Manager: Jennifer Collins
Media Editor: Christy Schaak
Director, Image Resource Center: Melinda Reo
Image Rights and Permissions Manager:
  Zina Arabia
Image Permissions Coordinator: Carolyn Gauntt
Image Researcher: Linda Sykes
Director, Creative Design: Leslie Osher
Interior and Cover Designer: Wanda Espana/
  Wee Design Group
Cover Illustration: Planet Earth Pictures/
  FPG International LLC

This book was set in 10/12 New Baskerville by Lithokraft and was printed and bound by Quebecor World.
Covers were printed by Phoenix Color Corp.

For permission to use copyrighted material, grateful
acknowledgment is made to the copyright holders
on pages 2009–2018, which are considered an
extension of this copyright page.

Pearson Education LTD.
Pearson Education Singapore, Pte. Ltd
Pearson Education, Canada, Ltd
Pearson Education–Japan
Pearson Education Australia PTY, Limited

Pearson Education North Asia Ltd
Pearson Educación de Mexico, S.A. de C.V.
Pearson Education Malaysia, Pte. Ltd
Pearson Education, Upper Saddle River, NJ

10 9 8 7 6 5 4 3 2 1
ISBN 0-13-048584-5 (student ed.)
ISBN 0-13-183819-9 (NASTA ed.)

Brief Contents

v

READING AND WRITING ABOUT **DRAMA**

SPECIAL WRITING TOPICS ABOUT **LITERATURE**

Contents

What Is Literature, and Why Do We Study It? **1** • *Types of Literature: The Genres,* **2** • *Reading Literature and Responding to It Actively,* **3**

GUY DE MAUPASSANT   *The Necklace,* **4**
To go to a ball, Mathilde Loisel borrows a necklace from a rich friend, but her rhapsodic evening has unforeseen consequences.

Reading and Responding in a Notebook or Computer File, **11** • *Writing Essays on Literary Topics,* **14** • *The Goal of Writing: To Show a Process of Thought,* **15** • *Three Major Stages in Thinking and Writing: Discovering Ideas, Making Initial Drafts, and Completing the Essay,* **16** • *The Discovery of Ideas ("Brainstorming"),* **17** • *Assembling Materials and Beginning to Write,* **22** • *Drafting the Essay,* **25** • *Writing a First Draft,* **28** • *Developing an Outline,* **30** • ***Demonstrative Student Essay (First Draft):*** *How Setting in "The Necklace" Is Related to the Character of Mathilde,* **31** • *Developing and Strengthening Essays Through Revision,* **32** • *Checking Development and Organization,* **36** • *Using Exact, Comprehensive, and Forceful Language,* **38** • ***Demonstrative Student Essay (Improved Draft):*** *How Maupassant Uses Setting in "The Necklace" to Show the Character of Mathilde,* **41** • *Essay Commentaries,* **43** • *Special Topics for Writing and Argument about the Writing Process,* **43**

READING AND WRITING ABOUT **FICTION**

8 TONE: THE EXPRESSION OF ATTITUDE IN FICTION   350

9 SYMBOLISM AND ALLEGORY:
KEYS TO EXTENDED MEANING   *393*

READING AND WRITING ABOUT **POETRY**

14   WORDS: THE BUILDING BLOCKS OF POETRY   635

15   CHARACTER AND SETTING: WHO, WHAT, WHERE, AND WHEN IN POETRY   664

**17   FIGURES OF SPEECH, OR METAPHORICAL LANGUAGE:
A SOURCE OF DEPTH AND RANGE IN POETRY**   725

18   TONE: THE CREATION OF ATTITUDE IN POETRY 758

19   PROSODY: SOUND, RHYTHM, AND RHYME IN POETRY   794

23   MEANING: IDEA AND THEME IN POETRY   955

24   THREE POETIC CAREERS: WILLIAM WORDSWORTH, EMILY DICKINSON, AND ROBERT FROST

STANZAIC POEMS

SONNETS

28   THE COMIC VISION: RESTORING THE BALANCE   1484

31 A CAREER IN DRAMA: TWO MAJOR PLAYS OF HENRIK IBSEN

✿ SPECIAL WRITING TOPICS ABOUT **LITERATURE**

32 WRITING AND DOCUMENTING THE RESEARCH ESSAY

Topical and Thematic Table of Contents

For analytical purposes, the following topical and thematic table of contents groups the selections into twenty-five separate subject categories. ("Hope and Renewal;" "Fidelity and Loyalty;" "Men;" and "America in Peace, War, and Tribulation" are new categories in the seventh edition.) The idea is that the topics will facilitate a thematic and focused study and comparison of a number of works. Obviously each of the works brings out many other issues than are suggested by the topics. For purposes of comparison, however, the topics invite analyses based on specific issues. Thus, the category "Women" suggests that the listed works may profitably be examined for what they have to say about the lives and problems specifically of women, just as the category "Men" suggests a concentration on the lives and problems specifically of men. The subject headings are suggestive only; they are by no means intended to dictate interpretations or approaches. We have accordingly assigned a number of works to two and often more categories. *A Dollhouse*, for example, does not easily fall into a single category.

Because the Topical and Thematic Table of Contents is to be as brief as possible, we use only the last names of authors and artists, although for authors with the same last names (e.g., Phyllis Webb, Charles Harper Webb; James Emanuel, Lynn Emanuel), we supply the complete name. In listing works we eliminate many but not all beginning definite and indefinite articles, and shorten most of the titles. Thus we refer to *A Certain Slant* (Dickinson), and to *That Time of Year* (Shakespeare) and so on, using recognizable short titles whenever possible rather than the full titles that appear in the regular Contents, in the text itself, and in the index. Of course, some titles are quite short, such as *Reconciliation* (Whitman), *Eating Poetry* (Strand), and *Everyday Use* (Walker). We include these in their entirety.

New in the seventh edition are references to works of art that are included in the three inserts. We expect that these will be usefully consulted for comparative purposes and that such comparisons will enhance the discussions of the various topics.

LOVE AND COURTSHIP

MEN

PAST AND PRESENT

RACE, ETHNICITY, AND NATIONALITY

Poems

Plays

Art

Preface to the Seventh Edition

Like the earlier editions of *Literature: An Introduction to Reading and Writing*, the new seventh edition is in part a carefully chosen anthology. Most of the works here are by American, British, and Canadian authors, but there are also a number of ancient and medieval writers, along with writers who lived in or came from France, Germany, Italy, Norway, Ceylon, and Indonesia, together with authors who represent backgrounds of Latino, American Indian, and Chinese culture. In total, 304 authors are represented, including ten anonymous authors. One hundred eighty-four of the authors—roughly sixty percent—were born after 1900. Of the eighty writers born since 1935, forty-two are women, or fifty-two percent. If one counts only the number of authors born after the end of World War II (1945), the percentage of women goes up dramatically to seventy percent.

The book includes a total of 505 separate works—sixty-two stories, 423 poems, and twenty plays and scenes. Each work is suitable for discussion either alone or in comparison. Ten stories, thirty-seven poems, and two dramas are new in this edition. For purposes of comparison, the works in two genres by a number of writers are included—specifically Atwood, Crane, Glaspell, Hughes, Poe, Shakespeare, Updike, and Walker. In addition, Faulkner and Munro are each represented by two stories, and Shakespeare and Ibsen are represented by two plays—Shakespeare in Chapters 27 and 28, and Ibsen in Chapter 31. There are four stories by Edith Wharton in Chapter 11, the chapter on the career in fiction. There are multiple selections of poems by many poets.

A BRIEF OVERVIEW OF THE SEVENTH EDITION

FLEXIBILITY. The seventh edition reaffirms a principle to which *Literature: An Introduction to Reading and Writing* is dedicated—flexibility. The earlier editions have been used for introduction-to-literature courses, genre courses, and both composition and composition-and-literature courses. Adaptability and flexibility have been the keys to this variety. Instructors can use the book for classroom discussions, panel discussions, essay or paragraph-length writing and study assignments, and special topics not covered in class.

FICTION.   The fiction section consists of ten chapters. Chapter 2 is a general introduction to fiction while Chapters 3-10—the "topical" chapters central to each section of the book—introduce students to such important topics as structure, character, point of view, and theme. Chapter 11 consists of four stories by Edith Wharton, and Chapter 12 contains seven stories for additional study and enjoyment.

Readers will note that some of the new stories are classic—like those by Faulkner, Petronius, Chekhov, and Wharton—and some, such as those by Munro and Bradbury, are well on their way to becoming classic. The new stories complement the fifty-two stories, such as those by Carver, Crane, Glaspell, Gilman, Hawthorne, Joyce, Laurence, Porter, and Twain, that are retained from the sixth edition.

POETRY.   The thirteen poetry chapters are arranged similarly to the fiction chapters. Chapter 13 is introductory. Chapters 14–23 deal with topics such as diction, symbolism, imagery, tone, and myth. Chapter 24 is the poetic careers chapter, consisting of selections by Wordsworth, Dickinson, and Frost. Chapter 25 contains 129 poems for additional study and enjoyment. Brief biographies of the anthologized poets are included in Appendix II to make the poetry section parallel with the drama and fiction sections.

Poetry selections are taken from poets of late medieval times to those of our own day, including poets such as the anonymous writer of "Sir Patrick Spens," Wyatt, Queen Elizabeth I, Shakespeare, Donne, Dryden, Pope, Gray, Wordsworth, Byron, Keats, Tennyson, Rossetti, Hopkins, Pound, Yeats, Eliot, Layton, Lowell, Brooks, Birney, and Clifton. Thirty-seven poems are new here. They represent a variety of American and British poets, most of whom are widely recognized. Agüeros, Carruth, Collins, Creeley, Davison, Dunn, Griffin, Kinnell, Merriam, Stevenson, and Terranova come readily to mind. Two of the poets were American presidents (Jimmy Carter and Abraham Lincoln). Younger poets, most of them with great distinctions to their credit, are Agüeros, Edelman, Harjo, Hospital, and Peacock. One of the poets new in the seventh edition is Micheal O'Siadhail (pronounced *me-hall oh-sheel*), who has achieved distinction not only for his poetry but also for his governmental service in his native Ireland. Of special note is the inclusion for the first time of a number of nineteenth-century poets who were chosen for poems illustrating various aspects of American life. (Please see the first category in the Topical and Thematic Table of Contents). These are Bryant, Emerson, Ingham, Lincoln, Melville, and Whittier. Along with the poems included for the first time, the seventh edition of *Literature: An Introduction to Reading and Writing* retains 386 poems that were included in the sixth edition.

DRAMA.   In the drama section Chapter 26 is introductory. Chapters 27 through 29 deal with tragedy, comedy, and realism and nonrealism. At the suggestion of a number of instructors who use film in their courses—a unique feature begun in the third edition—Chapter 30, on film, is retained, and the discussion matches those in the other chapters. The scenes from *Citizen Kane*, by Welles and Mankiewicz, and *The Turning Point*, by Laurents, have been retained.

Chapter 31 is the special career chapter on Henrik Ibsen. There is no "Plays for Additional Study and Enjoyment" chapter to match Chapters 12 and 25 because most plays are so lengthy that adding more would extend the book beyond reasonable limits within a one-volume format.

Nine of the longer plays from the previous edition have been kept in this edition because they are important in an introductory study of drama (*Oedipus the King, Hamlet, A Midsummer Night's Dream, Love Is the Doctor, Death of a Salesman, The Glass Menagerie, Mulatto, A Dollhouse, An Enemy of the People*). To this number, the important medieval *The Second Shepherds' Play* and Wilder's perennially popular *Our Town* have been added. These additions make the anthology more useful than in the past as the basis for a discussion of the history of dramatic literature. In an anthology of this scope, the seven short plays (*Am I Blue, The Bear, Before Breakfast, Tea Party, The Visitatio Sepulchri, The More the Merrier, Trifles*) are valuable because they may be covered in no more than one or two classroom hours, and also because they may be enlivened by having parts read aloud and acted by students. Indeed, the anonymous *Visitatio Sepulchri* and Keller's *Tea Party* are brief enough to permit classroom reading and discussion in a single period.

✳ ADDITIONAL FEATURES

CONTENTS. The Contents lists all the works and major discussion heads in the book. A new feature is the inclusion, following each entry, of a sentence containing a brief summation or impression of the work. It is hoped that these "guides" will interest students in approaching, anticipating, and reading the works.

TOPICAL AND THEMATIC TABLE OF CONTENTS. To make the seventh edition of *Literature: An Introduction to Reading and Writing* as flexible as possible, we have continued the Topical and Thematic Table of Contents. In this table, located immediately following the chapter-by-chapter Contents, a number of topics are provided, such as *Hope and Renewal; Women; Men; Women and Men; Conformity and Rebellion; Endings and Beginnings; Innocence and Experience*, and *Race, Ethnicity, and Nationality*. Under these topics, generous numbers of stories, poems, and plays are listed (many in a number of categories), to aid in the creation and study of topical or thematic units. In this edition, for the first time, references to the works of art in the Inserts are included along with the topics so that students may add visual references to their analyses of literature.

A special word is in order for the category "America in Peace, War, and Tribulation," which is first in the Topical and Thematic Table. After the attacks on the United States on September 11, 2001, it is fitting that a category of uniquely American topics be included for student analysis and discussion. Of course there cannot be a systematic and comprehensive examination of the background and thought that belongs to courses in American literature, but a selection of works that bear on American life and values is now particularly important. Some of the works describe an idealized America, but many also shed light on problems and issues that

America has faced in the past and is facing today. A few of the works concern our country at its beginning; some reflect the life of the frontier and the Civil War; others introduce issues of minority culture; still others introduce subjects such as war, misfortune, personal anguish, regret, healing, reverence for the land, the symbolic value of work, nostalgia, love, prejudice, and relationships between parents and children. It is our hope that students study the listed works broadly, as general human issues also dealing with the complexity of life in the United States today.

QUESTIONS. Following each anthologized selection in the detailed chapters are study questions designed to help students in their exploration and understanding of literature. Some questions are factual and may be answered quickly. Others provoke extended thought and classroom discussion, and may also serve for both in-class and out-of-class writing assignments. At the ends of twenty-six chapters we include a number of more general "Special Topics for Writing and Argument about (Character, Symbolism, Tragedy, etc.)." Many of these are comparison-contrast topics, and a number of them—at least one in each chapter—are assignments requiring creative writing (for example, "Write a poem," or "Compose a short scene"). What is unique about these topics is that students are asked not only to write creatively and argue cogently, but also to analyze their own creative processes. As already indicated, the seventh edition contains questions designed to add a research component to the study of the chapter topics.

DATES. To place the various works in historical context, we include the life dates for all authors. Along with the title of each anthologized work, we list the year of publication.

NUMBERING. For convenient reference, we have adopted a regular style of numbering the selections by fives:

Stories:	*every fifth **paragraph**.*
Poems:	*every fifth **line**.*
Poetic plays:	*every fifth **line**, starting at 1 with each new scene and act.*
Prose plays:	*every fifth **speech**, starting at 1 with each new scene and act.*

GLOSSES. For the poetry and poetic plays, we provide brief marginal glosses wherever they are needed. For all works, including poetry, we supply explanatory footnotes when more details are necessary. Words and phrases that are glossed or footnoted are highlighted by a small degree sign (°). Footnotes are located according to line, paragraph, or speech numbers.

THE GLOSSARY. In the discussions to the various chapters, key terms and concepts are **boldfaced**, and these are gathered alphabetically and explained briefly, with relevant page numbers in the text, in the comprehensive glossary following the appendices. Because the seventh edition of *Literature: An Introduction to Reading and Writing* may sometimes be used for reference, the glossary is also intended for general use.

BOXED DISCUSSIONS WITHIN THE CHAPTERS.   In some of the chapters, especially Chapters 1, 19, 26, and 32, separately boxed sections highlight brief but essential discussions of a number of important and related matters. The topics chosen for this treatment—such as the use of tenses in discussing a work, the use of authorial names, the terms "tenor" and "vehicle," useful ways to refer to parts of plays, and the concept of decorum—were based on the recommendations of instructors and students.

SPECIAL WRITING TOPICS.   In the seventh edition we have retained the section titled "Special Writing Topics about Literature," which follows the drama section. This section contains four chapters (32–35) that were formerly appendices, but on the advice of many readers they are now to be considered a main part of the book. These chapters, which contain general literary assignments, are arranged to place emphasis on research and recent critical theories.

PHOTOGRAPHS AND ART REPRODUCTIONS.   We also include a number of art reproductions and photographs, many within the chapters, but a number in special colored inserts. We hope that these reproductions, together with others that instructors might add, will encourage comparison-and-contrast discussions and essays about the relationship of literature and art. As already noted, the Topical and Thematic Table of Contents includes references to relevant art works.

DRAMATIZATIONS ON VIDEOTAPE AND DVD.   To strengthen the connection between fiction and dramatization, a number of stories are included that are available on videocassettes and also DVDs, which can be used as teaching tools for support and interpretation. References to some of the available dramatizations are included in the Instructor's Manual. In the introductions to many of the plays there is a listing of many of the cassette and DVD versions that can be brought into the classroom.

Revisions

There is little in the seventh edition that has not been reexamined, revised, or rewritten. Particularly noteworthy are the fourteen new demonstrative essays. Extensive revisions have also been made in the general introduction (Chapter 1); the introduction to poetry (Chapter 13); the introduction to drama (Chapter 26); the introductory sections on Dickinson and Frost (Chapter 24); the chapters on figures of speech (17) and prosody (19); and the chapters on research and taking examinations (32 and 34). The two appendices have also been changed and updated. The glossary has been corrected and amended in a number of places. Many of the current MLA recommendations for documenting electronic sources (2003), for example, are illustrated in Appendix I.

Throughout all the chapter discussions, the subheads have been changed from simple topics to complete sentences. This change has been made in the hope that pointed sentences will enable students to assimilate the following content more easily than before. Of special importance in each of the main chapters are the sections "Questions for Discovering Ideas" and "Strategies for Organizing Ideas," which have been revised in the light of the continuing goal to help students concentrate on their writing assignments.

✳ READING AND WRITING NOW AND IN THE FUTURE

Because writing is a major mode of thinking, it is an essential reinforcement of analytical and critical reading. Many people, when a particular work is named, will often admit that they remember that work well because they once wrote an essay about it when taking a literature class. It is an article of faith that students who write about what they read learn twice, for as they plan and develop their writing they necessarily grow as thinkers. Such an interlocking approach is the bedrock idea of the seventh edition of *Literature: An Introduction to Reading and Writing*. There is no chapter that does not contain abundant information and guides for writing. Moreover, we do not simply say what can be done with a topic of literary study, but we also show ways in which it might be done. Throughout the chapters there are thirty-one demonstrative essays that exemplify the strategies and methods brought out in the chapter. Following each of these essays is an analytical commentary showing how the writing principles of the discussion have been carried out.

A logical extension (and a major hope) of this combined approach is that the techniques students acquire in studying literature as a reading-writing undertaking will help them in every course they may ever take, and in whatever profession they follow. Students will always *read*—if not the authors contained here, then other authors, and certainly newspapers, letters, legal documents, memoranda, magazine articles, technical reports, business proposals, internet communications, and much more. Although students may never again need to write about topics like setting, structure, or prosody, they will certainly find a future need to *write*.

Indeed, the more effectively students learn to write about literature when taking their literature courses, the better they will be able to write later on—no matter what the topic. It is undeniable that the power to analyze problems and make convincing written and oral presentations is a major quality of leadership and success in all fields. To acquire the skills of disciplined reading and strong writing is therefore the best possible preparation that students can make for the future, whatever it may hold.

While we stress the value of our book as a teaching tool, we also emphasize that literature is to be enjoyed and loved. Sometimes we neglect the truth that study and delight are complementary, and that intellectual stimulation and emotional enjoyment develop not only from the immediate responses of pleasure, involvement, and sympathy, but also from the understanding, contemplation, and confidence generated by knowledge and developing skill. We therefore hope that the selections in the seventh edition of *Literature: An Introduction to Reading and Writing* will teach students about humanity, about their own perceptions, feelings, and lives, and about the timeless patterns of human existence. We hope they will take delight in such discoveries and grow as they make them. We see the book as a steppingstone to future achievement and to lifelong understanding and joy in great literature.

⁊ ACKNOWLEDGMENTS

As the book goes into the seventh edition, I wish to acknowledge the many people who at various times have offered helpful advice, information, and suggestions. To name them, as Dryden says in *Absalom and Achitophel*, is to praise them. They are Professors Eileen Allman, Brian Anderson, Peggy Cole, David Bady, Andrew Brilliant, Rex Butt, Stanley Coberly, Betty L. Dixon, Elizabeth Keats Flores, Alice Griffin, Loren C. Gruber, Robert Halli, Rebecca Heintz, Karen Holt, Claudia Johnson, Matthew Marino, Edward Martin, Evan Matthews, Pearl McHaney, Ruth Milberg-Kaye, Nancy Miller, JoAnna Stephens Mink, Ervin Nieves, Glen Nygreen, Michael Paull, Norman Prinsky, Bonnie Ronson, Dan Rubey, Margaret Ellen Sherwood, Beverly J. Slaughter, Keith Walters, Chloe Warner, Scott Westrem, Mardi Valgemae, Matthew Winston, and Ruth Zerner, and also Christel Bell, Linda Bridgers, Catherine Davis, Jim Freund, Edward Hoeppner, Anna F. Jacobs, Eleanor Tubbs, Brooke Mitchell, April Roberts, David Roberts, Braden Welborn, and Eve Zarin. I give special recognition and thanks to Ann Marie Radaskiewicz. The skilled assistance of Jonathan Roberts has been essential and invaluable at every stage of all the editions.

A number of other people have provided sterling guidance for the preparation of the seventh edition. They are Timothy C. Averill, Manchester Essex Regional High School; Barbara Bloy, Tufts University; Donna Campbell, Gonzaga University; Darren Chiang-Schulthesis, Fullerton College; Lawana Day, Pellissippi State Technical Community College; Bart Edelman, Glendale Community College; Barbara Goldstein, Hillsborough Community College; Karen L. Golightly, University of Memphis; Rosemary Johnsen, Michigan State University; Gay Lyons, Pellissippi State; Virginia L. Macdonald, Nicholls State University; Peter R. Malik, Alcorn State University; Dorothy Minor, Tulsa Community College; Ellen Nichols, San Diego Mesa Community College; Arlene Rodriguez, Springfield Technical Community College; William O. Shakespeare, Brigham Young University; and Caren Town, Georgia Southern University.

I wish especially to thank Carrie Brandon, who was Senior English Editor at Prentice Hall during most of the time I was working on the seventh edition. Her understanding, creativity, cheerfulness, and helpfulness have made working with her an honor and a pleasure. I also thank Yolanda de Rooy, President, Humanities and Social Sciences; Leah Jewell, Editor in Chief, English; and earlier Prentice Hall English editors, for their imagination and foresight, and also for their patience with me and support of me over the years. To Kathryn Graehl, whose work on the manuscript has been inestimably fine and who has saved me many times, I offer an extra salute of gratitude. Additional thanks are reserved for Joan Foley of Prentice Hall, our production editor, who has devoted her knowledge, intelligence, diligence, good humor, and skill to the many tasks needed to bring a book of this size to fruition. Thanks are also due to Mary Dalton-Hoffman for her superb work on securing permissions, and to Linda Sykes for research into the various photographs and illustrations. I also extend my gratitude to Rachel Falk, Senior Marketing Manager, and to Ann Marie McCarthy, Executive Managing Editor.

Special acknowledgement is due to my associate, Professor Henry E. Jacobs (1946–1986) of the University of Alabama. His energy and creativity were essential in planning and writing the first edition of *Literature: An Introduction to Reading and Writing*, but he was encompassed by fate and gloomy night before we could work together on subsequent revisions.

Edgar V. Roberts

N.B. The Prentice Hall Companion Web site offers many resources at **<www.prenhall.com/roberts>**. Here you will find a chapter-by-chapter guide through this text, as well as online quizzes that include instant scoring, a Syllabus Manager™ for instructors, and a message board where you may post questions or comments to a national audience. There is also an abundance of Web links to research specific authors, famous works written during numerous literary periods, and online literary journals.

Introduction:

Reading, Responding to, and Writing about Literature

 WHAT IS LITERATURE, AND WHY DO WE STUDY IT?

We use the word **literature,** in a broad sense, to mean compositions that tell stories, dramatize situations, express emotions, and analyze and advocate ideas. Before the invention of writing thousands of years ago, literary works were necessarily spoken or sung, and they were retained only as long as living people continued to repeat them. In some societies, the oral tradition of literature still exists, with many poems and stories designed exclusively for spoken delivery. Even in our modern age of writing and printing, much literature is still heard aloud rather than read silently. Parents delight their children with stories and poems; poets and story writers read their works directly before live audiences; plays and scripts are interpreted on stages and before movie and television cameras for the benefit of a vast public.

No matter how we assimilate literature, we gain much from it. In truth, readers often cannot explain why they enjoy reading, for goals and ideals are not easily articulated. There are, however, areas of general agreement about the value of systematic and extensive reading.

Literature helps us grow, both personally and intellectually. It opens doors for us. It stretches our minds. It develops our imagination, increases our understanding, and enlarges our power of sympathy. It helps us see beauty in the world around us. It links us with the cultural, philosophical, and religious world of which we are a part. It enables us to recognize human dreams and struggles in different places and times. It helps us develop mature sensibility and compassion for all living beings. It nurtures our ability to appreciate the beauty of order and arrangement— gifts that are also bestowed by a well-structured song, a beautifully painted canvas, or a well-chiseled piece of sculpture. It enables us to see worthiness in the aims of all people. It exercises our emotions through interest, concern, sympathy, tension, excitement, regret, fear, laughter, and hope. It encourages us to assist creative and talented people who need recognition and support. Through our cumulative experience in reading, literature shapes our goals and values by clarifying our own identities—both positively, through acceptance of the admirable in human beings, and negatively, through rejection of the sinister. It enables us to develop perspectives on events occurring locally and globally, and thereby it gives us understanding and control. It is one of the shaping influences of life. It makes us human.

TYPES OF LITERATURE: THE GENRES

Literature may be classified into four categories or *genres:* (1) prose fiction, (2) poetry, (3) drama, and (4) nonfiction prose. Usually the first three are classified as **imaginative literature.**

The genres of imaginative literature have much in common, but they also have distinguishing characteristics. **Prose fiction,** or **narrative fiction,** includes **myths, parables, romances, novels,** and **short stories.** Originally, *fiction* meant anything made up, crafted, or shaped, but today the word refers to prose stories based in the imaginations of authors. The essence of fiction is **narration,** the relating or recounting of a sequence of events or actions. Fictional works usually focus on one or a few major characters who change and grow (in their ability to make decisions, their awareness or insight, their attitude toward others, their sensitivity, and their moral capacity) as a result of how they deal with other characters and how they attempt to solve their problems. Although fiction, like all imaginative literature, can introduce true historical details, it is not real history, for its main purpose is to interest, stimulate, instruct, and divert, not to create a precise historical record.

If prose is expansive, **poetry** tends toward brevity. It offers us high points of emotion, reflection, thought, and feeling in what the English poet Wordsworth called "narrow room[s]." Yet in this context, it expresses the most powerful and deeply felt experiences of human beings, often awakening deep responses of welcome recognition: "Yes, I know what that's like. I would feel the same way. That's exactly right." Poems make us think, make us reflect, and generally instruct us. They can also arouse our emotions, surprise us, make us laugh or cry, and inspire us. Many poems become lifelong friends, and we visit them again and again for insight, understanding, laughter, or the quiet reflection of joy or sorrow.

Poetry's power lies not only in its words and thoughts, but also in its music, using rhyme and a variety of rhythms to intensify its emotional impact. Although poems themselves vary widely in length, individual lines are often short because poets distill the greatest meaning and imaginative power from their words through rhetorical devices such as **imagery** and **metaphor.** Though poetry often requires many **formal** and **metrical** restrictions, it is paradoxically the very restrictiveness of poetry that provides poets with great freedom. Traditionally important poetic forms include the fourteen-line **sonnet,**

ballads, blank verse, couplets, elegies, epigrams, hymns, limericks, odes, quatrains, songs or **lyrics, tercets** or **triplets, villanelles,** and the increasingly popular **haiku.** Many songs or lyrics have been set to music, and some were written expressly for that purpose. Some poems are long and **discursive,** like many poems by the American poet Walt Whitman. **Epic** poems, such as those by Homer and Milton, contain thousands of lines. Since the time of Whitman, many poets have abandoned rhymes and regular rhythms in favor of **free verse,** a far-ranging type of poetry growing out of content and the natural rhythms of spoken language.

Drama is literature designed for stage or film presentation by people—actors—for the benefit and delight of other people—an audience. The essence of drama is the development of **character** and **situation** through **speech** and **action.** Like fiction, drama may focus on a single character or a small number of characters, and it enacts fictional (and sometimes historical) events as if they were happening right before our eyes. The audience therefore is a direct witness to the ways in which characters are influenced and changed by events and by other characters. Although most modern plays use prose **dialogue** (the conversation of two or more characters), on the principle that the language of drama should resemble the language of ordinary people as much as possible, many plays from the past, such as those of ancient Greece and Renaissance England, are in poetic form.

Nonfiction prose consists of news reports, feature articles, essays, editorials, textbooks, historical and biographical works, and the like, all of which describe or interpret facts and present judgments and opinions. The goal of nonfiction prose is to present truths and conclusions about the factual world. Imaginative literature, although also grounded in facts, is less concerned with the factual record than with the revelation of truths about life and human nature. Recently another genre has been emphasized within the category of nonfiction prose. This is **creative nonfiction,** a type of literature that is technically nonfiction, such as diaries and journals, but which nevertheless involves a degree of imagination, and for this reason it is considered creative or imaginative.

❦ READING LITERATURE AND RESPONDING TO IT ACTIVELY

Sometimes we find it difficult, after we have finished reading a work, to express thoughts about it and to answer pointed questions about it. But more active and thoughtful reading gives us the understanding to develop well-considered answers. Obviously, we need to follow the work and to understand its details, but just as importantly, we need to respond to the words, get at the ideas, and understand the implications of what is happening. We rely on our own fund of knowledge and experience to verify the accuracy and truth of situations and incidents, and we try to articulate our own emotional responses to the characters and their problems.

To illustrate such active responding, we will examine "The Necklace" (1884) by the French writer Guy de Maupassant.[1] "The Necklace" is one of the best known of all stories, and it is included here with marginal notes like those that any reader might make during original and follow-up readings. Many notes, particularly at the beginning, are *assimilative*; that is, they record details about the action. But as the story progresses, the marginal comments are more concerned with conclusions about the story's meaning. Toward the end, the comments are full rather than minimal; they result not only from first responses but also from considered thought. Here, then, is Maupassant's "The Necklace."

GUY DE MAUPASSANT (1850–1893)

The Necklace ～⋖～✓⌣ 1884

Translated by Edgar V. Roberts

She was one of those pretty and charming women, born, as if by an error of destiny, into a family of clerks and copyists. She had no dowry, no prospects, no way of getting known, courted, loved, married by a rich and distinguished man. She finally settled for a marriage with a minor clerk in the Ministry of Education.

> "She" is pretty but poor, and has no chance in life unless she marries. Without connections, she has no entry into high society and marries an insignificant clerk.

She was a simple person, without the money to dress well, but she was as unhappy as if she had gone through bankruptcy, for women have neither rank nor race. In place of high birth or important family connections, they can rely only on their beauty, their grace, and their charm. Their inborn finesse, their elegant taste, their engaging personalities, which are their only power, make working-class women the equals of the grandest ladies.

> She is unhappy.

> A view of women who have no chance for an independent life and a career. In 1884, women had nothing more than this. Sad.

She suffered constantly, feeling herself destined for all delicacies and luxuries. She suffered because of her grim

[1]Henri-René-Albert-Guy de Maupassant (1850–1893) is considered one of the major nineteenth-century French naturalist writers. Scion of an aristocratic Norman family, he received his baccalaureate degree from a lycée at Le Havre, after which he began studying law. When the Franco-Prussian War broke out he served in the French army, including battlefield duty. After leaving the military he became a minor bureaucrat, first in the Ministry of Marine and then in the Ministry of Education (also the workplace of Loisel, the husband of "The Necklace").

As a youth Maupassant was an energetic oarsman, swimmer, and boatman—a power that he also devoted to his career as a writer. During the 1870s in Paris he had regularly submitted his literary efforts to the novelist Gustave Flaubert (1821–1880), a family friend who regarded him as a son and whose criticism both improved and encouraged him. In Maupassant's thirties, after the death of his mentor Flaubert, his career flourished. His first published volume was a collection of poems (*Des Vers*, 1880), which he had to withdraw after it created a scandal and a lawsuit because of its sexual openness. After this time, until his death in 1893, he produced thirty volumes—novels, poems, articles, travel books, and three hundred short stories. In addition to "The Necklace," a few of his better-known stories are "The Ball of Fat," "Mademoiselle Fifi," and "A Piece of String."

Maupassant was a meticulous writer, devoting much attention to the reality of everyday existence (hence his status as a naturalist writer). A number of his stories are about events occurring during the Franco-Prussian War. Some are about life among bureaucrats, some about peasant life in Normandy, and a large number, including "The Necklace," about Parisian life. His major stories are characterized by strong irony; human beings are influenced by forces they cannot control, and their wishes are often frustrated by their own defects. Under such circumstances, Maupassant's characters exhibit varying degrees of weakness, hypocrisy, vanity, insensitivity, callousness, and even cruelty, but those who are victimized are viewed with understanding and sympathy.

apartment with its drab walls, threadbare furniture, ugly curtains. All such things, which most other women in her situation would not even have noticed, tortured her and filled her with despair. The sight of the young country girl who did her simple housework awakened in her only a sense of desolation and lost hopes. She daydreamed of large, silent anterooms, decorated with oriental tapestries and lighted by high bronze floor lamps, with two elegant valets in short culottes dozing in large armchairs under the effects of forced-air heaters. She imagined large drawing rooms draped in the most expensive silks, with fine end tables on which were placed knickknacks of inestimable value. She dreamed of the perfume of dainty private rooms, which were designed only for intimate tête-à-têtes with the closest friends, who because of their achievements and fame would make her the envy of all other women.

She suffers because of her cheap belongings, wanting expensive things. She dreams of wealth and of how other women would envy her if she could display finery. But such luxuries are unrealistic and unattainable for her.

When she sat down to dinner at her round little table covered with a cloth that had not been washed for three days, in front of her husband who opened the kettle while declaring ecstatically, "Ah, good old boiled beef! I don't know anything better," she dreamed of expensive banquets with shining placesettings, and wall hangings portraying ancient heroes and exotic birds in an enchanted forest. She imagined a gourmet-prepared main course carried on the most exquisite trays and served on the most beautiful dishes, with whispered gallantries which she would hear with a sphinxlike smile as she dined on the pink meat of a trout or the delicate wing of a quail.

Her husband's taste is for plain things, while she dreams of expensive gourmet food. He has adjusted to his status. She has not.

5   She had no decent dresses, no jewels, nothing. And she loved nothing but these; she believed herself born only for these. She burned with the desire to please, to be envied, to be attractive and sought after.

She lives for her unrealistic dreams, and these increase her frustration.

She had a rich friend, a comrade from convent days, whom she did not want to see anymore because she suffered so much when she returned home. She would weep for the entire day afterward with sorrow, regret, despair, and misery.

She even thinks of giving up a rich friend because she is so depressed after visiting her.

Well, one evening, her husband came home glowing and carrying a large envelope.

"Here," he said, "this is something for you."

She quickly tore open the envelope and took out a card engraved with these words:

A new section in the story.

The CHANCELLOR OF EDUCATION *and*
MRS. GEORGE RAMPONNEAU
request that
MR. AND MRS. LOISEL
do them the honor of coming to dinner
at the Ministry of Education
on the evening of January 8.

An invitation to dinner at the Ministry of Education. A big plum.

10   Instead of being delighted, as her husband had hoped,   It only upsets her.
she threw the invitation spitefully on the table, muttering:

"What do you expect me to do with this?"

"But honey, I thought you'd be glad. You never get to go   Loisel really doesn't
out, and this is a special occasion! I had a lot of trouble getting   understand her. He can't
the invitation. Everyone wants one. The demand is high and   sympathize with her
not many clerks get invited. Everyone important will be there."   unhappiness.

She looked at him angrily and stated impatiently:

"What do you want me to wear to go there?"   She declares that she

15   He had not thought of that. He stammered: hasn't anything to wear.

"But your theater dress. That seems nice to me . . ."   He tries to persuade her

He stopped, amazed and bewildered, as his wife began   that her theater dress
to cry. Large tears fell slowly from the corners of her eyes to   might do for the occasion.
her mouth. He said falteringly:

"What's wrong? What's the matter?"

But with a strong effort she had recovered, and she answered calmly as she wiped her damp cheeks:

20   "Nothing, except that I have nothing to wear and therefore can't go to the party. Give your invitation to someone else
at the office whose wife will have nicer clothes than mine."

Distressed, he responded:

"Well, all right, Mathilde. How much would a new dress   Her name is Mathilde.
cost, something you could use at other times, but not any-   He volunteers to pay for a
thing fancy?"   new dress.

She thought for a few moments, adding things up and
thinking also of an amount that she could ask without getting an
immediate refusal and a frightened outcry from the frugal clerk.

Finally she responded tentatively: She is manipulating him.

25   "I don't know exactly, but it seems to me that I could get
by on four hundred francs."

He blanched slightly at this, because he had set aside   The dress will cost him his
just that amount to buy a shotgun for Sunday lark-hunts the   next summer's vacation.
next summer with a few friends in the Plain of Nanterre.   (He doesn't seem to have
                                                             included her in his plans.)
However, he said:

"All right, you've got four hundred francs, but make it a
pretty dress."

As the day of the party drew near, Mrs. Loisel seemed   A new section, the third in
sad, uneasy, anxious, even though her gown was all ready.   the story. The day of the
One evening her husband said to her: party is near.

30   "What's the matter? You've been acting funny for several days."

She answered:

"It's awful, but I don't have any jewels to wear, not a sin-   Now she complains that
gle gem, nothing to dress up my outfit. I'll look like a beggar.   she doesn't have any nice
I'd almost rather not go to the party."   jewelry. She is manipulating
                                             him again.
He responded:

"You can wear a corsage of cut flowers. This year it's all
the rage. For only ten francs you can get two or three gorgeous roses."

35   She was not convinced.

"No . . . there's nothing more humiliating than looking shabby in the company of rich women."

But her husband exclaimed:

"God, but you're silly! Go to your friend Mrs. Forrestier, and ask her to lend you some jewelry. You know her well enough to do that."

She uttered a cry of joy:

40   "That's right. I hadn't thought of that."

The next day she went to her friend's house and described her problem.

Mrs. Forrestier went to her mirrored wardrobe, took out a large jewel box, opened it, and said to Mrs. Loisel:

"Choose, my dear."

She saw bracelets, then a pearl necklace, then a Venetian cross of finely worked gold and gems. She tried on the jewelry in front of a mirror, and hesitated, unable to make up her mind about each one. She kept asking:

45   "Do you have anything else?"

"Certainly. Look to your heart's content. I don't know what you'd like best."

Suddenly she found a superb diamond necklace in a black satin box, and her heart throbbed with desire for it. Her hands shook as she picked it up. She fastened it around her neck, watched it gleam at her throat, and looked at herself ecstatically.

Then she asked, haltingly and anxiously:

"Could you lend me this, nothing but this?"

50   "Why yes, certainly."

She jumped up, hugged her friend joyfully, then hurried away with her treasure.

The day of the party came. Mrs. Loisel was a success. She was prettier than anyone else, stylish, graceful, smiling and wild with joy. All the men saw her, asked her name, sought to be introduced. All the important administrators stood in line to waltz with her. The Chancellor himself eyed her.

She danced joyfully, passionately, intoxicated with pleasure, thinking of nothing but the moment, in the triumph of her beauty, in the glory of her success, on cloud nine with happiness made up of all the admiration, of all the aroused desire, of this victory so complete and so sweet to the heart of any woman.

She did not leave until four o'clock in the morning. Her husband, since midnight, had been sleeping in a little empty room with three other men whose wives had also been enjoying themselves.

55   He threw, over her shoulders, the shawl that he had brought for the trip home—a modest everyday wrap, the poverty of which contrasted sharply with the elegance of her

---

She has a good point, but there seems to be no way out.

He proposes a solution: Borrow jewelry from Mrs. Forrestier, who is apparently the rich friend mentioned earlier.

Mathilde has her choice of her friend's jewels.

A "superb" diamond necklace. This is what the story has been building up to.

This is what she wants, just this.

She leaves with the "treasure." Things might be looking up for her.

A new section.

The party. Mathilde is a huge success.

Another judgment about women. Does the author mean that only women want to be admired? Don't men want admiration, too?

Loisel, with other husbands, is bored, while the wives are literally having a ball.

evening gown. She felt it and hurried away to avoid being noticed by the other women who luxuriated in rich furs.

Ashamed of her shabby everyday shawl, she rushes away to avoid being seen. She is forced back into the reality of her true situation. Her glamor is gone.

Loisel tried to hold her back:

"Wait a minute. You'll catch cold outdoors. I'll call a cab."

But she paid no attention and hurried down the stairs.
When they reached the street they found no carriages.
They began to look for one, shouting at cabmen passing by at
a distance.

They walked toward the Seine, desperate, shivering. Finally, on a quay, they found one of those old night-going buggies that are seen in Paris only after dark, as if they were
ashamed of their wretched appearance in daylight.

A comedown after the nice evening. They take a wretched-looking buggy home.

60   It took them to their door, on the Street of Martyrs, and
they sadly climbed the stairs to their flat. For her, it was finished. As for him, he could think only that he had to begin
work at the Ministry of Education at ten o'clock.

"Street of Martyrs." Is this name significant?

Loisel is down-to-earth.

She took the shawl off her shoulders, in front of the
mirror, to see herself once more in her glory. But suddenly
she cried out. The necklace was no longer around her neck!

SHE HAS LOST THE NECKLACE!

Her husband, already half undressed, asked:

"What's wrong?"

She turned toward him frantically:

65   "I . . . I . . . I no longer have Mrs. Forrestier's necklace."

He stood up, bewildered:

"What! . . . How! . . . It's not possible!"

And they looked in the folds of the gown, in the folds of
the shawl, in the pockets, everywhere. They found nothing.

They can't find it.

He asked:

70   "You're sure you still had it when you left the party?"

"Yes. I checked it in the vestibule of the Ministry."

"But if you'd lost it in the street, we would've heard it
fall. It must be in the cab."

"Yes, probably. Did you notice the number?"

"No. Did you see it?"

75   "No."

Overwhelmed, they looked at each other. Finally, Loisel
got dressed again:

"I'm going out to retrace all our steps," he said, "to see
if I can find the necklace that way."

And he went out. She stayed in her evening dress, without the energy to get ready for bed, stretched out in a chair,
drained of strength and thought.

He goes out to search for the necklace.

Her husband came back at about seven o'clock. He had
found nothing.

But is unsuccessful.

80   He went to Police Headquarters and to the newspapers
to announce a reward. He went to the small cab companies,
and finally he followed up even the slightest hopeful lead.

He really tries. He's doing his best.

She waited the entire day, in the same enervated state,
in the face of this frightful disaster.

Loisel came back in the evening, his face pale and haggard. He had found nothing.

"You'll have to write to your friend," he said, "that you broke a clasp on her necklace and that you're having it fixed. That'll give us time to look around."

Loisel's plan to explain delaying the return. He takes charge, is resourceful.

She wrote as he dictated.

85 By the end of the week they had lost all hope.

Things are hopeless.

And Loisel, looking five years older, declared:

"We'll have to see about replacing the jewels."

Note that Loisel does not even suggest that they explain things to Mrs. Forrestier.

The next day they took the case which had contained the necklace and went to the jeweler whose name was inside. He looked at his books:

They hunt for a replacement.

"I wasn't the one, Madam, who sold the necklace. I only made the case."

90 Then they went from jeweler to jeweler, searching for a necklace like the other one, racking their memories, both of them sick with worry and anguish.

In a shop in the Palais-Royal, they found a necklace of diamonds that seemed to them exactly like the one they were looking for. It was priced at forty thousand francs. They could buy it for thirty-six thousand.

A new diamond necklace will cost 36,000 francs, a monumental amount.

They got the jeweler to promise not to sell it for three days. And they made an agreement that he would buy it back for thirty-four thousand francs if the original was recovered before the end of February.

They make a deal with the jeweler. (Is Maupassant hinting that things might work out for them?)

Loisel had saved eighteen thousand francs that his father had left him. He would have to borrow the rest.

It will take all of Loisel's inheritance . . .

He borrowed, asking a thousand francs from one, five hundred from another, five louis° here, three louis there. He wrote promissory notes, undertook ruinous obligations, did business with finance companies and the whole tribe of loan sharks. He compromised himself for the remainder of his days, risked his signature without knowing whether he would be able to honor it; and, terrified by anguish over the future, by the black misery that was about to descend on him, by the prospect of all kinds of physical deprivations and moral tortures, he went to get the new necklace, and put down thirty-six thousand francs on the jeweler's counter.

. . . plus another 18,000 francs that must be borrowed at enormous rates of interest.

95 Mrs. Loisel took the necklace back to Mrs. Forrestier, who said with an offended tone:

"You should have brought it back sooner; I might have needed it."

Mrs. Forrestier is offended and complains about Mathilde's delay.

She did not open the case, as her friend feared she might. If she had noticed the substitution, what would she have thought? What would she have said? Would she not have taken her for a thief?

Is this enough justification for not telling the truth? It seems to be for the Loisels.

louis: a gold coin worth twenty francs.

Mrs. Loisel soon discovered the horrible life of the needy. She did her share, however, completely, heroically. That horrifying debt had to be paid. She would pay. They dismissed the maid; they changed their address; they rented an attic flat.

A new section, the fifth.

She learned to do the heavy housework, dirty kitchen jobs. She washed the dishes, wearing away her manicured fingernails on greasy pots and encrusted baking dishes. She handwashed dirty linen, shirts, and dish towels that she hung out on the line to dry. Each morning, she took the garbage down to the street, and she carried up water, stopping at each floor to catch her breath. And, dressed in cheap house dresses, she went to the fruit dealer, the grocer, the butchers, with her basket under her arms, haggling, insulting, defending her measly cash penny by penny.

They suffer to repay their debts. Mathilde accepts a cheap attic flat, and does all the heavy housework herself to save on domestic help.

She pinches pennies and haggles with the local merchants.

100 They had to make installment payments every month, and, to buy more time, to refinance loans.

They struggle to meet payments.

The husband worked evenings to make fair copies of tradesmen's accounts, and late into the night he made copies at five cents a page.

Mr. Loisel moonlights to make extra money.

And this life lasted ten years.

For ten years they struggle, but they endure.

At the end of ten years, they had paid back everything—everything—including the extra charges imposed by loan sharks and the accumulation of compound interest.

Another new section, the sixth of the story.

The Loisels have successfully paid back the loans. They have been quite virtuous.

Mrs. Loisel looked old now. She had become the strong, hard, and rude woman of poor households. Her hair unkempt, with uneven skirts and rough, red hands, she spoke loudly, washed floors with large buckets of water. But sometimes, when her husband was at work, she sat down near the window, and she dreamed of that evening so long ago, of that party, where she had been so beautiful and so admired.

Mrs. Loisel (why does the narrator not say "Mathilde"?) is roughened and aged by the work. But she has behaved "heroically" (¶ 98) and has shown her mettle.

105 What would life have been like if she had not lost that necklace? Who knows? Who knows? Life is so peculiar, so uncertain. How little a thing it takes to destroy you or to save you!

A moral? Our lives are shaped by small, uncertain things; we hang by a thread.

Well, one Sunday, when she had gone for a stroll along the Champs-Elysées to relax from the cares of the week, she suddenly noticed a woman walking with a child. It was Mrs. Forrestier, still youthful, still beautiful, still attractive.

The seventh part of the story, a scene on the Champs-Elysées. Mathilde sees Jeanne Forrestier for the first time in the previous ten years.

Mrs. Loisel felt moved. Would she speak to her? Yes, certainly. And now that she had paid, she could tell all. Why not?

She walked closer.

"Hello, Jeanne."

110 The other gave no sign of recognition and was astonished to be addressed so familiarly by this working-class woman. She stammered:

"But . . . Madam! . . . I don't know. . . . You must have made a mistake."

"No. I'm Mathilde Loisel."

Her friend cried out:

"Oh! . . . My poor Mathilde, you've changed so much."

115 "Yes. I've had some tough times since I saw you last; in fact hardships . . . and all because of you! . . ."

Jeanne notes Mathilde's changed appearance.

"Of me . . . how so?"

"You remember the diamond necklace that you lent me to go to the party at the Ministry of Education?"

"Yes. What then?"

"Well, I lost it."

120 "How, since you gave it back to me?"

"I returned another exactly like it. And for ten years we've been paying for it. You understand this wasn't easy for us, who have nothing. . . . Finally it's over, and I'm damned glad."

Mathilde tells Jeanne everything.

Mrs. Forrestier stopped her.

"You say that you bought a diamond necklace to replace mine?"

"Yes, you didn't notice it, eh? It was exactly like yours."

125 And she smiled with proud and childish joy.

Mrs. Forrestier, deeply moved, took both her hands.

"Oh, my poor Mathilde! But mine was only costume jewelry. At most, it was worth only five hundred francs! . . ."

SURPRISE! The lost necklace was not made of real diamonds, and the Loisels have slaved for no reason at all. But hard work and sacrifice probably brought out better qualities in Mathilde than she otherwise might have shown. Is this the moral of the story?

READING AND RESPONDING IN A NOTEBOOK OR COMPUTER FILE

The marginal comments printed with "The Necklace" demonstrate the active reading-responding process you should apply to everything you read. Use the margins in your text similarly to record your comments and questions, but plan also to record your more lengthy responses in a notebook, on note cards, on separate sheets of paper, or in a computer file. Be careful not to lose anything; keep all your notes. As you progress from work to work, you will find that your written or saved comments will be immensely important to you as your record, or journal, of your first impressions together with your more carefully considered and expanded thoughts.

In keeping your notebook, your objective should be to learn assigned works inside and out and then to say perceptive things about them. To achieve this goal, you need to read the work more than once. Develop a good note-taking system so that as you read, you will create a "memory bank" of your own knowledge. You can make withdrawals from this fund of ideas when you begin to write. As an aid in developing your own procedures for reading and "depositing" your ideas, you may wish to begin with the following *Guidelines for Reading*. Of course, you will want to modify these suggestions and add to them as you become a more experienced and disciplined reader.

GUIDELINES FOR READING

1. Observations for basic understanding
   a. Explain words, situations, and concepts. Write down words that are new or not immediately clear. Use your dictionary, and record the relevant meanings in your notebook. Write down special difficulties so that you can ask your instructor about them.
   b. Determine what is happening in the work. For a story or play, where do the actions take place? What do they show? Who is involved? Who is the major figure? Why is he or she major? What relationships do the characters have with one another? What concerns do the characters have? What do they do? Who says what to whom? How do the speeches advance the action and reveal the characters? For a poem, what is the situation? Who is talking, and to whom? What does the speaker say about the situation? Why does the poem end as it does and where it does?

2. Notes on first impressions
   a. Make a record of your reactions and responses. What did you think was memorable, noteworthy, funny, or otherwise striking? Did you worry, get scared, laugh, smile, feel a thrill, learn a great deal, feel proud, find a lot to think about?
   b. Describe interesting characterizations, events, techniques, and ideas. If you like a character or an idea, explain what you like, and do the same for characters and ideas you don't like. Is there anything else in the work that you especially like or dislike? Are parts easy or difficult to understand? Why? Are there any surprises? What was your reaction to them? Be sure to use your own words when writing your explanations.

3. Development of ideas and enlargement of responses
   a. Trace developing patterns. Make an outline or a scheme: What conflicts appear? Do these conflicts exist between people, groups, or ideas? How are the conflicts resolved? Is one force, idea, or side the winner? How do you respond to the winner or to the loser?
   b. Write expanded notes about characters, situations, and actions. What explanations need to be made about the characters? What is the nature of the situations (i.e., young people discover a damaged boat, and themselves, in the spring; a prisoner tries to hide her baby from a cruel guard; and so on)? What is the nature of the actions (i.e., a mother and daughter go shopping, a series of strangers intrude upon the celebration of a Christening, a woman is told that her husband has been killed in a train wreck, a group of children are taken to a fashionable toy store, and so on)? What are the people like, and what are their habits and customs? What sort of language do they use?
   c. Memorize important, interesting, and well-written passages. Copy them in full on note cards, and keep these in your pocket or purse. When walking to class, riding public transportation, or otherwise not occupying your time, learn them by heart. Please take memorization seriously.

d. Always write down questions that come up during your reading. You may raise these in class, and trying to write out your own answers will also aid your own study.

Sample Notebook Entries on Maupassant's "The Necklace"

The following entries illustrate how you can use the guidelines in your first thoughts about a work. You should try to develop enough observations and responses to be useful later, both for additional study and for developing essays. Notice that the entries are not only comments but also questions.

Early in the story, Mathilde seems to be spoiled. She and her husband are not well off, but she is unable to face her own situation.

She is a dreamer but seems harmless. Her daydreams about a fancy home, with all the expensive belongings, are not unusual. It would be unusual to find people who do not have such dreams.

She is embarrassed by her husband's taste for plain food. The storyteller contrasts her taste for trout and quail with Loisel's cheaper favorites.

When the Loisels get the invitation to the ball, Mathilde becomes difficult. Her wish for an expensive dress (the cost of Loisel's shotgun) creates a problem, and she creates another problem by wanting to wear fine jewelry.

Her change in character can be related to the places in the story: the Street of Martyrs, the dinner party scene, the attic flat. Also she fills the places she daydreams about with the most expensive things she can imagine.

Her success at the party shows that she has the charm the storyteller talks about in paragraph 2. She seems never to have had any other chance to exert her power.

The worst part of her personality is shown in rushing away from the party because she is ashamed of her shabby everyday shawl. Mathilde's unhappiness and unwillingness to adjust to her modest means cause the financial downfall of the Loisels. This disaster is her fault.

Borrowing the money to replace the necklace shows that both Loisel and Mathilde have a strong sense of honor. Making up the loss is good, even if it destroys them financially.

There are some nice touches, like Loisel's seeming to be five years older (paragraph 86) and his staying with the other husbands of women enjoying themselves (paragraph 54). These are well done.

It's too bad that Loisel and Mathilde don't confess to Jeanne that the jewels are lost. Their pride or their honor stops them—or perhaps their fear of being accused of theft.

Their ten years of slavish work (paragraphs 98–102) show how they have come down in life. Mathilde does all her work by hand, so she really does pitch in and is, as the narrator says, heroic.

The attic flat is important. Mathilde becomes loud and frumpy when living there (paragraph 99), but she also develops strength. She does what she has to. The earlier apartment and the elegance of her imaginary rooms had brought out her limitations.

The setting of the Champs-Elysées also reflects her character, for she feels free there to tell Jeanne about the disastrous loss and sacrifice (paragraph 121), producing the surprise ending.

The narrator's statement "How little a thing it takes to destroy you or to save you!" (paragraph 105) is full of thought. The necklace is little, but it makes a huge problem. This creates the story's irony.

Questions: Is this story more about the surprise ending or about the character of Mathilde? Is she to be condemned or admired? Does the outcome stem from the little things that make us or break us, as the narrator suggests, or from the difficulty of rising above one's economic class, which seems true, or both? What do the speaker's remarks about women's status mean? (Remember, the story was published in 1884.) This probably isn't relevant, but wouldn't Jeanne, after hearing about the substitution, give the full value of the necklace to the Loisels, and wouldn't they then be pretty well off?

These are reasonable, if fairly full, remarks and observations about "The Necklace." Use your notebook or journal similarly for all reading assignments. If your assignment is simply to learn about a work, general notes like these should be enough. If you are preparing for a test, you might write pointed observations more in line with what is happening in your class, and also write and answer your own questions (see Chapter 34, "Taking Examinations on Literature"). If you have a writing assignment, observations like these can help you focus more closely on your topic—such as character, idea, or setting. Whatever your purpose, always take good notes, and put in as many details and responses as you can. The notes will be invaluable to you as a mind refresher and as a wellspring of thought.

WRITING ESSAYS ON LITERARY TOPICS

Finished writing is the sharpened, focused expression of thought and study. It begins with the search for something to say—an idea. Not all ideas are equal; some are better than others, and getting good ideas is an ability that you will develop the more you think and write. As you discover ideas and explain them in words, you will also improve your perceptions and increase your critical faculties.

In addition, because literature itself contains the subject material (though not in a systematic way) of philosophy, religion, psychology, sociology, and politics, learning to analyze literature and to write about it will also improve your capacity to deal with these and other disciplines.

Writing Does Not Come Easily—for Anyone

A major purpose of your being in college, of which your composition and literature course is a vital part, is to develop your capacity to think and to express your thoughts clearly and fully. However, the process of creating a successfully argued essay—the actual process itself of writing—is not automatic. Writing begins in uncertainty and hesitation, and it becomes certain and confident—accomplished—only as a result of great care, applied thought, a certain amount of experimentation, the passage of time, and much effort. When you read complete, polished, well-formed pieces of writing, you might assume, as many of us do, that the writers wrote their successful versions the first time they tried, and never needed to make any changes and improvements at all. In an ideal world, perhaps, something like this could happen, but not in this one.

If you could see the early drafts of writing you admire, you would be surprised and startled—and also encouraged—to see that good writers are also human and that what they first write is often uncertain, vague, tangential, tentative, incomplete, and messy. Good writers do not always like their first drafts; nevertheless, they work with their efforts and build upon them. They reconsider their ideas and try to restate them, discard some details, add others, chop paragraphs in half and reassemble the parts elsewhere, throw out much (and then maybe recover some of it), revise or completely rewrite sentences, change words, correct misspellings, sharpen expressions, and add new material to tie all the parts together in a smooth, natural flow.

THE GOAL OF WRITING: TO SHOW A PROCESS OF THOUGHT

As you approach the task of writing, you should constantly realize that your goal should always be to *explain* the work you are analyzing. You should never be satisfied simply to restate the events in the work. Too often students fall easily into a pattern of retelling a story or play, or of summarizing the details of a poem. But nothing could be further from what is expected from good writing. You need to demonstrate your thought. Thinking is an active process that does not happen accidentally. Thinking requires that you develop ideas, draw conclusions, exemplify them and support them with details, and connect everything in a coherent manner. Your goal should constantly be to explain the results of your thinking—your ideas, your play of mind over the materials of a work, your insights, your conclusions. This is the ideal.

Approach each writing assignment with the following thoughts in mind: You should consider your reader as a person who has read the work, just as you have done. This person knows what is in the work, and therefore does not need you to restate what she or he already knows. Instead, the person needs to know what to think about it. Therefore, always, your task as a writer is to explain something about the work, to describe the thoughts that you can develop about it. Let us consider the story we have just read, Maupassant's "The Necklace." We have recognized that the main character, Mathilde Loisel, is a young Parisian housewife who is married to a minor clerk in the Ministry of Education. We know this, but if we are reading an essay about the story we will want to learn more. Let us then suppose that a first goal of one of your paragraphs is to explain the deep dissatisfaction Mathilde feels in the early part of the story. Your paragraph might go as follows:

> In the early part of the story Maupassant establishes that Mathilde is deeply dissatisfied with her life. Her threadbare furniture and drab walls are a cause of her unhappiness. Under these circumstances her daydreams of beautiful rooms staffed by "elegant valets," together with a number of rooms for intimate conversations with friends, multiply her dissatisfaction. The meager meals that she shares with her husband make her imagine sumptuous banquets that she feels are rightfully hers by birth but that are denied her because of her circumstances. The emphasis in these early scenes of the story is always on Mathilde's discontentment and frustration.

Notice here that your paragraph ties the story's events to the idea of Mathilde's unhappiness. The events are there, but you are explaining to us, as readers, that the events are directly related to Mathilde's unhappiness. The paragraph illustrates a process of thought. Here is another way in which you might use a thought to connect the same materials:

> In the early part of the story Maupassant emphasizes the economic difficulty of Mathilde's life. The threadbare furniture and ugly curtains, for example, highlight that there is no money to purchase better things. The same spareness of existence is shown by the meager meals that she shares with her husband. With the capacity to appreciate better things, Mathilde is forced by circumstances to make do with worse. Her dreams of sumptuous banquets are therefore natural, given her level of frustration with the life around her. In short, her unhappiness is an understandable consequence of her aversion to her plain and drab apartment and the tightness of money.

Here the details are substantially the same as in our first paragraph, but they are unified by a different idea, namely the economic constraints of Mathilde's life. What is important is that neither paragraph tells only the details. Instead the paragraphs illustrate the goal of writing with a purpose. Whenever you write, you should always be trying, as in these examples, to use a dominating thought or thoughts to shape the details in the work you are analyzing.

THREE MAJOR STAGES IN THINKING AND WRITING: DISCOVERING IDEAS, MAKING INITIAL DRAFTS, AND COMPLETING THE ESSAY

For both practiced and beginning writers alike, there are three basic stages of composition, and in each of these there are characteristic activities. In the beginning stage, writers try to find the details and thoughts that seem to be right for eventual inclusion in what they are hoping to write. The next (or middle) stage is characterized by written drafts, or sketches—ideas, sentences, paragraphs. The final or completion stage is the forming and ordering of what has previously been done—the creation and determination of a final essay. Although these stages occur in a natural order, they are not separate and distinct, but merge with each other and in effect are fused together. Thus, when you are close to finishing your essay you may find that you need something else, something more, something different. At this point you can easily re-create an earlier stage to discover new details and ideas. You might say that your work is always tentative until you regard it as finished or until you need to turn it in.

THE DISCOVERY OF IDEAS ("BRAINSTORMING")

With the foregoing general goal in mind, let us assume that you have read the work about which you are to write and have made notes and observations on which you are planning to base your thought. You are now ready to consider and plan what to include in your essay. This earliest stage of writing is unpredictable and somewhat frustrating because you are on a search. You do not know quite what you want, for you are reaching out for ideas and you are not yet sure what they are. This process of searching and discovery, sometimes also called brainstorming, requires you to examine any and every subject that your mind can produce.

Just as you are trying to reach for ideas, however, you also should try to introduce purpose and resolution into your thought. You have to zero in on something specific, and develop your ideas through this process. Although what you first write may seem indefinite, the best way to help your thinking is to put your mind, figuratively, into specific channels or grooves, and then to confine your thoughts within these boundaries. What matters is to get your mind going on a particular topic and to get your thoughts down on paper or onto a computer screen. Once you can see your thoughts in front of you, you can work with them and develop them. The following drawing can be helpful to you as an illustration of the various facets of a literary work, or ways of talking about it.

Consider the work you have read—story, poem, play—as the central circle, from which a number of points, like the rays of a star, shine out, some of them prominently, others less so. These points, or rays, are the various subjects, or topics, that you might decide to select in exploration, discovery, and discussion. Because some elements in a work may be more significant than others, the points are not all equal in size. Notice also that the points grow larger as they get nearer to the work, suggesting that once you select a point of discussion you may amplify that point with details and your own observations about the work.

There are many ways to consider literary works, but for now, as a way of getting started, you might choose to explore (1) the work's characters, (2) its historical period and background, (3) the social and economic conditions it depicts, (4) its major ideas, or (5) any of its artistic qualities.[2] These topics, of course, have many subtopics, but any one of them can help you in the concentration you will need for beginning your essay (and also for classroom discussion). All you need is one topic, just one; don't try everything at the same time. Let us see how our illustration can be revised to account for these topics. This time the number of points is reduced to illustrate the points or approaches we have just raised (with an additional and unnamed point to represent all the other approaches that might be used for other studies). These points represent your ways of discovering ideas about the work.

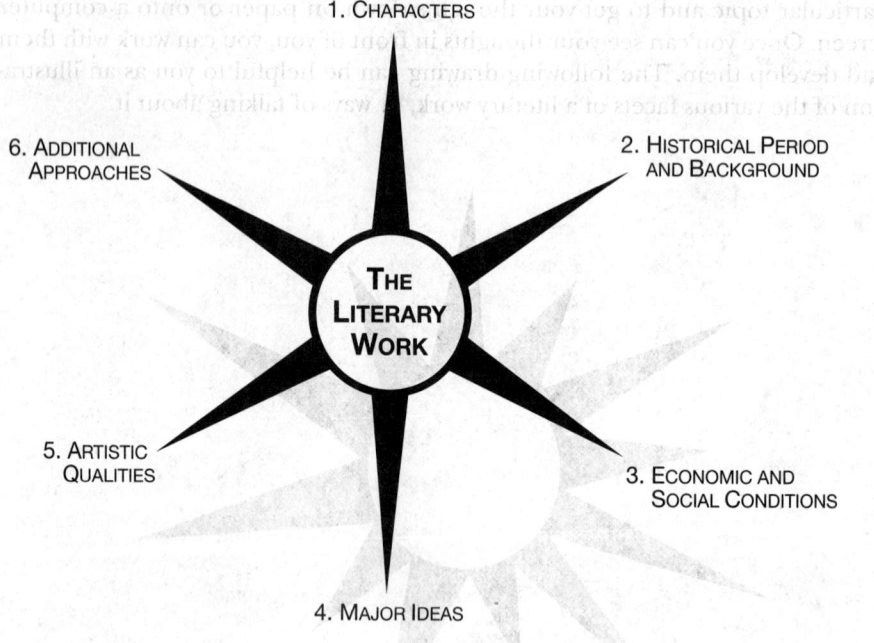

1. CHARACTERS

6. ADDITIONAL
APPROACHES

2. HISTORICAL PERIOD
AND BACKGROUND

THE
LITERARY
WORK

5. ARTISTIC
QUALITIES

3. ECONOMIC AND
SOCIAL CONDITIONS

4. MAJOR IDEAS

[2]Together with additional topics, these critical approaches are discussed in more detail in Chapter 33.

Study the Characters in the Work

It is not necessary to be a practicing psychologist to discuss the persons or characters that you find in a work (see also Chapter 4). You need only to raise issues about the characters and what they do and what they represent. What are the characters like at the work's beginning? What happens to them? Do they do anything that causes them to change, and how are they changed? Are the changes for good or for bad? Why do the characters do the things they do? What do they do correctly? What do they do incorrectly? Why? For example, Mathilde is wrong not to tell Jeanne about her losing the necklace. Such an immediate admission of truth would save her and her husband ten years of hardship and deprivation. But Mathilde doesn't tell the truth. Why not? What do we learn about her character because she avoids or ignores this admission? Is her avoidance understandable? Why?

THE NEED TO PRESENT AN ARGUMENT
WHEN WRITING ESSAYS ABOUT LITERATURE

As you write about literature, you should always keep trying to connect your explanations to a specific **argument;** that is, you are writing about a specific work, but you are trying to *prove*—or *demonstrate*—a point or idea about it. This book provides you with a number of separate subjects relating to the study of literature. As you select one of these and begin writing, however, you are not to explain just that such-and-such a story has a character who changes and grows, or that such-and-such a poem contains the thought that nature creates great beauty. Rather, you should demonstrate the importance of your topic to the work as a whole in relation to a specific point or argument. One example of an argument might be that a story's first-person point of view permits readers to draw their own conclusions about the speaker's character. Another argument might be that the poet's thought is shown in a poem's details about the bustling sounds and sights of animals in springtime.

Let us therefore repeat and stress that your writing should always have an argumentative edge—a goal of demonstrating the truth of your conclusions and clarifying and illuminating your idea about the topic and also about the work. It is here that the accuracy of your choices of details from the work, the soundness of your conclusions, and the cumulative weight of your evidence are essential. You cannot allow your main ideas to rest on one detail alone, but must support your conclusions by showing that the bulk of material leads to them and that they are linked in a reasonable chain of fact and logic. It is such clarification that is the goal of argumentation.

In discussing character, you might also wish to raise the issue of whether the people in the work do or do not do what might normally be expected from people in their circumstances. Do they correspond to type? The idea here is that certain attitudes and behaviors are typical of people at particular stages of life (e.g., children behaving like children, lovers dealing with their relationship, a young couple coping with difficult finances). Thus we might ask questions about whether the usual circumstances experienced by the characters affect them, either by limiting them in some way or by freeing them. What attitudes seem typical of the characters? How do these attitudes govern what the characters do, or don't do? For example, one of the most typical circumstances of life is marriage. According to the positive and ideal type of marriage, a husband and wife should be forthcoming with each other; they should tell each other things and should not conceal what is on their minds. If they have problems, they should discuss them and try to solve them together. In "The Necklace" we see that Mathilde and Loisel do not show these desired qualities, and their absence of communication can be seen as an element in their financial catastrophe. However, during their long years of trouble they work together, for they share a typical quality of honesty, and in this respect they fulfill their role, or type, as a married couple.

An analysis of typical attitudes themselves can also furnish you with material for discussion. For example, Mathilde, who is a member of the lower commercial class, has attitudes that are more appropriate to the upper or leisure class. There is no way that she can bridge this gap, and her frustration causes her to nag her husband to give her enough money to live out her dream, if only for a moment.

Determine the Work's Historical Period and Background

An obvious topic is the historical circumstances of the work. When was the work written? How well does it portray details about life at the time it appeared? What is historically unique about it? To what degree does it help you learn something about the past that you did not previously know? What actions in the work are like or unlike actions going on at the present time? What truthfulness to life do you discover in the work? In "The Necklace," for example, which was published more than a century ago, Mathilde's duty is to stay at home as a housewife—a traditional role—while her husband is the family breadwinner. After the loss of the necklace she can no longer afford domestic help, and she is compelled to do all her own housework and her own shopping. She has none of today's home conveniences such as a dishwasher, microwave, or car. Her husband, a clerk or secretary-copyist, spends his working day copying business records by hand, for at the period of the story there were no typewriters or word processors. Discussing matters like these might also help you with works written during modern times, because our own assumptions, artifacts, and habits will bear analysis and discussion.

Describe the Economic and Social Conditions Depicted in the Work

Closely related to the historical period, an obvious topic to pursue in many works is the economic and social condition of the characters. To what level of life, economically, do the characters belong? How are events in the work related to their condition? How does their money, or lack of it, limit what they do? How do their economic circumstances either restrict or liberate their imaginations? How do their jobs and their apparent income determine their way of life? If we ask some of these questions about "The Necklace," as we have seen, we find that Mathilde and her husband are greatly burdened by their lack of money, and also that their obligation to repay their huge loan drives them into economic want and sacrifice.

An important part of the economic and social analysis of literature is the consideration of female characters and what it means to be a woman. This is the feminist analysis of literature, which asks questions like these: What role is Mathilde compelled to take as a result of her sex and family background? How does Jeanne's way of life contrast with that of Mathilde? What can Mathilde do with her life? To what degree is she limited by her role as a housewife? Does she have any chance of an occupation outside the home? How does her economic condition cause her to yearn for better things? What causes her to borrow the necklace? What is her contribution, as a woman, to the repayment of the loans? Should Mathilde's limited life in "The Necklace" be considered as a political argument for greater freedom for women? Once you start asking questions like these, you will find that your thinking is developing along with your ideas for writing.

The feminist approach to the interpretation of literature has been well established, and it will usually provide you with a way to discuss a work. It is also possible, of course, to analyze what a work says about the condition of being a man, or being a child. Depending on the work, many of the questions important in a feminist approach are not dissimilar to those you might use if you are dealing with childhood or male adulthood.

One of the most important social and economic topics is that of race and ethnicity. What happens in the work that seems to occur mainly because of the race of the characters? Is the author pointing out any deprivations, any absence of opportunity, any oppression? What do the characters do under such circumstances? Do they succeed or not? Are they negative? Are they angry? Are they resolute and determined? Your aim in an inquiry of this type should be to concentrate on actions and ideas in the work that are clearly related to race.

Explain the Work's Major Ideas

One of the major ways of focusing on a work is to zero in on various ideas and values or issues to be discovered there. What ideas might we gain from the story of the lengthy but needless sacrifice and drudgery experienced by Mathilde and her husband? One obvious and acceptable idea is presented by the speaker, namely, that even the smallest, most accidental incident can cause immense consequences. This is an idea that we might expand and illustrate in an entire essay. Here are some other ideas that we also might pursue, all of them based on the story's actions:

- Many actions have unforeseeable and uncontrollable consequences.
- Lack of communication is a major cause of hardship.
- Adversity brings out a character's good qualities.
- Mutual effort enables people to overcome difficulties.

These ideas are all to be found in Maupassant's story. In other works, of course, we may find comparable ideas, in addition to other major ideas and issues.

Learn about and Describe the Work's Artistic Qualities

There are many possible topics for studying a work's artistic qualities, but basically here you may consider matters such as the work's plan or organization and the author's narrative method, writing style, or poetic techniques. Thus, in "The Necklace," we observe that almost the entire story develops with Mathilde at the center (narrative method; see also Chapter 5, on point of view). At first, the story brings us close to Mathilde, for we are told of her dissatisfaction and impatience with her surroundings. As the story progresses, the storyteller/speaker presents her person and actions more objectively and also more distantly. Another artistic approach would be to determine the story's pattern of development—how, chronologically, the loss of the necklace brings financial misfortune to the Loisels. We might also look for the author's inclusion of symbols in the story, such as the name of the street where the Loisels originally live, their move to an attic flat, or the roughness of Mathilde's hands as a result of her constant housework. There are many other ways to consider the formal aspects of a literary work.

ASSEMBLING MATERIALS AND BEGINNING TO WRITE

By this time you will already have been focusing on your topic and will have assembled much that you can put into your essay. You should now aim to develop paragraphs and sketches of what you will eventually include. There is much that you can do. You should think constantly of the point or argument you want to develop, but invariably digressions will occur, together with other difficulties—false starts, dead ends, total cessation of thought, digressions, despair, hopelessness, and general frustration. Remember, however, that it is important just to start. Jump right in and start writing anything at all—no matter how unacceptable your first efforts may seem—and force yourself to deal with the materials. The writing down of ideas does not commit you. You should not think that these first ideas are untouchable and holy just because you have written them on paper or on your computer screen. You can throw them out in favor of new ideas, you can make cross-outs and changes, and you can move paragraphs or even sections around as you wish. However, if you do not start writing, your first thoughts will remain locked in your mind and you will have nothing to work with. It is essential to accept the uncertainties in the writing process and make them work *for* you rather than *against* you.

Build on Your Original Notes

You need to get your mind going by mining your notebook or computer file for useful things you have already written. Thus, let us use an observation in our original set of notes—"The attic flat is important"—in reference to the poorer rooms where Mathilde and her husband live while they are paying back their creditors. With such a note as a start, you might develop a number of ideas to support an argument about Mathilde's character, as in the following:

The attic flat is important. Early in the story, in her apartment, Mathilde is dreamy and impractical. She seems delicate, but after losing the necklace, she is delicate no longer. She becomes a worker after they move to the flat. She does a lot more when living there.

In the flat, Mathilde has to sacrifice. She gives up her servant, washes greasy pots, climbs stairs carrying buckets of water, sloshes water around to clean floors, and does all the clothes washing by hand.

When living in the flat she gets stronger, but she also becomes loud and common. She argues with shopkeepers to get the lowest prices. She stops caring for herself. There is a reversal here, from incapable and well groomed to capable but coarse.

In this way, even in an assertion as basic as "The attic flat is important," the process of putting together details is a form of concentrated thought that leads you creatively forward. You can express thoughts and conclusions that you could not express at the beginning. Such an exercise in stretching your mind leads you to put elements of the work together in ways that create ideas for outstanding essays.

Trace Patterns of Action and Thought

You can also discover ideas by making a list or scheme for the story or main idea. What conflicts appear? Do these conflicts exist between people, groups, or ideas? How does the author resolve them? Is one force, idea, or side the winner? Why? How do you respond to the winner or to the loser? Using this method, you might make a list similar to this one:

> At the beginning, Mathilde is a fish out of water. She dreams of wealth, but her life is drab and her husband is dull.
>
> Fantasies make her even more dissatisfied; she punishes herself by thinking of a wealthy life.
>
> When the Loisels get the dinner invitation, Mathilde pouts and whines. Her husband feels discomfort when she manipulates him into buying her an expensive party dress.
>
> Her world of daydreams hurts her real life when her desire for wealth causes her to borrow the necklace. Losing the necklace is just plain bad luck.

These arguments all focus on Mathilde's character, but you may wish to trace other patterns you find in the story. If you start planning an essay about another pattern, be sure to account for all the actions and scenes that relate to your topic. Otherwise, you may miss a piece of evidence that could lead you to new conclusions.

Raise and Answer Your Own Questions

A habit you should always cultivate is to raise and answer questions as you read. The *Guidelines for Reading* will help you formulate questions (pp. 12–13), but you can raise additional questions like these:

- What is happening as the work unfolds? How does an action at the work's beginning bring about the work's later actions and speeches?
- Who are the main characters? What seems unusual or different about what they do in the work?
- What conclusions can be drawn about the work's actions, scenes, and situations? Explain these conclusions.
- What are the characters and speakers like? What do they do and say about themselves, their goals, the people around them, their families, their friends, their work, and the general circumstances of their lives?
- What kinds of words do the characters use: formal or informal words, slang or profanity?
- What literary conventions and devices have you discovered, and how do these affect the work? (When an author addresses readers directly, for example, that is a convention; when a comparison is used, that is a device, which might be either a metaphor or a simile.)

Of course, you can raise other questions as you reread the piece, or you can be left with one or two major questions that you decide to pursue.

Use the Plus-Minus, Pro-Con, or Either-Or Method for Putting Ideas Together

A common and very helpful method of discovering ideas is to develop a set of contrasts: plus-minus, pro-con, either-or. Let us suppose a plus-minus method of considering the following question about Mathilde: Should she be "admired" (plus) or "condemned" (minus)?

PLUS: ADMIRED?	MINUS: CONDEMNED?
After she cries when they get the invitation, she recovers with a "strong effort"—maybe she doesn't want her husband to feel bad.	She wants to be envied and admired only for being attractive and intriguing, not for more important qualities. She seems spoiled and selfish.
She scores a great victory at the dance. She really does have the power to charm and captivate.	She wastes her time in daydreaming about things she can't have, and she whines because she is unhappy.
Once she loses the necklace, she and her husband become poor and deprived. But she does "her share . . . completely, heroically" (paragraph 98) to make up for the loss.	Even though the Loisels live poorly, Mathilde manipulates her husband into giving her more money than they can afford for a party dress.
Even when she is poor, she dreams about that marvelous, shining moment at the great ball. This is pathetic, because Mathilde gets worse than she deserves.	She assumes that her friend Jeanne would think her a thief if she admitted losing the necklace. Shouldn't she have had more confidence in Jeanne?
At the end, after everything is paid back, and her reputation is secure, Mathilde confesses the loss to Jeanne.	She becomes loud and coarse and haggles about pennies, thus undergoing a cheapening of her person and manner.

By putting contrasting observations side by side in this way, you will find that ideas will start to come naturally and will be helpful to you when you begin writing, regardless of how you finally organize your essay. It's possible, for example, that you might develop either column as the argumentative basis of an essay, or you might use your notes to support the idea that Mathilde is too complex to be either wholly admired or wholly condemned. You might also want to introduce an entirely new topic of development, such as that Mathilde should be pitied rather than condemned or admired. In short, arranging materials in the plus-minus pattern is a powerful way to discover ideas—a truly helpful habit of promoting thought—that can lead to ways of development that you do not at first realize.

Use Your Writing to Develop Your Thinking

It is always important to write down what you are thinking for, as a principle, unwritten thought is incomplete thought. Make a practice of writing your observations about the work, in addition to any questions that occur to you. This is an exciting step in preliminary writing because it can be useful when you write later drafts. You will discover that looking at what you have written not only can enable you to correct and improve the writing you have done, but also can lead you to recognize that you need more. The process goes just about like this: "Something needs to be added here—important details that my reader will not have noticed, new support for my argument, a new idea that has just occurred to me, a significant connection to link my thoughts." If you follow such a process, you will be using your own written ideas to create new ideas. You will be advancing your own abilities as a thinker and writer.

The processes just described of searching for ideas, or brainstorming, are useful for you at any stage of composition. Even when you are fairly close to finishing your essay, you might suddenly recognize that you need to add something more (or subtract something you don't like). When that happens, you may return to the discovery or brainstorming process to initiate and develop new ideas and new arguments.

❧ DRAFTING THE ESSAY

As you use the brainstorming and focusing techniques, you are also in fact beginning your essay. You will need to revise your ideas as connections among them become more clear and as you reexamine the work to discover details to support the argument you are making. By this stage, however, you already have many of the raw materials you need for developing your topic.

Base Your Essay on a Central Idea or Central Argument

By definition, an essay *is an organized, connected, and fully developed set of paragraphs that expand on a* **central idea** *or* **central argument.** All parts of an essay should contribute to the reader's understanding of the idea. To achieve unity and completeness, each paragraph refers to the argument and demonstrates how selected details from the work relate to it and support it. The central idea helps you control and shape your essay, just as it also provides guidance for your reader.

A successful essay about literature is a brief but thorough (not exhaustive) examination of a literary work in light of topics like those we have already raised, such as character, background, economic conditions, circumstances of gender, major ideas, artistic qualities, or any additional topic such as point of view and symbolism. Central ideas or arguments might be (1) that a character is strong and tenacious, or (2) that the story shows the unpredictability of action, or (3) that the point of view makes the action seem "distant and objective," or (4) that a major symbol governs the actions and thoughts of the major characters. In essays on these topics, all materials must be tied to such central ideas or arguments. Thus, it is a fact that Mathilde in "The Necklace" endures ten years of slavish work and sacrifice as she and her husband accumulate enough money to repay their monumental debt. This we know, but it is not relevant to an essay on her character unless you connect it by a central argument showing how it demonstrates one of her major traits—her growing strength and perseverance.

Look through all of your ideas for one or two that catch your eye for development. In all the early stages of preliminary writing, the chances are that you have already discovered at least a few ideas that are more thought-provoking, or more important, than the others.

WRITING BY HAND, TYPEWRITER, OR WORD PROCESSOR

Thinking and writing are interdependent processes. If you don't get your thoughts into words in some way, your thinking will be incomplete. It is therefore vital for you to use the writing process as the means of developing your ideas. For many students, it is a psychological necessity to carry out this process by pencil, pen, or typewriter. If you are one of these students, make your written or typed responses on only one side of your paper or note cards. This strategy will enable you to spread your materials out and get an actual physical overview of them when you begin writing. Everything will be open to you; none of your ideas will be hidden on the back of the paper.

Today, word processing is thoroughly established as an indispensable tool for writers. The word processor can help you develop ideas, for it quickly enables you to eliminate unworkable thoughts and replace them with others. You can move sentences and paragraphs tentatively into new contexts, test how they look, and move them somewhere else if you choose.

In addition, with the rapid printers now available, you can print even the initial and tentative stages of writing. Using the printed draft, you can make additional notes, corrections, and suggestions for further development. With the marked-up draft as a guide, you can go back to the word processor and fill in your changes and improvements, repeating this procedure as often as you can. This facility makes the machine an incentive for improvement, right up to your final draft.

Word processing also helps you in the final preparation of your essays. Studies have shown that errors and awkward sentences are frequently found at the bottoms of pages prepared by hand or with a conventional typewriter. The reason is that writers hesitate to make improvements when they get near the end of a page because they shun the dreariness of starting the page over. Word processors eliminate this difficulty completely. Changes can be made anywhere in the draft, at any time, without damage to the final appearance of your essay.

Regardless of your writing method, you should always remember that unwritten thought is incomplete thought. You cannot lay everything out at once on the word processor's screen. You can see only a small part of what you are writing. Therefore, somewhere in your writing process, you need to prepare a complete draft of what you have written. A clean, readable draft permits you to gather everything together and to make even more improvements through revision.

Once you choose an idea you think you can work with, write it as a complete sentence that is essential to the argument of your essay. A simple phrase such as "setting and character" does not focus thought the way a sentence does. A sentence moves the topic toward new exploration and discovery because it combines a topic with an outcome, such as "The setting of 'The Necklace' reflects Mathilde's character." You can choose to be even more specific: "Mathilde's strengths and weaknesses are reflected in the real and imaginary places in 'The Necklace.' "

Now that you have phrased a single, central idea or argument for your essay, you also have established a guide by which you can accept, reject, rearrange, and change the ideas you have been planning to develop. You can now draft a few paragraphs (which you may base on some of the sketches you have already made; always use as much as you can of your early observations) to see whether your idea seems valid, or you can decide that it would be more helpful to make an outline or a list before you do more writing. In either case, you should use your notes for evidence to connect to your central idea. If you need to bolster your argument with more supporting details and ideas, go once again to the techniques of discovery and brainstorming.

Using the central idea that the changes in the story's settings reflect Mathilde's character might produce a paragraph like the following, which presents an argument about her negative qualities:

> The original apartment in the Street of Martyrs and the dream world of wealthy places both show negative sides of Mathilde's character. The real-life apartment, though livable, is shabby. The furnishings all bring out her discontent. The shabbiness makes her think only of luxuriousness, and having one servant girl causes her to dream of having many servants. The luxury of her dream life heightens her unhappiness with what she actually has.

In such a preliminary draft, in which the purpose is to connect details and thoughts to the major idea, many details from the story are used in support. In the final draft, this kind of support is essential.

Create a Thesis Sentence

With your central idea or argument as your focus, you can decide which of the earlier observations and ideas can be developed further. Your goal is to establish a number of major topics to support your argument and to express them in a **thesis sentence**—an organizing sentence that contains the major topics you plan to treat in your essay. Suppose you choose three ideas from your discovery stage of development. If you put the central idea at the left and the list of topics at the right, you have the shape of the thesis sentence. Note that the first two topics below are taken from the discovery paragraph:

CENTRAL IDEA	TOPICS
The setting of "The Necklace" reflects Mathilde's character.	1. First apartment
	2. Dream-life mansion rooms
	3. Attic flat

This arrangement leads to the following thesis statement or thesis sentence:

> Mathilde's character growth is related to her first apartment, her dream-life mansion rooms, and her attic flat.

You can revise the thesis sentence at any stage of the writing process if you find that you do not have enough evidence from the work to support it. Perhaps a new topic will occur to you, and you can include it, appropriately, as a part of your thesis sentence.

As we have seen, the central idea or central argument is the *glue* of the essay. The thesis sentence lists the parts to be fastened together—that is, the topics in which the central idea is to be demonstrated and argued. To alert your readers to your essay's structure, the thesis sentence is usually placed at the end of the introductory paragraph, just before the body of the essay.

WRITING A FIRST DRAFT

To write a first draft, you support the points of your thesis sentence with your notes and discovery materials. You can alter, reject, and rearrange ideas and details as you wish, as long as you change your thesis sentence to account for the changes (a major reason why many writers write their introductions last). The thesis sentence just shown contains three topics (it could be two, or four, or more) to be used in forming the body of the essay.

Begin Each Paragraph with a Topic Sentence

Just as the organization of the *entire essay* is based on the thesis, the form of each *paragraph* is based on its **topic sentence.** A topic sentence is an assertion about how a topic from the predicate of the thesis statement supports the argument contained or implied in the central idea. The first topic in our example is the relationship of Mathilde's character to her first apartment, and the resulting paragraph should emphasize this relationship. If your topic is the coarsening of her character during the ten-year travail, you can then form a topic sentence by connecting the trait with the location, as follows:

The attic flat reflects the coarsening of Mathilde's character.

Beginning with this sentence, the paragraph will present details that argue how Mathilde's rough, heavy housework changes her behavior, appearance, and general outlook.

USING VERB TENSES IN THE DISCUSSION OF LITERARY WORKS

Literary works spring into life with each and every reading. You may thus assume that everything happening takes place in the present, and when writing about literature you should use the *present tense of verbs*. It is correct to say "Mathilde and her husband *work* and *economize* [not *worked* and *economized*] for ten years to pay off the 18,000-franc debt they *undertake* [not *undertook*] to pay for the lost necklace."

When you consider an author's ideas, the present tense is also proper, on the principle that the words of an author are just as alive and current today (and tomorrow) as they were at the moment of writing, even if this same author has been dead for hundreds or even thousands of years.

Because it is incorrect to shift tenses inappropriately, you may encounter a problem when you refer to actions that have occurred prior to the time of the main action. An instance is Hemingway's "Soldier's Home" (Chapter 7), in which the main character is discontented and unsettled as a result of his combat experiences in Europe during World War I. In such a situation it is important to keep details in order, and thus you can use the past tense as long as you make the relationship clear between past and present, as in this example: "Krebs *cannot settle down* [present tense] because he *is always thinking* [present tense] about the actions he *went through* [past tense] during the fighting in Europe." This use of the past influencing the present is correct because it corresponds to the cause-and-effect relationship brought out in the story.

A problem also arises when you introduce historical or biographical details about a work or author. It is appropriate to use the *past tense* for such details if they genuinely do belong to the past. Thus it is correct to state "Shakespeare *lived* from 1564 to 1616," or that "Shakespeare *wrote* his tragedy *Hamlet* in about 1600–1601." It is also permissible to mix past and present tenses when you are treating historical facts about a literary work and are also considering it as a living text. Of prime importance is to keep things straight. Here is an example showing how past tenses (in bold) and present tenses (in italic) may be used when appropriate:

Because Hamlet **was** first **performed** in about 1601, Shakespeare most probably **wrote** it shortly before this time. In the play, a tragedy, Shakespeare *treats* an act of vengeance, but more importantly he *demonstrates* the difficulty of ever learning the exact truth. The hero, Prince Hamlet, *is* the focus of this difficulty, for the task of revenge *is assigned* to him by the Ghost of his father. Though the Ghost *claims* that his brother, Claudius, *is* his murderer, Hamlet *is* not able to verify this claim.

Here, the historical details are in the past tense, while all details about the play *Hamlet*, including Shakespeare as the creating author whose ideas and words are still alive, are in the present.

As a general principle, you will be right most of the time if you use the present tense exclusively for literary details and the past tense for historical details. When in doubt, however, *consult your instructor*.

Select Only One Topic—No More—for Each Paragraph

You should treat each separate topic in a single paragraph—one topic, one paragraph. However, if a topic seems especially difficult, long, and heavily detailed, you can divide it into two or more subtopics, each receiving a separate paragraph of its own—two or more subtopics, two or more separate paragraphs. Should you make this division, your topic then is really a section, and each paragraph in the section should have its own topic sentence.

Use Your Topic Sentence as the Basis of Your Paragraph Development

Once you choose a topic sentence, you can use it to focus your observations and conclusions. Let us see how our topic about the attic flat can be developed in a paragraph of argument:

> <u>The attic flat reflects the coarsening of Mathilde's character</u>. Maupassant emphasizes the burdens Mathilde endures to save money, such as mopping floors, cleaning greasy and encrusted pots and pans, taking out the garbage, and washing clothes and dishes by hand. This work makes her rough and coarse, an effect also shown by her giving up care of her hair and hands, wearing the cheapest dresses possible, haggling with the local shopkeepers, and becoming loud and penny-pinching. If at the beginning she is delicate and attractive, at the end she is unpleasant and coarse.

Here, details from the story are introduced to provide support for the topic sentence. All the subjects—the hard work, the lack of personal care, the wearing of cheap dresses, and the haggling with the shopkeepers—are introduced not to retell the story but rather to exemplify the argument the writer is making about Mathilde's character.

DEVELOPING AN OUTLINE

So far we have been creating an **outline**—that is, a skeletal plan of organization. Some writers never use any outline but prefer informal lists of ideas; others always rely on outlines. Still others insist that they cannot make an outline until they have finished writing. Regardless of your preference, your final essay should have a tight structure. Therefore, you should use a guiding outline to develop and shape your essay.

The outline we are concerned with here is the **analytical sentence outline.** This type is easier to create than it sounds. It consists of (1) an introduction, including the central idea and the thesis sentence, together with (2) topic sentences that are to be used in each paragraph of the body, followed by (3) a conclusion. When applied to the subject we have been developing, such an outline looks like this:

Title: *Setting in "The Necklace" Is Connected to Mathilde's Character*

1. **Introduction**
   a. *Central idea*: Maupassant uses setting to show Mathilde's character.
   b. *Thesis statement*: Her character growth is brought out by her first apartment, her daydreams about elegant rooms in a mansion, and her attic flat.
2. **Body**: *Topic sentences* a, b, and c (and d, e, and f, if necessary)
   a. Details about her first apartment explain her dissatisfaction and depression.
   b. Her daydreams about mansion rooms are like the apartment because they too make her unhappy.
   c. The attic flat reflects the coarsening of her character.
3. **Conclusion** *Topic sentence*: All details in the story, particularly the setting, are focused on the character of Mathilde.

The *conclusion* may be a summary of the body; it may evaluate the main idea; it may briefly suggest further points of discussion; or it may be a reflection on the details of the body.

Use the Outline in Developing Your Essay

The demonstrative essays included throughout this book are organized according to the principles of the analytical sentence outline. To emphasize the shaping effect of these outlines, all central ideas, thesis sentences, and topic sentences are underlined. In your own writing, you can underline or italicize these "skeletal" sentences as a check on your organization. Unless your instructor requires such markings, however, remove them in your final drafts.

❧ DEMONSTRATIVE STUDENT ESSAY (FIRST DRAFT)

The following demonstrative essay is a first draft of the subject we have been developing. It follows our outline, and it includes details from the story in support of the various topics. It is by no means, however, as good a piece of writing as it could be. The draft omits a topic, some additional details, and some new insights that are included in the second draft, which follows (pp. 41–42). It therefore reveals the need to make improvements through additional brainstorming and discovery-prewriting techniques.

How Setting in "The Necklace" Is Related to the Character of Mathilde

[1]   In "The Necklace" Guy de Maupassant does not give much detail about the setting. He does not even describe the necklace itself, which is the central object in his plot, but he says only that it is "superb" (paragraph 47). Rather, he uses the

setting to reflect the character of the central figure, Mathilde Loisel.* All his details are presented to bring out her traits. Her character growth is related to her first apartment, her dream-life mansion rooms, and her attic flat.†

[2] Details about her first apartment explain her dissatisfaction and depression. The walls are "drab," the furniture "threadbare," and the curtains "ugly" (paragraph 3). There is only a simple country girl to do the housework. The tablecloth is not changed daily, and the best dinner dish is boiled beef. Mathilde has no evening clothes, only a theater dress that she does not like. These details show her dissatisfaction about her life with her low-salaried husband.

[3] Her dream-life images of wealth are like the apartment because they too make her unhappy. In her daydreams about life in a mansion, the rooms are large, filled with expensive furniture and bric-a-brac, and draped in silk. She imagines private rooms for intimate talks, and big dinners with delicacies like trout and quail. With dreams of such a rich home, she feels even more despair about her modest apartment on the Street of Martyrs in Paris.

[4] The attic flat reflects the coarsening of Mathilde's character. Maupassant emphasizes the burdens she endures to save money, such as mopping floors, cleaning greasy and encrusted pots and pans, taking out the garbage, and washing clothes and dishes by hand. This work makes her rough and coarse, a fact also shown by her giving up care of her hair and hands, wearing the cheapest dresses possible, haggling with local shopkeepers, and becoming loud and penny-pinching. If at the beginning she is delicate and attractive, at the end she is unpleasant and coarse.

[5] In summary, Maupassant focuses everything in the story, including the setting, on the character of Mathilde. He does not include anything extra. Thus he says little about the big party scene, but emphasizes the necessary detail that Mathilde was a great "success" (paragraph 52). It is this detail that brings out some of her early attractiveness and charm (despite her more usual unhappiness). Thus in "The Necklace," Maupassant uses setting as a means to his end-- the story of Mathilde and her needless sacrifice.

DEVELOPING AND STRENGTHENING ESSAYS THROUGH REVISION

After finishing a first draft like this one, you may wonder what more you can do. You have read the work several times, used discovery and brainstorming techniques to establish ideas to write about, made an outline of your ideas, and written a full draft. How can you do better?

The best way to begin is to observe that a major mistake writers make when writing about literature is to do no more than retell a story or summarize an idea. Retelling a story shows only that you have read it, not that you have thought about it. Writing a good essay requires you to arrange a pattern of argument and thought.

---

*Central idea.
†Thesis sentence.

Use Your Own Order of References

There are many ways to escape the trap of summarizing stories and to set up a pattern of development. One way is to stress your own order when referring to parts of a work. Rearrange details to suit your own central idea or argument. It is often important to write first about the conclusion or middle. Should you find that you have followed the chronological order of the work instead of stressing your own order, you can use one of the preliminary writing techniques to figure out new ways to connect your materials. The principle is that you should introduce details about the work *only* to support the points you wish to make. Details for the sake of detail are unnecessary.

Use Literary Material as Evidence Supporting Your Argument

When you write, you are like a detective using clues as evidence for building a case, or a lawyer citing evidence to support an argument. Your goal is to convince your readers of your knowledge and the reasonableness of your conclusions. It is vital to use evidence convincingly so that your readers can follow your ideas. Let us look briefly at two drafts of a new example to see how writing can be improved by the pointed use of details. These are from drafts of an essay on the character of Mathilde.

PARAGRAPH 1

The major extenuating detail about Mathilde is that she seems to be isolated, locked away from other people. She and her husband do not talk to each other much, except about external things. He speaks about his liking for boiled beef, and she states that she cannot accept the big invitation because she has no nice dresses. Once she gets the dress, she complains because she has no jewelry. Even when borrowing the necklace from Jeanne Forrestier, she does not say much. When she and her husband discover that the necklace is lost, they simply go over the details, and Loisel dictates a letter of explanation, which Mathilde writes in her own hand. Even when she meets Jeanne on the Champs-Elysées, Mathilde does not say a great deal about her life but only goes through enough details about the loss and replacement of the necklace to make Jeanne exclaim about the needlessness of the ten-years sacrifice.

PARAGRAPH 2

The major flaw of Mathilde's character is that she is withdrawn and uncommunicative, apparently unwilling or unable to form an intimate relationship. For example, she and her husband do not talk to each other much, except about external things such as his taste for boiled beef and her lack of a party dress and jewelry. With such an uncommunicative marriage, one might suppose that she would be more open with her close friend, Jeanne Forrestier, but Mathilde does not say much even to her. This flaw hurts her greatly, because if she were more open she might have explained the loss and avoided the horrible sacrifice. This lack of openness, along with her self-indulgent dreaminess, is her biggest defect.

A comparison of these paragraphs shows that the first has more words than the second (156 compared to 119) but that it is more appropriate for a rough than a final draft because the writer does little more than retell the story.

Paragraph 1 is cluttered with details that do not support any conclusions. If you try to find what it says about Maupassant's actual use of Mathilde's solitary traits in "The Necklace," you will get little help. The writer needs to revise the paragraph by eliminating details that do not support the central idea.

On the other hand, the details in paragraph 2 actually do support the declared topic. Phrases such as "for example," "with such," and "this lack" show that the writer of paragraph 2 has assumed that the audience knows the story and now wants help in interpretation. Paragraph 2 therefore guides readers by connecting the details to the topic. It uses these details as evidence, *not* as a retelling of actions. By contrast, paragraph 1 recounts a number of relevant actions but does not connect them to the topic. More details, of course, could have been added to the second paragraph, but they are unnecessary because the paragraph develops the argument with the details used. There are many qualities that make good writing good, but one of the most important is shown in a comparison of the two paragraphs: *In good writing, no details are included unless they are used as supporting evidence in a pattern of thought and argument.*

Always Keep to Your Point; Stick to It Tenaciously

To show another distinction between first- and second-draft writing, let us consider a third example. The following *unrevised* paragraph, in which the writer assumes an audience that is interested in the relationship of economics to literature, is drawn from an essay on the idea of economic determinism in "The Necklace." In this paragraph the writer is trying to argue the point that economic circumstances underlie a number of incidents in the story. The idea is to assert that Mathilde's difficulties result not from character but rather from financial restrictions.

> More important than chance in governing life is the idea that people are controlled by economic circumstances. Mathilde, as is shown at the story's opening, is born poor. Therefore she doesn't get the right doors opened for her, and she settles down to marriage with a minor clerk, Loisel. With a vivid imagination and a burning desire for luxury, seeming to be born only for a life of ease and wealth, she finds that her poor home brings out her daydreams of expensive surroundings. She taunts her husband when he brings the big invitation, because she does not have a suitable (read "expensive") dress. Once she gets the dress it is jewelry she lacks, and she borrows that and loses it. The loss of the necklace means great trouble because it forces the Loisels to borrow heavily and to struggle financially for ten years.

This paragraph begins with an effective topic sentence, indicating that the writer has a good plan. The remaining part, however, shows how easily writers can be diverted from their objective. The flaw is that the material of the paragraph, while accurate, is not clearly connected to the topic. Once the second sentence is under way, the paragraph gets lost in a retelling of events, and the promising topic sentence is forgotten. The paragraph therefore shows that the use of detail alone will not support an intended meaning or argument. *Writers must do the connecting themselves to make sure that all relationships are explicitly clear.* This point cannot be overstressed.

Let us see how the problem can be treated. If the ideal paragraph can be schematized with line drawings, we might say that the paragraph's topic should be a straight line, moving toward and reaching a specific goal (the topic or argument of the paragraph), with an exemplifying line moving away from the straight line briefly to bring in evidence, but returning to the line to demonstrate the relevance of each new fact. Thus, the ideal scheme looks like this, with a straight line touched a number of times by an undulating line:

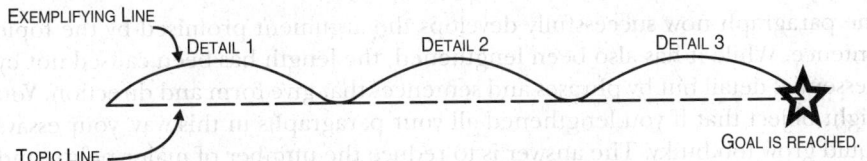

Notice that the exemplifying line, waving to illustrate how documentation or exemplification is to be used, always returns to the topic line.

A scheme for the faulty paragraph on "The Necklace," however, would look like this, with the line never returning but flying out into space:

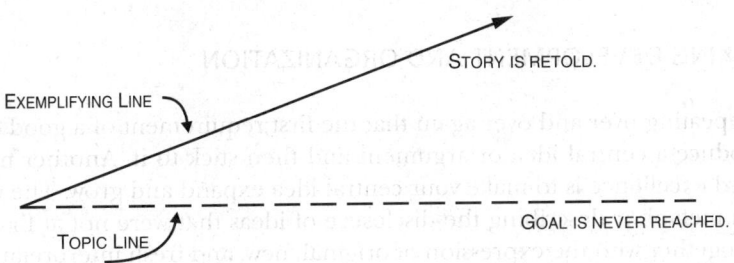

How might the faulty paragraph be improved? The best way is to remind the reader again and again of the topic and to use examples from the text in support.

As our model wavy-line diagram indicates, each time a topic is mentioned, the undulating line merges with the straight, or central-idea line. This relationship of argument to illustrative examples should prevail no matter what subject you write about, and you have to be tenacious in forming these connecting relationships. If you are analyzing *point of view*, for example, you should keep connecting your material to the speaker, or narrator, and the same applies to topics such as character, theme, or setting. According to this principle, we might revise the paragraph on economic determinism in "The Necklace" as follows. (Parts of sentences stressing the relationship of the examples to the topic of the paragraph are underlined.)

> *More important than chance in governing life is the idea that people are controlled by economic circumstances.* <u>As illustration</u>, the speaker begins by emphasizing that Mathilde, the main character, is born poor. Therefore she doesn't get the right doors opened for her, and she settles down to marriage with a minor clerk, Loisel.

<u>In keeping with the idea</u>, her vivid imagination and burning desire for luxury feed on her weakness of character as she feels deep unhappiness and depression because of the contrast between her daydreams of expensive surroundings and the poor home she actually has. <u>These straitened economic circumstances</u> inhibit her relationship with her husband, and she taunts him when he brings the big invitation because she does not have a suitable (read "expensive") dress. As a merging of her unrealistic dream life with actual reality, <u>her borrowing of the necklace suggests the impossibility of overcoming economic restrictions</u>. In the context of the idea, the ten-year sacrifice to pay for the lost necklace <u>demonstrates that being poor keeps people down, destroying their dreams and hopes of a better life.</u>

The paragraph now successfully develops the argument promised by the topic sentence. While it has also been lengthened, the length has been caused not by inessential detail but by phrases and sentences that give form and direction. You might object that if you lengthened all your paragraphs in this way, your essays would grow too bulky. The answer is to reduce the number of major points and paragraphs, on the theory that *it is better to develop a few topics pointedly than to develop many pointlessly*. Revising for the purpose of strengthening central and topic ideas requires that you either throw out some topics or else incorporate them as subpoints in the topics you keep. To control your writing in this way can result only in improvement.

✓ CHECKING DEVELOPMENT AND ORGANIZATION

It bears repeating over and over again that the first requirement of a good essay is to introduce a central idea or argument and then stick to it. Another major step toward excellence is to make your central idea expand and grow. The word *growth* is a metaphor describing the disclosure of ideas that were not at first noticeable, together with the expression of original, new, and fresh interpretations.

Try to Be Original

In everything you write, now and in the future, it is important that you try to be original. You might claim that originality is impossible because you are writing about someone else's work. "The author has said everything," might be the argument, "and therefore I can do little more than follow the story." This claim rests on the mistaken assumption that you have no choice in selecting material and no opportunity to have individual thoughts and make original contributions.

But you do have choices and opportunities to be original. You really do. One obvious area of originality is the development and formulation of your central idea. For example, a natural first response to "The Necklace" is "The story is about a woman who loses a borrowed necklace and endures hardship to help pay for it." But this response does not promise an argument because it refers only to events in the story and not to any idea. You can turn the sentence toward an argument, however, if you call the hardship "needless." Just this word alone demands that you explain the differences between needed and unneeded hardships, and your application of these differences to the heroine's plight would produce an original essay. Even better and more original insights could result if the topic of the budding essay were to connect the dreamy, withdrawn traits of the main character to her misfortunes. A resulting central idea might be "People themselves create their own difficulties." Such an argument would require you to define not only the personal but also the representative nature of Mathilde's experiences, an avenue of exploration that could produce much in the way of a fresh, original essay about "The Necklace."

You can also develop your ability to treat your subject originally if you plan the body of the essay to build up to what you think is your most important and incisive idea. As examples of such planning, the following brief outline suggests how a central idea can be widened and expanded:

Subject: *Mathilde Grows as a Character in "The Necklace"*

1. She has normal daydreams about a better life.
2. In trying to make her daydreams seem real, she takes a risk but then loses.
3. She develops by facing her mistake and working hard to correct it.

The list shows how a subject can be enlarged if you treat your exemplifying topic in increasing order of importance. In this case, the order moves from Mathilde's habit of daydreaming to her growing strength of character. The pattern shows how you can meet two primary standards of excellence in writing—organization and growth.

Clearly, you should always try to develop your central idea or argument. Constantly adhere to your topic, and constantly develop it. Nurture it and make it grow. Admittedly, in a short essay you will be able to move only a short distance with an idea or argument, but you should never be satisfied to leave the idea exactly where you found it. To the degree that you can learn to develop your ideas, you will receive recognition for increasingly original writing.

Write with Specific Readers in Mind

Whenever you write, you must decide how much detail to discuss. Usually you base this decision on your judgment of your readers. For example, if you assume that they have not read the work, you will need to include a short summary as background. Otherwise, they may not understand your argument.

Consider, too, whether your readers have any special interests or concerns. If they are particularly interested in politics, sociology, religion, or psychology, for example, you may need to select and develop your materials along one of these lines.

Your instructor will let you know who your audience is. Usually, it will be your instructor or your fellow students. They will be familiar with the work and will not expect you to retell a story or summarize an argument. Rather, they will want you to explain and interpret the work in the light of your main assertions about it. Thus, you can omit details that do not exemplify and support your argument, even if these details are important parts of the work. What you write should always be based on your developing idea together with your assessment of your readers.

USING EXACT, COMPREHENSIVE, AND FORCEFUL LANGUAGE

In addition to being original, organized, and well developed, the best writing is exact, comprehensive, and forceful. At any stage of the composition process, you should try to correct and improve your earliest sentences and paragraphs, which usually need to be rethought, reworded, and rearranged.

Try to make your sentences meaningful. First of all, ask yourself whether your sentences mean what you really intend, or whether you can make them more exact and therefore stronger. For example, consider these two sentences from essays about "The Necklace":

> It seems as though the main character's dreams of luxury cause her to respond as she does in the story.
> This incident, although it may seem trivial or unimportant, has substantial signifi-cance in the creation of the story; by this I mean the incident that occurred is es-sentially what the story is all about.

These sentences are inexact and vague and therefore are unhelpful. Neither of them goes anywhere. The first sentence is satisfactory up to the verb *cause*, but then it falls apart because the writer has lost sight of a thematic or argu-mentative purpose. It would be better to try to describe what the response *is* rather than to say nothing more than that some kind of response exists. To make the sentence more exact, we might try the following revision:

> Mathilde's dreams of luxury make her dissatisfied with her own possessions, and therefore she goes beyond her financial means to attend the big party.

With this revision, the writer could readily go on to consider the relationship of the early part of the story to the later parts. Without the revision, it is not clear where the writer might go.

The second sentence is vague because the writer has lost all contact with the main thread of argument. If we adopt the principle of trying to be exact, however, we can create more meaning and more promise:

> The accidental loss of the necklace, which is trivial though costly, supports the nar-rator's claim that major turns in life are produced not by earthshaking events but rather by minor ones.

In addition to working for exactness, try to make sentences—all sentences, but particularly thesis and topic sentences—complete and comprehensive. Con-sider the following sentence:

> The idea in "The Necklace" is that Mathilde and her husband work hard to pay for the lost necklace.

Although this sentence promises to describe an idea, it does no more than summarize the story's major action. It needs additional rethinking and rephrasing to make it more comprehensive, as in these two revisions:

> In "The Necklace" Maupassant brings out the necessity to overcome mistakes through hard work and responsibility.
>
> Maupassant's surprise ending in "The Necklace" symbolizes the need for always being truthful.

Both new sentences are connected to the action described by the original phrasing, "Mathilde and her husband work hard to pay for the lost necklace," although they point toward differing treatments. The first sentence concerns the virtue shown by the Loisels in their sacrifice. Because the second sentence includes the word *symbolizes*, an essay stemming from it would stress the Loisels' mistake in not confessing the loss. In dealing with the symbolic meaning of their failure, an essay developed along the lines of the second sentence would focus on the negative aspects of their characters, and an essay developed from the first sentence would stress their positive aspects. Both of the revised sentences, therefore, are more comprehensive than the original sentence and thus would help a writer get on the track toward a thoughtful and analytical essay.

Of course it is never easy to create fine sentences, but as a mode of improvement, you might use some self-testing mechanisms:

- *For treating story materials.* Always relate the materials to a point or argument. Do not say simply, "Mathilde works constantly for ten years to help pay off the debt." Instead, blend the material into a point, like this: "Mathilde's ten-year effort shows her resolution to overcome the horror of indebtedness," or "Mathilde's ten-year effort brings out her strength of character."
- *For responses and impressions.* Do not say simply, "The story's ending left me with a definite impression." Where does that sentence take you? Your readers want to know what your impression is, and therefore you need to describe it, as in the following: "The story's ending surprised me and also made me sympathetic to the major character," or "The story's ending struck me with the fact that life is unpredictable and unfair."
- *For ideas.* Make the idea clear and direct. Do not say, "Mathilde is living in a poor household," but rather use the story material to bring out an idea, as follows: "Mathilde's story shows that economic deprivation hurts one's quality of life."
- *For critical commentary.* Do not be satisfied with a statement such as "I found 'The Necklace' interesting." All right, the story is interesting, but what does that tell us? Instead, it is important to try to describe what was interesting and why it was interesting: "I found 'The Necklace' interesting because it shows how chance and bad luck may either make or destroy people's lives."

Good writing begins with attempts, like these, to rephrase sentences to make them really say something. If you always name and pin down descriptions, responses, and judgments, no matter how difficult the task seems, your sentences can be strong and forceful because you will be making them exact and comprehensive.

USING THE NAMES OF AUTHORS

For both men and women writers, you should typically include the author's *full name* in the *first sentence* of your essay. Here are model first sentences.

Shirley Jackson's "The Lottery" is a story featuring both suspense and horror.
"The Lottery," by Shirley Jackson, is a story featuring both suspense and horror.

For all later references, use only last names, such as *Jackson, Steinbeck, Lawrence*, or *Porter*. However, for the "giants" of literature, you should use the last names exclusively. In referring to writers like Shakespeare and Dickinson, for example, there is no need to include *William* or *Emily*.

In spite of today's informal standards, do not use an author's first name, as in "*Shirley* skillfully creates suspense and horror in 'The Lottery.'" Also, do not use a familiar title before the names of dead authors, such as "*Ms.* Jackson's 'The Lottery' is a suspenseful horror story," or "*Mr.* Shakespeare's idea is that information is uncertain." Use the last names alone.

As with all conventions, of course, there are exceptions. If you are referring to a childhood work of a writer, the first name might be appropriate, but be sure to shift to the last name when referring to the writer's mature works. If your writer has a professional or a noble title, such as "*Lord* Byron," "*Queen* Elizabeth," or "*Countess of* Winchelsea," it is not improper to use the title. Even then, however, the titles are commonly omitted for males, so that most references to Lord Byron and Alfred, Lord Tennyson, should be simply to "Byron" and "Tennyson."

Referring to living authors is somewhat problematical. Some journals and newspapers, like the *New York Times*, often use the respectful titles *Mr.* and *Ms.* in their reviews. However, scholarly journals, which are likely to remain on library shelves and websites for many decades, follow the general principle of beginning with the entire name and then using only the last name for subsequent references.

DEMONSTRATIVE STUDENT ESSAY (IMPROVED DRAFT)

If you refer again to the first draft of the essay about Maupassant's use of setting to illustrate Mathilde's character (pp. 31–32), you might notice that several parts of the draft need extensive reworking and revising. For example, paragraph 2 contains a series of short, unconnected comments, and the last sentence of that paragraph implies that Mathilde's dissatisfaction relates mainly to her husband rather than to her general circumstances. Paragraph 4 focuses too much on Mathilde's coarseness and not enough on her sacrifice and cooperation. The draft also ignores the fact that the story ends in another location, the Champs-Elysées, where Maupassant continues to demonstrate the nature of Mathilde's character. Finally, there is not enough support in this draft for the contention (in paragraph 5) that everything in the story is related to the character of Mathilde.

To discover how these issues can be more fully considered, the following revision of the earlier draft creates more introductory detail, includes an additional paragraph, and reshapes each of the paragraphs to stress the relationship of the central idea or argument to the topics of the various paragraphs. Within the limits of a short assignment, the essay illustrates all the principles of organization and unity that we have been discussing here.

How Maupassant Uses Setting in "The Necklace" to Show the Character of Mathilde

[1]   In "The Necklace" Guy de Maupassant uses setting to reflect the character and development of the main character, Mathilde Loisel.* As a result, his setting is not particularly vivid or detailed. He does not even describe the ill-fated necklace-- the central object in the story--but states only that it is "superb" (paragraph 47). In fact he includes descriptions of setting only if they illuminate qualities about Mathilde. Her changing character can be connected to the first apartment, the dream-life mansion rooms, the attic flat, and the public street.†

[2]   Details about the modest apartment of the Loisels on the Street of Martyrs indicate Mathilde's peevish lack of adjustment to life. Though everything is serviceable, she is unhappy with the "drab" walls, "threadbare" furniture, and "ugly" curtains (paragraph 3). She has domestic help, but she wants more servants than the simple country girl who does the household chores in the apartment. Her embarrassment and dissatisfaction are shown by details of her irregularly cleaned tablecloth and the plain and inelegant boiled beef that her husband adores. Even her best theater dress, which is appropriate for apartment life but which is inappropriate for more wealthy surroundings, makes her unhappy. All these details of the apartment establish that Mathilde's major trait at the story's beginning is maladjustment. She therefore seems unpleasant and unsympathetic.

        Like the real-life apartment, the impossibly wealthy setting of her daydreams about owning a mansion strengthens her unhappiness and her avoidance of reality. All the rooms of her fantasies are large and expensive, draped in silk and filled with nothing but the best furniture and bric-a-brac. Maupassant gives us the following description of her dream world:

[3]   She imagined a gourmet-prepared main course carried on the most exquisite trays and served on the most beautiful dishes, with whispered gallantries which she would hear with a sphinxlike smile as she dined on the pink meat of a trout or the delicate wing of a quail. (paragraph 4)

With such impossible dreams, her despair is complete. Ironically, this despair, together with her inability to live with reality, brings about her undoing. It makes her agree to borrow the necklace (which is just as unreal as her daydreams of wealth), and losing the necklace drives her into the reality of giving up her apartment and moving into the attic flat.

*Central idea.
†Thesis sentence.

[4]   Also ironically, the attic flat is related to the coarsening of her character while at the same time it brings out her best qualities of hard work and honesty. Maupassant emphasizes the drudgery of the work Mathilde endures to maintain the flat, such as walking up many stairs, washing floors with large buckets of water, cleaning greasy and encrusted pots and pans, taking out the garbage, washing clothes by hand, and haggling loudly with local shopkeepers. All this reflects her coarsening and loss of sensibility, also shown by her giving up hair and hand care and by wearing cheap dresses. The work she performs, however, makes her heroic (paragraph 98). As she cooperates to help her husband pay back the loans, her dreams of a mansion fade, and all she has left is the memory of her triumphant appearance at the Minister of Education's party. Thus the attic flat brings out her physical change for the worse at the same time that it also brings out her psychological change for the better.

[5]   Her walk on the Champs-Elysées illustrates another combination of traits--self-indulgence and frankness. The Champs-Elysées is the most fashionable street in Paris, and her walk to it is similar to her earlier indulgences in her daydreams of upper-class wealth. But it is on this street where she meets Jeanne, and it is her frankness in confessing to Jeanne that makes her completely honest. While the walk thus serves as the occasion for the story's concluding surprise and irony, Mathilde's being on the Champs-Elysées is totally in character, in keeping with her earlier reveries about luxury.

[6]   Other details in the story also have a similar bearing on Mathilde's character. For example, the story presents little detail about the party scene beyond the statement that Mathilde is a great "success" (paragraph 52)--a judgment that shows her ability to shine if given the chance. After she and Loisel accept the fact that the necklace cannot be found, Maupassant includes details about the Parisian streets, about the visits to loan sharks, and about the jewelry shops in order to bring out Mathilde's sense of honesty and pride as she "heroically" prepares to live her new life of poverty. Thus, in "The Necklace," Maupassant uses setting to highlight Mathilde's maladjustment, her needless misfortune, her loss of youth and beauty, and finally her growth as a responsible human being.

Commentary on the Essay

Several improvements to the first draft are seen here. The language of paragraph 2 has been revised to show more clearly the inappropriateness of Mathilde's dissatisfaction. In paragraph 3, the irony of the story is brought out, and the writer has connected the details to the central idea in a richer pattern of ideas, showing the effects of Mathilde's despair. Paragraph 5—new in the improved draft—includes additional details about how Mathilde's walk on the Champs-Elysées is related to her character. In paragraph 6, the fact that Mathilde is able "to shine" at the dinner party is interpreted according to the central idea. Finally, the conclusion is now much more specific, summarizing the change in Mathilde's character rather than saying simply that the setting reveals "her needless misfortune." In short, the second draft reflects the complexity of "The Necklace" better than the first draft. Because the writer has revised the first-draft ideas about the story, the final essay is tightly structured, insightful, and forceful.

✿ ESSAY COMMENTARIES

Throughout this book, the demonstrative essays are followed by short commentaries that show how the essays embody the chapter instructions and guidelines. For each essay that has a number of possible approaches, the commentary points out which one is employed, and when an essay uses two or more approaches, the commentary makes this fact clear. In addition, each commentary singles out one of the paragraphs for more detailed analysis of its argument and use of detail. The commentaries will hence help you develop the insights necessary to use the essays as aids in your own study and writing.

To sum up, follow these guidelines whenever you write about a story or any kind of literature:

- Never just retell the story or summarize the work. Bring in story materials only when you can use them as support for your central idea or argument.
- Throughout your essay, keep reminding your reader of your central idea.
- Within each paragraph, make sure that you stress your topic idea.
- Develop your subject. Make it bigger than it was when you began.
- Always make your statements exact, comprehensive, and forceful.
- And remember, never just retell the story or summarize the work.

Special Topics for Writing and Argument about the Writing Process

1. Write a brainstorming paragraph on the topic of anything in a literary work that you find especially good or interesting. Write as the thoughts occur to you; do not slow yourself down in an effort to make your writing seem perfect. You can make corrections and improvements later.

2. Using marginal and notebook notations, together with any additional thoughts, describe the way in which the author of a particular work has expressed important ideas and difficulties.

3. Create a plus-minus table to list your responses about a character or ideas in a work.

4. Raise questions about the actions of characters in a story or play in order to determine the various customs and manners of the society out of which the work is derived.

5. Analyze and explain the way in which the conflicts in a story or play are developed. What pattern or patterns do you find? Determine the relationship of the conflicts to the work's development, and fashion your idea of this relationship as an argument for a potential essay.

6. Basing your ideas on your marginal and notebook notations, select an idea and develop a thesis sentence from it, using your idea and a list of possible topics for an argument or central idea for an essay.

7. Using the thesis sentence you write for exercise 6, develop a brief topical outline for a full essay.

Reading *and* Writing

about

FICTION

Fiction: *An Overview*

Fiction originally meant anything *made up* or *shaped*. As we understand the word today, it refers to *short or long prose stories*—and it has retained this meaning since 1599, the first year for which we have a record for it in print. Fiction is distinguished from the works it imitates, such as *historical accounts, reports, biographies, autobiographies, letters,* and *personal memoirs* and *meditations.* While fiction often resembles these forms, it has a separate identity because it originates not in historical facts but in the imaginative and creative powers of the author. Writers of fiction may include historically accurate details, but their overriding goal is to tell a story and say something significant about life.

The essence of fiction, as opposed to drama, is **narration,** the recounting or telling of a sequence of events or actions. The earliest works of fiction relied almost exclusively on narration, with speeches or dialogue being reported rather than quoted directly. Much recent fiction includes extended passages of dialogue, thereby becoming more *dramatic* even though narration is still the primary mode.

Fiction is rooted in ancient legends and myths. Local priests told stories about their gods and heroes, as shown in some of the narratives of ancient Egypt. In the course of history, traveling storytellers would appear in a court or village to entertain listeners with tales of adventure in faraway countries. Although many of these were fictionalized accounts of events and people who may not ever have existed, they were largely accepted as fact or history. An especially long tale, an **epic,** was recited during a period of days. To aid their memories and to impress and entertain their listeners, the storytellers chanted their tales in poetry, often accompanying themselves on a stringed instrument.

Legends and epics also reinforced the local religions and power structures. Myths of gods like Zeus and Athena (Greece), Jupiter and Minerva (Rome), and Baal and Ishtar (Mesopotamia) abounded, together with stories of famous men and women like Oedipus, Helen of Troy, Hercules, Achilles, Odysseus,

Penelope, Aeneas, Romulus and Remus, Utu-Napishtim, Joseph, David, and Ruth. The ancient Macedonian king and general Alexander the Great (356–323 B.C.E.) developed many of his ideas about nobility and valor from *The Iliad*, Homer's epic about the Trojan War—and, we might add, from discussing the epic with his tutor, the philosopher Aristotle.

Perhaps nowhere is the moralistic-argumentative aspect of ancient storytelling better illustrated than in the **fables** of Aesop, a Greek who wrote in the sixth century B.C.E., and in the **parables** of Jesus as told in the Gospels of the New Testament (see Chapter 9). In these works, a short narrative provides an illustration of a religious, philosophic, or psychological conclusion.

Starting about eight hundred years ago, storytelling in Western civilization was developed to a fine art by writers such as Marie de France, a Frenchwoman who wrote in England near the end of the twelfth century; Giovanni Boccaccio (Italian, 1313–1375); and Geoffrey Chaucer (English, ca. 1340–1400). William Shakespeare (1564–1616) drew heavily on history and legend for the stories and characters in his plays.

⫶⋙ MODERN FICTION

Fiction in the modern sense of the word did not begin to flourish until the seventeenth and eighteenth centuries, when human beings of all social stations and ways of life became important literary topics. As one writer put it in 1709, human nature was not simple, and it could be explained only with reference to many complex motives such as "passion, humor, caprice, zeal, faction, and a thousand other springs."[1] Thus began the individual and psychological concerns that characterize fiction today. Indeed, fiction is strong because it is so real and personal. Most characters have both first and last names; the countries and cities in which they live are visualized as real places; and their actions and interactions are like those which readers themselves have experienced, could experience, or could readily imagine themselves experiencing.

Along with attention to character, fiction is also concerned with the significance of place on the lives of people. In the simplest sense, place or environment is a backdrop or setting within which characters speak, move, and act. But more broadly, environment comprises the social, economic, and political conditions that affect the outcomes of people's lives. Fiction is usually about the interactions among people, but it also involves these larger interactions—either directly or indirectly. Indeed, in a typical work of fiction there are always many forces, both small and large, that influence the ways in which characters meet and deal with their problems.

The first true works of fiction in Europe, however, were less concerned with society or politics than adventure. These were the lengthy Spanish and French **romances** of the sixteenth and seventeenth centuries. In English the word **novel** was borrowed from French and Italian to describe these works and

---

[1]Anthony Ashley Cooper, Third Earl of Shaftesbury, "Sensus Communis," III. 3.

to distinguish them from medieval and classical romances as something that was *new* (the meaning of *novel*). In England the word **story** was used along with *novel* in reference to the new literary form.

The increased levels of education and literacy in the eighteenth century facilitated the development of fiction. During the times of Shakespeare and John Dryden (1631–1700), the only way a writer could make a living from writing was either to be a member of the nobility or have a subsidy from a member of the nobility, or to have a play accepted at a theater and then receive either a direct payment or the proceeds of an "author's benefit." The paying audiences, however, were limited to people who lived within a short distance of the theater or who had the leisure and money to stay in town and attend the plays during the theater season.

Once great numbers of people could read for themselves, the paying audience for literature expanded. A writer could write a novel and receive money for it from a publisher, who could then profit from a wide sale. Readers could pick up the book when they wished, and they could finish it when they chose. Reading a novel could even be a social event, for people would gather together and read to each other as a means of sharing the reading experience. With this wider audience of people whom authors would never see or know, it became possible to develop an actual career out of writing. Fiction had arrived as a major genre of literature.

❧ THE SHORT STORY

Because novels were long, they took a long time to read—hours, days, even weeks. The American writer Edgar Allan Poe (1809–1849) addressed this problem and developed a theory of the **short story,** which he described in a review of Nathaniel Hawthorne's *Twice-Told Tales.* Poe was convinced that "worldly interests" prevented people from gaining the "totality" of comprehension and response that he believed reading should provide. A short, concentrated story (he called it "a brief prose tale" which could be read at a single sitting) was ideal for producing such a strong impression.

In the wake of the taste for short fiction after Poe, many writers have worked in the form. Today, stories are printed in many periodicals, such as *Harper's Magazine, The Atlantic Monthly*, and *Zoetrope,* and in many collections, such as *American Short Story Masterpieces.* Some of the better-established writers—William Faulkner, Ernest Hemingway, Shirley Jackson, Joyce Carol Oates, John Updike, Alice Walker, and Eudora Welty, to name only a small number—have published their stories in separate volumes.

❧ ELEMENTS OF FICTION I: VERISIMILITUDE AND *DONNÉE*

Fiction, along with drama, has a basis in **realism** or **verisimilitude.** That is, the situations or characters, although they are the **invention** of writers, are similar to those that many human beings experience, know, or think. Even **fantasy,** the creation of events that are dreamlike or fantastic, is anchored in the real world, however remotely. This connection of art and life has led some critics to label fiction, and also drama, as an art of **imitation.** Shakespeare's Hamlet states that an actor attempts to portray real human beings in realistic situations (to "hold a mirror up to Nature").

The same may also be said about writers of fiction, with the provisos that reality is not easily defined and that authors can follow many paths in imitating it. What matters in fiction is the way in which authors establish the ground rules for their works, whether with realistic or nonrealistic characters, places, actions, and physical and chemical laws. The assumption that authors make about the nature of their story material is called a **postulate** or a **premise**—what Henry James called a *donnée* (something given). The *donnée* of some stories is to resemble the everyday world as much as possible. Alice Walker's "Everyday Use" is such a story. In it a narrator describes her daughter's return to her poor and simple home, together with the subsequent clash of values represented by herself and her visiting daughter. The events of the story are common; they could happen in life just as Walker presents them.

Once a *donnée* is established, it governs the directions in which the story moves. Jackson's "The Lottery" (Chapter 5), for example, contains a premise or *donnée* that may be phrased like this: "Suppose that a small, ordinary town held a lottery in which the prize was not something good but instead was something bad." Everything in Jackson's story follows from this premise. At first we seem to be reading about innocent actions in a rural American community. By the end, however, in accord with the premise, the story enters the realms of nightmare.

In such ways authors may lead us into remote, fanciful, and symbolic levels of reality, as in Walter Van Tilburg Clark's "The Portable Phonograph" (Chapter 6), where the futuristic *donnée* is that world civilization has been destroyed in a global war. In Poe's "The Masque of the Red Death" (Chapter 6), the phantasmagoric *donnée* is that Death may assume a human but sinister shape. Literally nothing is out of bounds as long as the author makes clear the premise for the action.

Scenes and actions such as these, which are not realistic in our ordinary sense of the word, are normal in stories *as long as they follow the author's own stated or implied ground rules.* You may always judge a work by the standard of whether it is consistent with the premise, or the *donnée*, created by the writer.

In addition to referring to various levels of reality, the word *donnée* may also be taken more broadly. In *futuristic* and *science fiction*, for example, there is an assumption or *donnée* of certain situations and technological developments (e.g., interstellar space travel) that are not presently in existence. In a *love story*, the *donnée* is that two people meet and overcome an obstacle of some sort (usually not a serious one) on the way to fulfilling their love. Interesting variations of the love story are Robert Olen Butler's "Snow" (Chapter 12), James Joyce's "Araby" (Chapter 6), D. H. Lawrence's "The Horse Dealer's Daughter" (Chapter 10), and Alice Munro's "The Found Boat" (Chapter 7).

There are of course other types. A *growth* or *apprenticeship story*, for example, is about the development of a major character, such as Sarty in William

Faulkner's "Barn Burning" (Chapter 4) and Jackie in Frank O'Connor's "First Confession" (Chapter 7). In the *detective story*, a mysterious event is posited, and then an individual draws conclusions from the available evidence, as in Susan Glaspell's "A Jury of Her Peers" (Chapter 4), in which the correct detective work is done by two women, not by the legally authorized police investigators.

In addition to setting levels of reality and fictional types, authors may use other controls or springboards as their *données*. Sometimes an initial situation may be the occasion from which the story develops, such as the shopping trip in Joyce Carol Oates's "Shopping" (Chapter 4). Or the key may be a pattern of behavior, such as the boy's reactions to the people around him in O'Connor's "First Confession," or the solution of a mystery about a community icon as in Faulkner's "A Rose for Emily" (Chapter 3). There is always a shaping force, or a *donnée*, that guides the actions, and often a number of such controls operate at the same time.

ELEMENTS OF FICTION II: CHARACTER, PLOT, STRUCTURE, AND IDEA OR THEME

Works of fiction share a number of common elements. For reference here, the more significant ones are character, plot, structure, and idea or theme.

Character Brings Fiction to Life

Stories, like plays, are about characters, who are *not* real people but who are nevertheless *like* real people. A **character** may be defined as a reasonable facsimile of a human being, with all the good and bad traits of being human. Most stories are concerned with characters who are facing a major problem developing from misunderstanding, misinformation, unfocused ideals and goals, difficult situations, troubled relationships, and generally challenging situations. The characters may win, lose, or tie. They may learn and be the better for the experience or may miss the point and be unchanged.

It is a truism that modern fiction has accompanied the development of a psychological interest in human beings. Psychology itself has grown out of the philosophical and religious idea that people are not evil by nature, but rather that they have many inborn capacities—some of them good and others bad. People are not immune to problems in their lives, and they make many mistakes; they expend much effort in coping and adjusting. But they nevertheless are important and interesting and are therefore worth writing about, whether male or female; young or old; white, black, tan, or yellow; rich or poor; worker or industrialist; traveler or resident; doctor, librarian, mother, daughter, homemaker, prince, bartender, shepherd, or army lieutenant.

The range of fictional characters is vast: A married couple struggling to repay an enormous debt, a young man learning about sin and forgiveness, a woman recalling many conflicts with her mother, a man yearning for the return of the past, a woman surrounded by her insensitive and self-seeking brothers, a man making triumphs out of his blunders, a woman anticipating her first meeting with her long absent mother—all these, and more, may be found in fiction just as they may also be found in all levels and conditions of life. Because as human beings all of us share the same capacities for concern, involvement, sympathy, happiness, sorrow, exhilaration, and disappointment, we are able to find endless interest in such characters and their ways of coping with their circumstances.

Plot Is the Plan of Fiction

Fictional characters, who are drawn from life, go through a series of lifelike **actions** or **incidents,** which make up the story. In a well-done story, all the actions or incidents, speeches, thoughts, and observations are linked together to make up an entirety, sometimes called an **organic unity.** The essence of this unity is the development and resolution of a **conflict**—or conflicts—in which the **protagonist,** or central character, is engaged. The interactions of causes and effects as they develop **sequentially** or **chronologically** make up the story's **plot.** That is, a story's actions follow one another in time as the protagonist meets and tries to overcome opposing forces. Sometimes plot has been compared to a story's map, scheme, or blueprint.

Often the protagonist's struggle is directed against another character—an **antagonist.** Just as often, however, the struggle may occur between the protagonist and opposing groups, forces, ideas, and choices—all of which make up a collective antagonist. The conflict may be carried out wherever human beings spend their lives, such as a kitchen, a hotel, a shopping mall, a restaurant, a town square, a schoolroom, an ordinary living room, a church, an exclusive store, a vacation resort, a café, or a battlefield. The conflict may also take place internally, within the mind of the protagonist.

Structure Is the Knitting Together of Fiction

Structure refers to the way a story is assembled. Chronologically, all stories are similar because they move from beginning to end in accord with the time needed for *causes* to produce *effects.* But authors choose many different ways to put their stories together. Some stories are told in straightforward sequential order, and a description of the plot of such stories is identical to a description of the structure. Other stories, however, may get pieced together through out-of-sequence and widely separated episodes, speeches, secondhand reports, remembrances, accidental discoveries, dreams, nightmares, periods of delirium, fragments of letters, overheard conversations, and the like. In such stories, the plot and the structure diverge widely. Therefore, in dealing with the structure of stories, we emphasize not chronological order but the actual *arrangement* and *development* of the stories as they unfold, part by part. Usually we study an entire story, but we may also direct our attention toward the structure of a smaller aspect of arrangement such as an episode or passage of dialogue.

Idea or Theme Is the Vivifying Thought of Fiction

The word **idea** refers to the result or results of general and abstract thinking. Either directly or indirectly, fiction embodies ideas and themes that underlie and give life to stories and novels. The writers never need to state their ideas in specific words, but the strength of their works depends on the power with which they exemplify ideas and make them clear. Thus, writers of comic works are committed to the idea that human difficulties can be treated with humor. More serious works often show characters in the throes of difficult moral choices—the idea being that in a losing situation the only winners are those who maintain honor and self-respect. Mystery and suspense stories develop out of the idea that problems have solutions, although the solutions at first seem remote or even impossible. Even stories written for entertainment alone, some of which may at first seem devoid of ideas, stem out of an idea or position that the work itself makes clear. Writers may deal with the triumphs and defeats of life, the admirable and the despicable, the humorous and the pathetic, but whatever their goal, they are always expressing ideas about human experience. We may therefore raise questions such as these as we look for ideas in fiction: *What does this mean? Why does the author include it? What idea or ideas does it show? Why is it significant?*

Many works can be discussed in terms of the issues which they raise. An **issue** may involve a work's characters in direct or implicit argument or opposition, and also may bring out crucially important moments of decision about matters of private or public concern. In addition to the issues that the characters face, the works themselves may be considered for their more general issues.

Fictional ideas can also be considered as major **themes** that tie individual works together. Often an author makes the theme obvious, as in the Aesop fable in which a man uses an ax to kill a fly on another man's forehead. The theme of this fable might loosely be expressed in a sentence like "The cure should not be worse than the disease." A major theme in Maupassant's "The Necklace" (Chapter 1) is that people may be destroyed or saved by unlucky and unforeseeable events.

The process of determining and describing the themes or ideas in stories is never complete; there is always another theme that we can discuss, another issue that may be explored. Thus in "The Necklace," one might note the additional themes that adversity brings out worth, that telling the truth is better than concealing it, that envy often produces ill fortune, that people may build their lives on incorrect assumptions, and that good fortune is never recognized until it is lost. Indeed, one of the ways in which we judge stories is to determine the degree to which they embody a number of valid and important ideas.

ELEMENTS OF FICTION III: THE WRITER'S TOOLS

Narration Creates the Sequence and Logic of Fiction

Writers have a number of modes of presentation, or "tools," which they use in their stories. The principal tool (and the heart of fiction) is **narration,** the reporting of actions in sequential order. The object of narration is to *render* the story, to make it clear and to bring it alive to the reader's imagination through the movement of sentences through time. Unlike works of painting and sculpture, the reading and comprehension of a narration cannot be done in a single view. Jacques-Louis David's painting *The Death of Socrates,* for example (Insert I–2), is like a narrative because it tells a story—an actual historical occurrence. As related by Plato in the dialogue *Phaedo*, Socrates takes the cup of hemlock, which he will drink as the means of carrying out his own execution. David does include details that tell the story visually. In the rear of the painting some of Socrates' friends have said goodbye and are mounting stairs to leave. Two of the remaining men hold their heads in grief, and two turn toward a wall in despair. The jailer turns away from Socrates as he offers the cup of hemlock. Also, on the bed are the unlocked manacles that might have held Socrates, thus emphasizing that he could have obtained his freedom had he so chosen. In fact, however, it is only the moment of time prior to Socrates' drinking of the hemlock that David is able to capture in his painting. As a contrast, the writer of a narrative may include all the events leading up to and following such a moment, for a narration moves in a continuous line, from word to word, scene to scene, action to action, and speech to speech. As a result of this chronological movement, the reader's comprehension must necessarily also be chronological.

Style Is the Author's Skill in Bringing Language to Life

The medium of fiction and of all literature is language, and the manipulation of language—the **style**—is a primary skill of the writer. A mark of a good style is the use of active verbs and nouns that are **specific** and **concrete.** Even with the most active and graphic diction possible, writers can never render their incidents and scenes exactly, but they may be judged on how vividly and imaginatively they tell their stories.

Point of View Guides What We See and Understand in Fiction

One of the most important ways in which writers knit their stories together, and also an important way in which they try to interest and engage readers, is through the careful control of **point of view.** Point of view is the **voice** of the story, as revealed by the speaker who does the narrating. It is the way the story establishes its authenticity, either in reality or unreality. It may be regarded as the story's *focus,* the *angle of vision* from which things are not only seen and reported but also judged.

Basically, there are two kinds of points of view, but there are many, many variations, sometimes obvious and sometimes subtle. In the first, the **first-person point of view,** a fictitious observer tells us what he or she saw, heard, concluded, and thought. This viewpoint is characterized by the use of the pronoun *I* as the speaker refers to his or her position as an observer or commentator. The **speaker** or **narrator**—terms that are interchangeable—may sometimes seem to be the author speaking directly using an **authorial voice.** More often, however, the speaker is an independent character—a **persona** with characteristics that separate her or him from the author.

In common with all narrators, the first-person narrator establishes a clearly defined relationship to the story's events. Some narrators are deeply engaged in the action; others are only minor participants or observers; still others have had nothing to do with the action but are transmitting the reports of others who were more fully involved. Sometimes the narrator uses the *we* pronoun if he or she is or has been part of a group that has witnessed the action or participated in it. Often, too, the narrator might use *we* when referring to ideas and interpretations shared with the reader or listener—the idea being to draw readers into the story as much as possible.

The **third-person point of view** uses third-person pronouns (*she, he, it, they, her, him, them,* etc.).[2] The third-person point of view may be (1) **limited,** with the focus being on one particular character and what he or she does, says, hears, thinks, and otherwise experiences; (2) **omniscient,** with the possibility that the activities and thoughts of all the characters are open and fully known by the speaker; or (3) **dramatic,** or **objective,** in which the story is confined *only* to the reporting of actions and speeches, with no commentary and no revelation of the thoughts of any of the characters unless the characters themselves reveal their thoughts in a dramatic fashion.

Understanding point of view usually requires subtlety of perception—indeed, it may be one of the most difficult of all concepts in the study of fiction. In fuller perspective, therefore, we may think of it as the *total position* from which things are viewed, understood, and communicated. The position might be simply physical: *Where was the speaker located when the events occurred? Does the speaker give us a close or distant view of the events?* The position might also be personal or philosophical: *Do the events illustrate a personal opinion* (Maupassant's "The Necklace"), *embody a philosophical judgment* (Hawthorne's "Young Goodman Brown" [Chapter 9]), or *argue a theological principle* (St. Luke's "The Parable of the Prodigal Son" [Chapter 9])?

Point of view is one of the major ways by which authors make fiction vital. By controlling point of view, an author helps us make reasonable inferences about the story's actions. Authors use point of view to raise some of the same questions in fiction that perplex us in life. We need to evaluate what fictional narrators as well as real people tell us, for what they say is affected by their limitations, attitudes, opinions, and degree of candidness. The narrator of Mark Twain's "Luck," for example (Chapter 7), is convinced that his hero is a total nincompoop, and he tells the story to make us similarly convinced. But could we make a case that he might also be jealous of his boob hero, enough perhaps to omit some of the explanations that might give us a more complete, less biased picture? For readers, the perception of a fictional point of view can be as complex as life itself, and it may be as difficult—in fiction as in life—to evaluate our sources of information.

Description Creates the World of Fiction

Together with narration, a vital aspect of fiction is **description,** which is intended to cause readers to imagine or re-create the scenes and actions of the story. Description can be both physical (places and persons) and psychological (an emotion or set of emotions). Excessive description sometimes interrupts or postpones a story's actions, so many writers include only as much as is necessary to provide locations for what is happening in the story.

---

[2]The possibilities of a second-person point of view are discussed in Chapter 5.

Mood and **atmosphere** are important aspects of descriptive writing, and to the degree that descriptions are evocative, they may reach the level of **metaphor** and **symbolism.** These characteristics of fiction are a property of all literature, and you will also encounter them whenever you read poems and plays.

Dialogue Creates Interactions among Fictional Characters

Another major tool of the writer of fiction is **dialogue.** By definition, dialogue is the conversation of two people, but more than two characters may also participate. It is of course the major medium of the playwright, and it is one of the means by which fiction writers bring vividness and dramatic tension to their stories. Straight narration and description can do no more than make a second-hand assertion ("hearsay") that a character's thoughts and responses exist, but dialogue makes everything firsthand and real.

Dialogue is hence a means of *showing* rather than *reporting*. If characters feel pain or declare love, their own words may be taken as the expression of what is on their minds. Some dialogue may be terse and minimal. Other dialogue may be expanded, depending on the situation, the personalities of the characters, and the author's intent. Dialogue may concern any topic, including everyday and practical matters, personal feelings, reactions to the past, future plans, changing thoughts, sudden realizations, and political, social, philosophical, or religious ideas.

The language of dialogue indicates the intelligence, articulateness, educational levels, or emotional states of the speakers. Hence the author might use *grammatical mistakes, faulty pronunciation,* or *slang* to show a character of limited or disadvantaged background or a character who is trying to be seen in that light. *Dialect* shows the region from which the speaker comes, just as *accent* indicates a place of national origin. *Jargon* and *cliché* suggest self-inflation or intellectual limitations—usually reasons for laughter. The use of *private or intimate expressions* clearly shows people who are close to each other emotionally. Speech that is interrupted by *voiced pauses* (e.g., "er," "ah," "um," "y' know") or speech characterized by *inappropriate words* might show a character who is unsure or not in control. There are many possibilities in dialogue, but no matter what qualities you find, writers include dialogue to enable you to know their characters better.

Tone and Irony Guide Our Perceptions of Fictional Works

In every story we may consider **tone,** that is, the ways in which authors convey attitudes toward readers and also toward the work's subjects. **Irony,** one of the major components of tone, refers to language and situations that seem to reverse normal expectations. *Word choice* is the characteristic of **verbal irony,** in which what is meant is usually the opposite of what is said, as when we *mean* that people are doing badly even though we *say* that they are doing well. Broader forms of irony are *situational* and *dramatic.* **Situational irony** refers to circumstances in which bad things happen to good people, or in which rewards are not earned because forces beyond human comprehension seem to be in total control, making the world seem arbitrary and often absurd. In **dramatic irony** characters have only a nonexistent, partial, incorrect, or misguided understanding of what is happening to them, while both readers and other characters understand the situation more fully. Readers hence become concerned about the characters and hope that the characters will develop understanding quickly enough to avoid the problems bedeviling them and the pitfalls endangering them.

Symbolism and Allegory Show the Relevance of Fiction to the Larger World

In literature, even apparently ordinary things may acquire **symbolic** value; that is, everyday objects may be understood to have meanings that are beyond themselves, bigger than themselves. In fiction, many functional and essential incidents, objects, speeches, and characters may also be construed as symbols. Some symbols are widely recognized and therefore are considered as **cultural** or **universal.** Water, flowers, jewels, the sun, certain stars, the flag, altars, and minarets are examples of cultural symbols. Other symbols are **contextual;** that is, they take on symbolic meaning only in their individual works, as when in Maupassant's "The Necklace" Mathilde and her husband move into an attic flat, which may be taken as representative or symbolic of their loss of economic and social status.

When a complete story, in addition to maintaining its own narrative integrity, can be applied point by point to a parallel set of situations, it is an **allegory.** Many stories are not complete allegories, however, even though they may contain sections having allegorical parallels. For instance the Loisels' long servitude in Maupassant's "The Necklace" is similar to the lives and activities of many people who perform tasks for mistaken or meaningless reasons. "The Necklace" therefore has allegorical overtones even though it is not, in totality, an allegory.

Commentary Provides Us with an Author's Thoughts

Writers may also include **commentary, analysis,** or **interpretation,** in the expectation that readers need insight into the characters and their actions. When fiction was new, authors often expressed such commentary directly. Henry Fielding (1707–1754) divided his novels into "books" and included a chapter of personal and philosophical commentary at the beginning of each of these. In the next century, George Eliot (1819–1880) included many extensive passages of commentary in her novels.

Later writers have kept commentary at a minimum, preferring instead to concentrate on direct action and dialogue, thereby allowing readers to draw their own conclusions about meaning. In first-person narrations, however, you may expect the narrators to make their own personal comments. Such observations may be accepted at face value, but you should recognize that anything the speakers say is also a mode of character disclosure and therefore just as much a part of the total story as the narrative incidents.

The Elements Together Are Present in Works of Fiction

These, then, are the major tools of fiction, which authors usually employ simultaneously in their works. Thus, the story may be told by a character who is a witness, and thus it has a **first-person point of view.** The major **character,** the **protagonist,** goes through a series of **actions** as a result of a carefully arranged **plot.** Because of this plot, together with the author's chosen method of **narration,** the story will follow a certain kind of arrangement, or **structure,** such as a straightforward **sequence** or a disjointed series of **episodes.** The action may demonstrate the story's **theme** or **central idea.** The writer's **style** may be manifested in **ironic** expressions. The description of the character's actions may reveal **irony of situation,** while at the same time this situation is made vivid through **dialogue** in which the character is a participant. Because the plight of the character is like the plight of many persons in the world, it is an **allegory,** and the character herself or himself may be considered as a **symbol.**

Throughout each story we read, no matter what characteristics we are considering, it is most important to realize that a work of fiction is an entirety, a unity. Any reading of a story should be undertaken not to break things down into parts but to understand and assimilate the work *as a whole.* The separate analysis of various topics is thus a *means* to that end, *not* the end itself. The study of fiction, like the study of all literature, is designed to foster our growth and to increase our understanding of the human condition.

STORIES FOR STUDY

RAYMOND CARVER   (1938–1988)

Originally from Oregon, Carver lived in Washington and spent much of his adult life in California. He studied at Chico State and at the Iowa Writers Workshop. After doing blue-collar jobs for a time he worked as an editor and then, finally, as a teacher. Some of his collections are Will You Please Be Quiet, Please? *(1976) and* Cathedral *(1983).* Where I'm Calling From *(1988) collects earlier stories and adds a number of new ones.* Short Cuts *(1993) is a selection of ten stories that were woven together into a film (1993) by Robert Altman. Carver is considered a master of minimalism, that is, fiction that stresses only the essentials of action and description. Generally, his writing is economical, stripped to the bone. Many of his characters seem unusual if not odd or even cruel. For example, one of his brief stories, "Popular Mechanics," takes little more than a single page to depict how a couple breaking up is also about to break up (literally) their child. "Neighbors" is taken from* Where I'm Calling From.

Neighbors   1988

Bill and Arlene Miller were a happy couple. But now and then they felt they alone among their circle had been passed by somehow, leaving Bill to attend to his bookkeeping duties and Arlene occupied with secretarial chores. They talked about it sometimes, mostly in comparison with the lives of their neighbors, Harriet and Jim Stone. It seemed to the Millers that the Stones lived a fuller and brighter life. The Stones were always going out for dinner, or entertaining at home, or traveling about the country somewhere in connection with Jim's work.

The Stones lived across the hall from the Millers. Jim was a salesman for a machine-parts firm and often managed to combine business with pleasure trips, and on this occasion the Stones would be away for ten days, first to Cheyenne, then on to St. Louis to visit relatives. In their absence, the Millers would look after the Stones' apartment, feed Kitty, and water the plants.

Bill and Jim shook hands beside the car. Harriet and Arlene held each other by the elbows and kissed lightly on the lips.

"Have fun," Bill said to Harriet.

"We will," said Harriet. "You kids have fun too."   5

Arlene nodded.

Jim winked at her. "Bye, Arlene. Take good care of the old man."

"I will," Arlene said.

"Have fun," Bill said.

"You bet," Jim said, clipping Bill lightly on the arm. "And thanks again, you guys."   10

The Stones waved as they drove away, and the Millers waved too.

"Well, I wish it was us," Bill said.

"God knows, we could use a vacation," Arlene said. She took his arm and put it around her waist as they climbed the stairs to their apartment.

After dinner Arlene said, "Don't forget. Kitty gets liver flavor the first night." She stood in the kitchen doorway folding the handmade tablecloth that Harriet had bought for her last year in Santa Fe.

Bill took a deep breath as he entered the Stones' apartment. The air was already   15
heavy and it was vaguely sweet. The sunburst clock over the television said half past eight. He remembered when Harriet had come home with the clock, how she had crossed the hall to show it to Arlene, cradling the brass case in her arms and talking to it through the tissue paper as if it were an infant.

Kitty rubbed her face against his slippers and then turned onto her side, but jumped up quickly as Bill moved to the kitchen and selected one of the stacked cans from the gleaming drainboard. Leaving the cat to pick at her food, he headed for the bathroom. He looked at himself in the mirror and then closed his eyes and then looked again. He opened the medicine chest. He found a container of pills and read the label— Harriet Stone. One each day as directed—and slipped it into his pocket. He went back to the kitchen, drew a pitcher of water, and returned to the living room. He finished watering, set the pitcher on the rug, and opened the liquor cabinet. He reached in back for the bottle of Chivas Regal. He took two drinks from the bottle, wiped his lips on his sleeve, and replaced the bottle in the cabinet.

Kitty was on the couch sleeping. He switched off the lights, slowly closing and checking the door. He had the feeling he had left something.

"What kept you?" Arlene said. She sat with her legs turned under her, watching television.

"Nothing. Playing with Kitty," he said, and went over to her and touched her breasts.

"Let's go to bed, honey," he said.   20

The next day Bill took only ten minutes of the twenty-minute break allotted for the afternoon and left at fifteen minutes before five. He parked the car in the lot just as Arlene hopped down from the bus. He waited until she entered the building, then ran up the stairs to catch her as she stepped out of the elevator.

"Bill! God, you scared me. You're early," she said.

He shrugged. "Nothing to do at work," he said.

She let him use her key to open the door. He looked at the door across the hall before following her inside.

"Let's go to bed," he said.

"Now?" She laughed. "What's gotten into you?"   25

"Nothing. Take your dress off." He grabbed for her awkwardly, and she said, "Good God, Bill."

He unfastened his belt.

Later they sent out for Chinese food, and when it arrived they ate hungrily, without speaking, and listened to records.

"Let's not forget to feed Kitty," she said.   30

"I was just thinking about that," he said. "I'll go right over."

* * *

He selected a can of fish flavor for the cat, then filled the pitcher and went to water. When he returned to the kitchen, the cat was scratching in her box. She looked at him steadily before she turned back to the litter. He opened all the cupboards and examined the canned goods, the cereals, the packaged foods, the cocktail and wine glasses, the china, the pots and pans. He opened the refrigerator. He sniffed some celery, took two bites of cheddar cheese, and chewed on an apple as he walked into the bedroom. The bed seemed enormous, with a fluffy white bedspread draped to the floor. He pulled out a nightstand drawer, found a half-empty package of cigarettes and stuffed them into his pocket. Then he stepped to the closet and was opening it when the knock sounded at the front door.

He stopped by the bathroom and flushed the toilet on his way.

"What's been keeping you?" Arlene said. "You've been over here more than an hour."

"Have I really?" he said.   35

"Yes, you have," she said.

"I had to go to the toilet," he said.

"You have your own toilet," she said.

"I couldn't wait," he said.

That night they made love again.   40

In the morning he had Arlene call in for him. He showered, dressed, and made a light breakfast. He tried to start a book. He went out for a walk and felt better. But after a while, hands still in his pockets, he returned to the apartment. He stopped at the Stones' door on the chance he might hear the cat moving about. Then he let himself in at his own door and went to the kitchen for the key.

Inside it seemed cooler than his apartment, and darker too. He wondered if the plants had something to do with the temperature of the air. He looked out the window, and then he moved slowly through each room considering everything that fell under his gaze, carefully, one object at a time. He saw ashtrays, items of furniture, kitchen utensils, the clock. He saw everything. At last he entered the bedroom, and the cat appeared at his feet. He stroked her once, carried her into the bathroom, and shut the door.

He lay down on the bed and stared at the ceiling. He lay for a while with his eyes closed, and then he moved his hand under his belt. He tried to recall what day it was. He tried to remember when the Stones were due back, and then he wondered if they would ever return. He could not remember their faces or the way they talked and dressed. He sighed and with effort rolled off the bed to lean over the dresser and look at himself in the mirror.

He opened the closet and selected a Hawaiian shirt. He looked until he found Bermudas, neatly pressed and hanging over a pair of brown twill slacks. He shed his own clothes and slipped into the shorts and the shirt. He looked in the mirror again. He went to the living room and poured himself a drink and sipped it on his way back to the bedroom. He put on a blue shirt, a dark suit, a blue and white tie, black wing-tip shoes. The glass was empty and he went for another drink.

In the bedroom again, he sat on a chair, crossed his legs, and smiled, observing himself in the mirror. The telephone rang twice and fell silent. He finished the drink and took off the suit. He rummaged through the top drawers until he found a pair of panties and a brassiere. He stepped into the panties and fastened the brassiere, then looked through the closet for an outfit. He put on a black and white checkered skirt and tried to zip it up. He put on a burgundy blouse that buttoned up the front. He considered her shoes, but understood they would not fit. For a long time he looked out the living-room window from behind the curtain. Then he returned to the bedroom and put everything away.

He was not hungry. She did not eat much, either. They looked at each other shyly and smiled. She got up from the table and checked that the key was on the shelf and then she quickly cleared the dishes.

He stood in the kitchen doorway and smoked a cigarette and watched her pick up the key.

"Make yourself comfortable while I go across the hall," she said. "Read the paper or something." She closed her fingers over the key. He was, she said, looking tired.

He tried to concentrate on the news. He read the paper and turned on the television. Finally he went across the hall. The door was locked.

"It's me. Are you still there, honey?" he called.

After a time the lock released and Arlene stepped outside and shut the door. "Was I gone so long?" she said.

"Well, you were," he said.

"Was I?" she said. "I guess I must have been playing with Kitty."

He studied her, and she looked away, her hand still resting on the doorknob.

"It's funny," she said. "You know—to go in someone's place like that."

He nodded, took her hand from the knob, and guided her toward their own door. He let them into their apartment.

"It *is* funny," he said.

He noticed white lint clinging to the back of her sweater, and the color was high in her cheeks. He began kissing her on the neck and hair and she turned and kissed him back.

"Oh, damn," she said. "Damn, damn," she sang, girlishly clapping her hands. "I just remembered. I really and truly forgot to do what I went over there to do. I didn't feed Kitty or do any watering." She looked at him. "Isn't that stupid?"

"I don't think so," he said. "Just a minute. I'll get my cigarettes and go back with you."

She waited until he had closed and locked their door, and then she took his arm at the muscle and said, "I guess I should tell you. I found some pictures."

He stopped in the middle of the hall. "What kind of pictures?"

"You can see for yourself," she said, and she watched him.

"No kidding." He grinned. "Where?"

"In a drawer," she said. 65

"No kidding," he said.

And then she said, "Maybe they won't come back," and was at once astonished at her words.

"It could happen," he said. "Anything could happen."

"Or maybe they'll come back and . . ." but she did not finish.

They held hands for the short walk across the hall, and when he spoke she could 70 barely hear his voice.

"The key," he said. "Give it to me."

"What?" she said. She gazed at the door.

"The key," he said. "You have the key."

"My God," she said, "I left the key inside."

He tried the knob. It was locked. Then she tried the knob. It would not turn. Her 75 lips were parted, and her breathing was hard, expectant. He opened his arms and she moved into them.

"Don't worry," he said into her ear. "For God's sake, don't worry."

They stayed there. They held each other. They leaned into the door as if against a wind, and braced themselves.

QUESTIONS

1. Who is the speaker of "Neighbors"? On whom is the speaker's attention directed?

2. Who are the Millers? Do they seem normal at first? As the story progresses, do they seem to get odd? What happens to them?

3. Should the story be considered as realistic fiction, or would it be more appropriate to consider it as an illustration of life's absurdities?

LAURIE COLWIN (1944–1992)

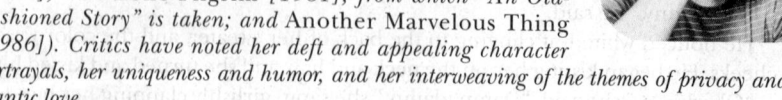

Colwin was born in New York and took her higher education at Bard and Columbia. During most of her brief life she worked as an editor and literary agent. Nevertheless she was quite busy as a writer in her own right, writing five novels (including Happy All the Time *[1978] and* Family Happiness *[1982]), two collections of essays, and three collections of stories (*Passion and Affect *[1974];* The Lone Pilgrim *[1981], from which "An Old-Fashioned Story" is taken; and* Another Marvelous Thing *[1986]). Critics have noted her deft and appealing character portrayals, her uniqueness and humor, and her interweaving of the themes of privacy and romantic love.*

An Old-Fashioned Story ~ ~ ~ 1981

The Rodkers had a son named Nelson, whom all the world called Nellie. The Leopolds had a daughter named Elizabeth. Marshall Rodker and Roger Leopold had been at college and law school together and courted wives who had been roommates at college.

Nelson was two years Elizabeth's senior, and he was a model child in every way. Elizabeth, on the other hand, began her life as a rebellious, spunky, and passionate child, but she was extraordinarily pretty, and such children are never called difficult: they are called original. It was the ardent hope of these people that their children might be friends and, when they grew up, would like each other well enough to marry.

In order to ensure their happy future, the children were brought together. If Elizabeth looked about to misbehave, Elinor Leopold placed her warm hand on Elizabeth's forearm and, with a little squeeze Elizabeth learned to dread, would say in tones of determined sweetness: "Darling, don't you want to see nice Nellie's chemistry set?" Elizabeth did not want to see it—or Nelson's stamp collection or his perfect math papers or the model city he had built with his Erector set. As she grew older, she did not want to dance with Nelson at dancing class or go to his school reception. But she did these things. That warm pressure on her forearm was as effective as a slap, although her compliance was not gained only by squeezes and horrified looks. Elizabeth had begun to have a secret life: she hated Nelson and she hated the Rodkers with secret fury. While she was too young to wonder if this loathing included her parents, she felt that if they forced Nelson upon her and chose the Rodkers for their dearest friends, they must in some way be against her. At the same time she realized that they were foolable to an amazing extent. If she smiled at Nelson, they were happy and considered her behavior impeccable. If she was rude, she spent weeks in pain—the pain of constant lectures. Thus, she learned to turn a cheerful face while keeping the fires of her dislike properly banked. The fact of the matter was that an afternoon of Nelson's stamp collection was good for two afternoons hanging around the park with her real friends.

Elizabeth's friends came down with measles, chicken pox, and mumps, but Elizabeth considered Nelson her childhood disease. As she got older, she began to feel that he had ruined her early years, but in her twenties she realized what an asset he had been. Without him she would never have learned to shield herself entirely from her parents. She learned from him how little it took to please: Nelson wrapped himself up warm when it was cold. He baked cookies for his mother's birthday. He played chess with his father. That, it appeared, sufficed—a very instructive lesson that was not lost on Elizabeth, who felt that beneath Nelson's clean, wavy hair lived a rat, a suck-up, a traitor to all children.

Nelson had an older brother named James. James was eight years Elizabeth's senior, and she regarded him as veritably ancient. James had been sent away to a progressive school for the brilliant and unmanageable children of the well-to-do. Here he learned to smoke, drive a car without a license, and play cards for money. When these traits became manifest, James was plucked from the libertine environment and sent to one of the nation's oldest and finest establishments for one last crack at making him an eventual leader of men. In this setting he drank beer, set off cherry bombs in trash cans, and hung around with town girls. By the time he was ready to graduate, he added to this sort of hell raising a penchant for seditious literature and came home spouting Marx,° Mao,° and Huysmans.°

At college he learned a great many more bad habits, including how to spend money, drink wine, seduce young women, and break some bone or other right before Thanksgiving vacation called him back to his family. In spite of this, he did extremely well

5

Marx: Karl Marx (1818–1883), founder of communism and writer of *The Communist Manifesto* (1848).

Mao: Mao Tse-tung (1893–1976), Chinese communist leader and author of *The Thoughts of Chairman Mao* (1967).

Huysmans: Joris-Karl Huysmans (1848–1907), French novelist, author of *Against the Grain* (1884), a novel about a young man's search for unique and exotic sensations.

and graduated with honors. The night of his graduation he was arrested with some of his unwholesome friends for disorderly conduct and was made to spend the night in jail. This was meant to scare him. The next morning he was released, his fingerprints in a manila envelope that he might know the kindness doled out by the police to young men who will someday be their elected leaders.

Elizabeth was kept abreast of James's evil career by her parents, who said that James was killing Marshall and breaking poor Harriet's heart. Nelson spoke of his brother as if he were some pathetic sort of animal.

Over a game of Scrabble, which, of course, Nelson was winning, he commented on the arrest.

"Poor Daddy and Mother. Jimmy got arrested, you know. They gave him back his fingerprints, but it will always be on his conscience, and if he's ever asked if he's been arrested, he'll have to say yes."

"Why will he?" Elizabeth said.

"Because it's true," said Nelson. "Besides, it's adolescent and silly. It's just as easy   10
not to get arrested as to get arrested." Nelson at the time was almost sixteen. He was a nice-looking, somewhat expressionless boy whom Elizabeth found more and more repulsive. All his clothes were clean. His hair was combed. Elizabeth knew that he underlined passages in books, a habit she found disgusting. When he read, he sat upright in his leather chair, under proper light with his book held at a proper angle. Elizabeth, who read under the covers with a flashlight, found his posture disgusting as well.

After a brief contemplation of the Scrabble board, Nelson made an ingenious play using the word "vugh," about which Elizabeth was doubtful but did not challenge. It was pointless to challenge Nelson. He was all-knowing and he never cheated. In fact, one of Harriet Rodker's favorite stories about him concerned a point of honor. Nelson, at seven, told his father that he had stolen two gum erasers from Mrs. Williamson's candy store. His father advised him to take them back. "But I can't," Nelson had said. "I was so upset about stealing them that I threw them away." Marshall Rodker then asked his son how he intended to make reparation—*if*, of course, was never at issue. Nelson had said, "I'll go to Mrs. Williamson and tell her what I did and pay her." This he did, and Mrs. Williamson swore she never knew a better boy than Nelson Rodker. Elizabeth was sure this was a true story but for one detail. She was certain that Nelson had not thrown the erasers away; she knew that he had eaten them. She was convinced that when his parents were out he made mashed potatoes from the *Joy of Cooking* so that he could eat them with his hands.

Nelson and Elizabeth went to brother-and-sister schools where Nelson distinguished himself. He won the Latin prize, the good citizen's award, the math medal, and scholar of the year. Meanwhile, James Rodker had dropped out of what little sight he permitted his parents by going to England, where it was thought he was studying economics or history. Only the Leopolds knew how scanty information was about James. At dinner parties his name and the subject of economic history were twined, but during Rodker-Leopold bridge games all was revealed. As Elizabeth stood with her ear to the library door, she learned that whenever the Rodkers went to London to see him, they found that he had just gone abroad, or, if he was in town, he turned up with Hindu or Oriental girls who were clearly his mistresses. Elizabeth longed for these bridge parties. James's career filled her with admiration. With Nelson constantly held over her head, it was hard for her not to have outright affection for anyone who behaved like a punk.

The beautiful daughters of the nervous well-to-do are tended like orchids, especially in a city like New York. Elizabeth was not allowed to take a public bus unaccompanied until she was thirteen. Her friends were carefully picked over. The little O'Connor girl was common; that her father had won a Pulitzer prize was of no matter. The little Jefferson boy was colored. It made no difference that his father was a diplomat. And so on. The only one of Elizabeth's friends Mrs. Leopold approved of was Holly Lukas, whose mother was an old friend. Holly was the only one to be dignified by a first name. Thus, Elizabeth never brought her real friends home, since, with the exception of Holly, they were all wrong: the children of broken homes, the sons and daughters of people with odd political or religious preferences or of blacklisted movie producers. Elizabeth learned the hard way that these children would not be made comfortable in her house. This might have put a crimp in Elizabeth's social life except that none of her friends wanted to entertain at home. They knew early on that the best place to conduct a private life was in public.

And then there was the Fifield Riding Academy incident. Like most girls her age, Elizabeth became horse crazy. She did not want to share this passion with her parents, who felt riding once a week was quite enough, so she made a deal with the stable that, in exchange for a free lesson, she would muck out the stalls on Tuesdays. This, however, was not known by her mother, who had her expensively outfitted. These riding clothes Elizabeth carried in a rucksack along with her real riding clothes—an old pair of blue jeans and a ratty sweater.

It was soon discovered that Elizabeth was coming home late one extra afternoon   15
each week stinking of horse. She was made to remove her jodhpurs at the service entrance and, when these garments were found to be relatively horseless, a search was made and the offending blue jeans rooted out. Mrs. Leopold then sat down to question her daughter. Elizabeth was mute. One word about manure and her riding days were over. But manure was not on Mrs. Leopold's mind and, in fact, when she learned that her spotless baby spent one weekday in the company of a pitchfork, she was much relieved.

She said, "Who works at the stable?"

Elizabeth said, "You know. Mr. Fifield. That girl, Franny Hatch, and some boys."

"What *boys?*"

"Oh, you know. Douglas Fifield and Buddy, the one who takes the little kids around the ring."

The questioning continued until Mrs. Leopold finally asked what she was really   20
after. "Did this Douglas or this Buddy ever try to touch you?"

Elizabeth was fourteen at the time, and it was clear that boys were not what worried Mrs. Leopold. It was Elizabeth herself. What wanton impulse would lead a girl to spend her time working in a stable?

Besides, parents of the time believed in companionship with their children. When Elizabeth discovered bird walking or skating, stationery embossed with birds or skates was ordered in case she wished to write to her relatives. This invasion of privacy, which radical students would later call co-option, looked harmless and well-meant and was practiced by most parents.

When Elizabeth went to college, she had her first taste of freedom. While similarly restrained girls went wild, Elizabeth reveled in being left alone and staying up late at night reading anything she liked. The Leopolds were not against reading, but Elizabeth's reading habits contributed to eyestrain and bad posture and, besides, all that reading made one lopsided. One must also sail, dress well, speak a foreign language, and be good at tennis. Since Elizabeth had never had the luxury to read undisturbed in her own house, she had little time at college to drink to excess or become promiscuous.

At home on holidays she was correctness itself. At twenty, in the middle of her first love affair, she was grown up enough to restrain herself from calling her beloved in Vermont, lest her parents find him on the telephone bill. Elizabeth's parents set great store on adult behavior. Had they known what sort of adult Elizabeth had become, great would have been their dismay. Elizabeth smiled beautifully and behaved in a flawless manner.

Her mother was not entirely happy. She felt, as mothers will, that her daughter was   25 not telling her the sort of things a daughter ought. She was vexed that Elizabeth was far away and none of her college chums could be conned. Mrs. Leopold knew she would have to wait for something to break: Elizabeth would want to go abroad to study, or to go to Africa, or she would turn up engaged to an awful boy. But Elizabeth did none of these things. She was graduated from college, came back to New York, and got a job.

Her decision to live in New York was not easily come by, but she loved New York and she wanted to enjoy it finally on her own terms. She went to her father's bank, and using as collateral a diamond-and-sapphire bracelet left to her by her grandmother, she borrowed enough money to rent an apartment on a little street in Greenwich Village and live until she had a salary. Through a friend of the O'Connor girl's Pulitzer-prize-winning father, she found a job at a publishing company and went to work.

Her parents were puzzled by this. The daughters of their friends were announcing their engagements in the *Times,* and those who joined the Peace Corps or had gone to graduate school were filed under the heading of "Useful Service," as if they had entered convents or dedicated themselves to the poor, following the example of Jane Addams,° who had after all come from a nice, rich family. Elizabeth further puzzled them by refusing to take a cent of their money, although Mrs. Leopold knew the truth: what you dole out to the young binds them to you. To have Elizabeth owing nothing was disconcerting, to say the least.

To even up the side, she called Elizabeth to see if she was comfortable in her little cramped apartment that doubtless had insufficient heat. In the summer she was sure Elizabeth was suffocating and offered an air conditioner. She worried that the cleaners in that part of town did shoddy work and brooded to Elizabeth about what young girls had for dinner.

Elizabeth was in a state of bliss. She could flop down on her bed with no lecture notes or required texts and read. Her friends, who had discovered many dangerous and exotic ways in which to cherish their freedom, found Elizabeth a little pathetic in this respect, but having the power to read what she liked was the ultimate liberty. Staying up all night exhausted her. Drink made her dizzy, drugs either disoriented her or made her sick, and she did not have a promiscuous nature. She did, however, have a lover.

The lover was her next-door neighbor, Roy Wayne Howard, a large man with an Ed-   30 wardian moustache. Roy was from central Ohio, and he was a fund raiser for the Center for Union Democracy. To this end he tried to hustle money. He found lawyers willing to donate their services. He had once been a hooded witness at the trial of some goons who had threatened an insurgent rank and file. Elizabeth, who was crazy about him, found him heroic.

Elizabeth had run into Roy in the neighborhood: They introduced themselves at the all-night grocery store. One evening Roy appeared at her door with a bottle of whisky and two glasses. He drank most of the whisky while he and Elizabeth sniped at one another. After several evenings of this sort, plus several afternoons watching football games on television and a meal at a crummy Spanish restaurant, they became lovers, and from then on they were on and off. When they were on, they went to prizefights, to bars, and to the jazz clubs Roy loved. After a month of this Roy ceased to appear. Ringing his

---

Jane Addams: Jane Addams (1860–1935), social worker, advocate of women's rights, and founder of Hull House in Chicago.

doorbell and confronting him turned out to be useless. Weeks would go by until they bumped into each other again and were on.

This kept up for a year. Elizabeth was in love with Roy, and this on-again, off-again business upset her. She discussed it with Holly Lukas.

"I can't bear it," Elizabeth wailed. "Why does he do this to me?"

"I would tell you," Holly said, "but you don't want to know."

"Yes, I do."

Holly, who was a great fan of Roy's, explained: "For a smart girl, Elizabeth, you have   35
a very selective intelligence. You're like your mother. You like to see a situation in the light that does you the most good. You think Roy is afraid of intimacy, which is a stylish thing to say, but the truth is that Roy is a little too fond of you, and when it occurs to him that there's nothing in it, he pulls back, for both your sakes."

"What do you mean, both our sakes?" said Elizabeth, who was reaching for her handkerchief.

"Roy is wonderful. Anyone with sense would love Roy. But Roy drinks too much. Roy dresses badly. Roy wants to be a solitary hero. Roy told you that his idea of happiness is to go off to an island in Lake Michigan with a transistor radio and a case of Scotch. You will never marry Roy, and Roy will never marry you. Since you're both old-fashioned, that's bound to catch up with you."

"Yes," said Elizabeth. "It's true. And if I hang around with Roy, I don't have to marry anyone else." Holly had told her this before.

"Absolutely," said Holly. "If you married Roy, both of you would be miserable. Face the fact that you're having a love affair that isn't unhappy but will not lead to anything."   40

Elizabeth knew the truth when she heard it, but still she went to prizefights and to bars with Roy intermittently.

Meanwhile, once every three weeks or so she had dinner with Nelson so if her mother said, "Aren't you seeing any nice young men?" she could truthfully answer, "I see Nelson."

Nelson called on a Wednesday to ask her out for Saturday. He always appeared in an elegant sports jacket and beautiful trousers. It was hard for Elizabeth to admit that he was good-looking, but he was. One night Nelson, who had been first in his class at law school, mentioned his volunteer prison work.

"You go into prisons looking like that?" she asked.

"Yes, and I wear my watch, too." Said watch was heavy and gold, a Rodker family relic.   45

"Those cons must really love you."

"Well, as a matter of fact, they do, because they get the services of a first-rate lawyer for free. And why should I change what I wear to go into a prison? I'd feel very condescended to if someone did that to me."

This prison-reform business was hard on Elizabeth. None of Nelson's attitudes were wrong and, worse, he never bragged. How she wished that he had turned out to be a corporate lawyer, voting Republican and talking about the creeping menace of socialism. Instead, he made a lot of money *and* did good works. There was nothing Elizabeth could pin on him.

Nelson always took her to a good restaurant and always paid for the meal, but he explained, "I'm told you're living on what you earn and, since what I earn is about three times what you earn, it's silly for you to split the check. If you wanted to be fair, you'd invite me for dinner. Your mother told my mother you're quite a good cook."

This was a sore subject with Elizabeth. She had invited her parents for dinner, after   50
concealing any incriminating thing in the house. Any trace of birth control was locked

away. Any book her mother might pick up and say, "Darling, are you reading *this?*" was hidden from view. All but several bottles of liquor were placed under the sink. No bottles would mean that Elizabeth had no social life. Too many would mean that she was either drinking to excess or hanging around with those who did.

Mrs. Leopold, who referred to these meals as "Elizabeth's bohemian dinners," said to her daughter, "I don't know where you learned to use spices in such an original way." Implying that Elizabeth never could have learned from her—and also that spices were common, and that real food, eaten by real people, was either plain American or French.

So Elizabeth had no intention of being fair and inviting Nelson for dinner. She figured he was probably a spy. Still, these dinners with him were not unpleasant, but after the pleasantest of them Elizabeth made sure that when Nelson left her at her door she changed her clothes and went next door to Roy Howard.

In early December Roy Howard moved away. He promised he would stay in touch, but Elizabeth began to cry. Roy said, "I love you in my own way but not in any way that will do any good." Then he gave her a kiss, and she knew he would continue to turn up intermittently. However, his moving brought her very low. She saw Nelson rather more often. He took her for drives in the country, or for walks, or out for dinner. He talked to her about her work and his own. He was an excellent time filler, and Elizabeth began to think of him as an old friend, one of those friends who connects you to your past. During a drive one afternoon he revealed to her that James was coming home for Christmas.

Coincidental with the departure of Roy Howard was an onslaught by her mother, who appeared one day at Elizabeth's office to take her out to lunch.

Soon Elizabeth was picking at a salad in a ladies' tearoom while her mother gently   55
grilled her. Why did she look so unwell and tired? Was she having trouble sleeping? Should she make an appointment with Dr. Goldhauer? Did her employers expect her to work herself into physical collapse? Mrs. Leopold had the knack of catching her daughter at her most vulnerable.

"I'm perfectly fine. It's just been a hectic week at work," Elizabeth said coldly.

Mrs. Leopold's eyes narrowed—a sign of war. War had once meant prohibition—of riding lessons and telephone calls. Now war meant a lecture, the only method left to Mrs. Leopold in her futile search for information. Basically, she wanted to know if Elizabeth was having romantic troubles, but since she would not ask, she came down hard on the issue of family loyalty and Elizabeth's lack of interest in the needs of others.

Elizabeth and Holly called these lectures "A Mother's Ten Commandments"—all of which they broke: Thou shalt tell thy mother everything. Thou shalt live very near thy mother. Thou shalt bring friends home for thy mother's approval. Thou shalt offer information about thy love life. Thou shalt dress according to thy mother's style. Thou shalt constantly be in debt to thy mother for sums large and small. Thou shalt have fierce family loyalty on all occasions. Thou shalt ask thy mother's opinion. Thou shalt confide thy troubles in thy mother so that thy mother may become hysterical. Thou shalt borrow thy mother's cleaning woman.

The lunch was not a success, and Elizabeth and her mother parted in terrible tempers.

One week later was the Rodkers' annual Christmas party, and Elizabeth was loaded   60
for bear. Her first step was the purchase of a black velvet dress that was low in the back, low in the front, and sleeveless. Next was the gardenia she wore in her hair. She looked quite beautiful, but her mother could not approve of the dress and she found the gardenia excessive. Nelson, however, found her ravishing and told her so. But Nelson's praise was not her goal: she was after James. She had decided that a little public bad behavior was exactly what she needed. It was time to get her mother off her back, outrage the Rodkers,

and put to rest once and for all her imitation of a well-composed young woman. She could also blitz what she considered their tidy plans for her: a safe marriage to nice Nelson, or someone very like him.

As soon as she had knocked back several glasses of champagne, she felt up to putting her plan in operation. This was to flirt slowly and blatantly with James. Then, if he was as dashing as she imagined, she would seduce him and then make it known. Before he went back to England, she would dump him. She was about to edge herself over to him when she felt that warm hand on her forearm.

"Darling, Harriet says you haven't said hello to her."

"Harriet can go to hell," said Elizabeth, so fortified by Piper Heidsieck that she ignored the threat of vengeance in her mother's eyes.

She approached James Rodker. Next to him the healthy Nelson palled. James looked haggard, tortured, just the sort of deep and troubled man you find in novels.

"Hello," she said with a big smile. "I haven't seen you since I was a little girl."   65

"Well, well, well," said James, "aren't you grown-up?" He turned her around and led her to a sofa.

"So you're Nellie's little pal," he said. "I've been hearing so much about you."

"I've always been hearing about you," Elizabeth said.

"Tell you what," said James, "as soon as the whole crowd is here, let's you and me sneak out for a drink and talk about all we've been hearing. What say?"

"All right," said Elizabeth, though this was not quite as she had planned. James had   70
jumped the gun on her.

But things worked out well enough. They made a public exit on the pretext of going out for a bag of ice and had the pleasure of watching Harriet Rodker's lips compress, but before she could speak, Elizabeth and James were out the door and into the elevator.

He took her to a bar around the corner, a dull, wood-paneled place—the sort of bar you can take your son to after a hockey game. They sat in a wooden booth and sipped their drinks in silence. James lit his pipe and smiled a knowing smile.

"So, here you are. The little number they've tucked away for brother Nellie," he said.

"I am not tucked away for anyone."

"No, on second thought, you wouldn't be. Girls like you play for higher stakes.   75
Love or income, or preferably both."

"I don't play for any stakes," Elizabeth said.

"How refreshingly young you are," said James. "Mother implored me to be kind to you."

"As opposed to what?"

"As opposed to dragging you by the hair, knocking you out, and catching a social disease, or giving you one."

"Have you had many social diseases?"   80

"Oh, several. I have contracted social diseases in Hong Kong, Saigon, and the town of High Wycombe." He set his dead pipe down on the table. "Little girls like you—I beg your pardon—women like you are meant to blush, or don't you blush any more? Probably not."

Elizabeth realized that the romantic James was rather drunk. He then began a long discourse on the subject of the nuclear family, quoting extensively in French from a sociologist Elizabeth had never heard of. Then he launched into an explanation of the English economy, and Elizabeth realized that for all that he was haggard he was extremely dull.

Suddenly he stared directly into Elizabeth's eyes.

"Have you the keys to your apartment?" he said, and, without waiting for an answer, continued, "Give them to me."

Elizabeth was old enough to have been flirted with and propositioned many times. 85
The men she liked best were straightforward, brave enough to state their intentions. The
keys James Rodker wanted he wanted to clean his pipe with, she was sure. The easy way
with which he made his request indicated to her that this was a well-used ploy. If you
forked over your keys, he cleaned his pipe. If you fluttered, James took this as encouragement and ended by using your keys to come and sleep with you. Elizabeth handed
over the keys and watched James dig the ashes out of his pipe.

"Clever girl," he said.

"I think we ought to go back," said Elizabeth, who was beginning to feel sleepy. She
was profoundly disappointed. James was not a man she wanted to flirt with, and she felt a
cold coming on.

"Not so fast," James said. "I'm going to tell you about all those things you've heard
about me." And he commenced to describe his college career, the flat he had inhabited
in London, the girls he had lived with in Paris, the bar girls he had slept with in Saigon,
his position on his paper, and the number of famous friends he had. Elizabeth had to
suppress a yawn.

"All right," said James, paying the bill. "Back to the arms of the family. Don't you
find it public-spirited of our lovely Nellie to work with the less fortunate?"

Elizabeth swallowed. "Nelson's all right." 90

"You, of course, are partisan," James said. "Nellie is an insect."

When they returned to the party, Elizabeth realized that they had been gone for
two hours and the smug smile James wore announced that they had been up to no good.

Elizabeth spent the next week in her apartment wrapped in a quilt. The cold she
had expected materialized. In addition to being ill, she was angry. From Holly she had
learned that James Rodker during his stay had not come home several nights and
dropped her name frequently. Thus, it was assumed that she and James were up to further evil doings. She said to Holly: "I know I set out to seduce him, but he's just too awful.
And besides, look at what he's done! He's set me up! He comes home to rub his parents'
nose in it and he used me!"

"Unthinkable," said Holly.

On the afternoon of New Year's Eve Elizabeth was curled up dozing under her 95
quilt. In a few hours she would dress and go to the boozy, happy party Holly gave each
New Year's. Elizabeth felt neither happy nor much in the mood for a party. She was
brooding heavily but was interrupted by the doorbell. She started—it might be Roy
Howard, who sometimes dropped by on whim. But it was not. It was Nelson Rodker.

"Hello," he said. "I was in the neighborhood and I heard you were sick, so I decided to drop by and see you."

This was most unlike Nelson. He was wearing a beautiful suit and gold cuff links.
The wind had blown his hair about and made his cheeks blaze. He looked healthy but
very serious.

"I guess you came to find out if I was sleeping with your brother," Elizabeth said.

"You're hardly the sort of girl to sleep with Jimmy. He's far too dull for you."

"How would you know?" 100

"I didn't come to fight with you or to check up on your behavior."

"You came as a kindly gesture to an ill friend."

"I came to see you because I wanted to."

"And to report back to our parents that I'm still alive and that James isn't hiding
under my bed?"

"Elizabeth, what is wrong with you? I always think of you as a free spirit and here   105
you chain me to my family."

"You are your family," Elizabeth said sulkily.

"I am most certainly not my family. I don't like my family and I never have. My family is silly, stuffy, and rigid. You're not the only one who behaved yourself and got out fast. What do you think I am?"

"A model boy," said Elizabeth.

Then Nelson did a most un-Nelson thing. He took the quilt from Elizabeth's shoulders, lifted her to her feet and gave her the sort of kiss she had never associated with Nelson or anyone like him.

"I came to tell you that I love you," said Nelson. "I've been wondering for months if   110
I love you because I was told to when I was a child or if I just love you. Well, I just love you."

They stood very close for a long time, the quilt lying at their feet.

"I don't know what to think," Elizabeth said.

"I want to know if you hate me because you expect it of yourself or if you actually hate me."

"I don't hate you," said Elizabeth.

"Do you think you could love me?"   115

Elizabeth discovered that her head was on his shoulder and that her arms were around his neck.

"It seems to make perfect sense," she said. "But things don't happen this way, do they?"

"Some old friends fall in love, all of a sudden," Nelson said.

"Whatever it is I feel, it seems to have hit me all at once. Or maybe it's crept up on me without my knowing."

"I'd like to take you to Holly's party," said Nelson.   120

"That's not for hours."

"Oh," said Nelson, "I'm sure we can find a way to pass the time."

"This will certainly amaze everyone," Elizabeth said.

"Only if we tell them," said Nelson. "A secret romance is one thing, but a secret romance worth keeping a secret is quite another. Just the thing for us, don't you think?"

They smiled ravishing smiles. As they stood with their arms entwined, they agreed   125
that it was just the perfect sort of thing for them.

QUESTIONS

1. Describe the situation in the two families. Who is Elizabeth? How completely is she developed as a character? To what degree is she unusual? How does she develop or change? What does she think of her family? What freedom does she covet most? What social conventions does she flaunt?

2. Who is Nelson? What is he like as a child? As an adult? What does Elizabeth think about him? Why is it important in the story's development for Elizabeth to misunderstand Nelson for most of their lives? What does Nelson think of his family? How different is he from his brother James?

3. Is the narrator named? Why or why not? How does the narrator's presentation shape your understanding of situations and characters?

4. What elements in the story are amusing? How does the narrator or speaker contribute to the humor?

5.   What surprise occurs at the story's end? What parts of the story might prepare readers for this conclusion? In light of the story's ending, consider the meaning of the title.

TIM O'BRIEN   (B. 1946)

William Timothy O'Brien was born in Minnesota and attended Macalester College in St. Paul. He saw duty in Vietnam during some of the more controversial times of that conflict, and after returning home he did graduate study, worked as a reporter, and became a writer. Among the works he has regularly published since the 1970s are If I Die in a Combat Zone, Box Me Up and Ship Me Home *(1973);* Northern Lights *(1974);* Going After Cacciato *(1978);* The Things They Carried *(1990), and* July, July *(2002). In his stories, which interweave fiction and autobiography, he realistically treats both the horrors of the Vietnam war and the ways in which returning veterans and their loved ones adjust to life after returning home. Because he portrays the lives and feelings of combat soldiers so well, he has been called one of the best American writers about war.*

The Things They Carried 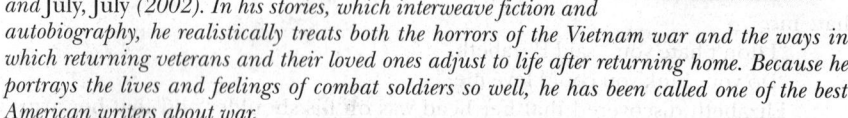 1990

First Lieutenant Jimmy Cross carried letters from a girl named Martha, a junior at Mount Sebastian College in New Jersey. They were not love letters, but Lieutenant Cross was hoping, so he kept them folded in plastic at the bottom of his rucksack. In the late afternoon, after a day's march, he would dig his foxhole, wash his hands under a canteen, unwrap the letters, hold them with the tips of his fingers, and spend the last hour of light pretending. He would imagine romantic camping trips into the White Mountains in New Hampshire. He would sometimes taste the envelope flaps, knowing her tongue had been there. More than anything, he wanted Martha to love him as he loved her, but the letters were mostly chatty, elusive on the matter of love. She was a virgin, he was almost sure. She was an English major at Mount Sebastian, and she wrote beautifully about her professors and roommates and midterm exams, about her respect for Chaucer and her great affection for Virginia Woolf. She often quoted lines of poetry; she never mentioned the war, except to say, Jimmy, take care of yourself. The letters weighed 10 ounces. They were signed Love, Martha, but Lieutenant Cross understood that Love was only a way of signing and did not mean what he sometimes pretended it meant. At dusk, he would carefully return the letters to his rucksack. Slowly, a bit distracted, he would get up and move among his men, checking the perimeter, then at full dark he would return to his hole and watch the night and wonder if Martha was a virgin.

The things they carried were largely determined by necessity. Among the necessities or near-necessities were P-38 can openers, pocket knives, heat tabs, wristwatches, dog tags, mosquito repellent, chewing gum, candy, cigarettes, salt tablets, packets of Kool-Aid, lighters, matches, sewing kits, Military Payment Certificates, C rations, and two or three canteens of water. Together, these items weighed between 15 and 20 pounds, depending upon a man's habits or rate of metabolism. Henry Dobbins, who was a big man, carried extra rations; he was especially fond of canned peaches in heavy syrup over pound cake. Dave Jensen, who practiced field hygiene, carried a toothbrush, dental floss, and several hotel-sized bars of soap he'd stolen on R&R in Sydney, Australia. Ted Lavender, who was scared, carried tranquilizers until he was shot in the head outside the village of Than Khe in mid-April. By necessity, and because it was SOP, they all carried steel helmets that weighed 5 pounds including the liner and camouflage cover. They carried the standard fatigue jackets and trousers. Very few carried underwear. On their feet they carried jungle boots—2.1 pounds—and Dave Jensen carried three pairs of socks and a can of Dr. Scholl's foot powder as a precaution against trench foot. Until he was shot, Ted Lavender carried six or seven ounces of premium dope, which for him was a necessity. Mitchell Sanders, the RTO, carried condoms. Norman Bowker carried a diary. Rat Kiley carried comic books. Kiowa, a devout Baptist, carried an illustrated New Testament that had been presented to him by his father, who taught Sunday school in Oklahoma City, Oklahoma. As a hedge against bad times, however, Kiowa also carried his grandmother's distrust of the white man, his grandfather's old hunting hatchet. Necessity dictated. Because the land was mined and booby-trapped, it was SOP for each man to carry a steel-centered, nylon-covered flak jacket, which weighed 6.7 pounds, but which on hot days seemed much heavier. Because you could die so quickly, each man carried at least one large compress bandage, usually in the helmet band for easy access. Because the nights were cold, and because the monsoons were wet, each carried a green plastic poncho that could be used as a raincoat or groundsheet or makeshift tent. With its quilted liner, the poncho weighed almost two pounds, but it was worth every ounce. In April, for instance, when Ted Lavender was shot, they used his poncho to wrap him up, then to carry him across the paddy, then to lift him into the chopper that took him away.

They were called legs or grunts.

To carry something was to hump it, as when Lieutenant Jimmy Cross humped his love for Martha up the hills and through the swamps. In its intransitive form, to hump meant to walk, or to march, but it implied burdens far beyond the intransitive.

Almost everyone humped photographs. In his wallet, Lieutenant Cross carried two photographs of Martha. The first was a Kodacolor snapshot signed Love, though he knew better. She stood against a brick wall. Her eyes were gray and neutral, her lips slightly open as she stared straight-on at the camera. At night, sometimes, Lieutenant Cross wondered who had taken the picture, because he knew she had boyfriends, because he loved her so much, and because he could see the shadow of the picture-taker spreading out against the brick wall. The second photograph had been clipped from the 1968 Mount Sebastian yearbook. It was an action shot—women's volleyball—and Martha was bent horizontal to the floor, reaching, the palms of her hands in sharp focus, the tongue taut, the expression frank and competitive. There was no visible sweat. She wore white gym shorts. Her legs, he thought, were almost certainly the legs of a virgin, dry and without hair, the left knee cocked and carrying her entire weight, which was just over one hundred pounds. Lieutenant Cross remembered touching that left knee. A dark theater, he remembered, and the movie was *Bonnie and Clyde*, and Martha wore a tweed skirt, and during the final scene, when he touched her knee, she turned and looked at him in a sad, sober way that made him pull his hand back, but he would always remember the feel of the tweed skirt and the knee beneath it and the sound of the gunfire that killed Bonnie and Clyde, how embarrassing it was, how slow and oppressive. He remembered kissing her good night at the dorm door. Right then, he thought, he should've done something brave. He should've carried her up the stairs to her room and tied her to the

5

bed and touched that left knee all night long. He should've risked it. Whenever he looked at the photographs, he thought of new things he should've done.

What they carried was partly a function of rank, partly of field specialty.

As a first lieutenant and platoon leader, Jimmy Cross carried a compass, maps, code books, binoculars, and a .45-caliber pistol that weighed 2.9 pounds fully loaded. He carried a strobe light and the responsibility for the lives of his men.

As an RTO, Mitchell Sanders carried the PRC-25 radio, a killer, 26 pounds with its battery.

As a medic, Rat Kiley carried a canvas satchel filled with morphine and plasma and malaria tablets and surgical tape and comic books and all the things a medic must carry, including M&M's for especially bad wounds, for a total weight of nearly 20 pounds.

As a big man, therefore a machine gunner, Henry Dobbins carried the M-60, which weighed 23 pounds unloaded, but which was almost always loaded. In addition, Dobbins carried between 10 and 15 pounds of ammunition draped in belts across his chest and shoulders. 10

As PFCs or Spec 4s, most of them were common grunts and carried the standard M-16 gas-operated assault rifle. The weapon weighed 7.5 pounds unloaded, 8.2 pounds with its full 20-round magazine. Depending on numerous factors, such as topography and psychology, the riflemen carried anywhere from 12 to 20 magazines, usually in cloth bandoliers, adding on another 8.4 pounds at minimum, 14 pounds at maximum. When it was available, they also carried M-16 maintenance gear—rods and steel brushes and swabs and tubes of LSA oil—all of which weighed about a pound. Among the grunts, some carried the M-79 grenade launcher, 5.9 pounds unloaded, a reasonably light weapon except for the ammunition, which was heavy. A single round weighed 10 ounces. The typical load was 25 rounds. But Ted Lavender, who was scared, carried 34 rounds when he was shot and killed outside Than Khe, and he went down under an exceptional burden, more than 20 pounds of ammunition, plus the flak jacket and helmet and rations and water and toilet paper and tranquilizers and all the rest, plus the unweighed fear. He was dead weight. There was no twitching or flopping. Kiowa, who saw it happen, said it was like watching a rock fall, or a big sandbag or something—just boom, then down—not like the movies where the dead guy rolls around and does fancy spins and goes ass over teakettle—not like that, Kiowa said, the poor bastard just flat-fuck fell. Boom. Down. Nothing else. It was a bright morning in mid-April. Lieutenant Cross felt the pain. He blamed himself. They stripped off Lavender's canteens and ammo, all the heavy things, and Rat Kiley said the obvious, the guy's dead, and Mitchell Sanders used his radio to report one U.S. KIA and to request a chopper. Then they wrapped Lavender in his poncho. They carried him out to a dry paddy, established security, and sat smoking the dead man's dope until the chopper came. Lieutenant Cross kept to himself. He pictured Martha's smooth young face, thinking he loved her more than anything, more than his men, and now Ted Lavender was dead because he loved her so much and could not stop thinking about her. When the dustoff arrived, they carried Lavender aboard. Afterward they burned Than Khe. They marched until dusk, then dug their holes, and that night Kiowa kept explaining how you had to be there, how fast it was, how the poor guy just dropped like so much concrete. Boom-down, he said. Like cement.

In addition to the three standard weapons—the M-60, M-16, and M-79—they carried whatever presented itself, or whatever seemed appropriate as a means of killing or staying alive. They carried catch-as-catch-can. At various times, in various situations, they carried M-14s and CAR-15s and Swedish Ks and grease guns and captured AK-47s and

Chi-Coms and RPGs and Simonov carbines and black market Uzis and .38-caliber Smith & Wesson handguns and 66 mm LAWs and shotguns and silencers and blackjacks and bayonets and C-4 plastic explosives. Lee Strunk carried a slingshot; a weapon of last resort, he called it. Mitchell Sanders carried brass knuckles. Kiowa carried his grandfather's feathered hatchet. Every third or fourth man carried a Claymore antipersonnel mine— 3.5 pounds with its firing device. They all carried fragmentation grenades—14 ounces each. They all carried at least one M-18 colored smoke grenade—24 ounces. Some carried CS or tear gas grenades. Some carried white phosphorus grenades. They carried all they could bear, and then some, including a silent awe for the terrible power of the things they carried.

In the first week of April, before Lavender died, Lieutenant Jimmy Cross received a good-luck charm from Martha. It was a simple pebble, an ounce at most. Smooth to the touch, it was a milky white color with flecks of orange and violet, oval-shaped, like a miniature egg. In the accompanying letter, Martha wrote that she had found the pebble on the Jersey shoreline, precisely where the land touched water at high tide, where things came together but also separated. It was this separate-but-together quality, she wrote, that had inspired her to pick up the pebble and to carry it in her breast pocket for several days, where it seemed weightless, and then to send it through the mail, by air, as a token of her truest feelings for him. Lieutenant Cross found this romantic. But he wondered what her truest feelings were, exactly, and what she meant by separate-but-together. He wondered how the tides and waves had come into play on that afternoon along the Jersey shoreline when Martha saw the pebble and bent down to rescue it from geology. He imagined bare feet. Martha was a poet, with the poet's sensibilities, and her feet would be brown and bare, the toenails unpainted, the eyes chilly and somber like the ocean in March, and though it was painful, he wondered who had been with her that afternoon. He imagined a pair of shadows moving along the strip of sand where things came together but also separated. It was phantom jealousy, he knew, but he couldn't help himself. He loved her so much. On the march, through the hot days of early April, he carried the pebble in his mouth, turning it with his tongue, tasting sea salt and moisture. His mind wandered. He had difficulty keeping his attention on the war. On occasion he would yell at his men to spread out the column, to keep their eyes open, but then he would slip away into daydreams, just pretending, walking barefoot along the Jersey shore, with Martha, carrying nothing. He would feel himself rising. Sun and waves and gentle winds, all love and lightness.

What they carried varied by mission.

When a mission took them to the mountains, they carried mosquito netting, machetes, canvas tarps, and extra bug juice.

If a mission seemed especially hazardous, or if it involved a place they knew to be bad, they carried everything they could. In certain heavily mined AOs, where the land was dense with Toe Poppers and Bouncing Betties, they took turns humping a 28-pound mine detector. With its headphones and big sensing plate, the equipment was a stress on the lower back and shoulders, awkward to handle, often useless because of the shrapnel in the earth, but they carried it anyway, partly for safety, partly for the illusion of safety.

On ambush, or other night missions, they carried peculiar little odds and ends. Kiowa always took along his New Testament and a pair of moccasins for silence. Dave Jensen carried night-sight vitamins high in carotene. Lee Strunk carried his slingshot; ammo, he claimed, would never be a problem. Rat Kiley carried brandy and M&M's candy. Until he was shot, Ted Lavender carried the starlight scope, which weighed 6.3 pounds with its aluminum carrying case. Henry Dobbins carried his girlfriend's panty-hose wrapped around his neck as a comforter. They all carried ghosts. When dark came, they would move out single file across the meadows and paddies to their ambush coordinates, where they would quietly set up the Claymores and lie down and spend the night waiting.

Other missions were more complicated and required special equipment. In mid-April, it was their mission to search out and destroy the elaborate tunnel complexes in the Than Khe area south of Chu Lai. To blow the tunnels, they carried one-pound blocks of pentrite high explosives, four blocks to a man, 68 pounds in all. They carried wiring, detonators, and battery-powered clackers. Dave Jensen carried earplugs. Most often, before blowing the tunnels, they were ordered by higher command to search them, which was considered bad news, but by and large they just shrugged and carried out orders. Because he was a big man, Henry Dobbins was excused from tunnel duty. The others would draw numbers. Before Lavender died there were 17 men in the platoon, and whoever drew the number 17 would strip off his gear and crawl in headfirst with a flashlight and Lieutenant Cross's .45-caliber pistol. The rest of them would fan out as security. They would sit down or kneel, not facing the hole, listening to the ground beneath them, imagining cobwebs and ghosts, whatever was down there—the tunnel walls squeezing in—how the flashlight seemed impossibly heavy in the hand and how it was tunnel vision in the very strictest sense, compression in all ways, even time, and how you had to wiggle in—ass and elbows—a swallowed-up feeling—and how you found yourself worrying about odd things: Will your flashlight go dead? Do rats carry rabies? If you screamed, how far would the sound carry? Would your buddies hear it? Would they have the courage to drag you out? In some respects, though not many, the waiting was worse than the tunnel itself. Imagination was a killer.

On April 16, when Lee Strunk drew the number 17, he laughed and muttered something and went down quickly. The morning was hot and very still. Not good, Kiowa said. He looked at the tunnel opening, then out across a dry paddy toward the village of Than Khe. Nothing moved. No clouds or birds or people. As they waited, the men smoked and drank Kool-Aid, not talking much, feeling sympathy for Lee Strunk but also feeling the luck of the draw. You win some, you lose some, said Mitchell Sanders, and sometimes you settle for a rain check. It was a tired line and no one laughed.

Henry Dobbins ate a tropical chocolate bar. Ted Lavender popped a tranquilizer and went off to pee.   20

After five minutes, Lieutenant Jimmy Cross moved to the tunnel, leaned down, and examined the darkness. Trouble, he thought—a cave-in maybe. And then suddenly, without willing it, he was thinking about Martha. The stresses and fractures, the quick collapse, the two of them buried alive under all that weight. Dense, crushing love. Kneeling, watching the hole, he tried to concentrate on Lee Strunk and the war, all the dangers, but his love was too much for him, he felt paralyzed, he wanted to sleep inside her lungs and breathe her blood and be smothered. He wanted her to be a virgin and not a virgin, all at once. He wanted to know her. Intimate secrets: Why poetry? Why so sad? Why that grayness in her eyes? Why so alone? Not lonely, just alone—riding her bike across campus or sitting off by herself in the cafeteria—even dancing, she danced alone—and it was the aloneness that filled him with love. He remembered telling her that one evening. How she nodded and looked away. And how, later, when he kissed her, she received the kiss without returning it, her eyes wide open, not afraid, not a virgin's eyes, just flat and uninvolved.

Lieutenant Cross gazed at the tunnel. But he was not there. He was buried with Martha under the white sand at the Jersey shore. They were pressed together, and the pebble in his mouth was her tongue. He was smiling. Vaguely, he was aware of how quiet the day was, the sullen paddies, yet he could not bring himself to worry about matters of security. He was beyond that. He was just a kid at war, in love. He was twenty-four years old. He couldn't help it.

A few moments later Lee Strunk crawled out of the tunnel. He came up grinning, filthy but alive. Lieutenant Cross nodded and closed his eyes while the others clapped Strunk on the back and made jokes about rising from the dead.

Worms, Rat Kiley said. Right out of the grave. Fuckin' zombie.

The men laughed. They all felt great relief.   25

Spook city, said Mitchell Sanders.

Lee Strunk made a funny ghost sound, a kind of moaning, yet very happy, and right then, when Strunk made that high happy moaning sound, when he went *Ahhooooo*, right then Ted Lavender was shot in the head on his way back from peeing. He lay with his mouth open. The teeth were broken. There was a swollen black bruise under his left eye. The cheekbone was gone. Oh shit, Rat Kiley said, the guy's dead. The guy's dead, he kept saying, which seemed profound—the guy's dead. I mean really.

The things they carried were determined to some extent by superstition. Lieutenant Cross carried his good-luck pebble. Dave Jensen carried a rabbit's foot. Norman Bowker, otherwise a very gentle person, carried a thumb that had been presented to him as a gift by Mitchell Sanders. The thumb was dark brown, rubbery to the touch, and weighed four ounces at most. It had been cut from a VC corpse, a boy of fifteen or sixteen. They'd found him at the bottom of an irrigation ditch, badly burned, flies in his mouth and eyes. The boy wore black shorts and sandals. At the time of his death he had been carrying a pouch of rice, a rifle and three magazines of ammunition.

You want my opinion, Mitchell Sanders said, there's a definite moral here.

He put his hand on the dead boy's wrist. He was quiet for a time, as if counting a   30
pulse, then he patted the stomach, almost affectionately, and used Kiowa's hunting hatchet to remove the thumb.

Henry Dobbins asked what the moral was.

Moral?

You know. *Moral*.

Sanders wrapped the thumb in toilet paper and handed it across to Norman Bowker. There was no blood. Smiling, he kicked the boy's head, watched the flies scatter, and said, It's like with that old TV show—Paladin. Have gun, will travel.

Henry Dobbins thought about it.   35

Yeah, well, he finally said. I don't see no moral.

There it *is*, man.

Fuck off.

They carried USO stationery and pencils and pens. They carried Sterno, safety pins, trip flares, signal flares, spools of wire, razor blades, chewing tobacco, liberated joss sticks and statuettes of the smiling Buddha, candles, grease pencils, *The Stars and Stripes*, fingernail clippers, Psy Ops leaflets, bush hats, bolos, and much more. Twice a week, when the resupply choppers came in, they carried hot chow in green mermite cans and large canvas bags filled with iced beer and soda pop. They carried plastic water containers, each with a two-gallon capacity. Mitchell Sanders carried a set of starched tiger fatigues for special occasions. Henry Dobbins carried Black Flag insecticide. Dave Jensen carried empty sandbags that could be filled at night for added protection. Lee Strunk carried tanning lotion. Some things they carried in common. Taking turns, they carried the big PRC-77 scrambler radio, which weighed 30 pounds with its battery. They shared the weight of memory. They took up what others could no longer bear. Often, they carried each other, the wounded or weak.

They carried infections. They carried chess sets, basketballs, Vietnamese-English dictionaries, insignia of rank, Bronze Stars and Purple Hearts, plastic cards imprinted with the Code of Conduct. They carried diseases, among them malaria and dysentery. They carried lice and ringworm and leeches and paddy algae and various rots and molds. They carried the land itself—Vietnam, the place, the soil—a powdery orange-red dust that covered their boots and fatigues and faces. They carried the sky. The whole atmosphere, they carried it, the humidity, the monsoons, the stink of fungus and decay, all of it, they carried gravity. They moved like mules. By daylight they took sniper fire, at night they were mortared, but it was not battle, it was just the endless march, village to village, without purpose, nothing won or lost. They marched for the sake of the march. They plodded along slowly, dumbly, leaning forward against the heat, unthinking, all blood and bone, simple grunts, soldiering with their legs, toiling up the hills and down into the paddies and across the rivers and up again and down, just humping, one step and then the next and then another, but no volition, no will, because it was automatic, it was anatomy, and the war was entirely a matter of posture and carriage, the hump was everything, a kind of inertia, a kind of emptiness, a dullness of desire and intellect and conscience and hope and human sensibility. Their principles were in their feet. Their calculations were biological. They had no sense of strategy or mission. They searched the villages without knowing what to look for, not caring, kicking over jars of rice, frisking children and old men, blowing tunnels, sometimes setting fires and sometimes not, then forming up and moving on to the next village, then other villages, where it would always be the same. They carried their own lives. The pressures were enormous. In the heat of early afternoon, they would remove their helmets and flak jackets, walking bare, which was dangerous but which helped ease the strain. They would often discard things along the route of march. Purely for comfort, they would throw away rations, blow their Claymores and grenades, no matter, because by nightfall the resupply choppers would arrive with more of the same, then a day or two later still more, fresh watermelons and crates of ammunition and sunglasses and woolen sweaters—the resources were stunning—sparklers for the Fourth of July, colored eggs for Easter—it was the great American war chest—the fruits of science, the smokestacks, the canneries, the arsenals at Hartford, the Minnesota forests, the machine shops, the vast fields of corn and wheat—they carried like freight trains; they carried it on their backs and shoulders—and for all the ambiguities of Vietnam, all the mysteries and unknowns, there was at least the single abiding certainty that they would never be at a loss for things to carry.

After the chopper took Lavender away, Lieutenant Jimmy Cross led his men into the village of Than Khe. They burned everything. They shot chickens and dogs, they trashed the village well, they called in artillery and watched the wreckage, then they marched for several hours through the hot afternoon, and then at dusk, while Kiowa explained how Lavender died, Lieutenant Cross found himself trembling.

He tried not to cry. With his entrenching tool, which weighed five pounds, he began digging a hole in the earth.

He felt shame. He hated himself. He had loved Martha more than his men, and as a consequence Lavender was now dead, and this was something he would have to carry like a stone in his stomach for the rest of the war.

All he could do was dig. He used his entrenching tool like an ax, slashing, feeling both love and hate, and then later, when it was full dark, he sat at the bottom of his foxhole and wept. It went on for a long while. In part, he was grieving for Ted Lavender, but mostly it was for Martha, and for himself, because she belonged to another world, which was not quite real, and because she was a junior at Mount Sebastian College in New Jersey, a poet and a virgin and uninvolved, and because he realized she did not love him and never would.

40

Like cement, Kiowa whispered in the dark. I swear to God—boom, down. Not a word.

I've heard this, said Norman Bowker.

A pisser, you know? Still zipping himself up. Zapped while zipping.

All right, fine. That's enough.

Yeah, but you had to see it, the guy just—

I *heard*, man. Cement. So why not shut the fuck *up?*

Kiowa shook his head sadly and glanced over at the hole where Lieutenant Jimmy Cross sat watching the night. The air was thick and wet. A warm dense fog had settled over the paddies and there was the stillness that precedes rain.

After a time Kiowa sighed.

One thing for sure, he said. The lieutenant's in some deep hurt. I mean that crying jag—the way he was carrying on—it wasn't fake or anything, it was real heavy-duty hurt. The man cares.

Sure, Norman Bowker said.

Say what you want, the man does care.

We all got problems.

Not Lavender.

No, I guess not, Bowker said. Do me a favor, though.

Shut up?

That's a smart Indian. Shut up.

Shrugging, Kiowa pulled off his boots. He wanted to say more, just to lighten up his sleep, but instead he opened his New Testament and arranged it beneath his head as a pillow. The fog made things seem hollow and unattached. He tried not to think about Ted Lavender, but then he was thinking how fast it was, no drama, down and dead, and how it was hard to feel anything except surprise. It seemed unchristian. He wished he could find some great sadness, or even anger, but the emotion wasn't there and he couldn't make it happen. Mostly he felt pleased to be alive. He liked the smell of the New Testament under his cheek, the leather and ink and paper and glue, whatever the chemicals were. He liked hearing the sounds of night. Even his fatigue, it felt fine, the stiff muscles and the prickly awareness of his own body, a floating feeling. He enjoyed not being dead. Lying there, Kiowa admired Lieutenant Jimmy Cross's capacity for grief. He wanted to share the man's pain, he wanted to care as Jimmy Cross cared. And yet when he closed his eyes, all he could think was Boom-down, and all he could feel was the pleasure of having his boots off and the fog curling in around him and the damp soil and the Bible smells and the plush comfort of night.

After a moment Norman Bowker sat up in the dark.

What the hell, he said. You want to talk, *talk.* Tell it to me.

Forget it.

No, man, go on. One thing I hate, it's a silent Indian.

For the most part they carried themselves with poise, a kind of dignity. Now and then, however, there were times of panic, when they squealed or wanted to squeal but couldn't, when they twitched and made moaning sounds and covered their heads and said Dear Jesus and flopped around on the earth and fired their weapons blindly and cringed and sobbed and begged for the noise to stop and went wild and made stupid promises to themselves and to God and to their mothers and fathers, hoping not to die. In different ways, it happened to all of them. Afterward, when the firing ended, they would blink and peek up. They would touch their bodies, feeling shame, then quickly hiding it. They would force themselves to stand. As if in slow motion, frame by frame, the world would take on the old logic—absolute silence, then the wind, then sunlight, then voices. It was the burden of being alive. Awkwardly, the men would reassemble themselves, first in private, then in groups, becoming soldiers again. They would repair the leaks in their eyes. They would check for casualties, call in dust-offs, light cigarettes, try to smile, clear their throats and spit and begin cleaning their weapons. After a time someone would shake his head and say, No lie. I almost shit my pants, and someone else would laugh, which meant it was bad, yes, but the guy had obviously not shit his pants, it wasn't that bad, and in any case nobody would ever do such a thing and then go ahead and talk about it. They would squint into the dense, oppressive sunlight. For a few moments, perhaps, they would fall silent, lighting a joint and tracking its passage from man to man, inhaling, holding in the humiliation. Scary stuff, one of them might say. But then someone else would grin or flick his eyebrows and say, Roger-dodger, almost cut me a new asshole, *almost.*

There were numerous such poses. Some carried themselves with a sort of wistful resignation, others with pride or stiff soldierly discipline or good humor or macho zeal. They were afraid of dying but they were even more afraid to show it.

They found jokes to tell.

They used a hard vocabulary to contain the terrible softness. *Greased* they'd say. *Offed, lit up, zapped while zipping.* It wasn't cruelty, just stage presence. They were actors. When someone died, it wasn't quite dying, because in a curious way it seemed scripted, and because they had their lines mostly memorized, irony mixed with tragedy, and because they called it by other names, as if to encyst and destroy the reality of death itself. They kicked corpses. They cut off thumbs. They talked grunt lingo. They told stories about Ted Lavender's supply of tranquilizers, how the poor guy didn't feel a thing, how incredibly tranquil he was.

There's a moral here, said Mitchell Sanders.

They were waiting for Lavender's chopper, smoking the dead man's dope.   70

The moral's pretty obvious, Sanders said, and winked. Stay away from drugs. No joke, they'll ruin your day every time.

Cute, said Henry Dobbins.

Mind blower, get it? Talk about wiggy. Nothing left, just blood and brains.

They made themselves laugh.

There it is, they'd say. Over and over—there it is, my friend, there it is—as if the repe-   75
tition itself were an act of poise, a balance between crazy and almost crazy, knowing without going, there it is, which meant be cool, let it ride, because Oh yeah, man, you can't change what can't be changed, there it is, there it absolutely and positively and fucking well *is.*

They were tough.

They carried all the emotional baggage of men who might die. Grief, terror, love, longing—these were intangibles, but the intangibles had their own mass and specific gravity, they had tangible weight. They carried shameful memories. They carried the common secret of cowardice barely restrained, the instinct to run or freeze or hide, and in many respects this was the heaviest burden of all, for it could never be put down, it required perfect balance and perfect posture. They carried their reputations. They carried the soldier's greatest fear, which was the fear of blushing. Men killed, and died, because they were embarrassed not to. It was what had brought them to the war in the first place, nothing positive, no dreams of glory or honor, just to avoid the blush of dishonor. They died so as not to die of embarrassment. They crawled into tunnels and walked point and advanced under fire. Each morning, despite the unknowns, they made their legs move. They endured. They kept humping. They did not submit to the obvious alternative, which was simply to close the eyes and fall. So easy, really. Go limp and tumble to the ground and let the muscles unwind and not speak and not budge until your buddies picked you up and lifted you into the chopper that would roar and dip its nose and carry you off to the world. A mere matter of falling, yet no one ever fell. It was not courage, exactly; the object was not valor. Rather, they were too frightened to be cowards.

By and large they carried these things inside, maintaining the masks of composure. They sneered at sick call. They spoke bitterly about guys who had found release by shooting off their own toes or fingers. Pussies, they'd say. Candy-asses. It was fierce, mocking talk, with only a trace of envy or awe, but even so the image played itself out behind their eyes.

They imagined the muzzle against flesh. So easy: squeeze the trigger and blow away a toe. They imagined it. They imagined the quick, sweet pain, then the evacuation to Japan, then a hospital with warm beds and cute geisha nurses.

And they dreamed of freedom birds.

At night, on guard, staring into the dark, they were carried away by jumbo jets. They felt the rush of takeoff. *Gone!* they yelled. And then velocity—wings and engines—a smiling stewardess—but it was more than a plane, it was a real bird, a big sleek silver bird with feathers and talons and high screeching. They were flying. The weights fell off; there was nothing to bear. They laughed and held on tight, feeling the cold slap of wind and altitude, soaring, thinking *It's over, I'm gone!*—they were naked, they were light and free—it was all lightness, bright and fast and buoyant, light as light, a helium buzz in the brain, a giddy bubbling in the lungs as they were taken up over the clouds and the war, beyond duty, beyond gravity and mortification and global entanglements—*Sin loi!* they yelled. *I'm sorry, motherfuckers, but I'm out of it, I'm goofed, I'm on a space cruise, I'm gone!*—and it was a restful, unencumbered sensation, just riding the light waves, sailing that big silver freedom bird over the mountains and oceans, over America, over the farms and great sleeping cities and cemeteries and highways and the golden arches of McDonald's, it was flight, a kind of fleeing, a kind of falling, falling higher and higher, spinning off the edge of the earth and beyond the sun and through the vast, silent vacuum where there were no burdens and where everything weighed exactly nothing—*Gone!* they screamed. *I'm sorry but I'm gone!*—and so at night, not quite dreaming, they gave themselves over to lightness, they were carried, they were purely borne.

On the morning after Ted Lavender died, First Lieutenant Jimmy Cross crouched at the bottom of his foxhole and burned Martha's letters. Then he burned the two photographs. There was a steady rain falling, which made it difficult, but he used heat tabs and Sterno to build a small fire, screening it with his body, holding the photographs over the tight blue flame with the tips of his fingers.

He realized it was only a gesture. Stupid, he thought. Sentimental, too, but mostly just stupid.

Lavender was dead. You couldn't burn the blame.

Besides, the letters were in his head. And even now, without photographs, Lieutenant Cross could see Martha playing volleyball in her white gym shorts and yellow T-shirt. He could see her moving in the rain.

When the fire died out, Lieutenant Cross pulled his poncho over his shoulders and ate breakfast from a can.

There was no great mystery, he decided.

In those burned letters Martha had never mentioned the war, except to say, Jimmy, take care of yourself. She wasn't involved. She signed the letters Love, but it wasn't love, and all the fine lines and technicalities did not matter. Virginity was no longer an issue. He hated her. Yes, he did. He hated her. Love, too, but it was a hard, hating kind of love.

The morning came up wet and blurry. Everything seemed part of everything else, the fog and Martha and the deepening rain.

He was a soldier, after all.   90

Half smiling, Lieutenant Jimmy Cross took out his maps. He shook his head hard, as if to clear it, then bent forward and began planning the day's march. In ten minutes, or maybe twenty, he would rouse the men and they would pack up and head west, where the maps showed the country to be green and inviting. They would do what they had always done. The rain might add some weight, but otherwise it would be one more day layered upon all the other days.

He was realistic about it. There was that new hardness in his stomach. He loved her but he hated her.

No more fantasies, he told himself.

Henceforth, when he thought about Martha, it would be only to think that she belonged elsewhere. He would shut down the daydreams. This was not Mount Sebastian, it was another world, where there were no pretty poems or midterm exams, a place where men died because of carelessness and gross stupidity. Kiowa was right. Boom-down, and you were dead, never partly dead.

Briefly, in the rain, Lieutenant Cross saw Martha's gray eyes gazing back at him.   95

He understood.

It was very sad, he thought. The things men carried inside. The things men did or felt they had to do.

He almost nodded at her, but didn't.

Instead he went back to his maps. He was now determined to perform his duties firmly and without negligence. It wouldn't help Lavender, he knew that, but from this point on he would comport himself as an officer. He would dispose of his good-luck pebble. Swallow it, maybe, or use Lee Strunk's slingshot, or just drop it along the trail. On the march he would impose strict field discipline. He would be careful to send out flank security, to prevent straggling or bunching up, to keep his troops moving at the proper pace and at the proper interval. He would insist on clean weapons. He would confiscate the remainder of Lavender's dope. Later in the day, perhaps, he would call the men together and speak to them plainly. He would accept the blame for what had happened to Ted Lavender. He would be a man about it. He would look them in the eyes, keeping his chin level, and he would issue the new SOPs in a calm, impersonal tone of voice, a lieutenant's voice, leaving no room for argument or discussion. Commencing immediately, he'd tell them, they would no longer abandon equipment along the route of march. They would police up their acts. They would get their shit together, and keep it together, and maintain it neatly and in good working order.

He would not tolerate laxity. He would show strength, distancing himself.   100

Among the men there would be grumbling, of course, and maybe worse, because their days would seem longer and their loads heavier, but Lieutenant Jimmy Cross reminded himself that his obligation was not to be loved but to lead. He would dispense with love; it was not now a factor. And if anyone quarreled or complained, he would simply tighten his lips and arrange his shoulders in the correct command posture. He might give a curt little nod. Or he might not. He might just shrug and say, Carry on, then they would saddle up and form into a column and move out toward the villages west of Than Khe.

QUESTIONS

1. What do we learn about Lieutenant Jimmy Cross? How do we learn about him? Why does he blame himself for Lavender's death? How does Kiowa misinterpret his emotions? How do his concerns unify the story? What other unifying elements does the story contain?

2. What is the effect of the repetitions in the story (the constant descriptions of how much things weigh, the regular need to carry things, the way in which Lavender died)?

3. Why is Mitchell Sanders unable to put into words the moral of the dead man's thumb? How would you describe the moral?

4. Analyze paragraph 39. Discuss the various burdens the men of the platoon must carry. What bearing does this paragraph have upon other parts of the story?

GAIUS PETRONIUS ARBITER (PETRONIUS, D. 66 A.D.)

An English version by Edgar V. Roberts

Historically, Petronius was a political figure in the court of the Roman Emperor Nero (ruled 54–68), who is best remembered for his reprisals against Roman Christians after the famous fire in Rome in 64 C.E. Petronius served as an ambassador and also as a consul (an office conferring the right to introduce legal cases in the Roman Senate). For a time he enjoyed imperial favor as one of Nero's inner circle. However, he was accused as being part of a conspiracy against Nero, and he was then was ordered by the emperor to commit suicide, which he had no choice but to do.

As a writer, Petronius is best known for his picaresque and satiric The Satiricon, *a lengthy work of which only a small part has survived. "The Widow of Ephesus" is taken from this work, which consists of a series of episodes and stories held together by the adventures of Encolpius, the narrator, and a group of his friends as they travel from town to town in southern Italy. The story of the Widow appears after a brawl that occurs on board the ship of Lichas, a wealthy sea captain whom Encolpius had earlier robbed, and his woman friend Tryphena, a courtesan with whom Encolpius has earlier had a brief affair. Encolpius and his friends, one of whom is Eumolpus, an elderly poet and raconteur, fight against Lichas and his crew. After the brawl, there is general joyousness on the ship, and the combatants settle down to hear the story of the Ephesian Widow. The speaker or narrator is Encolpius, who quotes Eumolpus's story.*

The Widow of Ephesus (from The Satyricon, Chs. 108–113) (65 C.E.)

We shook hands, chatted happily, and sang loudly while the entire ship rang with our noise. Sea birds landed on the yard-arms, and Eumolpus, who was drinking too much wine, decided to amuse us with a few stories. He began by insulting women. He called them weak because he claimed they were impetuous in love and would neglect even their own children while having an illicit affair. Moreover, he said that no woman he had ever known had the moral strength to resist a handsome man. He insisted that he did not get his ideas from legend or from historical accounts about evil women. Rather, he himself had actually seen what he was talking about, and he offered to tell us a true story in illustration. We immediately urged him on, and gave him our complete attention. This is the tale he told:

"Once upon a time in the city of Ephesus, on the Coast of Asia Minor, there lived a virtuous woman whose marital fidelity was so famous that women came from far and near just to get a glimpse of her. In the course of time, her husband got sick and died, and the newly widowed lady, all by herself, arranged his funeral and burial. At the funeral she was not satisfied only to follow the cortege in the usual way, by tearing her hair and beating her breasts. No, she actually accompanied the dead body right into the tomb, and after the coffin was placed in the vault in the custom of the Greeks, she began a vigil beside it, weeping and wailing both day and night.

"She was so rigorous in her duty that she neglected to eat, and she therefore became weaker by the hour. Neither her parents nor her closest relatives could persuade her to return home. Even the local politicians and judges could not convince her. She snubbed them, and so, with their dignity ruffled, they gave up trying.

"By this time this most amazing woman was already in the fifth day of her fast, to the sorrow of everyone in town, who believed that she would die at any moment. At her side was her faithful handmaiden, who shed as many tears as the mournful Widow did. This maiden also attended to practical matters such as refueling and relighting the torch whenever it was about to go out. Through all the city of Ephesus, from one end to another, no one talked about anything else. All the people from richest to poorest acknowledged the Widow as the supreme example of wifely love and duty. They had never seen or heard of anyone like her.

"But regular business in Ephesus also went on, and one day the Provincial Governor sentenced some local hoodlums to be crucified in the grounds next to the tomb in which the Widow stood vigil. On the night of the crucifixion a soldier was stationed there to keep away all relatives or friends who might have wanted to steal the bodies in order to bury them properly.

"As he stood guard, he saw the torchlight from the Widow's tomb, and he also heard her heartbreaking outcries. Now, curiosity is a weakness of humankind, and this soldier was typically human. He went down the stairs into the sepulchre to take a look. Imagine his shock at the sight of this pretty woman and the corpse of her husband! At first he thought he was seeing ghosts, or apparitions out of the Kingdom of Hades! But when he saw how the Widow mourned, and how she had scarred her face with her fingernails, he understood that she was near death. He therefore ran up to his station and got his supper, which he carried to her. He pleaded with the sorrowing woman to stop tearing herself apart with sobs. 'The same inescapable fate waits for all human beings,' he said, 'the final trip of all to the home of the dead.' He racked his brain for other customary words of condolence which are intended to heal the broken hearts of the bereaved.

"But the Widow, who was upset rather than consoled by this unexpected stranger, only tore at her bosom more violently, ripping out some of her hair and throwing it on the corpse. The soldier then kept repeating his soothing words, while at the same time he tempted her with the tasty food and drink of his supper. The first to yield was the Widow's handmaiden, who, tempted by the aromatic bouquet of the wine, gratefully accepted his generous offer.

"Brought back to life by the wine and the food, the handmaiden joined the soldier in his siege against the fortress of her mistress's self-sacrifice. She cried out, 'What good can it do anyone if you starve yourself to death, if you bury yourself alive, or if you yourself speed up your own last breath before your time has truly come? Remember what the poet Virgil said:

Do you believe that ashes or buried ghosts can feel?°

My Lady, come back to life, please! Give up this crazy notion of wifely duty and, as long as you are able, enjoy the light of the sun once more. Even your dead husband, if he could speak, would advise you to get on with your life.'

Do . . . feel: Aeneid, IV.34.

"Nobody is deaf when told to eat or to continue staying alive, and so the Widow, starving after her long fast, finally gave way. She refreshed herself with the food just as vigorously as her handmaiden had done.

"But everybody knows that one appetite follows another, and it should come as no   10
surprise that the soldier began wooing the Widow with the same tempting words he had used to rescue her from starvation. Although she was unparalleled for modesty, she recognized that he was an unusually handsome young man. He was also persuasive, and in addition the Widow's handmaiden quoted another line of Virgil to help him in his cause:

Would you hold out against a pleasure-giving passion?°

"Why make the story last longer? This woman stopped resisting, and she accepted the young soldier's love just as she had accepted his food. They spent the night together—and after that the next night, and the next, and the next. Naturally they kept the door of the tomb barred and bolted so that any strangers or friends passing by would conclude that the faithful wife had died upon the body of her husband.

"The soldier was enchanted both by the beauty of his new sweetheart and by their secret affair, and he bought her a few small presents out of his small pay. Every night, as soon as it was dark, he would steal away to the tomb with his gifts, and would stay there until morning.

"But one evening the parents of one of the crucified thieves took advantage of him. They watched him abandon his post to enjoy his night of love, and then they hurried to their son's cross, carried his body away, and had the final ceremony for the dead performed over it. When morning came and the soldier saw that the cross was empty, he fell into a cold sweat because he knew that the punishment for his dereliction of duty would be death. He told the Widow, and swore that he could not wait for the sentence of a court martial. He would, he said, commit suicide for his folly by falling on his sword. He then asked the Widow to put his body in the tomb after he was dead—as the final resting place not only her husband, but also for him, her lover. The Widow, however, was not only virtuous and dutiful, but she was also resourceful.

"'No,' she cried, 'heaven forbid that I should be forced by bad luck to stand vigil at the same time beside the bodies of the only two men in the world that I ever loved. I would rather hang up a dead man on the cross than permit a living man to die.'

"After these words she told him to take her husband's corpse from the vault, carry   15
it to the empty cross, nail it to the cross, and hoist it up. The soldier readily agreed to this practical scheme, and the next day everyone in town was asking how on earth the dead man had been able to climb onto the cross!"

As Eumolpus was finishing his story, Tryphena blushed until her face was red, and she tried to hide her embarrassment. The sailors were so amused that they rolled on the deck with laughter. While they laughed, Lichas sternly declared that the Provincial Governor should not have permitted such a farce. Indeed, Lichas said that the Governor's duty was to have restored the husband's corpse to the tomb, and then to have executed the Widow herself on the cross.

QUESTIONS

1.   Who tells the story? How is he introduced? What do you learn about him? What point does he make about his story?

Would . . . passion: Aeneid, IV.38.

2. Since there is an audience, some of whom react when the narrator is finished, what is their effect on the story?

3. What is the Widow's main virtue? How does she show this virtue upon her husband's death? What does abandoning her wish for self-sacrifice show about her?

4. Describe the soldier. In what ways does he show strength, earnestness, and fidelity?

5. Should the story be taken as a joke, as it apparently was intended, at the expense of the female protagonist and also an attack against women? What values might make it still seem a joke? What values might make it seem more serious than it was originally intended? In light of the misogynistic theme, to what degree are you able to like the story?

ALICE WALKER (B. 1944)

Walker was born in Georgia and attended Sarah Lawrence College, graduating in 1965. In addition to teaching at Yale, Wellesley, and other schools, she has edited and published fiction, poetry, and biography, and she received a Guggenheim Fellowship in 1977. Her main hobby is gardening. For her collection of poems Revolutionary Petunias *(1973), she received a Wall Book Award nomination. Her best-known novel,* The Color Purple *(1982), was made into a movie that won an Academy Award for 1985. A recent novel is* By the Light of My Father's Smile *(1998).*

Everyday Use ⊸ ⊱⊰⊷ 1973

for your grandmama

I will wait for her in the yard that Maggie and I made so clean and wavy yesterday afternoon. A yard like this is more comfortable than most people know. It is not just a yard. It is like an extended living room. When the hard clay is swept clean as a floor and the fine sand around the edges lined with tiny, irregular grooves, anyone can come and sit and look up into the elm tree and wait for the breezes that never come inside the house.

Maggie will be nervous until after her sister goes: she will stand hopelessly in corners, homely and ashamed of the burn scars down her arms and legs, eying her sister with a mixture of envy and awe. She thinks her sister has held life always in the palm of one hand, that "no" is a word the world never learned to say to her.

You've no doubt seen those TV shows° where the child who has "made it" is confronted, as a surprise, by her own mother and father, tottering in weakly from backstage. (A pleasant surprise, of course: What would they do if parent and child came on the show only to curse out and insult each other?) On TV mother and child embrace and smile into each other's faces. Sometimes the mother and father weep, the child wraps them in her arms and leans across the table to tell how she would not have made it without their help. I have seen these programs.

Sometimes I dream a dream in which Dee and I are suddenly brought together on a TV program of this sort. Out of a dark and soft-seated limousine I am ushered into a bright room filled with many people. There I meet a smiling, gray, sporty man like

TV shows: In the early days of television, a popular show was *This Is Your Life*, which the narrator describes exactly here.

Johnny Carson who shakes my hand and tells me what a fine girl I have. Then we are on the stage and Dee is embracing me with tears in her eyes. She pins on my dress a large orchid, even though she has told me once that she thinks orchids are tacky flowers.

In real life I am a large, big-boned woman with rough, man-working hands. In the winter I wear flannel nightgowns to bed and overalls during the day. I can kill and clean a hog as mercilessly as a man. My fat keeps me hot in zero weather. I can work outside all day, breaking ice to get water for washing; I can eat pork liver cooked over the open fire minutes after it comes steaming from the hog. One winter I knocked a bull calf straight in the brain between the eyes with a sledge hammer and had the meat hung up to chill before nightfall. But of course all this does not show on television. I am the way my daughter would want me to be: a hundred pounds lighter, my skin like an uncooked barley pancake. My hair glistens in the hot bright lights. Johnny Carson has much to do to keep up with my quick and witty tongue.

But that is a mistake, I know even before I wake up. Who ever knew a Johnson with a quick tongue? Who can even imagine me looking a strange white man in the eye? It seems to me I have talked to them always with one foot raised in flight, with my head turned in whichever way is farthest from them. Dee, though. She would always look anyone in the eye. Hesitation was no part of her nature.

"How do I look, Mama?" Maggie says, showing just enough of her thin body enveloped in pink skirt and red blouse for me to know she's there, hidden by the door.

"Come out into the yard," I say.

Have you ever seen a lame animal, perhaps a dog run over by some careless person rich enough to own a car, sidle up to someone who is ignorant enough to be kind to him? That is the way my Maggie walks. She has been like this, chin on chest, eyes on ground, feet in shuffle, ever since the fire that burned the other house to the ground.

Dee is lighter than Maggie, with nicer hair and a fuller figure. She's a woman now, though sometimes I forget. How long ago was it that the other house burned? Ten, twelve years? Sometimes I can still hear the flames and feel Maggie's arms sticking to me, her hair smoking and her dress falling off her in little black papery flakes. Her eyes seemed stretched open, blazed open by the flames reflected in them. And Dee, I see her standing off under the sweet gum tree she used to dig gum out of; a look of concentration on her face as she watched the last dingy gray board of the house fall in toward the red-hot brick chimney. Why don't you do a dance around the ashes? I'd wanted to ask her. She had hated the house that much.

I used to think she hated Maggie, too. But that was before we raised the money, the church and me, to send her to Augusta° to school. She used to read to us without pity; forcing words, lies, other folks' habits, whole lives upon us two, sitting trapped and ignorant underneath her voice. She washed us in a river of make-believe, burned us with a lot of knowledge we didn't necessarily need to know. Pressed us to her with the serious way she read, to shove us away at just the moment, like dimwits, we seemed about to understand.

Dee wanted nice things. A yellow organdy dress to wear to her graduation from high school; black pumps to match a green suit she'd made from an old suit somebody gave me. She was determined to stare down any disaster in her efforts. Her eyelids would not flicker for minutes at a time. Often I fought off the temptation to shake her. At sixteen she had a style of her own: and knew what style was.

Augusta: city in eastern Georgia, the location of Paine College.

Maggie is poor(?)

I never had an education myself. After second grade the school was closed down. Don't ask me why: in 1927 colored asked fewer questions than they do now. Sometimes Maggie reads to me. She stumbles along good-naturedly, but can't see well. She knows she is not bright. Like good looks and money, quickness passed her by. She will marry John Thomas (who has mossy teeth in an earnest face) and then I'll be free to sit here and I guess just sing church songs to myself. Although I never was a good singer. Never could carry a tune. I was always better at a man's job. I used to love to milk till I was hooked in the side° in '49. Cows are soothing and slow and don't bother you, unless you try to milk them the wrong way.

I have deliberately turned my back on the house. It is three rooms, just like the one that burned, except the roof is tin; they don't make shingle roofs any more. There are no real windows, just some holes cut in the sides, like the portholes on a ship, but not round and not square, with rawhide holding the shutters up on the outside. This house is in a pasture, too, like the other one. No doubt when Dee sees it she will want to tear it down. She wrote me once that no matter where we "choose" to live, she will manage to come see us. But she will never bring her friends. Maggie and I thought about this and Maggie asked me, "Mama, when did Dee ever *have* any friends?"

She has a few. Furtive boys in pink shirts hanging about on washday after school. Nervous girls who never laughed. Impressed with her they worshiped the well-turned phrase, the cute shape, the scalding humor that erupted like bubbles in lye. She read to them.

When she was courting Jimmy T she didn't have much time to pay to us, but turned all her faultfinding power on him. He *flew* to marry a cheap city girl from a family of ignorant flashy people. She hardly had time to recompose herself.

When she comes I will meet—but there they are!

Maggie attempts to make a dash for the house, in her shuffling way, but I stay her with my hand. "Come back here," I say. And she stops and tries to dig a well in the sand with her toe.

It is hard to see them clearly through the strong sun. But even the first glimpse of leg out of the car tells me it is Dee. Her feet were always neat-looking, as if God himself had shaped them with a certain style. From the other side of the car comes a short, stocky man. Hair is all over his head a foot long and hanging from his chin like a kinky mule tail. I hear Maggie suck in her breath. "Uhnnnh," is what it sounds like. Like when you see the wriggling end of a snake just in front of your foot on the road. "Uhnnnh."

Dee next. A dress down to the ground, in this hot weather. A dress so loud it hurts my eyes. There are yellows and oranges enough to throw back the light of the sun. I feel my whole face warming from the heat waves it throws out. Earrings gold, too, and hanging down to her shoulders. Bracelets dangling and making noises when she moves her arm up to shake the folds of the dress out of her armpits. The dress is loose and flows, and as she walks closer, I like it. I hear Maggie go "Uhnnnh" again. It is her sister's hair. It stands straight up like the wool on a sheep. It is black as night and around the edges are two long pigtails that rope about like small lizards disappearing behind her ears.

"Wa-su-zo-Tean-o!"° she says, coming on in that gliding way the dress makes her move. The short stocky yellow with the hair to his navel is all grinning and he follows up with "Asalamalakim,° my mother and my sister!" He moves to hug Maggie but she falls back, tight up against the back of my chair. I feel her trembling there and when I look up I see the perspiration falling off her chin.

15

20

---

hooked in the side: kicked by a cow.
Wa-su-zo-Tean-o: greeting used by black Muslims.
Asalamalakim: Muslim salutation meaning "Peace be with you."

"Don't get up," says Dee. Since I am stout it takes something of a push. You can see me trying to move a second or two before I make it. She turns, showing white heels through her sandals, and goes back to the car. Out she peeks next with a Polaroid. She stoops down quickly and lines up picture after picture of me sitting there in front of the house with Maggie cowering behind me. She never takes a shot without making sure the house is included. When a cow comes nibbling around the edge of the yard she snaps it and me and Maggie *and* the house. Then she puts the Polaroid in the back seat of the car, and comes up and kisses me on the forehead.

Meanwhile Asalamalakim is going through motions with Maggie's hand. Maggie's hand is as limp as a fish, and probably as cold, despite the sweat, and she keeps trying to pull it back. It looks like Asalamalakim wants to shake hands but wants to do it fancy. Or maybe he don't know how people shake hands. Anyhow, he soon gives up on Maggie.

"Well," I say, "Dee."

"No, Mama," she says. "Not 'Dee,' Wangero Leewanika Kemanjo!"   25

"What happened to 'Dee'?" I wanted to know.

"She's dead," Wangero said. "I couldn't bear it any longer, being named after the people who oppress me."

"You know as well as me you was named after your aunt Dicie," I said. Dicie is my sister. She named Dee. We called her "Big Dee" after Dee was born.

"But who was *she* named after?" asked Wangero.

"I guess after Grandma Dee," I said.   30

"And who was she named after?" asked Wangero.

"Her mother," I said, and saw Wangero was getting tired. "That's about as far back as I can trace it," I said. Though, in fact, I probably could have carried it back beyond the Civil War through the branches.

"Well," said Asalamalakim, "there you are."

"Uhnnnh," I heard Maggie say.

"There I was not," I said, "before 'Dicie' cropped up in our family, so why should I   35
try to trace it that far back?"

He just stood there grinning, looking down on me like somebody inspecting a Model A° car. Every once in a while he and Wangero sent eye signals over my head.

"How do you pronounce this name?" I asked.

"You don't have to call me by it if you don't want to," said Wangero.   40

"Why shouldn't I?" I asked. "If that's what you want us to call you, we'll call you."

"I know it might sound awkward at first," said Wangero.

"I'll get used to it," I said. "Ream it out again."

Well, soon we got the name out of the way. Asalamalakim had a name twice as long and three times as hard. After I tripped over it two or three times he told me to just call him Hakim-a-barber. I wanted to ask him was he a barber, but I didn't really think he was, so I didn't ask.

"You must belong to those beef-cattle peoples down the road," I said. They said "Asalamalakim" when they met you, too, but they didn't shake hands. Always too busy: feeding the cattle, fixing the fences, putting up salt-lick shelters,° throwing down hay. When the white folks poisoned some of the herd the men stayed up all night with rifles in their hands. I walked a mile and a half just to see the sight.

Model A car: the Ford car that replaced the Model T in the late 1920s. The Model A was proverbial for its quality and durability.

salt-lick shelters: shelters built to prevent rain from dissolving the large blocks of rock salt set up on poles for cattle.

Hakim-a-barber said, "I accept some of their doctrines, but farming and raising cattle is not my style." (They didn't tell me, and I didn't ask, whether Wangero (Dee) had really gone and married him.)

We sat down to eat and right away he said he didn't eat collards and pork was unclean. Wangero, though, went on through the chitlins and corn bread, the greens and everything else. She talked a blue streak over the sweet potatoes. Everything delighted her. Even the fact that we still used the benches her daddy made for the table when we couldn't afford to buy chairs.

"Oh, Mama!" she cried. Then turned to Hakim-a-barber. "I never knew how lovely these benches are. You can feel the rump prints," she said, running her hands underneath her and along the bench. Then she gave a sigh and her hand closed over Grandma Dee's butter dish. "That's it!" she said. "I knew there was something I wanted to ask you if I could have." She jumped up from the table and went over in the corner where the churn stood, the milk in it clabber° by now. She looked at the churn and looked at it.

"This churn top is what I need," she said. "Didn't Uncle Buddy whittle it out of a tree you all used to have?"

"Yes," I said.

"Uh huh," she said happily. "And I want the dasher, too."

"Uncle Buddy whittle that, too?" asked the barber.

Dee (Wangero) looked up at me.

"Aunt Dee's first husband whittled the dash," said Maggie so low you almost couldn't hear her. "His name was Henry, but they called him Stash."

"Maggie's brain is like an elephant's," Wangero said, laughing. "I can use the churn top as a centerpiece for the alcove table," she said, sliding a plate over the churn, "and I'll think of something artistic to do with the dasher."

When she finished wrapping the dasher the handle stuck out. I took it for a moment in my hands. You didn't even have to look close to see where hands pushing the dasher up and down to make butter had left a kind of sink in the wood. In fact, there were a lot of small sinks; you could see where thumbs and fingers had sunk into the wood. It was beautiful light yellow wood, from a tree that grew in the yard where Big Dee and Stash had lived.

After dinner Dee (Wangero) went to the trunk at the foot of my bed and started rifling through it. Maggie hung back in the kitchen over the dishpan. Out came Wangero with two quilts. They had been pieced by Grandma Dee and then Big Dee and me had hung them on the quilt frames on the front porch and quilted them. One was in the Lone Star pattern. The other was Walk Around the Mountain. In both of them were scraps of dresses Grandma Dee had worn fifty and more years ago. Bits and pieces of Grandpa Jarrell's Paisley shirts. And one teeny faded blue piece, about the size of a penny matchbox, that was from Great Grandpa Ezra's uniform that he wore in the Civil War.

"Mama," Wangero said sweet as a bird. "Can I have these old quilts?"

I heard something fall in the kitchen, and a minute later the kitchen door slammed.

"Why don't you take one or two of the others?" I asked, "These old things was just done by me and Big Dee from some tops your grandma pieced before she died."

"No," said Wangero. "I don't want those. They are stitched around the borders by machine."

"That'll make them last better," I said.

___

clabber: curdled, turned sour.

"That's not the point," said Wangero. "These are all pieces of dresses Grandma used to wear. She did all this stitching by hand. Imagine!" She held the quilts securely in her arms, stroking them.

"Some of the pieces, like those lavender ones, come from old clothes her mother handed down to her," I said, moving up to touch the quilts. Dee (Wangero) moved back just enough so that I couldn't reach the quilts. They already belonged to her.

"Imagine!" she breathed again, clutching them closely to her bosom.

"The truth is," I said, "I promised to give them quilts to Maggie, for when she marries John Thomas."

She gasped like a bee had stung her.

"Maggie can't appreciate these quilts!" she said. "She'd probably be backward enough to put them to everyday use."

"I reckon she would," I said. "God knows I been saving 'em for long enough with nobody using 'em. I hope she will!" I didn't want to bring up how I had offered Dee (Wangero) a quilt when she went away to college. Then she had told me they were old-fashioned, out of style.

"But they're *priceless!*" she was saying now, furiously; for she has a temper. "Maggie would put them on the bed and in five years they'd be in rags. Less than that!"

"She can always make some more," I said. "Maggie knows how to quilt."

Dee (Wangero) looked at me with hatred. "You just will not understand. The point is these quilts, *these* quilts!"

"Well," I said, stumped. "What would *you* do with them?"

"Hang them," she said. As if that was the only thing you *could* do with quilts.

Maggie by now was standing in the door. I could almost hear the sound her feet made as they scraped over each other.

"She can have them, Mama," she said, like somebody used to never winning anything, or having anything reserved for her. "I can 'member Grandma Dee without the quilts."

I looked at her hard. She had filled her bottom lip with checkerberry snuff and it gave her face a kind of dopey, hangdog look. It was Grandma Dee and Big Dee who taught her how to quilt herself. She stood there with her scarred hands hidden in the folds of her skirt. She looked at her sister with something like fear but she wasn't mad at her. This was Maggie's portion. This was the way she knew God to work.

When I looked at her like that something hit me in the top of my head and ran down to the soles of my feet. Just like when I'm in church and the spirit of God touches me and I get happy and shout. I did something I never had done before: hugged Maggie to me, then dragged her on into the room, snatched the quilts out of Miss Wangero's hands and dumped them into Maggie's lap. Maggie just sat there on my bed with her mouth open.

"Take one or two of the others," I said to Dee.

But she turned without a word and went out to Hakim-a-barber.

"You just don't understand," she said, as Maggie and I came out to the car.

"What don't I understand?" I wanted to know.

"Your heritage," she said. And then she turned to Maggie, kissed her, and said, "You ought to try to make something of yourself, too, Maggie. It's really a new day for us. But from the way you and Mama still live you'd never know it."

She put on some sunglasses that hid everything above the tip of her nose and her chin.

Maggie smiled; maybe at the sunglasses. But a real smile, not scared. After we watched the car dust settle I asked Maggie to bring me a dip of snuff. And then the two of us sat there just enjoying, until it was time to go in the house and go to bed.

QUESTIONS

1. Describe the narrator. Who is she? What is she like? Where and how does she live? What kind of life has she had? How does the story bring out her judgments about her two daughters?

2. Describe the narrator's daughters. How are they different physically and mentally? How have their lives been different?

3. Why did Dee change her name to "Wangero"? How is this change important, and how is it reflected in her attitude toward the family artifacts?

4. Describe the importance of the phrase "everyday use" (paragraph 66). How does this phrase highlight the conflicting values in the story?

JOY WILLIAMS (B. 1944)

Williams was born in Massachusetts and graduated from Marietta College and the University of Iowa. While still in her twenties she published her first stories. Among her novels are State of Grace *(1973),* The Changeling *(1978),* Breaking and Entering *(1988), and* The Quick and the Dead *(2002). Her story collection* Taking Care, *including the title story, appeared in 1982. Her varied interests are shown by the fact that she has published a history and guide to the Keys of Florida, her adopted home state. Among her distinctions are a judgeship of the PEN/Faulkner Award for Fiction, a Wallace Stegner Fellowship, a Guggenheim Fellowship, and the Rea Award for the Short Story (2002).*

Taking Care 1982

Jones, the preacher, has been in love all his life. He is baffled by this because as far as he can see, it has never helped anyone, even when they have acknowledged it, which is not often. Jones's love is much too apparent and arouses neglect. He is like an animal in a traveling show who, through some aberration, wears a vital organ outside the skin, awkward and unfortunate, something that shouldn't be seen, certainly something that shouldn't be watched working. Now he sits on a bed beside his wife in the self-care unit of a hospital fifteen miles from their home. She has been committed here for tests. She is so weak, so tired. There is something wrong with her blood. Her arms are covered with bruises where they have gone into the veins. Her hip, too, is blue and swollen where they have drawn out samples of bone marrow. All of this is frightening. The doctors are severe and wise, answering Jones's questions in a way that makes him feel hopelessly deaf. They have told him that there really is no such thing as a disease of the blood, for the blood is not a living tissue but a passive vehicle for the transportation of food, oxygen and waste. They have told him that abnormalities in the blood corpuscles, which his wife seems to have, must be regarded as symptoms of disease elsewhere in the body. They have shown him, upon request, slides and charts of normal and pathological blood cells which look to Jones like canapés. They speak (for he insists) of leukocytosis,° myelocytes° and megaloblasts.° None of this takes into account the love he has for his wife! Jones sits beside her

leukocytosis: elevated number of white blood cells.
myelocytes: nuclei of nerve cells.
megaloblasts: damaged red blood cells characteristic of anemia and leukemia.

in this dim pleasant room, wearing a grey suit and his clerical collar, for when he leaves her he must visit other parishioners who are patients here. This part of the hospital is like a motel. One may wear one's regular clothes. The rooms have ice-buckets, rugs and colorful bedspreads. How he wishes that they were traveling and staying overnight, this night, in a motel. A nurse comes in with a tiny paper cup full of pills. There are three pills, or rather, capsules, and they are not for his wife but for her blood. The cup is the smallest of its type that Jones has ever seen. All perspective, all sense of time and scale seem abandoned in this hospital. For example, when Jones turns to kiss his wife's hair, he nicks the air instead.

Jones and his wife have one child, a daughter, who, in turn, has a single child, a girl, born one-half year ago. Jones's daughter has fallen in with the stars and is using the heavens, as Jones would be the first to admit, more than he ever has. It has, however, brought her only grief and confusion. She has left her husband and brought the baby to Jones. She has also given him her dog. She is going to Mexico where soon, in the mountains, she will have a nervous breakdown. Jones does not know this, but his daughter has seen it in the stars and is going out to meet it. Jones quickly agrees to care for both the baby and the dog, as this seems to be the only thing his daughter needs from him. The day of the baby's birth is secondary to the position of the planets and the terms of houses, quadrants and gradients.° Her symbol is a bareback rider. To Jones, this is a graceful thought. It signifies audacity. It also means luck. Jones slips a twenty dollar bill in the pocket of his daughter's suitcase and drives her to the airport. The plane taxis down the runway and Jones waves, holding all their luck in his arms.

One afternoon, Jones had come home and found his wife sitting in the garden, weeping. She had been transplanting flowers, putting them in pots before the first frost came. There was dirt on her forehead and around her mouth. Her light clothes felt so heavy. Their weight made her body ache. Each breath was a stone she had to swallow. She cried and cried in the weak autumn sunshine. Jones could see the veins throbbing in her neck. "I'm dying," she said. "It's taking me months to die." But after he had brought her inside, she insisted that she felt better and made them both a cup of tea while Jones potted the rest of the plants and carried them down cellar. She lay on the sofa and Jones sat beside her. They talked quietly with one another. Indeed, they were almost whispering, as though they were in a public place surrounded by strangers instead of in their own house with no one present but themselves. "It's the season," Jones said. "In fall everything slows down, retreats. I'm feeling tired myself. We need iron. I'll go to the druggist right now and buy some iron tablets." His wife agreed. She wanted to go with him, for the ride. Together they ride, through the towns, for miles and miles, even into the next state. She does not want to stop driving. They buy sandwiches and milkshakes and eat in the car. Jones drives. They have to buy more gasoline. His wife sits close to him, her eyes closed, her head tipped back against the seat. He can see the veins beating on in her neck. Somewhere there is a dreadful sound, almost audible. "First I thought it was my imagination," his wife said. "I couldn't sleep. All night I would stay awake, dreaming. But it's not in my head. It's in my ears, my eyes. They ache. Everything. My tongue. My hair. The tips of my fingers are dead." Jones pressed her cold hand to his lips. He thinks of something mad and loving better than he—running out of control, deeply in the darkness of his wife. "Just don't make me go to the hospital," she pleaded. Of course she will go there. The moment has already occurred.

Jones is writing to his daughter. He received a brief letter from her this morning, telling him where she could be reached. The foreign postmark was so large that it almost

---

planets . . . gradients: terms used by believers in astrology to determine the future.

obliterated Jones's address. She did not mention either her mother or the baby, which makes Jones feel peculiar. His life seems increate as his God's life, perhaps even imaginary. His daughter tells him about the town in which she lives. She does not plan to stay there long. She wants to travel. She will find out exactly what she wants to do and then she will come home again. The town is poor but interesting and there are many Americans there her own age. There is a zoo right on the beach. Almost all the towns, no matter how small, have little zoos. There are primarily eagles and hawks in cages. And what can Jones reply to that? He writes *Everything is fine here. We are burning wood from the old apple tree in the fire place and it smells wonderful. Has the baby had her full series of polio shots? Take care.* Jones uses this expression constantly, usually in totally unwarranted situations, as when he purchases pipe cleaners or drives through toll booths. Distracted, Jones writes off the edge of the paper and onto the blotter. He must begin again. He will mail this on the way to the hospital. They have been taking X-rays for three days now but the pictures are cloudy. They cannot read them. His wife is now in a real sickbed with high metal sides. He sits with her while she eats her dinner. She asks him to take her good nightgown home and wash it with a bar of Ivory. They won't let her do anything now, not even wash out a few things. *You must take care.*

　　Jones is driving down a country road. It is the first snowfall of the season and he wants to show it to the baby who rides beside him in a small cushioned car seat all her own. Her head is almost on a level with his and she looks earnestly at the landscape, sometimes smiling. They follow the road that winds tightly between fields and deep pine woods. Everything is white and clean. It has been snowing all afternoon and is doing so still, but very very lightly. Fat snowflakes fall solitary against the windshield. Sometimes the baby reaches out for them. Sometimes she gives a brief kick and cry of joy. They have done their errands. Jones has bought milk and groceries and two yellow roses which lie wrapped in tissue and newspaper in the trunk, in the cold. He must buy two on Saturday as the florist is closed on Sunday. He does not like to do this but there is no alternative. The roses do not keep well. Tonight he will give one to his wife. The other he will pack in sugar water and store in the refrigerator. He can only hope that the bud will remain tight until Sunday when he brings it into the terrible heat of the hospital. The baby rocks against the straps of her small carrier. Her lips are pursed as she watches intently the fields, the grey stalks of crops growing out of the snow, the trees. She is warmly dressed and she wears a knitted orange cap. The cap is twenty-three years old, the age of her mother. Jones found it just the other day. It has faded almost to pink on one side. At one time, it must have been stored in the sun. Jones, driving, feels almost gay. The snow is so beautiful. Everything is white. Jones is an educated man. He has read Melville, who said that white is the colorless all-color of atheism from which we shrink.°

　　Jones does not believe this. He sees a holiness in snow, a promise. He hopes that his wife will know that it is snowing even though she is separated from the window by a curtain. Jones sees something moving across the snow, a part of the snow itself running. Although he is going slowly, he takes his foot completely off the accelerator. "Look, darling, a snowshoe rabbit." At the sound of his voice, the baby stretches open her mouth and narrows her eyes in soundless glee. The hare is splendid. So fast! It flows around invisible obstructions, something out of a kind dream. It flies across the ditch, its paws like paddles, faintly yellow, the color of raw wood. "Look, sweet," cries Jones, "How big he is!" But suddenly the hare is curved and falling, round as a ball, its feet and head tucked closely against its body. It strikes the road and skids upside down for several yards. The

5

---

　　colorless . . . shrink: quotation from Chapter 42, "The Whiteness of the Whale," of *Moby-Dick* (1851) by Herman Melville (1819–1891).

car passes around it, avoids it. Jones brakes and stops, amazed. He opens the door and trots back to the animal. The baby twists about in her seat as well as she can and peers after him. It is as though the animal had never been alive at all. Its head is broken in several places. Jones bends to touch its fur, but straightens again, not doing so. A man emerges from the woods, swinging a shotgun. He nods at Jones and picks the hare up by the ears. As he walks away, the hare's legs rub across the ground. There are small crystal stains on the snow. Jones returns to the car. He wants to apologize but he does not know to whom or for what. His life has been devoted to apologetics.° It is his profession. He is concerned with both justification and remorse. He has always acted rightly, but nothing has ever come of it. He gets in the car, starts the engine. "Oh, sweet," he says to the baby. She smiles at him, exposing her tooth. At home that night, after the baby's supper, Jones reads a story to her. She is asleep, panting in her sleep, but Jones tells her the story of al-Boraq,° the milk-white steed of Mohammed, who could stride out of the sight of mankind with a single step.

Jones sorts through a collection of records, none of which have been opened. They are still wrapped in cellophane. The jacket designs are subdued, epic. Names, instruments and orchestras are mentioned confidently. He would like to agree with their importance, for he knows that they have worth, but he is not familiar with the references. His daughter brought these records with her. They had been given to her by an older man, a professor she had been having an affair with. Naturally, this pains Jones. His daughter speaks about the men she has been involved with but no longer cares about. Where did these men come from? Where were they waiting and why have they gone? Jones remembers his daughter when she was a little girl, helping him rake leaves. What can he say? For years on April Fool's Day, she would take tobacco out of his humidor and fill it with corn flakes. Jones is full of remorse and astonishment. When he saw his daughter only a few weeks ago, she was thin and nervous. She had torn out almost all her eyebrows with her fingers from this nervousness. And her lashes. The roots of her eyes were white, like the bulbs of flowers. Her fingernails were crudely bitten, some bleeding below the quick. She was tough and remote, wanting only to go on a trip for which she had a ticket. What can he do? He seeks her in the face of the baby but she is not there. All is being both continued and resumed, but the dream is different. The dream cannot be revived. Jones breaks into one of the albums, blows the dust from the needle, plays a record. Outside it is dark. The parsonage is remote and the only buildings nearby are barns. The river cannot be seen. The music is Bruckner's *Te Deum.*° Very nice, Dedicated to God. He plays the other side. A woman, Kathleen Ferrier,° is singing in German. Jones cannot understand the words but the music stuns him. *Kindertotenlieder.*° It is devastating. In college he had studied only scientific German, The vocabulary of submarines, dirigibles and steam engines. Jones plays the record again and again, searching for his old grammer. At last he finds it. The wings of insects are between some of the pages. There are notes in pencil, written in his own young hand.

apologetics: the explanation and defense of religion, here, specifically, of Christianity.

al-Boraq: According to the Koran, the angel Gabriel brought the prophet Mohammed to the Islamic Seventh Heaven (made up of divine light) on the mystical horse Borak or al-Borak ("lightning").

Bruckner: Anton Bruckner (1824–1896), Austrian composer and organist. His *Te Deum* for chorus, soloists, and orchestra was completed in 1884. The long-play record is Columbia ML 4980.

Kathleen Ferrier: celebrated English contralto (1912–1953), who died of cancer.

Kindertotenlieder: "Songs of the Death of Children" (1902–1904), a cycle of five songs for voice and orchestra by Gustav Mahler (1860–1911), Austrian composer and conductor. Mahler's elder daughter died three years after he completed the work.

RENDER:

A. WAS THE TEACHER SATISFIED WITH YOU TODAY?

B. NO. HE IS NOT. MY ESSAY WAS GOOD BUT IT WAS NOT COPIED WELL.

C. I AM SORRY YOU WERE NOT INDUSTRIOUS THIS TIME FOR YOU GENERALLY ARE.

These lessons are neither of life or death. Why was he instructed in them? In the hospital, his wife waits to be translated, no longer a woman, the woman whom he loves, but a situation. Her blood moves mysteriously as constellations. She is under scrutiny and attack and she has abandoned Jones. She is a swimmer waiting to get on with the drowning. Jones is on the shore. In Mexico, his daughter walks along the beach with two men. She is acting out a play that has become her life. Jones is on the mountaintop. The baby cries and Jones takes her from the crib to change her. The dog paws the door. Jones lets him out. He settles down with the baby and listens to the record. He still cannot make out many of the words. The baby wiggles restlessly on his lap. Her eyes are a foal's eyes, navy-blue. She has grown in a few weeks to expect everything from Jones. He props her on one edge of the couch and goes to her small toy box where he keeps a bear, a few rattles and balls. On the way, he opens the door and the dog immediately enters. His heavy coat is cold, fragrant with ice. He noses the baby and she squeals.

Oft denk' ich, sie sind nur ausgegangen:
Bald werden sie wieder nach Hause gelangen!°

Jones selects a bright ball and pushes it gently in her direction.

It is Sunday morning and Jones is in the pulpit. The church is very old but the walls of the sanctuary have recently been painted a pale blue. In the cemetery adjoining, some of the graves are three hundred years old. It has become a historical landmark and no one has been buried there since World War I. There is a new place, not far away, which the families now use. Plots are marked not with stones but with small tablets, and immediately after any burial, workmen roll grassed sod over the new graves so that there is no blemish on the grounds, not even for a little while. Present for today's service are seventy-eight adults, eleven children and the junior choir. Jones counts them as the offertory is received. The church rolls say that there are three hundred fifty members but as far as Jones can see, everyone is here today. This is the day he baptizes the baby. He has made arrangements with one of the ladies to hold her and bring her up to the font at the end of the first hymn. The baby looks charming in a lacy white dress. Jones has combed her fine hair carefully, slicking it in a curl with water, but now it has dried and it sticks up awkwardly like the crest of a kingfisher. Jones bought the dress in Mammoth Mart, an enormous store which has a large metal elephant dressed in overalls dancing on the roof. He feels foolish at buying it there but he had gone to several stores and that is where he saw the prettiest dress. He blesses the baby with water from the silver bowl. He says, *We are saved not because we are worthy. We are saved because we are loved.* It is a brief ceremony. The baby, looking curiously at Jones, is taken out to the nursery. Jones begins his sermon. He can't remember when he wrote it, but here it is, typed, in front of him. *There is nothing wrong in what one does but there is something wrong in what one becomes.* He finds this questionable but goes on speaking. He has been preaching for thirty-four years. He is gaunt

Oft . . . gelangen: opening two lines of the fourth song in Mahler's *Kindertotenlieder,* from a poem by Friedrich Rückert (1788–1866): "Often I think they've just gone outside: / They'll get back home again soon!"

with belief. But his wife has a red cell count of only 2.3 millions. It is not enough! She is not getting enough oxygen! Jones is giving his sermon. Somewhere he has lost what he was looking for. He must have known once, surely. The congregation sways, like the wings of a ray in water. It is Sunday and for patients it is a holiday. The doctors don't visit. There are no tests or diagnoses. Jones would like to leave, to walk down the aisle and out into the winter, where he would read his words into the ground. Why can't he remember his life! He finishes, sits down, stands up to present communion. Tiny cubes of bread lie in a slumped pyramid. They are offered and received. Jones takes his morsel, hacked earlier from a sliced enriched loaf with his own hand. It is so dry, almost wicked. The very thought now sickens him. He chews it over and over again, but it lies unconsumed, like a mussel in his mouth.

Jones is waiting in the lobby for the results of his wife's operation. Has there ever been a time before dread? He would be grateful even to have dread back, but it has been lost, for a long time, in rapid possibility, probability and fact. The baby sits on his knees and plays with his tie. She woke very early this morning for her orange juice and then gravely, immediately, spit it all up. She seems fine now, however, her fingers exploring Jones's tie. Whenever he looks at her, she gives him a dazzling smile. He has spent most of the day fiercely cleaning the house, changing the bed-sheets and the pages of the many calendars that hang in the rooms, things he should have done a week ago. He has dusted and vacuumed and pressed all his shirts. He has laundered all the baby's clothes, soft small sacks and gowns and sleepers which froze in his hands the moment he stepped outside. And now he is waiting and watching his wristwatch. The tumor is precisely this size, they tell him, the size of his clock's face.

Jones has the baby on his lap and he is feeding her. The evening meal is lengthy and complex. First he must give her vitamins, then, because she has a cold, a dropper of liquid aspirin. This is followed by a bottle of milk, eight ounces, and a portion of strained vegetables. He gives her a rest now so that the food can settle. On his hip, she rides through the rooms of the huge house as Jones turns lights off and on. He comes back to the table and gives her a little more milk, a half jar of strained chicken and a few spoonfuls of dessert, usually cobbler, buckle or pudding. The baby enjoys all equally. She is good. She eats rapidly and neatly. Sometimes she grasps the spoon, turns it around and thrusts the wrong end into her mouth. Of course there is nothing that cannot be done incorrectly. Jones adores the baby. He sniffs her warm head. Her birth is a deep error, an abstraction. Born in wedlock but out of love. He puts her in the playpen and tends to the dog. He fills one dish with water and one with horsemeat. He rinses out the empty can before putting it in the wastebasket. The dog eats with great civility. He eats a little meat and then takes some water, then meat, then water. When the dog has finished, the dishes are as clean as though they'd been washed. Jones now thinks about his own dinner. He opens the refrigerator. The ladies of the church have brought brownies, vension, cheese and apple sauce. There are turkey pies, pork chops, steak, haddock and sausage patties. A brilliant light exposes all this food. There is so much of it. It must be used. A crust has formed around the punctures in a can of Pet. There is a clear bag of chicken livers stapled shut. There are large brown eggs in a bowl. Jones stares unhappily at the beads of moisture on cartons and bottles, at the pearls of fat on the cold cooked stew. He sits down. The room is full of lamps and cords. He thinks of his wife, her breathing body deranged in tubes, and begins to shake. All objects here are perplexed by such grief.

Now it is almost Christmas and Jones is walking down by the river, around an abandoned house. The dog wades heavily through the snow, biting it. There are petals of ice on the tree limbs and when Jones lingers under them, the baby puts out her hand and her mouth starts working because she would like to have it, the ice, the branch, everything.

His wife will be coming home in a few days, in time for Christmas. Jones has already put up the tree and brought the ornaments down from the attic. He will not trim it until she comes home. He wants very much to make a fine occasion out of opening the boxes of old decorations. The two of them have always enjoyed this greatly in the past. Jones will doubtlessly drop and smash a bauble, for he does every year. He tramps through the snow with his small voyager. She dangles in a shoulder sling, her legs wedged around his hip. They regard the rotting house seriously. Once it was a doctor's home and offices but long before Jones's time, the doctor, who was very respected, had been driven away because a town girl accused him of fathering her child. The story goes that all the doctor said was, "Is that so?" This incensed the town and the girl's parents, who insisted that he take the child as soon as it was born. He did and he cared for the child very well even though his practice was ruined and no one had anything to do with him. A year later the girl told the truth—that the actual father was a young college boy whom she was now going to marry. They wanted the child back, and the doctor willingly returned the infant to them. Of course it is a very old, important story. Jones has always appreciated it, but now he is annoyed at the man's passivity. He wife's sickness has changed everything for Jones. He will continue to accept but he will no longer surrender. Surely things are different for Jones now.

For insurance purposes, Jones's wife is brought out to the car in a wheelchair. She is thin and beautiful. Jones is grateful and confused. He has a mad wish to tip the orderly. Have so many years really passed? Is this not his wife, his love, fresh from giving birth? Isn't everything about to begin? In Mexico, his daughter wanders disinterestedly through a jewelry shop where she picks up a small silver egg. It opens on a hinge and inside are two figures, a bride and groom. Jones puts the baby in his wife's arms. At first the baby is alarmed because she cannot remember this person very well and she reaches for Jones, whimpering. But soon she is soothed by his wife's soft voice and she falls asleep in her arms as they drive. Jones has readied everything carefully for his wife's homecoming. The house is clean and orderly. For days he has restricted himself to only one part of the house so that his clutter will be minimal. Jones helps his wife up the steps to the door. Together they enter the shining rooms.

QUESTIONS

1. Describe the character of Jones. What is his major trait? How do you learn about it? Why does he continue to practice his profession and care for his family?

2. On the basis of this story, what can you say about the use of tenses in a narration? Why is the story told mainly in the present tense? What is the relationship here between past and present tense?

3. Explain why there are so few paragraphs in the story and why they are rather long. Why do you think Williams does not use more dialogue?

4. Explore the sad or depressing references and situations in the story (e.g., the ill wife, the dead rabbit, the daughter abandoning her child, the songs on the death of children). In the light of such references, how does the story make you think and feel?

RESPONDING TO LITERATURE: LIKES AND DISLIKES

People read for many reasons. In the course of daily affairs, they read signs, labels, price tags, recipes, or directions for assembling a piece of furniture or a toy. They read newspapers to learn about national, international, and local events. They read magazines to learn about important issues, celebrities, political figures, and biographical details about significant persons. Sometimes they read to pass the time or to take their minds off pressing problems or situations. Also, people read out of necessity—in school and in their work. They study for examinations in chemistry, biology, literature, psychology, and political science. They try to memorize noun paradigms and verb forms in a foreign language. They read to acquire knowledge in many areas, and they read to learn new skills, new information, and new ways to do their jobs better.

But, aside from incidental, leisurely, and obligatory reading, many people turn to imaginative literature, which they read because they like it and find it interesting. Even if they don't like everything they read equally, they nevertheless enjoy reading and usually pick out authors and types of literature that are appealing.

It is therefore worth considering those qualities of imaginative literature that at the primary level produce responses of pleasure (and also of displeasure). You either like or dislike a story, poem, or play. If you say no more than this, however, you have not said much. Analyzing and explaining your likes and dislikes requires you to describe the reasons for your responses. The goal should be to form your responses as judgments, which are usually *informed* and *informative*, rather than as simple reactions, which may be *uninformed* and *unexplained*.

Sometimes a reader's first responses are that a story or poem is either "okay" or else that it is "boring." These reactions usually mask an incomplete and superficial first reading. They are neither informative nor informed. As you study most works, however, you will be drawn into them and become interested and involved. To be interested in a poem, play, or story is to be taken into it emotionally. To be involved suggests that your emotions become wrapped up in the characters, problems, outcomes, ideas, and expressions of opinion and emotion. Both "interest" and "involvement" describe genuine responses to reading. Once you get interested and involved, your reading ceases to be a task or an assignment and grows into a pleasure.

Record Your Responses in Your Computer File, Notebook, or Journal

No one can tell you what you should or should not like, for your taste is uniquely your own. While your reading is still fresh, therefore, you should use your computer or a notebook to record your responses to a work and also your observations about it. Be frank in your judgment. Write down what you like or dislike, and explain the reasons for your responses, even if these are brief and incomplete. If, after later thought and fuller understanding, you change or modify your impressions, write down these changes too. Here is a journal entry that explains a favorable response to Maupassant's "The Necklace" (Chapter 1), the subject of the demonstrative student essay in this chapter:

> I like "The Necklace" because of the surprise ending. It isn't that I like Mathilde's bad luck, but I like the way Maupassant hides the most important fact in the story until the end. Mathilde does all that work and sacrifice for no reason at all, and the surprise ending makes this point strongly.

This paragraph could be developed as part of an essay. It is a clear statement of liking, followed by references to likable things in the story. This response pattern, which can be simply phrased as "I like [dislike] this work because . . . ," is a useful way to begin notebook or journal entries because it always requires that you explain your responses. (It is in this way, also, that you can begin to develop an argument about the work.) If at first you cannot explain the causes of your responses, at least make a brief list of the things you like or dislike. If you write nothing, you will likely forget your reactions. Recovering them later, either for discussion or writing, will be difficult.

STATING REASONS FOR FAVORABLE RESPONSES

Usually you can equate your interest in a work with liking it. You can be more specific about favorable responses by citing one or more of the following:

- You like and admire the characters and what they do and stand for. You get involved with them. When they are in danger, you are concerned; when they succeed, you are happy; when they speak, you like what they say.
- After you have read the last word in a story or play, you are sorry to part with these characters and wish that there were more to read about them and their activities.
- Even if you do not particularly like a character or the characters, you are nevertheless interested in the reasons for and outcomes of their actions.
- You get so interested and involved in the actions or ideas in the work that you do not want to put the work down until you have finished it.
- You like to follow the pattern of action or the development of the author's thoughts, so that you respond with appreciation upon finishing the work.
- You find that reading enables you to relax or to take your mind off a problem or a pressing responsibility.
- You learn something new—something you had never before known or thought about human beings and their ways of handling their problems.
- You learn about customs and ways of life in different places and times.
- You gain new insights into aspects of life that you thought you already understood.
- You feel happy or thrilled because of reading the work.
- You are amused, and you laugh often as you read.
- You like the author's descriptions of scenes, actions, ideas, and feelings.
- You find that many of the expressions are remarkable and beautiful, and are therefore worth remembering.

STATING REASONS FOR UNFAVORABLE RESPONSES

Although so far we have dismissed "okay" and "boring" and have stressed *interest, involvement,* and *liking,* it is important to know that disliking all or part of a work is normal and acceptable. You do not need to hide this response. Here, for example, are two short journal responses expressing dislike for Maupassant's "The Necklace":

> I do not like "The Necklace" because Mathilde seems spoiled, and I don't think she
> is worth reading about.

> "The Necklace" is not an adventure story, and I like reading only adventure stories.

These are both legitimate responses because they are based on a clear standard
of judgment. The first response stems from a distaste for an unlikable trait of
the main character, and the second from a preference for rapidly moving stories
that evoke interest in the dangers that main characters face and overcome.

Here is a paragraph-length notebook/journal entry that might be developed from the first response. Notice that the reasons for dislike are explained.
They would need only slightly more development for use in an essay.

> I dislike "The Necklace" because Mathilde seems spoiled, and I don't think she is
> worth reading about. She is a phony. She nags her husband because he is not rich.
> She never tells the truth. I dislike her for hurrying away from the party because she
> is ashamed that she might be seen in her threadbare shawl. She is foolish and dis-
> honest for not telling Jeanne Forrestier about losing the necklace. It's true that she
> works hard to pay the debt, but she also puts her husband through ten years of
> hardship. If Mathilde had faced facts, she might have had a better life. I do not like
> her and cannot like the story because of her.

As long as you include reasons for your dislike, as in the list and in the paragraph, you can use them again in considering the story more fully, when you will
surely also expand thoughts, focus your argument, include new details, pick new
topics for development as paragraphs, and otherwise modify your notebook
entry. You might even change your mind. However, even if you do not, it is better to record your original responses and reasons honestly than to force yourself
to say you like a story that you do not like.

Put Dislikes into a Larger Context

Although it is important to be honest about disliking a work, it is equally important to broaden your perspective and expand your taste. For example, a dislike
based on the preference for only mystery or adventure stories, if generally applied, would cause a person to dislike most works of literature. To maintain such
an attitude seems unnecessarily self-limiting.

If negative responses are put in a larger context, however, it is possible to
expand the capacity to like and appreciate good literature. For instance, some
readers might be preoccupied with their own concerns and therefore be uninterested in remote or "irrelevant" literary figures. However, if by reading about
literary characters they can gain insight into general problems of life, and therefore their own concerns, they can find something to like in just about any work.
Other readers might like sports and therefore not read anything but the daily
sports pages. What probably interests them about sports is competition, however, so if they can follow the competition or *conflict* in a literary work, they will
have discovered something to like in that work.

As an example, let us consider again the dislike based on a preference for
adventure stories and see whether this preference can be widened. Here are
some reasons for liking adventures:

1. Adventure has fast action.
2. It has danger and tension, and therefore interest.
3. It has daring, active, and successful characters.
4. It has obstacles that the characters work hard to overcome.

No one could claim that the first three points apply to "The Necklace," but the fourth point is promising. Mathilde, the major character, works hard to overcome an obstacle. She pitches in to help her husband pay the large debt. If you like adventures because the characters try to gain worthy goals, then you can also like "The Necklace" for the same reason. The principle here is clear: If a reason for liking a favorite work or type of work can be found in another work, then there is reason to like that new work.

The following paragraph shows a possible application of this "bridging" process of extending preferences. (The demonstrative student essay that begins on p. 104 is also developed along these lines.)

> I usually like only adventure stories, and therefore I disliked "The Necklace" at first because it is not adventure. But one of my reasons for liking adventure is that the characters work hard to overcome difficult obstacles, like finding buried treasure or exploring new places. Mathilde, Maupassant's main character in "The Necklace," also works hard to overcome an obstacle—economizing in order to help pay back the 18,000 francs that her husband borrows as part payment for the replacement necklace. I like adventure characters because they stick to things and win out. I see the same toughness in Mathilde. Her problems get more interesting as the story moves on after a slow beginning. I came to like the story.

The principle of "bridging" from like to like is worth restating and emphasizing: If a reason for liking a favorite work or type of work can be found in another work, then there is reason to like that new work. A person who adapts in such an open-minded way can redefine dislikes, no matter how slowly, and can consequently expand the ability to like and appreciate many kinds of literature.

An equally open-minded way to develop understanding and widen taste is to put dislikes in the following light: An author's creation of an unlikable character, situation, attitude, or expression may be deliberate. Your dislike might then result from the author's intentions. A first task of study, therefore, is to understand and explain the intention or plan. As you put the plan into your own words, you may find that you can like a work with unlikable things in it. Here is paragraph that traces this pattern of thinking, based again on "The Necklace":

> Maupassant apparently wants the reader to dislike Mathilde. At first, he shows her as unrealistic and spoiled. She lies to everyone and nags her husband. Her rushing away from the party so that no one can see her shabby shawl is a form of lying. But I like the story itself because Maupassant makes another kind of point. He does not hide her bad qualities, but he makes it clear that she herself is the cause of her trouble. If people like Mathilde never face the truth, they will get into bad situations. This is a good point, and I like the way Maupassant makes it. The entire story is therefore worth liking even though I still do not like Mathilde.

Both of these "bridging" analyses are consistent with the original negative reactions. In the first paragraph, the writer applies one of his principles of liking to include "The Necklace." In the second, the writer considers her initial dislike in the context of the work, and she discovers a basis for liking the story as a whole while still disliking the main character. The main concern in both responses is to keep an open mind despite initial dislike and then to see whether the unfavorable response can be more fully and broadly considered.

However, if you decide that your dislike overbalances any reasons you can find for liking, then you should explain your dislike. As long as you relate your response to the work accurately and measure it by a clear standard of judgment, your dislike of even a commonly liked work is not unacceptable. The important issue is not so much that you like or dislike a particular work but that you develop your own abilities to analyze and express your ideas.

WRITING ABOUT RESPONSES: LIKES AND DISLIKES

In developing an essay about your responses, begin by relying on your first reactions. Because it is not easy to reconstruct your first responses after a lapse of time, however, you will need your notebook/journal observations to guide you in the preliminary writing process. Develop your essay by stressing those characters, incidents, and ideas that interest (or do not interest) you.

As you plan your essay, your challenge will be to connect details from the work to your central idea or argument. That is, once you have begun by stating that you like (or dislike) the story, you might forget to highlight this response as you enumerate details. Therefore you need to stress your involvement in the work as you bring out evidence from it. You can show your attitudes by indicating approval (or disapproval), by commenting favorably (or unfavorably) on the details, by indicating things that seem new (or shopworn) and particularly instructive (or wrong), and by giving assent to (or dissent from) ideas or expressions of feeling.

Strategies for Organizing Ideas

Briefly describe the conditions that influence your response. Your central idea should be why you like or dislike the work. Your thesis sentence should include the major causes of your response, which are to be developed in the body.

The most common approach is to consider specific details that you like or dislike. The list on page 100 can help you articulate your responses. For example, you admired a particular character, or you got so interested in a story that you could not put it down, or you liked a particular passage in a poem or play, or you felt thrilled as you finished reading the work. Also, you may wish to develop a major idea, a fresh insight, or a particular outcome, as in the demonstrative paragraph on page 99, which shows a surprise ending as the cause of a favorable response.

A second approach (see p. 102) is to explain any changes in your responses about the work (i.e., negative to positive and vice versa). This approach requires that you isolate the causes of the change, but it does *not* require you to retell the story from beginning to end.

1. One way to deal with such a change—the "bridge" method of transferring prefer-ence from one type of work to another—is shown in the following demonstrative essay.

2. Another way is to explain a change in terms of a new awareness or understanding that you did not have on a first reading. Thus, for example, your first response to "The Necklace" might be unfavorable or neutral because the story may at first seem to move rather slowly. But further consideration might lead you to discover new insights that change your mind, such as the needs to overcome personal pride and to stop minor resentments from growing and festering. Your essay would then explain how these new insights have caused you to like the story.

In your conclusion you might summarize the reasons for your major re-sponse. You might also face any issues brought up by a change or modification of your first reactions. For example, if you have always held certain assumptions about your taste but like the work despite these assumptions, you may wish to talk about your own change or development. This topic is personal, but in an essay about your personal responses, discovery about yourself is legitimate and worthy.

DEMONSTRATIVE STUDENT ESSAY

Some Reasons for Liking Maupassant's "The Necklace"°

[1] To me, the most likable kind of reading is adventure. There are many rea-sons for my preference, but an important one is that adventure characters work hard to overcome obstacles. Because Guy de Maupassant's "The Necklace" is not adventure, I did not like it at first. But in one respect the story is like adventure: The major character, Mathilde Loisel, works hard with her husband for ten years to overcome a difficult obstacle (paying an overwhelming debt). Thus, because Mathilde does what adventure characters also do, the story is likable.* Mathilde's appeal results from her hard work, strong character, and sad fate, and also from the way our view of her changes.†

[2] Mathilde's hard work makes her seem good. Once she and her husband are faced with the huge debt of 18,000 francs, she works like a slave to pay it back. She gives up her servant and moves to a cheaper place. She does the household drudgery, wears cheap clothes, and haggles with shopkeepers. Just like the characters in adventure stories who do hard and unpleasant things, she does what she has to, and this makes her admirable.

[3] Her strong character shows her endurance, a likable trait. At first she is nag-ging and fussy, and she always dreams about wealth and tells lies, but she changes and gets better. She recognizes her blame in losing the necklace, and she has the toughness to help her husband redeem the debt. She sacrifices "heroically" (10, paragraph 98) by giving up her comfortable way of life, even though in the process she also loses her youth and beauty. Her jobs are not the exotic and glamorous ones of adventure stories, but her force of character makes her as likable as an adventure heroine.

°See pp. 4–11 for this story.
*Central idea. Mathilde's appeal results from her hard work, strong character, and sad fate, and also from the way our view of her changes.
†Thesis sentence.

[4] <u>Her sad fate also makes her likable</u>. In adventure stories the characters usually suffer as they do their jobs. Mathilde also suffers, but in a different way, because her suffering is permanent while the hardships of adventure characters are temporary. This fact makes her especially pitiable because all her sacrifices are not necessary. This unfairness invites the reader to take her side.

[5] <u>The most important quality promoting admiration is the way in which Maupassant shifts our view of Mathilde</u>. As she goes deeper into her hard life, Maupassant stresses her work and not the innermost thoughts he reveals at the beginning. In other words, the view into her character at the start, when she dreams about wealth, invites dislike; but the focus at the end is on her achievements, with never a complaint--even though she still has golden memories, as the narrator tells us.

> But sometimes, when her husband was at work, she sat down near the window, and she dreamed of that evening so long ago, of that party, where she had been so beautiful and so admired. (10, paragraph 104)

A major quality of Maupassant's changed emphasis is that Mathilde's fond memories do not lead to anything unfortunate. His shift in focus, from Mathilde's dissatisfaction to her sharing of responsibility and sacrifice, encourages the reader to like her.

[6] "The Necklace" is not an adventure story, but Mathilde has some of the good qualities of adventure characters. Also, the surprise revelation that the lost necklace was false is an unforgettable twist, and this makes her more deserving than she seems at first. Maupassant has arranged the story so that the reader finally admires Mathilde. <u>"The Necklace" is a skillfully told and likable story</u>.

WORK CITED

Maupassant, Guy de. "The Necklace." Trans. Edgar V. Roberts. <u>Literature: An Introduction to Reading and Writing</u>. Ed. Edgar V. Roberts and Henry E. Jacobs. 7th ed. Upper Saddle River: Prentice Hall, 2004. 4–11.

Commentary on the Essay

This essay demonstrates how a reader can develop appreciation by transferring a preference for one type of work to a work that does not belong to the type. In the essay, the "bridge" is an already established taste for adventure stories, and the grounds for liking "The Necklace" are that Mathilde, the main character, shares the admirable qualities of adventure heroes and heroines.

In paragraph 1, the introduction, the grounds for transferring preferences are established. Paragraph 2 deals with Mathilde's capacity to work hard, and paragraph 3 considers the equally admirable quality of endurance. The fourth paragraph describes how Mathilde's condition evokes sympathy and pity. These paragraphs hence explain the story's appeal by asserting that the main character is similar to admirable characters from works of adventure.

The fifth paragraph shows that Maupassant, as the story unfolds, alters the reader's perceptions of Mathilde from bad to good. For this reason, paragraph 5 marks a new direction from paragraphs 2, 3, and 4: It moves away from the topic material itself—Mathide's character—to Maupassant's *technique* in handling the topic material.

Paragraph 6, the conclusion, restates the comparison and also introduces the surprise ending as an additional reason for liking "The Necklace." With the body and conclusion together, therefore, the essay establishes five separate reasons as an argument to show the writer's approval of the story. Three of these, derived directly from the main character, constitute the major grounds for liking the story, and two are derived from Maupassant's techniques as an author.

Throughout the essay, the central idea or argument is brought out in words and expressions such as "likable," "Mathilde's appeal," "strong character," "she does what she has to," "pitiable," and "take her side." Many of these expressions were originally made in the writer's notebook; and, mixed as they are with details from the story, they make for continuity. It is this thematic development, together with details from the story as supporting evidence, that shows how an essay on the responses of liking and disliking can be both informed and informative.

Special Topics for Writing and Argument about Fiction

1. Describe the mixture of narration and dialogue in Walker's "Everyday Use." Why is there is a great deal of dialogue from paragraph 24 to the end (89–91)? On the basis of the mixture of dialogue and narration, what conclusions can you draw about the use that fiction makes of these elements?

2. Suppose that someone has told you that "The Things They Carried" is too detailed and realistic to be considered a story. Explain to this person why the assertion should be considered wrong. What elements of narrative, character, plot, point of view, idea, and description justify calling "The Things They Carried" a story?

3. In the last six months, what literary works did you read which you liked or disliked? Write a brief essay explaining your reasons for your positive or negative responses. To illustrate your arguments, you may make liberal references to these works, and, in addition, you may refer to films or TV shows that you have recently seen.

4. Consider the demonstrative likes/dislikes essay on Maupassant's "The Necklace." Do you accept the arguments in the essay? What other details and arguments can you think of for either liking or disliking the story?

5. Consider the narrative of "Neighbors" as an argument. How can you describe the argument? Is Carver arguing that people are civilized as long as they are being watched or instead that people, when unchecked, are irrational and uncivilized? What does the locked door signify in either argument?

6. Write contrasting paragraphs about a character (whom you know or about whom you have read). In the first, try to make your reader like the character. In the second, try to create a hostile response to the character. Write an additional paragraph explaining the ways in which you tried to create these opposite responses. How fair would it be for a reader to dislike your negative paragraph even though your hostile portrait is successful?

7. Write a brief episode or story that takes place in a historical period you believe you know well, being as factually accurate as you can. Introduce your own fictional characters as important "movers and shakers," and deal with their public or personal affairs or both. You may model your characters and episodes on historical persons, but you are free to exercise your imagination completely and construct your own characters.

Plot and Structure: *The Development and Organization of Stories*

CHAPTER 3

Stories and plays are made up mostly of **actions** or **incidents** that follow one another in chronological order. Finding a sequential or narrative order, however, is only the first step toward the more important consideration—the **plot,** or the controls governing the development of the actions.

PLOT: THE MOTIVATION AND CAUSATION OF FICTION

The English novelist E. M. Forster, in *Aspects of the Novel,* presents a memorable illustration of plot. To illustrate a bare set of actions, he proposes the following: "The king died, and then the queen died." He points out, however, that this sequence does not form a plot because it lacks *motivation* and *causation.* These he introduces in his next example: "The king died, and then the queen died of grief." The phrase "of grief" shows that one thing (grief) controls or overcomes another (the normal desire to live), and motivation and causation enter the sequence to form a plot. In a well-plotted story or play, one thing precedes or follows another not simply because time ticks away, but more importantly because *effects* follow *causes.* In a good work, nothing is irrelevant or accidental; everything is related and causative.

Determine the Conflict and Conflicts in a Story

The controlling impulse in a connected pattern of causes and effects is **conflict,** which refers to people or circumstances that a character must face and try to overcome. Conflicts bring out extremes of human energy, causing characters to engage in the decisions, actions, responses, and interactions that make up fictional literature.

In its most elemental form, a conflict is the opposition of two people. Their conflict may take the shape of anger, hatred, envy, argument, avoidance, political or moral opposition, gossip, lies, fighting, and many other attitudes and actions. Conflicts may also exist between groups, although conflicts between individuals are more identifiable and therefore more suitable for stories. Conflicts may also be abstract, such as when an individual opposes larger forces like natural objects, ideas, modes of behavior, or public opinion. A difficult or even impossible *choice*—a **dilemma**—is a natural conflict for an individual person. A conflict may also be brought out in ideas and opinions that clash. In short, conflict shows itself in many ways.

CONFLICT IS DIRECTLY RELATED TO DOUBT, TENSION, AND INTEREST.   Conflict is the major element of plot because opposing forces arouse *curiosity*, cause *doubt*, create *tension*, and produce *interest*. The same responses are the lifeblood of athletic competition. Consider which kind of athletic event is more interesting: (1) One team gets so far ahead that the winner is no longer in doubt, or (2) both teams are so evenly matched that the winner is in doubt until the final seconds. Obviously, games are uninteresting—as games—unless they develop as contests between teams of comparable strength. The same principle applies to conflicts in stories and dramas. There should be uncertainty about a protagonist's success or failure. Unless there is doubt, there is no tension, and without tension there is no interest.

FIND THE CONFLICTS TO DETERMINE THE PLOT.   To see a plot in operation, let us build on Forster's description. Here is a simple plot for a story of our own: "John and Jane meet, fall in love, and get married." This sentence contains a plot because it shows cause and effect (they get married *because* they fall in love), but with no conflict, the plot is not interesting. However, let us introduce conflicting elements into this common "boy meets girl" story:

> John and Jane meet at school and fall in love. They go together for two years and plan to marry, but a problem arises. Jane wants a career first, and after marriage she wants to be an equal contributor to the family. John understands Jane's wishes for equality, but he wants to get married first and let her finish her studies and have her career after they have children. Jane believes that John's plan is unacceptable because it constitutes a trap from which she cannot escape. This conflict interrupts their plans, and they part in anger and regret. Even though they still love each other, both marry other people and build separate lives and careers. Neither is happy even though they like and respect their spouses. The years pass, and, after children and grandchildren, Jane and John meet again. He is now divorced and she is a widow. Because their earlier conflict is no longer a barrier, they marry and try to make up for the past. Even their new happiness, however, is tinged with regret and reproach because of their earlier conflicts, their unhappy solution, their lost years, and their increasing age.

Here we have a true plot because our original "boy meets girl" topic now contains a major conflict from which a number of related conflicts develop. These conflicts lead to attitudes, choices, and outcomes that make the story interesting. The situation is lifelike; the conflicts rise out of realistic aims and hopes; the outcome is true to life.

⚘ THE STRUCTURE OF FICTION

Structure refers to the ways in which writers arrange materials in accord with the general ideas and purposes of their works. Unlike plot, which is concerned with conflict or conflicts, structure defines the layouts of works—the ways the story, play, or poem is shaped. Structure is about matters such as placement, balance, recurring themes, true and misleading conclusions, suspense, and the imitation of models or forms such as reports, letters, conversations, or confessions. A work might be divided into numbered sections or parts, or it might begin in a countryside (or one state) and conclude in a city (or another state), or it might develop a relationship between two people from their first introduction to their falling in love.

The importance of structure may be seen graphically in the art of the painter. As an example, Claude Lorrain's *Harbour at Sunset* (1639) pictures a lifelike scene comprising a harbor, ships, boats, buildings, and a shore on which people are engaging in activities such as working, chatting, transacting business, or fighting (Insert I–4). Near the horizon, the distant and glowing sun bathes the scene in light and is therefore the center of attention. This structuring of figures and background brings out contrasts between human beings, human artifacts and Nature, and human existence and the cosmos. Claude's painting suggests that, despite temporary human concerns, the source of life is like the sun—remote, vast, mysterious, and beautiful. In fiction, we find that organization and structure highlight many similar contrasts. To study structure is to study these arrangements and the purposes for which they are made.

⚘ FORMAL CATEGORIES OF STRUCTURE

Many aspects of structure are common to all genres of literature. Particularly for stories and plays, however, the following aspects form a skeleton, a pattern of development.

The Exposition Provides the Materials Necessary to Put the Plot into Operation

Exposition is the laying out, the putting forth, of the materials in the story—the main characters, their backgrounds, their characteristics, interests, goals, limitations, potentials, and basic assumptions. Exposition may not be limited to the beginning of the work, where it is most expected, but may be found anywhere. Thus, intricacies, twists, turns, false leads, blind alleys, surprises, and other quirks may be introduced to interest, intrigue, perplex, mystify, and please readers. Whenever something new arises, to the degree that it is new it is a part of exposition.

The Complication Marks the Beginning and the Growth of the Conflict

The **complication** is the onset and development of the major conflict—the plot. The major participants are the protagonist and antagonist, together with whatever ideas and values they represent, such as good or evil, freedom or oppression, independence or dependence, love or hate, intelligence or stupidity, or knowledge or ignorance.

The Crisis Marks the Decisions Made to End the Conflict

The **crisis** (Greek for "turning point") marks that part of the action where the conflict reaches its greatest tension. During the crisis, a decision or an action to resolve the conflict is undertaken, and therefore the crisis is the point at which curiosity, uncertainty, and tension are greatest. Usually the crisis is followed closely by the next stage, the *climax*. Often, in fact, the two are so close together that they are considered the same.

The Climax Is the Conclusion of the Conflict

Because the **climax** (Greek for *ladder*) is a consequence of the crisis, it is the story's *high point* and may take the shape of a decision, an action, an affirmation or denial, or an illumination or realization. It is the logical conclusion of the preceding actions; no new major developments follow it. In most stories, the climax occurs at the end or close to it. For example, in Crane's "The Blue Hotel," the climax is the Swede's verbal and physical encounter with the gambler. Everything that happens prior to this confrontation leads to it: the Swede's nervousness and suspicion, his odd behavior at the card table, his drunkenness, his pugnaciousness, his exultation after beating Johnnie, and his defiant exit from the Blue Hotel. The primitive power he thinks he has gained at the hotel causes him to antagonize the gambler—the story's climax—and thus to bring his existence to its sudden end.

The Resolution or Dénouement Finishes the Work and Releases the Tension

The **resolution** (a releasing or an untying) or **dénouement** (untying) is the completing of the story or play after the climax, for once the climax has occurred, the work's tension and uncertainty are finished, and most authors conclude quickly to avoid losing their readers' interest. For instance, the dénouement of "Blue Winds Dancing" comprises a few short details about the speaker's arrival at his home and the lodge, his description of his speaker's people, the dance, the drum beat, and finally his conclusion that he is home. Jamaica Kincaid ends "What I Have Been Doing Lately" with a resumption of the opening words of the story. Poe ends "The Masque of the Red Death" (Chapter 6) by asserting that the "illimitable" power of the Red Death has overcome the earth and all its occupants. In other words, after the story's major conflicts are finished, the dénouement brings the work to a satisfying and rapid ending.

FORMAL AND ACTUAL STRUCTURE

The structure just described is a *formal* one, an ideal pattern that moves directly from beginning to end. Few narratives and dramas follow this pattern exactly, however. A mystery story might hold back crucial details of exposition (because the goal is to mystify); a suspense story might keep the protagonist ignorant but provide readers with abundant details in order to maximize concern and tension about the outcome.

More realistic, less "artificial" stories might also contain structural variations. For example, Welty's "A Worn Path" produces a *double take* because of unique structuring. During most of the story the major character, Phoenix, seems to be in conflict with age, poverty, and environment. At the end, however, we are introduced to an additional difficulty—a new conflict—which enlarges our responses to include not just concern but also heartfelt anguish. "A Worn Path" is just one example of how a structural variation maximizes the impact of a work.

There are many other possible variants in structure. One of these is called **flashback,** or **selective recollection,** in which present circumstances are explained by the selective introduction of past events. The moment at which the flashback is introduced may be a part of the resolution of the plot, and the flashback might lead you into a moment of climax but then go from there to develop the details that are more properly part of the exposition. Let us again consider our brief story about John and Jane and use the flashback method of structuring the story:

> Jane is now old, and a noise outside causes her to remember the argument that forced her to part with John many years before. They were deeply in love, but their disagreement about her wishes for a career and equality split them apart. Then she pictures in her mind the years she and John have spent happily together after they married. She then contrasts her present happiness with her memory of her earlier, less happy marriage, and from there she recalls her youthful years of courtship with John before their disastrous conflict developed. Then she looks over at John, reading in a chair, and smiles. John smiles back, and the two embrace. Even then, Jane has tears on her face.

In this structure the action begins and remains in the present. Important parts of the past flood the protagonist's memory in flashback, though not in the order in which they happened. Memory might be used structurally in other ways. An example is Margaret Laurence's "The Loons" (Chapter 8), which is a narrative spoken (or thought) by a woman remembering her childhood and young adultood. The events of the story itself, however, develop through flashbacks—memories and hearsay reports about the life of a young Indian woman whose life was wasted and whose accidental death was essentially senseless. In short, this unique story builds its chronology through a series of intermittent and differing flashbacks.

Each narrative or drama has a unique structure. Some stories may be structured according to simple geography, as in Whitecloud's "Blue Winds Dancing" (a ride from California to Wisconsin) and Munro's "The Found Boat" (from a spring flood to an exploration on and beside a river [Chapter 7]). Parts or scenes might be carried on through conversations, as in Hemingway's "Soldier's Home" (Chapter 7) and Walker's "Everyday Use" (Chapter 2), or through a period of delirium, as in Katherine Anne Porter's "The Jilting of Granny Weatherall" (Chapter 9). A story may unfold in an apparently accidental way, with the characters making vital discoveries about the major characters, as in Glaspell's "A Jury of Her Peers" (Chapter 4). Additionally, parts of a work may be set out as fragments of conversation, as in St. Luke's "The Parable of the Prodigal Son" (Chapter 9), or as a ceremony, as in "Young Goodman Brown" (Chapter 9), or as an announcement of a party, as in "The Necklace" (Chapter 1). The possible variations in literary structures are infinite.

STORIES FOR STUDY

STEPHEN CRANE (1871–1900)

Born in New Jersey, Crane began writing stories at the age of eight, and by the time he was sixteen he was helping his brothers write for newspapers. He attended a number of colleges but did not graduate. While at Syracuse University he completed his first novel, Maggie: A Girl of the Streets, *which he published with borrowed money in 1893. During the remainder of his brief and turbulent life he worked as a writer and war correspondent. He spent a year in the West, and two of his better-known stories, "The Bride Comes to Yellow Sky" and "The Blue Hotel," came out of this experience. His best-known novel,* The Red Badge of Courage, *was published in 1895. "The Blue Hotel" was included in* The Monster and Other Stories *in 1899.*

The Blue Hotel   1899

I

The Palace Hotel at Fort Romper was painted a light blue, a shade that is on the legs of a kind of heron, causing the bird to declare its position against any background. The Palace Hotel, then, was always screaming and howling in a way that made the dazzling winter landscape of Nebraska seem only a grey swampish hush. It stood alone on the prairie, and when the snow was falling the town two hundred yards away was not visible. But when the traveller alighted at the railway station he was obliged to pass the Palace

Prairie Town
Palace Hotel
had to be looked at first
Edge of town
letting side a beside

Hotel before he could come upon the company of low clapboard houses which composed Fort Romper, and it was not to be thought that any traveller could pass the Palace Hotel without looking at it. Pat Scully, the proprietor, had proved himself a master of strategy when he chose his paints. It is true that on clear days, when the great transcontinental expresses, long lines of swaying Pullmans, swept through Fort Romper, passengers were overcome at the sight, and the cult that knows the brown-reds and the subdivisions of the dark greens of the East expressed shame, pity, horror, in a laugh. But to the citizens of this prairie town and to the people who would naturally stop there, Pat Scully had performed a feat. With this opulence and splendour, these creeds, classes, egotisms, that streamed through Romper on the rails day after day, they had no colour in common.

As if the displayed delights of such a blue hotel were not sufficiently enticing, it was Scully's habit to go every morning and evening to meet the leisurely trains that stopped at Romper and work his seductions upon any man that he might see wavering, gripsack in hand.

One morning, when a snow-crusted engine dragged its long string of freight cars and its one passenger coach to the station, Scully performed the marvel of catching three men. One was a shaky and quick-eyed Swede, with a great shining cheap valise; one was a tall bronzed cowboy, who was on his way to a ranch near the Dakota line; one was a little silent man from the East, who didn't look it, and didn't announce it. Scully practically made them prisoners. He was so nimble and merry and kindly that each probably felt it would be the height of brutality to try to escape. They trudged off over the creaking board sidewalks in the wake of the eager little Irishman. He wore a heavy fur cap squeezed tightly down on his head. It caused his two red ears to stick out stiffly, as if they were made of tin.

At last, Scully, elaborately, with boisterous hospitality, conducted them through the portals of the blue hotel. The room which they entered was small. It seemed to be merely a proper temple for an enormous stove, which, in the centre, was humming with god-like violence. At various points on its surface the iron had become luminous and glowed yellow from the heat. Beside the stove Scully's son Johnnie was playing High-Five° with an old farmer who had whiskers both grey and sandy. They were quarreling. Frequently the old farmer turned his face toward a box of sawdust—coloured brown from tobacco juice—that was behind the stove, and spat with an air of great impatience and irritation. With a loud flourish of words Scully destroyed the game of cards, and bustled his son upstairs with part of the baggage of the new guests. He himself conducted them to three basins of the coldest water in the world. The cowboy and the Easterner burnished themselves fiery red with this water, until it seemed to be some kind of metal-polish. The Swede, however, merely dipped his fingers gingerly and with trepidation. It was notable that throughout this series of small ceremonies the three travellers were made to feel that Scully was very benevolent. He was conferring great favours upon them. He handed the towel from one to another with an air of philanthropic impulse.

Afterward they went to the first room, and, sitting about the stove, listened to Scully's officious clamour at his daughters, who were preparing the midday meal. They reflected in the silence of experienced men who tread carefully amid new people. Nevertheless, the old farmer, stationary, invincible in his chair near the warmest part of the stove, turned his face from the sawdust-box frequently and addressed a glowing commonplace to the strangers. Usually he was answered in short but adequate sentences by either the cowboy or the Easterner. The Swede said nothing. He seemed to be

5

High-Five: the most commonly played card game in the United States before it was replaced in popularity by poker.

occupied in making furtive estimates of each man in the room. One might have thought that he had the sense of silly suspicion which comes to guilt. He resembled a badly frightened man.

Later, at dinner, he spoke a little, addressing his conversation entirely to Scully. He volunteered that he had come from New York, where for ten years he had worked as a tailor. These facts seemed to strike Scully as fascinating, and afterward he volunteered that he had lived at Romper for fourteen years. The Swede asked about the crops and the price of labour. He seemed barely to listen to Scully's extended replies. His eyes continued to rove from man to man.

Finally, with a laugh and a wink, he said that some of these Western communities were very dangerous; and after his statement he straightened his legs under the table, tilted his head, and laughed again, loudly. It was plain that the demonstration had no meaning to the others. They looked at him wondering and in silence.

II

As the men trooped heavily back into the front room, the two little windows presented views of a turmoiling sea of snow. The huge arms of the wind were making attempts—mighty, circular, futile—to embrace the flakes as they sped. A gate-post like a still man with a blanched face stood aghast amid this profligate fury. In a hearty voice Scully announced the presence of a blizzard. The guests of the blue hotel, lighting their pipes, assented with grunts of lazy masculine contentment. No island of the sea could be exempt in the degree of this little room with its humming stove. Johnnie, son of Scully, in a tone which defined his opinion of his ability as a card-player, challenged the old farmer of both grey and sandy whiskers to a game of High-Five. The farmer agreed with a contemptuous and bitter scoff. They sat close to the stove, and squared their knees under a wide board. The cowboy and the Easterner watched the game with interest. The Swede remained near the window, aloof, but with a countenance that showed signs of an inexplicable excitement.

The play of Johnnie and the grey-beard was suddenly ended by another quarrel. The old man arose while casting a look of heated scorn at his adversary. He slowly buttoned his coat, and then stalked with fabulous dignity from the room. In the discreet silence of all other men the Swede laughed. His laughter rang somehow childish. Men by this time had begun to look at him askance, as if they wished to inquire what ailed him.

A new game was formed jocosely. The cowboy volunteered to become the partner of Johnnie, and they all then turned to ask the Swede to throw in his lot with the little Easterner. He asked some questions about the game, and, learning that it wore many names, and that he had played it when it was under an alias, he accepted the invitation. He strode toward the men nervously, as if he expected to be assaulted. Finally, seated, he gazed from face to face and laughed shrilly. This laugh was so strange that the Easterner looked up quickly, the cowboy sat intent and with his mouth open, and Johnnie paused, holding the cards with still fingers.

Afterward there was a short silence. Then Johnnie said, "Well, let's get at it. Come on now!" They pulled their chairs forward until their knees were bunched under the board. They began to play, and their interest in the game caused the others to forget the manner of the Swede.

The cowboy was a board-whacker. Each time that he held superior cards he whanged them, one by one, with exceeding force, down upon the improvised table, and took the tricks with a glowing air of prowess and pride that sent thrills of indignation into the hearts of his opponents. A game with a board-whacker in it is sure to become intense. The countenances of the Easterner and the Swede were miserable whenever the cowboy

10

thundered down his aces and kings, while Johnnie, his eyes gleaming with joy, chuckled and chuckled.

Because of the absorbing play none considered the strange ways of the Swede. They paid strict heed to the game. Finally, during a lull caused by a new deal, the Swede suddenly addressed Johnnie: "I suppose there have been a good many men killed in this room." The jaws of the others dropped and they looked at him.

"What in hell are you talking about?" said Johnnie.

The Swede laughed again his blatant laugh, full of a kind of false courage and defiance. "Oh, you know what I mean all right," he answered. 15

"I'm a liar if I do!" Johnnie protested. The card was halted, and the men stared at the Swede. Johnnie evidently felt that as the son of the proprietor he should make a direct inquiry. "Now, what might you be drivin' at, mister?" he asked. The Swede winked at him. It was a wink full of cunning. His fingers shook on the edge of the board. "Oh, maybe you think I have been to nowheres. Maybe you think I'm a tenderfoot?"

"I don't know nothin' about you," answered Johnnie, "and I don't give a damn where you've been. All I got to say is that I don't know what you're driving at. There hain't never been nobody killed in this room."

The cowboy, who had been steadily gazing at the Swede, then spoke. "What's wrong with you, mister?"

Apparently it seemed to the Swede that he was formidably menaced. He shivered and turned white near the corners of his mouth. He sent an appealing glance in the direction of the little Easterner. During these moments he did not forget to wear his air of advanced pot-valour. "They say they don't know what I mean," he remarked mockingly to the Easterner.

The latter answered after prolonged and cautious reflection. "I don't understand 20 you," he said, impassively.

The Swede made a movement then which announced that he thought he had encountered treachery from the only quarter where he had expected sympathy, if not help. "Oh, I see you are all against me. I see——"

The cowboy was in a state of deep stupefaction. "Say," he cried, as he tumbled the deck violently down upon the board, "say, what are you gittin' at, hey?"

The Swede sprang up with the celerity of a man escaping from a snake on the floor. "I don't want to fight!" he shouted, "I don't want to fight!"

The cowboy stretched his long legs indolently and deliberately. His hands were in his pockets. He spat into the sawdust-box. "Well, who the hell thought you did?" he inquired.

The Swede backed rapidly toward a corner of the room. His hands were out pro- 25 tectingly in front of his chest, but he was making an obvious struggle to control his fright. "Gentlemen," he quavered. "I suppose I am going to be killed before I can leave this house! I suppose I am going to be killed before I can leave this house!" In his eyes was the dying-swan° look. Through the windows could be seen the snow turning blue in the shadow of dusk. The wind tore at the house, and some loose thing beat regularly against the clapboards like a spirit tapping.

A door opened, and Scully himself entered. He paused in surprise as he noted the tragic attitude of the Swede. Then he said. "What's the matter here?"

The Swede answered him swiftly and eagerly: "These men are going to kill me."

"Kill you!" ejaculated Scully. "Kill you! What are you talkin'?"

The Swede made the gesture of a martyr.

---

dying swan: Proverbially, a swan sings its most beautiful notes when it is about to die.

Scully wheeled sternly upon his son. "What is this, Johnnie?" 30

The lad had grown sullen. "Damned if I know," he answered. "I can't make no sense of it." He began to shuffle the cards, fluttering them together with an angry snap. "He says a good many men have been killed in this room, or something like that. And he says he's goin' to be killed here too. I don't know what ails him. He's crazy, I shouldn't wonder."

Scully then looked for explanation to the cowboy, but the cowboy simply shrugged his shoulders.

"Kill you?" said Scully again to the Swede. "Kill you? Man, you're off your nut."

"Oh, I know," burst out the Swede. "I know what will happen. Yes, I'm crazy—yes. Yes, of course, I'm crazy—yes. But I know one thing—" There was a sort of sweat of misery and terror upon his face. "I know I won't get out of here alive."

The cowboy drew a deep breath, as if his mind was passing into the last stages of 35
dissolution. "Well, I'm doggoned," he whispered to himself.

Scully wheeled suddenly and faced his son. "You've been troublin' this man!"

Johnnie's voice was loud with its burden of grievance. "Why, good Gawd, I ain't done nothin' to 'im."

The Swede broke in. "Gentlemen, do not disturb yourselves. I will leave this house. I will go away, because"—he accused them dramatically with his glance—"because I do not want to be killed."

Scully was furious with his son. "Will you tell me what is the matter, you young divil? What's the matter, anyhow? Speak out!"

"Blame it!" cried Johnnie in despair, "don't I tell you I don't know? He—he says we 40
want to kill him, and that's all I know. I can't tell what ails him."

The Swede continued to repeat: "Never mind, Mr. Scully; never mind. I will leave this house. I will go away, because I do not wish to be killed. Yes, of course, I am crazy—yes. But I know one thing! I will go away. I will leave this house. Never mind, Mr. Scully; never mind, I will go away."

"You will not go 'way," said Scully. "You will not go 'way until I hear the reason of this business. If anybody has troubled you I will take care of him. This is my house. You are under my roof, and I will not allow any peaceable man to be troubled here." He cast a terrible eye upon Johnnie, the cowboy, and the Easterner.

"Never mind, Mr. Scully; never mind. I will go away. I do not wish to be killed." The Swede moved toward the door which opened upon the stairs. It was evidently his intention to go at once for his baggage.

"No, no," shouted Scully peremptorily; but the white-faced man slid by him and disappeared. "Now," said Scully severely, "what does this mane?"°

Johnnie and the cowboy cried together: "Why, we didn't do nothin' to 'im!" 45

Scully's eyes were cold. "No," he said, "you didn't?"

Johnnie swore a deep oath. "Why, this is the wildest loon I ever see. We didn't do nothin' at all. We were just sittin' here playin cards, and he—"

The father suddenly spoke to the Easterner. "Mr. Blanc," he asked, "What has these boys been doin'?"

The Easterner reflected again. "I didn't see anything wrong at all," he said at last, slowly.

Scully began to howl, "But what does it mane?" He stared ferociously at his son. "I 50
have a mind to lather you for this, me boy."

Johnnie was frantic. "Well, what have I done?" he bawled at his father.

---

mane: mean. Scully speaks with a slight Irish brogue (see, for example, paragraphs 58, 70, and 114).

III

"I think you are tongue-tied," said Scully finally to his son, the cowboy, and the Easterner; and at the end of this scornful sentence he left the room.

Upstairs the Swede was swiftly fastening the straps of his great valise. Once his back happened to be half turned toward the door, and, hearing a noise there, he wheeled and sprang up, uttering a loud cry. Scully's wrinkled visage showed grimly in the light of the small lamp he carried. This yellow effulgence, streaming upward, coloured only his prominent features, and left his eyes, for instance, in mysterious shadow. He resembled a murderer.

"Man! man!" he exclaimed, "have you gone daffy?"

"Oh, no! Oh, no!" rejoined the other. "There are people in this world who know   55
pretty nearly as much as you do—understand?"

For a moment they stood gazing at each other. Upon the Swede's deathly pale cheeks were two spots brightly crimson and sharply edged, as if they had been carefully painted. Scully placed the light on the table and sat himself on the edge of the bed. He spoke ruminatively. "By cracky, I never heard of such a thing in my life. It's a complete muddle. I can't, for the soul of me, think how you ever got this idea into your head." Presently he lifted his eyes and asked: "And did you sure think they were going to kill you?"

The Swede scanned the old man as if he wished to see into his mind. "I did," he said at last. He obviously suspected that this answer might precipitate an outbreak. As he pulled on a strap his whole arm shook, the elbow wavering like a bit of paper.

Scully banged his hand impressively on the footboard of the bed. "Why, man, we're goin' to have a line of ilictric street-cars in this town next spring."

"'A line of electric street-cars,'" repeated the Swede, stupidly.

"And," said Scully, "there's a new railroad goin' to be built down from Broken Arm   60
to here. Not to mintion the four churches and the smashin' big brick schoolhouse. Then there's the big factory, too. Why, in two years Romper'll be a met-tro-*pol*-is."

Having finished the preparation of his baggage, the Swede straightened himself. "Mr. Scully," he said, with sudden hardihood, "how much do I owe you?"

"You don't owe me anythin'," said the old man, angrily.

"Yes, I do," retorted the Swede. He took seventy-five cents from his pocket and tendered it to Scully; but the latter snapped his fingers in disdainful refusal. However, it happened that they both stood gazing in a strange fashion at three silver pieces on the Swede's open palm.

"I'll not take your money," said Scully at last. "Not after what's been goin' on here." Then a plan seemed to strike him. "Here," he cried, picking up his lamp and moving toward the door. "Here! Come with me a minute."

"No," said the Swede, in overwhelming alarm.   65

"Yes," urged the old man. "Come on! I want you to come and see a picter—just across the hall—in my room."

The Swede must have concluded that his hour was come. His jaw dropped and his teeth showed like a dead man's. He ultimately followed Scully across the corridor, but he had the step of one hung in chains.

Scully flashed the light high on the wall of his own chamber. There was revealed a ridiculous photograph of a little girl. She was leaning against a balustrade of gorgeous decoration, and the formidable bang to her hair was prominent. The figure was as graceful as an upright sled-stake, and, withal, it was of the hue of lead. "There," said Scully, tenderly, "that's the picter of my little girl that died. Her name was Carrie. She had the purtiest hair you even saw! I was that found of her, she—"

Turning then, he saw that the Swede was not contemplating the picture at all, but, instead, was keeping keen watch on the gloom in the rear.

"Look, man!" cried Scully, heartily. "That's the picter of my little gal that died. Her name was Carrie. And then here's the picter of my oldest boy, Michael. He's a lawyer in Lincoln, an' doin' well. I gave that boy a grand eddication, and I'm glad for it now. He's a fine boy. Look at 'im now. Ain't he bold as blazes, him there in Lincoln, an' honoured an' respicted gintleman! An honoured and respicted gintleman," concluded Scully with a flourish. And, so saying, he smote the Swede jovially on the back. 70

The Swede faintly smiled.

"Now," said the old man, "there's only one more thing." He dropped suddenly to the floor and thrust his head beneath the bed. The Swede could hear his muffled voice. "I'd keep it under me piller if it wasn't for that boy Johnnie. Then there's the old woman—Where is it now? I never put it twice in the same place. Ah, now come out with you!"

Presently he backed clumsily from under the bed, dragging with him an old coat rolled into a bundle. "I've fetched him," he muttered. Kneeling on the floor, he unrolled the coat and extracted from its heart a large yellow-brown whiskey-bottle.

His first maneuver was to hold the bottle up to the light. Reassured, apparently, that nobody had been tampering with it, he thrust it with a generous movement toward the Swede.

The weak-kneed Swede was about to eagerly clutch this element of strength, but he suddenly jerked his hand away and cast a look of horror upon Scully. 75

"Drink," said the old man affectionately. He had risen to his feet, and now stood facing the Swede.

There was a silence. Then again Scully said: "Drink!"

The Swede laughed wildly. He grabbed the bottle, put it to his mouth; and as his lips curled absurdly around the opening and his throat worked, he kept his glance, burning with hatred, upon the old man's face.

IV

After the departure of Scully the three men, with the card-board still upon their knees, preserved for a long time an astounded silence. Then Johnnie said: "That's the dod-dangedest Swede I ever see."

"He ain't no Swede," said the cowboy, scornfully.

"Well, what is he then?" cried Johnnie. "What is he then?" 80

"It's my opinion," replied the cowboy deliberately, "he's some kind of a Dutch-man." It was a venerable custom of the country to entitle as Swedes all light-haired men who spoke with a heavy tongue. In consequence the idea of the cowboy was not without its daring. "Yes, sir," he repeated. "It's my opinion this feller is some kind of Dutchman."

"Well, he says he's a Swede, anyhow," muttered Johnnie, sulkily. He turned to the Easterner: "What do you think, Mr. Blanc?"

"Oh, I don't know," replied the Easterner.

"Well, what do you think makes him act that way?" asked the cowboy. 85

"Why, he's frightened." The Easterner knocked his pipe against the rim of the stove. "He's clear frightened out of his boots."

"What at?" cried Johnnie, and the cowboy together.

The Easterner reflected over his answer.

"What at?" cried the others again.

"Oh, I don't know, but it seems to me this man has been reading dime novels, and he thinks he's right out in the middle of it—the shootin' and stabbin' and all." 90

"But," said the cowboy, deeply scandalized, "this ain't Wyoming, ner none of them places. This is Nebrasker."

"Yes," added Johnnie, "an' why don't he wait till he gits *out West?*"

The travelled Easterner laughed. "It isn't different there even—not in these days. But he thinks he's right in the middle of hell."

Johnnie and the cowboy mused long.

"It's awful funny," remarked Johnnie at last.   95

"Yes," said the cowboy. "This is a queer game. I hope we don't git snowed in, because then we'd have to stand this here man bein' around with us all the time. That wouldn't be no good."

"I wish pop would throw him out," said Johnnie.

Presently they heard a loud stamping on the stairs, accompanied by ringing jokes in the voice of old Scully, and laughter, evidently from the Swede. The men around the stove stared vacantly at each other. "Gosh!" said the cowboy. The door flew open, and old Scully, flushed and anecdotal, came into the room. He was jabbering at the Swede, who followed him, laughing bravely. It was the entry of two roisterers from a banquet hall.

"Come now," said Scully sharply to the three seated men, "move up and give us a chance at the stove." The cowboy and the Easterner obediently sidled their chairs to make room for the new-comers. Johnnie, however, simply arranged himself in a more indolent attitude, and then remained motionless.

"Come! Git over, there," said Scully.   100

"Plenty of room on the other side of the stove," said Johnnie.

"Do you think we want to sit in the draught?" roared the father.

But the Swede here interposed with a grandeur of confidence. "No, no. Let the boy sit where he likes," he cried in a bullying voice to the father.

"All right! All right!" said Scully, deferentially. The cowboy and the Easterner exchanged glances of wonder.

The five chairs were formed in a crescent about one side of the stove. The Swede   105
began to talk; he talked arrogantly, profanely, angrily. Johnnie, the cowboy, and the Easterner maintained a morose silence, while old Scully appeared to be receptive and eager, breaking in constantly with sympathetic ejaculations.

Finally the Swede announced that he was thirsty. He moved in his chair, and said that he would go for a drink of water.

"I'll git it for you," cried Scully at once.

"No," said the Swede contemptuously. "I'll get it for myself." He arose and stalked with the air of an owner off into the executive parts of the hotel.

As soon as the Swede was out of hearing Scully sprang to his feet and whispered intensely to the others: "Upstairs he thought I was tryin' to poison 'im."

"Say," said Johnnie, "this makes me sick. Why don't you throw 'im out in the snow?"   110

"Why, he's all right now," declared Scully. "It was only that he was from the East, and he thought this was a tough place. That's all. He's all right now."

The cowboy looked with admiration upon the Easterner. "You were straight," he said. "You were on to that there Dutchman."

"Well," said Johnnie to his father, "he may be all right now, but I don't see it. Other time he was scared, but now he's too fresh."

Scully's speech was always a combination of Irish brogue and idiom, Western twang and idiom, and scraps of curiously formal diction taken from the storybooks and newspapers. He now hurled a strange mass of language at the head of his son. "What do I keep? What do I keep? What do I keep?" he demanded, in a voice of thunder. He slapped his knee impressively, to indicate that he himself was going to make reply, and that all should heed. "I keep a hotel," he shouted. "A hotel, do you mind? A guest under my roof has sacred privileges. He is to be intimidated by none. Not one word shall he hear that would prijudice him in favor of goin' away. I'll not have it. There's no place in this here town where they can say they iver took in a guest of mine because he was afraid to stay here." He wheeled suddenly upon the cowboy and the Easterner. "Am I right?"

"Yes, Mr. Scully," said the cowboy, "I think you're right."

"Yes, Mr. Scully," said the Easterner, "I think you're right."

115

V

At six-o'clock supper, the Swede fizzed like a fire-wheel. He sometimes seemed on the point of bursting into riotous song, and in all his madness he was encouraged by old Scully. The Easterner was encased in reserve; the cowboy sat in wide-mouthed amazement, forgetting to eat, while Johnnie wrathily demolished great plates of food. The daughters of the house, when they were obliged to replenish the biscuits, approached as warily as Indians, and, having succeeded in their purpose, fled with ill-concealed trepidation. The Swede domineered the whole feast, and he gave it the appearance of a cruel bacchanal. He seemed to have grown suddenly taller; he gazed, brutally disdainful, into every face. His voice rang through the room. Once when he jabbed out harpoon-fashion with his fork to pinion a biscuit, the weapon nearly impaled the hand of the Easterner, which had been stretched quietly out for the same biscuit.

After supper, as the men filed toward the other room, the Swede smote Scully ruthlessly on the shoulder. "Well, old boy, that was a good, square meal." Johnnie looked hopefully at his father; he knew that shoulder was tender from an old fall; and, indeed, it appeared for a moment as if Scully was going to flame out over the matter, but in the end he smiled a sickly smile and remained silent. The others understood from his manner that he was admitting his responsibility for the Swede's new viewpoint.

Johnnie, however, addressed his parent in an aside. "Why don't you license somebody to kick you downstairs?" Scully scowled darkly by way of reply.

When they were gathered about the stove, the Swede insisted on another game of High-Five. Scully gently deprecated the plan at first, but the Swede turned a wolfish glare upon him. The old man subsided, and the Swede canvassed the others. In his tone there was always a great threat. The cowboy and the Easterner both remarked indifferently that they would play. Scully said that he would presently have to go to meet the 6:58 train, and so the Swede turned menacingly upon Johnnie. For a moment their glances crossed like blades, and then Johnnie smiled and said, "Yes, I'll play."

120

They formed a square, with the little board on their knees. The Easterner and the Swede were again partners. As the play went on, it was noticeable that the cowboy was not board-whacking as usual. Meanwhile, Scully, near the lamp, had put on his spectacles and, with an appearance curiously like an old priest, was reading a newspaper. In time he went out to meet the 6:58 train, and, despite his precautions, a gust of polar wind whirled into the room as he opened the door. Besides scattering the cards, it chilled the players to the marrow. The Swede cursed frightfully. When Scully returned, his entrance disturbed a cosy and friendly scene. The Swede again cursed. But presently they were once more intent, their heads bent forward and their hands moving swiftly. The Swede had adopted the fashion of board-whacking.

Scully took up his paper and for a long time remained immersed in matters which were extraordinarily remote from him. The lamp burned badly, and once he stopped to adjust the wick. The newspaper, as he turned from page to page, rustled with a slow and comfortable sound. Then suddenly he heard three terrible words: "You are cheatin'!"

Such scenes often prove that there can be little of dramatic import in environment. Any room can present a tragic front: any room can be comic. This little den was now hideous as a torture-chamber. The new faces of the men themselves had changed it upon the instant. The Swede held a huge fist in front of Johnnie's face, while the latter looked steadily over it into the blazing orbs of his accuser. The Easterner had grown pallid: the cowboy's jaw had dropped in that expression of bovine amazement which was one of his important mannerisms. After the three words, the first sound in the room was made by Scully's paper as it floated forgotten to his feet. His spectacles had also fallen from his nose, but by a clutch he had saved them in air. His hand, grasping the spectacles, now remained poised awkwardly and near his shoulder. He stared at the card-players.

Probably the silence was while a second elapsed. Then, if the floor had been suddenly twitched out from under the men they could not have moved quicker. The five had projected themselves headlong toward a common point. It happened that Johnnie, in rising to hurl himself upon the Swede, had stumbled slightly because of his curiously instinctive care for the cards and the board. The loss of the moment allowed time for the arrival of Scully, and also allowed the cowboy time to give the Swede a great push which sent him staggering back. The men found tongue together, and hoarse shouts of rage, appeal, or fear burst from every throat. The cowboy pushed and jostled feverishly at the Swede, and the Easterner and Scully clung wildly to Johnnie; but through the smoky air, above the swaying bodies of the peace-compellers, the eyes of the two warriors ever sought each other in glances of challenge that were at once hot and steely.

Of course the board had been overturned, and now the whole company of   125
cards was scattered over the floor, where the boots of the men trampled the fat and painted kings and queens as they gazed with their silly eyes at the war that was waging above them.

Scully's voice was dominating the yells. "Stop now! Stop, I say! Stop, now—" Johnnie, as he struggled to burst through the rank formed by Scully and the Easterner, was crying. "Well, he says I cheated! He says I cheated! I won't allow no man to say I cheated! If he says I cheated, he's a——— ——!"

The cowboy was telling the Swede, "Quit, now! Quit, d'ye hear—"

The screams of the Swede never ceased: "He did cheat! I saw him! I saw him—"

As for the Easterner, he was importuning in a voice that was not heeded: "Wait a moment, can't you? Oh, wait a moment. What's the good of a fight over a game of cards? Wait a moment—"

In this tumult no complete sentences were clear. "Cheat"—"Quit"—"He says"—   130
these fragments pierced the uproar and rang out sharply. It was remarkable that, whereas Scully undoubtedly made the most noise, he was the least heard of any of the riotous band.

Then suddenly there was a great cessation. It was as if each man had paused for breath; and although the room was still lighted with the anger of men, it could be seen that there was no danger of immediate conflict, and at once Johnnie, shouldering his way forward, almost succeeded in confronting the Swede. "What did you say I cheated for? What did you say I cheated for? I don't cheat, and I won't let no man say I do!"

The Swede said, "I saw you! I saw you!"

"Well," cried Johnnie, "I'll fight any man what says I cheat!"

"No, you won't," said the cowboy. "Not here."

"Ah, be still, can't you?" said Scully, coming between them.   135

The quiet was sufficient to allow the Easterner's voice to be heard. He was repeating, "Oh, wait a moment, can't you? What's the good of a fight over a game of cards? Wait a moment!"

Johnnie, his red face appearing above his father's shoulder, hailed the Swede again. "Did you say I cheated?"

The Swede showed his teeth. "Yes."

"Then," said Johnnie, "we must fight."

"Yes, fight," roared the Swede. He was like a demoniac. "Yes, fight! I'll show you   140
what kind of a man I am! I'll show you who you want to fight! Maybe you think I can't
fight! Maybe you think I can't! I'll show you, you skin, you card-sharp! Yes, you cheated!
You cheated! You cheated!"

"Well, let's go at it, then, mister," said Johnnie coolly.

The cowboy's brow was beaded with sweat from his efforts in intercepting all sorts
of raids. He turned in despair to Scully. "What are you goin' to do now?"

A change had come over the Celtic visage of the old man. He now seemed all eagerness; his eyes glowed.

"We'll let them fight," he answered stalwartly. "I can't put up with it any longer. I've
stood this damned Swede till I'm sick. We'll let them fight."

VI

The men prepared to go out of doors. The Easterner was so nervous that he had great   145
difficulty in getting his arms into the sleeves of his new leather coat. As the cowboy
drew his fur cap down over his ears his hands trembled. In fact, Johnnie and old Scully
were the only ones who displayed no agitation. These preliminaries were conducted without words.

Scully threw open the door. "Well, come on," he said. Instantly a terrific wind
caused the flame of the lamp to struggle at its wick, while a puff of black smoke sprang
from the chimney-top. The stove was in mid-current of the blast, and its voice swelled to
equal the roar of the storm. Some of the scarred and bedabbled cards were caught up
from the floor and dashed helplessly against the farther wall. The men lowered their
heads and plunged into the tempest as into a sea.

No snow was falling, but great whirls and clouds of flakes, swept up from the
ground by the frantic winds, were streaming southward with the speed of bullets. The
covered land was blue with the sheen of an unearthly satin, and there was no other
hue save where, at the low, black railway station—which seemed incredibly distant—one
light gleamed like a tiny jewel. As the men floundered into a thigh-deep drift, it was
known that the Swede was bawling out something. Scully went to him, put a hand on his
shoulder, and projected an ear. "What's that you say?" he shouted.

"I say," bawled the Swede again. "I won't stand much show against this gang, I know
you'll all pitch on me."

Scully smote him reproachfully on the arm. "Tut, man!" he yelled. The wind tore
the words from Scully's lips and scattered them far alee.

"You are all a gang of—" boomed the Swede, but the storm also seized the remain-   150
der of this sentence.

Immediately turning their backs upon the wind, the men had swung around a corner to the sheltered side of the hotel. It was the function of the little house to preserve
here, amid this great devastation of snow, an irregular V-shape of heavily encrusted grass,
which crackled beneath the feet. One could imagine the great drifts piled against the
windward side. When the party reached the comparative peace of this spot it was found
that the Swede was still bellowing.

"Oh, I know what kind of a thing this is! I know you'll all pitch on me. I can't lick
you all!"

Scully turned upon him panther-fashion. "You'll not have to whip all of us. You'll
have to whip my son Johnnie. An' the man what troubles you durin' that time will have
me to dale with."

The arrangements were swiftly made. The two men faced each other, obedient to
the harsh commands of Scully, whose face, in the subtly luminous gloom, could be seen

set in the austere impersonal lines that are pictured on the countenances of the Roman veterans. The Easterner's teeth were chattering, and he was hopping up and down like a mechanical toy. The cowboy stood rock-like.

The contestants had not stripped off any clothing. Each was in his ordinary attire. Their fists were up, and they eyed each other in a calm that had the elements of leonine cruelty in it.   155

During this pause, the Easterner's mind, like a film, took lasting impressions of three men—the iron-nerved master of the ceremony; the Swede, pale, motionless, terrible; and Johnnie, serene yet ferocious, brutish yet heroic. The entire prelude had in it a tragedy greater than the tragedy of action, and this aspect was accentuated by the long, mellow cry of the blizzard, as it sped the tumbling and wailing flakes into the black abyss of the south.

"Now!" said Scully.

The two combatants leaped forward and crashed together like bullocks. There was heard the cushioned sound of blows, and of a curse squeezing out from between the tight teeth of one.

As for the spectators, the Easterner's pent-up breath exploded from him with a pop of relief, absolute relief from the tension of the preliminaries. The cowboy bounded into the air with a yowl. Scully was immovable as from supreme amazement and fear at the fury of the fight which he himself had permitted and arranged.

For a time the encounter in the darkness was such a perplexity of flying arms that   160
it presented no more detail than would a swiftly revolving wheel. Occasionally a face, as if illuminated by a flash of light, would shine out, ghastly and marked with pink spots. A moment later, the men might have been known as shadows, if it were not for the involuntary utterance of oaths that came from them in whispers.

Suddenly a holocaust of warlike desire caught the cowboy, and he bolted forward with the speed of a broncho. "Go it, Johnnie! go it! Kill him! Kill him!"

Scully confronted him. "Kape back," he said; and by his glance the cowboy could tell that this man was Johnnie's father.

To the Easterner there was a monotony of unchangeable fighting that was an abomination. This confused mingling was eternal to his sense, which was concentrated in a longing for the end, the priceless end. Once the fighters lurched near him, and as he scrambled hastily backward he heard them breathe like men on the rack.

"Kill him, Johnnie! Kill him! Kill him! Kill him!" The cowboy's face was contorted like one of those agony masks in museums.

"Keep still," said Scully, icily.   165

Then there was a sudden loud grunt, incomplete, cut short, and Johnnie's body swung away from the Swede and fell with sickening heaviness to the grass. The cowboy was barely in time to prevent the mad Swede from flinging himself upon his prone adversary. "No, you don't," said the cowboy, interposing an arm. "Wait a second."

Scully was at his son's side. "Johnnie! Johnnie, me boy!" His voice had a quality of melancholy tenderness. "Johnnie! Can you go on with it?" He looked anxiously down into the bloody, pulpy face of his son.

There was a moment of silence, and then Johnnie answered in his ordinary voice, "Yes, I—it—yes."

Assisted by his father he struggled to his feet. "Wait a bit now till you git your wind," said the old man.

A few paces away the cowboy was lecturing the Swede. "No, you don't! Wait a   170
second!"

The Easterner was plucking at Scully's sleeve. "Oh, this is enough," he pleaded. "This is enough! Let it go as it stands. This is enough!"

"Bill," said Scully, "git out of the road." The cowboy stepped aside. "Now." The combatants were actuated by a new caution as they advanced toward collision. They glared at each other, and then the Swede aimed a lightning blow that carried with it his entire weight. Johnnie was evidently half stupid from weakness, but he miraculously dodged, and his fist sent the over-balanced Swede sprawling.

The cowboy, Scully, and the Easterner burst into a cheer that was like a chorus of triumphant soldiery, but before its conclusion the Swede has scuffed agilely to his feet and come in berserk abandon at his foe. There was another perplexity of flying arms, and Johnnie's body again swung away and fell, even as a bundle might fall from a roof. The Swede instantly staggered to a little wind-waved tree and leaned upon it, breathing like an engine, while his savage and flamelit eyes roamed from face to face as the men bent over Johnnie. There was a splendour of isolation in his situation at this time which the Easterner felt once when, lifting his eyes from the man on the ground, he beheld that mysterious and lonely figure, waiting.

"Are you any good yet, Johnnie?" asked Scully in a broken voice.

The son gasped and opened his eyes languidly. After a moment he answered, 175
"No—I ain't—any good—any—more." Then, from shame, and bodily ill, he began to weep, the tears furrowing down through the blood-stains on his face. "He was too—too—too heavy for me."

Scully straightened and addressed the waiting figure.

"Stranger," he said, evenly, "it's all up with our side." Then his voice changed into that vibrant huskiness which is commonly the tone of the most simple and deadly announcements. "Johnnie is whipped."

Without replying, the victor moved off on the route to the front door of the hotel.

The cowboy was formulating new and unspellable blasphemies. The Easterner was startled to find that they were out in a wind that seemed to come direct from the shadowed arctic floes. He heard again the wail of the snow as it was flung to its grave in the south. He knew now that all this time the cold had been sinking into him deeper and deeper, and he wondered that he had not perished. He felt indifferent to the condition of the vanquished man.

"Johnnie, can you walk?" asked Scully. 180

"Did I hurt—hurt him any?" asked the son.

"Can you walk, boy? Can you walk?"

Johnnie's voice was suddenly strong. There was a robust impatience in it. "I asked you whether I hurt him any!"

"Yes, yes, Johnnie," answered the cowboy, consolingly; "he's hurt a good deal."

They raised him from the ground, and as soon as he was on his feet he went tottering 185
off, rebuffing all attempts at assistance. When the party rounded the corner they were fairly blinded by the pelting of the snow. It burned their faces like fire. The cowboy carried Johnnie through the drift to the door. As they entered, some cards again rose from the floor and beat against the wall.

The Easterner rushed to the stove. He was so profoundly chilled that he almost dared to embrace the glowing iron. The Swede was not in the room. Johnnie sank into a chair and, folding his arms on his knees, buried his face in them. Scully, warming one foot and then the other at a rim of the stove, muttered to himself with Celtic mournfulness. The cowboy had removed his fur cap, and with a dazed and rueful air he was running one hand through his tousled locks. From overhead they could hear the creaking of boards, as the Swede tramped here and there in his room.

The sad quiet was broken by the sudden flinging open of a door that led toward the kitchen. It was instantly followed by an inrush of women. They precipitated themselves upon Johnnie amid a chorus of lamentation. Before they carried their prey off to the kitchen, there to be bathed and harangued with that mixture of sympathy and abuse which is a feat of their sex, the mother straightened herself and fixed old Scully with an eye of stern reproach, "Shame be upon you, Patrick Scully!" she cried. "Your own son, too. Shame be upon you!"

"There, now! Be quiet, now!" said the old man, weakly.

"Shame be upon you, Patrick Scully!" The girls, rallying to this slogan, sniffed disdainfully in the direction of those trembling accomplices, the cowboy and the Easterner. Presently they bore Johnnie away, and left the three men to dismal reflection.

VII

"I'd like to fight this here Dutchman myself," said the cowboy, breaking a long silence.   190

Scully wagged his head sadly. "No, that wouldn't do. It wouldn't be right. It wouldn't be right."

"Well, why wouldn't it?" argued the cowboy. "I don't see no harm in it."

"No," answered Scully, with mournful heroism. "It wouldn't be right. It was Johnnie's fight, and now we mustn't whip the man just because he whipped Johnnie."

"Yes, that's true enough," said the cowboy; "but—he better not get fresh with me, because I couldn't stand no more of it."

"You'll not say a word to him," commanded Scully, and even then they heard the   195 tread of the Swede on the stairs. His entrance was made theatric. He swept the door back with a bang and swaggered to the middle of the room. No one looked at him. "Well," he cried, insolently, at Scully, "I s'pose you'll tell me now how much I owe you?"

The old man remained stolid. "You don't owe me nothin'."

"Huh!" said the Swede, "huh! Don't owe 'im nothin'."

The cowboy addressed the Swede. "Stranger, I don't see how you come to be so gay around here."

Old Scully was instantly alert. "Stop!" he shouted, holding his hand forth, fingers upward. "Bill, you shut up!"

The cowboy spat carelessly into the sawdust-box. "I didn't say a word, did I?"   200 he asked.

"Mr. Scully," called the Swede, "how much do I owe you?" It was seen that he was attired for departure, and that he had his valise in his hand.

"You don't owe me nothin'," repeated Scully in the same imperturbable way.

"Huh!" said the Swede. "I guess you're right. I guess if it was any way at all, you'd owe me somethin'. That's what I guess." He turned to the cowboy. "'Kill him! Kill him! Kill him!'" he mimicked, and then guffawed victoriously. "'Kill him!'" He was convulsed with ironical humour.

But he might have been jeering the dead. The three men were immovable and silent, staring with glassy eyes at the stove.

The Swede opened the door and passed into the storm, giving one derisive glance   205 backward at the still group.

As soon as the door was closed, Scully and the cowboy leaped to their feet and began to curse. They trampled to and fro, waving their arms and smashing into the air with their fists. "Oh, but that was a hard minute!" wailed Scully. "That was a hard minute! Him there leerin' and scoffin'! One bang at his nose was worth forty dollars to me that minute! How did you stand it, Bill?"

"How did I stand it?" cried the cowboy in a quivering voice. "How did I stand it? Oh!"

The old man burst into sudden brogue. "I'd loike to take that Swade," he wailed, "and hould 'im down on a shtone flure and bate 'im to a jelly wid a shtick!"

The cowboy groaned in sympathy. "I'd like to git him by the neck and hammer him"—he brought his hand down on a chair with a noise like a pistol-shot—"hammer that there Dutchman until he couldn't tell himself from a dead coyote!"

"I'd bate 'im until he—"   210

"I'd show *him* some things—"

And then together they raised a yearning, fanatic cry—"Oh-o-oh! if we only could—"

"Yes!"

"Yes!"

"And then I'd—"   215

"O-o-oh!"

VIII

The Swede, tightly gripping his valise, tacked across the face of the storm as if he carried sails. He was following a line of little naked, gasping trees which, he knew, must mark the way of the road. His face, fresh from the pounding of Johnnie's fists, felt more pleasure than pain in the wind and the driving snow. A number of square shapes loomed upon him finally, and he knew them as the houses of the main body of the town. He found a street and made travel along it, leaning heavily upon the wind whenever, at a corner, a terrific blast caught him.

He might have been in a deserted village. We picture the world as thick with conquering and elate humanity, but here, with the bugles of the tempest pealing, it was hard to imagine a peopled earth. One viewed the existence of man then as marvel, and conceded a glamour of wonder to these lice which were caused to cling to a whirling, fire-smitten, ice-locked, disease-stricken, space-lost bulb. The conceit of man was explained by this storm to be the very engine of life. One was a coxcomb not to die in it. However, the Swede found a saloon.

In front of it an indomitable red light was burning, and the snowflakes were made blood-colour as they flew through the circumscribed territory of the lamp's shining. The Swede pushed open the door of the saloon and entered. A sanded expanse was before him, and at the end of it four men sat about a table drinking. Down one side of the room extended a radiant bar, and its guardian was leaning upon his elbows listening to the talk of the men at the table. The Swede dropped his valise upon the floor and, smiling fraternally upon the barkeeper, said, "Gimme some whisky, will you?" The man placed a bottle, a whisky-glass, and a glass of ice-thick water upon the bar. The Swede poured himself an abnormal portion of whisky and drank it in three gulps. "Pretty bad night," remarked the bartender, indifferently. He was making the pretension of blindness which is usually a distinction of his class; but it could have been seen that he was furtively studying the half-erased blood-stains on the face of the Swede. "Bad night," he said again.

"Oh, it's good enough for me," replied the Swede, hardily, as he poured himself   220
some more whisky. The barkeeper took his coin and manoeuvred it through its reception by the highly nickelled cash-machine. A bell rang; a card labelled "20 cts." had appeared.

"No," continued the Swede, "this isn't too bad weather. It's good enough for me."

"So?" murmured the barkeeper, languidly.

The copious drams made the Swede's eyes swim, and he breathed a trifle heavier. "Yes, I like this weather. I like it. It suits me." It was apparently his design to impart a deep significance to these words.

"So?" murmured the bartender again. He turned to gaze dreamily at the scroll-like birds and bird-like scrolls which had been drawn with soap upon the mirrors in back of the bar.

"Well, I guess I'll take another drink," said the Swede, presently. "Have   225
something?"

"No, thanks; I'm not drinkin'," answered the bartender. Afterward he asked, "How
did you hurt your face?"

The Swede immediately began to boast loudly. "Why, in a fight. I thumped the soul
out of a man down here at Scully's hotel."

The interest of the four men at the table was at last aroused.

"Who was it?" said one.

"Johnnie Scully," blustered the Swede. "Son of the man what runs it. He will be   230
pretty near dead for some weeks, I can tell you. I made a nice thing of him. I did. He
couldn't get up. They carried him in the house. Have a drink?"

Instantly the men in some subtle way encased themselves in reserve. "No, thanks,"
said one. The group was of curious formation. Two were prominent local business men;
one was the district attorney; and one was a professional gambler of the kind known as
"square." But a scrutiny of the group would not have enabled an observer to pick the
gambler from the men of more reputable pursuits. He was, in fact, a man so delicate in
manner, when among people of fair class, and so judicious in his choice of victims, that in
the strictly masculine part of the town's life he had come to be explicitly trusted and admired. People called him a thoroughbred. The fear and contempt with which his craft
was regarded were undoubtedly the reason why his quiet dignity shone conspicuous
above the quiet dignity of men who might be merely hatters, billiard-markers, or grocery
clerks. Beyond an occasional unwary traveller who came by rail, this gambler was supposed to prey solely upon reckless and senile farmers, who, when flush with good crops,
drove into town in all the pride and confidence of an absolutely invulnerable stupidity.
Hearing at times in circuitous fashion of the despoilment of such a farmer, the important
men of Romper invariably laughed in contempt of the victim, and if they thought of the
wolf at all, it was with a kind of pride at the knowledge that he would never dare think of
attacking their wisdom and courage. Besides, it was popular that this gambler had a real
wife and two real children in a neat cottage in a suburb, where he led an exemplary
home life; and when any one even suggested a discrepancy in his character, the crowd immediately vociferated descriptions of this virtuous family circle. Then men who led exemplary home lives, and men who did not lead exemplary home lives, all subsided in a
bunch, remarking that there was nothing more to be said.

However, when a restriction was placed upon him—as, for instance, when a strong
clique of members of the new Pollywog Club refused to permit him, even as a spectator,
to appear in the rooms of the organization—the candour and gentleness with which he
accepted the judgment disarmed many of his foes and made his friends more desperately partisan. He invariably distinguished between himself and a respectable Romper man
so quickly and frankly that his manner actually appeared to be a continual broadcast
compliment.

And one must not forget to declare the fundamental fact of his entire position in
Romper. It is irrefutable that in all affairs outside his business, in all matters that occur
eternally and commonly between man and man, this thieving cardplayer was so generous, so just, so moral, that, in a contest, he could have put to flight the consciences of
nine tenths of the citizens of Romper.

And so it happened that he was seated in this saloon with the two prominent local
merchants and the district attorney.

The Swede continued to drink raw whisky, meanwhile babbling at the barkeeper   235
and trying to induce him to indulge in potations. "Come on. Have a drink. Come on.
What—no? Well, have a little one, then. By gawd, I've whipped a man tonight, and I want

to celebrate. I whipped him good, too. Gentlemen," the Swede cried to the men at the table, "have a drink?"

"Ssh!" said the barkeeper.

The group at the table, although furtively attentive, had been pretending to be deep in talk, but now a man lifted his eyes toward the Swede and said, shortly, "Thanks. We don't want any more."

At this reply the Swede ruffled out his chest like a rooster. "Well," he exploded, "it seems I can't get anybody to drink with me in this town. Seems so, don't it? Well!"

"Ssh!" said the barkeeper.

"Say," snarled the Swede, "don't you try to shut me up. I won't have it. I'm a gen-   240
tleman, and I want people to drink with me. And I want 'em to drink with me now. *Now*—do you understand?" He rapped the bar with his knuckles.

Years of experience had calloused the bartender. He merely grew sulky. "I hear you," he answered.

"Well," cried the Swede, "listen hard then. See those men over there? Well, they're going to drink with me, and don't you forget it. Now you watch."

"Hi!" yelled the barkeeper, "this won't do!"

"Why won't it?" demanded the Swede. He stalked over to the table, and by chance laid his hand upon the shoulder of the gambler. "How about this?" he asked wrathfully. "I asked you to drink with me."

The gambler simply twisted his head and spoke over his shoulder. "My friend, I   245
don't know you."

"Oh, hell!" answered the Swede, "come and have a drink."

"Now, my boy," advised the gambler, kindly, "take your hand off my shoulder and go 'way and mind your own business." He was a little, slim man, and it seemed strange to hear him use this tone of heroic patronage to the burly Swede. The other men at the table said nothing.

"What! You won't drink with me, you little dude? I'll make you, then! I'll make you!" The Swede had grasped the gambler frenziedly at the throat, and was dragging him from his chair. The other men sprang up. The barkeeper dashed around the corner of his bar. There was a great tumult, and then was seen a long blade in the hand of the gambler. It shot forward, and a human body, this citadel of virtue, wisdom, power, was pierced as easily as if it had been a melon. The Swede fell with a cry of supreme astonishment.

The prominent merchants and the district attorney must have at once tumbled out of the place backward. The bartender found himself hanging limply to the arm of a chair and gazing into the eyes of a murderer.

"Henry," said the latter, as he wiped his knife on one of the towels that hung be-   250
neath the bar rail, "you tell 'em where to find me. I'll be home, waiting for 'em." Then he vanished. A moment afterward the barkeeper was in the street dinning through the storm for help and, moreover, companionship.

The corpse of the Swede, alone in the saloon, had its eyes fixed upon a dreadful legend that dwelt atop the cash-machine: "This registers the amount of your purchase."

IX

Months later, the cowboy was frying pork over the stove of a little ranch near the Dakota line, when there was a quick thud of hoofs outside, and presently the Easterner entered with the letters and the papers.

"Well," said the Easterner at once, "the chap that killed the Swede has got three years. Wasn't much, was it?"

"He has? Three years?" The cowboy poised his pan of pork, while he ruminated upon the news. "Three years. That ain't much."

"No. It was a light sentence," replied the Easterner as he unbuckled his spurs. "Seems there was a good deal of sympathy for him in Romper." 255

"If the bartender had been any good," observed the cowboy, thoughtfully, "he would have gone in and cracked that there Dutchman on the head with a bottle in the beginnin' of it and stopped all this here murderin'."

"Yes, a thousand things might have happened," said the Easterner, tartly.

The cowboy returned his pan of pork to the fire, but his philosophy continued. "It's funny, ain't it? If he hadn't said Johnnie was cheatin' he'd be alive this minute. He was an awful fool. Game played for fun, too. Not for money. I believe he was crazy."

"I feel sorry for that gambler," said the Easterner.

"Oh, so do I," said the cowboy. "He don't deserve none of it for killin' who he did." 260

"The Swede might not have been killed if everything had been square."

"Might not have been killed?" exclaimed the cowboy. "Everythin' square? Why, when he said that Johnnie was cheatin' and acted like such a jackass? And then in the saloon he fairly walked up to git hurt?" With these arguments the cowboy browbeat the Easterner and reduced him to rage.

"You're a fool!" cried the Easterner, viciously. "You're a bigger jackass than the Swede by a million majority. Now let me tell you one thing. Let me tell you something. Listen! Johnnie *was* cheating!"

"'Johnnie,'" said the cowboy, blankly. There was a minute of silence, and then he said, robustly, "Why, no. The game was only for fun."

"Fun or not," said the Easterner, "Johnnie was cheating. I saw him. I know it. I saw 265 him. And I refused to stand up and be a man. I let the Swede fight it out alone. And you—you were simply puffing around the place wanting to fight. And then old Scully himself! We are all in it! This poor gambler isn't even a noun. He is a kind of an adverb. Every sin is the result of collaboration. We, five of us, have collaborated in the murder of this Swede. Usually there are from a dozen to forty women really involved in every murder, but in this case it seems to be only five men—you, I, Johnnie, old Scully; and that fool of an unfortunate gambler came merely as a culmination, the apex of a human movement, and gets all the punishment."

The cowboy, injured and rebellious, cried out blindly into this fog of mysterious theory: "Well, I didn't do anythin', did I?"

QUESTIONS

1. Describe the conflict in the story. Why is the Swede the major antagonist? How could he be seen as protagonist, instead of antagonist? Why do the others stress his identity as a Swede, and why is he never named?

2. Consider the Easterner's analysis (paragraph 90) as a plausible explanation of the Swede's behavior before the fight. How fully does this analysis explain these actions? How could the analysis be used in an argument that "The Blue Hotel" is a critique of conventional, dime-store views of the wild west?

3. Analyze the structure of the story. What relationship do the parts of abstract formal structure (described on pp. 111–12) have to the part divisions marked by Crane himself? Why is most of the story about events at the Blue Hotel, and why do events at the saloon, where the murder occurs, occupy only a small section? Explain, in relation to the story's structure, why we do not learn until the very end that Johnny actually *was* cheating.

4. How adequately does the Easterner's "noun-adverb" analysis in the concluding paragraphs explain the events of the story? Could such events be stopped at a certain point, or are they inevitable regardless of the Easterner's theory about collaborative control and responsibility?

WILLIAM FAULKNER (1897–1962)

Faulkner spent his childhood in Mississippi and became one of the foremost American novelists of the twentieth century. He twice received the Pulitzer Prize for Fiction (in 1955 and 1963), and he also received the Nobel Prize in Literature (in 1949). Throughout his extensive fiction about the special world that he named "Yoknapatawpha county," which is modeled on his own home area in Oxford, Mississippi, he treats life in the Southern United States as a symbol of humankind generally, emphasizing the decline of civilization and culture in the wake of the Civil War. Emily Grierson in "A Rose for Emily" is representative of this decline, for she maintains the appearances of status long after the substance is past. It is not unusual to find degraded, sullen, disturbed, and degenerate characters in Faulkner's fiction. In this respect Abner Snopes of "Barn Burning" (Chapter 4) is not untypical. The loyalty Snopes tries to exact from his son Sarty is one that excludes any allegiance to morality. Faulkner also uses the Snopes family as subjects in The Hamlet *(1940),* The Town *(1957), and* The Mansion *(1960).*

A Rose for Emily   1931

I

When Miss Emily Grierson died, our whole town went to her funeral: the men through a sort of respectful affection for a fallen monument, the women mostly out of curiosity to see the inside of her house, which no one save an old manservant—a combined gardener and cook—had seen in at least ten years.

It was a big, squarish frame house that had once been white, decorated with cupolas and spires and scrolled balconies in the heavily lightsome style of the seventies, set on what had once been our most select street. But garages and cotton gins had encroached and obliterated even the august names of that neighborhood; only Miss Emily's house was left, lifting its stubborn and coquettish decay above the cotton wagons and the gasoline pumps—an eyesore among eyesores. And now Miss Emily had gone to join the representatives of those august names where they lay in the cedar-bemused cemetery among the ranked and anonymous graves of Union and Confederate soldiers who fell at the battle of Jefferson.

Alive, Miss Emily had been a tradition, a duty, and a care; a sort of hereditary obligation upon the town, dating from that day in 1894 when Colonel Sartoris, the mayor—he who fathered the edict that no Negro woman should appear on the streets without an apron—remitted her taxes, the dispensation dating from the death of her father on into perpetuity. Not that Miss Emily would have accepted charity. Colonel Sartoris invented an involved tale to the effect that Miss Emily's father had loaned money to the town, which the town, as a matter of business, preferred this way of repaying. Only a man of Colonel Sartoris' generation and thought could have invented it, and only a woman could have believed it.

When the next generation, with its more modern ideas, became mayors and aldermen, this arrangement created some little dissatisfaction. On the first of the year they mailed her a tax notice. February came, and there was no reply. They wrote her a formal letter, asking her to call at the sheriff's office at her convenience. A week later the mayor wrote her himself, offering to call or to send his car for her, and received in reply a note on paper of an archaic shape, in a thin, flowing calligraphy in faded ink, to the effect that she no longer went out at all. The tax notice was also enclosed, without comment.

They called a special meeting of the Board of Aldermen. A deputation waited upon her, knocked at the door through which no visitor had passed since she ceased giving china-painting lessons eight or ten years earlier. They were admitted by the old Negro into a dim hall from which a stairway mounted into still more shadow. It smelled of dust and disuse—a close, dank smell. The Negro led them into the parlor. It was furnished in heavy, leather-covered furniture. When the Negro opened the blinds of one window, they could see that the leather was cracked; and when they sat down, a faint dust rose sluggishly about their thighs, spinning with slow motes in the single sun-ray. On a tarnished gilt easel before the fireplace stood a crayon portrait of Miss Emily's father.

They rose when she entered—a small, fat woman in black, with a thin gold chain descending to her waist and vanishing into her belt, leaning on an ebony cane with a tarnished gold head. Her skeleton was small and spare; perhaps that was why what would have been merely plumpness in another was obesity in her. She looked bloated, like a body long submerged in motionless water, and of that pallid hue. Her eyes, lost in the fatty ridges of her face, looked like two small pieces of coal pressed into a lump of dough as they moved from one face to another while the visitors stated their errand.

She did not ask them to sit. She just stood in the door and listened quietly until the spokesman came to a stumbling halt. Then they could hear the invisible watch ticking at the end of the gold chain.

Her voice was dry and cold. "I have no taxes in Jefferson. Colonel Sartoris explained it to me. Perhaps one of you can gain access to the city records and satisfy yourselves."

"But we have. We are the city authorities, Miss Emily. Didn't you get a notice from the sheriff, signed by him?"

"I received a paper, yes," Miss Emily said. "Perhaps he considers himself the sheriff ... I have no taxes in Jefferson."

"But there is nothing on the books to show that, you see. We must go by the—"

"See Colonel Sartoris. I have no taxes in Jefferson."

"But, Miss Emily—"

"See Colonel Sartoris." (Colonel Sartoris had been dead almost ten years.) "I have no taxes in Jefferson. Tobe!" The Negro appeared. "Show these gentlemen out."

II

So she vanquished them, horse and foot, just as she had vanquished their fathers thirty years before about the smell. That was two years after her father's death and a short time after her sweetheart—the one we believed would marry her—had deserted her. After her father's death she went out very little; after her sweetheart went away, people hardly saw her at all. A few of the ladies had the temerity to call, but were not received, and the only sign of life about the place was the Negro man—a young man then—going in and out with a market basket.

"Just as if a man—any man—could keep a kitchen properly," the ladies said; so they were not surprised when the smell developed. It was another link between the gross, teeming world and the high and mighty Griersons.

A neighbor, a woman, complained to the mayor, Judge Stevens, eighty years old. "But what will you have me do about it, madam?" he said.

"Why, send her word to stop it," the woman said. "Isn't there a law?"

"I'm sure that won't be necessary," Judge Stevens said. "It's probably just a snake or   20
a rat that nigger of hers killed in the yard. I'll speak to him about it."

The next day he received two more complaints, one from a man who came in diffident deprecation. "We really must do something about it, Judge. I'd be the last one in the world to bother Miss Emily, but we've got to do something." That night the Board of Aldermen met—three graybeards and one younger man, a member of the rising generation.

"It's simple enough," he said. "Send her word to have her place cleaned up. Give her a certain time to do it in, and if she don't . . ."

"Dammit, sir," Judge Stevens said, "will you accuse a lady to her face of smelling bad?"

So the next night, after midnight, four men crossed Miss Emily's lawn and slunk about the house like burglars, sniffing along the base of the brickwork and at the cellar openings while one of them performed a regular sowing motion with his hand out of a sack slung from his shoulder. They broke open the cellar door and sprinkled lime there, and in all the outbuildings. As they recrossed the lawn, a window that had been dark was lighted and Miss Emily sat in it, the light behind her, and her upright torso motionless as that of an idol. They crept quietly across the lawn and into the shadow of the locusts that lined the street. After a week or two the smell went away.

That was when people had begun to feel really sorry for her. People in our town,   25
remembering how old lady Wyatt, her great-aunt, had gone completely crazy at last, believed that the Griersons held themselves a little too high for what they really were. None of the young men were quite good enough for Miss Emily and such. We had long thought of them as a tableau, Miss Emily a slender figure in white in the background, her father a spraddled silhouette in the foreground, his back to her and clutching a horsewhip, the two of them framed by the back-flung front door. So when she got to be thirty and was still single, we were not pleased exactly, but vindicated; even with insanity in the family she wouldn't have turned down all of her chances if they had really materialized.

When her father died, it got about that the house was all that was left to her; and in a way, people were glad. At last they could pity Miss Emily. Being left alone, and a pauper, she had become humanized. Now she too would know the old thrill and the old despair of a penny more or less.

The day after his death all the ladies prepared to call at the house and offer condolence and aid, as is our custom. Miss Emily met them at the door, dressed as usual and with no trace of grief on her face. She told them that her father was not dead. She did that for three days, with the ministers calling on her, and the doctors, trying to persuade her to let them dispose of the body. Just as they were about to resort to law and force, she broke down, and they buried her father quickly.

We did not say she was crazy then. We believed she had to do that. We remembered all the young men her father had driven away, and we knew that with nothing left, she would have to cling to that which had robbed her, as people will.

III

She was sick for a long time. When we saw her again, her hair was cut short, making her look like a girl, with a vague resemblance to those angels in colored church windows— sort of tragic and serene.

The town had just let the contracts for paving the sidewalks, and in the summer after   30
her father's death they began the work. The construction company came with niggers and

mules and machinery, and a foreman named Homer Barron, a Yankee—a big, dark, ready man, with a big voice and eyes lighter than his face. The little boys would follow in groups to hear him cuss the niggers, and the niggers singing in time to the rise and fall of picks. Pretty soon he knew everybody in town. Whenever you heard a lot of laughing anywhere about the square, Homer Barron would be in the center of the group. Presently we began to see him and Miss Emily on Sunday afternoons driving in the yellow-wheeled buggy and the matched team of bays from the livery stable.

At first we were glad that Miss Emily would have an interest, because the ladies all said, "Of course a Grierson would not think seriously of a Northerner, a day laborer." But there were still others, older people, who said that even grief could not cause a real lady to forget *noblesse oblige* without calling it *noblesse oblige*. They just said, "Poor Emily. Her kinsfolk should come to her." She had some kin in Alabama; but years ago her father had fallen out with them over the estate of old lady Wyatt, the crazy woman, and there was no communication between the two families. They had not even been represented at the funeral.

And as soon as the old people said, "Poor Emily," the whispering began. "Do you suppose it's really so?" they said to one another. "Of course it is. What else could. . . ." This behind their hands; rustling of craned silk and satin behind jalousies closed upon the sun of Sunday afternoon as the thin, swift clop-clop-clop of the matched team passed: "Poor Emily."

She carried her head high enough—even when we believed that she was fallen. It was as if she demanded more than ever the recognition of her dignity as the last Grierson; as if it had wanted that touch of earthiness to reaffirm her imperviousness. Like when she bought the rat poison, the arsenic. That was over a year after they had begun to say "Poor Emily," and while the two female cousins were visiting her.

"I want some poison," she said to the druggist. She was over thirty then, still a slight woman, though thinner than usual, with cold, haughty black eyes in a face the flesh of which was strained across the temples and about the eyesockets as you imagine a lighthouse-keeper's face ought to look. "I want some poison," she said.

"Yes, Miss Emily. What kind? For rats and such? I'd recom—"   35

"I want the best you have. I don't care what kind."

The druggist named several. "They'll kill anything up to an elephant. But what you want is—"

"Arsenic," Miss Emily said. "Is that a good one?"

"Is . . . arsenic? Yes, ma'am. But what you want—"

"I want arsenic."   40

The druggist looked down at her. She looked back at him, erect, her face like a strained flag. "Why, of course," the druggist said. "If that's what you want. But the law requires you to tell what you are going to use it for."

Miss Emily just stared at him, her head tilted back in order to look him eye for eye, until he looked away and went and got the arsenic and wrapped it up. The Negro delivery boy brought her the package; the druggist didn't come back. When she opened the package at home there was written on the box, under the skull and bones: "For rats."

IV

So the next day we all said, "She will kill herself"; and we said it would be the best thing. When she had first begun to be seen with Homer Barron, we had said, "She will marry him." Then we said, "She will persuade him yet," because Homer himself had remarked—he liked men, and it was known that he drank with the younger men in the Elks' Club—that he was not a marrying man. Later we said, "Poor Emily" behind the jalousies as they passed on Sunday afternoon in the glittering buggy, Miss Emily with her head high and Homer Barron with his hat cocked and a cigar in his teeth, reins and whip in a yellow glove.

Then some of the ladies began to say that it was a disgrace to the town and a bad example to the young people. The men did not want to interfere, but at last the ladies forced the Baptist minister—Miss Emily's people were Episcopal—to call upon her. He would never divulge what happened during that interview, but he refused to go back again. The next Sunday they again drove about the streets, and the following day the minister's wife wrote to Miss Emily's relations in Alabama.

So she had blood-kin under her roof again and we sat back to watch developments. 45 At first nothing happened. Then we were sure that they were to be married. We learned that Miss Emily had been to the jeweler's and ordered a man's toilet set in silver, with the letters H. B. on each piece. Two days later we learned that she had bought a complete outfit of men's clothing, including a nightshirt, and we said, "They are married." We were really glad. We were glad because the two female cousins were even more Grierson than Miss Emily had ever been.

So we were not surprised when Homer Barron—the streets had been finished some time since—was gone. We were a little disappointed that there was not a public blowing-off, but we believed that he had gone on to prepare for Miss Emily's coming, or to give her a chance to get rid of the cousins. (By that time it was a cabal, and we were all Miss Emily's allies to help circumvent the cousins.) Sure enough, after another week they departed. And, as we had expected all along, within three days Homer Barron was back in town. A neighbor saw the Negro man admit him at the kitchen door at dusk one evening.

And that was the last we saw of Homer Barron. And of Miss Emily for some time. The Negro man went in and out with the market basket, but the front door remained closed. Now and then we would see her at a window for a moment, as the men did that night when they sprinkled the lime, but for almost six months she did not appear on the streets. Then we knew that this was to be expected too; as if that quality of her father which had thwarted her woman's life so many times had been too virulent and too furious to die.

When we next saw Miss Emily, she had grown fat and her hair was turning gray. During the next few years it grew grayer and grayer until it attained an even pepper-and-salt iron-gray, when it ceased turning. Up to the day of her death at seventy-four it was still that vigorous iron-gray, like the hair of an active man.

From that time on her front door remained closed, save for a period of six or seven years, when she was about forty, during which she gave lessons in china-painting. She fitted up a studio in one of the downstairs rooms, where the daughters and granddaughters of Colonel Sartoris' contemporaries were sent to her with the same regularity and in the same spirit that they were sent to church on Sundays with a twenty-five-cent piece for the collection plate. Meanwhile her taxes had been remitted.

Then the newer generation became the backbone and the spirit of the town, and 50 the painting pupils grew up and fell away and did not send their children to her with boxes of color and tedious brushes and pictures cut from the ladies' magazines. The front door closed upon the last one and remained closed for good. When the town got free postal delivery, Miss Emily alone refused to let them fasten the metal numbers above her door and attach a mailbox to it. She would not listen to them.

Daily, monthly, yearly we watched the Negro grow grayer and more stooped, going in and out with the market basket. Each December we sent her a tax notice, which would be returned by the post office a week later, unclaimed. Now and then we would see her in one of the downstairs windows—she had evidently shut up the top floor of the house—like the carven torso of an idol in a niche, looking or not looking at us, we could never tell which. Thus she passed from generation to generation—dear, inescapable, impervious, tranquil, and perverse.

And so she died. Fell ill in the house filled with dust and shadows, with only a doddering Negro man to wait on her. We did not even know she was sick; we had long since given up trying to get any information from the Negro. He talked to no one, probably not even to her, for his voice had grown harsh and rusty, as if from disuse.

She died in one of the downstairs rooms, in a heavy walnut bed with a curtain, her gray head propped on a pillow yellow and moldy with age and lack of sunlight.

V

The Negro met the first of the ladies at the front door and let them in, with their hushed, sibilant voices and their quick, curious glances, and then he disappeared. He walked right through the house and out the back and was not seen again.

The two female cousins came at once. They held the funeral on the second day, with the town coming to look at Miss Emily beneath a mass of bought flowers, with the crayon face of her father musing profoundly above the bier and the ladies sibilant and macabre; and the very old men—some in their brushed Confederate uniforms—on the porch and the lawn, talking of Miss Emily as if she had been a contemporary of theirs, believing that they had danced with her and courted her perhaps, confusing time with its mathematical progression, as the old do, to whom all the past is not a diminishing road but, instead, a huge meadow which no winter ever quite touches, divided from them now by the narrow bottle-neck of the most recent decade of years.

Already we knew that there was one room in that region above stairs which no one had seen in forty years, and which would have to be forced. They waited until Miss Emily was decently in the ground before they opened it.

The violence of breaking down the door seemed to fill this room with pervading dust. A thin, acrid pall as of the tomb seemed to lie everywhere upon this room decked and furnished as for a bridal: upon the valance curtains of faded rose color, upon the rose-shaded lights, upon the dressing table, upon the delicate array of crystal and the man's toilet things backed with tarnished silver, silver so tarnished that the monogram was obscured. Among them lay a collar and tie, as if they had just been removed, which, lifted, left upon the surface a pale crescent in the dust. Upon a chair hung the suit, carefully folded; beneath it the two mute shoes and the discarded socks.

The man himself lay in the bed.

For a long while we just stood there, looking down at the profound and fleshless grin. The body had apparently once lain in the attitude of an embrace, but now the long sleep that outlasts love, that conquers even the grimace of love, had cuckolded him. What was left of him, rotted beneath what was left of the nightshirt, had become inextricable from the bed in which he lay; and upon him and upon the pillow beside him lay that even coating of the patient and biding dust.

Then we noticed that in the second pillow was the indentation of a head. One of us lifted something from it, and leaning forward, that faint and invisible dust dry and acrid in the nostrils, we saw a long strand of iron-gray hair.

QUESTIONS

1. Who is Emily Grierson? What was the former position of her family in the town? What has happened to Emily after her father died? What are her economic circumstances? How does the deputation of alderman from the town of Jefferson treat her?

2. How do we learn about Emily? How do reports and rumors about her create the narrative of her life?

3. What has happened between Emily and Homer Barron? What is the significance, if any, of the fact that Homer is from the North?

4. Describe the plot of "A Rose for Emily." What contrasts and oppositions are developed in the story?

5. How does Faulkner shape the story's events to make Emily mysterious or enigmatic? In what ways does the ending come as a surprise?

JAMAICA KINCAID (b. 1949)

Jamaica Kincaid was born and educated in Antigua in the West Indies and now lives in Vermont. Her stories and novels are usually set in her native Antigua and often concern mother-daughter relationships, as in "Girl," one of her best-known (and very brief) stories. At the Bottom of the River (1983), from which "What I Have Been Doing Lately" is taken, was her first collection of stories. Novels are Annie John (1985), A Small Place (1988), Lucy (1990), and more recently The Autobiography of My Mother (1996). Although some critics are concerned that Kincaid's fiction contains less action than situation, all agree that she superbly renders the speech rhythms and simple, primal concerns of her native islands.

What I Have Been Doing Lately   1983

What I have been doing lately: I was lying in bed and the doorbell rang. I ran downstairs. Quick. I opened the door. There was no one there. I stepped outside. Either it was drizzling or there was a lot of dust in the air and the dust was damp. I stuck out my tongue and the drizzle or the damp dust tasted like government school ink. I looked north. I looked south. I decided to start walking north. While walking north, I noticed that I was barefoot. While walking north, I looked up and saw the planet Venus. I said, "It must be almost morning." I saw a monkey in a tree. The tree had no leaves. I said, "Ah, a monkey. Just look at that. A monkey." I walked for I don't know how long before I came up to a big body of water. I wanted to get across it but I couldn't swim. I wanted to get across it but it would take me years to build a bridge. Years passed and then one would take me I didn't know how long to build a bridge. Years passed and then one day, feeling like it, I got into my boat and rowed across. When I got to the other side, it was noon and my shadow was small and fell beneath me. I set out on a path that stretched out straight ahead. I passed a house, and a dog was sitting on the verandah but it looked the other way when it saw me coming. I passed a boy tossing a ball in the air but the boy looked the other way when he saw me coming. I walked and I walked but I couldn't tell if I walked a long time because my feet didn't feel as if they would drop off. I turned around to see what I had left behind me but nothing was familiar. Instead of the straight path, I saw hills. Instead of the boy with his ball, I saw tall flowering trees. I looked up and the sky was without clouds and seemed near, as if it were the ceiling in my house and, if I stood on a chair, I could touch it with the tips of my fingers. I turned around and looked ahead of me again. A deep hole had opened up before me. I looked in. The hole was deep and dark and I couldn't see the bottom. I thought, What's down there?, so on purpose I fell in. I fell and I fell, over and over, as if I were an old suitcase. On the sides of the deep hole I could see things written, but perhaps it was in a foreign language because I couldn't read them. Still I fell, for I don't know how long. As I fell I began to see that I didn't like the way falling made me feel. Falling made me feel sick and I missed all the people I had loved. I said, I don't want to fall anymore, and I reversed myself. I was standing again on the edge of the deep hole. I looked at the deep hole and I said, You can close up now, and it did. I walked some more without knowing distance. I only knew that I passed through days and nights, I only knew that I passed through rain and shine, light and darkness. I was never thirsty and I felt no pain. Looking at the horizon, I made a joke for myself: I said, "The earth has thin lips," and I laughed.

Looking at the horizon again, I saw a lone figure coming toward me, but I wasn't frightened because I was sure it was my mother. As I got closer to the figure, I could see that it wasn't my mother, but still I wasn't frightened because I could see that it was a woman.

When this woman got closer to me, she looked at me hard and then she threw up her hands. She must have seen me somewhere before because she said, "It's you. Just look at that. It's you. And just what have you been doing lately?"

I could have said, "I have been praying not to grow any taller."

I could have said, "I have been listening carefully to my mother's words, so as to make a good imitation of a dutiful daughter." 5

I could have said, "A pack of dogs, tired from chasing each other all over town, slept in the moonlight."

Instead, I said, What I have been doing lately: I was lying in bed on my back, my hands drawn up, my fingers interlaced lightly at the nape of my neck. Someone rang the doorbell. I went downstairs and opened the door but there was no one there. I stepped outside. Either it was drizzling or there was a lot of dust in the air and the dust was damp. I stuck out my tongue and the drizzle or the damp dust tasted like government school ink. I looked north and I looked south. I started walking north. While walking north, I wanted to move fast, so I removed the shoes from my feet. While walking north, I looked up and saw the planet Venus and I said, "If the sun went out, it would be eight minutes before I would know it." I saw a monkey sitting in a tree that had no leaves and I said, "A monkey. Just look at that. A monkey." I picked up a stone and I threw it at the monkey. The monkey, seeing the stone, quickly moved out of its way. Three times I threw a stone at the monkey and three times it moved away. The fourth time I threw the stone, the monkey caught it and threw it back at me. The stone struck me on my forehead over my right eye, making a deep gash. The gash healed immediately but now the skin on my forehead felt false to me. I walked for I don't know how long before I came to a big body of water. I wanted to get across, so when the boat came I paid my fare. When I got to the other side, I saw a lot of people sitting on the beach and they were having a picnic. They were the most beautiful people I had ever seen. Everything about them was black and shiny. Their skin was black and shiny. Their shoes were black and shiny. Their hair was black and shiny. The clothes they wore were black and shiny. I could hear them laughing and chatting and I said, I would like to be with these people, so I started to walk toward them, but when I got up close to them I saw that they weren't at a picnic and they weren't beautiful and they weren't chatting and laughing. All around me was black mud and the people all looked as if they had been made up out of the black mud. I looked up and saw that the sky seemed far away and nothing I could stand on would make me able to touch it with my fingertips. I thought, If only I could get out of this, so I started to walk. I must have walked for a long time because my feet hurt and felt as if they would drop off. I thought, If only just around the bend I would see my house and inside my house I would find my bed, freshly made at that, and in the kitchen I would find my mother or anyone else that I loved making me a custard. I thought, If only it was a Sunday and I was sitting in a church and I had just heard someone sing a psalm. I felt very sad so I sat down. I felt so sad that I rested my head on my own knees and smoothed my own head. I felt so sad I couldn't imagine feeling any other way again. I said, I don't like this. I don't want to do this anymore. And I went back to lying in bed, just before the doorbell rang.

QUESTIONS

1. Is the story told as if it were real or a dream? Why is the dreamlike quality introduced? How soon do you learn that the dreamlike narration has begun?

2. To what level of existence do the various descriptions and actions belong? In what ways do the actions and descriptions exceed everyday reality? Why does the author not introduce specific elements that might be considered appropriate in a world of dreams or in a future world?

3. Structurally, why does the story become repetitive at paragraph 7? What differences are there between the second narration and the first? Why does the story end with the third sound of the doorbell? What is the meaning of the repetitive actions?

4. Should this work be considered a story at all? What makes it a story? In what ways is it unlike a story?

EUDORA WELTY (1909–2001)

One of the major southern writers, Welty was born in Jackson, Mississippi. She attended the Mississippi State College for Women and the University of Wisconsin, and she began her writing career during the Great Depression. By 1943 she had published two major story collections, Curtain of Green *(1941, including "A Worn Path") and* The Wide Net *(1943). She is the author of many stories and was awarded the Pulitzer Prize in 1973 for her short novel* The Optimist's Daughter *(1972). "A Worn Path" received an O. Henry Award in 1941.*

A Worn Path   1941

It was December—a bright frozen day in the early morning. Far out in the country there was an old Negro woman with her head tied in a red rag, coming along a path through the pinewoods. Her name was Phoenix Jackson. She was very old and small and she walked slowly in the dark pine shadows, moving a little from side to side in her steps, with the balanced heaviness and lightness of a pendulum in a grandfather clock. She carried a thin, small cane made from an umbrella, and with this she kept tapping the frozen earth in front of her. This made a grave and persistent noise in the still air, that seemed meditative like the chirping of a solitary little bird.

She wore a dark striped dress reaching down to her shoe tops, and an equally long apron of bleached sugar sacks, with a full pocket: all neat and tidy, but everytime she took a step she might have fallen over her shoelaces, which dragged from her unlaced shoes. She looked straight ahead. Her eyes were blue with age. Her skin had a pattern all its own of numberless branching wrinkles and as though a whole little tree stood in the middle of her forehead, but a golden color ran underneath, and the two knobs of her cheeks were illuminated by a yellow burning under the dark. Under the rag her hair came down on her neck in the frailest of ringlets, still black, and with an odor like copper.

Now and then there was a quivering in the thicket. Old Phoenix said, "Out of my way, all you foxes, owls, beetles, jack rabbits, coons and wild animals! . . . Keep out from under these feet, little bob-whites. . . . Keep the big wild hogs out of my path. Don't let none of those come running my direction. I got a long way." Under her small black-freckled hand her cane, limber as a buggy whip, would switch at the brush as if to rouse up any hiding things.

On she went. The woods were deep and still. The sun made the pine needles almost too bright to look at, up where the wind rocked. The cones dropped as light as feathers. Down in the hollow was the mourning dove—it was not too late for him.

The path ran up a hill. "Seem like there is chains about my feet, time I get this far," she said, in the voice of argument old people keep to use with themselves. "Something always take a hold of me on this hill—pleads I should stay." 5

After she got to the top she turned and gave a full, severe look behind her where she had come. "Up through pines," she said at length. "Now down through oaks."

Her eyes opened their widest, and she started down gently. But before she got to the bottom of the hill a bush caught her dress.

Her fingers were busy and intent, but her skirts were full and long, so that before she could pull them free in one place they were caught in another. It was not possible to allow the dress to tear. "I in the thorny bush," she said. "Thorns, you doing your appointed work. Never want to let folks pass, no sir. Old eyes thought you was a pretty little *green* bush."

Finally, trembling all over, she stood free, and after a moment dared to stoop for her cane.

"Sun so high!" she cried, leaning back and looking, while the thick tears went over her eyes. "The time getting all gone here." 10

At the foot of this hill was a place where a log was laid across the creek.

"Now comes the trial," said Phoenix.

Putting her right foot out, she mounted the log and shut her eyes. Lifting her skirt, leveling her cane fiercely before her, like a festival figure in some parade, she began to march across. Then she opened her eyes and she was safe on the other side.

"I wasn't as old as I thought," she said.

But she sat down to rest. She spread her skirts on the bank around her and folded her hands over her knees. Up above her was a tree in a pearly cloud of mistletoe. She did not dare to close her eyes, and when a little boy brought her a plate with a slice of marble-cake on it she spoke to him. "That would be acceptable," she said. But when she went to take it there was just her own hand in the air. 15

So she left that tree, and had to go through a barbed-wire fence. There she had to creep and crawl, spreading her knees and stretching her fingers like a baby trying to climb the steps. But she talked loudly to herself: she could not let her dress be torn now, so late in the day, and she could not pay for having her arm or leg sawed off if she got caught fast where she was.

At last she was safe through the fence and risen up out in the clearing. Big dead trees, like black men with one arm, were standing in the purple stalks of the withered cotton field. There sat a buzzard.

"Who you watching?"

In the furrow she made her way along.

"Glad this is not the season for bulls." she said, looking sideways, "and the good Lord made his snakes to curl up and sleep in the winter. A pleasure I don't see no two-headed snake coming around that tree, where it come once. It took a while to get by him, back in the summer." 20

She passed through the old cotton and went into a field of dead corn. It whispered and shook and was taller than her head. "Through the maze now," she said, for there was no path.

Then there was something tall, black, and skinny there, moving before her.

At first she took it for a man. It could have been a man dancing in the field. But she stood still and listened, and it did not make a sound. It was as silent as a ghost.

"Ghost," she said sharply, "who be you the ghost of? For I have heard of nary death close by."

But there was no answer—only the ragged dancing in the wind.   25

She shut her eyes, reached out her hand, and touched a sleeve. She found a coat and inside that an emptiness, cold as ice.

"You scarecrow," she said. Her face lighted. "I ought to be shut up for good," she said with laughter. "My senses is gone. I too old, I the oldest people I ever know. Dance, old scarecrow," she said, "while I dancing with you."

She kicked her foot over the furrow, and with mouth drawn down, shook her head once or twice in a little strutting way. Some husks blew down and whirled in steamers about her skirts.

Then she went on, parting her way from side to side with the cane, through the whispering field. At last she came to the end, to a wagon track where the silver grass blew between the red ruts. The quail were walking around like pullets, seeming all dainty and unseen.

"Walk pretty," she said. "This is the easy place. This the easy going."   30

She followed the track, swaying through the quiet bare fields, through the little strings of trees silver in their dead leaves, past cabins silver from weather, with the doors and windows boarded shut, all like old women under a spell sitting there. "I walking in their sleep," she said, nodding her head vigorously.

In a ravine she went where a spring was silently flowing through a hollow log. Old Phoenix bent and drank. "Sweet-gum makes the water sweet," she said, and drank more. "Nobody know who made this well, for it was here when I was born."

The track crossed a swampy part where the moss hung as white as lace from every limb. "Sleep on, alligators, and blow your bubbles." Then the track went into the road.

Deep, deep the road went down between the high green-colored banks. Overhead the live-oaks met, and it was as dark as a cave.

A black dog with a lolling tongue came up out of the weeds by the ditch. She was   35
meditating, and not ready, and when he came at her she only hit him a little with her cane. Over she went in the ditch, like a little puff of milkweed.

Down there, her sense drifted away. A dream visited her, and she reached her hand up, but nothing reached down and gave her a pull. So she lay there and presently went to talking. "Old woman," she said to herself, "that black dog come up out of the weeds to stall you off, and now there he sitting on his fine tail smiling at you."

A white man finally came along and found her—a hunter, a young man, with his dog on a chain.

"Well, Granny!" he laughed. "What are you doing there?"

"Lying on my back like a June-bug waiting to be turned over, mister," she said, reaching up her hand.

He lifted her up, gave her a swing in the air, and set her down. "Anything broken,   40
Granny?"

"No sir, them old dead weeds is springy enough," said Phoenix, when she had got her breath. "I thank you for your trouble."

"Where do you live, Granny?" he asked, while the two dogs were growling at each other.

"Away back yonder, sir, behind the ridge. You can't even see it from here."

"On your way home?"

"No sir, I goin to town."

"Why, that's too far! That's as far as I walk when I come out myself, and I get something for my trouble." He patted the stuffed bag he carried, and there hung down a little closed claw. It was one of the bob-whites, with its beak hooked bitterly to show it was dead. "Now you go on home, Granny!"

"I bound to go to town, mister," said Phoenix. "The time come around."

He gave another laugh, filling the whole landscape. "I know you old colored people! Wouldn't miss going to town to see Santa Claus!"

But something held old Phoenix very still. The deep lines in her face went into a fierce and different radiation. Without warning, she had seen with her own eyes a flashing nickel fall out of the man's pocket onto the ground.

"How old are you, Granny?" he was saying.

"There is no telling, mister," she said, "no telling."

Then she gave a little cry and clapped her hands and said, "Git on away from here, dog! Look! Look at that dog!" She laughed as if in admiration. "He ain't scared of nobody. He a big black dog." She whispered, "Sic him!"

"Watch me get rid of that cur," said the man. "Sic him, Pete! Sic him!"

Phoenix heard the dogs fighting, and heard the man running and throwing sticks. She even heard a gunshot. But she was slowly bending forward by that time, further and further forward, the lids stretched down over her eyes, as if she were doing this in her sleep. Her chin was lowered almost to her knees. The yellow palm of her hand came out from the fold of her apron. Her fingers slid down and along the ground under the piece of money with the grace and care they would have in lifting an egg from under a setting hen. Then she slowly straightened up, she stood erect, and the nickel was in her apron pocket. A bird flew by. Her lips moved. "God watching me the whole time. I come to stealing."

The man came back, and his own dog panted about them. "Well, I scared him off that time," he said, and then he laughed and lifted his gun and pointed it at Phoenix.

She stood straight and faced him.

"Doesn't the gun scare you?" he said, still pointing it.

"No sir. I seen plenty go off closer by, in my day, and for less than what I done," she said, holding utterly still.

He smiled, and shouldered the gun. "Well, Granny," he said, "you must be a hundred years old, and scared of nothing. I'd give you a dime if I had any money with me. But you take my advice and stay home, and nothing will happen to you."

"I bound to go on my way, mister," said Phoenix. She inclined her head in the red rag. Then they went in different directions, but she could hear the gun shooting again and again over the hill.

She walked on. The shadows hung from the oak trees to the road like curtains. Then she smelled wood-smoke, and smelled the river, and she saw a steeple and the cabins on their steep steps. Dozens of little black children whirled around her. There ahead was Natchez shining. Bells were ringing. She walked on.

In the paved city it was Christmas time. There were red and green electric lights strung and crisscrossed everywhere, and all turned on in the daytime. Old Phoenix would have been lost if she had not distrusted her eyesight and depended on her feet to know where to take her.

She paused quietly on the sidewalk where people were passing by. A lady came along in the crowd, carrying an armful of red-, green-, and silver-wrapped presents; she gave off perfume like the red roses in hot summer, and Phoenix stopped her.

"Please, missy, will you lace up my shoe?" She held up her foot.

"What do you want, Grandma?"   65

"See my shoe," said Phoenix. "Do all right for out in the country, but wouldn't look right to go in a big building."

"Stand still then, Grandma," said the lady. She put her packages down on the sidewalk beside her and laced and tied both shoes tightly.

"Can't lace 'em with a cane," said Phoenix. "Thank you, missy. I doesn't mind asking a nice lady to tie up my shoe, when I gets out on the street."

Moving slowly and from side to side, she went into the big building, and into a tower of steps, where she walked up and around and around until her feet knew to stop.

She entered a door, and there she saw nailed up on the wall the document that had   70
been stamped with the gold seal and framed in the gold frame, which matched the dream that was hung up in her head.

"Here I be," she said. There was a fixed and ceremonial stiffness over her body.

"A charity case, I suppose," said an attendant who sat at the desk before her.

But Phoenix only looked above her head. There was sweat on her face, the wrinkles in her skin shone like a bright net.

"Speak up, Grandma," the woman said, "What's your name? We must have your history, you know. Have you been here before? What seems to be the trouble with you?"

Old Phoenix only gave a twitch to her face as if a fly were bothering her.   75

"Are you deaf?" cried the attendant.

But then the nurse came in.

"Oh, that's just old Aunt Phoenix," she said. "She doesn't come for herself—she has a little grandson. She makes these trips just as regular as clockwork. She lives away back off the Old Natchez Trace." She bent down. "Well, Aunt Phoenix, why don't you just take a seat? We won't keep you standing after your long trip." She pointed.

The old woman sat down, bolt upright in the chair.

"Now, how is the boy?" asked the nurse.   80

Old Phoenix did not speak.

"I said, how is the boy?"

But Phoenix only waited and stared straight ahead, her face very solemn and withdrawn into rigidity.

"Is his throat any better?" asked the nurse. "Aunt Phoenix, don't you hear me? Is your grandson's throat any better since the last time you came for the medicine?"

With her hands on her knees, the old woman waited, silent, erect, and motionless,   85
just as if she were in armor.

"You mustn't take up our time this way, Aunt Phoenix," the nurse said. "Tell us quickly about your grandson, and get it over. He isn't dead, is he?"

At last there came a flicker and then a flame of comprehension across her face, and she spoke.

"My grandson. It was my memory had left me. There I sat and forgot why I made my long trip."

"Forgot?" the nurse frowned. "After you came so far?"

Then Phoenix was like an old woman begging a dignified forgiveness for waking   90
up frightened in the night. "I never did go to school, I was too old at the Surrender," she said in a soft voice. "I'm an old woman without an education. It was my memory fail me. My little grandson, he is just the same, and I forgot it in the coming."

"Throat never heals, does it?" said the nurse, speaking in a loud, sure voice to old Phoenix. By now she had a card with something written on it, a little list. "Yes. Swallowed lye. When was it—January—two, three years ago—"

Phoenix spoke unasked now. "No missy, he not dead, he just the same. Every little while his throat begin to close up again, and he not able to swallow. He not get his breath. He not able to help himself. So the time come around, and I go on another trip for the soothing medicine."

"All right. The doctor said as long as you came to get it, you could have it," said the nurse. "But it's an obstinate case."

"My little grandson, he sit up there in the house all wrapped up, waiting by himself," Phoenix went on. "We is the only two left in the world. He suffer and it don't seem to put him back at all. He got a sweet look. He going to last. He wear a little patch quilt and peep out holding his mouth open like a little bird. I remembers so plain now. I not going to forget him again, no, the whole enduring time. I could tell him from all the others in creation."

"All right." The nurse was trying to hush her now. She brought her a bottle of medicine. "Charity," she said, making a check mark in a book.   95

Old Phoenix held the bottle close to her eyes, and then carefully put it into her pocket.

"I thank you," she said.

"It's Christmas time, Grandma," said the attendant. "Could I give you a few pennies out of my purse?"

"Five pennies is a nickel," said Phoenix stiffly.

"Here's a nickel," said the attendant.   100

Phoenix rose carefully and held out her hand. She received the nickel and then fished the other nickel out of her pocket and laid it beside the new one. She stared at her palm closely, with her head on one side.

Then she gave a tap with her cane on the floor.

"This is what come to me to do," she said, "I going to the store and buy my child a little windmill they sells, made out of paper. He going to find it hard to believe there such a thing in the world. I'll march myself back where he waiting, holding it straight up in this hand."

She lifted her free hand, gave a little nod, turned around, and walked out of the doctor's office. Then her slow step began on the stairs, going down.

QUESTIONS

1. From the description of Phoenix, what do you conclude about her economic condition? How do you know that she has taken the path through the woods before? Is she accustomed to being alone? What do you make of her speaking to animals, and of her imagining a boy offering her a piece of cake? What does her speech show about her education and background?

2. Describe the plot of the story. With Phoenix as the protagonist, what are the obstacles ranged against her? How might Phoenix be considered to be in the grip of large and indifferent social and political forces?

3. Comment on the meaning of this dialogue between Phoenix and the hunter:

   "Doesn't the gun scare you?" he said, still pointing it.

   "No, sir. I seen plenty go off closer by, in my day, and for less than what I done," she said, holding utterly still.

4. A number of responses might be made to this story, among them admiration for Phoenix, pity for her and her grandson and for the downtrodden generally, anger at her impoverished condition, and apprehension about her approaching senility. Do you share in any of these responses? Do you have any others?

TOM WHITECLOUD (1914–1972)

Thomas St. Germain Whitecloud was born in New York City. However, he spent much of his youth on the Lac du Flambeau Indian Reservation near Woodruff, Wisconsin, the town mentioned in paragraph 20 of "Blue Winds Dancing." After attending colleges in New Mexico and California, he received his degree in medicine from Tulane University. He lived in Louisiana and Texas throughout his medical career, and at the time of his death he was a consultant for the Texas Commission on Alcoholism and Drug Abuse for Indians. "Blue Winds Dancing,"
which can be considered as either a story or a fictionalized autobiographical fragment, received a prize in 1938 from both Scribner's Magazine, *in which it was published, and the Phi Beta Kappa National Honor Society.*

Blue Winds Dancing ⤳ ⤳ 1938

There is a moon out tonight. Moon and stars and clouds tipped with moonlight. And there is a fall wind blowing in my heart. Ever since this evening, when against a fading sky I saw geese wedge southward. They were going home. . . . Now I try to study, but against the pages I see them again, driving southward. Going home.

Across the valley there are heavy mountains holding up the night sky, and beyond the mountains there is home. Home, and peace, and the beat of drums, and blue winds dancing over snowfields. The Indian lodge will fill with my people, and our gods will come and sit among them. I should be there then. I should be at home.

But home is beyond the mountains, and I am here. Here where fall hides in the valleys, and winter never comes down from the mountains. Here where all the trees grow in rows; the palms stand stiffly by the roadsides, and in the groves the orange trees line in military rows, and endlessly bear fruit. Beautiful, yes; there is always beauty in order, in rows of growing things! But it is the beauty of captivity. A pine fighting for existence on a windy knoll is much more beautiful.

In my Wisconsin, the leaves change before the snows come. In the air there is the smell of wild rice and venison cooking; and when the winds come whispering through the forests, they carry the smell of rotting leaves. In the evenings, the loon calls, lonely; and birds sing their last songs before leaving. Bears dig roots and eat late fall berries, fattening for their long winter sleep. Later, when the first snows fall, one awakens in the morning to find the world white and beautiful and clean. Then one can look back over his trail and see the tracks following. In the woods there are tracks of deer and snowshoe rabbits, and long streaks where partridges slide to alight. Chipmunks make tiny footprints on the limbs and one can hear squirrels busy in hollow trees, sorting acorns. Soft lake waves wash the shores, and sunsets burst each evening over the lakes, and make them look as if they were afire.

That land which is my home! Beautiful, calm—where there is no hurry to get anywhere, no driving to keep up in a race that knows no ending and no goal. No classes where men talk and talk and then stop now and then to hear their own words come back to them from the students. No constant peering into the maelstrom of one's mind; no worries about grades and honors; no hysterical preparing for life until that life is half over; no anxiety about one's place in the thing they call Society.   5

I hear again the ring of axes in deep woods, the crunch of snow beneath my feet. I feel again the smooth velvet of ghost-birch bark. I hear the rhythm of the drums. . . . I am tired. I am weary of trying to keep up this bluff of being civilized. Being civilized means trying to do everything you don't want to, never doing anything you want to. It means dancing to the strings of custom and tradition; it means living in houses and never knowing or caring who is next door. These civilized white men want us to be like them—always dissatisfied—getting a hill and wanting a mountain.

Then again, maybe I am not tired. Maybe I'm licked. Maybe I am just not smart enough to grasp these things that go to make up civilization. Maybe I am just too lazy to think hard enough to keep up.

Still, I know my people have many things that civilization has taken from the whites. They know how to give; how to tear one's piece of meat in two and share it with one's brother. They know how to sing—how to make each man his own songs and sing them; for their music they do not have to listen to other men singing over a radio. They know how to make things with their hands, how to shape beads into design and make a thing of beauty from a piece of birch bark.

But we are inferior. It is terrible to have to feel inferior; to have to read reports of intelligence tests, and learn that one's race is behind. It is terrible to sit in classes and hear men tell you that your people worship sticks of wood—that your gods are all false, that the Manitou forgot your people and did not write them a book.

I am tired. I want to walk again among the ghost-birches. I want to see the leaves   10
turn in autumn, the smoke rise from the lodgehouses, and to feel the blue winds. I want to hear the drums; I want to hear the drums and feel the blue whispering winds.

There is a train wailing into the night. The trains go across the mountains. It would be easy to catch a freight. They will say he has gone back to the blanket; I don't care. The dance at Christmas. . . .

A bunch of bums warming at a tiny fire talk politics and women and joke about the Relief and the WPA and smoke cigarettes. These men in caps and overcoats and dirty overalls living on the outskirts of civilization are free, but they pay the price of being free in civilization. They are outcasts. I remember a sociology professor lecturing on adjustment to society; hobos and prostitutes and criminals are individuals who never adjusted, he said. He could learn a lot if he came and listened to a bunch of bums talk. He would learn that work and a woman and a place to hang his hat are all the ordinary man wants. These are all he wants, but other men are not content to let him want only these. He must be taught to want radios and automobiles and a new suit every spring. Progress would stop if he did not want these things. I listen to hear if there is any talk of communism or socialism in the hobo jungles. There is none. At best there is a sort of disgusted philosophy about life. They seem to think there should be a better distribution of wealth, or more work, or something. But they are not rabid about it. The radicals live in the cities.

I find a fellow headed for Albuquerque, and talk road-talk with him. "It is hard to ride fruit cars. Bums break in. Better to wait for a cattle car going back to the Middle West, and ride that." We catch the next east-bound and walk the tops until we find a cattle car. Inside, we crouch near the forward wall, huddle, and try to sleep. I feel peaceful and content at last. I am going home. The cattle car rocks. I sleep.

Morning and the desert. Noon and the Salton Sea, lying more lifeless than a mirage under a somber sun in a pale sky. Skeleton mountains rearing on the skyline, thrusting out of the desert floor, all rock and shadow and edges. Desert, Good country for an Indian reservation. . . .

Yuma and the muddy Colorado. Night again, and I wait shivering for the dawn.   15

Phoenix. Pima country. Mountains that look like cardboard sets on a forgotten stage. Tucson, Papago country. Giant cacti that look like petrified hitchhikers along the highways. Apache country. At El Paso my road-buddy decides to go on to Houston. I leave him, and head north to the mesa country. Las Cruces and the terrible Organ Mountains, jagged peaks that instill fear and wondering. Albuquerque. Pueblos along the Rio Grande. On the boardwalk there are some Indian women in colored sashes selling bits of pottery. The stone age offering its art to the twentieth century. They hold up a piece and fix the tourist with black eyes until, embarrassed, he buys or turns away. I feel suddenly angry that my people should have to do such things for a living. . . .

Santa Fe trains are fast, and they keep them pretty clean of bums. I decide to hurry and ride passenger coaltenders. Hide in the dark, judge the speed of the train as it leaves, and then dash out, and catch it. I hug the cold steel wall of the tender and think of the roaring fire in the engine ahead, and of the passengers back in the dining car reading their papers over hot coffee. Beneath me there is a blur of rails. Death would come quick if my hands should freeze and I fall. Up over the Sangre De Cristo range, around cliffs and through canyons to Denver. Bitter cold here, and I must watch out for Denver Bob. He is a railroad bull who has thrown bums from fast freights. I miss him. It is too cold, I suppose. On north to the Sioux country.

Small towns lit for the coming Christmas. On the streets of one I see a beam-shouldered young farmer gazing into a window filled with shining silver toasters. He is tall and wears a blue shirt buttoned, with no tie. His young wife by his side looks at him hopefully. He wants decorations for his place to hang his hat to please his woman. . . .

Northward again. Minnesota, and great white fields of snow; frozen lakes, and dawn running into dusk without noon. Long forests wearing white. Bitter cold, and one night the northern lights. I am nearing home.

I reach Woodruff at midnight. Suddenly I am afraid, now that I am but twenty miles   20
from home. Afraid of what my father will say, afraid of being looked on as a stranger by my own people. I sit by a fire and think about myself and all other young Indians. We just don't seem to fit in anywhere—certainly not among the whites, and not among the older people. I think again about the learned sociology professor and his professing. So many things seem to be clear now that I am away from school and do not have to worry about some man's opinion of my ideas. It is easy to think while looking at dancing flames.

Morning, I spend the day cleaning up, and buying some presents for my family with what is left of my money. Nothing much, but a gift is a gift, if a man buys it with his last quarter. I wait until evening, then start up the track toward home.

Christmas Eve comes in on a north wind. Snow clouds hang over the pines, and the night comes early. Walking along the railroad bed, I feel the calm peace of snowbound forests on either side of me. I take my time; I am back in a world where time does not mean so much now. I am alone; alone but not nearly so lonely as I was back on the campus at school. Those are never lonely who love the snow and the pines; never lonely when the pines are wearing white shawls and snow crunches coldly underfoot. In the woods I know there are the tracks of deer and rabbit; I know that if I leave the rails and go into the woods I shall find them. I walk along feeling glad because my legs are light and my feet seem to know that they are home. A deer comes out of the woods ahead of me, and stands silhouetted on the rails. The North, I feel, has welcomed me home. I watch him and am glad that I do not wish for a gun. He goes into the woods quietly, leaving only the design of his tracks in the snow. I walk on. Now and then I pass a field, white under the night sky, with houses at the far end. Smoke comes from the chimneys of the houses, and I try to tell what sort of wood each is burning by the smoke; some burn pine, others aspen, others tamarack. There is one from which comes black coal smoke that rises lazily and drifts out over the tops of the trees. I like to watch houses and try to imagine what might be happening in them.

Just as a light snow begins to fall I cross the reservation boundary; somehow it seems as though I have stepped into another world. Deep woods in a white-and-black winter night. A faint trail leading to the village.

The railroad on which I stand comes from a city sprawled by a lake—a city with a ...n people who walk around without seeing one another; a city sucking the life from ...untry around; a city with stores and police and intellectuals and criminals and ... apartment houses; a city with its politics and libraries and zoos.

Laughing, I go into the woods. As I cross a frozen lake I begin to hear the drums.   25
Soft in the night the drums beat. It is like the pulse beat of the world. The white line of
the lake ends at a black forest, and above the trees the blue winds are dancing.

I come to the outlying houses of the village. Simple box houses, etched black in the
night. From one or two windows soft lamplight falls on the snow. Christmas here, too, but
it does not mean much; not much in the way of parties and presents. Joe Sky will get
drunk. Alex Bodidash will buy his children red mittens and a new sled. Alex is a Carlisle
man, and tries to keep his home up to white standards. White standards. Funny that my
people should be ever falling farther behind. The more they try to imitate whites the
more tragic the result. Yet they want us to be imitation white men. About all we imitate
well are their vices.

The village is not a sight to instill pride, yet I am not ashamed; one can never be
ashamed of his own people when he knows they have dreams as beautiful as white snow
on a tall pine.

Father and my brother and sister are seated around the table as I walk in. Father stares
at me for a moment, then I am in his arms, crying on his shoulder. I give them the presents
I have brought, and my throat tightens as I watch my sister save carefully bits of red string
from the packages. I hide my feelings by wrestling with my brother when he strikes my shoulder in token of affection. Father looks at me, and I know he has many questions, but he
seems to know why I have come. He tells me to go alone to the lodge, and he will follow.

I walk along the trail to the lodge, watching the northern lights forming in the
heavens. White waving ribbons that seem to pulsate with the rhythm of the drums. Clean
snow creaks beneath my feet, and a soft wind sighs through the trees, singing to me.
Everything seems to say, "Be happy! You are home now—you are free. You are among
friends—we are your friends; we, the trees, and the snow, and the lights." I follow the trail
to the lodge. My feet are light, my heart seems to sing to the music, and I hold my head
high. Across white snow fields blue winds are dancing.

Before the lodge door I stop, afraid, I wonder if my people will remember me. I   30
wonder—"Am I Indian, or am I white?" I stand before the door a long time. I hear the ice
groan on the lake, and remember the story of the old woman under the ice, trying to get
out, so she can punish some runaway lovers. I think to myself, "If I am white I will not believe that story; If I am Indian, I will know that there is an old woman under the ice." I listen for a while, and I know that there is an old woman under the ice. I look again at the
lights, and go in.

Inside the lodge there are many Indians. Some sit on benches around the walls,
others dance in the center of the floor around a drum. Nobody seems to notice me. It
seems as though I were among a people I have never seen before. Heavy women with
long hair. Women with children on their knees—small children that watch with intent
black eyes the movements of the dancers, whose small faces are solemn and serene. The
faces of the old people are serene, too, and their eyes are merry and bright. I look at the
old men. Straight, dressed in dark trousers and beaded velvet vests, wearing soft moccasins. Dark, lined faces intent on the music. I wonder if I am at all like them. They dance
on, lifting their feet to the rhythm of the drums swaying lightly, looking upward. I look at
their eyes, and am startled at the rapt attention to the rhythm of the music.

The dance stops. The men walk back to the walls, and talk in low tones or with
their hands. There is little conversation, yet everyone seems to be sharing some secret. A
woman looks at a small boy wandering away, and he comes back to her.

Strange, I think and then remember. These people are not sharing words—they
are sharing a mood. Everyone is happy. I am so used to white people that it seems strange
so many people could be together without someone talking. These Indians are happy
because they are together, and because the night is beautiful outside, and the music is

beautiful. I try hard to forget school and white people, and be one of these—my people. I try to forget everything but the night, and it is a part of me that I am one with my people and we are all a part of something universal. I watch eyes, and see now that the old people are speaking to me. They nod slightly, imperceptibly, and their eyes laugh into mine. I look around the room. All the eyes are friendly; they all laugh. No one questions my being here. The drums begin to beat again, and I catch the invitation in the eyes of the old men. My feet begin to lift to the rhythm, and I look out beyond the walls into the night and see the lights. I am happy. It is beautiful. I am home.

QUESTIONS

1. Describe the first section of the story in terms of the structure. Could a case be made that this first section contains its own crisis and climax and that the rest of the story is really a resolution?

2. What do you learn in the first section about the conflict in the attitudes of the narrator? What is his attitude about "civilization"? What values make him think this way? If he is the protagonist, who or what is the antagonist?

3. What does the narrator mean by saying, "I am alone; alone but not nearly so lonely as I was back on the campus at school" (paragraph 22)?

4. What is meant by the dancing of the blue winds—what kind of wisdom? What is the place for such wisdom in a computerized, industrialized society?

WRITING ABOUT THE PLOT OF A STORY

An essay about plot is an analysis of the conflict and its developments. The organization of the essay should not be modeled on sequential sections and principal events, however, because these invite only a retelling of the story. Instead, the organization is to be developed from the important elements of conflict. As you look for ideas about plot, try to answer the following questions.

Questions for Discovering Ideas

* Who are the major and minor characters, and how do their characteristics put them in conflict? How can you describe the conflict or conflicts?
* How does the story's action grow out of the major conflict?
* If the conflict stems from contrasting ideas or values, what are these, and how are they brought out?
* What problems do the major characters face? How do the characters deal with these problems?
* How do the major characters achieve (or not achieve) their major goal(s)? What obstacles do they overcome? What obstacles overcome them or alter them?
* At the end, are the characters successful or unsuccessful, happy or unhappy, satisfied or dissatisfied, changed or unchanged, enlightened or ignorant? How has the resolution of the major conflict produced these results?

Strategies for Organizing Ideas

To keep your essay brief, be selective. Rather than describe everything a major character does, for example, stress the major elements in his or her conflict. Such an essay on Hemingway's "Soldier's Home" (Chapter 7) might emphasize the main character, Krebs, as he encounters the various problems that arise in his family as a result of his not wanting to settle down and go to work after returning from France after World War I. When there is a conflict between two major characters, the obvious approach is to focus equally on both. For brevity, however, emphasis might be placed on just one. Thus, an essay on the plot of "A Jury of Her Peers" (Chapter 4) might stress the things we learn about the major character, Minnie Wright, that are vital to to our considering her as the major participant in the story's conflict.

In addition, the plot may be analyzed more broadly in terms of impulses, goals, values, issues, and historical perspectives. Thus, you might emphasize the elements of chance working against Mathilde in Maupassant's "The Necklace" (Chapter 1) as a contrast to her dreams about wealth. A discussion of the plot of Poe's "The Masque of the Red Death" (Chapter 6) might stress the haughtiness of Prospero, the major character, because the plot could not develop without his egotism and pride.

The conclusion may contain a brief summary of the points you have made. It is also a fitting location to consider the effect or *impact* produced by the conflict. Additional ideas might focus on whether the author has arranged actions and dialogue to direct your favor toward one side or the other or whether the plot is possible or impossible, serious or comic, fair or unfair, or powerful or weak.

DEMONSTRATIVE STUDENT ESSAY (PLOT)

Plot in Faulkner's "A Rose for Emily"°

[1]   William Faulkner's "A Rose for Emily" may seem at first to be about a murder in a small Southern town, but even a first reading of the story reveals that the conflict does not arise from the search for a killer. It can't, because no one knows that a murder has even occurred until the murderess herself has died and been respectfully honored at her own funeral. Instead, incidents in the story indicate that the conflict is actually between those who are capable of change and those who are not, as well as those who want it and those who don't.* Both the major and minor events in the story's plot develop the idea that in the progress from an aristocratic but romanticized past to a more egalitarian present and future, there are unhealthy consequences for those who persist in clinging to the past.†

Faulkner begins to develop this conflict by relating several incidents that establish the story's main character, Emily Grierson, to be one of those older Southerners who are incapable of changing with the times. When Emily's father dies, for example, she refuses to accept his death. Some of the ladies of the town come to her home to offer their condolences:

She told them that her father was not dead. She did that for three days, with the ministers calling on her, and the doctors, trying to persuade her to let

°See pp. 130–35 for this story.
*Central idea.
†Thesis sentence.

them dispose of the body. Just as they were about to resort to law and force, she broke down, and they buried her father quickly. (132, paragraph 27)

[2]   This incident reveals that Emily cannot cope with big changes. Yet another incident--Emily's refusal to have a mailbox affixed to her house when the town gets free postal delivery (134, paragraph 50)--reveals that she cannot cope with smaller changes either. The event that most clearly reveals the unhealthy--and even disastrous--consequences of Emily's denial of change is her murder of her lover, who had apparently tried to end his relationship with her. The reader must piece the details together to understand what happened, but Faulkner provides enough information to indicate that Emily poisoned Homer Barron, who had said "that he was not a marrying man" (133, paragraph 43), and then kept his decomposing corpse in her bed, continuing to sleep beside it after she had become an old woman with gray hair. Emily does not want to progress, and she refuses all change--both good and bad--with all of her might. As a result, she resorts to murder to prevent change from occurring at all.

The past has an unhealthy grip on others, too, as brought out by two major plot incidents which show that Emily is not the only Jefferson resident who struggles with change. The first is the disagreement between Emily and the town's Board of Aldermen over the issue of her taxes. Emily claims that she owes no taxes because of an arrangement she made in 1894 with the town's former mayor, Colonel Sartoris. Her dispensation is overlooked until "the next generation, with its more modern ideas, became mayors and aldermen." These younger residents respond to her arrangement with "dissatisfaction" (131, paragraph 4), for [3]   in the egalitarian spirit of modern times, they believe that everyone in the town should be obliged to share the tax burden. True to form, Emily resists the idea that she should change. She repeats the statement "I have no taxes in Jefferson" four different times before finally ending the alderman's visit to her home (131, paragraphs 8–14). In this case, the younger and more modern townspeople try to force their newer and fairer standards upon Emily. Although their request is valid, Faulkner's narrator tells us that "she vanquished them" (131, paragraph 15). So even those who advocate needed change end up deferring to a relic from their past, and the unhealthy consequence is the continuation of inequality in Jefferson.

The second major incident that develops the clash between stagnation and progress is the townspeople's response to the awful smell that comes from Emily's house. When neighbors complain to the Board of Alderman, the issue pits the older residents against the younger ones, for the board is composed of "three graybeards and one younger man, a member of the rising generation" (132, paragraph 21). This younger man proposes to deal with the problem as though Emily is no one special: "'It's simple enough,' he said. 'Send her word to have her place cleaned up. Give her a certain time to do it in, and if she don't . . .'" (132, paragraph 22). His suggestion reflects a newer democratic spirit, one that does not defer to people on the basis of status or position. Eighty-year-old Judge Stevens, [4]   however, speaks for the other older aldermen when he reacts with horror to this suggestion: "'Dammit, sir,' Judge Stevens said, 'will you accuse a lady to her face of smelling bad?'" (132, paragraph 23). These older officials adhere to more old-fashioned, romantic notions of deference to ladies and to members of the old aristocracy. Once again, in the struggle between the past and the present, the status quo and progress, tradition is the winner. Emily (along with the past she represents) easily vanquishes the objections of the younger residents, for the aldermen agree only to sprinkle lime around her house secretly, under cover of darkness (132, paragraph 24). The result, however, is injustice, for an investigation into the smell that would have revealed its source to be a murdered corpse never takes place.

Without a doubt, in "A Rose for Emily" the characters who resist progress prevail over the ones who advocate it. And yet, two terrible consequences are the result of this opposition to change: A man is murdered and the killer escapes justice, all because the residents of the town, by consensus, defer to outdated and romantic notions from the past. Emily Grierson is not held--not by herself or by others--to the standards and rules that apply to everyone else in a democratic society. As a result, she ends up getting away with murder. Even so, Faulkner suggests that for those who cannot change, some pity may be in order, for the South's transformation completely overwhelms former aristocrats such as Emily. Faulkner is less sympathetic toward those like the older townspeople, however, who will not change, for as they seek to preserve the gentility of their heritage, they also perpetuate its flaws.

[5]

WORK CITED

Faulkner, William. "A Rose for Emily." Literature: An Introduction to Reading and Writing. Ed. Edgar V. Roberts and Henry E. Jacobs. 7th ed. Upper Saddle River: Prentice Hall, 2004. 130–35.

Commentary on the Essay

Because the subject is plot, this essay emphasizes the conflicting elements in Faulkner's "A Rose for Emily"—change and resistance to change—in the town of Jefferson. The first paragraph demonstrates how this conflict emerges only slowly in the story, inasmuch as the most lurid detail is not brought out until the story's end. Throughout the body of the essay, the conflict between change and nonchange is stressed as the major element of Faulkner's plot.

Note that the essay assumes that readers know the story already. Hence the essay is not a plot summary but is instead an analysis of a number of the elements making up the plot. Whatever summary is included is presented as evidence to support points about the plot of the story. As with any essay, it is important to realize that thematic thrust is the overriding need in the shaping of the essay.

Paragraph 2 of the body deals with three major plot incidents revealing how Emily is part of the old aristocracy and serves to crystallize resistance to change in Jefferson. Paragraph 3 demonstrates that many of the Jefferson townspeople are also resistant to change. This paragraph also asserts one of Faulkner's major ideas, namely, that this resistance to change has ill consequences. Paragraph 4 considers the issue of how the townspeople react to the terrible smell at the Grierson household, and thus Emily and her circumstances are a focal point for the town's evasion of the issue.

Paragraph 5 summarizes the conflicts of the plot and concludes with a modification of the central idea—that those resisting change are victors over those wanting change, and that the murder of Homer Barron is, symbolically, a negative comment on the town's way of dealing with the past.

❧ WRITING ABOUT STRUCTURE IN A STORY

Your essay should concern arrangement and shape. In form, the essay should not restate or summarize the part-by-part unfolding of the narrative or argument. Rather, it should explain why things are where they are: "Why is this here and not there?" is the fundamental question you need to answer. Thus it is possible to begin with a consideration of a work's crisis, and then to consider how the exposition and complication have built up to it. A vital piece of information, for example, might have been withheld in the story's earlier exposition (as in Ambrose Bierce's "An Occurrence at Owl Creek Bridge" [Chapter 5] and Faulkner's "A Rose for Emily") and introduced only at or near the conclusion. Therefore the crisis might be heightened because there would have been less suspense if the detail had been introduced earlier. Consider the following questions in planning to write about the story's structure.

Questions for Discovering Ideas

- If spaces or numbers divide the story into sections or parts, what structural importance do these parts have?
- If there are no marked divisions, what major sections can you find? (You might make divisions according to places where actions occur, various times of day, changing weather, or increasingly important events.)
- If the story departs in major ways from the formal structure of exposition, complication, crisis, climax, and resolution, what purpose do these departures serve?
- What variations in chronological order, if any, appear in the story (for example, gaps in the time sequence, flashbacks or selective recollection)? What effects are achieved by these variations?
- Does the story delay any crucial details of exposition? Why? What effect is achieved by the delay?
- Where does an important action or a major section (such as the climax) begin? End? How is it related to the other formal structural elements, such as the crisis? Is the climax an action, a realization, or a decision? To what degree does it relieve the work's tension? What is the effect of the climax on your understanding of the characters involved in it? How is this effect related to the arrangement of the climax?

Strategies for Organizing Ideas

Your essay should show why an entire story is arranged the way it is—to reveal the nature of a character's situation, to create surprise, or to evoke sympathy, reveal nobility (or depravity) of character, unravel apparently insoluble puzzles, express philosophical or political values, or bring out maximum humor. You might also, however, explain the structure of no more than a part of the story, such as the climax or the complication.

The essay is best developed in concert or agreement with what the work contains. The location of scenes is an obvious organizing element. Thus, essays on the structure of Hawthorne's "Young Goodman Brown" (Chapter 9) and Whitecloud's "Blue Winds Dancing" might be based on the fact that both take place outdoors (a dark forest for one and a series of railway locations and a winter scene for the other). Similarly, an essay might explore the structure of Maupassant's "The Necklace" (Chapter 1) by contrasting the story's indoor and outdoor locations. In Glaspell's "A Jury of Her Peers" (Chapter 4), much is made of the various parts of a kitchen in an early-twentieth-century Iowa farmhouse, and an essay might trace the structural importance of these.

Other ways to consider structure may be derived from a work's notable aspects, such as the growing suspense of Jackson's "The Lottery" (Chapter 5) or the revelations about the "sinfulness" of Goodman Brown's father and neighbors in Hawthorne's "Young Goodman Brown."

The conclusion should highlight the main parts of your essay. You may also deal briefly with the relationship of structure to the plot. If the work you have analyzed departs from chronological order, you might explain the causes and effects of this departure. Your aim should be to focus on the success of the work as it has been brought about by the author's choices in development.

DEMONSTRATIVE STUDENT ESSAY (STRUCTURE)

Scrambled Structure in Faulkner's "A Rose for Emily"°

[1]

The most notable incident in William Faulkner's story "A Rose for Emily" is that a murder has been committed in Jefferson, a small Southern town. One of Jefferson's most revered residents, Miss Emily Grierson, poisons her boyfriend, apparently because he has refused to make a long-term commitment to her. However, we readers, like the residents of Jefferson, do not discover that there has been a murder until the final sentences of the story. Although we are offered many clues about what happened, we don't understand their connections until the very end, when we're startled to realize that the reclusive, eccentric spinster not only killed her lover, but also slept beside his decomposing corpse for many years. We don't understand these clues until the end because Faulkner presents them in a mixed-up order.* His nonchronological account of specific incidents in the plot produces several intriguing effects. The scrambled order of events not only results in a concluding surprise, but the form of the story also echoes its content--the narration of isolated, seemingly unconnected events reflects the method of acquiring information in a small town and it also brings out the struggle between past and present generations.†

A major result of Faulkner's presentation of a scrambled order of events is to delay the the surprise ending. Faulkner's narrator tells us about the bad smell emanating from Emily's house (131, paragraph 16) before he introduces us to her

°See pp. 130–35 for this story.
*Central idea.
†Thesis sentence.

[2]   lover, Homer Barron, the sidewalk foreman from the North (133, paragraph 30). Then we learn that she buys rat poison (133, paragraph 42) and, after that, a man's toilet set engraved with the letters H. B. (134, paragraph 45). It is not until all these details are presented that we are told about Homer's disappearance, but we are also told that when he left there was no surprise in the town (134, paragraph 46). It's almost impossible for the reader to discern the cause and effect relationship between these incidents because they are not related in chronological order. Consequently, when Faulkner provides the final description of Homer's skeleton in Emily's bed, all the pieces of the puzzle instantly rearrange themselves in the reader's mind and click into place, producing a sudden, startling realization of what Emily had done (135, paragraphs 58–60).

[3]   <u>Furthermore, the scrambled order of events demonstrates Faulkner's use of the form of his story to reflect its content.</u> The nonchronological order of events realistically follows the way in which information travels in a small town, where gossip is passed along in bits and pieces, resulting in incomplete understanding. Faulkner's narrator relies on a variety of differenct sources to collect the details he presents, and he gives us these details not in the order of their happening, but rather in the order in which he learns of them. He is told about the foul smell by the mayor, who found out about it from one of Emily's neighbors and another unidentified man (132, paragraph 21). Many of the townspeople apparently reported that they observed Emily riding around town in a carriage with Homer Barron (133, paragraph 30). The ladies of the town surmise that she became mentally ill after the death of her father (133, paragraph 32). The druggist tells his story about her purchase of arsenic (133, paragraphs 34–41). The jeweler reveals her order of a man's toilet set (135, paragraph 45). These events, though they are all connected, do not seem to be connected when they are presented in the story. With this developing structure, each of the residents of Jefferson witnesses various details of Emily's life, but no one person knows everything. The narrator learns a little bit more from each person who sees or interacts with Emily, but their partial reports prevent any of them from making important connections, and so is it also with readers. The small-town tradition of ordinary gossip results in an incomplete picture of the truth until the last crucial detail is revealed.

[4]   <u>Faulkner also uses his scrambled presentation of detail to bring out the see-saw of emotions felt by the narrator, one of the younger generation, toward the past.</u> The vacillating emotions of the narrator are shaped by each of the incidents he relates, and in this way these emotions govern the form of the story. For example, the narrator expresses sympathy with "the next generation, with its more modern ideas" and democratic values (131, paragraph 4), but he also expresses feelings of pride, pity, and resentment toward Emily and her way of life. His description of Emily's house, "set on what had once been our most select street" (130, paragraph 2), displays his pride, but then her refusal to pay taxes provokes his resentment. He says that the younger generation felt "some little dissatisfaction" about an old municipal arrangement that relieved her of her tax burden (131, paragraph 4), yet he pities her when he learns of the foul smell. "That was when," he says, "people had begun to feel really sorry for her" (132, paragraph 25). But he reveals his resentment again when her father dies and people speculate that she will finally know what it's like to be without money and therefore she will be "humanized" (132, paragraph 26).

<u>As with the narrator, Faulkner's apparently disconnected narration of events also permits the presentation of the conflicting emotions of the younger, more</u>

[5] egalitarian generation toward their Southern ancestors. For the residents of Jefferson, Emily represents the aristocratic era of the old South--good aspects as well as bad--and she also invokes their ambiguous emotions about their heritage. Like most townspeople, the narrator feels pride in that heritage, but he also feels angry toward those in the wealthiest classes who assume that they are superior to everyone else. The narrator sums up all of these different emotions when he says, "Alive, Miss Emily had been a tradition, a duty, and a care; a sort of hereditary obligation upon the town" (130, paragraph 3). The conclusion of the story, coming unexpectedly though logically, makes the point that Emily has won the struggle between the generations because she has gotten away with murder, but only because of the uncertainty and ambiguity of the new generation as we see it presented piecemeal in the story.

[6] Faulkner thus relates the incidents of the story in a mixed-up order not only to build up to his concluding surprise, but also to give readers the same perspective as the townspeople. Clearly, Faulkner is a great storyteller and a master of his craft. His structural technique reinforces his overall message about the tensions between people of the past and the present. Though the new generation resents Emily, their respect and pity for her are the major causes by which Faulkner is able to construct his story of how a member of a past generation has committed a heinous crime without punishment.

WORK CITED

Faulkner, William. "A Rose for Emily." Literature: An Introduction to Reading and Writing. Ed. Edgar V. Roberts and Henry E. Jacobs. 7th ed. Upper Saddle River: Prentice Hall, 2004. 130–35.

Commentary on the Essay

As expressed in paragraph 1, this essay focuses on how Faulkner structures character and action in "A Rose for Emily" to achieve a surprise ending and also to contrast the older and newer generations in the American South. The essay's argument is that the parts of the story are placed where they are because they are also parts of Faulkner's artistic intentions. To unify the essay, the writer uses words and phrases such as "scrambled order of events," "*before* he introduces us," "Then we learn," "instantly rearrange," "where gossip is passed along," "apparently disconnected narration of events," and "unexpectedly though logically." All these expressions are intended not only for continuity, but also as a reminder that the essay is designed to show how and why Faulkner creates the story's structure as he has done it.

In the body, paragraph 2 presents a brief overview of how the apparently disconnected events build up to the surprise ending. Paragraph 3 stresses the story's realistic basis inasmuch as the details correspond closely to the significance of rumor, gossip, and casual observation in a small town. Together, then, paragraphs 2 and 3 account for the underlying causes of Faulkner's arrangement of the narrative.

In paragraph 4 the essay explains that Faulkner's form represents the attitudes of the narrator, and paragraph 5 deals with the same topic for the townsfolk. Paragraph 6 continues this idea and concludes the essay by emphasizing that the structure of "A Rose for Emily" permits Faulkner to dramatize the ambiguity with which the present generation of the South regards the previous generation.

Special Topics for Writing and Argument about Plot and Structure

1. Compare the structuring of the interior scenes in "A Rose for Emily," "Blue Winds Dancing," and "The Blue Hotel." How do these scenes bring out the conflicts of the stories? How do characters in the interiors contribute to plot developments? What is the relationship of these characters to the major themes of the stories?

2. Consider the surprises in "An Occurrence at Owl Creek Bridge" (Chapter 5), "The Story of an Hour" (Chapter 8), and "A Rose for Emily." How much preparation is made for the surprises? In retrospect, to what degree are the surprises not surprises at all but rather necessary outcomes of the preceding parts of the works?

3. Compare "Everyday Use" (Chapter 2) and "Blue Winds Dancing" as stories developing plots about clashing social and racial values. In what ways are the plots similar and different?

4. Analyze the repetitiveness in Kincaid's "What I Have Been Doing Lately." In what ways does the repetition seem to be a structural defect? In what ways does it seem to be an essential aspect of Kincaid's ideas as presented in the story?

5. Select a circumstance in your life that caused you doubt, difficulty, and conflict. Making yourself anonymous (give yourself a fictitious name and put yourself in a fictitious location), write a brief story about the occasion, stressing how your conflict began, how it affected you, and how you resolved it. You might choose to describe the details in chronological order, or you might begin the story in the present tense and introduce details in flashback.

6. William Faulkner is regarded as one of the major twentieth-century writers. How valid is this assertion? What in his works is particularly unique? Socially, are his typical fictional characters to be considered upper or lower class? What do critics say about his views on the nature of human existence? Are his views optimistic? Pessimistic? (You may discuss "A Rose for Emily" and also "Barn Burning" [Chapter 4] as representative works.) Use books and articles that you obtain from your library or over the Internet to substantiate your arguments.

Characters: *The People in Fiction*

Writers of fiction create narratives that enhance and deepen our understanding of human character and human life. In our own day, under the influences of pioneers like Freud, Jung, and Skinner, the science of psychology has influenced both the creation and the study of literature. It is well known that Freud buttressed some of his psychological conclusions by referring to literary works, especially plays by Shakespeare. Widely known films such as *Spellbound* and *The Snake Pit* have popularized the relationships between literary character and psychology. Without doubt, the presentation and understanding of character is a major aim of fiction (and literature generally).

In literature, a **character** is a verbal representation of a human being. Through action, speech, description, and commentary, authors portray characters who are worth caring about, cheering for, and even loving, although there are also characters you may laugh at, dislike, or even hate.

In a story or play emphasizing a major character, you may expect that each action or speech, no matter how small, is part of a total presentation of the complex combination of both the inner and the outer self that constitutes a human being. Whereas in life things may "just happen," in literature all actions, interactions, speeches, and observations are deliberate. Thus, you read about important actions like a long period of work and sacrifice (Maupassant's "The Necklace" [Chapter 1]), the strained relationship between a mother and her daughter (Oates's "Shopping"), acts of defiance and retribution (Poe's "The Masque of the Red Death" [Chapter 6]), or a young man's poignant dream of freedom (Bierce's "An Occurrence at Owl Creek Bridge" [Chapter 5]). By making such actions interesting, authors help you understand and appreciate not only their major characters but also life itself.

❦ CHARACTER TRAITS

In studying a literary character, try to determine the character's outstanding traits. A **trait** is a quality of mind or habitual mode of behavior that is evident in both active and passive ways, such as never repaying borrowed money, supplying moral support to friends and loved ones, being a person on whom people always rely, listening to the thoughts and problems of others, avoiding eye contact, taking the biggest portions, or always thinking oneself the center of attention. If we study the facial expression of Andrea del Verrocchio's bust of Lorenzo de' Medici, for example below, we can see that Verrocchio is presenting a negative view of his subject. Lorenzo's firm mouth, his fixed stare, and his closely knit eyebrows suggest his pride and ruthlessness. Sometimes, of course, the traits we encounter are minor and therefore negligible, but often a trait may be a person's *primary* characteristic (not only in fiction but also in life). Thus, characters may be ambitious or lazy, serene or anxious, aggressive or fearful, thoughtful or inconsiderate, open or secretive, confident or self-doubting, kind or cruel, quiet or noisy, visionary or practical, careful or careless, impartial or biased, straightforward or underhanded, "winners" or "losers," and so on.

    With this sort of list, to which you may add at will, you can analyze and develop conclusions about character. For example, Mathilde in Maupassant's "The Necklace" indulges in dreams of unattainable wealth and comfort and is so

"Bust of Lorenzo de'Medici," Florentine, fifteenth or sixteenth century; probably after a model by Andrea del Verocchio and O. Benintendi. (Photograph © Board of Trustees, National Gallery of Art, Washington, DC. Samuel H. Kress Collection.)

swept up in her visions that she scorns her comparatively good life with her reliable but dull husband. It is fair to say that this denial of reality is her major trait. It is also a major weakness, because Maupassant shows that her dream life harms her real life. By contrast, the boy Sarty of Faulkner's "Barn Burning" begins by telling the lies his father initially forces him to tell, but finally Sarty shows his increasing character strength by insisting on truth even if it means running away from his family. By similarly analyzing the actions, speeches, and thoughts of the literary characters you encounter, you can also draw conclusions about their qualities and strengths.

Distinguish Between Circumstances and Character Traits

When you study a fictional person, distinguish between circumstances and character, for circumstances have value *only if you show that they demonstrate important traits.* Thus, if our friend Sam wins a lottery, let us congratulate him on his luck; but the win does not say much about his *character*—not much, that is, unless you also point out that for several years he has been regularly spending hundreds of dollars each week for lottery tickets. In other words, making the effort to win a lottery *is* a character trait but winning (or losing) *is not.*

Or, let us suppose that an author stresses the neatness of one character and the sloppiness of another. If you accept the premise that people care for their appearance according to choice—and that choices develop from character—you can use these details to make conclusions about a person's self-esteem or the lack of it. In short, when reading about characters in literature, look beyond circumstances, actions, and appearances, and attempt to determine what these things show about character. Always try to get from the outside to the inside, for it is internal qualities—character—that determine external behavior.

✸ HOW AUTHORS DISCLOSE CHARACTER IN LITERATURE

Basically, authors rely on five ways of bringing characters to life. Remember that you must use your own knowledge and experience to make judgments about the qualities of the characters.

The Actions of Characters Reveal Their Qualities

What characters *do* is our best clue to understanding what they *are.* For example, taking care of an apartment belonging to a neighbor who has gone on a trip is part of ordinary existence for most people who do it, and it shows little about their characters except a desire to be helpful (this, in itself, may be a significant trait). But when Bill and Arlene Miller of Carver's "Neighbors" (Chapter 2) agree to take care of the apartment of the Stones, their neighbors, they cease being ordinary but somewhat strange folks and begin indulging all their incipient neuroses. By contrast, in Tan's "Two Kinds," the narrator Jing-Mei, after her turbulent childhood opposition to her mother's influences, reaches an emotional reconciliation with her past when playing the piano her mother had bought for her and given to her.

Like ordinary human beings, fictional characters do not necessarily understand how they may be changing or why they do the things they do. Nevertheless, their actions express their characters. Sarty of Faulkner's "Barn Burning" is such a character. He is developing a sense of rightness and responsibility, but he does not fully comprehend the causes of his growth. Actions may also signal qualities such as naiveté, weakness, deceit, a scheming personality, strong inner conflicts, sudden comprehension, or other growth or change. The actions of Abner Snopes in "Barn Burning" indicate a character of suspicion and resentment. Similarly, the strong inner conflict experienced by the two women in Glaspell's "A Jury of Her Peers" brings out their character strength. Theoretically, they have an overriding obligation to the law, but they discover that they have an even stronger personal obligation to the accused killer, Minnie. Hence they show their adaptability and their willingness to change their views under new circumstances.

The Author's Descriptions Tell Us about Characters

Appearance and environment reveal much about a character's social and economic status, and they also tell us about character traits. Mathilde in Maupassant's "The Necklace" dreams about wealth and unlimited purchasing power. Although her unrealizable desires destroy her way of life, they also cause her character strength to emerge. In Walker's "Everyday Use" (Chapter 3), the mother and younger daughter devote great care to the appearance of their poor and unpretentious house and the surrounding yard, and Walker's description of this care demonstrates their self-esteem and orderliness.

What Characters Say Reveals What They Are Like

Although the speeches of most characters are functional—essential to keeping the action moving along—they provide material from which you may draw conclusions. When the second traveler of Hawthorne's "Young Goodman Brown" (Chapter 9) speaks, for example, he reveals his devious and deceptive nature even though ostensibly he appears friendly. The lawmen in "A Jury of Her Peers" speak straightforwardly but without much understanding of the women in the story. Their speeches suggest that their characters are similarly straightforward, although their constant belittling of the two women indicates their inability to understand others.

Often, characters use speech to obscure their motives. The traveling potmender in Steinbeck's "The Chrysanthemums" (Chapter 9) is deceptive and guileful. His sole aim is to have Elisa give him some work to do, and we may consequently believe nothing of what he says. The Federal scout in Bierce's "An Occurrence at Owl Creek Bridge" (Chapter 5) is masquerading as a Confederate soldier, and in speaking with the major character Farquhar, who is a landowner and a Confederate loyalist, he speaks confidentially but deceivingly. The result of the scout's lies is that Farquhar is led to believe that he can safely burn the nearby bridge at Owl Creek. Farquhar makes the attempt, and of course he is caught by the Union troops.

What Others Say Tells Us about a Character

By studying what characters say about each other, you can enhance your understanding of the character being discussed. For example, the major character in Glaspell's "A Jury of Her Peers" is the farmwoman Minnie Wright. But Minnie never appears as a character, and we learn about her only through the conversations between Mrs. Hale and Mrs. Peters. It is from them that her character is revealed as an oppressed woman who has finally snapped and turned on her oppressor, her husband.

Ironically, speeches often indicate something other than what the speakers intend, perhaps because of prejudice, stupidity, or foolishness. Nora, in O'Connor's "First Confession" (Chapter 7), tells about Jackie's lashing out at her with a butterknife, but in effect she describes the boy's individuality just as she also discloses her own spitefulness.

The Author, Speaking as a Storyteller or an Observer, May Present Judgments about Characters

What the author, speaking as a work's authorial voice, says about a character is usually accurate, and the authorial voice can be accepted factually. However, when the authorial voice interprets actions and characteristics, as in Hawthorne's "Young Goodman Brown," the author himself or herself assumes the role of a reader or critic, whose opinions are therefore open to question. For this reason, authors frequently avoid interpretations and devote their skill to arranging events and speeches so that readers can draw their own conclusions.

❧ TYPES OF CHARACTERS: ROUND AND FLAT

No writer can present an entire life history of a protagonist, nor can each character in a story get "equal time" for development. Accordingly, some characters grow to be full and alive, while others remain shadowy. The British novelist and critic E. M. Forster, in *Aspects of the Novel,* calls the two major types "round" and "flat."

Round Characters Undergo Change

The basic trait of **round characters** is that we learn enough about them to permit us to conclude that they are full, lifelike, and memorable. Their roundness and fullness are characterized by both individuality and unpredictability. A complementary quality about round characters is therefore that they are **dynamic.** That is, they *recognize, change with,* or *adjust to* circumstances. Such changes may be shown in (1) an action or actions, (2) the realization of new strength and therefore the affirmation of previous decisions, (3) the acceptance of a new condition and the need for making changes, or (4) the discovery of unrecognized truths. We may consider Minnie Wright, in Glaspell's "A Jury of Her Peers," as dynamic. We learn that as a young woman she was happy and musical, though shy, but that she has been deprived and blighted by her twenty-year marriage. Finally, however, a particularly cruel action by her husband so enrages her that she breaks out of her subservient role and commits an act of violence. In short, her action shows her as a dynamic character capable of radical and earth-shaking change.

Because a round character plays a major role in a story, he or she is often called the **hero** or **heroine.** Some round characters are not particularly heroic, however, so it is preferable to use the more neutral word **protagonist** (the "first actor"). The protagonist is central to the action, moves against an **antagonist** (the "opposing actor"), and exhibits the ability to adapt to new circumstances.

Flat Characters Stay the Same

Unlike round characters, **flat characters** do not grow. They remain the same because they lack knowledge or insight, or because they are stupid or insensitive. They end where they begin and thus are **static,** not dynamic. Flat characters are not worthless in fiction, however, for they highlight the development of the round characters, as with the lawmen in Glaspell's "A Jury of Her Peers." Usually, flat characters are minor (e.g., relatives, acquaintances, functionaries), but not all minor characters are necessarily flat.

Sometimes flat characters are prominent in certain types of literature, such as cowboy, police, and detective stories, where the focus is less on character than on performance. Such characters might be lively and engaging, even though they do not develop or change. They must be strong, tough, and clever enough to perform recurring tasks such as solving a crime, overcoming a villain, or finding a treasure. The term **stock character** refers to characters in these repeating situations. To the degree that stock characters have many common traits, they are **representative** of their class or group. Such characters, with variations in names, ages, and sexes, have been constant in literature since the ancient Greeks. Some regular stock characters are the insensitive father, the interfering mother, the sassy younger sister or brother, the greedy politician, the resourceful cowboy or detective, the overbearing or henpecked husband, the submissive or nagging wife, the absent-minded professor, the angry police captain, the lovable drunk, and the town do-gooder.

Stock characters stay flat as long as they do no more than perform their roles and exhibit conventional and unindividual traits. When they possess no attitudes except those of their class, they are often called **stereotype** characters, because they all seem to have been cast in the same mold.

When authors bring characters into focus, however, no matter what roles they perform, the characters emerge from flatness and move into roundness. For example, Louise Mallard of Chopin's "The Story of an Hour" (Chapter 8) is a traditional housewife, and if she were no more than that she would be flat and stereotypical. After receiving the news that her husband has died, however, she quickly grows into a round character because of her sudden and unexpected exhilaration at the prospect of being widowed and free. A comparable character is Sarty of Faulkner's "Barn Burning." He is just a little boy, but he grows morally in opposition to his father's criminal acts. In sum, the ability to grow and develop and to be altered by circumstances makes characters round and dynamic. Absence of these traits makes characters flat and static.

⚡ REALITY AND PROBABILITY: VERISIMILITUDE

Characters in fiction should be true to life. Therefore their actions, statements, and thoughts must all be what human beings are *likely* to do, say, and think under the conditions presented in the literary work. This is the standard of **verisimilitude, probability,** or **plausibility.** One may readily admit that there are people *in life* who perform tasks or exhibit characteristics that are difficult or seemingly impossible (such as always leading the team to victory, always getting A+'s on every test, always being cheerful and helpful, or always understanding the needs of others). However, such characters in fiction would not be true to life because they do not fit within normal or usual behavior.

You should therefore distinguish between what characters may *possibly* do and what they *most frequently* or *most usually* do. Thus, in Maupassant's "The Necklace" it is possible that Mathilde could be truthful and tell her friend Jeanne Forrestier about the lost necklace. In light of Mathilde's pride and sense of self-respect, however, it is more in character for her and her husband to hide the loss and borrow money for a replacement, even though they must endure the harsh financial consequences for ten years. Granted the possibilities of the story (either self-sacrifice or the admission of a fault or a possible crime), the decision she makes with her husband is the more *probable* one.

Nevertheless, probability does not rule out surprise or even exaggeration. It is unusual that young Sarty tries to inform on his father in Faulkner's "Barn Burning," but it is not improbable because he has been developing a sense of morality throughout the story. Likewise, in Katherine Anne Porter's "The Jilting of Granny Weatherall" (Chapter 9) the accomplishments of Granny—such as fencing a hundred acres of farmland all by herself—do not seem impossible even if they do seem unlikely. But we learn that when she was young she became compulsively determined to overcome the ignominy of having been betrayed and deserted by her fiancé. It is therefore probable that she would be capable of a difficult achievement like building the fence.

Writers render probability of character in many ways. Works that attempt to mirror life—realistic, naturalistic, or "slice of life" stories like Joyce's "Araby" (Chapter 6)—set up a pattern of ordinary, everyday probability. Less realistic conditions establish different frameworks of probability, in which characters are *expected* to be unusual, as in Hawthorne's "Young Goodman Brown." Because a major way of explaining this story is that Brown is having a nightmarish psychotic trance, his bizarre and unnatural responses are probable. Equally probable is the way the doctors explain Louise Mallard's sudden death at the end of Chopin's "The Story of an Hour" even though their smug analysis is totally and comically wrong.

You might also encounter works containing *supernatural* figures such as the second traveler in "Young Goodman Brown" and the weeping and wailing woman in Tremblay's "The Thimble" (Chapter 9). You may wonder whether such characters are probable or improbable. Usually, gods and goddesses embody qualities of the best and most moral human beings, and devils like Hawthorne's guide take on attributes of the worst. However, you might remember that the devil is often given dashing and engaging qualities so that he can deceive gullible sinners and then drag them screaming into the fiery pits of hell. The friendliness of Brown's guide is therefore not an improbable trait. In judging characters of this or any other type, your best criteria are probability, consistency, and believability.

STORIES FOR STUDY

WILLA CATHER (1873–1947)

Willa Cather is acknowledged as one of America's foremost writers. Her life spanned the period from the decade after the Civil War to the conclusion of World War II. She was born in Virginia and as a girl was taken to Nebraska during mass migrations of homesteaders into the Midwest in the decades after the Civil War. She received a degree from the University of Nebraska in 1895 and spent time after that as a teacher in both Pittsburgh and New York. In 1911 she decided to become a writer, ultimately living in New York. During her career she published twelve novels and fifty-eight short stories. Her best-known novels are O Pioneers! *(1913),* My Antonía *(1918),* A Lost Lady *(1923), and* Death Comes for the Archbishop *(1927). She was the recipient of the Pulitzer Prize for 1923 for her novel* One of Ours. *"Paul's Case" was one of her earliest stories, appearing in her collection* The Troll Garden *(1905).*

Paul's Case ~<~'~' 1905

A Study in Temperament

It was Paul's afternoon to appear before the faculty of the Pittsburgh High School to account for his various misdemeanors. He had been suspended a week ago, and his father had called at the Principal's office and confessed his perplexity about his son. Paul entered the faculty room suave and smiling. His clothes were a trifle outgrown, and the tan velvet on the collar of his open overcoat was frayed and worn; but for all that there was something of the dandy about him, and he wore an opal pin in his neatly knotted black four-in-hand, and a red carnation in his buttonhole. This latter adornment the faculty somehow felt was not properly significant of the contrite spirit befitting a boy under the ban of suspension.

Paul was tall for his age and very thin, with high, cramped shoulders and a narrow chest. His eyes were remarkable for a certain hysterical brilliancy, and he continually used them in a conscious, theatrical sort of way, peculiarity offensive in a boy. The pupils were abnormally large, as though he were addicted to belladonna, but there was a glassy glitter about them which that drug does not produce.

When questioned by the Principal as to why he was there, Paul stated, politely enough, that he wanted to come back to school. This was a lie, but Paul was quite accustomed to lying; found it, indeed, indispensable for overcoming friction. His teachers were asked to state their respective charges against him, which they did with such a rancor and aggrievedness as evinced that this was not a usual case. Disorder and impertinence were among the offenses named, yet each of his instructors felt that it was scarcely possible to put into words the real cause of the trouble, which lay in a sort of hysterically defiant manner of the boy's; in the contempt which they all knew he felt for them, and which he seemingly made not the least effort to conceal. Once, when he had been making a synopsis of a paragraph at the blackboard, his English teacher had stepped to his side and attempted to guide his hand. Paul had started back with a shudder and thrust his hands violently behind him. The astonished woman could scarcely have been more hurt and embarrassed had he struck at her. The insult was so involuntary and definitely personal as to be unforgettable. In one way and another, he had made all his teachers, men and women alike, conscious of the same feeling of physical aversion. In one class he habitually sat with his hand shading his eyes; in another he always looked out of the window during the recitation; in another he made a running commentary on the lecture, with humorous intent.

His teachers felt this afternoon that his whole attitude was symbolized by his shrug and his flippantly red carnation flower, and they fell upon him without mercy, his English teacher leading the pack. He stood through it smiling, his pale lips parted over his white teeth. (His lips were continually twitching, and he had a habit of raising his eyebrows that was contemptuous and irritating to the last degree.) Older boys than Paul had broken down and shed tears under that ordeal, but his set smile did not once desert him, and his only sign of discomfort was the nervous trembling of the fingers that toyed with the buttons of his overcoat, and an occasional jerking of the other hand which held his hat. Paul was always smiling, always glancing about him, seeming to feel that people might be watching him and trying to detect something. This conscious expression, since it was as far as possible from boyish mirthfulness, was usually attributed to insolence or "smartness."

As the inquisition proceeded, one of his instructors repeated an impertinent remark of the boy's, and the Principal asked him whether he thought that a courteous speech to make to a woman. Paul shrugged his shoulders slightly and his eyebrows twitched.

"I don't know," he replied, "I didn't mean to be polite or impolite, either. I guess it's a sort of way I have, of saying things regardless."

The Principal asked him whether he didn't think that a way it would be well to get rid of. Paul grinned and said he guessed so. When he was told that he could go, he bowed gracefully and went out. His bow was like a repetition of the scandalous red carnation.

His teachers were in despair, and his drawing master voiced the feeling of them all when he declared there was something about the boy which none of them understood. He added, "I don't really believe that smile of his comes altogether from insolence; there's something sort of haunted about it. The boy is not strong, for one thing. There is something wrong about the fellow."

5

The drawing master had come to realize that, in looking at Paul, one saw only his white teeth and the forced animation of his eyes. One warm afternoon the boy had gone to sleep at his drawing board, and his master had noted with amazement what a white, blue-veined face it was; drawn and wrinkled like an old man's about the eyes, the lips twitching even in his sleep.

His teachers left the building dissatisfied and unhappy; humiliated to have felt so vindictive toward a mere boy, to have uttered this feeling in cutting terms, and to have set each other on, as it were, in the gruesome game of intemperate reproach. One of them remembered having seen a miserable street cat set at bay by a ring of tormentors.

As for Paul, he ran down the hill whistling the Soldiers' Chorus from *Faust*,° looking wildly behind him now and then to see whether some of his teachers were not there to witness his light-heartedness. As it was now late in the afternoon and Paul was on duty that evening as usher at Carnegie Hall,° he decided that he would not go home to supper.

When he reached the concert hall the doors were not yet open. It was chilly outside, and he decided to go up into the picture gallery—always deserted at this hour—where there were some of Raffaëlli's° gay studies of Paris streets and an airy blue Venetian scene or two that always exhilarated him. He was delighted to find no one in the gallery but the old guard, who sat in the corner, a newspaper on his knee, a black patch over one eye and the other closed. Paul possessed himself of the place and walked confidently up and down, whistling under his breath. After a while he sat down before a blue Rico° and lost himself. When he bethought him to look at his watch, it was after seven o'clock, and he rose with a start and ran downstairs, making a face at Augustus Caesar,° peering out from the cast-room, and an evil gesture at the Venus of Milo° as he passed her on the stairway.

When Paul reached the ushers' dressing-room half a dozen boys were there already, and he began excitedly to tumble into his uniform. It was one of the few that at all approached fitting, and Paul thought it very becoming—though he knew the tight, straight coat accentuated his narrow chest, about which he was exceedingly sensitive. He was always excited while he dressed, twanging all over to the tuning of the strings and preliminary flourishes of the horns in the music-room; but tonight he seemed quite beside himself, and he teased and plagued the boys until, telling him that he was crazy, they put him down on the floor and sat on him.

Somewhat calmed by his suppression, Paul dashed out to the front of the house to seat the early comers. He was a model usher. Gracious and smiling he ran up and down the aisles. Nothing was too much trouble for him; he carried messages and brought programs as though it were his greatest pleasure in life, and all the people in his section thought him a charming boy, feeling that he remembered and admired them. As the house filled, he grew more and more vivacious and animated, and the color came to his cheeks and lips. It was very much as though this were a great reception and Paul were the host. Just as the musicians came out to take their places, his English teacher arrived with checks for the seat which a prominent manufacturer had taken for the season. She betrayed some embarrassment when she handed Paul the tickets, and a *hauteur* which

10

Faust: the most popular opera of Charles Gounod (1818–1893), first produced in 1859.
Carnegie Hall: in Pittsburgh, not the more famous one in New York.
Raffaëlli: Jean-François Rafaëlli (1850–1924), impressionist painter, sculptor, and engraver, known for his scenes of Parisian life.
Rico: Martin Rico (1833–1908). Spanish painter, known for his landscapes.
Caesar . . . Milo: copies of the famous statues of Augustus in the Vatican Museum and the Venus de Milo in the Louvre.

subsequently made her feel very foolish. Paul was startled for a moment and had the feeling of wanting to put her out; what business had she here among all these fine people and gay colors? He looked her over and decided that she was not appropriately dressed and must be a fool to sit downstairs in such togs. The tickets had probably been sent her out of kindness, he reflected, as he put down a seat for her, and she had about as much right to sit there as he had.

When the symphony began Paul sank into one of the rear seats with a long sigh of relief, and lost himself as he had done before the Rico. It was not that symphonies, as such, meant anything in particular to Paul, but the first sigh of the instruments seemed to free some hilarious spirit within him; something that struggled there like the Genius in the bottle found by the Arab fisherman.° He felt a sudden zest of life; the lights danced before his eyes and the concert hall blazed into unimaginable splendor. When the soprano soloist came on, Paul forgot even the nastiness of his teacher's being there, and gave himself up to the peculiar intoxication such personages always had for him. The soloist chanced to be a German woman, by no means in her first youth, and the mother of many children; but she wore a satin gown and a tiara, and she had that indefinable air of achievement, that worldshine upon her, which always blinded Paul to any possible defects.

After a concert was over, Paul was often irritable and wretched until he got to sleep—and tonight he was even more than usually restless. He had the feeling of not being able to let down; of its being impossible to give up this delicious excitement which was the only thing that could be called living at all. During the last number he withdrew and, after hastily changing his clothes in the dressing-room, slipped out to the side door where the singer's carriage stood. Here he began pacing rapidly up and down the walk, waiting to see her come out.

Over yonder the Schenley, in its vacant stretch, loomed big and square through the fine rain, the windows of its twelve stories glowing like those of a lighted cardboard house under a Christmas tree. All the actors and singers of any importance stayed there when they were in the city, and a number of the big manufacturers of the place lived there in the winter. Paul had often hung about the hotel, watching the people go in and out, longing to enter and leave schoolmasters and dull care° behind him forever.

As last the singer came out, accompanied by the conductor, who helped her into her carriage and closed the door with a cordial *auf Wiedersehen*°—which set Paul to wondering whether she were not an old sweetheart of his. Paul followed the carriage over to the hotel, walking so rapidly as not to be far from the entrance when the singer alighted and disappeared behind the swinging glass doors which were opened by a Negro in a tall hat and a long coat. In the moment that the door was ajar, it seemed to Paul that he, too, entered. He seemed to feel himself go after her up the steps, into the warm, lighted building, into an exotic, a tropical world of shiny, glistening surfaces and basking ease. He reflected upon the mysterious dishes that were brought into the dining-room, the green bottles in buckets of ice, as he had seen them in the supper party pictures of the Sunday supplement. A quick gust of wind brought the rain down with sudden vehemence, and Paul was startled to find that he was still outside in the slush of the gravel driveway; that his boots were letting in the water and his scanty overcoat was clinging wet about him; that the lights in front of the concert hall were out, and that the rain was driving in sheets between him and the orange glow of the windows above him. There it was,

---

Arab fisherman: reference to the tale of "The Fisherman and the Jinni" from *The Arabian Nights.*
dull care: phrase from the popular seventeenth-century song "Begone, Dull Care."
auf Wiedersehen: German for "goodbye" (literally "until the seeing again").

what he wanted—tangibly before him, like the fairy world of Christmas pantomime; as the rain beat in his face, Paul wondered whether he were destined always to shiver in the black night outside looking up at it.

He turned and walked reluctantly toward the car° tracks. The end had to come some time; his father in his night-clothes at the top of the stairs, explanations that did not explain, hastily improvised fictions that were forever tripping him up, his upstairs room and its horrible yellow wallpaper, the creaking bureau with the greasy plush collar-box, and over his painted wooden bed the pictures of George Washington and John Calvin,° and the framed motto, "Feed my Lambs,"° which had been worked in red worsted by his mother, whom Paul could not remember.

Half an hour later, Paul alighted from the Negley Avenue car and went slowly down   20
one of the side streets off the main thoroughfare. It was a highly respectable street, where all the houses were exactly alike, and where business men of moderate means begot and reared large families of children, all of whom went to Sabbath-school and learned the shorter catechism, and were interested in arithmetic; all of whom were as exactly alike as their homes, and of a piece with the monotony in which they lived. Paul never went up Cordelia Street without a shudder of loathing. His home was next to the house of the Cumberland° minister. He approached it tonight with the nerveless sense of defeat, the hopeless feeling of sinking back forever into ugliness and commonness that he had always had when he came home. The moment he turned into Cordelia Street he felt the waters close above his head. After each of these orgies of living, he experienced all the physical depression which follows a debauch; the loathing of respectable beds, of common food, of a house permeated by kitchen odors; a shuddering repulsion for the flavorless, colorless mass of everyday existence; a morbid desire for cool things and soft lights and fresh flowers.

The nearer he approached the house, the more absolutely unequal Paul felt to the sight of it all; his ugly sleeping chamber, the cold bathroom with the grimy zinc tub, the cracked mirror, the dripping spigots; his father, at the top of the stairs, his hairy legs sticking out from his nightshirt, his feet thrust into carpet slippers. He was so much later than usual that there would certainly be inquiries and reproaches. Paul stopped short before the door. He felt that he could not be accosted by his father tonight; that he could not toss again on that miserable bed. He would not go in. He would tell his father that he had no car fare, and it was raining so hard he had gone home with one of the boys and stayed all night.

Meanwhile, he was wet and cold. He went around to the back of the house and tried one of the basement windows, found it open, raised it cautiously, and scrambled down the cellar wall to the floor. There he stood, holding his breath, terrified by the noise he had made; but the floor above him was silent, and there was no creak on the stairs. He found a soap-box and carried it over to the soft ring of light that streamed from the furnace door, and sat down. He was horribly afraid of rats, so he did not try to sleep, but sat looking distrustfully at the dark, still terrified lest he might have awakened his father. In such reactions, after one of the experiences which made days and nights out of the dreary blanks of the calendar, when his senses were deadened, Paul's head was always singularly clear. Suppose his father had heard him getting in at the window and had come down and shot him for a burglar? Then, again, suppose his father had come down,

---

car: streetcar.
John Calvin: John Calvin (1509–1564), a major theologian of the early Reformation in Switzerland.
"Feed my Lambs:" See John 21:15–17.
Cumberland: an independent, Evangelical branch of the Presbyterian Church, established in 1810.

pistol in hand, and he had cried out in time to save himself, and his father had been horrified to think how nearly he had killed him? Then, again, suppose a day should come when his father would remember that night, and wish there had been no warning cry to stay his hand? With this last supposition Paul entertained himself until daybreak.

The following Sunday was fine; the sodden November chill was broken by the last flash of autumnal summer. In the morning Paul had to go to church and Sabbath-school, as always. On seasonable Sunday afternoons the burghers of Cordelia Street usually sat out on their front "stoops," and talked to their neighbors on the next stoop, or called to those across the street in neighborly fashion. The men sat placidly on gay cushions placed upon the steps that led down to the sidewalk, while the women, in their Sunday "waists,"° sat in rockers on the cramped porches, pretending to be greatly at their ease. The children played in the streets; there were so many of them that the place resembled the recreation grounds of a kindergarten. The men on the steps—all in their shirt sleeves, their vests unbuttoned—sat with their legs well apart, their stomachs comfortably protruding, and talked of the prices of things, or told anecdotes of the sagacity of their various chiefs and overloads. They occasionally looked over the multitude of squabbling children, listened affectionately to their high-pitched, nasal voices, smiling to see their own proclivities reproduced in their offspring, and interspersed their legends of the iron kings with remarks about their son's progress at school, their grades in arithmetic, and the amounts they had saved in their toy banks. On this last Sunday of November, Paul sat all the afternoon on the lowest step of his "stoop," staring into the street, while his sisters, in their rockers, were talking to the minister's daughters next door about how many shirt-waists they had made in the last week, and how many waffles someone had eaten at the last church supper. When the weather was warm, and his father was in a particularly jovial frame of mind, the girls made lemonade, which was always brought out in a red-glass pitcher, ornamented with forget-me-nots in blue enamel. This the girls thought very fine, and the neighbors joked about the suspicious color of the pitcher.

Today Paul's father, on the top step, was talking to a young man who shifted a restless baby from knee to knee. He happened to be the young man who was daily held up to Paul as a model, and after whom it was his father's dearest hope that he would pattern. This young man was of a ruddy complexion, with a compressed, red mouth, and faded, near-sighted eyes, over which he wore thick spectacles, with gold bows that curved about his ears. He was clerk to one of the magnates of a great steel corporation, and was looked upon in Cordelia Street as a young man with a future. There was a story that, come five years ago— he was now barely twenty-six—he had been a trifle 'dissipated,' but in order to curb his appetites and save the loss of time and strength that a sowing of wild oats might have entailed, he had taken his chief's advice, oft reiterated to his employees, and at twenty-one had married the first woman whom he could persuade to share his fortunes. She happened to be an angular school mistress, much older than he, who also wore thick glasses, and who had now borne him four children, all nearsighted, like herself.

The young man was relating how his chief, now cruising in the Mediterranean, 25 kept in touch with all the details of the business, arranging his office hours on his yacht just as though he were at home, and "knocking off work enough to keep two stenographers busy." His father told, in turn, the plan his corporation was considering, of putting in an electric railway plant at Cairo. Paul snapped his teeth; he had an awful apprehension that they might spoil it all before he got there. Yet he rather liked to hear these legends of the iron kings, that were told and retold on Sundays and holidays; these stories of

waists: laced, close-fitting vests or jackets.

palaces in Venice, yachts on the Mediterranean, and high play at Monte Carlo appealed to his fancy, and he was interested in the triumphs of cash boys° who had become famous, though he had no mind for the cash-boy stage.

After supper was over, and he had helped to dry the dishes, Paul nervously asked his father whether he could go to George's to get some help in his geometry, and still more nervously asked for car fare. This latter request he had to repeat, as his father, on principle, did not like to hear requests for money, whether much or little. He asked Paul whether he could not go to some boy who lived nearer, and told him that he ought not to leave his school work until Sunday; but he gave him the dime. He was not a poor man, but he had a worthy ambition to come up in the world. His only reason for allowing Paul to usher was that he thought a boy ought to be earning a little.

Paul bounded upstairs, scrubbed the greasy odor of the dishwater from his hands with the ill-smelling soap he hated, and then shook over his fingers a few drops of violet water from the bottle he kept hidden in his drawer. He left the house with his geometry conspicuously under his arm, and the moment he got out of Cordelia Street and boarded a downtown car, he shook off the lethargy of two deadening days, and began to live again.

The leading juvenile of the permanent stock company which played at one of the downtown theaters was an acquaintance of Paul's, and the boy had been invited to drop in at the Sunday night rehearsals whenever he could. For more than a year Paul had spent every available moment loitering about Charley Edwards's dressing-room. He had won a place among Edwards's following not only because the young actor, who could not afford to employ a dresser, often found him useful, but because he recognized in Paul something akin to what churchmen term "vocation."

It was at the theater and at Carnegie Hall that Paul really lived; the rest was but a sleep and a forgetting.° This was Paul's fairy tale, and it had for him all the allurement of a secret love. The moment he inhaled the gassy, painty, dusty odor behind the scenes, he breathed like a prisoner set free, and felt within him the possibility of doing or saying splendid, brilliant things. The moment the cracked orchestra beat out the overture for *Martha,°* or jerked at the serenade from *Rigoletto,°* all stupid and ugly things slid from him, and his senses were deliciously, yet delicately fired.

Perhaps it was because, in Paul's world, the natural nearly always wore the guise of ugliness, that a certain element of artificiality seemed to him necessary in beauty. Perhaps it was because his experience of life elsewhere was so full of Sabbath-school picnics, petty economies, wholesome advice as to how to succeed in life, and the unescapable odors of cooking, that he found this existence so alluring, these smartly-clad men and women so attractive, that he was so moved by these starry apple orchards that bloomed perennially under the limelight. 30

It would be difficult to put it strongly enough how convincingly the stage entrance of that theater was for Paul the actual portal of Romance. Certainly none of the company ever suspected it, least of all Charley Edwards. It was very like the old stories that used to float about London of fabulously rich Jews, who had subterranean halls, with palms, and fountains, and soft lamps and richly apparelled women who never saw the disenchanting

---

cash boys: The Cash Boy, a novel by Horatio Alger (1832–1899), tells about the progress of a young boy from a $156 a year "cash boy" position to the inheritance of a million dollars.

a sleep and a forgetting: from "Intimations of Immortality," an ode by William Wordsworth (1770–1850), published in 1807. See Chapter 24.

Martha: opera by Friedrick von Flotow (1812–1883), first performed in 1847, the source of "The Last Rose of Summer."

Rigoletto: one of the best-known operas of Giuseppe Verdi (1813–1901), first performed in 1851.

light of London day. So, in the midst of that smoke-palled city, enamored of figures and grimy toil, Paul had his secret temple, his wishing-carpet, his bit of blue-and-white Mediterranean shore bathed in perpetual sunshine.

Several of Paul's teachers had a theory that his imagination had been perverted by garish fiction; but the truth was, he scarcely ever read at all. The books at home were not such as would either tempt or corrupt a youthful mind, and as for reading the novels that some of his friends urged upon him—well, he got what he wanted much more quickly from music; any sort of music, from an orchestra to a barrel organ. He needed only the spark, the indescribable thrill that made his imagination master of his senses, and he could make plots and pictures enough of his own. It was equally true that he was not stage-struck—not at any rate, in the usual acceptation of that expression. He had no desire to become an actor, any more than he had to become a musician. He felt no necessity to do any of these things; what he wanted was to see, to be in the atmosphere, float on the wave of it, to be carried out, blue league after blue league, away from everything.

After a night behind the scenes, Paul found the school-room more than ever repulsive; the bare floors and naked walls; the prosy men who never wore frock coats, or violets in their buttonholes; the women with their dull gowns, shrill voices, and pitiful seriousness about prepositions that govern the dative. He could not bear to have the other pupils think, for a moment, that he took these people seriously; he must convey to them that he considered it all trivial, and was there only by way of a joke, anyway. He had autograph pictures of all the members of the stock company which he showed to classmates, telling them the most incredible stories of his familiarity with these people, of his acquaintance with the soloists who came to Carnegie Hall, his suppers with them and the flowers he sent them. When these stories lost their effect, and his audience grew listless, he would bid all the boys good-by, announcing that he was going to travel for a while; going to Naples, to California, to Egypt. Then, next Monday, he would slip back, conscious and nervously smiling; his sister was ill, and he would have to defer his voyage until spring.

Matters went steadily worse with Paul at school. In the itch to let his instructors know how heartily he despised them, and how thoroughly he was appreciated elsewhere, he mentioned once or twice that he had no time to fool with theorems; adding—with a twitch of the eyebrows and a touch of that nervous bravado which so perplexed them—that he was helping the people down at the stock company; they were old friends of his.

The upshot of the matter was, that the Principal went to Paul's father, and Paul was taken out of school and put to work. The manager at Carnegie Hall was told to get another usher in his stead; the door-keeper at the theater was warned not to admit him to the house; and Charley Edwards remorsefully promised the boy's father not to see him again.

The members of the stock company were vastly amused when some of Paul's stories reached them—especially the women. They were hard-working women, most of them supporting indolent husbands or brothers, and they laughed rather bitterly at having stirred the boy to such fervid and florid inventions. They agreed with the faculty and with his father, that Paul's was a bad case.

The east-bound train was plowing through a January snowstorm; the dull dawn was beginning to show gray when the engine whistled a mile out of Newark.° Paul started up from the seat where he had lain curled in uneasy slumber, rubbed the breath-misted window glass with his hand, and peered out. The snow was whirling in curling eddies above the white bottom lands, and the drifts lay already deep in the fields and along the fences, while here and there the long dead grass and dried weed stalks protruded black above it.

Newark: New Jersey city within twenty miles of New York.

Lights shone from the scattered houses, and a gang of laborers who stood beside the track waved their lanterns.

Paul had slept very little, and he felt grimy and uncomfortable. He had made the all-night journey in a day coach because he was afraid if he took a Pullman he might be seen by some Pittsburgh business man who had noticed him in Denny & Carson's office. When the whistle woke him, he clutched quickly at his breast pocket, glancing about him with an uncertain smile. But the little, clay-bespattered Italians were still sleeping, the slatternly women across the aisle were in open-mouthed oblivion, and even the crumby, crying babies were for the nonce stilled. Paul settled back to struggle with his impatience as best he could.

When he arrived at the Jersey City° station, he hurried through his breakfast, manifestly ill at ease and keeping a sharp eye about him. After he reached the Twenty-third Street station° he consulted a cabman, and had himself driven to a men's furnishing establishment which was just opening for the day. He spent upward of two hours there, buying with endless reconsidering and great care. His new street suit he put on in the fitting-room; the frock coat and dress clothes he had bundled into the cab with his new shirts. Then he drove to a hatter's and a shoe house. His next errand was at Tiffany's, where he selected silver-mounted brushes° and a scarf-pin. He would not wait to have his silver marked, he said. Lastly, he stopped at a trunk shop on Broadway, and had his purchases packed into various traveling bags.

It was a little after one o'clock when he drove up to the Waldorf, and, after settling with the cabman, went into the office. He registered from Washington; said his mother and father had been abroad, and that he had come down to await the arrival of their steamer. He told his story plausibly and had no trouble, since he offered to pay for them in advance, in engaging his rooms; a sleeping-room, sitting room and bath.   40

Not once, but a hundred times Paul had planned this entry into New York. He had gone over every detail of it with Charley Edwards, and in his scrap book at home there were pages of description about New York hotels, cut from the Sunday papers.

When he was shown to his sitting room on the eighth floor, he saw at a glance that everything was as it should be; there was but one detail in his mental picture that the place did not realize, so he rang for the bell boy and sent him down for flowers. He moved about nervously until the boy returned, putting away his new linen and fingering it delightedly as he did so. When the flowers came, he put them hastily into water, and then tumbled into a hot bath. Presently he came out of his white bathroom, resplendent in his new silk underwear, and playing with the tassels of his red robe. The snow was whirling so fiercely outside his windows that he could scarcely see across the street; but within, the air was deliciously soft and fragrant. He put the violets and jonquils on the tabouret beside the couch, and threw himself down with a long sigh, covering himself with a Roman blanket. He was thoroughly tired; he had been in such haste, he had stood up to such a strain, covered so much ground in the last twenty-four hours, that he wanted to think how it had all come about. Lulled by the sound of the wind, the warm air, and the cool fragrance of the flowers, he sank into deep, drowsy retrospection.

It had been wonderfully simple; when they had shut him out of the theater and concert hall, when they had taken away his bone, the whole thing was virtually determined. The rest was a mere matter of opportunity. The only thing that at all surprised

---

Jersey City: New Jersey city on the Hudson River, directly across from the southern tip of Manhattan.
Twenty-third Street station: Paul's final destination in Manhattan.
brushes: hairbrushes.

him was his own courage—for he realized well enough that he had always been tormented by fear, a sort of apprehensive dread that, of late years, as the meshes of the lies he had
told closed about him, had been pulling the muscles of his body tighter and tighter. Until
now, he could not remember a time when he had not been dreading something. Even
when he was a little boy, it was always there—behind him or before, or on either side.
There had always been the shadowed corner, the dark place into which he dared not
look, but from which something seemed always to be watching him—and Paul had done
things that were not pretty to watch, he knew.

But now he had a curious sense of relief, as though he had at least thrown down
the gauntlet to the thing in the corner.

Yet it was but a day since he had been sulking in the traces; but yesterday afternoon   45
that he had been sent to the bank with Denny & Carson's deposit, as usual—but this time
he was instructed to leave the book to be balanced. There was above two thousand dollars
in checks, and nearly a thousand in the bank notes which he had taken from the book
and quietly transferred to his pocket. At the bank he had made out a new deposit slip.
His nerves had been steady enough to permit of his returning to the office, where he had
finished his work and asked for a full day's holiday tomorrow, Saturday, giving a perfectly
reasonable pretext. The bank book, he knew, would not be returned before Monday or
Tuesday, and his father would be out of town for the next week. From the time he slipped
the bank notes into his pocket until he boarded the night train for New York, he had not
known a moment's hesitation.

How astonishingly easy it had all been; here he was, the thing done; and this time
there would be no awakening, no figure at the top of the stairs. He watched the
snowflakes whirling by his window until he fell asleep.

When he awoke, it was four o'clock in the afternoon. He bounded up with a start;
one of his precious days gone already! He spent nearly an hour in dressing, watching
every stage of his toilet carefully in the mirror. Everything was quite perfect; he was exactly the kind of boy he had always wanted to be.

When he went downstairs, Paul took a carriage and drive up Fifth Avenue toward
the Park.° The snow had somewhat abated; carriages and tradesmen's wagons were hurrying soundlessly to and fro in the winter twilight; boys in woolen mufflers were shoveling
off the doorsteps; the avenue stages° made fine spots of color against the white street.
Here and there on the corners whole flower gardens blooming behind glass windows,
against which the snow flakes stuck and melted; violets, roses, carnations, lilies of the valley—somehow vastly more lovely and alluring that they blossomed thus unnaturally in
the snow. The Park itself was a wonderful stage winter-piece.

When he returned, the pause of the twilight had ceased, and the tune of the streets
had changed. The snow was falling faster, lights streamed from the hotels that reared
their many stories fearlessly up into the storm, defying the raging Atlantic winds. A long,
black stream of carriages poured down the avenue, intersected here and there by other
streams, tending horizontally. There were a score of cabs about the entrance of his hotel,
and his driver had to wait. Boys in livery were running in and out of the awning stretched
across the sidewalk, up and down the red velvet carpet laid from the door to the street.
Above, about, within it all, was the rumble and roar, the hurry and toss of thousands of
human beings as hot for pleasure as himself, and on every side of him towered the glaring affirmation of the omnipotence of wealth.

the Park: Central Park.
avenue stages: display windows.

The boy set his teeth and drew his shoulders together in a spasm of realization; the plot of all dramas, the text of all romances, the nerve-stuff of all sensations was whirling about him like the snowflakes. He burnt like a faggot in a tempest.

When Paul came down to dinner, the music of the orchestra floated up the elevator shaft to greet him. As he stepped into the thronged corridor, he sank back into one of the chairs against the wall to get his breath. The lights, the chatter, the perfumes, the bewildering medley of color—he had, for a moment, the feeling of not being able to stand it. But only for a moment; these were his own people, he told himself. He went slowly about the corridors, through the writing-rooms, smoking-rooms, reception-rooms, as though he were exploring the chambers of an enchanted palace, built and peopled for him alone.

When he reached the dining room he sat down at a table near a window. The flowers, the white linen, the many-colored wine glasses, the gay toilettes of the women, the low popping of corks, the undulating repetitions of the *Blue Danube*° from the orchestra, all flooded Paul's dream with bewildering radiance. When the roseate tinge of his champagne was added—that cold, precious, bubbling stuff that creamed and foamed in his glass—Paul wondered that there were honest men in the world at all. This was what all the world was fighting for, he reflected; this was what all the struggle was about. He doubted the reality of his past. Had he ever known a place called Cordelia Street, a place where fagged-looking business men boarded the early car? Mere rivets in a machine they seemed to Paul—sickening men, with combings of children's hair always hanging to their coats, and the smell of cooking in their clothes. Cordelia Street—Ah, that belonged to another time and country! Had he not always been thus, had he not sat here night after night, from as far back as he could remember, looking pensively over just such shimmering textures, and slowly twirling the stem of a glass like this one between his thumb and middle finger? He rather thought he had.

He was not in the least abashed or lonely. He had no special desire to meet or to know any of these people; all he demanded was the right to look on and conjecture, to watch the pageant. The mere stage properties were all he contended for. Nor was he lonely later in the evening, in his loge at the Opera. He was entirely rid of his nervous misgivings, of his forced aggressiveness, of the imperative desire to show himself different from his surroundings. He felt now that his surroundings explained him. Nobody questioned the purple,° he had only to wear it passively. He had only to glance down at his dress coat to reassure himself that here it would be impossible for anyone to humiliate him.

He found it hard to leave his beautiful sitting room to go to bed that night, and sat long watching the raging storm from his turret window. When he went to sleep, it was with the lights turned on in his bedroom; partly because of his old timidity, and partly so that, if he should wake in the night, there would be no wretched moment of doubt, no horrible suspicion of yellow wall-paper, or of Washington and Calvin above his bed.

On Sunday morning the city was practically snow-bound. Paul breakfasted late, and in the afternoon he fell in with a wild San Francisco boy, a freshman at Yale, who said he had run down for a "little flyer" over Sunday. The young man offered to show Paul the night side of the town, and the two boys went off together after dinner, not returning to the hotel until seven o'clock the next morning. They had started out in the confiding warmth of a champagne friendship, but their parting in the elevator was singularly cool. The freshman pulled himself together to make his train, and Paul went to bed. He woke

50

55

Blue Danube: Composed in 1866, "The Blue Danube" is perhaps the best-known waltz of Johann Strauss (1825–1899).

purple: that is, clothing fit for royalty.

at two o'clock in the afternoon, very thirsty and dizzy, and rang for ice water, coffee, and the Pittsburgh papers.

On the part of the hotel management, Paul excited no suspicion. There was this to be said for him, that he wore his spoils with dignity and in no way made himself conspicuous. His chief greediness lay in his ears and eyes, and his excesses were not offensive ones. His dearest pleasures were the gray winter twilights in his sitting room; his quiet enjoyment of his flowers, his clothes, his wide divan, his cigarette and his sense of power. He could not remember a time when he had felt so at peace with himself. The mere release from the necessity of petty lying, lying every day and every day, restored his self-respect. He had never lied for pleasure, even at school; but to make himself noticed and admired, to assert his difference from other Cordelia Street boys; and he felt a good deal more manly, more honest, even, now that he had no need for boastful pretensions, now that he could, as his actor friends used to say, "dress the part." It was characteristic that remorse did not occur to him. His golden days went by without a shadow, and he made each as perfect as he could.

On the eighth day after his arrival in New York, he found the whole affair exploited in the Pittsburgh papers, exploited with a wealth of detail which indicated that local news of a sensational nature was at a low ebb. The firm of Denny & Carson announced that the boy's father had refunded the full amount of his theft, and that they had no intention of prosecuting. The Cumberland minister had been interviewed, and expressed his hope of yet reclaiming the motherless lad, and Paul's Sabbath-school teacher declared that she would spare no effort to that end. The rumor had reached Pittsburgh that the boy had been seen in a New York hotel, and his father had gone East to find him and bring him home.

Paul had just come in to dress for dinner; he sank into a chair, weak in the knees, and clasped his head in his hands. It was to be worse than jail, even; the tepid waters of Cordelia Street were to close over him finally and forever. The gray monotony stretched before him in hopeless, unrelieved years; Sabbath-school, Young People's Meeting, the yellow-papered room, the damp dish-towels; it all rushed back upon him with sickening vividness. He had the old feeling that the orchestra had suddenly stopped, the sinking sensation that the play was over. The sweat broke out on his face, and he sprang to his feet, looked about him with his white, conscious smile, and winked at himself in the mirror. With something of the childish belief in miracles with which he had so often gone to class, all his lessons unlearned, Paul dressed and dashed whistling down the corridor to the elevator.

He had no sooner entered the dining room and caught the measure of the music, than his remembrance was lightened by his old elastic power of claiming the moment, mounting with it, and finding it all sufficient. The glare and glitter about him, the mere scenic accessories had again, and for the last time, their old potency. He would show himself that he was game, he would finish the thing splendidly. He doubted, more than ever, the existence of Cordelia Street, and for the first time he drank his wine recklessly. Was he not, after all, one of these fortunate beings? Was he not still himself, and in his own place? He drummed a nervous accompaniment to the music and looked about him, telling himself over and over that it had paid.

He reflected drowsily, to the swell of the violin and the chill sweetness of his wine, that he might have done it more wisely. He might have caught an outbound steamer and been well out of their clutches before now. But the other side of the world had seemed too far away and too uncertain then; he could not have waited for it; his need had been too sharp. If he had to choose over again, he would do the same thing tomorrow. He looked affectionately about the dining room, now gilded with a soft mist. Ah, it has paid indeed!

Paul was awakened the next morning by a painful throbbing in his head and feet. He had thrown himself across the bed without undressing, and had slept with his shoes

60

on. His limbs and hands were lead heavy, and his tongue and throat were parched. There came upon him one of those fateful attacks of clear-headedness that never occurred except when he was physically exhausted and his nerves hung loose. He lay still and closed his eyes and let the tide of realities wash over him.

His father was in New York: "stopping at some joint or other," he told himself. The memory of successive summers on the front stoop fell upon him like a weight of black water. He had not a hundred dollars left, and he knew now, more than ever, that money was everything, the wall that stood between all he loathed and all he wanted. The thing was winding itself up; he had thought of that on his first glorious day in New York, and had even provided a way to snap the threat. It lay on his dressing-table now; he had got it out last night when he came blindly up from dinner—but the shiny metal hurt his eyes, and he disliked the look of it, anyway.

He rose and moved about with a painful effort, succumbing now and again to attacks of nausea. It was the old depression exaggerated; all the world had become Cordelia Street. Yet somehow he was not afraid of anything, was absolutely calm; perhaps because he had looked into the dark corner at last, and knew. It was bad enough, what he saw there, but somehow not so bad as his long fear of it had been. He saw everything clearly now. He had a feeling that he had made the best of it, that he had lived the sort of life he was meant to live, and for half an hour he sat staring at the revolver. But he told himself that was not the way, so he went downstairs and took a cab to the ferry.

When Paul arrived at Newark, he got off the train and took another cab, directing the driver to follow the Pennsylvania tracks out of town. The snow lay heavy on the roadways and had drifted deep in the open fields. Only here and there the dead grass or dried weed stalks projected, singularly black, above it. Once well into the country, Paul dismissed the carriage and walked, floundering along the tracks, his mind a medley of irrelevant things. He seemed to hold in his brain an actual picture of everything he had seen that morning. He remembered every feature of both his drivers, the toothless old woman from whom he had bought the red flowers in his coat, the agent from whom he had got his ticket, and all of his fellow-passengers on the ferry. His mind, unable to cope with vital matters near at hand, worked feverishly and deftly at sorting and grouping these images. They made for him a part of the ugliness of the world, of the ache in his head, and the bitter burning on his tongue. He stopped and put a handful of snow into his mouth as he walked, but that, too, seemed hot. When he reached a little hillside, where the tracks ran through a cut some twenty feet below him, he stopped and sat down.

The carnations in his coat were drooping with the cold, he noticed; all their red glory over. It occurred to him that all the flowers he had seen in the show windows that first night must have gone the same way, long before this. It was only one splendid breath they had, in spite of their brave mockery at the winter outside the glass. It was a losing game in the end, it seemed, this revolt against the homilies by which the world is run. Paul took one of the blossoms carefully from his coat and scooped a little hole in the snow, where he covered it up. Then he dozed a while, from his weak condition, seeming insensible to the cold.

The sound of an approaching train woke him, and he started to his feet, remembering only his resolution, and afraid lest he should be too late. He stood watching the approaching locomotive, his teeth chattering, his lips drawn away from them in a frightened smile; once or twice he glanced nervously sidewise, as though he were being watched. When the right moment came, he jumped. As he fell, the folly of his haste occurred to him with merciless clearness, the vastness of what he had left undone. There flashed through his brain, clearer than ever before, the blue of Adriatic water, the yellow of Algerian sands.

He felt something strike his chest—his body was being thrown swiftly through the air, on and on, immeasurably far and fast, while his limbs gently relaxed. Then, because

65

the picture-making mechanism was crushed, the disturbing visions flashed into black, and Paul dropped back into the immense design of things.

QUESTIONS

1. Describe Paul as a character. How does he grow, or change? What are his strengths? Weaknesses? What do his preferences and annoyances show about him? What is shown by his meeting with the college boy in New York? Why is the story called "Paul's Case"?

2. Describe the speaker. How does the speaker describe Paul? The other characters? When does the speaker shift attention exclusively to Paul? Why?

3. What future does Paul see for himself? To what degree is his dislike of the life on Cordelia Street justified? Why does he think that forgiveness and correction would be worse for him than imprisonment? How can the story be seen as a criticism not of Paul but of early-twentieth-century society?

WILLIAM FAULKNER (1897–1962)

For a brief biography, please see Chapter 3, page 130.

Barn Burning ⟩⟨⟩⟨⟩⟨ 1939

The store in which the Justice of the Peace's court was sitting smelled of cheese. The boy, crouched on his nail keg at the back of the crowded room, knew he smelled cheese, and more; from where he sat he could see the ranked shelves close-packed with the solid, squat, dynamic shapes of tin cans whose labels his stomach read, not from the lettering which meant nothing to his mind but from the scarlet devils and the silver curve of fish— this, the cheese which he knew he smelled and the hermetic meat° which his intestines believed he smelled coming in intermittent gusts momentary and brief between the other constant one, the smell and sense just a little of fear because mostly of despair and grief, the old fierce pull of blood. He could not see the table where the Justice sat and before which his father and his father's enemy (*our enemy* he thought in that despair; *ourn! mine and his both! He's my father!*) stood, but he could hear them, the two of them that is, because his father had said no word yet:

"But what proof have you, Mr. Harris?"

"I told you. The hog got into my corn. I caught it up and sent it back to him. He had no fence that would hold it. I told him so, warned him. The next time I put the hog in my pen. When he came to get it I gave him enough wire to patch up his pen. The next time I put the hog up and kept it. I rode down to his house and saw the wire I gave him still rolled on to the spool in his yard. I told him he could have the hog when he paid me a dollar pound fee. That evening a nigger came with the dollar and got the hog. He was a strange nigger. He said, 'He say to tell you wood and hay kin burn.' I said, 'What?' 'That what he say to tell you,' the nigger said. 'Wood and hay kin burn.' That night my barn burned. I got the stock out but I lost the barn."

"Where is the nigger? Have you got him?"

"He was a strange nigger, I tell you. I don't know what became of him."   5

---

hermetic meat: canned meat.

"But that's not proof. Don't you see that's not proof?"

"Get that boy up here. He knows." For a moment the boy thought too that the man meant his older brother until Harris said. "Not him. The little one. The boy," and, crouching, small for his age, small and wiry like his father, in patched and faded jeans even too small for him, with straight, uncombed, brown hair and eyes gray and wild as storm scud, he saw the men between himself and the table part and become a lane of grim faces, at the end of which he saw the Justice, a shabby, collarless, graying man in spectacles, beckoning him. He felt no floor under his bare feet; he seemed to walk beneath the palpable weight of the grim turning faces. His father, stiff in his black Sunday coat donned not for the trial but for the moving, did not even look at him. *He aims for me to lie,* he thought, again with that frantic grief and despair. *And I will have to do hit.*

"What's your name, boy?" the Justice said.

"Colonel Sartoris Snopes," the boy whispered.

"Hey?" the Justice said. "Talk louder. Colonel Sartoris? I reckon anybody named for Colonel Sartoris in this country can't help but tell the truth, can they?" The boy said nothing. *Enemy! Enemy!* he thought; for a moment he could not even see, could not see that the Justice's face was kindly nor discern that his voice was troubled when he spoke to the man named Harris: "Do you want me to question this boy?" But he could hear, and during those subsequent long seconds there was absolutely no sound in the crowded little room save that of quiet and intent breathing it was as if he had swung outward at the end of a grape vine, over a ravine, and at the top of the swing had been caught in a prolonged instant of mesmerized gravity, weightless in time.

"No!" Harris said violently, explosively. "Damnation! Send him out of here!" Now time, the fluid world, rushed beneath him again, the voices coming to him again through the smell of cheese and sealed meat, the fear and despair and the old grief of blood:

"This case is closed. I can't find against you, Snopes, but I can give you advice. Leave this country and don't come back to it."

His father spoke for the first time, his voice cold and harsh, level, without emphasis: "I aim to. I don't figure to stay in a country among people who . . ." he said something unprintable and vile, addressed to no one.

"That'll do," the Justice said, "Take your wagon and get out of this country before dark. Case dismissed."

His father turned, and he followed the stiff black coat, the wiry figure walking a little stiffly, from where a Confederate provost's man's musket ball had taken him in the heel on a stolen horse thirty years ago, followed the two backs now, since his older brother had appeared from somewhere in the crowd, no taller than the father but thicker, chewing tobacco steadily, between the two lines of grim-faced men and out of the store and across the worn gallery and down the sagging steps and among the dogs and half-grown boys in the mild May dust, where as he passed a voice hissed:

"Barn burner!"

Again he could not see, whirling; there was a face in a red haze, moonlike, bigger than the full moon, the owner of it half again his size, he leaping in the red haze toward the face, feeling no blow, feeling no shock when his head struck the earth, scrabbling up and leaping again, feeling no blow this time either and tasting no blood, scrabbling up to see the other boy in full flight and himself already leaping into pursuit as his father's hand jerked him back, the harsh, cold voice speaking above him: "Go get in the wagon."

It stood in a grove of locusts and mulberries across the road. His two hulking sisters in their Sunday dresses and his mother and her sister in calico and sunbonnets were already in it, sitting on and among the sorry residue of the dozen and more movings which even the boy could remember—the battered stove, the broken beds and chairs, the clock

10

15

inlaid with mother-of-pearl, which would not run, stopped at some fourteen minutes past two o'clock of a dead and forgotten day and time, which had been his mother's dowry. She was crying, though when she saw him she drew her sleeve across her face and began to descend from the wagon. "Get back," the father said.

"He's hurt, I got to get some water and wash his . . ."

"Get back in the wagon." his father said. He got in too, over the tail-gate. His father 20 mounted to the seat where the older brother already sat and struck the gaunt mules two savage blows with the peeled willow, but without heat. It was not even sadistic; it was exactly that same quality which in later years would cause his descendants to over-run the engine before putting a motor car into motion, striking and reining back in the same movement. The wagon went on, the store with its quiet crowd of grimly watching men dropped behind; a curve in the road hid it. *Forever* he thought. *Maybe he's done satisfied now, now that he has . . .* stopping himself, not to say it aloud even to himself. His mother's hand touched his shoulder.

"Does hit hurt?" she said.

"Naw," he said. "Hit don't hurt. Lemme be."

"Can't you wipe some of the blood off before hit dries?"

"I'll wash tonight," he said. "Lemme be, I tell you."

The wagon went on. He did not know where they were going. None of them ever 25 did or ever asked, because it was always somewhere, always a house of sorts waiting for them a day or two days or even three days away. Likely his father had already arranged to make a crop on another farm before he. . . . Again he had to stop himself. He (the father) always did. There was something about his wolflike independence and even courage when the advantage was at least neutral which impressed strangers, as if they got from his latent ravening ferocity not so much a sense of dependability as a feeling that his ferocious conviction in the rightness of his own actions would be of advantage to all whose interest lay with his.

That night they camped, in a grove of oaks and beeches where a spring ran. The nights were still cool and they had a fire against it, of a rail lifted from a nearby fence and cut into lengths—a small fire, neat, niggard almost, a shrewd fire; such fires were his father's habit and custom always, even in freezing weather. Older, the boy might have remarked this and wondered why not a big one; why should not a man who had not only seen the waste and extravagance of war, but who had in his blood an inherent prodigality with material not his own, have burned everything in sight? Then he might have gone a step farther and thought that that was the reason; that niggard blaze was the living fruits of nights passed during those four years in the woods hiding from all men, blue or grey, with his strings of horses (captured horses, he called them). And older still, he might have divined the true reason: that the element of fire spoke to some deep mainspring of his father's being, as the element of steel or of powder spoke to other men, as the one weapon for the preservation of integrity, else breath were not worth the breathing, and hence to be regarded with respect and used with discretion.

But he did not think this now and he had seen those same niggard blazes all his life. He merely ate his supper beside it and was already half asleep over his iron plate when his father called him, and once more he followed the stiff back, the stiff and ruthless limp, up the slope and on to the starlit road where, turning, he could see his father against the stars but without face or depth—a shape black, flat, and bloodless as though cut from tin in the iron folds of the frockcoat which had not been made for him, the voice harsh like tin and without heat like tin:

"You were fixing to tell them. You would have told him." He didn't answer. His father struck him with the flat of his hand on the side of the head, hard but without heat,

No emotion

exactly as he had struck the two mules at the store, exactly as he would strike either of them with any stick in order to kill a horse fly, his voice still without heat or anger: "You're getting to be a man. You got to learn. You got to learn to stick to your own blood or you ain't going to have any blood to stick to you. Do you think either of them, any man there this morning, would? Don't you know all they wanted was a chance to get at me because they knew I had them beat? Eh?" Later, twenty years later, he was to tell himself, "If I had said they wanted only truth, justice, he would have hit me again." But now he said nothing. He was not crying. He just stood there. "Answer me," his father said.

"Yes," he whispered. His father turned.

"Get on to bed. We'll be there tomorrow."   30

Tomorrow they were there. In the early afternoon the wagon stopped before a paintless two-room house identical almost with the dozen others it had stopped before even in the boy's ten years, and again, as on the other dozen occasions, his mother and aunt got down and began to unload the wagon, although his two sisters and his father and brother had not moved.

"Likely hit ain't fitten for hawgs," one of the sisters said.

"Nevertheless, fit it will and you'll hog it and like it," his father said. "Get out of them chairs and help your Ma unload."

The two sisters got down, big, bovine, in a flutter of cheap ribbons; one of them drew from the jumbled wagon bed a battered lantern, the other a worn broom. His father handed the reins to the older son and began to climb stiffly over the wheel. "When they get unloaded, take the team to the barn and feed them." Then he said, and at first the boy thought he was still speaking to his brother: "Come with me."

"Me?" he said.

"Yes," his father said. "You."   35

"Abner," his mother said. His father paused and looked back—the harsh level stare beneath the shaggy, graying, irascible brows.

"I reckon I'll have a word with the man that aims to begin tomorrow owning me body and soul for the next eight months."

They went back up the road. A week ago—or before last night, that is—he would have asked where they were going, but not now. His father had struck him before last night but never before had he paused afterward to explain why; it was as if the blow and the following calm, outrageous voice still rang, repercussed, divulging nothing to him save the terrible handicap of being young, the light weight of his few years, just heavy enough to prevent his soaring free of the world as it seemed to be ordered but not heavy enough to keep footed solid in it, to resist it and try to chance the course of its events.

Presently he could see the grove of oaks and cedars and the other flowering trees   40
and shrubs where the house would be, though not the house yet. They walked beside a fence massed with honeysuckle and Cherokee roses and came to a gate swinging open between two brick pillars, and now, beyond a sweep of drive, he saw the house for the first time and at that instant he forgot his father and the terror and despair both, and even when he remembered his father again (who had stopped) the terror and despair did not return. Because, for all the twelve movings, they had sojourned until now in a poor country, a land of small farms and fields and houses, and he had never seen a house like this before. *Hit's big as a courthouse* he thought quietly, with a surge of peace and joy whose reason he could not have thought into words, being too young for that: *They are safe from him. People whose lives are a part of this peace and dignity are beyond his touch, he no more to them than a buzzing wasp: capable of stinging for a little moment but that's all; the spell of this peace and dignity rendering even the barns and stable and cribs which belong to it impervious to the puny flames he might contrive . . .* this, the peace and joy, ebbing for an instant as he looked again

at the stiff black back, the stiff and implacable limp of the figure which was not dwarfed by the house, for the reason that it had never looked big anywhere and which now, against the serene columned backdrop, had more than ever that impervious quality of something cut ruthlessly from tin, depthless, as though, sidewise to the sun, it would cast no shadow. Watching him, the boy remarked the absolutely undeviating course which his father held and saw the stiff foot come squarely down in a pile of fresh droppings where a horse had stood in the drive and which his father could have avoided by a simple change of stride. But it ebbed only for a moment, though he could not have thought this into words either, walking on in the spell of the house, which he could even want but without envy, without sorrow, certainly never with that ravening and jealous rage which unknown to him walked in the ironlike black coat before him: *Maybe he will feel it too. Maybe it will even change him now from what maybe he couldn't help but be.*

They crossed the portico. Now he could hear his father's stiff foot as it came down on the boards with clocklike finality, a sound out of all proportion to the displacement of the body it bore and which was not dwarfed either by the white door before it, as though it had attained to a sort of vicious and ravening minimum not to be dwarfed by anything—the flat, wide, black hat, the formal coat of broadcloth which had once been black but which had now that friction-glazed greenish cast of the bodies of old house flies, the lifted sleeve which was too large, the lifted hand like a curled claw. The door opened so promptly that the boy knew the Negro must have been watching them all the time, an old man with neat grizzled hair, in a linen jacket, who stood barring the door with his body, saying "Wipe yo foots, white man, fo you come in here. Major ain't home nohow."

"Get out of my way, nigger," his father said, without heat too, flinging the door back and the Negro also and entering, his hat still on his head. And now the boy saw the prints of the stiff foot on the doorsill and saw them appear on the pale rug behind the machinelike deliberation of the foot which seemed to bear (or transmit) twice the weight which the body compassed. The Negro was shouting "Miss Lula! Miss Lula!" somewhere behind them, then the boy, deluged as though by a warm wave by a suave turn of carpeted stair and a pendant glitter of chandeliers and a mute gleam of gold frames, heard the swift feet and saw her too, a lady—perhaps he had never seen her like before either—in a gray, smooth gown with lace at the throat and an apron tied at the waist and the sleeves turned back, wiping cake or biscuit dough from her hands with a towel as she came up the hall, looking not at his father at all but at the tracks on the blond rug with an expression of incredulous amazement.

"I tried," the Negro cried. "I tole him to . . ."

"Will you please go away?" she said in a shaking voice. "Major de Spain is not at home. Will you please go away?"

His father had not spoken again. He did not speak again. He did not even look at her. He just stood stiff in the center of the rug, in his hat, the shaggy iron-gray brows twitching slightly above the pebble-colored eyes as he appeared to examine the house with brief deliberation. Then with the same deliberation he turned; the boy watched him pivot on the good leg and saw the stiff foot drag round the arc of the turning, leaving a final long and fading smear. His father never looked at it, he never once looked down at the rug. The Negro held the door. It closed behind them, upon the hysteric and indistinguishable woman-wail. His father stopped at the top of the steps and scraped his boot clean on the edge of it. At the gate he stopped again. He stood for a moment, planted stiffly on the stiff foot, looking back at the house. "Pretty and white, ain't it?" he said. "That's sweat. Nigger sweat. Maybe it ain't white enough yet to suit him. Maybe he wants to mix some white sweat with it."

45

Two hours later the boy was chopping wood behind the house within which his mother and aunt and the two sisters (the mother and aunt, not the two girls, he knew that; even at this distance and muffled by walls the flat loud voices of the two girls emanated an incorrigible idle inertia) were setting up the stove to prepare a meal, when he heard the hooves and saw the linen-clad man on a fine sorrel mare, whom he recognized even before he saw the rolled rug in front of the Negro youth following on a fat bay carriage horse—a suffused, angry face vanishing, still at full gallop, beyond the corner of the house where his father and brother were sitting in the two tilted chairs; and a moment later, almost before he could have put the axe down, he heard the hooves again and watched the sorrel mare go back out of the yard, already galloping again. Then his father began to shout one of the sisters' names, who presently emerged backward from the kitchen door dragging the rolled rug along the ground by one end while the other sister walked behind it.

"If you ain't going to tote, go on and set up the wash pot," the first said.

"You, Sarty!" the second shouted. "Set up the wash pot!" His father appeared at the door, framed against that shabbiness, as he had been against that other bland perfection, impervious to either, the mother's anxious face at his shoulder.

"Go on," the father said. "Pick it up." The two sisters stooped, broad, lethargic; stooping, they presented an incredible expanse of pale cloth and a flutter of tawdry ribbons.

"If I thought enough of a rug to have to git hit all the way from France I wouldn't   50
keep hit where folks coming in would have to tromp on hit," the first said. They raised the rug.

"Abner," the mother said. "Let me do it."

"You go back and git dinner," his father said. "I'll tend to this."

From the woodpile through the rest of the afternoon the boy watched them, the rug spread flat in the dust beside the bubbling wash pot, the two sisters stooping over it with that profound and lethargic reluctance, while the father stood over them in turn, implacable and grim, driving them though never raising his voice again. He could smell the harsh homemade lye they were using; he saw his mother come to the door once and look toward them with an expression not anxious now but very like despair; he saw his father turn, and he fell to with the axe and saw from the corner of his eye his father raise from the ground a flattish fragment of field stone and examine it and return to the pot, and this time his mother actually spoke: "Abner. Abner. Please don't. Please, Abner."

Then he was done too. It was dusk; the whippoorwills had already begun. He could smell coffee from the room where they would presently eat the cold food remaining from the mid-afternoon meal, though when he entered the house he realized they were having coffee again because there was a fire on the hearth, before which the rug now lay spread over the backs of the two chairs. The tracks of his father's foot were gone. Where they had been were now long, water-cloudy scoriations resembling the sporadic course of a Lilliputian mowing machine.

It still hung there while they ate the cold food and then went to bed, scattered   55
without order or claim up and down the two rooms, his mother in one bed, where his father would later lie, the older brother in the other, himself, the aunt, and the two sisters on pallets on the floor. But his father was not in bed yet. The last thing the boy remembered was the depthless, harsh silhouette of the hat and coat bending over the rug and it seemed to him that he had not even closed his eyes when the silhouette was standing over him, the fire almost dead behind it, the stiff foot prodding him awake. "Catch up the mule," his father said.

When he returned with the mule his father was standing in the black door, the rolled rug over his shoulder. "Ain't you going to ride?" he said.

"No. Give me your foot."

He bent his knee into his father's hand, the wiry, surprising power flowed smoothly, rising, he rising with it, on to the mule's bare back (they had owned a saddle once; the boy could remember it though not when or where) and with the same effortlessness his father swung the rug up in front of him. Now in the starlight they retraced the afternoon's path, up the dusty road rife with honeysuckle, through the gate and up the black tunnel of the drive to the lightless house, where he sat on the mule and felt the rough warp of the rug drag across his thighs and vanish.

"Don't you want me to help?" he whispered. His father did not answer and now he heard again that stiff foot striking the hollow portico with that wooden and clocklike deliberation, that outrageous overstatement of the weight it carried. The rug, hunched, not flung (the boy could tell that even in the darkness) from his father's shoulder, struck the angle of wall and floor with a sound unbelievably loud, thunderous, then the foot again, unhurried and enormous; a light came on in the house and the boy sat, tense, breathing steadily and quietly and just a little fast, though the foot itself did not increase its beat at all, descending the steps now; now the boy could see him.

"Don't you want to ride now?" he whispered. "We kin both ride now," the light within the house altering now, flaring up and sinking. *He's coming down the stairs now,* he thought. He had already ridden the mule up beside the horse block; presently his father was up behind him and he doubled the reins over and slashed the mule across the neck, but before the animal could begin to trot the hard, thin arm came round him, the hard, knotted hand jerking the mule back to a walk.

In the first red rays of the sun they were in the lot, putting plow gear on the mules. This time the sorrel mare was in the lot before he heard it at all, the rider collarless and even bareheaded, trembling, speaking in a shaking voice as the woman in the house had done, his father merely looking up once before stooping again to the hame he was buckling, so that the man on the mare spoke to his stooping back:

"You must realize you have ruined that rug. Wasn't there anybody here, any of your women . . ." He ceased, shaking, the boy watching him, the older brother leaning now in the stable door, chewing, blinking slowly and steadily at nothing apparently. "It cost a hundred dollars. But you never had a hundred dollars. You never will. So I'm going to charge you twenty bushels of corn against your crop. I'll add it in your contract and when you come to the commissary you can sign it. That won't keep Mrs. de Spain quiet but maybe it will teach you to wipe your feet off before you enter her house again."

Then he was gone. The boy looked at his father, who still had not spoken or even looked up again, who was now adjusting the logger-head in the hame.

"Pap," he said. His father looked at him—the inscrutable face, the shaggy brows beneath which the gray eyes glinted coldly. Suddenly the boy went toward him, fast, stopping as suddenly. "You done the best you could!" he cried. "If he wanted hit done different why didn't he wait and tell you how? He won't git no twenty bushels! He won't git none! We'll get hit and hide hit! I kin watch . . ."

"Did you put the cutter back in that straight stock like I told you?"

"No, sir," he said.

"Then go do it."

That was Wednesday. During the rest of that week he worked steadily, at what was within his scope and some which was beyond it, with an industry that did not need to be driven nor even commanded twice; he had this from his mother, with the difference that some at least of what he did he liked to do, such as splitting wood with the half-size axe which his mother and aunt had earned, or saved money somehow, to present him with at Christmas. In company with the two older women (and on one afternoon even one of the sisters), he built pens for the shoat and the cow which were a part of his father's contract with the landlord, and one afternoon, his father being absent, gone somewhere on one of the mules, he went to the field.

They were running a middle buster now, his brother holding the plow straight while he handled the reins, and walking beside the straining mule, the rich black soil shearing cool and damp against his bare ankles, he thought *Maybe this is the end of it. Maybe even that twenty bushels that seems hard to have to pay for just a rug will be a cheap price for him to stop forever and always from being what he used to be;* thinking, dreaming now, so that his brother had to speak sharply to him to mind the mule: *Maybe he even won't collect the twenty bushels. Maybe it will all add up and balance and vanish—corn, rug, fire; the terror and grief, the being pulled two ways like between two teams of horses—gone, done with forever and ever.*

Then it was Saturday; he looked up from beneath the mule he was harnessing and saw his father in the black coat and hat. "Not that," his father said. "The wagon gear." And then, two hours later, sitting in the wagon bed behind his father and brother on the seat, the wagon accomplished a final curve, and he saw the weathered paintless store with its tattered tobacco- and patent-medicine posters and the tethered wagons and saddle animals below the gallery. He mounted the gnawed steps behind his father and brother, and there again was the lane of quiet, watching faces for the three of them to walk through. He saw the man in spectacles sitting at the plank table and he did not need to be told this was a Justice of the Peace; he sent one glare of fierce, exultant, partisan defiance at the man in collar and cravat now, whom he had seen but twice in his life, and that on a galloping horse, who now wore on his face an expression not of rage but of amazed unbelief which the boy could not have known was at the incredible circumstance of being sued by one of his own tenants, and came and stood against his father and cried at the Justice: "He ain't done it! He ain't burnt . . ." 70

"Go back to the wagon," his father said.

"Burnt?" the Justice said. "Do I understand this rug was burned too?"

"Does anybody here claim it was?" his father said. "Go back to the wagon." But he did not, he merely retreated to the rear of the room, crowded as that other had been, but not to sit down this time, instead, to stand pressing among the motionless bodies, listening to the voices:

"And you claim twenty bushels of corn is too high for the damage you did to the rug?"

"He brought the rug to me and said he wanted the tracks washed out of it. I washed the tracks out and took the rug back to him." 75

"But you didn't carry the rug back to him in the same condition it was in before you made the tracks on it."

His father did not answer, and now for perhaps half a minute there was no sound at all save that of breathing, the faint, steady suspiration of complete and intent listening.

"You decline to answer that, Mr. Snopes?" Again his father did not answer. "I'm going to find against you, Mr. Snopes. I'm going to find that you were responsible for the injury to Major de Spain's rug and hold you liable for it. But twenty bushels of corn seems a little high for a man in your circumstances to have to pay. Major de Spain claims it cost a hundred dollars. October corn will be worth about fifty cents. I figure that if Major de Spain can stand a ninety-five-dollar loss on something he paid cash for, you can stand a five-dollar loss you haven't earned yet. I hold you in damages to Major de Spain to the amount of ten bushels of corn over and above your contract with him, to be paid to him out of your crop at gathering time. Court adjourned."

It had taken no time hardly, the morning was but half begun. He thought they would return home and perhaps back to the field, since they were late, far behind all other farmers. But instead his father passed on behind the wagon, merely indicating with his hand for the older brother to follow with it, and crossed the road toward the black-smith shop opposite, pressing on after his father, overtaking him, speaking, whispering up at the harsh, calm face beneath the weathered hat: "He won't git no ten bushels nei-ther. He won't git one. We'll . . ." until his father glanced for an instant down on him, the face absolutely calm, the grizzled eyebrows tangled above the cold eyes, the voice almost pleasant, almost gentle:

"You think so? Well, we'll wait till October anyway." 80

The matter of the wagon—the setting of a spoke or two and the tightening of the tires—did not take long either, the business of the tires accomplished by driving the wagon into the spring branch behind the shop and letting it stand there, the mules nuz-zling into the water from time to time, and the boy on the seat with the idle reins, look-ing up the slope and through the sooty tunnel of the shed where the slow hammer rang and where his father sat on an upended cypress bolt, easily, either talking or listening, still sitting there when the boy brought the dripping wagon up out of the branch and halted it before the door.

"Take them on to the shade and hitch," his father said. He did so and returned. His father and the smith and a third man squatting on his heels inside the door were talking, about crops and animals; the boy, squatting too in the ammoniac dust and hoof-parings and scales of rust, heard his father tell a long and unhurried story out of the time before the birth of the older brother even when he had been a professional horse-trader. And then his father came up beside him where he stood before a tattered last year's circus poster on the other side of the store, gazing rapt and quiet at the scarlet horses, the in-credible poisings and convolutions of tulle and tights and the painted leers of comedi-ans, and said, "It's time to eat."

But not at home. Squatting beside his brother against the front wall, he watched his father emerge from the store and produce from a paper sack a segment of cheese and divided it carefully and deliberately into three with his pocket knife and produce crack-ers from the same sack. They all three squatted on the gallery and ate slowly, without talk-ing; then in the store again, they drank from a tin dipper tepid water smelling of the cedar bucket and of living beech trees. And still they did not go home. It was a horse lot this time, a tall rail fence upon and along which men stood and sat and out of which one by one horses were led, to be walked and trotted and then cantered back and forth along the road while the slow swapping and buying went on and the sun began to slant west-ward, they—the three of them—watching and listening, the older brother with his muddy eyes and his steady inevitable tobacco, the father commenting now and then on certain of the animals, to no one in particular.

It was after sundown when they reached home. They ate supper by lamplight, then, sitting on the doorstep, the boy watched the night fully accomplish, listening to the whip-poorwills and the frogs, when he heard his mother's voice: "Abner! No! No! Oh, God, Oh, God, Abner!" and he rose, whirled, and saw the altered light through the door where a can-dle stub now burned in a bottle neck on the table and his father, still in the hat and coat, at once formal and burlesque as though dressed carefully for some shabby and ceremonial vi-olence, emptying the reservoir of the lamp back into the five-gallon kerosene can from which it had been filled, while the mother tugged at his arm until he shifted the lamp to the other hand and flung her back, not savagely or viciously, just hard, into the wall, her hands flung out against the wall for balance, her mouth open and in her face the same quality of hopeless despair as had been in her voice. Then his father saw him standing in the door.

"Go to the barn and get that can of oil we were oiling the wagon with," he said. The 85
boy did not move. Then he could speak.

"What . . ." he cried. "What are you . . ."

"Go get that oil," his father said. "Go."

Then he was moving, running, outside the house, toward the stable: this the old habit, the old blood which he had not been permitted to choose for himself, which had been bequeathed him willy nilly and which had run for so long (and who knew where, battening on what of outrage and savagery and lust) before it came to him. *I could keep on,* he thought. *I could run on and on and never look back, never need to see his face again. Only I can't. I can't,* the rusted can in his hand now, the liquid sloshing in it as he ran back to the house and into it, into the sound of his mother's weeping in the next room, and handed the can to his father.

"Ain't you going to even send a nigger?" he cried. "At least you sent a nigger before!"

This time his father didn't strike him. The hand came even faster than the blow had, 90 the same hand which had set the can on the table with almost excruciating care flashing from the can toward him too quick for him to follow it, gripping him by the back of his shirt and on to tiptoe before he had seen it quit the can, the face stooping at him in breathless and frozen ferocity, the cold, dead voice speaking over him to the older brother who leaned against the table, chewing with that steady, curious, sidewise motion of cows:

"Empty the can into the big one and go on. I'll catch up with you."

"Better tie him up to the bedpost," the brother said.

"Do like I told you," the father said. Then the boy was moving, his bunched shirt and the hard, bony hand between his shoulder-blades, his toes just touching the floor, across the room and into the other one, past the sisters sitting with spread heavy thighs in the two chairs over the cold hearth, and to where his mother and aunt sat side by side on the bed, the aunt's arms about the mother's shoulders.

"Hold him," the father said. The aunt made a startled movement. "Not you," the father said. "Lennie. Take hold of him. I want to see you do it." His mother took him by the wrist. "You'll hold him better than that. If he gets loose don't you know what he is going to do? He will go up yonder." He jerked his head toward the road. "Maybe I'd better tie him."

"I'll hold him," his mother whispered. 95

"See you do then." Then his father was gone, the stiff foot heavy and measured upon the boards, ceasing at last.

Then he began to struggle. His mother caught him in both arms, he jerking and wrenching at them. He would be stronger in the end, he knew that. But he had not time to wait for it. "Lemme go!" he cried. "I don't want to have to hit you!"

"Let him go!" the aunt said. "If he don't go, before God, I am going up there myself!"

"Don't you see I can't?" his mother cried. "Sarty! Sarty! No! No! Help me, Lizzie!"

Then he was free. His aunt grasped at him but it was too late. He whirled, running, 100 his mother stumbled forward on to her knees behind him, crying to the nearer sister: "Catch him, Net! Catch him!" But that was too late too, the sister (the sisters were twins, born at the same time, yet either of them now gave the impression of being, encompassing as much living meat and volume and weight as any other two of the family) not yet having begun to rise from the chair, her head, face, alone merely turned, presenting to him in the flying instant an astonishing expanse of young female features untroubled by any surprise even, wearing only an expression of bovine interest. Then he was out of the room, out of the house, in the mild dust of the starlit road and the heavy rifeness of honeysuckle, the pale ribbon unspooling with terrific slowness under his running feet, reaching the gate at last and turning in, running, his heart and lungs drumming, on up the drive toward the lighted house, the lighted door. He did not knock, he burst in, sobbing for breath, incapable for the moment of speech; he saw the astonished face of the Negro in the linen jacket without knowing when the Negro had appeared.

"De Spain!" he cried, panted. "Where's . . ." then he saw the white man too emerging from a white door down the hall. "Barn!" he cried. "Barn!"

"What?" the white man said. "Barn?"

"Yes!" the boy cried. "Barn!"

"Catch him!" the white man shouted.

But it was too late this time too. The Negro grasped his shirt, but the entire sleeve, rotten with washing, carried away, and he was out that door too and in the drive again, and had actually never ceased to run even while he was screaming into the white man's face. 105

Behind him the white man was shouting. "My horse! Fetch my horse!" and he thought for an instant of cutting across the park and climbing the fence into the road, but he did not know the park nor how high the vine-massed fence might be and he dared not risk it. So he ran on down the drive, blood and breath roaring; presently he was in the road again though he could not see it. He could not hear either: the galloping mare was almost upon him before he heard her, and even then he held his course, as if the very urgency of his wild grief and need must in a moment more find him wings, waiting until the ultimate instant to hurl himself aside and into the weed-choked roadside ditch as the horse thundered past and on, for an instant in furious silhouette against the stars, the tranquil early summer night sky which, even before the shape of the horse and rider vanished, strained abruptly and violently upward: a long, swirling roar incredible and soundless, blotting the stars, and he springing up and into the road again, running again, knowing it was too late yet still running even after he heard the shot and, an instant later, two shots, pausing now without knowing he had ceased to run, crying "Pap! Pap!," running again before he knew he had begun to run, stumbling, tripping over something and scrabbling up again without ceasing to run, looking backward over his shoulder at the glare as he got up, running on among the invisible trees, panting, sobbing, "Father! Father!"

At midnight he was sitting on the crest of a hill. He did not know it was midnight and he did not know how far he had come. But there was no glare behind him now and he sat now, his back toward what he had called home for four days anyhow, his face toward the dark woods which he would enter when breath was strong again, small, shaking steadily in the chill darkness, hugging himself into the remainder of his thin, rotten shirt, the grief and despair now no longer terror and fear but just grief and despair. *Father. My father*, he thought. "He was brave!" he cried suddenly, aloud but not loud, no more than a whisper: "He was! He was in the war! He was in Colonel Sartoris' cav'ry!" not knowing that his father had gone to that war a private in the fine old European sense, wearing no uniform, admitting the authority of and giving fidelity to no man or army or flag, going to war as Malbrouck° himself did: for booty—it meant nothing and less than nothing to him if it were enemy booty or his own.

The slow constellations wheeled on. It would be dawn and then sun-up after a while and he would be hungry. But that would be tomorrow and now he was only cold, and walking would cure that. His breathing was easier now and he decided to get up and go on, and then he found that he had been asleep because he knew it was almost dawn, the night almost over. He could tell that from the whippoorwills. They were everywhere now among the dark trees below him, constant and inflectioned and ceaseless, so that, as

---

Malbrouck: hero of an old French ballad ("Malbrouck s'en va-t-en guerre"). The original Malbrouck, the English Duke of Marlborough (1650–1722) had been accused of profiteering during the War of the Spanish Succession (1702–1713).

the instant for giving over to the day birds drew nearer and nearer, there was no interval at all between them. He got up. He was a little stiff, but walking would cure that too as it would the cold, and soon there would be the sun. He went on down the hill, toward the dark woods within which the liquid silver voices of the birds called unceasing—the rapid and urgent beating of the urgent and quiring heart of the late spring night. He did not look back.

QUESTIONS

family

1. Explain why Sarty's character is round rather than flat. In what ways does he change and grow? What conflicts does he face? What does he learn? How does he feel about the things his father does? Why does he leave and "not look back" at the end?

2. In the Bible, 2 Samuel, Chapters 2 and 3, Abner, the cousin of King Saul, is a powerful commander, warrior, and king maker. He is loyal to the son of King Saul and fights against the supporters of King David. Abner's death makes it possible for David to become uncontested ruler. Why do you think that Faulkner chose the name Abner for the father of the Snopes family? What actions of Abner Snopes make him seem heroic? Antiheroic? Why?

3. When and where is the story occurring? How does Faulkner convey this information to you?

4. Describe the characters of Sarty's mother and sisters. What do you learn about them? To what extent do any of them exhibit growth or development?

5. At the story's end, who is the rider of the horse? Who fires the three shots? Why does Faulkner not tell us the result of the shooting? (In Book I of *The Hamlet*, Faulkner explains that Abner and his other son, Flem, escape.)

SUSAN GLASPELL (1882–1948)

For a brief biography, please see Chapter 26.

A Jury of Her Peers° ⤳⤳⤳ 1917

When Martha Hale opened the storm-door and got a cut of the north wind, she ran back for her big woolen scarf. As she hurriedly wound that round her head her eye made a scandalized sweep of her kitchen. It was no ordinary thing that called her away—it was probably further from ordinary than anything that had ever happened in Dickson County. But what her eye took in was that her kitchen was in no shape for leaving: her bread all ready for mixing, half the flour sifted and half unsifted.

She hated to see things half done; but she had been at that when the team from town stopped to get Mr. Hale, and then the sheriff came running in to say his wife wished Mrs. Hale would come too—adding, with a grin, that he guessed she was getting scary and wanted another woman along. So she had dropped everything right where it was.

"Martha!" now came her husband's impatient voice. "Don't keep folks waiting out here in the cold."

She again opened the storm-door, and this time joined the three men and the one woman waiting for her in the big two-seated buggy.

Glaspell's play *Trifles*, with which this story may be compared, appears in Chapter 26.

After she had the robes tucked around her she took another look at the woman who sat beside her on the back seat. She had met Mrs. Peters the year before at the county fair, and the thing she remembered about her was that she didn't seem like a sheriff's wife. She was small and thin and didn't have a strong voice. Mrs. Gorman, sheriff's wife before Gorman went out and Peters came in, had a voice that somehow seemed to be backing up the law with every word. But if Mrs. Peters didn't look like a sheriff's wife, Peters made it up in looking like a sheriff. He was to a dot the kind of man who could get himself elected sheriff—a heavy man with a big voice, who was particularly genial with the law-abiding, as if to make it plain that he knew the difference between criminals and non-criminals. And right there it came into Mrs. Hale's mind, with a stab, that this man who was so pleasant and lively with all of them was going to the Wrights' now as a sheriff.

"The country's not very pleasant this time of year," Mrs. Peters at last ventured, as if she felt they ought to be talking as well as the men.

Mrs. Hale scarcely finished her reply, for they had gone up a little hill and could see the Wright place now, and seeing it did not make her feel like talking. It looked very lonesome this cold March morning. It had always been a lonesome-looking place. It was down in a hollow, and the poplar trees around it were lonesome-looking trees. The men were looking at it and talking about what had happened. The county attorney was bending to one side of the buggy, and kept looking steadily at the place as they drew up to it.

"I'm glad you came with me," Mrs. Peters said nervously, as the two women were about to follow the men in through the kitchen door.

Even after she had her foot on the door-step, her hand on the knob, Martha Hale had a moment of feeling she could not cross that threshold. And the reason it seemed she couldn't cross it now was simply because she hadn't crossed it before. Time and time again it had been in her mind, "I ought to go over and see Minnie Foster"—she still thought of her as Minnie Foster, though for twenty years she had been Mrs. Wright. And then there was always something to do and Minnie Foster would go from her mind. But *now* she could come.

The men went over to the stove. The women stood close together by the door. Young Henderson, the county attorney, turned around and said, "Come up to the fire, ladies."

Mrs. Peters took a step forward, then stopped. "I'm not—cold," she said.

And so the two women stood by the door, at first not even so much as looking around the kitchen.

The men talked for a minute about what a good thing it was the sheriff had sent his deputy out that morning to make a fire for them, and then Sheriff Peters stepped back from the stove, unbuttoned his outer coat, and leaned his hands on the kitchen table in a way that seemed to mark the beginning of official business. "Now, Mr. Hale," he said in a sort of semi-official voice, "before we move things about, you tell Mr. Henderson just what it was you saw when you came here yesterday morning."

The county attorney was looking around the kitchen.

"By the way," he said, "has anything been moved?" He turned to the sheriff. "Are things just as you left them yesterday?"

Peters looked from cupboard to sink; from that to a small worn rocker a little to one side of the kitchen table.

"It's just the same."

"Somebody should have been left here yesterday," said the county attorney.

"Oh—yesterday," returned the sheriff, with a little gesture as of yesterday having been more than he could bear to think of. "When I had to send Frank to Morris Center for that man who went crazy—let me tell you. I had my hands full *yesterday*. I knew you could get back from Omaha by today, George, and as long as I went over everything here myself—"

"Well, Mr. Hale," said the county attorney, in a way of letting what was past and gone go, "tell just what happened when you came here yesterday morning."   20

Mrs. Hale, still leaning against the door, had that sinking feeling of the mother whose child is about to speak a piece. Lewis often wandered along and got things mixed up in a story. She hoped he would tell this straight and plain, and not say unnecessary things that would just make things harder for Minnie Foster. He didn't begin at once, and she noticed that he looked queer—as if standing in that kitchen and having to tell what he had seen there yesterday morning made him almost sick.

"Yes, Mr. Hale?" the county attorney reminded.

"Harry and I had started to town with a load of potatoes," Mrs. Hale's husband began.

Harry was Mrs. Hale's oldest boy. He wasn't with them now, for the very good reason that those potatoes never got to town yesterday and he was taking them this morning, so he hadn't been home when the sheriff stopped to say he wanted Mr. Hale to come over to the Wright place and tell the county attorney his story there, where he could point it all out. With all Mrs. Hale's other emotions came the fear now that maybe Harry wasn't dressed warm enough—they hadn't any of them realized how that north wind did bite. *Metaphor*

"We come along this road," Hale was going on, with a motion of his hand to the   25 road over which they had just come, "and as we got in sight of the house I says to Harry, 'I'm goin' to see if I can't get John Wright to take a telephone.' You see," he explained to Henderson, "unless I can get somebody to go in with me they won't come out this branch road except for a price *I* can't pay. I'd spoke to Wright about it once before; but he put me off, saying folks talked too much anyway, and all he asked was peace and quiet—guess you know about how much he talked himself. But I thought maybe if I went to the house and talked about it before his wife, and said all the women-folks liked the telephones, and that in this lonesome stretch of road it would be a good thing—well, I said to Harry that that was what I was going to say—though I said at the same time that I didn't know as what his wife wanted made much difference to John—"

Now there he was!—saying things he didn't need to say. Mrs. Hale tried to catch her husband's eye, but fortunately the county attorney interrupted with:

"Let's talk about that a little later, Mr. Hale. I do want to talk about that, but I'm anxious now to get along to just what happened when you got here."

When he began this time, it was very deliberately and carefully:

"I didn't see or hear anything. I knocked at the door. And still it was all quiet inside. I knew they must be up—it was past eight o'clock. So I knocked again, louder, and I thought I heard somebody say, 'Come in.' I wasn't sure—I'm not sure yet. But I opened the door—this door," jerking a hand toward the door by which the two women stood, "and there, in that rocker"—pointing to it—"sat Mrs. Wright."

Everyone in the kitchen looked at the rocker. It came into Mrs. Hale's mind that   30 that rocker didn't look in the least like Minnie Foster—the Minnie Foster of twenty years before. It was a dingy red, with wooden rungs up the back, and the middle rung was gone, and the chair sagged to one side.

"How did she—look?" the county attorney was inquiring.

"Well," said Hale, "she looked—queer."

"How do you mean—queer?"

As he asked it he took out a note-book and pencil. Mrs. Hale did not like the sight of that pencil. She kept her eye fixed on her husband, as if to keep him from saying unnecessary things that would go into that note-book and make trouble.

Hale did speak guardedly, as if the pencil had affected him too.　　35

"Well, as if she didn't know what she was going to do next. And kind of—done up."

"How did she seem to feel about your coming?"

"Why, I don't think she minded—one way or other. She didn't pay much attention. I said, 'Ho' do, Mrs. Wright? It's cold, ain't it?' And she said. 'Is it?'—and went on pleatin' at her apron.

"Well, I was surprised. She didn't ask me to come up to the stove, or to sit down, but just set there, not even lookin' at me. And so I said: 'I want to see John.'

"And then she—laughed. I guess you would call it a laugh.　　40

"I thought of Harry and the team outside, so I said, a little sharp, 'Can I see John?' 'No,' says she—kind of dull like. 'Ain't he home?' says I. Then she looked at me. 'Yes,' says she, 'he's home.' 'Then why can't I see him?' I asked her, out of patience with her now. 'Cause he's dead' says she, just as quiet and dull—and fell to pleatin' her apron. 'Dead?' says I, like you do when you can't take in what you've heard.

"She just nodded her head, not getting a bit excited, but rockin' back and forth.

"Why—where is he?' says I, not knowing *what* to say.

"She just pointed upstairs—like this"—pointing to the room above.

"I got up, with the idea of going up there myself. By this time I—didn't know what　　45 to do. I walked from there to here; then I says: 'Why, what did he die of?'

"'He died of a rope around his neck,' says she; and just went on pleatin' at her apron."

Hale stopped speaking, and stood staring at the rocker, as if he were still seeing the woman who had sat there the morning before. Nobody spoke; it was as if every one were seeing the woman who had sat there the morning before.

"And what did you do then?" the county attorney at last broke the silence.

"I went out and called Harry. I thought I might—need help. I got Harry in, and we went upstairs." His voice fell almost to a whisper. "There he was—lying over the—"

"I think I'd rather have you go into that upstairs," the county attorney interrupted,　　50 "where you can point it all out. Just go on now with the rest of the story."

"Well, my first thought was to get that rope off. It looked—"

He stopped, his face twitching.

"But Harry, he went up to him, and he said. 'No, he's dead all right, and we'd better not touch anything.' So we went downstairs.

"She was still sitting that same way. 'Has anybody been notified?' I asked. 'No,' says she, unconcerned.

"'Who did this, Mrs. Wright?' said Harry. He said it businesslike, and she stopped　　55 pleatin' at her apron. 'I don't know,' she says. 'You don't *know*?' says Harry. 'Weren't you sleepin' in the bed with him?' 'Yes,' says she, 'but I was on the inside.' 'Somebody slipped a rope round his neck and strangled him, and you didn't wake up?' says Harry. 'I didn't wake up,' she said after him.

"We may have looked as if we didn't see how that could be, for after a minute she said, 'I sleep sound.'

"Harry was going to ask her more questions, but I said maybe that weren't our business; maybe we ought to let her tell her story first to the coroner or the sheriff. So Harry went fast as he could over to High Road—the Rivers' place, where there's a telephone."

"And what did she do when she knew you had gone for the coroner?" The attorney got his pencil in his hand all ready for writing.

"She moved from that chair to this one over here"—Hale pointed to a small chair in the corner—"and just sat there with her hands held together and looking down. I got a feeling that I ought to make some conversation, so I said I had come in to see if John wanted to put in a telephone; and at that she started to laugh, and then she stopped and looked at me—scared."

At the sound of a moving pencil the man who was telling the story looked up.　　60

"I dunno—maybe it wasn't scared," he hastened: "I wouldn't like to say it was. Soon Harry got back, and then Dr. Lloyd came, and you, Mr. Peters, and so I guess that's all I know that you don't."

He said that last with relief, and moved a little, as if relaxing. Everyone moved a little. The county attorney walked toward the stair door.

"I guess we'll go upstairs first—then out to the barn and around there."

He paused and looked around the kitchen.

"You're convinced there was nothing important here?" he asked the sheriff. "Noth-　　65
ing that would—point to any motive?"

The sheriff too looked all around, as if to re-convince himself.

"Nothing here but kitchen things," he said, with a little laugh for the insignificance of kitchen things. _Trifles_

The county attorney was looking at the cupboard—a peculiar, ungainly structure, half closet and half cupboard, the upper part of it being built in the wall, and the lower part just the old-fashioned kitchen cupboard. As if its queerness attracted him, he got a chair and opened the upper part and looked in. After a moment he drew his hand away sticky.

"Here's a nice mess," he said resentfully.

The two women had drawn nearer, and now the sheriff's wife spoke.　　70

"Oh—her fruit," she said, looking to Mrs. Hale for sympathetic understanding. She turned back to the county attorney and explained: "She worried about that when it turned so cold last night. She said the fire would go out and her jars might burst.

Mrs. Peters' husband broke into a laugh.

"Well, can you beat the woman! Held for murder, and worrying about her preserves!"

The young attorney set his lips.

"I guess before we're through with her she may have something more serious than　　75
preserves to worry about."

"Oh, well," said Mrs. Hale's husband, with good-natured superiority, "women are used to worrying over trifles."

The two women moved a little closer together. Neither of them spoke. The county attorney seemed suddenly to remember his manners—and think of his future.

"And yet," said he, with the gallantry of a young politician. "for all their worries, what would we do without the ladies?"

The women did not speak, did not unbend. He went to the sink and began washing his hands. He turned to wipe them on the roller towel—whirled it for a cleaner place.

"Dirty towels! Not much of a housekeeper, would you say, ladies?"　　80

He kicked his foot against some dirty pans under the sink.

"There's a great deal of work to be done on a farm," said Mrs. Hale stiffly.

"To be sure. And yet"—with a little bow to her—"I know there are some Dickson County farm-houses that do not have such roller towels." He gave it a pull to expose its full length again.

"Those towels get dirty awful quick. Men's hands aren't always as clean as they might be."

"Ah, loyal to your sex, I see," he laughed. He stopped and gave her a keen look.　　85
"But you and Mrs. Wright were neighbors. I suppose you were friends, too."

Martha Hale shook her head.

"I've seen little enough of her of late years. I've not been in this house—it's more than a year."

"And why was that? You didn't like her?"

"I liked her well enough," she replied with spirit. "Farmers' wives have their hands full, Mr. Henderson. And then—" She looked around the kitchen.

"Yes?" he encouraged.

"It never seemed a very cheerful place," said she, more to herself than to him.

"No," he agreed; "I don't think anyone would call it cheerful. I shouldn't say she had the home-making instinct."

"Well, I don't know as Wright had, either," she muttered.

"You mean they didn't get on very well?" he was quick to ask.

"No; I don't mean anything," she answered, with decision. As she turned a little away from him, she added: "But I don't think a place would be any the cheerfuller for John Wright's bein' in it."

"I'd like to talk to you about that a little later, Mrs. Hale," he said. "I'm anxious to get the lay of things upstairs now."

He moved toward the stair door, followed by the two men.

"I suppose anything Mrs. Peters does'll be all right?" the sheriff inquired. "She was to take in some clothes for her, you know—and a few little things. We left in such a hurry yesterday."

The county attorney looked at the two women whom they were leaving alone there among the kitchen things.

"Yes—Mrs. Peters," he said, his glance resting on the woman who was not Mrs. Peters, the big farmer woman who stood behind the sheriff's wife. "Of course Mrs. Peters is one of us," he said, in a manner of entrusting responsibility. "And keep your eye out, Mrs. Peters, for anything that might be of use. No telling; you women might come upon a clue to the motive—and that's the thing we need."

Mr. Hale rubbed his face after the fashion of a showman getting ready for a pleasantry.

"But would the women know a clue if they did come upon it?" he said; and, having delivered himself of this, he followed the others through the stair door.

The women stood motionless and silent, listening to the footsteps, first upon the stairs, then in the room above them.

Then, as if releasing herself from something strange. Mrs. Hale began to arrange the dirty pans under the sink, which the county attorney's disdainful push of the foot had deranged.

"I'd hate to have men comin' into my kitchen," she said testily—"snoopin' round and criticizin'."

"Of course it's no more than their duty," said the sheriff's wife, in her manner of timid acquiescence.

"Duty's all right," replied Mrs. Hale bluffly; "but I guess that deputy sheriff that come out to make the fire might have got a little of this on." She gave the roller towel a pull. "Wish I'd thought of that sooner! Seems mean to talk about her for not having things slicked up, when she had to come away in such a hurry."

She looked around the kitchen. Certainly it was not "slicked up." Her eye was held by a bucket of sugar on a low shelf. The cover was off the wooden bucket, and beside it was a paper bag—half full.

Mrs. Hale moved toward it.

"She was putting this in there," she said to herself—slowly.

She thought of the flour in her kitchen at home—half sifted, half not sifted. She had been interrupted, and had left things half done. What had interrupted Minnie Foster? Why had that work been left half done? She made a move as if to finish it,—unfinished things always bothered her,—and then she glanced around and saw that Mrs. Peters was watching her—and she didn't want Mrs. Peters to get that feeling she had got of work begun and then—for some reason—not finished.

"It's a shame about her fruit," she said, and walked toward the cupboard that the county attorney had opened, and got on the chair, murmuring: "I wonder if it's all gone."

It was a sorry enough looking sight, but "Here's one that's all right," she said at last. She held it toward the light. "This is cherries, too." She looked again. "I declare I believe that's the only one."

With a sigh, she got down from the chair, went to the sink, and wiped off the bottle.

"She'll feel awful bad, after all her hard work in the hot weather. I remember the   115
afternoon I put up my cherries last summer."

She set the bottle on the table, and, with another sigh, started to sit down in the rocker. But she did not sit down. Something kept her from sitting down in that chair. She straightened—stepped back, and, half turned away, stood looking at it, seeing the woman who had sat there "pleatin' at her apron."

The thin voice of the sheriff's wife broke in upon her: "I must be getting those things from the front-room closet." She opened the door into the other room, started in, stepped back. "You coming with me, Mrs. Hale?" she asked nervously. "You—you could help me get them."

They were soon back—the stark coldness of that shut-up room was not a thing to linger in.

"My!" said Mrs. Peters, dropping the things on the table and hurrying to the stove.

Mrs. Hale stood examining the clothes the woman who was being detained in town   120
had said she wanted.

"Wright was close!"° she exclaimed, holding up a shabby black skirt that bore the marks of much making over. "I think maybe that's why she kept so much to herself. I s'pose she felt she couldn't do her part; and then, you don't enjoy things when you feel shabby. She used to wear pretty clothes and be lively—when she was Minnie Foster, one of the town girls, singing in the choir. But that—oh, that was twenty years ago."

With a carefulness in which there was something tender, she folded the shabby clothes and piled them at one corner of the table. She looked up at Mrs. Peters, and there was something in the other woman's look that irritated her.

"She don't care," she said to herself. "Much difference it makes to her whether Minnie Foster had pretty clothes when she was a girl."

Then she looked again, and she wasn't so sure; in fact, she hadn't at any time been perfectly sure about Mrs. Peters. She had that shrinking manner, and yet her eyes looked as if they could see a long way into things.

"This all you was to take in?" asked Mrs. Hale.   125

"No," said the sheriff's wife; "she said she wanted an apron. Funny thing to want," she ventured in her nervous little way, "for there's not much to get you dirty in jail, goodness knows. But I suppose just to make her feel more natural. If you're used to wearing an apron—. She said they were in the bottom drawer of this cupboard. Yes—here they are. And then her little shawl that always hung on the stair door."

She took the small gray shawl from behind the door leading upstairs, and stood a minute looking at it.

---

close: that is, frugal, tightfisted.

Suddenly Mrs. Hale took a quick step toward the other woman.

"Mrs. Peters!"

"Yes, Mrs. Hale?"

130

"Do you think she—did it?"

A frightened look blurred the other thing in Mrs. Peters' eyes.

"Oh, I don't know," she said, in a voice that seemed to shrink away from the subject.

"Well, I don't think she did," affirmed Mrs. Hale stoutly. "Asking for an apron, and her little shawl. Worryin' about her fruit."

"Mr. Peters says—." Footsteps were heard in the room above; she stopped, looked   135
up, then went on in a lowered voice: "Mr. Peters says—it looks bad for her. Mr. Henderson is awful sarcastic in a speech, and he's going to make fun of her saying she didn't—wake up."

For a moment Mrs. Hale had no answer. Then, "Well, I guess John Wright didn't wake up—when they was slippin' that rope under his neck," she muttered.

"No, it's *strange*," breathed Mrs. Peters. "They think it was such a—funny way to kill a man."

She began to laugh; at sound of the laugh, abruptly stopped.

"That's just what Mr. Hale said," said Mrs. Hale, in a resolutely natural voice. "There was a gun in the house. He says that's what he can't understand."

"Mr. Henderson said, coming out, that what was needed for the case was a motive.   140
Something to show anger—or sudden feeling."

"Well, I don't see any signs of anger around here," said Mrs. Hale, "I don't—" She stopped. It was as if her mind tripped on something. Her eye was caught by a dish-towel in the middle of the kitchen table. Slowly she moved toward the table. One half of it was wiped clean, the other half messy. Her eyes made a slow, almost unwilling turn to the bucket of sugar and the half empty bag beside it. Things begun—and not finished.

After a moment she stepped back, and said, in that manner of releasing herself: "Wonder how they're finding things upstairs? I hope she had it a little more red up° up there. You know,"—she paused, and feeling gathered,—"it seems kind of *sneaking*: locking her up in town and coming out here to get her own house to turn against her!"

"But, Mrs. Hale," said the sheriff's wife, "the law is the law."

"I s'pose 'tis," answered Mrs. Hale shortly.   145

She turned to the stove, saying something about that fire not being much to brag of. She worked with it a minute, and when she straightened up she said aggressively:

"The law is the law—and a bad stove is a bad stove. How'd you like to cook on this?"—pointing with the poker to the broken lining. She opened the oven door and started to express her opinion of the oven; but she was swept into her own thoughts, thinking of what it would mean, year after year, to have that stove to wrestle with. The thought of Minnie Foster trying to bake in that oven—and the thought of her never going over to see Minnie Foster—.

She was startled by hearing Mrs. Peters say: "A person gets discouraged—and loses heart."

The sheriff's wife had looked from the stove to the sink—to the pail of water which had been carried in from outside. The two women stood there silent, above them the footsteps of the men who were looking for evidence against the woman who had worked in that kitchen. That look of seeing into things, of seeing through a thing to something else, was in the eyes of the sheriff's wife now. When Mrs. Hale next spoke to her, it was gently:

red up: neat.

"Better loosen up your things, Mrs. Peters. We'll not feel them when we go out."   150

Mrs. Peters went to the back of the room to hang up the fur tippet she was wearing. A moment later she exclaimed, "Why, she was piecing a quilt," and held up a large sewing basket piled high with quilt pieces.

Mrs. Hale spread some of the blocks on the table.

"It's a log-cabin pattern," she said, putting several of them together, "Pretty, isn't it?"

They were so engaged with the quilt that they did not hear the footsteps on the stairs. Just as the stair door opened Mrs. Hale was saying:

"Do you suppose she was going to quilt it or just knot it?"   155

The sheriff threw up his hands.

"They wonder whether she was going to quilt it or just knot it!"

There was a laugh for the ways of women, a warming of hands over the stove, and then the county attorney said briskly:

"Well, let's go right out to the barn and get that cleared up."

"I don't see as there's anything so strange," Mrs. Hale said resentfully, after the out-   160
side door had closed on the three men—"our taking up our time with little things while we're waiting for them to get the evidence. I don't see as it's anything to laugh about."

"Of course they've got awful important things on their minds," said the sheriff's wife apologetically.

They returned to an inspection of the block for the quilt. Mrs. Hale was looking at the fine, even sewing, and preoccupied with thoughts of the woman who had done that sewing, when she heard the sheriff's wife say, in a queer tone:

"Why, look at this one."

She turned to take the block held out to her.

"The sewing," said Mrs. Peters, in a troubled way, "All the rest of them have been so   165
nice and even—but—this one. Why, it looks as if she didn't know what she was about!"

Their eyes met—something flashed to life, passed between them; then, as if with an effort, they seemed to pull away from each other. A moment Mrs. Hale sat there, her hands folded over that sewing which was so unlike all the rest of the sewing. Then she had pulled a knot and drawn the threads.

"Oh, what are you doing, Mrs. Hale?" asked the sheriff's wife, startled.

"Just pulling out a stitch or two that's not sewed very good," said Mrs. Hale mildly.

"I don't think we ought to touch things," Mrs. Peters said, a little helplessly.

"I'll just finish up this end," answered Mrs. Hale, still in that mild, matter-of-fact   170
fashion.

She threaded a needle and started to replace bad sewing with good. For a little while she sewed in silence. Then, in that thin, timid voice, she heard:

"Mrs. Hale!"

"Yes, Mrs. Peters?"

"What do you suppose she was so—nervous about?"

"Oh, *I* don't know," said Mrs. Hale, as if dismissing a thing not important enough   175
to spend much time on. "I don't know as she was—nervous. I sew awful queer sometimes when I'm just tired."

She cut a thread, and out of the corner of her eye looked up at Mrs. Peters. The small, lean face of the sheriff's wife seemed to have tightened up. Her eyes had that look of peering into something. But next moment she moved, and said in her thin, inde-cisive way:

"Well, I must get those clothes wrapped. They may be through sooner than we think. I wonder where I could find a piece of paper—and string."

"In that cupboard, maybe," suggested to Mrs. Hale, after a glance around.

One piece of the crazy sewing remained unripped. Mrs. Peter's back turned, Martha Hale now scrutinized that piece, compared it with the dainty, accurate sewing of the other blocks. The difference was startling. Holding this block made her feel queer, as if the distracted thoughts of the woman who had perhaps turned to it to try and quiet herself were communicating themselves to her.

Mrs. Peters' voice roused her.   180

"Here's a bird-cage," she said. "Did she have a bird, Mrs. Hale?"

"Why, I don't know whether she did or not." She turned to look at the cage Mrs. Peters was holding up. "I've not been here in so long." She sighed. "There was a man round last year selling canaries cheap—but I don't know as she took one. Maybe she did. She used to sing real pretty herself."

Mrs. Peters looked around the kitchen.

"Seems kind of funny to think of a bird here." She half laughed—an attempt to put up a barrier. "But she must have had one—or why would she have a cage? I wonder what happened to it."

"I suppose maybe the cat got it," suggested Mrs. Hale, resuming her sewing.   185

"No; she didn't have a cat. She's got that feeling some people have about cats—being afraid of them. When they brought her to our house yesterday, my cat got in the room, and she was real upset and asked me to take it out."

"My sister Bessie was like that," laughed Mrs. Hale.

The sheriff's wife did not reply. The silence made Mrs. Hale turn round. Mrs. Peters was examining the bird-cage.

"Look at this door," she said slowly. "It's broke. One hinge has been pulled apart."

Mrs. Hale came nearer.   190

"Looks as if someone must have been—rough with it."

Again their eyes met—startled, questioning, apprehensive. For a moment neither spoke nor stirred. Then Mrs. Hale, turning away, said brusquely:

"If they're going to find any evidence, I wish they'd be about it. I don't like this place."

"But I'm awful glad you came with me, Mrs. Hale." Mrs. Peters put the bird-cage on the table and sat down. "It would be lonesome for me—sitting here alone."

"Yes, it would, wouldn't it?" agreed Mrs. Hale, a certain determined naturalness in   195
her voice. She had picked up the sewing, but now it dropped in her lap, and she murmured in a different voice: "But I tell you what I *do* wish, Mrs Peters. I wish I had come over sometimes when she was here. I wish—I had."

"But of course you were awful busy, Mrs. Hale. Your house—and your children."

"I could've come," retorted Mrs. Hale shortly. "I stayed away because it weren't cheerful—and that's why I ought to have come. I"—she looked around—"I've never liked this place. Maybe because it's down in a hollow and you don't see the road. I don't know what it is, but it's a lonesome place, and always was. I wish I had come over to see Minnie Foster sometimes. I can see now—" She did not put it into words.

"Well, you mustn't reproach yourself," counseled Mrs. Peters. "Somehow, we just don't see how it is with other folks till—something comes up."

"Not having children makes less work," mused Mrs. Hale, after a silence, "but it makes a quiet house—and Wright out to work all day—and no company when he did come in. Did you know John Wright, Mrs. Peters?"

"Not to know him. I've seen him in town. They say he was a good man."   200

"Yes—good," conceded John Wright's neighbor grimly. "He didn't drink, and kept his word as well as most, I guess, and paid his debts. But he was a hard man, Mrs. Peters. Just to pass the time of day with him—." She stopped, shivered a little. "Like a raw wind that gets to the bone." Her eye fell upon the cage on the table before her, and she added, almost bitterly: "I should think she would've wanted a bird!"

Suddenly she leaned forward, looking intently at the cage. "But what do you s'pose went wrong with it?"

"I don't know," returned Mrs. Peters; "unless it got sick and died."

But after she said it she reached over and swung the broken door. Both women watched it as if somehow held by it.

"You didn't know—her?" Mrs. Hale asked, a gentler note in her voice.   205

"Not till they brought her yesterday," said the sheriff's wife.

"She—come to think of it, she was kind of like a bird herself. Real sweet and pretty, but kind of timid and—fluttery. How—she—did—change."

That held her for a long time. Finally, as if struck with a happy thought and relieved to get back to everyday things, she exclaimed:

"Tell you what, Mrs. Peters, why don't you take the quilt in with you? It might take up her mind."

"Why, I think that's a real nice idea, Mrs. Hale," agreed the sheriff's wife, as if she   210
too were glad to come into the atmosphere of a simple kindness. "There couldn't possibly be any objection to that, could there? Now, just what will I take? I wonder if her patches are in here—and her things?"

They turned to the sewing basket.

"Here's some red," said Mrs. Hale, bringing out a roll of cloth. Underneath that was a box. "Here, maybe her scissors are in here—and her things." She held it up. "What a pretty box! I'll warrant that was something she had a long time ago—when she was a girl."

She held it in her hand a moment; then, with a little sigh, opened it.

Instantly her hand went to her nose.

"Why—!"   215

Mrs. Peters drew nearer—then turned away.

"There's something wrapped up in this piece of silk," faltered Mrs. Hale.

"This isn't her scissors," said Mrs. Peters, in a shrinking voice.

Her hand not steady, Mrs. Hale raised the piece of silk. "Oh, Mrs. Peters!" she cried. "It's—"

Mrs. Peters bent closer.   220

"It's the bird," she whispered.

"But, Mrs. Peters!" cried Mrs. Hale. "*Look* at it! Its *neck*—look at its neck! It's all—other side *to*."

She held the box away from her.

The sheriff's wife again bent closer.

"Somebody wrung its neck," said she, in a voice that was slow and deep.   225

And then again the eyes of the two women met—this time clung together in a look of dawning comprehension, of growing horror. Mrs. Peters looked from the dead bird to the broken door of the cage. Again their eyes met. And just then there was a sound at the outside door.

Mrs. Hale slipped the box under the quilt pieces in the basket, and sank into the chair before it. Mrs. Peters stood holding to the table. The county attorney and the sheriff came in from outside.

"Well, ladies," said the county attorney, as one turning from serious things to little pleasantries, "have you decided whether she was going to quilt it or knot it?"

"We think," began the sheriff's wife in a flurried voice, "that she was going to— knot it."

He was too preoccupied to notice the change that came in her voice on that last.   230

"Well, that's very interesting, I'm sure," he said tolerantly. He caught sight of the bird-cage. "Has the bird flown?"

"We think the cat got it," said Mrs. Hale in a voice curiously even.

He was walking up and down, as if thinking something out.

"Is there a cat?" he asked absently.

Mrs. Hale shot a look up at the sheriff's wife.   235

"Well, not *now*," said Mrs. Peters. "They're superstitious, you know; they leave."

She sank into her chair.

The county attorney did not heed her. "No sign at all of anyone having come in from the outside," he said to Peters, in the manner of continuing an interrupted conversation. "Their own rope. Now let's go upstairs again and go over it, piece by piece. It would have to have been someone who knew just the—"

The stair door closed behind them and their voices were lost.

The two women sat motionless, not looking at each other, but as if peering into   240
something and at the same time holding back. When they spoke now it was as if they were afraid of what they were saying, but as if they could not help saying it.

"She liked the bird," said Martha Hale, low and slowly. "She was going to bury it in that pretty box."

"When I was a girl," said Mrs. Peters, under her breath, "my kitten—there was a boy took a hatchet, and before my eyes—before I could get there—" She covered her face an instant. "If they hadn't held me back I would have"—she caught herself, looked upstairs where footsteps were heard, and finished weakly—"hurt him."

Then they sat without speaking or moving.

"I wonder how it would seem," Mrs. Hale at last began, as if feeling her way over strange ground—"never to have had any children around?" Her eyes made a slow sweep of the kitchen, as if seeing what that kitchen had meant through all the years. "No, Wright wouldn't like the bird," she said after that—"a thing that sang. She used to sing. He killed that too." Her voice tightened.

Mrs. Peters moved uneasily.   245

"Of course we don't know who killed the bird."

"I knew John Wright," was Mrs. Hale's answer.

"It was an awful thing was done in this house that night, Mrs. Hale," said the sheriff's wife. "Killing a man while he slept—slipping a thing round his neck that choked the life out of him."

Mrs. Hale's hand went out to the bird cage.

"His neck. Choked the life out of him."   250

"We don't *know* who killed him," whispered Mrs. Peters wildly. "We don't *know*."

Mrs. Hale had not moved. "If there had been years and years of—nothing, then a bird to sing to you, it would be awful—still—after the bird was still."

It was as if something within her not herself had spoken, and it found in Mrs. Peters something she did not know as herself.

"I know what stillness is," she said, in a queer, monotonous voice. "When we homesteaded in Dakota, and my first baby died—after he was two years old—and me with no other then—"

Mrs. Hale stirred.   255

"How soon do you suppose they'll be through looking for the evidence?"

"I know what stillness is," repeated Mrs. Peters, in just that same way. Then she too pulled back. "The law has got to punish crime, Mrs. Hale," she said in her tight little way.

"I wish you'd seen Minnie Foster," was the answer, "when she wore a white dress with blue ribbons, and stood up there in the choir and sang."

The picture of that girl, the fact that she had lived neighbor to that girl for twenty years, and had let her die for lack of life, was suddenly more than she could bear.

"Oh, I *wish* I'd come over here once in a while!" she cried. "That was a crime! 260 Who's going to punish that?"

"We mustn't take on," said Mrs. Peters, with a frightened look toward the stairs.

"I might 'a' *known* she needed help! I tell you, it's *queer*, Mrs. Peters. We live close together, and we live far apart. We all go through the same things—it's all just a different kind of the same thing! If it weren't—why do you and I *understand?* Why do we *know*—what we know this minute?"

She dashed her hand across her eyes. Then, seeing the jar of fruit on the table, she reached for it and choked out:

"If I was you I wouldn't *tell* her her fruit was gone! Tell her it *ain't.* Tell her it's all right—all of it. Here—take this in to prove it to her! She—she may never know whether it was broke or not."

She turned away. 265

Mrs. Peters reached out for the bottle of fruit as if she were glad to take it—as if touching a familiar thing, having something to do, could keep her from something else. She got up, looked about for something to wrap the fruit in, took a petticoat from the pile of clothes she had brought from the front room, and nervously started winding that round the bottle.

"My!" she began, in a high; false voice, "it's a good thing the men couldn't hear us! Getting all stirred up over a little thing like a—dead canary." She hurried over that. "As if that could have anything to do with—with—My, wouldn't they *laugh?*"

Footsteps were heard on the stairs.

"Maybe they would," muttered Mrs. Hale—"maybe they wouldn't."

"No, Peters," said the county attorney incisively; "it's all perfectly clear, except the 270 reason for doing it. But you know juries when it comes to women. If there was some definite thing—something to show. Something to make a story about. A thing that would connect up with this clumsy way of doing it."

In a covert way Mrs. Hale looked at Mrs. Peters. Mrs. Peters was looking at her. Quickly they looked away from each other. The outer door opened and Mr. Hale came in.

"I've got the team° round now," he said. "Pretty cold out there."

"I'm going to stay here awhile by myself," the county attorney suddenly announced. "You can send Frank out for me, can't you?" he asked the sheriff. "I want to go over everything. I'm not satisfied we can't do better."

Again, for one brief moment, the two women's eyes found one another.

The sheriff came up to the table. 275

"Did you want to see what Mrs. Peters was going to take in?"

The county attorney picked up the apron. He laughed.

"Oh, I guess they're not very dangerous things the ladies have picked out."

Mrs. Hale's hand was on the sewing basket in which the box was concealed. She felt that she ought to take her hand off the basket. She did not seem able to. He picked up one of the quilt blocks which she had piled on to cover the box. Her eyes felt like fire. She had a feeling that if he took up the basket she would snatch it from him.

---

team: team of horses pulling the buggy in which the group had come.

But he did not take it up. With another little laugh, he turned away, saying: 280

"No; Mrs. Peters doesn't need supervising. For that matter, a sheriff's wife is married to the law. Ever think of it that way, Mrs. Peters?"

Mrs. Peters was standing beside the table. Mrs. Hale shot a look up at her; but she could not see her face. Mrs. Peters had turned away. When she spoke, her voice was muffled.

"Not—just that way," she said.

"Married to the law!" chuckled Mrs. Peters' husband. He moved toward the door into the front room, and said to the county attorney:

"I just want you to come in here a minute, George. We ought to take a look at these   285
windows."

"Oh—windows," said the county attorney scoffingly.

"We'll be right out, Mr. Hale," said the sheriff to the farmer, who was still waiting by the door.

Hale went to look after the horses. The sheriff followed the county attorney into the other room. Again—for one final moment—the two women were alone in that kitchen.

Martha Hale sprang up, her hands tight together, looking at that other woman, with whom it rested. At first she could not see her eyes, for the sheriff's wife had not turned back since she turned away at that suggestion of being married to the law. But now Mrs. Hale made her turn back. Her eyes made her turn back. Slowly, unwillingly, Mrs. Peters turned her head until her eyes met the eyes of the other woman. There was a moment when they held each other in a steady, burning look in which there was no evasion nor flinching. Then Martha Hale's eyes pointed the way to the basket in which was hidden the thing that would make certain the conviction of the other woman—that woman who was not there and yet who had been there with them all through that hour.

For a moment Mrs. Peters did not move. And then she did it. With a rush forward,   290
she threw back the quilt pieces, got the box, tried to put it in her handbag. It was too big. Desperately she opened it, started to take the bird out. But there she broke—she could not touch the bird. She stood there helpless, foolish.

There was the sound of a knob turning in the inner door. Martha Hale snatched the box from the sheriff's wife, and got it in the pocket of her big coat just as the sheriff and the county attorney came back into the kitchen.

"Well, Henry," said the county attorney facetiously, "at least we found out that she was not going to quilt it. She was going to—what is it you call it, ladies?"

Mrs. Hale's hand was against the pocket of her coat.

"We call it—knot it, Mr. Henderson."

QUESTIONS

1. Who is the central character? That is, on whom does the story focus?

2. Describe the differences between Mrs. Hale and Mrs. Peters, in terms of their status, backgrounds, and comparative strengths of character.

3. Why do the two women not voice their conclusions about the murderer? How does Glaspell show that they both know the murderer's identity, the reasons, and the method? Why do they both "cover up" at the story's conclusion?

JOYCE CAROL OATES (b. 1938)

An astoundingly productive and richly acclaimed author of more than twenty novels and many collections of stories and books of poems, Joyce Carol Oates received her education at Syracuse University and the University of Wisconsin. She began her teaching career at the University of Detroit and currently, in addition to various guest positions, is Distinguished Professor in the Humanities at Princeton University. Some of her many novels are With Shuddering Fall *(1964),* Angel of Light *(1981),* Solstice *(1985),* Foxfire *(1993), and* Middle Age: A Romance *(2001).*
A recent story collection is Faithless: Tales of Transgression *(2001). Among her many awards are a Guggenheim Fellowship, the Continuing Achievement Award of the O. Henry Award Prize Stories series, a National Book Award, and the Lotos Club Award of Merit. "Shopping" is taken from* Heat and Other Stories *(1991).*

Shopping ~~~~~~ *1991*

An old ritual, Saturday morning shopping. Mother and daughter. Mrs. Dietrich and Nola. Shops in the village, stores and boutiques at the splendid Livingstone Mall on Route 12: Bloomingdale's, Saks, Lord & Taylor, Bonwit's, Neiman-Marcus, and the rest. Mrs. Dietrich would know her way around the stores blindfolded but there is always the surprise of lavish seasonal displays, extraordinary holiday sales, the openings of new stores at the mall like Laura Ashley, Paraphernalia. On one of their mall days Mrs. Dietrich and Nola would try to get there at midmorning, have lunch around 1 P.M. at one or another of their favorite restaurants, shop for perhaps an hour after lunch, then come home. Sometimes the shopping trips were more successful than at other times, but you have to have faith, Mrs. Dietrich tells herself. Her interior voice is calm, neutral, free of irony. Even since her divorce her interior voice has been free of irony. You have to have faith.

Tomorrow morning Nola returns to school in Maine; today will be spent at the mall. Mrs. Dietrich has planned it for days—there are numerous things Nola needs, mainly clothes, a pair of good shoes; Mrs. Dietrich must buy a birthday present for one of her aunts; mother and daughter need the time together. At the mall, in such crowds of shoppers, moments of intimacy are possible as they rarely are at home. (Seventeen-year-old Nola, home on spring break for a brief eight days, seems always to be *busy*, always out with her *friends*, the trip to the mall has been postponed twice.) But Saturday, 10:30 A.M., they are in the car at last headed south on Route 12, a bleak March morning following a night of freezing rain; there's a metallic cast to the air and no sun anywhere in the sky but the light hurts Mrs. Dietrich's eyes just the same. "Does it seem as if spring will ever come? It must be twenty degrees colder up in Maine," she says. Driving in heavy traffic always makes Mrs. Dietrich nervous and she is overly sensitive to her daughter's silence, which seems deliberate, perverse, when they have so little time remaining together—not even a full day.

Nola asks politely if Mrs. Dietrich would like her to drive and Mrs. Dietrich says no, of course not, she's fine, it's only a few more miles and maybe traffic will lighten. Nola seems about to say something more, then thinks better of it. So much between them is precarious, chancy—but they've been kind to each other these past seven days. Nola's secrets remain her own and Mrs. Dietrich isn't going to pry; she's beyond that. She loves Nola with a fierce unreasoned passion stronger than any she felt for the man who had been her husband for thirteen years, certainly far stronger than any she ever felt for her own mother. Sometimes in weak despondent moods, alone, lonely, self-pitying, when she has had too much to drink, Mrs. Dietrich thinks she is in love with her daughter, but this is a thought she can't contemplate for long. And how Nola would snort in amused contempt, incredulous, mocking—"Oh, *Mother!*"—if she were told.

("Why do you make so much of things? Of people who don't seem to care about you?" Mr. Dietrich once asked. He had been speaking of one or another of their Livingstone friends, a woman in Mrs. Dietrich's circle; he hadn't meant to be insulting but Mrs. Dietrich was stung as if he'd slapped her.)

Mrs. Dietrich tries to engage her daughter in conversation of a harmless sort but 5
Nola answers in monosyllables; Nola is rather tired from so many nights of partying with her friends, some of whom attend the local high school, some of whom are home for spring break from prep schools—Exeter, Lawrenceville, Concord, Andover, Portland. Late nights, but Mrs. Dietrich doesn't consciously lie awake waiting for Nola to come home; they've been through all that before. Now Nola sits beside her mother looking wan, subdued, rather melancholy. Thinking her private thoughts. She is wearing a bulky quilted jacket Mrs. Dietrich has never liked, the usual blue jeans, black calfskin boots zippered tightly to mid-calf. Her delicate profile, thick-lashed eyes. Mrs. Dietrich must resist the temptation to ask, Why are you so quiet, Nola? What are you thinking? They've been through all that before.

Route 12 has become a jumble of small industrial parks, high-rise office and apartment buildings, torn-up landscapes: mountains of raw earth, uprooted trees, ruts and ditches filled with muddy water. Everywhere are yellow bulldozers, earth-movers, construction workers operating cranes, ACREAGE FOR SALE signs. When Mr. and Mrs. Dietrich first moved out to Livingstone from the city sixteen years ago this strength along Route 12 was quite attractive, mainly farmland, woods, a scattering of small suburban houses; now it has nearly all been developed. There is no natural sequence to what you see—buildings, construction work, leveled woods, the lavish grounds owned by Squibb. Though she has driven this route countless times, Mrs. Dietrich is never quite certain where the mall is and must be prepared for a sudden exit. She remembers getting lost the first several times, remembers the excitement she and her friends felt about the grand opening of the mall, stores worthy of serious shopping at last. Today is much the same. No, today is worse. Like Christmas when she was a small child, Mrs. Dietrich thinks. She'd hoped so badly to be happy she'd felt actual pain, a constriction in her throat like crying.

"*Are* you all right, Nola? You've been so quiet all morning," Mrs. Dietrich asks, half scolding. Nola stirs from her reverie, says she's fine, a just perceptible edge to her reply, and for the remainder of the drive there's some stiffness between them. Mrs. Dietrich chooses to ignore it. In any case she is fully absorbed in driving—negotiating a tricky exit across two lanes of traffic, then the hairpin curve of the ramp, the numerous looping drives of the mall. Then the enormous parking lot, daunting to the inexperienced, but Mrs. Dietrich always heads for the area behind Lord & Taylor on the far side of the mall, Lot D; her luck holds and she finds a space close in. "Well, we made it," she says, smiling happily at Nola. Nola laughs in reply—what does a seventeen-year-old's laughter *mean?*—*but* she remembers, getting out, to lock both doors on her side of the car. Even here at the Livingstone Mall unattended cars are no longer safe. The smile Nola gives Mrs. Dietrich across the car's roof is careless and beautiful and takes Mrs. Dietrich's breath away.

The March morning tastes of grit with an undercurrent of something acrid, chemical; inside the mall, beneath the first of the elegant brass-buttressed glass domes, the air is fresh and tonic, circulating from invisible vents. The mall is crowded, rather noisy—it *is* Saturday morning—but a feast for the eyes after that long trip on Route 12. Tall slender trees grow out of the mosaic-tiled pavement; there are beds of Easter lilies, daffodils, jonquils, tulips of all colors. There are cobblestone walkways, fountains illuminated from within, wide promenades as in an Old World setting. Mrs. Dietrich smiles with relief. She senses that Nola too is relieved, cheered. It's like coming home.

The shopping excursions began when Nola was a small child but did not acquire their special significance until she was twelve or thirteen years old and capable of serious, sustained shopping with her mother. Sometimes Mrs. Dietrich and Nola would shop with friends, another mother and daughter perhaps, sometimes Mrs. Dietrich invited one or two of Nola's school friends to join them, but she preferred to be alone with Nola and she believed Nola preferred to be alone with her. This was about the time when Mr. Dietrich moved out of the house and back into their old apartment building in the city—a separation, he'd called it initially, to give them perspective, though Mrs. Dietrich had no illusions about what "perspective" would turn out to entail—so the shopping trips were all the more significant. Not that Mrs. Dietrich and Nola spent very much money; they really didn't, *really* they didn't, when compared to friends and neighbors. And Mr. Dietrich rarely objected: the financial arrangement he made with Mrs. Dietrich was surprisingly generous.

At seventeen Nola is shrewd and discerning as a shopper, not easy to please, knowledgeable as a mature woman about certain aspects of fashion, quality merchandise, good stores. She studies advertisements, she shops for bargains. Her closets, like Mrs. Dietrich's, are crammed, but she rarely buys anything that Mrs. Dietrich thinks shoddy or merely faddish. Up in Portland, at the academy, she hasn't as much time to shop, but when she is home in Livingstone it isn't unusual for her and her girlfriends to shop nearly every day. Sometimes she shops at the mall with a boyfriend—but she prefers girls. Like all her friends she has charge accounts at the better stores, her own credit cards, a reasonable allowance. At the time of their settlement Mr. Dietrich said guiltily that it was the least he could do for them: if Mrs. Dietrich wanted to work part-time, she could (she was trained, more or less, in public relations of a small-scale sort); if not, not. Mrs. Dietrich thought, It's the most you can do for us too.

Near Baumgarten's entrance mother and daughter see a disheveled woman sitting by herself on one of the benches. Without seeming to look at her, shoppers are making a discreet berth around her, a stream following a natural course. Nola, taken by surprise, stares. Mrs. Dietrich has seen the woman from time to time at the mall, always alone, smirking and talking to herself, frizzed gray hair in a tangle, puckered mouth. Always wearing the same black wool coat, a garment of fairly good quality but shapeless, rumpled, stained, as if she sleeps in it. She might be anywhere from forty to sixty years of age. Once Mrs. Dietrich saw her make menacing gestures at children who were teasing her, another time she'd seen the woman staring belligerently at *her*. A white paste had gathered in the corners of her mouth.

"My God, that poor woman," Nola says. "I didn't think there were people like her here—I mean, I didn't think they would allow it."

"She doesn't seem to cause any disturbance," Mrs. Dietrich says. "She just sits. Don't stare, Nola, she'll see you."

"You've seen her here before? Here?"

"A few times this winter."

"Is she always like that?"

"I'm sure she's harmless, Nola. She just *sits*."

Nola is incensed, her pale blue eyes like washed glass. "I'm sure *she's* harmless, Mother. It's the harm the poor woman has to endure that is the tragedy."

Mrs. Dietrich is surprised and a little offended by her daughter's passionate tone but she knows enough not to argue. They enter Baumgarten's, taking their habitual route. So many shoppers! So much merchandise! Dazzling displays of tulips, chrome, neon, winking lights, enormous painted Easter eggs in wicker baskets. Nola speaks of the tragedy of women like that woman—the tragedy of the homeless, the mentally disturbed: bag ladies out on the street, outcasts of an affluent society—but she's soon distracted by the busyness on all sides, the attractive items for sale. They take the escalator up to the third floor, to the Clubhouse Juniors department, where Nola often buys things. From there they will move on to Young Collector, then to Act IV, then to Petite Corner, then one or another boutique and designer—Liz Claiborne, Christian Dior, Calvin Klein, Carlos Falchi, and the rest. And after Baumgarten's the other stores await, to be visited each in turn. Mrs. Dietrich checks her watch and sees with satisfaction that there's just enough time before lunch but not *too* much time. She gets ravenously hungry, shopping at the mall.

Nola is efficient and matter-of-fact about shopping, though she acts solely upon in-   20
stinct. Mrs. Dietrich likes to watch her at a short distance, holding items of clothing up to herself in the three-way mirrors, modeling things she thinks especially promising. A twill blazer, a dress with rounded shoulders and blouson jacket, a funky zippered jumpsuit in white sailcloth, a pair of straight-leg Evan Picone pants, a green leather vest: Mrs. Diet-rich watches her covertly. At such times Nola is perfectly content, fully absorbed in the task at hand; Mrs. Dietrich knows she isn't thinking about anything that would distress her. (Like Mr. Dietrich's betrayal. Like Nola's difficulties with her friends. Like her diffi-culties at school—as much as Mrs. Dietrich knows of them.) When Nola glances in her mother's direction Mrs. Dietrich pretends to be examining clothes for her own purposes. As if she's hardly aware of Nola. Once, at the mall, perhaps in this very store in this very department, Nola saw Mrs. Dietrich watching her and walked away angrily, and when Mrs. Dietrich caught up with her she said, "I can't stand it, Mother." Her voice was choked and harsh, a vein prominent in her forehead. "Let me go. For Christ's sake will you let me go." Mrs. Dietrich didn't dare touch her though she could see Nola was trem-bling. For a long terrible moment mother and daughter stood side by side near a display of bright brash Catalina beachwear while Nola whispered, "Let me go. *Let me go.*" How the scene ended Mrs. Dietrich can't recall—it erupts in an explosion of light, like a bad dream—but she knows better than to risk it again.

Difficult to believe that girl standing so poised and self-assured in front of the three-way mirror was once a plain, rather chunky, unhappy child. She'd been unpopular at school. Overly serious. Anxious. Quick to tears. Aged eleven she hid herself away in her room for hours at a time, reading, drawing pictures, writing little stories she could some-times be prevailed upon to read aloud to her mother, sometimes even to her father, though she dreaded his judgment. She went through a "scientific" phase a little later; Mrs. Dietrich remembers an ambitious bas-relief map of North America, meticulous il-lustrations for "photosynthesis," a pastel drawing of an eerie ball of fire labeled RED GIANT (a dying star?), which won a prize in a state competition for junior high students. Then for a season it was stray facts Nola confronted them with, often at the dinner table. Interrupting her parents' conversation to say brightly, "Did you know that Nero's favorite color was green? He carried a giant emerald and held it up to his eye to watch Christians being devoured by lions." And, "Did you ever hear of the raving ghosts of Siberia, with their mouths always open, starving for food, screaming?" And once at a large family gath-ering, "Did you all know that last week downtown a little baby's nose was chewed off by rats in his crib—a little *black* baby?" Nola meant only to call attention to herself, but you couldn't blame her listeners for being offended. They stared at her, not knowing what to say. What a strange child! What queer glassy-pale eyes! Mr. Dietrich told her curtly to leave the table; he'd had enough of the game she was playing and so had everyone else.

Nola stared at him, her eyes filling with tears. Game?

When they were alone Mr. Dietrich said angrily to Mrs. Dietrich, "Can't you control her in front of other people, at least?" Mrs. Dietrich was angry, too, and frightened. She said, "I *try*."

They sent her off aged fourteen to the Portland Academy up in Maine, and without their help she matured into a girl of considerable beauty. A heart-shaped face, delicate features, glossy red-brown hair scissor-cut to her shoulders. Five feet seven inches tall weighing less than one hundred pounds, the result of constant savage dieting. (Mrs. Dietrich, who has weight problems herself, doesn't dare inquire as to details. They've been through that already.) All the girls sport flat bellies, flat buttocks, jutting pelvic bones. Many, like Nola, are wound tight, high-strung as pedigreed dogs, whippets for instance, the breed that lives for running. Thirty days after they'd left her at the Portland Academy, Nola telephoned home at 11 P.M. one Sunday giggly and high, telling Mrs. Dietrich she adored the school she adored her suite-mates she adored most of her teachers particularly her riding instructor Tern, Tern the Terrier they called the woman because she was so fierce, such a character, eyes that bore right through your skull, wore belts with the most amazing silver buckles! Nola loved Tern but she wasn't *in* love—there's a difference!

Mrs. Dietrich broke down weeping, *that* time.   25

Now of course Nola has boyfriends. Mrs. Dietrich has long since given up trying to keep track of their names. And, in any case, the Paul of this spring isn't necessarily the Paul of last November, nor are all the boys necessarily students at the academy. There is even one "boy"—or young man—who seems to be married: who seems to be, in fact, one of the junior instructors at the school. (Mrs. Dietrich does not eavesdrop on her daughter's telephone conversations but there are things she cannot help overhearing.) Is your daughter on the pill? the women in Mrs. Dietrich's circle asked one another for awhile, guiltily, surreptitiously. Now they no longer ask.

But Nola has announced recently that she loathes boys—she's fed up.

She's never going to get married. She'll study languages in college, French, Italian, something exotic like Arabic, go to work for the American foreign service. Unless she drops out of school altogether to become a model.

"Do you think I'm too fat, Mother?" she asks frequently, worriedly, standing in front of the mirror, twisted at the waist to reveal her small round belly which, it seems, can't help being round: she bloats herself on diet Cokes all day long. "Do you think it *shows*?"

When Mrs. Dietrich was pregnant with Nola she'd been twenty-nine years old and   30
she and Mr. Dietrich had tried to have a baby for nearly five years. She'd lost hope, begun to despise herself; then suddenly it happened: like grace. Like happiness swelling so powerfully it can barely be contained. I can hear its heartbeat! her husband exclaimed. He'd been her lover then, young, vigorous, dreamy. Caressing the rock-hard belly, splendid white tight-stretched skin, that roundness like a warm pulsing melon. Never before so happy, and never since. Husband and wife. One flesh. Mr. Dietrich gave Mrs. Dietrich a reproduction on stiff glossy paper of Dante Gabriel Rossetti's *Beata Beatrix*, embarrassed, apologetic, knowing it was sentimental and perhaps a little silly but that was how he thought of her—so beautiful, rapturous, pregnant with their child. Her features were ordinarily pretty, her wavy brown hair cut short; Mrs. Dietrich looked nothing like the extraordinary woman in Rossetti's painting in her transport of ecstasy but she was immensely flattered and moved by her husband's gift, knowing herself adored, worthy of adoration. She told no one, but she knew the baby was to be a girl. It would be herself again, reborn and this time perfect.

Not until years later did she learn by chance that the woman in Rossetti's painting was in fact his dead wife Lizzy Siddal, who had killed herself with an overdose of laudanum after the stillbirth of their only child.

"Oh, Mother, isn't it *beautiful!*" Nola exclaims.

It is past noon. Past twelve-thirty. Mrs. Dietrich and Nola have made the rounds of a half dozen stores, traveled countless escalators, one clothing department has blended into the next and the chic smiling saleswomen have become indistinguishable, and Mrs. Dietrich is beginning to feel the urgent need for a glass of white wine. Just a glass. "Isn't it beautiful? It's *perfect*," Nola says. Her eyes glow with pleasure, her smooth skin is radiant. Modeling in the three-way mirror a queer little yellow-and-black striped sweater with a ribbed waist, punk style, mock cheap (though the sweater by Sergio Valente, even "drastically reduced," is certainly not cheap), Mrs. Dietrich feels the motherly obligation to register a mild protest, knowing Nola will not hear. She must have it and will have it. She'll wear it a few times, then retire it to the bottom of a drawer with so many other novelty sweaters, accumulated since sixth grade. (She's like her mother in that regard—can't bear to throw anything away. Clothes, shoes, cosmetics, records; once bought by Nola Dietrich they are hers forever, crammed in drawers and closets.)

"*Isn't* it beautiful?" Nola demands, studying her reflection in the mirror.

Mrs. Dietrich pays for the sweater on her charge account.   35

Next they buy Nola a good pair of shoes. And a handbag to go with them. In Paraphernalia where rock music blasts overhead and Mrs. Dietrich stands to one side, rather miserable, Nola chats companionably with two girls—tall, pretty, cutely made up—she'd gone to public school in Livingstone with. She says afterward with an upward rolling of her eyes, "God, I was afraid they'd latch onto us!" Mrs. Dietrich has seen women friends and acquaintances of her own in the mall this morning but has shrunk from being noticed, not wanting to share her daughter with anyone. She has a sense of time passing ever more swiftly, cruelly.

Nola wants to try on an outfit in Paraphernalia, just for fun, a boxy khaki-colored jacket with matching pants, fly front, zippers, oversized buttons, so aggressively ugly it must be chic, yes of course it *is* chic, "drastically reduced" from $245 to $219. An import by Julio Vicente and Mrs. Dietrich can't reasonably disapprove of Julio Vicente, can she. She watches Nola preening in the mirror, watches other shoppers watching her. My daughter. Mine. But of course there is no connection between them, they don't even resemble each other. A seventeen-year-old, a forty-seven-year-old. When Nola is away she seems to forget her mother entirely—doesn't telephone, certainly doesn't write. It's the way all their daughters are, Mrs. Dietrich's friends tell her. It doesn't *mean* anything. Mrs. Dietrich thinks how when she was carrying Nola, those nine long months, they'd been completely happy—not an instant's doubt or hesitation. The singular weight of the body. A state like trance you are tempted to mistake for happiness because the body is incapable of thinking, therefore incapable of anticipating change. Hot rhythmic blood, organs packed tight and moist, the baby upside down in her sac in her mother's belly, always present tense, always *now*. It was a shock when the end came so abruptly, but everyone told Mrs. Dietrich she was a natural mother, praised and pampered her. For a while. Then of course she'd had her baby, her Nola. Even now Mrs. Dietrich can't really comprehend the experience. *Giving birth. Had a baby. Was born.* Mere words, absurdly inadequate. She knows no more of how love ends than she knew as a child, she knows only of how love begins—in the belly, in the womb, where it is always present tense.

The morning's shopping has been quite successful, but lunch at La Crêperie doesn't go well. For some reason—surely there can be no reason?—lunch doesn't go well at all.

La Crêperie is Nola's favorite mall restaurant, always amiably crowded, bustling, a simulated sidewalk cafe with red-striped umbrellas, wrought-iron tables and chairs, menus in French, music piped in overhead. Mrs. Dietrich's nerves are chafed by the pretense of gaiety, the noise, the openness onto one of the mall's busy promenades where at any minute a familiar face might emerge, but she is grateful for her glass of chilled white wine—isn't it red wine that gives you headaches, hangovers?—white wine is safe. She orders a small tossed salad and a creamed chicken crepe and devours it hungrily—she *is* hungry—while Nola picks at her seafood crepe with a disdainful look. A familiar scene: mother watching while daughter pushes food around on her plate. Suddenly Nola is tense, moody, corners of her mouth downturned. Mrs. Dietrich wants to ask, What's wrong? She wants to ask, Why are you unhappy? She wants to smooth Nola's hair back from her forehead, check to see if her forehead is overly warm, wants to hug her close, hard. Why, why? What did I do wrong? Why do you hate me?

Calling the Portland Academy a few weeks ago Mrs. Dietrich suddenly lost control,   40
began crying. She hadn't been drinking and she hadn't known she was upset. A girl unknown to her, one of Nola's suitemates, was saying, "Please, Mrs. Dietrich, it's all right, I'm sure Nola will call you back later tonight—or tomorrow, Mrs. Dietrich? I'll tell her you called, all right, Mrs. Dietrich?" as embarrassed as if Mrs. Dietrich had been her own mother.

How love begins. How love ends.

Mrs. Dietrich orders a third glass of wine. This is a celebration of sorts, isn't it? Their last shopping trip for a long time. But Nola resists, Nola isn't sentimental. In casual defiance of Mrs. Dietrich she lights up a cigarette—yes, Mother, Nola has said ironically, since you stopped smoking *everybody* is supposed to stop—and sits with her arms crossed, watching streams of shoppers pass. Mrs. Dietrich speaks lightly of practical matters, tomorrow morning's drive to the airport and will Nola telephone when she gets to Portland to let Mrs. Dietrich know she has arrived safely? La Crêperie opens onto an atrium three stories high, vast, airy, lit with artificial sunlight, tastefully decorated with trees, potted spring flowers, a fountain, a gigantic white Easter bunny, cleverly mechanized, atop a nest of brightly painted wooden eggs. The bunny has an animated tail, an animated nose; paws, ears, eyes that move. Children stand watching it, screaming with excitement, delight. Mrs. Dietrich notes that Nola's expression is one of faint contempt and says, "It is noisy here, isn't it?"

"Little kids have all the fun," Nola says.

Then with no warning—though of course she'd been planning this all along—Nola brings up the subject of a semester in France, in Paris and Rouen, the fall semester of her senior year it would be; she has put in her application, she says, and is waiting to hear if she's been accepted. She smokes her cigarette calmly, expelling smoke from her nostrils in a way Mrs. Dietrich thinks particularly coarse. Mrs. Dietrich, who believed that particular topic was finished, takes care to speak without emotion. "I just don't think it's a very practical idea right now, Nola," she says. "We've been through it, haven't we? I—"

"I'm going," Nola says.   45

"The extra expense, for one thing. Your father—"

"If I get accepted, I'm going."

"Your father—"

"The hell with him too."

Mrs. Dietrich would like to slap her daughter's face. Bring tears to those steely eyes.   50
But she sits stiff, turning her wineglass between her fingers, patient, calm; she's heard all this before; she says, "Surely this isn't the best time to discuss it, Nola."

Mrs. Dietrich is afraid her daughter will leave the restaurant, simply walk away; that has happened before and if it happens today she doesn't know what she will do. But Nola sits unmoving, her face closed, impassive. Mrs. Dietrich feels her quickened heartbeat. It's like seeing your own life whirling in a sink, in a drain, one of those terrible dreams in which you're paralyzed—the terror of losing her daughter. Once after one of their quarrels Mrs. Dietrich told a friend of hers, the mother too of a teenaged daughter, "I just don't know her any longer; how can you keep living with someone you don't know?" and the woman said, "Eventually you can't."

Nola says, not looking at Mrs. Dietrich, "Why don't we talk about it, Mother."

"Talk about what?" Mrs. Dietrich asks.

"You know."

"The semester in France? Again?"   55

"No."

"What then?"

"You *know*."

"I don't know, really. Really!" Mrs. Dietrich smiles, baffled. She feels the corners of her eyes pucker white with strain.

Nola says, sighing, "How exhausting it is."   60

"How *what*?"

"How exhausting it is."

"What is?"

"You and me."

"What?"   65

"Being together."

"Being together how?"

"The two of us, like this—"

"But we're hardly ever together, Nola," Mrs. Dietrich says.

Her expression is calm but her voice is shaking. Nola turns away, covering her face   70
with a hand; for a moment she looks years older than her age—in fact exhausted. Mrs. Dietrich sees with pity that her daughter's skin is fair and thin and dry—unlike her own, which tends to be oily—it will wear out before she's forty. Mrs. Dietrich reaches over to squeeze her hand. The fingers are limp, ungiving. "You're going back to school tomorrow, Nola," she says. "You won't come home again until June twelfth. And you probably will go to France—if your father consents."

Nola gets to her feet, drops her cigarette to the flagstone terrace, and grinds it out beneath her boot. A dirty thing to do, Mrs. Dietrich thinks, considering there's an ashtray right on the table, but she says nothing. She dislikes La Crêperie anyway.

Nola laughs, showing her lovely white teeth. "Oh, the hell with him," she says. "Fuck Daddy, right?"

They separate for an hour, Mrs. Dietrich to Neiman-Marcus to buy a birthday gift for her elderly aunt, Nola to the trendy new boutique Pour Vous. By the time Mrs. Dietrich rejoins her daughter she's quite angry, blood beating hot and hard and measured in resentment; she has had time to relive old quarrels between them, old exchanges, stray humiliating memories of her marriage as well; these last-hour disagreements are the cruelest and they are Nola's specialty. She locates Nola in the rear of the boutique amid blaring rock music, flashing neon lights, chrome-edged mirrors, her face still hard, closed, prim, pale. She stands beside another teenaged girl, looking in a desultory way through a rack of blouses, shoving the hangers roughly along, taking no care when a blouse falls to the floor. Mrs. Dietrich remembers seeing Nola slip a pair of panty hose into her purse in a village shop because, she said afterward, the saleswoman was so damned slow coming to wait on her; fortunately Mrs. Dietrich was there, took the panty hose right out, and replaced it on the counter. No big deal, Mother, Nola said, don't have a stroke or something. Seeing Nola now, Mrs. Dietrich is charged with hurt, rage; the injustice of it, she thinks, the cruelty of it, and why, and why? And as Nola glances up, startled, not prepared to see her mother in front of her, their eyes lock for an instant and Mrs. Dietrich stares at her with hatred. Cold calm clear unmistakable hatred. She is thinking, Who are *you?* What have I to do with *you?* I don't know *you,* I don't love *you,* why should I?

Has Nola seen, heard? She turns aside as if wincing, gives the blouses a final dismissive shove. Her eyes look tired, the corners of her mouth downturned. Anxious, immediately repentant, Mrs. Dietrich asks if she has found anything worth trying on. Nola says with a shrug, "Not a thing, Mother."

On their way out of the mall Mrs. Dietrich and Nola see the disheveled woman in the black coat again, this time sitting prominently on a concrete ledge in front of Lord & Taylor's busy main entrance, shopping bag at her feet, shabby purse on the ledge beside her. She is shaking her head in a series of annoyed twitches as if arguing with someone but her hands are loose, palms up, in her lap. Her posture is unfortunate—she sits with her knees parted, inner thighs revealed, fatty, dead white, the tops of cotton stockings rolled tight cutting into the flesh. Again, streams of shoppers are making a careful berth around her. Alone among them Nola hesitates, seems about to approach the woman—Please don't, Nola, please! Mrs. Dietrich thinks—then changes her mind and keeps on walking. Mrs. Dietrich murmurs, "Isn't it a pity, poor thing, don't you wonder where she lives, who her family is?" but Nola doesn't reply. Her pace through the first floor of Lord & Taylor is so rapid that Mrs. Dietrich can barely keep up. 75

But she's upset. Strangely upset. As soon as they are in the car, packages and bags in the back seat, she begins crying.

It's childish helpless crying, as though her heart is broken. But Mrs. Dietrich knows it isn't broken; she has heard these very sobs before. Many times before. Still she comforts her daughter, embraces her, hugs her hard, hard. A sudden fierce passion. Vehemence. "Nola honey, Nola dear, what's wrong, dear? Everything will be all right, dear," she says, close to weeping herself. She would embrace Nola even more tightly except for the girl's quilted jacket, that bulky L. L. Bean thing she has never liked, and Nola's stubborn lowered head. Nola has always been ashamed, crying, frantic to hide her face. Strangers are passing close by the car, curious, staring. Mrs. Dietrich wishes she had a cloak to draw over her daughter and herself, so that no one would see.

QUESTIONS

1. Describe the characters of Mrs. Dietrich and Nola. What is the basis of the opposition between the two? Why does Nola seem to resent her mother? Should Nola's resentment be construed as a mark of her growth? Why do the two argue about the semester abroad? How does Mrs. Dietrich's attitude toward Nola seem to change in paragraph 73? Does her anger indicate a cessation of love for Nola?

2. Is this story more about Mrs. Dietrich or Nola? In what ways are the two women different? The same? Why does the story end as it does, in the car?

3. Explain the meaning of the vagabond woman at the beginning and ending of the story (paragraphs 11, 75). How should this woman be considered a symbol of the shortcomings of the way of life represented by the shopping mall?

4. Why is the story told in the present tense, with flashbacks into the past?

5. Consider the proposition "Never before so happy, and never since" (paragraph 30) as a theme of the story.

AMY TAN (b. 1952)

Amy Tan was born in Oakland, California, several years after her parents had left their native China to settle in the San Francisco Bay Area. Early in her life she exhibited talent as a writer, winning a first prize for essay writing at the age of eight. Her family endured the untimely deaths of her father and brother in 1967 and 1968, and the remaining family spent time afterward in Switzerland. She attended a number of U.S. colleges, including San Jose State University, where she graduated with honors in 1972 and received an M.A. in 1973. After graduating she did freelance business writing for companies such as IBM and Pacific Bell. *By 1985 she had decided to devote herself to the writing of fiction, and she launched her career in 1986 with the publication of her first short story, "End Game." In 1989 her* The Joy Luck Club, *an interlinked collection of stories, was published and enjoyed forty weeks on* the New York Times *list of best-sellers. Her other major books are* The Kitchen God's Wife *(1991),* The Hundred Secret Senses *(1995), and* The Bonesetter's Daughter *(2001), which had been earlier excerpted for publication in* The New Yorker. *Tan has also written two children's books,* The Moon Lady *(1992) and* SAGWA The Chinese Siamese Cat *(1994). She collaborates with the novelist Stephen King and the humorist Dave Barry in a "literary garage band, the Rock Bottom Remainders," which raises money for literacy causes and also for groups devoted to First Amendment rights. "Two Kinds" is taken from* The Joy Luck Club.

Two Kinds ~~~~~ 1989

My mother believed you could be anything you wanted to be in America. You could open a restaurant. You could work for the government and get good retirement. You could buy a house with almost no money down. You could become rich. You could become instantly famous.

"Of course you can be prodigy, too," my mother told me when I was nine. "You can be best anything. What does Auntie Lindo know? Her daughter, she is only best tricky."

America was where all my mother's hopes lay. She had come here in 1949 after losing everything in China: her mother and father, her family home, her first husband, and two daughters, twin baby girls. But she never looked back with regret. There were so many ways for things to get better.

We didn't immediately pick the right kind of prodigy. At first my mother thought I could be a Chinese Shirley Temple. We'd watch Shirley's old movies on TV as though they were training films. My mother would poke my arm and say, "*Ni kan*"—You watch. And I would see Shirley tapping her feet, or singing a sailor song, or pursing her lips into a very round O while saying, "Oh my goodness."

"*Ni kan*," said my mother as Shirley's eyes flooded with tears. "You already know 5 how. Don't need talent for crying!"

Soon after my mother got this idea about Shirley Temple, she took me to a beauty training school in the Mission district and put me in the hands of a student who could barely hold the scissors without shaking. Instead of getting big fat curls, I emerged with an uneven mass of crinkly black fuzz. My mother dragged me off to the bathroom and tried to wet down my hair.

"You look like Negro Chinese," she lamented, as if I had done this on purpose.

The instructor of the beauty training school had to lop off these soggy clumps to make my hair even again. "Peter Pan is very popular these days," the instructor assured my mother. I now had hair the length of a boy's, with straight-across bangs that hung at a slant two inches above my eyebrows. I liked the haircut and it made me actually look forward to my future fame.

In fact, in the beginning, I was just as excited as my mother, maybe even more so. I pictured this prodigy part of me as many different images, trying each one on for size. I was a dainty ballerina girl standing by the curtains, waiting to hear the right music that would send me floating on my tiptoes. I was like the Christ child lifted out of the straw manger, crying with holy indignity. I was Cinderella stepping from her pumpkin carriage with sparkly cartoon music filling the air.

In all of my imaginings, I was filled with a sense that I would soon become *perfect*. My mother and father would adore me. I would be beyond reproach. I would never feel the need to sulk for anything.

But sometimes the prodigy in me became impatient. "If you don't hurry up and get me out of here, I'm disappearing for good," it warned. "And then you'll always be nothing."

Every night after dinner, my mother and I would sit at the Formica kitchen table. She would present new tests, taking her examples from stories of amazing children she had read in *Ripley's Believe It or Not*, or *Good Housekeeping*, *Reader's Digest*, and a dozen other magazines she kept in a pile in our bathroom. My mother got these magazines from people whose houses she cleaned. And since she cleaned many houses each week, we had a great assortment. She would look through them all, searching for stories about remarkable children.

The first night she brought out a story about a three-year-old boy who knew the capitals of all the states and even most of the European countries. A teacher was quoted as saying the little boy could also pronounce the names of the foreign cities correctly.

"What's the capital of Finland?" my mother asked me, looking at the magazine story.

All I knew was the capital of California, because Sacramento was the name of the street we lived on in Chinatown. "Nairobi!" I guessed, saying the most foreign word I could think of. She checked to see if that was possibly one way to pronounce "Helsinki" before showing me the answer.

The tests got harder—multiplying numbers in my head, finding the queen of hearts in a deck of cards, trying to stand on my head without using my hands, predicting the daily temperatures in Los Angeles, New York, and London.

One night I had to look at a page from the Bible for three minutes and then report everything I could remember. "Now Jehoshaphat had riches° and honor in abundance and . . . that's all I remember, Ma," I said.

And after seeing my mother's disappointed face once again, something inside of me began to die. I hated the tests, the raised hopes and failed expectations. Before going to bed that night, I looked in the mirror above the bathroom sink and when I saw only my face staring back—and that it would always be this ordinary face—I began to cry. Such a sad, ugly girl! I made high-pitched noises like a crazed animal, trying to scratch out the face in the mirror.

And then I saw what seemed to be the prodigy side of me—because I had never seen that face before. I looked at my reflection, blinking so I could see more clearly. The girl staring back at me was angry, powerful. This girl and I were the same. I had new

10

15

Now Jehoshaphat had riches: Jing-Mei had been told to report on the Hebrew monarch Jehoshaphat as narrated in the eighteenth chapter of II Chronicles.

thoughts, willful thoughts, or rather thoughts filled with lots of won'ts. I won't let her change me, I promised myself. I won't be what I'm not.

So now on nights when my mother presented her tests, I performed listlessly, my   20
head propped on one arm. I pretended to be bored. And I was. I got so bored I started counting the bellows of the foghorns out on the bay while my mother drilled me in other areas. The sound was comforting and reminded me of the cow jumping over the moon. And the next day, I played a game with myself, seeing if my mother would give up on me before eight bellows. After a while I usually counted only one, maybe two bellows at most. At last she was beginning to give up hope.

Two or three months had gone by without any mention of my being a prodigy again. And then one day my mother was watching *The Ed Sullivan Show*° on TV. The TV was old and the sound kept shorting out. Every time my mother got halfway up from the sofa to adjust the set, the sound would go back on and Ed would be talking. As soon as she sat down, Ed would go silent again. She got up, the TV broke into loud piano music. She sat down. Silence. Up and down, back and forth, quiet and loud. It was like a stiff embraceless dance between her and the TV set. Finally she stood by the set with her hand on the sound dial.

She seemed entranced by the music, a little frenzied piano piece with this mesmerizing quality, sort of quick passages and then teasing lilting ones before it returned to the quick playful parts.

"*Ni kan*," my mother said, calling me over with hurried hand gestures, "Look here."

I could see why my mother was fascinated by the music. It was being pounded out by a little Chinese girl, about nine years old, with a Peter Pan haircut. The girl had the sauciness of a Shirley Temple. She was proudly modest like a proper Chinese child. And she also did this fancy sweep of a curtsy, so that the fluffy skirt of her white dress cascaded slowly to the floor like the petals of a large carnation.

In spite of these warning signs, I wasn't worried. Our family had no piano and we   25
couldn't afford to buy one, let alone reams of sheet music and piano lessons. So I could be generous in my comments when my mother bad-mouthed the little girl on TV.

"Play note right, but doesn't sound good! No singing sound," complained my mother.

"What are you picking on her for?" I said carelessly. "She's pretty good. Maybe she's not the best, but she's trying hard." I knew almost immediately I would be sorry I said that.

"Just like you," she said. "Not the best. Because you not trying." She gave a little huff as she let go of the sound dial and sat down on the sofa.

The little Chinese girl sat down also to play an encore of "Anitra's Dance" by Grieg.° I remember the song, because later on I had to learn how to play it.

Three days after watching *The Ed Sullivan Show*, my mother told me what my sched-   30
ule would be for piano lessons and piano practice. She had talked to Mr. Chong, who lived on the first floor of our apartment building. Mr. Chong was a retired piano teacher and my mother had traded housecleaning services for weekly lessons and a piano for me to practice on every day, two hours a day, from four until six.

The Ed Sullivan Show: Ed Sullivan (1902–1974), originally a newspaper columnist, hosted this popular variety television show from 1948 to 1971.

"*Anitra's Dance" by Grieg:* a portion of the suite composed for Ibsen's *Peer Gynt* by Norwegian composer Edvard Grieg (1843–1907).

When my mother told me this, I felt as though I had been sent to hell. I whined and then kicked my foot a little when I couldn't stand it anymore.

"Why don't you like me the way I am? I'm *not* a genius! I can't play the piano. And even if I could, I wouldn't go on TV if you paid me a million dollars!" I cried.

My mother slapped me. "Who ask you be genius?" she shouted. "Only ask you be your best. For you sake. You think I want you be genius? Hnnh! What for! Who ask you!"

"So ungrateful," I heard her mutter in Chinese. "If she had as much talent as she has temper, she would be famous now."

Mr. Chong, whom I secretly nicknamed Old Chong, was very strange, always tapping his fingers to the silent music of an invisible orchestra. He looked ancient in my eyes. He had lost most of the hair on top of his head and he wore thick glasses and had eyes that always looked tired and sleepy. But he must have been younger than I thought, since he lived with his mother and was not yet married.   35

I met Old Lady Chong once and that was enough. She had this peculiar smell like a baby that had done something in its pants. And her fingers felt like a dead person's, like an old peach I once found in the back of the refrigerator; the skin just slid off the meat when I picked it up.

I soon found out why Old Chong had retired from teaching piano. He was deaf. "Like Beethoven!" he shouted to me. "We're both listening only in our head!" And he would start to conduct his frantic silent sonatas.

Our lessons went like this. He would open the book and point to different things, explaining their purpose: "Key! Treble! Bass! No sharps or flats! So this is C major! Listen now and play after me!"

And then he would play the C scale a few times, a simple chord, and then, as if inspired by an old, unreachable itch, he gradually added more notes and running trills and a pounding bass until the music was really something quite grand.

I would play after him, the simple scale, the simple chord, and then I just played some nonsense that sounded like a cat running up and down on top of garbage cans. Old Chong smiled and applauded and then said, "Very good! But now you must learn to keep time!"   40

So that's how I discovered that Old Chong's eyes were too slow to keep up with the wrong notes I was playing. He went through the motions in half-time. To help me keep rhythm, he stood behind me, pushing down on my right shoulder for every beat. He balanced pennies on top of my wrists so I would keep them still as I slowly played scales and arpeggios. He had me curve my hand around an apple and keep that shape when playing chords. He marched stiffly to show me how to make each finger dance up and down, staccato like an obedient little soldier.

He taught me all these things, and that was how I also learned I could be lazy and get away with mistakes, lots of mistakes. If I hit the wrong notes because I hadn't practiced enough, I never corrected myself. I just kept playing in rhythm. And Old Chong kept conducting his own private reverie.

So maybe I never really gave myself a fair chance. I did pick up the basics pretty quickly, and I might have become a good pianist at that young age. But I was so determined not to try, not to be anybody different that I learned to play only the most earsplitting preludes, the most discordant hymns.

Over the next year, I practiced like this, dutifully in my own way. And then one day I heard my mother and her friend Lindo Jong both talking in a loud bragging tone of voice so others could hear. It was after church, and I was leaning against the brick wall wearing a dress with stiff white petticoats. Auntie Lindo's daughter, Waverly, who was about my age, was standing farther down the wall about five feet away. We had grown up together and shared all the closeness of two sisters squabbling over crayons and dolls. In other words, for the most part, we hated each other. I thought she was snotty. Waverly Jong had gained a certain amount of fame as "Chinatown's Littlest Chinese Chess Champion."

"She bring home too many trophy," lamented Auntie Lindo that Sunday. "All day   45
she play chess. All day I have no time do nothing but dust off her winnings." She threw a scolding look at Waverly, who pretended not to see her.

"You lucky you don't have this problem," said Auntie Lindo with a sigh to my mother.

And my mother squared her shoulders and bragged: "Our problem worser than yours. If we ask Jing-Mei wash dish, she hear nothing but music. It's like you can't stop this natural talent."

And right then, I was determined to put a stop to her foolish pride.

A few weeks later, Old Chong and my mother conspired to have me play in a talent show which would be held in the church hall. By then, my parents had saved up enough to buy me a secondhand piano, a black Wurlitzer spinet with a scarred bench. It was the showpiece of our living room.

For the talent show, I was to play a piece called "Pleading Child" from Schumann's   50
Scenes from Childhood.° It was a simple, moody piece that sounded more difficult than it was. I was supposed to memorize the whole thing, playing the repeat parts twice to make the piece sound longer. But I dawdled over it, playing a few bars and then cheating, looking up to see what notes followed. I never really listened to what I was playing. I daydreamed about being somewhere else, about being someone else.

The part I liked to practice best was the fancy curtsy: right foot out, touch the rose on the carpet with a pointed foot, sweep to the side, left leg bends, look up and smile.

My parents invited all the couples from the Joy Luck Club to witness my debut. Auntie Lindo and Uncle Tin were there. Waverly and her two older brothers had also come. The first two rows were filled with children both younger and older than I was. The littlest ones got to go first. They recited simple nursery rhymes, squawked out tunes on miniature violins, twirled Hula Hoops, pranced in pink ballet tutus, and when they bowed or curtsied, the audience would sigh in unison, "Awww," and then clap enthusiastically.

When my turn came, I was very confident. I remember my childish excitement. It was as if I knew, without a doubt, that the prodigy side of me really did exist. I had no fear whatsoever, no nervousness. I remember thinking to myself, This is it! This is it! I looked out over the audience, at my mother's blank face, my father's yawn. Auntie Lindo's stiff-lipped smile, Waverly's sulky expression. I had on a white dress layered with sheets of lace, and a pink bow in my Peter Pan haircut. As I sat down I envisioned people jumping to their feet and Ed Sullivan rushing up to introduce me to everyone on TV.

And I started to play. It was so beautiful. I was so caught up in how lovely I looked that at first I didn't worry how I would sound. So it was a surprise to me when I hit the first wrong note and I realized something didn't sound quite right. And then I hit another and another followed that. A chill started at the top of my head and began to trickle down. Yet I couldn't stop playing, as though my hands were bewitched. I kept thinking my fingers would adjust themselves back, like a train switching to the right track. I played this strange jumble through two repeats, the sour notes staying with me all the way to the end.

When I stood up, I discovered my legs were shaking. Maybe I had just been nervous   55
and the audience, like Old Chong, had seen me go through the right motions and had not heard anything wrong at all. I swept my right foot out, went down on my knee, looked up and smiled. The room was quiet, except for Old Chong, who was beaming and shouting, "Bravo! Bravo! Well done!" But then I saw my mother's face, her stricken face. The

---

Scenes from Childhood: Scenes from Childhood, or *Kinderszenen* (1836), is one of the best-known works for piano by Robert Schumann (1810–1856).

audience clapped weakly, and as I walked back to my chair, with my whole face quivering as I tried not to cry, I heard a little boy whisper loudly to his mother, "That was awful," and the mother whispered back, "Well, she certainly tried."

And now I realized how many people were in the audience, the whole world it seemed. I was aware of eyes burning into my back. I felt the shame of my mother and father as they sat stiffly throughout the rest of the show.

We could have escaped during intermission. Pride and some strange sense of honor must have anchored my parents to their chairs. And so we watched it all: the eighteen-year-old boy with a fake mustache who did a magic show and juggled flaming hoops while riding a unicycle. The breasted girl with white makeup who sang from *Madama Butterfly*° and got honorable mention. And the eleven-year-old boy who won first prize playing a tricky violin song that sounded like a busy bee.°

After the show, the Hsus, the Jongs, and the St. Clairs from the Joy Luck Club came up to my mother and father.

"Lots of talented kids," Auntie Lindo said vaguely, smiling broadly.

"That was somethin' else," said my father, and I wondered if he was referring to me   60
in a humorous way, or whether he even remembered what I had done.

Waverly looked at me and shrugged her shoulders. "You aren't a genius like me," she said matter-of-factly. And if I hadn't felt so bad, I would have pulled her braids and punched her stomach.

But my mother's expression was what devastated me: a quiet, blank look that said she had lost everything. I felt the same way, and it seemed as if everybody were now coming up, like gawkers at the scene of an accident, to see what parts were actually missing. When we got on the bus to go home, my father was humming the busy-bee tune and my mother was silent. I kept thinking she wanted to wait until we got home before shouting at me. But when my father unlocked the door to our apartment, my mother walked in and then went to the back, into the bedroom. No accusations. No blame. And in a way, I felt disappointed. I had been waiting for her to start shouting, so I could shout back and cry and blame her for all my misery.

I assumed my talent-show fiasco meant I never had to play the piano again. But two days later, after school, my mother came out of the kitchen and saw me watching TV.

"Four clock," she reminded me as if it were any other day. I was stunned, as though she were asking me to go through the talent-show torture again. I wedged myself more tightly in front of the TV.

"Turn off TV," she called from the kitchen five minutes later.   65

I didn't budge. And then I decided. I didn't have to do what my mother said anymore. I wasn't her slave. This wasn't China. I had listened to her before and look what happened. She was the stupid one.

She came out from the kitchen and stood in the arched entryway of the living room. "Four clock," she said once again, louder.

"I'm not going to play anymore," I said nonchalantly. "Why should I? I'm not a genius."

She walked over and stood in front of the TV. I saw her chest was heaving up and down in an angry way.

Madama Butterfly: The girl probably sang "Un Bel Di," the signature soprano aria from the opera *Madama Butterfly* by Giacomo Puccini (1858–1924).

busy bee: probably the well-known "Flight of the Bumblebee" by Nikolay Rimsky-Korsakov (1844–1908).

"No!" I said, and I now felt stronger, as if my true self had finally emerged. So this 70
was what had been inside me all along.

"No! I won't!" I screamed.

She yanked me by the arm, pulled me off the floor, snapped off the TV. She was frighteningly strong, half pulling, half carrying me toward the piano as I kicked the throw rugs under my feet. She lifted me up and onto the hard bench. I was sobbing by now, looking at her bitterly. Her chest was heaving even more and her mouth was open, smiling crazily as if she were pleased I was crying.

"You want me to be someone that I'm not!" I sobbed. "I'll never be the kind of daughter you want me to be!"

"Only two kinds of daughters," she shouted in Chinese. "Those who are obedient and those who follow their own mind! Only one kind of daughter can live in this house. Obedient daughter!"

"Then I wish I wasn't your daughter. I wish you weren't my mother," I shouted. As I 75
said these things I got scared. It felt like worms and toads and slimy things crawling out of my chest, but it also felt good, as if this awful side of me had surfaced, at last.

"Too late change this," said my mother shrilly.

And I could sense her anger rising to its breaking point. I wanted to see it spill over. And that's when I remembered the babies she had lost in China, the ones we never talked about. "Then I wish I'd never been born!" I shouted. "I wish I were dead! Like them."

It was as if I had said the magic words. Alakazam!—and her face went blank, her mouth closed, her arms went slack, and she backed out of the room, stunned, as if she were blowing away like a small brown leaf, thin, brittle, lifeless.

It was not the only disappointment my mother felt in me. In the years that followed, I failed her so many times, each time asserting my own will, my right to fall short of expectations. I didn't get straight As. I didn't become class president. I didn't get into Stanford. I dropped out of college.

For unlike my mother, I did not believe I could be anything I wanted to be. I could 80
only be me.

And for all those years, we never talked about the disaster at the recital or my terrible accusations afterward at the piano bench. All that remained unchecked, like a betrayal that was now unspeakable. So I never found a way to ask her why she had hoped for something so large that failure was inevitable.

And even worse, I never asked her what frightened me the most: Why had she given up hope?

For after our struggle at the piano, she never mentioned my playing again. The lessons stopped. The lid to the piano was closed, shutting out the dust, my misery, and her dreams.

So she surprised me. A few years ago, she offered to give me the piano, for my thirtieth birthday. I had not played in all those years. I saw the offer as a sign of forgiveness, a tremendous burden removed.

"Are you sure?" I asked shyly. "I mean, won't you and Dad miss it?" 85

"No, this your piano," she said firmly. "Always your piano. You only one can play."

"Well, I probably can't play anymore," I said. "It's been years."

"You pick up fast," said my mother, as if she knew this was certain. "You have natural talent. You could been genius if you want to."

"No I couldn't."

"You just not trying," said my mother. And she was neither angry nor sad. She said 90
it as if to announce a fact that could never be disproved. "Take it," she said.

But I didn't at first. It was enough that she had offered it to me. And after that, every time I saw it in my parents' living room, standing in front of the bay windows, it made me feel proud, as if it were a shiny trophy I had won back.

Last week I sent a tuner over to my parents' apartment and had the piano reconditioned, for purely sentimental reasons. My mother had died a few months before and I had been getting things in order for my father, a little bit at a time. I put the jewelry in special silk pouches. The sweaters she had knitted in yellow, pink, bright orange—all the colors I hated—I put those in moth-proof boxes. I found some old Chinese silk dresses, the kind with little slits up the sides. I rubbed the old silk against my skin, then wrapped them in tissue and decided to take them home with me.

After I had the piano tuned, I opened the lid and touched the keys. It sounded even richer than I remembered. Really, it was a very good piano. Inside the bench were the same exercise notes with handwritten scales, the same secondhand music books with their covers held together with yellow tape.

I opened up the Schumann book to the dark little piece I had played at the recital. It was on the left-hand side of the page, "Pleading Child." It looked more difficult than I remembered. I played a few bars, surprised at how easily the notes came back to me.

And for the first time, or so it seemed, I noticed the piece on the right-hand side. It 95 was called "Perfectly Contented." I tried to play this one as well. It had a lighter melody but the same flowing rhythm and turned out to be quite easy. "Pleading Child" was shorter but slower; "Perfectly Contented" was longer, but faster. And after I played them both a few times, I realized they were two halves of the same song.

QUESTIONS

1. What major characteristics about the narrator, Jing-Mei, are brought out in the story?

2. Describe the relationship between Jing-Mei and her mother. Why does Jing-Mei resist all efforts to develop her talents?

3. Characterize the mother. To what degree is she sympathetic? Unsympathetic? At the story's end, how does Jing-Mei feel about her mother?

4. What general details about the nature of first- and second-generation immigrants are presented in the story?

⫯ WRITING ABOUT CHARACTER

Usually your topic will be a major character in a story or drama, although you might also study one or more minor characters. After your customary overview, begin taking notes. List as many traits as you can, and also determine how the author presents details about the character through actions, appearance, speeches, comments by others, or authorial explanations. If you discover unusual traits, determine what they show. The following suggestions and questions will help you get started.

Questions for Discovering Ideas

• Who is the major character? What do you learn about this character from his or her own actions and speeches? From the speeches and actions of other characters? How else do you learn about the character?

- How important is the character to the work's principal action? Which characters oppose the major character? How do the major character and the opposing character(s) interact? What effects do these interactions create?
- What actions bring out important traits of the main character? To what degree is the character creating events, or just responding to them?
- Describe the main character's actions: Are they good or bad, intelligent or stupid, deliberate or spontaneous? How do they help you understand her or him? What to they show about the character as a person?
- Describe and explain the traits, both major and minor, of the character you plan to discuss. To what extent do the traits permit you to judge the character? What is your judgment?
- What descriptions (if any) of how the character looks do you discover in the story? What does this appearance demonstrate about him or her?
- In what ways is the character's major trait a strength—or a weakness? As the story progresses, to what degree does the trait become more (or less) prominent?
- Is the character round and dynamic? How does the character recognize, change with, or adjust to circumstances?
- If the character you are analyzing is flat or static, what function does he or she perform in the story (for example, by doing a task or by bringing out qualities of the major character)?
- If the character is a stereotype, to what type does he or she belong? To what degree does the character stay in the stereotypical role or rise above it? How?
- What do any of the other characters do, say, or think to give you understanding of the character you are analyzing? What does the character say or think about himself or herself? What does the storyteller or narrator say? How valid are these comments and insights? How helpful in providing insights into the character?
- Is the character lifelike or unreal? Consistent or inconsistent? Believable or not believable?

Strategies for Organizing Ideas

Sometimes when you have begun discussing a character you may find it easy to lapse into doing no more than presenting details of action without tying the actions to the character's traits and qualities. This is a trap to be avoided. Remember always to connect the actions and circumstances directly to characteristics—in other words to the character of the character. Do not be satisfied just to say what the character is doing, but tell your reader what the actions show about the character *as a person*—as a living, breathing individual with particular distinctness and unique identity. Always keep these thoughts in your mind when you discuss a literary character.

In your developing essay, identify the character you are studying, and refer to noteworthy problems in determining this character's qualities. Use your central idea and thesis sentence to create the form for the body of your essay. Consider one of the following approaches to organize your ideas and form the basis for your essay.

1. DEVELOP A CENTRAL TRAIT OR MAJOR CHARACTERISTIC, such as "a determination to preserve her children despite the constant threats around her" (Rosa of Ozick's "The Shawl" [Chapter 6]) or "the habit of seeing the world only on one's own terms" (Abner Snopes of "Barn Burning"). This kind of structure should be organized to show how the work brings out the trait. For example, one story might use dramatic speeches to bring the character to life (Minnie of "A Jury of Her Peers"). Another story might employ just the character's speech and actions (Tessie Hutchinson of Jackson's "The Lottery" [Chapter 5]). Studying the trait thus enables you to focus on the ways in which the author presents the character, and it also enables you to focus on separate parts of the work.

2. EXPLAIN A CHARACTER'S GROWTH OR CHANGE.   This type of essay describes a character's traits at the work's beginning and then analyzes changes or developments. It is important to stress the actual alterations as they emerge, but at the same time to avoid retelling the story. Additionally, you should not only describe the changing traits but also analyze how they are brought out within the work (such as the dream of Goodman Brown [Chapter 9] or Minnie Wright's twenty-year ordeal).

3. ORGANIZE YOUR ESSAY AROUND A NUMBER OF IMPORTANT BUT SEPARATE CHARACTERISTICS.   Most major characters exhibit not just one but many separate traits and qualities. Thus, for example, Paul of Cather's "Paul's Case" is a unique young man who exhibits qualities of general lack of concern for others, boredom, active dislike of his home life with his father, denial of reality, and self-destructiveness. Paul's character might be studied on the basis of these separate qualities provided that they are connected within the essay. (See the following demonstrative essay for an illustration of this type of development.)

4. ORGANIZE YOUR ESSAY AROUND CENTRAL ACTIONS, OBJECTS, OR QUOTATIONS THAT REVEAL PRIMARY CHARACTERISTICS.   Key incidents may stand out (such as walking on a fine rug with barnyard dirt on one's shoes), along with objects closely associated with the character being analyzed (such as a broken birdcage). There may be important quotations spoken by the character or by someone else in the work. Show how such elements serve as signposts or guides to understanding the character.

5. DEVELOP QUALITIES OF A FLAT CHARACTER OR CHARACTERS.   If the character is flat (such as the sisters in "Barn Burning" or the lawmen in "A Jury of Her Peers") you might develop topics such as the function and relative significance of the character, the group the character represents, the relationship of the flat character to the round ones, the importance of this relationship, and any additional qualities or traits. For a flat character, you should explain the circumstances or defects that keep the character from being round, as well as the importance of these shortcomings in the author's presentation of character.

In your conclusion, show how the character's traits are related to the work as a whole. If the person was good but came to a bad end, does this misfortune make him or her seem especially worthy? If the person suffers, does the suffering suggest any attitudes about the class or type of which he or she is a part? Or does it illustrate the author's general view of human life? Or both? Do the characteristics explain why the person helps or hinders other characters? How does your essay help to clear up first-reading misunderstandings?

DEMONSTRATIVE STUDENT ESSAY

The Character of the Mother in Amy Tan's "Two Kinds"°

[1]   The narrator of Tan's "Two Kinds" is Jing-Mei, a Chinese-American woman who tells the story as an adult looking back on her antagonism with her mother over a period of years in early adolescence, and it is through Jing-Mei's eyes alone that we learn of the mother. The mother is in effect a displaced person, removed from her home in China in 1949, and whose powerful energies and strong will are devoted to the "raised hopes" of the United States.* The story focuses on the mother-daughter conflicts resulting from the mother's wishes to make Jing-Mei excel in some activity or profession that will make her famous. Through Jing-Mei's descriptions and quotations, we infer that the mother is a loving and proud person with strong optimism about her new land, a belief in the value of hard work, and an inability to comprehend her second-generation daughter.†

[2]   The story makes clear, despite the narrator's frequent statements of childhood anger and dislike, that the mother is motivated by parental love, concern, and pride. She wishes nothing so much as her daughter's success. For example, at the story's end her offer of the piano is an expression of love. As she says in her broken English: "Always your piano. You only one can play" (217, paragraph 86). At another point the mother brags about her daughter's "natural talent" in music (215, paragraph 47), even though Jing-Mei calls this "foolish pride" (215, paragraph 48). After the mother has died, Jing-Mei puts away some of her personal effects, most notably a number of hand-knitted sweaters. Although Jing-Mei even then cannot resist explaining that she hates the colors (218, paragraph 92), it is clear that the knitting is to be taken as a sign of the mother's love. With all the heated disputes and antagonisms now a thing of the past, Jing-Mei seems to recognize and accept this love when she looks through the possessions, and also when she sits down to play the piano--her mother's gift--at which her mother so much wanted her to excel (218, paragraph 94).

[3]   Related to this love is the mother's optimistic and hopeful nature. In all the admittedly antagonistic mother-daughter interactions in this story, there is evidence of this hope. Jing-Mei tells us that her mother had come to America "after losing everything in China: her mother and father, her family home, her first husband, and two daughters, twin baby girls" (211, paragraph 3). Nevertheless, the mother does not brood on the past. No matter how much she might grieve privately, she accepts the optimistic idea that America, the new land, is a place of freedom from oppression where there are limitless opportunities for advancement. Success in business, a secure old age, home ownership, and national fame--all these are possibilities in which the mother, with her optimism about America, believes (211, paragraph 1).

Closely connected with the mother's optimism is her strong conviction about the value of work. By accepting America as the land of opportunity, she assumes that hard work is all that is needed to see the opportunity fulfilled (211,

°See pp. 211–18 for this story.
*Central idea.
†Thesis sentence.

paragraph 1). For herself, she is diligent in her work as a housecleaner, and in this way she practices her faith (212, paragraph 12). In the evenings she makes the same effort with Jing-Mei to nurture the girl's budding talents (212, paragraph 12). In trying to get Jing-Mei to learn mathematics, magic, weather prediction, geography, speed reading, and most importantly piano, the mother is acting on her faith that her daughter will find something in America that will turn her into a prodigy. It is this belief in the transforming power of work that leads to her constant prodding of Jing-Mei, and that also leads her to reproach Jing-Mei for not working hard enough. With all the force of the mother's characteristic beliefs in work being put on the shoulders of her daughter, however, the hopes are not realized. Instead, Jing-Mei describes a childhood filled with resentment and anger against her mother's exhortations to work and perform (211, paragraph 2).

[4]

Despite the mother's positive qualities, her principal flaw is her inability to comprehend her daughter. Her imagination simply does not permit her to understand that her daughter's thoughts are "filled with lots of won'ts" (213, paragraph 19), nor is the mother capable of understanding Jing-Mei's responses and feelings, for Jing-Mei tells us that "unlike my mother, I did not believe I could be anything I wanted to be. I could only be me" (217, paragraph 80). This conflict is one of personality, and it is also, likely, a difference in the culture of the two--a Chinese mother and an American daughter. As a parent, the mother demands the respect she believes children owe to older and wiser authority figures. In great anger after the disastrous recital, she declares her belief: "Only two kinds of daughters . . . . Those who are obedient and those who follow their own mind!'" (217, paragraph 74)--and she insists on obedience from her own child. So strong is the mother's desire to have Jing-Mei yield to her parental wishes that she half pulls and half carries Jing-Mei to the piano to resume her regular practice. In extreme bitterness and anger against her mother's inability to sympathize with her, Jing-Mei cruelly uses her mother's past as a weapon when she says she wishes she were dead like her mother's twin girls (217, paragraph 77). Because of this outburst, the mother's illusion of American success is deflated. All her hopes of making up for her lost life in China, along with the optimism that she has centered in her daughter, are dashed, and she backs "out of the room, stunned, as if she were blowing away like a small brown leaf, thin, brittle, lifeless" (217, paragraph 78).

[5]

And so the the mother quietly accepts new disappointment, even in her new land, because of her daughter. She has believed in renewal, and has thrown herself heart and soul into her dreams to make Jing-Mei a success. Obviously the mother's overriding character flaw, which she never realizes, is that she fails to recognize her daughter's individuality. She is unable to deal with this fact despite all her love, hard work, optimism, and willingness to assist. The mother and daughter are of course "two kinds," which means that they are two totally different and unadaptable characters. The "two kinds" may also mean that they are both alike in their stubbornness and desire for control, The result is that the daughter asserts herself even though she falls "short of expectations" (217, paragraph 79), while the mother silently retreats into resignation and disappointed hopes. Never do the mother and daughter discuss the breach that opens between them, and never does Jing-Mei hear her mother explain "why she had hoped for something so large that failure was inevitable" (217, paragraph 81).

[6]

WORK CITED

Tan, Amy. "Two Kinds." <u>Literature: An Introduction to Reading and Writing</u>. Ed. Edgar V. Roberts and Henry E. Jacobs. 7th ed. Upper Saddle River: Prentice Hall, 2003. 211–18.

Commentary on the Essay

The strategy of this essay is to use details from the story to bring out a number of the mother's separate traits. Hence the essay illustrates strategy 3 described on page 220. Other plans of development could also have been chosen, such as the mother's belief in the value of work (strategy 1); the change in the mother after the outbursts of anger at the piano (strategy 2); or the mother's separate reproaches to her daughter for not trying hard enough (another way to use strategy 3).

A major function of paragraph 1 of this essay is to explain how all judgments about the mother are gained exclusively through the words of the daughter, the narrator. The essay thus highlights how Tan uses presentation method 4 (see p. 161) as the means of rendering the mother's character.

The essay's argument is developed through a number of the mother's characteristics, namely her parental love (paragraph 2), her optimistic nature (paragraph 3), her high valuation of work (paragraph 4), and her failure to recognize her daughter's desire for individuality (paragraph 5). The concluding paragraph (6) summarizes a number of these details, and it also considers the irreconcilable character differences between the two.

As a study in composition, paragraph 3 demonstrates how discussion of a specific character trait, together with related details, contributes to the essay's development. The trait is the mother's optimistic nature (shown by her hope for a new life in America). Connecting details within the paragraph, selected from study notes, are the mother's belief in opportunity fueled by her uncritical understanding, through popular media, of some of the directions in which people might achieve success. The paragraph weaves together enough material to show the relationship between the mother's strong faith and her annoyance and reproachfulness, which lead to her emotional outburst against Jing-Mei—a climax producing the change that defines the mother as a round character.

Special Topics for Writing and Argument about Character

1. Compare the ways in which actions (or speeches, or the comments of others) are used to bring out the character traits of Sarty in "Barn Burning," Jing-Mei in "Two Kinds," Paul in "Paul's Case," and Mrs. Dietrich in "Shopping."

2. Compare the qualities and functions of two or more flat characters (e.g., the lawmen in Glaspell's "A Jury of Her Peers," the twins in Faulkner's "Barn Burning," the father and Old Chong in "Two Kinds." How do the flat characters bring out qualities of the major characters? What do you discover about their own character traits?

3. Using Sarty, Minnie Wright, and Jing-Mei as examples, describe the effects of circumstance on character. Under the rubric "circumstance" you may consider elements such as education, family, economic and social status, cultural background, and geographic isolation.

4. The word *case* commonly refers to legal investigations. It is used by Cather appropriately because Paul is first a problem student, and also, in the course of the story, a truant and a thief. Consider the possibility of applying the word *case* to the characters of Abner Snopes of Faulkner's "Barn Burning" and Minnie Wright of Glaspell's "A Jury of Her Peers." How aptly does the term apply to these characters? What crimes have they committed? What are the circumstances? To what degree are the characters guilty? Are there mitigating elements in their actions? Generally, how are they to be judged?

5. Compare the mother-daughter relationships in "Two Kinds" and "Shopping."

6. Topics for argument or brief essays:

   a. It often seems that fictional characters are under stress and also that they lead lives of great difficulty. How true is this claim? To what degree do the difficulties that characters experience bring out either good or bad qualities, or both?

   b. Develop this argument: To our friends and close relatives, we are round, but to ourselves and most other people, we are flat.

7. Write a brief essay comparing the changes or developments of two major or round characters in stories included in this chapter. You might deal with issues such as what the characters are like at the beginning; what conflicts they confront, deal with, or avoid; what qualities are brought out that signal the characters' changes or developments; and so on.

8. Write a brief story about an important decision you have made (e.g., choosing a school, beginning or leaving a job, declaring a major, starting or ending a friendship). Show how your qualities of character (to the extent that you understand yourself), together with your experiences, have gone into the decision. You may write more comfortably if you give yourself another name and describe your actions in the third person.

9. Using the card catalogue or computer catalogue in your library, find two critical studies of William Faulkner published by university presses. How fully do these studies describe and explain the characters living in Yoknapatawpha County, the imaginary place where Faulkner locates much of his fiction (see also "A Rose for Emily" [Chapter 3])? Referring to these studies, write a short research-based essay on the characters and activities of the Snopes family.

Point of View: *The Position or Stance of the Work's Narrator or Speaker*

The term **point of view** refers to the **speaker, narrator, persona,** or **voice** created by authors to tell stories, present arguments, and express attitudes and judgments. Point of view involves not only the speaker's physical position as an observer and recorder, but also the ways in which the speaker's social, political, and mental circumstances affect the narrative. For this reason, point of view is one of the most complex and subtle aspects of literary study.

Bear in mind that authors try not only to make their works vital and interesting but also to bring their presentations alive. The presentation is similar to a dramatic performance: In a play, the actors are always themselves, but in their roles they *impersonate* and temporarily *become* the characters whom they act. In fictional works, not only do authors impersonate or pretend to be characters who do the talking, but also they *create* these characters. One such character is Jackie, the narrator of Frank O'Connor's "First Confession" (Chapter 7), who is telling about events that occurred when he was a child. Because he is the subject as well as the narrator, he has firsthand knowledge of the actions, even though he also says things indicating that he, as an adult, has not fully assimilated his childhood experience. Another speaking character is Sammy of Updike's "A & P" (Chapter 7). Sammy is visualized as a real person describing an important event in his own life. We read Sammy's words, and we know that Sammy is a distinct though fictional character; but because Updike is the author we know that he is the one putting the words in Sammy's mouth. In Poe's "The Masque of the Red Death" (Chapter 6) we constantly hear the speaker's voice and are influenced not only by his narration but also by his attitudes.

Because of the ramifications of creating a narrative voice, point of view may also be considered as the centralizing or guiding intelligence in a work—the

understood
absorbed as
nourishment

mind that filters the fictional experience and presents only the most important details to create the maximum impact. It may be compared to the perspectives utilized by painters. As we noted in Chapter 3, Claude Lorrain's painting *Harbour at Sunset* (Insert I–4) puts all the buildings, ships, landscape, and foreground figures into the perspective of the distant sun's mysterious glow. A contrasting painting is Henri Matisse's *Harmony in Red/The Tablecloth* (Insert I–3)), which abandons the illusion of three dimensions while creating a perspective in which all the major details—chair, table, designs, still life, woman, and wall—are dominated not by dimensionality but rather by the color red. While Matisse concentrates on the connections of both life and color, Claude suggests that human artifacts and activities, however beautiful, are minor when compared with the vastness of the universe. In other words, the way reality is presented in each painting—the point of view or guiding intelligence presented by the painter—determines our perceptions and understanding of the painting. Similarly, the point of view or guiding intelligence created by the author of a literary work determines how we read, understand, and respond.

⁆ AN EXERCISE IN POINT OF VIEW: REPORTING AN ACCIDENT

As an exercise to show that point of view is derived from lifelike situations, let us imagine that there has been an auto accident. Two cars, driven by Alice and Bill, have collided, and the after-crash scene is represented in the drawing. How might this accident be described? What would Alice say? What would Bill say?

Now assume that Frank, who is Bill's best friend, and Mary, who knows neither Bill nor Alice, were witnesses. What might Frank say about who was responsible? What might Mary say? Additionally, assume that you are a reporter for a local newspaper and are sent to report on the accident. You know none of the people involved. How will your report differ from the other reports? Finally, to what degree are all the statements designed to persuade listeners and readers that the details and claims made in the respective reports are true?

The likely differences in the various reports may be explained by reference to point of view. Obviously, because both Alice and Bill are deeply involved—each of them is a major participant or what may be called a **major mover**—they will likely arrange their words to make themselves seem blameless. Frank, because he is Bill's best friend, will report things in Bill's favor. Mary will favor neither Alice nor Bill, but let us assume that she did not look up to see the colliding cars until she heard the crash. Thus, she did not see the accident happening but saw only the immediate aftereffects. Amid all this mixture of partial and impartial views of the action, to whom should we attribute the greatest reliability?

It seems clear that each person's report will have the "hidden agenda" of making herself or himself seem honest, objective, intelligent, impartial, and thorough. Thus, although both Alice and Bill may be truthful to the best of their abilities, it is unlikely that their reports will be reliable because they both have

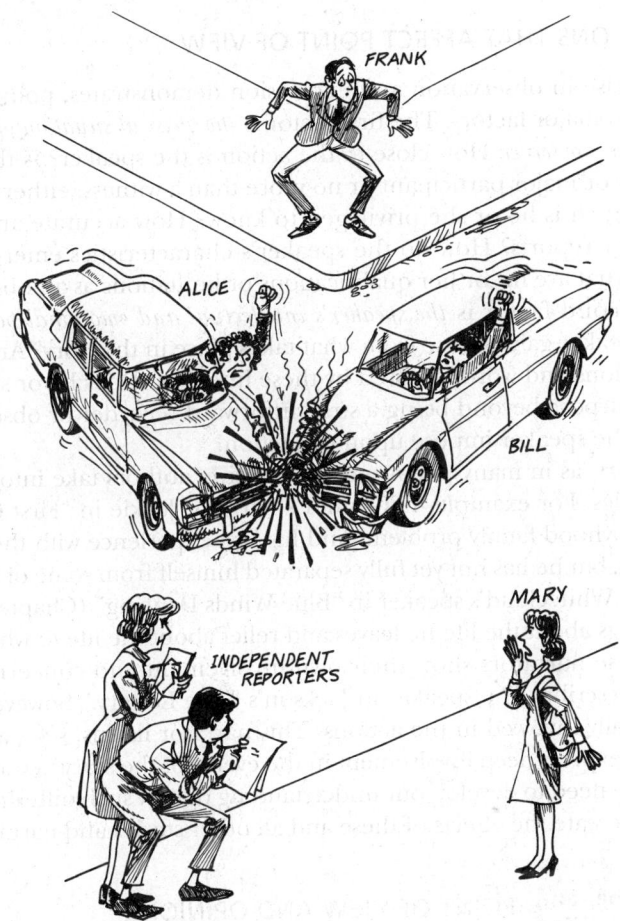

something to gain from avoiding responsibility for the accident. Also, Frank may be questionable as a witness because he is Bill's friend and may report things to Bill's advantage. Mary could be reliable, but she did not see everything; therefore she is unreliable not because of motivation but rather because of her location as a witness. Most likely, *your* account as an impartial reporter will be the most reliable and objective of all, because your major interest is to learn all the details and to report the truth accurately, with no concern about the personal interests of either Alice or Bill.

As you can see, the ramifications of describing actions are far-reaching, and the consideration of the various interests and situations is subtle. Indeed, of all the aspects of literature, point of view is the most complex because it is so much like life itself. On the one hand, point of view is intertwined with the many interests and wishes of humanity at large; on the other, it is linked to the enormous difficulty of uncovering and determining truth.

CONDITIONS THAT AFFECT POINT OF VIEW

As this exercise in observation and expression demonstrates, point of view depends on two major factors. The first factor is *the physical situation of the narrator, or speaker, as an observer.* How close to the action is the speaker? Is the speaker a major mover or major participant or no more than a witness, either close or distant? How much is he or she privileged to know? How accurate and complete are his or her reports? How do the speaker's characteristics emerge from the narration? What are his or her qualifications or limitations as an observer?

The second factor is *the speaker's intellectual and emotional position.* How might the speaker gain or lose from what takes place in the story? Are the speaker's observations and words colored by these interests? Does he or she have any persuasive purpose beyond being a straightforward recorder or observer? What values does the speaker impose upon the action?

In a story, as in many poems using narrative, authors take into account all these subtleties. For example, O'Connor's narrator Jackie in "First Confession" tells about boyhood family problems and his first experience with the sacrament of confession, but he has not yet fully separated himself from some of his youthful antagonisms. Whitecloud's speaker in "Blue Winds Dancing" (Chapter 3) is filled with misgivings about the life he leaves and relief about the life to which he is returning. These narrators show their own involvement and concern about the events they describe. The speaker in Jackson's "The Lottery," however, does not seem personally involved in the actions. This narrator listens, sees, and reports, but does not express deep involvement in the events of the story's country village. As readers, we need to develop our understanding of how such differing modes of presentation create the effects of these and all other stories and narrative poems.

POINT OF VIEW AND OPINIONS

Because *point of view* is often popularly understood to mean ideas, opinions, or beliefs, it must be stressed that the term is not directly synonymous with any of these. Point of view refers to a work's mode of narration, comprising narrator, language, audience, and perceptions of events and characters, while opinions and beliefs are thoughts and ideas that may or may not have anything to do with a narration.

One may grant, however, that the position from which people see and understand things (e.g., established positions of political party, religion, social philosophy, and morality) has a most definite bearing on how they think and therefore on their opinions and beliefs. Opinions also affect how people view reality, and opinions affect, if not control, what they say about reality. Therefore, opinions stem out of point of view and at the same time have an influence on point of view. A four-star general and a buck private will have different things to say about what happens on a wartime battlefield.

For our purposes in this chapter, however, a discussion of point of view should emphasize how the narration and dramatic situation of a work create and shape the work. If ideas seem to be particularly important in a story, your objective should be not to analyze and discuss the ideas as ideas, but rather to consider whether and how these ideas affect what the narrator concludes and says about the story's actions and situations.

❧ DETERMINING A WORK'S POINT OF VIEW

In your reading you will encounter a wide variety of points of view. To begin your analysis, first determine the work's grammatical voice (i.e., first, second, or third person). Then study the ways in which the subject, characterization, dialogue, and form interact with the point of view.

In the First-Person Point of View, the Narrator Tells about Events He or She Has Personally Witnessed

If the voice of the work is an "I," the author is using the **first-person point of view**—the impersonation of a fictional narrator or speaker who may be named or unnamed. In our hypothetical accident reports, both Alice and Bill are first-person speakers who are named. Similarly, the narrator of O'Connor's "First Confession" is named and identified. By contrast, the narrator of Américo Parédes' "The Hammon and the Beans" (Chapter 8) is an unnamed speaker. In Twain's "Luck" (Chapter 7), there are two unnamed first-person speakers (the first "I" introduces the second "I").

First-person speakers report events as though they have acquired their knowledge in a number of ways:

- What they themselves have done, said, heard, and thought (firsthand experience).
- What they have observed others doing and saying (firsthand witness).
- What others have said to them or otherwise communicated to them (secondhand testimony and hearsay).
- What they are able to infer or deduce from the information they have discovered (inferential information).
- What they are able to conjecture about how a character or characters might think and act, given their knowledge of a situation (conjectural, imaginative, or intuitive information).

THERE ARE MANY DIFFERENT KINDS OF FIRST-PERSON SPEAKERS.   Of all the points of view, the first person is the most independent of the author, because, as we have seen, the first-person speaker may have a unique identity, with name, job, and economic and social position. Often, however, the author creates a more anonymous but still independent first-person speaker, as with the unnamed speaker-narrator of Poe's "The Masque of the Red Death." There are also situations in which an "I" speaker is pluralized by "we" when the first person includes other characters. Such a first-person plural point of view lends reliability to the narrative, as in Zabytko's "Home Soil" (Chapter 10), because the characters included as "we," even if they are unidentified by the speaker, may be considered additional witnesses.

SOME FIRST-PERSON SPEAKERS ARE RELIABLE, AND OTHERS ARE UNRELIABLE.   When you encounter a first-person narrative (whether a story or narrative poem), determine the narrator's position and ability, prejudices or self-interest, and judgment of his or her readers or listeners. Most first-person speakers describing their own experiences are to be accepted as **reliable** and authoritative. But sometimes first-person speakers are **unreliable** because they may have interests or limitations that lead them to mislead, distort, or even lie. There is reason, for example, to question the reliability of the narrator of O'Connor's "First Confession." As an adult he is describing the events within his family and his after-school preparation sessions prior to his attending his first confession, but he is giving us his childhood memories, and he is not including the potential views of others about the ways in which things happened. Whether first-person speakers are reliable or unreliable, however, they are one of the means by which authors confer an authentic, lifelike aura to their works.

In the Second-Person Point of View, the Narrator Is Speaking to Someone Else Who Is Addressed as "You"

The **second-person point of view,** the least common of the points of view, offers the writer two major possibilities. In the first, a narrator (almost necessarily a first-person speaker) tells a listener what he or she has done and said at a past time. The actions might be a simple retelling of events, as when a parent tells a child about something the child did during infancy, or when a doctor tells a patient with amnesia about events before the causative injury. Also, the actions might also be subject to dispute and interpretation, as when a prosecuting attorney describes a crime for which a defendant is on trial or when a spouse lists grievances against an alienated spouse in a custody or divorce case. Still another situation of the second-person point of view might occur when an angry person accuses the listener of a betrayal or some other wrong. In such instances, it is worth bearing in mind that the point of view may possibly be considered first person rather than second, for the speaker is likely to be speaking subjectively about his or her own perception about the listener's actions.

The second possibility is equally complex. Some narrators seem to be addressing a "you" but are instead referring mainly to themselves—and to listeners only tangentially—in preference to an "I." In addition, some narrators follow the usage—not uncommon in colloquial speech—of the indefinite "you." In this use of point of view, the *you* (or *thou*) refers not to a specific listener but rather to anyone at all. In this way the writer avoids the more formal use of words like *one, a person,* or *people.* (Incidentally, the selection of *you* is non-gender-specific because it eliminates the need for pronouns such as *he, she,* or *he or she.*) A clever variation of the "you" point of view is seen in Lorrie Moore's "How to Become a Writer," in which the narrator is apparently describing her own experiences under the guise of giving directions to a listener interested in developing a writing career.

In the Third-Person Point of View, the Speaker Emphasizes the Actions and Speeches of Others

If events in the work are described in the third person (*he, she, it, they*), the author is using the **third-person point of view**. It is not always easy to characterize the voice in this point of view. Sometimes the speaker uses an "I," as in Poe's

"The Masque of the Red Death," and may seemingly be identical with the author, but at other times the author creates a distinct **authorial voice,** as in Faulkner's "Barn Burning" (Chapter 4). There are three variants of the third-person point of view: *dramatic* or *objective, omniscient,* and *limited omniscient.*

THE DRAMATIC OR OBJECTIVE POINT OF VIEW IS THE MOST BASIC METHOD OF NARRATION.   The most direct presentation of action and dialogue is the **dramatic** or **objective point of view** (also called **third-person objective**). It is the basic method of rendering action and speech that all the points of view share. The narrator of the dramatic point of view is an unidentified speaker who reports things in a way that is analogous to a hovering or tracking video camera or to what some critics have called "a fly on the wall (or tree)." Somehow, the narrator is always on the spot—in rooms, forests, village squares, moving vehicles, or even in outer space—to tell us what is happening and what is being said.

The dramatic presentation is limited *only* to what is said and what happens. The writer does not overtly draw conclusions or make interpretations, because the premise of the dramatic point of view is that readers, like a jury, can form their own interpretations if they are shown the right evidence. Jackson's "The Lottery"—a powerful example of the dramatic point of view—is an objective story about a bizarre small-town lottery. We, the readers, draw many conclusions about the story (such as that the people are tradition bound, insensitive, cruel, and so on), but because of the dramatic point of view, Jackson does not *state* any of these conclusions for us.

THE NARRATOR OF THE OMNISCIENT POINT OF VIEW CAN SEE ALL AND POTENTIALLY CAN DISCLOSE ALL.   The third-person point of view is **omniscient** (all-knowing) when the speaker not only presents action and dialogue but also reports what goes on in the minds of the characters. In our everyday real world, we never know, nor can we ever know, what other people are thinking. However, we always make assumptions about the thoughts of others, and these assumptions are the basis of the omniscient point of view. Authors use it freely but judiciously to explain responses, thoughts, feelings, and plans—an additional dimension that aids in the development of character. For example, in Maupassant's "The Necklace" (Chapter 1) the speaker takes an omniscient stance to explain the responses and thoughts of the major character and also, though to a lesser degree, of her husband.

THE NARRATOR OR SPEAKER IN THE LIMITED OR LIMITED-OMNISCIENT POINT OF VIEW FOCUSES ON THOUGHTS AND DEEDS OF A MAJOR CHARACTER.   More common than the omniscient and dramatic points of view is the **limited third person** or **limited omniscient third person,** in which the author concentrates on or *limits* the narration to the actions and thoughts of a major character. In our accident case, Frank, being Bill's friend, would be sympathetic to Bill; thus his report of the collision would likely be third-person limited, with Bill as the center of interest. Depending on whether a narration focuses on action or motivation, the limited third-person narrator may explore the mentality of the major character either lightly or in depth. The name given to the central figure on whom the third-person omniscient point of view is focused is the **point-of-view character.** Thus, Barrett Clare in Gilchrist's "The Song of Songs," Peyton Farquhar in "An Occurrence at Owl Creek Bridge," and Goodman Brown in Hawthorne's "Young Goodman Brown" (Chapter 9) are all point-of-view characters. Almost everything in these stories is there because the point-of-view characters see it, hear it, respond to it, think about it, imagine it entirely, do it or share in it, try to control it, or are controlled by it.

⋔ MINGLING POINTS OF VIEW

In some works, authors mingle points of view in order to imitate reality. For example, many first-person narrators use various types of the third-person point of view during much of their narration. Authors may also vary points of view to sustain interest, create suspense, or put the burden of response entirely upon readers. For example, Gilchrist in "The Song of Songs" preserves an almost exclusive focus on the major character, Barrett, until the final three paragraphs of the story, when there is a shift to a dramatic point of view as she meets her mother. As a result it appears that Barrett's emotional turmoil is at an end and that her life will be taking a positive and more normal turn. A comparable but contrasting change in point of view occurs at the end of Hawthorne's "Young Goodman Brown," where the narrator objectively and almost brutally summarizes Brown's loveless and morose life after his nightmare about evil. Similar changes occur in Bierce's "An Occurrence at Owl Creek Bridge," when the narrative shifts from close identification with the major character, Farquhar, to a remote and objective view of him at the story's conclusion.

POINT OF VIEW AND VERB TENSE

As demonstrated in this chapter, point of view refers to the ways narrators and speakers perceive and report actions and speeches. In the broadest sense, however, point of view may be considered as a total way of rendering truth, and for this reason the *tense* chosen by the narrators is important. Most narratives rely on the past tense: The actions happened in the past, and they are now over. The introduction of dialogue, however, even in a past-tense narration, dramatically brings the story into the present. Such dramatic rendering is accomplished by the dialogue concluding Maupassant's "The Necklace," for example, which emphasizes the immediacy of Mathilde's problems.

The narrator of a past-tense narrative may also introduce present-tense commentary during the narration—a strong means of signifying the importance of past events. Examples are in O'Connor's "First Confession," in which the narrator Jackie makes personal comments about the events he is describing, and in Mark Twain's "Luck," where the second narrator expresses amazement over the mistakes of the main character. In addition, as noted in Chapter 9, the narrators of parables and fables use past-tense narratives as vehicles for teaching current lessons in philosophy and religion.

In recent years a number of writers have used the present tense as their principal time reference. With the present tense, the narrative story or poem is rendered as a virtual drama that is unfolded moment by moment. In "Blue Winds Dancing," for instance, Whitecloud uses the present tense to emphasize the immediate experience as the narrator returns home. Joy Williams uses the present tense in "Taking Care" (Chapter 2) as a means not only of emphasizing the immediacy of the main character's situation, but also of demonstrating his future challenges.

Some writers intermingle tenses to show how time itself can be merged within the human mind, because our consciousness never exists only in the present but instead is a composite made up of past memories cresting upon a never-ending wave carrying us into the future. Thus at the end of Bierce's "An Occurrence at Owl Creek Bridge," the past-tense narration shifts into the present tense to demonstrate the vividness of the main character's perceptions just before his death.

❦ SUMMARY: GUIDELINES FOR POINT OF VIEW

The following guidelines summarize and further classify the types of points of view. Use them to distinguish differences and shades of variation in stories and poems.

1. **First person (*I, my, mine, me*, and sometimes *we, our*, and *us*).** First-person speakers are involved to at least some degree in the actions of the work. Such narrators may have (1) complete understanding, (2) partial or incorrect understanding, (3) no understanding at all, or (4) complete understanding with the motive to mislead or lie. Although the narrators described in guidelines 1 through 3 are usually **reliable** and tell the truth, they may also sometimes be **unreliable.** The only way to tell is to study the story closely. Obviously, 4 is by nature unreliable, but nevertheless might possibly be accepted (although critically) on matters of detail.

   a. *Major participant*
      i. Who tells his or her own story and thoughts as a major mover.
      ii. Who tells a story about others and also about herself or himself as one of the major movers.
      iii. Who tells a story mainly about others, and about himself or herself only tangentially.

   b. *Minor participant*, who tells a story about events experienced and witnessed.

   c. *Nonparticipating but identifiable speaker*, who learns about events in other ways (e.g., listening to participants through direct conversation, overhearing conversation, examining documents, hearing news reports, imagining what might have occurred). The narrative of such a speaker is a combination of fact and conjectural reconstruction.

2. **Second person (*you*, or possibly *thou*).** A rare point of view that occurs often enough to know about. It occurs (1) when the speaker (e.g., parent, psychologist) knows more about a character's actions than the character himself or herself; or (2) when the speaker (e.g., lawyer, spouse, friend, sports umpire, angry person) is explaining to another person (the "you") that person's disputable actions and statements. The speaker may also use "you" to mean (3) himself or herself or (4) anyone at all.

3. **Third person (*she, he, it, they*).** The speaker is outside the action and is mainly a reporter of actions and speeches. Some speakers may have unique and distinguishing traits even though no separate identity is claimed for them ("the unnamed third-person narrator"). Other third-person speakers who are not separately identifiable may represent the words and views of the authors themselves ("the authorial voice").

   a. *Dramatic or third-person objective.* The narrator reports only what can be seen and heard. The thoughts of characters are included only if they are spoken or written (dialogue, reported or overheard conversation, letters, reports, etc.).

   b. *Omniscient.* The omniscient speaker knows all, sees all, reports all, and when necessary, reveals the inner workings of the minds of any or all characters. Even an omniscient speaker, however, makes a mostly dramatic presentation.

   c. *Limited, or limited omniscient.* The focus is on the actions, responses, thoughts, and feelings of a single major character. Although the narration may concentrate on the character's actions, it may simultaneously probe deeply within the consciousness of the character.

STORIES FOR STUDY

AMBROSE BIERCE (1842–1914?)

Bierce was a native of Ohio, the youngest of nine children in the highly religious family of a poor farmer. When the Civil War began he enlisted in the Union army as a drummer boy and rose to the rank of major by the war's end. After the war he went to San Francisco to begin a career in journalism. At various times he reported, edited, and wrote reviews for papers such as the San Francisco Examiner *and the* San Francisco News-Letter. *After he married he and his wife spent five years in England, but eventually she left him and their two children died—events that had an embittering effect on him. In 1913 he traveled to Mexico, and nothing further is known about him; he is presumed to have died in revolutionary fighting there in 1914. Bierce published his first story in 1871 and later published two volumes of stories:* In the Midst of Life *(1892, originally published in 1891 as* Tales of Soldiers and Civilians, *which included "An Occurrence at Owl Creek Bridge"), and* Can Such Things Be? *(1893). He is perhaps best known for his sometimes cynical* The Devil's Dictionary *(1911). He favored the short story as a form over the novel on much the same grounds as Poe, namely that the story could be designed to produce a single effect. He believed that fiction should be realistic and should build to concluding twists and surprises—goals that are seen in "An Occurrence at Owl Creek Bridge." His complete works, which he edited himself, appeared in twelve volumes from 1909 to 1912.*

An Occurrence at Owl Creek Bridge   1891

A man stood upon a railroad bridge in northern Alabama, looking down into the swift water twenty feet below. The man's hands were behind his back, the wrists bound with a cord. A rope closely encircled his neck. It was attached to a stout cross-timber above his head and the slack fell to the level of his knees. Some loose boards laid upon the sleepers supporting the metals of the railway supplied a footing for him and his executioners—two private soldiers of the Federal army, directed by a sergeant who in civil life may have been a deputy sheriff. At a short remove upon the same temporary platform was an officer in the uniform of his rank, armed. He was a captain. A sentinel at each end of the bridge stood with his rifle in the position known as "support," that is to say, vertical in front of the left shoulder, the hammer resting on the forearm thrown straight across the chest—a formal and unnatural position, enforcing an erect carriage of the body. It did not appear to be the duty of these two men to know what was occurring at the center of the bridge; they merely blockaded the two ends of the foot planking that traversed it.

Beyond one of the sentinels nobody was in sight; the railroad ran straight away into a forest for a hundred yards, then, curving, was lost to view. Doubtless there was an outpost farther along. The other bank of the stream was open ground—a gentle acclivity topped with a stockade of vertical tree trunks, loopholed for rifles, with a single embrasure through which protruded the muzzle of a brass cannon commanding the bridge. Midway of the slope between the bridge and fort were the spectators—a single company of infantry in line, at "parade rest," the butts of the rifles on the ground, the barrels inclining slightly backward against the right shoulder, the hands crossed upon the stock. A lieutenant stood at the right of the line, the point of his sword upon the ground, his left hand resting upon his right. Excepting the group of four at the center of the bridge, not a man moved. The company faced the bridge, staring stonily, motionless. The sentinels, facing the banks of the stream, might have been statues to adorn the bridge. The captain stood with folded arms, silent, observing the work of his subordinates, but making no sign. Death is a dignitary who when he comes announced is to be received with formal manifestations of respect, even by those most familiar with him. In the code of military etiquette silence and fixity are forms of deference.

The man who was engaged in being hanged was apparently about thirty-five years of age. He was a civilian, if one might judge from his habit, which was that of a planter. His features were good—a straight nose, firm mouth, broad forehead, from which his long, dark hair was combed straight back, falling behind his ears to the collar of his well-fitting frock coat. He wore a mustache and pointed beard, but no whiskers; his eyes were large and dark gray, and had a kindly expression which one would hardly have expected in one whose neck was in the hemp. Evidently this was no vulgar assassin. The liberal military code makes provision for hanging many kinds of persons, and gentlemen are not excluded.

The preparations being complete, the two private soldiers stepped aside and each drew away the plank upon which he had been standing. The sergeant turned to the captain, saluted and placed himself immediately behind that officer, who in turn moved apart one pace. These movements left the condemned man and the sergeant standing on the two ends of the same plank, which spanned three of the cross-ties of the bridge. The end upon which the civilian stood almost, but not quite, reached a fourth. This plank had been held in place by the weight of the captain; it was now held by that of the sergeant. At a signal from the former the latter would step aside, the plank would tilt and the condemned man go down between two ties. The arrangement commended itself to his judgment as simple and effective. His face had not been covered nor his eyes bandaged. He looked a moment at his "unsteadfast footing," then let his gaze wander to the swirling water of the stream racing madly beneath his feet. A piece of dancing driftwood caught his attention and his eyes followed it down the current. How slowly it appeared to move! What a sluggish stream!

He closed his eyes in order to fix his last thoughts upon his wife and children. The water, touched to gold by the early sun, the brooding mists under the banks at some distance down the stream, the fort, the soldiers, the piece of driftwood—all had distracted him. And now he became conscious of a new disturbance. Striking through the thought of his dear ones was a sound which he could neither ignore nor understand, a sharp, distinct, metallic percussion like the stroke of a blacksmith's hammer upon the anvil; it had the same ringing quality. He wondered what it was, and whether immeasurably distant or near by—it seemed both. Its recurrence was regular, but as slow as the tolling of a death knell. He awaited each stroke with impatience and—he knew not why—apprehension. The intervals of silence grew progressively longer; the delays became maddening. With their greater infrequency the sounds increased in strength and sharpness. They hurt his ear like the thrust of a knife; he feared he would shriek. What he heard was the ticking of his watch. 5

He unclosed his eyes and saw again the water below him. "If I could free my hands," he thought, "I might throw off the noose and spring into the stream. By diving I could evade the bullets and, swimming vigorously, reach the bank, take to the woods and get away home. My home, thank God, is as yet outside their lines; my wife and little ones are still beyond the invader's farthest advance."

As these thoughts, which have here to be set down in words, were flashed into the doomed man's brain rather than evolved from it the captain nodded to the sergeant. The sergeant stepped aside.

II

Peyton Farquhar was a well-to-do planter, of an old and highly respected Alabama family. Being a slave owner and like other slave owners a politician he was naturally an original secessionist and ardently devoted to the Southern cause. Circumstances of an imperious nature, which it is unnecessary to relate here, had prevented him from taking service with the gallant army that had fought the disastrous campaigns ending with the fall of Corinth,° and he chafed under the inglorious restraint, longing for the release of his energies, the larger life of the soldier, the opportunity for distinction. That opportunity, he felt, would come, as it comes to all in war time. Meanwhile he did what he could. No service was too humble for him to perform in aid of the South, no adventure too perilous for him to undertake if consistent with the character of a civilian who was at heart a soldier, and who in good faith and without too much qualification assented to at least a part of the frankly villainous dictum that all is fair in love and war.

One evening while Farquhar and his wife were sitting on a rustic bench near the entrance to his grounds, a gray-clad soldier rode up to the gate and asked for a drink of water. Mrs. Farquhar was only too happy to serve him with her own white hands. While she was fetching the water her husband approached the dusty horseman and inquired eagerly for news from the front.

"The Yanks are repairing the railroads," said the man, "and are getting ready for another advance. They have reached the Owl Creek bridge, put it in order and built a stockade on the north bank. The commandant has issued an order, which is posted everywhere, declaring that any civilian caught interfering with the railroad, its bridges, tunnels or trains will be summarily hanged. I saw the order." 10

Corinth: In the northeast corner of Mississippi, near the Alabama state line, Corinth was the site of a battle in 1862 won by the Union army.

"How far is it to the Owl Creek bridge?" Farquhar asked.

"About thirty miles."

"Is there no force on this side of the creek?"

"Only a picket post half a mile out, on the railroad, and a single sentinel at this end of the bridge."

"Suppose a man—a civilian and student of hanging—should elude the picket   15 post and perhaps get the better of the sentinel," said Farquhar, smiling, "what could he accomplish?"

The soldier reflected. "I was there a month ago," he replied, "I observed that the flood of last winter had lodged a great quantity of driftwood against the wooden pier at this end of the bridge. It is now dry and would burn like tow."

The lady had now brought the water, which the soldier drank. He thanked her ceremoniously, bowed to her husband and rode away. An hour later, after nightfall, he repassed the plantation, going northward in the direction from which he had come. He was a Federal scout.

III

As Peyton Farquhar fell straight downward through the bridge he lost consciousness and was as one already dead. From this state he was awakened—ages later, it seemed to him— by the pain of a sharp pressure upon his throat, followed by a sense of suffocation. Keen, poignant agonies seemed to shoot from his neck downward through every fiber of his body and limbs. These pains appeared to flash along well-defined lines of ramification and to beat with an inconceivably rapid periodicity. They seemed like streams of pulsating fire heating him to an intolerable temperature. As to his head, he was conscious of nothing but a feeling of fulness—of congestion. These sensations were unaccompanied by thought. The intellectual part of his nature was already effaced; he had power only to feel, and feeling was torment. He was conscious of motion. Encompassed in a luminous cloud, of which he was now merely the fiery heart, without material substance, he swung through unthinkable arcs of oscillation, like a vast pendulum. Then all at once, with terrible suddenness, the light about him shot upward with the noise of a loud plash; a frightful roaring was in his ears, and all was cold and dark. The power of thought was restored; he knew that the rope had broken and he had fallen into the stream. There was no additional strangulation; the noose about his neck was already suffocating him and kept the water from his lungs. To die of hanging at the bottom of a river!—the idea seemed to him ludicrous. He opened his eyes in the darkness and saw above him a gleam of light, but how distant, how inaccessible! He was still sinking, for the light became fainter and fainter until it was a mere glimmer. Then it began to grow and brighten, and he knew that he was rising toward the surface—knew it with reluctance, for he was now very comfortable. "To be hanged and drowned," he thought, "that is not so bad; but I do not wish to be shot. No; I will not be shot; that is not fair."

He was not conscious of an effort, but a sharp pain in his wrist apprised him that he was trying to free his hands. He gave the struggle his attention, as an idler might observe the feat of a juggler, without interest in the outcome. What splendid effort—what magnificent, what superhuman strength! Ah, that was a fine endeavor! Bravo! The cord fell away; his arms parted and floated upward; the hands dimly seen on each side in the growing light. He watched them with a new interest as first one and then the other pounced upon the noose at his neck. They tore it away and thrust it fiercely aside, its undulations resembling those of a water snake. "Put it back, put it back!" He thought he shouted these words to his hands, for the undoing of the noose had been succeeded by the direst pang that he had yet experienced. His neck ached horribly; his brain was on fire; his heart, which had been fluttering faintly, gave a great leap, trying to force itself out at his mouth. His whole body was racked and wrenched with an insupportable anguish! But his disobedient hands gave no heed to the command. They beat the water vigorously with quick, downward strokes, forcing him to the surface. He felt his head emerge; his eyes were blinded by the sunlight; his chest expanded convulsively, and with a supreme and crowning agony his lungs engulfed a great draught of air, which instantly he expelled in a shriek!

He was now in full possession of his physical senses. They were indeed, preternaturally keen and alert. Something in the awful disturbance of his organic system had so exalted and refined them that they made record of things never before perceived. He felt the ripples upon his face and heard their separate sounds as they struck. He looked at the forest on the bank of the stream, saw the individual trees, the leaves and the veining of each leaf—saw the very insects upon them: the locusts, the brilliant-bodied flies, the gray spiders stretching their webs from twig to twig. He noted the prismatic colors in all the dewdrops upon a million blades of grass. The humming of the gnats that danced above the eddies of the stream, the beating of the dragon flies' wings, the strokes of the water-spiders' legs, like oars which had lifted their boat—all these made audible music. A fish slid along beneath his eyes and he heard the rush of its body parting the water. 20

He had come to the surface facing down the stream; in a moment the visible world seemed to wheel slowly round, himself the pivotal point, and he saw the bridge, the fort, the soldiers upon the bridge, the captain, the sergeant, the two privates, his executioners. They were in silhouette against the blue sky. They shouted and gesticulated, pointing at him. The captain had drawn his pistol, but did not fire; the others were unarmed. Their movements were grotesque and horrible, their forms gigantic.

Suddenly he heard a sharp report and something struck the water smartly within a few inches of his head, spattering his face with spray. He heard a second report, and saw one of the sentinels with his rifle at his shoulder, a light cloud of blue smoke rising from the muzzle. The man in the water saw the eye of the man on the bridge gazing into his own through the sights of the rifle. He observed that it was a gray eye and remembered having read that gray eyes were keenest, and that all famous marksmen had them. Nevertheless, this one had missed.

A counter-swirl had caught Farquhar and turned him half round; he was again looking into the forest on the bank opposite the fort. The sound of a clear, high voice in a monotonous singsong now rang out behind him and came across the water with a distinctness that pierced and subdued all other sounds, even the beating of the ripples in his ears. Although no soldier, he had frequented camps enough to know the dread significance of that deliberate, drawling, aspirated chant; the lieutenant on shore was taking a part in the morning's work. How coldly and pitilessly—with what an even, calm intonation, presaging, and enforcing tranquility in the men—with what accurately measured intervals fell those cruel words:

"Attention, company! . . . Shoulder arms! . . . Ready! . . . Aim! . . . Fire!"

Farquhar dived—dived as deeply as he could. The water roared in his ears like the voice of Niagara, yet he heard the dulled thunder of the volley and, rising again toward the surface, met shining bits of metal, singularly flattened, oscillating slowly downward. Some of them touched him on the face and hands, then fell away, continuing their descent. One lodged between his collar and neck; it was uncomfortably warm and he snatched it out. 25

As he rose to the surface, gasping for breath, he saw that he had been a long time under water; he was perceptibly farther down stream—nearer to safety. The soldiers had almost finished reloading; the metal ramrods flashed all at once in the sunshine as they were drawn from the barrels, turned in the air, and thrust into their sockets. The two sentinels fired again, independently and ineffectually.

The hunted man saw all this over his shoulder; he was now swimming vigorously with the current. His brain was as energetic as his arms and legs; he thought with the rapidity of lightning.

"The officer," he reasoned, "will not make that martinet's error a second time. It is as easy to dodge a volley as a single shot. He has probably already given the command to fire at will. God help me, I cannot dodge them all!"

An appalling plash within two yards of him was followed by a loud, rushing sound, *diminuendo*, which seemed to travel back through the air to the fort and died in an explosion which stirred the very river to its deeps! A rising sheet of water curved over him, fell down upon him, blinded him, strangled him! The cannon had taken a hand in the game. As he shook his head free from the commotion of the smitten water he heard the deflected shot humming through the air ahead, and in an instant it was cracking and smashing the branches in the forest beyond.

"They will not do that again," he thought; "the next time they will use a charge of grape. I must keep my eye upon the gun; the smoke will apprise me—the report arrives too late; it lags behind the missile. That is a good gun."   30

Suddenly he felt himself whirled round and round—spinning like a top. The water, the banks, the forests, the now distant bridge, fort and men—all were commingled and blurred. Objects were represented by their colors only; circular horizontal streaks of color—that was all he saw. He had been caught in a vortex and was being whirled on with a velocity of advance and gyration that made him giddy and sick. In a few moments he was flung upon the gravel at the foot of the left bank of the stream—the southern bank—and behind a projecting point which concealed him from his enemies. The sudden arrest of his motion, the abrasion of one of his hands on the gravel, restored him, and he wept with delight. He dug his fingers into the sand, threw it over himself in handfuls and audibly blessed it. It looked like diamonds, rubies, emeralds; he could think of nothing beautiful which it did not resemble. The trees upon the bank were giant garden plants; he noted a definite order in their arrangement, inhaled the fragrance of their blooms. A strange, roseate light shone through the spaces among their trunks and the wind made in their branches the music of Æolian harps. He had no wish to perfect his escape—was content to remain in that enchanting spot until retaken.

A whiz and rattle of grapeshot among the branches high above his head roused him from his dream. The baffled cannoneer had fired him a random farewell. He sprang to his feet, rushed up the sloping bank, and plunged into the forest.

All that day he traveled, laying his course by the rounding sun. The forest seemed interminable; nowhere did he discover a break in it, not even a woodman's road. He had not known that he lived in so wild a region. There was something uncanny in the revelation.

By nightfall he was fatigued, footsore, famishing. The thought of his wife and children urged him on. At last he found a road which led him in what he knew to be the right direction. It was as wide and straight as a city street, yet it seem untraveled. No fields bordered it, no dwelling anywhere. Not so much as the barking of a dog suggested human habitation. The black bodies of the trees formed a straight wall on both sides, terminating on the horizon in a point, like a diagram in a lesson in perspective. Overhead, as he looked up through this rift in the wood, shone great golden stars looking unfamiliar and grouped in strange constellations. He was sure they were arranged in some order which had a secret and malign significance. The wood on either side was full of singular noises, among which—once, twice, and again—he distinctly heard whispers in an unknown tongue.

His neck was in pain and lifting his hand to it found it horribly swollen. He knew   35
that it had a circle of black where the rope had bruised it. His eyes felt congested;
he could no longer close them. His tongue was swollen with thirst; he relieved its
fever by thrusting it forward from between his teeth into the cold air. How softly the
turf had carpeted the untraveled avenue—he could no longer feel the roadway beneath his feet!

Doubtless, despite his suffering, he had fallen asleep while walking, for now he
sees another scene—perhaps he has merely recovered from a delirium. He stands at
the gate of his own home. All is as he left it, and all bright and beautiful in the morning
sunshine. He must have traveled the entire night. As he pushes open the gate and passes up the wide white walk, he sees a flutter of female garments; his wife, looking fresh
and cool and sweet, steps down from the veranda to meet him. At the bottom of the
steps she stands waiting, with a smile of ineffable joy, an attitude of matchless grace and
dignity. Ah, how beautiful she is! He springs forward with extended arms. As he is
about to clasp her he feels a stunning blow upon the back of the neck; a blinding white
light blazes all about him with a sound like the shock of a cannon—then all is darkness
and silence!

Peyton Farquhar was dead; his body, with a broken neck, swung gently from side to
side beneath the timbers of the Owl Creek bridge.

QUESTIONS

1.   What is the situation in the story? What did Farquhar do to deserve his
     execution?

2.   Describe the various shifts in the story's point of view, particularly as indicated in
     paragraphs 5 and 37. How does Bierce make you aware of Farquhar's height-
     ened consciousness?

3.   According to Farquhar's perception of time, how long does it take him to get
     home after his escape (see paragraphs 33 and 36)?

4.   What evidence can you find to indicate that Farquhar is experiencing great pain,
     despite his feelings that he is escaping?

5.   What is the effect of the shift into the present tense in paragraph 36?

ELLEN GILCHRIST (b. 1935)

*A writer of novels, short stories, and poems, Gilchrist was born in
Mississippi and received her higher education at Vanderbilt and
Millsaps College. Among her novels are* The Annunciation
(1984) and I Cannot Get You Close Enough *(1990), which is
a collection of three novellas. Story collections are* In the Land of
Dreamy Dreams *(1981),* Drunk with Love *(1986), and* Light
Can Be Both Wave and Particle *(1989), from which "The Song
of Songs" is taken. Her newest collection is* "I, Rhoda Manning,
Go Hunting with My Daddy" and Other Stories *(2002).*

The Song of Songs   1989

It was Christmas morning. A bright clear day. Almost cool. The city of New Orleans lay in peace. Sleeeeep in heavenly peeeace. Sleep in heavenly peace."°

Strains of hymns from midnight mass echoed in the ears of the faithful. For unto us a child is born. Unto us a son is given.° The smell of lilies and candles. Morning.

Children were waking. Cats prowled the marble floors of the mansions of the Garden District and the lesser mansions of the Lower Garden District and the victorian houses of the university section.

Barrett Clare had slept like a baby on two Valiums and a Seconal, safe in the high bedroom of the biggest whitest house on State Street. She had fought for that house. If it had been up to him, Charlie Clare would have settled for the old Phipps place, that tacky brick box.

She opened her eyes. The sun was slanting in the wooden shutters, casting bright demarcations over everything on the floor, her red wool dress, her De Liso Debs, her satin, hand-embroidered slip, her underpants, her bra. She had slept alone in the walnut bed. I have always been alone, she thought, and rose from the bed, shaking off the fuzzy feeling of the drugs, worrying that Charles was already awake, looking for her. Her baby, her one and only love, her boy. Damn, she thought, and shook her head again. The Seconal was too much. That was going too far. Still, it was better than not sleeping. It was better than dreams.

She picked up the slacks she had been wearing the day before and squeezed them in her hand. She had been wearing them when the tall blond boy came with his terrible message. That nightmare. Only it was true. He had come out of nowhere at eleven o'clock in the morning on Christmas Eve to tell her where her mother was. Her real mother, the one that had borne her into the world and given her away. She never touched me, Barrett had told Gustave over and over. No, I know she didn't. I would remember if she had. No one can remember that far back, he would say, and move around ever so gradually in his old brown chair. An enormous response from Gustave. She never touched me, Barrett would insist. I know. I would know. They got me from the home when I was five days old. I weighed eight pounds. I was a huge baby. I was alone when I was born and I have been alone ever since. She had me and then she never even looked at me. Gustave would move again in his chair. When she talked of *it* at least he listened. Well, he always listened. He was a wonderful doctor. A member of the Academy. He was the best. The very best. The best that money could buy.

Where was he now that she needed him? Where had he gone to? How dare he leave town at Christmas. Why couldn't they find him? They could find him if they really wanted to. She sat down on the bed and rang his answering service.

"You know you can find him. You must tell him it's an emergency. Tell him it's Barrett, Barrett Clare. You must reach him for me. All right, I'll be waiting. Yes, please try." She hung up. Who do they think they are? Those answering-service people.

Amanda McCamey is my mother. I'll call her on the phone. The thought was like an arrow. It flew across the room and disappeared. No, it's her place to call me. If she knows where I am. Your mother is named Amanda McCamey and she is up in Arkansas and she is going to have a baby any day now. That is what the blond boy said. I am going there now. I will tell her that I told you.

I'll go too, she had answered. I will go and talk to her. You can't go, he said. She is going to have a baby. She doesn't know you know. She doesn't know I'm here.

Sleeeeep . . . peace: from the Christmas hymn "Silent Night."
For . . . given: chorus from *Messiah* (1741) by George Frideric Handel (1685–1759).

I want to tell someone, Barrett thought. I need to tell someone who my mother is. She is so beautiful. Didn't I touch her? That day at Loyola? When Brummette introduced us. I think I touched her. I think I shook her hand. She called me Shelley. She thought my name was Shelley. Why hasn't she called me if she knows who I am? Here is your mother, the blond boy said. And now I am taking her away.

A rush of fuzziness passed across her brain. She shook her head. She picked up Charlie's coat from the chair and started going through the pockets looking for a cigarette. He had come in from Vail at three or four. He had tried to get in bed with her. "It was a snowstorm, baby. They closed the airport. I couldn't help it."

"Get out of here, you bastard. Don't get near me."

"It's Christmas," he said.

"Go away, Charlie."

15

She went into the dressing room and washed her face and hands. She combed her hair. She looked deep into the mirror, searching her face for the face of her mother. It was there. Yes, anyone could see it. I could go on living, she thought. If it never would be Christmas. If I never had to hang that dead tree in the window. Well, Charles will be waking up. I must act normal. I must act like everything's okay. It's Christmas morning. She laughed at that. Suddenly her sadness and self-absorption seemed the silliest thing in all New Orleans.

She went downstairs and found Charles and Charlie in the breakfast room. Charlie still looked drunk. He was reading the paper. Charles had already started opening his presents. "Daddy slept with me," he said. "In my bed." He tore open a package containing a white shirt with his initials on the cuffs. He pulled it out of the package and took the pins out and tried it on. He was five years old, a sturdy wild little boy, excitable, hard to control.

The shirt was too big. The cuffs came down and hid his new Rolex watch. "It hides my watch," he said. "It doesn't fit. You have to take it back."

"You aren't supposed to be opening things yet," Charlie said. "I told you to wait for her. Is Lorraine coming, Barrett? Are we going to have breakfast?"

"She'll be here later. She has to cook for her family. I'll make breakfast. How was Vail?" He didn't answer. She rolled up the sleeves of her robe and set the table with red placemats and a set of Christmas china Charlie's sister had given them the year before. In a while she put a breakfast of bacon and eggs on the plates.

20

"Let's sit together now," she said. "Let's hold hands and say grace. Charles, do you want to say the prayer?" They were holding hands around the table. She could feel the thick wiry hair on Charlie's hand, tough reddish blond hair. Wire, she thought. Like his mind. A piece of wire. I'll put that in a poem.

At least there's Patsy, he was thinking. God love her soft little buns. God love her laughter.

"Lord make us thankful for these and all our many other blessings, for Christ's sake, amen. Ahh, men. That's what old maids say, isn't it, Daddy?"

"You all go on and eat," Barrett said. "I'm going upstairs for a while." She reached over and hugged the little boy. "I love you, Sweetie Pie," she said. "Don't you ever forget that." Charlie sighed and put butter on a biscuit. He took a bite and put the other half on Charles's plate. They were beautiful plates, white porcelain decorated with holly. "I love you too, Charlie," she said. "No matter what you do." She gave him a very small kiss on the cheek.

"Don't you want to see your presents?"

"Not yet," she said. She unrolled the sleeves of her robe and walked out of the kitchen past the painted porch swing. She was the only woman in town with a porch swing in her kitchen. She walked into the hall and up the stairs past the stained-glass window depicting

25

Saint George slaying the dragon. She walked into Charlie's room and took a pistol with handmade wooden handles out of a gun case and walked over to the window looking out on the avenue. Now I will pull the trigger and blow my old blue and brown coiled-up brains all over the Pande Camaroon and some will spill on the Andrew Wyeth and, why not, some of them can move out onto the balcony and festoon the iron railings. You know, they will say, those old railings New Orleans is so famous for? Yes, it will make a good story around town. It will make everybody's day. They'll forget themselves in the story of my willfulness.

She put the gun in her mouth and sucked the barrel. It was a game she liked to play. It was the only power she knew she had. The phone was ringing, a lovely ring, soft, like bells. Barrett took it down from its hanger on the wall. "Is this Barrett Clare?" the voice said. The voice was tearing into her ears. "This is Amanda McCamey. I am your mother. If this is Mrs. Charles Clare. If you are an adopted child, I am your mother. Oh, forgive me, oh, my God, forgive me. I need you so terribly dreadfully much. Will you talk to me? Will you let me talk to you?"

"This is me," she said. "I knew you would call me up. I've been waiting all day."

"I've been waiting all my life," the voice said. "Forgive me for calling you instead of coming there. I should have come. But I can't come for several days, perhaps a week. Will you come to me? Will you come to where I am? Will you bring your little boy? Your father will be here. I will have him here. He's the one that found you. I'll send him for you. Oh, yes, that's what I'll do."

"No," Barrett said. "Don't do that. I'll come today. Tell me where to go. Tell me how to get there." There was a sound on the other end, like sobbing, or something else, something she had never heard. "Don't cry," she said to her mother. "I am going to come to where you are as fast as I can get there. And I'm bringing Charles, my little boy. I will stay a long long time . . . I might come and stay forever. I might not ever leave. Can you hear me? I know you. Do you know that? I know who you are." 30

"How is that? How do you know?"

"I mean we met. At Loyola. Don Brummette introduced us. I used to read everything you wrote. I guess I had a crush on you that year."

"What do you look like? How could I not have known? I can't remember. So many things have happened today. A friend of mine was in a terrible wreck, someone I love. And everything else. Are you really coming here? You will come to me? You will come here?"

"I'm coming as soon as I can pack a bag and leave. I look like you. Yes, I think I look like you. We will look in a mirror. The two of us. We will look at one another. Tell me where you are. How to get there. How to go."

"Here's Katie," Amanda said. "She's my friend. She'll tell you what to do." 35

Then a woman named Katie got on the phone and told Barrett how to get to Fayetteville, Arkansas, from New Orleans, Louisiana. It was not that simple. "I'll be there this afternoon," Barrett said. "Tell my mother that I love her. Tell her I'll be there very soon." She put the phone back on the wall and picked the gun up off the dresser and walked across the room and put it back into the case and turned the key. Then she took the key and walked out on the balcony and threw it far out into the branches of a Japanese magnolia tree. Then she ran down the stairs to her husband and her child.

Charlie was sitting on the floor in a sea of wrapping paper drinking a brandy and playing with Charles. The great hanging tree for which the Clares were famous on State Street swayed softly above him. "Well," he said. "You're going to join us. How charming of you, Barrett."

"My mother just called me on the phone," she said. "My real mother. The one who had me. I'm going there today and taking Charles with me. Now get up please and help me. I want you to call and charter us a plane. She lives up in Arkansas. It's a long way and inaccessible. Do it right now, Charlie. This is not a joke. Something's happened to her. She needs me."

"Your mother?"

"Yes, my mother. Please get me a plane right now, Charlie. While I pack. Charles, you are going with me somewhere. We're going to see your grandmother. Your real grandmother. Someone you've never seen." The child did not move, but her husband, Charlie, got up. He came toward her, reaching out to her. "All right," he said. "That's wonderful. What else? What else can I do?"

"What will we wear?" Charles said. "What will we take to wear?"

"It doesn't matter what we wear," she said. "We're going to see my mother. My mother. I'm going to see my mother." She picked him up off the floor and hugged him fiercely and danced him around the room. I exist, she was singing inside her head. I am here. I am really here. Everything that happens from this day forward will be better. Whatever happens next will be better and better and better. My mother is waiting for me.

A woman named Katie met them at the airport and drove them to a house on top of a small mountain overlooking the university. "It was brave of you to come like this," Katie said. "What a brave thing to do."

"Where are we?" Charles said. "I don't know where we are."

Then they turned into a driveway and Barrett's mother was standing in the doorway of a small wooden house. A tall woman with hair that fell like a cascade almost to her waist. She walked out across the yard and took her daughter into her arms.

QUESTIONS

1. Describe the point of view of this story. Which character is the center of attention? Describe the narrator's attitude toward this character. What are the various ways in which this character is presented to us?

2. What is happening in Barrett's life? Why does she feel "alone ever since" she was born (paragraph 6)? What kind of relationship does she have with her husband, Charlie? Why does she go to her room and take out the gun? What does she do after she speaks with her mother?

3. Of what significance is it that the story takes place on Christmas day?

4. What view does the story present toward adoption and its effect on adopted children as adults?

SHIRLEY JACKSON (1919–1965)

Jackson was a native of California. She graduated from Syracuse University in New York and lived much of her life in Vermont. Although her life was short, she was a successful writer of novels, short stories, biographies, and children's fiction. Her stories often depict unusual, unreal, or bizarre events in common settings, of which "The Lottery" is a major example. She wrote the story in only two hours and submitted it to The New Yorker without major revisions. When it was published many readers raised questions about how to interpret the conclusion. Jackson steadfastly refused to explain, leaving readers to decide for themselves.

The Lottery   1948

The morning of June 27th was clear and sunny, with the fresh warmth of a full summer day; the flowers were blossoming profusely and the grass was richly green. The people of the village began to gather in the square, between the post office and the bank, around ten o'clock; in some towns there were so many people that the lottery took two days and had to be started on June 26th, but in this village, where there were only about three hundred people, the whole lottery took less than two hours, so it could begin at ten o'clock in the morning and still be through in time to allow the villagers to get home for noon dinner.

The children assembled first, of course. School was recently over for the summer, and the feeling of liberty sat uneasily on most of them; they tended to gather together quietly for a while before they broke into boisterous play, and their talk was still of the classroom and the teacher, of books and reprimands. Bobby Martin had already stuffed his pockets full of stones, and the other boys soon followed his example, selecting the smoothest and roundest stones; Bobby and Harry Jones and Dickie Delacroix—the villagers pronounced this name "Dellacroy"—eventually made a great pile of stones in one corner of the square and guarded it against the raids of the other boys. The girls stood aside, talking among themselves, looking over their shoulders at the boys, and the very small children rolled in the dust or clung to the hands of their older brothers or sisters.

Soon the men began to gather, surveying their own children, speaking of planting and rain, tractors and taxes. They stood together, away from the pile of stones in the corner, and their jokes were quiet and they smiled rather than laughed. The women, wearing faded house dresses and sweaters, came shortly after their menfolk. They greeted one another and exchanged bits of gossip as they went to join their husbands. Soon the women, standing by their husbands, began to call to their children, and the children came reluctantly, having to be called four or five times. Bobby Martin ducked under his mother's grasping hand and ran, laughing, back to the pile of stones. His father spoke up sharply, and Bobby came quickly and took his place between his father and his oldest brother.

The lottery was conducted—as were the square dances, the teen-age club, the Halloween program—by Mr. Summers, who had time and energy to devote to civic activities. He was a round-faced, jovial man and he ran the coal business, and people were sorry for him, because he had no children and his wife was a scold. When he arrived in the square, carrying the black wooden box, there was a murmur of conversation among the villagers, and he waved and called, "Little late today, folks." The postmaster, Mr. Graves, followed him, carrying a three-legged stool, and the stool was put in the center of the square and Mr. Summers set the black box down on it. The villagers kept their distance, leaving a space between themselves and the stool, and when Mr. Summers said, "Some of you fellows want to give me a hand?" there was a hesitation before two men, Mr. Martin and his oldest son, Baxter, came forward to hold the box steady on the stool while Mr. Summers stirred up the papers inside it.

The original paraphernalia for the lottery had been lost long ago, and the black box now resting on the stool had been put into use even before Old Man Warner, the oldest man in town, was born. Mr. Summers spoke frequently to the villagers about making a new box, but no one liked to upset even as much tradition as was represented by the black box. There was a story that the present box had been made with some pieces of the box that had preceded it, the one that had been constructed when the first people settled down to make a village here. Every year, after the lottery, Mr. Summers began talking again about a new box, but every year the subject was allowed to fade off without anything's being done. The black box grew shabbier each year; by now it was no longer

5

completely black but splintered badly along one side to show the original wood color, and in some places faded or stained.

Mr. Martin and his oldest son, Baxter, held the black box securely on the stool until Mr. Summers had stirred the papers thoroughly with his hand. Because so much of the ritual had been forgotten or discarded, Mr. Summers had been successful in having slips of paper substituted for the chips of wood that had been used for generations. Chips of wood, Mr. Summers had argued, had been all very well when the village was tiny, but now that the population was more than three hundred and likely to keep on growing, it was necessary to use something that would fit more easily into the black box. The night before the lottery, Mr. Summers and Mr. Graves made up the slips of paper and put them in the box, and it was then taken to the safe of Mr. Summers' coal company and locked up until Mr. Summers was ready to take it to the square next morning. The rest of the year, the box was put away, sometimes one place, sometimes another; it had spent one year in Mr. Graves's barn and another year underfoot in the post office, and sometimes it was set on a shelf in the Martin grocery and left there.

There was a great deal of fussing to be done before Mr. Summers declared the lottery open. There were the lists to make up—of heads of families, heads of households in each family, members of each household in each family. There was the proper swearing-in of Mr. Summers by the postmaster, as the official of the lottery; at one time, some people remembered, there had been a recital of some sort, performed by the official of the lottery, a perfunctory, tuneless chant that had been rattled off duly each year; some people believed that the official of the lottery used to stand just so when he said or sang it, others believed that he was supposed to walk among the people, but years and years ago this part of the ritual had been allowed to lapse. There had been, also, a ritual salute, which the official of the lottery had had to use in addressing each person who came up to draw from the box, but this also had changed with time, until now it was felt necessary only for the official to speak to each person approaching. Mr. Summers was very good at all this; in his clean white shirt and blue jeans, with one hand resting carelessly on the black box, he seemed very proper and important as he talked interminably to Mr. Graves and the Martins.

Just as Mr. Summers finally left off talking and turned to the assembled villagers, Mrs. Hutchinson came hurriedly along the path to the square, her sweater thrown over her shoulders, and slid into place in the back of the crowd. "Clean forgot what day it was," she said to Mrs. Delacroix, who stood next to her, and they both laughed softly. "Thought my old man was out back stacking wood," Mrs. Hutchinson went on, "and then I looked out the window and the kids was gone, and then I remembered it was the twenty-seventh and came a-running." She dried her hands on her apron, and Mrs. Delacroix said, "You're in time, though. They're still talking away up there."

Mrs. Hutchinson craned her neck to see through the crowd and found her husband and children standing near the front. She tapped Mrs. Delacroix on the arm as a farewell and began to make her way through the crowd. The people separated good-humoredly to let her through; two or three people said, in voices just loud enough to be heard across the crowd, "Here comes your Missus, Hutchinson," and "Bill, she made it after all." Mrs. Hutchinson reached her husband, and Mr. Summers, who had been waiting, said cheerfully, "Thought we were going to have to get on without you, Tessie." Mrs. Hutchinson said, grinning, "Wouldn't have me leave m'dishes in the sink, now, would you, Joe?," and soft laughter ran through the crowd as the people stirred back into position after Mrs. Hutchinson's arrival.

"Well, now," Mr. Summers said soberly, "guess we better get started, get this over with, so's we can go back to work. Anybody ain't here?"

"Dunbar," several people said. "Dunbar, Dunbar."

10

Mr. Summers consulted his list. "Clyde Dunbar," he said. "That's right. He's broke his leg, hasn't he? Who's drawing for him?"

"Me, I guess," a woman said, and Mr. Summers turned to look at her. "Wife draws for her husband," Mr. Summers said. "Don't you have a grown boy to do it for you, Janey?" Although Mr. Summers and everyone else in the village knew the answer perfectly well, it was the business of the official of the lottery to ask such questions formally. Mr. Summers waited with an expression of polite interest while Mrs. Dunbar answered.

"Horace's not but sixteen yet," Mrs. Dunbar said regretfully. "Guess I gotta fill in for the old man this year."

"Right," Mr. Summers said. He made a note on the list he was holding. Then he 15
asked, "Watson boy drawing this year?"

A tall boy in the crowd raised his hand. "Here," he said. "I'm drawing for m'mother and me." He blinked his eyes nervously and ducked his head as several voices in the crowd said things like "Good fellow, Jack," and "Glad to see your mother's got a man to do it."

"Well," Mr. Summers said, "guess that's everyone. Old Man Warner make it?"

"Here," a voice said, and Mr. Summers nodded.

A sudden hush fell on the crowd as Mr. Summers cleared his throat and looked at the list. "All ready?" he called. "Now, I'll read the names—heads of families first—and the men come up and take a paper out of the box. Keep the paper folded in your hand without looking at it until everyone has had a turn. Everything clear?"

The people had done it so many times that they only half listened to the directions; 20
most of them were quiet, wetting their lips, not looking around. Then Mr. Summers raised one hand high and said, "Adams." A man disengaged himself from the crowd and came forward. "Hi, Steve," Mr. Summers said, and Mr. Adams said, "Hi, Joe." They grinned at one another humorlessly and nervously. Then Mr. Adams reached into the black box and took out a folded paper. He held it firmly by one corner as he turned and went hastily back to his place in the crowd, where he stood a little apart from his family, not looking down at his hand.

"Allen," Mr. Summers said. "Anderson. . . . Bentham."

"Seems like there's no time at all between lotteries any more," Mrs. Delacroix said to Mrs. Graves in the back row. "Seems like we got through with the last one only last week."

"Time sure goes fast," Mrs. Graves said.

"Clark. . . . Delacroix."

"There goes my old man," Mrs. Delacroix said. She held her breath while her hus- 25
band went forward.

"Dunbar," Mr. Summers said, and Mrs. Dunbar went steadily to the box while one of the women said, "Go on, Janey," and another said, "There she goes."

"We're next," Mrs. Graves said. She watched while Mr. Graves came around from the side of the box, greeted Mr. Summers gravely, and selected a slip of paper from the box. By now, all through the crowd there were men holding the small folded papers in their large hands, turning them over and over nervously. Mrs. Dunbar and her two sons stood together, Mrs. Dunbar holding the slip of paper.

"Harburt. . . . Hutchinson."

"Get up there, Bill," Mrs. Hutchinson said, and the people near her laughed.

"Jones." 30

"They do say," Mr. Adams said to Old Man Warner, who stood next to him, "that over in the north village they're talking of giving up the lottery."

Old Man Warner snorted. "Pack of crazy fools," he said. "Listening to the young folks, nothing's good enough for *them*. Next thing you know, they'll be wanting to go back to living in caves, nobody work any more, live *that* way for a while. Used to be a saying about 'Lottery in June, corn be heavy soon.' First thing you know, we'd all be eating stewed chickweed and acorns. There's *always* been a lottery," he added petulantly. "Bad enough to see young Joe Summers up there joking with everybody."

"Some places have already quit lotteries," Mrs. Adams said.

"Nothing but trouble in *that*," Old Man Warner said stoutly. "Pack of young fools."

"Martin." And Bobby Martin watched his father go forward. "Overdyke. . . . Percy."   35

"I wish they'd hurry," Mrs. Dunbar said to her older son. "I wish they'd hurry."

"They're almost through," her son said.

"You get ready to run tell Dad," Mrs. Dunbar said.

Mr. Summers called his own name and then stepped forward precisely and selected a slip from the box. Then he called, "Warner."

"Seventy-seventh year I been in the lottery," Old Man Warner said as he went   40
through the crowd. "Seventy-seventh time."

"Watson." The tall boy came awkwardly through the crowd. Someone said, "Don't be nervous, Jack," and Mr. Summers said, "Take your time, son."

"Zanini."

After that, there was a long pause, a breathless pause, until Mr. Summers, holding his slip of paper in the air, said, "All right, fellows." For a minute, no one moved, and then all the slips of paper were opened. Suddenly, all the women began to speak at once, saying, "Who is it?" "Who's got it?" "Is it the Dunbars?" "Is it the Watsons?" Then the voices began to say, "It's Hutchinson. It's Bill," "Bill Hutchinson's got it."

"Go tell your father," Mrs. Dunbar said to her older son.

People began to look around to see the Hutchinsons. Bill Hutchinson was standing   45
quiet, staring down at the paper in his hand. Suddenly, Tessie Hutchinson shouted to Mr. Summers, "You didn't give him time enough to take any paper he wanted. I saw you. It wasn't fair!"

"Be a good sport, Tessie," Mrs. Delacroix called, and Mrs. Graves said, "All of us took the same chance."

"Shut up, Tessie," Bill Hutchinson said.

"Well, everyone," Mr. Summers said, "that was done pretty fast, and now we've got to be hurrying a little more to get done in time." He consulted his next list. "Bill," he said, "you draw for the Hutchinson family. You got any other households in the Hutchinsons?"

"There's Don and Eva," Mrs. Hutchinson yelled. "Make *them* take their chance!"

"Daughters draw with their husbands' families, Tessie," Mr. Summers said gently.   50
"You know that as well as anyone else."

"It wasn't *fair*," Tessie said.

"I guess not, Joe," Bill Hutchinson said regretfully. "My daughter draws with her husband's family, that's only fair. And I've got no other family except the kids."

"Then, as far as drawing for families is concerned, it's you," Mr. Summers said in explanation, "and as far as drawing for households is concerned, that's you, too. Right?"

"Right," Bill Hutchinson said.

"How many kids, Bill?" Mr. Summers asked formally.   55

"Three," Bill Hutchinson said. "There's Bill, Jr., and Nancy, and little Dave. And Tessie and me."

"All right, then," Mr. Summers said. "Harry, you got their tickets back?"

Mr. Graves nodded and held up the slips of paper. "Put them in the box, then," Mr. Summers directed. "Take Bill's and put it in."

"I think we ought to start over," Mrs. Hutchinson said, as quietly as she could. "I tell you it wasn't *fair*. You didn't give him time enough to choose. *Every*body saw that."

Mr. Graves had selected the five slips and put them in the box, and he dropped   60
all the papers but those onto the ground, where the breeze caught them and lifted
them off.

"Listen, everybody," Mrs. Hutchinson was saying to the people around her.

"Ready, Bill?" Mr. Summers asked, and Bill Hutchinson, with one quick glance
around at his wife and children, nodded.

"Remember," Mr. Summers said, "take the slips and keep them folded until each
person has taken one. Harry, you help little Dave." Mr. Graves took the hand of the little
boy, who came willingly with him up to the box. "Take a paper out of the box, Davy," Mr.
Summers said. Davy put his hand into the box and laughed. "Take just *one* paper," Mr.
Summers said. "Harry, you hold it for him." Mr. Graves took the child's hand and removed the folded paper from the tight fist and held it while little Dave stood next to him
and looked up at him wonderingly.

"Nancy next," Mr. Summers said. Nancy was twelve, and her school friends
breathed heavily as she went forward, switching her skirt, and took a slip daintily from
the box. "Bill, Jr.," Mr. Summers said, and Billy, his face red and his feet over-large, nearly knocked the box over as he got a paper out. "Tessie," Mr. Summers said. She hesitated
for a minute, looking around defiantly, and then set her lips and went up to the box. She
snatched a paper out and held it behind her.

"Bill," Mr. Summers said, and Bill Hutchinson reached into the box and felt   65
around, bringing his hand out at last with the slip of paper in it.

The crowd was quiet. A girl whispered, "I hope it's not Nancy," and the sound of
the whisper reached the edges of the crowd.

"It's not the way it used to be," Old Man Warner said clearly. "People ain't they way
they used to be."

"All right," Mr. Summers said. "Open the papers. Harry, you open little Dave's."

Mr. Graves opened the slip of paper and there was a general sigh through the
crowd as he held it up and everyone could see that it was blank. Nancy and Bill, Jr.,
opened theirs at the same time, and both beamed and laughed, turning around to the
crowd and holding their slips of paper above their heads.

"Tessie," Mr. Summers said. There was a pause, and then Mr. Summers looked at   70
Bill Hutchinson, and Bill unfolded his paper and showed it. It was blank.

"It's Tessie," Mr. Summers said, and his voice was hushed. "Show us her paper, Bill."

Bill Hutchinson went over to his wife and forced the slip of paper out of her hand.
It had a black spot on it, the black spot Mr. Summers had made the night before with the
heavy pencil in the coal-company office. Bill Hutchinson held it up, and there was a stir
in the crowd.

"All right, folks," Mr. Summers said. "Let's finish quickly."

Although the villagers had forgotten the ritual and lost the original black box, they
still remembered to use stones. The pile of stones the boys had made earlier was ready;
there were stones on the ground with the blowing scraps of paper that had come out of
the box. Mrs. Delacroix selected a stone so large she had to pick it up with both hands
and turned to Mrs. Dunbar. "Come on," she said. "Hurry up."

Mrs. Dunbar had small stones in both hands, and she said, gasping for breath, "I   75
can't run at all. You'll have to go ahead and I'll catch up with you."

The children had stones already, and someone gave little Davy Hutchinson a few
pebbles.

Tessie Hutchinson was in the center of a cleared space by now, and she held her
hands out desperately as the villagers moved in on her. "It isn't fair," she said. A stone hit
her on the side of the head.

Old Man Warner was saying, "Come on, come on, everyone." Steve Adams was in the front of the crowd of villagers with Mrs. Graves beside him.

"It isn't fair, it isn't right," Mrs. Hutchinson screamed, and then they were upon her.

QUESTIONS

1.　Describe the point of view of the story. What seems to be the position from which the narrator sees and describes the events? How much extra information does the narrator provide?

2.　What would the story be like if it were done with an omniscient point of view? With the first person? Could the story be as suspenseful as it is? In what other ways might the story be different with another point of view?

3.　Does the conclusion of "The Lottery" seem to come as a surprise? In retrospect, what hints earlier in the story tell about what is to come?

4.　A scapegoat, in the ritual of purification described in the Old Testament, was an actual goat that was released into the wilderness after having been ceremonially heaped with the "iniquities" of the people (Leviticus 16:22). What traces of such a ritual are suggested in "The Lottery"? Can you think of any other kinds of rituals that are retained today even though their purpose is now remote or even nonexistent?

5.　Is "The Lottery" a horror story or a surprise story, or neither or both? Explain.

LORRIE MOORE (b. 1957)

One of the youngest writers represented in this book, Lorrie Moore teaches at the University of Wisconsin. She was born in upstate New York and received a master of fine arts degree from Cornell. Following her first collection of stories, Self-Help *(1985), from which "How to Become a Writer" is taken, she published her first novel,* Anagrams, *in 1986. A recent work is* Like Life *(1991), a collection of eight stories taking its title from the last story, a grim portrait of life in a polluted, deteriorating future. She has received awards from the National Endowment for the Humanities and the Rockefeller Foundation, and her book* Birds of America *was nominated for the 1999 National Book Critics Circle fiction prize. Her fiction has been heralded for its combination of wry humor, deep feeling, and impending tragedy.*

How to Become a Writer ～＜～✓✓ 1985

First, try to be something, anything, else. A movie star/astronaut. A movie star/missionary. A movie star/kindergarten teacher. President of the World. Fail miserably. It is best if you fail at an early age—say, fourteen. Early, critical disillusionment is necessary so that at fifteen you can write long haiku sequences about thwarted desire. It is a pond, a cherry blossom, a wind brushing against sparrow wing leaving for mountain. Count the syllables. Show it to your mom. She is tough and practical. She has a son in Vietnam and a husband who may be having an affair. She believes in wearing brown because it hides spots. She'll look briefly at your writing, then back up at you with a face blank as a donut. She'll say: "How about emptying the dishwasher?" Look away. Shove the forks in the fork drawer.

Accidentally break one of the freebie gas station glasses. This is the required pain and suffering. This is only for starters.

In your high school English class look only at Mr. Killian's face. Decide faces are important. Write a villanelle about pores. Struggle. Write a sonnet. Count the syllables: nine, ten, eleven, thirteen. Decide to experiment with fiction. Here you don't have to count syllables. Write a short story about an elderly man and woman who accidentally shoot each other in the head, the result of an inexplicable malfunction of a shotgun which appears mysteriously in their living room one night. Give it to Mr. Killian as your final project. When you get it back, he has written on it: "Some of your images are quite nice, but you have no sense of plot." When you are home, in the privacy of your own room, faintly scrawl in pencil beneath his black-inked comments: "Plots are for dead people, pore-face."

Take all the babysitting jobs you can get. You are great with kids. They love you. You tell them stories about old people who die idiot deaths. You sing them songs like "Blue Bells of Scotland," which is their favorite. And when they are in their pajamas and have finally stopped pinching each other, when they are fast asleep, you read every sex manual in the house, and wonder how on earth anyone could ever do those things with someone they truly loved. Fall asleep in a chair reading Mr. McMurphy's *Playboy*. When the McMurphys come home, they will tap you on the shoulder, look at the magazine in your lap, and grin. You will want to die. They will ask you if Tracey took her medicine all right. Explain, yes, she did, that you promised her a story if she would take it like a big girl and that seemed to work out just fine. "Oh, marvelous," they will exclaim.

Try to smile proudly.

Apply to college as a child psychology major.   5

As a child psychology major, you have some electives. You've always liked birds. Sign up for something called "The Ornithological Field Trip." It meets Tuesdays and Thursdays at two. When you arrive at Room 134 on the first day of class, everyone is sitting around a seminar table talking about metaphors. You've heard of these. After a short, excruciating while, raise your hand and say diffidently, "Excuse me, isn't this Birdwatching One-oh-one?" The class stops and turns to look at you. They seem to all have one face—giant and blank as a vandalized clock. Someone with a beard booms out, "No, this is Creative Writing." Say: "Oh—right," as if perhaps you knew all along. Look down at your schedule. Wonder how the hell you ended up here. The computer, apparently, has made an error. You start to get up to leave and then don't. The lines at the registrar this week are huge. Perhaps you should stick with this mistake. Perhaps your creative writing isn't all that bad. Perhaps it is fate. Perhaps this is what your dad meant when he said, "It's the age of computers, Francie, it's the age of computers."

Decide that you like college life. In your dorm you meet many nice people. Some are smarter than you. And some, you notice, are dumber than you. You will continue, unfortunately, to view the world in exactly these terms for the rest of your life.

The assignment this week in creative writing is to narrate a violent happening. Turn in a story about driving with your Uncle Gordon and another one about two old people who are accidentally electrocuted when they go to turn on a badly wired desk lamp. The teacher will hand them back to you with comments: "Much of your writing is smooth and energetic. You have, however, a ludicrous notion of plot." Write another story about a man and a woman who, in the very first paragraph, have their lower torsos accidentally blitzed away by dynamite. In the second paragraph, with the insurance money, they buy a frozen yogurt stand together. There are six more paragraphs. You read the whole thing out loud in class. No one likes it. They say your sense of plot is outrageous and incompetent. After class someone asks you if you are crazy.

Decide that perhaps you should stick to comedies. Start dating someone who is funny, someone who has what in high school you called a "really great sense of humor" and what now your creative writing class calls "self-contempt giving rise to comic form." Write down all of his jokes, but don't tell him you are doing this. Make up anagrams of his old girlfriend's name and name all of your socially handicapped characters with them. Tell him his old girlfriend is in all of your stories and then watch how funny he can be, see what a really great sense of humor he can have.

Your child psychology advisor tells you you are neglecting courses in your major. What you spend the most time on should be what you're majoring in. Say yes, you understand.   10

In creative writing seminars over the next two years, everyone continues to smoke cigarettes and ask the same things: "But does it work?" "Why should we care about this character?" "Have you earned this cliché?" These seem like important questions.

On days when it is your turn, you look at the class hopefully as they scour your mimeographs for a plot. They look back up at you, drag deeply, and then smile in a sweet sort of way.

You spend too much time slouched and demoralized. Your boyfriend suggests bicycling. Your roommate suggests a new boyfriend. You are said to be self-mutilating and losing weight, but you continue writing. The only happiness you have is writing something new, in the middle of the night, armpits damp, heart pounding, something no one has yet seen. You have only those brief, fragile, untested moments of exhilaration when you know: you are a genius. Understand what you must do. Switch majors. The kids in your nursery project will be disappointed, but you have a calling, an urge, a delusion, an unfortunate habit. You have, as your mother would say, fallen in with a bad crowd.

Why write? Where does writing come from? These are questions to ask yourself. They are like: Where does dust come from? Or: Why is there war? Or: If there's a God, then why is my brother now a cripple?

These are questions that you keep in your wallet, like calling cards. These are questions, your creative writing teacher says, that are good to address in your journals but rarely in your fiction.   15

The writing professor this fall is stressing the Power of the Imagination. Which means he doesn't want long descriptive stories about your camping trip last July. He wants you to start in a realistic context but then to alter it. Like recombinant DNA. He wants you to let your imagination sail, to let it grow big-bellied in the wind. This is a quote from Shakespeare.

Tell your roommate your great idea, your great exercise of imaginative power: a transformation of Melville to contemporary life. It will be about monomania and the fish-eat-fish world of life insurance in Rochester, New York. The first line will be "Call me Fish-meal," and it will feature a menopausal suburban husband named Richard, who because he is so depressed all the time is called "Mopey Dick" by his witty wife Elaine. Say to your roommate: "Mopey Dick, get it?" Your roommate looks at you, like a buddy, and puts an arm around your burdened shoulders. "Listen, Francie," she says, slow as speech therapy. "Let's go out and get a big beer."

The seminar doesn't like this one either. You suspect they are beginning to feel sorry for you. They say: "You have to think about what is happening. Where is the story here?"

The next semester the writing professor is obsessed with writing from personal experience. You must write from what you know, from what has happened to you. He wants deaths, he wants camping trips. Think about what has happened to you. In three years there have been three things: you lost your virginity; your parents got divorced; and your brother came home from a forest ten miles from the Cambodian border with only half a thigh, a permanent smirk nestled into one corner of his mouth.

About the first you write: "It created a new space, which hurt and cried in a voice   20
that wasn't mine, 'I'm not the same anymore, but I'll be okay.'"

About the second you write an elaborate story of an old married couple who stumble upon an unknown land mine in their kitchen and accidentally blow themselves up. You call it: "For Better or for Liverwurst."

About the last you write nothing. There are no words for this. Your typewriter hums. You can find no words.

At undergraduate cocktail parties, people say, "Oh, you write? What do you write about?" Your roommate, who has consumed too much wine, too little cheese, and no crackers at all, blurts: "Oh, my god, she always writes about her dumb boyfriend."

Later on in life you will learn that writers are merely open, helpless texts with no real understanding of what they have written and therefore must half-believe anything and everything that is said of them. You, however, have not yet reached this stage of literary criticism. You stiffen and say, "I do not," the same way you said it when someone in the fourth grade accused you of really liking oboe lessons and your parents really weren't just making you take them.

Insist you are not very interested in any one subject at all, that you are interested in   25
the music of language, that you are interested in—in—syllables, because they are the atoms of poetry, the cells of the mind, the breath of the soul. Begin to feel woozy. Stare into your plastic wine cup.

"Syllables?" you will hear someone ask, voice trailing off, as they glide slowly toward the reassuring white of the dip.

Begin to wonder what you do write about. Or if you have anything to say. Or if there even is such a thing as a thing to say. Limit these thoughts to no more than ten minutes a day; like sit-ups, they can make you thin.

You will read somewhere that all writing has to do with one's genitals. Don't dwell on this. It will make you nervous.

Your mother will come visit you. She will look at the circles under your eyes and hand you a brown book with a brown briefcase on the cover. It is entitled: *How to Become a Business Executive*. She has also brought the *Names for Baby* encyclopedia you asked for; one of your characters, the aging clown–school teacher, needs a new name. Your mother will shake her head and say: "Francie, Francie, remember when you were going to be a child psychology major?"

Say: "Mom, I like to write."   30

She'll say: "Sure you like to write. Of course. Sure you like to write."

Write a story about a confused music student and title it: "Schubert Was the One with the Glasses, Right?" It's not a big hit, although your roommate likes the part where the two violinists accidentally blow themselves up in a recital room. "I went out with a violinist once," she says, snapping her gum.

Thank god you are taking other courses. You can find sanctuary in nineteenth-century ontological snags and invertebrate courting rituals. Certain globular mollusks have what is called "Sex by the Arm." The male octopus, for instance, loses the end of one arm when placing it inside the female body during intercourse. Marine biologists call it "Seven Heaven." Be glad you know these things. Be glad you are not just a writer. Apply to law school.

From here on in, many things can happen. But the main one will be this: you decide not to go to law school after all, and, instead, you spend a good, big chunk of your adult life telling people how you decided not to go to law school after all. Somehow you end up writing again. Perhaps you go to graduate school. Perhaps you work odd jobs and take writing courses at night. Perhaps you are working on a novel and writing down all the clever remarks and intimate personal confessions you hear during the day. Perhaps you are losing your pals, your acquaintances, your balance.

You have broken up with your boyfriend. You now go out with men who, instead of whispering "I love you," shout: "Do it to me, baby." This is good for your writing.

Sooner or later you have a finished manuscript more or less. People look at it in a vaguely troubled sort of way and say, "I'll bet becoming a writer was always a fantasy of yours, wasn't it?" Your lips dry to salt. Say that of all the fantasies possible in the world, you can't imagine being a writer even making the top twenty. Tell them you were going to be a child psychology major. "I bet," they always sigh, "you'd be great with kids." Scowl fiercely. Tell them you're a walking blade.

Quit classes. Quit jobs. Cash in old savings bonds. Now you have time like warts on your hands. Slowly copy all of your friends' addresses into a new address book.

Vacuum. Chew cough drops. Keep a folder full of fragments.

An eyelid darkening sideways.
World as conspiracy.
Possible plot? A woman gets on a bus.
Suppose you threw a love affair and nobody came.

At home drink a lot of coffee. At Howard Johnson's order the cole slaw. Consider how it looks like the soggy confetti of a map: where you've been, where you're going— "You Are Here," says the red star on the back of the menu.

Occasionally a date with a face blank as a sheet of paper asks you whether writers often become discouraged. Say that sometimes they do and sometimes they do. Say it's a lot like having polio.

"Interesting," smiles your date, and then he looks down at his arm hairs and starts to smooth them, all, always, in the same direction.

QUESTIONS

1. To whom does the "you" in the story refer? How strong a case may be made that the "you" refers really to "I," and that Francie is actually telling a story about herself?

2. In light of the title, how adequate are Francie's "directions" for becoming a writer?

3. Describe some of the comic elements of the story. What serious ideas about the development of a writer's profession undergird the story's humor?

ALICE MUNRO (b. 1931)

Munro, who is a writer almost exclusively of short stories, grew up in Western Ontario, twenty miles east of Lake Huron—the approximate geographical locales of "Meneseteung" and also of "The Found Boat" (Chapter 7). She received her higher eduacation at the University of Western Ontario, after which she married and moved to British Columbia, where she began her writing career. Her first collection was Dance of the Happy Shades *(1968), followed three years later by the novelistic* Lives of Girls and Women. *Later volumes are* Something I've Been Meaning to Tell You *(1974),* The Beggar Maid *(1978),* The Moons of Jupiter *(1982),* The Progress of Love *(1986),* Friend of My Youth *(1990),* Open Secrets *(1995),* Selected Stories *(1997),* The Love of a Good Woman *(1998), and* Hateship, Friendship, Courtship, Loveship, Marriage: Stories *(2002). Her stories are mainly regional and have a realistic basis in her own experiences. The stories are not autobiographical, however; her characters and their actions develop out of her powerful imagination and strong sympathy and compassion. Recipient of Canada's Governor-General's Award for her very first work, she has merited additional honors throughout her full and distinguished career. Among her most recent honors is the 1999 National Book Critics Circle Fiction Prize for* The Love of a Good Woman.

Meneseteung ⚘⚘⚘ 1988

Columbine, bloodroot,
And wild bergamot,
Gathering armfuls,
Giddily we go.

Offerings, the book is called. Gold lettering on a dull-blue cover. The author's full name underneath: Almeda Joynt Roth. The local paper, the *Vidette*, referred to her as "our poetess." There seems to be a mixture of respect and contempt, both for her calling and for her sex—or for their predictable conjuncture. In the front of the book is a photograph, with the photographer's name in one corner, and the date: 1865. The book was published later, in 1873.

The poetess has a long face; a rather long nose; full, somber dark eyes, which seem ready to roll down her cheeks like giant tears; a lot of dark hair gathered around her face in droopy rolls and curtains. A streak of gray hair plain to see, although she is, in this picture, only twenty-five. Not a pretty girl but the sort of woman who may age well, who probably won't get fat. She wears a tucked and braid-trimmed dark dress or jacket, with a lacy, floppy arrangement of white material—frills or a bow—filling the deep V at the neck. She also wears a hat, which might be made of velvet, in a dark color to match the dress. It's the untrimmed, shapeless hat, something like a soft beret, that makes me see artistic intentions, or at least a shy and stubborn eccentricity, in this young woman, whose long

neck and forward-inclining head indicate as well that she is tall and slender and somewhat awkward. From the waist up, she looks like a young nobleman of another century.
But perhaps it was the fashion.

"In 1854," she writes in the preface to her book, "my father brought us—my mother, my sister Catherine, my brother William, and me—to the wilds of Canada West (as it
then was). My father was a harness-maker by trade, but a cultivated man who could quote
by heart from the Bible, Shakespeare, and the writings of Edmund Burke. He prospered
in this newly opened land and was able to set up a harness and leather-goods store, and
after a year to build the comfortable house in which I live (alone) today. I was fourteen
years old, the eldest of the children, when we came into this country from Kingston,° a
town whose handsome streets I have not seen again but often remember. My sister was
eleven and my brother nine. The third summer that we lived here, my brother and sister
were taken ill of a prevalent fever and died within a few days of each other. My dear mother did not regain her spirits after this blow to our family. Her health declined, and after
another three years she died. I then became housekeeper to my father and was happy to
make his home for twelve years, until he died suddenly one morning at his shop.

"From my earliest years I have delighted in verse and I have occupied myself—and
sometimes allayed my griefs, which have been no more, I know, than any sojourner on
earth must encounter—with many floundering efforts at its composition. My fingers, indeed, were always too clumsy for crochet work, and those dazzling productions of embroidery which one sees often today—the overflowing fruit and flower baskets, the little
Dutch boys, the bonneted maidens with their watering cans—have likewise proved to
be beyond my skill. So I offer instead, as the product of my leisure hours, these rude
posies, these ballads, couplets, reflections."

Titles of some of the poems: "Children at Their Games," "The Gypsy Fair," "A Visit   5
to My Family," "Angels in the Snow," "Champlain at the Mouth of the Meneseteung,"
"The Passing of the Old Forest," and "A Garden Medley." There are some other, shorter
poems, about birds and wildflowers and snowstorms. There is some comically inten-
tioned doggerel about what people are thinking about as they listen to the sermon in
church.

"Children at Their Games": The writer, a child, is playing with her brother and sister—one of those games in which children on different sides try to entice and catch each
other. She plays on in the deepening twilight, until she realizes that she is alone, and
much older. Still she hears the (ghostly) voices of her brother and sister calling. *Come
over, come over, let Meda come over.* (Perhaps Almeda was called Meda in the family, or perhaps she shortened her name to fit the poem.)

"The Gypsy Fair": The Gypsies have an encampment near the town, a "fair," where
they sell cloth and trinkets, and the writer as a child is afraid that she may be stolen by
them, taken away from her family. Instead, her family has been taken away from her,
stolen by Gypsies she can't locate or bargain with.

"A Visit to My Family": A visit to the cemetery, a one-sided conversation.

"Angels in the Snow": The writer once taught her brother and sister to make "angels" by lying down in the snow and moving their arms to create wing shapes. Her brother always jumped up carelessly, leaving an angel with a crippled wing. Will this be made
perfect in Heaven, or will he be flying with his own makeshift, in circles?

Kingston: city in southeastern Ontario, on the St. Lawrence. The town of Meneseteung is visualized
as being about 200 miles west of Kingston.

"Champlain° at the mouth of the Meneseteung": This poem celebrates the popular, untrue belief that the explorer sailed down the eastern shore of Lake Huron and landed at the mouth of the major river.

"The Passing of the Old Forest": A list of all the trees—their names, appearance, and uses—that were cut down in the original forest, with a general description of the bears, wolves, eagles, deer, waterfowl.

"A Garden Medley": Perhaps planned as a companion to the forest poem. Catalogue of plants brought from European countries, with bits of history and legend attached, and final Canadianness resulting from this mixture.

The poems are written in quatrains or couplets. There are a couple of attempts at sonnets, but mostly the rhyme scheme is simple—*abab* or *abcb*. The rhyme used is what was once called "masculine" ("shore"/"before"), though once in a while it is "feminine" ("quiver"/"river"). Are those terms familiar anymore? No poem is unrhymed.

II

While roses cold as snow
Bloom where those "angels" lie,
Do they but rest below
Or, in God's wonder, fly?

In 1879, Almeda Roth was still living in the house at the corner of Pearl and Dufferin streets, the house her father had built for his family. The house is there today: the manager of the liquor store lives in it. It's covered with aluminum siding; a closed-in porch has replaced the veranda. The woodshed, the fence, the gates, the privy, the barn—all these are gone. A photograph taken in the eighteen-eighties shows them all in place. The house and fence look a little shabby, in need of paint, but perhaps that is just because of the bleached-out look of the brownish photograph. The lace-curtained windows look like white eyes. No big shade tree is in sight, and, in fact, the tall elms that overshadowed the town until the nineteen-fifties, as well as the maples that shade it now, are skinny young trees with the rough fences around them to protect them from the cows. Without the shelter of those trees, there is a great exposure—back yards, clotheslines, woodpiles, patchy sheds and barns and privies—all bare, exposed, provisional looking. Few houses would have anything like a lawn, just a patch of plantains and anthills and raked dirt. Perhaps petunias growing on top of a stump, in a round box. Only the main street is graveled; the other streets are dirt roads, muddy or dusty according to season. Yards must be fenced to keep animals out. Cows are tethered in vacant lots or pastured in back yards, but sometimes they get loose. Pigs get loose, too, and dogs roam free or nap in a lordly way on the boardwalks. The town has taken root, it's not going to vanish, yet it still has some of the look of an encampment. And, like an encampment, it's busy all the time—full of people, who, within the town, usually walk wherever they're going; full of animals, which leave horse buns, cowpats, dog turds, that ladies have to hitch up their skirts for; full of the noise of building and of drivers shouting at their horses and of the trains that come in several times a day.

I read about that life in the *Vidette*.

The population is younger than it is now, than it will ever be again. People past fifty usually don't come to a raw, new place. There are quite a few people in the cemetery already, but most of them died young, in accidents or childbirth or epidemics. It's youth

Champlain: The explorer Samuel de Champlain (1567–1635), a founder of Quebec, had traveled to the eastern regions of Lake Huron in 1615.

that's in evidence in town. Children—boys—rove through the streets in gangs. School is compulsory for only four months a year, and there are lots of occasional jobs that even a child of eight or nine can do—pulling flax, holding horses, delivering groceries, sweeping the boardwalk in front of stores. A good deal of time they spend looking for adventures. One day they follow an old woman, a drunk nicknamed Queen Aggie. They get her into a wheelbarrow and trundle her all over town, then dump her into a ditch to sober her up. They also spend a lot of time around the railway station. They jump on shunting cars and dart between them and dare each other to take chances, which once in a while result in their getting maimed or killed. And they keep an eye out for any strangers coming into town. They follow them, offer to carry their bags, and direct them (for a five-cent piece) to a hotel. Strangers who don't look so prosperous are taunted and tormented. Speculation surrounds all of them—it's like a cloud of flies. Are they coming to town to start up a new business, to persuade people to invest in some scheme, to sell cures or gimmicks, to preach on the street corners? All these things are possible any day of the week. Be on your guard, the *Vidette* tells people. These are times of opportunity and danger. Tramps, confidence men, hucksters, shysters, plain thieves, are traveling the roads, and particularly the railroads. Thefts are announced: money invested and never seen again, a pair of trousers taken from the clothesline, wood from the woodpile, eggs from the henhouse. Such incidents increase in the hot weather.

Hot weather brings accidents, too. More horses run wild then, upsetting buggies. Hands caught in the wringer while doing the washing, a man lopped in two at the sawmill, a leaping boy killed in a fall of lumber at the lumberyard. Nobody sleeps well. Babies wither with summer complaint, and fat people can't catch their breath. Bodies must be buried in a hurry. One day a man goes through the streets ringing a cowbell and calling "Repent! Repent!" It's not a stranger this time, it's a young man who works at the butcher shop. Take him home, wrap him in cold wet cloths, give him some nerve medicine, keep him in bed, pray for his wits. If he doesn't recover, he must go to the asylum.

Almeda Roth's house faces on Dufferin Street, which is a street of considerable respectability. On this street merchants, a mill owner, an operator of salt wells, have their houses. But Pearl Street, which her back windows overlook and her back gate opens onto, is another story. Workmen's houses are adjacent to hers. Small but decent row houses—that is all right. Things deteriorate toward the end of the block, and the next, last one becomes dismal. Nobody but the poorest people, the unrespectable and undeserving poor, would live there at the edge of a boghole (drained since then), called the Pearl Street Swamp. Bushy and luxuriant weeds grow there, makeshift shacks have been put up, there are piles of refuse and debris and crowds of runty children, slops are flung from doorways. The town tries to compel these people to build privies, but they would just as soon go in the bushes. If a gang of boys goes down there in search of adventure, it's likely they'll get more than they bargained for. It is said that even the town constable won't go down Pearl Street on a Saturday night. Almeda Roth has never walked past the row housing. In one of those houses lives the young girl Annie, who helps her with her housecleaning. That young girl herself, being a decent girl, has never walked down to the last block or the swamp. No decent woman ever would.

But that same swamp, lying to the east of Almeda Roth's house, presents a fine sight at dawn. Almeda sleeps at the back of the house. She keeps to the same bedroom she once shared with her sister Catherine—she would not think of moving to the larger front bedroom, where her mother used to lie in bed all day, and which was later the solitary domain of her father. From her window she can see the sun rising, the swamp mist filling with light, the bulky, nearest trees floating against that mist and the trees behind turning transparent. Swamp oaks, soft maples, tamarack, butternut.

III

Here where the river meets the inland sea,
Spreading her blue skirts from the solemn wood,
I think of birds and beasts and vanished men,
Whose pointed dwellings on these pale sands stood.

One of the strangers who arrived at the railway station a few years ago was Jarvis   20
Poulter, who now occupies the house next to Almeda Roth's—separated from hers by a
vacant lot, which he has bought, on Dufferin Street. The house is plainer than the Roth
house and has no fruit trees or flowers planted around it. It is understood that this is a
natural result of Jarvis Poulter's being a widower and living alone. A man may keep his
house decent, but he will never—if he is a proper man—do much to decorate it. Marriage forces him to live with more ornament as well as sentiment, and it protects him,
also, from the extremities of his own nature—from a frigid parsimony or a luxuriant
sloth, from squalor, and from excessive sleeping, drinking, smoking, or freethinking.°

In the interests of economy, it is believed, a certain estimable gentleman of our
town persists in fetching water from the public tap and supplementing his fuel supply by picking up the loose coal along the railway track. Does he think to repay the
town or the railway company with a supply of free salt?

This is the *Vidette*, full of sly jokes, innuendo, plain accusation, that no newspaper
would get away with today. It's Jarvis Poulter they're talking about though in other passages he is spoken of with great respect, as a civil magistrate, an employer, a churchman.
He is close, that's all. An eccentric, to a degree. All of which may be a result of his single
condition, his widower's life. Even carrying his water from the town tap and filling his
coal pail along the railway track. This is a decent citizen, prosperous: a tall—slightly
paunchy?—man in a dark suit with polished boots. A beard? Black hair streaked with
gray. A severe and self-possessed air, and a large pale wart among the bushy hairs of one
eyebrow? People talk about a young, pretty, beloved wife, dead in childbirth or some horrible accident, like a house fire or a railway disaster. There is no ground for this, but it
adds interest. All he has told them is that his wife is dead.

He came to this part of the country looking for oil. The first oil well in the world
was sunk in Lambton County, south of here, in the eighteen-fifties. Drilling for oil, Jarvis
Poulter discovered salt. He set to work to make the most of that. When he walks home
from church with Almeda Roth, he tells her about his salt wells. They are twelve hundred
feet deep. Heated water is pumped down into them, and that dissolves the salt. Then the
brine is pumped to the surface. It is poured into great evaporator pans over slow, steady
fires, so that the water is steamed off and the pure, excellent salt remains. A commodity
for which the demand will never fail.

"The salt of the earth," Almeda says.

"Yes," he says, frowning. He may think this disrespectful. She did not intend it so.   25
He speaks of competitors in other towns who are following his lead and trying to hog the
market. Fortunately, their wells are not drilled so deep, or their evaporating is not done
so efficiently. There is salt everywhere under this land, but it is not so easy to come by as
some people think.

Freethinking: an intellectual movement, begun in the eighteenth century, emphasizing reason and
denying the authority of religion and the supernatural. In the nineteenth century, there were organized
groups in America devoted to freethinking.

Does that not mean, Almeda says, that there was once a great sea?

Very likely, Jarvis Poulter says. Very likely. He goes on to tell her about other enterprises of his—a brickyard, a lime kiln. And he explains to her how this operates, and where the good clay is found. He also owns two farms, whose woodlots supply the fuel for his operations.

Among the couples strolling home from church on a recent, sunny Sabbath morning we noted a certain salty gentleman and literary lady, not perhaps in their first youth but by no means blighted by the frosts of age. May we surmise?

This kind of thing pops up in the *Vidette* all the time.

May they surmise, and is this courting? Almeda Roth has a bit of money, which her father left her, and she has her house. She is not too old to have a couple of children. She is a good enough housekeeper, with the tendency toward fancy iced cakes and decorated tarts which is seen fairly often in old maids. (Honorable mention at the Fall Fair.) There is nothing wrong with her looks, and naturally she is in better shape than most married women of her age, not having been loaded down with work and children. But why was she passed over in her earlier, more marriageable years, in a place that needs women to be partnered and fruitful? She was a rather gloomy girl—that may have been the trouble. The deaths of her brother and sister and then of her mother, who lost her reason, in fact, a year before she died, and lay in her bed talking nonsense—those weighed on her, so she was not lively company. And all that reading and poetry—it seemed more of a drawback, a barrier, an obsession, in the young girl than in the middle-aged woman, who needed something, after all, to fill her time. Anyway, it's five years since her book was published, so perhaps she has got over that. Perhaps it was the proud, bookish father, encouraging her?

Everyone takes it for granted that Almeda Roth is thinking of Jarvis Poulter as a husband and would say yes if he asked her. And she is thinking of him. She doesn't want to get her hopes up too much, she doesn't want to make a fool of herself. She would like a signal. If he attended church on Sunday evenings, there would be a chance, during some months of the year, to walk home after dark. He would carry a lantern. (There is as yet no street lighting in town.) He would swing the lantern to light the way in front of the lady's feet and observe their narrow and delicate shape. He might catch her arm as they step off the boardwalk. But he does not go to church at night.

Nor does he call for her, and walk with her to church on Sunday mornings. That would be a declaration. He walks her home, past his gate as far as hers; he lifts his hat then and leaves her. She does not invite him to come in—a woman living alone could never do such a thing. As soon as a man and woman of almost any age are alone together within four walls, it is assumed that anything may happen. Spontaneous combustion, instant fornication, an attack of passion. Brute instinct, triumph of the senses. What possibilities men and women must see in each other to infer such dangers. Or, believing in the dangers, how often they must think about the possibilities.

When they walk side by side she can smell his shaving soap, the barber's oil, his pipe tobacco, the wool and linen and leather smell of his manly clothes. The correct, orderly, heavy clothes are like those she used to brush and starch and iron for her father. She misses that job—her father's appreciation, his dark, kind authority. Jarvis Poulter's garments, his smell, his movement, all cause the skin on the side of her body next to him to tingle hopefully, and a meek shiver raises the hairs on her arms. Is this to be taken as a sign of love? She thinks of him coming into her—their—bedroom in his long underwear and his hat. She knows this outfit is ridiculous, but in her mind he does not look so; he

30

has the solemn effrontery of a figure in a dream. He comes into the room and lies down on the bed beside her, preparing to take her in his arms. Surely he removes his hat? She doesn't know, for at this point a fit of welcome and submission overtakes her, a buried gasp. He would be her husband.

One thing she has noticed about married women, and that is how many of them have to go about creating their husbands. They have to start ascribing preferences, opinions, dictatorial ways. Oh, yes, they say, my husband is very particular. He won't touch turnips. He won't eat fried meat. (Or he will only eat fried meat.) He likes me to wear blue (brown) all the time. He can't stand organ music. He hates to see a woman go out bareheaded. He would kill me if I took one puff of tobacco. This way, bewildered, sidelong-looking men are made over, made into husbands, heads of households. Almeda Roth cannot imagine herself doing that. She wants a man who doesn't have to be made, who is firm already and determined and mysterious to her. She does not look for companionship. Men—except for her father—seem to her deprived in some way, incurious. No doubt that is necessary, so that they will do what they have to do. Would she herself, knowing that there was salt in the earth, discover how to get it out and sell it? Not likely. She would be thinking about the ancient sea. That kind of speculation is what Jarvis Poulter has, quite properly, no time for.

Instead of calling for her and walking her to church, Jarvis Poulter might make another, more venturesome declaration. He could hire a horse and take her for a drive out to the country. If he did this, she would be both glad and sorry. Glad to be beside him, driven by him, receiving this attention from him in front of the world. And sorry to have the countryside removed for her—filmed over, in a way, by his talk and preoccupations. The countryside that she has written about in her poems actually takes diligence and determination to see. Some things must be disregarded. Manure piles, of course, and boggy fields full of high, charred stumps, and great heaps of brush waiting for a good day for burning. The meandering creeks have been straightened, turned into ditches with high, muddy banks. Some of the crop fields and pasture fields are fenced with big, clumsy uprooted stumps, others are held in a crude stitchery of rail fences. The trees have all been cleared back to the woodlots. And the woodlots are all second growth. No trees along the roads or lanes or around the farmhouses, except a few that are newly planted, young and weedy looking. Clusters of log barns—the grand barns that are to dominate the countryside for the next hundred years are just beginning to be built—and mean-looking log houses, and every four or five miles a ragged little settlement with a church and school and store and a blacksmith shop. A raw countryside just wrenched from the forest, but swarming with people. Every hundred acres is a farm, every farm has a family, most families have ten or twelve children. (This is the country that will send out wave after wave of settlers—it's already starting to send them—to northern Ontario and the West.) It's true that you can gather wildflowers in spring in the woodlots, but you'd have to walk through herds of horned cows to get to them.

IV

The Gypsies have departed.
Their camping-ground is bare.
Oh, boldly would I bargain now
At the Gypsy Fair.

Almeda suffers a good deal from sleeplessness, and the doctor has given her bromides and nerve medicine. She takes the bromides, but the drops gave her dreams that were too vivid and disturbing, so she has put the bottle by for an emergency. She told the doctor her eyeballs felt dry, like hot glass, and her joints ached. Don't read so much, he said, don't study; get yourself good and tired out with housework, take exercise. He believes that her troubles would clear up if she got married. He believes this in spite of the fact that most of his nerve medicine is prescribed for married women.

So Almeda cleans house and helps clean the church, she lends a hand to friends who are wallpapering or getting ready for a wedding, she bakes one of her famous cakes for the Sunday-school picnic. On a hot Saturday in August she decides to make some grape jelly. Little jars of grape jelly will make fine Christmas presents, or offerings to the sick. But she started late in the day and the jelly is not made by nightfall. In fact, the hot pulp has just been dumped into the cheesecloth bag, to strain out the juice. Almeda drinks some tea and eats a slice of cake with butter (a childish indulgence of hers), and that's all she wants for supper. She washes her hair at the sink and sponges off her body, to be clean for Sunday. She doesn't light a lamp. She lies down on the bed with the window wide open and a sheet just up to her waist, and she does feel wonderfully tired. She can even feel a little breeze.

When she wakes up, the night seems fiery hot and full of threats. She lies sweating on her bed, and she has the impression that the noises she hears are knives and saws and axes—all angry implements chopping and jabbing and boring within her head. But it isn't true. As she comes further awake she recognizes the sounds that she has heard sometimes before—the fracas of a summer Saturday night on Pearl Street. Usually the noise centers on a fight. People are drunk, there is a lot of protest and encouragement concerning the fight, somebody will scream "Murder!" Once, there was a murder. But it didn't happen in a fight. An old man was stabbed to death in his shack, perhaps for a few dollars he kept in the mattress.

She gets out of bed and goes to the window. The night sky is clear, with no moon and with bright stars. Pegasus° hangs straight ahead, over the swamp. Her father taught her that constellation—automatically, she counts its stars. Now she can make out distinct voices, individual contributions to the row. Some people, like herself, have evidently been wakened from sleep. "Shut up!" they are yelling. "Shut up that caterwauling or I'm going to come down and tan the arse off yez!"

But nobody shuts up. It's as if there were a ball of fire rolling up Pearl Street, shooting off sparks—only the fire is noise, it's yells and laughter and shrieks and curses, and the sparks are voices that shoot off alone. Two voices gradually distinguish themselves—a rising and falling howling cry and a steady throbbing, low-pitched stream of abuse that contains all those words which Almeda associates with danger and depravity and foul smells and disgusting sights. Someone—the person crying out, "Kill me! Kill me now!"— is being beaten. A woman is being beaten. She keeps crying, "Kill me! Kill me!" and sometimes her mouth seems choked with blood. Yet there is something taunting and triumphant about her cry. There is something theatrical about it. And the people around are calling out, "Stop it! Stop that!" or "Kill her! Kill her!" in a frenzy, as if at the theater or a sporting match or a prizefight. Yes, thinks Almeda, she has noticed that before—it is always partly a charade with these people; there is a clumsy sort of parody, an exaggeration, a missed connection. As if anything they did—even a murder—might be something they didn't quite believe but were powerless to stop.

Now there is the sound of something thrown—a chair, a plank?—and of a woodpile or part of a fence giving way. A lot of newly surprised cries, the sound of running, people getting out of the way, and the commotion has come much closer. Almeda can see

40

Pegasus: a constellation that is at its highest point (in early evening) in autumn. Its location here, in summer, indicates the lateness of the hour.

a figure in a light dress, bent over and running. That will be the woman. She has got hold of something like a stick of wood or a shingle, and she turns and flings it at the darker figure running after her.

"Ah, go get her!" the voices cry. "Go baste her one!"

Many fall back now; just the two figures come on and grapple, and break loose again, and finally fall down against Almeda's fence. The sound they make becomes very confused—gagging, vomiting, grunting, pounding. Then a long, vibrating, choking sound of pain and self-abasement, self-abandonment, which could come from either or both of them.

Almeda has backed away from the window and sat down on the bed. Is that the sound of murder she has heard? What is to be done, what is she to do? She must light a lantern, she must go downstairs and light a lantern—she must go out into the yard, she must go downstairs. Into the yard. The lantern. She falls over on her bed and pulls the pillow to her face. In a minute. The stairs, the lantern. She sees herself already down there, in the back hall, drawing the bolt of the back door. She falls asleep.

She wakes, startled, in the early light. She thinks there is a big crow sitting on her windowsill, talking in a disapproving but unsurprised way about the events of the night before. "Wake up and move the wheelbarrow!" it says to her, scolding, and she understands that it means something else by "wheelbarrow"—something foul and sorrowful. Then she is awake and sees that there is no such bird. She gets up at once and looks out the window.

Down against her fence there is a pale lump pressed—a body.

Wheelbarrow.

She puts a wrapper over her nightdress and goes downstairs. The front rooms are still shadowy, the blinds down in the kitchen. Something goes plop, plup, in a leisurely, censorious way, reminding her of the conversation of the crow. It's just the grape juice, straining overnight. She pulls the bolt and goes out the back door. Spiders have draped their webs over the doorway in the night, and the hollyhocks are drooping, heavy with dew. By the fence, she parts the sticky hollyhocks and looks down and she can see.

A woman's body heaped up there, turned on her side with her face squashed down into the earth. Almeda can't see her face. But there is a bare breast let loose, brown nipple pulled long like a cow's teat, and a bare haunch and leg, the haunch bearing a bruise as big as a sunflower. The unbruised skin is grayish, like a plucked, raw drumstick. Some kind of nightgown or all-purpose dress she has on. Smelling of vomit. Urine, drink, vomit.

Barefoot, in her nightgown and flimsy wrapper, Almeda runs away. She runs around the side of her house between the apple trees and the veranda; she opens the front gate and flees down Dufferin Street to Jarvis Poulter's house, which is the nearest to hers. She slaps the flat of her hand many times against the door.

"There is the body of a woman," she says when Jarvis Poulter appears at last. He is in his dark trousers, held up with braces, and his shirt is half unbuttoned, his face unshaven, his hair standing up on his head. "Mr. Poulter, excuse me. A body of a woman. At my back gate."

He looks at her fiercely. "Is she dead?"

His breath is dank, his face creased, his eyes bloodshot.

"Yes. I think murdered," says Almeda. She can see a little of his cheerless front hall. His hat on a chair. "In the night I woke up. I heard a racket down on Pearl Street," she says, struggling to keep her voice low and sensible. "I could hear this—pair. I could hear a man and a woman fighting."

He picks up his hat and puts it on his head. He closes and locks the front door, and puts the key in his pocket. They walk along the boardwalk and she sees that she is in her bare feet. She holds back what she feels a need to say next—that she is responsible, she could have run out with a lantern, she could have screamed (but who needed more screams?), she could have beat the man off. She could have run for help then, not now.

They turn down Pearl Street, instead of entering the Roth yard. Of course the body is still there. Hunched up, half bare, the same as before.

Jarvis Poulter doesn't hurry or halt. He walks straight over to the body and looks down at it, nudges the leg with the toe of his boot, just as you'd nudge a dog or a sow.

"You," he says, not too loudly but firmly, and nudges again.

Almeda tastes bile at the back of her throat.

"Alive," says Jarvis Poulter, and the woman confirms this. She stirs, she grunts weakly.   60

Almeda says, "I will get the doctor." If she had touched the woman, if she had forced herself to touch her, she would not have made such a mistake.

"Wait," says Jarvis Poulter. "Wait. Let's see if she can get up."

"Get up, now," he says to the woman. "Come on. Up, now. Up."

Now a startling thing happens. The body heaves itself onto all fours, the head is lifted—the hair all matted with blood and vomit—and the woman begins to bang this head, hard and rhythmically, against Almeda Roth's picket fence. As she bangs her head she finds her voice, and lets out an open-mouthed yowl, full of strength and what sounds like an anguished pleasure.

"Far from dead," says Jarvis Poulter. "And I wouldn't bother the doctor."   65

"There's blood," says Almeda as the woman turns her smeared face.

"From her nose," he says. "Not fresh." He bends down and catches the horrid hair close to the scalp to stop the head banging.

"You stop that now," he says. "Stop it. Gwan home now. Gwan home, where you belong." The sound coming out of the woman's mouth has stopped. He shakes her head slightly, warning her, before he lets go of her hair. "Gwan home!"

Released, the woman lunges forward, pulls herself to her feet. She can walk.

She weaves and stumbles down the street, making intermittent, cautious noises of   70
protest. Jarvis Poulter watches her for a moment to make sure that she's on her way. Then he finds a large burdock leaf, on which he wipes his hand. He says, "There goes your dead body!"

The back gate being locked, they walk around to the front. The front gate stands open. Almeda still feels sick. Her abdomen is bloated; she is hot and dizzy.

"The front door is locked," she says faintly. "I came out by the kitchen." If only he would leave her, she could go straight to the privy. But he follows. He follows her as far as the back door and into the back hall. He speaks to her in a tone of harsh joviality that she has never before heard from him. "No need for alarm," he says. "It's only the consequences of drink. A lady oughtn't to be living alone so close to a bad neighborhood." He takes hold of her arm just above the elbow. She can't open her mouth to speak to him, to say thank you. If she opened her mouth she would retch.

What Jarvis Poulter feels for Almeda Roth at this moment is just what he has not felt during all those circumspect walks and all his own solitary calculations of her probable worth, undoubted respectability, adequate comeliness. He has not been able to imagine her as a wife. Now that is possible. He is sufficiently stirred by her loosened hair—prematurely gray but thick and soft—her flushed face, her light clothing, which nobody but a husband should see. And by her indiscretion, her agitation, her foolishness, her need?

"I will call on you later," he says to her. "I will walk with you to church."

At the corner of Pearl and Dufferin streets last Sunday morning there was discov-   75
ered, by a lady resident there, the body of a certain woman of Pearl Street, thought

to be dead but only, as it turned out, dead drunk. She was roused from her heavenly—or otherwise—stupor by the firm persuasion of Mr. Poulter, a neighbour and a Civil magistrate, who had been summoned by the lady resident. Incidents of this sort, unseemly, troublesome, and disgraceful to our town, have of late become all too common.

V

I sit at the bottom of sleep,
As on the floor of the sea.
And fanciful Citizens of the Deep
Are graciously greeting me.

As soon as Jarvis Poulter has gone and she has heard her front gate close, Almeda rushes to the privy. Her relief is not complete, however, and she realizes that the pain and fullness in her lower body come from an accumulation of menstrual blood that has not yet started to flow. She closes and locks the back door. Then, remembering Jarvis Poulter's words about church, she writes on a piece of paper, "I am not well, and wish to rest today." She sticks this firmly into the outside frame of the little window in the front door. She locks that door, too. She is trembling, as if from a great shock or danger. But she builds a fire, so that she can make tea. She boils water, measures the tea leaves, makes a large pot of tea, whose steam and smell sicken her further. She pours out a cup while the tea is still quite weak and adds to it several dark drops of nerve medicine. She sits to drink it without raising the kitchen blind. There, in the middle of the floor, is the cheesecloth bag hanging on its broom handle between the two chair backs. The grape pulp and juice has stained the swollen cloth a dark purple. *Plop, plup* into the basin beneath. She can't sit and look at such a thing. She takes her cup, the teapot, and the bottle of medicine into the dining room.

She is still sitting there when the horses start to go by on the way to church, stirring up clouds of dust. The roads will be getting hot as ashes. She is there when the gate is opened and a man's confident steps sound on her veranda. Her hearing is so sharp she seems to hear the paper taken out of the frame and unfolded—she can almost hear him reading it, hear the words in his mind. Then the footsteps go the other way, down the steps. The gate closes. An image comes to her of tombstones—it makes her laugh. Tombstones are marching down the street on their little booted feet, their long bodies inclined forward, their expressions preoccupied and severe. The church bells are ringing.

Then the clock in the hall strikes twelve and an hour has passed.

The house is getting hot. She drinks more tea and adds more medicine. She knows that the medicine is affecting her. It is responsible for her extraordinary languor, her perfect immobility, her unresisting surrender to her surroundings. That is all right. It seems necessary.

Her surroundings—some of her surroundings—in the dining room are these: 80 walls covered with dark green garlanded wallpaper, lace curtains and mulberry velvet curtains on the windows, a table with a crocheted cloth and a bowl of wax fruit, a pinkish-gray carpet with nosegays of blue and pink roses, a sideboard spread with embroidered runners and holding various patterned plates and jugs and the silver tea things. A lot of things to watch. For every one of these patterns, decorations, seems charged with life, ready to move and flow and alter. Or possibly to explode. Almeda Roth's occupation throughout the day is to keep an eye on them. Not to prevent their alteration so much as to catch them at it—to understand it, to be a part of it. So much is going on in this room that there is no need to leave it. There is not even the thought of leaving it.

Of course, Almeda in her observations cannot escape words. She may think she can, but she can't. Soon this glowing and swelling begins to suggest words—not specific words but a flow of words somewhere, just about ready to make themselves known to her. Poems, even. Yes, again, poems. Or one poem. Isn't that the idea—one very great poem that will contain everything and, oh, that will make all the other poems, the poems she has written, inconsequential, mere trial and error, mere rags? Stars and flowers and birds and trees and angels in the snow and dead children at twilight—that is not the half of it. You have to get in the obscene racket on Pearl Street and the polished toe of Jarvis Poulter's boot and the plucked-chicken haunch with its blue-black flower. Almeda is a long way now from human sympathies or fears or cozy household considerations. She doesn't think about what could be done for that woman or about keeping Jarvis Poulter's dinner warm and hanging his long underwear on the line. The basin of grape juice has overflowed and is running over her kitchen floor, staining the boards of the floor, and the stain will never come out.

She has to think of so many things at once—Champlain and the naked Indians and the salt deep in the earth but as well as the salt the money, the money-making intent brewing forever in heads like Jarvis Poulter's. Also, the brutal storms of winter and the clumsy and benighted deeds on Pearl Street. The changes of climate are often violent, and if you think about it there is no peace even in the stars. All this can be borne only if it is channeled into a poem, and the word "channeled" is appropriate, because the name of the poem will be—it is "The Meneseteung." The name of the poem is the name of the river. No, in fact it is the river, the Meneseteung, that is the poem—with its deep holes and rapids and blissful pools under the summer trees and its grinding blocks of ice thrown up at the end of winter and its desolating spring floods. Almeda looks deep, deep into the river of her mind and into the tablecloth, and she sees the crocheted roses floating. They look bunchy and foolish, her mother's crocheted roses—they don't look much like real flowers. But their effort, their floating independence, their pleasure in their silly selves, does seem to her so admirable. A hopeful sign. *Meneseteung.*

She doesn't leave the room until dusk, when she goes out to the privy again and discovers that she is bleeding, her flow has started. She will have to get a towel, strap it on, bandage herself up. Never before, in health, has she passed a whole day in her nightdress. She doesn't feel any particular anxiety about this. On her way through the kitchen she walks through the pool of grape juice. She knows that she will have to mop it up, but not yet, and she walks upstairs leaving purple footprints and smelling her escaping blood and the sweat of her body that has sat all day in the closed hot room.

No need for alarm.

For she hasn't thought that crocheted roses could float away or that tombstones   85 could hurry down the street. She doesn't mistake that for reality, and neither does she mistake anything else for reality, and that is how she knows that she is sane.

VI

I dream of you by night,
I visit you by day.
Father, Mother,
Sister, Brother,
Have you no word to say?

April 22, 1903. At her residence, on Tuesday last, between three and four o'clock in the afternoon, there passed away a lady of talent and refinement whose pen, in days gone by, enriched our local literature with a volume of sensitive, eloquent verse. It is a sad misfortune that in later years the mind of this fine person had become somewhat clouded and her behaviour, in consequence, somewhat rash and unusual. Her attention to decorum and to the care and adornment of her person had suffered, to the degree that she had become, in the eyes of those unmindful of her former pride and daintiness, a familiar eccentric, or even, sadly, a figure of fun. But now all such lapses pass from memory and what is recalled is her excellent published verse, her labours in former days in the Sunday school, her dutiful care of her parents, her noble womanly nature, charitable concerns, and unfailing religious faith. Her last illness was of mercifully short duration. She caught cold, after having become thoroughly wet from a ramble in the Pearl Street bog. (It has been said that some urchins chased her into the water, and such is the boldness and cruelty of some of our youth, and their observed persecution of this lady, that the tale cannot be entirely discounted.) The cold developed into pneumonia, and she died, attended at the last by a former neighbour, Mrs. Bert (Annie) Friels, who witnessed her calm and faithful end.

January, 1904. One of the founders of our community, an early maker and shaker of this town, was abruptly removed from our midst on Monday morning last, whilst attending to his correspondence in the office of his company. Mr. Jarvis Poulter possessed a keen and lively commercial spirit, which was instrumental in the creation of not one but several local enterprises, bringing the benefits of industry, productivity, and employment to our town.

I looked for Almeda Roth in the graveyard. I found the family stone. There was just one name on it—Roth. Then I noticed two flat stones in the ground, a distance of a few feet—six feet?—from the upright stone. One of these said "Papa," the other "Mama." Farther out from these I found two other flat stones, with the names William and Catherine on them. I had to clear away some overgrowing grass and dirt to see the full name of Catherine. No birth or death dates for anybody, nothing about being dearly beloved. It was a private sort of memorializing, not for the world. There were no roses, either—no sign of a rosebush. But perhaps it was taken out. The grounds keeper doesn't like such things, they are a nuisance to the lawnmower, and if there is nobody left to object he will pull them out.

I thought that Almeda must have been buried somewhere else. When this plot was bought—at the time of the two children's deaths—she would still have been expected to marry, and to lie finally beside her husband. They might not have left room for her here. Then I saw that the stones in the ground fanned out from the upright stone. First the two for the parents, then the two for the children, but these were placed in such a way that there was room for a third, to complete the fan. I paced out from "Catherine" the same number of steps that it took to get from "Catherine" to "William," and at this spot I began pulling grass and scrabbling in the dirt with my bare hands. Soon I felt the stone and knew that I was right. I worked away and got the whole stone clear and I read the name "Meda." There it was with the others, staring at the sky.

I made sure I had got to the edge of the stone. That was all the name there was—   90
Meda. So it was true that she was called by that name in the family. Not just in the poem. Or perhaps she chose her name from the poem, to be written on her stone.

I thought that there wasn't anybody alive in the world but me who would know this, who would make the connection. And I would be the last person to do so. But perhaps this isn't so. People are curious. A few people are. They will be driven to find things out, even trivial things. They will put things together, knowing all along that they may be mistaken. You see them going around with notebooks, scraping the dirt off gravestones, reading microfilm, just in the hope of seeing this trickle in time, making a connection, rescuing one thing from the rubbish.

QUESTIONS

1. What do you learn about the speaker of this story? How does what you learn— particularly in paragraph 89—explain the narrator's concern with the story of Meda and Jarvis? How intimately does the speaker reveal the mind of Meda? What is the effect of paragraph 85?

2. What "facts" form the springboard for the story? As the speaker explains it, what firsthand experiences does she have with the places of the story? What effect do her experiences have on your perceptions of the characters?

3. Particularly considering paragraphs 14, 16, 31, and 86–87, explain the story's shifting or developing narration. You might deal with tense, documentation from the local newspaper, the speaker's involvement in the developing story, and Munro's imagination.

4. Describe the character development of Meda Roth. What effect does her poetry have on how you understand her? (Quotations from her poems appear at the beginnings of the sections.) Why does the episode of the beaten woman, and its immediate aftermath, cause a change in her attitude toward Jarvis?

5. Who is the subject of paragraphs 72–73? What is the effect of these paragraphs on Meda's story? Explain how one might claim that these paragraphs (a) interrupt the story or (b) are integral to it.

6. Why does Munro begin each of the story's sections with excerpts from Meda Roth's poetry? What do these examples add to your understanding of her character?

❦ WRITING ABOUT POINT OF VIEW

In your essay on point of view, you should explain how point of view contributes to making the work exactly as it is. As you prepare to write, therefore, consider language, authority and opportunity for observation, the involvement or detachment of the speaker, the selection of detail, interpretive commentaries, and narrative development. The following questions will help you get started.

Raise Questions to Discover Ideas

- How is the narration made to seem real or probable? Are the actions and speeches reported authentically, as they might be seen and reported in life?

- Is the narrator/speaker identifiable? What are the narrator's qualifications as an observer? How much of the story seems to result from the imaginative or creative powers of the narrator?

- How does the narrator/speaker perceive the time of the actions? If the predominant tense is the past, what relationship, if any, does the narrator establish between the past and the present (e.g., providing explanations, making conclusions)?

If the tense is present, what effect does this tense have on your understanding of the story?

- To what extent does the point of view make the work interesting and effective?

FIRST-PERSON POINT OF VIEW

- What situation prompts the speaker to tell the story or explain the situation? What does the story tell us about the experience and interests of the narrator/speaker?
- Is the speaker talking to the reader, a listener, or herself? How does her audience affect what she is saying? Is the level of language appropriate to her and the situation? How much does she tell about herself?
- To what degree is the narrator involved in the action (i.e., as a major participant or major mover, minor participant, or nonparticipating observer)? Does he make himself the center of humor or admiration? How? Does he seem aware of changes he undergoes?
- Does the speaker criticize other characters? Why? Does she seem to report fairly and accurately what others have told her?
- How reliable is the speaker? Does the speaker seem to have anything to hide? Does it seem that he may be using the story for self-justification or exoneration? What effect does this complexity have on the story?

SECOND-PERSON POINT OF VIEW

- What situation prompts the use of the second person? How does the speaker acquire the authority to explain things to the listener? How directly involved is the listener? What is the relationship between the speaker and listener? If the listener is indefinite, why does the speaker choose to use "you" as the basis of the narration?

THIRD-PERSON POINT OF VIEW

- Does the author speak in an authorial voice, or does it seem that the author has adopted a special but unnamed voice for the work?
- What is the speaker's level of language (e.g., formal and grammatical, informal or intimate and ungrammatical)? Are actions, speeches, and explanations made fully or sparsely?
- From what apparent vantage point does the speaker report action and speeches? Does this vantage point make the characters seem distant or close? How much sympathy does the speaker express for the characters?
- To what degree is your interest centered on a particular character? Does the speaker give you thoughts and responses of this character (limited third person)?
- If the work is third-person omniscient, how extensive is this omniscience (e.g., all the characters or just a few)? Generally, what limitations or freedoms can be attributed to this point of view?
- What special kinds of knowledge does the narrator assume that the listeners or readers possess (e.g., familiarity with art, religion, politics, history, navigation, music, current or past social conditions)?
- How much dialogue is used in the story? Is the dialogue presented directly, as dramatic speech, or indirectly, as past-tense reports of speeches? What is your perception of the story's events as a result of the use of dialogue?

TENSE

- What tense is used predominantly throughout the story? If a single tense is used throughout (e.g., present, past), what is the effect of this constant use of tense?
- Does the story demonstrate a mixture of tenses? Why are the tenses mixed? What purpose is served by these variations? What is the effect of this mixture?
- Is any special use made of the future tense? What is the effect of this use on the present and past circumstances of the characters?

Organize Your Essay about Point of View

Throughout your essay, you should develop your analysis of how the point of view determines such aspects as situation, form, general content, and language. The questions in the preceding section should help you decide how the point of view interacts with these other elements.

Begin by briefly stating the major influence of the point of view on the work. (*Examples:* "The omniscient point of view permits many insights into the major character," or "The first-person point of view permits the work to resemble an exposé of backroom political deals.") How does the point of view make the work interesting and effective? How will your analysis support your central idea?

A fruitful and imaginative way to build your analysis and argument is to explore how changing the point of view might affect the presentation of the story. Let us consider Welty's "A Worn Path" (Chapter 3), which limits its third-person point of view to the circumstances of Phoenix Jackson, whose walk to Natchez is a mission of mercy for her invalid grandson. With the third-person limited focus as we have it, we derive just enough information about Phoenix to understand and sympathize deeply with her plight. If she herself were the narrator, however, we would possibly get not an objective but rather a personalized view of her circumstances—and also perhaps a scattered and unfocused one—and the story would not be as powerful as it is. (Or it might become powerful through different means.) Two stories that would be vastly different if told from alternative perspectives are Oates's "Shopping" and Tan's "Two Kinds." Just suppose—for a moment—that "Shopping" were to limit its third-person narration to Nola, the daughter, rather than to Mrs. Dietrich, the mother. Such a different narration would focus on Nola's thoughts and interests, making Mrs. Dietrich appear arbitrary and unsympathetic. Conversely, suppose that "Two Kinds," which is the first-person narration of Jing-Mei, were to be told in the first person by Jing-Mei's mother. Certainly the mother would explain her ambitions for her daughter fully and reasonably, even though by the story's end Jing Mei does finally reach peace with her mother's memory.

You can see that this alternative approach to point of view requires creative imagination, for to carry it out you must, as it were, invade the author's space and speculate about the results of a point of view that the author did not choose. Considering such hypothetical alternative points of view deeply, however, will greatly enhance your analytical and critical abilities.

In your conclusion, evaluate the success of the point of view. Is it consistent, effective, truthful? What does it contribute to the nature and quality of the story? What particular benefits does the writer gain or lose (if anything) by as a result of the point of view?

DEMONSTRATIVE STUDENT ESSAY

Shirley Jackson's Dramatic Point of View in "The Lottery"°

[1]   The dramatic point of view in Shirley Jackson's "The Lottery" is essential to her success in rendering horror in the midst of the ordinary.* The story, however, is not only one of horror: It may also be called a surprise story, an allegory, or a portrayal of human insensitivity and cruelty. But the validity of all other claims for "The Lottery" hinges on the author's control over point of view to make the events develop out of a seemingly everyday, matter-of-fact situation--a control that could not be easily maintained with another point of view. The success of Jackson's point of view is achieved through her characterization, selection of details, and diction.†

[2]   Because of the dramatic point of view, Jackson succeeds in presenting the villagers as ordinary folks attending a normal, festive event--in contrast to the horror of their real purpose. The contrast depends on Jackson's speaker, who is emotionally uninvolved and who tells only enough about the three hundred townsfolk and their customs to permit the conclusion that they are normal, common people. The principal character is a local housewife, Tessie Hutchinson, but the speaker presents little about her except that she is just like everyone else--an important characteristic when she, like any other person being singled out for punishment, objects not to the lottery itself but to the "unfairness" of the drawing. The same commonness applies also to the other characters, whose brief conversations are recorded but not analyzed. This detached, reportorial method of making the villagers seem common and one-dimensional is fundamental to Jackson's dramatic point of view, and the cruel twist of the ending depends on the method.

[3]   While there could be much description, Jackson's speaker omits some of the important details to conceal the lottery's horrifying purpose. For example, the speaker presents enough information about the lottery to permit readers to understand its rules but does not disclose the grim prize for the "winner." The short saying "Lottery in June, corn be heavy soon" is mentioned as a remnant of a long-forgotten ritual, but the speaker does not explain anything more about this connection with scapegoatism and human sacrifice (248, paragraph 32). None of these references seems unusual as the narrator first presents them, and it is only the conclusion that reveals, in reconsideration, their shocking ghastliness.

Without doubt, a point of view other than the dramatic would spoil Jackson's concluding horror because it would require more explanatory detail. A first-person speaker, for example, would not be credible without explaining the situation and

---

°See pp. 244–50 for this story.
*Central idea.
†Thesis sentence.

revealing feelings that would give away the ending. Such an "I" speaker would need to say something like "The little boys gathered rocks but seemed not to be thinking about their forthcoming use in the stoning." But how would such detail affect the reader's response to the terrifying conclusion? Similarly, an omniscient narrator would need to include details about people's reactions (how could he or she be omniscient otherwise?). A more suitable alternative might be a limited om-

[4] niscient point of view confined to, say, a stranger in town or one of the local children. But any intelligent stranger would be asking "giveaway" questions, and any child but a tiny tot would know about the lottery's sinister outcome. Either hypothetical point-of-view character would therefore require revealing the information too soon. The only conclusion is that Jackson's point of view--the dramatic--is best for this story. Because it permits her naturally to hold back crucial details, it is essential for the suspenseful delay of horror.

Appropriate both to the suspenseful ending and also to the simple character of the villagers is the speaker's language. The words are accurate and descriptive but not elaborate. When Tessie Hutchinson appears, for example, she dries "her hands on her apron" (246, paragraph 8)--words that define her role as a housewife. Most of these simple, bare words may be seen as part of Jackson's technique of withholding detail to delay the reader's understanding. A prime example is the pile of stones, which is in truth a thoughtless and cruel preparation for the stoning, yet this conclusion cannot be drawn from the easy words describing it (245, paragraph 2):

[5] Bobby Martin had already stuffed his pockets full of stones, and the other boys soon followed his example, selecting the smoothest and roundest stones; Bobby and Harry Jones and Dickie Delacroix--the villagers pronounced this name "Dellacroy"--eventually made a great pile of stones in one corner of the square and guarded it against the raids of the other boys.

Both the nicknames and the connotation of boyhood games divert attention and obscure the horrible purpose of the stones. Even at the end, the speaker uses the word "pebbles" to describe the stones given to Tessie's son Davy (249, paragraph 76). The implication is that Davy is playing a game, not participating in the ritual stoning of his own mother!

Such masterly control over point of view is a major cause of Jackson's success in "The Lottery." Her narrative method is to establish the appearance of everyday, uneventful reality, which she maintains up to the beginning of the last scene. She is so successful that a reader's first response to the stoning is "Such

[6] an event could not take place among such common, earthy folks." Yet it is this reality that validates Jackson's vision. Horror is not to be found on moors and in haunted castles but among everyday people like Jackson's three hundred villagers. Without her control of the dramatic point of view, there could be little of this power of suggestion, and it would not be possible to claim such success for the story.

WORK CITED

Jackson, Shirley. "The Lottery." Literature: An Introduction to Reading and Writing. Ed. Edgar V. Roberts and Henry E. Jacobs. 7th ed. Upper Saddle River: Prentice Hall, 2004. 244–50.

Commentary on the Essay

The strategy of this essay is to argue for the importance of Jackson's dramatic point of view in building toward the shocking ending. Words of tribute throughout the essay are "success," "control," "essential," "appropriate," and "masterly". The introductory paragraph sets out three areas for exploration in the body: character, detail, and diction.

The body begins with paragraph 2, in which the aim is *not* to present a full character study (since the essay is not about character but point of view) but rather to discuss the ways in which the dramatic point of view *enables* the characters to be rendered. The argument of the paragraph is that the villagers are to be judged not as complete human beings but as "ordinary folks."

The second part of the body (paragraphs 3 and 4) emphasizes that the sparseness of detail permitted by the dramatic point of view aids Jackson in deferring conclusions about the horror of the drawing. Paragraph 4, which continues the topic of paragraph 3, shows how talking about alternative points of view may aid understanding of the story's actual point of view (see p. 245). The material for the paragraph is derived from notes speculating about whether Jackson's technique of withholding detail to build toward the concluding horror (the topic of paragraph 3) could be maintained with differing points of view. A combination of analysis and imagination is therefore at work in the paragraph.

The third section of the body (paragraph 5) emphasizes the idea that the flat, colorless diction defers awareness of what is happening; therefore, the point of view is vital in the story's surprise and horror. The concluding paragraph (6) emphasizes the way in which general response to the story, and also its success, are conditioned by the detached, dramatic point of view.

Special Topics for Writing and Argument about Point of View

1. Write a short narrative from the first-person point of view of one of these characters:

    a. Mathilde Loisel in "The Necklace" (Chapter 1): *I ruined ten years of my life by not telling the truth.*

    b. Old Man Warner in "The Lottery": *People ain't the way they used to be.*

    c. Faith in "Young Goodman Brown" (Chapter 9): *I don't understand why my husband is so sour and sullen all the time.*

    d. Charles in "The Song of Songs": *Why is Barrett making such a fuss about going to see her real mother?*

2. How would Hawthorne's story "Young Goodman Brown" (Chapter 9) be affected if told by a narrator with a different point of view (different knowledge, different interests, different purposes for telling the story), such as the narrators of "A Worn Path" (Chapter 3), Bierce's "An Occurrence at Owl Creek Bridge," and the second narrator of Mark Twain's "Luck" (Chapter 7)?

3. Recall a childhood occasion on which you were punished. Write an explanation of the punishment as though you were the adult who was in the position of punishing you. Be sure to consider your childhood self objectively, in the third

person. Present things from the viewpoint of the adult, and try to determine how the adult would have learned about your action, judged it, and decided on your punishment.

4.   Write an essay about the proposition that people often have something to gain when they speak and that therefore we need to be critical about what others tell us. Are they trying to change our judgments and opinions? Are they telling the truth? Are they leaving out any important details? Are they trying to sell us something? In your discussion, you may strengthen your ideas by referring to stories that you have been reading.

5.   In the reference section of your library, find two books on literary terms and concepts. How completely and clearly do these works explain the concept of point of view? With the aid of these books, together with the materials in this chapter, describe the interests and views of the narrators in Moore's "How to Become a Writer," Bierce's "An Occurrence at Owl Creek Bridge," or another story of your choice.

Setting: *The Background of Place, Objects, and Culture in Stories*

Like all human beings, literary characters do not exist in isolation. Just as they become human by interacting with other characters, they gain identity because of their cultural and political allegiances, their possessions, their jobs, and where they live, and move, and have their being. They are usually involved deeply with their environments, and their surroundings are causes of much of their motivation and many of their possible conflicts. Plays, stories, and narrative poems must therefore necessarily include descriptions of places, objects, and backgrounds—the **setting.**

❧ WHAT IS SETTING?

Setting is the natural, manufactured, political, cultural, and temporal environment, including everything that characters know and own. Characters may be either helped or hurt by their surroundings, and they may fight about possessions and goals. Further, as characters speak with each other, they reveal the degree to which they share the customs and ideas of their times.

Authors Use Three Basic Types of Settings

PUBLIC AND PRIVATE PLACES, TOGETHER WITH VARIOUS POS-SESSIONS, ARE IMPORTANT IN FICTION, AS IN LIFE. To reveal or highlight qualities of character, and also to make literature lifelike, authors include many details about objects and places of human manufacture, construction, and maintenance. Houses, both interiors and exteriors, are common, as are streets, alleys, public parks, garden paths, fences, confessionals, park benches, terraces, cemeteries, railway cars, trolley cars, historical landmarks, grocery stores, recital rooms, bridges, and the like. In addition, writers include references to objects such as walking sticks, baseballs, books, phonograph records, necklaces, money, guns, shawls, clocks, wallpaper, or hair ribbons. In Maupassant's "The Necklace" (Chapter 1) the loss of a comfortable home brings out the best in the major character by causing her to adjust to her economic reversal, whereas in Lawrence's "The Horse Dealer's Daughter" (Chapter 10) such a loss leads the major character to depression and attempted suicide. In Walker's "Everyday Use" (Chapter 2) a shabby but neat home reveals the narrator's strength of character.

Objects also enter directly into fictional action and character. The lives of the men in O'Brien's "The Things They Carried" (Chapter 2) absolutely depend on the myriad objects they must carry on their military missions. Trying on the neighbors' clothes is an indication of intense if not morbid peculiarity in Carver's "Neighbors" (Chapter 2). A broken birdcage reveals the pathetic but abusive husband–wife relationship in Glaspell's "A Jury of Her Peers" (Chapter 4).

OUTDOOR PLACES ARE SCENES OF MANY FICTIONAL ACTIONS.   The natural world is an obvious location for the action of many narratives and plays. It is therefore important to note natural surroundings (hills, shorelines, valleys, mountains, meadows, fields, trees, lakes, streams), living creatures (birds, dogs, horses, snakes), and also the times, seasons, and conditions in which things happen (morning or night, summer or winter, sunlight or cloudiness, wind or calmness, rain or shine, sunlight or darkness, summer or winter, snowfall or blizzard, heat or cold)—any or all of which may influence and interact with character, motivation, and conduct.

CULTURAL AND HISTORICAL CIRCUMSTANCES OFTEN FIGURE LARGELY IN FICTION.   Just as physical setting influences characters, so do historical and cultural conditions and assumptions. The broad cultural setting of Jackson's "The Lottery" (Chapter 5) is built on the persistence of a primitive belief despite the sophistication of our own modern and scientific age. The brutal oppressiveness and obscene prison-camp conditions in Ozick's "The Shawl" cause the major character to conceal a small child as the only way to keep that child alive. In Clark's "The Portable Phonograph" we see that an artistic and peaceful way of life breaks down when the culture on which it has historically depended has been destroyed.

THE LITERARY USES OF SETTING

Authors use setting to create meaning, just as painters include backgrounds and objects to render ideas. The contrasting settings of François Boucher's portrait *Madame de Pompadour*, for example, and Edward Hopper's *Automat* demonstrate how the same subject—a single female figure—can show divergent views of human life, one elegant and pampered, the other ordinary and forlorn (Insert II–2 and II–3).

Writers manipulate literary locations in a comparable way. For example, in Hawthorne's "Young Goodman Brown" (Chapter 9) a woodland path that is difficult to follow and that is filled with obstacles is a major topographical feature. The path is of course no more than ordinary, granted the time and circumstances of the story, but it also conveys the idea that life is difficult, unpredictable, treacherous, deceiving, and mysterious. Similarly, in Glaspell's "A Jury of Her Peers," the fixtures and utensils in the kitchen of the Wright farm indicate that Midwestern homesteads early in the twentieth century were bleak and oppressive.

The Setting Is Usually Essential and Vital in the Story

To study the setting in a narrative (or play), discover the important details and then try to explain their function. Depending on the author's purpose, the amount of detail may vary. Poe provides many graphic and also impressionistic details in "The Masque of the Red Death," so that we can follow, almost visually, the bizarre action at the story's end. In some works the setting is so intensely present, like the bleak living quarters in Clark's "The Portable Phonograph" and the various Dublin scenes in "Araby," that it is almost literally an additional participant in the action.

Setting Augments a Work's Realism and Credibility

One of the major purposes of literary setting is to establish **realism,** or **verisimilitude.** As the description of location and objects becomes particular and detailed, the events of the work become more believable. Maupassant places "The Necklace" in real locations in late-nineteenth-century Paris, and for this reason the story has all the semblance of having actually happened. Even futuristic, symbolic, and fantastic stories, as well as ghost stories, seem more believable if they include places and objects from everyday experience. Hawthorne's "Young Goodman Brown" and Michael Tremblay's "The Thimble" (Chapter 9) are such stories. Although these stories are by no means realistic, their credibility is enhanced because they take place in settings that have a basis in the world of reality.

Setting May Accentuate Qualities of Character

Setting may intersect with character as a means by which authors underscore the influence of place, circumstance, and time on human growth and change. Glaspell's setting in "A Jury of Her Peers" is the kitchen of the lonely, dreary Wright farm. This kitchen is a place of such hard work, oppression, and unrelieved joylessness that it explains the loss of Minnie's early brightness and promise and also helps us understand her angry act. (A blending of setting and character as seen in Maupassant's "The Necklace" is explored in the two drafts of the demonstrative essay in Chapter 1.)

The way characters respond and adjust to setting can reveal their strength or weakness. Peyton Farquhar's scheme to make an escape from his fate, even when it is literally dangling in front of him, suggests his character strength (Bierce's "An Occurrence at Owl Creek Bridge" [Chapter 5]). In contrast, Goodman Brown's Calvinistic religious conviction that human beings are totally depraved, which is confirmed to him by his nightmarish encounter, indicates the weakness and gullibility of his character (Hawthorne's "Young Goodman Brown").

Setting Is a Means by Which Authors Structure and Shape Their Works

Authors often use setting as one of the means of organizing their stories, as in Maupassant's "The Necklace." The story's final scene is believable because Mathilde leaves her impoverished home to take a nostalgic stroll on the Champs- Elysées, the most fashionable street in Paris. Without this change of setting, she could not have encountered Jeanne Forrestier again, for their usual ways of life would no longer bring them together. In short, the structure of the story depends on a normal and natural change of scene.

Another organizational application of place, time, and object is a **framing** or **enclosing setting,** when an author opens with a particular description and then returns to the same setting at the end. An example is Steinbeck's "The Chrysanthemums" (Chapter 9), which begins with the major character tending her flowers and ends with her seeing the destruction of some of these same flowers which she had given away. A comparable use of framing occurs in Hodgins' "The Concert Stages of Europe" (Chapter 8), in which the reference to a stiff paper piano keyboard opens and closes the story. In such ways, framing creates a formal completeness, just as it may underscore the author's depiction of the human condition.

Various Settings May Be Symbolic

If the scenes and materials of setting are highlighted or emphasized, they also may be taken as symbols through which the author expresses ideas. Such an emphasis is made in Ozick's "The Shawl," in which the shawl has the ordinary function of providing cover and warmth for the baby. Because it is so prominent, however, the shawl also suggests or symbolizes the attempt to preserve future generations, and because its loss also produces a human loss, it symbolizes the helplessness of the victims in Nazi extermination camps during World War II. In O'Brien's "The Things They Carried" (Chapter 2), the constant references to the weights of the objects symbolize how the men's lives depend on their own resources—their carried burdens.

Setting Is Used in the Creation of Atmosphere and Mood

Most actions *require* no more than a functional description of setting. Thus, taking a walk in a forest needs just the statement that there are many, or few, trees. However, if you find descriptions of shapes, light and shadows, animals, wind, and sounds, you may be sure that the author is creating an **atmosphere** or **mood** for the action (as in Clark's "The Portable Phonograph" and Hawthorne's "Young Goodman Brown"). There are many ways to develop moods. Descriptions of bright colors (red, orange, yellow) may contribute to a mood of happiness. The same colors in dim or eerie light, like the rooms in Poe's "The Masque of the Red Death," invoke gloom or augment hysteria. References to smells and sounds bring the setting to life further by asking additional sensory responses from the reader. The setting of a story in a small town or large city, in green or snow-covered fields, or in middle-class or lower-class residences may evoke responses to these places that contribute to the work's atmosphere.

Setting May Underscore a Work's Irony

Just as setting may reinforce character and theme, so it may establish expectations that are the opposite of what occurs. At the beginning of "The Lottery" (Chapter 5), for example, Jackson describes the plainness and folksiness of the assembling townspeople—details that make the conclusion ironic, for it is these same everyday folks who bring about the final horror. Irony is also a motif in Clark's "The Portable Phonograph" inasmuch as the lovely recorded music heard by the group of men sets in motion the incipient impulse toward violence with which the story closes. The ironic use of setting is by no means limited only to fiction, for it is of major significance in plays and poems. The dueling pistols in Chekhov's *The Bear* (Chapter 28) bring out the irony of the developing relationship between the major characters. These guns, which are designed for death, in fact become the means which prompt the characters to fall in love. A heavily ironic situation is created by Thomas Hardy in the poem "Channel Firing" (Chapter 13) when the noise of large guns at sea wakens the skeletons buried in an English churchyard. The irony is that those engaged in the gunnery practice, if "red war" gets still redder, will soon join the skeletons in the graveyard.

STORIES FOR STUDY

SANDRA CISNEROS (b. 1954)

Cisneros, a Mexican-American, was born in Illinois and was educated there. Her higher education was at Loyola University and the University of Iowa Writers' Workshop. She has been a "poet in the schools" in addition to teaching and also working as a college recruiter. She has held two NEA fellowships. The House on Mango Street, *which includes the title story included here, was the first of her books. It was first published in 1983 and reissued in 1991. Its audience has extended beyond readers of English, for it has been translated into eleven languages and has made her one of the widest selling and best-known Hispanic authors in the United States. Her* Woman Hollering Creek and Other Stories *was published in 1991, and her poetry volume* Loose Woman: Poems *appeared in 1991. She published* Hairs/Pelitos, *a book for small children, in 1997. In 2002 she published her second novel,* Caramelo, *which is based on the immigrant lives of her father and other members of her family.*

The House on Mango Street ～<～～～ 1983

We didn't always live on Mango Street. Before that we lived on Loomis on the third floor, and before that we lived on Keeler. Before Keeler it was Paulina, and before that I can't remember. But what I remember most is moving a lot. Each time it seemed there'd be one more of us. By the time we got to Mango Street we were six—Mama, Papa, Carlos, Kiki, my sister Nenny and me.

The house on Mango Street is ours and we don't have to pay rent to anybody or share the yard with the people downstairs or be careful not to make too much noise and there isn't a landlord banging on the ceiling with a broom. But even so, it's not the house we'd thought we'd get.

We had to leave the flat on Loomis quick. The water pipes broke and the landlord wouldn't fix them because the house was too old. We had to leave fast. We were using the washroom next door and carrying water over in empty milk gallons. That's why Mama and Papa looked for a house, and that's why we moved into the house on Mango Street, far away, on the other side of town.

They always told us that one day we would move into a house, a real house that would be ours for always so we wouldn't have to move each year. And our house would have running water and pipes that worked. And inside it would have real stairs, not hallway stairs, but stairs inside like the houses on T.V. And we'd have a basement and at least three washrooms so when we took a bath we didn't have to tell everybody. Our house would be white with trees around it, a great big yard and grass growing without a fence. This was the house Papa talked about when he held a lottery ticket and this was the house Mama dreamed up in the stories she told us before we went to bed.

But the house on Mango Street is not the way they told it at all. It's small and red with tight little steps in front and windows so small you'd think they were holding their breath. Bricks are crumbling in places, and the front door is so swollen you have to push hard to get in. There is no front yard, only four little elms the city planted by the curb. Out back is a small garage for the car we don't own yet and a small yard that looks smaller between the two buildings on either side. There are stairs in our house, but they're ordinary hallway stairs, and the house has only one washroom, very small. Everybody has to share a bedroom—Mama and Papa, Carlos and Kiki, me and Nenny.

Once when we were living on Loomis, a nun from my school passed by and saw me playing out front. The laundromat downstairs had been boarded up because it had been robbed two days before and the owner had painted on the wood YES WE'RE OPEN so as not to lose business.

Where do you live? she asked.

There, I said pointing up to the third floor.

You live *there*?

There. I had to look to where she pointed—the third floor, the paint peeling, wooden bars Papa had nailed on the windows so we wouldn't fall out. You live *there*? The way she said it made me feel like nothing. *There.* I lived *there.* I nodded.

I knew then I had to have a house. A real house. One I could point to. But this isn't it. The house on Mango Street isn't it. For the time being, Mama says. Temporary, says Papa. But I know how those things go.

5

10

QUESTIONS

1. Why is the speaker concerned with the nature of the houses she has lived in? What feeling does she show about these houses?

Character 1990

2. Describe the house on Mango Street. How does the condition of this house and the other houses explain the economic circumstances of the speaker's family?

3. What is the speaker like as a character? How do you learn about her? How much do you learn?

Thing-That

Character = Inner self
that determine
Thought
Speech
behavior

WALTER VAN TILBURG CLARK (1909–1971)

Clark was born in Maine, but he spent most of his life as a professor of English in the western United States. His best-known novel, The Ox-Bow Incident *(1940), which was popularized as a movie, deals with fairness and justice on the Nevada frontier. His other major novel was* The City of Trembling Leaves *(1945), a haunting story of initiation about a young man whose ambition it is to be a composer. "The Portable Phonograph" appeared in 1942, early in World War II, when American forces were being regularly defeated by the Japanese armies and navies in the South Pacific, and two years before the Allies invaded France. The atomic bomb was not known at this time, and hence the desolation envisioned in the story is the result of the "conventional" weaponry of bombs and tanks. Clark's stories were collected in* The Watchful Gods *(1950).*

The Portable Phonograph   1942

The red sunset, with narrow, black cloud strips like threats across it, lay on the curved horizon of the prairie. The air was still and cold, and in it settled the mute darkness and greater cold of night. High in the air there was wind, for through the veil of the dusk the clouds could be seen gliding rapidly south and changing shapes. A sensation of torment, of two-sided, unpredictable nature, arose from the stillness of the earth air beneath the violence of the upper air. Out of the sunset, through the dead, matted grass and isolated weed stalks of the prairie, crept the narrow and deeply rutted remains of a road. In the road, in places, there were crusts of shallow, brittle ice. There were little islands of an old oiled pavement in the road too, but most of it was mud, now frozen rigid. The frozen mud still bore the toothed impress of great tanks, and a wanderer on the neighboring undulations might have stumbled, in this light, into large, partially filled-in and weed-grown cavities, their banks channeled and beginning to spread into badlands. These pits were such as might have been made by falling meteors, but they were not. They were the scars of gigantic bombs, their rawness already made a little natural by rain, seed and time. Along the road there were rakish remnants of fence. There was also, just visible, one portion of tangled and multiple barbed wire still erect, behind which was a shelving ditch with small caves, now very quiet and empty, at intervals in its back wall. Otherwise there was no structure or remnant of a structure visible over the dome of the darkling earth, but only, in sheltered hollows, the darker shadows of young trees trying again.

Under the wuthering arch of the high wind a V of wild geese fled south. The rush of their pinions sounded briefly, and the faint, plaintive notes of their expeditionary talk. Then they left a still greater vacancy. There was the smell and expectation of snow, as there is likely to be when the wild geese fly south. From the remote distance, toward the red sky, came faintly the protracted howl and quick yap-yap of a prairie wolf.

North of the road, perhaps a hundred yards, lay the parallel and deeply intrenched course of a small creek, lined with leafless alders and willows. The creek was already silent under ice. Into the bank above it was dug a sort of cell, with a single opening, like the mouth of a mine tunnel. Within the cell there was a little red of fire, which showed dully through the opening, like a reflection or a deception of the imagination. The light came from the chary burning of four blocks of poorly aged peat, which gave off a petty warmth and much acrid smoke. But the precious remnants of wood, old fence posts and timbers from the long-deserted dugouts, had to be saved for the real cold, for the time when a man's breath blew white, the moisture in his nostrils stiffened at once when he stepped out, and the expansive blizzards paraded for days over the vast open, swirling and settling and thickening, till the dawn of the cleared day when the sky was a thin blue-green and the terrible cold, in which a man could not live for three hours unwarmed, lay over the uniformly drifted swell of the plain.

Around the smoldering peat four men were seated cross-legged. Behind them, traversed by their shadows, was the earth bench, with two old and dirty army blankets, where the owner of the cell slept. In a niche in the opposite wall were a few tin utensils which caught the glint of the coals. The host was rewrapping in a piece of daubed burlap, four fine, leather-bound books. He worked slowly and very carefully, and at last tied the bundle securely with a piece of grass-woven cord. The other three looked intently upon the process, as if a great significance lay in it. As the host tied the cord, he spoke. He was an old man, his long, matted beard and hair gray to nearly white. The shadows made his brows and cheekbones appear gnarled, his eyes and cheeks deeply sunken. His big hands, rough with frost and swollen by rheumatism, were awkward but gentle at their task. He was like a prehistoric priest performing a fateful ceremonial rite. Also his voice had in it a suitable quality of deep, reverent despair, yet perhaps, at the moment, a sharpness of selfish satisfaction.

"When I perceived what was happening," he said, "I told myself, 'It is the end. I cannot take much; I will take these.'"   5

"Perhaps I was impractical," he continued. "But for myself, I do not regret, and what do we know of those who will come after us? We are the doddering remnant of a race of mechanical fools. I have saved what I love; the soul of what was good in us here; perhaps the new ones will make a strong enough beginning not to fall behind when they become clever."

He rose with slow pain and placed the wrapped volumes in the niche with his utensils. The others watched him with the same ritualistic gaze.

"Shakespeare, the Bible, *Moby Dick,*° *The Divine Comedy,* "° one of them said softly. "You might have done worse; much worse."

"You will have a little soul left until you die," said another harshly. "That is more than is true of us. My brain becomes thick, like my hands." He held the big, battered hands, with their black nails, in the glow to be seen.

"I want paper to write on," he said. "And there is none."   10

The fourth man said nothing. He sat in the shadow farthest from the fire, and sometimes his body jerked in its rags from the cold. Although he was still young, he was sick, and coughed often. Writing implied a greater future than he now felt able to consider.

The old man seated himself laboriously, and reached out, groaning at the movement, to put another block of peat on the fire. With bowed heads and averted eyes, his three guests acknowledged his magnanimity.

"We thank you, Doctor Jenkins, for the reading," said the man who had named the books.

Moby-Dick: by Herman Melville (1819–1891), a classic American novel published in 1851.
   The Divine Comedy: by Dante (1265–1321), regarded as the supreme poem of the Italian Renaissance, circulated about 1300.

They seemed then to be waiting for something. Doctor Jenkins understood, but was loath to comply. In an ordinary moment he would have said nothing. But the words of *The Tempest*,° which he had been reading, and the religious attention of the three, made this an unusual occasion.

"You wish to hear the phonograph,"° he said grudgingly.   15

The two middle-aged men stared into the fire, unable to formulate and expose the enormity of their desire.

The young man, however, said anxiously, between suppressed coughs, "Oh, please," like an excited child.

The old man rose again in his difficult way, and went to the back of the cell. He returned and placed tenderly upon the packed floor, where the firelight might fall upon it, an old, portable phonograph in a black case. He smoothed the top with his hand, then opened it. The lovely green-felt-covered disk became visible.

"I have been using thorns as needles," he said. "But tonight, because we have a musician among us"—he bent his head to the young man, almost invisible in the shadow— "I will use a steel needle. There are only three left."

The two middle-aged men stared at him in speechless adoration. The one with the   20
big hands, who wanted to write, moved his lips, but the whisper was not audible.

"Oh, don't," cried the young man, as if he were hurt. "The thorns will do beautifully."

"No," the old man said. "I have become accustomed to the thorns—but they are not really good. For you; my young friend, we will have good music tonight.

"After all," he added generously, and beginning to wind the phonograph, which creaked, "they can't last forever."

"No, nor we," the man who needed to write said harshly. "The needle, by all means."

"Oh, thanks," said the young man. "Thanks," he said again, in a low, excited voice,   25
and then stifled his coughing with a bowed head.

"The records, though," said the old man when he had finished winding, "are a different matter. Already they are very worn. I do not play them more than once a week. One, once a week, that is what I allow myself.

"More than a week I cannot stand it; not to hear them," he apologized.

"No, how could you?" cried the young man. "And with them here like this."

"A man can stand anything," said the man who wanted to write, in his harsh, antagonistic voice.

"Please, the music," said the young man.   30

"Only the one," said the old man. "In the long run we will remember more that way."

He had a dozen records with luxuriant gold and red seals. Even in that light the others could see that the threads of the records were becoming worn. Slowly he read out the titles, and the tremendous, dead names of the composers and the artists and the orchestras. The three worked upon the names in their minds, carefully. It was difficult to select from such a wealth what they would at once most like to remember. Finally the man who wanted to write named Gershwin's "New York."°

The Tempest: Shakespeare's last play, first performed about 1611.

phonograph: Early phonographs, in use before electrically driven record players, had to be wound up by hand. They played records at a speed of 78 revolutions per minute and used steel needles that had to be changed very often. The phonograph is especially valuable to the characters in this story because they have no electricity.

George Gershwin (1898–1937): American composer who wrote in jazz idiom, not in the classical manner.

"Oh, no," cried the sick young man, and then could say nothing more because he had to cough. The others understood him, and the harsh man withdrew his selection and waited for the musician to choose.

The musician begged Doctor Jenkins to read the titles again, very slowly, so that he could remember the sounds. While they were read, he lay back against the wall, his eyes closed, his thin, horny hand pulling at his light beard, and listened to the voices and the orchestras and the single instruments in his mind.

When the reading was done he spoke despairingly. "I have forgotten," he com- 35
plained, "I cannot hear them clearly."

"There are things missing," he explained.

"I know," said Doctor Jenkins. "I thought that I knew all of Shelley° by heart. I should have brought Shelley."

"That's more soul than we can use," said the harsh man. "*Moby Dick* is better.

"By God, we can understand that," he emphasized.

The doctor nodded. 40

"Still," said the man who had admired the books, "we need the absolute if we are to keep a grasp on anything.

"Anything but these sticks and peat clods and rabbit snares," he said bitterly.

"Shelley desired an ultimate absolute," said the harsh man. "It's too much," he said. "It's no good; no earthly good."

The musician selected a Debussy° nocturne. The others considered and approved. They rose to their knees to watch the doctor prepare for the playing, so that they appeared to be actually in an attitude of worship. The peat glow showed the thinness of their bearded faces, and the deep lines in them, and revealed the condition of their garments. The other two continued to kneel as the old man carefully lowered the needle onto the spinning disk, but the musician suddenly drew back against the wall again, with his knees up, and buried his face in his hands.

At the first notes of the piano the listeners were startled. They stared at each other. 45
Even the musician lifted his head in amazement, but then quickly bowed it again, strainingly, as if he were suffering from a pain he might not be able to endure. They were all listening deeply, without movement. The wet, blue-green notes tinkled forth from the old machine, and were individual, delectable presences in the cell. The individual, delectable presences swept into a sudden tide of unbearably beautiful dissonance, and then continued fully the swelling and ebbing of that tide, the dissonant inpourings, and the resolutions, and the diminishments, and the little, quiet wavelets of interlude lapping between. Every sound was piercing and singularly sweet. In all the men except the musician, there occurred rapid sequences of tragically heightened recollection. He heard nothing but what was there. At the final, whispering disappearance, but moving quietly, so that the others would not hear him and look at him, he let his head fall back in agony, as if it were drawn there by the hair, and clenched the fingers of one hand over his teeth. He sat that way while the others were silent, and until they began to breathe again normally. His drawn-up legs were trembling violently.

Quickly Doctor Jenkins lifted the needle off, to save it, and not to spoil the recollection with scraping. When he had stopped the whirling of the sacred disk, he courteously left the phonograph open and by the fire, in sight.

Percy Bysshe Shelley (1792–1822): English poet who wrote poems about the soul, intellectual beauty, and mutability.

Claude Debussy (1862–1918): French composer. His *Nocturnes* for piano was first published in 1890.

The others, however, understood. The musician rose last, but then abruptly, and went quickly out at the door without saying anything. The others stopped at the door and gave their thanks in low voices. The doctor nodded magnificently.

"Come again," he invited, "in a week. We will have the 'New York.'"

When the two had gone together, out toward the rimmed road, he stood in the entrance, peering and listening. At first there was only the resonant boom of the wind overhead, and then, far over the dome of the dead, dark plain, the wolf cry lamenting. In the rifts of clouds the doctor saw four stars flying. It impressed the doctor that one of them had just been obscured by the beginning of a flying cloud at the very moment he heard what he had been listening for, a sound of suppressed coughing. It was not near by, however. He believed that down against the pale alders he could see the moving shadow.

With nervous hands he lowered the piece of canvas which served as his door, and pegged it at the bottom. Then quickly and quietly, looking at the piece of canvas frequently, he slipped the records into the case, snapped the lid shut, and carried the phonograph to his couch. There, pausing often to stare at the canvas and listen, he dug earth from the wall and disclosed a piece of board. Behind this there was a deep hole in the wall, into which he put the phonograph. After a moment's consideration, he went over and reached down his bundle of books and inserted it also. Then, guardedly, he once more sealed up the hole with the board and the earth. He also changed his blankets, and the grass-stuffed sack which served as a pillow, so that he could lie facing the entrance. After carefully placing two more blocks of peat on the fire, he stood for a long time watching the stretched canvas, but it seemed to billow naturally with the first gusts of a lowering wind. At last he prayed, and got in under his blankets, and closed his smoke-smarting eyes. On the inside of the bed, next to the wall, he could feel with his hand, the comfortable piece of lead pipe.

QUESTIONS

1. What kind of environment is described in the first three paragraphs of this story? What has happened before the story opens? To what extent do these paragraphs establish the tone and atmosphere of the story?

2. The first three descriptive paragraphs are loaded with adjectives. In the first, for example, we find *narrow, black, still, cold, mute, dead, isolated, shallow, brittle, old, frozen, tangled, quiet,* and *empty.* What do most of these adjectives contribute to the establishment of setting and, in turn, mood?

3. How is "the host's" home described? What do the details tell us about the host, humanity, and existence in the world of the story?

4. What record do the men choose to hear? What do the phonograph and the music represent to these men?

5. What does Dr. Jenkins do with his things after the men leave? How does he readjust his bed? Why does he do these things?

JOANNE GREENBERG (b. 1932)

Greenberg, a resident of Colorado, graduated from American University in Washington and also attended the University of London. Under the pseudonym "Hannah Green," she achieved wide recognition in 1964 with the novel I Never Promised You a Rose Garden, *which describes the struggles of a teenage girl against schizophrenia. In 1977, the story was made into a successful film, featuring Kathleen Quinlan. Greenberg's fiction reflects her deep concern for "problems of the less fortunate." She is a member of the National Association for the Deaf and has taught sign language. As a writer she has been prolific, producing nearly a dozen novels. "And Sarah Laughed" is taken from her collection* Rite of Passage *(1971) Newer works are* With the Snow Queen *(1991),* No Reck'ning Made *(1993), and* Where the Road Goes *(1998).*

And Sarah Laughed°   1971

She went to the window every fifteen minutes to see if they were coming. They would be taking the new highway cutoff; it would bring them past the south side of the farm; past the unused, dilapidated outbuildings instead of the orchards and fields that were now full and green. It would look like a poor place to the new bride. Her first impression of their farm would be of age and bleached-out, dried-out buildings on which the doors hung open like a row of gaping mouths that said nothing.

All day, Sarah had gone about her work clumsy with eagerness and hesitant with dread, picking up utensils to forget them in holding, finding them two minutes later a surprise in her hand. She had been planning and working ever since Abel wrote to them from Chicago that he was coming home with a wife. Everything should have been clean and orderly. She wanted the bride to know as soon as she walked inside what kind of woman Abel's mother was—to feel, without a word having to be said, the house's dignity, honesty, simplicity, and love. But the spring cleaning had been late, and Alma Yoder had gotten sick—Sarah had had to go over to the Yoders and help out.

Now she looked around and saw that it was no use trying to have everything ready in time. Abel and his bride would be coming any minute. If she didn't want to get caught shedding tears of frustration, she'd better get herself under control. She stepped over the pile of clothes still unsorted for the laundry and went out on the back porch.

The sky was blue and silent, but as she watched, a bird passed over the fields crying. The garden spread out before her, displaying its varying greens. Beyond it, along the creek, there was a row of poplars. It always calmed her to look at them. She looked today. She and Matthew had planted those trees. They stood thirty feet high now, stately as figures in a procession. Once—only once and many years ago—she had tried to describe in words the sounds that the wind made as it combed those trees on its way west. The little boy to whom she had spoken was a grown man now, and he was bringing home a wife. Married. . . .

Ever since he had written to tell them he was coming with his bride, Sarah had been going back in her mind to the days when she and Matthew were bride and groom and then mother and father. Until now, it hadn't seemed so long ago. Her life had flowed on past her, blurring the early days with Matthew when this farm was strange and new to her and when the silence of it was sharp and bitter like pain, not dulled and familiar like an echo of old age.

    5

And Sarah Laughed: See Genesis 18:12.

Matthew hadn't changed much. He was a tall, lean man, but he had had a boy's spareness then. She remembered how his smile came, wavered and went uncertainly, but how his eyes had never left her. He followed everything with his eyes. Matthew had always been a silent man; his face was expressionless and his body stiff with reticence, but his eyes had sought her out eagerly and held her and she had been warm in his look.

Sarah and Matthew had always known each other—their families had been neighbors. Sarah was a plain girl, a serious "decent" girl. Not many of the young men asked her out, and when Matthew did and did again, her parents had been pleased. Her father told her that Matthew was a good man, as steady as any woman could want. He came from honest, hardworking people and he would prosper any farm he had. Her mother spoke shyly of how his eyes woke when Sarah came into the room, and how they followed her. If she married him, her life would be full of the things she knew and loved, an easy, familiar world with her parents' farm not two miles down the road. But no one wanted to mention the one thing that worried Sarah: the fact that Matthew was deaf. It was what stopped her from saying yes right away; she loved him, but she was worried about his deafness. The things she feared about it were the practical things: a fall or a fire when he wouldn't hear her cry for help. Only long after she had put those fears aside and moved the scant two miles into his different world, did she realize that the things she had feared were the wrong things.

Now they had been married for twenty-five years. It was a good marriage—good enough. Matthew was generous, strong, and loving. The farm prospered. His silence made him seem more patient, and because she became more silent also, their neighbors saw in them the dignity and strength of two people who do not rail against misfortune, who were beyond trivial talk and gossip; whose lives needed no words. Over the years of help given and meetings attended, people noticed how little they needed to say. Only Sarah's friend Luita knew that in the beginning, when they were first married, they had written yearning notes to each other. But Luita didn't know that the notes also were mute. Sarah had never shown them to anyone, although she kept them all, and sometimes she would go up and get the box out of her closet and read them over. She had saved every scrap, from questions about the eggs to the tattered note he had left beside his plate on their first anniversary. He had written it when she was busy at the stove and then he'd gone out and she hadn't seen it until she cleared the table.

The note said: "I love you derest wife Sarah. I pray you have happy day all day your life."

When she wanted to tell him something, she spoke to him slowly, facing him, and he took the words as they formed on her lips. His speaking voice was thick and hard to understand and he perceived that it was unpleasant. He didn't like to use it. When he had to say something, he used his odd, grunting tone, and she came to understand what he said. If she ever hungered for laughter from him or the little meaningless talk that confirms existence and affection, she told herself angrily that Matthew talked through his work. Words die in the air; they can be turned one way or another, but Matthew's work prayed and laughed for him. He took good care of her and the boys, and they idolized him. Surely that counted more than all the words—words that meant and didn't mean—behind which people could hide.

Over the years she seldom noticed her own increasing silence, and there were times when his tenderness, which was always given without words, seemed to her to make his silence beautiful.

She thought of the morning she had come downstairs feeling heavy and off balance with her first pregnancy—with Abel. She had gone to the kitchen to begin the day, taking the coffeepot down and beginning to fill it when her eye caught something on the

10

kitchen table. For a minute she looked around in confusion. They had already laid away what the baby would need: diapers, little shirts and bedding, all folded away in the drawer upstairs, but here on the table was a bounty of cloth, all planned and scrimped for and bought from careful, careful study of the catalogue—yards of patterned flannel and plissé, coat wool and bright red corduroy. Sixteen yards of yellow ribbon for bindings. Under the coat wool was cloth Matthew had chosen for her; blue with a little gray figure. It was silk, and there was a card on which was rolled precisely enough lace edging for her collar and sleeves. All the long studying and careful planning, all in silence.

She had run upstairs and thanked him and hugged him, but it was no use showing delight with words, making plans, matching cloth and figuring which pieces would be for the jacket and which for sleepers. Most wives used such fussing to tell their husbands how much they thought of their gifts. But Matthew's silence was her silence too.

When he had left to go to the orchard after breakfast that morning, she had gone to their room and stuffed her ears with cotton, trying to understand the world as it must be to him, with no sound. The cotton dulled the outside noises a little, but it only magnified all the noises in her head. Scratching her cheek caused a roar like a downpour of rain; her own voice was like thunder. She knew Matthew could not hear his own voice in his head. She could not be deaf as he was deaf. She could not know such silence ever.

So she found herself talking to the baby inside her, telling it the things she would   15
have told Matthew, the idle daily things: Didn't Margaret Amson look peaked in town? Wasn't it a shame the drugstore had stopped stocking lump alum—her pickles wouldn't be the same.

Abel was a good baby. He had Matthew's great eyes and gentle ways. She chattered to him all day, looking forward to his growing up, when there would be confidences between them. She looked to the time when he would have his own picture of the world, and with that keen hunger and hope she had a kind of late blooming into a beauty that made people in town turn to look at her when she passed in the street holding the baby in the fine clothes she had made for him. She took Abel everywhere, and came to know a pride that was very new to her, a plain girl from a modest family who had married a neighbor boy. When they went to town, they always stopped over to see Matthew's parents and her mother.

Mama had moved to town after Pa died. Of course they had offered to have Mama come and live with them, but Sarah was glad she had gone to a little place in town, living where there were people she knew and things happening right outside her door. Sarah remembered them visiting on a certain spring day, all sitting in Mama's new front room. They sat uncomfortably in the genteel chairs, and Abel crawled around on the floor as the women talked, looking up every now and then for his father's nod of approval. After a while he went to catch the sunlight that was glancing off a crystal nut dish and scattering rainbow bands on the floor. Sarah smiled down at him. She too had a radiance, and, for the first time in her life, she knew it. She was wearing the dress she had made from Matthew's cloth—it became her and she knew that too, so she gave her joy freely as she traded news with Mama.

Suddenly they heard the fire bell ringing up on the hill: She caught Matthew's eye and mouthed, "Fire engines," pointing uphill to the firehouse. He nodded.

In the next minutes there was the strident, off-key blare as every single one of Arcadia's volunteer firemen—his car horn plugged with a matchstick and his duty before him—drove hellbent for the firehouse in an ecstasy of bell and siren. In a minute the ding-ding-ding-ding careened in deafening, happy privilege through every red light in town.

"Big bunch of boys!" Mama laughed. "You can count two Saturdays in good weath-   20
er when they don't have a fire, and that's during the hunting season!"

They laughed. Then Sarah looked down at Abel, who was still trying to catch the
wonderful colors. A madhouse of bells, horns, screaming sirens had gone right past them
and he hadn't cried, he hadn't looked, he hadn't turned. Sarah twisted her head sharply
away and screamed to the china cats on the whatnot shelf as loud as she could, but Abel's
eyes only flickered to the movement and then went back to the sun and its colors.

Mama whispered, "Oh, my dear God!"

Sarah began to cry bitterly, uncontrollably, while her husband and son looked on,
confused, embarrassed, unknowing.

The silence drew itself over the season and the seasons layered into years. Abel was
a good boy; Matthew was a good man.

Later, Rutherford, Lindsay, and Franklin Delano came. They too were silent. Heredi-   25
tary nerve deafness was rare, the doctors all said. The boys might marry and produce deaf
children, but it was not likely. When they started to school, the administrators and teachers
told her that the boys would be taught specially to read lips and to speak. They would not be
"abnormal," she was told. Nothing would show their handicap, and with training no one
need know that they were deaf. But the boys seldom used their lifeless voices to call to their
friends; they seldom joined games unless they were forced to join. No one but their mother
understood their speech. No teacher could stop all the jumping, turning, gum-chewing
schoolboys, or remember herself to face front from the blackboard to the sound-closed boys.
The lip-reading exercises never seemed to make plain differences—"man," "pan," "began."

But the boys had work and pride in the farm. The seasons varied their silence with
colors—crows flocked in the snowy fields in winter, and tones of golden wheat darkened
across acres of summer wind. If the boys couldn't hear the bedsheets flapping on the
washline, they could see and feel the autumn day. There were chores and holidays and
the wheel of birth and planting, hunting, fishing, and harvest. The boys were familiar in
town; nobody ever laughed at them, and when Sarah met neighbors at the store, they
praised her sons with exaggerated praise, well meant, saying that no one could tell, no
one could really tell unless they knew, about the boys not hearing.

Sarah wanted to cry to these kindly women that the simple orders the boys obeyed
by reading her lips were not a miracle. If she could ever hear in their long-practiced
robot voices a question that had to do with feelings and not facts, and answer it in words
that rose beyond the daily, tangible things done or not done, *that* would be a miracle.

Her neighbors didn't know that they themselves confided to one another from a
universe of hopes, a world they wanted half lost in the world that was; how often they
spoke pitting inflection against meaning to soften it, harden it, make a joke of it, curse by
it, bless by it. They didn't realize how they wrapped the bare words of love in gentle
humor or wild insults that the loved ones knew were ways of keeping the secret of love between the speaker and the hearer. Mothers lovingly called their children crow-bait,
mouse-meat, devils. They predicted dark ends for them, and the children heard the secrets beneath the words, heard them and smiled and knew, and let the love said-unsaid
caress their souls. With her own bitter knowledge Sarah could only thank them for well-
meaning and return to silence.

Standing on the back porch now, Sarah heard the wind in the poplars and she
sighed. It was getting on to noon. Warm air was beginning to ripple the fields. Matthew
would be ready for lunch soon, but she wished she could stand out under the warm sky
forever and listen to birds stitching sounds into the endless silence. She found herself
thinking about Abel again, and the bride. She wondered what Janice would be like. Abel

had gone all the way to Chicago to be trained in drafting. He had met her there, in the school. Sarah was afraid of a girl like that. They had been married quickly, without family or friends or toasts or gifts or questions. It hinted at some kind of secret shame. It frightened her. That kind of girl was independent and she might be scornful of a dowdy mother-in-law. And the house was still a mess.

From down the road, dust was rising. Matthew must have seen it too. He came over 　30 the rise and toward the house walking faster than usual. He'd want to slick his hair down and wash up to meet the stranger his son had become. She ran inside and bundled up the unsorted laundry, ran upstairs and pulled a comb through her hair, put on a crooked dab of lipstick, banged her shin, took off her apron and saw a spot on her dress, put the apron on again and shouted a curse to all the disorder she suddenly saw around her.

Now the car was crunching up the thin gravel of the driveway. She heard Matthew downstairs washing up, not realizing that the bride and groom were already at the house. Protect your own, she thought, and ran down to tell him. Together they went to the door and opened it, hoping that at least Abel's familiar face would comfort them.

They didn't recognize him at first, and he didn't see them. He and the tiny bride might have been alone in the world. He was walking around to open the door for her, helping her out, bringing her up the path to the house, and all the time their fingers and hands moved and spun meanings at which they smiled and laughed; they were talking somehow, painting thoughts in the air so fast with their fingers that Sarah couldn't see where one began and the other ended. She stared. The school people had always told her that such finger-talk set the deaf apart. It was abnormal; it made freaks of them. . . . How soon Abel had accepted someone else's strangeness and bad ways. She felt so dizzy she thought she was going to fall, and she was more bitterly jealous than she had ever been before.

The little bride stopped before them appealingly and in her dead, deaf-rote voice, said, "Ah-am pliizd to meet'ou." Sarah put out her hand dumbly and it was taken and the girl's eyes shone. Matthew smiled, and this time the girl spoke and waved her hands in time to her words, and then gave Matthew her hand. So Abel had told that girl about Matthew's deafness. It had never been a secret, but Sarah felt somehow betrayed.

They had lunch, saw the farm, the other boys came home from their summer school and met Janice. Sarah put out cake and tea and showed Abel and Janice up to the room she had made ready for them, and all the time the two of them went on with love-talk in their fingers; the jokes and secrets knitted silently between them, fears told and calmed, hopes spoken and echoed in the silence of a kitchen where twenty-five years of silence had imprisoned her. Always they would stop and pull themselves back to their good manners, speaking or writing polite questions and answers for the family; but in a moment or two, the talk would flag, the urgent hunger would overcome them and they would fight it, resolutely turning their eyes to Sarah's mouth. Then the signs would creep into their fingers, and the joy of talk into their faces, and they would fall before the conquering need of their communion.

Sarah's friend Luita came the next day, in the afternoon. They sat over tea with the 　35 kitchen window open for the cool breeze and Sarah was relieved and grateful to hold to a familiar thing now that her life had suddenly become so strange to her. Luita hadn't changed at all, thank God—not the hand that waved her tea cool or the high giggle that broke into generous laughter.

"She's darling!" Luita said after Janice had been introduced, and, thankfully, had left them. Sarah didn't want to talk about her, so she agreed without enthusiasm.

Luita only smiled back. "Sarah, you'll never pass for pleased with a face like that."

"It's just—just her ways," Sarah said. "She never even wrote to us before the wedding, and now she comes in and—and changes everything. I'll be honest, Luita, I didn't want Abel to marry someone who was deaf. What did we train him for, all those special classes? . . . *not* to marry another deaf person. And she hangs on him like a wood tick all day . . . ." She didn't mention the signs. She couldn't.

Luita said, "It's just somebody new in the house, that's all. She's important to you, but a stranger. Addie Purkhard felt the same way and you know what a lovely girl Velma turned out to be. It just took time. . . . She's going to have a baby, did she tell you?"

"Baby? Who?" Sarah cried, feeling cold and terrified.

"Why, *Velma.* A baby due about a month after my Dolores'."

It had never occurred to Sarah that Janice and Abel could have a baby. She wanted to stop thinking about it and she looked back at Luita whose eyes were glowing with something joyful that had to be said. Luita hadn't been able to see beyond it to the anguish of her friend.

Luita said, "You know, Sarah, things haven't been so good between Sam and me. . . ." She cleared her throat. "You know how stubborn he is. The last few weeks, it's been like a whole new start for us. I came over to tell you about it because I'm so happy, and I had to share it with you."

She looked away shyly, and Sarah pulled herself together and leaned forward, putting her hand on her friend's arm. "I'm so happy for you. What happened?"

"It started about three weeks ago—a night that neither of us could get to sleep. We hadn't been arguing; there was just that awful coldness, as if we'd both been frozen stiff. One of us started talking—just lying there in the dark. I don't even know who started, but pretty soon we were telling each other the most secret things—things we never could have said in the light. He finally told me that Dolores having a baby makes him feel old and scared. He's afraid of it, Sarah, and I never knew it, and it explains why he hates to go over and see them, and why he argues with Ken all the time. Right there beside me he told me so many things I'd forgotten or misunderstood. In the dark it's like thinking out loud—like being alone and yet together at the same time. I love him so and I came so close to forgetting it. . . ."

Sarah lay in bed and thought about Luita and Sam sharing their secrets in the dark. Maybe even now they were talking in their flower-papered upstairs room, moving against the engulfing seas of silence as if in little boats, finding each other and touching and then looking out in awe at the vastness all around them where they might have rowed alone and mute forever. She wondered if Janice and Abel fingered those signs in the dark on each other's body. She began to cry. There was that freedom, at least; other wives had to strangle their weeping.

When she was cried out, she lay in bed and counted all the good things she had: children, possessions, acres of land, respect of neighbors, the years of certainty and success. Then she conjured the little bride, and saw her standing in front of Abel's old car as she had at first—with nothing; all her virtues still unproven, all her fears still forming, and her bed in another woman's house. Against the new gold ring on the bride's finger, Sarah threw all the substance of her years to weigh for her. The balance went with the bride. It wasn't fair! The balance went with the bride because she had put that communion in the scales as well, and all the thoughts that must have been given and taken between them. It outweighed Sarah's twenty-five years of muteness; outweighed the house and barn and well-tended land, and the sleeping family keeping their silent thoughts.

The days went by. Sarah tortured herself with elaborate courtesy to Janice and politeness to the accomplice son, but she couldn't guard her own envy from herself and she found fault wherever she looked. Now the silence of her house was throbbing with her anger. Every morning Janice would come and ask to help, but Sarah was too restless to teach her, so Janice would sit for a while waiting and then get up and go outside to look for Abel. Then Sarah would decide to make coleslaw and sit with the chopping bowl in her lap, smashing the chopper against the wood with a vindictive joy that she alone could hear the sounds she was making, that she alone knew how savage they were and how satisfying.

At church she would see the younger boys all clean and handsome, Matthew greeting friends, Janice demure and fragile, and Abel proud and loving, and she would feel a terrible guilt for her unreasonable anger; but back from town afterwards, and after Sunday dinner, she noticed as never before how disheveled the boys looked, how ugly their hollow voices sounded. Had Matthew always been so patient and unruffled? He was like one of his own stock, an animal, a dumb animal.

Janice kept asking to help and Sarah kept saying there wasn't time to teach her.   50
She was amazed when Matthew, who was very fussy about his fruit, suggested to her that Janice might be able to take care of the grapes and, later, work in the orchard.

"I haven't time to teach her!"

"Ah owill teeech Ja-nuss," Abel said, and they left right after dinner in too much of a hurry.

Matthew stopped Sarah when she was clearing the table and asked why she didn't like Janice. Now it was Sarah's turn to be silent, and when Matthew insisted, Sarah finally turned on him. "You don't understand," she shouted. "You don't understand a thing!" And she saw on his face the same look of confusion she had seen that day in Mama's fussy front room when she had suddenly begun to cry and could not stop. She turned away with the plates, but suddenly his hand shot out and he struck them to the floor, and the voice he couldn't hear or control rose to an awful cry, "Ah ahm dehf! Ah ahm dehf!" Then he went out, slamming the door without the satisfaction of its sound.

If a leaf fell or a stalk sprouted in the grape arbor, Janice told it over like a set of prayers. One night at supper, Sarah saw the younger boys framing those dumb-signs of hers, and she took them outside and slapped their hands. "*We* don't do that!" she shouted at them, and to Janice later she said, "Those . . . signs you make—I know they must have taught you to do that, but out here . . . well, it isn't our way."

Janice looked back at her in a confusion for which there were no words.   55

It was no use raging at Janice. Before she had come there had never been anything for Sarah to be angry about. . . . What did they all expect of her? Wasn't it enough that she was left out of a world that heard and laughed without being humiliated by the love-madness they made with their hands? It was like watching them undressing.

The wind cannot be caught. Poplars may sift it, a rising bird can breast it, but it will pass by and no one can stop it. She saw the boys coming home at a dead run now, and they couldn't keep their hands from taking letters, words, and pictures from the fingers of the lovers. If they saw an eagle, caught a fish, or got scolded, they ran to their brother or his wife, and Sarah had to stand in the background and demand to be told.

One day Matthew came up to her and smiled and said, "Look." He put out his two index fingers and hooked the right down on the left, then the left down gently on the right. "Fwren," he said, "Ja-nuss say, fwren."

To Sarah there was something obscene about all those gestures, and she said, "I don't like people waving their hands around like monkeys in a zoo!" She said it very clearly so that he couldn't mistake it.

He shook his head violently and gestured as he spoke. "Mouth eat; mouth kiss,   60
mouth tawk! Fin-ger wohk; fin-ger tawk. E-ah" (and he grabbed his ear, violently), "e-ah dehf. *Mihn*," (and he rapped his head, violently, as if turning a terrible impatience against himself so as to spare her) "*mihn not* dehf!"

Later she went to the barn after something and she ran into Lindsay and Franklin Delano standing guilty, and when she caught them in her eye as she turned, she saw their hands framing signs. They didn't come into the house until it was nearly dark. Was their hunger for those signs so great that only darkness could bring them home? They weren't bad boys, the kind who would do a thing just because you told them not to. Did their days have a hunger too, or was it only the spell of the lovers, honey-honeying to shut out a world of moving mouths and silence?

At supper she looked around the table and was reassured. It could have been any farm family sitting there, respectable and quiet. A glance from the father was all that was needed to keep order or summon another helping. Their eyes were lowered, their faces composed. The hands were quiet. She smiled and went to the kitchen to fix the shortcake she had made as a surprise.

When she came back, they did not notice her immediately. They were all busy talking. Janice was telling them something and they all had their mouths ridiculously pursed with the word. Janice smiled in assent and each one showed her his sign and she smiled at each one and nodded, and the signers turned to one another in their joy, accepting and begging acceptance. Then they saw Sarah standing there; the hands came down, the faces faded.

She took the dinner plates away and brought in the dessert things, and when she went back to the kitchen for the cake, she began to cry. It was beyond envy now; it was too late for measuring or weighing. She had lost. In the country of the blind, Mama used to say, the one-eyed man is king. Having been a citizen of such a country, she knew better. In the country of the deaf, the hearing man is lonely. Into that country a girl had come who, with a wave of her hand, had given the deaf ears for one another, and had made Sarah the deaf one.

Sarah stood, staring at her cake and feeling for that moment the profundity of the silence which she had once tried to match by stuffing cotton in her ears. Everyone she loved was in the other room, talking, sharing, standing before the awful, impersonal heaven and the unhearing earth with pictures of his thoughts, and she was the deaf one now. It wasn't "any farm family," silent in its strength. It was a yearning family, silent in its hunger, and a demure little bride had shown them all how deep the hunger was. She had shown Sarah that her youth had been sold into silence. She was too old to change now. 65

An anger rose in her as she stared at the cake. Why should they be free to move and gesture and look different while she was kept in bondage to their silence? Then she remembered Matthew's mute notes, his pride in Abel's training, his face when he had cried, "I am deaf!" over and over. She had actually fought that terrible yearning, that hunger they all must have had for their own words. If they could all speak somehow, what would the boys tell her?

She knew what she wanted to tell them. That the wind sounds through the poplar trees, and people have a hard time speaking to one another even if they aren't deaf. Luita and Sam had to have a night to hide their faces while they spoke. It suddenly occurred to her that if Matthew made one of those signs with his hands and she could learn that sign, she could put her hands against his in the darkness, and read the meaning—that if she learned those signs she could hear him. . . .

She dried her eyes hurriedly and took in the cake. They saw her and the hands stopped, drooping lifelessly again; the faces waited mutely. Silence. It was a silence she could no longer bear. She looked from face to face. What was behind those eyes she loved? Didn't everyone's world go deeper than chores and bread and sleep?

"I want to talk to you," she said. "I want to talk, to know what you think." She put her hands out before her, offering them.

Six pairs of eyes watched her.   70
Janice said, "Mo-ther."
Eyes snapped away to Janice; thumb was under lip: the Sign.
Sarah followed them. "Wife," she said, showing her ring.
"Wife," Janice echoed, thumb under lip to the clasp of hands.
Sarah said, "I love. . . ."   75
  Janice showed her and she followed hesitantly and then turned to Matthew to give
and to be received in that sign.

QUESTIONS

1. Characterize Sarah. What do we learn about her character from the way she cares for her surroundings and tends to her tasks?

2. What kinds of detail about the appearance and circumstances of the farm appear in the story? Why are these details included?

3. Why does Greenberg not disclose right away that Matthew is deaf? Why does she withhold the same detail about Abel? How does Sarah respond when she learns that Abel is deaf?

4. What attitudes toward deafness and communication does Janice, with her mastery of sign language, bring out in Sarah? To what degree may her attitudes be considered a crisis? How does Sarah respond to the crisis? Why?

JAMES JOYCE (1882–1941)

Joyce, one of the greatest twentieth-century writers, was born in Ireland and received a vigorous and thorough education there. He left Ireland in 1902 and spent most of the rest of his life in Switzerland and France. His best-known works are Dubliners *(1914), A* Portrait of the Artist as a Young Man *(1914–1915),* Ulysses *(1922), and* Finnegans Wake *(1939). Much of his work has been called "fictionalized autobiography," a quality shown in "Araby," which is selected from* Dubliners. *As a young child, Joyce had lived on North Richmond Street, just like the narrator of the story. The bazaar that the narrator visits actually did take place in Dublin, from May 14 to 19, 1894, when Joyce was the same age as the narrator. It was called "Araby in Dublin" and was advertised as a "Grand Oriental Fete."*

Araby   1914

North Richmond Street,° being blind,° was a quiet street except at the hour when the Christian Brothers' School set the boys free. An uninhabited house of two storeys stood at the blind end, detached from its neighbours in a square ground. The other houses of the street, conscious of decent lives within them, gazed at one another with brown imperturbable faces.

North Richmond Street: name of a real street in Dublin on which Joyce lived as a boy.
blind: dead-end street.

The former tenant of our house, a priest, had died in the back drawing room. Air, musty from having long been enclosed, hung in all the rooms, and the waste room behind the kitchen was littered with old useless papers. Among these I found a few paper-covered books, the pages of which were curled and damp: *The Abbott*, by Walter Scott, *The Devout Communicant*° and *The Memoirs of Vidocq*.° I liked the last best because its leaves were yellow. The wild garden behind the house contained a central apple-tree and a few straggling bushes under one of which I found the late tenant's rusty bicycle-pump. He had been a very charitable priest; in his will he had left all his money to institutions and the furniture of his house to his sister.

When the short days of winter came dusk fell before we had well eaten our dinners. When we met in the street the houses had grown sombre. The space of sky above us was the colour of ever-changing violet and towards it the lamps of the street lifted their feeble lanterns. The cold air stung us and we played till our bodies glowed. Our shouts echoed in the silent street. The career of our play brought us through the dark muddy lanes behind the houses where we ran the gauntlet of the rough tribes from the cottages, to the back doors of the dark dripping gardens where odours arose from the ashpits, to the dark odorous stables where a coachman smoothed and combed the horse or shook music from the buckled harness. When we returned to the street light from the kitchen windows had filled the areas. If my uncle was seen turning the corner we hid in the shadow until we had seen him safely housed. Or if Mangan's sister came out on the doorstep to call her brother in to his tea we watched her from our shadow peer up and down the street. We waited to see whether she would remain or go in and, if she remained, we left our shadow and walked up to Mangan's steps resignedly. She was waiting for us, her figure defined by the light from the half-opened door. Her brother always teased her before he obeyed and I stood by the railings looking at her. Her dress swung as she moved her body and the soft rope of her hair tossed from side to side.

Every morning I lay on the floor in the front parlor watching her door. The blind was pulled down within an inch of the sash so that I could not be seen. When she came out on the doorstep my heart leaped. I ran to the hall, seized my books and followed her. I kept her brown figure always in my eye and, when we came near the point at which our ways diverged, I quickened my pace and passed her. This happened morning after morning. I had never spoken to her, except for a few casual words, and yet her name was like a summons to all my foolish blood.

Her image accompanied me even in places the most hostile to romance. On Saturday evenings when my aunt went marketing I had to go to carry some of the parcels. We walked through the flaring street, jostled by drunken men and bargaining women, amid the curses of labourers, the shrill litanies of shop-boys who stood on guard by the barrels of pigs' cheeks, the nasal chanting of street singers, who sang a *come-all-you* about O'Donovan Rossa,° or a ballad about the troubles in our native land. These noises converged in a single sensation of life for me: I imagined that I bore my chalice safely through the throng of foes. Her name sprang to my lips at moments in strange prayers and praises which I myself did not understand. My eyes were often full of tears (I could not tell why) and at times a flood from my heart seemed to pour itself out into my bosom. I thought little of the future. I did not know whether I would ever speak to her or not or,

5

The Devout Communicant: a book of meditations by Pacificus Baker, published 1873.
The Memoirs of Vidocq: published 1829, the story of François Vidocq, a Parisian chief of detectives.
O'Donovan Rossa: popular ballad about Jeremiah O'Donovan (1831–1915), a leader in the movement to free Ireland from English control. He was called "Dynamite Rossa."

if I spoke to her, how I could tell her of my confused adoration. But my body was like a harp and her words and gestures were like fingers running upon the wires.

One evening I went into the back drawing-room in which the priest had died. It was a dark rainy evening and there was no sound in the house. Through one of the broken panes I heard the rain impinge upon the earth, the fine incessant needles of water playing in the sodden beds. Some distant lamp or lighted window gleamed below me. I was thankful that I could see so little. All my senses seemed to desire to veil themselves and, feeling that I was about to slip from them, I pressed the palms of my hands together until they trembled, murmuring: *O love! O love!* many times.

At last she spoke to me. When she addressed the first words to me I was so confused that I did not know what to answer. She asked me was I going to *Araby*.° I forget whether I answered yes or no. It would be a splendid bazaar, she said; she would love to go.

—And why can't you? I asked.

While she spoke she turned a silver bracelet round and round her wrist. She could not go, she said, because there would be a retreat° that week in her convent. Her brother and two other boys were fighting for their caps and I was alone at the railings. She held one of the spikes, bowing her head towards me. The light from the lamp opposite our door caught the white curve of her neck, lit up her hair that rested there and, falling, lit up the hand upon the railing. It fell over one side of her dress and caught the white border of a petticoat, just visible as she stood at ease.

—It's well for you, she said.

—If I go, I said, I will bring you something.   10

What innumerable follies laid waste my waking and sleeping thoughts after that evening! I wished to annihilate the tedious intervening days. I chafed against the work of school. At night in my bedroom and by day in the classroom her image came between me and the page I strove to read. The syllables of the word *Araby* were called to me through the silence in which my soul luxuriated and cast an Eastern enchantment over me. I asked for leave to go to the bazaar on Saturday night. My aunt was surprised and hoped it was not some Freemason° affair. I answered few questions in class. I watched my master's face pass from amiability to sternness; he hoped I was not beginning to idle. I could not call my wandering thoughts together. I had hardly any patience with the serious work of life which, now that it stood between me and my desire, seemed to me child's play, ugly monotonous child's play.

On Saturday morning I reminded my uncle that I wished to go to the bazaar in the evening. He was fussing at the hall-stand, looking for the hatbrush, and answered me curtly:

—Yes, boy, I know.

As he was in the hall I could not go into the front parlour and lie at the window. I   15
left the house in bad humour and walked slowly towards the school. The air was pitilessly raw and already my heart misgave me.

When I came home to dinner my uncle had not yet been home. Still, it was early. I sat staring at the clock for some time and, when its ticking began to irritate me, I left the room. I mounted the staircase and gained the upper part of the house. The high cold empty gloomy rooms liberated me and I went from room to room singing. From the front window I saw my companions playing below in the street. Their cries reached me weakened and indistinct and, leaning my forehead against the cool glass, I looked over at the dark house where she lived. I may have stood there for an hour, seeing nothing but

---

Araby: the bazaar held in Dublin from May 14–19, 1894.
retreat: a special time set aside for concentrated religious instruction, discussion, and prayer.
Freemason: and therefore Protestant.

the brown-clad figure cast by my imagination, touched discreetly by the lamplight at the curved neck, at the hand upon the railing and at the border below the dress.

When I came downstairs again I found Mrs. Mercer sitting at the fire. She was an old garrulous woman, a pawnbroker's widow, who collected used stamps for some pious purpose. I had to endure the gossip of the tea-table. The meal was prolonged beyond an hour and still my uncle did not come. Mrs. Mercer stood up to go: she was sorry she couldn't wait any longer, but it was after eight o'clock and she did not like to be out late, as the night air was bad for her. When she had gone I began to walk up and down the room, clenching my fists. My aunt said:

—I'm afraid you may put off your bazaar for this night of Our Lord.

At nine o'clock I heard my uncle's latchkey in the halldoor. I heard him talking to himself and heard the hall-stand rocking when it had received the weight of his overcoat. I could interpret these signs. When he was midway through his dinner I asked him to give me the money to go to the bazaar. He had forgotten.

—The people are in bed and after their first sleep now, he said.   20

I did not smile. My aunt said to him energetically:

—Can't you give him the money and let him go? You've kept him late enough as it is.

My uncle said he was very sorry he had forgotten. He said he believed in the old saying: *All work and no play makes Jack a dull boy.* He asked me where I was going and, when I had told him a second time he asked me did I know *The Arab's Farewell to his Steed.*° When I left the kitchen he was about to recite the opening lines of the piece to my aunt.

I held a florin° tightly in my hand as I strode down Buckingham Street towards the station. The sight of the streets thronged with buyers and glaring with gas recalled to me the purpose of my journey. I took my seat in a third-class carriage of a deserted train. After an intolerable delay the train moved out of the station slowly. It crept onward among ruinous houses and over the twinkling river. At Westland Row Station a crowd of people pressed to the carriage doors; but the porters moved them back, saying that it was a special train for the bazaar. I remained alone in the bare carriage. In a few minutes the train drew up beside an improvised wooden platform. I passed out on to the road and saw by the lighted dial of a clock that it was ten minutes to ten. In front of me was a large building which displayed the magical name.

I could not find any sixpenny entrance and, fearing that the bazaar would be   25
closed, I passed in quickly through a turnstile, handing a shilling to a weary-looking man. I found myself in a big hall girdled at half its height by a gallery. Nearly all the stalls were closed and the greater part of the hall was in darkness. I recognized a silence like that which pervades a church after a service. I walked into the centre of the bazaar timidly. A few people were gathered about the stalls which were still open. Before a curtain, over which the words *Café Chantant* were written in coloured lamps, two men were counting money on a salver. I listened to the fall of the coins.

Remembering with difficulty why I had come I went over to one of the stalls and examined porcelain vases and flowered tea-sets. At the door of the stall a young lady was talking and laughing with two young gentlemen. I remarked their English accents and listened vaguely to their conversation.

—O, I never said such a thing!

—O, but you did!

—O, but I didn't!

The Arab's Farewell to his Steed: poem by Caroline Norton (1808–1877).
    florin: a two-shilling coin in the 1890s (when the story takes place), worth perhaps twenty dollars in today's money.

—Didn't she say that?   30
—Yes I heard her.
—O, there's a . . . fib!

Observing me the young lady came over and asked me did I wish to buy anything. The tone in her voice was not encouraging; she seemed to have spoken to me out of a sense of duty. I looked humbly at the great jars that stood like eastern guards at either side of the dark entrance to the stall and murmured:

—No, thank you.

The young lady changed the position of one of the vases and went back to the two   35
young men. They began to talk of the same subject. Once or twice the young lady glanced at me over her shoulder.

I lingered before her stall, though I knew my stay was useless, to make my interest in her wares seem the more real. Then I turned away slowly and walked down the middle of the bazaar. I allowed the two pennies to fall against the sixpence in my pocket. I heard a voice call from one end of the gallery that the light was out. The upper part of the hall was now completely dark.

Gazing up into the darkness I saw myself as a creature driven and derided by vanity; and my eyes burned with anguish and anger.

QUESTIONS

1. Describe what you consider to be the story's major idea.

2. How might the bazaar, "Araby," be considered symbolically in the story? To what extent does this symbol embody the story's central idea?

3. Consider the attitude of the speaker toward his home as indicated in the first paragraph. Why do you think the speaker uses the word *blind* to describe the dead-end street? What relationship exists between the speaker's pain at the end of the story to the ideas in the first paragraph?

4. Who is the narrator? About how old is he at the time of the story? About how old when he tells the story? What effect is produced by this difference in age between narrator-as-character and narrator-as-storyteller?

CYNTHIA OZICK (b. 1928)

Ozick has published three novels, Trust *(1966),* The Cannibal Galaxy *(1983), and* The Messiah of Stockholm *(1987); three short-story collections,* The Pagan Rabbi *(1971),* Bloodshed *(1976), and* Levitation *(1982); and frequent essays and reviews, among which is the collection* Fame and Folly *(1996). Among her many recognitions and awards, she serves on the Board of Advisers of the* American Poetry Review. *Her 1990 novella "Puttermesser Paired" was the first story featured in* Prize Stories 1992: The O. Henry Awards, *edited by William Abrahams. "The Shawl,"*
first published in the New Yorker *in 1980, was republished in* The Shawl *in 1989, with a companion story describing the heroine's experiences in the United States after surviving the death camp. Also, "The Shawl" was adapted as a play (1996).*

The Shawl ~≺≍≺⁓ 1980

Stella, cold, cold the coldness of hell. How they walked on the roads together, Rosa with Magda curled up between sore breasts, Magda wound up in the shawl. Sometimes Stella carried Magda. But she was jealous of Magda. A thin girl of fourteen, too small, with thin breasts of her own, Stella wanted to be wrapped in a shawl, hidden away, asleep, rocked by the march, a baby, a round infant in arms. Magda took Rosa's nipple, and Rosa never stopped walking, a walking cradle. There was not enough milk; sometimes Magda sucked air; then she screamed. Stella was ravenous. Her knees were tumors on sticks, her elbows chicken bones.

Rosa did not feel hunger; she felt light, not like someone walking but like someone in a faint, in trance, arrested in a fit, someone who is already a floating angel, alert and seeing everything, but in the air, not there, not touching the road. As if teetering on the tips of her fingernails. She looked into Magda's face through a gap in the shawl: a squirrel in a nest, safe, no one could reach her inside the little house of the shawl's windings. The face, very round, a pocket mirror of a face: but it was not Rosa's bleak complexion, dark like cholera, it was another kind of face altogether, eyes blue as air, smooth feathers of hair nearly as yellow as the Star sewn into Rosa's coat. You could think she was one of *their* babies.

Rosa, floating, dreamed of giving Magda away in one of the villages. She could leave the line for a minute and push Magda into the hands of any woman on the side of the road. But if she moved out of line they might shoot. And even if she fled the line for half a second and pushed the shawl-bundle at a stranger, would the woman take it? She might be surprised, or afraid; she might drop the shawl, and Magda would fall out and strike her head and die. The little round head. Such a good child, she gave up screaming, and sucked now only for the taste of the drying nipple itself. The neat grip of the tiny gums. One mite of a tooth tip sticking up in the bottom gum, how shining, an elfin tombstone of white marble gleaming there. Without complaining, Magda relinquished Rosa's teats, first the left, then the right; both were cracked, not a sniff of milk. The duct crevice extinct, a dead volcano, blind eye, chill hole, so Magda took the corner of the shawl and milked it instead. She sucked and sucked, flooding the threads with wetness. The shawl's good flavor, milk of linen.

It was a magic shawl, it could nourish an infant for three days and three nights. Magda did not die, she stayed alive, although very quiet. A peculiar smell, of cinnamon and almonds, lifted out of her mouth. She held her eyes open every moment, forgetting how to blink or nap, and Rosa and sometimes Stella studied their blueness. On the road they raised one burden of a leg after another and studied Magda's face. "Aryan," Stella said, in a voice grown as thin as a string; and Rosa thought how Stella gazed at Magda like a young cannibal. And the time that Stella said "Aryan," it sounded to Rosa as if Stella had really said "Let us devour her."

But Magda lived to walk. She lived that long, but she did not walk very well, partly because she was only fifteen months old, and partly because the spindles of her legs could not hold up her fat belly. It was fat with air, full and round. Rosa gave almost all her food to Magda, Stella gave nothing; Stella was ravenous, a growing child herself, but not growing much. Stella did not menstruate. Rosa did not menstruate. Rosa was ravenous, but also not; she learned from Magda how to drink the taste of a finger in one's mouth. They were in a place without pity, all pity was annihilated in Rosa, she looked at Stella's bones without pity. She was sure that Stella was waiting for Magda to die so she could put her teeth into the little thighs.

Rosa knew Magda was going to die very soon; she should have been dead already, but she had been buried away deep inside the magic shawl, mistaken there for the

5

shivering mound of Rosa's breasts; Rosa clung to the shawl as if it covered only herself. No one took it away from her. Magda was mute. She never cried. Rosa hid her in the barracks, under the shawl, but she knew that one day someone would inform; or one day someone, not even Stella, would steal Magda to eat her. When Magda began to walk Rosa knew that Magda was going to die very soon, something would happen. She was afraid to fall asleep; she slept with the weight of her thigh on Magda's body; she was afraid she would smother Magda under her thigh. The weight of Rosa was becoming less and less; Rosa and Stella were slowly turning into air.

Magda was quiet, but her eyes were horribly alive, like blue tigers. She watched. Sometimes she laughed—it seemed a laugh, but how could it be? Magda had never seen anyone laugh. Still, Magda laughed at her shawl when the wind blew its corners, the bad wind with pieces of black in it, that made Stella's and Rosa's eyes tear. Magda's eyes were always clear and tearless. She watched like a tiger. She guarded her shawl. No one could touch it; only Rosa could touch it. Stella was not allowed. The shawl was Magda's own baby, her pet, her little sister. She tangled herself up in it and sucked on one of the corners when she wanted to be very still.

Then Stella took the shawl away and made Magda die.

Afterward Stella said: "I was cold."

And afterward she was always cold, always. The cold went into her heart: Rosa saw that Stella's heart was cold. Magda flopped onward with her little pencil legs scribbling this way and that, in search of the shawl; the pencils faltered at the barracks opening, where the light began. Rosa saw and pursued. But already Magda was in the square outside the barracks, in the jolly light. It was the roll-call arena. Every morning Rosa had to conceal Magda under the shawl against a wall of the barracks and go out and stand in the arena with Stella and hundreds of others, sometimes for hours, and Magda, deserted, was quiet under the shawl, sucking on her corner. Every day Magda was silent, and so she did not die. Rosa saw that today Magda was going to die, and at the same time a fearful joy ran into Rosa's two palms, her fingers were on fire, she was astonished, febrile: Magda, in the sunlight, swaying on her pencil legs, was howling. Ever since the drying up of Rosa's nipples, ever since Magda's last scream on the road, Magda had been devoid of any syllable; Magda was a mute. Rosa believed that something had gone wrong with her vocal cords, with her windpipe, with the cave of her larynx; Magda was defective, without a voice; perhaps she was deaf; there might be something amiss with her intelligence; Magda was dumb. Even the laugh that came when the ash-stippled wind made a clown out of Magda's shawl was only the air-blown showing of her teeth. Even when the lice, head lice and body lice, crazed her so that she became as wild as one of the big rats that plundered the barracks at daybreak looking for carrion, she rubbed and scratched and kicked and bit and rolled without a whimper. But now Magda's mouth was spilling a long viscous rope of clamor.

"Maaaa—"

It was the first noise Magda had ever sent out from her throat since the drying up of Rosa's nipples.

"Maaaa . . . aaa!"

Again! Magda was wavering in the perilous sunlight of the arena, scrabbling on such pitiful little bent shins. Rosa saw. She saw that Magda was grieving for the loss of her shawl, she saw that Magda was going to die. A tide of commands hammered in Rosa's nipples: Fetch, get, bring! But she did not know which to go after first, Magda or the shawl. If she jumped out into the arena to snatch Magda up, the howling would not stop, because Magda would still not have the shawl; but if she ran back into the barracks to find the shawl, and if she found it, and if she came after Magda holding it and shaking it, then

10

she would get Magda back, Magda would put the shawl in her mouth and turn dumb again.

Rosa entered the dark. It was easy to discover the shawl. Stella was heaped under it, asleep in her thin bones. Rosa tore the shawl free and flew—she could fly, she was only air—into the arena. The sunheat murmured of another life, of butterflies in summer. The light was placid, mellow. On the other side of the steel fence, far away, there were green meadows speckled with dandelions and deep-colored violets; beyond them, even farther, innocent tiger lilies, tall, lifting their orange bonnets. In the barracks they spoke of "flowers," of "rain": excrement, thick turd-braids, and the slow stinking maroon water-fall that slunk down from the upper bunks, the stink mixed with a bitter fatty floating smoke that greased Rosa's skin. She stood for an instant at the margin of the arena. Sometimes the electricity inside the fence would seem to hum; even Stella said it was only an imagining, but Rosa heard real sounds in the wire: grainy sad voices. The farther she was from the fence, the more clearly the voices crowded at her. The lamenting voices strummed so convincingly, so passionately, it was impossible to suspect them of being phantoms. The voices told her to hold up the shawl, high; the voices told her to shake it, to whip with it, to unfurl it like a flag. Rosa lifted, shook, whipped, unfurled. Far off, very far, Magda leaned across her air-fed belly, reaching out with the rods of her arms. She was high up, elevated, riding someone's shoulder. But the shoulder that carried Magda was not coming toward Rosa and the shawl, it was drifting away, the speck of Magda was mov-ing more and more into the smoky distance. Above the shoulder a helmet glinted. The light tapped the helmet and sparkled it into a goblet. Below the helmet a black body like a domino and a pair of black boots hurled themselves in the direction of the electrified fence. The electric voices began to chatter wildly. "Maa-maa, maaamaaa," they all hummed together. How far Magda was from Rosa now, across the whole square, past a dozen barracks, all the way on the other side! She was no bigger than a moth.

All at once Magda was swimming through the air. The whole of Magda traveled through loftiness. She looked like a butterfly touching a silver vine. And the moment Magda's feathered round head and her pencil legs and balloonish belly and zigzag arms splashed against the fence, the steel voices went mad in their growling, urging Rosa to run and run to the spot where Magda had fallen from her flight against the electrified fence; but of course Rosa did not obey them. She only stood, because if she ran they would shoot, and if she tried to pick up the sticks of Magda's body they would shoot, and if she let the wolf's screech ascending now through the ladder of her skeleton break out, they would shoot; so she took Magda's shawl and filled her own mouth with it, stuffed it in and stuffed it in, until she was swallowing up the wolf's screech and tasting the cinna-mon and almond depth of Magda's saliva; and Rosa drank Magda's shawl until it dried.

QUESTIONS

1. Describe how Ozick presents the setting. Why do you not receive a clear picture of how things look? Why does Ozick present the details as she does?

2. In paragraph 15, what is on the other side of the fence? Explain Ozick's descrip-tion here. Why does Ozick include these details so close to the story's end?

3. What character is the center of interest in "The Shawl"? Why is she being treated as she is? What are her impressions of the conditions and circumstances around her? What are her responses to her hunger and deprivation?

4. Explain the function of the more unpleasant and brutal details. What do you need to know about the circumstances of the story to respond to these details?

EDGAR ALLAN POE (1809–1849)

Orphaned as an infant, Poe was brought up in the household of John Allan, a prospering Virginia merchant. He entered West Point in 1830, but was expelled in 1831. He then took up his literary career—poet, fiction writer, essayist, critic, and lecturer— which kept him fed but never secure. As a fiction writer he created the genres of detective story, murder story, horror story, and psychological story (sometimes overlapping in the same work). His fictional topics are uncanny and often weird, consisting of intricate punishments, live burials, mysterious substitutions of personality, journeys into unknown regions, trips to the moon, physical and psychological collapse, and strange and sometimes comic resurrections of the dead. In the decades after his death Poe was not highly regarded, but today, of all nineteenth-century American writers, he is the most widely read. His stature was fully acknowledged in 1986, when his name was placed in the Hall of Fame of American Authors.

The Masque of the Red Death   1842

The "Red Death" had long devastated the country. No pestilence had ever been so fatal, or so hideous. Blood was its Avatar° and its seal—the redness and the horror of blood. There were sharp pains, and sudden dizziness, and then profuse bleeding at the pores, with dissolution. The scarlet stains upon the body and especially upon the face of the victim, were the pest ban which shut him out from the aid and from the sympathy of his fellow-men. And the whole seizure, progress, and termination of the disease, were the incidents of half an hour.

But the Prince Prospero° was happy and dauntless and sagacious. When his dominions were half depopulated, he summoned to his presence a thousand hale and light-hearted friends from among the knights and dames of his court, and with these retired to the deep seclusion of one of his castellated abbeys. This was an extensive and magnificent structure, the creation of the prince's own eccentric yet august taste. A strong and lofty wall girdled it in. This wall had gates of iron. The courtiers, having entered, brought furnaces and massy hammers and welded the bolts. They resolved to leave means neither of ingress nor egress to the sudden impulses of despair or of frenzy from within. The abbey was amply provisioned. With such precautions the courtiers might bid defiance to contagion. The external world could take care of itself. In the meantime it was folly to grieve, or to think. The prince had provided all the appliances of pleasure. There were buffoons, there were improvisatori, there were ballet-dancers, there were musicians, there was Beauty, there was wine. All these and security were within. Without was the "Red Death."

It was toward the close of the fifth or sixth month of his seclusion, and while the pestilence raged most furiously abroad, that the Prince Prospero entertained his thousand friends at a masked ball of the most unusual magnificence.

It was a voluptuous scene, that masquerade. But first let me tell of the rooms in which it was held. There were seven—an imperial suite. In many palaces, however, such suites form a long and straight vista, while the folding doors slide back nearly to the walls

---

Avatar: model, incarnation, manifestation.
Prospero: that is, "prosperous." In Shakespeare's play *The Tempest*, the principal character is Prospero.

on either hand, so that the view of the whole extent is scarcely impeded. Here the case was very different; as might have been expected from the duke's love of the *bizarre*. The apartments were so irregularly disposed that the vision embraced but little more than one at a time. There was a sharp turn at every twenty or thirty yards, and at each turn a novel effect. To the right and left, in the middle of each wall, a tall and narrow Gothic window looked out upon a closed corridor which pursued the windings of the suite. These windows were of stained glass whose color varied in accordance with the prevailing hue of the decorations of the chamber into which it opened. That at the eastern extremity was hung, for example, in blue—and vividly blue were its windows. The second chamber was purple in its ornaments and tapestries, and here the panes were purple. The third was green throughout, and so were the casements. The fourth was furnished and lighted with orange—the fifth with white—the sixth with violet. The seventh apartment was closely shrouded in black velvet tapestries that hung all over the ceiling and down the walls, falling in heavy folds upon a carpet of the same material and hue. But in this chamber only, the color of the windows failed to correspond with the decorations. The panes here were scarlet—a deep blood color. Now in no one of the seven apartments was there any lamp or candelabrum, amid the profusion of golden ornaments that lay scattered to and fro or depended from the roof. There was no light of any kind emanating from lamp or candle within the suite of chambers. But in the corridors that followed the suite, there stood, opposite to each window, a heavy tripod, bearing a brazier of fire, that projected its rays through the tinted glass and so glaringly illumined the room. And thus were produced a multitude of gaudy and fantastic appearances. But in the western or black chamber the effect of the fire-light that streamed upon the dark hangings through the blood-tinted panes was ghastly in the extreme, and produced so wild a look upon the countenances of those who entered, that there were few of the company bold enough to set foot within its precincts at all.

It was in this apartment, also, that there stood against the western wall, a gigantic clock of ebony. Its pendulum swung to and fro with a dull, heavy, monotonous clang; and when the minute-hand made the circuit of the face, and the hour was to be stricken, there came from the brazen lungs of the clock a sound which was clear and loud and deep and exceedingly musical, but of so peculiar a note and emphasis that, at each lapse of an hour, the musicians of the orchestra were constrained to pause, momentarily, in their performance, to hearken to the sound; and thus the waltzers perforce ceased their evolutions; and there was a brief disconcert of the whole gay company; and, while the chimes of the clock yet rang, it was observed that the giddiest grew pale, and the more aged and sedate passed their hands over their brows as if in confused revery or meditation. But when the echoes had fully ceased, a light laughter at once pervaded the assembly; the musicians looked at each other and smiled as if at their own nervousness and folly, and made whispering vows, each to the other, that the next chiming of the clock should produce in them no similar emotion; and then, after the lapse of sixty minutes (which embrace three thousand and six hundred seconds of the Time that flies), there came yet another chiming of the clock, and then were the same disconcert and tremulousness and meditation as before.

But, in spite of these things, it was a gay and magnificent revel. The tastes of the duke were peculiar. He had a fine eye for colors and effects. He disregarded the *decora*° of mere fashion. His plans were bold and fiery, and his conceptions glowed with barbaric

decora: schemes, patterns.

lustre. There are some who would have thought him mad. His followers felt that he was not. It was necessary to hear and see and touch him to be *sure* that he was not.

He had directed, in great part, the movable embellishments of the seven chambers, upon occasion of this great fête,° and it was his own guiding taste which had given character to the masqueraders. Be sure they were grotesque. There were much glare and glitter and piquancy and phantasm—much of what has been since seen in "Hernani."° There were arabesque figures with unsuited limbs and appointments. There were delirious fancies such as the madman fashions. There were much of the beautiful, much of the wanton, much of the *bizarre*, something of the terrible, and not a little of that which might have excited disgust. To and fro in the seven chambers there stalked, in fact, a multitude of dreams. And these—the dreams—writhed in and about, taking hue from the rooms, and causing the wild music of the orchestra to seem as the echo of their steps. And, anon, there strikes the ebony clock which stands in the hall of the velvet. And then, for a moment, all is still, and all is silent save the voice of the clock. The dreams are stiff-frozen as they stand. But the echoes of the chime die away—they have endured but an instant—and a light, half-subdued laughter floats after them as they depart. And now again the music swells, and the dreams live, and writhe to and fro more merrily than ever, taking hue from the many-tinted windows through which stream the rays from the tripods. But to the chamber which lies most westwardly of the seven there are now none of the maskers who venture; for the night is waning away; and there flows a ruddier light through the blood-colored panes; and the blackness of the sable drapery appalls; and to him whose foot falls upon the sable carpet, there comes from the near clock of ebony a muffled peal more solemnly emphatic than any which reaches *their* ears who indulge in the more remote gaieties of the other apartments.

But these other apartments were densely crowded, and in them beat feverishly the heart of life. And the revel went whirlingly on, until at length there commenced the sounding of midnight upon the clock. And then the music ceased, as I have told; and the evolutions of the waltzers were quieted; and there was an uneasy cessation of all things as before. But now there were twelve strokes to be sounded by the bell of the clock; and thus it happened, perhaps that more of thought crept, with more of time, into the meditations of the thoughtful among those who revelled. And thus, too, it happened, perhaps, that before the last echoes of the last chime had utterly sunk into silence, there were many individuals in the crowd who had found leisure to become aware of the presence of a masked figure which had arrested the attention of no single individual before. And the rumor of this new presence having spread itself whisperingly around, there arose at length from the whole company a buzz, or murmur, expressive of disapprobation and surprise—then, finally, of terror, of horror, and of disgust.

In an assembly of phantasms such as I have painted, it may well be supposed that no ordinary appearance could have excited such sensation. In truth the masquerade license of the night was nearly unlimited; but the figure in question had out-Heroded Herod,° and gone beyond the bounds of even the prince's indefinite decorum. There are chords in the hearts of the most reckless which cannot be touched without emotion. Even with the utterly lost, to whom life and death are equally jests, there are matters of which no jest can be made. The whole company, indeed, seemed now deeply to feel that

---

fête: party, revel.
Hernani: tragedy by Victor Hugo (1802–1885), featuring elaborate scenes and costumes.
out-Heroded Herod: quoted from Shakespeare's *Hamlet*, Act 3, scene 2, line 13, in reference to extreme overacting.

in the costume and bearing of the stranger neither wit nor propriety existed. The figure was tall and gaunt, and shrouded from head to foot in the habiliments of the grave. The mask which concealed the visage was made so nearly to resemble the countenance of a stiffened corpse that the closest scrutiny must have had difficulty in detecting the cheat. And yet all this might have been endured, if not approved, by the mad revellers around. But the mummer had gone so far as to assume the type of the Red Death. His vesture was dabbled in *blood*—and his broad brow, with all the features of the face, was besprinkled with the scarlet horror.

When the eyes of Prince Prospero fell upon this spectral image (which, with a slow   10
and solemn movement, as if more fully to sustain its *rôle*, stalked to and fro among the waltzers) he was seen to be convulsed, in the first moment with a strong shudder either of terror or distaste; but, in the next, his brow reddened with rage.

"Who dares"—he demanded hoarsely of the courtiers who stood near him—"who dares insult us with this blasphemous mockery? Seize him and unmask him—that we may know whom we have to hang, at sunrise, from the battlements!"

It was in the eastern or blue chamber in which stood the Prince Prospero as he uttered these words. They rang throughout the seven rooms loudly and clearly, for the prince was a bold and robust man, and the music had become hushed at the waving of his hand.

It was in the blue room where stood the prince, with a group of pale courtiers by his side. At first, as he spoke, there was a slight rushing movement of this group in the direction of the intruder, who, at the moment was also near at hand, and now, with deliberate and stately step, made closer approach to the speaker. But from a certain nameless awe with which the mad assumptions of the mummer had inspired the whole party, there were found none who put forth hand to seize him; so that, unimpeded, he passed within a yard of the prince's person; and, while the vast assembly, as if with one impulse, shrank from the centres of the rooms to the walls, he made his way uninterruptedly, but with the same solemn and measured step which had distinguished him from the first, through the blue chamber to the purple—through the purple to the green—through the green to the orange—through this again to the white—and even thence to the violet, ere a decided movement had been made to arrest him. It was then, however, that the Prince Prospero, maddening with rage and the shame of his own momentary cowardice, rushed hurriedly through the six chambers, while none followed him on account of a deadly terror that had seized upon all. He bore aloft a drawn dagger, and had approached, in rapid impetuosity, to within three or four feet of the retreating figure, when the latter, having attained the extremity of the velvet apartment, turned suddenly and confronted his pursuer. There was a sharp cry—and the dagger dropped gleaming upon the sable carpet, upon which, instantly afterward, fell prostrate in death the Prince Prospero. Then, summoning the wild courage of despair, a throng of the revellers at once threw themselves into the black apartment, and, seizing the mummer, whose tall figure stood erect and motionless within the shadow of the ebony clock, gasped in unutterable horror at finding the grave cerements and corpse-like mask, which they handled with so violent a rudeness, untenanted by any tangible form.

And now was acknowledged the presence of the Red Death. He had come like a thief in the night.° And one by one dropped the revellers in the blood-bedewed halls of their revel, and died each in the despairing posture of his fall. And the life of the ebony

thief in the night: 2 Peter 3:10.

clock went out with that of the last of the gay. And the flames of the tripods expired. And Darkness and Decay and the Red Death held illimitable dominion over all.

QUESTIONS

1. What is happening throughout the country in this story? What does the Prince's reaction to these events tell us about him?

2. How do the details of number, color, and lighting help create the atmosphere and mood of the story?

3. Why do the color and window of the last room disturb the revellers? To what extent does this last room reflect the plot and ideas of the story?

4. What single object is located in this last room? How is this object described? What effect does its sound have on the revellers? What do you think Poe is suggesting by this object and its effects?

5. How are the nobles dressed for the masquerade? Why is the "masked figure" remarkable? How does Prospero react to him?

✾ WRITING ABOUT SETTING

In preparing to write about setting, determine the number and importance of locations, artifacts, and customs. Ask questions like the following:

- How extensive are the visual descriptions? Does the author provide such vivid and carefully arranged detail about surroundings that you could draw a map or plan? Or is the scenery vague and difficult to imagine?

- What connections, if any, are apparent between locations and characters? Do the locations bring characters together, separate them, facilitate their privacy, make intimacy and conversation difficult?

- How fully are objects described? How vital are they to the action? How important are they in the development of the plot or idea? How are they connected to the mental states of the characters?

- How important to plot and character are shapes, colors, times of day, clouds, storms, light and sun, seasons of the year, and conditions of vegetation?

- Are the characters poor, moderately well-off, or rich? How does their economic condition affect what happens to them, and how does it affect their actions and attitudes?

- What cultural, religious, and political conditions are brought out in the story? How do the characters accept and adjust to these conditions? How do the conditions affect the characters' judgments and actions?

- What is the state of houses, furniture, and objects (e.g., new and polished, old and worn, ragged and torn)? What connections can you find between these conditions and the outlook and behavior of the characters?

- How important are sounds or silences? To what degree is music or other sound important in the development of character and action?

- Do characters respect or mistreat the environment? If there is an environmental connection, how central is it to the story?

- What conclusions do you think the author expects you to draw as a result of the neighborhood, culture, and larger world of the story?

Strategies for Organizing Ideas

Begin by making a brief description of the setting or scenes of the work, specifying the amount and importance of detail. Choosing one of the approaches in the following list, describe the approach you plan to develop. As you gather material for your essay, however, you may need to combine your major approach with one or more of the others. Whatever approach for development you choose, be sure to consider setting not as an end in itself but rather as illustration and evidence for claims you are making about the particular story.

1. SETTING AND ACTION.   Explore the importance of setting in the work. How extensively is the setting described? Are locations essential or incidental to the actions? Does the setting serve as part of the action (e.g., places of flight or concealment; public places where people meet openly, or hidden places where they meet privately; natural or environmental conditions; seasonal conditions such as searing heat or numbing cold; customs and conventions)? Do any objects cause inspiration, difficulty, or conflict (for example, a bridge, a walking stick, a necklace, a fence, a hair ribbon, a dead bird)? How directly do these objects influence the action?

2. SETTING AND ORGANIZATION.   How is the setting connected to the various parts of the work? Does it undergo any changes as the action develops? Why are some parts of the setting more important than others? Is the setting used as a structural frame or enclosure for the story? How do objects, such as money, appliances, property, or physical location (e.g., a subway platform, a prison camp, a winter scene on a lake) influence the characters? How do descriptions made at the start become important in the action later on?

3. SETTING AND CHARACTER.   (For examples of this approach, see the two drafts of the demonstrative essay in Chapter 1.) Analyze the degree to which setting influences and interacts with character. Are the characters happy or unhappy where they live? Do they get into discussions or arguments about their home environments? Do they want to stay or leave? Do the economic, philosophical, religious, or ethnic aspects of the setting make the characters undergo changes? What jobs do the characters perform because of their ways of life? What freedoms or restraints do these jobs cause? How does the setting influence their decisions, transportation, speech habits, eating habits, attitudes about love and honor, and general behavior?

4. SETTING AND ATMOSPHERE.   To what extent does setting contribute to mood? Does the setting go beyond the minimum needed for action or character? How do descriptive words paint verbal pictures and evoke moods through references to colors, shapes, sounds, smells, or tastes? Does the setting establish a mood, say, of joy or hopelessness, plenty or scarcity? Do events happen in daylight or at night? Do the locations and activities of the characters suggest permanence or impermanence (like a return home, the creation of figures out of mud, the repair of a battered boat, the description of ocean currents, the building of a fence)? Are things warm and pleasant, or cold and harsh? What connection do you find between the atmosphere and the author's expressed or apparent thoughts about existence?

5. SETTING AND OTHER ASPECTS OF THE STORY. Does the setting reinforce the story's meaning? Does it establish irony about the circumstances and ideas in the story? If you choose this approach, consult the introductory paragraph in "The Literary Uses of Setting" earlier in this chapter. If you are interested in writing about the symbolic implications of a setting, consult Chapter 9.

To conclude, summarize your major points or write about related aspects of setting that you have not considered. Thus, if your essay treats the relationship of setting and action, your conclusion might mention connections of the setting with character or atmosphere. You might also point out whether your central idea about setting also applies to other major aspects of the story.

DEMONSTRATIVE STUDENT ESSAY

The Interaction of Story and Setting in James Joyce's "Araby"°

[1]   The narrator of Joyce's "Araby" is a young man telling a story about himself as an early adolescent first experiencing the overwhelming emotions that accompany sexual development. This intensely imaginative boy attaches his powerful feelings to the unnamed sister of Mangan, one of his playmates. Although he mainly worships her from afar, the two finally do speak, and he promises her that he will go to a Dublin bazaar called <u>Araby</u> and buy something for her. To him, the gift will be virtually a holy gift. In telling the story Joyce closely integrates the events themselves with the places in which they occur. <u>The setting not only serves as the place of the actions, but it is also suggestive of the boy's intense but confused emotions.</u>* <u>The aspects of setting are the outside scenes and the interior of his home, and also the negative views of the environment near his home and at the bazaar.</u>†

[2]   <u>Even before the boy goes to the bazaar, a number of elements of setting establish his ardent but silent affection for Mangan's sister.</u> When she is first introduced, the narrator and his friend Mangan are standing in "shadow," while she is described as standing in the light, "her figure defined by the light from the half-opened door" of her house, as though she is surrounded by a halo (295, paragraph 3). When she and the narrator first speak together about the Araby bazaar, the narrator says, "The light from the lamp opposite our door caught the white curve of her neck, lit up her hair that rested there and falling, lit up the hand upon the railing" (296, paragraph 9). These words of love and worship blend setting and subject matter, for the boy's feelings stem out of his vision of Mangan's sister at the entrance of the house. The interior light and the lamplight, which illuminate her in these two scenes, provide for him the hopeful but inarticulate vision that he might move permanently out of the shadow to be with her. Place, object, illumination, and imagination all blend in these early scenes and seem, as setting, to offer him the opportunities which he dreams that he might realize.

°See pp. 294–98 for this story.
*Central idea.
†Thesis sentence.

Additional aspects of setting also point to the boy's idealized feelings for the girl. The first of these is the local marketplace, where he accompanies his aunt to help carry parcels (his aunt and uncle are apparently his guardians). The circumstances here are "hostile to romance" (295, paragraph 5), for the streets are swarming with "drunken men and bargaining women, amid the curses of labourers, . . . and the shrill litanies of shop-boys" (295, paragraph 5). Despite this loud and boisterous environment, the narrator confesses that he indulges himself in the daydream of acting out his great love and devotion to Mangan's sister. "I imagined," he says, "that I bore my chalice safely through the throng of foes" (295, paragraph 5). In these passages the word chalice, and also the word litanies, reveals the religious overtones about the intensity of the narrator's boyhood love. Another significant location of setting is the back drawing room of his home, where a priest who once owned the house had died. In the total privacy of this room, listening to the sound of the rain hit the earth outside, the narrator as a boy experiences great depths of emotion that are mixed with religious fervor and prayer: "All my senses seemed to desire to veil themselves and, feeling that I was about to slip from them, I pressed the palms of my hands together until they trembled, murmuring: "O love! O love! many times" (296, paragraph 6).

[3]

An alternative pattern of settings in the story, however, complements the narrator's misgivings and disillusionment about his feelings. The very first sentence explains that the street on which he lived as a boy was "blind," a term meaning "dead-end" (294, paragraph 1). Even here at the beginning, then, the setting casts a pall over the narrator's idealized love, the implication of the setting being that the narrator's youthful imaginative power could have no outlet. In addition, the streets and alleys around his house are described as "dark," a word that Joyce uses three times to describe the scenes of early winter nights when the narrator and his friends play their childhood games of chase (295, paragraph 3). Darkness also pervades both the "gloomy rooms" of the boy's house (296, paragraph 16) and the home of Mangan's sister (296, paragraph 16). The darkness constantly surrounding the boy suggests the uncertainty and lack of direction of his feelings. The narrator himself explains that his attitudes were those of "confused adoration" (296, paragraph 5). This lack of knowledge and experience is reinforced by the "uninhabited house" at the end of his street, which is "detached from its neighbors" (294, paragraph 1), and by the "deserted" and "bare" third-class train car that carries the boy to the Araby bazaar (297, paragraph 24).

[4]

The setting within the bazaar is strongly influential in the boy's disillusionment. His aim has been to purchase "something" for Mangan's sister, a gesture that he believes is on the level of a holy obligation. But when he enters the building with "the magical name" (297, paragraph 24), he is struck not by the romance of the setting and the possibility of realizing his dreams, but rather by the closed stalls and the pervading darkness (297, paragraph 25). In addition, he finds that the place is bathed in "a silence like that which pervades a church after a service" (297, paragraph 25). Here the setting illustrates the boy's growing frustration and anger. When he goes to one of the few open stalls to shop for a gift, he notices "the great jars that stood like eastern guards at either side of the dark entrance to the stall" (298, paragraph 33). The young saleswoman there, who is rather unintelligent, is flirting with two men, but she leaves her flirtation to ask if she can help him. Interestingly, as she leaves him she changes "the position of one of the vases" (298, paragraph 35). This alteration of setting suggests a similar alteration in the boy's romantic ideals, for he concludes that his trip has been "useless" (298, paragraph 36). The darkness that immediately comes over the upper part of the

[5]

hall is suggestive of his "vanity" (298, paragraph 37), and it also suggests that his idealized love has fled to an emotional equivalent of the shadow where, earlier, he and Mangan waited for Mangan's sister to appear.

Without question the narrator as a boy is capable of intense imagination and the most deeply felt romantic enthusiasm, as is shown by the setting of doorlight and lamplight which forms a halo around Mangan's sister. But the negative objects and locations of setting, together with the narrator's youth,

[6] suggest the impossibility of his ever realizing his dreams. Ultimately, he concludes that he is a "creature driven and derided by vanity," a realization that overwhelms him with "anguish and anger" (298, paragraph 37). <u>The story ends on this note, and Joyce's use of setting throughout the story points toward the same conclusion.</u>

WORK CITED

Joyce, James. "Araby." <u>Literature: An Introduction to Reading and Writing.</u> Ed. Edgar V. Roberts and Henry E. Jacobs. 7th ed. Upper Saddle River: Prentice Hall, 2004. 294–98.

Commentary on the Essay

Because the topic of this essay is the setting of Joyce's "Araby," it is most important to note that, after a few sentences briefly describing the narrative, the essay focuses not on character, or point of view, but on setting. Setting is foremost. Whenever other aspects of the story become significant, the point of the essay is to emphasize these additional aspects to the story's setting.

The central idea of the essay is that the locations and some of the objects described in the story are linked with the major character's developing emotions. In its consideration of action and setting, the essay illustrates some aspects of strategy 1 described on page 307. In showing the connection between setting, character, and ideas, it illustrates strategies 3 and 5.

The introductory paragraph indicates the closeness of setting and story and lays out the areas to be developed. Paragraph 2 contains details showing the ways in which place and conditions of light establish the narrator's affections when he was a boy. Paragraph 3 brings out two major additional details of setting which illustrate the force of the narrator's boyhood emotions: in public, where he indulges his daydreams, and in private, where his desires take on an almost religious fervor. Paragraph 4 introduces a contrary patterning of setting in and about the boy's home which reinforces the negative aspects of the narrator's love. Paragraph 5 does the same for the setting of the Araby bazaar itself. The concluding paragraph encapsulates both the positive and negative aspects of setting and focuses on the story's conclusion as the climax of the narrator's boyhood disillusionment.

Special Topics for Writing and Argument about Setting

1. How do Dr. Jenkins and the young musician respond to the setting in "The Portable Phonograph"? How do they adjust to physical conditions? In light of this story, together with knowledge you have gained elsewhere from your reading and experience, what conclusions can you draw about the effects of warfare on character?

2. Compare and contrast how details of setting establish qualities and traits of the following female characters: Stella of "The Shawl," Mrs. Johnson of "Everyday Use" (Chapter 2), and the narrator of "The Yellow Wallpaper" (Chapter 12). To add to your comparison, you might discuss how the painters Boucher and Hopper portray background and dress to highlight the character of their female subjects (Insert II–2 and II–3).

3. In what ways might we say that both "The Masque of the Red Death" and "The Shawl" are inseparable from their settings? To answer this question, consider the relationship of character to place and circumstance. How could the actions of the stories happen without the locations in which they occur?

4. Consider the significance of place and character in either "The House on Mango Street" or "Araby."

5. Choose one story included in this chapter and rewrite a page or two, taking the characters out of their setting and placing them in an entirely new setting or in the setting of another story (you choose). Then write a brief analysis dealing with questions like these: How do you think your characters wuld be affected by their new settings? Do you make them change slowly or rapidly? Why? As a result of your rewriting, what can you conclude about the uses of setting in fiction?

6. Write a short narrative as though it is part of a story (which you may also wish to write for the assignment) using option *a* and/or *b*.

   a. Relate a natural setting or type of day to a mood—for example, a nice day to happiness and satisfaction, or a cold, cloudy, rainy day to sadness. Or create irony by relating the nice day to sadness or the rainy day to happiness.

   b. Indicate how an object or circumstance becomes the cause of conflict or reconciliation (such as the books and records in "The Portable Phonograph," the shawl in "The Shawl," the dirtied rug in "Barn Burning" [Chapter 4], or the newly tuned piano in "Two Kinds" [Chapter 4]).

7. In your library locate two books on the career of Edgar Allan Poe. On the basis of information you find in these sources, write a brief account of Poe's uses of setting and place to evoke atmosphere and to bring out qualities of human character.

Style: *The Words That Tell the Story*

Style, derived from the Latin word *stilus* (a writing instrument), means the way writers assemble words to tell the story, develop the argument, dramatize the play, or compose the poem. Sometimes style is distinguished from content, but it is wiser not to make this separation because style is best considered as the choice of words in the *service* of content. The written expression of a fictional action or scene, in other words, cannot be separated from the action or scene itself.

Style is also individual, because all authors put words together uniquely to fit the specific conditions in specific works. We can therefore speak of the style of Hemingway, for example, and of Mark Twain, even though both writers adapt words to situations. Thus an author can have a distinct style for narrative and descriptive passages, but a very different style for dialogue. For a visual comparison of styles, look again at the paintings by François Boucher and Edward Hopper in Chapter 6 (Insert II-2 and II-3). While the painters treat the same subject—a female figure—the *styles* are different: Boucher, a painter of the eighteenth century, achieves a beautiful, flattering image of his aristocratic subject; by contrast, Hopper, who lived in the twentieth, invests his more ordinary subject with an impression of emptiness and bleakness. These differing painting styles convey different outlooks on life. Similarly, writers vary their styles in the interest of content. In judging style the important criterion, therefore, is the author's *adaptability.* The more appropriately the words fit the situation, the better the style. The writer Jonathan Swift (1667–1745) defined style as the right words in the right places. Samuel Taylor Coleridge (1772–1834) defined prose style as words in their best order, and poetic style as the best words in their best order. We might add to these definitions that style also requires the right or best words at the right time and in the right circumstances.

❧ DICTION: THE WRITER'S CHOICE AND CONTROL OF WORDS

Diction refers to the qualities of the writer's word choices. The selection should be accurate and explicit, so that all actions, scenes, and ideas are clear. If a passage is effective—if it conveys an idea well or gets at the essence of an action vividly and powerfully—we can confidently say that the words are right. For example, a passage describing action should employ many active verbs, whereas a description of a place should contain nouns and adjectives indicating locations, relationships, colors, and shapes. An explanatory or reflective passage should include words that convey thoughts, states of mind and emotion, and conditions of various human relationships.

Formal, Neutral, and Informal Diction Create Unique Effects

One aspect of word choice is the degree of formality. There are three levels of diction: **formal** or *high*, **neutral** or *middle*, and **informal** or *low*. *Formal* or *high* diction consists of standard and also "elegant" words (frequently polysyllabic), the retention of correct word order, and the absence of contractions. The sentence "It is I," for example, is formal. The following sentences from Poe's "The Masque of the Red Death" (Chapter 6) demonstrate formal language:

> They resolved to leave means neither of ingress nor egress to the sudden impulses of despair or of frenzy from within. The abbey was amply provisioned. With such precautions the courtiers might bid defiance to contagion. (paragraph 2)

Note here the words *ingress, egress, amply provisioned, bid defiance,* and *contagion.* Though the sentences are brief and simple and all the words are accurate and apt, the italicized words are more "elegant" than those that most of us normally use. These words can thus be considered formal or high diction.

Neutral or *middle* diction is ordinary, everyday standard vocabulary, shunning longer words and using contractions when necessary. The sentence "It's me" is a neutral or middle example of what many people naturally say in preference to the more formal "It is I." Words in the neutral style can be thought of as clear window glass, with words in the formal or high style being more decorative, like stained glass. An example of neutral, middle diction is the following passage from Alice Munro's "The Found Boat":

> What surprised them in the second place was that when the boys did actually see what boat was meant, this old flood-smashed wreck held up in the branches, they did not understand that they had been fooled, that a joke had been played on them. They did not show a moment's disappointment, but seemed as pleased at the discovery as if the boat had been whole and new. They were already barefoot, because they had been wading in the water to get lumber, and they waded in here without a stop, surrounding the boat and appraising it and paying no attention even of an insulting kind to Eva and Carol who bobbed up and down on their log. Eva and Carol had to call to them. (paragraph 23)

The words of this passage are ordinary and easy. They are centered directly on the subject and do not draw attention to themselves. Even the longer words, like *surprised, disappointment, surrounding, appraising,* and *insulting,* would not be out of place in ordinary conversation, although *appraising* and *surrounding* would also be appropriate in a more formal passage.

Informal or *low* diction can range from *colloquial*—the language of relaxed, common activities—to the level of *substandard* or *slang* expressions. A person speaking to a close friend uses diction that would not be seemly in public and formal situations, and even in some social situations. Informal or low diction is thus correct for a good deal of narrative dialogue, depending, of course, on individual speakers. It is also a natural choice for stories told in the first-person point of view as though the speaker is talking directly to sympathetic and relaxed close friends. In Updike's "A & P," Sammy's first sentence illustrates informal, low diction:

> In walks these three girls in nothing but bathing suits.

Note the idiomatic and ungrammatical "In walks these three girls," a singular verb followed by a plural subject. Note also the colloquial use of *these* as a demonstrative adjective with no antecedent. This language suggests that the speaker is telling his story to a group of similar people, probably young men, who indulge in informal diction when talking among themselves.

Specific-General and Concrete-Abstract Diction Guides Readers to Perceptions of Numbers and Qualities

Another aspect of language is its degree of explicitness. **Specific** refers to words that bring real and genuine situations to mind. "My dog Teddie is barking" is specific. **General** statements refer to broad classes, such as "All people like pets" and "Dogs make good pets." There is an ascending order of generality from (1) very specific to (2) less specific to (3) general, as though the words themselves climb a stairway. Thus *peach* is a specific fruit. *Fruit* is specific but more general because it also includes apples, oranges, and all other fruits. *Dessert* is a still more general word, which can encompass all sweets, including fruits, peaches, and other confections such as ice cream. *Food* is more general yet, for the word includes everything eaten by living creatures. If you report that you are having "food" for dinner, you are facetiously general, but if you say that the main course is a charcoal-broiled loin steak with peaches and cream for dessert, you are seriously specific.

While *specific-general* refers to categories, *concrete-abstract* refers to qualities or conditions. **Concrete** words describe qualities of immediate perception. If you say "Ice cream is cold," the word *cold* is concrete because it describes a condition that you can feel, just as you can *taste* ice cream's sweetness and *feel* its creamy texture in your mouth. **Abstract** words refer to broader, less palpable qualities; they can therefore apply to many separate things. If we describe ice cream as *good* we are abstract, because *good* is far removed from ice cream itself and conveys no descriptive information about it. A vast number of things can be *good,* just as they can be *bad, fine,* "*cool,*" *excellent,* and so on.

Usually, writers of stories make most of their words specific and concrete to make us readily perceive actions, situations, objects, and scenes, for with more specificity and concreteness there is less ambiguity. Because exactness and vividness are goals of most fiction, specific and concrete words are the writer's basic tools, with general and abstract words being used sparingly.

The point, however, is not that abstract and general words have no place at all but rather that *words should be appropriate in the context*. Good writers control style to match their purposes. Observe, for example, Hemingway's diction in "Soldier's Home," a story about a young veteran who has just returned from World War I and is having difficulty adjusting to life back home. By combining specific and abstract language to convey this situation, Hemingway appropriately fits style to subject. In paragraph 6, for example (p. 320), he uses abstract terms to describe the mental state of Krebs, the young veteran. We read that Krebs feels "nausea in regard to experience that is the result of untruth or exaggeration," that he goes into the "easy pose of the old soldier" when he meets another veteran, and that he "lost everything" during his time abroad. Because the words are mainly abstract and general, it is not possible to determine the precise details underlying Krebs's uneasinesss.

By contrast, Hemingway's description of Krebs's daily activities as a recently returned veteran is specific: getting out of bed, walking to the library, eating lunch, reading on the front porch, and ambling down to the local pool hall. These details show that Krebs's activities are repetitive and meaningless. The two paragraphs therefore complement each other, with the specificity of paragraph 7 clarifying the abstraction of paragraph 6. In short, Hemingway skillfully combines abstract and specific words to build his portrait of a young man caught between two worlds—foreign warfare and peaceful life at home—and because of changing circumstances having no place in either.

Denotation and Connotation Refer to Stages of Meaning and Suggestion

Another way to understand style is to study the author's control of *denotation* and *connotation*. **Denotation** refers to what a word means, **connotation** to what the word suggests. For example, if a person in a social situation behaves in ways that are *friendly, warm, polite,* or *cordial,* these words all suggest slight differences in behavior because they have different connotations. Most of us prefer people who are friendly and warm rather than polite and cordial. Similarly, the words *dog* and *puppy* are close to each other denotatively, but *puppy* connotes more playfulness and cuteness than *dog*. Consider the connotations of words describing physical appearance. It is one thing to call a person *thin*, for example, but another to use the words *skinny, gaunt,* or *skeletal* and still something else to say *fit, trim, svelte, slim, shapely,* or *slender*.

Through the careful choice of words, not only for denotation but also for connotation, authors create unique effects even though they might be describing similar or even identical situations. Let us look briefly at Eudora Welty's description of Phoenix's walk through the woods in "A Worn Path" (Chapter 3):

> Her eyes were blue with age. Her skin had a pattern all its own of numberless branching wrinkles and as though a whole little tree stood in the middle of her forehead, but a golden color ran underneath, and the two knobs of her cheeks were illumined by a yellow burning under the dark. Under the rag her hair came down on her neck in the frailest of ringlets, still black, and with an odor like copper. (paragraph 2)

The description conveys a compelling note of admiration. Specifically, the words *golden color* and *illumined* would be appropriate in the description of delicate and lovely medieval illuminated book paintings; *frailest of ringlets, still black* suggests girlishness and personal care, despite Phoenix's advancing age and weakness. Comparably, in "A & P," Sammy's words describing the "queen" (paragraphs 2–4) suggest his admiration of both her sexual beauty and her grace. Shirley Jackson's less full description of Tessie Hutchinson (paragraph 8) in "The Lottery" (Chapter 5) reduces Tessie to no more than an average woman of the village. The meager details are that she has a "sweater thrown over her shoulders" and that she dries her hands "on her apron." All these descriptive examples demonstrate the ways in which connotation can complement an author's descriptive intentions.

RHETORIC: THE WRITER'S CHOICES OF EFFECTIVE ARRANGEMENTS AND FORMS

Rhetoric refers to the art of effective and persuasive writing and, more broadly, to the art of writing generally. In studying style, you can consider the rhetorical qualities of a passage. Some relatively straightforward basic approaches are (1) counting various elements in a passage and (2) analyzing the types of sentences.

Counting Permits Conclusions about Brevity or Expansiveness

Counting various elements is a quick and elementary way to begin the study of style. The number of words in a sentence; the number of verbs, adjectives, prepositions, and adverbs in a passage; or the number of syllables in relation to the total number of words—any of these can provide valuable clues about the style, especially if the count is related to other aspects of the passage. For illustration, let us say that Author A uses words mainly of one or two syllables, while Author B includes many words of three, four, and five syllables. Going further, let us say that A uses an average of twelve words per sentence and that B uses thirty-five. It would be fair to conclude that Author A is brief and Author B is more expansive. This is not to say that Author A's passage would be easier or superior, however, for a long string of short sentences with short words might seem choppy and tiresome. Remember that conclusions based on a count will provide tendencies of a particular author rather than absolutes.

THE USE OF PARTICULAR SENTENCE TYPES MAY GIVE CLUES IN DEFINING AND DESCRIBING AN AUTHOR'S STYLE

You can also study the rhetorical qualities of a passage by determining its various sentence types. Let us review the basic sentence types.

1. **Simple sentences** contain one subject and one verb, together with modifiers and complements. Usually simple sentences are short and are therefore appropriate for actions and declarations. Often they are idiomatic, particularly in dialogue.

Example: Nora sat in front of me by the confession box. (Frank O'Connor's "First Confession")

2. **Compound sentences** contain two simple sentences joined by a conjunction (*and, but, for, or, nor, so,* or *yet*) and a comma or by a semicolon without a conjunction. Frequently, compound sentences are formed by three or four simple sentences joined by conjunctions. Like simple sentences, compound sentences are appropriate for actions and declarations.

Example: Later he felt the need to talk but no one wanted to hear about it. (Hemingway's "Soldier's Home")

3. **Complex sentences** contain a main clause and a subordinate clause. Because of the subordinate clause, the complex sentence is suitable for describing cause-and-effect relationships in narrative and also for analysis and reflection.

Example: It was the Wawanash River, which every spring overflowed its banks. (Munro's "The Found Boat")

4. **Compound-complex sentences** contain two main clauses and a subordinate clause. In practice many authors produce sentences that contain a number of main and subordinate clauses.

Example: And yet, though the elder person was as simply clad as the younger, and as simple in manner too, he had an indescribable air of one who knew the world, and would not have felt abashed at the governor's dinner-table, or in King William's court, were it possible that his affairs should call him thither. (Hawthorne's "Young Goodman Brown" [Chapter 9]).

Parallelism Permits Balance, Order, and Economy of Diction

Parallelism is one of the most popular rhetorical devices. It refers to the repetition of the same grammatical form (nouns, verbs, phrases, clauses) to balance expressions, conserve words, and build climaxes. Here, for example, is a sentence by Poe from the story "The Masque of the Red Death":

There were much of the beautiful, much of the wanton, much of the *bizarre*, something of the terrible, and not a little of that which might have excited disgust. (paragraph 7)

Arrangements like this are called *parallel* because they can be laid out graphically, according to parts of speech, in parallel lines, as in the following:

There were much of the beautiful
    much of the wanton
    much of the *bizarre,*
    something of the terrible,
    and
    not a little of that which might have excited disgust.

Poe's parallel noun phrases (the last containing an adjective clause) moves in phases from beauty to terror and finally to disgust. Such an order marks a deliberate development leading to a climax, unlike the parallelism in the following sentence from the concluding paragraph of Clark's "The Portable Phonograph" (Chapter 6):

1　　　　2
Then quickly and quietly, looking at the piece of canvas frequently,

1　　　　　　　　　　2
he slipped the records into the case, snapped the lid shut,

3
and carried the phonograph to his couch.

Here there are two parallel adverbs at the beginning, both ending in *-ly*, and three past tense verbs ending in *-ed*, all of which have direct objects. The order here is time. Although the sentence is short, Clark uses parallelism to pack in a great deal of action.

You can also see parallel arrangements in individual sentences within a paragraph. In the following passage from Munro's "The Found Boat," for example, there are a number of identically formed sentences that sum up the exhilaration of adolescent boys and girls dashing naked to swim in a river. There are seven parallel clauses containing *they* followed by active verbs, which are underlined here:

> Nobody said a word this time, <u>they all bent and stripped themselves</u>. Eva, naked first, started running across the field, and then all the others ran, all five of them running bare through the knee-high hot grass, running towards the river. Not caring now about being caught but in fact leaping and yelling to call attention to themselves, if there was anybody to hear or see. <u>They felt</u> as if they were going to jump off a cliff and fly. <u>They felt</u> that something was happening to them different from anything that had happened before, and it had to do with the boat, the water, the sunlight, the dark ruined station, and each other. <u>They thought</u> of each other now hardly as names or people, but as echoing shrieks, reflections, all bold and white and loud and scandalous, and as fast as arrows. <u>They went running</u> without a break into the cold water and when it came almost to the tops of their legs <u>they fell on it and swam</u>. It stopped their noise. Silence, amazement, came over them in a rush. <u>They dipped and floated and separated</u>, sleek as mink. (paragraph 87)

You may not often encounter such readily detected parallel patterns, but you should always be alert to effective arrangements. You need not use technically correct names for the patterns you discover, as long as you focus on what you think is especially noteworthy.

STYLE IN GENERAL

If a story is good, you probably do not notice its style, for clear expressions and easy reading are marks of a writer's success. By studying style, however, you can discover and appreciate the author's achievement. The action described in a particular passage, the relationship of the passage to the entire work, the level of the diction, the vividness of the descriptions—all these should figure in your judgment.

In the paragraph from "The Found Boat," for example, Munro's masterly style can be perceived beyond the parallelism that we noted. The passage could be considered the climax of the story, which is, among other things, about emerging sexuality. In an almost ritualistic way, the paragraph describes the boys and girls running impetuously toward a river and diving in—a sexually symbolic action. Note that after the first two sentences of objective description, Munro's narrator presents us with four sentences of omniscient analysis describing the young people's feelings. If her intention had been to create searching psychological scrutiny, she might have selected words from the language of psychology (*libido, urge, sublimation,* and so on). Instead, she uses words that could have been in the vocabularies of the characters. Hence the young people feel "as if they were going to jump off a cliff and fly" and feel "that something was happening to them different from anything that had happened before." With these neutral words, the passage focuses on the excitement of the situation rather than on hidden psychological significance. In light of these considerations, Munro's style is exactly right—in fact, perfect.

Observations of this kind may not occur to you at first, but as long as you relate words to content, your analysis of style will be fruitful. The more you consider stories for style, the more you will discover your own analytical power.

STORIES FOR STUDY

ERNEST HEMINGWAY (1899–1961)

Hemingway was born in Illinois. During World War I he served in the Ambulance Corps in France, where he was wounded. In the 1920s he published The Sun Also Rises *(1926) and* A Farewell to Arms *(1929), and the resulting critical fame made him a major literary celebrity. He developed a sparse style in keeping with the elemental, stark lives of many of the characters he depicted. "Soldier's Home," from the collection* In Our Time *(1925), typifies that pared, annealed style. Notice the ambiguity and irony of the title. It may mean either "The soldier is home" or "The home of the soldier," but, ironically, the soldier's home no longer seems to be home.*

Soldier's Home   1925

Krebs went to the war from a Methodist college in Kansas. There is a picture which shows him among his fraternity brothers, all of them wearing exactly the same height and style collar. He enlisted in the Marines in 1917 and did not return to the United States until the second division returned from the Rhine in the summer of 1919.

There is a picture which shows him on the Rhine with two German girls and another corporal. Krebs and the corporal look too big for their uniforms. The German girls are not beautiful. The Rhine does not show in the picture.

By the time Krebs returned to his home town in Oklahoma the greeting of heroes was over. He came back much too late. The men from the town who had been drafted had all been welcomed elaborately on their return. There had been a great deal of hysteria. Now the reaction had set in. People seemed to think it was rather ridiculous for Krebs to be getting back so late, years after the war was over.

At first Krebs, who had been at Belleau Wood, Soissons, the Champagne, St. Mihiel and in the Argonne did not want to talk about the war at all. Later he felt the need to talk but no one wanted to hear about it. His town had heard too many atrocity stories to be thrilled by actualities. Krebs found that to be listened to at all he had to lie, and after he had done this twice he, too, had a reaction against the war and against talking about it. A distaste for everything that had happened to him in the war set in because of the lies he had told. All of the times that had been able to make him feel cool and clean inside himself when he thought of them; the times so long back when he had done the one thing, the only thing for a man to do, easily and naturally, when he might have done something else, now lost their cool, valuable quality and then were lost themselves.

His lies were quite unimportant lies and consisted in attributing to himself things other men had seen, done or heard of, and stating as facts certain apocryphal incidents familiar to all soldiers. Even his lies were not sensational at the pool room. His acquaintances, who had heard detailed accounts of German women found chained to machine guns in the Argonne forest and who could not comprehend, or were barred by their patriotism from interest in, any German machine gunners who were not chained, were not thrilled by his stories.

Krebs acquired the nausea in regard to experience that is the result of untruth or exaggeration, and when he occasionally met another man who had really been a soldier and they talked a few minutes in the dressing room at a dance he fell into the easy pose of the old soldier among other soldiers: that he had been badly, sickeningly frightened all the time. In this way he lost everything.

During this time, it was late summer, he was sleeping late in bed, getting up to walk down town to the library to get a book, eating lunch at home, reading on the front porch until he became bored and then walking down through the town to spend the hottest hours of the day in the cool dark of the pool room. He loved to play pool.

In the evening he practised on his clarinet, strolled down town, read and went to bed. He was still a hero to his two young sisters. His mother would have given him breakfast in bed if he had wanted it. She often came in when he was in bed and asked him to tell her about the war, but her attention always wandered. His father was non-committal.

Before Krebs went away to the war he had never been allowed to drive the family motor car. His father was in the real estate business and always wanted the car to be at his command when he required it to take clients out into the country to show them a piece of farm property. The car always stood outside the First National Bank building where his father had an office on the second floor. Now, after the war, it was still the same car.

Nothing was changed in the town except that the young girls had grown up. But they lived in such a complicated world of already defined alliances and shifting feuds that Krebs did not feel the energy or the courage to break into it. He liked to look at them, though. There were so many good-looking young girls. Most of them had their hair cut short. When he went away only little girls wore their hair like that or girls that were fast. They all wore sweaters and shirt waists with round Dutch collars. It was a pattern. He liked to look at them from the front porch as they walked on the other side of the street.

He liked to watch them walking under the shade of the trees. He liked the round Dutch collars above their sweaters. He liked their silk stockings and flat shoes. He liked their bobbed hair and the way they walked.

When he was in town their appeal to him was not very strong. He did not like them when he saw them in the Greek's ice cream parlor. He did not want them themselves really. They were too complicated. There was something else. Vaguely he wanted a girl but he did not want to have to work to get her. He would have liked to have a girl but he did not want to have to spend a long time getting her. He did not want to get into the intrigue and the politics. He did not want to have to do any courting. He did not want to tell any more lies. It wasn't worth it.

He did not want any consequences. He did not want any consequences ever again. He wanted to live along without consequences. Besides he did not really need a girl. The army had taught him that. It was all right to pose as though you had to have a girl. Nearly everybody did that. But it wasn't true. You did not need a girl. That was the funny thing. First a fellow boasted how girls meant nothing to him, that he never thought of them, that they could not touch him. Then a fellow boasted that he could not get along without girls, that he had to have them all the time, that he could not go to sleep without them.

That was all a lie. It was all a lie both ways. You did not need a girl unless you thought about them. He learned that in the army. Then sooner or later you always got one. When you were really ripe for a girl you always got one. You did not have to think about it. Sooner or later it would come. He had learned that in the army.

Now he would have liked a girl if she had come to him and not wanted to talk. But here at home it was all too complicated. He knew he could never get through it all again. It was not worth the trouble. That was the thing about French girls and German girls. There was not all this talking. You couldn't talk much and you did not need to talk. It was simple and you were friends. He thought about France and then he began to think about Germany. On the whole he had liked Germany better. He did not want to leave Germany. He did not want to come home. Still, he had come home. He sat on the front porch.

He liked the girls that were walking along the other side of the street. He liked the   15
look of them much better than the French girls or the German girls. But the world they were in was not the world he was in. He would like to have one of them. But it was not worth it. They were such a nice pattern. He liked the pattern. It was exciting. But he would not go through all the talking. He did not want one badly enough. He liked to look at them all, though. It was not worth it. Not now when things were getting good again.

He sat there on the porch reading a book on the war. It was a history and he was reading about all the engagements he had been in. It was the most interesting reading he had ever done. He wished there were more maps. He looked forward with a good feeling to reading all the really good histories when they would come out with good detail maps. Now he was really learning about the war. He had been a good soldier. That made a difference.

One morning after he had been home about a month his mother came into his bedroom and sat on the bed. She smoothed her apron.

"I had a talk with your father last night, Harold," she said, "and he is willing for you to take the car out in the evenings."

"Yeah?" said Krebs, who was not fully awake. "Take the car out? Yeah?"

"Yes. Your father has felt for some time that you should be able to take the car out   20
in the evenings whenever you wished but we only talked it over last night."

"I'll bet you made him," Krebs said.

"No. It was your father's suggestion that we talk the matter over."

"Yeah. I'll bet you made him," Krebs sat up in bed.

"Will you come down to breakfast, Harold?" his mother said.

"As soon as I get my clothes on," Krebs said. 25

His mother went out of the room and he could hear her frying something down-stairs while he washed, shaved and dressed to go down into the dining-room for break-fast. While he was eating breakfast his sister brought in the mail.

"Well, Hare," she said. "You old sleepy-head. What do you ever get up for?"

Krebs looked at her. He liked her. She was his best sister.

"Have you got the paper?" he asked.

She handed him *The Kansas City Star* and he shucked off its brown wrapper and 30 opened it to the sporting page. He folded *The Star* open and propped it against the water pitcher with his cereal dish to steady it, so he could read while he ate.

"Harold," his mother stood in the kitchen doorway, "Harold, please don't muss up the paper. You father can't read his *Star* if it's been mussed."

"I won't muss it," Krebs said.

His sister sat down at the table and watched him while he read.

"We're playing indoor° over at school this afternoon," she said. "I'm going to pitch."

"Good," said Krebs. "How's the old wing?" 35

"I can pitch better than lots of the boys. I tell them all you taught me. The other girls aren't much good."

"Yeah?" said Krebs.

"I tell them all you're my beau. Aren't you my beau, Hare?"

"You bet."

"Couldn't your brother really be your beau just because he's your brother?" 40

"I don't know."

"Sure you know. Couldn't you be my beau, Hare, if I was old enough and if you wanted to?"

"Sure. You're my girl now."

"Am I really your girl?"

"Sure." 45

"Do you love me?"

"Uh, huh."

"Will you love me always?"

"Sure."

"Will you come over and watch me play indoor?" 50

"Maybe."

"Aw, Hare, you don't love me. If you loved me, you'd want to come over and watch me play indoor."

Krebs's mother came into the dining-room from the kitchen. She carried a plate with two fried eggs and some crisp bacon on it and a plate of buckwheat cakes.

"You run along, Helen," she said. "I want to talk to Harold."

She put eggs and bacon down in front of him and brought in a jug of maple syrup 55 for the buckwheat cakes. Then she sat down across the table from Krebs.

"I wish you'd put down the paper a minute. Harold," she said.

Krebs took down the paper and folded it.

"Have you decided what you are going to do yet, Harold?" his mother said, taking off her glasses.

"No," said Krebs.

---

indoor: that is, a softball game played, of course, outdoors.

"Don't you think it's about time?" His mother did not say this in a mean way. She   60
seemed worried.

"I hadn't thought about it," Krebs said.

"God has some work for every one to do," his mother said. "There can be no idle
hands in His Kingdom."

"I'm not in His Kingdom," Krebs said.

"We are all of us in His Kingdom."

Krebs felt embarrassed and resentful as always.   65

"I've worried about you so much, Harold," his mother went on. "I know the temptations you must have been exposed to. I know how weak men are. I know what your own
dear grandfather, my own father, told us about the Civil War and I have prayed for you. I
pray for you all day long, Harold."

Krebs looked at the bacon fat hardening on his plate.

"Your father is worried, too," his mother went on. "He thinks you have lost your
ambition, that you haven't got a definite aim in life. Charley Simmons, who is just your
age, has a good job and is going to be married. The boys are all settling down; they're all
determined to get somewhere; you can see that boys like Charley Simmons are on their
way to being really a credit to the community."

Krebs said nothing.

"Don't look that way, Harold," his mother said. "You know we love you and I want   70
to tell you for your own good how matters stand. Your father does not want to hamper
your freedom. He thinks you should be allowed to drive the car. If you want to take some
of the nice girls out riding with you, we are only too pleased. We want you to enjoy yourself. But you are going to have to settle down to work, Harold. Your father doesn't care
what you start in at. All work is honorable as he says. But you've got to make a start at
something. He asked me to speak to you this morning and then you can stop in and see
him at his office."

"Is that all?" Krebs said.

"Yes. Don't you love your mother, dear boy?"

"No," Krebs said.

His mother looked at him across the table. Her eyes were shiny. She started crying.

"I don't love anybody," Krebs said.   75

It wasn't any good. He couldn't tell her, he couldn't make her see it. It was silly to
have said it. He had only hurt her. He went over and took hold of her arm. She was crying with her head in her hands.

"I didn't mean it," he said. "I was just angry at something. I didn't mean I didn't
love you."

His mother went on crying. Krebs put his arm on her shoulder.

"Can't you believe me, mother?"

His mother shook her head.   80

"Please, please, mother. Please believe me."

"All right," his mother said chokily. She looked up at him. "I believe you, Harold."

Krebs kissed her hair. She put her face up to him.

"I'm your mother," she said. "I held you next to my heart when you were a
tiny baby."

Krebs felt sick and vaguely nauseated.   85

"I know, Mummy," he said. "I'll try and be a good boy for you."

"Would you kneel and pray with me, Harold?" his mother asked.

They knelt down beside the dining-room table and Krebs's mother prayed.

"Now, you pray, Harold," she said.

"I can't," Krebs said.

"Try, Harold."

"I can't."

"Do you want me to pray for you?"

"Yes."

So his mother prayed for him and then they stood up and Krebs kissed his mother and went out of the house. He had tried so to keep his life from being complicated. Still, none of it had touched him. He had felt sorry for his mother and she had made him lie. He would go to Kansas City and get a job and she would feel all right about it. There would be one more scene maybe before he got away. He would not go down to his father's office. He would miss that one. He wanted his life to go smoothly. It had just gotten going that way. Well, that was all over now, anyway. He would go over to the schoolyard and watch Helen play indoor baseball.

QUESTIONS

1. Even though Hemingway is often praised for his specific writing, there are a number of vague passages in this story. Why does Hemingway include them? By what stylistic means does he control the vagueness?

2. Analyze Hemingway's sentences. What relationship is there between the things he describes and the length and complexity of his sentences?

3. Analyze Hemingway's descriptive style. What is the level of his diction? What words does he use for things and actions? How vivid are his descriptions?

4. Describe Harold Krebs. How do we learn about him? What does his relationship with his sister show about him? How does he change in the story?

ALICE MUNRO (b. 1931)

For a brief biography, please see Chapter 5, page 255.

The Found Boat   1974

At the end of Bell Street, McKay Street, Mayo Street, there was the Flood. It was the Wawanash River, which every spring overflowed its banks. Some springs, say one in every five, it covered the roads on that side of town and washed over the fields, creating a shallow choppy lake. Light reflected off the water made everything bright and cold, as it is in a lakeside town, and woke or revived in people certain vague hopes of disaster. Mostly during the late afternoon and early evening, there were people straggling out to look at it, and discuss whether it was still rising, and whether this time it might invade the town. In general, those under fifteen and over sixty-five were most certain that it would.

Eva and Carol rode out on their bicycles. They left the road—it was the end of Mayo Street, past any houses—and rode right into a field, over a wire fence entirely flattened by the weight of the winter's snow. They coasted a little way before the long grass stopped them, then left their bicycles lying down and went to the water.

"We have to find a log and ride on it," Eva said.

"Jesus, we'll freeze our legs off."

"Jesus, we'll freeze our legs off!" said one of the boys who were there too at the water's edge. He spoke in a sour whine, the way boys imitated girls although it was nothing like the way girls talked. These boys—there were three of them—were all in the same class as Eva and Carol at school and were known to them by name (their names being

Frank, Bud and Clayton), but Eva and Carol, who had seen and recognized them from the road, had not spoken to them or looked at them or, even yet, given any sign of knowing they were there. The boys seemed to be trying to make a raft, from lumber they had salvaged from the water.

Eva and Carol took off their shoes and socks and waded in. The water was so cold it sent pain up their legs, like blue electric sparks shooting through their veins, but they went on, pulling their skirts high, tight behind and bunched so they could hold them in front.

"Look at the fat-assed ducks in wading."

"Fat-assed fucks."

Eva and Carol, of course, gave no sign of hearing this. They laid hold of a log and climbed on, taking a couple of boards floating in the water for paddles. There were always things floating around in the Flood—branches, fence-rails, logs, road signs, old lumber; sometimes boilers, washtubs, pots and pans, or even a car seat or stuffed chair, as if somewhere the Flood had got into a dump.

They paddled away from shore, heading out into the cold lake. The water was per-   10
fectly clear, they could see the brown grass swimming along the bottom. Suppose it was the sea, thought Eva. She thought of drowned cities and countries. Atlantis. Suppose they were riding in a Viking boat—Viking boats on the Atlantic were more frail and narrow than this log on the Flood—and they had miles of clear sea beneath them, then a spired city, intact as a jewel irretrievable on the ocean floor.

"This is a Viking boat," she said. "I am the carving on the front." She stuck her chest out and stretched her neck, trying to make a curve, and she made a face, putting out her tongue. Then she turned and for the first time took notice of the boys.

"Hey, you sucks!" she yelled at them. "You'd be scared to come out here, this water is ten feet deep!"

"Liar," they answered without interest, and she was.

They steered the log around a row of trees, avoiding floating barbed wire, and got into a little bay created by a natural hollow of the land. Where the bay was now, there would be a pond full of frogs later in the spring, and by the middle of summer there would be no water visible at all, just a low tangle of reeds and bushes, green, to show that mud was still wet around their roots. Larger bushes, willows, grew around the steep bank of this pond and were still partly out of the water. Eva and Carol let the log ride in. They saw a place where something was caught.

It was a boat, or part of one. An old rowboat with most of one side ripped out, the   15
board that had been the seat just dangling. It was pushed up among the branches, lying on what would have been its side, if it had a side, the prow caught high.

Their idea came to them without consultation, at the same time:

"You guys! Hey, you guys!"

"We found you a boat!"

"Stop building your stupid raft and come and look at the boat!"

What surprised them in the first place was that the boys really did come, scram-   20
bling overland, half running, half sliding down the bank, wanting to see.

"Hey, where?"

"Where is it. I don't see no boat."

What surprised them in the second place was that when the boys did actually see what boat was meant, this old flood-smashed wreck held up in the branches, they did not understand that they had been fooled, that a joke had been played on them. They did not show a moment's disappointment, but seemed as pleased at the discovery as if the boat had been whole and new. They were already barefoot, because they had been wading in the water to get lumber, and they waded in here without a stop, surrounding the boat and appraising it and paying no attention even of an insulting kind to Eva and Carol who bobbed up and down on their log. Eva and Carol had to call to them.

"How do you think you're going to get it off?"

"It won't float anyway."   25

"What makes you think it will float?"

"It'll sink. Glub-blub-blub, you'll all be drownded."

The boys did not answer, because they were too busy walking around the boat, pulling at it in a testing way to see how it could be got off with the least possible damage. Frank, who was the most literate, talkative and inept of the three, began referring to the boat as *she*, an affectation which Eva and Carol acknowledged with fish-mouths of contempt.

"She's caught two places. You got to be careful not to tear a hole in her bottom. She's heavier than you'd think."

It was Clayton who climbed up and freed the boat, and Bud, a tall fat boy, who got   30
the weight of it on his back to turn it into the water so that they could half float, half carry it to shore. All this took some time. Eva and Carol abandoned their log and waded out of the water. They walked overland to get their shoes and socks and bicycles. They did not need to come back this way but they came. They stood at the top of the hill, leaning on their bicycles. They did not go on home, but they did not sit down and frankly watch, either. They stood more or less facing each other, but glancing down at the water and at the boys struggling with the boat, as if they had just halted for a moment out of curiosity, and staying longer than they intended, to see what came of this unpromising project.

About nine o'clock, or when it was nearly dark—dark to people inside the houses, but not quite dark outside—they all returned to town, going along Mayo Street in a sort of procession. Frank and Bud and Clayton came carrying the boat, upside-down, and Eva and Carol walked behind, wheeling their bicycles. The boys' heads were almost hidden in the darkness of the overturned boat, with its smell of soaked wood, cold swampy water. The girls could look ahead and see the street lights in their tin reflectors, a necklace of lights climbing Mayo Street, reaching all the way up to the standpipe. They turned onto Burns Street heading for Clayton's house, the nearest house belonging to any of them. This was not the way home for Eva or for Carol either, but they followed along. The boys were perhaps too busy carrying the boat to tell them to go away. Some younger children were still out playing, playing hopscotch on the sidewalk though they could hardly see. At this time of year the bare sidewalk was still such a novelty and delight. These children cleared out of the way and watched the boat go by with unwilling respect; they shouted questions after it, wanting to know where it came from and what was going to be done with it. No one answered them. Eva and Carol as well as the boys refused to answer or even look at them.

The five of them entered Clayton's yard. The boys shifted weight, as if they were going to put the boat down.

"You better take it round to the back where nobody can see it," Carol said. That was the first thing any of them had said since they came into town.

The boys said nothing but went on, following a mud path between Clayton's house and a leaning board fence. They let the boat down in the back yard.

"It's a stolen boat, you know," said Eva, mainly for the effect. "It must've belonged   35
to somebody. You stole it."

"You was the ones who stole it then," Bud said, short of breath. "It was you seen it first."

"It was you took it."

"It was all of us then. If one of us gets in trouble then all of us does."

"Are you going to tell anybody on them?" said Carol as she and Eva rode home, along the streets which were dark between the lights now and potholed from winter.

"It's up to you, I won't if you won't."   40

"I won't if you won't."

They rode in silence, relinquishing something, but not discontented.

The board fence in Clayton's back yard had every so often a post which supported it, or tried to, and it was on these posts that Eva and Carol spent several evenings sitting, jauntily but not very comfortably. Or else they just leaned against the fence while the boys worked on the boat. During the first couple of evenings neighborhood children attracted by the sound of hammering tried to get into the yard to see what was going on, but Eva and Carol blocked their way.

"Who said you could come in here?"

"Just us can come in this yard."   45

These evenings were getting longer, the air milder. Skipping was starting on the sidewalks. Further along the street there was a row of hard maples that had been tapped. Children drank the sap as fast as it could drip into the buckets. The old man and woman who owned the trees, and who hoped to make syrup, came running out of the house making noises as if they were trying to scare away crows. Finally, every spring, the old man would come out on his porch and fire his shotgun into the air, and then the thieving would stop.

None of those working on the boat bothered about stealing sap, though all had done so last year.

The lumber to repair the boat was picked up here and there, along back lanes. At this time of year things were lying around—old boards and branches, sodden mitts, spoons flung out with the dishwater, lids of pudding pots that had been set in the snow to cool, all the debris that can sift through and survive winter. The tools came from Clayton's cellar—left over, presumably, from the time when his father was alive—and though they had nobody to advise them the boys seemed to figure out more or less the manner in which boats are built, or rebuilt. Frank was the one who showed up with diagrams from books and *Popular Mechanics* magazines. Clayton looked at these diagrams and listened to Frank read the instructions and then went ahead and decided in his own way what was to be done. Bud was best at sawing. Eva and Carol watched everything from the fence and offered criticism and thought up names. The names for the boat that they thought of were: Water Lily, Sea Horse, Flood Queen, and Caro-Eve, after them because they had found it. The boys did not say which, if any, of these names they found satisfactory.

The boat had to be tarred. Clayton heated up a pot of tar on the kitchen stove and brought it out and painted slowly, his thorough way, sitting astride the overturned boat. The other boys were sawing a board to make a new seat. As Clayton worked, the tar cooled and thickened so that finally he could not move the brush any more. He turned to Eva and held out the pot and said, "You can go in and heat this on the stove."

Eva took the pot and went up the back steps. The kitchen seemed black after out-   50
side, but it must be light enough to see in, because there was Clayton's mother standing at the ironing board, ironing. She did that for a living, took in wash and ironing.

"Please may I put the tar pot on the stove?" said Eva, who had been brought up to talk politely to parents, even wash-and-iron ladies, and who for some reason especially wanted to make a good impression on Clayton's mother.

"You'll have to poke up the fire then," said Clayton's mother, as if she doubted whether Eva would know how to do that. But Eva could see now, and she picked up the lid with the stove-lifter, and took the poker and poked up a flame. She stirred the tar as it softened. She felt privileged. Then and later. Before she went to sleep a picture of Clayton came to her mind; she saw him sitting astride the boat, tar-painting, with such concentration, delicacy, absorption. She thought of him speaking to her, out of his isolation, in such an ordinary peaceful taking-for-granted voice.

On the twenty-fourth of May, a school holiday in the middle of the week, the boat was carried out of town, a long way now, off the road over fields and fences that had been repaired, to where the river flowed between its normal banks. Eva and Carol, as well as the boys, took turns carrying it. It was launched in the water from a cow-trampled spot between willow bushes that were fresh out in leaf. The boys went first. They yelled with triumph when the boat did float, when it rode amazingly down the river current. The boat was painted black, and green inside, with yellow seats, and a strip of yellow all the way around the outside. There was no name on it, after all. The boys could not imagine that it needed any name to keep it separate from the other boats in the world.

Eva and Carol ran along the bank, carrying bags full of peanut butter-and-jam sandwiches, pickles, bananas, chocolate cake, potato chips, graham crackers stuck together with corn syrup and five bottles of pop to be cooled in the river water. The bottles bumped against their legs. They yelled for a turn.

"If they don't let us they're bastards," Carol said, and they yelled together. "We   55
found it! We found it!"

The boys did not answer, but after a while they brought the boat in, and Carol and Eva came crashing, panting down the bank.

"Does it leak?"

"It don't leak yet."

"We forgot a bailing can," wailed Carol, but nevertheless she got in, with Eva, and Frank pushed them off, crying. "Here's to a Watery Grave!"

And the thing about being in a boat was that it was not solidly bobbing, like a log,   60
but was cupped in the water, so that riding in it was not like being on something in the water, but like being in the water itself. Soon they were all going out in the boat in mixed-up turns, two boys and a girl, two girls and a boy, a girl and a boy, until things were so confused it was impossible to tell whose turn came next, and nobody cared anyway. They went down the river—those who weren't riding, running along the bank to keep up. They passed under two bridges, one iron, one cement. Once they saw a big carp just resting, it seemed to smile at them, in the bridge-shaded water. They did not know how far they had gone on the river, but things had changed—the water had got shallower, and the land flatter. Across an open field they saw a building that looked like a house, abandoned. They dragged the boat up on the bank and tied it and set out across the field.

"That's the old station," Frank said. "That's Pedder Station." The others had heard this name but he was the one who knew, because his father was the station agent in town. He said that this was a station on a branch line that had been torn up, and that there had been a sawmill here, but a long time ago.

Inside the station it was dark, cool. All the windows were broken. Glass lay in shards and in fairly big pieces on the floor. They walked around finding the larger pieces of glass and tramping on them, smashing them, it was like cracking ice on puddles. Some partitions were still in place, you could see where the ticket window had been. There was a bench lying on its side. People had been here, it looked as if people came here all the time, though it was so far from anywhere. Beer bottles and pop bottles were lying around, also cigarette packages, gum and candy wrappers, the paper from a loaf of bread. The walls were covered with dim and fresh pencil and chalk writings and carved with knives.

I LOVE RONNIE COLES

I WANT TO FUCK

KILROY WAS HERE

RONNIE COLES IS AN ASS-HOLE

WHAT ARE YOU DOING HERE?

WAITING FOR A TRAIN

DAWNA MARY-LOU BARBARA JOANNE

It was exciting to be inside this large, dark, empty place, with the loud noise of breaking glass and their voices ringing back from the underside of the roof. They tipped the old beer bottles against their mouths. That reminded them that they were hungry and thirsty and they cleared a place in the middle of the floor and sat down and ate the lunch. They drank the pop just as it was, lukewarm. They ate everything there was and licked the smears of peanut butter and jam off the bread-paper in which the sandwiches had been wrapped.

They played Truth or Dare.

"I dare you to write on the wall, I am a Stupid Ass, and sign your name."

"Tell the truth—what is the worst lie you ever told?"

"Did you ever wet the bed?"

"Did you ever dream you were walking down the street without any clothes on?"

"I dare you to go outside and pee on the railway sign."

It was Frank who had to do that. They could not see him, even his back, but they knew he did it, they heard the hissing sound of his pee. They all sat still, amazed, unable to think of what the next dare would be.

"I dare everybody," said Frank from the doorway. "I dare—Everybody."

"What?"

"Take off all our clothes."

Eva and Carol screamed.

"Anybody who won't do it has to walk—has to *crawl*—around this floor on their hands and knees."

They were all quiet, till Eva said, almost complacently, "What first?"

"Shoes and socks."

"Then we have to go outside, there's too much glass here."

They pulled off their shoes and socks in the doorway, in the sudden blinding sun. The field before them was bright as water. They ran across where the tracks used to go.

"That's enough, that's enough," said Carol. "Watch out for thistles!"

"Tops! Everybody take off their tops!"

"I won't! We won't, will we, Eva?"

But Eva was whirling round and round in the sun where the track used to be. "I don't care, I don't care! Truth or Dare! Truth or Dare!"

She unbuttoned her blouse as she whirled, as if she didn't know what her hand was doing, she flung it off.

Carol took off hers. "I wouldn't have done it, if you hadn't!"

"Bottoms!"

Nobody said a word this time, they all bent and stripped themselves. Eva, naked first, started running across the field, and then all the others ran, all five of them running bare through the knee-high hot grass, running towards the river. Not caring now about being caught but in fact leaping and yelling to call attention to themselves, if there was anybody to hear or see. They felt as if they were going to jump off a cliff and fly. They felt that something was happening to them different from anything that had happened before, and it had to do with the boat, the water, the sunlight, the dark ruined station, and each other. They thought of each other now hardly as names or people, but as echoing shrieks, reflections, all bold and white and loud and scandalous, and as fast as arrows. They went running without a break into the cold water and when it came almost to the tops of their legs they fell on it and swam. It stopped their noise. Silence, amazement, came over them in a rush. They dipped and floated and separated, sleek as mink.

Eva stood up in the water her hair dripping, water running down her face. She was waist deep. She stood on smooth stones, her feet fairly wide apart, water flowing between her legs. About a yard away from her Clayton also stood up, and they were blinking the water out of their eyes, looking at each other. Eva did not turn or try to hide; she was quivering from the cold of the water, but also with pride, shame, boldness, and exhilaration.

Clayton shook his head violently, as if he wanted to bang something out of it, then bent over and took a mouthful of river water. He stood up with his cheeks full and made a tight hole of his mouth and shot the water at her as if it was coming out of a hose, hitting her exactly, first one breast and then the other. Water from his mouth ran down her body. He hooted to see it, a loud self-conscious sound that nobody would have expected, from him. The others looked up from wherever they were in the water and closed in to see.

Eva crouched down and slid into the water, letting her head go right under. She   90
swam, and when she let her head out, downstream, Carol was coming after her and the boys were already on the bank, already running into the grass, showing their skinny backs, their white, flat buttocks. They were laughing and saying things to each other but she couldn't hear, for the water in her ears.

"What did he do?" said Carol.

"Nothing."

They crept in to shore. "Let's stay in the bushes till they go," said Eva. "I hate them anyway. I really do. Don't you hate them?"

"Sure," said Carol, and they waited, not very long, until they heard the boys still noisy and excited coming down to the place a bit upriver where they had left the boat. They heard them jump in and start rowing.

"They've got all the hard part, going back," said Eva, hugging herself and shivering   95
violently. "Who cares? Anyway. It never was our boat."

"What if they tell?" said Carol.

"We'll say it's all a lie."

Eva hadn't thought of this solution until she said it, but as soon as she did she felt almost light-hearted again. The ease and scornfulness of it did make them both giggle, and slapping themselves and splashing out of the water they set about developing one of those fits of laughter in which, as soon as one showed signs of exhaustion, the other would snort and start up again, and they would make helpless—soon genuinely helpless—faces at each other and bend over and grab themselves as if they had the worst pain.

QUESTIONS

1. Consider the details used in passages of description in the story. What kinds of details are included?

2. What is the level of diction in the dialogue of the story? From the dialogue, what do you learn about the various speakers?

3. Study paragraph 10. What does the paragraph tell you about Eva as a limited-point-of-view center of interest? How?

4. Consider the last paragraph in the story as a paragraph of action. What verbs are used, and how well do they help you visualize and imagine the sounds of the scene? What is the effect of the verb "snort"?

5. From the lifestyle and artifacts mentioned, what do you learn about the time of the events and the economic level of the town? What is the effect of the facts that it is early springtime, that the water is still cold, but that in May the water is swimmable? What are the implications for summer?

FRANK O'CONNOR (1903–1966)

Frank O'Connor, the nom de plume *of Michael O'Donovan, was an only child of poor parents in County Cork, Ireland. He began writing when young, and for a time he was a director of Ireland's national theater. His output as a writer was considerable, with sixty-seven stories appearing in the posthumous* Collected Stories *of 1981. A meticulous writer, he was constantly revising his work. "First Confession," for example, went through a number of stages before the final version included here.*

First Confession   1951

All the trouble began when my grandfather died and my grandmother—my father's mother—came to live with us. Relations in the one house are a strain at the best of times, but, to make matters worse, my grandmother was a real old countrywoman and quite unsuited to the life in town. She had a fat, wrinkled old face, and, to Mother's great indignation, went round the house in bare feet—the boots had her crippled, she said. For dinner she had a jug of porter° and a pot of potatoes with—sometimes—a bit of salt fish, and she poured out the potatoes on the table and ate them slowly, with great relish, using her fingers by way of a fork.

Now, girls are supposed to be fastidious, but I was the one who suffered most from this. Nora, my sister, just sucked up to the old woman for the penny she got every Friday out of the old-age pension, a thing I could not do. I was too honest, that was my trouble; and when I was playing with Bill Connell, the sergeant-major's son, and saw my grandmother steering up the path with the jug of porter sticking out from beneath her shawl I was mortified. I made excuses not to let him come into the house, because I could never be sure what she would be up to when we went in.

When Mother was at work and my grandmother made the dinner I wouldn't touch it. Nora once tried to make me, but I hid under the table from her and took the bread-knife with me for protection. Nora let on to be very indignant (she wasn't, of course, but she knew Mother saw through her, so she sided with Gran) and came after me. I lashed out at her with the bread-knife, and after that she left me alone. I stayed there till Mother came in from work and made my dinner, but when Father came in later Nora said in a shocked voice: "Oh, Dadda, do you know what Jackie did at dinner-time?" Then, of course, it all came out; Father gave me a flaking; Mother interfered, and for days after that he didn't speak to me and Mother barely spoke to Nora. And all because of that old woman! God knows, I was heart-scalded.

Then, to crown my misfortune, I had to make my first confession and communion. It was an old woman called Ryan who prepared us for these. She was about the one age with Gran; she was well-to-do, lived in a big house on Montenotte, wore a black cloak and bonnet, and came every day to school at three o'clock when we should have been going home, and talked to us of hell. She may have mentioned the other place as well, but that could only have been by accident, for hell had the first place in her heart.

She lit a candle, took out a new half-crown, and offered it to the first boy who would hold one finger—only one finger!—in the flame for five minutes by the school clock. Being always very ambitious I was tempted to volunteer, but I thought it might look

5

---

porter: *a dark-brown beer.*

Irish   *Catholic*

fear   *Ambition* —   *What about the suffering in —?*

greedy. Then she asked were we afraid of holding one finger—only one finger!—in a little candle flame for five minutes and not afraid of burning all over in roasting hot furnaces for all eternity. "All eternity! Just think of that! A whole lifetime goes by and it's
nothing, not even a drop in the ocean of your sufferings." The woman was really interesting about hell, but my attention was all fixed on the half-crown. At the end of the lesson she put it back in her purse. It was a great disappointment; a religious woman like
that, you wouldn't think she'd bother about a thing like a half-crown.

Another day she said she knew a priest who woke one night to find a fellow he did-
n't recognize leaning over the end of his bed. The priest was a bit frightened—naturally
enough—but he asked the fellow what he wanted, and the fellow said in a deep, husky
voice that he wanted to go to confession. The priest said it was an awkward time and
wouldn't it do in the morning, but the fellow said that last time he went to confession,
there was one sin he kept back, being ashamed to mention it, and now it was always on
his mind. Then the priest knew it was a bad case, because the fellow was after making a
bad confession and committing a mortal sin. He got up to dress, and just then the cock
crew in the yard outside, and—lo and behold!—when the priest looked round there was
no sign of the fellow, only a smell of burning timber, and when the priest looked at his
bed didn't he see the print of two hands burned in it? That was because the fellow had
made a bad confession. This story made a shocking impression on me.

But the worst of all was when she showed us how to examine our conscience. Did
we take the name of the Lord, our God, in vain? Did we honour our father and our mother? (I asked her did this include grandmothers and she said it did.) Did we love our
neighbours as ourselves? Did we covet our neighbour's goods? (I thought of the way I felt
about the penny that Nora got every Friday.) I decided that, between one thing and another, I must have broken the whole ten commandments, all on account of that old
woman, and so far as I could see, so long as she remained in the house I had no hope of
ever doing anything else.

I was scared to death of confession. The day the whole class went I let on to have a
toothache, hoping my absence wouldn't be noticed; but at three o'clock, just as I was
feeling safe, along comes a chap with a message from Mrs. Ryan that I was to go to confession myself on Saturday and be at the chapel for communion with the rest. To make it
worse, Mother couldn't come with me and sent Nora instead.

Now, that girl had ways of tormenting me that Mother never knew of. She held my
hand as we went down the hill, smiling sadly and saying how sorry she was for me, as if she
were bringing me to the hospital for an operation.

"Oh, God help us!" she moaned. "Isn't it a terrible pity you weren't a good boy?
Oh, Jackie, my heart bleeds for you! How will you ever think of all your sins? Don't forget
you have to tell him about the time you kicked Gran on the shin."

"Lemme go!" I said, trying to drag myself free of her. "I don't want to go to confession at all."

"But sure, you'll have to go to confession, Jackie," she replied in the same regretful
tone. "Sure, if you didn't the parish priest would be up to the house, looking for you.
'Tisn't, God knows, that I'm not sorry for you. Do you remember the time you tried to kill
me with the bread-knife under the table? And the language you used to me? I don't know
what he'll do with you at all, Jackie. He might have to send you up to the bishop."

I remember thinking bitterly that she didn't know the half of what I had to tell—if
I told it. I knew I couldn't tell it, and understood perfectly why the fellow in Mrs. Ryan's
story made a bad confession; it seemed to me a great shame that people wouldn't stop
criticizing him. I remember that steep hill down to the church, and the sunlit hillsides

10

beyond the valley of the river, which I saw in the gaps between the houses like Adam's last glimpse of Paradise.°

Then, when she had manœuvered me down the long flight of steps to the chapel yard, Nora suddenly changed her tone. She became the raging malicious devil she really was.

"There you are!" she said with a yelp of triumph, hurling me through the church door. "And I hope he'll give you the penitential psalms, you dirty little caffler."

I knew then I was lost, given up to eternal justice. The door with the coloured-glass panels swung shut behind me, the sunlight went out and gave place to deep shadow, and the wind whistled outside so that the silence within seemed to crackle like ice under my feet. Nora sat in front of me by the confession box. There were a couple of old women ahead of her, and then a miserable-looking poor devil came and wedged me in at the other side, so that I couldn't escape even if I had the courage. He joined his hands and rolled his eyes in the direction of the roof, muttering aspirations in an anguished tone, and I wondered had he a grandmother too. Only a grandmother could account for a fellow behaving in that heartbroken way, but he was better off than I, for he at least could go and confess his sins; while I would make a bad confession and then die in the night and be continually coming back and burning people's furniture.

Nora's turn came, and I heard the sound of something slamming, and then her voice as if butter wouldn't melt in her mouth, and then another slam, and out she came. God, the hypocrisy of women! Her eyes were lowered, her head was bowed, and her hands were joined very low down on her stomach, and she walked up the aisle to the side altar looking like a saint. You never saw such an exhibition of devotion, and I remembered the devilish malice with which she had tormented me all the way from our door, and wondered were all religious people like that, really. It was my turn now. With the fear of damnation in my soul I went in, and the confessional door closed of itself behind me.

It was pitch-dark and I couldn't see priest or anything else. Then I really began to be frightened. In the darkness it was a matter between God and me, and He had all the odds. He knew what my intentions were before I even started; I had no chance. All I had ever been told about confession got mixed up in my mind, and I knelt to one wall and said: "Bless me, father, for I have sinned; this is my first confession." I waited for a few minutes, but nothing happened, so I tried it on the other wall. Nothing happened there either. He had me spotted all right.

It must have been then that I noticed the shelf at about one height with my head. It was really a place for grown-up people to rest their elbows, but in my distracted state I thought it was probably the place you were supposed to kneel. Of course, it was on the high side and not very deep, but I was always good at climbing and managed to get up all right. Staying up was the trouble. There was room only for my knees, and nothing you could get a grip on but a sort of wooden moulding a bit above it. I held on to the moulding and repeated the words a little louder, and this time something happened all right. A slide was slammed back; a little light entered the box, and a man's voice said: "Who's there?"

"'Tis me, father," I said for fear he mightn't see me and go away again. I couldn't see him at all. The place the voice came from was under the moulding, about level with my knees, so I took a good grip of the moulding and swung myself down till I saw the astonished face of a young priest looking up at me. He had to put his head on one side to see me, and I had to put mine on one side to see him, so we were more or less talking to one another upside-down. It struck me as a queer way of hearing confessions, but I didn't feel it my place to criticize.

20 "Bless me, father, for I have sinned; this is my first confession," I rattled off all in one breath, and swung myself down the least shade more to make it easier for him.

2 "What are you doing up there?" he shouted in an angry voice, and the strain the politeness was putting on my hold of the moulding, and the shock of being addressed in such an uncivil tone, were too much for me. I lost my grip, tumbled, and hit the door an unmerciful wallop before I found myself flat on my back in the middle of the aisle. The people who had been waiting stood up with their mouths open. The priest opened the door of the middle box and came out, pushing his biretta back from his forehead; he looked something terrible. Then Nora came scampering down the aisle.

22 "Oh, you dirty little caffler!" she said. "I might have known you'd do it. I might have known you'd disgrace me. I can't leave you out of my sight for one minute."

23 Before I could even get to my feet to defend myself she bent down and gave me a clip across the ear. This reminded me that I was so stunned I had even forgotten to cry, so that people might think I wasn't hurt at all, when in fact I was probably maimed for life. I gave a roar out of me.

24 "What's all this about?" the priest hissed, getting angrier than ever and pushing Nora off me. "How dare you hit the child like that, you little vixen?"   25

25 "But I can't do my penance with him, father," Nora cried, cocking an outraged eye up to him.

26 "Well, go and do it, or I'll give you some more to do," he said, giving me a hand up. "Was it coming to confession you were, my poor man?" he asked me.

"'Twas, father," said I with a sob.

27 "Oh," he said respectfully, "a big hefty fellow like you must have terrible sins. Is this your first?"

30 "'Tis, father," said I.   30

29 "Worse and worse," he said gloomily. "The crimes of a lifetime. I don't know will I get rid of you at all today. You'd better wait now till I'm finished with these old ones. You can see by the looks of them they haven't much to tell."

"I will, father," I said with something approaching joy.

The relief of it was really enormous. Nora stuck out her tongue at me from behind his back, but I couldn't even be bothered retorting. I knew from the very moment that man opened his mouth that he was intelligent above the ordinary. When I had time to think, I saw how right I was. It only stood to reason that a fellow confessing after seven years would have more to tell than people that went every week. The crimes of a lifetime, exactly as he said. It was only what he expected, and the rest was the cackle of old women and girls with their talk of hell, the bishop, and the penitential psalms. That was all they knew. I started to make my examination of conscience, and barring the one bad business of my grandmother it didn't seem so bad.

The next time, the priest steered me into the confession box himself and left the shutter back the way I could see him get in and sit down at the further side of the grille from me.

"Well, now," he said, "what do they call you?"   35

"Jackie, father," said I.

"And what's a-trouble to you, Jackie?"

"Father," I said, feeling I might as well get it over while I had him in good humour, "I had it all arranged to kill my grandmother."

He seemed a bit shaken by that, all right, because he said nothing for quite a while.

"My goodness," he said at last, "that'd be a shocking thing to do. What put that into 40
your head?"

"Father," I said, feeling very sorry for myself, "she's an awful woman."

"Is she?" he asked. "What way is she awful?"

"She takes porter, father," I said, knowing well from the way Mother talked of it that
this was a mortal sin, and hoping it would make the priest take a more favourable view of
my case.

"Oh, my!" he said, and I could see he was impressed.

"And snuff, father," said I. 45

"That's a bad case, sure enough, Jackie," he said.

"And she goes round in her bare feet, father," I went on in a rush of self-pity, "and
she knows I don't like her, and she gives pennies to Nora and none to me, and my da
sides with her and flakes me, and one night I was so heart-scalded I made up my mind I'd
have to kill her."

"And what would you do with the body?" he asked with great interest.

"I was thinking I could chop that up and carry it away in a barrow I have," I said.

"Begor, Jackie," he said, "do you know you're a terrible child?" 50

"I know, father," I said, for I was just thinking the same thing myself. "I tried to kill
Nora too with a bread-knife under the table, only I missed her."

"Is that the little girl that was beating you just now?" he asked.

"'Tis, father."

"Someone will go for her with a bread-knife one day, and he won't miss her,"
he said rather cryptically. "You must have great courage. Between ourselves, there's a
lot of people I'd like to do the same to but I'd never have the nerve. Hanging is an
awful death."

"Is it, father?" I asked with the deepest interest—I was always very keen on hanging. 55
"Did you ever see a fellow hanged?"

"Dozens of them," he said solemnly. "And they all died roaring."

"Jay!" I said.

"Oh, a horrible death!" he said with great satisfaction. "Lots of fellows I saw killed
their grandmothers too, but they all said 'twas never worth it."

He had me there for a full ten minutes talking, and then walked out the chapel
yard with me. I was genuinely sorry to part with him, because he was the most entertaining character I'd ever met in the religious line. Outside, after the shadow of the church,
the sunlight was like the roaring of waves on a beach; it dazzled me; and when the frozen
silence melted and I heard the screech of trams on the road my heart soared. I knew now
I wouldn't die in the night and come back, leaving marks on my mother's furniture. It
would be a great worry to her, and the poor soul had enough.

Nora was sitting on the railing, waiting for me, and she put on a very sour puss 60
when she saw the priest with me. She was made jealous because a priest had never come
out of the church with her.

"Well," she asked coldly, after he left me, "what did he give you?"

"Three Hail Marys," I said.

"Three Hail Marys," she repeated incredulously. "You mustn't have told him
anything."

"I told him everything," I said confidently.

"About Gran and all?" 65

"About Gran and all."

(All she wanted was to be able to go home and say I'd made a bad confession.)

"Did you tell him you went for me with the bread-knife?" she asked with a frown.
"I did to be sure."
"And he only gave you three Hail Marys?"　　　　70
"That's all."
She slowly got down from the railing with a baffled air. Clearly, this was beyond her. As we mounted the steps back to the main road she looked at me suspiciously.
"What are you sucking?" she asked.
"Bullseyes." *exact target direct hit*
"Was it the priest gave them to you?"　　　　75
"'Twas."
"Lord God," she wailed bitterly, "some people have all the luck! 'Tis no advantage to anybody trying to be good. I might just as well be a sinner like you."

QUESTIONS

1. Describe Jackie as a narrator. What is the level of his language? To whom does he seem to be speaking or writing? What elements of language do you find in the story that seem characteristically Irish?

2. Describe Jackie's character. How old do you think he is at the time of the narration? Is there evidence that he has grown as a person since the time of the story's events? Do you think his attitudes have changed about his grandmother? His parents? His sister? Mrs. Ryan? The priest?

3. Is Jackie's confession a "good" one? Whose religion seems more appealing, Mrs. Ryan's or the priest's?

4. To what degree are the relationships within Jackie's family either ordinary or unusual?

5. "First Confession" is a funny story. What contributions are made to the humor by the situations? The language?

MARK TWAIN (1835–1910)

Mark Twain (born Samuel Clemens) is one of the literary giants of nineteenth- and early-twentieth-century America. Largely because of his use of colloquial and regional English in Huckleberry Finn, *he was acknowledged by Hemingway as a founder of American literature. He was born in Missouri and spent much of his youth as a Mississippi River pilot, Confederate soldier, journalist, and miner. In 1863 he adopted "Mark Twain" as his nom de plume. His most famous works are the novels* Tom Sawyer *(1876) and* Huckleberry Finn *(1884–1885).* Huckleberry Finn *is today the subject of controversy for characterizations some people consider racist, even though more than a century has passed since its publication. "Luck" is a brief story (Twain calls it a "sketch") illustrating Twain's art of comic debunking, a characteristic that he also shows in works such as* The Innocents Abroad *and the short critical essay "Fenimore Cooper's Literary Offenses." The technique in "Luck" is to present an inside, private view of a person of high reputation and in effect to show that "the emperor has no clothes."*

Guest at banquet

Luck[1] ~~~~~ 1891

It was at a banquet in London in honor of one of the two or three conspicuously illustrious English military names of this generation. For reasons which will presently appear, I will withhold his real name and titles and call him Lieutenant-General Lord Arthur Scoresby, V.C., K.C.B., etc., etc. What a fascination there is in a renowned name! There sat the man, in actual flesh, whom I had heard of so many thousands of times since that day, thirty years before, when his name shot suddenly to the zenith from a Crimean battlefield,° to remain forever celebrated. It was food and drink to me to look, and look, and look at that demi-god; scanning, searching, noting: the quietness, the reserve, the noble gravity of his countenance; the simple honesty that expressed itself all over him; the sweet unconsciousness of his greatness—unconsciousness of the hundreds of admiring eyes fastened upon him, unconsciousness of the deep, loving, sincere worship welling out of the breasts of those people and flowing toward him.

—starts telling

The clergyman at my left was an old acquaintance of mine—clergyman now, but had spent the first half of his life in the camp and field and as an instructor in the military school at Woolwich. Just at the moment I have been talking about a veiled and singular light glimmered in his eyes and he leaned down and muttered confidentially to me—indicating the hero of the banquet with a gesture:

"Privately—he's an absolute fool."

This verdict was a great surprise to me. If its subject had been Napoleon, or Socrates, or Solomon, my astonishment could not have been greater. Two things I was well aware of: that the Reverend was a man of strict veracity and that his judgment of men was good. Therefore I knew, beyond doubt or question, that the world was mistaken about this hero: he *was* a fool. So I meant to find out, at a convenient moment, how the Reverend, all solitary and alone, had discovered the secret.

Some days later the opportunity came, and this is what the Reverend told me: 5

About forty years ago I was an instructor in the military academy at Woolwich. I was present in one of the sections when young Scoresby underwent his preliminary examination. I was touched to the quick with pity, for the rest of the class answered up brightly and handsomely, while he—why, dear me, he didn't know *anything*, so to speak. He was evidently good, and sweet, and lovable, and guileless; and so it was exceedingly painful to see him stand there, as serene as a graven image, and deliver himself of answers which were veritably miraculous for stupidity and ignorance. All the compassion in me was aroused in his behalf. I said to myself, when he comes to be examined again he will be flung over, of course; so it will be simply a harmless act of charity to ease his fall as much as I can. I took him aside and found that he knew a little of Caesar's history; and as he didn't know anything else, I went to work and drilled him like a galley-slave on a certain line of stock questions concerning Caesar which I knew would be used. If you'll believe me, he went through with flying colors on examination day! He went through on that purely superficial "cram," and got compliments too, while others, who knew a thousand times more than he, got plucked. By some strangely lucky accident—an accident not likely to happen twice in a century—he was asked no question outside of the narrow limits of his drill.

It was stupefying. Well, all through his course I stood by him, with something of the sentiment which a mother feels for a crippled child; and he always saved himself—just by miracle, apparently.

---

[1]This is not a fancy sketch. I got it from a clergyman who was an instructor at Woolwich forty years ago, and who vouched for its truth. [Twain's note.]

Crimean battlefield: In the Crimean War (1853–1856), England was one of the allies that fought against Russia.

Now, of course, the thing that would expose him and kill him at last was mathematics. I resolved to make his death as easy as I could; so I drilled him and crammed him, and crammed him and drilled him, just on the line of questions which the examiners would be most likely to use, and then launched him on his fate. Well, sir, try to conceive of the result: to my consternation, he took the first prize! And with it he got a perfect ovation in the way of compliments.

Sleep? There was no more sleep for me for a week. My conscience tortured me day and night. What I had done I had done purely through charity, and only to ease the poor youth's fall. I never had dreamed of any such preposterous results as the thing that had happened. I felt as guilty and miserable as Frankenstein. Here was a wooden-head whom I had put in the way of glittering promotions and prodigious responsibilities, and but one thing could happen: he and his responsibilities would all go to ruin together at the first opportunity.

The Crimean War had just broken out. Of course there had to be a war, I said to myself. We couldn't have peace and give this donkey a chance to die before he is found out. I waited for the earthquake. It came. And it made me reel when it did come. He was actually gazetted to a captaincy in a marching regiment! Better men grow old and gray in the service before they climb to a sublimity like that. And who could ever have foreseen that they would go and put such a load of responsibility on such green and inadequate shoulders? I could just barely have stood it if they had made him a cornet; but a captain—think of it! I thought my hair would turn white.

Consider what I did—I who so loved repose and inaction. I said to myself, I am responsible to the country for this, and I must go along with him and protect the country against him as far as I can. So I took my poor little capital that I had saved up through years of work and grinding economy, and went with a sigh and bought a cornetcy in his regiment, and away we went to the field.

And there—oh, dear, it was awful. Blunders?—why he never did anything *but* blunder. But, you see, nobody was in the fellow's secret. Everybody had him focused wrong, and necessarily misinterpreted his performance every time. Consequently they took his idiotic blunders for inspirations of genius. They did, honestly! His mildest blunders were enough to make a man in his right mind cry; and they did make me cry—and rage and rave, too, privately. And the thing that kept me always in a sweat of apprehension was the fact that every fresh blunder he made increased the luster of his reputation! I kept saying to myself, he'll get so high that when discovery does finally come it will be like the sun falling out of the sky.

He went right along, up from grade to grade, over the dead bodies of his superiors, until at last, in the hottest moment of the battle of——down went our colonel, and my heart jumped into my mouth, for Scoresby was next in rank! Now for it, said I: we'll all land in Sheol in ten minutes, sure.

The battle was awfully hot; the allies were steadily giving way all over the field. Our regiment occupied a position that was vital; a blunder now must be destruction. At this crucial moment, what does this immortal fool do but detach the regiment from its place and order a charge over a neighboring hill where there wasn't a suggestion of an enemy! "There you go!" I said to myself; "this *is* the end at last."

And away we did go, and were over the shoulder of the hill before the insane movement could be discovered and stopped. And what did we find? An entire and unsuspected Russian army in reserve! And what happened? We were eaten up? That is necessarily what would have happened in ninety-nine cases out of a hundred. But no; those Russians argued that no single regiment would come browsing around there at such a time. It must be the entire English army, and that the sly Russian game was detected and blocked, so they turned tail, and away they went, pell-mell, over the hill and down into the field, in wild confusion, and we after them; they themselves broke the solid Russian center in the

10

15

field, and tore through, and in no time there was the most tremendous rout you ever saw, and the defeat of the allies was turned into a sweeping and splendid victory! Marshall Canrobert looked on, dizzy with astonishment, admiration, and delight; and sent right off for Scoresby, and hugged him, and decorated him on the field in presence of all the armies!

And what was Scoresby's blunder that time? Merely the mistaking his right hand for his left—that was all. An order had come to him to fall back and support our right; and, instead, he fell *forward* and went over the hill to the left. But the name he won that day as a marvelous military genius filled the world with his glory, and that glory will never fade while history books last.

He is just as good and sweet and lovable and unpretending as a man can be, but he doesn't know enough to come in when it rains. Now that is absolutely true. He is the supremest ass in the universe; and until half an hour ago nobody knew it but himself and me. He has been pursued, day by day and year by year, by a most phenomenal astonishing luckiness. He has been a shining soldier in all our wars for a generation; he has littered his whole military life with blunders, and yet has never committed one that didn't make him a knight or a baronet or a lord or something. Look at his breast; why, he is just clothed in domestic and foreign decorations. Well, sir, every one of them is the record of some shouting stupidity or other; and, taken together, they are proof that the very best thing in all this world that can befall a man is to be born lucky. I say again, as I said at the banquet, Scoresby's an absolute fool.

QUESTIONS

1. Describe Twain's style as a writer of narrative prose. What kinds of detail does he present? Does he give you enough detail about the battle during the Crimean War, for example, to justify an assertion that he describes action vividly? Or does he confine his detail to illuminate the life of Scoresby?

2. What elements in the story are amusing? How does the development of humor depend on Twain's arrangement of words?

3. Study the first paragraph. What does Twain intend after the "look, and look, and look" phrase? Why do you think he begins the story with such a description, which might even be called heroic? Contrast this paragraph with paragraph 12, where the word *blunder* is repeated.

4. Who begins the story? Who finally tells it? How does the second narrator learn about Scoresby? How does he summarize Scoresby's career?

JOHN UPDIKE (b. 1932)

Updike was born and reared in Pennsylvania during the Great Depression. His parents were diligent about his education, and in 1950 he received a scholarship for study at Harvard, graduating in 1954. He worked for the New Yorker *for two years before deciding to devote himself exclusively to his own writing, but since then he has remained a frequent contributor of stories and poems to that magazine. In 1959, he published his first story collection,* The Same Door, *and his first novel,* The Poorhouse Fair. *In 1960, with* Rabbit, Run, *he began his extensive* Rabbit *chronicles. In 1981 he received the Pulitzer Prize for* Rabbit Is Rich. *His collected poems were published in 1993, and he is continually productive in writing new stories and poems. Today he is considered one of the best of America's major writers of fiction and poetry.*

A & P° 〜〜〜〜 *1961*

In walks these three girls in nothing but bathing suits. I'm in the third checkout slot, with my back to the door, so I don't see them until they're over by the bread. The one that caught my eye first was the one in the plaid green two-piece. She was a chunky kid, with a good tan and a sweet broad soft-looking can with those two crescents of white just under it, where the sun never seems to hit, at the top of the backs of her legs. I stood there with my hand on a box of HiHo crackers trying to remember if I rang it up or not. I ring it up again and the customer starts giving me hell. She's one of these cash-register-watchers, a witch about fifty with rouge on her cheekbones and no eyebrows, and I know it made her day to trip me up. She'd been watching cash registers for fifty years and probably never seen a mistake before.

By the time I got her feathers smoothed and her goodies into a bag—she gives me a little snort in passing, if she'd been born at the right time they would have burned her over in Salem—by the time I get her on her way the girls had circled around the bread and were coming back, without a pushcart, back my way along the counters, in the aisle between the checkouts and the Special bins. They didn't even have shoes on. There was this chunky one, with the two-piece—it was bright green and the seams on the bra were still sharp and her belly was still pretty pale so I guessed she just got it (the suit)—there was this one, with one of those chubby berry-faces, the lips all bunched together under her nose, this one, and a tall one, with black hair that hadn't quite frizzed right, and one of these sunburns right across under the eyes, and a chin that was too long—you know, the kind of girl other girls think is very "striking" and "attractive" but never quite makes it, as they very well know, which is why they like her so much—and then the third one, that wasn't quite so tall. She was the queen. She kind of led them, the other two peeking around and making their shoulders round. She didn't look around, not this queen, she just walked straight on slowly, on these long white prima-donna legs. She came down a little hard on her heels, as if she didn't walk in her bare feet that much, putting down her heels and then letting the weight move along to her toes as if she was testing the floor with every step, putting a little deliberate extra action into it. You never know for sure how girls' minds work (do you really think it's a mind in there or just a little buzz like a bee in a glass jar?) but you got the idea she had talked the other two into coming in here with her, and now she was showing them how to do it, walk slow and hold yourself straight.

She had on a kind of dirty-pink—beige, maybe, I don't know—bathing suit with a little nubble all over it and, what got me, the straps were down. They were off her shoulders looped loose around the cool tops of her arms, and I guess as a result the suit had slipped a little on her, so all around the top of the cloth there was this shining rim. If it hadn't been there you wouldn't have known there could have been anything whiter than those shoulders. With the straps pushed off, there was nothing between the top of the suit and the top of her head except just *her*, this clean bare plane of the top of her chest down from the shoulder bones like a dented sheet of metal tilted in the light. I mean, it was more than pretty.

She had sort of oaky hair that the sun and salt had bleached, done up in a bun that was unraveling, and a kind of prim face. Walking into the A & P with your straps down, I suppose it's the only kind of face you *can* have. She held her head so high her neck, coming up out of those white shoulders, looked kind of stretched, but I didn't mind. The longer her neck was, the more of her there was.

A & P: the Great Atlantic and Pacific Tea Company, a large grocery chain established in 1859 and still flourishing in 18 states, with more than 800 A & P stores in the United States and 200 in Canada.

She must have felt in the corner of her eye me and over my shoulder Stokesie in the second slot watching, but she didn't tip. Not this queen. She kept her eyes moving across the racks, and stopped, and turned so slow it made my stomach rub the inside of my apron, and buzzed to the other two, who kind of huddled against her for relief, and then they all three of them went up the cat-and-dog-food-breakfast-cereal-macaroni-rice-raisins-seasonings-spreads-spaghetti-soft-drinks-crackers-and-cookies aisle. From the third slot I look straight up this aisle to the meat counter, and I watched them all the way. The fat one with the tan sort of fumbled with the cookies, but on second thought she put the package back. The sheep pushing their carts down the aisle—the girls were walking against the usual traffic (not that we have one-way signs or anything)—were pretty hilarious. You could see them, when Queenie's white shoulders dawned on them, kind of jerk, or hop, or hiccup, but their eyes snapped back to their own baskets and on they pushed. I bet you could set off dynamite in an A & P and the people would by and large keep reaching and checking oatmeal off their lists and muttering "Let me see, there was a third thing, began with A, asparagus, no ah, yes, applesauce!" or whatever it is they do mutter. But there was no doubt, this jiggled them. A few houseslaves in pin curlers even looked around after pushing their carts past to make sure what they had seen was correct.

You know, it's one thing to have a girl in a bathing suit down on the beach, where what with the glare nobody can look at each other much anyway, and another thing in the cool of the A & P, under the fluorescent lights, against all those stacked packages, with her feet paddling along naked over our checkerboard green-and-cream rubber-tile floor.

"Oh Daddy," Stokesie said beside me. "I feel so faint."

"Darling," I said. "Hold me tight." Stokesie's married, with two babies chalked up on his fuselage already, but as far as I can tell that's the only difference. He's twenty-two, and I was nineteen this April.

"Is it done?" he asks, the responsible married man finding his voice. I forgot to say he thinks he's going to be manager some sunny day, maybe in 1990 when it's called the Great Alexandrov and Petrooshki° Tea Company or something.

What he meant was, our town is five miles from the beach, with a big summer colony out on the Point, but we're right in the middle of town, and the women generally put on a shirt or shorts or something before they get out of the car into the street. And anyway these are usually women with six children and varicose veins mapping their legs and nobody, including them, could care less. As I say, we're right in the middle of town, and if you stand at our front doors you can see two banks and the Congregational church and the newspaper store and three real-estate offices and about twenty-seven old freeloaders tearing up Central Street because the sewer broke again. It's not as if we're on the Cape,° we're north of Boston and there's people in this town haven't seen the ocean for twenty years.

The girls had reached the meat counter and were asking McMahon something. He pointed, they pointed, and they shuffled out of sight behind a pyramid of Diet Delight peaches. All that was left for us to see was old McMahon patting his mouth and looking after them sizing up their joints. Poor kids, I began to feel sorry for them, they couldn't help it.

10

Great Alexandrov and Petrooshki: apparently a reference to the possibility that someday Russia might rule the United States.

the Cape: Cape Cod, the southeastern area of Massachusetts, a place of many resorts and beaches.

Now here comes the sad part of the story, at least my family says it's sad, but I don't think it's so sad myself. The store's pretty empty, it being Thursday afternoon, so there was nothing much to do except lean on the register and wait for the girls to show up again. The whole store was like a pinball machine and I didn't know which tunnel they'd come out of. After a while they come around out of the far aisle, around the light bulbs, records at discount of the Caribbean Six or Tony Martin Sings or some such gunk you wonder they waste the wax on, sixpacks of candy bars, and plastic toys done up in cellophane that fall apart when a kid looks at them anyway. Around they come, Queenie still leading the way, and holding a little gray jar in her hand. Slots Three through Seven are unmanned and I could see her wondering between Stokes and me, but Stokesie with his usual luck draws an old party in baggy gray pants who stumbles up with four giant cans of pineapple juice (what do these bums *do* with all that pineapple juice? I've often asked myself) so the girls come to me. Queenie puts down the jar and I take it into my fingers icy cold. Kingfish Fancy Herring Snacks in Pure Sour Cream: 49¢. Now her hands are empty, not a ring or a bracelet, bare as God made them, and I wonder where the money's coming from. Still with that prim look she lifts a folded dollar bill out of the hollow at the center of her nubbed pink top. The jar went heavy in my hand. Really, I thought that was so cute.

Then everybody's luck begins to run out. Lengel comes in from haggling with a truck full of cabbages on the lot and is about to scuttle into that door marked MANAGER behind which he hides all day when the girls touch his eye. Lengel's pretty dreary, teaches Sunday school and the rest, but he doesn't miss that much. He comes over and says, "Girls, this isn't the beach."

Queenie blushes, though maybe it's just a brush of sunburn I was noticing for the first time, now that she was so close. "My mother asked me to pick up a jar of herring snacks." Her voice kind of startled me, the way voices do when you see the people first, coming out so flat and dumb yet kind of tony, too, the way it ticked over "pick up" and "snacks." All of a sudden I slid right down her voice into her living room. Her father and the other men were standing around in ice-cream coats and bow ties and the women were in sandals picking up herring snacks on toothpicks off a big glass plate and they were all holding drinks the color of water with olives and sprigs of mint in them. When my parents have somebody over they get lemonade and if it's a real racy affair Schlitz in tall glasses with "They'll Do It Every Time"° cartoons stenciled on.

"That's all right," Lengel said. "But this isn't the beach." His repeating this struck   15
me as funny, as if it had just occurred to him, and he had been thinking all these years the A & P was a great big dune and he was the head lifeguard. He didn't like my smiling—as I say he doesn't miss much—but he concentrates on giving the girls that sad Sunday-school-superintendent stare.

Queenie's blush is no sunburn now, and the plump one in plaid, that I liked better from the back—a really sweet can—pipes up, "We weren't doing any shopping. We just came in for the one thing."

"That makes no difference," Lengel tells her, and I could see from the way his eyes went that he hadn't noticed she was wearing a two-piece before. "We want you decently dressed when you come in here."

"We *are* decent," Queenie says suddenly, her lower lip pushing, getting sore now that she remembers her place, a place from which the crowd that runs the A & P must look pretty crummy. Fancy Herring Snacks flashed in her very blue eyes.

"They'll Do It Every Time": syndicated daily and Sunday cartoon created by Jimmy Hatlo.

"Girls, I don't want to argue with you. After this come in here with your shoulders covered. It's our policy." He turns his back. That's policy for you. Policy is what the king-pins want. What the others want is juvenile delinquency.

All this while, the customers had been showing up with their carts but, you know, sheep, seeing a scene, they had all bunched up on Stokesie, who shook open a paper bag as gently as peeling a peach, not wanting to miss a word. I could feel in the silence everybody getting nervous, most of all Lengel, who asks me, "Sammy, have you rung up their purchase?"

I thought and said "No" but it wasn't about that I was thinking. I go through the punches, 4, 9, GROC, TOT—it's more complicated than you think, and after you do it often enough, it begins to make a little song, that you hear words to, in my case "Hello (*bing*) there, you (*gung*) hap-py *pee*-pul (*splat*)!"—the *splat* being the drawer flying out. I un-crease the bill, tenderly as you may imagine, it just having come from between the two smoothest scoops of vanilla I had ever known were there, and pass a half and a penny into her narrow pink palm, and nestle the herrings in a bag and twist its neck and hand it over, all the time thinking.

The girls, and who'd blame them, are in a hurry to get out, so I say "I quit" to Lengel quick enough for them to hear, hoping they'll stop and watch me, their unsus-pected hero. They keep right on going, into the electric eye; the door flies open and they flicker across the lot to their car, Queenie and Plaid and Big Tall Goony-Goony (not that as raw material she was so bad), leaving me with Lengel and a kink in his eyebrow.

"Did you say something, Sammy?"

"I said I quit."

"I thought you did."

"You didn't have to embarrass them."

"It was they who were embarrassing us."

I started to say something that came out "Fiddle-de-doo." It's a saying of my grand-mother's, and I know she would have been pleased.

"I don't think you know what you're saying," Lengel said.

"I know you don't," I said. "But I do." I pull the bow at the back of my apron and start shrugging it off my shoulders. A couple customers that had been heading for my slot begin to knock against each other, like scared pigs in a chute.

Lengel sighs and begins to look very patient and old and gray. He's been a friend of my parents for years. "Sammy, you don't want to do this to your Mom and Dad," he tells me. It's true, I don't. But it seems to me that once you begin a gesture it's fatal not to go through with it. I fold the apron, "Sammy" stitched in red on the pocket, and put it on the counter, and drop the bow tie on top of it. The bow tie is theirs, if you've ever won-dered. "You'll feel this for the rest of your life," Lengel says, and I know that's true, too, but remembering how he made that pretty girl blush makes me so scrunchy inside I punch the No Sale tab and the machine whirs "pee-pul" and the drawer splats out. One advantage to this scene taking place in summer, I can follow this up with a clean exit, there's no fumbling around getting your coat and galoshes, I just saunter into the electric eye in my white shirt that my mother ironed the night before, and the door heaves itself open, and outside the sunshine is skating around on the asphalt.

I look around for my girls, but they're gone, of course. There wasn't anybody but some young married screaming with her children about some candy they didn't get by the door of a powder-blue Falcon° station wagon. Looking back in the big windows, over the bags of peat moss and aluminum lawn furniture stacked on the pavement, I could see

Falcon: small car that had recently been introduced by the Ford Motor Company.

Lengel in my place in the slot, checking the sheep through. His face was dark gray and his back stiff, as if he'd just had an injection of iron, and my stomach kind of fell as I felt how hard the world was going to be to me hereafter.

QUESTIONS

1. From Sammy's language, what do you learn about his view of himself? About his educational and class level? The first sentence, for example, is grammatically incorrect in standard English but not uncommon in colloquial English. Point out and explain similar passages.

2. Consider the first eleven paragraphs as exposition, in which you learn about the location, the issues, and the participants in the story's conflict. Is there anything inessential in this section? Do you learn enough to understand the story? How might someone other than Sammy present the material?

3. How do you learn that Sammy is an experienced "girl watcher"? What does *he think* he thinks about most girls? To what degree is this estimate inconsistent with what he finally does after the girls leave?

4. Why does Sammy say "I quit" so abruptly? What does he mean when he says that the world is going to be hard to him after his experience at the A & P?

❦ WRITING ABOUT STYLE

As you set out to develop your materials and ideas, consider the selected passage in the context of the entire story. If you can answer questions such as the following, you will readily assemble materials for your essay on the style of a passage from a story.

Questions for Discovering Ideas

*   Use a dictionary to discover the meaning of any words you do not recognize. Are there any unusual words? Any especially difficult or uncommon words? Do any of the words distract you as you read?

*   Are the words the most common ones that might be used? Can you think of more difficult ones? Easier ones? More accurate ones? How many words are particularly short (one or two syllables)? How many are long (three syllables and more)?

*   How varied are the sentence lengths? Do you find mostly short sentences (five to twenty words) or mostly long ones (twenty-one and longer), or is there a mixture of long and short sentences? What relationships do you find between the nature of the material and the lengths of the sentences?

*   Are the sentences simple, compound, or complex? What is the connection between sentence types and the topics? What variations do you discover within sentences at the beginning, middle, and end of the story?

*   Can you easily visualize and imagine the situations described by the words? If you find it easy, or hard, to what degree does your success or difficulty stem from the level of diction?

- For passages describing *action*, how vivid are the words? How do they help you picture the action? How do they hold your attention?

- For passages describing *exterior or interior scenery*, how specific are the words? How much detail does the writer provide? Should there be more or fewer words? How spatial are the descriptions of scenery? How many words are devoted to colors, shapes, and sizes?

- For passages of *dialogue*, what does the level of speech indicate about the characters doing the talking? How do a person's speeches establish her or his character? For what purposes does the author use formal or informal diction? How much slang do you find? Why is it there?

- What words belong only to particular occupations or ways of life (e.g., foreign words, specialized or technical words referring to things like horses, airplanes, flowers, medicine, psychology, and warfare)? What use do speakers make of contractions?

- What noteworthy rhetorical devices do you find? How many sentences are *periodic* as opposed to *loose*? What effect is gained by this sentence or sentences? What other rhetorical devices have you discovered? How are they used? What is their effect?

Strategies for Organizing Ideas

To describe and evaluate the style of the passage, first consider the style in relationship to the story. For example, suppose the speaker has just returned home after a long and painful journey, or has just finished a race with a close competitor, or is recalling an event of the long-distant past, or is anticipating future happiness or frustration. Keep such conditions in mind throughout your analysis.

To focus your essay, either single out one aspect of style or discuss everything, depending on the length of the assignment. Be sure to treat topics like *levels of diction*, categories like *specific-general* and *concrete-abstract*, the degree of *simplicity* or *complexity*, *length*, *numbers* of words, and *denotation-connotation*. In discussing rhetorical aspects, go as far as you can with the terminology at your command. For example, at a minimum, you should be able to consider simple-compound-complex for sentence types and parallelism for rhetorical devices. If you can draw attention to the elements in a parallel structure by using grammatical terms, do so. If you can detect the ways in which the sentences are kept simple or made complex, describe these ways. Be sure to use examples from the passage to illustrate your claims.

Your essay should reflect your awareness of style at your own stage of development as a reader. Later, when you have gained sharper perceptions and a wider descriptive vocabulary, you will be able to write more detailed and expert analyses.

In your conclusion, try to evaluate the author's style. To what extent has your analysis increased or reinforced your appreciation of the author's technique? Does the passage take on any added importance as a result of your study? Is there anything elsewhere in the work comparable to the content, words, or ideas that you have discussed in the passage?

Numbers for Easy Reference

Include a copy of your passage at the beginning of your essay, as in the demonstrative essay that follows. For your reader's convenience, number the sentences in the passage, and use these numbers when you refer to them.

> ### NUMBERS FOR EASY REFERENCE
>
> In preparing your essay, make a copy of the entire passage just as it appears in the text. Include the copy at the beginning, as in the sample essay. For your reader's convenience, number lines in poetry and sentences in prose.

DEMONSTRATIVE STUDENT ESSAY

A Study of the Style of Paragraph 31 of Updike's "A & P"°

[1] Lengel sighs and begins to look very patient and old and gray. [2] He's been a friend of my parents for years. [3] "Sammy, you don't want to do this to your Mom and Dad," he tells me. [4] It's true, I don't. [5] But it seems to me that once you begin a gesture it's fatal not to go through with it. [6] I fold the apron, "Sammy" stitched in red on the pocket, and put it on the counter, and drop the bow tie on top of it. [7] The bow tie is theirs, if you've ever wondered. [8] "You'll feel this for the rest of your life," Lengel says, and I know that's true, too, but remembering how he made that pretty girl blush makes me so scrunchy inside I punch the No Sale tab and the machine whirs "pee-pul" and the drawer splats out. [9] One advantage to this scene taking place in summer, I can follow this up with a clean exit, there's no fumbling around getting your coat and galoshes, I just saunter into the electric eye in my white shirt that my mother ironed the night before, and the door heaves itself open, and outside the sunshine is skating around on the asphalt.

[1] The first-person narrator of John Updike's "A & P" is Sammy, a nineteen-year-old who is working as a checkout cashier at a midtown A & P north of Boston and five miles from the ocean. Updike gives Sammy an informal and colloquial style of speech, as though Sammy is telling this story to a few of his close friends (he speaks to his "you" listeners in paragraph 2 [340]). He uses slang expressions and idioms, such as referring to the bottom of one of the girls in bathing suits as a "can" (340 and 342, paragraphs 1 and 16) and pointing out that another store employee was "sizing up their joints" (341, paragraph 11). Along with additional slang words like "chunky" (340, paragraph 1), he employs colorful language such as "feathers smoothed" (340, paragraph 2) and "flicker across" (343, paragraph 22). His syntax is informal and also at times ungrammatical. For example, he tells his listeners that "there's people in this town haven't seen the ocean for twenty years" (341, paragraph 10), a sentence which omits a "who" clause marker and also makes a subject-verb agreement error. Sammy is not above a mild curse, either, for he states early in the story that a "customer starts giving me hell" (340, paragraph 1).

°See pp. 339–44 for this story.

[2] The paragraph under consideration, the next to the last one in the story, describes Sammy's gesture supporting the three girls who wear only their bathing suits when shopping in the A & P. Lengel, the store manager, has told them that they must be "decently dressed" in the store (342, paragraph 17), and Sammy then makes his direct and simple gesture, the completion of which is described in paragraph 31 (343). He takes off his apron and tie and leaves the store, an act that climaxes the comedy of this nineteen-year-old giving up his job in protest against the prudery represented by his boss. <u>The paragraph thus crystallizes the story's movement from restrictiveness to freedom and growth.</u>* <u>Sammy's speech is grounded in the colloquialism of his background, and it also demonstrates both his skill as an observer and his budding moral perceptiveness.</u>†

[3] <u>An important characteristic of Sammy's diction is his connection to the limited world that he is growing away from.</u> Just as he does elsewhere in the story, he mixes past and present tenses, a common method of ordinary colloquial speech. Here he tells his story of past events completely in the present tense, although he also correctly uses two past and two perfect tenses in the appropriate places (sentences 2, 7, 8, and 9). In addition, his use of the slang words "scrunchy" and "splats" (sentence 8) are evidence of the lack of sophistication and polish of his background.

[4] <u>Although Sammy's language in the paragraph thus reveals his background and shortcomings as a speaker, there are also words that show his skill.</u> His memory of Lengel's checkout-counter advice reflects his objectivity and accuracy. Also, his observations about Lengel in sentences 1 and 8 show considerable understanding of Lengel and sympathy with Lengel as a person. Some of the paragraph is devoted to description, and Sammy's words here are economical and to the point, ably appropriate for the subject matter, as in the opening sentence, "Lengel sighs and begins to look very patient and old and gray." Sammy's most skillful and imaginative language is contained in the last sentence, in which he observes that "the door heaves itself open" and that the sun is "skating around on the asphalt" in the parking lot (sentence 9). The language of these observations truly demonstrates Sammy's skill as an observer.

[5] <u>Quite important about Sammy's diction is that it also reflects the growth of his perceptiveness, both of himself and also of the greater world around him.</u> He understands that his gesture is significant, but he does not--or cannot--express its significance beyond indicating that he was embarrassed at the way in which Lengel had admonished the "pretty girl" (sentence 8). Sammy is capable, however, of analyzing the drama of his exit, and of discussing an alternative view of how it might have been done in another season. Thus, in describing his gesture, he states that in the summer, when the story takes place, "there's no fumbling around getting your coat and galoshes." Interestingly, in the final sentence of the paragraph his language is much less colloquial and much more standard than it had been earlier. His use of "saunter" as a description of his walk to the door suggests a degree of defiance just as it also indicates his ability to make appropriate word choices in explaining himself.

There are other potential issues implicit in Sammy's language, such as those of young against old or of sexual admiration and appreciation against conventional respectability. Although these issues are major in the story, they are not

---

*Central idea.
†Thesis sentence.

[6] as prominent in the paragraph. Importantly, the paragraph corresponds to the emergence of Sammy's bravery and daring, even if he expends these virtues on nothing more than suddenly quitting his job. <u>This stylistic analysis shows the paragraph to be a packed one, vital in the narrative itself, and also touching on the important issues underlying Sammy's chivalric protest against the store's dress code</u>. In all these respects, the paragraph provides an anticipation of the final word about Sammy's life--"hereafter" (344, paragraph 32)--a formal word from his vocabulary, and one that we as readers might never have expected when we first began reading the story's opening sentence.

WORK CITED

Updike, John. "A & P." <u>Literature: An Introduction to Reading and Writing</u>. Ed. Edgar V. Roberts and Henry E. Jacobs. 7th ed. Upper Saddle River: Prentice Hall, 2004. 339–44.

Commentary on the Essay

This essay shows how separate stylistic topics can be unified. Important in this objective are the transitions from paragraph to paragraph, such as "Just as he does elsewhere," "thus reveals his background and shortcomings," "it also reflects," "In all these respects," and "other potential issues." These transitional phrases enable the reader to move easily from one topic to the next.

The beginning of the essay demonstrates the importance of relating the passage being studied to the story as a whole. The first paragraph of the essay locates the context of the paragraph to be analyzed, and the final words connect the paragraph to both the opening and ending of the story.

In the body, paragraph 2 goes quickly over the context of the paragraph, and it contains the central idea about Sammy's development as a character, together with the thesis sentence indicating the three topics of style to be brought out in support of the central idea. Paragraph 3 concentrates on those aspects of Updike's style for Sammy which demonstrate Sammy's limited background, while paragraph 4 considers how the style shows Sammy's observational skill. Paragraph 5 asserts that the paragraph being analyzed shows that Sammy is growing in his awareness both of the world around him and also of himself. Paragraph 6, the last of the body, briefly considers other issues in the style of the analyzed paragraph, and it shows how this paragraph anticipates Sammy's continued growth.

Special Topics for Writing and Argument about Style

1. In "Luck" there are two narrators. What purposes do these narrators serve? How do they differ in style (word choices, expressions of opinion, use of questions)?

2. Write an essay that answers the following questions: To what degree are the narrative and descriptive styles of "Soldier's Home" appropriate to the nature of the story? What would be the effect on the story if Hemingway had used the style of

Faulkner in "Barn Burning" (Chapter 4), or Updike in "A & P," or Whitecloud in "Blue Winds Dancing" (Chapter 3)?

3. Stories like Munro's "The Found Boat" and Crane's "The Blue Hotel" (Chapter 3) are characterized by full descriptions, so that the reader needs to imagine few details. How appropriate would similarly full descriptions be in stories like Hemingway's "Soldier's Home" and Twain's "Luck"?

4. Compare the narrative style in O'Connor's "First Confession" and Updike's "A & P." What level of diction do the narrators use? What characteristics are brought out by the speech of these narrators? How much dialogue is employed in each story? What does the dialogue bring out about the narrators? To what degree, if any, does the style indicate any changes that might be taking place in the narrators?

5. Write two brief character sketches, or a description of an action, to be included in a longer story. Make the first favorable and the second negative. Analyze your word choices in the contrasting accounts: What kinds of words do you select, and on what principles do you select them? What kinds of words might you select if you wanted to create a neutral account? On the basis of your answers, what can you conclude about the development of a fiction writer's style?

6. Munro's "The Found Boat" and Gilman's "The Yellow Wallpaper" (Chapter 12) feature the psychological makeup of their major characters. Write an essay considering the nature and effectiveness of the psychological portraiture in these stories.

7. Using your library's card or computer catalogue, or else a university press book about Hemingway containing a substantial bibliography, list five works about Hemingway as a writer of fiction. Study at least one of the books, and write a brief summary of the author's discussion of Hemingway's style (i.e., Hemingway's descriptions, diction, brevity, dialogue).

CHAPTER

8

Tone: *The Expression of Attitude in Fiction*

Tone refers to the methods by which writers and speakers reveal attitudes or feelings. It is an aspect of all spoken and written statements, whether declarations of earnest love, requests to pass a dinner dish, letters asking parents for money, or official government notices threatening penalties if taxes and fines are not paid. Because tone is often equated with *attitude*, it is important to realize that tone refers not so much to attitudes themselves but instead *to those techniques and modes of presentation that reveal or create attitudes.*

As a literary concept, *tone* is adapted from the phrase *tone of voice* in speech. Tone of voice reflects attitudes toward a particular object or situation, and also toward listeners. Let us suppose that Mary has a difficult assignment, and she expects to work on it all day. Things go well, and she finishes quickly. She happily tells her friend Anne, "I'm so pleased. I needed only two hours for that." Then she decides to buy tickets for a popular play and must wait through a long and slow line. After getting her tickets, she tells the people at the end of the line, "I'm so pleased. I needed only two hours for that." The sentences are exactly the same, but by changing her emphasis and vocal inflection, Mary indicates her disgust and impatience with her long wait and also shows her sympathy with the people still in line. By controlling the *tone* of her statements, in other words, Mary conveys attitudes of satisfaction at one time and indignation and also sympathy at another.

Tone and the expression of attitude are vital components of all forms of communication. In Bierstadt's painting *Among the Sierra Nevada Mountains, California,* for example (Insert II–4), we find suggestions of a major philosophy of existence. At the top of the painting the sky and the mountains are troubled and indistinguishable. But below the waterfall at the center, the earthly scene is pictured as being calm and tranquil, and the deer and birds in the foreground represent the life that has wondrously and mysteriously emerged from the celestial mix. These details reveal

Bierstadt's attitude of both awe and admiration for the universe and the earth he portrays.

As the example about Mary indicates, an attitude itself can be summarized with a word or phrase (satisfaction or indignation, love or contempt, deference or command, and so on), but the study of tone examines those aspects of situation, language, action, and background that *bring out* the attitude. In Welty's "A Worn Path" (Chapter 3), for example, the attendant offers Phoenix "a few pennies," but Phoenix wants more. Being a recipient of charity but also being an independent sort, Phoenix makes the following response:

> "Five pennies is a nickel," said Phoenix stiffly. (paragraph 99)

This request is indirect, but it is nevertheless demanding. Although Phoenix is not a literary master, she is a master of tone in this conversational situation.

❧ TONE AND ATTITUDES

In most literary works, attitudes point in a number of directions, so that tone becomes a highly complex matter. The following things to look for, however, should help you in understanding and describing literary tone.

Determine the Writer's Attitude Toward the Material

By reading a story carefully, we may deduce the author's attitude or attitudes toward the subject matter. In "The Story of an Hour," for example, Kate Chopin sympathetically portrays a young wife's secret wishes for freedom, just as she also humorously reveals the unwitting smugness that often pervades men's relationships with women. In "The Hammon and the Beans," Parédes shows revulsion against the effects of poverty, and also pity for the dead young girl who might have been saved with proper health care. Joy Williams in "Taking Care" (Chapter 2) reveals deep admiration for Jones, her major character. "Rape Fantasies" reveals Atwood's amused affection for Estelle, the narrator. All these stories exhibit various types of **irony,** which is one of the most significant aspects of authorial tone.

Discover the Writer's Attitude Toward Readers

Authors recognize that readers participate in the creative act and that all elements of a story—word choice, characterization, allusions, levels of reality—must take readers' responses into account (see the discussion of reader-response criticism in Chapter 33). When Hawthorne's woodland guide in "Young Goodman Brown" (Chapter 9) refers to "King Philip's War," for example, Hawthorne assumes that his readers know that this seventeenth-century war was inhumanly greedy and cruel. By not explaining this part of history, he indicates respect for the knowledge of his readers, and he also assumes their agreement with his interpretation. Updike in "A & P" (Chapter 7) assumes that readers understand his use of Sammy's diction to reveal Sammy as a perceptive and independent but insecure young man. Authors always make such considerations about readers by implicitly complimenting them on their knowledge and also by satisfying their curiosity and desire to be interested, stimulated, and pleased.

Determine Other Dominant Attitudes

Beyond general authorial tone, you will discover many internal and dramatically rendered expressions of attitude. For example, the speaker of Laurence's "The Loons" is a woman describing her memory of a childhood summer vacation when her family was accompanied by Piquette, an Indian girl who had nowhere else to go. The narrator asks Piquette to "come and play," and Piquette responds scornfully, "I ain't a kid." The narrator's immediate reaction is to reject Piquette completely, but on mature reflection she decides to gain Piquette's trust. This change of attitude is the ultimate cause of the speaker's decision to tell Piquette's story, and therefore it is also the cause of the story's focus on the pathos of change and loss.

element evoking pity →

In addition, as characters interact, their tone dramatically shows their judgments about other characters and situations. A complicated control of tone occurs at the end of Glaspell's "A Jury of Her Peers" (Chapter 4), where the two major characters, Mrs. Hale and Mrs. Peters, begin covering up incriminating evidence about Minnie Wright. When Mrs. Peters agrees to this obstruction of justice, however, she speaks not about illegality but rather about the possible embarrassment of the action.

> "My!" she began, in a high, false voice, "it's a good thing the men couldn't hear us! Getting all stirred up over a little thing like a—dead canary." She hurried over that. "As if that could have anything to do with—with—My, wouldn't they *laugh*?" (paragraph 267)

Notice that her words reveal her knowledge that men scoff at feminine concerns, like Minnie's quilting knots, and therefore she openly anticipates the men's amusement. The reader, however, knows that she is joining Mrs. Hale in hiding evidence.

⚘ TONE AND HUMOR

A major aspect of tone is humor. Everyone likes to laugh, and shared laughter is part of good human relationships; but not everyone can explain why things are funny. Laughter resists close analysis; it is unplanned, personal, idiosyncratic, and unpredictable. Nonetheless, there are a number of common elements.

1. THERE MUST BE SOMETHING TO LAUGH AT.   Laughter is commonly *directed at* a person, thing, situation, custom, habit of speech or dialect, or arrangement of words. Because laughter requires an object or "butt," it is sometimes classified as *homicidal* (general laughter against something or someone), *fratricidal* (laughter against someone close), and *suicidal* (laughter against oneself).

2. LAUGHTER STEMS OUT OF DISPROPORTION OR *INCONGRUITY*. We normally know what to expect under given conditions, and anything **contrary to these expectations is incongruous** and may therefore generate laughter. A traditional joke about the prototypical absent-minded professor has the professor lighting his pipe with a flaming hundred-dollar bill. Such behavior is inappropriate or incongruous—and therefore funny—because it violates our expectations about ordinary and normal care of money. A student in a language class once wrote about a "*congregation* of verbs" and also about parts of speech as "nouns, verbs, and *proverbs.*" The student meant the *conjugation* of verbs, of course, and also (maybe) either *adverbs* or *pronouns*, but somehow his understanding slipped and he created a comic incongruity. Such inadvertent verbal errors are called **malapropisms,** after Mrs. Malaprop, a character in Richard Brinsley Sheridan's play *The Rivals* (1775). In the literary creation of malapropisms, the tone is directed against the speaker, for the amusement of both readers and author alike.

3. SAFETY AND/OR GOOD WILL PREVENTS HARM AND ENSURES HUMOR. Seeing a person slip on a banana peel and hurtle through the air can cause laughter, but only if we ourselves are not that person, for laughter depends on insulation from danger and pain. In comic situations that involve physical abuse—falling down stairs or being hit in the face by cream pies—the abuse never harms the participants. The incongruity of such situations causes laughter, and the immunity from pain and injury prevents a response of horror. Good will enters into humor in romantic comedy or in any other work in which we are drawn into general sympathy with the major figures, such as Elizabeth and Nelson in Colwin's "An Old-Fashioned Story" (Chapter 2). As the author leads the characters toward recognizing that they love each other, our involvement produces happiness, smiles, and (perhaps) even sympathetic laughter.

4. UNFAMILIARITY, NEWNESS, AND UNIQUENESS PRODUCE THE SPONTANEITY WHICH PROMPTS LAUGHTER. Laughter depends on seeing something new or unique, on experiencing something familiar in a new light, and on gaining flashes of insight. It is always spontaneous, even when readers already know what they are laughing at. Indeed, the task of the comic writer is to develop ordinary materials to that point when spontaneity frees readers to laugh. Thus you can read and reread O'Connor's "First Confession" (Chapter 7) and laugh each time because, even though you know what will happen, the story shapes your acceptance of how reconciliation penetrates a wall of anger and guilt. Young Jackie's comic troubles with his sister and grandmother are always comic because his experiences are so spontaneous and incongruous.

TONE AND IRONY

The capacity to have more than one attitude toward someone or something is a uniquely human trait. We know that people are not perfect, but we love a number of them anyway. Therefore we speak to them not only with love and praise, but also with banter and criticism. On occasion, you have probably given mildly insulting greeting cards to your loved ones, not to affront them but to amuse them. You share smiles and laughs, and at the same time you also remind them of your affection.

The word *irony* describes such contradictory statements or situations. Irony is natural to human beings who are aware of life's ambiguities and complexities. It develops from the realization that life does not always measure up to promise, that friends and loved ones are sometimes angry at each other, that the universe contains incomprehensible mysteries, that the social and political structure is often oppressive rather than liberating, that doubt exists even in the certainty of knowledge and faith, and that human character is built through chagrin, regret, and pain as much as through emulation and praise. In expressing an idea ironically, writers pay the greatest compliment to their audience, for they assume that readers have sufficient intelligence and skill to discover the real meaning of quizzical or ambiguous statements and situations.

The Four Major Kinds of Irony Are Verbal, Situational, Cosmic, and Dramatic

VERBAL IRONY DEPENDS ON THE INTERPLAY OF WORDS. In **verbal irony,** one thing is said, but the opposite is meant. In the example opening this chapter, Mary's ironic expression of pleasure after her two-hour wait for tickets really means that she is disgusted. There are important types of verbal irony. In **understatement,** the expression does not fully describe the importance of a situation and therefore makes its point by implication. For example, in Bierce's "An Occurrence at Owl Creek Bridge" (Chapter 5) the condemned man, Farquhar, contemplates the apparatus designed by the soldiers to hang him. His response is described by the narrator: "The arrangement commended itself to his judgment as simple and effective" (paragraph 4). These words would be appropriate for the appraisal of ordinary machinery, but because the apparatus is going to kill Farquhar, his understated observation is ironic.

By contrast, in **overstatement** or **hyperbole,** the words are obviously and inappropriately excessive, and readers or listeners therefore understand that the true meaning is considerably less than what is said. An example is the priest's exaggerated dialogue with Jackie in "First Confession" (Chapter 7, paragraphs 38–50). Though the priest makes incongruously hyperbolic comments on Jackie's plans for slaughtering his grandmother, readers know that he means no such thing. The gulf between what is said and what is meant produces smiles and chuckles.

Often verbal irony is ambiguous, having double meaning or **double entendre.** Midway through "Young Goodman Brown" (Chapter 9), for example, the woodland guide leaves Brown alone with the advice "when you feel like moving again, there is my staff to help you along" (paragraph 40). The word "staff" is ambiguous, for in the story we are told that it refers to the staff that resembles a "serpent" (paragraph 13). The word therefore suggests that the devilish guide is leaving Brown not only with a real staff but also with the spirit of evil. Ambiguity (and irony) inhere in the word "staff" because of the divine and well-known staff of the Twenty-Third Psalm, a staff that gives comfort (i.e., "Thy rod and thy staff, they comfort me"). Ambiguity, of course, can be used in relation to any topic. Double entendre is often used in statements about sexuality for the amusement of listeners or readers.

SITUATIONAL IRONY FILLS THE GAP BETWEEN HOPE AND REALITY. **Situational irony,** or **irony of situation,** refers to the chasm between what we hope for or expect and what actually happens. It is often pessimistic because it emphasizes that human beings usually have little or no control over their lives or anything else. The forces of opposition can be psychological, social, cultural, political, or environmental. Thus in Atwood's "Rape Fantasies" the narrator, Estelle, states her inability to understand why men cannot be satisfied by human relationships with women rather than rapacious ones. "Rape Fantasies" is not a sociological document, but Estelle's uneasiness underscores the irony of the political and social conditions that produce rape. Although situational irony often involves disaster, it need not always do so. For example, a happier occurrence of situational irony is in Chekhov's play *The Bear* (Chapter 28), for the two characters shift from anger to love as they fall into the grips of emotions that are "bigger than both of them."

COSMIC IRONY STEMS FROM THE POWER OF CHANCE AND FATE. A special kind of situational irony that emphasizes the pessimistic and fatalistic side of life is **cosmic irony** or **irony of fate.** By the standard of cosmic irony, the universe is indifferent to individuals, who are subject to blind chance, accident, uncontrollable emotions, perpetual misfortune, and misery. Even if things temporarily go well, people's lives end badly, and their best efforts do not rescue them or make them happy. A work illustrating cosmic irony is Glaspell's "A Jury of Her Peers," which develops out of the stultifying conditions of farm life experienced by Minnie Wright. She has no profession, no other hope, no other life except the lonely, dreary farm—nothing. After close to two decades of wretchedness, she buys a canary that warbles for her to make her life pleasant. Within a year, her boorish husband wrings the bird's neck, and she in turn wreaks vengeance against him. Her situation is cosmically ironic, for the implication of "A Jury of Her Peers" is that human beings are caught in a web of disastrous circumstances from which there is no escape.

DRAMATIC IRONY RESULTS FROM MISUNDERSTANDING AND LACK OF KNOWLEDGE. Like cosmic irony, **dramatic irony** is a special kind of situational irony. It happens when a character either has no information about a situation or else misjudges it, but readers (and often some of the other characters) see everything completely and correctly. As might be expected, dramatic irony is derived from drama, and the quintessentially ironic model is found in Sophocles' ancient Greek play *Oedipus the King* (Chapter 27). In this play, everyone—other characters and readers alike—knows the truth long before Oedipus knows it. It is important to recognize that dramatic irony can also be found in fiction (and in poetry). It is seen in Chopin's "The Story of an Hour," where the doctors are ignorant of Louise's reaction to the reports of her husband's death. The story's readers, however, do indeed know and understand her feelings, and therefore they also know that the doctors reveal their own pompous vanity as they misdiagnose the cause of her sudden death.

STORIES FOR STUDY

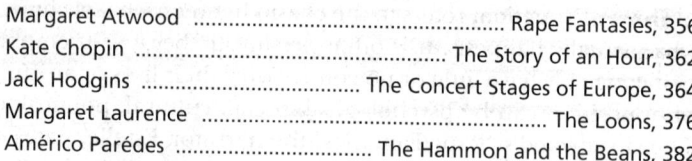

MARGARET ATWOOD (b. 1939)

Atwood is one of Canada's premier writers, having published many books of poetry, a number of novels and stories, and much criticism. In addition, she is editor of The Oxford Book of Canadian Verse *(1982). One of her most widely recognized works is the anti-utopian novel* The Handmaid's Tale *(1986), which describes a futuristic nightmare society of fear and repression for women. This story was adapted as a movie in 1990. The stories in a collection,* Wilderness Tips *(1992), reflect regret and diminished hopes, unlike the more comic topics of her story "Rape Fantasies" and her poem "Siren Song." The scope of her work may be inferred from more recent publications:* The Robber Bride *(1993),* Good Bones and Simple Murders *(1994),* Poems *(1994),* Princess Prunella and the Purple Peanut *(1995),* Morning in the Burned House *(1995), and* The Blind Assassin *(2001).*

Rape Fantasies   1977

The way they're going on about it in the magazines you'd think it was just invented, and not only that but it's something terrific, like a vaccine for cancer. They put it in capital letters on the front cover, and inside they have these questionnaires like the ones they used to have about whether you were a good enough wife or an endomorph or an ectomorph, remember that? with the scoring upside down on page 73, and then these numbered do-it-yourself dealies, you know? RAPE, TEN THINGS TO DO ABOUT IT, like it was ten new hairdos or something. I mean, what's so new about it?

So at work they all have to talk about it because no matter what magazine you open, there it is, staring you right between the eyes, and they're beginning to have it on the television, too. Personally I'd prefer a June Allyson° movie anytime but they don't make them any more and they don't even have them that much on the Late Show. For instance, day before yesterday, that would be Wednesday, thank god it's Friday as they say, we were sitting around in the women's lunch room—the *lunch* room, I mean you'd think you could get some peace and quiet in there—and Chrissy closes up the magazine she's been reading and says, "How about it, girls, do you have rape fantasies?"

June Allyson: actress (b. 1917) known for her bright smile and scratchy voice. She specialized in "sweet" movie and musical roles, 1943–1959, and for a long time she appeared in TV commercials.

The four of us were having our game of bridge the way we always do, and I had a bare twelve points counting the singleton with not that much of a bid in anything. So I said one club, hoping Sondra would remember about the one club convention, because the time before when I used that she thought I really meant clubs and she bid us up to three, and all I had was four little ones with nothing higher than a six, and we went down two and on top of that we were vulnerable. She is not the world's best bridge player. I mean, neither am I but there's a limit.

Darlene passed but the damage was done, Sondra's head went round like it was on ball bearings and she said, "*What* fantasies?"

"Rape fantasies," Chrissy said. She's a receptionist and she looks like one; she's   5
pretty but cool as a cucumber, like she's been painted all over with nail polish, if you know what I mean. Varnished. "It says here all women have rape fantasies."

"For Chrissake, I'm eating an egg sandwich," I said, "and I bid one club and Darlene passed."

"You mean, like some guy jumping you in an alley or something," Sondra said. She was eating her lunch, we all eat our lunches during the game, and she bit into a piece of that celery she always brings and started to chew away on it with this thoughtful expression in her eyes and I knew we might as well pack it in as far as the game was concerned.

"Yeah, sort of like that," Chrissy said. She was blushing a little, you could see it even under her makeup.

"I don't think you should go out alone at night," Darlene said, "you put yourself in a position," and I may have been mistaken but she was looking at me. She's the oldest, she's forty-one though you wouldn't know it and neither does she, but I looked it up in the employees' file. I like to guess a person's age and then look it up to see if I'm right. I let myself have an extra pack of cigarettes if I am, though I'm trying to cut down. I figure it's harmless as long as you don't tell. I mean, not everyone has access to that file, it's more or less confidential. But it's all right if I tell you, I don't expect you'll ever meet her, though you never know, it's a small world. Anyway.

"For *heaven's* sake, it's only *Toronto*," Greta said. She worked in Detroit for three   10
years and she never lets you forget it, it's like she thinks she's a war hero or something, we should all admire her just for the fact that she's still walking this earth, though she was really living in Windsor° the whole time, she just worked in Detroit. Which for me doesn't really count. It's where you sleep, right?

"Well, do you?" Chrissy said. She was obviously trying to tell us about hers but she wasn't about to go first, she's cautious, that one.

"I certainly don't," Darlene said, and she wrinkled up her nose, like this, and I had to laugh. "I think it's disgusting." She's divorced, I read that in the file too, she never talks about it. It must've been years ago anyway. She got up and went over to the coffee machine and turned her back on us as though she wasn't going to have anything more to do with it.

"Well," Greta said. I could see it was going to be between her and Chrissy. They're both blondes, I don't mean that in a bitchy way but they do try to outdress each other. Greta would like to get out of Filing, she'd like to be a receptionist too so she could meet more people. You don't meet much of anyone in Filing except other people in Filing. Me, I don't mind it so much, I have outside interests.

"Well," Greta said, "I sometimes think about, you know my apartment? It's got this little balcony, I like to sit out there in the summer and I have a few plants out there. I never bother that much about locking the door to the balcony, it's one of those sliding

---

Windsor: city south of Detroit, noted as the only place where any portion of Canada is south of the United States.

glass ones, I'm on the eighteenth floor for heaven's sake, I've got a good view of the lake and the CN Tower and all. But I'm sitting around one night in my housecoat, watching TV with my shoes off, you know how you do, and I see this guy's feet, coming down past the window, and the next thing you know he's standing on the balcony, he's let himself down by a rope with a hook on the end of it from the floor above, that's the nineteenth, and before I can even get up off the chesterfield he's inside the apartment. He's all dressed in black with black gloves on"—I knew right away what show she got the black gloves off because I saw the same one—"and then he, well, you know."

"You know what?" Chrissy said, but Greta said, "And afterwards he tells me that he   15
goes all over the outside of the apartment building like that, from one floor to another, with his rope and his hook . . . and then he goes out to the balcony and tosses his rope, and he climbs up it and disappears."

"Just like Tarzan," I said, but nobody laughed.

"Is that all?" Chrissy said. "Don't you ever think about, well, I think about being in the bathtub, with no clothes on . . ."

"So who takes a bath in their clothes?" I said, you have to admit it's stupid when you come to think of it, but she just went on, ". . . with lots of bubbles, what I use is Vitabath, it's more expensive but it's so relaxing, and my hair pinned up, and the door opens and this fellow's standing there. . . ."

"How'd he get in?" Greta said.

"Oh, I don't know, through a window or something. Well, I can't very well get out   20
of the bathtub, the bathroom's too small and besides he's blocking the doorway, so I just *lie* there, and he starts to very slowly take his own clothes off, and then he gets into the bathtub with me."

"Don't you scream or anything?" said Darlene. She'd come back with her cup of coffee, she was getting really interested. "I'd scream like bloody murder."

"Who'd hear me?" Chrissy said. "Besides, all the articles say it's better not to resist, that way you don't get hurt."

"Anyway you might get bubbles up your nose," I said, "from the deep breathing," and I swear all four of them looked at me like I was in bad taste, like I'd insulted the Virgin Mary or something. I mean, I don't see what's wrong with a little joke now and then. Life's too short, right?

"Listen," I said, "those aren't *rape* fantasies. I mean, you aren't getting *raped*, it's just some guy you haven't met formally who happens to be more attractive than Derek Cummins"—he's the Assistant Manager, he wears elevator shoes or at any rate they have these thick soles and he has this funny way of talking, we call him Derek Duck—"and you have a good time. Rape is when they've got a knife or something and you don't want to."

"So what about you, Estelle," Chrissy said, she was miffed because I laughed at her   25
fantasy, she thought I was putting her down. Sondra was miffed too, by this time she'd finished her celery and she wanted to tell about hers, but she hadn't got in fast enough.

"All right, let me tell you one," I said. "I'm walking down this dark street at night and this fellow comes up and grabs my arm. Now it so happens that I have a plastic lemon in my purse, you know how it always says you should carry a plastic lemon in your purse? I don't really do it, I tried it once but the darn thing leaked all over my cheque-book, but in this fantasy I have one, and I say to him, 'You're intending to rape me, right?' and he nods, so I open my purse to get the plastic lemon, and I can't find it! My purse is full of all this junk, Kleenex and cigarettes and my change purse and my lipstick and my driver's licence, you know the kind of stuff: so I ask him to hold out his hands, like this, and I pile all this junk into them and down at the bottom there's the plastic lemon, and I can't get the top off. So I hand it to him and he's very obliging, he twists the top off and hands it back to me, and I squirt him in the eye."

I hope you don't think that's too vicious. Come to think of it, it is a bit mean, especially when he was so polite and all.

"*That's* your rape fantasy?" Chrissy says, "I don't believe it."

"She's a card," Darlene says, she and I are the ones that've been here the longest and she never will forget the time I got drunk at the office party and insisted I was going to dance under the table instead of on top of it, I did a sort of Cossack number° but then I hit my head on the bottom of the table—actually it was a desk—when I went to get up, and I knocked myself out cold. She's decided that's the mark of an original mind and she tells everyone new about it and I'm not sure that's fair. Though I did do it.

"I'm being totally honest," I say. I always am and they know it. There's no point in being anything else, is the way I look at it, and sooner or later the truth will out so you might as well not waste the time, right? "You should hear the one about the Easy-Off Cleaner."   30

But that was the end of the lunch hour, with one bridge game shot to hell, and the next day we spent most of the time arguing over whether to start a new game or play out the hands we had left over from the day before, so Sondra never did get a chance to tell about her rape fantasy.

It started me thinking though, about my own rape fantasies. Maybe I'm abnormal or something, I mean I have fantasies about handsome strangers coming in through the window too, like Mr. Clean, I wish one would, please god somebody without flat feet and big sweat marks on his shirt, and over five feet five, believe me being tall is a handicap though it's getting better, tall guys are starting to like someone whose nose reaches higher than their belly button. But if you're being totally honest you can't count those as rape fantasies. In a real rape fantasy, what you should feel is this anxiety, like when you think about your apartment building catching on fire and whether you should use the elevator or the stairs or maybe just stick your head under a wet towel, and you try to remember everything you've read about what to do but you can't decide.

For instance, I'm walking along this dark street at night and this short, ugly fellow comes up and grabs my arm, and not only is he ugly, you know, with a sort of puffy nothing face, like those fellows you have to talk to in the bank when your account's overdrawn—of course I don't mean they're all like that—but he's absolutely covered in pimples. So he gets me pinned against the wall, he's short but he's heavy, and he starts to undo himself and the zipper gets stuck. I mean, one of the most significant moments in a girl's life, it's almost like getting married or having a baby or something, and he sticks the zipper.

So I say, kind of disgusted, "Oh for Chrissake," and he starts to cry. He tells me he's never been able to get anything right in his entire life, and this is the last straw, he's going to go jump off a bridge.

"Look," I say, I feel so sorry for him, in my rape fantasies I always end up feeling   35
sorry for the guy, I mean there has to be something *wrong* with them, if it was Clint Eastwood° it'd be different but worse luck it never is. I was the kind of little girl who buried dead robins, know what I mean? It used to drive my mother nuts, she didn't like me touching them, because of the germs I guess. So I say, "Listen, I know how you feel. You really should do something about those pimples, if you got rid of them you'd be quite good looking, honest; then you wouldn't have to go around doing stuff like this. I had them myself once," I say, to comfort him, but in fact I did, and it ends up I give him

---

Cossack number: a Ukrainian folk dance movement performed in a squatting position, with much hand clapping.

Clint Eastwood: born 1930, star of many tough-guy detective and western movies; most famous as "Dirty Harry" (1971).

the name of my old dermatologist, the one I had in high school, that was back in Leamington,° except I used to go to St. Catharine's for the dermatologist. I'm telling you, I was really lonely when I first came here; I thought it was going to be such a big adventure and all, but it's a lot harder to meet people in a city. But I guess it's different for a guy.

Or I'm lying in bed with this terrible cold, my face is all swollen up, my eyes are red and my nose is dripping like a leaky tap, and this fellow comes in through the window and *he* has a terrible cold too, it's a new kind of flu that's been going around. So he says, "I'b goig do rabe you"—I hope you don't mind me holding my nose like this but that's the way I imagine it—and he lets out this terrific sneeze, which slows him down a bit, also I'm no object of beauty myself, you'd have to be some kind of pervert to want to rape someone with a cold like mine, it'd be like raping a bottle of LePages mucilage the way my nose is running. He's looking wildly around the room, and I realize it's because he doesn't have a piece of Kleenex! "Id's ride here," I say, and I pass him the Kleenex, god knows why he even bothered to get out of bed, you'd think if you were going to go around climbing in windows you'd wait till you were healthier, right? I mean, that takes a certain amount of energy. So I ask him why doesn't he let me fix him a NeoCitran and scotch, that's what I always take, you still have the cold but you don't feel it, so I do and we end up watching the Late Show together. I mean, they aren't all sex maniacs, the rest of the time they must lead a normal life. I figure they enjoy watching the Late Show just like anybody else.

I do have a scarier one though . . . where the fellow says he's hearing angel voices that're telling him he's got to kill me, you know, you read about things like that all the time in the papers. In this one I'm not in the apartment where I live now, I'm back in my mother's house in Leamington and the fellow's been hiding in the cellar, he grabs my arm when I go downstairs to get a jar of jam and he's got hold of the axe too, out of the garage, that one is really scary. I mean, what do you say to a nut like that?

So I start to shake but after a minute I get control of myself and I say, is he sure the angel voices have got the right person, because I hear the same angel voices and they've been telling me for some time that I'm going to give birth to the reincarnation of St. Anne who in turn has the Virgin Mary and right after that comes Jesus Christ and the end of the world, and he wouldn't want to interfere with that, would he? So he gets confused and listens some more, and then he asks for a sign and I show him my vaccination mark, you can see it's sort of an odd-shaped one, it got infected because I scratched the top off, and that does it, he apologizes and climbs out the coal chute° again, which is how he got in in the first place, and I say to myself there's some advantage in having been brought up a Catholic even though I haven't been to church since they changed the service into English,° it just isn't the same, you might as well be a Protestant. I must write to Mother and tell her to nail up that coal chute, it always has bothered me. Funny, I couldn't tell you at all what this man looks like but I know exactly what kind of shoes he's wearing, because that's the last I see of him, his shoes going up the coal chute, and they're the old-fashioned kind that lace up the ankles, even though he's a young fellow. That's strange, isn't it?

Let me tell you though I really sweat until I see him safely out of there and I go upstairs right away and make myself a cup of tea. I don't think about that one much. My mother always said you shouldn't dwell on unpleasant things and I generally agree with that, I mean, dwelling on them doesn't make them go away. Though not dwelling on them doesn't make them go away either, when you come to think of it.

Leamington: in Ontario on the north shore of Lake Erie, southeast of Windsor.

coal chute: trough for delivering coal from a truck into a basement coal bin. Estelle's remark indicates that the chute was not fastened over the opening to the bin, thus permitting an illegal entry.

into English: In accord with the Second Vatican Council (1962–1965), the Latin Mass was replaced by vernacular languages in the late 1960s.

Sometimes I have these short ones where the fellow grabs my arm but I'm really a Kung-Fu° expert, can you believe it, in real life I'm sure it would just be a conk on the head and that's that, like getting your tonsils out, you'd wake up and it would be all over except for the sore places, and you'd be lucky if your neck wasn't broken or something, I could never even hit the volleyball in gym and a volleyball is fairly large, you know?—and I just go *zap* with my fingers into his eyes and that's it, he falls over, or I flip him against a wall or something. But I could never really stick my fingers in anyone's eyes, could you? It would feel like hot jello and I don't even like cold jello, just thinking about it gives me the creeps. I feel a bit guilty about that one, I mean how would you like walking around knowing someone's been blinded for life because of you?

But maybe it's different for a guy.

The most touching one I have is when the fellow grabs my arm and I say, sad and kind of dignified, "You'd be raping a corpse." That pulls him up short and I explain that I've just found out I have leukaemia and the doctors have only given me a few months to live. That's why I'm out pacing the streets alone at night, I need to think, you know, come to terms with myself. I don't really have leukaemia but in the fantasy I do, I guess I chose that particular disease because a girl in my grade four class died of it, the whole class sent her flowers when she was in the hospital. I didn't understand then that she was going to die and I wanted to have leukaemia too so I could get flowers. Kids are funny, aren't they? Well, it turns out that he has leukaemia himself, and *he* only has a few months to live, that's why he's going around raping people, he's very bitter because he's so young and his life is being taken from him before he's really lived it. So we walk along gently under the street lights, it's spring and sort of misty, and we end up going for coffee, we're happy we've found the only other person in the world who can understand what we're going through, it's almost like fate, and after a while we just sort of look at each other and our hands touch, and he comes back with me and moves into my apartment and we spend our last months together before we die, we just sort of don't wake up in the morning, though I've never decided which one of us gets to die first. If it's him I have to go on and fantasize about the funeral, if it's me I don't have to worry about that, so it just about depends on how tired I am at the time. You may not believe this but sometimes I even start crying. I cry at the end of movies, even the ones that aren't all that sad, so I guess it's the same thing. My mother's like that too.

The funny thing about these fantasies is that the man is always someone I don't know, and the statistics in the magazines, well, most of them anyway, they say it's often someone you do know, at least a little bit, like your boss or something—I mean, it wouldn't be *my* boss, he's over sixty and I'm sure he couldn't rape his way out of a paper bag, poor old thing, but it might be someone like Derek Duck, in his elevator shoes, perish the thought—or someone you just met, who invites you up for a drink, it's getting so you can hardly be sociable any more, and how are you supposed to meet people if you can't trust them even that basic amount? You can't spend your whole life in the Filing Department or cooped up in your own apartment with all the doors and windows locked and the shades down. I'm not what you would call a drinker but I like to go out now and then for a drink or two in a nice place, even if I am by myself, I'm with Women's Lib on that even though I can't agree with a lot of the other things they say. Like here for instance, the waiters all know me and if anyone, you know, bothers me . . . I don't know why I'm telling you all this, except I think it helps you get to know a person, especially at first, hearing some of the things they think about. At work they call me the office worry wart,

---

Kung-Fu: elaborate self-defense system developed in China, similar to karate.

but it isn't so much like worrying, it's more like figuring out what you should do in an emergency, like I said before.

Anyway, another thing about it is that there's a lot of conversation, in fact I spend most of my time, in the fantasy that is, wondering what I'm going to say and what he's going to say, I think it would be better if you could get a conversation going. Like, how could a fellow do that to a person he's just had a long conversation with, once you let them know you're human, you have a life too, I don't see how they could go ahead with it, right? I mean, I know it happens but I just don't understand it, that's the part I really don't understand.

QUESTIONS

1. What elements of the various rape fantasies are comic? How is the comedy brought out (e.g., through subject matter, circumstances of description, attitudes and understanding of the characters, comments by the narrator)?

2. What do the various fantasies of Estelle have in common, and what do they show about her? How does Atwood control the tone so as to keep Estelle from considering rape as a problem in psychology or criminology?

3. Describe the story's tone. How does tone affect your perception of Estelle?

4. Consider the tone of the very last paragraph. What is Atwood's apparent attitude toward the subject? How is it tempered by her attitude toward Estelle?

5. Studies point out that rape is an act of violence. What do the women in the story do to deflect the seriousness of the potential violence involved?

KATE CHOPIN (1851–1904)

Born in St. Louis, Chopin lived in Louisiana from the time of her marriage until 1882. After her husband's death she returned to St. Louis and began to write. She published two collections of stories based on the life she had known back in Louisiana: Bayou Folk *(1894) and* A Night in Acadie *(1897). However, she became best known for her major novel,* The Awakening *(1899), which aroused negative reactions because it mentioned taboo subjects like adultery and miscegenation. Indeed, the critical disapproval was so intense that Chopin published no further works, even though she was at the height of her literary power and lived five years after the controversy.*

The Story of an Hour   1894

Knowing that Mrs. Mallard was afflicted with a heart trouble, great care was taken to break to her as gently as possible the news of her husband's death.

It was her sister Josephine who told her, in broken sentences: veiled hints that revealed in half concealing. Her husband's friend Richards was there, too, near her. It was he who had been in the newspaper office when intelligence of the railroad disaster was received, with Brently Mallard's name leading the list of "killed." He had only taken the time to assure himself of its truth by a second telegram, and had hastened to forestall any less careful, less tender friend in bearing the sad message.

She did not hear the story as many women have heard the same, with a paralyzed inability to accept its significance. She wept at once, with sudden, wild abandonment, in her sister's arms. When the storm of grief had spent itself she went away to her room alone. She would have no one follow her.

There stood, facing the open window, a comfortable, roomy armchair. Into this she sank, pressed down by a physical exhaustion that haunted her body and seemed to reach into her soul.

She could see in the open square before her house the tops of trees that were all aquiver with the new spring life. The delicious breath of rain was in the air. In the street below a peddler was crying his wares. The notes of a distant song which some one was singing reached her faintly, and countless sparrows were twittering in the eaves.

There were patches of blue sky showing here and there through the clouds that had met and piled one above the other in the west facing her window.

She sat with her head thrown back upon the cushion of the chair, quite motionless, except when a sob came up into her throat and shook her, as a child who has cried itself to sleep continues to sob in its dreams.

She was young, with a fair, calm face, whose lines bespoke repression and even a certain strength. But now there was a dull stare in her eyes, whose gaze was fixed away off yonder on one of those patches of blue sky. It was not a glance of reflection, but rather in-dicated a suspension of intelligent thought.

There was something coming to her and she was waiting for it, fearfully. What was it? She did not know; it was too subtle and elusive to name. But she felt it, creeping out of the sky, reaching toward her through the sounds, the scents, the color that filled the air.

Now her bosom rose and fell tumultuously. She was beginning to recognize this thing that was approaching to possess her, and she was striving to beat it back with her will—as powerless as her two white slender hands would have been.

When she abandoned herself a little whispered word escaped her slightly parted lips. She said it over and over under her breath: "free, free, free!" The vacant stare and the look of terror that had followed it went from her eyes. They stayed keen and bright. Her pulses beat fast, and the coursing blood warmed and relaxed every inch of her body.

She did not stop to ask if it were or were not a monstrous joy that held her. A clear and exalted perception enabled her to dismiss the suggestion as trivial.

She knew that she would weep again when she saw the kind, tender hands folded in death; the face that had never looked save with love upon her, fixed and gray and dead. But she saw beyond that bitter moment a long procession of years to come that would be-long to her absolutely. And she opened and spread her arms out to them in welcome.

There would be no one to live for during those coming years; she would live for herself. There would be no powerful will bending hers in that blind persistence with which men and women believe they have a right to impose a private will upon a fellow-creature. A kind intention or a cruel intention made the act seem no less a crime as she looked upon it in that brief moment of illumination.

And yet she had loved him—sometimes. Often she had not. What did it matter! What could love, the unsolved mystery, count for in face of this possession of self-assertion which she suddenly recognized as the strongest impulse of her being!

"Free! Body and soul free!" she kept whispering.

Josephine was kneeling before the closed door with her lips to the keyhole, im-ploring for admission. "Louise, open the door! I beg; open the door—you will make yourself ill. What are you doing, Louise? For heaven's sake open the door."

"Go away. I am not making myself ill." No; she was drinking in a very elixir of life through that open window.

Her fancy was running riot along those days ahead of her. Spring days, and summer days, and all sorts of days that would be her own. She breathed a quick prayer that life might be long. It was only yesterday she had thought with a shudder that life might be long.

She arose at length and opened the door to her sister's importunities. There was a   20
feverish triumph in her eyes, and she carried herself unwittingly like a goddess of Victory. She clasped her sister's waist, and together they descended the stairs. Richards stood
waiting for them at the bottom.

Some one was opening the front door with a latchkey. It was Brently Mallard who
entered, a little travel-stained, composedly carrying his grip-sack and umbrella. He had
been far from the scene of accident, and did not even know there had been one. He
stood amazed at Josephine's piercing cry: at Richards' quick motion to screen him from
the view of his wife.

But Richards was too late.

When the doctors came they said she had died of heart disease—of joy that kills.

QUESTIONS

1. What do we learn about Louise's husband? How has he justified her responses?
   How are your judgments about him controlled by the context of the story?

2. Analyze the tone of paragraph 5. How is the imagery here (and in the following
   paragraphs) appropriate for her developing mood?

3. What is the apparent attitude of the narrator toward the institution of marriage,
   and what elements of tone make this apparent?

4. What do Louise's sister and Richards have in common? How do their attitudes
   contribute to the irony of the story?

5. Consider the tone of the last paragraph. What judgment is being made about
   how men view their importance to women?

JACK HODGINS (b. 1938)

*Both a novelist and short-story writer, Hodgins is a native of
British Columbia. His works, some quite realistic and others tinged
with the aura of "magic realism," are derived from his knowledge of
the people and the countryside of this area. Among his novels are*
The Invention of the Word *(1977),* The Resurrection of
Joseph Bourne *(1979),* The Honorary Patron *(1987), and*
The Macken Charm *(1995). He has also written works for children and is the editor of three anthologies. His ideas about writing
fiction are the substance of* A Passion for Narrative, *which was
published in 1993. His story collections are* Spit Delaney's Island *(1977) and* The Barclay
Family Theater *(1981), in which Hodgins included "The Concert Stages of Europe."*

The Concert Stages of Europe ⸻⸺⸻ 1978

Now I know Cornelia Horncastle would say I'm blaming the wrong person. I know that. I
know too that she would say thirty years is a long time to hold a grudge, and that if I needed someone to blame for the fact that I made a fool of myself in front of the whole district
and ruined my life in the process, then I ought to look around for the person who gave
me my high-flown ideas in the first place. But she would be wrong; because there is no
doubt I'd have led a different sort of life if it weren't for her, if it weren't for that piano
keyboard her parents presented her with on her eleventh birthday. And everything—
everything would have been different if that piano keyboard hadn't been the kind made

out of stiff paper that you unfolded and laid out across the kitchen table in order to do your practising.

I don't suppose there would have been all that much harm in her having the silly thing, if only my mother hadn't got wind of it. What a fantastic idea, she said. You could learn to play without even making a sound! You could practise your scales without having to hear that awful racket when you hit a wrong note! A genius must have thought of it, she said. Certainly someone who'd read his Keats: *Heard melodies are sweet, but those unheard are sweeter.* "And don't laugh," she said, "because Cornelia Horncastle is learning to play the piano and her mother doesn't even have to miss an episode of *Ma Perkins* while she does it."

That girl, people had told her, would be giving concerts in Europe some day, command performances before royalty, and her parents hadn't even had to fork out the price of a piano. It was obvious proof, if you needed it, that a person didn't have to be rich to get somewhere in this world.

In fact, Cornelia's parents hadn't needed to put out even the small amount that paper keyboard would have cost. A piano teacher named Mrs. Humphries had moved onto the old Dendoff place and, discovering that almost no one in the district owned a piano, gave the keyboard to the Horncastles along with a year's free lessons. It was her idea, apparently, that when everyone heard how quickly Cornelia was learning they'd be lining up to send her their children for lessons. She wanted to make the point that having no piano needn't stop anyone from becoming a pianist. No doubt she had a vision of paper keyboards in every house in Waterville, of children everywhere thumping their scales out on the kitchen table without offending anyone's ears, of a whole generation turning silently into Paderewskis without ever having played a note.

They would, I suppose, have to play a real piano when they went to her house for 5 lessons once a week, but I was never able to find out for myself, because all that talk of Cornelia's marvellous career on the concert stages of Europe did not prompt my parents to buy one of those fake keyboards or sign me up for lessons with Mrs. Humphries. My mother was born a Barclay, which meant she had a few ideas of her own, and Cornelia's glorious future prompted her to go one better. We would buy a *real* piano, she announced. And I would be sent to a teacher we could trust, not to that newcomer. If those concert stages of Europe were ever going to hear the talent of someone from the stump ranches of Waterville, it wouldn't be Cornelia Horncastle, it would be Barclay Desmond. Me.

My father nearly choked on his coffee. "But Clay's a boy!"

"So what?" my mother said. *All* those famous players used to be boys. What did he think Chopin was? Or Tchaikovsky?

My father was so embarrassed that his throat began to turn a dark pink. Some things were too unnatural even to think about.

But eventually she won him over. "Think how terrible you'd feel," she said, "if he ended up in the bush, like you. If Mozart's father had worked for the Comox Logging Company and thought piano-playing was for sissies, where would the world be today?"

My father had no answer to that. He'd known since before his marriage that though 10 my mother would put up with being married to a logger, expecting every day to be made a widow, she wouldn't tolerate for one minute the notion that a child of hers would follow him up into those hills. The children of Lenora Barclay would enter the professions.

She was right, he had to agree; working in the woods was the last thing in the world he wanted for his sons. He'd rather they take up ditch-digging or begging than have to work for that miserable logging company, or take their orders from a son-of-a-bitch like Tiny Beechman, or get their skulls cracked open like Stanley Kirck. It was a rotten way to make a living, and if he'd only had a decent education he could have made something of himself.

Of course, I knew he was saying all this just for my mother's benefit. He didn't really believe it for a minute. My father loved his work. I could tell by the way he was always talking about Ab Jennings and Shorty Cresswell, the men he worked with. I could tell by the excitement that mounted in him every year as the time grew near for the annual festival of loggers' sports where he usually won the bucking contest. It was obvious, I thought, that the man really wanted nothing more in this world than that one of his sons should follow in his footsteps. And much as I disliked the idea, I was sure that I was the one he'd set his hopes on. Kenny was good in school. Laurel was a girl. I was the obvious choice. I even decided that what he'd pegged me for was high-rigger. I was going to be one of those men who risked their necks climbing hundreds of feet up the bare lonely spar tree to hang the rigging from the top. Of course I would fall and kill myself the first time I tried it, I knew that, but there was no way I could convey my hesitation to my father since he would never openly admit that this was really his goal for me.

And playing the piano on the concert stages of Europe was every bit as unattractive. "Why not Kenny?" I said, when the piano had arrived, by barge, from Vancouver.

"He's too busy already with his school work," my mother said. Kenny was hoping for a scholarship, which meant he got out of just about everything unpleasant.

"What about Laurel?"

"With her short fat fingers?"

In the meantime, she said, though she was no piano-player herself (a great sigh here for what might have been), she had no trouble at all identifying which of those ivory keys was the all-important Middle C and would show it to me, to memorize, so that I wouldn't look like a total know-nothing when I showed up tomorrow for my first lesson. She'd had one piano lesson herself as a girl, she told me, and had learned all about Mister Middle C, but she'd never had a second lesson because her time was needed by her father, outside, helping with the chores. Seven daughters altogether, no sons, and she was the one who was the most often expected to fill the role of a boy. The rest of them had found the time to learn chords and chromatic scales and all those magic things she'd heard them practising while she was scrubbing out the dairy and cutting the runners off strawberry plants. They'd all become regular show-offs in one way or another, learning other instruments as well, putting on their own concerts and playing in dance bands and earning a reputation all over the district as entertaining livewires—The Barclay Sisters. And no one ever guessed that all the while she was dreaming about herself at that keyboard, tinkling away, playing beautiful music before huge audiences in elegant theatres.

"Then it isn't me that should be taking lessons," I said. "It's you."

"Don't be silly." But she walked to the new piano and pressed down one key, a black one, and looked as if I'd tempted her there for a minute. "It's too late now," she said. And then she sealed my fate: "But I just know that you're going to be a great pianist."

When my mother "just knew" something, that was as good as guaranteeing it already completed. It was her way of controlling the future and, incidentally, the rest of us. By "just knowing" things, she went through life commanding the future to fit into certain patterns she desired while we scurried around making sure that it worked out that way so she'd never have to be disappointed. She'd had one great disappointment as a girl—we were never quite sure what it was, since it was only alluded to in whispers with far-off looks—and it was important that it never happen again. I was trapped.

People were always asking what you were going to be when you grew up. As if your wishes counted. In the first six years of my life the country had convinced me it wanted me to grow up and get killed fighting Germans and Japanese. I'd seen the coils of barbed wire along the beach and knew they were there just to slow down the enemy while I went looking for my gun. The teachers at school obviously wanted me to grow up and become

15

20

a teacher just like them, because as far as I could see nothing they ever taught me could be of any use or interest to a single adult in the world except someone getting paid to teach it to someone else. My mother was counting on my becoming a pianist with a swallow-tail coat and standing ovations. And my father, despite all his noises to the contrary, badly wanted me to climb into the crummy every morning with him and ride out those gravelly roads into mountains and risk my life destroying forests.

I did not want to be a logger. I did not want to be a teacher. I did not want to be a soldier. And I certainly did not want to be a pianist. If anyone had ever asked me what I did want to be when I grew up, in a way that meant they expected the truth, I'd have said quite simply that what I wanted was to be a Finn.

Our new neighbours, the Korhonens, were Finns. And being a Finn, I'd been told, meant something very specific. A Finn would give you the shirt off his back, a Finn was as honest as the day is long, a Finn could drink anybody under the table and beat up half a dozen Germans and Irishmen without trying, a Finn was not afraid of work, a Finn kept a house so clean you could eat off the floors. I knew all these things before ever meeting our neighbours, but as soon as I had met them I was able to add a couple more generalizations of my own to the catalogue: Finnish girls were blonde and beautiful and flirtatious, and Finnish boys were strong, brave, and incredibly intelligent. These conclusions were reached immediately after meeting Lilja Korhonen, whose turned-up nose and blue eyes fascinated me from the beginning, and Larry Korhonen, who was already a teenager and told me for starters that he was actually Superman, having learned to fly after long hours of practice off their barn roof. Mr. and Mrs. Korhonen, of course, fitted exactly all the things my parents had told me about Finns in general. And so I decided my ambition in life was to be just like them.

I walked over to their house every Saturday afternoon and pretended to read their coloured funnies. I got in on the weekly steam-bath with Larry and his father in the sauna down by the barn. Mr. Korhonen, a patient man whose eyes sparkled at my eager attempts, taught me to count to ten—*yksi, kaksi, kolme, nelja, viisi, kuusi, seitseman, kahdeksan, yhdeksan, kymmenen*. I helped Mrs. Korhonen scrub her linoleum floors and put down newspapers so no one could walk on them, then I gorged myself on cinnamon cookies and *kala loota* and coffee sucked through a sugar cube. If there was something to be caught from just being around them, I wanted to catch it. And since being a Finn seemed to be a full-time occupation, I didn't have much patience with my parents, who behaved as if there were other things you had to prepare yourself for.

The first piano teacher they sent me to was Aunt Jessie, who lived in a narrow, cramped house up a gravel road that led to the mountains. She'd learned to play as a girl in Toronto, but she had no pretensions about being a real teacher, she was only doing this as a favour to my parents so they wouldn't have to send me to that Mrs. Humphries, an outsider. But one of the problems was that Aunt Jessie—who was no aunt of mine at all, simply one of those family friends who somehow get saddled with an honorary family title—was exceptionally beautiful. She was so attractive, in fact, that even at the age of ten I had difficulty keeping my eyes or my mind on the lessons. She exuded a dreamy sort of delicate femininity; her soft, intimate voice made the hair on the back of my neck stand on end. Besides that, her own playing was so much more pleasant to listen to than my own stumbling clangs and clunks that she would often begin to show me how to do something and become so carried away with the sound of her own music that she just kept right on playing through the rest of my half-hour. It was a simple matter to persuade her to dismiss me early every week so that I'd have a little time to play in the creek that ran past the back of her house, poling a homemade raft up and down the length of her property while her daughters paid me nickels and candies for a ride. At the end of a year my

25

parents suspected I wasn't progressing as fast as I should. They found out why on the day I fell in the creek and nearly drowned, had to be revived by a distraught Aunt Jessie, and was driven home soaked and shivering in the back seat of her old Hudson.

Mr. Korhonen and my father were huddled over the taken-apart cream separator on the verandah when Aunt Jessie brought me up to the door. My father, when he saw me, had that peculiar look on his face that was halfway between amusement and concern, but Mr. Korhonen laughed openly. "That boy lookit like a drowny rat."

I felt like a drowned rat too, but I joined his laughter. I was sure this would be the end of my piano career, and could hardly wait to see my mother roll her eyes to the ceiling, throw out her arms, and say, "I give up."

She did nothing of the sort. She tightened her lips and told Aunt Jessie how disappointed she was. "No wonder the boy still stumbles around on that keyboard like a blindfolded rabbit; he's not going to learn the piano while he's out risking his life on the *river!*"

When I came downstairs in dry clothes Aunt Jessie had gone, no doubt wishing she'd left me to drown in the creek, and my parents and the Korhonens were all in the kitchen drinking coffee. The Korhonens sat at either side of the table, smoking hand-rolled cigarettes and squinting at me through the smoke. Mrs. Korhonen could blow beautiful white streams down her nostrils. They'd left their gumboots on the piece of newspaper just inside the door, of course, and wore the same kind of grey work-socks on their feet that my father always wore on his. My father was leaning against the wall with both arms folded across his chest inside his wide elastic braces, as he sometimes did, swishing his mug gently as if he were trying to bring something up from the bottom. My mother, however, was unable to alight anywhere. She slammed wood down into the fire-box of the stove, she rattled dishes in the sink water, she slammed cupboard doors, she went around the room with the coffee pot, refilling mugs, and all the while she sang the song of her betrayal, cursing her own stupidity for sending me to a friend instead of to a professional teacher, and suddenly in a flash of inspiration dumping all the blame on my father: "If you hadn't made me feel it was somehow pointless I wouldn't have felt guilty about spending more money!"

From behind the drifting shreds of smoke Mr. Korhonen grinned at me. Sucked laughter between his teeth. "Yust *teenk*, boy, looks like-it you're saved!"   30

Mrs. Korhonen stabbed out her cigarette in an ashtray, picked a piece of tobacco off her tongue, and composed her face into the most serious and ladylike expression she could muster. "Yeh! Better he learn to drive the tractor." And swung me a conspirator's grin.

"Not on your life," my mother said. Driving a machine may have been a good enough ambition for some people, she believed, but the Barclays had been in this country for four generations and she knew there were a few things higher. "What we'll do is send him to a real teacher. Mrs. Greensborough."

Mrs. Greensborough was well known for putting on a public recital in town once a year, climaxing the program with her own rendition of Grieg's Piano Concerto—so beautiful that all went home, it was said, with tears in their eyes. The problem with Mrs. Greensborough had nothing to do with her teaching. She was, as far as I could see, an excellent piano teacher. And besides, there was something rather exciting about playing on her piano, which was surrounded and nearly buried by a thousand tropical plants and dozens of cages full of squawking birds. Every week's lesson was rather like putting on a concert in the midst of the Amazon jungle. There was even a monkey that swung through the branches and sat on the top of the piano with the metronome between its paws. And Mrs. Greensborough was at the same time warm and demanding, complimentary and hard to please—though given a little, like Aunt Jessie, to taking off on long passages of her own playing, as if she'd forgotten I was there.

It took a good hour's hard bicycling on uphill gravel roads before I could present myself for the lesson—past a dairy farm, a pig farm, a turkey farm, a dump, and a good long stretch of bush—then more washboard road through heavy timber where driveways disappeared into the trees and one dog after another lay in wait for its weekly battle with my right foot. Two spaniels, one Irish setter, and a bulldog. But it wasn't a spaniel or a setter or even a bulldog that met me on the driveway of the Greensborough's chicken farm, it was a huge German shepherd that came barking down the slope the second I had got the gate shut, and stuck its nose into my crotch. And kept it there, growling menacingly, the whole time it took me to back him up to the door of the house. There was no doubt in my mind that I would come home from piano lesson one Saturday minus a few parts. Once I had got to the house, I tried to get inside quickly and shut the door in his face, leaving him out there in the din of cackling hens; but he always got his nose between the door and the jamb, growled horribly and pushed himself inside so that he could lie on the floor at my feet and watch me hungrily the whole time I sat at the kitchen table waiting for Ginny Stamp to finish off her lesson and get out of there. By the time my turn came around my nerves were too frayed for me to get much benefit out of the lesson.

Still, somehow I learned. That Mrs. Greensborough was a marvellous teacher, my   35
mother said. The woman really knew her stuff. And I was such a fast-learning student that it took less than two years for my mother to begin thinking it was time the world heard from me.

"Richy Ryder," she said, "is coming to town."

"What?"

"Richy Ryder, CJMT. *The Talent Show.*"

I'd heard the program. Every Saturday night Richy Ryder was in a different town somewhere in the province, hosting his one-hour talent contest from the stage of a local theatre and giving away free trips to Hawaii.

Something rolled over in my stomach.   40

"And here's the application form right here," she said, whipping two sheets of paper out of her purse to slap down on the table.

"No thank you," I said. If she thought I was going in it, she was crazy.

"Don't be silly. What harm is there in trying?" My mother always answered objections with great cheerfulness, as if they were hardly worth considering.

"I'll make a fool of myself."

"You play beautifully," she said. "It's amazing how far you've come in only two years.   45
And besides, even if you don't win, the experience would be good for you."

"You have to go door-to-door ahead of time, begging for pledges, for money."

"Not begging," she said. She plunged her hands into the sink, peeling carrots so fast I couldn't see the blade of the vegetable peeler. "Just giving people a chance to vote for you. A dollar a vote." The carrot dropped, skinned naked, another one was picked up. She looked out the window now toward the barn and, still smiling, delivered the argument that never failed. "I just know you'd win it if you went in, I can feel it in my bones."

"Not this time!" I shouted, nearly turning myself inside out with the terror. "Not this time. I just can't do it."

Yet somehow I found myself riding my bicycle up and down all the roads around Waterville, knocking at people's doors, explaining the contest, and asking for their money and their votes. I don't know why I did it. Perhaps I was doing it for the same reason I was tripping over everything, knocking things off tables, slamming my shoulder into doorjambs; I just couldn't help it, everything had gone out of control. I'd wakened one morning that year and found myself six feet two inches tall and as narrow as a fence stake. My feet were so far away they seemed to have nothing to do with me. My hands flopped around on the ends of those lanky arms like fish, something alive. My legs had grown so fast the bones in my knees parted and I had to wear elastic bandages to keep from falling apart. When I turned a corner on my bicycle, one knee would bump the handlebar, throwing me into the ditch. I was the same person as before, apparently, saddled with this new body I didn't know what to do with. Everything had gone out of control. I seemed to have nothing to do with the direction of my own life. It was perfectly logical that I should end up playing the piano on the radio, selling myself to the countryside for a chance to fly off to Hawaii and lie on the sand under the whispering palms.

There were actually two prizes offered. The all-expense, ten-day trip to Hawaii would go to the person who brought in the most votes for himself, a dollar a vote. But lest someone accuse the radio station of getting its values confused, there was also a prize for the person judged by a panel of experts to have the most talent. This prize, which was donated by Nelson's Hardware, was a leatherette footstool.

"It's not the prize that's important," people told me. "It's the chance to be heard by all those people."

I preferred not to think of all those people. It seemed to me that if I were cut out to be a concert pianist it would be my teacher and not my parents encouraging me in this thing. Mrs. Greensborough, once she'd forked over her two dollars for two votes, said nothing at all. No doubt she was hoping I'd keep her name out of it.

But it had taken no imagination on my part to figure out that if I were to win the only prize worth trying for, the important thing was not to spend long hours at the keyboard, practising, but to get out on the road hammering at doors, on the telephone calling relatives, down at the General Store approaching strangers who stopped for gas. Daily piano practice shrank to one or two quick run-throughs of "The Robin's Return," school homework shrank to nothing at all, and home chores just got ignored. My brother and sister filled in for me, once in a while, so the chickens wouldn't starve to death and the woodbox would never be entirely empty, but they did it gracelessly. It was amazing, they said, how much time a great pianist had to spend out on the road, meeting his public. Becoming famous, they said, was more work than it was worth.

And becoming famous, I discovered, was what people assumed I was after. "You'll go places," they told me. "You'll put this place on the old map." I was a perfect combination of my father's down-to-earth get-up-and-go and my mother's finer sensitivity, they said. How wonderful to see a young person with such high ambition!

"I always knew this old place wouldn't be good enough to hold you," my grandmother said as she fished out a five-dollar bill from her purse. But my mother's sisters, who appeared from all parts of the old farmhouse in order to contribute a single collective vote, had some reservations to express. Eleanor, the youngest, said she doubted I'd be able to carry it off, I'd probably freeze when I was faced with a microphone, I'd forget what a piano was for. Christina announced she was betting I'd faint, or have to run out to the bathroom right in the middle of my piece. And Mabel, red-headed Mabel who'd played accordion once in an amateur show, said she remembered a boy who made such a fool of himself in one of these things that he went home and blew off his head. "Don't be so morbid," my grandmother said. "The boy probably had no talent. Clay here is destined for higher things."

From behind her my grandfather winked. He seldom had a chance to contribute more than that to a conversation. He waited until we were alone to stuff a five-dollar bill in my pocket and squeeze my arm.

I preferred my grandmother's opinion of me to the aunts'. I began to feed people lies so they'd think that about me—that I was destined for dizzying heights. I wanted to be a great pianist, I said, and if I won that trip to Hawaii I'd trade it in for the money so

50

55

that I could go off and study at the Toronto Conservatory. I'd heard of the Toronto Conservatory only because it was printed in big black letters on the front cover of all those yellow books of finger exercises I was expected to practise.

I don't know why people gave me their money. Pity, perhaps. Maybe it was impossible to say no to a six-foot-two-inch thirteen-year-old who trips over his own bike in front of your house, falls up your bottom step, blushes red with embarrassment when you open the door, and tells you he wants your money for a talent contest so he can become a Great Artist. At any rate, by the day of the contest I'd collected enough money to put me in the third spot. I would have to rely on pledges from the studio audience and phone-in pledges from the radio audience to rocket me up to first place. The person in second place when I walked into that theatre to take my seat down front with the rest of the contestants was Cornelia Horncastle.

I don't know how she managed it so secretly. I don't know where she found the people to give her money, living in the same community as I did, unless all those people who gave me their dollar bills when I knocked on their doors had just given her two the day before. Maybe she'd gone into town, canvassing street after street, something my parents wouldn't let me do on the grounds that town people already had enough strangers banging on their doors every day. Once I'd got outside the vague boundaries of Waterville I was to approach only friends or relatives or people who worked in the woods with my dad, or stores that had—as my mother put it—done a good business out of us over the years. Cornelia Horncastle, in order to get herself secretly into that second place, must have gone wild in town. Either that or discovered a rich relative.

She sat at the other end of the front row of contestants, frowning over the sheets of music in her hands. A short nod and a quick smile were all she gave me. Like the other contestants, I was kept busy licking my dry lips, rubbing my sweaty palms together, wondering if I should whip out to the bathroom one last time, and rubbernecking to get a look at people as they filled up the theatre behind us. Mrs. Greensborough, wearing dark glasses and a big floppy hat, was jammed into the far corner at the rear, studying her program. Mr. and Mrs. Korhonen and Lilja came partway down the aisle and found seats near the middle. Mr. Korhonen winked at me. Larry, who was not quite the hero he had once been, despite the fact that he'd recently beat up one of the teachers and set fire to the bus shelter, came in with my brother Kenny—both of them looking uncomfortable—and slid into a back seat. My parents came all the way down front, so they could look back up the slope and pick out the seats they wanted. My mother smiled as she always did in public, as if she expected the most delightful surprise at any moment. They took seats near the front. Laurel was with them, reading a book.

My mother's sisters—with husbands, boyfriends, a few of my cousins—filled up the entire middle section of the back row. Eleanor, who was just a few years older than myself, crossed her eyes and stuck out her tongue when she saw that I'd turned to look. Mabel pulled in her chin and held up her hands, which she caused to tremble and shake. Time to be nervous, she was suggesting, in case I forgot. Bella, Christina, Gladdy, Frieda—all sat puffed up like members of a royal family, or the owners of this theatre, looking down over the crowd as if they believed every one of these people had come here expressly to watch their nephew and for no other reason. "Look, it's the Barclay girls," I heard someone behind me say. And someone else: "Oh, *them*." The owner of the first voice giggled. "It's a wonder they aren't all entered in this thing, you know how they like to perform." A snort. "They *are* performing, just watch them." I could tell by the muffled "Shhh" and the rustling of clothing that one of them was nudging the other and pointing at me, at the back of my neck. "One of them's son." When I turned again, Eleanor stood up in the aisle by her seat, did a few steps of a tap dance, and quickly sat down. In case I was tempted to take myself seriously.

When my mother caught my eye, she mouthed a silent message: stop gawking at the audience, I was letting people see how unusual all this was to me, instead of taking it in my stride like a born performer. She indicated with her head that I should notice the stage.

As if I hadn't already absorbed every detail. It was exactly as she must have hoped. A great black concert grand with the lid lifted sat out near the front of the stage, against a painted backdrop of palm trees along a sandy beach, and—in great scrawled letters— the words "Richy Ryder's CJMT Talent Festival." A long blackboard leaned against one end of the proscenium arch, with all the contestants' names on it and the rank order of each. Someone named Brenda Roper was in first place. On the opposite side of the stage, a microphone seemed to have grown up out of a heap of pineapples. I felt sick.

Eventually Richy Ryder came out of whatever backstage room he'd been hiding in and passed down the row of contestants, identifying us and telling us to get up onto the stage when our turns came without breaking our necks on those steps. "You won't be nervous, when you get up there," he said. "I'll make you feel at ease." He was looking off somewhere else as he said it, and I could see his jaw muscles straining to hold back a yawn. And he wasn't fooling me with his "you won't be nervous" either, because I knew without a doubt that the minute I got up on that stage I would throw up all over the piano.

Under the spotlight, Richy Ryder acted like a different person. He did not look the least bit like yawning while he told the audience the best way of holding their hands to get the most out of applause, cautioned them against whistling or yelling obscenities, painted a glorious picture of the life ahead for the talented winner of this contest, complimented the audience on the number of happy, shiny faces he could see out there in the seats, and told them how lucky they were to have this opportunity of showing off the fine young talent of the valley to all the rest of the province. I slid down in my seat, sure that I would rather die than go through with this thing.

65

The first contestant was a fourteen-year-old girl dressed up like a gypsy, singing something in a foreign language. According to the blackboard she was way down in ninth place, so I didn't pay much attention until her voice cracked open in the middle of a high note and she clutched at her throat with both hands, a look of incredulous surprise on her face. She stopped right there, face a brilliant red, and after giving the audience a quick curtsey hurried off the stage. A great beginning, I thought. If people were going to fall to pieces like that through the whole show no one would even notice my upchucking on the Heintzman. I had a vision of myself dry-heaving the whole way through "The Robin's Return."

Number two stepped up to the microphone and answered all of Richy Ryder's questions as if they were some kind of test he had to pass in order to be allowed to perform. Yes sir, his name was Roger Casey, he said with a face drawn long and narrow with seriousness, and in case that wasn't enough he added that his father was born in Digby, Nova Scotia, and his mother was born Esther Romaine in a little house just a couple of blocks up the street from the theatre, close to the Native Sons' Hall, and had gone to school with the mayor though she'd dropped out of Grade Eight to get a job at the Safeway cutting meat. And yes sir, he was going to play the saxophone because he'd taken lessons for four years from Mr. D. P. Rowbottom on Seventh Street though he'd actually started out on the trumpet until he decided he didn't like it all that much. He came right out to the edge of the stage, toes sticking over, leaned back like a rooster about to crow, and blasted out "Softly As in a Morning Sunrise" so loud and hard that I thought his bulging eyes would pop right out of his head and his straining lungs would blast holes through that red-and-white shirt. Everyone moved forward, tense and straining, waiting for something terrible to happen—for him to fall off the stage or explode or go sailing off into the air from the force of his own fantastic intensity—but he stopped suddenly and everyone fell back exhausted and sweaty to clap for him.

The third contestant was less reassuring. A kid with talent. A smart-aleck ten-year-old with red hair, who told the audience he was going into show business when he grew up, started out playing "Swanee River" on his banjo, switched in the middle of a bar to a mouth organ, tap-danced across the stage to play a few bars on the piano, and finished off on a trombone he'd had stashed away behind the palm tree. He bowed, grinned, flung himself around the stage as if he'd spent his whole life on it, and looked as if he'd do his whole act again quite happily if the audience wanted him to. By the time the tremendous applause had died down my jaw was aching from the way I'd been grinding my teeth the whole time he was up there. The audience would not have gone quite so wild over him, I thought, if he hadn't been wearing a hearing aid and a leg brace.

Then it was my turn. A strange calm fell over me when my name was called, the kind of calm that I imagine comes over a person about to be executed when his mind finally buckles under the horror it has been faced with, something too terrible to believe in. I wondered for a moment if I had died. But no, my body at least hadn't died, for it transported me unbidden across the front of the audience, up the staircase (with only a slight stumble on the second step, hardly noticeable), and across the great wide stage of the theatre to stand facing Richy Ryder's enormous expanse of white smiling teeth, beside the microphone.

"And you are Barclay Philip Desmond," he said.   70

"Yes," I said.

And again "yes," because I realized that not only had my voice come out as thin and high as the squeal of a dry buzz-saw, but the microphone was at least a foot too low. I had to bend my knees to speak into it.

"You don't live in town, do you?" he said. He had no intention of adjusting that microphone. "You come from a place called . . . Waterville. A logging and farming settlement?"

"Yes," I said.

And again "yes" because while he was speaking my legs had straightened up, I'd returned to my full height and had to duck again for the microphone.   75

He was speaking to me but his eyes, I could see, were busy keeping all that audience gathered together, while his voice and his mind were obviously concentrated on the thousands of invisible people who were crouched inside that microphone, listening, the thousands of people who—I imagined now—were pulled up close to their sets all over the province, wondering if I was actually a pair of twins or if my high voice had some peculiar way of echoing itself, a few tones lower.

"Does living in the country like that mean you have to milk the cows every morning before you go to school?"

"Yes."

And again "yes."

I could see Mrs. Greensborough cowering in the back corner. I promise not to   80
mention you, I thought. And the Korhonens, grinning. I had clearly passed over into another world they couldn't believe in.

"If you've got a lot of farm chores to do, when do you find the time to practise the piano?"

He had me this time. A "yes" wouldn't be good enough. "Right after school," I said, and ducked to repeat. "Right after school. As soon as I get home. For an hour."

"And I just bet," he said, throwing the audience an enormous wink, "that like every other red-blooded country kid you hate every minute of it. You'd rather be outside playing baseball."

The audience laughed. I could see my mother straining forward; she still had the all-purpose waiting-for-the-surprise smile on her lips but her eyes were frowning at the master of ceremonies. She did not approve of the comment. And behind that face she was no doubt thinking to herself "I just know he's going to win" over and over so hard that she was getting pains in the back of her neck. Beside her, my father had a tight grin on his face. He was chuckling to himself, and sliding a look around the room to see how the others were taking this.

Up at the back, most of my aunts—and their husbands, their boyfriends—had tilt- 85
ed their chins down to their chests, offering me only the tops of their heads. Eleanor, however, had both hands behind her neck. She was laughing harder than anyone else.

Apparently I was not expected to respond to the last comment, for he had another question as soon as the laughter had died. "How old are you, son?"

"Thirteen."

For once I remembered to duck the first time.

"Thirteen. Does your wife like the idea of your going on the radio like this?"

Again the audience laughed. My face burned. I felt tears in my eyes. I had no con- 90
trol over my face. I tried to laugh like everyone else but realized I probably looked like an idiot. Instead, I frowned and looked embarrassed and kicked at one shoe with the toe of the other.

"Just a joke," he said, "just a joke." The jerk knew he'd gone too far. "And now seri- ously, one last question before I turn you loose on those ivories over there."

My heart had started to thump so noisily I could hardly hear him. My hands, I real- ized, had gone numb. There was no feeling at all in my fingers. How was I ever going to play the piano?

"What are you going to be when you grow up?"

The thumping stopped. My heart stopped. A strange, cold silence settled over the world. I was going to die right in front of all those people. What I was going to be was a corpse, dead of humiliation, killed in a trap I hadn't seen being set. What must have been only a few seconds crawled by while something crashed around in my head, trying to get out. I sensed the audience, hoping for some help from them. My mother had settled back in her seat and for the first time that surprise-me smile had gone. Rather, she looked confident, sure of what I was about to say.

And suddenly, I was aware of familiar faces all over that theatre. Neighbours. 95
Friends of the family. My aunts. People who had heard me answer that question at their doors, people who thought they knew what I wanted.

There was nothing left of Mrs. Greensborough but the top of her big hat. My fa- ther, too, was looking down at the floor between his feet. I saw myself falling from that spar tree, high in the mountains.

"Going to be?" I said, turning so fast that I bumped the microphone with my hand, which turned out after all not to be numb.

I ducked.

"Nothing," I said. "I don't know. Maybe . . . maybe nothing at all."

I don't know who it was that snorted when I screwed up the stool, sat down, and 100
stood up to screw it down again. I don't know how well I played, I wasn't listening. I don't know how loud the audience clapped, I was in a hurry to get back to my seat. I don't know what the other contestants did, I wasn't paying any attention except when Cornelia Horncastle got up on the stage, told the whole world she was going to be a professional pianist, and sat down to rattle off Rachmaninoff's Rhapsody on a Theme of Paganini as if she'd been playing for fifty years. As far as I know it may have been the first time she'd ever heard herself play it. She had a faint look of surprise on her face the whole time, as if she couldn't quite get over the way the keys went down when you touched them.

As soon as Cornelia came down off the stage, smiling modestly, and got back into her seat, Richy Ryder announced a fifteen-minute intermission while the talent judges made their decision and the studio audience went out into the lobby to pledge their money and their votes. Now that the talent had been displayed, people could spend their money according to what they'd heard rather than according to who happened to come knocking on their door. Most of the contestants got up to stretch their legs but I figured I'd stood up once too often that night and stayed in my seat. The lower exit was not far away; I contemplated using it; I could hitch-hike home and be in bed before any of the others got out of there.

I was stopped, though, by my father, who sat down in the seat next to mine and put a greasy carton of popcorn in my lap.

"Well," he said, "that's that."

His neck was flushed. This must have been a terrible evening for him. He had a carton of popcorn himself and tipped it up to gather a huge mouthful. I had never before in my life, I realized, seen my father eat popcorn. It must have been worse for him than I thought.

Not one of the aunts was anywhere in sight! I could see my mother standing in the far aisle, talking to Mrs. Korhonen. Still smiling. She would never let herself fall apart in public, no matter what happened. My insides ached with the knowledge of what it must have been like right then to be her. I felt as if I had just betrayed her in front of the whole world. Betrayed everyone.   105

"Let's go home," I said.

"Not yet. Wait a while. Might as well see this thing to the end."

True, I thought. Wring every last drop of torture out of it.

He looked hard at me a moment, as if he were trying to guess what was going on in my head. And he did, he did, he always knew. "My old man wanted me to be a doctor," he said. "My mother wanted me to be a florist. She liked flowers. She thought if I was a florist I'd be able to send her a bouquet every week. But what does any of that matter now?"

Being part of a family was too complicated. And right then I decided I'd be a loner. No family for me. Nobody whose hearts could be broken every time I opened my mouth. Nobody expecting anything of me. Nobody to get me all tangled up in knots trying to guess who means what and what is it that's really going on inside anyone else. No temptations to presume I knew what someone else was thinking or feeling or hoping for.   110

When the lights had flickered and dimmed, and people had gone back to their seats, a young man with a beard came out onto the stage and changed the numbers behind the contestants' names. I'd dropped to fifth place, and Cornelia Horncastle had moved up to first. She had also, Richy Ryder announced, been awarded the judges' footstool for talent. The winner of the holiday in sunny Hawaii would not be announced until the next week, he said, when the radio audience had enough time to mail in their votes.

"And that," my mother said when she came down the aisle with her coat on, "is the end of a long and tiring day." I could find no disappointment showing in her eyes, or in the set of her mouth. Just relief. The same kind of relief that I felt myself. "You did a good job," she said, "and thank goodness it's over."

As soon as we got in the house I shut myself in the bedroom and announced I was never coming out. Lying on my bed, I tried to read my comic books but my mind passed from face to face all through the community, imagining everyone having a good laugh at the way my puffed-up ambition had got its reward. My face burned. Relatives, the aunts, would be ashamed of me. Eleanor would never let me forget. Mabel would remind me of the boy who'd done the only honourable thing, blown off his head. Why wasn't I doing the same? I lay awake the whole night, torturing myself with these thoughts. But when morning came and the hunger pains tempted me out of the bedroom as far as the breakfast table, I decided the whole wretched experience had brought one benefit with it: freedom from ambition. I wouldn't worry any more about becoming a pianist for my mother.

Nor would I worry any more about becoming a high-rigger for my father. I was free at last to concentrate on pursing the only goal that ever really mattered to me: becoming a Finn.

Of course I failed at that too. But then neither did Cornelia Horncastle become a great pianist on the concert stages of Europe. In fact, I understand that once she got back from her holiday on the beaches of Hawaii she announced to her parents that she was never going to touch a piano again as long as she lived, ivory, or cardboard, or any other kind. She had already, she said, accomplished all she'd ever wanted from it. And as far as I know, she's kept her word to this day.

QUESTIONS

1. Describe the attitude of Barclay Desmond toward his own experience as a young pianist and recitalist. Why does the story devote so much attention to Richy Ryder's introductory questions to Clay? Might Clay's experience have been different if he could have had a different kind of introduction?

2. How does Hodgins make the story comic? Describe the uses of farce, verbal humor, and fancifulness. Even though Clay makes himself the object of much humor, what is your attitude toward him at the story's end?

3. In what ways is the story serious? How seriously do you treat Clay's statements about his own ambitions (see paragraphs 22, 94–99, 113)?

4. Why do you think Clay begins and ends by referring to Cornelia Horncastle? In what ways do you think Clay is similar to Cornelia, and also different from her?

MARGARET LAURENCE (1926–1987)

Laurence was born in Neepawa, Manitoba, and was educated in Winnipeg, the provincial capital. She spent her twenties in Somalia and Ghana, and one of her earliest writing efforts was to make translations from the Somali language. Eventually she lived in both England and Canada. After publication of her first novel, This Side Jordan *(1960), and her first collection of stories,* The Tomorrow-Tamer *(1964), she wrote prolifically, her most acclaimed work being her novels and stories dramatizing the lives of women in Manawaka, her fictionalized name for Neepawa. The best known of the Manawaka novels is* The Diviners *(1974). Laurence also wrote travel books, collections of essays, and children's stories; her autobiographical memoir* Dance on the Earth *was published in 1989, two years after her death. "The Loons" is taken from* A Bird in the House *(1970), her collection of eight Manawaka stories.*

The Loons   1970

Just below Manawaka, where the Wachakwa River ran brown and noisy over the pebbles, the scrub oak and grey-green willow and chokecherry bushes grew in a dense thicket. In a clearing at the centre of the thicket stood the Tonnerre family's shack. The basis of this dwelling was a small square cabin made of poplar poles and chinked with mud, which had been built by Jules Tonnerre some fifty years before, when he came back from Batoche with a bullet in his thigh, the year that Riel was hung and the voices of the Metis entered their long silence. Jules had only intended to stay the winter in the Wachakwa Valley, but the family was still there in the thirties, when I was a child. As the Tonnerres had increased, their settlement had been added to, until the clearing at the foot of the town hill was a chaos of lean-tos, wooden packing cases, warped lumber, discarded car tyres, ramshackle chicken coops, tangled strands of barbed wire and rusty tin cans.

The Tonnerres were French halfbreeds, and among themselves they spoke a *patois* that was neither Cree nor French. Their English was broken and full of obscenities. They did not belong among the Cree of the Galloping Mountain reservation, further north, and they did not belong among the Scots-Irish and Ukrainians of Manawaka, either. They were, as my Grandmother MacLeod would have put it, neither flesh, fowl, nor good salt herring. When their men were not working at odd jobs or as section hands on the C.P.R., they lived on relief. In the summers, one of the Tonnerre youngsters, with a face that seemed totally unfamiliar with laughter, would knock at the doors of the town's brick houses and offer for sale a lard-pail full of bruised wild strawberries, and if he got as much as a quarter he would grab the coin and run before the customer had time to change her mind. Sometimes old Jules, or his son Lazarus, would get mixed up in a Saturday-night brawl, and would hit out at whoever was nearest, or howl drunkenly among the offended shoppers on Main Street, and then the Mountie would put them for the night in the barred cell underneath the Court House, and the next morning they would be quiet again.

Piquette Tonnerre, the daughter of Lazarus, was in my class at school. She was older than I, but she had failed several grades, perhaps because her attendance had always been sporadic and her interest in schoolwork negligible. Part of the reason she had missed a lot of school was that she had had tuberculosis of the bone, and had once spent many months in hospital. I knew this because my father was the doctor who had looked after her. Her sickness was almost the only thing I knew about her, however. Otherwise, she existed for me only as a vaguely embarrassing presence, with her hoarse voice and her clumsy limping walk and her grimy cotton dresses that were always miles too long. I was neither friendly nor unfriendly towards her. She dwelt and moved somewhere within my scope of vision, but I did not actually notice her very much until that peculiar summer when I was eleven.

"I don't know what to do about that kid," my father said at dinner one evening. "Piquette Tonnerre, I mean. The damn bone's flared up again. I've had her in hospital for quite a while now, and it's under control all right, but I hate like the dickens to send her home again."

"Couldn't you explain to her mother that she has to rest a lot?" my mother said.   5

"The mother's not there," my father replied. "She took off a few years back. Can't say I blame her. Piquette cooks for them, and she says Lazarus would never do anything for himself as long as she's there. Anyway, I don't think she'd take much care of herself, once she got back. She's only thirteen, after all. Beth, I was thinking—what about taking her up to Diamond Lake with us this summer? A couple of months rest would give that bone a much better chance."

My mother looked stunned.

"But Ewen—what about Roddie and Vanessa?"

"She's not contagious," my father said. "And it would be company for Vanessa."

"Oh dear," my mother said in distress, "I'll bet anything she has nits in her hair."   10

"For Pete's sake," my father said crossly, "do you think Matron would let her stay in the hospital for all this time like that? Don't be silly, Beth."

Grandmother MacLeod, her delicately featured face as rigid as a cameo, now brought her mauve-veined hands together as though she were about to begin a prayer.

"Ewen, if that half-breed youngster comes along to Diamond Lake, I'm not going," she announced. "I'll go to Morag's for the summer."

I had trouble in stifling my urge to laugh, for my mother brightened visibly and quickly tried to hide it. If it came to a choice between Grandmother MacLeod and Piquette, Piquette would win hands down, nits or not.

"It might be quite nice for you, at that," she mused. "You haven't seen Morag for   15
over a year, and you might enjoy being in the city for a while. Well, Ewen dear, you do
what you think best. If you think it would do Piquette some good, then we'll be glad to
have her, as long as she behaves herself."

So it happened that several weeks later, when we all piled into my father's old Nash,
surrounded by suitcases and boxes of provisions and toys for my ten-month-old brother,
Piquette was with us and Grandmother MacLeod, miraculously, was not. My father would
only be staying at the cottage for a couple of weeks, for he had to get back to his practice,
but the rest of us would stay at Diamond Lake until the end of August.

Our cottage was not named, as many were, "Dew Drop Inn," or "Bide-a-Wee," or
"Bonnie Doon." The sign on the roadway bore in austere letters only our name, MacLeod.
It was not a large cottage, but it was on the lakefront. You could look out the windows and
see, through the filigree of the spruce trees, the water glistening greatly as the sun caught
it. All around the cottage were ferns, and sharp-branched raspberry bushes, and moss that
had grown over fallen tree trunks. If you looked carefully among the weeds and grass, you
could find wild strawberry plants which were in white flower now and in another month
would bear fruit, the fragrant globes hanging like miniature scarlet lanterns on the thin
hairy stems. The two gray squirrels were still there, gossiping at us from the tall spruce beside the cottage, and by the end of the summer they would again be tame enough to take
pieces of crust from my hands. The broad moose antlers that hung above the back door
were a little more bleached and fissured after the winter, but otherwise everything was the
same. I raced joyfully around my kingdom, greeting all the places I had not seen for a year.
My brother, Roderick, who had not been born when we were here last summer, sat on the
car rug in the sunshine and examined a brown spruce cone, meticulously turning it round
and round in his small and curious hands. My mother and father toted the luggage from
car to cottage, exclaiming over how well the place had wintered, no broken windows,
thank goodness, no apparent damage from storm-felled branches or snow.

Only after I had finished looking around did I notice Piquette. She was sitting on
the swing, her lame leg held stiffly out, and her other foot scuffing the ground as she
swung slowly back and forth. Her long hair hung black and straight around her shoulders, and her broad coarse-featured face bore no expression—it was blank, as though she
no longer dwelt within her own skull, as though she had gone elsewhere. I approached
her very hesitantly.

"Want to come and play?"

Piquette looked at me with a sudden flash of scorn.

"I ain't a kid," she said.   20

Wounded, I stamped angrily away, swearing I would not speak to her for the rest of
the summer. In the days that followed, however, Piquette began to interest me, and I
began to want to interest her. My reasons did not appear bizarre to me. Unlikely as it may
seem, I had only just realised that the Tonnerre family, whom I had always heard called
half-breeds, were actually Indians, or as near as made no difference. My acquaintance
with Indians was not extensive. I did not remember ever having seen a real Indian, and
my new awareness that Piquette sprang from the people of Big Bear and Poundmaker, of
Tecumseh, of the Iroquois who had eaten Father Brebeuf's heart—all this gave her an instant attraction in my eyes. I was a devoted reader of Pauline Johnson at this age, and
sometimes would orate aloud and in an exalted voice, *West Wind, blow from your prairie
nest; Blow from the mountains, blow from the west*—and so on. It seemed to me that Piquette
must be in some way a daughter of the forest, a kind of junior prophetess of the wilds,
who might impart to me, if I took the right approach, some of the secrets which she undoubtedly knew—where the whippoorwill made her nest, how the coyote reared her
young, or whatever it was that it said in Hiawatha.

I set about gaining Piquette's trust. She was not allowed to go swimming, with her bad leg, but I managed to lure her down to the beach—or rather, she came because there was nothing else to do. The water was always icy, for the lake was fed by springs, but I swam like a dog, thrashing my arms and legs around at such speed and with such an output of energy that I never grew cold. Finally, when I had had enough, I came out and sat beside Piquette on the sand. When she saw me approaching, her hand squashed flat the sand castle she had been building, and she looked at me sullenly, without speaking.

"Do you like this place?" I asked, after a while, intending to lead on from there into the question of forest lore.

Piquette shrugged. "It's okay. Good as anywhere."   25

"I love it," I said. "We come here every summer."

"So what?" Her voice was distant, and I glanced at her uncertainly, wondering what I could have said wrong.

"Do you want to come for a walk?" I asked her. "We wouldn't need to go far. If you walk just around the point there, you come to a bay where great big reeds grow in the water, and all kinds of fish hang around there. Want to? Come on."

She shook her head.

"Your dad said I ain't supposed to do no more walking than I got to."   30

I tried another line.

"I bet you know a lot about the woods and all that, eh?" I began respectfully.

Piquette looked at me from her large dark unsmiling eyes.

"I don't know what in hell you're talkin' about," she replied. "You nuts or somethin'? If you mean where my old man, and me, and all them live, you better shut up, by Jesus, you hear?"

I was startled and my feelings were hurt, but I had a kind of dogged perseverance.   35
I ignored her rebuff.

"You know something, Piquette? There's loons here, on this lake. You can see their nests just up the shore there, behind those logs. At night, you can hear them even from the cottage, but it's better to listen from the beach. My dad says we should listen and try to remember how they sound, because in a few years when more cottages are built at Diamond Lake and more people come in, the loons will go away."

Piquette was picking up stones and snail shells and then dropping them again.

"Who gives a good goddamn?" she said.

It became increasingly obvious that, as an Indian, Piquette was a dead loss. That evening I went out by myself, scrambling through the bushes that overhung the steep path, my feet slipping on the fallen spruce needles that covered the ground. When I reached the shore, I walked along the firm damp sand to the small pier that my father had built, and sat down there. I heard someone else crashing through the undergrowth and the bracken, and for a moment I thought Piquette had changed her mind, but it turned out to be my father. He sat beside me on the pier and we waited, without speaking.

At night the lake was like black glass with a streak of amber which was the path of   40
the moon. All around, the spruce trees grew tall and close-set, branches blackly sharp against the sky, which was lightened by a cold flickering of stars. Then the loons began their calling. They rose like phantom birds from the nests on the shore, and flew out onto the dark still surface of the water.

No one can ever describe that ululating sound, the crying of the loons, and no one who has heard it can ever forget it. Plaintive, and yet with a quality of chilling mockery, those voices belonged to a world separated by aeons from our neat world of summer cottages and the lighted lamps of home.

"They must have sounded just like that," my father remarked, "before any person ever set foot here."

Then he laughed. "You could say the same, of course, about sparrows, or chipmunks, but somehow it only strikes you that way with the loons."

"I know," I said.

Neither of us suspected that this would be the last time we would ever sit here together on the shore, listening. We stayed for perhaps half an hour, and then we went back to the cottage. My mother was reading beside the fireplace. Piquette was looking at the burning birch log, and not doing anything.   45

"You should have come along," I said, although in fact I was glad she had not.

"Not me," Piquette said. "You wouldn' catch me walkin' way down there jus' for a bunch of squawkin' birds."

Piquette and I remained ill at ease with one another. I felt I had somehow failed my father, but I did not know what was the matter, nor why she would not or could not respond when I suggested exploring the woods or playing house. I thought it was probably her slow and difficult walking that held her back. She stayed most of the time in the cottage with my mother, helping her with the dishes or with Roddie, but hardly ever talking. Then the Duncans arrived at their cottage, and I spent my days with Mavis, who was my best friend. I could not reach Piquette at all, and I soon lost interest in trying. But all that summer she remained as both a reproach and a mystery to me.

That winter my father died of pneumonia, after less than a week's illness. For some time I saw nothing around me, being completely immersed in my own pain and my mother's. When I looked outward once more, I scarcely noticed that Piquette Tonnerre was no longer at school. I do not remember seeing her at all until four years later, one Saturday night when Mavis and I were having Cokes in the Regal Café. The jukebox was booming like tuneful thunder, and beside it, leaning lightly on its chrome and its rainbow glass, was a girl.

Piquette must have been seventeen then, although she looked about twenty. I   50
stared at her, astounded that anyone could have changed so much. Her face, so stolid and expressionless before, was animated now with a gaiety that was almost violent. She laughed and talked very loudly with the boys around her. Her lipstick was bright carmine, and her hair was cut short and frizzily permed. She had not been pretty as a child, and she was not pretty now, for her features were still heavy and blunt. But her dark and slightly slanted eyes were beautiful, and her skin-tight skirt and orange sweater displayed to enviable advantage a soft and slender body.

She saw me, and walked over. She teetered a little, but it was not due to her once-tubercular leg, for her limp was almost gone.

"Hi, Vanessa." Her voice still had the same hoarseness. "Long time no see, eh?"

"Hi," I said. "Where've you been keeping yourself, Piquette?"

"Oh, I been around," she said. "I been away almost two years now. Been all over the place—Winnipeg, Regina, Saskatoon. Jesus, what I could tell you! I come back this summer, but I ain't stayin'. You kids goin' to the dance?"

"No," I said abruptly, for this was a sore point with me. I was fifteen, and thought I   55
was old enough to go to the Saturday-night dances at the Flamingo. My mother, however, thought otherwise.

"Y'oughta come," Piquette said. "I never miss one. It's just about the on'y thing in this jerkwater town that's any fun. Boy, you couldn' catch me stayin' here. I don' give a shit about this place. It stinks."

She sat down beside me, and I caught the harsh over-sweetness of her perfume.

"Listen, you wanna know something, Vanessa?" she confided, her voice only slightly blurred. "Your dad was the only person in Manawaka that ever done anything good to me."

I nodded speechlessly. I was certain she was speaking the truth. I knew a little more than I had that summer at Diamond Lake, but I could not reach her now any more than I had then. I was ashamed, ashamed of my own timidity, the frightened tendency to look the other way. Yet I felt no real warmth towards her—I only felt that I ought to, because of that distant summer and because my father had hoped she would be company for me, or perhaps that I would be for her, but it had not happened that way. At this moment, meeting her again, I had to admit that she repelled and embarrassed me, and I could not help despising the self-pity in her voice. I wished she would go away. I did not want to see her. I did not know what to say to her. It seemed that we had nothing to say to one another.

"I'll tell you something else," Piquette went on. "All the old bitches an' biddies in this town will sure be surprised. I'm gettin' married this fall—my boyfriend, he's an English fella, works in the stockyards in the city there, a very tall guy, got blond wavy hair. Gee, is he ever handsome. Got this real classy name. Alvin Gerald Cummings—some handle, eh? They call him Al."

For the merest instant, then, I saw her. I really did see her, for the first and only time in all the years we had both lived in the same town. Her defiant face, momentarily, became unguarded and unmasked, and in her eyes there was a terrifying hope.

"Gee, Piquette—" I burst out awkwardly, "that's swell. That's really wonderful. Congratulations—good luck—I hope you'll be happy—"

As I mouthed the conventional phrases, I could only guess how great her need must have been, that she had been forced to seek the very things she so bitterly rejected.

When I was eighteen, I left Manawaka and went away to college. At the end of my first year, I came back home for the summer. I spent the first few days in talking non-stop with my mother, as we exchanged all the news that somehow had not found its way into letters—what had happened in my life and what had happened here in Manawaka while I was away. My mother searched her memory for events that concerned people I knew.

"Did I ever write you about Piquette Tonnerre, Vanessa?" she asked one morning.

"No, I don't think so," I replied. "Last I heard of her, she was going to marry some guy in the city. Is she still there?"

My mother looked perturbed, and it was a moment before she spoke, as though she did not know how to express what she had to tell and wished she did not need to try.

"She's dead," she said at last. Then, as I stared at her, "Oh, Vanessa, when it happened, I couldn't help thinking of her as she was that summer—so sullen and gauche and badly dressed. I couldn't help wondering if we could have done something more at that time—but what could we do? She used to be around in the cottage there with me all day, and honestly, it was all I could do to get a word out of her. She didn't even talk to your father very much, although I think she liked him, in her way."

"What happened?" I asked.

"Either her husband left her, or she left him," my mother said. "I don't know which. Anyway, she came back here with two youngsters, both only babies—they must have been born very close together. She kept house, I guess, for Lazarus and her brothers, down in the valley there, in the old Tonnerre place. I used to see her on the street sometimes, but she never spoke to me. She'd put on an awful lot of weight, and she looked a mess, to tell you the truth, a real slattern, dressed any old how. She was up in court a couple of times—drunk and disorderly, of course. One Saturday night last winter, during the coldest weather, Piquette was alone in the shack with the children. The Tonnerres made home brew all the time, so I've heard, and Lazarus said later she'd been drinking most of the day when he and the boys went out that evening. They had an old woodstove there—you know the kind, with exposed pipes. The shack caught fire. Piquette didn't get out, and neither did the children."

I did not say anything. As so often with Piquette, there did not seem to be anything to say. There was a kind of silence around the image in my mind of the fire and the snow, and I wished I could put from my memory the look that I had seen once in Piquette's eyes.

I went up to Diamond Lake for a few days that summer, with Mavis and her family. The MacLeod cottage had been sold after my father's death, and I did not even go to look at it, not wanting to witness my long-ago kingdom possessed now by strangers. But one evening I went down to the shore by myself.

The small pier which my father had built was gone, and in its place there was a large and solid pier built by the government, for Galloping Mountain was now a national park, and Diamond Lake had been re-named Lake Wapakata, for it was felt that an Indian name would have a greater appeal to tourists. The one store had become several dozen, and the settlement had all the attributes of a flourishing resort—hotels, a dance-hall, cafés with neon signs, the penetrating odours of potato chips and hot dogs.

I sat on the government pier and looked out across the water. At night the lake at least was the same as it had always been, darkly shining and bearing within its black glass the streak of amber that was the path of the moon. There was no wind that evening, and every-thing was quiet all around me. It seemed too quiet, and then I realized that the loons were no longer here. I listened for some time, to make sure, but never once did I hear that long-drawn call, half mocking and half plaintive, spearing through the stillness across the lake.

I did not know what had happened to the birds. Perhaps they had gone away to   75
some far place of belonging. Perhaps they had been unable to find such a place, and had simply died out, having ceased to care any longer whether they lived or not.

I remembered how Piquette had scorned to come along, when my father and I sat there and listened to the lake birds. It seemed to me now that in some unconscious and totally unrecognised way, Piquette might have been the only one, after all, who had heard the crying of the loons.

QUESTIONS

1. Describe the narrator. Granted the passage of time in the story, why is it essential for the narrator to be approximately the same age as Piquette?

2. How does the narrator's attitude toward Piquette change as the story develops (see especially paragraph 61)? As a result of this change, what happens to your attitude toward Piquette?

3. Describe what happens to the lake and the loons and how these conditions reflect the circumstances of Piquette's life (see paragraphs 1, 6, 16, 17, 36–45, 72–73). If one assumes that in a previous age Piquette would have inherited the traditions of the Cree Indians, what is Piquette's legacy in the changing modern world?

AMÉRICO PARÉDES (1915–1999)

Parédes was a Mexican-American storyteller, folklorist, essayist, and poet, closely identified with Mexican-Americans living in Texas, his native state. He received his Ph.D. at the University of Texas in 1956 and also taught there for many years. His dissertation was published in 1958 as With His Pistol in His Hand, *a study of an early-twentieth-century popular ballad about a fugitive, Gregorio Cortés. Deeply interested in the culture of the "lower border," he was one of the leaders of the Chicano movement in cultural-literary studies. He edited the* Journal of American Folklore *and also edited* Folklore and Culture on the Texas-Mexican Border *(1993). Among his honors was a Guggenheim Fellowship in 1962 and the Aztec Eagle medal from the Mexican government in 1991. "The Hammon and the Beans" was first published in the* Texas Observer *in 1963 and was republished in* The Hammon and the Beans and Other Stories *in 1994.*

The Hammon and the Beans   ~ ~ ~ ~   1963

Once we lived in one of my grandfather's houses near Fort Jones.° It was just a block from the parade grounds, a big frame house painted a dirty yellow. My mother hated it, especially because of the pigeons that cooed all day about the eaves. They had fleas, she said. But it was a quiet neighborhood at least, too far from the center of town for automobiles and too near for musical, night-roaming drunks.

At this time Jonesville-on-the-Grande was not the thriving little city that it is today. We told off our days by the routine on the post. At six sharp the flag was raised on the parade grounds to the cackling of the bugles, and a field piece thundered out a salute. The sound of the shot bounced away through the morning mist until its echoes worked their way into every corner of town. Jonesville-on-the-Grande woke to the cannon's roar, as if to battle, and the day began.

At eight the whistle from the post laundry sent us children off to school. The whole town stopped for lunch with the noon whistle, and after lunch everybody went back to work when the post laundry said that it was one o'clock, except for those who could afford to be old-fashioned and took the siesta. The post was the town's clock, you might have said, or like some insistent elder person who was always there to tell you it was time.

At six the flag came down, and we went to watch through the high wire fence that divided the post from the town. Sometimes we joined in the ceremony, standing at salute until the sound of the cannon made us jump. That must have been when we had just studied about George Washington in school, or recited "The Song of Marion's Men"° about Marion the Fox and the British cavalry that chased him up and down the broad Santee. But at other times we stuck out our tongues and jeered at the soldiers. Perhaps the night before we had hung at the edges of a group of old men and listened to tales about Aniceto Pizaña and the "border troubles,"° as the local paper still called them when it referred to them gingerly in passing.

It was because of the border troubles, ten years or so before, that the soldiers had come back to old Fort Jones. But we did not hate them for that; we admired them even, at least sometimes. But when we were thinking about the border troubles instead of Marion the Fox we hooted them and the flag they were lowering, which for the moment was theirs alone, just as we would have jeered an opposing ball team, in a friendly sort of way. On these occasions even Chonita would join in the mockery, though she usually ran home at the stroke of six. But whether we taunted or saluted, the distant men in khaki uniforms went about their motions without noticing us at all.

The last word from the post came in the night when a distant bugle blew. At nine it was all right because all the lights were on. But sometimes I heard it at eleven when

5

Fort Jones: The setting of Fort Jones and Jonesville-on-the-Grande in Texas is fictional. The story takes place in the mid-1920s, one of the most turbulent periods of Mexican history and only a few years after the deaths of two of the greatest heroes of the Mexican revolution—Pancho Villa (1877–1923) and Emiliano Zapata (ca. 1879–1919).

"Song of Marion's Men": a poem by William Cullen Bryant (1794–1878) about Colonel Francis Marion (ca. 1732–1795), who was a leader of irregular guerrilla forces in South Carolina during the Revolutionary War. Because of his hit-and-run tactics, involving his hiding in the swamps near the "broad Santee" river in South Carolina, Marion was nicknamed the "Swamp Fox."

border troubles: The most serious border incidents occurred in 1916, when Pancho Villa was responsible for deaths of Americans on both sides of the border. He made repeated raids into New Mexico and Texas.

everything was dark and still, and it made me feel that I was all alone in the world. I would even doubt that I was me, and that put me in such a fright that I felt like yelling out just to make sure I was really there. But next morning the sun shone and life began all over again. With its whistles and cannon shots and bugles blowing. And so we lived, we and the post, side by side with the wire fence in between.

The wandering soldiers whom the bugle called home at night did not wander in our neighborhood, and none of us ever went into Fort Jones. None except Chonita. Every evening when the flag came down she would leave off playing and go down towards what was known as the "lower" gate of the post, the one that opened not on Main Street but against the poorest part of town. She went into the grounds and to the mess halls and pressed her nose against the screens and watched the soldiers eat. They sat at long tables calling to each other through food-stuffed mouths.

"Hey bud, pass the coffee!"

"Give me the ham!"

"Yeah, give me the beans!"   10

After the soldiers were through the cooks came out and scolded Chonita, and then they gave her packages with things to eat.

Chonita's mother did our washing, in gratefulness—as my mother put it— for the use of a vacant lot of my grandfather's which was a couple of blocks down the street. On the lot was an old one-room shack which had been a shed long ago, and this Chonita's father had patched up with flattened-out pieces of tin. He was a laborer. Ever since the end of the border troubles there had been a development boom in the Valley, and Chonita's father was getting his share of the good times. Clearing brush and building irrigation ditches he sometimes pulled down as much as six dollars a week. He drank a good deal of it up, it was true. But corn was just a few cents a bushel in those days. He was the breadwinner, you might say, while Chonita furnished the luxuries.

Chonita was a poet too. I had just moved into the neighborhood when a boy came up to me and said, "Come on! Let's go hear Chonita make a speech."

She was already on top of the alley fence when we got there, a scrawny little girl of about nine, her bare dirty feet clinging to the fence almost like hands. A dozen other kids were there below her, waiting. Some were boys I knew at school; five or six were her younger brothers and sisters.

"Speech! Speech!" they all cried. "Let Chonita make a speech! Talk in English,   15
Chonita!"

They were grinning and nudging each other except for her brothers and sisters, who looked up at her with proud serious faces. She gazed out beyond us all with a grand, distant air and then she spoke.

"Give me the hammon and the beans!" she yelled. "Give me the hammon and the beans!"

She leaped off the fence and everybody cheered and told her how good it was and how she could talk English better than the teachers at the grammar school.

I thought it was a pretty poor joke. Every evening almost, they would make her get up on the fence and yell, "Give me the hammon and the beans!" And everybody would cheer and make her think she was talking English. As for me, I would wait there until she got it over with so we could play at something else. I wondered how long it would be before they got tired of it all. I never did find out because just about that time I got the chills and fever, and when I got up and around Chonita wasn't there anymore.

In later years I thought of her a lot, especially during the thirties when I was grow-   20
ing up. Those years would have been just made for her. Many's the time I have seen her

in my mind's eyes, in the picket lines demanding not bread, not cake, but the hammon and the beans. But it didn't work out that way.

One night Doctor Zapata came into our kitchen through the back door. He set his bag on the table and said to my father, who had opened the door for him, "Well, she is dead."

My father flinched. "What was it?" he asked.

The doctor had gone to the window and he stood with his back to us, looking out toward the light of Fort Jones. "Pneumonia, flu, malnutrition, worms, the evil eye," he said without turning around. "What the hell difference does it make?"

"I wish I had known how sick she was," my father said in a very mild tone. "Not that it's really my affair, but I wish I had."

The doctor snorted and shook his head.   25

My mother came in and I asked her who was dead. She told me. It made me feel strange but I did not cry. My mother put her arm around my shoulders. "She is in Heaven now," she said. "She is happy."

I shrugged her arm away and sat down in one of the kitchen chairs.

"They're like animals," the doctor was saying. He turned round suddenly and his eyes glistened in the light. "Do you know what that brute of a father was doing when I left? He was laughing! Drinking and laughing with his friends."

"There's no telling what the poor man feels," my mother said.

My father made a deprecatory gesture. "It wasn't his daughter anyway."   30

"No?" the doctor said. He sounded interested.

"This is the woman's second husband," my father explained. "First one died before the girl was born, shot and hanged from a mesquite limb. He was working too close to the tracks the day the Olmito train was derailed."

"You know what?" the doctor said. "In classical times they did things better. Take Troy, for instance. After they stormed the city they grabbed the babies by the heels and dashed them against the wall. That was more humane."

My father smiled. "You sound very radical. You sound just like your relative down there in Morelos."°

"No relative of mine," the doctor said. "I'm a conservative, the son of a conserva-   35
tive, and you know that I wouldn't be here except for that little detail."

"Habit," my father said. "Pure habit, pure tradition. You're a radical at heart."

"It depends on how you define radicalism," the doctor answered. "People tend to use words too loosely. A dentist could be called a radical, I suppose. He pulls up things by the roots."

My father chuckled.

"Any bandit in Mexico nowadays can give himself a political label," the doctor went on, "and that makes him respectable. He's a leader of the people."

"Take Villa, now—" my father began.   40

"Villa was a different type of man," the doctor broke in.

"I don't see any difference."

The doctor came over to the table and sat down. "Now look at it this way," he began, his finger in front of my father's face. My father threw back his head and laughed.

"You'd better go to bed and rest," my mother told me. "You're not completely well, you know."

So I went to bed, but I didn't go to sleep, not right away. I lay there for a long time   45
while behind my darkened eyelids Emiliano Zapata's cavalry charged down to the broad

Morelos: the home state of Zapata.

Santee, where there were grave men with hoary hairs.° I was still awake at eleven when the cold voice of the bugle went gliding in and out of the dark like something that couldn't find its way back to wherever it had been. I thought of Chonita in Heaven, and I saw her in her torn and dirty dress, with a pair of bright wings attached, flying round and round like a butterfly shouting, "Give me the hammon and the beans!"

Then I cried. And whether it was the bugle, or whether it was Chonita or what, to this day I do not know. But cry I did, and I felt much better after that.

QUESTIONS

1. How does Parédes establish the setting of the story? What is the significance of the fort? Of the "dirty yellow" paint? Of the vacant lot and the shack?

2. Is Chonita a round or flat character? To what extent does the author make her symbolic and representative?

3. What is the tone of the story (some possibilities: ironic, cynical, resigned, bitter, resentful)? What techniques does Parédes use to control the tone?

4. How does Doctor Zapata's attitude toward Chonita's death, and the words he uses to announce it, help to control the tone?

5. How does the tale of Chonita's brief life and her death fit into the political, social, and broadly human framework of the story?

6. Near the end of Bryant's "Song of Marion's Men" (lines 53–56) the following four lines appear:

> And lovely ladies greet our band [i.e., of soldiers]
> With kindliest welcoming,
> And smiles like those of summer,
> And tears like those of spring.

Contrast these lines with the narrator's vision of Chonita in heaven.

❦ WRITING ABOUT TONE

Begin with a careful reading, noting those elements of the work that convey attitudes. Consider whether the work genuinely creates the attitudes it is designed to evoke. In Poe's "The Masque of the Red Death" (Chapter 6), for example, do the bizarre rooms of Prince Prospero's "castellated abbey" clearly determine the Prince's pride and defiance? In Laurence's "The Loons," does the narrator provide sufficient information about Piquette to permit genuine sympathy for her plight? In "The Hammon and the Beans," does the conclusion justify the narrator's recovery of "better" feelings? Developing responses to questions such as these will help you in creating ideas for your essay.

---

grave men with hoary hairs: Cf. lines 49–52 of Bryant's "Song of Marion's Men":

Grave men there are by broad Santee,
　Grave men with hoary hairs;
Their hearts are all with Marion,
　For Marion are their prayers.

Questions for Discovering Ideas

- How strongly do you respond to the story? What attitudes can you identify and characterize? What elements in the story elicit your concern, indignation, fearfulness, anguish, amusement, or sense of affirmation?
- What causes you to sympathize or not to sympathize with the characters, situations, or ideas? What makes the circumstances in the work admirable or understandable (or deplorable)?
- What does the dialogue suggest about the author's attitudes toward the characters? How does it influence your attitudes? What qualities of diction permit and encourage your responses?
- To what degree, if any, does the story supersede any previous ideas you might have had about the same or similar subject matter? What do you think created the changes in your attitude?
- What role does the narrator/speaker play in your attitudes toward the story material? Does the speaker seem intelligent or stupid, friendly or unfriendly, sane or insane, or idealistic or pragmatic?
- In an amusing or comic story, what elements of plot, character, and diction are particularly comic? How strongly do you respond to humor-producing situations? Why?
- What ironies do you find in the story (verbal, situational, cosmic, dramatic)? How is the irony connected to philosophies of marriage, family, society, politics, religion, or morality?
- To what extent are the characters controlled by fate, social or racial discrimination, limitations of intelligence, economic and political inequality, and limited opportunity?
- Do any words seem unusual or noteworthy, such as words in dialect, polysyllabic words, or foreign words or phrases that the author assumes you know? Are there any especially connotative or emotive words? What do these words suggest about the author's apparent assumptions about the readers?

Strategies for Organizing Ideas

Your goal is to show how the author establishes the dominant moods of the story—for example, the pathos of "The Loons" or the comedy of "Rape Fantasies." Some possibilities are the use or misuse of language, the exposé of a pretentious speaker, the use of exact and specific descriptions, the isolation of a major character, the failure of plans, and the continuance of naiveté in a disillusioned world. Some of the things to discuss are these.

1. AUDIENCE, SITUATION, AND CHARACTERS. Is any person or group directly addressed by the speaker? What attitude is expressed (love, respect, condescension, confidentiality, confidence, etc.)? What is the basic situation in the story? Do you find irony? If so, what kind is it? What does the irony show (optimism or pessimism, for example)? How is the situation controlled to shape your responses? That is, can actions, situations, or characters be seen as expressions of attitude or as embodiments of certain favorable or unfavorable ideas or positions? What is the nature of the speaker or persona? Why does the persona speak exactly as he or she does? How is the persona's character manipulated to show apparent authorial attitudes and to elicit reader response? Does the story promote respect, admiration, dislike, or other feelings about character or situation? How?

2. DESCRIPTIONS, DICTION. Your concern here is not to analyze descriptions or diction for themselves alone but to relate these matters to attitude. *For descriptions:* To what degree do descriptions of natural scenery and conditions (snowstorms, cold, rain, ice, intense sunlight) convey an attitude that complements or opposes the circumstances of the characters? Are there any systematic references to colors, sounds, or noises that collectively reflect an attitude? *For diction:* Do connotative meanings of words (see Chapter 7) control response in any way? To what degree does the diction require readers to have a large or technical vocabulary? Do speech patterns or the use of dialect evoke attitudes about speakers or their condition of life? Is the level of diction normal, standard, or substandard, or is the language filled with slang? What is the effect of such a level? Are there unusual or particularly noteworthy expressions? If so, what attitudes do these show? Does the author use verbal irony? To what effect?

3. HUMOR. Is the story funny? How funny, how intense? How is the humor achieved? Does the humor develop out of incongruous situations or language or both? What is the underlying basis of attack in the humor? Are the objects of laughter still respected or loved, even though they cause amusement?

4. IDEAS. Are any ideas advocated, defended mildly, or attacked? How does the author clarify his or her attitude toward these ideas—directly, by statement, or indirectly, through understatement, overstatement, or a character's speeches? In what ways does the story assume a common ground of assent between author and reader? That is, what common assumptions do you find about behavior, religion, politics, morality, and so on? Is it easy to give assent (temporary or permanent) to these ideas, or is any concession needed by the reader to approach the story? For example, a major subject of O'Connor's "First Confession" (Chapter 7) is the preparation for a child going to first confession in the Catholic faith. Not everyone can relate to this situation, but even a skeptical reader can find common ground in the psychological situation of the story or in the desire to learn as much as possible about human beings.

5. UNIQUE CHARACTERISTICS OF THE STORY. Each story has unique properties that contribute to the tone. In Atwood's "Rape Fantasies" the center of interest is the narrator, Estelle, and the ideas about rape she expresses both in conversation and narration. The speaker of Hodgins's "The Concert Stages of Europe" demonstrates a willingness to describe embarrassing situations that someone else might omit or mitigate. In other stories you might discover a recurring word or phrase that seems special. For example, the narrator of Mark Twain in "Luck" (Chapter 7) develops a passage centering on the word *blunder* and thereby makes his attitude clear about the boob hero, Scoresby (paragraph 12).

In the conclusion, first summarize your main points and then go on to redefinitions, explanations, or afterthoughts, together with ideas reinforcing earlier points. You might also mention some other major aspect of the story's tone that you did not develop in the body.

DEMONSTRATIVE STUDENT ESSAY

Chopin's Use of Irony in "The Story of an Hour"°

[1]   "The Story of an Hour" is a remarkably short short story that exhibits Kate Chopin's complex control over tone. <u>There are many ironies in the story, which grow out of error, misunderstanding, incorrect expectation, and a certain degree of pompous pride.</u>* In addition, the story raises an ironic question about the nature of marriage as an institution. All this is a great deal for so brief a story, yet it is all there. <u>The story contains a rich mixture of situational, cosmic, and dramatic irony.</u>†

[2]   <u>The focal point of the story's situational irony is Louise Mallard, the central character.</u> Not much is disclosed about her character, her major circumstances being that she is obviously a faithful and dedicated housewife and that she suffers from heart disease. She is made inconsolable when she is told that her husband has died. She is a loving wife, and she weeps convulsively and then retreats to her room in order to be private in her grief. Previously unknown and unsuspected feelings then come upon her--feelings that she is now "free." In other words, she realizes that her marriage has put her in bondage, even though at the same time she recognizes that her husband "had never looked save with love upon her" (363, paragraph 13). For the first time she recognizes the gap between her life and her hidden hopes and expectations, virtually a definition of situational irony.

[3]   <u>Both situational and cosmic ironies are focused on the people closest to Louise, namely her sister Josephine and Brently Mallard's friend Richards.</u> They are kindly, and have the best intentions toward her. Richards verifies the truth of the telegram before coming to the Mallard household with the news, and then he first tells Josephine. In turn, Josephine breaks the news gently to Louise, in "veiled hints that revealed in half concealing" (362, paragraph 2), so as to forestall the shock that would bring on a fatal heart attack. Josephine is successful, and her concern causes her to beg Louise to come out of her room, for Josephine believes that Louise will make herself ill with grief (363, paragraph 17). With these best intentions, of course, Josephine becomes the inadvertent cause of bringing Louise in sight of the front door just as Brently Mallard enters it, and the shock of seeing him brings about the fatal heart attack. Thus, through no fault of her own, Josephine brings about the blow of fate that she and Richards have tried to avoid.

[4]   <u>Another major cosmic irony in the story results from the inaccuracy and unreliability of information.</u> At the time of the story (1894), the best and most modern method of sending information over distances was by telegraph. Richards is in the newspaper office "when intelligence of the railroad disaster was received, with Brently Mallard's name leading the list of 'killed'" (362, paragraph 2). Since the news could never have come so rapidly in the days before telegraphy was common, we may suppose that Louise would never have heard the news of the death in a previous age, and therefore would never have experienced the emotional crisis brought about by the inaccurate news. The error of information may be caused

°See pp. 362–64 for this story.
*Central idea.
†Thesis sentence.

by human mistakes, but the consequences are cosmic for Louise--and, one might add, for her unsuspecting husband, who enters the house only to witness his wife's sudden death.

This irony-filled story also contains dramatic irony that may be found in two major details. None of the characters understands what Louise begins feeling as she sits upstairs. Their experience and their imagination simply make it impossible to comprehend her feelings. This failure of understanding is particularly sad with regard to Josephine and Richards, for these two are the closest ones to her. Thus in effect, Louise dies alone even though she is surrounded by the people who love her most. In the case of the doctors who diagnose the cause of Louise's **[5]** death, the lack of understanding is bitterly ironic:

> When the doctors came they said she had died of heart disease--of joy that kills. (364, paragraph 23)

The pompous doctors find it impossible to imagine the true reason for Louise's shock, for, they obviously think, what other reason than joy at seeing her restored husband could bring about such a powerful assault on her system? "The Story of an Hour," of course, ends on this grim but also somewhat comic note.

The story's crowning situational irony is the discrepancy between normal and conventional ideas of marriage as ideal and the reality of marriage as fact. One senses the authorial voice insisting strongly on uncomfortable reality when Louise contemplates a future life free of the need for satisfying anyone else:

> **[6]** There would be no powerful will bending hers in that blind persistence with which men and women believe they have a right to impose a private will upon a fellow-creature. (363, paragraph 14)

Louise's marriage has not been bad, but the story at this point straightforwardly goes to the heart of the conflict between personal freedom and marital obligation. Chopin's phrase "blind persistence" is particularly effective here in establishing an attitude of disapproval if not of protest.

Even though "The Story of an Hour" may thus be considered as a tract against marriage, it is above all a superbly crafted story. In just twenty-three paragraphs it introduces a complex number of ironies revolving about the crisis created by the mistakes and misunderstandings of a single hour. It is the sudden **[7]** coming together of all the ironies that crash in on Louise Mallard and destroy her. In her case, these ironies come into full play only when she believes that her husband has been killed and then quickly discovers that he is alive. In life, for most people, such crises may never come into play. As a general principle, the story's major irony is that even the best and most enviable circumstances of life contain inherent imperfections, unarticulated frustration, and potential unhappiness.

WORK CITED

Chopin, Kate. "The Story of an Hour." Literature: An Introduction to Reading and Writing. Ed. Edgar V. Roberts and Henry E. Jacobs. 7th ed. Upper Saddle River: Prentice Hall, 2004. 362–64.

⚜ COMMENTARY ON THE ESSAY

The topic of this essay on tone is Chopin's complex use of irony. Throughout the essay, a good deal of the story's action is used to exemplify the sorts of irony being discussed. Links and connections within the essay are brought out by phrases like "even though," "also," "the crowning situational irony," "another," and "both."

Paragraph 1, the introduction, contains the central idea that announces the causes producing irony. The thesis sentence indicates that the combination of situational, cosmic, and dramatic irony will be explored in the body. Paragraph 2 demonstrates how situational irony applies to the circumstances of the major character, Louise. Paragraph 3 shows how both situational and cosmic irony enter into the story through Louise's sister Josephine and Brently's friend Richards. An additional element of cosmic irony is discussed in paragraph 4. This irony is made to seem particularly unfortunate because the telegraphic errors are totally modern and could never have occurred in a pretechnological age.

In paragraph 5, the story's dramatic irony is introduced. This irony results from the lack of understanding by those closest to Louise and from the pompous intellectual blindness of the examining physicians. Paragraph 6 introduces Chopin's major idea criticizing marriage as an institution. Connected to the thematic purpose of the essay, however, this idea is shown to be integrated with the story's major situational irony. The final paragraph, 7, pays tribute to the story as a story, and speculates about how Chopin deals truthfully with difficult issues of life and marriage.

Special Topics for Writing and Argument about Tone

1. Write an essay comparing and contrasting attitudes toward two or more of the following female characters: Louise in "The Story of an Hour," Piquette in "The Loons," Mathilde in "The Necklace" (Chapter 1), and Phoenix in "A Worn Path" (Chapter 3). How does the author's presentation control your understanding of them? What details of tone are important in a feminist approach to these works?

2. Consider a short story in which the narrator is the central character (for example, "The Concert Stages of Europe," "A & P" (Chapter 7), "First Confession" (Chapter 7), "Everyday Use" (Chapter 2), and "Blue Winds Dancing" (Chapter 3). Write an essay showing how the language of the narrator affects your attitudes toward him or her (that is, your sympathy for the narrator, your interest in the narrative, your feelings toward the other characters and what they do). Be sure to emphasize the relationship between the narrator's language and your responses.

3. Describe the attitude of Estelle, the narrator in "Rape Fantasies," toward sexual molestation. How does her character influence the tone of the story (e.g., treating the subject of rape in an amusing, uncomprehending, or serious manner)?

4. In "The Hammon and the Beans," how does Parédes express irony about the fact that Mexican-American children are taught United States history but learn nothing about the Mexican political movements represented by Villa and Zapata?

5. Write a fragment of a story of your own about, for example, a student, a supervisor, or a politician. Treat your main character with dramatic irony; that is, your character thinks he or she knows all the details about a situation but really does not (e.g., a male student declares interest in a female student without realizing that she is already engaged; a supervisor expresses distrust in one of the best workers in the firm; a politician accuses an opponent of actions that were initiated not by the opponent but by a supporter). Through what actions, words, and situations do you make your irony clear?

6. In your school library, consult the most recent copy of the *MLA International Bibliography of Books and Articles on the Modern Languages and Literatures*, and make a short list of books and articles on Margaret Atwood or Kate Chopin. Consult at least three of the works you have listed, and using these, together with your own insights, write a short description of the writer's irony (comic or serious) and social criticism.

Symbolism and Allegory:
Keys to Extended Meaning

Symbolism and **allegory,** like metaphors and similes (see Chapter 17), are modes that expand meaning. They are literary devices developed from the connections that real-life people make between their own existence and particular objects, places, or occurrences, through either experience or reading: A man might remember making a vital realization about honesty and morality during a rowboat ride as a boy. A failed examination might cause a woman to study harder than ever before and therefore to excel. A bereaved mother might associate personal grief with ordinary packing boxes. The significance of details like these can be meaningful not just at the time they occur but throughout an entire lifetime. Merely bringing them to mind or speaking about them unlocks their meanings, implications, and consequences. It is as though the reference alone can be the equivalent of pages of explanation and analysis.

From this principle, both symbolism and allegory are derived. By highlighting details as *symbols,* and stories or parts of stories as *allegories,* writers expand their meaning while keeping their works within reasonable lengths.

❧ SYMBOLISM

The words **symbol** and **symbolism** are derived from the Greek word meaning "to throw together" (*syn,* "together," and *ballein,* "to throw"). A symbol creates a direct meaningful equation between (1) a specific object, scene, character, or action and (2) ideas, values, persons, or ways of life. In effect, a symbol is a *substitute* for the elements being signified, much as the flag stands for the ideals of the nation.

In painting and sculpture, symbols are easily recognized, for to tell a story visually, the artist must make every object count. In the anonymous fresco *Hercules and the Infant Telephus* from ancient Herculaneum, for example, the painter has depicted a crucial event in the life of the mythical hero Hercules—the choice he had to make early in his life between pleasure or toil (Insert II-1). By symbolically turning his head away from the seated figure representing Pleasure, Hercules is rejecting the life of ease that she symbolizes. Instead, his life will be one of work, hardship, battle, victory, and glory, as symbolized by the lion, the eagle, and the sheaf of arrows. The image of his child, Telephus, whom he later abandons and who is being suckled by a donkey, symbolizes Hercules' insensitivity, verging on cruelty, which became a part of his single-minded existence as a warrior and hero.

When we first encounter a symbol in a story (also in poems and plays), it may seem to carry no more weight than its surface or obvious meaning. It can be a description of a character, an object, a place, an action, or a situation, and it may function normally and usefully in this capacity. What makes a symbol symbolic, however, is its capacity to signify additional levels of meaning—major ideas, simple or complex emotions, or philosophical or religious qualities or values. There are two types of symbols—*cultural* and *contextual.*

Cultural Symbols Are Derived from Our Cultural and Historical Heritage

Many symbols are *generally* or *universally* recognized and are therefore **cultural** (also called **universal**). They embody ideas and emotions that writers and readers share as heirs of the same historical and cultural tradition. When using cultural symbols, a writer assumes that readers already know what the symbols represent. An example is the character Sisyphus of ancient Greek myth. As a punishment for trying to overcome death not just once but twice, Sisyphus is doomed by the underworld gods to roll a large boulder up a high hill forever. Just as he gets the boulder to the top, it rolls down, and then he is fated to roll it up again—and again—and again—because the boulder always rolls back. The plight of Sisyphus has been interpreted as a symbol of the human condition: In spite of constant struggle, a person rarely if ever completes anything. Work must always be done over and over from day to day and from generation to generation, and the same problems confront humanity throughout all time. Because of such fruitless effort, life seems to have little or no meaning. Nevertheless, there is hope: People who confront their tasks, as Sisyphus does, stay involved and active, and their work makes their lives meaningful. A writer referring to Sisyphus would expect us to understand that this ancient mythological figure symbolizes these conditions.

Similarly, ordinary water, because living creatures cannot live without it, is recognized as a symbol of life. It has this meaning in the ceremony of baptism, and it conveys this meaning and dimension in a variety of literary contexts. Thus, a spouting fountain might symbolize optimism (as upwelling, bubbling life), and a stagnant pool might symbolize the pollution and diminution of life. Water is also a universal symbol of sexuality, and its condition or state can symbolize various romantic relationships. For instance, stories in which lovers meet near a turbulent stream, a roaring waterfall, a mud puddle, a beach with high breakers, a stormy sea, a calm lake, or a wide and gently flowing river symbolically represent love relationships that range from uncertainty to serenity.

Contextual Symbols Are Symbolic Only in Individual Works

Objects and descriptions that are not universal symbols can be symbols *only if they are made so within individual works*. These are **contextual, private,** or **authorial** symbols. Unlike cultural symbols, contextual symbols derive their meanings from the context and circumstances of individual works. For example, the standing clock in Poe's "The Masque of the Red Death" (Chapter 6) is a large timepiece that in the story symbolizes not only the passage of time but also the sinister forces of death. Similarly, Elisa's chrysanthemums in Steinbeck's "The Chrysanthemums" seem at first nothing more than prized flowers. As the story progresses, however, they gain symbolic significance. The traveling tinsmith's apparent interest in them is the wedge he uses to get a small mending job from Elisa. Her description of the care needed in planting and tending them suggests that they symbolize her kindness, love, orderliness, femininity, and motherliness.

Like Poe's clock, Steinbeck's chrysanthemums are a major contextual symbol. But there is not necessarily any carryover of symbolic meaning. In other stories, clocks and flowers are not symbolic unless the authors of these stories deliberately give them a symbolic charge. Further, if they are symbolic, they can be given different meanings than in the Poe and Steinbeck stories.

Determine What Is Symbolic (and Not Symbolic)

In determining whether a particular object, action, or character is a symbol, you need to judge the importance that the author gives to it. If the element is prominent and also maintains a constancy of meaning, you can justify interpreting it as a symbol. For example, the loons of Laurence's "The Loons" (Chapter 8) are water birds that ordinarily inhabit lakeshores, and their absence at the story's end is an expected result of the increased number of lakeside residences described in the story. Although the loons are ordinary, they are also symbolic, for the story is about loss and change (the death of the narrator's father and Piquette, the loss of the way of life of the Indians, the changes accompanying increased population). Here, the importance of the birds has invested them with symbolic meaning. Importance is therefore a key to the determination of symbolism, as at the end of Welty's "A Worn Path" (Chapter 3). Phoenix, Welty's major character, plans to spend all her money for a toy windmill for her sick grandson. Readers will note that the windmill is small and fragile, like her life and that of her grandson, but that Phoenix wants to give the boy a little pleasure despite their poverty and hopelessness. For these reasons the windmill is a contextual or authorial symbol of Phoenix's strong character, generous nature, and pathetic existence.

ALLEGORY

An **allegory** is like a symbol because it transfers and broadens meaning. The term is derived from the Greek word *allegorein* (from *allos*, "other," and *ēgorein*, "to speak in public") which means "to say something beyond what is commonly understood." Allegory, however, is more sustained than symbolism. An allegory is to a symbol as a motion picture is to a still picture. In form, an allegory is a complete and self-sufficient narrative, but it also signifies another series of conditions or events. Although some stories are allegories from beginning to end, many stories that are not allegories can nevertheless contain brief sections or episodes that are *allegorical*. Allegories are often concerned with morality and especially with religion, but we may also find political and social allegories. To the degree that literary works are true not only because of the lives of their main characters but also because of life generally, one might maintain that much literature may be considered allegorical even though the authors did not plan their works as allegories.

Understand the Applications and Meaning of Allegory

Allegories and the allegorical method are more than literary exercises. Without question, readers and listeners learn and memorize stories and tales more easily than moral lessons, and therefore allegory is a favorite method of teaching morality. In addition, thought and expression have not always been free and also safe. The threat of censorship and the danger of political or economic reprisal have sometimes caused authors to express their views indirectly in the form of allegory rather than to name names and write openly, thereby risking political prosecution, accusations of libel, or even bodily harm. Hence, the double meanings of many allegories are based not just in literary type but also in the reality of circumstances in our difficult world.

In studying allegory, determine whether all or part of a work can have an extended, allegorical meaning. The popularity of George Lucas's film *Star Wars* and its sequels (in videotape and newly refurbished rereleases) and also its "prequel" (*The Phantom Menace*), for example, is attributable at least partly to its being an allegory about the conflict between good and evil. Obi Wan Kenobi (intelligence) assists Luke Skywalker (heroism, boldness) and instructs him in "the Force" (moral or religious faith). Thus armed and guided, Skywalker opposes the powers of Darth Vader (evil) to rescue the Princess Leia (purity and goodness) with the aid of the latest spaceships and weaponry (technology). The story has produced a set of popular adventure films, accompanied by dramatic music and ingenious visual and sound effects. With the obvious allegorical overtones, however, it stands for any person's quest for self-fulfillment.

To apply a part of the allegory more specifically, consider that for a time the evil Vader imprisons Skywalker and that Skywalker must exert all his skill and strength to get free and overcome Vader. In the allegorical application of the episode, this imprisonment signifies those moments of doubt, discouragement, and depression that people experience while trying to better themselves through education, work, self-improvement, friendship, marriage, and so on.

Almost from the beginning of recorded literature, similar heroic deeds have been represented in allegorical forms. From ancient Greece, the allegorical hero Jason sails the *Argo* to distant lands to gain the Golden Fleece (those who take risks are rewarded). From Anglo-Saxon England, the hero Beowulf saves King Hrothgar's throne by killing Grendel and his monstrous mother (victory comes to those who rely on the forces of good). From seventeenth-century England, Bunyan's *The Pilgrim's Progress* tells how the hero Christian overcomes difficulties and temptations while traveling from this world to the next (belief, perseverance, and resistance to temptation save the faithful). As long as the parallel connections are close and consistent, such as those mentioned here, an allegorical interpretation is valid.

FABLE, PARABLE, AND MYTH

Closely related to symbolism and allegory in the ability to extend and expand meaning are three additional forms—*fable, parable,* and *myth.*

FABLE. The **fable** (from Latin *fabula,* a story or narration) is an old, brief, and popular form. Often but not always, fables are about animals who possess human traits (such fables are called **beast fables**). Past collectors and editors of fables have attached "morals" or explanations to the brief stories, as is the case with Aesop, the most enduringly popular of fable writers. Tradition has it that Aesop was a slave who composed fables in ancient Greece. His fable "The Fox and the Grapes" signifies the trait of belittling things we cannot have. More recent popular contributions to the fable tradition include Walt Disney's "Mickey Mouse," Walt Kelly's "Pogo," and Berke Breathed's "Bloom County." The adjective *fabulous* refers to the collective body of fables of all sorts, even though the word is often used as little more than a vague term of approval.

PARABLE. A **parable** (from Greek *parabolé,* a "setting beside" or comparison) is a short, simple allegory with a moral or religious bent. Parables are most often associated with Jesus, who used them to embody unique religious insights and truths. For example, his parables "The Prodigal Son" and "The Good Samaritan," as recorded by Luke, are interpreted to show God's understanding, forgiveness, concern, and love.

MYTH. A **myth** (from Greek *muthos,* a story or plot) is a traditional story that embodies and codifies the religious, philosophical, and cultural values of the civilization in which it is composed. Usually the central figures of mythical stories are heroes, gods, and demigods, such as Zeus, Hera, Prometheus, Athena, Sisyphus, Oedipus, and Atalanta from ancient Greece. Most myths are of course fictional, but some are based in historical truth. They are by no means confined to the past, for the word *myth* can also refer to abstractions and ideas that people today hold collectively, such as the concept of never-ending economic growth or the idea that all problems can be solved by science. Sometimes the words *myth* and *mythical* are used with the meaning "fanciful" or "untrue." Such disparagement is misleading because the truths of mythology are not to be found literally in the myths themselves but rather in their symbolic and allegorical interpretations.

∤ ALLUSION IN SYMBOLISM AND ALLEGORY

Cultural or universal symbols and allegories often allude to other works from our cultural heritage, such as the Bible, ancient history and literature, and works of the British and American traditions. Sometimes understanding a story may require knowledge of history and current politics.

If the meaning of a symbol is not immediately clear to you, you will need a dictionary or other reference work. The scope of your college dictionary will surprise you. If you cannot find an entry there, however, try one of the major encyclopedias, or ask your reference librarian, who can direct you to shelves loaded with helpful books. A few excellent guides are *The Oxford Companion to Classical Literature* (ed. M. C. Howatson and Ian Chilvers), *The Oxford Companion to English Literature* (ed. Margaret Drabble), William Rose Benét's *The Reader's Encyclopedia*, Timothy Gantz's *Early Greek Myth: A Guide to Literary and Artistic Sources*, and Richmond Y. Hathorn's *Greek Mythology*. Useful aids in finding biblical references are *Cruden's Complete Concordance*, which in various editions has been a reliable guide since 1737, and *The New Strong's Exhaustive Concordance of the Bible*, which has been revised and expanded regularly since it was first published in 1890. These concordances list all the major words used in the Bible (King James version), so you can easily locate the chapter and verse of any and all biblical passages. If you still have trouble after using sources like these, see your instructor.

STORIES FOR STUDY

AESOP (ca. 6th c. B.C.E.)

Not much is known about the ancient fabulist Aesop. According to tradition, he was a freed slave who lived from about 620 to 560 B.C.E. Aristotle claimed that he had been a public defender, but there is no other evidence that he existed at all. In fact, versions of some of the fables were known a millennium before his time. Aesop might therefore be considered as much a collector as a creator of fables.

The Fox and the Grapes *(ca. 6th C. B.C.E.)*

A hungry Fox came into a vineyard where there hung delicious clusters of ripe Grapes; his mouth watered to be at them; but they were nailed up to a trellis so high, that with all his springing and leaping he could not reach a single bunch. At last, growing tired and disappointed, "Let who will take them!" says he, "they are but green and sour; so I'll e'en let them alone."

Teaches a moral

QUESTIONS

1. How much do you learn about the characteristics of the fox? How are these characteristics related to the moral or message of the fable?

2. What is the conflict in the fable? What is the resolution?

3. In your own words, explain the meaning of the fable. Is the "sour grapes" explanation a satisfactory excuse, or is it a rationalization for failure?

4. From your reading of "The Fox and the Grapes," explain the characteristics of the fable as a type of literature.

THE MYTH OF ATALANTA

The story of Atalanta is an anonymous myth that was known throughout both the ancient Greek and Roman worlds. Because communication in ancient times was uncertain, there were variations in some of the details of the story, such as the names of Atalanta's father and her suitors. However, there was general agreement about the details of her story, which was told by many different writers, such as Apollodorus, Aelian, and Pacuvius. The best-known ancient text of the story appears in Ovid's Metamorphoses. *The story included here is slightly adapted from the brief but comprehensive version by Richmond Y. Hathorn (Greek Mythology, 1977).*

Atalanta *(5th–1st C. B.C.E.)*

There was once a man from Arcadia, in southern Greece, who hoped very much for a son, and when his wife gave birth to a daughter, he abandoned the child in the woods. A she-bear that lived there suckled the baby, until some hunters chanced on the child and reared it, calling it Atalanta [i.e., "the invincible one"]. Atalanta grew up to be a true daughter of the wilderness, an incomparable hunter, being instructed by the Goddess of the Hunt, Artemis, herself. Atalanta was a runner who could outrace any man, and a skillful wrestler, on one occasion defeating the hero Peleus at Pelias' funeral games. She tried also to go on the expedition with the Argonauts to recover the Golden Fleece, but she was turned away by Jason, who was afraid of the trouble a beautiful young woman might cause in a crew of young men.

Then Atalanta took part in the hunting of the Calydonian Boar, falling in love with the Calydonian Prince Meleager and being loved in return. But as this love brought about Meleager's death and as Atalanta was already inclined toward celibacy because of her allegiance to Artemis, she resolved on leading a solitary manless life henceforth, especially because the oracle at Delphi warned her that marriage would cause her whole nature to be changed. So when she gave birth to Meleager's child on her way back from Calydon to Arcadia, she kept it a secret and exposed the baby boy on Mount Parthenion. This child, called Parthenopaeous, was found by the same shepherds who had found and reared Telephus (the son of Hercules and the Princess Auge), and he grew up to be Telephus' companion in early adventures. Eventually Parthenopaeous met his death in the war of the Seven against Thebes.

Meanwhile Atalanta had returned to her old hunting haunts, fighting off attacks of satyrs and discouraging the proposals of mortal men by stipulating that each suitor should compete with her in a race, in which she would be armed with a spear. The condition was that if she overtook her opponent she might stab him to death. And in this way she had disposed of three suitors, cutting off their heads and displaying them beside the racecourse.

There was a young Arcadian named Milanion, who hated women as much as Atalanta hated men, and who was as fond of the chase as she was. He encountered Atalanta frequently during his hunts, and imperceptibly he fell in love with her. More and more he put himself in her way, until he was faithfully following her around, carrying her hunting-nets and enduring her endless disdain. Once when a centaur, Hylaeus, whom Atalanta had rejected, attacked her in anger, Milanion intervened, receiving the blows of the centaur's club and even being wounded by one of the centaur's arrows while protecting Atalanta with his body. Atalanta killed the man-beast, and then nursed the injured Milanion back to health, her feeling for him growing warmer all the while.

Still there was no way of winning Atalanta short of defeating her in the footrace; so in spite of all her discouragements Milanion challenged her. But before the day of the race he prayed to Aphrodite, the Goddess of Love, for aid, and the Goddess plucked three golden apples from the Garden of the Hesperides and instructed him in their use. When the race had begun and Atalanta was drawing near, Milanion dropped one golden apple and the young woman stopped to pick it up. Again she drew near, and again he dropped an apple, the Goddess causing them to weigh heavily in Atalanta's bosom. So when the third apple was dropped and picked up, Milanion was able to reach the goal unscathed and to claim Atalanta as his bride.

But in the flush of his victory and her willing defeat they both forgot to give thanks to Aphrodite. The Goddess punished them by inflicting a rage of lust on both of them, so that they lost all control of themselves. Passing by a sanctuary of Cybele, the Great Mother of Gods, they fell immediately to lovemaking in the holy grotto near the holy temple. They behaved with such abandon that the very statues averted their eyes. The Great Mother was incensed and thought of killing them at once, but instead she changed Milanion into a Lion and Atalanta into a lioness and made them the team that draws her chariot.

5

QUESTIONS

1. What abilities does Atalanta have? How does she try to preserve her independence?

2. Why does Atalanta vow to shun men? What causes her to change her mind? What finally happens to her?

3. Consider the symbolic significance of Atalanta's name, the golden apples, the chopping off of the heads of slow-running suitors, the father's abandonment of Atalanta, the exposure of the infant Parthenopaeus, the battle with the centaur, the way in which Atalanta loses the race, and the lovemaking in the holy grotto of the Great Mother of Gods.

ANITA SCOTT COLEMAN (1890–1960)

Coleman, a writer of stories, poems, and essays, was born in Mexico and educated in New Mexico. Her mother had been a slave who had been bought out of slavery by her father. She published mainly in magazines. "Unfinished Masterpieces," for example, was published in Crisis: A Record of the Darker Races, *the magazine begun in 1910 that heralded the development of the Harlem Renaissance.*

Unfinished Masterpieces   1927

There are days which stand out clearly like limpid pools beside the dusty road; when your thoughts, crystal clear as water, are pinioned in loveliness like star-points. Solitary days, which come often, if you are given to browsing in fields of past adventure; or rarely, if you are seldom retrospective; and not at all, if you are too greatly concerned with rushing onward to a nebulous future. Days whereupon your experiences glimmer before you waveringly like motion-pictures and the people you have known stroll through the lanes of memory, arrayed in vari-colored splendor or in amusing disarray. Days like these are to be revered, for they have their humors and their whimsicalities. Hurry your thoughts and the gathering imageries take flight. Perplexity but makes the lens of introspection blur. And of annoyance beware, for it is an evil vapor that disseminates and drowns the visions in the sea of grim realities. Such days must be cultivated. Scenes for their reception must be set. Cushions perhaps, and warmth of fire. Above all, the warmth of sweet content. Ease and comfort, comfort and ease and moods of receptivity. Then hither, come hither the places and the people we have known, the associations that withstand time's effacements. Backward ho, through the mazes of the past.

STOP! "Why howdy, Dora Johns." Darling playmate of my child-years. With wooly hair a length too short for even pigtails. Mud-spatters upon your funny black face. Mud-spatters all over your dress and your little black hands mud-spattered too.

Why? What? Come on and see. And lo! I am a child again.

Hand in hand, unmindful of her muddy ones, we skip around the old ramshackle house, back to the furthest corner of an unkempt yard, impervious to the tin cans, the ash-heap, the litter, the clutter that impedes our way, our eyes upon, our thoughts bent upon one small clean-swept corner, where there is mud. More mud and water in a battered tin can. And row after row of mud. No, not mud—not merely mud, but things made out of mud. Row on row, drying in the sun.

Carefully, I sit down, doubling up, to be as small as possible, for only this corner where mud things are drying is clean and corners are seldom, if ever, quite large enough. Besides, I must not touch the things made out of mud. If the dried ones fall, they break. If the moist ones are molested, be it with ever so gentle a finger, they lose their shape. Moreover I must not disturb Dora.

Her little hands are busied with the mud. Little moulder's fingers are deftly plying their skill. Her child's face is alight. What has splashed her grave child's face with such a light? I wondered. I wonder now. The glitter of brittle talent, a gleam of sterling genius or the glow from artistic fires burning within the soul of a little black child?

Little Dora shaping figures out of mud. Vases and urns, dolls and toys, flying birds and trotting horses, frisking dogs and playing kittens, marvelous things out of mud. Crying aloud as though dealt a blow if one of the dried mud-figures is broken. Working in mud for endless hours, while the neighbor children play. Their hilarious merriment dropping like bombs into the quiet of our clean-swept corner. Deadly missiles seeking to find a mark. The insistent halloes of futile mirth forever bubbling on the other side of a high-board fence. The dividing fence and upon one side the clean-swept corner and the row on row of mud things drying in the sun. And Dora seeming not to heed the seething bubbles upon the other side, shaping, shaping marvelous things out of mud.

Yet, Oh Dora, now that the day is ours, will you not say, "When did the bombs of futile mirth strike their target? When did the tin-cans and the rags and the old ash-heap crowd you out from your clean-swept corner? What rude hand caused the dried mud shapes to fall and break? Who set a ruthless foot in the midst of your damp mud things?" Or were you too plastic, as plastic as your mud? You dare not tell. Only this you can whisper into the mists of our today. You are one of the Master's unfinished shapes which He will some day gather to mould anew into the finished masterpiece.

A lump of mud. Now, there is a sobriquet for you—you funny, funny man. Mr. William Williams. I saw you but once. We chanced to meet in the home of a mutual friend. I thought you so very funny then. Uncouth and very boorish, but ever, when these pageants of the past, these dumb shows of inarticulate folks arise before me upon retrospective days, you appear garbed in the tatters of pathos.

"I am fifty-one years old," you kept repeating. How pitiful those fifty-one years are. 10
You wear a child's simplicity, the sort that is so sad to see upon a man. Fifty-one and penniless. Fifty-one and possessed of naught else but the clothing you wore. Fifty-one and no place on earth you might call home. You confessed to being a vagabond though "bum" was the term you used and you were very proud of your one accomplishment, an ability to avoid all labour.

"I've given no man a full day's honest work in all my fifty-one years," you boasted. "I gambles. I ain't no cotton-pickin' nigger." Your one and only boast after holding life, the fathomless fountain of eternal possibilities, in your possession for fifty-one priceless years.

Nevertheless you have lived and so intensely. You held us against our will. Clustered around you, listening to you talk. Relating clippings as it were from the scrap-book of your life.

Tales of the road, of the only places you knew. Roads leading away from plantations where the cotton waited to be picked by numberless "cotton-pickin' niggers." Roads leading to pool halls and gambling dens. Roads beginning and roads ending in "riding the roads," carrying backward and forward, here and yon through the weird goblin land of the South's black belt.

With a hardened casualness you told stories that revolted and at the same time cheered us with an all sufficing glow of thankfulness that life had spared us the sordidness of yours. Offhandily, you gave us humorous skits that tempered our laughter with wishes that we might know at least a bit of such a droll existence as had been yours. With magical words you painted pictures so sharply they cut scars upon our hearts. You drew others so filled with rollicking delight their gladsomeness was contagious. With the nonchalance of a player shuffling cards you flipped your characters before us, drawn directly from the cesspool of your contacts and spellbound we listened.

Someone remarked how wonderful you talked and you replied, "Once, I sorter 15
wanted to write books. Once, I uster read a heaps. See times when I was broke and nobody would stake me for a game. I'd lay around and read. I've read the Bible through and through and every Police Gazette I could lay my hands on. Yes, suh, I've read a heap. And I've wished a lot'er times I'd sense enough to write a book."

Lump of mud. Containing the you, the splendid artist in you, the soul of you, the unfinished you in the ungainly lump of you, awaiting the gathering-up to be molded anew into the finished masterpiece.

August Renoir (1841-1919), *The Umbrellas (Les Parapluies)*, c. 1881-1886. National Gallery, London. (© Art Resource, New York)

Jacques-Louis David (1748-1825), *The Death of Socrates*, 1787. Oil on canvas, 51 X 77.25 in./129.5 X 196.2 cm. Signed and dated: L. David (on bench at right); L.D./MDCCLXXXVII (lower left). The Metropolitan Museum of Art, New York. Catherine Lorillard Wolfe Collection, Wolfe Fund, 1931. 31.45. (Photograph © 1995 The Metropolitan Museum of Art)

Henri Matisse (1869-1954), *Harmony in Red (The Tablecloth)*, 1908-1909. Hermitage, St. Petersburg. (Scala/Art Resource, New York. © 2003 Succession H. Matisse, Paris/Artists Rights Society [ARS], New York)

Claude Lorrain (1600-1682), *Harbour at Sunset* (*Seaport at Sunset*), 1639. Oil on canvas. Louvre, Paris. (© Erich Lessing/Art Resource, New York)

Pablo Picasso (1881-1973), *Guernica*, 1937. Oil on canvas, 350 X 782 cm. Museo Nacional Centro de Arte Reina Sofia, Madrid. (© Estate of Pablo Picasso/Artists Rights Society [ARS], New York)

James Abbott McNeill Whistler (1834-1903), *The Little White Girl, Symphony in White, No. 2,* 1864. Oil on canvas, 76.5 X 51.1 cm. (© Tate Gallery, London/Art Resource, New York)

Martin Johnson Heade (American, 1819-1904), *Approaching Storm: Beach Near Newport*, c. 1861–1862. Oil on canvas, 28 X 58 3/8 in./71.12 X 148.27 cm. Courtesy Museum of Fine Arts, Boston. Gift of Maxim Karolik for the M. and M. Karolik Collection of American Paintings, 1815–1865. 45.889. Reproduced with permission. (© 2003 Museum of Fine Arts, Boston. All rights reserved.)

Pieter Brueghel the Elder (c. 1525-1569), *Peasants' Dance*, 1568. Oil on oak wood, 114 X 164 cm. Kunsthistorisches Museum, Vienna. (© Erich Lessing/Art Resource, New York)

What a day! Here is my friend at whose fire-side I have lingered beholding Mr. William Williams, great lump of mud. To be sure, she also is an unfinished production. Though it is apparent that the Master had all but done when she slipped from his hands and dropped to earth to lie groping like the rest of us thereon.

Let us sit here together, friend, and enjoy this day.

I shall try to discover what recent gift you have given to the poor the while you are quietly stitching upon the garments, linens and scarlet, with which to clothe your household. Sit here and smile with the welcoming light in your eyes, knowing that your door is open to such as William Williams and Dora Johns, the Dora who is become as the mud beneath one's feet. Kind mistress of the widely opened door where white and black, rich and poor, of whatever caste or creed may enter and find comfort and ease and food and drink.

QUESTIONS

1. What talents do Dora and William possess? Why have they not lived up to their talents? What has kept them down? Why are they "unfinished masterpieces"?

2. How may Dora and William be seen as symbols? What do they symbolize?

3. Characterize the narrator. What attitude does she exhibit toward the lack of fulfillment of the major characters (see particularly paragraph 19)? How might the story have been different if the narrator had shown hostility, for example, or extreme bitterness?

NATHANIEL HAWTHORNE (1804–1864)

Hawthorne, a friend and associate of the fourteenth president of the United States, Franklin Pierce, is one of the great American writers of the nineteenth century. His most famous work is The Scarlet Letter *(1850), the sale of which gave him a degree of independence. During the administration of President Pierce (1853–1857), Hawthorne served as American consul in Liverpool, England, and this opportunity enabled him to travel extensively in Europe. Throughout his writing there runs a conflict between freedom and conventionality, with those choosing freedom sometimes suffering from the guilt that their choice brings. "Young Goodman Brown," which is one of the early stories that he included in* Twice-Told Tales *(1837, 1842), embodies this conflict*

Young Goodman Brown  1835

Young Goodman Brown came forth at sunset, into the street of Salem village,° but put his head back, after crossing the threshold, to exchange a parting kiss with his young wife. And Faith, as the wife was aptly named, thrust her own pretty head into the street, letting the wind play with the pink ribbons of her cap, while she called to Goodman Brown.

"Dearest heart," whispered she, softly and rather sadly, when her lips were close to his ear, "prithee, put off your journey until sunrise, and sleep in your own bed tonight. A lone woman is troubled with such dreams and such thoughts, that she's afeared of herself, sometimes. Pray, tarry with me this night, dear husband, of all nights in the year!"

Salem village: in Massachusetts, about fifteen miles north of Boston. The time of the story is the late seventeenth or early eighteenth century.

"My love and my Faith," replied young Goodman Brown, "of all nights in the year, this one night must I tarry away from thee. My journey, as thou callest it, forth and back again, must needs be done 'twixt now and sunrise. What, my sweet, pretty wife, dost thou doubt me already, and we but three months married!"

"Then God bless you!" said Faith with the pink ribbons, "and may you find all well, when you come back."

"Amen!" cried Goodman Brown. "Say thy prayers, dear Faith, and go to bed at dusk, and no harm will come to thee."   5

So they parted; and the young man pursued his way, until, being about to turn the corner by the meeting-house, he looked back and saw the head of Faith still peeping after him, with a melancholy air, in spite of her pink ribbons.

"Poor little Faith!" thought he, for his heart smote him. "What a wretch am I, to leave her on such an errand! She talks of dreams, too. Methought, as she spoke, there was trouble in her face, as if a dream had warned her what work is to be done tonight. But no, no! 't would kill her to think it. Well; she's a blessed angel on earth; and after this one night, I'll cling to her skirts and follow her to Heaven."

With this excellent resolve for the future, Goodman Brown felt himself justified in making more haste on his present evil purpose. He had taken a dreary road, darkened by all the gloomiest trees of the forest, which barely stood aside to let the narrow path creep through, and closed immediately behind. It was all as lonely as could be; and there is this peculiarity in such a solitude, that the traveller knows not who may be concealed by the innumerable trunks and the thick boughs overhead; so that, with lonely footsteps, he may yet be passing through an unseen multitude.

"There may be a devilish Indian behind every tree," said Goodman Brown to himself; and he glanced fearfully behind him, as he added, "What if the devil himself should be at my very elbow!"

His head being turned back, he passed a crook of the road, and looking forward again, beheld the figure of a man, in grave and decent attire, seated at the foot of an old tree. He arose at Goodman Brown's approach, and walked onward, side by side with him.   10

"You are late, Goodman Brown," said he. "The clock of the Old South° was striking, as I came through Boston; and that is full fifteen minutes agone."

"Faith kept me back awhile," replied the young man, with a tremor in his voice, caused by the sudden appearance of his companion, though not wholly unexpected.

It was now deep dusk in the forest, and deepest in that part of it where these two were journeying. As nearly as could be discerned, the second traveller was about fifty years old, apparently in the same rank of life as Goodman Brown, and bearing a considerable resemblance to him, though perhaps more in expression than features. Still, they might have been taken for father and son. And yet, though the elder person was as simply clad as the younger, and as simple in manner too, he had an indescribable air of one who knew the world, and would not have felt abashed at the governor's dinner-table, or in King William's° court, were it possible that his affairs should call him thither. But the only thing about him that could be fixed upon as remarkable, was his staff, which bore the likeness of a great black snake, so curiously wrought, that it might almost be seen to twist and wriggle itself like a living serpent. This, of course, must have been an ocular deception, assisted by the uncertain light.

Old South: The Old South Church, in Boston, is still there.
King William: William III was king of England from 1688 to 1701 (the time of the story). William IV was king from 1830 to 1837 (the period when Hawthorne wrote the story).

"Come, Goodman Brown!" cried his fellow-traveller, "this is a dull pace for the beginning of a journey. Take my staff, if you are so soon weary."

"Friend," said the other, exchanging his slow pace for a full stop, "having kept   15
covenant by meeting thee here, it is my purpose now to return whence I came. I have scruples, touching the matter thou wot'st of.°

"Sayest thou so?" replied he of the serpent, smiling apart. "Let us walk on, nevertheless, reasoning as we go, and if I convince thee not, thou shalt turn back. We are but a little way in the forest, yet."

"Too far, too far!" exclaimed the goodman, unconsciously resuming his walk. "My father never went into the woods on such an errand, nor his father before him. We have been a race of honest men and good Christians, since the days of the martyrs.° And shall I be the first of the name of Brown that ever took this path and kept—"

"Such company, thou wouldst say," observed the elder person, interrupting his pause. "Well said, Goodman Brown! I have been as well acquainted with your family as ever a one among the Puritans; and that's no trifle to say. I helped your grandfather, the constable, when he lashed the Quaker woman so smartly through the streets of Salem. And it was I that brought your father a pitch-pine knot, kindled at my own hearth, to set fire to an Indian village, in King Philip's war.° They were my good friends, both; and many a pleasant walk have we had along this path, and returned merrily after midnight. I would fain be friends with you, for their sake."

"If it be as thou sayest," replied Goodman Brown, "I marvel they never spoke of these matters. Or, verily, I marvel not, seeing that the least rumor of the sort would have driven them from New England. We are a people of prayer, and good works to boot, and abide no such wickedness."

"Wickedness or not," said the traveller with twisted staff, "I have a very general ac-   20
quaintance here in New England, The deacons of many a church have drunk the communion wine with me; the selectmen, of divers towns, make me their chairman; and a majority of the Great and General Court are firm supporters of my interest. The governor and I, too—but these are state secrets."

"Can this be so!" cried Goodman Brown, with a stare of amazement at his undisturbed companion. "Howbeit, I have nothing to do with the governor and council; they have their own ways, and are no rule for a simple husbandman like me. But, were I to go on with thee, how should I meet the eye of that good old man, our minister, at Salem village? Oh, his voice would make me tremble, both Sabbath-day and lecture-day!"

Thus far, the elder traveller had listened with due gravity, but now burst into a fit of irrepressible mirth, shaking himself so violently, that his snakelike staff actually seemed to wriggle in sympathy.

"Ha! ha! ha!" shouted he, again and again; then composing himself, "Well, go on, Goodman Brown, go on; but, prithee, don't kill me with laughing!"

"Well, then, to end the matter at once," said Goodman Brown, considerably nettled, "there is my wife, Faith. It would break her dear little heart; and I'd rather break my own!"

---

thou wot'st: you know.

days of the martyrs: the martyrdoms of Protestants in England during the reign of Queen Mary (1553–1558).

King Philip's war: This war (1675–1676), infamous for the atrocities committed by the New England settlers, resulted in the suppression of Indian tribal life and prepared the way for unlimited settlement of New England by European immigrants. "Philip" was the English name of Chief Metacomet of the Wampanoag tribe.

"Nay, if that be the case," answered the other, "e'en go thy ways, Goodman Brown.   25
I would not, for twenty old women like the one hobbling before us, that Faith should
come to any harm."

As he spoke, he pointed his staff at a female figure on the path, in whom Goodman
Brown recognized a very pious and exemplary dame, who had taught him his catechism
in youth, and was still his moral and spiritual adviser, jointly with the minister and Deacon Gookin.

"A marvel, truly, that Goody° Cloyse should be so far in the wilderness, at nightfall!" said he. "But, with your leave, friend, I shall take a cut through the woods, until we
have left this Christian woman behind. Being a stranger to you, she might ask whom I was
consorting with, and whither I was going."

"Be it so," said his fellow-traveller. "Betake you to the woods, and let me keep the
path."

Accordingly, the young man turned aside, but took care to watch his companion,
who advanced softly along the road, until he had come within a staff's length of the old
dame. She, meanwhile, was making the best of her way, with singular speed for so aged a
woman, and mumbling some indistinct words, a prayer, doubtless, as she went. The traveller put forth his staff, and touched her withered neck with what seemed the serpent's tail.

"The devil!" screamed the pious old lady.   30

"Then Goody Cloyse knows her old friend?" observed the traveller, confronting
her, and leaning on his writhing stick.

"Ah, forsooth, and is it your worship, indeed?" cried the good dame. "Yea, truly is
it, and in the very image of my old gossip,° Goodman Brown, the grandfather of the silly
fellow that now is. But, would your worship believe it? My broomstick hath strangely disappeared, stolen, as I suspect, by that unhanged witch, Goody Cory,° and that, too, when
I was all anointed with the juice of smallage and cinquefoil and wolf's-bane—"°

"Mingled with fine wheat and the fat of a new-born babe," said the shape of old
Goodman Brown.

"Ah, your worship knows the recipe," cried the old lady, cackling aloud. "So, as I
was saying, being all ready for the meeting, and no horse to ride on, I made up my mind
to foot it; for they tell me there is a nice young man to be taken into communion tonight.
But now your good worship will lend me your arm, and we shall be there in a twinkling."

"That can hardly be," answered her friend. "I will not spare you my arm, Goody   35
Cloyse, but here is my staff, if you will."

So saying, he threw it down at her feet, where, perhaps, it assumed life, being one
of the rods which its owner had formerly lent to the Egyptian Magi.° Of this fact, however, Goodman Brown could not take cognizance. He had cast up his eyes in astonishment,
and looking down again, beheld neither Goody Cloyse nor the serpentine staff, but his
fellow-traveller alone, who waited for him as calmly as if nothing had happened.

"That old woman taught me my catechism!" said the young man; and there was a
world of meaning in this simple comment.

They continued to walk onward, while the elder traveller exhorted his companion
to make good speed and persevere in the path, discoursing so aptly, that his arguments
seemed rather to spring up in the bosom of his auditor, than to be suggested by himself.

Goody: shortened form of "goodwife," a respectful name for a married woman of low rank. A
"Goody Cloyse" was one of the women sentenced to execution by Hawthorne's great-grandfather, Judge
John Hathorne.
   gossip: from "good sib" or "good relative."
   Goody Cory: name of a woman who was also sent to execution by Judge Hathorne.
   smallage and cinquefoil and wolf's-bane: plants commonly used by witches in making ointments.
   lent to the Egyptian Magi: See Exodus 7:10–12.

As they went he plucked a branch of maple, to serve for a walking-stick, and began to strip it of the twigs and little boughs, which were wet with evening dew. The moment his fingers touched them, they became strangely withered and dried up, as with a week's sunshine. Thus the pair proceeded, at a good free pace, until suddenly, in a gloomy hollow of the road, Goodman Brown sat himself down on the stump of a tree, and refused to go any farther.

"Friend," said he, stubbornly, "my mind is made up. Not another step will I budge on this errand. What if a wretched old woman do choose to go to the devil, when I thought she was going to Heaven! Is that any reason why I should quit my dear Faith, and go after her?"

"You will think better of this by and by," said his acquaintance, composedly. "Sit here and rest yourself a while; and when you feel like moving again, there is my staff to help you along."   40

Without more words, he threw his companion the maple stick, and was as speedily out of sight as if he had vanished into the deepening gloom. The young man sat a few moments by the roadside, applauding himself greatly, and thinking with how clear a conscience he should meet the minister, in his morning walk, nor shrink from the eye of good old Deacon Gookin. And what calm sleep would be his, that very night, which was to have been spent so wickedly, but purely and sweetly now, in the arms of Faith! Amidst these pleasant and praise-worthy meditations, Goodman Brown heard the tramp of horses along the road, and deemed it advisable to conceal himself within the verge of the forest, conscious of the guilty purpose that had brought him thither, though now so happily turned from it.

On came the hoof-tramps and the voices of the riders, two grave old voices, con-versing soberly as they drew near. These mingled sounds appeared to pass along the road, within a few yards of the young man's hiding-place; but owing, doubtless, to the depth of the gloom, at that particular spot, neither the travellers nor their steeds were visible. Though their figures brushed the small boughs by the wayside, it could not be seen that they intercepted, even for a moment, the faint gleam from the strip of bright sky, athwart which they must have passed. Goodman Brown alternately crouched and stood on tiptoe, pulling aside the branches, and thrusting forth his head as far as he durst, without dis-cerning so much as a shadow. It vexed him the more, because he could have sworn, were such a thing possible, that he recognized the voices of the minister and Deacon Gookin, jogging° along quietly, as they were wont to do, when bound to some ordination or eccle-siastical council. While yet within hearing, one of the riders stopped to pluck a switch.

"Of the two, reverend Sir," said the voice like the deacon's, "I had rather miss an ordi-nation dinner than to-night's meeting. They tell me that some of our community are to be here from Falmouth and beyond, and others from Connecticut and Rhode Island; besides several of the Indian powwows,° who, after their fashion, know almost as much deviltry as the best of us. Moreover, there is a goodly young woman to be taken into communion."

"Mighty well, Deacon Gookin!" replied the solemn old tones of the minister. "Spur up, or we shall be late. Nothing can be done, you know, until I get on the ground."

The hoofs clattered again, and the voices, talking so strangely in the empty air,   45
passed on through the forest, where no church had ever been gathered, nor solitary Christian prayed. Whither, then, could these holy men be journeying, so deep into the heathen wilderness? Young Goodman Brown caught hold of a tree, for support, being ready to sink down on the ground, faint and over-burthened with the heavy sickness of his heart. He looked up to the sky, doubting whether there really was a Heaven above him. Yet, there was the blue arch, and the stars brightening in it.

jogging: riding a horse at a slow trot.
powwow: a Narragansett Indian word describing a priest or cult leader who led ritual ceremonies of dance, incantation, and magic.

"With Heaven above, and Faith below, I will yet stand firm against the devil!" cried Goodman Brown.

While he still gazed upward, into the deep arch of the firmament, and had lifted his hands to pray, a cloud, though no wind was stirring, hurried across the zenith, and hid the brightening stars. The blue sky was still visible, except directly overhead, where this black mass of cloud was sweeping swiftly northward. Aloft in the air, as if from the depths of the cloud, came a confused and doubtful sound of voices. Once, the listener fancied that he could distinguish the accents of town's people of his own, men and women, both pious and ungodly, many of whom he had met at the communion-table, and had seen others rioting at the tavern. The next moment, so indistinct were the sounds, he doubted whether he had heard aught but the murmur of the old forest, whispering without a wind. Then came a stronger swell of those familiar tones, heard daily in the sunshine, at Salem village, but never, until now, from a cloud at night. There was one voice, of a young woman, uttering lamentations, yet with an uncertain sorrow, and entreating for some favor, which, perhaps, it would grieve her to obtain. And all the unseen multitude, both saints and sinners, seemed to encourage her onward.

"Faith!" shouted Goodman Brown, in a voice of agony and desperation; and the echoes of the forest mocked him, crying—"Faith! Faith!" as if bewildered wretches were seeking her, all through the wilderness.

The cry of grief, rage, and terror was yet piercing the night, when the unhappy husband held his breath for a response. There was a scream, drowned immediately in a louder murmur of voices fading into far-off laughter, as the dark cloud swept away, leaving the clear and silent sky above Goodman Brown. But something fluttered lightly down through the air, and caught on the branch of a tree. The young man seized it and beheld a pink ribbon.

"My Faith is gone!" cried he, after one stupefied moment. "There is no good on earth, and sin is but a name. Come, devil! for to thee is this world given." 50

And maddened with despair, so that he laughed loud and long, did Goodman Brown grasp his staff and set forth again, at such a rate, that he seemed to fly along the forest path, rather than to walk or run. The road grew wilder and drearier, and more faintly traced, and vanished at length, leaving him in the heart of the dark wilderness, still rushing onward, with the instinct that guides mortal man to evil. The whole forest was peopled with frightful sounds; the creaking of the trees, the howling of wild beasts, and the yell of Indians; while, sometimes, the wind tolled like a distant church bell, and sometimes gave a broad roar around the traveller, as if all Nature were laughing him to scorn. But he was himself the chief horror of the scene, and shrank not from its other horrors.

"Ha! ha! ha!" roared Goodman Brown, when the wind laughed at him. "Let us hear which will laugh loudest! Think not to frighten me with your deviltry! Come witch, come wizard, come Indian powwow, come devil himself! and here comes Goodman Brown. You may as well fear him as he fear you!"

In truth, all through the haunted forest, there could be nothing more frightful than the figure of Goodman Brown. On he flew, among the black pines, brandishing his staff with frenzied gestures, now giving vent to an inspiration of horrid blasphemy, and now shouting forth such laughter, as set all the echoes of the forest laughing like demons around him. The fiend in his own shape is less hideous than when he rages in the breast of man. Thus sped the demoniac on his course, until, quivering among the trees, he saw a red light before him, as when the felled trunks and branches of a clearing have been set on fire, and throw up their lurid blaze against the sky, at the hour of midnight. He paused, in a lull of the tempest that had driven him onward, and heard the swell of what seemed a hymn, rolling solemnly from a distance, with the weight of many voices. He knew the tune. It was a familiar one in the choir of the village meeting-house. The verse died heavily away, and was lengthened by a chorus, not of human voices, but of all the sounds of the be-nighted wilderness, pealing in awful harmony together. Goodman Brown cried out; and his cry was lost to his own ear, by its unison with the cry of the desert.

In the interval of silence, he stole forward, until the light glared full upon his eyes. At one extremity of an open space, hemmed in by the dark wall of the forest, arose a rock, bearing some rude, natural resemblance either to an altar or a pulpit, and sur-rounded by four blazing pines, their tops aflame, their stems untouched, like candles at an evening meeting. The mass of foliage, that had overgrown the summit of the rock, was all on fire, blazing high into the night, and fitfully illuminating the whole field. Each pen-dent twig and leafy festoon was in a blaze. As the red light arose and fell, a numerous con-gregation alternately shone forth, then disappeared in shadow, and again grew, as it were, out of the darkness, peopling the heart of the solitary woods at once.

"A grave and dark-clad company!" quoth Goodman Brown.   55

In truth, they were such. Among them, quivering to-and-fro, between gloom and splendor, appeared faces that would be seen, next day, at the council-board of the province, and others which, Sabbath after Sabbath, looked devoutly heavenward, and benignantly over the crowded pews, from the holiest pulpits in the land. Some affirm that the lady of the governor was there. At least, there were high dames well known to her, and wives of honored husbands, and widows a great multitude, and ancient maidens, all of excellent re-pute, and fair young girls, who trembled lest their mothers should espy them. Either the sudden gleams of light, flashing over the obscure field, bedazzled Goodman Brown, or he recognized a score of the church members of Salem village, famous for their especial sanc-tity. Good old Deacon Gookin had arrived, and waited at the skirts of that venerable saint, his reverend pastor. But, irreverently consorting with these grave, reputable, and pious peo-ple, these elders of the church, these chaste dames and dewy virgins, there were men of dis-solute lives and women of spotted fame, wretches given over to all mean and filthy vice, and suspected even of horrid crimes. It was strange to see, that the good shrank not from the wicked, nor were the sinners abashed by the saints. Scattered, also, among their pale-faced enemies, were the Indian priests, or powwows, who had often scared their native forest with more hideous incantations than any known to English witchcraft.

"But, where is Faith?" thought Goodman Brown; and, as hope came into his heart, he trembled.

Another verse of the hymn arose, a slow and mournful strain, such as the pious love, but joined to words which expressed all that our nature can conceive of sin, and darkly hint-ed at far more. Unfathomable to mere mortals is the lore of fiends. Verse after verse was sung, and still the chorus of the desert swelled between, like the deepest tone of a mighty organ. And, with the final peal of that dreadful anthem, there came a sound, as if the roar-ing wind, the rushing streams, the howling beasts, and every other voice of the unconverted wilderness were mingling and according with the voice of guilty man, in homage to the prince of all. The four blazing pines threw up a loftier flame, and obscurely discovered shapes and visages of horror on the smoke-wreaths, above the impious assembly. At the same moment, the fire on the rock shot redly forth, and formed a glowing arch above its base, where now appeared a figure. With reverence be it spoken, the apparition bore no slight similitude, both in garb and manner, to some grave divine of the New England churches.

"Bring forth the converts!" cried a voice, that echoed through the field and rolled into the forest.

At the word, Goodman Brown stepped forth from the shadow of the trees, and ap-   60
proached the congregation, with whom he felt a loathful brotherhood, by the sympathy of all that was wicked in his heart. He could have well-nigh sworn, that the shape of his own dead father beckoned him to advance, looking downward from a smoke-wreath, while a

woman, with dim features of despair, threw out her hand to warn him back. Was it his mother? But he had no power to retreat one step, nor to resist, even in thought, when the minister and good old Deacon Gookin seized his arms, and led him to the blazing rock. Thither came also the slender form of a veiled female, led between Goody Cloyse, that pious teacher of the catechism, and Martha Carrier, who had received the devil's promise to be queen of hell. A rampant hag was she! And there stood the proselytes, beneath the canopy of fire.

"Welcome, my children," said the dark figure, "to the communion of your race! Ye have found, thus young, your nature and your destiny. My children, look behind you!"

They turned; and flashing forth, as it were, in a sheet of flame, the fiend-worshippers were seen; the smile of welcome gleamed darkly on every visage.

"There," resumed the sable form, "are all whom ye have reverenced from youth. Ye deemed them holier than yourselves, and shrank from your own sin, contrasting it with their lives of righteousness and prayerful aspirations heavenward. Yet, here are they all, in my worshipping assembly! This night it shall be granted you to know their secret deeds; how hoary-bearded elders of the church have whispered wanton words to the young maids of their households; how many a woman, eager for widow's weeds, has given her husband a drink at bedtime, and let him sleep his last sleep in her bosom; how beardless youths have made haste to inherit their father's wealth; and how fair damsels—blush not, sweet ones!—have dug little graves in the garden, and bidden me, the sole guest, to an infant's funeral. By the sympathy of your human hearts for sin, ye shall scent out all the places—whether in church, bed-chamber, street, field, or forest—where crime has been committed, and shall exult to behold the whole earth one stain of guilt, one mighty blood-spot. Far more than this! It shall be yours to penetrate, in every bosom, the deep mystery of sin, the fountain of all wicked arts, and which inexhaustibly supplies more evil impulses than human power—than my power, at its utmost!—can make manifest in deeds. And now, my children, look upon each other."

They did so; and, by the blaze of the hell-kindled torches, the wretched man beheld his Faith, and the wife her husband, trembling before that unhallowed altar.

"Lo! there ye stand, my children," said the figure, in a deep and solemn tone, almost sad, with its despairing awfulness, as if his once angelic nature° could yet mourn for our miserable race. "Depending upon one another's hearts, ye had still hoped that virtue were not all a dream! Now are ye undeceived!—Evil is the nature of mankind. Evil must be your only happiness. Welcome, again, my children, to the communion of your race!"

"Welcome!" repeated the fiend-worshippers, in one cry of despair and triumph.

And there they stood, the only pair, as it seemed, who were yet hesitating on the verge of wickedness, in this dark world. A basin was hollowed, naturally, in the rock. Did it contain water, reddened by the lurid light? or was it blood? or, perchance, a liquid flame? Herein did the Shape of Evil dip his hand, and prepare to lay the mark of baptism upon their foreheads, that they might be partakers of the mystery of sin, more conscious of the secret guilt of others, both in deed and thought, than they could now be of their own. The husband cast one look at his pale wife, and Faith at him. What polluted wretches would the next glance show them to each other, shuddering alike at what they disclosed and what they saw!

"Faith! Faith!" cried the husband. "Look up to Heaven, and resist the Wicked One!"

Whether Faith obeyed, he knew not. Hardly had he spoken, when he found himself amid calm night and solitude, listening to a roar of the wind, which died heavily away through the forest. He staggered against the rock, and felt it chill and damp, while a hanging twig, that had been all on fire, besprinkled his cheek with the coldest dew.

The next morning, young Goodman Brown came slowly into the street of Salem village staring around him like a bewildered man. The good old minister was taking a walk

65

70

---

once angelic nature: Lucifer ("light bearer"), another name for the Devil, led the traditional revolt of the angels and was thrown into hell as his punishment. See Isaiah 14:12–15.

along the grave-yard, to get an appetite for breakfast and meditate his sermon, and bestowed a blessing, as he passed, on Goodman Brown. He shrank from the venerable saint, as if to avoid an anathema. Old Deacon Gookin was at domestic worship, and the holy words of his prayer were heard through the open window. "What God doth the wizard pray to?" quoth Goodman Brown. Goody Cloyse, that excellent old Christian, stood in the early sunshine, at her own lattice, catechising a little girl, who had brought her a pint of morning's milk. Goodman Brown snatched away the child, as from the grasp of the fiend himself. Turning the corner by the meetinghouse, he spied the head of Faith, with the pink ribbons, gazing anxiously forth, and bursting into such joy at the sight of him that she skipt along the street, and almost kissed her husband before the whole village. But Goodman Brown looked sternly and sadly into her face, and passed on without a greeting.

Had Goodman Brown fallen asleep in the forest, and only dreamed a wild dream of a witch-meeting?

Be it so, if you will. But, alas! it was a dream of evil omen for young Goodman Brown. A stern, a sad, a darkly meditative, a distrustful, if not a desperate man did he become, from the night of that fearful dream. On the Sabbath day, when the congregation were singing a holy psalm, he could not listen, because an anthem of sin rushed loudly upon his ear, and drowned all the blessed strain. When the minister spoke from the pulpit, with power and fervid eloquence, and with his hand on the open Bible, of the sacred truths of our religion, and of saint-like lives and triumphant deaths, and of future bliss or misery unutterable, then did Goodman Brown turn pale, dreading lest the roof should thunder down upon the gray blasphemer and his hearers. Often, awaking suddenly at midnight, he shrank from the bosom of Faith, and at morning or eventide, when the family knelt down in prayer, he scowled, and muttered to himself, and gazed sternly at his wife, and turned away. And when he had lived long, and was borne to his grave, a hoary corpse, followed by Faith, an aged woman, and children and grandchildren, a goodly procession, besides neighbors not a few, they carved no hopeful verse upon his tombstone; for his dying hour was gloom.

QUESTIONS

1. Near the end of the story the narrator asks the following: "Had Goodman Brown fallen asleep in the forest, and only dreamed a wild dream of a witch-meeting?" What is the answer? If Goodman Brown's visions come out of his own dreams (mind, subconscious), what do they tell us about him?

2. Is Goodman Brown round or flat? To what extent is he a symbolic "everyman" or representative of humankind?

3. Consider Hawthorne's use of symbolism, such as sunset and night, the walking stick, the witches' sabbath, the marriage to Faith, and the vague shadows amid the darkness, together with other symbols that you may find.

4. What details establish the two settings? What characterizes Salem? The woods? Why might we be justified in seeing the forest as a symbolic setting?

5. To what extent are the people, objects, and events in Goodman Brown's adventure invested with enough *consistent* symbolic resonance to justify calling his episode in the woods an allegory? Consider Brown's wife, Faith, as an allegorical figure. What do you make of Brown's statements "I'll cling to her skirts and follow her to Heaven" (paragraph 7) and "Faith kept me back awhile" (paragraph 12)? In this same light, consider the other characters Brown meets in the forest, the sunset, the walk into the forest, and the staff "which bore the likeness of a great black snake" (paragraph 13).

ST. LUKE (1st c. c.e.)

Although little is known about St. Luke, evidence in Colossians, Philemon, and 2 Timothy indicates that a man named Luke was the "beloved physician" and traveling companion of the apostle Paul, who journeyed in the Mediterranean area during the middle of the first century c.e. Scholars indicate that Luke built his gospel from the Gospel of St. Mark and also from written sources known as "Q" some of which were also used by St. Matthew. Luke also relied on other sources that were available only to him. In addition to his gospel, Luke is also accepted as the author of the Acts of the Apostles.

The Parable of the Prodigal Son (Luke 15:11–32) ⤞⤝⤟ (ca. 90 c.e.)

11 And he [Jesus] said, A certain man had two sons:

12 And the younger of them said to *his* father, Father, give me the portion of goods that falleth *to me*. And he divided unto them *his* living.°

13 And not many days after the younger son gathered all together, and took his journey into a far country,° and there wasted his substance with riotous living.

14 And when he had spent all, there arose a mighty famine in that land; and he began to be in want.

15 And he went and joined himself to a citizen of that country; and he sent him into his fields to feed swine.°

16 And he would fain have filled his belly with the husks° that the swine did eat: and no man gave unto him.

17 And when he came to himself, he said, How many hired servants of my father's have bread enough and to spare, and I perish with hunger!

18 I will arise and go to my father, and will say unto him, Father, I have sinned against heaven, and before thee.

19 And am no more worthy to be called thy son: make me as one of thy hired servants.

20 And he arose, and came to his father. But when he was yet a great way off, his father saw him, and had compassion, and ran, and fell on his neck, and kissed him.

21 And the son said unto him, Father, I have sinned against heaven, and in thy sight, and am no more worthy to be called thy son.

22 But the father said to his servants, Bring forth the best robe, and put *it* on him; and put a ring on his hand, and shoes on *his* feet:

23 And bring hither the fatted calf,° and kill *it;* and let us eat, and be merry:

24 For this my son was dead, and is alive again; he was lost, and is found. And they began to be merry.

25 Now his elder son was in the field: and as he came and drew nigh to the house, he heard music and dancing.

26 And he called one of the servants, and asked what these things meant.

27 And he said unto him, Thy brother is come; and thy father hath killed the fatted calf, because he hath received him safe and sound.

28 And he was angry, and would not go in: therefore came his father out, and intreated him.

---

divided . . . his living: one-third of the father's estate; the son had to renounce all further claim.

for country: countries of the Jewish dispersal, or diaspora, in the areas bordering the Mediterranean Sea.

feed swine: In Jewish custom, pigs were unclean.

husks: pods of the carob tree, the eating of which was thought to be penitential.

fatted calf: grain-fed calf.

29 And he answering said to *his* father, Lo, these many years do I serve thee, neither transgressed I at any time thy commandment: and yet thou never gavest me a kid, that I might make merry with my friends:

30 But as soon as this thy son was come, which hath devoured thy living with harlots, thou hast killed for him the fatted calf.

31 And he said unto him, Son, thou art ever with me, and all that I have is thine.

32 It was meet° that we should make merry, and be glad: for this thy brother was dead, and is alive again: and was lost, and is found.

QUESTIONS

1. Describe the character of the Prodigal Son. Is he flat or round, representative or individual? Why is it necessary that the character be considered representatively, even though he has individual characteristics?

2. What is the plot? What is the antagonism against which the Prodigal Son contends? Why is it necessary that the brother resent the brother's return?

3. What is the resolution of the parable? Why is there no "they lived happily ever after" ending?

4. Using verse numbers, analyze the structure of the parable. What determines your division of the parts? Do these parts coincide with the development of the plot? Describe the relationship of plot to structure in the parable.

5. What is the point of view here? How does the emphasis shift with verse 22?

6. On the basis of the fact that there are many characteristics here of many stories you have read, write a description of the parable as a type of literature.

KATHERINE ANNE PORTER (1894–1980)

Porter was a native of Texas but made her home in many places during her life, spending considerable time in Mexico and Germany. She established her reputation with her early collections Flowering Judas *(1930) and* Pale Horse, Pale Rider *(1939), which gained praise for her analyses and insights into human character. A later collection of stories was* The Leaning Tower *(1944). Her major novel,* Ship of Fools, *appeared in 1962 and was made into a motion picture. She was awarded the Pulitzer Prize for fiction and also the National Book Award in 1966 for her* The Collected Stories. *"The Jilting of Granny Weatherall" first appeared in* Flowering Judas.

The Jilting of Granny Weatherall 1930

She flicked her wrist neatly out of Doctor Harry's pudgy careful fingers and pulled the sheet up to her chin. The brat ought to be in knee breeches. Doctoring around the country with spectacles on his nose! "Get along now, take your schoolbooks and go. There's nothing wrong with me."

meet: appropriate.

Doctor Harry spread a warm paw like a cushion on her forehead where the forked green vein danced and made her eyelids twitch. "Now, now, be a good girl, and we'll have you up in no time."

"That's no way to speak to a woman nearly eighty years old just because she's down. I'd have you respect your elders, young man."

"Well, Missy, excuse me." Doctor Harry patted her cheek. "But I've got to warn you, haven't I? You're a marvel, but you must be careful or you're going to be good and sorry."

"Don't tell me what I'm going to be. I'm on my feet now, morally speaking. It's Cor- 5
nelia. I had to go to bed to get rid of her."

Her bones felt loose, and floated around in her skin, and Doctor Harry floated like a balloon around the foot of the bed. He floated and pulled down his waistcoat and swung his glasses on a cord. "Well, stay where you are, it certainly can't hurt you."

"Get along and doctor your sick," said Granny Weatherall. "Leave a well woman alone. I'll call for you when I want you. . . . Where were you forty years ago when I pulled through milk-leg and double pneumonia? You weren't even born. Don't let Cornelia lead you on." she shouted, because Doctor Harry appeared to float up to the ceiling and out. "I pay my own bills, and I don't throw my money away on nonsense!"

She meant to wave good-by, but it was too much trouble. Her eyes closed of themselves, it was like a dark curtain drawn around the bed. The pillow rose and floated under her, pleasant as a hammock in a light wind. She listened to the leaves rustling outside the window. No, somebody was swishing newspapers: no, Cornelia and Doctor Harry were whispering together. She leaped broad awake, thinking they whispered in her ear.

"She was never like this, *never* like this!" "Well, what can we expect?" "Yes, eighty years old. . . ."

Well, and what if she was? She still had ears. It was like Cornelia to whisper around 10
doors. She always kept things secret in such a public way. She was always being tactful and kind. Cornelia was dutiful; that was the trouble with her. Dutiful and good: "So good and dutiful," said Granny, "that I'd like to spank her." She saw herself spanking Cornelia and making a fine job of it.

"What'd you say, Mother?"

Granny felt her face tying up in hard knots.

"Can't a body think, I'd like to know?"

"I thought you might want something."

"I do. I want a lot of things. First off, go away and don't whisper." 15

She lay and drowsed, hoping in her sleep that the children would keep out and let her rest a minute. It had been a long day. Not that she was tired. It was always pleasant to snatch a minute now and then. There was always so much to be done, let me see: tomorrow.

Tomorrow was far away and there was nothing to trouble about. Things were finished somehow when the time came; thank God there was always a little margin over for peace: then a person could spread out the plan of life and tuck in the edges orderly. It was good to have everything clean and folded away, with the hair brushes and tonic bottles sitting straight on the white embroidered linen: the day started without fuss and the pantry shelves laid out with rows of jelly glasses and brown jugs and white stone-china jars with blue whirligigs and words painted on them: coffee, tea, sugar, ginger, cinnamon, allspice: and the bronze clock with the lion on top nicely dusted off. The dust that lion could collect in twenty-four hours! The box in the attic with all those letters tied up, well she'd have to go through that tomorrow. All those letters—George's letters and John's letters and her letters to them both—lying around for the children to find afterwards made her uneasy. Yes, that would be tomorrow's business. No use to let them know how silly she had been once.

While she was rummaging around she found death in her mind and it felt clammy and unfamiliar. She had spent so much time preparing for death there was no need for bringing it up again. Let it take care of itself now. When she was sixty she had felt very old, finished, and went around making farewell trips to see her children and grandchildren, with a secret in her mind: This is the very last of your mother, children! Then she made her will and came down with a long fever. That was all just a notion like a lot of other things, but it was lucky too, for she had once for all got over the idea of dying for a long time. Now she couldn't be worried. She hoped she had better sense now. Her father had lived to be one hundred and two years old and had drunk a noggin of strong hot toddy on his last birthday. He told the reporters it was his daily habit, and he owed his long life to that. He had made quite a scandal and was very pleased about it. She believed she'd just plague Cornelia a little.

"Cornelia! Cornelia!" No footsteps, but a sudden hand on her cheek. "Bless you, where have you been?"

"Here, mother."   20

"Well, Cornelia, I want a noggin of hot toddy."

"Are you cold, darling?"

"I'm chilly, Cornelia. Lying in bed stops the circulation. I must have told you that a thousand times."

Well, she could just hear Cornelia telling her husband that Mother was getting childish and they'd have to humor her. The thing that most annoyed her was that Cornelia thought she was deaf, dumb, and blind. Little hasty glances and tiny gestures tossed around her and over her head saying. "Don't cross her, let her have her way, she's eighty years old," and she sitting there as if she lived in a thin glass cage. Sometimes Granny almost made up her mind to pack up and move back to her own house where nobody could remind her every minute that she was old. Wait, wait, Cornelia, till your own children whisper behind your back!

In her day she had kept a better house and had got more work done. She wasn't   25
too old yet for Lydia to be driving eighty miles for advice when one of the children jumped the track, and Jimmy still dropped in and talked things over: "Now, Mammy, you've a good business head, I want to know what you think of this? . . ." Old Cornelia couldn't change the furniture around without asking. Little things, little things! They had been so sweet when they were little. Granny wished the old days were back again with the children young and everything to be done over. It had been a hard pull, but not too much for her. When she thought of all the food she had cooked, and all the clothes she had cut and sewed, and all the gardens she had made—well, the children showed it. There they were, made out of her, and they couldn't get away from that. Sometimes she wanted to see John again and point to them and say, Well, I didn't do so badly, did I? But that would have to wait. That was for tomorrow. She used to think of him as a man, but now all the children were older than their father, and he would be a child beside her if she saw him now. It seemed strange and there was something wrong in the idea. Why, he couldn't possibly recognize her. She had fenced in a hundred acres once, digging the post holes herself and clamping the wires with just a negro boy to help. That changed a woman. John would be looking for a young woman with the peaked Spanish comb in her hair and the painted fan. Digging post holes changed a woman. Riding country roads in the winter when women had their babies was another thing: sitting up nights with sick horses and sick negroes and sick children and hardly ever losing one. John, I hardly ever lost one of them! John would see that in a minute, that would be something he could understand, she wouldn't have to explain anything!

It made her feel like rolling up her sleeves and putting the whole place to rights again. No matter if Cornelia was determined to be everywhere at once, there were a great many things left undone on this place. She would start tomorrow and do them. It was good to be strong enough for everything, even if all you made melted and changed and slipped under your hands, so that by the time you finished you almost forgot what you were working for. What was it I set out to do? she asked herself intently, but she could not remember. A fog rose over the valley, she saw it marching across the creek swallowing the trees and moving up the hill like an army of ghosts. Soon it would be at the near edge of the orchard, and then it was time to go in and light the lamps. Come in children, don't stay out in the night air.

Lighting the lamps had been beautiful. The children huddled up to her and breathed like little calves waiting at the bars in the twilight. Their eyes followed the match and watched the flame rise and settle in a blue curve, then they moved away from her. The lamp was lit, they didn't have to be scared and hang on to mother any more. Never, never, never more. God, for all my life I thank Thee. Without Thee, my God, I could never have done it. Hail, Mary, full of grace.

I want you to pick all the fruit this year and see that nothing is wasted. There's always someone who can use it. Don't let good things rot for want of using. You waste life when you waste good food. Don't let things get lost. It's bitter to lose things. Now, don't let me get to thinking, not when I am tired and taking a little nap before supper. . . .

The pillow rose about her shoulders and pressed against her heart and the memory was being squeezed out of it: oh, push down the pillow, somebody: it would smother her if she tried to hold it. Such a fresh breeze blowing and such a green day with no threats in it. But he had not come, just the same. What does a woman do when she has put on the white veil and set out the white cake for a man and he doesn't come? She tried to remember. No, I swear he never harmed me but in that. He never harmed me but in that . . . and what if he did? There was the day, the day, but a whirl of dark smoke rose and covered it, crept up and over into the bright field where everything was planted so carefully in orderly rows. That was hell, she knew hell when she saw it. For sixty years she had prayed against remembering him and against losing her soul in the deep pit of hell, and now the two things were mingled in one and the thought of him was a smoky cloud from hell that moved and crept in her head when she had just got rid of Doctor Harry and was trying to rest a minute. Wounded vanity, Ellen, said a sharp voice in the top of her mind. Don't let your wounded vanity get the upper hand of you. Plenty of girls get jilted. You were jilted, weren't you. Then stand up to it. Her eyelids wavered and let in streamers of blue-gray light like tissue paper over her eyes. She must get up and pull the shades down or she'd never sleep. She was in bed again and the shades were not down. How could that happen? Better turn over, hide from the light, sleeping in the light gave you nightmares. "Mother, how do you feel now?" and a stinging wetness on her forehead. But I don't like having my face washed in cold water!

Hapsy? George? Lydia? Jimmy? No, Cornelia, and her features were swollen and full of little puddles. "They're coming, darling, they'll all be here soon." Go wash your face, child, you look funny.

Instead of obeying, Cornelia knelt down and put her head on the pillow. She seemed to be talking but there was no sound. "Well, are you tongue-tied? Whose birthday is it? Are you going to give a party?"

Cornelia's mouth moved urgently in strange shapes. "Don't do that, you bother me, daughter."

"Oh, no, Mother, Oh, no . . ."

Nonsense. It was strange about children. They disputed your every word. "No what, Cornelia?"

"Here's Doctor Harry."

"I won't see that boy again. He just left five minutes ago."

"That was this morning, Mother. It's night now. Here's the nurse."

"This is Doctor Harry, Mrs. Weatherall. I never saw you look so young and happy!"

30

35

"Ah, I'll never be young again—but I'd be happy if they'd let me lie in peace and get rested."

She thought she spoke up loudly, but no one answered. A warm weight on her fore- 40
head, a warm bracelet on her wrist, and a breeze went on whispering, trying to tell her
something. A shuffle of leaves in the everlasting hand of God. He blew on them and they
danced and rattled. "Mother, don't mind, we're going to give you a little hypodermic."
"Look here, daughter, how do ants get in this bed? I saw sugar ants yesterday." Did you
send for Hapsy too?

It was Hapsy she really wanted. She had to go a long way back through a great many
rooms to find Hapsy standing with a baby on her arm. She seemed to herself to be Hapsy
also, and the baby on Hapsy's arm was Hapsy and himself and herself, all at once, and
there was no surprise in the meeting. Then Hapsy melted from within and turned flimsy
as gray gauze and the baby was a gauzy shadow, and Hapsy came up close and said, "I
thought you'd never come," and looked at her very searchingly and said, "You haven't
changed a bit!" They leaned forward to kiss, when Cornelia began whispering from a long
way off, "Oh, is there anything you want to tell me? Is there anything I can do for you?"

Yes, she had changed her mind after sixty years and she would like to see George. I
want you to find George. Find him and be sure to tell him I forgot him. I want him to
know I had my husband just the same and my children and my house like any other
woman. A good house too and a good husband that I loved and fine children out of him.
Better than I hoped for even. Tell him I was given back everything he took away and
more. Oh, no, oh, God, no, there was something else besides the house and the man and
the children. Oh, surely they were not all? What was it? Something not given back. . . .
Her breath crowded down under her ribs and grew into a monstrous frightening shape
with cutting edges; it bored up into her head, and the agony was unbelievable: Yes, John,
get the doctor now, no more talk, my time has come.

When this one was born it should be the last. The last. It should have been born
first, for it was the one she had truly wanted. Everything came in good time. Nothing left
out, left over. She was strong, in three days she would be as well as ever. Better, A woman
needed milk in her to have her full health.

"Mother, do you hear me?"

"I've been telling you—"   45

"Mother, Father Connolly's here."

"I went to Holy Communion only last week. Tell him I'm not so sinful as all that."

"Father just wants to speak to you."

He could speak as much as he pleased. It was like him to drop in and inquire about
her soul as if it were a teething baby, and then stay on for a cup of tea and a round of cards
and gossip. He always had a funny story of some sort, usually about an Irishman who made
his little mistakes and confessed them, and the point lay in some absurd thing he would
blurt out in the confessional showing his struggles between native piety and original sin.
Granny felt easy about her soul. Cornelia, where are your manners? Give Father Connolly
a chair. She had her secret comfortable understanding with a few favorite saints who
cleared a straight road to God for her. All as surely signed and sealed as the papers for the
new Forty Acres. Forever . . . heirs and assigns forever. Since the day the wedding cake was
not cut, but thrown out and wasted. The whole bottom dropped out of the world, and
there she was blind and sweating with nothing under her feet and the walls falling away.
His hand had caught her under the breast, she had not fallen, there was the freshly polished floor with the green rug on it, just as before. He had cursed like a sailor's parrot and
said. "I'll kill him for you." Don't lay a hand on him, for my sake leave something to God.
"Now, Ellen, you must believe what I tell you . . ."

So there was nothing, nothing to worry about any more, except sometimes in the   50
night one of the children screamed in a nightmare, and they both hustled out shaking
and hunting for the matches and calling, "There, wait a minute, here we are!" John, get
the doctor now. Hapsy's time has come. But there was Hapsy standing by the bed in a
white cap. "Cornelia, tell Hapsy to take off her cap. I can't see her plain."

Her eyes opened very wide and the room stood out like a picture she had seen
somewhere. Dark colors with the shadow rising towards the ceiling in long angles. The
tall black dresser gleamed with nothing on it but John's picture, enlarged from a little
one, with John's eyes very black when they should have been blue. You never saw him, so
how do you know how he looked? But the man insisted the copy was perfect, it was very
rich and handsome. For a picture, yes, but it's not my husband. The table by the bed had
a linen cover and a candle and a crucifix. The light was blue from Cornelia's silk lampshades. No sort of light at all, just frippery. You had to live forty years with kerosene lamps
to appreciate honest electricity. She felt very strong and she saw Doctor Harry with a rosy
nimbus around him.

"You look like a saint, Doctor Harry, and I vow that's as near as you'll ever come to it."

"She's saying something."

"I heard you, Cornelia. What's all this carrying-on?"

"Father Connolly's saying—"   55

Cornelia's voice staggered and bumped like a cart in a bad road. It rounded corners
and turned back again and arrived nowhere. Granny stepped up in the cart very lightly
and reached for the reins, but a man sat beside her and she knew him by his hands, driving the cart. She did not look in his face, for she knew without seeing, but looked instead
down the road where the trees leaned over and bowed to each other and a thousand birds
were singing a Mass. She felt like singing too, but she put her hand in the bosom of her
dress and pulled out a rosary, and Father Connolly murmured Latin in a very solemn
voice and tickled her feet. My God, will you stop that nonsense? I'm a married woman.
What if he did run away and leave me to face the priest by myself? I found another a whole
world better. I wouldn't have exchanged my husband for anybody except St. Michael himself, and you may tell him that for me with a thank you in the bargain.

Light flashed on her closed eyelids, and a deep roaring shook her. Cornelia, is that
lightning? I hear thunder. There's going to be a storm. Close all the windows. Call the
children in . . . "Mother, here we are, all of us." "Is that you, Hapsy?" "Oh, no, I'm Lydia.
We drove as fast as we could." Their faces drifted above her, drifted away. The rosary fell
out of her hands and Lydia put it back. Jimmy tried to help, their hands fumbled together, and Granny closed two fingers around Jimmy's thumb. Beads wouldn't do, it must be
something alive. She was so amazed her thoughts ran round and round. So, my dear
Lord, this is my death and I wasn't even thinking about it. My children have come to see
me die. But I can't, it's not time. Oh, I always hated surprises. I wanted to give Cornelia
the amethyst set—Cornelia, you're to have the amethyst set, but Hapsy's to wear it when
she wants, and, Doctor Harry, do shut up. Nobody sent for you. Oh, my dear Lord, do
wait a minute. I meant to do something about the Forty Acres, Jimmy doesn't need it and
Lydia will later on with that worthless husband of hers. I meant to finish the altar cloth
and send six bottles of wine to Sister Borgia for her dyspepsia. I want to send six bottles of
wine to Sister Borgia, Father Connolly, now don't let me forget.

Cornelia's voice made short turns and tilted over and crashed. "Oh, Mother, oh,
Mother, oh, Mother. . . ."

"I'm not going, Cornelia. I'm taken by surprise. I can't go."

You'll see Hapsy again. What about her? "I thought you'd never come." Granny   60
made a long journey outward, looking for Hapsy. What if I don't find her? What then?

Her heart sank down and down, there was no bottom to death, she couldn't come to the end of it. The blue light from Cornelia's lampshade drew into a tiny point in the center of her brain, it flickered and winked like an eye, quietly it fluttered and dwindled. Granny lay curled down within herself, amazed and watchful, staring at the point of light that was herself; her body was now only a deeper mass of shadow in an endless darkness and this darkness would curl around the light and swallow it up. God, give a sign!

For the second time there was no sign. Again no bridegroom and the priest in the house. She could not remember any other sorrow because this grief wiped them all away. Oh, no, there's nothing more cruel than this—I'll never forgive it. She stretched herself with a deep breath and blew out the light.

QUESTIONS

1. What are Granny's circumstances in the story? What is happening to her? How do we learn about her and her past life? What evidence do you see in the story that Granny is hallucinating and becoming delirious?

2. What sort of person is Granny? Would you call her admirable? Why or why not? In what ways is Granny associated with light? Would it be fair to claim that Granny has been a giver of light during her life? In what way is light symbolic?

3. What is the meaning of "jilting" as it applies to Granny? To what degree does Granny feel "jilted" at the end of her life? How has jilting colored and symbolized her life? How has she overcome it?

4. Explain the story's point of view. (See also Chapter 5.) To what degree does the narrator enter Granny's mind to explain what is happening to her?

5. Who is Hapsy? What is the significance of Hapsy to Granny? What has apparently happened to her?

JOHN STEINBECK (1902–1968)

Steinbeck was born in Salinas, California, and for a time attended Stanford University. In the 1920s, while working at jobs such as surveying, picking fruit, and hatching trout, he began his writing career. A number of stories and novels preceded his best-known novel, The Grapes of Wrath *(1939), for which he was awarded the Pulitzer Prize in 1940. He received the Nobel Prize in literature in 1962. His fiction, often set in rural areas, features a realistic and pessimistic view of life. A number of his novels have been made into films, the best known of which is* The Grapes of Wrath. *His home in Salinas is open to the visiting public.*

The Chrysanthemums ～〈～′～′ 1937

The high grey-flannel fog of winter closed off the Salinas Valley° from the sky and from all the rest of the world. On every side it sat like a lid on the mountains and made of the great valley a closed pot. On the broad, level land floor the gang plows bit deep and left the black earth shining like metal where the shares had cut. On the foothill ranches

---

Salinas Valley: in Monterey County, California, about 50 miles south of San Jose.

across the Salinas River, the yellow stubble fields seemed to be bathed in pale cold sunshine, but there was no sunshine in the valley now in December. The thick willow scrub along the river flamed with sharp and positive yellow leaves.

It was a time of quiet and of waiting. The air was cold and tender. A light wind blew up from the southwest so that the farmers were mildly hopeful of a good rain before long; but fog and rain do not go together.

Across the river, on Henry Allen's foothill ranch there was little work to be done, for the hay was cut and stored and the orchards were plowed up to receive the rain deeply when it should come. The cattle on the higher slopes were becoming shaggy and rough-coated.

Elisa Allen, working in her flower garden, looked down across the yard and saw Henry, her husband, talking to two men in business suits. The three of them stood by the tractor shed, each man with one foot on the side of the little Fordson.° They smoked cigarettes and studied the machines as they talked.

Elisa watched them for a moment and then went back to her work. She was thirty-   5
five. Her face was lean and strong and her eyes were as clear as water. Her figure looked blocked and heavy in her gardening costume, a man's black hat pulled low down over her eyes, clodhopper shoes, a figured print dress almost completely covered by a big corduroy apron with four big pockets to hold the snips, the trowel and scratcher, the seeds and the knife she worked with. She wore heavy leather gloves to protect her hands while she worked.

She was cutting down the old year's chrysanthemum stalks with a pair of short and powerful scissors. She looked down toward the men by the tractor shed now and then. Her face was eager and mature and handsome; even her work with the scissors was over-eager, over-powerful. The chrysanthemum stems seemed too small and easy for her energy.

She brushed a cloud of hair out of her eyes with the back of her glove, and left a smudge of earth on the cheek in doing it. Behind her stood the neat white farm house with red geraniums close-banked around it as high as the windows. It was a hard-swept looking little house, with hard-polished windows, and a clean mud-mat on the front steps.

Elisa cast another glance toward the tractor shed. The strangers were getting into their Ford coupe. She took off a glove and put her strong fingers down into the forest of new green chrysanthemum sprouts that were growing around the old roots. She spread the leaves and looked down among the close-growing stems. No aphids were there, no sowbugs or snails or cutworms. Her terrier fingers destroyed such pests before they could get started.

Elisa started at the sound of her husband's voice. He had come near quietly, and he leaned over the wire fence that protected her flower garden from cattle and dogs and chickens.

"At it again," he said. "You've got a strong new crop coming."   10

Elisa straightened her back and pulled on the gardening glove again. "Yes. They'll be strong this coming year." In her tone and on her face there was a little smugness.

"You've got a gift with things," Henry observed. "Some of those yellow chrysanthemums you had this year were ten inches across. I wish you'd work out in the orchard and raise some apples that big."

Her eyes sharpened. "Maybe I could do it, too. I've a gift with things, all right. My mother had it. She could stick anything in the ground and make it grow. She said it was having planters' hands that knew how to do it."

"Well, it sure works with flowers," he said.

Fordson: a tractor manufactured by the Ford Motor Company, with large steel-lugged rear wheels.

"Henry, who were those men you were talking to?"   15

"Why, sure, that's what I came to tell you. They were from the Western Meat Company. I sold those thirty head of three-year-old steers. Got nearly my own price, too."

"Good," she said. "Good for you."

"And I thought," he continued, "I thought how it's Saturday afternoon, and we might go to Salinas for dinner at a restaurant, and then to a picture show—to celebrate, you see."

"Good," she repeated. "Oh, yes. That will be good."

Henry put on his joking tone. "There's fights tonight. How'd you like to go to the   20
fights?"

"Oh, no," she said breathlessly. "No, I wouldn't like fights."

"Just fooling, Elisa. We'll go to a movie. Let's see. It's two now. I'm going to take Scotty and bring down those steers from the hill. It'll take us maybe two hours. We'll go in town about five and have dinner at the Cominos Hotel. Like that?"

"Of course I'll like it. It's good to eat away from home."

"All right, then. I'll go get up a couple of horses."

She said, "I'll have plenty of time to transplant some of these sets, I guess."   25

She heard her husband calling Scotty down by the barn. And a little later she saw the two men ride up the pale yellow hillside in search of the steers.

There was a little square sandy bed kept for rooting the chrysanthemums. With her trowel she turned the soil over and over, and smoothed it and patted it firm. Then she dug ten parallel trenches to receive the sets. Back at the chrysanthemum bed she pulled out the little crisp shoots, trimmed off the leaves of each one with her scissors and laid it on a small orderly pile.

A squeak of wheels and plod of hoofs came from the road. Elisa looked up. The country road ran along the dense bank of willows and cottonwoods that bordered the river, and up this road came a curious vehicle, curiously drawn. It was an old spring-wagon, with a round canvas top on it like the cover of a prairie schooner. It was drawn by an old bay horse and a little grey-and-white burro. A big stubble-bearded man sat between the cover flaps and drove the crawling team. Underneath the wagon, between the hind wheels, a lean and rangy mongrel dog walked sedately. Words were painted on the canvas in clumsy, crooked letters. "Pots, pans, knives, sisors, lawn mores. Fixed." Two rows of articles and the triumphantly definitive "Fixed" below. The black paint had run down in little sharp points beneath each letter.

Elisa, squatting on the ground, watched to see the crazy, loose-jointed wagon pass by. But it didn't pass. It turned into the farm road in front of her house, crooked old wheels skirling and squeaking. The rangy dog darted from between the wheels and ran ahead. Instantly the two ranch shepherds flew out at him. Then all three stopped, and with stiff and quivering tails, with taut straight legs, with ambassadorial dignity, they slowly circled, sniffing daintily. The caravan pulled up to Elisa's wire fence and stopped. Now the newcomer dog, feeling outnumbered, lowered his tail and retired under the wagon with raised hackles and bared teeth.

The man on the wagon seat called out. "That's a bad dog in a fight when he gets   30
started."

Elisa laughed. "I see he is. How soon does he generally get started?"

The man caught up her laughter and echoed it heartily. "Sometimes not for weeks and weeks," he said. He climbed stiffly down, over the wheel. The horse and the donkey dropped like unwatered flowers.

Elisa saw that he was a very big man. Although his hair and beard were greying, he did not look old. His worn black suit was wrinkled and spotted with grease. The laughter had disappeared from his face and eyes the moment his laughing voice ceased. His eyes were dark and they were full of the brooding that gets in the eyes of teamsters and of sailors. The calloused hands he rested on the wire fence were cracked, and every crack was a black line. He took off his battered hat.

"I'm off my general road, ma'am," he said. "Does this dirt road cut over across the river to the Los Angeles highway?"

Elisa stood up and shoved the thick scissors in her apron pocket. "Well, yes, it does,   35
but it winds around and then fords the river. I don't think your team could pull through the sand."

He replied with some asperity, "It might surprise you what them beasts can pull through."

"When they get started?" she asked.

He smiled for a second. "Yes. When they get started."

"Well," said Elisa, "I think you'll save time if you go back to the Salinas road and pick up the highway there."

He drew a big finger down the chicken wire and made it sing. "I ain't in any hurry,   40
ma'am. I go from Seattle to San Diego and back every year. Takes all my time. About six months each way. I aim to follow nice weather."

Elisa took off her gloves and stuffed them in the apron pocket with the scissors. She touched the under edge of her man's hat, searching for fugitive hairs. "That sounds like a nice kind of a way to live," she said.

He leaned confidentially over the fence. "Maybe you noticed the writing on my wagon. I mend pots and sharpen knives and scissors. You got any of them things to do?"

"Oh, no," she said quickly. "Nothing like that." Her eyes hardened with resistance.

"Scissors is the worst thing," he explained. "Most people just ruin scissors trying to sharpen 'em, but I know how. I got a special tool. It's a little bobbit kind of thing, and patented. But it sure does the trick."

"No. My scissors are all sharp."   45

"All right, then. Take a pot," he continued earnestly, "a bent pot, or a pot with a hole. I can make it like new so you don't have to buy no new ones. That's saving for you."

"No," she said shortly. "I tell you I have nothing like that for you to do."

His face fell to an exaggerated sadness. His voice took on a whining undertone. "I ain't had a thing to do today. Maybe I won't have no supper tonight. You see I'm off my regular road. I know folks on the highway clear from Seattle to San Diego. They save their things for me to sharpen up because they know I do it so good and save them money."

"I'm sorry," Elisa said irritably. "I haven't anything for you to do."

His eyes left her face and fell to searching the ground. They roamed about until   50
they came to the chrysanthemum bed where she had been working. "What's them plants, ma'am?"

The irritation and resistance melted from Elisa's face. "Oh, those are chrysanthemums, giant whites and yellows. I raise them every year, bigger than anybody around here."

"Kind of a long-stemmed flower? Looks like a quick puff of colored smoke?" he asked.

"That's it. What a nice way to describe them."

"They smell kind of nasty till you get used to them," he said.

"It's a good bitter smell," she retorted, "not nasty at all."   55

He changed his tone quickly. "I like the smell myself."

"I had ten-inch blooms this year," she said.

The man leaned farther over the fence. "Look. I know a lady down the road a piece, has got the nicest garden you ever seen. Got nearly every kind of flower but no chrysantheums. Last time I was mending a copper-bottom washtub for her (that's hard job but I do it good), she said to me, 'If you ever run acrost some nice chrysantheums I wish you'd try to get me a few seeds.' That's what she told me."

Elisa's eyes grew alert and eager. "She couldn't have known much about chrysan-themums. You can raise them from seed, but it's much easier to root the little sprouts you see there."

"Oh," he said. "I s'pose I can't take none to her, then." 60

"Why yes you can," Elisa cried. "I can put some in damp sand, and you can carry them right along with you. They'll take root in the pot if you keep them damp. And then she can transplant them."

"She'd sure like to have some, ma'am. You say they're nice ones?"

"Beautiful," she said. "Oh, beautiful." Her eyes shone. She tore off the battered hat and shook out her dark pretty hair. "I'll put them in a flower pot, and you can take them right with you. Come into the yard."

While the man came through the picket gate Elisa ran excitedly along the geranium-bordered path to the back of the house. And she returned carrying a big red flower pot. The gloves were forgotten now. She kneeled on the ground by the starting bed and dug up the sandy soil with her fingers and scooped it into the bright new flower pot. Then she picked up the little pile of shoots she had prepared. With her strong fingers she pressed them into the sand and tamped around them with her knuckles. The man stood over her. "I'll tell you what to do," she said. "You remember so you can tell the lady."

"Yes, I'll try to remember." 65

"Well, look. These will take root in about a month. Then she must set them out, about a foot apart in good rich earth like this, see?" She lifted a handful of dark soil for him to look at. "They'll grow fast and tall. Now remember this. In July tell her to cut them down, about eight inches from the ground."

"Before they bloom?" he asked.

"Yes, before they bloom." Her face was tight with eagerness. "They'll grow right up again. About the last of September the buds will start."

She stopped and seemed perplexed. "It's the budding that takes the most care," she said hesitantly. "I don't know how to tell you." She looked deep into his eyes, search-ingly. Her mouth opened a little, and she seemed to be listening. "I'll try to tell you," she said. "Did you ever hear of planting hands?"

"Can't say I have, ma'am." 70

"Well, I can only tell you what it feels like. It's when you're picking off the buds you don't want. Everything goes right down into your fingertips. You watch your fingers work. They do it themselves. You can feel how it is. They pick and pick the buds. They never make a mistake. They're with the plant. Do you see? Your fingers and the plant. You can feel that, right up your arm. They know. They never make a mistake. You can feel it. When you're like that you can't do anything wrong. Do you see that? Can you understand that?"

She was kneeling on the ground looking up at him. Her breast swelled passionately.

The man's eyes narrowed. He looked away self-consciously. "Maybe I know," he said. "Sometimes in the night in the wagon there—"

Elisa's voice grew husky. She broke in on him. "I've never lived as you do, but I know what you mean. When the night is dark—why, the stars are sharp-pointed, and there's quiet. Why, you rise up and up! Every pointed star gets driven into your body. It's like that. Hot and sharp and—lovely."

Kneeling there, her hand went out toward his legs in the greasy black trousers. Her 75 hesitant fingers almost touched the cloth. Then her hand dropped to the ground. She crouched low like a fawning dog.

He said, "It's nice, just like you say. Only when you don't have no dinner, it ain't."

She stood up then, very straight, and her face was ashamed. She held the flower pot out to him and placed it gently in his arms. "Here. Put it in your wagon, on the seat, where you can watch it. Maybe I can find something for you to do."

At the back of the house she dug in the can pile and found two old and battered aluminum saucepans. She carried them back and gave them to him. "Here, maybe you can fix these."

His manner changed. He became professional. "Good as new I can fix them." At the back of his wagon he set a little anvil, and out of an oily tool box dug a small machine hammer. Elisa came through the gate to watch him while he pounded out the dents in the kettles. His mouth grew sure and knowing. At a difficult part of the work he sucked his under-lip.

"You sleep right in the wagon?" Elisa asked.   80

"Right in the wagon, ma'am. Rain or shine. I'm dry as a cow in there."

"It must be nice," she said. "It must be very nice. I wish women could do such things."

"It ain't the right kind of a life for a woman."

Her upper lip raised a little, showing her teeth. "How do you know? How can you tell?" she said.

"I don't know ma'am," he protested. "Of course I don't know. Now here's your ket-   85
tles, done. You don't have to buy no new ones."

"How much?"

"Oh, fifty cents'll do. I keep my prices down and my work good. That's why I have all them satisfied customers up and down the highway."

Elisa brought him a fifty-cent piece from the house and dropped it in his hand. "You might be surprised to have a rival some time. I can sharpen scissors, too. And I can beat the dents out of little pots. I could show you what a woman might do."

He put his hammer back in the oily box and shoved the little anvil out of sight. "It would be a lonely life for a woman, ma'am, and a scarey life, too, with animals creeping under the wagon all night." He climbed over the single-tree, steadying himself with a hand on the burro's white rump. He settled himself in the seat, picked up the lines. "Thank you kindly, ma'am," he said. "I'll do like you told me; I'll go back and catch the Salinas road."

"Mind," she called, "if you're long in getting there, keep the sand damp."   90

"Sand, ma'am? . . . Sand? Oh, sure. You mean round the chrysantheums. Sure I will." He clucked his tongue. The beasts leaned luxuriously into their collars. The mongrel dog took his place between the back wheels. The wagon turned and crawled out the entrance road and back the way it had come, along the river.

Elisa stood in front of her wire fence watching the slow progress of the caravan. Her shoulders were straight, her head thrown back, her eyes half-closed, so that the scene came vaguely into them. Her lips moved silently, forming the words "Good-bye—good-bye." Then she whispered, "That's a bright direction. There's a glowing there." The sound of her whisper startled her. She shook herself free and looked about to see whether anyone had been listening. Only the dogs had heard. They lifted their heads toward her from their sleeping in the dust, and then stretched out their chins and settled asleep again. Elisa turned and ran hurriedly into the house.

In the kitchen she reached behind the stove and felt the water tank. It was full of hot water from the noonday cooking. In the bathroom she tore off her soiled clothes and flung them into the corner. And then she scrubbed herself with a little block of pumice, legs and thighs, loins and chest and arms, until her skin was scratched and red. When she had dried herself she stood in front of a mirror in her bedroom and looked at her body.

She tightened her stomach and threw out her chest. She turned and looked over her shoulder at her back.

After a while she began to dress, slowly. She put on her newest under-clothing and her nicest stockings and the dress which was the symbol of her prettiness. She worked carefully on her hair, pencilled her eyebrows and rouged her lips.

Before she was finished she heard the little thunder of hoofs and the shouts of   95
Henry and his helper as they drove the red steers into the corral. She heard the gate bang shut and set herself for Henry's arrival.

His step sounded on the porch. He entered the house calling "Elisa, where are you?"

"In my room, dressing. I'm not ready. There's hot water for your bath. Hurry up. It's getting late."

When she heard him splashing in the tub, Elisa laid his dark suit on the bed, and shirt and socks and tie beside it. She stood his polished shoes on the floor beside the bed. Then she went to the porch and sat primly and stiffly down. She looked toward the river road where the willow-line was still yellow with frosted leaves so that under the high grey fog they seemed a thin band of sunshine. This was the only color in the grey afternoon. She sat unmoving for a long time. Her eyes blinked rarely.

Henry came banging out of the door, shoving his tie inside his vest as he came. Elisa stiffened and her face grew tight. Henry stopped short and looked at her. "Why— why, Elisa. You look so nice!"

"Nice? You think I look nice? What do you mean by 'nice'?"   100

Henry blundered on. "I don't know. I mean you look different, strong and happy."

"I am strong? Yes, strong. What do you mean 'strong'?"

He looked bewildered. "You're playing some kind of a game," he said helplessly. "It's a kind of a play. You look strong enough to break a calf over your knee, happy enough to eat it like watermelon."

For a second she lost her rigidity. "Henry! Don't talk like that. You didn't know what you said." She grew complete again. "I'm strong," she boasted. "I never knew before how strong."

Henry looked down toward the tractor shed, and when he brought his eyes back   105
to her, they were his own again. "I'll get out the car. You can put on your coat while I'm starting."

Elisa went into the house. She heard him drive to the gate and idle down his motor, and then she took a long time to put on her hat. She pulled it here and pressed it there. When Henry turned the motor off she slipped into her coat and went out.

The little roadster bounced along on the dirt road by the river, raising the birds and driving the rabbits into the brush. Two cranes flapped heavily over the willow-line and dropped into the river-bed.

Far ahead on the road Elisa saw a dark speck. She knew.

She tried not to look as they passed it, but her eyes would not obey. She whispered to herself sadly. "He might have thrown them off the road. That wouldn't have been much trouble, not very much. But he kept the pot," she explained. "He had to keep the pot. That's why he couldn't get them off the road."

The roadster turned a bend and she saw the caravan ahead. She swung full around   110
toward her husband so she could not see the little covered wagon and the mismatched team as the car passed them.

In a moment it was over. The thing was done. She did not look back. She said loudly, to be heard above the motor, "It will be good, tonight, a good dinner."

"Now you're changed again," Henry complained. He took one hand from the wheel and patted her knee. "I ought to take you in to dinner oftener. It would be good for both of us. We get so heavy out on the ranch."

"Henry," she asked, "could we have wine at dinner?"

"Sure we could. Say! That will be fine."

She was silent for a little while; then she said, "Henry, at those prize fights, do the 115
men hurt each other very much?"

"Sometimes a little, not often. Why?"

"Well, I've read how they break noses, and blood runs down their chests. I've read
how the fighting gloves get heavy and soggy with blood."

He looked around at her. "What's the matter, Elisa? I didn't know you read things
like that." He brought the car to a stop, then turned to the right over the Salinas River
bridge.

"Do any women ever go to the fights?" she asked.

"Oh, sure, some. What's the matter, Elisa? Do you want to go? I don't think you'd 120
like it, but I'll take you if you really want to go."

She relaxed limply in the seat. "Oh, no. No. I don't want to go. I'm sure I don't."
Her face was turned away from him. "It will be enough if we can have wine. It will be plenty." She turned up her coat collar so he could not see that she was crying weakly—like an
old woman.

QUESTIONS

1. What point of view is used in the story? What are the advantages of this point of
   view?

2. Consider the symbolism of the setting in this story with respect to the Salinas Valley, the time of year, and the description of the Allen house. What do these
   things tell us about Elisa Allen and her world?

3. To what extent is Steinbeck's description of Elisa in paragraphs 5 and 6 symbolic? What is she wearing? What do her clothes hide or suppress?

4. What do the chrysanthemums symbolize for Elisa? What do they symbolize *about*
   her? What role do these flowers play in her life?

5. How does Elisa's character or sense of self change during the episode in which
   she washes and dresses for dinner? To what extent is this washing-dressing
   episode symbolic? How would you explain the symbolism?

6. Consider the symbolic impact of Elisa's seeing the chrysanthemum sprouts at
   the roadside. What does her reaction tell us about her values?

MICHEL TREMBLAY (b. 1942)

*Tremblay, a French-Canadian native of Montreal, is both a
dramatist and writer of fiction. He is known as an experimental
and avant-garde writer. In one of his plays, for example
(Albertine, en cinq temps [1984]), five actresses play one character at various times of life. His innovativeness and boldness extend to his treating subjects such as incest, transvestitism, and
prostitution. His works are strongly symbolic and, as with "The
Thimble," allegorical. He has written a number of novels, including the autobiographical* The Fat Woman Next Door Is Preg-
nant *(1981). His collection of stories* Contes pour buveurs attardés *(1966; translated as*
Stories for Late-Night Drinkers, *1974) included "The Thimble."*

The Thimble ✎✎✎✎ 1996

Translated by Jay Bochner

If Bobby Stone had known what was to happen that day, he probably would never have got out of bed. And . . . well, the catastrophe might have been avoided.

Bobby Stone wasn't bad fellow. He worked in an office, drank in moderation, went to mass every Sunday, and had a weakness for plump women. He was neither old nor young, though he wore a hat to cover an expanding bald spot.

Bobby Stone had not the slightest inkling that he was going to be the cause of the catastrophe.

"Now, now, my dear lady, please stop this silly game. People are looking at us!" He was right. A throng of loafers had gathered around them and some were beginning to eye Bobby Stone reproachfully, because this woman was weeping and wailing. "Sir, I beg of you," she cried, "take it! Take it! I give it to you. It's yours!" But Bobby Stone didn't want it; he didn't want to have anything to do with it. "What do you expect me to do with it?" he said. "And besides, it's a . . . thing that belongs to women." More and more people gathered on the sidewalk and Bobby Stone began to sweat. He took out his handkerchief to wipe his forehead, but he didn't remove his hat. *She's crazy. That's it, she's crazy. And all those people looking at us. But I don't want to have her thimble!*

A man emerged from the crowd and grabbed Bobby Stone by the collar. "So," he said, breathing a rotten smell into his face, "we make women cry in the middle of the street?" Bobby Stone was trembling. "But Mister, I don't know this woman! She wants to give me her thimble, and I don't want her thimble, I don't. . . ." Really, Bobby Stone had had enough. In an abrupt surge of courage—or was it cowardice?—he slammed his fist into the face of the man who was threatening him and took off, knocking over two or three people who tried to stop him.

As you might have expected, he worked very poorly that day. The columns of figures swayed on the page, and when he closed his eyes Bobby Stone saw the strange woman offering him the thimble. "It is yours."

The five o'clock bell rang. Bobby Stone slumped in his desk chair, his tie undone and one hand on his chest. *I never would have believed such a stupid incident. . . . Oh, no that's too much, following me to my office!* But it was no vision this time; his eyes were wide open. She was sitting in the chair directly in front of him on the other side of his desk. "If you do not take it immediately," said the woman, "I will have to forbid you from taking it, and then you'll run after me to steal it from me. I'm telling you, you'll steal it from me." Bobby Stone, mad with fear, jumped up and ran towards the door. "Very well then," the woman cried out, "I forbid you to take my thimble!" Bobby Stone stopped short. Oh, what a fine thimble, such a fine beautiful thimble! Made out of plastic with tiny dimples in it. A fine thimble! He must have this thimble. Nothing else in the world existed outside of this pink and yellow thimble. He ran after the woman, who pretended to flee but was careful to lose ground all the while. . . .

Smack! And another! You bitch! So, you wanted to keep it all to yourself, did you? The thimble for you and nothing for me! This is for you. Some good kicks, you see, and the back of my hand, and a few with the knee. . . .

When he left the building his clothes were all mussed and there was some blood on his fingernails, but he had the thimble. It was his and no one—but no one, do you hear?—would ever be able to take it from him. He knew the secret of the thimble now. Before she died the woman had whispered, "In the thimble . . . in the thimble . . . I have locked the universe."

When he awoke the next morning Bobby Stone remembered nothing. He found a pink and yellow thimble on his night-table. What an ugly thimble! He threw it in the garbage. But before he left for the office Bobby Stone tore a loose button from his overcoat. He found some thread and a needle and thought of the thimble at the bottom of the garbage pail. He went and got it. And so as not to prick himself while he sewed on his coat button, Bobby Stone pushed his little finger into the little thimble. He squashed the entire universe.

QUESTIONS

1. Why does the story begin with a premonition of "catastrophe"? What is the catastrophe? To what degree is the narrative realistic or unrealistic?

2. What does the woman say is the significance of the thimble? What does Bobby do with the thimble after he takes it from her? Might some other object have worked as well, for purposes of the story?

3. Explain the story as an allegory of desire, denial, and the consequences of these emotions. What happens when Bobby puts his finger into the thimble? Is there a scientific basis for this happening, and if so, what is it? What is the allegorical meaning?

4. What elements of "The Thimble" may be compared with Aesop's "The Fox and the Grapes"?

❦ WRITING ABOUT SYMBOLISM OR ALLEGORY

To discover possible parallels that determine the presence of symbolism or allegory, consider the following questions.

Questions for Discovering Ideas

A. SYMBOLISM

- What cultural or universal symbols can you discover in names, objects, places, situations, or actions in a work (e.g., the character Faith, the woods, and the walking stick in "Young Goodman Brown"; the lumps of mud in "Unfinished Masterpieces"; the bleakness of the weather in "The Chrysanthemums"; or the straying young man in "The Parable of the Prodigal Son")?

- What contextual symbolism can be found in a work? What makes you think it is symbolic? What is being symbolized? How definite or direct is the symbolism? How systematically is it used? How necessary to the work is it? To what degree does it strengthen the work? How strongly does the work stand on its own without the reading for symbolism?

- Is it possible to make parallel lists to show how qualities of a particular symbol match the qualities of a character or action? Here is such a list for the toy windmill in Welty's "A Worn Path" (Chapter 3).

QUALITIES OF THE WINDMILL	COMPARABLE QUALITIES IN PHOENIX AND HER LIFE
1. Cheap	1. Poor, but she gives all she has for the windmill
2. Breakable	2. Old, and not far from death
3. A gift	3. Generous

4. Not practical	4. Needs relief from reality and practicality
5. Colorful	5. Needs something new and cheerful

B. ALLEGORY

- How clearly does the author point you toward an allegorical reading (i.e., through names and allusions, consistency of narrative, literary context)?
- How consistent is the allegorical application? Does the entire work, or only a part, embody the allegory? On what basis do you draw these conclusions?
- How complete is the allegorical reading? How might the allegory yield to a diagram such as the following one on Hawthorne's "Young Goodman Brown," which shows how characters, actions, objects, and ideas correspond allegorically?

Young Goodman Brown	Brown Himself	Citizens of the Village	The Forest Figure (Father), the Devil	Faith	The Forest Meeting	Retreat into Suspicion and Distrust
Allegorical application to morality and faith	Potential for good	Culture and religious reinforcement	Forces of evil and deceit	Salvation and love; ideals to be rescued and preserved	Attack on ideals; incentive to disillusionment	Destruction of faith; doubt, spiritual negligence, loss of certainty, increase of gloom and suspicion
Allegorical application to personal and general concerns	Individual in pursuit of goals	External support for personal strength and growth	Obstacles to overcome, or by which to be overcome	Personal involvement, steadiness, happiness, religious conviction	Susceptibility to deceit, lack of conviction, misunderstanding, misinterpretation of others	Failure, depression, discouragement, disappointment, bitterness

C. OTHER FORMS

- What enables you to identify the story as a parable or fable? What lesson or moral is either clearly stated or implicit?
- What mythological identification is established in the work? What do you find in the story (names, situations, etc.) that enables you to determine its mythological significance? How is the myth to be understood? What symbolic value does the myth have? What current and timeless application does it have?

Strategies for Organizing Ideas

Relate the central idea of your essay to the meaning of the major symbols or allegorical thrust of the story. An idea about "Young Goodman Brown," for example, is that fanaticism darkens and limits the human soul. An early incident in the story provides symbolic support for this idea. Specifically, when Goodman Brown enters the woods, he resolves "to stand firm against the devil," and he then looks up toward "Heaven above him." As he looks, a "black mass of cloud" appears to hide "the brightening stars" (paragraph 47). Within the limits of our central idea, the cloud can be seen as a symbol, just like the widening path or the night walk itself. Look for ways to make solid connections like this when you designate something as a symbol or allegory.

Also, your essay will need to include justifications for your symbols or allegorical parallels. In "The Masque of the Red Death" (Chapter 6), for example, Prince Prospero's seemingly impregnable "castellated abbey" is a line of defense against the plague. But the Red Death in a human shape easily invades the castle and conquers Prospero and his ill-fated guests. If you treat the abbey as a symbol, it is important to apply it to measures that people take (medicine, escapist activity, etc.) to keep death distant and remote. In the same way, in describing the allegorical elements in "Young Goodman Brown," you need to establish a comprehensive statement such as the following: People lose ideals and forsake principles not because they are evil but because they misunderstand the people around them (see the second demonstrative essay that follows).

For the body of your essay there are a number of strategies for discussing symbolism and allegory. You might use one exclusively, or a combination.

SYMBOLISM.   If you want to write about symbolism, you might consider the following points.

1. THE MEANING OF A MAJOR SYMBOL.   Identify the symbol and what it stands for. Then answer questions such as these: Is the symbol cultural or contextual? How do you decide? How do you derive your interpretation of the symbolic meaning? What is the extent of the meaning? Does the symbol undergo modification or new applications if it reappears in the work? How does the symbol affect your understanding of the work? Does the symbol bring out any ironies? How does the symbol add strength and depth to the work?

2. THE DEVELOPMENT AND RELATIONSHIP OF SYMBOLS.   For two or more symbols, consider issues such as these: How do the symbols connect with each other (like night and the cloud in "Young Goodman Brown" as symbols of a darkening mind)? What additional meanings do the symbols provide? (The windmill and the medicine in "A Worn Path," for example, are ironic because the windmill suggests cheer while the medicine suggests hopelessness.) Do the symbols control the form of the work? How? (For example, at the beginning of Steinbeck's "The Chrysanthemums," the barren wintry countryside is compared to a "closed pot," and at the ending Elisa learns that the tinsmith has dumped the earth out of the pot which she had given to him as a gift. In a similar vein, Joyce's "Araby" [Chapter 6] begins with the "blind" or dead-end street and ends with the darkness of the closed bazaar.) Can these comparable objects and conditions be viewed symbolically in relationship to the development of the two stories? Other issues are whether the symbols fit naturally or artificially into the context of the story or whether and how the writer's symbols create unique quality or excellence.

ALLEGORY.   When writing about allegory, you might use one of the following approaches.

1. THE APPLICATION AND MEANING OF THE ALLEGORY. What is the subject of the story (allegory, fable, parable, myth)? How can it be more generally applied to ideas or to qualities of human character, not only of its own time but also of our own? What other versions of the story do you know, if any? Does it illustrate, either closely or loosely, particular philosophies or religious views? If so, what are these? How do you know?

2. THE CONSISTENCY OF THE ALLEGORY. Is the allegory used consistently throughout the story, or is it used intermittently? Explain and illustrate this use. Would it be correct to call your story *allegorical* rather than an *allegory*? Can you determine how parts of the story are introduced for their allegorical importance? Examples are the increasingly dark pathway home in Bierce's "An Occurrence at Owl Creek Bridge" (Chapter 5) and the frozen preserves in Glaspell's "A Jury of Her Peers" (Chapter 4), which are allegorical equivalents of life's destructive difficulties, and the Parisian street in Maupassant's "The Necklace" (Chapter 1), which corresponds to the temptation to live beyond one's means.

In concluding, you might summarize main points, describe general impressions, explain the impact of the symbolic or allegorical methods, indicate personal responses, or suggest further lines of thought and application. You might also assess the quality and appropriateness of the symbolism or allegory (such as Hawthorne's "Young Goodman Brown" opening in darkness and closing in gloom).

DEMONSTRATIVE STUDENT ESSAY (SYMBOLISM)

Symbols of Light and Darkness in "The Jilting of Granny Weatherall"°

[1] In Katherine Anne Porter's "The Jilting of Granny Weatherall," Ellen Weatherall--Granny Weatherall--is lying on her deathbed, and things in the story are described as they are being filtered through her conscious and unconscious mind. For sixty of her eighty years of life, Granny has been a tower of strength for those around her, but now she is succumbing to a series of more and more powerful strokes, climaxed by the "deep roaring" of the terminal, killing stroke (418, paragraph 57). As she gets closer and closer to her last moments, she fades in and out of awareness, and she finally loses contact with her adult children who are keeping vigil around her. Near the end, as she receives extreme unction from her priest, she does not understand what is happening to her (418, paragraph 56). During this final period of her life, while she sometimes makes contact with those around her, her mind wanders within her memories of beliefs, hopes, plans, fears, embarrassments, sorrows, intentions, and convictions. <u>Her mental associations reveal her personality as a valiant and triumphant woman who has met and overcome the major obstacles and challenges of her life.</u>

° See pp. 413–19 for this story.

[2]   She has been constant in her religious duties, and religious concerns are never far from her mind. For example, one of her last thoughts is that she wants to send six bottles of wine to a Sister Borgia (418, paragraph 57). In her delirium her thoughts touch on her gratefulness for her life of hard work and service, and also on her love for her children, even including a child, Hapsy, whom she apparently lost in childbirth but whom she imagines as having lived to adulthood (Hapsy seems to be the "something not given back" that she tries to remember [417, paragraph 42]). Significantly, as Granny's thoughts "spread out the plan of life and tuck in the edges orderly" (414, paragraph 17) her memories are dominated by biblical symbols of light and darkness.* The symbols of light crystallize her convictions and ideals, while the symbols of darkness express her lifelong fears and anxieties.†

[3]   Light, whiteness, and brightness symbolize the safety, security, and inner peace that Granny seeks but has not always found. Several times she brings to mind that during her lifetime she has made a ceremony out of lighting the household lamps to dispel the darkness, thus acting out many actions reminiscent of the Bible, such as the books of Genesis and Exodus. She remembers that when fog began to move toward her house, "marching across the creek swallowing the trees and moving up the hill like an army of ghosts," her regular reaction was "to go in and light the lamps" (416, paragraph 26). She also remembers, "Lighting the lamps had been beautiful" when her children were small (416, paragraph 27). These memories suggest that she has habitually sought the symbol of light to dispel what she has perceived as threatening darkness. After the rooms had been illumined by lamp light, the children would no longer be frightened: "they didn't have to be scared and hang on to mother any more. Never, never, never more" (416, paragraph 27). Furthermore, when Granny contemplates having chased the darkness of their fears away with light, she associates the light with divine protection and guidance. She likes strong, bright light, not the blue light shining from her daughter Cornelia's silk lampshades, which she believes are "[n]o sort of light at all, just frippery" (418, paragraph 51). Although darkness always looms nearby, Granny has constantly found comfort in surrounding herself with light and brightness, symbols that reflect her need for order and peace of mind.

[4]   In contrast, images of darkness, smoke, and fog suggest the fear, doubt, despair, and instability that Granny associates with life's uncertainties and with the prospect of abandonment. We learn that at the age of twenty she experienced the most crushing event of her life. On the day of her intended marriage, her fiancé, George, jilted her at the altar. She was inconsolable: "The whole bottom dropped out of the world, and there she was blind and sweating with nothing under her feet and the walls falling away" (417, paragraph 49). When she remembers this day of sorrow and betrayal, dark images flow into her mind--disturbing symbols of horror and rejection: "There was the day, the day, but a whirl of dark smoke rose and covered it, crept up and over into the bright field. . . . That was hell, she knew hell when she saw it" (416, paragraph 29). Even her marriage with John, who died young and left her as a widow to rear their children, has not lessened her pain and regret. On her deathbed, after sixty years of "pray[ing] against remembering him [George] and against losing her soul in the deep pit of hell" (416, paragraph 29), another symbol of darkness indicates that she has never

*Central idea.
†Thesis sentence.

truly recovered from her feelings of rejection: "the thought of him was a smoky cloud from hell that moved and crept in her head" (416, paragraph 29). These symbols of darkness bring out the shattering horror of Granny's early pain.

At the end of the story, the combination of references to light and dark symbolizes the second "jilting" that Granny experiences. After Porter establishes that darkness symbolizes doubt and despair and that light symbolizes safety and security, she uses both symbols to show Granny's state of mind in the final moments before her death. Granny visualizes a "point of light that was herself" which is being consumed by darkness (419, paragraph 60). Through repetition, Porter stresses the negative symbolism of darkness, for Granny's "body was now only a deeper mass of shadow in an endless darkness and this darkness would curl around the light and swallow it up" (419, paragraph 60). As the darkness overwhelms her, she cries out to God to give her a saving and healing sign of divine

[5] presence. But "[f]or the second time there was no sign" (419, paragraph 61)--a direct echo of Matthew 12:39 ("there shall no sign be given"). It is safe to assume that Granny feels the despair of darkness as she lies dying, for her thoughts of George as bridegroom merge with her thoughts of God as bridegroom, and she feels jilted by the second just as by the first. Despite her despair, however, the true status of her soul is demonstrated by what we have learned throughout the story about the energy and devotion of her life. Her achievement as the center of her family is accurately summed up by her brief prayer as she remembers lighting the lamps, which is to her the symbol of divine love: "God, for all my life I thank thee. Without Thee, my God, I could never have done it" (416, paragraph 27).

The symbols are of course not only symbols, but they also have a basis in the actual reality of light and darkness. Thus at one point Granny remarks that she should "hide from the light" and that "sleeping in the light gave you nightmares" (416, paragraph 29). It appears that here, at least, reality is more significant than symbolism. When Granny approaches the very end of the "hard pull" of her life, she despairs because of the "cruel" realization that she has received no divine sign. The last words of the story describe her last moment of life: "She

[6] stretched herself with a deep breath and blew out the light." This ending is final and inescapable, and at first we might conclude that Granny's light is gone and that the darkness she feared has overcome her. Another Biblical quotation, however, may put the two symbols into additional perspective, for we learn in Isaiah that in the long run both light and darkness are divine, for God says. "I form the light, and create darkness" (Isaiah 45:7). This is a dimension of Granny's life that goes beyond symbolism.

WORK CITED

Porter, Katherine Anne. "The Jilting of Granny Weatherall." Literature: An Introduction to Reading and Writing. Ed. Edgar V. Roberts and Henry E. Jacobs. 7th ed. Upper Saddle River: Prentice Hall, 2004. 413–19.

Commentary on the Essay about Symbolism

This essay illustrates the principles of analysis described in the second part of the guide for considering symbolism. Connection within the essay may be seen in the continuity of topic from paragraph 1 to paragraph 2, and also from paragraph 4 to paragraph 5. Additionally, some of the individual words and phrases providing continuity are "in contrast," "another," "despite," "however," and "not only . . . but also."

Paragraph 1 establishes the nature of the story and also the qualities of the major character, Granny Weatherall. Paragraph 2 introduces her religious outlook, and it also contains the central idea, about the significance of symbolic light and darkness in the story. The concluding thesis sentence indicates that the body of the essay will treat the meanings of both symbols.

In the body, paragraph 3 introduces the idea that both symbols are common in the Bible, and that therefore they are a natural function of Granny's religious fidelity. Paragraph 4 is a contrast with the preceding paragraph because it explains that Granny was jilted at age twenty and that she has always associated this horrible memory with darkness. Paragraph 5 emphasizes that to Granny, the darkness seems to be victorious as she assumes that she has been deserted by God just as she had been jilted when she was young. Paragraph 6 concludes the essay by (1) treating the reality of light and dark in the story, thus pointing out that the symbols are not consistently used symbolically; and (2) introducing the biblical idea that Granny is in God's hands, whether in lightness or darkness.

DEMONSTRATIVE STUDENT ESSAY (ALLEGORY)

The Allegory of Hawthorne's "Young Goodman Brown"°

[1] Nathaniel Hawthorne's "Young Goodman Brown" is a nightmarish narrative. It allegorizes the process by which something good--religion--becomes a justification for intolerance and prejudice. The major character, Young Goodman Brown of colonial Salem, begins as a presumably pious and holy person, but he takes a walk into a nearby darkening forest of suspicion and sanctimoniousness. The process is portrayed by Hawthorne as being originated by the devil himself, who leads Goodman Brown into the night, which becomes increasingly evil and sinful. By the end of the allegory Brown is transformed into an unforgiving, antisocial, dour, and dreary misanthrope.

[2] Hawthorne's choice of location for the story reminds us that it was in Salem, in the late seventeenth century, that religious zealousness became so extreme that a number of witch trials and public hangings took place solely on the basis of suspicion and false accusation. This setting indicates that Hawthorne's immediate allegorical target is the overzealous pursuit of religious principles. And so Goodman Brown's trip takes him not only into the gloom of night but it also marks a descent into the darkest dungeons of his soul.*

While the story directly details elements in the growth of religious zealotry, Hawthorne's allegory may also be applied more generally to the ways in which people uncritically follow any ideal which leads them to distrust and suspect others. The allegory is thus relevant to those who swallow political slogans, who believe in their own racial or ethnic superiority, or who justify superpatriotism and

°See pp. 403–411 for this story.
*Central idea.

[3]   supernationalism. As such persons persuade themselves of their own supremacy they ignore the greater need for love, understanding, toleration, cooperation, and forgiveness. Hawthorne's allegory is a realistic portrait of how people get into such a mental state, with Goodman Brown as the example of the attitude. Such people push ahead even against their own good nature and background, and they develop their prejudices through delusion, mistrust, and suspicion.[†]

Young Goodman Brown's pathway into the night is not a direct plunge into evil, but Hawthorne shows that Brown is not without good nature because he has misgivings about what he is doing. Many times early in the story we learn that he has doubts about the "evil purpose" of his allegorical walk. At the very beginning Faith calls him back and pleads with him to stay the night with her (403, paragraph 2), but even so, he leaves her. As he walks away he thinks of himself as "a wretch" for doing so (404, paragraph 7). He excuses himself with a promise that once the evening is over he will stick with Faith forever after, an "excellent resolve for the future," as the narrator ironically states (404, paragraph 8). When Goodman Brown is reproached by the devil for being late--we conclude that Brown's purpose was to keep this diabolical appointment--he gives the excuse "Faith kept me back a while" (404, paragraph 12), a sentence of ironic double meaning. Once he has kept his appointment with the devil, he states his intention to go no farther because he has "scruples" which remind him that "it is my purpose now to return whence I came" (405, paragraph 15). When he alludes to his family's proud and virtuous heritage, the devil finds his naive and idealistic claims deeply amusing. Even when Goodman Brown is standing before the altar of profanation deep within the forest, he appeals to Faith, "Look up to Heaven, and resist the Wicked One!" (410, paragraph 68). All this hesitation represents a true conscience in Goodman Brown even though he ignores it as he progresses deeper into the forest of sin. His failure--and failure it is--is his inability or unwillingness to persist in making his own insight and conscience his guides of conduct.

It is important to remember that Goodman Brown is favored by his background, which might reasonably be expected to have kept him on a true path of goodness. Almost as a claim of entitlement he cries out, "With Heaven above, and Faith below, I will yet stand firm against the devil" (408, paragraph 46). He also cries out for Faith even when he hears a voice resembling hers that is "uttering lamentations" within the darkening woods (408, paragraph 47). When he sees Faith's pink ribbon mysteriously flutter down, he exclaims, "My Faith is gone!" (408, paragraph 50). These instances show allegorically that Goodman Brown's previous way of life has given him the right paths to follow and the right persons in whom to believe. Even as he is most sorely tempted when he is standing before the "unhallowed altar" (410, paragraph 64), he asks the question "But, where is Faith?" as though he could reclaim the innocence that he has previously known (409, paragraph 57). Just as he has ignored his conscience, he also ignores the power of his background, and it is such neglect that fuels his change into "the demoniac" (408, paragraph 53) who abandons himself to "the instinct that guides mortal man to evil" (408, paragraph 51).

Another major element in Goodman Brown's allegorical path into darkness is that he is persuaded in his own imagination that virtually all the people he

[4]

[5]

[†]Thesis sentence.

knows have yielded their lives to sin and are therefore unworthy. In the grips of this distorted view of others, he believes not what he sees but what he thinks he is seeing. Thus he witnesses the encounter between the devil and Goody Cloyse shortly after he enters the forest, but what he sees is not the good woman who taught him his catechism but rather a witch who is bent on evil and who is on speaking terms with the devil. He ignores the fact that he too is on friendly terms with the devil (the image of his own father) and therefore, while ignoring the log in his own eye, he condemns Goody Cloyse for the speck in hers. After his transfor-

[6] mation, when he walks back into his village from his allegorical walk into evil, he "snatche[s] away" a child from Goody Cloyse as though she were preaching the words of the devil and not God (411, paragraph 70). He cannot believe that others possess goodness as long he is convinced by the devil's words that "the whole earth [is] one stain of guilt, one mighty blood-spot" (410, paragraph 63). For this reason he condemns both his minister and Deacon Gookin, whose conspiratorial voices he imagines that he overhears on the pathway through the forest. In short, the process of Hawthorne's allegory about the growth of harmful pietism demonstrates that travelers on the pathway to prejudice accept suspicion and mistrust without trying to get at the whole truth and without recognizing that judgment is not in human but rather is in divine hands.

As Hawthorne allegorizes the development of religious discrimination, he makes clear that, like any kind of discrimination, mistrust and suspicion form its basis. Certainly, as the devil claims, human beings commit many criminal and depraved sins (410, paragraph 63), but this does not mean that all human beings are equally at fault, and that they are beyond love and redemption. The key for Goodman Brown is that he exceeds his judgmental role and bases his condemnation of others solely on his own hasty and mistrustful conclusions. As long as

[7] he has faith he will not falter, but when he leaves his faith, or believes that he has lost his faith, he is adrift and will see only evil wherever he looks. For this reason he permits suspicion and loathing to distort his previous love for his wife and neighbors, and he becomes harsh and desperate forever after. Hawthorne devotes the concluding paragraph of the story to a brief summary of Brown's life after the fateful night. This conclusion completes the allegorical cycle beginning with Brown's initiation into evil and extending to his "dying hour" of "gloom" and his unhopeful tombstone (411, paragraph 72).

Hawthorne's "Young Goodman Brown" allegorizes the paradox of how noble beliefs become ignoble. Goodman Brown dies in gloom because he believes that his wrong vision is true. His form of evil is the hardest to stop because wrongdoers who are convinced of their own goodness are beyond reach. In view

[8] of such self-righteous evil, whether cloaked in the apparent virtues of Puritanism or of some other blindly rigorous doctrine, Hawthorne writes, "The fiend in his own shape is less hideous than when he rages in the breast of man" (408, paragraph 53). Young Goodman Brown is one of the many who are convinced that they alone walk in light, but who really create darkness.

WORK CITED

Hawthorne, Nathaniel. "Young Goodman Brown." Literature: An Introduction to Reading and Writing. Ed. Edgar V. Roberts and Henry E. Jacobs. 7th ed. Upper Saddle River: Prentice Hall, 2004. 403–11.

Commentary on the Essay about Allegory

This essay deals with a major idea in "Young Goodman Brown," and it therefore illustrates the first approach described earlier (p. 431). Unity in the essay is achieved by a number of means. For example, paragraph 2 extends a topic in paragraph 1. Also, a phrase in sentence 2 of paragraph 1 is echoed in sentence 1 of paragraph 8. Making additional connections within the essay are individual words such as "another," "while," "therefore," and the repetition of words throughout the essay that are contained in the thesis sentence.

The first three paragraphs of the essay consitute an extended introduction to the topics of paragraphs 4 through 8, for they establish "Young Goodman Brown" as an allegory. Paragraph 1 briefly treats the allegorical nature of the narrative. Paragraph 2 relates the historical basis of the topic to Hawthorne's purpose in writing the story, and it concludes with the essay's central idea. Paragraph 3 broadens the scope of Hawthorne's allegory by showing that it includes zealousness wherever it might appear. Paragraph 3 also concludes with the essay's thesis sentence.

Paragraph 4, the first in the body, deals with an important aspect of the allegory, and one that makes it particularly relevant and timely even today— namely, that people of basically good nature may grow to practice evil ways under the pretense of goodness. Similarly, paragraph 5 points out that such people usually come from good backgrounds and have benefited from good influences during their lives.

Paragraphs 6 and 7 locate the origins of evil in two major human qualities,— first, the belief in one's own delusions; and second, the mental confusion that results from the conviction that appearance is more real and believable than reality itself. Paragraph 8 concludes the essay on the note that the finished "product"—a person who has become suspicious and misguided—demonstrates how good ideas, when pushed to the extreme by false imagination, can backfire.

Special Topics for Writing and Argument about Symbolism and Allegory

1. Compare and contrast the symbolism in Munro's "The Found Boat" (Chapter 7), Porter's "The Jilting of Granny Weatherall," Steinbeck's "The Chrysanthemums," and Tremblay's "The Thimble." To what degree do the stories rely on contextual symbols? On universal symbols? On the basis of your comparison, what is the case for asserting that realism and fantasy are directly related to the nature of the symbolism employed by the writer?

2. Why do writers who advocate moral, philosophical, or religious issues frequently use symbolism or allegory? In treating this question, you might introduce references from "The Parable of the Prodigal Son," Tremblay's "The Thimble," and Hawthorne's "Young Goodman Brown."

3. Write an essay on the allegorical method of one or more of the parables included in the Gospel of St. Luke, such as "The Bridegroom" (5:34–35), "The Garments and the Wineskins" (5:36–39), "The Sower" (8:4–15), "The Good

Samaritan" (10:25–37), "The Prodigal Son" (15:11–32), "The Ox in the Well" (14:5–6), "The Watering of Animals on the Sabbath" (13:15–17), "The Rich Fool" (12:16–21), "Lazarus" (16:19–31), "The Widow and the Judge" (18:1–8), and "The Pharisee and the Publican" (18:9–14).

4. Consider the story of Atalanta, first as a myth about male dominance in man-woman relationships and second as a myth about the obstacles to a woman's freedom and independence.

5. Write your own brief story using a widely recognized cultural symbol such as the flag (patriotism, love of country, a certain type of politics), water (life, sexuality, regeneration), or the population explosion (the end of life on earth). By arranging actions and dialogue, make clear the issues conveyed by your symbol, and also try to resolve conflicts the symbol might raise among your characters.

6. Write a brief story in which you develop your own contextual symbol. You might, for example, demonstrate how holding a job brings out character strengths that are not at first apparent or how neglecting to care for the inside or outside of a house indicates a character's decline. The principle is to take something that can at first seem normal and ordinary, then to make that thing symbolic as you develop your story.

7. Using the card or computer catalogue of your library, discover a recent critical-biographical book or books about Hawthorne. Explain what the book says about Hawthorne's uses of symbolism. To what extent does the book relate Hawthorne's symbolism to his religious and family heritage?

Idea or Theme: *The Meaning and the Message in Fiction*

The word **idea** refers to the result or results of general and abstract thinking. Synonymous words are *concept, thought, opinion,* and *principle.* In literary study the consideration of ideas relates to *meaning, interpretation, explanation,* and *significance.* Although ideas are usually extensive and complex, separate ideas can be named by words such as *right, good, love, piety, liberty, causation, wilderness,* and, not surprisingly, *idea* itself.

IDEAS AND ASSERTIONS

Although single words alone can name ideas, we must put these words into operation in *sentences* or *assertions* before they can advance our understanding. Good operational sentences about ideas are not the same as ordinary conversational statements such as "It's a nice day." An observation of this sort may be true (depending on the weather), but it gives us no ideas and does not stimulate our minds. Rather, a sentence asserting an idea should initiate a thought or argument about the day's quality, such as "A nice day requires light breezes, blue sky, a warm sun, and relaxation." Because this sentence makes an assertion about the word "nice," it allows us to consider and develop the idea of a nice day.

In studying literature, always express ideas as assertions. For example, you might state that an idea in Lawrence's "The Horse Dealer's Daughter" is "love," but it would be difficult to discuss anything more unless you make an assertion that promises an argument, such as "This story demonstrates the idea that love is irresistible and irrational." This assertion would lead you to explain the unlikely love that bursts out in the story. Similarly, for Welty's "A Worn Path" (Chapter 3) an assertion like the following would advance further argument: "Phoenix embodies the idea that caring for others gives no reward but the continuation of the duty itself."

Although we have noted only one idea in these two works, most stories contain many ideas. When one of the ideas seems to be the major one, it is called the **theme.** In practice, the words *theme* and *major idea* are the same.

IDEAS AND ISSUES

A word that is often used as an equivalent to *idea* is **issue,** which may be defined as an open and unsettled point about which there may be argument or contention. On political matters, issues are usually about what courses of action to take, such as whether a new bridge should be built, or whether more money should be spent on schools. Often, however, the issues revolve about the theoretical basis on which to proceed. To this extent, issues are identical with ideas. The nature of issue as a concept—because issues develop out of situations—is particularly helpful in the study of literature. Sometimes issues are not stated and we as readers make inferences from the work or works we are discussing. What do we find there? What do we take away from the work? Have we understood the issue properly? How do we define the issue as an idea? The answers to such questions frequently lead us directly into discussions of ideas. Thus in Zabytko's "Home Soil" we find the topic of behavior in past wars, but a major issue is the assertion that people can never forget wrongs that they have committed, even in past wars that have been justifiable. The idea is that human beings are not capable of living with intense guilt. In Bambara's "The Lesson" we find the issue of economic inequality and political injustice. (See the demonstrative essay at the end of this chapter.) Here the idea is that economic inequality results in an unacceptably high human cost.

IDEAS AND VALUES

Literature embodies **values** along with ideas. *Value,* of course, commonly refers to the price of something, but in the realm of ideas and principles, it is a standard of what is desired, sought, esteemed, and treasured. For example, *democracy* refers to our political system, but it is also a complex idea of representative government that we esteem most highly, and so also do we esteem concepts like honor, cooperation, generosity, and love. A vital idea/value is *justice,* which, put most simply, involves equality before the law and also the fair evaluation of conduct that is deemed unacceptable or illegal. Such an idea of justice is a major topic of Glaspell's "A Jury of Her Peers" (Chapter 4). Glaspell dramatizes the story of a farm wife who, for twenty years, endures her husband's intimidation and her abject circumstances of life, but finally rises up to strangle her husband in his sleep. By a rigid concept of justice as guilt-conviction-punishment, the wife, Minnie Wright, is guilty and should be convicted and punished. But justice as an idea also involves a full and fair consideration of the circumstances and motivation of wrongdoing, and it is such a consideration that Mrs. Hale and Mrs. Peters make during their examination of Minnie's kitchen. Many of their speeches showing their sympathy to Minnie are equivalent to a jurylike deliberation. Their final decision is in effect a verdict, and their covering up of Minnie's crime is evidence for their implied idea that justice, to be most highly valued, should be tempered with understanding—even if they do not use these exact words when they discuss Minnie's situation. In short, the idea of justice underlying Glaspell's "A Jury of Her Peers" also involves a deeply felt value.

A graphic connection of ideas and values is seen in Picasso's massive painting *Guernica* (Insert I-5)). The painting superbly illustrates the agony of Guernica, the Spanish town bombed by Nazi planes in 1937. The agonized horse and the screaming man, the disembodied head and arms, the mother holding her dead infant—all convey the idea that war is an unspeakable crime against humanity. Picasso's condemnation of war and the man responsible for the slaughter at Guernica, Francisco Franco, is also clear. That Picasso wanted his values to be understood is confirmed by his instruction that the painting was not to be displayed in Spain until after Franco died.

THE PLACE OF IDEAS IN LITERATURE

Because writers of poems, plays, and stories are usually not systematic philosophers, it is not appropriate to go "message hunting" as though their works contained nothing but ideas. Indeed, there is great benefit and pleasure to be derived from just savoring a work—following the patterns of narrative and conflict, getting to like the characters, understanding the work's implications and suggestions, and listening to the sounds of the author's words—to name only a few of the reasons for which literature is treasured.

Nevertheless, ideas are vital to understanding and appreciating literature: Writers have ideas and want to communicate them. For example, in "The Horse Dealer's Daughter" Lawrence presents us with a man and a woman who fall suddenly and unpredictably in love. This love is unusual, and the story is therefore effective, but the story is also provocative because it raises the idea that love pushes aside other decisions that people make. Gaines in "The Sky Is Gray" describes the extraordinary difficulty and pain experienced by a young child and his mother when trying to see a dentist, but the story embodies *ideas* about the need for equality, the strength of human character, and the beauty of human kindness.

Distinguish Between Ideas and Actions

As you analyze works for ideas, it is important to avoid the trap of confusing ideas and actions. Such a trap is contained in the following sentence about O'Connor's "First Confession" (Chapter 7): "The major character, Jackie, misbehaves at home and tries to stab his sister with a bread knife." This sentence successfully describes a major action in the story, but it does not express an *idea* that connects characters and events, and for this reason it obstructs understanding. Some possible connections might be achieved with sentences like these:

"'First Confession' illustrates the idea that family life may produce anger and potential violence" or " 'First Confession' shows that compelling children to accept authority may produce effects that are the opposite of adult intentions." A study based on these connecting formulations could be focused on ideas and would not be sidetracked into doing no more than retelling O'Connor's story.

Distinguish Between Ideas and Situations

You should also distinguish between ideas and situations. For example, in Joyce's "Araby" (Chapter 6) the narrator describes his frustration and embarrassment at the Araby bazaar in Dublin. This is a *situation,* but it is not the *idea* brought out by the situation. Joyce's idea here is rather that immature love causes unreal dreams and hopes that result in disappointment and self-reproach. If you are able to distinguish a story's various situations from the writer's major idea or ideas, you will be able to focus on ideas and therefore sharpen your own thinking.

❧ HOW TO FIND IDEAS

Ideas are not as obvious as characters or setting. To determine an idea, you need to consider the meaning of what you read and then to develop explanatory and comprehensive assertions. Your assertions need not be the same as those that others might make. People notice different things, and individual formulations vary. In Chopin's "The Story of an Hour" (Chapter 8), for example, an initial expression of some of the story's ideas might take any of the following forms: (1) Partners in even a good marriage can have ambivalent feelings about their married life. (2) An accident can lead a wife to think negative but previously unrecognized thoughts. (3) Even those closest to a person may never realize that person's innermost feelings. Although any one of these choices could be a basic idea in the study of "The Story of an Hour," they have in common the main character's surprising feelings of release when she is told that her husband has been killed. In discovering ideas, you should follow a similar process—making a number of formulations for an idea and then selecting one for further development.

As you read, be alert to the different ways in which authors convey ideas. One author might prefer an indirect way through a character's speeches, whereas another may prefer direct statements. In practice, authors can employ any or all the following methods.

1. STUDY THE AUTHORIAL VOICE. Although authors mainly render action, dialogue, and situation, they sometimes state ideas to guide us and deepen our understanding. In the second paragraph of Maupassant's "The Necklace" (Chapter 1), for example, the authorial voice presents the idea that women have only charm and beauty to get on in the world. Ironically, Maupassant uses the story to show that for the major character Mathilde, nothing is effective, for her charm cannot prevent disaster. Hawthorne, in "Young Goodman Brown" (Chapter 9), expresses this powerful idea: "The fiend in his own shape is less hideous than when he rages in the breast of man" (paragraph 53). This statement is made by the narrator just when the major character, Goodman Brown, is speeding through "the benighted wilderness" on his way to the satanic ritual. Although the idea is complex and will bear extensive discussion, its essential aspect is that the causes of evil originate within human beings themselves, and the implication is that we alone are responsible for all our actions, whether good or evil.

2. STUDY THE FIRST-PERSON SPEAKER. First-person narrators or speakers frequently express ideas along with their depiction of actions and situations, and they also make statements from which you can make inferences about ideas. (See also Chapter 5.) Because what they say is part of a dramatic presentation, they can be right or wrong, well-considered or thoughtless, good or bad, or brilliant or half-baked, depending on the speaker. In Zabytko's "Home Soil" the narrator considers the idea that war causes regret and guilt, no matter when it is fought or who fights in it. A somewhat half-baked speaker, yet an interesting one, is Sammy, the narrator of Updike's "A & P" (Chapter 7), who seems engulfed in intellectual commonplaces, particularly in his insinuation about the intelligence of women. In his defense, however, Sammy *acts* on the worthy idea that people have the freedom and right to wear any clothes they please. If the speaker seems to possess limited understanding or inadequate consideration of what he or she is saying, like Estelle in Atwood's "Rape Fantasies" (Chapter 8), you may nevertheless still study and evaluate such a speaker's ideas. Estelle, for example, tends to trivialize the seriousness of rape, but the ideas she expresses about the relationships between men and women are worthy of consideration.

3. STUDY THE STATEMENTS MADE BY CHARACTERS. In many stories, characters express their own views, which can be right or wrong, admirable or contemptible. When you consider such dramatic speeches, you must do considerable interpreting and evaluating yourself. For example, Old Man Warner in "The Lottery" (Chapter 5) states that the lottery is valuable even though we learn from the narrator that the beliefs underlying it have long been forgotten. Because Warner is a zealous and noisy person, however, his words show that outdated ideas continue to do harm even when there is strong reason to throw them out and adopt new ones. The unnamed young man in the dentist's office in "The Sky Is Gray" speaks in contradictions, but when he amplifies them we learn a number of his ideas about the failure of America to live up to its professed principles of equality. The men in Glaspell's "A Jury of Her Peers" express conventional masculine ideas about the need for men to control women. The story itself, however, demonstrates the shortcomings and pomposity of their thought.

4. STUDY THE WORK'S FIGURES OF SPEECH. Figurative language is one of the major components of poetry, but it also abounds in prose fiction (see also Chapter 17). In Joyce's "Araby," for example, the narrator uses a beautiful figure of speech to describe his youthful admiration for his friend's sister. He says that his body "was like a harp and her words and gestures were like fingers running upon the wires." Another notable figure occurs in Glaspell's "A Jury of Her

Peers," when a character compares John Wright, the murdered husband, with "a raw wind that gets to the bone" (paragraph 201). With this figurative language, Glaspell conveys the idea that bluntness, indifference, and cruelty create great personal damage.

5. STUDY HOW CHARACTERS MAY STAND FOR IDEAS. Characters and their actions can often be equated with certain ideas and values. The power of Mathilde's story in Maupassant's "The Necklace" (Chapter 1), for example, enables us to explain that she represents the idea that unrealizable dreams can invade and damage the real world. Two diverse or opposed characters can embody contrasting ideas, as with Louise and Josephine of Chopin's "The Story of an Hour." Each woman can be taken to represent differing views about the role of women in marriage. In effect, characters who stand for ideas can assume symbolic status, as in Hawthorne's "Young Goodman Brown," where the protagonist symbolizes the alienation accompanying zealousness, or in Ozick's "The Shawl" (Chapter 6), where the small child Magda embodies the vulnerability and helplessness of human beings in the face of dehumanizing state brutality. Such characters can be equated directly with particular ideas, and to talk about them is a shorthand way of talking about the ideas.

6. STUDY THE WORK ITSELF AS AN EMBODIMENT OF IDEAS. One of the most important ways in which authors express ideas is to interlock them within all parts and aspects of the work. The art of painting is instructive here, for a painting can be taken in with a single view that comprehends all the aspects of color, form, action, and expression, which can also be considered separately. Thus, we may again refer to the broken and distorted figures in Picasso's *Guernica*, (Insert I-5), which can be viewed together, and which emphasize the idea that war creates unspeakable horror and suffering for both human beings, animals, and the land itself. In the same way, when a work is considered in its totality, the various parts collectively can embody major ideas, as in Gaines's "The Sky Is Gray," where Gaines dramatizes the urgency of ending racial barriers. He does not use these exact words, but the story powerfully embodies this idea. The third section of Bierce's "An Occurrence at Owl Creek Bridge" (Chapter 5) is based on the idea that under great stress the human mind operates with lightning speed. Most works represent ideas in a similar way. Even "escape literature," which ostensibly enables readers to forget immediate problems, contains conflicts between good and evil, love and hate, good spies and bad, earthlings and aliens, and so on. Thereby, such works *do* embody ideas, even though their avowed intention is not to make readers think but rather to help them forget.

STORIES FOR STUDY

TONI CADE BAMBARA (1939–1995)

Bambara (an African tribal name that Toni Cade appropriated from an old manuscript) was brought up in Harlem and Bedford Stuyvesant in New York. She received a B.A. from Queens College and an M.A. in American Studies from the City College of New York. For a time she was a social worker, and later she taught at many schools, including Rutgers, Duke, and the Scribe Video Center in Philadelphia. She also collaborated in the writing of television documentaries, including a life of W.E.B. DuBois. In her fiction she treats the subjects of the black and also the female experience. She avoids using this material for political purposes, however, even though the subjects could easily fall within the political realm. Instead, she deals with her characters on the human level, trying to offer her readers "nourishment." Story Collections are Gorilla, My Love *(1972), from which "The Lesson" is taken, and* The Sea Birds Are Still Alive *(1977). Her novels are* The Salt Eaters *(1980) and* If Blessing Comes *(1987).*

The Lesson ⚶⚶⚶ 1972

Back in the days when everyone was old and stupid or young and foolish and me and Sugar were the only ones just right, this lady moved on our block with nappy hair and proper speech and no makeup. And quite naturally we laughed at her, laughed the way we did at the junk man who went about his business like he was some big-time president and his sorry-ass horse his secretary. And we kinda hated her too, hated the way we did the winos who cluttered up our parks and pissed on our handball walls and stank up our hallways and stairs so you couldn't halfway play hide-and-seek without a goddamn gas mask. Miss Moore was her name. The only woman on the block with no first name. And she was black as hell, cept for her feet, which were fish-white and spooky. And she was always planning these boring-ass things for us to do, us being my cousin, mostly, who lived on the block cause we all moved North the same time and to the same apartment then spread out gradual to breathe. And our parents would yank our heads into some kinda shape and crisp up our clothes so we'd be presentable for travel with Miss Moore, who always looked like she was going to church, though she never did. Which is just one of the things the grownups talked about when they talked behind her back like a dog. But when she came calling with some sachet she'd sewed up or some gingerbread she'd made or some book, why then they'd all be too embarrassed to turn her down and we'd get handed over all spruced up. She'd been to college and said it was only right that she should take responsibility for the young ones education, and she not even related by marriage or blood. So they'd go for it. Specially Aunt Gretchen. She was the main gofer in the family. You got some ole dumb shit foolishness you want somebody to go for, you send for Aunt Gretchen. She been screwed into the go-along for so long, it's a blood-deep natural thing with her. Which is how she got saddled with me and Sugar and Junior in the first place while our mothers were in a la-de-da apartment up the block having a good ole time.

So this one day Miss Moore rounds us all up at the mailbox and it's purdee° hot and she's knockin herself out about arithmetic. And school suppose to let up in summer I heard, but she don't never let up. And the starch in my pinafore scratching the shit outta me and I'm really hating this nappy-head bitch and her goddamn college degree. I'd much rather go to the pool or to the show where it's cool. So me and Sugar leaning on the mailbox being surly, which is a Miss Moore word. And Flyboy checking out what everybody brought for lunch. And Fat Butt already wasting his peanut-butter-and-jelly

---

purdee: pretty.

sandwich like the pig he is. And Junebug punchin on Q.T.'s arm for potato chips. And Rosie Giraffe shifting from one hip to the other waiting for somebody to step on her foot or ask her if she from Georgia so she can kick ass, preferably Mercedes'. And Miss Moore asking us do we know what money is, like we a bunch of retards. I mean real money, she say, like it's only poker chips or Monopoly papers we lay on the grocer. So right away I'm tired of this and say so. And would much rather snatch Sugar and go to the Sunset and terrorize the West Indian kids and take their hair ribbons and their money too. And Miss Moore files that remark away for next week's lesson on brotherhood, I can tell. And finally I say we oughta get to the subway cause it's cooler and besides we might meet some cute boys. Sugar done swiped her mama's lipstick, so we ready.

So we heading down the street and she's boring us silly about what things cost and what our parents make and how much goes for rent and how money ain't divided up right in this country. And then she gets to the part about we all poor and live in the slums, which I don't feature. And I'm ready to speak on that, but she steps out in the street and hails two cabs just like that. Then she hustles half the crew in with her and hands me a five-dollar bill and tells me to calculate 10 percent tip for the driver. And we're off. Me and Sugar and Junebug and Flyboy hangin out the window and hollering to everybody, putting lipstick on each other cause Flyboy a faggot anyway, and making farts with our sweaty armpits. But I'm mostly trying to figure how to spend this money. But they all fascinated with the meter ticking and Junebug starts laying bets as to how much it'll read when Flyboy can't hold his breath no more. Then Sugar lays bets as to how much it'll be when we get there. So I'm stuck. Don't nobody want to go for my plan, which is to jump out at the next light and run off to the first bar-b-que we can find. Then the driver tells us to get the hell out cause we there already. And the meter reads eighty-five cents. And I'm stalling to figure out the tip and Sugar say give him a dime. And I decide he don't need it bad as I do, so later for him. But then he tries to take off with Junebug foot still in the door so we talk about his mama something ferocious. Then we check out that we on Fifth Avenue and everybody dressed up in stockings. One lady in a fur coat, hot as it is. White folks crazy.

"This is the place," Miss Moore say, presenting it to us in the voice she uses at the museum. "Let's look in the windows before we go in."

"Can we steal?" Sugar asks very serious like she's getting the ground rules squared away before she plays. "I beg your pardon," say Miss Moore, and we fall out. So she leads us around the windows of the toy store and me and Sugar screamin, "This is mine, that's mine, I gotta have that, that was made for me, I was born for that," till Big Butt drowns us out.

"Hey, I'm going to buy that there."

"That there? You don't even know what it is, stupid."

"I do so," he say punchin on Rosie Giraffe. "It's a microscope."

"Whatcha gonna do with a microscope, fool?"

"Look at things."

"Like what, Ronald?" ask Miss Moore. And Big Butt ain't got the first notion. So here go Miss Moore gabbing about the thousands of bacteria in a drop of water and the somethinorother in a speck of blood and the million and one living things in the air around us is invisible to the naked eye. And what she say that for? Junebug go to town on that "naked" and we rolling. Then Miss Moore ask what it cost. So we all jam into the window smudgin it up and the price tag say $300. So then she ask how long'd take for Big Butt and Junebug to save up their allowances. "Too long," I say. "Yeh," adds Sugar, "outgrown it by that time." And Miss Moore say no, you never outgrow learning instruments. "Why, even medical students and interns and," blah, blah, blah. And we ready to choke Big Butt for bringing it up in the first damn place.

5

10

"This here costs four hundred eighty dollars," say Rosie Giraffe. So we pile up all over her to see what she pointin out. My eyes tell me it's a chunk of glass cracked with something heavy, and different-color inks dripped into the splits, then the whole thing put into a oven or something. But for $480 it don't make sense.

"That's a paperweight made of semi-precious stones fused together under tremendous pressure," she explains slowly, with her hands doing the mining and all the factory work.

"So what's a paperweight?" asks Rosie Giraffe.

"To weigh paper with, dumbbell," say Flyboy, the wise man from the East.   15

"Not exactly," say Miss Moore, which is what she say when you warm or way off too. "It's to weigh paper down so it won't scatter and make your desk untidy." So right away me and Sugar curtsy to each other and then to Mercedes who is more the tidy type.

"We don't keep paper on top of the desk in my class," say Junebug, figuring Miss Moore crazy or lyin one.

"At home, then," she say. "Don't you have a calendar and a pencil case and a blotter and a letter-opener on your desk at home where you do your homework?" And she know damn well what our homes look like cause she nosys around in them every chance she gets.

"I don't even have a desk," say Junebug. "Do we?"

"No. And I don't get no homework neither," says Big Butt.   20

"And I don't even have a home," say Flyboy like he do at school to keep the white folks off his back and sorry for him. Send this poor kid to camp posters, is his specialty.

"I do," says Mercedes. "I have a box of stationery on my desk and a picture of my cat. My godmother bought the stationery and the desk. There's a big rose on each sheet and the envelopes smell like roses."

"Who wants to know about your smelly-ass stationery," say Rosie Giraffe fore I can get my two cents in.

"It's important to have a work area all your own so that. . . ."

"Will you look at this sailboat, please," say Flyboy, cuttin her off and pointin to the   25
thing like it was his. So once again we tumble all over each other to gaze at this magnificent thing in the toy store which is just big enough to maybe sail two kittens across the pond if you strap them to the posts tight. We all start reciting the price tag like we in assembly. "Handcrafted sailboat of fiberglass at one thousand one hundred ninety-five dollars."

"Unbelievable," I hear myself say and am really stunned. I read it again for myself just in case the group recitation put me in a trance. Same thing. For some reason this pisses me off. We look at Miss Moore and she lookin at us, waiting for I dunno what.

"Who'd pay all that when you can buy a sailboat set for a quarter at Pop's, a tube of glue for a dime, and a ball of string for eight cents? It must have a motor and a whole lot else besides," I say. "My sailboat cost me about fifty cents."

"But will it take water?" say Mercedes with her smart ass.

"Took mine to Alley Pond Park once," say Flyboy. "String broke. Lost it. Pity."

"Sailed mine in Central Park and it keeled over and sank. Had to ask my father for   30
another dollar."

"And you got the strap," laugh Big Butt. "The jerk didn't even have a string on it. My old man wailed on his behind."

Little Q.T. was staring hard at the sailboat and you could see he wanted it bad. But he too little and somebodyd just take it from him. So what the hell. "This boat for kids, Miss Moore?"

"Parents silly to buy something like that just to get all broke up," say Rosie Giraffe.

"That much money it should last forever," I figure.

"My father'd buy it for me if I wanted it."   35

"Your father, my ass," say Rosie Giraffe getting a chance to finally push Mercedes.

"Must be rich people shop here," say Q.T.

"You are a very bright boy," say Flyboy. "What was your first clue?" And he rap him on the head with the back of his knuckles, since Q.T. the only one he could get away with. Though Q.T. liable to come up behind you years later and get his licks in when you half expect it.

"What I want to know is," I says to Miss Moore though I never talk to her, I wouldn't give the bitch that satisfaction, "is how much a real boat costs? I figure a thousand'd get you a yacht any day."

"Why don't you check that out," she says, "and report back to the group?" Which really pains my ass. If you gonna mess up a perfectly good swim day least you could do is have some answers. "Let's go in," she say like she got something up her sleeve. Only she don't lead the way. So me and Sugar turn the corner to where the entrance is, but when we get there I kinda hang back. Not that I'm scared, what's there to be afraid of, just a toy store. But I feel funny, shame. But what I got to be shamed about? Got as much right to go in as anybody. But somehow I can't seem to get hold of the door, so I step away from Sugar to lead. But she hangs back too. And I look at her and she looks at me and this is ridiculous. I mean, damn, I have never ever been shy about doing nothing or going nowhere. But then Mercedes steps up and then Rosie Giraffe and Big Butt crowd in behind and shove, and next thing we all stuffed into the doorway with only Mercedes squeezing past us, smoothing out her jumper and walking right down the aisle. Then the rest of us tumble in like a glued-together jigsaw done all wrong. And people lookin at us. And it's like the time me and Sugar crashed into the Catholic church on a dare. But once we got in there and everything so hushed and holy and the candles and the bowin and the handkerchiefs on all the drooping heads, I just couldn't go through with the plan. Which was for me to run up to the altar and do a tap dance while Sugar played the nose flute and messed around in the holy water. And Sugar kept givin me the elbow. Then later teased me so bad I tied her up in the shower and turned it on and locked her in. And she'd be there till this day if Aunt Gretchen hadn't finally figured I was lyin about the boarder takin a shower.

Same thing in the store. We all walkin on tiptoe and hardly touchin the games and puzzles and things. And I watched Miss Moore who is steady watchin us like she waitin for a sign. Like Mama Drewery watches the sky and sniffs the air and takes note of just how much slant is in the bird formation. Then me and Sugar bump smack into each other, so busy gazing at the toys, 'specially the sailboat. But we don't laugh and go into our fat-lady bump-stomach routine. We just stare at that price tag. Then Sugar run a finger over the whole boat. And I'm jealous and want to hit her. Maybe not her, but I sure want to punch somebody in the mouth.

"Whatcha bring us here for, Miss Moore?"

"You sound angry, Sylvia. Are you mad about something?" Givin me one of them grins like she tellin a grown-up joke that never turns out to be funny. And she's lookin very closely at me like maybe she plannin to do my portrait from memory. I'm mad, but I won't give her that satisfaction. So I slouch around the store bein very bored and say, "Let's go."

Me and Sugar at the back of the train watchin the tracks whizzin by large then small then gettin gobbled up in the dark. I'm thinking about this tricky toy I saw in the store. A clown that somersaults on a bar then does chin-ups just cause you yank lightly at his leg. Cost $35. I could see me askin my mother for a $35 birthday clown. "You wanna who that costs what?" she'd say, cocking her head to the side to get a better view of the hole in my head. Thirty-five dollars could buy new bunk beds for Junior and Gretchen's boy. Thirty-five dollars and the whole household could go visit Granddaddy Nelson in the country. Thirty-five dollars would pay for the rent and the piano bill too. Who are these people that spend that much for performing clowns and $1000 for toy sailboats? What kinda work they do and

40

how they live and how come we ain't in on it? Where we are is who we are. Miss Moore always pointin out. But it don't necessarily have to be that way, she always adds then waits for somebody to say that poor people have to wake up and demand their share of the pie and don't none of us know what kind of pie she talking about in the first damn place. But she ain't so smart cause I still got her four dollars from the taxi and she sure ain't gettin it. Messin up my day with this shit. Sugar nudges me in my pocket and winks.

Miss Moore lines us up in front of the mailbox where we started from, seem   45
like years ago, and I got a headache for thinkin so hard. And we lean all over each other so we can hold up under the draggy-ass lecture she always finishes us off with at the end before we thank her for borin us to tears. But she just looks at us like she readin tea leaves. Finally she say, "Well, what did you think of F.A.O. Schwarz?"

Rosie Giraffe mumbles, "White folks crazy."

"I'd like to go there again when I get my birthday money," says Mercedes, and we shove her out the pack so she has to lean on the mailbox by herself.

"I'd like a shower. Tiring day," say Flyboy.

Then Sugar surprises me by sayin, "You know, Miss Moore, I don't think all of us here put together eat in a year what that sailboat costs." And Miss Moore lights up like somebody goosed her. "And?" she say, urging Sugar on. Only I'm standin on her foot so she don't continue.

"Imagine for a minute what kind of society it is in which some people can spend on   50
a toy what it would cost to feed a family of six or seven. What do you think?"

"I think," say Sugar pushing me off her feet like she never done before, cause I whip her ass in a minute, "that this is not much of a democracy if you ask me. Equal chance to pursue happiness means an equal crack at the dough, don't it?" Miss Moore is besides herself and I am disgusted with Sugar's treachery. So I stand on her foot one more time to see if she'll shove me. She shuts up, and Miss Moore looks at me, sorrowfully I'm thinkin. And somethin weird is goin on, I can feel it in my chest.

"Anybody else learn anything today?" lookin dead at me. I walk away and Sugar has to run to catch up and don't even seem to notice when I shrug her arm off my shoulder.

"Well, we got four dollars anyway," she says.

"Uh hunh."

"We could go to Hascombs and get half a chocolate layer and then go to the Sun-   55
set and still have plenty money for potato chips and ice cream sodas."

"Uh hunh."

"Race you to Hascombs," she say.

We start down the block and she gets ahead which is O.K. by me cause I'm going to the West End and then over to the Drive to think this day through. She can run if she want to and even run faster. But ain't nobody gonna beat me at nuthin.

QUESTIONS

1. Who is Miss Moore? Why does she take an interest in the neighborhood children? Where does she take them? How does she attempt to teach them?

2. Describe Sylvia, the narrator, as a character. Why does she keep $4 of the five-dollar bill given her by Miss Moore? What does she mean by "ain't nobody gonna beat me at nuthin" in the story's final paragraph?

3. Describe the level of language of the narrator. Is she writing the story or speaking it? How do you know?

4. Consider paragraphs 44–50. What ideas about equality and inequality are brought out in the story? Do you think the children will remember the "lesson" or that they will forget it? Why?

ANTON CHEKHOV (1860–1904)

For a brief biography, please see Chapter 28, page 1570.

Lady with Lapdog 1899

Translated by David Magarshack

The appearance on the front of a new arrival—a lady with a lapdog—became the topic of general conversation. Dmitry Dmitrich Gurov, who had been a fortnight in Yalta and got used to its ways, was also interested in new arrivals. One day, sitting on the terrace of Vernet's restaurant, he saw a young woman walking along the promenade; she was fair, not very tall, and wore a toque; behind her trotted a white pomeranian.

Later he came across her in the park and in the square several times a day. She was always alone, always wearing the same toque, followed by the white pomeranian. No one knew who she was, and she became known simply as the lady with the lapdog.

"If she's here without her husband and without any friends," thought Gurov, "it wouldn't be a bad idea to strike up an acquaintance with her."

He was not yet forty, but he had a twelve-year-old daughter and two schoolboy sons. He had been married off when he was still in his second year at the university, and his wife seemed to him now to be almost twice his age. She was a tall, black-browed woman, erect, dignified, austere, and, as she liked to describe herself, a "thinking person." She was a great reader, preferred the new "advanced" spelling, called her husband by the more formal "Dimitry" and not the familiar "Dmitry"; and though he secretly considered her not particularly intelligent, narrow-minded, and inelegant, he was afraid of her and disliked being at home. He had been unfaithful to her for a long time, he was often unfaithful to her, and that was why, perhaps, he almost always spoke ill of women, and when men discussed women in his presence, he described them as the lower breed.

He could not help feeling that he had had enough bitter experience to have the right to call them as he pleased, but all the same without the lower breed he could not have existed a couple of days. He was bored and ill at ease among men, with whom he was reticent and cold, but when he was among women he felt at ease, he knew what to talk about with them and how to behave, even when he was silent in their company he experienced no feeling of constraint. There was something attractive, something elusive in his appearance, in his character and his whole person that women found interesting and irresistible; he was aware of it, and was himself drawn to them by some irresistible force. 5

Long and indeed bitter experience had taught him that every new affair, which at first relieved the monotony of life so pleasantly and appeared to be such a charming and light adventure, among decent people and especially among Muscovites,° who are so irresolute and so hard to rouse, inevitably developed into an extremely complicated problem and finally the whole situation became rather cumbersome. But at every new meeting with an attractive woman he forgot all about this experience, he wanted to enjoy life so badly and it all seemed so simple and amusing.

And so one afternoon, while he was having dinner at a restaurant in the park, the woman in the toque walked in unhurriedly and took a seat at the table next to him. The way she looked, walked and dressed, wore her hair, told him that she was of good social standing, that she was married, that she was in Yalta for the first time, that she was alone and bored. . . . There was a great deal of exaggeration in the stories about the laxity of

---

Muscovites: That is, natives of Moscow.

morals among the Yalta visitors, and he dismissed them with contempt, for he knew that such stories were mostly made up by people who would gladly have sinned themselves if they had had any idea how to go about it; but when the woman sat down at the table three yards away from him he remembered these stories of easy conquests and excursions to the mountains and the tempting thought of a quiet and fleeting affair, an affair with a strange woman whose very name he did not know, suddenly took possession of him.

He tried to attract the attention of the dog by calling softly to it, and when the pomeranian came up to him he shook a finger at it. The pomeranian growled. Gurov again shook a finger at it.

The woman looked up at him and immediately lowered her eyes.

"He doesn't bite," she said and blushed.

"May I give him a bone?" he asked, and when she nodded, he said amiably: "Have you been long in Yalta?"

"About five days."

"And I am just finishing my second week here."

They said nothing for the next few minutes.

"Time flies," she said without looking at him, "and yet it's so boring here."

"That's what one usually hears people saying here. A man may be living in Belev and Zhizdra or some other God-forsaken hole and he isn't bored, but the moment he comes here all you hear from him is 'Oh, it's so boring! Oh, the dust!' You'd think he'd come from Granada!"

She laughed. Then both went on eating in silence, like complete strangers; but after dinner they strolled off together, and they embarked on the light playful conversation of free and contented people who do not care where they go or what they talk about. They walked, and talked about the strange light that fell on the sea; the water was of such a soft and warm lilac, and the moon threw a shaft of gold across it. They talked about how close it was after a hot day. Gurov told her that he lived in Moscow, that he was a graduate in philology but worked in a bank, that he had at one time thought of singing in a private opera company but had given up the idea, that he owned two houses in Moscow. . . . From her he learnt that she had grown up in Petersburg, but had got married in the town of S——, where she had been living for the past two years, that she would stay another month in Yalta, and that her husband, who also needed a rest, might join her. She was quite unable to tell him what her husband's job was, whether he served in the offices of the provincial governor or the rural council, and she found this rather amusing herself. Gurov also found out that her name and patronymic were Anna Sergeyevna.

Later, in his hotel room, he thought about her and felt sure that he would meet her again the next day. It had to be. As he went to bed he remembered that she had only recently left her boarding school, that she had been a schoolgirl like his own daughter; he recalled how much diffidence and angularity there was in her laughter and her conversation with a stranger—it was probably the first time in her life she had found herself alone, in a situation when men followed her, looked at her, and spoke to her with only one secret intention, an intention she could hardly fail to guess. He remembered her slender, weak neck, her beautiful grey eyes.

"There's something pathetic about her, all the same," he thought as he fell asleep.

II

A week had passed since their first meeting. It was a holiday. It was close indoors, while in the streets a strong wind raised clouds of dust and tore off people's hats. All day long one felt thirsty, and Gurov kept going to the terrace of the restaurant, offering Anna Sergeyevna fruit drinks and ices. There was nowhere to go.

In the evening, when the wind had dropped a little, they went to the pier to watch the arrival of the steamer. There were a great many people taking a walk on the landing pier; some were meeting friends, they had bunches of flowers in their hands. It was there that two peculiarities of the Yalta smart set at once arrested attention: the middle-aged women dressed as if they were still young girls and there was a great number of generals.

Because of the rough sea the steamer arrived late, after the sun had set, and she had to swing backwards and forwards several times before getting alongside the pier. Anna Sergeyevna looked at the steamer and the passengers through her lorgnette, as though trying to make out some friends, and when she turned to Gurov her eyes were sparkling. She talked a lot, asked many abrupt questions, and immediately forgot what it was she had wanted to know; then she lost her lorgnette in the crowd of people.

The smartly dressed crowd dispersed; soon they were all gone, the wind had dropped completely, but Gurov and Anna were still standing there as though waiting to see if someone else would come off the boat. Anna Sergeyevna was no longer talking. She was smelling her flowers without looking at Gurov.

"It's a nice evening," he said. "Where shall we go now? Shall we go for a drive?"

She made no answer.   25

Then he looked keenly at her and suddenly put his arms round her and kissed her on the mouth. He felt the fragrance and dampness of the flowers and immediately looked around him fearfully: had anyone seen them?

"Let's go to your room," he said softly.

And both walked off quickly.

It was very close in her hotel room, which was full of the smell of the scents she had bought in a Japanese shop. Looking at her now, Gurov thought: "Life is full of strange encounters!" From his past he preserved the memory of carefree, good-natured women, whom love had made gay and who were grateful to him for the happiness he gave them, however short-lived; and of women like his wife, who made love without sincerity, with unnecessary talk, affectedly, hysterically, with such an expression, as though it were not love or passion, but something much more significant; and of two or three very beautiful, frigid women, whose faces suddenly lit up with a predatory expression, an obstinate desire to take, to snatch from life more than it could give; these were women no longer in their first youth, capricious, unreasoning, despotic, unintelligent women, and when Gurov lost interest in them, their beauty merely aroused hatred in him and the lace trimmings on their negligés looked to him then like the scales of a snake.

But here there was still the same diffidence and angularity of inexperienced   30
youth—an awkward feeling; and there was also the impression of embarrassment, as if someone had just knocked at the door. Anna Sergeyevna, this lady with the lapdog, apparently regarded what had happened in a peculiar sort of way, very seriously, as though she had become a fallen woman—so it seemed to him, and he found it odd and disconcerting. Her features lengthened and drooped, and her long hair hung mournfully on either side of her face; she sank into thought in a despondent pose, like a woman taken in adultery in an old painting.

"It's wrong," she said. "You'll be the first not to respect me now."

There was a watermelon on the table. Gurov cut himself a slice and began to eat it slowly. At least half an hour passed in silence.

Anna Sergeyevna was very touching; there was an air of pure, decent, naive woman about her, a woman who had very little experience of life; the solitary candle burning on the table scarcely lighted up her face, but it was obvious that she was unhappy.

"But, darling, why should I stop respecting you?" Gurov asked. "You don't know yourself what you're saying."

"May God forgive me," she said, and her eyes filled with tears. "It's terrible."   35

"You seem to wish to justify yourself."

"How can I justify myself? I am a bad, despicable creature. I despise myself and have no thought of justifying myself. I haven't deceived my husband, I've deceived myself. And not only now. I've been deceiving myself for a long time. My husband is, I'm sure, a good and honest man, but, you see, he is a flunkey. I don't know what he does at his office, all I know is that he is a flunkey. I was only twenty when I married him, I was eaten up by curiosity, I wanted something better. There surely must be a different kind of life, I said to myself. I wanted to live. To live, to live! I was burning with curiosity. I don't think you know what I am talking about, but I swear I could no longer control myself, something was happening to me, I could not be held back, I told my husband I was ill, and I came here. . . . Here too I was going about as though in a daze, as though I was mad, and now I've become a vulgar worthless woman whom everyone has a right to despise."

Gurov could not help feeling bored as he listened to her; he was irritated by her naive tone of voice and her repentance, which was so unexpected and so out of place; but for the tears in her eyes, he might have thought that she was joking or play-acting.

"I don't understand," he said gently, "what it is you want."

She buried her face on his chest and clung close to him.   40

"Please, please believe me," she said. "I love a pure, honest life. I hate immorality. I don't know myself what I am doing. The common people say 'the devil led her astray,' I too can now say about myself that the devil has led me astray."

"There, there . . ." he murmured.

He gazed into her staring, frightened eyes, kissed her, spoke gently and affectionately to her, and gradually she calmed down and her cheerfulness returned; both of them were soon laughing.

Later, when they went out, there was not a soul on the promenade, the town with its cypresses looked quite dead, but the sea was still roaring and dashing itself against the shore; a single launch tossed on the waves, its lamp flickering sleepily.

They hailed a cab and drove to Oreanda.   45

"I've just found out your surname, downstairs in the lobby," said Gurov. "Von Diederitz. Is your husband a German?"

"No. I believe his grandfather was German. He is of the Orthodox faith himself."

In Oreanda they sat on a bench not far from the church, looked down on the sea, and were silent. Yalta could scarcely be seen through the morning mist. White clouds lay motionless on the mountain tops. Not a leaf stirred on the trees, the cicadas chirped, and the monotonous, hollow roar of the sea, coming up from below, spoke of rest, of eternal sleep awaiting us all. The sea had roared like that down below when there was no Yalta or Oreanda, it was roaring now, and it would go on roaring as indifferently and hollowly when we were here no more. And in this constancy, in this complete indifference to the life and death of each one of us, there is perhaps hidden the guarantee of our eternal salvation, the never-ceasing movement of life on earth, the never-ceasing movement towards perfection. Sitting beside a young woman who looked so beautiful at the break of day, soothed and enchanted by the sight of all that fairy-land scenery—the sea, the mountains, the clouds, the wide sky—Gurov reflected that, when you came to think of it, everything in the world was really really beautiful, everything but our own thoughts and actions when we lose sight of the higher aims of existence and our dignity as human beings.

Someone walked up to them, a watchman probably, looked at them, and went away. And there seemed to be something mysterious and also beautiful in this fact, too. They could see the Theodosia boat coming towards the pier, lit up by the sunrise, and with no lights.

"There's dew on the grass," said Anna Sergeyevna, breaking the silence.   50

"Yes. Time to go home."

They went back to town.

After that they met on the front every day at twelve o'clock, had lunch and dinner together, went for walks, admired the sea. She complained of sleeping badly and of her heart beating uneasily, asked the same questions, alternately worried by feelings of jealousy and by fear that he did not respect her sufficiently. And again and again in the park or in the square, when there was no one in sight, he would draw her to him and kiss her passionately. The complete idleness, these kisses in broad daylight, always having to look round for fear of someone watching them, the heat, the smell of the sea, and the constant looming into sight of idle, well-dressed, and well-fed people seemed to have made a new man of him; he told Anna Sergeyevna that she was beautiful, that she was desirable, made passionate love to her, never left her side, while she was often lost in thought and kept asking him to admit that he did not really respect her, that he was not in the least in love with her and only saw in her a vulgar woman. Almost every night they drove out of town, to Oreanda or to the waterfall; the excursion was always a success, and every time their impressions were invariably grand and beautiful.

They kept expecting her husband to arrive. But a letter came from him in which he wrote that he was having trouble with his eyes and implored his wife to return home as soon as possible. Anna Sergeyevna lost no time in getting ready for her journey home.

"It's a good thing I'm going," she said to Gurov. "It's fate."   55

She took a carriage to the railway station, and he saw her off. The drive took a whole day. When she got into the express train, after the second bell, she said:

"Let me have another look at you. . . . One last look. So."

She did not cry, but looked sad, just as if she were ill, and her face quivered.

"I'll be thinking of you, remembering you," she said. "Good-bye. You're staying, aren't you? Don't think badly of me. We are parting for ever. Yes, it must be so, for we should never have met. Well, good-bye. . . ."

The train moved rapidly out of the station; its lights soon disappeared, and a   60
minute later it could not even be heard, just as though everything had conspired to put a quick end to this sweet trance, this madness. And standing alone on the platform gazing into the dark distance, Gurov listened to the chirping of the grasshoppers and the humming of the telegraph wires with a feeling as though he had just woken up. He told himself that this had been just one more affair in his life, just one more adventure, and that it too was over, leaving nothing but a memory. He was moved and sad, and felt a little penitent that the young woman, whom he would never see again, had not been happy with him; he had been amiable and affectionate with her, but all the same in his behavior to her, in the tone of his voice and in his caresses, there was a suspicion of light irony, the somewhat coarse arrogance of the successful male, who was, moreover, almost twice her age. All the time she called him good, wonderful, high-minded; evidently she must have taken him to be quite different from what he really was, which meant that he had involuntarily deceived her.

At the railway station there was already a whiff of autumn in the air; the evening was chilly.

"Time I went north, too," thought Gurov, as he walked off the platform. "High time!"

III

At home in Moscow everything was already like winter: the stoves were heated, and it was still dark in the morning when the children were getting ready to go to school and having breakfast, so that the nurse had to light the lamp for a short time. The frosts had set in. When the first snow falls and the first day one goes out for a ride in a sleigh, one is glad to see the white ground, the white roofs, the air is so soft and wonderful to breathe, and one remembers the days of one's youth. The old lime trees and birches, white with rime, have such a benignant look, they are nearer to one's heart than cypresses and palms, and beside them one no longer wants to think of mountains and the sea.

Gurov had been born and bred in Moscow, and he returned to Moscow on a fine frosty day; and when he put on his fur coat and warm gloves and took a walk down Petrovka Street, and when on Saturday evening he heard the church bells ringing, his recent holiday trip and the places he had visited lost their charm for him. Gradually he became immersed in Moscow life, eagerly reading three newspapers a day and declaring that he never read Moscow papers on principle. Once more, he could not resist the attraction of restaurants, clubs, banquets, and anniversary celebrations, and once more he felt flattered that well-known lawyers and actors came to see him and that in the Medical Club he played cards with a professor as his partner. Once again he was capable of eating a whole portion of the Moscow speciality of sour cabbage and meat served in a frying-pan. . . .

Another month and, he thought, nothing but a memory would remain of Anna Sergeyevna; he would remember her as through a haze and only occasionally dream of her with a wistful smile, as he did of the others before her. But over a month passed, winter was at its height, and he remembered her as clearly as though he had only parted from her the day before. His memories haunted him more and more persistently. Every time the voices of his children doing their homework reached him in his study in the stillness of the evening, every time he heard a popular song or some music in a restaurant, every time the wind howled in the chimney—it all came back to him: their walks on the pier, early morning with the mist on the mountains, the Theodosia boat, and the kisses. He kept pacing the room for hours remembering it all and smiling, and then his memories turned into daydreams and the past mingled in his imagination with what was going to happen. He did not dream of Anna Sergeyevna, she accompanied him everywhere like his shadow and followed him wherever he went. Closing his eyes, he saw her as clearly as if she were before him, and she seemed to him lovelier, younger, and tenderer than she had been; and he thought that he too was much better than he had been in Yalta. In the evenings she gazed at him from the bookcase, from the fireplace, from the corner— he heard her breathing, the sweet rustle of her dress. In the street he followed women with his eyes, looking for anyone who resembled her. . . .

He was beginning to be overcome by an overwhelming desire to share his memories with someone. But at home it was impossible to talk of his love, and outside his home there was no one he could talk to. Not the tenants who lived in his house, and certainly not his colleagues in the bank. And what was he to tell them? Had he been in love then? Had there been anything beautiful, poetic, edifying, or even anything interesting about his relations with Anna Sergeyevna? So he had to talk in general terms about love and women, and no one guessed what he was driving at, and his wife merely raised her black eyebrows and said:

"Really, Dimitry, the role of a coxcomb doesn't suit you at all!"

One evening, as he left the Medical Club with his partner, a civil servant, he could not restrain himself, and said:

"If you knew what a fascinating woman I met in Yalta!"

The civil servant got into his sleigh and was about to be driven off, but suddenly he turned round and called out:

"I say!"

"Yes?"

"You were quite right: the sturgeon was a bit off."

These words, so ordinary in themselves, for some reason hurt Gurov's feelings: they seemed to him humiliating and indecent. What savage manners! What faces! What stupid nights! What uninteresting, wasted days! Crazy gambling at cards, gluttony, drunk-enness, endless talk about one and the same thing. Business that was of no use to anyone and talk about one and the same thing absorbed the greater part of one's time and ener-gy, and what was left in the end was a sort of dock-tailed, barren life, a sort of nonsensical existence, and it was impossible to escape from it, just as though you were in a lunatic asy-lum or a convict chain gang!

Gurov lay awake all night, fretting and fuming, and had a splitting headache the   75
whole of the next day. The following nights too he slept badly, sitting up in bed thinking, or walking up and down his room. He was tired of his children, tired of the bank, he did not feel like going out anywhere or talking about anything.

In December, during the Christmas holidays, he packed his things, told his wife that he was going to Petersburg to get a job for a young man he knew, and set off for the town of S———. Why? He had no very clear idea himself. He wanted to see Anna Sergeyev-na, to talk to her, to arrange a meeting, if possible.

He arrived in S———in the morning and took the best room in a hotel, with a fit-ted carpet of military grey cloth and an inkstand grey with dust on the table, surmounted by a horseman with raised hand and no head. The hall porter supplied him with all the necessary information: Von Diederitz lived in a house of his own in Old Potter's Street, not far from the hotel. He lived well, was rich, kept his own carriage horses, the whole town knew him. The hall-porter pronounced the name: Dridiritz.

Gurov took a leisurely walk down Old Potter's Street and found the house. In front of it was a long grey fence studded with upturned nails.

"A fence like that would make anyone wish to run away," thought Gurov, scanning the windows and the fence.

As it was a holiday, he thought, her husband was probably at home. It did not mat-   80
ter either way, though, for he could not very well embarrass her by calling at the house. If he were to send in a note it might fall into the hands of the husband and ruin everything. The best thing was to rely on chance. And he kept walking up and down the street and along the fence, waiting for his chance. He watched a beggar enter the gate and the dogs attack him; then, an hour later, he heard the faint indistinct sounds of a piano. That must have been Anna Sergeyevna playing. Suddenly the front door opened and an old woman came out, followed by the familiar white pomeranian. Gurov was about to call to the dog, but his heart began to beat violently and in his excitement he could not remember its name.

He went on walking up and down the street, hating the grey fence more and more, and he was already saying to himself that Anna Sergeyevna had forgotten him and had perhaps been having a good time with someone else, which was indeed quite natural for a young woman who had to look at that damned fence from morning till night. He went back to his hotel room and sat on the sofa for a long time, not knowing what to do, then he had dinner and after dinner a long sleep.

"How stupid and disturbing it all is," he thought, waking up and staring at the dark windows: it was already evening. "Well, I've had a good sleep, so what now? What am I going to do tonight?"

He sat on a bed covered by a cheap grey blanket looking exactly like a hospital blanket, and taunted himself in vexation:

"A lady with a lapdog! Some adventure, I must say! Serves you right!"

At the railway station that morning he had noticed a poster announcing in huge   85
letters the first performance of *The Geisha Girl* at the local theatre. He recalled it now, and decided to go to the theatre.

"Quite possibly she goes to first nights," he thought.

The theatre was full. As in all provincial theatres, there was a mist over the chandeliers and the people in the gallery kept up a noisy and excited conversation; in the first row of the stalls stood the local dandies with their hands crossed behind their backs; here, too, in the front seat of the Governor's box, sat the Governor's daughter, wearing a feather boa, while the Governor himself hid modestly behind the portière so that only his hands were visible; the curtain stirred, the orchestra took a long time tuning up. Gurov scanned the audience eagerly as they filed in and occupied their seats.

Anna Sergeyevna came in too. She took her seat in the third row, and when Gurov glanced at her his heart missed a beat and he realized clearly that there was no one in the world nearer and dearer or more important to him than that little woman with the stupid lorgnette in her hand, who was in no way remarkable. That woman lost in a provincial crowd now filled his whole life, was his misfortune, his joy, and the only happiness that he wished for himself. Listening to the bad orchestra and the wretched violins played by second-rate musicians, he thought how beautiful she was. He thought and dreamed.

A very tall, round-shouldered young man with small whiskers had come in with Anna Sergeyevna and sat down beside her; he nodded at every step he took and seemed to be continually bowing to someone. This was probably her husband, whom in a fit of bitterness at Yalta she had called a flunkey. And indeed there was something of a lackey's obsequiousness in his lank figure, his whiskers, and the little bald spot on the top of his head. He smiled sweetly, and the gleaming insignia of some scientific society which he wore in his buttonhole looked like the number on a waiter's coat.

In the first interval the husband went out to smoke and she was left in her seat. 90 Gurov, who also had a seat in the stalls, went up to her and said in a trembling voice and with a forced smile:

"Good evening!"

She looked up at him and turned pale, then looked at him again in panic, unable to believe her eyes, clenching her fan and lorgnette in her hand and apparently trying hard not to fall into a dead faint. Both were silent. She sat and he stood, frightened by her embarrassment and not daring to sit down beside her. The violinists and the flautist began tuning their instruments, and they suddenly felt terrified, as though they were being watched from all the boxes. But a moment later she got up and walked rapidly towards one of the exits; he followed her, and both of them walked aimlessly along corridors and up and down stairs. Figures in all sorts of uniforms—lawyers, teachers, civil servants, all wearing badges—flashed by them; ladies, fur coats hanging on pegs, the cold draught bringing with it the odour of cigarette-ends. Gurov, whose heart was beating violently, thought:

"Oh, Lord, what are all these people, that orchestra, doing here?"

At that moment, he suddenly remembered how after seeing Anna Sergeyevna off he had told himself that evening at the station that all was over and that they would never meet again. But how far they still were from the end!

She stopped on a dark, narrow staircase with a notice over it: "To the Upper Circle." 95

"How you frightened me!" she said, breathing heavily, still looking pale and stunned. "Oh, dear, how you frightened me! I'm scarcely alive. Why did you come? Why?"

"But, please, try to understand, Anna," he murmured hurriedly. "I beg you, please, try to understand. . . ."

She looked at him with fear, entreaty, love, looked at him intently, so as to fix his features firmly in her mind.

"I've suffered so much," she went on, without listening to him. "I've been thinking of you all the time. The thought of you kept me alive. And yet I tried so hard to forget you—why, oh, why did you come?"

On the landing above two schoolboys were smoking and looking down, but Gurov   100
did not care. He drew Anna Sergeyevna towards him and began kissing her face, her lips,
her hands.

"What are you doing? What are you doing?" she said in horror, pushing him away.
"We've both gone mad. You must go back tonight, this minute. I implore you, by all that's
sacred. . . . Somebody's coming!"

Somebody was coming up the stairs.

"You must go back," continued Anna Sergeyevna in a whisper. "Do you hear? I'll
come to you in Moscow. I've never been happy, I'm unhappy now, and I shall never be
happy, never! So please don't make me suffer still more. I swear I'll come to you in
Moscow. But now we must part. Oh, my sweet, my darling, we must part!"

She pressed his hand and went quickly down the stairs, looking back at him all the
time, and he could see from the expression in her eyes that she really was unhappy.
Gurov stood listening for a short time, and when all was quiet he went to look for his coat
and left the theatre.

IV

Anna Sergeyevna began going to Moscow to see him. Every two or three months she left   105
the town of S——, telling her husband that she was going to consult a Moscow gynaecol-
ogist, and her husband believed and did not believe her. In Moscow she stayed at the Slav
Bazaar and immediately sent a porter in a red cap to inform Gurov of her arrival. Gurov
went to her hotel, and no one in Moscow knew about it.

One winter morning he went to her hotel as usual (the porter had called with his
message at his house the evening before, but he had not been in). He had his daughter
with him, and he was glad of the opportunity of taking her to school, which was on the
way to the hotel. Snow was falling in thick wet flakes.

"It's three degrees above zero," Gurov was saying to his daughter, "and yet it's snowing. But then, you see, it's only warm on the earth's surface, in the upper layers of the atmosphere the temperature's quite different."

"Why isn't there any thunder in winter, Daddy?"

He explained that, too. As he was speaking, he kept thinking that he was going to
meet his mistress and not a living soul knew about it. He led a double life: one for all who
were interested to see, full of conventional truth and conventional deception, exactly like
the lives of his friends and acquaintances; and another which went on in secret. And by a
kind of strange concatenation of circumstances, possibly quite by accident, everything
that was important, interesting, essential, everything about which he was sincere and did
not deceive himself, everything that made up the quintessence of his life, went on in secret, while everything that was a lie, everything that was merely the husk in which he hid
himself to conceal the truth, like his work at the bank, for instance, his discussions at the
club, his ideas of the lower breed, his going to anniversary functions with his wife—all
that happened in the sight of all. He judged others by himself, did not believe what he
saw, and was always of the opinion that every man's real and most interesting life went on
in secret, under cover of night. The personal, private life of an individual was kept a secret, and perhaps that was partly the reason why civilized man was so anxious that his personal secrets should be respected.

Having seen his daughter off to her school, Gurov went to the Slav Bazaar. He took   110
off his fur coat in the cloakroom, went upstairs, and knocked softly on the door. Anna
Sergeyevna, wearing the grey dress he liked most, tired out by her journey and by the suspense of waiting for him, had been expecting him since the evening before; she was pale,

looked at him without smiling, but was in his arms the moment he went into the room. Their kiss was long and lingering, as if they had not seen each other for two years.

"Well," he asked, "how are you getting on there? Anything new?"

"Wait, I'll tell you in a moment. . . . I can't."

She could not speak because she was crying. She turned away from him and pressed her handkerchief to her eyes.

"Well, let her have her cry," he thought, sitting down in an armchair. "I'll wait."

Then he rang the bell and ordered tea; while he was having his tea, she was still standing there with her face to the window. She wept because she could not control her emotions, because she was bitterly conscious of the fact that their life was so sad: they could only meet in secret, they had to hide from people, like thieves! Was not their life ruined?

"Please stop crying!" he said.

It was quite clear to him that their love would not come to an end for a long time, if ever. Anna Sergeyevna was getting attached to him more and more strongly, she worshipped him, and it would have been absurd to tell her that all this would have to come to an end one day. She would not have believed it, anyway.

He went up to her and took her by the shoulders, wishing to be nice to her, to make her smile; and at that moment he caught sight of himself in the looking glass.

His hair was already beginning to turn grey. It struck him as strange that he should have aged so much, that he should have lost his good looks in the last few years. The shoulders on which his hands lay were warm and quivering. He felt so sorry for this life, still so warm and beautiful, but probably soon to fade and wilt like his own. Why did she love him so? To women he always seemed different from what he was, and they loved in him not himself, but the man their imagination conjured up and whom they had eagerly been looking for all their lives; and when they discovered their mistake they still loved him. And not one of them had ever been happy with him. Time had passed, he had met women, made love to them, parted from them, but not once had he been in love; there had been everything between them, but no love.

It was only now, when his hair was beginning to turn grey, that he had fallen in love properly, in good earnest for the first time in his life.

He and Anna Sergeyevna loved each other as people do who are very dear and near, as man and wife or close friends love each other; they could not help feeling that fate itself had intended them for one another, and they were unable to understand why he should have a wife and she a husband; they were like two migrating birds, male and female, who had been caught and forced to live in separate cages. They had forgiven each other what they had been ashamed of in the past, and forgave each other everything in their present, and felt that this love of theirs had changed them both.

Before, when he felt depressed, he had comforted himself by all sorts of arguments that happened to occur to him on the spur of the moment, but now he had more serious things to think of, he felt profound compassion, he longed to be sincere, tender. . . .

"Don't cry, my sweet," he said. "That'll do, you've had your cry. . . . Let's talk now, let's think of something."

Then they had a long talk. They tried to think how they could get rid of the necessity of hiding, telling lies, living in different towns, not seeing one another for so long. How were they to free themselves from their intolerable chains?

"How? How?" he asked himself, clutching at his head. "How?"

And it seemed to them that in only a few more minutes a solution would be found and a new, beautiful life would begin; but both of them knew very well that the end was still a long, long way away and that the most complicated and difficult part was only just beginning.

QUESTIONS

1. Describe the structure of this story. How might it be divided into parts? What conflict is developed in the course of the story? Where are the crisis and climax?

2. What characteristics of Gurov are brought out in the story? How does he change as the story develops? In what way does his change mark an improvement in his character?

3. Compare ideas about love in this story and in Lawrence's "The Horse Dealer's Daughter." What effect does love have on individuals? How does it affect Gurov? How does it affect Anna? How does the story differentiate between infatuation and love? Do the stories indicate that love solves problems, or that love creates problems?

4. In what locations does the story take place? How might these locations be said to symbolize the relationship between Gurov and Anna? Of what importance is the lapdog?

ERNEST J. GAINES (b. 1933)

A native of Louisiana, Gaines has spent much of his life in San Francisco. Since 1964, when he published his first novel, Catherine Carmier, *he has written a number of novels chronicling the lives of southern blacks, the best known of which is* The Autobiography of Miss Jane Pittman *(1971), which was translated into German in 1975. A recent novel is* A Lesson Before Dying *(1993). Two important recent publications featuring interviews with him are* Porch Talk with Ernest Gaines, *edited by Marcia Gau (1990), and* Conversations with Ernest Gaines, *edited by John Lowe (1995). "The Sky Is Gray" is selected from his 1968 collection of stories,* Bloodline.

The Sky Is Gray ⸜⟵⸝⸍ 1968

1

Go'n be coming in a few minutes. Coming round that bend down there full speed. And I'm go'n get out my handkerchief and wave it down, and we go'n get on it and go.

I keep on looking for it, but Mama don't look that way no more. She's looking down the road where we just come from. It's a long old road, and far's you can see you don't see nothing but gravel. You got dry weeds on both sides, and you got trees on both sides, and fences on both sides, too. And you got cows in the pastures and they standing close together. And when we was coming out here to catch the bus I seen the smoke coming out of the cows's noses.

I look at my mama and I know what she's thinking. I been with Mama so much, just me and her, I know what she's thinking all the time. Right now it's home—Auntie and them. She's thinking if they got enough wood—if she left enough there to keep them warm till we get back. She's thinking if it go'n rain and if any of them go'n have to go out in the rain. She's thinking 'bout the hog—if he go'n get out, and if Ty and Val be able to get him back in. She always worry like that when she leaves the house. She don't worry too much if she leave me there with the smaller ones, 'cause she know I'm go'n look after them and look after Auntie and everything else. I'm the oldest and she say I'm the man.

I look at my mama and I love my mama. She's wearing that black coat and that black hat and she's looking sad. I love my mama and I want put my arm round her and tell her. But I'm not supposed to do that. She say that's weakness and that's crybaby stuff, and she don't want no crybaby round her. She don't want you to be scared, either. 'Cause Ty's scared of ghosts and she's always whipping him. I'm scared of the dark, too, but I make 'tend I ain't. I make 'tend I ain't 'cause I'm the oldest, and I got to set a good sample for the rest. I can't ever be scared and I can't ever cry. And that's why I never said nothing 'bout my teeth. It's been hurting me and hurting me close to a month now, but I never said it. I didn't say it 'cause I didn't want act like a crybaby, and 'cause I know we didn't have enough money to go have it pulled. But, Lord, it been hurting me. And look like it wouldn't start till at night when you was trying to get yourself little sleep. Then soon 's you shut your eyes—ummm-ummm, Lord, look like it go right down to your heartstring.

"Hurting, hanh?" Ty'd say.   5

I'd shake my head, but I wouldn't open my mouth for nothing. You open your mouth and let that wind in, and it almost kill you.

I'd just lay there and listen to them snore. Ty there, right 'side me, and Auntie and Val over by the fireplace. Val younger than me and Ty, and he sleeps with Auntie. Mama sleeps round the other side with Louis and Walker.

I'd just lay there and listen to them, and listen to that wind out there, and listen to that fire in the fireplace. Sometimes it'd stop long enough to let me get little rest. Sometimes it just hurt, hurt, hurt. Lord, have mercy.

2

Auntie knowed it was hurting me. I didn't tell nobody but Ty, 'cause we buddies and he ain't go'n tell nobody. But some kind of way Auntie found out. When she asked me, I told her no, nothing was wrong. But she knowed it all the time. She told me to mash up a piece of aspirin and wrap it in some cotton and jugg it down in that hole. I did it, but it didn't do no good. It stopped for a little while, and started right back again. Auntie wanted to tell Mama, but I told her, "Uh-uh." 'Cause I knowed we didn't have any money, and it just was go'n make her mad again. So Auntie told Monsieur Bayonne, and Monsieur Bayonne came over to the house and told me to kneel down 'side him on the fireplace. He put his finger in his mouth and made the Sign of the Cross on my jaw. The tip of Monsieur Bayonne's finger is some hard, 'cause he's always playing on that guitar. If we sit outside at night we can always hear Monsieur Bayonne playing on his guitar. Sometimes we leave him out there playing on the guitar.

Monsieur Bayonne made the Sign of the Cross over and over on my jaw, but that   10
didn't do no good. Even when he prayed and told me to pray some, too, that tooth still hurt me.

"How you feeling?" he say.

"Same," I say.

He kept on praying and making the Sign of the Cross and I kept on praying, too.

"Still hurting?" he say.

"Yes, sir."   15

Monsieur Bayonne mashed harder and harder on my jaw. He mashed so hard he almost pushed me over on Ty. But then he stopped.

"What kind of prayers you praying, boy?" he say.

"Baptist," I say.

"Well, I'll be—no wonder that tooth still killing him. I'm going one way and he pulling the other. Boy, don't you know any Catholic prayers?"

"I know 'Hail Mary,'" I say.   20

"Then you better start saying it."

"Yes, sir."

He started mashing on my jaw again, and I could hear him praying at the same time. And, sure enough, after while it stopped hurting me.

Me and Ty went outside where Monsieur Bayonne's two hounds was and we started playing with them. "Let's go hunting," Ty say. "All right," I say; and we went on back in the pasture. Soon the hounds got on a trail, and me and Ty followed them all 'cross the pasture and then back in the woods, too. And then they cornered this little old rabbit and killed him, and me and Ty made them get back, and we picked up the rabbit and started on back home. But my tooth had started hurting me again. It was hurting me plenty now, but I wouldn't tell Monsieur Bayonne. That night I didn't sleep a bit, and first thing in the morning Auntie told me to go back and let Monsieur Bayonne pray over me some more. Monsieur Bayonne was in his kitchen making coffee when I got there. Soon 's he seen me he knowed what was wrong.

"All right, kneel down there 'side that stove," he say. "And this time make sure you   25
pray Catholic. I don't know nothing 'bout that Baptist, and I don't want know nothing 'bout him."

3

Last night Mama say, "Tomorrow we going to town."

"It ain't hurting me no more," I say. "I can eat anything on it."

"Tomorrow we going to town," she say.

And after she finished eating, she got up and went to bed. She always go to bed early now. 'Fore Daddy went in the Army,° she used to stay up late. All of us sitting out on the gallery or round the fire. But now, look like soon 's she finish eating she go to bed.

This morning when I woke up, her and Auntie was standing 'fore the fireplace. She   30
say: "Enough to get there and back. Dollar and a half to have it pulled. Twenty-five for me to go, twenty-five for him. Twenty-five for me to come back, twenty-five for him. Fifty cents left. Guess I get little piece of salt meat with that."

"Sure can use it," Auntie say. "White beans and no salt meat ain't white beans."

"I do the best I can," Mama say.

They was quiet after that, and I made 'tend I was still asleep.

"James, hit the floor," Auntie say.

I still made 'tend I was asleep. I didn't want them to know I was listening.   35

"All right," Auntie say, shaking me by the shoulder. "Come on. Today's the day."

I pushed the cover down to get out, and Ty grabbed it and pulled it back.

"You, too, Ty," Auntie say.

"I ain't getting no teef pulled," Ty say.

"Don't mean it ain't time to get up," Auntie say. "Hit it, Ty."   40

Ty got up grumbling.

"James, you hurry up and get in your clothes and eat your food," Auntie say. "What time y'all coming back?" she say to Mama.

"That 'leven o'clock bus," Mama say. "Got to get back in that field this evening."

"Get a move on you, James," Auntie say.

I went in the kitchen and washed my face, then I ate my breakfast. I was having   45
bread and syrup. The bread was warm and hard and tasted good. And I tried to make it last a long time.

Ty came back there grumbling and mad at me.

Daddy went in the Army: The time of the story is about 1942, early in World War II, when millions of men were being drafted into the armed services.

"Got to get up," he say. "I ain't having to teefes pulled. What I got to be getting up for?"

Ty poured some syrup in his pan and got a piece of bread. He didn't wash his hands, neither his face, and I could see that white stuff in his eyes.

"You the one getting your teef pulled," he say. "What I got to get up for. I bet if I was getting a teef pulled, you wouldn't be getting up. Shucks; syrup again. I'm getting tired of this old syrup. Syrup, syrup, syrup. I'm go'n take with the sugar diabetes. I want me some bacon sometime."

"Go out in the field and work and you can have your bacon," Auntie say. She stood   50
in the middle door looking at Ty. "You better be glad you got syrup. Some people ain't got that—hard's time is."

"Shucks," Ty say. "How can I be strong."

"I don't know too much 'bout your strength," Auntie say; "but I know where you go'n be hot at, you keep that grumbling up. James, get a move on you; your mama waiting."

I ate my last piece of bread and went in the front room. Mama was standing 'fore the fireplace warming her hands. I put on my coat and my cap, and we left the house.

4

I look down there again, but it still ain't coming. I almost say, "It ain't coming yet," but I keep my mouth shut. 'Cause that's something else she don't like. She don't like for you to say something just for nothing. She can see it ain't coming. I can see it ain't coming, so why say it ain't coming. I don't say it, I turn and look at the river that's back of us. It's so cold the smoke's just raising up from the water. I see a bunch of pool-doos not too far out—just on the other side of the lilies. I'm wondering if you can eat pool-doos.° I ain't too sure, 'cause I ain't never ate none. But I done ate owls and blackbirds, and I done ate redbirds,° too. I didn't want kill the redbirds, but she made me kill them. They had two of them back there. One in my trap, one in Ty's trap. Me and Ty was go'n play with them and let them go, but she made me kill them 'cause we needed the food.

"I can't," I say. "I can't."   55

"Here," she say. "Take it."

"I can't," I say. "I can't. I can't kill him, Mama, please."

"Here," she say. "Take this fork, James."

"Please, Mama, I can't kill him," I say.

I could tell she was go'n hit me. I jerked back, but I didn't jerk back soon enough.   60
"Take it," she say.

I took it and reached in for him, but he kept on hopping to the back.

"I can't, Mama," I say. The water just kept on running down my face. "I can't," I say.

"Get him out of there," she say.

I reached in for him and he kept on hopping to the back. Then I reached in far-   65
ther, and he pecked me on the hand.

"I can't, Mama," I say.

She slapped me again.

I reached in again, but he kept on hopping out my way. Then he hopped to one side and I reached there. The fork got him on the leg and I heard his leg pop. I pulled my hand out 'cause I had hurt him.

"Give it here," she say, and jerked the fork out my hand.

---

pool-doos: Pool-doo is a local Louisiana pronunciation of French *poule d'eau,* or "bird of water." It refers to a marsh hen, or bird of the rail family—most likely the American coot.
redbirds: cardinals.

She reached in and got the little bird right in the neck. I heard the fork go in his neck, and I heard it go in the ground. She brought him out and helt him right in front of me. 70
"That's one," she say. She shook him off and gived me the fork. "Get the other one."
"I can't, Mama," I say, "I'll do anything, but don't make me do that."
She went to the corner of the fence and broke the biggest switch over there she could find. I knelt 'side the trap, crying.
"Get him out of there," she say.
"I can't, Mama." 75
She started hitting me 'cross the back. I went down on the ground, crying.
"Get him," she say.
"Octavia?" Auntie say.
'Cause she had come out of the house and she was standing by the tree looking at us.
"Get him out of there," Mama say. 80
"Octavia," Auntie say, "explain to him. Explain to him. Just don't beat him. Explain to him."
But she hit me and hit me and hit me.
I'm still young—I ain't no more than eight; but I know now; I know why I had to do it. (They was so little, though. They was so little. I 'member how I picked the feathers off them and cleaned them and helt them over the fire. Then we all ate them. Ain't had but a little bitty piece each, but we all had a little bitty piece, and everybody just looked at me 'cause they was so proud.) Suppose she had to go away? That's why I had to do it. Suppose she had to go away like Daddy went away? Then who was go'n look after us? They had to be somebody left to carry on. I didn't know it then, but I know it now. Auntie and Monsieur Bayonne talked to me and made me see.

5

Time I see it I get out my handkerchief and start waving. It's still 'way down there, but I keep waving anyhow. Then it come up and stop and me and Mama get on. Mama tell me go sit in the back while she pay. I do like she say, and the people look at me. When I pass the little sign that say "White" and "Colored," I start looking for a seat. I just see one of them back there, but I don't take it, 'cause I want my mama to sit down herself. She comes in the back and sit down, and I lean on the seat. They got seats in the front, but I know I can't sit there, 'cause I have to sit back of the sign. Anyhow, I don't want sit there if my mama go'n sit back here.
They got a lady sitting 'side my mama and she looks at me and smiles little bit. I 85 smile back, but I don't open my mouth, 'cause the wind'll get in and make that tooth ache. The lady take out a pack of gum and reach me a slice, but I shake my head. The lady just can't understand why a little boy'll turn down gum, and she reach me a slice again. This time I point to my jaw. The lady understands and smiles little bit, and I smile little bit, but I don't open my mouth, though.
They got a girl sitting 'cross from me. She got on a red overcoat and her hair's plaited in one big plait. First, I make 'tend I don't see her over there, but then I start looking at her little bit. She make 'tend she don't see me, either, but I catch her looking that way. She got a cold, and every now and then she h'ist that little handkerchief to her nose. She ought to blow it, but she don't. Must think she's too much a lady or something.
Every time she h'ist that little handkerchief, the lady 'side her say something in her ear. She shakes her head and lays her hands in her lap again. Then I catch her kind of looking where I'm at. I smile at her little bit. But think she'll smile back? Uh-uh. She just

turn up her little old nose and turn her head. Well, I show her both of us can turn us head. I turn mine too and look out at the river.

The river is gray. The sky is gray. They have pool-doos on the water. The water is wavy, and the pool-doos go up and down. The bus go round a turn, and you got plenty trees hiding the river. Then the bus go round another turn, and I can see the river again.

I look toward the front where all the white people sitting. Then I look at that little old gal again. I don't look right at her, 'cause I don't want all them people to know I love her. I just look at her little bit, like I'm looking out that window over there. But she knows I'm looking that way, and she kind of look at me, too. The lady sitting 'side her catch her this time, and she leans over and says something in her ear.

"I don't love him nothing," that little old gal says out loud.   90

Everybody back there hear her mouth, and all of them look at us and laugh.

"I don't love you, either," I say. "So you don't have to turn up your nose, Miss."

"You the one looking," she say.

"I wasn't looking at you," I say. "I was looking out that window, there."

"Out that window, my foot," she say. "I seen you. Everytime I turned round you was   95
looking at me."

"You must of been looking yourself if you seen me all them times," I say.

"Shucks," she say, "I got me all kind of boyfriends."

"I got girlfriends, too," I say.

"Well, I just don't want you getting your hopes up," she say.

I don't say no more to that little old gal 'cause I don't want have to bust her in the   100
mouth. I lean on the seat where Mama sitting, and I don't even look that way no more. When we get to Bayonne, she jugg her little old tongue out at me. I make 'tend I'm go'n hit her, and she duck down 'side her mama. And all the people laugh at us again.

6

Me and Mama get off and start walking in town. Bayonne is a little bitty town. Baton Rouge is a hundred times bigger than Bayonne. I went to Baton Rouge once—me, Ty, Mama, and Daddy. But that was 'way back yonder, 'fore Daddy went in the Army. I wonder when we go'n see him again. I wonder when. Look like he ain't ever coming back home. . . . Even the pavement all cracked in Bayonne. Got grass shooting right out the sidewalk. Got weeds in the ditch, too; just like they got at home.

It's some cold in Bayonne. Look like it's colder than it is home. The wind blows in my face, and I feel that stuff running down my nose. I sniff. Mama says use that handkerchief. I blow my nose and put it back.

We pass a school and I see them white children playing in the yard. Big old red school, and them children just running and playing. Then we pass a café, and I see a bunch of people in there eating. I wish I was in there 'cause I'm cold. Mama tells me keep my eyes in front where they belong.

We pass stores that's got dummies, and we pass another café, and then we pass a shoe shop, and that bald-head man in there fixing on a shoe. I look at him and I butt into that white lady, and Mama jerks me in front and tells me stay there.

We come up to the courthouse, and I see the flag waving there. This flag ain't like   105
the one we got at school. This one here ain't got but a handful of stars.° One at school

---

handful of stars: The Confederate flag contains thirteen stars. At the time of the story, the American flag had forty-eight.

got a big pile of stars—one for every state. We pass it and we turn and there it is—the dentist office. Me and Mama go in, and they got people sitting everywhere you look. They even got a little boy in there younger than me.

Me and Mama sit on that bench, and a white lady come in there and ask me what my name is. Mama tells her and the white lady goes on back. Then I hear somebody hollering in there. Soon's that little boy hear him hollering, he starts hollering, too. His mama pats him and pats him, trying to make him hush up, but he ain't thinking 'bout his mama.

The man that was hollering in there comes out holding his jaw. He is a big old man and he's wearing overalls and a jumper.

"Got it, hanh?" another man asks him.

The man shakes his head—don't want open his mouth.

"Man, I thought they was killing you in there," the other man says. "Hollering like   110
a pig under a gate."

The man don't say nothing. He just heads for the door, and the other man follows him.

"John Lee," the white lady says. "John Lee Williams."

The little boy juggs his head down in his mama's lap and holler more now. His mama tells him go with the nurse, but he ain't thinking 'bout his mama. His mama tells him again, but he don't even hear her. His mama picks him up and takes him in there, and even when the white lady shuts the door I can still hear little old John Lee.

"I often wonder why the Lord let a child like that suffer," a lady says to my mama. The lady's sitting right in front of us on another bench. She's got on a white dress and a black sweater. She must be a nurse or something herself, I reckon.

"Not us to question," a man says.   115

"Sometimes I don't know if we shouldn't," the lady says.

"I know definitely we shouldn't," the man says. The man looks like a preacher. He's big and fat and he's got on a black suit. He's got a gold chain, too.

"Why?" the lady says.

"Why anything?" the preacher says.

"Yes," the lady says. "Why anything?"   120

"Not us to question," the preacher says.

The lady looks at the preacher a little while and looks at Mama again.

"And look like it's the poor who suffers the most," she says. "I don't understand it."

"Best not to even try," the preacher says. "He works in mysterious ways—wonders to perform."°

Right then little John Lee bust out hollering, and everybody turn they head to listen.   125

"He's not a good dentist," the lady says. "Dr. Robillard is much better. But more expensive. That's why most of the colored people come here. The white people go to Dr. Robillard. Y' all from Bayonne?"

"Down the river," my mama says. And that's all she go'n say, 'cause she don't talk much. But the lady keeps on looking at her, and so she says, "Near Morgan."

"I see," the lady says.

7

"That's the trouble with the black people in this country today," somebody else says. This one here's sitting on the same side me and Mama's sitting, and he is kind of sitting in front of that preacher. He looks like a teacher or somebody that goes to college. He's got on a

---

He works . . . perform: an allusion to the well-known hymn "God moves in a mysterious way / His wonders to perform," by William Cowper (1731–1800).

suit, and he's got a book that he's been reading. "We don't question is exactly our problem," he says. "We should question and question and question—question everything."

The preacher just looks at him a long time. He done put a toothpick or something in his mouth, and he just keeps on turning it and turning it. You can see he don't like that boy with that book.

"Maybe you can explain what you mean," he says.

"I said what I meant," the boy says. "Question everything. Every stripe, every star, every word spoken. Everything."

"It 'pears to me that this young lady and I was talking 'bout God, young man," the preacher says.

"Question Him, too," the boys says.

"Wait," the preacher says. "Wait now."

"You heard me right," the boy says. "His existence as well as everything else. Everything."

The preacher just looks across the room at the boy. You can see he's getting madder and madder. But mad or no mad, the boy ain't thinking 'bout him. He looks at that preacher just 's hard 's the preacher looks at him.

"Is this what they coming to?" the preacher says. "Is this what we educating them for?"

"You're not educating me," the boy says. "I wash dishes at night so that I can go to school in the day. So even the words you spoke need questioning."

The preacher just looks at him and shakes his head.

"When I come in this room and seen you there with your book, I said to myself, 'There's an intelligent man.' How wrong a person can be."

"Show me one reason to believe in the existence of a God," the boy says.

"My heart tells me," the preacher says.

" 'My heart tells me,' " the boys says. " 'My heart tells me.' Sure, 'My heart tells me.' And as long as you listen to what your heart tells you, you will have only what the white man gives you and nothing more. Me, I don't listen to my heart. The purpose of the heart is to pump blood throughout the body, and nothing else."

"Who's your paw, boy?" the preacher says.

"Why?"

"Who is he?"

"He's dead."

"And you mom?"

"She's in Charity Hospital with pneumonia. Half killed herself, working for nothing."

"And 'cause he's dead and she's sick, you mad at the world?"

"I'm not mad at the world. I'm questioning the world. I'm questioning it with cold logic, sir. What do words like Freedom, Liberty, God, White, Colored mean? I want to know. That's why you are sending us to school, to read and to ask questions. And because we ask these questions, you call us mad. No sir, it is not us who are mad."

"You keep saying 'us'?"

" 'Us.' Yes—us. I'm not alone."

The preacher just shakes his head. Then he looks at everybody in the room—everybody. Some of the people look down at the floor, keep from looking at him. I kind of look 'way myself, but soon 's I know he done turn his head, I look that way again.

"I'm sorry for you," he says to the boy.

"Why?" the boy says. "Why not be sorry for yourself? Why are you so much better off than I am? Why aren't you sorry for these other people in here? Why not be sorry for the lady who had to drag her child into the dentist office? Why not be sorry for the lady sitting on that bench over there? Be sorry for them. Not for me. Some way or the other I'm going to make it."

"No, I'm sorry for you," the preacher says.

"Of course, of course," the boy says, nodding his head. "You're sorry for me because I rock that pillar you're leaning on."

"You can't ever rock the pillar I'm leaning on, young man. It's stronger than anything man can ever do." 160

"You believe in God because a man told you to believe in God," the boy says. "A white man told you to believe in God. And why? To keep you ignorant so he can keep his feet on your neck."

"So now we the ignorant?" the preacher says.

"Yes," the boy says. "Yes." And he opens his book again.

The preacher just looks at him sitting there. The boy done forgot all about him. Everybody else make 'tend they done forgot the squabble, too.

Then I see that preacher getting up real slow. Preacher's a great big old man and 165 he got to brace himself to get up. He comes over where the boy is sitting.

He just stands there a little while looking down at him, but the boy don't raise his head.

"Get up, boy," preacher says.

The boy looks up at him, then he shuts his book real slow and stands up. Preacher just hauls back and hit him in the face. The boy falls back 'gainst the wall, but he straightens himself up and looks right back at that preacher.

"You forgot the other cheek," he says.°

The preacher hauls back and hit him again on the other side. But this time the boy 170 braces himself and don't fall.

"That hasn't changed a thing," he says.

The preacher just looks at the boy. The preacher's breathing real hard like he just run up a big hill. The boy sits down and opens his book again.

"I feel sorry for you," the preacher says. "I never felt so sorry for a man before."

The boy makes 'tend he don't even hear that preacher. He keeps on reading his book. The preacher goes back and gets his hat off the chair.

"Excuse me," he says to us. "I'll come back some other time. Y'all, please excuse me." 175

And he looks at the boy and goes out the room. The boy h'ist his hand up to his mouth one time to wipe 'way some blood. All the rest of the time he keeps on reading. And nobody else in there say a word.

8

Little John Lee and his mama come out the dentist office, and the nurse calls somebody else in. Then little bit later they come out, and the nurse calls another name. But fast's she calls somebody in there, somebody else comes in the place where we sitting, and the room stays full.

The people coming in now, all of them wearing big coats. One of them says something 'bout sleeting, another one says he hope not. Another one says he think it ain't nothing but rain. 'Cause, he says, rain can get awful cold this time of year.

All round the room they talking. Some of them talking to people right by them, some of them talking to people clear 'cross the room, some of them talking to anybody'll listen. It's a little bitty room, no bigger than us kitchen, and I can see everybody in there. The little old room's full of smoke, 'cause you got two old men smoking pipes over by that side door. I think I feel my tooth thumping me some, and I hold my breath and wait. I wait and wait, but it don't thump me no more. Thank God for that.

other cheek: Matthew 5:39.

I feel like going to sleep, and I lean back 'gainst the wall. But I'm scared to go to   180
sleep. Scared 'cause the nurse might call my name and I won't hear her. And Mama
might go to sleep, too, and she'll be mad if neither one of us heard the nurse.

I look up at Mama. I love my mama. I love my mama. And when cotton come I'm go'n
get her a new coat. And I ain't go'n get a black one, either. I think I'm go'n get her a red one.

"They got some books over there," I say. "Want read one of them?"

Mama looks at the books, but she don't answer me.

"You got yourself a little man there," the lady says.

Mama don't say nothing to the lady, but she must've smiled, 'cause I seen the lady   185
smiling back. The lady looks at me a little while, like she's feeling sorry for me.

"You sure got that preacher out here in a hurry," she says to that boy.

The boy looks up at her and looks in his book again. When I grow up I want be just
like him. I want clothes like that and I want keep a book with me, too.

"You really don't believe in God?" the lady says.

"No," he says.

"But why?" the lady says.   190

"Because the wind is pink," he says.

"What?" the lady says.

The boy don't answer her no more. He just reads in his book.

"Talking 'bout the wind is pink," that old lady says. She's sitting on the same bench
with the boy and she's trying to look in his face. The boy makes 'tend the old lady ain't
even there. He just keeps on reading. "Wind is pink," she says again. "Eh, Lord, what children go'n be saying next?"

The lady 'cross from us bust out laughing.   195

"That's a good one," she says. "The wind is pink. Yes sir, that's a good one."

"Don't you believe the wind is pink?" the boy says. He keeps his head down in the book.

"Course I believe it, honey," the lady says. "Course I do." She looks at us and winks
her eye. "And what color is grass, honey?"

"Grass? Grass is black."

She bust out laughing again. The boy looks at her.   200

"Don't you believe grass is black?" he says.

The lady quits her laughing and looks at him. Everybody else looking at him, too.
The place quiet, quiet.

"Grass is green, honey," the lady says. "It was green yesterday, it's green today, and
it's go'n be green tomorrow."

"How do you know it's green?"

"I know because I know."   205

"You don't know it's green," the boy says. "You believe it's green because someone
told you it was green. If someone had told you it was black you'd believe it was black."

"It's green," the lady says. "I know green when I see green."

"Prove it's green," the boy says.

"Sure, now," the lady says. "Don't tell me it's coming to that."

"It's coming to just that," the boy says. "Words mean nothing. One means no more   210
than the other."

"That's what it all coming to?" that old lady says. That old lady got on a turban and
she got on two sweaters. She got a green sweater under a black sweater. I can see the
green sweater 'cause some of the buttons on the other sweater's missing.

"Yes, ma'am," the boy says. "Words mean nothing. Action is the only thing. Doing.
That's the only thing."

"Other words, you want the Lord to come down here and show Hisself to you?" she says.

"Exactly, ma'am," he says.

"You don't mean that, I'm sure?" she says.   215

"I do, ma'am," he says.

"Done, Jesus," the old lady says, shaking her head.

"I didn't go 'long with that preacher at first," the other lady says; "but now—I don't know. When a person say the grass is black, he's either a lunatic or something's wrong."

"Prove to me that it's green," the boy says.

"It's green because the people say it's green."   220

"Those same people say we're citizens of these United States," the boy says.

"I think I'm a citizen," the lady says.

"Citizens have certain rights," the boy says. "Name me one right that you have. One right, granted by the Constitution, that you can exercise in Bayonne."

The lady don't answer him. She just looks at him like she don't know what he's talking 'bout. I know I don't.

"Things changing," she says.   225

"Things are changing because some black men have begun to think with their brains and not their hearts," the boy says.

"You trying to say these people don't believe in God?"

"I'm sure some of them do. Maybe most of them do. But they don't believe that God is going to touch these white people's hearts and change things tomorrow. Things change through action. By no other way."

Everybody sit quiet and look at the boy. Nobody says a thing. Then the lady 'cross the room from me and Mama just shakes her head.

"Let's hope that not all your generation feel the same way you do," she says.   230

"Think what you please, it doesn't matter," the boy says. "But it will be men who listen to their heads and not their hearts who will see that your children have a better chance than you had."

"Let's hope they ain't all like you, though," the old lady says. "Done forgot the heart absolutely."

"Yes ma'am, I hope they aren't all like me," the boy says. "Unfortunately, I was born too late to believe in your God. Let's hope that the ones who come after will have your faith—if not in your God, then in something else, something definitely that they can lean on. I haven't anything. For me, the wind is pink, the grass is black."

9

The nurse comes in the room where we all sitting and waiting and says the doctor won't take no more patients till one o'clock this evening.° My mama jumps up off the bench and goes up to the white lady.

"Nurse, I have to go back in the field this evening," she says.   235

"The doctor is treating his last patient now," the nurse says. "One o'clock this evening."

"Can I at least speak to the doctor?" my mama asks.

"I'm his nurse," the lady says.

"My little boy's sick," my mama says. "Right now his tooth almost killing him."

The nurse looks at me. She's trying to make up her mind if to let me come in. I   240
look at her real pitiful. The tooth ain't hurting me at all, but Mama say it is, so I make 'tend for her sake.

---

evening: local dialect for *afternoon.*

"This evening," the nurse says, and goes on back in the office.

"Don't feel 'jected, honey," the lady says to Mama. "I been round them a long time—they take you when they want to. If you was white, that's something else; but we the wrong color."

Mama don't say nothing to the lady, and me and her go outside and stand 'gainst the wall. It's cold out there. I can feel that wind going through my coat. Some of the other people come out of the room and go up the street. Me and Mama stand there a little while and we start walking. I don't know where we going. When we come to the other street we just stand there.

"You don't have to make water, do you?" Mama says.

"No, ma'am," I say.   245

We go on up the street. Walking real slow. I can tell Mama don't know where she's going. When we come to a store we stand there and look at the dummies. I look at a little boy wearing a brown overcoat. He's got on brown shoes, too. I look at my old shoes and look at his'n again. You wait till summer, I say.

Me and Mama walk away. We come up to another store and we stop and look at them dummies, too. Then we go on again. We pass a café where the white people in there eating. Mama tells me keep my eyes in front where they belong, but I can't help from seeing them people eat. My stomach starts to growling 'cause I'm hungry. When I see people eating, I get hungry; when I see a coat, I get cold.

A man whistles at my mama when we go by a filling station. She makes 'tend she don't even see him. I look back and I feel like hitting him in the mouth. If I was bigger, I say; if I was bigger, you'd see.

We keep on going. I'm getting colder and colder, but I don't say nothing. I feel that stuff running down my nose and I sniff.

"That rag," Mama says.   250

I get it out and wipe my nose. I'm getting cold all over now—my face, my hands, my feet, everything. We pass another little café, but this'n for white people, too, and we can't go in there, either. So we just walk. I'm so cold now I'm 'bout ready to say it. If I knowed where we was going I wouldn't be so cold, but I don't know where we going. We go, we go, we go. We walk clean out of Bayonne. Then we cross the street and we come back. Same thing I seen when I got off the bus this morning. Same old trees, same old walk, same old weeds, same old cracked pave—same old everything.

I sniff again.

"That rag," Mama says.

I wipe my nose real fast and jugg that handkerchief back in my pocket 'fore my hand gets too cold. I raise my head and I can see David's hardware store. When we come up to it, we go in. I don't know why, but I'm glad.

It's warm in there. It's so warm in there you don't ever want to leave. I look for the   255
heater, and I see it over by them barrels. Three white men standing round the heater talking in Creole.° One of them comes over to see what my mama want.

"Got any axe handles?" she says.

Me, Mama and the white man start to the back, but Mama stops me when we come up to the heater. She and the white man go on. I hold my hands over the heater and look at them. They go all the way to the back, and I see the white man pointing to the axe handles 'gainst the wall. Mama takes one of them and shakes it like she's trying to figure how much it weighs. Then she rubs her hand over it from one end to the other end. She turns it over and looks at the other side, then she shakes it again, and shakes her

---

Creole: the French Cajun dialect in Louisiana.

head and puts it back. She gets another one and she does it just like she did the first one, then she shakes her head. Then she gets a brown one and do it that, too. But she don't like this one, either. Then she gets another one, but 'fore she shakes it or anything, she looks at me. Look like she's trying to say something to me, but I don't know what it is. All I know is I done got warm now and I'm feeling right smart better. Mama shakes this axe handle just like she did the others, and shakes her head and says something to the white man. The white man just looks at his pile of axe handles, and when Mama pass him to come to the front, the white man just scratch his head and follows her. She tells me come on and we go on out and start walking again.

We walk and walk, and no time at all I'm cold again. Look like I'm colder now 'cause I can still remember how good it was back there. My stomach growls and I suck it in to keep Mama from hearing it. She's walking right 'side me, and it growls so loud you can hear it a mile. But Mama don't say a word.

10

When we come up to the courthouse, I look at the clock. It's got quarter to twelve. Mean we got another hour and a quarter to be out here in the cold. We go and stand 'side a building. Something hits my cap and I look up at the sky. Sleet's falling.

I look at Mama standing there. I want stand close 'side her, but she don't like that.   260
She say that's crybaby stuff. She say you got to stand for yourself, by yourself.

"Let's go back to that office," she says.

We cross the street. When we get to the dentist office I try to open the door, but I can't. I twist and twist, but I can't. Mama pushes me to the side and she twist the knob, but she can't open the door, either. She turns 'way from the door. I look at her, but I don't move and I don't say nothing. I done seen her like this before and I'm scared of her.

"You hungry?" she says. She says it like she's made at me, like I'm the cause of everything.

"No, ma'am," I say.

"You want eat and walk back, or you rather don't eat and ride?"   265

"I ain't hungry," I say.

I ain't just hungry, but I'm cold, too. I'm so hungry and cold I want to cry. And look like I'm getting colder and colder. My feet done got numb. I try to work my toes, but I don't even feel them. Look like I'm go'n die. Look like I'm go'n stand right here and freeze to death. I think 'bout home. I think 'bout Val and Auntie and Ty and Louis and Walker. It's 'bout twelve o'clock and I know they eating dinner now. I can hear Ty making jokes. He done forgot 'bout getting up early this morning and right now he's probably making jokes. Always trying to make somebody laugh. I wish I was right there listening to him. Give anything in the world if I was home round the fire.

"Come on," Mama says.

We start walking again. My feet so numb I can't hardly feel them. We turn the corner and go on back up the street. The clock on the courthouse starts hitting for twelve.

The sleet's coming down plenty now. They hit the pave and bounce like rice. Oh,   270
Lord; oh, Lord, I pray. Don't let me die, don't let me die, don't let me die, Lord.

11

Now I know where we going. We going back of town where the colored people eat. I don't care if I don't eat. I been hungry before. I can stand it. But I can't stand the cold.

I can see we go'n have a long walk. It's 'bout a mile down there. But I don't mind. I know when I get there I'm go'n warm myself. I think I can hold out. My hands numb in my pockets and my feet numb, too, but if I keep moving I can hold out. Just don't stop no more, that's all.

The sky's gray. The sleet keeps on falling. Falling like rain now—plenty, plenty. You can hear it hitting the pave. You can see it bouncing. Sometimes it bounces two times 'fore it settles.

We keep on going. We don't say nothing. We just keep on going, keep on going.

I wonder what Mama's thinking. I hope she ain't mad at me. When summer come I'm go'n pick plenty cotton and get her a coat. I'm go'n get her a red one.

I hope they'd make it summer all the time. I'd be glad if it was summer all the time—but it ain't. We got to have winter, too. Lord, I hate the winter. I guess everybody hate the winter.

I don't sniff this time. I get out my handkerchief and wipe my nose. My hand's so cold I can hardly hold the handkerchief.

I think we getting close, but we ain't there yet. I wonder where everybody is. Can't see a soul but us. Look like we the only two people moving round today. Must be too cold for the rest of the people to move round in.

I can hear my teeth. I hope they don't knock together too hard and make that bad one hurt. Lord, that's all I need, for that bad one to start off.

I hear a church bell somewhere. But today ain't Sunday. They must be ringing for a funeral or something.

I wonder what they doing at home. They must be eating. Monsieur Bayonne might be there with his guitar. One day Ty played with Monsieur Bayonne's guitar and broke one of the strings. Monsieur Bayonne was some mad with Ty. He say Ty wasn't go'n ever 'mount to nothing. Ty can go just like Monsieur Bayonne when he ain't there. Ty can make everybody laugh when he starts to mocking Monsieur Bayonne.

I used to like to be with Mama and Daddy. We used to be happy. But they took him in the Army. Now, nobody happy no more. . .I be glad when Daddy comes home.

Monsieur Bayonne say it wasn't fair for them to take Daddy and give Mama nothing and give us nothing. Auntie say, "Shhh, Etienne. Don't let them hear you talk like that." Monsieur Bayonne say, "It's God truth. What they giving his children? They have to walk three and a half miles to school hot or cold. That's anything to give for a paw? She's got to work in the field rain or shine just to make ends meet. That's anything to give for a husband?" Auntie say, "Shhh, Etienne, shhh." "Yes, you right," Monsieur Bayonne say. "Best don't say it in front of them now. But one day they go'n find out. One day." "Yes, I suppose so," Auntie say. "Then what, Rose Mary?" Monsieur Bayonne say. "I don't know, Etienne," Auntie say. "All we can do is us job, and leave everything else in His hand. . . ."

We getting closer, now. We getting closer. I can even see the railroad tracks.

We cross the tracks, and now I see the café. Just to get in there, I say. Just to get in there. Already I'm starting to feel little better.

12

We go in. Ahh, it's good. I look for the heater; there 'gainst the wall. One of them little brown ones. I just stand there and hold my hands over it. I can't open my hands too wide 'cause they almost froze.

Mama's standing right 'side me. She done unbuttoned her coat. Smoke rises out of the coat, and the coat smells like a wet dog.

I move to the side so Mama can have more room. She opens out her hands and rubs them together. I rub mine together, too, 'cause this keeps them from hurting. If you let them warm too fast, they hurt you sure. But if you let them warm just little bit at a time, and you keep rubbing them, they be all right every time.

They got just two more people in the café. A lady back of the counter, and a man on this side the counter. They been watching us even since we come in.

Mama gets out the handkerchief and count up the money. Both of us know how 290 much money she's got there. Three dollars. No, she ain't got three dollars, 'cause she had to pay us way up here. She ain't got but two dollars and a half left. Dollar and a half to get my tooth pulled, and fifty cents for us to go back on, and fifty cents worth of salt meat.

She stirs the money round with her finger. Most of the money is change 'cause I can hear it rubbing together. She stirs it and stirs it. Then she looks at the door. It's still sleeting. I can hear it hitting 'gainst the wall like rice.

"I ain't hungry, Mama," I say.

"Got to pay them something for they heat," she says.

She takes a quarter out the handkerchief and ties the handkerchief up again. She looks over her shoulder at the people, but she still don't move. I hope she don't spend the money. I don't want her spending it on me. I'm hungry, I'm almost starving I'm so hungry, but I don't want her spending the money on me.

She flips the quarter over like she's thinking. She's must be thinking 'bout us walk- 295 ing back home. Lord, I sure don't want walk home. If I thought it'd do any good to say something, I'd say it. But Mama makes up her own mind 'bout things.

She turns 'way from the heater right fast, like she better hurry up and spend the quarter 'fore she change her mind. I watch her go toward the counter. The man and the lady look at her, too. She tells the lady something and the lady walks away. The man keeps on looking at her. Her back's turned to the man, and she don't even know he's standing there.

The lady puts some cakes and a glass of milk on the counter. Then she pours a cup of coffee and sets it 'side the other stuff. Mama pays her for the things and comes on back where I'm standing. She tells me sit down at the table 'gainst the wall.

The milk and the cake's for me; the coffee's for Mama. I eat slow and I look at her. She's looking outside at the sleet. She's looking real sad. I say to myself, I'm go'n make all this up one day. You see, one day, I'm go'n make all this up. I want say it now; I want tell her how I feel right now; but Mama don't like for us to talk like that.

"I can't eat all this," I say.

They ain't got but just three little old cakes there. I'm so hungry right now, the 300 Lord knows I can eat a hundred times three, but I want my mama to have one.

Mama don't even look my way. She knows I'm hungry, she knows I want it. I let it stay there a little while, then I get it and eat it. I eat just on my front teeth, though, 'cause if cake touch that back tooth I know what'll happen. Thank God it ain't hurt me at all today.

After I finish eating I see the man go to the juke box. He drops a nickel in it, then he just stand there a little while looking at the record: Mama tells me keep my eyes in front where they belong. I turn my head like she say, but then I hear the man coming toward us.

"Dance, pretty?" he says.

Mama gets up to dance with him. But 'fore you know it, she done grabbed the little man in the collar and done heaved him 'side the wall. He hit the wall so hard he stop the juke box from playing.

"Some pimp," the lady back of the counter says. "Some pimp." 305

The little man jumps up off the floor and starts toward my mama. 'Fore you know it, Mama done sprung open her knife and she's waiting for him.

"Come on," she says. "Come on. I'll gut you from your neighbo° to your throat. Come on."

neighbo: navel.

I go up to the little man to hit him, but Mama makes me come and stand 'side her. The little man looks at me and Mama and goes on back to the counter.

"Some pimp," the lady back of the counter says. "Some pimp." She starts laughing and pointing at the little man. "Yes sir, you a pimp, all right. Yes sirree."

13

"Fasten that coat, let's go," Mama says.   310

"You don't have to leave," the lady says.

Mama don't answer the lady, and we right out in the cold again. I'm warm right now—my hands, my ears, my feet—but I know this ain't go'n last too long. It done sleet so much now you got ice everywhere you look.

We cross the railroad tracks, and soon's we do, I get cold. That wind goes through this little old coat like it ain't even there. I got on a shirt and a sweater under the coat, but that wind don't pay them no mind. I look up and I can see we got a long way to go. I wonder if we go'n make it 'fore I get too cold.

We cross over to walk on the sidewalk. They got just one sidewalk back here, and it's over there.

After we go just a little piece, I smell bread cooking. I look, then I see a baker shop.   315
When we get closer, I can smell it more better. I shut my eyes and make 'tend I'm eating. But I keep them shut too long and I butt up 'gainst a telephone post. Mama grabs me and see if I'm hurt. I ain't bleeding or nothing and she turns me loose.

I can feel I'm getting colder and colder, and I look up to see how far we still got to go. Uptown is 'way up yonder. A half mile more, I reckon. I try to think of something. They say think and you won't get cold. I think of that poem, "Annabel Lee."° I ain't been to school in so long—this bad weather—I reckon they done passed "Annabel Lee" by now. But passed it or not, I'm sure Miss Walker go'n make me recite it when I get there. That woman don't never forget nothing. I ain't never seen nobody like that in my life.

I'm still getting cold. "Annabel Lee" or no "Annabel Lee," I'm still getting cold. But I can see we getting closer. We getting there gradually.

Soon's we turn the corner, I see a little old white lady up in front of us. She's the only lady on the street. She's all in black and she's got a long black rag over her head.

"Stop," she says.

Me and Mama stop and look at her. She must be crazy to be out in all this bad   320
weather. Ain't got but a few other people out there, and all of them's men.

"Y'all done ate?" she says.

"Just finish," Mama says.

"Y'all must be cold then?" she says.

"We headed for the dentist," Mama says. "We'll warm up when we get there."

"What dentist?" the old lady says. "Mr. Bassett?"   325

"Yes, ma'am," Mama says.

"Come on in," the old lady says. "I'll telephone him and tell him y'all coming."

Me and Mama follow the old lady in the store. It's a little bitty store, and it don't have much in there. The old lady takes off her head rag and folds it up.

"Helena?" somebody calls from the back.

"Yes, Alnest?" the old lady says.   330

"Did you see them?"

"*Annabel Lee*": poem (1849) by Edgar Allan Poe (1809–1849). See Chapter 19.

"They're here. Standing beside me."

"Good. Now you can stay inside."

The old lady looks at Mama. Mama's waiting to hear what she brought us in here for. I'm waiting for that, too.

"I saw y'all each time you went by," she says. "I came out to catch you, but you were gone." 335

"We went back of town," Mama says.

"Did you eat?"

"Yes, ma'am."

The old lady looks at Mama a long time, like she's thinking Mama might be just saying that. Mama looks right back at her. The old lady looks at me to see what I have to say. I don't say nothing. I sure ain't going 'gainst my mama.

"There's food in the kitchen," she says to Mama. "I've been keeping it warm." 340

Mama turns right around and starts for the door.

"Just a minute," the old lady says. Mama stops. "The boy'll have to work for it. It isn't free."

"We don't take no handout," Mama says.

"I'm not handing out anything," the old lady says. "I need my garbage moved to the front. Ernest has a bad cold and can't go out there."

"James'll move it for you," Mama says. 345

"Not unless you eat," the old lady says. "I'm old, but I have my pride, too, you know."

Mama can see that she ain't go'n beat this old lady down, so she just shakes her head.

"All right," the old lady says. "Come into the kitchen."

She leads the way with that rag in her hand. The kitchen is a little bitty little old thing, too. The table and the stove just 'bout fill it up. They got a little room to the side. Somebody in there laying 'cross the bed—'cause I can see one of his feet. Must be the person she was talking to: Ernest or Alnest—something like that.

"Sit down," the old lady says to Mama. "Not you," she says to me. "You have to move the cans." 350

"Helena?" the man says in the other room.

"Yes, Alnest?" the old lady says.

"Are you going out there again?"

"I must show the boy where the garbage is, Alnest," the old lady says.

"Keep that shawl over your head," the old man says. 355

"You don't have to remind me, Alnest. Come, boy," the old lady says.

We go out in the yard. Little old back yard ain't no bigger than the store or the kitchen. But it can sleet here just like it can sleet in any big back yard. And 'fore you know it, I'm trembling.

"There," the old lady says, pointing to the cans. I pick up one of the cans and set it right back down. The can's so light, I'm go'n see what's inside of it.

"Here," the old lady says. "Leave that can alone."

I look back at her standing there in the door. She's got that black rag wrapped 360 round her shoulders, and she's pointing one of her little old fingers at me.

"Pick it up and carry it to the front," she says. I go by her with the can, and she's looking at me all the time. I'm sure the can's empty. I'm sure she could've carried it herself—maybe both of them at the same time. "Set it on the sidewalk by the door and come back for the other one," she says.

I go and come back, and Mama looks at me when I pass her. I get the other can and take it to the front. It don't feel a bit heavier than that first one. I tell myself I ain't go'n be nobody's fool, and I'm go'n look inside this can to see just what I been hauling. First,

I look up the street, then down the street. Nobody coming. Then I look over my shoulder toward the door. That little old lady done slipped up there quiet 's mouse, watching me again. Look like she knowed what I was go'n do.

"Ehh, Lord," she says. "Children, children. Come in here, boy, and go wash your hands."

I follow her in the kitchen. She points toward the bathroom, and I go in there and wash up. Little bitty old bathroom, but it's clean, clean. I don't use any of her towels; I wipe my hands on my pants legs.

When I come back in the kitchen, the old lady done dished up the food. Rice, gravy, meat—and she even got some lettuce and tomato in a saucer. She even got a glass of milk and a piece of cake there, too. It looks so good, I almost start eating 'fore I say my blessing.

"Helena?" the old man says.

"Yes, Alnest?"

"Are they eating?"

"Yes," she says.

"Good," he says. "Now you'll stay inside."

The old lady goes in there where he is and I can hear them talking. I look at Mama. She's eating slow like she's thinking. I wonder what's the matter now. I reckon she's thinking 'bout home.

The old lady comes back in the kitchen.

"I talked to Dr. Bassett's nurse," she says. "Dr. Bassett will take you as soon as you get there."

"Thank you, ma'am," Mama says.

"Perfectly all right," the old lady says. "Which one is it?"

Mama nods toward me. The old lady looks at me real sad. I look sad, too.

"You're not afraid, are you?" she says.

"No, ma'am," I say.

"That's a good boy," the old lady says. "Nothing to be afraid of. Dr. Bassett will not hurt you."

When me and Mama get through eating, we thank the old lady again.

"Helena, are they leaving?" the old man says.

"Yes, Alnest."

"Tell them I say good-bye."

"They can hear you, Alnest."

"Good-bye both mother and son," the old man says. "And may God be with you."

Me and Mama tell the old man good-bye, and we follow the old lady in the front room. Mama opens the door to go out, but she stops and comes back in the store.

"You sell salt meat?" she says.

"Yes."

"Give me two bits worth."

"That isn't very much salt meat," the old lady says.

"That's all I have," Mama says.

The old lady goes back of the counter and cuts a big piece off the chunk. Then she wraps it up and puts it in a paper bag.

"Two bits," she says.

"That looks like awful lot of meat for a quarter," Mama says.

"Two bits," the old lady says. "I've been selling salt meat behind this counter twenty-five years. I think I know what I'm doing."

"You got a scale there," Mama says.

"What?" the old lady says.

"Weigh it," Mama says.

"What?" the old lady says. "Are you telling me how to run my business?"

"Thanks very much for the food," Mama says.   400

"Just a minute," the old lady says.

"James," Mama says to me. I move toward the door.

"Just one minute, I said," the old lady says.

Me and Mama stop again and look at her. The old lady takes the meat out of the bag and unwraps it and cuts 'bout half of it off. Then she wraps it up again and juggs it back in the bag and gives the bag to Mama. Mama lays the quarter on the counter.

"Your kindness will never be forgotten," she says. "James," she says to me.   405

We go out, and the old lady comes to the door to look at us. After we go a little piece I look back, and she's still there watching us.

The sleet's coming down heavy, heavy now, and I turn up my coat collar to keep my neck warm. My mama tells me turn it right back down.

"You not a bum," she says. "You a man."

QUESTIONS

1. What does Gaines establish by using the eight-year-old boy, James, as the narrator who tells the story in the present tense and in his own dialect?

2. Why does James describe the family's need to kill and eat the small birds?

3. What is the major action in the story? What is the result of James and his mother Octavia taking the trip to the dentist? What is gained by the delays, which require the boy and his mother to wait in the office and then to walk out into the cold and sleet?

4. What is the significance of the discussions of suffering occasioned by the protesting child in the dentist's office? What ideas does the young man present (section 7)? When the minister hits him and reproaches him, what is demonstrated about the old and new ideas professed by African-Americans?

5. What values are represented by the elderly couple in the store? Why doesn't the woman phone Dr. Robillard, the "better" but "more expensive" dentist? Why doesn't Octavia accept the portion of salt meat the woman first offers her? What causes the woman to cut the salt meat in half?

D. H. LAWRENCE (1885–1930)

Lawrence was born in an English mining community, but he received a sufficient education to enable him to become a teacher and writer. He fictionalized the early years of his life in the novel Sons and Lovers *(1913). His most controversial work,* Lady Chatterley's Lover, *was printed privately in Italy in 1928 but was not published in an uncut version in the United States until the 1960s. He shocked his contemporaries with his emphasis on the importance of sexuality, an idea that is central to "The Horse Dealer's Daughter." He was afflicted with tuberculosis and lived in a number of warm, sunny places, including Italy, New Zealand, and New Mexico, in an attempt to restore his health. Nevertheless, his illness claimed him in 1930, when he was only forty-five years old.*

The Horse Dealer's Daughter ~~~~~ 1922

"Well, Mabel, and what are you going to do with yourself?" asked Joe, with foolish flippancy. He felt quite safe himself. Without listening for an answer, he turned aside, worked a grain of tobacco to the tip of his tongue, and spat it out. He did not care about anything, since he felt safe himself.

The three brothers and the sister sat round the desolate breakfast table, attempting some sort of desultory consultation. The morning's post had given the final tap to the family fortunes, and all was over. The dreary dining-room itself, with its heavy mahogany furniture, looked as it were waiting to be done away with.

But the consultation amounted to nothing. There was a strange air of ineffectuality about the three men, as they sprawled at table, smoking and reflecting vaguely on their own condition. The girl was alone, a rather short, sullen-looking young woman of twenty-seven. She did not share the same life as her brothers. She would have been good-looking, save for the impassive fixity of her face, "bulldog," as her brothers called it.

There was a confused tramping of horses' feet outside. The three men all sprawled round in their chairs to watch. Beyond the dark holly-bushes that separated the strip of lawn from the high-road, they could see a cavalcade of shire horses swinging out of their own yard, being taken for exercise. This was the last time. These were the last horses that would go through their hands. The young men watched with critical, callous look. They were all frightened at the collapse of their lives, and the sense of disaster in which they were involved left them no inner freedom.

Yet they were three fine, well-set fellows enough. Joe, the eldest, was a man of thirty-   5
three, broad and handsome in a hot, flushed way. His face was red, he twisted his black moustache over a thick finger, his eyes were shallow and restless. He had a sensual way of uncovering his teeth when he laughed, and his bearing was stupid. Now he watched the horses with a glazed look of helplessness in his eyes, a certain stupor of downfall.

The great draught-horses swung past. They were tied head to tail, four of them, and they heaved along to where a lane branched off from the highroad, planting their great hoofs floutingly in the fine black mud, swinging their great rounded haunches sumptuously, and trotting a few sudden steps as they were led into the lane, round the corner. Every movement showed a massive, slumbrous strength, and a stupidity which held them in subjection. The groom at the head looked back, jerking the leading rope. And the cavalcade moved out of sight up the lane, the tail of the last horse, bobbed up tight and stiff, held out taut from the swinging great haunches as they rocked behind the hedges in a motionlike sleep.

Joe watched with glazed hopeless eyes. The horses were almost like his own body to him. He felt he was done for now. Luckily, he was engaged to a woman as old as himself, and therefore her father, who was steward of a neighbouring estate, would provide him with a job. He would marry and go into harness. His life was over, he would be a subject animal now.

He turned uneasily aside, the retreating steps of the horses echoing in his ears. Then, with foolish restlessness, he reached for the scraps of bacon-rind from the plates, and making a faint whistling sound, flung them to the terrier that lay against the fender. He watched the dog swallow them, and waited till the creature looked into his eyes. Then a faint grin came on his face, and in a high, foolish voice he said:

"You won't get much more bacon, shall you, you little b———?"

The dog faintly and dismally wagged its tail, then lowered its haunches, circled   10
round, and lay down again.

There was another helpless silence at the table. Joe sprawled uneasily in his seat, not willing to go till the family conclave was dissolved. Fred Henry, the second brother,

Joe like animals that is controlled

What can Women do housemaid Stay with Sister Train for Nurse

was erect, clean-limbed, alert. He had watched the passing of the horses with more *sang-froid.*° If he was an animal, like Joe, he was an animal which controls, not one which is controlled. He was master of any horse, and he carried himself with a well-tempered air of mastery. But he was not master of the situations of life. He pushed his coarse brown moustache upwards, off his lip, and glanced irritably at his sister, who sat impassive and inscrutable.

"You'll go and stop with Lucy for a bit, shan't you?" he asked. The girl did not answer.

"I don't see what else you can do," persisted Fred Henry.

"Go as a skivvy,"° Joe interpolated laconically.

The girl did not move a muscle.

"If I was her, I should go in for training for a nurse," said Malcolm, the youngest of   15
them all. He was the baby of the family, a young man of twenty-two, with a fresh, jaunty *museau.*°

But Mabel did not take any notice of him. They had talked at her and round her for so many years, that she hardly heard them at all. *Shut them out*

The marble clock on the mantel-piece softly chimed the half-hour, the dog rose uneasily from the hearthrug and looked at the party at the breakfast table. But still they sat on in ineffectual conclave.

"Oh, all right," said Joe suddenly, *à propos* of nothing. "I'll get a move on."

He pushed back his chair, straddled his knees with a downward jerk, to get them   20
free, in horsey fashion, and went to the fire. Still he did not go out of the room; he was curious to know what the others would do or say. He began to charge his pipe, looking down at the dog and saying, in a high, affected voice:

"Going wi' me? Going wi' me are ter? Tha'rt goin' further than tha counts on just now, dost hear?"

The dog faintly wagged its tail, the man stuck out his jaw and covered his pipe with his hands, and puffed intently, losing himself in the tobacco, looking down all the while at the dog, with an absent brown eye. The dog looked up at him in mournful distrust. Joe stood with his knees stuck out, in real horsey fashion.

"Have you had a letter from Lucy?" Fred Henry asked of his sister.

"Last week," came the neutral reply.

"And what does she say?"   25

There was no answer.

"Does she *ask* you to go and stop there?" persisted Fred Henry.

"She says I can if I like."

"Well, then, you'd better. Tell her you'll come on Monday."

This was received in silence.   30

"That's what you'll do then, is it?" said Fred Henry, in some exasperation.

But she made no answer. There was a silence of futility and irritation in the room. Malcolm grinned fatuously. *Foolishly*

"You'll have to make up your mind between now and next Wednesday," said Joe loudly, "or else find yourself lodgings on the kerbstone."

The face of the young woman darkened, but she sat on immutable.

"Here's Jack Fergusson!" exclaimed Malcolm, who was looking aimlessly out of the   35
window.

---

sang-froid: unconcern (literally, cold blood).
skivvy: British slang for housemaid.
museau: French for nose, snout.

"Where?" exclaimed Joe, loudly.

"Just gone past."

"Coming in?"

Malcolm craned his neck to see the gate.

"Yes," he said.   40

There was a silence. Mabel sat on like one condemned, at the head of the table. Then a whistle was heard from the kitchen. The dog got up and barked sharply. Joe opened the door and shouted:

"Come on."

After a moment, a young man entered. He was muffled up in overcoat and a purple woolen scarf, and his tweed cap, which he did not remove, was pulled down on his head. He was of medium height, his face was rather long and pale, his eyes looked tired.

"Hello, Jack! Well, Jack!" exclaimed Malcolm and Joe. Fred Henry merely said "Jack!"

"What's doing?" asked the newcomer, evidently addressing Fred Henry.   45

"Same. We've got to be out by Wednesday—Got a cold?"   *stop = stay*

"I have—got it bad, too."

"Why don't you stop in?"

"*Me* stop in? When I can't stand on my legs, perhaps I shall have a chance." The young man spoke huskily. He had a slight Scotch accent.

"It's a knock-out, isn't it," said Joe boisterously, "if a doctor goes round croaking   50 with a cold. Looks bad for the patients, doesn't it?"   *So this looks bad*

The young doctor looked at him slowly.   *Done one side of the blw.*

"Anything the matter with *you*, then?" he asked, sarcastically.   *sick & stop by.*

"Not as I know of. Damn your eyes, I hope not. Why?"

"I thought you were very concerned about the patients, wondered if you might be one yourself."   *burning*

"Damn it, no, I've never been patient to no flaming doctor, and hope I never shall   55 be," returned Joe.

At this point Mabel rose from the table, and they all seemed to become aware of her existence. She began putting the dishes together. The young doctor looked at her, but did not address her. He had not greeted her. She went out of the room with the tray, her face impassive and unchanged.

"When are you off then, all of you?" asked the doctor.

"I'm catching the eleven-forty," replied Malcolm. "Are you goin' down wi' th' trap, Joe?"

"Yes, I've told you I'm going down wi' th' trap, haven't I?"

"We'd better be getting her in then.—So long, Jack, if I don't see you before I go,"   60 said Malcolm, shaking hands.

He went out, followed by Joe, who seemed to have his tail between his legs.

"Well, this is the devil's own," exclaimed the doctor, when he was left alone with Fred Henry. "Going before Wednesday, are you?"

"That's the orders," replied the other.

"Where, to Northampton?"

"That's it."   65

"The devil!" exclaimed Fergusson, with quiet chagrin.

And there was silence between the two.

"All settled up, are you?" asked Fergusson.

trap: small wagon.

"About."

There was another pause.

"Well, I shall miss yer, Freddy boy," said the young doctor.

"And I shall miss thee, Jack," returned the other.

"Miss you like hell," mused the doctor.

Fred Henry turned aside. There was nothing to say. Mabel came in again, to finish clearing the table.

"What are *you* going to do then, Miss Pervin?" asked Fergusson. "Going to your sister's, are you?"

Mabel looked at him with her steady, dangerous eyes, that always made him uncomfortable, unsettling his superficial ease.

"No," she said.

"Well, what in the name of fortune *are* you going to do? Say what you *mean* to do," cried Fred Henry, with futile intensity.

But she only averted her head, and continued her work. She folded the white tablecloth, and put on the chenille cloth.

"The sulkiest bitch that ever trod!" muttered her brother.

But she finished her task with perfectly impassive face, the young doctor watching her interestedly all the while. Then she went out.

Fred Henry stared after her, clenching his lips, his blue eyes fixing in sharp antagonism, as he made a grimace of sour exasperation.

"You could bray her into bits, and that's all you'd get out of her," he said, in a small, narrowed tone.

The doctor smiled faintly.

"What's she *going* to do then?" he asked.

"Strike me if *I* know!" returned the other.

There was a pause. Then the doctor stirred.

"I'll be seeing you to-night, shall I?" he said to his friend.

"Ay—where's it to be? Are we going over to Jessdale?"

"I don't know. I've got such a cold on me. I'll come round to the Moon and Stars, anyway."

"Let Lizzie and May miss their night for once, eh?"

"That's it—if I feel as I do now."

"All's one—"

The two young men went through the passage and down to the back door together. The house was large, but it was servantless now, and desolate. At the back was a small bricked house-yard, and beyond that a big square, gravelled fine and red, and having stables on two sides. Sloping, dank, winter-dark fields stretched away on the open sides.

But the stables were empty. Joseph Pervin, the father of the family, had been a man of no education, who had become a fairly large horse dealer. The stables had been full of horses, there was a great turmoil and come-and-go of horses and of dealers and grooms. Then the kitchen was full of servants. But of late things had declined. The old man had married a second time, to retrieve his fortunes. Now he was dead and everything was gone to the dogs, there was nothing but debt and threatening.

For months, Mabel had been servantless in the big house, keeping the home together in penury for her ineffectual brothers. She had kept house for ten years. But previously, it was with unstinted means. Then, however brutal and coarse everything was, the sense of money had kept her proud, confident. The men might be foul-mouthed, the women in the kitchen might have bad reputations, her brothers might have illegitimate children. But so long as there was money, the girl felt herself established, and brutally proud, reserved.

Animal pride that dominated each family member

Isolated from other women

No company came to the house, save dealers and coarse men. Mabel had no associates of her own sex, after her sister went away. But she did not mind. She went regularly to church, she attended to her father. And she lived in the memory of her mother, who had died when she was fourteen, and whom she had loved. She had loved her father, too, in a different way, depending upon him, and feeling secure in him, until at the age of fifty-four he married again. And then she had set hard against him. Now he had died and left them all hopelessly in debt.

Planning suicide

hopeless

She had suffered badly during the period of poverty. Nothing, however, could shake the curious sullen, animal pride that dominated each member of the family. Now, for Mabel, the end had come. Still she would not cast about her. She would follow her own way just the same. She would always hold the keys of her own situation. Mindless and persistent, she endured from day to day. Why should she think? Why should she answer anybody? It was enough that this was the end, and there was no way out. She need not pass any more darkly along the main street of the small town, avoiding every eye. She need not demean herself any more, going into the shops and buying the cheapest food. This was at an end. She thought of nobody, not even of herself. Mindless and persistent, she seemed in a sort of ecstasy to be coming nearer to her fulfilment, her own glorification, approaching her dead mother, who was glorified.°

In the afternoon she took a little bag, with shears and sponge and a small scrubbing brush, and went out. It was a grey, wintry day, with saddened, dark-green fields and an atmosphere blackened by the smoke of foundries not far off. She went quickly, darkly along the causeway, heeding nobody, through the town to the churchyard.

There she always felt secure, as if no one could see her, although as a matter of fact she was exposed to the stare of everyone who passed along under the churchyard wall. Nevertheless, once under the shadow of the great looming church, among the graves, she felt immune from the world, reserved within the thick churchyard wall as in another country.   100

Carefully she clipped the grass from the grave, and arranged the pinky-white, small chrysanthemums in the tin cross. When this was done, she took an empty jar from a neighbouring grave, brought water, and carefully, most scrupulously sponged the marble headstone and the coping-stone.

grief of mother's loss

It gave her sincere satisfaction to do this. She felt in immediate contact with the world of her mother. She took minute pains, went through the park in a state bordering on pure happiness, as if in performing this task she came into a subtle, intimate connection with her mother. For the life she followed here in the world was far less real than the world of death she inherited from her mother.

The doctor's house was just by the church. Fergusson, being a mere hired assistant, was slave to the countryside. As he hurried now to attend to the outpatients in the surgery, glancing across the graveyard with his quick eye, he saw the girl at her task at the grave. She seemed so intent and remote, it was like looking into another world. Some mystical element was touched in him. He slowed down as he walked, watching her as if spell-bound.

She lifted her eyes, feeling him looking. Their eyes met. And each looked again at once, each feeling, in some way, found out by the other. He lifted his cap and passed on down the road. There remained distinct in his consciousness, like a vision, the memory of her face, lifted from the tombstone in the churchyard, and looking at him with slow, large, portentous eyes. It *was* portentous, her face. It seemed to mesmerise him. There was a heavy power in her eyes which laid hold of his whole being, as if he had drunk some powerful drug. He had been feeling weak and done before. Now the life came back into him, he felt delivered from his own fretted, daily self.

who was glorified: See Romans 8:17, 30.

He finished his duties at the surgery as quickly as might be, hastily filling up the bottles of the waiting people with cheap drugs. Then, in perpetual haste, he set off again to visit several cases in another part of his round, before teatime. At all times he preferred to walk, if he could, but particularly when he was not well. He fancied the motion restored him.

The afternoon was falling. It was grey, deadened, and wintry, with a slow, moist, heavy coldness sinking in and deadening all the faculties. But why should he think or notice? He hastily climbed the hill and turned across the dark-green fields, following the black cinder-track. In the distance, across a shallow dip in the country, the small town was clustered like smouldering ash, a tower, a spire, a heap of low, raw, extinct houses. And on the nearest fringe of the town, sloping into the dip, was Oldmeadow, the Pervins' house. He could see the stables and the outbuildings distinctly, as they lay towards him on the slope. Well, he would not go there many more times! Another resource would be lost to him, another place gone: the only company he cared for in the alien, ugly little town he was losing. Nothing but work, drudgery, constant hastening from dwelling to dwelling among the colliers and the iron-workers. It wore him out, but at the same time he had a craving for it. It was a stimulant to him to be in the homes of the working people, moving as it were through the innermost body of their life. His nerves were excited and gratified. He could come so near, into the very lives of the rough, inarticulate, powerfully emotional men and women. He grumbled, he said he hated the hellish hole. But as a matter of fact it excited him, the contact with the rough, strongly-feeling people was a stimulant applied direct to his nerves.

Below Oldmeadow, in the green, shallow, soddened hollow of fields, lay a square, deep pond. Roving across the landscape, the doctor's quick eye detected a figure in black passing through the gate of the field, down towards the pond. He looked again. It would be Mabel Pervin. His mind suddenly became alive and attentive.

Why was she going down there? He pulled up on the path on the slope above, and stood staring. He could just make sure of the small black figure moving in the hollow of the failing day. He seemed to see her in the midst of such obscurity, that he was like a clairvoyant, seeing rather with the mind's eye than with ordinary sight. Yet he could see her positively enough, whilst he kept his eye attentive. He felt, if he looked away from her, in the thick, ugly falling dusk, he would lose her altogether.

He followed her minutely as she moved, direct and intent, like something transmitted rather than stirring in voluntary activity, straight down the field towards the pond. There she stood on the bank for a moment. She never raised her head. Then she waded slowly into the water.

He stood motionless as the small black figure walked slowly and deliberately towards the centre of the pond, very slowly, gradually moving deeper into the motionless water, and still moving forward as the water got up to her breast. Then he could see her no more in the dusk of the dead afternoon.

"There!" he exclaimed. "Would you believe it?"

And he hastened straight down, running over the wet, soddened fields, pushing through the hedges, down into the depression of callous wintry obscurity. It took him several minutes to come to the pond. He stood on the bank, breathing heavily. He could see nothing. His eyes seemed to penetrate the dead water. Yes, perhaps that was the dark shadow of her black clothing beneath the surface of the water.

He slowly ventured into the pond. The bottom was deep, soft clay, he sank in, and the water clasped dead cold round his legs. As he stirred he could smell the cold, rotten clay that fouled up into the water. It was objectionable in his lungs. Still, repelled and yet not heeding, he moved deeper into the pond. The cold water rose over his thighs, over his loins, upon his abdomen. The lower part of his body was all sunk in the hideous cold element. And the bottom was so deeply soft and uncertain, he was afraid of pitching with his mouth underneath. He could not swim, and was afraid.

105

110

He crouched a little, spreading his hands under the water and moving them round, trying to feel for her. The dead cold pond swayed upon his chest. He moved again, a little deeper, and again, with his hands underneath, he felt all around under the water. And he touched her clothing. But it evaded his fingers. He made a desperate effort to grasp it.

And so doing he lost his balance and went under, horribly, suffocating in the foul earthy water, struggling madly for a few moments. At last, after what seemed an eternity, he got his footing, rose again into the air and looked around. He gasped, and knew he was in the world. Then he looked at the water. She had risen near him. He grasped her clothing, and drawing her nearer, turned to take his way to land again.

He went very slowly, carefully, absorbed in the slow progress. He rose higher, climbing out of the pond. The water was not only about his legs; he was thankful, full of relief to be out of the clutches of the pond. He lifted her and staggered on to the bank, out of the horror of wet, grey clay.

He laid her down on the bank. She was quite unconscious and running with water. He made the water come from her mouth, he worked to restore her. He did not have to work very long before he could feel the breathing begin again in her; she was breathing naturally. He worked a little longer. He could feel her live beneath his hands; she was coming back. He wiped her face, wrapped her in his overcoat, looked round into the dim, dark-grey world, then lifted her and staggered down the bank and across the fields.

It seemed an unthinkably long way, and his burden so heavy he felt he would never get to the house. But at last he was in the stable-yard, and then in the house-yard. He opened the door and went into the house. In the kitchen he laid her down on the hearthrug, and called. The house was empty. But the fire was burning in the grate.

Then again he kneeled to attend to her. She was breathing regularly, her eyes were wide open as if conscious, but there seemed something missing in her look. She was conscious in herself, but unconscious of her surroundings.

He ran upstairs, took blankets from a bed, and put them before the fire to warm. 120 Then he removed her saturated, earthy-smelling clothing, rubbed her dry with a towel, and wrapped her naked in the blankets. Then he went into the dining-room, to look for spirits. There was a little whiskey. He drank a gulp himself, and put some into her mouth.

The effect was instantaneous. She looked full into his face, as if she had been seeing him for some time, and yet had only just become conscious of him.

"Dr. Fergusson?" she said.

"What?" he answered.

He was divesting himself of his coat, intending to find some dry clothing upstairs. He could not bear the smell of the dead, clayey water, and he was mortally afraid for his own health.

"What did I do?" she asked. 125

"Walked into the pond," he replied. He had begun to shudder like one sick, and could hardly attend to her. Her eyes remained full on him, he seemed to be going dark in his mind, looking back at her helplessly. The shuddering became quieter in him, his life came back in him, dark and unknowing, but strong again.

"Was I out of my mind?" she asked, while her eyes were fixed on him all the time.

"Maybe, for the moment," he replied. He felt quiet, because his strength had come back. The strange fretful strain had left him.

"Am I out of my mind now?" she asked.

"Are you?" he reflected a moment. "No," he answered truthfully, "I don't see that 130 you are." He turned his face aside. He was afraid, now, because he felt dazed, and felt dimly that her power was stronger than his, in this issue. And she continued to look at him fixedly all the time. "Can you tell me where I shall find some dry things to put on?" he asked.

"Did you dive into the pond for me?" she asked.

"No," he answered. "I walked in. But I went in overhead as well."

There was silence for a moment. He hesitated. He very much wanted to go upstairs to get into dry clothing. But there was another desire in him. And she seemed to hold him. His will seemed to have gone to sleep, and left him, standing there slack before her. But he felt warm inside himself. He did not shudder at all, though his clothes were sodden on him.

"Why did you?" she asked.

"Because I didn't want you to do such a foolish thing," he said.   135

"It wasn't foolish," she said, still gazing at him as she lay on the floor, with a sofa cushion under her head. "It was the right thing to do. *I* knew best, then."

"I'll go and shift these wet things," he said. But still he had not the power to move out of her presence, until she sent him. It was as if she had the life of his body in her hands, and he could not extricate himself. Or perhaps he did not want to.

Suddenly she sat up. Then she became aware of her own immediate condition. She felt the blankets about her, she knew her own limbs. For a moment it seemed as if her reason were going. She looked round, with wild eye, as if seeking something. He stood still with fear. She saw her clothing lying scattered.

"Who undressed me?" she asked, her eyes resting full and inevitable on his face.

"I did," he replied, "to bring you round."   140

For some moments she sat and gazed at him awfully, her lips parted.

"Do you love me then?" she asked.

He only stood and stared at her, fascinated. His soul seemed to melt.

She shuffled forward on her knees, and put her arms round him, round his legs, as he stood there, pressing her breasts against his knees and thighs, clutching him with strange, convulsive certainty, pressing his thighs against her, drawing him to her face, her throat, as she looked up at him with flaring, humble eyes of transfiguration, triumphant in first possession.

"You love me," she murmured, in strange transport, yearning and triumphant and   145
confident. "You love me. I know you love me, I know."

And she was passionately kissing his knees, through the wet clothing, passionately and indiscriminately kissing his knees, his legs, as if unaware of everything.

He looked down at the tangled wet hair, the wild, bare, animal shoulders. He was amazed, bewildered, and afraid. He had never thought of loving her. He had never wanted to love her. When he rescued her and restored her, he was a doctor, and she was a patient. He had had no single personal thought of her. Nay, this introduction of the personal element was very distasteful to him, a violation of his professional honour. It was horrible to have her there embracing his knees. It was horrible. He revolted from it, violently. And yet—and yet—he had not the power to break away.

She looked at him again, with the same supplication of powerful love, and that same transcendent, frightening light of triumph. In view of the delicate flame which seemed to come from her face like a light, he was powerless. And yet he had never intended to love her. He had never intended. And something stubborn in him could not give way.

"You love me," she repeated, in a murmur of deep, rhapsodic assurance. "You love me."

Her hands were drawing him, drawing him down to her. He was afraid, even a little   150
horrified. For he had, really, no intention of loving her. Yet her hands were drawing him towards her. He put out his hand quickly to steady himself, and grasped her bare shoulder. A flame seemed to burn the hand that grasped her soft shoulder. He had no intention of loving her: his whole will was against his yielding. It was horrible—And yet

wonderful was the touch of her shoulder, beautiful the shining of her face. Was she perhaps mad? He had a horror of yielding to her. Yet something in him ached also.

He had been staring away at the door, away from her. But his hand remained on her shoulder. She had gone suddenly very still. He looked down at her. Her eyes were now wide with fear, with doubt, the light was dying from her face, a shadow of terrible greyness was returning. He could not bear the touch of her eyes' question upon him, and the look of death behind the question.

With an inward groan he gave way, and let his heart yield towards her. A sudden gentle smile came on his face. And her eyes, which never left his face, slowly, slowly filled with tears. He watched the strange water rise in her eyes, like some slow fountain coming up. And his heart seemed to burn and melt away in his breast.

He could not bear to look at her any more. He dropped on his knees and caught her head with his arms and pressed her face against his throat. She was very still. His heart, which seemed to have broken, was burning with a kind of agony in his breast. And he felt her slow, hot tears wetting his throat. But he could not move.

He felt the hot tears wet his neck and the hollows of his neck, and he remained motionless, suspended through one of man's eternities. Only now it had become indispensable to him to have her face pressed close to him; he could never let her go again. He could never let her head go away from the close clutch of his arm. He wanted to remain like that for ever, with his heart hurting him in a pain that was also life to him. Without knowing, he was looking down on her damp, soft brown hair.

Then, as it were suddenly, he smelt the horrid stagnant smell of the water. And at   155
the same moment she drew away from him and looked at him. Her eyes were wistful and *fearful*
unfathomable. He was afraid of them, and he fell to kissing her, not knowing what he was
doing. He wanted her eyes not to have that terrible, wistful, unfathomable look.

When she turned her face to him again, a faint delicate flush was glowing, and there was again dawning that terrible shining of joy in her eyes, which really terrified him, and yet which he now wanted to see, because he feared the look of doubt still more.

"You love me?" she said, rather faltering.

"Yes." The word cost him a painful effort. Not because it wasn't true. But because it was too newly true, the *saying* seemed to tear open again his newly-torn heart. And he hardly wanted it to be true, even now.

She lifted her face to him, and he bent forward and kissed her on the mouth gently, with the one kiss that is an eternal pledge. And as he kissed her his heart strained again in his breast. He never intended to love her. But now it was over. He had crossed over the gulf to her, and all that he had left behind had shrivelled and become void.

After the kiss, her eyes again slowly filled with tears. She sat still, away from him,   160
with her face drooped aside, and her hands folded in her lap. The tears fell very slowly. There was complete silence. He too sat there motionless and silent on the hearthrug. The strange pain of his heart that was broken seemed to consume him. That he should love her? That this was love! That he should be ripped open in this way!—Him, a doctor!— How they would all jeer if they knew!—It was agony to him to think they might know.

In the curious naked pain of the thought he looked again to her. She was sitting there drooped into a muse. He saw a tear fall, and his heart flared hot. He saw for the first time that one of her shoulders was quite uncovered, one arm bare, he could see one of her small breasts; dimly, because it had become almost dark in the room.

"Why are you crying?" he asked, in an altered voice.

She looked up at him, and behind her tears the consciousness of her situation for the first time brought a dark look of shame to her eyes.

"I'm not crying, really," she said, watching him half frightened.

He reached his hand, and softly closed it on her bare arm.   165

"I love you! I love you!" he said in a soft, low vibrating voice, unlike himself.

She shrank, and dropped her head. The soft, penetrating grip of his hand on her arm distressed her. She looked up at him.

"I want to go," she said. "I want to go and get you some dry things."

"Why?" he said. "I'm all right."

"But I want to go," she said. "And I want you to change your things."   170

He released her arm, and she wrapped herself in the blanket, looking at him rather frightened. And still she did not rise.

"Kiss me," she said wistfully.

He kissed her, but briefly, half in anger.

Then, after a second, she rose nervously, all mixed up in the blanket. He watched her in her confusion, as she tried to extricate herself and wrap herself up so that she could walk. He watched her relentlessly, as she knew.

And as she went, the blanket trailing, and as he saw a glimpse of her feet and her   175
white leg, he tried to remember her as she was when he had wrapped her in the blanket. But then he didn't want to remember, because she had been nothing to him then, and his nature revolted from remembering her as she was when she was nothing to him.

A tumbling muffled noise from within the dark house startled him. Then he heard her voice:—"There are clothes." He rose and went to the foot of the stairs, and gathered up the garments she had thrown down. Then he came back to the fire, to rub himself down and dress. He grinned at his own appearance, when he had finished.

The fire was sinking, so he put on coal. The house was now quite dark, save for the light of a street-lamp that shone in faintly from beyond the holly trees. He lit the gas with matches he found on the mantel-piece. Then he emptied the pockets of his own clothes, and threw all his wet things in a heap into the scullery. After which he gathered up her sodden clothes, gently, and put them in a separate heap on the copper-top in the scullery.

It was six o'clock on the clock. His own watch had stopped. He ought to be back to the surgery. He waited, and still she did not come down. So he went to the foot of the stairs and called:

"I shall have to go."

Almost immediately he heard her coming down. She had on her best dress of black   180
voile, and her hair was tidy, but still damp. She looked at him—and in spite of herself, smiled.

"I don't like you in those clothes," she said.

"Do I look a sight?" he answered.

They were shy of one another.

"I'll make you some tea," she said.

"No, I must go."   185

"Must you?" And she looked at him again with the wide, strained, doubtful eyes. And again, from the pain of his breast, he knew how he loved her. He went and bent to kiss her, gently, passionately, with his heart's painful kiss.

"And my hair smells so horrible," she murmured in distraction. "And I'm so awful, I'm so awful! Oh, no, I'm too awful." And she broke into bitter, heartbroken sobbing. "You can't want to love me, I'm horrible."

"Don't be silly, don't be silly," he said, trying to comfort her, kissing her, holding her in his arms. "I want you, I want to marry you, we're going to be married, quickly, quickly—to-morrow if I can."

But she only sobbed terribly, and cried.

"I feel awful. I feel awful. I feel I'm horrible to you."   190

"No, I want you, I want you," was all he answered blindly, with that terrible intonation which frightened her almost more than her horror lest he should *not* want her.

QUESTIONS

1. What idea is Lawrence illustrating by the breakup of the Pervin household?
2. What does the comparison of Joe Pervin and the draft horses mean with regard specifically to Joe, and generally to people without love?
3. What kind of person is Mabel? How do her brothers treat her? How does she feel about her brothers? What dilemma does she face as the story begins?
4. What effect does Mabel have on Fergusson as he watches her in her home, in the churchyard, and at the pond? What does this effect contribute to Lawrence's ideas about love?
5. What do Mabel and Fergusson realize as he revives and warms her? How do their responses signify their growth as characters?
6. Why does the narrator tell us at the story's end that Fergusson "had no intention of loving" Mabel? What idea does this repeated assertion convey?
7. In this story, there is an extensive exploration of the ambiguous feelings of both Fergusson and Mabel after they realize their love. Why does Lawrence explore these feelings so extensively?

IRENE ZABYTKO (b. 1954)

Irene Zabytko was born in Chicago's Ukrainian neighborhood and took her undergraduate and graduate study at Vermont College. A proficient speaker of Ukrainian, she has lived in Ukraine and taught English-language courses there. She is a past winner of the PEN Syndicated Fiction Project, and has held fellowships at the He-lene Wurlitzer Foundation, the Hambidge Center, the Virginia Center for the Creative Arts and Sciences, and the Millay Colony for the Arts. She has been heard on "The Sound of Writing" pro-gram of National Public Radio. Her fiction has appeared in Catholic Girls *(1992) and* Earth Tones *(1994). She is the author of* The Sky Unwashed *(Algonquin Books of Chapel Hill, 2000), a novel based on the nuclear accident in Chernobyl, Russia during the 1980s. Recently she published* When Luba Leaves Home: Stories *(Algonquin Books of Chapel Hill, 2003).*

Home Soil   1992

I watch my son crack his knuckles, oblivious to the somber sounds of the Old Slavonic hymns the choir behind us is singing.

We are in the church where Bohdan, my son, was baptized nineteen years ago. It is Sunday. The pungent smell of frankincense permeates the darkened atmosphere of this cathedral. Soft sun rays illuminate the stained-glass windows. I sit near the one that shows Jesus on the cross looking down on some unidentifiable Apostles who are kneeling beneath His nailed feet. In the background, a tiny desperate Judas swings from a rope, the thirty pieces of silver thrown on the ground.

There is plenty of room in my pew, but my son chooses not to sit with me. I see him staring at the round carapace of a ceiling, stoic icons staring directly back at him. For the remainder of the Mass, he lightly drums his nervous fingers on top of the cover of *My Divine Friend*, the Americanized prayer book of the Ukrainian service. He took bongo lessons before he graduated high school, and learned the basic rolls from off a record, "Let's Swing with Bongos." I think it was supposed to make him popular with the girls at parties. I also think he joined the army because he wanted the virile image men in uniforms have that the bongos never delivered. When he returned from Nam, he mentioned after one of our many conversational silences that he lost the bongos, and the record is cracked, with the pieces buried somewhere deep inside the duffel bag he still hasn't unpacked.

Bohdan, my son, who calls himself Bob, has been back for three weeks. He looks so "American" in his green tailored uniform: his spit-shined vinyl dress shoes tap against the red-cushioned kneelers. It was his idea to go to church with me. He has not been anywhere since he came home. He won't even visit my garden.

Luba, my daughter, warned me he would be moody. She works for the Voice of   5
America and saw him when he landed from Nam in San Francisco. "Just don't worry, *tato*,"° she said to me on the telephone. "He's acting weird. Culture shock."

"Explain what you mean."

"Just, you know, strange." For a disc jockey, and a bilingual one at that, she is so inarticulate. She plays American jazz and tapes concerts for broadcasts for her anonymous compatriots in Ukraine. That's what she was doing when she was in San Francisco, taping some jazz concert. Pure American music for the huddled gold-toothed youths who risk their *komsomol* privileges and maybe their lives listening to these clandestine broadcasts and to my daughter's sweet voice. She will never be able to visit our relatives back there because American security won't allow it, and she would lose her job. But it doesn't matter. After my wife died, I have not bothered to keep up with anyone there, and I don't care if they have forgotten all about me. It's just as well.

I noticed how much my son resembled my wife when I first saw him again at the airport. He was alone, near the baggage claim ramp. He was taller than ever, and his golden hair was bleached white from the jungle sun. He inherited his mother's high cheekbones, but he lost his baby fat, causing his cheeks to jut out from his lean face as sharp as the arrowheads he used to scavenge for when he was a kid.

We hugged briefly. I felt his medals pinch through my thin shirt. "You look good, son," I lied. I avoided his eyes and concentrated on a pin shaped like an open parachute that he wore over his heart.

"Hi, *tato*," he murmured. We spoke briefly about his flight home from San Francis-   10
co, how he'd seen Luba. We stood apart, unlike the other soldiers with their families who were hugging and crying on each other's shoulders in a euphoric delirium.

He grabbed his duffle bag from the revolving ramp and I walked behind him to see if he limped or showed any signs of pain. He showed nothing.

"Want to drive?" I asked, handing him the keys to my new Plymouth.

"Nah," he said. He looked around at the cars crowding the parking lot, and I thought he seemed afraid. "I don't remember how the streets go anymore."

An usher in his best borscht-red polyester suit waits for me to drop some money into the basket. It is old Pan° Medved, toothless except for the prominent gold ones he flashes at me as he pokes me with his basket.

---

tato: "Father" or "Dad."
Pan: a term of respect for adult males, the equivalent of *Mr.*

"*Nu*, give," he whispers hoarsely, but loud enough for a well-dressed woman with   15
lacquered hair who sits in front of me to turn around and stare in mute accusation.

I take out the gray and white snakeskin wallet Bohdan brought back for me, and
transfer out a ten dollar bill. I want the woman to see it before it disappears into the basket. She smiles at me and nods.

Women always smile at me like that. Especially after they see my money and find
out that I own a restaurant in the neighborhood. None of the Ukies° go there; they don't
eat fries and burgers much. But the "jackees"—the Americans—do when they're sick of
eating in the cafeteria at the plastics factory. My English is pretty good for a D.P., and no
one has threatened to bomb my business because they accuse me of being a no-god bo-
hunk commie. Not yet anyway.

But the women are always impressed. I usually end up with the emigrés—some of
them Ukrainians. The Polish women are the greediest for gawdy trinkets and for a man
to give them money so that they can return to their husbands and children in Warsaw. I
like them the best anyway because they laugh more than the other women I see, and they
know how to have a good time.

Bohdan knows nothing about my lecherous life. I told the women to stay clear after
my son arrived. He is so lost with women. I think he was a virgin when he joined the army,
but I'm sure he isn't now. I can't ask him.

After mass ends, I lose Bohdan in the tight clusters of people leaving their pews   20
and genuflecting toward the iconostasis. He waits for me by the holy water front. It looks
like a regular porcelain water fountain but without a spout. There is a sponge in the
basin that is moistened with the holy water blessed by the priests here. Bohdan stands
towering over the font, dabs his fingers into the sponge, but doesn't cross himself the way
he was taught to do as a boy.

"What's the matter?" I ask in English. I hope he will talk to me if I speak to him in
his language.

But Bohdan ignores me and watches an elderly woman gingerly entering the door
of the confessional. "What she got to say? Why is she going in there?"

"Everyone has sins."

"Yeah, but who forgives?"

"God forgives," I say. I regret it because it makes me feel like a hypocrite whenever   25
I parrot words I still find difficult to believe.

We walk together in the neighborhood; graffiti visible in the alley-ways despite the
well-trimmed lawns with flowers and "bathtub" statues of the Blessed Mary smiling benev-
olently at us as we pass by the small bungalows. I could afford to move out of here, out of
Chicago and into some nearby cushy suburb, Skokie or something. But what for? Some
smart Jewish lawyer or doctor would be my next door neighbor and find out that I'm a
Ukie and complain to me about how his grandmother was raped by Petliura.° I've heard
it before. Anyway, I like where I am. I bought a three-flat apartment building after my
wife died and I live in one of the apartments rent-free. I can walk to my business, and see
the past—old women in babushkas sweeping the sidewalks in front of their cherished
gardens; men in Italian-made venetian-slat sandals and woolen socks rushing to a chess
match at the Soyuiez, a local meeting place where the D.P.s sit for hours rehashing the
war over beers and chess.

Ukies: Ukrainian Americans.

Petliura: Simeon Petliura (1879–1926), an anti-Bolshevik Ukrainian leader who was accused of responsibility for Jewish pogroms during World War I. When his forces were defeated by the Russians he
went into exile in Paris, where he was ultimately assassinated by a Jewish nationalist.

Bohdan walks like a soldier. Not exactly a march, but a stiff gait that a good posture in a rigid uniform demands. He looks masculine, but tired and worn. Two pimples are sprouting above his lip where a faint moustache is starting.

"Want a cigarette?" I ask. Soldiers like to smoke. During the forties, I smoked that horrible cheap tobacco, *mahorka*. I watch my son puff heavily on the cigarette I've given him, with his eyes partially closed, delicately cupping his hands to protect it from the wind. In my life, I have seen so many soldiers in that exact pose; they all look the same. When their faces are contorted from sucking the cigarette, there is an unmistakable shadow of vulnerability and fear of living. That gesture and stance are more eloquent than the blood and guts war stories men spew over their beers.

Pan Medved, the battered gold-toothed relic in the church, has that look. Pan Holewski, one of my tenants, has it too. I would have known it even if he never openly displayed his old underground soldier's cap that sits on a bookshelf in the living room between small Ukrainian and American flags. I see it every time I collect the rent.

I wish Bohdan could tell me what happened to him in Vietnam. What did he do? What was done to him? Maybe now isn't the time to tell me. He may never tell me. I never told anyone either.   30

I was exactly his age when I became a soldier. At nineteen, I was a student at the university in L'vov, which the Poles occupied. I was going to be a poet, to study poetry and write it, but the war broke out, and my family could not live on the romantic epics I tried to publish, so I was paid very well by the Nazis to write propaganda pamphlets. "Freedom for Ukrainians" I wrote—"Freedom for our people. Fight the Poles and Russians alongside our German brothers" and other such dreck. I even wrote light verse that glorified Hitler as the protector of the free Ukrainian nation that the Germans promised us. My writing was as naïve as my political ideas.

My new career began in a butcher shop, commandeered after the Polish owner was arrested and shot. I set my battered Underwood typewriter atop an oily wooden table where crescents of chicken feathers still clung between the cracks. Meat hooks that once held huge sides of pork hung naked in a back room, and creaked ominously like a deserted gallows whenever anyone slammed the front door. Every shred of meat had been stolen by looters after the Germans came into the city. Even the little bell that shopkeepers kept at the entrance was taken. But I was very comfortable in my surroundings. I thought only about how I was to play a part in a historical destiny that my valiant words would help bring about. That delusion lasted only about a week or so until three burly Nazis came in. "*Schnell!*" they said to me, pushing me out of my chair and pointing to the windows where I saw crowds chaotically swarming about. Before I could question the soldiers, one of them shoved a gun into my hands and pushed me out into the streets. I felt so bewildered until the moment I pointed my rifle at a man who was about—I thought—to hit me with a club of some sort. Suddenly, I felt such an intense charge of power, more so than I had ever felt writing some of my best poems. I was no longer dealing with abstract words and ideas for a mythological cause; I was responsible for life and death.

I enjoyed that power, until it seeped into my veins and poisoned my soul. It was only an instant, a brief interlude, a matter of hours until that transformation occurred. I still replay that scene in my mind almost forty years after it happened, no matter what I am doing, or who I am with.

I think she was a village girl. Probably a Jew, because on that particular day, the Jews were the ones chosen to be rounded up and sent away in cattle cars. Her hair was golden red, short and wavy as was the style, and her neck was awash in freckles. It was a crowded station in the center of the town, not far from the butcher shop. There were Germans shouting and women crying and church bells ringing. I stood with that German regulation rifle I hardly knew how to handle, frozen because I was too lightheaded and excited.

I too began to yell at people and held the rifle against my chest, and I was very much aware of how everyone responded to my authority.

Then, this girl appeared in my direct line of vision. Her back was straight, her shoulders tensed; she stopped in the middle of all the chaos. Simply stopped. I ran up and pushed her. I pushed her hard, she almost fell. I kept pushing her, feeling the thin material of her cheap wool jacket against my chapped eager hand; her thin muscles forced forward by my shoves. Once, twice, until she toppled into the open door of a train and fell toward a heap of other people moving deeper into the tiny confines of the stinking cattle car. She never turned around.

I should have shot her. I should have spared her from whatever she had to go through. I doubt she survived. I should have tried to find out what her name was, so I could track down her relatives and confess to them. At least in that way, they could have spat at me in justice and I would have finally received the absolution I will probably never find in this life.

* * *

I don't die. Instead, I go to the garden. It is Sunday evening. I am weeding the crop of beets and cabbages I planted in the patch in my backyard. The sun is lower, a breeze kicks up around me, but my forehead sweats. I breathe in the thick deep earth smells as the dirt crumbles and rotates against the blade of my hoe. I should destroy the honeysuckle vine that is slowly choking my plants, but the scent is so sweet, and its intoxicating perfume reminds me of a woman's gentleness.

I hoe for a while, but not for long, because out of the corner of my eye, I see Bohdan sitting on the grass tearing the firm green blades with his clenched hands. He is still wearing his uniform, all except the jacket, tie, and cap. He sits with his legs apart, his head down, ignoring the black flies that nip at his ears.

I wipe my face with a bright red bandana, which I brought with me to tie up the stalks of my drooping sunflowers. "Bohdan," I say to my son. "Why don't we go into the house and have a beer. I can finish this another time." I look at the orange sun. "It's humid and there's too many flies—means rain will be coming."

My son is quietly crying to himself.

"*Tato*, I didn't know anything," he cries out. "You know, I just wanted to jump out from planes with my parachute. I just wanted to fly . . ."

"I should have stopped you," I say more to myself than to him. Bohdan lets me stroke the thin spikes of his army regulation crew-cut which is soft and warm and I am afraid of how easily my hand can crush his skull.

I rock him in my arms the way I saw his mother embrace him when he was afraid to sleep alone.

There is not much more I can do right now except to hold him. I will hold him until he pulls away.

QUESTIONS

1. Where does the narrator live now, and what does he do? What do you learn about his past? What event remains fixed in his memory? Why?

2. What ideas about the exercise of power during warfare are brought out by the narrator's speaking of "the absolution I will probably never find in this life" (paragraph 36)?

3. Why is the narrator's son Bohdan in tears (paragraph 40)? How are Bohdan's experiences parallel with the narrator's? What ideas underlie this paralleling of experience?

4.   What is the significance of the narrator's saying "I am afraid of how easily my hand can crush his skull" (paragraph 42)?

❧ WRITING ABOUT A MAJOR IDEA IN FICTION

Most likely you will write about a major idea or theme, but you may also get interested in one of your story's other ideas. As you begin brainstorming and developing your first drafts, consider questions such as the following.

Questions for Discovering Ideas

GENERAL IDEAS

- What ideas do you discover in the work? How do you discover them (through action, character depiction, scenes, language)?
- To what do the ideas pertain? To the individuals themselves? To individuals and society? To religion? To social, political, or economic justice?
- How balanced are the ideas? If a particular idea is strongly presented, what conditions and qualifications are also presented (if any)? What contradictory ideas are presented?
- Are the ideas limited to members of any groups represented by the characters (age, race, nationality, personal status)? Or are the ideas applicable to general conditions of life? Explain.
- Which characters in their own right represent or embody ideas? How do their actions and speeches bring these ideas out?
- If characters state ideas directly, how persuasive is their expression, how intelligent and well considered? How germane are the ideas to the work? How germane to more general conditions?
- With children, young adults, or the old, how do the circumstances express or embody an idea?

A SPECIFIC IDEA

- What idea seems particularly important in the work? Why? Is it asserted directly, indirectly, dramatically, ironically? Does any one method predominate? Why?
- How pervasive in the work is the idea (throughout or intermittent)? To what degree is it associated with a major character or action? How does the structure of the work affect or shape your understanding of the idea?
- What value or values are embodied in the idea? Of what importance are the values to the work's meaning?
- How compelling is the idea? How could the work be appreciated without reference to any idea at all?

Strategies for Organizing Ideas

Narrative and dramatic elements have a strong bearing on ideas in well-written stories, poems, and plays. In this sense, an idea is like a key in music or like a continuous thread tying together actions, characters, statements, symbols, and dialogue. As readers, we can trace such threads throughout the entire fabric of the work.

As you write about ideas, you may find yourself relying most heavily on the direct statements of the authorial voice or on a combination of these and your interpretation of characters and action, or you might focus exclusively on a first-person speaker and use his or her ideas to develop your analysis. Always make clear the sources of your details and distinguish the sources from your own commentary.

In your essay, your general goal is to describe an idea and show its importance in the story. Each separate work will invite its own approach, but here are a number of strategies you might use to organize your essay:

1. *Analyze the idea as it applies to character. Example:* "Minnie Wright embodies the idea that living with cruelty and insensitivity leads to alienation, unhappiness, despair, and even to violence" ("A Jury of Her Peers" [Chapter 4]).

2. *Show how actions bring out the idea. Example:* "That Mabel and Dr. Fergusson fall in love rather than go their separate ways indicates Lawrence's idea that love literally rescues human lives."

3. *Show how dialogue and separate speeches bring out the idea. Example:* "The priest's responses to Jackie's confession embody the idea that kindness and understanding are the best means to encourage religious and philosophical commitment" ("First Confession" [Chapter 7]).

4. *Show how the story's structure is determined by the idea. Example:* "The idea that horror can exist in ordinary things leads to a structure in which Jackson (in 'The Lottery' [Chapter 5]) introduces seemingly commonplace people, builds suspense about an impending misfortune, and develops a conclusion of mob insensitivity and cruelty."

5. *Treat variations or differing manifestations of the idea. Example:* "The idea that zealousness leads to harm is shown in Brown's nightmarish distortion of reality, his rejection of others, and his dying gloom" ("Young Goodman Brown" [Chapter 9]).

6. *Deal with a combination of these (together with any other significant aspect). Example:* "The idea in 'Araby' (Chapter 6) that devotion is complex and contradictory is shown in the narrator's romantic mission as a carrier of parcels, his outcries to love in the back room of his house, and his self-reproach and shame at the story's end." (Here the idea is traced through both speech and action.)

Your conclusion might begin with a summary, together with your evaluation of the validity or force of the idea. If you have been convinced by the author's ideas, you might say that the author has expressed the idea forcefully and convincingly, or else you might show the relevance of the idea to current conditions. If you are not persuaded by the idea, you should demonstrate its shortcomings or limitations. If you wish to mention a related idea, whether in the story you have studied or in some other story, you might introduce that here, but be sure to stress the connections.

DEMONSTRATIVE STUDENT ESSAY

Toni Cade Bambara's Idea of Justice and Economic Equality in "The Lesson"°

[1]
Bambara's story presents its "lesson" in an unexpected way. The lesson does not take place in a classroom, but rather it evolves as part of a day's excursion taken by a group of young Harlem children. When the lesson comes, it memorably embodies ideas about justice and economic equality.* There are few ideas more important than these, whether presented in discourse and editorials, as is usual, or, in this story, in fiction. They have a bearing on every phase of politics and economics, and no politicians can ignore them and still hope for election. Bambara's story is therefore timely and significant. Her ideas are carried out in the children's observations and also in the general discussion after the trip, and they are also made apparent in Sylvia, who is the major character and also the narrator.†

[2]
The leader of the children is Miss Moore, the educated woman from the South who among other things is trying to educate Sylvia and her friends about the concept of money and justice. She pays the group's taxi fare to F.A.O. Schwarz, the best-known and most expensive toy store in New York City. The children are shrewdly observant, and they see things from the perspective of the have-nots vewing and commenting on the haves. They groan and make jokes about the unreachably expensive toys on view at the store--a microscope, a paperweight, and a sailboat--and Sylvia makes mental notes about an expensive performing toy clown. Although the children don't know the words, they are making observations about the idea of conspicuous consumption. Some of the more perceptive children become more articulate, however, during their brief meeting with Miss Moore once they return home. She asks for their responses and ideas, in the hopes that their own thoughts are more valuable than a direct lecture. The "lesson" takes its most dramatic form when Sugar, Sylvia's friend, summarizes the ideas that the group has been feeling at the store. She first says, in a very complex sentence, "You know, Miss Moore, I don't think all of us here put together eat in a year what that sailboat costs" (449, paragraph 49). Sugar's second observation expresses a more openly political idea: "this is not much of a democracy if you ask me. Equal chance to pursue happiness means an equal crack at the dough, don't it?" (449, paragraph 51). These are not the observations of a professional economist, but they directly and successfully put the case for greater equality of opportunity and justice.

[3]
These economic ideas in "The Lesson" are also focused on Sylvia, the narrator. Along with the other children, she can be considered as a case study of how society is hurt by economic and social inequality. With a powerful sense of self, and with a strong and inquiring spirit, she should have already benefited from many opportunities for improvement. Instead, her thoughts constantly take a negative turn. She feels superior to others; she is critical of her Aunt Gretchen, who is raising her;

°See pp. 445–49 for this story.
*Central idea.
†Thesis sentence.

she talks back to Miss Moore and other grown-ups (445, paragraph 1); she is self-ish; she is unkind and even vicious (445–46, paragraph 2); she is sullen and also unresponsive. If one wanted an example of the ill effects of inequality, Sylvia would be it. Because of the adversity of her background, she is reduced to negativity.

[4]   Yet Sylvia, in addition to her strong sense of self, has great intelligence and perception. As the children ride the subway home, she thinks over the day's events and shows that she understands the economic and justice issues that the trip has brought to her mind. As she compares the prices of the toys she has seen to the amounts her family pays for necessities, she thinks, "Who are these people that spend [. . . $35] for performing clowns and $1000 for toy sailboats?" (448, paragraph 44). She also has the intellectual power to feel a strong need "to think this day through" (449, paragraph 58). Yet, in keeping with Bambara's focus on the idea of injustice, Sylvia's mind is drawn away from such productive thinking to a consideration of the money she has taken from Miss Moore ($4). She also thinks of herself and her ideas of dominance as she says there "ain't nobody gonna beat me at nuthin" (449, paragraph 58). This last sentence is her final thought in the story, and it is a pathetic reminder that her mind has been turned by her circumstances toward anger and her wish for superiority. Surely she exemplifies the ill consequences of inequality and injustice.

[5]   The major and most truthful aspect of Bambara's presentation of economic and justice issues is that the growth from childhood to thoughtful adulthood is made difficult if not impossible by inequality of opportunity and economic circumstances. Bambara demonstrates this difficulty by implying that many of the children will never improve their lives, and that even the most able will have a high hill to climb. Obstacles in the way of their ever realizing the idea of equality are that they do not perceive the inequality which is keeping them down, and also that they have little idea of what to do to improve themselves for, as Sylvia observes, "don't none of us know what kind of pie she talking about in the first damn place" (449, paragraph 44). One might hope that, on a general scale, people like Sylvia may find a better path for their lives.

WORK CITED

Bambara, Toni Cade. "The Lesson." Literature: An Introduction to Reading and Writing. Ed. Edgar V. Roberts and Henry E. Jacobs. 7th ed. Upper Saddle River: Prentice Hall, 2004. 445–49.

Commentary on the Essay

This essay follows strategy 6 (p. 495) by showing how separate components of the story exhibit the idea's pervasiveness. Throughout, citations of characters, actions, and speeches, together with observations about the story's organization, are used as evidence for the various conclusions about the story's main ideas. Transitions within the essay are effected by words and phrases like "also," "yet," "however," and "are also focused," all of which emphasize the continuity of the topic.

Paragraph 1 asserts that the story's major action—the trip from Harlem to F.A.O. Schwarz in Manhattan—brings out Bambara's idea about the harmful effects on people, specifically children, of economic injustic.

The argument of paragraph 2 is that the the plainspokenness of the children provides a brief analysis of inequality as it applies to expensive toys. Paragraphs 3 and 4 indicate that the "lesson" is applicable to Sylvia, the story's narrator. The connection with paragraph 2 is that while this paragraph is general, the treatment in paragraphs 3 and 4 is personal. Paragraph 5 concludes the essay on the note of the difficulties that rise when children must contend with the injustice of poverty and economic equality.

Special Topics for Writing and Argument about Ideas

1. Compare two stories containing similar themes. *Examples:* Chekhov's "Lady with Lapdog" and Lawrence's "The Horse Dealer's Daughter," Zabytko's "Home Soil" and Hemingway's "Soldier's Home" (Chapter 7), Ozick's "The Shawl" (Chapter 6) and Clark's "The Portable Phonograph" (Chapter 6), Faulkner's "Barn Burning" (Chapter 4) and Munro's "The Found Boat" (Chapter 7), Chopin's "The Story of an Hour" (Chapter 8) and Gilman's "The Yellow Wallpaper" (Chapter 12). For help in developing your essay, consult Chapter 35 on the technique of comparison-contrast.

2. Consider "The Sky Is Gray" as an example of the idea of economic determinism. That is, to what degree are the circumstances and traits of the characters, particularly James, controlled and limited by their economic status? According to the idea, how likely is it that the characters can ever rise above their circumstances?

3. Write an essay criticizing the ideas in a story in this anthology which you dislike or to which you are indifferent. With what statements in the story do you disagree? What actions? What characters? How do your own beliefs and values cause you to dislike the story's ideas? How might the story be changed to illustrate ideas with which you would agree?

4. Select an idea that particularly interests you, and write a story showing how characters may or may not live up to the idea. If you have difficulty getting started, try one of these possible ideas:
   a. Interest and enthusiasm are hard to maintain for long.
   b. People always want more than they have or need.
   c. The concerns of adults are different from those of children.
   d. It is awkward to confront another person about a grievance.
   e. Making a romantic or career decision is hard because it requires a change in life's directions.

5. Using books that you discover in the card or computer catalogue in your college or local library, search for discussions of only one of the following topics, and write a brief report on what you find.
   a. D. H. Lawrence or Thomas Hardy on the power of the working classes.
   b. James Joyce on the significance of religion.
   c. Cynthia Ozick on the effects of the Holocaust.
   d. Ernest Hemingway on individualism and self-realization.
   e. Stephen Crane on the power of chance in life.
   f. The ideas underlying Poe's concept of the short story as a form.
   g. Nathaniel Hawthorne on the significance of religion, both good and bad.

A Career in Fiction: *A Collection of Stories by Edith Wharton*

✤ LIFE AND CAREER

By birth, Edith Wharton (Edith Newbold Jones, 1862–1937) was a member of the American social elite. She spent much of her "babyhood" with her parents in Europe, becoming proficient in French, German, and Italian. When the family returned to the United States, young Edith spent many hours in the library of their New York home, reading her father's collection of five to six hundred books. She wrote that she had "free access" to "poetry & history," but, curiously, was prohibited from reading novels without permission. She quickly assimilated what she called the "realm of words," and came to regard it as her "own native country." By the age of ten she began writing, particularly enjoying the writing of sermons. Her mother was pleased to have a budding author in the family, and paid to have a collection of Edith's juvenile poems published privately.

A young woman of Edith's class was expected to marry a man firmly established within the social structure, and then to spend a life of leisurely visits and international travel. Accordingly, when the time came, she entertained a number of suitors. Her favorite was Walter Berry, a man of intelligence and taste who eventually became an international lawyer and who remained friends with her throughout his life. Although she unquestionably loved him, no marriage ensued. Instead, in 1885 she married Edward ("Teddy") Wharton, a Bostonian whose chief qualities seem to have been that he loved small dogs (she adored small dogs, and there are many photographs of her and her dogs) and that he moved in the same social circle as the Jones family. The couple lived in Rhode Island and New York, and for a number of years they enjoyed their estate home, "The Mount," that they built near Lenox, Massachusetts.

Early in the marriage, Wharton began developing her literary career. A number of stories and fledgling novels were followed by one of her best novels,

House of Mirth (1905), and by this time she had become widely recognized as a writer of considerable power. While she was growing as a writer, however, her marriage with Teddy was coming apart. In 1913, after Teddy had embezzled a large amount of her money, she sued him for divorce on the grounds of adultery, even though divorce at that time was unusual enough to raise questions about her reputation—a subject that she explored in a number of her works, notable among them "The Other Two," which is included in this chapter.

After her divorce she went to live in France, where she spent the rest of her life—in Paris itself on the Rue de Varenne (which still bears a plaque describing her residence there), at a villa near Paris (the "Pavillon Colombe"), and also at a chateau on the French Riviera. When World War I broke out in 1914, she enthusiastically joined the war effort, touring the front to determine the needs of soldiers, and establishing rescue organizations for refugees. For this effort, which cost her considerable time and treasure, she was made a Chevalier of the Legion of Honor by the French government in 1916. After the war she resumed her writing, receiving a Pulitzer Prize for *The Age of Innocence* in 1921, and a Gold Medal for "special Distinction in Literature" from the American Academy of Arts and Letters in 1929. She was also a popular success, and a number of her works were adapted for Hollywood films. In 1937 she was crippled by a terminal stroke, and at her interment in the Cimetière des Gonards, near Versailles, her coffin was attended by an honor guard of French war veterans.

STORIES

While Wharton's birth placed her among the American social elite, her achievement ranked her among one of America's major writers and enabled her to cultivate the friendship of leading figures like Henry James, Bernard Berenson, Jean Cocteau, André Gide, Percy Lubbock, Logan Piersall Smith, and President Theodore Roosevelt. Throughout her career she wrote many novels, both long and short, along with books on gardening, travel, and architecture. But she never stopped writing short stories. Her earliest significant work was a story, and her last work, published posthumously, was also a story. Her completed stories total eighty-six, a considerable output.

In her critical work about stories, "Telling a Short Story," Wharton tells us that the special aim of the short-story writer is to create "situations" from which to drive "a shaft . . . straight into the heart of experience." This observation suggests a major difference between the story and the novel: The novel should emphasize character development and change, whereas the story should aim at achieving a powerful effect. Her stories regularly render the actions of individuals—particularly women—under the pressure of situations and the need to make decisions. She was able to create virtually entire lives for her characters and to render their reactions and feelings as they cope with experience. She stated that characters usually appeared in her imagination fully named and well realized, and that she often had more characters in her mind than she had stories and novels into which to put them. She also said that she had to take the

Edith
Wharton

characters as they revealed themselves to her. If she tried to change their names, she also lost the characters.

Wharton's best stories reveal the frustrations and the emotional subtleties of male–female relationships, and the ironic contrasts between outer appearance and inner reality that these relationships force on people. She exploits such a contrast in "The Muse's Tragedy," one of her earliest stories (1899). At the very end of "Roman Fever," one of her last stories (1934), she reveals how the lifelong amiability of two middle-aged women is tinged with previously unvoiced jealousy and resentfulness. Wharton also successfully uncovers the amusing aspects of male–female relationships. For example, "The Other Two"

(1904), which her biographer and editor R. W. B. Lewis calls "very likely the best story Mrs. Wharton ever wrote," is a subtly comic treatment of embarrassments and adjustments following divorce and remarriage.

In addition, Wharton admired ghost stories and wrote a substantial number of them. To her, a good ghost story was no mere "treatise on the sources of the supernatural." It was, rather, a work producing the chill and shudder evoked by "the peculiar category of the eerie." Therefore, instead of dealing with the macabre, her ghost stories explore the borders between conscious and unconscious levels of reality—with, admittedly, an emphasis on the sinister and the destructive. Usually her ghosts reflect characteristics of individuals within the story, as in "The Eyes" (1910) and "The Triumph of Night" (1914). The ghost story included here, "Pomegranate Seed" (1931), is representative, for it dramatizes—but never explains—how the everyday world that we do see is clutched by the "eerie" world that we do not see. Thematically, the story parallels the conclusion of *The Age of Innocence* (1921), in which the dead past is so strong that it continues to shape the living present.

Wharton lived to be seventy-five and wrote professionally for more than forty of those years. Even during World War I, when she was preoccupied with her relief work, she produced a novella, *Summer* (1916), which demonstrated her continued commitment to her craft as a writer. In the area of life she explores in her fiction—that inner emotional world stemming out of close personal relationships—she is a master. To read her stories is to be convinced that hers was indeed the kind of "first-rate mind" that could "perceive the differences underneath" the surfaces of life that Walter Berry described to her in the days of their courtship. Few writers have created so sensitive a portrayal of human feelings.

⚘ BIBLIOGRAPHIC SOURCES

Wharton's autobiographical writings, *A Backward Glance* and *Life and I*, are included in *Edith Wharton: Novellas and Other Writings* (1990), edited by Cynthia Griffin Wolff. A complete edition of her stories is the Library of America two-volume *Edith Wharton: Collected Stories* (1891–1910) and (1911–1937), published in 2001 and selected and annotated by Maureen Howard. Of equal importance is *The Collected Short Stories of Edith Wharton* (two volumes, 1968), edited by R. W. B. Lewis. These volumes also contain a comprehensive introduction and a useful classification of the stories. The standard biography, *Edith Wharton: A Biography* (1975), is also by Lewis. Eleanor Dwight's *Edith Wharton: An Extraordinary Life* (1994) is a fully illustrated biography. Wharton's letters are collected in *The Letters of Edith Wharton* (1988), edited by R. W. B. Lewis and Nancy Lewis. The index to the letters provides a key to Wharton's own comments about her various works. A convenient collection of twenty stories is *The Muse's Tragedy and Other Stories by Edith Wharton* (1990), edited by Candace Waid. Cynthia Griffin Wolff has edited *Roman Fever and Other Stories* (1997). Wharton's own introduction to the ghost story is contained in Edith Wharton, *The Ghost Stories of Edith Wharton* (1973). Significant criticism may be found in Janet Beer, *Edith Wharton* (2002); Millicent Bell, ed., *The Cambridge*

Companion to Edith Wharton (1995); Josephine Donovan, *After the Fall: The Demeter-Persephone Myth in Wharton, Cather, and Glasgow* (1989); Judith Fryer, *Felicitous Space: The Imaginative Structures of Edith Wharton and Willa Cather* (1986); Wendy Gimbel, *Edith Wharton: Orphancy and Survival* (1984); Susan Goodman, *Wharton's Women: Friends and Rivals* (1990); Irving Howe, ed., *Edith Wharton: A Collection of Critical Essays* (1962); Blake Nevius, *Edith Wharton: A Study of Her Fiction* (1953); Mary E. Papke, *Verging on the Abyss: The Social Fiction of Kate Chopin and Edith Wharton* (1990); Geoffrey Walton, *Edith Wharton, A Critical Interpretation* (1982); Cynthia Griffin Wolff, *A Feast of Words: The Triumph of Edith Wharton* (1977); and Sarah Bird Wright, *Edith Wharton A to Z: The Essential Guide to the Life and Work* (1998).

WRITING TOPICS

1. Wharton's idea that the past continues to hold power over the present.
2. Wharton's use of irony.
3. Wharton's views of the relationship of men and women.
4. The social background of the stories (customs of travel, work, husband–wife behavior, work habits).
5. The persistence of innocence within the fabric of experience.
6. Wharton's creation of reality (houses, jobs, social position, personal relationships, etc.).
7. Wharton's use of point of view, and the selection of multiple points of view within her stories.
8. Wharton's use of dramatic dialogue and indirect discourse.
9. Wharton's treatment of women, in their relationships with men and their connection with the world at large.
10. Wharton's use of allusions and symbols. These may be both real (e.g., the Roman Forum, the pouring of coffee, mysterious letters on tables, geographical and topographic locations, etc.) and artificial (the myth of Persephone, literary reputations, works of art, etc.).

FOUR STORIES OF EDITH WHARTON ARRANGED IN CHRONOLOGICAL ORDER

The Muse's Tragedy ➤✦✧✦✧➤ 1899

Danyers afterwards liked to fancy that he had recognized Mrs. Anerton at once; but that, of course, was absurd, since he had seen no portrait of her—she affected a strict anonymity, refusing even her photograph to the most privileged—and from Mrs. Memorall, whom he revered and cultivated as her friend, he had extracted but the one impressionist phrase: "Oh, well, she's like one of those old prints where the lines have the value of color."

He was almost certain, at all events, that he had been thinking of Mrs. Anerton as he sat over his breakfast in the empty hotel restaurant, and that, looking up on the approach of the lady who seated herself at the table near the window, he had said to himself, *"That might be she."*

Ever since his Harvard days—he was still young enough to think of them as immensely remote—Danyers had dreamed of Mrs. Anerton, the Silvia of Vincent Rendle's immortal sonnet cycle, the Mrs. A. of the *Life and Letters*. Her name was enshrined in some of the noblest English verse of the nineteenth century—and of all past or future centuries, as Danyers, from the standpoint of a maturer judgment, still believed. The first reading of certain poems—of the *Antinous*, the *Pia Tolomei*, the *Sonnets to Silvia*—had been epochs in Danyers' growth, and the verse seemed to gain in mellowness, in amplitude, in meaning as one brought to its interpretation more experience of life, a finer emotional sense. When, in his boyhood, he had felt only the perfect, the almost austere beauty of form, the subtle interplay of vowel sounds, the rush and fullness of lyric emotion, he now thrilled to the close-packed significance of each line, the allusiveness of each word—his imagination lured hither and thither on fresh trails of thought, and perpetually spurred by the sense that, beyond what he had already discovered, more marvelous regions lay waiting to be explored. Danyers had written, at college, the prize essay on Rendle's poetry (it chanced to be the moment of the great man's death); he had fashioned the fugitive verse of his own Storm and Stress period on the forms which Rendle had first given to English meter, and when two years later the *Life and Letters* appeared, and the Silvia of the sonnets took substance as Mrs. A., he had included in his worship of Rendle the woman who had inspired not only such divine verse but such playful, tender, incomparable prose.

Danyers never forgot the day when Mrs. Memorall happened to mention that she knew Mrs. Anerton. He had known Mrs. Memorall for a year or more, and had somewhat contemptuously classified her as the kind of woman who runs cheap excursions to celebrities; when one afternoon she remarked, as she put a second lump of sugar in his tea:

"Is it right this time? You're almost as particular as Mary Anerton."   5

"Mary Anerton?"

"Yes, I never *can* remember how she likes her tea. Either it's lemon with sugar, or lemon without sugar, or cream without either, and whichever it is must be put into the cup before the tea is poured in; and if one hasn't remembered, one must begin over again. I suppose it was Vincent Rendle's way of taking his tea and has become a sacred rite."

"Do you *know* Mrs. Anerton?" cried Danyers, disturbed by this careless familiarity with the habits of his divinity.

"And did I once see Shelley plain? Mercy, yes! She and I were at school together—she's an American, you know. We were at a pension near Tours for nearly a year; then she went back to New York, and I didn't see her again till after her marriage. She and Anerton spent a winter in Rome while my husband was attached to our Legation there, and she used to be with us a great deal." Mrs. Memorall smiled reminiscently. "It was *the* winter."

"The winter they first met?"   10

"Precisely—but unluckily I left Rome just before the meeting took place. Wasn't it too bad? I might have been in the *Life and Letters. You* know he mentions that stupid Madame Vodki, at whose house he first saw her."

"And did you see much of her after that?"

"Not during Rendle's life. You know she has lived in Europe almost entirely, and though I used to see her off and on when I went abroad, she was always so engrossed, so preoccupied, that one felt one wasn't wanted. The fact is, she cared only about his friends—she separated herself gradually from all her own people. Now, of course, it's different; she's desperately lonely; she's taken to writing to me now and then; and last year, when she heard I was going abroad, she asked me to meet her in Venice, and I spent a week with her there."

"And Rendle?"

Mrs. Memorall smiled and shook her head. "Oh, I never was allowed a peep at him; none of her old friends met him, except by accident. Ill-natured people say that was the reason she kept him so long. If one happened in while he was there, he was hustled into Anerton's study, and the husband mounted guard till the inopportune visitor had departed. Anerton, you know, was really much more ridiculous about it than his wife. Mary was too clever to lose her head, or at least to show she'd lost it—but Anerton couldn't conceal his pride in the conquest. I've seen Mary shiver when he spoke of Rendle as *our poet*. Rendle always had to have a certain seat at the dinner table, away from the draft and not too near the fire, and a box of cigars that no one else was allowed to touch, and a writing table of his own in Mary's sitting room—and Anerton was always telling one of the great man's idiosyncrasies: how he never would cut the ends of his cigars, though Anerton himself had given him a gold cutter set with a star sapphire, and how untidy his writing table was, and how the housemaid had orders always to bring the wastepaper basket to her mistress before emptying it, lest some immortal verse should be thrown into the dustbin."

"The Anertons never separated, did they?"

"Separated? Bless you, no. He never would have left Rendle! And besides, he was very fond of his wife."

"And she?"

"Oh, she saw he was the kind of man who was fated to make himself ridiculous, and she never interfered with his natural tendencies."

From Mrs. Memorall, Danyers further learned that Mrs. Anerton, whose husband had died some years before her poet, now divided her life between Rome, where she had a small apartment, and England, where she occasionally went to stay with those of her friends who had been Rendle's. She had been engaged, for some time after his death, in editing some juvenilia which he had bequeathed to her care; but that task being accomplished, she had been left without definite occupation, and Mrs. Memorall, on the occasion of their last meeting, had found her listless and out of spirits.

"She misses him too much—her life is too empty. I told her so—I told her she ought to marry."

"Oh!"

"Why not, pray? she's a young woman still—what many people would call young," Mrs. Memorall interjected, with a parenthetic glance at the mirror. "Why not accept the inevitable and begin over again? All the King's horses and all the King's men won't bring Rendle to life—and besides, she didn't marry him when she had the chance."

Danyers winced slightly at this rude fingering of his idol. Was it possible that Mrs. Memorall did not see what an anticlimax such a marriage would have been? Fancy Rendle "making an honest woman" of Silvia; for so society would have viewed it! How such a reparation would have vulgarized their past—it would have been like "restoring" a masterpiece; and how exquisite must have been the perceptions of the woman who, in defiance of appearances, and perhaps of her own secret inclination, chose to go down to posterity as Silvia rather than as Mrs. Vincent Rendle!

Mrs. Memorall, from this day forth, acquired an interest in Danyers' eyes. She was like a volume of unindexed and discursive memoirs, through which he patiently plodded in the hope of finding embedded amid layers of dusty twaddle some precious allusion to the subject of his thought. When, some months later, he brought out his first slim volume, in which the remodeled college essay on Rendle figured among a dozen somewhat overstudied "appreciations," he offered a copy to Mrs. Memorall; who surprised him, the next time they met, with the announcement that she had sent the book to Mrs. Anerton.

Mrs. Anerton in due time wrote to thank her friend. Danyers was privileged to read the few lines in which, in terms that suggested the habit of "acknowledging" similar tributes, she spoke of the author's "feeling and insight," and was "so glad of the opportunity," etc. He went away disappointed, without clearly knowing what else he had expected.

The following spring, when he went abroad, Mrs. Memorall offered him letters to everybody, from the Archbishop of Canterbury to Louise Michel. She did not include Mrs. Anerton, however, and Danyers knew, from a previous conversation, that Silvia objected to people who "brought letters." He knew also that she traveled during the summer, and was unlikely to return to Rome before the term of his holiday should be reached, and the hope of meeting her was not included among his anticipations.

The lady whose entrance broke upon his solitary repast in the restaurant of the Hotel Villa d'Este had seated herself in such a way that her profile was detached against the window, and thus viewed, her domed forehead, small arched nose, and fastidious lip suggested a silhouette of Marie Antoinette. In the lady's dress and movements—in the very turn of her wrist as she poured out her coffee—Danyers thought he detected the same fastidiousness, the same air of tacitly excluding the obvious and unexceptional. Here was a woman who had been much bored and keenly interested. The waiter brought her a *Secolo*, and as she bent above it Danyers noticed that the hair rolled back from her forehead was turning gray; but her figure was straight and slender, and she had the invaluable gift of a girlish back.

The rush of Anglo-Saxon travel had not set toward the lakes, and with the exception of an Italian family or two, and a hump-backed youth with an *abbé*, Danyers and the lady had the marble halls of the Villa d'Este to themselves.

When he returned from his morning ramble among the hills he saw her sitting at   30
one of the little tables at the edge of the lake. She was writing, and a heap of books and newspapers lay on the table at her side. That evening they met again in the garden. He had strolled out to smoke a last cigarette before dinner, and under the black vaulting of ilexes, near the steps leading down to the boat landing, he found her leaning on the parapet above the lake. At the sound of his approach she turned and looked at him. She had thrown a black lace scarf over her head, and in this somber setting her face seemed thin and unhappy. He remembered afterwards that her eyes, as they met his, expressed not so much sorrow as profound discontent.

To his surprise she stepped toward him with a detaining gesture.

"Mr. Lewis Danyers, I believe?"

He bowed.

"I am Mrs. Anerton. I saw your name on the visitors' list and wished to thank you for an essay on Mr. Rendle's poetry—or rather to tell you how much I appreciated it. The book was sent to me last winter by Mrs. Memorall."

She spoke in even melancholy tones, as though the habit of perfunctory utterance   35
had robbed her voice of more spontaneous accents; but her smile was charming.

They sat down on a stone bench under the ilexes, and she told him how much pleasure his essay had given her. She thought it the best in the book—she was sure he had put more of himself into it than into any other; was she not right in conjecturing that he had been very deeply influenced by Mr. Rendle's poetry? *Pour comprendre il faut aimer,*° and it seemed to her that, in some ways, he had penetrated the poet's inner meaning more completely than any other critic. There were certain problems, of course, that he had left untouched; certain aspects of that many-sided mind that he had perhaps failed to seize.

Pour comprendre il faut aimer: To understand, one must love.

"But then you are young," she concluded gently, "and one could not wish you, as yet, the experience that a fuller understanding would imply."

II

She stayed a month at Villa d'Este, and Danyers was with her daily. She showed an unaffected pleasure in his society; a pleasure so obviously founded on their common veneration of Rendle, that the young man could enjoy it without fear of fatuity. At first he was merely one more grain of frankincense on the altar of her insatiable divinity; but gradually a more personal note crept into their intercourse. If she still liked him only because he appreciated Rendle, she at least perceptibly distinguished him from the herd of Rendle's appreciators.

Her attitude toward the great man's memory struck Danyers as perfect. She neither proclaimed nor disavowed her identity. She was frankly Silvia to those who knew and cared; but there was no trace of the Egeria in her pose.° She spoke often of Rendle's books, but seldom of himself; there was no posthumous conjugality, no use of the possessive tense, in her abounding reminiscences. Of the master's intellectual life, of his habits of thought and work, she never wearied of talking. She knew the history of each poem; by what scene or episode each image had been evoked; how many times the words in a certain line had been transposed; how long a certain adjective had been sought, and what had at last suggested it; she could even explain that one impenetrable line, the torment of critics, the joy of detractors, the last line of *The Old Odysseus.*

Danyers felt that in talking of these things she was no mere echo of Rendle's thought. If her identity had appeared to be merged in his it was because they thought alike, not because he had thought for her. Posterity is apt to regard the women whom poets have sung as chance pegs on which they hung their garlands; but Mrs. Anerton's mind was like some fertile garden wherein, inevitably, Rendle's imagination had rooted itself and flowered. Danyers began to see how many threads of his complex mental tissue the poet had owed to the blending of her temperament with his; in a certain sense Silvia had herself created the *Sonnets to Silvia.* 40

To be the custodian of Rendle's inner self, the door, as it were, to the sanctuary, had at first seemed to Danyers so comprehensive a privilege that he had the sense, as his friendship with Mrs. Anerton advanced, of forcing his way into a life already crowded. What room was there, among such towering memories, for so small an actuality as his? Quite suddenly, after this, he discovered that Mrs. Memorall knew better: his fortunate friend was bored as well as lonely.

"You have had more than any other woman!" he had exclaimed to her one day: and her smile flashed a derisive light on his blunder. Fool that he was, not to have seen that she had not had enough! That she was young still—do years count?—tender, human, a woman; that the living have need of the living.

After that, when they climbed the alleys of the hanging park, resting in one of the little ruined temples, or watching, through a ripple of foliage, the remote blue flash of the lake, they did not always talk of Rendle or of literature. She encouraged Danyers to speak of himself; to confide his ambitions to her; she asked him the questions which are the wise woman's substitute for advice.

"You must write," she said, administering the most exquisite flattery that human lips could give.

Egeria in her pose: In ancient Roman mythology Egeria was so distraught by the death of her lover, Numa, that she melted into tears and was turned by the goddess Diana into a fountain.

Of course he meant to write—why not do something great in his turn? His best, at least; with the resolve, at the outset, that his best should be *the* best. Nothing less seemed possible with that mandate in his ears. How she had divined him; lifted and disentangled his groping ambitions; laid the awakening touch on his spirit with her creative *Let there be light!* 45

It was his last day with her, and he was feeling very hopeless and happy.

"You ought to write a book about *him*," she went on gently.

Danyers started; he was beginning to dislike Rendle's way of walking in unannounced.

"You ought to do it," she insisted. "A complete interpretation—a summing up of his style, his purpose, his theory of life and art. No one else could do it as well."

He sat looking at her perplexedly. Suddenly—dared he guess? 50

"I couldn't do it without you," he faltered.

"I could help you—I would help *you*, *of* course."

They sat silent, both looking at the lake.

It was agreed, when they parted, that he should rejoin her six weeks later in Venice. There they were to talk about the book.

III

Lago d'Iseo, August 14th

When I said good-bye to you yesterday I promised to come back to Venice in a week: was to give you your answer then. I was not honest in saying that; I didn't mean to go back to Venice or to see you again. I was running away from you—and I mean to keep on running! If you won't, I must. Somebody must save you from marrying a disappointed woman of—well, you say years don't count, and why should they, after all, since you are not to marry me? 55

That is what I dare not go back to say. *You are not to marry me.* We have had our month together in Venice (such a good month, was it not?) and now you are to go home and write a book—any book but the one we—didn't talk of!—and I am to stay here, attitudinizing among my memories like a sort of female Tithonus.° The dreariness of this enforced immortality!

But you shall know the truth. I care for you, or at least for your love, enough to owe you that.

You thought it was because Vincent Rendle had loved me that there was so little hope for you. I had had what I wanted to the full; wasn't that what you said? It is just when a man begins to think he understands a woman that he may be sure he doesn't! It is because Vincent Rendle *didn't love me* that there is no hope for you. I never had what I wanted, and never, never, never will I stoop to wanting anything else.

Do you begin to understand? It was all a sham then, you say? No, it was all real as far as it went. You are young—you haven't learned, as you will later, the thousand imperceptible signs by which one gropes one's way through the labyrinth of human nature; but didn't it strike you, sometimes, that I never told you any foolish little anecdotes about him? His trick, for instance, of twirling a paper knife round and round between his thumb and forefinger while he talked; his mania for saving the backs of notes; his greediness for wild strawberries, the little pungent Alpine ones; his childish delight in acrobats and jugglers; his way of always calling me *you—dear you*, every letter began—I never told you a word of all that, did I? Do you suppose I could have helped telling you, if he had loved me? These

---

Tithonus: Tithonus was the son of Laomedon, king of Troy. Aurora, the goddess of the Dawn, fell in love with him, and he asked her for the gift of immortality. This she granted, but Tithonus had not asked for eternal youth, and so as time went by he developed all the infirmities of advancing age.

little things would have been mine, then, a part of my life—of our life—they would have slipped out in spite of me (it's only your unhappy woman who is always reticent and dignified). But there never was any "our life"; it was always "our lives" to the end. . . .

If you knew what a relief it is to tell someone at last, you would bear with me, you would let me hurt you! I shall never be quite so lonely again, now that someone knows. 60

Let me begin at the beginning. When I first met Vincent Rendle I was not twenty-five. That was twenty years ago. From that time until his death, five years ago, we were fast friends. He gave me fifteen years, perhaps the best fifteen years, of his life. The world, as you know, thinks that his greatest poems were written during those years; I am supposed to have "inspired" them, and in a sense I did. From the first, the intellectual sympathy between us was almost complete; my mind must have been to him (I fancy) like some perfectly tuned instrument on which he was never tired of playing. Someone told me of his once saying of me that I "always understood"; it is the only praise I ever heard of his giving me. I don't even know if he thought me pretty, though I hardly think my appearance could have been disagreeable to him, for he hated to be with ugly people. At all events he fell into the way of spending more and more of his time with me. He liked our house; our ways suited him. He was nervous, irritable; people bored him and yet he disliked solitude. He took sanctuary with us. When we traveled he went with us; in the winter he took rooms near us in Rome. In England or on the Continent he was always with us for a good part of the year. In small ways I was able to help him in his work; he grew dependent on me. When we were apart he wrote to me Continually—he liked to have me share in all he was doing or thinking; he was impatient for my criticism of every new book that interested him; I was a part of his intellectual life. The pity of it was that I wanted to be something more. I was a young woman and I was in love with him—not because he was Vincent Rendle, but just because he was himself!

People began to talk, of course—I was Vincent Rendle's Mrs. Anerton; when the *Sonnets to Silvia* appeared, it was whispered that I was Silvia. Wherever he went, I was invited; people made up to me in the hope of getting to know him; when I was in London my doorbell never stopped ringing. Elderly peeresses, aspiring hostesses, lovesick girls and struggling authors overwhelmed me with their assiduities. I hugged my success, for I knew what it meant—they thought that Rendle was in love with me! Do you know, at times, they almost made me think so too? Oh, there was no phase of folly I didn't go through. You can't imagine the excuses a woman will invent for a man's not telling her that he loves her—pitiable arguments that she would see through at a glance if any other woman used them! But all the while, deep down, I knew he had never cared. I should have known it if he had made love to me every day of his life. I could never guess whether he knew what people said about us—he listened so little to what people said; and cared still less, when he heard. He was always quite honest and straightforward with me; he treated me as one man treats another; and yet at times I felt he *must* see that with me it was different. If he did see, he made no sign. Perhaps he never noticed—I am sure he never meant to be cruel. He had never made love to me; it was no fault of his if I wanted more than he could give me. The *Sonnets to Silvia*, you say? But what are they? A cosmic philosophy, not a love poem; addressed to Woman, not to a woman!

But then, the letters? Ah, the letters! Well, I'll make a clean breast of it. You have noticed the breaks in the letters here and there, just as they seem to be on the point of growing a little—warmer? The critics, you may remember, praised the editor for his commendable delicacy and good taste (so rare in these days!) in omitting from the correspondence all personal allusions, all those *details intimes* which should be kept sacred from the public gaze. They referred, of course, to the asterisks in the letters to Mrs. A. Those letters I myself prepared for publication; that is to say, I copied them out for the editor, and every now and then I put in a line of asterisks to make it appear that some-thing had been left out. You understand? The asterisks were a sham—*there was nothing to leave out.*

No one but a woman could understand what I went through during those years—the moments of revolt, when I felt I must break away from it all, fling the truth in his face and never see him again; the inevitable reaction, when not to see him seemed the one un-endurable thing, and I trembled lest a look or word of mine should disturb the poise of our friendship; the silly days when I hugged the delusion that he *must* love me, since every-body thought he did; the long periods of numbness, when I didn't seem to care whether he loved me or not. Between these wretched days came others when our intellectual ac-cord was so perfect that I forgot everything else in the joy of feeling myself lifted up on the wings of his thought. Sometimes, then, the heavens seemed to be opened.

All this time he was so dear a friend! He had the genius of friendship, and he spent   65
it all on me. Yes, you were right when you said that I have had more than any other woman. *Il faut de l'adresse pour aimer,*° Pascal says; and I was so quiet, so cheerful, so frankly affectionate with him, that in all those years I am almost sure I never bored him. Could I have hoped as much if he had loved me?

You mustn't think of him, though, as having been tied to my skirts. He came and went as he pleased, and so did his fancies. There was a girl once (I am telling you every-thing), a lovely being who called his poetry "deep" and gave him *Lucile* on his birthday. He followed her to Switzerland one summer, and all the time that he was dangling after her (a little too conspicuously, I always thought, for a Great Man), he was writing to *me* about his theory of vowel combinations—or was it his experiments in English hexameter? The letters were dated from the very places where I knew they went and sat by waterfalls together and he thought out adjectives for her hair. He talked to me about it quite frankly afterwards. She was perfectly beautiful and it had been a pure delight to watch her; but she would talk, and her mind, he said, was "all elbows." And yet, the next year, when her marriage was announced, he went away alone, quite suddenly . . . and it was just afterwards that he published *Love's Viaticum.*° Men are queer!

After my husband died—I am putting things crudely, you see—I had a return of hope. It was because he loved me, I argued, that he had never spoken; because he had al-ways hoped some day to make me his wife; because he wanted to spare me the "re-proach." Rubbish! I knew well enough, in my heart of hearts, that my one chance lay in the force of habit. He had grown used to me; he was no longer young; he dreaded new people and new ways; *il avait pris son pli.*° Would it not be easier to marry me?

I don't believe he ever thought of it. He wrote me what people call "a beautiful let-ter," he was kind, considerate, decently commiserating; then, after a few weeks, he slipped into his old way of coming in every afternoon, and our interminable talks began again just where they had left off. I heard later that people thought I had shown "such good taste" in not marrying him.

So we jogged on for five years longer. Perhaps they were the best years, for I had given up hoping. Then he died.

After his death—this is curious—there came to me a kind of mirage of love. All the   70
books and articles written about him, all the reviews of the *Life*, were full of discreet allu-sions to Silvia. I became again the Mrs. Anerton of the glorious days. Sentimental girls and dear lads like you turned pink when somebody whispered, "That was Silvia you were

---

Il faut de l'adresse pour aimer: To love one must have skill.
Love's Viaticum: Ways of Loving; Advice to Those on Love's Journey.
il avait pris son pli: he was set in his ways.

talking to." Idiots begged for my autograph—publishers urged me to write my reminiscences of him—critics consulted me about the reading of doubtful lines. And I knew that, to all these people, I was the woman Vincent Rendle had loved.

After a while that fire went out too and I was left alone with my past. Alone—quite alone; for he had never really been with me. The intellectual union counted for nothing now. It had been soul to soul, but never hand in hand, and there were no little things to remember him by.

Then there set in a kind of Arctic winter. I crawled into myself as into a snow hut. I hated my solitude and yet dreaded anyone who disturbed it. That phase, of course, passed like the others. I took up life again, and began to read the papers and consider the cut of my gowns. But here was one question that I could not be rid of, that haunted me night and day. Why had he never loved me? Why had I been so much to him, and no more? Was I so ugly, so essentially unlovable, that though a man might cherish me as his mind's comrade, he could not care for me as a woman? I can't tell you how that question tortured me. It became an obsession.

My poor friend, do you begin to see? I had to find out what some other man thought of me. Don't be too hard on me! Listen first—consider. When I first met Vincent Rendle I was a young woman, who had married early and led the quietest kind of life; I had had no "experiences." From the hour of our first meeting to the day of his death I never looked at any other man, and never noticed whether any other man looked at me. When he died, five years ago, I knew the extent of my powers no more than a baby. Was it too late to find out? Should I never know why?

Forgive me—forgive me. You are so young; it will be an episode, a mere "document," to you so soon! And, besides, it wasn't as deliberate, as cold-blooded as these disjointed lines have made it appear. I didn't plan it, like a woman in a book. Life is so much more complex than any rendering of it can be. I liked you from the first—I was drawn to you (you must have seen that)—I wanted you to like me; it was not a mere psychological experiment. And yet in a sense it was that, too—I must be honest. I had to have an answer to that question; it was a ghost that had to be laid.

At first I was afraid—oh, so much afraid—that you cared for me only because I was Silvia, that you loved me because you thought Rendle had loved me. I began to think there was no escaping my destiny.

How happy I was when I discovered that you were growing jealous of my past; that you actually hated Rendle! My heart beat like a girl's when you told me you meant to follow me to Venice.

After our parting at Villa d'Este my old doubts reasserted themselves. What did I know of your feeling for me, after all? Were you capable of analyzing it yourself? Was it not likely to be two-thirds vanity and curiosity, and one-third literary sentimentality? You might easily fancy that you cared for Mary Anerton when you were really in love with Silvia—the heart is such a hypocrite! Or you might be more calculating than I had supposed. Perhaps it was you who had been flattering my vanity in the hope (the pardonable hope!) of turning me, after a decent interval, into a pretty little essay with a margin.

When you arrived in Venice and we met again—do you remember the music on the lagoon, that evening, from my balcony?—I was so afraid you would begin to talk about the book—the book, you remember, was your ostensible reason for coming. You never spoke of it, and I soon saw your one fear was I might do so—might remind you of your object in being with me. Then I knew you cared for me! yes, at that moment really cared! We never mentioned the book once, did we, during that month in Venice?

I have read my letter over; and now I wish that I had said this to you instead of writing it. I could have felt my way then, watching your face and seeing if you understood.

But, no, I could not go back to Venice; and I could not tell you (though I tried) while we were there together. I couldn't spoil that month—my one month. It was so good, for once in my life, to get away from literature.

You will be angry with me at first—but, alas! not for long. What I have done would have been cruel if I had been a younger woman; as it is, the experiment will hurt no one but myself. And it will hurt me horribly (as much as, in your first anger, you may perhaps wish), because it has shown me, for the first time, all that I have missed.   80

QUESTIONS

1. Why is the story titled "The Muse's Tragedy"? What is the tragedy? Who is the tragic character?

2. Describe the circumstances of Rendle and Mrs. Anerton—the poet and "Silvia." How convincing is Wharton's portrayal of these circumstances? How does Danyers get involved in the situation?

3. What sort of person is Mrs. Anerton? Why does she praise Rendle? Why is she critical of him? Why does she say "Men are queer!" (paragraph 66)?

4. How do Danyers's attitudes toward Mrs. Anerton change? How do her attitudes toward him develop? What is the outcome of these changes?

5. Explain why Wharton changes the point of view in section 3. What events have occurred between sections 2 and 3? What thoughts does Mrs. Anerton have about these events? Why does not Wharton give Danyers the opportunity to express his thoughts about these events?

6. Mrs. Anerton writes: "It is just when a man begins to think he understands a woman that he may be sure he doesn't!" (paragraph 58). How is this sentence applicable to the story? What general application might it have?

The Other Two ~ ~ ~ ~ 1904

Waythorn, on the drawing-room hearth, waited for his wife to come down to dinner.

It was their first night under his own roof, and he was surprised at his thrill of boyish agitation. He was not so old, to be sure—his glass gave him little more than the five-and-thirty years to which his wife confessed—but he had fancied himself already in the temperate zone; yet here he was listening for her step with a tender sense of all it symbolized, with some old trail of verse about the garlanded nuptial doorposts floating through his enjoyment of the pleasant room and the good dinner just beyond it.

They had been hastily recalled from their honeymoon by the illness of Lily Haskett, the child of Mrs. Waythorn's first marriage. The little girl, at Waythorn's desire, had been transferred to his house on the day of her mother's wedding, and the doctor, on their arrival, broke the news that she was ill with typhoid, but declared that all the symptoms were favorable. Lily could show twelve years of unblemished health, and the case promised to be a light one. The nurse spoke as reassuringly, and after a moment of alarm Mrs. Waythorn had adjusted herself to the situation. She was very fond of Lily—her affection for the child had perhaps been her decisive charm in Waythorn's eyes—but she had the perfectly balanced nerves which her little girl had inherited, and no woman ever wasted less tissue in unproductive worry. Waythorn was therefore quite prepared to see her come in presently, a little late because of a last look at Lily, but as serene and well-appointed as if her good-night kiss had been laid on the brow of health. Her composure was restful to him; it acted as ballast to his somewhat unstable sensibilities. As he pictured her bending over the child's bed he thought how soothing her presence must be in illness: her very step would prognosticate recovery.

His own life had been a gray one, from temperament rather than circumstance, and he had been drawn to her by the unperturbed gaiety which kept her fresh and elastic at an age when most women's activities are growing either slack or febrile. He knew what was said about her; for, popular as she was, there had always been a faint undercurrent of detraction. When she had appeared in New York, nine or ten years earlier, as the pretty Mrs. Haskett whom Gus Varick had unearthed somewhere—was it in Pittsburgh or Utica—society, while promptly accepting her, had reserved the right to cast a doubt on its own indiscrimination. Inquiry, however, established her undoubted connection with a socially reigning family, and explained her recent divorce as the natural result of a runaway match at seventeen; and as nothing was known of Mr. Haskett it was easy to believe the worst of him.

Alice Haskett's remarriage with Gus Varick was a passport to the set whose recognition she coveted, and for a few years the Varicks were the most popular couple in town. Unfortunately the alliance was brief and stormy, and this time the husband had his champions. Still, even Varick's staunchest supporters admitted that he was not meant for matrimony, and Mrs. Varick's grievances were of a nature to bear the inspection of the New York courts. A New York divorce is in itself a diploma of virtue, and in the semiwidowhood of this second separation Mrs. Varick took on an air of sanctity, and was allowed to confide her wrongs to some of the most scrupulous ears in town. But when it was known that she was to marry Waythorn there was a momentary reaction. Her best friends would have preferred to see her remain in the role of the injured wife, which was as becoming to her as crepe to a rosy complexion. True, a decent time had elapsed, and it was not even suggested that Waythorn had supplanted his predecessor. People shook their heads over him, however, and one grudging friend, to whom he affirmed that he took the step with his eyes open, replied oracularly: "Yes—and with your ears shut." 5

Waythorn could afford to smile at these innuendoes. In the Wall Street phrase, he had "discounted" them. He knew that society has not yet adapted itself to the consequences of divorce, and that till the adaptation takes place every woman who uses the freedom the law accords her must be her own social justification. Waythorn had an amused confidence in his wife's ability to justify herself. His expectations were fulfilled, and before the wedding took place Alice Varick's group had rallied openly to her support. She took it all imperturbably: she had a way of surmounting obstacles without seeming to be aware of them, and Waythorn looked back with wonder at the trivialities over which he had worn his nerves thin. He had the sense of having found refuge in a richer, warmer nature than his own, and his satisfaction, at the moment, was humorously summed up in the thought that his wife, when she had done all she could for Lily, would not be ashamed to come down and enjoy a good dinner.

The anticipation of such enjoyment was not, however, the sentiment expressed by Mrs. Waythorn's charming face when she presently joined him. Though she had put on her most engaging tea gown she had neglected to assume the smile that went with it, and Waythorn thought he had never seen her look so nearly worried.

"What is it?" he asked. "Is anything wrong with Lily?"

"No; I've just been in and she's still sleeping." Mrs. Waythorn hesitated. "But something tiresome has happened."

He had taken her two hands, and now perceived that he was crushing a paper between them. 10

"This letter?"

"Yes—Mr. Haskett has written—I mean his lawyer has written."

Waythorn felt himself flush uncomfortably. He dropped his wife's hands.

"What about?"

"About seeing Lily. You know the courts—"   15

"Yes, yes," he interrupted nervously.

Nothing was known about Haskett in New York. He was vaguely supposed to have remained in the outer darkness from which his wife had been rescued, and Waythorn was one of the few who were aware that he had given up his business in Utica and followed her to New York in order to be near his little girl. In the days of his wooing, Waythorn had often met Lily on the doorstep, rosy and smiling, on her way "to see papa."

"I am so sorry," Mrs. Waythorn murmured.

He roused himself. "What does he want?"

"He wants to see her. You know she goes to him once a week."   20

"Well—he doesn't expect her to go to him now, does he?"

"No—he has heard of her illness; but he expects to come here."

"*Here?*"

Mrs. Waythorn reddened under his gaze. They looked away from each other.

"I'm afraid he has the right. . . . You'll see. . . ." She made a proffer of the letter.   25

Waythorn moved away with a gesture of refusal. He stood staring about the softly-lighted room, which a moment before had seemed so full of bridal intimacy.

"I'm so sorry," she repeated. "If Lily could have been moved—"

"That's out of the question," he returned impatiently.

"I suppose so."

Her lip was beginning to tremble, and he felt himself a brute.   30

"He must come, of course," he said. "When is—his day?"

"I'm afraid—tomorrow."

"Very well. Send a note in the morning."

The butler entered to announce dinner.

Waythorn turned to his wife. "Come—you must be tired. It's beastly, but try to for-   35
get about it," he said, drawing her hand through his arm.

"You're so good, dear. I'll try," she whispered back.

Her face cleared at once, and as she looked at him across the flowers, between the rosy candleshades, he saw her lips waver back into a smile.

"How pretty everything is!" she sighed luxuriously.

He turned to the butler. "The champagne at once, please. Mrs. Waythorn is tired."

In a moment or two their eyes met above the sparkling glasses. Her own were quite   40
clear and untroubled: he saw that she had obeyed his injunction and forgotten.

II

Waythorn, the next morning, went downtown earlier than usual. Haskett was not likely to come till the afternoon, but the instinct of flight drove him forth. He meant to stay away all day—he had thoughts of dining at his club. As his door closed behind him he reflected that before he opened it again it would have admitted another man who had as much right to enter it as himself, and the thought filled him with a physical repugnance.

He caught the "elevated" at the employees' hour, and found himself crushed between two layers of pendulous humanity. At Eighth Street the man facing him wriggled out, and another took his place. Waythorn glanced up and saw that it was Gus Varick. The men were so close together that it was impossible to ignore the smile of recognition on Varick's handsome overblown face. And after all—why not? They had always been on good terms, and Varick had been divorced before Waythorn's attentions to his wife began. The two exchanged a word on the perennial grievance of the congested trains, and when a seat at their side was miraculously left empty the instinct of self-preservation made Waythorn slip into it after Varick.

The latter drew the stout man's breath of relief. "Lord—I was beginning to feel like a pressed flower." He leaned back, looking unconcernedly at Waythorn. "Sorry to hear that Sellers is knocked out again."

"Sellers?" echoed Waythorn, starting at his partner's name.

Varick looked surprised. "You didn't know he was laid up with the gout?"   45

"No. I've been away—I only got back last night." Waythorn felt himself reddening in anticipation of the other's smile.

"Ah—yes; to be sure. And Sellers' attack came on two days ago. I'm afraid he's pretty bad. Very awkward for me, as it happens, because he was just putting through a rather important thing for me."

"Ah?" Waythorn wondered vaguely since when Varick had been dealing in "important things." Hitherto he had dabbled only in the shallow pools of speculation, with which Waythorn's office did not usually concern itself.

It occurred to him that Varick might be talking at random, to relieve the strain of their propinquity. That strain was becoming momentarily more apparent to Waythorn, and when, at Cortlandt Street, he caught sight of an acquaintance and had a sudden vision of the picture he and Varick must present to an initiated eye, he jumped up with a muttered excuse.

"I hope you'll find Sellers better," said Varick civilly, and he stammered back: "If I   50
can be of any use to you—" and let the departing crowd sweep him to the platform.

At his office he heard that Sellers was in fact ill with the gout, and would probably not be able to leave the house for some weeks.

"I'm sorry it should have happened so, Mr. Waythorn," the senior clerk said with affable significance. "Mr. Sellers was very much upset at the idea of giving you such a lot of extra work just now."

"Oh, that's no matter," said Waythorn hastily. He secretly welcomed the pressure of additional business, and was glad to think that, when the day's work was over, he would have to call at his partner's on the way home.

He was late for luncheon, and turned in at the nearest restaurant instead of going to his club. The place was full, and the waiter hurried him to the back of the room to capture the only vacant table. In the cloud of cigar smoke Waythorn did not at once distinguish his neighbors: but presently, looking about him, he saw Varick seated a few feet off. This time, luckily, they were too far apart for conversation, and Varick, who faced another way, had probably not even seen him; but there was an irony in their renewed nearness.

Varick was said to be fond of good living, and as Waythorn sat dispatching his hur-   55
ried luncheon he looked across half enviously at the other's leisurely degustation of his meal. When Waythorn first saw him he had been helping himself with critical deliberation to a bit of Camembert at the ideal point of liquefaction, and now, the cheese removed, he was just pouring his *café double* from its little two-storied earthen pot. He poured slowly, his ruddy profile bent over the task, and one beringed white hand steadying the lid of the coffeepot; then he stretched his other hand to the decanter of cognac at his elbow, filled a liqueur glass, took a tentative sip, and poured the brandy into his coffee cup.

Waythorn watched him in a kind of fascination. What was he thinking of—only of the flavor of the coffee and the liqueur? Had the morning's meeting left no more trace in his thoughts than on his face? Had his wife so completely passed out of his life that even this odd encounter with her present husband, within a week after her remarriage, was no more than an incident in his day? And as Waythorn mused, another idea struck him: had

Haskett ever met Varick as Varick and he had just met? The recollection of Haskett perturbed him, and he rose and left the restaurant, taking a circuitous way out to escape the placid irony of Varick's nod.

It was after seven when Waythorn reached home. He thought the footman who opened the door looked at him oddly.

"How is Miss Lily?" he asked in haste.

"Doing very well, sir. A gentleman—"

"Tell Barlow to put off dinner for half an hour," Waythorn cut him off, hurrying   60
upstairs.

He went straight to his room and dressed without seeing his wife. When he reached the drawing room she was there, fresh and radiant. Lily's day had been good; the doctor was not coming back that evening.

At dinner Waythorn told her of Sellers' illness and of the resulting complications. She listened sympathetically, adjuring him not to let himself be overworked, and asking vague feminine questions about the routine of the office. Then she gave him the chronicle of Lily's day; quoted the nurse and doctor, and told him who had called to inquire. He had never seen her more serene and unruffled. It struck him, with a curious pang, that she was very happy in being with him, so happy that she found a childish pleasure in rehearsing the trivial incidents of her day.

After dinner they went to the library, and the servant put the coffee and liqueurs on a low table before her and left the room. She looked singularly soft and girlish in her rosy-pale dress, against the dark leather of one of his bachelor armchairs. A day earlier the contrast would have charmed him.

He turned away now, choosing a cigar with affected deliberation.

"Did Haskett come?" he asked, with his back to her.   65

"Oh, yes—he came."

"You didn't see him, of course?"

She hesitated a moment. "I let the nurse see him."

That was all. There was nothing more to ask. He swung round toward her, applying a match to his cigar. Well, the thing was over for a week, at any rate. He would try not to think of it. She looked up at him, at trifle rosier than usual, with a smile in her eyes.

"Ready for your coffee, dear?"   70

He leaned against the mantelpiece, watching her as she lifted the coffeepot.

The lamplight struck a gleam from her bracelets and tipped her soft hair with brightness. How light and slender she was, and how each gesture flowed into the next! She seemed a creature all compact of harmonies. As the thought of Haskett receded, Waythorn felt himself yielding again to the joy of possessorship. They were his, those white hands with their flitting motions, his the light haze of hair, the lips and eyes. . . .

She sat down the coffeepot, and reaching for the decanter of cognac, measured off a liqueur glass and poured it into his cup.

Waythorn uttered a sudden exclamation.

"What is the matter?" she said, startled.   75

"Nothing: only—I don't take cognac in my coffee."

"Oh, how stupid of me," she cried.

Their eyes met, and she blushed a sudden agonized red.

III

Ten days later, Mr. Sellers, still housebound, asked Waythorn to call on his way downtown.

The senior partner, with his swaddled foot propped up by the fire, greeted his associate with an air of embarrassment.   80

"I'm sorry, my dear fellow; I've got to ask you to do an awkward thing for me."

Waythorn waited, and the other went on, after a pause apparently given to the arrangement of his phrases: "The fact is, when I was knocked out I had just gone into a rather complicated piece of business for—Gus Varick."

"Well?" said Waythorn, with an attempt to put him at his ease.

"Well—it's this way: Varick came to me the day before my attack. He had evidently had an inside tip from somebody, and had made about a hundred thousand. He came to me for advice, and I suggested his going in with Vanderlyn."

"Oh, the deuce!" Waythorn exclaimed. He saw in a flash what had happened. The investment was an alluring one, but required negotiation. He listened quietly while Sellers put the case before him, and, the statement ended, he said: "You think I ought to see Varick?"

"I'm afraid I can't as yet. The doctor is obdurate. And this thing can't wait. I hate to ask you, but no one else in the office knows the ins and outs of it."

Waythorn stood silent. He did not care a farthing for the success of Varick's venture, but the honor of the office was to be considered, and he could hardly refuse to oblige his partner.

"Very well," he said, "I'll do it."

That afternoon, apprised by telephone, Varick called at the office. Waythorn, waiting in his private room, wondered what the others thought of it. The newspapers, at the time of Mrs. Waythorn's marriage, had acquainted their readers with every detail of her previous matrimonial ventures, and Waythorn could fancy the clerks smiling behind Varick's back as he was ushered in.

Varick bore himself admirably. He was easy without being undignified, and Waythorn was conscious of cutting a much less impressive figure. Varick had no experience of business, and the talk prolonged itself for nearly an hour while Waythorn set forth with scrupulous precision the details of the proposed transaction.

"I'm awfully obliged to you," Varick said as he rose. "The fact is I'm not used to having much money to look after, and I don't want to make an ass of myself—" He smiled, and Waythorn could not help noticing that there was something pleasant about his smile. "It feels uncommonly queer to have enough cash to pay one's bills. I'd have sold my soul for it a few years ago!"

Waythorn winced at the allusion. He had heard it rumored that a lack of funds had been one of the determining causes of the Varick separation, but it did not occur to him that Varick's words were intentional. It seemed more likely that the desire to keep clear of embarrassing topics had fatally drawn him into one. Waythorn did not wish to be outdone in civility.

"We'll do the best we can for you," he said. "I think this is a good thing you're in."

"Oh, I'm sure it's immense. It's awfully good of you—" Varick broke off, embarrassed. "I suppose the thing's settled now—but if—"

"If anything happens before Sellers is about, I'll see you again," said Waythorn quietly. He was glad, in the end, to appear the more self-possessed of the two.

The course of Lily's illness ran smooth, and as the days passed Waythorn grew used to the idea of Haskett's weekly visit. The first time the day came round, he stayed out late, and questioned his wife as to the visit on his return. She replied at once that Haskett had merely seen the nurse downstairs, as the doctor did not wish anyone in the child's sickroom till after the crisis.

The following week Waythorn was again conscious of the recurrence of the day, but had forgotten it by the time he came home to dinner. The crisis of the disease came a few days later, with a rapid decline of fever, and the little girl was pronounced out of danger.

In the rejoicing which ensued the thought of Haskett passed out of Waythorn's mind, and one afternoon, letting himself into the house with a latchkey, he went straight to his library without noticing a shabby hat and umbrella in the hail.

In the library he found a small effaced-looking man with a thinnish gray beard sitting on the edge of a chair. The stranger might have been a piano tuner, or one of those mysteriously efficient persons who are summoned in emergencies to adjust some detail of the domestic machinery. He blinked at Waythorn through a pair of gold-rimmed spectacles and said mildly: "Mr. Waythorn, I presume? I am Lily's father."

Waythorn flushed. "Oh—" he stammered uncomfortably. He broke off, disliking to appear rude. Inwardly he was trying to adjust the actual Haskett to the image of him projected by his wife's reminiscences. Waythorn had been allowed to infer that Alice's first husband was a brute.

"I am sorry to intrude," said Haskett, with his over-the-counter politeness.   100

"Don't mention it," returned Waythorn, collecting himself. "I suppose the nurse has been told?"

"I presume so. I can wait," said Haskett. He had a resigned way of speaking, as though life had worn down his natural powers of resistance.

Waythorn stood on the threshold, nervously pulling off his gloves.

"I'm sorry you've been detained. I will send for the nurse," he said; and as he opened the door he added with an effort: "I'm glad we can give you a good report of Lily." He winced as the we slipped out, but Haskett seemed not to notice it.

"Thank you, Mr. Waythorn. It's been an anxious time for me."   105

"Ah, well, that's past. Soon she'll be able to go to you." Waythorn nodded and passed out.

In his own room he flung himself down with a groan. He hated the womanish sensibility which made him suffer so acutely from the grotesque chances of life. He had known when he married that his wife's former husbands were both living, and that amid the multiplied contacts of modern existence there were a thousand chances to one that he would run against one or the other, yet he found himself as much disturbed by his brief encounter with Haskett as though the law had not obligingly removed all difficulties in the way of their meeting.

Waythorn sprang up and began to pace the room nervously. He had not suffered half as much from his two meetings with Varick. It was Haskett's presence in his own house that made the situation so intolerable. He stood still, hearing steps in the passage.

"This way, please," he heard the nurse say. Haskett was being taken upstairs, then: not a corner of the house but was open to him. Waythorn dropped into another chair, staring vaguely ahead of him. On his dressing table stood a photograph of Alice, taken when he had first known her. She was Alice Varick then—how fine and exquisite he had thought her! Those were Varick's pearls about her neck. At Waythorn's instance they had been returned before her marriage. Had Haskett ever given her any trinkets—and what had become of them, Waythorn wondered? He realized suddenly that he knew very little of Haskett's past or present situation; but from the man's appearance and manner of speech he could reconstruct with curious precision the surroundings of Alice's first marriage. And it startled him to think that she had, in the background of her life, a phase of existence so different from anything with which he had connected her. Varick, whatever his faults, was a gentleman, in the conventional, traditional sense of the term: the sense which at that moment seemed, oddly enough, to have most meaning to Waythorn. He and Varick had the same social habits, spoke the same language, understood the same allusions. But this other man . . . it was grotesquely uppermost in Waythorn's mind that Haskett had worn a made-up tie attached with an elastic. Why should that ridiculous detail symbolize the whole man? Waythorn was exasperated by his own paltriness, but the fact of the tie expanded, forced itself on him, became as it were the key to Alice's past. He could see her, as Mrs. Haskett, sitting in a "front parlor" furnished in plush, with a pianola, and copy of *Ben Hur* on the center table. He could see her going to the theater with Haskett or perhaps even to a "Church Sociable"—she in a "picture hat" and Haskett in a black frock coat, a little creased, with the made-up tie on an elastic. On the way home they would stop and look at the illuminated shop windows, lingering over the photographs of New York actresses. On Sunday afternoons Haskett would take her for a walk, pushing Lily ahead of them in a white enameled perambulator, and Waythorn had a vision of the people they would stop and talk to. He could fancy how pretty Alice must have looked, in a dress adroitly constructed from the hints of a New York fashion paper, and how she must have looked down on the other women, chafing at her life, and secretly feeling that she belonged in a bigger place.

For the moment his foremost thought was one of wonder at the way in which she had   110
shed the phase of existence which her marriage with Haskett implied. It was as if her whole aspect, every gesture, every inflection, every allusion, were a studied negation of that period of her life. If she had denied being married to Haskett she could hardly have stood more convicted of duplicity than in this obliteration of the self which had been his wife.

Waythorn started up, checking himself in the analysis of her motives. What right had he to create a fantastic effigy of her and then pass judgment on it? She had spoken vaguely of her first marriage as unhappy, had hinted, with becoming reticence, that Haskett had wrought havoc among her young illusions. . . . It was a pity for Waythorn's peace of mind that Haskett's very inoffensiveness shed a new light on the nature of those illusions. A man would rather think that his wife has been brutalized by her first husband than that the process has been reversed.

IV

"Mr. Waythorn, I didn't like that French governess of Lily's."

Haskett, subdued and apologetic, stood before Waythorn in the library, revolving his shabby hat in his hand.

Waythorn, surprised in his armchair over the evening paper, stared back perplexedly at his visitor.

"You'll excuse my asking to see you," Haskett continued. "But this is my last visit,   115
and I thought if I could have a word with you it would be a better way than writing to Mrs. Waythorn's lawyer."

Waythorn rose uneasily. He did not like the French governess either; but that was irrelevant.

"I am not so sure of that," he returned stiffly; "but since you wish it I will give your message to—my wife." He always hesitated over the possessive pronoun in addressing Haskett.

The latter sighed. "I don't know as that will help much. She didn't like it when I spoke to her."

Waythorn turned red. "When did you see her?" he asked.

"Not since the first day I came to see Lily—right after she was taken sick. I re-   120
marked to her then that I didn't like the governess."

Waythorn made no answer. He remembered distinctly that, after that first visit, he had asked his wife if she had seen Haskett. She had lied to him then, but she had respected his wishes since; and the incident cast a curious light on her character. He was sure she would not have seen Haskett that first day if she had divined that Waythorn would object, and the fact that she did not divine it was almost as disagreeable to the latter as the discovery that she had lied to him.

"I don't like the woman," Haskett was repeating with mild persistency. "She ain't straight. Mr. Waythorn—she'll teach the child to be underhand. I've noticed a change in Lily—she's too anxious to please—and she don't always tell the truth. She used to be the straightest child, Mr. Waythorn—" He broke off, his voice a little thick. "Not but what I want her to have a stylish education," he ended.

Waythorn was touched. "I'm sorry, Mr. Haskett; but frankly, I don't quite see what I can do."

Haskett hesitated. Then he laid his hat on the table, and advanced to the hearthrug, on which Waythorn was standing. There was nothing aggressive in his manner, but he had the solemnity of a timid man resolved on a decisive measure.

"There's just one thing you can do, Mr. Waythorn," he said. "You can remind Mrs. Waythorn that, by the decree of the courts, I am entitled to have a voice in Lily's bringing-up." He paused, and went on more deprecatingly: "I'm not the kind to talk about enforcing my rights, Mr. Waythorn. I don't know as I think a man is entitled to rights he hasn't known how to hold on to; but this business of the child is different. I've never let go there—and I never meant to."   125

The scene left Waythorn deeply shaken. Shamefacedly, in indirect ways, he had been finding out about Haskett; and all that he had learned was favorable. The little man, in order to be near his daughter, had sold out his share in a profitable business in Utica, and accepted a modest clerkship in a New York manufacturing house. He boarded in a shabby street and had few acquaintances. His passion for Lily filled his life. Waythorn felt that this exploration of Haskett was like groping about with a dark lantern in his wife's past; but he saw now that there were recesses his lantern had not explored. He had never inquired into the exact circumstances of his wife's first matrimonial rupture. On the surface all had been fair. It was she who had obtained the divorce, and the court had given her the child. But Waythorn knew how many ambiguities such a verdict might cover. The mere fact that Haskett retained a right over his daughter implied an unsuspected compromise. Waythorn was an idealist. He always refused to recognize unpleasant contingencies till he found himself confronted with them, and then he saw them followed by a spectral train of consequences. His next days were thus haunted, and he determined to try to lay the ghosts by conjuring them up in his wife's presence.

When he repeated Haskett's request a flame of anger passed over her face; but she subdued it instantly and spoke with a slight quiver of outraged motherhood.

"It is very ungentlemanly of him," she said.

The word grated on Waythorn. "That is neither here nor there. It's a bare question of rights."

She murmured: "It's not as if he could ever be a help to Lily—"   130

Waythorn flushed. This was even less to his taste. "The question is," he repeated, "what authority has he over her?"

She looked downward, twisting herself a little in her seat. "I am willing to see him— I thought you objected," she faltered.

In a flash he understood that she knew the extent of Haskett's claims. Perhaps it was not the first time she had resisted them.

"My objecting has nothing to do with it," he said coldly; "if Haskett has a right to be consulted you must consult him."

She burst into tears, and he saw that she expected him to regard her as a victim.   135

Haskett did not abuse his rights. Waythorn had felt miserably sure that he would not. But the governess was dismissed, and from time to time the little man demanded an interview with Alice. After the first outburst she accepted the situation with her usual adaptability. Haskett had once reminded Waythorn of the piano tuner, and Mrs. Waythorn, after a month or two, appeared to class him with that domestic familiar. Waythorn could not but respect the father's tenacity. At first he had tried to cultivate the suspicion that Haskett might be "up" to something, that he had an object in securing a foothold in the house. But in his heart Waythorn was sure of Haskett's single-mindedness; he even guessed in the latter a mild contempt for such advantages as his relation with the Waythorns might offer. Haskett's sincerity of purpose made him invulnerable, and his successor had to accept him as a lien on the property.

Mr. Sellers was sent to Europe to recover from his gout, and Varick's affairs hung on Waythorn's hands. The negotiations were prolonged and complicated; they necessitated frequent conferences between the two men, and the interests of the firm forbade Waythorn's suggesting that his client should transfer his business to another office.

Varick appeared well in the transaction. In moments of relaxation his coarse streak appeared, and Waythorn dreaded his geniality; but in the office he was concise and clearheaded, with a flattering deference to Waythorn's judgment. Their business relations being so affably established, it would have been absurd for the two men to ignore each other in society. The first time they met in a drawing room, Varick took up their intercourse in the same easy key, and his hostess' grateful glance obliged Waythorn to respond to it. After that they ran across each other frequently, and one evening at a ball Waythorn, wandering through the remoter rooms, came upon Varick seated beside his wife. She colored a little, and faltered in what she was saying; but Varick nodded to Waythorn without rising, and the latter strolled on.

In the carriage, on the way home, he broke out nervously: "I didn't know you spoke to Varick."

Her voice trembled a little. "It's the first time—he happened to be standing near   140
me; I didn't know what to do. It's so awkward, meeting everywhere—and he said you had been very kind about some business."

"That's different," said Waythorn.

She paused a moment. "I'll do just as you wish," she returned pliantly. "I thought it would be less awkward to speak to him when we meet."

Her pliancy was beginning to sicken him. Had she really no will of her own—no theory about her relation to these men? She had accepted Haskett—did she mean to accept Varick? It was "less awkward," as she had said, and her instinct was to evade difficulties or to circumvent them. With sudden vividness Waythorn saw how the instinct had developed. She was "as easy as an old shoe"—a shoe that too many feet had worn. Her elasticity was the result of tension in too many different directions. Alice Haskett—Alice Varick—Alice Waythorn—she had been each in turn, and had left hanging to each name a little of her privacy, a little of her personality, a little of the inmost self where the unknown god abides.

"Yes—it's better to speak to Varick," said Waythorn wearily.

V

The winter wore on, and society took advantage of the Waythorns' acceptance of Varick.   145
Harassed hostesses were grateful to them for bridging over a social difficulty, and Mrs. Waythorn was held up as a miracle of good taste. Some experimental spirits could not resist the diversion of throwing Varick and his former wife together, and there were those who thought he found a zest in the propinquity. But Mrs. Waythorn's conduct remained irreproachable. She neither avoided Varick nor sought him out. Even Waythorn could not but admit that she had discovered the solution of the newest social problem.

He had married her without giving much thought to that problem. He had fancied that a woman can shed her past like a man. But now he saw that Alice was bound to hers both by the circumstances which forced her into continued relation with it, and by the traces it had left on her nature. With grim irony Waythorn compared himself to a member of a syndicate. He held so many shares in his wife's personality and his predecessors were his partners in the business. If there had been any element of passion in the transaction he would have felt less deteriorated by it. The fact that Alice took her change of husbands like a change of weather reduced the situation to mediocrity. He could have forgiven her for blunders, for excesses; for resisting Haskett, for yielding to Varick; for anything but her acquiescence and her tact. She reminded him of a juggler tossing knives; but the knives were blunt and she knew they would never cut her.

And then, gradually, habit formed a protecting surface for his sensibilities. If he paid for each day's comfort with the small change of his illusions, he grew daily to value the comfort more and set less store upon the coin. He had drifted into a dulling propinquity with Haskett and Varick and he took refuge in the cheap revenge of satirizing the situation. He even began to reckon up the advantages which accrued from it, to ask himself if it were not better to own a third of a wife who knew how to make a man happy than a whole one who had lacked opportunity to acquire the art. For it was an art, and made up, like all others, of concessions, eliminations and embellishments; of lights judiciously thrown and shadows skillfully softened. His wife knew exactly how to manage the lights, and he knew exactly to what training she owed her skill. He even tried to trace the source of his obligations, to discriminate between the influences which had combined to produce his domestic happiness; he perceived that Haskett's commonness had made Alice worship good breeding, while Varick's liberal construction of the marriage bond had taught her to value the conjugal virtues; so that he was directly indebted to his predecessors for the devotion which made his life easy if not inspiring.

From this phase he passed into that of complete acceptance. He ceased to satirize himself because time dulled the irony of the situation and the joke lost its humor with its sting. Even the sight of Haskett's hat on the hall table had ceased to touch the springs of epigram. The hat was often seen there now, for it had been decided that it was better for Lily's father to visit her than for the little girl to go to his boardinghouse. Waythorn, having acquiesced in this arrangement, had been surprised to find how little difference it made. Haskett was never obtrusive, and the few visitors who met him on the stairs were unaware of his identity. Waythorn did not know how often he saw Alice, but with himself Haskett was seldom in contact.

One afternoon, however, he learned on entering that Lily's father was waiting to see him. In the library he found Haskett occupying a chair in his usual provisional way. Waythorn always felt grateful to him for not leaning back.

"I hope you'll excuse me, Mr. Waythorn," he said rising. "I wanted to see Mrs. Waythorn about Lily, and your man asked me to wait here till she came in." 150

"Of course," said Waythorn, remembering that a sudden leak had that morning given over the drawing room to the plumbers.

He opened his cigar case and held it out to his visitor, and Haskett's acceptance seemed to mark a fresh stage in their intercourse. The spring evening was chilly, and Waythorn invited his guest to draw up his chair to the fire. He meant to find an excuse to leave Haskett in a moment; but he was tired and cold, and after all the little man no longer jarred on him.

The two were enclosed in the intimacy of their blended cigar smoke when the door opened and Varick walked into the room. Waythorn rose abruptly. It was the first time that Varick had come to the house, and the surprise of seeing him, combined with the singular inopportuneness of his arrival, gave a new edge to Waythorn's blunted sensibilities. He stared at his visitor without speaking.

Varick seemed too preoccupied to notice his host's embarrassment.

"My dear fellow," he exclaimed in his most expansive tone, "I must apologize for   155
tumbling in on you in this way, but I was too late to catch you downtown, and so I
thought—"

He stopped short, catching sight of Haskett, and his sanguine color deepened to a
flush which spread vividly under his scant blond hair. But in a moment he recovered
himself and nodded slightly. Haskett returned the bow in silence, and Waythorn was still
groping for speech when the footman came in carrying a tea table.

The intrusion offered a welcome vent to Waythorn's nerves. "What the deuce are
you bringing this here for?" he said sharply.

"I beg your pardon, sir, but the plumbers are still in the drawing room, and Mrs.
Waythorn said she would have tea in the library." The footman's perfectly respectful tone
implied a reflection on Waythorn's reasonableness.

"Oh, very well," said the latter resignedly, and the footman proceeded to open the
folding tea table and set out its complicated appointments. While this interminable
process continued the three men stood motionless, watching it with a fascinated stare, till
Waythorn, to break the silence, said to Varick, "Won't you have a cigar?"

He held out the case he had just tendered to Haskett, and Varick helped himself   160
with a smile. Waythorn looked about for a match, and finding none, proffered a light
from his own cigar. Haskett, in the background, held his ground mildly, examining his
cigar tip now and then, and stepping forward at the right moment to knock its ashes into
the fire.

The footman at last withdrew, and Varick immediately began: "If I could just say
half a word to you about this business—"

"Certainly," stammered Waythorn; "in the dining room—"

But as he placed his hand on the door it opened from without, and his wife appeared on the threshold.

She came in fresh and smiling, in her street dress and hat, shedding a fragrance
from the boa which she loosened in advancing.

"Shall we have tea in here, dear?" she began; and then she caught sight of Varick.   165
Her smile deepened, veiling a slight tremor of surprise.

"Why, how do you do?" she said with a distinct note of pleasure.

As she shook hands with Varick she saw Haskett standing behind him. Her smile
faded for a moment, but she recalled it quickly, with a scarcely perceptible side glance at
Waythorn.

"How do you do, Mr. Haskett?" she said, and shook hands with him a shade less
cordially.

The three men stood awkwardly before her, till Varick, always the most self-
possessed, dashed into an explanatory phrase.

"We—I had to see Waythorn a moment on business," he stammered, brick-red   170
from chin to nape.

Haskett stepped forward with his air of mild obstinacy. "I am sorry to intrude; but
you appointed five o'clock—" he directed his resigned glance to the timepiece on the
mantel.

She swept aside their embarrassment with a charming gesture of hospitality.

"I'm so sorry—I'm always late; but the afternoon was so lovely." She stood drawing
off her gloves, propitiatory and graceful, diffusing about her a sense of ease and familiarity in which the situation lost its grotesqueness. "But before talking business," she added
brightly, "I'm sure everyone wants a cup of tea."

She dropped into her low chair by the tea table, and the two visitors, as if drawn by
her smile, advanced to receive the cups she held out.

She glanced about for Waythorn, and he took the third cup with a laugh.   175

QUESTIONS

1. Describe the story's tone. How does Wharton develop the comic possibilities of the relationships between Alice and the three men?

2. What kind of a person is Waythorn? How does he slowly begin to accept the other two? How does he finally recognize the relationship of his own happiness to Alice's earlier marriages with the other two?

3. What is the difference between Alice's description of the other two and Waythorn's own experience with them?

4. Why does Wharton limit the point of view to Waythorn, while preserving dramatic objectivity about both Alice and the other two?

Pomegranate Seed[1]   1931

Charlotte Ashby paused on her doorstep. Dark had descended on the brilliancy of the March afternoon, and the grinding rasping street life of the city was at its highest. She turned her back on it, standing for a moment in the old-fashioned, marble-flagged vestibule before she inserted her key in the lock. The sash curtains drawn across the panes of the inner door softened the light within to a warm blur through which no details showed. It was the hour when, in the first months of her marriage to Kenneth Ashby, she had most liked to return to that quiet house in a street long since deserted by business and fashion. The contrast between the soulless roar of New York, its devouring blaze of lights, the oppression of its congested traffic, congested houses, lives, minds and this veiled sanctuary she called home, always stirred her profoundly. In the very heart of the hurricane she had found her tiny islet—or thought she had. And now, in the last months, everything was changed, and she always wavered on the doorstep and had to force herself to enter.

While she stood there she called up the scene within: the hall hung with old prints, the ladderlike stairs, and on the left her husband's long shabby library, full of books and pipes and worn armchairs inviting to meditation. How she had loved that room! Then, upstairs, her own drawing-room, in which, since the death of Kenneth's first wife, neither furniture nor hangings had been changed, because there had never been money enough, but which Charlotte had made her own by moving furniture about and adding more books, another lamp, a table for the new reviews. Even on the occasion of her only visit to the first Mrs. Ashby—a distant, self-centered woman, whom she had known very slightly—she had looked about her with an innocent envy, feeling it to be exactly the drawing-room she would have liked for herself; and now for more than a year it had been hers to deal with as she chose—the room to which she hastened back at dusk on winter days, where she sat reading by the fire, or answering notes at the pleasant roomy desk, or going over her stepchildren's copy books, till she heard her husband's step.

Sometimes friends dropped in; sometimes—oftener—she was alone; and she liked that best, since it was another way of being with Kenneth, thinking over what he had said when they parted in the morning, imagining what he would say when he sprang up the stairs, found her by herself and caught her to him.

Now, instead of this, she thought of one thing only—the letter she might or might not find on the hall table. Until she had made sure whether or not it was there, her mind had no room for anything else. The letter was always the same—a square grayish envelope with "Kenneth Ashby, Esquire," written on it in bold but faint characters. From the first it had struck Charlotte as peculiar that anyone who wrote such a firm hand should trace the letters so lightly; the address was always written as though there were not enough ink in the pen, or the writer's wrist were too weak to bear upon it. Another curious thing was that, in spite of its masculine curves, the writing was so visibly feminine. Some hands are sexless, some masculine, at first glance; the writing on the gray envelope, for all its strength and assurance, was without doubt a woman's. The envelope never bore anything but the recipient's name; no stamp, no address. The letter was presumably delivered by hand—but by whose? No doubt it was slipped into the letter box, whence the parlour maid, when she closed the shutters and lit the lights, probably extracted it. At any rate, it was always in the evening, after dark, that Charlotte saw it lying there. She thought of the letter in the singular, as "it," because, though there had been several since her marriage—seven, to be exact—they were so alike in appearance that they had become merged in one another in her mind, become one letter, become "it."

The first had come the day after their return from their honeymoon—a journey   5
prolonged to the West Indies, from which they had returned to New York after an absence of more than two months. Re-entering the house with her husband, late on that first evening—they had dined at his mother's—she had seen, alone on the hall table, the gray envelope. Her eye fell on it before Kenneth's, and her first thought was: "Why, I've seen that writing before"; but where she could not recall. The memory was just definite enough for her to identify the script whenever it looked up at her faintly from the same pale envelope; but on that first day she would have thought no more of the letter if, when her husband's glance lit on it, she had not chanced to be looking at him. It all happened in a flash—his seeing the letter, putting out his hand for it, raising it to his shortsighted eyes to decipher the faint writing, and then abruptly withdrawing the arm he had slipped through Charlotte's, and moving away to the hanging light, his back turned to her. She had waited—waited for a sound, an exclamation; waited for him to open the letter; but he had slipped it into his pocket without a word and followed her into the library. And there they sat down by the fire and lit their cigarettes, and he had remained silent, his head thrown back broodingly against the armchair, his eyes fixed on the hearth, and presently had passed his hand over his forehead and said: "Wasn't it unusually hot at my mother's tonight? I've got a splitting head. Mind if I take myself off to bed?"

That was the first time. Since then Charlotte had never been present when he had received the letter. It usually came before he got home from his office, and she had to go upstairs and leave it lying there. But even if she had not seen it, she would have known it had come by the change in his face when he joined her—which, on those evenings, he seldom did before they met for dinner. Evidently, whatever the letter contained, he wanted to be by himself to deal with it; and when he reappeared he looked years older, looked emptied of life and courage, and hardly conscious of her presence. Sometimes he was silent for the rest of the evening; and if he spoke, it was usually to hint some criticism of her household arrangements, suggest some change in the domestic administration, to ask, a little nervously, if she didn't think Joyce's nursery governess was rather young and flighty, or if she herself always saw to it that Peter—whose throat was delicate—was properly wrapped up when he went to school. At such times Charlotte would remember the friendly warnings she had received when she became engaged to Kenneth Ashby: "Marrying a heartbroken widower! Isn't that rather risky? You know Elsie Ashby absolutely dominated him"; and how she had jokingly replied: "He may be glad of a little liberty for a change." And in this respect she had been right. She had needed no one to tell her, during the first months, that her husband was perfectly happy with her. When they came back from their protracted honeymoon the same friends said: "What have you done to

Kenneth? He looks twenty years younger"; and this time she answered with careless joy: "I suppose I've got him out of his groove."

But what she noticed after the gray letters began to come was not so much his nervous tentative fault-finding—which always seemed to be uttered against his will as the look in his eyes when he joined her after receiving one of the letters. The look was not unloving, not even indifferent; it was the look of a man who had been so far away from ordinary events that when he returns to familiar things they seem strange. She minded that more than the fault-finding.

Though she had been sure from the first that the handwriting on the gray envelope was a woman's, it was long before she associated the mysterious letters with any sentimental secret. She was too sure of her husband's love, too confident of filling his life, for such an idea to occur to her. It seemed far more likely that the letters—which certainly did not appear to cause him any sentimental pleasure—were addressed to the busy lawyer than to the private person. Probably they were from some tiresome client—women, he had often told her, were nearly always tiresome as clients—who did not want her letters opened by his secretary and therefore had them carried to his house. Yes; but in that case the unknown female must be unusually troublesome, judging from the effect her letters produced. Then again, though his professional discretion was exemplary, it was odd that he had never uttered an impatient comment, never remarked to Charlotte, in a moment of expansion, that there was a nuisance of a woman who kept badgering him about a case that had gone against her. He had made more than one semi-confidence of the kind—of course without giving names or details; but concerning this mysterious correspondent his lips were sealed.

There was another possibility: what is euphemistically called an "old entanglement." Charlotte Ashby was a sophisticated woman. She had few illusions about the intricacies of the human heart; she knew that there were often old entanglements. But when she had married Kenneth Ashby, her friends, instead of hinting at such a possibility, had said: "You've got your work cut out for you. Marrying a Don Juan is a sinecure to it. Kenneth's never looked at another woman since he first saw Elsie Corder. During all the years of their marriage he was more like an unhappy lover than a comfortably contented husband. He'll never let you move an armchair or change the place of a lamp; and whatever you venture to do, he'll mentally compare with what Elsie would have done in your place."

Except for an occasional nervous mistrust as to her ability to manage the children—a mistrust gradually dispelled by her good humor and the children's obvious fondness for her—none of these forebodings had come true. The desolate widower, of whom his nearest friends said that only his absorbing professional interests had kept him from suicide after his first wife's death, had fallen in love, two years later, with Charlotte Gorse, and after an impetuous wooing had married her and carried her off on a tropical honeymoon. And ever since he had been as tender and loverlike as during those first radiant weeks. Before asking her to marry him he had spoken to her frankly of his great love for his first wife and his despair after her sudden death; but even then he had assumed no stricken attitude, or implied that life offered no possibility of renewal. He had been perfectly simple and natural, and had confessed to Charlotte that from the beginning he had hoped the future held new gifts for him. And when, after their marriage, they returned to the house where his twelve years with his first wife had been spent, he had told Charlotte at once that he was sorry he couldn't afford to do the place over for her, but that he knew every woman had her own views about furniture and all sorts of household arrangements a man would never notice, and had begged her to make any changes she saw fit without bothering to consult him. As a result, she made as few as possible; but his way of beginning their new life in the old setting was so frank and unembarrassed that it put her immediately at her ease, and she was almost sorry to find that

10

the portrait of Elsie Ashby, which used to hang over the desk in his library, had been transferred in their absence to the children's nursery. Knowing herself to be the indirect cause of this banishment, she spoke of it to her husband; but he answered; "Oh, I thought they ought to grow up with her looking down on them." The answer moved Charlotte, and satisfied her; and as time went by she had to confess that she felt more at home in her house, more at ease and in confidence with her husband, since that long coldly beautiful face on the library wall no longer followed her with guarded eyes. It was as if Kenneth's love had penetrated to the secret she hardly acknowledged to her own heart—her passionate need to feel herself the sovereign even of his past.

With all this stored-up happiness to sustain her, it was curious that she had lately found herself yielding to a nervous apprehension. But there the apprehension was; and on this particular afternoon—perhaps because she was more tired than usual, or because of the trouble of finding a new cook or, for some other ridiculously trivial reason, moral or physical—she found herself unable to react against the feeling. Latchkey in hand, she looked back down the silent street to the whirl and illumination of the great thoroughfare beyond, and up at the sky already aflare with the city's nocturnal life. "Outside there," she thought, "sky-scrapers, advertisements, telephones, wireless, airplanes, movies, motors, and all the rest of the twentieth century; and on the other side of the door something I can't explain, can't relate to them. Something as old as the world, as mysterious as life. . . . Nonsense! What am I worrying about? There hasn't been a letter for three months now—not since the day we came back from the country after Christmas. . . . Queer that they always seem to come after our holidays! . . . Why should I imagine there's going to be one tonight!"

No reason why, but that was the worst of it—one of the worsts!—that there were days when she would stand there cold and shivering with the premonition of something inexplicable, intolerable, to be faced on the other side of the curtained panes; and when she opened the door and went in, there would be nothing; and on other days when she felt the same premonitory chill, it was justified by the sight of the gray envelope. So that ever since the last had come she had taken to feeling cold and premonitory every evening, because she never opened the door without thinking the letter might be there.

Well, she'd had enough of it; that was certain. She couldn't go on like that. If her husband turned white and had a headache on the days when the letter came, he seemed to recover afterward; but she couldn't. With her the strain had become chronic, and the reason was not far to seek. Her husband knew from whom the letter came and what was in it; he was prepared beforehand for whatever he had to deal with, and master of the situation, however bad; whereas she was shut out in the dark with her conjectures.

"I can't stand it! I can't stand it another day!" she exclaimed aloud, as she put her key in the lock. She turned the key and went in; and there, on the table, lay the letter.

II

She was almost glad of the sight. It seemed to justify everything, to put a seal of definiteness on the whole blurred business. A letter for her husband; a letter from a woman—no doubt another vulgar case of "old entanglement." What a fool she had been ever to doubt it, to rack her brains for less obvious explanations! She took up the envelope with a steady contemptuous hand, looked closely at the faint letters, held it against the light and just discerned the outline of the folded sheet within. She knew that now she would have no peace till she found out what was written on that sheet.

Her husband had not come in; he seldom got back from his office before half-past six or seven, and it was not yet six. She would have time to take the letter up to the drawing-room, hold it over the teakettle which at that hour always simmered by the fire

15

in expectation of her return, solve the mystery and replace the letter where she had found it. No one would be the wiser, and her gnawing uncertainty would be over. The alternative, of course, was to question her husband; but to do that seemed even more difficult. She weighed the letter between thumb and finger, looked at it again under the light, started up the stairs with the envelope—and came down again and laid it on the table.

"No, I evidently can't," she said, disappointed.

What should she do, then? She couldn't go up alone to that warm welcoming room, pour out her tea, look over her correspondence, glance at a book or review—not with that letter lying below and the knowledge that in a little while her husband would come in, open it and turn into the library alone, as he always did on the days when the gray envelope came.

Suddenly she decided. She would wait in the library and see for herself; see what happened between him and the letter when they thought themselves unobserved. She wondered the idea had never occurred to her before. By leaving the door ajar, and sitting in the corner behind it, she could watch him unseen. . . . Well, then, she would watch him! She drew a chair into the corner, sat down, her eyes on the crack, and waited.

As far as she could remember, it was the first time she had ever tried to surprise another person's secret, but she was conscious of no compunction. She simply felt as if she were fighting her way through a stifling fog that she must at all costs get out of.   20

At length she heard Kenneth's latchkey and jumped up. The impulse to rush out and meet him had nearly made her forget why she was there; but she remembered in time and sat down again. From her post she covered the whole range of his movements—saw him enter the hall, draw the key from the door and take off his hat and overcoat. Then he turned to throw his gloves on the hall table, and at that moment he saw the envelope. The light was full on his face, and what Charlotte first noted there was a look of surprise. Evidently he had not expected the letter—had not thought of the possibility of its being there that day. But though he had not expected it, now that he saw it he knew well enough what it contained. He did not open it immediately, but stood motionless, the color slowly ebbing from his face. Apparently he could not make up his mind to touch it; but at length he put out his hand, opened the envelope, and moved with it to the light. In doing so he turned his back on Charlotte, and she saw only his bent head and slightly stooping shoulders. Apparently all the writing was on one page, for he did not turn the sheet but continued to stare at it for so long that he must have reread it a dozen times—or so it seemed to the woman breathlessly watching him. At length she saw him move; he raised the letter still closer to his eyes, as though he had not fully deciphered it. Then he lowered his head, and she saw his lips touch the sheet.

"Kenneth!" she exclaimed, and went out into the hall.

The letter clutched in his hand, her husband turned and looked at her. "Where were you?" he said, in a low bewildered voice, like a man waked out of his sleep.

"In the library, waiting for you." She tried to steady her voice: "What's the matter! What's in that letter? You look ghastly."

Her agitation seemed to calm him, and he instantly put the envelope into his pock-   25
et with a slight laugh. "Ghastly? I'm sorry. I've had a hard day in the office—one or two complicated cases. I look dog-tired, I suppose."

"You didn't look tired when you came in. It was only when you opened that letter—"

He had followed her into the library, and they stood gazing at each other. Charlotte noticed how quickly he had regained his self-control; his profession had trained him to rapid mastery of face and voice. She saw at once that she would be at a disadvantage in any attempt to surprise his secret, but at the same moment she lost all desire to maneuvre, to trick him into betraying anything he wanted to conceal. Her wish was still to penetrate the mystery, but only that she might help him to bear the burden it implied. "Even if it is another woman," she thought.

"Kenneth," she said, her heart beating excitedly, "I waited here on purpose to see you come in. I wanted to watch you while you opened that letter."

His face, which had paled, turned to dark red; then it paled again. "That letter? Why especially that letter?"

"Because I've noticed that whenever one of those letters comes it seems to have such a strange effect on you."

A line of anger she had never seen before came out between his eyes, and she said to herself: "The upper part of his face is too narrow; this is the first time I ever noticed it."

She heard him continue, in the cool and faintly ironic tone of the prosecuting lawyer making a point: "Ah; so you're in the habit of watching people open their letters when they don't know you're there?"

"Not in the habit. I never did such a thing before. But I had to find out what she writes to you, at regular intervals, in those gray envelopes."

He weighed this for a moment; then: "The intervals have not been regular," he said.

"Oh, I daresay you've kept a better account of the dates than I have," she retorted, her magnanimity vanishing at his tone. "All I know is that every time that woman writes to you—"

"Why do you assume it's a woman?"

"It's a woman's writing. Do you deny it?"

He smiled. "No, I don't deny it. I asked only because the writing is generally supposed to look more like a man's."

Charlotte passed this over impatiently. "And this woman—what does she write to you about?"

Again he seemed to consider a moment. "About business."

"Legal business?"

"In a way, yes. Business in general."

"You look after her affairs for her?"

"Yes."

"You've looked after them for a long time?"

"Yes. A very long time."

"Kenneth, dearest, won't you tell me who she is?"

"No. I can't." He paused and brought out, as if with a certain hesitation: "Professional secrecy."

The blood rushed from Charlotte's heart to her temples. "Don't say that—don't!"

"Why not?"

"Because I saw you kiss the letter."

The effect of the words was so disconcerting that she instantly repented having spoken them. Her husband, who had submitted to her cross-questioning with a sort of contemptuous composure, as though he were humouring an unreasonable child, turned on her a face of terror and distress. For a minute he seemed unable to speak; then, collecting himself with an effort, he stammered out: "The writing is very faint; you must have seen me holding the letter close to my eyes to try to decipher it."

"No; I saw you kissing it." He was silent. "Didn't I see you kissing it?"

He sank back into indifference. "Perhaps."

"Kenneth! You stand there and say that—to me?"

"What possible difference can it make to you? The letter is on business, as I told you. Do you suppose I'd lie about it? The writer is a very old friend whom I haven't seen for a long time."

"Men don't kiss business letters, even from women who are very old friends, unless they have been their lovers, and still regret them."

He shrugged his shoulders slightly and turned away, as if he considered the discussion at an end and were faintly disgusted at the turn it had taken.

"Kenneth!" Charlotte moved toward him and caught hold of his arm.

He paused with a look of weariness and laid his hand over hers. "Won't you believe   60
me?" he asked gently.

"How can I? I've watched these letters come to you—for months now they've been coming. Ever since we came back from the West Indies—one of them greeted me the very day we arrived. And after each one of them I see their mysterious effect on you, I see you disturbed, unhappy, as if someone were trying to estrange you from me."

"No, dear; not that. Never!"

She drew back and looked at him with passionate entreaty. "Well, then, prove it to me, darling. It's so easy!"

He forced a smile. "It's not easy to prove anything to a woman who's once taken an idea into her head."

"You've only got to show me the letter."   65

His hand slipped from hers and he drew back and shook his head.

"You won't?"

"I can't."

"Then the woman who wrote it is your mistress."

"No, dear. No."   70

"Not now, perhaps. I suppose she's trying to get you back, and you're struggling, out of pity for me. My poor Kenneth!"

"I swear to you she never was my mistress."

Charlotte felt the tears rushing to her eyes. "Ah, that's worse, then—that's hopeless! The prudent ones are the kind that keep their hold on a man. We all know that." She lifted her hands and hid her face in them.

Her husband remained silent; he offered neither consolation nor denial, and at length, wiping away her tears, she raised her eyes almost timidly to his.

"Kenneth, think! We've been married such a short time. Imagine what you're mak-   75
ing me suffer. You say you can't show me this letter. You refuse even to explain it."

"I've told you the letter is on business. I will swear to that too."

"A man will swear to anything to screen a woman. If you want me to believe you, at least tell me her name. If you'll do that, I promise you I won't ask to see the letter."

There was a long interval of suspense, during which she felt her heart beating against her ribs in quick admonitory knocks, as if warning her of the danger she was incurring.

"I can't," he said at length.

"Not even her name?"   80

"No."

"You can't tell me anything more?"

"No."

Again a pause; this time they seemed both to have reached the end of their arguments and to be helplessly facing each other across a baffling waste of incomprehension.

Charlotte stood breathing rapidly, her hands against her breast. She felt as if she   85
had won a hard race and missed the goal. She had meant to move her husband and had succeeded only in irritating him; and this error of reckoning seemed to change him into a stranger, a mysterious incomprehensible being whom no argument or entreaty of hers could reach. The curious thing was that she was aware in him of no hostility or even

impatience, but only of a remoteness, an inaccessibility, far more difficult to overcome. She felt herself excluded, ignored, blotted out of his life. But after a moment or two, looking at him more calmly, she saw that he was suffering as much as she was. His distant guarded face was drawn with pain; the coming of the gray envelope, though it always cast a shadow, had never marked him as deeply as this discussion with his wife.

Charlotte took heart; perhaps, after all, she had not spent her last shaft. She drew nearer and once more laid her hand on his arm. "Poor Kenneth! If you knew how sorry I am for you—"

She thought he winced slightly at this expression of sympathy, but he took her hand and pressed it.

"I can think of nothing worse than to be incapable of loving long," she continued; "to feel the beauty of a great love and to be too unstable to bear its burden."

He turned on her a look of wistful reproach. "Oh, don't say that of me. Unstable!"

She felt herself at last on the right tack, and her voice trembled with excitement as she went on: "Then what about me and this other woman? Haven't you already forgotten Elsie twice within a year?" 90

She seldom pronounced his first wife's name; it did not come naturally to her tongue. She flung it out now as if she were flinging some dangerous explosive into the open space between them, and drew back a step, waiting to hear the mine go off.

Her husband did not move; his expression grew sadder, but showed no resentment. "I have never forgotten Elsie," he said.

Charlotte could not repress a faint laugh. "Then, you poor dear, between the three of us—"

"There are not—" he began; and then broke off and put his hand to his forehead.

"Not what?" 95

"I'm sorry; I don't believe I know what I'm saying. I've got a blinding headache." He looked wan and furrowed enough for the statement to be true, but she was exasperated by his evasion.

"Ah, yes; the gray-envelope headache!"

She saw the surprise in his eyes. "I'd forgotten how closely I've been watched," he said coldly. "If you'll excuse me, I think I'll go up and try an hour in the dark, to see if I can rid myself of this neuralgia."

She wavered; then she said, with desperate resolution: "I'm sorry your head aches. But before you go I want to say that sooner or later this question must be settled between us. Someone is trying to separate us, and I don't care what it costs me to find out who it is." She looked him steadily in the eyes. "If it costs me your love, I don't care! If I can't have your confidence I don't want anything from you."

He still looked at her wistfully. "Give me time." 100

"Time for what? It's only a word to say."

"Time to show you that you haven't lost my love or my confidence."

"Well, I'm waiting."

He turned toward the door, and then glanced back hesitatingly. "Oh, do wait, my love," he said, and went out of the room.

She heard his tired step on the stairs and the closing of his bedroom door above. 105 Then she dropped into a chair and buried her face in her folded arms. Her first movement was one of compunction; she seemed to herself to have been hard, unhuman, unimaginative. "Think of telling him that I didn't care if my insistence cost me his love! The lying rubbish!" She started up to follow him and unsay the meaningless words. But she was checked by a reflection. He had had his way, after all; he had eluded all attacks on his secret, and now he was shut up alone in his room, reading that other woman's letter.

III

She was still reflecting on this when the surprised parlor-maid came in and found her. No, Charlotte said, she wasn't going to dress for dinner; Mr. Ashby didn't want to dine. He was very tired and had gone up to his room to rest; later she would have something brought on a tray to the drawing-room. She mounted the stairs to her bedroom. Her dinner dress was lying on the bed, and at the sight the quiet routine of her daily life took hold of her and she began to feel as if the strange talk she had just had with her husband must have taken place in another world, between two beings who were not Charlotte Gorse and Kenneth Ashby, but phantoms projected by her fevered imagination. She recalled the year since her marriage—her husband's constant devotion; his persistent, almost too insistent tenderness; the feeling he had given her at times of being too eagerly dependent on her, too searchingly close to her, as if there were not air enough between her soul and his. It seemed preposterous, as she recalled all this, that a few moments ago she should have been accusing him of an intrigue with another woman! But, then, what—

Again she was moved by the impulse to go up to him, beg his pardon and try to laugh away the misunderstanding. But she was restrained by the fear of forcing herself upon his privacy. He was troubled and unhappy, oppressed by some grief or fear; and he had shown her that he wanted to fight out his battle alone. It would be wiser, as well as more generous, to respect his wish. Only, how strange, how unbearable, to be there, in the next room to his, and feel herself at the other end of the world! In her nervous agitation she almost regretted not having had the courage to open the letter and put it back on the hall table before he came in. At least she would have known what his secret was, and the bogy might have been laid. For she was beginning now to think of the mystery as something conscious, malevolent: a secret persecution before which he quailed, yet from which he could not free himself. Once or twice in his evasive eyes she thought she had detected a desire for help, an impulse of confession, instantly restrained and suppressed. It was as if he felt she could have helped him if she had known, and yet had been unable to tell her!

There flashed through her mind the idea of going to his mother. She was very fond of old Mrs. Ashby, a firm-fleshed clear-eyed old lady, with an astringent bluntness of speech which responded to the forthright and simple in Charlotte's own nature. There had been a tacit bond between them ever since the day when Mrs. Ashby senior, coming to lunch for the first time with her new daughter-in-law, had been received by Charlotte downstairs in the library, and glancing up at the empty wall above her son's desk, had remarked laconically: "Elsie gone, eh?" adding, at Charlotte's murmured explanation: "Nonsense. Don't have her back. Two's company." Charlotte, at this reading of her thoughts, could hardly refrain from exchanging a smile of complicity with her mother-in-law; and it seemed to her now that Mrs. Ashby's almost uncanny directness might pierce to the core of this new mystery. But here again she hesitated, for the idea almost suggested a betrayal. What right had she to call in any one, even so close a relation, to surprise a secret which her husband was trying to keep from her? "Perhaps, by and by, he'll talk to his mother of his own accord," she thought, and then ended: "But what does it matter? He and I must settle it between us."

She was still brooding over the problem when there was a knock on the door and her husband came in. He was dressed for dinner and seemed surprised to see her sitting there, with her evening dress lying unheeded on the bed.

"Aren't you coming down?"

"I thought you were not well and had gone to bed," she faltered.

He forced a smile. "I'm not particularly well, but we'd better go down." His face, though still drawn, looked calmer than when he had fled upstairs an hour earlier.

110

"There it is; he knows what's in the letter and has fought his battle out again, whatever it is," she reflected, "while I'm still in darkness." She rang and gave a hurried order that dinner should be served as soon as possible—just a short meal, whatever could be got ready quickly, as both she and Mr. Ashby were rather tired and not very hungry.

Dinner was announced, and they sat down to it. At first neither seemed able to find a word to say; then Ashby began to make conversation with an assumption of ease that was more oppressive than his silence. "How tired he is! How terribly overtired!" Charlotte said to herself, pursuing her own thoughts while he rambled on about municipal politics, aviation, an exhibition of modern French painting, the health of an old aunt and the installing of the automatic telephone. "Good heavens, how tired he is!"

When they dined alone they usually went into the library after dinner, and Charlotte curled herself up on the divan with her knitting while he settled down in his armchair under the lamp and lit a pipe. But this evening, by tacit agreement, they avoided the room in which their strange talk had taken place, and went up to Charlotte's drawing-room.

They sat down near the fire, and Charlotte said: "Your pipe?" after he had put down his hardly tasted coffee.

He shook his head. "No, not tonight."

"You must go to bed early; you look terribly tired. I'm sure they overwork you at the office."

"I suppose we all overwork at times."

She rose and stood before him with sudden resolution. "Well, I'm not going to have you use up your strength slaving in that way. It's absurd. I can see you're ill." She bent over him and laid her hand on his forehead. "My poor old Kenneth. Prepare to be taken away soon on a long holiday."

He looked up at her, startled. "A holiday?"

"Certainly. Didn't you know I was going to carry you off at Easter? We're going to start in a fortnight on a month's voyage to somewhere or other. On any one of the big cruising steamers." She paused and bent closer, touching his forehead with her lips. "I'm tired, too, Kenneth."

He seemed to pay no heed to her last words, but sat, his hands on his knees, his head drawn back a little from her caress, and looked up at her with a stare of apprehension. "Again? My dear, we can't; I can't possibly go away."

"I don't know why you say 'again,' Kenneth; we haven't taken a real holiday this year."

"At Christmas we spent a week with the children in the country."

"Yes, but this time I mean away from the children, from servants, from the house. From everything that's familiar and fatiguing. Your mother will love to have Joyce and Peter with her."

He frowned and slowly shook his head. "No, dear; I can't leave them with my mother."

"Why, Kenneth, how absurd; she adores them. You didn't hesitate to leave them with her for over two months when we went to the West Indies."

He drew a deep breath and stood up uneasily. "That was different."

"Different? Why?"

"I mean, at that time I didn't realize"—He broke off as if to choose his words and then went on: "My mother adores the children, as you say. But she isn't always very judicious. Grandmothers always spoil children. And she sometimes talks before them without thinking." He turned to his wife with an almost pitiful gesture of entreaty. "Don't ask me to, dear."

Charlotte mused. It was true that the elder Mrs. Ashby had a fearless tongue, but she was the last woman in the world to say or hint anything before her grandchildren at which the most scrupulous parent could take offense. Charlotte looked at her husband in perplexity.

"I don't understand."

He continued to turn on her the same troubled and entreating gaze. "Don't try to," he muttered.

"Not try to?"   135

"Not now—not yet." He put up his hands and pressed them against his temples. "Can't you see that there's no use in insisting? I can't go away, no matter how much I might want to."

Charlotte still scrutinized him gravely. "The question is, do you want to?"

He returned her gaze for a moment; then his lips began to tremble, and he said, hardly above his breath: "I want—anything you want."

"And yet—"

"Don't ask me. I can't leave—I can't!"   140

"You mean that you can't go away out of reach of those letters!"

Her husband had been standing before her in an uneasy half-hesitating attitude; now he turned abruptly away and walked once or twice up and down the length of the room, his head bent, his eyes fixed on the carpet.

Charlotte felt her resentfulness rising with her fears. "It's that," she persisted. "Why not admit it? You can't live without them."

He continued his troubled pacing of the room; then he stopped short, dropped into a chair and covered his face with his hands. From the shaking of his shoulders, Charlotte saw that he was weeping. She had never seen a man cry, except her father after her mother's death, when she was a little girl; and she remembered still how the sight had frightened her. She was frightened now; she felt that her husband was being dragged away from her into some mysterious bondage, and that she must use up her last atom of strength in the struggle for his freedom, and for hers.

"Kenneth—Kenneth!" she pleaded, kneeling down beside him. "Won't you listen   145
to me? Won't you try to see what I'm suffering? I'm not unreasonable, darling; really not. I don't suppose I should ever have noticed the letters if it hadn't been for their effect on you. It's not my way to pry into other people's affairs; and even if the effect had been different—yes, yes; listen to me—if I'd seen that the letters made you happy, that you were watching eagerly for them, counting the days between their coming, that you wanted them, that they gave you something I haven't known how to give—why, Kenneth, I don't say I shouldn't have suffered from that, too; but it would have been in a different way, and I should have had the courage to hide what I felt, and the hope that some day you'd come to feel about me as you did about the writer of the letters. But what I can't bear is to see how you dread them, how they make you suffer, and yet how you can't live without them and won't go away lest you should miss one during your absence. Or perhaps," she added, her voice breaking into a cry of accusation—"perhaps it's because she's actually forbidden you to leave. Kenneth, you must answer me! Is that the reason? Is it because she's forbidden you that you won't go away with me?"

She continued to kneel at his side, and raising her hands, she drew his gently down. She was ashamed of her persistence, ashamed of uncovering that baffled disordered face, yet resolved that no such scruples should arrest her. His eyes were lowered, the muscles of his face quivered; she was making him suffer even more than she suffered herself. Yet this no longer restrained her.

"Kenneth, is it that? She won't let us go away together?"

Still he did not speak or turn his eyes to her; and a sense of defeat swept over her. After all, she thought, the struggle was a losing one. "You needn't answer. I see I'm right," she said.

Suddenly, as she rose, he turned and drew her down again. His hands caught hers and pressed them so tightly that she felt her rings cutting into her flesh. There was something frightened, convulsive in his hold; it was the clutch of a man who felt himself slipping over a precipice. He was staring up at her now as if salvation lay in the face she bent above him. "Of course we'll go away together. We'll go wherever you want," he said in a low confused voice; and putting his arm about her, he drew her close and pressed his lips on hers.

IV

Charlotte had said to herself: "I shall sleep tonight," but instead she sat before her fire   150
into the small hours, listening for any sound that came from her husband's room. But he, at any rate, seemed to be resting after the tumult of the evening. Once or twice she stole to the door and in the faint light that came in from the street through his open window she saw him stretched out in heavy sleep—the sleep of weakness and exhaustion. "He's ill," she thought—"he's undoubtedly ill. And it's not overwork; it's this mysterious persecution."

She drew a breath of relief. She had fought through the weary fight and the victory was hers—at least for the moment. If only they could have started at once—started for anywhere! She knew it would be useless to ask him to leave before the holidays; and meanwhile the secret influence—as to which she was still so completely in the dark—would continue to work against her, and she would have to renew the struggle day after day till they started on their journey. But after that everything would be different. If once she could get her husband away under other skies, and all to herself, she never doubted her power to release him from the evil spell he was under.

Lulled to quiet by the thought, she too slept at last.

When she woke, it was long past her usual hour, and she sat up in bed surprised and vexed at having overslept herself. She always liked to be down to share her husband's breakfast by the library fire; but a glance at the clock made it clear that he must have started long since for his office. To make sure, she jumped out of bed and went into his room; but it was empty. No doubt he had looked in or on her before leaving, seen that she still slept, and gone downstairs without disturbing her; and their relations were sufficiently loverlike for her to regret having missed their morning hour.

She rang and asked if Mr. Ashby had already gone. Yes, nearly an hour ago, the maid said. He had given orders that Mrs. Ashby should not be waked and that the children should not come to her till she sent for them. . . . Yes, he had gone up to the nursery himself to give the order. All this sounded usual enough; and Charlotte hardly knew why she asked: "And did Mr. Ashby leave no other message?"

Yes, the maid said, he did; she was so sorry she'd forgotten. He'd told her, just as he   155
was leaving, to say to Mrs. Ashby that he was going to see about their passages, and would she please be ready to sail tomorrow?

Charlotte echoed the woman's "Tomorrow," and sat staring at her incredulously. "Tomorrow—you're sure he said to sail tomorrow?"

"Oh, ever so sure, ma'am. I don't know how I could have forgotten to mention it."

"Well, it doesn't matter. Draw my bath, please." Charlotte sprang up, dashed through her dressing, and caught herself singing at her image in the glass as she sat brushing her hair. It made her feel young again to have scored such a victory. The other woman vanished to a speck on the horizon, as this one, who ruled the foreground, smiled back at the reflection of her lips and eyes. He loved her, then—he loved her as passionately as ever. He had divined what she had suffered, had understood that their happiness depended on their getting away at once, and finding each other again after yesterday's desperate groping in the fog. The nature of the influence that had come between them did not much matter to Charlotte now; she had faced the phantom and dispelled it. "Courage—that's the secret! If only people who are in love weren't always so afraid of risking their happiness by looking it in the eyes." As she brushed back her light abundant hair it waved electrically above her head, like the palms of victory. Ah, well, some women knew how to manage men, and some didn't—and only the fair—she gaily paraphrased— deserved the brave!° Certainly she was looking very pretty.

The morning danced along like a cockleshell on a bright sea—such a sea as they would soon be speeding over. She ordered a particularly good dinner, saw the children off to their classes, had her trunks brought down, consulted with the maid about getting out summer clothes—for of course they would be heading for heat and sunshine—and wondered if she oughtn't to take Kenneth's flannel suits out of camphor. "But how absurd," she reflected, "that I don't yet know where we're going!" She looked at the clock, saw that it was close on noon, and decided to call him up at his office. There was a slight delay; then she heard his secretary's voice saying that Mr. Ashby had looked in for a moment early, and left again almost immediately. . . . Oh, very well; Charlotte would ring up later. How soon was he likely to be back? The secretary answered that she couldn't tell; all they knew in the office was that when he left he had said he was in a hurry because he had to go out of town.

Out of town! Charlotte hung up the receiver and sat blankly gazing into new dark- 160
ness. Why had he gone out of town? And where had he gone? And of all days, why should he have chosen the eve of their suddenly planned departure? She felt a faint shiver of apprehension. Of course he had gone to see that woman—no doubt to get her permission to leave. He was as completely in bondage as that; and Charlotte had been fatuous enough to see the palms of victory on her forehead. She burst into a laugh and, walking across the room, sat down again before her mirror. What a different face she saw! The smile on her pale lips seemed to mock the rosy vision of the other Charlotte. But gradually her color crept back. After all, she had a right to claim the victory, since her husband was doing what she wanted, not what the other woman exacted of him. It was natural enough, in view of his abrupt decision to leave the next day, that he should have arrangements to make, business matters to wind up; it was not even necessary to suppose that his mysterious trip was a visit to the writer of the letters. He might simply have gone to see a client who lived out of town. Of course they would not tell Charlotte at the office; the secretary had hesitated before imparting even such meager information as the fact of Mr. Ashby's absence. Meanwhile she would go on with her joyful preparations, content to learn later in the day to what particular island of the blest she was to be carried.

The hours wore on, or rather were swept forward on a rush of eager preparations. At last the entrance of the maid who came to draw the curtains roused Charlotte from her labors, and she saw to her surprise that the clock marked five. And she did not yet know where they were going the next day! She rang up her husband's office and was told that Mr. Ashby had not been there since the early morning. She asked for his partner, but the partner could add nothing to her information, for he himself, his suburban train having been behind time, had reached the office after Ashby had come and gone. Charlotte stood perplexed; then she decided to telephone to her mother-in-law. Of course Kenneth, on the eve of a month's absence, must have gone to see his mother. The mere fact that the children—in spite of his vague objections—would certainly have to be left with old Mrs. Ashby, made it obvious that he would have all sorts of matters to

---

brave: Inverted from "Only the brave deserve the fair," a famous line from John Dryden's poem "Alexander's Feast."

decide with her. At another time Charlotte might have felt a little hurt at being excluded from their conference, but nothing mattered now but that she had won the day, that her husband was still hers and not another woman's. Gaily she called up Mrs. Ashby, heard her friendly voice, and began: "Well, did Kenneth's news surprise you? What do you think of our elopement?"

Almost instantly, before Mrs. Ashby could answer, Charlotte knew what her reply would be. Mrs. Ashby had not seen her son, she had had no word from him and did not know what her daughter-in-law meant. Charlotte stood silent in the intensity of her surprise. "But then, where has he been?" she thought. Then, recovering herself, she explained their sudden decision to Mrs. Ashby, and in doing so, gradually regained her own self-confidence, her conviction that nothing could ever again come between Kenneth and herself. Mrs. Ashby took the news calmly and approvingly. She, too, had thought that Kenneth looked worried and overtired, and she agreed with her daughter-in-law that in such cases change was the surest remedy. "I'm always so glad when he gets away. Elsie hated traveling; she was always finding pretexts to prevent his going anywhere. With you, thank goodness, it's different." Nor was Mrs. Ashby surprised at his not having had time to let her know of his departure. He must have been in a rush from the moment the decision was taken; but no doubt he'd drop in before dinner. Five minutes' talk was really all they needed. "I hope you'll gradually cure Kenneth of his mania for going over and over a question that could be settled in a dozen words. He never used to be like that, and if he carried the habit into his professional work he'd soon lose all his clients. . . . Yes, do come in for a minute, dear, if you have time; no doubt he'll turn up while you're here." The tonic ring of Mrs. Ashby's voice echoed on reassuringly in the silent room while Charlotte continued her preparations.

Toward seven the telephone rang, and she darted to it. Now she would know! But it was only from the conscientious secretary, to say that Mr. Ashby hadn't been back, or sent any word, and before the office closed she thought she ought to let Mrs. Ashby know. "Oh, that's all right. Thanks a lot!" Charlotte called out cheerfully, and hung up the receiver with a trembling hand. But perhaps by this time, she reflected, he was at his mother's. She shut her drawers and cupboards, put on her hat and coat and called up to the nursery that she was going out for a minute to see the thildren's grandmother.

Mrs. Ashby lived near by, and during her brief walk through the cold spring dusk Charlotte imagined that every advancing figure was her husband's. But she did not meet him on the way, and when she entered the house she found her mother-in-law alone. Kenneth had neither telephoned nor come. Old Mrs. Ashby sat by her bright fire, her knitting needles flashing steadily through her active old hands, and her mere bodily presence gave reassurance to Charlotte. Yes, it was certainly odd that Kenneth had gone off for the whole day without letting any of them know; but, after all, it was to be expected. A busy lawyer held so many threads in his hands that any sudden change of plan would oblige him to make all sorts of unforeseen arrangements and adjustments. He might have gone to see some client in the suburbs and been detained there; his mother remembered his telling her that he had charge of the legal business of a queer old recluse somewhere in New Jersey, who was immensely rich but too mean to have a telephone. Very likely Kenneth had been stranded there.

But Charlotte felt her nervousness gaining on her. When Mrs. Ashby asked her at what hour they were sailing the next day and she had to say she didn't know—that Kenneth had simply sent her word he was going to take their passages—the uttering of the words again brought home to her the strangeness of the situation. Even Mrs. Ashby conceded that it was odd; but she immediately added that it only showed what a rush he was in.

"But, mother, it's nearly eight o'clock! He must realize that I've got to know when we're starting tomorrow."

"Oh, the boat probably doesn't sail till evening. Sometimes they have to wait till midnight for the tide. Kenneth's probably counting on that. After all, he has a level head."

Charlotte stood up. "It's not that. Something has happened to him."

Mrs. Ashby took off her spectacles and rolled up her knitting. "If you begin to let yourself imagine things—"

"Aren't you in the least anxious?"

"I never am till I have to be. I wish you'd ring for dinner, my dear. You'll stay and dine? He's sure to drop in here on his way home."

Charlotte called up her own house. No, the maid said, Mr. Ashby hadn't come in and hadn't telephoned. She would tell him as soon as he came that Mrs. Ashby was dining at his mother's. Charlotte followed her mother-in-law into the dining-room and sat with parched throat before her empty plate, while Mrs. Ashby dealt calmly and efficiently with a short but carefully prepared repast. "You'd better eat something, child, or you'll be as bad as Kenneth. . . . Yes, a little more asparagus, please, Jane."

She insisted on Charlotte's drinking a glass of sherry and nibbling a bit of toast; then they returned to the drawing-room, where the fire had been made up, and the cushions in Mrs. Ashby's armchair shaken out and smoothed. How safe and familiar it all looked; and out there, somewhere in the uncertainty and mystery of the night, lurked the answer to the two women's conjectures, like an indistinguishable figure prowling on the threshold.

At last Charlotte got up and said: "I'd better go back. At this hour Kenneth will certainly go straight home."

Mrs. Ashby smiled indulgently. "It's not very late, my dear. It doesn't take two sparrows long to dine."

"It's after nine." Charlotte bent down to kiss her. "The fact is, I can't keep still."

Mrs. Ashby pushed aside her work and rested her two hands on the arms of her chair. "I'm going with you," she said, helping herself up.

Charlotte protested that it was too late, that it was not necessary, that she would call up as soon as Kenneth came in, but Mrs. Ashby had already rung for her maid. She was slightly lame, and stood resting on her stick while her wraps were brought. "If Mr. Kenneth turns up, tell him he'll find me at his own house," she instructed the maid as the two women got into the taxi which had been summoned. During the short drive Charlotte gave thanks that she was not returning home alone. There was something warm and substantial in the mere fact of Mrs. Ashby's nearness, something that corresponded with the clearness of her eyes and the texture of her fresh firm complexion. As the taxi drew up she laid her hand encouragingly on Charlotte's. "You'll see; there'll be a message."

The door opened at Charlotte's ring and the two entered. Charlotte's heart beat excitedly; the stimulus of her mother-in-law's confidence was beginning to flow through her veins.

"You'll see—you'll see," Mrs. Ashby repeated.

The maid who opened the door said no, Mr. Ashby had not come in, and there had been no message from him.

"You're sure the telephone's not out of order?" his mother suggested; and the maid said, well, it certainly wasn't half an hour ago; but she'd just go and ring up to make sure. She disappeared, and Charlotte turned to take off her hat and cloak. As she did so her eyes lit on the hall table, and there lay a gray envelope, her husband's name faintly traced on it. "Oh!" she cried out, suddenly aware that for the first time in months she had entered her house without wondering if one of the gray letters would be there.

"What is it, my dear?" Mrs. Ashby asked with a glance of surprise.

170

175

180

Charlotte did not answer. She took up the envelope and stood staring at it as if she could force her gaze to penetrate to what was within. Then an idea occurred to her. She turned and held out the envelope to her mother-in-law.

"Do you know that writing?" she asked.

Mrs. Ashby took the letter. She had to feel with her other hand for her eyeglasses, and when she had adjusted them she lifted the envelope to the light. "Why!" she exclaimed; and then stopped. Charlotte noticed that the letter shook in her usually firm hand. "But this is addressed to Kenneth," Mrs. Ashby said at length, in a low voice. Her tone seemed to imply that she felt her daughter-in-law's question to be slightly indiscreet.

"Yes, but no matter," Charlotte spoke with sudden decision. "I want to know—do you know the writing?"

Mrs. Ashby handed back the letter. "No," she said distinctly.

The two women had turned into the library. Charlotte switched on the electric light and shut the door. She still held the envelope in her hand.

"I'm going to open it," she announced.

She caught her mother-in-law's startled glance. "But, dearest—a letter not addressed to you? My dear, you can't!"

"As if I cared about that—now!" She continued to look intently at Mrs. Ashby. "This letter may tell me where Kenneth is."

Mrs. Ashby's glossy bloom was effaced by a quick pallor; her firm cheeks seemed to shrink and wither. "Why should it? What makes you believe—It can't possibly—"

Charlotte held her eyes steadily on that altered face. "Ah, then you do know the writing?" she flashed back.

"Know the writing? How should I? With all my son's correspondents. . . . What I do know is—" Mrs. Ashby broke off and looked at her daughter-in-law entreatingly, almost timidly.

Charlotte caught her by the wrist. "Mother! What do you know? Tell me! You must!"

"That I don't believe any good ever came of a woman's opening her husband's letters behind his back."

The words sounded to Charlotte's irritated ears as flat as a phrase culled from a book of moral axioms. She laughed impatiently and dropped her mother-in-law's wrist. "Is that all? No good can come of this letter, opened or unopened. I know that well enough. But whatever ill comes, I mean to find out what's in it." Her hands had been trembling as they held the envelope, but now they grew firm, and her voice also. She still gazed intently at Mrs. Ashby. "This is the ninth letter addressed in the same hand that has come for Kenneth since we've been married. Always these same gray envelopes. I've kept count of them because after each one he has been like a man who has had some dreadful shock. It takes him hours to shake off their effect. I've told him so. I've told him I must know from whom they come, because I can see they're killing him. He won't answer my questions; he says he can't tell me anything about the letters; but last night he promised to go away with me—to get away from them."

Mrs. Ashby, with shaking steps, had gone to one of the armchairs and sat down in it, her head drooping forward on her breast. "Ah," she murmured.

"So now you understand—"

"Did he tell you it was to get away from them?"

"He said, to get away—to get away. He was sobbing so that he could hardly speak. But I told him I knew that was why."

"And what did he say?"

"He took me in his arms and said he'd go wherever I wanted."

"Ah, thank God!" said Mrs. Ashby. There was a silence, during which she continued   205
to sit with bowed head, and eyes averted from her daughter-in-law. At last she looked up
and spoke. "Are you sure there have been as many as nine?"

"Perfectly. This is the ninth. I've kept count."

"And he has absolutely refused to explain?"

"Absolutely."

Mrs. Ashby spoke through pale contracted lips. "When did they begin to come? Do
you remember?"

Charlotte laughed again. "Remember? The first one came the night we got back   210
from our honeymoon."

"All that time?" Mrs. Ashby lifted her head and spoke with sudden energy. "Then—
Yes, open it."

The words were so unexpected that Charlotte felt the blood in her temples, and her
hands began to tremble again. She tried to slip her finger under the flap of the envelope,
but it was so tightly stuck that she had to hunt on her husband's writing table for his ivory
letter-opener. As she pushed about the familiar objects his own hands had so lately
touched, they sent through her the icy chill emanating from the little personal effects of
someone newly dead. In the deep silence of the room the tearing of the paper as she slit
the envelope sounded like a human cry. She drew out the sheet and carried it to the lamp.

"Well?" Mrs. Ashby asked below her breath.

Charlotte did not move or answer. She was bending over the page with wrinkled
brows, holding it nearer and nearer to the light. Her sight must be blurred, or else dazzled by the reflection of the lamplight on the smooth surface of the paper, for, strain her
eyes as she would, she could discern only a few faint strokes, so faint and faltering as to be
nearly undecipherable.

"I can't make it out," she said.   215

"What do you mean, dear?"

"The writing's too indistinct. . . . Wait."

She went back to the table and, sitting down close to Kenneth's reading lamp,
slipped the letter under a magnifying glass. All this time she was aware that her mother-
in-law was watching her intently.

"Well?" Mrs. Ashby breathed.

"Well, it's no clearer. I can't read it."   220

"You mean the paper is an absolute blank?"

"No, not quite. There is writing on it. I can make out something like 'mine'—oh,
and 'come.' It might be 'come.' "

Mrs. Ashby stood up abruptly. Her face was even paler than before. She advanced
to the table and, resting her two hands on it, drew a deep breath. "Let me see," she said,
as if forcing herself to a hateful effort.

Charlotte felt the contagion of her whiteness. "She knows," she thought. She
pushed the letter across the table. Her mother-in-law lowered her head over it in silence,
but without touching it with her pale wrinkled hands.

Charlotte stood watching her as she herself, when she had tried to read the letter,   225
had been watched by Mrs. Ashby. The latter fumbled for her glasses, held them to her
eyes, and bent still closer to the outspread page, in order, as it seemed, to avoid touching
it. The light of the lamp fell directly on her old face, and Charlotte reflected what depths
of the unknown may lurk under the clearest and most candid lineaments. She had never
seen her mother-in-law's features express any but simple and sound emotions—cordiality,
amusement, a kindly sympathy; now and again a flash of wholesome anger. Now
they seemed to wear a look of fear and hatred, of incredulous dismay and almost cringing

defiance. It was as if the spirits warring within her had distorted her face to their own likeness. At length she raised her head. "I can't—I can't," she said in a voice of childish distress.

"You can't make it out either?"

She shook her head, and Charlotte saw two tears roll down her cheeks.

"Familiar as the writing is to you?" Charlotte insisted with twitching lips.

Mrs. Ashby did not take up the challenge. "I can make out nothing—nothing."

"But you do know the writing?"   230

Mrs. Ashby lifted her head timidly; her anxious eyes stole with a glance of apprehension around the quiet familiar room. "How can I tell? I was startled at first. . . ."

"Startled by the resemblance?"

"Well, I thought—"

"You'd better say it out, mother! You knew at once it was *her* writing?"

"Oh, wait, my dear—wait."   235

"Wait for what?"

Mrs. Ashby looked up; her eyes, travelling slowly past Charlotte, were lifted to the
blank wall behind her son's writing table.

Charlotte, following the glance, burst into a shrill laugh of accusation. "I needn't
wait any longer! You've answered me now! You're looking straight at the wall where her
picture used to hang!"

Mrs. Ashby lifted her hand with a murmur of warning. "Sh-h."

"Oh, you needn't imagine that anything can ever frighten me again!" Charlotte   240
cried.

Her mother-in-law still leaned against the table. Her lips moved plaintively. "But
we're going mad—we're both going mad. We both know such things are impossible."

Her daughter-in-law looked at her with a pitying stare. "I've known for a long time
now that everything was possible."

"Even this?"

"Yes, exactly this."

"But this letter—after all, there's nothing in this letter—"   245

"Perhaps there would be to him. How can I tell? I remember his saying to me once
that if you were used to a handwriting the faintest stroke of it became legible. Now I see
what he meant. He was used to it."

"But the few strokes that I can make out are so pale. No one could possibly read
that letter."

Charlotte laughed again. "I suppose everything's pale about a ghost," she said
stridently.

"Oh, my child—my child—don't say it!"

"Why shouldn't I say it, when even the bare walls cry it out? What difference does it   250
make if her letters are illegible to you and me? If even you can see her face on that blank
wall, why shouldn't he read her writing on this blank paper? Don't you see that she's
everywhere in this house, and the closer to him because to everyone else she's become invisible?" Charlotte dropped into a chair and covered her face with her hands. A turmoil
of sobbing shook her from head to foot. At length a touch on her shoulder made her
look up, and she saw her mother-in-law bending over her. Mrs. Ashby's face seemed to
have grown still smaller and more wasted, but it had resumed its usual quiet look.
Through all her tossing anguish, Charlotte felt the impact of that resolute spirit.

"Tomorrow—tomorrow. You'll see. There'll be some explanation tomorrow."

Charlotte cut her short. "An explanation? Who's going to give it, I wonder?"

Mrs. Ashby drew back and straightened herself heroically. "Kenneth himself will,"
she cried out in a strong voice. Charlotte said nothing, and the old woman went on: "But

meanwhile we must act; we must notify the police. Now, without a moment's delay. We must do everything—everything."

Charlotte stood up slowly and stiffly; her joints felt as cramped as an old woman's. "Exactly as if we thought it could do any good to do anything?"

Resolutely Mrs. Ashby cried: "Yes!" and Charlotte went up to the telephone and un-   255
hooked the receiver.

QUESTIONS

1. What does the title mean? How does the title determine the story's events?
2. Wharton includes many similes and comparisons in the story, such as "she felt that her husband was being dragged away from her into some mysterious bondage" (paragraph 144), and "her joints felt as cramped as an old woman's" (paragraph 254), and "It was as if the spirits warring within her had distorted her face to their own likeness" (paragraph 225). How do such comparisons and similes contribute to the ghostliness of "Pomegranate Seed"?
3. Why does Wharton not explain the origin of the letters? What would be the effect on the story if she had made this explanation?
4. In what ways does the ghost plot depend on the character traits of Charlotte and Kenneth?
5. How may "Pomegranate Seed" be read symbolically and allegorically?

Roman Fever ⫸⟨⟨⟨⟨⟨   1934

From the table at which they had been lunching two American ladies of ripe but well-cared-for middle age moved across the lofty terrace of the Roman restaurant and, leaning on its parapet, looked first at each other, and then down on the outspread glories of the Palatine and the Forum, with the same expression of vague but benevolent approval.

As they leaned there a girlish voice echoed up gaily from the stairs leading to the court below. "Well, come along, then," it cried, not to them but to an invisible companion, "and let's leave the young things to their knitting;" and a voice as fresh laughed back: "Oh, look here, Babs, not actually *knitting*—" "Well, I mean figuratively," rejoined the first. "After all, we haven't left our poor parents much else to do . . ." and at that point the turn of the stairs engulfed the dialogue.

The two ladies looked at each other again, this time with a tinge of smiling embarrassment, and the smaller and paler one shook her head and colored—slightly.

"Barbara!" she murmured, sending an unheard rebuke after the mocking voice in the stairway.

The other lady, who was fuller, and higher in color, with a small determined nose   5
supported by vigorous black eyebrows, gave a good-humored laugh. "That's what our daughters think of us!"

Her companion replied by a deprecating gesture. "Not of us individually. We must remember that. It's just the collective modern idea of Mothers. And you see—" Half-guiltily she drew from her handsomely mounted black hand-bag a twist of crimson silk run through by two fine knitting needles. "One never knows," she murmured. "The new system has certainly given us a good deal of time to kill; and sometimes I get tired just looking—even at this." Her gesture was now addressed to the stupendous scene at their feet.

The dark lady laughed again, and they both relapsed upon the view, contemplating it in silence, with a sort of diffused serenity which might have been borrowed from the spring effulgence of the Roman skies. The luncheon-hour was long past, and the two had their end of the vast terrace to themselves. At its opposite extremity a few groups, detained by a lingering look at the outspread city, were gathering up guidebooks and fumbling for tips. The last of them scattered, and the two ladies were alone on the air-washed height.

"Well, I don't see why we shouldn't just stay here," said Mrs. Slade, the lady of the high color and energetic brows. Two derelict basket-chairs stood near, and she pushed them into the angle of the parapet, and settled herself in one, her gaze upon the Palatine. "After all, it's still the most beautiful view in the world."

"It always will be, to me," assented her friend Mrs. Ansley, with so slight a stress on the "me" that Mrs. Slade, though she noticed it, wondered if it were not merely accidental, like the random underlinings of old-fashioned letter-writers.

"Grace Ansley was always old-fashioned," she thought; and added aloud, with a retrospective smile: "It's a view we've both been familiar with for a good many years. When we first met here we were younger than our girls are now. You remember?"   10

"Oh, yes, I remember," murmured Mrs. Ansley, with the same undefinable stress— "There's that head-waiter wondering," she interpolated. She was evidently far less sure than her companion of herself and of her rights in the world.

"I'll cure him of wondering," said Mrs. Slade, stretching her hand toward a bag as discreetly opulent-looking as Mrs. Ansley's. Signing to the head-waiter, she explained that she and her friend were old lovers of Rome, and would like to spend the end of the afternoon looking down on the view—that is, if it did not disturb the service? The head-waiter, bowing over her gratuity, assured her that the ladies were most welcome, and would be still more so if they would condescend to remain for dinner. A full moon night, they would remember.

Mrs. Slade's black brows drew together, as though references to the moon were out-of-place and even unwelcome. But she smiled away her frown as the head-waiter retreated. "Well, why not? We might do worse. There's no knowing, I suppose, when the girls will be back. Do you even know back from *where*? *I* don't!"

Mrs. Ansley again colored slightly. "I think those young Italian aviators we met at the Embassy invited them to fly to Tarquinia for tea. I suppose they'll want to wait and fly back by moonlight."

"Moonlight—moonlight! What a part it still plays. Do you suppose they're as sentimental as we were?"   15

"I've come to the conclusion that I don't in the least know what they are," said Mrs. Ansley. "And perhaps we didn't know much more about each other."

"No, perhaps we didn't."

Her friend gave her a shy glance. "I never should have supposed you were sentimental, Alida."

"Well, perhaps I wasn't." Mrs. Slade drew her lids together in retrospect; and for a few moments the two ladies, who had been intimate since childhood, reflected how little they knew each other. Each one, of course, had a label ready to attach to the other's name; Mrs. Delphin Slade, for instance, would have told herself, or any one who asked her, that Mrs. Horace Ansley, twenty-five years ago, had been exquisitely lovely—no, you wouldn't believe it, would you? . . . though, of course, still charming, distinguished. . . . Well, as a girl she had been exquisite; far more beautiful than her daughter Barbara, though certainly Babs, according to the new standards at any rate, was more effective— had more *edge*, as they say. Funny where she got it, with those two nullities as parents. Yes; Horace Ansley was—well, just the duplicate of his wife. Museum specimens of old New York. Good-looking, irreproachable, exemplary. Mrs. Slade and Mrs. Ansley had lived opposite each other—actually as well as figuratively—for years. When the drawing-room curtains in No. 20 East 73rd Street were renewed, No. 23, across the way, was always aware of it. And of all the movings, buyings, travels, anniversaries, illnesses—the tame chronicle of an estimable pair. Little of it escaped Mrs. Slade. But she had grown bored with it by the time her husband made his big *coup* in Wall Street, and when they bought in upper Park Avenue had already begun to think: "I'd rather live opposite a speak-easy for a change; at least one might see it raided." The idea of seeing Grace raided was so amusing that (before the move) she launched it at a woman's lunch. It made a hit, and went the rounds—she sometimes wondered if it had crossed the street, and reached Mrs. Ansley. She hoped not, but didn't much mind. Those were the days when respectability was at a discount, and it did the irreproachable no harm to laugh at them a little.

A few years later, and not many months apart, both ladies lost their husbands. There was an appropriate exchange of wreaths and condolences, and a brief renewal of intimacy in the half-shadow of their mourning; and now, after another interval, they had run across each other in Rome, at the same hotel, each of them the modest appendage of a salient daughter. The similarity of their lot had again drawn them together, lending itself to mild jokes, and the mutual confession that, if in old days it must have been tiring to "keep up" with daughters, it was now, at times, a little dull not to.

No doubt, Mrs. Slade reflected, she felt her unemployment more than poor Grace ever would. It was a big drop from being the wife of Delphin Slade to being his widow. She had always regarded herself (with a certain conjugal pride) as his equal in social gifts, as contributing her full share to the making of the exceptional couple they were: but the difference after his death was irremediable. As the wife of the famous corporation lawyer, always with an international case or two on hand, every day brought its exciting and unexpected obligation: the impromptu entertaining of eminent colleagues from abroad, the hurried dashes on legal business to London, Paris or Rome, where the entertaining was so handsomely reciprocated; the amusement of hearing in her wake: "What, that handsome woman with the good clothes and the eyes is Mrs. Slade—*the* Slade's wife? Really? Generally the wives of celebrities are such frumps."

Yes; being *the* Slade's widow was a dullish business after that. In living up to such a husband all her faculties had been engaged; now she had only her daughter to live up to, for the son who seemed to have inherited his father's gifts had died suddenly in boyhood. She had fought through that agony because her husband was there, to be helped and to help; now, after the father's death, the thought of the boy had become unbearable. There was nothing left but to mother her daughter; and dear Jenny was such a perfect daughter that she needed no excessive mothering. "Now with Babs Ansley I don't know that I should be so quiet," Mrs. Slade sometimes half-enviously reflected; but Jenny, who was younger than her brilliant friend, was that rare accident, an extremely pretty girl who somehow made youth and prettiness seem as safe as their absence. It was all perplexing—and to Mrs. Slade a little boring. She wished that Jenny would fall in love—with the wrong man, even; that she might have to be watched, outmaneuvred, rescued. And instead, it was Jenny who watched her mother, kept her out of draughts, made sure that she had taken her tonic.

Mrs. Ansley was much less articulate than her friend, and her mental portrait of Mrs. Slade was slighter, and drawn with fainter touches. "Alida Slade's awfully brilliant; but not as brilliant as she thinks," would have summed it up; though she would have added, for the enlightenment of strangers, that Mrs. Slade had been an extremely dashing girl; much more so than her daughter, who was pretty, of course, and clever in a way, but had none of her mother's—well, "vividness," someone had once called it. Mrs. Ansley would take up current words like this, and cite them in quotation marks, as unheard-of audacities. No: Jenny was not like her mother. Sometimes Mrs. Ansley thought Alida Slade was disappointed; on the whole she had had a sad life. Full of failures and mistakes; Mrs. Ansley had always been rather sorry for her. . . .

20

So these two ladies visualized each other, each through the wrong end of her little telescope.

II

For a long time they continued to sit side by side without speaking. It seemed as though, to both, there was a relief in laying down their somewhat futile activities in the presence of the vast Memento Mori which faced them. Mrs. Slade sat quite still, her eyes fixed on the golden slope of the Palace of the Caesars, and after a while Mrs. Ansley ceased to fidget with her bag, and she too sank into meditation. Like many intimate friends, the two ladies had never before had occasion to be silent together, and Mrs. Ansley was slightly embarrassed by what seemed, after so many years, a new stage in their intimacy, and one with which she did not yet know how to deal.

25

Suddenly the air was full of that deep clangor of bells which periodically covers Rome with a roof of silver. Mrs. Slade glanced at her wristwatch. "Five o'clock already," she said, as though surprised.

Mrs. Ansley suggested interrogatively: "There's bridge at the Embassy at five."

For a long time Mrs. Slade did not answer. She appeared to be lost in contemplation, and Mrs. Ansley thought the remark had escaped her. But after a while she said, as if speaking out of a dream: "Bridge, did you say? Not unless you want to. . . . But I don't think I will, you know."

"Oh, no," Mrs. Ansley hastened to assure her. "I don't care to at all. It's so lovely here; and so full of old memories, as you say." She settled herself in her chair, and almost furtively drew forth her knitting. Mrs. Slade took sideway note of this activity, but her own beautifully cared-for hands remained motionless on her knee.

"I was just thinking," she said slowly, "what different things Rome stands for to each generation of travelers. To our grandmothers, Roman fever; to our mothers, sentimental danger—how we used to be guarded!—to our daughters, no more dangers than the middle of Main Street. They don't know it—but how much they're missing!" The long golden light was beginning to pale, and Mrs. Ansley lifted her knitting a little closer to her eyes. "Yes; how we were guarded!"

30

"I always used to think," Mrs. Slade continued, "that our mothers had a much more difficult job than our grandmothers. When Roman fever stalked the streets it must have been comparatively easy to gather in the girls at the danger hour; but when you and I were young, with such beauty calling us, and the spice of disobedience thrown in, and no worse risk than catching cold during the cool hour after sunset, the mothers used to be put to it to keep us in—didn't they?"

She turned again toward Mrs. Ansley, but the latter had reached a delicate point in her knitting. "One, two, three—slip two; yes, they must have been," she assented, without looking up.

Mrs. Slade's eyes rested on her with a deepened attention. "She can knit—in the face of *this*! How like her. . . ."

Mrs. Slade leaned back, brooding, her eyes ranging from the ruins which faced her to the long green hollow of the Forum, the fading glow of the church fronts beyond it, and the outlying immensity of the Colosseum. Suddenly she thought: "It's all very well to say that our girls have done away with sentiment and moonlight. But if Babs Ansley isn't out to catch that young aviator—the one who's a Marchese—then I don't know anything. And Jenny has no chance beside her. I know that too. I wonder if that's why Grace Ansley likes the two girls to go everywhere together? My poor Jenny as a foil—!" Mrs. Slade gave a hardly audible laugh, and at the sound Mrs. Ansley dropped her knitting.

"Yes—?"   35

"I—oh, nothing. I was only thinking how your Babs carries everything before her. That Campolieri boy is one of the best matches in Rome. Don't look so innocent, my dear—you know he is. And I was wondering, ever so respectfully, you understand, wondering how two such exemplary characters as you and Horace had managed to produce anything quite so dynamic." Mrs. Slade laughed again, with a touch of asperity.

Mrs. Ansley's hands lay inert across her needles. She looked straight out at the great accumulated wreckage of passion and splendor at her feet. But her small profile was almost expressionless. At length she said: "I think you overrate Babs, my dear."

Mrs. Slade's tone grew easier. "No; I don't. I appreciate her. And perhaps envy you. Oh, my girl's perfect; if I were a chronic invalid I'd—well, I think I'd rather be in Jenny's hands. There must be times . . . but there! I always wanted a brilliant daughter . . . and never quite understood why I got an angel instead."

Mrs. Ansley echoed her laugh in a faint murmur. "Babs is an angel too."

"Of course—of course! But she's got rainbow wings. Well, they're wandering by the sea   40 with their young men; and here we sit . . . and it all brings back the past a little too acutely."

Mrs. Ansley had resumed her knitting. One might almost have imagined (if one had known her less well, Mrs. Slade reflected) that, for her also, too many memories rose from the lengthening shadows of those august ruins. But no; she was simply absorbed in her work. What was there for her to worry about? She knew that Babs would almost certainly come back engaged to the extremely eligible Campolieri. "And she'll sell the New York house, and settle down near them in Rome, and never be in their way . . . she's much too tactful. But she'll have an excellent cook, and just the right people in for bridge and cocktails . . . and a perfectly peaceful old age among her grandchildren."

Mrs. Slade broke off this prophetic flight with a recoil of self-disgust. There was no one of whom she had less right to think unkindly than of Grace Ansley. Would she never cure herself of envying her? Perhaps she had begun too long ago.

She stood up and leaned against the parapet, filling her troubled eyes with the tranquilizing magic of the hour. But instead of tranquilizing her the sight seemed to increase her exasperation. Her gaze turned toward the Colosseum. Already its golden flank was drowned in purple shadow, and above it the sky curved crystal clear, without light or color. It was the moment when afternoon and evening hang balanced in mid-heaven.

Mrs. Slade turned back and laid her hand on her friend's arm. The gesture was so abrupt that Mrs. Ansley looked up, startled.

"The sun's set. You're not afraid, my dear?"   45

"Afraid—?"

"Of Roman fever or pneumonia? I remember how ill you were that winter. As a girl you had a very delicate throat, hadn't you?"

"Oh, we're all right up here. Down below, in the Forum, it does get deathly cold, all of a sudden . . . but not here."

"Ah, of course you know because you had to be so careful." Mrs. Slade turned back to the parapet. She thought: "I must make one more effort not to hate her." Aloud she said: "Whenever I look at the Forum from up here I remember that story about a great-aunt of yours, wasn't she? A dreadfully wicked great-aunt?"

"Oh yes; Great-aunt Harriet. The one who was supposed to have sent her young sis-   50 ter out to the Forum after sunset to gather a night-blooming flower for her album. All our great-aunts and grandmothers used to have albums of dried flowers."

Mrs. Slade nodded. "But she really sent her because they were in love with the same man—"

"Well, that was the family tradition. They said Aunt Harriet confessed it years afterward. At any rate, the poor little sister caught the fever and died. Mother used to frighten us with the story when we were children."

"And you frightened me with it, that winter when you and I were here as girls. The winter I was engaged to Delphin."

Mrs. Ansley gave a faint laugh. "Oh, did I? Really frightened you? I don't believe you're easily frightened."

"Not often; but I was then. I was easily frightened because I was too happy. I wonder if you know what that means?"   55

"I—yes . . ." Mrs. Ansley faltered.

"Well, I suppose that was why the story of your wicked aunt made such an impression on me. And I thought: 'There's no more Roman fever, but the Forum is deathly cold after sunset—especially after a hot day. And the Colosseum's even colder and damper.'"

"The Colosseum—?"

"Yes. It wasn't easy to get in, after the gates were locked for the night. Far from easy. Still, in those days it could be managed; it was managed, often. Lovers met there who couldn't meet elsewhere. You knew that?"

"I—I daresay. I don't remember."   60

"You don't remember? You don't remember going to visit some ruins or other one evening, just after dark, and catching a bad chill? You were supposed to have gone to see the moon rise. People always said that expedition was what caused your illness."

There was a moment's silence; then Mrs. Ansley rejoined: "Did they? It was all so long ago."

"Yes. And you got well again—so it didn't matter. But I suppose it struck your friends—the reason given for your illness, I mean—because everybody knew you were so prudent on account of your throat, and your mother took such care of you. . . . You *had* been out late sight-seeing, hadn't you, that night?"

"Perhaps I had. The most prudent girls aren't always prudent. What made you think of it now?"

Mrs. Slade seemed to have no answer ready. But after a moment she broke out: 65
"Because I simply can't bear it any longer—!"

Mrs. Ansley lifted her head quickly. Her eyes were wide and very pale. "Can't bear what?"

"Why—your not knowing that I've always known why you went."

"Why I went—?"

"Yes. You think I'm bluffing, don't you? Well, you went to meet the man I was engaged to—and I can repeat every word of the letter that took you there."

While Mrs. Slade spoke Mrs. Ansley had risen unsteadily to her feet. Her bag, her   70
knitting and gloves, slid in a panic-stricken heap to the ground. She looked at Mr. Slade as though she were looking at a ghost.

"No, no—don't," she faltered out.

"Why not? Listen, if you don't believe me. 'My one darling, things can't go on like this. I must see you alone. Come to the Colosseum immediately after dark tomorrow. There will be somebody to let you in. No one whom you need fear will suspect'—but perhaps you've forgotten what the letter said?"

Mrs. Ansley met the challenge with an unexpected composure. Steadying herself against the chair she looked at her friend, and replied: "No; I know it by heart too."

"And the signature? 'Only your D. S.' Was that it? I'm right, am I? That was the letter that took you out that evening after dark?"

Mrs. Ansley was still looking at her. It seemed to Mrs. Slade that a slow struggle was   75
going on behind the voluntarily controlled mask of her small quiet face. "I shouldn't have
thought she had herself so well in hand," Mrs. Slade reflected, almost resentfully. But at
this moment Mrs. Ansley spoke, "I don't know how you knew. I burnt that letter at once."

"Yes; you would, naturally—you're so prudent!" The sneer was open now. "And if you
burnt the letter you're wondering how on earth I know what was in it. That's it, isn't it?"

Mrs. Slade waited, but Mrs. Ansley did not speak.

"Well, my dear, I know what was in that letter because I wrote it!"

"You wrote it?"

"Yes."   80

The two women stood for a minute staring at each other in the last golden light.
Then Mrs. Ansley dropped back into her chair. "Oh," she murmured, and covered her
face with her hands.

Mrs. Slade waited nervously for another word or movement. None came, and at
length she broke out: "I horrify you."

Mrs. Ansley's hands dropped to her knee. The face they uncovered was streaked with
tears. "I wasn't thinking of you. I was thinking—it was the only letter I ever had from him!"

"And I wrote it. Yes; I wrote it! But I was the girl he was engaged to. Did you happen
to remember that?"

Mrs. Ansley's head drooped again. "I'm not trying to excuse myself. . . . I   85
remembered. . . ."

"And still you went?"

"Still I went."

Mrs. Slade stood looking down on the small bowed figure at her side. The flame of
her wrath had already sunk, and she wondered why she had ever thought there would be
any satisfaction in inflicting so purposeless a wound on her friend. But she had to justify
herself.

"You do understand? I'd found out—and I hated you, hated you. I knew you were in
love with Delphin—and I was afraid; afraid of you, of your quiet ways, your sweetness . . .
your . . . well, I wanted you out of the way, that's all. Just for a few weeks; just till I was sure
of him. So in a blind fury I wrote that letter. . . . I don't know why I'm telling you now."

"I suppose," said Mrs. Ansley slowly, "it's because you've always gone on hating me."   90

"Perhaps. Or because I wanted to get the whole thing off my mind." She paused.
"I'm glad you destroyed the letter. Of course I never thought you'd die."

Mrs. Ansley relapsed into silence, and Mrs. Slade, leaning above her, was conscious
of a strange sense of isolation, of being cut off from the warm current of human communion. "You think me a monster!"

"I don't know. . . . It was the only letter I had, and you say he didn't write it?"

"Ah, how you care for him still!"

"I cared for that memory," said Mrs. Ansley.   95

Mrs. Slade continued to look down on her. She seemed physically reduced by the
blow—as if, when she got up, the wind might scatter her like a puff of dust. Mrs. Slade's
jealousy suddenly leapt up again at the sight. All these years the woman had been living
on that letter. How she must have loved him, to treasure the mere memory of its ashes!
The letter of the man her friend was engaged to. Wasn't it she who was the monster?

"You tried your best to get him away from me, didn't you? But you failed; and I kept
him. That's all."

"Yes. That's all."

"I wish now I hadn't told you. I'd no idea you'd feel about it as you do; I thought
you'd be amused. It all happened so long ago, as you say; and you must do me the justice
to remember that I had no reason to think you'd ever taken it seriously. How could I,

when you were married to Horace Ansley two months afterward? As soon as you could get out of bed your mother rushed you off to Florence and married you. People were rather surprised—they wondered at its being done so quickly; but I thought I knew. I had an idea you did it out of pique—to be able to say you'd got ahead of Delphin and me. Girls have such silly reasons for doing the most serious things. And your marrying so soon convinced me that you'd never really cared."

"Yes. I suppose it would," Mrs. Ansley assented. 100

The clear heaven overhead was emptied of all its gold. Dusk spread over it, abruptly darkening the Seven Hills. Here and there lights began to twinkle through the foliage at their feet. Steps were coming and going on the deserted terrace—waiters looking out of the doorway at the head of the stairs, then reappearing with trays and napkins and flasks of wine. Tables were moved, chairs straightened. A feeble string of electric lights flickered out. Some vases of faded flowers were carried away, and brought back replenished. A stout lady in a dust-coat suddenly appeared, asking in broken Italian if any one had seen the elastic band which held together her tattered Baedeker. She poked with her stick under the table at which she had lunched, the waiters assisting.

The corner where Mrs. Slade and Mrs. Ansley sat was still shadowy and deserted. For a long time neither of them spoke. At length Mrs. Slade began again: "I suppose I did it as a sort of joke—"

"A joke?"

"Well, girls are ferocious sometimes, you know. Girls in love especially. And I remember laughing to myself all that evening at the idea that you were waiting around there in the dark, dodging out of sight, listening for every sound, trying to get in.—Of course I was upset when I heard you were so ill afterward."

Mrs. Ansley had not moved for a long time. But now she turned slowly toward her 105 companion. "But I didn't wait. He'd arranged everything. He was there. We were let in at once," she said.

Mrs. Slade sprang up from her leaning position. "Delphin there? They let you in?—Ah, now you're lying!" she burst out with violence.

Mrs. Ansley's voice grew clearer, and full of surprise. "But of course he was there. Naturally he came—"

"Came? How did he know he'd find you there? You must be raving!"

Mrs. Ansley hesitated, as though reflecting. "But I answered the letter. I told him I'd be there. So he came."

Mrs. Slade flung her hands up to her face. "Oh, God—you answered! I never 110 thought of your answering. . . ."

"It's odd you never thought of it, if you wrote the letter."

"Yes. I was blind with rage."

Mrs. Ansley rose, and drew her fur scarf about her. "It is cold here. We'd better go. I'm sorry for you," she said as she clasped the fur about her throat.

The unexpected words sent a pang through Mrs. Slade. "Yes; we'd better go." She gathered up her bag and cloak. "I don't know why you should be sorry for me," she muttered.

Mrs. Ansley stood looking away from her toward the dusky secret mass of the Colos- 115 seum. "Well—because I didn't have to wait that night."

Mrs. Slade gave an unquiet laugh. "Yes; I was beaten there. But I oughtn't to begrudge it to you, I suppose. At the end of all these years. After all, I had everything; I had him for twenty-five years. And you had nothing but that one letter that he didn't write."

Mrs. Ansley was again silent. At length she turned toward the door of the terrace. She took a step, and turned back, facing her companion.

"I had Barbara," she said, and began to move ahead of Mrs. Slade toward the stairway.

QUESTIONS

1. What is meant by "Roman fever"? What ambiguity can you find in the phrase? How has Roman fever influenced the lives of the two women, Alida and Grace? Why is its influence still continuing at the time of the story?

2. Explain how Wharton plants clues throughout the story to establish the situation between Alida and Grace. To what degree is the final speech a surprise?

3. Describe the story's point of view. What benefit for the story is gained because the thoughts of Grace Ansley, except perhaps in paragraph 25, are not disclosed except dramatically?

4. Describe the two women and their rivalry, both past and present. How does their conversation constitute a development of their characters and their relationship? A number of critics have stated that the conclusion leaves the two women alienated and bitter. How true is this claim?

❧ EDITED SELECTIONS FROM CRITICISM OF EDITH WHARTON

The following selections are intended to supply details and ideas for essays on Wharton's stories. For a selective bibliography, consult the *Bibliographic Sources* section (pp. 502–503), which may be augmented with your college library catalogue and the most recent volumes of the *MLA International Bibliography* available in your library's reference room. You might also consult the comprehensive "Appendix VI: Bibliography" in Sarah Bird Wright, *Edith Wharton A to Z: The Essential Guide to the Life and Work* (New York: Facts on File, 1998, pp. 309–18).

In these passages of selected criticism the bracketed page numbers refer to the original pagination of the sources. Footnotes in the sources have been deleted. Excisions from the sources are indicated by bracketed ellipses.

1. Introductory Detail and Commentary by R. W. B. Lewis[2]

In the eight years after her first publication, though she wrote a dozen stories, she later repudiated a number of them, and held back others until her first collection of short fiction, *The Greater Inclination*, in 1899, which contained some expert tales . . . . [vii]

But in 1900 alone, Edith Wharton brought out seven stories. It is fair to say that after that, except during the formidably distracting interlude of the First World War, her fiction-writing energy never let up. A couple more statistics may be added. Between 1900 and the outbreak of the war in 1914, Edith Wharton produced almost fifty short stories, an average of three or four a year. And this during a period in her private life which saw the abandonment and sales of her American homes, her permanent expatriation to France and a Faubourg St. Germain apartment, the end of her marriage in a painful divorce, and a passionate, disturbing love affair with Morton Fullerton, an American journalist based in Paris—all elements one can find reflected overtly or obscurely in the stories produced. Between the end of the war and her death in 1937, Edith Wharton [viii]

---

[2]R. W. B. Lewis, Introduction, *The Selected Short Stories of Edith Wharton*, by Edith Wharton, ed. R. W. B. Lewis (New York: Scribner's, 1991) vii–xx.

wrote twenty-four stories, one or two a year; but in those same years, it should be remembered, she brought out nine novels (*The Age of Innocence* and *A Mother's Recompense* among them), four novellas (the splendid durable *Old New York* foursome), a book of poems, a collection of critical essays, and an autobiography. "You are a wonder," her editor once said to her. "Do you marvel that I bow low before such energy?"

In the prewar years, Edith Wharton's stories were published in the influentially genteel magazines, with their appeal to cultivated upper-class taste and their solid if limited readership: the excellent *Scribner's Magazine* for the most part; the *Century* or *Harper's* if *Scribner's* was booked up. Financial figures are more readily available for Mrs. Wharton's novels than for her stories, but it is a reasonable guess that she received about $300 per story in the early 1900s. Her wares increased steadily in value. After the success of her first novel, *The Valley of Decision* in 1902, which brought in $10,000 in royalties in a matter of months, the Scribner's publishing house willingly gave her a $5,000 advance on her next novel, *The House of Mirth.* This became the fastest-selling novel in the history of Scribners and earned its author $30,000 in sixty days. (It is safe to multiply any of these figures by ten to get a sense of the contemporary equivalent.) Edith Wharton was now getting $700 and more for a short story. The sum would be more like $1,500 by 1913; and in 1925, to glance forward, a mild little anecdote called "Miss Mary Pask," which Edith Wharton wrote in a single afternoon on the terrace of her Riviera winter home while recovering from the grippe, netted her $1,800.

That story appeared in the up-and-coming monthly, the *Pictorial Review,* and in fact, [ix] by this stage Edith Wharton had moved from what would later be called "quality publishing" into the world of (relatively) big literary money. She had shifted over from Scribner's to Appleton & Company in 1912 for her novel *The Reef,* in response to Appleton's offer of a $15,000 advance; and for stories and serials, she turned to magazines of large, even mass circulation: the *Pictorial Review,* the *Saturday Evening Post,* and *Hearst's International-Cosmopolitan.* In 1920 the *Pictorial Review* paid $18,000 for magazine rights to *The Age of Innocence.* Edith Wharton belatedly realized what she had let herself in for when she discovered the first installment flanked by advertisements for soap flakes and Sani-Flush, a detergent for cleaning toilet bowls. She understood further when the editor notified her casually that several installments would have to be trimmed to make space for illustrations and further ads. "I cannot consent to have my work treated as prose by the yard," she declared wrathfully.

She won that particular case, but there is no doubt that Edith Wharton after 1920 wrote and sold a number of flimsy fictional concoctions for large sums of money—to pay the expenses of her elegant manner of life, her travels, her lavishly hospitable homes in southern France and outside of Paris, and her many private charities. Even during the depths of the Depression, though she had trouble placing her more serious work, she received $2,000 from the *Saturday Evening Post* for the forgettable "A Glimpse," and $5,000 from Hearst's for the negligable if likable "Charm Incorporated" (neither of these is in this volume). When in 1934 Edith Wharton flew into a temper with Appleton-Century (as it had been renamed) over its allegedly poor advertising and generally inadequate treatment of her books, the senior editor replied with a long financial statement demonstrating that the house had paid her almost $580,000—for royalites on novels, serial rights, short stories, motion picture and dramatic rights—over the last fourteen years of their association. In present terms the amount would be reckoned in millions.

But the creative picture must not be falsified. It is true that Edith Wharton's only collection of stories in the 1920s, *Here and Beyond* in 1926, contained nothing but potboilers, to borrow the title of one of her own early tales (though the story "Bewitched" had a second life on television not long ago). . . . Almost literally to the day she died—she sent on her story "All Souls"' to her agent only a few months before her death in the summer of 1937—Edith Wharton maintained the high level and the remarkable variety that had characterized her achievement in the writing of short stories for forty-six years. . . .

The expanded attention to Edith Wharton, as it happens, coincided with a marked increase of stress in American criticism at large on the historically and socially conditioned. Among the several Edith Whartons that have come into view, perhaps the most visible at the moment is the delineator as well as the victim of class distinctions, the analyst of a marketplace culture, and the historian of women as social beings in modern America.

Lewis on "The Other Two"

As to the validity of this profile, one need look no further than "The Other Two," the best [x] story of its kind that Edith Wharton ever wrote, and one made to order for the social or even sociological critic. It comes to us through the fluctuating and maturing consciousness of a New York investment broker, Waythorn, his wife's third husband. The first husband, Haskett, is a lower-class figure; he looks like a piano tuner, has an "over-the-counter politeness," and an uncultivated manner of speech, and worst of all, for Waythorn, he wears a made-up tie with an elastic. The second husband, Gus Varick, a florid man-about-town, is, in Waythorn's reflection and "whatever his faults," "a gentleman, in the conventional, traditional sense of the term." Varick visits Waythorn's Wall Street office to consult about a $100,000 investment, and the two men establish affable business relations.

But Waythorn comes to realize Varick's essential crudity of character and social manner, even as he grows aware of Haskett's probity and humanity. His social education completes itself in his understanding of his wife Alice and her curious pliancy toward both her former husbands. In an idiom nicely blending the financial with the erotic, he muses that "He held so many shares in his wife's personality, and his predecessors were his partners in the business." But a larger proposition (though of course it conveys Waythorn's way of thinking not less than an insight into his wife) is carried in an astonishing, evolving figure that draws upon consumer tactics, sexual innuendo, and the psychology of personality to move into the realm of the mythopoetic:

> She was "as easy as an old shoe"—a shoe that too many feet had worn. Her elastici-   [xi]
> ty was the result of tension in too many directions. Alice Haskett—Alice Varick—
> Alice Waythorn—she had been each in turn, and had left hanging to each name a
> little of her privacy, a little of her personality, a little of the inmost self where the
> unknown gods abide.

Lewis on "Roman Fever"

With "The Other Two," as [a] luminous exercise . . . in social realism, we can place . . .   [xi] "Roman Fever." . . . The softly spoken but breathtaking last line of "Roman Fever" (in Edith Wharton's final collection *The World Over* in 1936) discloses with a kind of formal perfection a situation that has silently endured for more than two decades. . . .

Lewis on "Pomegranate Seed" and Wharton's Ghost Stories

Edith Wharton's imagination tended persistently toward the mythic: toward an enlarge-   [xiv] ment, even a mystifying of the human, through suggestions of the ritualistic and the ancient in common human experience. "The Legend," in 1910, provides a fascinating and problematic instance of the tendency. . . .

The mythic aspect of "The Legend" lurks in the narrative as a possibility of mean- [xv]
ing, a matter of names and rhythms, and a title that may or may not point beyond the legendary philosopher himself to some ancient seasonal rite. In "Pomegranate Seed" of
1931, the myth encloses the tale.

Kenneth Ashby, after the death of his first wife, is happily married to Charlotte
Gorse, the two of them occupying a comfortable old-fashioned house in New York. But
soon after their honeymoon, there begin to arrive in the dusk of winter days letters addressed to Ashby in a nearly illegible but visibly feminine hand. The letters have a disintegrating effect on Ashby, though he will say nothing about them. In the wake of one of
them, he disappears; and it is conjectured by Charlotte and her mother-in-law, amid frissons of terror and disbelief, that the letters have been summonses from the dead wife,
and that Ashby has gone to join her.

When asked about the story's title, Edith Wharton told her editor that it came from
"classical mythology," and explained: "When Persephone left the under-world to re-visit
her mother Demeter, her husband Hades, lord of the infernal regions, gave her a pomegranate seed to eat, because he knew that if he did so she would never be able to remain
among the living, but would be drawn back to the company of the dead." In the opening
section of the old legend, in Ovid's Metamorphoses and elsewhere, the maiden Persephone is espied by Hades, who abducts her, carries her down to the world below, and
there makes her his queen. Her mother Demeter, the earth-goddess, searches the world
for her, and eventually secures her release—but only for half of each year. More than
likely, the myth was a narrative working-out of the death, or ground-burial, of the corn
seed in one season and birth or growth in another.

Edith Wharton was obsessed by the Persephone myth throughout her literary life.
References to it, and the Eleusinian mysteries associated with it, turn up in her letters,
notebooks, and stories. In two of her early tales, *The Touchstone* and "Copy," novels entitled *Pomegranate Seed* are attributed to the women writers involved; and Edith Wharton
herself wrote a short poetic drama of that name published in *Scribner's* in 1912. In this interesting, modest effort, chiefly a dialogue between the temporarily reunited Demeter
and Persephone, the daughter, who bears an "estranging darkness" on her brow, declares
forthrightly:

> I, that have eaten of the seed of death, [xvi]
> And with the dead die daily, am become
> Of their undying kindred.

She announces her preference for that dark world over the sunlit earthworld of her
mother. Her last words are: "Free me. I hear the voices of my dead."

The pomegranate seeds in the Whartonian story appear to be the letters from the
former Mrs. Ashby; by consuming them, that is by reading them, Kenneth Ashby has
made it imperative, even irresistible for him to spend a portion of his time in the dead
woman's company. Part of the story's technical brilliance is that we know about that wife,
as we know everything else, only through the disturbed consciousness of Charlotte, for
whom she is simply "a distant, self-centered woman." The reader is invited to participate
in the serious game of interpretation. For this reader, we have a ghostly metaphor of masculine yielding, of masochistic submission to female power of the sexual and psychological variety.

Such a reading has, in any case, the advantage of bringing "Pomegranate Seed" in [xvii]
line with other Edith Wharton ghost stories: "The Lady's Maid's Bell," "Kerfol," "Mr. Jones,"
"The Eyes," "All Souls'." The mythic is quiescent in some of these stories, which may be

seen rather as fictional strategies—something Edith Wharton shared with other writers in the Anglo-American Victorian age—for dealing with intensities of sexual behavior by distancing them into the spectral and legendary. So distanced, the behavior could be dealt with more freely than the proprieties normally allowed. In "The Lady's Maid's Bell," the brutish physical demands made by one Brampton upon his frail fastidious wife (and with which the maid, the bell, and the ghostliness are implicated) can be referred to, in tightlipped fashion, by the servant Hartley: "I turned sick," she remembers, peering back into the far past, "to think what some ladies have to endure and hold their tongues about." In "Kerfol," an American visitor, puzzled by a cluster of silent small dogs he encounters in the courtyard of an old house in Brittany, is led to discover the seventeenth-century drama of the house, a drama of sexual torment, monstrous revenge, and madness. In "Mr. Jones," an Englishwoman, taking possession through inheritance of a six-hundred-year-old country mansion, ferrets out the poignant tale, dating back to the 1820s, of its former mistress: the deaf-and-dumb heiress Juliana, whom her heartless husband kept in solitary confinement under the iron guard of his caretaker Mr. Jones. For permitting this secret history to be known, the present-day housekeeper, Mrs. Clemm, is strangled to death by the ghost of Mr. Jones.

The housekeeper's name, incidentally, is the same as that of Edgar Allan Poe's housekeeper in Baltimore, after Poe had married that Mrs. Clemm's daughter Virginia. The use of it is no doubt Edith Wharton's gesture of kinship to one of the two American writers (Hawthorne was the other) whom she acknowledged as her precursors in what (in her 1925 essay "Telling a Short Story") she called "the peculiar category of the eerie. [...]"

2. David Galens on "Pomegranate Seed" and "Roman Fever"[3]

Point of View of "Pomegranate Seed"

The narrative point of view in Wharton's "Pomegranate Seed" is third-person limited. In a work of fiction related from a third-person limited point of view, the narrator is not a character in the story, but someone outside of it who refers to the characters as "he," "she," and "they." This outside narrator, however, is not omniscient (or all-knowing), but is limited in knowledge to the perceptions of one or more of the characters in the story. The narrator of "Pomegranate Seed," and therefore its reader, sees the events of the story through the eyes of Charlotte Ashby, even though it is not Charlotte herself who tells the story. The story's readers never have more information than Charlotte does at any point in the narrative, and are thus more fully involved in the story's mystery than they might have been if it were told by an omniscient narrator. [216]

Setting of "Pomegranate Seed"

"Pomegranate Seed" takes place in two locations in 1930s New York City: Kenneth Ashby's house and the nearby residence of his mother. Wharton makes clear that the Ashbys' neighborhood is a relatively quiet one; theirs is a "street long since deserted by business and fashion." Even from this quiet street, however, "the soulless roar of New York" is apparent to Charlotte's ears. "Pomegranate Seed" is the only one of Wharton's ghost stories to have an urban setting, and Wharton may have placed the story there as a sort of challenge to herself as a writer. [216]

[3]David Galens, gen. ed., *Short Stories for Students: Presenting Analysis, Context, and Criticism on Commonly Studied Short Stories* (Detroit: Gale, 2002).

Allusion in "Pomegranate Seed"

The title, "Pomegranate Seed," is an allusion to the Greek myth of Persephone. Daughter [216] of Zeus and Demeter, the goddess of the harvest, Persephone is abducted by Hades, the god of death, and carried off to the underworld. At Zeus's insistence, Hades agrees to release Persephone on the condition that she has eaten no food while in the underworld. Unfortunately Persephone has eaten six pomegranate seeds in Hades's garden, and for that reason is allowed to return to the world of the living for no more than six months at a time. This can be likened to Wharton's story, in that Kenneth is pulled between the underworld and the world above: between Elsie, who is dead—or in the underworld—and Charlotte, who is flesh and blood and belongs to the world familiar to Kenneth, the land of the living.

Ghost Stories and History regarding "Pomegranate Seed"

In one important way, the historical considerations that readers bring to the interpreta- [217] tion of other kinds of fiction do not apply to ghost stories. Ghost stories deal with situations that are outside of nature and, for that reason, outside of history. Ghosts and the emotions with which audiences read stories about ghosts exist in a realm that is not much affected by history, politics, and economy. At the same time, of course, writers live and work inside history, and the media with which writers practice their craft—language and literary genre—are very much shaped by historical factors. For these reasons, and not because Elsie Ashby's ghost is in some recognizable way a ghost of the 1930s, Wharton's "Pomegranate Seed" is a story whose historical and cultural background may be profitably explored.

For one thing, "Pomegranate Seed" is a story that presents its setting and characters as being very much up to date. It is Wharton's only urban ghost story, taking place amid what she calls the "soulless roar of New York." Much of the story's action is presented as dialogue exchanged over the telephone—a work of technology that was still something of a novelty when the story was first published by the *Ladies' Home Journal* in 1931. Kenneth Ashby, the remarried widower who is haunted by his first wife's mysterious letters, is a lawyer with a bustling career in the metropolis. Clearly, much of the story's effect is derived from the intrusion of something so old-fashioned as a ghost upon the lives of the modern-day Ashbys.

The Ashbys, however, seem to be curiously exempt from what worried Americans most at the time of the story's first publication: the Great Depression. Beginning with the Stock Market Crash of 1929 and lasting until the early 1940s, the Depression left more than 16 million people unemployed and reduced the U.S. Gross National Product by almost fifty percent. For many Americans it was a time of lost hope, skepticism toward government, and brutal poverty. Wharton herself suffered some financial reverses after 1929 as the New York real estate in which her money was invested declined in value, and as the magazines to which she sold her work were forced to reduce the sums they paid contributors.

Setting of "Roman Fever"

"Roman Fever" is among Edith Wharton's last writings and caps off her noteworthy ca- [303] reer. "Roman Fever" was first published in *Liberty* magazine in 1934, and it was included in Wharton's final collection of short stories, *The World Over*, in 1936. Several reviewers of this final collection from newspapers and magazines throughout the nation called special attention to "Roman Fever." Since then, however, the story has received little critical attention. The few critics who have written about the story describe it as artistic, complex, and reflective of Wharton's moral landscape.

"Roman Fever" is set in Rome, Italy, around the mid-1920s. On the one hand, the ruins of Rome become the focus of Wharton's skill at descriptive writing. On the other hand, the ruins of Rome remind both women of an earlier time spent in Rome together when their friendship and rivalry both began. More generally Wharton shows the kind of life a woman of independent means could lead in Rome at that time.

The setting of Rome is contrasted with the home neighborhood of the two women on Manhattan's East Side in New York. Mrs. Slade and Mrs. Ansley have lived across the street from each other so close that each woman knows all the mundane details of the other's everyday life. But this setting is too confining to allow them to communicate their true feelings. It is only in Rome that Mrs. Slade feels able to reveal the truth to Mrs. Ansley.

Point of View of "Roman Fever"

The story is told from a third-person, omniscient point of view. This means that readers [303] see and hear what the characters see and hear, and that readers are also privy to their thoughts. However, in this case, the interior life, motivations, and reactions of Mrs. Slade are revealed to a greater extent than those of Mrs. Ansley's. For example, readers know that Mrs. Slade decides to tell the truth about the letter Delphin was supposed to have written 25 years ago because she is envious of her rival and dislikes her, though at the same time she believes she is a good person. Readers also know that she regrets her words after she has said them. On the other hand, not much is revealed about Mrs. Ansley's motivation. Readers do not know, for instance, why Mrs. Ansley decides to reveal the truth about Barbara's parentage.

Structure of "Roman Fever"

Although the story is relatively brief, it is divided into two sections. The first section pro- [303] vides the background and history of Mrs. Slade and Mrs. Ansley. The second section develops the theme of the rivalry between the two women, concluding with the truth about Barbara's parentage. The two parts also represent the past and the present.

In the first part of the story, Mrs. Slade notes Mrs. Ansley's odd emphasis on the personal pronoun *me* when she talks about the view of Rome from the terrace. She also notes Mrs. Ansley's emphasis on the personal pronoun *I* when she says "I remember" in response to Mrs. Slade's comment about the summer they spent in Rome as girls. Although Mrs. Slade attributes this emphasis to Mrs. Ansley's being old-fashioned, the emphasis really alludes to Mrs. Ansley's fond memories of the time she spent with Delphin.

In the second part of the story, Mrs. Slade's musings show that she is gearing up to- [304] ward something more significant than a simple conversation about malaria. At one point, she watches Mrs. Ansley knitting and thinks, "She can knit—in the face of *this!*" The reader wonders what *this* refers to, since up to this point the women are simply having a casual conversation about the past.

Symbolism and Imagery in "Roman Fever"

Wharton makes use of a number of symbols and images to reinforce the emotions of the [304] story. The ruins that the two women are gazing at of the Palatine, the Forum, and the Colosseum symbolize the ruins of these women's perceptions of themselves and each other. Mrs. Ansley calmly knits, which would seem to be the staid activity of a middle-aged woman, but what she is knitting is described as "a twist of crimson silk." Her knitting can be said to represent the passionate and more frivolous side of her nature. Also, the women's actions can be viewed symbolically, to indicate their feelings toward the conversation and each other. As soon as Mrs. Slade starts to talk about their shared past, Mrs. Ansley lifts her knitting "a little closer to her eyes," thus shielding herself and her reactions from Mrs. Slade. However, when Mrs. Slade learns that Mrs. Ansley did meet Delphin at the Colosseum, it is Mrs. Slade who must cover her face and hide her deepest emotions. In fact, by the end of the story, the power structure has changed, as shown by Mrs. Ansley's actions. After revealing the truth about Barbara's father, she "began to move ahead of Mrs. Slade toward the stairway."

3. Alice Hall Petry on "Roman Fever"[4]

Probably Edith Wharton's best-known short story is "Roman Fever," the product of a 1934 [312] trip to Rome, and the most enduring tale from her uneven late collection entitled *The World Over* (1936). It is curious that so widely-anthologized a work has generated such a paucity of critical interest, and even more curious that the few appraisals which it has received have been so tepid: Geoffrey Walton, for example, simply dismisses it as "a very light little comedy that can be taken as a kind of farewell skit on the decorum of the great days." More appreciative are Cynthia Griffin Wolff and Marilyn Jones Lyde, both of whom [313] without explaining the bases of their appraisals find the story to be one of Wharton's best works. But "Roman Fever" is considerably more substantial than Walton's remark would suggest, and Wolff's and Lyde's appraisals can and should be explored at length. One way that we can begin to appreciate the complex art of "Roman Fever" is to examine Wharton's handling of what might at first appear to be a minor element in the story: the act of knitting.

That knitting will occupy a special position in "Roman Fever" is signified at the outset by the simple fact that it is the first matter to receive attention in the story. Grace Ansley and Alida Slade overhear their young daughters discussing them:

> . . . let's leave the young things to their knitting"; and a voice as fresh laughed back: "Oh, look here, Babs, not actually *knitting*—" "Well, I mean figuratively," rejoined the first. "After all, we haven't left our poor parents much else to do . . ."

Since Wharton had asserted in the brief introductory paragraph that Grace and Alida were "two American ladies of ripe but well-cared-for middle age", it is apparent that their daughters' appraisal of them as "young things" is mocking. The implication clearly is that the ladies are physically, emotionally, and intellectually capable of nothing more than the traditionally passive, repetitive, and undemanding task of knitting. By having the daughters patronize their mothers in this fashion, Wharton is predisposing the reader to perceive the ladies as stereotypical matrons; and the rest of the story will be devoted to obliterating this stereotype, to exposing the intense passions which have been seething in both women for more than twenty-five years.

A major rupture in the stereotype is the simple fact that (the daughters' remarks notwithstanding) Alida Slade does not knit at all. This unexpected situation focuses the reader's attention more intensely on Grace Ansley, whose apparently passionate devotion to knitting ultimately will enable us to probe the psyches of both women and to reconstruct the remarkable events of a generation before. The complex relationship between

---

[4]Alice Hall Petry, "A Twist of Crimson Silk: Edith Wharton's 'Roman Fever,' " *Studies in Short Fiction* 24. 2 (1987): 163–66, *Short Stories for Students: Presenting Analysis, Context, and Criticism on Commonly Studied Short Stories,* David Galens, gen. ed. (Detroit: Gale, 2002). Pagination refers to *Short Stories for Students.*

Grace and knitting is evident in her first action in the story: "Half-guiltily she drew from her handsomely mounted black hand-bag a twist of crimson silk run through by two fine knitting needles". The sentence presents two distinct aspects of Grace's character. The phrase "half-guiltily" is in keeping with the persona she has presented to the world throughout her adult life. "Smaller and paler" than the assertive Alida, Grace is "evidently far less sure than her companion of herself and of her rights in the world". The "evidently" is eloquent, for although Grace may seem embarrassed by her hobby, the physical objects themselves tell a far different story about her: she has chosen "crimson" silk, an insistently passionate color; and the skein has been "run through" by needles, a startlingly assertive image. The sensuality and forcefulness suggested by her knitting materials will help to render plausible her passionate moonlight tryst with Delphin Slade twenty-five years earlier, as well as her capacity to stand up to the vicious taunts of Alida, the "dark lady" of the piece.

Quite early in the story, then, knitting has ceased to be a general symbol of complacent middle-age: it is rapidly becoming a complex personal emblem for Grace, and in fact one may gauge Grace's mental state according to how she manipulates her knitting materials. This element first becomes obvious in the second portion of the story, wherein Grace recognizes instinctively that she and Alida have reached, "after so many years, a new stage in their intimacy, and one with which she did not yet know how to deal". That intimacy is far from positive: both women recognize that Alida is very much in control of the situation, steadily steering the conversation to the matter of the love triangle in which they had been involved so many years before. Grace's response to Alida's catty remark that Rome is "so full of old memories" is to begin knitting: "She settled herself in her chair, and almost furtively drew forth her knitting. Mrs. Slade took sideway note of this activity, but her own beautifully cared-for hands remained motionless on her knee". The aggressive Alida needs nothing to occupy her hands, but the guilt-ridden Grace—predisposed to "fidget"—uses her knitting as a physical means of containing her growing stress, of maintaining some semblance of order in a situation not in her control. As Alida continues to press her advantage, ironically lamenting how much modern girls were "missing" out on in disease-free, twentieth-century Rome, Grace "lifted her knitting a little closer to her eyes" not simply because "the long golden light was beginning to pale", but also because it serves as a physical barrier behind which to protect herself from Alida's probing. Closely aligned with this, the knitting offers Grace an ideal excuse for responding neither immediately nor extensively to Alida's painful interrogation. Further, it enables her to avoid making eye contact with her tormentor. . . . Alida's palpable annoyance suggests that Grace's knitting is more than just an evasion tactic: those needles are effective psychological weapons against a woman who is deliberately tormenting her for having once loved Delphin Slade. In fine, the fact that Grace knits under duress indicates that she is vastly different from the pale, cringing matron of the story's opening paragraphs. . . . [314]

4. Sarah Bird Wright on "The Muse's Tragedy" and "Roman Fever"[5]

Wright on "The Muse's Tragedy"

"The Muse's Tragedy" draws on many of Wharton's Italian travels and prefigures her volume on Italian villas and gardens. For instance, in *Italian Villas and Their Gardens*, she describes the Villa d'Este at Cernobbio on Lake Como, admiring the fluted descending [177]

[5]Sarah Bird Wright, *Edith Wharton A to Z: The Essential Guide to the Life and Work* (New York: Facts on File, 1998).

water basins and carved entablature and statuary in the gardens. She detects in the gardens at the Villa d'Este "much of the Roman spirit—the breadth of design, the unforced inclusion of natural features, and that sensitiveness to the quality of the surrounding landscape that characterizes the great gardens of the Campagna. . . . She thus invests the hillside ruins on Lake Como with the spirit of early Rome, and, moreover, links them with the ruins on the Campagna. In the story, Danyers takes a "morning ramble" among the hills and he and Mrs. Anerton converse leaning over the parapet above the lake; they later climb to the ruined temples above the villa.

Edith Wharton's editor at Scribner's, William Crary Brownell, wrote her that the book had been "appreciated so much in so many directions that I have heard of . . . that you can assuredly plume yourself on having joined the 'note' of universality to that of distinction. . . ." Reviewers praised the entire volume of stories; several linked Edith Wharton with Henry James, which she considered a tribute at that early stage of her career [i.e., in 1899]. "What," asked the reviewer for the *Critic*, "is 'The Muse's Tragedy' but *The Tragic Muse* turned other end to?" . . . (In James's novel [*The Tragic Muse*, 1890], Nicholas Dormer, son of an English statesman, gives up fortune, position and marriage to his beautiful cousin to become a portrait painter; he is inspired by the example of his "muse," the actress Miriam Rooth). John D. Barry, of *Literary World*, found the story the finest in the volume [i.e., Wharton's collection of stories *The Greater Inclination*, which included "The Muse's Tragedy" and which was published in 1899].

Wright on "Roman Fever"

Percy Hutchison, writing in the *New York Times Book Review*, called the story "as memorable a short story as Mrs. Wharton has ever done" and "as sharp-cut as a diamond, and as hard of surface." Joseph Reilly, reviewing the volume for *Catholic World*, believed the story to be one of the best she ever wrote. [R. W. B.] Lewis calls it a "brilliant piece of short fiction" and believes it reveals" a serenity that pervades the narrative in a long atmospheric glow." John Gerlach considers the ending successful in "making the story whole" and "deepening it"; it "clarifies and binds together the beginning and the middle, revealing what in retrospect is both latent and inevitable . . . what is calm is so only as a means of concealing volcanic truth."   [215]

5. Janet Beer on Edith Wharton's Stories[6]

Janet Beer on Wharton, the Short Story, and the Relationship of Wharton's Stories to Naturalist Writers

Throughout her career Edith Wharton was a prolific writer of short stories and novellas; her first published fiction was a short-story collection entitled *The Greater Inclination* (1899) and the last book of new fiction she published before her death was also a collection of tales, *The World Over* (1936). Her experimentations with the form of the short story and the novella shadowed her work in the writing of full-length fictions; she was able to tease out problems of genre, style, setting, and theme in the shorter fiction, working with the historical, the gothic and ghostly, with manners and with local colour in ways that were of direct use to her in the structuring and management of material in her longer narratives.   [36]

Wharton often reflected, in correspondence and in her critical writing, on the characteristics and the utility of the short-story form; it was a genre in which she felt comfortable and confident. In a letter to Robert Grant, written in response to his comments on her novel *The Fruit of the Tree*, published in 1907, she says:

[6]Janet Beer, *Edith Wharton* (Horndon: Northcote House, 2002).

> As soon as I look at a subject from the novel-angle I see it in its relation to a larger whole, in all its remotest connotations; & I can't help trying to take them in, at the cost of the smaller realism that I arrive at, I think, better in my short stories. This is the reason why I have always obscurely felt that I didn't know how to write a novel. I feel it more clearly after each attempt, because it is in such sharp contrast to the sense of authority with which I take hold of a short story.

Wharton not only used the short story as a benchmark against which to judge her success or otherwise with the full-length novel, however. She relished working inventively within the constraints of the short story form whilst also pushing it to its limits in the novella. . . .   [37]
[38]
    Many of Wharton's early short-story collections have titles that steer the reader towards a consideration of the work and ideas of the natural and social scientists as significant influences in the fiction. In her own copy of *Evolution and Effort* (1895) by Edmond Kelly she underlines the meaning of the phrase 'the greater inclination', the title of her first published collection of short fiction. Her next volume was entitled *Crucial Instances* (1901), which is a quotation from a discussion of 'The Laws of Inheritance' in Charles Darwin's 1871 *The Descent of Man*, a text to which she pays even more direct tribute in the title of her third collection, *The Descent of Man and Other Stories* (1904). These are not chance or casual allusions to the work of Darwin and others: Wharton . . . was profoundly influenced by social and natural science, and her language and themes reflect the reading she did in the subject. . . .

    Wharton's setting in the majority of her short fiction may well be the comfortable   [39]
homes of the leisure classes, but she is not necessarily treating lives that are much more sophisticated than those depicted in the work of the leading naturalist writers of her age.
. . .

    Wharton claims, as she always claimed, that content and form, style and setting, are   [40]
inextricably linked and that they are matters of individual choice and even aptitude for the artist. In 'The Great American Novel' [an essay of 1927] she is simply enumerating another version of the method advocated by Darwin for investigating 'The Laws of Inheritance'—here in the section from which she derives the title of her second volume of short stories: 'As it was impossible even to estimate in how large a number of cases throughout the animal kingdom these two propositions held good, it occurred to me to investigate some striking or crucial instances, and to rely on the result.' In the writing of her short stories, in particular, she sought to depict the 'crucial instances' through which she could shed some light on the human condition. Again, Wharton's ambitions are not discernibly distinct from those of the Naturalist writers, who are described, here in Donna Campbell's words, as being concerned with 'the accurate and detailed representation of ordinary human beings, a fascination with tracing the workings of heredity, and a belief in the shaping power of the environment.' Wharton is, however, primarily ab-   [41]
sorbed by relations between men and women and, centrally, the impact upon the institution of marriage of social change and—in particular—the expansion of opportunities for women. . . .

Beer on "The Other Two"

The story 'The Other Two' features a woman who has, using the restricted means at her   [41]
disposal, managed to find a way to adapt and change, in order to improve her social standing and economic position. . . . Wharton shows Mr Waythorn becoming aware of his own complicity in the professionalization of Alice's role as a bride/wife; what attracted him to her—her ability to be the perfectly and endlessly obliging partner—is also what ultimately arouses his contempt, a contempt that is directed as much towards himself as

towards her. Alice, however, is an index of the evolving nature of the social constitution. She is welcomed as an agent of change because no change is overtly signalled; hostesses do not even have to adjust their guest lists to avoid inviting husbands two and three to the same event. Alice Waythorn is an example from a society in the process of 'adaptation', being perfectly 'adapted' herself to move on up the social register, learning, if not 'to shed her past like a man', then to gloss over its continuing difficulties with the successful practice of the 'art . . . of concessions, eliminations and embellishments; of lights judiciously thrown and shadows skilfully softened'.

Beer on "Pomegranate Seed"

In substantial numbers of her stories her protagonists have to find ways and means to live [43] with the knowledge of their own emotional, moral, or aesthetic insufficiencies. . . . In her ghost stories, a genre to which she returned regularly throughout her career, Wharton often uses the device of the prior event or act as the inspiration for or cause of the su- [44] pernatural intervention. In 'Afterward', published in 1910, . . . the ghost of a wronged business partner comes to claim the life of Ned Boyne; in 'Kerfol', published in 1916 . . . the tyrannical Lord of Kerfol is savaged to death by a pack of ghost dogs, dogs he had murdered one by one; in the late story 'Pomegranate Seed', published in the *Saturday Evening Post* in 1931, Kenneth Ashby is denied any future prospect of happiness in a second marriage by his dead wife, Elsie, who seeks to reassert her former dominance over him from beyond the grave. . . .

Seven Stories for Additional Study and Enjoyment

RAY BRADBURY (Ray Douglas Spaulding, b. 1920)

Known especially for his work in science fiction, Bradbury was born in Illinois, and as a boy he moved with his family to Los Angeles. Early on he made a decision to become a writer, and he began by writing stories and articles in popular magazines. Since that time he has received wide recognition and innumerable awards. His first of his many collections of stories was Dark Carnival *(1947). In 2001 his* Collected Short Stories *appeared, and in 2002 his* One More for the Road: A New Short Story Collection *was published. His best-known novel is* Fahrenheit 451 *(1953), about a future time in which all thought is prohibited, all books are banned, and most people are confined to staying inside at night and doing little more than watching television.* Fahrenheit 451 *is one of his three works that have been made into major motion pictures, the other two being* The Illustrated Man *(1951) and* Something Wicked This Way Comes *(1962). Bradbury has written successful collections of poems and children's stories, and, using a number of noms de plume, he has also written extensively for film and television. With the movie director John Huston, he wrote the filmscript for* Moby Dick *(1956), which was awarded an Oscar.*

Zero Hour ⟩⟨⟨⟩⟨⟨⟩ 1947

Oh, it was to be so jolly! What a game! Such excitement they hadn't known in years. The children catapulted this way and that across the green lawns, shouting at each other, holding hands, flying in circles, climbing trees, laughing.

Overhead, the rockets flew and beetle-cars whispered by on the streets, but the children played on. Such fun, such tremulous joy, such tumbling and hearty screaming.

Mink ran into the house, all dirt and sweat. For her seven years she was loud and strong and definite. Her mother,

Mrs. Morris, hardly saw her as she yanked out drawers and rattled pans and tools into a large sack.

"Heavens, Mink, what's going on?"

"The most exciting game ever!" gasped Mink, pink-faced.

"Stop and get your breath," said the mother.

"No, I'm all right," gasped Mink. "Okay I take these things, Mom?"

"But don't dent them," said Mrs. Morris.

"Thank you, thank you!" cried Mink, and boom! she was gone, like a rocket. Mrs. Morris surveyed the fleeing tot. "What's the name of the game?"

"Invasion!" said Mink. The door slammed.

In every yard on the street children brought out knives and forks and pokers and old stove pipes and can-openers.

It was an interesting fact that this fury and bustle occurred only among the younger children. The older ones, those ten years and more, disdained the affair and marched scornfully off on hikes or played a more dignified version of hide-and-seek on their own.

Meanwhile, parents came and went in chromium beetles. Repair men came to repair the vacuum elevators in houses, to fix fluttering television sets or hammer upon stubborn food-delivery tubes. The adult civilization passed and repassed the busy youngsters, jealous of the fierce energy of the wild tots, tolerantly amused at their flourishings, longing to join in themselves.

"This and this and this," said Mink, instructing the others with their assorted spoons and wrenches. "Do that, and bring that over here. No! Here, ninnie! Right. Now, get back while I fix this—" Tongue in teeth, face wrinkled in thought. "Like that. See?"

"Yayyy!" shouted the kids.

Twelve-year-old Joseph Connors ran up.

"Go away," said Mink straight at him.

"I wanna play," said Joseph.

"Can't!" said Mink.

"Why not?"

"You'd just make fun of us."

"Honest, I wouldn't."

"No. We know you. Go away or we'll kick you."

Another twelve-year-old boy whirred by on little motor-skates. "Aye, Joe! Come on! Let them sissies play!"

Joseph showed reluctance and a certain wistfulness. "I want to play," he said.

"You're old," said Mink, firmly.

"Not that old," said Joe sensibly.

"You'd only laugh and spoil the Invasion."

The boy on the motor-skates made a rude lip noise. "Come on, Joe! Them and their fairies! Nuts!"

Joseph walked off slowly. He kept looking back, all down the block.

Mink was already busy again. She made a kind of apparatus with her gathered equipment. She had appointed another little girl with a pad and pencil to take down notes in painful slow scribbles. Their voices rose and fell in the warm sunlight.

All around them the city hummed. The streets were lined with good green and peaceful trees. Only the wind made a conflict across the city, across the country, across the continent. In a thousand other cities there were trees and children and avenues, business men in their quiet offices taping their voices, or watching televisors. Rockets hovered like darning needles in the blue sky. There was the universal quiet conceit and

easiness of men accustomed to peace, quite certain there would never be trouble again.
Arm in arm, men all over earth were a united front. The perfect weapons were held in
equal trust by all nations. A situation of incredibly beautiful balance had been brought
about. There were no traitors among men, no unhappy ones, no disgruntled ones; therefore the world was based upon a stable ground. Sunlight illumined half the world and the
trees drowsed in a tide of warm air.

Mink's mother, from her upstairs window, gazed down.

The children.

She looked upon them and shook her head. Well, they'd eat well, sleep well, and   35
be in school on Monday. Bless their vigorous little bodies. She listened.

Mink talked earnestly to someone near the rose-bush—though there was no one
there.

These odd children. And the little girl, what was her name? Anna? Anna took notes
on a pad. First, Mink asked the rose-bush a question, then called the answer to Anna.

"Triangle," said Mink.

"What's a tri," said Anna with difficulty, "angle?"

"Never mind," said Mink.

"How you spell it?" asked Anna.   40

"T-R-I—" spelled Mink, slowly, then snapped. "Oh, spell it yourself!" She went on to
other words. "Beam," she said.

"I haven't got tri," said Anna, "angle down yet!"

"Well, hurry, hurry!" cried Mink.

Mink's mother leaned out the upstairs window: "A-N-G-L-E," she spelled down at   45
Anna.

"Oh, thanks, Mrs. Morris," said Anna.

"Certainly," said Mink's mother and withdrew, laughing, to dust the hall with an
electro-duster-magnet.

The voices wavered on the shimmery air. "Beam," said Anna. Fading.

"Four-nine-seven-A-and-B-and-X," said Mink, far away, seriously. "And a fork and a
string and a—hex-hex-agony . . . hexagonal!"

At lunch, Mink gulped milk at one toss and was at the door. Her mother slapped   50
the table.

"You sit right back down," commanded Mrs. Morris. "Hot soup in a minute." She
poked a red button on the kitchen butler and ten seconds later something landed with a
bump in the rubber receiver. Mrs. Morris opened it, took out a can with a pair of aluminum holders, unsealed it with a flick and poured hot soup into a bowl.

During all this, Mink fidgeted. "Hurry, Mom! This is a matter of life and death!
Aw—!"

"I was the same way at your age. Always life and death. I know."

Mink banged away at the soup.

"Slow down," said Mom.

"Can't," said Mink. "Drill's waiting for me."   55

"Who's Drill? What a peculiar name," said Mom.

"You don't know him," said Mink.

"A new boy in the neighborhood?" asked Mom.

"He's new all right," said Mink. She started on her second bowl.   60

"Which one is Drill?" asked Mom.

"He's around," said Mink, evasively. "You'll make fun. Everybody pokes fun. Gee,
darn."

"Is Drill shy?"

"Yes. No. In a way. Gosh, Mom, I got to run if we want to have the Invasion!"

"Who's invading what?"

"Martians invading Earth—well, not exactly Martians. They're—I don't know. From up." She pointed with her spoon.

"And *inside*," said Mom, touching Mink's feverish brow.

Mink rebelled. "You're laughing! You'll kill Drill and everybody."

"I didn't mean to," said Mom. "Drill's a Martian?"

"No. He's—well—maybe from Jupiter or Saturn or Venus. Anyway, he's had a hard time."

"I imagine." Mrs. Morris hid her mouth behind her hand.

"They couldn't figure a way to attack Earth."

"We're impregnable," said Mom, in mock-seriousness.

"That's the word Drill used! Impreg—That was the word, Mom."

"My, my. Drill's a brilliant little boy. Two-bit words."

"They couldn't figure a way to attack, Mom. Drill says—he says in order to make a good fight you got to have a new way of surprising people. That way you win. And he says also you got to have help from your enemy."

"A fifth column," said Mom.

"Yeah. That's what Drill said. And they couldn't figure a way to surprise Earth or get help."

"No wonder. We're pretty darn strong," laughed Mom, cleaning up. Mink sat there, staring at the table, seeing what she was talking about.

"Until, one day," whispered Mink, melodramatically, "they thought of children!"

"*Well*!" said Mrs. Morris brightly.

"And they thought of how grown-ups are so busy they never look under rosebushes or on lawns!"

"Only for snails and fungus."

"And then there's something about dim-dims."

"Dim-dims?"

"Dimens-shuns."

"Dimensions?"

"Four of 'em. And there's something about kids under nine and imagination. It's real funny to hear Drill talk."

Mrs. Morris was tired. "Well, it must be funny. You're keeping Drill waiting now. It's getting late in the day and, if you want to have your Invasion before your supper bath, you'd better jump."

"Do I have to take a bath?" growled Mink.

"You do. Why is it children hate water? No matter what age you live in children hate water behind the ears!"

"Drill says I won't have to take baths," said Mink.

"Oh, he does, does he?"

"He told all the kids that. No more baths. And we can stay up till ten o'clock and go to two televisor shows on Saturday 'stead of one!"

"Well, Mr. Drill better mind his p's and q's. I'll call up his mother and—"

Mink went to the door. "We're having trouble with guys like Pete Britz and Dale Jerrick. They're growing up. They make fun. They're worse than parents. They just won't believe in Drill. They're so snooty, cause they're growing up. You'd think they'd know better. They were little only a coupla years ago. I hate them worst. We'll kill them first."

"Your father and I, last?"

"Drill says you're dangerous. Know why? Cause you don't believe in Martians! They're going to let us run the world. Well, not just us, but the kids over in the next block, too. I might be queen." She opened the door. "Mom?"

"Yes?"

"What's—lodge . . . ick?"   100

"Logic? Why, dear, logic is knowing what things are true and not true."

"He mentioned that," said Mink. "And what's im—pres—sion—able?" It took her a minute to say it.

"Why, it means—" Her mother looked at the floor, laughing gently. "It means—to be a child, dear."

"Thanks for lunch!" Mink ran out, the stuck her head back in. "Mom, I'll be sure you won't be hurt, much, really!"

"Well, thanks," said Mom.   105

Slam went the door.

At four o'clock the audio-visor buzzed. Mrs. Morris flipped the tab. "Hello, Helen!" she said, in welcome.

"Hello Mary. How are things in New York?"

"Fine, how are things in Scranton? You look tired."

"So do you. The children. Underfoot," said Helen.

Mrs. Morris sighed, "My Mink, too. The super Invasion."   110

Helen laughed. "Are your kids playing that game, too?"

"Lord, yes. Tomorrow it'll be geometrical jacks and motorized hopscotch. Were we this bad when we were kids in '48?"

"Worse. Japs and Nazis. Don't know how my parents put up with me. Tomboy."

"Parents learn to shut their ears."   115

A silence.

"What's wrong, Mary?" asked Helen.

Mrs. Morris' eyes were half-closed; her tongue slid slowly, thoughtfully over her lower lip. "Eh?" She jerked. "Oh, nothing. Just thought about that. Shutting ears and such. Never mind. Where were we?"

"My boy Tim's got a crush on some guy named—Drill, I think it was."

"Must be a new password. Mink likes him, too."   120

"Didn't know it got as far as New York. Word of mouth, I imagine. Looks like a scrap drive. I talked to Josephine and she said her kids—that's in Boston—are wild on this new game. It's sweeping the country."

At this moment, Mink trotted into the kitchen to gulp a glass of water. Mrs. Morris turned. "How're things going?"

"Almost finished," said Mink.

"Swell," said Mrs. Morris. "What's that?"

"A yo-yo," said Mink. "Watch."   125

She flung the yo-yo down its string. Reaching the end, it—

It vanished.

"See?" said Mink. "Ope!" Dibbling her finger she made the yo-yo reappear and zip up the string.

"Do that again," said her mother.

"Can't. Zero hour's five o'clock! 'Bye."   130

Mink exited, zipping her yo-yo.

On the audio-visor, Helen laughed. "Tim brought one of those yo-yo's in this morning, but when I got curious he said he wouldn't show it to me, and when I tried to work it, finally, it wouldn't work."

"You're not impressionable," said Mrs. Morris.

"What?"

"Never mind. Something I thought of. Can I help you, Helen?"   135

"I wanted to get the black-and-white cake recipe—"

The hour drowsed by. The day waned. The sun lowered in the peaceful blue sky. Shadows lengthened on the green lawns. The laughter and excitement continued. One little girl ran away, crying.

Mrs. Morris came out the front door.

"Mink, was that Peggy Ann crying?"

Mink was bent over in the yard, near the rose-bush. "Yeah. She's a scarebaby. We 140 won't let her play, now. She's getting too old to play. I guess she grew up all of a sudden."

"Is that why she cried? Nonsense. Give me a civil answer, young lady, or inside you come!"

Mink whirled in consternation, mixed with irritation. "I can't quit now. It's almost time. I'll be good. I'm sorry."

"Did you hit Peggy Ann?"

"No, honest. You ask her. It was something—well, she's just a scaredypants."

The ring of children drew in around Mink where she scowled at her work with 145 spoons and a kind of square-shaped arrangement of hammers and pipes. "There and there," murmured Mink.

"What's wrong?" said Mrs. Morris.

"Drill's stuck. Half way. If we could only get him all the way through, it'll be easier. Then all the others could come through after him."

"Can I help?"

"No'm, thanks, I'll fix it."

"All right. I'll call you for your bath in half an hour. I'm tired of watching you." 150

She went in and sat in the electric-relaxing chair, sipping a little beer from a half-empty glass. The chair massaged her back. Children, children. Children and love and hate, side by side. Sometimes children loved you, hated you, all in half a second. Strange children, did they ever forget or forgive the whippings and the harsh, strict words of command? She wondered. How can you ever forget or forgive those over and above you, those tall and silly dictators?

Time passed. A curious, waiting silence came upon the street, deepening.

Five o'clock. A clock sang softly somewhere in the house, in a quiet, musical voice, "Five o'clock . . . five o'clock. Time's awasting. Five o'clock," and purred away into silence.

Zero hour.

Mrs. Morris chuckled in her throat. Zero hour. 155

A beetle-car hummed into the driveway. Mr. Morris. Mrs. Morris smiled. Mr. Morris got out of the beetle, locked it and called hello to Mink at her work. Mink ignored him. He laughed and stood for a moment watching the children in their business. Then he walked up the front steps.

"Hello, darling."

"Hello, Henry."

She strained forward on the edge of the chair, listening. The children were silent. Too silent.

He emptied his pipe, refilled it. "Swell day. Makes you glad to be alive." 160

Buzz.

"What's that?" asked Henry.

"I don't know." She got up, suddenly, her eyes widening. She was going to say something. She stopped it. Ridiculous. Her nerves jumped. "Those children haven't anything dangerous out there, have they?" she said.

"Nothing but pipes and hammers. Why?"

"Nothing electrical?" 165

"Heck, no," said Henry. "I looked."

She walked to the kitchen. The buzzing continued. "Just the same you'd better go tell them to quit. It's after five. Tell them—" Her eyes widened and narrowed. "Tell them to put off their Invasion until tomorrow." She laughed, nervously.

The buzzing grew louder.

"What are they up to? I'd better go look, all right."

The explosion!   170

The house shook with dull sound. There were other explosions in other yards on other streets.

Involuntarily, Mrs. Morris screamed. "Up this way!" she cried, senselessly, knowing no sense, no reason. Perhaps she saw something from the corners of her eyes, perhaps she smelled a new odor or heard a new noise. There was no time to argue with Henry to convince him. Let him think her insane. Yes, insane! Shrieking, she ran upstairs. He ran after her to see what she was up to. "In the attic!" she screamed. "That's where it is!" It was only a poor excuse to get him in the attic in time—oh God, in time!

Another explosion outside. The children screamed with delight, as if at a great fireworks display.

"It's not in the attic!" cried Henry. "It's outside!"

"No, no!" Wheezing, gasping, she fumbled at the attic door. "I'll show you. Hurry!   175 I'll show you!"

They tumbled into the attic. She slammed the door, locked it, took the key, threw it into a far, cluttered corner.

She was babbling wild stuff now. It came out of her. All the subconscious suspicion and fear that had gathered secretly all afternoon and fermented like a wine in her. All the little revelations and knowledges and sense that had bothered her all day and which she had logically and carefully and sensibly rejected and censored. Now it exploded in her and shook her to bits.

"There, there," she said, sobbing against the door. "We're safe until tonight. Maybe we can sneak out, maybe we can escape!"

Henry blew up, too, but for another reason. "Are you crazy? Why'd you throw that key away! Damn it, honey!"

"Yes, yes, I'm crazy, if it helps, but stay here with me!"   180

"I don't know how in hell I can get out!"

"Quiet. They'll hear us. Oh, God, they'll find us soon enough—"

Below them, Mink's voice. The husband stopped. There was a great universal humming and sizzling, a screaming and giggling. Downstairs, the audio-televisor buzzed and buzzed insistently, alarmingly, violently. Is that Helen calling? thought Mrs. Morris. And is she calling about what I think she's calling about?

Footsteps came into the house. Heavy footsteps.

"Who's coming in my house?" demanded Henry, angrily. "Who's tramping around   185 down there?"

Heavy feet. Twenty, thirty, forty, fifty of them. Fifty persons crowding into the house. The humming. The giggling of the children. "This way!" cried Mink, below.

"Who's downstairs?" roared Henry. "Who's there!"

"Hush, oh, nonononono!" said his wife, weakly, holding him. "Please, be quiet. They might go away."

"Mom?" called Mink, "Dad?" A pause. "Where are you?"

Heavy footsteps, heavy, heavy, very HEAVY footsteps came up the stairs. Mink lead-   190 ing them.

"Mom?" A hesitation. "Dad?" A waiting, a silence.

Humming. Footsteps toward the attic. Mink's first.

They trembled together in silence in the attic, Mr. and Mrs. Morris. For some reason the electric humming, the queer cold light suddenly visible under the door crack, the strange odor and the alien sound of eagerness in Mink's voice, finally got through to Henry Morris, too. He stood, shivering, in the dark silence, his wife beside him.

"Mom! Dad!"

Footsteps. A little humming sound. The attic lock melted. The door opened. Mink   195
peered inside, tall blue shadows behind her.

"Peek-a-boo," said Mink.

ROBERT OLEN BUTLER (b. 1945)

Butler was born in Granite City, Illinois, and was educated at Northwestern and Iowa (M.A., 1969). He served in Army Intelligence in Vietnam from 1969–1972 and became proficient in the Vietnamese language. After his discharge he worked in a steel mill, drove a cab, and taught high school. At the present time he lives in Louisiana, where he teaches at McNeese State University. He has been prolific as a novelist and story writer ever since the first of his nine novels, The Alleys of Eden, *was published in 1981 after it had been rejected by twenty-one publishers. He has had many honors, including a Guggenheim Fellowship in fiction and a grant from the National Endowment for the Arts. For* A Good Scent from a Strange Mountain *(1993), a collection of stories about Vietnam and its aftermath, he received the Pulitzer Prize in fiction for 1993. He has written for movies and television. His most recent collection of stories is* Tabloid Dreams *(1996) and his most recent novel is* Mr. Spaceman *(1999). The story "Snow" is taken from* A Good Scent from a Strange Mountain.

Snow ~~~~ 1992

I wonder how long he watched me sleeping. I still wonder that. He sat and he did not wake me to ask about his carry-out order. Did he watch my eyes move as I dreamed? When I finally knew he was there and I turned to look at him, I could not make out his whole face at once. His head was turned a little to the side. His beard was neatly trimmed, but the jaw it covered was long and its curve was like a sampan sail and it held my eyes the way a sail always did when I saw one on the sea. Then I raised my eyes and looked at his nose. I am Vietnamese, you know, and we have a different sense of these proportions. Our noses are small and his was long and it also curved, gently, a reminder of his jaw, which I looked at again. His beard was dark gray, like he'd crawled out of a charcoal kiln. I make these comparisons to things from my country and village, but it is only to clearly say what this face was like. It is not that he reminded me of home. That was the farthest thing from my mind when I first saw Mr. Cohen. And I must have stared at him in those first moments with a strange look because when his face turned full to me and I could finally lift my gaze to his eyes, his eyebrows made a little jump like he was asking me, What is it? What's wrong?

I was at this same table before the big window at the front of the restaurant. The Plantation Hunan does not look like a restaurant, though. No one would give it a name like that unless it really was an old plantation house. It's very large and full of antiques. It's quiet right now. Not even five, and I can hear the big clock—I had never seen one till I came here. No one in Vietnam has a clock as tall as a man. Time isn't as important as that in Vietnam. But the clock here is very tall and they call it Grandfather, which I like, and Grandfather is ticking very slowly right now, and he wants me to fall asleep again. But I won't.

This plantation house must feel like a refugee. It is full of foreign smells, ginger and Chinese pepper and fried shells for wonton, and there's a motel on one side and a gas station on the other, not like the life the house once knew, though there are very large oak trees surrounding it, trees that must have been here when this was still a plantation. The house sits on a busy street and the Chinese family who owns it changed it from Plantation Seafood into a place that could hire a Vietnamese woman like me to be a waitress. They are very kind, this family, though we know we are different from each other. They are Chinese and I am Vietnamese and they are very kind, but we are both here in Louisiana and they go somewhere with the other Chinese in town—there are four restaurants and two laundries and some people, I think, who work as engineers at the oil refinery. They go off to themselves and they don't seem to even notice where they are.

I was sleeping that day he came in here. It was late afternoon of the day before Christmas. Almost Christmas Eve. I am not a Christian. My mother and I are Buddhist. I live with my mother and she is very sad for me because I am thirty-four years old and I am not married. There are other Vietnamese here in Lake Charles, Louisiana, but we are not a community. We are all too sad, perhaps, or too tired. But maybe not. Maybe that's just me saying that. Maybe the others are real Americans already. My mother has two Vietnamese friends, old women like her, and her two friends look at me with the same sadness in their faces because of what they see as my life. They know that once I might have been married, but the fiancé I had in my town in Vietnam went away in the Army and though he is still alive in Vietnam, the last I heard, he is driving a cab in Hô Chí Minh City and he is married to someone else. I never really knew him, and I don't feel any loss. It's just that he's the only boy my mother ever speaks of when she gets frightened for me.

I get frightened for me, too, sometimes, but it's not because I have no husband. That Christmas Eve afternoon I woke slowly. The front tables are for cocktails and for waiting for carry-out, so the chairs are large and stuffed so that they are soft. My head was very comfortable against one of the high wings of the chair and I opened my eyes without moving. The rest of me was still sleeping, but my eyes opened and the sky was still blue, though the shreds of cloud were turning pink. It looked like a warm sky. And it was. I felt sweat on my throat and I let my eyes move just a little and the live oak in front of the restaurant was quivering—all its leaves were shaking and you might think that it would look cold doing that, but it was a warm wind, I knew. The air was thick and wet, and cutting through the ginger and pepper smell was the fuzzy smell of mildew.

Perhaps it was from my dream but I remembered my first Christmas Eve in America. I slept and woke just like this, in a Chinese restaurant. I was working there. But it was in a distant place, in St. Louis. And I woke to snow. The first snow I had ever seen. It scared me. Many Vietnamese love to see their first snow, but it frightened me in some very deep way that I could not explain, and even remembering that moment—especially as I woke from sleep at the front of another restaurant—frightened me. So I turned my face sharply from the window in the Plantation Hunan and that's when I saw Mr. Cohen.

I stared at those parts of his face, like I said, and maybe this was a way for me to hide from the snow, maybe the strangeness that he saw in my face had to do with the snow. But when his eyebrows jumped and I did not say anything to explain what was going on inside me, I could see him wondering what to do. I could feel him thinking: Should I ask her what is wrong or should I just ask her for my carry-out? I am not an especially shy person, but I hoped he would choose to ask for the carry-out. I came to myself with a little jolt and I stood up and faced him—he was sitting in one of the stuffed chairs at the next table. "I'm sorry," I said, trying to turn us both from my dreaming. "Do you have an order?"

5

He hesitated, his eyes holding fast on my face. These were very dark eyes, as dark as the eyes of any Vietnamese, but turned up to me like this, his face seemed so large that I had trouble taking it in. Then he said, "Yes. For Cohen." His voice was deep, like a movie actor who is playing a grandfather, the kind of voice that if he asked what it was that I had been dreaming, I would tell him at once.

But he did not ask anything more. I went off to the kitchen and the order was not ready. I wanted to complain to them. There was no one else in the restaurant, and everyone in the kitchen seemed like they were just hanging around. But I don't make any trouble for anybody. So I just went back out to Mr. Cohen. He rose when he saw me, even though he surely also saw that I had no carry-out with me.

"It's not ready yet," I said. "I'm sorry."   10

"That's okay," he said, and he smiled at me, his gray beard opening and showing teeth that were very white.

"I wanted to scold them," I said. "You should not have to wait for a long time on Christmas Eve."

"It's okay," he said. "This is not my holiday."

I tilted my head, not understanding. He tilted his own head just like mine, like he wanted to keep looking straight into my eyes. Then he said, "I am Jewish."

I straightened my head again, and I felt a little pleasure at knowing that his   15
straightening his own head was caused by me. I still didn't understand, exactly, and he clearly read that in my face. He said, "A Jew doesn't celebrate Christmas."

"I thought all Americans celebrated Christmas," I said.

"Not all. Not exactly." He did a little shrug with his shoulders, and his eyebrows rose like the shrug, as he tilted his head to the side once more, for just a second. It all seemed to say, What is there to do, it's the way the world is and I know it and it all makes me just a little bit weary. He said, "We all stay home, but we don't all celebrate."

He said no more, but he looked at me and I was surprised to find that I had no words either on my tongue or in my head. It felt a little strange to see this very American man who was not celebrating the holiday. In Vietnam we never miss a holiday and it did not make a difference if we were Buddhist or Cao Đài or Catholic. I thought of this Mr. Cohen sitting in his room tonight alone while all the other Americans celebrated Christmas Eve. But I had nothing to say and he didn't either and he kept looking at me and I glanced down at my hands twisting at my order book and I didn't even remember taking the book out. So I said, "I'll check on your order again," and I turned and went off to the kitchen and I waited there till the order was done, though I stood over next to the door away from the chatter of the cook and the head waiter and the mother of the owner.

Carrying the white paper bag out to the front, I could not help but look inside to see how much food there was. There was enough for two people. So I did not look into Mr. Cohen's eyes as I gave him the food and rang up the order and took his money. I was counting his change into his palm—his hand, too, was very large—and he said, "You're not Chinese, are you?"

I said, "No. I am Vietnamese," but I did not raise my face to him, and he went away.   20

Two days later, it was even earlier in the day when Mr. Cohen came in. About four-thirty. The grandfather had just chimed the half hour like a man who is really crazy about one subject and talks of it at any chance he gets. I was sitting in my chair at the front once again and my first thought when I saw Mr. Cohen coming through the door was that he would think I am a lazy girl. I started to jump up, but he saw me and he motioned with his hand for me to stay where I was, a single heavy pat in the air, like he'd just laid this large hand of his on the shoulder of an invisible child before him. He said, "I'm early again."

"I am not a lazy girl," I said.

"I know you're not," he said and he sat down in the chair across from me.

"How do you know I'm not?" This question just jumped out of me. I can be a cheeky girl sometimes. My mother says that this was one reason I am not married, that this is why she always talks about the boy I was once going to marry in Vietnam, because he was a shy boy, a weak boy, who would take whatever his wife said and not complain. I myself think this is why he is driving a taxi in Hô Chí Minh City. But as soon as this cheeky thing came out of my mouth to Mr. Cohen, I found that I was afraid. I did not want Mr. Cohen to hate me.

But he was smiling. I could even see his white teeth in this smile. He said, "You're right. I have no proof."

"I am always sitting here when you come in," I said, even as I asked myself, Why are you rubbing on this subject?

I saw still more teeth in his smile, then he said, "And the last time you were even sleeping."

I think at this I must have looked upset, because his smile went away fast. He did not have to help me seem a fool before him. "It's all right," he said. "This is a slow time of day. I have trouble staying awake myself. Even in court."

I looked at him more closely, leaving his face. He seemed very prosperous. He was wearing a suit as gray as his beard and it had thin blue stripes, almost invisible, running through it. "You are a judge?"

"A lawyer," he said.

"You will defend me when the owner fires me for sleeping."

This made Mr. Cohen laugh, but when he stopped, his face was very solemn. He seemed to lean nearer to me, though I was sure he did not move. "You had a bad dream the last time," he said.

How did I know he would finally come to ask about my dream? I had known it from the first time I'd heard his voice. "Yes," I said. "I think I was dreaming about the first Christmas Eve I spent in America. I fell asleep before a window in a restaurant in St. Louis, Missouri. When I woke, there was snow on the ground. It was the first snow I'd ever seen. I went to sleep and there was still only a gray afternoon, a thin little rain, like a mist. I had no idea things could change like that. I woke and everything was covered and I was terrified."

I suddenly sounded to myself like a crazy person. Mr. Cohen would think I was lazy and crazy both. I stopped speaking and I looked out the window. A jogger went by in the street, a man in shorts and a T-shirt, and his body glistened with sweat. I felt beads of sweat on my own forehead like little insects crouching there and I kept my eyes outside, wishing now that Mr. Cohen would go away.

"Why did it terrify you?" he said.

"I don't know," I said, though this wasn't really true. I'd thought about it now and then, and though I'd never spoken them, I could imagine reasons.

Mr. Cohen said, "Snow frightened me, too, when I was a child. I'd seen it all my life, but it still frightened me."

I turned to him and now he was looking out the window.

"Why did it frighten you?" I asked, expecting no answer.

But he turned from the window and looked at me and smiled just a little bit, like he was saying that since he had asked this question of me, I could ask him, too. He answered, "It's rather a long story. Are you sure you want to hear it?"

"Yes," I said. Of course I did.

"It was far away from here," he said. "My first home and my second one. Poland and then England. My father was a professor in Warsaw. It was early in 1939. I was eight years old and my father knew something was going wrong. All the talk about the corridor

25

30

35

40

to the sea was just the beginning. He had ears. He knew. So he sent me and my mother to England. He had good friends there. I left that February and there was snow everywhere and I had my own instincts, even at eight. I cried in the courtyard of our apartment building. I threw myself into the snow there and I would not move. I cried like he was sending us away from him forever. He and my mother said it was only for some months, but I didn't believe it. And I was right. They had to lift me bodily and carry me to the taxi. But the snow was in my clothes and as we pulled away and I scrambled up to look out the back window at my father, the snow was melting against my skin and I began to shake. It was as much from my fear as from the cold. The snow was telling me he would die. And he did. He waved at me in the street and he grew smaller and we turned a corner and that was the last I saw of him."

Maybe it was foolish of me, but I thought not so much of Mr. Cohen losing his father. I had lost a father, too, and I knew that it was something that a child lives through. In Vietnam we believe that our ancestors are always close to us, and I could tell that about Mr. Cohen, that his father was still close to him. But what I thought about was Mr. Cohen going to another place, another country, and living with his mother. I live with my mother, just like that. Even still.

He said, "So the snow was something I was afraid of. Every time it snowed in England I knew that my father was dead. It took a few years for us to learn this from others, but I knew it whenever it snowed."

"You lived with your mother?" I said.

"Yes. In England until after the war and then we came to America. The others from Poland and Hungary and Russia that we traveled with all came in through New York City and stayed there. My mother loved trains and she'd read a book once about New Orleans, and so we stayed on the train and we came to the South. I was glad to be in a place where it almost never snowed."

I was thinking how he was a foreigner, too. Not an American, really. But all the talk about the snow made this little chill behind my thoughts. Maybe I was ready to talk about that. Mr. Cohen had spoken many words to me about his childhood and I didn't want him to think I was a girl who takes things without giving something back. He was looking out the window again, and his lips pinched together so that his mouth disappeared in his beard. He seemed sad to me. So I said, "You know why the snow scared me in St. Louis?"

He turned at once with a little humph sound and a crease on his forehead between his eyes and then a very strong voice saying, "Tell me," and it felt like he was scolding himself inside for not paying attention to me. I am not a vain girl, always thinking that men pay such serious attention to me that they get mad at themselves for ignoring me even for a few moments. This is what it really felt like and it surprised me. If I was a vain girl, it wouldn't have surprised me. He said it again: "Tell me why it scared you."

I said, "I think it's because the snow came so quietly and everything was underneath it, like this white surface was the real earth and everything had died—all the trees and the grass and the streets and the houses—everything had died and was buried. It was all lost. I knew there was snow above me, on the roof, and I was dead, too."

"Your own country was very different," Mr. Cohen said.

It pleased me that he thought just the way I once did. You could tell that he wished there was an easy way to make me feel better, make the dream go away. But I said to him, "This is what I also thought. If I could just go to a warm climate, more like home. So I came down to New Orleans, with my mother, just like you, and then we came over to Lake Charles. And it is something like Vietnam here. The rice fields and the heat and the way the storms come in. But it makes no difference. There's no snow to scare me here, but I still sit alone in this chair in the middle of the afternoon and I sleep and I listen to the grandfather over there ticking."

I stopped talking and I felt like I was making no sense at all, so I said, "I should check on your order."

Mr. Cohen's hand came out over the table. "May I ask your name?"

"I'm Miss Giàu," I said.

"Miss Giàu?" he asked, and when he did that, he made a different word, since   55
Vietnamese words change with the way your voice sings them.

I laughed. "My name is Giàu, with the voice falling. It means 'wealthy' in Vietnamese. When you say the word like a question, you say something very different. You say I am Miss Pout."

Mr. Cohen laughed and there was something in the laugh that made me shiver just a little, like a nice little thing, like maybe stepping into the shower when you are covered with dust and feeling the water expose you. But in the back of my mind was his carry-out and there was a bad little feeling there, something I wasn't thinking about, but it made me go off now with heavy feet to the kitchen. I got the bag and it was feeling different as I carried it back to the front of the restaurant. I went behind the counter and I put it down and I wished I'd done this a few moments before, but even with his eyes on me, I looked into the bag. There was one main dish and one portion of soup.

Then Mr. Cohen said, "Is this a giau I see on your face?" And he pronounced the word exactly right, with the curling tone that made it "pout."

I looked up at him and I wanted to smile at how good he said the word, but even wanting to do that made the pout worse. I said, "I was just thinking that your wife must be sick. She is not eating tonight."

He could have laughed at this. But he did not. He laid his hand for a moment on   60
his beard, he smoothed it down. He said, "The second dinner on Christmas Eve was for my son passing through town. My wife died some years ago and I am not remarried."

I am not a hard-hearted girl because I knew that a child gets over the loss of a father and because I also knew that a man gets over the loss of a wife. I am a good girl, but I did not feel sad for Mr. Cohen. I felt very happy. Because he laid his hand on mine and he asked if he could call me. I said yes, and as it turns out, New Year's Eve seems to be a Jewish holiday. Vietnamese New Year comes at a different time, but people in Vietnam know to celebrate whatever holiday comes along. So tonight Mr. Cohen and I will go to some restaurant that is not Chinese, and all I have to do now is sit here and listen very carefully to Grandfather as he talks to me about time.

JOHN CHIOLES (b. 1940)

Chioles, a Greek-American, is known for works about his native country. One is a collection and translation, with Dinos Siotis, Twenty Contemporary Greek Poets *(1979). The other is* Athens, Capital City (Athenes, Ville Capitale), *a description of the history, art, and architecture of Athens (1985). In the early 1990s, with Alexander Damianikos, he was involved in developing audiocassettes titled* Arab and Islam, Hellenism, *and* Reformation. *His moving story "Before the Firing Squad" was included in* The Available Press/PEN Short Story Collection, *with an introduction by Anne Tyler (1985). He has also published in the Greek language.*

The time of "Before the Firing Squad" is World War II, about 1944, during the closing days of the German occupation of Greece. The physical setting is an area of the Peloponnesus (i.e., Southern Greece) not far from the site of ancient Sparta. Chioles mentions the Arkadian Mountains and also the area of Mani to the south (paragraph 2). Mani is the middle of the three peninsulas forming the southern part of the Peloponnesus. (Ancient Sparta, of course, was known for the discipline and ferocity of its armies and for the fact that in the Peloponnesian War in the fifth century B.C.E. it defeated the forces of Athens.)

Before the Firing Squad   1985

The sound at first was a low moan, and you knew the momentum would build as soon as the hand-cranked siren, managed by teenaged boys, would pick up speed. No matter where I was, my knees turned to jelly, my pulse quickened, instinctively I would look up the hill to the bell tower of the church feeling betrayed that I could not be up there; at least there, watching the crank turn, the sound didn't frighten me. But the watch at the bell tower was for the older boys. You had to be at least twelve. From atop, where the giant bell hung, the boys kept a lookout for movement of vehicles; on a clear day they could see seven kilometers in the distance, beyond the bend.

Their convoys came from the main road. The moment they turned the bend that brings you full face with the town, their approach would echo against the side of the mountain. A hollow reverberation. The siren had by then stopped, to be replaced now by the rumbling of their trucks and heavy artillery. A moan of a different kind. The boys would run from the bell tower down the narrow streets to their homes. In no time, the dissonance of the enemy, something as ugly, efficient, and foreign to these parts as the unclean death they brought, appeared and disappeared, taking away the sun, leaving behind clouds of dust. They rarely stopped. But if they did, it could only bring down the reign of terror on all our heads. Mostly, though, they rode through on their way to Mani, where they would embark on ships bound for North Africa. To that end, they would ride roughshod over the Arkadian Mountains. What interested them most was to make sure they passed through the towns and hamlets without incident or delay, ready to crush any attempt at interference.

Their garrison of twelve soldiers stationed in the town wore mustard-colored uniforms, not the sinister black kind worn by the ones in the convoys.° These soldiers seemed very young and curiously happy. Everyone said they spoke a softer kind of German, without the harsh sounds of those northern peoples; most of them knew ancient Greek even, and liked the lilting songs of Homer. Their weapons were limited and not always in evidence. The whole town was ready to swear that these youths had never fought even a skirmish, let alone been in a war. My father used to call them Hitler's boy-soldiers, sent to promote a peaceful occupation, playing on the conscience of the partisans, counting on their decency. And, a curious thing, these young soldiers were never ambushed; none of them died in the everyday activity along these mountains, the daily sabotaging of the main artery, the only asphalt road leading down to the sea. While killing was the order of the day during that spring—ten townspeople executed for the death of one dark-uniformed German—these twelve had become practically the mascots of the town.

"I don't want you talking to this Fritz so much," Father said one day. "Everybody treats him like one of us. It isn't right." All the nice Germans we called Fritz and all the mean ones Ludwig; except that Fritz was really the name of my friend.

"He's harmless," I said. "And sometimes he brings his ration of chocolate and biscuits to share."   5

"He's the enemy," Father retorted the way he did when he would have no more discussion.

---

mustard colored . . . black kind: The mustard-colored uniforms are those of the regular German army. The black uniforms belong to the Waffen SS, whose members were infamous for their cruelty.

But the siren prevented any further talk. They came late in the afternoon of that day. My father was caught unawares. One convoy had already passed earlier, and he had run to the mountain and back again. They rarely had more than one a day. His reflexes were so swift that he practically knocked me over when he jumped to his feet.

"Put your warm sweater on and let's go." He had never taken me with him before. Women and children never ran to the mountain. The siren was for the men, whether they were part of the road sabotage teams or not. My father often stayed in the mountains for days; we never knew what he did there. "Hurry, we have no time. We'll take the back way so Fritz will not spot us. Your mother will know I've taken you with me."

The small garrison, our German mascots, lived across the street from us. They had requisitioned the best two-storied house, using the ground floor as offices and the second floor as living quarters. They were fully aware of the siren, but they pretended it came from the partisan stronghold in the mountain. Some said they even welcomed it; it gave them time to put on battle outfits, grab their guns, and move, a fierce-looking patrol, along the road. They never asked about the men of each household; their frequent absences from home they were content to believe had to do with working in the fields and vineyards. So Fritz had never asked about my father. Much like any of my friends, he was shy in his presence and avoided passing by whenever it was obvious Father was at home. Often he would come over to show us photos of his parents and his sisters, tell my mother how homesick he was, express joy or sadness whenever he would receive mail from home. And always my mother would find something to give him by way of comfort, a bunch of grapes or chestnuts or a few raisins. But whenever Father was at home it was understood he would never come over. He seemed no more than a boy and was treated much like the rest of us.

"Run faster! They're getting greedy today, and they could be mean." As we ran   10
through brush foliage I would scrape my legs and thought how nice it will be when I get to wear long trousers in another year or so.

"When we get on top I'll pick some wild tea leaves and chamomile buds for Mother. We don't have to come right back, do we?"

"We'll stay as long as we have to. Till they're gone." My father's furrowed brow told me this was not a usual run. The enemy was changing its routine; that meant everything would become unpredictable.

"Whoever is not alert, and doesn't expect the worst, will never know the unexpected when it comes his way," my father was saying to his friends when we reached the thick forest of pines. Below us, like ants in the distance, carefully covered heavy artillery rolled along the asphalt road. The atmosphere was highly charged. An unusually large number of people had taken to the mountain. The mood had changed as the sun went away and a cold mid-afternoon chill set in. All the world turned dark green and it smelled of rain, even the canvas covering the moving guns and trucks below took on the color of running oil in the absence of the sun.

"It's best to do nothing for a couple of days. They'll have patrols everywhere," one of the older men was saying to Father.

"We could've blown the far bridge yesterday. We should have been warned   15
about this."

"Maybe this is only the beginning of moving out their heavy stuff. It's up to us."

My presence in this adult conversation went unnoticed. Yet I knew I should not be hearing what was being said. So I slipped away quietly. Nearby, some goats beat their grazing rhythm on the bushes; they made the acanthus bob up and down. I had no time to wonder why the goats seemed so nervous. Just then I stepped on a dried branch which flew up at me, my feet got tangled, and I came tumbling a good ten meters down the slope. Though I was stunned, I felt hardly any pain. But the fear was real, for I heard the pounding of a machine-gun and felt the whistle of bullets flying above my head. I stayed down, hardly breathing. The machine-gun, rattling but unable to pin down movement in the vast forest, moved on along a horizontal line, then stopped.

As the moan of the convoy became more distant, I felt my father's hand lifting me up. I was more ashamed than hurting. Not until I stood upright did I see the blood running down my leg and a whole patch of skin from my knee hanging upside down.

"It's nothing" my father said, and quickly used his handkerchief to patch it up.

"It doesn't hurt any," I said.   20

"It will. Why did you come this far? Didn't we say we never come into full view of the road?"

"I fell down."

"You'll be all right. I'm going to have to send you home with your cousins. Your mother should take care of that knee."

I said nothing but followed sheepishly the downward path, my father's handkerchief tied behind my left knee. He had made the knot too tight and I felt a numbing pain but did not let on to my older cousins. Father had whispered something to them, that they should take care of me, I guessed, so I did not want to show I needed looking after.

At home there was commotion; our window was open. Mother had been putting   25
my baby sister to sleep; she had lit the oil lamp. Across the way, the German soldiers were playing phonograph records, their usual sad music. (Only, Fritz had told me many times that their music was not at all funereal as the townspeople thought—it was happy and exultant, he'd say; still, it sounded sad to me.) Nobody got wind that I limped into the house at dusk. Stealth was always my strong point.

When Mother saw me, there was an uproar and a lot to answer for. I explained quickly, and, seeing that my wound was still bleeding, she softened her tone as to the mystery of my whereabouts all afternoon.

"Here, sit down. Let's have a look."

I clenched my teeth while she cleaned the whole knee with a sponge. It stung good and sharp now.

"You must be starved, too. Fritz has brought you a surprise. Uncover that bowl on the table. It's all for you."

A bowl of food, rice with bits of chicken, cubed chunks of meat in a thick white   30
soup. Never had I eaten anything so tasty before. It came from a fancy tin that my friend received on special occasions. If each of us had to cherish one memory of food that would make our taste buds water, Fritz's bowl of chicken with rice on that evening would be mine. I felt no pain from the leg while I ate to my heart's content, nor did I notice that he had come to the window, looking in, and already my mother had silently shown him my knee. In no time, he returned with a first-aid kit and set about to dress the wound. He spoke admonishingly to me in German, but also found the right phrases in Greek to let me know he was unhappy with me.

"Children don't become partisans, you know." But his smile gave him away. He only meant I should be careful. Then he became serious again. Whenever he looked serious his eyebrows went from the straw color of his hair to a darker shade and he looked older. Even his eyes did not keep their blue but went dark like the sea.

It seemed a cloud hung over the fate of the twelve German soldiers of our town. They would be transferred soon. They might be taken to the front lines. Everything was becoming very unpredictable, he was telling my mother. I had never seen Fritz so sad before. He hung his head low as he pulled out of his trouser pocket a letter he had just received from his mother. She lived, he told us, in a big city in his country that was being bombed constantly now, and they had even less to eat than we did.

"I do not know if I will see them again."

"You will, you will. All this will soon be over and you'll get to go home. You'll see," my mother consoled as best she could.

The next morning the news was out. The whole town became concerned. If they left, would they be replaced by the black-uniformed ones? What would be in store for us? The neighborhood around us began to treat them like departing friends; they offered them sweets, dried fruits and nuts, and whatever parting hospitality they could. In their turn, the boy-soldiers responded with moist eyes, uncertain, and very scared of the weeks ahead. My mother always said, remembering those last few hours, not one of them looked a day over sixteen.

An old philosopher who dwelled along the dusty plains of Asia Minor once said there will come a Great Year whose summer will be a World Conflagration. That's just what happened to us that summer. On the very day they came to collect their soldiers and depart for good, they also set fire to nearly every house in the town.

Activity along the mountains had been fierce lately. The far bridge had been blown up; so had the narrow pass beyond. The siren howled urgently at full speed on that day. When they turned the bend they began to slow down, rolling into town at a snail's pace to cover for their foot soldiers, who darted off the road, torches in hand, setting fire to every house, every barn, every haystack in sight. That way they took a long time to get to us who lived near the square; but we had seen the smoke and the flames and we knew what was in store for us.

My mother refused to run away, hoping, with children in hand, she might at least save the house. But as the confusion around us got worse, the shooting in all directions, the trails of smoke, the terror-filled sounds of homes bursting open under the flame—no one could possibly be reasoned with, no one caught up in such careening panic. Every black Ludwig looked like a madman in passionate play with fire. During these terrible moments Fritz was nowhere to be seen.

We stood at the door of our house and watched the commotion all around us, until a burst from an automatic hit near our feet and we were routed and shown the way to the open space in the middle of the square. While she held the baby and I held on to her sleeve, my mother shuffled us to the gathering place. We never looked behind. But we knew. All around the square the trucks were moving slowly, never at rest, making a terrible din, which drowned out the cries of the dozen or so women and children huddled in the middle. We were shoved against them, and for the first time I saw a number of our town mascots, the boysoldiers, armed to the teeth, some guarding us, some being given stern orders by an officer while others were already jumping onto the moving trucks with all their gear.

The officer pointed in our direction and began to scream an order to his subordinates. Three of them rushed over to our group and kneaded us all into a straight line. I saw to my horror that Fritz was one of them. His eyes were dark and furious, hardly anyone recognized him; his whole body and movements had taken on a different shape. I felt a crushing disappointment. He looked old now like the others.

Their mission accomplished, the three ran back to the officer. He gave them what seemed final instructions and climbed into the cab of his moving truck. The three raced to set up just ahead of us a machine-gun with tripod at the front of the barrel. One of them brought the ammunition, and I saw Fritz reach into the box and bring out a magazine, which he loaded onto the gun. Just then, whistles began blowing, those piercing kind they use at train platforms to signal an imminent departure. They didn't want to remain sitting targets for the partisans, so they had to make haste.

Suddenly the motors got louder; speed was only seconds away. Fritz, now arguing with the other two soldiers, appeared even more fierce. They were pushing to get behind the machine-gun, but he seemed to win out. While they rushed to jump on the trucks, he

fell on his belly and hugged the gun, groping for the trigger. We were all frozen with fear. I searched for his eyes in utter disbelief. Time fled and backtracked toward me again. I was aware only that the trucks were moving faster, that Fritz was frozen in his place, his right hand now on the ground, too far from the latch of the trigger. Then in a flash he jumped up, lifted the gun from its tripod, and let it sing half across the sky, while in the same motion he chased the last truck, leaping headfirst into it. His torso, writhing wildly to get his weight into the truck, was the last thing I saw of Fritz, who had in those last dancerlike movements transformed his body once more into the boy that he really was, waving good-bye at us with his legs.

STEPHEN DIXON (b. 1936)

A New York native, Dixon received his B.A. from the City College of New York in 1958. His first collections of stories were No Relief *(1976) and* Quite Contrary *(1979). Early in 1992, his novel* Frog *was under consideration for the PEN/Faulkner Award for Fiction. His selected short stories appeared in 1994, followed in the next year by his novel* Interstate. *Among many distinctions are the O. Henry Award and the Pushcart Prize. "All Gone" (1990) is somewhat like Dixon's novel* Too Late *(1978), in which the protagonist, Art, goes in search of his lost woman friend Donna. His search reveals the city as a bizarre and dangerous place, reminiscent of Eliot's experience on the subway platform in "All Gone."*

All Gone ~~~~~ 1990

He says goodbye, we kiss at the door, he rings for the elevator, I say "I'll call you when I find out about the tickets," he says "Anytime, as I'll be in all day working on that book jacket I'm behind on," waves to me as the elevator door opens and I shut the door.

I find out about the tickets and call him and he doesn't answer. Maybe he hasn't gotten home yet, though he usually does in half an hour. But it's Saturday and the subway's always much slower on weekends, and I call him half an hour later and he doesn't answer.

He could have got home and I missed him because he right away might have gone out to buy some necessary art supply or something, and I call him an hour later and he doesn't answer. I do warm-ups, go out and run my three miles along the river, come back and shower and call him and he doesn't answer. I dial him every half hour after that for the next three hours and then call Operator and she checks and says his phone's in working order.

I call his landlord and say "This is Maria Pierce, Eliot Schulter's good friend for about the last half-year—you know me. Anyway, could you do me a real big favor and knock on his door? I know it's an inconvenience but he's only one flight up and you see, he should be home and doesn't answer and I've been phoning and phoning him and am getting worried. I'll call you back in fifteen minutes. If he's in and for his own reasons didn't want to answer the phone or it actually is out of order, could you have him call me at home?"

I call the landlord back in fifteen minutes and he says "I did what you said and he didn't answer. That would've been enough for me. But you got me worried also, so I went downstairs for his duplicate keys and opened his door just a ways and yelled in for him and then walked in and he wasn't there, though his place looked okay."

"Excuse me, I just thought of something. Was his night light on?"

"You mean the little small-watt-bulb lamp on his fireplace mantel?"

5

"That's the one. He always keeps it on at night to keep away burglars who like to jump in from his terrace."

"What burglars jumping in from where? He was never robbed that I know."

"The tenant before him said she was. Was it on?"

"That's different. Yes. I thought he'd forgotten about the light, so I shut if off. I was thinking about his electricity cost, but you think I did wrong?"

"No. It only means he never got home. Thanks."

I call every half hour after that till around six, when he usually comes to my apartment. But he never comes here without our first talking on the phone during the afternoon about all sorts of things: how our work's going, what the mail brought, what we might have for dinner that evening and do later and if there's anything he can pick up on the way here and so on. The concert's at eight and I still have to pick up the tickets from my friend who's giving them to me and can't go herself because her baby's sick and her husband won't go without her. I call her and say "I don't see how we can make the concert. Eliot's not here, hasn't called, doesn't answer his phone and from what his landlord said, I doubt he ever got home after he left me this morning."

"Does he have any relatives or close friends in the city for you to call?"

"No, he would have gone to his apartment directly—I know him. He had important work to finish, and the only close person other than myself to him is his mother in Seattle."

"Maybe he did get home but got a very sudden call to drop everything and fly out to her, so he didn't have the time to phone you, or when he did, your line was busy."

"No, we're close enough that he'd know it would worry me. He'd have called from the airport, someplace."

"Your line still could have been busy all the times you were trying to get him. But I'm sure everything's okay, and don't worry about the tickets. Expensive as they are, I'll put them down as a total loss. Though if you are still so worried about him, phone the police in his neighborhood or even his mother in Seattle."

"Not his mother. There's no reason and I'd just worry her and Eliot would get angry at me. But the police is a good idea."

I call the police station in his precinct. The officer who answers says "We've nothing on a Mr. Schulter. But being that you say he left your apartment this morning, phone your precinct station," and she gives me the number. I call it and the officer on duty says "Something did come in today about someone of his name—let me think."

"Oh no."

"Hey, take it easy. It could be nothing. I'm only remembering that I saw an earlier bulletin, but what it was went right past me. What's your relationship to him before I start searching for it?"

"His closest friend. We're really very very close and his nearest relative is three thousand miles from here."

"Well, I don't see it in front of me. I'll locate it, though don't get excited when I'm away. It could be nothing. I might even be wrong. It was probably more like a Mr. Fullter or Schulton I read about, but not him. Want me to phone you back?"

"I'll wait, thanks."

"Let me take your number anyway, just in case I get lost."

He goes, comes back in a minute. "Now take it easy. It's very serious. He had no I.D. on him other than this artist society card with only his signature on it, which we were checking into, so we're grateful you called."

"Please, what is it?"

"According to this elderly witness, he was supposedly thrown on the subway tracks this morning and killed."

I scream, break down, hang up, pound the telephone table with my fists, the officer   30
calls back and says "If you could please revive yourself, Miss, we'd like you to come to the
police station here and then, if you could by the end of the night sometime, to the
morgue to identify your friend."

I say no, I could never go to the morgue, but then go with my best friend. She stays
outside the body room when I go in, look and say "That's him." Later I call Eliot's mother and the next day her brother comes to the city and takes care of the arrangements to
have Eliot flown to Seattle and his apartment closed down and most of his belongings
sold or given away or put on the street. The uncle asks if I'd like to attend the funeral, but
doesn't mention anything about providing air fare or where I would stay. Since I don't
have much money saved and also think I'll be out of place there and maybe even looked
down upon by his family I've never seen, I stay here and arrange on that same funeral day
a small ceremony in the basement of a local church, where I and several of our friends
and his employers speak about Eliot and read aloud excerpts of his letters to a couple of
us and listen to parts of my opera records he most liked to play and for a minute bow our
heads, hold hands and pray.

According to that elderly witness, Eliot was waiting for a train on the downtown
platform of my stop when he saw a young man speaking abusively to a girl of about fifteen. When the girl continued to ignore him, he made several obscene gestures and said
he was going to throw her to the platform and force her to do all sorts of sordid things to
him and if he couldn't get her to do them there because people were watching, then in
the men's room upstairs. The girl was frightened and started to walk away. The young
man grabbed her wrist, started to twist it, stopped and said he would rip her arm off if she
gave him a hard time, but didn't let go. There were a few people on the platform. Nobody said anything or tried to help her and in fact all of them except Eliot and this elderly man eventually moved to the other end of the platform or at least away from what
was going on. Then Eliot went over to the young man, who was still holding the girl by
her wrist, and very politely asked him to let her alone. Something like "Excuse me, I
don't like to interfere in anyone's problems. But if this young lady doesn't want to be
bothered by you, then I would really think you'd let her go."

"Listen, I know her, so mind your business," the young man said and she said to
Eliot "No he don't." Then out of nowhere a friend of the young man ran down the subway stairs and said to him "What's this chump doing, horning in on your act?" The elderly man got up from a bench and started for the upstairs to get help. "You stay right here,
grandpa," the first young man said, "or you'll get thrown on your back too." The elderly
man stopped. Eliot said to the young men "Please, nobody should be getting thrown on
their backs. And I hate to get myself any more involved in this but for your own good you
fellows ought to go now or just leave everybody here alone."

"And for your own good," one of the young men said, "you'd be wiser moving your
ass out of here."

"I can only move it once I know this girl's out of danger with you two."   35

"She'll be plenty out of danger when you move your ass out of here, now move."

"Believe me, I'd like to, but how can I? Either you leave her completely alone now
or I'll have to get the police."

That's when they jumped him, beat him to the ground and, when he continued to
fight back with his feet, fists and butting his head, picked him up and threw him on the
tracks. He landed on his head and cracked his skull and something like a blood clot suddenly shot through to the brain, a doctor later said. The girl had already run away. The
young men ran the opposite way. The elderly man shouted at Eliot to get up, then at people to jump down to the tracks to help Eliot up, then ran in the direction the young men
went to the token booth upstairs and told the attendant inside that an unconscious man

was lying on the tracks and for her to do something quick to prevent a train from running over him. She phoned from the booth. He ran back to the platform and all the way to the other end of it yelling to the people around him "Stop the train. Man on the tracks, stop the local train." When the downtown local entered the station a minute later, he and most of the people along the platform screamed and waved the motorman to stop the train because someone was on the tracks. The train came to a complete stop ten feet from Eliot. A lot of the passengers were thrown to the floor and the next few days a number of them sued the city for the dizzy spells and sprained fingers and ripped clothes they said they got from the sudden train stop and also for the days and weeks they'd have to miss from their jobs because of their injuries. Anyway, according to that same doctor who examined Eliot at the hospital, he was dead a second or two after his head hit the train rail.

For a week after the funeral I go into my own special kind of mourning: seeing nobody, never leaving the apartment or answering phone calls, eating little and drinking too much, but mostly just sleeping or watching television while crying and lying in bed. Then I turn the television off, answer every phone call, run along the river for twice as many miles than I usually do, go out for a big restaurant dinner with a friend and return to my job.

The Saturday morning after the next Saturday after that I sit on the bench near the　40 place on the subway platform where Eliot was thrown off. I stay there from eight to around one, on the lookout for the two young men. I figure they live in the neighborhood and maybe every Saturday have a job or something to go to downtown and after a few weeks they'll think everything's forgotten about them and their crime and they can go safely back to their old routines, like riding the subway to work at the station nearest their homes. The descriptions I have of them are the ones the elderly witness gave. He said he was a portrait painter or used to be and so he was absolutely exact about their height, age, looks, mannerisms and hair color and style and clothes. He also made detailed drawings of the men for the police, which I have copies of from the newspaper, and which so far haven't done the police any good in finding them.

What I'm really looking out for besides those descriptions are two young men who will try and pick up or seriously annoy or molest a teen-age girl on the platform or do that to any reasonably young woman, including me. If I see them and I'm sure it's them I'll summon a transit policeman to arrest them and if there's none around then I'll follow the young men, though discreetly, till I see a policeman. And if they try and molest or terrorize me on the bench and no policeman's around, I'll scream at the top of my lungs till someone comes and steps in, and hopefully a policeman. But I just want those two young men caught, that's all, and am willing to risk myself a little for it, and though there's probably not much chance of it happening, I still want to give it a good try.

I do this every Saturday morning for months. I see occasional violence on the platform, like a man slapping his woman friend in the face or a mother hitting her infant real hard, but nothing like two or even one man of any description close to those young men terrorizing or molesting a woman or girl or even trying to pick one up. I do see men, both old and young, and a few who look no more than nine years old or ten, leer at women plenty as if they'd like to pick them up or molest them. Some men, after staring at a woman from a distance, then walk near to her when the train comes just to follow her through the same door into the car. But that's as far as it goes on the platform. Maybe when they both get in the car and especially when it's crowded, something worse happens. I know that a few times a year when I ride the subway, a pull or poke from a man has happened to me.

A few times a man has come over to the bench and once even a woman who looked manly and tried to talk to me, but I brushed them off with silence or a remark. Then one morning a man walks over when I'm alone on the bench and nobody else is around. I'm not worried, since he has a nice face and is decently dressed and I've seen him before here waiting for the train and all it seems he wants now is to sit down. He's a big man, so I move over a few inches to the far end of the bench to give him more room.

"No," he says, "I don't want to sit—I'm just curious. I've seen you in this exact place almost every Saturday for the last couple of months and never once saw you get on the train. Would it be too rude—"

"Yes."

"All right. I won't ask it. I'm sorry."

"No, go on, ask it. What is it you want to know? Why I sit here? Well I've been here every Saturday for more than three months straight, if you're so curious to know, and why you don't see me get on the car is none of your business, okay?"

"Sure," he says, not really offended or embarrassed. "I asked for and got it and should be satisfied. Excuse me," and he walks away and stands near the edge of the platform, never turning around to me. When the local comes, he gets on it.

Maybe I shouldn't have been that sharp with him, but I don't like to be spoken to by men I don't know, especially in subways.

Next Saturday around the same time he comes downstairs again and stops by my bench.

"Hello," he says.

I don't say anything and look the other way.

"Still none of my business why you sit here every Saturday like this?"

I continue to look the other way.

"I should take a hint, right?"

"Do you think that's funny?"

"No."

"Then what do you want me to do, call a policeman?"

"Of course not. I'm sorry and I am being stupid."

"Look, I wouldn't call a policeman. You seem okay. You want to be friendly or so it seems. You're curious besides, which is good. But to me it is solely my business and not yours why I am here and don't want to talk to you and so forth and I don't know why you'd want to persist in it."

"I understand," and he walks away, stays with his back to me and gets on the train when it comes.

Next Saturday he walks down the stairs and stays near the platform edge about ten feet away reading a book. Then he turns to me and seems just about to say something and I don't know what I'm going to say in return, if anything, because he does seem polite and nice and intelligent and I actually looked forward a little to seeing and speaking civilly to him, when the train comes. He waves to me and gets on it. I lift my hand to wave back but quickly put it down. Why start?

Next Saturday he runs down the stairs to catch the train that's pulling in. He doesn't even look at me this time, so in a rush is he to get on the car. He gets past the doors just before they close and has his back to me when the train leaves. He must be late for someplace.

The next Saturday he comes down the stairs and walks over to me with two containers of coffee or tea while the train's pulling in. He keeps walking to me while the train doors open, close, and the train goes. I look at the advertisement clock. He's about fifteen minutes earlier than usual.

"How do you like your coffee if I can ask, black or regular? Or maybe you don't want any from me, if you do drink coffee, which would of course be all right too."

"Regular, but I don't want any, thanks."

"Come on, take it, it's not toxic and I can drink my coffee any old way. And it'll perk you up, not that you need perking up and certainly not from me," and he gives me a container. "Sugar?" and I say "Really, this is—" and he says "Come on: sugar?" and I nod and he pulls out of his jacket pocket a couple of sugar packets and a stirring stick. "I just took these on the way out of the shop without waiting for a bag, don't ask me why. The stick's probably a bit dirty, do you mind?" and I shake my head and wipe the stick though there's nothing on it. "Mind if I sit and have my coffee also?" and I say "Go ahead. It's not my bench and all that and I'd be afraid to think what you'd pull out of your pocket if I said no—probably your own bench and cocktail table," and he says "Don't be silly," and sits.

He starts talking about the bench, how the same oak one has been here for at least thirty years because that's how long he's lived in the neighborhood, then about the coffee, that it's good though always from the shop upstairs a little bitter, then why he happens to see me every Saturday: that he's recently divorced and has a child by that marriage who he goes to in Brooklyn once a week to spend the whole day with. He seems even nicer and more intelligent than I thought and comfortable to be with and for the first time I think he's maybe even goodlooking when before I thought his ears stuck out too far and he had too thin a mouth and small a nose. He dresses well anyway and has a nice profile and his hair's stylish and neat and his face shaven clean which I like and no excessive jewelry or neck chain which I don't and in his other jacket pocket are a paperback and small ribbon-wrapped package, the last I guess a present for his little girl.

His train comes and when the doors open I say "Shouldn't you get on it?" and he says "I'll take the next one if you don't mind," and I say "I don't think it's up to me to decide," and he hunches his shoulders and gives me that expression "Well I don't know what to say," and the train goes and when it's quiet again he continues the conversation, now about what I think of something that happened in Africa yesterday which he read in the paper today. I tell him I didn't read it and that maybe when I do read my paper it won't be the same as his and so might not have that news story and he says "What paper you read?" and I tell him and he says "Same one—front page, left-hand column," and I say "Anyway, on Saturdays I don't, and for my own reasons, have time for the newspaper till I get home later and really also don't have the time to just sit here and talk," and he says "Of course, of course," but seriously, as if he believes me, and we're silent for a while, drinking our coffees and looking at the tracks.

We hear another train coming and I say "I think you better get on this one," and he says "Okay. It's been great and I hope I haven't been too much of a nuisance," and I say "You really haven't at all," and he says "Mind if I ask your name?" and I say "Your train," and he yells to the people going into the subway car "Hold the door," and gets up and says to me "Mine's Vaughn," and shakes my hand and says "Next week," and runs to the train with his container and he's not past the door a second when the man who kept it open for him lets it close. 70

I picture him on his way to Brooklyn, reading his book, later in Prospect Park with his daughter as he said they would do if the good weather holds up and in an indoor ice-skating rink if it doesn't, and then go back to my lookout. People spit and throw trash on the tracks, a drunk or crazy man urinates on the platform, a boy defaces the tile wall with a marker pen and tells me to go shoot myself when I very politely suggest he stop, there's almost a fight between a man trying to get off the train and the one blocking his way who's trying to get on, which I doubt would have happened if both sides of the double door had opened, but again no sign of my two young men.

Vaughn's not there the next Saturday and the Saturday after that and the third Saturday he's not there I begin thinking that I'm thinking more about him than I do of anybody or thing and spending more time looking at the staircase and around the platform form him than I do for those young men. I've gradually lost interest in finding them and over the last four months my chances have gotten worse and worse that I'll even recognize them if they ever do come down here and as far as their repeating that harassing-the-girl incident at this particular station, well forget it, and I leave the station at noon instead of around my usual two and decide that was my last Saturday there.

A month later I meet Vaughn coming out of a supermarket when I'm going in. He's pulling a shopping cart filled with clean laundry at the bottom and two big grocery bags on top. It's Saturday, we're both dressed in T-shirts and shorts for the warm weather now, and I stop him by saying "Vaughn, how are you?" He looks at me as if he doesn't remember me. "Maybe because you can't place me anywhere else but on a subway bench. Maria Pierce. From the subway station over there."

"That's right. Suddenly your face was familiar, but you never gave me your name. What's been happening?" and I say "Nothing much I guess," and he says "You don't wait in subway stations anymore for whatever you were waiting for those days?" and I say "How would you know? You stopped coming yourself there and to tell you the truth I was sort of looking forward to a continuation of that nice chat we last had."

"Oh, let me tell you what went wrong. My ex-wife, giving me a day's notice, changed jobs and locations and took my daughter to Boston with her. I could have fought it, but don't like arguments. I only get to see her when I get up there, which hasn't happened yet, and maybe for August if I want." 75

"That's too bad. I remember how devoted you were."

"I don't know it's so bad. I'm beginning to enjoy my freedom every Saturday, as much as I miss my kid. But I got to go. Ice cream in the bag will soon be melting," and he says goodbye and goes.

If I knew his last name I might look him up in the phone book and call him and say something like "Since we live in the same neighborhood, would you care to have a cup of coffee one of these days? I owe you one and I'll even, if you're still curious, let you in on my big secret why I every Saturday for months waited at our favorite subway station." Then I think no, even if I did have his phone number. I gave him on the street a couple of openings to make overtures about seeing me again and he didn't take them because he didn't want to or whatever his reasons but certainly not because of his melting ice cream.

Several weeks later I read in the newspaper that those two young men got caught. They were in the Eighth Street subway station and tried to molest a policewoman dressed like an artist with even a sketchbook and drawing pen, and two plain-clothesmen were waiting nearby. The police connected them up with Eliot's death. The two men later admitted to being on my subway platform that day but said they only started a fight with him because he tried to stop one of them from making a date with a girl the young man once knew. They said they told Eliot to mind his business, he refused, so they wrestled him to the ground and then said he could get up if he didn't make any more trouble. Eliot said okay, got up and immediately swung at them, missed, lost his footing and before either of them could grab him away, fell to the tracks. They got scared and ran to the street. They don't know the girl's last name or where she lives except that it's somewhere in the Bronx.

I buy all the newspapers that day and the next. One of them has a photo of the 80 young men sticking their middle fingers up to the news photographers. They don't look anything like the young men I was on the lookout for, so either the witness's description of them or the printing of the photograph was bad, because I don't see how they could have physically changed so much in just a few months.

I continue to read the papers for weeks after that, hoping to find something about the young men going to trial, but don't. Then a month later a co-worker of mine who knew about Eliot and me says she saw on the television last night that the young men were allowed to plead guilty to a lesser charge of negligent manslaughter or something and got off with a jail term of from one to three years. "It seems the elderly man, that main witness to Eliot's murder, died of a fatal disease a while ago and the young woman witness could never be found. As for molesting the policewoman, that charge was dropped, though the news reporter never said why."

ANDRE DUBUS (1936–1999)

Dubus was born in Louisiana and received degrees from McNeese State College and the University of Iowa. He taught at Bradford College in Massachusetts before he was struck and disabled by a speeding automobile. He lived northwest of Boston near the Merrimack River, an area he often employed as the setting in his ficiton. The stories in his Selected Stories *(1988), from which "The Curse" is taken, touch the darker areas of human existence, but nevertheless have a compelling force. In "They Now Live in Texas," for example, a woman sees a horror ghost movie on her VCR and then awaits her own demons. In another story, "Townies," a drifting, purposeless young man kills his girlfriend and then achieves a curious serenity as he waits for the police. Dubus's last short story collection was* Dancing After Hours *(1996). He also worked in the longer form of the novella and published several novellas in* We Don't Live Here Anymore *(1984). He gained many honors, among them a Guggenheim Fellowship and a MacArthur Fellowship.*

The Curse ~ ✦✧✦ ~ 1988

Mitchell Hayes was forty-nine years old, but when the cops left him in the bar with Bob, the manager, he felt much older. He did not know what it was like to be very old, a shrunken and wrinkled man, but he assumed it was like this: fatigue beyond relieving by rest, by sleep. He also was not a small man: his weight moved up and down in the hundred and seventies and he was five feet, ten inches tall. But now his body seemed short and thin. Both stood at one end of the bar; he was a large blackhaired man, and there was nothing in front of him but an ash tray he was using. He looked at Mitchell at the cash register and said: "Forget it. You heard what Smitty said."

Mitchell looked away, at the front door. He had put the chairs upside down on the table. He looked from the door past Bob to the empty space of floor at the rear; sometimes people danced there, to the jukebox. Opposite Bob, on the wall behind the bar, was a telephone; Mitchell looked at it. He had told Smitty there were five guys and when he moved to the phone one of them stepped around the corner of the bar and shoved him: one hand against Mitchell's chest, and it pushed him backward; he nearly fell. That was when they were getting rough with her at the bar. When they took her to the floor Mitchell looked once at her sounds, then looked down at the duckboard he stood on, or at the belly or chest of a young man in front of him.

He knew they were not drunk. They had been drinking before they came to his place, a loud popping of motorcycles outside, then walking into the empty bar, young and sunburned and carrying helmets and wearing thick leather jackets in August. They stood in front of Mitchell and drank drafts. When he took their first order he thought they were on drugs and later, watching them, he was certain. They were not relaxed, in the way of most drinkers near closing time. Their eyes were quick, alert as wary animals, and they spoke loudly, with passion, but their passion was strange and disturbing, because they were only chatting, bantering. Mitchell knew nothing of the effects of drugs, so could not guess what was in their blood. He feared and hated drugs because of his work and because he was the stepfather of teenagers: a boy and a girl. He gave last call and served them and leaned against the counter behind him.

Then the door opened and the girl walked in from the night, a girl he had never seen, and she crossed the floor toward Mitchell. He stepped forward to tell her she had missed last call, but before he spoke she asked for change for the cigarette machine. She was young, he guessed nineteen to twenty-one, and deeply tanned and had dark hair. She was sober and wore jeans and a dark blue tee shirt. He gave her the quarters but she was standing between two of the men and she did not get to the machine.

When it was over and she lay crying on the cleared circle of floor, he left the bar   5
and picked up the jeans and tee shirt beside her and crouched and handed them to her. She did not look at him. She lay the clothes across her breasts and what Mitchell thought of now as her wound. He left her and dialed 911, then Bob's number. He woke up Bob. Then he picked up her sneakers from the floor and placed them beside her and squatted near her face, her crying. He wanted to speak to her and touch her, hold a hand or press her brow, but he could not.

The cruiser was there quickly, the siren coming east from town, then slowing and deepening as the car stopped outside. He was glad Smitty was one of them; he had gone to high school with Smitty. The other was Dave, and Mitchell knew him because it was a small town. When they saw the girl Dave went out to the cruiser to call for an ambulance, and when he came back he said two other cruisers had those scumbags and were taking them in. The girl was still crying and could not talk to Smitty and Dave. She was crying when a man and woman lifted her onto a stretcher and rolled her out the door and she vanished forever in a siren.

Bob came in while Smitty and Dave were sitting at the bar drinking coffee and Smitty was writing his report; Mitchell stood behind the bar. Bob sat next to Dave as Mitchell said: "I could have stopped them, Smitty."

"That's our job," Smitty said. "You want to be in the hospital now?"

Mitchell did not answer. When Smitty and Dave left, he got a glass of Coke from the cobra and had a cigarette with Bob. They did not talk. Then Mitchell washed his glass and Bob's cup and they left, turning off the lights. Outside Mitchell locked the front door, feeling the sudden night air after almost ten hours of air conditioning. When he had come to work the day had been very hot, and now he thought it would not have happened in winter. They had stopped for a beer on their way somewhere from the beach; he had heard them say that. But the beach was not the reason. He did not know the reason, but he knew it would not have happened in winter. The night was cool and now he could smell trees. He turned and looked at the road in front of the bar. Bob stood beside him on the small porch.

"If the regulars had been here," Bob said.   10

He turned and with his hand resting on the wooden rail he walked down the ramp to the ground. At his car he stopped and looked over its roof at Mitchell.

"You take it easy," he said.

Mitchell nodded. When Bob got in his car and left, he went down the ramp and drove home to his house on a street that he thought was neither good nor bad. The houses were small and there were old large houses used now as apartments for families. Most of the people had work, most of the mothers cared for their children, and most of the children were clean and looked like they lived in homes, not caves like some he saw in town.

He worried about the older kids, one group of them anyway. They were idle. When he was a boy in a town farther up the Merrimack River, he and his friends committed every mischievous act he could recall on afternoons and nights when they were idle. His stepchildren were not part of that group. They had friends from the high school. The front porch light was on for him and one in the kitchen at the rear of the house. He went in the front door and switched off the porch light and walked through the living and dining rooms to the kitchen. He got a can of beer from the refrigerator, turned out the light, and sat at the table. When he could see, he took a cigarette from Susan's pack in front of him.

Down the hall he heard Susan move on the bed then get up and he hoped it wasn't for the bathroom but for him. He had met her eight years ago when he had given up on ever marrying and having kids, then one night she came into the bar with two of her girl friends from work. She made six dollars an hour going to homes of invalids, mostly what she called her little old ladies, and bathing them. She got the house from her marriage, and child support the guy paid for a few months till he left town and went south. She came barefoot down the hall and stood in the kitchen doorway and said: "Are you all right?"

"No."   15

She sat across from him, and he told her. Very soon she held his hand. She was good. He knew if he had fought all five of them and was lying in pieces in a hospital bed she would tell him he had done the right thing, as she was telling him now. He liked her strong hand on his. It was a professional hand and he wanted from her something he had never wanted before: to lie in bed while she bathed him. When they went to bed he did not think he would be able to sleep, but she kneeled beside him and massaged his shoulders and rubbed his temples and pressed her hands on his forehead. He woke to the voices of Marty and Joyce in the kitchen. They had summer jobs, and always when they woke him he went back to sleep till noon, but now he got up and dressed and went to the kitchen door. Susan was at the stove, her back to him, and Marty and Joyce were talking and smoking. He said good morning, and stepped into the room.

"What are you doing up?" Joyce said.

She was a pretty girl with her mother's wide cheekbones and Marty was a tall good-looking boy, and Mitchell felt as old as he had before he slept. Susan was watching him. Then she poured him a cup of coffee and put it at his place and he sat, Marty said: "You getting up for the day?"

"Something happened last night. At the bar." They tried to conceal their excitement, but he saw it in their eyes. "I should have stopped it. I think I *could* have stopped it. That's the point. There were these five guys. They were on motorcycles but they weren't bikers. Just punks. They came in late, when everybody else had gone home. It was a slow night anyway. Everybody was at the beach."

"They rob you?" Marty said.   20

"No. A girl came in. Young. Nice looking. You know: just a girl, minding her business." They nodded, and their eyes were apprehensive.

"She wanted cigarette change, that's all. Those guys were on dope. Coke or something. You know: they were flying in place."

"Did they rape her?" Joyce said.

"Yes, honey."   25

"The *fuckers*."

Susan opened her mouth then closed it and Joyce reached quickly for Susan's pack of cigarettes. Mitchell held his lighter for her and said: "When they started getting rough with her at the bar I went for the phone. One of them stopped me. He shoved me, that's all. I should have hit him with a bottle."

Marty reached over the table with his big hand and held Mitchell's shoulder.

"No, Mitch. Five guys that mean. And coked up or whatever. No way. You wouldn't be here this morning."

"I don't know. There was always a guy with me. But just one guy, taking turns." 30

"Great," Joyce said. Marty's hand was on Mitchell's left shoulder; she put hers on his right hand.

"They took her to the hospital," he said. "The guys are in jail."

"They are?" Joyce said.

"I called the cops. When they left."

"You'll be a good witness," Joyce said. 35

He looked at her proud face.

"At the trial," she said.

The day was hot but that night most of the regulars came to the bar. Some of the younger ones came on motorcycles. They were a good crowd: they all worked, except the retired ones and no one ever bothered the women, not even the young ones with their summer tans. Everyone talked about it: some had read the newspaper story, some had heard the story in town, and they wanted to hear it from Mitchell. He told it as often as they asked but he did not finish it because he was working hard and could not stay with any group of customers long enough.

He watched their faces. Not one of them, even the women, looked at him as if he had not cared enough for the girl, or was a coward. Many of them even appeared sympathetic, making him feel for moments that he was a survivor of something horrible, and when that feeling left him he was ashamed. He felt tired and old, making drinks and change, moving and talking up and down the bar. At the stool at the far end Bob drank coffee and whenever Mitchell looked at him he smiled or nodded and once raised his right fist, with the thumb up.

Reggie was drinking too much. He did that two or three times a month and 40 Mitchell had to shut him off and Reggie always took it humbly. He was a big gentle man with a long brown beard. But tonight shutting off Reggie demanded from Mitchell an act of will, and when the eleven o'clock news came on the television and Reggie ordered another shot and a draft, Mitchell pretended not to hear him. He served the customers at the other end of the bar, where Bob was. He could hear Reggie calling: Hey Mitch; shot and a draft, Mitch. Mitchell was close to Bob now. Bob said softly: "He's had enough."

Mitchell nodded and went to Reggie, leaned closer to him so he could speak quietly, and said: "Sorry, Reggie. Time for coffee. I don't want you dead out there."

Reggie blinked at him.

"Okay, Mitch." He pulled some bills from his pocket and put them on the bar. Mitchell glanced at them and saw at least a ten dollar tip. When he rang up Reggie's tab the change was sixteen dollars and fifty cents, and he dropped the coins and shoved the bills into the beer mug beside the cash register. The mug was full of bills, as it was on most nights, and he kept his hand in there, pressing Reggie's into the others, and saw the sunburned young men holding her down on the floor and one kneeling between her legs, spread and held, and he heard their cheering voices and her screaming and groaning and finally weeping and weeping and weeping, until she was the siren crying then fading into the night. From the floor behind him, far across the room, he felt her pain and terror and grief, then her curse upon him. The curse moved into his back and spread down and up his spine, into his stomach and legs and arms and shoulders until he quivered with it. He wished he were alone so he could kneel to receive it.

CHARLOTTE PERKINS GILMAN (1860–1935)

Born in 1860, Gilman did not begin writing seriously until after the birth of her daughter in the 1880s, which was followed by her "nervous breakdown." Attempting to establish her independence, she left her husband in 1890 and went to California, where she launched what was to become a distinguished career as an advocate for women's rights. For many decades she lectured and wrote extensively, her touchstone work being Women and Economics *(1898), in which she championed the need for women's financial independence. Among her many writings were* Concerning Children *(1900),* Human Work *(1904), and* His Religion and Hers *(1923). In the 1930s she became incurably ill, and with death facing her, she took her own life in 1938.*

The Yellow Wallpaper°   1892

It is very seldom that mere ordinary people like John and myself secure ancestral halls for the summer.

A colonial mansion, a hereditary estate, I would say a haunted house and reach the height of romantic felicity—but that would be asking too much of fate!

Still I will proudly declare that there is something queer about it.

Else, why should it be let so cheaply? And why have stood so long untenanted?

John laughs at me, of course, but one expects that.   5

John is practical in the extreme. He has no patience with faith, an intense horror of superstition, and he scoffs openly at any talk of things not to be felt and seen and put down in figures.

John is a physician, and *perhaps*—(I would not say it to a living soul, of course, but this is dead paper and a great relief to my mind)—*perhaps* that is one reason I do not get well faster.

You see, he does not believe I am sick! And what can one do?

If a physician of high standing, and one's own husband, assures friends and relatives that there is really nothing the matter with one but temporary nervous depression—a slight hysterical tendency—what is one to do?

My brother is also a physician, and also of high standing, and he says the same   10
thing.

So I take phosphates or phosphites—whichever it is—and tonics, and air and exercise, and journeys, and am absolutely forbidden to "work" until I am well again.

Personally, I disagree with their ideas.

Personally, I believe that congenial work, with excitement and change, would do me good.

But what is one to do?

I did write for a while in spite of them; but it *does* exhaust me a good deal—having   15
to be so sly about it, or else meet with heavy opposition.

The Yellow Wallpaper: The story is based on the "rest cure" developed after the Civil War by the famous Philadelphia physician S. Weir Mitchell (1829–1914); see paragraph 83. The Mitchell treatment required confining the patient to a hospital, hotel, or some other remote residence. Once isolated, the patient was to have complete bed rest, increased food intake, iron supplements, exercise, and sometimes massage and electric shock therapy. Gilman had experienced Mitchell's "cure," and sent a copy of this story to him as criticism. After receiving the story Mitchell modified his methods.

I sometimes fancy that in my condition, if I had less opposition and more society and stimulus—but John says the very worst thing I can do is to think about my condition, and I confess it always makes me feel bad.

So I will let it alone and talk about the house.

The most beautiful place! It is quite alone, standing well back from the road, quite three miles from the village. It makes me think of English places that you read about, for there are hedges and walls and gates that lock, and lots of separate little houses for the gardeners and people.

There is a *delicious* garden! I never saw such a garden—large and shady, full of box-bordered paths, and lined with long grape-covered arbors with seats under them.

There were greenhouses, but they are all broken now.   20

There was some legal trouble, I believe, something about the heirs and co-heirs; anyhow, the place has been empty for years.

That spoils my ghostliness, I am afraid, but I don't care—there is something strange about the house—I can feel it.

I even said so to John one moonlight evening, but he said what I felt was a draught, and shut the window.

I get unreasonably angry with John sometimes. I'm sure I never used to be so sensitive. I think it is due to this nervous condition.

But John says if I feel so I shall neglect proper self-control; so I take pains to control   25
myself—before him, at least, and that makes me very tired.

I don't like our room a bit. I wanted one downstairs that opened onto the piazza and had roses all over the window, and such pretty old-fashioned chintz hangings! But John would not hear of it.

He said there was only one window and not room for two beds, and no near room for him if he took another.

He is very careful and loving, and hardly lets me stir without special direction.

I have a schedule prescription for each hour in the day; he takes all care from me, and so I feel basely ungrateful not to value it more.

He said he came here solely on my account, that I was to have perfect rest and all   30
the air I could get. "Your exercise depends on your strength, my dear," said he, "and your food somewhat on your appetite; but air you can absorb all the time." So we took the nursery at the top of the house.

It is a big, airy room, the whole floor nearly, with windows that look all ways, and air and sunshine galore. It was nursery first, and then playroom and gymnasium, I should judge, for the windows are barred for little children, and there are rings and things in the walls.

The paint and paper look as if a boys' school had used it. It is stripped off—the paper—in great patches all around the head of my bed, about as far as I can reach, and in a great place on the other side of the room low down. I never saw a worse paper in my life. One of those sprawling, flamboyant patterns committing every artistic sin.

It is dull enough to confuse the eye in following, pronounced enough constantly to irritate and provoke study, and when you follow the lame uncertain curves for a little distance they suddenly commit suicide—plunge off at outrageous angles, destroy themselves in unheard-of contradictions.

The color is repellent, almost revolting: a smouldering unclean yellow, strangely faded by the slow-turning sunlight. It is a dull yet lurid orange in some places, a sickly sulphur tint in others.

No wonder the children hated it! I should hate it myself if I had to live in this   35
room long.

There comes John, and I must put this away—he hates to have me write a word.

We have been here two weeks, and I haven't felt like writing before, since that first day.

I am sitting by the window now, up in this atrocious nursery, and there is nothing to hinder my writing as much as I please, save lack of strength.

John is away all day, and even some nights when his cases are serious.

I am glad my case is not serious!   40

But these nervous troubles are dreadfully depressing.

John does not know how much I really suffer. He knows there is no reason to suffer, and that satisfies him.

Of course it is only nervousness. It does weigh on me so not to do my duty in any way!

I meant to be such a help to John, such a real rest and comfort, and here I am a comparative burden already!

Nobody would believe what an effort it is to do what little I am able—to dress and   45
entertain, and order things.

It is fortunate Mary is so good with the baby. Such a dear baby!

And yet I *cannot* be with him, it makes me so nervous.

I suppose John never was nervous in his life. He laughs at me so about this wallpaper!

At first he meant to repaper the room, but afterward he said that I was letting it get the better of me, and that nothing was worse for a nervous patient than to give way to such fancies.

He said that after the wallpaper was changed it would be the heavy bedstead, and   50
then the barred windows, and then that gate at the head of the stairs, and so on.

"You know the place is doing you good," he said, "and really, dear, I don't care to renovate the house just for a three months' rental."

"Then do let us go downstairs," I said. "There are such pretty rooms there."

Then he took me in his arms and called me a blessed little goose, and said he would go down cellar, if I wished, and have it whitewashed into the bargain.

But he is right enough about the beds and windows and things.

It is as airy and comfortable a room as anyone need wish, and, of course, I would   55
not be so silly as to make him uncomfortable just for a whim.

I'm really getting quite fond of the big room, all but that horrid paper.

Out of one window I can see the garden—those mysterious deep-shaded arbors, the riotous old-fashioned flowers, and bushes and gnarly trees.

Out of another I get a lovely view of the bay and a little private wharf belonging to the estate. There is a beautiful shaded lane that runs down there from the house. I always fancy I see people walking in these numerous paths and arbors, but John has cautioned me not to give way to fancy in the least. He says that with my imaginative power and habit of story-making, a nervous weakness like mine is sure to lead to all manner of excited fancies, and that I ought to use my will and good sense to check the tendency. So I try.

I think sometimes that if I were only well enough to write a little it would relieve the press of ideas and rest me.

But I find I get pretty tired when I try.   60

It is so discouraging not to have any advice and companionship about my work. When I get really well, John says we will ask Cousin Henry and Julia down for a long visit; but he says he would as soon put fireworks in my pillow-case as to let me have those stimulating people about now.

I wish I could get well faster.

But I must not think about that. This paper looks to me as if it *knew* what a vicious influence it had!

There is a recurrent spot where the pattern lolls like a broken neck and two bulbous eyes stare at you upside down.

I get positively angry with the impertinence of it and the everlastingness. Up and down and sideways they crawl, and those absurd unblinking eyes are everywhere. There is one place where two breadths didn't match, and the eyes go all up and down the line, one a little higher than the other.

I never saw so much expression in an inanimate thing before, and we all know how much expression they have! I used to lie awake as a child and get more entertainment and terror out of blank walls and plain furniture than most children could find in a toy-store.

I remember what a kindly wink the knobs of our big old bureau used to have, and there was one chair that always seemed like a strong friend.

I used to feel that if any of the other things looked too fierce I could always hop into that chair and be safe.

The furniture in this room is no worse than inharmonious, however, for we had to bring it all from downstairs. I suppose when this was used as a playroom they had to take the nursery things out, and no wonder! I never saw such ravages as the children have made here.

The wallpaper, as I said before, is torn off in spots, and it sticketh closer than a brother°—they must have had perseverance as well as hatred.

Then the floor is scratched and gouged and splintered, the plaster itself is dug out here and there, and this great heavy bed, which is all we found in the room, looks as if it had been through the wars.

But I don't mind it a bit—only the paper.

There comes John's sister. Such a dear girl as she is, and so careful of me! I must not let her find me writing.

She is a perfect and enthusiastic housekeeper, and hopes for no better profession. I verily believe she thinks it is the writing which made me sick!

But I can write when she is out, and see her a long way off from these windows.

There is one that commands the road, a lovely shaded winding road, and one that just looks off over the country. A lovely country, too, full of great elms and velvet meadows.

This wallpaper has a kind of sub-pattern in a different shade, a particularly irritating one, for you can only see it in certain lights, and not clearly then.

But in the places where it isn't faded and where the sun is just so—I can see a strange, provoking, formless sort of figure that seems to skulk about behind that silly and conspicuous front design.

There's sister on the stairs!

Well, the Fourth of July is over! The people are all gone, and I am tired out. John thought it might do me good to see a little company, so we just had Mother and Nellie and the children down for a week.

Of course I didn't do a thing. Jennie sees to everything now.

But it tired me all the same.

John says if I don't pick up faster he shall send me to Weir Mitchell° in the fall.

But I don't want to go there at all. I had a friend who was in his hands once, and she says he is just like John and my brother, only more so!

Besides, it is such an undertaking to go so far.

sticketh closer than a brother: Proverbs 18:24.
Weir Mitchell: See note on page 590.

I don't feel as if it was worthwhile to turn my hand over for anything, and I'm getting dreadfully fretful and querulous.

I cry at nothing, and cry most of the time.

Of course I don't when John is here, or anybody else, but when I am alone.

And I am alone a good deal just now. John is kept in town very often by serious cases, and Jennie is good and lets me alone when I want her to.

So I walk a little in the garden or down that lovely lane, sit on the porch under the roses, and lie down up here a good deal. 90

I'm getting really fond of the room in spite of the wallpaper. Perhaps *because* of the wallpaper.

It dwells in my mind so!

I lie here on this great immovable bed—it is nailed down, I believe—and follow that pattern about by the hour. It is as good as gymnastics, I assure you. I start, we'll say, at the bottom, down in the corner over there where it has not been touched, and I determine for the thousandth time that I *will* follow that pointless pattern to some sort of a conclusion.

I know a little of the principle of design, and I know this thing was not arranged on any laws of radiation, or alternation, or repetition, or symmetry, or anything else that I ever heard of.

It is repeated, of course, by the breadths, but not otherwise. 95

Looked at in one way, each breadth stands alone; the bloated curves and flourishes—a kind of "debased Romanesque" with delirium tremens go waddling up and down in isolated columns of fatuity.

But, on the other hand, they connect diagonally, and the sprawling outlines run off in great slanting waves of optic horror, like a lot of wallowing sea-weeds in full chase.

The whole thing goes horizontally, too, at least it seems so, and I exhaust myself trying to distinguish the order of its going in that direction.

They have used a horizontal breadth for a frieze, and that adds wonderfully to the confusion.

There is one end of the room where it is almost intact, and there, when the crosslights fade and the low sun shines directly upon it, I can almost fancy radiation after all—the interminable grotesque seems to form around a common center and rush off in headlong plunges of equal distraction. 100

It makes me tired to follow it. I will take a nap, I guess.

I don't know why I should write this.

I don't want to.

I don't feel able.

And I know John would think it absurd. But I *must* say what I feel and think in some way—it is such a relief! 105

But the effort is getting to be greater than the relief.

Half the time now I am awfully lazy, and lie down ever so much. John says I mustn't lose my strength, and has me take cod liver oil and lots of tonics and things, to say nothing of ale and wine and rare meat.

Dear John! He loves me very dearly, and hates to have me sick. I tried to have a real earnest reasonable talk with him the other day, and tell him how I wish he would let me go and make a visit to Cousin Henry and Julia.

But he said I wasn't able to go, nor able to stand it after I got there; and I did not make out a very good case for myself, for I was crying before I had finished.

It is getting to be a great effort for me to think straight. Just this nervous weakness, I suppose. 110

And dear John gathered me up in his arms, and just carried me upstairs and laid me on the bed, and sat by me and read to me till it tired my head.

He said I was his darling and his comfort and all he had, and that I must take care of myself for his sake, and keep well.

He says no one but myself can help me out of it, that I must use my will and self-control and not let any silly fancies run away with me.

There's one comfort—the baby is well and happy, and does not have to occupy this nursery with the horrid wallpaper.

If we had not used it, that blessed child would have! What a fortunate escape! 115 Why, I wouldn't have a child of mine, an impressionable little thing, live in such a room for worlds.

I never thought of it before, but it is lucky that John kept me here after all; I can stand it so much easier than a baby, you see.

Of course I never mention it to them any more—I am too wise—but I keep watch for it all the same.

There are things in that wallpaper that nobody knows about but me, or ever will.

Behind that outside pattern the dim shapes get clearer every day.

It is always the same shape, only very numerous. 120

And it is like a woman stooping down and creeping about behind that pattern. I don't like it a bit. I wonder—I begin to think—I wish John would take me away from here!

It is so hard to talk with John about my case, because he is so wise, and because he loves me so.

But I tried it last night.

It was moonlight. The moon shines in all around just as the sun does.

I hate to see it sometimes, it creeps so slowly, and always comes in by one window 125 or another.

John was asleep and I hated to waken him, so I kept still and watched the moonlight on that undulating wallpaper till I felt creepy.

The faint figure behind seemed to shake the pattern, just as if she wanted to get out.

I got up softly and went to feel and see if the paper *did* move, and when I came back John was awake.

"What is it, little girl?" he said. "Don't go walking about like that—you'll get cold."

I thought it was a good time to talk, so I told him that I really was not gaining here, 130 and that I wished he would take me away.

"Why, darling!" said he. "Our lease will be up in three weeks, and I can't see how to leave before.

"The repairs are not done at home, and I cannot possibly leave town just now. Of course, if you were in any danger, I could and would, but you really are better, dear, whether you can see it or not. I am a doctor, dear, and I know. You are gaining flesh and color, your appetite is better, I feel really much easier about you."

"I don't weigh a bit more," said I, "nor as much; and my appetite may be better in the evening when you are here but it is worse in the morning when you are away!"

"Bless her little heart!" said he with a big hug. "She shall be as sick as she pleases! But now let's improve the shining hours by going to sleep, and talk about it in the morning!"

"And you won't go away?" I asked gloomily. 135

"Why, how can I, dear? It is only three weeks more and then we will take a nice little trip of a few days while Jennie is getting the house ready. Really, dear, you are better!"

"Better in body perhaps—" I began, and stopped short, for he sat up straight and looked at me with such a stern, reproachful look that I could not say another word.

"My darling," said he, "I beg of you, for my sake and for our child's sake, as well as for your own, that you will never for one instant let that idea enter your mind! There is nothing so dangerous, so fascinating, to a temperament like yours. It is a false and foolish fancy. Can you not trust me as a physician when I tell you so?"

So of course I said no more on that score, and we went to sleep before long. He thought I was asleep first, but I wasn't, and lay there for hours trying to decide whether that front pattern and the back pattern really did move together or separately.

On a pattern like this, by daylight, there is a lack of sequence, a defiance of law, that is a constant irritant to a normal mind.   140

The color is hideous enough, and unreliable enough, and infuriating enough, but the pattern is torturing.

You think you have mastered it, but just as you get well under way in following, it turns a back-somersault and there you are. It slaps you in the face, knocks you down, and tramples upon you. It is like a bad dream.

The outside pattern is a florid arabesque, reminding one of a fungus. If you can imagine a toadstool in joints an interminable string of toadstools, budding and sprouting in endless convolutions—why, that is something like it.

That is, sometimes!

There is one marked peculiarity about this paper, a thing nobody seems to notice   145
but myself, and that is that it changes as the light changes.

When the sun shoots in through the east window—I always watch for that first long, straight ray—it changes so quickly than I never can quite believe it.

That is why I watch it always.

By moonlight—the moon shines in all night when there is a moon—I wouldn't know it was the same paper.

At night in any kind of light, in twilight, candlelight, lamplight, and worst of all by moonlight, it becomes bars! The outside pattern, I mean, and the woman behind it is as plain as can be.

I didn't realize for a long time what the thing was that showed behind, that dim   150
sub-pattern, but now I am quite sure it is a woman.

By daylight she is subdued, quiet. I fancy it is the pattern that keeps her so still. It is so puzzling. It keeps me quiet by the hour.

I lie down ever so much now. John says it is good for me, and to sleep all I can.

Indeed he started the habit by making me lie down for an hour after each meal.

It is a very bad habit, I am convinced, for you see, I don't sleep.

And that cultivates deceit, for I don't tell them I'm awake—oh, no!   155

The fact is I am getting a little afraid of John.

He seems very queer sometimes, and even Jennie has an inexplicable look.

It strikes me occasionally, just as a scientific hypothesis, that perhaps it is the paper!

I have watched John when he did not know I was looking, and come into the room suddenly on the most innocent excuses, and I've caught him several times *looking at the paper!* And Jennie too. I caught Jennie with her hand on it once.

She didn't know I was in the room, and when I asked her in a quiet, a very quiet   160
voice, with the most restrained manner possible, what she was doing with the paper, she turned around as if she had been caught stealing, and looked quite angry—asked me why I should frighten her so!

Then she said that the paper stained everything it touched, that she had found yellow smooches on all my clothes and John's and she wished we would be more careful!

Did not that sound innocent? But I know she was studying that pattern, and I am determined that nobody shall find it out but myself.

Life is very much more exciting now than it used to be. You see, I have something more to expect, to look forward to, to watch. I really do eat better, and am more quiet than I was.

John is so pleased to see me improve! He laughed a little the other day, and said I seemed to be flourishing in spite of my wallpaper.

I turned it off with a laugh. I had no intention of telling him it was *because* of the   165
wallpaper—he would make fun of me. He might even want to take me away.

I don't want to leave now until I have found it out. There is a week more, and I think that will be enough.

I'm feeling so much better!

I don't sleep much at night, for it is so interesting to watch developments; but sleep a good deal during the daytime.

In the daytime it is tiresome and perplexing.

There are always new shoots on the fungus, and new shades of yellow all over it. I   170
cannot keep count of them, though I have tried conscientiously.

It is the strangest yellow, that wallpaper! It makes me think of all the yellow things I ever saw—not beautiful ones like buttercups, but old, foul, bad yellow things.

But there is something else about that paper—the smell! I noticed it the moment we came into the room, but with so much air and sun it was not bad. Now we have had a week of fog and rain, and whether the windows are open or not, the smell is here.

It creeps all over the house.

I find it hovering in the dining-room, skulking in the parlor, hiding in the hall, lying in wait for me on the stairs.

It gets into my hair.   175

Even when I go to ride, if I turn my head suddenly and surprise it—there is that smell!

Such a peculiar odor, too! I have spent hours in trying to analyze it, to find what it smelled like.

It is not bad—at first—and very gentle, but quite the subtlest, most enduring odor I ever met.

In this damp weather it is awful. I wake up in the night and find it hanging over me.

It used to disturb me at first. I thought seriously of burning the house—to reach   180
the smell.

But now I am used to it. The only thing I can think of that it is like is the *color* of the paper! A yellow smell.

There is a very funny mark on this wall, low down, near the mopboard. A streak that runs round the room. It goes behind every piece of furniture, except the bed, a long, straight, even *smooch*, as if it had been rubbed over and over.

I wonder how it was done and who did it, and what they did it for. Round and round and round—round and round and round—it makes me dizzy!

I really have discovered something at last.

Through watching so much at night, when it changes so, I have finally found out.   185

The front pattern *does* move—and no wonder! The woman behind shakes it!

Sometimes I think there are a great many women behind, and sometimes only one, and she crawls around fast, and her crawling shakes it all over.

Then in the very bright spots she keeps still, and in the very shady spots she just takes hold of the bars and shakes them hard.

And she is all the time trying to climb through. But nobody could climb through that pattern—it strangles so; I think that is why it has so many heads.

They get through and then the pattern strangles them off and turns them upside   190
down, and makes their eyes white!

If those heads were covered or taken off it would not be half so bad.

I think that woman gets out in the daytime!

And I'll tell you why—privately—I've seen her!

I can see her out of every one of my windows!

It is the same woman, I know, for she is always creeping, and most women do not   195
creep by daylight.

I see her in that long shaded lane, creeping up and down. I see her in those dark
grape arbors, creeping all around the garden.

I see her on that long road under the trees, creeping along, and when a carriage
comes she hides under the blackberry vines.

I don't blame her a bit. It must be very humiliating to be caught creeping by daylight!

I always lock the door when I creep by daylight. I can't do it at night, for I know
John would suspect something at once.

And John is so queer now that I don't want to irritate him. I wish he would take an-   200
other room! Besides, I don't want anybody to get that woman out at night but myself.

I often wonder if I could see her out of all the windows at once.

But, turn as fast as I can, I can only see out of one at a time.

And though I always see her, she *may* be able to creep faster than I can turn! I have
watched her sometimes away off in the open country, creeping as fast as a cloud shadow
in a wind.

If only that top pattern could be gotten off from the under one! I mean to try it, little by little.

I have found out another funny thing, but I shan't tell it this time! It does not do to   205
trust people too much.

There are only two more days to get this paper off, and I believe John is beginning
to notice. I don't like the look in his eyes.

And I heard him ask Jennie a lot of professional questions about me. She had a
very good report to give.

She said I slept a good deal in the daytime.

John knows I don't sleep very well at night, for all I'm so quiet!

He asked me all sorts of questions, too, and pretended to be very loving and kind.   210

As if I couldn't see through him!

Still, I don't wonder he acts so, sleeping under this paper for three months.

It only interests me, but I feel sure John and Jennie are affected by it.

Hurrah! This is the last day, but it is enough. John is to stay in town over night, and
won't be out until this evening.

Jennie wanted to sleep with me—the sly thing; but I told her I should undoubtedly   215
rest better for a night all alone.

That was clever, for really I wasn't alone a bit! As soon as it was moonlight and that
poor thing began to crawl and shake the pattern, I got up and ran to help her.

I pulled and she shook. I shook and she pulled, and before morning we had peeled
off yards of that paper.

A strip about as high as my head and half around the room.

And then when the sun came and that awful pattern began to laugh at me, I declared I would finish it today!

We go away tomorrow, and they are moving all my furniture down again to leave   220
things as they were before.

Jennie looked at the wall in amazement, but I told her merrily that I did it out of
pure spite at the vicious thing.

She laughed and said she wouldn't mind doing it herself, but I must not get tired.

How she betrayed herself that time!

But I am here, and no person touches this paper but Me—not *alive!*

She tried to get me out of the room—it was too patent! But I said it was so quiet 225
and empty and clean now that I believed I would lie down again and sleep all I could, and
not to wake me even for dinner—I would call when I woke.

So now she is gone, and the servants are gone, and the things are gone, and there is
nothing left but that great bedstead nailed down, with the canvas mattress we found on it.

We shall sleep downstairs tonight, and take the boat home tomorrow.

I quite enjoy the room, now it is bare again.

How those children did tear about here!

This bedstead is fairly gnawed! 230

But I must get to work.

I have locked the door and thrown the key down into the front path.

I don't want to go out, and I don't want to have anybody come in, till John comes.

I want to astonish him.

I've got a rope up here that even Jennie did not find. If that woman does get out, 235
and tries to get away, I can tie her!

But I forgot I could not reach far without anything to stand on!

This bed will *not* move!

I tried to lift and push it until I was lame, and then I got so angry I bit off a little
piece at one corner—but it hurt my teeth.

Then I peeled off all the paper I could reach standing on the floor. It sticks horribly and the pattern just enjoys it! All those strangled heads and bulbous eyes and waddling fungus growths just shriek with derision!

I am getting angry enough to do something desperate. To jump out of the window 240
would be admirable exercise, but the bars are too strong even to try.

Besides I wouldn't do it. Of course not. I know well enough that a step like that is
improper and might be misconstrued.

I don't like to *look* out of the windows even—there are so many of those creeping
women, and they creep so fast.

I wonder if they all came out of that wallpaper as I did?

But I am securely fastened now by my well-hidden rope—you don't get *me* out in
the road there!

I suppose I shall have to get back behind the pattern when it comes night, and that 245
is hard!

It is so pleasant to be out in this great room and creep around as I please!

I don't want to go outside. I won't, even if Jennie asks me to.

For outside you have to creep on the ground, and everything is green instead of
yellow.

But here I can creep smoothly on the floor, and my shoulder just fits in that long
smooch around the wall, so I cannot lose my way.

Why, there's John at the door! 250

It is no use, young man, you can't open it!

How he does call and pound!

Now he's crying to Jennie for an axe.

It would be a shame to break down that beautiful door!

"John, dear!" said I in the gentlest voice. "The key is down by the front steps, under 255
a plantain leaf!"

That silenced him for a few moments.

Then he said, very quietly indeed, "Open the door, my darling!"

"I can't," said I. "The key is down by the front door under a plantain leaf!" And then I said it again, several times, very gently and slowly, and said it so often that he had to go and see, and he got it of course, and came in. He stopped short by the door.

"What is the matter?" he cried. "For God's sake, what are you doing!"

I kept on creeping just the same, but I looked at him over my shoulder.   260

"I've got out at last," said I, "in spite of you and Jane. And I've pulled off most of the paper, so you can't put me back!"

Now why should that man have fainted? But he did, and right across my path by the wall, so that I had to creep over him every time!

TILLIE OLSEN (b. ca. 1913)

Tillie Olsen was born in 1912 or 1913 in Nebraska. Although she did not have an extensive formal education, she has been the recipient of five honorary degrees and a number of other honors, including a Guggenheim Fellowship. Her early efforts at writing were tentative, and after the mid-1930s she put her career on hold while she devoted herself to her four daughters, "everyday jobs," and marriage. In the 1950s she resumed writing, lecturing, and advocating feminist and minority issues, all of which have characterized her career since then. Her total output has not been great, for her work has been deliberate, careful, and slow. In 1974 she completed her long-developing novel, Yonnondio, From the Thirties, *which she had begun while in her teens (she had published a single chapter from the novel in 1934). The subject of the novel, which could be considered as a virtual life's work, is a working-class family during the depression years. "I Stand Here Ironing" is from her 1956 prize-winning collection* Tell Me a Riddle *(1961). If one judges the story as being related to Olsen's own experiences, it is visualized as happening in about 1951, when the narrator, the mother, is thirty-eight, and Emily, the daughter, is nineteen.*

I Stand Here Ironing ✎✎✎ 1953–1954

I stand here ironing, and what you asked me moves tormented back and forth with the iron.

"I wish you would manage the time to come in and talk with me about your daughter. I'm sure you can help me understand her. She's a youngster who needs help and whom I'm deeply interested in helping."

"Who needs help.". . . . Even if I came, what good would it do? You think because I am her mother I have a key, or that in some way you could use me as a key? She has lived for nineteen years. There is all that life that has happened outside of me, beyond me.

And when is there time to remember, to sift, to weigh, to estimate, to total? I will start and there will be an interruption and I will have to gather it all together again. Or I will become engulfed with all I did not do, with what should have been and what cannot be helped.

She was a beautiful baby. The first and only one of our five that was beautiful at   5
birth. You do not guess how new and uneasy her tenancy in her now-loveliness. You did not know her all those years she was thought homely, or see her poring over her baby pictures, making me tell her over and over how beautiful she had been—and would be, I would tell her—and was now, to the seeing eye. But the seeing eyes were few or nonexistent. Including mine.

I nursed her. They feel that's important nowadays. I nursed all the children, but with her, with all the fierce rigidity of first motherhood, I did like the books then said. Though her cries battered me to trembling and my breasts ached with swollenness, I waited till the clock decreed.

Why do I put that first? I do not even know if it matters, or if it explains anything.

She was a beautiful baby. She blew shining bubbles of sound. She loved motion, loved light, loved color and music and textures. She would lie on the floor in her blue overalls patting the surface so hard in ecstasy her hands and feet would blur. She was a miracle to me, but when she was eight months old I had to leave her daytimes with the woman downstairs to whom she was no miracle at all, for I worked or looked for work and for Emily's father, who "could no longer endure" (he wrote in his good-bye note) "sharing want with us."

I was nineteen. It was the pre-relief, pre-WPA world of the depression. I would start running as soon as I got off the streetcar, running up the stairs, the place smelling sour, and awake or asleep to startle awake, when she saw me she would break into a clogged weeping that could not be comforted, a weeping I can hear yet.

After a while I found a job hashing at night so I could be with her days, and it was   10
better. But it came to where I had to bring her to his family and leave her.

It took a long time to raise the money for her fare back. Then she got chicken pox and I had to wait longer. When she finally came, I hardly knew her, walking quick and nervous like her father, looking like her father, thin, and dressed in a shoddy red that yellowed her skin and glared at the pockmarks. All the baby loveliness gone.

She was two. Old enough for nursery school they said, and I did not know then what I know now—the fatigue of the long day, and the lacerations of group life in the kinds of nurseries that are only parking places for children.

Except that it would have made no difference if I had known. It was the only place there was. It was the only way we could be together, the only way I could hold a job.

And even without knowing, I knew. I knew the teacher that was evil because all these years it has curdled into my memory, the little boy hunched in the corner, her rasp, "why aren't you outside, because Alvin hits you? that's no reason, go out, scaredy." I knew Emily hated it even if she did not clutch and implore "don't go Mommy" like the other children, mornings.

She always had a reason why we should stay home. Momma, you look sick.   15
Momma, I feel sick. Momma, the teachers aren't there today, they're sick. Momma, we can't go, there was a fire there last night. Momma, it's a holiday today, no school, they told me.

But never a direct protest, never rebellion. I think of our others in their three-, four-year-oldness—the explosions, the tempers, the denunciations, the demands—and I feel suddenly ill. I put the iron down. What in me demanded that goodness in her? And what was the cost, the cost to her of such goodness?

The old man living in the back once said in his gentle way: "You should smile at Emily more when you look at her." What *was* in my face when I looked at her? I loved her. There were all the acts of love.

It was only with the others I remembered what he said, and it was the face of joy, and not of care or tightness or worry I turned to them—too late for Emily. She does not smile easily, let alone almost always as her brothers and sisters do. Her face is closed and sombre, but when she wants, how fluid. You must have seen it in her pantomimes, you spoke of her rare gift for comedy on the stage that rouses a laughter out of the audience so dear they applaud and applaud and do not want to let her go.

Where does it come from, that comedy? There was none of it in her when she came back to me that second time, after I had had to send her away again. She had a new daddy now to learn to love, and I think perhaps it was a better time.

Except when we left her alone nights, telling ourselves she was old enough. 20

"Can't you go some other time, Mommy, like tomorrow?" she would ask. "Will it be just a little while you'll be gone? Do you promise?"

The time we came back, the front door open, the clock on the floor in the hall. She rigid awake. "It wasn't just a little while. I didn't cry. Three times I called you, just three times, and then I ran downstairs to open the door so you could come faster. The clock talked loud. I threw it away, it scared me what it talked."

She said the clock talked loud again that night I went to the hospital to have Susan. She was delirious with the fever that comes before red measles, but she was fully conscious all the week I was gone and the week after we were home when she could not come near the new baby or me.

She did not get well. She stayed skeleton thin, not wanting to eat, and night after night she had nightmares. She would call for me, and I would rouse from exhaustion to sleepily call back: "You're all right, darling, go to sleep, it's just a dream," and if she still called, in a sterner voice, "now go to sleep, Emily, there's nothing to hurt you." Twice, only twice, when I had to get up for Susan anyhow, I went in to sit with her.

Now when it is too late (as if she would let me hold and comfort her like I do the 25 others) I get up and go to her at once at her moan or restless stirring. "Are you awake, Emily? Can I get you something?" And the answer is always the same: "No, I'm all right, go back to sleep, Mother."

They persuaded me at the clinic to send her away to a convalescent home in the country where "she can have the kind of food and care you can't manage for her, and you'll be free to concentrate on the new baby." They still send children to that place. I see pictures on the society page of sleek young women planning affairs to raise money for it, or dancing at the affairs, or decorating Easter eggs or filling Christmas stockings for the children.

They never have a picture of the children so I do not know if the girls still wear those gigantic red bows and the ravaged looks on the every other Sunday when parents can come to visit "unless otherwise notified"—as we were notified the first six weeks.

Oh it is a handsome place, green lawns and tall trees and fluted flower beds. High up on the balconies of each cottage the children stand, the girls in their red bows and white dresses, the boys in white suits and giant red ties. The parents stand below shrieking up to be heard and the children shriek down to be heard, and between them the invisible wall "Not To Be Contaminated by Parental Germs or Physical Affection."

There was a tiny girl who always stood hand in hand with Emily. Her parents never came. One visit she was gone. "They moved her to Rose Cottage" Emily shouted in explanation. "They don't like you to love anybody here."

She wrote once a week, the labored writing of a seven-year-old. "I am fine. How is 30 the baby. If I write my leter nicly I will have a star. Love." There never was a star. We wrote every other day, letters she could never hold or keep but only hear read—once. "We simply do not have room for children to keep any personal possessions," they patiently explained when we pieced one Sunday's shrieking together to plead how much it would mean to Emily, who loved so to keep things, to be allowed to keep her letters and cards.

Each visit she looked frailer. "She isn't eating," they told us.

(They had runny eggs for breakfast or mush with lumps, Emily said later, I'd hold it in my mouth and not swallow. Nothing ever tasted good, just when they had chicken.)

It took us eight months to get her released home, and only the fact that she gained back so little of her seven lost pounds convinced the social worker.

I used to try to hold and love her after she came back, but her body would stay stiff, and after a while she'd push away. She ate little. Food sickened her, and I think much of life too. Oh she had physical lightness and brightness, twinkling by on skates, bouncing like a ball up and down up and down over the jump rope, skimming over the hill; but these were momentary.

She fretted about her appearance, thin and dark and foreign-looking at a time   35 when every little girl was supposed to look or thought she should look a chubby blonde replica of Shirley Temple. The doorbell sometimes rang for her, but no one seemed to come and play in the house or be a best friend. Maybe because we moved so much.

There was a boy she loved painfully through two school semesters. Months later she told me how she had taken pennies from my purse to buy him candy. "Licorice was his favorite and I brought him some every day, but he still liked Jennifer better'n me. Why, Mommy?" The kind of question for which there is no answer.

School was a worry to her. She was not glib or quick in a world where glibness and quickness were easily confused with ability to learn. To her overworked and exasperated teachers she was an overconscientious "slow learner" who kept trying to catch up and was absent entirely too often.

I let her be absent, though sometimes the illness was imaginary. How different from my now-strictness about attendance with the others. I wasn't working. We had a new baby, I was home anyhow. Sometimes, after Susan grew old enough, I would keep her home from school, too, to have them all together.

Mostly Emily had asthma, and her breathing, harsh and labored, would fill the house with a curiously tranquil sound. I would bring the two old dresser mirrors and her boxes of collections to her bed. She would select beads and single earrings, bottle tops and shells, dried flowers and pebbles, old postcards and scraps, all sorts of oddments; then she and Susan would play Kingdom, setting up landscapes and furniture, peopling them with action.

Those were the only times of peaceful companionship between her and Susan. I   40 have edged away from it, that poisonous feeling between them, that terrible balancing of hurts and needs I had to do between the two, and did so badly, those earlier years.

Oh there are conflicts between the others too, each one human, needing, demanding, hurting, taking—but only between Emily and Susan, no, Emily toward Susan that corroding resentment. It seems so obvious on the surface, yet it is not obvious. Susan, the second child, Susan, golden- and curly-haired and chubby, quick and articulate and assured, everything in appearance and manner Emily was not; Susan, not able to resist Emily's precious things, losing or sometimes clumsily breaking them; Susan telling jokes and riddles to company for applause while Emily sat silent (to say to me later: that was *my* riddle, Mother, I told it to Susan); Susan, who for all the five years' difference in age was just a year behind Emily in developing physically.

I am glad for that slow physical development that widened the difference between her and her contemporaries, though she suffered over it. She was too vulnerable for that terrible world of youthful competition, of preening and parading, of constant measuring of yourself against every other, of envy, "If I had that copper hair," "If I had that skin. . . ." She tormented herself enough about not looking like the others, there was enough of the unsureness, the having to be conscious of words before you speak, the constant caring—what are they thinking of me? without having it all magnified by the merciless physical drives.

Ronnie is calling. He is wet and I change him. It is rare there is such a cry now. That time of motherhood is almost behind me when the ear is not one's own but must always be racked and listening for the child cry, the child call. We sit for a while and I hold him, looking out over the city spread in charcoal with its soft aisles of light, "*Shoogily*," he breathes and curls closer. I carry him back to bed, asleep. *Shoogily*. A funny word, a family word, inherited from Emily, invented by her to say: *comfort.*

In this and other ways she leaves her seal, I say aloud. And startle at my saying it. What do I mean? What did I start to gather together, to try and make coherent? I was at the terrible, growing years. War years. I do not remember them well. I was working, there were four smaller ones now, there was not time for her. She had to help be a mother, a housekeeper, and shopper. She had to set her seal. Mornings of crisis and near hysteria trying to get lunches packed, hair combed, coats and shoes found, everyone to school or Child Care on time, the baby ready for transportation. And always the paper scribbled on by a smaller one, the book looked at by Susan then mislaid, the homework not done. Running out to that huge school where she was one, she was lost, she was a drop; suffering over the unpreparedness, stammering and unsure in her classes.

There was so little time left at night after the kids were bedded down. She would   45
struggle over books, always eating (it was in those years she developed her enormous appetite that is legendary in our family) and I would be ironing, or preparing food for the next day, or writing V-mail to Bill, or tending the baby. Sometimes, to make me laugh, or out of her despair, she would imitate happenings or types at school.

I think I said once: "Why don't you do something like this in the school amateur show?" One morning she phoned me at work, hardly understandable through the weeping: "Mother, I did it. I won, I won; they gave me first prize; they clapped and clapped and wouldn't let me go."

Now suddenly she was Somebody, and as imprisoned in her difference as she had been in anonymity.

She began to be asked to perform at other high schools, even in colleges, then at city and statewide affairs. The first one we went to, I only recognized her that first moment when thin, shy, she almost drowned herself into the curtains. Then: Was this Emily? The control, the command, the convulsing and deadly clowning, the spell, then the roaring, stamping audience, unwilling to let this rare and precious laughter out of their lives.

Afterwards: You ought to do something about her with a gift like that—but without money or knowing how, what does one do? We have left it all to her, and the gift has as often eddied inside, clogged and clotted, as been used and growing.

She is coming. She runs up the stairs two at a time with her light graceful step, and I   50
know she is happy tonight. Whatever it was that occasioned your call did not happen today.

"Aren't you ever going to finish the ironing, Mother? Whistler painted his mother in a rocker. I'd have to paint mine standing over an ironing board." This is one of her communicative nights and she tells me everything and nothing as she fixes herself a plate of food out of the icebox.

She is so lovely. Why did you want me to come in at all? Why were you concerned? She will find her way.

She starts up the stairs to bed. "Don't get me up with the rest in the morning." "But I thought you were having midterms." "Oh, those," she comes back in, kisses me, and says quite lightly, "in a couple of years when we'll all be atom-dead they won't matter a bit."

She has said it before. She *believes* it. But because I have been dredging the past, and all that compounds a human being is so heavy and meaningful in me, I cannot endure it tonight.

I will never total it all. I will never come in to say: She was a child seldom smiled at. 55
Her father left me before she was a year old. I had to work her first six years when there
was work, or I sent her home and to his relatives. There were years she had care she
hated. She was dark and thin and foreign-looking in a world where the prestige went to
blondeness and curly hair and dimples, she was slow where glibness was prized. She was a
child of anxious, not proud, love. We were poor and could not afford for her the soil of
easy growth. I was a young mother, I was a distracted mother. There were the other children pushing up, demanding. Her younger sister seemed all that she was not. There were
years she did not want me to touch her. She kept too much in herself, her life was such
she had to keep too much in herself. My wisdom came too late. She has much to her and
probably little will come of it. She is a child of her age, of depression, of war, of fear.

Let her be. So all that is in her will not bloom—but in how many does it? There is
still enough left to live by. Only help her to know—help make it so there is cause for her
to know—that she is more than this dress on the ironing board, helpless before the iron.

Reading *and* Writing

about

POETRY

Meeting Poetry: *An Overview*

Our words **poem** and **poetry** are derived from the Greek word *poiein,* "to create or make," the idea being that poetry is a created artifact, a structure that develops from the human imagination and that is expressed rhythmically in words. Although **poet** originally meant the writer of any kind of literature, we now use the word exclusively to mean a person who writes poems. *Poetry* and *poem* describe a wide variety of spoken and written forms, styles, and patterns, and also a wide variety of subjects. In light of this variety, we believe that the best way to understand poetry is to experience it—read it, study it, savor it, think about it, dream about it, learn it, memorize it, mull it over, talk about it with others, ask questions about it, enjoy it, love it. The more experience with poetry you have, the more you will develop your own ideas and definitions of just what poetry is, and the deeper will be your understanding and the greater your appreciation.

❦ THE NATURE OF POETRY

We begin with a poem based in the lives of students and teachers alike.

BILLY COLLINS (b. 1941)

Schoolsville   1985

Glancing over my shoulder at the past,
I realize the number of students I have taught
is enough to populate a small town.

I can see it nestled in a paper landscape,
chalk dust flurrying down in winter,   5
nights dark as a blackboard.

The population ages but never graduates.
On hot afternoons they sweat the final in the park
and when it's cold they shiver around stoves
reading disorganized essays out loud.   10
A bell rings on the hour and everybody zigzags
in the streets with their books.

I forgot all their last names first and their
first names last in alphabetical order.
But the boy who always had his hand up   15
is an alderman and owns the haberdashery.
The girl who signed her papers in lipstick
leans against the drugstore, smoking,
brushing her hair like a machine.

Their grades are sewn into their clothes   20
like references to Hawthorne.°   *i.e.,* The Scarlet Letter
The A's stroll along with other A's.
The D's honk whenever they pass another D.

All the creative writing students recline
on the courthouse lawn and play the lute.   25
Wherever they go, they form a big circle.

Needless to say, I am the mayor.
I live in the white colonial at Maple and Main.
I rarely leave the house. The car deflates
in the driveway. Vines twirl around the porchswing.   30

Once in a while a student knocks on the door
with a term paper fifteen years late
or a question about Yeats or double-spacing.
And sometimes one will appear in a window pane
to watch me lecturing the wall paper,   35
quizzing the chandelier, reprimanding the air.

QUESTIONS

1. What recognizable school experiences does the poem mention? Why is "Schoolsville" the title?
2. Describe the speaker. How does he indicate affection for students?
3. What details indicate that the poem is fantasy and not reality? To what degree is the poem humorous?
4. Compare the details of this poem with those in Roethke's "Dolor" (Chapter 14). What similarities do you find in the choice and appropriateness of detail? What differences?
5. Each poem you read may help you understand, and therefore define, poetry. How might this poem help you begin making a definition?

"Schoolsville" reveals the variety and freedom of poetry. Unlike poems that are set out in strict line lengths, rhythms, and rhymes, "Schoolsville," though arranged in lines, does not follow measured rhythmical or rhyming patterns. The language is not difficult, the descriptions are straightforward, and the scenes seem both real and amusing. Many details—such as the "chalk dust flurrying down" like snow, "the girl who signed her papers in lipstick," and the students forming a circle when they meet—are outrightly funny. But the poem moves from apparent reality to something beyond reality. Unifying the poem is the fanciful idea that school life is, like life generally, at once comical, serious, memorable, and poignant.

We may contrast "Schoolsville" with the following poem, "Hope," by Lisel Mueller, which deals with a topic—hope—that is common to us all, a topic that governs both our present and future behavior. What is unique, however, is that the poet provides us with thoughts about the nature of hope that might never have occurred to us. In this sense the poem fulfills the creative goal of poetry to lead us and guide us.

Hope desire with expectation of fulfillment.

LISEL MUELLER (b. 1924)

Hope   1976

It hovers in dark corners
before the lights are turned on,
    it shakes sleep from its eyes
    and drops from mushroom gills,
        it explodes in the starry heads   5
        of dandelions turned sages,
            it sticks to the wings of green angels
            that sail from the tops of maples.

It sprouts in each occluded eye
of the many-eyed potato,   10
    it lives in each earthworm segment
    surviving cruelty,

it is the motion that runs
from the eyes to the tail of a dog,
    it is the mouth that inflates the lungs
    of the child that has just been born.   15

It is the singular gift — *The gift given to each individual*
we cannot destroy in ourselves,
the argument that refutes death,
the genius that invents the future,
all we know of God.   20

Watery part of blood that circulates
blood—ved liquid that, carries and
in the heart,
Veins

It is the serum which makes us swear
not to betray one another;
it is in this poem, trying to speak.

QUESTIONS

1. How does the poem illustrate the meaning of hope? How true or adequate are the specific locations where hope may be found? How do these locations provide the grounds for a broadened understanding of hope?

2. What does the poet mean by saying that hope is a "singular gift / we cannot destroy in ourselves" and that hope is a "serum" that prevents people from betraying each other?

3. According to the illustrations in the poem, how strong is the connection between hope and life? Can anything or anyone be without hope?

4. Why does the poet write "trying to speak" rather than "speaking" in the final line?

    "Hope" demonstrates that poetry is inseparable from life and living. We regularly hope for fine weather, good luck, happier times, love, successful academic and athletic performance, more money, more and better friendships, successful and rewarding careers, and so on. But Mueller takes us on a new and unexpected trip. Her speaker reminds us that hope exists in common things around us where we have never even imagined it might be, such as the fluttering seeds ("angels") of maple trees, the expanding lungs of a newborn baby, and "the genius that invents the future." Hope may even be found in the blind eyes of a potato which, when planted in lowly garden dirt, possess an indomitable wish for growth. The poem makes these ordinary things extraordinary. Mueller even leaves us with a speculative and unusual conclusion, giving life to hope by stating that hope speaks simultaneously with poetry itself. All these connections, which Mueller naturally and easily creates for us, cause us to say yes, to agree that hope exists in every obscure and out-of-the-way part of existence. Like all good poetry, "Hope" leads us into thoughts which we have not only not considered, but which we have never even dreamed about.

    We should always recognize that good poems, regardless of their topic, have similar power. To see this, let us look at another poem, by the seventeenth-century English poet Robert Herrick.

ROBERT HERRICK (1591–1664)

Here a Pretty Baby Lies   1648

Here a pretty baby lies
Sung asleep with lullabies:
Pray be silent, and not stir
Th'easy earth that covers her.

QUESTIONS

1. What situation is described in this poem? To what degree is this situation either ordinary or unusual?

2. How does the final line change your perception of the first three lines? How does it change your response to the poem?

3. Consider the double meanings of the following words and phrases: "Here . . . lies"; "Sung asleep"; "lullabies"; "stir."

Nothing in the first three lines of this short poem seems anything other than ordinary. A scene is described that takes place over and over again everywhere in the world. A baby is sleeping quietly, and we are told to make no sounds that would awaken her. But the last line hits us with a hammer, making us realize that nothing in the poem is what we understood at first. We immediately change our initial impressions and realize that the baby is not just sleeping but dead, lying not in a cradle but in a coffin; that the lullabies are not the lullabies sung by a loving mother but the religious songs sung at a funeral ceremony; and that the stirring is not just making noise but disturbing the still-loose earth that has just been shoveled onto the baby's grave. The effect of this very simple poem has legitimately been called overwhelming.

The three poems we have just seen have much in common; they are serious, engaging, original, and powerful. The first, however, is amusing and slightly perplexing; the second is serious and thought-provoking; the third is sad and deeply moving. There are no other poems like them. Once we have read them, we will never forget them. Even if we never read them again (but we should), they will echo in our minds as time passes, sometimes with great power and impact, sometimes with less. In reading them again we may rediscover our original responses, and often we may have entirely new responses to them. In short, these poems live, and as long as we too live, they will be a permanent part of our minds.

Preliminary Ideas about Poetry Can Help Understanding

As "Schoolsville," "Hope," and "Here a Pretty Baby Lies" demonstrate, all good poems are unique, and all good poems broaden our comprehension and add layers to our understandings. Like living itself, the experience of poetry is a developing process, but nevertheless, it is possible to offer a number of preliminary statements as a guide to understanding. To begin with, poems are imaginative works expressed in words that are used with the utmost compression, force, and economy. Unlike prose, which is expansive if not exhaustive, many poems are brief. But poetry is also comprehensive, offering us high points of thought, feeling, reflection, and resolution. Poems may be formed in just about any coherent and developed shape, from a line of a single word to lines of twenty, thirty, or more words; and these lines may be organized into any number of repeating or nonrepeating patterns. Some poems make us think, give us new and unexpected insights, and generally instruct us. Other poems arouse our emotions, surprise us, amuse us, and inspire us. Ideally, reading and understanding poetry should prompt us to reexamine, reinforce, and reshape our ideas, our attitudes, our feelings, and our lives. Let us hear what Robert Frost concluded about poetry: "Read it a hundred times: it will forever keep its freshness as a metal keeps its fragrance. It can never lose its sense of a meaning that once unfolded by surprise as it went."[1] Always be alert for the surprise of poetry.

🎵 POETRY OF THE ENGLISH LANGUAGE

Today, most nations of the world have their own literatures, including poetry, with their own unique histories and characteristics. In this anthology, however, we are concerned primarily, but not exclusively, with poetry in our own language by American, British, and Canadian poets.

The earliest poems in English date back to the period of *Old English* (450–1100). Many of these early English poems reflect the influence of Christianity. Indeed, the most famous poem, the epic *Beowulf*, was probably interpreted as a Christian allegory even though it concerns the secular themes of adventure, courage, and war. Ever since the *Middle English* period (1100–1500), poets have written about many other subjects, although religious themes have remained important. Today, we find poetry on virtually all topics, including worship, music, love, society, sports, individuality, sexuality, warfare, strong drink, government, and politics; some poems treat special and unusual topics such as fishing, machines, buildings, computers, exotic birds, and car crashes.

In short, poetry is in a flourishing condition in all its many forms. Commonly held moral principles are instilled by the use of well-known brief poems, epigrams, rhymes, and jingles, such as "Work. / Don't shirk," "A good beginning / Is half the winning," and "A stitch in time / Saves nine." Many people, such as poets themselves and teachers, read poetry or parts of poems aloud in front of audiences of students, friends, families, and general audiences. Many others read poetry silently in private for their own benefit. Nursery rhymes are one of the important means by which children learn the vocabulary and rhythms of our language. Poems that are set to music and sung aloud are especially powerful.

---

[1]"The Figure a Poem Makes," in *Complete Poems of Robert Frost 1949* (New York: Holt, 1949), p. viii.

Francis Scott Key's "The Star-Spangled Banner," which he wrote during a battle in the War of 1812, is our national anthem and is sung before sports competitions and many other events. More recently, musical groups like the Beatles, U2, and Smashing Pumpkins, along with singer Bruce Springsteen, have given poetic expression to ideas that huge masses of people have taken to heart. Ever since the 1960s, people devoted to civil rights have been unified and strengthened by the simple lyrics of "We Shall Overcome," not only in the United States but throughout the world. During the national crisis following the attacks on the World Trade Center and the Pentagon in 2001, many people turned to "America the Beautiful" and "God Bless America" as songs that stir the heart. The strength and vitality of poetry could be similarly documented time and time again.

❦ HOW TO READ A POEM

With poetry, as with any other literary form, the more effort we put into understanding, the greater will be our reward. Poems are often about subjects that we have never experienced directly. We have never met the poet, never had his or her exact experiences, and never thought about things in exactly the same way. To recapture the experience of the poem, we need to understand the language, ideas, attitudes, and frames of reference that bring the poem to life.

We must therefore read all poems carefully, thoughtfully, sympathetically. The economy and compression of poetry mean that every part of the poem must carry some of the impact and meaning, and thus every part repays careful attention. Try to interact with the poem. Do not expect the poem (or the poet) to do all the work. The poem contributes its language, imagery, rhythms, ideas, and all the other aspects that make it poetry, but you, the reader, will need to open your mind and your heart to the poem's impact. You have to use your imagination and let it happen.

There is no single technique for reading, absorbing, and appreciating poetry. In Chapter 1 we offer a number of guidelines for studying any work of literature (pp. 12–13). In addition to following the guidelines, read each poem more than once and keep in mind these objectives.

1. READ STRAIGHT THROUGH TO GET A GENERAL SENSE OF THE POEM.   In this first reading, do not stop to puzzle out hard passages or obscure words; just read through from beginning to end. The poem is probably not as hard as you might at first think.

2. TRY TO UNDERSTAND THE POEM'S MEANING AND ORGANIZATION.   As you read and reread the poem, study these elements.

- *The title.* The title is almost always informative. The title of Collins's "Schoolsville" suggests that the poem will contain a somewhat flippant treatment of school life. The title of Frost's "Stopping by Woods on a Snowy Evening" suggests that the poem will present ideas derived from a natural scene of cold and darkness.

- *The speaker.* Poems are dramatic, having points of view just like prose fiction. First-person speakers talk from the "inside" because they are directly involved in the action (like the speaker in Collins's "Schoolsville"). Other speakers are "outside" observers demonstrating the third-person limited and omniscient points of view, as in the anonymous "Sir Patrick Spens" (see also Chapter 5).

- *The meanings of all words, whether familiar or unfamiliar.* The words in many poems are immediately clear, as in Herrick's "Here a Pretty Baby Lies," but other poems may contain unfamiliar words and references that need looking up. You will need to consult dictionaries, encyclopedias, and other sources until you gain a grasp of the poem's content. If you have difficulty with meanings even after using your sources, ask your instructor.

- *The poem's setting and situation.* Some poems establish their settings and circumstances vividly. Frost's "Stopping by Woods on a Snowy Evening" describes an evening scene in which the speaker stops his sleigh by a woods so that he can watch snow falling amid the trees. Although not all poems are so clear, you should learn as much as you can about setting and situation in every poem you read.

- *The poem's basic form and development.* Some poems, like the anonymous "Sir Patrick Spens," are narratives; others, like Northrup's "Ogichidag," are personal statements; still others may be speeches to another person, like Herrick's "Here a Pretty Baby Lies." The poems may be laid out in a sonnet form or may develop in two-line sequences (couplets). They may contain stanzas, as in Mueller's "Hope," each unified by a particular action or thought. Try to determine the form and to trace the way in which the poem unfolds, part by part.

- *The poem's subject and theme.* The **subject** indicates the general or specific topic, while the **theme** refers to the idea or ideas that the poem explores. Jarrell's "The Death of the Ball Turret Gunner" announces its subject in the title. However, you must usually infer the theme. Jarrell's theme is the repulsive ugliness of war, the poignancy of untimely death, the callousness of the living toward the dead, and the suddenness with which war forces young people to face cruelty and horror.

3. READ THE POEM ALOUD, SOUNDING EACH WORD CLEARLY. Although this step may seem unnecessary, reading aloud will enable you to judge the effect of sound, rhythm, and rhyme. If you read Jarrell's "The Death of the Ball Turret Gunner" aloud, for example, you will notice the impact of rhyming *froze* with *hose* and the suggestion of the percussive sounds of cannon fire in the repeated and rhyming *l*, *a*, and *k* sounds of *black flak*. (For further discussion of sounds in poetry, see Chapter 19.)

4. PREPARE A PARAPHRASE OF THE POEM, AND MAKE AN EXPLICATION OF THE IDEAS AND THEMES. A **paraphrase** (discussed later in this chapter) is a restatement of the poem in your own words which helps crystallize your understanding. An **explication,** which is both an explanation and an interpretation, goes beyond paraphrase to consider significance—either of brief passages or of the entire poem.

❦ STUDYING POETRY

Let us now look in detail at a poem, in this case one that tells a story. It was composed as a song, or ballad, sometime during the late Middle Ages or early Renaissance, when most people got information about the outside world from strolling balladeers who sang the news to them (there were no newspapers, and besides, few people could read). It tells a story that is probably true, or at least based on a real event.

ANONYMOUS

Sir Patrick Spens ⟋⟍⟋⟍⟋⟍⟋   Fifteenth century

The king sits in Dumferline° town,
   Drinking the blood-red wine:
"O where will I get a good sailor
   To sail this ship of mine?"

Up and spoke an eldern° knight   *old, senior* 5
   Sat° at the king's right knee: *Who sat*
"Sir Patrick Spens is the best sailor
   That sails upon the sea."

The king has written a braid° letter   *large, commanding*
   And signed it wi'° his hand,   *with* 10
And sent it to Sir Patrick Spens,
   Was° walking on the sand.   *Who was*

The first line that Sir Patrick read,
   A loud laugh laughèd he;
The next line that Sir Patrick read,   15
   A tear blinded his eye.

"O who is this has° done this deed,   *who has*
   This ill deed done to me,
To send me out this time o'° the year,   *of*
   To sail upon the sea?   20

"Make haste, make haste, my merry men all,
   Our good ship sails the morn."°   *in the morning*
"O say not so, my master dear,
   For I fear a deadly storm.

Late late yestere'en° I saw the new moon   *yesterday evening* 25
   With the old moon in her arm,
And I fear, I fear, my dear master,
   That we will come to harm."

SIR PATRICK SPENS. 1 *Dumferline*: a town on the Firth of Forth, in Scotland.

O our Scots nobles were right loath
  To wet their cork-heeled shoon,°   *shoes*   30
But long ere a'° the play were played   *all*
  Their hats they swam aboon.°   *about (in the water)*

O long, long may their ladies sit
  Wi' their fans into their hand,
Or e'er they see Sir Patrick Spens   35
  Come sailing to the land.

O long, long may the ladies stand,
  Wi' their gold combs in their hair,
Waiting for their own dear lords,
  For they'll see them no more.   40

Half o'er, half o'er to Aberdour°
  It's fifty fathom deep,
And there lies good Sir Patrick Spens,
  Wi' the Scots lords at his feet.

41 *Aberdour*: Aberdeen, on the east coast of Scotland on the North Sea, about eighty miles north of Dumferline.

QUESTIONS

1. What action does the poem describe? Who are the principal individual figures? What groups of people are involved with and concerned about the action?

2. What do you learn about the principal figure, Sir Patrick Spens? Why does he follow the king's orders rather than his own judgment?

3. What conflicts do you find in the poem? Do they seem personal or political?

4. What emotions are conveyed in the last two stanzas? Since the poem does not explain why the king sends Sir Patrick and his men to sea, how might the emotions have been expressed more strongly?

5. Describe the poem's use of dialogue. How many people speak? How do the speeches assist in conveying the poem's action?

    "Sir Patrick Spens" is a **narrative ballad.** A narrative tells a story, and the term *ballad* defines the poem's shape or form. The first two stanzas set up the situation: The king needs a captain and crew to undertake a vital mission, and an old knight—one of the king's close advisers—suggests choosing Sir Patrick Spens, who is obviously distinguished and reliable. The rest of the poem focuses on the feelings and eventual death of Sir Patrick and his men. The third stanza provides a transition from the king to Sir Patrick. The king orders Sir Patrick to embark on an important sea voyage, and Sir Patrick reads the order. At first he laughs—probably sardonically, because Sir Patrick's response is that an order to go to sea during an obvious time of danger is nothing more than a grim joke. But when he realizes that the order is real, he foresees disaster. Our sense of impending calamity is increased when we learn that Sir Patrick's crew is also frightened (lines 23–28).

The shipwreck, described in the eighth stanza, is presented with ironic understatement. There is no description of the storm or of the crew's panic, nor does the speaker describe the masts splitting or the ship sinking under the waves. Although these horrors are omitted, the floating hats are grim evidence of destruction and death. The remainder of the poem continues in this vein of understatement. In the ninth and tenth stanzas the focus shifts back to the land, and to the ladies who will wait a "long, long" time (forever) for Sir Patrick and his men to return. The poem ends with a vision of Sir Patrick and the "Scots lords" lying "fifty fathom deep."

On first reflection, "Sir Patrick Spens" tells a sad tale without complications. The subject seems to describe no more than Sir Patrick's unfortunate drowning, along with his crew and the Scots noblemen. One might therefore claim that the poem does not have a clear theme. Even the irony of the floating hats and the waiting ladies is straightforward and unambiguous.

However, you might consider how the poem appeals to our imaginations through its suggestions of the contradictions and conflicts between authority and individuals. Sir Patrick knows the danger, yet he still obeys the king. In addition, in lines 5, 17 to 20, and 31 there is a suggestion of political infighting. The "eldern knight" is in effect responsible for dooming the ship. Moreover, the "play" being "played" suggests that a political game is taking place over and beyond the grim game of the men caught in the deadly storm (if Sir Patrick knows the danger, would not the knight also know it, and would not this knight also know the consequences of choosing Sir Patrick?). These political motives are not spelled out, but they are implied. Thus the poem is not only a sad tale but also a poignant dramatization of how power operates, of how a loyal person responds to a tragic dilemma, and of the pitiful consequences of that response.

In reading poetry, then, let the poem be your guide. Get all the words, try to understand dramatic situations, follow the emotional cues the poet gives you, and try to explain everything that is happening. Let the poem trigger your imagination. If you find implications that you believe are important, as with the political overtones of "Sir Patrick Spens," use details from the poem to support your observations. Resist the temptation to "uncover" unusual or farfetched elements in the poem (such as that hope is a tiny spirit that inhabits human beings, trees, and vegetables in the blink of an eye, or that the "man he killed" was literally the speaker's brother). *Draw only those conclusions that the poem itself supports.*

POEMS FOR STUDY

EMILY DICKINSON (1830–1886)

For a photo, see p. 1012.

Because I Could Not Stop for Death (J712, F479) — 1890 (ca. 1863)

Because I could not stop for Death –
He kindly stopped for me –
The Carriage held but just Ourselves –
And Immortality.

We slowly drove – He knew no haste   5
And I had put away
My labor and my leisure too,
For His Civility –

We passed the School, where Children strove
At Recess – in the Ring –   10
We passed the Fields of Gazing Grain –
We passed the Setting Sun –

Or rather – He passed Us –
The Dews drew quivering and chill –
For only Gossamer,° my Gown –   *thin fabric*   15
My Tippet° – only Tulle° –   *cape, scarf; thin silk*

We passed before a House that seemed
A Swelling of the Ground –
The Roof was scarcely visible –
The Cornice – in the Ground –   20

Since then – tis Centuries – and yet
Feels shorter than the Day
I first surmised the Horses' Heads
Were toward Eternity –

QUESTIONS

1. Who is the speaker, and what is she like? Why couldn't she stop for Death? What perspective does her present position give the poem?
2. In what unusual ways does the poem characterize death?
3. What does the carriage represent? Where is it headed? Who are the riders? What is meant by the things the carriage passes?
4. What is represented by the house in line 17? Why does the poet use the word "House" in preference to some other word?

ROBERT FRANCIS (1901–1987)

Catch 1950

Two boys uncoached are tossing a poem together,
Overhand, underhand, backhand, sleight of hand, every hand,
Teasing with attitudes, latitudes, interludes, altitudes,
High, make him fly off the ground for it, low, make him stoop,
Make him scoop it up, make him as-almost-as-possible miss it,   5
Fast, let him sting from it, now, fool him slowly,
Anything, everything tricky, risky, nonchalant,
Anything under the sun to outwit the prosy,
Over the tree and the long sweet cadence down,
Over his head, make him scramble to pick up the meaning,   10
And now, like a posy, a pretty one plump in his hands.

QUESTIONS

1. Describe the language of "Catch." How does the poet establish that there are two meanings to most of the words in the game of catch played by the "boys"?
2. How accurately does the poem describe a game of ordinary catch in which the participants are throwing a baseball? How interesting would a game of catch be if the participants stood still and merely threw the ball back and forth to each other? How interesting would poetry be if the poet did not create variety just as the catch players vary their throws?
3. How well does the analogy of the game of catch explain why poetry sometimes requires extra efforts of understanding?

ROBERT FROST (1874–1963)

For a photo, see p. 1049.

Stopping by Woods on a Snowy Evening 1923

Whose woods these are I think I know.
His house is in the village though;
He will not see me stopping here
To watch his woods fill up with snow.

My little horse must think it queer
To stop without a farmhouse near
Between the woods and frozen lake
The darkest evening of the year.

He gives his harness bells a shake
To ask if there is some mistake.
The only other sound's the sweep
Of easy wind and downy flake.

The woods are lovely, dark and deep,
But I have promises to keep,
And miles to go before I sleep,
And miles to go before I sleep.

5

10

15

QUESTIONS

1. What do we learn about the speaker? Where is he? What is he doing?
2. What is the setting (place, weather, time) of this poem?
3. Why does the speaker want to watch the "woods fill up with snow"?
4. What evidence suggests that the speaker is embarrassed or self-conscious about stopping? Consider the words "though" in line 2 and "must" in line 5.
5. The last stanza offers two alternative attitudes and courses of action. What are they? Which does the speaker choose?
6. To what extent do the sound and rhyme of this poem contribute to its impact? Note especially the *s* sounds in line 11 and the *w* sounds in line 12.

THOMAS HARDY (1840–1928)

The Man He Killed 1902

"Had he and I but met
By some old ancient inn,
We should have sat us down to wet
Right many a nipperkin!°   *half-pint cup*

"But ranged as infantry,
And staring face to face,
I shot at him as he at me,
And killed him in his place.

"I shot him dead because—
Because he was my foe.
Just so: my foe of course he was;
That's clear enough; although

"He thought he'd 'list,° perhaps,   *enlist*
Off-hand like—just as I—
Was out of work—had sold his traps° —   *possessions*
No other reason why.

5

10

15

"Yes; quaint and curious war is!
You shoot a fellow down
You'd treat if met where any bar is,
   Or help to half-a-crown."°   20

THE MAN HE KILLED. 20 *half a crown*: at the time, the equivalent of $20 or $30.

QUESTIONS

1.   Who and what is the speaker? What do you learn about him from his language?

2.   What situation and event is the speaker recalling and relating?

3.   What is the effect produced by repeating the word "because" in lines 9 and 10 and using the word "although" in line 12?

4.   What is the speaker's attitude toward his "foe" and toward what he has done?

5.   What point, if any, does this poem make about war? How are this poem and Jarrell's "The Death of the Ball Turret Gunner" similar and different?

JOY HARJO (b. 1951)

Eagle Poem   1990

To pray you open your whole self
To sky, to earth, to sun, to moon
To one whole voice that is you.
And know there is more
That you can't see, can't hear,   5
Can't know except in moments
Steadily growing, and in languages
That aren't always sound but other
Circles of motion.
Like eagle that Sunday morning   10
Over Salt River. Circled in blue sky
In wind, swept our hearts clean
With sacred wings.
We see you, see ourselves and know
That we must take the utmost care   15
And kindness in all things.
Breathe in, knowing we are made of
All this, and breathe, knowing
We are truly blessed because we
Were born, and die soon within a   20
True circle of motion,
Like eagle rounding out the morning
Inside us.
We pray that it will be done
In beauty.   25
In beauty.

QUESTIONS

1. What is meant by the requirement that "to pray you open your whole self / To sky, to earth, to sun, to moon"? What is the meaning of lines 4–9?

2. Why is the eagle significant to the speaker? Of what importance is the figure that the eagle makes?

3. Why does the poet repeat the phrase "In beauty" at the poem's end? (For comparison, see the Navajo Healing Prayer from the Beautyway Chant, Chapter 25.)

RANDALL JARRELL (1914–1965)

The Death of the Ball Turret Gunner°   1945

From my mother's sleep I fell into the State
And I hunched in its belly till my wet fur froze.°
Six miles from earth, loosed from its dream of life,
I woke to black flak° and the nightmare fighters.
When I died they washed me out of the turret with a hose.   5

THE DEATH OF THE BALL TURRET GUNNER. *Ball Turret Gunner:* High-altitude bombers in World War II (1941–1945) contained a revolvable gun turret both at the top and at the bottom, from which a machine-gunner could shoot at attacking fighter planes. Gunners in these turrets were sometimes mutilated by the gunfire of attacking planes.   2 *froze:* The stratospheric below-zero temperatures caused the moisture in the gunner's breath to freeze as it contacted the collar of his flight jacket.   4 *flak:* the round, black explosions of antiaircraft shells fired at bombers from the ground, an acronym of the German word *Fliegerabwehrkanone.*

QUESTIONS

1. Who is the speaker? Where has he been, and what has he been doing? What has happened to him?

2. In the first line, what is the poet saying about the age of the speaker and the opportunities he had for living before he was killed? How may this line be read politically and polemically?

3. What is a turret? What is your response to the last line?

LOUIS MACNEICE (1907–1963)

Snow   1935

The room was suddenly rich and the great bay-window was
Spawning snow and pink roses against it
Soundlessly collateral and incompatible:
World is suddener than we fancy it.

World is crazier and more of it than we think,
Incorrigibly plural. I peel and portion
A tangerine and spit the pips and feel
The drunkenness of things being various.   5

And the fire flames with a bubbling sound for world
Is more spiteful and gay than one supposes—   10
On the tongue on the eyes on the ears in the palms of one's hands—
There is more than glass between the snow and the huge roses.

QUESTIONS

1. Where is the speaker at the time of the poem? What is the contrast between the roses and the snow? Why is this contrast important?

2. What words describe snow in lines 1–3? What words in lines 4, 5, 6, 8, 10 describe the world generally? Why does the speaker choose these words rather than more descriptive ones?

3. What does the last line suggest?

4. What similarities and differences do you find between "Snow" and Frost's "Stopping by Woods on a Snowy Evening"?

JIM NORTHRUP (b. 1943)

Ogichidag°   1993

I was born in war, WW Two.
Listened as the old men told stories
of getting gassed in the trenches, WW One.
Saw my uncles come back from
Guadalcanal, North Africa,   5
and the Battle of the Bulge.
Memorized the war stories
my cousins told of Korea.
Felt the fear in their voices.
Finally it was my turn,   10
my brothers too.
Joined the marines in time
for the Cuban Missile Crisis.
Heard the crack of rifles
in the rice paddies south of Da Nang.   15
Watched my friends die there
then tasted the bitterness of
the only war America ever lost.
My son is now a warrior.
Will I listen to his war stories   20
or cry into his open grave?

OGICHIDAG. The title is the Ojibway word for "warriors."

QUESTIONS

1. What battles are mentioned in the poem, and over what period of time do these battles extend?

2. How does the speaker state that he learned about the battles? Why is this method of gaining knowledge important? What experience has the speaker had with war?

3. Why does the speaker finish the poem by referring to his son? In relationship to the poem's structure, why is the concluding question important?

NAOMI SHIHAB NYE (b. 1952)

Where Children Live ⸙ 1982

Homes where children live exude a pleasant rumpledness,
like a bed made by a child, or a yard littered with balloons.

To be a child again one would need to shed details
till the heart found itself dressed in the coat with a hood.
Now the heart has taken on gloves and mufflers,   5
the heart never goes outside to find something to "do."
And the house takes on a new face, dignified.
No lost shoes blooming under bushes.
No chipped trucks in the drive.
Grown-ups like swings, leafy plants, slow-motion back and forth.   10
While the yard of a child is strewn with the corpses
of bottle-rockets and whistles,
anything whizzing and spectacular, brilliantly short-lived.

Trees in children's yards speak in clearer tongues.
Ants have more hope. Squirrels dance as well as hide.   15
The fence has a reason to be there, so children can go in and out.
Even when the children are at school, the yards glow
with the leftovers of their affection,
the roots of the tiniest grasses curl toward one another
like secret smiles.   20

QUESTIONS

1. How accurately does the poem present the "pleasant rumpledness" of children?
2. What is the speaker's view of the comparative dependence or independence of children? What does the speaker think of children?
3. Sometimes poems about children can be overly sentimental. How well does this poem present sentiment about children? Does it go too far, or is it about right?

WILLIAM SHAKESPEARE (1564–1616)

For a drawing, see p. 1306.

Sonnet 55: Not Marble, Nor the Gilded Monuments ⸙ 1609

Not marble, nor the gilded monuments
Of princes, shall outlive this powerful rhyme;
But you shall shine more bright in these contents
Than unswept stone, besmeared with sluttish time.
When wasteful war shall statues overturn,   5
And broils root out the work of masonry,

Nor° Mars his° sword nor war's quick fire shall burn   *Neither; Mars's*
The living record of your memory.
'Gainst death and all-oblivious enmity
Shall you pace forth; your praise shall still find room   10
Even in the eyes of all posterity
That wear this world out to the ending doom.°   *Judgment Day*
So, till the judgment that yourself arise,
You live in this, and dwell in lovers' eyes.

QUESTIONS

1. Who is the speaker of the poem, and who is being addressed?
2. What powers of destruction does the speaker mention? What, according to the speaker, will survive these powers?
3. What does "the living record of your memory" (line 8) mean?
4. What is the poem's subject? Theme?

ELAINE TERRANOVA (b. 1939)

Rush Hour ⋙⋘ 1995

Odd, the baby's scabbed face peeking over
the woman's shoulder. The little girl
at her side with her arm in a cast,
wearing a plain taffeta party dress.
The woman herself who is in shorts and sunglasses   5
among commuters in the underground station. Her body
that sags and tenses at the same time.

The little girl has not once moved
to touch her or to be touched.
Even on the train, she never turns and says,   10
"Mommy." Sunlight bobs over her blond head
inclining toward the window. The baby
is excited now. "Loo, loo, loo, loo,"
he calls, a wet crescendo. "He's pulling
my hair," the little girl at last cries out.   15

A kind man comes up the aisle to see
the baby. He stares at those rosettes of blood
and wants to know what's wrong with him.
The woman says a dog bit him. "It must have been
a big dog, then." "Oh, no. A neighbor's little dog."   20
The man says, "I hope they put that dog to sleep."
The woman is nearly pleading. "It was an accident. He didn't
mean to do it." The conductor, taking tickets,

asks the little girl how she broke her arm.
But the child looks out to the big, shaded houses.   25
The woman says, "She doesn't like to talk
about that." No one has seen what is behind

her own dark glasses. She pulls the children to her.
Maybe she is thinking of the arm raised over them,
its motion that would begin like a blessing.   30

QUESTIONS

1. What clues early in the poem indicate that the woman and her children are victims of domestic abuse?

2. Why does the mother not appeal for help when the two men, the "kind man" and the conductor, inquire about the injuries of the children? What is the irony of the raised arm in the last two lines? What is the pathos of the mother's situation?

3. Describe the attitude of the speaker telling the story of the poem. Why does the speaker do no more than describe details, and not actually rail against domestic abuse?

— practice

🎵 WRITING A PARAPHRASE OF A POEM

restating the text giving the meaning different words

Paraphrasing is especially useful in the study of poetry. It fixes both the general shape and the details of a poem in your mind, and it also reveals the poetic devices at work. A comparison of the original poem with the paraphrase highlights the techniques and the language that make the poem effective.

To paraphrase a poem, rewrite it in prose, in your own words. Decide what details to include—a number that you determine partly by the length of the poem and partly by the total length of your paraphrase. When you deal with lyrics, sonnets, and other short poems, you may include all the details, and thus your paraphrase may be as long as the work, or longer. Paraphrases of long poems, however, will be shorter than the originals because some details must be summarized briefly while others may be cut entirely.

It is vital to make your paraphrase accurate and also to use *only your own words.* To make sure that your words are all your own, read through the poem several times. Then, put the poem out of sight and write your paraphrase. Once you've finished, check yourself both for accuracy and vocabulary. If you find that you've borrowed too many of the poem's words, choose other words that mean the same thing, or else use quotation marks to set off the original words (but do not overuse quotations).

Above all, remain faithful to the poem, but *avoid drawing conclusions and giving unnecessary explanations.* It would be wrong in a paraphrase of Jarrell's "The Death of the Ball Turret Gunner," for example, to state, "This poem makes a forceful argument against the brutal and wasteful deaths caused by war." This assertion states the poem's *theme*, but it *does not* describe the poem's actual content.

Organizing Your Paraphrase

The organization of your paraphrase should reflect the poem's form or development. Include material in the order in which it occurs. With short poems, organize your paraphrase to reflect the poem's development line by line or stanza by stanza. In paraphrasing Shakespeare's "Not Marble, Nor the Gilded Monuments," for example, you should deal with each four-line group in sequence and then consider the final couplet. With longer poems, look for natural divisions such as groups of related stanzas, verse paragraphs, or other possible organizational units. In every situation, the poem's shape should determine the form of your paraphrase.

DEMONSTRATIVE STUDENT PARAPHRASE

A Paraphrase of Thomas Hardy's "The Man He Killed"°

[1]   If the man I killed had met me in an inn, we would have sat down together and had many drinks. Because we belonged to armies of warring foot soldiers lined up on a battlefield, however, we shot at each other, and my shot killed him.

[2]   The reason I killed him, I think, was that he and I were enemies--just that. But as I think of it, I realize that he had enlisted in just the way I did. Maybe he did it on a whim, or maybe he had lost his job and sold everything he owned. There was no other reason to enlist.

[3]   Being at war is unusual and strange. Instead of buying a man a drink, or helping him out with a little money, you have to kill him.

Commentary on the Essay

Because Hardy's poem is short, the paraphrase attempts to include all its details. The organization closely follows the poem's development. Paragraph 1, for example, restates the contents of the first two stanzas. Paragraph 2 restates the third and fourth stanzas. Finally, the last paragraph separately paraphrases the last stanza, which contains the reflections made by the poem's "I" speaker. This paragraph concludes the paraphrase just as the last stanza concludes the poem.

Notice that the essay does not abstract details from the poem, such as "The dead man might have become a good friend in peacetime" in paraphrasing stanza 5; nor does it extend details, such as "We would have gotten acquainted, had drinks together, told many stories, and done quite a bit of laughing" for stanza 1 (both stanzas, however, actually do suggest these details). Although the paraphrase reflects the poem's strong antiwar sentiments, an interpretive sentence like "By his very directness, the narrator brings out the senselessness and brutality of warfare" would be out of place. What is needed is a short restatement of the poem to demonstrate the essay writer's understanding of the poem's content, and no more.

WRITING AN EXPLICATION OF A POEM

Explication goes beyond the assimilation required for a paraphrase and thus provides you with the opportunity to show your understanding. But there is no need to explain everything in the poem. A complete, or total, explication would

°See p. 622 for this poem.

theoretically require you to explain the meaning and implications of each word and every line—a technique that obviously would be exhaustive (and exhausting). It would also be self-defeating, for explicating everything would prohibit you from using your judgment and deciding what is important.

A more manageable and desirable technique is therefore the **general explication,** which devotes attention to the meaning of individual parts in relationship to the entire work, as in the discussion of "Sir Patrick Spens" (p. 617). You might think of a general explication as your explanation or "reading" of the poem. Because it does not require you to go into exhaustive detail, you will need to be selective and to consider only those details that are significant in themselves and vital to your own thematic development.

Questions for Discovering Ideas

- What does the title contribute to the reader's understanding?
- Who is speaking? Where is the speaker when the poem is happening?
- What is the situation? What has happened in the past, or what is happening in the present, that has brought about the speech?
- What difficult, special, or unusual words does the poem contain? What references need explaining? How does an explanation assist in the understanding of the poem?
- How does the poem develop? Is it a personal statement? Is it a story?
- What is the main idea of the poem? What details make possible the formulation of the main idea?

Strategies for Organizing Ideas

Your general explication demonstrates your ability to (1) follow the essential details of the poem (the same as in a paraphrase), (2) understand the issues and the meaning the poem reveals, (3) explain some of the relationships of content to technique, and (4) note and discuss especially important or unique aspects of the poem.

In your introduction, use your central idea to express a general view of the poem, which your essay will bear out. The discussion of the anonymous "Sir Patrick Spens" (p. 617) suggests some possible central ideas, namely that (1) the poem highlights a conflict between self-preservation and obedience to authority, and (2) innocent people may be caught in political infighting. In the following demonstrative student essay explicating Hardy's "The Man He Killed," the central idea is that war is senseless.

In the body of your essay, first explain the poem's content—not with a paraphrase but with a description of the poem's major organizing elements. Hence, if the speaker of the poem is "inside" the poem as a first-person involved "I," you do not need to reproduce this voice yourself in your description. Instead, *describe* the poem in your own words, with whatever brief introductory phrases you find necessary, as in the second paragraph of the following demonstrative essay.

Next, explicate the poem in relation to your central idea. Choose *your own* order of discussion, depending on your topics. You should, however, keep stressing your central idea with each new topic. Thus, you might wish to follow your description by discussing the poem's meaning, or even by presenting two or more possible interpretations. You might also wish to refer to significant techniques. For example, in the anonymous "Sir Patrick Spens" a noteworthy technique is the unintroduced quotations (i.e., quotations appearing without any "he said" or "quoth he" phrases) as the ballad writer's means of dramatizing the commands and responses of Sir Patrick and his doomed crew.

You might also introduce special topics, such as the crewman who explains that there will be bad luck because the new moon has "the old moon in her arm" (line 26). Such a reference to superstition might include the explanation of the crewman's assumptions, the relationship of his uneasiness to the remainder of the poem, and also how the ballad writer keeps the narrative brief. In short, discuss those aspects of meaning and technique that bear upon your central idea.

In your conclusion, you may repeat your major idea to reinforce your essay's thematic structure. Because your essay is a general explication, there will be parts of the poem that you will not have discussed. You might therefore mention what might be gained from an exhaustive discussion of various parts of the poem (do not, however, begin to exhaust any subject in the conclusion of your essay). The last stanza of Hardy's "The Man He Killed," for example, contains the words "quaint and curious" in reference to war. These words are unusual, particularly because the speaker might have chosen *hateful, senseless, destructive,* or other similarly descriptive words. Why did Hardy have his speaker make such a choice? With brief attention to such a problem, you may conclude your essay.

DEMONSTRATIVE STUDENT ESSAY

An Explication of Thomas Hardy's "The Man He Killed"°

[1] Hardy's "The Man He Killed" exposes the senselessness of war.* It does this through a silent contrast between the needs of ordinary people, as represented by a young man--the speaker--who has killed an enemy soldier in battle, and the antihuman and unnatural deaths of war. Of major note in this contrast are the speaker's circumstances, his language, his sense of identity with the dead man, and his concerns and wishes.†

The speaker begins by contrasting the circumstances of warfare with those of peace. He does not identify himself, but his speech reveals that he is common and ordinary--a person, one of "the people," who enjoys drinking in a bar and who

°See p. 622 for this poem.
*Central idea.
†Thesis sentence.

[2] prefers friendship and helpfulness to violence. If he and the man he killed had met in an inn, he says, they would have shared many drinks, but because they met on a battlefield they shot at each other, and he killed the other man. The speaker tries to justify the killing but can produce no stronger reason than that the dead man was his "foe." Once he states this reason, he again thinks of the similarities between himself and the dead man, and then he concludes that warfare is "quaint and curious" (line 17) because it forces a man to kill another man whom he would have befriended if they had met during peacetime.

[3] To make the irony of warfare clear, the poem uses easy, everyday language to bring out the speaker's ordinary qualities. His manner of speech is conversational, as in "We should have sat us down" (line 3), "'list" (for "enlist," line 13), and his use of "you" in the last stanza. Also, his word choices, shown in words like "nipperkin," "traps," and "fellow" (lines 4, 15, and 18), are common and informal, at least in British usage. This language is important because it establishes that the speaker is an average man whom war has thrown into an unnatural role.

[4] As another means of stressing the stupidity of war, the poem makes clear that the two men--the live soldier who killed and the dead soldier who was killed-- were so alike that they could have been brothers or even twins. They had similar ways of life, similar economic troubles, similar wishes to help other people, and similar motives in enlisting in the army. Symbolically, the "man he killed" is the speaker himself, and hence the killing may be considered a form of suicide. The poem thus raises the question of why two people who are almost identical should be shoved into opposing battle lines in order to kill each other. This question is rhetorical, for the obvious answer is that there is no good reason.

[5] Because the speaker (and also, very likely, the dead man) is shown as a person embodying the virtues of friendliness and helpfulness, Hardy's poem is a strong disapproval of war. Clearly, political reasons for violence as policy are irrelevant to the characters and concerns of the men who fight. They, like the speaker, would prefer to follow their own needs rather than remote and meaningless ideals. The failure of complex but irrelevant political explanations is brought out most clearly in the third stanza, in which the speaker tries to give a reason for shooting the other man. Hardy's use of punctuation--the dashes--stresses the fact that the speaker has no commitment to the cause he served when killing. Thus the speaker stops at the word "because--" and gropes for a reason (line 9). Not being articulate, he can say only "Because he was my foe. / Just so: my foe of course he was; / That's clear enough" (lines 10–12). These short bursts of words indicate that he cannot explain things to himself or to anyone else except in the most obvious and trite terms, and in apparent embarrassment he inserts "of course" as a way of emphasizing hostility even though he clearly felt none toward the man he killed.

[6] A reading thus shows the power of the poem's dramatic argument. Hardy does not establish closely detailed reasons against war as a policy but rather dramatizes the idea that all political arguments are unimportant in view of the central and glaring brutality of war--killing. Hardy's speaker is not able to express deep feelings; rather he is confused because he is an average sort who wants only to live and let live and to enjoy a drink in a bar with friends. But this very commonness stresses the point that everyone is victimized by war--both those who die and those who kill. The poem is a powerful argument for peace and reconciliation.

WORK CITED

Hardy, Thomas. "The Man He Killed." <u>Literature: An Introduction to Reading and Writing</u>. Ed. Edgar V. Roberts and Henry E. Jacobs. 7th ed. Upper Saddle River: Prentice Hall, 2004. 622–23.

Commentary on the Essay

This explication begins by stating a central idea about "The Man He Killed," then indicates the topics to follow that will develop the idea. Although nowhere does the speaker state that war is senseless, the essay takes the position that the poem embodies this idea. A more detailed examination of the poem's themes might develop the idea by discussing the ways in which individuals are caught up in social and political forces, or the contrast between individuality and the state. In this essay, however, the simple statement of the idea is enough.

Paragraph 2 describes the major details of the poem, with guiding phrases like "The speaker begins," "he says," and "he again thinks." Thus the paragraph goes over the poem, like a paraphrase, but explains how things occur, as is appropriate for an explication. Paragraph 3 is devoted to the speaker's words and idioms, with the idea that his conversational manner is part of the poem's contrasting method of argument. If these brief references to style were more detailed, this topic could be more fully developed as an aspect of Hardy's implied argument against war.

Paragraph 4 extends paragraph 3 inasmuch as it points out the similarities of the speaker and the man he killed. If the situation were reversed, the dead man might say exactly the same things about the present speaker. This affinity underscores the suicidal nature of war. Paragraph 5 treats the style of the poem's fourth stanza. In this context, the treatment is brief. The last paragraph reiterates the main idea and concludes with a tribute to the poem as an argument.

The entire essay therefore represents a reading and explanation of the poem's high points. It stresses a particular interpretation and briefly shows how various aspects of the poem bear it out.

Special Topics for Writing and Argument about the Nature of Poetry

1. Skim the titles of poems listed in the table of contents of this book. Judging by the subjects of those poems, describe and discuss the possible range of subject matter for poetry. What topics seem most suitable? Why? Do any topics seem to be ruled out? Why? What additional subject matter would you suggest as possible topics for poems?

2. How accurate is the proposition that poetry is a particularly compressed form of expression? To support your position, you might refer to poems such as Dickinson's "Because I Could Not Stop for Death," Francis's "Catch," and Frost's "Stopping by Woods on a Snowy Evening."

3. Consider the subject of war as brought out in Jarrell's "The Death of the Ball Turret Gunner," Hardy's "The Man He Killed," and Northrop's "Ogichidag."

What ideas are common to the poems? What ideas are distinct and unique? On the basis of your comparison, consider the use of poetry as a vehicle for the expression of moral and political ideas.

4.   Write two poems of your own about your future plans. In one, assume that the world is stable and will go on forever. In the other, assume that a large asteroid is out of orbit and is hurtling toward earth at great speed, and a collision six months from now will bring untold destruction and may even end life on earth. After composing your poems, write a brief explanation of how and why they differ in terms of language, references, and attitudes toward friends, family, country, religion, and so on.

5.   Consult the brief section on reader-response criticism in Chapter 33. Then write an essay about your responses to one poem, or a number of poems, in this chapter. Assume that your own experiences are valuable guides for your judgment. In the poems that you have read, what has had a bearing on your experiences? What in your own experiences has given you insights into the poems? Try to avoid being anecdotal; instead, try to find a relationship between your experiences and the poetry.

6.   In the reference section of your library, find two books (anthologies, encyclopedias, introductions, dictionaries of literary terms) about the general subject of poetry. On the basis of how these two sources define and explain poetry, write a brief essay telling a person younger than you what to expect from the reading of poems.

Words: *The Building Blocks of Poetry*

Words are the spoken and written signifiers of thoughts, objects, and actions. They are also the building blocks of both poetry and prose, but poetry is unique because by its nature it uses words with the utmost economy. The words of poetry create rhythm, rhyme, meter, and form. They define the poem's speaker, the characters, the setting, and the situation, and they also carry its ideas and emotions. For this reason, each poet searches for perfect and indispensable words, words that convey all the compressed meanings, overtones, and emotions that each poem requires, and also the words that sound right and look right.

Life—and poetry—might be simpler (but less interesting) if there were an exact one-to-one correspondence between words and the objects or ideas they signify. Such close correspondences exist in artificial language systems such as chemical equations and computer languages. This identical correlation, however, is not characteristic of English or any other natural language. Instead, words have the independent and glorious habit of attracting and expressing a vast array of different meanings.

Even if we have not thought much about language, most of us know that words are sometimes ambiguous, and much literature is built on ambiguity. For instance, in Shakespeare's *Romeo and Juliet*, when Mercutio says, "Seek for me tomorrow and you shall find me a grave man," the joke works because *grave* has two separate meanings, both of which come into play. In reading poetry, we recognize that poets rejoice in this shifting and elusive but also rich nature of language.

CHOICE OF DICTION: SPECIFIC AND CONCRETE, GENERAL AND ABSTRACT

Because poets always try to use only the exactly right words, they constantly make conscious and subconscious decisions about diction. One of the major categories of their choice is diction that is either specific and concrete or general and abstract.

Specific language refers to objects or conditions that can be perceived or imagined, and **general** language signifies broad classes of persons, objects, and phenomena. **Concrete** diction describes conditions or qualities that are exact and particular; **abstract** diction refers to qualities that are rarefied and theoretical. In practice, poems using specific and concrete words tend to be visual, familiar, and compelling. By contrast, poems that use general and abstract words tend to be detached and cerebral, and they often deal with universal questions or emotions.

These distinctions become clear when we compare Housman's "Loveliest of Trees" and Eberhart's "The Fury of Aerial Bombardment." Many of the terms and images that Housman uses, such as "cherry. . . / hung with bloom" and "threescore years and ten," are specific and concrete; they evoke exact time and clear visualization. By contrast, Eberhart's terms, such as "infinite spaces" and "eternal truth," are general and abstract, and it is therefore hard to define them with clarity and exactness. This contrast, which by no means implies that Housman's poem is superior to Eberhart's, reflects differences in word choices for different objectives.

Most poets employ mixtures of words in these categories because in many poems they draw general observations and abstract conclusions from specific situations and concrete responses. They therefore interweave their words to fit their situations and ideas, as in Roethke's "Dolor," which uses specific and concrete words to define a series of abstract emotional states.

❄ LEVELS OF DICTION

Like ordinary speakers and writers of prose, poets choose words from the category of the three levels of diction: high or formal, middle or neutral, and low or informal. Often, the high and middle levels are considered standard or "right" while low language is dismissed as substandard or "wrong." In poetry, however, none of the classes is more correct than any other, for what counts is that they all function according to the poet's wishes, from broadly formal and intellectual to ordinary and popular.

High or Formal Diction Is Elevated and Elaborate

High or **formal diction** exactly follows the rules of syntax, seeking accuracy of expression even if unusually elevated or complex words are brought into play. Beyond "correctness," formal language is characterized by complex words and a lofty tone. In general, formal diction freely introduces words of French, Latin, and Greek derivation, some of which are quite long, so some people might think that formal language is "difficult." Graves uses formal diction in "The Naked and the Nude" when the speaker asserts that the terms in the title are "By lexicographers construed / As synonyms that should express / The same deficiency of dress." The Latinate words, italicized here, stiffen and generalize the passage: We find *lexicographers* instead of *dictionary writers, construed* (from Latin) instead of *thought* (native English), *express* (from Latin) instead of *say* or *show* (native English), and *deficiency* (Latin) instead of *lack* (English). It is simply a fact that our language contains thousands of words that were originally French, Latin, or Greek and that many of these are long and abstract. But not all words of this sort are necessarily long, nor are they abstract and stiff. Many of our short words, for example, are French in origin, such as *class, face, fort, paint, bat, tend, gain, cap, trace, order,* and *very.* A good college-level dictionary contains brief descriptions of word origins, or etymologies; as an exercise, you might trace the origins of a number of words in a poem.

Middle or Neutral Diction Stresses Simplicity

Middle or **neutral diction** maintains the correct language and word order of formal diction but avoids elaborate words and elevated tone just as it avoids idioms, colloquialisms, contractions, slang, jargon, and fads of speech. For example, Emily Dickinson's "Because I Could Not Stop for Death" (Chapter 13) is almost entirely in middle diction.

Low or Informal Diction Is the Language of Common, Everyday Use

Low or **informal diction** is relaxed and unself-conscious, the language of people buying groceries, gasoline, and pizza, and of people who may be "hanging out" while guzzling beer or soda pop. Poems using informal diction include common and simple words, idiomatic expressions, substandard expressions, foreign expressions, slang, "swearwords" or "cusswords," grammatical "errors," and contractions. Informal diction is seen in Hardy's "The Man He Killed" (Chapter 13), in which the speaker uses words and phrases like "many a nipperkin," "He thought he'd 'list," and "Off-hand like."

SPECIAL TYPES OF DICTION

Depending on their subjects and purposes, poets (and writers of prose) may wish to introduce four special types of diction into their poems: *idiom, dialect, slang,* and *jargon.*

Idiom Refers to Unique Forms of Diction and Word Order

The words **idiom** and **idioms,** originally meaning "making one's own," refer to words, phrases, and expressions that are common and acceptable in a particular language, even though they might, upon analysis, seem peculiar or illogical. Standard English idioms are so ingrained into our thought that we do not notice them. Poems automatically reflect these idioms. Thus, for example, a poet may "think *of*" an idea, speak of "living *in*" a house, talk of "going *out* to play," or describe a woman "lovely *as* chandeliers." Poets hardly have choices about such idioms as long as they are using standard English. Real choice occurs when poets select idioms that are unusual or even ungrammatical, as in phrases like "had he and I but met," "we was happy," and "except that You than He." Idioms like these enable poets to achieve levels of ordinary and colloquial diction, depending on their purposes.

Dialect Refers to Regional and Group Usage and Pronunciation

Although we recognize English as a common language, in practice the language is made up of many habits of speech or **dialects** that are characteristic of many groups, regions, and nations. In addition to "general American," we can recognize many common dialects such as Southern, Midwestern, New England, Brooklynese, American Black English, Yiddish English, and Texan, together with "upper" British, Cockney, and Scottish and Australian English. Dialect is concerned with whether we refer to a *pail* (general American) or a *bucket* (Southern); or sit down on a *sofa* (Eastern) or a *couch* (general American) or *davenport* (Midwestern); or drink *soda* (Eastern), *pop* (Midwestern), *soda pop* (a confused Midwesterner living in the East, or a confused Easterner living in the Midwest), or *tonic* (Bostonian). Burns's "Green Grow the Rashes, O" and Hardy's "The Ruined Maid" illustrate the poetic use of dialect.

Slang Refers to Informal and Substandard Vocabulary and Idiom

Much of the language that people use every day is **slang.** Sometimes slang is impermanent, appearing among certain speakers and then vanishing. The use of the word *bad* to mean "good" illustrates how a new slang meaning can develop, and even stay for a time, and then diminish in use. This is not to say that slang is not persistent, for permanent slang forms a significant part of the language. There is a continuous word stock of substandard or "impolite" words, some of which are so-called four-letter words, that everyone knows but speaks only privately. There are also innumerable slang expressions. For example, we have many slang phrases describing dying, such as *kick the bucket, croak, be wasted, buy the farm, be burked, be disappeared,* and *be offed.* A nonnative speaker of English, unfamiliar with our slang, would have difficulty understanding that a person who "kicked the bucket," "bought the farm," or "was offed" had actually died.

Even though slang is a permanent part of our language, it is usually confined to colloquial or conversational levels. (Interestingly, people with perfect command of standard English regularly use slang in private among their friends and acquaintances.) If slang is introduced into a standard context, therefore, it mars and jars, as in Cummings's "Buffalo Bill's Defunct" (Chapter 20), where the speaker refers to Buffalo Bill as a "blueeyed boy." Because the poem deals with the universality of death, the phrase, which usually refers to a young man on the make, ironically underscores this intention.

Jargon Is the Special Language and Terminology of Groups

Particular groups develop **jargon**—specialized words and expressions which are usually employed by members of specific professions or trades, such as astronauts, doctors, lawyers, computer experts, plumbers, and football players. Without an initiation, people ordinarily cannot understand the special meanings. Although jargon at its worst befuddles rather than informs, it is significant when it becomes part of mainstream English or is used in literature. Poets may introduce jargon for special effects. For example, Paul Zimmer, in "The Day Zimmer Lost Religion" (Chapter 25), wryly uses the phrase "ready for Him now," a boxing expression that describes a fighter in top condition. Linda Pastan uses "gives me an A" and "I'm dropping out," both phrases from school life, to create comic effects in "Marks" (Chapter 25). Another poem employing jargon is Eberhart's "The Fury of Aerial Bombardment," which uses technical terms for firearms to establish the authenticity of the poem's references and therefore to reinforce the poem's judgments about warfare.

DECORUM: THE MATCHING OF SUBJECT AND WORD

A vital literary concept is **decorum** ("beautiful," "appropriate"); that is, words and subjects should be in perfect accord—formal words for serious subjects, and informal words for low subjects and comedy. In Shakespeare's *A Midsummer Night's Dream*, for example, the nobles usually speak poetry and the "mechanicals" speak prose (Chapter 28). When the nobility are relaxed and in the forest, however, they also speak prose. Decorum governs such choices of language.

In the eighteenth century, writers aimed to make the English language as dignified as ancient Latin, which was the international language of discourse. They therefore asserted that only formal diction was appropriate for poetry; common life and colloquial language were excluded except in drama and popular ballads. These rules of decorum required standard and elevated language rather than common words and phrases. The development of scientific terminology during the eighteenth century also influenced language. In the scientific mode, poets of the time used descriptive phrases like "lowing herd" for cattle (Thomas Gray) and "finny prey" for fish (Alexander Pope). In this vein, Thomas Gray observed the dependence of color on light in the line "cheerful fields resume their green attire" from the "Sonnet on the Death of Richard West."

Pope, one of the greatest eighteenth-century poets, maintained these rules of decorum—and also made fun of them—in his mock-epic poem *The Rape of the Lock*, and more fully in the mock-critical work *Peri Bathous, or The Art of Sinking in Poetry*. In *The Rape of the Lock*, he refers to a scissors as a "glittering forfex." Similarly, in the following couplet he elevates the simple act of pouring coffee.

From silver spouts the grateful liquors glide,
While China's earth receives the smoking tide.

Since Wordsworth transformed poetic diction early in the nineteenth century, the topics and language of people of all classes, with a special stress on common folk, have become a feature of poetry. Poets have continued to follow rules of decorum, however, inasmuch as the use of colloquial diction and even slang is a necessary consequence of popular subject matter.

ᗷ SYNTAX

Syntax refers to word order and sentence structure. Normal English word order is firmly fixed in a *subject-verb-object* sequence. At the simplest level, we say, "A dog (*subject*) bites (*verb*) a man (*object*)." This order is so central to our communication that any change significantly affects meaning: "A dog bites a man" is not the same as "A man bites a dog."

Much of the time, poets follow normal word order, as in "The Lamb," where Blake creates a simple, easy order in keeping with the poem's purpose of presenting a childlike praise of God. Many modern poets such as Mark Strand go out of their way to create ordinary, everyday syntax, on the theory that a poem's sentence structures should not get in the way of the reader's perceptions.

Yet, just as good poets always explore the limits of ideas, so also do they sometimes explore the many possibilities of syntax, as in line 7 of Donne's "Batter My Heart": "Reason, Your viceroy in me, me should defend." In prose, this sentence would read "Reason, who is Your viceroy in me, should defend me." But note that Donne drops the "who is," and that he also puts the direct object "me" before and not after the verb. The resulting emphasis on the pronoun *me* is appropriate to the personal–divine relationship that is the topic of the sonnet. The alteration also meets the demand of the poem's rhyme scheme. A set of particularly noteworthy syntactic variations occurs in Roethke's "Dolor." The poet uses an irregular and idiosyncratic combination of objects, phrases, and appositives to create ambiguity and uncertainty underscoring the idea that school and office routines are aimless and depressing.

Some of the other means by which poets shape word order to create emphasis are an aspect of **rhetoric. Parallelism** is the most easily recognized rhetorical device. A simple form of parallelism is **repetition,** as with the phrase "who made thee" in Blake's "The Lamb." Through the use of the same grammatical forms, though in different words, parallelism produces lines or portions of lines that impress our minds strongly, as in this passage from Robinson's "Richard Cory," in which there are four parallel past-tense verbs (italicized here).

So on we *worked*, and *waited* for the light,
And *went* without the meat, and *cursed* the bread;

The final two lines of this poem demonstrate how parallelism may embody **antithesis**—a contrasting situation or idea that brings out surprise and climax.

And Richard Cory, one calm summer night,
Went home and *put* a bullet through his head.

A major quality of parallelism is the packing of words (the *economy* and *compression* of poetry), for by using a parallel structure the poet makes a single word or phrase function a number of times, with no need for repetition. The opening verb phrase "have known" in Roethke's "Dolor," though used once, controls six parallel direct objects. At the end of Donne's "Batter My Heart," parallelism (along with antithesis) permits Donne to omit the italicized words added and bracketed in the last line here.

> for I,
> Except You enthrall° me, never shall be free, *unless; enslave*
> Nor [*shall I*] ever [*be*] chaste, except You ravish me.

Note also that parallelism and antithesis make possible the unique *a b b a* ordering of these two lines, with the pattern "enthrall" (verb) "free" (adjective) "chaste" (adjective) "ravish" (verb). This rhetorical pattern is called **antimetabole** or **chiasmus** and is a common pattern of creating emphasis.

♦ DENOTATION AND CONNOTATION

To achieve the maximum impact, poets depend not just on the simplest, most essential meanings of words but also on the suggestions and associations that words bring to us. For this reason, control over denotation and connotation (see also Chapter 7) is so important that it has been called the very soul of the poet's art.

Denotation Refers to Standard, Most Commonly Recognized Meanings

The ordinary dictionary meaning of a word—**denotation**—indicates conventional correspondences between words and objects or ideas. Although we might expect denotation to be straightforward, most English words have multiple denotations. The noun *house*, for example, can refer to a *building*, a *family*, a *branch of Congress*, a *theater*, a *theater audience*, a *sorority* or *fraternity*, an *astrological classification*, or a *brothel*. Although context usually makes the denotation of *house* more specific, the various meanings confer a built-in ambiguity in this simple word.

Denotation presents problems because with the passing of time, new meanings emerge and old ones are shed. In poems written in the eighteenth century and earlier, there are many words that have changed so completely that a modern dictionary is not much help. In Marvell's "To His Coy Mistress" (Chapter 21), for example, the speaker asserts that his "vegetable love should grow / Vaster than empires, and more slow." At first reading, "vegetable" may seem to refer to something like a giant, loving turnip. When we turn to a current dictionary, we discover that *vegetable* is an adjective meaning "plantlike," but *plantlike love* does not get us much beyond *vegetable love*. A reference to the *Oxford English Dictionary* (*OED*), however, tells us that *vegetable* was used as an adjective in the seventeenth century to mean "living or growing like a plant." Thus we find out that "vegetable love" means love that grows slowly but steadily larger.

Connotation Refers to a Word's Emotional, Psychological, Social, and Historical Overtones

The life of language, and the most difficult to control, is a result of **connotation.** Almost no word is without it. For instance, according to the dictionary, the words *childish* and *childlike* denote the state of being like a child. Nevertheless, they connote or imply different sets of characteristics. *Childish* suggests a person who is bratty, stubborn, immature, silly, and petulant, whereas *childlike* suggests that a person may be innocent, charming, and unaffected. These different meanings are based entirely on connotations, for the denotations make little distinction.

Connotation affects us in almost everything we hear and read. We constantly encounter the manipulation of connotation in advertising, for example. The manipulation may be as sophisticated as the current use of the word *lite* or *light* to describe foods and drinks. In all such products, *lite* denotes "dietetic," "low-calorie," or even "weak." The distinction—and the selling point—is found in connotation. Imagine how difficult it would be to sell a drink called "dietetic beer" or "weak beer." *Light* and *lite*, however, carry none of the negative connotations and, instead, suggest products that are pleasant, sparkling, bright, and healthy.

Poets always try to make individual words carry as many appropriate and effective denotations and connotations as possible. Put another way, poets use *packed* or *loaded* words that carry a broad range of meaning and association. With this in mind, read the following poem by Robert Graves.

ROBERT GRAVES (1895–1985)

The Naked and the Nude ⌣⌣⌣ 1957

For me, the naked and the nude
(By lexicographers° construed
As synonyms that should express
The same deficiency of dress
Or shelter) stand as wide apart   5
As love from lies, or truth from art.

Lovers without reproach will gaze
On bodies naked and ablaze;
The Hippocratic° eye will see
In nakedness, anatomy;   10
And naked shines the Goddess when
She mounts her lion among men.

The nude are bold, the nude are sly
To hold each treasonable eye.
While draping by a showman's trick   15
Their dishabille° in rhetoric,

THE NAKED AND THE NUDE. 2 *lexicographers*: writers of dictionaries.   9 *Hippocratic*: medical; the adjective derives from Hippocrates (ca. 460–377 B.C.E.), the ancient Greek who is considered the "father of medicine."   16 *dishabille*: being carelessly or partly dressed.

They grin a mock-religious grin
Of scorn at those of naked skin.

The naked, therefore, who compete
Against the nude may know defeat;
Yet when they both together tread
The briary pastures of the dead,
By Gorgons° with long whips pursued,
How naked go the sometime nude!   20

23 *Gorgons*: mythological female monsters with snakes for hair.

QUESTIONS

1. How does the speaker explain the denotations and connotations of "naked" and "nude" in the first stanza? What is indicated by the fact that the word *naked* is derived from Old English *nacod* while *nude* comes from Latin *nudus*?

2. What examples of "the naked" and "the nude" do the second and third stanzas provide? What do the examples have in common?

3. How do the connotations of words like "sly," "draping," "dishabille," "rhetoric," and "grin" contribute to the poem's ideas about "the nude"?

4. What does "briary pastures of the dead" mean in line 22?

This poem explores the connotative distinctions between the title words, *naked* and *nude*, which share a common denotation. The title also suggests that the poem is about human customs, for if the speaker were considering the words alone, he would say "naked" and "nude" instead of "*the* naked and *the* nude." The speaker's use of *the* signifies a double focus on both language and human perspectives. In the first five lines the poem establishes that the two key words should be "synonyms that should express / The same deficiency of dress" (lines 3–4). By introducing elevated and complex words such as "lexicographers" and "construed," however, Graves implies that the connection between "the naked" and "the nude" is sophisticated and artificial.

In the rest of the poem, Graves develops this distinction, linking the word *naked* to virtues of love, truth, innocence, and honesty, while connecting *nude* to artifice, hypocrisy, and deceit. At the end, he visualizes a classical underworld in which all pretentiousness will disappear, and the nude will lose their sophistication and become merged with the naked. The implication is that artifice will vanish in the face of eternal reality. A thorough study of the words in the poem bears out the consistency of Graves's idea.

POEMS FOR STUDY

WILLIAM BLAKE (1757–1827)

The Lamb ～⌒～⌒ 1789

Little Lamb, who made thee?
  Dost thou know who made thee?
Gave thee life & bid thee feed,
By the stream & o'er the mead;
Gave thee clothing of delight,   5
Softest clothing wooly bright;
Gave thee such a tender voice,
Making all the vales rejoice!
  Little Lamb who made thee?
  Dost thou know who made thee?   10

  Little Lamb I'll tell thee,
  Little Lamb I'll tell thee!
He is called by thy name,
For he calls himself a Lamb:
He is meek & he is mild,   15
He became a little child:
I a child & thou a lamb,
We are called by his name.
  Little Lamb God bless thee.
  Little Lamb God bless thee.   20

QUESTIONS

1. Who or what is the speaker in this poem? The listener? How are they related?
2. What is the effect of repetition in the poem?
3. How would you characterize the diction in this poem? High, middle, or low? Abstract or concrete? How is it consistent with the speaker?

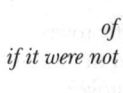

4. What are the connotations of "softest," "bright," "tender," "meek," and "mild"? What do these words imply about the Creator?

5. Describe the characteristics of God imagined in this poem. Contrast the image here with the image of God in Donne's "Batter My Heart."

ROBERT BURNS (1756–1796)

Green Grow the Rashes, O   1787

1

There's naught but care on ev'ry han',°   *hand*
    In every hour that passes, O;
What signifies the life o'° man   *of*
    An' 'twere na° for the lasses, O?   *if it were not*
Chorus:
Green grow the rashes,° O;   *rushes*   5
Green grow the rashes, O;
The sweetest hours that e'er I spend
    Are spent among the lasses, O!

2

The war'ly° race may riches chase,   *worldly*
    An' riches still may fly them, O;   10
An' tho' at last they catch them fast,
    Their hearts can ne'er enjoy them, O.
Chorus.

3

But gie me a cannie° hour at e'en,°   *give me a happy; evening*
    My arms about my dearie, O,
An' war'ly cares an' war'ly men   15
    May a' gae tapsalteerie,° O!   *all go topsy-turvy*
Chorus.

4

For you sae douce° ye sneer at this,   *so sober, so straitlaced*
    Ye're naught but senseless asses, O;
The wisest man the warl' e'er° saw,   *world ever*
    He dearly loved the lasses, O.   20
Chorus.

5

Auld Nature swears the lovely dears
    Her noblest work she classes, O;
Her prentice han'° she tried on man,   *apprentice hand*
    An' then she made the lasses, O.
Chorus.

QUESTIONS

1. Who is the speaker? What is he like? What is his highest value? How seriously do you take his pronouncements?

2. How does the speaker justify his feelings? How does he compare his interests with those of other people?

3. What is the speaker's explanation of the origins of men and women? How might this explanation have been received in 1787, the year of publication, when most people accepted the creation story as told in Genesis?

LEWIS CARROLL (1832–1898)

Jabberwocky° ⸙⸜⸝⸍⸌ 1871

'Twas brillig, and the slithy toves
    Did gyre and gimble in the wabe;
All mimsy were the borogoves,
    And the mome raths outgrabe.

"Beware the Jabberwock, my son!   5
    The jaws that bite, the claws that catch!
Beware the Jubjub bird, and shun
    The frumious Bandersnatch!"

He took his vorpal sword in hand;
    Long time the manxome foe he sought—   10
So rested he by the Tumtum tree,
    And stood awhile in thought.

And, as in uffish thought he stood,
    The Jabberwock, with eyes of flame,
Came whiffling through the tulgey wood,   15
    And burbled as it came!

One, two! One, two! And through and through
    The vorpal blade went snicker-snack!
He left it dead, and with its head
    He went galumphing back.   20

"And hast thou slain the Jabberwock?
    Come to my arms, my beamish boy!
O frabjous day! Callooh! Callay!"
    He chortled in his joy.

'Twas brillig, and the slithy toves   25
    Did gyre and gimble in the wabe;
All mimsy were the borogoves,
    And the mome raths outgrabe.

JABBERWOCKY. The poem, which appears in the first chapter of *Through the Looking Glass,* is full of non-sense words that Carroll made up with the sound (rather than the sense) in mind. Alice admits that the poem makes some sense even though she does not know the words: "It seems very pretty . . . but it's rather hard to understand! . . . Somehow it seems to fill my head with ideas—only I don't exactly know what they are!"

QUESTIONS

1. Summarize in your own words the story that this poem tells.

2.   Humpty Dumpty begins to explain or explicate this poem for Alice in Chapter 6
     of *Through the Looking Glass*. He explains that " 'brillig' means four o'clock in the
     afternoon—the time when you begin *broiling* things for dinner." He also explains
     that " 'slithy' means 'lithe' and 'slimy.' 'Lithe' is the same as 'active.' You see it's
     like a portmanteau—there are two meanings packed into one word." Go
     through the poem and determine what combinations of words are packed into
     these portmanteau words. *Brillig*, for example, might be seen as a combination
     of *broiling, brilliant,* and *light.*

HAYDEN CARRUTH (b. 1921)

An Apology for Using the Word "Heart" in Too Many Poems 1959

What does it mean? Lord knows; least of all I.
   Faced with it, schoolboys are shy,
And grown-ups speak it at moments of excess
   Which later seem more or less
Unfeasible. It is equivocal, sentimental,   5
   Debatable, really a sort of lentil—
Neither pea nor bean. Sometimes it's a muscle,
   Sometimes courage or at least hustle,
Sometimes a core or center, but mostly it's
   A sound that slushily fits   10
The meters of popular songwriters without
   Meaning anything. It is stout,
Leonine, chicken, great, hot, warm, cold,
   Broken, whole, tender, bold,
Stony, soft, green, blue, red, white,   15
   Faint, true, heavy, light,
Open, down, shallow, etc. No wonder
   Our superiors thunder
Against it. And yet in spite of a million abuses
   The word survives; its uses   20
Are such that it remains virtually indispensable
   And, I think, defensible.
The Freudian terminology is awkward or worse,
   And suggests so many perverse
Etiologies that it is useless; but "heart" covers   25
   The whole business, lovers
To monks, i.e., the capacity to love in the fullest
   Sense. Not even the dullest
Reader misapprehends it, although locating
   It is a matter awaiting   30
Someone more ingenious than I. But given
   This definition, driven
Though it is out of a poet's necessity, isn't
   The word needed at present
As much as ever, if it is well written and said,   35
   With the heart and the head?

QUESTIONS

1. How much attention is given in this poem to the meanings of the word "heart"? How accurate are the definitions? Why does the poet title the poem "An Apology . . ."?

2. Would it be fair to describe some of the definitions as "flippant"? Why? How do we know that the poet is being serious?

3. Why does Carruth say, "Not even the dullest / Reader misapprehends it" [i.e., the word "heart"]? How true is this claim?

[handwritten: Page 959]

E. E. CUMMINGS (1894–1962)

next to of course god america i ⟍⟍⟍⟍ 1926

"next to of course god america i
love you land of the pilgrims' and so forth oh
say can you see by the dawn's early my
country 'tis of centuries come and go
and are no more what of it we should worry   5
in every language even deafanddumb
thy sons acclaim your glorious name by gorry
by jingo by gee by gosh by gum
why talk of beauty what could be more beautiful than these heroic happy dead   10
who rushed like lions to the roaring slaughter
they did not stop to think they died instead
then shall the voice of liberty be mute?"

He spoke.   And drank rapidly a glass of water

[handwritten annotations: Historical overtone; read page 767; Satiric poem; reveals speakers shortcoming for readers amusement; pg 760]

QUESTIONS

1. What is the form of this poem? What is the rhyme scheme? What does Cummings achieve by not using capitalization and punctuation?

2. Who is the speaker? What characteristics and capacities does he show? How do you respond to him?

3. What ideas does the poem bring out? In what ways does the speaker parody the speakers that one is likely to hear on the Fourth of July throughout the United States? What is Cummings saying not only about the speakers but also about the crowds that listen to such speeches?

[handwritten: satirical imitation; Satire = literary ridicule done with humor]

JOHN DONNE (1572–1631)

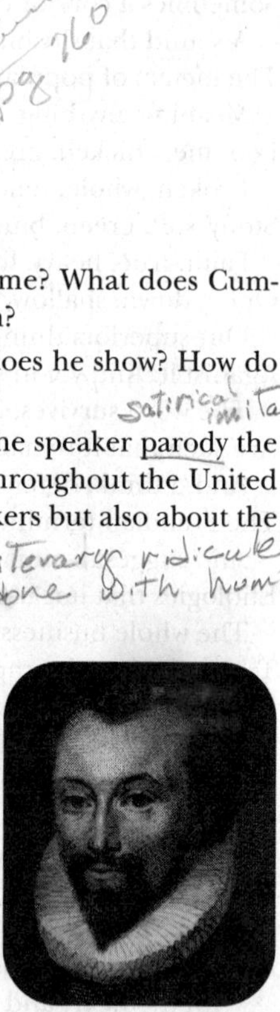

Holy Sonnet 14: Batter My Heart,
Three-Personed God ⟍⟍⟍⟍ 1633

Batter my heart, three-personed God; for You
As yet but knock, breathe, shine, and seek to mend;
That I may rise and stand, o'erthrow me, and bend
Your force to break, blow, burn and make me new.
I, like an usurped° town, to another due,   *conquered*   5

Labor to admit You, but Oh, to no end;
Reason, Your viceroy in me, me should defend,
But is captived, and proves weak or untrue.
Yet dearly I love You, and would be loved fain,°   *gladly*
But am betrothed unto Your enemy.   10
Divorce me, untie or break that knot again;
Take me to You, imprison me, for I,
Except You enthrall me, never shall be free,
Nor ever chaste, except you ravish me.

QUESTIONS

1. What kind of God is suggested by the words "batter," "knock," "overthrow," and "break"? What does "three-personed God" mean?

2. With which person of God might the verbs "knock" and "break" be associated? The verbs "breathe" and "blow"? The verbs "shine" and "burn"?

3. What is the effect of the altered word order at the ends of lines 7 and 9?

4. Explain the words "enthrall" (line 13) and "ravish" (line 14) to resolve the apparent paradox or contradiction in the last two lines.

RICHARD EBERHART (b. 1904)

The Fury of Aerial Bombardment   1947

You would think the fury of aerial bombardment
Would rouse God to relent; the infinite spaces
Are still silent. He looks on shock-pried faces.
History, even, does not know what is meant.

You would feel that after so many centuries   5
God would give man to repent; yet he can kill
As Cain could, but with multitudinous will,
No farther advanced than in his ancient furies.

Was man made stupid to see his own stupidity?
Is God by definition indifferent, beyond us all?   10
Is the eternal truth man's fighting soul
Wherein the Beast ravens in its own avidity?

Of Van Wettering I speak, and Averill,
Names on a list, whose faces I do not recall
But they are gone to early death, who late in school   15
Distinguished the belt feed lever from the belt holding pawl.

QUESTIONS

1. Who or what is the speaker in this poem? What does the last stanza tell you about him? (Eberhart was a gunnery instructor during World War II.)

2. What type and level of diction predominates in lines 1–12? What observations about God are made in these lines? Compare the image of God presented here with the one found in Donne's "Batter My Heart, Three-Personed God" and Blake's "The Lamb." What similarities or differences do you find?

3. How does the level and type of diction change in the last stanza? What is the effect of these changes? How is jargon used here?

4. Compare this poem with Thomas Hardy's "Channel Firing" (p. 710). How are the ideas in the poems similar?

BART EDELMAN (b. 1951)

Chemistry Experiment ⤳⟨⟨⟨⟨   2001

We listened intently to the professor,
Followed each one of her instructions,
Read through the textbook twice,
Wore lab coats and safety goggles,
Mixed the perfect chemical combinations   5
In the proper amounts and order.
It was all progressing smoothly;
We thought we were a complete success.
And then the flash of light,
The loud, perplexing explosion,   10
The black rope of smoke,
Rising freely above our singed hair.
Someone in another lab down the hallway
Phoned the local fire department
Which arrived lickety-split   15
With the hazardous waste crew,
And they assessed the accident,
Deciding we were out of danger.
It was the talk of the campus
For many weeks afterwards.   20
We, however, became so disillusioned
That we immediately dropped the course
And slowly retreated from each other.
The very idea we could have done
More damage than we actually did—   25
Blown up ourselves and the building
From the base of its foundation—
Shook us, like nothing had before.
And even now, years later,
When anyone still asks about you,   30
I get this sick feeling in my stomach
And wonder what really happened
To all that elementary matter.

QUESTIONS

1. What events are recounted in this poem? How may the narrative be placed into sections? Who is the listener or implied reader of the poem?

2. What level of language is contained here? Study lines 13-18. How does the diction change here? Why?

3. Why does the poem end as it does? What connection does this conclusion have with the previous parts of the poem? Why might this incident have caused the participants to have lost contact with each other?

THOMAS GRAY (1716–1771)

Sonnet on the Death of Richard West ≻⌢≺⌣⌢⌣⌢⌣≺ *(1742) 1775*

In vain to me the smiling mornings shine,
    And redd'ning Phoebus° lifts his golden fire;
The birds in vain their amorous descant° join, *gladly*
    Or cheerful fields resume their green attire:°
These ears, alas! for other notes repine; 5
    A different object do these eyes require.
My lonely anguish melts no heart but mine,
    And in my breast the imperfect joys expire.
Yet morning smiles the busy race to cheer,
    And new-born pleasure brings to happier men; 10
The fields to all their wonted tribute bear;°
    To warm their little loves the birds complain:°
I fruitless mourn to him that cannot hear,
    And weep the more because I weep in vain.

SONNET ON THE DEATH OF RICHARD WEST. 2 *Phoebus:* Apollo, the Sun God 4 *resume their green attire:* During the darkness of night, the "cheerful fields" have no color, but in the light of the morning sun they become green again. 11 *The fields . . . bear:* The fields contribute their customary harvest to benefit all creation. 12 *complain:* sing love songs.

QUESTIONS

1. What is the poem's subject, the speaker or the dead friend? How effective is the poem as a lament or dirge?

2. Describe the poem's level of diction. Why does the speaker use phrases like "smiling mornings" (line 1), "redd'ning Phoebus" (2), "golden fire" (2), "resume their green attire" (4), and "notes" (5)? How common are these phrases? What is their effect?

3. Consider the syntax in lines 5, 6, 9, 10, 11, and 12. What is unusual about the word order in these lines? What is the effect of this word order?

4. In the 1800 Preface to *Lyrical Ballads*, William Wordsworth printed this poem. He italicized lines 6–8 and 13 and 14 and wrote, "It will easily be perceived, that the only part of this Sonnet which is of any value is the lines printed in Italics; it is equally obvious, that . . . the language of these lines does in no respect differ from that of prose." What does Wordsworth's criticism mean? To what degree is it justified?

A. E. HOUSMAN (1859–1936)

Loveliest of Trees, the Cherry Now   1896

Loveliest of trees, the cherry now
Is hung with bloom along the bough,
And stands about the woodland ride°   *path*
Wearing white for Eastertide.

Now, of my threescore years and ten,   5
Twenty will not come again,
And take from seventy springs a score,
It only leaves me fifty more.

And since to look at things in bloom
Fifty springs are little room,   10
About the woodland I will go
To see the cherry hung with snow.

QUESTIONS

1. How old is the speaker? How can you tell? Why does he assume he will live seventy years ("threescore years and ten")?

2. How would you describe the speaker's perception or sense of time? What is the effect of the words "only" (line 8) and "little" (line 10)?

3. What ideas about time, beauty, and life does this poem explore? What does it suggest about the way we should live?

CAROLYN KIZER (b. 1925)

Night Sounds   1984

imitated from the Chinese

The moonlight on my bed keeps me awake;
Living alone now, aware of the voices of evening,
A child weeping at nightmares, the faint love-cries of a woman,
Everything tinged by terror or nostalgia.

No heavy, impassive back to nudge with one foot   5
While coaxing, "Wake up and hold me,"
When the moon's creamy beauty is transformed
Into a map of impersonal desolation.

But, restless in this mock dawn of moonlight
That so chills the spirit, I alter our history;   10
You were never able to lie quite peacefully at my side,
Not the night through. Always withholding something.

Awake before morning, restless and uneasy,
Trying not to disturb me, you would leave my bed

While I lay there rigidly, feigning sleep.   15
Still—the night was nearly over, the light not as cold
As a full cup of moonlight.

And there were the lovely times when, to the skies' cold *No*
You cried to me, *Yes!* Impaled me with affirmation.
Now when I call out in fear, not in love, there is no answer.   20
Nothing speaks in the dark but the distant voices,
A child with the moon in his face, a dog's hollow cadence.

QUESTIONS

1. To what degee may this poem be considered confessional? What is being confessed?

2. Who is the "you" of the poem? What has happened between the speaker and the "you"? With what contrasts does the speaker conclude the poem? How are these contrasts related to the relationship between the speaker and the "you"?

3. What situation and impressions are brought about by these words in the first stanza: "moonlight," "weeping," "nightmares," "tinged," "terror," "nostalgia"?

4. What is the effect of the participles in stanzas 1–4 ("living," "coaxing," "withholding," "trying," "feigning")?

MAXINE KUMIN (b. 1925)

Hello, Hello Henry   1982

My neighbor in the country, Henry Manley,
with a washpot warming on his woodstove,
with a heifer and two goats and yearly chickens,
has outlasted Stalin, Roosevelt and Churchill
but something's stirring in him in his dotage.   5

Last fall he dug a hole and moved his privy
and a year ago in April reamed his well out.
When the country sent a truck and poles and cable,
his daddy ran the linemen off with birdshot
and swore he'd die by oil lamp, and did.   10

Now you tell me that all yesterday in Boston
you set your city phone at mine, and had it ringing
inside a dead apartment for three hours
room after empty room, to keep yours busy.
I hear it in my head, that ranting summons.   15

That must have been about the time that Henry
walked up two miles, shy as a girl come calling,
to tell me he has a phone now, 264, ring two.
It rang one time last week—wrong number.
He'd be pleased if one day I would think to call him.   20

Hello, hello Henry? Is that you?

QUESTIONS

1. What is the poem's level of diction? What does this level contribute to your response to the poem?

2. What words in this poem are appropriate for a country location? What do the words show about Henry Manley, and about the conditions on his farm?

3. Who is the speaker? What does the selection of words indicate about the speaker's character and state of mind?

4. How does the listener enter into the poem's action in the third stanza? What is the meaning of the listener's action?

DENISE LEVERTOV (1923–1997)

Of Being ~<~✓~ *1997*

I know this happiness
Is provisional:

     the looming presences—
     great suffering, great fear—

     withdraw only   5
     into peripheral vision:

but ineluctable this shimmering
of wind in the blue leaves:

this flood of stillness
widening the lake of sky: 10

this need to dance,
this need to kneel:

       this mystery:

QUESTIONS

1. What is meant by "this happiness / Is provisional"?

2. What is it that withdraws (line 5)? How does the poet connect withdrawing with the poem's title?

3. What do the words "peripheral vision," "ineluctable," "blue leaves," "flood of stillness," and "lake of sky" contribute to your understanding of the "mystery" with which the poem closes? What is noteworthy about these words?

4. Why does the poet end the poem with a colon rather than a period?

HENRY REED (1914–1986)

Naming of Parts ~<~✓~ *1946*

To-day we have naming of parts. Yesterday,
We had daily cleaning. And to-morrow morning,
We shall have what to do after firing. But to-day,
To-day we have naming of parts. Japonica

[handwritten marginalia, top left: "Spring / move or shoot up suddenly"; "Swivel – on swing on turn on a pivot"]

Glistens like coral in all of the neighboring gardens,   5
    And to-day we have naming of parts.

This is the lower sling swivel. And this
Is the upper sling swivel, whose use you will see,
When you are given your slings. And this is the piling swivel,
Which in your case you have not got. The branches   10
Hold in the gardens their silent, eloquent gestures,
    Which in our case we have not got.

[handwritten marginalia, right: "garden gun"; "sling-strap"; "sling – valuables"; "easing of manner"]

This is the safety-catch, which is always released
With an easy flick of the thumb. And please do not let me
See anyone using his finger. You can do it quite easy   15
If you have any strength in your thumb. The blossoms
Are fragile and motionless, never letting anyone see
    Any of them using their finger.

And this you can see is the bolt. The purpose of this
Is to open the breech, as you see. We can slide it   20
Rapidly backwards and forwards: we call this
Easing the spring. And rapidly backwards and forwards
The early bees are assaulting and fumbling the flowers:
    They call it easing the Spring.

[handwritten marginalia, right: "breech - rear end of body"; "rear end of a firearm"]

They call it easing the Spring: it is perfectly easy   25
If you have any strength in your thumb: like the bolt,
And the breech, and the cocking-piece, and the point of balance,
Which in our case we have not got; and the almond-blossom
Silent in all of the gardens and the bees going backwards and forwards,
    For to-day we have naming of parts.   30

[handwritten marginalia, bottom: "Jargon - special vocabulary of a group -"]

QUESTIONS

1. There may be two speakers in this poem, or one speaker repeating the words of another and adding his own thoughts. What two voices do you hear?

2. What is the setting? The situation? How do these affect the speaker?

3. How and why is jargon used in the poem? With what set of "parts" is the jargon initially associated? How does this change?

4. How are phrases like "easing the spring" (lines 22, 24, 25) and "point of balance" (27) used ambiguously? What is the effect of repetition?

[handwritten marginalia: "having more than one interpretation"]

EDWIN ARLINGTON ROBINSON (1869–1935)

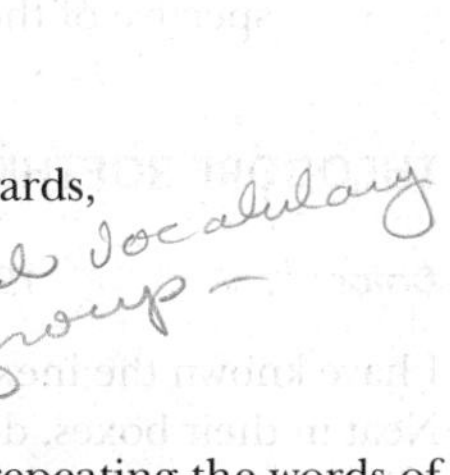

Richard Cory   1897

Whenever Richard Cory went down town,
We people on the pavement looked at him:
He was a gentleman from sole to crown,
Clean favored, and imperially slim.

And he was always quietly arrayed,   5
And he was always human when he talked;

But still he fluttered pulses when he said,
'Good-morning,' and he glittered when he walked.

And he was rich—yes, richer than a king—
And admirably schooled in every grace: 10
In fine, we thought that he was everything
To make us wish that we were in his place.

So on we worked, and waited for the light,
And went without the meat, and cursed the bread;
And Richard Cory, one calm summer night,   15
Went home and put a bullet through his head.

QUESTIONS

1. What is the effect of using "down town," "pavement," "meat," and "bread" in connection with the people who admire Richard Cory?

2. What are the connotations and implications of the name "Richard Cory"? Of the word "gentleman"?

3. Why does the poet use "sole to crown" instead of "head to toe" and "imperially slim" instead of "very thin" to describe Cory?

4. What effect does repetition produce in this poem? Consider especially the six lines that begin with "And."

5. What positive characteristic does Richard Cory possess (at least from the perspective of the speaker) besides wealth?

THEODORE ROETHKE (1907–1963)

Dolor 1943

I have known the inexorable sadness of pencils,
Neat in their boxes, dolor of pad and paper-weight,
All the misery of manila folders and mucilage,
Desolation in immaculate public places,
Lonely reception room, lavatory, switchboard,   5
The unalterable pathos of basin and pitcher,
Ritual of multigraph, paper-clip, comma,
Endless duplication of lives and objects.
And I have seen dust from the walls of institutions,
Finer than flour, alive, more dangerous than silica,   10
Sift, almost invisible, through long afternoons of tedium,
Dropping a fine film on nails and delicate eyebrows,
Glazing the pale hair, the duplicate grey standard faces.

QUESTIONS

1. What does "dolor" mean? What words objectify the concept?
2. Why does "Dolor" not contain the fourteen lines usual in a sonnet?
3. What institutions, conditions, and places does the speaker associate with "dolor"? What do these have in common?
4. Describe the relationships of sentence structures and lines in "Dolor."

STEPHEN SPENDER (1909–1995)

I Think Continually of Those Who Were Truly Great ~ ~ ~ ~ ~ *1934*

I think continually of those who were truly great.
Who, from the womb, remembered the soul's history
Through corridors of light where the hours are suns,
Endless and singing. Whose lovely ambition
Was that their lips, still touched with fire,   5
Should tell of the spirit clothed from head to foot in song.
And who hoarded from the spring branches
The desires falling across their bodies like blossoms.

What is precious is never to forget
The delight of the blood drawn from ageless springs   10
Breaking through rocks in worlds before our earth;
Never to deny its pleasure in the simple morning light,
Nor its grave evening demand for love;
Never to allow gradually the traffic to smother
With noise and fog the flowering of the spirit.   15

QUESTIONS

1. How does this poem cause you to reconsider what is usually understood by the word "great"? What are the principal characteristics of people "who were truly great"?

2. Why does Spender use the words "were great" rather than "are great"? What difference, if any, does this distinction make to Spender's definition of greatness?

3. What is the meaning of phrases like "delight of the blood," "in worlds before our earth," "hours are suns," "still touched with fire"? What other phrases need similar thought and explanation?

4. How practical is the advice of the poem in the light of its definitions of "great" and "precious"? Why should the practicality or impracticality of these definitions probably not be considered in your judgment of the poem?

WALLACE STEVENS (1879–1955)

Disillusionment of Ten O'Clock ~ ~ ~ ~ ~ *1923*

The houses are haunted
By white night-gowns.
None are green,
Or purple with green rings,
Or green with yellow rings,   5
Or yellow with blue rings.
None of them are strange,
With socks of lace
And beaded ceintures.°   *belts*
People are not going   10

To dream of baboons and periwinkles.
Only, here and there, an old sailor,
Drunk and asleep in his boots,
Catches tigers
In red weather.   15

QUESTIONS

1.   Is the "Ten O'Clock" here morning or night? How can you tell?

2.   What do "haunted" and "white night-gowns" suggest about the people who live in the houses? What do the negative images in lines 3–9 suggest?

3.   To whom are these people contrasted in lines 12–15?

4.   What are the connotations of "socks with lace" and "beaded ceintures"? With which character in the poem would you associate these things?

5.   What is the effect of using words and images like "baboons," "periwinkles," "tigers," and "red weather" in lines 11–15? Who will dream of these things?

6.   Explain the term "disillusionment" and explore its relation to the point that this poem makes about dreams, images, and imagination.

MARK STRAND (b. 1934)

Eating Poetry   ✎✎✎✎✎   1968

Ink runs from the corners of my mouth.
There is no happiness like mine.
I have been eating poetry.

The librarian does not believe what she sees.
Her eyes are sad   5
and she walks with her hands in her dress.

The poems are gone.
The light is dim.
The dogs are on the basement stairs and coming up.

Their eyeballs roll,   10
their blond legs burn like brush.
The poor librarian begins to stamp her feet and weep.

She does not understand.
When I get on my knees and lick her hand,
She screams.   15

I am a new man.
I snarl at her and bark.
I romp with joy in the bookish dark.

QUESTIONS

1.   In the first three lines, which words tell you the poem is not to be taken literally?

2.   What is the serious topic of the poem? What words indicate its serious intent?

3.   What is the comic topic? Which words tell you that the poem's action is comic?

WRITING ABOUT DICTION AND SYNTAX IN POETRY

Study your poem carefully, line by line, to gain a general sense of its meaning. Try to establish how diction and syntax may be connected to elements such as tone, character, and idea. As you develop your ideas, look for effective and consistent patterns of word choice, connotation, repetition, and syntactic patterns that help create and reinforce the conclusions you have drawn about the poem. Ask questions like those that follow.

Questions for Discovering Ideas

- Who is the speaker? What is the speaker's profession or way of life? How does the speaker's background affect his or her power of observation? How does the background affect his or her level of speech?
- Who is the listener? How does the listener affect what the speaker says?
- What other characters are in the poem? How are their actions described? How accurate and fair do you think these descriptions are?
- Is the level of diction in the poem elevated, neutral, or informal, and how does this level affect your perception of the speaker, subject, and main idea or ideas?
- What patterns of diction or syntax do you discover in the poem? (*Example:* Consider words related to situation, action, setting, or particular characters.) How ordinary or unusual are these words? Which, if any, are unusual enough to warrant further examination?
- Does the poem contain many "loaded" or connotative words in connection with any single element, such as setting, speaker, or theme?
- Does the poem contain a large number of general and abstract or specific and concrete words? What is the effect of these choices?
- Does the poem contain dialect? Colloquialisms? Jargon? If so, how does this special diction shape your response to the poem?
- What is the nature of the poem's syntax? Is there any unusual word order? What seems to be the purpose or effect of syntactic variations?
- Has the poet used any striking patterns of sentence structure such as parallelism or repetition? If so, what is the effect?

Strategies for Organizing Ideas

When you narrow your examination to one or two specific areas of diction or syntax, you should list important words, phrases, and sentences, and investigate the full range of meaning and effect that the examples produce. Begin grouping examples that work in similar ways or produce similar effects. Eventually you may be able to develop the related examples as units or sections for your essay.

Your central idea should emerge from your investigation of the specific diction or syntax that you find most fruitful and interesting. Let the poem be your guide. Since diction and syntax contribute to the poem's impact and meaning, try to connect your thesis and examples to your other conclusions. If you are writing about Stevens's "Disillusionment of Ten O'Clock," for example, your central idea might assert that Stevens uses words describing colors (i.e., "white," "green," "purple," "yellow," "blue," "red") to contrast life's visual reality with the psychological "disillusionment" of the "houses," "People," and "old sailor." Such a formulation makes a clear connection of diction to meaning.

There are many different ways to organize your material. If you deal with only one aspect of diction, such as connotative words, you might treat these in the order in which they appear in the poem. When you deal with two or three different aspects of diction and syntax, however, you might devote a series of paragraphs to related examples of multiple denotation, then connotation, and finally jargon (assuming the presence of jargon in the poem). In such an instance, your organization would be controlled by the types of material under consideration rather than by the order in which the words occur.

Alternatively, you might deal with the impact of diction or syntax on a series of other elements, such as character, setting, or situation. Such an essay would focus on a single type of lexical or syntactic device as it relates to these different elements in sequence. Thus, you might discuss the link between connotation and character, then setting, and finally situation. Whatever organization you select, keep in mind that each poem will suggest its own avenues of exploration and strategies of organization.

In your conclusion summarize your ideas about the impact of the poem's diction or syntax. You might also consider the larger implications of your ideas in connection with the thoughts and emotions evoked by your reading.

DEMONSTRATIVE STUDENT ESSAY

Extraordinary Definitions in Stephen Spender's "I Think Continually of Those Who Were Truly Great"°

[1] In the two-stanza poem "I Think Continually of Those Who Were Truly Great," Spender considers the meaning of true greatness. He begins the poem as though the speaker has been talking to an unnamed person who has spoken about greatness as the word is usually understood. The poem itself might then be considered a one-sided response by the speaker in which he presents his own definition of greatness, with particular emphasis on the truly in "truly great." The poem creates a different and new concept of greatness.* Spender develops his argument in two parts, each of which is knitted together by particular attitudes and grammatical structures.†

Because the poem concentrates on new definitions, it is important to discuss how Spender treats the ideas that readers might have about greatness. Usually the type of person most readers think of as great is a leader of some sort--a king, a president, an emperor, a general, or a financial mogul. It is this understanding that Spender is contradicting in the poem. Readers find that he says

---

°See p. 657 for this poem.
*Central idea.
†Thesis sentence.

[2]   nothing about leadership, nor are there any references at all to specific great persons. Instead, Spender goes beyond usual definitions and asks readers to consider the meaning of greatness in a deeply individual and personal way. His first
line is designed to catch the interest of readers, just as the rest of the poem is designed to surprise and lead them. Something unusual is being said--something
new, something extraordinary.

The first stanza of the poem presents a set of positive qualities that define
true greatness. Spender carries out his definitions within three clauses that modify and therefore define the word "great" ("who . . . remembered," "whose . . . ambition / was," and "who hoarded"). Interestingly, the speaker's reference to "history"
(line 2) immediately puts readers on guard because it does not refer to history as
a record of human accomplishments. Rather, the history of greatness is the
"soul's" history, having no written record but composed of "corridors of light . . .

[3]   Endless and singing." The unusual idea here is that song, not business, gives
form to the world through persons who become great by connecting themselves
with the very origins of life. Going on, Spender provides a new definition of "tell"
(line 6). Usually people telling about greatness describe politics, economics, or
world domination, but in this poem the telling is about the "spirit." Spender introduces readers to the concept of hoarding, but, as with telling, readers discover
that the truly great do not hoard wealth but rather accept and hoard "desires"
(lines 7–8).

The key words in Spender's first stanza, in short, go beyond their commonly used economic and political meanings and refer instead to feelings and spirituality. Readers thus consider the poem's references as being not to documented
history but rather to a deeper remembrance of a preexisting condition of glory.

[4]   Spender's redefined meaning of greatness means that those who are great can
tune themselves into the basic song of the human spirit. The words redefining
"great" therefore enable readers to expand their understanding of greatness into
new and unexamined areas of thought.

The second stanza of the poem is unified by three negatives, which are
cast within infinitive phrases ("never to forget," "never to deny," and "never to
allow") which define the word "precious" in line 9. As in the first stanza, Spender
uses a common definition as a starting point: What is precious--a necessary part
of greatness--is not a large bank account but rather the connection with ageless
springs of human delight. Of highest value is the joy that has been in our human

[5]   blood long before our world was created, existing in unknown worlds going back
to the moment of divine creation. Preciousness also consists of accepting the
pleasure of morning light and the more sober ("grave") needs of evening love
(line 13). Spender's third definition of what is precious (lines 14–15) is the insistence that people should allow their spirit to flower despite the smothering grind of
daily business ("the traffic"). In all these thoughts about what is precious, readers
are faced with new definitions and new ways of seeing.

It is clear that the poem presents readers with the possibility of greatness in
accord with Spender's unique definitions. Such greatness asks readers to forge a
new being for themselves. From the poem, readers may conclude that this new

[6]   being is a free spirit who achieves greatness through song, who finds joy in the
morning light of endless and rhythmical sunshine, and who willingly accepts
pleasure in desires and love. Greatness, in short, is the ability to reconnect oneself with the very springs of existence.

"I Think Continually of Those Who Were Truly Great," then, is a defining and
also a guiding poem. It presents readers with a set of ordinary words defined in a

[7] completely new way. Readers find no advice to abandon the needs of ordinary living but rather are told of a need to reconsider and freshen their assumptions of what to expect from life. The poem suggests to readers that everyone can become great by resisting the grind of daily living ("the traffic") and re-connecting with the age-old sources of human strength. Even if people are never in positions of political or military leadership--the usual avenue of greatness--they can reestablish such connections. Thus Spender's poem reaffirms life by offering new ways for readers to think about becoming "truly great."

WORK CITED

Spender, Stephen. "I Think Continually of Those Who Were Truly Great." Literature: An Introduction to Reading and Writing. Ed. Edgar V. Roberts and Henry E. Jacobs. 7th ed. Upper Saddle River: Prentice Hall, 2004. 657.

Commentary on the Essay

This essay considers how Spender redefines the two major words within the poem: "great" and "precious," as well as how he redefines other words (e.g., "history," "tell"). In addition it deals with how Spender's syntax unifies the poem's two major parts. Finally, it attempts to treat the subject matter of the poem in the light of reader responses (see Chapter 33). Note that throughout the essay there are references to readers, their expectations, and their responses. A major element of the essay is that Spender leads readers to new understanding along the pathway of usual or commonly accepted understanding.

The opening paragraph makes assertions about the poem's dramatic situation and also about Spender's goal of redefining the key word "great." The body of the essay deals with definition and redefinition. Because the poem is concerned with redefinition, paragraph 2 describes how the word "great" is usually understood. On this basis, paragraphs 3 and 4 move ahead to consider how the poem redefines this word.

The next two paragraphs (5 and 6) focus on the meaning of "precious," which Spender uses as an equivalent to greatness. The examples are examined here in the order in which they appear in the poem. Thus, paragraph 5 shows how Spender establishes three areas of life that are particularly precious, unlike the large bank account that is usually understood to confer preciousness. Paragraph 6 extends this idea by considering the implications of a reevaluated existence in the light of Spender's redefinition.

The conclusion in paragraph 7 reasserts that Spender's definitions are designed to show readers the ways to personal, not public, greatness and that therefore everyone and not just a few may become great. In this way, the words examined in the essay are linked to the poem's reaffirmation of life.

Special Topics for Writing and Argument about the Words of Poetry

1. Using Eberhart's "The Fury of Aerial Bombardment" in this chapter, together with poems by Jarrell (Chapter 13) and Owen (Chapters 16, 18), study the words that these poets use to indicate the weapons and actions of warfare. In an essay, consider these questions: What shared details make the poems similar? What separate details make them different? How do the poets use word choices to make their points about war as action, tragedy, and horror?

2. Write an essay considering the sound qualities of the invented words in "Jabberwocky." Some obvious choices are "brillig," "frumious," "vorpal," and "manxome," but you are free to choose any or all of them. What is the relationship between the sound and apparent meaning of these words? What effect do the surrounding normal words and normal word order have on the special words? How does Carroll succeed in creating a narrative "structure" even though the key words are, on the surface, nonsense?

3. Analyze Robinson's use of diction in "Richard Cory." Be sure to discuss the words he uses to describe the populace. How are these words different from his words for Cory? What is the nature of the diction describing Cory's final action?

4. Write a brief essay discussing the use of connotation in Cummings's "next to of course god america i," Kumin's "Hello, Hello Henry," Levertov's "Of Being," Roethke's "Dolor," and Strand's "Eating Poetry." What particularities of meaning do the poets introduce? How does their control of connotation contribute to the various ideas you discover in the poems?

5. Compare the words describing natural scenes in Gray's "Sonnet on the Death of Richard West" and Wordsworth's "Daffodils." Which poem seems more specific and direct in its depiction of Nature?

6. Write a short poem describing a violent crime and commenting on it. Then, assume that you are the "alleged perpetrator" of the crime, and write another poem on the same topic. Even though you describe the same situation, how do your words differ, and why have you made these different choices? Explain the other different word choices you have made. You might also discuss words that you considered using but rejected.

7. Find a book or books in your library about the works of Gray, Roethke, Robinson, Wordsworth, or another poet represented in this chapter. How fully do these sources discuss the style of these poets? Write a brief report explaining how the writers of the book or books deal with poetic diction.

CHAPTER

15

Characters and Setting: *Who, What, Where, and When in Poetry*

Poets, like other writers, bring their works alive through the interactions of fictional characters who experience love and hatred, pleasure and pain, and most of the other conditions and situations of life. Just as in fiction, poetic characters are defined by what they say, what they do, and how they react, and also by what other characters say about them. Not all poetry is narrative, however. Hence we will study character in poems in relation to someone or something else—such as the interactions of speakers with listeners or with the reader, the inner conflicts of a speaker discussing the state of his or her spirit, and conditions such as love, hate, acceptance, disagreement, emulation, decision making, and action—brought out in personal, social, and political life.

In addition, we will examine the **setting** of a poem as one of the major means of measuring character (see also Chapter 6). Poetic protagonists, like those in stories, are necessarily influenced by their possessions, the places they inhabit, the conditions of their lives, and the times in which they live. The period that people have spent in a relationship, their relative wealth or poverty, their surroundings, their social and economic circumstances—all have a bearing on their characters. Poems therefore abound with references to events and situations and also to objects such as beaches, forests, battlefields, graveyards, teaspoons, melons, museums, and paintings.

CHARACTERS IN POETRY

The Speaker or Persona Is the Voice of the Poem

The most significant character in poetry is the **speaker,** also called the **persona** (plural *personae*, a term that comes from the Etruscan-Latin word meaning "mask"). In prose fiction, we also use *speaker* and *persona,* but we often prefer the word *narrator* because of the obvious role of storyteller. This distinction emphasizes the personal and psychological importance of poetic speakers. Sometimes the speaker is a distinct character, with individual traits and well-imagined circumstances, as in Browning's "My Last Duchess," Piercy's "Wellfleet Sabbath," and Marlowe's "The Passionate Shepherd to His Love." In Dickinson's "Because I Could Not Stop for Death" (Chapter 13) the speaker is especially unique, for she states that she has been dead for hundreds of years and is now looking back from eternity to the occasion of her death.

Not all poetic speakers have separate identities, for some embody a position or stance that the poet selects to present detail or advance an argument. The poet is thus the undeniable speaker, but the voice we hear may be considered as a brief dramatization of the poet's personality or need. Donne in "Batter My Heart" (Chapter 14) adopts such a stance—a supplicant or penitent praying for divine favor. In this sonnet Donne is not creating a separate dramatic character in deep religious anguish, but is expressing his own hope and fear.

Expectedly, poets use many sorts of speakers to voice their poems. In this anthology, there are poems spoken by kings and dukes, husbands and wives, lovers and killers, shepherds and secretaries, believers and nonbelievers, adults and children, and almost every other kind of person you can imagine. In addition, you meet speakers who are mythological heroes and heroines, dead people, skeletons, ordinary people, machines, philosophers, lovers, former slaves, and ghosts. In fact, speakers do not have to be human; they can be animals, clouds, buildings, computers, or whatever the poet's imagination may create.

INSIDE SPEAKERS USE THE FIRST PERSON VOICE AND ARE INVOLVED IN THE POEM'S ACTIONS. A poetic speaker may be *inside* or *outside* the poem, depending on the **point of view** used by the poet (see Chapter 5). If the point of view is first person, the speaker is *inside* the poem. Here is such a poem, written by an unknown late-medieval poet.

ANONYMOUS

Western Wind, When Wilt Thou Blow　　　*Fifteenth century?*

Western wind, when wilt thou blow
The small rain down can rain?
Christ, if my love were in my arms,
And I in my bed again.

In this poem the "my" and "I" pronouns indicate that the speaker is *inside* the poem speaking in the first person, wishing for warm spring rains and the renewal of life and love that is signaled by spring.

OUTSIDE SPEAKERS USE THE THIRD PERSON AND ARE OBJECTIVE ABOUT THE POEM'S ACTIONS. The speaker is *outside* the poem, however, if the third person is used.

In such poems, the speaker is not involved with the action; he or she describes what is happening to others, as in this anonymous Scots ballad.

ANONYMOUS

Bonny George Campbell ⸜⸝⸌⸍   *Late sixteenth century*

High upon Highlands
  And low upon Tay,°
Bonny George Campbell
  Rode out on a day.

But toom° came his saddle,   *empty*   5
  All bloody to see,
Oh, home came his good horse,
  But never came he.

Down came his old mother,
  Greeting full sair°   *weeping full sore*   10
And down came his bonny wife,
  Wringing her hair.

Saddled, and bridled,
  And booted rode he;
And home came his good horse,   15
  But never came he.

"My meadow lies green,
  And my corn is unshorn,°   *grain is not harvested*
My barn is to build°   *yet to be built*
And my babe is unborn."   20

Saddled, and bridled,
  And booted rode he;
Toom home came the saddle,
  But never came he.

BONNY GEORGE CAMPBELL. 2 *Tay:* Loch Tay, a lake in Perth County, in central Scotland, about sixty miles north of Glasgow.

QUESTIONS

1. What can you deduce about the character, social status, way of life, and feelings of the three persons mentioned in the poem?
2. Why must you infer the exact nature of what happened to Bonny George Campbell?
3. Who is the speaker of the fifth stanza? What effect has Campbell's absence had on this speaker?

    In this ballad the speaker limits his or her perspective to the people left behind who loved Campbell. They do not know his fate beyond what they infer from the bloody saddle—nor do we, because the speaker does not tell us. However, the speaker does describe the effects of the loss upon Campbell's mother and wife, even quoting the wife's lamentation because Campbell's absence has deprived her of husband and breadwinner. By avoiding entering the poem as an "I," the speaker maintains objectivity and lets the details speak for themselves.

ADDITIONAL INFORMATION ABOUT SPEAKERS MAY BE GAINED FROM OTHER DETAILS IN POEMS. There is a great deal more to learn about poetic speakers. An obvious place to begin is the title. Take, for example, Marlowe's "The Passionate Shepherd to His Love," which reveals that the speaker is a young shepherd and that he is passionately in love.

We can also learn from the speaker's diction. In Housman's "Loveliest of Trees" (Chapter 14), the speaker reveals that he is twenty years old, that he doesn't think his remaining fifty years (assuming a lifetime of seventy years, the biblical life expectancy) will give him enough time to experience and observe life fully, that he enjoys the flowering of spring, that he knows enough about church rituals to claim that the whiteness of cherry blossoms coincides with the liturgical color of white for Easter, and that he is meditative and somber rather than extroverted and hilarious. All this is quite a bit of information from so short a poem.

If we look at all poems with the same care, we will discover many other details. Grammatical forms and word levels may define the speaker's social class or educational level (see Chapter 14). Similarly, the selection of topics may indicate the speaker's emotional state, self-esteem, knowledge, attitudes, habits, hobbies, and much more.

The Person with Whom or to Whom the Speaker Is Talking Is the Listener

The second type of character in poetry is the **listener**—a person, not the reader, whom the speaker addresses directly and who is therefore "inside" the poem. Occasionally we find poems in the form of a **dialogue** between two persons, so that the characters are *both* speakers and listeners, as in Randall's "Ballad of Birmingham" (Chapter 20). Whatever the form, the speaker–listener relationship creates drama and tension. In effect, we as readers are an audience, hearing either conversational exchanges or one-way conversations. The speakers of course identify themselves with the "I" pronoun and address their listeners with the pronouns "thou-thy-thee" and "you-your-yours."

In some poems the listener is passive, merely hearing the speaker's words without response, as in Marlowe's "The Passionate Shepherd to His Love" and Glück's "Snowdrops." In a variation of this situation the listener may not be present, but may instead be the speaker's intended recipient. In this case the speaker is like a letter writer and the listener is the "addressee." Such a listener is the "thou-thee-thine" of Ben Jonson's well-known "Drink to Me, Only, with Thine Eyes."

BEN JONSON (1573–1637)

Drink to Me, Only, with Thine Eyes   *1616*

Drink to me, only, with thine eyes,
   And I will pledge° with mine;   *drink a toast*
Or leave a kiss but in the cup,
   And I'll not look for wine.
The thirst that from the soul doth° rise   *does*   5
   Doth ask a drink divine:
But might I of Jove's nectar° sup
   I would not change° for thine.   *exchange it [i.e., nectar]*

I sent thee, late,° a rosy wreath,   *lately, a short time ago*
   Not so much honoring thee,   10
As giving it a hope, that there
   It could not withered be.
But thou thereon did'st only breathe,
   And sent'st it back to me:
Since when° it grows, and smells, I swear,   *that time, then*   15
   Not of itself, but thee.

DRINK TO ME, ONLY, WITH THINE EYES. 7 *Jove's nectar:* Jove, or Jupiter, was the principal Roman god. Nectar (a word meaning "overcoming death") was the drink of the gods; a human being who drank it would become immortal.

QUESTIONS

1. Who is the speaker? What do you learn about him, his knowledge, his wit, and his concern for the listener?

2. What has the speaker sent to the listener? What did she do, and why is he still writing to her?

3. How can the poem be seen as an attempt to "top" the listener's disdain? Explain why the speaker seems just as interested in showing his wittiness as in complimenting the listener.

    This poem demonstrates that the listener has not been passive; she has returned the speaker's gift and thus has spurned him. Therefore the poem may be seen at least partly as the speaker's attempt, by demonstrating his wit, to ingratiate himself with the listener. In similar poems involving a speaker and a silent listener, we should consider both the dramatic situation and the listener's stated and implied responses.

    A related but distinct type of situation involving a listener is the **dramatic monologue,** in which the speaker talks directly to an on-the-spot listener whose reactions may directly affect the course of the poem. Browning's "My Last Duchess" is such a poem, in which the speaker, the duke, addresses an envoy of a "count," a "you" listener, who has been given the task of arranging financial terms about the dowry to be given by the count when the duke marries the count's daughter.

    Ultimately, we as readers are the listeners of all poems. In this capacity we are the poet's uninvolved, outside audience. Thus, in poems like Hardy's

"The Workbox" (Chapter 18) and Browning's "My Last Duchess," we are a virtual hearing and viewing audience, and in a poem like Housman's "Loveliest of Trees" (Chapter 14) we are outside listeners, eavesdropping as the speaker meditates on time, death, and beauty. Sometimes, however, the poet may address us directly in our role as readers, as in this brief dedicatory poem that Ben Jonson uses to begin his book of epigrams published in 1616.

BEN JONSON (1573–1637)

To the Reader ⸙⸙⸙⸙⸙ *1616*

Pray thee, take care, that tak'st my book in hand,
To read it well: that is, to understand.

In this couplet Jonson establishes intimacy with us as readers by using the second-person singular pronoun *thee*. Though we are clearly *outside* the poem, Jonson invites us *inside* by asking us to read well and understand all his forthcoming poems. As much as a poet can, he therefore closes the distance that exists between poem and reader.

Only rarely do poets address us directly, as Jonson does. For this reason it is important to determine what is meant when a poet uses the "you" pronoun (see also Chapter 5, p. 230). Sometimes the "you" suggests that we are on-the-spot listeners and even colleagues or chums of poetic speakers, but more often the "you" is a conversational way by which the speaker refers to himself or herself. Hardy's speaker in "The Man He Killed" (Chapter 13), for example, uses an indirect "you" in this way, and thereby he establishes our assent to the idea that war is "quaint and curious." Even when we are invited to become inside listeners in this way, however, our responses do not enter the poem structurally, and therefore our role as spectators or witnesses does not change. We remain an audience of outside listeners.

Poems Are Sometimes Little Dramas with Major and Minor Participants

Because many poems are dramatic, they often involve a third type of character—major or minor participants. We learn about these characters from appearance, speech, action, and reaction. In the anonymous "Sir Patrick Spens" (p. 617), for example, we learn from Sir Patrick's outcry that he is distressed, but from his action that he is obedient. In Hardy's "Channel Firing" (Chapter 16) we learn that the ages-old skeletons are sorry that they sacrificed personal enjoyment when they were alive because their strict living did nothing to improve humankind.

Most poetic speakers are reliable reporters about the actions and characters of the major and minor participants. For example, the speaker-narrator of the anonymous "Sir Patrick Spens" is honest and straightforward, and his assessment of Sir Patrick is reliable. But we should also be aware that poetic speakers, as in all fiction, can have interests beyond those of reportorial accuracy. A speaker who uses language for distortion and intimidation is the duke in Browning's "My Last Duchess."

His words make clear that he is a liar and that we must look beyond his distortions to learn the character of the duchess and the nature of their life together.

Not all participants, of course, are human. Poets frequently include descriptions of the animal and vegetable kingdom, such as swimmers (large game fish, otters, people [sometimes]), flyers (orioles, bluejays, swans, ravens, nightingales, larks), walkers and runners (bears, deer, lambs, lions, woodchucks, tigers), and growers (petunias, roses, leaves, birch trees). Although some of these animals and vegetables are given character traits, as with the horse in Frost's "Stopping by Woods on a Snowy Evening" (Chapter 13) and the boobies in Tate's "The Blue Booby" (Chapter 25), they are mainly pictorial or symbolic.

SETTING AND CHARACTER IN POETRY

The people in poetry do not exist in a vacuum. When they speak and act, they reflect the time, place, thought, social conventions, and general circumstances of their lives. Love poetry, for example, is not about desire alone but rather about love within the possible ranges provided by culture and environment. Religion, economic circumstances, leisure, and the condition of the natural world may all enter into a lover's pronouncements. Thus, the speaker of Marlowe's "The Passionate Shepherd to His Love" daydreams about spending time in open nature with his love, sharing the songs of birds and the sights of "valleys, groves, hills, and fields." Here the setting of an Arcadian dream world—without work, want, or illness—reinforces his desire. In contrast, the speaker of Cowper's "The Poplar Field" speaks about Nature as the occasion to meditate on change and, ultimately, death. Cowper cites examples of how the woodsman's axe has caused the inhabitants of a once ideal world to flee, such as the winds and the blackbird that formerly sang in the leaves of the trees that have now been "felled." Thus, one poem deals directly with the reality of change while the other ignores it, although both poems yearn for an ideal natural world.

As in Cowper's "The Poplar Field," settings readily occasion personal, political, philosophical, and religious thought. Gray's "Elegy Written in a Country Churchyard" shows how important such thought can be when it is integrated into poetry. Here the approaching "darkness" causes the speaker to think of the "rude forefathers of the hamlet" in their churchyard graves. This thought leads him to speculate about how death cuts off those who are talented and potentially great. The interaction here is complex, interweaving character and history with natural and cultural situations and images. A poem similarly connecting character and setting is Wordsworth's "Lines Composed a Few Miles above Tintern Abbey" (Chapter 24). This poem, based on the relationship of the past, present, and future of the speaker to the natural scenes he describes, is a model of how poetic setting and character can be fused.

It is no exaggeration to say that setting interacts with character in endless numbers of ways. Thus in Browning's "My Last Duchess," the duke's display of valuable art creates a setting that exposes his greed and cruelty. In "London," Blake introduces bleak sights and anguished sounds that evoke a response of repulsion and rejection. As the representation of a philosophical judgment, the setting of Arnold's "Dover Beach" demonstrates changeability and impermanence. The speaker's solution is to establish personal fidelity as a fixture against change, dissolution, and brutality. To greater or lesser degrees, most poems offer similar connections of setting and character.

POEMS FOR STUDY

MATTHEW ARNOLD (1822–1888)

Dover Beach   1867 (1849)

The sea is calm tonight.
The tide is full, the moon lies fair
Upon the straits—on the French coast the light
Gleams and is gone; the cliffs of England stand,
Glimmering and vast, out in the tranquil bay.   5
Come to the window, sweet is the night air!
Only, from the long line of spray
Where the sea meets the moon-blanched land,
Listen! you hear the grating roar
Of pebbles which the waves draw back, and fling,   10
At their return, up the high strand,
Begin, and cease, and then again begin,
With tremulous cadence slow, and bring
The eternal note of sadness in.

Sophocles long ago   15
Heard it on the Aegean, and it brought
Into his mind the turbid ebb and flow
Of human misery; we
Find also in the sound a thought,
Hearing it by this distant northern sea.   20

The Sea of Faith
Was once, too, at the full, and round earth's shore
Lay like the folds of a bright girdle furled.
But now I only hear
Its melancholy, long, withdrawing roar,   25
Retreating, to the breath
Of the night wind, down the vast edges drear
And naked shingles° of the world.   beaches

Ah, love, let us be true
To one another! for the world, which seems   30
To lie before us like a land of dreams,
So various, so beautiful, so new,
Hath really neither joy, nor love, nor light,
Nor certitude, nor peace, nor help for pain;
And we are here as on a darkling plain   35
Swept with confused alarms of struggle and flight,
Where ignorant armies clash by night.

QUESTIONS

1. What words and details establish the setting?
2. Where are the speaker and listener? What can they see? Hear?
3. What sort of movement may be topographically traced in the first six lines of the poem, so that the scene finally focuses on the speaker and the listener?
4. What is meant by comparing the English Channel to the Aegean Sea, and relating the Aegean surf to the thought of Sophocles?
5. What faith remains after the loss of religious faith? Defend the claim that the faith is the speaker's commitment to personal fidelity rather than love.

WILLIAM BLAKE (1757–1827)   *For a drawing, see p. 644.*

London   1794

I wander thro' each charter'd° street,
Near where the charter'd Thames does flow,
And mark in every face I meet
Marks of weakness, marks of woe.

In every cry of every Man,   5
In every Infant's cry of fear,
In every voice, in every ban,°   *public pronouncement*
The mind-forg'd manacles I hear.

LONDON. 1 *charter'd:* privileged, licensed, authorized.

How the Chimney-sweeper's cry
Every blackning Church appalls;° 10
And the hapless Soldier's sigh
Runs in blood down Palace walls.

But most thro' midnight streets I hear
How the youthful Harlot's curse
Blasts the new-born Infant's tear, 15
And blights with plagues the Marriage hearse.

10 *appalls:* weakens, makes pale, shocks.

QUESTIONS

1. What does London represent to the speaker? How do the persons who live there contribute to the poem's ideas about the state of humanity?

2. What sounds does the speaker mention as a part of the London scene? Characterize these sounds in relation to the poem's main idea.

3. Because of the tension in the poem between civilized activity (as represented in the chartering of the street and the river) and free human impulses, explain how the poem might be considered revolutionary.

4. The poem appeared in *Songs of Experience*, published in 1794. Explain the appropriateness of Blake's including the poem in a collection so named.

ROBERT BROWNING (1812–1889)

My Last Duchess°   1842

FERRARA

That's my last Duchess painted on the wall,
Looking as if she were alive. I call
That piece a wonder, now: Frà Pandolf's° hands
Worked busily a day, and there she stands. 5
Will't please you sit and look at her? I said
"Frà Pandolf" by design, for never read
Strangers like you that pictured countenance,
The depth and passion of its earnest glance,
But to myself they turned (since none puts by
The curtain I have drawn for you, but I) 10
And seemed as they would ask me, if they durst,°   *dared*
How such a glance came there; so, not the first
Are you to turn and ask thus. Sir, 'twas not
Her husband's presence only, called that spot
Of joy into the Duchess' cheek: perhaps 15
Frà Pandolf chanced to say "Her mantle laps
Over my lady's wrist too much," or "Paint

MY LAST DUCHESS. The poem is based on incidents in the life of Alfonso II, duke of Ferrara, whose first wife died in 1561. Some claimed she was poisoned. The duke negotiated his second marriage to the daughter of the count of Tyrol through an agent.   3 *Frà Pandolf:* an imaginary painter who is also a monk.

little compliment

Must never hope to reproduce the faint
Half-flush that dies along her throat": such stuff
Was courtesy, she thought, and cause enough   20
For calling up that spot of joy. She had
A heart—how shall I say?—too soon made glad,
Too easily impressed; she liked whate'er
She looked on, and her looks went everywhere.
Sir, 'twas all one! My favor at her breast,   25
The dropping of the daylight in the West,
The bough of cherries some officious fool
Broke in the orchard for her, the white mule
She rode with round the terrace—all and each
Would draw from her alike the approving speech,
Or blush, at least. She thanked men—good! but thanked   30
Somehow—I know not how—as if she ranked
My gift of a nine-hundred-years-old name
With anybody's gift. Who'd stoop to blame
This sort of trifling? Even had you skill   35
In speech—(which I have not)—to make your will
Quite clear to such a one, and say, "Just this
Or that in you disgusts me; here you miss,
Or there exceed the mark"—and if she let
Herself be lessoned so, nor plainly set   40
Her wits to yours, forsooth, and made excuse
—E'en then would be some stooping; and I choose
Never to stoop. Oh sir, she smiled, no doubt,
Whene'er I passed her; but who passed without
Much the same smile? This grew; I gave commands;   45
Then all smiles stopped together. There she stands
As if alive. Will't please you rise? We'll meet
The company below, then. I repeat,
The Count your master's known munificence
Is ample warrant that no just pretense   50
Of mine for dowry will be disallowed;
Though his fair daughter's self, as I avowed
At starting, is my object. Nay, we'll go
Together down, sir. Notice Neptune,° though,
Taming a sea horse, thought a rarity,   55
Which Claus of Innsbruck° cast in bronze for me!

She was happy person

go down stairs

points to statue

54 *Neptune:* Roman god of the sea.   56 *Claus of Innsbruck:* an imaginary sculptor.

QUESTIONS

1. Who dominates the conversation in this poem? Who is the listener? What is the purpose of the "conversation"? Why does the speaker avoid dealing with the purpose until near the poem's end?

2. What third character does the speaker describe? In what ways are his descriptions accurate or inaccurate? What judgment do you think Browning wants you to make of the speaker? Why?

3. How does the speaker's language illustrate his attitude toward his own power? In light of this attitude, what do you think Browning's point is in the poem?

WILLIAM COWPER (1731–1800)

The Poplar Field ⌐⌐⌐⌐ 1782

The poplars are felled,° farewell to the shade   *cut down*
And the whispering sound of the cool colonnade.
The winds play no longer, and sing in the leaves,
Nor Ouse° on his bosom their image receives.

Twelve years have elapsed since I last took a view   5
Of my favourite field and the bank where they grew,
And now in the grass behold they are laid,
And the tree is my seat that once lent me a shade.

The blackbird has fled to another retreat
Where the hazels afford him a screen from the heat,   10
And the scene where his melody charmed me before,
Resounds with his sweet-flowing ditty no more.

My fugitive years are all hasting away,
And I must ere long lie as lowly as they,
With a turf on my breast, and a stone at my head,   15
Ere another such grove shall arise in its stead.

'Tis a sight to engage me, if any thing can,
To muse on the perishing pleasures of man;
Though his life be a dream, his enjoyments, I see,
Have a being less durable even than he.   20

THE POPLAR FIELD. 4 *Ouse:* river in northern England, near which Cowper lived.

QUESTIONS

1. What situation does the speaker describe? How has the scene changed from what he knew twelve years before? Why does the speaker refer to the passage of time? What kind of person is he?
2. How has the situation affected the blackbird? Why does the speaker care?
3. How does the scene affect the speaker? What idea does he express about what has occurred?

LOUISE GLÜCK (b. 1943)

Snowdrops ⌐⌐⌐⌐ 1992

Do you know what I was, how I lived? You know
what despair is; then
winter should have meaning for you.

I did not expect to survive,
earth suppressing me. I didn't expect   5
to waken again, to feel

in damp earth my body
able to respond again, remembering
after so long how to open again
in the cold light
of earliest spring—   10

afraid, yes, but among you again
crying yes risk joy

in the raw wind of the new world.

QUESTIONS

1. How much does the speaker say about her previous condition? What does she say about how she has changed? What has happened to make her change? To what degree, if any, has the speaker's change altered her general view of the world?

2. How much about her circumstances does the speaker leave vague? Why? Why is the poem titled "Snowdrops"? What is the meaning of the phrase "yes risk joy"?

3. Why does the poet not capitalize the first words in each line?

THOMAS GRAY (1716–1771)

Elegy Written in a Country Churchyard ⨯⟨⟩⨯⟨⨯ 1751

The curfew tolls the knell of parting day,
  The lowing herd wind slowly o'er the lea,
The ploughman homeward plods his weary way,
  And leaves the world to darkness and to me.

Now fades the glimm'ring landscape on the sight,   5
  And all the air a solemn stillness holds,
Save where the beetle wheels his droning flight,
  And drowsy tinklings lull the distant folds;

Save that from yonder ivy-mantled tower
  The moping owl does to the moon complain   10
Of such as wand'ring near her secret bower
  Molest her ancient solitary reign.

Beneath those rugged elms, that yew-tree's shade,
  Where heaves the turf in many a mold'ring heap,
Each in his narrow cell forever laid,   15
  The rude forefathers of the hamlet sleep.

The breezy call of incense-breathing morn,
  The swallow twitt'ring from the straw-built shed,
The cock's shrill clarion, or the echoing horn,°   *hunting horn*
  No more shall rouse them from their lowly bed.   20

For them no more the blazing hearth shall burn,
  Or busy housewife ply her evening care;

No children run to lisp their sire's return,
   Or climb his knees the envied kiss to share.

Oft did the harvest to their sickle yield,   25
   Their furrow oft the stubborn glebe° has broke;   *church land*
How jocund did they drive their team afield!
   How bowed the woods beneath their sturdy stroke!

Let not Ambition mock their useful toil
   Their homely joys, and destiny obscure;   30
Nor Grandeur hear with a disdainful smile
   The short and simple annals of the poor.

The boast of heraldry, the pomp of power,
   And all that beauty, all that wealth e'er gave,
Awaits alike th'inevitable hour.   35
   The paths of glory lead but to the grave.

Nor you, ye proud, impute to these the fault,
   If mem'ry o'er their tomb no trophies raise,
Where through the long-drawn aisle and fretted vault
   The pealing anthem swells the note of praise.   40

Can storied urn or animated bust
   Back to its mansion call the fleeting breath?
Can Honor's voice provoke the silent dust,
   Or Flatt'ry soothe the dull cold ear of death?

Perhaps in this neglected spot is laid   45
   Some heart once pregnant with celestial fire;
Hands that the rod of empire might have swayed,
   Or waked to ecstasy the living lyre.

But Knowledge to their eyes her ample page
   Rich with the spoils of time did ne'er unroll;   50
Chill Penury repressed their noble rage,
   And froze the genial current of the soul.

Full many a gem of purest ray serene,
   The dark unfathomed caves of ocean bear;
Full many a flower is born to blush unseen,   55
   And waste its sweetness on the desert air.

Some village Hampden,° that with dauntless breast
   The little tyrant of his fields withstood;
Some mute inglorious Milton here may rest,
   Some Cromwell guiltless of his country's blood.   60

Th'applause of list'ning senates to command,
   The threats of pain and ruin to despise,
To scatter plenty o'er a smiling land,
   And read their hist'ry in a nation's eyes.

ELEGY WRITTEN IN A COUNTRY CHURCHYARD. 57 *Hampden:* John Hampden (1594–1643), English statesman who defended the rights of the people against King Charles I and who died in the English Civil War of
1642–1646.

Their lot forbade: nor circumscribed alone   65
  Their growing virtues, but their crimes confined;
Forbade to wade through slaughter to a throne,
  And shut the gates of mercy on mankind,

The struggling pangs of conscious truth to hide,
  To quench the blushes of ingenuous shame,   70
Or heap the shrine of luxury and pride
  With incense kindled at the Muse's flame.

Far from the madding° crowd's ignoble strife,   *raving*
  Their sober wishes never learned to stray;
Along the cool sequestered vale of life   75
  They kept the noiseless tenor of their way.

Yet ev'n these bones from insult to protect
  Some frail memorial still erected nigh,
With uncouth° rhymes and shapeless sculpture decked,   *uneducated, unsophisticated*
  Implores the passing tribute of a sigh.   80

Their names, their years, spelt by th'unlettered Muse,
  The place of fame and elegy supply;
And many a holy text around she strews,
  That teach the rustic moralist to die.

For who to dumb forgetfulness a prey,   85
This pleasing anxious being e'er resigned,
Left the warm precincts of the cheerful day,
  Nor cast one longing ling'ring look behind?

On some fond breast the parting soul relies,
  Some pious drops the closing eye requires;
Ev'n from the tomb the voice of Nature cries,   90
  Ev'n in our ashes live their wonted fires.

For thee, who mindful of th'unhonored dead
  Dost in these lines their artless tale relate;
If chance, by lonely contemplation led,   95
  Some kindred spirit shall inquire thy fate.

Haply some hoary-headed swain may say,
  "Oft have we seen him at the peep of dawn
Brushing with hasty steps the dews away
  To meet the sun upon the upland lawn.   100

"There, at the foot of yonder nodding beech
  That wreathes its old fantastic° roots so high,   *fancifully extravagant, grotesque*
His listless length at noontide would he stretch
  And pore upon the brook that babbles by.

"Hard by yon wood, now smiling as in scorn,   105
  Mutt'ring his wayward fancies he would rove,
Now drooping, woeful wan, like one forlorn,
  Or crazed with care, or crossed in hopeless love.

"One morn I missed him on the 'customed hill,
  Along the heath and near his fav'rite tree;
Another came; nor yet beside the rill,
  Nor up the lawn, nor at the wood was he;   110

"The next with dirges due in sad array
  Slow through the church-way path we saw him borne.
Approach and read (for thou canst read) the lay,
  Graved on the stone beneath you aged thorn."   115

THE EPITAPH

Here rests his head upon the lap of earth
  A youth to fortune and to fame unknown;
Fair Science frowned not on his humble birth,
  And Melancholy marked him for her own.   120

Large was his bounty, and his soul sincere,
  Heav'n did a recompense as largely send:
He gave to mis'ry all he had, a tear:
  He gain'd from Heav'n ('twas all he wished) a friend.

No farther seek his merits to disclose,   125
  Or draw his frailties from their dread abode
(There they alike in trembling hope repose),
  The bosom of his Father and his God.

QUESTIONS

1. What is the time of day of the speaker's meditation? What is happening in nature as the poem opens? Whom is the speaker addressing?

2. Who are the people buried in the church graveyard? What point does Gray make about the contributions they might have made if they had not died?

3. How does Gray's use of sights and sounds complement the poem's mood?

4. Who is "thee" (line 93)? What happens to him? Why is he included in the poem?

THOMAS HARDY (1840–1928)

For a photo, see p. 622.

The Ruined Maid 1866

"O 'melia,° my dear, this does everything crown!°;   *i.e., Amelia*
Who could have supposed I should meet you in Town?
And whence such fair garments, such prosperi-ty"—
"O didn't you know I'd been ruined," said she.

—"You left us in tatters, without shoes or socks,   5
Tired of digging potatoes, and spudding up docks;°   *digging up weeds*
And now you've gay bracelets and bright feathers three!"
"Yes: that's how we dress when we're ruined," said she.

THE RUINED MAID. 1 *does everything crown:* crowns everything; is a great surprise.

—"At home in the barton° you said 'thee' and 'thou,'
And 'thik oon,' and 'theäs oon,' and 't'other';° but now   10
Your talking quite fits 'ee° for high compa-ny!"—   *thee*
"Some polish is gained with one's ruin," said she.

—"Your hands were like paws then, your face blue and bleak
But now I'm bewitched by your delicate cheek,
And your little gloves fit as on any la-dy!"—   15
"We never do work when we're ruined," said she.

—"You used to call home-life a hag-ridden dream,
And you'd sigh, and you'd sock°; but at present you seem   *moan, groan*
To know not of megrims° or melancho-ly!"—   *migraine headaches*
"True. One's pretty lively when ruined," said she.   20

—"I wish I had feathers, a fine sweeping gown,
And a delicate face, and could strut about Town!"—
"My dear—a raw country girl, such as you be,
Cannot quite expect that. You ain't ruined," said she.

9 *At home in the barton:* when you lived at home on the farm.   9–10 *'thee' . . . 't'other':* i.e., you spoke familiarly in the country dialect (using the second-person pronoun), saying "thik oon" for "that one" and
"theäs oon" for "this one."

QUESTIONS

1. Who are the two speakers? How have they come together? What are their pres-
    ent economic circumstances? Who is 'melia (Amelia)? Does she seem to be
    bragging to the first speaker? Why has not the first speaker learned about 'melia
    earlier, before their encounter in town?

2. How aware of her situation is 'melia? Is she happy or unhappy about it? How
    completely has she shed her country habits of speech?

3. What double meaning does the word "ruined" have in this poem? To what ex-
    tent does Hardy use the poem to challenge conventional moral judgments?

C. DAY LEWIS (1904–1972)

Song ⌐ ⌐ ⌐ ⌐ ⌐   *1935*

Come, live with me and be my love,
And we will all the pleasures prove
Of peace and plenty, bed and board,
That chance employment may afford.

I'll handle dainties on the docks   5
And thou shalt read of summer frocks:
At evening by the sour canals
We'll hope to hear some madrigals.

Care on thy maiden brow shall put
A wreath of wrinkles, and thy foot   10

Be shod with pain: not silken dress
But toil shall tire thy loveliness.

Hunger shall make thy modest zone
And cheat fond death of all but bone—
If these delights thy mind may move,
Then live with me and be my love.

15

QUESTIONS

1. What is the connection and contrast between this poem and Marlowe's "Passionate Shepherd to His Love"?
2. To what other poems in this chapter is this poem related? How?
3. Who is the speaker in this poem? The listener?
4. What is the effect of words like "chance employment" (line 4), "read" (line 6), and "hope" (line 8)?

CHRISTOPHER MARLOWE (1564–1593)

The Passionate Shepherd to His Love ✳ 1599

Come live with me and be my love,
And we will all the pleasures prove°   *test, try out*
That valleys, groves, hills, and fields,
Woods, or steepy mountain yields.

And we will sit upon the rocks,   5
Seeing the shepherds feed their flocks,
By shallow rivers to whose falls
Melodious birds sing madrigals.

And I will make thee beds of roses
And a thousand fragrant posies,   10
A cap of flowers, and a kirtle°   *long dress*
Embroidered all with leaves of myrtle;

A gown made of the finest wool
Which from our pretty lambs we pull;
Fair lined slippers for the cold,   15
With buckles of the purest gold;

A belt of straw and ivy buds,
With coral clasps and amber studs;
And if these pleasures may thee move,
Come live with me, and be my love.   20

The shepherds' swains° shall dance and sing   *lovers*
For thy delight each May morning:
If these delights thy mind may move,
Then live with me and be my love.

QUESTIONS

1. Describe the speaker. What does he do? What is he like? What does he want?
2. Who is the listener? What is the relationship between speaker and listener?
3. What sort of life does the speaker offer the listener?
4. What is the speaker's understanding of reality?

JOYCE CAROL OATES (b. 1938)

For a photo, see p. 202.

Loving 1970

A balloon of gauze around us,
sheerest gauze: it is a balloon of skin
around us, fine light-riddled skin,
invisible.

If we reach out to pinch its walls it floats from us—   5
it eludes us wetly, this sac.

 It is warmed by a network of veins
fine as hairs and invisible.
The veins pulsate and expand to the width
of eyelashes.   10
In them blood floats weightless as color.
The warm walls sink upon us when we love
each other, and are blinded by the heavier skin
that closes over our eyes.

We are in here together.   15
Outside, people are walking in a landscape—
it is a city landscape, it is theirs.
Their shouts and laughter come to us in broken sounds.
Their strides take them everywhere in daylight.
If they turn suddenly toward us we draw back—   20
the skin shudders wetly, finely—
will we be torn into two people?

The balloon will grow up around us again
as if breathed out of us, moist and sticky and light
as skin, more perfect than our own skin,   25
invisible.

QUESTIONS

1. What does the speaker mean by a "balloon of gauze around us"? How does she define this balloon? What does she mean by "We are in here together" (line 15)?
2. Why does the speaker refer to veins and blood and "warm walls" in discussing the subject of loving? How common are these references to love? How appropriate is the language?
3. How would you characterize the speaker's attitudes about love? To what does the final stanza refer?

MARGE PIERCY (b. 1934)

Wellfleet° Sabbath ✦ 1988

The hawk eye of the sun slowly shuts.
The breast of the bay is softly feathered
dove grey. The sky is barred like the sand
when the tide trickles out.

The great doors of the sabbath are swinging
open over the ocean, loosing the moon
floating up slow distorted vast, a copper
balloon just sailing free.   5

The wind slides over the waves, patting
them with its giant hand, and the sea   10
stretches its muscles in the deep,
purrs and rolls over.

The sweet beeswax candles flicker
and sigh, standing between the phlox
and the roast chicken. The wine shines   15
its red lantern of joy.

Here on this piney sandspit, the Shekinah°
comes on the short strong wings of the seaside
sparrow raising her song and bringing
down the fresh clean night.   20

WELLFLEET SABBATH. *Wellfleet:* a seaside town close to the northern tip of Cape Cod, Massachusetts.
17 *Shekinah:* in the Jewish faith, a visible sign or manifestation of divinity.

QUESTIONS

1. Who is the speaker? Where is she? What is the special occasion? Who, if anyone, is being addressed?
2. What attributes do the speaker's descriptions confer upon the exterior natural world? How do these attributes, together with the interior scene, contribute to the speaker's apparent mood?
3. Who, if anyone, is being addressed? What is the reader's relationship to the poem?

AL PURDY (1918–2000)

Poem ✦ 1971

You are ill and so I lead you away
and put you to bed in the dark room
—you lie breathing softly and I hold your hand
feeling the fingertips relax as sleep comes

You will not sleep more than a few hours   5
and the illness is less serious than my anger or cruelty
and the dark bedroom is like a foretaste of other darknesses

to come later which all of us must endure alone
but here I am permitted to be with you

After a while in sleep your fingers clutch tightly   10
and I know that whatever may be happening
the fear coiled in dreams or the bright trespass of pain
there is nothing at all I can do except hold your hand
and not go away

QUESTIONS

1. What is the dramatic situation of this poem? Who is speaking to whom? What is
    their relationship?

2. What is the condition of the speaker? Of the listener? What traits of character
    does the speaker exhibit?

SIR WALTER RALEIGH (1552–1618)

The Nymph's Reply to the Shepherd ~~~~~ 1600

If all the world and love were young,
And truth in every shepherd's tongue,
These pretty pleasures might me move
To live with thee and be thy love.

Time drives the flocks from field to fold°   *fenced field*   5
When rivers rage and rocks grow cold,
And Philomel° becometh dumb;   *the nightingale*
The rest complains of cares to come.

The flowers do fade, and wanton fields
To wayward winter reckoning yields;   10
A honey tongue, a heart of gall,
Is fancy's spring, but sorrow's fall.

Thy gowns, thy shoes, thy beds of roses,
Thy cap, thy kirtle,° and thy posies°   *long dress; flowers and poems*
Soon break, soon wither, soon forgotten—   15
In folly ripe, in reason rotten.

Thy belt of straw and ivy buds,
Thy coral clasps and amber studs,
All these in me no means can move
To come to thee and be thy love.   20

But could youth last and love still° breed,   *always*
Had joys no date nor age no need,
Then these delights my mind might move
To live with thee and be thy love.

QUESTIONS

1.   Who is the speaker? What do we learn about the speaker? Who is the listener?
2.   How are the ideas of love and the world in this poem different from those in Marlowe's poem?
3.   To what extent is this poem a parody (an imitation that makes fun) of Marlowe's poem? To what extent is it a refutation of Marlowe's poem?
4.   Determine the steps of the speaker's logical argument in this poem.

CHRISTINA ROSSETTI (1830–1894)

A Christmas Carol ~~~~ 1872

In the bleak mid-winter
  Frosty wind made moan,
Earth stood hard as iron,
  Water like a stone;
Snow had fallen, snow on snow,   5
  Snow on snow,
In the bleak mid-winter
  Long ago.

Our God, Heaven cannot hold Him
  Nor earth sustain;   10
Heaven and earth shall flee away
  When He comes to reign:
In the bleak mid-winter
  A stable-place sufficed°   *see Luke 2:7*
The Lord God Almighty   15
  Jesus Christ.

Enough for Him whom cherubim
  Worship night and day,
A breastful of milk
  And a mangerful of hay;   20
Enough for Him whom angels
  Fall down before,
The ox and ass and camel
  Which adore.

Angels and archangels   25
  May have gathered there,
Cherubim and seraphim
  Throng'd the air,
But only His mother
  In her maiden bliss   30
Worshipped the Beloved
  With a kiss.

What can I give Him,

Poor as I am?
If I were a shepherd°   *see Luke 2:8–20*   35
  I would bring a lamb,
If I were a wise man°   *see Matthew 2:1–12*
  I would do my part,—
Yet what I can I give Him,
  Give my heart.   40

QUESTIONS

1. Why does Rossetti stress the bitterness and bleakness of the winter setting in this poem?

2. Why does the speaker stress the simplicity of the birthplace of "The Lord God Almighty"? What is the origin and tradition of this setting?

3. How does the fourth stanza prepare you for the speaker's description of her own condition in the fifth stanza?

4. How are the objects considered gifts by the speaker a part of the setting traditionally associated with the birth of Jesus? How does the speaker's gift reveal her character and condition?

JANE SHORE (b. 1947)

A Letter Sent to Summer   1977

Oh summer if you would only come
with your big baskets of flowers,
dropping by like an old friend
just passing through the neighborhood!

If you came to my door disguised   5
as a thirsty biblical angel
I'd buy all your hairbrushes and magazines!
I'd be more hospitable
than any ancient king.

I'd personally carry your luggage in,   10
Your monsoons. Your squadrons of bugs,
Your plums and lovely melons.
Let the rose let out its long long sigh
And Desire return to the hapless rabbit.

This request is also in my own behalf.   15
Inside my head it is always snowing,
even when I sleep. When I wake up,
and still you have not arrived,
I curl back into my blizzard of linens.

Not like winter's buckets of whitewash.   20
Please wallpaper my bedroom
with leafy vegetables and farms.

If you knocked right now,
I would not interfere.
Start near the window.   25
Start right here.

QUESTIONS

1. Describe the speaker. What do you learn about her and how she is responding to
    the time of year?

2. Describe what summer means to the speaker. What attributes does she give to
    summer? What contrasts are brought out by references to "bugs" and "mon-
    soons" in addition to "plums" and "the rose"?

3. What does the phrase "always snowing" contribute to your understanding of the
    speaker's yearning for summer?

MAURA STANTON (b. 1946)

Childhood ~ ~ ~ ~ *1984*

I used to lie on my back, imagining
A reverse house on the ceiling of my house
Where I could walk around in empty rooms
All by myself. There was no furniture
Up there, only a glass globe on the floor.   5
And knee-high barriers at every door.
The low silled windows opened on blue air.
Nothing hung in the closet; even the kitchen
Seemed immaculate, a place for thought.
I liked to walk across the swirling plaster   10
Into the parts of the house I couldn't see.
The hum from the other house, now my ceiling,
Reached me only faintly. I'd look up
To find my brothers watching old cartoons,
Or my mother vacuuming the ugly carpet.   15
I'd stare amazed at unmade beds, the clutter,
Shoes, half-dressed dolls, the telephone,
Then return dizzily to my perfect floorplan
Where I never spoke or listened to anyone.

I must have turned down the wrong hall,   20
Or opened a door that locked shut behind me,
For I live on the ceiling now, not the floor.
This is my house, room after empty room.
How do I ever get back to the real house
Where my sisters spill milk, my father calls,   25
And I am at the table, eating cereal?
I fill my white rooms with furniture,
Hang curtains over the piercing blue outside.
I lie on my back. I strive to look down,

This ceiling is higher than it used to be,   30
The floor so far away I can't determine
Which room I'm in, which year, which life.

QUESTIONS

1. How do the first four lines introduce the poem? To what degree is the situation normal? Unusual? Humorous?

2. How accurate is the imaginative explanation of details about the ceiling? About the rooms of the house?

3. How does line 20 constitute a shift in the poem? What purpose is served by these final thirteen lines?

4. Characterize the speaker. How does she explain what has happened to her? In relationship to her opening sentence, explain the last four lines.

JAMES WRIGHT (1927–1980)

A Blessing   1963

Just off the highway to Rochester, Minnesota,
Twilight bounds softly forth on the grass.
And the eyes of those two Indian ponies
Darken with kindness.
They have come gladly out of the willows   5
To welcome my friend and me.
We step over the barbed wire into the pasture
Where they have been grazing all day, alone.
They ripple tensely, they can hardly contain their happiness
That we have come.   10
They bow shyly as wet swans. They love each other.
There is no loneliness like theirs.
At home once more,
They begin munching the young tufts of spring in the darkness.
I would like to hold the slenderer one in my arms.   15
For she has walked over to me
And nuzzled my left hand.
She is black and white,
Her mane falls wild on her forehead,
And the light breeze moves me to caress her long ear   20
That is delicate as the skin over a girl's wrist.
Suddenly I realize
That if I stepped out of my body I would break
Into blossom.

QUESTIONS

1. What has happened just before the poem opens? Account for the poet's use of the present tense in his descriptions.

2. Is the setting specific or general? What happens as the poem progresses?

3. What realization overtakes the speaker? How does this realization constitute a "blessing," and what does it show about his character?

4. Why is it necessary for the poet to include all the detail of the first twenty-one lines before the realization of the last three?

WRITING ABOUT CHARACTER AND SETTING IN POETRY

Writing about character and setting involves many of the same considerations whether you deal with prose fiction or poetry. You might therefore review the material on character presented in Chapter 4. However, there are some important differences between the two writing tasks. One of these is the way you find out about characters. In prose fiction, you can usually judge a character by the details about his or her actions, words, thoughts, appearance, and opinions. In poetry, the speaker is less likely to provide full details. Consequently, many conclusions must be inferred from the speaker's suggestions and hints.

Another difference between fiction and poetry concerns the types of character. Fiction presents a broad range of writing options: You may write about the protagonist, the antagonist, the narrator, or any of the incidental characters. In poetry you are usually limited to the speaker or to one of the characters described by the speaker (although you may sometimes be able to discuss the listener, too). In writing about Browning's "My Last Duchess," for example, you learn enough about both the duke and the duchess to write about either.

In planning and prewriting, you should find out as much as you can about the characters and their relationship to their situations; that is, to the action, emotion, ideas, setting, and other characters. Answering the following questions will help you to focus your ideas.

Questions for Discovering Ideas

About the Speaker

*   Who is the speaker? What is he or she doing? What does he or she say about himself or herself? About others?
*   What conclusions can you draw about occurrences involving the speaker that took place before the poem begins?
*   How reliable is the speaker as an observer and reporter? What knowledge enables the speaker to make judgments and opinions?
*   What do the speaker's word choices reveal about his or her education and social standing? How does the language reveal his or her assumptions?
*   What tone of voice is suggested in the speaker's presentation?
*   How deeply is the speaker involved with the action of the poem? What connection does she or he make with the other characters? With the poem's actions?

About Other Characters

*   How vividly does the poem describe action, appearance, emotions, responses, and ideas? How strong a picture do you get of any other character (characters)?
*   How does each significant character respond to the surroundings described and implied in the poem?

- What is the character trying to gain or learn?
- How is the character affected by others, and how do others respond to her or to him?
- What degree of control does the character exert, and what does his or her effort tell you?
- How does the character speak and behave, and what do you learn from these words and actions?

Strategies for Organizing Ideas

When you write about a single character, formulate a central idea that focuses on his or her personality or status. If you are writing about the duke in Browning's "My Last Duchess," for example, your idea might be that he is arrogant, cruel, greedy, and power-mad. In writing about Sir Patrick Spens (Chapter 13), your idea would likely be about his self-sacrificing fidelity to the king. If the topic is a set of characters, the central idea should express some relationship or commonality among them. Thus the grieving characters in the anonymous "Bonny George Campbell" show their love for Campbell, and the characters in Blake's "London" illustrate the withering effects of discriminatory law and religion.

Consider organizing your essay along the lines of one of the following approaches.

1. CHARACTER AS REVEALED BY ACTION. Often the speaker describes himself or herself as a major character or major mover. What does the action reveal about this speaker? In Shore's "A Letter Sent to Summer," the speaker indicates that she would be willing to buy "hairbrushes and magazines" from Summer. What does this proposed action demonstrate? In Gray's "Elegy Written in a Country Churchyard," the speaker enters the churchyard at sunset, and his action causes him to think of life, glory, fame, fortune, and religious dedication. What do his speculations and conclusions reveal about his character?

In a parallel way, the speaker of Glück's "Snowdrops" may be an animated snowdrop (snowflake) that has undergone a transformation from winter to spring. Or the speaker may be a person describing what appears to be an episode of depression that coincided with the fall of snow in winter. The spring-time recovery is accompanied by the words "suppressing," "remembering," "earth," and "damp earth." What do these words, and the use of the word "risk" near the poem's end, suggest about the speaker's character and her relationship with the cyclical patterns of nature?

2. CHARACTER AS REVEALED BY INTERACTION. Poems based in a dramatic situation yield best to this treatment. Browning's "My Last Duchess" is a fine example, as are Hardy's "Channel Firing" (Chapter 16) and Jonson's "Drink to Me, Only, with Thine Eyes." The situation in Purdy's "Poem" is that the speaker is talking directly to a listener who seems gravely ill. What does the speaker's attitude toward the listener reveal about his character? In this and other poems, what do you learn about relationships and how they have affected the poetic characters?

3. CHARACTER AS REVEALED BY CIRCUMSTANCE OR SETTING. The essay based on the interrelationship of character and setting assumes that time, place, artifact, money, family, culture, and history influence character and motivation, and also that individual and collective traits are developed as people try to control their surroundings. For instance, the speaker of Wright's "A Blessing" describes the thrill of looking at a roadside pasture, and at the end of the poem he feels as though he is about to "break / Into blossom." What enables him to reach this joyful conclusion? Why does he feel safe rather than frightened? Why does he believe in the benevolence of the two ponies, and, in turn, why do the ponies treat him with affection? What aspects of character enable him to step over the barbed wire without fear and to believe that the experience is really a "blessing"? Would such an experience have been possible at a more suspicious, less civilized time, when people stepping uninvited onto property might have been considered intruders and peppered with buckshot? In short, how has setting in the broadest sense entered into the speaker's character?

In dealing with the interrelationship of character and external situation, you might be able to organize the body of your essay by relying on certain aspects of the setting. Thus you might select the details about past, present, and future time in Gray's "Elegy Written in a Country Churchyard." Similarly, the details about the roaring surf and the dim lights in Arnold's "Dover Beach" can provide thematic links for a discussion of the speaker's sense of alienation, loss, and dedication. In such ways, you may use aspects of setting not only as topics to shed light on character but also to guide and shape your essay.

Whatever strategy you choose, remember that your organization will finally be determined by your poem. Each poem suggests its own avenues of exploration, directing your thought and organization.

In your conclusion you might summarize your major points about the character or characters, or you might tie your ideas into an assessment of the poem as a whole. Thus, you might briefly discuss the connection between character and character, character and environment, character and death, character and greed, character and love, and so on, and deal with these topics generally as you write your final sentences.

DEMONSTRATIVE STUDENT ESSAY

The Character of the Duke in Browning's "My Last Duchess"°

In this dramatic monologue, Browning skillfully develops the character of his speaker, who holds the high position of Duke of Ferrara (in Italy) during the sixteenth century, a period of aristocratic absolutism. Because the duke is at the top of the aristocracy, he exerts absolute control, whether for good or for bad. [1] Browning's duke is bad; not only is he bad, but he is totally evil.* He reveals this

°See pp. 673–74 for this poem.
*Central idea.

evil in his one-way conversation with the listener, who is an envoy of a less powerful aristocrat, the count, whose daughter the duke is claiming in marriage. The duke's evil character is brought out by his indulgence in power, his intimidation of others, his manipulation of his dead wife, and his general contempt for others.[†]

[2]

The duke's indulgence in power, the basis of his evil, is apparent in his use of indirect speech. On the surface, Browning makes him seem intelligent, civilized, and friendly. The duke begins speaking by pointing out to his listener the beauty of a painting of his "last Duchess," but his entire speech--comprising the entire poem--reveals the horror of his self-indulgence. His indirect but threatening description of how he treated the duchess shows that he delights in evil. When he says "I gave commands; / Then all smiles stopped together" (lines 45-46), he is actually bragging about how he had the duchess killed. He is coldly horrible, the more so because he masks his evil with quiet words and a love of good art.

[3]

Another horrible quality is the way the duke intimidates people. At first it seems that he is doing no more than telling about his dead wife, but the poem makes clear that he is intimidating both his listener and also the count, the listener's master. The last nine lines (48-56) indicate that his monologue should have been a dialogue, in which he should have negotiated the terms for the dowry he is to receive from the count. The fact that he has talked only about how he got rid of his "last Duchess" shows his arrogance. Thus, there is no mention of dowry until lines 48-53, when the duke states that he will make a "just pretense" for a dowry which of course the count will honor (for "just pretense," read a demand for all the count's money and land). In addition, the duke's commands, "Will't please you rise? We'll meet / The company below, then," indicate that the negotiation that never began is now over and that the envoy is totally in his power. This is intimidation of the most ruthless and inhuman sort.

The duke's evil nature is also brought out in his description of the duchess. If we study his words to determine what the duchess was really like, we conclude that she was even-tempered and pleasant to all--the soul of graciousness and courtesy. In fact, it would be hard to say that she was anything but perfect. But the duke, rather than indicating pleasure with her, states that she was ungrateful because she was not submissive. He complains that the smile she gave to others was the same as the smile she gave to him (it probably was not; we may conclude that her smile to him probably covered fear):

[4]

> O sir, she smiled, no doubt,
> Whene'er I passed her; but who passed without
> Much the same smile? (lines 43-45)

These lines show that the duke is a manipulator and that the poor duchess was in an impossible situation. Very likely he would have complained also if she had smiled only at him and not at others--thereby leaving herself open to the duke's perverted judgment that she did not show the graciousness toward others that he expected from his wife. No matter how good she was, there was no way for her to have pleased him. He would have manipulated her into an unfavorable position that would have justified his giving the "commands" to remove her.

Perhaps the worst of this monster's traits is the contempt he shows for people by thinking of them not as human beings but rather as things. Most notable is

[†]Thesis sentence.

[5] the way he thinks of the duchess; he calls her painting a "piece" (line 3) to hang on a wall, looking "as if she were alive" (line 2). He does not even name her, or recognize her humanity by calling her "the <u>late</u> Duchess," and he speaks about the bronze statue of Neptune "taming a sea horse" (line 55) as being equal to her. This same contempt for people is shown in his claim that his interest in the count's daughter is the "fair daughter's self" (line 52), while the rest of the poem makes clear that he wants only wealth and power out of the new marriage. Oddly, also, he seems to think of himself less as a person than as a "nine-hundred-years-old name" (line 33), and it is this intangible distinction that he prizes above his own humanity. In other words, he views even himself with contempt.

[6] Browning's duke, then, is a person with absolute power but without the kindness and understanding to use it for anyone but himself. His complaints about the dead Duchess are meaningless, for they are no more than pretexts for cruel self-indulgence. He is at the top of the aristocratic power structure, and therefore he is able to do what he wants without reprisal. People must defer to him and obey him, but only because he makes everyone afraid. His intimidation, his manipulation, his lust for power--all govern him, and leave him unable to look at human beings as anything more than pawns in his game for control. <u>He is an example of the saying that absolute power corrupts absolutely, and his character is therefore a frightening portrait of evil</u>.

WORK CITED

Browning, Robert. "My Last Duchess." <u>Literature: An Introduction to Reading and Writing</u>. Ed. Edgar V. Roberts and Henry E. Jacobs. 7th ed. Upper Saddle River: Prentice Hall, 2004. 673–74.

Commentary on the Essay

Because the subject of the discussion, the duke, is the speaker, the essay is based partially on details presented by him, but it is also partially based on interpretations. The principal subject matter is the interaction of the duke and the subject of the poem—the "last Duchess"—in addition to his interaction with the listener, who is a representative of an inferior aristocrat, and whom he therefore treats with contempt. Elements of setting are also introduced to illuminate the duke's character: his works of art, his absolute power, his pride in his name and title, and his wealth. The essay thus demonstrates how character can be analyzed with reference to (1) interactions between persons and persons and also (2) the connections of persons with their surroundings.

The central idea is that the duke is evil. This point is made in paragraph 1, with sufficient accompanying detail to explain that the duke's position enables him to exercise absolute power. Paragraph 2 discloses that indulgence in power is one of the duke's primary evil traits, while paragraphs 3, 4, and 5 bring out traits of intimidation, manipulation, and contempt. The final paragraph summarizes but also asserts that the duke's justifications for killing his wife are irrelevant to his real motives of greed and lust for power.

As the essay develops, transitions are effected by words such as "another," "also," "worst," and "then." The assertions in the essay are supported by references to specific details from the poem, quotations from the poem (with line numbers noted), and interpretations of details.

Special Topics for Writing and Argument about Character and Setting in Poetry

1. Write an essay comparing the speakers of the "passionate shepherd" poems (by Marlowe, Raleigh, and Lewis). How are the speakers alike, and how are they different? How do their words and references indicate their characters? How do the speakers influence your judgments of the poems in which they appear?

2. Write an essay discussing the relationships between location, thought, and character as asserted in the poems by Arnold, Blake, Cowper, Hardy, Shore, and Wordsworth. What importance do place and time have on the opportunity for life and the development of character? How do responses to time, historical period, and place influence ideas about how to live?

3. Consider Piercy's "Wellfleet Sabbath," Gray's "Elegy Written in a Country Churchyard," Rossetti's "A Christmas Carol," and Wright's "A Blessing" as poems embodying a type or types of religious experience. What common or similar circumstances occasion the religious reflections in the poems? What common ideas and conclusions do the poems express? What philosophical or sectarian differences do you find? On the basis of your study, explain typical patterns of religious experience. (For ideas about how to approach this topic, you may wish to consult Chapter 35 and also the section titled "Archetypal Criticism" in Chapter 33.)

4. Write a short poem, biographical or autobiographical, showing how a certain time, place, or experience has shaped a present quality of character and/or a certain decision about life, friendships, and goals.

5. Use your library to locate two university press books about Robert Browning. Analyze the extent to which they discuss Browning's use of dramatic monologue. With the aid of what you discover, write a brief essay on Browning's use of the dramatic monologue as a means of disclosing character.

Imagery: *The Poem's Link to the Senses*

16

In literature, **imagery** refers to words that trigger your imagination to recall and recombine **images**—memories or mental pictures of sights, sounds, tastes, smells, sensations of touch, and motions. The process is active and even vigorous, for when words and descriptions produce images, you are using your personal experiences with life and language to help you understand the works you are reading. You are re-creating the work *in your own way* through the controlled stimulation produced by the writer's words. Imagery is therefore one of the strongest modes of literary expression because it provides a channel to your active imagination, and along this channel, writers bring their works directly to your mind and consciousness.

For example, reading the word *lake* may trigger in your mind a memory of an actual lake. Your mental picture—or image—may be a distant view of calm waters reflecting a blue sky, a nearby view of gentle waves rippling in the wind, your splashing as you wade or dive into the water, a close-up view of a sandy lake bottom from a boat, or an overhead view of a sun-drenched shoreline. Similarly, the words *rose, apple, hot dog, malted milk,* and *pizza* all cause you to recollect these objects and, in addition, may cause you to recall their smells and tastes. Active and graphic words like *run, jog, row, swim, vault,* and *dive* stimulate you to picture yourself performing these actions, or they may bring to mind moving images of someone else doing them.

𝕍 RESPONSES AND THE WRITER'S USE OF DETAIL

In studying imagery, we try to comprehend and explain our imaginative reconstruction of the pictures and impressions evoked by the work's images. We let the poet's words simmer and percolate in our minds. To get our imaginations stirring, we might follow a description by Samuel Taylor Coleridge in lines 37–41 of "Kubla Khan."

A damsel with a dulcimer
In a vision once I saw:
It was an Abyssinian maid,
And on her dulcimer she played
Singing of Mount Abora.

We do not read about the color of the young woman's clothing or learn anything else about her appearance except that she is playing a stringed instrument, a dulcimer, and that she is singing a song about a mountain in a foreign, remote land. But Coleridge's image is enough. From it we can visualize a vivid, exotic picture of a young woman from a distant land singing, together with impressions of the loveliness of her song (even though we never hear it or understand it). The image lives.

THE RELATIONSHIP OF IMAGERY TO IDEAS AND ATTITUDES

Images do more than elicit impressions. By the *authenticating* effects of the vision and perceptions underlying them, they give you new ways of seeing the world and of strengthening your old ways of seeing it. Shakespeare, in Sonnet 116: "Let Me Not to the Marriage of True Minds" (Chapter 20), develops the idea that love provides people with consistency of purpose in their lives. Rather than stating the idea directly, he uses images of a landmark or lighthouse and also of a fixed star—sights with which we as his readers are familiar.

. . . it [love] is an ever fixéd mark
That looks on tempests and is never shaken;
It is the star to every wandering bark
Whose worth's unknown, although his° height be taken.   *its*

These images form a link with readers that is clear and also verifiable by observation. Such uses of imagery comprise one of the strongest means by which writers reinforce ideas.

In addition, as you form mental pictures and impressions from a poet's images, you respond with appropriate attitudes and feelings. Thus the phrase "Beside the lake, beneath the trees," from Wordsworth's poem "Daffodils" (Chapter 24) prompts both the visualization of a wooded lakeshore and the related pleasantness of outdoor relaxation and happiness. A contrasting visualization is to be found in Hubert von Herkomer's painting *Hard Times* (next page), in which all the images—the tired faces, the heavy load, the tools, the bleak road, the leafless trees—point toward the harsh life of the worker and his family, causing a response of sadness and sympathy. Imagery used in a more negative way is found in Ray Durem's "I Know I'm Not Sufficiently Obscure," which triggers disturbing responses through images of blood, lynching, and "cold Korean mud." By using such imagery, artists and poets create sensory vividness, and they also influence and control our attitudes as readers.

Sir Hubert von Herkomer, *Hard Times*. (Copyright Manchester City Art Gallery.)

TYPES OF IMAGERY

Visual Imagery Is the Language of Sight

Sight is the most significant of our senses, for it is the key to our remembrance of other impressions. Therefore, the most frequently occurring literary imagery is to things we can visualize either exactly or approximately—**visual images.** In the three-stanza poem "Cargoes," John Masefield creates mental pictures or images of oceangoing merchant vessels from three periods of human history.

JOHN MASEFIELD (1878–1967)

Cargoes   1902

Quinquereme° of Nineveh° from distant Ophir,°
Rowing home to haven in sunny Palestine,
With a cargo of ivory,
And apes and peacocks,°
Sandalwood, cedarwood,° and sweet white wine.   5

CARGOES. 1 *quinquereme:* the largest of the ancient ships. It was powered by three tiers of oars and was named "quinquereme" because five men operated each vertical oar station. The top two oars were each taken by two men, while one man alone took the bottom oar. *Nineveh:* the capital of ancient Assyria, and an "exceeding great city" (Jonah 3:3). *Ophir:* Ophir probably was in Africa and was known for its gold (1 Kings 10:22; 1 Chron. 29:4). Masefield quotes from some of the biblical verses in his first stanza.   4 *apes and peacocks:* 1 Kings 10:22 and 2 Chron. 9:21   5 *cedarwood:* 1 Kings 9:11.   6 *Isthmus:* the Isthmus of Panama.

Stately Spanish galleon coming from the Isthmus,°
Dipping through the Tropics by the palm-green shores,
With a cargo of diamonds,
Emeralds, amethysts,
Topazes, and cinnamon, and gold moidores.°   10
Dirty British coaster with a salt-caked smoke-stack,
Butting through the Channel in the mad March days,
With a cargo of Tyne coal,°
Road-rails, pig-lead,
Firewood, iron-ware, and cheap tin trays.   15

10 *moidores:* coins used in Portugal and Brazil at the time the New World was being explored.   13 *Tyne coal:* coal from Newcastle upon Tyne, in northern England, renowned for its coal production.

QUESTIONS

1. Consider the images of life during three periods of history: ancient Israel at the time of Solomon (ca. 950 B.C.E.), sixteenth-century Spain, and modern England. What do these images tell you about Masefield's interpretation of modern commercial life?

2. To what senses do most of the images refer (e.g., sight, taste)?

3. The poem contains no complete sentences. Why do you think Masefield included only verbals ("rowing," "dipping," "butting") to begin the second line of each stanza, rather than finite verbs?

4. In historical reality, the quinquereme was likely rowed by slaves, and the Spanish galleon likely carried riches stolen from Central American natives. How might these unpleasant details affect the impressions otherwise achieved in the first two stanzas?

Masefield's images are vivid as they stand and need no further amplification. For us to reconstruct them imaginatively, we do not need ever to have seen the ancient biblical lands or waters, or ever to have seen or handled the cheap commodities on a modern merchant ship. We have seen enough in our lives to *imagine* places and objects like these, and hence Masefield is successful in fixing his visual images in our minds.

Auditory Imagery Is the Language of Sound

Auditory images trigger our experiences with sound. For such images, let us consider Wilfred Owen's "Anthem for Doomed Youth," which is about the death of soldiers in warfare and the sorrow of their loved ones.

WILFRED OWEN (1893–1918)

Anthem for Doomed Youth ⌣ ⌣ ⌣ ⌣ ⌣   1920

What passing-bells° for these who die as cattle?
Only the monstrous anger of the guns.
Only the stuttering rifles' rapid rattle
Can patter out their hasty orisons.°   *prayers*

No mockeries for them from prayers or bells, 5
Nor any voice of mourning save the choirs—
The shrill, demented choirs of wailing shells;
And bugles calling for them from sad shires.°
What candles may be held to speed them all?
Not in the hands of boys, but in their eyes 10
Shall shine the holy glimmers of good-byes.
The pallor of girls' brows shall be their pall;
Their flowers the tenderness of patient minds,
And each slow dusk a drawing-down of blinds.

ANTHEM FOR DOOMED YOUTH. 1 *passing-bells:* church bells tolling upon the entry of a funeral cortege into a church cemetery. 8 *shires:* British counties.

QUESTIONS

1. What type of imagery predominates in the first eight lines? How does the imagery change in the last six lines?

2. Contrast the images of death at home and death on the battlefield. How does this contrast affect your experience and understanding of the poem?

3. Consider these images: "holy glimmers of good-byes," "pallor of girls' brows," "patient minds," "drawing-down of blinds." What relationship do the people defined by these images have to the doomed youth?

The poem begins with the question of "What passing-bells" may be tolled "for these who die as cattle." Owen's speaker is referring to the traditional tolling of a church bell to announce a burial. The images of these ceremonial sounds suggest a period of peace and order, when there is time to pay respect to the dead. But the poem points out that the only sound for those who have fallen in battle is the "rapid rattle" of "stuttering" rifles—not the solemn, dignified sounds of peace but the horrifying noises of war. Owen's auditory images evoke corresponding sounds in our imaginations, and they help us to experience the poem and to hate the uncivilized depravity of war.

Olfactory, Gustatory, and Tactile Imagery Refers to Smell, Taste, and Touch

In addition to sight and sound, you will find images from the other senses: smell, taste, and touch. Shakespeare includes an olfactory image of sweet perfumes in Sonnet 130: "My Mistress' Eyes Are Nothing Like the Sun," and the odor of roses is suggested in Burns's "A Red, Red Rose" (Chapter 17).

Gustatory images are also common, though less frequent than those referring to sight and sound. Lines 5 and 10 of Masefield's "Cargoes," for example, include images of "sweet white wine" and "cinnamon." Although the poem refers to these commodities as cargoes, the words themselves also register in our minds as gustatory images because they evoke our sense of taste.

Images of touch and texture are not as common because touch is difficult to render except in terms of effects. The speaker of Amy Lowell's "Patterns" (Chapter 25), for example, uses tactile imagery when imagining a never-to-happen embrace with her fiancé, who we learn has been killed on a wartime battlefield. Her imagery in lines 51–52 records the effect of the embrace ("bruised"), whereas her internalized feelings are expressed in metaphors ("aching, melting"):

And the buttons of his waistcoat bruised my body as he clasped me
Aching, melting, unafraid.

Tactile images are not uncommon in love poetry, where references to touch and feeling are natural.

Kinetic and Kinesthetic Imagery Refers to Motion and Activity

References to movement are also images. Images of general motion are **kinetic** (remember that *motion pictures* are called "cinema"; note the closeness of *kine* in *kinetic* and *cine* in *cinema*), whereas the term ***kinesthetic*** is applied to human or animal movement. Imagery of motion is closely related to visual images, for motion is most often seen. Masefield's "British coaster" is a visual image, but when it goes "Butting through the channel," this reference to motion makes it also kinetic. When Hardy's skeletons sit upright at the beginning of "Channel Firing," the image is kinesthetic, as is the action of Lowell's speaker in "Patterns" walking in the garden after hearing about her fiancé's death. Both types are seen at the conclusion of the following poem, Elizabeth Bishop's "The Fish."

ELIZABETH BISHOP (1911–1979)

The Fish ⟋⟍⟋⟍⟋ *1946*

I caught a tremendous fish
and held him beside the boat
half out of water, with my hook
fast in a corner of his mouth.
He didn't fight.
He hadn't fought at all.
He hung a grunting weight,
battered and venerable
and homely. Here and there
his brown skin hung in strips
like ancient wallpaper,
and its pattern of darker brown

5

10

was like wallpaper:
shapes like full-blown roses
stained and lost through age.
He was speckled with barnacles,   15
fine rosettes of lime,
and infested
with tiny white sea-lice,
and underneath two or three   20
rags of green weed hung down.
While his gills were breathing in
the terrible oxygen
—the frightening gills,
fresh and crisp with blood,   25
that can cut so badly—
I thought of the coarse white flesh
packed in like feathers,
the big bones and the little bones,
the dramatic reds and blacks   30
of his shiny entrails,
and the pink swim-bladder
like a big peony.
I looked into his eyes
which were far larger than mine   35
but shallower, and yellowed,
the irises backed and packed
with tarnished tinfoil
seen through the lenses
of old scratched isinglass.°   *a thin sheet of mica*   40
They shifted a little, but not
to return my stare.
—It was more like the tipping
of an object toward the light.
I admired his sullen face,   45
the mechanism of his jaw,
and then I saw
that from his lower lip
—if you could call it a lip—
grim, wet, and weaponlike,   50
hung five old pieces of fish-line,
or four and a wire leader
with the swivel still attached,
with all their five big hooks
grown firmly in his mouth.   55
A green line, frayed at the end
where he broke it, two heavier lines,
and a fine black thread
still crimped from the strain and snap
when it broke and he got away.   60
Like medals with their ribbons

frayed and wavering,   65
a five-haired beard of wisdom
trailing from his aching jaw.
I stared and stared
and victory filled up
the little rented boat,
from the pool of bilge   70
where oil had spread a rainbow
around the rusted engine
to the bailer rusted orange,
the sun-cracked thwarts,   75
the oarlocks on their strings,
the gunnels—until everything
was rainbow, rainbow, rainbow!
And I let the fish go.

QUESTIONS

1. Describe the poem's images of action. What is unusual about them?

2. What impression does the fish make upon the speaker? Is the fish beautiful? ugly? Why is the fish described in such detail?

3. What do the "five old pieces of fish-line" indicate?

4. How is the rainbow formed around the boat's engine? Why does the speaker refer to the "pool of bilge"? What does the rainbow mean to the speaker?

5. What right does the speaker have to keep the fish? Why does she choose to relinquish this right?

The kinetic images at the end of "The Fish" are those of victory filling the boat (difficult to visualize) and the oil spreading to make a rainbow in the bilgewater (easy to visualize). The kinesthetic images are readily imagined—the speaker's staring, observing, and letting the fish go—and they are vivid and real. The final gesture is the necessary outcome of the observed contrast between the deteriorating artifacts of human beings and the natural world of the fish, and it is a vivid expression of the right of the natural world to exist without human intervention. In short, Bishop's kinetic and kinesthetic images are designed to objectivize the need for freedom not only for human beings but for all the earth and animated Nature.

The areas from which kinetic and kinesthetic imagery can be derived are too varied and unpredictable to describe. Occupations, trades, professions, businesses, recreational activities—all these might furnish images. One poet introduces references from gardening, another from money and banking, another from modern real estate developments, another from the falling of leaves in autumn, another from life in the jungle, another from life in the home. The freshness, newness, and surprise of much poetry result from the many and varied areas from which writers draw their images.

POEMS FOR STUDY

WILLIAM BLAKE (1757–1827)   *For a drawing, see p. 644.*

The Tyger°   1794

Tyger! Tyger! burning bright
In the forests of the night,
What immortal hand or eye
Could frame thy fearful symmetry?

In what distant deeps or skies   5
Burnt the fire of thine eyes?
On what wings dare he aspire?
What the hand, dare seize the fire?

And what shoulder, & what art,
Could twist the sinews of thy heart?   10
And when thy heart began to beat,
What dread hand? & what dread feet?

What the hammer? what the chain?
In what furnace was thy brain?

THE TYGER. The title refers not only to a tiger but to any large, wild, ferocious cat.

What the anvil? what dread grasp   15
Dare its deadly terrors clasp?

When the stars threw down their spears,
And water'd heaven with their tears,
Did he smile his work to see?
Did he who made the Lamb make thee?   20

Tyger! Tyger! burning bright
In the forests of the night,
What immortal hand or eye
Dare frame thy fearful symmetry?

QUESTIONS

1. What do the associations of the image of "burning" suggest? Why is the burning done at night rather than day? What does night suggest?

2. Describe the kinesthetic images of lines 5–20. What ideas is Blake's speaker representing by these images? What attributes does the speaker suggest may belong to the blacksmith-type initiator of these actions?

3. Line 20 presents the kinesthetic image of a creator. What is implied about the mixture of good and evil in the world? What answer does the poem offer? Why does Blake phrase this line as a question rather than an assertion?

4. The sixth stanza repeats the first stanza with only one change of imagery of action. Contrast these stanzas, stressing the difference between "could" (line 4) and "dare" (24).

ELIZABETH BARRETT BROWNING (1806–1861)

Sonnets from the Portuguese: Number 14 ⤛⤜⤝⤞   1850

If thou must love me, let it be for nought
Except for love's sake only. Do not say
"I love her for her smile—her look—her way
Of speaking gently—for a trick of thought
That falls in well with mine, and certes° brought   *certainly*   5
A sense of pleasant ease on such a day"—
For these things in themselves, Belovèd, may
Be changed, or change for thee,— and love, so wrought,°   *created*
May be unwrought so. Neither love me for
Thine own dear pity's wiping my cheeks dry,—   10
A creature might forget to weep, who bore
Thy comfort long, and lose thy love thereby!
But love me for love's sake, that evermore
Thou mayst love on, through love's eternity.

QUESTIONS

1. Who is the speaker of this poem? Why might you conclude that the speaker is female?

2. What images does the speaker use to indicate possible causes for loving? What kinds of images are they? How does the speaker explain why they should be rejected?

3. How does the idea of lines 1, 13, and 14 build upon the ideas in the rest of the poem?

SAMUEL TAYLOR COLERIDGE (1772–1834)

Kubla Khan   1816

In Xanadu did Kubla Khan
A stately pleasure dome decree:
Where Alph,° the sacred river, ran
Through caverns measureless to man
   Down to a sunless sea.   5
So twice five miles of fertile ground
With walls and towers were girdled round:
And there were gardens bright with sinuous rills,
Where blossomed many an incense-bearing tree;
And here were forest ancient as the hills,   10
Enfolding sunny spots of greenery.

But oh! that deep romantic chasm which slanted
Down the green hill athwart a cedarn cover!
A savage place! as holy and enchanted
As e'er beneath a waning moon was haunted   15
By woman wailing for her demon lover!
And from this chasm, with ceaseless turmoil seething,
As if this earth in fast thick pants were breathing,
A mighty fountain momently was forced:
Amid whose swift half-intermitted burst   20
Huge fragments vaulted like rebounding hail,
Or chaffy grain beneath the thresher's flail:
And 'mid these dancing rocks at once and ever
It flung up momently the sacred river.
Five miles meandering with a mazy motion   25
Through wood and dale the sacred river ran,
Then reached the caverns measureless to man,
And sank in tumult to a lifeless ocean:
And 'mid this tumult Kubla heard from far
Ancestral voices prophesying war!   30
The shadow of the dome of pleasure

KUBLA KHAN. 3 *Alph:* possibly a reference to the river Alpheus in Greece, as described by the ancient writers Virgil and Pausanias.

Floated midway on the waves;
Where was heard the mingled measure
From the fountain and the caves.
It was a miracle of rare device,
A sunny pleasure dome with caves of ice!   35

    A damsel with a dulcimer
    In a vision once I saw:
    It was an Abyssinian maid,
    And on her dulcimer she played   40
    Singing of Mount Abora.°
Could I revive within me
Her symphony and song,
To such a deep delight 'twould win me,
That with music loud and long,   45
I would build that dome in air,
That sunny dome! those caves of ice!
And all who heard should see them there,
And all should cry, Beware! Beware!
His flashing eyes, his floating hair!   50
Weave a circle round him thrice,
And close your eyes with holy dread,
For he on honeydew hath fed,
And drunk the milk of Paradise.

41 *Mount Abora:* a mountain of Coleridge's imagination. But see John Milton's *Paradise Lost*, IV. 268–284.

QUESTIONS

1. How many of the poem's images might be sketched or visualized? Which ones would be panoramic landscapes? Which might be close-ups?

2. What is the effect of auditory images such as "wailing," "fast thick pants," "tumult," "ancestral voices prophesying war," and "mingled measure"?

3. When Coleridge was writing this poem, he was recalling it from a dream. At line 54 he was interrupted, and when he resumed he could write no more. How might an argument be made that the poem is finished?

4. How do lines 35–36 establish the pleasure dome as a place of mysterious oddity? What is the effect of the words "miracle" and "rare"? The effect of combining the images "sunny" and "caves of ice"?

5. Why does the speaker yearn for the power of the singing Abyssinian maid? What kinesthetic images end the poem? How are these images important in the speaker's desire to reconstruct the vision of the pleasure dome?

RAY DUREM (1915–1963)

I Know I'm Not Sufficiently Obscure ⸻ 1962

I know I'm not sufficiently obscure
to please the critics—nor devious enough.
Imagery escapes me.

I cannot find those mild and gracious words
To clothe the carnage.   5
Blood is blood and murder's murder.
What's a lavender word for lynch?
Come, you pale poets, wan, refined and dreamy:
Here is a black woman working out her guts
in a white man's kitchen   10
for little money and no glory.
How should I tell that story?
There is a black boy, blacker still from death,
face down in the cold Korean mud.
Come on with your effervescent jive   15
explain to him why he ain't alive.
Reword our specific discontent
into some plaintive melody,
a little whine, a little whimper,
not too much—and no rebellion!   20
God, no! Rebellion's much too corny.
You deal with finer feelings,
very subtle—an autumn leaf
hanging from a tree—I see a body!

QUESTIONS

1. Who is the "you" listener addressed by the speaker (lines 8, 15, 22)? Why does the speaker admit that he is "not sufficiently obscure"? What issue is he dealing with by this admission?

2. In line 3 the speaker says, "Imagery escapes me." How does the rest of the poem contradict this statement?

3. Consider the images in lines 7, 13, and 23–24. To what degree are these images timely? Dated?

T. S. ELIOT (1888–1965)

Introductory performance

Preludes ~~~~~~ 1910

I

The winter evening settles down
With smell of steaks in passageways.
Six o'clock.
The burnt-out ends of smoky days.   *Street*
And now a gusty shower wraps   5
The grimy scraps
Of withered leaves about your feet
And newspapers from vacant lots;
The showers beat
On broken blinds and chimney-pots,   10
And at the corner of the street

A lonely cab-horse steams and stamps.
And then the lighting of the lamps.

II

The morning comes to consciousness
Of faint stale smells of beer   15
From the sawdust-trampled street
With all its muddy feet that press
To early coffee-stands.
With the other masquerades
That time resumes,   20
One thinks of all the hands
That are raising dingy shades
In a thousand furnished rooms.

III

You tossed a blanket from the bed,
You lay upon your back, and waited;
You dozed, and watched the night revealing   25
The thousand sordid images
Of which your soul was constituted;
They flickered against the ceiling.
And when all the world came back
And the light crept up between the shutters   30
And you heard the sparrows in the gutters,
You had such a vision of the street,
As the street hardly understands;
Sitting along the bed's edge, where   35
You curled the papers from your hair,
Or clasped the yellow soles of feet
In the palms of both soiled hands.

IV

His soul stretched tight across the skies
That fade behind a city block,   40
Or trampled by insistent feet
At four and five and six o'clock;
And short square fingers stuffing pipes,
And evening newspapers, and eyes
Assured of certain certainties,   45
The conscience of a blackened street
Impatient to assume the world.

I am moved by fancies that are curled
Around these images, and cling:
The notion of some infinitely gentle   50
Infinitely suffering thing.

Wipe your hand across your mouth, and laugh;
The worlds revolve like ancient women
Gathering fuel in vacant lots.

QUESTIONS

1. From what locations are the images in the first stanza derived? How do the images shift in the second stanza? What is the connection between the images in the second and third stanzas?

2. Who is the "you" in the third stanza? What images are associated with this listener?

3. Who is the "His" of the fourth stanza? How do the images develop in this stanza? What is meant particularly in the images of lines 46–47?

4. What is the nature of the <u>bodily imagery</u> in the poem? The urban imagery? What impressions do these images cause?

5. In lines 48–51, what does the speaker conclude? How do the last two unnumbered stanzas constitute a contrast of attitude?

SUSAN GRIFFIN (b. 1943)

Love Should Grow Up Like a Wild Iris in the Fields   1972

Love should grow up like a wild iris in the fields,
unexpected, after a terrible storm, opening a purple
mouth to the rain, with not a thought to the future,
ignorant of the grass and the graveyard of leaves
around, forgetting its own beginning. Love should   5
grow like a wild iris
but does not.
Love more often is to be found in kitchens at the dinner hour,
tired out and hungry, lingers over tables in houses where
the walls record movements; while the cook is probably angry,   10
and the ingredients of the meal are budgeted, while
a child cries feed me now and her mother not quite
hysterical says over and over, wait just a bit, just a bit.
Love should grow up in the fields like a wild iris
but never does   15
really startle anyone, was to be expected, was to be
predicted, is almost absurd, goes on from day to day, not quite
blindly, gets taken to the cleaners every fall, sings old
songs over and over, and falls on the same piece of rug that
never gets tacked down, gives up, wants to hide, is not   20
brave, knows too much, is not like an
iris growing wild but more like
staring into space
in the street
not quite sure   25
which door it was, annoyed about the sidewalk being
slippery, trying all the doors, thinking
if love wished the world to be well, it would be well.
Love should
grow up like a wild iris, but doesn't, it comes from   30
the midst of everything else, sees like the iris

of an eye, when the light is right,
feels in blindness and when there is nothing else is
tender, blinks, and opens
face up to the skies.   35

QUESTIONS

1. Contrast the locations of the images in the first seven lines and in the next eight. How do the ideas of the poet depend on this contrast in locations?

2. Note the difference in the mood of the verbs, from the "should" clause in the first six lines to the declarative present verb in line 7. Also, note the present tense verbs from lines 8–13, and then the "should" again in line 14. What is the effect of this differing use of verbs?

3. Trace the image of the wild iris throughout the poem. Why is the iris wild, and not cultivated? How does the iris grow? What is the effect of the change in the image of the iris from the flower to the eye (line 32)?

4. How is the sentence in lines 30–31 ("it comes from/the midst of everything else") related to the ideas and images in the rest of the poem?

THOMAS HARDY (1840–1928)   *For a photo, see p. 622.*

Channel Firing ⌣ ⌣ ⌣ ⌣ 1914

That night your great guns, unawares,
Shook all our coffins° as we lay,
And broke the chancel window-squares,
We thought it was the Judgment Day

And sat upright. While drearisome   5
Arose the howl of wakened hounds:
The mouse let fall the altar-crumb,
The worms drew back into the mounds,

The glebe° cow drooled. Till God called, "No;
It's gunnery practice out at sea   10
Just as before you went below;
The world is as it used to be:

"All nations striving strong to make
Red war yet redder. Mad as hatters
They do no more for Christés sake   15
Than you who are helpless in such matters.

"That this is not the judgment hour
For some of them's a blessed thing,
For if it were they'd have to scour
Hell's floor for so much threatening. . . .   20

CHANNEL FIRING. 2 *coffins:* It has been common practice in England for hundreds of years to bury people in the floors or basements of churches. 9 *glebe:* a parcel of land adjoining and belonging to a church. Cows were grazed there to keep the grass short.

"Ha, ha. It will be warmer when
I blow the trumpet (if indeed
I ever do; for you are men,
And rest eternal sorely need)."

So down we lay again. "I wonder,   25
Will the world ever saner be,"
Said one, "than when He sent us under
In our indifferent century!"

And many a skeleton shook his head.
"Instead of preaching forty year,"   30
My neighbor Parson Thirdly said,
"I wish I had stuck to pipes and beer."

Again the guns disturbed the hour,
Roaring their readiness to avenge,
As far inland as Stourton Tower,°   35
And Camelot,° and starlit Stonehenge.°

35 *Stourton Tower:* tower commemorating King Alfred the Great's defeat of the Danes in A.C.E. 879.
36 *Camelot:* legendary seat of King Arthur's court. *Stonehenge:* group of standing stones on Salisbury
Plain, probably built as a place of worship before 1000 B.C.E. Stonehenge today is one of England's most famous landmarks.

QUESTIONS

1. Who is the speaker in this poem? What is the setting? The situation?
2. To whom does the "your" in line 1 refer? The "our" in line 2?
3. What has awakened the speaker and his companions? What mistake have they
    made?
4. What three other voices are heard in the poem? How are their traits revealed?
5. What ideas about war and the nature of humanity does this poem explore?

GEORGE HERBERT (1593–1633)

The Pulley   1633

When God at first made man,
Having a glass of blessings standing by,
"Let us," said he, "pour on him all we can.
Let the world's riches, which dispersed lie,
    Contract into a span."°

So strength first made a way;   5
Then beauty flowed, then wisdom, honor, pleasure.
When almost all was out, God made a stay,
Perceiving that, alone of all his treasure,
    Rest° in the bottom lay.

THE PULLEY. 4 *into a span:* that is, within the control of human beings.   10 *rest:* (1) repose, security; (2) all
that remains.

"For if I should," said he,   10
"Bestow this jewel also on my creature,
    He would adore my gifts instead of me.
And rest in Nature, not the God of Nature;
        So both should losers be.

    "Yet let him keep the rest,   15
But keep them with repining restlessness.
    Let him be rich and weary, that at least,
If goodness lead him not, yet weariness
        May toss him to my breast."

QUESTIONS

1. Describe the dramatic scene of the poem. Who is doing what?
2. What are the particular "blessings" that God confers on humanity, according to
    the speaker? Why should these be considered blessings?
3. Consider the image of the pulley as the means, or device (through "repining
    restlessness"), by which God compels people to become worshipful.
4. Analyze and discuss the meaning of the kinetic images signified by the words
    "pour," "flowed," "rest," and "toss."

GERARD MANLEY HOPKINS (1844–1889)

Spring   1877

Nothing is so beautiful as Spring—
    When weeds, in wheels, shoot long and lovely and lush;
    Thrush's eggs look little low heavens, and thrush
Through the echoing timber does so rinse and wring
The ear, it strikes like lightnings to hear him sing;   5
    The glassy peartree leaves and blooms, they brush
    The descending blue; that blue is all in a rush
With richness; the racing lambs too have fair their fling.

What is all this juice and all this joy?
    A strain of the earth's sweet being in the beginning   10
In Eden garden.— Have, get, before it cloy,
    Before it cloud, Christ, lord, and sour with sinning,
Innocent mind and Mayday in girl and boy,
    Most, O maid's child, thy choice and worthy the winning.

QUESTIONS

1. What images does the speaker mention as support for his first line, "Nothing is
    so beautiful as Spring"? Are these images those that you would normally expect?
    To what degree do they seem to be new or unusual?

2. What images of motion and activity do you find in the poem? Are these mainly static or dynamic? What do these suggest about the speaker's view of spring?
3. What is the relationship between "Eden garden" in line 11 and the scene described in lines 1–8? To what extent are spring and "Innocent mind and May-day" a glimpse of the Garden of Eden?
4. Christ is mentioned in lines 12 and 14 (as "maid's child"). Do these references seal the poem off from readers who are not Christian? Why or why not?

DENISE LEVERTOV (1923–1997)   *For a photo, see p. 654.*

A Time Past ~~~~~ 1975

The old wooden steps to the front door
where I was sitting that fall morning
when you came downstairs, just awake,
and my joy at sight of you (emerging
into golden day—   5
                              the dew almost frost)
pulled me to my feet to tell you
how much I loved you:

those wooden steps
are gone now, decayed   10
replaced with granite,
hard, gray, and handsome.
The old steps live
only in me:
my feet and thighs   15
remember them, and my hands
still feel their splinters.
Everything else about and around that house
brings memories of others—of marriage,
of my son. And the steps do too: I recall   20
sitting there with my friend and her little son who died,
or was it the second one who lives and thrives?
And sitting there 'in my life,' often, alone or with my husband.
Yet that one instant,
your cheerful, unafraid, youthful, 'I love you too,'   25
the quiet broken by no bird, no cricket, gold leaves
spinning in silence down without
any breeze to blow them,
                              is what twines itself
in my head and body across those slabs of wood   30
that were warm, ancient, and now
wait somewhere to be burnt.

QUESTIONS

1. Describe the visual imagery of the poem. What tactile imagery is associated with the steps? What other images are part of the speaker's memory?

2. How is the image of the "old wooden steps" developed in the poem? What has happened to the wooden steps? What meaning may be derived from their having been replaced by the granite steps? How are these steps tied to the speaker's "time past"?

3. Why do you think the speaker expressly denies the recollection of any sounds of bird or cricket?

THOMAS LUX (b. 1946)

The Voice You Hear When You Read Silently　1997

THE VOICE YOU HEAR WHEN YOU READ SILENTLY
is not silent, it is a speaking-
out-loud voice in your head: it is *spoken*,
a voice is *saying* it
as you read. It's the writer's words,　　　　　　　　　　　　　　5
of course, in a literary sense
his or her "voice" but the sound
of that voice is the sound of *your* voice.
Not the sound your friends know
or the sound of a tape played back　　　　　　　　　　　　　10
but your voice
caught in the dark cathedral
of your skull, your voice heard
by an internal ear informed by internal abstracts
and what you know by feeling,　　　　　　　　　　　　　　15
having felt. It is your voice
saying, for example, the word "barn"
that the writer wrote
but the "barn" you say
is a barn you know or knew. The voice　　　　　　　　　　　20
in your head, speaking as you read,
never says anything neutrally—some people
hated the barn they knew,
some people love the barn they know
so you hear the word loaded　　　　　　　　　　　　　　25
and a sensory constellation
is lit: horse-gnawed stalls,
hayloft, black heat tape wrapping
a water pipe, a slippery
spilled *chirrr* of oats from a split sack,　　　　　　　　　30
the bony, filthy haunches of cows . . . .
And "barn" is only a noun—no verb
or subject has entered into the sentence yet!
The voice you hear when you read to yourself
is the clearest voice: you speak it　　　　　　　　　　　35
speaking to you.

QUESTIONS

1. What is meant by the "constellation" being lit when the reader reads a word, in this case "barn"? How does "constellation" explain the development of the barn image in lines 26–30?

2. Why is the "voice you hear when you read silently / . . . not silent"?

3. Describe the meaning and associations of "the dark cathedral / of your skull" in lines 11–12. What is particularly significant about the use of "cathedral" in these lines?

MICHEAL O'SIADHAIL (b. 1947)

Abundance ~~~~~ 1995

(for Marie)

To be there, childlike, when it happens.
Nothing I've ever earned or achieved.
Delight. Sudden quivers of abundance.

A whole glorious day with a friend.
Brunch. This honeyed bread. Talk.   5
All the time in the world to spend.

Those icy stings and a gladdened vein,
an autumn swim tingling my nape,
dousing pleasure on a sleepy brain.

Watching children on a bandstand floor;   10
some irrepressible urge to celebrate,
squealing, tramping, pleasing for more.

November birches with leaves of apricot,
After a long walk in the frosty air,
to warm our palms around a coffee-pot.   15

Waves and moments of energy released.
I hoard them. A child with sweets and cakes
chortles at prospects of a midnight feast.

So much is that might never have been.

QUESTIONS

1. Describe the images that the speaker equates with abundance. What is the location of these images? From the images, what idea about abundance does the speaker convey?

2. What types of images are developed in the poem? What tactile images does the speaker introduce? What gustatory images?

3. Why does the poet describe images of autumn scenes and activities, rather than images from spring days?

4. What is the meaning of the poem's last line? In what way does the line stem out of the preceding six stanzas?

P. K. PAGE (b. 1917)

Photos of a Salt Mine 1954

How innocent their lives look,
how like a child's
dream of caves and winter, both combined;
the steep descent to whiteness
and the stope°   5
with its striated walls
their folds all leaning as if pointing to
the greater whiteness still,
that great white bank
with its decisive front,   10
that seam upon a slope,
salt's lovely ice.

And wonderful underfoot the snow of salt
the fine
particles a broom could sweep,   15
one thinks
muckers might make angels in its drifts
as children do in snow,
lovers in sheets,
lie down and leave imprinted where they lay   20
a feathered creature holier than they.

And in the outworked stopes
with lamps and ropes
up miniature matterhorns
the miners climb   25
probe with their lights
the ancient folds of rock—
syncline and anticline°—
and scoop from darkness an Aladdin's cave:
rubies and opals glitter from its walls.   30

PHOTOS OF A SALT MINE. 5 *stope:* a mining excavation taking the form of huge steps.   27 *syncline and anticline:* A syncline is a U-shaped formation of rock strata; an anticline is a formation bending down from a high point.

But hoses douse the brilliance of these jewels,
melt fire to brine.
Salt's bitter water trickles thin and forms,
slow fathoms down,
a lake within a cave,   35
lacquered with jet—
white's opposite.
There grey on black the boating miners float
to mend the stays and struts of that old stope
and deeply underground   40
their words resound,
are multiplied by echo, swell and grow
and make a climate of a miner's voice.

So all the photographs like children's wishes
are filled with caves or winter,   45
innocence
has acted as a filter,
selected only beauty from the mine.
Except in the last picture,
it is shot   50
from an acute high angle. In a pit
figures the size of pins are strangely lit
and might be dancing but you know they're not.
Like Dante's vision of the nether hell
men struggle with the bright cold fires of salt,   55
locked in the black inferno of the rock:
the filter here, not innocence but guilt.

QUESTIONS

1. What "filter" conditions the images in the first 47 lines? What characterizes the images in this section of the poem?

2. What beauties does the poet bring out through such images? What impressions does she convey with images like "miniature matterhorns," "brilliance of these jewels," "lacquered with jet," and "striated walls"?

3. What "filter" conditions the images in the last nine lines? What significance should be placed on the "figures the size of pins" (line 51)? How do the images of "pit," "nether hell," and "black inferno" suggest the poet's view of the lives imposed on the people working in such a mine?

4. What images of motion and activity do you find in the poem? What ideas do these images convey?

EZRA POUND (1885–1972)

In a Station of the Metro°   1916

The apparition of these faces in the crowd;
Petals on a wet, black bough.

IN A STATION OF THE METRO. *Metro:* the Paris subway.

QUESTIONS

1. Is the image of the <u>wet</u>, <u>black</u> bough happy or sad? If the petals were on a tree in the sunlight, what would be the effect?
2. What is the meaning of the image suggested by "apparition"? Does it suggest a positive or negative view of human life?
3. This poem contains only two lines. Is it proper to consider it as a poem nevertheless? If it is not a poem, what is it?

[margin handwritten notes: "sad", "Ghost", "disembodied Soul"]

FRIEDRICH RÜCKERT (1788–1866)

If You Love for the Sake of Beauty *⌐⌐⌐⌐* *1823*

Anonymous Translator

If you love for the sake of beauty, O never love me!
Love the sun, which has bright golden hair.
If you love for the sake of youth, O never love me!
Love the spring, which is reborn each year.
If you love for the sake of wealth, O never love me!   5
Love the mermaid, whose pearls are rich and clear.
If you love for the sake of love alone, O yes then, love me!
Love me as I love you—forever!

QUESTIONS

1. What is the poem's situation? Who is speaking? Who is the listener?
2. How do the images in lines 2, 4, and 6 exemplify the abstract concepts in lines 1, 3, and 5? How does the speaker use these images to reinforce his or her negative requests?
3. How may the final two lines be considered a climax of the poem?

WILLIAM SHAKESPEARE (1564–1616)   *For a drawing, see p. 1306.*

Sonnet 130: My Mistress' Eyes Are Nothing Like the Sun *⌐⌐⌐⌐* *1609*

My mistress' eyes are nothing like the sun;
Coral is far more red than her lips' red;
If snow be white, why then her breasts are dun;
If hairs be wires, black wires grow on her head.
I have seen roses damasked,° red and white,   *set in an elaborate bouquet*   5
But no such roses see I in her cheeks;
And in some perfumes is there more delight
Than in the breath that from my mistress reeks.
I love to hear her speak, yet well I know

That music hath a far more pleasing sound; 10
I grant I never saw a goddess go;
My mistress, when she walks, treads on the ground.
And yet, by heaven, I think my love as rare
As any she belied with false compare.

QUESTIONS

1. To what does the speaker negatively compare his mistress's eyes? Lips? Breasts? Hair? Cheeks? Breath? Voice? Walk? What kinds of images are created in these negative comparisons?

2. What conventional images does this poem ridicule? What sort of poem is Shakespeare mocking by using the negative images in lines 1–12?

3. In the light of the last two lines, do you think the speaker intends the images as insults? If not as insults, how should they be taken?

4. Are most of the images auditory, olfactory, visual, or kinesthetic? Explain.

5. What point does this poem make about love poetry? About human relationships? How does the imagery contribute to the development of both points?

WRITING ABOUT IMAGERY

Questions for Discovering Ideas

In preparing to write, you should develop a set of thoughtful notes dealing with issues such as the following:

- What type or types of images prevail in the work? Visual (shapes, colors)? Auditory (sounds)? Olfactory (smells)? Tactile (touch and texture)? Gustatory (taste)? Kinetic or kinesthetic (motion)? Or is the imagery a combination?

- To what degree do the images reflect either the poet's actual observation or the poet's reading and knowledge of fields such as science or history?

- How well do the images stand out? How vivid are they? How does the poet make the images vivid?

- Within a group of images, say, visual or auditory, do the images pertain to one location or area rather than another (e.g., natural scenes rather than interiors, snowy scenes rather than grassy ones, loud and harsh sounds rather than quiet and soothing ones)?

- What explanation is needed for the images? (Images might be derived from the classics or the Bible, the Vietnam War or World War II, the behaviors of four-footed creatures or birds or fish, and so on.)

- What effect do the circumstances described in the poem (e.g., conditions of brightness or darkness, warmth or cold) have on your responses to the images? What purpose do you think the poet achieves by controlling these responses?

- How well are the images integrated within the poem's argument or development?

Answering questions like these will provide you with a sizable body of ready-made material that you can convert directly to your essay.

Strategies for Organizing Ideas

Connect a brief overview of the poem to your plan for the body of your essay, noting perhaps that the writer uses images to strengthen ideas about war, character, or love or that the writer relies predominantly on images of sight, sound, and action. You might deal with just one of the following aspects, or you may combine your approaches, as you wish.

1. IMAGES SUGGESTING IDEAS AND/OR MOODS. Such an essay should emphasize the effects of the imagery. What ideas or moods are evoked by the images? (The auditory images beginning Owen's "Anthem for Doomed Youth," for example, all point toward a condemnation of the brutality of war. The visual images in "Spring," by Hopkins, all point toward a sense of earthly and also divine growth and lushness.) Do the images promote approval or disapproval? Cheerfulness? Melancholy? Are the images drab, exciting, vivid? How? Why? Are they conducive to humor or surprise? How does the writer achieve these effects? Are the images consistent, or are they ambiguous? (The images in Masefield's "Cargoes" indicate first approval and then disapproval, with no ambiguity. By contrast, Shakespeare's images in "My Mistress' Eyes" might be construed as insults, but in context, they are really compliments.)

2. THE TYPES OF IMAGES. Here the emphasis is on the categories of images themselves. Is there a predominance of a particular type of image (e.g., visual or auditory), or is there a blending? Is there a bunching of types at particular points in the poem or story? If so, why? Is there any shifting as the work develops (for example, in Owen's "Anthem for Doomed Youth" the auditory images first suggest loudness and harshness, but later images describe quietness and sorrow)? Are the images appropriate, granted the nature and apparent intent of the work? Do they assist in making the ideas seem convincing? If any images seem inappropriate, is the inappropriateness intentional or inadvertent? What is the effect of the inappropriate imagery?

3. SYSTEMS OF IMAGES. Here the emphasis should be on the areas from which the images are drawn. This is another way of considering the appropriateness of the imagery: Is there a pattern of similar or consistent images, such as dark and dreary urban scenes (Eliot's "Preludes") or color and activity (Hopkins's "Spring")? Do all the images adhere consistently to a particular frame of reference, such as a sunlit garden (Lowell's "Patterns" [Chapter 25]), an extensive recreational forest and garden (Coleridge's "Kubla Khan"), a front stair (Levertov's "A Time Past"), or a forest at night (Blake's "The Tyger")? What is unusual or unique about the set of images? What unexpected or new responses do they produce?

Your conclusion, in addition to restating your major points, is the place for additional insights. It would not be proper to go too far in new directions here, but you might briefly take up one or more of the ideas that you have not developed in the body. In short, what have you learned from your study of imagery in the poem?

DEMONSTRATIVE STUDENT ESSAY

Imagery in T. S. Eliot's "Preludes"°

[1] T. S. Eliot's poem "Preludes" offers a series of generally depressing images of inhabitants of modern cities.* The first stanza sets the scene by describing a wet, wintry urban street scene. The second stanza moves indoors to describe the actions of the residents "in a thousand furnished rooms" (line 23). The third stanza zooms in even closer to focus on one particular "you" (lines 24-38). Then the fourth stanza expands outward again to the action on the street. This alternation of images from outside to inside and then back to outside follows Eliot's use of specific images to communicate his pessimistic ideas about modern urban life. Four types of images suggest Eliot's view that modern city dwellers are spiritually impoverished and that they suffer from a sense of meaningless and purposelessness.†

[2] Numerous images of the human body focus on the commonness and anti-heroism of most modern human beings. Eliot's speaker refers to "feet" four different times (lines 7, 17, 37, 41)--not the mind, not the soul, but the feet. In the third stanza, the soles of a woman's feet are described as "yellow" (line 37), a color not of health but of sickness. And throughout the poem these feet are not marching heroically to a stirring martial tune, nor do they carry runners to victory, dance brilliantly to happy music, walk purposefully with children in tow, or carry a political leader to a podium to deliver an important speech. No, these feet trudge through city streets as though they are just going through the motions: they "press" to "coffee-stands," presumably at lunch and break times (lines 17-18), and their only insistence occurs "At four and five and six o'clock" (line 42) when businesses close for the day and people are in a rush to leave their purposeless jobs and get home to their equally purposeless lives. The feet are also destructive, for they not only trample the sawdust in the street (line 16), but in the fourth stanza they might somehow be thought to be trampling on a soul (lines 39–41).

[3] Eliot's speaker zooms in on other specific parts of the body, too, including hands, fingers, eyes, and a mouth. The hands and fingers, like the feet, seem to be just going through the motions of raising shades or stuffing pipes (lines 21–22, 43). The eyes are "Assured of certain certainties" (line 45), a phrase which suggests that they focus only on the concrete and tangible world and avoid the consideration of faith and mystery. The mouth needs to be wiped (line 52) as though it is dirty--or perhaps foamy from beer. Such bodily images indicate that modern-day people are immersed in the physical world, and they also suggest that this focus amounts to a destructive anomie that is dulling their souls and robbing them of meaningful lives.

While the bodily images suggest modern antiheroism, comparable images of dirt and squalor indicate that the world of cities is soiled and impoverished. Tree leaves are not fresh and green, but they are fallen and have become "grimy scraps" (line 6), blown by the wind, together with the pages of discarded

---

°See p. 707 for this poem.
*Central idea.
†Thesis sentence.

newspapers of meaningless headlines and news articles (line 8). The urban streets are "muddy" (line 17) and the shades in people's homes are "dingy" (line 22). The hands of a woman described in the third stanza are "soiled" (line 38). People wake up in the morning to the "faint stale smells of beer" (line 15) from the previous night's binging. All these images indicate a lack of cleanliness, and others stem from deterioration and neglect: The window blinds are "broken" (line 10), and even the songs of sparrows come from "the gutters" (line 32). In this dirty, broken-down world, an individual soul is constituted, according to Eliot's speaker, of a "thousand sordid images" (line 27). Clearly, the lack of spiritual life is represented in the squalid physical world.

[4]

Not only is this world filthy and tawdry, it is also gloomy and unenlightened, and the city-dwellers' spiritual void is reflected in images of darkness. The first stanza begins in the darkness of an early winter evening (line 1), but even the relatively short days are described as "smoky" (line 4). Morning comes in the second and third stanzas, but in the third stanza the woman who rises from bed is disconcerted by the "thousand sordid images" (line 27) that have "flickered against the ceiling" during the night (line 29). The light of day has to creep "up between the shutters" (line 31), an image that suggests it is uninvited and unwelcome.

[5]

A final set of images suggests that, in addition to being dirty, cheap, and dark, this urban world--both natural and human--is one of spiritual bankruptcy and enervation. The poem is set in winter (line 1), a cold, lifeless, and colorless season when the leaves have fallen from the branches to be blown about aimlessly on the streets and sidewalks. Evenings are described as the "burnt-out ends of smoky days" (line 4)--an image suggesting that human effort, day by day, amounts to no more than a foul-smelling cigarette butt. Twice, Eliot's speaker mentions vacant lots (lines 8, 54), an image conveying the idea that the outside world consists of both emptiness and wasted space scattered with undifferentiated litter. Such images of disuse and depletion are consistent with the poem's emphasis on spiritual stagnation.

[6]

It would seem that these images present an unrelieved set of gloomy and hopeless images, but the poem also contains slight signs--glimmers--of something more positive. In lines 46 and 47 the speaker introduces the image of the "conscience of a blackened street" which is "Impatient to assume the world." These lines do not make up a complete sentence, but rather form a fragment, and therefore the potentially positive associations and implications are tentative and maybe even illusory. Even so, the word "conscience" suggests something spiritual that may survive and even emerge despite the image of the "blackened street" on which people live. In addition, in the final stanza, Eliot's speaker explains, "I am moved by fancies that are curled / Around these images, and cling" (48–49). Specifically, they put him in mind of "some infinitely gentle / Infinitely suffering thing" (50–51). Something better, then, may be present, and may be redemptive through infinite gentleness in the face of all the tawdriness of modern humanity. But the poet's final words are that his speaker has been given no more than a fleeting image of a better world, and so the poem's negative images prevail. All we can do, we are told, is to take what comes and not expect too much, for the world has always been like this, even from ancient times, revolving in its orbit while people go about their tasks of daily survival and drudgery.

[7]

WORK CITED

Eliot, T.S. "Preludes." Literature: An Introduction to Reading and Writing. Ed. Edgar V. Roberts and Henry E. Jacobs. 7th ed. Upper Saddle River: Prentice Hall, 2004. 707–708.

Commentary on the Essay

This essay illustrates the third strategy for writing about imagery (p. 720), referring to the various locations that make up sets of images developed by Eliot in "Preludes." This method permits the introduction of imagery drawn from identifiable visual classes, specifically, negative images of the human bodyand negative images of street life and the time of day. The introductory paragraph of the essay presents the central idea that Eliot uses his images to lead to his gloomy view of modern urban life. The thesis sentence indicates that the essay will discuss four different types of images.

Paragraphs 2, 3, and 4 form a connected group stressing Eliot's use of images which focus on various parts of the human body. In particular, paragraph 2 uses the words "sickness," "trudge," "purposeles," and "destructive" to characterize the negative mental pictures prompted by the images. Although the paragraph indicates downside responses to the images, it does not go beyond the limits of the images themselves. The idea is that Eliot invites these responses.

Paragraph 5 stresses a second type of image in the poem, namely, images that refer to darkness and connect it to the psychological darkness and sordidness of individuals inhabiting the modern city.

The sixth paragraph demonstrates an additional class of image that denotes a whittling away of the human spirit. Here the images of winter, deciduous leaf fall, evening, and vacant lots are cited for the ways in which they cumulatively bring out this impression. The last paragraph deals with the images and thoughts about redemption brought out in the poem. The idea of the paragraph is that the images are so fleeting that they do not counterbalance the prevailing negative images of the rest of the poem.

Special Topics for Writing and Argument about Imagery in Poetry

1. Compare the images of war in Owen's "Anthem for Doomed Youth" and Hardy's "Channel Firing." Describe the differing effects of the images. How are the images used? How effectively do these images aid in the development of the attitudes toward war expressed in each poem?

2. Basing your work on the poems in this chapter by Blake, Coleridge, Griffin, Hopkins, and O'Siadhail, write an essay discussing the poetic use of images drawn from the natural world. What sorts of references do the poets make? What attitudes do they express about the details they select? What is the relationship

between the images and religious views? What judgments about topics such as Nature, God, humanity, and friendship do the poets show by their images?

3. Considering the imagery of Eliot's "Preludes," write an essay explaining the power of imagery. As you develop your thoughts, be sure to consider the dramatic nature of Eliot's images and to account for the impressions and ideas that they create. You may also wish to introduce references to images from other poems that are relevant to your points.

4. Write a comparison of the imagery in Elizabeth Browning's "If Thou Must Love Me" and Rückert's "If You Love for the Sake of Beauty." Even though the poems are on virtually identical subjects, how does the selection of images contribute toward making each poem distinct?

5. Write a poem describing one of these:
   a. Athletes who have just completed an exhausting run.
   b. Children getting out of school for the day.
   c. Your recollection of having been lost as a child.
   d. A cat that always sits down right on your schoolwork.
   e. A particularly good meal you had recently.
   f. The best concert you ever attended.
   g. Driving to work or school on a rainy or snowy day.

   Then, write an analysis of the images you selected for your poem, and explain your choices. What details stand out in your mind? What do you recall best—sight, smell, sound, action? What is the relationship between your images and the ideas you express in your poem?

6. Study the reproduction of Herkomer's painting *Hard Times* (p. 697). Then write an essay comparing and contrasting the artistic techniques with Hopkins's poem "Spring" and Pound's "In a Station of the Metro," along with other poems that you may wish to include. What similarities and differences do you find in subject matter, treatment, arrangement, and general idea? On the basis of your comparison, what relationships do you perceive between poetic and painterly technique?

7. Use the retrieval system (computer or card catalogue) in your library to research the topic of imagery in Shakespeare (see *imagery* or *style and imagery*). How many titles do you find? Over how many years have these works been published? Take one of the books out, and write a brief report on one of the chapters. What topics are discussed? What types of imagery are introduced? What relationship does the author make between imagery and content?

Figures of Speech, or Metaphorical Language: *A Source of Depth and Range in Poetry*

Figures of speech, metaphorical language, figurative language, figurative devices, and **rhetorical figures** are terms describing organized patterns of comparison that deepen, broaden, extend, illuminate, and emphasize meaning. First and foremost, the use of figures of speech is a major characteristic by which great literature provides us with fresh and original ways of thinking, feeling, and understanding. Although figurative language is sometimes called "ornate," as though it were unnecessarily decorative, it is not uncommon in conversational speech, and it is essential in literary thought and expression. Unlike the writing of the social and "hard" sciences, imaginative literature does not purport to be direct and absolute, offering a direct correspondence of words and things. Yes, literature presents specific and accurate descriptions and explanations, but it also moves in areas of implication and suggestiveness through the use of figurative language, which enables writers to amplify their ideas while still employing relatively small numbers of words. Such language is therefore a sine qua non in imaginative literature, particularly poetry, where it compresses thought, deepens understanding, and shapes response.

    The two most important figures of speech, and the most easily recognized, are metaphors and similes. There are also many other metaphorical figures, some of which are paradox, anaphora, apostrophe, personification, synecdoche and metonymy, pun (or paronomasia), synesthesia, overstatement, and understatement. All these figures are modes of comparison, and they may be expressed in single words, phrases, clauses, or entire structures.

indispensable Condition or qualification

METAPHORS AND SIMILES: THE MAJOR FIGURES OF SPEECH

A Metaphor Shows That Something Unknown Is Identical to Something Known

A **metaphor** (a "carrying out a change") equates known objects or actions with something that is unknown or to be explained (e.g., "Your words are music to my ears," "You are the sunshine of my life," "My life is a squirrel cage"). The equation of the metaphor not only explains and illuminates the thing—let us choose Judith Minty's concept of marital inseparability in "Conjoined"— but also offers distinctive and original and often startling ways of seeing it and thinking about it. Thus Minty draws her metaphor of a married couple from the joining of two onions under one onion skin. Here the metaphor is unique and surprising, and yet on examination it is right and natural, and even somewhat comic.

Metaphors are inseparable from language. In a heavy storm, for example, trees may be said to bow constantly as the wind blows against them. *Bow* is a metaphor because the word usually refers to performers' bending forward to acknowledge the applause of an audience and to indicate their gratitude for the audience's approval. The metaphor therefore asks us to equate our knowledge of theater life (something known) to a weather occurrence (something to be explained). A comparable reference to theater life creates one of the best-known metaphors to appear in Shakespeare's plays: "All the world's a stage, / And all the men and women merely players." Here, Shakespeare's character Jacques (JAY-queez) from Act 2, scene 7 of *As You Like It*, identifies human life exactly with stage life. In other words, the things said and done by stage actors are also said and done by living people in real life. It is important to recognize that Shakespeare's metaphor does not state that the world is *like* a stage but that it literally *is* a stage.

A Simile Shows That Something Unknown Is Similar to Something Known

A **simile** (a "showing of likeness or resemblance") illustrates the similarity or comparability of the known to something unknown or to be explained. Whereas a metaphor merges identities, a simile focuses on resemblances (e.g., "Your words are like music to me," "You are like sunshine in my life," "I feel like a squirrel in a cage"). Similes are distinguishable from metaphors because they are introduced by *like* with nouns and *as* (also *as if* and *as though*) with clauses. If Minty had written that a married couple is like "The onion in my cupboard," her comparison would have been a simile.

Let us consider one of the best-known similes in poetry, from "A Valediction: Forbidding Mourning" by the seventeenth-century poet John Donne. This is a dramatic poem spoken by a lover about to go on a trip. His loved one is sorrowful, and he attempts to console her by claiming that even when he is gone, he will remain with her in spirit. The following stanza contains the famous simile embodying this idea.

> Our two souls therefore, which are one,
> Though I must go, endure not yet
> A breach,° but an expansion   *break, separation*
> Like gold to airy thinness beat.

The simile compares the souls of the speaker and his loved one to gold, a metal both valuable and malleable. By the simile, the speaker asserts that the impending departure will not be a separation but rather a thinning out, so that the relationship of the lovers will remain constant and rich even as the distance between them increases. Because the comparison is introduced by *like*, the emphasis of the figurative language is on the similarity of the lovers' love to gold (which is always gold even when it is thinned out by the goldsmith's hammer), not on the identification of the two.

CHARACTERISTICS OF METAPHORICAL LANGUAGE

In Chapter 16, we saw that imagery stimulates the imagination and recalls memories (images) of sights, sounds, tastes, smells, sensations of touch, and motions. Metaphors and similes go beyond literal imagery to introduce perceptions and comparisons that can be unusual, unpredictable, and surprising, as in Donne's simile comparing the lovers' relationship to gold. The comparison emphasizes the bond between the two lovers; the reference to gold shows how valuable the bond is; the unusual and original comparison is one of the elements that make the poem striking and memorable.

To see metaphorical language in further operation, let us take a commonly described condition—happiness. In everyday speech, we might use the sentence "She was happy" to state that a particular character was experiencing joy and excitement. The sentence is of course accurate, but it is not interesting. A more vivid way of saying the same thing is to use an image of action, such as "She jumped for joy." But another and better way of communicating joy is the following simile: "She felt as if she had just won the lottery." Because readers easily understand the disbelief, excitement, exhilaration, and delight that such an event would bring, they also understand—and feel—the character's happiness. It is the simile that evokes this perception and enables each reader to personalize the experience, for no simple description could help a reader comprehend the same degree of emotion.

As a parallel poetic example, let us look at John Keats's sonnet "On First Looking into Chapman's Homer," which Keats wrote soon after reading the translation of Homer's great epics *The Iliad* and *The Odyssey* by the Renaissance poet George Chapman. Keats, one of the greatest of all poets himself, describes his enthusiasm about Chapman's successful and exciting work.

JOHN KEATS (1795–1821) *Tenor is the* [handwritten]

On First Looking into Chapman's Homer° 1816·

Much have I travell'd in the realms of gold°   *the world of great art*
   And many goodly states and kingdoms seen:
   Round many western islands° have I been   *ancient literature*
Which bards in fealty to Apollo° hold.
Oft of one wide expanse° had I been told   *epic poetry*   5
   That deep-brow'd Homer ruled as his demesne°;   *realm, estate*
   Yet did I never breathe its pure serene°
Till I heard Chapman speak out loud and bold:
Then felt I like some watcher of the skies
   When a new planet swims into his ken°   *range of vision*   10
Or like stout Cortez° when with eagle eyes
   He star'd at the Pacific—and all his men
Look'd at each other with a wild surmise°—   *conjecture, supposition*
   Silent, upon a peak in Darien.

[handwritten margin notes: "used Vehicle is description of astronomical and geographical discovery"]

ON FIRST LOOKING INTO CHAPMAN'S HOMER. George Chapman (c. 1560–1634) published his translations of Homer's *Iliad* in 1612 and *Odyssey* in 1614–15. 4 *bards . . . Apollo*: writers who are sworn subjects of Apollo, the Greek god of light, music, poetry, prophecy, and the sun. 7 *serene*: a clear expanse of air; also grandeur, clarity; rulers were also sometimes called "serene majesty." 11 *Cortez*: Hernando Cortès (1485–1547), a Spanish general and the conqueror of Mexico. Keats confuses him with Vasco de Balboa (c. 1475–1519), the first European to see the Pacific Ocean (in 1510) from Darien, an early name for the Isthmus of Panama.

As a first step in understanding the power of metaphorical language, we can briefly paraphrase the sonnet's content.

> I have enjoyed much art and read much poetry, and I have been told that Homer is the best writer of all. However, I did not appreciate his works until I first read them in Chapman's clear and forceful translation. This discovery was exciting and awe-inspiring.

If all Keats had written had been a paragraph like this one, we would pay little attention to it, for it conveys no excitement or wonder. But the last six lines of the sonnet contain two memorable similes ("like some watcher of the skies" and "like stout Cortez") that stand out and demand a special effort of imagination. To appreciate these similes fully, we need to imagine what it would be like to be an astronomer as he or she discovers a previously unknown planet, and what it would have been like to be one of the first European explorers to see the Pacific Ocean. As we imagine ourselves in these roles, we get a sense of the amazement, excitement, exhilaration, and joy that would accompany such discoveries. With that experience comes the realization that the world—the universe—is far bigger and more astonishing than we had ever dreamed. Metaphorical language therefore makes strong demands on our creative imaginations. It bears repeating that as we develop our own mental pictures under the stimulation of metaphors and similes, we also develop appropriately associated attitudes and feelings. Let us consider once more Keats's metaphor "realms of gold," which invites us both to imagine brilliant and shining kingdoms and also to join Keats in valuing and loving not

just poetry but all literature. The metaphorical "realms of gold" act upon our minds, liberating our imaginations, directing our understanding, and evoking our feelings. In such a way, reading and responding to the works of writers like Keats produces both mental and emotional experiences that were previously hidden to us. Poets constantly give us something new, and they increase our power to think and know. They enlarge us.

VEHICLE AND TENOR

To describe the relationship between a writer's ideas and the metaphors and similes chosen to objectify them, two useful terms have been coined by I. A. Richards (in *The Philosophy of Rhetoric* [1929]). First is the **vehicle**, or the specific words of the metaphor or simile. Second is the **tenor,** which is the totality of ideas and attitudes not only of the literary speaker but also of the author. For example, the tenor of Donne's simile in "A Valediction: Forbidding Mourning" is the inseparable love and unbreakable connection of the two lovers; the vehicle is the hammering of gold "to airy thinness." Similarly, the tenor of the similes in the sestet of Keats's sonnet "On First Looking into Chapman's Homer" is awe and wonder; the vehicle is the description of astronomical and geographical discovery.

OTHER FIGURES OF SPEECH

A Paradox Uses an Apparent Error or Contradiction to Reveal Truth

A **paradox** is "a thought beyond a thought," a figurative device through which something apparently wrong or contradictory is shown to be truthful and non-contradictory. The phrase "I, a child, very old" in Whitman's "Facing West from California's Shores" is a paradox. The obvious contradiction is that no one can be old and young at the same time, but this contradiction can be reconciled if we realize that even as people get older they still retain many of the qualities of children (such as enthusiasm and hope). Thus Whitman's contradiction is not contradictory (is this clause a paradox?) and the speaker may genuinely be "a child, very old." The second line of Sir Thomas Wyatt's sonnet "I Find No Peace" embodies two paradoxes. One opposes fear with hope, the other fire with ice: "I fear and hope, I burn and freeze like ice." These paradoxes genuinely reflect the contradictory states of people in love—wanting love ("hope," "burn") but also being uncertain and unsure about the relationship ("fear," "freeze"). The paradoxes thus highlight the truth that love is a complex and sometimes unsettling emotion.

Anaphora Provides Weight and Emphasis Through Repetition

Anaphora ("to carry again or repeat") is the repetition of the same word or phrase throughout a work or a section of a work in order to lend weight and emphasis. An example occurs in Blake's "The Tyger" (Chapter 16), when the interrogative word *what is* used five times to emphasize the mystery of evil (italics added).

What the hammer? *what* the chain?
In *what* furnace was thy brain?
What the anvil? *what* dread grasp
Dare its deadly terrors clasp?

Anaphora is the most obvious feature of Muriel Rukeyser's "Looking at Each Other," where the word *yes* begins each of the poem's twenty-five lines.

Apostrophe Creates the Drama of a Speaker Addressing an Audience

In an apostrophe (a "turning away," or redirection of attention) a speaker addresses a real or imagined listener who is not present. It is like a public speech, with readers as audience, and it therefore makes a poem dramatic. An apostrophe enables the speaker to develop ideas that might arise naturally on a public occasion, as in Wordsworth's sonnet "London, 1802," which is addressed to the long-dead English poet Milton. In the following sonnet by Keats, "Bright Star," the speaker addresses a distant and inanimate star, yet through apostrophe he proceeds as though the star has human understanding and divine power.

JOHN KEATS (1795–1821)   *For a drawing, see p. 728.*

Bright Star   1838 (1819)

Bright star! would I were steadfast as thou art—
  Not in lone splendor hung aloft the night,
And watching, with eternal lids apart,
  Like Nature's patient, sleepless eremite,°   hermit
The moving waters at their priestlike task
  Of pure ablution round earth's human shores,   5
Or gazing on the new soft-fallen mask
  Of snow upon the mountains and the moors;
No—yet still steadfast, still unchangeable,
  Pillowed upon my fair love's ripening breast,
To feel forever its soft fall and swell,   10
  Awake forever in a sweet unrest,
    Still, still to hear her tender-taken breath,
    And so live ever—or else swoon to death.

QUESTIONS

1. With what topic is the speaker concerned in this sonnet? How does he compare himself with the distant star?

2. What qualities does the speaker attribute specifically to the star? What role does he seem to assign to it? In light of this role, and the qualities needed to serve in it, how might the star be compared to a divine and benign presence?

3. In light of the emphasis on the words "forever" and "ever" in lines 11–14, how appropriate is the choice of the star as the subject of the apostrophe in the poem?

In this sonnet the speaker addresses the star as though it is a person or god, an object of adoration, and the poem is therefore like a petitional prayer. The star is idealized with qualities that the speaker wishes to establish in himself,

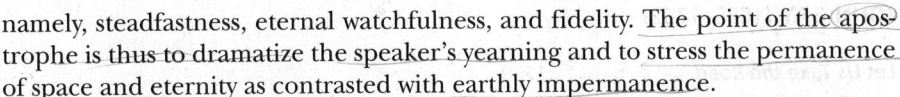

namely, steadfastness, eternal watchfulness, and fidelity. The point of the apostrophe is thus to dramatize the speaker's yearning and to stress the permanence of space and eternity as contrasted with earthly impermanence.

Personification Is the Attribution of Human Traits to Abstractions or to Nonhuman Objects

A close neighbor of apostrophe is **personification,** another dramatic figurative device through which poets explore relationships to environment, ideals, and inner lives. In "Bright Star," as we have just seen, Keats personifies the star addressed by the speaker. Shakespeare's speaker in Sonnet 146, "Poor Soul, the Center of My Sinful Earth" (Chapter 25), personifies his own soul as he speaks of earthly and heavenly concerns. Other important uses of personification are seen in Shelley's "Ode to the West Wind" (Chapter 19) and also in Keats's "To Autumn" (Chapter 17) and "Ode on a Grecian Urn" (Chapter 23).

Synecdoche and Metonymy Transfer Meanings by Parts and Associations

These figures are close in purpose and effect. **Synecdoche** ("taking one thing out of another") is a device in which a part stands for the whole or a whole for a part, like the expression "all hands aboard," which describes the whole of a ship's crew by their hands, that part of them that performs work. **Metonymy** (a "transfer of name") substitutes one thing for another with which it is closely identified, as when "Hollywood" is used to mean the movie industry, or when "the White House" signifies the policies and activities of the U.S. president. The purpose of both figures of speech is the creation of new insights and ideas, just like metaphors and similes.

Synecdoche is seen in Keats's "To Autumn," where the gourd and hazel shells, which are single instances of ripe produce, stand for the entire autumnal harvest. In Wordsworth's "London, 1802," the phrase "thy heart" (line 13) is a synecdoche in which a part—the heart—refers to the complete person. Metonymy is seen again in Keats's "To Autumn," when the "granary floor" (line 14), the place where grain is stored, bears the transferred meaning of the entire autumnal harvest.

Pun, or Paronomasia, Shows That Words with Similar or Identical Sounds Have Different Meanings

A pun ("a point or a puncture") or paronomasia ("something beside a name") is wordplay stemming from the fact that words with different meanings have surprisingly similar or even identical sounds and that some individual words have surprisingly differing and even contradictory meanings. Because puns are sometimes considered outrageous and often require a little bit of thinking, people may groan when they hear them (even while they enjoy them). Also, because many puns seem to play only with sound, they have not always enjoyed critical acclaim. Good puns can always be relished because they work with sounds to reveal ideas. John Gay, for example, creates clever puns in the following song, sung chorally by the gang of thieves in *The Beggar's Opera* (1728), a play which, incidentally, marked the beginning of the modern musical comedy tradition.

JOHN GAY (1685–1732)

Let Us Take the Road   1728

Let us take the road.
  Hark! I hear the sound of coaches!
  The hour of attack approaches,
To your arms, brave boys, and load.
    See the ball I hold! [*holding up a bullet*]   5
  Let the chemists° toil like asses,   *alchemists*
  Our fire their fire surpasses,°   *Our [gun]fire is better than their [forge] fire.*
  And turns all our lead to gold.

QUESTIONS

1. What traits are shown by the singers of this poem? Why do they not seem frightening, despite their admission that they are holdup men?

2. Describe the puns in the poem. What kind of knowledge is needed to explain them fully? How many puns are there? How are they connected? Why do the puns seem both witty and outrageous?

      Here "fire," "lead," and "gold" are puns. Lead was the "base" or "low" metal that the medieval alchemists ("chemists") tried to transform into ingots of gold, using the heat from their fires. The puns develop because the gang of cutthroats singing the song is about to go out to rob travelers at gunpoint. Hence their bullets are their lead, which they will transform into the gold coins they steal. Their fire is not the fire of alchemists, but rather pistol fire. Through these puns, Gay's villains charm us by their wit and delight in their villainy, even though in real life they would scare us to death.

Synesthesia Demonstrates the Oneness or Unity of Feelings

In **synesthesia** (the "bringing together of feelings") a poet describes a feeling or perception with words that usually refer to different or even opposite feelings or perceptions. Keats uses synesthesia extensively, as, for example, in the "Ode to a Nightingale" (Chapter 20), where a plot of ground is "melodious," a draught of wine tastes of "Dance, and Provençal song, and sunburnt mirth," and beaded bubbles of wine are "winking at the brim" of a glass.

Overstatement and Understatement Are Means of Creating Emphasis

Two important devices creating emphasis are overstatement (or hyperbole) and understatement. **Overstatement,** also called the overreacher, is exaggeration for effect. In "London, 1802," for example, Wordsworth declares that England "is a fen / Of stagnant waters." That is, the country and its people collectively make up a stinking, polluted marsh, a muddy dump. What Wordsworth establishes by this overstatement is his judgment that England in 1802 was so morally and politically rotten that it needed a writer like Milton to unite the people around noble ideas.

In contrast with overstatement, **understatement** is the deliberate underplaying or undervaluing of a thing. One of the most famous poetic understatements is in Marvell's "To His Coy Mistress" (Chapter 21).

The grave's a fine and private place,
But none, I think, do there embrace.

Here Marvell, through understatement, wittily and grimly emphasizes the eternity of death by contrasting the motionless privacy of the grave with the active privacy of a trysting place.

POEMS FOR STUDY

JACK AGÜEROS (b. 1934)

Sonnet for You, Familiar Famine ⤳⤳⤳ *1996*

Nobody's waiting for any apocalypse to meet you, Famine!

We know you. There isn't a corner of our round world
where you don't politely accompany someone to bed each
night. In some families, you're the only one sitting
at the table when the dinner bell tolls. "He's not so   5
bad," say people who have plenty and easily tolerate you.
They argue that small portions are good for us, and
are just what we deserve. There's an activist side to
you, Famine. You've been known to bring down governments,
yet you never get any credit for your political reforms.   10

Don't make the mistake I used to make of thinking fat
people are immune to Famine. Famine has this other ugly
side. Famine knows that the more you eat the more you
long. That side bears his other frightening name, Emptiness.

QUESTIONS

1. What figure of speech does the poet use in this poem? What situation does the poem address?

2. What is the purpose of using this figure for the poem rather than a more direct analysis of the causes and effects of hunger?

3. What powers does the speaker attribute to Famine? How correct is his assessment of these powers?

ROBERT BURNS (1759–1796)

For a drawing, see p. 645.

A Red, Red Rose ⤳⤳⤳ *1796*

O my Luve's like a red, red rose,
  That's newly sprung in June:
O my Luve's like the melodie
  That's sweetly play'd in tune.

As fair art thou, my bonnie lass,   5
  So deep in luve am I;
And I will luve thee still, my Dear,
  Till a'° the seas gang° dry.   *all; go*

Till a' the seas gang dry, my Dear,
  And the rocks melt wi'° the sun: *with*   10
And I will luve thee still, my Dear,
  While the sands o'° life shall run.   *of*

And fare thee weel, my only Luve!
  And fare thee weel, awhile!
And I will come again, my Luve,
  Tho' it were ten thousand mile!

QUESTIONS

1. In light of the character and background of the speaker, do the two opening similes seem common or unusual? If they are just ordinary, does that fact diminish their value? How and why?

2. Describe the shift of listener envisioned after the first stanza. How are the last three stanzas related to the first?

3. Consider the metaphors concerning time and travel. How do the metaphors assist you in comprehending the speaker's character?

JOHN DONNE (1572–1631)   *For a drawing, see p. 648.*
For a drawing, see p. 648.

A Valediction: Forbidding Mourning   1633

As virtuous men pass mildly away,
　And whisper to their souls to go,
Whilst some of their sad friends do say
　The breath goes now, and some say, No;

So let us melt, and make no noise,   5
　No tear-floods, nor sigh-tempests move,
'Twere profanation of our joys
　To tell the laity° our love.

Moving of th'earth° brings harm and fears,   *earthquakes*
　Men reckon what it did and meant: 10
But trepidation° of the spheres,
　Though greater far, is innocent.

Dull sublunary lovers' love
　(Whose soul is sense°) cannot admit
Absence, because it doth remove   15
　Those things which elemented it.

But we by a love so much refined
　That our selves know not what it is,
Inter-assured of the mind,
　Care less, eyes, lips, and hands to miss.   20

Our two souls therefore, which are one,
　Though I must go, endure not yet
A breach, but an expansion
　Like gold to airy thinness beat.°

A VALEDICTION: FORBIDDING MOURNING. 7, 8 *profanation . . . laity:* as though the lovers are priests of love, whose love is a mystery.   11 *trepidation:* Before Sir Isaac Newton explained the precession of the equinoxes, it was assumed that the positions of heavenly bodies should be constant and perfectly circular. The clearly observable irregularities (caused by the slow wobbling of the earth's axis) were explained by the concept of *trepidation,* or a trembling or oscillation that occurred in the outermost of the spheres surrounding the earth.   14 *soul is sense:* lovers whose attraction is totally physical.   24 *gold to airy thinness beat:* a reference to the malleability of gold.

If they be two, they are two so   25
   As stiff twin compasses° are two;
Thy soul, the fixt foot, makes no show
   To move, but doth, if th'other do.

And though it in the center sit,
   Yet when the other far doth roam,   30
It leans and harkens after it,
   And grows erect, as that comes home.

Such wilt thou be to me, who must
   Like th'other foot, obliquely run;
Thy firmness draws my circle just,°   35
   And makes me end where I begun.

26 *compasses:* a compass used for drawing circles.   35 *just:* perfectly round.

QUESTIONS

1.   What is the situation envisioned as the occasion for the poem? Who is talking to whom? What is their relationship?

2.   What is the intention of the first two stanzas? What is the effect of the phrases "tear-floods" and "sigh-tempests"?

3.   Describe the effect of the opening simile about men on their deathbeds.

4.   What is the metaphor of the third stanza (lines 9–12)? In what sense might the "trepidation of the spheres" be less harmful than the parting of the lovers?

5.   In lines 13–20 there is a comparison making the love of the speaker and his sweetheart superior to the love of average lovers. What is the basis for the speaker's claim?

6.   What is the comparison begun by the word "refined" in line 17 and continued by the simile in line 24?

ABBIE HUSTON EVANS (1881–1983)

The Iceberg Seven-eighths Under ⋗⟨⟨⟨⟨⟨⟩ 1961

Under the sky at night, stunned by our guesses,
We know incredibly much and incredibly little.
Wrapped in the envelope of gossamer air,
A clinging mote whirled round in a blizzard of stars,
A chaff-cloud of great suns that has not settled,   5
By the barn's black shoulder where the gibbous moon
Hangs low, no other light making a glimmer
In the dark country, hearing the breathing of cattle—
I do not need that anyone should tell me
Most real goes secret, sunken, nigh-submerged: 10
Yet does it dazzle with its least part showing,
Like the iceberg seven-eighths under.

QUESTIONS

1. How does the simile of the "iceberg seven-eighths under" explain the "Most real" that "goes secret"? In what way is this simile, together with line 11, an extension of the idea in line 2?

2. What metaphors does the poet use to describe the earth and the people ("We") on it?

3. Explain the contrast between the metaphors of night and darkness (lines 1, 6, 8) and the use of the word "dazzle" in line 11. How does the poem express awe about the visible universe?

THOMAS HARDY (1840–1928)   *For a photo, see p. 622.*

The Convergence of the Twain   ⤏⤏   1912

Lines on the Loss of the "Titanic"°

I

> In a solitude of the sea
> Deep from human vanity,
> And the Pride of Life that planned her, stilly couches she.

II

> Steel chambers, late the pyres
> Of her salamandrine fires,°   5
> Cold Currents thrid,° and turn to rhythmic tidal lyres.   *thread, instrumental strings*

III

> Over the mirrors meant
> To glass the opulent
> The sea-worm crawls—grotesque, slimed, dumb, indifferent.

IV

> Jewels in joy designed   10
> To ravish the sensuous mind
> Lie lightless, all their sparkles bleared and black and blind.

THE CONVERGENCE OF THE TWAIN. The *Titanic*, the largest passenger ship in existence at the time, and considered unsinkable, was sunk after a collision with an iceberg on its maiden voyage in April 1912. The loss was particularly notable because some of the passengers were among the world's social elite, and 1,500 people were lost because there were not enough lifeboats for everyone. In 1985 the wreck of the ship was discovered on the ocean floor 13,000 feet down, and some of the ship's artifacts have been re-covered. The loss of the *Titanic* has become legendary. 4–5 *Steel chambers . . . salamandrine fires* The idea here is that the "steel chambers" of the ship's furnaces were built to resist the high heat of the coal fires, much like the salamander of ancient myth, which could live through fire.

V

Dim moon-eyed fishes near
Gaze at the gilded gear
And query: "What does this vaingloriousness down here?"   15

VI

Well: while was fashioning
This creature of cleaving wing,
The Immanent Will that stirs and urges everything

VII

Prepared a sinister mate
For her—so gaily great—   20
A Shape of Ice, for the time far and dissociate.

VIII

And as the smart ship grew
In stature, grace, and hue,
In shadowy silent distance grew the Iceberg too.

IX

Alien they seemed to be: 25
No mortal eye could see
The intimate welding of their later history.

X

Or sign that they were bent
By paths coincident
On being anon twin halves of one august event.   30

XI

Till the Spinner of the Years
Said "Now!" And each one hears,
And consummation comes, and jars two hemispheres.

QUESTIONS

1. What human attributes does Hardy ascribe to the *Titanic?* What pronoun does
    he regularly use in reference to the ship? What is the name of this figure
    of speech?

2. What are the meanings of "vanity" (line 2), "Pride of Life" (line 3), and "vain-
    gloriousness" (line 15) in relation to the speaker's judgment of the meaning of
    the *Titanic?*

3. Why does Hardy introduce the phrases "Spinner of the Years" (line 31) and "Im-
    manent Will" (line 18)?

4. What is the idea of calling the iceberg the "sinister mate" of the *Titanic* (line 19)? What irony results from this phrase, and from the word "consummation" in line 33?

JOY HARJO (b. 1951)

For a photo, see p. 623.

Remember ⤳⤳⤳ 1983

Remember the sky that you were born under,
know each of the star's stories.
Remember the moon, know who she is. I met her
in a bar once in Iowa City.
Remember the sun's birth at dawn, that is the   5
strongest point of time. Remember sundown
and the giving away to night.
Remember your birth, how your mother struggled
to give you form and breath. You are evidence of
her life, and her mother's, and hers.   10
Remember your father. He is your life, also.
Remember the earth whose skin you are:
red earth, black earth, yellow earth, white earth
brown earth, we are earth.
Remember the plants, trees, animal life who all have their   15
tribes, their families, their histories, too. Talk to them,
listen to them. They are alive poems.
Remember the wind. Remember her voice. She knows the
origin of this universe. I heard her singing Kiowa war
dance songs at the corner of Fourth and Central once.   20
Remember that you are all people and that all people
are you.
Remember that you are this universe and that this
universe is you.
Remember that all is in motion, is growing, is you.   25
Remember that language comes from this.
Remember the dance that language is, that life is.
Remember.

QUESTIONS

1. How many times is the word "remember" repeated in this poem? What is the name of this figure of speech? What is the effect of the repetitions?

2. Who is the speaker, and who is the listener? What is the apparent purpose of stating all the things that the listener is being asked to remember? What is the implication of the word "remember," inasmuch as many of the things designated for remembrance happened before the listener was alive or was old enough to have a memory?

3. What is meant by "the earth whose skin you are" in line 12? Explain the paradox of "you are all people and . . . all people / are you" in lines 21–22.

LANGSTON HUGHES (1902–1967)

For a photo, see p. 1608.

Harlem   1951

What happens to a dream deferred?
Does it dry up
like a raisin in the sun?
Or fester like a sore—
And then run?
Does it stink like rotten meat?   5
Or crust and sugar over—
like a syrupy sweet?

Maybe it just sags
like a heavy load.   10

Or does it explode?

QUESTIONS

1. In the light of the black experience with the "American Dream," what do you
    think is meant by the phrase "dream deferred"?

2. Explain the structure of the poem in terms of the speaker's questions and an-
    swers. How is the structure here similar to the one in Blake's "The Tyger"
    (p. 703)?

3. Explain the similes in lines 3, 4, 6, 8, and 10. Why are these apt comparisons?
    What sorts of human actions are implied in these figures?

4. What is the meaning of the metaphor in line 11? Why do you think Hughes
    shifted from similes to a metaphor in this line?

JOHN KEATS (1795–1821)

For a drawing, see p. 728.

To Autumn   1820

Season of mists and mellow fruitfulness!
    Close bosom-friend of the maturing sun;
Conspiring with him to load and bless
    With fruit the vines that round the thatch-eaves run;
To bend with apples the mossed cottage-trees,   5
    And fill all fruit with ripeness to the core;
        To swell the gourd, and plump the hazel shells
With a sweet kernel; to set budding more,
    And still more, later flowers for the bees,
    Until they think warm days will never cease,   10
        For Summer has o'erbrimmed their clammy cells.

Who hath not seen thee oft amid thy store?
    Sometimes whoever seeks abroad may find
Thee sitting careless on a granary floor,
    Thy hair soft-lifted by the winnowing wind,   15
Or on a half-reaped furrow sound asleep,
Drowsed with the fume of poppies, while thy hook

Spares the next swath and all its twinèd flowers;
And sometimes like a gleaner thou dost keep
    Steady thy laden head across a brook;   20
    Or by a cider-press, with patient look,
    Thou watchest the last oozings hours by hours.

Where are the songs of Spring? Ay, where are they?
    Think not of them, thou hast thy music too,—
While barrèd clouds bloom the soft-dying day,   25
    And touch the stubble-plains with rosy hue;
Then in a wailful choir the small gnats mourn
    Among the river sallows, borne aloft
    Or sinking as the light wind lives or dies;
And full-grown lambs loud bleat from hilly bourn;   30
    Hedge-crickets sing; and now with treble soft
    The redbreast whistles from a garden-croft;
    And gathering swallows twitter in the skies.

QUESTIONS

1.   How is personification used in the first stanza? How does it change in the second? What is the effect of such personification?

2.   How does Keats structure the poem to accord with his apostrophe to autumn? That is, in what ways can the stanzas be distinguished by the type of discourse addressed to the season?

3.   Analyze Keats's metonymy in the first stanza and synecdoche in the second. What effects does he achieve with these devices?

4.   How, through the use of images, does Keats develop his idea that autumn is a season of "mellow fruitfulness"?

JANE KENYON (1947–1995)

Portrait of a Figure Near Water   ⤳   1996

Rebuked, she turned and ran
uphill to the barn. Anger, the inner
arsonist, held a match to her brain.
She observed her life: against her will
it survived the unwavering flame.   5

The barn was empty of animals.
Only a swallow tilted
near the beams, and bats
hung from the rafters
the roof sagged between.   10

Her breath became steady
where, years past, the farmer cooled
the big tin amphorae of milk.

The stone trough was still
filled with water: she watched it
and received its calm.   15

So it is when we retreat in anger
we think we burn alone
and there is no balm.
Then water enters, though it makes
no sound.   20

QUESTIONS

1.   What do you think has happened before the poem opens? What sort of rebuke
     has the woman received? What does it lead her to do?
2.   What is the effect of "tilted" (line 7), and why does the speaker draw attention to the
     roof sagging between the rafters (line 10)? Why does the writer call the large milk
     cans "amphorae" (line 13)? How do these word choices affect the poem's context?
3.   What is the metaphorical sense of anger as "the inner / arsonist" (lines 2–3)? In
     what way is the water in the stone trough for animals metaphorical? What
     metaphorical meanings should be attributed to water?

HENRY KING (1592–1669)

Sic Vita° ⤳⤳⤳ 1657

Like to the falling of a star,
Or as the flights of eagles are,
Or like the fresh spring's gaudy hue,
Or silver drops of morning dew,
Or like a wind that chafes the flood,
Or bubbles which on water stood: 5
Even such is man, whose borrowed light
Is straight called in, and paid to night.
  The wind blows out, the bubble dies;
  The spring entombed in autumn lies: 10
  The dew dries up, the star is shot;
  The flight is past, and man forgot.

SIC VITA (Latin). Such is life.

QUESTIONS

1.   How many similes do you find in lines 1–6? Describe the range of references;
     that is, from what sources are the similes derived? What do all these similes (and
     references) have in common?
2.   Explain the two metaphors in lines 7–8. (One is brought out by the words "bor-
     rowed," "called in," and "paid," the other by "light" and "night.")
3.   Explain the continuation in lines 9–12 of the similes in 1–6. Do you think that
     these last four lines are essential, or might the poem have been successfully con-
     cluded with line 8? Explain.
4.   What point does this poem make about humanity? In what ways do the similes in
     the poem help explore these ideas and bring them to life?

JUDITH MINTY (b. 1937)

Conjoined ✥ 1981

a marriage poem

The onion in my cupboard, a monster, actually
two joined under one transparent skin:
each half-round, then flat and deformed
where it pressed and grew against the other.

An accident, like the two-headed calf rooted   5
in one body, fighting to suck at its mother's teats;
or like those other freaks, Chang and Eng,° twins
joined at the chest by skin and muscle, doomed
to live, even make love, together for sixty years.

Do you feel the skin that binds us   10
together as we move, heavy in this house?
To sever the muscle could free one,
but might kill the other. Ah, but men
don't slice onions in the kitchen, seldom see
what is invisible. We cannot escape each other.   15

CONJOINED. 7 *Chang and Eng:* born in 1811, the original and most famous Siamese twins. Although they were never separated, they nevertheless fathered twenty-two children. They died in 1874.

QUESTIONS

1. What are the two things—the "us" and "we" of lines 10 and 11—that are conjoined? Since this is "a marriage poem," might they be the man and the woman? Why might they also be considered as the body and soul of the speaker; or the desire to be married and subordinated, on the one hand, and to be free and in control of destiny, on the other?

2. Explore the metaphor of the onion and the similes of the two-headed calf and the Siamese twins. Why do you think the poet introduces the words "monster," "accident," and "freaks" into these figures in lines 1, 5, and 7? In what sense do you believe that these words are applicable to the nature and plight of women?

3. Is it true that *all* "men / don't slice onions in the kitchen, seldom see / what is invisible"? Explain.

MARGE PIERCY (b. 1934)   *For a photo, see p. 683.*

A Work of Artifice ✥ 1973

The bonsai tree
in the attractive pot
could have grown eighty feet tall

on the side of a mountain
till split by lightning.   5
But a gardener
carefully pruned it.
It is nine inches high.
Every day as he
whittles back the branches   10
the gardener croons,
It is your nature
to be small and cozy,
domestic and weak;
how lucky, little tree,   15
to have a pot to grow in.
With living creatures
one must begin very early
to dwarf their growth:
the bound feet,   20
the crippled brain,
the hair in curlers,
the hands you
love to touch.

QUESTIONS

1. What is a bonsai tree? In what ways is it an apt metaphor for women? The tree
   "could have grown eighty feet tall." What would be the comparable growth and
   development of a woman?

2. What do you make of the gardener's song (lines 12–16)? If the bonsai tree were
   able to respond, would it accept the gardener's consolation? What conclusions
   about women's lives are implied by the metaphor of the tree?

3. How does the poem shift at line 17? To what extent do the next images (lines
   20–24) embody women's lives? How are the images metaphorical?

SYLVIA PLATH (1932–1963)

Metaphors   1960

I'm a riddle in nine syllables,
An elephant, a ponderous house,
A melon strolling on two tendrils.
O red fruit, ivory, fine timbers!
This loaf's big with its yeasty rising.   5
Money's new-minted in this fat purse.
I'm a means, a stage, a cow in calf.
I've eaten a bag of green apples,
Boarded the train there's no getting off.

QUESTIONS

1. What evidence can you find in the poem that the speaker is a woman?

2. The speaker calls herself a "riddle in nine syllables." What is the answer to the riddle? Why nine syllables (as opposed to eight or ten)? In what sense is the poem also a riddle? How are the answers to both riddles related?

3. Which of the metaphors do you find amusing, shocking, or demeaning? What do these suggest about the speaker's attitude toward herself?

4. What aspect of the speaker's condition is captured in the "bag of green apples" metaphor (line 8)? What two meanings are suggested by the "stage" metaphor (line 7)? Why is the "train" metaphor (line 9) appropriate to the speaker's condition and the results of that condition?

MURIEL RUKEYSER (1913–1980)

Looking at Each Other ～＜～～～ 1978

Yes, we were looking at each other
Yes, we knew each other very well
Yes, we had made love with each other many times
Yes, we had heard music together
Yes, we had gone to the sea together   5
Yes, we had cooked and eaten together
Yes, we had laughed often day and night
Yes, we fought violence and knew violence
Yes, we hated the inner and outer oppression
Yes, that day we were looking at each other   10
Yes, we saw the sunlight pouring down
Yes, the corner of the table was between us
Yes, bread and flowers were on the table
Yes, our eyes saw each other's eyes
Yes, our mouths saw each other's mouth   15
Yes, our breasts saw each other's breasts
Yes, our bodies entire saw each other
Yes, it was beginning in each
Yes, it threw waves across our lives
Yes, the pulses were becoming very strong   20
Yes, the beating became very delicate
Yes, the calling the arousal
Yes, the arriving the coming
Yes, there it was for both entire
Yes, we were looking at each other   25

QUESTIONS

1. What is the dramatic situation of the poem? What sort of listener is the speaker addressing?

2. Describe the rhetorical device at work here. How many different words are being repeated?

3. What is the effect of the repetitions? What is their relationship to the emotions and experiences that the speaker is describing?

WILLIAM SHAKESPEARE (1564–1616)
For a drawing, see p. 1306.

Sonnet 18: Shall I Compare Thee to a Summer's Day? 1609

Shall I compare thee to a summer's day?	
Thou art more lovely and more temperate:	
Rough winds do shake the darling° buds of May,	*dear, cherished*
And summer's lease hath all too short a date:	
Sometime too hot the eye of heaven° shines	*the sun* 5
And often is his° gold complexion dimmed;	*its*
And every fair from fair sometime declines,	
By chance, or nature's changing course, untrimmed;	
But thy eternal summer shall not fade,	
Nor lose possession of that fair thou owest;°	*owns, possess* 10
Nor shall Death brag thou wand'rest in his shade,	
When in eternal lines to time thou growest:	
So long as men can breathe, or eyes can see,	
So long lives this, and this gives life to thee.	

QUESTIONS

1. What is the dramatic situation of the poem? Who is speaking to whom?
2. What do the metaphors in lines 1–8 assert? Why does the speaker emphasize life's brevity?
3. Describe the shift in topic beginning in line 9. How do these lines both deny and echo the subject of lines 1–8?
4. What relationship do the last two lines have to the rest of the poem? What is the meaning of "this" (line 14)? What sort of immortality does Shakespeare exalt in the sonnet?

WILLIAM SHAKESPEARE (1564–1616)
For a drawing, see p. 1306.

Sonnet 30: When to the Sessions of Sweet Silent Thought 1609

When to the sessions° of sweet silent thought	*holding of court*
I summon° up remembrance of things past,	
I sigh the lack of many a thing I sought,	
And with old woes new wail my dear time's waste:°	
Then can I drown an eye (un-used to flow)	5
For precious friends hid in death's dateless° night,	*endless*
And weep afresh love's long since canceled° woe,	*paid in full*
And moan th'expense° of many a vanished sight.	*cost, loss*

SONNET 30. *2 summon:* to issue a summons to appear at a legal hearing. revive old sorrows about lost opportunities and express sorrow for them again. *4 old woes . . . waste:*

Then can I grieve at grievances foregone,
And heavily° from woe to woe tell° o'er   *sadly; count*   10
The sad account of fore-bemoanèd moan,
Which I new pay, as if not paid before.
   But if the while I think on thee (dear friend)
   All losses are restored, and sorrows end.

QUESTIONS

1.   Explain the metaphor of "sessions" and "summon" in lines 1–2. Where are the "sessions" being held? What is a "summons" for remembrance?

2.   What is the metaphor brought out by the word "canceled" in line 7? In what sense might a "woe" of love be canceled? Explain the metaphor of "expense" in line 8.

3.   What type of transaction does Shakespeare refer to in the metaphor of lines 9–12? What understanding does the metaphor provide about the sadness and regret that a person feels about past mistakes and sorrows?

4.   What role does the speaker assign to the "dear friend" of line 13 in relation to the metaphors of the poem?

ELIZABETH TUDOR, QUEEN ELIZABETH I (1533–1603)

On Monsieur's Departure ⤳⤳⤳ *ca. 1560 (1964)*

I grieve° and dare not show my discontent,   *I am unhappy*
I love and yet am forced to seem to hate,
I do, yet dare not say I ever meant,
I seem stark mute but inwardly do prate.°   *chatter endlessly*
   I am and not, I freeze and yet am burned,   5
   Since from myself another self I turned.

My care° is like my shadow in the sun,   *loved one*
Follows me flying, flies when I pursue it,
Stands and lies by me, doth what I have done.
His too familiar care° doth make me rue it.   *alternativeness, love*   10
   No means I find to rid him from my breast,
   Till by the end of things it be supprest.

Some gentler passion slide into my mind,
For I am soft and made of melting snow;
Or be more cruel, love, and so be kind.   15
Let me or float or sink, be high or low.
   Or let me live with some more sweet content.
   Or die and so forget what love ere meant.

QUESTIONS

1.   What is the significance of "Monsieur's Departure"? How does this detail prompt the patterns of thought in the poem?

2.   Explain the speaker's use of antithesis in the poem to explain her ambivalent situation. How seriously should we take the ideas in lines 12 and 18? Assuming

that this is a deeply personal and private lyric, why, granted the speaker's royal status, does she express such contradictory feelings?

3. What is the meaning of the shadow simile in lines 7–10? How well does this comparison reveal her situation?

4. What is explained by the paradoxes in lines 5 and 15?

MONA VAN DUYN (b. 1921)

Earth Tremors Felt in Missouri ~ ‹~·~·˺ 1964

The quake last night was nothing personal,
you told me this morning. I think one always wonders,
unless, of course, something is visible: tremors
that take us, private and willy-nilly, are usual.

But the earth said last night that what I feel,   5
you feel; what secretly moves you, moves me.
One small, sensuous catastrophe
makes inklings letters, spelled in a worldly tremble.

The earth, with others on it, turns in its course
as we turn toward each other, less than ourselves, gross, 10
mindless, more than we were. Pebbles, we swell
to planets, nearing the universal roll,
in our conceit even comprehending the sun,
whose bright ordeal leaves cool men woebegone.

QUESTIONS

1. In what ways is this poem intensely personal, a "confessional" poem? How does the poem develop materials that might be considered less personal and more public?

2. Why does the speaker equate herself and her listener with the earth? Granted that this metaphor is apt, what is then meant by "earth tremors," "quake last night," "Pebbles, we swell / to planets," and "comprehending the sun"?

3. What feelings are brought out in the last line through the words "ordeal" and "woebegone"?

4. Compare the use of the earth/person metaphor as it is used in this poem and in Donne's "The Good Morrow" (Chapter 25).

WALT WHITMAN (1819–1892)

Facing West from California's Shores ~ ‹~·~·˺ 1860

Facing west from California's shores,
Inquiring, tireless, seeking what is yet unfound,
I, a child, very old, over waves, towards the house of maternity,°
    the land of migrations, look afar,
Look off the shores of my Western sea, the circle almost circled;

For starting westward from Hindustan,° from the vales of Kashmir,   5
From Asia, from the north, from the God, the sage, and the hero,
From the south, from the flowery peninsulas° and the spice islands,°
Long having wandered since, round the earth having wandered
Now I face home again, very pleased and joyous.
(But where is what I started for so long ago?   10
And why is it yet unfound?)

FACING WEST FROM CALIFORNIA'S SHORES.   3 *house of maternity:* Asia, then considered the cradle of
human civilization.   5 *Hindustan:* India.   7 *flowery peninsulas:* south India, south Burma, and the Maylay
peninsula.   7 *spice islands:* the Molucca Islands of Indonesia.

QUESTIONS

1.   What major paradox, or apparently contradictory situation, is described in this
     poem? How does the poet bring out this paradox? What has the speaker been
     seeking? Where has he looked for it?

2.   Describe the meaning of the phrase "a child, very old"; "where is what I started
     for"; "the circle almost circled." In what ways are these phrases paradoxical?

3.   Why does the speaker twice use the word "unfound" (lines 2, 11)? How might
     the word be considered a theme of the poem?

WILLIAM WORDSWORTH (1770–1850)   *For a drawing, see p. 987.*

London, 1802 ━━━━━ *1807 (1802)*

Milton! thou should'st be living at this hour:
England hath need of thee: she is a fen°   bog, marsh
Of stagnant waters: altar, sword, and pen,
Fireside, the heroic wealth of hall and bower,
Have forfeited their ancient English dower°   widow's inheritance   5
Of inward happiness. We are selfish men;
Oh! raise us up, return to us again;
And give us manners,° virtue, freedom, power.
Thy soul was like a star, and dwelt apart:
Thou hadst a voice whose sound was like the sea: 10
Pure as the naked heavens, majestic, free,
So didst thou travel on life's common way,
In cheerful godliness; and yet thy heart
The lowliest duties on herself did lay.

LONDON, 1802.   8 *manners:* customs, moral codes of social and political conduct.

QUESTIONS

1.   What is the effect of Wordworth's apostrophe to Milton? What elements of Mil-
     ton's career as a writer does Wordsworth emphasize?

2.   In lines 3 and 4, the device of metonymy is used. How does Wordsworth judge
     the respective institutions represented by the details?

3.   Consider the use of overstatement, or hyperbole, from lines 2–6. What effect does Wordsworth achieve by using the device as extensively as he does here?

4.   What effect does Wordsworth make through his use of overstatement in his praise of Milton in lines 9–14? What does he mean by the metonymic references to "soul" (line 9) and "heart" (line 13)?

SIR THOMAS WYATT (1503–1542)

I Find No Peace   1557

I find no peace, and all my war is done,
  I fear and hope, I burn and freeze like ice;
  I fly above the wind yet can I not arise;
  And naught I have and all the world I season.
That looseth nor locketh holdeth me in prison,°   5
  And holdeth me not, yet I can scape° nowise;   escape
  Nor letteth me live nor die at my devise,°   choice
  And yet of death it giveth none occasion.
Without eyen° I see, and without tongue I plain;°   eyes
  I desire to perish, and yet I ask health;   10
  I love another, and thus I hate myself;
I feed me in sorrow, and laugh in all my pain.
  Likewise displeaseth me both death and life°
  And my delight is causer of this strife.

I FIND NO PEACE. 5 *that . . . prison:* that is, "that which neither lets me go nor contains me holds me in prison." At the time of Wyatt, -*eth* was used for the third person singular present tense. 9 *plain:* express desires about love. 13 *Likewise . . . life:* literally, "it is displeasing to me, in the same way, both death and life." That is, "both death and life are equally distasteful to me."

QUESTIONS

1.   What situation is the speaker reflecting upon? What metaphors and similes express his feelings? How successful are these figures?

2.   How many paradoxes are in the poem? What is their cumulative effect? What is the topic of the paradoxes in lines 1–4? In lines 5–8? Why does the speaker declare that hating himself is a consequence of loving another? Why is it ironic that his "delight" is the "causer of this strife"?

3.   To what extent do you think the paradoxes express the feelings of a person in love, particularly because in the sixteenth century, the free and unchaperoned meetings of lovers were not easily arranged?

✍ WRITING ABOUT FIGURES OF SPEECH

Begin by determining the use, line by line, of metaphors, similes, or other rhetorical figures. Obviously, similes are the easiest figures to recognize because they introduce comparisons with the word *like* or *as*. Metaphors can be recognized because the topics are discussed not as themselves but as other topics. If the poems speak of falling leaves or law courts, but the subjects are memory or increasing age, you are looking at metaphors. Similarly, if the poet is addressing an absent person or a natural object, or if you find clear double meanings in words, you may have apostrophe, personification, or puns.

Questions for Discovering Ideas

- What figures of speech does the work contain? Where do they occur? Under what circumstances? How extensive are they?
- How do you recognize them? Are they signaled by a single word or phrase, such as "desert places" in Frost's "Desert Places" (Chapter 20), or are they more extensively detailed, as in Shakespeare's Sonnet 30, "When to the Sessions of Sweet Silent Thought"?
- How vivid are the figures? How obvious? How unusual? What kind of effort is needed to understand them in context?
- Structurally, how are the figures developed? How do they rise out of the situation envisioned in the poem? To what degree are the figures integrated into the poem's development of ideas? How do they relate to other aspects of the poem?
- Is one type of figure used in a particular section while another type predominates in another section? Why?
- If you have discovered a number of figures, what relationships can you find among them (such as the judicial and financial connections in Shakespeare's "When to the Sessions of Sweet Silent Thought")?
- How do the figures of speech broaden, deepen, or otherwise assist in making the ideas in the poem forceful?
- In general, how appropriate and meaningful are the figures of speech in the poem? What effect do the figures have on the poem's tone, and on your understanding and appreciation of the poem?

Strategies for Organizing Ideas

For this essay, two types of compositions are possible. One is a full-scale essay. The other, because some rhetorical figures may occupy only a small part of the poem, is a single paragraph. Let us consider the single paragraph first.

1. A PARAGRAPH.   For a single paragraph you need only one topic, such as the hyperbole used in the opening of "London, 1802." The goal is to deal with the single figure and its relationship to the poem's main idea. Thus the essay should describe the figure and discuss its meaning and implications. It is important to begin with a comprehensive topic sentence, such as one that explains the cleverness of the puns in Gay's "Let Us Take the Road" or the use of paradox in Wyatt's "I Find no Peace."

2. A FULL-LENGTH ESSAY.   One type of essay might examine just one figure, if the figure is pervasive enough in the poem to justify a full treatment. Most often, the poet's use of metaphors and similes is suitable for extensive discussion. A second type of essay might explore the meaning and effect of two or more figures, with the various parts of the body of the essay being taken up with each figure. The unity of this second kind of essay is achieved by the linking of a series of two or three different rhetorical devices to a single idea or emotion.

In the introduction, relate the quality of the figures to the general nature of the work. Thus, metaphors and similes of suffering might be appropriate to a religious, redemptive work, while those of sunshine and cheer might be right for a romantic one. If there is any discrepancy between the metaphorical language and the topic, you could consider that contrast as a possible central idea, for it would clearly indicate the writer's ironic perspective. Suppose that the topic of the poem is love, but the figures put you in mind of darkness and cold: What would the writer be saying about the quality of love? You should also try to justify any claims that you make about the figures. For example, one of the similes in Coleridge's "Kubla Khan" (Chapter 16) compares the sounds of a "mighty fountain" to the breathing of the earth in "fast thick pants." How is this simile to be taken? As a reference to the animality of the earth? As a suggestion that the fountain, and the earth, are dangerous? Or simply as a comparison suggesting immense, forceful noise? How do you explain your answer or answers? Your introduction is the place to establish ideas and justifications of this sort.

The following approaches for discussing rhetorical figures are not mutually exclusive, and you may combine them as you wish. Most likely, your essay will bring in most of the following classifications.

1. *Interpret the meaning and effect of the figures.* Here you explain how the figures enable you to make an interpretation. In the second stanza of "A Valediction: Forbidding Mourning," for example, the following metaphor introduces church hierarchy and religious mystery to explain lovers and their love.

> 'Twere profanation of our joys
> To tell the laity our love.

Here Donne emphasizes the mystical relationship of two lovers, drawing the metaphor from the religious tradition whereby any popular explanation of religious mysteries is considered a desecration. A directly explanatory approach, such as this, requires that metaphors, similes, or other figures be expanded and interpreted, including the explanation of necessary references and allusions.

2. *Analyze the frames of reference and their appropriateness to the subject matter.* Here you classify and locate the sources and types of the references and determine the appropriateness of these to the poem's subject matter. Ask questions similar to those you might ask in a study of imagery: Does the writer refer extensively to nature, science, warfare, politics, business, reading (e.g., Shakespeare's metaphor equating personal reverie with courtroom proceedings)? Does the metaphor seem appropriate? How? Why?

3. *Focus on the interests and sensibilities of the poet.* In a way this approach is like strategy 2, but the emphasis here is on what the selectivity of the writer might show about his or her vision and interests. You might begin by listing the figures in the poem and then determining the sources, just as you would do in discussing the sources of images generally. But then you should raise questions like the following: Does the writer use figures derived from one sense rather than another (i.e., sight, hearing, taste, smell, touch)? Does he or she record color, brightness, shadow, shape, depth, height, number, size, slowness, speed, emptiness, fullness, richness, drabness? Has the writer relied on the associations of figures of sense? Do metaphors and similes referring to green plants and trees, to red roses, or to rich fabrics, for example, suggest that life is full and beautiful, or do references to touch suggest amorous warmth? This approach is designed to help you draw conclusions about the author's taste or sensibility.

4. *Examine the effect of one figure on the other figures and ideas of the poem.* The assumption of this approach is that each literary work is unified and organically whole, so that each part is closely related and inseparable from everything else. Usually it is best to pick a figure that occurs at the beginning of the poem and then determine how this figure influences your perception of the rest of the poem. Your aim is to consider the relationship of part to parts and part to whole. The beginning of Donne's "A Valediction: Forbidding Mourning," for example, contains a simile comparing the parting of the speaker and his listener to the quiet dying of "virtuous men." What is the effect of this comparison upon the poem? To help you with questions like this, you might substitute a totally different detail, such as, here, the violent death of a condemned criminal, or the slaughter of a domestic animal, rather than the deaths of "virtuous men." Such suppositions, which would clearly be out of place, may help you understand and then explain the poet's figures of speech.

In your conclusion, summarize your main points, describe your general impressions, try to describe the impact of the figures, indicate your personal responses, or show what might further be done along the lines you have been developing. If you know other works by the same writer, or other works by other writers who use comparable or contrasting figures, you might explain the relationship of the other work or works to your present analysis.

DEMONSTRATIVE STUDENT PARAGRAPH

Wordsworth's Use of Overstatement in "London, 1802"°

[1]   Through overstatement in "London, 1802," Wordsworth emphasizes his tribute to Milton as a master of idealistic thought.* The speaker's claim that England is "a fen / Of stagnant waters" (lines 2-3) is overstated, as is the implication that people ("We") in England have no "manners, virtue, freedom, power" (lines 6, 8). With the overstatements, however, Wordsworth implies that the nation's well-being depends on the constant flow of creative thoughts by persons of great ideas. Because Milton was clearly the greatest of these, in the view of Wordsworth's speaker, the overstatements stress the need for leadership. Milton is the model, and the overstated criticism lays the foundation in the real political and moral world for the rebirth of another Milton. Thus, through overstatement, Wordsworth emphasizes Milton's importance and in this way pays tribute to him.

°See p. 749 for this poem.
*Central idea.

Commentary on the Paragraph

This paragraph deals with a single rhetorical figure, in this case Wordsworth's overstatements in "London, 1802." Although most often the figure of speech will be fairly obvious, as this one in "London, 1802" is, prominence is not a requirement. In addition, there is no need to write an excessively long paragraph. The goal here is not to describe all the details of Wordsworth's overstatement, but to show how the figure affects his tribute to Milton. For this reason the paragraph illustrates clear and direct support of the major point.

DEMONSTRATIVE STUDENT ESSAY

Personification in Hardy's "The Convergence of the Twain"°

[1] Shortly after the luxury ocean liner Titanic sank in 1912, killing more than 1,500 people, Thomas Hardy wrote "The Convergence of the Twain." This poem, which is subtitled "Lines on the Loss of the 'Titanic,'" does not try to describe the sinking but focuses instead on the ship when at the bottom, on the building of the ship, and on the iceberg, the ship's "sinister mate" (line 19) that "grew" at the same time the ship was being built. Hardy does not refer to the fashionable passengers who died, nor does he mention the members of the crew who were killed. Interestingly though, the poem still includes, through the personification of inanimate and nonhuman objects, many human characteristics.* By the use of personification Hardy develops the idea that the sinking of the Titanic is cause for pondering the immense power of the universe and also the fatuousness of human pride and vanity.†

[2] Both the Titanic and the iceberg that it struck are personified in the poem. Hardy gives the ship the attributes of a woman by referring to it with the feminine pronouns "she" and "her" (lines 3, 5, 20), thus following the traditional custom of referring to large ships as female. He adds elegance to the personification by describing the Titanic as "gaily great" (line 20) with "stature" and "grace" (line 23). After the ship sinks, she "couches" on the ocean floor (line 3), a word that normally describes the human action of reclining or lying down.

[3] Ironically, the iceberg is also personified, but as the Titanic's "sinister mate" (line 19) and not as a fashionably acceptable husband. Hardy continues to develop the human attributes of both ship and iceberg by describing them, even though they seem "alien" to one another (line 25), as "twin halves" (line 30). Both display the human ability to hear (line 32), and Hardy ironically describes their collision as the disastrous "consummation" of their union (line 33). By thus personifying the ship and the iceberg, Hardy introduces the metaphor that the convergence of ship and natural object formed a bizarre marriage. The personification also emphasizes the major roles of the ship and the iceberg in a cosmic event that "jars two

°See pp. 737–38 for this poem.
*Central idea.
†Thesis sentence.

hemispheres" (i.e., earth and heaven; line 33). The implication of the "consummation" is that while human beings plan and create, their power is futile when compared to immense and uncontrollable universal power, which has somehow brought the two together.

[4] The exact nature of universal power is not made clear in the poem, for Hardy does not provide explanations with names like God or Fate or Destiny to describe them. In fact, Hardy speaks ironically if not jestingly of divine power. He refers to "The Immanent Will" (line 18), a vague term for divinity, and "the Spinner of the Years" (line 31), which is not a conventional religious term. Hardy's use of capitalization for these personifications indicates that they are names for a superior force or being, but the names themselves lead more to puzzlement than to definiteness. "The Immanent Will," Hardy's speaker states, is a personification "that stirs and urges everything" (line 18), even though events affecting human life are mysterious. So is it also with the "Spinner of the Years" (line 31), a personification reminiscent of Lachesis, the ancient Fate who spun out the threads of life for all living beings. However, this power has a "will," like a human being, and it "spins," a human action. Furthermore, it acts as another character in the drama, one operating in secrecy, outside the scope of human awareness, who arranges for the other characters to be brought together. It is this "Will" that has "prepared" the iceberg and then left it to grow (line 24), and it is the "Spinner of the Years" that says the word "Now!' " (line 32) to cause the collision of ship and iceberg as though the two had been drawing together throughout all time. Clearly, by using personification to characterize mysteries beyond human comprehension, Hardy suggests that this "convergence of the twain" was somehow destined to happen.

[5] But why does the universal power create this destiny? Two other instances of personification in the poem suggest the motive. First of all, although the sunken Titanic is now "Deep from human vanity" (line 2), the third line of the poem refers to the "Pride of Life that planned" the ship. Thus, human pride is personified as the builders of a ship supposedly so grand and advanced that it could not sink. But the ship did sink, and the personified "fishes" in the fifth stanza make the observation that the product of pride is now meaningless and vain. These fish perform the human actions of gazing "at the gilded gear" of the shipwreck and then of asking the question "What does this vaingloriousness down here?" (lines 14-15). The fishes' question leads readers to the inescapable conclusion that even the proudest of human efforts are nothing much more than rusting scrap metal in the scale of the larger universe.

[6] It seems that Hardy's personifications in this poem are functional and appropriate in light of the disastrous sinking of the Titanic. As a matter of historical record, there were contributing causes, such as the ship's high speed at night even though it was traveling through waters known to contain icebergs, and such as the builders' miscalculations about the ship's hull design, but the ultimate causes of the calamity itself cannot be known. Even the obvious religious and philosophical answers are not satisfying. It would have been possible for Hardy to develop the idea that Divinity rules human affairs, or that the many deaths were tragic, or that the wreck served some purpose of punishment for the human pride that led to the original building of the ship. But Hardy introduces the poem's personifications to explain the mystery in human terms, and he only hints at the traditional answers. To do anything else would have made the poem more positive, perhaps, but it would have implied that explanations are available even though they really are not.

WORK CITED

Hardy, Thomas. "The Convergence of the Twain." <u>Literature: An Introduction to Reading and Writing</u>. 7th ed. Ed. Edgar V. Roberts and Henry E. Jacobs. 7th ed. Upper Saddle River: Prentice Hall, 2004. 737–38.

Commentary on the Essay

This essay begins with a treatment of Hardy's personification of the ship and the iceberg that sank her. The goal of the essay is to explain how the personifications enable Hardy to treat the topic fully but also ironically. The essay therefore illustrates strategy 1 described on page 752.

In addition to providing a brief description of the poem, the introduction brings out the central idea and the thesis sentence. Paragraph 2 deals with the personification of the ship. The iceberg is explained as a personification in paragraph 3. Paragraph 3 also demonstrates that the personifications of ship and iceberg permit Hardy to introduce the metaphor of a marriage between the two. Paragraph 4 considers the more perplexing personifications of divinity and fate, which underlay the sinking according to Hardy's construction of the disaster. Paragraph 5 deals with two additional personifications, namely the human attributes to the fish swimming around the wreck. Also in paragraph 5, human pride is personified as the as the creator of the ship. Paragraph 6 deals with the issues of Hardy's use of personification. The idea is that this figure of speech, pursued throughout the poem, permits the poet to deal with the disaster in human terms inasmuch as any other explanation is not possible.

Throughout the essay, transitions are brought about by linking words and phrases. In paragraph 3, for example, the words "also personified" and "but as" move the reader from paragraph 2 to the new content. In paragraph 4, the phrase effecting the transition is the repeitition of "universal power." The opening sentence of paragraph 6 is in effect a summarizing sentence which extends the topic by treating the effect of the personifications throughout the poem.

Special Topics for Writing and Argument about Figures of Speech in Poetry

1. Study the simile of the "stiff twin compasses" in Donne's "A Valediction: Forbidding Mourning." Using such a compass or a drawing of one, write an essay that demonstrates the accuracy, or lack of it, of Donne's descriptions. What light does the simile shed on the relationship of two lovers? How does it emphasize any or all of these aspects of love: closeness, immediacy, extent, importance, duration, intensity?

2. Consider some of the metaphors and similes in the poems included in this chapter. Write an essay that answers the following questions. How effective are the figures you select? (Examples: the bonsai tree [Piercy], the Siamese twins [Minty], the explosive [Hughes], the summer's day [Shakespeare].) What insights do the figures provide within the contexts of their respective poems? How appropriate are they? Might they be expanded more fully, and if they were, what would be the effect?

3.   Consider some of the other rhetorical figures in the poems of this chapter. Write an essay describing the importance of figures of speech in creating emphasis and in extending and deepening the ideas of poetry. Here are some possible topics.

     a.   Paradox in Wyatt's "I Find No Peace" or Whitman's "Facing West from California's Shores."

     b.   The simile of the compass in Donne's "A Valediction."

     c.   Metaphor in Minty's "Conjoined" or Piercy's "A Work of Artifice."

     d.   Metaphor and simile in Evans's "The Iceberg Seven-eighths Under" or in Hardy's "The Convergence of the Twain."

     e.   Anaphora in Rukeyser's "Looking at Each Other" or in Harjo's "Remember."

     f.   A comparison of contrasts and paradoxes in Elizabeth I's "On Monsieur's Departure" and Wyatt's "I Find No Peace."

     g.   Similes in King's "Sic Vita" or Hughes's "Harlem." Personification in the poems by Wordsworth, Keats, or Agüeros. Metonymy in Keats's "To Autumn."

4.   Write a poem in which you create a governing metaphor or simile. Examples: "My girlfriend/boyfriend is like (a) an opening flower, (b) a difficult book, (c) an insoluble mathematical problem, (d) a bill that cannot be paid, (e) a slow-moving chess game." "Teaching a person how to do a particular job is like (a) shoveling heavy snow, (b) climbing a mountain during a landslide, (c) having someone force you underwater when you're gasping for breath." When you finish, describe the relationship between your comparison and the development and structure of your poem.

5.   In your library's reference section, find the third edition of J. A. Cuddon's *A Dictionary of Literary Terms and Literary Theory* (1991) or some other dictionary of literary terms. Study the entries for metaphysical and conceit, and write a brief report on these sections. You might attempt to answer questions like these: What is meant by the word *conceit*? What are some of the kinds of conceit the reference work discusses? What is a metaphysical conceit? Who are some of the writers considered metaphysical? In the "metaphysical" entry, of what importance is John Donne?

CHAPTER

18

Tone: *The Creation of Attitude in Poetry*

Tone (see also Chapter 8), a term derived from the phrase *tone of voice*, describes the shaping of attitudes in poetry. Each poet's choice of words governs the reader's responses, as do the participants and situations in the poem. In addition, the poet shapes responses through denotation and connotation, seriousness or humor, irony, metaphors, similes, understatement, overstatement, and other figures of speech (see Chapter 17). Of major importance is the poem's speaker. How much self-awareness does the speaker show? What is his or her background? What relationship does the speaker establish with listeners and readers? What does the speaker assume about the readers and about their knowledge? How do these assumptions affect the ideas and the diction?

To compare poetic tone with artistic tone, see the reproduction of Fernand Léger's painting *The City* (Insert II-8). A viewer's response to the painting depends on the relationships of the various shapes to Léger's arrangement and color. The signs, stairs, pole, and human figures in the painting are all common in modern cities. By cutting them up or leaving them partially hidden, Léger creates an atmosphere suggesting that contemporary urban life is truncated, sinister, and even threatening.

The same control applies to poetic expression. The sentences must be just long enough to achieve the poet's intended effect—no shorter and no longer. In a conversational style there should be no formal words, just as in a formal style there should be no slang, no rollicking rhythms, and no frivolous rhymes—that is, unless the poet deliberately wants readers to be startled or shocked. In all the features that contribute to a poem's tone, the poet's consistency of intention is primary. Any unintentional deviations will cause the poem to sink and the poet to fail.

TONE, CHOICE, AND RESPONSE

Remember that a major objective of poets is to stimulate, enrich, and inspire readers. Poets may begin their poems with a brief idea, a vague feeling, or a fleeting impression. Then, in the light of their developing design, they *choose* what to say—the form of their material and the words and phrases to express their ideas. The poem "Theme for English B" by Langston Hughes illustrates this process in almost outline form. Hughes's speaker lays out many interests that he shares with his intended reader, his English teacher, for the poem is imagined to be a response to a classroom assignment. In this way Hughes encourages all readers to accept his ideas of human equality (see the demonstrative student essay, p. 789).

page 773

In the long run, readers might not accept all the ideas in any poem, but the successful poem gains agreement—at least for a time—because the poet's control over tone is right. Each poem attempts to evoke total responses, which might be destroyed by any lapses in tone. Let us look at a poem in which the tone misses, and misses badly.

CORNELIUS WHUR (1782–1853)

The First-Rate Wife ~ ⌇ ⌇ ~ *1837*

This brief effusion I indite,
   And my vast wishes send,
That thou mayst be directed right,
And have ere long within thy sight
   A most *enchanting* friend!   5

The *maiden* should have *lovely face,*
   And be of *genteel mien;*
If not, within thy dwelling place,
There may be vestige of disgrace,
   Not much admired—when seen.   10

Nor will thy dearest be complete
   Without *domestic* care;
If otherwise, howe'er discreet,
Thine eyes will very often meet
   What none desire to share!   15

And further still—thy future *dear,*
   Should have some *mental* ray;
If not, thou mayest drop a tear,
Because no *real sense* is there
   To charm life's dreary day!   20

QUESTIONS

1. What kind of person is the poem's speaker? The listener? What is the situation? What requirements does the speaker create for the "first-rate wife"?

2. Describe the poem's tone. How does the speaker's character influence the tone? In light of the tone, to what degree can the poem be considered insulting?

3. How might lines 14 and 15 be interpreted as a possible threat if the woman as a wife does not keep the house clean and straight?

In this poem the speaker is talking to a friend or associate and is explaining his requirements for a "first-rate wife." From his tone, he clearly regards getting married as little more than hiring a pretty housekeeper. In the phrase "some *mental* ray," for example, the word *some* does not mean "a great deal" but is more like "*at least* some," as though nothing more could be expected of a woman. Even allowing for the fact that the poem was written early in the nineteenth century and represents a benighted view of women and marriage, "The First-Rate Wife" offends most readers. Do you wonder why you've never heard of Cornelius Whur before?

⫯⫰ TONE AND THE NEED FOR CONTROL

"The First-Rate Wife" demonstrates the need for the poet to be in control over all facets of the poem. The speaker must be aware of his or her situation and should not, like Whur's speaker, demonstrate any smugness or insensitivity, unless the poet is deliberately revealing the shortcomings of the speaker by dramatizing them for the reader's amusement, as E. E. Cummings does in the poem "next to of course god america i" (Chapter 14). In a poem with well-controlled tone, details and situations should be factually correct; observations should be logical and fair, and also comprehensive and generally applicable. The following poem, based on battlefield conditions in World War I, illustrates a masterly control over tone.

WILFRED OWEN (1893–1918)

Dulce et Decorum Est° ⸱‐⸱ ⟨⸱⟩⸱‐⸱ 1920

Bent double, like old beggars under sacks,
Knock-kneed, coughing like hags, we cursed through sludge,
Till on the haunting flares we turned our backs
And towards our distant rest began to trudge.
Men marched asleep. Many had lost their boots   5
But limped on, blood-shod. All went lame; all blind;
Drunk with fatigue; deaf even to the hoots
Of tired, outstripped Five-Nines° that dropped behind.

Gas!° GAS! Quick, boys!—An ecstasy of fumbling,
Fitting the clumsy helmets° just in time;   10

But someone still was yelling out and stumbling
And flound'ring like a man in fire or lime . . .
Dim, through the misty panes and thick green° light,
As under a green sea, I saw him drowning.

In all my dreams, before my helpless sight,   15
He plunges at me, guttering, choking, drowning.

If in some smothering dreams you too could pace
Behind the wagon that we flung him in.
And watch the white eyes writhing in his face,
His hanging face, like a devil's sick of sin;   20
If you could hear, at every jolt, the blood
Come gargling from the froth-corrupted lungs,
Obscene as cancer, bitter as the cud
Of vile, incurable sores on innocent tongues.—
My friend, you would not tell with such high zest   25
To children ardent for some desperate glory,
The old Lie: Dulce et decorum est
Pro patria mori.

DULCE ET DECORUM EST. The Latin title comes from Horace's *Odes,* Book 3, line 13: *Dulce et decorum est
pro patria mori* ("It is sweet and honorable to die for the fatherland").   8 *Five-Nines:* Artillery shells that
made a hooting sound just before landing.   9 *Gas:* Chlorine gas was used as an antipersonnel weapon in
1915 by the Germans at Ypres, in Belgium.   10 *helmets:* Soldiers carried gas masks as normal battle equipment.   13 *thick green:* The chlorine gas used in gas attacks has a greenish-yellow color.

QUESTIONS

1. What is the scene described in lines 1–8? What expressions does the speaker use to indicate his attitude toward the conditions?

2. What does the title of the poem mean? What attitude or conviction does it embody?

3. Does the speaker really mean "my friend" in line 25? In what tone of voice might this phrase be spoken?

4. What is the tonal relationship between the patriotic fervor of the Latin phrase and the images of the poem? How does the tonal contrast create the dominant tone of the poem?

The tone of "Dulce et Decorum Est" never lapses. The poet intends the description to evoke a response of horror and shock, for he contrasts the strategic goals of warfare with the speaker's up-close experience of terror in battle. The speaker's language skillfully emphasizes first the dreariness and fatigue of warfare (with words like "sludge," "trudge," "lame," and "blind") and second the agony of violent death from chlorine gas (embodied in the participles "guttering," "choking," "drowning," "smothering," and "writhing"). With these details established, the concluding attack against the "glory" of war is difficult to refute, even if warfare is undertaken to defend or preserve one's country. Although the details about the agonized death may distress or discomfort a sensitive reader, they are not designed to do that alone but instead are integral to the poem's argument. Ultimately, it is the contrast between the high ideals of the Latin phrase and the ugliness of battlefield death that creates the dominant tone of the poem. The Latin phrase treats war and death in the abstract; the poem makes images of battle and death vividly real. The resultant tone is that of controlled bitterness and irony.

❧ TONE AND COMMON GROUNDS OF ASSENT

Not all those reading Owen's poem will deny that war is sometimes necessary; the issues of politics and warfare are far too complex for that. But the poem does show another important aspect of tone—namely, the degree to which the poet judges and tries to control responses through the establishment of a *common ground of assent.* An appeal to a bond of commonly held interests, concerns, and assumptions is essential if a poet is to maintain an effective tone. Owen, for example, does not create arguments against the necessity of a just war. Instead, he bases the poem on realistic details about the choking, writhing, spastic death suffered by the speaker's comrade, and he appeals to emotions that everyone, pacifist and militarist alike, would feel—horror at the contemplation of violent death. Even assuming a widely divergent audience, in other words, the *tone* of the poem is successful because it is based on commonly acknowledged facts and commonly felt emotions. Knowing a poem like this one, even advocates of a strong military would need to defend their ideas on the grounds of *preventing* just such needless, ugly deaths. Owen carefully considers the responses of his readers, and he regulates speaker, situation, detail, and argument in order to make the poem acceptable for the broadest possible spectrum of opinion.

TONE IN CONVERSATION AND POETRY

Many readers think that tone is a subtle and difficult subject, but it is nevertheless true that in ordinary situations we master tone easily and expertly (see Chapter 8). We constantly use standard questions and statements that deal with tone, such as "What do you mean by that?" "What I'm saying is this . . .," and "Did I hear you correctly?" together with other comments that extend to humor and, sometimes, to hostility. In poetry we do not have everyday speech situations; we have only the poems themselves and are guided by the materials they provide us. Some poems are straightforward and unambiguous, but in other poems feeling and mood are essential to our understanding. In Hardy's "The Workbox" (p. 764), for example, the husband's gift to his wife indicates not love but suspicion. Also, the husband's relentless linking of the dead man's coffin to the gift reveals his underlying anger. Pope, in the passage from the "Epilogue to the Satires" included in this chapter, satirically describes deplorable habits and customs of his English contemporaries in the 1730s. His concluding lines (of the passage and also of the poem) emphasize his scorn:

Yet may this verse (if such a verse remain)
Show there was one who held it in disdain.

The speaker of Ondaatje's "Late Movies with Skyler" describes how he and Skyler watch the late show. The activities described in the poem clearly establish a friendly and companionable bond between the two men. Poems of course may also reveal respect and wonder, as shown in the last six lines of Keats's "On First Looking into Chapman's Homer" (Chapter 17). By attending carefully to the details of such poems, you can draw conclusions about poetic tone that are as accurate as those you draw in normal speech situations.

TONE AND IRONY

Irony is a mode of indirection, a means of making a point by emphasizing a discrepancy or opposite (see also Chapter 8). Thus Owen uses the title "Dulce et Decorum Est" to emphasize that death in warfare is not sweet and honorable but rather demeaning and horrible. The title ironically reminds us of eloquent holiday speeches at the tombs of unknown soldiers, but as we have seen, it also reminds us of the reality of the agonized death of Owen's soldier. As an aspect of tone, therefore, irony is a powerful way of conveying attitudes, for it draws your attention to at least two ways of seeing a situation, enabling you not only to *understand* but also to *experience*. Poetry shares with fiction the various kinds of ironies that afflict human beings. These are *verbal irony, situational irony,* and *dramatic irony.*

Verbal Irony, Through Word Selection, Emphasizes Ambiguities and Discrepancies

At almost any point in a poem, a poet may introduce the ironic effects of language itself—**verbal irony.** The poem "she being Brand / -new," by E. E. Cummings, is built on the double meanings derived from the procedures of breaking in a new car. Indeed, the entire poem is a virtuoso piece of double entendre. Another example of verbal irony is seen in Theodore Roethke's "My Papa's Waltz," in which the speaker uses the name of this graceful and stately dance to describe his childhood memories of his father's whirling him around the kitchen in wild, boisterous drunkenness.

Life's Anomalies and Uncertainties Underlie Situational Irony

Situational irony is derived from the discrepancies between the ideal and the actual. People would like to live their lives in terms of a standard of love, friendship, honor, success, and general excellence, but the irony is that the reality of their lives often falls far short of such standards. Whereas in fiction ironic situations emerge from extended narrative, in poetry such situations are usually at a high point or climax, and we must infer the narrative circumstances that have gone on before. Thomas Hardy, in "The Workbox," skillfully exploits an ironic situation between a husband and a wife.

THOMAS HARDY (1840–1928)

The Workbox   1914

"See, here's the workbox, little wife,
  That I made of polished oak."
He was a joiner,° of village° life;   *cabinetmaker*
  She came of borough° folk.

He holds the present up to her   5
  As with a smile she nears
And answers to the profferer,
  "'Twill last all my sewing years!"

"I warrant it will. And longer too.
  'Tis a scantling° that I got   10
Off poor John Wayward's coffin, who
  Died of they knew not what.

"The shingled pattern that seems to cease
  Against your box's rim
Continues right on in the piece   15
  That's underground with him.

"And while I worked it made me think
  Of timber's varied doom:
One inch where people eat and drink,
  The next inch in a tomb.   20

"But why do you look so white, my dear,
  And turn aside your face?
You knew not that good lad, I fear,
  Though he came from your native place?"

"How could I know that good young man,   25
  Though he came from my native town,
When he must have left far earlier than
  I was a woman grown?"

"Ah, no. I should have understood!
  It shocked you that I gave   30
To you one end of a piece of wood
  Whose other is in a grave?"

"Don't, dear, despise my intellect.
  Mere accidental things
Of that sort never have effect   35
  On my imaginings."

Yet still her lips were limp and wan,
  Her face still held aside,
As if she had known not only John,
  But known of what he died.   40

THE WORKBOX.   3, 4 *village, borough:* A village was small and rustic; a borough was larger and more sophisticated.   10 *scantling:* a small leftover piece of wood.

QUESTIONS

1. Who does most of the speaking here? What does the speaker's tone show about the characters of the husband and the wife? What does the tone indicate about the poet's attitude toward them?

2. What do lines 21–40 indicate about the wife's knowledge of John and about her earlier relationship with him? Why does she deny such knowledge? What does the last stanza show about her? Why is John's death kept a mystery?

3. In lines 17–20, what irony is suggested by the fact that the wood was used both for John's coffin and the workbox?

4. Why is the husband's irony more complex than he realizes? What do his words and actions show about his character?

5. The narrator, or poet, speaks only in lines 3–7 and 37–40. How much of his explanation is essential? How much shows his attitude? How might the poem have been more effectively concluded?

"The Workbox" is a domestic drama of deception, cruelty, and sadness. The complex details are evidence of situational irony, that is, an awareness that human beings do not control their lives but are rather controlled by powerful forces—in this case by both death and earlier feelings and commitments. Beyond this domestic irony, Hardy also emphasizes symbolically the direct connection that death has with the living. As a result of the husband's gift made of the wood with which he has also made a coffin for the dead man, the wife will never escape being reminded of this man. Within the existence imagined in the poem, she will have to live with regret and the constant need to deny her true emotions, and her situation is therefore endlessly ironic.

Dramatic Irony Is Built on the Ignorance of Characters and the Greater Knowledge of Readers

In addition to the situational irony of "The Workbox," the wife's deception reveals that the husband is in a situation of **dramatic irony.** He does not know the circumstances of his wife's past, and he does not actually *know*—though he suspects—that his wife is not being truthful about her earlier relationship with the dead man, but the poem is sufficient to enable readers to draw the right conclusions. By emphasizing the wood, the husband is apparently trying to make his wife uncomfortable, even to the point of extracting a confession from her, but he has only his suspicions, and he therefore remains unsure of the truth and also of his wife's feelings. Because of these uncertainties Hardy has deftly used dramatic irony to create a poem of great complexity and pathos.

TONE AND SATIRE

Satire, an important genre in the study of tone, is designed to expose human follies and vices. In method, a satiric poem may be bitter and vituperative, but often it employs humor and irony, on the grounds that anger turns readers away while a comic tone more easily wins agreement. The speaker of a satiric poem either may attack folly and vice directly, or it may dramatically embody the folly or vice and thus serve as an illustration of the subject of satire. An example of the first type is the following short poem by Alexander Pope, in which the speaker directly attacks a listener who has claimed to be a poet but whom the speaker considers a fool. The speaker cleverly uses insult as the tone of attack.

ALEXANDER POPE (1688–1744)

Epigram from the French 1732

Sir, I admit your general rule
That every poet is a fool:
But you yourself may serve to show it,
That every fool is not a poet.

QUESTIONS

1. What has the listener said before the poem begins? How does the speaker build on the listener's previous comment?
2. Considering this poem as a brief satire, describe the nature of satiric attack and the corresponding tone of attack.
3. Look at the pattern "poet," "fool," "fool," "poet." This is a rhetorical pattern (*a, b, b, a*) called chiasmus or antimetabole. What does the pattern contribute to the poem's effectiveness?

An example of the second type of satiric poem is another of Pope's epigrams, in which the speaker is an actual embodiment of the subject being attacked.

ALEXANDER POPE (1688–1744)

Epigram, Engraved on the Collar of a Dog which I Gave to His Royal Highness 1738

I am his Highness' dog at Kew:°   *the royal palace near London*
Pray tell me sir, whose dog are you?

QUESTIONS

1. Who or what is the subject of the satiric attack?
2. What attitude is expressed toward social pretentiousness?

Here the speaker is, comically, the king's dog, and the listener is an unknown dog. Pope's satire is directed not against canines, however, but against human beings who pretentiously prize class above everything. The first line ridicules those who claim social status that is derived, not earned. The second implies an unwillingness to recognize the listener until the question of rank is resolved. Pope, by using the dog as a speaker, reduces such snobbishness to an absurdity. A similar satiric poem attacking pretentiousness is "next to of course god america i" by E. E. Cummings (Chapter 14), in which the speaker voices a set of patriotic platitudes and in doing so illustrates cummings's satiric point that most speeches of this sort are empty-headed. Satiric tone may thus range widely, being sometimes objective, comic, and distant; sometimes deeply concerned and scornful; and sometimes dramatic, ingenuous, and revelatory. Always, however, the satiric mode aims toward confrontation and exposé.

POEMS FOR STUDY

JIMMY CARTER (b. 1924)

I Wanted to Share My Father's World ✂ ✂ ✂ 1995

This is a pain I mostly hide,
but ties of blood, or seed, endure,
and even now I feel inside
the hunger for his outstretched hand,
a man's embrace to take me in,
the need for just a word of praise.

I despised the discipline
he used to shape what I should be,

5

not owning up that he might feel
his own pain when he punished me.   10

I didn't show my need to him,
since his response to an appeal
would not have meant as much to me,
or been as real.

From those rare times when we did cross   15
the bridge between us, the pure joy
survives.

      I never put aside
the past resentments of the boy
until, with my own sons, I shared   20
his final hours, and came to see
what he'd become, or always was—
the father who will never cease to be
alive in me.

QUESTIONS

1. This poem is about the remembered attitudes of President Carter's speaker toward his father. What is the nature of these attitudes? To what degree are these attitudes of sons to fathers either usual or unusual? Why does the speaker state in line 1, "This is a pain I mostly hide"?

2. Why does the speaker use the words "despised" (line 7) and "resentments" (line 18)? Why does he mention "those rare times" in line 15?

3. What is the tone of the last stanza? Why does the speaker refer to going with his own sons to share the "final hours" of his father? What is the tone of the final two lines?

LUCILLE CLIFTON (b. 1936)

homage to my hips   1987

these hips are big hips
they need space to
move around in.
they don't fit into little
petty places. these hips   5
are free hips.
they don't like to be held back.
these hips have never been enslaved.
they go where they want to go.
they do what they want to do.   10
these hips are mighty hips.
these hips are magic hips.
i have known them
to put a spell on a man and
spin him like a top!   15

QUESTIONS

1.   What is unusual about the subject matter? Considering that some people are embarrassed to mention their hips, what attitudes does the speaker express here?

2.   How do the words "enslaved," "want to go," "want to do," "mighty," and "spell" define the poem's ideas about the relationship between mentality and physicality?

3.   To what degree is this a comic poem? What about the subject and the diction makes the poem funny?

BILLY COLLINS (b. 1941)   *For a photo, see p. 610.*

The Names°   ⌐⌐⌐⌐   2002

Yesterday, I lay awake in the palm of the night.
A fine rain stole in, unhelped by any breeze,
And when I saw the silver glaze on the windows,
I started with A, with Ackerman, as it happened,
Then Baxter and Calabro,   5
Davis and Eberling, names falling into place
As droplets fell through the dark.

Names printed on the ceiling of the night.
Names slipping around a watery bend.
Twenty-six willows on the banks of a stream.   10

In the morning, I walked out barefoot
Among thousands of flowers
Heavy with dew like the eyes of tears,
And each had a name—
Fiori inscribed on a yellow petal   15
Then Gonzalez and Han, Ishikawa and Jenkins.

Names written in the air
And stitched into the cloth of the day.
A name under a photograph taped to a mailbox.
Monogram on a torn shirt,   20
I see you spelled out on storefront windows
And on the bright unfurled awnings of this city.
I say the syllables as I turn a corner—
Kelly and Lee,
Medina, Nardella, and O'Connor.   25

When I peer into the woods,
I see a thick tangle where letters are hidden
As in a puzzle concocted for children.
Parker and Quigley in the twigs of an ash,
Rizzo, Schubert, Torres, and Upton,   30
Secrets in the boughs of an ancient maple.

THE NAMES. This poem was read by Professor Collins before a joint session of the United States Congress held in New York city on September 6, 2002. It was first published earlier that day in the *New York Times.*

Names written in the pale sky.
Names rising in the updraft amid buildings.
Names silent in stone
Or cried out behind a door.
Names blown over the earth and out to sea.   35

 In the evening—weakening light, the last swallows.
A boy on a lake lifts his oars.
A woman by a window puts a match to a candle,
And the names are outlined on the rose clouds—
Vanacore and Wallace,   40
(let X stand, if it can, for the ones unfound)
Then Young and Ziminsky, the final jolt of Z.

 Names etched on the head of a pin.
One name spanning a bridge, another undergoing a tunnel.
A blue name needled into the skin.   45
Names of citizens, workers, mothers and fathers,
The bright-eyed daughter, the quick son.
Alphabet of names in green rows in a field.
Names in the small tracks of birds.
Names lifted from a hat   50
Or balanced on the tip of the tongue.
Names wheeled into the dim warehouse of memory.
So many names, there is barely room on the walls of the heart.

N.B. In light of the topic of this poem, questions seem superfluous.

E. E. CUMMINGS (1894–1962)   *For a photo, see p. 648.*

she being Brand / -new   1926

she being Brand

-new;and you
know consequently a
little stiff i was
careful of her and(having   5

thoroughly oiled the universal
joint tested my gas felt of
her radiator made sure her springs were O.

K.)i went right to it flooded-the-carburetor cranked her

up,slipped the   10
clutch(and then somehow got into reverse she
kicked what
the hell)next
minute i was back in neutral tried and

again slo-wly;bare,ly nudg.   ing(my   15

lev-er Right-
oh and her gears being in

A 1 shape passed
from low through
second-in-to-high like
greasedlightning)just as we turned the corner of Divinity   20

avenue i touched the accelerator and give

her the juice,good

                    (it

was the first ride and believe i we was   25
happy to see how nice she acted right up to
the last minute coming back down by the Public
Gardens i slammed on

the   30
internalexpanding
&
externalcontracting
brakes Bothatonce and

brought allofher tremB   35
-ling
to a:dead.

stand-
;Still)

QUESTIONS

1.   How extensive is the verbal irony, the double entendre, in this poem? This poem is considered comic. Do you agree? Why or why not? This poem might also be considered sexist. Do you agree? Why or why not?

2.   How do the spacing and alignment affect your reading of the poem? How does the unexpected and sometimes absent punctuation—such as in line 15, "again slo-wly;bare,ly nudg. ing(my"—contribute to the humor?

3.   Can this poem in any respect be called off-color or bawdy? How might you refute such charges in light of the tone the speaker uses to equate a first sexual experience with the breaking in of a new car?

MARI EVANS

I Am a Black Woman ✦ 1970

I am a black woman
the music of my song
some sweet arpeggio of tears
is written in a minor key
and I   5
can be heard humming in the night
Can be heard
    humming
in the night

I saw my mate leap screaming to the sea   10
and I/with these hands/cupped the lifebreath
from my issue in the canebreak
I lost Nat's swinging body° in a rain of tears

and heard my son scream all the way from Anzio°
for Peace he never knew. . . . I   15

learned Da Nang° and Pork Chop Hill°
in anguish
Now my nostrils know the gas
and these trigger tire/d fingers
seek the softness in my warrior's beard   20
I
am a black woman
tall as a cypress
strong
beyond all definition still   25
defying place
and time
and circumstance
  assailed
    impervious   30
      indestructible

Look
  on me and be
renewed

I AM A BLACK WOMAN. 13 *Nat's swinging body:* Nat Turner was hanged in 1831 for leading a slave revolt in Southampton, Virginia. 14 *Anzio:* seacoast town in Italy, the scene of fierce fighting between the Allies and the Germans in 1943 during World War II. 16 *Da Nang:* major American military base in South Vietnam, frequently attacked during the Vietnam War. *Park Chop Hill:* site of a bloody battle between UN and Communist forces during the Korean War (1950–1953).

QUESTIONS

1. What attitude is indicated by the phrase "sweet arpeggio of tears"? How does "in a minor key" complete both the idea and the comparison?

2. What phrases and descriptions does the speaker use to indicate her attitudes of anguish, despair, pain, and indignation?

3. In the last fourteen lines, what contrasting attitude is expressed? How does the speaker make this attitude clear? On balance, is the poem optimistic or pessimistic? Why?

SEAMUS HEANEY (b. 1939)

Mid-term Break ⚞⚞⚞⚞ 1966

I sat all morning in the college sick bay
Counting bells knelling classes to a close.
At two o'clock our neighbors drove me home.

In the porch I met my father crying— 5
He had always taken funerals in his stride—
And Big Jim Evans saying it was a hard blow.

The baby cooed and laughed and rocked the pram
When I came in, and I was embarrassed
By old men standing up to shake my hand

And tell me they were "sorry for my trouble," 10
Whispers informed strangers I was the eldest,
Away at school, as my mother held my hand

In hers and coughed out angry tearless sighs.
At ten o'clock the ambulance arrived
With the corpse, stanched and bandaged by the nurses. 15

Next morning I went up into the room. Snowdrops
And candles soothed the bedside; I saw him
For the first time in six weeks. Paler now,

Wearing a poppy bruise on his left temple,
He lay in the four foot box as in his cot. 20
No gaudy scars, the bumper knocked him clear.

A four foot box, a foot for every year.

QUESTIONS

1. What is the situation of the poem? Who is the speaker? Why has he been called home? What are his responses to the circumstances at home?

2. How old was the speaker's brother at the time of the accident? How do you know? When you read line 19, what do you at first make of the "poppy bruise"?

3. Describe your responses to the last four lines of the poem the first time you read them. What clues in the earlier part of the poem prepare you for these final three lines? Do they sufficiently prepare you, or does the final line come as a surprise? Why is the poem unrhymed until the final two lines?

LANGSTON HUGHES (1902–1967)

For a photo, see p. 1608.

Theme for English B ✂╌╌╌ 1959

The instructor said,

Go home and write
a page tonight.
And let that page come out of you—
Then, it will be true. 5

I wonder if it's that simple?

I am twenty-two, colored, born in Winston-Salem.
I went to school there, then Durham, then here

to this college on the hill above Harlem.°
I am the only colored student in my class.   10
The steps from the hill lead down to Harlem,
through a park, then I cross St. Nicholas,
Eighth Avenue, Seventh, and I come to the Y,
the Harlem Branch Y, where I take the elevator
up to my room, sit down, and write this page: — *Colon*   15

It's not easy to know what is true for you or me
at twenty-two, my age. But I guess I'm what
I feel and see and hear. Harlem, I hear you:
hear you, hear me—we two—you, me talk on this page.
(I hear New York, too.) Me—who? *am I   do I ever exist*   20

Well, I like to eat, sleep, drink, and be in love.
I like to work, read, learn, and understand life.
I like a pipe for a Christmas present,
or records—Bessie,° bop,° or Bach.°

I guess being colored doesn't make me not like   25
the same things other folks like who are other races.
So will my page be colored that I write?
Being me, it will not be white.
But it will be
a part of you, instructor.   30
You are white—
yet a part of me, as I am a part of you.
That's American.

Sometimes perhaps you don't want to be a part of me.
Nor do I often want to be a part of you.   35
But we are, that's true!
As I learn from you,
I guess you learn from me—
although you're older—and white—
and somewhat more free.   40

This is my page for English B.

(marginal handwritten notes: "Here is paper now he's writing"; "after writing another"; "his writing / the instructor reading")

THEME FOR ENGLISH B. 9 *college . . . Harlem:* a reference to Columbia University in the Columbia Heights section of New York City. The other streets and buildings mentioned in lines 11–14 refer to specific places in the same vicinity.   24 *Bessie:* Bessie Smith (ca. 1898–1937), American jazz singer, famed as the "Empress of the Blues." *bop:* a type of popular music that was in vogue in the 1940s through the 1960s. *Bach:* Johann Sebastian Bach (1685–1750), German composer, considered the master of the baroque style of music.

QUESTIONS

1. What is the tone of the speaker's self-assessment? What does the tone indicate about his feelings toward the situation in the class and at the Y?

2. What tone is implicit in the fact that the speaker, in response to a theme assignment, has composed a poem rather than a prose essay?

3. What is the tone of lines 21–24, where the speaker indicates his likes? In what way may the characteristics brought out in these lines serve as an argument for social and political equality?

4. How does the tone in lines 27–40, particularly lines 34–36, prevent the statements of the speaker from becoming overly assertive or strident?

X. J. KENNEDY (b. 1929)

John while swimming in the ocean   1986

John while swimming in the ocean
Rubbed sharks' backs with suntan lotion.
Now those sharks have skin of bronze
In their bellies—namely, John's.

QUESTIONS

1. What is the "action" of the poem? Why is it ludicrous?
2. What do the rhymes contribute to the poem's comic tone?
3. Describe the poem's attitude toward beach and ocean culture.

ABRAHAM LINCOLN (1809–1865)

My Childhood's Home°   1844

My childhood's home I see again,
   And sadden with the view;
And still, as memory crowds my brain,
   There's pleasure in it too.

O Memory! thou midway world   5
   'Twixt earth and paradise,
Where things decayed and loved ones lost
   In dreamy shadows rise,

And, freed from all that's earthly vile,
   Seem hallowed, pure, and bright,   10
Like scenes in some enchanted isle
   All bathed in liquid light.

As dusky mountains please the eye
   When twilight chases day;
As bugle-notes that, passing by,   15
   In distance die away.

As leaving some grand waterfall,
   We, lingering, list its roar—

MY CHILDHOOD'S HOME. In 1844, while on a political campaign in Indiana, Lincoln visited the home where he had been raised and where his mother and sister were buried. The occasion prompted him to write this poem.

So memory will hallow all
  We've known, but know no more.   20

Near twenty years have passed away
  Since here I bid farewell
To woods and fields, and scenes of play,
  And playmates loved so well.

Where many were, but few remain   25
  Of old familiar things;
But seeing them, to mind again
  The lost and absent brings.

The friends I left the parting day,
  How changed, as time has sped!   30
Young childhood grown, strong manhood gray,
  And half of all are dead.

I hear the loved survivors tell
  How nought from death could save
Till every sound appears a knell,   35
  And every spot a grave.

I range the fields with pensive tread
  And pace the hollow rooms,
And feel (companion of the dead)
  I'm living in the tombs.   40

QUESTIONS

1. How does Lincoln's speaker explain the importance of memory? How is the sentence "So memory will hallow all / We've known, but know no more" (lines 19–20) related to the descriptions and ideas that follow?
2. Do stanzas 6 and 7 seem exaggerated, self-indulgent, or sentimental? What seems to forestall this criticism of the ideas here?
3. What leads the speaker to the conclusion he makes in the last two lines?

SHARON OLDS (b. 1942)

The Planned Child ~ ~ ~ ~ ~ 1996

I hated the fact that they had planned me, she had taken
a cardboard out of his shirt from the laundry
as if sliding the backbone up out of his body,
and made a chart of the month and put
her temperature on it, rising and falling
to know the day to make me—I would have   5
liked to have been conceived in heat,
in haste, by mistake, in love, in sex,
not on cardboard, the little x on the
rising line that did not fall again.   10

But when a friend was pouring wine
and said that I seem to have been a child who had been wanted,
I took the wine against my lips
as if my mouth were moving along   15
that valved wall in my mother's body, she was
bearing down, and then breathing from the mask, and then
bearing down, pressing me out into
the world that was not enough for her without me in it,
not the moon, the sun, Orion   20
cartwheeling across the dark, not
the earth, the sea—none of it
was enough, for her, without me.

QUESTIONS

1. Who is the speaker? What is she like? What is she talking about? Why does she
    begin the poem talking about something she hated?

2. What change of attitudes is described by the poem? Why does the poem seem to
    require such a change?

3. What attitude is expressed in the concluding global, planetary, solar, and stellar
    references? Why does the speaker state that, to her mother, she has more value
    than this image?

4. What unique qualities of perception and expression does the speaker exhibit?
    Have you ever read a poem before in which details about conception and child-
    birth have been so prominent? Why are these details included in this poem?

MICHAEL ONDAATJE (b. 1943)

Late Movies with Skyler ～く～く～ 1979

All week since he's been home
he has watched late movies alone
terrible one star films and then staggering
through the dark house to his bed
waking at noon to work on the broken car   5
he has come home to fix.

21 years old and restless
back from logging on Vancouver Island
with men who get rid of crabs with Raid
    2 minutes bending over in agony   10
    and then into the showers!

Last night I joined him for *The Prisoner of Zenda*
a film I saw three times in my youth
and which no doubt influenced me morally.
Hot coffee bananas and cheese   15
we are ready at 11.30 for adventure.

At each commercial Sky
breaks into midnight guitar practice
head down playing loud and intensely
till the movie comes on and the music suddenly stops.   20
Skyler's favourite hour's when he's usually alone
cooking huge meals of anything in the frying pan
thumbing through *Advanced Guitar* like a bible.
We talk during the film
and break into privacy during commercials   25
or get more coffee or push
the screen door open and urinate under the trees.

Laughing at the dilemmas of 1920 heroes
suggestive lines, cutaways to court officials
who raise their eyebrows at least 4 inches   30
when the lovers kiss . . .
only the anarchy of the evil Rupert of Hentzau°
is appreciated
                    And still somehow
by 1.30 we are moved   35
as Stewart Granger° girl-less and countryless
rides into the sunset with his morals and his horse.
The perfect world is over. Banana peels
orange peels ash trays guitar books.
2 a.m. We stagger through   40
into the slow black rooms of the house.
I lie in bed fully awake. The darkness
breathes to the pace of a dog's snoring.
The film is replayed to sounds
of an intricate blues guitar.   45
Skyler is Rupert then the hero.
He will leave in a couple of days
for Montreal or the Maritimes.
In the movies of my childhood the heroes
after skilled swordplay and moral victories   50
leave with absolutely nothing
to do for the rest of their lives.

LATE MOVIES WITH SKYLER. 32 *Rupert of Hentzau*: evil character in the *Prisoner of Zenda* (1952).
35 *Stewart Granger*: British actor (1913–1993) who appeared as the king in *The Prisoner of Zenda*.

QUESTIONS

1. What value does the speaker place on old movies? What details does he intro-
    duce to contrast the world of movies with the world around him? What effect do
    the activities during the commercials have on the value of the film to Skyler and
    the speaker?
2. Who is Skyler? Where has he been? What has he been doing? What will he be
    doing in the future? What is the speaker's attitude toward Skyler and his activities?

3. What comic details can you discover in the poem? What makes them comic? How does this humor affect the speaker's sympathy for Skyler and for himself?

4. Describe the tone of the last four lines. In what way are the lines relevent to Skyler and to the speaker? To what degree are these lines integral to the poem?

ROBERT PINSKY (b. 1940)

Dying   ～ ⌣ ⌣ ⌣́   1984

Nothing to be said about it, and everything—
The change of changes, closer or further away:
The Golden Retriever next door, Gussie, is dead,

Like Sandy, the Cocker Spaniel from three doors down
Who died when I was small; and every day   5
Things that were in my memory fade and die.

Phrases die out: first, everyone forgets
What doornails are; then after certain decades
As a dead metaphor, "*dead as a doornail*" flickers

And fades away. But someone I know is dying—   10
And though one might say glibly, "everyone is,"
The different pace makes the difference absolute.

The tiny invisible spores in the air we breathe,
That settle harmlessly on our drinking water
And on our skin, happen to come together,   15

With certain conditions on the forest floor,
Or even a shady corner of the lawn—
And overnight the fleshy, pale stalks gather,

The colorless growth without a leaf or flower;
And around the stalks, the summer grass keeps growing   20
With steady pressure, like the insistent whiskers

That grow between shaves on a face, the nails
Growing and dying from the toes and fingers
At their own humble pace, oblivious

As the nerveless moths, that live their night or two—   25
Though like a moth a bright soul keeps on beating,
Bored and impatient in the monster's mouth.

QUESTIONS

1. What details about death does the poem introduce? How are they connected in the poem's development? What is the effect of these details on the tone of the poem?

2. What is meant by line 12, "The different pace makes the difference absolute"? How strongly does this statement counter the phrase "everyone is" in line 11?

3. Up until line 25 this poem can be considered negative or even despairing. What is the effect of lines 26 and 27 on this negative tone? What is the meaning of the phrase "monster's mouth" in these last two lines?

ALEXANDER POPE (1685–1744)

From *Epilogue to the Satires, Dialogue I* Lines 137–172 ⤳⟨⟨⟨⟨⟨ 1738

Virtue may choose the high or low degree,
'Tis just alike to Virtue, and to me;
Dwell in a monk, or light upon a king,
She's still the same, beloved, contented thing.   140
Vice is undone, if she forgets her birth,
And stoops from angels to the dregs of earth:
But 'tis the Fall degrades her to a whore;
Let Greatness own her, and she's mean no more:°
Her birth, her beauty, crowds and courts confess,°   145
Chaste matrons praise her, and grave bishops bless:
In golden chains the willing world she draws,
And hers the gospel is, and hers the laws:
Mounts the tribunal, lifts her scarlet head,
And sees pale Virtue carted° in her stead!   150
Lo! at the wheels of her triumphal car,°   *carriage*
Old England's genius, rough with many a scar,
Dragged in the dust! his arms hang idly round,
His flag inverted trails along the ground!°
Our youth, all liveried o'er with foreign gold,   155
Before her dance; behind her crawl the old!
See thronging millions to the pagod° run,
And offer country, parent, wife, or son!
Hear her black trumpet through the land proclaim,
That "not to be corrupted is the shame."   160
In soldier, churchman, patriot, man in power,
'Tis avarice all, ambition is no more!
See, all our nobles begging to be slaves!
See all our fools aspiring to be knaves!
The wit of cheats, the courage of a whore,   165
Are what ten thousand envy and adore.
All, all look up, with reverential awe,

EPILOGUE TO THE SATIRES, DIALOGUE I. **144** *mean no more:* i.e., if the rich and powerful follow vice, vice is no longer low but fashionable. **145** *Her birth . . . confess:* i.e., under the dictates of fashion, both crowds and courts claim that Vice is both high-born and beautiful. **150** *carted:* It was an eighteenth-century punishment to display prostitutes in a cart; in addition, condemned criminals were carried in a cart from prison to Tyburn, in London, where they were hanged. **152–154** *Old England's genius . . . along the ground:* i.e., the spirit of England is humiliated by being tied to Vice's triumphal carriage and then dragged along the ground. The idea is that corrupt politicians have sacrificed England's defensive power for their own gain. **157** *pagod:* i.e., a pagoda, a symbol of how people have forsaken their own religion and adopted foreign religions.

On crimes that scape,° or triumph o'er the law: *escape*
While truth, worth, wisdom, daily they decry—
"Nothing is sacred now but villainy."   170
  Yet may this verse (if such a verse remain)
Show there was one who held it in disdain.

QUESTIONS

1. The entire poem is in the form of a dialogue, in which these concluding lines
    are identified as being spoken by "P" (Pope). Should readers therefore take
    these lines as an expression of Pope's own ideas? In your answer, pay special at-
    tention to the final couplet.

2. Explain this poem as social satire. What is attacked? What evidence does the
    speaker advance to support his case that society has deserted virtue and religion?

3. Describe the poem's tone. What specific charges does the speaker make against
    the prevailing sociopolitical structure?

4. How timely is the poem? To what degree might such charges be advanced in our
    society today?

SALVATORE QUASÍMODO (1901–1968)

Auschwitz°   ⸻   *1983*

Translated by Jack Bevan

Far from the Vistula,° along the northern plain,
love, in a death-camp there at Auschwitz:
on the pole's rust and tangled fencing, rain
funeral cold.
No tree, no birds in the grey air   5
or above our thought, but limp
pain that memory leaves
to its silence without irony or anger.
You ask no elegies or idylls: only
the meaning of our destiny, you, here,   10
hurt by the mind's war,
uncertain at the clear
presence of life. For life is here
in every No that seems a certainty:
here we shall hear the angel weep, the monster, hear   15
our future time
beating the hereafter that is here, forever
in motion, not an image

AUSCHWITZ. *Auschwitz* is the German name for the town of Oswiecim in southern Poland, site of the
most notorious of the German concentration-extermination camps in World War II. There were two major
camps—Auschwitz itself, a former Polish army camp, and nearby Birkenau, which contained many temporary barracks for worker-prisoners, together with gas chambers and crematoria for the extermination of
hundreds of thousands of victims.   1 *Vistula:* The Vistula River rises in the northern Carpathian Mountains,
south of Auschwitz.

of dreams, of possible pity.
Here are the myths, the metamorphoses.   20
Lacking the name of symbols or a god,
they are history, earth places,
they are Auschwitz, love. How suddenly
the dear forms of Alpheus and Arethusa°
changed into shadow-smoke!   25

Out of that hell hung with a white
inscription "work will make you free"°
there came the endless smoke
of many thousand women thrust at dawn
out of the kennels up to the firing-wall,   30
or, screaming for mercy to water, choked,
their skeleton mouths under the jets of gas.

You, soldier, will find them in your annals
taking the forms of animals and rivers,
or are you too, now, ash of Auschwitz,   35
medal of silence?
Long tresses in glass urns can still be seen
bound up with charms, and an infinity
of ghostly little shoes and shawls of Jews:°
relics of a time of wisdom,   40
of man whose knowledge takes the shape of arms,
they are the myths, our metamorphoses.

Over the plains where love and sorrow
and pity rotted, there in the rain
a No inside us beat;   45
a No to death that died at Auschwitz
never from the pit of ashes
to show itself again.

24 *Alpheus and Arethusa:* a river and fountain in Greece. In ancient mythology, Alpheus, who loved Arethusa, was transformed into the river (bearing his name) to be united with Arethusa, who was transformed into the fountain (bearing her name).   27 *work will make you free:* a translation of the large metal sign *Arbeit macht frei*, which crested the main gate of Auschwitz and is still on display there. A copy of the sign is displayed in the Holocaust Museum in Washington, D.C.   37–39 *Long tresses . . . shawls of Jews:* Today the barracks at Auschwitz house permanent displays that include the hair, shoes, eyeglasses, luggage, and clothing of thousands of the victims.

QUESTIONS

1. Compare the tone of the first ten lines with that of the last six. What differences do you notice? How does the idea of the last three lines answer the question posed in lines 9 and 10?

2. Even though the speaker is referring to the deadliest of all the camps, what does he mean by "For life is here / in every No that seems a certainty" (lines 13–14)?

3. In line 20 the speaker mentions ancient myths about metamorphoses or transformations. What type of metamorphosis is linked to the death camps in lines 26–42? What attitudes are brought out by this linkage?

ANNE RIDLER (1912–2001)

Nothing Is Lost   1994

Nothing is lost.
We are too sad to know that, or too blind;
Only in visited moments do we understand:
    It is not that the dead return—
        They are about us always, though unguessed.   5

    This penciled Latin verse
You dying wrote me, ten years past and more,
Brings you as much alive to me as the self you wrote it for,
    Dear father, as I read your words
        With no word but Alas.   10

    Lines in a letter, lines in a face
Are faithful currents of life: the boy has written
His parents across his forehead, and as we burn
    Our bodies up each seven years,
        His own past self has left no plainer trace.   15

    Nothing dies.
The cells pass on their secrets, we betray them
Unknowingly: in a freckle, in the way
    We walk, recall some ancestor,
        And Adam in the color of our eyes.   20

    Yes, on the face of the new born,
Before the soul has taken full possession,
There pass, as over a screen, in succession
    The images of other beings:
        Face after face looks out, and then is gone.   25

    Nothing is lost, for all in love survive.
I lay my cheek against his sleeping limbs
To feel if he is warm, and touch in him
    Those children whom no shawl could warm,
        No arms, no grief, no longing could revive.   30

    Thus what we see, or know,
Is only a tiny portion, at the best,
Of the life in which we share; an iceberg's crest
    Our sunlit present, our partial sense,
        With deep supporting multitudes below.   35

QUESTIONS

1. What is unusual about the phrase "nothing dies" (line 16)? How successfully
   does the poet explain and exemplify the idea?

2. In what ways does the "face of the new born" reflect the "images of other beings"
   (lines 21–24)? How might the "color of our eyes" demonstrate that we are descended from Adam (line 20)? How true is it that "all in love survive" (line 26)?

3. In what ways might this poem offer comfort to readers who believe strongly in the concept of their own uniqueness and originality?

THEODORE ROETHKE (1907–1963)

For a photo, see p. 656.

My Papa's Waltz 1942

The whiskey on your breath
Could make a small boy dizzy;
But I hung on like death:
Such waltzing was not easy.

We romped until the pans   5
Slid from the kitchen shelf;
My mother's countenance
Could not unfrown itself.

The hand that held my wrist
Was battered on one knuckle;   10
At every step you missed
My right ear scraped a buckle.

You beat time on my head
With a palm caked hard by dirt,
Then waltzed me off to bed   15
Still clinging to your shirt.

QUESTIONS

1. What is the tone of the speaker's opening description of his father? What is the tone of the phrases "like death" and "such waltzing"?

2. What is the "waltz" the speaker describes? What is the tone of his words describing it in lines 5–15?

3. What does the reference to his "mother's countenance" contribute to the tone? What situation is suggested by the selection of the word "unfrown"?

4. What does the tone of the physical descriptions of the father contribute to your understanding of the speaker's attitude toward his childhood experiences as his father's dancing partner?

JONATHAN SWIFT (1667–1745)

A Description of the Morning 1709

Now hardly here and there a hackney-coach
Appearing, showed the ruddy morn's approach.
Now Betty from her master's bed had flown,
And softly stole to discompose her own.

"kennel's edge
= edge of gutter

The slip-shod 'prentice from his master's door
Had pared the dirt, and sprinkled round the floor.
Now Moll had whirled her mop with dextrous airs,
Prepared to scrub the entry and the stairs.
The youth with broomy stumps began to trace
The kennel's edge,° where wheels had worn the place.   10
The small-coal man° was heard with cadence deep,   *charcoal seller*
Till drowned in shriller notes of chimney-sweep.
Duns° at his lordship's gate began to meet;— *note formal Solitutudo*   *bill collectors*
And brickdust Moll had screamed through half the street.
The turnkey° now his flock returning sees,   15
Duly let out a-nights to steal for fees.
The watchful bailiffs take their silent stands,
And schoolboys lag° with satchels in their hands.

A DESCRIPTION OF THE MORNING. 10 *kennel's edge:* that is, the edge of the gutter. Swift annotated this line "To find old Nails."   15 *turnkey:* an entrepreneur, operating a jail for profit, who allowed prisoners to go free at night so that they might bring him a night's booty to pay for the necessities provided them in jail.   18 *schoolboys lag:* cf. Shakespeare's *As You Like It*, 2.7.145–147.

QUESTIONS

1. What images of life in early-eighteenth-century London are presented in this poem? Who is "Betty"? Why is she discomposing her bed? Are such images to be considered ordinary, heroic, or antiheroic? Why?

2. Why does Swift conclude with the reference to "schoolboys" lagging "with satchels in their hands"? Why would it not have been preferable to conclude with reference to adult behavior?

3. How do you know that Swift's poem is satiric? What is being satirized?

page 765   *designed to expose human follies and vices!*

DAVID WAGONER (b. 1926)

My Physics Teacher   1981

He tried to convince us, but his billiard ball
Fell faster than his pingpong ball and thumped
To the floor first, in spite of Galileo.°
The rainbows from his prism skidded off-screen
Before we could tell an infra from an ultra.   5
His hand-cranked generator refused to spit
Sparks and settled for smoke. The dangling pith
Ignored the attractions of his amber wand,
No matter how much static he rubbed and dubbed
From the seat of his pants, and the housebrick   10
He lowered into a tub of water weighed

(Eureka!) more than the overflow.°

He believed in a World of Laws, where problems had answers,
Where tangible objects and intangible forces
Acting thereon could be lettered, numbered, and crammed   15
Through our tough skulls for lifetimes of homework.
But his only uncontestable demonstration
Came with our last class: he broke his chalk
On a formula, stooped to catch it, knocked his forehead
On the eraser-gutter, staggered slewfoot, and stuck   20
One foot forever into the wastebasket.

MY PHYSICS TEACHER. 3–12 *Galileo . . . overflow:* These lines describe classic classroom demonstrations in physics. Galileo first formulated the law of uniform falling bodies. Newton explained that a prism divides light into the colors of the rainbow. ("Infra" refers to infrared light; "ultra" to ultraviolet.) Sparks leaping across the space between two wires graphically demonstrate electrical generation and power. The motion of dried pith toward a charged piece of amber demonstrates the magnetic power of static electricity. Archimedes explained how the weight of a floating object is the same as the weight of water it displaces, and also how the volume of an immersed object (not the weight) is the same as the volume of displaced water. The physics teacher did not understand this distinction. (According to legend, Archimedes made this discovery when taking a bath, and then shouted *"Eureka!"* ["I have found it"].)

QUESTIONS

1. What idea underlies the physics teacher's use of classroom demonstrations? What is the speaker's apparent response to this idea?

2. What happens to these demonstrations? Why are these failures comic and farci-cal? What effect do the poem's farcical actions have upon the validity of the teacher's ideas?

C. K. WILLIAMS (b. 1936)

Dimensions   1969

There is a world somewhere else that is unendurable.
Those who live in it are helpless in the hands of the elements,
they are like branches in the deep woods in wind
that whip their leaves off and slice the heart of the night
and sob. They are like boats bleating wearily in fog.   5

But here, no matter what, we know where we stand.
We know more or less what comes next. We hold out.
Sometimes a dream will shake us like little dogs, a fever
hang on so we're not ourselves or love wring us out,
but we prevail, we certify and make sure, we go on.   10

There is a world that uses its soldiers and widows
for flour, its orphans for building stone, its legs for pens.
In that place, eyes are softened and harmless like God's
and all blend in the traffic of their tragedy and pass by
like people. And sometimes one of us, losing the way,   15
will drift over the border and see them there, dying,
laughing, being revived. When we come home, we are half way.
Our screams heal the torn silence. We are like scars.

QUESTIONS

1. Why should this poem be called ironic? Should the irony be called situational? Cosmic? Why?

2. What is intended by the poem's title? What is the implication of the first line? What irony does the line bring out? Describe the irony of the second stanza (lines 6–10).

3. What is meant by "losing the way" and drifting "over the border" (lines 15–16)? What is the meaning and the irony of the last three lines? What does it mean to be "like scars" (line 18)?

WILLIAM BUTLER YEATS (1865–1939)

When You Are Old ⫻⫻⫻⫻⫻ *1893*

When you are old and grey and full of sleep,
And nodding by the fire, take down this book,
And slowly read, and dream of the soft look
Your eyes had once, and of their shadows deep;

How many loved your moments of glad grace,   5
And loved your beauty with love false or true,
But one man loved the pilgrim soul in you,
And loved the sorrows of your changing face;

And bending down beside the glowing bars,
Murmur, a little sadly, how Love fled   10
And paced upon the mountains overhead
And hid his face amid a crowd of stars.

QUESTIONS

1. What is the speaker of this poem like? How does the speaker describe himself?

2. To whom is the speaker speaking? What are you asked to conclude about the past relationship between the speaker and the listener?

3. Describe the dominant attitudes expressed by the speaker. What words might describe the poem's tone?

⫻⫻ WRITING ABOUT TONE IN POETRY

Be careful to note those elements of the work that touch particularly on attitudes or authorial consideration. For example, you may be studying Hughes's "Theme for English B," where it is necessary to consider the force of the poet's claim for equality. How serious is the claim? Does the speaker's apparent matter-of-factness make him seem less than enthusiastic? Or does this tone indicate that equality is so fundamental a right that its realization should be an everyday part of life? Devising and answering such questions can help you understand the degree to which authors show control of tone. Similar questions apply when you study internal qualities such as style and characterization.

Questions for Discovering Ideas

- What is the speaker like? Is he or she intelligent, observant, friendly, idealistic, realistic, trustworthy? How do you think you should respond to the speaker's characteristics?

- Do all the speeches seem right for the speaker and situation? Are all descriptions appropriate, all actions believable?

- If the work is comic, at what is the comedy directed? At situations? At characters? At the speaker himself or herself? What is the poet's apparent attitude toward the comic objects?

- Does the writer ask you to (1) sympathize with those in misfortune, (2) rejoice with those who have found happiness, (3) lament the human condition, (4) become angry against unfairness and inequality, (5) admire examples of noble human behavior, or (6) have another appropriate emotional response?

- Do any words seem unusual or especially noteworthy, such as dialect, polysyllabic words, foreign words or phrases that the author assumes you know, or especially connotative words? What is the effect of such words on the poem's tone?

Strategies for Organizing Ideas

The goal of your essay is to examine all aspects bearing on the tone. Consider the following topics.

1. THE AUDIENCE, SITUATION, AND CHARACTERS.   Is any person or group directly addressed by the speaker? What attitude is expressed (love, respect, condescension, confidentiality, confidence, etc.)? What is the basic situation in the work? What is the nature of the speaker or persona? What is the relationship of the speaker to the material? What is the basis of the speaker's authority? Does the speaker give you the whole truth? Is he or she trying to withhold anything? Why? How is the speaker's character manipulated to show apparent authorial attitude and to stimulate responses? Do you find any of the various sorts of irony? If so, what does the irony show (optimism or pessimism, for example)? How is the situation controlled to shape your responses? That is, can actions, situations, or characters be seen as expressions of attitude or as embodiments of certain favorable or unfavorable ideas or positions? How does the work promote respect, admiration, dislike, or other feelings about character or situation?

2. DESCRIPTIONS AND DICTION.   Your concern here is to relate attitudes to the poet's use of language and description. Are there any systematic references, such as to colors, sounds, noises, natural scenes, and so on, that collectively reflect an attitude? Do connotative meanings of words control response in any way? Is any special knowledge of references or unusual words expected of readers? What is the extent of this knowledge? Do speech or dialect patterns indicate attitudes about speakers or their condition of life? Are speech patterns normal and standard or slang and substandard? What is the effect of these patterns? Are there unusual or particularly noteworthy expressions? If so, what attitudes do these show? Does the author use verbal irony? To what effect?

3. HUMOR. Is the work funny? How funny, how intense? How is the humor achieved? Does the humor develop out of incongruous situations or language, or both? Is there an underlying basis of attack in the humor, or are the objects of laughter still respected or even loved despite having humor directed against them?

4. IDEAS. Ideas may be advocated, defended mildly, attacked, or ridiculed. Which attitude is present in the work you have been studying? How does the poet make his or her attitude clear—directly, by statement, or indirectly, through understatement, overstatement, or the language of a character? In what ways does the work assume a common ground of assent between author and reader? That is, are there apparently common assumptions about religious views, political ideas, moral and behavioral standards, and so on? Are these common ideas readily acceptable, or is any concession needed by the reader to approach the work? For example, a major subject of Arnold's "Dover Beach" (Chapter 15) is that absolute belief in the truth of Christianity has been lost. This subject may not be important to everyone, but even an irreligious reader or a follower of another faith may find common ground in the poem's psychological situation or in the desire to learn as much as possible about so important an institution as religion.

5. UNIQUE CHARACTERISTICS. Each work has unique properties that contribute to the tone. For example, Roethke's "My Papa's Waltz" is a brief narrative in which the speaker's recollected feelings about his father's boisterously drunken behavior must be inferred from understatement. Hardy's "Channel Firing" (Chapter 16) develops from the comic but also absurd idea that the sounds of cannons being fired from ships at sea are so loud they could wake up the dead. Be alert for such special circumstances in the poem you are considering, and as you plan and develop your essay take them into account.

Your conclusion may summarize your main points and from there go on to any needed definitions, explanations, or afterthoughts, together with ideas reinforcing earlier points. If you have changed your mind or have made new realizations, briefly explain these. Finally, you might mention some other major aspect of the work's tone that you did not develop in the body.

DEMONSTRATIVE STUDENT ESSAY

The Tone of Confidence in "Theme for English B" by Langston Hughes°

"Theme for English B" grows from the situational irony of racial differences as seen by the speaker, an African-American college student. This situation might easily produce bitterness, anger, outrage, or vengefulness. However, the poem

°See p. 773 for this poem.

[1] contains none of these. It is not angry or indignant; it is not an appeal for revenge or revolution. It is rather a declaration of personal independence and individuality. The tone is one of objectivity, daring, occasional playfulness, but above all, confidence.* These attitudes are made plain in the speaker's situation, the ideas, the poetic form, the diction, and the expressions.[†]

[2] Hughes's poetic treatment is objective, factual, and personal, not emotional or political. The poem contains a number of factual details: The speaker is black in an otherwise all-white college English class. He has come from North Carolina and is now living alone at the Harlem YMCA, away from family and roots. He is also, at 22, an "older" student in the first-year classroom. All this is evidence of disadvantage, yet the speaker does no more than present the facts objectively, without comment.

[3] Hughes's thoughts about equality--the idea underlying the poem--are presented in the same objective, cool manner. The speaker writes to his instructor as an equal, not as an inferior. His idea is that all people are the same, regardless of race or background. In defining himself, therefore, he does not deal in abstractions, but emphasizes that he, like everyone else, has ordinary likes and needs, and that his abilities and activities are like those of everyone else. By causing the speaker to avoid emotionalism and controversy, Hughes makes counterarguments difficult if not impossible.

[4] The argument for equality is carried out even in Hughes's actual use of the poetic form. The title here is the key, for it does not promise the most exciting of topics. Normally, in fact, one would expect nothing much more than a short prose theme in response to an English assignment, but a poem is unexpected and therefore daring and original, particularly one like this that touches on the topic of equality and identity. The wit, originality, and skill of the speaker's use of the form itself demonstrate the self-confidence and self-sufficiency that underlie the theoretical claim for equality.

Hughes's diction is also in keeping with the poem's confidence and daring. Almost all the words are short and simple--of no more than one or two syllables--showing the speaker's confidence in the truth and power of his ideas. This high proportion of short words reflects a conscious attempt to keep the diction clear and direct. A result is that Hughes avoids any possible ambiguities, as the following words show:

[5]
> Well, I like to eat, sleep, drink, and be in love.
> I like to work, read, learn, and understand life.
> I like a pipe for a Christmas present,
> or records--Bessie, bop, or Bach. (lines 21-24)

With the exception of what it means to "understand life," these words are free of emotional overtones. They reflect the speaker's confident belief that equality should replace inequality and prejudice.

A number of the speaker's phrases and expressions also show this same confidence. Although most of the language is simple and descriptive, it is also playful and ironic. In lines 18-20 there seems to be a deliberate use of confusing

*Central idea.
[†]Thesis sentence.

language to bring about a verbal merging of the identities of the speaker, the instructor, Harlem, and the greater New York area:

> Harlem, I hear you:
> hear you, hear me--we two--you, me talk on this page.
> (I hear New York, too.) Me--who? (lines 18-20)

[6] One may also find a certain whimsicality in the way in which the speaker treats the irony of the black-white situation:

> So will my page be colored that I write? (line 27)

Underlying this last expression is an awareness that, despite the claim that people are equal and are tied to each other by common humanity, there are also strong differences among individuals. The speaker is confidently asserting grounds for independence as well as equality.

[7] <u>Thus, an examination of "Theme for English B" reveals vitality and confidence</u>. The poem is a statement of trust and an almost open challenge on the personal level to the unachieved ideal of equality. Hughes makes this point through the deliberate simplicity of the speaker's words and descriptions. Yet the poem is not without irony, particularly at the end, where the speaker mentions that the instructor is "somewhat more free" than he is. "Theme for English B" is complex and engaging. It shows the speaker's confidence through objectivity, daring, and playfulness.

WORK CITED

Hughes, Langston. "Theme for English B." <u>Literature: An Introduction to Reading and Writing</u>. Ed. Edgar V. Roberts and Henry E. Jacobs. 7th ed. Upper Saddle River: Prentice Hall, 2004. 773–74.

Commentary on the Essay

Because this essay embodies a number of approaches by which tone may be studied in any work (situation, common ground, diction, special characteristics), it is typical of many essays that use a combined, eclectic approach. The central idea is that the dominant attitude in "Theme for English B" is the speaker's confidence, and that this confidence is shown in the similar but separable attitudes of objectivity, daring, and playfulness.

Paragraph 2 deals with situational irony in relation to the social and political circumstance of racial discrimination (see approach 1, p. 788). Paragraph 3 considers the objectivity with which Hughes considers the idea of equality (approach 4).

Paragraph 4 shows how a topic that might ordinarily be taken for granted, in this case the basic form or genre of expression, can be seen as a unique feature of tone (approach 5). The paragraph contrasts the *expected* student response (no more than a brief prose essay) with the *actual* response (the poem itself, with its interesting twists and turns). Since the primary tone of the poem is that of self-confidence, which is the unspoken basis for the speaker's assertion of independence and equality, the paragraph stresses that the form itself embodies this attitude.

Paragraphs 5 and 6 consider how Hughes's word choices exhibit his attempts at clarity, objectivity, playfulness, and confidence (approach 2). The attention given in these paragraphs to Hughes's simple, direct diction is justified by its importance in the poem's tone.

The concluding paragraph stresses again the attitude of confidence in the poem and also notes additional attitudes of trust, challenge, irony, daring, and playfulness.

Special Topics for Writing and Argument about Tone in Poetry

1. Consider "homage to my hips," "she being Brand / -new," "The Workbox," and "The First-Rate Wife" as poems about love. What similarities do you find? That is, do the poets state that love creates joy, satisfaction, distress, embarrassment, trouble? How does the tone of each of the poems enable you to draw your conclusions? What differences do you find in the ways the poets either control or do not control tone?

2. Consider these same poems from a feminist viewpoint (see Chapter 33). What importance and value do the poems give to women? How do they view women's actions? Generally, what praise or blame do the poems deserve because of their treatment of women?

3. a. Consider the tone of Roethke's "My Papa's Waltz." Some readers have concluded that the speaker is expressing fond memories of his childhood experiences with his father. Others believe that the speaker is ambiguous about the father and that he blocks out remembered pain as he describes the father's boisterousness in the kitchen. Basing your conclusion on the tone of the poem alone, how should the poem be interpreted?

   b. In your library, find two critical biographies about Theodore Roethke published by university presses. What do these books disclose about Roethke's childhood and his family, particularly his father? On the basis of what you learn, should your interpretation of the tone of "My Papa's Waltz" be changed or unchanged? Why?

4. Write a poem about a person or occasion that has made you either glad or angry. Try to create the same feelings in your reader, but create these feelings through your rendering of situation and your choices of the right words. (*Possible topics:* a social injustice, an unfair grade, a compliment you have received on a task well done, the landing of a good job, the winning of a game, a rise in the price of gasoline, a good book or movie, and so on.)

5. What judgments about modern city life do you think Léger conveys in his painting *The City* (Insert II-8)? If the tone of paintings can be considered similar to poetic tone, in what ways is *The City* comparable to the presentation of detail in Eliot's "Preludes" (Chapter 16), Blake's "London" (Chapter 15), Sandburg's

"Chicago" (Chapter 25), and Swift's "A Description of the Morning"—together with any other poems you wish to include?

6. How does Ondaatje establish a companionable relationship between the speaker and Skyler in "Late Movies with Skyler"? In what way is this relationship connected to the tone of the poem?

7. Explain how the details and ideas in Ridler's "Nothing Is Lost" shape the poem's tone. What is the effect of the stanzaic pattern and the rhymes on your understanding and on your responses to the poem's ideas? In terms of ideas and tone, how does this poem compare with Pinsky's "Dying"?

8. Quasímodo's "Auschwitz" concerns one of the twentieth century's central evils, the most abhorrent of the Nazi death camps, about which people have expressed anger, horror, indignation, outrage, disgust, hatred, and vengefulness. To what degree do you find these attitudes in Quasímodo's poem? How do such attitudes, or others, govern the poem's tone?

Prosody: *Sound, Rhythm, and Rhyme in Poetry*

19

Prosody (the pronunciation of a song or poem) is the general word describing the study of poetic sounds and rhythms. Common alternative words are **metrics, versification, mechanics of verse,** and the **music of poetry.** Most readers, when reading poetry aloud, interpret the lines and develop an appropriate speed and expressiveness of delivery—a proper *rhythm.* Indeed, some people think of rhythm and sound as the *music* of poetry because they convey musical rhythms and tempos. Like music, poetry often requires a regular beat. The tempo and loudness of poetry may vary freely, however, and a reader may stop at any time to repeat the sounds and to think about the words and ideas. It is the music of poetry that makes the speaking and hearing of poetry dramatic, exciting, and inspiring.

In considering prosody, we should recognize that poets, being especially attuned to language, blend words and ideas together so that "the sound" becomes "an echo to the sense" (Pope, *An Essay on Criticism*). The consequence of this idea is that *prosodic technique cannot be separated from a poem's content.* For this reason, the study of prosody aims to determine how poets control their words so that the sound of a poem complements its expression of emotions and ideas.

✿ IMPORTANT DEFINITIONS FOR STUDYING PROSODY

To understand and discuss prosody, you need to be able to explain the various sounds of both speech and poetry. Let us grant that the subject is technical, detailed, and also subtle, and as a result, the study of vocal production can take, and has taken, entire careers. A basic knowledge of spoken sound, however, will enable you to analyze that aspect of the poet's craft that pertains to qualities of pronunciation and rhythm.

Vowel Sounds Create the Flow of Poetic Speech

The continuous stream of speech, whether conversation, oratory, or poetry, is provided mainly by **vowel sounds.** A vowel (from the Latin word *vox*, or "voice") results from vibrations resonating in the space between the tongue and the top of the mouth. As our tongues go up or down or forward or backward, or as they curl or flatten out, and as our lips move synchronously with our tongues, we form vowels. Some vowels are "long," such as $\bar{e}$ (fl*ee*), $\bar{a}$, (st*a*y), $\bar{o}$ (*o*pen), and $\overline{oo}$ (f*oo*d). Others are "short," such as $\breve{\imath}$ (f*i*t), $\breve{u}$ (f*u*n), and $\breve{e}$ (s*e*t). Some vowels are called "front" (e.g., s*ee*, pl*a*y) and some are called "back" (kn*ow*ing, m*oo*n), depending on the position of the tongue in the production of the sound. Some are rounded (h*ō*pe, h*ō̄*op) because their production requires pursed lips, but more are unrounded (gr*ee*n, sw*i*m).

Many of our English vowel sounds are pronounced as a **schwa,** or minimal vowel sound, despite their spellings (e.g., the *e* in "th*e* boy," the *a* in "*a*lone"). Thus, "*a*bout," "stag*e*s," "rap*i*d," "nati*o*n," and "circ*u*s" contain the vowels *a, e, i, o,* and *u,* but all the italicized letters make the same schwa sound, which in pronunciation receives a light stress.

Of special importance is the **diphthong** (two voices, two sounds), that is, a meaningful sound that begins with one vowel sound and then is completed by the movement to another vowel sound. The three English diphthongs are *i* (try, appl*i*ance), *ou* (h*ou*se, sh*ou*t), and *oi* (f*oi*l, empl*oy*).

Consonant Sounds Are Meaningful Sounds Produced Through the Creation of Vocal Obstructions in the Mouth

Consonant sounds ("sounds made at the same time [as vowels]") result from the touching and near touching of various parts of the mouth (lips, tongue, teeth, palate), thus producing meaningful sounds obstructing the flow of vowel sound. Some consonants are continuous (e.g., *m, h, sh*), while others are momentary (*t, k*). In combination, consonants and vowels make for understandable speech. The consonants are classified into three major groups.

1. STOP SOUNDS, ALSO CALLED *PLOSIVES*, ARE PERCUSSIVE AND ABRUPT.   There are six stop sounds, which are made by the momentary stoppage and release of breath either when the lips touch each other (*p* and *b*) or when the tongue touches the palate (*k* and *g*) or the alveolar ridge above the teeth (*t* and *d*).

2. CONTINUANT SOUNDS ARE SMOOTH AND FLOWING.   They are produced by the steady release of the breath in conjunction with various positions of the tongue in relation to the lips, teeth, and palate, as in *n, ng, l, r, th* (as in *thorn*), *th* (as in *the*), *f, v, s, z, sh* (as in *sharp*), and *zh* (as in plea*s*ure); or with the touching of the lower lip and upper teeth for the sounds *f* and *v*; or with the touching of both lips for the sound *m.* Two special sounds called *affricates* begin with the stops *t* and *d* and then become the continuants *sh* and *zh* (as in *chew* and *judge*).

3. SEMIVOWEL SOUNDS ARE MORE LIKE CONSONANTS THAN VOWELS.   They are midway between vowels and consonants, and they have in common that they move from an originating sound and then move to another vowel sound. They are *w* (*w*agon, *w*in, *w*eather), *y* (*y*es, *y*oung, un*i*on), and *h* (*h*ope, *h*eap).

Consonants may be either voiced or voiceless. Voiced consonants are produced with the vibration of the vocal chords (e.g., *b, d, g, v, z, zh*), and voiceless consonants are produced by the breath alone, in this way being whispered sounds (e.g., *p, t, k, f, s, sh*). Among the semivowels, *w* and *y* are voiced, but *h* is voiceless.

Nasal consonants result from the release of sound through the nose. Three consonants require the stoppage of the breath in the mouth so that the sound can be released through the nose. The consonants, called *nasals,* are *n, m,* and *ng* (as in su*n*, su*m*, and su*ng*). In English, the *n* and *m* sounds may begin and end words or may appear in the middle of a word, whereas the *ng* sound may appear in the middle or end but may not begin a word. The nasals affect the pronunciation of adjoining consonants, as in words like *mountain* and *student,* in which the *t* and *d* sounds are released nasally by many speakers of English. Adjoining consonants also affect the pronunciation of the nasal, as in words like *sink* and *think,* in which the concluding *k* sound causes the preceding nasal to be an *ng* sound, as in *sing* and *thing,* even though the sound is spelled with an *n* alone.

◆ SEGMENTS: INDIVIDUALLY MEANINGFUL SOUNDS

Individual sounds in combination make up syllables and words, and separate words in combination make up lines of poetry. Syllables and words are made up of **segments,** or individually meaningful sounds (which linguists call *segmental phonemes*). In the word *top,* there are three segments: *t, o,* and *p.* When you hear these three sounds in order, you recognize the word *top,* as distinguished from, say, *tape* and *type.* It takes three alphabetical letters—*t, o,* and *p*—to spell (or *graph*) *top,* because each letter is identical with a segment. Quite often, however, English uses more than one letter to spell a segment. For example, in the word *enough,* there are four segments (*e, n, u, f*), although six letters are required for the correct spelling: *e, n, ou,* and *gh.* The last two segments (*u* and *f*) require two letters each (two letters forming one segment are called a *digraph*). In the word *through* there are three segments but *seven* letters. To be spelled correctly in this word, the $\overline{oo}$ segment must have four letters (*ough*). Note, however, that in the word *flute,* the $\overline{oo}$ segment requires only one letter, *u.* When we study the effects of various segments in relationship to poetic rhythm, we deal with **sound;** usually our concern is with prosodic devices such as **alliteration, assonance,** and **rhyme.**

When segments are meaningfully combined, they make up syllables and words. A **syllable,** in both prose and poetry, consists of a single meaningful strand of sound such as the article *a* in "*a* table," the stem *lin* in "*lin*en," and the entire word *screech.* The article *a,* which is both a syllable and a word, has only one segment; *lin,* the first syllable of a two-syllable word, contains three segments (*lin* does not occur alone but is used in combinations such as *lin*gerie and *lin*oleum);

screech is a complete word of one syllable consisting of the five segments *s, k, r, ee,* and *tch.* The past tense of *screech* (*screeched*) adds one meaningful sound, *t,* and two letters, *ed,* but this additional sound does not create a new syllable. The understanding of what constitutes syllables is important because poetic rhythm is determined by the positions of heavily stressed and less heavily stressed syllables.

Distinguish Between Spellings and the Actual Sounds of Words

It is important—vital—to understand the differences between spelling, or **graphics,** and pronunciation, or **phonetics.** Not all English sounds are spelled and pronounced in the same way, as with *top.* Thus the letter *s* has three very different sounds in the words *sweet, sugar,* and *flows: s, sh* ("*sh*arp"), and *z.* On the other hand, the words *shape, ocean, nation, sure, fissure, Eschscholtzia,* and *machine* use different combinations of letters to spell the *sh* sound.

Vowel sounds may also be spelled in different ways. The *e* sound, for example, can be spelled *i* in *machine, ee* in *speed, ea* in *eat, e* in *even,* and *y* in *funny,* yet the vowel sounds in *eat, break,* and *bear* are not the same even though they are spelled the same. Remember this: With both consonants and vowel sounds, *do not confuse spellings with sounds.*

POETIC RHYTHM

Rhythm in speech is a combination of vocal speeds, rises and falls, starts and stops, vigor and slackness, and relaxation and tension. In ordinary speech and in prose, rhythm is not as important as the flow of ideas. In poetry, rhythm is significant because poetry is emotionally charged, compact, and intense. Poets invite us to change speeds while reading—to slow down and linger over some words and sounds and to pass rapidly over others. They also invite us to give more-than-ordinary vocal stress or emphasis to certain syllables and less stress to others. The more intense syllables are called **heavy-stress** syllables, and it is the heavy stresses that determine the **accent** or **beat** of a poetic line. The less intense syllables receive **light stress.** In traditional verse, poets select patterns called **feet,** which consist of a regularized relationship of heavy stresses to light stresses.

Scansion Is the Systematic Study of Poetic Rhythm

To study the patterns of versification in any poem, you **scan** the poem. The act of scanning—**scansion**—enables you to discover how the poem establishes a prevailing metrical pattern, and also how and why there are variations in the pattern.

DETERMINE STRESSES, OR BEATS. In the scansion of a poem, it is important to use a commonly recognized notational system to record stresses or accents. A *heavy* or *primary* stress (also called an **accented syllable**) is indicated by a prime mark or acute accent (´), or it may be indicated by capital letters, as in "To BE or NOT to BE." A *light* stress (also called an **unaccented syllable**) is indicated by a bowl-like half circle called a **breve** (˘) or sometimes by a raised circle or degree sign (°). If you are using capital letters to indicate a heavy stress, use lowercase letters to indicate the light stress, as in "When I con-SID-er HOW my LIGHT is SPENT." To separate one foot from another, a **virgule** or slash (/) is used. Thus, the following line, from Coleridge's "The Rime of the Ancient Mariner," may be schematized formally in this way.

WA - ter, / WA - ter, / EV - ery WHERE, /

Here the virgules or slashes show that the line contains two two-syllable feet followed by a single three-syllable foot.

DETERMINE THE METER OR MEASURE.   A major part of scansion is the determination of a poem's **meter,** or the number of feet in its lines. Lines containing five feet are **pentameter,** four are **tetrameter,** three are **trimeter,** two are **dimeter,** and one is **monometer.** (To these may be added the less common line lengths **hexameter,** a six-foot line; **heptameter** or **the septenary,** seven feet; and **octameter,** eight feet.) In terms of accent or beat, a trimeter line has three beats (heavy stresses), a pentameter line five beats, and so on.

❧ THE MAJOR METRICAL FEET

You are now ready to scan poems and to determine the patterns of metrical feet, which measure the relationships of syllables and stresses. In English the names of the feet are derived from Greek poetry. We may classify them as feet of two syllables, three syllables, and one syllable (or imperfect).

The Two-Syllable Foot

1. IAMB *(LIGHT/HEAVY)*.   The most important poetic foot in English is the **iamb** (a word of unknown origin), which contains a light stress followed by a heavy stress:

the WINDS

The iamb is the most important and most common foot because it most nearly duplicates natural speech while also elevating speech to poetry. It is the most versatile of English poetic feet, and it is capable of great variation. Even within the same line, iambic feet vary in intensity, so that they may support or undergird the shades of meaning designed by the poet. For example, in this line of iambic pentameter from Wordsworth's sonnet "The World Is Too Much with Us," each foot is unique.

The WINDS / that WILL / be HOWL - / ing AT / all HOURS, /

Even though "will" and "at" receive the heavy stress in their individual iambic positions, they are not as strongly emphasized as "winds," "howl-," and "hours" (indeed, they are also less strong than "all," which is in the light-stress position in the concluding iamb). Such variability, approximating the stresses and rhythms of actual speech, makes the iamb suitable for both serious and light verse, and it therefore helps poets to focus attention on ideas and emotions. If they use it with skill, it never becomes monotonous, for it does not distract readers by drawing attention to its own rhythm.

2. TROCHEE *(Heavy/Light).*   The **trochee** (*running*), sometimes called the **choree** (*dancing*), consists of a heavy accent followed by a light one.

FLOW - er

Rhythmically, most two-syllable English words are trochaic (tro-KAY-ick), as may be seen in words like *author, early, follow, major, morning, often, singing, snowfall, something, story, water, walking, willow,* and *window.* A major exception is seen in many two-syllable words beginning with prefixes, such as *sublime, because,* and *impel.* Another exception is found in two-syllable words that are borrowed from another language but are still pronounced as in the original language, as with *machine, technique, garage,* and *chemise,* all of which are recent importations from French, in which an iambic structure prevails. Illustrating the strength of trochaic rhythms in English, however, the final stresses in many French words borrowed hundreds of years ago now accent the next-to-last syllable, as with *apartment, cherry, expression, language, lesson, nation,* and *very.*

Because trochaic rhythm has often been called *falling, dying, light,* or *anticlimactic,* and because iambic rhythm has been called *rising, elevating, serious,* and *climactic,* poets have preferred the iambic foot. They therefore have arranged various placements of single- and multiple-syllable words, and have also used a variety of other means, so that the heavy-stress syllable is at the end of the foot, as in Shakespeare's

With - IN / his BEND - / ing SICK - / le's COM - / pass COME, /

in which three successive trochaic words (*bending, sickle's,* and *compass*) are arranged to match the iambic meter.

3. SPONDEE *(Heavy/Heavy).*   The **spondee** (originally two long notes played at the pouring of an offering)—also called a **hovering accent**—consists of two successive, equally heavy accents, as in "men's eyes" in Shakespeare's line

When IN / dis - GRACE / with FOR - / tune AND / MEN'S EYES

The spondee is mainly a substitute foot in English verse because successive spondees usually become iambs or trochees. An entire poem written in spondees would be unlikely within traditional metrical patterns and ordinary English syntax (but see Brooks's poem "We Real Cool"). As a substitute, however, the spondee creates emphasis. The usual way to indicate the spondaic foot is to link the two syllables together with chevronlike marks like this:

MEN'S EYES

4. PYRRHIC *(LIGHT/LIGHT).* The **pyrrhic** (a foot, a war dance) consists of two unstressed syllables, even though one of them may be in a normally stressed position, as in "on their" in this line from Pope's *Pastorals*.

Now SLEEP - / ing FLOCKS / on their / SOFT FLEE - / ces LIE. /

The pyrrhic is made up of weakly accented words such as prepositions (e.g., *on, to*) and articles (*the, a*). Like the spondee, it is a substitute foot for an iamb or a trochee. An entire poem could not be in pyrrhics because the pyrrhics, like spondees, would be resolved as trochees and iambs. As a substitute foot, however, the pyrrhic acts as a rhythmic catapult to move the reader swiftly to the next heavy-stress syllable, and therefore it undergirds the ideas conveyed by more important words.

The Three-Syllable Foot

1. DACTYL *(HEAVY/LIGHT/LIGHT).* The **dactyl** (after the shape of a finger, which has a long joint and two shorter joints) has a heavy stress followed by two lights.

GREEN as our / HOPE in it, / WHITE as our / FAITH in it. / (Swinburne)

2. ANAPEST *(LIGHT/LIGHT/HEAVY).* The **anapest** ("beaten back," or "turned around"; the reverse of a dactyl) consists of two light accents followed by a heavy accent.

by the DAWN'S / ear - ly LIGHT. / (Key)

The Imperfect Foot

A single stressed syllable (´) by itself or an unstressed syllable (˘) by itself creates an **imperfect foot.** This foot is a variant or substitute occurring in a poem in which one of the major feet forms the metrical pattern. The second line of Key's "The Star-Spangled Banner," for example, is anapestic, but it contains an imperfect foot at the end.

What so PROUD - / ly we HAILED / at the TWI - /light's last GLEAM - / ing. /

SPECIAL METERS

In many poems you will find meters other than those described above. Poets like Browning, Tennyson, Poe, and Swinburne introduce special or unusual meters. Other poets manipulate pauses or **caesurae** (discussed later) to create the effects of unusual meters. For these reasons, you should know about metrical feet such as the following:

1. **Amphibrach** (short at both ends). A light, heavy, and light:

   Ah FEED me / and FILL me / with PLEAS - ure. / (Swinburne)

2. **Amphimacer** (long at both ends) *or* **Cretic** (a song from the Island of Crete). A heavy, light, and heavy:

   LOVE is BEST. /   (Browning)

3. **Bacchius** or **Bacchic** (pertaining to Bacchus, the god of wine and conviviality). A light stress followed by two heavy stresses:

   Some LATE LARK / [SING - ing]. /   (Henley)

4. **Dipodic measure** (literally, "two feet" combining to make one) or **syzygy** (a yoking together), or **double duple** meter. Dipodic measure develops in longer lines when a poet submerges two regular feet under a stronger beat, so that a "galloping" or "rollicking" rhythm results. The following line from Masefield's "Cargoes," for example, may be scanned as trochaic hexameter, with the concluding foot being an iamb.

   QUIN - que / REME of / NIN - e - / VEH from / DIS-tant / o - PHIR, /

   In reading, however, a stronger beat is superimposed, which makes one foot out of two—dipodic measure or syzygy.

   QUIN - quer - eme of / NIN - e - veh from / DIS - tant o – PHIR, /

SUBSTITUTION

Most regular poems (i.e., poems written according to the "rules" of prosody) follow a formal pattern that may be analyzed according to the feet we have been describing here. Too much formal regularity, however, sometimes makes for monotony, and so for interest and emphasis (and also, especially, because of the natural rhythms of English speech), poets frequently alter and enlarge the regular patterns through the **substitution** of a dominant foot by a variant foot. Thus in an iambic line the poet may insert a spondee or an anapest and by this means may provide a wider and more conversational rhythmical range than the unvarying use of the poem's chosen pattern can achieve. As an example, the pattern of Swift's "A Description of the Morning" (Chapter 18) is iambic pentameter (i.e., five iambs per line). However, Swift introduces a formal substitution at the beginning of the following line.

DUNS at / his LORD - / ship's GATE / be - GAN / to MEET; /

The first foot is a trochee, and the strong accent on *Duns* enables Swift to stress his comic assertion that even a member of the nobility, who supposedly has the money to pay his bills, does not do so and therefore is dunned by bill collectors. Note also that the light accent on *at* enables the voice to move rapidly through *at his lord-*. Thus, although the first two feet are a trochee and an iamb, the rhythmical effect is that of an imperfect foot followed by an anapest. This simple substitution helps Swift to emphasize and satirize the unglamorous side of London life early in the eighteenth century.

When studying rhythm, your main concern in noting substitutions is to determine the formal metrical pattern and then to analyze the variations on this pattern and their principal techniques and effects. Always try to show how these variations have enabled the poet to get points across and to achieve emphasis.

❧ ACCENTUAL, STRONG-STRESS, AND "SPRUNG" RHYTHMS

The foregoing descriptions of poetic feet will enable the analysis of most so-called traditional poetry. A number of poets, however, stretch the bounds of traditional feet, and use generally unmeasured rhythms derived from accentual or strong stresses. Such lines are historically linked to the poetry of Old English (see Chapter 13, p. 614). At that time, each line was divided in two, with two major stresses, also alliterated, occurring in each half. In the nineteenth century, Gerard Manley Hopkins (1844–1889) developed what he called "sprung" rhythm, a rhythm in which the major stresses would be released or **sprung** from the line. The method is complex, but a primary characteristic is the placement together of one-syllable stressed words, as in this line from "Pied Beauty"(Chapter 25).

With SWIFT, SLOW; SWEET, SOUR; a - DAZZ - le, DIM;

Here a number of elements combine to create six major stresses. Many of Hopkins's lines combine alliteration and strong stresses in this way to create the same heavy emphasis.

A parallel instance of strongly stressed lines is seen in "We Real Cool" by Brooks. In this poem the effect is achieved by the exclusive use of monosyllabic stressed words combined with internal rhyme, repetition, and alliteration.

THE CAESURA: THE PAUSE CREATING VARIETY AND NATURAL RHYTHMS IN POETRY

Whenever we speak, we run words together rapidly, without pause, but we do stop briefly and almost unnoticeably between significant units or phrases. Intelligible conversation could not take place without these pauses, which, both grammatically and rhythmically, create separate units of meaning called **cadence groups.** In poetry using a regular meter, the cadence groups operate just as they do in prose to make ideas clear. That is, while we follow the poetic measures, we also pause briefly at the ends of phrases, and we pause longer, for emphasis, at the ends of sentences. In scansion, the name of these pauses, which linguists call *junctures*, is **caesura** (a "cutting off"), pluralized as **caesurae.** When writing out our scansion of a line, we use two diagonal slashes or virgules (//) to indicate a caesura so that the caesura can be distinguished from the single virgule separating feet. Often the caesura coincides with the end of a foot, as at the end of the second iamb in this line by William Blake ("To Mrs. Anna Flaxman").

> With hands / di - vine // he mov'd / the gen - / tle Sod. /

The caesura, however, may fall within a foot, and there may be more than one in a line, as within the second and third iambs in this line by Ben Jonson from a poem of praise about a country estate named "Penshurst."

> Thou ART / not, // PENS - / hurst, // BUILT / to EN - / vious SHOW. /

When a caesura ends a line, usually marked by a comma, semicolon, or period, that line is **end-stopped,** as in this famous line opening Keats's "Endymion."

> A thing / of beau - / ty // is / a joy / for - ev - er. //

If a line has no punctuation at the end and the thought carries over to the next line, it is called **run-on.** A term also used to indicate run-on lines is **enjambement.** The following passage, a continuation of the line from Keats, contains three run-on lines.

> Its loveliness increases; // it will never
> Pass into nothingness; // but still will keep
> A bower quiet for us, // and a sleep
> Full of sweet dreams, // . . .

It is important to recognize that the formal rhythms of poetry are superimposed on the rhythms of natural speech, creating a tension between the two. By manipulating the placement of caesurae, the pauses that fall randomly in speech, poets create many of the variant rhythms that are provided by formal substitution. If the poet ends a cadence group within a foot, the pause, or caesura, may cause us actually to *hear* trochees, amphibrachs, and other variant feet even though the line may scan correctly and regularly in the established meter. This type of *de facto* variation is **rhetorical substitution.** A noteworthy example in an iambic pentameter line is this one from the first Epistle of Pope's *Essay on Man.*

His AC - / tions', // PAS - / sions', // BE - / ing's, // USE / and END. /

This is the second line in a "heroic" couplet, which theoretically requires that there should be only a single caesura following the fourth syllable. In this line, however, Pope provides us with great rhythmical variety. He uses not one but rather three caesurae, each of them producing an emphatic pause or juncture. Pope's line is regularly iambic, but the effect is different in actual reading or speaking. Because of the caesurae after the third, fifth, and seventh syllables, the rhythm produces an amphibrach, a trochee, another trochee, and an amphimacer. The effect is a skillful line containing two inner two-syllable feet, framed by two three-syllable feet, thus:

His AC - tions', // PAS - sions', // BE - ing's, // USE and END.
TROCHEE   TROCHEE   AMPHIMACER   AMPHIBRACH

The spoken substitutions effected by the caesurae in this regular line produce the effect of substitution—rhetorical substitution—and therefore tension and interest. Never believe that Pope did not know what he was doing with words and rhythms.

⸙ SEGMENTAL POETIC DEVICES

Once you have completed your analysis of rhythms, you should consider the segmental poetic devices in the poem. Usually these devices are used to create emphasis, but sometimes in context they may echo or imitate actions and objects. The segmental devices most common in poetry are *assonance, alliteration, onomatopoeia,* and *euphony and cacophony.*

Identical Vowel Sounds Create Assonance

Assonance is the repetition of identical *vowel* sounds in different words—for example, the short *ĭ* in "sw*i*ft Cam*i*lla sk*i*ms." It is a strong means of emphasis, as in the following line, where the *u* sound connects the two words *lull* and *slumber,* and the short *ĭ* connects *him, in,* and *his.*

And more, to l*u*ll h*i*m *i*n h*i*s sl*u*mber soft. (Spenser)

Identical Consonant Sounds Create Alliteration

Like assonance, **alliteration** is a means of highlighting ideas by words containing the same consonant sound—for example, the repeated *m* in Spenser's "*M*ixed with a *m*ur*m*uring wind," or the *s* sound in Edmund Waller's praise of Oliver Cromwell, "Your never-failing *s*word made war to cea*s*e," which emphasizes the connection between the words *sword* and *cease*.

There are two kinds of alliteration. Most commonly, alliteration is regarded as the repetition of identical consonant sounds that begin syllables in close patterns—for example, in Pope's lines "La*b*orious, heavy, *b*usy, *b*old, and *b*lind," "While *p*ensive *p*oets *p*ainful vigils keep," and "*b*razen *b*rainless *b*rothers." When used judiciously, alliteration gives strength to ideas by emphasizing key words, but too much *c*an *c*ause *c*omi*c* and *c*atastrophi*c* *c*onse*qu*ences.

The second form of alliteration occurs when a poet repeats identical or similar consonant sounds that do not begin syllables but nevertheless create a pattern—for example, the *z* segment in the line "In the*s*e place*s* free*z*ing bree*z*es ea*s*ily cau*s*e snee*z*es," or the *m*, *b*, and *p* segments (all of which are made *bilabially*, that is, with both lips) in "The *m*iserably *m*u*mb*ling and *m*o*m*entously *m*ur*m*uring *b*eggar *p*ro*p*els *p*egs and *p*e*bb*les in the *b*u*bb*ling *p*ool." Such clearly designed patterns are hard to overlook.

Verbal Imitation of Real Sounds Is Onomatopoeia, or "Poetic Sound Effects"

Onomatopoeia is a blend of consonant and vowel sounds designed to *imitate* or *suggest* a situation or an action. It is made possible in poetry because many English words are **echoic** in origin; that is, they are verbal echoes of the actions they describe, such as *buzz, bump, slap,* and so on. In "The Bells," Poe uses such words *826* to create onomatopoeia. Through the combined use of assonance and alliteration, he imitates the kinds of bells that he celebrates. Thus, wedding bells sound softly with "m*o*lten g*o*lden n*o*tes" (*o*), while alarm bells "*cl*ang and *cl*ash and roar" (*kl*). David Wagoner includes imitative words like *tweedledy, thump,* and *wheeze* to suggest the sounds of the music produced by the protagonist of his "March for a One-Man Band." *835*   *the music*

Pleasing Sounds Create Euphony and Harsh Sounds Create Cacophony

Words describing smooth or jarring sounds, particularly those resulting from consonants, are euphony and cacophony. **Euphony** ("good sound") refers to words containing consonants that permit an easy and smooth flow of spoken sound. Although there is no rule that some consonants are inherently more pleasant than others, students of poetry often cite sounds like *m, n, ng, l, v,* and *z,* together with *w* and *y,* as being especially easy on the ears. The opposite of euphony is **cacophony** ("bad sound"), in which percussive and choppy sounds make for vigorous and noisy pronunciation, as in tongue twisters like "*black* bug's blood" and "shuffling shellfish fashioned by a selfish sushi chef." Obviously, unintentional cacophony is a mark of imperfect control. When a poet deliberately creates it for effect, however, as in Pope's "The hoarse, rough verse should like the torrent roar" (*An Essay on Criticism*), and in Coleridge's "Huge fragments vaulted like rebounding hail, / Or chaffy grain beneath the thresher's flail" ("Kubla Khan"), cacophony is a mark of poetic skill. Although poets generally aim at easily flowing, euphonious lines, cacophony does have a place, always depending on the poet's intention and subject matter.

RHYME: THE DUPLICATION AND SIMILARITY OF SOUNDS

Rhyme refers to words containing identical final syllables. One type of rhyme involves words with identical concluding vowel sounds, or assonance, as in *day, weigh, hey, bouquet, fiancé,* and *matinee*. A second type of rhyme is created by assonance combined with identical consonant sounds, as in *ache, bake, break,* and *opaque*; or *turn, yearn, fern, spurn,* and *adjourn;* or *apple* and *dapple;* or *slippery* and *frippery*. Rhymes like these, because their rhyming sounds are identical, are called **exact rhymes.** It is important to note that rhymes result from *sound* rather than from spelling; words do not have to be spelled the same way or look alike to rhyme. All the words rhyming with *day,* for example, are spelled differently, but because they all contain the same ā, sound, they rhyme.

Rhyme, above all, gives delight. It also strengthens a poem's psychological impact. Through its network of similar sounds that echo and resonate in our minds, it promotes memory by clinching feelings and ideas. It has been an important aspect of poetry for hundreds of years, and, although many poets have shunned it because they find it restrictive and artificial, it is closely connected with how well particular poems move us or leave us flat. There are few restrictions on the types of words that poets may choose in making rhymes. Nouns may be rhymed with verbs, adjectives, adverbs, and other nouns or with any other rhyming word, regardless of part of speech.

Most often, rhymes are placed at the ends of lines. Two successive lines may rhyme, for example, or rhymes may appear in alternating lines. It is also possible to introduce rhyming words at intervals of four, five, or more lines. If rhyming sounds are too far away from each other, however, it is difficult for readers to recall them and they therefore lose their effectiveness. Sometimes poets use rhyme within individual lines—**internal rhyme.** Poe uses internal rhyme effectively in the concluding stanzas of "Annabel Lee," where he rhymes the words *ever dissever; beams, dreams; rise, eyes;* and *tide* and *side*. Internal rhyme is not common, but you should be alert for it and make note of it when it occurs.

Poets who are skillful and original rhymers are able to create fresh, unusual, and surprising turns of thought. We can therefore judge poets on their use of rhyme. Often poets become quite creative rhymers, putting together words like *bent 'em* and *Tarentum* or *masterly* and *dastardly*. Some rhymers, whom an anonymous sixteenth-century critic called a "rakehelly rout of ragged rhymers," are satisfied with easy rhymes, or **cliché rhymes,** like *trees* and *breeze* (a rhyme that

Alexander Pope criticized in 1711 in *An Essay on Criticism*). But good rhymes and good poets go together, in creative cooperation. The seventeenth-century poet John Dryden, who wrote volumes of rhyming couplets, acknowledged that the need to find rhyming words inspired ideas he had not anticipated. In this sense, rhyme has been—and still is—a vital element of poetic creativity.

RHYME AND METER

The effects of rhyme are closely bound to rhythm and meter. There is general agreement that rhymes coinciding with a strong accent are conducive to serious subjects. Commensurately, rhymes coinciding with syllables of light stress are appropriate for light and comic subject matter. There is no hard-and-fast rule about such matters, for the effects of rhyme always result from the poet's skill, regardless of rhymes. There is enough truth in the observations, however, to warrant considering the relationship of rhyme and accent.

Rising Rhymes Form the Climaxing Syllables of Iambs and Anapests

The most significant type of **rising rhyme** is **iambic rhyme,** which utilizes one-syllable words in an iambic foot (like *the west* and *in rest, more strong* and *ere long*) and two-syllable words in which the accent falls on the second syllable (like *away* and *today, demand* and *command.* Such rhymes are also called **heavy-stress rhyme** or **accented rhyme.** Iambic rhyme is illustrated in the opening lines of Robert Frost's "Stopping by Woods on a Snowy Evening" (Chapter 13; italics added).

> Whose woods / these are / I think / I *KNOW.* // *Iambic rhyme*
> His house / is in / the vil- / lage *THOUGH;* //

Here, the rhyming sounds are produced by one-syllable words—*know* and *though*—that occur in the final heavy-stress positions of the lines. The rhyme climaxing a final syllable can also involve spondees, as in lines 9–12 of Shakespeare's "Sonnet 18: Shall I Compare Thee to a Summer's Day?" (Chapter 17; italics added).

But thy eternal summer shall *not fade,*
Nor lose possession of that fair *thou owest;*
Nor shall Death brag thou wand'rest in *his shade,*
When in eternal lines to time *thou growest:*

Byron, in the anapestic poem "The Destruction of Sennacherib" (Chapter 25), uses rising rhymes inasmuch as the anapest consists of two light accents followed by a heavy accent.

The Assyrian came down like the wolf *on the fold,*
And his cohorts were gleaming in pur*ple and gold.*

Falling Rhymes Conclude with One or Two or More Lightly Stressed Syllables

Rhymes using words of two or more syllables in which the heavy stress is followed by light syllables are **trochaic rhyme** or **double rhyme** for two-syllable rhymes, **dactylic rhyme** or **triple rhyme** for three-syllable rhymes. Less technically, these types of rhymes are also called **falling rhymes** or **dying rhymes** because the intensity of pronunciation decreases on the light accent or accents following the heavy accent. Falling rhyme is seen in lines 2 and 4 of "Miniver Cheevy" by Edwin Arlington Robinson (italics added).

> Miniver Cheevy, child of scorn
>   Grew lean while he assailed the _seasons_;
> He wept that he was ever born,
>   And he had _reasons_.

falling rhymes

Here the double rhyme undergirds the humor of the passage, thus helping to make Miniver Cheevy seem self-centered and pathetic.

Double rhymes can also be used to bring out irony or anticlimax, as in "a-dying" and "flying" in Browning's "Soliloquy of the Spanish Cloister" (Chapter 25, lines 53-56; italics added). *1078*

> If I trip him just _a-dying_,
>   Sure of heaven as sure can be,
> Spin him round and send him _flying_
>   Off to hell, a Manichee?

Browning uses trochaic rhymes freely throughout this poem, including the rhyming of English and Latin words ("rose-acacia" and "_Plena gratiã_"). The effect of such rhymes is to complement Browning's exposé of the anger and hypocrisy of the speaker, a monk, who condemns no one but himself as he inveighs against a saintly fellow monk. *Inveighs- protests or complains forcefully*

Dactylic or **triple rhyme,** even more than trochaic rhyme, is light or humorous because it tends to minimize the subject matter and maximize the rhythm, as in Eliot's "Macavity: The Mystery Cat," where Eliot rhymes _Macavity_ with _gravity, depravity,_ and _suavity._ These are comic rhymes, totally in keeping with the nature of the poem's feline hero. Ogden Nash makes great use of such rhymes in "Very Like a Whale." There, among other ingenious and amusing rhymes, we see _better for_ rhymed with _metaphor,_ and _experience_ with _Assyrians._ How many of us could come up with rhymes like these?

 815

Variations in Rhyme Extend the Boundaries of Rhyming Poetry

Unlike poets writing in other languages (such as Italian, which offers virtually endless rhyming possibilities because most Italian words end in vowel sounds), English poets are limited in selecting rhymes because our language is short in identical word terminations. To compensate for this shortfall of English rhymes, a tradition has grown that many English words may be rhymed even if their sounds do not duplicate each other exactly.

Rhymes may therefore be created out of words with similar but not identical sounds—**inexact rhyme.** In most inexact rhymes, either the vowel segments are different while the consonants are the same, or vice versa. In addition to inexact rhyme, this type of rhyme is variously called **slant rhyme, near rhyme, half rhyme, off rhyme, analyzed rhyme,** or **suspended rhyme.** In employing slant rhyme, a poet can pair *bleak* with *broke* or *could* with *solitude.* Emily Dickinson uses slant rhyme extensively in "To Hear an Oriole Sing"; in the second stanza of the poem she rhymes *bird, unheard,* and *crowd. Bird* and *unheard* form an exact rhyme, but the vowel and consonant shift in *Crowd* produces a slant rhyme.

Another common variation is **eye rhyme** or **sight rhyme.** In eye rhyme, the sounds to be eye-rhymed are *identical in spelling* but *different in pronunciation.* Entire words may be eye-rhymed, so that *wind* (verb) may be joined to *wind* (noun), and *cóntest* (noun) may be used with *contést* (verb). In most eye rhymes, however, it is only the relevant parts of words that must be spelled identically. Thus *stove* may pair with *prove* and *above,* and *bough* may match *cough, dough, enough,* and *through,* despite all the differing pronunciations The following lines contain eye rhyme.

Although his claim was not to praise but *bury,*
His speech for Caesar roused the crowd to *fury.*

The different pronunciations of *bury* and *fury* make clear the contrast between exact rhyme and eye rhyme. In exact rhyme, identical sound is crucial; spelling is usually the same but may be different as long as the sounds remain identical. In eye rhyme, the eye-rhyming patterns must be spelled identically but the sounds must be different.

An additional variation is **identical rhyme**; that is, the same words are placed into rhyming positions, such as *veil* and *veil* or *stone* and *stone.* Perhaps the most extreme variation is **vowel rhyme,** in which poets put words ending in vowels into rhyming positions, as in *day* and *sky* or *key* and *play.*

RHYME SCHEMES

A **rhyme scheme** refers to a poem's pattern of rhyming sounds, which can be schematized by alphabetical letters. The first rhyming sounds, such as *love* and *dove,* are marked with an *a*; the next rhyming sounds, such as *swell* and *fell,* receive a *b*; the next sounds, such as *first* and *burst,* receive a *c*; and so on. Thus, a pattern of lines ending with the words *love, moon, thicket; dove, June, picket;* and *above, croon, wicket* can be schematized as *a b c, a b c, a b c.*

To formulate a rhyme scheme or pattern, you include the meter and the number of feet in each line as well as the letters indicating rhymes. Here is such a formulation.

Iambic pentameter: *a b a b, c d c d, e f e f*

This scheme shows that all the lines in the poem are iambic, with five feet in each line. Commas are used here to mark a stanzaic pattern of three 4-line units, or **quatrains,** with the rhymes falling on the first and third, and the second and fourth, lines of each quatrain.

Should the number of feet in the lines of a poem or **stanza** vary, you show this fact by using a number in front of each letter.

Iambic: *4a 3b 4a 3b 5a 5a 4b*

This formulation shows an intricate pattern of rhymes and line lengths in a stanza of seven lines. The first, third, fifth, and sixth lines rhyme and vary from four to five feet. The second, fourth, and seventh lines also rhyme and vary from three to four feet.

The absence of a rhyme sound is indicated by an *x*. Thus, you formulate the rhyme scheme of **ballad measure** like this:

Iambic: *4x 3a 4x 3a*

The formulation shows that the quatrain alternates iambic tetrameter (four feet) with iambic trimeter (three feet). In this ballad quatrain, only lines 2 and 4 rhyme; there is no end rhyme in lines 1 and 3.

POEMS FOR STUDY

GWENDOLYN BROOKS (1917–2000)

We Real Cool  1959

Spondee

The Pool Players.
Seven at the Golden Shovel.

We real cool. We
Left school. We

Lurk late. We
Strike straight. We

Sing sin. We   5
Thin gin. We

Jazz June. We
Die soon.

QUESTIONS

1.   What is the major idea of the poem? Who is the speaker? How is the last sentence a climax? How is this sentence consistent with the declarations in lines 1–7? How is the poet's attitude made clear?

2.   Describe the patterning of stresses in the poem. Explain the absence of light stresses. What method is employed to achieve the constant strong stresses?

ROBERT BROWNING (1812–1889)   *For a photo, see p. 673.*

Porphyria's Lover° 1836

The Rain set early in to-night,
   The sullen wind was soon awake,
It tore the elm-tops down for spite,
   And did its worst to vex the lake:
   I listened with heart fit to break.   5
When glided in Porphyria; straight
   She shut the cold out and the storm,
And kneeled and made the cheerless grate
   Blaze up, and all the cottage warm;
   Which done, she rose, and from her form   10
Withdrew the dripping cloak and shawl,
   And laid her soiled gloves by, untied
Her hat and let the damp hair fall,
   And, last, she sat down by my side
   And called me. When no voice replied,   15
She put my arm about her waist,
   And made her smooth white shoulder bare,

PORPHYRIA'S LOVER. When Browning published this poem in his *Dramatic Lyrics* of 1842, he grouped it with another poem under the title "Madhouse Cells."

And all her yellow hair displaced,
  And, stooping, made my cheek lie there,
  And spread, o'er all, her yellow hair.   20
Murmuring how she loved me—she
  Too weak, for all her heart's endeavor,
To set its struggling passion free
  From pride, and vainer ties dissever,
  And give herself to me forever,   25
But passion sometimes would prevail,
  Nor could to-night's gay feast restrain
A sudden thought of one so pale
  For love of her, and all in vain:
  So, she was come through wind and rain.   30
Be sure I looked up at her eyes
  Happy and proud; at last I knew
Porphyria worshipped me: surprise
  Made my heart swell, and still it grew
  While I debated what to do.   35
That moment she was mine, mine, fair,
  Perfectly pure and good: I found
A thing to do, and all her hair
  In one long yellow string I wound
  Three times her little throat around   40
And strangled her. No pain felt she;
  I am quite sure she felt no pain.
As a shut bud that holds a bee,
  I warily oped her lids: again
  Laughed the blue eyes without a stain.   45
And I untightened next the tress
  About her neck; her cheek once more
Blushed bright beneath my burning kiss:
  I propped her head up as before
  Only, this time my shoulder bore   50
Her head, which droops upon it still:
  The smiling rosy little head,
So glad it has its utmost will,
  That all it scorned at once is fled,
  And I, its love, am gained instead!   55
Porphyria's love: she guessed not how
  Her darling one wish would be heard.
And thus we sit together now,
  And all night long we have not stirred,
  And yet God has not said a word!   60

QUESTIONS

1.   What is the situation in this poem? Who is the speaker? Where is he at the time he is speaking? To whom is he speaking?

2.   Who is Porphyria? What has happened after her meeting with the speaker?

3. Explain the speaker's mental state. What evidence do you find for asserting that he is unstable? What is his justification for strangling Porphyria?

4. Describe the pattern of rhymes in the poem. What is the prevailing metrical pattern? What variations seem consistent with the speaker's mental condition?

5. Why do you suppose Browning chose circumstances like these for the subject of a poem?

EMILY DICKINSON (1830–1886)

For a photo, see p. 1012.

To Hear an Oriole Sing (F402, J526) 1891 (ca. 1862)

[handwritten: Slant rhyme 809 this poem]

To hear an Oriole sing
May be a common thing –
Or only a divine.

It is not of the Bird *[handwritten: rhyme]*
Who sings the same, unheard,   5
As unto Crowd –

The Fashion of the Ear
Attireth that it hear
In Dun, or fair –

So whether it be Rune,   10
Or whether it be none
Is of within.

The "Tune is in the Tree –"
The Skeptic – showeth me –
"No Sir! In Thee!"   15

QUESTIONS

1. What can you deduce about the speaker? The listener? Who speaks in line 13? To whom is line 15 addressed?

2. Formulate the rhyme scheme of this poem. How does it help subdivide the poem into cohesive units of thought? To what extent does it unify the poem?

3. Locate all the slant rhymes in this poem. What effect do these have on your reading and perception? How is the rhyme here like the oriole's song?

4. To what degree does rhyme reinforce meaning? Note especially the rhyme words in the final stanza.

JOHN DONNE (1572–1631)

For a drawing, see p. 648.

The Sun Rising 1633

Busy old fool, unruly Sun,
Why dost thou thus,

[handwritten margin notes: savage-insolent, contemptuously, rude]

[handwritten left margin: Pedantic—one who is Too concerned with or shows off his learning]

Through windows, and through curtains call on us?
Must to thy motions lovers' seasons run?
    Saucy pedantic wretch, go chide° ~ *scold*   5
    Late school boys and sour prentices,°   *apprentices*
Go tell Court-huntsmen, that the King will ride,
Call country ants to harvest offices;° ~ *duties*   *duties*
Love, all alike, no season knows, nor clime,° *climate*   *climate*
Nor hours, days, months, which are the rags of time.   10

[handwritten: fall harvest]
[handwritten: auto]

    Thy beams, so° reverend, and strong   *[handwritten: Think?]*
    Why shouldst thou think?°
I could eclipse and cloud them with a wink,
But that I would not lose her sight so long;
    If her eyes have not blinded thine,   15
    Look, and tomorrow late, tell me,
Whether both the Indias of spice and Mine°
Be where thou leftst them, or lie here with me.
Ask for those kings whom thou saw'st yesterday,
And thou shalt hear, All here in one bed lay.   20

[handwritten: East indies / West indies]

    She'is° all States, and all Princes, I,
    Nothing else is.
Princes do but play us; compared to this,
All honor's mimic; all wealth alchemy.°
    Thou, sun, art half as happy'as° we,   25
    In that the world's contracted thus;
Thine age asks ease, and since thy duties be
To warm the world, that's done in warming us.
Shine here to us, and thou art everywhere;
This bed thy center° is, these walls, thy sphere.   30

[handwritten: Trochee - poetic foot with alternating accents]

THE SUN RISING. 8 *Call . . . offices*: i.e., Notify the country's ants to carry out the duty of eating the harvest of grain and produce. 11, 12 *Thy beams . . . think?*: i.e., why shouldst thou think that thy beams are so reverend and strong? 17 *Indias of spice and Mine*: The India of "spice" is the East Indies; the India of "Mine" (gold) is the West Indies. 21 *She'is*: For scansion, these two words are to be considered one syllable ("shé's"). 24 *all wealth alchemy*: i.e., all wealth is false because it has been created by alchemists. 25 *happy'as*: to be scanned as a trochee ("háppyàz"). 30 *center*: the earth, around which the sun revolves (according the the Ptolemaic view of the solar system).

QUESTIONS

1.   What is the speaker like? How deeply does he seem to be in love? How does he feel about love? What evidence do you find that the speaker has a good sense of humor?

2.   To whom is the poem addressed? What is the speaker's attitude toward this listener?

3.   What solar, seasonal, geographical, and political metaphors are developed in the poem?

4.   What is the poem's rhyme scheme? What is the metrical norm of the lines? What variations on this norm do you find in the poem?

T.S. ELIOT (1888–1965)

For a photo, see p. 707.

Macavity: The Mystery Cat   1939

Macavity's a Mystery Cat: he's called the Hidden Paw—
For he's the master criminal who can defy the Law.
He's the bafflement of Scotland Yard, the Flying Squad's despair:
For when they reach the scene of the crime—*Macavity's not there!*

Macavity, Macavity, there's no one like Macavity,   5
He's broken every human law, he breaks the law of gravity.
His powers of levitation would make a fakir stare,
And when you reach the scene of crime—*Macavity's not there!*
You may seek him in the basement, you may look up in the air—
But I tell you once and once again, *Macavity's not there!*   10

Macavity's a ginger cat, he's very tall and thin;
You would know him if you saw him, for his eyes are sunken in.
His brow is deeply lined with thought, his head is highly domed;
His coat is dusty from neglect, his whiskers are uncombed.
He sways his head from side to side, with movements like a snake;   15
And when you think he's half asleep, he's always wide awake.

Macavity, Macavity, there's no one like Macavity,
For he's a fiend in feline shape, a monster of depravity.
You may meet him in a by-street, you may see him in the square—
But when a crime's discovered, then *Macavity's not there!*   20

He's outwardly respectable. (They say he cheats at cards.)
And his footprints are not found in any file of Scotland Yard's.
And when the larder's looted, or the jewel-case is rifled,
Or when the milk is missing, or another Peke's been stifled,°
Or the greenhouse glass is broken, and the trellis past repair—   25
Ay, there's the wonder of the thing! *Macavity's not there!*

And when the Foreign Office find a Treaty's gone astray,
Or the Admiralty lose some plans and drawings by the way,
There may be a scrap of paper in the hall or on the stair—
But it's useless to investigate—*Macavity's not there!*   30
And when the loss has been disclosed, the Secret Service say:
"It *must* have been Macavity!"—but he's a mile away.
You'll be sure to find him resting, or a-licking of his thumbs,
Or engaging in doing complicated long division sums.

Macavity, Macavity, there's no one like Macavity,   35
There never was a Cat of such deceitfulness and suavity.
He always has an alibi, and one or two to spare:
At whatever time the deed took place—MACAVITY WASN'T THERE!
And they say that all the Cats whose wicked deeds are widely known
(I might mention Mungojerrie, I might mention Griddlebone)   40
Are nothing more than agents for the Cat who all the time
Just controls their operations: the Napoleon of Crime!

MACAVITY: THE MYSTERY CAT. 24 *Peke's been stifled:* A Pekinese dog (a small animal, with silky hair) has been found dead.

QUESTIONS

1. What are some of Macavity's major "crimes" as a master criminal and "mystery cat"? How, if the "crimes" had been attributed to a human being, would they be grievous wrongs? Since they are attributed to a cat, how do they add to the comic qualities of the poem?

2. What is the basic metrical foot of the poem? How many feet are contained in each of the lines? What is the norm?

3. Once you begin reading and getting into the lines, what new kind of pattern emerges? How many major stresses appear in each line? In light of the nature of the poem, how is the dipodic rhythm appropriate?

RALPH WALDO EMERSON (1803–1882)

Concord Hymn ˌ⏑⏑ˈ 1837

Sung at the completion of the Battle Monument, July 4, 1837

By the rude bridge that arched the flood,
   Their flag to April's breeze unfurled,
Here once the embattled farmers stood,
   And fired the shot heard round the world.

The foe long since in silence slept;   5
   Alike the conqueror silent sleeps;
And Time the ruined bridge has swept
   Down the dark stream which seaward creeps.

On the green bank, by this soft stream,
   We set to-day a votive stone;   10
That memory may their deed redeem,
   When, like our sires, our sons are gone.

Spirit, that made those spirits dare
   To die, and leave their children free,
Bid Time and Nature gently spare   15
   The shaft we raise to them and thee.

QUESTIONS

1. Line 4 is one of the best-known lines of American poetry. Why is it so well known? Discuss the rhythm of the line. Where are the heavy accents? What complication occurs in the phrase "heard round"?

2. Discuss line 7. What does Emerson do grammatically to get his idea across and also to create the verbal "swept" to rhyme with "slept"?

3. Describe Emerson's use of alliteration and assonance in the poem.

ISABELLA GARDNER (1915–1981)

At a Summer Hotel   *1979*

I am here with my bountiful womanful child
to be soothed by the sea not roused by these roses roving wild.
My girl is gold in the sun and bold in the dazzling water,
She drowses on the blond sand and in the daisy fields my daughter
dreams. Uneasy in the drafty shade I rock on the veranda   5
reminded of Europa Persephone Miranda.°

AT A SUMMER HOTEL. 6 *Europa Persephone Miranda:* Europa was a princess in Greek mythology who attracted the attention of Zeus, the king of the gods. He took the form of a bull and carried her over the sea to Crete. She bore him three sons. Persephone, in Greek mythology, was the daughter of Zeus and Demeter, the goddess of fertility. She attracted the attention of Hades, the god of the underworld, who forcibly carried her off and married her. Miranda is an innocent young woman in Shakespeare's play *The Tempest* who was exiled on an island for twelve years with her father, Prospero. One of his servants, the beastlike Caliban, attempted to rape her.

QUESTIONS

1. Why is the speaker "uneasy" (line 5)? How do the references to Europa, Persephone, and Miranda help define this uneasiness?
2. To what extent do alliteration and repetition unify the lines and make the sound echo sense? Note especially the *ful* sounds in line 1, the *s* and *r* sounds in line 2, and the *d* and *dr* sounds in lines 4–5.
3. What is the effect of internal rhyme in this poem?
4. What kind of rhyme (rising or falling, exact or slant) is in lines 1–2? To what extent does this rhyme highlight the poem's central idea? What rhyme is in lines 3–6? How does this rhyme affect the poem's tone and impact?

ROBERT HERRICK (1591–1674)

Upon Julia's Voice   *1648*

So smooth, so sweet, so silv'ry is thy voice,
As, could they hear, the damned would make no noise,
But listen to thee (walking in thy chamber)
Melting melodious words, to lutes of amber.

QUESTIONS

1. How do the words "silv'ry" and "amber" contribute to the praise of Julia's voice? How powerful does the speaker claim her voice is?
2. What is the "joke" of the poem? How can the praise of Julia's voice be interpreted as general praise for Julia herself?
3. How and where is alliteration used in the poem? Which of the alliterative sounds best complement the words praising the sweetness of Julia's voice?

GERARD MANLEY HOPKINS (1844–1889)

For a photo, see p. 712.

God's Grandeur 1877

The world is charged with the grandeur of God.
  It will flame out, like shining from shook foil;
  It gathers to a greatness, like the ooze of oil
Crushed. Why do men then now not reck his rod?°
Generations have trod, have trod, have trod;   5
  And all is seared with trade; bleared, smeared with toil;
  And wears man's smudge and shares man's smell: the soil
Is bare now, nor can foot feel, being shod.
And for all this, nature is never spent;
  There lives the dearest freshness deep down things;   10
And though the last lights off the black West went
  Oh, morning, at the brown brink eastward, springs—
Because the Holy Ghost over the bent
  World broods with warm breast and with ah! bright wings.

GOD'S GRANDEUR. 4 *reck his rod:* God as king holds a scepter, making official laws through scriptures which people ("men") disobey.

QUESTIONS

1. What is the contrast between the assertions in lines 1–4 and 5–8 (the octave)? How do lines 9–14 (the sestet) develop out of this contrast?

2. Analyze Hopkins's use of alliteration. What alliterative patterns occur? How do these affect meter and emphasis? On the basis of your analysis, describe "sprung rhythm" as used by Hopkins.

3. What instances of assonance, repetitions, and internal rhyme do you find?

LANGSTON HUGHES (1902–1967)

For a photo, see p. 1608.

Let America Be America Again 1936

Let America be America again.
Let it be the dream it used to be.
Let it be the pioneer on the plain
Seeking a home where he himself is free.

(America never was America to me.)   5

Let America be the dream the dreamers dreamed—
Let it be that great strong land of love
Where never kings connive nor tyrants scheme
That any man be crushed by one above.

(It never was America to me.)   10

O, let my land be a land where Liberty
Is crowned with no false patriotic wreath,

But opportunity is real, and life is free,
Equality is in the air we breathe.

(There's never been equality for me,   15
Nor freedom in this "homeland of the free.")

Say who are you that mumbles in the dark?
And who are you that draws your veil across the stars?
I am the poor white, fooled and pushed apart,
I am the Negro bearing slavery's scars.   20
I am the red man driven from the land,
I am the immigrant clutching the hope I seek—
And finding only the same old stupid plan
Of dog eat dog, of mighty crush the weak.

I am the young man, full of strength and hope,   25
Tangled in that ancient endless chain
Of profit, power, gain, of grab the land!
Of grab the gold! Of grab the ways of satisfying need!
Of work the men! Of take the pay!
Of owning everything for one's own greed!   30

I am the farmer, bondsman to the soil.
I am the worker sold to the machine.
I am the Negro, servant to you all.
I am the people, worried, hungry, mean—
Hungry yet today despite the dream.   35
Beaten yet today—O, Pioneers!
I am the man who never got ahead,
The poorest worker bartered through the years.

Yet I'm the one who dreamt our basic dream
In the Old World while still a serf of kings,   40
Who dreamt a dream so strong, so brave, so true,
That even yet its mighty daring sings
In every brick and stone, in every furrow turned
That's made America the land it has become.
O, I'm the man who sailed those early seas   45
In search of what I meant to be my home—
For I'm the one who left dark Ireland's shore,
And Poland's plain, and England's grassy lea,
And torn from Black Africa's strand I came
To build a "homeland of the free."   50
The free?

A dream—
Still beckoning to me!

O, let America be America again—
The land that never has been yet—   55
And yet must be—
The land where *every* man is free.
The land that's mine—
The poor man's, Indian's, Negro's, ME—

Who made America, 60
Whose sweat and blood, whose faith and pain,
Whose hand at the foundry, whose plow in the rain,
Must bring back our mighty dream again.
Sure, call me any ugly name you choose—
The steel of freedom does not stain. 65
From those who live like leeches on the people's lives,
We must take back our land again,
America!

O, yes,
I say it plain,
America never was America to me, 70
And yet I swear this oath—
America will be!
An ever-living seed,
Its dream 75
Lies deep in the heart of me.

We, the people, must redeem
Our land, the mines, the plants, the rivers,
The mountains and the endless plain—
All, all the stretch of these great green states— 80
And make America again!

QUESTIONS

1. In light of the poet's ideas, what is the effect of the changing stanzaic patterns? After the opening, fairly regular quatrains, why do the groupings become irregular?

2. What is the effect of the refrains in lines 5, 10, and 15–16? Why does the poet stop using the refrain after the third quatrain and not bring it out again until line 71?

3. Describe the use of alliteration. In phrases like "pushed apart" and "slavery's scars," together with other phrases, how does the alliteration emphasize the poet's ideas?

4. Describe the use of assonance, rhyme, and slant rhyme. What is gained by the slant rhymes?

JOHN HALL INGHAM (1860–ca. 1925)

George Washington ⚘ 1900

This was the man God gave us when the hour
Proclaimed the dawn of Liberty begun;
Who dared a deed and died when it was done
Patient in triumph, temperate in power,—
Not striving like the Corsican° to tower 5
To heaven, nor like great Philip's greater son°

To win the world and weep for worlds unwon,
Or lose the star to revel in the flower.
The lives that serve the eternal verities
Alone do mold mankind. Pleasure and pride   10
Sparkle awhile and perish, as the spray
Smoking across the crests of cavernous seas
Is impotent to hasten or delay
The everlasting surges of the tide.

GEORGE WASHINGTON. 5 *Corsican:* Napoleon I (1769–1821), General and Emperor of France from 1804–1814. 7 *great Philip's greater son:* Alexander the Great, King of Macedonia (356-323 B.C.E.), who conquered all the known world in the short years of his reign. There was a tradition, derived from Plutarch's *Life*, that Alexander wept because there were no more worlds for him to conquer.

QUESTIONS

1. For what reasons does the poet extoll Washington? Explain the symbolism of line 8, "Or lose the star to revel in the flower." What is the sense of the simile in the last five lines of the poem?

2. Trace the patterning of alliteration and assonance in the poem. How effectively does the poet use these devices? Are they appropriate, or might some think they are overly obvious?

3. In line 3 there occurs a pattern called *consonance*, in which words have the same beginning and ending consonant sounds ("*dared* a *deed* and *died*"). Why do you think the poet includes this pattern here?

PHILIP LEVINE (b. 1928)

A Theory of Prosody   1988

When Nellie, my old pussy
cat, was still in her prime,
she would sit behind me
as I wrote, and when the line
got too long she'd reach   5
one sudden black foreleg down
and paw at the moving hand,
the offensive one. The first
time she drew blood I learned
it was poetic to end   10
a line anywhere to keep her
quiet. After all, many mornings
she'd gotten to the chair
long before I was even up.
Those nights I couldn't sleep   15
she'd come and sit in my lap
to calm me. So I figured
I owed her the short cat line.
She's dead now almost nine years,

and before that there was one
during which she faked attention
and I faked obedience.
Isn't that what it's about–
pretending there's an alert cat
who leaves nothing to chance.

20

25

QUESTIONS

1. Why is this poem comic? How effective a "theory of prosody" is contained in the poem? What is suggested by the syllable break in line 12? How seriously are we to take the final lines?

2. What is the relationship between the speaker and his cat, Nellie? How true is it that cats sitting at a table with their masters and mistresses sometimes take a swipe at what they are writing?

3. Compare this poem with Robert Frost's "A Considerable Speck" (Chapter 24). In what ways do the poets seem to be having a good time? Nevertheless, what truths about writing are they advancing in the poems?

HENRY WADSWORTH LONGFELLOW (1807–1882)

The Sound of the Sea ◜◞◟◞◞ *1875*

The sea awoke at midnight from its sleep,
  And round the pebbly beaches far and wide
  I heard the first wave of the rising tide
Rush onward with uninterrupted sweep;
A voice out of the silence of the deep,
  A sound mysteriously multiplied
  As of a cataract from the mountain's side,
Or roar of winds upon a wooded steep.
  So comes to us at times, from the unknown
    And inaccessible solitudes of being,
      The rushing of the sea-tides of the soul;
And inspirations, that we deem our own,
  Are some divine foreshadowing and foreseeing
    Of things beyond our reason or control.

5

10

QUESTIONS

1. What is the analogy on which this poem is based? How does the form of the poem follow this analogy? Is the poem to be considered philosophical, mystical, or religious? Why does the poet conclude with the idea of "things beyond our reason or control"?

2. Describe the form of this poem, its rhyme scheme, and its use of rhyme.

3. What is the basic meter of the poem? Describe variations gained through substitution.

4.   Describe the effects of alliteration and assonance in the poem. How do these prosodic devices complement the meanings of the affected words?

HERMAN MELVILLE (1819–1891)

Shiloh: A Requiem°   1862

Skimming lightly, wheeling still,
    The swallows fly low
Over the field in clouded days,
    The forest field of Shiloh—
Over the field where April rain   5
Solaced the parched one stretched in pain
Through the pause of night
That followed the Sunday fight
    Around the church of Shiloh—
The church so lone, the log-built one,   10
That echoed to many a parting groan
        And natural prayer
Of dying foemen mingled there—
Foemen at morn, but friends at eve—
    Fame or country least their care: 15
(What like a bullet can undeceive!)
    But now they lie low,
While over them the swallows skim,
    And all is hushed at Shiloh.

SHILOH. One of the earliest major battles of the Civil War, the Battle of Shiloh, in southwestern Tennessee, also called the Battle of Pittsburg Landing, took place in April 1862. It was a remarkably bloody but substantially indecisive conflict, with 10,000 casualties on each side.

QUESTIONS

1.   Why is it difficult to determine the dominant meter in this poem? What do you think the dominant meter is? What types of metrical feet can you find here?

2.   What connection can you make between the indeterminate meter and Melville's subject?

3.   What rhymes does Melville create for "Shiloh"? What is the effect of these rhymes? What other rhymes does Melville introduce? How do these rhymes link together his ideas?

4.   What irony is expressed in line 14: "Foemen at morn, but friends at eve"?

OGDEN NASH (1902–1971)

Very Like a Whale°   1934

One thing that literature would be greatly the better for
Would be a more restricted employment by authors of simile and metaphor.
Authors of all races, be they Greeks, Romans, Teutons or Celts,

Can't seem just to say that anything is the thing it is but have to go out of their
    way to say that it is like something else.
What does it mean when we are told   5
That the Assyrian came down like a wolf on the fold?
In the first place, George Gordon Byron° had had enough experience
To know that it probably wasn't just one Assyrian, it was a lot of Assyrians.
However, as too many arguments are apt to induce apoplexy and thus hinder longevity,
We'll let it pass as one Assyrian for the sake of brevity.   10
Now then, this particular Assyrian; the one whose cohorts were gleaming in purple
    and gold,
Just what does the poet mean when he says he came down like a wolf on the fold?
In heaven and earth more than is dreamed of in our philosophy there are a great
    many things,
But I don't imagine that among them there is a wolf with purple and gold cohorts
    or purple and gold anythings.
No, no, Lord Byron, before I'll believe that this Assyrian was actually like a wolf   15
    I must have some kind of proof;
Did he run on all fours and did he have a hairy tail and a big red mouth and big
    white teeth and did he say Woof woof woof?
Frankly I think it very unlikely, and all you were entitled to say, at the very most,
Was that the Assyrian cohorts came down like a lot of Assyrian cohorts about to
    destroy the Hebrew host.
But that wasn't fancy enough for Lord Byron, oh dear me no, he had to invent a lot of
    figures of speech and then interpolate them.
With the result that whenever you mention Old Testament soldiers to people they say Oh   20
    yes, they're the ones that a lot of wolves dressed up in gold and purple ate them.
That's the kind of thing that's being done all the time by poets, from Homer to
    Tennyson;
They're always comparing ladies to lilies° and veal to venison.
How about the man who wrote,
Her little feet stole in and out like mice beneath her petticoat?°
Wouldn't anybody but a poet think twice   25
Before stating that his girl's feet were mice?
Then they always say things like that after a winter storm
The snow is a white blanket. Oh it is, is it, all right then, you sleep under a six-inch
    blanket of snow and I'll sleep under a half-inch blanket of unpoetical blanket
    material and we'll see which one keeps warm.
And after that maybe you'll begin to comprehend dimly
What I meant by too much metaphor and simile.   30

VERY LIKE A WHALE. See *Hamlet*, 3.2.358.   *7 George Gordon Byron:* See Byron, "The Destruction of Sennacherib" (Chapter 25), which Nash is satirizing in this poem.   *22 ladies to lilies:* See Campion, "Cherry Ripe," stanza 1 (Chapter 25); and also Burns, "A Red, Red Rose" (Chapter 17).   *24 little feet . . . petticoat:* In Sir John Suckling's "A Ballad upon a Wedding" (1641), the following lines appear: "Her feet beneath her petticoat / Like little mice stole in and out." Also in a poem by Robert Herrick complimenting the feet of Susanna Southwell (1648), he wrote: "Her pretty feet / Like snails did creep."

QUESTIONS

1.   How serious is Nash when he states that literature would be improved if poets
would remove simile and metaphor from their works? How just is his "criticism"
of metaphor in line 4?

2. Explain how Nash achieves humor in this poem. How does the ending of the first line indicate that the subject matter is to be considered with a smile?

3. Describe Nash's rhymes in this poem. What types of rhymes do you find here? In what ways are some of the rhymes comic? How original are Nash's rhymes?

EDGAR ALLAN POE (1809–1849)   *For a drawing, see p. 302.*

Annabel Lee   1849

It was many and many a year ago,
    In a kingdom by the sea,
That a maiden there lived whom you may know
    By the name of Annabel Lee;
And this maiden she lived with no other thought   5
    Than to love and be loved by me.

She was a child and *I* was a child,
    In this kingdom by the sea,
But we loved with a love that was more than love—
    I and my Annabel Lee—   10
With a love that the wingèd seraphs of Heaven
    Coveted her and me.

And this was the reason that, long ago,
    In this kingdom by the sea,
A wind blew out of a cloud by night   15
    Chilling my Annabel Lee;
So that her high-born kinsmen came
    And bore her away from me,
To shut her up in a sepulchre
    In this kingdom by the sea.   20

The angels, not half so happy in Heaven,
    Went envying her and me:—
Yes! that was the reason (as all men know,
    In this kingdom by the sea)
That the wind came out of the cloud chilling   25
    And killing my Annabel Lee.

But our love it was stronger by far than the love
    Of those who were older than we—
    Of many far wiser than we—
And neither the angels in Heaven above   30
    Nor the demons down under the sea
Can ever dissever my soul from the soul
    Of the beautiful Annabel Lee:—

For the moon never beams without bringing me dreams
    Of the beautiful Annabel Lee;   35
And the stars never rise but I feel the bright eyes
    Of the beautiful Annabel Lee:

And so all the night-tide, I lie down by the side
Of my darling, my darling, my life and my bride
   In her sepulchre there by the sea—   40
    In her tomb by the side of the sea.

QUESTIONS

1. How does the speaker explain the death of Annabel Lee? What is his attitude about the cause of her death? How does this judgment explain the actions he describes at the poem's end?

2. What basic meter does the poet establish in the poem? What variations do you find on this pattern?

3. Why do stanzas 3, 5, and 6 contain more lines than stanzas 1, 2, and 4? Why does stanza 5 contain seven lines, concluding with a dash?

4. Describe the poem's internal rhymes, repetitions, assonances, and alliterations. What is their effect? Why did Poe include them?

EDGAR ALLAN POE (1809–1849)   *For a drawing, see p. 302.*

The Bells ⌣⌣⌣⌣ 1849

I

    Hear the sledges with the bells—   *silver sledge*
        Silver bells!
What a world of merriment their melody foretells!
How they tinkle, tinkle, tinkle,
    In the icy air of night!   5
While the stars that oversprinkle
All the heavens, seem to twinkle
    With a crystalline delight;
      Keeping time, time, time,
      In a sort of Runic rhyme,
To the tintinnabulation that so musically wells   10
    From the bells, bells, bells, bells,
      Bells, bells, bells—
From the jingling and the tinkling of the bells.

II

    Hear the mellow wedding bells—   *golden bells*   15
        Golden bells!
What a world of happiness their harmony foretells!
    Through the balmy air of night
    How they ring out their delight!—
      From the molten-golden notes,
      And all in tune,   20
    What a liquid ditty floats

To the turtle-dove that listens, while she gloats
    On the moon!
  Oh, from out the sounding cells,   25
What a gush of euphony voluminously wells!
    How is swells!
    How it dwells
  On the Future!—how it tells
  Of the rapture that impels   30
  To the swinging and the ringing
    Of the bells, bells, bells—
Of the bells, bells, bells, bells,
    Bells, bells, bells—
To the rhyming and the chiming of the bells!   35

III

  Hear the loud alarum bells—   *brass*
    Brazen bells!
What a tale of terror, now, their turbulency tells!
  In the startled ear of night
  How they scream out their affright!   40
    Too much horrified to speak,
    They can only shriek, shriek,
      Out of tune,
In a clamorous appealing to the mercy of the fire,
In a mad expostulation with the deaf and frantic fire,   45
    Leaping higher, higher, higher,
    With a desperate desire,
  And a resolute endeavor
  Now—now to sit, or never,
By the side of the pale-faced moon,   50
    Oh, the bells, bells, bells!
    What a tale their terror tells
    Of Despair!
  How they clang, and clash, and roar!
  What a horror they outpour   55
On the bosom of the palpitating air!
    Yet the ear, it fully knows,
    By the twanging
    And the clanging,
    How the danger ebbs and flows;   60
  Yet the ear distinctly tells,
    In the jangling
    And the wrangling,
  How the danger sinks and swells,
By the sinking or the swelling in the anger of the bells—   65
    Of the bells—
  Of the bells, bells, bells, bells,
    Bells, bells, bells—
In the clamor and the clangor of the bells!

IV

Hear the tolling of the bells—   70
    Iron bells!
What a world of solemn thought their monody compels!
  In the silence of the night,
  How we shiver with affright
At the melancholy menace of their tone!   75
  For every sound that floats
  From the rust within their throats
    Is a groan.
    And the people—ah, the people—
    They that dwell up in the steeple,   80
      All alone,
  And who tolling, tolling, tolling,
    In that muffled monotone,
  Feel a glory in so rolling
    On the human heart a stone—   85
    They are neither man nor woman—
    They are neither brute nor human—
      They are Ghouls:—
    And their king it is who tolls:—
    And he rolls, rolls, rolls,   90
      Rolls
    A paean from the bells!
  And his merry bosom swells
     With the paean of the bells!
    And he dances, and he yells;   95
Keeping time, time, time,
In a sort of Runic rhyme,
    To the paean of the bells—
    Of the bells:
Keeping time, time, time,   100
In a sort of Runic rhyme,
    To the throbbing of the bells—
   Of the bells, bells, bells—
    To the sobbing of the bells;
Keeping time, time, time,   105
   As he knells, knells, knells,
  In a happy Runic rhyme,
    To the rolling of the bells—
   Of the bells, bells, bells:—
    To the tolling of the bells—   110
Of the bells, bells, bells, bells,
   Bells, bells, bells—
To the moaning and the groaning of the bells.

QUESTIONS

1.   What kinds of bells does Poe extol in each of the stanzas? What metals and images does he associate with each type of bell? How appropriate are these? Why do you think the stanzas become progressively longer?

2. What segmental sounds does Poe utilize as imitative of the various bells? What differences in vowels are observable between the silver sledge bells, for example, and the brass ("brazen") alarum bells? Between the vowels describing the iron bells and the golden bells?

3. What is the effect of the repetition of the word "bells" throughout? What onomatopoeic effect is created by these repetitions?

4. Describe the pattern of rhymes in this poem.

ALEXANDER POPE (1685–1744)

From *An Essay on Man, Epistle I* (lines 17–90) ⁓◁~⁓ 1734

I. Say first, of God above, or man.° below,	men; humanity
What can we reason but from what we know?	
Of man, what see we but his station here,	
From which to reason, or to which refer?	20
Through worlds unnumbered though the God be known,	
'Tis ours to trace him° only in our own.	God
He who through vast immensity can pierce,	
See worlds on worlds compose one universe,	
Observe how system into system runs,	25
What other planets circle other suns,	
What varied being peoples every star,	
May tell why Heaven has made us as we are.	
But of this frame the bearings and the ties,	
The strong connections, nice dependencies,	30
Gradations just, has thy pervading soul	
Looked through? or can a part contain the whole?	
Is the great chain that draws all to agree,	
And drawn supports, upheld by God, or thee?	
II. Presumptuous man! the reason wouldst thou find,	35
Why formed so weak, so little, and so blind?	
First, if thou canst, the harder reason guess,	
Why formed no weaker, blinder, and no less!	
Ask of thy mother earth, why oaks are made	
Taller or stronger than the weeds they shade!	40
Or ask of yonder argent fields above,	
Why Jove's satellites are less than Jove!	
Of systems possible, if 'tis confessed	
That wisdom infinite must form the best,	
Where all must full or not coherent be,	45
And all that rises, rise in due degree;	
Then, in the scale of reasoning life, 'tis plain,	
There must be, somewhere, such a rank as man:	
And all the question (wrangle e'er so long)	
Is only this, if God has placed him wrong.	50
Respecting man, whatever wrong we call,	
May, must be right, as relative to all.	
In human works, though labored on with pain,	

A thousand movements scarce one purpose gain;
In God's, one single can its end produce;   55
Yet serves to second too some other use.
So man, who here seems principal alone,
Perhaps acts second to some sphere unknown,
Touches some wheel, or verges to some goal;
'Tis but a part we see, and not a whole.   60
    When the proud steed shall know why man restrains
His fiery course, or drives him o'er the plains:
When the dull ox, why now he breaks the clod,
Is now a victim, and now Egypt's god:
Then shall man's pride and dullness comprehend   65
His actions', passions', being's, use and end;
Why doing, suffering, checked, impelled; and why
This hour a slave, the next a deity.
    Then say not man's imperfect, Heaven in fault;
Say rather, man's as perfect as he ought: 70
His knowledge measured to his state and place;
His time a moment, and a point his space.
If to be perfect in a certain sphere,
What matter, soon or late, or here or there?
The blessed today is as completely so,   75
As who began a thousand years ago.
    III. Heaven from all creatures hides the book of fate,
All but the page prescribed, their present state;
From brutes what men, from men what spirits know,
Or who could suffer being here below?   80
The lamb thy riot dooms to bleed today,
Had he thy reason, would he skip and play?
Pleased to the last, he crops the flowery food,
And licks the hand just raised to shed his blood.
Oh blindness to the future! kindly given,   85
That each may fill the circle marked by Heaven:
Who sees with equal eye, as God of all,
A hero perish, or a sparrow fall,
Atoms or systems into ruin hurled,
And now a bubble burst, and now a world.   90

QUESTIONS

1. What is the topic of the passage? How appropriate is it to present such material
    in the form of couplets? How does Pope use the couplet to develop his thought
    in the poem?

2. Analyze five or six of the couplets. On the basis of your study, what principles of
    the couplet does Pope follow? You might consider the average lengths of words
    and the use of iambs, caesurae, and end-stopped lines.

3. Describe Pope's use of rhyme. What types of words does he rhyme? How helpful
    are the rhymes in the emphasis of Pope's ideas?

EDWIN ARLINGTON ROBINSON (1869–1935)   *For a photo, see p. 655.*

For a photo, see p. 655.

Miniver Cheevy   1910

Miniver Cheevy, child of scorn,
  Grew lean while he assailed the seasons;
He wept that he was ever born,
  And he had reasons.

Miniver loved the days of old   5
  When swords were bright and steeds were prancing;
The vision of a warrior bold
  Would set him dancing.

Miniver sighed for what was not,
  And dreamed, and rested from his labors;   10
He dreamed of Thebes° and Camelot,°
  And Priam's° neighbors.

Miniver mourned the ripe renown
  That made so many a name so fragrant;
He mourned Romance, now on the town,   15
  And Art, a vagrant.

Miniver loved the Medici,°
  Albeit he had never seen one;
He would have sinned incessantly
  Could he have been one.   20

Miniver cursed the commonplace
  And eyed a khaki suit with loathing;
He missed the medieval grace
  Of iron clothing.

Miniver scorned the gold he sought,   25
  But sore annoyed was he without it;
Miniver thought, and thought, and thought,
  And thought about it.

Miniver Cheevy, born too late,
  Scratched his head and kept on thinking;   30
Miniver coughed, and called it fate,
  And kept on drinking.

MINIVER CHEEVY. 11 *Thebes:* a city in Greece prominent in Greek legend and mythology in connection with Cadmus and Oedipus. *Camelot:* legendary seat of the Round Table and capital of Britain during the reign of King Arthur. 12 *Priam's:* Priam was the king of Troy during the Trojan War. 17 *Medici:* wealthy Italian family that ruled Florence from the fifteenth to the eighteenth century. During the Renaissance, Lorenzo de'Medici was an important patron of the arts.

QUESTIONS

1. What is the speaker's attitude toward the central character? How does rhyme
    help define this attitude?

2.   How does repetition reinforce the image of the central character and the speaker's attitude? Consider the beginning of each stanza and lines 27–28.

3.   What rhyme predominates in lines 2 and 4 of each stanza? How does this rhyme help make sound echo sense?

PERCY BYSSHE SHELLEY (1792–1822)

Ode to the West Wind   1820

I

O wild West Wind, thou breath of Autumn's being,
Thou, from whose unseen presence the leaves dead
Are driven, like ghosts from an enchanter fleeing,

Yellow, and black, and pale, and hectic° red,
Pestilence-stricken multitudes: O Thou,   5
Who chariotest to their dark wintry bed

The winged seeds, where they lie cold and low,
Each like a corpse within its grave, until
Thine azure sister of the Spring° shall blow

Her clarion o'er the dreaming earth, and fill   10
(Driving sweet buds like flocks to feed in air)
With living hues and odours plain and hill:

Wild Spirit, which art moving everywhere;
Destroyer and Preserver; hear, O hear!

II

Thou on whose stream, 'mid the steep sky's commotion,   15
Loose clouds like Earth's decaying leaves are shed,
Shook from the tangled boughs of Heaven and Ocean,

Angels of rain and lightning: there are spread
On the blue surface of thine aery surge,
Like the bright hair uplifted from the head   20

Of some fierce Maenad,° even from the dim verge
Of the horizon to the zenith's height,
The locks of the approaching storm. Thou Dirge

Of the dying year, to which this closing night
Will be the dome of a vast sepulchre,   25
Vaulted with all thy congregated might

ODE TO THE WEST WIND 4 *hectic:* a tubercular fever that produced flushed cheeks.   9 *Spring:* the wind that will blow in the spring.   21 *Maenad:* a frenzied female worshipper of Dionysus, the god of wine and fertility in Greek mythology.

Of vapours,° from whose solid atmosphere   *clouds*
Black rain and fire and hail will burst: O hear!

III

Thou who didst waken from his summer dreams
The blue Mediterranean, where he lay,   30
Lulled by the coil of his crystalline streams,

Beside a pumice isle in Baiae's bay,°
And saw in sleep old palaces and towers
Quivering within the wave's intenser day,

All overgrown with azure moss and flowers   35
So sweet, the sense faints picturing them! Thou
For whose path the Atlantic's level powers

Cleave themselves into chasms, while far below
The sea-blooms and the oozy woods which wear
The sapless foliage of the ocean, know   40

Thy voice, and suddenly grow grey with fear,
And tremble and despoil themselves: O hear!

IV

If I were a dead leaf thou mightest bear;
If I were a swift cloud to fly with thee;
A wave to pant beneath thy power, and share   45

The impulse of thy strength, only less free
Than thou, O Uncontrollable! If even
I were as in my boyhood, and could be

The comrade of thy wanderings over Heaven,
As then, when to outstrip thy skiey speed   50
Scarce seemed a vision; I would ne'er have striven

As thus with thee in prayer in my sore need,
Oh! lift me as a wave, a leaf, a cloud!
I fall upon thorns of life! I bleed!

A heavy weight of hours has chained and bowed   55
One too like thee: tameless, and swift, and proud.

V

Make me thy lyre,° even as the forest is:
What if my leaves are falling like its own!
The tumult of thy mighty harmonies

---

32 *Baiae's bay:* a bay of the Mediterranean Sea west of Naples, famous for the elaborate villas built on the shore by Roman emperors.   57 *lyre:* an Aeolian harp, a musical device that is sounded by the wind blowing across strings.

Will take from both a deep, autumnal tone,   60
Sweet though in sadness. Be thou, Spirit fierce,
My spirit! Be thou me, impetuous one!

Drive my dead thoughts over the universe
Like withered leaves to quicken a new birth!
And, by the incantation of this verse,   65

Scatter, as from an unextinguished hearth
Ashes and sparks, my words among mankind!
Be through my lips to unawakened Earth

The trumpet of a prophecy! O Wind,
If Winter comes, can Spring be far behind?   70

QUESTIONS

1. To what extent are the speaker's thoughts and feelings organized by the poem's
    five sections? What is the logical progression from section to section?

2. What aspect of the natural world does the wind affect in the first section of the
    poem? The second stanza? The third? What does the West Wind symbolize? Why
    does the speaker state, "Make me thy lyre"?

3. Formulate the structure (meter and rhyme scheme) of the stanzas. How many
    times (and where) is the *e* rhyme of the first stanza repeated as a rhyming sound?
    What is the effect of this repetition?

4. Describe Shelley's use of alliteration and assonance in the poem.

ALFRED, LORD TENNYSON (1809–1892)

From *Idylls of the King: The Passing of Arthur* (lines 344–393)   1869 (1842)

But, as he walked, King Arthur panted hard,
Like one that feels a nightmare on his bed   345
When all the house is mute. So sighed the King,
Muttering and murmuring at his ear, "Quick, quick!
I fear it is too late, and I shall die."
But the other swiftly strode from ridge to ridge,
Clothed with his breath, and looking, as he walked,   350
Larger than human on the frozen hills.
He heard the deep behind him, and a cry
Before. His own thought drove him like a goad.
Dry clashed his harness in the icy caves
And barren chasms, and all to left and right   355
The bare black cliff clanged round him, as he based
His feet on juts of slippery crag that rang
Sharp-smitten with the dint of armèd heels—
And on a sudden, lo! the level lake,
And the long glories of the winter moon.   360

Then saw they how there hove a dusky barge,
Dark as a funeral scarf from stem to stern,
Beneath them; and descending they were ware°   *aware*

That all the decks were dense with stately forms,
Black-stoled, black-hooded, like a dream—by these
Three Queens with crowns of gold; and from them rose
A cry that shivered to the tingling stars,
And, as it were one voice, an agony
Of lamentation, like a wind that shrills
All night in a waste land, where no one comes,
Or hath come, since the making of the world.

   Then murmured Arthur, "Place me in the barge."
So to the barge they came. There those three Queens
Put forth their hands, and took the King, and wept.
But she, that rose the tallest of them all
And fairest, laid his head upon her lap,
And loosed the shattered casque,° and chafed his hands,   *helmet*
And called him by his name, complaining loud,
And dropping bitter tears against a brow
Striped with dark blood: for all his face was white
And colorless, and like the withered moon
Smote by the fresh beam of the springing east;
And all his greaves and cuisses° dashed with drops   *pieces of armor*
Of onset;° and the light and lustrous curls—   *blood*
That made his forehead like a rising sun
High from the dais-throne—were parched with dust:
Or, clotted into points and hanging loose,
Mixed with the knightly growth that fringed his lips.
So like a shattered column lay the King:
Not like that Arthur who, with lance in rest,
From spur to plume a star of tournament,
Shot through the lists at Camelot, and charged
Before the eyes of ladies and of kings.

365

370

375

380

385

390

QUESTIONS

1. How does Tennyson develop the mood of depression and loss associated with the dying of Arthur? What is the effect of the concluding simile?

2. Analyze the patterns of assonance and alliteration in the passage. What patterns are developed most extensively? What effects are thus achieved?

3. Describe Tennyson's use of onomatopoeia in lines 349–360, 369–371, and 380–383. What segments contribute to this effect?

DAVID WAGONER (b. 1926)

March for a One-Man Band   1983

He's *a boom a blat* in the uniform
Of an army *tweedledy* band *a toot*
Complete with medals *a honk* cornet
Against *a thump* one side of his lips

[handwritten annotations in margins: "arrogance → showing an offensive sense of superiority", "Soldier", "Sound made by ... gunshot", "protagonist", "Chief character in the story", "838"]

And the other stuck with *a sloop a tweet*
A whistle *a crash* on top of *a crash*
A helmet *a crash* a cymbal a drum
At his *bumbledy* knee and a *rimshot* flag
A *click* he stands at attention *a wheeze*
And plays the Irrational Anthem *bang.* — *gunshot*   10

[handwritten: "not based on reason"]

QUESTIONS

[handwritten: "feeling opinion mood"]   *[handwritten: "Totally consumed in self"]*

1. What attitude does the speaker convey about the one-man band? Why is the Anthem "Irrational" rather than "National"?

2. Describe the onomatopoeic effect of the italicized percussive words. What is the purpose of the rhythms that these words cause?

3. What ambiguity is suggested by the *bang* of line 10? How does this ambiguity make the poem seem more than simply an entertaining display of sounds?

♪ WRITING ABOUT PROSODY

Because studying prosody requires a specific detail and description, it is best to limit your study to a short poem or to a short passage from a long poem. A sonnet, a stanza of a lyric poem, or a fragment from a long poem will often be sufficient. If you choose a fragment, it should be self-contained, such as an entire speech or a short episode or scene.

The analysis of even a short poem, however, can grow long because of the need to describe word positions and stresses and also to determine the various effects. For this reason you do not have to exhaust your topic. Try to make your discussion representative of the prosody of your poem or passage.

Your first reading in preparation for your essay should be for comprehension. On second and third readings, make notes of sounds, accents, and rhymes by reading the poem aloud. To perceive sounds, one student helped herself by reading aloud in an exaggerated way in front of a mirror. If you have privacy or are not self-conscious, you might do the same. Let yourself go a bit. As you dramatize your reading (maybe even in front of fellow students), you will find that heightened levels of reading also accompany the poet's expression of important ideas. Mark these spots for later analysis and discussion so that you will be able to make strong assertions about the relationship of sound to sense.

Carry out your study of the passage in the following way. What counts in this preliminary study of prosody is that your analyses be clear enough to provide help in developing your actual discussion.

• Determine the formal pattern of feet. You may wish to use lower case letters for light stresses, and capital letters for heavy stresses, as in "And ON / a SUD - / den, LO! / the LEV - / el LAKE." The capital letters really make the strong accents clear. Or, you may wish to use a short acute accent or stress mark for heavily stressed syllables (´) and the breve for unaccented or lightly stressed syllables (˘), as in "And ó / a súd / den Lo! / the lev - / el Láke." Use chevrons to mark spondees, as in

his own / thought drove / him

- Indicate the separate feet by a diagonal slash or virgule (/). Indicate caesurae and end-of-line pauses by double virgules (//).
- Be sure to mark the formal and rhetorical substitutions that you discover.
- Do the same for alliteration, assonance, onomatopoeia, and rhyme. You might wish to draw lines connecting the repeating sounds, for these effects will be close together in the poem, and your connections will dramatize this closeness.

Once you have analyzed the various effects in your poem and have recorded these on your work sheets and in your notes, you will be ready to formulate a central idea and organization. The focus of your essay should reflect the most significant features of prosody in relationship to some other element of the poem, such as speaker, tone, or ideas.

Strategies for Organizing Ideas

In preparing for your essay, try to establish ideas about the following. Above all, it is important to keep foremost the connections of prosody to the subject of the poem or passage you are studying.

Is there any characteristic, any particular rhythm, that might help to establish a character, as in Browning's "Porphyria's Lover" (see the demonstrative student essay)? Are there varying rhythmic lengths that might create particular emphases on visual or auditory images, as Poe does in "The Bells"? Does the poet include, say, a number of monosyllabic words in close order to create an imitation of special speech patterns, as Brooks does in "We Real Cool"?

Can you find evidence that prosody is being used as an organizational element? In an Italian or Petrarchan sonnet, for example, the rhymes are important in tying together the development of ideas. In a Shakespearean sonnet there are three 4-line groups (quatrains), each containing the development of a particular idea or image or symbol, and the concluding two lines rhyme and at the same time create a "cap" or idea tying the previous ideas together. (This aspect of prosody is also important in the consideration of poetic form, described in Chapter 20.)

Can you show that the variation of dominant poetic feet is done in such a way that strong stresses fall on words that are therefore made especially important? This characteristic is of course a major aspect of poetry. In "The Sun Rising," for example, Donne begins with a trochaic substitution: "Busy old fool, . . ." This trochee creates what is in effect an opening outburst against the sun, as though it is a meddling peeping Tom. It makes for humor at the beginning, and it also makes the poem dramatic and conversational—all of which Donne clearly intended.

In rhyming poems, what is the effect of the rhyme? What is the patterning of the rhymes? What is their effect on your perception of the merging of sound and idea? What sorts of words are rhymed—nouns, verbs, adjectives, a combination of these? Are the rhymes especially clever, as in Eliot's "Macavity: The Mystery Cat," or unusual, as in Gardner's "At a Summer Hotel"? Generally, what are the rhymes like? How do they "clinch" or connect ideas? What part does rhyme play in the poem's development?

Try to describe the poet's use of segmental (sound) devices, specifically assonance and alliteration. Hopkins uses alliteration powerfully in "God's Grandeur." One can find this device everywhere in the poem, but in line 2 it is especially noteworthy: "It will flame out, like shining from shook foil," in which the predominant *f* and *sh* sounds enable Hopkins in the stressing of his simile about the grandeur of divine creation. A few lines later Hopkins uses assonance with similar power: "Why do men then now not reck his rod?" Alliteration aside, the *eh* sounds in "men," "then," and "reck" make the poem exemplary in the connections of prosody and topic.

What connection can you make between the general prosodic characteristics of the poem and the dominant mood or manner? The percussiveness of Wagoner's "March for a One-Man Band" is integral to his boisterous views of his subject. The rollicking rhythms of Eliot's "Macavity" are a fine example of the ways in which rhythms underscore the lightness and humor of the topic. The same is true of Nash's "Very Like a Whale," in which the rhythm is a major element in the comic tone, together with lines of varying length and clever and unexpected rhymes. The truncated line lengths of Levine's "A Theory of Prosody" are essential in the poem's comic minimization of some aspects of poetic theory.

What significance can you find in the ways in which the poet has put together elements like euphony, cacophony, and onomatopoeia? It is difficult to overlook Tennyson's euphonious line "And the long glories of the winter moon." Tennyson creates onomatopoeia in describing a noble warrior climbing down a precipitous hill: "The bare black cliff clanged round him, . . ."; Shelley in "Ode to the West Wind" creates cacophony in describing "old palaces and towers / Quivering within the wave's intenser day." How do poets create such effects?

After a brief description of the poem (such as that it is a sonnet, a two-stanza lyric, a dipodic burlesque poem, and so on), establish the scope of your essay. Your central idea will outline the thought that you wish to carry out through your prosodic analysis, such as that regularity of meter is consistent with a happy, firm vision of love or life; or that frequent spondees emphasize the solidity of the speaker's wish to love; or that particular sounds echo some of the poem's actions.

Depending on your assignment, you should state in your introduction, beyond the essential details about the poem or passage, those aspects of prosody you plan to discuss. It might be all aspects of rhythm or sound, or perhaps just one, such as the poet's use of regular meter, a particular substitution, alliteration, or assonance. It is possible, for example, to devote an entire essay to (1) regular meter; (2) one particular variation in meter, such as the anapest or spondee; (3) rhyme; (4) assonance; (5) alliteration; (6) euphony or cacophony; or (7) onomatopoeia. For brevity, the demonstrative essay treats rhyme, rhythm, and segmental effects together.

The body of your essay may include all the following elements or just one, depending on your instructor's assignment.

1. RHYTHM.   Establish the formal metrical pattern. What is the dominant metrical foot and line length? Are some lines shorter than the pattern? What relationship do the variable lengths have with the subject matter? If the poem is a lyric or a sonnet, are important words and syllables successfully placed in stressed positions in order to achieve emphasis? Try to relate line lengths to exposition, development of ideas, and rising or falling emotions. It is also important to look for either repeating or varying metrical patterns as the subject matter reaches peaks or climaxes. Generally, deal with the relationship between the formal rhythmical pattern and the poet's ideas and attitudes.

When noting substitutions, analyze the formal variations and the principal effects of these. If you concentrate on only one substitution, describe any apparent pattern in its use, that is, its locations, recurrences, and effects on meaning.

2. SEGMENTAL EFFECTS.   Here you might be discussing, collectively or separately, the use and effects of assonance, alliteration, onomatopoeia, and cacophony and euphony. Be sure to establish that the instances you choose really occur systematically enough in the poem to form a pattern. Illustrate sounds by including relevant words within parentheses. You might write separate paragraphs on alliteration, assonance, and any other seemingly important pattern. Also, because space is always at a premium, you might concentrate on only one noteworthy effect, like a certain pattern of assonance, rather than on everything. Throughout your discussion, always keep foremost the relationship between content and sound.

REFERRING TO SOUNDS IN POETRY

To make illustrations clear, emphasize the sounds to which you are calling attention. If you use an entire word to illustrate a sound, underline or italicize only the sound, not the entire word, and put the word within quotation marks (for example, "The poet uses a t ['tip,' 'top,' and 'terrific']"). When you refer to entire words containing particular segments, however, underline or italicize these words (for example, "The poet uses a t in tip, top, and terrific," or "The poet uses a t in tip, top, and terrific).

3. RHYME.   Your discussion of rhyme should describe the major features of the poem's rhymes, specifically the scheme and variants, the lengths and rhythms of the rhyming words, and noteworthy segmental characteristics. In discussing the grammar of the rhymes, note the kinds of words (i.e., verbs, nouns, etc.) used for rhymes: Are they all the same? Does one form predominate? Is there variety? Can you determine the grammatical positions of the rhyming words? How may these characteristics be related to the idea or theme of the poem?

Another avenue of exploration might be to study the qualities of the rhyming words. Are the words specific? Concrete? Abstract? Are there any striking rhymes? Any surprises? Any rhymes that are particularly clever and witty? Do any rhymes give unique comparisons or contrasts? How?

Generally, note any striking or unique rhyming effects. Without becoming overly subtle or far-fetched, you can make valid and interesting conclusions. Do any sounds in the rhyming words appear in patterns of assonance or alliteration elsewhere in the poem? Do the rhymes contribute to onomatopoeia in the poem? Broadly, what aspects of rhyme are uniquely effective because they blend fully with the poem's thought and mood?

In your conclusion, try to develop a short evaluation of the poet's prosodic performance. If we accept the premise that poetry is designed not only to stimulate emotions but also to provide information and transfer attitudes, to what degree do the prosodic techniques of your poem contribute to these goals? Without going into excessive detail (and writing another essay), what more can you say here? What has been the value of your study to your understanding and appreciating the poem? If you think your analysis has helped you to develop new awareness of the poet's craft, it would be appropriate to state what you have learned.

DEMONSTRATIVE STUDENT ESSAY

Rhyme, Rhythm, and Sound in Browning's "Porphyria's Lover"°

[1]   In Robert Browning's dramatic monologue "Porphyria's Lover," the "lover" is the speaker--unfortunately for Porphyria, for he is murderously insane. He is speaking early in the morning, and he tells his listeners about the events of the night, his last night with Porphyria, a golden-haired beauty who had "come through wind and rain" (line 30) from some "gay feast" (line 27) to meet him for a romantic rendezvous. Shockingly, he states that he killed her rather than accept her living love. He states that he strangled her because that is the way he could hold her without the fear of her ever leaving him. Further, he is able to rationalize murdering her by assuring his listeners that by this action he has given Porphyria her "utmost will" (line 53), her "darling one wish" (line 57), that she give herself to him forever instead of being diverted by her "pride, and vainer ties" (line 24). His belief in divine approval for this act is shown in his claim that "God has not said a word" (line 60), a particularly sick statement. The way he tells his tale is expressive of his dangerous mentality.* Specifically, the rhymes, rhythms, and sounds within the poem all reflect the disturbance of this demented killer.[†]

[2]   Browning uses the rhymes of the poem to reflect the speaker's agitated state of mind. Although the four-stress iambic lines are not divided into stanzas, they are actually grouped into twelve sets of five by the rhyme scheme--a b a b b. While this grouping is symmetrical overall, the extra rhyming line concluding each group skews what is otherwise a neatly alternating pattern of rhymes. This asymmetrical fifth line is consistent with how the speaker's ostensibly balanced and calm description of his grisly crime reveals the abnormal imbalances in his thought.

In addition, the rhyming sounds themselves indicate the speaker's irrationality. For the most part, the rhyming sounds are separate and are unrepeated

---

°See p. 811 for this poem.
*Central idea.
[†]Thesis sentence.

among the different groups of lines. Only two of the five-line groups include rhyming sounds that appear in a previous group: in the ninth group, the rhyming words she and bee (lines 41, 43) duplicate the sounds of she and free in the fifth group (lines 21, 23), and the rhyming words pain, again, and stain (lines 42, 44-45) echo the sixth group's restrain, vain, and rain (lines 27, 29-30). (This assumes that Browning pronounced "again" as a word rhyming with the others.) Significant-

[3] ly, the group that repeats rhyming sounds from previous groups is the one that contains the speaker's description of his killing Porphyria and then, in a particularly depraved action, lifting her eyelids and finding that her blue eyes were still laughing. The earlier groups that are linked through rhyme to this description are the ones in which he concludes that his love for her is "all in vain" (line 29) because she is "too weak" to cut the ties that bind her to whatever life she has had away from him (lines 22-25). Thus, the connection created by the rhyming sounds reinforces the cause-and-effect relationship between the speaker's deranged assessment of his wish to possess Porphyria totally and the act of murder that he believes has fulfilled his wish.

The meter, too, can be seen to reflect the speaker's troubled state. The poem's basic iambic tetrameter is not a "heroic" measure like iambic pentameter, but is a measure that is often used for satiric and more common subjects. The meter can be seen in the poem's first five lines:

> The RAIN / set EAR - / ly IN / to - NIGHT,
> The SUL - / len WIND / was SOON / a - WAKE,
> It TORE / the ELM - / tops DOWN / for SPITE,
> And DID / its WORST / to VEX / the LAKE:
> i LIST - / ened WITH / heart FIT / to BREAK.

However, a number of lines in the poem, such as lines 41-45, vary this rhythm with spondees that may be taken as evidence of the speaker's inner turbulence when describing his actions. (Here only the spondees are marked.)

[4] And strangled her. No pain felt she;

I am quite sure she felt no pain.

As a shut bud that holds a bee,
I warily oped her lids: again

Laughed the blue eyes without a stain.

The spondees here suggest a disruption of order, which is appropriate in light of the speaker's tortured admission that only after he has killed her is Porphyria "without a stain"--that is, pure.

Another notable group contains the lines in which he assumes the ability to read Porphyria's mind, and then states that no matter how strongly she was "murmuring" that she loved him, she nevertheless was too proud and too vain to give herself to him totally.

Murmuring how she loved me--she

[5]

> Too weak, for all her heart's endeavor,
> To set its struggling passion free
> From pride, and vainer ties dissever,
> And give herself to me forever. (lines 21–25)

In this group there is only one regular line, the middle one (line 23). The others show irregularity either through the use of spondees or, at the line ends, amphibrachs (endeavor, dissever, forever). It is clear that these are not just variations in rhythm, but that they are instead demonstrative of the speaker's weakened mental state.

In addition, one may find in the poem a good deal of assonance and alliteration, usually on words and phrases in which the speaker's abnormality is specially brought out. Thus, in lines 36 and 37 we have alliteration on m and p sounds in "That moment she was mine, mine, fair, / Perfectly pure. . . ." Under other circumstances, in other poems, alliteration is used as a way of emphasizing key words and ideas, but here the alliteration seems definitely to suggest the speaker's excitement when recalling his weird and diseased fantasy about possessing Porphyria. The same excitement and agitation can be seen in the use of the b alliteration in line 48. It should be stressed that here the speaker is confessing to [6]tright necrophilia. After he has strangled Porphyria, opened her eyes, and loosened her hair, he kisses her, and he then states that she "Blushed bright beneath my burning kiss." These b sounds, which occur four times in the line, are indicative of the speaker's excitement when he describes his kiss. Earlier, he also has included words with stress on the b sound: "As a shut bud that holds a bee." In these same words, "shut bud," one may also find assonance on the uh sound. Assonance occurs again, on the eh sound, in lines 46–49: "next," "tress," "neck," and "head." This same assonance on eh occurs again in five lines of the next group (51–55). It would appear that this killer becomes especially expressive when his emotions are heightened by the memory of his grisly act.

The poem's subtle cacophony, too, reflects the speaker's mad, agitated frame of mind. This can be seen in the first five lines which, although they establish the regularity of the meter, contain words about the storm that better reveal the speaker's anger and hatred than an actual storm. Importantly, the sounds in a number of these words are percussive, and their cacophony suggests his agitation: "tore," "spite," "worst," "vex" (i.e., veks), "heart fit," and "break." This man is not shouting and raving, but he definitely is totally controlled by his weird compulsiveness. Thus, the hissing s sounds in a number of words in the first five lines suggest that the sounds of the words emerging into his consciousness to describe the wind and storm are like the raging tempest in his mind: "sullen," "soon," "tops," "spite," "worst," "vex" (i.e., veks), "listened."

[8]   "Porphyria's Lover" is a masterly poem in which subject and style fuse together in a most meaningful way. The meter is for the most part regular, but it contains variations that may be taken to highlight the speaker's disturbance. So also is it with Browning's control over his use of segmental devices, which are brought out in lines in which the speaker describes his insane act of murdering his sweetheart, whose only mistake was to fall in love and be faithful. In virtually every way, the poem's irregularities and variations complement the speaker's delirium and also his moments of pathological exhilaration.

WORK CITED

Browning, Robert. "Porphyria's Lover." Literature: An Introduction to Reading and Writing. Ed. Edgar V. Roberts and Henry E. Jacobs. 7th ed. Upper Saddle River: Prentice Hall, 2004. 811–12.

Commentary on the Essay

This essay presents a relatively full treatment of the prosody of Browning's "Porphyria's Lover." It is to be understood that there could be further analysis of the poem's prosody. If such analysis did no more than lengthen the essay, however, without adding significantly to the conclusions, it would be, in effect, superfluous.

Paragraph 1 is introductory and is concerned with establishing the poem's content—an essential purpose considering the extremity of the speaker's character. The central idea makes the connection between his madness and "the way he tells his tale."

The discussion of prosody itself begins in paragraphs 2 and 3 with the description of the poem's rhymes. A principal idea here is that the fifth rhyming line of each five-line group, together with other characteristics of the rhyme, is to be construed as suggestive of the speaker's abnormal imbalances.

In paragraphs 4 and 5 the topic shifts to the poem's rhythms. Here, the use of the spondee and the uncommon amphibrach is to be considered not as substitutions inserted for emphasis or variety but rather as evidence of the disruptions in the speaker's thoughts. In paragraph 6 the topic is assonance and alliteration, which normally also are segmental elements that thrust individual words and lines into positions of emphasis. Here, however, the devices are shown to indicate the speaker's excitement at the memory of possessing Porphyria and kissing her after killing her.

Paragraph 7 introduces the poem's "subtle cacophony" as made apparent in the first stanza, in which, even before we suspect the speaker of any wrongdoing, he describes the wind in words featuring sharp and painful sounds—words that can be interpreted to show that he is ascribing a malign influence to the rainstorm. The idea in the essay, here, is that the malignity is not a function of Nature but rather of himself. The last paragraph, 8, is a summarizing statement speaking about the fusing together of subject and style and also asserting that the irregularities and variations in the poem are consistent with the speaker's disturbed mind.

Of greatest importance for the clarity of the essay, there are many supporting examples. Some of these are embodied within the essay, and others are set off in block style, accurately marked, and numbered by line. In any essay about prosody, readers are likely to be unsure of the validity of the writer's observations unless such examples are provided and are clearly located within the poem.

Special Topics for Writing and Argument about Rhythm and Rhyme in Poetry

1. For Shakespeare's Sonnet 73, "That Time of Year Thou May'st in Me Behold" (Chapter 20), analyze the ways in which Shakespeare creates iambics. What is the relationship of lightly accented syllables to the heavily accented ones? Where does Shakespeare use articles (*the*), pronouns (*this, his*), prepositions (*upon, against, of*), relative clause markers (*which, that*), and adverb clause markers (*as, when*) in relation to syllables of heavy stress? On the basis of this study, how would you characterize Shakespeare's control of the iambic foot?

2. Eliot's "Macavity: The Mystery Cat," Robinson's "Miniver Cheevy," Poe's "The Bells," Nash's "Very Like a Whale," and Gardner's "At a Summer Hotel" all include falling rhymes. What is the effect of this rhyming pattern in the poems? To what degree do the poems achieve seriousness despite the fact that falling rhyme is often used generally to complement humorous and light verse?

3. Compare the sounds used in Poe's "The Bells" with those of Wagoner's "March for a One-Man Band." What effects are achieved by each poet? What is the relationship in each poem between sound and content? Which poem do you prefer on the basis of sound? Why?

4. Analyze the rhymes in two of the following poems: Shakespeare's Sonnet No. 73, Hopkins's "God's Grandeur," Poe's "Annabel Lee," Shelley's "Ode to the West Wind," or the passage from Pope's "Essay on Man." What is interesting or unique about the various rhyming words? What relationships can you discover between the rhymes and the topics of the poems?

5. Compare one of the rhyming poems with one of the nonrhyming poems included in this chapter. What differences in reading and sound can you discover as a result of the use or nonuse of rhyme? What benefits does rhyme give to the poem? What benefits does nonrhyme give?

6. Analyze Hardy's use of rhymes in "Channel Firing" (Chapter 16). What effects does Hardy create by using trochaic rhyme, like *hatters* and *matters*, and also by using dactyllic rhyme, like *saner be* and *century*? What is the relationship of such rhymes to the heavy-stress rhymes in the poem?

7. Write a short poem of your own using rhymes with trochaic words or dactylic words such as *computer, emetic, scholastic, remarkable, along with me, inedible, moron, anxiously, emotion, fishing*, and so on. If you have trouble with exact rhymes, see what you can do with slant rhymes and eye rhymes. The idea is to use your ingenuity.

8. Using the topical index in your library, take out a book on prosody, such as Harvey Gross's *Sound and Form in Modern Poetry* (1968) or *The Structure of Verse* (1966), or Gay Wilson Allen's *American Prosody* (1935, reprinted 1966). Select a topic (e.g., formal or experimental prosody) or a poet (e.g., Arnold, Blake, Browning, Frost, Shakespeare) and write a summary of the ideas and observations that the writers make on your subject. What relationship do the writers make about prosody and the poet's ideas? How does prosody enter into the writer's thought? Into the ways in which the poets emphasize ideas and images?

Form: *The Shape of the Poem*

Open form - structure and technique

Because poetry is compressed and highly rhythmical, it always exists under self-imposed restrictions, or conventions. Traditionally, many poets have chosen a variety of clearly recognizable shapes or forms—*closed-form* poetry. Since the middle of the nineteenth century, however, many poets have rejected the more regular patterns in favor of poems that appear more free and spontaneous—*open-form* poetry. These terms refer to the structure and technique of the poems, not to content or ideas.

CLOSED-FORM POETRY

Closed-form poetry is written in specific and traditional patterns of lines produced through *line length, meter, rhyme, and line groupings.* In the closed form (and also in the open form), the **line** is, loosely, the poetic equivalent of the prose sentence. A prime characteristic of the closed-form line, as opposed to a sentence, is that its length should be measured or restricted. Various numbers of lines may be grouped together through rhyme and other means to form a **stanza,** which is the poetic equivalent of a paragraph in prose. Individual lines may coincide exactly with sentences, although quite often sentences stretch out over two or more lines. Stanzas consist of groups of lines that are both connected and also separated by developments of subject, idea, or expression of feeling.

Over the centuries English and American poets have appropriated and evolved many closed forms. Among the most important of these are *blank verse,* the *couplet,* the *tercet* or *triplet, terza rima,* the *villanelle,* the *quatrain,* the *sonnet,* the *song* or *lyric,* the *ode,* the *ballad,* the *elegy,* and *common measure* or the *hymnal stanza,* together with forms like *haiku,* the *epigram,* the *epitaph,* the *limerick,* the *clerihew,* and the *double dactyl.*

Blank Verse Consists of Five Unrhymed Iambic Lines

One of the most common closed forms in English is **blank verse,** or unrhymed iambic pentameter, which represents the adaptation and fusion of sentences to poetic form. The great advantage of blank verse is that it resembles normal speech but at the same time it maintains poetic identity. It is suitable for relatively short poems, but it may also extend for hundreds or even thousands of lines. It is the most adaptable line of English poetry. The master of blank verse is Shakespeare, who used it extensively in his plays. Since Shakespeare, poets of English have used blank verse again and again. Milton used it in his masterly long epic *Paradise Lost.* Wordsworth was fond of blank verse and used it in some of his best-known poems. Let us look at a passage from his autobiographical poem *The Prelude* (1850) to see his blank verse in action.

> Wisdom and Spirit of the universe!
> Thou Soul that art the eternity of thought,
> That givest to forms and images a breath
> And everlasting motion, not in vain
> By day or star-light thus from my first dawn
> Of childhood didst thou intertwine for me
> The passions that build up our human soul;
> Not with the mean and vulgar works of man,
> But with high objects, with enduring things—
> With life and nature, purifying thus
> The elements of feeling and of thought,
> And sanctifying, by such discipline,
> Both pain and fear, until we recognise
> A grandeur in the beatings of the heart. (Book I, lines 401–414)

While these lines are linked together to make up the entire passage, each one creates an identifiable unit of thought and grammatical coherence. This clearly significant thought presented within the iambic rhythm creates the distinction that we expect from poetry.

The Couplet Consists of Two Lines Connected by Thought and Rhyme

The **couplet** contains two rhyming lines and is the shortest distinct closed form. The two lines are usually identical in length and meter. Some couplets are short. Even lines in monometer (one major stress), like "Some play / All day," make up a couplet. However, most English couplets are in iambic tetrameter (four stresses) or iambic pentameter (five stresses), and they have been a regular feature of English poetry ever since Chaucer used them in the fourteenth century. In the seventeenth and eighteenth centuries, the iambic pentameter couplet was considered appropriate for epic, or heroic, poetry. For this reason it is often called the **heroic couplet.** Because these centuries are considered the "neo-classic" age of literature, the form is also called the **neoclassic couplet.** It was used with consummate skill by Dryden (1631–1700) and Pope (1688–1744).

(handwritten top margin: np to pg 31?)

(handwritten: Parallelism - A figure of speech which the same grammatical forms are repeated)

Usually, the heroic couplet expresses a complete idea and is grammatically self-sufficient. It thrives on the rhetorical strategies of **parallelism** and **antithesis.** Look, for example, at these two couplets from "The Rape of the Lock," Pope's well-known mock-epic poem (1711).

(handwritten: Couplet = 2 lines of verse that rhyme)

Here Britain's statesmen oft the fall foredoom
Of foreign tyrants, and of nymphs at home;
Here thou, great Anna! whom three realms obey,
Dost sometimes counsel take—and sometimes tea.

(handwritten: nymphs - lesser goddess in ancient mythology)

These lines describe activities at Hampton Court, the royal palace and residence of Queen Anne (reigned 1701–1714). Notice that the first couplet allows Pope to link "Britain's statesmen" with two parallel but also <u>antithetical</u> events: the fall of nations and the "fall" of young women. Similarly, the second heroic couplet allows for the parallel and comic linking of royal meetings of state ("counsel") and teatime (in the early eighteenth century, *tea* was pronounced "tay"). The example thus demonstrates how the heroic couplet may contrast amusing and ironic actions and situations.

(handwritten: Antithetical - direct opposites)

The Tercet or Triplet Consists of Three Lines

A three-line stanza is called a **tercet** or **triplet.** Tercets may be written in any uniform line length or meter and most commonly contain three rhymes (*a a a, b b b*, and so on), which are, in effect, short stanzas. The following poem by Tennyson is in iambic tetrameter triplets.

(handwritten: iambic = 2 syllable foot)

(handwritten: 3 line stanza set; a line consisting of 4 metrical feet; crag = steep cliff)

ALFRED, LORD TENNYSON (1809–1892)

The Eagle 1851

He clasps the crag with crooked hands;
Close to the sun in lonely lands,
Ring'd with the azure world, he stands.

(handwritten: Azure = blue of the sky)

The wrinkled sea beneath him crawls;
He watches from his mountain walls,
And like a thunderbolt he falls.

5

In the first tercet, we view the eagle as though at a distance. In the second, the perspective shifts, and we see through the eagle's eyes and follow his actions. In this tercet the verbs are active: the sea "crawls" and the eagle "falls." While the two tercets and the shift in perspective divide the poem, alliteration pulls things back together. This is especially true of the *k* sound in "clasps," "crag," "crooked," "close," and "crawls" and the *w* sound in "with," "world," "watches," and "walls."

There are two important variations on the tercet pattern, each requiring a high degree of ingenuity and control. The first tercet variation is **terza rima,** in which stanzas are interlocked through a pattern that requires the center termination in one tercet to be rhymed twice in the next: *a b a, b c b, c d c, d e d,* and so on. You can see an example of terza rima in Shelley's "Ode to the West Wind" (Chapter 19).

The most complex variation of the tercet pattern is the **villanelle,** a nineteen-line form containing six tercets, rhymed *a b a,* and concluded by four lines. The first and third lines of the first tercet are repeated alternately in subsequent tercets as a refrain and also are used in the concluding four lines. For examples see Elizabeth Bishop's "One Art," Theodore Roethke's "The Waking," and Dylan Thomas's "Do Not Go Gentle into That Good Night."

The Quatrain Is a Unit of Four Lines

The most common and adaptable stanzaic building block is the four-line **quatrain.** This stanza has been popular for hundreds of years and has lent itself to many variations. Like couplets and tercets, quatrains may be written in any line length and meter; even the line lengths within a quatrain may vary. The determining factor is the rhyme scheme, and even that is variable, depending on the form and the poet's aims. Quatrains may be rhymed *a a a a,* but they can also be rhymed *a b a b, a b b a, a a b a,* or even *a b c b.* Quatrains are basic components of many traditional closed forms, most notably ballads and sonnets, and they are significant in many religious hymns.

The Sonnet Is a Versatile Poem of Fourteen Lines

The **sonnet,** consisting of fourteen lines, is one of the most popular and durable closed poetic forms. Initially it was an Italian form (*sonnetto* means "little song") created by the medieval Italian poet Petrarch (1304–1374), who wrote collections or *cycles* of sonnets. The sonnet form as made famous by Petrarch is called the **Italian sonnet** or **Petrarchan sonnet** in Petrarch's honor. The form and style of Petrarchan sonnets were adapted to English poetry in the early sixteenth century, and with variations they have been used ever since. As a form, the Petrarchan sonnet is in iambic pentameter, and it contains two quatrains (the **octave**) and two tercets (the **sestet**). In terms of structure and meaning, the octave presents a problem or situation that is resolved in the sestet, as in Milton's "When I Consider How My Light Is Spent." The rhyme scheme of the Petrarchan octave is fixed in an *a b b a, a b b a* pattern. The sestet offers a number of different rhyming possibilities, including *c d c, c d c* and *c d e, c d e.*

Shakespeare was the most original adapter of the sonnet tradition. Recognizing that there are fewer rhyming words in English than in Italian, he developed the **Shakespearean sonnet** or **English sonnet** on seven rhymes (in the pattern *a b a b, c d c d, e f e f, g g*) rather than the five rhymes of the Italian sonnet. As indicated by the rhyme scheme, the Shakespearean sonnet contains three quatrains and a concluding couplet. The pattern of thought therefore shifts from the octave-sestet organization of the Italian sonnet to a four-part argument on a single thought or emotion. Each Shakespearean quatrain contains a separate development of the sonnet's central idea or problem, and the couplet provides a climax and resolution.

The Song or Lyric Is a Stanzaic Poem of Variable Measure and Length

The **song** or **lyric** is a stanzaic form that was originally designed to be sung to a repeating melody, although not all lyrics are written specifically for music. Even so, the line lengths and rhyme schemes of the first stanza are duplicated in all subsequent stanzas, as though for repeated singing to the same tune. The stanzas of a lyric may be built from any combination of single lines, couplets, triplets, and quatrains. The line lengths may shift, and a great deal of metrical variation is common.

There is theoretically no limit to the number of stanzas in a lyric, although there are usually no more than five or six. A. E. Housman's "Loveliest of Trees" 652 (Chapter 14), for example, is made up of three quatrains containing two couplets each. It is in iambic tetrameter and rhymes *a a b b*. The second and third stanzas repeat the same pattern of rhyme, *c c d d, e e f f*. Lyrics can have very complex and ingenious stanzaic structures. Donne's "The Canonization" (Chapter 21) for instance, contains five stanzas that repeat the following pattern: *iambic: 5a 4b 5b 5a 4c 4c 4c 4a 3a*. This nine-line stanza contains three different rhymes and three different line lengths. Nevertheless, the same intricate pattern is repeated in each of the five stanzas.

The Ode Is a Complex and Extensive Stanzaic Poem

The **ode** is a more variable stanzaic form than the lyric, with varying line lengths and intricate rhyme schemes. Usually the topics of odes are meditative and philosophical, but there is no set topic material, just as there is no set form. Some odes have repeating patterns, while others offer no duplication and introduce a new structure in each stanza. Poets have developed their own structures according to their needs. Keats's great odes were particularly congenial to his ideas, as in "Ode to a Nightingale," which consists of eight stanzas in iambic pentameter with the repeating form *a b a b c d e 3c d e*. Although many odes have been set to music, most do not fit repeating melodies.

The Elegy Is a Poem about Death and Its Meaning for the Living

The **elegy** ("lament") has had a long and rich history in other languages extending back to ancient times, and it has defined a number of topics, but for our purposes it is a poem of lament. Usually the topic is the death of a specific person, but it is also generally concerned with mortality and the negative or tragic aspects of life. In English the most notable elegy is Milton's "Lycidas" (1638), which he wrote in observance of the death by drowning of a "learned friend" with whom he had gone to school. Milton also composed this poem as a

pastoral, that is, a poem describing rural lives and concerns, with direct allegorical implications for the lives of urban city-dwellers. So that you may get a sense of this poem, here are the opening twenty-four lines.

Yet once more, O ye laurels, and once more	
Ye myrtles brown, with ivy never sere,°	*dry, withered*
I come to pluck your berries° harsh and crude,	*to write this poem*
And with forced fingers rude,	
Shatter your leaves before the mellowing year.	5
Bitter constraint, and sad occasion dear,	
Compels me to disturb your season due;	
For Lycidas is dead, dead ere his prime,	
Young Lycidas, and° hath not left his peer:	*who*
Who would not sing for Lycidas? he knew	10
Himself to sing, and build the lofty rhyme.	
He must not float upon his watery bier	
Unwept, and welter to the parching wind,	
Without the meed° of some melodious tear.	*gift, honor*
Begin then, sisters° of the sacred well,	*the muses* 15
That from beneath the seat of Jove° doth spring,	*God (Jupiter)*
Begin, and somewhat loudly sweep the string.	
Hence with denial vain, and coy excuse,	
So may some gentle muse	
With lucky° words favor my destined urn,	*providential, inspired* 20
And as he passes turn,	
And bid fair peace be to my sable shroud.	
For we were nursed upon the self-same hill,	
Fed the same flock; by fountain, shade, and rill.°	*i.e., we went to the same school*

Today few people think of the traditional formalities of elegiac writing, and prefer to understand poems as elegies if they concern death, mortality, and grief. Thus, Collins's "The Names" (Chapter 18), Dryden's "To the Memory of Mr. Oldham," Pinsky's "Dying" (Chapter 18), Ransom's "Bells for John Whiteside's Daughter" (Chapter 25), cummings' "Buffalo Bill's Defunct," and Dickinson's "The Bustle in a House" (Chapter 24), to name just a few poems in this book, might, broadly, all be considered elegies.

Ballads Consist of Many Narrative Quatrains

The **ballad,** which fuses narrative description with dramatic dialogue, originated in folk literature and is one of the oldest closed forms in English poetry. Ballads consist of many quatrains in which lines of iambic tetrameter alternate with iambic trimeter. Normally, only the second and fourth lines of each stanza rhyme, in the pattern *x a x a, x b x b, x c x c,* and so on. The ballad was designed for singing, like the anonymous "Sir Patrick Spens" (Chapter 13). Popular ballad tunes were used over and over again by later balladeers, often as many as forty and fifty times, and many of the tunes have survived to the present day and are still popular, for example, "Barbara Allan" (Chapter 25).

Common Measure, or the Hymnal Stanza, Is a Poem Consisting of a Number of Quatrains

Common measure, a quatrain form, is similar to the ballad stanza. It shares with the ballad the alternation of four-beat and three-beat iambic lines but adds a second rhyme to the first and third lines of each quatrain: *a b a b, c d c d,* and so on. Because the measure is often used in hymns, it is sometimes called the **hymnal stanza.** Many of Emily Dickinson's poems, including "Because I Could Not Stop for Death" (Chapter 13), are in common measure.

The Haiku Is a Complete Poem of Seventeen Syllables

The **haiku** originated in Japan, where it has been a favorite genre for hundreds of years. It traditionally imposes strict rules on the writer: (1) There should be three lines (a tercet) of five, seven, and five syllables per line, for a total of seventeen syllables. (2) The topic should be derived from nature. (3) The poem should embody a unique observation or insight. Today, English-language poets have adapted the haiku but have taken liberties with the subject matter and have often reduced the syllable count. Whether the traditional pattern is varied or not, however, the haiku must be short, simple, objective, clear, and (often) symbolic. The following anonymous haiku illustrates some of these qualities.

Spun in High, Dark Clouds

Spun in high, dark clouds,
Snow forms vast webs of white flakes
And drifts lightly down.

The central metaphor equates gathering snow with the webs of silkworms or spiders. To supply tension, the lines contrast "high" with "down" and "dark" with "white." Because of the enforced brevity, the diction is simple and, except for the word "forms," of English derivation (the word *form* was originally French). In addition, the words are mainly monosyllabic, and the poem therefore fills the seventeen-syllable form with sixteen words.

There Are Additional but Less Significant Closed-Form Types

Many other closed forms have enjoyed long popularity. One of these, the **epigram,** is a short and witty poem that usually makes a humorous or satiric point. Epigrams are two to four lines long and are often written in couplets. The form was developed by the Roman poet Martial (ca. 40–103 C.E.) and has always been popular. Humorous **epitaphs,** brief lines composed to mark the death of someone, can also be epigrams.

Another popular type is the **limerick,** a five-line form popularized by the English artist and humorist Edward Lear (1812–1888). Like the epigram, limericks are comic and usually bawdy, their humor being reinforced by falling rhymes.

Comic closed forms continue to be devised by enterprising writers. The **clerihew,** a two-couplet form invented in the late nineteenth century by Edmund Clerihew Bentley (1875–1956), is related to the epigram. A final illustration of closed-form humor is the **double dactyl,** devised in the 1960s by Anthony Hecht and Paul Pascal. The form is related to the epigram, limerick, and clerihew, and it has rules that govern the meter, line length, and specific topic material.

Poets Use the Closed Form to Shape and Polish Meaning

Although many contemporary poets consider closed forms restrictive and even stultifying, the closed form has always provided both a framework and a challenge for poets to express new and fresh ideas, attitudes, and feelings. Let us look at the way Shakespeare uses the sonnet form to shape thoughts and emotions.

WILLIAM SHAKESPEARE (1564–1616)   *For a drawing, see p. 1306.*

Closed form

Sonnet 116: Let Me Not to the Marriage of True Minds   1609

Sonnet - iambic pentameter | five metrical feet | 14 lines

Let me not to the marriage of true minds
Admit impediments.° Love is not love
Which alters when it alteration finds,
Or bends with the remover to remove:
Oh, no! it is an ever-fixèd mark,
That looks on tempests and is never shaken;
It is the star to every wandering bark,
Whose worth's unknown, although his height° be taken   *its altitude*
Love's not Time's fool,° though rosy lips and cheeks   *slave*
Within his° bending sickle's compass come;   *Time's*
Love alters not with his brief hours and weeks,
But bears it out even to the edge of doom.°   *the Last Judgment*
If this be error and upon me proved,
I never writ, nor no man ever loved.

SONNET 116. *2 impediments:* a reference to "The Order of Solemnization of Matrimony" in the Anglican Church's *Book of Common Prayer:* "I require that if either of you know of any impediment why ye may not be lawfully joined together in Matrimony, ye do now confess it."

QUESTIONS   *line restricted or measured* *Traditional English meter line grouping* *The development of an idea*

1. Describe the restrictions of this closed form. How is the poem's argument structured by the form?
2. What is the poem's meter? Rhyme scheme? Structure?
3. Describe the varying ideas about love explored in the three quatrains.
4. What does the concluding couplet contribute to the poem's argument about love?

Even if we did not know that the poem is Shakespeare's, we would instantly recognize it as a Shakespearean sonnet. It is in iambic pentameter and contains three quatrains and a concluding couplet, rhyming *a b a b, c d c d, e f e f, g g.* The sonnet form provides the organization for the poem's argument—that real love is a "marriage of true minds" existing independent of earthly time and change. Each quatrain advances a new perspective on this idea.

This is not to say that Shakespeare exhausts the subject or that he wants to. The ideas in the third quatrain, for example, about how love transcends time, could be greatly expanded. A philosophical analysis of the topic might deal extensively with Platonic ideas about reality—whether it exists in *particulars* or *universals.* Similarly, the poem's very last line, if it became the topic of a prose inquiry, might include the introduction of evidence about the poet's own writing, and also about many examples of human love. But the two lines are enough, granted the restrictions of the form, and more would be superfluous. One might add that most readers find Shakespeare's poem interesting and vital, while extensive philosophical discourses often drop into laps as readers fall asleep.

The closed poetic form therefore may be viewed as a complex consequence of poetic compression. No matter what form a poet chooses—couplet, sonnet, song, ballad, ode—that form imposes restrictions, and it therefore challenges and shapes the poet's thought. The poet of the closed form shares with all writers the need to make ideas seem logical and well supported, but the challenge of the form is to make all this happen *within the form itself.* The thought must be developed clearly and also fully, and there should be no lingering doubts once the poem is completed. The words must be the most fitting and exact ones that could be selected. When we look at good poems in the closed form, in short, we may be sure that they represent the ultimate degree of poetic thought, discipline, and skill.

OPEN-FORM POETRY

Among the closed forms, as we have seen, the ode is the form that gives poets great opportunity for variability and expansion. The ode is thus the closed form that is most nearly related, in spirit, to **open-form poetry,** but the open form eliminates the restrictions of the closed form. Each open-form poem is unique and unpredictable. Poetry of this type was once termed **free verse** (from the French *vers libre*) to signify its liberation from regular metrics and its embrace of spoken rhythms. But open-form poetry is not therefore disorganized or chaotic. Open-form poets have instead created new ways to arrange words and lines, new ways to express thoughts and feelings, and new ways to order poetic experience.

Poets writing in the open form attempt to fuse form and content by stressing speechlike rhythms, creating a natural and easy-flowing word order, altering and varying line lengths according to the importance of ideas, and creating emphasis through the control of shorter and longer pauses. They often isolate individual words, phrases, and clauses as single lines, freely emphasize their ideas through the manipulation of spaces separating words and sentences, and sometimes even break up individual words in separate lines to highlight their importance. Sometimes they create poems that look exactly like prose and that are printed in blocks and paragraphs instead of stanzas or lines, as with "Museum" by Robert Hass. Such **prose poems** rely on a progression of images and the cadences of language.

Open-Form Poetry Is Free in Form and Variable in Content

An early example of open-form poetry is Walt Whitman's "Reconciliation." This poem was included in *Drum Taps*, a collection of fifty-three poems about the poet's reactions to Civil War battles in Virginia.

WALT WHITMAN (1819–1892)   *For a photo, see p. 748.*

Reconciliation   1865, 1881

Word over all, beautiful as the sky,
Beautiful that war and all its deeds of carnage must in time be utterly lost,
That the hands of the sisters Death and Night incessantly softly wash again,
      and ever again, this soiled world;
For my enemy is dead, a man divine as myself is dead,
I look where he lies white-faced and still in the coffin—I draw near,   5
Bend down and touch lightly with my lips the white face in the coffin.

QUESTIONS

1. How do individual lines, varying line lengths, punctuation, pauses, and cadences create rhythm and organize the images and ideas in this poem?
2. How do alliteration, assonance, and the repetition of words unify the poem and reinforce its content?
3. What is the "word" referred to in line 1? What does the speaker find "beautiful" about this "word" and the passage of time?
4. What instances of personification can you find? What do these personified figures do? What does the speaker do in lines 5–6? Why does he do this?

"Reconciliation" shows the power of open-form poetry. There is no dominant meter, rhyme scheme, or stanza pattern. Instead, Whitman uses individual lines and varying line lengths to organize and emphasize the images, ideas, and emotions. He also uses repetition, alliteration, and assonance to make internal line connections.

Without going into every aspect of the poem, one may note the unifying elements in the first few lines. The "word over all" (i.e., reconciliation, peace) is linked to the second line by the repetition of the words "beautiful" and "all," while "beautiful" is grammatically complemented by the clauses "that . . . lost" (line 2) and "That . . . world" (line 3). The reconciling word is thus connected to the image of the two personified figures, Death and Night, who "wash" war and carnage (bloodshed) out of "this soiled world."

In the third line, unity and emphasis are created through the repetition of "again" and the alliteration on the *ly* sound of "incessant*ly*"and "soft*ly*," the *s* sound in "sisters," "incessantly," "softly," and "soil'd," and the *d* sound in "hands," "Death," "soil'd," and "World." One may also note the unifying assonance patterns of *i* in "its," "in," "sisters," "incessantly," and "this," and *i* in "sky," "time," and "Night." The pauses, or junctures, of the line create internal rhythms that coincide with the thought.

> That the hands // of the sisters // Death and Night // incessantly softly //
> wash again and ever again // this soiled world.

This selective analysis demonstrates that open-form poetry creates its own unity. While some of the unifying elements, such as alliteration and assonance, are also a property of closed-form poetry, many are unique to poetry of the open form, such as the repetitions, the reliance on grammatical structures, and the control of rhythms. The concept of the open form is that the topic itself shapes the number of lines, the line lengths, and the physical appearance on the page. Unity is there—development is there—but the open form demands that there be as many shapes and forms as there are topics.

VISUAL AND CONCRETE POETRY

In **visual poetry,** also called **shaped verse** and **picture poetry,** poets not only emphasize the idea and emotion of their subject but also fashion the poem into a recognizable shape on the page, as with the figure of a cone in Charles Harper Webb's "The Shape of History." Some visual poetry seeks to balance the pleasures of seeing with those of hearing. Other visual poetry, however, abandons sound completely and invests all its impact in our perception of the visual image or picture.

Visual poetry is not a recent development. The Chinese have been producing it for thousands of years, and there are surviving examples from ancient Greece. In the seventeenth century, traditional English poets were manipulating the lines of their poems to represent wings, altars, squares, triangles, stars, and the like. This type of poetry was often more ingenious than significant. Exceptional poets, however, produced shaped verse in which the visual image and the meaning strikingly echo each other.

After World War II, picture poems experienced a revival when visual poetry reentered the literary landscape with the birth of a new movement called **concrete poetry.** Poets in this tradition focus on the medium in which the poem is created. With printed work, this means that the poets pay far more attention to the visual arrangement of letters, words, lines, and white space than they do to content. Concrete poetry represents a fusion of writing with painting or graphic design, and the emphasis is on the visual.

Visual Poetry Connects Language and Visual Form

In reading visual and concrete poems, you should seek correspondences between images and poetic ideas. Describe the shape of the poem and the figures it resembles, the varying line lengths, the placement of individual words and phrases, and the use of space. A superb example of seventeenth-century visual poetry is George Herbert's "Easter Wings," a religious poem that offers two differing but related shapes.

GEORGE HERBERT (1593–1633)   *For a photo, see p. 610.*

Easter Wings   1633

Lord, who createdst man in wealth and store,°   *abundance*
   Though foolishly he lost the same,
      Decaying more and more
         Till he became
           Most poor: 5
           With thee
         O let me rise
      As larks, harmoniously,
   And sing this day thy victories:
Then shall the fall° further the flight in me.   10

My tender age in sorrow did I begin:
   And still with sicknesses and shame
      Thou didst so punish sin,
         That I became
           Most thin.   15
           With thee
         Let me combine,
      And feel this day thy victory;°
   For, if I imp° my wing on thine,
Affliction shall advance the flight in me.   20

EASTER WINGS. 10 *fall:* the biblical account of how sin and death were introduced as a punishment for humankind after Adam and Eve disobeyed God. See also line 2.   18 *victory:* I Corinthians 15:54–57.   19 *imp:* to repair a falcon's wing or tail by grafting on feathers.

QUESTIONS

1.   What does the poem look like when viewed straight on? When viewed sideways, with the left side at the top? How do these two images echo and emphasize the poem's content?

2.   How does the typographical arrangement echo the sense? In lines 5 and 15, for example, how are typography, shape, and meaning fused?

3.   What do lines 1–5 tell you about humanity's spiritual history, according to Herbert? What do lines 11–15 tell you about the speaker's spiritual state? How are these parallel?

    This poem is an admission of sin and a prayer for redemption. It compares humanity's loss of Eden ("wealth and store") to the speaker's spiritual state as a petitioner seeking salvation. When viewed straight on, each stanza resembles an altar. Sideways, the stanzas resemble the wings of two angels. The images are thus linked with the title of the poem, and they connote contrition, prayer, grace, and angelic reward.

The correspondence between shape and meaning goes even further. Herbert reinforces the ideas by the careful manipulation of line lengths. Thus, in discussing humanity's spiritual history, the original "wealth and store" of Eden are described in the poem's longest line (line 1). As the fall from grace is described, the lines get progressively shorter (and the picture becomes narrower) until humanity's fallen state is described in one of the shortest lines, "Most poor" (line 5). This same pattern is repeated in lines 11–15 to portray the "sickness and shame" that have made the speaker spiritually "Most thin." In the second half of both stanzas, this pattern is reversed; the lines expand to complement the speaker's prayers for grace and salvation. The full lengths of lines 10 and 20 depict the speaker's hope of a victorious redemption—in effect the restoration of the divine favor described in line 1.

POEMS FOR STUDY

ELIZABETH BISHOP (1911–1979)

One Art   1976

The art of losing isn't hard to master;
so many things seem filled with the intent
to be lost that their loss is no disaster.

Lose something every day. Accept the fluster
of lost door keys, the hour badly spent.   5
The art of losing isn't hard to master.

Then practice losing farther, losing faster:
places, and names, and where it was you meant
to travel. None of these will bring disaster.

I lost my mother's watch. And look! my last, or   10
next-to-last, of three loved houses went.
The art of losing isn't hard to master.

I lost two cities, lovely ones. And, vaster,
some realms I owned, two rivers, a continent.
I miss them, but it wasn't a disaster.   15

—Even losing you (the joking voice, a gesture
I love) I shan't have lied. It's evident
the art of losing's not too hard to master
though it may look like (*Write* it!) like disaster.

QUESTIONS

1. This poem is written in a traditional closed form called the villanelle (originally
    an Italian peasant song), which was developed in France during the Middle
    Ages. A villanelle is nineteen lines long. Fairly strict rules govern the length and
    structure of stanzas, the rhyme scheme, and the repetition of complete lines. Try
    to formulate these rules. For comparison, see Roethke's "The Waking" and
    Thomas's "Do Not Go Gentle into That Good Night."

2. On what idea is the poem based? What evidence does the speaker produce about
    losing? What feelings does she express about her losses?

3. How could the speaker have lost "two cities"? What other things has she lost
    which justify her claim that "the art of losing isn't hard to master"? What might
    she mean by having lost the "you" to whom the poem is addressed?

BILLY COLLINS (b. 1941)   *For a photo, see p. 610.*

Sonnet   1999

All we need is fourteen lines, well, thirteen now,
and after this next one just a dozen
to launch a little ship on love's storm-tossed seas,
then only ten more left like rows of beans.

How easily it goes unless you get Elizabethan   5
and insist the iambic bongos must be played
and rhymes positioned at the ends of lines,
one for every station of the cross.
But hang on here while we make the turn
into the final six where all will be resolved,   10
where longing and heartache will find an end,
where Laura will tell Petrarch to put down his pen,
take off those crazy medieval tights,
blow out the lights, and come at last to bed.

QUESTIONS

1. Why is this poem amusing? What makes it amusing?
2. What is the effect of lines 6 and 7? Why does the speaker refer to "every station of the cross" in line 8?
3. What is the "little ship" that is to be launched on "love's storm-tossed seas"? To what tradition of the sonnet form is this a reference?
4. Why does the poet conclude the poem with a description of a scene between Petrarch and Laura?

E. E. CUMMINGS (1894–1962)   *For a photo, see p. 648.*

Buffalo Bill's Defunct°   ⟶⟨⟩⟶⟨⟩⟶⟨⟩   1923

Buffalo Bill's
defunct
          who used to
          ride a watersmooth-silver
                                        stallion   5
and break onetwothreefourfive pigeonsjustlikethat
                                        Jesus

he was a handsome man
                        and what i want to know is
how do you like your blueeyed boy   10
Mister Death

BUFFALO BILL'S DEFUNCT. The poem has no title; it is usually referred to as "Portrait" or by its first two lines. Buffalo Bill (William F. Cody, 1846–1917) was an American plainsman, hunter, army scout, sharpshooter, and showman whose Wild West show began touring the world in 1883; he became a symbol of the Wild West.

QUESTIONS

1. What is the effect of devoting a whole line to "Buffalo Bill's" (line 1), "defunct" (line 2), "stallion" (line 5), "Jesus" (line 7), and "Mister Death" (line 11)? How does this technique reflect and emphasize the content of the poem?
2. How does the typographical arrangement of line 6 contribute to the fusion of sound and sense? What other examples of this technique do you find?

3. Explain the denotations and connotations of *defunct*. What would be lost (or gained) by using the term *dead* or *deceased* instead?

4. To what extent is this poem a "portrait" of Buffalo Bill? What do we learn about him? Is the portrait respectful, mocking, or something in between?

JOHN DRYDEN (1631–1700)

To the Memory of Mr. Oldham° ⟶⟨⟩⟶ *1684*

Farewell, too little and too lately known,
Whom I began to think and call my own:
For sure our souls were near allied, and thine
Cast in the same poetic mold with mine.
One common note on either lyre did strike,   5
And knaves and fools we both abhorred alike.
To the same goal did both our studies drive;
The last set out the soonest did arrive.
Thus Nisus° fell upon the slipp'ry place,
While his young friend performed and won the race.   10
O early ripe! to thy abundant store
What could advancing age have added more?
It might (what nature never gives the young)
Have taught the numbers of thy native tongue.
But satire needs not those, and wit will shine   15
Through the harsh cadence of a rugged line;
A noble error, and but seldom made,
When poets are by too much force betrayed.
Thy gen'rous fruits, though gathered ere their prime,
Still showed a quickness; and maturing time   20
But mellows what we write to the dull sweets of rhyme.
Once more, hail and farewell;° farewell, thou young.
But ah too short, Marcellus° of our tongue;
Thy brows with ivy and with laurels° bound;
But fate and gloomy night encompass thee around.   25

TO THE MEMORY OF MR. OLDHAM. John Oldham (1653–1683) was a young poet whom Dryden admired. 9 *Nisus*: a character in Virgil's *Aeneid* who slipped in a pool of blood while running a race, thus allowing his best friend to win. 22 *hail and farewell*: an echo of the Latin phrase "ave atque vale" spoken by gladiators about to fight. 23 *Marcellus*: a Roman general who was adopted by the Emperor Augustus as his successor but died at the age of twenty. 24 *laurels*: a plant sacred to Apollo, the Greek god of poetry; the traditional prize given to poets is a wreath of laurel.

QUESTIONS

1. What is the meter of this poem? Rhyme scheme? Closed form? How does the form control the tempo? Why is this tempo appropriate?

2. What does the speaker reveal about himself in lines 1–10? About Oldham? About his relationship with Oldham? What did the two have in common?

3. What is the effect of Dryden's frequent classical allusions? What pairs of rhyming words most effectively clinch ideas?

CAROLYN FORCHÉ (b. 1950)

The Colonel ~~~~~ 1978

What you have heard is true. I was in his house. His wife carried a tray of coffee and sugar. His daughter filed her nails, his son went out for the night. There were daily papers, pet dogs, a pistol on the cushion beside him. The moon swung bare on its black cord over the house. On the television was a cop show. It was in English. Broken bottles were embedded in the walls around the house to scoop the kneecaps from a man's legs   5
or cut his hands to lace. On the windows there were gratings like those in liquor stores. We had dinner, rack of lamb, good wine, a gold bell was on the table for calling the maid. The maid brought green mangoes, salt, a type of bread. I was asked how I enjoyed the country. There was a brief commercial in Spanish. His wife took everything away. There was some talk then of how difficult it had become to govern. The parrot   10
said hello on the terrace. The colonel told it to shut up, and pushed himself from the table. My friend said to me with eyes: say nothing. The colonel returned with a sack used to bring groceries home. He spilled many human ears on the table. They were like dried peach halves. There is no other way to say this. He took one of them in his hands, shook it in our faces, dropped it into a water glass. It came alive there. I am tired of   15
fooling around he said. As for the rights of anyone, tell your people they can go fuck themselves. He swept the ears to the floor with his arm and held the last of his wine in the air. Something for your poetry, no? he said. Some of the ears on the floor caught this scrap of his voice. Some of the ears on the floor were pressed to the ground.

QUESTIONS

1. Why does the poet use the prose poem form for this poem?
2. What is the character of the colonel? How can he be gracious, and then abusive, at the same time? What atrocities has he committed or ordered committed?
3. Why does the speaker include details about the walls about the house? What do the walls show about the mentality of those within the walls? Explain the meaning of the last sentence.

ROBERT FROST (1874–1963)

For a photo, see p. 1049.

*861
Allusion*

Desert Places ~~~~~ 1936

Snow falling and night falling fast, oh, fast
In a field I looked into going past,
And the ground almost covered smooth in snow,
But a few weeds and stubble showing last.

The woods around it have it—it is theirs.   5
All animals are smothered in their lairs.
I am too absent-spirited to count;
The loneliness includes me unawares.

And lonely as it is that loneliness
Will be more lonely ere it will be less—   10

A blanker whiteness of benighted snow
With no expression, nothing to express.

They cannot scare me with their empty spaces
Between stars—on stars where no human race is.
I have it in me so much nearer home   15
To scare myself with my own desert places.

QUESTIONS

1. What is the meter? The rhyme scheme? The form?

2. What setting and situation are established in lines 1–4? What does the snow affect here? What does it affect in lines 5–8? In lines 9–12?

3. What different kinds of "desert places" is this poem about? Which kind is the most important? Most frightening?

4. How does the type of rhyme (rising or falling) change in the last stanza? How does this change affect the tone and impact of the poem?

5. How does the stanzaic pattern of this poem organize the progression of the speaker's thoughts, feelings, and conclusions?

ALLEN GINSBERG (1926–1997)

A Supermarket in California ～≺≍∽⌣∼ 1955

What thoughts I have of you tonight, Walt Whitman,° for
I walked down the sidestreets under the trees with a headache
self-conscious looking at the full moon.
   In my hungry fatigue, and shopping for images, I went
into the neon fruit supermarket, dreaming of your enumerations!°   5
   What peaches and what penumbras! Whole families
shopping at night! Aisles full of husbands! Wives in the
avocados, babies in the tomatoes!—and you, Garcia Lorca,° what
were you doing down by the watermelons?

   I saw you, Walt Whitman, childless, lonely old grubber,   10
poking among the meats in the refrigerator and eyeing the
grocery boys.
   I heard you asking questions of each: Who killed the pork
chops? What price bananas? Are you my Angel?
   I wandered in and out of the brilliant stacks of cans   15
following you, and followed in my imagination by the store
detective.
   We strode down the open corridors together in our solitary
fancy tasting artichokes, possessing every frozen delicacy, and
never passing the cashier.   20

A SUPERMARKET IN CALIFORNIA. 1 *Walt Whitman:* American poet (1819–1892) who experimented with open forms and significantly influenced the development of twentieth-century poetry.   5 *enumerations:* Many of Whitman's poems contain long lists.   8 *Garcia Lorca:* Spanish surrealist poet and playwright (1896–1936) whose later poetry became progressively more like prose.

Where are we going, Walt Whitman? The doors close in
an hour. Which way does your beard point tonight?
   (I touch your book and dream of our odyssey in the supermarket
and feel absurd.)
   Will we walk all night through solitary streets? The trees   25
add shade to shade, lights out in the houses, we'll both be
lonely.

   Will we stroll dreaming of the lost America of love past blue
automobiles in driveways, home to our silent cottage?
   Ah, dear father, graybeard, lonely old courage-teacher,   30
what America did you have when Charon° quit poling his ferry
and you got out on a smoking bank and stood watching the
boat disappear on the black waters of Lethe?°

31 *Charon*: boatman in Greek mythology who ferried the souls of the dead across the river Styx into Hades,
the underworld.   33 *Lethe*: the river of forgetfulness in Hades. The dead drank from this river and forgot
their former lives.

QUESTIONS

1.   Where is the speaker? What is he doing? What is his condition?
2.   What effect is produced by placing Whitman and Lorca in the market?
3.   To what extent do we find Whitman-like enumerations in this work? What is the
effect of such enumerations?
4.   Why is this a poem? What poetic devices are employed here? To what extent
might it make more sense to consider this prose rather than poetry?

NIKKI GIOVANNI (b. 1943)

Nikki-Rosa ⌇⌇⌇⌇⌇ 1968

childhood remembrances are always a drag
if you're Black
you always remember things like living in Woodlawn°
with no inside toilet
and if you become famous or something   5
they never talk about how happy you were to have your mother
all to yourself and
how good the water felt when you got your bath from one of those
big tubs that folk in chicago barbecue in
and somehow when you talk about home   10
it never gets across how much you
understood their feelings
as the whole family attended meetings about Hollydale

NIKKI-ROSA. 3 *Woodlawn*: a predominantly black suburb of Cincinnati, Ohio.

and even though you remember
your biographers never understand   15
your father's pain as he sells his stock
and another dream goes
and though you're poor it isn't poverty that
concerns you
and though they fought a lot   20
it isn't your father's drinking that makes any difference
but only that everybody is together and you
and your sister have happy birthdays and very good christmasses
and I really hope no white person ever has cause to write about me
because they never understand Black love is Black wealth and they'll   25
probably talk about my hard childhood and never understand that
all the while I was quite happy

QUESTIONS

1. To what extent do individual lines, caesurae, and cadences create a rhythm and reinforce the sense of this poem?

2. What points does the speaker make about childhood in general, the childhoods of blacks, and her own childhood?

3. What ideas about the ways in which whites understand or misunderstand blacks does this poem explore?

Prose poems
block form 853 bottom
854 top

ROBERT HASS (b. 1941)

Museum ⟶⟨⟩⟨⟩ 1989

On the morning of the Käthe Kollwitz° exhibit, a young man and woman come into
the museum restaurant. She is carrying a baby; he carries the air-freight edition of the
Sunday *New York Times*. She sits in a high-backed wicker chair, cradling the infant in
her arms. He fills a tray with fresh fruit, rolls, and coffee in white cups and brings it to
the table. His hair is tousled, her eyes are puffy. They look like they were thrown down   5
into sleep and then yanked out of it like divers coming up for air. He holds the baby.
She drinks coffee, scans the front page, butters a roll and eats it in their little corner in
the sun. After a while, she holds the baby. He reads the *Book Review* and eats some fruit.
Then he holds the baby while she finds the section of the paper she wants and eats
fruit and smokes. They've hardly exchanged a look. Meanwhile, I have fallen in love with   10
this equitable arrangement, and with the baby who cooperates by sleeping. All around
them are faces Käthe Kollwitz carved in wood of people with no talent or capacity for suffering who are suffering the numbest kinds of pain: hunger, helpless terror. But this
young couple is reading the Sunday paper in the sun, the baby is sleeping, the green has
begun to emerge from the rind of the cantaloupe, and everything seems possible.   15

MUSEUM. 1 *Käthe Kollwitz*: Kollwitz (1867–1945) was a German artist well known for her sculptures and
engravings portraying the misery of poverty and war.

QUESTIONS

1. Does this poem contain material that you ordinarily think of as poetic? What seems "poetic"? "Unpoetic"? Why?
2. Why does Hass not present the poem in lines? On what principle (topical, grammatical) might you set it up in line form? How might its being in lines change the way you read it as well as see it?
3. How does the poem contrast the young couple and their baby with the art of Käthe Kollwitz?
4. In the light of this poem, how seriously should we take the final statement ("and everything seems possible")?

GEORGE HERBERT (1593–1633)

Virtue° ⸙⸙⸙ 1633

Sweet day, so cool, so calm, so bright,
The bridal of the earth and sky:
The dew shall weep thy fall tonight;
    For thou must die.   5

Sweet rose, whose hue, angry° and brave,°   *red; splendid*
Bids the rash° gazer wipe his eye:
Thy root is ever in its grave,
    And thou must die.

Sweet spring, full of sweet days and roses,   10
A box where sweets° compacted lie: *perfumes*
My music shows ye have your closes,°
    And all must die.

Only a sweet and virtuous soul,
Like seasoned timber, never gives;°   15
But though the whole world turn to coal,°
    Then chiefly lives.

VIRTUE. The title can allude to (a) divine Power operating both outside and inside an individual; (b) a characteristic quality or property; (c) conformity to divine and moral laws. 6 *rash:* eager or sympathetic. 11 *closes:* A close is the conclusion of a musical composition. 14 *never gives:* i.e., never gives in, never deteriorates and collapses (like rotted timber). 15 *turn to coal:* the burned-out residue of the earth and universe after the universal fire on Judgment Day.

QUESTIONS

1. What is the rhyme scheme of this poem? The meter? The form?
2. What points does the speaker make about the day, the rose, spring, and the "sweet and virtuous soul"?

WILLIAM HEYEN (b. 1940)

Mantle° ⌣⌣⌣⌣   1980

         Mantle ran so hard, they said,
           he tore his legs to pieces,
             What is this but spirit?

         52 homers in '56, the triple crown.
I was a high school junior, batting   5
           fourth behind him in a dream.

         I prayed for him to quit, before
his lifetime dropped below .300.
           But he didn't, and it did.

         He makes Brylcreem commercials now,   10
models with open mouths draped around him
           as they never were in Commerce, Oklahoma,

             where the sandy-haired, wide-shouldered boy
             stood up against his barn,
             lefty for an hour (Ruth, Gehrig),   15

                then righty (DiMaggio),
            as his father winged them in,
              and the future blew toward him,

                   now a fastball, now a slow
                 curve hanging   20
                 like a model's smile.

MANTLE. Mickey Mantle (1931–1995), a Yankee outfielder from 1951–1968. A switch hitter, he hit eighteen world series home runs (a record) and 536 career home runs. He was the American League's most valuable player in 1956, the year he won the triple crown (line 4).

QUESTIONS

1. Describe the shape of the poem, being careful to study the last stanza. Why is this shape appropriate for a famous baseball player?

2. How does the poet use Mantle as a symbol in this poem?

3. Who are Ruth, Gehrig, and DiMaggio? In what ways are they like Mantle?

JOHN HOLLANDER (b. 1929)

Swan and Shadow ～⌒～⌒~ 1969

```
                          Dusk
                        Above the
                    water hang the
                           loud
                           flies
                          Here                                              5
                          O so
                          gray
                          then
                          What               A pale signal will appear    10
                          When               Soon before its shadow fades
                        Where                Here in this pool of opened eye
                        In us        No Upon us As at the very edges
                     of where we take shape in the dark air
                       this object bares its image awakening             15
                       ripples of recognition that will
                       brush darkness up into light
 even after this bird this hour both drift by atop the perfect sad instant now
                       already passing out of sight
                       toward yet-untroubled reflection                  20
                       this image bears its object darkening
                       into memorial shades Scattered bits of
                       light          No of water Or something across
                       water          Breaking up No Being regathered
                       soon           Yet by then a swan will have        25
                       gone           Yes out of mind into what
                          vast
                          pale
                          hush
                          of a
                         place                                           30
                          past
              sudden dark as
                       if a swan
                       sang                                              35
```

QUESTIONS

1. How effectively and consistently does the shape image reinforce the meaning?

2. What specific words, phrases, and lines are emphasized by the typographical arrangement? To what extent does this effect give added impact to the poem?

3. How well does the structure echo the verbal images of the poem?

4. Do you find Hollander's experiment with shaped verse as successful as Herbert's in "Easter Wings" (p. 856)? If so, demonstrate how it succeeds. If not, explain why.

JOHN KEATS (1795–1821) *note 889*

For a drawing, see p. 728.

Ode to a Nightingale ⌐⌐⌐⌐⌐ 1819

1

My heart aches, and a drowsy numbness pains
  My sense, as though of hemlock° I had drunk,   *a poisonous herb*
Or emptied some dull opiate to the drains
  One minute past, and Lethe-wards° had sunk:
'Tis not through envy of thy happy lot,   5
  But being too happy in thine happiness,—
    That thou, light-winged Dryad° of the trees,
      In some melodious plot
    Of beechen green, and shadows numberless,
Singest of summer in full-throated ease.   10

2

O, for a draught of vintage! that hath been
  Cool'd a long age in the deep-delvèd earth,
Tasting of Flora° and the country green,
  Dance, and Provencal song, and sunburnt mirth!
O for a beaker full of the warm South,   15
  Full of the true, the blushful Hippocrene,°
    With beaded bubbles winking at the brim,
      And purple-stainèd mouth;
    That I might drink, and leave the world unseen,
And with thee fade away into the forest dim: 20

3

Fade far away, dissolve, and quite forget
  What thou among the leaves hast never known,
The weariness, the fever, and the fret
  Here, where men sit and hear each other groan;
Where palsy shakes a few, sad, last gray hairs,   25
  Where youth grows pale, and spectre-thin, and dies;
    Where but to think is to be full of sorrow
      And leaden-eyed despairs,
    Where Beauty cannot keep her lustrous eyes,
Or new Love pine at them beyond to-morrow.   30

4

Away! away! for I will fly to thee,
  Not charioted by Bacchus° and his pards,°   *leopards*

ODE TO A NIGHTINGALE. 4 *Lethe-wards:* toward the river of forgetfulness in Hades, the underworld of Greek mythology. 7 *Dryad:* in Greek mythology, a semidivine tree spirit. 13 *Flora:* the Roman goddess of flowers. 16 *Hippocrene:* the fountain of the Muses on Mt. Helicon in Greek mythology; the phrase thus refers to both the waters of poetic inspiration and a cup of wine. 32 *Bacchus:* the Greek god of wine. See Chapter 28.

But on the viewless wings of Poesy,°   *poetry*
   Though the dull brain perplexes and retards:
Already with thee! tender is the night,   35
    And haply the Queen-Moon is on her throne,
      Cluster'd around by all her starry Fays;°   *fairies*
        But here there is no light,
   Save what from heaven is with the breezes blown
   Through verdurous glooms and winding mossy ways.   40

5

I cannot see what flowers are at my feet,
   Nor what soft incense hangs upon the boughs,
But, in embalmed° darkness, guess each sweet   *fragrant*
    Wherewith the seasonable month endows
The grass, the thicket, and the fruit-tree wild;   45
    White hawthorn, and the pastoral eglantine;°   *honeysuckle*
      Fast fading violets cover'd up in leaves;
        And mid-May's eldest child,
   The coming musk-rose, full of dewy wine,
    The murmurous haunt of flies on summer eves.   50

6

Darkling° I listen; and, for many a time   *in the dark*
   I have been half in love with easeful Death,
Call'd him soft names in many a musèd rhyme,
   To take into the air my quiet breath;
Now more than ever seems it rich to die,   55
   To cease upon the midnight with no pain,
    While thou art pouring forth thy soul abroad
      In such an ecstasy!
   Still wouldst thou sing, and I have ears in vain—
    To thy high requiem become a sod.   60

7

Thou wast not born for death, immortal Bird!
   No hungry generations tread thee down;
The voice I hear this passing night was heard
   In ancient days by emperor and clown:
Perhaps the self-same song that found a path   65
    Through the sad heart of Ruth,° when, sick for home,
      She stood in tears amid the alien corn;°   *wheat, grain*
        The same that oft-times hath
   Charm'd magic casements, opening on the foam
    Of perilous seas, in faery lands forlorn.   70

66 *Ruth:* the widow of Boaz in the biblical Book of Ruth.

8

Forlorn! the very word is like a bell
  To toll me back from thee to my sole self!
Adieu! the fancy° cannot cheat so well   *imagination*
  As she is fam'd to do, deceiving elf.
Adieu! adieu! thy plaintive anthem fades   75
  Past the near meadows, over the still stream,
    Up the hill-side; and now 'tis buried deep
      In the next valley-glades:
Was it a vision, or a waking dream?
  Fled is that music:—Do I wake or sleep?   80

QUESTIONS

1. Formulate the structure (meter of each line and rhyme scheme) of the stanzas. What traditional form is employed here?

2. What is the speaker's mental and emotional state in stanza 1? What similes are employed to describe this condition?

3. What does the speaker want in stanza 2? Whom does he want to join? Why? From what aspects of the world (stanza 3) does he want to escape?

4. How do the speaker's mood and perspective change in stanza 4? How does he achieve this transition? What characterizes the world that the speaker enters in stanza 5? What senses are employed to describe this world?

5. What does the speaker establish about the nightingale's song in stanza 7? What does the song come to symbolize?

CLAUDE MCKAY (1890–1948)

In Bondage ⤳⟨⟨⟩⟨⟩ 1922

I would be wandering in distant fields
Where man, and bird, and beast, lives leisurely,
And the old earth is kind, and ever yields
Her goodly gifts to all her children free;
Where life is fairer, lighter, less demanding,   5
And boys and girls have time and space for play
Before they come to years of understanding—
Somewhere I would be singing, far away.
For life is greater than the thousand wars
Men wage for it in their insatiate lust,   10
And will remain like the eternal stars,
When all that shines to-day is drift and dust.

But I am bound with you in your mean graves,
O black men, simple slaves of ruthless slaves.

QUESTIONS

1. What is the meter of this poem? The rhyme scheme? The form? To what extent does the form organize the speaker's thoughts?

2. Lines 1–8 present a conditional (rather than actual) situation that the speaker desires. What word signals this nature? What is the speaker's wish?

3.   What point does the speaker make about life in lines 9–12?

4.   How does the couplet undermine the rest of the poem? What single word conveys this reversal? How effectively do the rhymes clinch the poem's meaning? What is the speaker telling us about the lives of African Americans?

JOHN MILTON (1608–1674)

On His Blindness (When I Consider How My Light Is Spent)°   1655

When I consider how my light is spent
  Ere half my days, in this dark world and wide,
  And that one talent° which is death to hide,
  Lodged with me useless, though my soul more bent
To serve therewith my Maker, and present   5
  My true account, lest he returning chide;
  "Doth God exact day-labor, light denied?"
  I fondly° ask; but Patience to prevent°   *foolishly; forestall*
That murmur, soon replies, "God doth not need
  Either man's work or his own gifts; who best   10
  Bear his mild yoke, they serve him best. His state
Is kingly. Thousands at his bidding speed
  And post o'er land and ocean without rest;
  They also serve who only stand and wait."

ON HIS BLINDNESS (WHEN I CONSIDER HOW MY LIGHT IS SPENT). Milton began to go blind in the late 1640s and was completely blind by 1651.   3 *talent*: both a skill and a reference to the talents discussed in the parable in Matthew 25:14–30.

QUESTIONS

1.   What is the meter of this poem? The rhyme scheme? The closed form?

2.   To what extent do the two major divisions of this form organize the poem's ideas?

3.   What problem is raised in the octave? What are the speaker's complaints? Who is the speaker in the sestet? How are the earlier conflicts resolved?

4.   Explore the word *talent* and relate its various meanings to the poem as a whole.

DUDLEY RANDALL (1914–2000)

Ballad of Birmingham°   1966

(On the bombing of a church in Birmingham, Alabama, 1963)

"Mother dear, may I go downtown
Instead of out to play,
And march the streets of Birmingham
In a Freedom March today?"

"No, baby, no, you may not go,   5
For the dogs are fierce and wild,
And clubs and hoses, guns and jails
Aren't good for a little child."

"But, mother, I won't be alone.
Other children will go with me,   10
And march the streets of Birmingham
To make our country free."

"No, baby, no, you may not go,
For I fear those guns will fire.
But you may go to church instead   15
And sing in the children's choir."

She has combed and brushed her night-dark hair,
And bathed rose petal sweet,
And drawn white gloves on her small brown hands,
And white shoes on her feet.   20

The mother smiled to know her child
Was in the sacred place,
But that smile was the last smile
To come upon her face.

For when she heard the explosion,   25
Her eyes grew wet and wild.
She raced through the streets of Birmingham
Calling for her child.

She clawed through bits of glass and brick,
Then lifted out a shoe   30
"Oh, here's the shoe my baby wore,
But, baby, where are you?"

BALLAD OF BIRMINGHAM. Four black children were killed when the 16th Street Baptist Church in Birmingham, Alabama, was bombed in 1963. A man was finally indicted for the murders in 1977 and convicted in 1982. There was an additional conviction in 2002.

QUESTIONS

1. Formulate the structure (meter, rhyme scheme, stanza form) of this poem. What traditional closed form is employed here?

2. Who is the speaker in stanzas 1 and 3? In stanzas 2 and 4? How are quotation and repetition employed to create tension?

3. What ironies do you find in the mother's assumptions? In the poem as a whole? In the society pictured in the poem?

4. Compare the poem to "Sir Patrick Spens" (p. 617) and to "Barbara Allan" (p. 1069). How are the structures of all three alike? To what extent do all three deal with the same type of subject matter?

THEODORE ROETHKE (1908–1963)

For a photo, see p. 656.

The Waking 〜 1953

I wake to sleep, and take my waking slow.
I feel my fate in what I cannot fear.
I learn by going where I have to go.

We think by feeling. What is there to know?
I hear my being dance from ear to ear.   5
I wake to sleep, and take my waking slow.

Of those so close beside me, which are you?
God bless the Ground! I shall walk softly there,
And learn by going where I have to go.

Light takes the Tree; but who can tell us how?   10
The lowly worm climbs up a winding stair;
I wake to sleep, and take my waking slow.

Great Nature has another thing to do
To you and me; so take the lively air,
And, lovely, learn by going where to go.   15

This shaking keeps me steady. I should know.
What falls away is always. And is near.
I wake to sleep, and take my waking slow.
I learn by going where I have to go.

QUESTIONS

1. Compare the form of this poem with the poems by Bishop and Thomas in this chapter.

2. In what way or ways does the speaker "wake to sleep"? What other apparent contradictions does the speaker develop in this poem? Why might a reader conclude that the poem is positive rather than negative?

3. What does the speaker mean by saying that he learns "by going where I have to go"? In what way does "always" fall away (line 17)?

WILLIAM SHAKESPEARE (1564–1616)

For a drawing, see p. 1306.

Sonnet 73: That Time of Year Thou May'st in Me Behold 〜 1609

That time of year thou may'st in me behold
When yellow leaves, or none, or few, do hang
Upon those boughs which shake against the cold,
Bare ruined choirs,° where late the sweet birds sang.

SONNET 73. 4 *choirs*: the part of a church just in front of the altar.

In me thou see'st the twilight of such day   5
As after sunset fadeth in the west;
Which by and by black night doth take away,
Death's second self,° that seals up all in rest.
In me thou see'st the glowing of such fire,
That on the ashes of his° youth doth lie,   *its*   10
As the death-bed whereon it must expire,
Consumed with that which it was nourished by.°
This thou perceivest, which makes thy love more strong,   *final*
To love that well which thou must leave ere long.   *— Couplet*

8 *Death's . . . self:* That is, night is a mirror image of death inasmuch as it brings the sleep of rest just as death brings the sleep of actual death.   12 *Consumed . . . by:* That is, the ashes of the fuel burned at the fire's height now prevent the fire from continuing, and in fact extinguish it.

QUESTIONS

1. Describe the content of lines 1–4, 5–8, and 9–12. What connects these three sections? How does the concluding couplet relate to the first twelve lines?

2. Analyze the iambic pentameter of the poem. Consider the spondees in lines 2 ("do hang"), 4 ("bare ru-" and "birds sang"), 5 ("such day"), 7 ("black night"), 8 ("death's sec-"), 9 ("such fire"), 10 ("doth lie"), 11 ("death-bed"), 13 ("more strong"), and 14 ("ere long"). What is the effect of these substitutions on the poem's ideas?

3. How does the enjambement of lines 1–3 and 5–6 permit these lines to seem to conclude *as lines* even though grammatically they carry over to form sentences?

4. In lines 2, 5, 6, and 9, where does Shakespeare place the caesurae? What relationship is there between the rhythms produced by these caesurae and the content of lines 1–12? In lines 13 and 14, how do the rising stressed caesurae relate to the content?

PERCY BYSSHE SHELLEY (1792–1822)

Ozymandias   ⌣ ⌣ ⌣   1818

I met a traveller from an antique land,
Who said—"Two vast and trunkless legs of stone
Stand in the desert. . . . Near them, on the sand,
Half sunk, a shattered visage lies, whose frown,
And wrinkled lip, and sneer of cold command,   5
Tell that its sculptor well those passions read
Which yet survive, stamped on these lifeless things,
The hand that mocked them, and the heart that fed;
And on the pedestal, these words appear;
'My name is Ozymandias, King of Kings,   10
Look on my Works, ye Mighty, and despair!'
Nothing beside remains. Round the decay
Of that colossal Wreck, boundless and bare
The lone and level sands stretch far away."

QUESTIONS

1.   What is the meter of this poem? The rhyme scheme? What traditional closed form is modified here? How do the modifications affect the poem?

2.   To what extent are content and meaning shaped by the closed form? What is described in the octave? In the sestet?

3.   Characterize Ozymandias (thought to be Ramses II, pharaoh of Egypt, who died in 1225 B.C.E.) from the way he is portrayed in this poem.

MAY SWENSON (1919–1989)

Women ⨯⟶⟵⨯ 1968

Women	Or they	
should be	should be	
pedestals	little horses	
moving	those wooden	
pedestals	sweet	5
moving	oldfashioned	
to the	painted	
motions	rocking	
of men	horses	

the gladdest things in the toyroom   10

The	feelingly	
pegs	and then	
of their	unfeelingly	
ears	To be	
so familiar	joyfully	15
and dear	ridden	
to the trusting	rockingly	
fists	ridden until	
To be chafed	the restored	

egos dismount and the legs stride away   20

Immobile	willing	
sweetlipped	to be set	
sturdy	into motion	
and smiling	Women	
women	should be	25
should always	pedestals	
be waiting	to men	

QUESTIONS

1.   Is this poem an instance of closed-form, open-form, or visual poetry? In what different ways or sequences can it be read? How do the different sequences change the meaning?

2.   How well does the image of the poem reinforce its meaning? Would the effect be different if the columns of words were straight instead of undulating?

3. To what extent do repetition and alliteration help to organize the poem and underscore its sense? Note especially *w, m, f, r,* and *s* sounds.

4. What does this poem *say* that women should be? Does it mean what it says? How are men characterized? In what way is this poem ironic?

DYLAN THOMAS (1914–1953)

Do Not Go Gentle into That Good Night   1951

Do not go gentle into that good night,
Old age should burn and rave at close of day;
Rage, rage against the dying of the light.

Though wise men at their end know dark is right,
Because their words had forked no lightning they
Do not go gentle into that good night.   5

Good men, the last wave by, crying how bright
Their frail deeds might have danced in a green bay,
Rage, rage against the dying of the light.

Wild men who caught and sang the sun in flight,
And learn, too late, they grieved it on its way,   10
Do not go gentle into that good night.

Grave men, near death, who see with blinding sight
Blind eyes could blaze like meteors and be gay,
Rage, rage against the dying of the light.   15

And you, my father, there on the sad height,
Curse, bless, me now with your fierce tears, I pray.
Do not go gentle into that good night.
Rage, rage against the dying of the light.

QUESTIONS

1. What conclusions do you make about the speaker, listener, and situation in this poem?

2. What connotative words do you find here? Consider "dying," the "good" of "good night," "gentle," "Curse, bless, me now with your fierce tears, I pray," and "grave."

3. What five different kinds of men does the speaker discuss in stanzas 2–5? What do they have in common? Of what value are they to the speaker's father (line 16)?

4. Compare the form of this poem with the poems by Bishop and Roethke in this chapter.

JEAN TOOMER (1894–1967)

Reapers ～＜ン✓ノ 1923

Black reapers with the sound of steel on stones
Are sharpening scythes. I see them place the hones
In their hip-pockets as a thing that's done,
And start their silent swinging, one by one.
Black horses drive a mower through the weeds,   5
And there, a field rat, startled, squealing bleeds,
His belly close to ground. I see the blade,
Blood-stained, continue cutting weeds and shade.

QUESTIONS

1. What is the poem's meter? The rhyme scheme? The form? What is the difference between Toomer's use of the form and Dryden's?

2. How do the images of this poem relate to each other? How does the image of the bleeding field rat and the "blood-stained" blade heighten the impact?

3. How does alliteration unify this poem and make sound echo sense? Note especially the *s* and *b* sounds and the phrase "silent swinging."

CHARLES HARPER WEBB (b. 1952)

The Shape of History ～＜ン✓ノ 1995

Turning and turning in the widening gyre . . .°

Today's paper is crammed full of news: pages and pages on the Somalia
Famine, the Balkan Wars, Gays in the Military. On this date a year ago,
only 1/365 of "The Year's Top Stories" happened. *Time* magazine fits a
decade into one thin retrospective. Barely enough occurred a century
   ago to fill one sub-chapter in a high school text. 500 years ago, one   5
      or two things happened every 50 years. 5000 years ago, a city
         was founded, a grain cultivated, a civilization toppled every
            other century. Still farther back, the years march by in
               groups like graduates at a big state university: 10,000 to
                  20,000 BC; 50,000–100,000 BC; 1–10 million BC.   10
                  Before that, things happened once an Era: Mam-
                     mals in the Cenozoic, Dinosaurs in the Meso-
                        zoic, Forests in the Paleozoic, Protozoans in
                           the Pre-Cambrian. Below that, at the
                              very base of time's twisting gyre, its   15
                                 cornucopia, its ram's-horn trum-
                                    pet, its tornado tracking across
                                       eternity, came what Christ-
                                       ians call Creation, astro-
                                          physicists call the Big   20
                                          Bang. Then, for tril-
                                             lions of years,
                                                nothing at
                                                   all.

THE SHAPE OF HISTORY. *Turning . . . gyre:* See line 1 of Yeats's "The Second Coming," p. 913.

QUESTIONS

1. What shape does the poet give to history? How accurate is this shape?
2. How do the lengths of the first and final two lines graphically show how civilization has grown? What "top stories" are mentioned in the first few lines? How representative of modern news are these stories? How long will it take for such stories to be replaced by new, similar stories?
3. In the light of the epigraph by Yeats, what does the speaker apparently think will happen in the future?
4. Considering the content and the diminishing shape of the poem's twenty-four lines, what do you think is meant by "nothing at / all"?

PHYLLIS WEBB (b. 1927)

Poetics Against the Angel of Death° ⤳⤳⤳ *1962*

I am sorry to speak of death again
(some say I'll have a long life)
but last night Wordsworth's 'Prelude'°   5
suddenly made sense—I mean the measure,
the elevated tone, the attitude
of private Man speaking to public men.
Last night I thought I would not wake again
but now with this June morning I run ragged to elude   10
the Great Iambic Pentameter
who is the Hound of Heaven° in our stress
because I want to die
writing Haiku
or, better,
long lines, clean and syllabic as knotted bamboo. Yes!

POETICS AGAINST THE ANGEL OF DEATH. *Angel of Death:* See Byron's "The Destruction of Sennacherib," stanza 3 (Chapter 25).   3 *Wordsworth's 'Prelude':* See Chapter 24.   10 *Hound of Heaven (The):* a long poem (1893) by Francis Thompson (1859–1907) about attempting to evade God's love.

QUESTIONS

1. In the poem itself, what is meant by the "Angel of Death"?
2. What attitude does the speaker express about iambic pentameter? How does the speaker explain this attitude? How defensible is the attitude?
3. For what poetic forms does the speaker express a preference? Why? How does the form of this poem bear out the preference?

WILLIAM CARLOS WILLIAMS (1883–1963)

The Dance ⟶⟨⟨⟨⟩⟩⟩ *1944*

In Brueghel's° great picture, The Kermess,
the dancers go round, they go round and
around, the squeal and the blare and the
tweedle of bagpipes, a bugle and fiddles
tipping their bellies (round as the thick-sided   5
glasses whose wash they impound)
their hips and their bellies off balance
to turn them. Kicking and rolling about
the Fair Grounds, swinging their butts, those
shanks must be sound to bear up under such   10
rollicking measures, prance as the dance
in Breughel's great picture, The Kermess.

THE DANCE. 1 *Brueghel's:* Pieter Brueghel (ca. 1525–1569), a Flemish painter. *Peasants' Dance (The Kermess)* shows peasants dancing in celebration of the anniversary of the founding of a church (*church mass*). See Insert I-8.

QUESTIONS

1. What effect is produced by repeating the first line as the last line?
2. How do repetition, alliteration, assonance, onomatopoeia, and internal rhyme affect the tempo, feeling, and meaning of the poem? How do the numerous participles (like "tipping," "kicking," "rolling") make sound echo sense?
3. What words are capitalized? What effect is produced by omitting the capital letters at the beginning of each line? How does this typographical choice reinforce the sound and the sense of the poem?
4. Most of the lines of this poem are run-on rather than end-stopped, and many of them end with fairly weak words such as *and, the, about,* and *such.* What effect is produced through these techniques?
5. How successful is Williams in making the words and sentence rhythms echo the visual rhythms in Breughel's painting? Why is this open form more appropriate to the images of the poem than any closed form could be?

❦ WRITING ABOUT FORM IN POETRY

An essay about form in poetry should demonstrate a relationship between a poem's sense and its form. Do not discuss form or shape in isolation, for such an essay would be no more than a detailed description. The first thing to do as you go about determining what you want to say is to examine the poem's main ideas. Consider the various elements that contribute to the poem's impact and effectiveness: the speaker, listener, setting, situation, diction, imagery, and rhetorical devices. Once you understand these, it will be easier to establish a connection between form and content.

It will be helpful to prepare a work sheet that highlights the elements you wish to discuss. For closed forms, these elements will be rhyme scheme, meter, line lengths, and stanzaic patterns. They may also include significant words and phrases that connect stanzas. The work sheet for an open-form poem should indicate variables such as rhythm and phrases, the use of pauses, significant words that are isolated or emphasized through typography, and patterns of repeated sounds, words, phrases, and images.

Questions for Discovering Ideas

Closed Form

- What is the principal meter? Line length? Rhyme scheme? To what extent do these establish and/or reinforce the form?
- What is the form of each stanza or unit? How many stanzas or divisions does the poem contain? How does the poem establish a pattern? How is the pattern repeated?
- What is the form of the poem (e.g., couplet, tercet, ballad, villanelle, sonnet)? In what ways is the poem traditional, and what variations does it introduce? What is the effect of the variations?
- How effectively does the structure create or reinforce the poem's internal logic? What topical, logical, or thematic progressions unite the various parts of the poem?
- To what extent does the form organize the images of the poem? Are key images developed within single units or stanzas? Do images recur in several units?
- To what extent does the form organize and bring out the poem's ideas or emotions?

Open Form

- What does the poem look like on the page? What is the relationship of its shape to its meaning?
- How does the poet use variable line lengths, spaces, punctuation, capitalization, and the like to shape the poem? How do these variables contribute to the poem's sense and impact?
- What rhythms are built into the poem through language or typography? How are these relevant to the poem's content?
- What is the poem's progression of ideas, images, and/or emotions? How is the logic created and what does it contribute?
- How does form or typography isolate or group, and thus emphasize, various words and phrases? What is the effect of such emphasis?
- What patterns do you discover of words and sounds? To what degree do the patterns create order and structure? How are they related to the sense of the poem?

Strategies for Organizing Ideas

In developing your central idea, you should illustrate the connections between form and meaning. For example, in planning an essay on Randall's "Ballad of Birmingham" you might develop your ideas according to the speeches that are a normal feature of the ballad form. The poem's first part is a dialogue between mother and child about the hazard of the local streets and the safety of the local church. In the second part, after the explosion, the mother runs toward the church and calls for her child, who, ironically, will never again engage with her in further dialogue. Another plan is needed for an essay on Williams's "The Dance"; such a plan might link the lively, bustling movement of the dancers pictured in Brueghel's painting (Insert I-8) to the rhythms, repetitions, and run-on lines of the poem. Still another plan would be needed for a discussion of Heyen's "Mantle," the form of which requires enough stanzas of approximately equal length to make up the pattern of a pitched ball (what is this pattern?).

Your introduction may contain general remarks about the poem, but it should focus on the connection between form and substance. Describe the ways in which structure and content interact together, with a brief listing of your specific topics.

Early in the body, describe the formal characteristics of your poem, using schemes and numbers (as in paragraph 2 of the demonstrative student essay). With closed forms, your description should detail such standard features as the traditional form, meter, rhyme scheme, stanzaic structure, and number of stanzas. With open-form poetry, you should focus on the most striking and significant features of the verse (as in the brief discussion of Whitman's "Reconciliation" on pp. 854–55).

Be sure to integrate your discussion of both form and content. It may be that you have uncovered a good deal of information about technical features such as alliteration or rhyme, or you may wish to stress how words, phrases, and clauses develop a pattern of ideas. Remember that you are not making a paraphrase or a general explication, but instead are showing how the poet uses form—either an open or a closed one—in the service of meaning. The order in which you deal with your topics is entirely your decision.

The conclusion of your essay might contain additional relevant observations about shape or structure. It might also summarize your argument. Here, as in all essays about literature, make sure to reach an actual conclusion rather than simply a stopping point.

DEMONSTRATIVE STUDENT ESSAY

Form and Meaning in George Herbert's "Virtue"°

Herbert's devotional four-stanza poem "Virtue" (1633) contrasts the mortality of worldly things with the immortality of the "virtuous soul." This is not an uncommon topic in religious poetry and hymns, and there is nothing unusual about this contrast. What is unusual, however, is the simplicity and directness of Herbert's expressions and the way in which he integrates his ideas within his stanzaic song pattern. Each part of the poem organizes the images logically and underscores the supremacy of life over death.* Through control over line and stanza groupings, rhyme scheme, and repeated sounds and words, Herbert's stanzas create a structural and visual distinction between the "sweet" soul and the rest of creation.†

[1]

°See p. 865 for this poem.
*Central idea.
†Thesis sentence.

[2]   Herbert's control over lines within the stanzas is particularly strong. Each stanza follows the same basic a b a b rhyme scheme. Since some rhyme sounds and words are repeated throughout the first three stanzas, however, the structure of the poem can be formulated as 4a 4b 4a 2b; 4c 4b 4c 2b; 4d 4b 4d 2b; 4e 4f 4e 2f. Each stanza thus contains three lines of iambic tetrameter with a final line of iambic dimeter--an unusual pattern that creates a unique emphasis. In the first three stanzas, the dimeter lines repeat the phrase "must die," while in the last stanza the contrast is made on the words "Then chiefly lives." These rhythms require a sensitive reading, and they powerfully underscore Herbert's idea that death is conquered by eternal life.

[3]   Like individual lines, Herbert's stanzaic structure provides the poem's pattern of organization and logic. The first stanza focuses on the image of the "Sweet day," comparing the day to "The bridal of the earth and sky" (line 2) and asserting that the day inevitably "must die." Similarly, the second stanza focuses on the image of a "Sweet rose" and asserts that it too "must die." The third stanza shifts to the image of "Sweet spring." Here the poet blends the images of the first two stanzas into the third by noting that the "Sweet spring" is "full of sweet days and roses" (line 9). The stanza concludes with the summarizing claim that "all must die." In this way, the third stanza is the climax of Herbert's imagery of beauty and mortality. The last stanza introduces a new image--"a sweet and virtuous soul"-- and an assertion that is the opposite of the ideas expressed in the previous three stanzas. Although the day, the rose, and the spring "must die," the soul "never" deteriorates, but "chiefly lives" even "though the whole world turn to coal" (line 15). With its key image of the "virtuous soul," this last stanza marks the logical conclusion of Herbert's argument. His pattern of organization allows this key image of permanence to be separated structurally from the images of impermanence.

[4]   This structural organization of images and ideas is repeated and reinforced by other techniques. Herbert's rhyme scheme, for example, links the first three stanzas while isolating the fourth. That the b rhyme is repeated at the ends of the second and fourth lines of each of the first three stanzas makes these stanzas into a complete unit. The fourth stanza, however is different in both content and rhyme. The stanza introduces the concept of immortality, and it also introduces entirely new rhymes, replacing the b rhyme with an f rhyme. Thus the rhyme scheme, by sound alone, parallels the poem's imagery and logic.

[5]   As a complement to the rhyming sounds, the poem also demonstrates organizing patterns of assonance. Most notable is the oo sound, which is repeated throughout the first three stanzas in the words "cool," "dew," "whose," "hue," "root," and "music." In Herbert's time, the sound might still have been prominent in the word "thou," so that in the first three stanzas the oo, which is not unlike a moan (certainly appropriate to things that die), is repeated eight times. In the last stanza there is a stress on the o sound, in "only," "soul," "though," "whole," and "coal." While oh may also be a moan, in this context it is more like an exclamation, in keeping with the triumph contained in the final line.

[6]   Herbert's repetition of key words and phrases also distinguishes the first three stanzas from the last stanza. Each of the first three stanzas begins with "sweet" and ends with "must die." These repetitions stress both the beauty and the mortality of worldly things. In the last stanza, however, this repetition is abandoned, just as the stress on immortality transcends mortality. The "Sweet" that begins each of the first three stanzas is replaced by "Only" (line 13). Similarly, "must die" is replaced with "chiefly lives." Both substitutions separate this final stanza from the

three previous stanzas. More important, the shift in the verbal pattern emphasizes the conceptual transition from death to the virtuous soul's immortality.

[7]   The lyric form of Herbert's "Virtue" provides an organizational pattern for the poem's images and ideas. At the same time, the stanzaic pattern and the rhyme scheme allow the poet to draw a strong distinction between the corruptible world and the immortal soul. The closed form of this poem is not arbitrary or incidental; it is an integral way of asserting the importance of the key image, the "sweet and virtuous soul."

WORK CITED

Herbert, George "Virtue." Literature: An Introduction to Reading and Writing. Ed. Edgar V. Roberts and Henry E. Jacobs. 7th ed. Upper Saddle River: Prentice Hall, 2004. 865.

Commentary on the Essay

The introductory paragraph establishes the groundwork of the essay—the treatment of form in relationship to content. The main idea is that each part of the poem represents a complete blending of image, logic, and meaning.

Paragraph 2 , the first in the body, demonstrates how the poem's schematic formulation is integrated into Herbert's contrast of death and life. In this respect the paragraph demonstrates how a formal enumeration can be integrated within an essay's thematic development.

The focus of paragraph 3 is the organization of both images and ideas from stanza to stanza. Paragraph 4 begins with a transitional sentence that repeats part of the essay's central idea and, at the same time, connects it to paragraph 3. In the same way, paragraph 4 is closely tied to both paragraphs 1 and 3. The main topic here, the rhyme scheme of "Virtue," is introduced in the second sentence. This paragraph also asserts that rhythm also reinforces the division between mortality and immortality. On much the same topic, paragraph 5 introduces Herbert's use of assonance, which can be seen as integral in the poem's blending of form and content.

Paragraph 6 takes up the last structural element described in the introduction—repeated key words and phrases. The idea is that these repetitions emphasize the distinction in the poem between mortality and immortality.

Paragraph 7, the conclusion, provides a brief overview and summation of the essay's argument. In addition, it concludes that form in "Virtue" is neither arbitrary nor incidental but rather an integral part of the poem's meaning.

Special Topics for Writing and Argument about Poetic Form

1.   Describe the use of the ode form as exemplified by Shelley's "Ode to the West Wind" (Chapter 19) and Keats's "Ode to a Nightingale." What patterns of regularity do you find? What differences do you find in the form and content of the poems? How do you account for these differences?

2. How do Cummings, Milton, Thomas, Randall, and Dryden use different forms to consider the subject of death (in "Buffalo Bill's Defunct," "Lycidas," "Do Not Go Gentle into that Good Night," "Ballad of Birmingham," and "To the Memory of Mr. Oldham")? What differences in form and treatment do you find? What similarities do you find, despite these differences?

3. Consider the structural arrangement and shaping of the following works: Brueghel's painting *Peasants' Dance (La Kermesse)* (Insert I-8), Hass's "Museum," Heyen's "Mantle," Hollander's "Swan and Shadow," Webb's "The Shape of History," and Williams's "The Dance." How do painter and poets utilize topic, arrangement, shape, and space to draw attention to their main ideas? How do the shaped and prose poems (Hass, Heyen, Hollander, and Webb) blend poetic and artistic techniques?

4. Compare and contrast the use of the villanelle by Bishop ("One Art"), Roethke ("The Waking"), and Thomas ("Do Not Go Gentle into that Good Night"). What topics do the poets develop? Why do the poets choose the villanelle as their poetic form? What lines do they repeat? What is the effect of this repetition?

5. Compare Brooks's "We Real Cool" and Hopkins's "God's Grandeur" (both in Chapter 19). How do these poems sound when read aloud? What can you say about each poet's use of strong stresses in order to achieve emphasis?

6. Compare the sonnets in this chapter by Shakespeare, Shelley, Milton, and Collins. In what ways are the poetic forms of Shakespeare, Milton, and Shelley similar? Different? How may Collins's poem be read as a commentary on the sonnet forms of the other poets?

7. Write a visual poem, and explain the principles on which you develop your lines. Here are some possible topics (just to get you started): a "boom box," a cat, a dog, a car, a football, a snow shovel, a giraffe. After finishing your poem, write a short essay that considers these questions: What are the strengths and limitations of the visual form, according to your experience? How does the form help make your poem serious or comic? How does it encourage creative language and original development of ideas?

8. Write a haiku. Be sure to fit your poem to the 5–7–5 pattern of syllables. What challenges and problems do you encounter in this form? Once you have completed your haiku (which, to be traditional, should be on a topic concerned with nature), try to cut the number of syllables to 4–5–4. Explain how you establish the first haiku pattern, and also explain how you go about cutting the total number of syllables. Be sure to explain what kinds of words you use (length, choice of diction, etc.).

9. Using a computer reference system or regular card catalogue, depending on availability in your college library, look up one of the following topics: "ballads, England," "concrete poetry," or "blank verse." How many references are included under these listings? What sorts of topics are included under the basic topic?

Symbolism and Allusion: *Windows to Wide Expanses of Meaning*

Symbolism refers to the use of symbols in works of art and in all other forms of expression. As we noted in Chapter 9, a **symbol** has meaning in and of itself, but it is also understood to represent something else, like the flag for the country or the school song for the school. Symbols occur in stories as well as in poems, but poetry relies more heavily on symbols because it is more concise and because it comprises more forms than fiction, which is restricted to narratives.

Most of the words we use every day are symbols, for they stand for various objects without actually being those objects. When we say *horse*, for example, or *tree*, or *run*, these words are symbols of horses and trees and people running. They direct our minds to real horses, real trees, and real actions in the real world that we have seen and can therefore easily imagine. In literature, however, symbolism implies a special relationship that expands our ordinary understanding of words, descriptions, and arguments.

SYMBOLISM AND MEANINGS

Symbolism goes beyond the close referral of word to thing; it is more like a window through which one can glimpse the extensive world outside. Because poetry is compact, its descriptions and portrayals of experience are brief. Symbolism is therefore one of its primary characteristics. It is a shorthand way of referring to extensive ideas or attitudes that otherwise would be inappropriate to include in the brief format of a poem. Thus the speaker of Yeats's poem "The Wild Swans at Coole" (Chapter 25) refers to a large flock of swans as symbols of a permanent beauty that transcends his own life's experiences of change and weariness. The hearts of the swans "have not grown old" and have not altered, as he has, during the previous years. This idea could easily be developed through many observations about the impermanence of life and the permanence of Nature, but Yeats is less conerned with details than with the symbolism of the birds. They are "Mysterious, beautiful" and will continue to "Delight men's eyes" long after they have flown beyond the speaker's vision and understanding.

Symbolism Extends Meaning Beyond Normal Connotation

The use of symbols is a way of moving outward, a means of extending and crystallizing information and ideas. For example, at the time of William Blake (1757–1827), the word *tiger* meant both a large, wild cat and also the specific animal we know today as a tiger. The word's connotation therefore links it with wildness and predation. As a symbol in "The Tyger" (Chapter 16), however, Blake uses the animal as a stand-in for what he considers cosmic negativism—the savage, wild forces that undermine the progress of civilization. Thus the tiger as a symbol is more meaningful than either the denotation or the connotation of the word would indicate. A visual comparison can be made with Francisco Goya's painting *The Colossus* (Insert II-8), in which the giant pugilistic figure above the tiny figures in the landscape represents the combination of anger, defiance, and ruthlessness that is unleashed and unchecked during times of war.

Cultural or Universal Symbols Are Widely Recognized

Many symbols, wherever they are used, possess a ready-made, clearly agreed upon meaning. These are **cultural** or **universal symbols** (also discussed in Chapter 9). Many such symbols, like the tiger, are drawn directly from nature. Other natural universal symbols are springtime and morning, which signify beginnings, growth, hope, optimism, and love. If such symbols were to be introduced into a poem about the suddenness and irevocability of death, however, they would be ironic, for their presence would emphasize the contrast between death and life.

Cultural symbols are drawn from history and custom, such as the many Judeo-Christian religious symbols that appear in poetry. References to the lamb, Eden, Egyptian bondage, shepherds, exile, the Temple, blood, water, bread, the cross, and wine—all Jewish and/or Christian symbols—occur over and over again. Sometimes these symbols are prominent in a purely devotional context. In other contexts, however, they may be contrasted with symbols of warfare and corruption to show how extensively people neglect their moral and religious obligations.

Contextual, Private, or Authorial Symbols Are Operative as Symbols Only Within Individual Works

Symbols that are not widely or universally recognized are termed **contextual, private,** or **authorial symbols** (also discussed in Chapter 9). Some of these have a natural relationship with the objects and ideas being symbolized. Let us consider snow, which is cold and white and covers everything when it falls. A poet can exploit this quality and make snow a symbol. At the beginning of the long poem "The Waste Land," T. S. Eliot does exactly that; he refers to snow as a symbol of retreat from life, a withdrawal into an intellectual and moral hibernation. Another poem symbolizing snow is the following one. Here the poet refers to snow as a both a literal and figurative link between the living and the dead.

VIRGINIA SCOTT (b. 1938)

Snow ⸱⸱⸳⸳⸳ 1977

A doe stands at the roadside,
spirit of those who have lived here
and passed known through our memory.
The doe stands at the edge of the icy road,
then darts back into the woods.   5

Snow falling,
mother-spirit hovering,
white on the drops in the road and fields,
light from the windows
of the old house   10
brightening the snow.

Presences: mother,
grandmother,
here in their place
at the foot of *ben lomond*,   15
green trees black in the hemlock night.

The doe stands at the edge of the icy road,
then darts back into the woods.

Golden Grove, New Brunswick, Canada
January 5, 1977

QUESTIONS

1. How is snow described in the poem? How and where is it seen? As a symbol, what does it signify in relationship to the doe, the memory of other people, the mother-spirit, the old house, the light, the presences, the mountains, and the trees?

2. Explain the structural purpose for which the doe is mentioned three times in the poem, with lines 17 and 18 repeating 4 and 5. As a symbol, what do you think the doe signifies?

3. What are the relationships described in the poem between memory of the past and existence in the present? What does the symbolism contribute to your understanding of these relationships?

This poem describes a real circumstance at a real place at a real time; the poet has even provided an actual location and date, just as we do when writing a letter. We can therefore presume that the snow is real snow, falling in the evening just as lights go on in the nearby houses. This detail by itself would be sufficient as a realistic image, but as Scott develops the poem, the snow symbolizes the link between the speaker's memory of the past and perception of the present. The reality of the moment is suffused with the memory of the people—"mother, / grandmother"—who "lived here." The poet is meditating on the idea that individuals, though they may often be by themselves, like the speaker, are never alone as long as they have a vivid memory of the past. Symbolically, the past and present are always connected, just as the snow covers the scene.

At the poem's conclusion, the doe darting into the woods suggests a linking of present and future (i.e., as long as there are woods, does will dart into them). Both the snow and the deer are private and contextual symbols, for they are established and developed within the poem, and they do not have the same symbolic value elsewhere. Through the symbolism, therefore, the poet has converted a private moment into an idea of general significance.

Similarly, references to other ordinary materials may be symbolic if the poet emphasizes them sufficiently, as in Keats's "La Belle Dame Sans Merci," which opens and closes with the image of withered sedge, or grass. What might seem like nothing more than a natural detail becomes additionally important because it can be understood to symbolize the loss and bewilderment felt by people when loved ones seem to be faithless and destructive rather than loyal and supportive.

The meanings of symbols may be placed on a continuum of qualities from good to bad, high to low, favorable to unfavorable. For example, Cummings's old balloonman of "in Just-" (Chapter 22) is on the positive end, symbolizing the irresistible and joyful call of growth and sexuality. Outright horror is suggested by the symbol of the rough beast slouching toward Bethlehem in Yeats's "The Second Coming." Although this mythical beast shares the same birthplace with Jesus, the commonality is ironic because the beast represents the extremes of anger, hatred, and brutality that in Yeats's judgment were dominant in modern politics.

THE FUNCTION OF SYMBOLISM IN POETRY

Poets do not simply jam symbols into a poem artificially and arbitrarily. Rather, symbols are structurally important and meaningful first and are secondarily (and essentially) symbolic. We therefore find symbols in single words, and also in actions, scenes and settings, characters and characterizations, and various situations.

Many Words Are Automatically Symbolic

With general and universal symbols, a single word is often sufficient, as with references to the lamb, shepherd, cross, blood, bread, and wine; or to summer and winter; or to drought and flood, morning and night, heat and shade, storm and calm, or feast and famine. One of the most famous of all birds, the nightingale, is an example of a single word being instantly symbolic. Because of this bird's beautiful song, it symbolizes natural, unspoiled beauty as contrasted with the contrived attempts by human beings to create beauty. Keats *868* refers to the bird in this way in his "Ode to a Nightingale" (Chapter 20), and his speaker compares human mortality with the virtually eternal beauty of this singer.

Another word also referring to a species of bird as a symbol is *geese.* Because migratory geese fly south in the fall, they symbolize the loss of summer abundance, seasonal change, alteration, and loss, with accompanying feelings of regret and sorrow. Because they return north in the spring, however, they also symbolize regeneration, newness, anticipation, and hope. These contrasting symbolic values are important in Jorie Graham's "The Geese" and Mary Oliver's *900* "Wild Geese." Graham emphasizes that the geese are "crossing" overhead but nevertheless that human affairs of "the everyday" continue despite the changes symbolized by the geese. In contrast, Oliver emphasizes geese as symbols of renewal, for the geese returning in spring suggest that "the world offers itself to your imagination."

Symbolism Is to Be Seen in Actions

Not only words but also actions may be presented as symbols. In Scott's "Snow," as we have just observed, the doe darting into the darkening woods symbolizes renewal and the mystery of life. In Hardy's "In Time of 'The Breaking of Na-*902* tions,'" the action of the man plowing a field symbolizes the continued life and vitality of the folk, the people, despite the political wrangling and military warfare that constantly rage in the world.

Symbolism Is to Be Seen in Settings and Scenes

While settings and scenes may be no more than just that—settings and scenes— the poet may develop them as symbols. We may note a symbolic setting in Wilbur's "Year's End." Wilbur draws our attention to a little dog, curled up as if sleeping, and its (presumable) owners, all of whom were killed by falling lava when the eruption of Mount Vesuvius destroyed Pompeii, the ancient Roman town, in 79 C.E. In the poem's context, this scene symbolizes the incompleteness of human achievements, a condition not only of present life but also of ancient *906* life. Keats, in "La Belle Dame Sans Merci," introduces the "elfin grot" (grotto) of the "lady in the meads." This grotto is an unreal, magical, womblike location symbolizing both the allure and the disappointment that sometimes characterize sexual attraction.

Symbolism Is to Be Seen in Characters

Poets also devise characters or people as symbols representing ideas or values, like the balloonman in Cummings's "in Just-." Although the balloonman is only mentioned, and not described or visualized, Cummings includes enough detail about him to make him a symbol of the primitive vitality, joy, and sexuality that calls children out of childhood. The "fairy's child" of Keats's "La Belle Dame Sans Merci" is a symbol of the mystery of love. The figures in Hardy's "In Time of 'The Breaking of Nations' " symbolize the power of average, ordinary people to endure even "Though Dynasties pass."

Symbolism Is to Be Seen in Situations

A poem's situations, circumstances, and conditions may also be symbolic. The position of the young gunner in the World War II bomber, six miles above the earth (Jarrell's "The Death of the Ball Turret Gunner" [Chapter 13]), makes him vulnerable and helpless, and his death symbolizes the condition of humankind in the modern age of fear and anxiety, when life is threatened by global war and technologically expert destructiveness. In "she being Brand / -new" (Chapter 18) cummings cleverly uses the situation of the speaker's breaking in a new automobile as the symbol of another kind of encounter involving the speaker.

ALLUSIONS AND MEANING

Just as symbolism enriches meaning, so also do **allusions** (see also Chapter 9), which take the form of (1) unacknowledged brief quotations from other works and (2) references to historical events and any aspect of human culture—art, music, literature, and so on. The use of allusions is a means of connecting new literary works with the broader cultural tradition of which the works are a part. In addition, allusions presuppose a common bond of knowledge between the poet and the reader. On the one hand, poets making allusions compliment the past, and on the other, they salute readers able to discover how the meanings of the allusions are transformed in the new context.

Allusions Add Dimension to Poetry

An allusion carries with it the entire context of the work from which it is drawn. Perhaps the richest sources of references and stories are the King James Bible and the plays of Shakespeare. Keats introduces a biblical allusion in "Ode to a Nightingale" (Chapter 20), where he refers to the story of Ruth, who was "sick for home" while standing "in tears amid the alien corn." This allusion is particularly rich, because Ruth became the mother of Jesse. According to the Gospel of Matthew, it was from the line of Jesse that King David was born, and it was from the house of David that Jesus was born. Thus Keats's nightingale is not only a symbol of natural beauty, but through the biblical allusion it symbolizes regeneration and redemption, much in keeping with Keats's assertion that the bird is "not born for death." In Yeats's "The Second Coming," we encounter an allusion to Shakespeare's *Macbeth*. Yeats uses the phrase "blood-dimmed tide," which refers to Macbeth's soliloquy in the second act of *Macbeth*. In the play, after murdering Duncan, Macbeth asks if there is enough water in Neptune's ocean to wash the blood from his hands. His immediate, guilt-ridden response is that

Duncan's blood will instead turn the green water to red. This image of crime being bloody enough to stain the ocean's water is thus the allusive context of Yeats's "blood-dimmed tide."

Once works become well known, as with the Bible and the plays of Shakespeare, they may in turn become a source of allusions for subsequent writers. Such a well-known work is Frost's "Stopping by Woods on a Snowy Evening" (Chapter 13), which contains an oft-quoted last line: "And miles to go before I sleep." This line is so universally recognized that it has become a symbol of completing tasks and fulfilling responsibilities. Isabella Gardner alludes to the Frost line in her "Collage of Echoes," for example, a poem which contains a number of allusions.

Allusions may be discovered in no more than a single word or phrase in a poem, provided that the expression is unusual enough or associative enough to bear the weight of the reference. Scott's "Snow," for example, speaks of "green trees black in the hemlock night." Of course, the word *hemlock* refers to a common evergreen tree observed by the speaker, but a distillation of hemlock was also the poison drunk by Socrates when the ancient Athenians executed him, as described in Plato's dialogue *Phaedo*.[1] Because of this association, any use of the word *hemlock* can be construed as an allusion to the death of Socrates and the abuse of legal authority. Another allusion to hemlock occurs in the beginning lines of "Ode to a Nightingale," in which Keats refers to hemlock. His speaker declares that a "drowsy numbness" has overtaken him "as though of hemlock . . . [he] had drunk." As the poem continues, we realize that Keats's allusion refers to the way in which death might open a new plane of existence for the speaker—a life of immortal beauty. Thus Keats builds the single-word allusion into new ideas about the nature of death.

Phrases and also descriptions and situations may also signal allusions, as in Josephine Jacobsen's "Tears," where the following sentence occurs: "Yet the globe is salt/with that savor." This is an allusion to the book of Matthew, 5:13: "Ye are the salt of the earth: but if the salt have lost his savour, wherewith shall it be salted?" This biblical passage refers to the need for believers to retain their faith, for without such faith they are "good for nothing, but to be cast out." However, Jacobsen is discussing something different, namely the endlessness of grief as a condition of life, with the continuing facts of sorrow remaining on the earth as a silent legacy. By making this allusion, Jacobsen adds to her idea the implication that, throughout human history, sorrow and tears have been a result of the loss of faith and love in human relationships.

Allusions are therefore an important means by which poets broaden the context and deepen meaning. The issues a poet raises in a new poem, in other words, are important not only there but are linked through allusion to issues raised earlier by other thinkers or brought out by previous events, places, or persons. With connections made through allusions, poets clarify

[1]To see Jacques-Louis David's painting of this scene, see Insert I-2.

their own ideas. Allusion is hence not literary "theft" but is rather a means of enrichment.

🌿 STUDYING FOR SYMBOLS AND ALLUSIONS

As you study poetry, remember that symbols and allusions do not come marked with special notice and fanfare. Your decision to call something symbolic must be based on the circumstances of the poem. Let us say that the poet introduces a major item of importance at a climactic part of the poem, or that the poet introduces a description that is unusual or noteworthy, such as the connection between "stony sleep" and the "rough beast" in Yeats's "The Second Coming." When such a connection occurs, the element may no longer be taken literally but should be read as a symbol.

Even after you have found a connection such as this, however, you will need to discover and understand symbolic meaning. For instance, in the context of Yeats's "The Second Coming," the phrase "rough beast" might refer to the person or persons hinted at in traditional interpretations of the New Testament as the "Antichrist." In a secular frame of reference, the associations of blankness and pitilessness suggest brutality and suppression. Still further, however, if the last hundred years had not been a period in which millions of people were persecuted and exterminated in military and secret police operations, even these associations might make the "rough beast" quizzical but not necessarily symbolic. But because of the rightness of the application, together with the traditional biblical associations, the figure clearly should be construed as a symbol of heartless persecution and brutality.

As you can see, the interpretation of a symbol requires that you consider, in some depth, the person, object, situation, or action being considered as symbolic. If the element can be seen as general and representative—characteristic of the condition of a large number of human beings—it assumes symbolic significance. As a rule, the more ideas that you can associate with the element, the more likely it is to be a symbol.

As for allusions, the identification of an allusion is usually simple. A word, situation, or phrase either is an allusion or it is not, and hence the matter is easily settled once a source is located. The problem comes in determining how the allusion affects the context of the poem you are reading. Thus we understand that in the poem "Snow," Scott alludes to Frost's "Desert Places" (Chapter 20, p. 861) by borrowing Frost's phrase "Snow falling." Once this allusion is established, its purpose must still be learned. Thus, on the one hand, the allusion might mean that the situation in "Snow" is the same as in Frost's poem, namely, that the speaker is making observations about interior blankness—the "desert places" of the mind, or soul. On the other hand, the poet may be using the allusion in a new sense, and this indeed is the case. Whereas Frost uses the falling snow to suggest coldness of spirit, Scott uses it, more warmly, to connect the natural scene to the memory of family. In other words, once the presence of an allusion is established, the challenge of reading and understanding still continues.

POEMS FOR STUDY

EMILY BRONTË (1818–1848)

No Coward Soul Is Mine ↗︎⟨⟩↙︎ 1850 (1846)

No coward soul is mine,
No trembler in the world's storm-troubled sphere:
   I see Heaven's glories shine,
And faith shines equal, arming me from fear.

   O God within my breast,   5
Almighty, ever-present Deity!
   Life—that in me has rest,
As I—undying Life—have power in Thee!

   Vain are the thousand creeds
That move men's hearts, unutterably vain,   10
   Worthless as withered weeds,
Or idle froth amid the boundless main,°   *i.e., oceans throughout the world*

   To waken doubt in one
Holding so fast by Thine infinity;
   So surely anchored on   15
The steadfast rock of immortality.

   With wide-embracing love
Thy spirit animates eternal years,
   Pervades and broods above,
Changes, sustains, dissolves, creates, and rears.   20

Though earth and man were gone,
And suns and universes ceased to be,
   And Thou wert left alone,°   *If Thou were to be left [totally] alone*
Every existence would exist in Thee.

There is not room for Death,   25
Nor atom that his might could render void:
   Thou—THOU art Being and Breath,
And what THOU art may never be destroyed.

QUESTIONS

1.   Why does the speaker assert in the first stanza that "No coward soul is mine"? Why does she raise this issue? Why might someone consider a soul like hers cowardly? Does the speaker make a convincing argument for the poem's first line?

2.   Who is "God within my breast" of the poem? What connection or lack of connection does this "Thee/THOU/THY" have with the "thousand creeds / That move men's hearts" of lines 9 and 10?

3.   In general, what is the breadth and scope of the symbolic references in this poem? Compare the symbolism of the "storm-troubled sphere" in stanza one, and of the vanished world, suns, universes, and even humanity in stanza six.

4.   What is the meaning and connection of the symbols "withered weeds" (line 11) and "idle froth" (line 12)? To what extent does the speaker, in lines 9–12, seem to be denigrating conventional religious faiths? How does the grammatical connection between stanzas three and four help in the understanding of these stanzas?

5.   What does the speaker apparently mean, in lines 23–24, by the statement "And Thou wert left alone, / Every existence would exist in Thee"?

6.   Describe the symbolism implied in the word "arming" in the first stanza. Against what does the speaker need arming? Who or what is arming her soul? What do "infinity" (line 14) and "immortality" (line 16) contribute to her expressed sense of her own personal strength?

AMY CLAMPITT (1920–1994)

Beach Glass ⟋⟍⟋⟍ 1983

While you walk the water's edge,
turning over concepts
I can't envision, the honking buoy
serves notice that at any time
the wind may change,   5
the reef-bell clatters
its treble monotone, deaf as Cassandra°
to any note but warning. The ocean,
cumbered by no business more urgent
than keeping open old accounts   10
that never balanced,
goes on shuffling its millenniums
of quartz, granite, basalt.

BEACH GLASS. 7 *Cassandra:* mythical Trojan prophetess who accurately foretold future disasters but whom no one believed.

It behaves
toward the permutations of novelty— 15
driftwood and shipwreck, last night's
beer cans, split oil, the coughed-up
residue of plastic—with random
impartiality, playing catch or tag
or touch-last like a terrier, 20
turning the same thing over and over,
over and over. For the ocean, nothing
is beneath consideration.

The houses
of so many mussels and periwinkles
have been abandoned here, it's hopeless 25
to know which to salvage. Instead
I keep a lookout for beach glass—
amber of Budweiser, chrysoprase°
of Almadén and Gallo, lapis
by way of (no getting around it, 30
I'm afraid) Phillips'
Milk of Magnesia, with now and then a rare
translucent turquoise or blurred amethyst
of no known origin. 35

The process
goes on forever: they came from sand,
they go back to gravel,
along with the treasuries
of Murano,° the buttressed 40
astonishments of Chartres,°
which even now are readying
for being turned over and over as gravely
and gradually as an intellect
engaged in the hazardous 45
redefinitions of structures
no one has yet looked at.

29 *chrysoprase:* a gold-green gemstone.   40 *Murano:* a Venetian island famous for its glass.   41 *Chartres:* the medieval cathedral of Chartres, France, which is unique because of the incredible beauty of its stained glass windows.

QUESTIONS

1. What is the symbolic idea of the poet's description of the buoy near the shore? How does the reference to Cassandra support the poem's meaning?

2. What life forms, now jetsam, does the speaker observe on the shore? What human artifacts have been cast ashore? Why does she choose to collect some of these artifacts? Why does she use words like "chrysoprase," "lapis," and "amethyst" in reference to these objects?

3. What is the meaning of the last stanza? What is the purpose of the poem's symbolic contrast between the beach glass and the glass from Murano and Chartres? What do these objects symbolize?

ARTHUR HUGH CLOUGH (1819–1861)

Say Not the Struggle Nought Availeth ⤳⟨⤳⟨⤳ 1849

Say not the struggle nought availeth,
  The labour and the wounds are vain,
The enemy faints not, nor faileth,°
  And as things have been they remain.°

                                                 See Isaiah 40:28–31

If hopes were dupes, fears may be liars°;   5
  It may be, in yon smoke concealed,
Your comrades chase e'en now the fliers,°   *soldiers in retreat*
  And, but for you, possess the field.°   *have control over the battlefield*

For while the tired waves, vainly breaking,
  Seem here no painful inch to gain,   10
Far back, through creeks and inlets making,
  Comes silent, flooding in, the main.°   *i.e., the ocean*

And not by eastern windows only,
  When daylight comes, comes in the light,
In front, the sun climbs slow, how slowly,   15
  But westward, look, the land is bright.

SAY NOT THE STRUGGLE NOUGHT AVAILETH. *1–4 Say . . . remain:* In more direct syntax, the title sentence may be construed as "Do not say that the struggle [of life] is of no value." Lines 2, 3, and 4 are each direct objects of the opening verb "Say not." *5 If hopes . . . liars:* i.e., If one grants that hope is unreal and therefore deceptive, one may also grant that fear is unreal and therefore equally deceptive.

QUESTIONS

1. How many separate symbols are there in this poem? From what topics are they drawn? Why does Clough allude to some of the words in Isaiah?

2. Consider this poem as a persuasive argument against feelings of personal depression and desolation. How does Clough use symbols as the basis of his argument that the listener should overcome his/her despair?

3. Why does Clough end the poem, in line 16, with the observation that the sun shining in the East illuminates the West? Why does Clough draw attention to the slowness of the ascendant sun? Additionally, to what degree might "westward" be considered as a symbol of immortality because it is the location of the setting sun?

PETER DAVISON (b. 1928)

Delphi° ⤳⟨⤳⟨⤳ 1964

The crackle of parched grass bent by wind
Is the only music in the grove
Except the gush of the Pierian Spring.°
Eagles are often seen, but through a glass
Their naked necks declare them to be vultures.   5

The place is sacred with a sanctity
Now faded, like a kerchief washed too often.
There lies the crevice where the priestesses
Hid in the crypt and drugged themselves and spoke
Until in later years the ruling powers   10
Bribed them to prophesy what was desired.
Till then the Greeks took pride in hopelessness
And, though they sometimes wrestled with their gods,°
They never won a blessing or a name
But only knowledge.   15
                    I shall never know myself
Enough to know what things I half believe
And, half believing, only half deny.

DELPHI. In ancient Greece, Delphi was the location of the Temple of Apollo, the home of the famous oracle. Fumes issuing from an underground opening, around which the temple was built, would overcome the
priestess, always named Pythia, and she would then deliver prophecies to priests, who would them pass
them on, in prose, to inquiring people who wished to know the future. These people of course would have
previously made an offering to the Temple.   3 *Pierian Spring:* A famous spring near Delphi, on the western
slope of Mount Olympus, sacred to the Muses. Consider Alexander Pope's lines from *An Essay on Criticism:*
"A little learning is a dangerous thing;/Drink deep, or taste not, the Pierian Spring."   13 *wrestled with their
gods:* See Genesis 32:24–32.

QUESTIONS

1. What is the topic of this poem? Why is the poem titled "Delphi"?

2. What is the meaning of the final three lines? How do they relate to the previous
    part of the poem? Why does the speaker include them?

3. Explain the allusions to Delphi, the "crevice where the priestesses/Hid in the
    crypt," and the reference to Genesis in lines 13–15.

JOHN DONNE (1572–1631)   *For a drawing, see p. 648.*

The Canonization° ⚬⚬⚬ 1633

For Godsake hold your tongue, and let me love,
    Or chide my palsy, or my gout,
My five gray hairs, or ruin'd fortune flout,
    With wealth your state, your mind with Arts improve,°
        Take you a course,° get you a place,°   5
        Observe His Honor,° or his grace,°
Or the King's real, or his stampèd face
    Contemplate,° what you will, approve,°
        So you will let me love.

THE CANONIZATION. *The Canonization:* the making of saints.   4 *With wealth . . . improve:* i.e., Improve
your state with wealth and your mind with arts.   5 *Take you a course:* take up a career.   *place:* a political
appointment.   6 *His Honor:* any important courtier.   *his grace:* a person of greatest eminence, such as a
bishop or the king.   7, 8 *Or . . . contemplate:* i.e., Or contemplate either the king's real face (at court) or
stamped face (on coins).   8 *What . . . approve:* Try anything you like (i.e., "Mind your own business").

Alas, alas, who's injured by my love?   10
  What merchant's ships have my sighs drown'd?
Who says my tears have overflow'd his ground?
  When did my colds a forward spring° remove?
    When did the heats which my veins fill°
    Add one more to the plaguy Bill?°
Soldiers find wars, and Lawyers find out still   15
  Litigious men, which quarrels move,
  Though she and I do love.

Call us what you will, we are made such by love;
  Call her one, me another fly,°
We'are Tapers° too, and at our own cost die,°   20
And we in us find the 'Eagle and the Dove.°   *candles*
  The Phoenix riddle° hath more wit
  By us, we two, being one, are it.
So, to one neutral thing both sexes fit,
  We die and rise the same, and prove   25
Mysterious° by this love.

We can die by it, if not live by love,
  And if unfit for tombs and hearse
Our legend be, it will be fit for verse;   30
  And if no piece of Chronicle we prove,
    We'll build in sonnets pretty rooms;
    As well a well wrought urn becomes
The greatest ashes, as half-acre tombs,
  And by these hymns, all shall approve   35
  Us *Canoniz'd* for love:°

And thus invoke° us; "You whom reverend love   *pray to saints*
  Made one another's hermitage;°
You, to whom love was peace, that now is rage;
  Who did the whole world's soul extract, and drove   40
    Into the glasses of your eyes
    So made such mirrors, and such spies,
That they did all to you epitomize,°
  Countries, towns, courts: Beg from above
  A pattern of your love!"   45

13 *a forward spring:* an early spring (season).   14 *the heats . . . fill:* i.e., "the heats (fevers) that fill my veins." Donne apparently wrote this line before the discovery of blood circulation was announced by William Harvey in 1616.   15 *plaguy Bill:* a regularly published list of deaths caused by the plague.   20 *fly:* a butterfly or moth (and apparently superficial and light-headed).   21 *at . . . die:* It was supposed that sexual climax shortened life.   22 *the 'Eagle and the Dove:* masculine and feminine symbols.   23 *Phoenix riddle:* In ancient times the phoenix, a mythical bird that lived for a thousand years, was supposed to die and rise five hundred years later from its own ashes; hence the phoenix symbolized immortality and the renewal of life and desire. See Chapter 22.   27 *Mysterious:* unknowable to anyone but God, and therefore quintessentially holy.   35, 36 *by these hymns . . . Canoniz'd for love:* The idea is that later generations will remember the lovers and elevate them to the sainthood of a religion of love. Because the lovers' love is recorded so powerfully in the speaker's poems ("sonnets" in line 33), these later generations will use the poems as hymns in their worship of love.   38 *Made . . . hermitage:* made a religious retreat for each other.   40–43 *Who did . . . epitomize:* An allusion to reputed alchemical processes, and therefore to be understood approximately like this: "Who extracted the whole world's soul and, through your eyes, assimilated this soul into yours, so that you, whose eyes saw and reflected each other, embodied the love and desire felt by all human beings."

QUESTIONS

1. What is the situation of the poem? Whom is the speaker addressing? Why does he begin as he does? How does he defend his love?

2. What symbols do you find in the poem? What are the symbols? What is being symbolized?

3. What mythic and religious mysteries are linked with sexual love in the third stanza? What does "canonization" mean? What canonizes and immortalizes the lovers? How does the "canonization" symbolize the poem's idea about the nature of love?

4. What will future lovers ask of these saints of love? Of what use will the speaker's poem be at that time? What do you think of the speaker's claim about love?

STEPHEN DUNN (b. 1939)

Hawk ～＜～✓～ *1989*

What a needy, desperate thing
to claim what's wild for oneself,
yet the hawk circling above the pines
looks like the same one I thought

might become mine after it crashed   5
into the large window and lay
one wing spread, the other loosely
tucked, then no, not dead, got up

dazed, and in minutes was gone.
Now once again   10
this is its sky, this its woods.
The tasty small birds it loves

have seen their God and know
the suddenness of such love
as we know lightning or flash flood.   15
If hawks can learn, this hawk learned

what's clear can be hard
down where the humans live,
and that the hunting isn't good
where the air is such a lie.   20

It glides above the pines and I
turn back into the room, the hawk book
open on the cluttered table
to Cooper's Hawk

and the unwritten caption   25
that to be wild
means nothing you do or have done
needs to be explained.

QUESTIONS

1. Why does the speaker consider the issue of owning or not owning the hawk that crashed into his window?

2. In what way is the hawk significant? How can a reader justify considering it as a symbol? What does the bird symbolize?

3. What is the meaning of the final four lines? How true are the lines? If "to be wild" needs no explanation, what does it mean, in contrast, to be civilized?

ISABELLA GARDNER (1915–1981)

Collage of Echoes ～＜～／～ 1979

I have no promises to keep
Nor miles to go before I sleep,°
For miles of years I have made promises
and (mostly) kept them.
    It's time I slept.
Now I lay me down to sleep°
With no promises to keep.   5
    My sleaves are ravelled°
    I have travelled.°

COLLAGE OF ECHOES. 2 *miles to go before I sleep:* See Robert Frost, "Stopping by Woods on a Snowy Evening" (p. 621), lines 13–16.   6 *Now I lay me down to sleep:* from the child's prayer: Now I lay me down to sleep; / I pray the Lord my soul to keep. / If I should die before I wake, / I pray the Lord my soul to take 8 *My sleaves are ravelled:* See *Macbeth,* II.2.37: "Sleep that knits up the ravelled sleave of care."   9 *I have travelled:* See Keats, "On First Looking into Chapman's Homer" (p. 728).

QUESTIONS

1. Given the allusions in the poem, what do you conclude about the speaker's judgment of the reader's knowledge of literature?

2. How reliant is "Collage of Echoes" upon the contexts being echoed? How do the echoes assist in enabling enjoyment and appreciation of the poem?

3. In relation to the speaker's character as demonstrated in the poem, consider the phrases "(mostly) kept them," "With no promises to keep," and "My sleaves are ravelled." What do they show about the speaker's self-assessment? In what way might these phrases be considered comic?

JORIE GRAHAM (b. 1954)

The Geese ～＜～／～ 1980

Today as I hang out the wash I see them again, a code
as urgent as elegant,
tapering with goals.
For days they have been crossing. We live beneath these geese

as if beneath the passage of time, or a most perfect heading.   5
Sometime I fear their relevance.
Closest at hand,
between the lines,

the spiders imitate the paths the geese won't stray from,
imitate them endlessly to no avail: 10
things will not remain connected,
will not heal,

and the world thickens with texture instead of history,
texture instead of place.
Yet the small fear of the spiders   15
binds and binds

the pins to the lines, the lines to the eaves, to the pincushion bush,
as if, at any time, things could fall further apart
and nothing could help them
recover their meaning. And if these spiders had their way,   20

chainlink over the visible world,
would we be in or out? I turn to go back in.
There is a feeling the body gives the mind
of having missed something, a bedrock poverty, like falling

without the sense that you are passing through one world,   25
that you could reach another
anytime. Instead the real
is crossing you,

your body an arrival
you know is false but can't outrun. And somewhere in between   30
these geese forever entering and
these spiders turning back

this astonishing delay, the everyday, takes place.

QUESTIONS

1. What is the dominant tense of the poem? What effect does this tense have on the speaker's conclusions?

2. What action does the speaker perform in the course of the poem? What is the relationship between this action and the final lines?

3. What do the geese symbolize? What do the spiders symbolize? How are these symbols contrasted?

4. The first half of this poem, particularly lines 11 and 18, is reminiscent of Yeats's "The Second Coming" (p. 913). In your judgment, what use does Graham make of this allusion?

THOMAS HARDY (1840–1928)

For a photo, see p. 622.

In Time of "The Breaking of Nations"° ✦✦✦ 1916 (1915)

Only a man harrowing clods
  In a slow silent walk,
With an old horse that stumbles and nods
  Half asleep as they stalk.

Only thin smoke without flame   5
  From the heaps of couch grass:°   *quack grass*
Yet this will go onward the same
  Though Dynasties pass.

Yonder a maid and her wight°
  Come whispering by;   *fellow*
War's annals will fade into night   10
  Ere their story die.

IN TIME OF "THE BREAKING OF NATIONS." See Jeremiah 51:20, "with you I break nations in pieces."

QUESTIONS

1. What does Hardy symbolize by the man, horse, smoke, and couple? How realistic and vivid are these symbols? Are they universal or contextual?

2. How does Hardy show that the phrase "breaking of nations" is to be taken symbolically? What meaning is gained by the biblical allusion of this phrase?

3. Contrast the structure of stanza 1 with that of stanzas 2 and 3. How does the form of stanzas 2 and 3 enable Hardy to emphasize the main idea?

4. How does the speaker show his evaluation of the life of the common people? You might consider that at the time (1915), World War I was raging in Europe.

GEORGE HERBERT (1593–1633)

The Collar° ✦✦✦ 1633

I struck the board, and cry'd, "No more;
  I will abroad!
What? shall I ever sigh and pine?
My lines and life are free; free as the road,
  Loose as the wind, as large as store,   5
    Shall I be still in suit?°
Have I no harvest but a thorn°
  To let me blood, and not restore
What I have lost with cordial fruit?
    Sure there was wine   10

THE COLLAR. *collar:* (a) the collar worn by a member of the clergy; (b) the collar of the harness of a draft animal such as a horse; (c) a restraint placed on prisoners; (d) a pun on *choler* (yellow bile), a bodily substance that was thought to cause quick rages.   **6** *in suit:* waiting upon a person of power to gain favor or position.   **7** *thorn:* See Mark 15:17.

Before my sighs did dry it: there was corn
    Before my tears did drown it.
Is the year only lost to me?
    Have I no bays° to crown it?
No flowers, no garlands gay? all blasted?   15
    All wasted?
Not so, my heart: but there is fruit,
    And thou hast hands.
Recover all thy sigh-blown age
On double pleasures: leave thy cold dispute   20
Of what is fit, and not; forsake thy cage;
    Thy rope of sands,
Which petty thoughts have made, and made to thee
    Good cable, to enforce and draw,
        And be thy law,   25
While thou didst wink and wouldst not see.
    Away; take heed:
    I will abroad.
Call in thy death's head there: tie up thy fears.
    He that forbears   30
To suit° and serve his need,   *follow*
    Deserves his load."
But as I rav'd and grew more fierce and wild
    At every word,
Me thought I heard one calling, "Child:"   35
    And I replied, *"My Lord."*

14 *bays:* laurel crowns to signify victory and honor.

QUESTIONS

1. What is the opening situation? Why is the speaker angry? Against what role in life is he complaining?

2. In light of the many possible meanings of *collar* (see note), explain the title as a symbol in the poem.

3. Explain the symbolism of the thorn (line 7), blood (line 8), wine (line 10), bays (line 14), flowers and garlands (line 15), cage (line 21), rope of sands (line 22), death's head (line 29), and the dialogue in lines 35 and 36.

JOSEPHINE JACOBSEN (b. 1908)

Tears   1981

Tears leave no mark on the soil
or pavement; certainly not in sand
or in any known rain forest;
never a mark on stone.
One would think that no one in Persepolis°   5
or Ur° ever wept.

You would assume that, like Alice,°
we would all be swimming, buffeted
in a tide of tears.
But they disappear. Their heat goes.   10
Yet the globe is salt
with that savor.°

The animals want no part in this.
The hare both screams and weeps
at her death, one poet says.   15
The stag, at death, rolls round drops
down his muzzle; but he is in
Shakespeare's forest.°

These cases are mythically rare.
No, it is the human being who persistently   20
weeps; in some countries, openly, in others, not.
Children who, even when frightened, weep most hopefully;
women, licensed weepers.°
Men, in secret, or childishly; or nobly.

Could tears not make a sea of their mass?   25
It could be salt and wild enough;
it could rouse storms and sink ships,
erode, erode its shores:
tears of rage, of love, of torture,
of loss. Of loss.   30

Must we see the future
in order to weep? Or the past?
Is that why the animals
refuse to shed tears?
But what of the present, the tears of the present?   35
The awful relief, like breath

after strangling? The generosity
of the verb "to shed"?
They are a classless possession
yet are not found in the museum   40
of even our greatest city.
Sometimes what was human, turns
into an animal, dry-eyed.

TEARS. *5, 6 Persepolis . . . Ur:* Persepolis was the capital city of ancient Persia (now Iran). Ur, on the Persian Gulf, was the capital city of the ancient Sumerian Empire. Today, both cities survive only in ruins. The Hebrew patriarch Abraham traveled from "Ur of the Chaldees" to settle in the land of Canaan, the "promised land." *7 Alice:* In Lewis Carroll's *Alice in Wonderland* (Ch. 2), Alice sheds tears, and then is reduced in size and almost drowns in her own teardrops. *11–12 Yet . . . savor:* Matthew 5:13. *14–18 The hare . . . forest:* In the poem *Autumn* by James Thomson (1700–1748), lines 401–457, a cruel hunt of the hare and the stag is described. It is the stag who sheds "big round tears" and "groans in anguish" when dying. Jacobsen's allusion to Shakespeare—to whom Thomson is also alluding—is *As You Like It*, 2.1.29–43. *23 licensed weepers:* In certain countries, such as Greece, professional "weepers" weep and cry aloud at funerals.

QUESTIONS

1. What does the poem's major symbol, tears, mean? What significance does the poem attribute to tears? Why are tears sometimes disregarded?

2. How does the poem apply the symbol to various cultures and conditions?

3. How do tears differentiate human beings from animals? What is the symbolic value of this difference? In light of the contrast, what is the meaning of the last two lines?

4. Explain the poem's use of allusions (i.e., Persepolis, Ur, the New Testament, *Alice in Wonderland*, professional mourners, Shakespeare).

ROBINSON JEFFERS (1887–1962)

The Purse-Seine   ⸙   *1937*

1

Our sardine fishermen work at night in the dark of the moon;
    daylight or moonlight
They could not tell where to spread the net, unable to see the
    phosphorescence of the shoals of fish.
They work northward from Monterey, coasting Santa Cruz;
    off New Year's Point or off Pigeon Point
The look-out man will see some lakes of milk-color light on the seas's night-purple;
    he points, and the helmsman
Turns the dark prow, the motorboat circles the gleaming shoal and drifts out   5
    her seine-net. They close the circle
And purse the bottom of the net, then with great labor haul it in.

2

                         I cannot tell you
How beautiful the scene is, and a little terrible, then, when the crowded fish
Know they are caught, and wildly beat from one wall to the other of their closing destiny
    the phosphorescent
Water to a pool of flame, each beautiful slender body sheeted with flame, like a   10
    live rocket
A comet's tail wake of clear yellow flame; while outside the narrowing
Floats and cordage of the net great sea-lions come up to watch, sighing in the dark; the
    vast walls of night
Stand erect to the stars.

3

                     Lately I was looking from a night mountain-top
On a wide city, the colored splendor, galaxies of light: how could I help but recall the   15
    seine-net
Gathering the luminous fish? I cannot tell you how beautiful the city appeared, and a
    little terrible.
I thought, We have geared the machines and locked all together into interdependence;
    we have built the great cities; now

There is no escape. We have gathered vast populations incapable of free survival,
   insulated
From the strong earth, each person in himself helpless, on all dependent. The circle is
   closed, and the net
Is being hauled in. They hardly feel the cords drawing, yet they shine already. The   20
   inevitable mass-disasters
Will not come in our time nor in our children's, but we and our children
Must watch the net draw narrower, government take all powers—or revolution, and the
   new government
Take more than all, add to kept bodies kept souls—or anarchy, the mass-disasters.

                                           4

                              These things are Progress;
Do you marvel our verse is troubled or frowning, while it keeps its reason? Or it lets go,   25
   lets the mood flow
In the manner of the recent young men into mere hysteria, splintered gleams, crackled
   laughter. But they are quite wrong.
There is no reason for amazement: surely one always knew that cultures decay, and life's
   end is death.

QUESTIONS

1. Describe how the purse-seine is used to haul in the sardines. What is the speaker's reaction to the scene as described in stanza 2?

2. How does the speaker explain that the purse-seine is a symbol? What does it symbolize? What do the sardines symbolize?

3. Compare the ideas of Jeffers with those of Yeats in "The Second Coming." Are the ideas of Jeffers more or less methodical?

4. Is the statement at the end to be taken as a fact or as a resigned acceptance of that fact? Does the poem offer any solution to the problem?

5. How can the sea-lions of line 12, and their sighs, be construed as a symbol?

JOHN KEATS (1795–1821)   *For a drawing, see p. 728.*

La Belle Dame Sans Merci: A Ballad°   1820 (1819)

                                           1

O what can ail thee, knight at arms,
   Alone and palely loitering?
The sedge has wither'd from the lake,
   And no birds sing.

                                           2

O what can ail thee, knight at arms,
   So haggard and so woe-begone?   5

LA BELLE DAME SANS MERCI. French for "The beautiful lady without pity" (that is, "The heartless woman"). "La Belle Dame Sans Merci" is the title of a medieval poem by Alain Chartier; Keats's poem bears no other relationship to the medieval poem, which was thought at the time to have been by Chaucer.

The squirrel's granary is full,
  And the harvest's done.

3

I see a lily on thy brow
  With anguish moist and fever dew,   10
And on thy cheeks a fading rose
  Fast withereth too.

4

I met a lady in the meads,°   *Symbol of mystery of love page 890*   *meadows*
  Full beautiful, a fairy's child;
Her hair was long, her foot was light,   15
  And her eyes were wild.

5

I made a garland for her head,
  And bracelets too, and fragrant zone;°   *belt*
She look'd at me as she did love,
  And made sweet moan.   20

6

I set her on my pacing steed,
  And nothing else saw all day long,
For sidelong would she bend, and sing
  A fairy's song.

7

She found me roots of relish° sweet,   *magical potion*   25
  And honey wild, and manna° dew,   *see Exodus 16:14–36*
And sure in language strange she said—
  I love thee true.

8

She took me to her elfin grot,°   *grotto*
  And there she wept, and sigh'd full sore,   30
And there I shut her wild wild eyes
  With kisses four.

9

And there she lullèd me asleep,
  And there I dream'd—Ah! woe betide!
The latest° dream I ever dream'd   *last*   35
  On the cold hill's side.

10

I saw pale kings, and princes too,
  Pale warriors, death pale were they all;

They cried—"La belle dame sans merci
  Hath thee in thrall!"°   *slavery*   40

11

I saw their starv'd lips in the gloam
  With horrid warning gapèd wide,
And I awoke and found me here
  On the cold hill's side.

12

And this is why I sojourn here,   45
  Alone and palely loitering,
Though the sedge is wither'd from the lake,
  And no birds sing.

QUESTIONS

1. Who is the speaker of stanzas 1–3? Who speaks after that?
2. In light of the dreamlike content of the poem, how can the knight's experience be viewed as symbolic? What is being symbolized?
3. Consider "relish" (line 25), "honey" (line 26), and "manna" (line 26) as symbols. Are they realistic or mythical? What does the allusion to manna signify? What is symbolized by the "pale kings, and princes too" and "Pale warriors" (lines 37–38)?
4. Consider the poem's setting as symbols of the knight's state of mind.

X.J. KENNEDY (b. 1929)

Old Men Pitching Horseshoes   1985

Back in a yard where ringers groove a ditch,
These four in shirtsleeves congregate to pitch
Dirt-burnished iron. With appraising eye,
One sizes up a peg, hoists and lets fly—
A clang resounds as though a smith had struck   5
Fire from a forge. His first blow, out of luck,
Rattles in circles. Hitching up his face,
He swings, and weight once more inhabits space,
Tumbles as gently as a new-laid egg.
Extended iron arms surround their peg
Like one come home to greet a long-lost brother.   10
Shouts from one outpost. Mutters from the other.
Now changing sides, each withered pitcher moves
As his considered dignity behooves
Down the worn path of earth where August flies
And sheaves of air in warm distortions rise.   15
To stand ground, fling, kick dust with all the force
Of shoes still hammered to a living horse.

Old men
Pitching
horseshoes

outpost—remote military post

Marvell ~ To His Coy Mistress   909

Congregate—assemble

QUESTIONS

1. How does the poet indicate that the pitching of horseshoes is symbolic? As symbols, why are old men chosen rather than young men?

2. Discuss the effects of the words "congregate," "outpost," "withered," "sheaves," "kick dust," and "force." What do these words contribute to the poem's symbolism?

3. Compare the topic of this poem with the concluding lines of T. S. Eliot's "Preludes" (p. 707), especially the last two lines. How is the symbolism of these poems similar? Different?

ANDREW MARVELL (1621–1678)

962

To His Coy Mistress   1681

Had we but world enough, and time,
This coyness, lady, were no crime.
We would sit down, and think which way
To walk, and pass our long love's day.
Thou by the Indian Ganges° side   5
Shouldst rubies find; I by the tide
Of Humber° would complain. I would
Love you ten years before the flood,°   Noah's flood
And you should, if you please, refuse
Till the conversion of the Jews.°   10
My vegetable love should grow
Vaster than empires and more slow;
An hundred years should go to praise
Thine eyes, and on thy forehead gaze;
Two hundred to adore each breast,   15
But thirty thousand to the rest;
An age at least to every part,
And the last age should show your heart.
For, lady, you deserve this state,
Nor would I love at lower rate.   20
  But at my back I always hear
Time's wingèd chariot hurrying near;
And yonder all before us lie
Deserts of vast eternity.
Thy beauty shall no more be found,   25
Nor, in thy marble vault, shall sound
My echoing song; then worms shall try
That long-preserved virginity,
And your quaint honor turn to dust,
And into ashes all my lust: 30
The grave's a fine and private place,

geographic

geographic
and
religious
allusion

religious

religious

TO HIS COY MISTRESS. 5 *Ganges:* a large river that runs across most of India.   7 *Humber:* a small river that runs through the north of England to the North Sea.   10 *Jews:* Traditionally, this conversion is supposed to occur just before the Last Judgment.

But none, I think, do there embrace.
   Now therefore, while the youthful hue
Sits on thy skin like morning dew,
And while thy willing soul transpires   35
At every pore with instant fires,
Now let us sport us while we may,
And now, like amorous birds of prey,
Rather at once our time devour
Than languish in his slow-chapped° power.   *slow-jawed* 40
Let us roll all our strength and all
Our sweetness up into one ball,
And tear our pleasures with rough strife
Thorough° the iron gates of life: *through*
Thus, though we cannot make our sun   45
Stand still, yet we will make him run.

QUESTIONS

1. In lines 1–20 the speaker sets up a hypothetical situation and the first part of a pseudological proof: If *A* then *B*. What specific words indicate the logic of this section? What hypothetical situation is established?

2. How do geographic and biblical allusions affect our sense of time and place?

3. In lines 21–32 the speaker refutes the hypothetical condition set up in the first twenty lines. What word indicates that this is a refutation? How does imagery help create and reinforce meaning here?

4. The last part of the poem (lines 33–46) presents the speaker's "logical" conclusion. What words indicate that this is a conclusion? What is the conclusion?

MARY OLIVER (b. 1935)   page 910

Wild Geese   1986

You do not have to be good.
You do not have to walk on your knees
for a hundred miles through the desert, repenting.
You only have to let the soft animal of your body
   love what it loves.   5
Tell me about despair, yours, and I will tell you mine.
Meanwhile the world goes on.
Meanwhile the sun and the clear pebbles of the rain
are moving across the landscapes,
over the prairies and the deep trees,   10
the mountains and the rivers.
Meanwhile the wild geese, high in the clean blue air,
are heading home again.
Whoever you are, no matter how lonely,   15
the world offers itself to your imagination,
calls to you like the wild geese, harsh and exciting—
over and over announcing your place
in the family of things.

QUESTIONS

1. What idea is contained in the first five lines? What ideas are expressed in lines 6–12? In what ways are lines 13–17 a climax of the poem? How does this last section build on the poem's earlier parts?

2. What is symbolized by the references to "the sun and the clear pebbles of the rain," and so on, in lines 7–10? Do these symbols suggest futility or hope?

3. What do the wild geese symbolize (lines 11–12, 15)? How is the symbol of the geese a response to the poem's first six lines? How well would the words *acceptance, self-knowledge,* or *adjustment* describe the poem's ideas? What other words would be better or more suitable? Why?

JUDITH VIORST (b. 1931)

A Wedding Sonnet for the Next Generation° ⟩‑⟨‑⟩‑⟩ 2000

He might compare you to a summer's day,°
Declaring you're far fairer in his eyes.
She might, with depth and breadth and many sighs,
Count all the ways she loves you, way by way.°

He might say when you're old and full of sleep,   5
He'll cherish still the Pilgrim soul in you.°
She might—oh, there are poems so fine, so true,
To help you speak of love and vows to keep.

Words help. And you are writing your own poem.
It doesn't always scan or always rhyme.   10
It mingles images of the sublime
With plainer words: Respect. Trust. Comfort. Home.

How very rich is love's vocabulary
When friends, dear friends, best friends decide to marry.

A WEDDING SONNET FOR THE NEXT GENERATION. 1 *summer's day:* See Shakespeare, "Shall I Compare Thee to a Summer's Day?" (Chapter 17). 3, 4 *She might . . . way by way:* See Elizabeth Barrett Browning, "How Do I Love Thee" (Chapter 25). 5, 6 *He might say . . . Pilgrim soul in you:* See Yeats, "When You Are Old" (Chapter 18).

QUESTIONS

1. Why does the poem speak of "the Next Generation" in the title? What is the form of the poem? Why do the first lines alternate between "he" and "she"?

2. What is the meaning and effect of the allusions in lines 1–6? Why does Viorst introduce these allusions? What assumptions does she make about her audience for this poem?

3. How does the poem change in the last six lines? How does the language shift in these lines?

4. What does it mean to say "you are writing your own poem"? How are the final two lines related to the previous parts of the poem?

WALT WHITMAN (1819–1892)

For a photo, see p. 748.

A Noiseless Patient Spider ～く～く～ 1868

A noiseless patient spider,
I marked where on a little promontory it stood isolated,
Marked how to explore the vacant vast surrounding,
It launched forth filament, filament, filament out of itself,
Ever unreeling them, ever tirelessly speeding them.   5

And you O my soul where you stand,
Surrounded, detached, in measureless oceans of space,
Ceaselessly musing, venturing, throwing, seeking the spheres
      to connect them,
Till the bridge you will need be formed, till the ductile anchor hold,
Till the gossamer thread you fling catch somewhere, O my soul.   10

QUESTIONS

1. The subject of the second stanza is seemingly unrelated to the subject of the
   first. How are these stanzas related?
2. In what way does the spider's web symbolize the soul and the poet's view of the
   isolation of human beings? How does the web symbolize the soul's ceaseless
   "musing . . . seeking" and the attempt "to connect"?
3. Explain why the second stanza is not a complete sentence. How might this grammatical feature be related to the spider's web? To the poet's idea that life requires striving but does not offer completeness?

RICHARD WILBUR (b. 1921)

Poem notes
Symbolic setting
889

Year's End ～く～く～ 1950

Now winter downs the dying of the year,
And Night is all a settlement of snow;
From the soft street the rooms of houses show
A gathered light, a shapen atmosphere,
Like frozen-over lakes whose ice is thin   5
And still allows some stirring down within.

I've known the wind by water banks to shake
The late leaves down, which frozen where they fell
And held in ice as dancers in a spell
Fluttered all winter long into a lake;   10
Graved on the dark in gestures of descent,
They seemed their own most perfect monument.

There was perfection in the death of ferns
Which laid their fragile cheeks against the stone
A million years. Great mammoths overthrown   15
Composedly have made their long sojourns,

Like palaces of patience, in the gray
And changeless lands of ice. And at Pompeii°

[handwritten: Scene]

[handwritten: Incompleteness of human achievement]

The little dog lay curled and did not rise
But slept the deeper as the ashes rose   20
And found the people incomplete, and froze
The random hands, the loose unready eyes
Of men expecting yet another sun
To do the shapely thing they had not done.

These sudden ends of time must give us pause.   25
We fray into the future, rarely wrought

[handwritten: Symbols]

Save in the tapestries of afterthought.
More time, more time. Barrages of applause
Come muffled from a buried radio.
The New-year bells are wrangling with the snow.   30

YEAR'S END. 18 *Pompeii:* the southern Italian Roman city covered by lava during the eruption of Mount
Vesuvius in 79 c.e. Many people and animals died trying to escape the lava flow and were covered over
where they fell. Modern excavators created statues of these fallen figures by using plaster to fill in cavities
left by their bodies. One of these was the "little dog" mentioned in line 19.

QUESTIONS

1. What natural and historical symbols does Wilbur introduce in the poem? What
    ideas do the symbols present about time and the use people make of time?

2. Describe Wilbur's use of two-word groups united by assonance and consonance
    in the poem (e.g., "P*e*ople incompl*e*te," "*d*owns the *d*ying," "*still* . . . *stirring*").
    How effective are these groups in drawing your attention to Wilbur's meaning?

3. Describe the symbols in the final stanza ("fray into the future," "tapestries of af-
    terthought," "muffled from a buried radio"). Why does the poem conclude with
    the symbols of "New-year bells" and "snow"?

4. Consider the meaning of line 25. How can this line be interpreted so that the
    poem may have either positive or negative views of human activity?

WILLIAM BUTLER YEATS (1865–1939)

The Second Coming° ⌣ ⌣ ⌣ ⌣ ⌣   1920 (1919)

[handwritten: read 890]
[handwritten: Allusions + meaning]

Turning and turning in the widening gyre°
The falcon cannot hear the falconer;

[handwritten: would Trade center]

Things fall apart; the center cannot hold;

[handwritten: Theory of]

Mere anarchy is loosed upon the world,
The blood-dimmed tide° is loosed, and everywhere   5
The ceremony of innocence is drowned;
The best lack all conviction, while the worst
Are full of passionate intensity.

[handwritten: book of revelation - Bible]

Surely some revelation is at hand;
Surely the Second Coming is at hand.   10
The Second Coming! Hardly are those words out

handwritten: Here is the image *handwritten: have a vision* *handwritten: Spirit of the world*

When a vast image out of *Spiritus Mundi°* *handwritten: Spirit of the world*
Troubles my sight: somewhere in sands of the desert
A shape with lion body and the head of a man,° *handwritten: sphinx*
A gaze blank and pitiless as the sun,   15
Is moving its slow thighs, while all about it
Reel shadows of the indignant desert birds.
The darkness drops again; but now I know   *handwritten: Allusion 2000 years symbol*
That twenty centuries of stony sleep   *handwritten: birth of Christ*
Were vexed to nightmare by a rocking cradle, *handwritten: birth of antichrist*
And what rough beast, its hour come round at last,   *handwritten: End of 2000 year now*   20
Slouches towards Bethlehem to be born?   *handwritten: yeats theory*

handwritten left margin: Vision is over   New Testament expand Christ return

THE SECOND COMING. The phrase "second coming" has been traditionally used to refer to expectations of the return of Jesus for the salvation of believers, as described in the New Testament. The prophecies foretold that Christ's return would be preceded by famine, epidemics, wars between nations, and general civil disturbance. Yeats believed that human history could be measured in cycles of approximately 2,000 years (see line 19, "twenty centuries"). According to this system, the birth of Jesus ended the Greco-Roman cycle and in 1919, when Yeats wrote "The Second Coming," it appeared to him that the Christian period was ending and a new era was about to take its place. The New Testament expectation was that Jesus would reappear. Yeats, by contrast, holds that the disruptions of the twentieth century were preceding a takeover by the forces of evil.   1 *gyre:* a radiating spiral, cone, or vortex. Yeats used the intersecting of two of these shapes as a visual symbol of his cyclic theory. As one gyre spiraled and widened out, to become dissipated, one period of history would end; at the same time a new gyre, closer to the center, would begin and spiral in a reverse direction to the starting point of the old gyre. A drawing of this plan looks like this:

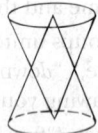

The falcon of line 2 is at the broadest, centrifugal point of one gyre, symbolically illustrating the end of a cycle. The "indignant desert birds" of line 17 "reel" in a tighter circle, symbolizing the beginning of the new age in the new gyre.   5 *blood-dimmed tide:* quotation from Shakespeare's *Macbeth,* II.2.60–63. 12 *Spiritus Mundi:* literally, the spirit of the world, a collective human consciousness that furnished writers and thinkers with a common fund of images and symbols. Yeats referred to this collective repository as "a great memory passing on from generation to generation,"   14 *lion body and the head of a man:* that is, the Sphinx, which in ancient Egypt symbolized the pharaoh as a spirit of the sun. Because of this pre-Christian origin, the reincarnation of a sphinx could therefore represent qualities associated in New Testament books like Revelation (11, 13, 17), Mark (13:14–20), and 2 Thessalonians (2:1–12) with a monstrous, superhuman, satanic figure. For a picture of the Sphinx, see p. 945.

QUESTIONS

1. Consider the following as symbols: the "gyre," the "falcon," the "blood-dimmed tide," the "ceremony of innocence," the "worst" who are "full of passionate intensity." What ideas and values do these symbolize in the poem?

2. Why does Yeats capitalize the phrase "Second Coming"? To what does this phrase refer? Explain the irony of Yeats's use of the phrase in this poem.

3. Contrast the symbols of the falcon of line 2 and the desert birds of line 17. Considering that these are realistically presented, how does the realism contribute to their identity as symbols?

4. What is symbolized by the sphinx being revealed as a "rough beast"? What is the significance of the beast's going "towards Bethlehem to be born"?

Hercules and the Infant Telephus. A Roman fresco from Herculaneum. Museo Archeologico Nazionale, Naples. (© Scala/Art Resource, New York)

François Boucher (1703-1770), *Madame de Pompadour*. Paper on canvas, 60 X 45.5 cm. Louvre, Paris. (© Erich Lessing/Art Resource, New York)

Edward Hopper (1882–1967), *Automat*, 1927. Oil on canvas, 28 1/8 X 36 in. Des Moines Art Center Permanent Collections; purchased with funds from the Edmundson Art Foundation, Inc. 1958.2. (Photograph by Michael Tropea, Chicago)

Albert Bierstadt (1830-1902), *Among the Sierra Nevada Mountains, California*, 1868. Oil on canvas, 71 X 120 in./183 X 305 cm. (© Smithsonian American Art Museum, Washington, DC/Art Resource, New York)

Thomas Cole (1801-1848), *View from Mount Holyoke, Northampton, Massachusetts, After a Thunderstorm (The Oxbow)*, 1836. Oil on canvas, 51 1/2 in. high X 76 in. wide/130.8 X 193 cm. Signed and dated: T. Cole 1836 (lower left). The Metropolitan Museum of Art, New York. Gift of Mrs. Russell Sage, 1908 (08.228). (Photograph © 1995 The Metropolitan Museum of Art)

Charles Wysocki (1928-2002), *Old Glory Farms*, c. 1975. (© Charles Wysocki, Inc.)

Henri Matisse (1869-1954), *Icarus* from *Jazz* series, 1947. New York Public Library, Astor Lenox, and Tilden Foundation, Spencer Collection/Art Resource, New York. (© 2003 Succession H. Matisse, Paris/Artists Rights Society [ARS], New York)

Fernand Leger (1881-1955), *The City*, 1919. Oil on canvas, 91 X 177 1/2 in. The Philadelphia Museum of Art, Philadelphia. A. E. Gallatin Collection. (© 2004 Artists Rights Society [ARS], New York/ADAGP, Paris)

Francisco de Goya y Lucientes (1746-1828), *The Colossus*, 1808-1810. Oil on canvas, 116 X 105 cm. Museo del Prado, Madrid. (© Erich Lessing/Art Resource, New York)

WRITING ABOUT SYMBOLISM AND ALLUSION IN POETRY

As you read the poem to be studied, take notes and make all the observations you can about the presence of symbols or allusions or both. Explanatory notes will help you establish basic information, but you also need to explain meanings and create interpretations in your own words. Use a dictionary for understanding words or phrases that require further study. For allusions, you might check out original sources to determine original contexts. Use the footnotes that your text supplies, and ask your instructor. Try to determine the ways in which your poem is similar to, or different from, the original work or source, and then determine the purpose served by the allusion.

Questions for Discovering Ideas

Cultural or Universal Symbols

- What symbols that you can characterize as cultural or universal can you discover in names, objects, places, situations, or actions in the poem (e.g., nightingales, hemlock, a thorn, two lovers, Bethlehem)?

- How are these symbols used? What do they mean, both specifically, in the poem, and universally, in a broader context? What would the poem be like without the symbolic meaning?

Contextual Symbols

- What contextual symbols can you locate in the poem (e.g., withered sedge, a flock of birds, a doe running into a woods)? How are these symbols used specifically in the poem? What would the poem be like if the contextual symbol were not taken to be symbolic?

- What causes you to conclude that the symbols are truly symbolic? What is being symbolized? What do the symbols mean? How definite or direct is the symbolism?

- Is the symbolism used systematically throughout the poem, or is it used only once? How does the symbolism affect the poem's ideas or emotions?

Allusions

- Granted your knowledge of literature, science, geography, television, the Bible, film, popular culture, and other fields of knowledge, what allusions do you recognize?

- Do you find other references in these or other categories? What do the allusions mean in their original context? What do they mean within the poem?

- Do you see any possible allusions that you are not sure about? What help do you find in the explanatory notes in the text you are using? Consult a dictionary, such as *The Oxford Dictionary of Allusions*, or another reference work to discover the nature of these allusions. See Chapter 9. If you have questions, be sure to ask your reference librarian for assistance.

Strategies for Organizing Ideas

Begin with a brief description of the poem and of the symbolism or allusions in it. A symbol might be central to the poem, or an allusion might be introduced at a particularly important point. Your central idea might take you in a number of

directions: You might conclude that the symbolism is based on objects like flowers and natural scenes, or that it stems out of an action or set of actions, or that
it is developed from an initial situation such as a time of the day or year. The
symbols may be universal or contextual; they may be applicable particularly to
personal life or to political or social life. Allusions may emphasize the differences between your poem and the work or event being alluded to, or they may
highlight the circumstances of your poem. Also, you might make a point that
the symbols and/or allusions make the poem seem optimistic, or pessimistic,
and so on.

Here are some possible approaches for your essay, which may be combined as need arises.

1. THE MEANING OF SYMBOLS OR ALLUSIONS. This approach is the most natural
one to take for an essay on symbolism or allusion. If you have discovered a symbol or symbols or allusions, explain the meaning as best you can. What is the
poem's major idea? How do you know that your interpretation is valid? How do
the poem's symbols and allusions contribute to your interpretation? How pervasive, how applicable, are these devices? If you have discovered many symbols and
allusions, which ones predominate? What do they mean? Why are some more
important than others? What connects them with each other and with the
poem's main ideas? How are you able to make conclusions about all this?

2. THE EFFECT OF SYMBOLS OR ALLUSIONS ON THE POEM'S FORM. Here the goal is
to determine how symbolism or allusion is related to the poetic structure.
Where does the symbol occur? If it is early, how do the following parts relate to
the ideas borne by the symbol? What logical or chronological function does the
symbol serve in the poem's development? Is the symbol repeated, and if so, to
what effect? If the symbol is introduced later, has it been anticipated earlier?
How do you know? Can the symbol be considered climactic? What might the
structure of the poem have been like if the symbolism had not been used? (Answering this question can help you judge how the symbol influences the poem's
structure.) Many of these same questions might also be applied to an allusion or
allusions. In addition, for an allusion, it is important to compare the contexts of
the work you are studying and the original to determine how the poet uses the
allusion as a part of the poem's form or structure.

3. THE RELATIONSHIP BETWEEN THE LITERAL AND THE SYMBOLIC. The object here is
to describe the literal nature of the symbols, and then to determine their appropriateness to the poem's context. If the symbol is part of a narrative, what is its
literal function? If the symbol is a person, object, or setting, what physical aspects are described? Are colors included? Shapes? Sizes? Sounds? In light of this
description, how applicable is the symbol to the ideas it embodies? How appropriate is the literal condition to the symbolic condition? The answers to questions like these should lead not so much to a detailed account of the meaning of
the symbols but rather to an account of their appropriateness to the topics and
ideas of the poem.

4. THE IMPLICATIONS AND RESONANCES OF SYMBOLS AND ALLUSIONS. This type of
essay is more personal than the others, for it is devoted to the suggestions and

associations—the "implications and resonances"—that the poem's symbols and allusions bring out. The object of the essay is to describe your own responses or chain of thinking that the poem sets in motion. You are therefore free to move in your own direction as long as you base your discussion on the symbols and allusions in the poem. If the poet is speaking in general terms about the end of an era, for example, as with the symbol of the "rough beast" in Yeats's "The Second Coming" and the giant fishnets in Jeffers's "The Purse-Seine," then you could apply these symbols to your own thinking.

Your conclusion might contain a summary of your main points. If your poem is rich in symbols or allusions, you might also consider some of the elements that you have not discussed in the body and try to tie these together with those you have already discussed. It would also be appropriate to introduce any new ideas you developed as a result of your study.

DEMONSTRATIVE STUDENT ESSAY

Symbolism in Oliver's "Wild Geese"°

[1]
     Mary Oliver's "Wild Geese" can be understood as an extended answer to the issue raised in its first line. This idea, to be refuted, is unusual--one might almost say startling--because it is stated so baldly: "You do not have to be good." Not many poems begin with a line like that. <u>The rest of the poem is developed through a series of symbols asserting the idea that there is a more significant kind of goodness.</u>* Essentially, the argument is to shun traditional habits of contrition and repentance, and instead to embrace the idea that goodness is to be realized through the animal and human spirit to be found within oneself and to be seen and heard everywhere in Nature. <u>Oliver demonstrates this idea first through a traditional but negative symbol, and second through a series of positive symbols of the natural world.</u>†

     <u>The first symbol in the poem negatively symbolizes traditional but ineffective approaches to creating goodness within oneself.</u> The picture is that of a hermit-like person actively suffering for contrition's sake:

[2]
     You do not have to walk on your knees
     for a hundred miles through the desert, repenting. (lines 2–3)

The notion of "repenting" symbolizes the historical misconception that human beings must endure punishment in atonement for their despair, guilt, and sinfulness. The vision of knees in the desert thus symbolizes the deeply ingrained idea that self-denial and suffering are necessary for goodness and inner peace.

°See p. 910 for this poem.
*Central idea.
†Thesis sentence.

Before going on with the more detailed symbolism of the poem, Oliver introduces another element of the conversation the speaker is having with the listener who has spoken before the poem begins, but who now just listens. <u>The idea is that goodness can be found within "the soft animal of your body"</u>:

[3]

> You only have to let the soft animal of your body
> love what it loves. (lines 4–5)

It is not clear just what sort of animal is described, but the word "animal" is based the action of breathing, the principal characteristic of living beings. The essence of life is therefore the "soft animal" of the self, which here symbolizes the ethics that are a consequence of love.

[4]

A second part of the poem begins with the seventh line, "Meanwhile the world goes on." <u>The idea here is that there is a larger existence than the one that is defined by human concepts of goodness or repentance, guilt or despair.</u> The speaker's argument is carried on totally with a cumulative set of symbols derived from the natural world. These are "the sun and the clear pebbles of the rain" which are visualized as "moving across" the world--over "prairies," "deep trees," "mountains," and "rivers" (lines 8–11), all of which suggest vast expanses of land and wilderness. Because of their virtual infiniteness, these natural objects make human concerns seem small and insignificant. Thus, as symbols, they signify the need for a larger perspective and a more broad dedication than human beings have usually made.

[5]

<u>In this context the poet introduces the symbol of "the wild geese, high in the clean blue air"</u> (line 12). The geese, part of the general symbol of the world going on, are migrating homeward. The idea is somewhat mystical, but nevertheless the symbolism provides a clear analogy for human beings living in our modern troubled and troubling civilization. We are part of the universe, the world. We live here and belong here, just as the wild geese do. We tend to forget our place here, however, as we lose perspective and become enmeshed in cultural concerns which lead us only to guilt and loneliness (line 14). The need is to listen to the inner animal, the outer world, which has a strong pull on us if only we will let it consume our imaginations, just as the wild geese symbolize the world's power to restore the world's creatures to home and to a sense of belonging.

[6]

<u>The "world," in the symbolic fabric of the poem, is an active participant in the process.</u> It "offers itself to your imagination, / calls to you like the wild geese, harsh and exciting--" (lines 15–16). The idea of the symbol is that we, like the wild geese, need to let our imaginations follow the call. While people are traditionally preoccupied with despair, the sentient and nonsentient elements of nature are simply <u>being</u>. We could be like that if only we could perceive the symbolic meaning of the world around us. If we pay attention to the trees and the sun and the rain, we too will experience the strength of being a part of nature, and our morality will follow as a matter of course because we in fact have a definite place "in the family of things" (line 18) just as the geese return home to lead their lives in the landscapes of the world.

WORK CITED

Oliver, Mary. "Wild Geese." <u>Literature: An Introduction to Reading and Writing</u>. Ed. Edgar V. Roberts and Henry E. Jacobs. 7th ed. Upper Saddle River: Prentice Hall, 2004. 910.

Commentary on the Essay

This essay conforms to first strategy for writing about symbolism (p. 916) inasmuch as it involves a concentrated explanation of the symbolism in Oliver's "Wild Geese"—symbolism which is mainly drawn from the world of Nature.

The introduction briefly characterizes the rather shocking opening line and goes on to assert that the rest of the poem is developed through a succession of symbols. The central idea is responsive to the opening line, namely, that the poem is to introduce symbols of "a more significant kind of goodness," and the thesis sentence states that in the body there will be a discussion of a negative symbol and a set of more positive symbols.

Paragraphs 3 through 6 consider the meanings of the poem's three major symbols—the "soft animal" (3), rain, land, and wilderness (4), and the "wild geese" (5). The final paragraph, 6, deals with the issue of goodness and the different kind of "good" brought out in the poem's symbolism (that is, being part of the "family of things").

Special Topics for Writing and Argument about Symbolism and Allusion in Poetry

1. Analyze the ways in which Keats, Herbert, and Jeffers use symbols to convey the fact and idea of capture and thralldom ("La Belle Dame Sans Merci," "The Collar," and "The Purse-Seine"). What major symbols do the three poets use? How appropriate is each symbol in its respective poem? How do the poets use the symbols to focus on the problems they present in their poems?

2. Describe the differences in the ways in which Graham, Viorst, and Yeats use allusions in "The Geese," "A Wedding Sonnet for the Next Generation," and "The Second Coming." How completely can we understand these poems without an explanation of the allusions? How extensive should explanations be? To what extent does the allusiveness make the poems difficult? Challenging? Interesting? Enriching?

3. Compare the use of religious symbols in Donne's "The Canonization" and Herbert's "The Collar." What are the locations from which the poets draw their symbols? How do the symbols figure into the major ideas and arguments of the poems?

4. Describe the nature of the symbols in Cummings's "in Just-" (Chapter 22), Hardy's "In Time of 'The Breaking of Nations,'" and Whitman's "A Noiseless Patient Spider." What parallels in general topic matter do you discover? How do the poets make the poems diverge, despite the common qualities of the symbols?

5. Write a poem in which you develop a major symbol, as Jeffers does in "The Purse-Seine" and Cowper does in "The Poplar Field." To get yourself started, you might consider symbols like these:

    - A littered street or sidewalk
    - A new SUV, or an all-terrain vehicle
    - Coffee hour after church
    - An athletic competition
    - A computer

- The checkout counter at the neighborhood supermarket
- The family dog looking out a window as children leave for school
- A handgun

Write an essay describing the process of your creation. How do you begin? How much detail is necessary? How many conclusions do you need to bring out about your symbol? When do you think you have said enough? Too much? How do you decide?

6. Write a poem in which you make your own allusions to your own experiences, such as attending school, participating in an activity, joining a team, reading a book, identifying with a movie character, or going to a recent artistic or political event. What assumptions do you make about your reader when you bring out your allusions? How do you make the allusion (i.e., by a quotation, a name, a title, an indirect reference)? How does your allusion deepen your meaning? How does your allusion increase your own power of expression?

7. Write an essay describing the use of animals and birds as symbols in this chapter's poems by Graham, Jeffers, Oliver, and Whitman. How do the poets show the symbolic connection of the animals to human affairs? How faithfully do they consider the animals as animals?

8. From your library, take out a university press study of Yeats or Jeffers. How much detail is devoted in the study to either poet's use of symbols? How pervasively is symbolism employed by the poet? How does the poet use symbolism to express ideas about science or nationalism? What other use or uses does the poet make of symbolism?

Myths: *Systems of Symbolic Allusion in Poetry*

Our word *myth* is derived from the Greek word *muthos* or *mythos,* meaning a story, narrative, or plot. Usually, we think of a **myth** as a story that deals with the relationships of gods to humanity (the myths of Prometheus or Odysseus), with battles among gods (the myth of Zeus and Chronos) or heroes (the myth of Achilles and Hector), or with heroic quests (the myth of Jason and the Argonauts). In addition, a myth may be a set of beliefs or assumptions among societies (the myth of the American frontier, the myth of endless progress, the myth of the Lorelei). **Mythology** refers collectively to stories and beliefs, either of a particular society (*Greek mythology*) or of a number of societies (*the mythology of the Ancient Near East*). A system of beliefs and religious or historical doctrine is a **mythos** (the *Islamic mythos* or the *Buddhist mythos*). Although we usually think that myths are ancient, and of course many are, the meanings of myths are not limited exclusively to the past. Old myths profoundly influence our modern consciousness, and they, together with new assumptions and mythical ways of seeing and understanding, continue not only to affect our daily lives but also to shape our local and national political policies.

MYTHOLOGY AS AN EXPLANATION OF HOW THINGS ARE

Throughout the ages, people have developed myths because they want to know who they are, where they have been, where they are going, how the world got the way it is, and whether anyone up there cares. Mythical stories and characters provide answers to such questions. They comprise narrative systems that explain the history, culture, religion, and collective psychology of individual societies and civilizations. They also satisfy our need to understand and humanize conditions that are otherwise mysterious and frightening.

Although many myths originated in primitive times, they still, today, provide a wealth of material and allusion in literature and art. The world around us seems more rich, awesome, and divine when we know that many events, places, creatures, trees, and flowers are important in the beautiful stories and legends that we have inherited from the past.

Myths and Science Are Not the Same

Myths and the sciences overlap, since both attempt to provide explanations for the universe. At the beginning of civilization, almost all the vital questions were answered by myths, such as those about gods, the creation of the earth and humanity, lightning and thunder, earthquakes and volcanoes, sexuality, birth, good, evil, and death.

As Western civilization became progressively more educated and sophisticated, particularly after the time of Copernicus (1473–1543), scientific discoveries replaced myths as the means of explaining the "how" of life and existence. Thus we understand today that lightning and thunder are produced by electrically charged clouds, not by the great and powerful gods Zeus and Thor hurling lightning bolts from the sky (but lightning is still not a thoroughly understood phenomenon). Wherever volcanoes erupt, we know that the cause is molten rock under great pressure deep within the earth's crust being vented violently through fissures in the volcano, not the anger of the Hawaiian goddess Pele.

Even though myths are not scientific, they should not be dismissed. It is true that we know an immense amount scientifically about *how* things happen, but we do not really know *why* they happen. For instance, although physicists and theorists tell us a great deal about the early stages of the universe and the development of galaxies, quasars, black holes, stars, the solar system, and our earth, they do not even approach answering the imponderable religious and philosophical questions about causes that myths attempt to explain.

Mythical Stories and Concepts Have Great Power

Myths are ingrained in our minds and in our speech. For example, we *know* with scientific certainty that we have daylight when our city or town faces the sun directly, and that we have night when we are turned away from the sun and are in the earth's shadow. Nevertheless, we continue to use the phrases "the sun rises" and "the sun sets" to explain day and night, as though we still believed the myth that the earth is flat and that the sun circles around it. Such mythically originated language is inseparable from our minds. Even the belief that science and technology can solve all earthly problems may be seen as a myth. Human beings, in short, are **mythopoeic**—that is, not only do we live with myths, but we habitually create them.

We should therefore realize that myths express truth symbolically even if mythical heroes and stories themselves are scientifically or historically no more than fabrications. The truths are not to be found in mythical lore itself but rather in what they show about our earthly existence. Thus, when we read about the problems of the ancient Theban king Oedipus, we can safely assume that the

specific details of his life (if he actually ever did live) did not happen just as Sophocles dramatizes them in *Oedipus the King*. But we find in the play a powerful rendering of how human beings make mistakes and how they must pay for them. In short, the truth of the Oedipus myth is psychological, not literal and historical.

Myths Explain Our Circumstances in the World and the Universe

We can broaden our consideration by adding that myths also imply a special perspective about how people see their place and purpose. This kind of myth may be constructive and generative. Thus, at one time most North Americans accepted the myth that Nature was limitless and hostile and in need of being conquered. With this concept in mind, settlers moved into every available corner of the land—to build, farm, create industries, and establish new ways of life. Without such an inspiring myth, people might have stayed put, and the nation would never have achieved its current prominence.

This is not to say that all myths are positive; indeed, some myths are destructive. Thus, the once-positive myth of hostile and inexhaustible Nature has led us into the massive problems we face today with environmental exploitation and degradation. There is need for a different myth—a myth declaring that the earth is no longer inimical and in need of taming, but rather that the earth is beautiful, tender, and fragile and is in need of preservation and conservation.

The Ansel Adams photograph "Forest Floor, Yosemite Valley" is a visual embodiment of this more tolerant and loving myth of Nature (p. 923).

Mythological Themes or Motifs Are Common to Many Cultures

Since myths address our human need to know, it is not surprising to find that many civilizations, separated by time and space, have parallel myths, such as the many stories accounting for the creation of the universe. The details of these myths are different, but the *patterns* are similar inasmuch as they all posit both an original time and act of creation and a creator god or gods who also take part in human history. The principal god is perceived as a shaper, a modeler, a divine artisan, who has fashioned the orderly systems we find in the world, such as life, daylight, ecological dependence, tides, warmth, fertility, harvests, morality, and social stability.

One of the most crucial of all myths involves sin, disobedience, and evil, which are usually blamed for winter, natural calamities, illness, and death. A corollary of the myth is that a god-hero or goddess-heroine must undergo a sacrifice to atone for sin and to ensure the renewed vitality of spring. In *The Golden Bough,* a massive collection and analysis of mythic stories, Sir James Frazer (1854–1941) compares a series of mythical death-renewal motifs. Among such sacrificed and reborn gods are Thammuz (Babylonia), Attis (Phrygia), Osiris (Egypt), and Adonis, Dionysus, and Persephone (Greece). Again, the specific myths take different forms, but they reflect the same mysteries, fears, and hopes.

Scholars and anthropologists like Frazer were among the first to observe the interrelationships among myths produced by diverse cultures. The Swiss psychoanalyst Carl Gustav Jung (1875–1961) offered an explanation for this duplication. He noticed that images, characters, and events similar to those in literature, mythology, and religion also occurred in the dreams of his patients. He termed these recurring images **archetypes** (from the Greek word meaning "model" or "first mold") and developed a theory that all human beings share a universal or collective unconsciousness. Even if Jung's theory is ignored, the fact remains that types of mythic creatures such as dragons and centaurs, archetypal mother-daughter and father-son stories, and narratives involving sacrifices, heroic quests, and trips to the underworld recur throughout various mythologies and pervade our literature.[1]

MYTHOLOGY AND LITERATURE

When writing was invented approximately four to five thousand years ago, the first written works recorded oral mythologies; that is, the mythologies had already existed for long periods of time before they were written down. The ancient Greek poet Homer, for example (perhaps a mythical figure himself), told about the mythical gods and heroes of the Trojan War. Homer did not actually write (tradition says he was blind), but other writers recorded and transmitted

---

[1]See also Chapter 33 for a further discussion of archetypes.

his epics. The Latin writer Ovid (43 B.C.E.–17 C.E.) knew a large body of mythology and wrote poetic stories based on it. The result of this assimilation of myth into poetry was a combination of literature and religion that served the double purpose of teaching and entertaining. In this way, poets throughout antiquity used mythology as a mine for ideas, images, and symbols.

Although almost two thousand years have passed since Ovid lived, writers and artists still rely on mythology. In every generation since the earliest Anglo-Saxon poems and legends, poets of English have retold and updated mythological stories. Indeed, most of the poems in this chapter are from the twentieth century. Modern poetry utilizing mythology, however, is no longer designed to reinforce the dominant religion. Instead, it uses mythology to link past and present, to dramatize important concerns, and to symbolize universal patterns of thought.

Most Western poets who use mythological material in their verse turn to long-standing bodies of myth, particularly those of Greco-Roman, Norse-Teutonic, and Judeo-Christian origin. These systems of mythology are **universal** or **public,** since they are part of a vast common heritage. Like *cultural symbols,* they make up a reservoir of material that all writers are free to employ.

References to Mythology Are Common in Poetry

When poets make references to a myth, as in poems like Tennyson's "Ulysses" and Parker's "Penelope," both of which refer to the myth of Odysseus (Ulysses), they assume that readers already understand something about the stories and characters. With these poems, readers are expected to know enough of Homer's *Odyssey* to recall that this hero fought in the Trojan War for ten years and then was forced to spend an additional ten years in attempting to return to Ithaca, the island kingdom which he ruled. In other words, during most of his reign he was a warrior and adventurer—an absentee ruler—but at the same time his queen, Penelope, stayed at home.

Although you might have enough background in mythology to understand a poet's mythological references, you may sometimes need to fill in or reinforce your knowledge. A good place to start is a dictionary or general encyclopedia, where you will find brief identifications of mythic figures and a key to further reading. Eventually you will want access to more detailed information. Excellent books that retell the stories of Greco-Roman mythology are Richmond Hathorn's *Greek Mythology,* M. C. Howatson's *The Oxford Companion to Classical Literature,* and Timothy Gantz's *Early Greek Myth: A Guide to Literary and Artistic Sources.* Bulfinch's *The Age of Fable* and Edith Hamilton's *Mythology* are respected traditional books. Charles Mills Gayley's *The Classic Myths in English Literature and in Art* has been a standard and revered book for more than a century. There are also many classical dictionaries, such as the *Oxford Classical Dictionary,* that are immensely useful. Early in the nineteenth century, John Keats learned much of his mythology from John Lemprière's *A Classical Dictionary: Containing A Copious Account of all The Proper Names Mentioned in Ancient Authors.* Many libraries have this book on their reference shelves, and your use of it will both inform you and impress you with a sense of bibliographical history. Not all mythology is classical. Should you want to understand references to the myths of Paul Bunyan and Johnny Appleseed, for example, you would want a collection of American folktales. References to Odin, Thor, the Valkyries, or Loki should lead you to a collection of Norse-Teutonic mythology.

Myths Are Often Vital in Poetry

We are now ready to look at a poem that is built upon a myth. The poem is by William Butler Yeats, and it draws on Greco-Roman mythology.

WILLIAM BUTLER YEATS (1865–1939)

Leda and the Swan ⟶ ⟵ ⟶ ⟶ *1924 (1923)*

A sudden blow: the great wings beating still
Above the staggering girl, her thighs caressed
By the dark webs, her nape caught in his bill,
He holds her helpless breast upon his breast.

How can those terrified vague fingers push   5
The feathered glory from her loosening thighs?
And how can body, laid in that white rush,
But feel the strange heart beating where it lies?

A shudder in the loins engenders there
The broken wall, the burning roof and tower   10
And Agamemnon dead.
                              Being so caught up,
So mastered by the brute blood of the air,
Did she put on his knowledge with his power
Before the indifferent beak could let her drop?   15

QUESTIONS

1. What mythic event does the poem retell? Who was Leda? The swan? Who were Leda's children? What events are alluded to in lines 10 and 11?

2. How is Leda described? What words suggest her helplessness? What phrases suggest the swan's mystery and divinity?

3. What question is raised in the last two lines? To what extent does the poem provide an answer to this question?

Yeats's sonnet focuses on a specific event of ancient Greek mythology: Zeus, king of the gods, having taken the form of a swan, raped Leda, a Spartan queen. According to the myth, this violent event was a starting point not only of Greek civilization but also of the angers and troubles of humanity in general. One of the children born of the rape was Helen of Troy, whose abduction by Paris precipitated the Trojan War. Yeats's phrase "The broken wall, the burning roof and tower" refers to the Greek destruction of Troy. Another child was

Clytemnestra, married to Agamemnon, king of Mycenae and leader of the allied Greek forces. Because Agamemnon had sacrificed their daughter Iphigeneia as a part of the war effort, Clytemnestra vowed revenge and had him murdered when he returned home from the Trojan War.

After a graphic recounting of the swan's attack on Leda and a brief reference to the sack of Troy and Agamemnon's death, Yeats's concluding lines raise a central issue stemming from the myth. While Leda took on some of Zeus's divine power with the rape (through the process of childbearing), the poem asks whether she also "put on" some of his divine knowledge—whether she acquired Zeus's foreknowledge of the fall of Troy, the murder of Agamemnon, and, by extension, the subsequent events in history. Of course, the question is rhetorical and the answer is negative.

If all Yeats's poem did were to question the ancient myth in this way, it would be of limited interest for modern readers. But it does more than that; it directs our attention to concerns of today. Thus, we may conclude from Yeats's use of the myth that human beings, like Leda, do not have foreknowledge, but have only their own culture, experience, and intelligence as their guides. If divine beings exist, they have no interest in human affairs, but are rather uninvolved and "indifferent" (line 14). By extension the myth suggests that the burden of civilization is on human beings themselves and that if knowledge and power are ever to be combined for constructive goals, that blending must be a human achievement.

Yeats thus employs mythic material in this sonnet to raise a searching question about the nature of existence, knowledge, and power. The historical process is embodied in the rape, the children born out of it, and their troubles. As the central figure of the myth, Leda is the focal point of circumstances and concerns that have extended from the distant past to the present, and that will likely extend into the future.

A poem of great interest because it is not only based on the ancient myth of Leda, but also is deliberately connected to "Leda and the Swan," is Mona Van Duyn's sixteen-line "Leda."

MONA VAN DUYN (b. 1921)

Leda ～＜～✓✓ 1970

"Did she put on his knowledge with his power
Before the indifferent beak could let her drop?"

Not even for a moment. He knew, for one thing, what he was.
When he saw the swan in her eyes he could let her drop.
In the first look of love men find their great disguise,
and collecting these rare pictures of himself was his life.

Her body became the consequence of his juice,
while her mind closed on a bird and went to sleep.
Later, with the children in school, she opened her eyes
and saw her own openness, and felt relief.

5

In men's stories her life ended with his loss.
She stiffened under the storm of his wings to a glassy shape,　　10
stricken and mysterious and immortal. But the fact is,
she was not, for such an ending, abstract enough.

She tried for a while to understand what it was
that had happened, and then decided to let it drop.
She married a smaller man with a beaky nose,　　15
And melted away in the storm of everyday life.

QUESTIONS

1. What relationship does this poem have to Yeats's "Leda and the Swan"?
2. Why does Van Duyn refer to "men's stories" in line 9? What sort of story is she telling in this poem? What use is she making here of the Leda myth? Why does she conclude the poem as she does?
3. Why does Van Duyn use sixteen lines for her poem, rather than casting it in the form of a sonnet? What rhyming pattern and repetitive pattern does Van Duyn use in this poem?

Van Duyn quotes Yeats's final two lines, and the beginning of her poem is a direct answer to these lines. She puts the scene not in ancient classical times, but rather in the context of modern life, and the issues of the poem are the ways in which women's lives differ from men's. It is in such a way that Van Duyn has taken the original myth, alluded to the famous poem of Yeats, and added her own ideas to both ancient and modern treatments. As these poems demonstrate, mythology could hardly be more alive and vital in modern poetry.

Because myths thus embody recurring issues, they have great value for modern readers. Muriel Rukeyser's "Myth," for example, uses the ancient myth about Oedipus to shed light amusingly on misperceptions about male–female relationships. Edward Field's "Icarus" (one of a number of Icarus poems we include here) uses the ancient Icarus myth to decry the impact of modern society upon individuals. In these and in other poems based in mythology, you may look for such original ways in which poets receive something old and make it new. Myths do not belong only to the past but are alive and well in the present.

The poems in this chapter feature mythical material about Odysseus and Icarus, to which are added a number of poems based on other myths. Although the poems delve into ancient mythology for their subjects, they are remarkably different; each offers its own meaning, impact, and poetic experience. The poets shape their mythic material to illustrate and symbolize ideas about pride, daring, disillusionment, suffering, indignation, creativity, idealism, and indifference to the plights of others, and therefore the poems demonstrate how myths can be used for original effects in new poetic contexts. As you study the poems, consider these general questions along with the questions following the poems.

1. How completely does the poem deal with the myth? What is included? What is excluded? What does the poet expect that you should know about the myth? How does the poet create a variation on the myth beyond the original?

2. Why do modern poets treat mythical subjects? Do they simply interpret or reinterpret ancient stories, or do they use the ancient stories to shed light on modern circumstances? Why? How?

SEVEN POEMS RELATED TO THE MYTH OF ODYSSEUS

Odysseus (Ulysses) was the mythical king of the island realm of Ithaca and one of the principal Greek generals in the Trojan War. He spent ten years fighting at Troy, and after the Greek victory he set sail for home. He encountered so many obstacles and delays, however, and his return took so long—an additional ten years—that traveling and adventure became a way of life with him. When he sailed near the Sirens, who lured sailors to death with the beauty of their songs, he resisted their attraction by having himself lashed to the mast of his ship. For a year he was confined on the island of Aeaea by Circe, a sorceress. Circe turned his men into swine, but he escaped this transformation by taking a magical herb. For seven years he was held by the nymph Calypso on the island of Ogygia. There were many other adventures, all described in Homer's *Odyssey*.

During his long absence, his kingdom was entrusted to his wife, Penelope. Penelope was dutiful and faithful, but she was besieged by crowds of suitors, each of whom sought to take over the Ithacan kingdom by marrying her. She promised to accept one of the suitors when she finished making a shroud for her father-in-law. During the day she wove the shroud, but at night she unraveled her day's work, in this way delaying the need to fulfill her promise to remarry. By the time the suitors discovered her ruse, Odysseus had returned. With the help of his son Telemachus, he slaughtered all the suitors and restored himself as king.

POEMS FOR STUDY

MARGARET ATWOOD (b. 1939)

Siren Song   1974

This is the one song everyone
would like to learn: the song
that is irresistible:

the song that forces men
to leap overboard in squadrons   5
even though they see the beached skulls

the song nobody knows
because anyone who has heard it
is dead, and the others can't remember.

Shall I tell you the secret   10
and if I do, will you get me
out of this bird suit?

I don't enjoy it here
squatting on this island
looking picturesque and mythical   15

with these two feathery maniacs,
I don't enjoy singing
this trio, fatal and valuable.

I will tell the secret to you,
to you, only to you.   20
Come closer. This song

is a cry for help: Help me!
Only you, only you can,
you are unique

at last. Alas   25
it is a boring song
but it works every time.

QUESTIONS

1. Who were the Sirens in Greek mythology? What effect did their song have?

2. Who is the speaker in this poem? What is the effect of her colloquial diction? What does she tell you about her song?

3. Who is the "you" referred to in lines 10–24? What does the speaker say about her life? What "works every time"? To what extent is the conclusion amusing?

LOUISE GLÜCK (b. 1943)

For a photo, see p. 675.

Penelope's Song   1996

Little soul, little perpetually undressed one,
do now as I bid you, climb
the shelf-like branches of the spruce tree;
wait at the top, attentive, like
a sentry or look-out. He will be home soon;   5
it behooves you to be
generous. You have not been completely

perfect either; with your troublesome body
you have done things you shouldn't
discuss in poems. Therefore   10
call out to him over the open water, over the bright water
with your dark song, with your grasping,
unnatural song—passionate,
like Maria Callas.° Who
wouldn't want you? Whose most demonic appetite   15
could you possibly fail to answer? Soon
he will return from wherever he goes in the meantime,
suntanned from his time away, wanting
his grilled chicken. Ah, you must greet him,
you must shake the boughs of the tree   20
to get his attention,
but carefully, carefully, lest
his beautiful face be marred
by too many falling needles.

PENELOPE'S SONG. 14 *Maria Callas*: Callas (1923–1977) was one of the best-known sopranos of the twentieth century, famous for her acting and her fiery interpretations of operatic heroines.

QUESTIONS

1. Who is the speaker of this poem? To whom is she speaking? What does she tell herself that she might not tell a companion or friend?

2. Describe your response to the poem if the speaker is Penelope, planning to welcome Odysseus after his twenty-year adventure in Troy and on the high seas.

3. Describe your response if the speaker is a modern woman planning to welcome her husband after he has spent Sunday afternoon seeing a professional football game. How does the poem seem to change under these circumstances?

4. If such were the circumstances, what use is Glück making of the Odysseus myth?

W.S. MERWIN (b. 1927)

Odysseus   1960

Always the setting forth was the same,
Same sea, same dangers waiting for him
As though he had got nowhere but older.
Behind him on the receding shore
The identical reproaches, and somewhere   5
Out before him, the unravelling patience
He was wedded to. There were the islands
Each with its woman and twining welcome
To be navigated, and one to call "home."
The knowledge of all that he betrayed   10
Grew till it was the same whether he stayed
Or went. Therefore he went. And what wonder
If sometimes he could not remember

Which was the one who wished on his departure
Perils that he could never sail through,
And which, improbable, remote, and true,
Was the one he kept sailing home to?

15

QUESTIONS

1. What aspects of the Odysseus myth are evoked in this poem? What point does the poem make about Odysseus's experiences?

2. To what extent is Odysseus symbolic of a specific kind of life and attitude toward life? How does our knowledge of Odysseus contribute to the impact and meaning of the poem?

3. Compare this poem with Parker's "Penelope." How is the same mythic material used toward different ends in these poems?

4. Compare this poem with Tennyson's "Ulysses." Explain how and why the same mythic figure can be used to convey such different ideas.

DOROTHY PARKER (1893–1967)

Penelope ⌐⌐ 1936

960

In the pathway of the sun,
  In the footsteps of the breeze,
Where the world and sky are one,
  He shall ride the silver seas,
    He shall cut the glittering wave.

5

I shall sit at home, and rock;
Rise, to heed a neighbor's knock;
Brew my tea, and snip my thread;
Bleach the linen for my bed.
    They will call him brave.

This underscore the powerful irony

10

QUESTIONS

1. How does the speaker describe her life? How is her life different from that of the male figure described in lines 1–5?

2. To what extent is Penelope a symbol? What does she symbolize? How does our knowledge of the myth deepen our response to this symbolism?

LINDA PASTAN (b. 1932)

The Suitor ⌐⌐ 1988

There is always a story
that no one bothers to tell:
the younger son of a younger son,

hardly a suitor at all, sits
at the sharp edge of the table   5
among the boisterous men, not hungry
except for a glimpse of Penelope,
a woman wasted, he thinks—
those pale arms, that hair
a web she might have woven   10
around her own head.
Sometimes he tries to speak
to the son° who looks at him wonderingly,   *Telemachus*
but doesn't answer.
How could Odysseus have left?   15
he asks himself, but is grateful
for the chance to pretend
it could be him she'll choose.
He almost knows it must end badly,
though his will be a minor tributary   20
in that unplumbed sea
of wasted blood.

QUESTIONS

1. Why does Pastan choose a young man as the suitor of the poem? Who are the "boisterous men," and what is the suitor's relationship to them?

2. How does the suitor feel about Penelope? What does he have to gain by being a part of the suitors seeking her hand in marriage?

3. What will be the suitor's fate? Why does Pastan close on the note of "wasted blood"?

ALFRED, LORD TENNYSON (1809–1892)

Ulysses 1842 (1833)

It little profits that an idle king,
By this still hearth, among these barren crags,
Matched with an aged wife, I mete and dole
Unequal laws° unto a savage race,   *rewards and punishments*
That hoard, and sleep, and feed, and know not me.   5

I cannot rest from travel; I will drink
Life to the lees.° All times I have enjoyed   *dregs*
Greatly, have suffered greatly, both with those
That loved me, and alone; on shore, and when
Through scudding drifts the rainy Hyades°   10
Vexed the dim sea. I am become a name;
For always roaming with a hungry heart
Much have I seen and known—cities of men

ULYSSES. 10 *Hyades:* nymphs who were placed among the stars by Zeus, the king of the gods. The name means "rain," and the rising of the stars was thought to precede a storm.

And manners, climates, councils, governments,
Myself not least, but honored of them all—   15
And drunk delight of battle with my peers,
Far on the ringing plains of windy Troy.
I am a part of all that I have met;
Yet all experience is an arch wherethrough
Gleams that untraveled world whose margin fades   20
Forever and forever when I move.
How dull it is to pause, to make an end,
To rust unburnished, not to shine in use!
As though to breathe were life! Life piled on life
Were all too little, and of one to me   25
Little remains; but every hour is saved
From that eternal silence, something more,
A bringer of new things; and vile it were
For some three suns to store and hoard myself,
And this gray spirit yearning in desire   30
To follow knowledge like a sinking star,
Beyond the utmost bound of human thought.

    This is my son, mine own Telemachus,
To whom I leave the scepter and the isle—°
Well-loved of me, discerning to fulfill   35
This labor, by slow prudence to make mild
A rugged people, and through soft degrees
Subdue them to the useful and the good.
Most blameless is he, centered in the sphere
Of common duties, decent not to fail   40
In offices of tenderness, and pay
Meet° adoration to my household gods,   *appropriate*
When I am gone. He works his work, I mine.

    There lies the port; the vessel puffs her sail;
There gloom the dark, broad seas. My mariners,   45
Souls that have toiled, and wrought, and thought with me—
That ever with a frolic welcome took
The thunder and the sunshine, and opposed
Free hearts, free foreheads—you and I are old;
Old age hath yet his honor and his toil.   50
Death closes all; but something ere the end,
Some work of noble note, may yet be done,
Not unbecoming men that strove with Gods.
The lights begin to twinkle from the rocks;
The long day wanes; the slow moon climbs; the deep   55
Moans round with many voices. Come, my friends,
'Tis not too late to seek a newer world.
Push off, and sitting well in order smite
The sounding furrows; for my purpose holds
To sail beyond the sunset, and the baths   60
Of all the western stars, until I die.

34 *isle:* Ithaca, the island realm ruled by Odysseus.

It may be that the gulfs will wash us down;
It may be we shall touch the Happy Isles,°
And see the great Achilles,° whom we knew.

   Though much is taken, much abides; and though   65
We are not now that strength which in old days
Moved earth and heaven, that which we are, we are—
One equal temper of heroic hearts,
Made weak by time and fate, but strong in will
To strive, to seek, to find, and not to yield.   70

63 *Happy Isles:* the Elysian Fields, dwelling place of mortals who have been made immortal by the gods.
64 *Achilles:* Greek hero of the Trojan War who killed Hector and was, in turn, killed by Paris.

QUESTIONS

1. Who is the speaker of the poem? What is his attitude toward his life in Ithaca? What key phrases and adjectives in lines 1–5 establish this attitude?

2. Who is Telemachus? What is the speaker's attitude toward him? How are the speaker and Telemachus different?

3. What aspects of Ulysses are emphasized in this poem? To what extent does he become symbolic? What does he symbolize?

PETER ULISSE (b. 1944)

Odyssey: 20 Years Later   *1995*

I battled Trojans with Odysseus.
Bludgeoning the eye of Polyphemus
I meandered past Scylla and Charybdis,
descended into Hades, outwitted Calypso.
I ate of the lotus, and forgot.   5
Twenty years I roamed—

Wandering Jew, Prodigal Son, opener
of doors in empty streets I
embraced strangers like a lover's quest,
searched for the beautiful which   10
alone
could make a life complete.
I released hands in bedrooms,
turned to St. Augustine

It is only now I feel the pull   15
of salmon swimming up current,
turtles drawn to Galapagos,
fowls finding a path through
a thousand mile sky,
only now I understand   20
Odyssey not as Cyclops, Sirens,

or unfavorable winds but

simply as
coming home.

QUESTIONS

1. Who is the "I" of line 1? How does this line reveal the identity of the "I"? How is this speaker different from the speaker of Tennyson's "Ulysses"? What do the final lines tell you about the speaker's and Odysseus's journeys?
2. Consider the speaker's description of having duplicated the actions performed by Odysseus and other ancient figures. What ideas does the speaker present about the repetitive or cyclical nature of human experience?
3. What autobiographical or confessional details are contained in lines 13–19? What educational experiences are alluded to in these lines?

SEVEN POEMS RELATED TO THE MYTH OF ICARUS

Icarus was the son of Daedalus, the greatest master of applied science in ancient Greek myth. The story begins with Minos, king of Crete, who also ruled Athens and the rest of the Greek world. Each year (or, according to other versions of the story, every nine years) Minos compelled the Athenians to make a tribute of seven young people to be sacrificed to the Minotaur, an enormously powerful monster, half man and half bull, who was the source of Cretan military and political power. Needing to control the monster by confining him, Minos hired Daedalus to build an enclosure—a labyrinth—as a prison. Daedalus completed this job and then asked royal leave to return home, but Minos wanted to benefit further from the skills of Daedalus. Accordingly, Minos imprisoned Daedalus in the labyrinth together with his son, Icarus. Angered by the King's overbearing treatment, Daedalus got revenge by aiding the Athenian hero, Theseus, in killing the Minotaur and thereby in freeing Athens from the burden of the living tribute. Daedalus then exerted his great inventiveness to carry out an aerial escape from the labyrinth. He made two pairs of wings out of wax and feathers—one pair for himself and one for Icarus. Daedalus flew safely away and eventually made his home in Sicily. Icarus, however, flew too close to the sun. The wax melted and the wings fell apart. Icarus fell into the Icarian Sea (named after him), and he drowned.

POEMS FOR STUDY

BRIAN ALDISS (b. 1925)

Flight 063 ⤴⤷⤵⤴ 1994

Why always speak of Icarus' fall?—
That legendary plunge
Amid a shower of tallow
And feathers and the poor lad's
Sweat? And that little splash   5
Which caught the eye of Brueghel°
While the sun remained
Aloof within its private zone?

   That fall remains
Suspended in the corporate mind.   10
Yet as our Boeing flies
High above the Arctic Circle

Into the sun's eye, think—
Before the fall the flight was.
(So with Adam—just before   15
The Edenic Fall, he had
That first taste of Eve.)

Dinner is served aboard Flight 063.
We eat from plastic trays, oblivious
To the stratosphere.   20

But Icarus—his cliff-top jump,
The leap of heart, the blue air scaled—
His glorious sense of life
Imperiled. Time   25
Fell far below, the everyday
Was lost in his ascent.

Up, up, he sailed, unheeding
Such silly limitations as
The melting point of wax.

FLIGHT 063. 6 *Brueghel*: Pieter Brueghel or Breughel (ca. 1525–1569) was a Flemish painter whose subjects include the Nativity ("the miraculous birth"), the Crucifixion ("the dreadful martyrdom"), and the fall of Icarus. His *Landscape with the Fall of Icarus* is reproduced in color in Insert III-4.

QUESTIONS

1. What attitude toward Icarus does the speaker present (see lines 21–26)? What emotions does he attribute to Icarus during the beginning of the flight? What is the significance of line 14 ("Before the fall the flight was")?

2. What do the words "dinner" and "oblivious" suggest about modern attitudes toward flight?

3. Why does the speaker emphasize the word "think" (line 13)? Why is the melting point of wax a "silly" limitation?

W. H. AUDEN (1907–1973)

Musée des Beaux Arts°   1940

About suffering they were never wrong,
The Old Masters: how well they understood
Its human position; how it takes place
While someone else is eating or opening a window or just
    walking dully along;
How, when the aged are reverently, passionately waiting   5
For the miraculous birth, there always must be
Children who did not specially want it to happen, skating
On a pond at the edge of the wood:
They never forgot
That even the dreadful martyrdom must run its course   10
Anyhow in a corner, some untidy spot
Where the dogs go on with their doggy life and the torturer's horse
Scratches its innocent behind on a tree.
In Brueghel's *Icarus*, for instance: how everything turns away
Quite leisurely from the disaster; the ploughman may   15
Have heard the splash, the forsaken cry,
But for him it was not an important failure; the sun shone
As it had to on the white legs disappearing into the green
Water; and the expensive delicate ship that must have seen
Something amazing, a boy falling out of the sky,   20
Had somewhere to get to and sailed calmly on.

MUSÉE DES BEAUX ARTS. "Museum of Fine Arts."

QUESTIONS

1. What does the speaker say about the perceptions of the "Old Masters" to suffering? What use does Auden make of the Brueghel painting?

2. What concern do those close to Icarus's fall show toward the fall and the drowning? In the light of this concern, what ideas does the poem express about the ultimate importance of heroism and great occurrences?

3. Compare this poem with Frost's "Out, Out—" (Chapter 24). What does each poet indicate about the attitudes of people toward the suffering of others? Would you characterize these poems as painfully truthful? Ironic? Disillusioned?

EDWARD FIELD (b. 1924)

Icarus   1963

Only the feathers floating around the hat
Showed that anything more spectacular had occurred
Than the usual drowning. The police preferréd to ignore
The confusing aspects of the case,

And the witnesses ran off to a gang war.   5
So the report filed and forgotten in the archives read simply
"Drowned," but it was wrong: Icarus
Had swum away, coming at last to the city
Where he rented a house and tended the garden.

"That nice Mr. Hicks" the neighbors called him,   10
Never dreaming that the gray, respectable suit
Concealed arms that had controlled huge wings
Nor that those sad, defeated eyes had once
Compelled the sun. And had he told them
They would have answered with a shocked, uncomprehending stare.   15
No, he could not disturb their neat front yards;
Yet all his books insisted that this was a horrible mistake:
What was he doing aging in a suburb?
Can the genius of the hero fall
To the middling stature of the merely talented?   20

And nightly Icarus probes his wound
And daily in his workshop, curtains carefully drawn,
Constructs small wings and tries to fly
To the lighting fixture on the ceiling:
Fails every time and hates himself for trying.   25

He had thought himself a hero, had acted heroically,
And dreamt of his fall, the tragic fall of the hero;
But now rides commuter trains,
Serves on various committees,
And wishes he had drowned.   30

QUESTIONS

1. What twist on the Icarus myth occurs in this poem?

2. How does Field undercut the heroic myth of Icarus? What happens to Icarus after he rents a house and tends his garden? What does Icarus, the daily suburban commuter with "sad, defeated eyes," wish at the poem's end?

3. What level of language does Field use in this poem? How does this language complement the poem's antiheroic view of Icarus?

MURIEL RUKEYSER (1913–1980)   *For a photo, see p. 745.*

Waiting for Icarus   1973

He said he would be back and we'd drink wine together
He said that everything would be better than before
He said we were on the edge of a new relation
He said he would never again cringe before his father
He said that he was going to invent full-time   5
He said he loved me that going into me

He said was going into the world and the sky
He said all the buckles were very firm
He said the wax was the best wax
He said Wait for me here on the beach   10
He said Just don't cry

I remember the gulls and the waves
I remember the islands going dark on the sea
I remember the girls laughing
I remember they said he only wanted to get away from me   15
I remember mother saying: Inventors are like poets,
               a trashy lot
I remember she told me those who try out inventions are worse
I remember she added: Women who love such are the worst of all
I have been waiting all day, or perhaps longer.   20
I would have liked to try those wings myself.
It would have been better than this.

QUESTIONS

1. Who is speaking? How long has she been waiting for Icarus? When is she speaking? Does she know what has happened to Icarus?

2. In what ways is the speaker's narration a complaint? What does she complain about? How do the things she says bring ancient and modern circumstances to a common level?

3. To what degree is this poem humorous? What effect does Rukeyser's use of anaphora (see p. 729) have on the development of the poem?

ANNE SEXTON (1928–1974)

To a Friend Whose Work Has Come to Triumph°   1962

Consider Icarus, pasting those sticky wings on,
testing that strange little tug at his shoulder blade,
and think of that first flawless moment over the lawn
of the labyrinth. Think of the difference it made!
There below are the trees, as awkward as camels;   5
and here are the shocked starlings pumping past
and think of innocent Icarus who is doing quite well:
larger than a sail, over the fog and the blast
of the plushy ocean, he goes. Admire his wings!
Feel the fire at his neck and see how casually   10
he glances up and is caught, wondrously tunneling
into that hot eye. Who cares that he fell back to the sea?
See him acclaiming the sun and come plunging down
while his sensible daddy goes straight into town.

TO A FRIEND WHOSE WORK HAS COME TO TRIUMPH. The title alludes to and reverses the title of a poem by William Butler Yeats, "To a Friend Whose Has Come to Nothing" (1914).

QUESTIONS

1. Describe the contrast made in this poem between Icarus and Daedalus ("his sensible daddy"). What achievement does the speaker attribute to Icarus? Does the speaker seem to like or dislike Icarus?

2. In relation to line 12, what is the significance of the poem's title? In what sense has Icarus's life been a model for "Triumph"?

3. What tone is indicated by phrases like "sticky wings," "strange little tug," "awkward as camels," "plushy ocean," "hot eye," and "sensible daddy"?

STEPHEN SPENDER (1909–1995)

Icarus ～〈 ～ ～ 1933

He will watch the hawk with an indifferent eye
  Or pitifully;
Nor on those eagles that so feared him, now
  Will strain his brow;
Weapons men use, stone, sling and strong-thewed bow   5
  He will not know.

This aristocrat, superb of all instinct,
  With death close linked
Had paced the enormous cloud, almost had won
  War on the sun;   10
Till now, like Icarus mid-ocean-drowned,
  Hands, wings, are found.

QUESTIONS

1. Describe the structure of this poem. How many lines does Spender devote to the character of Icarus? Why does he consider Icarus an aristocrat?

2. Why does he say that Icarus had "almost" won a "War on the sun"? What modern lesson does Spender draw from the story of Icarus?

3. Why does the first stanza contain future tense verbs, and why in the second stanza do the verbs shift to past perfects ("had paced," "had won"), a present perfect ("are found"), and a past participle ("linked")?

WILLIAM CARLOS WILLIAMS (1883–1963)

Landscape with the Fall of Icarus ～〈 ～ ～ 1962

According to Brueghel°
when Icarus fell
it was spring

a farmer was ploughing
his field   5
the whole pageantry

of the year was
awake tingling
near

the edge of the sea   10
concerned
with itself

sweating in the sun
that melted
the wings' wax   15

unsignificantly
off the coast
there was

a splash quite unnoticed
this was   20
Icarus drowning

LANDSCAPE WITH THE FALL OF ICARUS. 1 *Brueghel:* See the note for line 6 in Aldiss's "Flight 063" (p. 937).
Also see Insert III-4.

QUESTIONS

1. As the speaker presents the actual fall of Icarus as contained in Brueghel's painting, how significant is Icarus himself?

2. The poem is in tercets (three-line groups), and no line has more than four
   words. What is the effect of these sparse lines on the seriousness of Icarus's situation? Why does the poem not contain more detail?

3. Why does the speaker mention other things, specifically, the season, the farmer,
   the act of ploughing, the "tingling" pageant "of the year," and the shoreline—before he describes the splash in the last three lines?

4. Compare the view of Icarus in this poem with the views of Aldiss, Auden, Field,
   and Spender.

✴ THREE POEMS RELATED TO THE MYTH OF THE PHOENIX

In ancient myth, the phoenix was a gold and red Arabian bird resembling an
eagle. At the end of a long period—some accounts say five hundred years,
others say fifteen hundred—the phoenix would be mysteriously consumed
by fire. A new phoenix would then reconstitute itself from the ashes of the
old, and a new life cycle would begin. According to the myth, this process
continued indefinitely. Because of this constant renewal, many religions
have considered the phoenix story optimistically, as a symbol of life overcoming death.

POEMS FOR STUDY

AMY CLAMPITT (1920–1994)

Berceuse° ⌣⌣⌣ 1982

Listen to Gieseking° playing a Berceuse
of Chopin°—the mothwing flutter
light as ash, perishable as burnt paper—

and sleep, now the furnaces of Auschwitz°
are all out, and tourists go there.   5
The purest art has slept with turpitude,

we all pay taxes. Sleep. The day of waking
waits, cloned from the phoenix—
a thousand replicas in upright silos,

nurseries of the ultimate enterprise.   10
Decay will undo what it can, the rotten
fabric of our repose connives with doomsday.

Sleep on, scathed felicity. Sleep, rare
and perishable relic. Imagining's no shutter
against the absolute, incorrigible sunrise.   15

BERCEUSE. *Berceuse:* a lullaby or cradle song.   1 *Gieseking:* Walter Gieseking (1895–1956), famous French pianist.   2 *Chopin:* Frédéric Chopin (1810–1849), Polish composer and pianist.   4 *Auschwitz:* World War II Nazi death camp near Kraków, Poland. See also Quasímodo's poem "Auschwitz" (p. 781).

QUESTIONS

1. In what ways is this poem pessimistic? How does the speaker contrast the best and worst aspects of human life?

2. What is meant by line 6? What irony is contained in the image of the phoenix (stanza 3)? What objects are replicated in the "upright silos"?

3. What are the "felicity" and "relic" of lines 13 and 14? Why should these "sleep" (see also line 7)? What is meant by the "absolute, incorrigible sunrise" of line 15?

DENISE LEVERTOV (1923–1997)

For a photo, see p. 654.

Hunting the Phoenix ⟩⟨⟩⟨⟩⟨ 1987

Leaf through discolored manuscripts,
make sure no words
lie thirsting, bleeding,
waiting for rescue. No:
old loves half-   5
articulated, moments forced
out of the stream of perception
to play 'statue',
and never released—
they had no blood to shed.   10
You must seek
the ashy nest itself
if you hope to find
charred feathers, smouldering flightbones,
and a twist of singing flame   15
rekindling.

QUESTIONS

1. What use is Levertov making here of the phoenix myth? How does the poem's
    organization make the references to the phoenix clear?

2. What is the speaker referring to that might be recorded in "discolored manu-
    scripts"? What might be the things that have "no blood to shed"?

3. Why, in the last six lines, does the speaker introduce a reference to "the ashy
    nest"? What is meant by the poem's advice to seek this nest? What is the promise
    if one does seek out the nest?

MAY SARTON (1912–1995)

The Phoenix° Again ⟩⟨⟩⟨⟩⟨ 1988

On the ashes of this nest
Love wove with deathly fire
The phoenix takes its rest
Forgetting all desire.

After the flame, a pause,   5
After the pain, rebirth.
Obeying nature's laws
The phoenix goes to earth.

You cannot call it old
You cannot call it young.   10
No phoenix can be told,
This is the end of song.

THE PHOENIX AGAIN. *Phoenix:* See the note to line 23 of John Donne's "The Canonization" (p. 897).

It struggles now alone
Against death and self-doubt,
But underneath the bone   15
The wings are pushing out.

And one cold starry night
Whatever your belief
The phoenix will take flight
Over the seas of grief   20

To hear her thrilling song
To stars and waves and sky
For neither old nor young
The phoenix does not die.

QUESTIONS

1.   What is the phoenix? What does it signify?

2.   What significance does the phoenix have for the speaker? What personal situation does the speaker seem to be describing? Why does the speaker invoke the details of the phoenix's return to life after death?

3.   Compare Sarton's use of the phoenix with the uses by Donne in "The Canonization" (p. 897) and Clampitt in "Berceuse" (p. 943).

❦ TWO POEMS RELATED TO THE MYTH OF OEDIPUS

For the story of Oedipus, see the introduction to *Oedipus the King* by Sophocles (Chapter 27).

The Great Sphinx, Gîza, Egypt. (Foto Marburg/Art Resource, New York, NY.)

POEMS FOR STUDY

MURIEL RUKEYSER (1913–1980)   *For a photo, see p. 745.*

Myth 1978

Long afterward, Oedipus, old and blinded, walked the
roads.   He smelled a familiar smell.   It was
the Sphinx.   Oedipus said, "I want to ask one question.
Why didn't I recognize my mother?"   "You gave the
wrong answer," said the Sphinx.   "But that was what   5
made everything possible," said Oedipus.   "No," she said.
"When I asked, What walks on four legs in the morning,
two at noon, and three in the evening, you answered,
Man.   You didn't say anything about woman."
"When you say Man," said Oedipus, "you include women   10
too. Everyone knows that."   She said, "That's what
you think."

QUESTIONS

1. Who was Oedipus? The Sphinx? According to this poem, what was wrong with
   Oedipus's answer to the Riddle of the Sphinx?
2. What elements and techniques in this work allow you to consider it a poem?
3. What two myths and meanings of *myth* are embodied in the title?
4. To what extent does the poem's colloquial language revitalize the mythic material?

JOHN UPDIKE (b. 1932)   *For a photo, see p. 339.*

On the Way to Delphi 1978

Oedipus slew his father near this muddy field
the bus glides by as it glides by many another,
and Helicon° is real; the Muses hid and dwelled
on a hill, less than a mountain, that we could climb
if the bus would stop and give us the afternoon.   5

ON THE WAY TO DELPHI. 3 *Helicon:* a mountain in southwestern Greece. In ancient Greek mythology,
Helicon was the home of the Nine Muses.

From these small sites, now overrun by roads and fame,
dim chieftains stalked into the world's fog and grew huge.
Where shepherds sang their mistaken kings, stray factories
mar with cement and smoke the lean geology
that wants to forget—*has* forgotten—the myths it bred. 10

We pass some slopes where houses, low, of stone, blend in
like utterings on the verge of sleep—accretions scarce
distinguishable from scree,° on the uphill way rocks, rubble
to architecture and law. No men are visible.
All out: Parnassus.° The oracle's voice is wild. 15

13 *scree:* piles of loose rock at the base of a mountain or hill.   15 *Parnassus:* a mountain sacred to Dionysus, Apollo, and the Muses. The geography of the poem indicates that the speaker's reflections take place
on a tour bus ride from Athens north and west to Delphi, which is at the foot of Mount Parnassus.

QUESTIONS

1. What is the situation of the speaker of this poem? Where is he? What is he doing? What prompts his observations about Oedipus and the sacred mountains of ancient Greece?

2. Why does the speaker observe that the field is "muddy" near where Oedipus killed his father?

3. In the second stanza, what prompts the contrast between the present and the mythical past? What does it mean to say that modern people have forgotten the ancient myths? What is symbolic about the low houses that are similar to "scree"?

✿ TWO POEMS RELATED TO THE MYTH OF PAN

Pan was the ancient Greek god of hunters, shepherds, country folk generally, and domestic animals. He was also a god of fertility and in this capacity was recognized for his lasciviousness. His name coincides with the Greek word meaning "all," and consequently he was sometimes given the attributes of a single, comprehensive, all-encompassing god. Because shepherds necessarily went far from home with their sheep, roaming woodlands, valleys, hills, and mountainsides, Pan was associated with distant, dangerous, and solitary locations, where shrines were built for him. Because of this association with shepherds and their life, he was visualized as having the body of a man but the horns, ears, thighs, tail, and legs of a goat. Shepherds, to divert themselves on their pastoral journeying, played a flute, called a syrinx, made up of seven reeds, and Pan was the reputed inventor of this instrument. He was called *Faunus* by the Romans, who celebrated a festival in his name each year in February (a month of purification). This was known as the *Lupercalia*, a festival held for general fertility. The festival also permitted a certain amount of license, for naked or lightly clad young men who held light whips cut from the skins of sacrificial goats would lash female spectators to ensure their fertility, all in the name of Pan or Faunus.

POEMS FOR STUDY

E. E. CUMMINGS (1894–1962)

For a photo, see p. 648.

in Just- 〜 〜 1923

in Just-
spring   when the world is mud-
luscious the little
lame balloonman

whistles   far   and wee   5

and eddieandbill come
running from marbles and
piracies and it's
spring

when the world is puddle-wonderful   10

the queer
old balloonman whistles
far   and   wee
and bettyandisbel come dancing

from hop-scotch and jump-rope and   15

it's
spring
and
    the
        goat-footed   20

balloonMan   whistles
far
and
wee

QUESTIONS

1. Who is the balloonman? What mythical figure does he represent? How do you know? What characteristics does this balloonman/balloonMan have? What does the balloonman's whistle symbolize?

2. Besides the balloonman, there are four other characters in the poem. Who are they? Why does Cummings run their names together? What impulses are acting on these characters that are regarded as attributable to Pan?

3. Read the poem aloud. Taking into account the spacing and alignment, how does the physical arrangement on the page influence your perceptions not only of the poem's content but also of its rhythm? *dark*

4. Explain the following as symbols: "spring," "mud-luscious," "puddle-wonderful," and "hop-scotch." *fertility growth*

JOHN CHIPMAN FARRAR (1896–1974)

Song for a Forgotten Shrine to Pan ✕✕✕ 1919

Come to me, Pan, with your wind-wild laughter,
  Where have you hidden your golden reed?
Pipe me a torrent of tune-caught madness,
  Come to me, Pan, in my lonely need

Where are the white-footed youths and the maidens,   5
  Garlanded, rosy-lipped, lyric with spring?
They tossed me poppies, tall lilies and roses
  And now but the winds their soft blown petals bring.

Where are the fauns and the nymphs and the satyrs?
  Where are the voices that sang in the trees?   10
Beauty has fled like a wind-startled nestling,
  Beauty, O Pan, and your sweet melodies.

Come to me! Come to me! God of mad music,
  Come to me, child of the whispering night.
Bring to all silences, torrents of music,   15
  People all shadows with garlands of light.

QUESTIONS

1. Why does the title indicate that the Shrine to Pan is "forgotten"? What does the speaker mean by "my lonely need" in line 4?

2. What attributes of Pan are brought out in the poem? Why does the speaker use the phrase "Come to me" five times in the poem? What does he yearn for?

3. Why does the poet introduce a rhythm involving two light stresses followed by a heavy stress (anapests)? How is this prevailing rhythm consistent with the poem's topic?

✿ WRITING ABOUT MYTHS IN POETRY

An essay on myths in poetry will normally connect the mythic material in a poem to some other element, such as speaker, character, action, tone, setting, situation, imagery, form, or meaning. This approach suggests a two-part exploration of the poem, one concerned with its general sense, and the other with the ways in which myths shape and control that sense.

As you study the poem, look for the ways in which myth enriches the poem and focuses its meaning. The following questions should be helpful to you.

Questions for Discovering Ideas

- To what extent does the title identify the mythic content of the poem and thus provide a key for understanding?

- How much of the poem's action, setting, and situation are borrowed from mythology? What is the significance of the action in the myth? What does this action symbolize? How does the poet reshape the action and its significance?

- To what extent does our understanding of the myth explain the poem's speaker, characters, situations, and ideas? What characters, including the speaker, are drawn from mythology?

- In what ways are these characters symbolic (see Chapter 17)? What aspects of this symbolism are carried into the poem? How does the poem either maintain or change the symbolism?

- How do the various formal elements of the poem, such as diction, rhyme, meter, and form, reshape the mythic material and affect the meaning and impact of the myth?

- How does the tone of the poem either reinforce or undercut the ideas and implications of the original myth? Cite specific words and phrases that lead you to your conclusions.

- Does the rhyme (if any) lead us to consider the mythic content as serious or comic?

- Generally, how does the mythic content help develop and clarify the poem?

Strategies for Organizing Ideas

A main challenge in writing about myths is to develop a focus or central idea. If, for example, you find that the poem retells a myth in order to make a point about history or society, you should fashion your major idea to reflect that connection. Similarly, if the poem employs a mythical speaker or character to convey ideas about war or heroism, your essay should focus on the links among myth, character, and those ideas.

When you formulate a central idea, draft it as a complete sentence that conveys the full scope of your ideas. It is not enough merely to assert that a given poem contains a great deal of mythic material. If you are writing about Yeats's "Leda and the Swan," for example, you might be tempted to form a central idea that argues, "Yeats's 'Leda and the Swan' retells the myth of Leda's rape by Zeus and the consequences of that event." That sentence does not tell the reader anything about the *way* the Leda myth works in the poem, nor does it provide a basis for any discussion beyond summary and paraphrase. A more effective formulation would be the following: "In Yeats's 'Leda and the Swan,' the myth of Leda's rape by Zeus and the consequences of that rape illustrate the process of history and also question the connection between knowledge and power." This sentence points to a specific connection between mythological content and the poem's effect, and it gives a shaping direction to the essay.

In your introductory paragraph or paragraphs, you should briefly summarize the significant parts of your poem's mythical elements, together with any noteworthy details about the poem's form or circumstances of composition. Your aim should be to focus on the poem (and the mythic material within the poem) rather than on the myth itself. Thus, you should link the mythical elements with other aspects of the poem and make assertions about the effects of this connection. To organize the body of your essay, you can employ various strategies like the following:

1. You might echo the organization of the poem, shaping the central paragraphs so as to reflect the poem's line-by-line or stanza-by-stanza logic.

2. You might choose an organization based on a series of different mythic elements or figures. For instance, if a poem alludes to Odysseus; his wife, Penelope; and his son, Telemachus, you might devote paragraphs to the way each figure shapes the poem's impact and meaning.

3. You might use the relevant elements of poetry as the focal points of organization. Thus, if you argue that diction, rhyme, and tone shape the mythological material to produce significant effects, you would deal with each element in turn.

To bring your essay to a convincing and assertive close, you might summarize your major points. At the same time, you might draw your reader's attention to the significance of your observations and to any further implications of the ways in which the myth is integrated into the poem you have studied.

DEMONSTRATIVE STUDENT ESSAY

Myth and Meaning in Dorothy Parker's "Penelope"°

[1]   Dorothy Parker's short lyric poem "Penelope" uses mythic allusion and symbolism to criticize conventional ideas about the roles of women and men. Her speaker is the mythic figure Penelope, the wife of King Odysseus of the ancient realm of Ithaca. Not only is Penelope the speaker, but she is also the poem's major figure. <u>Parker uses Penelope to assert that society has consistently misjudged and undervalued women's lives.</u>* <u>Parker's assertions are brought out through the poem's title, its mythic resonance, its diction, and its view of the representative lives of both Odysseus and Penelope.</u>†

[2]   <u>The key to the poem's use of myth is the title, "Penelope."</u> As the only place where the poem's mythological speaker is named, the title alludes to Homer's Odyssey, which tells that Penelope endures a twenty-year wait while her husband is at war and at sea. Her seemingly endless wait is filled with trouble. Her palace is occupied by boorish suitors who assume that Odysseus is dead and that his

---

°See p. 932 for this poem.
*Central idea.
†Thesis sentence.

kingship is vacant. They therefore demand that Penelope choose a new husband. Only Penelope and Telemachus, her son, cling to the hope that Odysseus is still alive. She keeps the arrogant suitors at bay by promising to marry one of them after she finishes weaving a shroud for Odysseus's father. To delay this event, she works at the loom by day and unravels the work by night.

[3] Although the title refers directly to Penelope, the poem itself also deals with Odysseus. Lines 1–5 evoke the king's adventures in Penelope's phrases "He shall ride the silver seas" (line 4) and "He shall cut the glittering wave" (line 5). Because Odysseus is not identified by name but only by the pronoun "he," readers might see this male figure as a symbol of all men who choose to lead their principal lives outside the home. The adjectives "silver" and "glittering" connote splendor and glory, while the verbs "ride" and "cut" suggest resoluteness and boldness. In addition, the phrases "pathway of the sun" (line 1) and "footsteps of the breeze" (line 2) add romance and mystery. In the same lines, however, one may perceive that the wife is providing a subtle undercutting of her absent husband's heroism. The phrase "ride the silver seas," for example, suggests that some of the Homeric lines are clichés. The implication is that an overglorified image of active heroes like Odysseus is both exaggerated and inaccurate.

[4] Just as this language has general implications for men, the language about Penelope herself is significant for women. In lines 6–9 she, as the speaker, contrasts the restrictedness of her life with the freedom of male lives. Here we find no adjectives at all; the woman's existence is thus rendered factually, without adornment of any sort. In addition, the verbs represent passive and domestic activities: "sit," "rock," "rise," "brew," "snip," and "bleach." These last two verbs are especially effective. The phrase "snip my thread" (line 8) is the only allusion to Penelope's unhappy existence. It refers to her daring deception of the suitors through her nightly unraveling of the shroud. At the same time, "snip" is contrasted with the verb "cut" used earlier in the poem. While the words are synonyms, their connotations are different because "cut" implies violence while "snip" suggests careful and delicate activity. "Bleach" is equally connotative. Although the word refers directly to "the linen for my bed," it is consistent with the view that the circumstances of Penelope's life are faded and colorless.

[5] The poem's final line ironically clarifies Penelope's attitude toward the different roles of men and women. Penelope asserts, "They will call him brave." "They" refers to society, to the world at large, and to generations of readers who have admired Odysseus in Homer's Iliad and Odyssey. The meter of the line--a concluding spondee--places a great emphasis on the word him, thus demonstrating the speaker's realization, and the poet's assertion, that society ignores or dismisses the quiet bravery of women. In myth and in life, the woman's role demands just as much courage and conviction as the man's.

[6] "Penelope" thus employs mythic figures and events to criticize the historical perception of the roles of men and women. Odysseus, the mythical and typical male, is presented as a heroic figure, but he too is human, and his adventures are tinged with overdramatization. Parker's point is not to demean him, however, but rather to emphasize that women, too, have their own heroism. Biology and destiny may have traditionally confined women at home to keep house and to weave tapestries while men are granted the freedom to find adventure in far-off lands. But waiting at home while meeting domestic challenges takes courage too. Penelope and Odysseus lived at a time of the old ways, but if Parker's poem is understood properly, it is time for new ways to begin. Penelope is right to express annoyance

and irony when considering the judgment of history. Our knowledge of her courageous survival in Ithaca during the absence of Odysseus adds significantly to the
truth and depth of her feelings.

WORK CITED

Parker, Dorothy. "Penelope." <u>Literature: An Introduction to Reading and Writing</u>.
Ed. Edgar V. Roberts and Henry E. Jacobs. 7th ed. Upper Saddle River:
Prentice Hall, 2004. 932.

Commentary on the Essay

This essay shows how the poet uses the Penelope–Odysseus myth to shed new
light on conventional attitudes about men and women. As a guide for your own
writing aims, therefore, the essay illustrates how the mythological material can
lead to ideas for development.

Athough the body of the essay follows the organization of the poem itself,
it is not a summary of the poem. Thus, paragraph 2 focuses on the title, paragraph 3 on lines 1–5, paragraph 4 on lines 6–9, and paragraph 5 on the last line.
Each of the paragraphs also advances a specific aspect of the essay's central idea.
In paragraph 2, Penelope is identified and the relevant mythic material is reviewed. The information in this paragraph is logically necessary for the remainder of the essay.

In paragraph 3, the title and its mythic importance introduce Odysseus
and the symbol of the heroic male. Here, the point is that Parker's diction for
her speaker undercuts the active male image while seeming to glorify it. The
first sentence of paragraph 4 provides a transition from Odysseus and heroic
males to Penelope and the perceived passiveness of women. Again, the essay explores the way Parker's diction and mythic allusion demonstrate that there is
more to the lives of women than usually is claimed. Paragraph 5 looks at the
poem's final line in relation to the contrasted lives of "heroic" men and "passive"
women. Here, the essay shows how tone and meter reveal the speaker's attitude
toward these contrasting lives and society's misperception of them.

The conclusion goes quickly over the essay's basic points, and it emphasizes how the poem, with its ancient myth, brings new light to a traditional problem. In paragraph 6 the writer has concluded with some brief comments that
deal with the poem's ideas and their current importance.

Special Topics for Writing and Argument about Myths in Poetry

1. In Atwood's "Siren Song," Glück's "Penelope's Song," Merwin's "Odysseus,"
    Parker's "Penelope," Pastan's "The Suitor," Tennyson's "Ulysses," and Ulisse's
    "Odyssey: 20 Years Later," the poets evoke the same myth but for different pur-
    poses. What are these purposes? What views do you find about adventure, do-
    mesticity, and sexuality? What attitudes toward figures in the myth (Odysseus,

Penelope, Calypso, the Sirens, Circe) do the poets bring out? How do word choice, selection of detail, and point of view influence each poet's conclusions?

2. The myth of Icarus is used by Aldiss, Auden, Field, Rukeyser, Sexton, Spender, and Williams. Basing your conclusions on two or more of the poems in this group, what similarities and differences can you describe? How do the poets present the myth? How do they use the myth to create unusual or surprising endings, and to comment on contemporary but also permanent attitudes about life and the sufferings of others?

3. What point does Rukeyser's "Myth" make about both men and women and their attitudes toward each other? How does our knowledge of the Oedipus myth (see Sophocles' play *Oedipus the King* [Chapter 27]) help clarify these aspects of the poem? In what respects is the poem contemporary?

4. Compare and contrast (a) the use of the phoenix myth by Clampitt, Levertov, and Sarton, or (b) the use of the mythology of the god Pan by Cummings and Farrar.

5. In your library, choose a book on myths, such as Kenneth McLeish, *Myth: Myths and Legends of the World Explored* (1996), or Richard Erdoes and Alfonso Ortiz, *American Indian Myths and Legends* (1984). Select a story from among the many myths described there (e.g., Oedipus, Jason, Prometheus, Antigone, Sisyphus, Beaver stealing fire from the Pines, Coyote placing the stars, A Tale of Elder Brother). To these you might add biblical stories (e.g., the fight between God and Satan, Noah, Leviathan, Joseph and his brothers, the Hebrew captivity in Egypt, the Exodus, the Babylonian captivity) and other legends and actual historical stories (Robin Hood, Paul Bunyan, Davy Crockett, the Amistad event, the forty-niners, the Civil War, the Lone Ranger, the log cabin, the Rough Riders, etc.). Write a poem based on the story you choose. Try to present your own view about the importance, timeliness, intelligence, and truth of your story. What kinds of detail do you select? How do you give the figures mythic status? How do you make your own attitudes apparent by your arrangement of detail and your word choice?

Meaning: *Idea and Theme in Poetry*

[handwritten annotations: Idea refers to the result of general & abstract thinking. Motif – something that moves –]

When we talk about understanding poetry, we frequently use the words *idea, theme, motif,* and *meaning* (see also Chapter 10). Usually **idea** refers to a *concept, principle, scheme, method,* or *plan.* An idea may yield to extensive description and definition, such as the *idea of goodness,* the *idea of time,* and so on. When we use the word **theme** we refer to an idea, image, principle, or **motif** that, like a melody in music, is embodied, repeated, and developed within a literary work.

Going up the scale from idea, theme, and motif, we arrive at **meaning,** the word referring comprehensively to the ideas expressed within the poem—the poem's sense or message. For example, in the poem "Daffodils" (Chapter 24) Wordsworth begins with a description of how on a walk he saw large numbers ("a host") of daffodils blooming "beside a lake, beneath the trees." He goes on to describe his impressions upon seeing daffodils in bloom, and, at the poem's end, he points out how the remembered vision of this scene gives him spiritual joy and comfort.

For oft, when on my couch I lie
In vacant or in pensive mood,
They flash upon that inward eye
Which is the bliss of solitude;
And then my heart with pleasure fills,
And dances with the daffodils. (lines 19–24)

By drawing general conclusions about his experience in this way, Wordsworth develops his theme and brings out the idea that intimate contact with natural scenes provides energy and creative renewal for his mind and spirit.

❦ MEANING, POWER, AND POETIC THOUGHT

Poetry achieves much of its power through the expression of ideas. Such power is shown in Dryden's "A Song for St. Cecilia's Day," an ode, written in 1687, that

[handwritten marginal note: Friday 1/2 hrs, Saturday 1¼ hrs, Sunday – 1½, Monday – 3 hr, Tuesday 3 hr, Wed 3 hr]

[handwritten: 96⁵]

exalts music, harmony, and the divine creation. Dryden's complex ideas are based on analogy and comparison, starting with the belief that in the very beginning of time (which was thought to be much more recent in his day than in ours), the divine principles of order and harmony created the universe out of a primeval chaos of "jarring atoms." Expanding this idea by analogy, Dryden asserts that the earthly counterpart of this creative heavenly harmony is music. In other words, just as harmony is the principle that began the "universal frame" of creation, so musical harmony is the principle that creates order and civilization on earth. In both the past and the present, then, harmony has been essential to human life and all life. It will be similarly essential in the future and even beyond, for musical harmony will continue triumphantly throughout eternity after our visible universe ends. These ideas combine biblical theology, late-seventeenth-century science, Dryden's understanding of music and musical instruments, and his reasoning based on analogy. For this reason the poem may not seem up to date by modern standards. However, we might consider that the discovery of universal principles of order has always been sought by scientists from Pythagoras to Newton to Einstein to Hubble, and that order and regularity are postulates of musical theory and composition. Dryden's idea about the vitality of harmony is therefore still current and contemporary, and his emphasis on this idea makes the poem both true and powerful. Modern readers can still learn from reading "A Song for St. Cecilia's Day" and can still be inspired by it.

This example also introduces the fact that poetry involves a unique form of thinking. Usually the direct presentation of ideas is concerned with organization, method, science, instruction, and reasoning and logic. Poetry is at once all and none of these things. It is both organized and methodical, but it usually advocates neither organization nor method; it is distant from science, but it often incorporates scientific details (see David Wagoner's "My Physics Teacher" [Chapter 18] and Donne's "A Valediction: Forbidding Mourning" [Chapter 17]); it is always instructive even though pleasure, not instruction, is its primary aim; and it establishes patterns that follow reason and logic even though it is not primarily ratiocinative or logical. It is true that poetry benefits from the thinking processes necessary for discursive prose (such as reports, articles, and persuasive speeches); its underlying thinking processes are additionally linked with association, suggestion, indirection, implication, analogy, metaphor, symbol, paradox, and ambiguity.

Expressing ideas is only one of a number of poetic aims, for poems may take the shape of narration, description, dialogue, observation, persuasive speech, self-analysis, confession, imaginary situations, and much else. In this respect, poetry as an instrument for ideas is like both music and painting. Music expresses ideas through complex melodic development, instrumentation, key, harmony or disharmony, and dynamics. Painting relies on ranges of color, light and shadow, action, expression, and arrangement. Both music and painting depend on nonlogical, nonverbal types of thought. Because poetry employs words, it is similar to more discursive presentations of ideas. But it is unique because it is an art form, and a poet controls words and ideas within the poem just as a painter controls paint on the canvas to make a meaningful picture, or a composer controls individual notes to create meaningful music.

❦ ISSUES IN DETERMINING THE MEANING OF POEMS

Our Understandings May Be Restricted by Time

A major issue in understanding poetic meaning lies in the nature of poetry it-self: Poetry, like all literature and also like music, is a *time art*. Each poem's de-veloping meaning depends on the poem itself, our interaction with it, and the passage of time. Naturally, our power of absorption sometimes lags. The early lines recede in our minds as we encounter the new words, images, ideas, sym-bols, sounds, and rhythms of later and concluding lines. The result is that we cannot express the poem's meaning comprehensively at a given single moment.

Personal Concerns May Divert Our Attention

Our own concerns and preoccupations also influence the impact that poems may have on us. We may not always be ready to reach out to the poem we are reading. Almost without warning, parts that we think we understand escape our compre-hension, and lines that we may have read inattentively yesterday burst upon us with great meaning and power today. As a public example of this fact, former pres-ident Dwight D. Eisenhower once introduced a new legislative proposal by quot-ing the following couplet from *An Essay on Criticism* by Alexander Pope.

Be not the first by whom the new are tried,
Nor yet the last to lay the old aside.

Everyone who studies Pope's poem reads these lines, which refer to the need for being cautious about immediately forsaking old approaches and accepting new ones. But President Eisenhower—or more likely someone on his staff—thought the lines provided a meaningful justification for new legislation. Here we have a clear example of how meaning may emerge as time and circumstance change.

The Uniqueness and Autonomy of Poetry Limit Our Interpretive Power

When we interpret a poem for its meaning, it is important to recognize the lim-itations of our effort. What we say about a poem is no more than that. It demon-strates our own perception and understanding, but only the poem itself contains its *entire* meaning. Individual poems are made up of separate parts, each part with its own meaning, and the various parts together make up the whole, so that the poem is an artifact intricately connected to the poet's mind, the circumstances of composition, and the historical period of the poem's ori-gin. As we continue to raise questions about individual poems—as one of the best ways to understand them—we recognize that our understanding often falls short of our efforts to comprehend and explain.

Yet even after we complete our analysis and determine what we consider to be a poem's meaning, the poem is still independent. Consider the conclusion of Keats's "Ode on a Grecian Urn," some of the most frequently quoted lines in poetry.

When old age shall this generation waste,
   Thou shalt remain, in midst of other woe
Than ours, a friend to man, to whom thou say'st,
"Beauty is truth, truth beauty,"—that is all
   Ye know on earth, and all ye need to know.

The meaning of these lines has been analyzed and discussed ever since Keats wrote them. Their meaning will continue to be discussed as long as people read and talk about poetry, yet it still eludes us even as we feel that we know what it means (see also p. 982). Perhaps no other passage so clearly shows that poems always possess their own identity and integrity. Poetic meaning is like the dancer who was once asked why she danced. Her response was that if she could explain her reasons in words, she would no longer need to dance. In other words, no matter how well we follow a poem's intricate themes or motifs, or how comprehensively we determine its meaning, the poem is still out there—dancing.

MEANING AND POETIC TECHNIQUES

Even if we grant the unlikelihood of grasping a poem's entire meaning at a single instant, there is still much that we can do to increase our understanding. We can study each poem's ideas and relate these ideas to the intellectual and emotional impact of the poem. In effect, meaning involves us in a transfer of thought and experience from the poet's mind to our own, for reading poetry is a cooperative venture between poet and reader. It is no exaggeration to say that the structure and development of a poem are intended to produce a corresponding development of thoughts, reactions, considerations, and emotions in readers. To get at meaning is to get at all the ways in which poetry brings these effects about.

An initial understanding of meaning can be gained by a close, sentence-by-sentence reading. But for most poems the meaning emerges as a result of comprehending not only the direct statements but also the results of the poet's technique. In other chapters we have studied many of the elements of technique that the poet uses: those of speaker; character, setting and action; diction; imagery and figures of speech; tone; rhythm, meter, sound, and rhyme; structure and form; and symbol and allusion. A brief reminder of the techniques may be helpful here.

The Speaker Provides a Starting Point for Our Understanding of a Poem

It is important that we learn the identity and circumstances of the speaker (see Chapter 15). The speaker of Hardy's "Channel Firing"(Chapter 16), for example, is a skeleton who has been wakened in his grave by the noise of battleship guns being fired on the nearby sea. The speaker in Olds's "35/10" is a mother brushing her daughter's hair. The attitudes and ironies so essential to the meanings of these poems would not be clear if we did not know who these speakers are and what they are doing at the "time" the action of the poems is occurring. Similarly, we need to know whether a speaker is trustworthy or untrustworthy. The speaker of "next to of course god america i" by Cummings (Chapter 14), for example, demonstrates his unreliability because he voices nothing but political platitudes. Without knowing it, he is funny, because Cummings makes the speaker's words parody the occasional speeches of politicians from the earliest times to our own. As these various examples show, each poem contains its own unique speaker, whose character has a vital bearing on poetic content and meaning.

Character, Setting, and Action Are Dramatic Elements of Meaning

Here are three important elements to observe and to study, for all of these can be considered as parts of the drama of poetry. A poem describing the painted scenes on an ancient Greek vase (Keats's "Ode on a Grecian Urn"), for example, conveys a different meaning from one giving details about a walk through the woodland in spring (Housman's "Loveliest of Trees" [Chapter 14]) or one that tells about an adult speaker searching the shadows of memory for a vision of dead childhood friends (Justice's "On the Death of Friends in Childhood"). All three of these poems introduce the subject of death, but their radically different contexts and actions produce a new perspective, a different emotional response, a new experience, and a different meaning.

The Selection of Words Shapes Our Perception of Ideas

The words of a poem—denotation, connotation, and syntax (see Chapter 14)— are basic to a poem's total meaning and impact. In Robert Herrick's "To the Virgins, to Make Much of Time," for example, the speaker advises virgins to gather "rosebuds," which could easily be interpreted as an invitation to promiscuous sexuality. However, the poem concludes on the advice to "go marry," and thereby it places the urgency of sex in the context of socially and religiously approved behavior. By contrast, in Ben Jonson's "To Celia," the speaker urges "sports of love" and "love's fruit" but provides no additional context. Thus the diction of "To Celia" primarily stresses seduction, while the diction of "To the Virgins" provides happy but mature advice about life, even though both poems belong to the *carpe diem* ("seize the day") tradition of love poetry.

Imagery and Figures of Speech Provide an Interpretative Basis of Ideas

Imagery, metaphor, simile, and other figures of speech (see Chapters 16 and 17) make abstract ideas and situations concrete and immediate. We have stressed how Keats creates the excitement of discovery through his simile of the "watcher of the skies" in "On First Looking into Chapman's Homer" (Chapter 17). Beyond such uses, a poet may introduce imagery and metaphorical language to reinforce or to negate what appears to be the speaker's major thrust. In Owen's "Dulce et Decorum Est," for example (Chapter 18), soldiers are described as "Bent double, like old beggars under sacks." The simile is consistent with the rest of the poem;

it defines the speaker's abhorrence of the destructiveness of war, and it shapes the poem's sense that war is humiliating, dehumanizing, and vicious.

The Tone of a Poem Enables Us to Measure and Balance Ideas

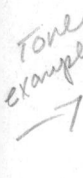

A poem's tone (see Chapter 18) has a significant effect on the ways in which we perceive its ideas, as in "On the Death of Friends in Childhood" by Justice, where the sentences "We shall not ever meet them" and "let us seek them there in the shadows" show the speaker's unambiguous sorrow and regret over the loss of childhood friends and the potentially rewarding experience they might have offered him. Tone may sometimes create ambiguity, however, or it may even work against the stated purpose of the speaker, as in the duke's mentioning the marriage settlement in "My Last Duchess" (Chapter 15). The duke speaks of the count's "known munificence" as justification for his "just" claims, while we conclude that the duke will make confiscatory demands. Through irony, therefore, Browning shows the duke's smugness, cruelty, and inhumanity.

Prosody (Meter, Sound, and Rhyme) Distinguishes and Emphasizes Ideas

Prosodic devices are integral aspects of poetic meaning (see Chapter 19). Rhythm and meter are often controlled to emphasize important words and therefore to shape our perception of major ideas. In Dorothy Parker's "Penelope" (Chapter 22) the concluding line is "They will call him brave." The meter literally demands a strong accent on "him," thus underscoring the poem's powerful irony (i.e., "They will call *him* brave [but not me, even though I have been equally brave]"). Rhyme and other segmental effects may be employed to point up ideas, regulate the tone, and thus shape meaning. The strong, single-word rhymes in the final stanza of Larkin's "Next, Please," for example ("black," "back"; "wake," "break"), are integrated with heavy alliteration (the *b* and *br* sounds) and concluding palatal stops (the *k* sounds) to bring the poem to a powerful conclusion. The employment of such effects, in fact, is one of the best single poetic techniques for helping readers' memories, and therefore for both establishing and emphasizing ideas.

Structure and Form Permit Us to Follow the Development of Ideas

The form of a poem (see Chapter 20) orders and shapes its developing meaning. The units or stanzas usually reflect specific steps in a poetic argument or in the logical buildup from details to ideas. Such is the case in Dryden's "A Song for St. Cecilia's Day." In this closed-form ode, with stanzas of irregular length depending on the subject, the ideas begin with Dryden's opening paean to heavenly harmony and grow toward the concluding tribute to the universal and cosmological power of music. In Judith Viorst's open-form poem "True Love," the stanzas wryly complement the poem's movement from marital irritations and frustrations to the assertion of the meaning of "true love."

JUDITH VIORST (b. 1931)

open form

For a photo, see p. 911.

True Love 1968

Stanza

It is true love because
I put on eyeliner and a concerto and make pungent observations about the great issues
    of the day
Even when there's no one here but him,
And because
I do not resent watching the Green Bay Packers   5
Even though I am philosophically opposed to football,
And because
When he is late for dinner and I know he must be either having an affair or lying dead
    in the middle of the street,
I always hope he's dead.

It's true love because   10
If he said quit drinking martinis but I kept drinking them and the next morning I
    couldn't get out of bed,
He wouldn't tell me he told me,
And because
He is willing to wear unironed undershorts
Out of respect for the fact that I am philosophically opposed to ironing,   15
And because
If his mother was drowning and I was drowning and he had to choose one of us to save,
He says he'd save me.

It's true love because
When he went to San Francisco on business while I had to stay home with the painters   20
    and the exterminator and the baby who was getting the chicken pox,
He understood why I hated him,
And because
When I said that playing the stock market was juvenile and irresponsible and then the
    stock I wouldn't let him buy went up twenty-six points,
I understood why he hated me,
And because   25
Despite cigarette cough, tooth decay, acid indigestion, dandruff, and other features of
    married life that tend to dampen the fires of passion,
We still feel something
We can call
True love.

TRUE LOVE. See Shakespeare's *A Midsummer Night's Dream*, 1.1.132: "The course of true love never did
run smooth."

QUESTIONS

1. What does the poet mean by "true love"?

2. What situations described here are antiromantic? What importance do they have
in the speaker's idea of the wife–husband relationship?

3. What comic situations and statements does the poem contain? How do these elements contribute to the poem's tone and meaning?

4. Explain why lines 2, 8, 11, 17, 20, 23, and 26 are the poem's longest lines. In what ways is the meaning of these lines contrasted with the meaning of the shorter lines?

Symbol, Allusion, and Myth Broaden the Scope of a Poem's Ideas

Poets employ symbol and allusion, and they use mythical materials (see Chapters 21 and 22) as a shorthand way of conveying complex ideas and a great deal of information as quickly and economically as possible. For instance, in Herrick's "To the Virgins, to Make Much of Time," two symbols—rosebuds and flowers—point beyond themselves to youth and the brevity of life as well as to sexuality, marriage, family, and full involvement in life. Allusion can be equally important, as in Marvell's "To His Coy Mistress," where we find that geographic and biblical allusions are integral to the poem's developing argument. The use of myth puts poems in a broad historical context. Poems devoted entirely to mythical subjects, such as Parker's "Penelope" and Field's "Icarus" (Chapter 22), may render unexpected insights into human problems. Even a brief reference to a myth, such as Dryden's lines about Orpheus in "A Song for St. Cecilia's Day," serve to introduce complex thoughts and enrich the total meaning of a poem.

Admittedly, these topics form a large number of variables to consider when you study each poem's central idea and meaning. However, with increasing experience as a disciplined reader, you will do much of this step-by-step analysis naturally and routinely. A point to remember about analyzing poetic meaning is that you can draw upon your available knowledge to develop your understanding.

POEMS FOR STUDY

ROBERT CREELEY (b. 1926)

"Do you think . . ."   1972

Do you think that if
you once do what you want
to do you will want not to do it.

Do you think that if
there's an apple on the table   5
and somebody eats it, it
won't be there anymore.

Do you think that if
two people are in love with one another,
one or the other has got to be   10
less in love than the other at
some point in the otherwise happy relationship.

Do you think that if
you once take a breath, you're by
that committed to taking the next one   15
and so on until the very process of
breathing's an endlessly expanding need
almost of its own necessity forever.

Do you think that if
no one knows then whatever   20
it is, no one will know and
that will be the case, like
they say, for an indefinite
period of time if such time
can have a qualification of such time.   25

Do you know anyone,
really. Have you been, really,
much alone. Are you lonely,
now, for example. Does anything
really matter to you, really, or   30
has anything mattered. Does each
thing tend to be there, and then not
to be there, just as if that were it.

Do you think that if
I said, *I love you*, or anyone   35
said it, or you did. Do you
think that if you had all
such decisions to make and could
make them. Do you think that
if you did. That you really   40
would have to think it all into
reality, that world, each time, new.

QUESTIONS

1. Even though each of the stanzas of this poem begins with a question, why does the poet not include question marks?

2. Are the questions to be considered as riddles, or as statements? How difficult is the language and punctuation in this poem, as in the final nine lines?

3. Write a brief essay dealing with the issues in one of the stanzas. Stanza 3, for example, considers the question of degrees of love. What is the idea of this stanza (or any of the stanzas)? What light does the stanza shed on your thinking about the subject?

CARL DENNIS (b. 1939)

The God Who Loves You ⤙⤚ 2001

<pre>
It must be troubling for the god who loves you
To ponder how much happier you'd be today
Had you been able to glimpse your many futures.
It must be painful for him to watch you on Friday evenings
Driving home from the office, content with your week—   5
Three fine houses sold to deserving families—
Knowing as he does exactly what would have happened
Had you gone to your second choice for college,
Knowing the roommate you'd have been allotted
Whose ardent opinions on painting and music   10
Would have kindled in you a lifelong passion.
A life thirty points above the life you're living
On any scale of satisfaction. And every point
A thorn in the side of the god who loves you.
You don't want that, a large-souled man like you   15
Who tries to withhold from your wife the day's disappointments
So she can save her empathy for the children.
And would you want this god to compare your wife
With the woman you were destined to meet on the other campus?
It hurts you to think of him ranking the conversation   20
You'd have enjoyed over there higher in insight
Than the conversation you're used to.
And think how this loving god would feel
Knowing that the man next in line for your wife
Would have pleased her more than you ever will   25
Even on your best days, when you really try.
Can you sleep at night believing a god like that
Is pacing his cloudy bedroom, harassed by alternatives
You're spared by ignorance? The difference between what is
And what could have been will remain alive for him   30
Even after you cease existing, after you catch a chill
Running out in the snow for the morning paper,
Losing eleven years that the god who loves you
Will feel compelled to imagine scene by scene
</pre>

Unless you come to the rescue by imagining him   35
No wiser than you are, no god at all, only a friend
No closer than the actual friend you made at college,
The one you haven't written in months. Sit down tonight
And write him about the life you can talk about
With a claim to authority, the life you've witnessed,   40
Which for all you know is the life you've chosen.

QUESTIONS

1. Who is the speaker? What is he like? How do you know? What sort of life has the
    listener led? What other kinds of lives might he have led?

2. What is the poem's topic? What ideas is the speaker presenting? To what degree
    are these ideas perplexing, or perhaps even frustrating? What is achieved by the
    considering such ideas?

3. Explain the following lines: "The difference between what is / And what could
    have been will remain alive for him / Even after you cease existing, . . ." (lines
    29–31). What qualities of "the god who loves you" is the poem bringing out
    here?

JOHN DRYDEN (1631–1700)

A Song for St. Cecilia's Day°   1687

I

From harmony, from heavenly harmony
        This universal frame began:
    When Nature underneath a heap
            Of jarring atoms lay,
    And could not heave her head,
The tuneful voice was heard from high,   5
        "Arise, ye more than dead."
Then cold, and hot, and moist, and dry°
In order to their stations leap,
        And Music's pow'r obey.   10
From harmony, from heavenly harmony
        This universal frame began:
        From harmony to harmony
Through all the compass of the notes it ran,
The diapason° closing full in Man.°   15

SONG FOR ST. CECILIA'S DAY. *St. Cecilia:* St. Cecilia, the patron saint of music, was traditionally considered the creator of the pipe organ. In London after 1683, she was celebrated annually on November 22 by the performance of a poem set to orchestral and choral music. Dryden wrote two poems for the occasion: this one in 1687, and the longer "Alexander's Feast" in 1697. The best-known version of the "Song for St. Cecilia's Day" is by Georg Frederic Handel.   8 *cold . . . dry:* Before the modern classification of elements, it was supposed that there were four "elements" having four primary qualities: earth = cold, fire = hot, water = moist, and air = dry.   15 *diapason:* the organ stop determining keys and chords; thus, metaphorically, the quality that created and shaped humankind.   15 *Man:* the human race.

II

What passion cannot Music raise and quell!
 When Jubal° struck the corded shell,
 His listening brethren stood around,
 And, wondering, on their faces fell
 To worship that celestial sound: 20
Less than a god they thought there could not dwell
 Within the hollow of that shell,
 That spoke so sweetly and so well.
What passion cannot Music raise and quell!

III

 The trumpet's loud clangor   25
  Excites us to arms
 With shrill notes of anger
  And mortal alarms.
 The double double double beat
  Of the thundering drum   30
Cries, "Hark! the foes come;
Charge, charge, 'tis too late to retreat."

IV

 The soft complaining flute
 In dying notes discovers
 The woes of hopeless lovers,   35
Whose dirge is whispered by the warbling lute.

V

 Sharp violins proclaim
Their jealous pangs, and desperation,
Fury, frantic indignation,
Depth of pains, and height of passion   40
 For the fair, disdainful dame.

VI

 But O! what art can teach,
 What human voice can reach
The sacred organ's praise?
 Notes inspiring holy love,   45
Notes that wing their heavenly ways
 To mend the choirs above.

VII

Orpheus° could lead the savage race
And trees unrooted left their place,

17 *Jubal:* "the father of all such as handle the harp and organ" (Genesis 4:21). 48 *Orpheus:* in Greek myth, the
greatest of all musicians. His playing tamed wild animals, and trees uprooted themselves to go and hear him.

Sequacious of the lyre;   50
But bright Cecilia raised the wonder higher:
When to her organ vocal breath was given,
An angel heard, and straight appeared,
   Mistaking earth for heaven.

GRAND CHORUS

As from the power of sacred lays   55
 The spheres began to move,
And sung the great Creator's praise
 To all the blessed above;
So, when the last and dreadful hour
This crumbling pageant shall devour   60
The trumpet shall be heard on high,
The dead shall live, the living die,
And Music shall untune the sky.°

63 *And Music shall untune the sky:* The harmony of the sky (i.e., heavenly harmony) will be replaced eternally by musical harmony.

QUESTIONS

1. What is the central idea of "A Song for St. Cecilia's Day"? In light of this idea, what is the major attribute of the creator God (whom Dryden does not specifically mention)? Why does the angel mistake earth for heaven (stanza VII)? How is this example related to the poem's major idea?

2. Through what attribute is music related to the created universal order? How is music analogous to the ordering principles of creation? How long will music continue to exist? Why?

3. What powers are attributed to the various instruments? When is vocal music introduced? What is its effect?

4. Should Dryden's ideas in the poem be considered outdated? To what degree are the ideas still important and valid?

DONALD HALL (b. 1928)

Whip-poor-will   1981

As the last light
of June withdraws
the whip-poor-will sings
his clear brief notes

by the darkening house, then   5
rises abruptly from sandy
ground, a brown bird

in the near-night, soaring
over shed and woodshed
to far dark fields. When
he returns at dawn,   10
in my sleep I hear
his three syllables make
a man's name, who slept
fifty years in this bed   15
and ploughed these fields:
Wes-ley-Wells° . . . *Wes-*
ley-Wells . . .
            It is good
to wake early in high
summer with work to do,   20
and look out the window
at a ghost bird lifting away
to drowse all morning
in his grassy hut.   25

WHIP-POOR-WILL. 17 *Wes-ley-Wells:* the name of the poet's grandfather.

QUESTIONS

1. What is a whippoorwill? How does its song figure into the poem's development?
    Why does the speaker stress that he hears the name *Wesley Wells* not when waking
    but when asleep?

2. Who was Wesley Wells? What connection is established between him and the
    home and life of the speaker?

3. Why is so much attention given to the flying and singing habits of the bird?

4. How comparable is this poem to Keats's "Ode to a Nightingale" (p. 868)? How
    do birds and their songs serve to bring out major ideas in both poems?

ROBERT HERRICK (1591–1674)

To the Virgins, to Make Much of Time   1648

Gather ye rosebuds while ye may,
    Old time is still a-flying;
And this same flower that smiles today
    Tomorrow will be dying.

The glorious lamp of heaven, the sun,   5
    The higher he's a-getting,
The sooner will his race be run,
    And nearer he's to setting.

That age is best which is the first,
    When youth and blood are warmer;   10
But being spent, the worse, and worst
    Times still succeed the former.

Then be not coy, but use your time,
  And, while ye may, go marry;
For, having lost but once your prime,   15
  You may forever tarry.

QUESTIONS

1. What does the title of this poem tell us? What can we deduce about the speaker? To whom is the poem addressed?

2. What point does this poem make about time? Life? Love?

3. How does symbolism help shape the message and meaning of the poem? Consider especially "rosebuds," "flower," and "the sun."

4. How do rhyme and tone help create and focus the meaning of this poem?

5. This type of poem is called *carpe diem* (Latin for "seize the day" or "enjoy the present"). Compare this poem with Jonson's "To Celia" and Marvell's "To His Coy Mistress," which are also *carpe diem* poems. How are the tone and message of this poem similar to and different from those in the poems by Jonson and Marvell?

LANGSTON HUGHES (1902–1967)   *For a photo, see p. 1608.*

The Negro Speaks of Rivers   1926

I've known rivers:
I've known rivers ancient as the world and older than the flow of human blood in
    human veins.

My soul has grown deep like the rivers.

I bathed in the Euphrates when dawns were young.
I built my hut near the Congo and it lulled me to sleep.   5

I looked upon the Nile and raised the pyramids above it.
I heard the singing of the Mississippi when Abe Lincoln went down to New Orleans,
    and I've seen its muddy bosom turn all golden in the sunset.

I've known rivers:
Ancient, dusky rivers.

My soul has grown deep like the rivers.   10

QUESTIONS

1. What does the speaker mean by stating that his soul has grown deep like the rivers? Does the speaker refer to himself individually, or to his race collectively, or to both?

2. What is meant by the citation of the Euphrates, the Congo, the Nile, and the Mississippi? To what civilizations does the speaker refer? What idea about the history of blacks is implied by these rivers?

3. How do the repeated and echoed lines (8–10 repeating and echoing 1–3) affect your understanding of the poem's ideas? Why does the poet conclude the poem in this way?

BEN JONSON (1572–1632)

To Celia°   1606

Come my Celia, let us prove,°	*try*
While we may, the sports of love;	
Time will not be ours forever;	
He at length our good will sever.	
Spend not then his gifts in vain.	5
Suns that set may rise again;	
But if once we lose this light,	
'Tis with us perpetual night,	
Why should we defer our joys?	
Fame° and rumor are but toys.	*reputation* 10
Cannot we delude the eyes	
Of a few poor household spies,	
Or his° easier ears beguile,	*Celia's husband*
So removed by our wile?	
'Tis no sin love's fruit to steal;	15
But the sweet theft to reveal,	
To be taken, to be seen,	
These have crimes accounted been.	

TO CELIA. The poem is from Jonson's play *Volpone:* it is spoken by Volpone (the name means "the fox") to Celia, a married woman whom he is trying to seduce.

QUESTIONS

1. What is the speaker like? What is his attitude toward time? Love? Celia?
2. What is personified in lines 3–5? What power does this force have?
3. How is the idea of "seizing the day" relevant to the first eight lines of this poem?
4. How does the speaker's argument change in the last ten lines? What assertions does the poem make about time, love, reputation, and crime?
5. What is the tone of the poem? How does it affect the meaning?

DONALD JUSTICE (b. 1925)

On the Death of Friends in Childhood   1960

We shall not ever meet them bearded in heaven,
Nor sunning themselves among the bald of hell;
If anywhere, in the deserted schoolyard at twilight,
Forming a ring, perhaps, or joining hands
In games whose very names we have forgotten,   5
Come, memory, let us seek them there in the shadows.

QUESTIONS

1. What is the subject of this poem: the living, or the dead? How accurate is the title as a guide to subject and theme?
2. What point (if any) does this poem make about death? Time? Memory? The living?

3. How do imagery, diction, rhetoric and tone contribute to the total meaning of this poem? Consider phrases like "bearded in heaven" and "sunning themselves among the bald of hell." What is personified in the last line?

"The Krater of Thanagra," fourth century b.c.e., showing a wedding procession and musicians. National Museum, Athens, Greece. Alinari/Art Resource, New York, NY.

JOHN KEATS (1795–1821)   *For a drawing, see p. 728.*

Ode on a Grecian Urn° ⌒⌒⌒⌒ *1820 (1819)*

1

Thou still unravish'd bride of quietness,
    Thou foster-child of silence and slow time,
Sylvan historian, who canst thus express
A flowery tale more sweetly than our rhyme:

ODE ON A GRECIAN URN. The imaginary Grecian urn to which the poem is addressed combines design motifs from many different existing urns. This imaginary one is decorated with a border of leaves and trees, men (or gods) chasing women, a young musician sitting under a tree, lovers, and a priest and congregation leading a heifer to sacrifice.

What leaf-fring'd legend° haunts about thy shape   *border and tale*   5
   Of deities or mortals, or of both,
      In Tempe° or the dales of Arcady?°
   What men or gods are these? What maidens loth?
What mad pursuit? What struggle to escape?
      What pipes and timbrels? What wild ecstasy?   10

2

Heard melodies are sweet, but those unheard
   Are sweeter; therefore, ye soft pipes, play on;
Not to the sensual ear, but, more endear'd,
   Pipe to the spirit ditties of no tone:
Fair youth, beneath the trees, thou canst not leave   15
   Thy song, nor ever can those trees be bare;
      Bold lover, never, never canst thou kiss,
Though winning near the goal—yet, do not grieve;
      She cannot fade, though thou hast not thy bliss,
      For ever wilt thou love, and she be fair!   20

3

Ah, happy, happy boughs! that cannot shed
   Your leaves, nor ever bid the spring adieu;
And, happy melodist, unwearied,
   For ever piping songs for ever new;
More happy love! more happy, happy love!   25
   For ever warm and still to be enjoy'd,
      For ever panting, and for ever young;
All breathing human passion far above,
   That leaves a heart high-sorrowful and cloy'd,
      A burning forehead, and a parching tongue.   30

4

Who are these coming to the sacrifice?
   To what green altar, O mysterious priest,
Lead'st thou that heifer lowing at the skies,
   And all her silken flanks with garlands drest?
What little town by river or sea shore,   35
   Or mountain-built° with peaceful citadel,   *built on a mountain*
      Is emptied of this folk, this pious morn?
And, little town, thy streets for evermore
   Will silent be; and not a soul to tell
      Why thou art desolate, can e'er return.   40

5

O Attic shape! Fair attitude! with brede°   *braid, pattern*
   Of marble men and maidens overwrought,°   *ornamented*
With forest branches and the trodden weed;

7 *Tempe:* a beautiful rustic valley in Greece. *Arcady:* refers to the valleys of Arcadia, a state in ancient Greece known for its beauty and peacefulness.

Thou, silent form, dost tease us out of thought
As doth eternity: Cold Pastoral!   45
   When old age shall this generation waste,
      Thou shalt remain, in midst of other woe
   Than ours, a friend to man, to whom thou say'st,
"Beauty is truth, truth beauty,"—that is all
      Ye know on earth, and all ye need to know.   50

QUESTIONS

1. What is the dramatic situation? What does the speaker see and do?

2. What does the speaker call the urn in the first stanza? What is suggested in these lines about the urn's relationship to time and change? To poetry?

3. What are "unheard" melodies (line 11) and "ditties of no tone" (line 14)? Why are these "sweeter" than songs heard by "the sensual ear" (line 13)? What central contrast is created through this comparison?

4. What do the trees, the musician, and the lovers have in common? How are they all related to the real world of time and change?

PHILIP LARKIN (1922–1985)

Next, Please ⌐⌐⌐⌐ 1955

Always too eager for the future, we
Pick up bad habits of expectancy.
Something is always approaching; every day
Till then we say,

Watching from a bluff the tiny, clear,   5
Sparkling armada of promises draw near.
How slow they are! And how much time they waste,
Refusing to make haste!

Yet still they leave us holding wretched stalks
Of disappointment, for, though nothing balks   10
Each big approach, leaning with brasswork prinked,°   *adorned*
Each rope distinct,

Flagged, and the figurehead with golden tits
Arching our way, it never anchors; it's
No sooner present than it turns to past.   15
Right to the last

We think each one will heave to and unload
All good into our lives, all we are owed
For waiting so devoutly and so long.
But we are wrong: 20

Only one ship is seeking us, a black-
Sailed unfamiliar, towing at her back
A huge and birdless silence. In her wake
No waters breed or break.

QUESTIONS

1. What is the subject of the poem? The theme? What point does it make about time, expectation, human nature, and the way we live our lives?

2. What cliché does the extended metaphor that begins in the second stanza ironically revitalize and reverse? How does this metaphor make the total meaning of the poem clearer and more palpable?

3. How do meter, rhyme, and diction help create meaning? Consider, for example, the metrical variation in the fourth line of each stanza, rhyming pairs such as "waste-haste" and "wake-break," or words such as "bluff" and "armada."

4. Compare this poem to the three *carpe diem* poems in this chapter, including Marvell's "To His Coy Mistress." To what extent is "Next, Please" a *carpe diem* poem?

ARCHIBALD MACLEISH (1892–1982)

Ars Poetica   1926

A poem should be palpable and mute
As a globed fruit,

Dumb
As old medallions to the thumb,

Silent as the sleeve-worn stone   5
Of casement ledges where the moss has grown—

A poem should be wordless
As the flight of birds

                              * * *

A poem should be motionless in time
As the moon climbs.   10

Leaving, as the moon releases
Twig by twig the night-entangled trees,

Leaving, as the moon behind the winter leaves,
Memory by memory the mind—

A poem should be motionless in time   15
As the moon climbs.

                              * * *

A poem should be equal to:
Not true.

For all the history of grief
An empty doorway and a maple leaf

For love   20
The leaning grasses and two lights above the sea—

A poem should not mean
But be.

QUESTIONS

1. What do lines 1–8 assert about a poem? How do the similes make this assertion clear and concrete?

2. How do you resolve the paradoxes that a poem may be both "mute" and "dumb," and also "silent" and "wordless"?

3. How do symbolism and simile clarify the claims about poetry in lines 9–16? How can something be "motionless" and also "climb"?

4. What does the third section (lines 17–24) state about a poem? Why are the symbols of grief and love included here?

5. To what extent does "Ars Poetica" illustrate its own definition of poetry?

EVE MERRIAM (1916–1992)

Reply to the Question: "How Can You Become A Poet?" 1976

take the leaf of a tree
trace its exact shape
the outside edges
and inner lines

memorize the way it is fastened to the twig 5
(and how the twig arches from the branch)
how it springs forth in April
how it is panoplied in July

by late August
crumple it in your hand 10
so that you smell its end-of-summer sadness

chew its woody stem

listen to its autumn rattle

watch as it atomizes in the November air

then in winter 15
when there is no leaf left
                    invent one

QUESTIONS

1. What idea about poetic creation is advanced in the first eleven lines of this poem? Why do you think the poet suggests that so many things be done with the leaf of a tree?

2. What senses does the poet indicate that the reader should exercise on the way to becoming a poet?

3. What is the idea contained in the last three lines? What is the relationship between the actual leaf and the invented leaf?

SHARON OLDS (b. 1942)   *For a photo, see p. 776.*

35/10 ❧❧❧❧ 1984

Brushing out my daughter's dark
silken hair before the mirror
I see the grey gleaming on my head,
the silver-haired servant behind her. Why is it
just as we begin to go   5
they begin to arrive, the fold in my neck
clarifying as the fine bones of her
hips sharpen? As my skin shows
its dry pitting, she opens like a small
pale flower on the tip of a cactus;   10
as my last chances to bear a child
are falling through my body, the duds among them,
her full purse of eggs, round and
firm as hard-boiled yolks, is about
to snap its clasp. I brush her tangled   15
fragrant hair at bedtime. It's an old
story—the oldest we have on our planet—
the story of replacement.

QUESTIONS

1. Who is the speaker in this poem? What is she doing? What is the setting?
2. How does the speaker contrast her own state of being to her daughter's stage of life? How are images, metaphors, and similes used to clarify this contrast? How does this contrast help convey the poem's meaning?
3. What point does this poem make about life and nature? To what extent does the last sentence clarify (or overclarify) the poem's theme?

LINDA PASTAN (b. 1932)

Ethics ❧❧❧❧ 1980

In ethics class so many years ago
our teacher asked this question every fall:
if there were a fire in a museum
which would you save, a Rembrandt painting
or an old woman who hadn't many   5
years left anyhow? Restless on hard chairs
caring little for pictures or old age
we'd opt one year for life, the next for art
and always half-heartedly. Sometimes
the woman borrowed my grandmother's face   10
leaving her usual kitchen to wander
some drafty, half-imagined museum.
One year, feeling clever, I replied

why not let the woman decide herself?
Linda, the teacher would report, eschews   15
the burdens of responsibility.
This fall in a real museum I stand
before a real Rembrandt, old woman,
or nearly so, myself. The colors
within this frame are darker than autumn,   20
darker even than winter—the browns of earth,
though earth's most radiant elements burn
through the canvas. I know now that woman
and painting and season are almost one
and all beyond saving by children.   25

QUESTIONS

1. What can we surmise about the speaker in this poem? How does this knowledge contribute to our understanding of theme?

2. What are the two settings, situations, and actions presented here? How are they related? How much time has passed between them? How does the contrast between them help create meaning?

3. How has the passage of time changed the speaker's attitudes? What does she now realize about "woman / and painting and season" (lines 23–24)? About children?

4. What is the subject of this poem? The theme? What point does it make about art, life, time, and values?

MOLLY PEACOCK (b. 1947)

Desire ≻≺≻≺ 1984

It doesn't speak and it isn't schooled,
like a small foetal animal with wettened fur.
It is the blind instinct for life unruled,
visceral frankincense and animal myrrh.
It is what babies bring to kings,   5
an eyes-shut, ears-shut medicine of the heart
that smells and touches endings and beginnings
without the details of time's experienced *part-*
fit-into-part-fit-into-part. Like a paw,
it is blunt; like a pet who knows you   10
and nudges your knee with its snout—but more raw
and blinder and younger and more divine, too,
than the tamed wild—it's the drive for what is real,
deeper than the brain's detail: the drive to feel.

QUESTIONS

1. In line 4, what is the meaning of the references to frankincense and myrrh? Why does line 5 introduce a reference to "what babies bring to kings"? What ideas about desire does the poet seem to be suggesting by using these references?

2. What thoughts about desire does the poet introduce in the poem's last six lines, particularly the concluding couplet? Why is desire compared to "a pet who knows you"?

3. In view of the poem's topic, what reason can you give to explain why the poet does not begin every line with a capital letter?

ANNE STEVENSON (b. 1933)

The Spirit Is Too Blunt an Instrument _ ⌒ ⌒ _ 1987

The spirit is too blunt an instrument
to have made this baby.
Nothing so unskilful as human passions
could have managed the intricate
exacting particulars: the tiny   5
blind bones with their manipulating tendons,
the knee and the knucklebones, the resilient
fine meshings of ganglia and vertebrae
in the chain of the difficult spine.

Observe the distinct eyelashes and sharp crescent   10
fingernails, the shell-like complexity
of the ear with its firm involutions
concentric in miniature to the minute
ossicles.° Imagine the   *delicate bones of the ear*
infinitesimal capillaries, the flawless connections   15
of the lungs, the invisible neural filaments
through which the completed body
already answers to the brain.

Then name any passion or sentiment
possessed of the simplest accuracy.   20
No. No desire or affection could have done
with practice what habit
has done perfectly, indifferently,
through the body's ignorant precision.
It is left to the vagaries of the mind to invent   25
love and despair and anxiety
and their pain.

QUESTIONS

1. What idea about the creation and composition of a human being is being developed in lines 5–18? What knowledge does the poet expect of her readers?

2. Why does the poet speak of "the body's ignorant precision" in line 24? What is meant by this phrase? How important is the idea in the context of the poem?

3. What is meant by "the vagaries of the mind" in line 25? What is Stevenson's purpose in introducing this idea?

WRITING ABOUT THEME AND MEANING IN POETRY

The prewriting process for this essay includes reading and rereading, developing your initial ideas about the poem, testing those ideas against the poem itself, formulating a tentative central idea for your essay, and organizing your observations into coherent units. Always keep foremost that your essay should connect the poem's theme and meaning to other poetic elements, such as speaker, imagery, metaphor, symbol, and tone.

Questions for Discovering Ideas

- What does the title of the poem tell you about subject and meaning?
- What do you learn about the speaker? How does the speaker shape and communicate ideas?
- How do the other characters (if any) affect the poem's meaning?
- What impact do setting, situation, and action have on theme?
- How do diction, imagery, metaphor, simile, and other figures of speech affect the ideas? How are multiple denotations and connotations employed? To what extent are special types of diction or word order used?
- Describe the tone of the poem. What effect does the tone have on the ideas?
- What role do rhythm, meter, sound, and rhyme play in shaping and emphasizing important words and ideas?
- How does the poem's form shape its ideas? What effect does the form have on your response?
- How do symbol, allusion, or myth contribute to the poem's ideas?

You will find poems for which all these questions are relevant, for some poets employ every element and device in the poetic repertory to develop their meaning. Other poems touch on only a few of these areas. Look for major elements that have the strongest impact on the poem's ideas and on your consideration of the poem as an emotional and intellectual experience.

Strategies for Organizing Ideas

Be careful to distinguish between *subject* and *theme*. For example, in planning to discuss the ideas of Larkin's "Next, Please," you might write the following: "Larkin's 'Next, Please' makes a clear assertion about human habits of expectation." This sentence describes the poem's *subject*, and it might even be a good beginning sentence for your essay. It is not, however, a good central idea because it tells the reader nothing about the poem's theme or meaning. A better central idea might be "Larkin's 'Next, Please' exposes the futility of ignoring the present while anticipating the future." This sentence summarizes the theme of the poem and makes a strong statement on which to build an effective essay.

Next, focus on the relationship between your idea and the ways in which the poem creates meaning. Use the information you gain from answering the questions for discovering ideas in the preceding section. Thus, if you find that a poem's theme is established through symbol and allusion, you should make this connection by relating meaning to these elements. Such a plan might be (1) theme, (2) theme and symbol, and (3) theme and allusion. Or it might be that the poet's meaning is made plain through a dominant image or metaphor. You might then plan to develop the idea part by part, showing how the metaphor develops it, or you might want to stress the metaphor itself as it grows and develops as support for the poem's idea, as in the demonstrative student essay that follows.

In your introductory paragraph, before stating your central idea, bring out any points that are relevant to the poem and your essay. If your poem is about life at the front in World War I, for example, or if the speaker is a woman walking along a sandy beach, it is important to make these basic facts clear right at the beginning.

As you organize and develop your paragraphs, keep in mind the following structural patterns. They will be useful for almost all the poems you encounter.

1. The poem may convey meaning through direct statement. In such a case you might organize your essay to reflect the line-by-line or sentence-by-sentence structure of the poem itself.

2. You might find that the speaker's reasoning or argument most effectively creates meaning. To follow such a pattern of logic, for example, would be useful in an essay about the meaning of Andrew Marvell's "To His Coy Mistress" (Chapter 21).

3. The poet's use of a *single element* (such as a metaphor, simile, or myth) or a set of consistent references (such as discussions of explorers, bankers, darkness, or rain) might bring out the poem's meaning. Your organization might reflect how the element is used in the poem.

4. Finally, it might be that a number of *different poetic elements* (e.g., rhythm, rhyme, metaphor, level of diction, imagery) work together to shape theme and impact. The structure of an essay dealing with such elements can be based on a sequential discussion of each element as it contributes to meaning.

Please note that these four structural patterns can be modified and combined. To accommodate the specific poem you are considering, you should always be ready to adjust whatever plan you choose.

In your conclusion, you might pull all the strands of the essay together and reaffirm the connection between the poem's method and meaning. This is most conveniently done through a summary of your major points. The conclusion is also the place where you can consider additional aspects of the poem's ideas. Your reactions and thoughts upon reading the poem often suggest additional ideas for inclusion in your essay. Similarly, you might want to consider the extent to which your own circumstances (such as age, interests, political views, religion) help determine your understanding of the poem.

DEMONSTRATIVE STUDENT ESSAY

Meaning in Keats's "Ode on a Grecian Urn"°

[1]   John Keats's "Ode on a Grecian Urn" explores the incomprehensible vastness and mystery of art and imagination. <u>Specifically, the poem offers Keats's belief that the beauty of art stimulates the human imagination, which leads to the contemplation of significant, though often unknowable, subjects.</u>* <u>Keats develops this theme through his use of speaker and situation, figurative language, style, and the direct but difficult statements of his final, famous stanza.</u>†

[2]   <u>The speaker and situation of the poem are developed together as an interplay of the speaker's thoughts with the everlastingly silent urn.</u> One may imagine the dramatic situation: The speaker is standing in front of a display featuring the urn. He is a keen observer, and he muses about the many details on the urn's surface. As he ponders, his thoughts re-create the urn almost as a living thing, which he addresses in a lengthy apostrophe, offering words of praise, wonder, and speculation. He raises questions about the decorative scenes that he sees painted on the urn:

What men or gods are these? What maidens loth?
What mad pursuit? What struggle to escape?
What pipes and timbrels? What wild ecstasy? (lines 8–10)

Throughout the poem the speaker continues to alternate his questions with arguments about the advantages of being a character frozen upon the urn in a moment of endless time. However, the speaker is demonstrating that a "conversation" is taking place. As he studies the urn, its beautiful illustrations stimulate his imagination and cause him to begin a dialogue within himself about the transience of human life and the permanence of art. Keats's apostrophe, then, is a recreation of what goes on in the mind of one who follows art to the farthest reaches of contemplation. Because the vase is mute, both about its origin and its originator, the apostrophe also suggests the absence of answers to the largest questions human beings can ask about the meaning of life and the nature of eternity.

[3]   <u>Also in the first stanza, Keats develops his theme through a number of metaphors about the urn.</u> In the poem's first line, the speaker calls the urn a "still unravish'd bride of quietness." This comparison indicates that, in spite of its antiquity, the urn presents all the eagerness and anticipation of youth, and it therefore suggests that art transcends both time and change. In the poem's second line, the urn is seen as a "foster-child of silence and slow time." This metaphor, too, suggests that this work of art is still as youthful and fresh as a child. In addition, because the urn is a "foster child" not only of silence but also of "slow time," it is a product of the realm of art, where time stands still, fixed in a moment

---

°See p. 971 for this poem.
*Central idea.
†Thesis sentence.

forever, despite the constant change and impermanence of human life. Next, the urn is addressed as a "sylvan historian" that tells a story even better than a poem can (lines 3–4). While "sylvan" refers to the trees and leaves that decorate the urn, the metaphor of "historian" indicates that art is both a record of history and a teller of historical tales. It records past deeds, ideas, insights, and views of existence, for all to see and consider, and from which to learn. Thus, all three major metaphors develop the idea that human life is transitory but that art touches that great, vast, endless realm of permanence which is otherwise unattainable for human beings.

[4]
The speaker asserts that the painted pictures on the urn continue to develop this contrast. In the second stanza he notes a piper sitting and playing beneath leafy trees (lines 15–16) and a "bold lover" trying to win a kiss from a maiden (lines 17–18). Keats's style is vital here, with his emphasis on words indicating timelessness, such as "never," "ever," "for ever," and "for evermore." Thus, the piper can never leave his song (lines 15–16), the trees can never "be bare" (line 16), the lover will never achieve his goal (lines 17–18), and the maiden will "For ever" be fair (line 20). In the third stanza, the "happy boughs" will never shed their leaves, "nor ever bid the spring adieu" (lines 21–22); the piper will never tire of playing (line 23); and lovers "for ever young" (line 27) will experience love that is "For ever warm" (line 26). In the third stanza, the streets of a little town "emptied of its folk" will "for evermore" be silent (line 37–38). The diction emphasizes that all these scenes are frozen in time, forever unchanging, forever beautiful, unlike real life, in which everything is always aging and changing.

[5]
But Keats also suggests that because these scenes are perpetuated by art, they stimulate the human imagination in a way that actual physical sensations cannot. This is the idea brought out in the sentence "Heard melodies are sweet, but those unheard / Are sweeter" (lines 11–12). The image of the piper playing "ditties of no tone" (line 14) speaks not to the speaker's "sensual ear" (line 13) but to his "spirit" (line 14). These are not easy ideas, and any attempt to render them fully falls short of what Keats is saying. One cannot escape the conclusion that he is thinking that "ditties of no tone" go mysteriously beyond ordinary music in the ordinary world. These silent songs exceed our comprehension, and therefore the silent piper on the urn is directly linked to forces and impulses about which we will always remain ignorant. In real life, the piper would be playing perhaps no more than an everyday tune, which we might or might not like, but in his place on the urn, this piper is universal and transcendent.

[6]
In the final stanza the speaker's contemplation of these images leads to concluding statements about the poem's theme. There, he continues the apostrophe to the urn: "Thou, silent form, dost tease us out of thought / As doth eternity" (44–45). In other words, art provokes our thoughts, but our understandings will remain incomplete. The phrase "tease us out of thought" suggests that the meaning of art, like life--like eternity--goes beyond our limited powers of speech and imagination. Next, the speaker asserts that

> When old age shall this generation waste,
>   Thou shalt remain, in midst of other woe
>   Than ours, a friend to man, to whom whou say'st,
> "Beauty is truth, truth beauty,"--that is all
>   Ye know on earth, and all ye need to know. (lines 46–50)

[7]   These lines make up a summarizing and comprehensive statement, which we can accept as true on the highest and most abstract level. It would seem that Keats's idea is that truth and beauty represent a distillation and refinement of human actions and thoughts. By this standard, a scientific theory, well established in fact and logic, is also beautiful. The same beauty can be found in honest conversations between people, or in the fulfillment of a correctly executed task, or in the construction of a new house, or in the accurate discovery of a new invention. The idea is that no matter what things we do, there is always something beautiful and true that exists beyond the actual results of our achievements. As long as our goal is to follow truth, without any subterfuge or questionable motivation, the ultimate goal--beauty--is attainable through the medium of art and creativity. Keats's Grecian urn, as a work of art, and as the occasion of this great poem about art, represents an ideal that points us toward a standard by which all things can be measured, even though we may never be able to articulate this meaning that transcends everything we are capable of learning.

WORK CITED

Keats, John. "Ode on a Grecian Urn." Literature: An Introduction to Reading and Writing. Ed. Edgar V. Roberts and Henry E. Jacobs. 7th ed. Upper Saddle River: Prentice Hall, 2004. 971.

Commentary on the Essay

The essay illustrates the need to combine and adjust strategies of organization in dealing with a specific poem. It combines a focus on metaphor, imagery, and diction, with equal interest in the poem's dramatic situation, combined with elements of close reading at the essay's end. (The essay thus represents a modification and combination of organization strategies 3 and 4 on page 980.)

Paragraph 2 deals with the poem's situation, which is visualized as the musings of the speaker in front of a display of the urn. This discussion provides the foundation for the essay's subsequent treatment of theme and meaning.

Paragraphs 3 through 7 treat the connection between metaphor and meaning. Paragraph 3 introduces a number of metaphors by which Keats illustrates the power of the original artist of the urn. Paragraph 4 examines the way that the urn presents pictures that emphasize the endlessness of eternity. Important here is the stylistic emphasis on words like "ever" and "forever."

Paragraph 5 deals with the implications of the pictured musician, piping "ditties of no tone." In paragraph 6 the transcendence of the piper is connected to the thought that the urn can tease the spectator out of thought. The continuation of this idea is brought out in paragraph 7, which treats the meaning of the poem's concluding five lines. The value of this paragraph is that it is more than a summary, leaving the reader with new thoughts.

Special Topics for Writing and Argument about Meaning in Poetry

1. Compare two or all of the following as *carpe diem* poems: Jonson's "To Celia," Herrick's "To the Virgins," Marvell's "To His Coy Mistress," and Larkin's "Next, Please." How well does each poem express the central idea of the *carpe diem* tradition? What are the similarities and differences of the tone and ideas? If the poems involve invitations to seduction, how do they transcend their topic to deal with ideas and values?

2. On the basis of ideas about age, change, and the loss of time and life, compare Justice's "On the Death of Friends in Childhood," Marvell's "To His Coy Mistress," Olds's "35/10," and Pastan's "Ethics." How do the ideas of the poems merge, even though they are about different subjects? Which of the poems do you prefer? Why?

3. Basing your discussion on the poems of Viorst and Pastan in this chapter, explain how comic humor can be employed as a vehicle for serious ideas. How do the poets introduce humor into their poems? What relationship does the humor have to ideas? How might the expression of ideas be better (or worse) if the poems were serious and not comic?

4. Write your own poem in which you stress a particular idea. You might write about a friend or acquaintance who has endured an illness, performed an important service, admitted a mistake or failure, or succeeded in a task. Other possible topics are a social, religious, or political issue or some aspect of education, work, or community life. When you finish, explain how you go about making the situation clear to your reader, and explain how you use the situation to bring out your ideas. Do not neglect the title as one of the means of expressing ideas.

5. In the reference section of your library, select a guide to ideas, such as Philip P. Wiener, ed., *Dictionary of the History of Ideas: Studies of Selected Pivotal Ideas* (1973). Read about one or more of the following: *allegory, beauty, holy, idea, love, realism, sublime*. Explain the depth and application of the idea. What writers are associated with the idea? How does the author of the article demonstrate the idea's development? Describe how the author of the article emphasizes and exemplifies the idea.

Three Poetic Careers:
William Wordsworth,
Emily Dickinson, and Robert Frost

In Chapters 13 through 23 we have considered poetry in terms of its elements and effects. In this chapter we examine collections of poems by three major poets: William Wordsworth (1770–1850), Emily Dickinson (1830–1886), and Robert Frost (1874–1963). Wordsworth, whose first poems were published late in the eighteenth century, was one of the first Romantic poets in England. He stands at the crossroad between classicism and modernity. Dickinson and Frost are both American poets and New Englanders. Dickinson is one of the most prominent poetic voices of the nineteenth century, and Frost is recognized as a poetic giant of the twentieth century. Although the poems included here comprise only a fraction of the work of each of these major poets, it has been our goal to select enough poems to illustrate the central concerns and major characteristics that are to be found in the study of their poetic careers.

WILLIAM WORDSWORTH (1770–1850)

Life and Work

William Wordsworth was born in 1770 in the Lake District of northern England. He had three brothers and one sister. His father, John Wordsworth, was an attorney who urged him to memorize many poems of the great English poets. His mother died when he was eight years old, and the children were separated. Wordsworth went to a school at Hawkshead, near Lake Windermere, where he was an undistinguished pupil but enjoyed a good deal of personal freedom. Having little money but boundless energy, he became a tireless walker, to which he attributed the "indomitable vigour" of his adult life. He walked everywhere. During his lifetime he walked more than 100,000 miles— and not slowly, either. As he walked various English and European countrysides, often covering as much as forty miles a day, he met and conversed with many local people, an experience that is reflected in his poetry.

Wordsworth's thirteenth year was marked by the death of his father, who, unwisely, had loaned his life savings to his employer, Sir James Lowther, who later became the first Lord Lonsdale. Representatives of the children appealed to Lord Lonsdale to restore the money, but this honorable gentleman rebuffed every claim. Not until Lonsdale died, when Wordsworth was in his early thirties, was restitution finally made. Once Wordsworth received his share of the inheritance, life became somewhat easier for him.

In 1787, four years after his father's death and fifteen years before his belated inheritance, his uncles enabled him to enter Cambridge University. He found classes uninteresting, but he read voraciously, and between terms he went walking. In 1790 he took a walking tour of France and the Alps with a friend, Robert Jones, and in 1791, the year he graduated, he walked with Jones throughout Wales.

For a time after his graduation Wordsworth lived in France, then at the height of its revolution, and he shared the idealistic possibilities of the new age based on trust "in the People." Later he described his youthful optimism: "Bliss was it in that dawn to be alive, / But to be young was very Heaven!" (*The Prelude*, XI.108–09). Eventually, however, he was disillusioned by the excesses of the Reign of Terror and the militarism of Napoleon.

While in France, Wordsworth began an affair with Annette Vallon, a woman who held royalist sympathies. In 1793 the couple had a daughter, Caroline. Wordsworth wanted to marry Annette, but his money ran out and he had to return home the same year. Also in 1793, England and France went to war, and Wordsworth was unable to return to France. After the war, in 1802, he and Annette agreed that they had grown too separate from each other to undertake a successful marriage. They parted as friends, and Wordsworth, who had just come into his inheritance, provided for the care of their daughter.

In Wordsworth's post-Cambridge years he spent much time deciding what to do with his life, his options being poetry (his preference), the clergy, the law, or the military. Fortune intruded on his behalf, because for a time in 1795 he had cared for a good friend, Raisley Calvert, who was dying. Calvert believed in Wordsworth's future as a poet and expressed his gratitude by leaving Wordsworth a bequest of £ 900. This substantial sum enabled Wordsworth to take a home in the south of England, where he was joined by his sister Dorothy, who remained his housekeeper, friend, and lifelong confidante. Here he met Samuel Taylor Coleridge, a young man with similar interests and enthusiasms. The two men walked and talked together for many months, developing plans for a magazine and then for a book of poems.

Their collaboration resulted in one of the most significant books in English literature despite its inauspicious title: *Lyrical Ballads, with a Few Other Poems*, published in 1798. The collection contained twenty-three poems, four by Coleridge (including "The Rime of the Ancient Mariner") and nineteen by Wordsworth. Although *Lyrical Ballads* did not create a great general stir, many poetry readers bought it, and Wordsworth and Coleridge soon issued new, expanded editions. For the 1800 edition, Wordsworth included his landmark "Preface," in which he lays out his poetic credo.

William Wordsworth

After Wordsworth and Annette separated amicably in 1802, he married a woman he had known since childhood, Mary Hutchinson. The couple moved into Dove Cottage, Wordsworth's home in Grasmere, in the Lake District. Eventually they had five children, and in 1813 they took up permanent residence at nearby Rydal Mount. Along with growing recognition as a poet, Wordsworth attained financial security when he was appointed revenue collector in the Lake District. Years later he received an annual government pension of £ 300. In 1843 he was named poet laureate, an honor he held until his death in 1850.

Wordsworth published his poetry regularly throughout his lifetime, the most notable publications, after *Lyrical Ballads*, being *Poems in Two Volumes* in 1807, *The Excursion* in 1814, and his collected poems in 1815. His long autobiographical poem *The Prelude*, which he wrote and revised for more than five decades, was not published until after his death in 1850. In later years, Dove Cottage, Wordsworth's first residence in Grasmere, has become a shrine. Rebuilt and greatly enlarged, the home is now operated as a national historic trust. Rydal Mount is similarly open to visitors.

Wordsworth and Romanticism

Both Wordsworth and Coleridge, are acknowledged as the originators of English Romantic poetry. It must be said that the writers living in the so-called Romantic period (1798–1832) did not describe themselves as romantics; the term was conferred by later critics. There are many ways to explain Romanticism–and little agreement about any of them—but essence of Romanticism is a belief in the power and validity of human emotions as a means of knowing and as a guide to life. The result is a strong emphasis on the individual and also on common people, regardless of station, since all people are capable of learning through emotional experiences. Whereas previous periods considered a ruling class the proper center of power and human interest, the Romantic believed that this center exists among all people. Romanticism undoubtedly reflected many ideas of the period—the Protestant Reformation, with its emphasis on the sanctity of individual conscience and its skepticism toward hierarchy; the influences of the American and French Revolutions, with their emphasis on the "common man" and representative government; the cultivation of sensibility in aesthetics, with its focus on individual feelings; and the growth of scientific research and experimentation as opposed to the acceptance of authoritarian dicta.

ROMANTICISM AND NATURE.   Wordsworth has always been considered a poet of nature. In his own life he spent much time outdoors in all seasons, and he records innumerable experiences in the natural world. He can therefore be considered a topographic or landscape poet. But his object is not to record details but rather to emphasize the meaning of nature. His descriptions of natural scenes are therefore impressionistic and interpretive. For example, when he considers a remembered vision of daffodils, a vision that filled him with joy, he describes them as "fluttering and dancing in the breeze" and outdoing "the sparkling waves in glee." He clearly states his belief that nature provides evidence for universal power, a power that he seeks to assimilate within himself through feeling and imagination. The concluding lines from "The Tables Turned" (1798) illustrate this idea.

Come forth, and bring with you a heart
That watches and receives.

Because Wordsworth is one of those with a heart that receives, he frequently writes of his excitement upon seeing the beauty of nature. He describes such a feeling in the following brief poem.

My Heart Leaps Up   1802

My heart leaps up when I behold
   A rainbow in the sky.
So was it when my life began;
So is it now I am a man;
So be it when I shall grow old,
   Or let me die!
The Child is the father of the Man;
And I could wish my days to be
Bound each to each by natural piety.

His great paean to nature, the distillation of this kind of experience, occurs in lines 93 to 102 of "Lines Composed a Few Miles above Tintern Abbey" (1798).

              And I have felt
A presence that disturbs me with the joy

5

Of elevated thoughts; a sense sublime
Of something far more deeply interfused,
Whose dwelling is the light of setting suns,
And the round ocean, and the living air,
And the blue sky, and in the mind of man:
A motion and a spirit, that impels
All thinking things, all objects of all thought,
And rolls through all things. . . .

ROMANTICISM, THE SELF, AND THE MORAL SENSE.   In some writers, the consequence of Romanticism is extreme egotism. One certainly finds self-centeredness in Wordsworth, whose own experiences, responses, and emotions are his major subject. There is, however, a tempering sense that individual emotions are not self-indulgent but rather that they lead to self-realization and to a genial moral philosophy that he describes in "Tintern Abbey" as a "cheerful faith, that all which we behold / Is full of blessings" (lines 133–34).

His poetry embodies this particular type of Romanticism. Believing that all lives are worthy of study and understanding, Wordsworth wrote many poems that treat topics of ordinary life, over which is cast an imaginative and moral perspective. Examples from *Lyrical Ballads* are an old huntsman, a little girl who cannot understand death, a betrayed woman who forever laments her abandonment, and a man who can never get warm because he once denied a few sticks of firewood to an aged woman. These subjects illustrate Wordsworth's broad concern with the meaning of the common events of everyday life.

But his most characteristic poems are those in which he concentrates on individual experience as illustrated by his own life and thought. Wordsworth looks at his life as a revelation—even a divine revelation—and therefore as holy. For him, poetry of personal testimony and self-concern is justifiable and even necessary. His longest poem, which is about himself, is the posthumously published *The Prelude*, his exhaustive autobiographical self-analysis focused on the growth of his own poetic imagination. This long work is unique in English literature. In the ode "Intimations of Immortality" (1807), Wordsworth is equally concerned with his own change and development. In this poem he traces the emergence of "the philosophic mind." Perhaps Wordsworth's most serene description of himself is "Lines Composed a Few Miles above Tintern Abbey." In this poem the speaker, whom we may take to be Wordsworth himself, describes how his moral sense has been evoked and shaped by his lifelong experiences with nature.

Romanticism and Wordsworth's Theory of Composition

Wordsworth's Romanticism, then, is based on the idea that human emotions are good and moral and that they are authoritative and trustworthy. In particular, poets—that is, persons of powerful intuition and imagination—are specially inspired recipients of universal wisdom, and their poetry is the record of their inspiration, set down for others to appreciate and recognize as paralleling their own experience. His brief preface to "Tintern Abbey" best tells the story.

No poem of mine was composed under circumstances more pleasant for me to re-member than this. I began it upon leaving Tintern, after crossing the Wye, and concluded it just as I was entering Bristol in the evening, after a ramble of four or five days, with my Sister. Not a line of it was altered and not any part of it written down till I reached Bristol.

Of major significance is Wordsworth's claim that he altered "not a line," for his belief is that the entire poem was inspired, and that he received it through his own intuition and imagination. He clarifies these ideas in the "Pref-ace" to the second edition of *Lyrical Ballads*, in which he states that poetic com-position is produced by "emotion recollected in tranquillity." That is, the poet, living life as all of us do, finds that the memory of past experiences comes to mind involuntarily, through random associations, and that in times of relax-ation and meditation this recollection causes the poet to reexperience the ac-companying emotions. Such reflection is the basis of poetry, for the renewal of once-felt emotions inspires the poet to begin writing. Although the outline of this process is clear, the specifics of recollection are unknown, unknowable, and unpredictable—mysterious—and therefore, for a Romantic, the act of poetic creation is evidence for a transcendent source of wisdom.

This view of poetic composition is similar to the idea of "negative capabili-ty" of John Keats (1795–1821). According to Keats, writing in 1817, negative ca-pability is a capacity to accept and preserve ideas without critical interference because poetic thoughts come to the poet through a "penetralium of mystery."[1] This is a quintessentially Romantic idea of composition, and it explains why at least some of the Romantics believed that poetry should be preserved without change or revision. Because the poetic process exceeds normal human under-standing, it should be hallowed and left unaltered. We should not conclude that Wordsworth never scratched out words and lines or added others. He rewrote poems all the time. But he believed that his original thoughts and ideas should be retained because they came to him from a mysterious and transcendent power. His revisions were therefore intended to bring his poems into line with his original inspiration.

Wordsworth's Poetic Diction

Wordsworth's poetry marks a unique turn that reflects not only developing dem-ocratic ideals but also the emphasis on direct and everyday language that had been a major goal of the scientific revolution begun more than a century earlier with the founding of the English Royal Society (1661). His ideas about poetic diction are found in his "Preface." He seeks to use words as denotatively as pos-sible, and his aim is that the words should be "the real language of men in a state of vivid sensation." (He repeats the phrase "real language" a number of times.)

[1]Hyder Rollins, ed., *The Letters of John Keats, 1814 – 1821* (Cambridge: Harvard, 1972), I.193 – 194. Keats explains negative capability as a state "when a man is capable of being in uncertainties, Mysteries, doubts, without any irritable reaching after fact & reason." *Penetralium* (more correctly, *penetralia*) refers to an innermost and holy area, usually said of a religious sanctuary, but Keats clearly uses the word to mean an unseen, remote, mysterious, and divine center of inspiration.

His aim is to "look steadily" at his subject and to use the vocabulary of prose as his poetic medium, for, as he says, "there neither is, nor can be, any *essential* difference between the language of prose and metrical composition."

Wordsworth's theory about poetic language is consistent with his ideas about the nature of poetry: The poet's obligation is to render experiences accurately and to express them without resorting to traditional poetic conventions, which tend to divert the poem from its goal of re-creating the experiences. The object of poets, in short, is to connect their own imaginations with the imaginations of readers and to enable readers to duplicate or share the poet's heightened awareness. Such a theory of poetic language constitutes a marked change in poetic practice and theory, one we see continuing in much modern poetry.

Bibliographic Sources

The standard edition of Wordsworth is Ernest De Selincourt and Helen Darbishire, eds., *The Poetical Works of William Wordsworth* in five volumes (Oxford: Clarendon, 1940–49; Volumes I–III were revised from 1952–54). Cornell University Press has been publishing *The Cornell Wordsworth* in separate volumes since 1975. These volumes are based on manuscript as well as published versions of the poems, and they are considered definitive. Standard one-volume editions are Andrew J. George, ed., *The Complete Poetical Works of Wordsworth* (Boston: Houghton Mifflin, 1932; frequently reprinted); Stephen Gill, ed., *William Wordsworth: A Life* (Oxford: Oxford UP, 1989); and John O. Hayden, ed., *William Wordsworth: The Poems*, 2 vols. (London: Penguin, 1977, rpt. 1989). The works first published in *Lyrical Ballads* are available in R. L. Brett and A. R. Jones, eds., *Lyrical Ballads: Wordsworth and Coleridge; The Text of the 1798 Edition with the Additional 1800 Poems and Prefaces* (New York: Barnes and Noble, 1963). Readily available selections of the poetry are the Penguin Classics edition by John O. Hayden, ed., *William Wordsworth: Selected Poems* (New York: Penguin, 1994); and Nicholas Roe, ed., *William Wordsworth: Selected Poetry* (London: Penguin, 1992). Another excellent selection is Jack Stillinger, ed., *William Wordsworth: Selected Poems and Prefaces*, Riverside Editions (Boston: Houghton Mifflin, 1965).

A brief critical biography is by Russell Noyes, *William Wordsworth*, 1971, revised by John O. Hayden (New York: Twayne, 1991). A fully illustrated brief biography (photographs, drawings, paintings) is F. E. Halliday, *Wordsworth and His World* (New York: Viking, 1970). A recent biography is Kenneth R. Johnston, *The Hidden Wordsworth: Poet, Lover, Rebel, Spy* (New York: Norton, 1999). Lane Cooper's *A Concordance to the Poems of Wordsworth* (London, 1911) is essential for studying Wordsworth's words and therefore his ideas.

Significant criticism is found in F. W. Bateson, *Wordsworth: A Re-Interpretation*, 2nd ed. (London: Longmans, 1956); Richard E. Brantley, *Wordsworth's "Natural Methodism"* (New Haven: Yale UP, 1975); Helen Darbishire, *The Poet Wordsworth* (Oxford: Clarendon, 1950, rpt. 1980); Alan Grob, *The Philosophic Mind: A Study of Wordsworth's Poetry and Thought*, 1797–1805 (Columbus: Ohio State UP, 1973); John O. Hayden, *William Wordsworth and the Mind of Man: The Poet as Thinker* (Bibliophile Press, 1993); Thomas McFarland, *William*

Wordsworth: Intensity and Achievement (Oxford: Clarendon, 1992); John L. Mahoney, *Wordsworth and the Critics: The Development of a Critical Reputation* (Camden House, 2000); John Purkis, *A Preface to Wordsworth* (New York: Scribner, 1970); and Duncan Wu, *Wordsworth: An Inner Life* (Oxford: Blackwell, 2001). Useful collections of selected criticism are Meyer H. Abrams, ed., *Wordsworth: A Collection of Critical Essays* (Englewood Cliffs: Prentice Hall, 1972); Jack M. Davis, ed., *Discussions of William Wordsworth* (Boston: Heath, 1964); and Harold Bloom, ed., *William Wordsworth* (New York: Chelsea House, 1985). Lionel Trilling's *The Liberal Imagination: Essays on Literature and Society* (New York: Doubleday, 1953, rpt. 1976) contains a superb essay, "The Immortality Ode."

Special Topics for Writing and Argument about the Poetry of William Wordsworth

1. The speakers of Wordsworth's poems: characteristics, observations, insights, philosophy.

2. Political ideas in Wordsworth's sonnets: attitudes toward freedom, human dignity. Implications for a democratic form of government.

3. The ideas and structure of "Ode: Intimations of Immortality from Recollections of Early Childhood."

4. Wordsworth's use of symbols: childhood, natural scenes, city vistas.

5. Wordsworth's poetic diction: description, action, introspection.

6. Wordsworth's (a) blank verse, (b) stanzaic poetry, (c) sonnets. His use of rhythm and rhyme.

7. Wordsworth's "cheerful faith": the moral effect of experience, the thoughts that lie too deep for tears.

8. Wordsworth's introduction of events of common life into his poetry.

9. Wordsworth's theory of poetic composition: the nature of the poet, the relationship of the poet to his audience, memory, emotion recollected in tranquillity.

10. Wordsworth as a topographic and landscape poet: description, response, meaning.

POEMS BY WILLIAM WORDSWORTH

BLANK VERSE POEMS

STANZAIC POEMS

BLANK VERSE POEMS

From *The Prelude, Book I*, Lines 301–474 ~ ~ ~ ~ 1850

    Fair seed-time had my soul, and I grew up
Fostered alike by beauty and by fear:
Much favoured in my birth-place, and no less
In that beloved Vale to which erelong
We were transplanted—there were we let loose   305
For sports of wider range. Ere I had told
Ten birth-days, when among the mountain slopes
Frost, and the breath of frosty wind, had snapped
The last autumnal crocus, 'twas my joy
With store of springes o'er my shoulder hung   310
To range the open heights where woodcocks run
Along the smooth green turf. Through half the night,
Scudding away from snare to snare, I plied
That anxious visitation;—moon and stars
Were shining o'er my head. I was alone,   315
And seemed to be a trouble to the peace
That dwelt among them. Sometimes it befel
In these night wanderings, that a strong desire
O'erpowered my better reason, and the bird
Which was the captive of another's toil   320
Became my prey; and when the deed was done
I heard among the solitary hills
Low breathings coming after me, and sounds
Of undistinguishable motion, steps
Almost as silent as the turf they trod.   325

    Nor less when spring had warmed the cultured Vale,
Roved we as plunderers where the mother-bird
Had in high places built her lodge; though mean

Our object and inglorious, yet the end
Was not ignoble. Oh! when I have hung   330
Above the raven's nest, by knots of grass
And half-inch fissures in the slippery rock
But ill sustained, and almost (so it seemed)
Suspended by the blast that blew amain,
Shouldering the naked crag, oh, at that time   335
While on the perilous ridge I hung alone,
With what strange utterance did the loud dry wind
Blow through my ear! the sky seemed not a sky
Of earth—and with what motion moved the clouds!

    Dust as we are, the immortal spirit grows   340
Like harmony in music; there is a dark
Inscrutable workmanship that reconciles
Discordant elements, makes them cling together
In one society. How strange that all
The terror, pains, and early miseries,   345
Regrets, vexations, lassitudes interfused
Within my mind, should e'er have borne a part,
And that a needful part, in making up
The calm existence that is mine when I
Am worthy of myself! Praise to the end!   350
Thanks to the means which Nature deigned to employ;
Whether her fearless visitings, or those
That came with soft alarm, like hurtless light
Opening the peaceful clouds; or she may use
Severer interventions, ministry   355
More palpable, as best might suit her aim.

    One summer evening (led by her) I found
A little boat tied to a willow tree
Within a rocky cave, its usual home.
Straight I unloosed her chain, and stepping in   360
Pushed from the shore. It was an act of stealth
And troubled pleasure, nor without the voice
Of mountain-echoes did my boat move on;
Leaving behind her still, on either side,
Small circles glittering idly in the moon,   365
Until they melted all into one track
Of sparkling light. But now, like one who rows,
Proud of his skill, to reach a chosen point
With an unswerving line, I fixed my view
Upon the summit of a craggy ridge,   370
The horizon's utmost boundary; for above
Was nothing but the stars and the grey sky.
She was an elfin pinnace; lustily
I dipped my oars into the silent lake,
And, as I rose upon the stroke, my boat   375
Went heaving through the water like a swan;
When, from behind that craggy steep till then

The horizon's bound, a huge peak, black and huge,
As if with voluntary power instinct
Upreared its head. I struck and struck again,   380
And growing still in stature the grim shape
Towered up between me and the stars, and still,
For so it seemed, with purpose of its own
And measured motion like a living thing,
Strode after me. With trembling oars I turned,   385
And through the silent water stole my way
Back to the covert of the willow tree;
There in her mooring-place I left my bark,—
And through the meadows homeward went, in grave
And serious mood; but after I had seen   390
That spectacle, for many days, my brain
Worked with a dim and undetermined sense
Of unknown modes of being; o'er my thoughts
There hung a darkness, call it solitude
Or blank desertion. No familiar shapes   395
Remained, no pleasant images of trees,
Of sea or sky, no colours of green fields;
But huge and mighty forms, that do not live
Like living men, moved slowly through the mind
By day, and were a trouble to my dreams.   400

    Wisdom and Spirit of the universe!
Thou Soul that art the eternity of thought,
That givest to forms and images a breath
And everlasting motion, not in vain
By day or star-light thus from my first dawn   405
Of childhood didst thou intertwine for me
The passions that build up our human soul;
Not with the mean and vulgar works of man,
But with high objects, with enduring things—
With life and nature, purifying thus   410
The elements of feeling and of thought,
And sanctifying, by such discipline,
Both pain and fear, until we recognise
A grandeur in the beatings of the heart.
Nor was this fellowship vouchsafed to me   415
With stinted kindness. In November days,
When vapours rolling down the valley made
A lonely scene more lonesome, among woods,
At noon and 'mid the calm of summer nights,
When, by the margin of the trembling lake,   420
Beneath the gloomy hills homeward I went
In solitude, such intercourse was mine;
Mine was it in the fields both day and night,
And by the waters, all the summer long.

    And in the frosty season, when the sun   425
Was set, and visible for many a mile

The cottage windows blazed through twilight gloom,
I heeded not their summons: happy time
It was indeed for all of us—for me
It was a time of rapture! Clear and loud   430
The village clock tolled six,—I wheeled about,
Proud and exulting like an untired horse
That cares not for his home. All shod with steel,
We hissed along the polished ice in games
Confederate, imitative of the chase   435
And woodland pleasures,—the resounding horn,
The pack loud chiming, and the hunted hare.
So through the darkness and the cold we flew,
And not a voice was idle; with the din
Smitten, the precipices rang aloud;   440
The leafless trees and every icy crag
Tinkled like iron; while far distant hills
Into the tumult sent an alien sound
Of melancholy not unnoticed, while the stars
Eastward were sparkling clear, and in the west   445
The orange sky of evening died away.
Not seldom from the uproar I retired
Into a silent bay, or sportively
Glanced sideway, leaving the tumultuous throng,
To cut across the reflex of a star   450
That fled, and, flying still before me, gleamed
Upon the glassy plain; and oftentimes,
When we had given our bodies to the wind,
And all the shadowy banks on either side
Came sweeping through the darkness, spinning still   455
The rapid line of motion, then at once
Have I, reclining back upon my heels,
Stopped short; yet still the solitary cliffs
Wheeled by me—even as if the earth had rolled
With visible motion her diurnal round!   460
Behind me did they stretch in solemn train,
Feebler and feebler, and I stood and watched
Till all was tranquil as a dreamless sleep.

    Ye Presences of Nature in the sky
And on the earth! Ye Visions of the hills!   465
And Souls of lonely places! can I think
A vulgar hope was yours when ye employed
Such ministry, when ye through many a year
Haunting me thus among my boyish sports,
On caves and trees, upon the woods and hills,   470
Impressed upon all forms the characters
Of danger or desire; and thus did make
The surface of the universal earth
With triumph and delight, with hope and fear,
Work like a sea?   475

Lines Composed a Few Miles above Tintern Abbey on Revisiting the Banks of the Wye During a Tour, June 13, 1798° *1798*

Five years have past; five summers, with the length
Of five long winters! and again I hear
These waters, rolling from their mountain-springs
With a soft inland murmur.—Once again
Do I behold these steep and lofty cliffs,   5
That on a wild secluded scene impress
Thoughts of more deep seclusion, and connect
The landscape with the quiet of the sky.
The day is come when I again repose

Here, under this dark sycamore, and view   10
These plots of cottage-ground, these orchard-tufts,
Which at this season, with their unripe fruits,
Are clad in one green hue, and lose themselves
'Mid groves and copses. Once again I see
These hedge-rows, hardly hedge-rows, little lines   15
Of sportive wood run wild; these pastoral farms,
Green to the very door; and wreaths of smoke
Sent up, in silence, from among the trees!
With some uncertain notice, as might seem
Of vagrant dwellers in the houseless woods,   20
Or of some Hermit's cave, where by his fire
The Hermit sits alone.
                        These beauteous forms,
Through a long absence, have not been to me
As is a landscape to a blind man's eye:
But oft, in lonely rooms, and 'mid the din   25
Of towns and cities, I have owed to them
In hours of weariness, sensations sweet,
Felt in the blood, and felt along the heart;
And passing even into my purer mind,
With tranquil restoration:—feelings too   30
Of unremembered pleasure: such, perhaps,
As have no slight or trivial influence
On that best portion of a good man's life,
His little, nameless, unremembered acts
Of kindness and of love. Nor less, I trust,   35
To them I may have owed another gift,
Of aspect more sublime; that blessed mood,
In which the burden of the mystery,
In which the heavy and the weary weight
Of all this unintelligible world,   40
Is lightened:—that serene and blessed mood,
In which the affections gently lead us on,—

LINES COMPOSED ABOVE TINTERN ABBEY. Wordsworth first visited the valley of the Wye in southwest
England in August 1793 at age twenty-three. On this second visit he was accompanied by his sister Dorothy
(the "Friend" in line 115).

Until, the breath of this corporeal frame
And even the motion of our human blood
Almost suspended, we are laid asleep   45
In body, and become a living soul:
While with an eye made quiet by the power
Of harmony, and the deep power of joy,
We see into the life of things.
                                    If this
Be but a vain belief, yet, oh!—how oft—   50
In darkness and amid the many shapes
Of joyless daylight; when the fretful stir
Unprofitable, and the fever of the world,
Have hung upon the beatings of my heart—
How oft, in spirit, have I turned to thee,   55
O sylvan Wye! thou wanderer thro' the woods,
How often has my spirit turned to thee!
    And now, with gleams of half extinguished thought,
With many recognitions dim and faint,
And somewhat of a sad perplexity,   60
The picture of the mind revives again:
While here I stand, not only with the sense
Of present pleasure, but with pleasing thoughts
That in this moment there is life and food
For future years. And so I dare to hope,   65
Though changed, no doubt, from what I was when first
I came among these hills; when like a roe
I bounded o'er the mountains, by the sides
Of the deep rivers, and the lonely streams,
Wherever nature led: more like a man   70
Flying from something that he dreads, than one
Who sought the thing he loved. For nature then
(The coarser pleasures of my boyish days,
And their glad animal movements all gone by)
To me was all in all.—I cannot paint   75
What then I was. The sounding cataract
Haunted me like a passion: the tall rock,
The mountain, and the deep and gloomy wood,
Their colours, and their forms, were then to me
An appetite; a feeling and a love,   80
That had no need of a remoter charm,
By thought supplied, nor any interest
Unborrowed from the eye.—That time is past,
And all its aching joys are now no more,
And all its dizzy raptures. Not for this   85
Faint I, nor mourn nor murmur; other gifts
Have followed; for such loss, I would believe,
Abundant recompense. For I have learned
To look on nature, not as in the hour
Of thoughtless youth; but hearing oftentimes   90
The still, sad music of humanity,

Nor harsh nor grating, though of ample power
To chasten and subdue. And I have felt
A presence that disturbs me with the joy
Of elevated thoughts; a sense sublime   95
Of something far more deeply interfused,
Whose dwelling is the light of setting suns,
And the round ocean, and the living air,
And the blue sky, and in the mind of man;
A motion and a spirit, that impels   100
All thinking things, all objects of all thought,
And rolls through all things. Therefore am I still
A lover of the meadows and the woods,
And mountains; and of all that we behold
From this green earth; of all the mighty world   105
Of eye, and ear,—both what they half create,
And what perceive; well pleased to recognize
In nature and the language of the sense,
The anchor of my purest thoughts, the nurse,
The guide, the guardian of my heart, and soul   110
Of all my moral being.
                    Nor perchance,
If I were not thus taught, should I the more
Suffer my genial spirits to decay:
For thou art with me here upon the banks
Of this fair river; thou my dearest Friend,   115
My dear, dear Friend; and in thy voice I catch
The language of my former heart, and read
My former pleasures in the shooting lights
Of thy wild eyes. Oh! yet a little while
May I behold in thee what I was once,   120
My dear, dear Sister! and this prayer I make,
Knowing that Nature never did betray
The heart that loved her; 'tis her privilege,
Through all the years of this our life, to lead
From joy to joy: for she can so inform   125
The mind that is within us, so impress
With quietness and beauty, and so feed
With lofty thoughts, that neither evil tongues,
Rash judgments, nor the sneers of selfish men,
Nor greetings where no kindness is, nor all   130
The dreary intercourse of daily life,
Shall e'er prevail against us, or disturb
Our cheerful faith that all which we behold
Is full of blessings. Therefore let the moon
Shine on thee in thy solitary walk;   135
And let the misty mountain-winds be free
To blow against thee: and, in after years,
When these wild ecstasies shall be matured
Into a sober pleasure; when thy mind
Shall be a mansion for all lovely forms,   140

Thy memory be as a dwelling-place
For all sweet sounds and harmonies; oh! then,
If solitude, or fear, or pain, or grief,
Should be thy portion, with what healing thoughts
Of tender joy wilt thou remember me,   145
And these my exhortations! Nor, perchance—
If I should be where I no more can hear
Thy voice, nor catch from thy wild eyes these gleams
Of past existence—wilt thou then forget
That on the banks of this delightful stream   150
We stood together; and that I, so long
A worshipper of Nature, hither came
Unwearied in that service: rather say
With warmer love—oh! with far deeper zeal
Of holier love. Nor wilt thou then forget,   155
That after many wanderings, many years
Of absence, these steep woods and lofty cliffs,
And this green pastoral landscape, were to me
More dear, both for themselves and for thy sake!

❦ STANZAIC POEMS

Daffodils (I Wandered Lonely as a Cloud) ⤝⤚⤝⤚ 1807 (1804)

I wandered lonely as a cloud
That floats on high o'er vales and hills,
When all at once I saw a crowd,
A host, of golden daffodils;
Beside the lake, beneath the trees,   5
Fluttering and dancing in the breeze.

Continuous as the stars that shine
And twinkle on the milky way,
They stretched in never-ending line
Along the margin of a bay: 10
Ten thousand saw I at a glance,
Tossing their heads in sprightly dance.

The waves beside them danced; but they
Out-did the sparkling waves in glee:
A poet could not but be gay,   15
In such a jocund° company: *cheerful, merry*
I gazed—and gazed—but little thought
What wealth the show to me had brought:

For oft, when on my couch I lie
In vacant or in pensive mood,   20
They flash upon that inward eye
Which is the bliss of solitude;
And then my heart with pleasure fills,
And dances with the daffodils.

Wordsworth's note: "Written at Town-end, Grasmere. Daffodils grew and still grow on the margin of Ullswater, and probably may be seen to this day as beautiful in the month of March, nodding their golden heads beside the dancing and foaming waves." Wordsworth also pointed out that lines 21 and 22, the "best lines," were by his wife, Mary.

Lines Written in Early Spring   *1798*

I heard a thousand blended notes,
While in a grove I sate° reclined,   *sat*
In that sweet mood when pleasant thoughts
Bring sad thoughts to the mind.

To her fair works did Nature link   5
The human soul that through me ran;
And much it grieved my heart to think
What man has made of man.

Through primrose tufts, in that green bower,
The periwinkle° trailed its wreaths;   10
And 'tis my faith that every flower
Enjoys the air it breathes.

The birds around me hopped and played,
Their thoughts I cannot measure—
But the least motion which they made,   15
It seemed a thrill of pleasure.

The budding twigs spread out their fan,
To catch the breezy air;
And I must think, do all I can,
That there was pleasure there.   20

If this belief from heaven be sent,
If such be Nature's holy plan,
Have I not reason to lament
What man has made of man?

LINES WRITTEN IN EARLY SPRING. 10 *periwinkle:* a trailing evergreen plant with blue or white flowers.

Ode: Intimations of Immortality from Recollections of Early Childhood   *1807*

> *The Child is Father of the Man;*
> *And I could wish my days to be*
> *Bound each to each by natural piety.*

I

There was a time when meadow, grove, and stream,
The earth, and every common sight,
          To me did seem
          Apparelled in celestial light,
The glory and the freshness of a dream.   5
It is not now as it hath been of yore;—
          Turn wheresoe'er I may,

By night or day,
The things which I have seen I now can see no more.

II

The Rainbow comes and goes,
And lovely is the Rose;
The Moon doth with delight   10
Look round her when the heavens are bare;
Waters on a starry night
Are beautiful and fair;
The sunshine is a glorious birth;
But yet I know, where'er I go,   15
That there hath past away a glory from the earth.

III

Now, while the birds thus sing a joyous song,
And while the young lambs bound
As to the tabor's sound,
To me alone there came a thought of grief: 20
A timely utterance gave that thought relief,
And I again am strong:
The cataracts blow their trumpets from the steep;
No more shall grief of mine the season wrong;   25
I hear the Echoes through the mountains throng,
The Winds come to me from the fields of sleep,
And all the earth is gay;
Land and sea
Give themselves up to jollity,   30
And with the heart of May
Doth every Beast keep holiday;—
Thou Child of Joy,
Shout round me, let me hear thy shouts, thou happy   35
Shepherd-boy!

IV

Ye blessèd Creatures, I have heard the call
Ye to each other make; I see
The heavens laugh with you in your jubilee;
My heart is at your festival,
My head hath its coronal,   40
The fulness of your bliss, I feel—I feel it all.
Oh evil day! if I were sullen
While Earth herself is adorning,
This sweet May-morning,   45
And the Children are culling
On every side,
In a thousand valleys far and wide,
Fresh flowers; while the sun shines warm,
And the Babe leaps up on his Mother's arm:—   50

I hear, I hear, with joy I hear!
　　—But there's a Tree, of many, one,
A single Field which I have looked upon,
Both of them speak of something that is gone:
　　　The Pansy at my feet
　　　Doth the same tale repeat:
Whither is fled the visionary gleam?
Where is it now, the glory and the dream?

V

Our birth is but a sleep and a forgetting:
The Soul that rises with us, our life's Star,　　　　　　　　　60
　　　Hath had elsewhere its setting,
　　　　And cometh from afar:
　　　Not in entire forgetfulness,
　　　And not in utter nakedness,
But trailing clouds of glory do we come　　　　　　　　　65
　　　From God, who is our home:
Heaven lies about us in our infancy!
Shades of the prison-house begin to close
　　　Upon the growing Boy,
　　　　But He　　　　　　　　　70
Beholds the light, and whence it flows,
　　　He sees it in his joy;
The Youth, who daily farther from the east
　　　Must travel, still is Nature's Priest,
　　　And by the vision splendid　　　　　　　　　75
　　　Is on his way attended;
At length the Man perceives it die away,
And fade into the light of common day.

VI

Earth fills her lap with pleasures of her own;
Yearnings she hath in her own natural kind,　　　　　　　80
And, even with something of a Mother's mind,
　　　And no unworthy aim,
　　　The homely Nurse doth all she can
To make her Foster-child, her Inmate Man,
　　　Forget the glories he hath known,　　　　　　　85
And that imperial palace whence he came.

VII

Behold the Child among his new-born blisses,
A six years' Darling of a pigmy size!
See, where 'mid work of his own hand he lies,
Fretted by sallies of his mother's kisses,　　　　　　　90
With light upon him from his father's eyes!
See, at his feet, some little plan or chart,
Some fragment from his dream of human life,

Shaped by himself with newly-learnèd art;
 A wedding or a festival,   95
 A mourning or a funeral;
  And this hath now his heart,
  And unto this he frames his song:
  Then will he fit his tongue
To dialogues of business, love, or strife;   100
 But it will not be long
 Ere this be thrown aside,
 And with new joy and pride
The little Actor cons another part;
Filling from time to time his 'humorous stage'   105
With all the Persons, down to palsied Age,
That Life brings with her in her equipage;
 As if his whole vocation
   Were endless imitation.

VIII

Thou, whose exterior semblance doth belie   110
  Thy Soul's immensity;
Thou best Philosopher, who yet dost keep
Thy heritage, thou Eye among the blind,
That, deaf and silent, read'st the eternal deep,
Haunted for ever by the eternal mind,—   115
  Mighty Prophet! Seer blest!
  On whom those truths do rest,
Which we are toiling all our lives to find,
In darkness lost, the darkness of the grave;
Thou, over whom thy Immortality   120
Broods like the Day, a Master o'er a Slave,
A Presence which is not to be put by;
Thou little Child, yet glorious in the might
Of heaven-born freedom on thy being's height,
Why with such earnest pains dost thou provoke   125
The years to bring the inevitable yoke,
Thus blindly with thy blessedness at strife?
Full soon thy Soul shall have her earthly freight,
And custom lie upon thee with a weight,
Heavy as frost, and deep almost as life!   130

IX

  O joy! that in our embers
  Is something that doth live,
  That nature yet remembers
  What was so fugitive!
The thought of our past years in me doth breed   135
Perpetual benediction: not indeed
For that which is most worthy to be blest;

Delight and liberty, the simple creed
Of Childhood, whether busy or at rest,
With new-fledged hope still fluttering in his breast:— 140
    Not for these I raise
    The song of thanks and praise;
But for those obstinate questionings
Of sense and outward things,
Fallings from us, vanishings; 145
  Blank misgivings of a Creature
Moving about in worlds not realized,
High instincts before which our mortal Nature
Did tremble like a guilty Thing surprised:
    But for those first affections, 150
    Those shadowy recollections,
  Which, be they what they may,
Are yet the fountain light of all our day,
Are yet a master light of all our seeing;
  Uphold us, cherish, and have power to make 155
Our noisy years seem moments in the being
Of the eternal Silence: truths that wake,
    To perish never;
  Which neither listlessness, nor mad endeavour,
    Nor Man nor Boy, 160
Nor all that is at enmity with joy,
Can utterly abolish or destroy!
    Hence in a season of calm weather
    Though inland far we be,
Our Souls have sight of that immortal sea 165
    Which brought us hither,
  Can in a moment travel thither,
And see the Children sport upon the shore,
And hear the mighty waters rolling evermore.

       X

Then sing, ye Birds, sing, sing a joyous song! 170
    And let the young Lambs bound
    As to the tabor's sound!
We in thought will join your throng,
    Ye that pipe and ye that play,
    Ye that through your hearts today 175
    Feel the gladness of the May!
What though the radiance which was once so bright
Be now for ever taken from my sight,
    Though nothing can bring back the hour
Of splendour in the grass, of glory in the flower; 180
    We will grieve not, rather find
    Strength in what remains behind;
    In the primal sympathy
    Which having been must ever be;
    In the soothing thoughts that spring 185

Out of human suffering;
 In the faith that looks through death,
In years that bring the philosophic mind.

XI

And O, ye Fountains, Meadows, Hills, and Groves,
Forebode not any severing of our loves!
Yet in my heart of hearts I feel your might;   190
I only have relinquished one delight
To live beneath your more habitual sway.
I love the Brooks which down their channels fret,
Even more than when I tripped lightly as they;   195
The innocent brightness of a new-born Day
  Is lovely yet;
The Clouds that gather round the setting sun
Do take a sober colouring from an eye
That hath kept watch o'er man's mortality;   200
Another race hath been, and other palms are won.
Thanks to the human heart by which we live,
Thanks to its tenderness, its joys, and fears,
To me the meanest flower that blows can give
Thoughts that do often lie too deep for tears.   205

Expostulation and Reply 1798

"Why, William, on that old grey stone,
Thus for the length of half a day,
Why, William, sit you thus alone,
And dream your time away?

"Where are your books?—that light bequeathed   5
To Beings else forlorn and blind!
Up! up! and drink the spirit breathed
From dead men to their kind.

"You look round on your Mother Earth,
As if she for no purpose bore you;   10
As if you were her first-born birth,
And none had lived before you!"

One morning thus, by Esthwaite lake,
When life was sweet, I knew not why,
To me my good friend Matthew spake,   15
And thus I made reply.

"The eye—it cannot choose but see;
We cannot bid the ear be still;
Our bodies feel, where'er they be,
Against or with our will.   20

"Nor less I deem that there are Powers
Which of themselves our minds impress;

That we can feed this mind of ours
In a wise passiveness.

"Think you, 'mid all this mighty sum   25
Of things for ever speaking,
That nothing of itself will come,
But we must still be seeking?

"—Then ask not wherefore, here, alone,   30
Conversing as I may,
I sit upon this old grey stone,
And dream my time away."

The Tables Turned ⤳⟜⟜⟜ 1798

An Evening Scene on the Same Subject

Up! up! my Friend, and quit your books;
Or surely you'll grow double:
Up! up! my Friend, and clear your looks;
Why all this toil and trouble?

The sun, above the mountain's head,   5
A freshening lustre mellow
Through all the long green fields has spread,
His first sweet evening yellow.

Books! 'tis a dull and endless strife:
Come, hear the woodland linnet,   10
How sweet his music! on my life,
There's more of wisdom in it.

And hark! how blithe the throstle sings!
He, too, is no mean preacher:
Come forth into the light of things,   15
Let Nature be your Teacher.

She has a world of ready wealth,
Our minds and hearts to bless—
Spontaneous wisdom breathed by health,
Truth breathed by cheerfulness.   20

One impulse from a vernal wood
May teach you more of man,
Of moral evil and of good,
Than all the sages can.

Sweet is the lore which Nature brings;   25
Our meddling intellect
Mis-shapes the beauteous forms of things:—
We murder to dissect.

Enough of Science and of Art;
Close up those barren leaves;   30

Come forth, and bring with you a heart
That watches and receives.

Stepping Westward ⇢ ⤙⤚ ⤙⤚ 1807

"*What, you are stepping westward?*"—"*Yea.*"
—'Twould be a *wildish* destiny,
If we, who thus together roam
In a strange Land, and far from home,
Were in this place the guests of Chance: 5
Yet who would stop, or fear to advance,
Though home or shelter he had none,
With such a sky to lead him on?

The dewy ground was dark and cold;
Behind, all gloomy to behold;   10
And stepping westward seemed to be
A kind of *heavenly* destiny:
I liked the greeting; 'twas a sound
Of something without place or bound;
And seemed to give me spiritual right   15
To travel through that region bright.

The voice was soft, and she who spake
Was walking by her native lake:
The salutation had to me
The very sound of courtesy: 20
Its power was felt; and while my eye
Was fixed upon the glowing Sky,
The echo of the voice enwrought
A human sweetness with the thought
Of travelling through the world that lay   25
Before me in my endless way.

Wordsworth's note: While my Fellow-traveller and I were walking by the side of Loch Ketterine, one fine
evening after sunset, in our road to a Hut where, in the course of our Tour, we had been hospitably entertained some weeks before, we met, in one of the loneliest parts of that solitary region, two well-dressed
Women, one of whom said to us, by way of greeting, "What, you are stepping westward?"

The Solitary Reaper ⇢ ⤙⤚ ⤙⤚ 1807

Behold her, single in the field,
Yon solitary Highland Lass!
Reaping and singing by herself;
Stop here, or gently pass!

Alone she cuts and binds the grain,   5
And sings a melancholy strain;
O listen! for the Vale profound
Is overflowing with the sound.

No Nightingale did ever chaunt
More welcome notes to weary bands   10

Of travelers in some shady haunt,
Among Arabian sands;
A voice so thrilling ne'er was heard
In springtime from the Cuckoo bird,
Breaking the silence of the seas   15
Among the farthest Hebrides.°

Will no one tell me what she sings?°
Perhaps the plaintive numbers flow
For old, unhappy, far-off things,
And battles long ago;   20
Or is it some more humble lay,
Familiar matter of today?
Some natural sorrow, loss, or pain,
That has been, and may be again?

Whate'er the theme, the Maiden sang   25
As if her song could have no ending;
I saw her singing at her work,
And o'er the sickle bending—

I listened, motionless and still;
And, as I mounted up the hill,   30
The music in my heart I bore,
Long after it was heard no more.

THE SOLITARY REAPER. 16 *Hebrides:* a group of islands off the west coast of Scotland.   17 *Will . . . sings:*
The speaker does not understand Scots Gaelic, the language in which the woman sings.

❦ SONNETS*

Composed upon Westminster Bridge, September 3, 1802 ⸙⸙⸙ 1807

Earth has not any thing to show more fair:
Dull would he be of soul who could pass by
A sight so touching in its majesty:
This City now doth, like a garment, wear
The beauty of the morning; silent, bare,   5
Ships, towers, domes, theatres, and temples lie
Open unto the fields, and to the sky;
All bright and glittering in the smokeless air.
Never did sun more beautifully steep
In his first splendour, valley, rock, or hill;   10
Ne'er saw I, never felt, a calm so deep!
The river glideth at his own sweet will:
Dear God! the very houses seem asleep;
And all that mighty heart is lying still!

*See also "London, 1802," p. 749.

I Grieved for Buonaparté, with a Vain ⟶⟨⟨⟨ 1807

I grieved for Buonaparté, with a vain
And an unthinking grief! The tenderest mood
Of that Man's mind—what can it be? what food
Fed his first hopes? what knowledge could *he* gain?
'Tis not in battles that from youth we train   5
The Governor who must be wise and good,
And temper with the sternness of the brain
Thoughts motherly, and meek as womanhood.
Wisdom doth live with children round her knees:
Books, leisure, perfect freedom, and the talk   10
Man holds with week-day man in the hourly walk
Of the mind's business: these are the degrees
By which true Sway doth mount; this is the stalk
True Power doth grow on; and her rights are these.

It Is a Beauteous Evening, Calm and Free ⟶⟨⟨⟨ 1807

It is a beauteous evening calm and free,
The holy time is quiet as a Nun
Breathless with adoration; the broad sun
Is sinking down in its tranquillity;
The gentleness of heaven broods o'er the Sea:
Listen! the mighty Being is awake,   5
And doth with his eternal motion make
A sound like thunder—everlastingly.
Dear Child! dear Girl! that walkest with me here,
If thou appear untouched by solemn thought,
Thy nature is not therefore less divine: 10
Thou liest in Abraham's bosom all the year;
And worshipp'st at the Temple's inner shrine,
God being with thee when we know it not.

London, 1802, 749 (See Chapter 17.)

On the Extinction of the Venetian Republic ⟶⟨⟨⟨ 1807

Once did She hold the gorgeous east in fee;
And was the safeguard of the west: the worth
Of Venice did not fall below her birth,
Venice, the eldest Child of Liberty.
She was a maiden City, bright and free;   5
No guile seduced, no force could violate;
And, when she took unto herself a Mate,
She must espouse the everlasting Sea.
And what if she had seen those glories fade,
Those titles vanish, and that strength decay;   10
Yet shall some tribute of regret be paid
When her long life hath reached its final day:
Men are we, and must grieve when even the Shade
Of that which once was great, is passed away.

Scorn Not the Sonnet ~~~~~ 1827

Scorn not the Sonnet; Critic, you have frowned,
Mindless of its just honours, with this key
Shakespeare unlocked his heart; the melody
Of this small lute gave ease to Petrarch's wound;
A thousand times this pipe did Tasso sound;   5
With it Camoëns soothed an exile's grief;
The Sonnet glittered a gay myrtle leaf
Amid the cypress with which Dante crowned
His visionary brow: a glow-worm lamp,
It cheered mild Spenser, called from Faery-land   10
To struggle through dark ways; and, when a damp
Fell round the path of Milton, in his hand
The Thing became a trumpet; whence he blew
Soul-animating strains—alas, too few!

To Toussaint L'Ouverture ~~~~~ 1807

Toussaint,° the most unhappy man of men!
Whether the whistling Rustic tend his plough
Within thy hearing, or thy head be now
Pillowed in some deep dungeon's earless den;—
O miserable Chieftain! where and when   5
Wilt thou find patience? Yet die not; do thou
Wear rather in thy bonds a cheerful brow:
Though fallen thyself, never to rise again,
Live, and take comfort. Thou hast left behind
Powers that will work for thee, air, earth, and skies;   10
There's not a breathing of the common wind
That will forget thee; thou hast great allies;
Thy friends are exultations, agonies,
And love, and man's unconquerable mind.

TO TOUSSAINT L'OUVERTURE. 1 *Toussaint.* Haitian revolutionary leader imprisoned by Napoleon.

EMILY DICKINSON (1830–1886)

Life and Work

Emily Elizabeth Dickinson, who is acknowledged as one of America's greatest poets, was born on December 10, 1830. She was raised in Amherst, Massachusetts, which in the nineteenth century was a small and tradition-bound town. Dominating the Dickinson family was Emily's father, Edward, a lawyer, a legislator, and also a rigorous Calvinist, whose concept of life was stern religious observance and obedience to God's laws. Emily was taken to Sunday School, but late in her teens she declined to pronounce herself a believing Christian. She spent a number of years at primary school and eventually studied classics at Amherst Academy. She also

Emily Dickinson

enrolled at the South Hadley Seminary for Women (now Mount Holyoke College), but her parents withdrew her after a year because of ill health.[2]

During these years of childood and youth, she led a normally active life. She saw many people, liked school and her teachers, wrote essays, acquired a number of good friends, gossiped, sang at the piano to her own accompaniment, treasured spring flowers, amused her friends with impromptu stories, studied theology, read Pope's *An Essay on Man,* and planned to become the "Belle of Amherst" at the age of seventeen. She also began writing poetry, which consisted mainly of occasional verses and valentines.

After leaving school she returned home. She was to spend the rest of her life there, sharing in family and household duties. In 1856 she won a second prize at the local fair for her recipe for rye and Indian bread. She took occasional trips, including long stays in Boston in 1864 and 1865 to be treated for an undisclosed eye ailment. Eventually, however, she stopped traveling altogether.

She included a number of men among her friends and correspondents. One was Benjamin Newton, a law student whom she met in 1848 and who undertook to guide her reading. This guidance was cut short, however, because Newton married, moved away, and died of tuberculosis in 1853. The second

---

[2]It would appear that there are four reliable likenesses of Emily Dickinson. The first is a painting of her and her brother and sister, done by Otis A. Bullard in about 1840, showing Emily at the age of about nine. There is a silhouette of her at the age of about fourteen. The first and most reliable photo is a daguerreotype taken of her at about the age of sixteen. This is the photo that is always duplicated. Still another photograph has come to light that may show Dickinson at the age of about thirty to thirty-five. As yet the photo, an albumen print with Dickinson's name on the back, has not been authenticated, but it is fair to say that its resemblance to the authentic photo is uncanny. See *The New Yorker,* May 22, 2000, pp. 30–31. This photo is included in Alfred Habegger, *My Wars Are Laid Away in Books* (2001), where all the likenesses are included. Habegger believes that the photo is authentic. Richard B. Sewall includes a photograph of a young woman as the frontispiece to the second volume of his *The Life of Emily Dickinson* (1974), and he duplicates this same photo on page 752 of the one-volume *Life* of 1980. On the back of the original is written "Emily Dickenson 1860" in an unknown hand, and the features of the portrayed woman are consistent with those in the daguerrotype of Dickinson at sixteen. Although it is tempting to consider this photograph genuine, the attribution has not been validated.

man was Reverend Charles Wadsworth, a Philadelphia minister whom she met in 1854. She regarded him as an intellectual adviser and her "dearest earthly friend." Her poetic activity increased considerably during the time she knew and corresponded with him, particularly after he left for San Francisco in 1862 to accept a ministerial call. The two saw each other only once more, in 1880, when he returned for a visit.

After Wadsworth's departure, Dickinson began corresponding with Thomas Higginson, a literary critic and Civil War hero who had written an article encouraging young writers. She sent him some of her poetry and asked if her verses "breathed" enough to warrant publication. She may have viewed Higginson as another mentor, but she soon discovered that his literary judgments were stultifying. Indeed, some critics conclude that his inability to understand her poetic methods was a major reason she did not publish collections of her poems during her lifetime. He visited her in August of 1870 and noted her nervousness and her girlish energy (she was thirty-nine at the time). He listened more than he spoke, believing that to interrupt her would cause her to withdraw from conversation. Later he wrote that she exhibited a unique capacity to drain his "nerve power" and that he was therefore glad he did not live near her. Ironically, Higginson became one of the first editors of her work after her death in 1886.

Still another man of importance to her, to whom she wrote often, was Otis Lord, a judge who had been her father's closest friend (her father died in 1874). Lord was a regular guest in the Dickinson household. He and Dickinson seem to have loved each other, for he proposed marriage to her in 1878. She did not love him sufficiently to accept his offer, but afterward the two remained on good terms.

Although Dickinson had written poems since her school days, she did not devote herself to poetry until her late twenties—beginning in about 1858. After this time her poetic output expanded, almost miraculously. Many of her poems are quite short, consisting of no more than a single stanza, but some are much longer. No more than ten of them were published during her lifetime, mostly against her wishes. Instead, her "publication" consisted of making fair copies of the poems in longhand that is quite difficult to read. In the privacy of her own room she put numbers of poems together in what were later called "fascicles," which consisted of folded sheets of stationery bound with thread. These handwritten copies were for her eyes only, although she frequently sent copies in letters and also sent batches of poems to friends. The poems she didn't prepare carefully for her fascicles were kept in little packets. She locked away all these private literary treasures, which were discovered only after her death.

In total, 1,775 to 1,789 of her poems have been recovered. The figure 1,775 is the number of poems included by Thomas H. Johnson in *The Complete Poems of Emily Dickinson* (1955), the first major complete edition of Dickinson's poetry. The figure 1,789 is the number included by Ralph W. Franklin in *The Poems of Emily Dickinson: Variorum Edition* (1998). Both editions are based on exhaustive studies of all the documentary evidence available at the times when the editors were doing their research. Beyond these major scholarly editions, a number of brief poems have been recently mined from Dickinson's letters and published, in 1993, as 498 new poems, on the theory that parts of the letters reach a succinctness and rhythm more characteristic of poetry than prose.

These poems are short, some being no more than two lines long. If one accepts them as additional Dickinson poems, they bring the total count above 2,280.

At the same time as Dickinson was creating this overwhelmingly large body of poetry, she also became reclusive. She removed herself from much of life's business, and she took to wearing only white dresses. Naturally, such behavior created interest and speculation. One of the stories about her was that her reclusiveness was so extreme that even when she gave gingerbread to local children she stayed at an upper window and lowered the sweets in a basket so that she might not be seen. Another was that she concealed herself behind doors when speaking to visitors (see "I Cannot Live with You," line 47). At first, she was not housebound, for she shared both outside and inside household work, and she visited nearby friends. But by the time she was forty she refused invitations, staying almost entirely inside the family house. One of her major tasks was caring for her parents until they died. When she became an invalid herself during the last year of her life, she was cared for by her younger sister Lavinia. She died in May 1886.

Poetic Characteristics

Dickinson's most productive years were between 1862 and 1865, when she wrote at least 760 poems. This amazingly high number is hard to account for on biographical grounds. As much as one can say is that, by her thirties, she had matured as an observer, thinker, and poet and that she compulsively turned to verse as the expression of her thought and meditation. What Dickinson sought in poetry—both what she read and what she wrote—was intensity more than form. When Thomas Higginson visited her in 1870, she declared her views positively. She said that if she was reading a book and found that

it makes my whole body so cold no fire ever can warm me I know *that* is poetry. If I feel physically as if the top of my head were taken off, I know *that* is poetry. These are the only way I know it. Is there any other way.

In her poetry she successfully achieves such intensity. Her poems are energetic, imaginative, astoundingly creative, and also economical. Within a small number of lines she covers vast distances. Who but Dickinson, for example, could conceive the first line of "I Heard a Fly Buzz–When I Died," and even more, who could progress from this opening to the concluding sentence, "I could not see to see"? Because she covers so much territory, her style is sometimes elliptical and obscure, producing a rapid interplay of thoughts and images. Her diction is neutral, with a number of formal words that may be taken as evidence of her reading and general knowledge. In her desire for accuracy she regularly referred to Webster's *Dictionary*, one of the books she kept at her side. This fact has caused critics to observe that reading her poetry often requires the aid of a dictionary.

Her sentences are regularly broken by interjections and sentence fragments. She uses these grammatical irregularities deliberately, just as she employs capital letters to emphasize words. In addition, she indulges in eccentricities of punctuation. Because her poems are mostly private monologues, she usually ignores periods and commas, instead adopting dashes and exclamation points to mark rhythm and vocal modulations. To suggest varying degrees of expressiveness, she uses dashes of differing lengths, although printed texts obscure this subtlety.

Dickinson's earliest experiences with the poetry of others was with the quatrain form (see Chapter 20), which abounds in Protestant hymnals of the time. It is thus no surprise that in her own poems she frequently uses common measure and the ballad stanza. She is no metronomic observer of meter, however, for many of her stanzaic forms are irregular. She achieves flexibility and originality by shortening many lines, varying many of the meters, and freely inserting midline caesurae, or brief pauses. She is a skilled rhymer, preferring exact rhymes but also using slant rhymes, eye rhymes, vowel rhymes, and repeated-word rhymes (*identical rhyme*). These irregularities, which confounded Dickinson's first editors, have since been recognized as important and effective elements of her poetic craft.

Poetic Subjects

Although, as we have seen, a surprising amount of biographical information is available about Dickinson, the key details are missing—the connections between events in her life and her poems. For example, it seems obvious that a real and powerful sadness underlies the poignant conclusion of "Safe in Their Alabaster Chambers," just as a sense of personal inadequacy or reproach may have caused her to write "I Felt a Funeral in My Brain." We can only guess, however, about the specific situations that led her to write such poems.

Nevertheless, the general occasions inspiring some of her poems are clear. The world she lived in was small, and she found subjects in her surroundings: house, garden, yard, and village. A lowly snake is the topic of one of her poems—one of the few published when she was alive—as are butterflies, a singing oriole, and a vibrating hummingbird. She even wrote a poem about the railroad locomotives servicing Amherst. Sometimes no more than a recollection, a single word, a concept, or a paradox that arose from her own interior monologue enabled her to originate poems. Such inspirations account for topics such as a haunted mind, a memory, a state of solitude, the nature of truth and beauty, the condition of self-reliance, the angle of winter light. For one of the poems, "My Triumph Lasted Till the Drums," one may postulate a connection with her thoughts about the Civil War. She was at the height of her poetic power during this time, and she expresses feelings about the horrors of the war in these ironic lines: "A Bayonet's contrition / Is nothing to the Dead."

Dickinson's poems on death and dying probably had occasional sources also, even though these sources may be far removed from the time and circumstance of the poems. One of Dickinson's dearest childhood friends was Sophia Holland, who died in 1844. Perhaps the loss of Sophia was one of her memories when she wrote "I Never Lost as Much But Twice" and "This World Is Not Conclusion," together with her other poems on death.

Emily Dickinson's room at the family homestead in Amherst, Massachusetts, where she wrote much of her poetry.

Much of her other poetry may have a similar if remote occasional origin. She wrote poems about love and the psychology of personal relationships, even though she never married or had a love affair that we know about. We may therefore wonder about the internal necessity that caused her to write poems like "Wild Nights–Wild Nights!" and "I Cannot Live with You," which portray states of sexual ecstasy and final renunciation. And what sorts of personal experience and introspection underlay such poems as "After Great Pain, a Formal Feeling Comes," "The Soul Selects Her Own Society," and "One Need Not Be a Chamber – To Be Haunted"?

In the absence of specific details linking her life to her poetry, therefore, the occasions of her poems must remain no more than peripherally relevant—themselves unseen, though in the effects they remain. We are left to conclude that her inspiration rose from within herself. She is a personal, contemplative, confessional poet, whether she herself is the omnipresent "I" of her poems or whether the "I" is an objective speaker to whom she assigns all the strength of her imagination and her dreams. This speaker possesses bright wit, clever and engaging playfulness, acute powers of observation, deep sensitivity, intense introspection, and tender responsiveness. She is alive, quick, and inventive. She enjoys riddles. She leads readers into new and unexplored regions of thought and feeling.

All these characteristics are to be discovered everywhere in her poetry. Her speaker expresses a vital joy and delirious energy in the quizzical poem "I Taste a Liquor Never Brewed," an insouciant bluffness in "I'm Nobody! Who Are You?," inner terror in "One Need Not Be a Chamber – To Be Haunted," and overwhelming tenderness and regret at the end of "The Bustle in a House." In

the last stanza of "I Cannot Live with You" she captures the deep anguish of a relationship that is ending.

So We must meet apart –
You there – I – here –
With just the Door ajar
That Oceans are – and Prayer –
And that White Sustenance –
Despair –

She is also reverent, and a number of poems introduce the topics of God, immortality, scripture, and the final judgment. But she is sometimes saucy and flippant about religion. Going to church on Sunday, for example, was expected of
the dutiful Christian, but she explains why she prefers staying home with "a
Bobolink for a Chorister."

So instead of getting to Heaven, at last –
I'm going, all along.

Undeniably, Dickinson's external daily life was uneventful. Her inner life
was anything but uneventful, however, for she was always reflecting and thinking. What we know about her is that her inquiring and restless mind was the
source of her compulsive poetic strength, and that her poetry expresses the vital
personal feelings and psychological insights that emerged from her thoughts
about life, love, death, Nature, and God. It is not possible to read her poems
without revering her as a person and as a poet.

Bibliographic Sources

After Dickinson died, her sister, Lavinia, was astonished to find the many fascicles and packets of poems that she had left. Lavinia recognized the significance
of this work and eventually turned much of it over to Thomas Higginson and
Mabel L. Todd for editing and publication. They published three separate volumes of Dickinson's verse (in 1890, 1891, and 1896), each containing about a
hundred poems. In these volumes, the editors eliminated slant rhymes,
smoothed out the meter, revised those metaphors that struck them as outrageous, and regularized the punctuation.

These well-intentioned editorial "adjustments" remained intact until 1955,
when the Harvard University Press published Thomas H. Johnson's three-vol-
ume complete edition. Johnson also published a single-volume edition of the
poems in 1961 and, in addition, a paperback selection titled *Final Harvest: Emily
Dickinson's Poems* (1961). Johnson's pioneering edition has been followed by the
ambitious and comprehensive *The Poems of Emily Dickinson: Variorum Edition* in
three volumes (Cambridge: Harvard UP, 1998), edited by Ralph W. Franklin,
who also edited the facsimile edition of the handwritten poems, *The Manuscript
Books of Emily Dickinson* (Cambridge: Harvard UP, 1981). Franklin's edition has
also been published in one volume as *The Poems of Emily Dickinson: Reading Edition* (Cambridge: Harvard UP, 1999). The poems that have been extracted from

Dickinson's letters, which we have already mentioned, were edited by William H. Shurr, with Anna Dunlap and Emily Grey Shurr, as *New Poems of Emily Dickinson* (Chapel Hill: U of North Carolina P, 1993).

Definitive biographies of Dickinson are Richard B. Sewall, *The Life of Emily Dickinson* (New York: Farrar, 1974; rpt. [Harvard UP] 1980; rpt. 1994), Alfred Habegger, *My Wars Are Laid Away in Books: The Life of Emily Dickinson* (New York: Random House, 2001), and Cynthia Griffin Wolff, *Emily Dickinson* (New York: Knopf, 1986). A useful book containing biographical, critical, and many other details is Jane Donahue Eberwein, ed., *An Emily Dickinson Encyclopedia* (Westport: Greenwood, 1998). The numbers of important critical studies are legion. Some of these are Albert J. Gelpi, *Emily Dickinson: The Mind of the Poet* (Cambridge: Harvard UP, 1966); Joanne F. Diehl, *Dickinson and the Romantic Imagination* (Princeton: Princeton UP, 1981); David Porter, *Dickinson, the Modern Idiom* (Cambridge: Harvard UP, 1981); Susan Juhasz, *The Undiscovered Continent: Emily Dickinson and the Space of the Mind* (Bloomington: U of Indiana P, 1983); E. Miller Budick, *Emily Dickinson and the Life of Language: A Study in Symbolic Poetics* (Baton Rouge: Louisiana State UP, 1985); Donna Dickenson, *Emily Dickinson* (Leamington Spa: Berg, 1985); Sharon Leder and Andrea Abbott, *The Language of Exclusion: The Poetry of Emily Dickinson and Christina Rossetti* (New York: Greenwood, 1987); Cristanne Miller, *Emily Dickinson: A Poet's Grammar* (Cambridge: Harvard UP, 1987); Elizabeth Phillips, *Emily Dickinson: Personae and Performance* (University Park: Pennsylvania State UP, 1988); Joanne Dobson, *Dickinson and the Strategies of Reticence* (Bloomington: U of Indiana P, 1989); Paula Bennett, *Emily Dickinson: Woman Poet* (Iowa City: U of Iowa P, 1990); Gary Lee Stonum, *The Dickinson Sublime* (Madison: U of Wisconsin P, 1990); Joan Kirkby, *Emily Dickinson* (New York: St. Martin's, 1991); Judith Farr, *The Passion of Emily Dickinson* (Cambridge: Harvard UP, 1992); Claudia Ottlinger, *The Death-Motif in the Poetry of Emily Dickinson and Christina Rossetti* (Frankfurt: Lang, 1996); and Paul Crumbley, *Inflections of the Pen: Dash and Voice in Emily Dickinson* (Lexington: U of Kentucky P, 1996).

Collections of essays on Dickinson are Paul J. Ferlazzo, ed., *Critical Essays on Emily Dickinson* (Boston: Hall, 1958, a historical collection); Richard B. Sewall, ed., *Emily Dickinson: A Collection of Critical Essays* (Englewood Cliffs: Prentice Hall, 1963); Judith Farr, ed., *Emily Dickinson: A Collection of Critical Essays* (Upper Saddle River: Prentice Hall, 1996), and Gudrun Grabher et al., eds. *The Emily Dickinson Handbook* (Amherst: U of Massachusetts P, 1998). One of the hour-long programs in the PBS *Voices and Visions* series (1987) features Dickinson's work.

Special Topics for Writing and Argument about the Poetry of Emily Dickinson

1. Dickinson's characteristic brevity in the explanation of situations and the expression of ideas.

2. Dickinson's use of personal but not totally disclosed subject matter.

3. Dickinson's use of imagery and symbolism: sources, types, meanings. Her humor and irony.

4. Dickinson's ideas about love, separation, personal pain, war, death, faith, religion, science, the soul.

5. Dickinson's power as a poet.

6. Dickinson's poems as they appear on the page: the relationship of meaning to lines, stanzas, capitalization, punctuation, the use of the dash.

7. The structuring of a number of Dickinson's poems: subject, development, conclusions.

8. The character of the speaker in a number of Dickinson's poems: personality, things noticed, accuracy of conclusions. If there appears to be a listener in the poems, what effect does this listener have on the speaker?

9. Dickinson's verse forms and use of rhymes.

10. Themes of exhilaration, sorrow, pity, triumph, and regret in Dickinson.

For ease in locating the selections included here, the poems are arranged alphabetically by the first significant words in first lines. There are two numbers following the title of each poem. The first number (e.g., J501) refers to the poem numbers in Thomas H. Johnson's *The Complete Poems of Emily Dickinson*. Critics since Johnson's edition have unanimously employed these numbers. The second number (e.g., F373) refers to the new numbering in Ralph W. Franklin's *The Poems of Emily Dickinson: Variorum Edition*. It would appear that future Dickinson criticism will need to include both numbers if the poem under discussion is to be properly identified, as with the following title: *After Great Pain, a Formal Feeling Comes (J341, F372)*.

The texts are based on Franklin's edition. Typographically, we have also followed Franklin's edition in treating the dash; as in the following line, *After great pain, a formal feeling comes –*. Many past editions have utilized a longer dash, as in *After great pain, a formal feeling comes—*.

POEMS BY EMILY DICKINSON

After Great Pain, a Formal Feeling Comes (J341, F372) ⟩⟨⟩⟨⟩ 1929 *(ca. 1862)*

After great pain, a formal feeling comes –
The Nerves sit ceremonious, like Tombs –
The Stiff Heart questions 'was it He, that bore,'
And 'Yesterday, or Centuries before'?

The Feet, mechanical, go round –   5
A Wooden way
Of Ground, or Air, or Ought° –   *anything, nothing*
Regardless grown,
A Quartz contentment, like a stone –

This is the Hour of Lead –   10
Remembered, if outlived,
As Freezing persons, recollect the Snow –
First – Chill – then Stupor – then the letting go –

Because I Could Not Stop for Death (J712, F479), 620 (See Chapter 13.)

The Bustle in a House (J1078, F1108) ⟩⟨⟩⟨⟩ 1890 *(ca. 1865)*

The Bustle in a House
The Morning after Death
Is solemnest of industries
Enacted upon Earth –

The Sweeping up the Heart   5
And putting Love away
We shall not want to use again
Until Eternity –

The Heart Is the Capital of the Mind (J1354, F1381) ⟩⟨⟩⟨⟩ 1929 *(ca. 1875)*

The Heart is the Capital of the Mind –
The Mind is a single State –
The Heart and the Mind together make
A single Continent.

One – is the Population –   5
Numerous enough –

This ecstatic Nation
Seek – it is Yourself –

I Cannot Live with You (J640, F706)   1890 (ca. 1863)

I cannot live with You –
It would be Life –
And Life is over there –
Behind the Shelf

The Sexton keeps the Key to –   5
Putting up
Our Life – His Porcelain –
Like a Cup –

Discarded of the Housewife –
Quaint – or Broke –   10
A newer Sevres° pleases –   *a fine French porcelain*
Old Ones crack –

I could not die – with You –
For One must wait
To shut the Other's Gaze down –   15
You – could not –

And I – Could I stand by
And see You – freeze –
Without my Right of Frost –
Death's privilege?   20

Nor could I rise – with You –
Because Your Face
Would put out Jesus' –
That New Grace

Glow plain – and foreign   25
On my homesick eye –
Except that You than He
Shone closer by –

They'd judge Us – How –
For You – served Heaven – You know,   30
Or sought to –
I could not –

Because You saturated sight –
And I had no more eyes
For sordid excellence   35
As Paradise

And were You lost, I would be –
Though my name
Rang loudest
On the Heavenly fame –   40

And were You – saved –
And I – condemned to be
Where You were not
That self – were Hell to Me –

So We must meet apart –   45
You there – I – here –
With just the Door ajar
That Oceans are – and Prayer –
And that White Sustenance –
Despair –   50

I Died for Beauty – but Was Scarce (J449, F448)   1890 (ca. 1862)

I died for Beauty – but was scarce
Adjusted in the Tomb
When One who died for Truth, was lain
In an adjoining Room –

He questioned softly "Why I failed"?   5
"For Beauty", I replied –
"And I – for Truth – Themselves are One –
We Brethren, are", He said –

And so, as Kinsmen, met a Night –
We talked between the Rooms –   10
Until the Moss had reached our lips –
And covered up – Our names –

I Felt a Funeral in My Brain (J280, F340)   1896 (ca. 1862)

I felt a Funeral, in my Brain,
And Mourners to and fro
Kept treading – treading – till it seemed
That Sense was breaking through –

And when they all were seated,   5
A Service, like a Drum –
Kept beating – beating – till I thought
My mind was going numb –

And then I heard them lift a Box
And creak across my Soul   10
With those same Boots of Lead, again,
Then Space – began to toll,

As all the Heavens were a Bell,
And Being, but an Ear,
And I, and Silence, some strange Race   15
Wrecked, solitary, here –

And then a Plank in Reason, broke,
And I dropped down, and down –
And hit a World, at every plunge,
And Finished knowing – then –   20

I Heard a Fly Buzz – When I Died (J465, F591) 1896 (ca. 1863)

I heard a Fly buzz – when I died –
The Stillness in the Room
Was like the Stillness in the Air –
Between the Heaves of Storm –

The Eyes around – had wrung them dry –   5
And Breaths were gathering firm
For that last Onset – when the King
Be witnessed – in the Room –

I willed my Keepsakes – Signed away
What portion of me be   10
Assignable – and then it was
There interposed a Fly –

With Blue – uncertain – stumbling Buzz –
Between the light – and me –
And then the Windows failed – and then   15
I could not see to see –

I Like to See It Lap the Miles (J585, F383) 1891 (ca. 1862)

I like to see it lap the Miles –
And lick the Valleys up –
And stop to feed itself at Tanks –
And then – prodigious step

Around a Pile of Mountains –   5
And supercilious peer
In Shanties – by the sides of Roads –
And then a Quarry pare

To fit it's sides
And crawl between   10
Complaining all the while
In horrid – hooting stanza –
Then chase itself down Hill –

And neigh like Boanerges° –
Then – prompter than a Star   15
Stop – docile and omnipotent
At it's own stable door –

I LIKE TO SEE IT LAP THE MILES. 14 *Boanerges:* a surname meaning "the sons of thunder" that appears in Mark 3:17.

I'm Nobody! Who Are You? (J288, F260) 1891 (ca. 1861)

I'm Nobody! Who are you?
Are you – Nobody – too?
Then there's a pair of us!
Don't tell! they'd banish us – you know!

How dreary – to be – Somebody!
How public – like a Frog –
To tell your name – the livelong June –
To an admiring Bog!

5

I Never Lost as Much But Twice (J49, F39) ⟶⟵⟶⟵ 1890 (ca. 1858)

I never lost as much but twice –
And that was in the sod.
Twice have I stood a beggar
Before the door of God!

Angels – twice descending
Reimbursed my store –
Burglar! Banker – Father!
I am poor once more!

5

I Taste a Liquor Never Brewed (J214, F207) ⟶⟵⟶⟵ 1861, 1890 (ca. 1860)

I taste a liquor never brewed –
From Tankards scooped in Pearl –
Not all the Frankfort Berries°   *grapes*
Yield such an Alcohol!

Inebriate of Air – am I –   5
And Debauchee of Dew –
Reeling – thro endless summer days –
From inns of Molten Blue –

When "Landlords" turn the drunken Bee
Out of the Foxglove's door –
When Butterflies – renounce their "drams" –   10
I shall but drink the more!

Till Seraphs swing their Snowy Hats –
And Saints – to windows run –
To see the little Tippler   15
From Manzanilla° come!

I TASTE A LIQUOR NEVER BREWED. 16 *Manzanilla:* a pale sherry from Spain. Dickinson may also have been thinking of Manzanillo, a Cuban city known for rum.

Much Madness Is Divinest Sense (J435, F620) ⟶⟵⟶⟵ 1890 (ca. 1863)

Much Madness is divinest Sense –
To a discerning Eye –
Much Sense – the starkest Madness –
'Tis the Majority
In this, as all, prevail –   5
Assent – and you are sane –
Demur – you're straightway dangerous –
And handled with a Chain –

My Life Closed Twice Before It's Close (J1732, F1773)   1896

My life closed twice before it's close;
It yet remains to see
If Immortality unveil
A third event to me,

So huge, so hopeless to conceive   5
As these that twice befell.
Parting is all we know of heaven,
And all we need of hell.

My Triumph Lasted Till the Drums (J1227, F1212)   1935 (ca. 1871)

My Triumph lasted till the Drums
Had left the Dead alone
And then I dropped my Victory
And chastened stole along
To where the finished Faces   5
Conclusion turned on me
And then I hated Glory
And wished myself were They.

What is to be is best descried
When it has also been –   10
Could Prospect taste of Retrospect
The Tyrannies of Men
Were Tenderer, diviner
The Transitive toward –
A Bayonet's contrition   15
Is nothing to the Dead.

One Need Not Be a Chamber – To Be Haunted (J670, F407)   1891 (ca. 1862, 1864)

One need not be a chamber – to be Haunted –
One need not be a House –
The Brain has Corridors – surpassing
Material Place –

Far safer, of a midnight meeting   5
External Ghost
Than it's interior confronting –
That cooler Host –

Far safer, through an Abbey gallop,
The Stones a'chase –   10
Than unarmed, one's a'self encounter –
In lonesome Place –

Ourself behind ourself, concealed –
Should startle most –
Assassin hid in our Apartment   15
Be Horror's least –

The Body – borrows a Revolver –
He bolts the Door –
O'erlooking a superior spectre –
Or More –   20

Safe in Their Alabaster Chambers (J216, F124)   1862 (ca. 1859)

Safe in their Alabaster Chambers –
Untouched by Morning –
And untouched by Noon –
Lie the meek members of the Resurrection –
Rafter of Satin – and Roof of Stone!   5

Grand go the Years – in the Crescent – above them –
Worlds scoop their Arcs –
And Firmaments – row –
Diadems – drop – and Doges° – surrender –
Soundless as dots – on a Disc of snow –   10

SAFE IN THEIR ALABASTER CHAMBERS. 9 *Doges:* Rulers of Venice and Genoa, Italian city-states during the Renaissance.

Some Keep the Sabbath Going to Church (J324, F236)   1864 (ca. 1861)

Some keep the Sabbath going to Church –
I keep it, staying at Home –
With a Bobolink for a Chorister –
And an Orchard, for a Dome –

Some keep the Sabbath in Surplice –
I, just wear my Wings –
And instead of tolling the Bell, for Church,
Our little Sexton – sings.   5

God preaches, a noted Clergyman –
And the sermon is never long.
So instead of getting to Heaven, at last –
I'm going, all along.   10

The Soul Selects Her Own Society (J303, F409)   1890 (ca. 1862)

The Soul selects her own Society –
Then – shuts the Door –
To her divine Majority –
Present no more –

Unmoved – she notes the Chariots – pausing –   5
At her low Gate –
Unmoved – an Emperor be kneeling
Opon° her Mat –   *upon*

I've known her – from an ample nation –
Choose One –   10

Then – close the Valves of her attention –
Like Stone –

Success Is Counted Sweetest (J67, F112)   1864 (ca. 1859)

Success is counted sweetest
By those who ne'er succeed.
To comprehend a nectar
Requires sorest need.

Not one of all the purple Host   5
Who took the Flag today
Can tell the definition
So clear of Victory

As he defeated – dying –
On whose forbidden ear   10
The distant strains of triumph
Burst agonized and clear!

Tell All the Truth but Tell It Slant (J1129, F1263)   1945 (ca. 1872)

Tell all the truth but tell it slant –
Success in Circuit lies
Too bright for our infirm Delight
The Truth's superb surprise
As Lightning to the Children eased   5
With explanation kind
The Truth must dazzle gradually
Or every man be blind –

There's a Certain Slant of Light (J258, F320)   1890 (ca. 1862)

There's a certain Slant of light,
Winter Afternoons –
That oppresses, like the Heft
Of Cathedral Tunes –

Heavenly Hurt, it gives us –   5
We can find no scar,
But internal difference –
Where the Meanings, are –

None may teach it – Any –
'Tis the Seal Despair –   10
An imperial affliction
Sent us of the Air –

When it comes, the Landscape listens –
Shadows – hold their breath –
When it goes, 'tis like the Distance   15
On the look of Death –

This World Is Not Conclusion (J501, F373) ⚘ *1896, 1945 (ca. 1862)*

This World is not Conclusion.
A Species stands beyond –
Invisible, as Music –
But positive, as Sound –
It beckons, and it baffles –   5
Philosophy, dont know –
And through a Riddle, at the last –
Sagacity, must go –
To guess it, puzzles scholars –
To gain it, Men have borne   10
Contempt of Generations
And Crucifixion, shown –
Faith slips – and laughs, and rallies –
Blushes, if any see –
Plucks at a twig of Evidence –   15
And asks a Vane, the way –
Much Gesture, from the Pulpit –
Strong Hallelujahs roll –
Narcotics cannot still the Tooth
That nibbles at the soul –   20

To Hear an Oriole Sing (J526, F402), 813 (See Chapter 19.)

Wild Nights – Wild Nights! (J249, F269) ⚘ *1891 (ca. 1861)*

Wild Nights – Wild Nights!
Were I with thee
Wild Nights should be
Our luxury!

Futile – the winds –   5
To a Heart in port –
Done with the Compass –
Done with the Chart!

Rowing in Eden –
Ah – the Sea!   10
Might I but moor – tonight –
In thee!

❧ EDITED SELECTIONS FROM CRITICISM OF DICKINSON'S POETRY, WITH AN EMPHASIS ON POEMS INCLUDED IN THIS CHAPTER

The following selections are intended to supply details and ideas for essays on Dickinson's poems. For a selective bibliography, consult the "Bibliographic Sources" section (p. 1017), which may be augmented with your college library catalogue and the most recent volumes of the *MLA International Bibliography* available in the reference room of your library. The bracketed page numbers refer to the original pagination of the sources included here. Footnotes in the sources have been deleted.

From "The Flower, the Bee, and the Spider"*

"Tell all the Truth," Emily instructed herself, "but tell it slant— / Success in Circuit lies." [144] When she said that "every suggestion is Dimension," she was really referring to what she called on another occasion "the circumference of Expression," and was thereby assigning to form and style all the connotations of the word "circumference": self contained full-ness and totality; precision of outline and bounds; circuitous definition of center and di-mension. In her mind the Bible, unlike poetry, spoke "with the Centre, not with the Circumference" of expression, because the Bible made emphatic, direct statements about God (the omnipresent Center) in God's own words, whereas poetry could only speak roundabout in her own words. So clearly did she realize that the particular style and form which a poet used was a projection of himself and his experience that she re-jected—politely and gratefully but adamantly—every piece of practical literary advice that "Preceptor" Higginson offered.

What, then, was the basic element in the peculiar and distinctive style which Emily Dickinson made? Emerson had said that organic form depended on making every nu-ance of relation into a new word; the poet named things "sometimes after their appear-ance, sometimes after their essence," and gave "to every one its own name and not another's, thereby rejoicing the intellect, which delights in detachment or boundary." We might often want more conciseness and particularity in Emerson's style, but Emily's [145] friend Dr. Holland expressed a popular contemporary view when he observed of Emer-son's writing: "There is no more spare language on his ideas, than there is flesh on his bones corporeal. A word less on the one, or an atom less on the other, and there would be a fatal catastrophe." In his journal Thoreau had formulated this same first command-ment for the stylist: "By your few words show how insufficient would be many words. . . . In breadth we may be patterns of conciseness, but in depth we may well be prolix." Emily Dickinson refined this tendency toward exactness and condensation even further. If Emerson and Thoreau wrote at their best in well-wrought and precisely tooled sentences, then Emily Dickinson compressed language into finely honed and deliberately placed words. Her mind did not move in abstract or even sequential logic, and so her lan-guage—whether in verse or prose—does not depend on its sweep or smoothness or exu-berance or delicately woven texture or even on its syntactical coherence. Indeed, the very confusion of the syntax—a fairly common occurrence, actually—forces the reader to concentrate on the basic verbal units and derive the strength and meaning largely from the circumference of words.

Therefore, while as the poet-seer she could bewail the inadequacy of words for the vision, as poet-craftsman she reveled time and again in the breadth and depth enclosed in one mighty word:

> Could mortal lip divine
> The undeveloped Freight
> Of a delivered syllable
> 'Twould crumble with the weight.   [J1409, F1456]

*From Albert J. Gelpi, *Emily Dickinson: The Mind of the Poet* (Cambridge: Harvard UP, 1966).

Moreover, her concern was not just with the density or weight of the words but with the "life and palpitation" which Thoreau called for:

> A word is dead
> When it is said,
> Some say.
> I say it just
> Begins to live
> That day.   [J1212, F278]

The vigorous word lived primarily in itself—in its sensual concreteness or its conceptual precision or its connotative resonance or its metaphorical implications—but secondarily it lived in its effect on the verse pattern—that is, in its contribution to rhyme, rhythm, alliteration, and so on. "How lovely," Emily exclaimed to Mrs. Holland, "are the wiles of Words!" . . .

A good indication of her formalism is her insatiable and unabating interest in the [147] wiles of words. Emily told Higginson that for some years her lexicon had been her only companion, and throughout her life she pored over the dictionary as zealously as she read her Bible. From the native strength of words and from her experiments in expanding their scope she fashioned a unique language (Higginson thought it "spasmodic" and "uncontrolled.") She chose words with stinging freshness; she flavored speech with earthy New England colloquialisms; she often dropped the "s" of the third-person singular of the present tense to suggest the enduring quality of the action; she emphasized nouns by the striking addition or omission of the preceding article; she sometimes used singular nouns where plurals were expected and vice versa; she made parts of speech perform unorthodox functions, used words in startling contexts, coined words when none seemed available or apt. Like Ezra Pound, William Carlos Williams, Marianne Moore, and E. E. Cummings, Emily Dickinson sought to speak the uniqueness of her experience in a personal tongue by reconstituting and revitalizing—at the risk of eccentricity—the basic verbal unit.

For the framework in which to set her words, Emily Dickinson came naturally to depend on the standard hymn stanzas. She was familiar with them from church and was otherwise quite unsophisticated in the technicalities of metrics. The quatrains of short lines (mostly three and four beats) imposed the necessity for conciseness and control, and the association with the meetinghouse suggested (whether she realized it or not) the [148] religious basis of her poetic calling. Without relaxing the rigid formality of the quatrains she gave them variety and adaptability through the flexibility of the rhythms (marked by those dots and dashes that serve as breathing points) and through the atonality of slant rimes and the internal harmonics of the vowels and consonants. She had worked out a stanza which was prescribed without monotony and which could be skillfully worked within strict limits.

Take for example this carefully constructed quatrain:

> The Clock strikes one that just struck two—
> Some schism in the Sum—
> A Vagabond from Genesis
> Has wrecked the Pendulum—   [J1569, F1598]

All the words are monosyllables accept for three trisyllabic words (Vagabond, Genesis, Pendulum), and these are reiterated in the trisyllabic rime "in the Sum" and in the three words beginning with "s" in the second line. The tone of the bell "strikes one" in the monosyllables and especially in the words "Clock," "strikes," "struck," and "wrecked." The "two" mentioned at the end of the first line is repeated in the "Some" and "Sum" of the second, which are in turn split by "schism." In the poem which begins "When Bells stop ringing—Church—begins—" (P 633 [J633, F601]) . . . the slow, solemn pace suggests the motionlessness which is the subject of the poem. Another quatrain is built on the tonal possibilities of the letter "o," on which every change is rung:

> The blonde Assassin passes on—
> The Sun proceeds unmoved
> To measure off another Day
> For an Approving God.   [J1624, F1668]

A more complex sound pattern becomes a chamber of echoes, in which "b," "l," and "e" tumble in rapid succession and the short "i" 's of the first line are picked up in the last:

> Admonished by her buckled lips
> Let every babbler be
> The only secret people keep
> Is Immortality.   [J1748, F1776]

This sort of analysis might best be left to the explorations of the individual reader of the poetry, especially since the point is by now plain. Like a good American craftsman, Emily Dickinson whittled her materials, within the limits of a rather strict form, into something of beauty and use. Moreover, the qualities of her style attest to the qualities of her consciousness; at its best the writing is terse, compact, concrete—and yet oblique, cryptic, surrendering its secret only in lightning-flashes of word and metaphor.

From "Orthodox Modernisms"*

Dickinson's power derives partly from a cluster of techniques, from certain themes, and [222] from tonal qualities that we consider modern and admire for their apparent newness. Her work is a catalogue of these modernisms, conventional to us now in their familiarity and so commonly known in her repertoire that a summary here will suffice. She possessed an intuitive knack for exploiting the capacity of language under certain distortions or tensions to arrest, illuminate, pierce, astonish. Her wonderfully engaging first lines range from the controlled audacity of flatness and understatement ("Before I got my eye put out") to marvelous lines of great syntactic pressure involving mystery, lure, expectation, and which play sophisticatedly with line-end novelty and grammatical deception.

The animated lexical selection that is the heart of her craft comprises violations sometimes of great daring. She surprised with her language and, when it was not so deliberately concocted as to be coy or patent, it brings off its risks and shocks in a modern way. A corpse in poem 287 [J287, F259] is "This Pendulum of snow" and death's finality is in "Decades of Arrogance." Elsewhere her lexical surprises manage a careful deflation and austerity that dehumanize, objectify, as in these sciential lines about a corpse:

> The busy eyes—congealed—
> It straightened—that was all . . .
> It multiplied indifference

*From David Porter, *Dickinson, the Modern Idiom* (Cambridge: Harvard UP, 1981).

Dry and hard, spare in a Poundian sense, this cold language forms into an analytical instrument of great accuracy. There is also word parading of the sort we now admire as well in Marianne Moore. In Dickinson's little known poem about a June bug, the polysyllables [223] thump against the single-syllable vernacular:

> From Eminence remote
> Drives ponderous perpendicular
>
> . . . .
>
> Depositing his Thunder
> He hoists abroad again—
> A Bomb upon the Ceiling
> Is an improving thing
> It keeps conjecture flourishing—   [J1128, F1150]

Dickinson interrupted nineteenth-century poetic discourse with a vernacular so direct it seemed crude to her first public. She disarmingly called it in poem 373 [J373, F575] "my simple speech" and "plain word." It was in fact flattened speech, a *talking* that was depoetizing; and an escape from pomposity. Into her poems and particularly into those outrageous first lines came a natural breath and diction that created the illusion and the impact of real speech acts. . . .

Most modern, perhaps, among Dickinson's techniques is her use of language [225] realms as constitutive elements in analytical structure. She makes the language medium itself objective and able to cut like a tool, managing this in at least three ways: vernacular diction inserted in formal language for its cross-cut effect; deploying Anglo-Saxon abruptness against the formalities of Latinate diction (this has been much noticed); and cleverly treating a subject with an alien lexical set. An instance of this last, as I have noted elsewhere, is characterizing God in the language of law or commerce. Dickinson, intuitively audacious in this, makes one language subset cut against and criticize another level of lexical selection, making a drama of language itself as if lexicons were themselves characters. Here is God silently measured by cold legalisms.

> I read my sentence—steadily—
> Reviewed it with my eyes,
> To see that I made no mistake
> In it's extremest clause—
> The Date, and manner, of the shame—
> And then the Pious Form
> That "God have mercy" on the Soul
> The Jury voted Him—   [J412, F432]

Besides such strategies of diction choice at which she was so adept, Dickinson employed other techniques that we call modern. As noted, she elided syntax (for various reasons), omitted transitions, and dropped structural and even syntactical copulas. This habit of withholding connective material produces curiously vexatious ways we now choose to see as modern: discontinuity of structure and story, and remystification of phenomena that seem simple and clear, and those extinguishings of meaning by which we experience complexity and feel the intractable quality of existence again. Beyond this, Dickinson's habitual brevity seems modern in its glimpses and incompleteness. These are notes raised to literature, notation as authentic response. Wayward in punctuation, the poems disregard nicety and neglect finish. They have an aura of spontaneity and the status of randomness which, as when we look at impressionist or action painting, we find [226] congenial and not a counterfeiting of sensation and reality. Like Hardy, but apparently less knowingly, her poetry was revolutionary because it avoided the jeweled line. It was more a making of the irregular line through a rough simplicity and by drastic reduction. Indeed, sometimes the print version of her manuscripts unavoidably makes a modern line disposition.

> And Life was not so
> Ample I
> Could finish – Enmity—   [J478, F763]

Her partial rhymes and the structural instability and shifts in poems contribute to this impatient art.

Dickinson's rift vision, the ability to make language cut into the disparities between concept and reality, between the expectation and the actuality—this creation in language of cruel parallax—effects a disruption and penetration that we also call modern. It appeals to our suspicion of wholeness and seamless compatible meaning. This effect is behind Harold Bloom's accurate observation that Dickinson, as much as any modern, made the visible world a little hard to see.

The several techniques emphasized here as modern are well known and often displayed as the true source of Dickinson's modernity. Yet we shall see that her modernity operated at a more fundamental level than this. For now it is clear that these several conventional modernisms, what have now become part of the technical orthodoxy of modernist verse in English, contribute to the powerful effect that is indubitably of our time: the estrangement from outer reality and the resistance of common words to definitive meaning. The estrangement is accomplished by the compact, unsustained, raw power of language at the surface of her clipped-off poems.

In her themes, as well, Dickinson is with the moderns. Her language, animated by her selective cleverness, together with the snapshot brevity of her hymn form, courted instability and change and spotted the vulnerability of settled states. This is why sunsets evoked some of her best imagistic effort. The spectacle of day's end was intensely, exaggeratedly visual, it was naturally associated with death, and it was recurrent novelty, change taking place before the eyes. The sunset was thus a visual allegory for what most [227] centrally engaged this poet.

Her preoccupation with change led to more desperate visions of mutability where the price of each moment of transport qualified every ecstasy, showing by her allegorical terms the furrow that threatens every glow. Unlike Emerson and Whitman, Dickinson brought into view with her strange and critical metaphors the opaque being of man, the "mysterious peninsula" as she called it, the unmanageable, excruciatingly sensitive, and needful portion that was her preoccupation.

She possessed a modernist knowledge of the mind's hidden places, what she called "That awful stranger Consciousness," terrifying to face. Equipped with her estranging language, she raised to the reader's awareness the intricate workings out of sight, careful not to "Mistake the Outside for the in" as she said. It is this interior life, in (for this recluse) the inevitable metaphor of the house, that is "haunted" and is the crucial spot where we enact our ignorance of ourselves and the world. Here is the "interior Confronting," where "Unarmed, one's a'self encounter." Now become an orthodox element of modern themes—what Irving Howe has called a modern fondness for the signs of psychic division—the interior life and the language to see it were the particular loci of Dickinson's attention. Encountering the self both dictated the strategies of her language and was the act in which her language had its circumstantial reflection.

"I felt a Funeral in my Brain" [J280, F340] is the first coolly targeted modern interior in American poetry, and it is handled adroitly with modernist attention not to moral judgment but to judgment-free description. There is no emotional slither, to use Pound's term, or didactic assertion as in other poems such as "Bound—a trouble / And lives can bear it!" or "A Weight with Needles on the pounds," but rather psychological interiority seen minutely. The funeral-in-the-brain poem, representative of a substantial cluster of Dickinson's works on psychic distress, manifested two generations in advance the doctrine of imagism that Pound defined as the transfer of a complex of emotions in an instant of time.

It was Dickinson diving into the wreck and her devastated speaker indeed "wrecked" in the poem. Assurance of diction and line is firm. The poem has structure and lexical cohesion of a high order for Dickinson, and it is this firmness that operates so effectively against the subject matter of instability and disintegration. It is a superb per- [228] formance, thoroughly modernist in its dark vision clinically portrayed.

Such language . . . made visible a new category of psychic suffering. Minutely observant, its figure of the interior funeral sustained, the poem moves with impressive directness into its surrealist transformation at the line "Then Space—began to toll." The familiar terms make new equations: Heaven is a Bell, Being an ear, and Silence a strange Race, and the wreck itself an annihilating silence. The surreal landscape, haunted with Dickinson's sense of exclusion and ignorance, unfolds, at least to the somewhat redundant last stanza, with a sure finality of language and wholeness of vision. In its cold-blooded, unflinching way as well as in the interior location of its action, the poem is supremely modernist. From the broader view of the Dickinson canon, we see how her concern with the interior reflects an equally modern concern with intense self-consciousness extending even to self-torture and the poetry of breakdown. . . .

The protomodernist image of the durable face of technological violence, of assault [229] masked by dehumanized visages, is related in terror to another theme of Dickinson's that is hardly depictable by such momentary frissons. That is her vision of the *absence of an end*. I find this the most frightful of all Dickinson's modernist themes because it involves the pathological extremity of her familiar images such as this, of death in life, that ends an eight-line poem of utter inertness.

> I take my living place
> As one commuted led—
> A Candidate for Morning Chance
> But dated with the Dead.   [J1194, F1209]

The smell of nihilism rises from more than a few poems, sometimes in a complete flatness of tune where her theme is the loss that drains every gain: note the eight lines that tick off loss beginning "Finding is the first Act / The second, loss" [J870, F910]. Associated with this theme of lost purpose and the absence of an end is a fearful corollary: the prevention of ripeness, of completion and thereby of knowledge and identity. It is the vision we saw in "What ripeness after that": that is, a life of incompletion, of ignorance, of need without assuaging. It can stand for the quintessential modernist condition—until with Dickinson we find ourselves going deeper . . .

Particular tones in Dickinson's poetry are also part of her commonly recognized mod- [230] ernism. Currents of doubt and the snowman moments give certain poems a psychological desperation that was unfamiliar to much nineteenth-century poetry. The sharply discrepant tone in poems, their directness of statement, and the audacity of their attack on conventional belief and easy-going piety are elements that would have given offense in her own time and so did not appear in the first editions of her poetry in the 1890s. Her colloquial and irreverently casual heresy at times ("It's easy to invent a Life"), her deliberate inelegance in a primitive offbeat diction ("It is simple to ache in the Bone or the Rind"), and the seemingly sophisticated skepticism in offhand phrases ("Our Savior, by a Hair") combine to give a considerable portion of the poetry a discordant tone that undercuts the poetry of unquestioned assent with which her contemporaries filled the verse books of the day.

Satire and irreverence along a gamut from mild asides to bitter attack are also modernist elements that form part of our critical orthodoxy and the surfaces by which Dickinson can be labeled a modern. In the poem beginning "There's been a Death, in [231] the opposite house" [J389, F547] she creates a gentle satire on the impersonal organization that swings into action at a death, with its ritual movements and the professional mourners who take charge. In such verse of casual irreverence, the understatement and vernacular ease effectively counterpoint the regular common meter that arranges them. Deft lexical selection provides the edge that cuts in in the modern way. Her lines on the aurora borealis, where the common expectation would be for "paint" and "tint," Dickinson slips all askew by substituting "infection" and "taint":

> The North—Tonight . . .
> Infects my simple spirit
> With Taints of Majesty   [J290, F319]

She deflated a generically solemn occasion by unobtrusive negation and the one unexpected word "soldered":

> I've seen a Dying Eye
> Run round and round a Room . . .
> And then—be soldered down
> Without disclosing what it be
> 'Twere blessed to have seen   [J547, F648]

Her language pierced theological pomposities with strokes of marvelous wit, as here with out-of-place words from the public hall set off against Resurrection:

> No crowd that has occurred
> Exhibit—I suppose
> That General Attendance
> That Resurrection – does   [J515, F653]

Dickinson's modernist tones include the confessional one. She excelled in creat- [232] ing a sense of private immediacy because, by the strategy of seemingly autobiographical speech acts, she reproduced in writing the speaking voice. Archibald MacLeish has written most knowingly on the unique voice by which we identify her. It is language signifying emotional experience close at hand that impresses us. The voice, quotation marks invisible, contradicts a reader's conscious awareness of the deliberately written text. This way in which Dickinson *did* speak out to strangers produces what we take to be an immediate proximity to the mind. The flattened conversational tone depoetizes experience and gives it a confessional authenticity of the sort we are familiar with in our own time.

> To Ache is human—not polite—
> The Film upon the eye
> Mortality's Old Custom—
> Just locking up—to Die   [J479, F458]

Toughness of attitude and candor couched in unstudied inelegance are further tonal qualities by which twentieth-century readers have assigned Dickinson to the origins of modernism along with Whitman. The blunt tones sound frequently along her lines, as here in this bald assertion that seems to have no poetic pretentions: "Men die—externally— / It is a truth—of Blood" [J531, F584].

Boldly secular content and skeptical tone quite disjunct from the orderly arrangement of the hymn form make an ironic combination. The poems produce that most modern of all attitudes, the ironicalization of experience. Beyond that, the disjunction and tonal qualities together effect a modernist estrangement, dissonance, and thus a critical perspective. Her bruskness deromanticizes, as in the moon poem that begins "I watched the Moon around the House." Dickinson's daring comes out most clearly if her moon is put alongside the famous protoimagist poem on the moon by T. E. Hulme. Dickinson's lines have in their more compact shape a greater bravado. It is part of what she shares with poets who followed her.

> like a Head—a Guillotine
> Slide carelessly away—
> like a Stemless Flower—
> Upheld in rolling Air—   [J629, F593]

The best summing up of these tonal qualities we now see as a modern set is in that [233] phrase *the ironicalization of experience*. The tonal undercutting, the evasion of stock sincerity, the protective irreverence and throwaway understatement, thus making the hymn form play a different tune: all these effects, even if there were behind them no perspective of mind much more fundamental, would withal make Dickinson a modern. Neither sophisticated nor sustained, hers was a poetic cunning working by stealth of language and subversion of form to create surprise by strangeness. Out of these strategies came a disordering of experience, a new confession of our precarious status.

From "The Landscape of the Spirit"*

Dickinson's poems frequently assert her sense of the mind's actuality with images of cav- [14] erns and corridors [J777, F877; J670, F407], windows and doors [J303, F409; J657, F466], [15] even cellars [J1182, F1234]. Because she took the mind to be her dwelling place, it is appropriate that she use these domestic figurative correspondences to describe it. Yet her poems using such architectural analogues go beyond pointing out how a mind might be like a house. They set out to show, as well, what happens in a mind that is as a house, so that the solidity which door and window frame provide grants substance both to the setting and to the events occurring within. The architectural vocabulary usually portrays the mind as an enclosed space, its confinement responsible for power, safety, yet fearful confrontation.

Poem 303 is a strong statement about the power of the self alone. The soul is shown living within a space defined by door, gate, and mat. The external world, with its nations and their rulers, is kept outside.

> The soul selects her own Society—
> Then—shuts the Door—
> To her divine Majority—
> Present no more—

*From Suzanne Juhasz, "The Undiscovered Continent:" *Emily Dickinson and The Space of the Mind* (Bloomington: Indiana UP, 1983).

Unmoved—she notes the Chariots—pausing—
At her low Gate—
Unmoved—an Emperor be kneeling
Upon her Mat—

I've known her—from an ample nation—
Choose One—
Then—close the Valves of her attention—
Like Stone—

Traditional ideas about power are reversed here. Not control over vast populations but the ability to construct a world for oneself comprises the greatest power, a god-
like achievement, announces the opening stanza. Not only is the soul alone "divine," but
it is also identified as "Society" and "Majority": the poem also challenges our ideas about
what constitutes a social group. Consequently, the enclosed space of the soul's house is
more than adequate for a queenly life, and ambassadors of the external world's glories,
even emperors, can easily be scorned. Yet while the speaker claims her equality with
those most powerful in the outer world—they may be emperors, but she is "divine Majority,"—at the same time she asserts her difference from them; for her domestic vocabulary of door, low gate and mat establishes her dwelling as not a grand palace but rather
a simple house.

While associating power with the enclosed space of the mind, the poem also im- [16]
plies how isolation is confinement, too. When the soul turns in upon her own concerns,
she closes "the Valves of her attention— / Like Stone—."

Valves permit the flow of whatever they regulate in one direction only: here from outside to inside. Either of the halves of a double door or any of the leaves of a folding door
are valves. Valves seen as doors reinforce the poem's house imagery, while their association
with stone makes the walls separating soul from world so solid as to be, perhaps, prison-like.

Prison-like because they allow no escape from the kinds of conflict, the kinds of terror, even, that must occur within. Poem 670 [J670, F407] exaggerating the architectural
vocabulary, compares the chambers of the mind to the haunted castle of gothic fiction, a
stereotypical setting for horror.

One need not be a Chamber—to be Haunted—
One need not be a House—
The Brain has Corridors—surpassing
Material Place—

Far safer, of a Midnight Meeting
External Ghost
Than its interior Confronting—
That Cooler Host.

Far safer, through an Abbey gallop,
The stones a'chase—
Than Unarmed, one's a'self encounter—
In lonesome Place—

Ourself behind ourself, concealed—
Should startle most—
Assassin hid in our Apartment
Be Horror's least.

> The Body—borrows a Revolver—
> He bolts the Door—
> O'erlooking a superior spectre—
> Or More—

The poem assumes that the mind is substantial, possessing corridors and chambers, because it is the dwelling place of "oneself." The extended comparison that is developed, between two kinds of dwellings, two binds of hauntings, is for the purpose of dramatizing how there can be something more frightening than the most frightening situation usually imaginable.   [17]

Both the second and third stanzas begin with the same phrase: "Far safer." Safer are the supernatural events of gothic castles, meeting ghosts at midnight; we are warned about "interior confronting," the everyday moments of the mind, another lonesome place, when "one's a'self encounter." One clue to the degree of difference in horror is the word, "Unarmed." We come prepared to find ghosts in spooky old castles, but not in what Dickinson calls in another poem "That polar privacy / A soul admitted to itself" [J1695, F1696].

There is, in fact, no way one can be armed against this particular kind of ghost. The murderer seeking to kill the body can be vanquished—one can borrow a revolver, bolt the door. But this assassin is hidden within oneself—is oneself. There is no escape. As Dickinson comments in poem 894 [J894, F1076], "Of Consciousness, her awful Mate / The Soul cannot be rid."

In the final stanza [of poem J670, F407] the quintessence of this horror is revealed. The rhetoric of the poem has been dramatic as well as concrete. Two dramas, in fact, have been enacted and contrasted. The external self has been venturing into lonesome abbeys, discovering hidden assassins in her chamber, even as the internal self has become aware of the existence of the "Cooler Host." Now the two plots turn into one. The self, who is, after all, body and mind at once, bolts the door, only to discover that she has locked herself in with herself. Adventuring in the external world, one need not confront one's own consciousness. But when one turns from "Horror's least" to live in the mind, that "superior spectre" can never be avoided again.

Because consciousness is self-confrontation, it establishes a "society" within, of "ourself" with "ourself." To represent the conflict and struggle engendered here, poem 642 uses an architectural vocabulary that provides a setting, fortress, for a drama of siege and defense. Yet even as "One need not be a Chamber—to be Haunted—" constructs a comparison between external and internal ghost stories only to conflate them, so the following poem's distinctions between inner and outer, protagonist and antagonist, turn out to be fictions.

> Me from Myself—to banish—
> Had I Art—
> Impregnable my Fortress
> Unto All Heart—
>
> But since Myself—assault Me—
> How have I peace
> Except by subjugating
> Consciousness?
>
> And since We're mutual Monarch
> How this be
> Except by Abdication—
> Me—of Me—?   [J642, F709]

The speaker of the poem "Myself" wishes for the ability to banish from her castle an enemy, called "Me." In the second stanza she admits to the complexity of the problem; more than skill is required to maintain the defense, because there is a profound connection between the combatants. Reversing their titles—"Me" is now the speaker, "Myself" the opponent—the poem acknowledges their interchangeability while at the same time continuing to deal with them as separate entities. The enemy is also identified as "Heart" in the first stanza, "Consciousness" in the second. That these are as much aspects of "Me" as they are of "Myself" the poem will not yet admit.

Although we know that the poem is discussing one person and not two, its dramatic fiction of attacker and attacked creates a situation that is surely war, albeit civil. When the dichotomy itself is collapsed in the final stanza, the effect is to intensify the situation, the pain, the impossibility of victory. "Mutual Monarch," the antagonists are revealed to be in actuality both within. There is nobody without. Without doesn't matter. Victory is impossible, is not a mere matter of "art," because enemy and friend are one. "Consciousness" is the self's awareness of itself and could be vanquished only through the annihilation of self, which would leave no victor, since no self is left. The very naming of the characters in this drama articulates and also anticipates this conclusion. If in stanza one the defender was Myself, the attacker, Me; and in stanza two the attacker was Myself, the defender, Me; in the final stanza they, as mutual Monarch, are "Me" and "Me."

The poem's structure dramatizes an experienced conflict. If the fictional dichotomy of within and without is necessary so that we might understand the problem, so is the final denial of the fiction, that we might better understand the conclusion: that self-consciousness means precisely the encounter of the self with itself, and that this is a perpetual struggle.

From "The American Plain Style"*

In a still broader sense of influence, the American idiom itself, in both its literary and daily [143] forms, may have contributed to Dickinson's use of a style that is biblical in origin. By the mid-nineteenth century Puritan "plain style" had become the language of self-expression, the trusted idiom in America, although—or perhaps because—it had lost its bolstering [144] doctrinal and political contexts. According to Perry Miller's "An American Language," the plain style's demand that one speak from personal knowledge and as comprehensibly as possible made it the natural mode of discourse for a people living "in the wilderness:" and, by the late eighteenth century, attempting to form a democracy. All American writers, he claims, have had to deal with the consequences of this wholesale adoption of the principles and techniques of plain style. Because of its pervasiveness, Dickinson would inevitably have used language to some extent within its dictates. For epistemological reasons also, Dickinson may have felt some affinity for this style. Miller describes the plain style as inherently "defiant"—a style that both proclaims authority for the word and places the word's authority in individuals' articulate examinations of the truth; the style encourages practical discourse on theoretical or spiritual truths. Hence, it can as easily be turned against the idea of an authoritative God as it can be used to support that idea. Authority of language lies with the "plainest" (that is, apparently most artless yet still most commanding) speaker. The Puritans kept the style's implicit defiance in check by subordinating their word to God's Word; the latter was the law which theirs attempted to interpret and reflect. Emerson, Miller claims, partially maintained this check on defiance through his romantic belief in Nature as the origin of language, while Thoreau released the defiance of this style in his prose, "glory[ing] in his participation in the community of sin."

*From Christanne Miller, *Emily Dickinson: A Poet's Grammar* (Cambridge: Harvard UP, 1987).

More covertly than Thoreau, Dickinson does the same. Her very disguise of defiance, however, may also stem in part from inherent characteristics of the plain style, which demands the simplicity reflected in its name but paradoxically also a kind of reticence that may prevent its complete message from being articulated. Ideally, the plain speaker "convey[s] the emphasis, the hesitancies, the searchings of language as it is spoken"; plainness lies in the apparent artlessness of the speaker's or writer's use of the word. Partly as a consequence, writers in the plain style leave much unsaid, and they claim that their discourse says even less than it does. Using words sparingly leaves much to implication, and making modest claims for a text may disguise the authority its author in fact feels. Thus the plain style frequently underplays its own importance and seriousness; even when it most anarchically expresses the perception of the individual, it maintains the guise of saying little, and that only matter-of-factly. Hence, while speaking "plain" truth, an individual may confound every doctrine that the Puritans held true and [145] believed the plain style must express. As Miller puts it: "The forthright method [plain style] proved to be . . . the most subversive power that the wicked could invoke against those generalities it had, long ago, been designed to protect." Through reticence, indirection, and disguised claims for the authority of her word, Dickinson manipulates characteristics of the plain use of language in poetry that contradict Puritan convictions about the individual's relation to God and His Word. The style that affirms God's truth for the Puritans, and denies that God's power is the only good (while still celebrating it) for Thoreau, becomes ironic with Dickinson: while appearing to affirm or naively question, she denies the trustworthiness of any superhuman power. . . .

It is in her attitude toward language and toward communication itself as much as in her characteristic manipulations of the word that Dickinson differs from her contem- [146] poraries and predecessors who wrote in plain style. Like them, she emphasizes the bare force of the word, eschewing elaborate syntax, modifiers, and extended conceits. Like them, she tends to stress the word's direct mediation between the individual and the world (for them, God). Like them, but to an unusual extreme, she makes small claims for her writing: her poems are "a letter to the World"; she is often a girl, or (like) a daisy, bird, spider, or gnat. Even when she has volcanic power, she generally appears harmless and unimportant: "A meditative spot— / An acre for a Bird to choose / Would be the General thought—" [J1677, F1743]. Dickinson, however, senses a different need for both plainness and reticence from those who believe in a natural or divine law of language. The word has two faces for her. Its effect may be epiphanic and it may come to her as a "gift," revealing "That portion of the Vision" she could not find without the help of "Cherubim" [J1126, F1243]. This is the language of poetry, of pure communication, "Like signal esoteric sips / Of the communion Wine" [J1452, F1476], or a "word of Gold" [J430, F388]. At other times the word is all but meaningless—an "Opinion" [J797, F849], an empty term. In a letter to Bowles she writes: "The old words are *numb*—and there *a'nt* any *new* ones—Brooks—are useless—in *Freshettime*—" (L 252). Her trick as poet is to make the old words new. To do this, she trusts "Philology," not God or Nature, and when she succeeds in doing this she feels that she has been lucky.

To Dickinson's mind, success in speaking plainly, in creating a word "that breathes" [J1651, F1715] does not prove spiritual salvation or make her a candidate for fame, partly because her sense of moral superiority depends on overthrowing the notion that God or the world can save her. The economical use of the words of ordinary life gives language its power. Speaking indirectly or subversively disguises the poet's usurpation of moral judgment from divine or human law, and thus saves her to speak again. As Perry Miller suggests, in Dickinson's poetry the pull between plainness and reticence subverts the whole idea of plainness. Because her meanings are not plain, they cannot be expressed plainly despite her use of simple words; her plainest speech *is* that of indirection.

As this conception of language implies, for Dickinson there is no stable relation between spiritual truth, the facts of existence, and the terms of language. Names are not adequate to things, and the function of language is not primarily to name. Things are perceived and understood through their relations to the rest of the world and by the process of cumulative, even contradictory, definition rather than by categorization or labeling. Dickinson has greater affinity with the lexicographer, the scientist of language seeking to clarify each word's various meanings, than she does with the Romantic *Ur*-poet   [148] Adam. Her language stresses the relation between object and its effects or relations in an active world; meaning, for her, is not fixed by rules or even by her own previous perception of the world. The principles of Dickinson's world do not have to do with immutable properties and distinctions.

Dickinson manifests her belief in the flux or instability of relationship in the narratives of her poems more obviously than in her use of language. For example, the figures of her poems often change positions relative to each other, or prove to be undifferentiable rather than separate identities. In "The Moon is distant from the Sea," first "She" is the moon and "He" the water, then she becomes "the distant Sea—" and his are the ordering "Amber Hands—" of light [J429, F387]; the "single Hound" attending the Soul proves to be "It's own identity." [J822, F817]; in an early poem, she and her playmate Tim turn out to be "I—'Tim'—and—Me!" [J196, F231]. In a late poem, desired object, self, and "Messenger" are indistinguishable in both their presence and their absence; in a mockery of simplicity, all have the same name:

We send the Wave to find the Wave—
An Errand so divine,
The Messenger enamored too,
Forgetting to return,
We make the wise distinction still,
Soever made in vain,
The sagest time to dam the sea is when the sea is gone—   [J1604, F1643]

Although this poem may be read as an elaboration of a truism—that one must give to receive, or that some losses cannot be prevented—it also ironically suggests that distinguishing present and absent sea (loved "Wave" from our own) is "vain." The "wise distinction" persists in failing to recognize the absurdity of damming what is not there and cannot be kept anyway. We attempt to conserve only what we have already lost.

Similarly, in "The Sea said 'Come' to the Brook" [J1210, F1275], the grown Brook takes the same form and title as the Sea that wanted to keep it small, as if to prove that the existence of one sea does not prevent the growth of innumerable physically indistinguishable others. In the last stanza it is not immediately clear which "Sea" is which:

The Sea said "Go" to the Sea—
The Sea said "I am he
You cherished"—"Learned Waters—
Wisdom is stale—to Me"

In countless other poems, unspecified and multiply referential "it" or "this" is as meaningful a subject for speculation as any clearly delineated event or object. Metaphor serves as the primary tool of definition and explanation because it allows for the greatest flexibility in its reference to fact.

From "The Histrionic Imagination"*

Dickinson recognized, early in her career, the value of the dramatic monologue and learned to use it with skill. A well-known poem, dated about 1858 or 1859 when the apprenticeship was nearing its end, serves both as an example in which she has not quite mastered the form but is alert to its efficacy and as a work in which she draws on her own experience but changes it in the act of speaking about it.

> I never lost as much but twice,
> And that was in the sod.
> Twice have I stood a beggar
> Before the door of God!
>
> Angels—twice descending
> Reimbursed my store—
> Burglar! Banker—Father!
> I am poor once more!   [J49, F39]

The story line of the verse is addressed to an imagined interlocutor on the subject of the power of God; when the poet allows the speaker to address God directly, however, the break in point of view discloses that Dickinson has not yet learned to integrate narration and drama. The austerely restricted language of the narrative is right for the recollection of painful loss in contrast to the defiant and improvident moment when the persona forgets the unidentified listener and turns in line seven to revile God directly, but an experienced poet does not lose awareness of the audience assumed in a monologue even when the character being depicted rages on.   [83]

Despite the violation of point of view, or perhaps because of it, the supplicant's outburst continues to reverberate in our ears as we listen to the falling strain of a voice quickly regaining control and we believe we have overheard Emily Dickinson herself quarreling with God. When we find in a second poem, "Going to Heaven!" (#79, [J79, F128] c. 1859), that the persona, a young girl who both hopes to go and is glad she isn't going to heaven, says, "If you sh'd get there first / Save just a little place for me / Close to the two I lost—," we look elsewhere for the experiences about which *she* is talking in the angry indictment of God. Who, among the people she loved, we ask, died during Dickinson's childhood and youth? And what other personal loss is of the enormity of death? Because neither poem gives any clues, we search the biography for them.

There was more anguish in the life of young Emily Dickinson than "I never lost as much but twice" enumerates. She recalled, in a letter of March 28, 1846, to Abiah Root, whose schoolmate had just died, an experience of early sorrow. The opening words of the recollection prefigure the idiomatic cadence in which the poem begins. She wrote: "I have never lost but one friend near my age & with whom my thoughts & her own were the same. It was before you came to Amherst. My friend was Sophia Holland. She was too lovely for earth & she was transplanted from earth to heaven. . . . Then it seemed to me I should die too." Emily, who was fourteen at the time of the death of her friend in the spring of 1844, gave way to "a fixed melancholy," told no one the cause of her grief, and was not well. Her parents sent her to Boston, where she stayed with relatives for a month and her health improved so that her "spirits were better." In May 1846, her maternal grandfather, Joel Norcross, died; there is no record of how she felt about him, but she

*From Elizabeth Phillips, *Emily Dickinson: Personae and Performance* (University Park: Pennsylvania State UP, 1988).

went again in August to Boston for her health. In May 1848, during her seventeenth year, Jacob Holt, a friend about whom she anxiously asked more than once in letters from Holyoke, died at the age of twenty-six; he wrote some rather commonplace poems, one of which she copied in her Bible. There were, also, other persons who are usually suggested as "the two" she lost in death. Since the emotions of loss became more complex as she matured, they well may be fused beyond one's ability to extricate them in the poem.

Leonard Humphrey, who was principal of the Amherst Academy in 1846 – 47, Emily's last year there, died at the age of twenty-six in November 1850; reporting the death of her "master" to Abiah, Emily mourned but did not give way to melancholy: "my rebellious thoughts," she asserted, "are many." Thereafter, Ben Newton, who introduced her to Emerson's poetry in 1850, left Amherst for Worcester, married in 1851, and died at the age of thirty-two on March 24, 1853. He taught her to read, she said, and was, "the first of my own friends." Had she forgotten Sophia Holland, who has not counted in explanations of the poet's loss? [84]

Additional comments in the letters seem to lend support to readers who identify "the two she lost as Humphrey and Newton (Or are they "three": Holt, Humphrey, and Newton?) Writing on April 25, 1862, to Higginson, the poet said: "When a little Girl, I had a friend who taught me Immortality—but venturing too near, himself—he never returned—Soon after, my Tutor, died—and for several years, my Lexicon was my only companion." As if she were explaining "I never lost as much but twice," which Higginson had not seen, she added: "Then I found one more—but he was not contented I be his scholar—so he left the Land." This remark causes further speculation about whether the final loss in the poem is a kind different from that "in the sod." Casual readers then want to hear a name such as Charles Wadsworth or Samuel Bowles, neither of whom had "left the land" before or during the year in which Dickinson made a final copy of the verse ending with the dramatic cry: "Burglar! Banker—Father! / I am poor once more!"

There is not only too much evidence but too much uncertainty about what to choose from it for ascertaining the specific provocations of the poem's dramatic script. Nevertheless, if the letters to Abiah Root began the account of the incremental sorrow that is Dickinson's subject, one can say the soliloquy depends on events that are autobiographical but is not a literal recording of any one among them. The poet was rather finding words to make emotions *sound* true.

The recurrent experience of separations and loss may well be the source of another poem, which is more lyrical than dramatic. The emphasis is again on emotions related to a life "closed twice," but beyond the term "parting" there is no evidence that permits one to identity the events to which the persona refers. If the experiences are personal, they have been transmuted into flawless lines:

My life closed twice before its close—
It yet remains to see
If Immortality unveil
A third event to me [85]

So huge, so hopeless to conceive
As these that twice befell.
Parting is all we know of heaven,
And all we need of hell.   [J1732, F1773, n.d.]

Although there is no autograph copy or date of composition for this justly famous poem, it points up Dickinson's practice of trying out different aspects of a theme in order to realize the perfection of form inherent in it. The poet ceased, moreover, to be an amateur in exploiting the possibilities of the dramatic monologue, which became the genre for a number of equally memorable Dickinson texts.

From "The Gothic Mode: 'Tis so appalling—it exhilarates—'"*

Emily Dickinson's gothic poems are perhaps her most startling challenge to the symbolic [87] order. They are transgressive poems of great energy which explore taboo states usually excluded from consideration. In these poems the speakers spare the reader no excess in their relish of the macabre, as a selection of first lines suggests: 'As by the dead we love to sit' [J88, F78]; 'Do People moulder equally, / They bury, in the Grave?' [J432, F390] or 'If I may have it, when it's dead.' [J577, F431]. In many poems, the dead simply refuse to Lie down; witty, garrulous corpses relentlessly address the reader from deathbed or grave: 'Twas just this time, last year, I died' [J445, F344]; 'I heard a Fly buzz—when I died—' [J465, F591], 'I died for Beauty—' [J449, F448]. In others the speaker confronts an unknown self and experiences 'A doubt if it be Us' [J859, F903].

The Gothic poems fall into three main categories: those in which the speaker encounters unknown forces within the self; those in which the walking dead are women and continue Dickinson's explorations of gender; and those in which death is welcomed as a liberation from the confinements of the symbolic order. These poems challenge the ideals and propriety of the social order; they are disturbing because they question the certainty and rightness of its interpretations of the world. Madness suggests that there are forces [88] within that are beyond its jurisdiction; human identity is not ultimately fixed, coherent, controlled, knowable. The dissolution of death is a permanent reminder of the fragility and artificiality of the social order and its rigid conventions.

The nineteenth century saw the articulation of the idea of the unconscious and Dickinson's poems participate in that impulse. Dickinson was acutely aware of what Edward Young had referred to as 'the stranger within thee'. In his book *Night Thoughts* (1742–5), which was used as one of the textbooks at Amherst Academy, Young writes that reason is but 'a baffled counsellor': man looks within and finds 'an awful stranger'. Dickinson was similarly aware of an alien aspect to consciousness, writing in Poem 894: 'Of Consciousness, her awful Mate / The Soul cannot be rid—' [J894, F1076]. Sometimes consciousness was an oppressive companion:

> I do not know the man so bold
> He dare in lonely Place
> That awful stranger Consciousness
> Deliberately face—   [Poem J1323, F1325]

Several poems explore the encounter of the self with a stranger within. In Poem 670 [J670, F407], the internal ghost is an awesome force to be reckoned with:

> One need not be a Chamber—to be Haunted—
> One need not be a House—
> The Brain has Corridors—surpassing
> Material Place—
> Far safer, of a Midnight Meeting
> External Ghost
> Than its interior Confronting—   [89]
> That Cooler Host.

*From Joan Kirkby, *Emily Dickinson* (New York: St. Martin's, 1991).

Far safer, through an Abbey gallop,
The Stones a'chase—
Than Unarmed, one's a' self encounter—
In lonesome Place—

Ourself behind ourself, concealed—
Should startle most—
Assassin hid in our Apartment
Be Horror's least.

The Body—borrows a Revolver—
He bolts the Door—
O'erlooking a superior spectre—
Or More—

In this poem the mind itself is seen as more terrifying and dangerous than a haunted house; it has dark, unknown corridors surpassing 'Material place'. The encounter with one's concealed self is more dangerous than ghost, or graveyard, or assassin; they are 'Horror's least.' These could be fled on horseback, locked out or vanquished with revolver, but there is no escape from the self. Indeed the self hidden within the self is 'a superior spectre / —Or More', suggesting some terror greater than any hitherto conceived. The mind has within itself the potential for insurrection and dissolution. . . .

Dickinson's most famous Poem 712 [J712, F479] 'Because I could not stop for   [98]
Death—' deals with a similar moment in which a woman is severed from her chosen tasks and carried off by an anonymous gentleman called 'Death'. Once again the fair theme of love is associated with 'a thought so mean'. However, this poem makes explicit the fact that the advent of the gentleman caller is nothing short of death for the woman. While this poem is usually read as a poem about death, revealing Dickinson's playfully macabre vision of death as a gentleman caller, it is a poem that identifies the gentleman caller as death; for him woman is expected to put away both her labour and her leisure. Like the woman in Poem 732 [J732, F857] she is expected to rise 'to His Requirement' and drop 'The Playthings of Her Life / To take the honorable Work / Of Woman, and of Wife—'.

Because I could not stop for Death—
He kindly stopped for me
The Carriage held but just Ourselves—
And Immortality.

We slowly drove—He knew no haste
And I had put away
My labor and my leisure too,
For His Civility—

We passed the School, where Children strove
At Recess—in the Ring—
We passed the Fields of Gazing Grain—   [99]
We passed the Setting Sun—

Or rather—He passed Us—
The Dews drew quivering and chill—
For only Gossamer, my Gown—
My Tippet—only Tulle—

> We paused before a House that seemed
> A Swelling of the Ground—
> The Roof was scarcely visible—
> The Cornice—in the Ground—
>
> Since then—'tis Centuries—and yet
> Feels shorter than the Day
> I first surmised the Horses' Heads
> Were toward Eternity—

The first stanza suggests that the female speaker is so deeply engaged in her own life that she does not wish to stop, but it also suggests the passivity of female desire. Courting is a male prerogative; she must wait to be called upon, but once chosen a surrender that is both quick and total is expected. She must give up her work and her leisure 'For His Civility'. He has all the privileges of authority; he nominates the time of execution but is regarded as 'kindly' and civil. That the death coach contains the new couple—'And Immortality'—suggests something of the enormous duration of the marriage journey. However, it also suggests that male authority extends into eternity; both earthly life and after life are in his hands; indeed that hypothesis underpins his authority here.

The second stanza highlights the slowness and solemnity of this journey to a bridal house that strongly resembles a grave. Like the anonymous 'He' in Poem 315 [J315, F477] 'He fumbles at your Soul', 'He knew no haste'. She is assumed to have no interest or activity separate from his. Rather like the woman in Poem 273 [J273, F330] 'He put the Belt around my life—', she begins to sense her 'Lifetime folding up—'. As the journey progresses the speaker becomes increasingly aware that she has lost all agency and volition. Like the woman in Poem 443 [J443, F522] her 'ticking' has stopped. The fields of grain are 'gazing' at her; the setting sun 'passed Us'. In her bridal finery she experiences a mortal chill: 'For only Gossamer, my Gown— / My Tippet—only Tulle—'. Indeed the fine silk veil around her neck is a kind of noose; like the bride in Poem 1072 [J1072, F194] she is 'Born—Bridalled—Shrouded— / In a day—'. The wedding house turns out to be her grave; it is lowly and scarcely undifferentiated from the ground. Since this deathly bridal day, it seems like 'Centuries' and 'Eternity'. Dickinson's poem suggests the eternity of death-in-life endured after marriage, what the woman in Poem 443 [J443, F522] refers to as 'Miles on Miles of Nought—'. [100]

In this poem woman is interrupted from her independent activities and brought to a house that seems 'A Swelling of the Ground', inevitably suggesting the house of biological destiny, the womb as tomb. There is the suggestion in the poem that female autonomy would threaten the existing order; a woman with her own work and her own leisure may be too busy 'to stop' for connubial death. In Poem 1445 [J1445, F1470] 'Death is the supple Suitor', images of death and courtship are interwined in similar fashion; it is 'a stealthy Wooing'; a coach carries the woman away to 'Troth unknown' and 'Kindred as responsive / As Porcelain'.

Dickinson's most striking gothic poems are those in which the dead address the speaker from deathbed or grave. These poems bear out Gillian Beer's view that 'Ghost stories are to do with the insurrection, not the resurrection of the dead. It is the element of 'the insurrectionary' and 'the uncontrollable' that confounds. It goes without saying that these poems are disconcerting. Death is the ultimate taboo and the corpse 'the ultimate impurity', 'the most sickening waste'. Yet Dickinson's speakers provocatively play on graves, sit by the dead, wonder if corpses moulder equally. In drawing near the corpse, the object that marks the limit between life and death, Dickinson invokes a place that is outside the rule of the symbolic order. In these poems, death marks the dissolution of the social order and becomes an emblem of liberation from its oppressive and artificial [101] conventions. The corpse highlights the frailty of the symbolic order. As Julia Kristeva writes, a 'decaying body, lifeless, completely turned into dejection, blurred between the inanimate and the inorganic . . . the corpse represents fundamental pollution.' It is 'above all the opposite of the spiritual, of the symbolic, and of divine law.'

In Poem 465 [J465, F591] Dickinson presents a speaker beyond the limit of the symbolic order; she has 'Signed away / What portion of me be / Assignable—' and is henceforth to nature, a decomposing body subject only to the fly. The poem highlights the radical distance between the dying, who awaits the dissolution of the human into the undifferentiated matter of the corpse, and the living, who remain entirely bound up in the trappings of the social order, property, keepsakes, and the law of the father—'the King' who is to be 'witnessed—in the Room—'.

> I heard a Fly buzz—when I died—
> The Stillness in the Room
> Was like the Stillness in the Air—
> Between the Heaves of Storm—
>
> The Eyes around—had wrung them dry—
> And Breaths were gathering firm
> For that last Onset—when the King
> Be witnessed—in the Room—
>
> I willed my Keepsakes—Signed away   [102]
> What portion of me be
> Assignable—and then it was
> There interposed a Fly—
>
> With Blue—uncertain stumbling Buzz—
> Between the light—and me—
> And then the Windows failed—and then
> I could not see to see—   [J465, F591]

At the moment of death, the speaker's attention is deflected by the buzz of a fly, lowly earthly representative of physical decay. For the dying person that simple presence erases all other concerns, social and religious alike. However, the living reaffirm their allegiance to the symbolic order. They turn their attention away from the dying person and what is represented by death to an affirmation of their faith; they prepare themselves to witness God's presence in the room, his taking of the dying person.

While the living await the 'King' and the re-inscription of the social order, the dying person awaits the fly and a decomposition of the self into corporeal waste. She has willed her keepsakes and signed away the portion of her with meaning in the social order, that is property, gender, social identity. The use of sign and assignable is significant in this context. In death the subject relinquishes the power to sign, to signify, to mark with characters, and to assign, to transfer or designate by writing. The corpse is outside the sign, outside the system of differences inscribed by the social order. The dead body is disconcertingly free of its rules, systems, distinctions and limits. In death there is also a dissolution of the gender-marked body. The corpse is an 'it', as the speaker notes in Poem 389 [J389, F547] 'There's been a Death, in the Opposite House':

> Somebody flings a Mattress out—
> The Children hurry by—
> They wonder if *it* died—on that   [103]
> I used to—when a Boy—

The buzzing fly blocks out the light of distinction and differentiation. The buzz of the fly is the antithesis of human language with its discrete units of modulated sounds. That the blue of the sky is transposed to the buzz of the fly suggests a further scrambling of the senses. Indeed the windows fail, which suggests a total breakdown of the social framing of experience. Windows are artificial barriers between inside and outside, nature and culture; windows frame and limit vision. However, in death the social framing of experience ends. There is darkness and a dissolution of all the restricting categories and hierarchies on which the social order is based.

A similar dynamics informs Poem 449 [J449, F448] which is Dickinson's witty retort to the closing lines of Keats' 'Ode on a Grecian Urn': 'Beauty is Truth, Truth Beauty,—that is all / Ye know on earth and all ye need to know.' In Dickinson's poem death deposes pomp.

> I died for Beauty—but was scarce
> Adjusted in the Tomb
> When One who died for Truth, was lain
> In an adjoining Room—
>
> He questioned softly "Why I failed"?
> "For Beauty", I replied—
> "And I—for Truth—Themself are One—
> We Brethren, are", He said—
>
> And so, as Kinsmen, met a Night—
> We talked between the Rooms—
> Until the Moss had reached our lips—
> And covered up—our names—

The concepts and abstractions of the symbolic order avail for little here. The fact of phys- [104]
ical decomposition overtakes the speaker practically in mid sentence. The moss covers up the speakers' names and makes the differences for which they died irrelevant. Each corpse has died as she thought in significance, for a large life ordering abstraction whose significance would continue after death. However, death marks the dissolution of the whole system of differences on which the social order is based. The moss like the fly signals the dissolution of the symbolic order as well as the decay of the body; the moss seals the lips, the locus of speech, and covers up 'our names—'.

ROBERT FROST (1874 – 1963)

Life and Work

Robert Lee Frost (1874 – 1963) published his first book of poems, *A Boy's Will*, when he was living in England in 1913. At this time he was unrecognized and unknown in the United States. Ezra Pound wrote that "it is a sinister thing that so American . . . a talent . . . should have to be exported before it can find due encouragement and recognition." Time, of course, made Frost the most visible and admired American poet of his day. He eventually received twenty-five honorary degrees and four Pulitzer Prizes. Although there was no officially recognized national poet until the 1980s, when the poet laureateships were

Robert Frost in 1915

established through the Library of Congress, he came as close as possible to being America's official poet when he read "The Gift Outright" at the inauguration of President John F. Kennedy in January 1961. Writing in 1999, Joyce Carol Oates declared that "Frost's influence is so pervasive in American poetry, like Whitman's, as to be beyond assessment."[3] His collected poetic works continue to earn him this recognition.

Although in his person, and in his poetry, Frost presented himself as the quintessential New Englander, he was born on March 26, 1874, in California, where he spent his first ten years of life. His father, William Frost, had gone to San Francisco to take a job with the *San Francisco Bulletin*, and he and his wife Belle had their two children there. When William died in 1885, Frost's mother returned east to Lawrence, Massachusetts, where Frost attended high school, studied classics, and began writing poetry. He graduated in 1892 as co-valedictorian with Elinor White, whom he married in 1895. After high school he attended Dartmouth College for seven weeks and then turned to newspaper work and teaching school. Two years after his marriage, he enrolled at Harvard (1897 – 1899), aiming at a specialty in classical literature. He had hoped to take courses with William James, but he was disappointed because James was on leave during the years of Frost's attendance. However, Frost was able to take a class taught by the famous philosopher George Santayana. Personal reasons, including an unwillingness to submit to rigorous academic discipline, led him to end his student days at Harvard without taking a degree.

The image that one gains of Frost at this time is that he had enormous capability, powerful energy, much anxiety and self-doubt, and uncertain focus. In later years he stated that his early interests inclined him toward a career in archaeology, astronomy, farming, or teaching Latin. It does not seem that he had

[3]*American Poetry Review*, Vol. 28, No. 6 (Nov/Dec 1999): 9.

any vision of himself as the poet and man of letters he was to become. Even at the height of his fame he minimized his poetic achievement by telling an audience at Amherst College that all he ever wanted from his poetic career was to write "a few little poems it'd be hard to get rid of. That's all I ask."[4]

Much of Frost's early uncertainty resulted from his need to support his growing family. He gravitated toward farming as a way of life that would take up his physical energies and also give him the chance to think and to write. Fortunately, he had a supportive grandfather, William Frost, Sr., who backed up affection with financial support. In 1900 William Senior gave Robert a farm in Derry, New Hampshire, and for the next twelve years the poet lived in Derry, raised chickens and apples, wrote poetry, and taught English at Pinkerton Academy. His life was hard but satisfying, but, as he later said, he was "not much of a farmer." He preferred to sit up late at night to study, and then to sleep until noon. He did not see it as his obligation to get up with the sun and then go about the endless tasks needed for successful farming. He was also an unusual farmer because he had been acquiring an immense amount of erudition, including the study of Latin and Greek poets and large numbers of Shakespeare's sonnets. It was during this time in Derry, in the first decade of the twentieth century, that he wrote many of his most famous poems, either in completed form or in draft. He sent many of these poems to magazines but was unsuccessful in getting them published.

By 1912 he was aching to devote himself to writing but was extremely discouraged with the way things were going. According to the terms of Grandfather Frost's gift, however, he was permitted to sell the farm and use the money for his own purposes. Because he believed that he might make a better start abroad, he planned a move to England, one of the many moves he was to make in his life. He also told the joke that he might be poor abroad without embarrassing his relatives and friends. Once he landed in England, his poetic career was energized. He found a publisher who liked his poems and put him under contract. Almost overnight he emerged from obscurity through the publication of his first two poetic volumes, *A Boy's Will* (1913) and *North of Boston* (1914), which were favorably reviewed and which started to earn him acclaim in the United States. He also met a number of emerging and established poets, including Pound, Eliot, and Yeats.

Just as in 1913 he had been anxious to move abroad, early in 1915 he was anxious to return home. World War I had been declared, and he believed life would be better and safer in the United states. Once he got back he took up residence on a farm near Franconia, New Hampshire. His life after this time was one of increasing professional success together with a heavy burden of personal anxiety and grief. He and his wife had already lost two of their children in infancy. In addition, their daughter Marjorie died in 1934, and their son Carol,

---

[4]*Amherst Alumni News* (April 1954), quoted in Jay Parini, *Robert Frost: A Life* (New York: Holt, 1999), p. 391.

who suffered severe bouts of depression, committed suicide in 1940. Elinor herself died in 1938. In addition, Frost was constantly stretching his finances to help his remaining adult children as they attempted to create their own lives. There is no question that the man who was becoming the most successful poet of his generation was also a person who suffered intensely in private.

But it must be emphasized that Frost's career as a poet flourished beyond his early hopes. In 1916 he published *Mountain Interval,* a book containing "The Road Not Taken," "Birches," and "Out, Out—." He soon was in constant demand as a teacher and speaker. Amherst College created the position of poet-in-residence for him, an honor that would continue for much of his life. He also regularly lectured at Michigan, Harvard, Yale, and Dartmouth. Stories abound about his brilliance in front of audiences, both large and small. Seminars that he began teaching in the afternoon would stretch late into the evening as he captivated his students with his insights and his immense knowledge. He was popular not only with students. With the development of television after 1950, Frost took to the new medium with great enthusiasm. With his memorable appearance and voice, he was interviewed on many early television shows, and as a result he became perhaps the most widely recognizable poet in the history of literature.

As he gained all these successes as a teacher and lecturer, his poetic output remained constant and regular. In 1923 he published *Selected Poems* and *New Hampshire.* The latter collection, for which he won a Pulitzer Prize, contains some of his best-known work: "Stopping by Woods on a Snowy Evening," "Fire and Ice," and "Nothing Gold Can Stay." Throughout his career there were many additional collections. *West Running Brook* appeared in 1928, *Collected Poems* in 1930. Additional collections were *A Further Range* (1936), *A Witness Tree* (1942), *Steeple Bush* (1947), *Complete Poems* (1949), *Aforesaid* (1954), and *In the Clearing* (1962).

Poetic Characteristics

Early in his career and throughout his long public experience as a speaker and lecturer, Frost cultivated his persona as a philosophical, wry, and wise country poet. This is the friendly, almost avuncular voice we most regularly hear, the one that expresses knowledge and concern for the land, history, and human nature. Even with this genial persona, however, there are complicated undertones of wit and irony. There is also what Randall Jarrell called "The Other Frost," the often agonized and troubled spirit whose voice is heard in poems such as "Acquainted with the Night" and "Fire and Ice."

Regardless of the voice we hear, Frost preferred traditional poetic forms and rhythms, and he disapproved of free verse so strongly that he once asserted that writing it was like playing tennis without a net. He possessed complete knowledge of traditional forms (he knew much Latin poetry by heart). We therefore find that he uses conventional rhyme schemes and clear meters with traditional metrical substitutions in much of his poetry, together with closed forms such as couplets, sonnets (with interesting varying rhyme patterns), terza rima, quatrains, stanzas, and blank verse (see Chapter 20). Tension in the poems is created through the contrast of traditional form and Frost's character-istic conversational style. His diction is informal, plain, and colloquial, and his phrases are simple and direct. He uses and refines the natural speech patterns and rhythms of New England, polishing the language of everyday life, and blending speech and formal patterns into a compact and unique poetic texture.

Structurally, Frost's poems typically move in a smooth, uninterrupted flow from an event or an object, through a metaphor, to an idea. Within this pattern, he usually describes a complete event rather than a single vision. The heart of the process is the image or metaphor. Frost's metaphors are sparse and careful; they are brought sharply into focus and skillfully interwoven within each poem. Frost himself saw metaphors as the beginning of the process. In *Education by Po-etry* (1931) he states that "poetry begins in trivial metaphors, pretty metaphors, 'grace' metaphors, and goes on to the profoundest thinking that we have. Poet-ry provides the one permissible way of saying one thing and meaning another." In "The Figure a Poem Makes," a brief essay that he wrote as the Preface to *The Complete Poems of Robert Frost* of 1949, he goes on further to describe what to him was the poetic process: "The figure a poem makes. It begins in delight and ends in wisdom. The figure is the same as for love. No one can really hold that the ec-stasy should be static and stand still in one place. It begins in delight, it inclines to the impulse, it assumes direction with the first line laid down, it runs a course of lucky events, and ends in a clarification of life—not necessarily a great clarifi-cation, such as sects and cults are founded on, but in a momentary stay against confusion."

Poetic Subjects

Frost's poems are usually based in everyday life and rural settings. Poems are oc-casioned by flowers, stone fences, rain, snow, birch trees, falling leaves, a spider, a tree branch, birds, a hired man, a garden, children, wood chopping, apple picking, piano playing, sleigh riding, and hay cutting, to name just a few of the topics. However, the Frostian poetic structure always moves from such subjects toward philosophical generalizations about life and death, survival and respon-sibility, and nature and humanity. As he said in "The Figure a Poem Makes," the "delight" of poetry "is in the surprise of remembering something I didn't know I knew."

One of Frost's major appeals is that his poems are easily accessible. They are by no means simplistic, however, but run deep, as seen, for example, in poems like "The Road Not Taken" and "Misgiving." They also may be complex and ambiguous, as in "Mending Wall," in which the philosophies of the speaker and his fence-repairing neighbor are well presented and contrasted. Readers often conclude that the speaker's wish to remove barriers is the poem's major idea, but the neighbor's argument for maintaining them is equally strong. Fur-ther, in "Desert Places" (Chapter 20) we are presented with a chilling view of the infinite desert within the human spirit. In "Acquainted with the Night," Frost's sophisticated urban speaker tells us of the night of the city and also presents hints about the dark night of the soul.

Bibliographic Sources

Frost's complete works are in Richard Poirier and Mark Richardson, eds., *Robert Frost: Collected Poems, Prose, & Plays* (1995), and in Edward Connery Lathem, ed., *The Poetry of Robert Frost: The Collected Poems* (1969, frequently reprinted, most recently in 2002), which is also available in a paperback edition (2002). Of great use is Edward Connery Lathem's *A Concordance to the Poetry of Robert Frost* (rpt. 1994). Twelve of Frost's lectures have been preserved in Reginald Cook, *Robert Frost, A Living Voice* (Amherst: U of Massachusetts P, 1974). The standard biography, although often hostile, is by Lawrance Thompson, in three volumes: *Robert Frost: The Early Years; The Years of Triumph*; and *The Later Years* (New York: Holt Rinehart, 1966 – 1977). The last volume was completed after Thompson's death by Roy H. Winnick. A superb recent biography is Jay Parini, *Robert Frost: A Life* (New York: Holt, 1999).

Useful criticism includes George Nitchie, *Human Values in the Poetry of Robert Frost* (Durham: Duke UP, 1960); Reuben Brower, *The Poetry of Robert Frost: Constellations of Intention* (New York: Oxford UP, 1963); Philip L. Gerber, *Robert Frost* (Boston: Twayne, 1966, rpt. 1982); Richard Poirier, *Robert Frost: The Work of Knowing* (Palo Alto: Stanford UP, 1990); John Kemp, *Robert Frost and New England: The Poet as Regionalist* (Princeton: Princeton UP, 1979); Richard Wakefield, *Robert Frost and the Opposing Lights of the Hour* (New York: Lang, 1985); James Potter, *A Robert Frost Handbook* (University Park: Pennsylvania State UP, 1980); Harold Bloom, ed., *Robert Frost* (New York: Chelsea House, 1986; a collection of critical essays); George Monteiro, *Robert Frost and the New England Renaissance* (Lexington: U of Kentucky P, 1988); Judith Oster, *Toward Robert Frost: The Reader and the Poet* (Athens: U of Georgia P, 1991); George F. Bagby, *Frost and the Book of Nature* (Knoxville: U of Tennessee P, 1993); and Katherine Kearns, *Robert Frost and a Poetics of Appetite* (New York: Cambridge UP, 1994). One of the hour-long programs in the PBS *Voices and Visions* series (1987) features his work.

Special Topics for Writing and Argument about the Poetry of Robert Frost

1. The nature of Frost's topics (situations, scenes, actions) and his use of them for observation, narration, and metaphor.

2. Frost's assessment of the human situation: work, love, death, choices, diminution of life, Stoicism, keeping or not keeping boundaries.

3. Frost's speaker: character, experiences, recollections, and reflections. In developing his subjects, to what degree does the speaker take a possible listener into account?

4. Frost as poet of ideas: his vision of the way things are or should be.

5. Frost as "confessional" poet: misgivings, the admission of personal errors/fears.

6. Frost's use of narration and description in his poetry.

7. The structuring of Frost's poems: situation, observation, and generalization.

8. Frost's poetic diction: level and relationship to topic; conversational style.

9. Poetic forms in Frost: rhythm, meter, rhyme, and line and stanza patterns.

10. Frost's wry humor.

POEMS BY ROBERT FROST (CHRONOLOGICALLY ARRANGED)

A Line-Storm Song   1913

The line-storm clouds fly tattered and swift.
    The road is forlorn all day,
Where a myriad snowy quartz stones lift,
    And the hoof-prints vanish away.
The roadside flowers, too wet for the bee,   5
    Expend their bloom in vain.
Come over the hills and far with me,
    And be my love in the rain.

The birds have less to say for themselves
    In the wood-world's torn despair   10
Than now these numberless years the elves,
    Although they are no less there:
All song of the woods is crushed like some
    Wild, easily shattered rose.
Come, be my love in the wet woods, come,   15
    Where the boughs rain when it blows.

There is the gale to urge behind
    And bruit our singing down,
And the shallow waters aflutter with wind
    From which to gather your gown.   20
What matter if we go clear to the west,
    And come not through dry-shod?

For wilding brooch shall wet your breast
    The rain-fresh goldenrod.

Oh, never this whelming east wind swells   25
    But it seems like the sea's return
To the ancient lands where it left the shells
    Before the age of the fern;
And it seems like the time when after doubt
    Our love came back amain.   30
Oh, come forth into the storm and rout
    And be my love in the rain.

The Tuft of Flowers   1913

I went to turn the grass once after one
Who mowed it in the dew before the sun.

The dew was gone that made his blade so keen
Before I came to view the leveled scene

I looked for him behind an isle of trees;   5
I listened for his whetstone on the breeze.

But he had gone his way, the grass all mown,
And I must be, as he had been,—alone,

"As all must be," I said within my heart,
"Whether they work together or apart."   10

But as I said it, swift there passed me by
On noiseless wing a bewildered butterfly,

Seeking with memories grown dim o'er night
Some resting flower of yesterday's delight.

And once I marked his flight go round and round,   15
As where some flower lay withering on the ground.

And then he flew as far as eye could see,
And then on tremulous wing came back to me.

I thought of questions that have no reply,
And would have turned to toss the grass to dry.   20

But he turned first, and led my eye to look
At a tall tuft of flowers beside a brook,

A leaping tongue of bloom the scythe had spared
Beside a reedy brook the scythe had bared.

The mower in the dew had loved them thus,   25
By leaving them to flourish, not for us,

Nor yet to draw one thought of ours to him,
But from sheer morning gladness at the brim.

The butterfly and I had lit upon,
Nevertheless, a message from the dawn,   30

That made me hear the wakening birds around,
And hear his long scythe whispering to the ground,

And feel a spirit kindred to my own;
So that henceforth I worked no more alone;

But glad with him, I worked as with his aid,   35
And weary, sought at noon with him the shade.

And dreaming, as it were, held brotherly speech
With one whose thought I had not hoped to reach.

"Men work together," I told him from the heart,
"Whether they work together or apart."   40

Mending Wall ⌐⌐⌐⌐ 1914

Something there is that doesn't love a wall,
That sends the frozen-ground-swell under it,
And spills the upper boulders in the sun;
And makes gaps even two can pass abreast.
The work of hunters is another thing: 5
I have come after them and made repair
Where they have left not one stone on a stone,
But they would have the rabbit out of hiding,
To please the yelping dogs. The gaps I mean,
No one has seen them made or heard them made,   10
But at spring mending-time we find them there.
I let my neighbor know beyond the hill;
And on a day we meet to walk the line
And set the wall between us once again.
We keep the wall between us as we go.   15
To each the boulders that have fallen to each.
And some are loaves and some so nearly balls
We have to use a spell to make them balance:
'Stay where you are until our backs are turned!'
We wear our fingers rough with handling them.   20
Oh, just another kind of outdoor game,
One on a side. It comes to little more:
There where it is we do not need the wall:
He is all pine and I am apple orchard.
My apple trees will never get across   25
And eat the cones under his pines, I tell him.
He only says, "Good fences make good neighbors."
Spring is the mischief in me, and I wonder

If I could put a notion in his head:
"*Why* do they make good neighbors? Isn't it   30
Where there are cows? But here there are no cows."
Before I built a wall I'd ask to know
What I was walling in or walling out,
And to whom I was like to give offense.
Something there is that doesn't love a wall,   35
That wants it down. I could say "Elves" to him,
But it's not elves exactly, and I'd rather
He said it for himself. I see him there
Bringing a stone grasped firmly by the top
In each hand, like an old-stone savage armed.   40
He moves in darkness as it seems to me,
Not of woods only and the shade of trees.
He will not go behind his father's saying,
And he likes having thought of it so well
He says again, "Good fences make good neighbors."   45

Birches ⌐⌐⌐⌐⌐ *1915*

When I see birches bend to left and right
Across the lines of straighter darker trees,
I like to think some boy's been swinging them.
But swinging doesn't bend them down to stay
As ice-storms do. Often you must have seen them   5
Loaded with ice a sunny winter morning
After a rain. They click upon themselves
As the breeze rises, and turn many-colored
As the stir cracks and crazes their enamel.
Soon the sun's warmth makes them shed crystal shells   10
Shattering and avalanching on the snow-crust—
Such heaps of broken glass to sweep away
You'd think the inner dome of heaven had fallen.
They are dragged to the withered bracken by the load,
And they seem not to break; though once they are bowed   15
So low for long, they never right themselves:
You may see their trunks arching in the woods
Years afterwards, trailing their leaves on the ground
Like girls on hands and knees that throw their hair
Before them over their heads to dry in the sun.   20
But I was going to say when Truth broke in
With all her matter-of-fact about the ice-storm
I should prefer to have some boy bend them
As he went out and in to fetch the cows—
Some boy too far from town to learn baseball,   25
Whose only play was what he found himself,
Summer or winter, and could play alone.
One by one he subdued his father's trees

By riding them down over and over again
Until he took the stiffness out of them,
And not one but hung limp, not one was left   30
For him to conquer. He learned all there was
To learn about not launching out too soon
And so not carrying the tree away
Clear to the ground. He always kept his poise   35
To the top branches, climbing carefully
With the same pains you use to fill a cup
Up to the brim, and even above the brim.
Then he flung outward, feet first, with a swish,
Kicking his way down through the air to the ground.   40
So was I once myself a swinger of birches.
And so I dream of going back to be.
It's when I'm weary of considerations,
And life is too much like a pathless wood
Where your face burns and tickles with the cobwebs   45
Broken across it, and one eye is weeping
From a twig's having lashed across it open.
I'd like to get away from earth awhile
And then come back to it and begin over.
May no fate willfully misunderstand me   50
And half grant what I wish and snatch me away
Not to return. Earth's the right place for love:
I don't know where it's likely to go better.
I'd like to go by climbing a birch tree,
And climb black branches up a snow-white trunk   55
Toward Heaven, till the tree could bear no more,
But dipped its top and set me down again.
That would be good both going and coming back.
One could do worse than be a swinger of birches.

The Road Not Taken ⤳⟨⤳⟨⟨⟨ 1915

Two roads diverged in a yellow wood,
And sorry I could not travel both
And be one traveler, long I stood
And looked down one as far as I could
To where it bent in the undergrowth;   5

Then took the other, as just as fair,
And having perhaps the better claim,
Because it was grassy and wanted wear;
Though as for that the passing there
Had worn them really about the same,   10

And both that morning equally lay
In leaves no step had trodden black.
Oh, I kept the first for another day!
Yet knowing how way leads on to way,
I doubted if I should ever come back.   15

I shall be telling this with a sigh
Somewhere ages and ages hence:
Two roads diverged in a wood, and I—
I took the one less traveled by,
And that has made all the difference.   20

"Out, Out—"   *~<~·~·*   1916

The buzz saw snarled and rattled in the yard
And made dust and dropped stove-length sticks of wood,
Sweet-scented stuff when the breeze drew across it.
And from there those that lifted eyes could count
Five mountain ranges one behind the other   5
Under the sunset far into Vermont.
And the saw snarled and rattled, snarled and rattled,
As it ran light, or had to bear a load.
And nothing happened: day was all but done.
Call it a day, I wish they might have said   10
To please the boy by giving him the half hour
That a boy counts so much when saved from work.
His sister stood beside them in her apron
To tell them "Supper." At the word, the saw,
As if to prove saws knew what supper meant,   15
Leaped out at the boy's hand, or seemed to leap—
He must have given the hand. However it was,
Neither refused the meeting. But the hand!
The boy's first outcry was rueful laugh,
As he swung toward them holding up the hand   20
Half in appeal, but half as if to keep
The life from spilling. Then the boy saw all—
Since he was old enough to know, big boy
Doing a man's work, though a child at heart—
He saw all spoiled. "Don't let him cut my hand off—   25
The doctor, when he comes. Don't let him, sister!"
So. But the hand was gone already.
The doctor put him in the dark of ether.
He lay and puffed his lips out with his breath.
And then—the watcher at his pulse took fright.   30
No one believed. They listened at his heart.
Little – less – nothing! – and that ended it.
No more to build on there. And they, since they
Were not the one dead, turned to their affairs.

The Oven Bird   *~<~·~·*   1916

There is a singer everyone has heard,
Loud, a mid-summer and a mid-wood bird,
Who makes the solid tree trunks sound again.

He says that leaves are old and that for flowers
Mid-summer is to spring as one to ten.   5
He says the early petal-fall is past
When pear and cherry bloom went down in showers
On sunny days a moment overcast;
And comes that other fall we name the fall.
He says the highway dust is over all.   10
The bird would cease and be as other birds
But that he knows in singing not to sing.
The question that he frames in all but words
Is what to make of a diminished thing.

Fire and Ice ❀ 1920

Some say the world will end in fire,
Some say in ice.
From what I've tasted of desire
I hold with those who favor fire.
But if it had to perish twice,   5
I think I know enough of hate
To say that for destruction ice
Is also great
And would suffice.

Stopping by Woods on a Snowy Evening (1923), 621 (See Chapter 13.)

Misgiving ❀ 1923

All crying, "We will go with you, O Wind!"
The foliage follow him, leaf and stem;
But a sleep oppresses them as they go,
And they end by bidding him stay with them.

Since ever they flung abroad in spring   5
The leaves had promised themselves this flight,
Who now would fain seek sheltering wall,
Or thicket, or hollow place for the night.

And now they answer his summoning blast
With an ever vaguer and vaguer stir,   10
Or at utmost a little reluctant whirl
That drops them no further than where they were.

I only hope that when I am free
As they are free to go in quest
Of the knowledge beyond the bounds of life   15
It may not seem better to me to rest.

Nothing Gold Can Stay ❀ 1923

Nature's first green is gold,
Her hardest hue to hold.
Her early leaf's a flower;

But only so an hour.
Then leaf subsides to leaf.   5
So Eden sank to grief,
So dawn goes down to day.
Nothing gold can stay.

Acquainted with the Night ~~~~ 1928

I have been one acquainted with the night.
I have walked out in rain—and back in rain.
I have outwalked the furthest city light.

I have looked down the saddest city lane.
I have passed by the watchman on his beat   5
And dropped my eyes, unwilling to explain.

I have stood still and stopped the sound of feet
When far away an interrupted cry
Came over houses from another street,

But not to call me back or say good-by,   10
And further still at an unearthly height,
One luminary clock against the sky

Proclaimed the time was neither wrong nor right.
I have been one acquainted with the night.

Desert Places (1936), 861 (See Chapter 20.)

Design ~~~~ 1936

I found a dimpled spider, fat and white,
On a white heal-all,° holding up a moth
Like a white piece of rigid satin cloth—
Assorted characters of death and blight
Mixed ready to begin the morning right,   5
Like the ingredients of a witches' broth—
A snow-drop spider, a flower like a froth,
And dead wings carried like a paper kite.

What had that flower to do with being white,
The wayside blue and innocent heal-all?   10
What brought the kindred spider to that height,
Then steered the white moth thither in the night?
What but design of darkness to appall?—
If design govern in a thing so small.

DESIGN 2 *heal-all:* a flower, usually blue, thought to have healing powers.

The Silken Tent ~~~~ 1936

She is as in a field a silken tent
At midday when a sunny summer breeze
Has dried the dew and all its ropes relent,

So that in guys it gently sways at ease,
And its supporting central cedar pole,   5
That is its pinnacle to heavenward
And signifies the sureness of the soul,
Seems to owe naught to any single cord,
But strictly held by none, is loosely bound
By countless silken ties of love and thought   10
To everything on earth the compass round,
And only by one's going slightly taut
In the capriciousness of summer air
Is of the slightest bondage made aware.

The Strong Are Saying Nothing ~✦~ 1937

The soil now gets a rumpling soft and damp,
And small regard to the future of any weed.
The final flat of the hoe's approval stamp
Is reserved for the bed of a few selected seed.

There is seldom more than a man to a harrowed piece.   5
Men work alone, their lots plowed far apart,
One stringing a chain of seed in an open crease,
And another stumbling after a halting cart.

To the fresh and black of the squares of early mold
The leafless bloom of a plum is fresh and white;   10
Though there's more than a doubt if the weather is not too cold
For the bees to come and serve its beauty aright.

Wind goes from farm to farm in wave on wave,
But carries no cry of what is hoped to be.
There may be little or much beyond the grave,   15
But the strong are saying nothing until they see.

The Gift Outright ~✦~ 1941

The land was ours before we were the land's.
She was our land more than a hundred years
Before we were her people. She was ours
In Massachusetts, in Virginia,
But we were England's, still colonials,   5
Possessing what we still were unpossessed by,
Possessed by what we now no more possessed.
Something we were withholding made us weak
Until we found out that it was ourselves
We were withholding from our land of living,   10
And forthwith found salvation in surrender.
Such as we were we gave ourselves outright
(The deed of gift was many deeds of war)
To the land vaguely realizing westward,
But still unstoried, artless, unenhanced,   15
Such as she was, such as she would become.

A Considerable Speck   1942

(Microscopic)

A speck that would have been beneath my sight
On any but a paper sheet so white
Set off across what I had written there.
And I had idly poised my pen in air
To stop it with a period of ink   5
When something strange about it made me think.
This was no dust speck by my breathing blown,
But unmistakably a living mite
With inclinations it could call its own.
It paused as with suspicion of my pen,   10
And then came racing wildly on again
To where my manuscript was not yet dry;
Then paused again and either drank or smelt—
With loathing, for again it turned to fly.
Plainly with an intelligence I dealt.   15
It seemed too tiny to have room for feet,
Yet must have had a set of them complete
To express how much it didn't want to die.
It ran with terror and with cunning crept.
It faltered: I could see it hesitate;   20
Then in the middle of the open sheet
Cower down in desperation to accept
Whatever I accorded it of fate.
I have none of the tenderer-than-thou
Collectivistic regimenting love   25
With which the modern world is being swept
But this poor microscopic item now!
Since it was nothing I knew evil of
I let it lie there till I hope it slept.
I have a mind myself and recognize   30
Mind when I meet with it in any guise.
No one can know how glad I am to find
On any sheet the least display of mind.

Take Something like a Star°   1943

O Star (the fairest one in sight),
We grant your loftiness the right
To some obscurity of cloud—
It will not do to say of night,
Since dark is what brings out your light.   5
Some mystery becomes the proud.
But to be wholly taciturn

TAKE SOMETHING LIKE A STAR. Earlier versions of this poem used the title "Choose Something like a Star."

In your reserve is not allowed.
Say something to us we can learn
By heart and when alone repeat.   10
Say something! And it says, "I burn,"
But say with what degree of heat.
Talk Fahrenheit, talk Centigrade.
Use language we can comprehend.
Tell us what elements you blend.   15
It gives us strangely little aid,
But does tell something in the end.
And steadfast as Keats' Eremite,
Not even stooping from its sphere,
It asks a little of us here.   20
It asks of us a certain height,
So when at times the mob is swayed
To carry praise or blame too far,
We may take something like a star
To stay our minds on and be staid.   25

One Hundred Twenty-Nine Poems for Additional Study and Enjoyment

A. R. AMMONS (1926–2001)

80-Proof   1975

A fifth of me's me:
the rest's chaser:
35 lbs.'s
my true self: but
chuck 10 lbs. or so for bones,   5
what's left's
steaks & chops &
chicken fat,
two-over-easy & cream-on-the-side:
strip off a sheath of hide,   10
strip out nerves & veins
& permeable membranes,
what's left's a greasy spot:
the question's
whether   15
to retain
the shallow stain
or go 100% spiritual
and fifth by fifth
achieve a whole,   20
highly transcendental.

MAYA ANGELOU (b. 1928)

My Arkansas   1978

There is a deep brooding
in Arkansas.
Old crimes like moss pend
from poplar trees.
The sullen earth°   *See p. 1138, line 12.*   5
is much too
red for comfort.

Sunrise seems to hesitate
and in that second
lose its
incandescent aim, and   10
dusk no more shadows
than the noon.
The past is brighter yet.

Old hates and
ante-bellum° lace are rent   15

MY ARKANSAS. 16 *ante-bellum:* before the U.S. Civil War (1861–1865).

but not discarded.
Today is yet to come
in Arkansas.
It writhes. It writhes in awful   20
waves of brooding.

ANONYMOUS

Barbara Allan ⸙⸝⸜⸝⸌   Sixteenth century

It was in and about the Martinmas° time,   *November 11*
   When the green leaves were a-fallin',
That Sir John Graeme in the West Country
   Fell in love with Barbara Allan.

He sent his man down through the town   5
   To the place where she was dwellin':
"O haste and come to my master dear,
   Gin° ye be Barbara Allan."   *if*

O slowly, slowly rose she up,
   To the place where he was lyin',   10
And when she drew the curtain by:
   "Young man, I think you're dyin'."

"O it's I'm sick, and very, very sick,
   And 'tis all for Barbara Allan."
"O the better for me ye shall never be,   15
   Though your heart's blood were a-spillin'."

"O dinna ye mind,° young man," said she,   *don't you recall*
   "When ye the cups were fillin',
That ye made the healths° go round and round,   *toasts*
   And slighted Barbara Allan?"   20

He turned his face unto the wall,
   And death with him was dealin':
"Adieu, adieu,° my dear friends all,   *farewell*
   And be kind to Barbara Allan."

And slowly, slowly, rose she up,   25
   And slowly, slowly left him;
And sighing said she could not stay,
   Since death of life had reft him.°   *since death had bereft him of life*

She had not gone a mile but twa,°   *two*
   When she heard the dead-bell knellin',   30
And every jow° that the dead-bell ga'ed°   *stoke; made*
   It cried, "Woe to Barbara Allan!"

"O mother, mother, make my bed,
   O make it soft and narrow:
Since my love died for me today,   35
   I'll die for him tomorrow."

ANONYMOUS (NAVAJO)

Healing Prayer from the Beautyway Chant ⌇⌇⌇ Traditional

Out of the East, Beauty has come home,
Out of the South, Beauty has come home,
Out of the West, Beauty has come home,
Out of the North, Beauty has come home,
Out of the highest heavens and the lowest lands,   5
   Beauty has come home.
    Everywhere around us, Beauty has come home.
As we live each day, everything evil will leave us.
   We will be entirely healed,
   Our bodies will exult in the fresh winds,   10
   Our steps will be firm.
As we live each day,
   Everything before us will be Beautiful;
   Everything behind us will be Beautiful;
   Everything above us will be Beautiful;
   Everything below us will be Beautiful;   15
   Everything around us will be Beautiful;
   All our thoughts will be Beautiful;
   All our words will be Beautiful;
   All our dreams will be Beautiful.
We will be forever restored, forever whole.   20
All things will be Beautiful forever.

ANONYMOUS

Lord Randal ⌇⌇⌇ Sixteenth century

"Oh, where have you been, Lord Randal, my son?
Oh, where have you been, my handsome young man?"
"Oh, I've been to the wildwood; mother, make my bed soon,
I'm weary of hunting and I fain° would lie down."   *gladly*

"And whom did you meet there, Lord Randal, my son?   5
And whom did you meet there, my handsome young man?"
"Oh, I met with my true love; mother, make my bed soon,
I'm weary of hunting and I fain would lie down."

"What got you for supper, Lord Randal, my son?
What got you for supper, my handsome young man?"   10
"I got eels boiled in broth; mother, make my bed soon,
I'm weary of hunting and I fain would lie down."

"And who got your leavings, Lord Randal, my son?
And who got your leavings, my handsome young man?"
"I gave them to my dogs; mother, make my bed soon,   15
I'm weary of hunting and I fain would lie down."

"And what did your dogs do, Lord Randal, my son?
And what did your dogs do, my handsome young man?"
"Oh, they stretched out and died; mother, make my bed soon,   20
I'm weary of hunting and I fain would lie down."

"Oh, I fear you are poisoned, Lord Randal, my son,
Oh, I fear you are poisoned, my handsome young man."
"Oh, yes, I am poisoned; mother, make my bed soon,
For I'm sick at my heart and I fain would lie down."

"What will you leave your mother, Lord Randal, my son?   25
What will you leave your mother, my handsome young man?"
"My house and my lands; mother, make my bed soon,
For I'm sick at my heart and I fain would lie down."

"What will you leave your sister, Lord Randal, my son?
What will you leave your sister, my handsome young man?"   30
"My gold and my silver; mother, make my bed soon,
For I'm sick at my heart and I fain would lie down."

"What will you leave your brother, Lord Randal, my son?
What will you leave your brother, my handsome young man?"
"My horse and my saddle; mother, make my bed soon,   35
For I'm sick at my heart and I fain would lie down."

"What will you leave your true-love, Lord Randal, my son?
What will you leave your true-love, my handsome young man?"
"A halter to hang her; mother, make my bed soon,
For I'm sick at my heart and I want to lie down."   40

ANONYMOUS

The Three Ravens   ⌇⌇⌇⌇   Sixteenth century

There were three ravens sat on a tree,
  Down a down, hay down, hay down,
There were three ravens sat on a tree,
  With a down,
There were three ravens sat on a tree,   5
They were as black as they might be,
  With a down, derry, derry, derry, down, down.°

The one of them said to his mate,
"Where shall we our breakfast take?

"Down in yonder green field   10
There lies a knight slain under his shield.

"His hounds they lie down at his feet,
So well they can their master keep.

THE THREE RAVENS. 7 *down:* In singing this ballad, the first line of each stanza is repeated three times and
the refrain is repeated as in stanza 1.

"His hawks they fly so eagerly,°   *fiercely*
There's no fowl° dare him come nigh."   *bird*   15

Down there comes a fallow° doe,   *light brown*
As great with young as she might go,°   *walk*

She lifted up his bloody head,
And kissed his wounds that were so red.

She got him up upon her back,
And carried him to earthen lake.°   20
                                      pit

She buried him before the prime,°   *morning prayer service*
She was dead herself ere evensong time.°
God send every gentleman
Such hawks, such hounds, and such a lemman.°   *mistress*   25

23 *evensong time:* the time for the evening prayer service.

MARGARET ATWOOD (b. 1939)

Variation on the Word Sleep ⸎ 1981

I would like to watch you sleeping,
which may not happen.
I would like to watch you,
sleeping. I would like to sleep
with you, to enter
your sleep as its smooth dark wave   5
slides over my head

and walk with you through that lucent
wavering forest of bluegreen leaves
with its watery sun & three moons
towards the cave where you must descend,   10
towards your worst fear

I would like to give you the silver
branch, the small white flower, the one
word that will protect you
from the grief at the center   15
of your dream, from the grief
at the center. I would like to follow
you up the long stairway
again & become
the boat that would row you back   20
carefully, a flame
in two cupped hands
to where your body lies
beside me, and you enter
it as easily as breathing in   25

I would like to be the air
that inhabits you for a moment
only. I would like to be that unnoticed
& that necessary.
  30

W. H. AUDEN (1907–1973)

For a photo, see p. 938.

The Unknown Citizen ⁓⁓⁓ 1940

(To JS/07/M/378
This Marble Monument
Is Erected by the State)

He was found by the Bureau of Statistics to be
One against whom there was no official complaint,
And all the reports on his conduct agree
That, in the modern sense of an old-fashioned word, he was a saint,
For in everything he did he served the Greater Community. 5

Except for the War till the day he retired
He worked in a factory and never got fired,
But satisfied his employers, Fudge Motors Inc.
Yet he wasn't a scab° or odd in his views.   *strikebreaker*
For his Union reports that he paid his dues, 10
(Our report on his Union shows it was sound)
And our Social Psychology workers found
That he was popular with his mates° and liked a drink.   *co-workers*
The Press are convinced that he bought a paper every day
And that his reactions to advertisements were normal in every way. 15
Policies taken out in his name prove that he was fully insured,
And his Health-card shows he was once in hospital but left it cured.
Both Producers Research and High-Grade Living declare
He was fully sensible to the advantages of the Installment Plan
And had everything necessary to the Modern Man, 20
A phonograph, a radio, a car and a frigidaire.
Our reseachers into Public Opinion are content
That he held the proper opinions for the time of year;
When there was peace, he was for peace; when there was war, he went.
He was married and added five children to the population, 25
Which our Eugenist says was the right number for a parent of his generation,
And our teachers report that he never interfered with their education.
Was he free? Was he happy? The question is absurd:
Had anything been wrong, we should certainly have heard.

WENDELL BERRY (b. 1934)

Another Descent ⁓⁓⁓ 1985

Through the weeks of deep snow
we walked above the ground
on fallen sky, as though we did
not come of root and leaf, as though
we had only air and weather 5
for our difficult home.

But now
as March warms, and the rivulets
run like birdsong on the slopes,
and the branches of light sing in the hills,
slowly we return to earth.   10

EARLE BIRNEY (1904–1995)

Can. Lit.° ⤢✦⤡ *1962*

(or them able leave her ever)

since we'd always sky about
when we had eagles they flew out
leaving no shadow bigger than wren's
to trouble even our broodiest hens
too busy bridging loneliness   5
to be alone
we hacked in railway ties
what Emily° etched in bone

we French & English never lost
our civil war   10
endure it still
a bloody civil bore

the wounded sirened off
no Whitman° wanted
it's only by our lack of ghosts   15
we're haunted

CAN LIT. The title is an abbreviation for "Canadian Literature." 8 *Emily:* Emily Dickinson (1830–1886),
American poet (see pp. 1011–1048). 14 *Whitman:* Walt Whitman (1819–1892), American poet.

LOUISE BOGAN (1879–1970)

Women ⤢✦⤡ *1923*

Women have no wilderness in them,
They are provident instead,
Content in the tight hot cell of their hearts
To eat dusty bread.

They do not see cattle cropping red winter grass,   5
They do not hear
Snow water going down under culverts
Shallow and clear.

They wait, when they should turn to journeys,
They stiffen, when they should bend.
They use against themselves that benevolence
To which no man is friend.

They cannot think of so many crops to a field
Or of clean wood cleft by an axe.
Their love is an eager meaninglessness
Too tense, or too lax.

They hear in every whisper that speaks to them
A shout and a cry.
As like as not, when they take life over their door-sills
They should let it go by.

ARNA BONTEMPS (1902–1973)

A Black Man Talks of Reaping 1940

I have sown beside all waters in my day.
I planted deep, within my heart the fear
that wind or fowl would take the grain away.
I planted safe against this stark, lean year.

I scattered seed enough to plant the land
in rows from Canada to Mexico
but for my reaping only what the hand
can hold at once is all that I can show.

Yet what I sowed and what the orchard yields
my brother's sons are gathering stalk and root;
small wonder then my children glean in fields
they have not sown, and feed on bitter fruit.

ANNE BRADSTREET (1612–1672)

To My Dear and Loving Husband 1678

If ever two were one, then surely we.
If ever man were loved by wife, then thee;
If ever wife was happy in a man,
Compare with me ye women if you can.
I prize thy love more than whole mines of gold,
Or all the riches that the East doth hold.
My love is such that rivers cannot quench,
Nor ought but love from thee give recompense.
Thy love is such I can no way repay;

The heavens reward thee manifold, I pray.   10
Then while we live, in love let's so persever,
That when we live no more we may live ever.

GWENDOLYN BROOKS (1917–2000)   *For a photo, see p. 811.*

Primer for Blacks ⤙⤙⤚⤚ 1980

Blackness
is a title,
is a preoccupation,
is a commitment Blacks
are to comprehend—   5
and in which you are
to perceive your Glory.

The conscious shout
of all that is white is
"It's Great to be white."   10
The conscious shout
of the slack in Black is
"It's Great to be white."
Thus all that is white
has white strength and yours.   15

The word Black
has geographic power,
pulls everybody in:
Blacks here—
Blacks there—   20
Blacks wherever they may be.
And remember, you Blacks, what they told you—
remember your Education:
"one Drop—one Drop
maketh a brand new Black."   25
      'Oh mighty Drop.
——And because they have given us kindly
so many more of our people.

Blackness
stretches over the land.
Blackness—   30
the Black of it,
the rust-red of it,
the milk and cream of it,
the tan and yellow-tan of it,
the deep-brown middle-brown high-brown of it,   35
the "olive" and ochre of it—
Blackness
marches on.

The huge, the pungent object of our prime out-ride   40
is to Comprehend,
to salute and to Love the fact that we are Black,
which *is* our "ultimate Reality,"
which is the lone ground
from which our meaningful metamorphosis,   45
from which our prosperous staccato,
group of individual, can rise.

Self-shriveled Blacks.
Begin with gaunt and marvelous concession:
YOU are our costume and our fundamental bone.   50

        All of you—
        You COLORED ones,
        you NEGRO ones,
those of you who proudly cry
        "I'm half INDian"—   55
        those of you who proudly screech
        "I'VE got the blood of George WASHington in
            MY veins"—

ALL of you—   60
        you proper Blacks,
you half-Blacks,
you wish-I-weren't Blacks,
Niggeroes and Niggerenes.

You.

ELIZABETH BARRETT BROWNING (1806–1861)

Sonnets from the Portuguese: Number 43 ⤳⤳ *1850*

How do I love thee? Let me count the ways.
I love thee to the depth and breadth and height
My soul can reach, when feeling out of sight
For the ends of Being and ideal Grace.
I love thee to the level of every day's   5
Most quiet need, by sun and candlelight.
I love thee freely, as men strive for Right;
I love thee purely, as they turn from Praise.
I love thee with the passion put to use
In my old griefs, and with my childhood's faith.   10
I love thee with a love I seemed to lose
With my lost saints,—I love thee with the breath,
Smiles, tears, of all my life!—and, if God choose,
I shall but love thee better after death.

ROBERT BROWNING (1812–1889)

For a drawing, see p. 673.

Soliloquy of the Spanish Cloister ~ ~ ~ ~ 1842

1

Gr-r-r—there go, my heart's abhorrence!
    Water your damned flowerpots, do!
If hate killed men, Brother Lawrence,
    God's blood, would not mine kill you!
What? your myrtle bush wants trimming?   5
    Oh, that rose has prior claims—
Needs its leaden vase filled brimming?
    Hell dry you up with its flames!

2

At the meal we sit together:
    Salve tibi:° I must hear   *Hail to thee!*   10
Wise talk of the kind of weather,
    Sort of season, time of year:
Not a plenteous cork-crop: scarcely
    Dare we hope oak-galls, I doubt:
What's the Latin name for "parsley"?   15
    What's the Greek name for Swine's Snout?

3

Whew! We'll have our platter burnished,
    Laid with care on our own shelf!
With a fire-new spoon we're furnished,
    And a goblet for ourself,   20
Rinsed like something sacrificial
    Ere 'tis fit to touch our chaps°   *jaws*
Marked with L. for our initial!
    (He-he! There his lily snaps!)

4

Saint, forsooth! While brown Dolores   25
    Squats outside the Convent bank
With Sanchicha, telling stories,
    Steeping tresses in the tank,
Blue-black, lustrous, thick like horsehairs,
    —Can't I see his dead eye glow,   30
Bright as 'twere a Barbary corsair's?°   *pirate's*
    (That is, if he'd let it show!)

5

When he finishes refection,°   *dinner*
    Knife and fork he never lays
Cross-wise, to my recollection,   35

As do I, in Jesu's praise.
I the Trinity illustrate,
    Drinking watered orange-pulp—
In three sips the Arian° frustrate;   *Anti-Trinitarian (a heretic)*
    While he drains his at one gulp.   40

6

Oh, those melons? If he's able
    We're to have a feast! so nice!
One goes to the Abbot's table,
    All of us get each a slice.
How go on your flowers? None double?   45
    Not one fruit-sort can you spy?
Strange!—And I, too, at such trouble,
    Keep them close-nipped on the sly!

7

There's a great text in Galatians,°   *perhaps 3:10 or 5:19–21*
    Once you trip on it, entails   50
Twenty-nine distinct damnations,
    One sure, if another fails:
If I trip him just a-dying,
    Sure of heaven as sure can be,   55
Spin him round and send him flying
    Off to hell, a Manichee?°   *heretic*

8

Or, my scrofulous° French novel   *pornographic*
    On gray paper with blunt type!
Simply glance at it, you grovel
    Hand and foot in Belial's° gripe: *the Devil*   60
If I double down its pages
    At the woeful sixteenth print,
When he gathers his greengages,
    Ope a sieve and slip it in't?

9

Or, there's Satan!—one might venture   65
    Pledge one's soul to him, yet leave
Such a flaw in the indenture°   *contract*
    As he'd miss till, past retrieve,
Blasted lay that rose-acacia
    We're so proud of! *Hy, Zy, Hine* . . .   70
'St, there's Vespers! *Plena gratia*°   *full of grace*
    Ave, Virgo!° Gr-r-r—you swine!   *Hail, Virgin!*

WILLIAM CULLEN BRYANT (1794–1878)

To Cole, the Painter, Departing for Europe ⌐≺≺≺⌐ 1829

Thine eyes shall see the light of distant skies;
   Yet, Cole! thy heart shall bear to Europe's strand
   A living image of our own bright land,
Such as upon thy glorious canvas lies;
Lone lakes—savannas where the bison roves—   5
   Rocks rich with summer garlands—solemn streams—
   Skies where the desert eagle wheels and screams—
Spring bloom and autumn blaze of boundless groves.

Fair scenes shall greet thee where thou goest—fair,
   But different—everywhere the trace of men,   10
   Paths, homes, graves, ruins, from the lowest glen
To where life shrinks from the fierce Alpine air.
   Gaze on them, till the tears shall dim thy sight,
   But keep that earlier, wilder image bright.

GEORGE GORDON, LORD BYRON (1788–1824)

The Destruction of Sennacherib° ⌐≺≺≺⌐ 1815

The Assyrian came down like the wolf on the fold,
And his cohorts were gleaming in purple and gold;
And the sheen of their spears was like stars on the sea,
When the blue wave rolls nightly on deep Galilee.

Like the leaves of the forest when summer is green,   5
That host with their banners at sunset were seen:
Like the leaves of the forest when autumn hath blown,
That host on the morrow lay withered and strown.

For the Angel of Death spread his wings on the blast,
And breathed in the face of the foe as he passed;   10
And the eyes of the sleepers waxed deadly and chill,
And their hearts but once heaved—and for ever grew still!

And there lay the steed with his nostril all wide,
But through it there rolled not the breath of his pride;
And the foam of his gasping lay white on the turf,   15
And cold as the spray of the rock-beating surf.

And there lay the rider distorted and pale,
With the dew on his brow, and the rust on his mail;
And the tents were all silent, the banners alone,
The lances unlifted, the trumpet unblown.   20

THE DESTRUCTION OF SENNACHERIB. Sennacherib was king of the ancient Near Eastern empire of Assyria from 705 to 681 B.C.E. He laid seige to Jerusalem in about 702 B.C.E., even though King Hezekiah had already rendered tribute to Assyria. According to 2 Kings 19:35–36, a miracle occurred to save the besieged Hebrews: "the angel of the Lord went out and smote . . . [185,000 Assyrian soldiers]; and when they [the Hebrews] arose early in the morning, behold, they [the Assyrians] were all dead corpses." See p. 823 for some of Ogden Nash's parodies of this poem.

And the widows of Ashur° are loud in their wail,
And the idols are broke in the temple of Baal;°
And the might of the Gentile, unsmote by the sword,
Hath melted like snow in the glance of the Lord!

21 *Ashur:* the land of the Assyrians.   22 *Baal:* a god who supposedly controlled weather and storms.

THOMAS CAMPION (1567–1620)

Cherry Ripe ⫽⫻⫶⫻⫽ 1617

There is a garden in her face,
Where roses and white lilies grow;
A heavenly paradise is that place,
Wherein all pleasant fruits do flow.
There cherries grow, which none may buy   5
Till "Cherry ripe" themselves do cry.

Those cherries fairly do enclose
Of orient pearl a double row;
Which when her lovely laughter shows,
They look like rosebuds filled with snow.   10
Yet them nor peer nor prince can buy
Till "Cherry ripe" themselves do cry.

Her eyes like angels watch them still;
Her brows like bended bows do stand,
Threatening with piercing frowns to kill   15
All that attempt, with eye or hand,
Those sacred cherries to come nigh
Till "Cherry ripe" themselves do cry.

LUCILLE CLIFTON (b. 1936)

For a photo, see p. 768.

this morning (for the girls of eastern high school) ⫽⫻⫶⫻⫽ 1987

this morning
this morning
          i met myself

coming in
                                                            5
a bright
jungle girl
shining
quick as a snake
a tall   10
tree girl a
me girl

          i met myself
this morning
coming in

and all day
i have been
a black bell
ringing
i survive   15

        survive   20

survive

LUCILLE CLIFTON (b. 1936)

For a photo, see p. 768.

the poet ~ 1987

i beg my bones to be good but
they keep clicking music and
i spin in the center of myself
a foolish frightful woman
moving my skin against the wind and   5
tap dancing for my life.

LEONARD COHEN (b. 1934)

'The killers that run . . .' ~ 1972

The killers that run
      the other countries
are trying to get us
to overthrow the killers
      that run our own   5
I for one
prefer the rule
      of our native killers
I am convinced
      the foreign killer   10
will kill more of us
than the old familiar killer does
      Frankly I don't believe
anyone out there
really wants us to solve   15
our social problems
      I base this all on how I feel
about the man next door
I just hope he doesn't
      get any uglier   20
Therefore I am a patriot
I don't like to see
      a burning flag
because it excites

the killers on either side   25
to unfortunate excess
which goes on gaily
            quite unchecked
until everyone is dead

BILLY COLLINS (b. 1941)

For a photo, see p. 610.

Days >·<~·~·~ 1995

Each one *is* a gift, no doubt.
mysteriously placed in your waking hand
or set upon your forehead
moments before you open your eyes.

Today begins cold and bright,   5
the ground heavy with snow
and the thick masonry of ice.
the sun glinting off the turrets of clouds.

Through the calm eye of the window
everything is in its place   10
but so precariously
this day might be resting somehow

on the one before it,
all the days of the past stacked high
like the impossible tower of dishes   15
entertainers used to build on stage.

No wonder you find yourself
perched on the top of a tall ladder
hoping to add one more.
Just another Wednesday   20

you whisper,
then holding your breath,
place this cup on yesterday's saucer
without the slightest clink.

FRANCES CORNFORD (1886–1960)

From a Letter to America on a Visit to Sussex: Spring 1942 >·<~·~·~ 1942

How simply violent things
Happen, is strange.
How strange it was to see
In the soft Cambridge sky our Squadron's wings,
And hear the huge hum in the familiar grey.   5
And it was odd today

On Ashdown Forest that will never change,
To find a gunner in the gorse, flung down,
Well-camouflaged, and bored and lion-brown.
A little further by those twisted trees   10
(As if it rose on humped preposterous seas
Out of a Book of Hours) up a bank
Like a large dragon, purposeful though drunk,
Heavily lolloped, swayed and sunk,
A tank.   15
All this because manoeuvres had begun.
But now, but soon,
At home on any usual afternoon,
High overhead
May come the Erinyes° winging   *the furies in Greek mythology* 20
Or here the boy may lie beside his gun,
His mud-brown tunic gently staining red,
While larks get on with their old job of singing.

STEPHEN CRANE (1871–1900)

Do Not Weep, Maiden, for War Is Kind ⤠⥽⥼⤔ *1896, 1899 (1895)*

Do not weep, maiden, for war is kind.
Because your lover threw wild hands toward the sky
And the affrighted steed ran on alone,
Do not weep.
War is kind.   5

  Hoarse, booming drums of the regiment
  Little souls who thirst for fight,
  These men were born to drill and die
  The unexplained glory flies above them
  Great is the battle-god, great, and his kingdom—   10
  A field where a thousand corpses lie.

Do not weep, babe, for war is kind.
Because your father tumbled in the yellow trenches,
Raged at his breast, gulped and died,
Do not weep.
War is kind.   15

  Swift, blazing flag of the regiment
  Eagle with crest of red and gold,
  These men were born to drill and die
  Point for them the virtue of slaughter   20
  Make plain to them the excellence of killing
  And a field where a thousand corpses lie.

Mother whose head hung humble as a button
On the bright splendid shroud of your son,
Do not weep.
War is kind.   25

E. E. CUMMINGS (1894–1962)

For a photo, see p. 648.

if there are any heavens ≻≺≺↙↙↙ 1931

if there are any heavens my mother will(all by herself)have
one.   It will not be a pansy heaven nor
a fragile heaven of lilies-of-the-valley but
it will be a heaven of blackred roses

my father will be (deep like a rose   5
tall like a rose)

standing near my

swaying over her
(silent)
with eyes which are really petals and see   10

nothing with the face of a poet really which
is a flower and not a face with
hands
which whisper
This is my beloved my   15

           (suddenly in sunlight

he will bow,

& the whole garden will bow)

JAMES DICKEY (1923–1997)

Kudzu ≻≺≺↙↙↙ 1964

Japan invades. Far Eastern vines
Run from the clay banks they are

 Supposed to keep from eroding,
Up telephone poles,
Which rear, half out of leafage,   5
As though they would shriek,
Like things smothered by their own
Green, mindless, unkillable ghosts.
In Georgia, the legend says
That you must close your windows   10

At night to keep it out of the house.
The glass is tinged with green, even so,

As the tendrils crawl over the fields.
The night the kudzu has
Your pasture, you sleep like the dead.   15
Silence has grown Oriental
And you cannot step upon ground:
Your leg plunges somewhere

It should not, it never should be,
Disappears, and waits to be struck   20

Anywhere between sole and kneecap:
For when the kudzu comes,

The snakes do, and weave themselves
Among its lengthening vines,
Their spade heads resting on leaves,   25
Growing also, in earthly power
And the huge circumstance of concealment.
One by one the cows stumble in,
Drooling a hot green froth,
And die, seeing the wood of their stalls   30

Strain to break into leaf.
In your closed house, with the vine

Tapping your window like lightning,
You remember what tactics to use.
In the wrong yellow fog-light of dawn   35
You herd them in, the hogs,
Head down in their hairy fat,
The meaty troops, to the pasture.
The leaves of the kudzu quake
With the serpents' fear, inside   40

The meadow ringed with men
Holding sticks, on the country roads.

The hogs disappear in the leaves.
The sound is intense, subhuman,
Nearly human with purposive rage.   45
There is no terror
Sound from the snakes.
No one can see the desperate, futile
Striking under the leaf heads.
Now and then, the flash of a long   50

Living vine, a cold belly,
Leaps up, torn apart, then falls
Under the tussling surface.
You have won, and wait for frost,
When, at the merest touch   55
Of cold, the kudzu turns
Black, withers inward and dies,
Leaving a mass of brown strings
Like the wires of a gigantic switchboard.
You open your windows,   60

With the lightning restored to the sky
And no leaves rising to bury

You alive inside your frail house,
And you think, in the opened cold,
Of the surface of things and its terrors,   65

And of the mistaken, mortal
Arrogance of the snakes
As the vines, growing insanely sent
Great powers into their bodies
And the freedom to strike without warning: 70

From them, though they killed
Your cattle, such energy also flowed

To you from the knee-high meadow
(It was as though you had
A green sword twined among   75
The veins of your growing right arm—
Such strength as you would not believe
If you stood alone in a proper
Shaved field among your safe cows—):
Came in through your closed   80

Leafy windows and almighty sleep
And prospered, till rooted out.

JAMES DICKEY (1923–1997)

The Lifeguard   1962

In a stable of boats I lie still,
From all sleeping children hidden.
The leap of a fish from its shadow
Makes the whole lake instantly tremble.
With my foot on the water, I feel   5
The moon outside

Take on the utmost of its power.
I rise and go out through the boats.
I set my broad sole upon silver,
On the skin of the sky, on the moonlight,   10
Stepping outward from earth onto water
In quest of the miracle

This village of children believed
That I could perform as I dived
For one who had sunk from my sight.   15
I saw his cropped haircut go under.
I leapt, and my steep body flashed
Once, in the sun.

Dark drew all the light from my eyes.
Like a man who explores his death   20
By the pull of his slow-moving shoulders,
I hung head down in the cold,
Wide-eyed, contained, and alone
Among the weeds,

And my fingertips turned into stone   25
From clutching immovable blackness.
Time after time I leapt upward
Exploding in breath, and fell back
From the change in the children's faces
At my defeat.   30

Beneath them I swam to the boathouse
With only my life in my arms
To wait for the lake to shine back
At the risen moon with such power
That my steps on the light of the ripples   35
Might be sustained.

Beneath me is nothing but brightness
Like the ghost of a snowfield in summer.
As I moved toward the center of the lake,
Which is also the center of the moon,
I am thinking of how I may be   40
The saviour of one

Who has already died in my care.
The dark trees fade from around me.
The moon's dust hovers together.
I call softly out, and the child's   45
Voice answers through blinding water.
Patiently, slowly,

He rises, dilating to break
The surface of stone with his forehead.
He is one I do not remember   50
Having ever seen in his life.
The ground I stand on is trembling
Upon his smile.

I wash the black mud from my hands.
On a light given off by the grave   55
I kneel in the quick of the moon
At the heart of a distant forest
And hold in my arms a child
Of water, water, water.   60

JAMES DICKEY (1923–1997)

The Performance ❧ 1967

The last time I saw Donald Armstrong
He was staggering oddly off into the sun,
Going down, off the Philippine Islands.
I let my shovel fall, and put that hand

Above my eyes, and moved some way to one side   5
That his body might pass through the sun,

And I saw how well he was not
Standing there on his hands,
On his spindle-shanked forearms balanced,
Unbalanced, with his big feet looming and waving   10
In the great, untrustworthy air
He flew in each night, when it darkened.

Dust fanned in scraped puffs from the earth
Between his arms, and blood turned his face inside out,
To demonstrate its suppleness   15
Of veins, as he perfected his role.
Next day, he toppled his head off
On an island beach to the south,

And the enemy's two-handed sword
Did not fall from anyone's hands   20
At that miraculous sight,
As the head rolled over upon
Its wide-eyed face, and fell
Into the inadequate grave

He had dug for himself, under pressure.   25
Yet I put my flat hand to my eyebrows
Months later, to see him again
In the sun, when I learned how he died,
And imagined him, there,
Come, judged, before his small captors,   30

Doing all his lean tricks to amaze them—
The back somersault, the kip-up—
And at last, the stand on his hands,
Perfect, with his feet together,
His head down, evenly breathing,   35
As the sun poured up from the sea

And the headsmen broke down
In a blaze of tears, in that light
Of the thin, long human frame
Upside down in its own strange joy,   40
And, if some other one had not told him,
Would have cut off the feet

Instead of the head,
And if Armstrong had not presently risen
In kingly, round-shouldered attendance,   45
And then knelt down in himself
Beside his hacked, glittering grave, having done
All things in this life that he could.

JOHN DONNE (1572–1631)

For a drawing, see p. 648.

The Good Morrow ⌇⌁⌇⌁ 1633

I wonder, by my troth, what thou and I
Did, till we loved! Were we not weaned till then,
But sucked on country pleasures, childishly?
Or snorted we in the seven sleepers' den?°
T'was so; But this, all pleasures fancies be.   5
If ever any beauty I did see,
Which I desired, and got, t'was but a dream of thee.

And now good morrow to our waking souls,
Which watch not one another out of fear;
For love all love of other sights controls,°   10
And makes one little room an everywhere.
Let sea-discoverers to new worlds have gone,
Let maps to other, worlds on worlds have shown,°
Let us possess one world; each hath one, and is one.

My face in thine eye, thine in mine appears,°   15
And true plain hearts do in the faces rest;
Where can we find two better hemispheres
Without sharp North, without declining West?
Whatever dies was not mixed equally;
If our two loves be one, or thou and I   20
Love so alike, that none do slacken, none can die.°

THE GOOD MORROW. 4 *seven sleepers' den:* a reference to the miraculous legend of the Seven Sleepers of Ephesus, in Asia Minor. Seven young nobles fled Ephesus to avoid religious persecution by the Emperor Decius (ca. 250 C.E.). They took refuge in a cave and were sealed inside. They then slept for either 230 or 309 years, and they emerged praising God. After they died, their remains were taken to St. Victor's Church in Marseilles, France, where they were encrypted.   10 *For love . . . controls:* i.e., Love is so powerful that it eliminates fear and makes everything in the world worthy of love.   13, 14 *let sea-discoverers . . . shown:* i.e., let sea-explorers discover new worlds, and let maps show other new worlds to other discovers.   15 *My face . . . appears:* Each face is reflected in the pupils of the other lover's eyes.   19–21 *Whatever . . . can die:* Scholastic philosophy argued that elements which are united in perfect balance will never change or decay; hence, such a mixture cannot die. Donne's analogy suggests—humorously—that the love of the lovers is too pure to die, and that they may therefore go on making love forever.

JOHN DONNE (1572–1631)

For a drawing, see p. 648.

Holy Sonnet 10: Death Be Not Proud ⌇⌁⌇⌁ 1633

Death, be not proud, though some have callèd thee
Mighty and dreadful, for thou art not so;
For those whom thou think'st thou dost overthrow
Die not, poor Death, nor yet canst thou kill me.
From rest and sleep, which but thy pictures° be,   *imitations*   5
Much pleasure; then from thee much more must flow,
And soonest our best men with thee do go,
Rest of their bones, and soul's delivery.
Thou art slave to fate, chance, kings, and desperate men,

And dost with poison, war, and sickness dwell, 10
And poppy° or charms can make us sleep as well   *opium*
And better than thy stroke; why swell'st° thou then?   *puff up with pride*
One short sleep past, we wake eternally°   *i.e., we will live eternally*
And death shall be no more; Death, thou shalt die.

JOHN DONNE (1572–1631)

For a drawing, see p. 648.

A Hymn to God the Father ~~~~~ 1633

Wilt Thou forgive that sin where I begun,
　　Which is my sin, though it were done before?
Wilt Thou forgive those sins through which I run,
　　And do them still, though still I do deplore?
　　　　When Thou hast done, Thou hast not done,   5
　　　　　　For I have more.

Wilt Thou forgive that sin by which I won
　　Others to sin and made my sin their door?
Wilt Thou forgive that sin which I did shun
　　A year or two, but wallowed in a score?   10
　　　　When Thou hast done, Thou hast not done,
　　　　　　For I have more.

I have a sin of fear, that when I have spun
　　My last thread, I shall perish on the shore;
Swear by Thy Self, that at my death Thy sun   15
　　Shall shine as it shines now and heretofore;
　　　　And, having done that, Thou hast done,
　　　　　　I have no more.

MICHAEL DRAYTON (1563–1631)

Since There's No Help ~~~~~ 1619

Since there's no help, come let us kiss and part;
Nay, I have done, you get no more of me,
And I am glad, yea glad with all my heart
That thus so cleanly I myself can free;
Shake hands forever, cancel all our vows,   5
And when we meet at any time again,
Be it not seen in either of our brows
That we one jot of former love retain.
Now at the last gasp of love's latest breath,
When, his pulse failing, passion speechless lies,   10
When faith is kneeling by his bed of death,
And innocence is closing up his eyes;
Now if thou wouldst, when all have given him over,
From death to life thou mightst him yet recover.

PAUL LAURENCE DUNBAR (1872–1906)

Sympathy ⤙⤚⤛⤜ 1895

I know what the caged bird feels, alas!
When the sun is bright on the upland slopes;
When the wind stirs soft through the springing grass
And the river flows like a stream of glass;
When the first bird sings and the first bud opes,   5
And the faint perfume from its chalice steals—
I know what the caged bird feels!

I know why the caged bird beats his wing
Till its blood is red on the cruel bars;
For he must fly back to his perch and cling   10
When he fain would be on the bough a-swing;
And a pain still throbs in the old, old scars
And they pulse again with a keener sting—
I know why he beats his wing!

I know why the caged bird sings, ah me,   15
When his wing is bruised and his bosom sore,
When he beats his bars and would be free;
It is not a carol of joy or glee,
But a prayer that he sends from his heart's deep core,
But a plea, that upward to Heaven he flings—   20
I know why the caged bird sings!

T. S. ELIOT (1888–1965)   *For a photo, see p. 707.*

The Love Song of J. Alfred Prufrock° 1915 (1910–1911)

> *S'io credesse che mia risposta fosse°*
> *A persona che mai tornasse al mondo,*
> *Questa fiamma staria senza piu scosse.*
> *Ma per ciò che giammai di questo fondo*
> *Non tornò vivo alcun, s'i'odo il vero,*
> *Senza tema d'infamia ti rispondo.*

Let us go then, you and I
When the evening is spread out against the sky
Like a patient etherized upon a table;
Let us go, through certain half-deserted streets,
The muttering retreats   5
Of restless nights in one-night cheap hotels
And sawdust restaurants with oyster shells;
Streets that follow like a tedious argument

THE LOVE SONG OF J. ALFRED PRUFROCK. The poem is a monologue spoken by Prufrock; the name is invented but suggests a businessman. EPIGRAPH: The Italian epigraph is quoted from Dante's *Inferno* (Canto 27, lines 61–66) and is spoken by a man who relates his evil deeds to Dante because he assumes that Dante will never return to the world: "If I believed that my response were made to a person who would ever revisit the world, this flame would stand motionless. But since none has ever returned from this depth alive, if I hear the truth, I answer you without fear of infamy."

Of insidious intent
To lead you to an overwhelming question . . .   10
Oh, do not ask, "What is it?"
Let us go and make our visit.

In the room the women come and go
Talking of Michelangelo.°   15

The yellow fog that rubs its back upon the windowpanes,
The yellow smoke that rubs its muzzle on the windowpanes
Licked its tongue into the corners of the evening,
Lingered upon the pools that stand in drains,
Let fall upon its back the soot that falls from chimneys,
Slipped by the terrace, made a sudden leap,   20
And seeing that it was a soft October night,
Curled once about the house, and fell asleep.

And indeed there will be time
For the yellow smoke that slides along the street,
Rubbing its back upon the windowpanes;   25
There will be time, there will be time°
To prepare a face to meet the faces that you meet;
There will be time to murder and create,
And time for all the works and days° of hands
That lift and drop a question on your plate;   30
Time for you and time for me,
And time yet for a hundred indecisions,
And for a hundred visions and revisions,
Before the taking of a toast and tea.

In the room the women come and go   35
Talking of Michelangelo.

And indeed there will be time
To wonder, "Do I dare?" and, "Do I dare?"
Time to turn back and descend the stair,
With a bald spot in the middle of my hair—   40
(They will say: "How his hair is growing thin!")
My morning coat, my collar mounting firmly to the chin,
My necktie rich and modest, but asserted by a simple pin—
(They will say: "But how his arms and legs are thin!")
Do I dare   45
Disturb the universe?
In a minute there is time
For decisions and revisions which a minute will reverse.

For I have known them all already, known them all—
Have known the evenings, mornings, afternoons,   50
I have measured out my life with coffee spoons;
I know the voices dying with a dying fall°

14 *Michelangelo:* one of the greatest Italian Renaissance painters and sculptors (1475–1564). The name
suggests that the women are cultured, or at least pretending to be so.   26 *time:* an allusion to Andrew
Marvell's "To His Coy Mistress" (p. 909).   29 *works and days:* the title of a poem about farming by the
Greek poet Hesiod. Here the phrase ironically refers to social gestures.   52 *dying fall:* an allusion to a
speech by Orsino in Shakespeare's *Twelfth Night* (1.1.4).

Beneath the music from a farther room.
  So how should I presume?

And I have known the eyes already, known them all—   55
The eyes that fix you in a formulated phrase,
And when I am formulated, sprawling on a pin,
When I am pinned and wriggling on the wall,
Then how should I begin
To spit out all the butt-ends of my days and ways?   60
And how should I presume?

And I have known the arms already, known them all—
Arms that are braceleted and white and bare
(But in the lamplight, downed with light brown hair!)
Is it perfume from a dress   65
That makes me so digress?
Arms that lie along a table, or wrap about a shawl.
    And should I then presume?
    And how should I begin?

                    * * * * *

Shall I say, I have gone at dusk through narrow streets   70
And watched the smoke that rises from the pipes
Of lonely men in shirt-sleeves, leaning out of windows? . . .

I should have been a pair of ragged claws
Scuttling across the floors of silent seas.

                    * * * * *

And the afternoon, the evening, sleeps so peacefully!   75
Smoothed by long fingers,
Asleep . . . tired . . . or it malingers,°
Stretched on the floor, here beside you and me.
Should I, after tea and cakes and ices,
Have the strength to force the moment to its crisis?   80
But though I have wept and fasted, wept and prayed,
Though I have seen my head (grown slightly bald) brought in upon a platter,°
I am no prophet—and here's no great matter;
I have seen the moment of my greatness flicker,
And I have seen the eternal Footman hold my coat, and snicker,   85
And in short, I was afraid.

And would it have been worth it, after all,
After the cups, the marmalade, the tea,
Among the porcelain, among some talk of you and me,
Would it have been worth while,   90
To have bitten off the matter with a smile,
To have squeezed the universe into a ball°
To roll it toward some overwhelming question,
To say: "I am Lazarus,° come from the dead,
Come back to tell you all, I shall tell you all"—   95

77 *malingers:* pretends to be ill.   82 *platter:* as was the head of John the Baptist; see Mark 6:17–28 and
Matthew 14:3–11.   92 *ball:* another allusion to Marvell's "Coy Mistress."   94 *Lazarus:* See John 11:1–44.

If one, setling a pillow by her head,
   Should say: "That is not what I meant at all.
   That is not it, at all."

And would it have been worth it, after all,   100
Would it have been worth while,
After the sunsets and the dooryards and the sprinkled streets,
After the novels, after the teacups, after the skirts that trail along the floor—
And this, and so much more?—
It is impossible to say just what I mean!
But as if a magic lantern threw the nerves in patterns on a screen: 105
Would it have been worth while
If one, setling a pillow or throwing off a shawl,
And turning toward the window, should say:
   "That is not it at all,
   That is not what I meant, at all."   110

* * * * *

No! I am not Prince Hamlet,° nor was meant to be;
Am an attendant lord, one that will do
To swell a progress,° start a scene or two,
Advise the prince; no doubt, an easy tool,
Deferential, glad to be of use,   115
Politic, cautious, and meticulous;
Full of high sentence,° but a bit obtuse;
At times, indeed, almost ridiculous—
Almost, at times, the Fool.

I grow old . . . I grow old . . .   120
I shall wear the bottoms of my trousers rolled.°

Shall I part my hair behind? Do I dare to eat a peach?
I shall wear white flannel trousers, and walk upon the beach.
I have heard the mermaids singing, each to each.

I do not think that they will sing to me.   125

I have seen them riding seaward on the waves
Combing the white hair of the waves blown back
When the wind blows the water white and black.

We have lingered in the chambers of the sea
By sea-girls wreathed with seaweed red and brown   130
Till human voices wake us, and we drown.

111 *Prince Hamlet:* the hero of Shakespeare's play *Hamlet.*   113 *swell a progress:* enlarge a royal procession.   117 *sentence:* ideals, opinions, sentiment.   121 *rolled:* a possible reference to pants cuffs, which
were becoming fashionable in 1910.

JAMES EMANUEL (b. 1921)

The Negro ⁓⟨⟩⟨⟩⁓ 1968

Never saw him.
Never can.
Hypothetical,
Haunting man:

Eyes a-saucer,   5
Yessir bossir,
Dice a-clicking,
Razor flicking.

The-ness froze him
In a dance.   10
A-ness never
Had a chance.

LYNN EMANUEL (b. 1949)

Like God ⌁⌁⌁ *1998*

you hover above the page staring
down on a small town. By its roads
some scenery loafs in a hammock of
sleepy prose and here is a mongrel
loping and here is a train pulling into   5
a station in three long sentences and
here are the people in galoshes waiting.
But you know this story and it is not
about those travelers and their galoshes,
but about your life, so, like a diver   10
climbing over the side of a boat and
down into the ocean, you climb, sentence
by sentence, into this story on this page.

You have been expecting yourself
as the woman who purrs by in a dress   15
by Patou, and a porter manacled to
the luggage, and a matron bulky as
the *Britannia*, and there, haunting
her ankles like a piece of ectoplasm
that barks is, once again, that small   20
white dog from chapter twenty.
These are your fellow travelers and
you become part of their logjam of
images of hats and umbrellas and
Vuitton luggage, you are a face   25
behind or inside these faces, a
heartbeat in the volley of these
heartbeats, as you choose, out of all
the passengers, the journey of a man
with a mustache scented faintly with   30
Prince Albert. "He must be a secret
sensualist," you think and your awareness
drifts to his trench coat, worn, softened,

and flabby, a coat with a lobotomy, just
as the train arrives at a destination.   35

No, you would prefer another stop
in a later chapter where the climate is
affable and sleek. But most of
the passengers are disembarking, and
you did not choose to be in the story   40
of the white dress. You did not choose
the story of the matron whose bosom
is like the prow of a ship and who is
launched toward lunch at The Hotel Pierre,
or even the story of the dog-on-a-leash,   45
even though this is now your story:
the story of the man-who-had-to-
take-the-train and walk the dark road
described hurriedly by someone sitting
at the café so you could discover it,   50
although you knew all along it would
be there, you, who have been hovering
above this page, holding the book in
your hands, like God, reading.

CHIEF DAN GEORGE (1899–1981)

The Beauty of the Trees ⸙⸙⸙⸙⸙ 1974

The beauty of the trees,
the softness of the air,
the fragrance of the grass,
    speaks to me.

The summit of the mountain,   5
the thunder of the sky,
the rhythm of the sea,
    speaks to me.

The faintness of the stars,
the freshness of the morning,
the dewdrop on the flower,   10
    speaks to me.

The strength of fire,
the taste of salmon,
the trail of the sun,   15
and the life that never goes away,
    they speak to me.

And my heart soars.

NIKKI GIOVANNI (b. 1943)

Woman ❧❦❧ 1978

she wanted to be a blade
of grass amid the fields
but he wouldn't agree
to be the dandelion

she wanted to be a robin singing 5
through the leaves
but he refused to be
her tree

she spun herself into a web   *Action*
    and looking for a place to rest 10
turned to him
but he stood straight
declining to be her corner

she tried to be a book
but he wouldn't read 15
she turned herself into a bulb
but he wouldn't let her grow

she decided to become   *New behavior*
a woman   *Changed!*
and though he still refused   *Accountable* 20
to be a man
she decided it was all
right

MARILYN HACKER (b. 1942)

Sonnet Ending with a Film Subtitle ❧❦❧ 1979

For Judith Landry

Life has its nauseating ironies:
The good die young, as often has been shown;
Chaste spouses catch Venereal Disease;
And feminists sit by the telephone.
Last night was rather bleak, tonight is starker. 5
I may stare at the wall till half-past-one.
My friends are all convinced Dorothy Parker
Lives, but is not well, in Marylebone.°   *a district in London*
I wish that I could imitate my betters
And fortify my rhetoric with guns. 10
Some day we women all will break our fetters
And raise our daughters to be Lesbians.
(I wonder if the bastard kept my letters?)
Here follow untranslatable French puns.

JOHN HAINES (b. 1936)

Little Cosmic Dust Poem 1985

Out of the debris of dying stars,
this rain of particles
that waters the waste with brightness;
the sea-wave of atoms hurrying home,
collapse of the giant,   5
unstable guest who cannot stay;

the sun's heart reddens and expands,
his mighty aspiration is lasting,
as the shell of his substance
one day will be white with frost.   10

In the radiant field of Orion°
great hordes of stars are forming,
just as we see every night,
fiery and faithful to the end.

Out of the cold and fleeing dust   15
that is never and always,
the silence and waste to come—
this arm, this hand,
my voice, your face, this love.

LITTLE COSMIC DUST POEM. 11 *Orion:* a prominent winter constellation. Recent observations have led scientists to conclude that stars are being formed in the nebulous area in the "sword" of the constellation.

DONALD HALL (b. 1928)

Scenic View 1981

Every year the mountains
get paler and more distant—
trees less green, rock piles
disappearing—as emulsion
from a billion Kodaks   5
sucks color out.
In fifteen years
Monadnock and Kearsarge,
the Green Mountains
and the White, will turn   10
invisible, all
tint removed
atom by atom to albums
in Medford and Greenwich,
while over the valleys   15
the still intractable granite
rears with unseeable peaks
fatal to airplanes.

DANIEL HALPERN (b. 1945)

Snapshot of Hué ⸱⸱⸱⸱⸱ 1982

For Robert Stone

They are riding bicycles on the other side
of the Perfume River.

A few months ago the bridges were down
and there was no one on the streets.

There were the telling piles on corners,   5
debris that contained a little of everything.

There was nothing not under cover—
even the sky remained impenetrable

day after day. And if you were seen
on the riverbank you were knocked down.   10

It is clear today. The litter in the streets
has been swept away. It couldn't have been

that bad, one of us said, the river barely moving,
the bicycles barely moving, the sun posted above.

DANIEL HALPERN (b. 1945)

Summer in the Middle Class ⸱⸱⸱⸱⸱ 1991

All over America
it's suddenly
mid-July
We're chasing
our sons around   5
the yard
with balls and sticks
We are lumbering
because we are overweight
and a little older   10
being survivors
of the baby boom
making good the legacy
At sundown
a million barbecues ignite   15
as if from a single match
Webers
Crestlines
international hibachis
and the sad slabs of meat   20

begin to emerge
from their various marinades
the tables get set
and the mosquitoes awaken
for the evening meal   25

When they have finished
what is rightfully theirs
the children are removed
from the tables
and the adults open   30
another bottle or can of beer
The evenings are special
this time of year
the heat finally bearable
the coals a coolish grey   35
dying into themselves
It's what happens in unison
that makes America America
the lights going off
the fluorescent show   40
of t.v. coming on
and then
the total darkness

H. S. (SAM) HAMOD (b. 1936)

Leaves ~~~~~ *1973*

For Sally

Tonight, Sally and I are making stuffed
grapeleaves, we get out a package, it's
drying out, I've been saving it in the freezer, it's
one of the last things my father ever picked in this
life—they're over five years old   5
and up to now
we just kept finding packages of them in the
freezer, as if he were still picking them
somewhere packing them
carefully to send to us   10
making sure they didn't break into pieces.

                              * * *

"To my Dar Garnchildn
Davd and Lura
from Thr Jido"
twisted on tablet paper   15

between the lines
in this English lettering
hard for him even to print,
I keep this small torn record,
this piece of paper stays in the upstairs storage,   20
one of the few pieces of American
my father ever wrote. We find his Arabic letters
all over the place, even in the files we find
letters to him in English, one I found from Charles Atlas
telling him, in 1932,   25
"Of course, Mr. Hamod, you too can build
your muscles like mine . . ."

                          * * *

Last week my mother told me, when I was
asking why I became a poet, "But don't you remember,
your father made up poems, don't you remember him   30
singing in the car as we drove—those were poems."
Even now, at night, I sometimes
get out the Arabic grammar book
though it seems so late.

FRANCES E. W. HARPER (1825–1911)

She's Free! ⤙⥈⤚ 1854

How say that by law we may torture and chase
A woman whose crime is the hue of her face?—
With her step on the ice, and her arm on her child,
The danger was fearful, the pathway was wild. . . .
But she's free! yes, free from the land where the slave,   5
From the hand of oppression, must rest in the grave;
Where bondage and blood, where scourges and chains,
Have placed on our banner indelible stains. . . .

The bloodhounds have miss'd the scent of her way,
The hunter is rifled and foiled of his prey,   10
The cursing of men and clanking of chains
Make sounds of strange discord on Liberty's plains. . . .
Oh! poverty, danger and death she can brave,
For the child of her love is no longer a slave.

MICHAEL S. HARPER (b. 1938)

Called ⤙⥈⤚ 1975

Digging the grave
through black dirt,
gravel and rocks

that will hold her down,
we speak of her heat   5
which has driven her out
over the highway
in her first year.

A fly glides from her mouth
as we take her four legs,   10
and the great white neck
muddled at the lakeside
bends gracefully into the arc
of her tongue, colorless, now,
and we set her in the bed   15
of earth and rock
which will hold her as the sun
sets over her shoulders.

You had spoken of her brother,
100 lbs or more,   20
and her slight frame
from the diet of chain
she had broken;
on her back
as the spade cools her brow   25
with black dirt, rocks,
sand, white tongue,
what pups does she hold
that are seeds unspayed
in her broken body;   30
what does her brother say
to the seed gone out over
the prairie, on the hunt
of the unreturned:
and what do we say   35
to the master of the dog dead,
heat, highway, this bed
on the shoulder
of the road west
where her brother called, calls   40

ROBERT HASS (b. 1941)

Spring Rain ⋰⋱⋰ 1989

Now the rain is falling, freshly, in the intervals between sunlight,

a Pacific squall started no one knows where, drawn east as the drifts of
warm air make a channel;

it moves its own way, like water or the mind,

and spills this rain passing over. The Sierras will catch it as last snow   5
flurries before summer, observed only by the wakened marmots at ten
thousand feet,

and we will come across it again as larkspur and penstemon sprouting
along a creek above Sonora Pass next August,

where the snowmelt will have trickled into Dead Man's Creek and the   10
creek spilled into the Stanislaus and the Stanislaus into the San Joaquin
and the San Joaquin into the slow salt marshes of the bay.

That's not the end of it: the gray jays of the mountains eat larkspur seeds,
which cannot propagate otherwise.

To simulate the process, you have to soak gathered seeds all night in the   15
acids of coffee

and then score them gently with a very sharp knife before you plant them
in the garden.

ROBERT HAYDEN (1913–1980)

Those Winter Sundays ⸙⸙⸙ 1962

Sundays too my father got up early
and put his clothes on in the blueblack cold,
then with cracked hands that ached
from labor in the weekday weather made
banked fires blaze. No one ever thanked him.   5
I'd wake and hear the cold splintering, breaking,
When the rooms were warm, he'd call,
and slowly I would rise and dress,
fearing the chronic angers of that house,

Speaking indifferently to him,
who had driven out the cold   10
and polished my good shoes as well.
What did I know, what did I know
of love's austere and lonely offices?

GEORGE HERBERT (1593–1633)

Love (III)° ⸙⸙⸙ 1633

Love bade me welcome: yet my soul drew back,
    Guilty of dust and sin.
But quick-eyed Love, observing me grow slack
    From my first entrance in,
Drew nearer to me, sweetly questioning   5
    If I lacked° anything.

"A guest," I answered, "worthy to be here":
    Love said, "You shall be he."
"I, the unkind, ungrateful? Ah, my dear,
    I cannot look on thee."   10
Love took my hand, and smiling did reply,
    "Who made the eyes but I?"

"Truth, Lord; but I have marred them; let my shame
    Go where it doth deserve."
"And know you not," says Love, "who bore the blame?"   15
    "My dear, then I will serve."
"You must sit down," says Love, "and taste my meat."°
    So I did sit and eat.

LOVE (III). CF. I John 4:8: "He that loveth not knoweth not God; for God is love." wanted; the phrase is a standard question asked by innkeepers. 6 *lacked:* wanted; the phrase is a standard question asked by innkeepers. 17 *and taste my meat:* Job 12:11: "Doth not the ear try words? and the mouth taste his meat?" Here, *meat* refers simply to food in general. 17–18 *You must sit down . . . eat:* Luke 13:37: "Blessed are those servants, whom the Lord when he cometh shall find watching: verily I say unto you, that he shall gird himself, and make them to sit down to meat, and will come forth and serve them."

WILLIAM HEYEN (b. 1940)

The Hair: Jacob Korman's Story ⸙ 1980

Ten kilometers from Warsaw,
I arrived in Rembertow where
hundreds of Jews had lived
until the wheel turned: *Judenrein.*°   *cleansed; rid of Jews*

You think they let themselves be taken?   5
They would not fill the trucks.
Men were shot trying to pull guns
from the guards' hands.

and hands of dead women
clutched hair, hair of SS guards   10
blood-patched hair everywhere,
a *velt mit hor,* a field of hair

A. D. HOPE (1907–2000)

Advice to Young Ladies ⸙ 1970

A.U.C.° 334: about this date
For a sexual misdemeanor, which she denied,
The vestal virgin Postumia was tried.
Livy records it among affairs of state.

They let her off: it seems she was perfectly pure;   5
The charge arose because some thought her talk
Too witty for a young girl, her ways, her walk
Too lively, her clothes too smart to be demure.

The Pontifex Maximus, summing up the case,
Warned her in future to abstain from jokes,   10
To wear less modish and more pious frocks.
She left the court reprieved, but in disgrace.

What then? With her the annalist is less
Concerned than what the men achieved that year;
Plots, quarrels, crimes, with oratory to spare!   15
I see Postumia with her dowdy dress,

Stiff mouth and listless step; I see her strive
To give dull answers. She had to knuckle down.
A vestal virgin who scandalized that town
Had fair trial, then they buried her alive.   20

Alive, bricked up in suffocating dark,
A ration of bread, a pitcher if she was dry
Preserved the body they did not wish to die
Until her mind was quenched to the last spark.

How many the black maw has swallowed in its time!   25
Spirited girls who would not know their place.
Talented girls who found that the disgrace
Of being a woman made genius a crime;

How many others, who would not kiss the rod
Domestic bullying broke, or public shame?   30
Pagan or Christian, it was much the same:
Husbands, Saint Paul declared, rank next to God.

Livy and Paul, it may be, never knew
That Rome was doomed; each spoke of her with pride.
Tacitus, writing after both had died,   35
Showed that whole fabric rotten through and through.

Historians spend their lives and lavish ink
Explaining how great commonwealths collapse
From great defects of policy—perhaps
The cause is sometimes simpler than they think.   40

It may not seem so grave an act to break
Postumia's spirit as Galileo's, to gag
Hypatia as crush Socrates, or drag
Joan as Giordano Bruno to the stake.

Can we be sure: Have more states perished, then,   45
For having shackled the enquiring mind,
Than those who, in their folly not less blind,
Trusted the servile womb to breed free men?

ADVICE TO YOUNG LADIES. 1 *A.U.C.*: A.U.C. stands for *ab urbe condita*, "from the founding of the city." A.U.C.
334 therefore means 334 years after the founding of ancient Rome.

GERARD MANLEY HOPKINS (1844–1889)   *For a photo, see p. 712.*

Pied Beauty ~~~~~~ *1918 (1877)*

Glory be to God for dappled things—
   For skies of couple-colour as a brinded° cow;
     For rose-moles all in stipple upon trout that swim;
Fresh-firecoal chestnut-falls;° finches' wings;
   Landscape plotted and pieced°—fold,° fallow,° and plough;
     And áll trádes, their gear and tackle and trim.   5

All things counter,° original, spare,° strange;
   Whatever is fickle, freckled (who knows how?)
     With swift, slow; sweet, sour; adazzle, dim;
He fathers-forth whose beauty is past change: 10
Praise him.

PIED BEAUTY. 2 *Brinded:* brindled, that is, grey with dark spots.   4 *chestnut-falls:* the meat of a roasted chestnut.   5 *pieced:* divided into fields of different colors, depending on the crops or use. *fold:* an enclosed field for animals. *fallow:* a plowed but unplanted field.   7 *counter:* opposed, as in contrasting patterns. *spare:* rare.

GERARD MANLEY HOPKINS (1844–1889)   *For a photo, see p. 712.*

The Windhover° ~~~~~~ *1918 (1877)*

To Christ Our Lord

I caught this morning morning's minion,° king-   *darling*
   dom of daylight's dauphin,° dapple-dawn-drawn Falcon, in his riding
   Of the rolling level underneath him steady air, and striding
High there, how he rung upon the rein of a wimpling wing
In his ecstasy! then off, off forth on swing,   5
   As a skate's heel sweeps smooth on a bow-bend: the hurl and gliding
   Rebuffed the big wind. My heart in hiding
Stirred for a bird,—the achieve of, the mastery of the thing!

Brute beauty and valour and act, oh, air, pride, plume, here
   Buckle!° AND the fire that breaks from thee then, a billion   *join*   10
Times told lovelier, more dangerous. O my chevalier!°   *knight*
   No wonder of it: shéer plód makes plough down sillion°
Shine, and blue-beak embers, ah my dear,
   Fall, gall themselves, and gash gold-vermilion.

THE WINDHOVER. The poem's title refers to a kestrel—or falcon—that glides or hovers in the wind. 2 *dauphin:* prince, heir to the throne of France.   12 *sillion:* the ridge of earth between two plowed furrows in a field.

CAROLINA HOSPITAL (b. 1957)

Dear Tia ✦✦✦✦ 1988

I do not write.
The years have frightened me away.
My life in a land so familiarly foreign,
a denial of your presence.
Your name is mine.   5
One black and white photograph of your youth,
all I hold on to.
One story of your past.

The pain comes not from nostalgia.
I do not miss your voice urging me in play,   10
your smile,
or your pride when others called you my mother.
I cannot close my eyes and feel your soft skin;
listen to your laughter;
smell the sweetness of your bath   15
I write because I cannot remember at all.

JULIA WARD HOWE (1819–1910)

Battle Hymn of the Republic ✦✦✦✦ 1862

Mine eyes have seen the glory of the coming of the Lord;
He is trampling out the vintage where the grapes of wrath are stored:
He hath loosed the fateful lightning of His terrible swift sword;
   His truth is marching on!
    Glory! glory! hallelujah!   5
    Glory! glory! hallelujah!
    Glory! glory! hallelujah!
     Our God is marching on!

I have seen Him in the watch-fire of a hundred circling camps,
They have builded Him an altar in the evening dews and damps;   10
I can read His righteous sentence by the dim and flaring lamps;
   His day is marching on!
    Glory! etc.

I have read a fiery gospel writ in burnished rows of steel:
"As ye deal with my contemners so with you my grace shall deal!"   15
Let the Hero born of woman crush the serpent with his heel,
   Since God is marching on!
    Glory! etc.

He has sounded forth the trumpet that shall never call retreat;
He is sifting out the hearts of men before His judgment seat;   20
Oh! be swift, my soul, to answer Him, be jubilant, my feet!
   Our God is marching on!
    Glory! etc.

In the beauty of the lilies Christ was born across the sea,
With a glory in his bosom that transfigures you and me;   25
As he died to make men holy, let us die to make men free.
   While God is marching on!
     Glory! etc.

LANGSTON HUGHES (1902–1967)   *For a photo, see p. 1608.*

Negro ⟋⟍⟍⟋ 1958

I am a Negro:
   Black as the night is black,
   Black like the depths of my Africa.

I've been a slave:
   Caesar told me to keep his door-steps clean.   5
   I brushed the boots of Washington.

I've been a worker:
   Under my hand the pyramids arose.
   I made mortar for the Woolworth Building.

I've been a singer: 10
   All the way from Africa to Georgia
   I carried my sorrow songs.
   I made ragtime.

I've been a victim:
   The Belgians cut off my hands in the Congo.   15
   They lynch me still in Mississippi.

I am a Negro:
   Black as the night is black,
   Black like the depths of my Africa.

ROBINSON JEFFERS (1887–1962)   *For a photo, see p. 905.*

The Answer ⟋⟍⟍⟋ 1937

Then what is the answer?—Not to be deluded by dreams.
To know that great civilizations have broken down into violence, and their tyrants come,
   many times before.
When open violence appears, to avoid it with honor or choose the least ugly faction;
   these evils are essential.
To keep one's own integrity, be merciful and uncorrupted and not wish for evil; and not
   be duped
By dreams of universal justice or happiness. These dreams will not be fulfilled.   5
To know this, and know that however ugly the parts appear the whole remains beautiful.
   A severed hand

Is an ugly thing, and man dissevered from the earth and stars and his history . . . for
    contemplation or in fact . . .
Often appears atrociously ugly. Integrity is wholeness, the greatest beauty is
Organic wholeness, the wholeness of life and things, the divine beauty of the universe.
    Love that, not man
Apart from that, or else you will share man's pitiful confusions, or drown in despair
    when his days darken.   10

GALWAY KINNELL (b. 1927)

After Making Love We Hear Footsteps   *1980*

For I can snore like a bullhorn
or play loud music
or sit up talking with any reasonably sober Irishman
and Fergus will only sink deeper
into his dreamless sleep, which goes by all in one flash,   5
but let there be that heavy breathing
or a stifled come-cry anywhere in the house
and he will wrench himself awake
and make for it on the run—as now, we lie together,
after making love, quiet, touching along the length of our bodies,   10
familiar touch of the long-married,
and he appears—in his baseball pajamas, it happens,
the neck opening so small
he has to screw them on, which one day may make him wonder
about the mental capacity of baseball players—   15
and flops down between us and hugs us and snuggles himself to sleep,
his face gleaming with satisfaction at being this very child.

In the half darkness we look at each other
and smile
and touch arms across his little, startlingly muscled body—   20
this one whom habit of memory propels to the ground of his making,
sleeper only the mortal sounds can sing awake,
this blessing love gives again into our arms.

MAXINE KUMIN (b. 1925)   *For a photo, see p. 653.*

Woodchucks   *1972*

Gassing the woodchucks didn't turn out right.
The knockout bomb from the Feed and Grain Exchange
was featured as merciful, quick at the bone
and the case we had against them was airtight,
both exits shoehorned shut with puddingstone,   5
but they had a sub-sub-basement out of range.

Next morning they turned up again, no worse
for the cyanide than we for our cigarettes
and state-store Scotch, all of us up to scratch.
They brought down the marigolds as a matter of course   10
and then took over the vegetable patch
nipping the broccoli shoots, beheading the carrots.

The food from our mouths, I said, righteously thrilling
to the feel of the .22, the bullet's neat noses.
I, a lapsed pacifist fallen from grace   15
puffed with Darwinian pieties° for killing,
now drew a bead on the littlest woodchuck's face.
He died down in the everbearing roses.

Ten minutes later I dropped the mother. She
flipflopped in the air and fell, her needle teeth   20
still hooked in a leaf of early Swiss chard.
Another baby next. O one-two-three
the murderer inside me rose up hard,
the hawkeye killer came on stage forthwith.

There's one chuck left. Old wily fellow, he keeps   25
me cocked and ready day after day after day.
All night I hunt his humped-up form. I dream
I sight along the barrel in my sleep.
If only they'd all consented to die unseen
gassed underground the quiet Nazi way.°   30

WOODCHUCKS. 16 *Darwinian pieties:* Charles Darwin (1809–1892) was a British naturalist who formulated the theory of evolution; the piety is "survival of the fittest."   30 *gassed . . . way:* a reference to the extermination of millions of people in gas chambers by the Nazis during World War II.

IRVING LAYTON (b. 1912)

Rhine Boat Trip° ⸎⸎⸎ 1977

The castles on the Rhine
are all haunted
by the ghosts of Jewish mothers
looking for their ghostly children

And the clusters of grapes   5
in the sloping vineyards
are myriads of blinded eyes
staring at the blind sun

The tireless Lorelei:°
can never comb from their hair   10

RHINE BOAT TRIP. The title refers to the Rhine River, which flows through Germany.   9 *Lorelei:* legendary seductive nymphs who lived in the cliffs overlooking the Rhine, and whose singing lured sailors to shipwreck.

the crimson beards
of murdered rabbis

However sweetly they sing
one hears only
the low wailing of cattle-cars°
moving invisibly across the land

15

---

15 *cattle-cars:* railroad cars designed to transport cattle but used by the Nazis to transport Jews from the cities of Europe to extermination camps.

LI-YOUNG LEE (b. 1957)

A Final Thing ⚡ 1990

I am that last, that
final thing, the body
in a white sheet listening,

the whole of me trained,
curled like one great ear on
a sound, a noise I know, a

5

woman talking
in another room,
the woman I love; and

though I can't hear
her words, by their voicing
I can guess

10

she is telling a story,

using a voice which speaks to another,
weighted with that other's attention,
and avowing it
by deepening in intention.

15

Rich with the fullness of what's declared,
this voice points
away from itself
to some place

20

in the hearer,
sends the hearer back
to himself
to find what he knows.

25

A saying full of hearing,
a murmuring full of telling
and compassion for the listener
and for what's told,

now interrupted by a second voice,   30

thinner, higher, uncertain,
Querying, it seems
an invitation to be met,
stirring anticipation, embodying
incompletion of time and the day.   35

My son, my first-born, and his mother
are involved in a story no longer only theirs,
for I am implicated,
all three of us now
clinging to expectancy, riding sound and air.   40

Will my first morning of heaven be this?
No. And this is not
my last morning on earth.
I am simply last
in my house   45

to waken, and the first
sound I hear
is the voice of one I love
speaking to one we love.
I hear it through the bedroom wall;   50

something, someday, I'll close my eyes to recall.

ALAN P. LIGHTMAN (b. 1948)

In Computers ~~~~ 1982 (1981)

In the magnets of computers will
    be stored

Blend of sunset over wheat
    fields.
Low thunder of gazelle.   5
Light, sweet wind on high
    ground.
Vacuum stillness spreading from
    a thick snowfall.

Men will sit in rooms   10
upon the smooth, scrubbed earth
or stand in tunnels on the moon
and instruct themselves in how it
    was.
Nothing will be lost.   15
Nothing will be lost.

LIZ LOCHHEAD (b. 1947)

The Choosing ⸌⸜⸍⸜⸌⸍ 1984

We were first equal Mary and I
with same coloured ribbons in mouse-coloured hair
and with equal shyness,
we curtseyed to the lady councillor
for copies of Collins' Children's Classics.   5
First equal, equally proud.

Best friends too Mary and I
a common bond in being cleverest (equal)
in our small school's small class.
I remember   10
the competition for top desk
or to read aloud the lesson
at school service.
And my terrible fear
of her superiority at sums.   15
I remember the housing scheme
where we both stayed.
The same houses, different homes,
where the choices were made.

I don't know exactly why they moved,   20
but anyway they went.
Something about a three-apartment
and a cheaper rent.
But from the top deck of the high-school bus
I'd glimpse among the others on the corner   25
Mary's father, mufflered, contrasting strangely
with the elegant greyhounds by his side.
He didn't believe in high school education,
especially for girls,
or in forking out for uniforms.   30

Ten years later on a Saturday—
I am coming from the library—
sitting near me on the bus,
Mary
with a husband who is tall,   35
curly haired, has eyes
for no one else but Mary.
Her arms are round the full-shaped vase
that is her body.
Oh, you can see where the attraction lies   40
in Mary's life—
not that I envy her, really.

And I am coming from the library
with my arms full of books.

I think of those prizes that were ours for the taking   45
and wonder when the choices got made
we don't remember making.

AUDRE LORDE (1934–1992)

Every Traveler Has One Vermont Poem   (1986)

Spikes of lavender aster under Route 91
hide a longing or confession
"I remember when air was invisible"
from Chamberlin Hill down to Lord's Creek
tree mosses point the way home.   5

Two nights of frost
and already the hills are turning
curved green against the astonished morning
sneeze-weed and ox-eye daisies
nor caring I am a stranger   10
making a living choice.

Tanned boys I do not know
on their first proud harvest
wave from their father's tractor
one smiles as we drive past   15
the other hollers
nigger
into cropped and fragrant air.

AMY LOWELL (1874–1925)

Patterns   1916

I walk down the garden paths,
And all the daffodils
Are blowing, and the bright blue squills.
I walk down the patterned garden-paths
In my stiff, brocaded gown.   5
With my powdered hair and jewelled fan,
I too am a rare
Pattern. As I wander down
The garden paths.
My dress is richly figured,   10
And the train
Makes a pink and silver stain
On the gravel, and the thrift
Of the borders.
Just a plate of current fashion   15

Tripping by in high-heeled, ribboned shoes.
Not a softness anywhere about me,
Only whalebone° and brocade.
And I sink on a seat in the shade
Of a lime tree. For my passion   20
Wars against the stiff brocade.
The daffodils and squills
Flutter in the breeze
As they please.
And I weep;   25
For the lime-tree is in blossom
And one small flower has dropped upon my bosom.

And the plashing of waterdrops
In the marble fountain
Comes down the garden-paths.   30
The dripping never stops.

Underneath my stiffened gown
Is the softness of a woman bathing in a marble basin,
A basin in the midst of hedges grown
So thick, she cannot see her lover hiding,   35
But she guesses he is near,
And the sliding of the water
Seems the stroking of a dear
Hand upon her.
What is Summer in a fine brocaded gown!   40
I should like to see it lying in a heap upon the ground.
All the pink and silver crumpled up on the ground.

I would be the pink and silver as I ran along the paths,
And he would stumble after,
Bewildered by my laughter.   45
I should see the sun flashing from his sword-hilt and buckles on his shoes.
I would choose
To lead him in a maze along the patterned paths,
A bright and laughing maze for my heavy-booted lover.
Till he caught me in the shade,   50
And the buttons of his waistcoat bruised my body as he clasped me,
Aching, melting, unafraid.
With the shadows of the leaves and the sundrops,
And the plopping of the waterdrops,
All about us in the open afternoon—   55
I am very like to swoon
With the weight of this brocade,
For the sun sifts through the shade.

Underneath the fallen blossom
In my bosom,   60
Is a letter I have hid.

PATTERNS. 18 *whalebone:* Baleen from whales was used to make corsets for women because it was strong and flexible, like an early plastic.

It was brought to me this morning by a rider from the Duke.
Madam, we regret to inform you that Lord Hartwell
Died in action Thursday se'nnight.°
As I read it in the white, morning sunlight,   65
The letters squirmed like snakes.
"Any answer, Madam," said my footman.
"No," I told him.
"See that the messenger takes some refreshment.

No, no answer."   70
And I walked into the garden,
Up and down the patterned paths,
In my stiff, correct brocade.
The blue and yellow flowers stood up proudly in the sun,
Each one.   75
I stood upright too,
Held rigid to the pattern
By the stiffness of my gown.
Up and down I walked.
Up and down.   80

In a month he would have been my husband.
In a month, here, underneath this lime,
We would have broken the pattern;
He for me, and I for him,
He as Colonel, I as Lady,   85
On this shady seat.
He had a whim
That sunlight carried blessing.
And I answered, "It shall be as you have said."
Now he is dead.   90

In Summer and In Winter I shall walk
Up and down
The patterned garden-paths
In my stiff, brocaded gown.
The squills and daffodils   95
Will give peace to pillared roses, and to asters, and to snow.
I shall go
Up and down,
In my gown.
Gorgeously arrayed,   100
Boned and stayed.
And the softness of my body will be guarded from embrace
By each button, hook, and lace.
For the man who should loose me is dead,
Fighting with the Duke in Flanders,°   105
In a pattern called a war.
Christ! What are patterns for?

---

64 *se'nnight:* seven nights, hence a week ago.   **105** *Flanders:* a place of frequent warfare in Belgium. The speaker's clothing (lines 5, 6) suggests the time of the Duke of Marlborough's Flanders campaigns of 1702–1710. The Battle of Waterloo (1815) was also fought nearby under the Duke of Wellington. During World War I, fierce fighting against the Germans occurred in Flanders in 1914 and 1915, with great loss of life.

GWENDOLYN MAC EWAN (1941–1987)

Dark Pines under Water ⟋⟨⟍⟍⟋ 1969

This land like a mirror turns you inward
And you become a forest in a furtive lake;
The dark pines of your mind reach downward,
You dream in the green of your time,
Your memory is a row of sinking pines.   5

Explorer, you tell yourself this is not what you came for
Although it is good here, and green;
You had meant to move with a kind of largeness,
You had planned a heavy grace, an anguished dream.

But the dark pines of your mind dip deeper   10
And you are sinking, sinking, sleeper
In an elementary world;
There is something down there and you want it told.

HEATHER MCHUGH (b. 1948)

Lines ⟋⟨⟍⟍⟋ 1981

Some are waiting, some can't wait.
The stores are full of necessities.

The sun dies down, the graveyard
grows, the subway is a wind
instrument with so many stops, but
even the underground comes
to an end, and all those flights   5
of fancy birds settle for one
telephone wire, the one on which
just now, the man in utterly
unheard-of love has caught
the word goodbye. He puts   10
the receiver back in the cradle
and stands. Outside his window
an old man with a hearing-aid walks   15
without aim, happy just to be alive.

CLAUDE MCKAY (1890–1948)

The White City ⟋⟨⟍⟍⟋ 1922

I will not toy with it nor bend an inch.
Deep in the secret chambers of my heart
I muse my life-long hate, and without flinch

I bear it nobly as I live my part.
My being would be a skeleton, a shell,   5
If this dark Passion that fills my every mood,
And makes my heaven in the white world's hell,
Did not forever feed me vital blood.
I see the mighty city through a mist—
The strident trains that speed the goaded mass,   10
The poles and spires and towers vapor-kissed,
The fortressed port through which the great ships pass,
The tides, the wharves, the dens I contemplate,
Are sweet like wanton loves because I hate.

W. S. MERWIN (b. 1927)

Listen ⤙⤛⤜⤝ 1988

Listen
with the night falling we are saying thank you
we are stopping on the bridges to bow from the railings
we are running out of the glass rooms
with our mouths full of food to look at the sky   5
and say thank you
we are standing by the water looking out
in different directions

back from a series of hospitals back from a mugging
after funerals we are saying thank you   10
after the news of the dead
whether or not we knew them we are saying thank you
looking up from tables we are saying thank you
in a culture up to its chin in shame
living in the stench it has chosen we are saying thank you   15

over telephones we are saying thank you
in doorways and in the backs of cars and in elevators
remembering wars and the police at the back door
and the beatings on stairs we are saying thank you
in the banks that use us we are saying thank you   20

with the animals dying around us
our lost feelings we are saying thank you
with the forests falling faster than the minutes
of our lives we are saying thank you
with the words going out like cells of a brain   25
with the cities growing over us like the earth
we are saying thank you faster and faster
with nobody listening we are saying thank you
we are saying thank you and waving
dark though it is   30

EDNA ST. VINCENT MILLAY (1892–1950)

What Lips My Lips Have Kissed, and Where, and Why 1923

What lips my lips have kissed, and where, and why,
I have forgotten, and what arms have lain
Under my head till morning; but the rain
Is full of ghosts tonight, that tap and sigh
Upon the glass and listen for reply,   5
And in my heart there stirs a quiet pain
For unremembered lads that not again
Will turn to me at midnight with a cry.
Thus in the winter stands the lonely tree,
Nor knows what birds have vanished one by one,   10
Yet knows it boughs more silent than before:
I cannot say what loves have come and gone,
I only know that summer sang in me
A little while, that in me sings no more.

N. SCOTT MOMADAY (b. 1934)

The Bear 1992

What ruse of vision,
escarping the wall of leaves,
    rending incision
into countless surfaces,

    would cull and color   5
his somnolence, whose old age
    has outworn valor,
all but the fact of courage?

    Seen, he does not come,
move, but seems forever there,   10
    dimensionless, dumb
in the windless noon's hot glare.

    More scarred than others
these years since the trap maimed him,
    pain slants his withers,   15
drawing up the crooked limb.

    Then he is gone, whole,
without urgency, from sight,
    as buzzards control,
imperceptibly, their flight.   20

HOWARD NEMEROV (1920–1991)

Life Cycle of Common Man   1960

Roughly figured, this man of moderate habits,
This average consumer of the middle class,
Consumed in the course of his average life span
Just under half a million cigarettes,
Four thousand fifths of gin and about   5
A quarter as much vermouth; he drank
Maybe a hundred thousand cups of coffee,
And counting his parents' share it cost
Something like half a million dollars
To put him through life. How many beasts   10
Died to provide him with meat, belt and shoes
Cannot be certainly said.

                      But anyhow,
It is in this way that a man travels through time,
Leaving behind him a lengthening trail   15
Of empty bottles and bones, of broken shoes,
Frayed collars and worn out or outgrown
Diapers and dinnerjackets, silk ties and slickers.

Given the energy and security thus achieved,
He did . . .? What? The usual things, of course,   20
The eating, dreaming, drinking and begetting,
And he worked for the money which was to pay
For the eating, et cetera, which were necessary
If he were to go on working for the money, et cetera,
But chiefly he talked. As the bottles and bones   25
Accumulated behind him, the words proceeded
Steadily from the front of his face as he
Advanced into the silence and made it verbal.
Who can tally the tale of his words? A lifetime
Would barely suffice for their repetition;   30
If you merely printed all his commas the result
Would be a very large volume, and the number of times
He said "thank you" or "very little sugar, please,"
Would stagger the imagination. There were also
Witticisms, platitudes, and statements beginning   35
"It seems to me" or "As I always say."
Consider the courage in all that, and behold the man
Walking into deep silence, with the ectoplastic
Cartoon's balloon of speech proceeding
Steadily out of the front of his face, the words   40
Borne along on the breath which is his spirit
Telling the numberless tale of his untold Word
Which makes the world his apple, and forces him to eat.

JIM NORTHRUP (b. 1943)

wahbegan° ⤳⤳⤳ *1993*

Didja ever hear a sound
smell something
taste something
that brought you back
to Vietnam, instantly?   5
Didja ever wonder
when it would end?
It ended for my brother.
He died in the war
but didn't fall down   10
for fifteen tortured years.
His flashbacks are over,
another casualty whose name
will never be on the Wall.
Some can find peace   15
only in death.
The sound of his
family crying hurt.
The smell of the flowers
didn't comfort us.   20
The bitter taste
in my mouth
still sours me.
How about a memorial
for those who made it   25
through the war
but still died
before their time?

wahbegan. The title is an Ojibway name.

MARY OLIVER (b. 1935)

Ghosts ⤳⤳⤳ *1983*

1

Have you noticed?

2

Where so many millions of powerful bawling beasts
lay down on the earth and died
it's hard to tell now
what's bone, and what merely
was once.   5

The golden eagle, for instance,
has a bit of heaviness in him;
moreover the huge barns
seem ready, sometimes, to ramble off   10
toward deeper grass.

3

1805
near the Bitterroot Mountains:
a man named Lewis kneels down
on the prairie watching   15
a sparrow's nest cleverly concealed in the wild hyssop
and lined with buffalo hair. The chicks,
not more than a day hatched, lean
quietly into the thick wool as if
content, after all,   20
to have left the perfect world and fallen,
helpless and blind
into the flowered fields and the perils
of this one.

4

In the book of the earth it is written: 25
nothing can die.

In the book of the Sioux it is written:
they have gone away into the earth to hide.
Nothing will coax them out again
but the people dancing.   30

5

Said the old-timers:
the tongue
is the sweetest meat.

Passengers shooting from train windows
could hardly miss, they were   35
that many.

Afterward the carcasses
stank unbelievably, and sang with flies, ribboned
with slopes of white fat,
black ropes of blood—hellhunks   40
in the prairie heat.

6

Have you noticed? how the rain
falls soft as the fall
of moccasins. *Have you noticed?*

how the immense circles still,   45
stubbornly, after a hundred years,
mark the grass where the rich droppings
from the roaring bulls
fell to the earth as the herd stood
day after day, moon after moon   50
in their tribal circle, outwaiting
the packs of yellow-eyed wolves that are also
have you noticed? gone now.

7

Once only, and then in a dream,
I watched while, secretly
and with the tenderness of any caring woman,   55
a cow gave birth
to a red calf, tongued him dry and nursed him
in a warm corner
of the clear night
in the fragrant grass   60
in the wild domains
of the prairie spring, and I asked them,
in my dream I knelt down and asked them
to make room for me.   65

SIMON ORTIZ (b. 1941)

A Story of How a Wall Stands ⟶≺⌒⌒⟶ 1976

> At Aacqu there is a wall almost 400 years old which
> supports hundreds of tons of dirt and bones—it's a
> graveyard built on a steep incline—and it looks like
> it's about to fall down the incline but will not for a long time.

My father, who works with stone,
says, "That's just the part you see,
the stones which seem to be
just packed in on the outside,"
and with his hands put the stone and mud   5
in place. "Underneath
what looks like loose stone,
there is stone woven together."
He ties one hand over the other,
fitting like the bones of his hands   10
and fingers. "That's what is
holding it together."

"It is built that carefully,"
he says, "the mud mixed
to a certain texture," patiently   15

"with the fingers," worked
in the palm of his hand. "So that
placed between the stones, they hold
together for a long, long time."

He tells me those things,   20
the story of them worked
with his fingers, in the palm
of his hands, working the stone
and the mud until they become
the wall that stands a long, long time.   25

LINDA PASTAN (b. 1932)

Marks ᵉᵉᵉ 1978

My husband gives me an A
for last night's supper,
an incomplete for my ironing,
a B plus in bed.
My son says I am average,   5
an average mother, but if
I put my mind to it
I could improve.
My daughter believes
in Pass/Fail and tells me   10
I pass. Wait 'til they learn
I'm dropping out.

MARGE PIERCY (b. 1936)   For a photo, see p. 683.

The Secretary Chant ᵉᵉᵉ 1973

My hips are a desk.
From my ears hang
chains of paper clips.
Rubber bands form my hair.
My breasts are wells of mimeograph ink.   5
My feet bear casters.
Buzz. Click.
My head is a badly organized file.
My head is a switchboard
where crossed lines crackle.   10
Press my fingers
and in my eyes appear
credit and debit.
Zing. Tinkle.
My navel is a reject button.   15
From my mouth issue canceled reams.

Swollen, heavy, rectangular
I am about to be delivered
of a baby
Xerox machine.
File me under W   20
because I wonce
was
a woman.

MARGE PIERCY (b. 1936)   *For a photo, see p. 683.*

Will We Work Together? ⸻ 1980

You wake in the early grey
morning in bed alone and curse
me, that I am only
sometimes there. But when
I am with you, I light   5
up the corners, I am bright
as a fireplace roaring
with love, every bone in my back
and my fingers is singing
like a tea kettle on the boil.   10
My heart wags me, a big dog
with a bigger tail. I am
a new coin printed with
your face. My body wears
sore before I can express   15
on yours the smallest part
of what moves me. Words
shred and splinter.
I want to make with you
some bold new thing   20
to stand in the marketplace,
the statue of a goddess
laughing, armed and wearing
flowers and feathers. Like sheep
of whose hair is made   25
blankets and coats, I want
to force from this fierce sturdy
rampant love some useful thing.

SYLVIA PLATH (1932–1963)   *For a photo, see p. 744.*

Last Words ⸻ 1971 (1961)

I do not want a plain box, I want a sarcophagus
With tigery stripes, and a face on it
Round as the moon, to stare up.
I want to be looking at them when they° come

Picking among the dumb minerals, the roots,   5
I see them already—the pale, star-distance faces.
Now they are nothing, they are not even babies.
I imagine them without fathers or mothers, like the first gods.
They will wonder if I was important.
I should sugar and preserve my days like fruit!   10
My mirror is clouding over—
A few more breaths, and it will reflect nothing at all.
The flowers and the faces whiten to a sheet.

I do not trust the spirit. It escapes like steam
In dreams, through mouth-hole or eye-hole. I can't stop it.   15
One day it won't come back. Things aren't like that.
They stay, their little particular lusters
Warmed by much handling. They almost purr.
When the soles of my feet grow cold,
The blue eye of my turquoise will comfort me.   20
Let me have my copper cooking pots, let my rouge pots
Bloom about me like night flowers, with a good smell.
They will roll me up in bandages, they will store my heart
Under my feet in a neat parcel.°
I shall hardly know myself. It will be dark,   25
And the shine of these small things sweeter than the face of Ishtar.°

LAST WORDS. **4** *they:* possibly archeologists exploring the speaker's tomb or stone coffin ("sarcophagus").
19–24 *When . . . parcel:* The objects and procedures here refer to the household goods normally entombed
with a body in ancient Egypt, and also to the preparation of a mummy.   **27** *Ishtar:* ancient Babylonian
goddess of fertility, love, and war.

SYLVIA PLATH (1932–1963)   *For a photo, see p. 744.*

Mirror   1965 (1961)

I am silver and exact. I have no preconceptions.
Whatever I see I swallow immediately
Just as it is, unmisted by love or dislike.
I am not cruel, only truthful—
The eye of a little god, four-cornered.   5
Most of the time I meditate on the opposite wall.
It is pink, with speckles. I have looked at it so long
I think it is a part of my heart. But it flickers.
Faces and darkness separate us over and over.

Now I am a lake. A woman bends over me,   10
Searching my reaches for what she really is.
Then she turns to those liars, the candles or the moon.
I see her back, and reflect it faithfully.
She rewards me with tears and an agitation of hands.
I am important to her. She comes and goes.   15
Each morning it is her face that replaces the darkness.
In me she has drowned a young girl, and in me an old woman
Rises toward her day after day, like a terrible fish.

KATHA POLLITT (b. 1949)

Archaeology ⌁⌁⌁⌁ 1981

"Our real poems are already in us
and all we can do is dig."
—Jonathan Galassi

You knew the odds on failure from the start,
that morning you first saw, or thought you saw,
beneath the heartstruck plains of a second-rate country
the outline of buried cities. A thousand to one
you'd turn up nothing more than the rubbish heap   5
of a poor Near Eastern backwater:
a few chipped beads,
splinters of glass and pottery, broken tablets
whose secret lore, laboriously deciphered,
would prove to be only a collection of ancient grocery lists.   10
Still, the train moved away from the station without you.

How many lives ago
was that? How many choices?
Now that you've got your bushelful of shards
do you say, *give me back my years*   15
or wrap yourself in the distant
glitter of desert stars,
telling yourself it was foolish after all
to have dreamed of uncovering
some fluent vessel, the bronze head of a god?   20
Pack up your fragments. Let the simoom°   *a desert sandstorm*
flatten the digging site. Now come
the passionate midnights in the museum basement
when out of that random rubble you'll invent
the dusty market smelling of sheep and spices,   25
streets, palmy gardens, courtyards set with wells
to which, in the blue of evening, one by one
come strong veiled women, bearing their perfect jars.

EZRA POUND (1885–1972)   *For a photo, see p. 717.*

The River-Merchant's Wife: A Letter° ⌁⌁⌁⌁ 1926 (1915)

While my hair was still cut straight across my forehead
I played about the front gate, pulling flowers.
You came by on bamboo stilts, playing horse,
You walked about my seat, playing with blue plums.
And we went on living in the village of Chokan:°   5
Two small people, without dislike or suspicion.

THE RIVER-MERCHANTS WIFE: A LETTER. Freely translated from the Chinese of Li Po (701–762).
5 *Chokan:* a suburb of Nanking, China.

At fourteen I married My Lord you.
I never laughed, being bashful.
Lowering my head, I looked at the wall.
Called to, a thousand times, I never looked back. 10

At fifteen I stopped scowling,
I desired my dust to be mingled with yours
Forever and forever and forever.
Why should I climb the look out?

At sixteen you departed, 15
You went into far Ku-tō-en,° by the river of swirling eddies,
And you have been gone five months.
The monkeys make sorrowful noise overhead.

You dragged your feet when you went out.
By the gate now, the moss is grown, the different mosses, 20
Too deep to clear them away!
The leaves fall early this autumn, in wind.
The paired butterflies are already yellow with August

Over the grass in the West garden;
They hurt me, I grow older. 25
If you are coming down through the narrows of the river Kiang,
Please let me know beforehand,
And I will come out to meet you
As far as Chō-fŭ-sa.°

16 *Ku-tō-en.* an island several hundred miles up the Kiang River from Nanking.   29 *Chō-fŭ-sa.* a beach near *Ku-tō-en.*

JOHN CROWE RANSOM (1888–1974)

Bells for John Whiteside's Daughter 〰〰〰 1924

There was such speed in her little body,
And such lightness in her footfall,
It is no wonder her brown study
Astonishes us all.

Her wars were bruited in our high window. 5
We looked among orchard trees and beyond
Where she took arms against her shadow,
Or harried unto the pond.

The lazy geese, like a snow cloud
Dripping their snow on the green grass, 10
Tricking and stopping, sleepy and proud,
Who cried in goose, Alas,

For the tireless heart within the little
Lady with rod that made them rise
From their noon apple-dreams and scuttle 15
Goose-fashion under the skies!

But now go the bells, and we are ready,
In one house we are sternly stopped
To say we are vexed at her brown study,
Lying so primly propped. 20

JOHN RAVEN (b. 1936)

Assailant ⤳⟨⟩⤳ 1969

He jumped me while I was asleep.
He was big and fat.
I been in many fights before,
but never one like that.
The only way I could survive, 5
was to get my hat . . .
His *name*?
Officers, I ain't talkin' 'bout no man;
I'm talkin' 'bout a rat!

ADRIENNE RICH (b. 1929)

Diving into the Wreck ⤳⟨⟩⤳ 1973

First having read the book of myths,
and loaded the camera,
and checked the edge of the knife-blade,
I put on
the body armor of black rubber 5
the absurd flippers
the grave and awkward mask.
I am having to do this
not like Cousteau with his
assiduous team 10
aboard the sun-flooded schooner
but here alone.

There is a ladder.
The ladder is always there
hanging innocently
close to the side of the schooner. 15
We know what it is for,1
we who have used it.
otherwise
it is a piece of maritime floss
some sundry equipment. 20

I go down.
Rung after rung and still

the oxygen immerses me
the blue light
the clear atoms
of our human air.
I go down.
My flippers cripple me,
I crawl like an insect down the ladder
and there is no one
to tell me when the ocean
will begin.

First the air is blue and then
it is bluer and then green and then
black I am blacking out and yet
my mask is powerful
it pumps my blood with power
the sea is another story
the sea is not a question of power
I have to learn alone
to turn my body without force
in the deep element.

And now: it is easy to forget
what I came for
among so many who have always
lived here
swaying their crenellated fans
between the reefs
and besides
you breathe differently down here.

I came to explore the wreck.
The words are purposes.
The words are maps.
I came to see the damage that was done
and the treasures that prevail.
I stroke the beam of my lamp
slowly along the flank
of something more permanent
than fish or weed

the thing I came for:
the wreck and not the story of the wreck
the thing itself and not the myth
the drowned face always staring
toward the sun
the evidence of damage
worn by salt and sway into this threadbare beauty
the ribs of the disaster
curving their assertion
among the tentative haunters.

25

30

35

40

45

50

55

60

65

70

This is the place.
And I am here, the mermaid whose dark hair
streams black, the merman in his armored body.
We circle silently
about the wreck   75
we dive into the hold.
I am she: I am he

whose drowned face sleeps with open eyes
whose breasts still bear the stress
whose silver, copper, vermeil cargo lies   80
obscurely inside barrels
half-wedged and left to rot
we are the half-destroyed instruments
that once held to a course
the water-eaten log   85
the fouled compass

We are, I am, you are
by cowardice or courage
the one who find our way
back to this scene   90
carrying a knife, a camera
a book of myths
in which
our names do not appear.

THEODORE ROETHKE (1908–1963)

For a photo, see p. 656.

The Light Comes Brighter   ⌒⌒⌒⌒   1941

The light comes brighter from the east; the caw
Of restive crows is sharper on the ear.
A walker at the river's edge may hear
A cannon crack announce an early thaw.

The sun cuts deep into the heavy drift,   5
Though still the guarded snow is winter-sealed,
At bridgeheads buckled ice begins to shift,
The river overflows the level field.

Once more the trees assume familiar shapes,
As branches loose last vestiges of snow.   10
The water stored in narrow pools escapes
In rivulets; the cold roots stir below.

Soon field and wood will wear an April look,
The frost be gone, for green is breaking now;
The ovenbird will match the vocal brook,   15
The young fruit swell upon the pear-tree bough.

And soon a branch, part of a hidden scene,
The leafy mind, that long was tightly furled,
Will turn its private substance into green,
And young shoots spread upon our inner world.   20

LUIS OMAR SALINAS (b. 1937)

In a Farmhouse   ~~~~~   *1973*

Fifteen miles
out of Robstown
with the Texas sun
fading in the distance
I sit in the bedroom   5
profoundly,
animated by the day's work
in the cottonfields.

I made two dollars and
thirty cents today   10
I am eight years old
and I wonder
how the rest of the Mestizos°
do not go hungry
and if one were to die   15
of hunger
what an odd way
to leave for heaven.

IN A FARMHOUSE. 13 *Mestizos:* persons of mixed Spanish and Amerindian ancestry.

SONIA SANCHEZ (b. 1934)

rite on: white america   ~~~~~   *1970*

this country might have
been a pio
     neer land
once.
     but.   there ain't   5
no mo
      indians   blowing
custer's° mind
          with a different
image of america.   10
                this country

rite on: white america. 8 *custer's:* General George Armstrong Custer (1839–1876) was killed in his "last stand" at the Little Bighorn in Montana during a battle with Sioux Indians.

might have
              needed shoot/
outs/ daily/
           once.
                 but there ain't
no mo real/ white/   allamerican
                       bad/guys.
just
      u & me.
                blk/ and un/armed.
this country might have
been a pion
              eer land.   once.
                                       and it still is.

check out
          the falling
gun/shells   on our blk/tomorrows.

CARL SANDBURG (1878–1967)

Chicago 1916

   Hog Butcher for the World,
   Tool Maker, Stacker of Wheat,
   Player with Railroads and the Nation's Freight Handler;
   Stormy, husky, brawling,
   City of the Big Shoulders:

They tell me you are wicked and I believe them, for I have
   seen your painted women under the gas lamps luring
   the farm boys.
And they tell me you are crooked and I answer: Yes, it is true I have seen the gunman
   kill and go free to kill again.
And they tell me you are brutal and my reply is: On the faces of women and children I
   have seen the marks of wanton hunger.
And having answered so I turn once more to those who sneer at this my city, and I give
   them back the sneer and say to them:
Come and show me another city with lifted head singing so proud to be alive and coarse
   and strong and cunning.
Flinging magnetic curses amid the toil of piling job on job, here is a tall bold slugger set
   vivid against the little soft cities;
Fierce as a dog with tongue lapping for action, cunning as a savage pitted against the
   wilderness,
   Bareheaded,
   Shoveling,
   Wrecking,
   Planning,
   Building, breaking, rebuilding,
Under the smoke, dust all over his mouth, laughing with white teeth,

Under the terrible burden of destiny laughing as a young man laughs,
Laughing even as an ignorant fighter laughs who has never lost a battle,   20
Bragging and laughing that under his wrist is the pulse, and under his ribs the heart of
   the people,
         Laughing!
Laughing the stormy, husky, brawling laughter of Youth, half-naked, sweating, proud to
   be Hog Butcher, Tool Maker, Stacker of Wheat, Player with Railroads and Freight
   Handler to the Nation.

SIEGFRIED SASSOON (1886–1967)

Dreamers ⌇⌇⌇⌇   1918

Soldiers are citizens of death's grey land,
   Drawing no dividend from time's to-morrows.
In the great hour of destiny they stand,
   Each with his feuds, and jealousies, and sorrows.

Soldiers are sworn to action; they must win   5
   Some flaming, fatal climax with their lives.
Soldiers are dreamers; when the guns begin
   They think of firelit homes, clean beds, and wives.

I see them in foul dug-outs, gnawed by rats,
   And in the ruined trenches, lashed with rain,   10
Dreaming of things they did with balls and bats,
   And mocked by hopeless longing to regain
Bank-holidays,° and picture shows, and spats,
   And going to the office in the train.

Dreamers 13 *Bank-holidays:* legal holidays in Great Britain.

GJERTRUD SCHNACKENBERG (b. 1953)

The Paperweight ⌇⌇⌇⌇   1982

The scene within the paperweight is calm,
A small white house, a laughing man and wife,
Deep snow. I turn it over in my palm
And watch it snowing in another life,

Another world, and from this scene learn what   5
It is to stand apart: she serves him tea
Once and forever, dressed from head to foot
As she is always dressed. In this toy, history

Sifts down through the glass like snow, and we
Wonder if her single deed tells much   10
Or little of the way she loves, and whether he
Sees shadows in the sky. Beyond our touch,

Beyond our lives, they laugh, and drink their tea.
We look at them just as the winter night

With its vast empty spaces bends to see
Our isolated little world of light, 15

Covered with snow, and snow in clouds above it,
And drifts and swirls too deep to understand.
Still I must try to think a little of it,
With so much winter in my head and hand. 20

ALAN SEEGER (1886–1916)

I Have a Rendezvous with Death   1916

I have a rendezvous with Death
At some disputed barricade,
When Spring comes back with rustling shade
And apple blossoms fill the air—
I have a rendezvous with Death
When Spring brings back blue days and fair. 5

It may be he shall take my hand
And lead me into his dark land
And close my eyes and quench my breath—
It may be I shall pass him still. 10

I have a rendezvous with Death
On some scarred slope of battered hill,
When Spring comes round again this year
And the first meadow flowers appear.

God knows 'twere better to be deep
Pillowed in silk and scented down, 15
Where Love throbs out in blissful sleep,
Pulse nigh to pulse and breath to breath,
Where hushed awakenings are dear. . . .
But I've a rendezvous with Death
At midnight in some flaming town, 20
When Spring trips north again this year,
And I to my pledged word am true,
I shall not fail that rendezvous.

BRENDA SEROTTE (b. 1946)

My Mother's Face   1991

Dressing for work
I glanced in the mirror
startled to see my mother's face
white, with the mouth turned down
her red frizzled hair 5

wild in all directions.
She turned sideways
to study my dress
standing tiptoe like I do
craning her long neck   10
in a futile attempt to see my feet.
Then without warning, the tears
rolling from the outer corners down
past slightly pitted cheeks
past that inverted smile   15
into the cave of her bosom
which heaved a sigh so forlorn
so weighted with loss
that had I not been standing silent
I would have surely thought it was me.   20

WILLIAM SHAKESPEARE (1564–1616)   *For a drawing, see p. 1306.*

Fear No More the Heat o' the Sun°   ⟜⟜⟜   1623 (ca. 1609)

Fear no more the heat o' the sun,
   Nor the furious winter's rages;
Thou thy worldly task hast done,
   Home art gone, and ta'en° thy wages: *taken*
Golden lads and girls all must,   5
As° chimney-sweepers, come to dust.   *like*

Fear no more the frown o' the great;
   Thou art past the tyrant's stroke;
Care no more to clothe and eat;
   To thee the reed is as the oak;   10
The scepter, learning, physic, must
All follow this, and come to dust.

Fear no more the lightning flash,
   Nor the all-dreaded thunder stone,°
Fear not slander, censure rash;   15
   Thou hast finished joy and moan:°   *sadness*
All lovers young, all lovers must
Consign to thee, and come to dust.

No exorciser harm thee!
Nor no witchcraft charm thee!   20
Ghost unlaid forbear thee!
Nothing ill come near thee!
Quiet consummation have;
And renownéd be thy grave!

FEAR NO MORE THE HEAT O' THE SUN. A dirge or lament sung over the supposedly dead body of Imogen
in Act 4 of Shakespeare's *Cymbeline.*   14 *thunder stone:* The sound of thunder was believed to be caused
by stones falling from the sky.

WILLIAM SHAKESPEARE (1564–1616)

For a drawing, see p. 1306.

Sonnet 29: When in Disgrace with Fortune and Men's Eyes ⟶ ⟨⟩ ⟨⟩ 1609

When, in disgrace with Fortune and men's eyes,
I all alone beweep my outcast state,
And trouble deaf heaven with my bootless° cries,   *futile, useless*
And look upon myself and curse my fate,
Wishing me like to one more rich in hope,   5
Featured like him, like him with friends possessed,
Desiring this man's art and that man's scope,
With what I most enjoy contented least;
Yet in these thoughts myself almost despising,
Haply I think on thee, and then my state,   10
(Like to the lark at break of day arising)
From sullen earth sings hymns at heaven's gate,
For thy sweet love remembered such wealth brings
That then I scorn to change my state with kings.

WILLIAM SHAKESPEARE (1564–1616)

For a drawing, see p. 1306.

Sonnet 146: Poor Soul, The Center of My Sinful Earth ⟶ ⟨⟩ ⟨⟩ 1609

Poor soul, the center of my sinful earth,
Thrall° to these rebel powers that thee array,°   *captive*
Why dost thou pine within and suffer dearth
Painting thy outward walls so costly gay?
Why so large cost having so short a lease,   5
Dost thou upon thy fading mansion spend?
Shall worms, inheritors of this excess,
Eat up thy charge? Is this thy body's end?
Then, soul, live thou upon thy servant's loss,°
And let that pine to aggravate thy store;°   10
Buy terms° divine in selling hours of dross°   *periods; refuse*
Within be fed, without be rich no more:
So shalt thou feed on Death, that feeds on men,
And Death once dead, there's no more dying then.

POOR SOUL. 2 *array:* surround or dress out, as in a military formation. 9 *thy servant's loss:* the loss of the body. 10 *let . . . store:* let the body ("that") dwindle ("pine") to increase ("aggravate") the riches ("store") of the soul.

KARL SHAPIRO (1913–2000)

Auto Wreck ⟶ ⟨⟩ ⟨⟩ 1941

Its quick soft silver bell beating, beating,
And down the dark one ruby flare
Pulsing out red light like an artery,

personification
animal

The ambulance at top speed floating down
Past beacons and illuminated clocks   *metaphors*   5
Wings in a heavy curve, dips down,
And brakes speed, entering the crowd.
The doors leap open, emptying light;
Stretchers are laid out, the mangled lifted
And stowed into the little hospital.   *describes*   10
Then the bell, breaking the hush, tolls once,
And the ambulance with its terrible cargo
Rocking, slightly rocking, moves away,
As the doors, an afterthought, are closed.

We are deranged, walking among the cops   15
Who sweep glass and are large and composed.   *now reflecting on*
One is still making notes under the light.
One with a bucket douches ponds of blood
Into the street and gutter.
One hangs lanterns on the wrecks that cling,   20
Empty husks of locusts, to iron poles.   *almost like hissy*
Our throats were tight as tourniquets,
Our feet were bound with splints, but now,
Like convalescents intimate and gauche,
We speak through sickly smiles and warn   25
With the stubborn saw of common sense,   *grimace*   *sickly smile*
The grim joke and the banal resolution.   *"morbid curiosity"*
The traffic moves around with care,   *attracted to accident*
But we remain, touching a wound
That opens to our richest horror.   30
Already old, the question Who shall die?
Becomes unspoken Who is innocent?
logic   For death in war is done by hands;
Suicide has cause and stillbirth, logic;
And cancer, simple as a flower, blooms.   35
But this invites the occult mind,
Cancels our physics with a sneer,
And spatters all we knew of dénouement   *Unusual message of great poem*
Across the expedient and wicked stones.

LESLIE MARMON SILKO (b. 1948)

Where Mountain Lion Lay Down with Deer   1974

I climb the black rock mountain
   stepping from day to day
          silently.
I smell the wind for my ancestors
   pale blue leaves
   crushed wild mountain smell.   5

Returning
  up the gray stone cliff
  where I descended
        a thousand years ago.   10

Returning to faded black stone
  where mountain lion lay down with deer.
It is better to stay up here

                  watching wind's reflection
                  in tall yellow flowers.   15
The old ones who remember me are gone
        the old songs are all forgotten
and the story of my birth.
How I danced in snow-frost moonlight
        distant stars to the end of the Earth,   20
How I swam away
        in freezing mountain water
        narrow mossy canyon tumbling down
                out of the mountain
                out of the deep canyon stone   25

      down
            the memory
                  spilling out
                  into the world.

DAVE SMITH (b. 1942)

Bluejays ⤞⤝⤞⤝ 1981

She tries to call them down,
quicknesses of air.
They bitch and scorn,
they roost away from her.

It isn't that she's brutal.   5
She's just a girl. Worse,
her touch is total.
Her play is dangerous.

Darkly they spit each at each,
from tops of pine and spruce.
Her words are shy and sweet,   10
but it's no use.

Ragged, blue, shrill,
they dart around like boys.
They fear the beautiful   15
but do not fly away.

STEVIE SMITH (1902–1971)

Not Waving But Drowning   1957

Nobody heard him, the dead man,
But still he lay moaning:
I was much further out than you thought
And not waving but drowning.

Poor chap, he always loved larking   5
And now he's dead
It must have been too cold for him his heart gave way,
They said.

Oh, no no no, it was too cold always
(Still the dead one lay moaning)   10
I was much too far out all my life
And not waving but drowning.

W. D. SNODGRASS (b. 1926)

These Trees Stand . . .   1960

These trees stand very tall under the heavens.
While *they* stand, if I walk, all stars traverse
This steep celestial gulf their branches chart.
Though lovers stand at sixes and at sevens
While civilizations come down with the curse,   5
Snodgrass is walking through the universe.

I can't make any world go around *your* house.
But note this moon. Recall how the night nurse
Goes ward-rounds, by the mild, reflective art
Of focusing her flashlight on her blouse.   10
Your name's safe conduct into love or verse;
Snodgrass is walking through the universe.

Your name's absurd, miraculous as sperm
And as decisive. If you can't coerce
One thing outside yourself, why you're the poet!   15
What irrefrangible atoms whirl, affirm
Their destiny and form Lucinda's skirts!
She can't make up your mind. Soon as you know it,
Your firmament grows touchable and firm.
If all this world runs battlefield or worse,   20
Come, let us wipe our glasses on our shirts:
Snodgrass is walking through the universe.

CATHY SONG (b. 1955)

Lost Sister ~~~~~ 1983

1

In China,
even the peasants
named their first daughters
Jade—°
the stone that in the far fields   5
could moisten the dry season,
could make men move mountains
for the healing green of the inner hills
glistening like slices of winter melon.
And the daughters were grateful: 10
they never left home.
To move freely was a luxury
stolen from them at birth.
Instead, they gathered patience,
learning to walk in shoes   15
the size of teacups,°
without breaking—
the arc of their movements
as dormant as the rooted willow,
as redundant as the farmyard hens.   20
But they traveled far
in surviving,
learning to stretch the family rice,
to quiet the demons,
the noisy stomachs.   25

2

There is a sister
across the ocean,
who relinquished her name,
diluting jade green
with the blue of the Pacific.   30
Rising with a tide of locusts,
she swarmed with others
to inundate another shore.
In America,
there are many roads   35
and women can stride along with men.

But in another wilderness,
the possibilities,

LOST SISTER. 4. *Jade:* Both the mineral and the name are considered signs of good fortune and health in China. 16 *teacups:* Traditionally, girls' feet were bound at the age of seven in China because minuscule feet were considered beautiful and aristocratic. The binding inhibited the natural growth of the feet and made it painful and difficult to walk.

the loneliness,
can strangulate like jungle vines.
The meager provisions and sentiments
of once belonging—   40
fermented roots, Mah-Jongg° tiles and firecrackers—
set but a flimsy household
in a forest of nightless cities.
A giant snake rattles above,   45
spewing black clouds into your kitchen.

Dough-faced landlords
slip in and out of your keyholes,
making claims you don't understand,   50
tapping into your communication systems
of laundry lines and restaurant chains.

You find you need China:
your one fragile identification,
a jade link   55
handcuffed to your wrist.
You remember your mother
who walked for centuries,
footless—
and like her,   60
you have left no footprints,
but only because
there is an ocean in between,
the unremitting space of your rebellion.

43. *Mah-Jongg:* a Chinese game played with 144 domino-like tiles marked in suits, counters, and dice.

GARY SOTO (b. 1952)

Oranges   ✕︽᷄᷅᷄᷅   1984

The first time I walked
With a girl, I was twelve,
Cold, and weighted down
With two oranges in my jacket.
December. Frost cracking   5
Beneath my steps, my breath
Before me, then gone,
As I walked toward
Her house, the one whose
Porch light burned yellow   10
Night and day, in any weather.
A dog barked at me, until
She came out pulling
At her gloves, face bright
With rouge. I smiled,   15
Touched her shoulder, and led

Her down the street, across
A used car lot and a line
Of newly planted trees,
Until we were breathing
Before a drugstore. We   20
Entered, the tiny bell
Bringing a saleslady
Down a narrow aisle of goods.
I turned to the candies
Tiered like bleachers,   25
And asked what she wanted—
Light in her eyes, a smile
Starting at the corners
Of her mouth. I fingered
A nickel in my pocket,   30
And when she lifted a chocolate
That cost a dime,
I didn't say anything.
I took the nickel from
My pocket, then an orange,   35
And set them quietly on
The counter. When I looked up,
The lady's eyes met mine,
And held them, knowing
Very well what it was all   40
About.
        Outside,
A few cars hissing past,
Fog hanging like old
Coats between the trees.   45
I took my girl's hand
In mine for two blocks,
Then released it to let
Her unwrap the chocolate.
I peeled my orange   50
That was so bright against
The gray of December
That, from some distance,
Someone might have thought   55
I was making a fire in my hands.

GARY SOTO (b. 1952)

Kearney Park ⤳⤳⤳ *1985*

True Mexicans or not, let's open our shirts
And dance, a spark of heels

Chipping at the dusty cement. The people
Are shiny like the sea, turning
To the clockwork of rancheras,   5
The accordion wheezing, the drum-tap
Of work rising and falling.
Let's dance with our hats in hand.
The sun is behind the trees,
Behind my stutter of awkward steps   10
With a woman who is a brilliant arc of smiles,
An armful of falling water. Her skirt
Opens and closes. My arms
Know no better but to flop
On their own, and we spin, dip   15
And laugh into each other's faces—
Faces that could be famous
On the coffee table of my abuelita.°   *little grandmother*
But grandma is here, at the park, with a beer
At her feet, clapping   20
And shouting, "Dance, hijo,° dance!"   *son, child*
Laughing, I bend, slide, and throw up
A great cloud of dust,
Until the girl and I are no more.

WILLIAM STAFFORD (1914–1993)

Traveling Through the Dark   1960

Traveling through the dark I found a deer
dead on the edge of the Wilson River road.
It is usually best to roll them into the canyon:
that road is narrow; to swerve might make more dead.

By glow of the tail-light I stumbled back of the car   5
and stood by the heap, a doe, a recent killing;
she had stiffened already, almost cold.
I dragged her off; she was large in the belly.

My fingers touching her side brought me the reason—
her side was warm; her fawn lay there waiting,   10
alive, still, never to be born.
Beside that mountain road I hesitated.

The car aimed ahead its lowered parking lights;
under the hood purred the steady engine.
I stood in the glare of the warm exhaust turning red;   15
around our group I could hear the wilderness listen.
I thought hard for us all—my only swerving—,
then pushed her over the edge into the river.

GERALD STERN (b. 1925)

Burying an Animal on the Way to New York ~ ~ ~ ~ 1977

Don't flinch when you come across a dead animal lying on the road;
you are being shown the secret of life.
Drive slowly over the brown flesh;
you are helping to bury it.
If you are the last mourner there will be no caress   5
at all from the crushed limbs
and you will have to slide over the dark spot imagining
the first suffering all by yourself
Shreds of spirit and little ghost fragments will be spread out
for two miles above the white highway.   10
Slow down with your radio off and your window open
to hear the twittering as you go by.

WALLACE STEVENS (1879–1955)   *For a photo, see p. 657.*

The Emperor of Ice-Cream ~ ~ ~ ~ 1923

Call the roller of big cigars,
The muscular one, and bid him whip
In kitchen cups concupiscent curds.
Let the wenches dawdle in such dress
As they are used to wear, and let the boys   5
Bring flowers in last month's newspapers.
Let be be finale° of seem.
The only emperor is the emperor of ice-cream.
Take from the dresser of deal,°
Lacking the three glass knobs, that sheet   10
On which she embroidered fantails° once

And spread it so as to cover her face.
If her horny feet protrude, they come
To show how cold she is, and dumb.
Let the lamp affix its beam.   15
The only emperor is the emperor of ice-cream.

THE EMPEROR OF ICE-CREAM. 7 *finale:* the grand conclusion.   9 *deal:* unfinished pine or fir used to make
cheap furniture.   11 *fantails:* fantail pigeons.

MAY SWENSON (1919–1989)

Question ~ ~ ~ ~ 1978

Body my house
my horse my hound
what will I do
when you are fallen

Where will I sleep
How will I ride
What will I hunt

Where can I go
without my mount
all eager and quick   10
How will I know
in thicket ahead
is danger or treasure
when Body my good
bright dog is dead   15

How will it be
to lie in the sky
without roof or door
and wind for an eye

With cloud for shift   20
how will I hide?

JAMES TATE (b. 1943)

The Blue Booby   1969

The blue booby lives
on the bare rocks
of Galápagos°
and fears nothing.
It is a simple life: 5
they live on fish,
and there are few predators.
Also, the males do not
make fools of themselves
chasing after the young   10
ladies. Rather,
they gather the blue
objects of the world
and construct from them
a nest—an occasional   15
Gaulois° package,
a string of beads,
a piece of cloth from
a sailor's suit. This
replaces the need for   20
dazzling plumage;
in fact, in the past
fifty million years

THE BLUE BOOBY. 3 *Galápagos:* islands in the Pacific Ocean on the equator about six hundred miles west of Ecuador where many unique species of animals live.   16 *Gaulois:* a brand of French cigarettes with a blue package.

the male has grown
considerably duller,
nor can he sing well.   25
The female, though,
asks little of him—
the blue satisfies her
completely, has   30
a magical effect
on her. When she returns
from her day of
gossip and shopping,
she sees he has found her   35
a new shred of blue foil:
for this she rewards him
with her dark body,
the stars turn slowly
in the blue foil beside them   40
like the eyes of a mild savior.

DYLAN THOMAS (1914–1953)   *For a photo, see p. 876.*

A Refusal to Mourn the Death, by Fire, of a Child in London ⪼⪻⪼⪻ 1946

Never until the mankind making
Bird beast and flower
Fathering and all humbling darkness
Tells with silence the last light breaking
And the still hour   5
Is come of the sea tumbling in harness

And I must enter again the round
Zion of the water bead
And the synagogue of the ear of corn
Shall I let pray the shadow of a sound   10
Or sow my salt seed
In the least valley of sackcloth to mourn

The majesty and burning of the child's death.
I shall not murder
The mankind of her going with a grave truth   15
Nor blaspheme down the stations of the breath
With any further
Elegy of innocence and youth.

Deep with the first dead lies London's daughter,
Robed in the long friends,   20
The grains beyond age, the dark veins of her mother,
Secret by the unmourning water

Of the riding Thames.°
After the first death, there is no other.

A REFUSAL TO MOURN. 23 *Thames:* the River Thames, which flows through London.

CHASE TWICHELL (b. 1950)

Blurry Cow 1983

Two cows stand transfixed
by a trough of floating leaves,
facing as if into the camera,
black and white. One stamps
at the hot sting of a deerfly.   5

Seen from the window of a train,
the hoof lifts forever
over hay crosshatched by speed,
and the scales of the haunches
balance. The rest is lost: 10
the head a sudden slur of light,
the dog loping along the tracks
toward a farm yard
where a woman wavers
in her mirage of laundry.   15
A blurry cow, of all things,
strays into the mind's eye,
the afterimage
of this day on earth.

JOHN UPDIKE (b. 1932)   *For a photo, see p. 339.*

Perfection Wasted 1990

And another regrettable thing about death
is the ceasing of your own brand of magic,
which took a whole life to develop and market—
the quips, the witticisms, the slant
adjusted to a few, those loved ones nearest   5
the lip of the stage, their soft faces blanched
in the footlight glow, their laughter close to tears,
their tears confused with their diamond earrings,
their warm pooled breath in and out with your heartbeat,
their response and your performance twinned.   10
The jokes over the phone. The memories packed
in the rapid-access file. The whole act.
Who will do it again? That's it: no one;
imitators and descendants aren't the same.

TINO VILLANUEVA (b. 1941)

Day-Long Day ❧ ❧ ❧ ❧ 1972

> Again the drag of pisca,° pisca . . . pisca . . .
> Daydreams border on sun-fed hallucinations,
> eyes and hands automatically discriminate
> whiteness of cotton from field of vision.
> Pisca, pisca.
> > "Un Hijo del Sol, "°
> > Genaro Gonzales°

Third-generation timetable.
Sweat day-long dripping into open space;
sun blocks out the sky, suffocates the only breeze.
From el amo desgraciado,° a sentence:

"I wanna bale a day, and the boy here   5
don't hafta go to school."

                            * * *

In time-binding motion—
a family of sinews and backs,
row-trapped,
zigzagging through summer-long rows
of cotton: Lubbock by way of Wharton.°   10

"Está como si escupieran fuego,"° a mother moans
in sweat-patched jeans,
stooping
with unbending dreams.
"Estudia para que no seas burro como nosotros,"°   15
our elders warn, their gloves and cuffs
leaf-stained by seasons.

                            * * *

Bronzed and blurry-eyed by
the blast of degrees,
we blend into earth's rotation.   20
And sweltering toward Saturday, the
day-long day is sunstruck by 6:00 P.M.
One last chug-a-lug from a water jug
old as granddad.
Day-long sweat dripping into open space: 25
Wharton by way of Lubbock.

DAY-LONG DAY. EPIGRAPH: *pisca:* picking cotton. *Un Hijo del Sol:* a Son of the Sun. *Genaro Gonzales:* Hispanic author, born 1949.   4 *el amo desgraciado:* the despicable boss.   11 *Lubbock . . . Wharton:* cities on opposite sides of Texas.   12 *Está . . . fuego:* "It's as if they are spewing fire."   16 *Estudia . . . nosotros:* "Study so that you will not be a burro like us."

SHELLY WAGNER (b. ca. 1950)

The Boxes   1991

When I told the police I couldn't find you,
they began a search that included everything—
even the boxes in the house:
the footlockers of clothes in the attic,
the hamper in the bathroom,   5
and the Chinese lacquered trunk by the sofa.
They made me raise every lid.
I told them you would never stay in a box,
not with all the commotion.
You would have jumped out,   10
found your flashlight
and joined the search.

Poor Thomas, taking these men
who don't know us
through our neighbors' garages   15
where you never played,
hoping they were right
and we were wrong
and he would find you and
snatch you home by the hand   20

so the police cars could
get out of our driveway
and the divers would
get out of our river
because it was certainly   25
past our bedtime.
We would double-bolt our doors
like always,
say longer prayers than usual
and go to bed. But during the night   30
I would have sat till morning
beside my sleeping boys.

But that's not what happened.
Thomas is still here, now older.
I still go to his room   35
when he is sleeping
just to look at him.
I still visit the cemetery,
not as often,
but the urge is the same: 40
to lie down on the grass,
put my arm around the hump of ground
and tell you, "Get out of this box!
Put a stop to this commotion. Come home.
You should be in bed."   45

ALICE WALKER (b. 1944)

Revolutionary Petunias ⋰⋰⋰ 1972

Sammy Lou of Rue
sent to his reward
the exact creature who
murdered her husband,
using a cultivator's hoe   5
with verve and skill;
and laughed fit to kill
in disbelief
at the angry, militant
pictures of herself   10
the Sonneteers quickly drew:
not any of them people that
she knew.
A backwoods woman
her house was papered with   15
funeral home calendars and
faces appropriate for a Mississippi
Sunday School. She raised a George,
a Martha, a Jackie and a Kennedy. Also
a John Wesley Junior.°   20
"Always respect the word of God,"
she said on her way to she didn't
know where, except it would be by
electric chair, and she continued
"Don't yall forgit to *water*   25
my purple petunias."

REVOLUTIONARY PETUNIAS. 18–20 *George . . . Junior:* The children are named after George and Martha Washington, Jackie and John Fitzgerald Kennedy (1917–1963, thirty-fifth U.S. president), and John Wesley (1703–1791), English evangelical preacher who founded Methodism.

EDMUND WALLER (1606–1687)

Go, Lovely Rose ⋰⋰⋰ 1645

  Go, lovely rose!
Tell her that wastes her time and me
  That now she knows,
When I resemble° her to thee,   *compare*
How sweet and fair she seems to be.   5

  Tell her that's young,
And shuns to have her graces spied,

That hadst thou sprung
In deserts, where no men abide,
Thou must have uncommended died. 10

Small is the worth
Of beauty from the light retired;
  Bid her come forth,
Suffer herself to be desired,
And not blush so to be admired. 15

Then die! that she
The common fate of all things rare
  May read in thee;
How small a part of time they share
That are so wondrous sweet and fair. 20

ROBERT PENN WARREN (1905–1989)

Heart of Autumn ⌃⌃⌃⌃ 1978

Wind finds the northwest gap, fall comes.
Today, under gray cloud-scud and over gray
Wind-flicker of forest, in perfect formation, wild geese
Head for a land of warm water, the *boom*, the lead pellet.

Some crumple in air, fall. Some stagger, recover control, 5
Then take the last glide for a far glint of water. None
Knows what has happened. Now, today, watching
How tirelessly *V* upon *V* arrows the season's logic,

Do I know my own story? At least, they know
When the hour comes for the great wing-beat. Sky-strider, 10
Star-strider—they rise, and the imperial utterance,
Which cries out for distance, quivers in the wheeling sky.

That much they know, and in their nature know
The path of pathlessness, with all the joy
Of destiny fulfilling its own name. 15
I have known time and distance, but not why I am here.

Path of logic, path of folly, all
The same—and I stand, my face lifted now skyward,
Hearing the high beat, my arms outstretched in the tingling
Process of transformation, and soon tough legs, 20

With folded feet, trail in the sounding vacuum of passage,
And my heart is impacted with a fierce impulse
To unwordable utterance—
Toward sunset, at a great height.

BRUCE WEIGL (b. 1949)

Song of Napalm ━━━━ 1985

For My Wife

After the storm, after the rain stopped pounding,
We stood in the doorway watching horses
Walk off lazily across the pasture's hill.
We stared through the black screen,
Our vision altered by the distance   5
So I thought I saw a mist
Kicked up around their hooves when they faded
Like cut-out horses
Away from us.
The grass was never more blue in that light, more   10
Scarlet; beyond the pasture
Trees scraped their voices in the wind, branches
Criss-crossed the sky like barbed-wire
But you said they were only branches.

Okay. The storm stopped pounding.   15
I am trying to say this straight: for once
I was sane enough to pause and breathe
Outside my wild plans and after the hard rain
I turned my back on the old curses, I believed
They swung finally away from me . . .   20

But still the branches are wire
And thunder is the pounding mortar,
Still I close my eyes and see the girl
Running from her village, napalm
Stuck to her dress like jelly,   25
Her hands reaching for the no one
Who waits in waves of heat before her.

So I can keep on living,
So I can stay here beside you,
I try to imagine she runs down the road and wings   30
Beat inside her until she rises
Above the stinking jungle and her pain
Eases, and your pain, and mine.
But the lie swings back again.
The lie works only as long as it takes to speak   35
And the girl runs only so far
As the napalm allows
Until her burning tendons and crackling
Muscles draw her up
Into that final position   40
Burning bodies so perfectly assume. Nothing

Can change that; she is burned behind my eyes
And not your good love and not the rain-swept air
And not the jungle green
Pasture unfolding before us can deny it.   45

PHILLIS WHEATLEY (1754–1784)

On Being Brought from Africa to America ~~~~ 1773

'Twas mercy brought me from my *Pagan* land,
Taught my benighted soul to understand
That there's a God, that there's a *Saviour* too:
Once I redemption neither sought nor knew.
Some view our sable race with scornful eye,   5
"Their colour is a diabolic die."
Remember, *Christians*, *Negroes*, black as *Cain*,
May be refin'd, and join th' angelic train.

WALT WHITMAN (1819–1892)   For a photo, see p. 748.

Beat! Beat! Drums! ~~~~ 1861

Beat! beat! drums!—blow! bugles! blow!
Through the windows—through doors—burst like a ruthless force,
Into the solemn church, and scatter the congregation,
Into the school where the scholar is studying;
Leave not the bridegroom quiet—no happiness must he have now with his bride,   5
Nor the peaceful farmer any peace, plowing his field or gathering his grain,
So fierce you whir and pound you drums—so shrill you bugles blow.

Beat! beat! drums!—blow! bugles! blow!
Over the traffic of cities—over the rumble of wheels in the streets;
Are beds prepared for sleepers at night in the houses? no sleepers must sleep in   10
     those beds,
No bargainers' bargains by day—no brokers or speculators—would they continue?
Would the talkers be talking? would the singer attempt to sing?
Would the lawyer rise in the court to state his case before the judge?
Beat! beat! drums—blow! bugles! blow!
Then rattle quicker, heavier drums—you bugles wilder blow.   15
Make no parley—stop for no expostulation,
Mind not the timid—mind not the weeper or prayer,
Mind not the old man beseeching the young man,
Let not the child's voice be heard, nor the mother's entreaties,
Make even the trestles to shake the dead where they lie awaiting the hearses,   20
So strong you thump O terrible drums—so loud you bugles blow.

WALT WHITMAN (1819–1892)

For a photo, see p. 748.

Dirge for Two Veterans ⤳⤳⤳ 1865

The last sunbeam
Lightly falls from the finished Sabbath,
On the pavement here, and there beyond it is looking,
    Down a new-made double grave.

Lo, the moon ascending,   5
Up from the east the silvery round moon,
Beautiful over the house-tops, ghastly, phantom moon,
    Immense and silent moon.

I see a sad procession,
And I hear the sound of coming full-keyed bugles,   10
All the channels of the city streets they're flooding,
    As with voices and with tears.

I hear the great drums pounding
And the small drums steady whirring,
And every blow of the great convulsive drums,   15
    Strikes me through and through.

For the son is brought with the father,
(In the foremost ranks of the fierce assault they fell,
Two veterans son and father dropped together,
    And the double grave awaits them.)   20

Now nearer blow the bugles,
And the drums strike more convulsive,
And the daylight o'er the pavement quite has faded,
    And the strong dead-march enwraps me.

In the eastern sky up-buoying,   25
The sorrowful vast phantom moves illumined,
('Tis some mother's large transparent face,
    In heaven brighter growing.)

O strong dead-march you please me!
O moon immense with your silvery face you soothe me!   30
O my soldiers twain! O my veterans passing to burial!
    What I have I also give you.

The moon gives you light,
And the bugles and the drums give you music,
And my heart, O my soldiers, my veterans,   35
    My heart gives you love.

WALT WHITMAN (1819–1892)   *For a photo, see p. 748.*

Full of Life Now   1857

Full of life now, compact, visible,
I, forty years old the eighty-third year of the States,
To one a century hence or any number of centuries hence,
To you yet unborn these, seeking you.

When you read these I that was visible am become invisible,   5
Now it is you, compact, visible, realizing my poems, seeking me,
Fancying how happy you were if I could be with you and become your comrade;
Be it as if I were with you. (Be not too certain but I am now with you.)

WALT WHITMAN (1819–1892)   *For a photo, see p. 748.*

I Hear America Singing   1867

I hear America singing, the varied carols I hear:
Those of mechanics—each one singing his, as it should be, blithe and strong;
The carpenter singing his, as he measures his plank or beam,
The mason singing his, as he makes ready for work, or leaves off work;
The boatman singing what belongs to him in his boat—the deckhand singing on the
     steamboat deck;   5
The shoemaker singing as he sits on his bench—the hatter singing as he stands;
The wood cutter's song—the ploughboy's on his way in the morning, or at noon
     intermissions, or at sundown;
The delicious singing of the mother—or of the young wife at work—or of the girl
     sewing or washing—
Each singing what belongs to him or her and to none else;
The day what belongs to the day—at night, the part of young fellows, robust, friendly,   10
Singing, with open mouths, their strong melodious songs.

JOHN GREENLEAF WHITTIER (1807–1892)

The Bartholdi Statue°   1886

The land, that, from the rule of kings,
     In freeing us, itself made free,
Our Old World Slister, to us brings
     Her sculptured Dream of Liberty:

THE BARTHOLDI STATUE. The Statue of Liberty, by Frédéric Auguste Bartholdi (1834–1904) was dedicated in October, 1886. The Compte de Rochambeau (1725–1807) was a general commanding the French forces at Yorktown in 1781, and his efforts were helpful and decisive in defeating the English.

Unlike the shapes on Egypt's sands   5
   Uplifted by the toil-worn slave,
On Freedom's soil with freemen's hands
   We rear the symbol free hands gave.

O France, the beautiful! to thee
   Once more a debt of love we owe: 10
In peace beneath thy Colors three,
   We hail a later Rochambeau!

Rise, stately Symbol! holding forth
   Thy light and hope to all who sit
In chains and darkness! Belt the earth   15
   With watch-fires from thy torch uplit!

Reveal the primal mandate still
   Which Chaos heard and ceased to be,
Trace on mid-air th'Eternal Will
   In signs of fire: "Let Man be free!"   20

Shine far, shine free, a guiding light
   To Reason's ways and Virtue's aim,
A lightning-flash the wretch to smite
   Who shields his licence with thy name!

RICHARD WILBUR (b. 1921)

For a photo, see p. 912.

April 5, 1974 ◦╶◦╴◦╶◦ 1976

The air was soft, the ground still cold.
In the dull pasture where I strolled
Was something I could not believe.
Dead grass appeared to slide and heave,
Though still too frozen-flat to stir,   5
And rocks to twitch, and all to blur.
What was this rippling of the land?
Was matter getting out of hand
And making free with natural law?
I stopped and blinked, and then I saw   10
A fact as eerie as a dream.
There was a subtle flood of steam
Moving upon the face of things.
It came from standing pools and springs
And what of snow was still around;   15
It came of winter's giving ground
So that the freeze was coming out,
As when a set mind, blessed by doubt,
Relaxes into mother-wit.
Flowers, I said, will come of it.   20

WILLIAM CARLOS WILLIAMS (1883–1963)

For a photo, see p. 941.

The Red Wheelbarrow 1923

so much depends
upon

a red wheel
barrow

glazed with rain   5
water

beside the white
chickens.

WILLIAM BUTLER YEATS (1865–1939)

The Wild Swans at Coole 1919

The trees are in their autumn beauty,
The woodland paths are dry,
Under the October twilight the water
Mirrors a still sky;
Upon the brimming water among the stones   5
Are nine-and-fifty swans.

The nineteenth autumn has come upon me
Since I first made my count;
I saw, before I had well finished,
All suddenly mount   10
And scatter wheeling in great broken rings
Upon their clamorous wings.

I have looked upon those brilliant creatures,
And now my heart is sore.
All's changed since I, hearing at twilight,   15
The first time on this shore,
The bell beat of their wings above my head,
Trod with a lighter tread.

Unwearied still, lover by lover,
They paddle in the cold   20
Companionable streams or climb the air;
Their hearts have not grown old;
Passion or conquest, wander where they will,
Attend upon them still.

But now they drift on the still water,   25
Mysterious, beautiful;
Among what rushes will they build,

By what lake's edge or pool
Delight men's eyes when I awake some day
To find they have flown away?   30

PAUL ZIMMER (b. 1934)

The Day Zimmer Lost Religion   ⤳ ⟨⤳⤳⟩   1973

The first Sunday I missed Mass on purpose
I waited all day for Christ to climb down
Like a wiry flyweight° from the cross and
Club me on my irreverent teeth, to wade into
My blasphemous gut and drop me like a   5
Red hot thurible,° the devil roaring in
Reserved seats until he got the hiccups.

It was a long cold way from the old days
When cassocked and surpliced° I mumbled Latin
At the old priest and rang his obscure bell.   10
A long way from the dirty wind that blew
The soot like venial sins° across the schoolyard
Where God reigned as a threatening,
One-eyed triangle high in the fleecy sky.

The first Sunday I missed Mass on purpose   15
I waited all day for Christ to climb down
Like the playground bully, the cuts and mice
Upon his face agleam, and pound me
Till my irreligious tongue hung out.
But of course He never came, knowing that   20
I was grown up and ready for Him now.

THE DAY ZIMMER LOST RELIGION. 3 *flyweight:* a boxer weighing less than 112 pounds.   6 *thurible:* a censer, a container in which incense is burned.   9 *cassocked and surpliced:* wearing the traditional garb of an altar boy during Mass.   12 *venial sins:* minor inadvertent sins.

Reading *and* Writing

about

DRAMA

The Dramatic Vision: *An Overview*

Drama has much in common with the other genres of literature. Like fiction, drama focuses on one or a few major characters who enjoy success or endure failure as they face challenges and deal with other characters. Many plays are written in prose, as is fiction, on the principle that the language of drama should resemble the language of life as much as possible. Drama is also like poetry because both genres develop situations through speech and action. Indeed, a great number of plays, particularly those of past ages, exist as poetry. The dramatists of ancient Athens employed intricate poetic forms in their plays. Many European plays from the Renaissance through the nineteenth century were written in blank verse or rhymed couplets, a tradition of poetic drama preserved by twentieth-century dramatists such as T. S. Eliot and Christopher Fry.

As separate genres, however, there are necessarily major differences among drama, fiction, and poetry. Fiction is distinguished from drama because the essence of fiction is narration—the relating or recounting of a sequence of events or actions, the actual telling of a story. Poetry is unlike both drama and fiction because it exists in many formal and informal shapes, and it is usually the shortest of the genres. Although we usually read poetry silently and alone, it is also frequently read aloud before groups. Unlike both fiction and poetry, drama is literature designed for impersonation by people—actors—for the benefit and delight of other people—an audience.

Symbolism language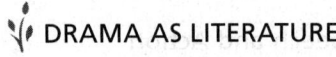

DRAMA AS LITERATURE

Drama is a unique genre because it can be presented and discussed both as literature—drama itself—and as performance—the production of plays in the theater. The major literary aspects of drama are the *text, language, characters, plot, structure, point of view, tone, symbolism, and theme or meaning*. All these elements have remained constant throughout the history of drama.

In addition, drama written in poetic forms, such as Shakespeare's *Hamlet* and *A Midsummer Night's Dream*, includes elements such as meter and rhyme.

The Text Is the Printed (or Handwritten) Play

The text of a play is in effect a plan for bringing the play into action on the stage. The most notable features of the text are dialogue, monologue, and stage directions. **Dialogue** is the conversation of two or more characters. A **monologue** is spoken by a single character who is usually alone onstage. **Stage directions** are the playwright's instructions about facial and vocal expression, movement and action, gesture and "body language," stage appearance, lighting, and similar matters. In addition, some dramatists, such as George Bernard Shaw and Tennessee Williams, provide introductions and explanations for their plays. Such material may be considered additional directions for interpretation and staging.

Language, Imagery, and Style Bring the Play to Life

What we learn about characters, relationships, and conflicts is conveyed in dramatic language. Through dialogue, and sometimes through soliloquy and aside, characters use language to reveal intimate details about their lives and their deepest thoughts—their loves, hatreds, hopes, and plans.

To bring such revelations before the audience, dramatists employ words that have wide-ranging connotations and that acquire many layers of meaning. Such is the case with the many variations of the phrase "well liked" in Arthur Miller's *Death of a Salesman*. Similarly, playwrights can introduce metaphors and symbols that contribute significantly to the play's meaning and impact. Again in *Death of a Salesman*, the abandoned auto trip and the imminence of an auto accident are central symbols.

Dramatists also make sure that the words of their characters fit the circumstances, the time, and the place of the play. Miller's Willy Loman speaks the language of modern America, and Shakespeare's Hamlet speaks Elizabethan blank verse, almost academic prose, and "one-liner" remarks. In addition, dramatists employ accents, dialects, idiom, jargon, and clichés to indicate character traits. The gravediggers in *Hamlet* speak in a Renaissance English lower-class dialect that distinguishes them from the aristocratic characters in the play.

Characters Talk Themselves Alive Through Speech and Action

Drama necessarily focuses on its **characters,** who are persons the playwright creates to embody the play's actions, ideas, and attitudes. Of course characters are characters, no matter where we find them, and many of the character types that populate drama are also inhabitants of fiction. The major quality of characters in drama, however, is that they become alive through speech and action. To understand them we must listen to their words and watch and interpret how they react both to their circumstances and to the characters around them. They are also sometimes described and discussed by other characters, but primarily they are rendered dramatically.

Drama is not designed to present the full life stories of its characters. Rather, the plots of drama bring out intense and highly focused oppositions or conflicts in which the characters are engaged. In accord with such conflicts, most major dramatic characters are considered as protagonists and antagonists. The **protagonist** (the first or leading struggler or actor), usually the central character, is opposed by the **antagonist** (the one who struggles against). A classic conflict is seen in Shakespeare's *Hamlet*, in which Prince Hamlet, the protagonist, tries first to confirm and then to punish the crime committed by King Claudius, his uncle and the play's antagonist.

Just as in fiction, drama presents us with both round and flat characters. A **round, dynamic, developing,** and **growing character,** like Shakespeare's Hamlet and Ibsen's Nora, possesses great **motivation.** The round character profits from experience and undergoes a development in awareness, insight, understanding, moral capacity, and the ability to make decisions. A **flat, static, fixed,** and **unchanging character,** like those who enter close to the end of Stanley Kauffmann's *The More the Merrier,* does not undergo any change or growth. There is no rule, however, that flat characters must be dull. They can be charming, vibrant, entertaining, and funny, but even if they are memorable in these ways, they remain fixed and static.

Dramatic characters can also be considered as realistic, nonrealistic, stereotyped (or stock), ancillary, and symbolic. **Realistic characters** are designed to seem like individualized women and men; they are given thoughts, desires, motives, personalities, and lives of their own. **Nonrealistic characters** are often undeveloped and symbolic. An interesting example is Torvald Helmer of Ibsen's *A Dollhouse.* In terms of his assumptions and expectations, he is nonrealistic for most of the play, but he becomes sadly realistic when he recognizes the disastrous effects of his previous outlook on life and marriage. He is unique because he does not so much grow as undergo an almost instant change.

Throughout the ages, drama and other types of literature have relied on **stereotype** or **stock characters,** that is, unindividualized characters whose actions and speeches make them seem to have been taken from a mold. The general types developed in the comedy of ancient Athens and Rome, and in the drama of the Renaissance, are the *stubborn father,* the *romantic hero* and *heroine,* the *clever male servant,* the *saucy maidservant,* the *braggart soldier,* the *bumpkin,* the *trickster,* the *victim,* the *insensitive husband,* the *shrewish wife,* and the *lusty youth.* Modern drama continues these stereotypes, and it has also invented many of its own, such as the *private eye,* the *stupid bureaucrat,* the *corrupt politician,* the *independent pioneer,* the *kindly prostitute,* the *loner cowboy,* and the *town sheriff who never loses the draw in a showdown.*

There are also **ancillary characters** who set off or highlight the protagonist and who provide insight into the action. The first type, the **foil,** has been a feature of drama since its beginnings in ancient Athens. The foil is a character who is to be compared and contrasted with the protagonist. Laertes and Fortinbras are foils in *Hamlet.* Because of the play's circumstances, Laertes is swept into destruction along with Hamlet, whereas Fortinbras picks up the pieces and gets life moving again after the final death scene. The second type is the **choric figure,** who is loosely connected to the choruses of ancient drama. Usually the choric figure is a single character, often a confidant of the protagonist, such as Hamlet's friend Horatio. When the choric figure expresses ideas about the play's major issues and actions, he or she is called a **raisonneur** (the French word meaning "reasoner") or **commentator.**

Any of the foregoing types of characters can also be **symbolic** in the context of individual plays. They can symbolize ideas, moral values, religious concepts, ways of life, or some other abstraction. For instance, Linda in *Death of a Salesman* symbolizes helplessness before destructive forces, while Fred Higgins in *Mulatto* symbolizes the cynicism, indifference, cruelty, and misuse of responsibility that accompany the concept of racial supremacy.

Action, Conflict, and Plot Make Up a Play's Development

Plays are made up of a series of sequential and related **actions** or **incidents.** The actions are connected by **chronology**—the logic of time—and the term given to the principles underlying this ordered chain of actions and reactions is **plot,** which is a connected plan or pattern of causation. The impulse controlling the connections is **conflict,** which refers to people or circumstances—the antagonist—that the protagonist tries to overcome. Most dramatic conflicts are vividly apparent because the clashes of wills and characters take place onstage, right in front of our eyes. Conflicts can also exist between groups, although conflicts between individuals are more identifiable and therefore more common in plays.

Dramatic plots can be simplified and schematized, but most of them are as complicated as life itself. Special complications result from a **double** or **multiple plot**—two or more different but related lines of action. Usually one of these plots is the **main plot,** but the **subplot** can be independently important and sometimes even more interesting. Such a situation occurs in *A Midsummer Night's Dream,* where the exploits of Bottom and the "mechanicals," which form just one of the four strands of plot, are so funny that they often steal the show in productions of the play.

Structure Is the Play's Pattern of Organization

The way a play is arranged or laid out is its **structure.** With variations, many traditional plays contain elements that constitute a structure of *five stages:* (1) *exposition* or *introduction,* (2) *complication* and *development,* (3) *crisis* or *climax,* (4) *falling action,* and (5) *dénouement, resolution,* or *catastrophe.* In the nineteenth century, the German novelist and critic Gustav Freytag (1816–1895) visualized this pattern as a pyramid (though he used six elements rather than five). In the so-called **Freytag pyramid,** the exposition and complication lead up to a high point of tension—the crisis or climax—followed by the falling action and the catastrophe.

This pyramidal pattern of organization can be observed to greater or lesser degrees throughout many plays. Some plays follow the pattern closely, but often there is uncertainty about when one phase of the structure ends and the next one begins. In addition, words defining some of the stages are variable. Even though students of drama agree about the meaning of the first two stages, the terms for the final three are not used with precision. With these reservations, the Freytag pyramid is valuable in the analysis of dramatic plot structure.

The Freytag Pyramid

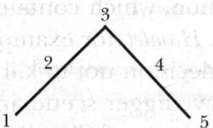

1. Exposition or Introduction
2. Complication and Development
3. Crisis or Climax
4. Falling Action
5. Dénouement, Resolution, or Catastrophe

1. THE EXPOSITION OR INTRODUCTION BRINGS OUT EVERYTHING WE NEED TO KNOW TO UNDERSTAND AND FOLLOW WHAT IS TO HAPPEN IN THE PLAY. In the first part of a drama, the dramatist introduces the play's background, characters, situations, and conflicts. Although exposition is occasionally presented through direct statements to the audience, the better method is to render it dramatically. Both major and minor characters thus perform the task of exposition through dramatic dialogue—describing situations, actions, and plans, and also explaining the traits and motives of other characters. In such a way, Sophocles in *Oedipus the King* provides expository material in the prologue featuring Oedipus, the Priest, and Creon; Eugene O'Neill in *Before Breakfast* dramatizes the exposition in the early actions and speeches of the major character, Mrs. Rowland. In *Hamlet*, Horatio's explanations to Barnardo and Marcellus provide vital information about circumstances in the Danish court.

2. THE COMPLICATION AND DEVELOPMENT MARK THE ONSET OF THE PLAY'S MAJOR CONFLICTS. In this second stage, also called the **rising action,** we see the beginning of difficulties that seem overwhelming and insoluble, as in *Hamlet*, where we learn in the exposition that a death of the king has occurred before the play opens. **Complication** develops as the characters try to learn answers to some of the following perplexing questions: Was the death a murder? If so, who did it? How was it done? How can the murderer be identified? Is the man suspected of the murder truly guilty? What should be done about the murder? What punishment should there be? In *A Midsummer Night's Dream*, less serious complications result from the **development** of issues like these: Can young lovers overcome parental opposition? Can a bumbling group of amateur actors successfully perform a play before the highest social group in the nation? Can a squabble among supernatural beings be brought to a peaceful conclusion?

3. THE CRISIS OR CLIMAX IS THE CULMINATION OF THE PLAY'S CONFLICTS AND COMPLICATIONS—THE INTENSE MOMENTS OF DECISION. The uncertainty and anxiety of the complication lead to the third stage, the **crisis** ("turning point") or **climax** ("high point"). In this third stage, all the converging circumstances compel the hero or heroine to recognize what needs to be done to resolve the play's major conflict. Another way of considering the crisis or climax is to define it as that point in the play when uncertainty ends and inevitability begins, as when Hamlet vows vengeance after drawing conclusions about the King's reaction to the player scene.

4. THE FALLING ACTION IS A TIME OF AVOIDANCE AND DELAY.   The downward slope of the pyramid is the **falling action,** which contains complicating elements deferring the play's conclusion. In *Hamlet,* for example, a number of scenes make up the falling action: Hamlet's decision not to kill Claudius at prayer, Hamlet's departure for England, the gravedigger scene and the conflicts at Ophelia's grave, and the murderous conspiracy of Claudius and Laertes. In *Oedipus the King,* Oedipus continues to seek confirming evidence about the death of his father, although by the end of Episode 3—the climax—he has all the information he needs to determine that he himself is the murderer.

5. THE DÉNOUEMENT IS THE END, THE LOGICAL OUTCOME OF WHAT HAS GONE BEFORE.
In the **dénouement** ("unraveling") or **resolution** ("untying"), also called the **catastrophe** ("overturning"), all tragic protagonists undergo suffering or death, all mysteries are explained, all conflicts are resolved, all mistakes are corrected, all dastardly schemes are defeated, all long-lost children are identified, all obstacles to love are overcome, all deserving characters are rewarded, and the play ends. In short, the function of the dénouement is to end complications and conflicts, not to create new ones. It is important to observe that the word *catastrophe* for the final dramatic stage should not necessarily be construed in the sense of a calamity, even though most tragic catastrophes are calamitous. It is probably best, however, to use the words *dénouement* and *resolution* as general descriptions of a play's final stage and to reserve *catastrophe* for tragedies.

Of great significance is that the various points of the pyramid define an abstract model that is applicable to most plays—tragedy, comedy, and tragicomedy alike. Since the time of Shakespeare, however, most dramatists writing in English have been concerned less with dramatic form than with dramatic effect. As a result, many plays in English do not perfectly follow the pattern charted in the Freytag pyramid. You should therefore be prepared for plays that conceal or delay essential parts of the exposition; create a number of separate crises and climaxes; crowd the climax, falling action, and dénouement into a short space at the play's end; or modify the formal pattern in other significant ways.

Point of View Focuses on a Play's Major Character (or Characters) and Ideas

In fiction, the concept of **point of view** refers to the narrative *voice* of the story, the speaker or guiding intelligence through which the characters and actions are presented (see Chapter 5). In drama, the term refers generally to a play's **perspective** or focus—the ways in which dramatists direct attention to the play's characters and their concerns. In the theater, dramatists govern our responses visually by putting major characters onstage and keeping them there. That these characters are always speaking and moving before our eyes makes us devote our attention to them, become involved with them, and see things pretty much as they see things. For example, once the opening speeches of *Hamlet* are over, the play focuses directly on Hamlet and never wavers, even after he lies dead on the stage in the last act. In O'Neill's *Before Breakfast,* the entire play is a monologue spoken by Mrs. Rowland, and we therefore see things from her perspective even though we recognize her limitations and shortcomings.

The dramatist can also keep characters and issues in our minds by causing other characters to speak about them. Thus when each of the major characters in *The More the Merrier* leaves the stage, the onstage characters discuss their persons, their qualities, and their intentions.

Tone or Atmosphere Creates Mood and Attitude

Authors of plays have unique ways of conveying tone beyond those used by poets and fiction writers (see Chapter 8). Some of these are vocal ranges, stage gestures (such as rolling one's eyes, throwing up one's hands, staring at another character, holding one's forehead in despair, jumping for joy, making side remarks, and staggering in grief). Even silence, intensive stares, and shifting glances can be effective means for creating moods and controlling attitudes.

Whereas the voices and actions of actors establish mood on the stage, we do not have these guides in reading. There are written guides, however, to dramatic tone: Sometimes a playwright uses stage directions as an indication of tone, as Ibsen does in *A Dollhouse*, directing the inflections of a speaker's voice with the stage direction that she is shaking her head when speaking. Similarly, Hughes suggests the mood of one of his characters in *Mulatto* with the direction that he "runs" to his mother and hugs her "teasingly."

When such directions are absent—and usually they are—we need to take the diction, tempo, imagery, and context as clues to the tone of specific speeches and whole plays. In the opening scene of *Hamlet*, Shakespeare uses short and rapidly delivered sentences to create a mood of fearfulness, anxiety, and apprehensiveness. This opening passage anticipates the Ghost's forthcoming charge of murder against Claudius, and it also prepares us for the ominous events to come in the rest of the play.

One of the most common methods playwrights employ to control the tone of the play is **dramatic irony.** This type of **situational** (as opposed to **verbal**) irony refers to circumstances in which characters have only a partial, incorrect, or misguided understanding of what is happening, while both readers and other characters understand the situation completely. Readers hence become concerned about the characters and hope that they will develop understanding quickly enough to avoid the problems bedeviling them and the threats endangering them. The classic example of dramatic irony occurs in Sophocles' *Oedipus the King:* As Oedipus condemns the murderer of his father, he also unwittingly condemns himself.

Dramatists Frequently Introduce Symbolism and Allegory

In drama, as in fiction and poetry, the meaning of a **symbol** extends beyond its surface meaning (see Chapters 9 and 21). Dramatic symbols, which can be characters, settings, objects, actions, situations, or statements, can be both cultural or contextual. **Cultural** or **universal symbols**—such as crosses, flags, snakes, and flowers—are generally understood by the audience or reader regardless of the context in which they appear. In Act 5 of *Hamlet*, for example, we readily accept Yorick's skull as a symbol of death. **Contextual** or **private symbols** develop their impact only within the context of a specific play or even a particular scene. We often don't realize at first that such objects or actions are symbolic; they acquire symbolic meaning only through context and continued action. In the living-room setting of Hughes's *Mulatto*, for instance, there is a vestibule "leading to the porch." There is nothing unusual about this location, but as the play develops we realize that it symbolizes how the rights and privileges of whites on the plantation are denied to the African Americans who work there.

When a play offers consistent and sustained symbols that refer to general human experiences, that play can be construed as an **allegory**, or at least as being **allegorical**. For example, Ibsen's *A Dollhouse* can be considered allegori-cally as an expression of the shortcomings of any way of life in which a grown person is infantilized and therefore is prevented from realizing the mature and independent life that she is entitled to seek as an adult.

Subject and Theme Are the Complex of Ideas Presented by the Dramatist

Most playwrights do not aim to propagandize their audience, but nevertheless they do embody ideas in their plays. The aspects of humanity a playwright ex-plores constitute the play's **subject**. Plays can be *about* love, religion, hatred, war, ambition, death, envy, or anything else that is part of the human condition.

The ideas that the play dramatizes make up the play's **theme** or meaning. A play might explore the idea that love will always find a way or that marriage can be destructive, that pride always leads to disaster, or that grief can be con-quered through strength and a commitment to life. Full, evening-long plays can contain many thematic strands. Ibsen creates such complexity in *A Dollhouse*, in which he deals with themes of selfless devotion, egotism, pompousness, hypocrisy, betrayal, and women's self-determination. Even short plays can have complex themes, as in O'Neill's *Before Breakfast*, which explores the themes that anger can be stronger than love, that deceit is a consequence of alienation, and that despair and fear can conquer the normal wish to live.

PERFORMANCE: THE UNIQUE ASPECT OF DRAMA

As we read and talk about drama, we should always remind ourselves that *plays are meant to be acted*. It is **performance** that makes a play immediate, exciting, and powerful. The elements of performance are the *actors*, the *director* and the *producer*, the *stage*, *sets* or *scenery*, *lighting*, *costumes* and *makeup*, and the *audience*.

Actors Bring the Play to Our Eyes and Ears

Good actors are trained and have the experience to exert their intelligence, emotions, imaginations, voices, and bodies to bring their roles into our pres-ence. Actors speak as they imagine the characters might speak—earnestly, ea-gerly, calmly, excitedly, prayerfully, exultantly, sorrowfully, or angrily. When they respond, they respond as they imagine the characters might respond—with surprise, expectation, approval, happiness, irony, acceptance, rejection, resignation, or resolution. When they move about the stage according to patterns called **blocking,** they move as they imagine the characters might move—slowly, swiftly, smoothly, hesitatingly, furtively, stealthily, or clumsily, and gesturing broadly or subtly. Actors also frequently engage in **stage business**—gestures or movements that make the play dynamic, spontaneous, and often funny.

The Director and the Producer Create and Support the Play's Production

In the theater, all aspects of performance are shaped and supervised by the **director** and the **producer.** The producer, the one with the money, is responsible for financing and arranging the production. Working closely with the producer is the director, who is probably the most significant member of the entire dramatic production. The director cooperates closely with the actors and guides them in speaking, responding, standing, and moving in ways that are consistent with his or her vision of the play. When a play calls for special effects (for example, the Ghost in *Hamlet*) both the producer and the director work with specialists such as musicians, choreographers, and sound and lighting technicians to enhance and enliven the performance.

The Stage Is the Location of Both Speech and Action

Most modern theaters feature an interior **proscenium stage**—a picture-frame stage that is like a room with one wall missing so that the audience can look in on the action. In most proscenium stages, a large curtain representing the missing wall is usually opened and closed to indicate the beginning and ending of acts. Members of the audience who are seated centrally before the stage are close to the action, but people seated at the sides, to the rear, behind a tall person, or in the balcony are to greater or lesser degrees removed from the vital and up-close involvement that is desirable in good theater. There is no question that such remoteness is a built-in disadvantage of many proscenium stages.

Modern theater designers have therefore experimented with stage designs inspired by theaters of the past. One notable success has been to revive the shape of the ancient Greek amphitheater (with seats rising from the stage in an expanding half-circle), a structure employed in theaters like the Tyrone Guthrie in Minneapolis and at the Shakespeare Festival Theatre in Ashland, Oregon. Because seats for the audience ascend in semicircular tiers around three sides of the stage, most of the audience is closer to the action—and better able to see—than in a theater with a proscenium stage. The audience is also, therefore, more closely involved in the dramatic action.

Like many other modern theaters, these theaters feature a **thrust stage** or **apron stage** (like the **platform stage** used in the time of Shakespeare), which enlarges the proscenium stage with an acting area projecting into the audience by twenty or more feet. It is on this apron that a good deal of the acting occurs. Closely related to the apron stage is **theater-in-the-round,** a stage open on all sides like a boxing ring, surrounded by the audience. Productions for both types of stages are especially lively because the actors usually enter and leave through the same doorways and aisles used by the audience.

Sets (Scenery) Create the Play's Location and Appearance

Most productions use **sets** (derived from the phrase "set scenes," i.e., fixed scenes) or **scenery** to establish the action in place and time, to underscore the ideas of the director, and to determine the level of reality of the production. Sets are constructed and decorated to indicate a specific place (a living room, a kitchen, a throne room, a forest, a graveyard) or a detached and indeterminate place with a specific atmosphere (an open plain, a vanished past, a nightmarish future). When we first see the stage at the beginning of a performance, it is the scenery that we see, bringing the play to life through walls, windows, stairways, furniture, furnishings, and painted locations.

In most proscenium stages, the sets establish a permanent location or **scene** resembling a framed picture. All characters enter this setting, and they leave once they have achieved their immediate purpose. Such a fixed scene is established in *Oedipus the King*, which is set entirely in front of the royal palace of ancient Thebes, and in *Before Breakfast*, set in an apartment kitchen. Generally, one-act plays rely on a single setting and a short imagined time of action. Many full-length plays also confine the action to a single setting despite the longer imagined time during which the action takes place.

Because sets are usually elaborate and costly, many producers use single fixed-scene sets that are flexible and easily changed. Some productions employ a single, neutral set throughout the play and then mark scene changes with the physical introduction of movable **properties** (or **props**)—chairs, tables, beds, flower vases, hospital curtain-enclosures, trees, shovels, skulls, and so on. The use of props to mark separate scenes is a necessity in modern productions of plays that require constant scene changes, like *Hamlet*. Interestingly, many productions make scene changes an integral part of the drama by having costumed stage-hands, or even the actors themselves, carry props on and off the stage. In a 1995 New York production of *Hamlet*, for example, Hamlet himself (performed by Ralph Fiennes) carried in the chairs needed for the spectators of the player scene.

The constant changing of scenery is sometimes avoided by the use of a **unit set**—a series of platforms, rooms, stairs, and exits that form the locations for all the play's actions, as in Miller's *Death of a Salesman*. The movement of the characters from place to place within the unit set marks the shifting scenes and changing topics.

Like characters, the setting can be realistic or nonrealistic. A **realistic setting,** sometimes called a **naturalistic setting,** requires extensive construction and properties, for the object is to create as lifelike a stage as possible. In O'Neill's *Before Breakfast*, for example, the setting is a realistic copy of a tacky early-twentieth-century New York apartment kitchen. By contrast, a **nonrealistic setting** is nonrepresentational and often symbolic. Sometimes a realistic play can be made suggestive and expressive through the use of a nonrealistic setting.

Lighting Creates Clarity, Emphasis, and Mood

In ancient and medieval times, plays were performed in daylight, and hence no artificial illumination was required. With the advent of indoor theaters and evening performances, **lighting** became a necessity. At first, artificial lighting was provided by lanterns, candelabras, sconces, and torches (yes, some theaters burned down), and indirect lighting was achieved by reflectors and valances— all of which were used with great ingenuity and effect. Later, gaslight and lime-light lamps replaced the earlier open flames.

The evolution of theater lighting reached its climax with the development of electric lights in the nineteenth century. Today, dramatic performances are enhanced by virtually all the technical features of our electronic age, including specialized lamps, color filters, spotlights, dimmers, and simulated fires. This dazzling technology, which employs hundreds or even thousands of lights of varying intensity in unlimited combination, is used to highlight individual characters, to isolate and emphasize various parts of the stage, to establish times, and generally to shape the moods of individual scenes. Lighting can also divide the stage or a unit set into different acting areas simply through the illumination of one section and the darkening of the rest, as in productions of plays like Miller's *Death of a Salesman.* The result is that lighting has become an integral element of set design, especially when the dramatist uses a **scrim** (a curtain that becomes transparent when illuminated from behind), which permits great variety in the portrayal of scenes and great rapidity in scene changes. In our day it is a rare stage indeed that does not contain an elaborate, computerized, and complicated (and expensive) lighting system.

Costumes and Makeup Establish the Nature and Appearance of the Actors

Actors make plays vivid by wearing **costumes** and using **makeup,** which help the audience understand a play's time period together with the occupations, mental outlooks, and socioeconomic conditions of the characters. Costumes, which include not only dress but items such as jewelry, good-luck charms, swords, firearms, and canes, can be used realistically (farm women in plain clothes, a salesman in a business suit, a king in rich robes) or symbolically (a depressed character wearing black). Makeup usually enhances an actor's facial features, just as it can fix the illusion of youth or age or emphasize a character's joy or sorrow.

The Audience Responds to the Performance and Helps to Shape It

To be complete, plays require an interaction of actors and **audience.** Drama enacts fictional or historical events as if they were happening in the present, and members of the audience—whether spectators or readers—are direct witnesses to the dramatic action from start to finish. The audience most definitely has a creative impact on theatrical performances. Although audiences are made up of people who otherwise do not know each other, they have a common bond of interest in the play. Therefore, even though they are isolated by the darkness of the theater in which they sit, they respond communally. Their reactions (e.g., laughter, gasps, applause) provide instant feedback to the actors and thus continually influence the delivery and pace of the performance. For this reason, drama *in the theater* is the most immediate and accessible of the literary arts. There is no intermediary between the audience and the stage action—no narrator, as in prose fiction, and no speaker, as in poetry.

DRAMA FROM ANCIENT TIMES TO OUR OWN: TRAGEDY, COMEDY, AND ADDITIONAL FORMS

Today, people interested in drama have more options than at any other time in human history. There is professional live theater in many major cities, and touring theatrical troupes reach areas with smaller populations. Many cities and towns have amateur community theaters, and so also with many schools and churches. Movie theaters and multiplexes are flourishing. Television has brought film versions of plays to the home screen, together with innumerable situation comedies ("sitcoms"), continuous narrative dramas (including soap operas), made-for-TV films, documentary dramas ("docudramas"), short skits on comedy shows, and many other types. All these different genres ultimately spring from the drama that was developed twenty-six hundred years ago in Athens, the leading ancient Greek city-state. Although subsequent centuries have produced many variations, the types the Athenians created are still as important today as they were then. They are tragedy and comedy.[1]

Tragedy and Comedy Originated in Ancient Greece

During the sixth century B.C.E., drama first arose from choral presentations the Athenians held during religious festivals celebrating Dionysus, the god of wine, conviviality, sexual vitality, ecstasy, fertility, and freedom. The choruses were made up of young men who sang or chanted lengthy songs that the Athenians called **dithyrambs;** the choruses also performed interpretive dance movements during the presentations. The dithyrambs were not dramatizations but rather recitations, which became dramatic when a member of the chorus was designated to step forward and impersonate—*act*—one of the heroes. Soon, additional men from the choruses took acting roles, and the focus of the performances shifted from the choral group to individual actors. Greek **tragedy** as we know it had come into being. It was this pattern of drama that during the fifth century B.C.E. produced a golden age of tragedy. Most of the tragedies have been lost, and only a small but very significant number of plays by the three greatest Athenian dramatists—Aeschylus, Sophocles, and Euripides—have survived.

Not long after the emergence of tragedy, comedy became an additional feature of the festivals. Because the ancient Athenians encouraged free speech,

---

[1]Fuller discussions of tragedy and comedy are presented in Chapters 27 and 28.

at least for males, the comedy writers created a boisterous, lewd, and freely critical type of burlesque comedy that later critics called **Old Comedy.** The eleven surviving plays of Aristophanes represent this tradition. In the fourth century B.C.E., after Athenian power and freedom had declined because of the debilitating wars with Sparta at the end of the fifth century, this type of comedy was replaced by **Middle Comedy,** a more social, discreet, and international drama, and then by **New Comedy,** a type of play featuring the development of situation, plot, and character. The best-known writer of New Comedy was Menander, whose plays were long thought to be totally lost. In the last hundred years, however, a number of fragments of his work have been discovered, including one play in its entirety.

Both of these Greek dramatic types have proved long-lasting. The introduction of subject matter about loss in the earliest tragedies has led to today's common understanding that tragedy dramatizes an individual's fall from a secure and elevated position to social or personal defeat. Likewise, what we usually consider typical comedies are directly linked to the pattern of ancient New Comedy: plays that dramatize the regeneration of individuals who begin in insecurity and end with the overcoming of troubles and the anticipation of happiness.

Tragedy and Comedy Were of Less Significance in Ancient Rome

The two Athenian dramatic forms were adopted by the Romans during the periods of the Republic (before 29 B.C.E.) and the Empire (after 29 B.C.E.). Although Republican Rome produced writers of note who created comedies (Plautus, ca. 254–184 B.C.E., and Terence, ca. 195 or 185–159 B.C.E.), the only significant playwright of imperial times was the tragedian Seneca (4 B.C.E.–65 C.E.), who wrote "closet dramas"—that is, plays designed to be read but not performed.

Ancient Drama Faded Along with the Breakup of the Western Roman Empire

As the Roman Empire in western Europe disintegrated in the fifth century C.E., many of its institutions, including the theater, disintegrated with it. In the next five centuries, often called the Dark Ages, Europe fell into feudalism, characterized by political decentralization and social fragmentation. The intellectuals of the period—most of them clergy—were creating Christian theology and establishing the growing church while abandoning the memories and records of the past, of which drama was a major element. As far as we know, there were no public theaters, no patrons able or willing to support public performances, no popular audiences with the money to pay for admission, no official permission by secular and religious authorities to perform plays, and no practicing dramatists—in short, there was no organized theater. It is hard to believe, however, that the human need for stories and fantasies did not remain. Tales and songs were unquestionably passed on from parents to children and community to community throughout these otherwise dreary centuries.

feudalism—medieval political order in which land is granted in return for service

Medieval Drama Developed as a Part of Church Services

When drama emerged hundreds of years after the fall of Rome, it had little to do with the Greek and Roman dramatic tradition because it was a creation of the Christian church. It was at some point in the tenth century—approximately when the medieval period or Middle Ages were emerging from the Dark Ages— that the clergy started to realize the potentiality of dramatic presentations within the mass. It was then that dramatic **tropes** (short interludes performed in conjunction with the mass, either with or without musical accompaniment) developed in the churches. These tropes were not considered as separate dramas, however, but were integrated within regular services.

The earliest tropes were written for Easter rituals. The prototype of the Easter trope, which is included here, represented the discovery of the empty tomb as evidence of Christ's resurrection. This is the *Visitatio Sepulchri*, or *The Visit to the Sepulcher*, often known as the *Quem Quaeritis* ("Whom are you seeking") trope. This is considered the first European drama, from which all subsequent dramas have developed. Authored by persons who are unknown and forever unknowable, the trope was in Latin and was chanted not for the people but for cloistered monks and priests. It was enacted many times both on the continent and the British Isles, and in later centuries it became a regular feature of Easter worship. It has survived in a variety of forms in medieval manuscripts. Some versions contain detailed directions about performance, and some are cast in a question-and-answer format.

Although the *Quem Quaeritis* trope was a part of ritual, it clearly involved impersonation—and therefore drama—to the degree that priests and monks represented the persons and scenes contained in the gospel accounts of the resurrection. The heart of the trope is that the Angel at the tomb announces the resurrection to the three Marys, who then leave to proclaim the news.

ANONYMOUS

The Visit to the Sepulcher (Visitatio Sepulchri) ⸱⸢⸟⸿⸾⸿⸽ *Tenth Century* C.E.

[CAST OF CHARACTERS]

> [The Angel at the Tomb]
> [Mary the Mother of James and Joseph]
> [Mary Magdalen]
> [Mary of Bethany, the Sister of Martha and Lazarus*]

[SCENE: *The Sepulcher in which Christ was entombed after the Crucifixion. The* ANGEL, *dressed in white and holding a palm leaf, enters and sits beside a location curtained off to represent the tomb.*

*Although gospel accounts are substantially in accord about the first two Marys, there is no agreement about the third woman, who is named "Salome" by Mark and "Joanna" by Luke. None of the gospel accounts of the resurrection indicates that Mary of Bethany was the third Mary. Nevertheless, medieval tradition fixed a tradition that there was a third Mary, and that it was Mary of Bethany, probably on the authority of John 12:7, where Jesus implies that this Mary will be one of those to anoint his dead body.

Behind the curtain is a table or other surface representing a burial slab on which there is a linen sheet (i.e., the burial shroud supplied by Joseph of Aramathea). The three MARYs enter, carrying vessels [thuribles] as though they are intending to anoint Christ's body with aromatic oils and spices. At first they do not see the tomb, and they wander about until they do. Then they stop in front of the ANGEL]

ANGEL. Whom are you seeking in this sepulcher, O followers of Christ?

THE THREE HOLY WOMEN. [*Speaking together.*] Jesus of Nazareth, who was crucified, O heavenly one.

ANGEL. [*Pulling back the curtain to show the empty tomb.*] He is not here. He has been resurrected, as was predicted. Go forth, tell everyone that he is risen. Spread the news!

THE THREE HOLY WOMEN. [*Kneeling and singing.*] Alleluia! Today Christ the Lord, the Son of God, the Mighty Lion, has been resurrected! Thanks be to God! Tell it to all the world!

ANGEL. Come and see the place where the Lord was laid.

[*The Three Holy Women examine the empty tomb and, with the ANGEL, display the burial shroud.*]

ANGEL. Alleluia! Alleluia! Hurry, tell the disciples that the Lord has risen! Alleluia! Alleluia!

[*He exits, singing alleluias.*]

THE THREE HOLY WOMEN. [*Rejoicing, and singing in unison.*] The Lord, who hung on the tree for us, has risen from the grave! Alleluia!

[*They exit, joyfully repeating these lines.*]

QUESTIONS

1. What dramatic characteristics, as opposed to the obvious theology, do you find in this brief play?

2. Describe the play's dramatic actions. What sorts of movement would have been carried out? How extensive might have been the use of properties?

3. How do you suppose this play would have affected people attending the service in which it was performed?

Comparable Dramatic Ceremonies Followed the *Visitatio Sepulchri*

During the eleventh and twelfth centuries, the *Visit to the Sepulcher* ceremony became more elaborate, with additional characters and actions such as the race by Peter and John to the tomb and Mary Magdalen's recognition of the risen Christ after having first confused him for a gardener. Some of the ceremonies, which were eventually performed before congregations, became extensive enough to require a lengthy performance. Historians of drama observe that this Easter ceremony was *dramatic liturgy* rather than *liturgical drama*, but any congregations present would likely have ignored this distinction. Instead they would have welcomed the ceremony as something totally new, vital, dramatic, and exciting.

In addition to the Easter pageantry, the church also developed special Christmas ceremonies such as those for the Three Wise Men, the Shepherds, the scene at the stable, the ranting Herod, and the Slaughter of the Innocents

(Innocents Day was December 28). These ceremonies were observed as regular parts of Easter and Christmas rituals for hundreds of years after their beginnings in the tenth century.

A New Kind of Drama, the Corpus Christi Play, Grew Independently of the Church

Growing out of the religious dramatic tradition, a full-blown religious and civic drama developed in the fourteenth century. This was the Corpus Christi (i.e., "Body of Christ") play, which evolved just as the drama of ancient Athens had developed out of religious festivals for the god Dionysus in the sixth century B.C.E.[2] The major expression of the new religious drama came during the celebration of Corpus Christi Day, a celebration of the doctrine of transubstantiation (i.e., during mass, Eucharistic bread and wine were said to become transformed miraculously into the real body and blood of Christ).

Corpus Christi Day regularly featured local processions devoted to the worship of the Eucharist, and in this way it brought religious celebration into the streets and before the public. Because the feast occurred at the end of the liturgical year, it coincided with the beginning of good weather. The winter and spring rains abated, daylight hours lengthened, short trips from country villages to nearby towns became possible, and people could spend an entire day outside and still be comfortable.

The goal of the new Corpus Christi, or mystery plays, was to create a complete sequence or **cycle** of plays dramatizing the biblical accounts of world history from the Creation to Judgment Day. The plays were produced by the local craft guilds, the members of whom were master tradesmen. Hence the plays were also known as *mysteries*, or *mystery plays*. Naturally, the guild masters wanted to boost the prestige of their towns and their own wealth and power. They therefore welcomed this annual religious celebration that attracted customers and patrons. Although there were as yet no professional acting companies like the one that Shakespeare joined in the late sixteenth century, the annual staging of the Corpus Christi plays required large numbers of participants. The planning by the local guilds was therefore complex and challenging; the result was an engaging and inspiring drama.

As the Corpus Christi feasts grew in importance, the plays became a highlight of town life in the early summer. By the fifteenth century as many as forty towns had their own cycles. Some were large and elaborate; some—probably those performed in the smaller towns—were modest. Often the performances took place not only on Corpus Christi Thursday but also on Friday and Saturday, thus creating an extensive religious and secular celebration. Although the texts of most of these plays have been lost, cycles from four towns have been preserved. These cycles, named after the towns that presented them, contain more than 150 plays.

---

[2]See pp. 1258–61.

English Replaced Latin as the Language of the Corpus Christi Plays

A major influence on the Corpus Christi drama—with profound implications for later drama—was the increasing importance of the English language at this time. During the two centuries following the Norman conquest in 1066, the ruling and intellectual languages of England had been French and Latin. By the fourteenth century, however, things were changing: English had been enriched with as many as 10,000 French words (a huge number of which we still retain) and was reasserting its role as the major language of England. More and more, the governing classes were committed to England—having a centuries-long tradition there—and used English as the language of intellectual and political discourse. Native writers began looking with increased favor on English as a literary language. A new literature in English—including drama—was ripe for development.

In this chapter, *The Second Shepherds' Play* by the "Wakefield Master" is representative of the Corpus Christi or mystery play.

Other Religious Dramas Originated after the Corpus Christi Plays

In the course of time, additional types of religious dramas were developed. One of these was the **miracle play,** a devotional dramatization of the lives of saints. In addition, the **morality play** was developed as a genre instructing the faithful in the proper way to lead a devotional life. The most famous of these, in about 1500, was *Everyman*, which even today retains a good deal of interest and power.

In the Renaissance, Ancient and Medieval Traditions Fused to Create a New Secular Drama

In the sixteenth century, drama became liberated from these religious foundations and began rendering the twists and turns of more secular human conflicts. It was also at this time that the drama of ancient Greece and Rome was rediscovered. Therefore, the performing tradition growing out of the medieval church was combined with the surviving ancient tragedies and comedies to create an entirely new drama that quickly reached its highest point in the plays of Shakespeare. In this way, tragedy and comedy, the forms originated by the Athenians, had a revival during the Renaissance in Europe.[3]

New Types of Drama Have Developed Since the Renaissance

Renaissance drama was by no means a copy of ancient forms, however, even though a number of sixteenth- and seventeenth-century playwrights, including Shakespeare, reworked many of the ancient plays. The plays of Renaissance

[3]The Renaissance revival of drama also transformed the theater into a business. Earlier drama had been a product of the church and religious life, but during the Renaissance, actors and theater people found that they could make a living in the theater. Although at first there was little money in acting and in writing plays, some of the theater managers were able to do quite well. Shakespeare himself was a theater manager as well as a dramatist and minor actor. He earned enough from his shares in the Globe Theatre to retire in 1611 and leave London to spend his remaining days in his native Stratford-upon-Avon.

England, and later the plays of the United States, offer mixtures of tragedy and comedy. For example, some of Shakespeare's comedies treat disturbing and potentially destructive topics, just as many of his tragedies include scenes that are farcical, witty, and ironic. When the patterns and emotions are truly mixed, the play is called a **tragicomedy,** a term first used by the Roman playwright Plautus. In many ways tragicomedy is the dominant form of twentieth-century drama.

Additional types of drama that evolved from tragedy and comedy include farce, melodrama, and social drama. The major purpose of **farce,** which was also a strong element in the Athenian Old Comedy, is to make audiences laugh. Typically, it is crammed full of extravagant dialogue, stage business, and slapstick, with exaggerated emotions and rapid extremes of action. The "mechanicals" in Shakespeare's *A Midsummer Night's Dream* offer us a good example of farce, and the characters appearing at the end of Kauffmann's *The More the Merrier* are introduced in a farcical manner.

Resembling tragedy but stepping back from tragic outcomes is **melodrama,** a form in which most situations and characters are so exaggerated that they seem ridiculous. In its pure form, melodrama brings characters to the brink of ruin but saves them through the superhuman resources of a hero who always arrives just in time to pay the mortgage, save the business, and rescue the heroine while the grumbling villain flees the stage muttering "Curses, foiled again," or words to this effect.

The nineteenth century saw the creation of a form of topical drama known as **social drama** (sometimes called **problem drama**), a type that still exists as serious drama today. This type of play explores social problems and the individual's place in society. The plays can be tragic, comic, or mixed. Examples of social drama are Ibsen's *A Dollhouse* and Miller's *Death of a Salesman.*

Despite all these terms and types, keep in mind that classification is not the goal of reading or seeing plays. It is less important to identify the melodramatic elements in O'Neill's *Before Breakfast* or the farcical elements in Kauffmann's *The More the Merrier* than it is to understand and share the experiences and ideas that each play offers.

READING PLAYS

As we have noted, drama relies heavily on actors and directors to bring it to life. You might therefore ask why we bother to read plays without seeing them performed. The most obvious answer is that we may never get the chance actually to *see* a professional or amateur performance of a particular play. But we also read plays to familiarize ourselves with important literature. Plays are not simply maps to theatrical production; they are a significant and valuable part of our literary heritage. Dramas like Sophocles' *Oedipus the King*, Shakespeare's *Hamlet*, and Miller's *Death of a Salesman* have become cultural touchstones. Finally, we read plays in order to have the time to study and understand them. Only through reading do we have the opportunity to look at the parts that make up the whole and to determine how they fit together to create a moving and meaningful experience.

Reading a play, as opposed to attending a performance, carries both advantages and disadvantages. The major disadvantage is that we lack the immediacy of live theater. We do not see a majestic palace or a run-down living room, the rich robes of a king or the pathetic rags of a beggar, a vital and smiling young person or a tired and tearful old person. We do not hear the lovers flirting, the servants complaining, the soldiers boasting, the opponents threatening, the conspirators plotting; nor do we hear fanfares of trumpets or the sounds of a wedding ceremony or a funeral procession.

The major advantage of reading is that we can consider each element in the play at length, and we can "stage" the play in our imagination. In the theater, the action proceeds at the director's pace. There is no opportunity to turn back to an interesting scene or to reconsider an important speech. In addition, a performance always represents someone else's interpretation. The director and the actors have already made choices that emphasize certain avenues of exploration and cut off others. Reading a play lets us avoid these drawbacks—provided that we read attentively and with understanding. We can read at our own tempo, turn back and reread a particular speech or scene, or explore those implications or ideas that strike us as interesting.

Try to use the advantages of reading and study to compensate for the disadvantages. You have time and freedom to read carefully, reflect deeply, and follow your thoughts. Rely on your experiences in watching theatrical productions, movies, and television to enhance your reading. Use your imagination. Stage the play as fully as you can in the theater of your mind. Become the director, producer, set designer, lighting technician, costume designer, and all the actors. Build whatever mental sets you like, dress your actors as you see fit, and move the characters across the stage of your mind. Enjoy.

PLAYS FOR STUDY

SUSAN GLASPELL, *TRIFLES*

Susan Glaspell, a writer of both plays and fiction, was a native of Iowa. She was educated at Drake University and the University of Chicago. In her thirties she moved to the Northeast and became interested in theater. Along with her husband, George Cook, she was a founder and director of the Provincetown Players of Cape Cod in 1914. The organization encouraged lesser-known young dramatists and was often experimental, but nevertheless it became successful enough to justify the opening of a second theater in New York. The first offerings of the theater were many one-act plays, featuring the earlier works of Glaspell herself, Eugene O'Neill, Edna Ferber, Edmund Wilson, and Edna St. Vincent Millay.

The five principal actors arrive in the cold and bleak kitchen of the Wright farm at the beginning of Glaspell's *Trifles* in the original 1916 production, featuring Marjorie Vonnegut, Elinor M. Cox, John Kind, Arthur Hohl, and T. W. Gibson.

Glaspell wrote or coauthored over ten plays for the Provincetown Players, including Suppressed Desires *(1914),* Close the Book *(1917),* Women's Honor *(1918),* Tickless Time *(1918),* Bernice *(1919, her first full-length play),* The Inheritors *(1921), and* The Verge *(1921). After 1922, however, she gave up the theater and turned almost exclusively to fiction. The exception was* Alison's House *(1930), a play loosely based on the life and family of Emily Dickinson, for which she won a Pulitzer Prize.*

Glaspell deals with diverse topics in her drama, including misunderstood parentage, the effects of psychoanalysis, rejection of the machine age, the function and importance of honor, the tensions between political conservatives and liberals, and the onset of psychosis. Running through much of her work are strongly feminist ideas, based on a critique of the power—personal, social, and political—that men possess and that women are denied. Usually, Glaspell focuses on the negative and destructive effects that male–female relationships have on women, but she also stresses the ways in which women cope with their circumstances. To maintain character integrity and to preserve their domestic strength, they are forced into roles that are characterized not by direct but by indirect action.

Trifles, Glaspell's best-known drama, displays these characteristics. She wrote it in ten days for the Provincetown Players, who produced the play in 1916. Its inspiration was a murder trial she had covered while working as a reporter for a Des Moines newspaper before moving to the Northeast. In 1917 she refashioned the material for the short story "A Jury of Her Peers," with which *Trifles* can be compared (see p. 188). Although Glaspell preserves a considerable amount of dramatic dialogue in the story, the additions and changes she makes are indicative of the differences between drama and fiction.

Trifles concerns a murder investigation, but the play is not a mystery. Soon after the characters enter and go about their business, the two women characters begin to uncover the circumstances that reveal the killer and the nature of the crime. Once the facts are established, however, the action focuses on the significant details of motive. Indeed, the heart of the play consists of the contrasting ways in which the men and the women attempt to uncover and understand the motive. The men—the county attorney and the sheriff, accompanied by Hale—look for signs of violent rage, and they move onstage and offstage throughout the house in their search. The women—Mrs. Hale and Mrs. Peters—stay onstage and draw their conclusions from the ordinary, everyday details of a farm woman's kitchen. It is finally the women, not the men, who realize the true power that comes from understanding. Their realization—as well as their strength—leads them to their final decisions about how to judge the killer and treat the evidence.

The language that Glaspell gives to her characters is in keeping with the plain and simple lives the characters lead: simple, specific, and unadorned. Of the two groups, the women are more direct in the expression of their ideas. Once they realize the gravity of the situation they are exploring, however, they become indirect, but only because they fear to speak the words that describe the truths they have discovered. By contrast, the men usually talk convivially and smugly about the crime and their own roles in life, patronizingly among themselves about the women, and almost scornfully to the women about womanly concerns.

SUSAN GLASPELL (1882–1948)

Trifles ~ 1916

CAST OF CHARACTERS

George Henderson, *county attorney*
Henry Peters, *sheriff*
Lewis Hale, *a neighboring farmer*
Mrs. Peters
Mrs. Hale

SCENE. *The kitchen in the now abandoned farmhouse of JOHN WRIGHT, a gloomy kitchen, and left without having been put in order—unwashed pans under the sink, a loaf of bread outside the bread-box, a dish-towel on the table—other signs of incompleted work. At the rear the outer door opens and the SHERIFF comes in followed by the COUNTY ATTORNEY and HALE. The SHERIFF and HALE are men in middle life, the COUNTY ATTORNEY is a young man; all are much bundled up and go at once to the stove. They are followed by the two women—the SHERIFF'S wife first; she is a slight wiry woman, a thin nervous face. MRS. HALE is larger and would ordinarily be called more comfortable looking, but she is disturbed now and looks fearfully about as she enters. The women have come in slowly, and stand close together near the door.*

COUNTY ATTORNEY. [*Rubbing his hands.*] This feels good. Come up to the fire, ladies.

MRS. PETERS. [*After taking a step forward*] I'm not—cold.

SHERIFF. [*Unbuttoning his overcoat and stepping away from the stove as if to mark the beginning of official business.*] Now, Mr. Hale, before we move things about, you explain to Mr. Henderson just what you saw when you came here yesterday morning.

COUNTY ATTORNEY. By the way, has anything been moved? Are things just as you left them yesterday?

SHERIFF. [*Looking about.*] It's just the same. When it dropped below zero last night I thought I'd better send Frank out this morning to make a fire for us—no use getting pneumonia with a big case on, but I told him not to touch anything except the stove—and you know Frank.

COUNTY ATTORNEY. Somebody should have been left here yesterday.

SHERIFF. Oh—yesterday. When I had to send Frank to Morris Center for that man who went crazy—I want you to know I had my hands full yesterday. I knew you could get back from Omaha by today and as long as I went over everything here myself—

5

COUNTY ATTORNEY. Well, Mr. Hale, tell just what happened when you came here yesterday morning.

HALE. Harry and I had started to town with a load of potatoes. We came along the road from my place and as I got here I said, "I'm going to see if I can't get John Wright to go in with me on a party telephone." I spoke to Wright about it once before and he put me off, saying folks talked too much anyway, and all he asked was peace and quiet—I guess you know about how much he talked himself; but I thought maybe if I went to the house and talked about it before his wife, though I said to Harry that I didn't know as what his wife wanted made much difference to John—

COUNTY ATTORNEY. Let's talk about that later, Mr. Hale. I do want to talk about 10
that, but tell now just what happened when you got to the house.

HALE. I didn't hear or see anything; I knocked at the door, and still it was all quiet inside. I knew they must be up, it was past eight o'clock. So I knocked again, and I thought I heard somebody say, "Come in." I wasn't sure, I'm not sure yet, but I opened. the door—this door [*Indicating the door by which the two women are still standing.*] and there in that rocker—[*Pointing to it.*] sat Mrs. Wright.

[*They all look at the rocker.*]

COUNTY ATTORNEY. What—was she doing?

HALE. She was rockin' back and forth. She had her apron in her hand and was kind of—pleating it.

COUNTY ATTORNEY. And how did she—look?

HALE. Well, she looked queer. 15

COUNTY ATTORNEY. How do you mean—queer?

HALE. Well, as if she didn't know what she was going to do next. And kind of done up.

COUNTY ATTORNEY. How did she seem to feel about your coming?

HALE. Why, I don't think she minded—one way or other. She didn't pay much attention. I said, "How do, Mrs. Wright, it's cold, ain't it?" And she said, "Is it?"—and went on kind of pleating at her apron. Well, I was surprised; she didn't ask me to come up to the stove, or to set down, but just sat there, not even looking at me, so I said, "I want to see John." And then she—laughed. I guess you would call it a laugh. I thought of Harry and the team outside, so I said a little sharp: "Can't I see John?" "No," she says, kind o' dull like. "Ain't he home?" says I. "Yes," says she, "he's home." "Then why can't I see him?" I asked her, out of patience. "'Cause he's dead," says she. "*Dead?*" says I. She just nodded her head, not getting a bit excited, but rockin' back and forth. "Why—where is he?" says I, not knowing what to say. She just pointed upstairs—like that. [*Himself pointing to the room above.*] I got up, with the idea of going up there. I walked from there to here—then I says, "Why, what did he die of?" "He died of a rope round his neck," says she, and just went on pleatin' at her apron. Well, I went out and called Harry. I thought I might—need help. We went upstairs and there he was lyin'—

COUNTY ATTORNEY. I think I'd rather have you go into that upstairs, where you can 20
point it all out. Just go on now with the rest of the story.

HALE. Well, my first thought was to get that rope off. It looked . . . [*Stops, his face twitches.*] . . . but Harry, he went up to him, and he said, "No, he's dead all right, and we'd better not touch anything." So we went back downstairs. She was still sitting that same way. "Has anybody been notified?" I asked. "No," says she, unconcerned. "Who did this, Mrs. Wright?" said Harry. He said it businesslike—and she stopped pleatin' of her apron. "I don't know," she says. "You don't *know?*" says Harry. "No," says she. "Weren't you sleepin' in the bed with him?" says Harry. "Yes," says she, "but I was on the inside." "Somebody slipped a rope round his neck and strangled him and you didn't wake up?" says Harry. "I didn't wake up," she said after him. We must 'a looked as if we didn't see how that could be, for after a minute she said, "I sleep sound." Harry was going to ask her more questions but I said maybe we ought to let her tell her story first to the coroner, or the sheriff, so Harry went fast as he could to Rivers' place, where there's a telephone.

COUNTY ATTORNEY.   And what did Mrs. Wright do when she knew that you had gone for the coroner?

HALE.   She moved from that chair to this one over here [*Pointing to a small chair in the corner.*] and just sat there with her hands held together and looking down. I got a feeling that I ought to make some conversation, so I said I had come in to see if John wanted to put in a telephone, and at that she started to laugh, and then she stopped and looked at me—scared. [*The COUNTY ATTORNEY, who has had his notebook out, makes a note.*] I dunno, maybe it wasn't scared. I wouldn't like to say it was. Soon Harry got back, and then Dr. Lloyd came, and you, Mr. Peters, and so I guess that's all I know that you don't.

COUNTY ATTORNEY.   [*Looking around.*] I guess we'll go upstairs first—and then out to the barn and around there. [*To the SHERIFF.*] You're convinced that there was nothing important here—nothing that would point to any motive.

SHERIFF.   Nothing here but kitchen things.   25

[*The COUNTY ATTORNEY, after again looking around the kitchen, opens the door of a cupboard closet. He gets up on a chair and looks on a shelf. Pulls his hand away, sticky.*]

COUNTY ATTORNEY.   Here's a nice mess.

[*The women draw nearer.*]

MRS. PETERS.   [*To the other woman.*] Oh, her fruit; it did freeze. [*To the LAWYER.*] She worried about that when it turned so cold. She said the fire'd go out and her jars would break.

SHERIFF.   Well, can you beat the women! Held for murder and worryin' about her preserves.

COUNTY ATTORNEY.   I guess before we're through she may have something more serious than preserves to worry about.

HALE.   Well, women are used to worrying over trifles.   30

[*The two women move a little closer together.*]

COUNTY ATTORNEY.   [*With the gallantry of a young politician.*] And yet, for all their worries, what would we do without the ladies? [*The women do not unbend. He goes to the sink, takes a dipperful of water from the pail and pouring it into a basin, washes his hands. Starts to wipe them on the roller-towel, turns it for a cleaner place.*] Dirty towels! [*Kicks his foot against the pans under the sink.*] Not much of a housekeeper, would you say, ladies?

MRS HALE.   [*Stiffly.*] There's a great deal of work to be done on a farm.

COUNTY ATTORNEY.   To be sure. And yet [*With a little bow to her.*] I know there are some Dickson county farmhouses which do not have such roller towels.

[*He gives it a pull to expose its full length again.*]

MRS HALE.   Those towels get dirty awful quick. Men's hands aren't always as clean as they might be.

COUNTY ATTORNEY.   Ah, loyal to your sex, I see. But you and Mrs. Wright were   35
neighbors. I suppose you were friends, too.

MRS HALE.   [*Shaking her head.*] I've not seen much of her of late years. I've not been in this house—it's more than a year.

COUNTY ATTORNEY.   And why was that? You didn't like her?

MRS HALE.   I liked her all well enough. Farmers' wives have their hands full, Mr. Henderson. And then—

COUNTY ATTORNEY.   Yes—?

MRS HALE.   [*Looking about.*] It never seemed a very cheerful place.   40

COUNTY ATTORNEY.   No—it's not cheerful. I shouldn't say she had the homemaking instinct.

MRS HALE.   Well. I don't know as Wright had, either.

COUNTY ATTORNEY.   You mean that they didn't get on very well?

MRS HALE.   No, I don't mean anything. But I don't think a place'd be any cheerfuller for John Wright's being in it.

COUNTY ATTORNEY.   I'd like to talk more of that a little later. I want to get the lay of   45
things upstairs now.

[*He goes to the left, where three steps lead to a stair door.*]

SHERIFF.   I suppose anything Mrs. Peters does'll be all right. She was to take in some clothes for her, you know, and a few little things. We left in such a hurry yesterday.

COUNTY ATTORNEY.   Yes, but I would like to see what you take, Mrs. Peters, and keep an eye out for anything that might be of use to us.

MRS. PETERS.   Yes, Mr. Henderson.

[*The women listen to the men's steps on the stairs, then look about the kitchen.*]

MRS HALE.   I'd hate to have men coming into my kitchen, snooping around and criticising.

[*She arranges the pans under the sink which the Lawyer had shoved out of place.*]

MRS. PETERS.   Of course it's no more than their duty.   50

MRS HALE.   Duty's all right, but I guess that deputy sheriff that came out to make the fire might have got a little of this on. [*Gives the roller towel a pull.*] Wish I'd thought of that sooner. Seems mean to talk about her for not having things slicked up when she had to come away in such a hurry.

MRS. PETERS.   [*Who had gone to a small table in the left rear corner of the room, and lifted one end of a towel that covers a pan.*] She had bread set.

[*Stands still.*]

MRS. HALE.   [*Eyes fixed on a loaf of bread beside the breadbox, which is on a low shelf at the other side of the room. Moves slowly toward it.*] She was going to put this in there. [*Picks up loaf, then abruptly drops it. In a manner of returning to familiar things.*] It's a shame about her fruit. I wonder if it's all gone. [*Gets up on the chair and looks.*] I think there's some here that's all right, Mrs. Peters. Yes—here; [*Holding it toward the window.*] this is cherries, too. [*Looking again.*] I declare I believe that's the only one. [*Gets down, bottle in her hand. Goes to the sink and wipes it off on the outside.*] She'll feel awful bad after all her hard work in the hot weather. I remember the afternoon I put up my cherries last summer.

[*She puts the bottle on the big kitchen table, center of the room. With a sigh, is about to sit down in the rocking-chair. Before she is seated realizes what chair it is; with a slow look at it, steps back. The chair which she has touched rocks back and forth.*]

MRS. PETERS. Well, I must get those things from the front room closet. [*She goes to the door at the right, but after looking into the other room, steps back.*] You coming with me, Mrs. Hale? You could help me carry them.

[*They go in the other room; reappear, MRS. PETERS carrying a dress and skirt, MRS. HALE following with a pair of shoes.*]

MRS. PETERS. My, it's cold in there.   55

[*She puts the clothes on the big table and hurries to the stove.*]

MRS. HALE. [*Examining the skirt.*] Wright was close. I think maybe that's why she kept so much to herself. She didn't even belong to the Ladies Aid. I suppose she felt she couldn't do her part, and then you don't enjoy things when you feel shabby. She used to wear pretty clothes and be lively, when she was Minnie Foster, one of the town girls singing in the choir. But that—oh, that was thirty years ago. This all you was to take in?

MRS. PETERS. She said she wanted an apron. Funny thing to want, for there isn't much to get you dirty in jail, goodness knows. But I suppose just to make her feel more natural. She said they was in the top drawer in this cupboard. Yes, here. And then her little shawl that always hung behind the door. [*Opens stair door and looks.*] Yes, here it is.

[*Quickly shuts door leading upstairs.*]

MRS. HALE. [*Abruptly moving toward her.*] Mrs. Peters?
MRS. PETERS. Yes, Mrs. Hale?
MRS. HALE. Do you think she did it?   60
MRS. PETERS. [*In a frightened voice.*] Oh, I don't know.
MRS. HALE. Well, I don't think she did. Asking for an apron and her little shawl. Worrying about her fruit.
MRS. PETERS. [*Starts to speak, glances up, where footsteps are heard in the room above. In a low voice.*] Mr. Peters says it looks bad for her. Mr. Henderson is awful sarcastic in a speech and he'll make fun of her sayin' she didn't wake up.
MRS. HALE. Well, I guess John Wright didn't wake when they was slipping that rope under his neck.
MRS. PETERS. No, it's strange. It must have been done awful crafty and still. They   65
say it was such a—funny way to kill a man, rigging it all up like that.
MRS. HALE. That's just what Mr. Hale said. There was a gun in the house. He says that's what he can't understand.
MRS. PETERS. Mr. Henderson said coming out that what was needed for the case was a motive; something to show anger, or—sudden feeling.
MRS. HALE. [*Who is standing by the table.*] Well, I don't see any signs of anger around here. [*She puts her hand on the dish towel which lies on the table, stands looking down at table, one half of which is clean, the other half messy.*] It's wiped to here. [*Makes a move as if to finish work, then turns and looks at loaf of bread outside the breadbox. Drops towel. In that voice of coming back to familiar things.*] Wonder how they are finding things upstairs. I hope she had it a little more red-up° up there. You know, it seems kind of *sneaking*. Locking her up in town and then coming out here and trying to get her own house to turn against her!
MRS. PETERS. But Mrs. Hale, the law is the law.
MRS. HALE. I s'pose 'tis. [*Unbuttoning her coat.*] Better loosen up your things,   70
Mrs. Peters. You won't feel them when you go out.

68 *red-up:* neat, arranged in order.

[*Mrs. Peters takes off her fur tippet,° goes to hang it on hook at back of room, stands looking at the under part of the small corner table.*]

MRS. PETERS.   She was piecing a quilt.

[*She brings the large sewing basket and they look at the bright pieces.*]

MRS. HALE.   It's log cabin pattern. Pretty, isn't it? I wonder if she was goin' to quilt it or just knot it?

[*Footsteps have been heard coming down the stairs. The Sheriff enters followed by Hale and the County Attorney.*]

SHERIFF.   They wonder if she was going to quilt it or just knot it!

[*The men laugh; the women look abashed.*]

COUNTY ATTORNEY.   [*Rubbing his hands over the stove.*] Frank's fire didn't do much up there, did it? Well, let's go out to the barn and get that cleared up.

[*The men go outside.*]

MRS. HALE.   [*Resentfully.*] I don't know as there's anything so strange, our takin'   75
up our time with little things while we're waiting for them to get the evidence. [*She sits down at the big table smoothing out a block with decision.*] I don't see as it's anything to laugh about.
MRS. PETERS.   [*Apologetically.*] Of course they've got awful important things on their minds.

[*Pulls up a chair and joins Mrs. Hale at the table.*]

MRS. HALE.   [*Examining another block.*] Mrs. Peters, look at this one. Here, this is the one she was working on, and look at the sewing! All the rest of it has been so nice and even. And look at this! It's all over the place! Why, it looks as if she didn't know what she was about!

[*After she has said this they look at each other, then start to glance back at the door. After an instant Mrs. Hale has pulled at a knot and ripped the sewing.*]

MRS. PETERS.   Oh, what are you doing, Mrs. Hale?
MRS. HALE.   [*Mildly.*] Just pulling out a stitch or two that's not sewed very good.
[*Threading a needle.*] Bad sewing always made me fidgety.
MRS. PETERS.   [*Nervously.*] I don't think we ought to touch things.   80
MRS. HALE.   I'll just finish up this end. [*Suddenly stopping and leaning forward.*]
Mrs. Peters?
MRS. PETERS.   Yes, Mrs. Hale?
MRS. HALE.   What do you suppose she was so nervous about?
MRS. PETERS.   Oh—I don't know. I don't know as she was nervous. I sometimes sew awful queer when I'm just tired. [*Mrs. Hale starts to say something, looks at Mrs. Peters, then goes on sewing.*] Well I must get these things wrapped up. They may be through sooner

70 S.D. *tippet:* scarf-like garment of fur or wool for the neck and shoulders.

than we think. [*Putting apron and other things together.*] I wonder where I can find a piece of paper, and string.

MRS. HALE.   In that cupboard, maybe.   85

MRS. PETERS.   [*Looking in cupboard.*] Why, here's a bird-cage. [*Holds it up.*] Did she have a bird, Mrs. Hale?

MRS. HALE.   Why, I don't know whether she did or not—I've not been here for so long. There was a man around last year selling canaries cheap, but I don't know as she took one; maybe she did. She used to sing real pretty herself.

MRS. PETERS.   [*Glancing around.*] Seems funny to think of a bird here. But she must have had one, or why would she have a cage? I wonder what happened to it?

MRS. HALE.   I s'pose maybe the cat got it.

MRS. PETERS.   No, she didn't have a cat. She's got that feeling some people have   90
about cats—being afraid of them. My cat got in her room and she was real upset and asked me to take it out.

MRS. HALE.   My sister Bessie was like that. Queer, ain't it?

MRS. PETERS.   [*Examining the cage.*] Why, look at this door. It's broke. One hinge is pulled apart.

MRS. HALE.   [*Looking too.*] Looks as if someone must have been rough with it.

MRS. PETERS.   Why, yes.

[*She brings the cage forward and puts it on the table.*]

MRS. HALE.   I wish if they're going to find any evidence they'd be about it. I don't   95
like this place.

MRS. PETERS.   But I'm awful glad you came with me, Mrs. Hale. It would be lonesome for me sitting here alone.

MRS. HALE.   It would, wouldn't it? [*Dropping her sewing.*] But I tell you what I do wish, Mrs. Peters. I wish I had come over sometimes when *she* was here. I—[*Looking around the room.*]—wish I had.

MRS. PETERS.   But of course you were awful busy, Mrs. Hale—your house and your children.

MRS. HALE.   I could've come. I stayed away because it weren't cheerful—and that's why I ought to have come. I—I've never liked this place. Maybe because it's down in a hollow and you don't see the road. I dunno what it is, but it's a lonesome place and always was. I wish I had come over to see Minnie Foster sometimes. I can see now—

[*Shakes her head.*]

MRS. PETERS.   Well, you mustn't reproach yourself, Mrs. Hale. Somehow we just   100
don't see how it is with other folks until—something comes up.

MRS. HALE.   Not having children makes less work—but it makes a quiet house, and Wright out to work all day, and no company when he did come in. Did you know John Wright, Mrs. Peters?

MRS. PETERS.   Not to know him; I've seen him in town. They say he was a good man.

MRS. HALE.   Yes—good; he didn't drink, and kept his word as well as most, I guess, and paid his debts. But he was a hard man, Mrs. Peters. Just to pass the time of day with him—[*Shivers.*] Like a raw wind that gets to the bone. [*Pauses, her eye falling on the cage.*] I should think she would 'a wanted a bird. But what do you suppose went with it?

MRS. PETERS.   I don't know, unless it got sick and died.

[*She reaches over and swings the broken door, swings it again, both women watch it.*]

MRS. HALE.   You weren't raised round here, were you? [*Mrs. PETERS shakes her*   105
head.] You didn't know—her?

MRS. PETERS.   Not till they brought her yesterday.

MRS. HALE.   She—come to think of it, she was kind of like a bird herself—real
sweet and pretty, but kind of timid and—fluttery. How—she—did—change. [*Silence; then
as if struck by a happy thought and relieved to get back to everyday things.*] Tell you what, Mrs. Peters, why don't you take the quilt in with you? It might take up her mind.

MRS. PETERS.   Why, I think that's a real nice idea, Mrs. Hale. There couldn't possibly be any objection to it, could there? Now, just what would I take? I wonder if her patches are in here—and her things.

[*They look in the sewing basket.*]

MRS. HALE.   Here's some red. I expect this has got sewing things in it. [*Brings out
a fancy box.*] What a pretty box. Looks like something somebody would give you. Maybe
her scissors are in here. [*Opens box. Suddenly puts her hand to her nose.*] Why— [*Mrs. PETERS
bends nearer, then turns her face away.*] There's something wrapped up in this piece of silk.

MRS. PETERS.   Why, this isn't her scissors.   110

MRS. HALE.   [*Lifting the silk.*] Oh, Mrs. Peters—it's—

[*Mrs. Peters bends closer.*]

MRS. PETERS.   It's the bird.

MRS. HALE.   [*Jumping up.*] But, Mrs. Peters—look at it! Its neck! Look at its neck!
It's all—other side *to.*

MRS. PETERS.   Somebody—wrung—its—neck.

[*Their eyes meet. A look of growing comprehension, of horror. Steps are heard outside. MRS. HALE
slips box under quilt pieces, and sinks into her chair. Enter SHERIFF and COUNTY ATTORNEY.
MRS. PETERS rises.*]

COUNTY ATTORNEY.   [*As one turning from serious things to little pleasantries.*] Well,   115
ladies, have you decided whether she was going to quilt it or knot it?

MRS. PETERS.   We think she was going to—knot it.

COUNTY ATTORNEY.   Well, that's interesting, I'm sure. [*Seeing the bird-cage.*] Has the
bird flown?

MRS. HALE.   [*Putting more quilt pieces over the box.*] We think the—cat got it.

COUNTY ATTORNEY.   [*Preoccupied.*] Is there a cat?

[*MRS. HALE glances in a quick covert way at MRS. PETERS.*]

MRS. PETERS.   Well, not *now.* They're superstitious, you know. They leave.   120

COUNTY ATTORNEY.   [*To SHERIFF PETERS, continuing an interrupted conversation.*] No
sign at all of anyone having come from the outside. Their own rope. Now let's go up
again and go over it piece by piece. [*They start upstairs.*] It would have to have been someone who knew just the—

[*MRS. PETERS sits down. The two women sit there not looking at one another, but as if peering into
something and at the same time holding back. When they talk now it is in the manner of feeling their
way over strange ground, as if afraid of what they are saying, but as if they cannot help saying it.*]

MRS. HALE.   She liked the bird. She was going to bury it in that pretty box.

MRS. PETERS.   [*In a whisper.*] When I was a girl—my kitten—there was a boy took a hatchet, and before my eyes—and before I could get there—[*Covers her face an instant.*] If they hadn't held me back I would have—[*Catches herself, looks upstairs where steps are heard, falters weakly.*]—hurt him.

MRS. HALE.   [*With a slow look around her.*] I wonder how it would seem never to have had any children around. [*Pause.*] No, Wright wouldn't like the bird—a thing that sang. She used to sing. He killed that, too.

MRS. PETERS.   [*Moving uneasily.*] We don't know who killed the bird.   125

MRS. HALE.   I knew John Wright.

MRS. PETERS.   It was an awful thing was done in this house that night, Mrs. Hale. Killing a man while he slept, slipping a rope around his neck that choked the life out of him.

MRS. HALE.   His neck. Choked the life out of him.

[*Her hand goes out and rests on the bird-cage.*]

MRS. PETERS.   [*With rising voice.*] We don't know who killed him. We don't know.

MRS. HALE.   [*Her own feeling not interrupted.*] If there'd been years and years of   130
nothing, then a bird to sing to you, it would be awful—still, after the bird was still.

MRS. PETERS.   [*Something within her speaking.*] I know what stillness is. When we homesteaded in Dakota, and my first baby died—after he was two years old, and me with no other then—

MRS. HALE.   [*Moving.*] How soon do you suppose they'll be through, looking for the evidence?

MRS. PETERS.   I know what stillness is. [*Pulling herself back.*] The law has got to punish crime, Mrs. Hale.

MRS. HALE.   [*Not as if answering that.*] I wish you'd seen Minnie Foster when she wore a white dress with blue ribbons and stood up there in the choir and sang. [*A look around the room.*] Oh, I *wish* I'd come over here once in a while! That was a crime! That was a crime! Who's going to punish that?

MRS. PETERS.   [*Looking upstairs.*] We mustn't—take on.   135

MRS. HALE.   I might have known she needed help! I know how things can be— for women. I tell you, it's queer, Mrs. Peters. We live close together and we live far apart. We all go through the same things—it's all just a different kind of the same thing. [*Brushes her eyes, noticing the bottle of fruit, reaches out for it.*] If I was you I wouldn't tell her her fruit was gone. Tell her it *ain't*. Tell her it's all right. Take this in to prove it to her. She—she may never know whether it was broke or not.

MRS. PETERS.   [*Takes the bottle, looks about for something to wrap it in; takes petticoat from the clothes brought from the other room, very nervously begins winding this around the bottle. In a false voice.*] My, it's a good thing the men couldn't hear us. Wouldn't they just laugh! Getting all stirred up over a little thing like a—dead canary. As if that could have anything to do with—with—wouldn't they *laugh!*

[*The men are heard coming down stairs.*]

MRS. HALE.   [*Under her breath.*] Maybe they would—maybe they wouldn't.

COUNTY ATTORNEY.   No, Peters, it's all perfectly clear except a reason for doing it. But you know juries when it comes to women. If there was some definite thing. Something to show—something to make a story about—a thing that would connect up with this strange way of doing it—

[*The women's eyes meet for an instant. Enter* HALE *from outer door.*]

HALE.   Well, I've got the team° around. Pretty cold out there. 140

COUNTY ATTORNEY.   I'm going to stay here a while by myself. [*To the* SHERIFF.] You can send Frank out for me, can't you? I want to go over everything. I'm not satisfied that we can't do better.

SHERIFF.   Do you want to see what Mrs. Peters is going to take in?

[*The* COUNTY ATTORNEY *goes to the table, picks up the apron, laughs.*]

COUNTY ATTORNEY.   Oh, I guess they're not very dangerous things the ladies have picked out. [*Moves a few things about, disturbing the quilt pieces which cover the box. Steps back.*] No, Mrs. Peters doesn't need supervising. For that matter, a sheriff's wife is married to the law. Ever think of it that way, Mrs. Peters?

MRS. PETERS.   Not—just that way.

SHERIFF.   [*Chuckling.*] Married to the law. [*Moves toward the other room.*] I just want 145 you to come in here a minute, George. We ought to take a look at these windows.

COUNTY ATTORNEY.   [*Scoffingly.*] Oh, windows!

SHERIFF.   We'll be right out, Mr. Hale.

[HALE *goes outside. The* SHERIFF *follows the* COUNTY ATTORNEY *into the other room. Then* MRS. HALE *rises, hands tight together, looking intensely at* MRS. PETERS, *whose eyes make a slow turn, finally meeting* MRS. HALE'S. *A moment* MRS. HALE *holds her, then her own eyes point the way to where the box is concealed. Suddenly* MRS. PETERS *throws back quilt pieces and tries to put the box in the bag she is wearing. It is too big. She opens box, starts to take bird out, cannot touch it, goes to pieces, stands there helpless. Sound of a knob turning in the other room.* MRS. HALE *snatches the box and puts it in the pocket of her big coat. Enter* COUNTY ATTORNEY *and* SHERIFF.]

COUNTY ATTORNEY.   [*Facetiously.*] Well, Henry, at least we found out that she was not going to quilt it. She was going to—what is it you call it, ladies?

MRS. HALE.   [*Her hand against her pocket.*] We call it—knot it, Mr. Henderson.

CURTAIN

QUESTIONS

1.   How does the first entrance of the characters establish a distinction between the men and women in the play? What is suggested by the different reactions of the men and women to the frozen preserves?

2.   What does Mr. Hale report to the County Attorney in his extended narrative? How observant is he? How accurate?

3.   What is needed for a strong legal case against Minnie? What does the Sheriff conclude about the kitchen? What do his conclusions tell you about the men?

4.   What are the women's conclusions about the bad sewing? What does Mrs. Hale do about it? At this point, what might she be thinking about the murder?

5.   Of what importance are Mrs. Hale's descriptions (a) of Minnie as a young woman and (b) of the Wrights' marriage?

6.   What do the women deduce from the broken birdcage and the dead bird? How are these symbolic, and what do they symbolize?

140 *team:* team of horses drawing a wagon.

7. How did Minnie Wright murder her husband? What hints lead you to this solution? What information permits the women to make the right inferences about the crime and the method of strangulation?

8. What does Mrs. Hale do with the "trifles" of evidence? Why? How is her reaction to the evidence different from that of Mrs. Peters? What conflict develops between these women? How is it resolved?

9. Why does Mrs. Hale feel guilty about her relationship with Minnie Wright? To what degree does her guilt shape her decisions and actions?

GENERAL QUESTIONS

1. To what does the title of this play refer? How does this irony of the word *trifles* help shape the play's meaning?

2. What are the men like? Are they round characters or flat? How observant are they? What is their attitude toward their jobs? Toward their own importance? Toward the women and "kitchen things"?

3. What is Mrs. Hale like? How observant is she? What is her attitude toward the men and their work, and toward herself?

4. Some critics argue that Minnie is the play's most important character, even though she never appears onstage. Do you agree? Why do you think Glaspell did not make Minnie a speaking character?

5. How is symbolism employed to establish and underscore the play's meaning? Consider especially the birdcage, the dead bird, and the repeated assertion that Mrs. Wright was going to "knot" (tie) rather than "quilt" (sew) the quilt.

STANLEY KAUFFMANN, *THE MORE THE MERRIER*

Stanley Kauffmann is a native New Yorker who received his higher education at New York University, graduating in 1935. In addition to the creation of a large number of plays, his professional activities have included acting, stage managing, editing, directing, writing stories and novels, writing screenplays, running a weekly television program about the art of film, and teaching. He is perhaps best known today as one of America's foremost theater and movie critics. For a time he wrote reviews for The New York Times, *and for decades he has been a regular reviewer for* The New Republic, *also doing reviews for* The Saturday Review *and* The Atlantic Monthly. *He was a recipient of the George Jean Nathan Award for drama criticism in 1973, and he has taught at Yale, the Graduate Center of The City University of New York, and Hunter College. His early years in the theater gave him both a theoretical and practical knowledge of drama. Over a twelve-year period beginning in 1933, he wrote more than twenty comedies. Some of these were full-length productions, such as* How She Managed Her Marriage (1935) *and* The True Adventure (1935); *a greater number consisted of one act, such as* The Singer in Search of a King (1935). *In addition to writing under his own name, he used the pseudonym Spranger Barry for a small number of plays.*

The More the Merrier is a brief and entertaining piece in the tradition of romantic farce. The play begins conventionally, with the two main characters agreeing to marry. In their action and dialogue, they demonstrate that they are smitten both with each other and with the idea of a perfect marriage that promises the new beginning of a separate and better life. When Simon enters, however, the subject matter begins to verge on social drama. The dialogue between Emily and Simon shifts the play away from the previous borderline frivolousness, for as they speak they introduce a more serious treatment of motivation and the causes and occasions of human relationships. Despite the fact that these characters are part of the upper-crust, social-club level of society, the dimensions of their lives include great concern and uncertainty about genuinely human problems. The farcical mixup closing the play, together with the dialogue between the offstage characters at the final curtain, underscores the fact that while human beings may aspire to separateness and individuality, they can grow, mature, and live their lives only as integral members of society.

STANLEY KAUFFMANN (b. 1916)

The More the Merrier   1940

CAST OF CHARACTERS

> Emily Stringer
> Raphael Thumb
> Simon Latchflake
> Vesta Frimpole
> A Woman's Voice
> A Man's Voice

PLACE. *A room with people in it.*

TIME. *An evening of their lives.*

SCENE. *A room, furnished enough to suggest the real, bare enough to be fantastic. Immediately on the rising of the curtain we should get a definite hint that the place is as improbable as the play. There is a door back center, a door right, and a door left.*

RAPHAEL *is kneeling for the seated* EMILY, *anxiously awaiting an answer to the question he has just asked.*

> EMILY.   Yes.
> RAPHAEL.   You—you will?
> EMILY.   Yes.
> RAPHAEL.   Darling! [*He embraces her. They kiss.*] Darling!   5
> EMILY.   Sweetheart! [*They kiss again.*] Dear, you'd better get up. It's hard to kiss you, leaning over like this.
> RAPHAEL.   Sorry, honeybunch. [*He gets to his feet, leans over her, and kisses her again.*] How wonderful. How delicious. How unbelievable.
> EMILY.   [*Her hands on his cheek.*] Dear, silly Raphael. Didn't you know?
> RAPHAEL.   I could only hope, Emily!
> EMILY.   [*Leaning forward.*] Raphael. [*They kiss.*]   10
> RAPHAEL.   When shall it be?
> EMILY.   As soon as possible.

RAPHAEL. Tomorrow—tonight—

EMILY. [*Laughs.*] Oh, my rash, impetuous boy! No, not tomorrow; not for at least a month. I'll have to shop for a trousseau, and it will take three weeks to cry the banns°—

RAPHAEL. The banns?

EMILY. The banns are so cute—and then we'll have our wedding, a beautiful wedding. 15

RAPHAEL. A symbol of the beginning of a beautiful new life.

EMILY. Yes.

RAPHAEL. [*Thinking.*] Emily.

EMILY. [*Leaning forward with pouted lips, thinking he wants to kiss her.*] Raphael. [*He does nothing. She stares at him.*] Well.

RAPHAEL. Oh—excuse me— [*He is jarred out of his thoughtfulness and kisses her.*] I 20
was about to say: it will really be a new life, won't it?

EMILY. A wonderful new life.

RAPHAEL. Cut off from everyone else.

EMILY. Just us two.

RAPHAEL. Just us two. [*Thinking, again.*] Emily.

EMILY. [*Leaning forward.*] Raphael. 25

RAPHAEL. Oh—er—yes, dear. [*He kisses her.*] I was about to say: it will really be cut off from everyone else, won't it? I mean, to me that's always been the marvelous thing about marriage. It—it separates you from the rest of the world; gives you a life apart.

EMILY. It will be as if we were born again.

RAPHAEL. No old ties?

EMILY. No old ties, no old bonds. You and I together, apart from the world.

RAPHAEL. Oh—[*Clasping her hands.*] —oh, if you only knew how wonderful that 30
sounds. I have often thought to myself, "Raphael Thumb, you must make a fresh start. You are slipping. You must cut loose from the past. You must take a fresh grip." Our marriage will be that fresh grip, dear.

EMILY. A very fresh grip, sweetest. Raphael.

RAPHAEL. [*Leaning forward.*] Emily.

EMILY. Sit back, dear. I only want to ask you a question.

RAPHAEL. Oh. Of Course. [*He relaxes.*]

EMILY. Raphael, what is it you want to cut loose from? 35

RAPHAEL. My past.

EMILY. You have a past?

RAPHAEL. Haven't you?

EMILY. It all depends. Do you mean past with a small "p" or a capital "P"?

RAPHAEL. A small "p," I hope. 40

EMILY. Well, yes, I have.

RAPHAEL. So have I. But even more than forgetting the past, I want to lose all the things and people that disappoint me. You know, dear, when we're very young, we—we form ideals of friendship and living, and we're never quite able to adhere to them. Consequently, we're usually looking for a chance to wipe the slate clean and begin over again. That's what marriage is for. That's why I'm so happy.

EMILY. [*Leaning forward.*] Raphael.

RAPHAEL. [*Puzzled.*] Er—is it a question, dear—or—

---

13 *banns*: declarations made in church, usually Anglican, of an intent to marry. According to convention, the banns must be declared on three successive Sundays before a marriage is permitted.

EMILY. Not a question. [*They kiss.*] Our marriage will be just like pulling two straight, untangled threads out of a jumbled skein.   45

RAPHAEL. There are so many things I despise. Cigars, for instance. I'll never smoke cigars again.

EMILY. Lipstick, for another instance. I'll never use it again.

RAPHAEL. And the people I never want to see again! Susan Tellow . . . and Arnold Brunt.

EMILY. Lucy Fishpocket . . . and Seymour Prazey.

RAPHAEL. How about Bertie Moxpitch?   50

EMILY. And Adelaide Jarbus.

RAPHAEL. And Prissie Yemling.

EMILY. And Lester Warbeak.

RAPHAEL. Dorothy Hosepull!

EMILY. Chesterton Keith!   55

RAPHAEL. I hate them all.

EMILY. We'll never see them again. We'll be too busy being married.

RAPHAEL. Ah, my life feels purged already. Emily.

EMILY. [*Leaning forward.*] Raphael. [*They kiss.*]

RAPHAEL. We two. Alone.   60

EMILY. Sweetiekins.

RAPHAEL. Honey lamb.

[*Yes, they kiss again.*]

EMILY. Raphael, when did you discover that you loved me? Or was it gradual?

RAPHAEL. Oh, it was sudden. Very sudden. I remember the day exactly. It was just seven months ago at Sarah Bullhorn's birthday party. I glimpsed you coming through the doorway with a lemon sherbet in your hand, and—

EMILY. It couldn't have been lemon. I hate lemon.   65

RAPHAEL. Well, perhaps it was orange. But anyway, that was the moment.

EMILY. [*Hugging him.*] Sweetist Babykins!

RAPHAEL. My own! And when did you learn you loved me?

EMILY. The first time I danced with you. You're the only man I've ever known whose hands aren't hot and sweaty by eleven p.m.

RAPHAEL. Angelest!   70

EMILY. Ducky diddle!

[*Right. Another kiss.*]

RAPHAEL. And now we're each other's. Alone. Isn't love wonderful?

EMILY. Wonderful. It's like a cold shower or a swift swim. It simply kills everything mean and dirty in you and gives you a new outlook on life.

RAPHAEL. Us—

EMILY. Emily and Raphael.   75

RAPHAEL. Alone forever. [*A knock at the door back center.*] Who can that be?

EMILY. I haven't the faintest.

RAPHAEL. Shall I answer?

EMILY. [*After a moment's pouting deliberation.*] No, let him go away.

RAPHAEL. [*Sighing happily.*] Ah! Now, where were we?   80

EMILY. I think you were about to kiss me again.

RAPHAEL. That must have been it. Well— [*He leans forward. Another knock.*] He hasn't gone.

EMILY. Persistent wretch.

RAPHAEL. Hadn't I better answer?

EMILY. Not until you've kissed me again. 85

RAPHAEL. My ownest. My own, own darling.

EMILY. My heart's treasure.

[*They kiss. Simultaneously, the doorbell rings. It has a really hideous sound.*]

RAPHAEL. Drat that man!

EMILY. [*Reclining languidly, her back to the door.*] I suppose you'd better answer, dear.

RAPHAEL. Yes, lamikins. [*As he goes to the door, the bell rings again.*] All right, all right. Wait a moment, can't you? [*Muttering.*] People who don't know when other people want to 90 be alone— [*He opens the door. SIMON LATCHFLAKE stands there, his overcoat up around his ears, his hat down over his brows. You'd never have recognized him if we hadn't told you.*] Who is it?

SIMON. [*In a voice slightly muffled by his coat.*] Me. It's me.

RAPHAEL. [*Recognizing him.*] Oh, it's you, old man! Well, for goodness' sake, come in! However on earth did you know I was here? How did you find me? Come in.

[*SIMON enters. The door is shut behind him.*]

SIMON. Oh, I managed to find you.

RAPHAEL. I'm glad you did. Old man, congratulate me. This is the happiest day of my life. I want you to meet the girl who's just promised to be mine alone. Emily, darling.

EMILY. [*Going to them.*] Yes, dear.

RAPHAEL. Emily, I want you to meet my old friend— 95

EMILY. Simon Latchflake.

SIMON. Yes.

RAPHAEL. What?

SIMON. [*Nods.*] Simon Latchflake.

EMILY. Oh. 100

RAPHAEL. Well!

EMILY. [*Whispering.*] Is it you?

RAPHAEL. Yes, it's he; but how did you know?

EMILY. Oh, dear. Tonight of all nights.

SIMON. Rather disappointing, isn't it, Emily? 105

RAPHAEL. Emily! I say, would someone mind very much explaining just what— what—

SIMON. Shall I explain, Emily?

EMILY. Yes, you'd better explain—now.

RAPHAEL. Well, the first thing is—

SIMON. —to take off my coat. [*Which he does.*] 110

RAPHAEL. [*With a tinge of the sardonic.*] Oh, make yourself at home.

SIMON. Thank you.

RAPHAEL. Will you be seated?

SIMON. Not yet.

RAPHAEL. I shall sit. Emily? 115

EMILY. No, no. Hurry, Simon. Explain.

SIMON. Well, Raphael, I called at your home tonight to take you along to the club for a game of billiards. Your butler told me you'd gone to visit a lady, a lady you'd been visiting frequently, a Miss Emily Stringer. That was a jolt, I can tell you. Then when he told me how you'd been prancing and dancing around the house before you left, I knew you'd come here to propose. I followed at once and tried to arrive before it was too late. There's the whole thing in a nutshell.

RAPHAEL. That's only the nutshell. What I want to know is, what was the jolt. How did Emily come to know you and you her?

SIMON.   Raphael, old man, this is going to be a shock. Here goes. Not many
months ago, I stood in your shoes.   120

RAPHAEL.   What! You mean—

SIMON.   Yes. Miss Stringer was engaged to me.

RAPHAEL.   Wha—Em—Emily, is this true?

EMILY.   Yes, Raphael, too true.

RAPHAEL.   But I—I don't understand.   125

EMILY.   Raphael, dear, it was before I knew you.

RAPHAEL.   Oh, of course. But—phew! And we were going to shut out the rest of
the world. The first man who calls is my friend and your former fiancé. [*Sternly, to Simon.*]
Even so, how dare you presume to follow me and try to stop me?

SIMON.   Ah, Raphael, you don't know this woman as I know her.

RAPHAEL.   Stop! I won't hear a word against Emily.

EMILY.   Thank you, dear.

RAPHAEL.   Even though she was once engaged to you, I hold the highest opinion   130
of her.

EMILY.   *Thank* you dear.

RAPHAEL.   But what's the matter with her?

SIMON.   Well, take tonight for instance. Haven't you noticed something wrong already?

RAPHAEL.   [*Troubled.*] Why—er—

SIMON.   Fool! Utter fool!   135

RAPHAEL.   [*Worried by the fact that he may have missed something.*] I—I can't think of
anything—

SIMON.   I'm here. That's what's wrong. I'm here.

RAPHAEL.   That's very wrong. But it's not her fault.

SIMON.   Oh, yes, it is. And it's only a sample of what your future life will be. I know
what you were talking about before I came . . . how you were going to seclude yourself   140
from the world, how you were going to live alone. But, with this woman, that's impossible.
Her life is knotted up with thousands of other people. She has hundreds of close friends.
I'm only one of them. We keep coming. I came tonight.

RAPHAEL.   But you came—

SIMON.   Nevertheless, it's a sample.

RAPHAEL.   You mean, I'd never have—

SIMON.   With this woman, you'll never have what you want most from marriage;
you'll never have the chance to break loose from the old . . . you'll never begin anew.

EMILY.   What's the matter with having friends?

SIMON.   Nothing, if you like it. But for a man like Raphael, who has ideals, who's   145
dissatisfied with his past life and wants to begin a better one beginning with marriage,
you're the wrong woman.

RAPHAEL.   Really, you know, you—er—have no right—

SIMON.   Raphael, old man. I have the great right—the desire for your welfare.

EMILY.   Raphael, are you going to listen to him?

RAPHAEL.   Well, dear, you can't deny that he speaks from experience. I—I don't
exactly know.   150

EMILY.   You don't love me.

RAPHAEL.   Oh, I do, I do. But I—I really ought to think it over. You see, one of my
principal reasons for marrying—well, I must be sure.

SIMON.   That's all I want to hear. Raphael, old man, you're saved. Now you go right home and—

EMILY.   No, no!

RAPHAEL.   No, no!

SIMON.   Well, then, go inside and have a nice long talk with yourself.   155

RAPHAEL.   All right. [*Turning back tentatively.*] I wish I had something to smoke.

SIMON.   Have you promised to give up cigars? [*RAPHAEL nods.*] The usual thing. Here. [*He gives RAPHAEL a terribly long cigar.*] Take this, and don't come back till you've finished it.

RAPHAEL.   All right. [*He starts right, turns and looks back dubiously.*] All right. [*He exits.*]

EMILY.   [*Angrily.*] Well, he can think it over, if he wants to. I'm not to be bandied about this way. After he's finished that cigar, perhaps I won't be so anxious to take *him.*   160

SIMON.   Good.

EMILY.   And you—what a beast you are! Not satisfied to wound my pride a year ago, you come here tonight to interfere with my happiness.

SIMON.   [*Taking a mirror from his pocket.*] Here, you look terrible. It's the kissing that's done it, I suppose. Fix yourself up.

EMILY.   You mind your own— [*Glancing in the mirror.*] I wish I had a lipstick.

SIMON.   [*Taking one from his pocket.*] Here.

EMILY.   [*Coldly.*] Thank you. [*She makes the necessary adjustments and turns away. He*   165 *replaces the instruments of war in his pocket.*]

SIMON.   Do you know why I came here tonight and told those things to Raphael?

EMILY.   You said it was because—

SIMON.   That's not the reason. That was only to discourage him. I came because— well—I've reconsidered the matter. I want to marry you.

EMILY.   Indeed! Isn't that just too flattering!

SIMON.   Emily, I love you.   170

EMILY.   Liar.

SIMON.   Well, at least I want to marry you.

EMILY.   Why?

SIMON.   Oh, I'm sick of the old life: new girl every week, parties, dances, bright conversations. I want to settle down.   175

EMILY.   [*Mockingly.*] Oh, but you forget. I'm a girl who has thousands of ties with the past. There'd be no escape with me.

SIMON.   I could take you away.

EMILY.   From my habits?

SIMON.   From people. We'll make new habits.

EMILY.   No, thank you. I'll marry the man I love, the man who loves me. That's Raphael.   180

SIMON.   [*Cajolingly.*] You were engaged to me once.

EMILY.   Once was enough. Simon, you're a fool.

SIMON.   Am I?

EMILY.   For two reasons. First, for thinking you could discourage Raphael. Two minutes alone with him and I'll have him back again. Second, about this new life, turning over a new leaf.

SIMON.   Raphael believes it, too.

EMILY.   Yes, and I encourage him in it because it makes him happy to think about   185 it; but I don't really believe it. Our lives are too closely caught up with other people and other things ever to extract them completely. When I was a child, someone put chewing gum in my hair. Have you ever tried to take chewing gum out of your hair?

SIMON.   No!

EMILY.   Well, it can't be done. You have to cut off the hair.

SIMON.   Who cares. I say that a new life—

EMILY.   No. The chains of our old lives are linked and cross-linked. Pull one, pull all.   190

SIMON.   But, Emily—

EMILY.   The proof? See how entangled our lives are: mine and yours; yours and Raphael's; and Raphael's back again with mine.

SIMON.   Coincidence, mere coincidence. I happened to know you and Raphael happened to know you; and he and I happened to be friends. It—it just happened.

EMILY.   Everything just happens. Don't you see? And there's probably someone else whose life is tied up with all three of ours, although we don't know it. Nobody lives alone.

[*A knock at the door.*]

SIMON.   Don't answer.

EMILY.   Why not?   195

SIMON.   I have a horrible feeling that it's the person you just described, someone who knows all three of us.

EMILY.   [*Going to the door.*] We'll see.

SIMON.   Wait! Things are complicated enough! Don't make them worse! Wait!

[*But Emily has opened the door. VESTA FRIMPOLE is there.*]

EMILY.   Vesta!

VESTA.   Emily!   200

SIMON.   Vesta!

VESTA.   Simon!

EMILY.   Another thread.

SIMON.   I told you. [*To VESTA.*] How—how did you—

VESTA.   I phoned your home. They told me you were at this address. I didn't know   205 that Emily lived here. How are you, Emily, dear? I haven't seen you in ages.

EMILY.   I'm fine, dear. How are you?

VESTA.   Oh, I can't complain. Has Simon been proposing to you?

EMILY.   Yes.

VESTA.   Have you accepted him?

EMILY.   No.   210

VESTA.   Good. [*Kneeling to SIMON.*] Simon, will you marry me?

SIMON.   For Heaven's sake, get up.

VESTA.   Will you?

SIMON.   Oh, get up!

VESTA.   [*Rising.*] All right, dear, don't be angry. I only did it to prove that I'm sincere.   215

EMILY.   Shall I leave?

SIMON.   No! [*To VESTA.*] Why on earth do you want to marry me?

VESTA.   Oh, I don't know. I'm sort of tired of the old life; I want to turn over a new leaf—

EMILY.   [*Bored.*] Mother, mother, pin a rose on me.

SIMON.   For I'm to be Queen of the May.°   220

VESTA.   What?

---

221 *Queen of the May:* See Tennyson's "The May Queen" (1833).

SIMON.   We've been through all that.
EMILY.   It won't work.
VESTA.   But why—
SIMON.   Too many people!   225
EMILY.   Too many ties!
SIMON.   No clean starts!
EMILY.   Better make the best of it.
SIMON.   Chewing gum in the hair.
VESTA.   But I don't understand. Why couldn't we—   230
SIMON.   Everyone knows everyone else, and everyone's past is brought up into his
future every day of his life. That's why.
VESTA.   No, I still don't understand—

[*Raphael comes in right.*]

RAPHAEL.   This cigar is pretty bad. Do I have to—
VESTA.   Raphael Thumb!
RAPHAEL.   Vesta Frimpole!   235
EMILY.   What!
SIMON.   I'm not surprised.
RAPHAEL.   Emily, I might as well tell you the truth immediately. Vesta and I were
engaged once.
VESTA.   Indeed we were.
SIMON.   [*To Vesta.*] Now do you understand?   240
VESTA.   But—but—
RAPHAEL.   [*To Vesta.*] What a pleasant surprise to see you here.
VESTA.   Oh—thanks.
SIMON.   Cease the amenities. Raphael, have you made up your mind?
RAPHAEL.   Yes. The unexpected sight of Vesta has made it up for me.   245
EMILY.   [*Fearfully.*] Raphael—you mean—
RAPHAEL.   I mean I realize now that there is no escape from the past, and I shall
marry you anyway.
EMILY.   Beloved!
RAPHAEL.   Adored one!
                                                                                 250

[*They embrace.*]

VESTA.   [*Coyly.*] Simon!
SIMON.   No!
VESTA.   Simon—
SIMON.   No!
VESTA.   [*Wheedlingly.*] Simon—   255
SIMON.   Oh—

[*They embrace, too. Suddenly there is a knock on the door center.*]

RAPHAEL.   Don't open. [*He goes to the switch next to the door and plunges the room into
comparative darkness, leaving just enough light for us to see their faces. Then he looks through the
keyhole.*] Oh, it's no one you know. A friend of mine. Name of Bussbones.
ALL THE OTHERS.   Arthur Bussbones? [*They look at each other.*]
RAPHAEL.   [*Wearily.*] Oh, dear. [*Another glance through the keyhole.*] Look! A cab's

stopping at the corner! Someone's getting out. It looks like that Vetborough girl.

THE OTHERS. Virginia Vetborough? [*They look at each other again. More knocking at the door.*]

260

EMILY.   There's only one chance for us! Don't open the door! [*She goes to the door, quietly turns the key in the lock and hands it to* RAPHAEL.] Swallow the key!

RAPHAEL.   What?

EMILY.   Please?

SIMON.   For all of us. Please.

VESTA.   To lock out the past. It's our only chance.

RAPHAEL.   Oh—very well. [*He swallows the key.*] Hm. Not as bad as I expected. Now what?

265

SIMON.   We must escape. We have a locked door across our lives, separating us from the past. It's a headstart, small but nevertheless real. We must capitalize it. You take Emily that way; Vesta and I will go this way; and may we never meet again.

RAPHAEL.   Amen.

SIMON.   Come, Vesta dear.

VESTA.   [*Cooingly.*] All right, darling.

RAPHAEL.   [*In the shadows.*] Wait a minute, I'm Raphael. Hey Simon, you've got Emily.

270

SIMON.   Excuse me, Emily.

EMILY.   Quite all right.

SIMON.   [*Tentatively.*] Vesta?

VESTA.   Yes, dear.

SIMON.   Come, Vesta.

RAPHAEL.   Emily?

275

EMILY.   Yes, dear.

RAPHAEL.   Come, Emily.

[*One pair tiptoes to the right, the other to the left. More knocking at the door.*]

ONE PAIR.   [*Fingers to lips.*] Ssh!

THE OTHER PAIR.   [*Likewise.*] Ssh!

[*All exit. A woman's footsteps approach the front door. More knocking. Voices are heard outside.*]

280

A WOMAN.   Isn't anyone home?

A MAN.   I don't think so. I've been knocking several minutes. No one answers. By the way, madam, don't I know you? Aren't you Virginia Vetborough?

A WOMAN.   Why, Arthur Bussbones! Of all people!

A MAN.   Well, well!

285

[*They laugh.*]

A WOMAN.   And how have you been since we broke off our engagement?

[*They continue to chatter; but you have the idea.*]

CURTAIN

QUESTIONS

1.   Who are the two main characters in the play? What are they doing as the play opens? What beliefs do they reveal about love and marriage?

2.   Who is Simon? When does he enter? What is his interest in interrupting the con-

versation between Raphael and Emily?

3. What do Emily and Simon discuss after Raphael has left the stage? Why does Kauffmann have Emily discuss these matters with Simon when Raphael is not present?

4. In what way is the attitude toward marriage expressed by Vesta similar to the attitude of Simon? How are they "made for each other"?

5. Describe the language spoken by the characters in the play. What particular types of phrases do they use to indicate their affection? To what degree does this language seem out of date?

6. What changes or developments do the characters undergo in the course of the play, particularly with regard to attitudes about the possibilities of marriage?

7. What attitudes toward the material of the play and toward the audience are revealed in the stage directions? How seriously does the dramatist take the characters and their attitudes?

8. Why does the play end with the conversation of Virginia Vetborough and Arthur Bussbones after the major characters have left the stage?

GENERAL QUESTIONS

1. How generally true is Simon's claim, made about Emily, that our lives are "knotted up with thousands of other people" (speech 140), and Emily's point that "Our lives are too closely caught up with other people and other things ever to extract them completely" (speech 186)? How do these ideas relate to the intention of Raphael and Emily that their married life will give them a life "apart" from the lives of everyone else?

2. Describe the idea that "mere coincidence" and simple happenstance rather than decisiveness governs some of the most significant aspects of personal life (speeches 193, 194). What are the implications of this idea for relationships of love and marriage? Are love and marriage no more than accidental, the result of chance happenings? What is the role of deliberation in such circumstances of life?

3. How does this play illustrate the ways in which dramatists express ideas even through the substance of apparently light and "improbable" romantic farce?

BETTY KELLER, *TEA PARTY*

Betty Keller, a Canadian, has brought a wide variety of experience to her work for the theater, including such unlikely jobs as insurance adjuster, farmer, photographer's assistant, and prison matron. She served as a teacher for many theatrical workshops in Vancouver, including four years with Playhouse Holiday. She taught drama and theater at the Windsor Secondary School in North Vancouver until 1974, the year she published Improvisations in Creative Drama, *the collection of short plays and sketches from which* Tea Party *is selected. She also taught at Simon Fraser University and the University of British Columbia. She was the founder/ producer of the western Canadian writers festival and workshop program* The Festival of the Written Arts *from 1983 to 1994. In addition to her work in drama, she has written biographi-*

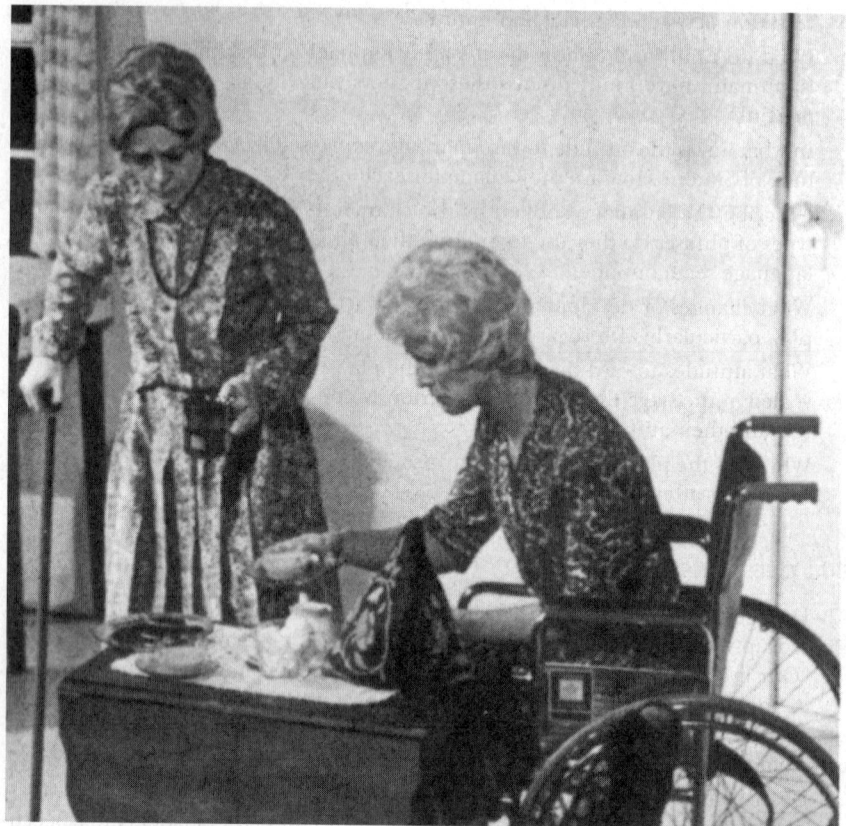

Alma (standing) and Hester (in the wheel chair) discuss what they will do if their newsboy comes in for some tea in Keller's *Tea Party*. The actors are Fran Burnside and Sandie McGinnis in the production by the Driftwood Players in February, 1987.

cal and historical works, including Pauline: A Biography of Pauline Johnson *(1982);* Black Wolf: The Life of Ernest Thompson Seton *(1984);* On the Shady Side: Vancouver 1886–1914 *(1986);* Sea Silver: Inside British Columbia's Salmon Farming Industry *(1996); and* Bright Seas and Pioneer Spirits: The Sunshine Coast *(1996).*

Brief as *Tea Party* is, it illustrates the power of drama to depict character and situation and to convey emotion. The main characters are two lonely elderly sisters who have outlived their friends and relatives and have no one except the people who occasionally come to their house to perform various services, such as delivering the paper and reading the meters. The sketch presents their plight deftly and succinctly, touching with great tenderness on the pathos of their loneliness.

Tea Party is too short to present difficult choices for the characters, and hence they hardly get the opportunity to go through the responses and changes that are found in full-length plays. Both Alma and Hester are individualized, however, as they carry on a minor controversy about names and dates from their long-vanished past. Beyond this, in Alma's last speech, which ends the dramatic sketch, one might find a hint of the awareness and recognition that we expect of round, developed characters. Even though the paperboy is not a speaking part, his unkindness to the sisters is shown clearly, and in this way Keller dramatizes the poignant situation of persons whom life has passed by. It is difficult to find a play that conveys so much of life and feeling in so short a span of time and action.

BETTY KELLER (b. 1930)

Tea Party   *1974*

CHARACTERS

> Alma Evans: *seventy-five years old, small and spare framed. Her clothing is simple but not outdated, her grey hair cut short and neat. She walks with the aid of a cane, although she would not be classed as a cripple.*
> Hester Evans: *seventy-nine years old. There is little to distinguish her physically from her sister, except perhaps a face a little more pinched and pain-worn. She sits in a wheelchair; but although her legs may be crippled, her mind certainly is not.*
> The Boy: *in his early teens, seen only fleetingly.*

SCENE. *The sitting room of the Evans sisters' home. The door to the street is on the rear wall Upstage Left,° a large window faces the street Upstage Center. On the right wall is the door to the kitchen; on the left, a door to the remainder of the house. Downstage Left is an easy chair, Upstage Right a sofa, Downstage Right a tea trolley. The room is crowded with the knickknacks gathered by its inhabitants in three-quarters of a century of living.*

[*At rise, ALMA is positioning HESTER's wheelchair Upstage Left. ALMA's cane is on HESTER's lap.*]

> HESTER.   That's it.

[*ALMA takes her cane from HESTER. They both survey the room.*]

> ALMA.   I think I'll sit on the sofa . . . at the far end.
> HESTER.   Yes. That will be cosy. Then he can sit on this end between us.

[*ALMA sits on the Downstage Right end of the sofa. They both study the effect.*]

> ALMA.   But then he's too close to the door, Hester!

[*HESTER nods, absorbed in the problem.*]

> ALMA.   [*Moving to the Upstage Left end of sofa.*] Then I'd better sit here.
> HESTER.   But now he's too far away from me, Alma.   5

[*ALMA stands; both of them study the room again.*]

> ALMA.   But if I push the tea trolley in front of you, he'll have to come to you, won't he?
> HESTER.   Oh, all right, Alma. You're sure it's today?
> ALMA.   [*Pushing the tea trolley laden with cups and napkins, etc. to HESTER.*] The first Thursday of the month.
> HESTER.   You haven't forgotten the chocolate biscuits?°
> ALMA.   No dear, they're on the plate. I'll bring them in with the tea. [*Goes to the*   10

Upstage Left: To visualize stage locations, assume that the stage directions are described from the viewpoint of an actor facing the audience. Thus "Right" is actually to the left of the audience, and "Left" is right. "Downstage" refers to the front of the stage, while "Upstage" is the back. The terms *down* and *up* were established at a time when stages were tilted toward the audience, so that spectators at floor level could have as complete a view as possible of the entire stage.   10 *chocolate biscuits:* chocolate cookies.

window, peering up the street to the Right.]

HESTER. And cocoa?

ALMA. I remembered.

HESTER. You didn't remember for Charlie's visit.

ALMA. Charlie drinks tea, Hester. I didn't make cocoa for him because he drinks tea.

HESTER. Oh, He didn't stay last time anyway.

ALMA. It was a busy day. . . .

HESTER. Rushing in and out like that. I was going to tell him about father and the *Bainbridge* . . . and he didn't stay.

ALMA. What about the *Bainbridge?*

HESTER. Her maiden voyage out of Liverpool . . . when father was gone three months and we thought he'd gone down with her.

ALMA. That wasn't the *Bainbridge.*

HESTER. Yes, it was. It was the *Bainbridge.* I remember standing on the dock in the snow when she finally came in. That was the year I'd begun first form, and I could spell out the letters on her side.

ALMA. It was her sister ship, the *Heddingham.*

HESTER. The *Bainbridge.* You were too young to remember. Let's see, the year was . . .

ALMA. Mother often told the story. It was the *Heddingham* and her engine broke down off Cape Wrath beyond the Hebrides.

HESTER. It was 1902 and you were just four years old.

ALMA. The *Heddingham,* and she limped into port on January the fifth.

HESTER. January the fourth just after nine in the morning, and we stood in the snow and watched the *Bainbridge* nudge the pier, and I cried and the tears froze on my cheeks.

ALMA. The *Heddingham.*

HESTER. Alma, mother didn't cry, you know. I don't think she ever cried. My memory of names and places is sharp so that I don't confuse them as some others I could mention, but sometimes I can't remember things like how people reacted. But I remember that day. There were tears frozen on my cheeks but mother didn't cry.

ALMA. [*Nodding.*] She said he didn't offer a word of explanation. Just marched home beside her.

HESTER. [*Smiling.*] He never did say much . . . . Is he coming yet?

ALMA. No, can't be much longer though. Almost half past four.

HESTER. Perhaps you'd better bring in the tea. Then it will seem natural.

ALMA. Yes dear, I know. [*Exits out door Upstage Right.*] Everything's ready.

HESTER. What will you talk about?

ALMA. [*Re-entering with the teapot*] I thought perhaps . . . [*Carefully putting down the teapot.*] . . . perhaps brother George!

HESTER. And the torpedo? No, Alma, he's not old enough for that story!

ALMA. He's old enough to know about courage. I thought I'd show him the medal, too. [*She goes to the window, peers both ways worriedly, then carries on towards the kitchen.*]

HESTER. Not yet? He's late to-night. You're sure it's today?

ALMA. He'll come. It's the first Thursday. [*Exit.*]

HESTER. You have his money?

ALMA. [*Returning with the plate of biscuits.*] I've got a twenty dollar bill, Hester.

HESTER. Alma!

ALMA.   Well, we haven't used that one on him. It was Dennis, the last one, who always had change. We could get two visits this way, Hester.   45

HESTER.   Maybe Dennis warned him to carry change for a twenty.

ALMA.   It seemed worth a try. [*Goes to the window again.*] Are you going to tell him about the *Heddingham?*

HESTER.   The *Bainbridge.* Maybe . . . or maybe I'll tell him about the day the Great War ended. Remember, Alma, all the noise, the paper streamers . . .

ALMA.   And father sitting silent in his chair.

HESTER.   It wasn't the same for him with George gone. Is he coming yet?

ALMA.   No dear, maybe he's stopped to talk somewhere. [*Looking to the right.*] . . .   50
No . . . no, there he is, on the Davis' porch now!

HESTER.   I'll pour then. You get the cocoa, Alma.

ALMA.   [*Going out.*] It's all ready, I just have to add hot water.

HESTER.   Don't forget the marshmallows!

ALMA.   [*Reappearing*] Oh, Hester, what if he comes in and just sits down closest to the door? He'll never stay!   55

HESTER.   You'll have to prod him along. For goodness sakes, Alma, get his cocoa!

[*ALMA disappears.*]

HESTER.   He must be nearly here. He doesn't go to the Leschynskis, and the Black-burns don't get home till after six.

ALMA.   [*Returning with the cocoa.*] Here we are! Just in . . .

[*The BOY passes the window. There is a slapping sound as the newspaper lands on the porch.*]

[*ALMA and HESTER look at the door and wait, hoping to hear a knock, but they both know the truth. Finally, ALMA goes to the door, opens it and looks down at the newspaper.*]

ALMA.   He's gone on by.

HESTER.   You must have had the day wrong.

ALMA.   No, he collected at the Davis'.   60

HESTER.   [*After a long pause.*] He couldn't have forgotten us.

ALMA.   [*Still holding the cocoa, she turns from the door.*] He's collecting at the Kerighan's now. [*She closes the door and stands forlornly.*]

HESTER.   Well, don't stand there with that cocoa! You look silly. [*ALMA brings the cocoa to the tea trolley.*] Here's your tea. [*ALMA takes the cup, sits on the Upstage Left end of the sofa. There is a long silence.*]

HESTER.   I think I'll save that story for the meter man.

ALMA.   The *Heddingham?*   65

HESTER.   The *Bainbridge.*

ALMA.   [*After a pause.*] They don't read the meters for two more weeks.

SLOW BLACKOUT

QUESTIONS

1.   What is the play's major conflict? The minor conflict?

2.   Why do the two sisters discuss their seating arrangements for the paperboy? How do we learn that they have made these arrangements before?

3.　What does Alma's plan for the twenty-dollar bill show about her? What does the discussion about both the money and the paperboys indicate about their own self-awareness?

4.　How does controversy about the names *Bainbridge* and *Heddingham* help you understand the two sisters?

GENERAL QUESTIONS

1.　How does Keller's description of the sets aid you in understanding the action? The normal tasks of the women? From the setting of this play, what are your conclusions about the relationship of objects and spatial arrangements to the action and development of drama?

2.　Consider the women, particularly with regard to their age. In the light of their health and their isolation, how does *Tea Party* present the circumstances of the aged? How can the play be constructed as a sociological/political argument, with the elderly as the focus?

EUGENE O'NEILL, *BEFORE BREAKFAST*

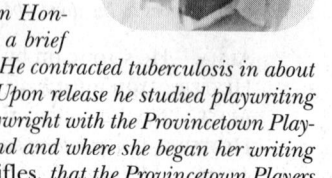

Eugene O'Neill is one of America's great playwrights. He wrote more than forty plays and won three Pulitzer Prizes. He is still the only American dramatist to have received the Nobel Prize for literature (1936).

O'Neill was born in New York, the son of a well-known actor, and was educated sporadically as his parents traveled from city to city on theatrical tours. Eventually he studied at Princeton, but he left to go to work, first in a mail-order house and then in Honduras, where he engaged in prospecting. He then began a brief career as a seaman, traveling on both sides of the Atlantic. He contracted tuberculosis in about 1912, and while in a sanitarium he began to write plays. Upon release he studied playwriting at Harvard, but by 1916 he had left to try his luck as a playwright with the Provincetown Players, the same company that Susan Glaspell had helped found and where she began her writing career. It was in 1916, the same year that Glaspell wrote Trifles, *that the Provincetown Players produced O'Neill's first drama,* Bound East for Cardiff.

O'Neill maintained a close connection with the Provincetown Players for several years, providing them with ten one-act plays between 1916 and 1920. Among these were Thirst *(1916),* Before Breakfast *(1916),* Fog *(1917),* The Long Voyage Home *(1917),* Ile *(1917), and* The Rope *(1917). His later (and longer) works include* The Emperor Jones *(1920),* Anna Christie *(1921),* Desire Under the Elms *(1924),* Strange Interlude *(1928),* Mourning Becomes Electra *(1931), and* The Iceman Cometh *(1946). O'Neill also wrote an autobiographical play,* Long Day's Journey into Night *(1936), that at his request was withheld until after his death. Staged on Broadway in 1956, it received the Pulitzer Prize in drama (O'Neill's third Pulitzer); it was later made into a film starring Katherine Hepburn.*

Before Breakfast, though one of O'Neill's earliest plays, shows his characteristic control of point of view, conflict, character, and setting. The play was first staged in December 1916 by the Provincetown Players in New York City's Greenwich Village (where Christopher Street, the address of the Rowlands' apartment, is located). The play contains little action, and yet it is charged with conflict. The plot is simple and straightforward—a wife onstage berates her offstage husband for twenty minutes. The conflict between them is long-standing and bitter, and it is resolved in the play's horrifying conclusion.

Above all, *Before Breakfast* illustrates O'Neill's skillful control over the dramatic point of view. By giving Mrs. Rowland every word spoken on the stage, O'Neill causes the audience to

Mrs. Rowland (Lona Leigh) attends to the coffee in the 2001 Provincetown Playhouse, New York City, production of *Before Breakfast*, directed by Stephen Kennedy Murphy, lights by Matthew E. Adelson, and set by Roger Hanna.

understand everything as it is filtered through her mind. Indeed, the play is a bravura piece for a gifted actress. Because Mrs. Rowland dominates the stage so completely, it is tempting to see her character as one of constantly nagging spitefulness. It is to O'Neill's credit, however, that she is not without basic strength, and that her bitterness is not without cause. Alfred, the unseen and unheard offstage husband, has contributed to their estranged relationship.

Of particular note in indicating the impasse that the characters have reached are O'Neill's extensive stage directions describing the setting. We learn that the Rowlands' flat is in Greenwich Village, the traditional New York home of artists, poets, and actors. On the one hand, therefore, the flat suggests Alfred's artistic aspirations, but on the other, the poverty of the surroundings indicates the sad truth that such dreams cannot be sustained unless someone pays the rent.

The language of Mrs. Rowland, the only speaking character in the play, indicates both her lack of education and her intense dissatisfaction. Phrases such as "I got," "like I was," "liable" for "likely," and "sewing my fingers off" suggest that her knowledge of language has not been derived from education and study. Her speech also suggests the social gulf that originally separated her from Alfred, a gulf that they tried to bridge in their marriage but which now has opened up irretrievably. A number of other phrases embody the taunts that Mrs. Rowland directs at Alfred ("pawn, pawn, pawn," "like a man," "a fine life," "in trouble," etc.).

EUGENE O'NEILL (1888–1953)

Before Breakfast ✂ 1916

CHARACTERS

 Mrs. Rowland, *the wife*
 Mr. Alfred Rowland, *the husband*

SCENE. *A small room serving both as kitchen and dining room in a flat on Christopher Street, New York City. In the rear, to the right, a door leading to the outer hallway. On the left of the doorway, a sink, and a two-burner gas stove. Over the stove, and extending to the left wall, a wooden closet for dishes, etc. On the left, two windows looking out on a fire escape where several potted plants are dying of neglect. Before the windows, a table covered with oilcloth. Two cane-bottomed chairs are placed by the table. Another stands against the wall to the right of door in rear. In the right wall, rear, a doorway leading into a bedroom. Farther forward, different articles of a man's and a woman's clothing are hung on pegs. A clothes line is strung from the left corner, rear, to the right wall, forward.*

It is about eight-thirty in the morning of a fine, sunshiny day in the early fall.

MRS. ROWLAND enters from the bedroom, yawning, her hands still busy putting the finishing touches on a slovenly toilet by sticking hairpins into her hair which is bunched up in a drab-colored mass on top of her round head. She is of medium height and inclined to a shapeless stoutness, accentuated by her formless blue dress, shabby and worn. Her face is characterless, with small regular features and eyes of a nondescript blue. There is a pinched expression about her eyes and nose and her weak, spiteful mouth. She is in her early twenties but looks much older.

She comes to the middle of the room and yawns, stretching her arms to their full length. Her drowsy eyes stare about the room with the irritated look of one to whom a long sleep has not been a long rest. She goes wearily to the clothes hanging on the right and takes an apron from a hook. She ties it about her waist, giving vent to an exasperated "damn" when the knot fails to obey her clumsy fingers. Finally gets it tied and goes slowly to the gas stove and lights one burner. She fills the coffee pot at the sink and sets it over the flame. Then slumps down into a chair by the table and puts a hand over her forehead as if she were suffering from headache. Suddenly her face brightens as though she had remembered something, and she casts a quick glance at the dish closet; then looks sharply at the bedroom door and listens intently for a moment or so.

MRS. ROWLAND. [*In a low voice.*] Alfred! Alfred! [*There is no answer from the next room and she continues suspiciously in a louder tone.*] You needn't pretend you're asleep. [*There is no reply to this from the bedroom, and, reassured, she gets up from her chair and tiptoes cautiously to the dish closet. She slowly opens one door, taking great care to make no noise, and slides out, from their hiding place behind the dishes, a bottle of Gordon gin and a glass. In doing so she disturbs the top dish, which rattles a little. At this sound she starts guiltily and looks with sulky defiance at the doorway to the next room.*]

[*Her voice trembling.*] Alfred!

[*After a pause, during which she listens for any sound, she takes the glass and pours out a large drink and gulps it down; then hastily returns the bottle and glass to their hiding place. She closes the closet door with the same care as she had opened it, and, heaving a great sigh of relief, sinks down into her chair again. The large dose of alcohol she has taken has an almost immediate effect. Her features become more animated, she seems to gather energy, and she looks at the bedroom door with a hard, vindictive smile on her lips. Her eyes glance quickly about the room and are fixed on a man's coat and vest which hang from a hook at right. She moves stealthily over to the open doorway and stands there, out of sight of anyone inside, listening for any movement.*]

[*Calling in a half-whisper.*] Alfred!

[*Again there is no reply. With a swift movement she takes the coat and vest from the hook and returns with them to her chair. She sits down and takes the various articles out of each pocket but quickly puts them back again. At last, in the inside pocket of the vest, she finds a letter.*]

[*Looking at the handwriting—slowly to herself.*] Hmm! I knew it.

[*She opens the letter and reads it. At first her expression is one of hatred and rage, but as she goes on to the end it changes to one of triumphant malignity. She remains in deep thought for a moment, staring before her, the letter in her hands, a cruel smile on her lips. Then she puts the letter back in the pocket of the vest, and still careful not to awaken the sleeper, hangs the clothes up again on the same hook, and goes to the bedroom door and looks in.*]

[*In a loud, shrill voice.*] Alfred! [*Still louder.*] Alfred! [*There is a muffled, yawning groan from the next room.*] Don't you think it's about time you got up? Do you want to stay in bed all day? [*Turning around and coming back to her chair.*] Not that I've got any doubts about your being lazy enough to stay in bed forever. [*She sits down and looks out of the window, irritably.*] Goodness knows what time it is. We haven't even got any way of telling the time since you pawned your watch like a fool. The last valuable thing we had, and you knew it. It's been nothing but pawn, pawn, pawn, with you—anything to put off getting a job, anything to get out of going to work like a man.

[*She taps the floor with her foot nervously, biting her lips.*]

[*After a short pause.*] Alfred! Get up, do you hear me? I want to make that bed before I go out. I'm sick of having this place in a continual muss on your account. [*With a certain vindictive satisfaction.*] Not that we'll be here long unless you manage to get some money some place. Heaven knows I do my part—and more—going out to sew every day while you play the gentleman and loaf around bar rooms with that good-for-nothing lot of artists from the Square.°

[*A short pause during which she plays nervously with a cup and saucer on the table.*]

And where are you going to get money, I'd like to know? The rent's due this week and you know what the landlord is. He won't let us stay a minute over our time. You say you *can't* get a job. That's a lie and you know it. You never even look for one. All you do is moon around all day writing silly poetry and stories that no one will buy—and no wonder they won't. I notice I can always get a position, such as it is; and it's only that which keeps us from starving to death.

[*Gets up and goes over to the stove—looks into the coffee pot to see if the water is boiling; then comes back and sits down again.*]

You'll have to get money to-day some place. I can't do it all, and I won't do it all. You've got to come to your senses. You've got to beg, borrow, or steal it somewheres. [*With a contemptuous laugh.*] But where, I'd like to know? You're too proud to beg, and/you've borrowed the limit, and you haven't the nerve to steal.

[*After a pause—getting up angrily.*] Aren't you up yet, for heaven's sake? It's just like you to go to sleep again, or pretend to. [*She goes to the bedroom door and looks in.*] Oh, you are up. Well, it's about time. You needn't look at me like that. Your airs don't fool me a bit any more. I know you too well—better than you think I do—you and your goings-on. [*Turning away from the door—meaningly.*] I know a lot of things, my dear. Never mind what I know, now. I'll tell you before I go, you needn't worry. [*She comes to the middle of the room and stands there, frowning.*]

[*Irritably.*] Hmm! I suppose I might as well get breakfast ready—not that there's anything much to get. [*Questioningly.*] Unless you have some money? [*She pauses for an*

6 *Square:* Washington Square, at the center of Greenwich Village.

answer from the next room which does not come.] Foolish question! [*She gives a short, hard laugh.*] I ought to know you better than that by this time. When you left here in such a huff last night I knew what would happen. You can't be trusted for a second. A nice condition you came home in! The fight we had was only an excuse for you to make a beast of yourself. What was the use pawning your watch if all you wanted with the money was to waste it in buying drink?

[*Goes over to the dish closet and takes out plates, cups, etc., while she is talking.*]

Hurry up! It don't take long to get breakfast these days, thanks to you. All we got this morning is bread and butter and coffee; and you wouldn't even have that if it wasn't for me sewing my fingers off. [*She slams the loaf of bread on the table with a bang.*]

The bread's stale. I hope you'll like it. *You* don't deserve any better, but I don't see why *I* should suffer.

[*Going over to the stove.*] The coffee'll be ready in a minute, and you needn't expect me to wait for you.

[*Suddenly with great anger.*] What on earth are you doing all this time? [*She goes over to the door and looks in.*] Well, you're *almost* dressed at any rate. I expected to find you back in bed. That'd be just like you. How awful you look this morning! For heaven's sake, shave! You're disgusting! You look like a tramp. No wonder no one will give you a job. I don't blame them—when you don't even look halfway decent. [*She goes to the stove.*] There's plenty of hot water right here. You've got no excuse. [*Gets a bowl and pours some of the water from the coffee pot into it.*] Here.

[*He reaches his hand into the room for it. It is a sensitive hand with slender fingers. It trembles and some of the water spills on the floor.*]

[*Tauntingly.*] Look at your hand tremble! You'd better give up drinking. You can't   15
stand it. It's just your kind that get the D.T.'s. *That would be* the last straw! [*Looking down at the floor.*] Look at the mess you've made of this floor—cigarette butts and ashes all over the place. Why can't you put them on a plate? No, you wouldn't be considerate enough to do that. You never think of me. You don't have to sweep the room and that's all you care about.

[*Takes the broom and commences to sweep viciously, raising a cloud of dust. From the inner room comes the sound of a razor being stropped.*] °

[*Sweeping.*] Hurry up! It must be nearly time for me to go. If I'm late I'm liable to lose my position, and then I couldn't support you any longer. [*As an afterthought she adds sarcastically.*] And then you'd have to go to work or something dreadful like that. [*Sweeping under the table.*] What I want to know is whether you're going to look for a job today or not. You know your family won't help us any more. They've had enough of you, too. [*After a moment's silent sweeping.*] I'm about sick of all this life. I've a good notion to go home, if I wasn't too proud to let them know what a failure you've been—you, the millionaire Rowland's only son, the Harvard graduate, the poet, the catch of the town— Huh! [*With bitterness.*] There wouldn't be many of them now envy my catch if they knew the truth. What has our marriage been, I'd like to know? Even before your *millionaire* father died owing everyone in the world money, you certainly never wasted any of your

---

15 S.D. *stropped:* Alfred is using a leather strap to sharpen a straight razor, the kind barbers still use, with a very sharp steel blade that is hinged to a handle.

time on your wife. I suppose you thought I'd ought to be glad you were *honorable* enough to marry me—after getting me into trouble. You were ashamed of me with your fine friends because my father's only a grocer, that's what you were. At least he's honest, which is more than any one could say about yours. [*She is sweeping steadily toward the door. Leans on her broom for a moment.*]

You hoped every one'd think you'd been forced to marry me, and pity you, didn't you? You didn't hesitate much about telling me you loved me, and making me believe your lies, before it happened, did you? You made me think you didn't want your father to buy me off as he tried to do. I know better now. I haven't lived with you all this time for nothing. [*Somberly.*] It's lucky the poor thing was born dead, after all. What a father you'd have been!

[*Is silent, brooding moodily for a moment—then she continues with a sort of savage joy.*]

But I'm not the only one who's got you to thank for being unhappy. There's one other, at least, and *she* can't hope to marry you now. [*She puts her head into the next room.*] How about Helen? [*She starts back from the doorway, half frightened.*]

Don't look at me that way! Yes, I read her letter. What about it? I got a right to. I'm your wife. And I know all there is to know, so don't lie. You needn't stare at me so. You can't bully me with your superior airs any longer. Only for me you'd be going without breakfast this very morning. [*She sets the broom back in the corner—whiningly.*] You never did have any gratitude for what I've done. [*She comes to the stove and puts the coffee into the pot.*] The coffee's ready. I'm not going to wait for you. [*She sits down in her chair again.*]

[*After a pause—puts her hand to her head—fretfully.*] My head aches so this morning.   20
It's a shame I've got to go to work in a stuffy room all day in my condition. And I would-n't if you were half a man. By rights I ought to be lying on my back instead of you. You know how sick I've been this last year; and yet you object when I take a little something to keep up my spirits. You even didn't want me to take that tonic I got at the drug store. [*With a hard laugh.*] I know you'd be glad to have me dead and out of your way; then you'd be free to run after all these silly girls that think you're such a wonderful, misun-derstood person—this Helen and the others. [*There is a sharp exclamation of pain from the next room.*]

[*With satisfaction.*] There! I knew you'd cut yourself. It'll be a lesson to you. You know you oughtn't to be running around nights drinking with your nerves in such an awful shape. [*She goes to the door and looks in.*]

What makes you so pale? What are you staring at yourself in the mirror that way for? For goodness sake, wipe that blood off your face! [*With a shudder.*] It's horrible. [*In relieved tones.*] There, that's better. I never could stand the sight of blood. [*She shrinks back from the door a little.*] You better give up trying and go to a barber shop. Your hand shakes dreadfully. Why do you stare at me like that? [*She turns away from the door.*] Are you still mad at me about that letter? [*Defiantly.*] Well, I had a right to read it. I'm your wife. [*She comes to the chair and sits down again. After a pause.*]

I knew all the time you were running around with someone. Your lame excuses about spending the time at the library didn't fool me. Who is this Helen, anyway? One of those artists? Or does she write poetry, too? Her letter sounds that way. I'll bet she told you your things were the best ever, and you believed her, like a fool. Is she young and pretty? I was young and pretty, too, when you fooled me with your fine, poetic talk; but life with you would soon wear anyone down. What I've been through!

[*Goes over and takes the coffee off the stove.*] Breakfast is ready. [*With a contemptuous glance.*] Breakfast! [*Pours out a cup of coffee for herself and puts the pot on the table.*] Your coffee'll be cold. What are you doing—still shaving, for heaven's sake? You'd better give it up. One of these mornings you'll give yourself a serious cut. [*She cuts off bread and butters it. During the following speeches she eats and sips her coffee.*]

I'll have to run as soon as I've finished eating. One of us has got to work. [*Angrily.*]   25
Are you going to look for a job to-day or aren't you? I should think some of your fine friends would help you, if they really think you're so much. But I guess they just like to hear you talk. [*Sits in silence for a moment.*]

I'm sorry for this Helen, whoever she is. Haven't you got any feelings for other people? What will her family say? I see she mentions them in her letter. What is she going to do—have the child—or go to one of those doctors? That's a nice thing, I must say. Where can she get the money? Is she rich? [*She waits for some answer to this volley of questions.*]

Hmm! You won't tell me anything about her, will you? Much I care. Come to think of it, I'm not so sorry for her after all. She knew what she was doing. She isn't any schoolgirl, like I was, from the looks of her letter. Does she know you're married? Of course, she must. All your friends know about your unhappy marriage. I know they pity you, but they don't know my side of it. They'd talk different if they did.

[*Too busy eating to go on for a second or so.*]

This Helen must be a fine one, if she knew you were married. What does she expect, then? That I'll divorce you and let her marry you? Does she think I'm crazy enough for that—after all you've made me go through? I guess not! And you can't get a divorce from me and you know it. No one can say *I've* ever done anything wrong. [*Drinks the last of her cup of coffee.*]

She deserves to suffer, that's all I can say. I'll tell you what I think; I think your Helen is no better than a common street-walker, that's what I think. [*There is a stifled groan of pain from the next room.*]

Did you cut yourself again? Serves you right. [*Gets up and takes off her apron.*] Well,   30
I've got to run along. [*Peevishly.*] This is a fine life for me to be leading! I won't stand for your loafing any longer. [*Something catches her ear and she pauses and listens intently.*] There! You've overturned the water all over everything. Don't say you haven't. I can hear it dripping on the floor. [*A vague expression of fear comes over her face.*] Alfred! Why don't you answer me?

[*She moves slowly toward the room. There is the noise of a chair being overturned and something crashes heavily to the floor. She stands, trembling with fright.*]

Alfred! Alfred! Answer me! What is it you knocked over? Are you still drunk?
[*Unable to stand the tension a second longer she rushes to the door of the bedroom.*]
Alfred!

[*She stands in the doorway looking down at the floor of the inner room, transfixed with horror. Then she shrieks wildly and runs to the other door, unlocks it and frenziedly pulls it open, and runs shrieking madly into the outer hallway.*]

[*The curtain falls.*]

QUESTIONS

1. What does the setting tell you about the Rowlands?
2. How is Mrs. Rowland described in the opening stage directions? How does O'Neill use adjectives to shape your initial response to her? How does the rest of the play sustain or alter this image?

3.   How does Mrs. Rowland speak to Alfred? What does she complain about? What does she accuse Alfred of being and doing?

4.   What happened during Mrs. Rowland's premarital affair with Alfred? Why didn't she let Alfred's father "buy her off"?

5.   Where is the play's crisis? Which character comes to a crisis? What leads you to conclude that the character and play have reached a crisis?

6.   Mrs. Rowland precipitates the climax by discussing Alfred's affair. What do we learn about Helen? What pushes Alfred over the edge?

GENERAL QUESTIONS

1.   How does the setting define the characters, their relationship, and their life? What details of setting are most significant?

2.   Is Mrs. Rowland flat or round? Static or dynamic? Individualized or stereotyped? Why does she have no first name?

3.   Why is Alfred Rowland kept off stage (except for his hand) and given no dialogue? How does this affect the play?

4.   Alfred is presented from his wife's point of view. How accurate is this portrait? To what degree does Alfred justify his wife's accusations?

5.   Why does O'Neill present the history of Alfred's family and his relationship with Mrs. Rowland out of chronological order? What is the effect of this method of presentation?

THE WAKEFIELD MASTER, *THE SECOND SHEPHERDS' PLAY* *(SECUNDA PAGINA PASTORUM)*

Wakefield is a town in Yorkshire in northern England, about forty miles south of York. In the fourteenth century York was a major city and also the religious center of the area because the archbishopric and cathedral of York were established there. By contrast, Wakefield was insignificant. Anyone from Wakefield wanting to see the springtime Corpus Christi plays[4] had to journey over poor or nonexistent roads to York, for little of importance was happening in Wakefield. By the fifteenth century, however, Wakefield gained prominence in woolen manufacture. Eventually the Wakefield tradesmen became prosperous enough to establish and support their own cycle of Corpus Christi plays. They apparently began by borrowing a number of plays from the York cycle, and to this core of plays the local writers soon added their own versions.

Most importantly, early in the history of the Wakefield cycles, a master dramatist, the "Wakefield Master," emerged. He wrote six of the surviving Wakefield plays in their entirety. These are The Killing of Abel, Noah, The First Shepherds' Play, The Second Shepherds' Play, The Slaughter of the Innocents *(featuring the ranting of King Herod), and* The Buffeting *(or* Coliphizatio*). He also wrote major portions of two others,* The Scourging *(or* Flagellatio*) and* The Last Judgment. *No factual biographical material exists about the Wakefield Master. Historians speculate that he flourished between 1425 and 1450. He was probably a priest or monk, for he demonstrates knowledge not only of the Vulgate Bible but also of church traditions.*

[4]See pp. 1178–79.

Certainly the Wakefield Master had a powerful imagination, as *The Second Shepherds' Play* shows. He developed his plot from the second chapter of Luke, which contains the brief story of the angel appearing to the shepherds and of the Christ child being wrapped in swaddling clothes and lying in a manger. Luke contains little detail beyond this. But the Master freely expands this text. He brings the shepherds to life by presenting the circumstances of their lives, their complaints and grievances, and their hardships. As a part of his realization of the shepherds he presents a bold and probably risky satiric attack on the political and social conditions of his day. Even bolder is the Mak episode, which the Master derived from an earlier medieval story. The climax of the episode, culminating at Jill's cradle containing the stolen sheep, is a parodic parallel of the holy manger scene with which the play concludes. Although Mak has been driven by circumstances to petit larceny, the Master gives him realistic traits of cheekiness, ingenuity, adaptability, hypocrisy, and religious uncertainty and devotion.

One of the Master's major characteristics is his use of realistic and frank diction, as can be seen in the boisterous language with which the shepherds abuse Mak when they first meet him. But the Master also shows unusual understanding and sensitivity, which he brings out in the First Shepherd's complaint and in Mak's touching prayer when he first appears on the stage. The tone of the concluding speeches by Mary and the shepherds is one of simple devotion, in keeping with the lives of the main characters. Clearly the Master knew and understood the people who formed his audience, and in his dramatization he demonstrated that biblical characters were people just like them, with the same foibles and troubles, likewise in need of the salvation promised by their religion.

The Wakefield Master was a poet and metrist of consummate skill. He wrote in a unique nine-line stanza that identifies his writing throughout the Wakefield cycle. Each stanza begins with four 4-beat lines rhyming both internally and externally (*a b, a b, a b, a b*; these can be considered as eight lines rather than four). The fifth line of the stanza rhymes with the ninth line, and three separately rhyming short lines appear as lines 6, 7, and 8. Although the most important element of the longer lines is the stressed beat, many beats are formed around triple rhythms, mostly anapests, but also including dactyls and amphibrachs (see Chapter 19). In the shorter lines the Master often employs iambs and trochees. He also uses alliteration (examples: "to grant ere he go," "I am set for to spin," etc.) but does not do so systematically.

In the following version for today's students, the original stanzaic form has been maintained. The internal rhymes of the first four lines (the original *a* rhymes) have been dropped, but, when possible, the Master's end rhymes have been retained (the original *b* rhymes). Linguistic changes since the fifteenth century have made it impossible to use the Master's rhyming words, but an attempt has been made to transfer a number of the original internal rhymes to the line endings (with a consequent shift of the ideas in the lines). Barring this solution, new rhyming words have been introduced, consistent with the subject matter of the individual stanzas.

Much of the Master's fifteenth-century language has gone out of use, and much of it is compressed and difficult, so that the original text requires extensive glossing and explanatory footnotes. To avoid such notes, and also to make the present text as self-sufficient as possible, a small number of lines have been extended to five and sometimes to six beats, and many of the shorter lines have been expanded. The footnotes explain matters that modernization cannot accommodate. The list of characters is expanded here, along with the addition of explanatory stage directions [all within brackets]. The goal of these changes is to attempt to make the play as lively for modern readers as it was for Wakefield audiences in the fifteenth century.

THE WAKEFIELD MASTER (flourished. ca. 1425–1450)

The Second Shepherds' Play ca. 1425–1450, in a manuscript of ca. 1460–1485

A modernized reading edition

CHARACTERS

First Shepherd (Coll [Colin]), *the head shepherd in rank, bitter about economic inequality and the aristocratic power structure.*

Second Shepherd (Gib [Gibbon]), *the second-ranking shepherd, unhappy with the institution of marriage, and particularly with his own wife.*

Third Shepherd (Daw [David]), *a superstitious youth, impulsive and outspoken, and dissatisfied because of his subordinate status.*

Mak, *a poor cottager and petty thief, unable to comprehend his place in the universe.*

Jill (Gill [Gillian]), *his wife, generally unhappy with her role in life, but opportunistic in assisting Mak.*

Angel, *a divine messenger (traditionally the Angel Gabriel) sent to tell the shepherds about the divine birth.*

Mary, *the mother of the Christ Child.*

Joseph *(a nonspeaking part).*

Ram *(a nonspeaking part for a child costumed as a ram).*

Sheep *(nonspeaking parts for children costumed as sheep).*

Star *(a nonspeaking part for an actor holding a large star).*

Animals *(nonspeaking parts for adults and children costumed as horses, cows, goats, dogs, cats, pigs, ducks, chickens, etc.).*

[SCENE: *One half of the stage is a field where the shepherds tend their sheep. The other half contains the cottage of MAK and his wife, JILL. This cottage can be modified to represent the stable and manger of Luke 2:7 and 2:16. The season is winter.*]

Here begins the second pageant. (Incipit Alia eorundem.—Ms.)°

[*Enter COLL, the FIRST SHEPHERD, followed by a number of sheep. He is cold, and claps his hands, stamps his feet, etc., in an attempt to stay warm.*]

FIRST SHEPHERD.   Lord, this winter is cold, and I'm thinly wrapped.
My body is stiff, so long have I napped.
My numbing legs buckle, my fingers are chapped.
There's nothing that's right now, for I am all strapped
     In sorrow.   5
   In storms and in tempest,
   Now in the East, now in the west,
   Woe to all those who can never find rest
     Mid-day nor morrow!

S.D. 0.1 *Incipit Alia eorundem*: Literally, "Here begins the second." The stage directions in Latin are part of the original manuscript. The bracketed stage directions have been added throughout this version. The original Latin directions are included in parentheses following the unbracketed translations.

We wretched shepherds, who walk on the moor,   10
In faith, we've almost been tossed out the door!
The way things are standing, no wonder we're poor,
For the profit from land is as bare as the floor.
      It can't be forgot.   15
    We have been blamed,
    Overtaxed, and hand-tamed.
    We've been humbled and maimed
      By the gentry, that landowning lot.

These lords rob us of rest. Curse them all, by Mary!°
Their followers and yes-men,° they make our plows tarry.   20
Some say that's for the best; we find it contrary.
Thus are workers oppressed, so that all will miscarry
      In striving for life.
    Thus they hold us under;
    Thus they bring us asunder.   25
    It would be a great wonder
      If we ever could thrive.

Once a man gets painted sleeves and fine brooches, nowadays,°
Woe to the worker who grieves or gainsays!
None dare to object, such power he plays.   30
Yet none can believe any word that he says—
      Not even a single letter.
    He develops his influence
    With boasting and arrogance,
    And does all with the countenance°   35
      Of lords that are greater.

When one of these gallants, with pride all aglow,
Comes to borrow my wagon, and also my plow,°
His wishes have power. Grant them I must ere he go.
Thus live we in pain, and in anger and woe   40
      By night and by day.
    He'll have what he wishes.
    What's mine, alas, his is.
    I'll sleep with the fishes
      If once I say nay.   45

It makes me feel good, as I walk thus, and groan
To speak of this world, in manner of moan.

---

19 *by Mary:* Historically, the shepherds should make no references to the Christian religion since the religion did not develop until two generations after the time of the play's action. Nevertheless, the Wakefield Master disregards historical accuracy by giving his characters the everyday speech of the late fifteenth century. Thus there are many references to the Cross, Jesus, the Saints, etc.   20 *Their followers and yes-men:* The manuscript has "These men that ar lord-fest." That is, subordinates of the lord of the manor; their task was to collect tribute and to impose the lord's wishes upon the tenants.   28 *When . . . nowadays:* The official regalia worn by officials representing the lord of the manor.   35 *countenance:* The support given by the manorial lord for enforcing the actions of his officials.   38 *When . . . plow:* With the authority of the manorial lord, an official could commandeer implements and materials belonging to the tenants.

To my sheep I will shift, and guard them alone,
There perch on a ridge, or sit on a stone,
    Full soon,   50
For I think, pardee,°
We'll get more company
Of true men, if they be,
    Before it be noon.

[*The First Shepherd moves upstage, with his sheep. Gib, the Second Shepherd, enters. At first the two shepherds do not see each other.*]

SECOND SHEPHERD.   Bless us and keep us! What does it all mean?   55
Why fares this world thus? It's as bad as we've seen.
Lord, this winter is spiteful; the winds are too keen.
And the cold is so frightful it's freezing my spleen—
    No lie.
Now in dry, now in wet,   60
Now in snow, now in sleet,
    When my shoes have been frozen right onto my feet,
    Relief is not nigh.

But, as far as I know, or yet as I go
Those poor men who marry must suffer much woe,   65
With sorrow unending. It often falls so.
Silly old Copyle, our hen, to and fro
    She cackles.
But when she starts to cluck,
Or to groan or to croak,   70
Woe to our poor strutting cock,
    For he's in her shackles.°

Those men who are wed have lost all their will.
Even in comfort, they swallow this pill.
God knows that they're led both full hard and full ill!   75
In bower and bed, they keep quiet and still.
    For me—I'll secure it—
My part I have found;
My lesson is sound:
    "Woe to him who is bound,   80
    For he must endure it."

But in our times now—it's marvel to me—
I think my soul shatters, these wonders to see—
When Fate forces widowers, to make such things be,
Some men will have two wives, and some will have three,   85
    Within their door!°

---

51 *pardee:* "By God" (from the French *par dieu*).   69–72 *But when . . . shackles:* The Second Shepherd's idea is that when the hen starts clucking, she has laid an egg, and that the cock, or rooster, falls correspondingly more under her power.   82–86 *But in . . . door!* The Second Shepherd finds it hard to believe that some men choose to embark upon second and even third marriages, thus losing the independence they have regained after the deaths of their previous wives.

One wife alone is sufficient for woe.
But believe what I say, for I know:
With every *new* marriage that men undergo,
    Their feelings grow ever more sore!   90

[*He speaks directly to the audience.*]

Young men, when wooing, by our Redeemer God without spot,
Be wary of wedding—may this ne'er be forgot:
"If I'd known" is a phrase that is empty of thought.
Long lives of lament have most weddings brought,
    And griefs punitive,   95
    With many sharp pangs intertwined.
    For in only an hour you find
    Troubles that bitterly torment your mind
        As long as you live.

My wifely companion, by holiest epistle,   100
Is rough as a briar, and sharp as a thistle.
Her face is like brine, and her brow's like a bristle.
She chants loud—and clearly—when she wets her whistle,
    To sing out her pater-noster.
    She's as big as a whale;   105
    She has a gallon of gall.
    By Him Who died for us all,
        I wish I had run till I lost her.

[*The First Shepherd steps forward.*]

FIRST SHEPHERD [*pointing to the audience*].
    May God guard these people!
[*To the* SECOND SHEPHERD.]   So mutely you stand!
SECOND SHEPHERD.   The devil's in your belly; you deserve reprimand.   110
Have you seen Daw anywhere?
FIRST SHEPHERD.   Yes, on a lea-land
He was blowing his horn. He's just now at hand,
        Not far.
        Stand still.
SECOND SHEPHERD.   Why?
FIRST SHEPHERD.   He's now coming, think I.   115
SECOND SHEPHERD.   He'll tell us a lie,
        Unless we take care,

[*The first two shepherds conceal themselves. The* THIRD SHEPHERD, DAW, *enters, accompanied by sheep.*]

THIRD SHEPHERD.   Guard me, you crosses of Christ and Saint Nicholas!
Of these I have need. All is worse than it was.
Those who can, now take heed. Let the world pass;   120
It is always in danger, and brittle as glass,
        And the earth itself trembles and slides.
    The world has never fared so,
    With signs and with portents below.

Some tell of weal, but more tell of woe, 125
 And nothing is stable, besides.

Never since Noah have such floods been seen!
It blew and rained roughly then. Storms were so keen!
Some stammered, and some stood in doubt, as I ween.
May God now make everything good. I say as I mean. 130
 For think now; just ponder
 The floods make everything drown
 Both in field and in town,
 And bear all things down.
  And this is a sign and a wonder.

We that walk in the nights—our livestock to keep— 135
See the strangest of sights when all other men sleep.

[*He notices the first two shepherds, but does not speak to them.*]

 Yet methinks my heart lightens; I see my pals peep.
 I'll pretend that they're monsters! I'll scatter my sheep
  As though I have seen Beelzebub. 140
 To trick's my intent.

[*He frightens his sheep away loudly.*]

  But, as I walk on this bent,
  I might quickly repent
   The toes that I stub.

[*The FIRST and SECOND SHEPHERDS come forward. The THIRD SHEPHERD continues speaking.*]

[*To the FIRST SHEPHERD.*] Ah, Sir, may God save your soul.
[*To the SECOND SHEPHERD.*]   And master mine. 145
 I would like a stiff drink, and then go to dine.
FIRST SHEPHERD.   Christ's curse, you're a knave, nothing better than swine!
SECOND SHEPHERD.   What, the boy wants to rave!
[*To the THIRD SHEPHERD.*]   You must wait, and don't whine,
  Because we have already eaten.
  Bad luck on your pate! 150
[*To the audience.*]   Though this rascal is late
  He believes he's in state
   For a meal—but only if he'll do the treating!

THIRD SHEPHERD.   Such servants as I—those who slave and who sweat—
 Get no more than a pittance, which makes me upset. 155
 While our masters sleep safely, we're weary and wet.
 And our food and our drink? They come too slowly yet.
  I do not exaggerate.
  Both our lady and sire
  Though we've run in the mire 160
  Can lower the sum of our hire,
   And pay us our wages too late.

But hear my truth, master. Here's what I decide:
I'll do just what's required for the pay they provide.
I'll work a bit, Sir, then play when I'm not occupied. 165

    For I've ne'er had a supper so fill my inside,
        That it stopped me from work in these fields.
    Why should I care a whit?
    With my staff, I can quit.
    "A cheap bargain"—this all people admit—   170
        "Produces no yields."

FIRST SHEPHERD.   You'd be a bad one to go out a wooing
    With a man of small means, with not much for spending.

SECOND SHEPHERD.   Peace, boy, I say! Enough of this jangling,
    Or I'll fill you with fear, by the Heaven's great King,   175
        For your double tongue.
    Where are our sheep, boy? We're angry, I warn.

THIRD SHEPHERD.   Sir, this same day, at morn
    I left them down in the corn
        At the time when lauds were rung.°   180

    Their pasture is good. They cannot go wrong.

FIRST SHEPHERD.   That is right. By the Cross, these nights are so long!
    Yet I wish, e'er we leave, we could sing us a song.

SECOND SHEPHERD.   I agree, that with music, our souls will get strong.

THIRD SHEPHERD.   I grant.   185

FIRST SHEPHERD.   My tenor voice will make the tune fly.

SECOND SHEPHERD.   And I'll take the treble so high.

THIRD SHEPHERD.   The mid part is mine, I'll never deny.
    Let's hear how you chant.

[*They sing.° When their song is done,*] MAK *enters, wearing a cloak over his clothing.* (Tunc intrat MAK in clamide se super togam vestitus.—Ms.) [*The shepherds do not see* MAK *at first, but they hear and react to his words.*]

MAK. [*Prays*].   Lord, for Thy seven names.° Lord, Who mad'st the moon shine,   190
    Who mad'st more stars than I count, I don't know my place in
        Thy world divine.
    I am confused. My mind cannot fathom Thy design.
    Now, God, I wish I were in heaven, for there no children weep
        or pine
        In eternal stillness.

FIRST SHEPHERD   Who's that wailing so?   195

MAK [*still praying*].   God, if only Thou knewest my woe,
    As I walk on this moor here below!
    My life is an illness!

---

180 *At the time when lauds were rung:* The earliest canonical hour and service of the liturgical day. 189 S.D. *They sing*: The manuscript does not include the text of the song. In light of the earlier complaints made by the shepherds, however, the topic was probably the difficulty of the shepherding life. Martial Rose, in *The Wakefield Mystery Plays* (New York: Norton, 1961), suggests extant medieval music that would be appropriate for musical occasions in the play (p. 52).   190 *seven names*: Traditionally, God was known by seven names, such as *Lord, The Lord God,* and *God the Father.* In Christian numerology, seven, like three, was considered a particularly significant and holy number (e.g., the *seven* sacraments, the *seven* cardinal virtues, the *seven* champions of Christendom, the *seven* stars, etc.).

[*The shepherds come forward and confront* MAK.]

SECOND SHEPHERD. Mak, where have you been? Give us tidings.
THIRD SHEPHERD. Is that Mak? We must look then quite close to our things.   200

The THIRD SHEPHERD *takes* MAK'*s cloak away from him. (Et accipit clamidem ab ipso.—Ms.)*

MAK. [*He protests in a cultured accent, as though he is an aristocrat. He pretends not to
  recognize the shepherds.*]
                    What, I'm a yeoman, I tell you, of Kings.
                    The self and the same, sent from great lordings,
                              And those on high.
                              Fie on you! Go hence!
                              Away! Out of my presence!   205
                              I demand the respect and the reverence
                                   Due to such as I!

FIRST SHEPHERD.   Your accent is strange. Is your brain in the shade?
SECOND SHEPHERD.   Mak, what does this mean? Why such a charade?
THIRD SHEPHERD.   Be hanged by the devil, you low renegade!   210
MAK.   I'll make a complaint, and see you all flayed,
                                      At my word!
                                 Your crimes I'll expose.
FIRST SHEPHERD.   But, Mak, it's not truth you'll disclose.
                                 Give up your accent, and your silly pose,   215
                                      And go sit on a turd!°

SECOND SHEPHERD.   Mak, the devil in your eye! I'll give you a bashing!
THIRD SHEPHERD.   Don't you know me, by God? What you need is a lashing!
MAK. [*Turns submissive under their threats.*]   I knew you all three! Joking is only my fashion!
                                 You're fine people, by God.
FIRST SHEPHERD.   Oh, you just saved yourself from a thrashing!   220
SECOND SHEPHERD.   You're such a fool it makes me weep!
                                 Your goings at night, in furtive formation,
                                 Give you a rascally rogue's reputation,
                                 In practice a real proclamation,
                                      That you're out stealing sheep.   225

MAK.   I'm honest as steel; this is common admission.
                                 But I have a sickness that's just like perdition.
                                 My digestion won't work. It is out of condition.
THIRD SHEPHERD. [*aside.*]   "The devil does not die at home." That's no superstition!
MAK.   Therefore   230
                                 Full sore I am, and ill.
                                 You may turn me to stone, silent and still,
                                 If I've eaten my fill
                                      In the last month or more.

215–216 *Give up . . . on a turd!*: The original is "Now take outt that Sothren tothe, / And sett in a
torde!" Because Wakefield is in the north of England, the "Southren tothe" refers to a dialect of the
southernmost part of England.

| FIRST SHEPHERD. | But how fares your wife? Is she well, by my hood? | 235 |

MAK. She does nothing but sprawl at the fire, by the rood!
She's also a drunkard, with a houseful of brood
Bad luck to whatever she'll do that is good.°
    Hear more now that's true:
    Her gluttony's wild.   240
    And each year—I'm beguiled—
    She bears a new child,
      And some years it's two.

Ev'n if I prospered, with wealth to disburse,
I'd lose house and home, which none can reimburse   245
And she is not worth it; she's only a curse.
No one can know, or imagine, a woman that's worse
    Than this slut without sense.
    Now do you see what I prefer?
    To give, at her death mass, all in my coffer—   250
    Tomorrow, or sooner, to offer
      All of my pence.°

[*The shepherds laugh at* MAK'S *outburst. They soon grow sleepy. They yawn, stretch, etc.*]

SECOND SHEPHERD. I'm worn out with watching like none in this shire.
Now I must sleep, ev'n if I had more for my hire.

THIRD SHEPHERD. I'm cold and I'm naked, and I'd like a fire. [*Lies down.*]   255

FIRST SHEPHERD. I'm weary, exhausted, and run in the mire.
[*To the Second Shepherd*]   You, keep the watch true! [*Lies down and immediately
      falls asleep.*]

SECOND SHEPHERD. Nay, I'll lie down too, just in the rear.
I need as much sleep as anyone here. [*Lies down and sleeps.*]

THIRD SHEPHERD [*Angered at being left alone to watch.*]
    In the eyes of my parents, I was as dear   260
      As any of you.

But, Mak, come over here! Between us lie down.

MAK.   I'm afraid I would get in your way. On that you would frown.
[*Lies down and pretends to sleep. The* THIRD SHEPHERD *falls asleep.*]

[*Two lines, rhyming with "down" and "frown," are missing here from the manuscript, which resumes with the last five lines of the stanza, spoken by* MAK.]

MAK.   No doubt.
    From my head to my toe,   265
    Manus tuas commendo,
    Poncio Pilato.°
    Christ's Cross, bear me out.

---

    238 *Bad luck . . . good:* Mak directs his curse not against a good action, but rather against his wife.
His point is that she will never do anything good. Therefore he can safely render his curse because he believes that it is an empty one.   249–252 *Now . . . pence:* Mak's idea is that he would give everything he
owns to see his wife dead.   266–277 *Manus . . . Poncio Pilato:* "Into thy hands I commend [*myself*], Pontius
Pilate." Mak's bad Latin is a joke by the Wakefield Master. Mak is quoting one of the seven last words of
Christ on the cross, as recorded in Luke 24:36, but Mak forgets—or does not know—that Jesus commends
his spirit to God and not to Pilate.

The shepherds being asleep, MAK rises, and speaks the next lines alone. (Tunc surgit, pastoribus dormientibus, et dicit.—Ms.)

Now's the time for a man like me, lacking in gold,
To be stealthy and stalk within the sheepfold,   270
And nimbly then work.—But he can't be too bold.
If they find sheep are missing they'll snuff him dead cold
  At the ending.
  Now it's time forth to fare.
  But he needs to take care   275
  If success be his prayer,
   But as yet has nothing for spending.

[MAK chants the lines of the next stanza, and makes movements and gestures as though he is weaving a spell over the sleeping shepherds.]

A circle about you I'll draw, as round as the moon.
Until I have finished my task—ev'n though it be noon—
It's here you must lie, stone still, in a swoon.   280
And these words I will say, in a magical rune.
  With all that I have of might:
  Over your heads my hands arise!
  Out goes your vision! Now dark are your eyes!
  You'll no more your sight utilize,   285
   Till I make things clear and bright!

[The shepherds begin snoring.]

My Lord, they sleep sound! Their noise you can hear!
Though now I'll learn herding, it's not my career.
The flock may be scared, yet I'll nip that sheep here.

[He stalks a large, bold-looking ram, the leader of the flock.]
  Come here! Come on!

[The ram runs to him and nuzzles him.]   He's here! I'm changing to cheer   290
  From sorrow. *[Examines the ram.]*
  He's a fat sheep, strong and well set.
  With the fairest and finest of fleece, I will bet!
  I will soon pay them back—unless I forget—
   But this one I will borrow.   295

[He picks up the ram and carries it across the stage to his house. He knocks on the door.]

How, Jill, are you in? Get us some light!

WIFE.   Who makes such a din at this time of the night?
I'm doing my job, which is spinning. I hope not I might
Lose a penny from these interruptions. I curse them on sight!
  This we cannot ignore: 300
  A housewife whose working has been
  Interrupted as though it's routine,
  Can finish no work that can ever be seen—
   Not even the tiniest chore.

MAK.   Good Wife, open the door. Don't you see what I bring?   305
WIFE.   Unlock it yourself, for all that I care!

[*MAK enters. JILL speaks ironically.*] Ah, come in, my sweeting!

MAK.   Sweeting indeed! You don't care how long I've been standing.

WIFE.   By your uncovered neck, you are likely to swing!

MAK.   Just hear what I say!
               I'm worth my omelet,   310
               For when it counts, I can get
               More than the workers who slavishly sweat
               All the long day!

[*Shows the ram to her.*]

               Jill, just see what I found! Was ever such grace?

WIFE.   It'd be a foul blot to be hanged for the case.   315

MAK.   I've often escaped, Jill, a much faster chase.

WIFE.   "If too long to water you carry a vase,"
               They say, "At last,
               It comes home all broken."

MAK.   Indeed, I do know that token.   320
               But let's keep this whole thing unspoken.
               Just come and help, fast.

[*MAK gets a knife and prepares to kill the sheep.*]

               This ram should be slaughtered. I'd sure like to eat,
               Because for a year I've not tasted sheep meat.

WIFE.   But, if they come when you're cutting, and hear the sheep bleat—   325

MAK.   Then I might be caught! God, how that makes me sweat!
                   So go now and lock
                   The gate at the front.

WIFE.   Yes, Mak,
               But if they should come then around by the back—

MAK.   Then I will suffer, from this shepherd pack,   330
               Full many a devilish hard knock.

WIFE.   I've thought of a scheme, because *you* have none.—
               We'll hide him right here, until they are gone.
               In my cradle let's put him.—

[*They put the ram in the cradle.*]   —I'll stay here alone,
               And lie down as though I'm in childbed, and groan.   335

MAK.   Get ready and start.
               And I'll make our story seem right—
               That you've given birth to a male child tonight.

WIFE.   Now, then, it's my great delight
               That I was brought up so smart!   340

               This clever disguise, by my great brain amassed,
               Shows that a woman's plans can't be surpassed.
               —But we might be spied on. —Hide now! Get away fast!

MAK.   I must be there when they wake; else blows a cold blast.
               Now I'll go there to sleep.   345

[*MAK crosses the stage to the sleeping shepherds.*]

               This goodly group is still sleeping sound.
               I'll sneak in beside them, right here on the ground.

If I do things right, it will never be found
That I took their sheep.

[*He lies down and pretends to sleep. The* FIRST *and* SECOND SHEPHERDS *wake up, stretch, yawn, etc.*]

FIRST SHEPHERD.   *Resurrex a mortruis!* Strength, come back to my hand!   350
                         Judas carnas dominus!° I'm too sleepy to stand!
                         By Jesus, my foot is asleep! I'm thirsty! It's food I demand!
                         I thought we had lain down on fair English land.

SECOND SHEPHERD.   Oh me!
                         Lord, I surely have slept well.   355
                         I'm fresh as an eel.
                         I'm easy and light—so much, that I feel
                         Like a leaf on a tree.

[*The* THIRD SHEPHERD *wakes up, crying out as though having a nightmare.*]

THIRD SHEPHERD.   A blessing upon us! Just see my bones quake!
                         My heart's in my throat! See me shudder and shake!   360
                         Who's making this noise in my head? I fear I might break!
                         Run! Run for your 'lives!

[*He dashes about frantically, but soon settles down, and calls out to the other two shepherds.*]

                         Hark, fellows, now wake!
                         There were four of us when the sun set!
                         Have you seen whether Mak is still here?

FIRST SHEPHERD.   We were up before you were astir.   365

SECOND SHEPHERD.   Man, to God I swear and aver,
                         He hasn't gone anywhere yet.

THIRD SHEPHERD.   I dreamt that I saw him all dressed in wolf skin.

FIRST SHEPHERD. [*Aside.*] Many are like that now: "Sheep without, wolf within."

THIRD SHEPHERD.   We were sleeping, and he, with a snare for this sin,   370
                         Trapped a fat sheep—silent, without any din.

SECOND SHEPHERD.   Be still!
                         It's only a dream! Is that understood?
                         It's nothing but fantasy, by the Rood!

FIRST SHEPHERD.   Now, God, turn all to good,   375
                         If it be Thy will.

[*The Shepherds begin rousing* MAK, *who pretends that his limbs are asleep, that his neck is stiff, etc. He utters appropriate groans and cries. They seem sympathetic and offer help to him.*]

SECOND SHEPHERD.   Get up, Mak, for shame! You've been sleeping too long!

MAK.   May Christ's holy name be amid this fine throng!
                         What is this? By Saint James, my foot's going wrong!
                         I'll be all right soon! —Ah! It feels like my neck has been wrung!   380
                         You're being so kind.
                         Much thanks. Since yesterday midnight—

350–351 *Resurrex . . . dominus:* Incorrect Latin like that spoken by Mak in line 266. These misquotations were perhaps designed to confirm the Third Shepherd's later admission that the shepherds are "unlettered" (line 707). The quotation in line 350 is a corruption of "*Resurrexit a mortuis*" ("He arose from the dead"), from the Apostle's Creed. The quotation in line 351, meaning something like "Judas [is] God's meat," is apparently a misquotation of the opening of Psalm 47:6, "*Laudes canas domino*" ("Sing praises to the Lord").

I swear by Saint Steven so bright—
A nightmare has made me unright,
    Almost out of my mind.   385

I dreamed that my Jill was in labor, and that she then had—
At the rooster's first cry—a bouncing young lad,
To make my flock larger. What could this be but bad?
I've such trouble already, I've nearly gone mad!
    Oh, my head!   390
    My houseful of kids puts my life in chains!
    I wish that the devil would knock out their brains!
    Woe to the father with so many pains,
        And therefore without any bread!

By your leave, I must go home to Jill, as I planned.   395
Look me over. I've nothing in sleeve or in hand!
I'd never offend you, or steal on your land.

[*He leaves for his cottage at the other side of the stage.*]

THIRD SHEPHERD.   A curse on your journey!

[*To the other shepherds.*]
            —Here we can no longer stand,
    But must learn, on this morn,
    If our sheep are all still in full store.   400

FIRST SHEPHERD.   I'll be the one to go out before.
    Soon again, let us meet.

SECOND SHEPHERD.   Yes, but where?

THIRD SHEPHERD.   At the Crooked Thorn.°

[*The shepherds leave separately to look for their sheep. MAK knocks at the door of his house and shouts to his wife, who is inside.*]

MAK.   Open the door! Who's inside? How long must I wait?

WIFE.   Who's making this racket?

[*Opens the door and recognizes MAK.*]   May the waning moon curse you
            both early and late.°   405

MAK.   [*Entering the house.*]
    What cheer, Jill? It's I, Mak, your husband, your mate!

WIFE.   [*Pretends to be experiencing a vision in which MAK is being hanged.*]
    It's the devil I see—a rope round his neck and meeting his fate
        For he is Sir Guile.
    Lo, you'll see him and hear him moan!
    It's the pain in his throat that's making him groan!   410
    Then my weaving I must postpone—

[*Aside*]   But just for a little while!

MAK. [*Aside.*]   Do you hear what she'll say just to keep her high pose?
But in fact she lives idly—just scratching her toes.

---

403 *the Crooked thorn:* A landmark between Wakefield and Horbury, a village three miles to the southwest. This reference is one of the details that have led scholars to conclude that Wakefield was the probable location of the Wakefield cycle of plays. (See also the note to line 455.)   405 *May . . . late:* The text has "Now walk in the wenyand!" Since ancient times, the waning moon had been considered unlucky and even deadly. There were many superstitions. A child born during the wane, for example, could not live to puberty. Crops planted during the wane would not grow. Human blood would weaken during the wane, and therefore people would be susceptible to severe illnesses.

WIFE.   Who wanders? Who wakes? Who comes? Who goes?   415
Who brews? Who bakes? Who makes me hoarse, and offends
    my repose?
        Be sure, then,
    It's a truth to behold—
    Now in hot, now in cold,
    Empty and woeful is every household   420
        Where lives not a woman.

But how did things go with the herdsmen, Mak?

MAK.   The words that they uttered, when I started back,
Were to see if their sheep were still all in the pack.
They're sure to be mad when they learn of their lack,   425
        Pardee!
    But howso the game goes,
    I'll be their suspect, or so I suppose,
    It's me that they'll noisily then accuse,
        And cry out against me.   430

But now you must do what you promised.

WIFE.   Depend on me, too.
I'll swaddle him right in my cradle—a great switcheroo.
I could help even better with more derring-do.

[*Puts the ram in the cradle and wraps it as though it were a newborn child.*]

Now I'll lie down. Put these covers on me.

[*Gets into bed.*]
MAK.   I will, by what's true.
[*Begins covering her.*]
WIFE.   Don't forget my behind!   435
If Coll and his mates see aught that's amiss
They'll blast us until they have sent us to bliss!

MAK.   Should they see the sheep I'll shout "Haroo! Hey, what's this?"
    To confuse them about what they find.

WIFE.   Sharpen your ears for their call; they'll be coming anon.   440
Make everything ready. Start then to sing by yourself alone.
Sing "Lullay, lullay!" and I will then groan
And cry out, by the wall, on Mary and John,
        In wailing full sore.
    And when you hear the shepherds at last;   445
    Start singing your lullabies hard and fast.
    —If I am dealing you any false cast,
        Trust me no more.

[*MAK listens for the shepherds while JILL remains silent in bed. The shepherds enter on the other side of the stage.*]

THIRD SHEPHERD.   Ah, Coll, good morn! Why sleep you not?
FIRST SHEPHERD.   Alas, that I ever was born! We have a foul blot!   450
Of our fattest of rams we've been shorn!
THIRD SHEPHERD.   Lord and Mary, this pains my thought!

SECOND SHEPHERD.	Who could do us such scorn? This is so huge a spot!
FIRST SHEPHERD.	A rascal, I think, *entre nous.*

       I searched, with the dogs that I keep,
       Through Horbery Shrogs° wide and deep.   455
       And, guarding our fifteen young sheep,
          I found only a single ewe.°

THIRD SHEPHERD.	Now hear, if you will. By Saint Thomas of Kent,°

       Either Mak or else Jill was at that event!

FIRST SHEPHERD.	Peace, man, be still! I saw when he went. 460

       You slander him ill. You ought to repent
          In good speed.

SECOND SHEPHERD.	Now, as I dream to be wealthy,

       Or if death itself should overtake me,
       Still I would say it was indeed he   465
          That did this same deed.

THIRD SHEPHERD.	Let's go thither, I think, and run on our feet.

       I will not eat a meal, till the truth I do meet.

FIRST SHEPHERD.	Nor savor a drink, till the facts are complete.
SECOND SHEPHERD.	I'll not rest again till true knowledge I greet. 470

          My brother,
       I swear to you now, by my honor so bright,
       Until I see Mak, and gain total insight,
       Wherever I've slept for a single night,
          I'll not sleep another.   475

[*The shepherds walk to* MAK'S *cottage.* MAK, *seeing them, raucously begins singing a lullaby, and signals for* JILL *to begin groaning. Together, they make a loud and terrible discord.*]

THIRD SHEPHERD.	Will you hear how they're croaking? Sir Mak likes to croon.
FIRST SHEPHERD.	I've never heard bawling so clear out of tune!

       Call on him.

SECOND SHEPHERD.	Mak, hey Mak! Undo your door soon!
MAK.	Who is that who is talking as if it were noon,

          In a voice raised aloft?   480
          Who is there? Who is it, I say?

THIRD SHEPHERD.	It's good fellows you'd see, if it only were day.

[MAK *opens the door, holding his finger to his lips as a sign of quiet. He speaks softly, as though he is in a sickroom.*]

MAK.	As far as you may,

          You good men, please speak soft

       By this sick woman's head, in the grips of disease.   485
       I'd rather be dead, than do aught to displease.

---

455 *Horbery Shrogs:* A grazing area near Horbury (see the note to line 403).   456–457 *guarding . . . ewe:* That is, the dominant ram (taken by Mak) which ordinarily protected the fifteen sheep, was not to be found. Only a single female (ewe) was in its place. The First Shepherd's meaning is that the sheep are un-protected and in danger.   458 *Saint Thomas of Kent:* That is, Saint Thomas á Becket.

WIFE.   [*Speaks quietly, as though in pain.*]
　　　　　　　　　　　　Oh! Move away there! I can't breathe with ease.
　　　　　　　　　　　　Each step that you take gives my head a great squeeze,
　　　　　　　　　　　　　　So tight!
FIRST SHEPHERD.　　　　　　Tell us now, Mak, if you may,　　　　　　　　490
　　　　　　　　　　　　How are things going, I say?
MAK.　　　　　　　　　　Are you staying in town just for today?
　　　　　　　　　　　　How will you be faring this night?

　　　　　　　　　　　　You've run in the mire, and your clothes are still wet.
　　　　　　　　　　　　I'll make you a fire, if you'll come here and sit.　　495
[*Begins to prepare a fire.*]

　　　　　　　　　　　　It's a nurse I desire. Do you know of one yet?
　　　　　　　　　　　　Well paid is my hire. Remember my dream? This is it!
　　　　　　　　　　　　　　Things have now come full season.
　　　　　　　　　　　　I have many children—a lot, not a few—
　　　　　　　　　　　　More than enough, and even more, too.　　　　500
　　　　　　　　　　　　But, as they say, we must drink as we brew,
　　　　　　　　　　　　　　And that is but reason.

　　　　　　　　　　　　Please eat ere you go. You're so hot you'll combust.
SECOND SHEPHERD.　　　　No, neither eating nor drinking can soothe our disgust.
MAK.　　　　　　　　　　Why, Sir, does something disturb you?
THIRD SHEPHERD.　　　　　　　　　　　Yes, a ram in our trust,　　505
　　　　　　　　　　　　To our great loss, was stolen while grazing, and we are nonplussed!
MAK.　　　　　　　　　　　　Sirs, have a drink to unwind!
　　　　　　　　　　　　If *I'd* been there you'd have not heard *me* snore!
　　　　　　　　　　　　Some villain, I'm sure, I'd have beaten full sore!
FIRST SHEPHERD.　　　　　By Mary now, some think you *were*.　　　　510
　　　　　　　　　　　　And this is what troubles our mind.

SECOND SHEPHERD.　　　　Mak, some of us think that it's *you* it should be.
THIRD SHEPHERD.　　　　　Either it's you or your spouse—so say we.
MAK.　　　　　　　　　　Now, if you have suspicion of Jill, or of me,
　　　　　　　　　　　　Come search through our house, and then you can see　515
　　　　　　　　　　　　　　Who made off with this woolly head.
　　　　　　　　　　　　You'll see that I stole not a thing.
　　　　　　　　　　　　Neither heifer nor bull° did I bring.
　　　　　　　　　　　　And Jill, my wife, has not gone out visiting
　　　　　　　　　　　　　　Since she lay down on her bed.　　　　520

　　　　　　　　　　　　As I'm true and I'm honest, to God here I pray
[*Points to the cradle.*]
　　　　　　　　　　　　That this is the first meal I'll eat on this day.
FIRST SHEPHERD.　　　　　Mak, by heaven's bliss eternal, hear now, I say:
　　　　　　　　　　　　"They learn early to steal who cannot say nay."
[*The shepherds begin to search the cottage.*]
WIFE.　　　　　　　　　　　　　　Oh!—It's a faint I have felt!　　525
　　　　　　　　　　　　Out of my house, thieves, leave us alone!

---

518 *heifer nor bull:* These terms are applicable to sheep as well as cattle.

	You come to rob us—to take what we own!	
MAK.	Have you no pity when hearing her groan?	
	Your hearts should now melt.	

[*The shepherds approach the cradle, causing JILL to cry out and moan.*]

WIFE.	Out, thieves, from my child! It's you I abhor!	530
MAK.	If you knew how she labored, your hearts would be sore.	
	You do wrong—here's my warning—to come thus before	
	A woman recovering from pain.	

[*Appears to be deeply grieved and in sorrow.*]

| | I cannot say more. | |
| WIFE. [*Cries out*]. | Ah!—I'm suffering so in my middle! | |

[*To the shepherds.*]

	I pray to our Lord God so mild,	535
	If ever it's you I've beguiled,	
	I will eat this newborn child	
	That lies in this cradle.	

MAK.	For God's pain, woman! Peace! Do not cry out so!	
	You'll injure your brain, and you'll put me in woe!	540
SECOND SHEPHERD.	I think our ram's slain. Don't you think this also?	
THIRD SHEPHERD.	Our work here is vain. We might as well go,	
	Damn it all! What matters	
	Is this: Here I can find the meat of no sheep,	
	Neither tender nor tough, in nothing shallow or deep.	545
	Nothing salted or fresh do they keep,	
	But these two empty platters.	

[*The THIRD SHEPHERD holds up two plates. Being close to the cradle, he gets a whiff of the ram, and makes gestures of disgust.*]

	I've never smelled livestock, so tame or so wild,	
	As I'm hoping for bliss, that stank just like this child.	
WIFE.	No, as God blesses me with my baby so mild.	550
FIRST SHEPHERD.	We suspected you wrongly. We were falsely beguiled.	
SECOND SHEPHERD	[*to MAK, standing by the cradle*].	
	Sir, now we are done.	
	Sir, for him may Our Lady ne'er fail!	
	May I ask if your child is a male?	
MAK.	The finest of lords would always prevail,	555
	If this child were *his* son.	
	When he awakens, he dances and skips—a joy to see.	
THIRD SHEPHERD.	Long may his hips be in tempo, and happy may he always be.	
	But who were his godparents, who gave the Church guarantee?	
MAK.	May their just lips speak wisdom.	
FIRST SHEPHERD. [*Aside.*]	Hark now, he's lying to me!	560
MAK.	May God's grace make them free from all woes.	
	They are Parkyn, and Gybon Waller, I say,	
	And gentle John Horne,° as the faithful pray.	

562–563 *Gybon Waller . . . John Horne: Parkyn and Gybon Waller were* the second and first shepherds in *The First Shepherds' Play* by the Wakefield Master. Obviously, John Horne was a well known dancer.

He gives us excitement each holiday
With his dancing toes.   565

SECOND SHEPHERD.   Mak, let us be friends, for we are all one.
MAK.   We together! I give you my pledge! [*Aside.*] But whatever I get
must still be hard won.

[*To the shepherds, jovially.*] Farewell, all three! [*Aside, angrily.*] I'll be glad when you're gone!

[*The shepherds leave* MAK'S *cottage and walk toward their field at the other side of the stage.*]

THIRD SHEPHERD.   Fair words there may be, but love is there none
This year.   570
FIRST SHEPHERD.   Did you give the fair child anything?
SECOND SHEPHERD.   I swear, not even a single farthing!
THIRD SHEPHERD.   Fast again then will I now fling.
Wait for me here.

[*The* THIRD SHEPHERD *hurries back to* MAK'S *cottage and speaks to* MAK.]

Mak, take it not ill, if I come to your child, this paragon.   575
MAK.   Nay, I'm offended, and foul have you done.
THIRD SHEPHERD.   I'll not grieve the child, that little day-star one.
Mak, with your leave, let me give your son
But sixpence.
[*Puts money into the cradle.*]
MAK.   Nay, go away! He sleeps.   580
[*The sheep begins bleating.*]
THIRD SHEPHERD.   Methinks he peeps!
MAK.   When he wakens he weeps!
I pray you, go hence!

[*MAK tries to usher the THIRD SHEPHERD out. But the other shepherds return, and all the shepherds gather around the cradle.*]

THIRD SHEPHERD.   Let me give him a kiss, and lift up the clout.
[*Raises the covering and looks within the cradle.*]
What the devil is this? He has a long snout!   585
FIRST SHEPHERD.   He's badly defective. We shouldn't be snooping about.
SECOND SHEPHERD.   "When the woof is ill-spun," they say, "nothing good can come out."
[*Looks in the cradle.*]
Ah, so! Look what's been done!
He is like to our sheep!
THIRD SHEPHERD.   How, Gib? May I peep?   590
FIRST SHEPHERD.   I swear, "The truth will creep
Where it cannot run!"
SECOND SHEPHERD.   This was a bold cheat, at which I'm aghast!
A diabolical fraud!
THIRD SHEPHERD.   Yes, Sirs, it was, but it's past.
Let's bind this scoundrel, and burn him fast.   595
[*To Jill.*]   Ah, you false witch, you'll hang at the last!
So you will.

[*To the other shepherds.*]

Do you see how they swaddle
His four feet in the middle.

| | I never saw, in a cradle, | 600 |
| | A hornèd lad so ill. | |

MAK.	I bid you all peace! Let things alone here!	
	It was I who begat him! The woman who bore him is there!	
FIRST SHEPHERD.	[*Sarcastically.*]	
	What devil's name did you give him? "Mak?" [*Holds up the ram.*]	
	Look, God, at Mak's heir!	
SECOND SHEPHERD.	Leave off our mocking. May God alone judge this affair.	605
	But I'll say this much: I know what I saw.	
WIFE.	As pretty a child is he	
	As ever sat on a woman's knee;	
	A dearest darling—God's gift to me—	
	To fill us with laughter and awe.	610

THIRD SHEPHERD.	[*Lifting the ram's ear.*] I see here our brand. That's a clear token!	
MAK.	I tell you, sirs, listen! The child's nose was broken!	
	A clergyman told me a spell had been spoken!	
FIRST SHEPHERD.	But this is all false! My revenge I'll be working!	
	I'll get me a weapon! [*Searches about.*]	615
WIFE.	The child was possessed by an elf!°	
	I saw it myself!	
	When the clock struck twelve,	
	He became misshapen!	

SECOND SHEPHERD.	[*To MAK and JILL.*]	
	You're guilty together—"cuts from the same stalk."	620
THIRD SHEPHERD.	Let's do them to death for their false double-talk.	

[*The shepherds menace MAK with clubs, ropes, etc. He is frightened and gives up his lies about the ram.*]

MAK. [*Points to a tree stump.*]	If I once more offend, chop my head on this block!	
	I ask for your mercy.	
FIRST SHEPHERD.	Sirs, follow my lead, and don't balk:	
	In dealing with Mak's great trespass,	
	To dispute or argue is not our need.	625
	Neither fighting nor backbiting, let us proceed.	
	But get all this done with the greatest of speed,	
	And toss him in canvas!	

[*With much clamor, the shepherds drag MAK outside the cottage. They throw him up and catch him a number of times in a blanket. MAK and JILL shout and moan in protest.*]

| FIRST SHEPHERD. | My God, I'm so sore I'm about to break! | |
| | In faith, I can do no more. I need rest! I ache! | 630 |

[*The shepherds release MAK, who along with JILL runs to his cottage. The shepherds pick up their ram and walk back to their field.*]

| SECOND SHEPHERD. | Ugh! Like a seven-score sheep, ° he made my arms shake. | |
| | I'll sleep anywhere soundly, ev'n through an earthquake. | |

---

616 *elf:* Until Shakespeare made elves and fairies seem charming and amusing in *A Midsummer Night's Dream,* these supernatural creatures were considered harmful.   631 *seven-score sheep:* That is, an extremely large sheep, weighing 140 pounds or more.

THIRD SHEPHERD.	Now I pray you,	
	Let us lie down on this green.	
FIRST SHEPHERD.	I think those thieves were so obscene!	635
THIRD SHEPHERD.	Why should you still feel such spleen?	
	Sleep. Do as I tell you!	

[*The shepherds lie down and fall immediately asleep. The* ANGEL *enters and sings the text of Luke 2:14, "Gloria in Excelsis Deo, et in terra pax hominibus bonae voluntatis" ("Glory to God in the Highest, and on earth peace to persons of good will.") The shepherds wake up and are "sore afraid" (Luke 2:9), demonstrating their fear by scurrying frantically to find hiding places.*]

ANGEL.	Rise, herdsmen kind, for now He is born	640
	Who shall take from the fiend what from Adam was shorn.	
	That demon to grind this night He is born.	
	God is made your friend—here on this morn!	
	God now requests	
	To Bethlehem town you must go to see.	
	There lies that Child so dear and free	
	In a lowly crib of poverty	645
	Between two beasts.° [*Exit.*]	

FIRST SHEPHERD.	I never yet heard so celestial a sound!	
	It was a great marvel! The voice did astound!	
SECOND SHEPHERD.	He spoke of God's Son, way up in heav'n bound!	
	So brightly he shone that the woods all about and around	
	Did as in daylight appear!°	650
THIRD SHEPHERD.	He spoke of a boy that is born this day	
	In Bethlehem town, I say.	

[*An Angel appears above the shepherds, carrying a large star.*]

FIRST SHEPHERD.	Lo! Yon star° does this message convey.	
	Let us seek him there.	655
SECOND SHEPHERD.	Say, did you hear how well he sang his song?	
	His voice was perfect.	
THIRD SHEPHERD.	Yea, marry, three breves to a long.	
	Nothing was lacking. No crotchet° was wrong.	
FIRST SHEPHERD.	Just as he sang it, we'll follow along.	
	I think I remember it well.	660
SECOND SHEPHERD.	Let's see how you croon	
	Can you bark at the moon?	
THIRD SHEPHERD.	Hold your tongues! Be done with *that* tune!	
FIRST SHEPHERD.	Follow my lead, let your voices swell!	

638–646 *Rise . . . beasts:* The angel's speech is a free expansion of Luke 2:10–12.   649–650 *So bright-ly he shone . . . appear:* See Luke 2:9.   654 *star:* See Matthew 2:2–10. There is no reference to a star in the Gospel of Luke.   657–658 *breves, long, crotchet:* Medieval terms of musical notation. A *breve* (short) was the basic note, and the *long* was the equivalent of either two or three *breves*, depending on the tempo. The *crotchet* had the length of an eighth of a *breve* or a *quarter* of a *semi* or *half breve* (a *half breve* is, today, the equivalent of a whole note). Today, the *crotchet* is simply a "quarter note." From line 657 we may conclude that the Angel's song was counted in threes (in accord with the concept of the Holy Trinity?).

[*The shepherds sing the "Gloria" that the* ANGEL *had sung.*]

SECOND SHEPHERD.   He said now to Bethlehem make our journey.   665
    Let's linger no longer. No more should we tarry.

THIRD SHEPHERD.   Leave sadness. Our song should be mirthful and merry.
    Of gladness eternal we're beneficiary
        Without ambiguity.

FIRST SHEPHERD.   Hie we thither, therefore,   670
    Though we're weary and wet to the core,
    Both the lady and child we'll adore.
        Let's go now with great assiduity.

[*The shepherds laugh and chat as they begin walking. The* SECOND SHEPHERD, *who is holding a book, quiets them (line 674) and pronounces the following speech loudly and clearly.*]

SECOND SHEPHERD.   We find prophecy in the books—stop making this din!—
    Of David and Isaiah° and other scholars therein.   675
    By clergy they prophesied that in a virgin
    Should He have birth and life, to redeem us from sin,
        And slake it.
    To relieve our race from woe.
    For Isaiah said so: 680
    Ecce virgo
    Concipiet° a child that is naked.

THIRD SHEPHERD.   Full glad may we be, to adore, on that day
    That One, lovely to see, Whom all powers obey.
    Lord, should it come thus to me, for once and for aye,   685
    Then I'd kneel on my knee, and words I would say
        To that child.
    —But the angel said
    In a crib he was laid,
    He was poorly arrayed,   690
        Both meek and mild.

FIRST SHEPHERD.   Patriarchs and prophets, who the past did adorn,
    They yearned to have seen this Child that is born.
    They are gone now full clean; their hope is forlorn.
    We shall see Him, I ween, before it be morn—   695
        God's sign and token.
    When I see Him and kneel,
    Then I'll know that it's real.
    It's as true as fine steel,
        What the prophets have spoken.   700

    It's to poor folk like us that the child would appear.
    His messenger found us, then told us of cheer.

---

675 *David and Isaiah:* Books of the Hebrew Scriptures that were interpreted as prophesies of Christ. In Psalm 89 (the Psalms were traditionally attributed to David), God swears to grant David and his seed the "throne to all generations" (verse 4). Because of this Psalm, Jesus, being of the House of David, was considered the kingly heir of God's promise. Isaiah 7:14 was the text that was interpreted as a prophecy of the Virgin birth.   681–682 *Ecce virgo / Concipiet:* See Isaiah 7:14.

SECOND SHEPHERD.   Go we now forth, let us fare.

[*The* ANGEL *carries the star to a point above the stable.* MARY *and* JOSEPH *are at the manger, where the child is lying. They are surrounded by animals, including the sheep of the earlier scenes. The shepherds walk to the stable.*]

                                      The place is now near.
THIRD SHEPHERD.   I'm ready and eager. Together we'll go in right there [*points*],
                             To that manger under the star so bright.   705

[*Before entering, the shepherds kneel and pray.*]

                           Lord, we're unlettered, all of us three,
                           We ask Thee now, if Thy will it be,
                           To grant that our presents be worthy
                                To give the Child strength and delight.

[*The shepherds enter the stable. Each shepherd kneels at the manger while presenting his gift.*]

FIRST SHEPHERD.   Hail, comely and clean, hail, young child!   710
                           Hail, maker, I mean, born of maiden so mild!
                           Thou hast conquered, I ween, that warlock so wild—
                           That falsest beguiler of humans, *he* goes now beguiled!
[*Looks at the child, and is enraptured.*]
                                Look, his smile so merry is!
                                Look, he laughs, my sweeting!   715
                                A well fair meeting!
                                I have given my greeting.
                                     Have a bob of cherries.°

[*The* FIRST SHEPHERD *places a cluster of cherries at the manger.*]

SECOND SHEPHERD.   Hail, sovereign Savior, for Thou hast us sought!
                           Hail, noble freedom and flower, That all things hast wrought!   720
                           Hail, full of favor, Who mad'st all out of naught!
                           Hail! I kneel and I cower. A bird have I brought
                                     To my child.° [*Places a birdcage at the manger.*]
                                Hail, little tiny mop!
                                Of our creed Thou art top!   725
                                I would drink of Thy cup,°
                                     Little day-star so mild.

THIRD SHEPHERD.   Hail, darling dear, so full of Godhead!
                           I pray Thee be near when I am in need!
                           Hail! Sweet is Thy cheer! But it makes my heart bleed   730
                           To see Thee lie here in Thy clothing so poor indeed.

---

     718 *bob of cherries:* Because the time of the action is winter, the First Shepherd's offering of a bunch of fresh cherries symbolizes the promise of abundant life, even when most of Nature is moribund.   723–724 *A bird . . . child:* With their power of flight, birds have traditionally symbolized the soul's release from earth. In ancient Rome, for example, captive eagles were freed during imperial funerals to symbolize the apotheosis of the emperors. The Second Shepherd's bird therefore suggests the power of religion to confer immortality.   726 *cup:* i.e., the Eucharist cup, the central element of the Corpus Christi celebrations.

And Thou art without pence!
What I have here is only a ball.
Put forth Thy hand, and give it I shall.
Have it for play as Thou growest up tall,   735
And use it for tennis.° [*Puts the ball in the manger.*]

MARY. [*to the shepherds*]. The Father celestial, God omnipotent
Who in seven days made all, His Son now has sent.
He called me by name, and o'ershadowed° me ere He went.
I conceived the child thus, by God's mighty intent.   740
And now He is born.
May He keep you from woe.
I shall pray to Him so.
Tell it forth as you go,
And remember this morn.   745

FIRST SHEPHERD. Farewell, Lady, so fair to behold,
With Thy child on Thy knee!
SECOND SHEPHERD. But He lies here so cold!

[*Kneels, and gives his cloak to cover the child.*]

Lord, be it well with me! Now we'll go, Thou may'st behold.
THIRD SHEPHERD. Forsooth, already it seems that this tale has been told
Full often in thankful voice.   750
FIRST SHEPHERD. What grace we have found!
SECOND SHEPHERD. Come forth! Our souls are unbound!
THIRD SHEPHERD. Let us sing with great sound!
Make a joyful noise!

[*They leave, singing a song of praise. MARY, JOSEPH, and the animals remain at the manger as a tableau in the light of the star, while a chorus takes up and completes the song of the shepherds.*]

The end of the Shepherds' Play. (*Explicit pagina Pastorum.*—Ms.)

QUESTIONS

1. Lines 1–189: What characteristics of each of the shepherds are established through the speeches they make when they first appear?

2. Lines 190–198: Why does the Wakefield Master introduce Mak in solitary prayer before the shepherds come forward and begin their discussions with him? What do you learn about Mak from this prayer?

3. Lines 199–261: What circumstances of life does Mak complain about? Why does Mak behave as he does when the shepherds first confront him? What attitudes

---

736 *tennis:* In the fifteenth century, tennis was a game not of the people but of the aristocracy and royalty. It was played in an indoor court—unlike the current outdoor game of "lawn tennis" developed in the nineteenth century—and only those who could afford the facilities were able to play. The Third Shepherd's offering of the ball is therefore symbolic of the Christ child's kingly status. Tennis balls at the time were solid, not hollow like tennis balls today, and were made of tightly wound strips of cloth bound together with twine and a tough outer covering.   739 *o'ershadowed:* See Luke 1:35.

toward him do the shepherds show? What are Mak's complaints? Which ones are realistic, and which are more properly conventional and/or farcical?

4. Lines 262–277: What character traits of Mak are established by this speech?

5. Lines 278–295: Explain why Mak casts a spell over the shepherds. What do you think the fifteenth-century audience would have thought about this spell? Why does Mak profess that he will pay the shepherds back for the ram he is stealing?

6. Lines 296–349: Why does Jill apparently show differing attitudes about Mak? What is the purpose of her proverb in lines 317–318? From Jill's reaction, what do you conclude about Mak's normal activities? Describe Jill's plan for hiding the stolen ram.

7. Lines 350–403: When the shepherds awake, what evidence do they have that Mak has been up to any mischief? Why does Mak describe his dream? Why does Mak offer to let the shepherds inspect him before he leaves?

8. Lines 404–448: Why do Mak and Jill badger each other at the opening of this section? Why does Jill seem to have a vision of Mak's being hanged? What plans do both Mak and Jill make to anticipate the coming of the shepherds to look for their ram?

9. Lines 449–475: How have the shepherds discovered the missing ram? What do they resolve to do? Why do they suspect Mak of being the thief?

10. Lines 476–574: Describe the farcical nature of the activities in this section. Describe the irony of Mak (522) and Jill (536–538) in their oaths to eat the "child" in their cradle if they have seen the missing ram. How do Mak and Jill try to cause the shepherds to leave? Why do the shepherds leave and then return?

11. Lines 575–628: How does each shepherd react to their discovery that the "child" in the cradle has a long snout? To what degree are their responses normal and realistic? What characteristics of the shepherds are brought out by their responses? How do Mak and Jill maintain that the ram is really a human child? What punishment do the shepherds inflict on Mak?

12. Lines 629–673: What biblical elements are contained in this section? What parts are to be attributed to the dramatist? When the shepherds listen to the angel, what might be gained by having them listen prayerfully? What might be gained by having them moan, groan, and seek safety from the heavenly voice? Why do you think the shepherds repeat the song of the angel?

13. Lines 674–709: What message does the Wakefield Master convey in this section and in lines 737–745? How does the tone of this concluding section differ from the earlier sections of the play?

14. Lines 710–754: What gifts do the shepherds present to the Christ child? What is the meaning of their gifts? Contrast the nature of their gifts with the gifts of the Three Wise Men as described in Matthew 2:11.

GENERAL QUESTIONS

1. According to the Gospel of Luke, which the Wakefield Master is following, the text of a shepherds' play might begin with line 629, with the shepherds and the angel. Why do you think the Wakefield Master includes all the action that has gone on before, and why does he use the biblically based section only as the play's last scene? What would the play be like if the material of the first 628 lines were omitted, and if the material following line 629 became the substance of the play?

2. Characterize each of the shepherds. How are they similar and different? When they discover the ram in the cradle, what differences in character are exhibited?

3. Characterize Mak. To what degree can he be considered a realistic character? What elements of farce overshadow the realistic aspects of his character? Why should the modern critical claim be maintained that Mak is a pioneering creation—the most thoroughly realized character to have appeared in English drama to the date of the play?

4. How does the scene in Mak's cottage parallel the manger scene with which the play closes? Inasmuch as the scene is a parody of the manger scene, how does the scene escape the charge that it might be considered irreverent and immoral?

5. Describe this as a folk play. What elements of everyday life do you discover here? What strictly human, day-to-day affairs? In your answer you might also consider the importance of line 701: "It's to poor folk like us that the child would appear."

6. What is the significance of the First Shepherd's complaints about the political and economic structure of which he is a part?

✿ WRITING ABOUT THE ELEMENTS OF DRAMA

Although some aspects of drama, such as lighting and stage movement, are purely theatrical, drama shares a number of elements with fiction and poetry. The planning and the writing processes for essays about drama are therefore similar to those used for essays on the other genres. As you plan, select a play and an appropriate element or series of elements. It would be inappropriate, for example, to attempt an essay about character development in *Tea Party* (pp. 1205–1208) because this play is too short to probe the two characters deeply.

Once you select the play, choose a focus, which will be your central idea. For example, you might argue that a character is flat, static, nonrealistic, or symbolic of good or evil. Or, to assert relationships among elements, you might claim that a play's meaning is shaped and emphasized through setting or through conflict.

Topics for Discovering Ideas

PLOT, ACTION, CONFLICT. (See also Chapter 3.) In planning an essay on plot or structure, demonstrate how actions and conflicts unfold. In addition, link this concern to other dramatic elements, such as tone or theme. In general, this topic breaks down into three areas—conflict, plot, and structure. For conflict, determine what the conflicts are, which one is central, and how it is resolved. What kind of conflict is it? Does it suggest any general behavioral patterns? For plot, determine the separate stages of development. What is the climax? The dénouement? How are they anticipated or foreshadowed? In examining plot structures and patterns, determine whether the play has a subplot or second plot. If so, how is it related to the main plot? Is a significant pattern of action repeated? If so, what is the effect? To what extent do these parallel or repetitive patterns influence theme and meaning? How do they control your responses?

CHARACTERS. (See also Chapter 4.) Focus on a significant figure and formulate a central idea about his or her personality, function, or meaning. Is the character round or flat? Static or dynamic? Individualized or stereotyped? Realistic or nonrealistic? Symbolic? How is the character described in the stage directions? By other characters? By himself or herself? What does he or she do, think, say? What is the character's attitude toward the environment? The action? Other characters? Himself or herself? To what extent does he or she articulate and/or embody key ideas in the play?

POINT OF VIEW AND PERSPECTIVE. (See also Chapter 5.) In many plays, such as *Hamlet* (Chapter 27) and *Before Breakfast,* the playwright presents the action from the perspective of an individual character. The audience therefore sees things as this character sees the same things, influences them, and is influenced by them. When you deal with such a technique, consider how the perspective affects the play's structure and meaning. Why is this point of view useful or striking? What does it suggest about character? Theme? To what extent does your reaction to the play correspond with or diverge from this perspective?

Another feature of perspective is that characters may speak directly to the audience, in a *soliloquy,* or indirectly, in a *monologue.* In dealing with these perspectives, consider whether you sympathize with the character doing the speaking. What information does the character convey? What is he or she trying to prove? What is the tone of the speech? What do these devices contribute to your response? Generally, what does the perspective contribute to your understanding of the play?

SETTING, SETS, AND PROPS. (See also Chapter 6.) Normally, you will not write about setting and properties in isolation; such an essay would simply produce a detailed description of the setting(s) and objects. Instead, a discussion of setting in drama should be linked to another element, such as character, mood, or meaning. Such an essay will demonstrate the ways in which setting(s) and objects help establish the time, place, characters, lifestyle, values, or ideas.

When dealing with a single setting, pay close attention to the opening stage directions and any other directions or dialogue that describe the environment or objects. In plays with multiple settings, you will normally select one or two for examination. Ask yourself whether the setting is realistic or nonrealistic and to what extent it may be symbolic. What details and objects are specified? What do these tell you about the time, the place, and the characters and their way of life and values? To what extent does the setting contribute to the play's tone, atmosphere, impact, and meaning?

DICTION, IMAGERY, AND STYLE. (See also Chapters 7, 14, and 16.) As with setting, try to connect the devices of language to some other element such as tone, character, or meaning. Investigate the play's levels of diction and types of dialect, jargon, slang, or clichés. To what extent do these techniques define the characters and support or undercut their ideas? What connotative words or phrases are repeated? Which are spoken at particularly significant moments? What striking or consistent threads of imagery, metaphor, tone, or meaning do you find? How do all these aspects of language shape your reaction?

REFERRING TO PLAYS AND PARTS OF PLAYS

Italicize or <u>underline</u> the titles of plays as you would do for book titles. In referring to speeches, assume that your reader may have a text different from yours. Therefore, provide the information necessary for finding the exact location, regardless of text.

In the body of your essay, for a play with act, scene, and line or speech numbers, refer to *Act* (Arabic numeral), *scene* (Arabic numeral), and *line* or *speech* number (Arabic numeral), separated by commas. For clarity, spell out these words: *Hamlet accuses his mother of offenses against his father in Act 3, scene 4, line 9,* or *Claudius defends his own status as king in Act 4, scene 5, lines 120–23.*

In direct quotations, including block quotations (set apart from your own writing), write the Arabic numbers in parentheses following the quotation, as in (*3.1.33*). Use periods to separate these numbers. When no word precedes the last number, this number is understood to refer to a line; in such a case, for clarity, it is best to spell out that you are referring to a speech number: (*2.1.speech 4*). The principle you should follow is that your reference should leave no doubts in your reader's mind.

When a play is divided into acts but not scenes, or if the play contains only one act, spell out the details completely. Thus, in a play like *Death of a Salesman*, which contains two acts and an epilogue, you may refer to *Act 1, speech 348* or *Epilogue, speech 5*. If the play contains no act numbers but only numbered scenes, spell things out similarly: *scene 1, speech 29*. When referring to a one-act play like *The More the Merrier*, use the speech number: *speech 265*.

For stage directions, use the line or speech number immediately preceding the direction, and abbreviate *stage direction* as *S.D.*: *scene 1, speech 16 S.D.* Your reader will then know that you are referring to the stage direction following speech 16 in scene 1. If there are stage directions at the opening of the play before the speeches begin (as in *Before Breakfast*), use a zero and then a decimal point followed by an Arabic numeral to refer to the paragraph of directions. Thus *0.3 S.D.* refers to the third paragraph of directions at the play's beginning.

For prefaces, scene directions, and casts of characters. Not all of the plays have prefatory material, but if there is a preface, refer to it as though you are considering a stage direction, as in *Miller reminds us to be "aware of towering angular shapes" in the introductory remarks to Act 1 (0.2 S.D).*

For scene directions at the beginning of acts or scenes, use the most specific style to make the circumstances clear: *The scene directions for Act 1 of Ibsen's* A Dollhouse *describe the comfortable home of the Helmer family,* or *In the section marked "The Setting" beginning Act 1 of* Mulatto, *Hughes states that Colonel Norwood's living room is "long outdated" (0.2 S.D.).*

For the cast of characters, the same principle applies. Spell out what you mean, such as the *cast of characters*, the *Characters* list, or the *Dramatis Personae*, as in *"In the 'Characters' list of* Mulatto, *Hughes indicates that Colonel Norwood is a 'commanding' person."* The important thing about referring to parts of plays is that you be clear and exact. The guidance offered here will cover most situations, but complications and exceptions will occur. When they do, always ask your instructor what to do and what systems of reference to use.

TONE AND ATMOSPHERE.   (See also Chapters 8 and 18.) Try to deal with *how* the tone is established and *what impact* it has on the play's meaning. Seek those devices the playwright employs to control your attitudes toward individual characters, situations, and outcomes. Look for clues in stage directions, diction, imagery, rhetorical devices, tempo, and context. Is tone articulated directly? Or indirectly, through irony? Also try to establish the presence of dramatic irony: To what extent do you (as a reader or spectator) know more than many of the onstage characters?

SYMBOLISM AND ALLEGORY.   (See also Chapters 9 and 17.) Try to determine the characters, objects, settings, situations, actions, words or phrases, and/or costumes that seem to be symbolic. What do they symbolize, and how do you know that they are symbolic? Are they universal or contextual? Is the symbolism extensive and consistent enough to form an allegorical system? If so, what are the two levels of meaning addressed by the allegory? To what extent does the symbolism or allegory shape the play's meaning and your responses to it?

THEME.   (See also Chapters 10 and 23.) The questions and areas of concern listed above should help you in discussing theme. Try to connect theme with various other aspects of the play such as character, conflict, action, setting, language, or symbolism. What key ideas does the play explore, and what aspects of the play convey these ideas most emphatically? In dealing with each topic and question, isolate the elements and devices that have the strongest impact on meaning.

Strategies for Organizing Ideas

For an essay on drama, you might choose from a number of strategies. If you are writing about loneliness and frustration in Keller's *Tea Party*, for example, you might select a number of objects or occurrences as the launching point for your discussion. Some of these might be the tea trolley and the sofa, the bringing in of the cocoa, or the paperboy's rapid movement past the window. In discussing the crimes of Claudius in Shakespeare's *Hamlet*, you might choose (1) the testimony of the Ghost to Hamlet, (2) Claudius's reaction to the players' scene, (3) his speech as he is praying, and (4) his poisoning of the cup, showing how these actions convincingly establish his villainy. For such essays, you might devote separate paragraphs to each element, or you might use two or more paragraphs for each element as you develop your ideas further.

Similar strategies can be found for every possible type of essay on drama. In dealing with character in Keller's *Tea Party*, for example, you might claim that a number of symbolic props help to establish and reinforce the characters of the two aged sisters and their loneliness. You might then use separate paragraphs to discuss these related symbols, such as Hester's wheelchair, the arrangement of the furniture, the preparation for serving tea. Similarly, in writing about language in plays like Anton Chekhov's *The Bear* (Chapter 28), you would establish how the particular play connects qualities of speech to revelations about topics such as character and idea. Thus, Smirnov's constant use of exclamations, shouts, and profanity, at least until shortly before the play's end, establish his irascibility.

DEMONSTRATIVE STUDENT ESSAY

Eugene O'Neill's Use of Negative Descriptions and Stage Directions in *Before Breakfast*° as a Means of Revealing Character

[1]   In the one-act play <u>Before Breakfast</u>, O'Neill dramatizes the suicidal crisis and climax of a worsening husband-wife relationship. The story is clear. Mrs. Rowland, when still a young girl, was naive and opportunistic. She seduced and then married Alfred Rowland, who was the heir of his father's millions. Her resulting pregnancy ended in stillbirth. As if this were not enough, Alfred's father died not a millionaire, but a pauper. <u>During the years of these disappointments, Mrs. Rowland has lost whatever pleasantness she once possessed and has descended into a state of personal neglect, alcoholism, and selfishness.</u>* <u>To bring out these traits early in the play, O'Neill relies on negative descriptions and stage directions.</u>†

[2]   <u>The descriptions of Mrs. Rowland's personal neglect emphasize her loss of self-esteem.</u> The directions indicate that she has allowed her figure to become "a shapeless stoutness" and that she has piled her hair into a "drab-colored mass." This neglect of her physical person is capped off, according to O'Neill's description, by her blue dress, which is "shabby and worn" and "formless" (1210, 0.3 S.D.). Clearly, the shabbiness and excessive wear may result from poverty and thus show little about her character, but the formlessness of the dress indicates a characteristic lack of concern about appearance, also shown by her stoutness and her hair. This slovenliness shows how she wants to appear in public, because she is dressed and ready to go to work for the day. O'Neill's negative descriptions thus define her lack of self-respect.

    <u>Similarly uncomplimentary, O'Neill's directions about her sneakiness reveal her dependence on alcohol.</u> A serious sign of distress, even though it might also be funny onstage, is the direction indicating that she takes out a bottle of gin that she keeps hidden in a "dish closet" (1210, speech 1 S.D.). With this stage direction O'Neill symbolizes the weakest trait of the secret drinker, which he also shows in the direction that Mrs. Rowland brightens up once she has taken a stiff jolt of gin:

[3]   The large dose of alcohol she has taken has an almost immediate effect. Her features become more animated, she seems to gather energy, and she looks at the bedroom with a hard, vindictive smile on her lips. (1210, speech 3 S.D.)

    It is safe to assume that these stage directions, on the morning of the play's action, would also have applied to her behavior on many previous mornings. In short, O'Neill is telling us that Mrs. Rowland is a secret alcoholic.

[4]   <u>The furtiveness of her drinking also shows up in her search of Alfred's clothing, which also shows her selfishness and bitterness.</u> When she methodically empties his pockets and uncovers the letter that we soon learn is from his mistress, the stage directions show that she unhesitatingly reads the letter. Then O'Neill directs the actress to form "a cruel smile on her lips" as she thinks about what to do with this new information (1211, speech 4 S.D.). As with the drinking, we see Mrs. Rowland rifling through Alfred's things only this once, but the action suggests that this secretive prying is a regular feature of her life. However, it is her discovery on <u>this</u> morning--before breakfast--that is the key to the action, because her extensive monologue against her husband, which constitutes most of the play,

°See pp. 1209–1214 for this play.
*Central idea.
†Thesis sentence.

allows her to vent all her hatred by reproaching him about his lack of work, his neglect of her, the time he spends with friends, and his love affair.

[5]
While O'Neill uses these stage directions and descriptions to convey Mrs. Rowland's unpleasantness, he provides balance in her speeches and additional actions. He makes her a master of harangue, but there is nothing either in the directions or in her speeches to indicate that she wants to drive Alfred to suicide. Indeed, her horror at his suicide is genuine--just as it concludes the play with an incredible shock. In addition, on the positive side, her speeches show that despite her alcoholism and anger she is actually functioning in the outside world--as a seamstress--and that it is she who provides the meager money on which the couple is living (1211, speech 6). In addition, she is working despite the fact that she has been feeling ill for a period of time (1213, speech 20). She also has enough concern for Alfred to bring him hot water for shaving (1212, speech 14 S.D.).

[6]
It is clear that O'Neill wants us to conclude that if Mrs. Rowland were a supportive person, Alfred might not be the nervous alcoholic who cuts his throat in the bathroom. However, the play does not make clear that he ever could have been better, even with the maximum support of a perfect wife. Certainly, Mrs. Rowland is not supportive. The stage directions and speeches show that she is limited by her weakness and bitterness. With such defects of character, she has unquestionably never given Alfred any support at all, and probably never could. Everything that O'Neill tells us about her indicates that she is petty and selfish, and that she originally married Alfred expecting to receive and not to give.

[7]
As things stand at the beginning of the play, Alfred is at the brink of despair, and Mrs. Rowland's bitter and reproachful speeches drive him to self-destruction. Despite all the malice that O'Neill attributes to her character through the stage descriptions and directions, however, it is not possible to say that she is the sole cause of Alfred's suicide. O'Neill shows that Mrs. Rowland is an unpleasant, spiteful, and messy whiner, but it is not possible to reach any further conclusions.

WORK CITED

Eugene O'Neill, Before Breakfast. Literature: An Introduction to Reading and Writing. Ed. Edgar V. Roberts and Henry E. Jacobs. 7th ed. Upper Saddle River: Prentice Hall, 2004. 1209-1214.

Commentary on the Essay

This essay shows how dramatic conventions can be considered in reference to the analysis of character. Although the essay refers briefly to Mrs. Rowland's speeches, it stresses those descriptions and directions that O'Neill designs specifically for the actress performing the role. The essay thus indicates one way to discuss a play, as distinguished from a story or poem.

The introductory paragraph contains enough of the story about Mrs. Rowland and her husband to help the reader make sense of the subsequent material about the stage directions and descriptions. Throughout the essay, paragraph transitions are effected by words such as *similarly, also, while,* and *then.*

Paragraph 2, the first of the body, deals with O'Neill's stage directions concerning Mrs. Rowland's slovenly appearance and personal care. Paragraphs 3 and 4 are concerned with directions about her behavior—first her drinking and then her search of Alfred's clothing. Paragraph 5 briefly attempts to consider how O'Neill uses Mrs. Rowland's speeches and other actions to balance the totally negative portrait he builds up through the negative stage directions.

Paragraphs 6 and 7 close the essay. Paragraph 6 considers how the stage directions lead no further than the conclusion that the Rowlands' marriage is a terrible one. Paragraph 7 continues the argument of paragraph 6, with the additional thought that O'Neill's stage directions do not justify concluding that Mrs. Rowland's spiteful character is the cause of her husband's suicide.

Special Topics for Writing and Argument about the Elements of Drama

1. *Tea Party* might be considered sentimental, on the grounds that the two elderly characters are presented to evoke sympathy and anguish, not to resemble the life of real persons. Write an essay defending the play against this judgment, being sure to make references to Keller's characterizations and her development of character.

2. Compare Kauffmann's play *The More the Merrier*, Hardy's poem "The Workbox" (p. 764), and Lawrence's story "The Horse Dealer's Daughter" (p. 478). To what common social level do the characters belong? How do they apparently function within this level? What common concerns about personal life do you discover in the three sets of characters? What common patterns do the play and the story reveal about the previous lives and concerns of the characters? (For a method of treating comparison and contrast, see Chapter 35.)

3. *Before Breakfast* is set in an apartment in Greenwich Village in lower Manhattan around 1916. It was performed in Greenwich Village in December 1916. Write an essay that deals with the following questions.
   a. What do you make of this convergence of settings—artistic and realistic?
   b. What did O'Neill assume about his original audience's reaction to the setting?

4. Compare the treatment of the religious scenes in *The Second Shepherds' Play* and *The Visit to the Sepulcher*. Why do you suppose the *Shepherds' Play* is longer and more full of detail about the lives of the shepherds?

5. Write an essay on one of the following topics. Before you begin writing, read Chapter 33 for suggestions on how to proceed.
   a. The viewpoint of the men in *Trifles*.
   b. A feminist analysis of Mrs. Rowland in *Before Breakfast*.
   c. A close formal (New Critical) analysis of the dialogue (speeches 16–194) between Emily and Simon in *The More the Merrier*.
   d. The two sisters as archetypal old people in *Tea Party*.

6. On the basis of the plays included in this chapter, write an essay dealing with the characteristics of the dramatic form. Consider topics such as dialogue, monologue, soliloquy, action, vocal ranges, staging, comparative lengths of plays, pauses in speech, stage directions, laughter, seriousness, and the means by which the dramatists engage the audience in characters and situations.

7. Using the catalogue in your library, look up the category *Drama—Criticism* or *Drama—History and Criticism*, whichever title your library uses. You will find there a number of categories, such as the relationship of drama to (a) elements, (b) history, (c) origin, (d) philosophy, (e) production, (f) religion, (g) stagecraft, and (h) themes. Develop a short bibliography on one of these topics and take out two or three of the relevant books. Describe them briefly, and explain—and criticize if possible—the principal ideas in one of the chapters.

The Tragic Vision:
Affirmation Through Loss

Tragedy is drama in which a major character undergoes a loss but also achieves illumination or a new perspective. It is considered the most elevated literary form because it concentrates affirmatively on the religious and cosmic implications of its major character's misfortunes. In ancient Greece, it originated as a key element in Athenian religious festivals during the decades before Athens became a major military, economic, and cultural power during the fifth century B.C.E.

Tragedy, however, was not religious in a sectarian sense. It did not dramatize religious doctrines and did not present a consistent religious view. To the Athenians, religion connected the past with the present and with the gods, and through this connection it served to enrich individuals, society, and the state.

Originally, tragedy in Athens was associated with the worship of a specific god—Dionysus, one of the twelve principal Athenian deities who, it was thought, transformed human personality, freed people from care and grief, assured their fertility, and provided them with joy. To elevate this god in the eyes of his fellow Athenians, the Athenian tyrant Peisistratus (ruled 560–527 B.C.E.) added the worship of Dionysus to the regular religious festivals that the Athenians held in honor of their gods.[1]

[1]Ancient religion is difficult for us to understand because of our completely different religious traditions and the passage of 2,500 years of history. In its origins, Greek religion was local in nature—a by-product of the geographic isolation of the various Greek city-states. Collective public worship of a centralized god within centrally located religious buildings—like the churches, temples, and mosques we know today—did not then exist. Instead, the Greeks believed in many gods with varying powers and interests who could travel invisibly and at will from place to place within their dominions. Consequently the Greeks erected many separate local shrines and sanctuaries, which were considered holy to particular gods and where people might place offerings and say prayers. Large temples built in important city-states like Athens and Corinth were dedicated to gods, such as Zeus, Athena, and Apollo, that important citizens especially revered. Even then, the temples were not designed for mass worship, but rather were considered resident sanctuaries for the gods themselves. The major space in the temples was a holy-of-holies reserved only for the god. To make public this essentially private worship, the Greek city-states held religious festivals such as the Athenian celebrations of Dionysus and Athena.

∿ THE ORIGINS OF TRAGEDY

From the standpoint of drama, the most significant of these Dionysiac festivals were the Lenaia and the Great or City Dionysia. The **Lenaia** was a short celebration held in January (the Greek month *Gamelion*), and the **City Dionysia** for Great Dionysia) was a weeklong event in March–April (*Elaphebolion*, the month of stags). In the sixth century B.C.E., ceremonies held during the festival of the City Dionysia began to include tragedy, although not in the form that has been transmitted to us. The philosopher and critic Aristotle (384–322 B.C.E.), writing almost two hundred years after tragedy first appeared, claimed that the first tragedies developed from a choral ode called a **dithyramb**—an ode or song that was sung or chanted and also danced by large choruses at the festivals.[2] According to Aristotle, the first tragedies were choral improvisations originating with "the authors of the Dithyramb" (*Poetics* IV.12, p. 19).

The Stories of Tragedy Were Drawn from Tales of Prehistoric Times

From Aristotle's claim, we can conclude that tragedy soon took on the characteristics and conventions that elevated it. For subject matter, writers turned to well-known myths about the heroes and demigods of the prehistoric period between the vanished age of bronze and the living age of iron. These myths described individual adventures and achievements, including epic explorations and battles that had taken place principally during the time of the Trojan War. Like the stories in the Bible, the Greek myths illustrated divine–human relationships and also served as examples or models of heroic behavior. With very few exceptions, these myths became the fixed tragic subject matter. Indeed, Aristotle called them the "received legends" that by his time had become the "usual subjects of tragedy" (*Poetics* IX.8, p. 37).

The mythical heroes—many of whom were objects of cult worship—were kings, queens, princes, and princesses. They engaged in conflicts; they suffered; and, often, they died. Though great and noble, they were nevertheless human, and a common critical judgment is that they were dominated by **hubris** or **hybris** (arrogant pride, insolence, contemptuous violence), which was manifested in destructive actions such as deceit, subterfuge, lying, betrayal, revenge, cruelty, murder, suicide, patricide, infanticide, and self-mutilation. By truthfully demonstrating the faults of these heroes along with their greatness, the writers of

---

[2]S. H. Butcher, *Aristotle's Theory of Poetry and Fine Art*, 4th ed. (New York: Dover, 1951), p. 19 (VI.12). All parenthetical references to Aristotle are from this edition, but see also Stephen Halliwell, *The Poetics of Aristotle: Translation and Commentary* (Chapel Hill: U of North Carolina P, 1987). The origin of the word *dithyramb* is obscure. Some ancient etymologists claimed that the word was derived from the legendary "double birth" of Dionysus. This derivation is based on the idea that dithyramb is a compound (*dis*, "two," and *thyra*, "door") referring to the myth that Zeus removed Dionysus from the womb of his mother, Semele, and then placed the fetus within his thigh. When Zeus removed Dionysus, the god had "come through the door" of birth twice. This derivation, however, has been disputed. For a description of the origin of comedy during the festivals for Dionysus, see Chapter 28.

tragedy also invoked philosophical and religious issues that provided meaning and value in the face of misfortune and suffering.

The Word *Tragedy* Underwent an Elevation in Meaning

One of the genuine puzzles about tragedy is the word itself, which combines the Greek words *tragos* ("goat") and *oide* ("ode" or "song")—a "goat ode" or "goat song." This meaning raises the question of how so unlikely a word is linked to the tragic form. One often-repeated answer is that the word was first applied to choral ceremonials performed at the ritual sacrifice of a goat. Another is that the word described a choral competition in which a goat was the prize.

A more persuasive recent answer is that the word *tragedy* stemmed from the word *tragoidoi*, or "billy goat singers," which was applied pejoratively to the young men (*ephebes*) in the choruses.[3] The ephebes were military trainees between the ages of eighteen and twenty. Those trainees who were best at close-order drill were selected as choral members because the dramatic choruses required precision movements. Because they were young, however, they were still likened to goats.[4] Indeed, at first tragedy was apparently not called *tragodia* (tragedy) at all, but rather *tragoidoi*, as though the chorus members were more important than the speeches they recited. This explanation is consistent with the improvisatory origins of tragedy that Aristotle describes. In the decades following its beginnings, the genre grew in importance, quality, and stature, and the word *tragedy* underwent the accompanying elevation that it still possesses.

Tragedy Evolved from a Choral Form to a Dramatic Form

Because the surviving Athenian plays are dominated by acting parts, modern readers sometimes conclude that the chorus parts annoyingly interrupt the main action. It may be surprising to recognize that in the beginning there were no individual actors at all, only choruses. The introduction of actors—and their eventual domination—was one of the improvisations that Aristotle associates with the evolution of tragedy. We can surmise that during a festival performance of an unknown choral ode, the chorus leader stepped forward to deliver lines introducing and linking the choral speeches. Because of this special function, the new speaker—called a **hypocrites** (hip-POCK-rih-tayss), which became the word for actor—was soon separated and distinguished from the chorus.

The next essential step was *impersonation*, or the assuming of a role. The *hypocrites* would represent a hero, and the chorus would represent groups such as townspeople, worshipers, youths, or elders. With the commencement of such role-playing, genuine drama had begun. According to tradition, the first

[3]For this argument, see John J. Winkler, "'The Ephebes' Song: *Tragodia and Polis*," in John J. Winkler and Froma I. Zeitlin, eds., *Nothing to Do with Dionysos? Athenian Drama in Its Social Context* (Princeton: Princeton UP, 1990), pp. 20–62. For a discussion of the military nature of the ancient Greek city-state, see Paul Rahe, "The Martial Republics of Classical Greece," *The Wilson Quarterly*, vol. 17, no. 1 (Winter 1993): 58–70.   [4]There is nothing unusual about this comparison. In English a common everyday word for a child is *kid*, which is the standard word (along with *kit*) for a young goat and also other young animals.

hypocrites or actor—and therefore the acknowledged founder of the acting profession—was the writer and choral leader Thespis, in about 536–533 B.C.E., during the time of Peisistratus.

THE ORIGIN OF TRAGEDY IN BRIEF

In the sixth century B.C.E., tragedy originated in Athens at the time of the City Dionysia, one of the major religious festivals held to celebrate Dionysus, a liberating god and one of the twelve major gods of the city. As a genre, tragedy first featured improvisations upon a type of choral ode called a *dithyramb*. It then evolved, as Aristotle says, "by slow degrees" (*Poetics* IV.12, p. 19), developing new elements as they seemed appropriate and necessary.

One of the vital new elements was an emphasis on the misfortune or death of a major character.* This emphasis resulted *not* from a preconceived theoretical design, however, but rather from the reality of suffering in the lives of the heroic subjects. As writers of tragedy developed the cosmic and religious implications of such adversity, performances offered philosophic, religious, moral, and civic benefits, and therefore, presumably, simply attending the performance of a tragedy came to be regarded as the fulfillment of a religious obligation.

Because tragedy was originally linked to the choral dithyrambs, it is important to stress that *tragedy began as a form for choruses, not for actors*. Even after actors became dominant in the plays, the chorus was important enough for Aristotle to state that "the chorus should be regarded as one of the actors" (XVIII.7, p. 69).

*Although the tragic protagonist often dies at the play's end, the extant Athenian tragedies do not follow this pattern rigidly. It is true that the major figures suffer, and sometimes they die, but often they escape punishment entirely, and they may even receive divine pardon.

THE ANCIENT COMPETITIONS IN TRAGEDY

Once Thespis set the pattern of action involving actor and chorus, the writing of tragedies as a competition within the Dionysiac festivals became institutionalized.

The Tragic Dramatists Competed for the Honor of Having Their Plays Performed

Early each summer, a number of dramatists vied for the honor of having their plays performed at the next City Dionysia, to be held the following spring. They prepared three tragedies (a **trilogy**)[5] together with a **satyr** play (a boisterous burlesque) and submitted the four works to the Eponymous Archon, one of the city's two principal magistrates and the man for whom the year was named. The three best submissions were approved, or "given a chorus," for performance at the festival. On the last day of the festival, after the performances were over, the

---

[5]In the earliest dramas, the trilogies shared a common subject, as may be seen in the *Oresteia* of Aeschylus, which is a cycle of three plays on the subject of the royal house of Agamemnon. But by the time of Sophocles and Euripides, connected trilogies were no longer required. Sophocles' *Oedipus the King* and *Oedipus at Colonus*, for example, were submitted at widely different times.

archon awarded a prize to the tragic playwright voted best for that year. There was also a prize for the best writer of a comedy. The winner's prize was not money, but rather a crown of ivy and the glory of triumph.

The Three Greatest Athenian Tragic Playwrights Were Aeschylus, Sophocles, and Euripides

To gain the honor of victory during the centuries of the competitions, many writers of tragedy composed and submitted many plays. The total number must have been exceedingly large, certainly in the high hundreds and likely in the thousands. Most of these have long since vanished because many of the writers were insignificant and also because there were no more than a few copies of each play, all handwritten on perishable papyrus scrolls.

A small number of works by three tragic playwrights, however, have survived. These dramatists are **Aeschylus** (525–456 B.C.E.), who added a second actor; **Sophocles** (ca. 496–406/5 B.C.E.), who added a third actor, created scene design, and enlarged the chorus from twelve to fifteen; and **Euripides** (ca. 484–406 B.C.E.). Although these three playwrights did not win prizes every time they entered the competitions, a consensus grew that they were the best, and by the middle of the fourth century B.C.E. their works were recognized as classics. Although tragedies had originally been intended for only one performance—at the festival for which they competed—an exception was made for these three dramatists, whose tragedies were then performed repeatedly both in Athens and elsewhere in the Greek-speaking world.

The combined output of the three classic playwrights was slightly more than three hundred plays, of which three-fourths were tragedies and one-fourth were satyr plays. As many as eight hundred years after the end of the fifth century B.C.E., these plays, together with many other Greek tragedies, satyr plays, and comedies, were available to readers who could afford to buy copies or to pay scribes to copy them.[6] However, with the increasing dominance of Christianity, the plays fell into neglect because they were considered pagan and also because vellum or parchment, which made up the pages of the books (*codices*) that replaced papyrus scrolls, was enormously expensive and was reserved for Christian works. Most of the unique and priceless copies of Athenian plays were subsequently destroyed or thrown out with the garbage.

Thirty-Three Tragedies by the Three Great Athenian Tragedians Have Survived to the Present Day

The Greek dramatic tradition might have vanished entirely had it not been for the efforts of Byzantine scholars during the ninth century C.E., when Constantinople became the center of a revival of interest in classical Greek language and

---

[6]In the third century B.C.E., a complete hand-copied set of Greek plays was apparently deposited in the Egyptian Royal Library that formed a part of the Ptolemaic museum and palace of Alexandria, but at some point all the holdings were lost, thrown away, or destroyed, just as the palace and museum were destroyed. In modern Alexandria, the location of the ancient library is not exactly known. See Luciano Canfora, *The Vanished Library: A Wonder of the Ancient World* (Berkeley: U of California P, 1990).

literature. A primary characteristic of this revival was the copying and preservation of important texts—including those of the major Greek writers. We may conclude that the scholars copied as many of the plays as they could locate, and that they tried to shelter their copies in the supposedly secure monastery libraries.

However, security was impossible to maintain during those centuries. Fire, neglect, time, political destabilization, and pillage (such as the sack of Constantinople by Christian Crusaders in 1204) took an enormous toll on the Byzantine manuscript collections. Even so, seven tragedies by Aeschylus, seven by Sophocles, and ten by Euripides somehow were saved from destruction.[7] Additionally, in the fourteenth century, a scholar named Demetrius Triclinius made a lucky find of scrolls containing nine more plays by Euripides (part of what was once a complete set), bringing the total of Euripidean plays to nineteen. Therefore, of all the hundreds upon hundreds of plays written by all the Greek tragic playwrights, thirty-three still survive intact. These plays make up the complete Greek tragedy as we know it.[8]

There is, however, just a little more: Many ancient writers often quoted brief passages from plays that were not otherwise preserved, and these portions therefore still exist. Moreover, collectors living in ancient Egypt owned many copies of the plays, and not everything from these collections was lost. In recent centuries, papyrus and vellum fragments—some quite extensive—have been recovered by archaeologists from such unlikely locations as ancient Egyptian rubbish heaps, tombs, and the linings of coffins.

ARISTOTLE AND THE NATURE OF TRAGEDY

Because Aristotle's *Poetics* (*Peri Poietikes*), the first section of his major critical work, survives substantially intact from antiquity, he is in effect the Western world's first critic and aesthetician. From him, later critics derived the various "rules" of tragic composition. He also wrote a second part of the *Poetics* concerning comedy. This second work is lost, but enough fragments and summaries survive to permit a partial hypothetical reconstruction.[9] Aristotle also considered aspects of literature in parts of other philosophical works, principally the *Ethics* and the *Politics*. In addition he, along with his students, assembled a complete catalogue of Greek tragedy from its beginnings to his own time (the

---

[7]Many standard reference works contain the assertion that these twenty-four plays were selected by an unnamed Byzantine schoolmaster for use in the Byzantine schools, and that this anthology was widely adopted and exclusively used thereafter. This claim would explain why the anthologized plays were preserved while unanthologized plays were lost. L. D. Reynolds and N. G. Wilson, in their authoritative *Scribes and Scholars: A Guide to the Transmission of Greek and Latin Literature*, 3rd ed. (Oxford UP, 1991), question this hypothesis. They point out that there is no historical record that such an anthology was ever made, that modern scholars are in truth ignorant "of the origin of the selection," and that therefore "it is perhaps best to abandon the idea that a conscious act of selection by an individual was a primary factor in determining the survival of texts" (p. 54).　[8]The survival of Greek drama was under constant threat until the first printed editions were published at the beginning of the sixteenth century.　[9]See Richard Janko, trans., *Aristotle, Poetics I with the Tractatus Coislinianus, A Hypothetical Reconstruction of Poetics II, the Fragments of the On Poets* (Indianapolis: Hackett, 1987), pp. 47–55.

Didaskaliae). He was therefore able to base his criticism on virtually the entire body of Greek tragedy, including written copies of many plays that he had probably never seen performed. No one before or since has had more firsthand knowledge of Greek tragedy. His criticism is therefore especially valuable because it rests not only on his acute powers of observation, but also on his unique and encyclopedic knowledge.

As we have seen, Aristotle states that tragedy grew out of improvisations related to dithyrambic choral odes. He adds that once tragedy reached its "natural" or ideal form it stopped evolving (*Poetics* IV.12, p. 19). His criticism is designed to explain the ideal characteristics of tragedy. Throughout the *Poetics* he stresses concepts of exactitude, proportion, appropriateness, and control. His famous definition of tragedy is in accord with these concepts. In the sixth chapter of the *Poetics*, he states that tragedy is "an imitation of an action that is serious, complete, and of a certain magnitude; in language embellished with each kind of artistic ornament, the several kinds being found in separate parts of the play; in the form of action, not of narrative; through pity and fear effecting the proper purgation of these emotions" (VI.2, p. 23).

To Aristotle, the Key to Tragedy Is the Concept of Catharsis

The last part of this definition—that purgation or **catharsis** is the end or goal of tragedy—crystallizes the earlier parts. In Aristotle's view, tragedy arouses the disturbing emotions of pity and fear (*eleos* and *phobos*), and, through the experience of the drama, brings about a "proper purgation" or purification of these emotions. Originally, the word *catharsis* was a medical term, and therefore many interpreters argue that tragedy produces a therapeutic effect through an actual purging or "vomiting" of emotions—a sympathetic release of feelings that produces emotional relief and encourages psychological health. In other words, tragedy heals.

A complementary view is that tragic catharsis has a larger public and moral purpose. In this sense, Aristotle's description of tragedy is an implicit argument defending literature itself against the strong disapproval of his teacher, Plato.[10] Both master and pupil accepted the premise that human beings behave thoughtlessly and stupidly as a result of uncontrolled emotion. While in the grip of deep feelings, people cannot be virtuous and can do no good for others because they make bad decisions that produce bad personal, social, political, military, and moral results. Consequently, if individual temperance and public justice are to prevail, there is a universal need to moderate and regulate the emotions. Because Plato states that the emotionalism of literature is untrue, undignified, and also unreasonable, he denies that literature can address this need.

But in the *Poetics* and in relevant parts of other works, Aristotle shows that tragedy indeed addresses this need, and does so through the effect of catharsis. By arousing the powerful feelings of pity and fear, tragedy trains or develops the

---

[10]See Janko, especially pp. xvi–xx, and Butcher's discussion on pp. 245–251 of *Aristotle's Theory of Poetry and Fine Art*.

emotions so that people become *habituated* to measuring, shaping, and channeling their feelings—controlling them, and not being controlled by them. Through catharsis, people are led to the development of an emotional mean, a condition of poise and balance among emotional forces, and they achieve this balanced state harmlessly because in the artistic context of tragedy they are immune to the damage such emotions may do in actual life. Tragedy therefore assists in the development of moral virtue, for people who have experienced the emotional catharsis or regulation of tragedy will be led to love and hate correctly, to direct their loyalties correctly, and also to make correct decisions and take correct actions, both for themselves and, more significantly, for the public.

It is important to stress Aristotle's idea that catharsis is also brought about by other literary genres, especially comedy and epic, as well as by music. In other words, artistic works have in common that they cleanse or purify the emotions. It is through the continuous and renewed shaping and regulating of feelings—catharsis—that tragedy, like literature broadly, encourages moral virtue, and therefore on both philosophical and religious grounds it is defensible and necessary.

The Tragic Plot Is Structured to Arouse and Shape Emotions

In the light of the concept of catharsis, Aristotle's description of the formal aspects and characteristics of tragedy can be seen as an outline of the ways in which these characteristics first arouse the emotions and then regulate and shape them.

THE TRAGIC PLOT REQUIRES THE REPRESENTATION OF A SINGLE MAJOR ACTION. Aristotle concedes that tragedy is not true in the sense that history is true. He therefore stresses that a tragic plot, or **muthos,** is not an exact imitation or duplication of life, but rather a **representation** or *mimesis.* The concept of representation acknowledges both the moral role of the writer and the artistic freedom needed to create works conducive to proper responses. A tragic plot therefore consists of a self-contained and concentrated single action. Anything outside this action, such as unrelated incidents in the life of the major character, is not to be contained in the play. The action of *Oedipus the King,* for example, is focused on Oedipus's determination as king of Thebes to free his city from the pestilence that is destroying it. Although other aspects of his life are introduced in the play's dialogue because they are relevant to the action, they are reported rather than dramatized. Only those incidents integral to the action are included in the play.

TRAGIC RESPONSES ARE BROUGHT TO A HEAD THROUGH REVERSAL, RECOGNITION, AND SUFFERING. Aristotle's discussion of the three major elements of tragic plot is particularly significant. The elements all appear near the conclusion of a tragic play because they are the probable and inevitable results of the early elements of exposition and complication. First is the "**reversal** of the situation" (*peripeteia*) from apparent good to bad, or a "change [usually also a surprise] by which the action veers round to its opposite," as in *Oedipus the King,* where the outcome is the reverse of what Oedipus intends and expects (XI.1, p. 41). Even if the outcome is unhappy—especially if it is unhappy—it is "the right ending" (XIII.6, p. 47) because it is the most tragic; that is, it evokes the greatest degree of pity and fear.

Second is "a change from ignorance to knowledge, producing love or hate between the persons destined by the poet for good or bad fortune." Aristotle calls this change *anagnorisis* or **recognition** (XI.2, p. 41). In the best and most powerful tragedies, according to him, the reversal and the recognition occur together and create surprise. Aristotle considers recognition to be the discovery of the true identity and involvement of persons, the establishment of guilt or innocence, and the revelation of previously unknown details, for "it is upon such situations that the issues of good or bad fortune will depend" (XI.4, p. 41). One might add that recognition is of major importance because ideally, upon discovering the truth, the protagonist acknowledges errors and accepts responsibility. In *Oedipus the King*, Oedipus ultimately recognizes his own guilt even though during most of the play he has been trying to evade it. He then becomes the agent of his own punishment. Because such recognition illustrates that human beings have the strength to preserve their integrity even in adversity, it is one of the elements making tragedy the highest of all literary forms.

Aristotle describes the third part of plot as a "scene of suffering" (*pathos*) which he defines as "a destructive or painful action, such as death on the stage, bodily agony, wounds, and the like" (XI.6, p. 43). He stresses that the destructive or painful action, including death, should be caused by "those who are near or dear to one another" (XIV.4, pp. 49–50). That is, violence should occur within a royal household or family rather than against a hostile foe. Because the trust, love, and protectiveness that one hopes for in a family is replaced by treachery, hate, and mayhem, the suffering of the tragic protagonist is one of the major ways in which tragedy arouses fear and pity.

To Aristotle, Additional Tragic Requirements Are Seriousness, Completeness, and Artistic Balance

The first part of Aristotle's definition, asserting that a tragedy is "serious, complete, and of a certain magnitude," can be seen as a vital aspect of his analysis of how tragedy shapes responses. The term **serious,** or noble or elevated, concerns the play's tone and level of life, in contrast with the boisterousness and ribaldry of Athenian comedies. While comedy represents human character as less serious than it is, tragedy shows it as more serious (II.4, p. 13). Seriousness is also a consequence of the political and cosmological dimensions of the issues in which the heroic characters are engaged. By **complete,** we understand that a tragedy must be shaped and perfected into a logical and finished whole. The beginning, the middle, and the ending must be so perfectly placed that changing or removing any part would spoil the work's integrity (VII.2-3, p. 31). By stating that a tragedy should be of a "certain" or proportional **magnitude,** Aristotle refers to a balance of length and subject matter. The play should be short enough to "be easily embraced by the memory" and long enough to "admit of a change . . . from good fortune to bad" (VII.5–7, p. 33). In other words, everything is artistically balanced; nothing superfluous is included, and nothing essential is omitted.

For Aristotle, Appropriate Diction and Song Are Necessary in Tragedy

For modern readers, Aristotle's description of tragic structure is more easily understood than his discussion of tragic language. His statement about tragic poetry—that it is the "mere metrical arrangement of the words" (VI.4, p. 25)—is clear as far as it goes, for the plays themselves show that the tragic playwrights used poetic forms deliberately and exactly. These characteristics, however, do not survive translation into modern English. As for **song** (*melos*), Aristotle's claim that it is "a term whose sense everyone understands" (VI.4, p. 25) is not illuminating. What is therefore significant about his discussion of verse and song is his statement that the "several kinds of artistic ornament are to be found in separate parts of the play" (VI.2, p. 23). That is, where verse is appropriate, the tragic playwrights include poetry as a means of elevating the drama; where music and song are appropriate, they include these to increase beauty and intensify the drama. As with the other aspects of tragedy, therefore, placement, balance, and appropriateness are the most fitting standards of judgment.

The Tragedy's Hero Is the Focus of Sympathetic Tragic Emotions

Aristotle's description of the tragic protagonist or hero, though not included in his definition of tragedy, is integral to the concept of catharsis and therefore to his description of tragedy. As with the other parts of his analysis, he demonstrates the exact effects and limits of the topic—the perfected balance of form necessary to bring about proper tragic responses. To this end, he states that we, as normally imperfect human beings, are able to sympathize with a "highly renowned and prosperous" protagonist because that protagonist is also imperfect—a person who exists between extremes, just "like ourselves" (XIII.2, p. 45). The misfortunes of this noble protagonist are caused not by "vice" or "depravity" but rather by "some great error or frailty" (XIII.4, p. 47). Aristotle's word for such shortcomings is *hamartia*, which is often translated as **tragic flaw**, and it is this flaw that makes the protagonist human—neither a saint nor a villain. If the protagonist were a saint (one who is "eminently good and just"), his or her suffering would be undeserved and unfair, and our pity would be overwhelmed by indignation and anger—not a proper tragic reaction. Nor could we pity a villain experiencing adversity and pain, for we would judge the suffering to be deserved, and our primary response would then be satisfaction—also not a proper reaction. Therefore, an ideal tragedy is fine-tuned to control our emotions exactly, producing horror and fear because the suffering protagonist is a person like ourselves, and pity because the suffering far exceeds what the protagonist deserves.

ARISTOTLE'S VIEW OF TRAGEDY IN BRIEF

Aristotle's definition of tragedy hinges on his idea that tragedy, as a dramatic form, is designed to evoke powerful emotions and thereby, through catharsis, to serve both a salutary and ethical purpose. The tragic incidents and plot must be artistically construct-ed to produce the "essential tragic effect" (VI.12, p. 27). Therefore Aristotle stresses that plot and incidents, arranged for this effect, form the end or goal—the "chief thing of all"—of tragedy (VI.10, p. 27).

IRONY IN TRAGEDY

Implicit in the excessiveness of tragic suffering is the idea that the universe is mysterious and often unfair and that unseen but powerful forces—fate, fortune, circumstances, and the gods—directly intervene in human life. Ancient Athen-ian belief was that the gods give rewards or punishments to suit their own pur-poses, which mortals cannot understand, bring about, or prevent. For example, in *Prometheus Bound* (attributed to Aeschylus), the god Hephaestus binds Prometheus to a rock in the Scythian Mountains as punishment for having given fire and technology to humankind. (A good deed produces suffering.) Con-versely, in *Medea*, Euripides shows that the god Apollo permits Medea to escape after killing her own children. (An evil deed produces reward.)

Situational and Cosmic Irony Are Essential in Tragedy

These examples illustrate the pervasiveness of situational and cosmic irony in tragedy. Characters are thrust into situations that are caused by others or that they themselves unwittingly cause. When they try to act responsibly and nobly to relieve their situations, their actions do not produce the expected results—this is consistent with Aristotle's idea of reversal—and usually things come out badly. For example, Oedipus brings suffering on himself just when he succeeds—and *because* he succeeds—in rescuing his city. Whether on the personal or cosmic level, therefore, there is no escape—no way to evade responsibility, and no way to change the universal laws that thrust human beings into such situations.

Situational and cosmic irony is not confined to ancient tragedies. Shake-speare's tragic hero Hamlet speaks about the "divinity that shapes our ends," thus expressing the unpredictability of hopes, plans, and achievements, and also the wisdom of resignation. In *Death of a Salesman*, Miller's hero, Willy Loman, is gripped not so much by divine power as by time—the agent of destruction being the inexorable force of economic circumstances.

The Tragic Dilemma Confronts the Problem of Free Will vs. Fate

These ironies are related to what is called the **tragic dilemma**—a situation that forces the tragic protagonist to make a difficult choice. The tragic dilemma has also been called a "lose-lose" situation. Thus, Oedipus cannot shirk his duty as king of Thebes because that would be ruinous. He therefore tries to eliminate his city's affliction, but that course also is ruinous. In other words, the choices posed in a tragic dilemma seemingly permit freedom of will, but the consequences of any choice demonstrate the inescapable fact that powerful forces, perhaps even fate or inevitability, baffle even the most reasonable and noble intentions. As Hamlet states, "O cursèd spite, / That ever I was born to set it right" (1.5. 188–89).

Dramatic Irony Focuses Attention on the Tragic Limitations of Human Vision and Knowledge

It is from a perspective of something like divinity that we as readers or spectators perceive the action of tragedies. We are like the gods because we always know more than the characters. Such dramatic irony permits us, for example, to know what Oedipus does not know: In defensive rage, he killed his real father, and he himself is therefore his city's bane. Similar dramatic irony can be found in Shakespeare's *Hamlet,* for we realize that Claudius murdered Hamlet's father while Hamlet himself has only unconfirmable suspicions of this truth. The underlying basis of dramatic irony in real life is of course that none of us can know our own futures exactly, and few if any can anticipate accident, illness, and all the social, economic, and political adversity that may distress or destroy our way of life.

[margin handwritten note: bane- poison Cause of Woe]

❧ THE ANCIENT ATHENIAN AUDIENCE AND THEATER

Athenian audiences of the fifth century B.C.E., predominantly free men but also a small number of women, took their theater seriously. Indeed, as young men many citizens had taken active parts in the parades and choruses. Admission was charged for those able to pay, but subsidies allowed poorer people to attend as well. Rich Athenians, as a duty (*liturgeia*) to the state, underwrote the costs of the productions—except for three professional actors who were paid by the government. Each wealthy man, for his contribution, was known as a *choragos,* or choral sponsor. To gain public recognition, the choragos sometimes performed as the leader of the chorus.

Ancient Athenian Theater Originated in the Marketplace, or Agora

In the beginning, tragic performances were given specially designated space in the Athenian *agora,* or marketplace. In the center of the performing area was an altar dedicated to Dionysus, around which the choruses danced and chanted. Wooden risers were set up for the spectators.

Ancient Greek Plays Were Performed in the Athenian Theater of Dionysus

By the early fifth century B.C.E., a half-circular outdoor theater (*theatron,* or "place for seeing") was constructed at the base of the hill at the southern base of the Acropolis in the area sacred to Dionysus (see the photograph, Insert III-1).

Ancient theater at Epidauros, Greece.

All later performances of tragedies were held at this **Theater of Dionysus,** which held as many as fourteen thousand people (the comic dramatist Aristophanes indicated that thirteen thousand were in attendance at one of his plays). In the earliest days of the theater, most spectators sat on the sloping ground, but eventually wooden and then stone benches were constructed in the rising semicircle, with more elegant seating for dignitaries in front. Although the Theater was outdoors, the acoustics were sufficiently good to permit audiences to hear both the chorus and the actors, provided that the audience remained reasonably quiet during performances.

THE *ORCHESTRA* WAS THE FOCAL POINT OF BOTH SIGHT AND SOUND. Centered at the base of the hill—the focus of attention—was a round area modeled on the one that had been used in the agora. This was the *orchestra* (or-KESS-tra) or "dancing place," which was about sixty-five feet in diameter. Here, each chorus sang its odes and performed its dance movements to the rhythm of a double-piped flute (*aulos*), an instrument that was also used to mark the step in military drill. In the center was a permanent altar.

THE *SKENE* WAS A VERSATILE BUILDING USED FOR BOTH ACTION AND ENTRANCES. Behind the *orchestra* was a building for actors, costumes, and props called the *skene* ("tent"), from which is derived our modern word *scene*. Originally a tent or hut, the *skene* was later made of wood and decorated to provide backdrops for the various plays. Some theater historians argue that the stage itself was a wooden platform (*proskenion* or proscenium) in front of the *skene* to elevate the actors and set them off from the chorus. At the center of the *skene* a double door for entrances and exits opened out to the stage and the *orchestra.* Through this door a large platform (*ekkyklyma*) could be rolled out to show interior scenes. There was no curtain.

View of modern production of Sophocles' *Oedipus at Colonus* at the Theater of Epidauros (see also p. 1259). Note the size of the orchestra, the formation and gestures of the chorus (fifteen members, in masks, together with the choral leader), the central altar, the reconstructed skene, and the single actor on the proscenium.

The roof of the *skene* was sometimes used as a place of action (as in Aeschylus's *Agamemnon*). A *mechane* (may-KAH-nay), or crane, was also located there so that actors playing gods could be swung up, down, and around as a mark of divine power. It was this crane that gave rise to the phrase ***theos apo mechanes,*** or, in Latin, ***deus ex machina*** ("a god out of the machine"), terms that refer to an artificial and/or illogical action or device introduced at a play's end to bring otherwise impossible conflicts to a satisfactory solution.

THE ACTORS PERFORMED IN ALL STAGE AND ORCHESTRA AREAS, AND THE CHORUS PERFORMED IN THE ORCHESTRA. The performing space for the actors was mainly in front of the *skene*. The space for the chorus was the entire *orchestra*. The chorus entered the *orchestra*—and left it at the end of the play—along the aisles between the retaining wall of the hillside seats and the front of the *skene*. Each of these lateral walkways was known as a *parados* ("way in"), the name also given to the chorus's entry scene. The actors often used the *skene* for entrances and exits, but they were also free to use either of the walkways.

THE THEATER WAS REPAIRED AND RESTORED A NUMBER OF TIMES IN ANTIQUITY. In the centuries after it was built, the Theater of Dionysus was remodeled and restored a number of times. Aeschylus' trilogy the *Oresteia* was performed in 458 B.C.E., for example, not long after a renovation. The ruins existing on the south slope of the Acropolis today are not those of the theater known by Sophocles, but rather those of a Roman restoration. A better sense of how the theater looked during the time of Sophocles can be gained from the Theater of Epidaurus, which has been preserved in excellent condition (see the photographs, pp. 1259 and 1260) and which even in antiquity was considered one of the best Greek theaters.

ANCIENT GREEK TRAGIC ACTORS AND THEIR COSTUMES

The task of the three competing playwrights who had been "given a chorus" by the archon to stage their works during the City Dionysia (and later during the Lenaia) was to plan, choreograph, and direct the productions, usually with the aid of professionals. By performance time, the dramatists would already have spent many months preparing the three assigned actors and fifteen choristers. They also would have directed rehearsals for a small number of auxiliary chorus members and other silent extras in roles such as servants and soldiers.

Costumes Distinguished the Actors from the Chorus

All these participants needed costumes. The chorus members were lightly clad, for ease of movement, and were apparently barefoot. The main actors wore the identifying costumes of tragedy, namely, sleeved robes, boots, and masks. Their robes were heavily decorated and embroidered. Their calf-high leather boots, called *kothornoi* or, in English, **buskins,** were like the elegant boots worn by the patron god Dionysus in painting and statuary. During the following centuries, the buskins became elevator shoes that made the tragic actors taller, in keeping with their heroic stature.

Masks Worn by Chorus and Actors Helped the Audience Recognize and Distinguish the Characters

A vital aspect of ancient tragic costuming was the use of conventionalized plaster and linen **masks,** which were designed to identify and delineate characters. These were of particular help for those in the audience who sat at increasing distances away and up from the orchestra and stage, and who therefore would have had trouble seeing facial expressions. As many as twenty-eight different kinds of masks were in use for the tragic productions. Each mask portrayed a distinct facial type and expression (e.g., king, queen, young woman, old man). The choristers wore identical masks for their group roles. Apparently the masks covered the entire head, except for openings for seeing, breathing, and speaking. They included a high headdress and, when necessary, a beard.

The masks, along with costume changes, gave the actors great versatility. Each actor could assume a number of different roles simply by entering the *skene*, changing mask and costume, and reentering as a new character. Thus, in *Oedipus the King* a single actor could represent the seer Tiresias and later reappear as the Messenger. The masks even made it possible for two actors, or even all three, to perform as the same character in separate parts of the play if the need arose.

۱⁄ PERFORMANCE AND THE FORMAL ORGANIZATION OF GREEK TRAGEDY

On performance days, the competing playwrights staged their plays from morning to afternoon, first the tragedies, then the satyr plays (and after these, comedies by other writers). Because plays were performed with a minimum of scenery and props, dramatists used dialogue to establish times and locations. Each tragedy was performed in the order of the formally designated sections that modern editors have marked in the printed texts. It is therefore possible to describe the production of a play in terms of these structural divisions.

The First Part Was the *Prologue,* the Play's Exposition

There was considerable variety in the performance of the **prologue.** Sometimes it was given by a single actor, speaking as either a mortal or a god. In *Oedipus the King,* Sophocles used all three actors for the prologue (Oedipus, the Priest, and Creon), speaking to themselves and also to the extras acting as the Theban populace.

The Second Part Was the *Parados,* the Entry of the Chorus into the Orchestra

Once the chorus members entered the orchestra, they remained there until the play's end. Because they were required to project their voices to spectators in the top seats, they both sang and chanted their lines. They also moved rhythmically in a number of stanzaic *strophes* (turns), *antistrophes* (counterturns), and *epodes* (units following the songs). These dance movements, regulated by the rhythm of the *aulos* or flute as in military drill, were done in straight-line formations of five or three, but we do not know whether the chorus stopped or continued moving when delivering their lines. After the **parados,** the choristers would necessarily have knelt or sat at attention, in this way focusing on the activities of the actors and, when necessary, responding as a group.

The Play's Principal Action Consisted of Four Episodes and Stasimons

With the chorus as a model audience, the drama itself was developed in four full sections or acting units. The major part of each section was the **episode.** Each episode featured the actors, who presented both action and speech, including swift one-line interchanges known as **stichomythy.**[11] The following second part of the acting section was called a *stasimon* (plural *stasima*), performed by the chorus in the *orchestra.* Like the *parados,* the *stasima* required dance movements, along with the chanting and singing of strophes, antistrophes, and

---

[11]For example, at the end of the first episode of *Oedipus the King,* Oedipus goes into the *skene*—the palace—while a servant leads Tiresias off along the *parados,* thus indicating that he is leaving Thebes entirely.

epodes. The topics concerned the play's developing action, although over time the *stasima* became more general and therefore less integral to the play.

The Play Concluded with the Exodos

When the last of the four episode-*stasimon* sections had been completed, the *exodos* (literally, "a way out"), or the final section, commenced. It contained the resolution of the drama, the exit of the actors, and the last pronouncements, dance movements, and exit of the chorus.

The Role of the Chorus Was Diminished as Greek Tragedy Evolved

We know little about tragic structure at the very beginning of the form, but Athenian tragedies of the fifth century B.C.E. followed the pattern just described. Aeschylus, the earliest of the Athenian writers of tragedy, lengthened the episodes, thus emphasizing the actors and minimizing the chorus (*Poetics* IV.13, p. 19). Sophocles made the chorus even less important. Euripides, Sophocles's younger contemporary, concentrated on the episodes, making the chorus almost incidental. In later centuries, dramatists dropped the choral sections completely, establishing a precedent for the five-act structure adopted by Roman dramatists and later by Renaissance dramatists.

PLAYS FOR STUDY

Thoughts 1257

SOPHOCLES, *OEDIPUS THE KING*

Sophocles was born between 500 and 494 B.C.E. into an affluent Athenian family. He began acting and singing early, and he served as a choral leader in the celebrations for the defeat of the Persians at Marathon in 480 B.C.E. In 468 he won highest festival honors for the first play he submitted for competition, Triptolemos. *He wrote at least 120 plays, approximately 90 of them tragedies, and he won the prize a record 24 times. He was also an active citizen. He was twice elected general of his tribe, and he served as a priest in the cult of Asclepius, the god of healing. Because of his dramatic and public achievements, he was venerated during his lifetime, and after his death in 406–405 B.C.E., a cult was established in his honor.*

When *Oedipus the King* was first performed between 430 and 425 B.C.E., most of the audience would have known the general outlines of the story inasmuch as it was one of the "received legends" of tragedy: the antagonism of the gods Hephaestus and Hera toward Cadmus of Thebes (of whom Oedipus was a descendant); the prophecy that the Theban king Laius would be killed by his own son; the exposure of the newly born Oedipus on a mountainside; his rescue by a well-meaning shepherd; his youth spent as the adopted son of King Polybus and Queen Merope of Corinth; his trip to Delphi to learn his origins; his impetuous murder of Laius (a stranger to him); his solution of the Sphinx's riddle; his ascension as king of Thebes and his marriage to Queen Jocasta, his mother; his reign as king; the plague that afflicted Thebes; his attempts at restoration; and Jocasta's suicide when the truth of Oedipus' past is revealed.

Although these details were commonly known, there was disagreement about the outcome of Oedipus' life. One version told that he remarried, had four children with his new wife, reigned long and successfully, died in battle, and was finally worshiped as a hero. Sophocles, however, dramatizes a version—either borrowed or of his own creation—that tells of Oedipus' self-imposed punishment.

As we have said, Aristotle prized *Oedipus the King* so highly that he used it to illustrate many of his principles of tragedy. Of particular interest is that the play embodies the so-called three **unities,** which are implicit in the *Poetics* although Aristotle does not stress them. Sophocles creates *unity of place* by using the front of the royal palace of Thebes as the location for the entire action. He creates *unity of action* by dramatizing only those activities leading to Oedipus' recognition of the true scourge of the city. Finally, he creates *unity of time* because the stage or action time coincides with real-life time. In fact, the play's time is considerably shorter than the "single revolution of the sun" (*sic*) that Aristotle recommends as the proper period for a complete tragic action (V.4, p.23). Above all, *Oedipus the King* meets Aristotle's requirements for one of the very best plays because of the skill with which Sophocles makes Oedipus' recognition of his guilt coincide exactly with the disastrous reversal of his fortunes (XI.2, p. 41).

[handwritten margin note: Scourge Whip punishment]

SOPHOCLES (ca. 496–406 B.C.E.)

Oedipus the King ~ < ~ < ~ 430–425 B.C.E.

Translated by Thomas Gould

CHARACTERS

> Oedipus,° *The King of Thebes*
> Priest of Zeus, *Leader of the Suppliants*
> Creon, *Oedipus's Brother-in-law*
> Chorus, *a Group of Theban Elders*
> Choragos, *Spokesman of the Chorus*
> Tiresias, *a blind Seer or Prophet*
> Jocasta, *The Queen of Thebes*
> Messenger, *from Corinth, once a Shepherd*
> Herdsman, *once a Servant of Laius*
> Second Messenger, *a Servant of Oedipus*

Oedipus: The name means "swollen foot." It refers to the mutilation of Oedipus's feet by his father, Laius, before the infant was sent to Mount Cithaeron to be put to death by exposure.

MUTES

> Suppliants, *Thebans seeking Oedipus's help*
> Attendants, *for the Royal Family*
> Servants, *to lead Tiresias and Oedipus*
> Antigone, *Daughter of Oedipus and Jocasta*
> Ismene, *Daughter of Oedipus and Jocasta*

[*The action takes place during the day in front of the royal palace in Thebes. There are two altars (left and right) on the Proscenium and several steps leading down to the Orchestra. As the play opens, Thebans of various ages who have come to beg Oedipus for help are sitting on these steps and in part of the Orchestra. These suppliants are holding branches of laurel or olive which have strips of wool° wrapped around them. Oedipus enters from the palace (the central door of the Skene).*]

PROLOGUE

OEDIPUS.   My children, ancient Cadmus'° newest care,
      why have you hurried to those seats, your boughs
      wound with the emblems of the suppliant?
      The city is weighed down with fragrant smoke,
      with hymns to the Healer° and the cries of mourners.   5
      I thought it wrong, my sons, to hear your words
      through emissaries, and have come out myself,
      I, Oedipus, a name that all men know.

[*OEDIPUS addresses the PRIEST.*]

      Old man—for it is fitting that you speak
      for all—what is your mood as you entreat me,   10
      fear or trust? You may be confident
      that I'll do anything. How hard of heart
      if an appeal like this did not rouse my pity!
PRIEST.   You, Oedipus, who hold the power here,
      you see our several ages, we who sit   15
      before your altars—some not strong enough
      to take long flight, some heavy in old age,
      the priests, as I of Zeus,° and from our youths
      a chosen band. The rest sit with their windings
      in the markets, at the twin shrines of Pallas,°   20
      and the prophetic embers of Ismēnos.°
      Our city, as you see yourself, is tossed
      too much, and can no longer lift its head
      above the troughs of billows red with death.
      It dies in the fruitful flowers of the soil,   25
      it dies in its pastured herds, and in its women's
      barren pangs. And the fire-bearing god°

    0.1 S.D. *wool:* Branches wrapped with wool are traditional symbols of prayer or supplication.
Cadmus: Oedipus's great-great-grandfather (although he does not know this) and the founder of Thebes.
5 *Healer:* Apollo, god of prophecy, light, healing, justice, purification, and destruction. 18 *Zeus:* father
and king of the gods.   20 *Pallas:* Athena, goddess of wisdom, arts, crafts, and war. 21 *Ismēnos:* a reference to the temple of Apollo near the river Ismenos in Thebes. Prophecies were made here by "reading"
the ashes of the altar fires.   27 *fire-bearing god:* contagious fever viewed as a god.

has swooped upon the city, hateful plague,
and he has left the house of Cadmus empty.
Black Hades° is made rich with moans and weeping.   30
Not judging you an equal of the gods,
do I and the children sit here at your hearth,
but as the first of men, in troubled times
and in encounters with divinities.
You came to Cadmus' city and unbound   35
the tax we had to pay to the harsh singer,°   *— The Sphinx, a monster with a lion body woman head and wing*
did it without a helpful word from us,
with no instruction; with a god's assistance
you raised up our life, so we believe.
Again now Oedipus, our greatest power,   40
we plead with you, as suppliants, all of us,
to find us strength, whether from a god's response,
or learned in some way from another man.
I know that the experienced among men
give counsels that will prosper best of all.   45
Noblest of men, lift up our land again!
Think also of yourself; since now the land
calls you its Savior for your zeal of old,
oh let us never look back at your rule
as men helped up only to fall again!   50
Do not stumble! Put our land on firm feet!
The bird of omen was auspicious then,
when you brought that luck; be that same man again!
The power is yours; if you will rule our country,
rule over men, not in an empty land.   55
A towered city or a ship is nothing
if desolate and no man lives within.
OEDIPUS.   Pitiable children, oh I know, I know
the yearnings that have brought you. Yes, I know
that you are sick. And yet, though you are sick,   60
there is not one of you so sick as I.
For your affliction comes to each alone,
for him and no one else, but my soul mourns
for me and for you, too, and for the city.
You do not waken me as from a sleep,   65
for I have wept, bitterly and long,
tried many paths in the wanderings of thought,

---

30 *Black Hades:* refers to both the underworld, where the spirits of the dead go, and the god of the underworld. 36 *harsh singer:* the Sphinx, a monster with a woman's head, a lion's body, and wings. The "tax" that Oedipus freed Thebes from was the destruction of all the young men who failed to solve the Sphinx's riddle and were subsequently devoured. The Sphinx always asked the same riddle: "What goes on four legs in the morning, two legs at noon, and three legs in the evening, and yet is weakest when supported by the largest number of feet?" Oedipus discovered the correct answer—man, who crawls in infancy, walks in his prime, and uses a stick in old age—and thus ended the Sphinx's reign of terror. The Sphinx destroyed herself when Oedipus answered the riddle. Oedipus's reward for freeing Thebes of the Sphinx was the throne and the hand of the recently widowed Jocasta. (A photograph of the Sphinx built in ancient Egypt, at Giza, appears on p. 945.)

and the single cure I found by careful search
I've acted on: I sent Menoeceus' son,
Creon, brother of my wife, to the Pythian   70
halls of Phoebus,° so that I might learn
what I must do or say to save this city.
Already, when I think what day this is,
I wonder anxiously what he is doing.
Too long, more than is right, he's been away.   75
But when he comes, then I shall be a traitor
if I do not do all that the god reveals.

PRIEST.   Welcome words! But look, those men have signaled
   that it is Creon who is now approaching!
OEDIPUS.   Lord Apollo! May he bring Savior Luck,   80
   a Luck as brilliant as his eyes are now!
PRIEST.   His news is happy, it appears. He comes,
   forehead crowned with thickly berried laurel.°
OEDIPUS.   We'll know, for he is near enough to hear us.

[Enter CREON along one of the Parados.]

   Lord, brother in marriage, son of Menoeceus!   85
   What is the god's pronouncement that you bring?
CREON.   It's good. For even troubles, if they chance
   to turn out well, I always count as lucky.
OEDIPUS.   But what was the response? You seem to say
   I'm not to fear—but not to take heart either.   90
CREON.   If you will hear me with these men present,
   I'm ready to report—or go inside.

[CREON moves up the steps toward the palace.]

OEDIPUS.   Speak out to all! The grief that burdens me
   concerns these men more than it does my life.
CREON.   Then I shall tell you what I heard from the god.   95
   The task Lord Phoebus sets for us is clear:
   drive out pollution sheltered in our land,
   and do not shelter what is incurable.
OEDIPUS.   What is our trouble? How shall we cleanse ourselves?
CREON.   We must banish or murder to free ourselves   100
   from a murder that blows storms through the city.
OEDIPUS.   What man's bad luck does he accuse in this?
CREON.   My Lord, a king named Laius ruled our land
   before you came to steer the city straight.
OEDIPUS.   I know. So I was told—I never saw him.   105
CREON.   Since he was murdered, you must raise your hand
   against the men who killed him with their hands.
OEDIPUS.   Where are they now? And how can we ever find
   the track of ancient guilt now hard to read?

   70–71 *Pythian . . . Phoebus:* the temple of Phoebus Apollo's oracle or prophet at Delphi.   83 *laurel:*
Creon is wearing a garland of laurel leaves, sacred to Apollo.

CREON.   In our own land, he said. What we pursue,
    that can be caught; but not what we neglect.   110
OEDIPUS.   Was Laius home, or in the countryside—
    or was he murdered in some foreign land?
CREON.   He left to see a sacred rite, he said;
    He left, but never came home from his journey.   115
OEDIPUS.   Did none of his party see it and report—
    someone we might profitably question?
CREON.   They were all killed but one, who fled in fear,
    and he could tell us only one clear fact.
OEDIPUS.   What fact? One thing could lead us on to more   120
    if we could get a small start on our hope.
CREON.   He said that bandits chanced on them and killed him—
    with the force of many hands, not one alone.
OEDIPUS.   How could a bandit dare so great an act—
    unless this was a plot paid off from here!   125
CREON.   We thought of that, but when Laius was killed,
    we had no one to help us in our troubles.
OEDIPUS.   It was your very kingship that was killed!
    What kind of trouble blocked you from a search?
CREON.   The subtle-singing Sphinx asked us to turn   130
    from the obscure to what lay at our feet.
OEDIPUS.   Then I shall begin again and make it plain.
    It was quite worthy of Phoebus, and worthy of you,
    to turn our thoughts back to the murdered man,
    and right that you should see me join the battle   135
    for justice to our land and to the god.
    Not on behalf of any distant kinships,
    it's for myself I will dispel this stain.
    Whoever murdered him may also wish
    to punish me—and with the selfsame hand.   140
    In helping him I also serve myself.
    Now quickly, children: up from the altar steps,
    and raise the branches of the suppliant!
    Let someone go and summon Cadmus' people:
    say I'll do anything.

                        [*Exit an* ATTENDANT *along one of the Parados.*]

                 Our luck will prosper   145
    if the god is with us, or we have already fallen.
PRIEST.   Rise, my children; that for which we came,
    he has himself proclaimed he will accomplish.
    May Phoebus, who announced this, also come
    as Savior and reliever from the plague.   150

[*Exit* OEDIPUS *and* CREON *into the Palace. The* PRIEST *and the* SUPPLIANTS *exit left and right along the Parados. After a brief pause, the* CHORUS *(including the* CHORAGOS*) enters the Orchestra from the Parados.*]

[Handwritten annotations: "Entry and first lyrical ode ot the Chorus" above Parados; "father + king of the gods" above line 151; "Delphi" next to Pytho; "Appolo" next to Delian Healer; "goddess of Virginity Childbirth" next to Artemis]

PARADOS

Strophe 1°

CHORUS.   Voice from Zeus,° sweetly spoken, what are you
    that have arrived from golden
Pytho° to our shining
Thebes? I am on the rack, terror
      shakes my soul.   155
Delian Healer,° summoned by "iē!"
I await in holy dread what obligation, something new
or something back once more with the revolving years,
    you'll bring about for me.
Oh tell me, child of golden Hope,   160
    deathless Response!

Antistrophe 1

I appeal to you first, daughter of Zeus,
    deathless Athena,
    and to your sister who protects this land,
    Artemis,° whose famous throne is the whole circle   165
    of the marketplace,
and Phoebus, who shoots from afar: iō!
Three-fold defenders against death, appear!
If ever in the past, to stop blind ruin
    sent against the city,   170
you banished utterly the fires of suffering,
    come now again!

Strophe 2

Ah! Ah! Unnumbered are the miseries
I bear. The plague claims all
our comrades. Nor has thought found yet a spear   175
by which a man shall be protected. What our glorious
earth gives birth to does not grow. Without a birth
from cries of labor
    do the women rise.
One person after another   180
    you may see, like flying birds,
faster than indomitable fire, sped
to the shore of the god that is the sunset.°

Antistrophe 2

And with their deaths unnumbered dies the city.
Her children lie unpitied on the ground,   185

---

    151 *Strophe:* Strophe and antistrophe (line 162) are stanzaic units referring to movements, countermovements, and gestures that the Chorus performed while singing or chanting in the orchestra. See pp. 1260 and 1262.   151 *Voice from Zeus:* a reference to Apollo's prophecy. Zeus taught Apollo how to prophesy.   153 *Pytho:* Delphi.   156 *Delian Healer:* Apollo.   165 *Artemis:* goddess of virginity, childbirth, and hunting.   183 *god . . . sunset:* Hades, god of the underworld.

spreading death, unmourned.
Meanwhile young wives, and gray-haired mothers with them,
on the shores of the altars, from this side and that,
suppliants from mournful trouble,
    cry out their grief.   190
A hymn to the Healer shines,
the flute a mourner's voice.
Against which, golden goddess, daughter of Zeus,
    send lovely Strength.

Strophe 3

Cause raging Ares°—who,   195
    armed now with no shield of bronze,
burns me, coming on amid loud cries—
to turn his back and run from my land,
with a fair wind behind, to the great
    hall of Amphitrite,° *Atlantic Ocean*   200
or to the anchorage that welcomes no one,
Thrace's troubled sea!
If night lets something get away at last,
    it comes by day.
Fire-bearing god   205
    you who dispense the might of lightning,
Zeus! Father! Destroy him with your thunderbolt!

[*Enter Oedipus from the palace.*]

Antistrophe 3 *Apollo*

Lycēan Lord!° From your looped
    bowstring, twisted gold,
I wish indomitable missiles might be scattered   210
and stand forward, our protectors; also fire-bearing
radiance of Artemis, with which
    she darts across the Lycian mountains.
I call the god whose head is bound in gold,
with whom this country shares its name,   215
Bacchus,° wine-flushed, summoned by "euoi!,"
    Maenads' comrade,
to approach ablaze
    with gleaming . . . . . .
pine, opposed to that god-hated god.   220

EPISODE 1

OEDIPUS.   I hear your prayer. Submit to what I say
    and to the labors that the plague demands
    and you'll get help and a relief from evils.

---

195 *Ares*: god of war and destruction.   200 *Amphitrite*: the Atlantic Ocean.   208 *Lycēan Lord*:
Apollo.   216 *Bacchus*: Dionysus, god of fertility and wine.

I'll make the proclamation, though a stranger
to the report and to the deed. Alone,   225
had I no key, I would soon lose the track.
Since it was only later that I joined you,
to all the sons of Cadmus I say this:
whoever has clear knowledge of the man
who murdered Laius, son of Labdacus,   230
I command him to reveal it all to me—
nor fear if, to remove the charge, he must
accuse himself: his fate will not be cruel—
he will depart unstumbling into exile.
But if you know another, or a stranger,   235
to be the one whose hand is guilty, speak:
I shall reward you and remember you.
But if you keep your peace because of fear,
and shield yourself or kin from my command,
hear you what I shall do in that event: 240
I charge all in this land where I have throne
and power, shut out that man—no matter who—
both from your shelter and all spoken words,
nor in your prayers or sacrifices make
him partner, not allot him lustral° water.   245
All men shall drive him from their homes: for he
is the pollution that the god-sent Pythian
response has only now revealed to me.
In this way I ally myself in war
with the divinity and the deceased.°   250
And this curse, too, against the one who did it,
whether alone in secrecy, or with others:
may he wear out his life unblest and evil!
I pray this, too: if he is at my hearth
and in my home, and I have knowledge of him,   255
may the curse pronounced on others come to me.
All this I lay to you to execute,
for my sake, for the god's, and for this land
now ruined, barren, abandoned by the gods.
Even if no god had driven you to it,   260
you ought not to have left this stain uncleansed,
the murdered man a nobleman, a king!
You should have looked! But now, since, as it happens,
It's I who have the power that he had once,
and have his bed, and a wife who shares our seed,   265
and common bond had we had common children
(had not his hope of offspring had back luck—
but as it happened, luck lunged at his head);
because of this, as if for my own father,
I'll fight for him, I'll leave no means untried,   270

245 *lustral:* purifying.   250 *the deceased:* Laius.

to catch the one who did it with his hand,
for the son of Labdacus, of Polydôrus,
of Cadmus before him, and of Agênor.° *— refers to Laios by citing his heritage*
This prayer against all those who disobey:
the gods send out no harvest from their soil,   275
nor children from their wives. Oh, let them die
victims of this plague, or of something worse.
Yet for the rest of us, people of Cadmus,
we the obedient, may Justice, our ally,
and all the gods, be always on our side!   280

CHORAGOS.   I speak because I feel the grip of your curse:
the killer is not I. Nor can I point
to him. The one who set us to this search,
Phoebus, should also name the guilty man.

OEDIPUS.   Quite right, but to compel unwilling gods—   285
no man has ever had that kind of power.

CHORAGOS.   May I suggest to you a second way?

OEDIPUS.   A second or a third—pass over nothing!

CHORAGOS.   I know of no one who sees more of what
Lord Phoebus sees than Lord Tiresias.   290
My Lord, one might learn brilliantly from him.

OEDIPUS.   Nor is this something I have been slow to do.
At Creon's word I sent an escort—twice now!
I am astonished that he has not come.

CHORAGOS.   The old account is useless. It told us nothing.   295

OEDIPUS.   But tell it to me. I'll scrutinize all stories.

CHORAGOS.   He is said to have been killed by travelers.

OEDIPUS.   I have heard, but the one who did it no one sees.

CHORAGOS.   If there is any fear in him at all,
he won't stay here once he has heard that curse.   300

OEDIPUS.   He won't fear words: he had no fear when he did it.

[*Enter* TIRESIAS *from the right, led by a* SERVANT *and two of Oedipus's* ATTENDANTS.]

CHORAGOS.   Look there! There is the man who will convict him!
It's the god's prophet they are leading here.
one gifted with the truth as no one else.

OEDIPUS.   Tiresias, master of all omens—   305
public and secret, in the sky and on the earth—
your mind, if not your eyes, sees how the city
lives with a plague, against which Thebes can find
no Saviour or protector, Lord, but you.
For Phoebus, as the attendants surely told you,   310
returned this answer to us: liberation
from the disease would never come unless
we learned without a doubt who murdered Laius—
put them to death, or sent them into exile.
Do not begrudge us what you may learn from birds   315
or any other prophet's path you know!

272–273 *son . . . Agênor:* refers to Laius by citing his genealogy.

Care for yourself, the city, care for me,
care for the whole pollution of the dead!
We're in your hands. To do all that he can
to help another is man's noblest labor.   320

TIRESIAS.   How terrible to understand and get
no profit from the knowledge! I knew this,
but I forgot, or I had never come.

OEDIPUS.   What's this? You've come with very little zeal.

TIRESIAS.   Let me go home! If you will listen to me,   325
You will endure your troubles better—and I mine.

OEDIPUS.   A strange request, not very kind to the land
that cared for you—to hold back this oracle!

TIRESIAS.   I see your understanding comes to you
inopportunely. So that won't happen to me . . .   330

OEDIPUS.   Oh, by the gods, if you understand about this,
don't turn away! We're on our knees to you.

TIRESIAS.   None of you understands! I'll never bring
my grief to light—will not speak of yours.

OEDIPUS.   You know and won't declare it! Is your purpose   335
to betray us and to destroy this land?

TIRESIAS.   I will grieve neither of us. Stop this futile
cross-examination. I'll tell you nothing!

OEDIPUS.   Nothing? You vile traitor! You could provoke
a stone to anger! You still refuse to tell?   340
Can nothing soften you, nothing convince you?

TIRESIAS.   You blamed anger in me—you haven't seen.
Can nothing soften you, nothing convince you?

OEDIPUS.   Who wouldn't fill with anger, listening
to words like yours which now disgrace this city?   345

TIRESIAS.   It will come, even if my silence hides it.

OEDIPUS.   If it will come, then why won't you declare it?

TIRESIAS.   I'd rather say no more. Now if you wish,
respond to that will all your fiercest anger!

OEDIPUS.   Now I am angry enough to come right out   350
with this conjecture: you, I think, helped plot
the deed; you did it—even if your hand
cannot have struck the blow. If you could see,
I should have said the deed was yours alone.

TIRESIAS.   Is that right! Then I charge you to abide   355
by the decree you have announced: from this day
say no word to either these or me,
for you are the vile polluter of this land!

OEDIPUS.   Aren't you appalled to let a charge like that
come bounding forth? How will you get away?   360

TIRESIAS.   You cannot catch me. I have the strength of truth.

OEDIPUS.   Who taught you this? Not your prophetic craft!

TIRESIAS.   You did. You made me say it. I didn't want to.

OEDIPUS.   Say what? Repeat it so I'll understand.

TIRESIAS.   I made no sense? Or are you trying me?   365

OEDIPUS.   No sense I understood. Say it again!

TIRESIAS.　　I say you are the murderer you seek.

OEDIPUS.　　Again that horror! You'll wish you hadn't said that.

TIRESIAS.　　Shall I say more, and raise your anger higher?

OEDIPUS.　　Anything you like! Your words are powerless.　　370

TIRESIAS.　　You live, unknowing, with those nearest to you
　　　in the greatest shame. You do not see the evil.

OEDIPUS.　　You won't go on like that and never pay!

TIRESIAS.　　I can if there is any strength in truth.

OEDIPUS.　　In truth, but not in you! You have no strength,　　375
　　　blind in your ears, your reason, and your eyes.

TIRESIAS.　　Unhappy man! Those jeers you hurl at me
　　　before long all these men will hurl at you.

OEDIPUS.　　You are the child of endless night; it's not
　　　for me or anyone who sees to hurt you.　　380

TIRESIAS.　　It's not my fate to be struck down by you.
　　　Apollo is enough. That's his concern.

OEDIPUS.　　Are these inventions Creon's or your own?

TIRESIAS.　　No, your affliction is yourself, not Creon.

OEDIPUS.　　Oh success!—in wealth, kingship, artistry,　　385
　　　in any life that wins much admiration—
　　　the envious ill will stored up for you!
　　　to get at my command, a gift I did not
　　　seek, which the city put into my hands,
　　　my loyal Creon, colleague from the start,　　390
　　　longs to sneak up in secret and dethrone me.
　　　So he's suborned this fortuneteller—schemer!
　　　deceitful beggar-priest!—who has good eyes
　　　for gains alone, though in his craft he's blind.
　　　Where were your prophet's powers ever proved?　　395
　　　Why, when the dog who chanted verse° was here,
　　　did you not speak and liberate this city?
　　　Her riddle wasn't for a man chancing by
　　　to interpret; prophetic art was needed,
　　　but you had none, it seems—learned from birds　　400
　　　or from a god. I came along, yes I,
　　　Oedipus the ignorant, and stopped her—
　　　by using thought, not augury from birds.
　　　And it is I whom you may wish to banish,
　　　so you'll be close to the Creontian throne.　　405
　　　You—and the plot's concocter—will drive out
　　　pollution to your grief; you look quite old
　　　or you would be the victim of that plot!

CHORAGOS.　　It seems to us that this man's words were said
　　　in anger, Oedipus, and yours as well.　　410
　　　Insight, not angry words, is what we need,
　　　the best solution to the god's response.

TIRESIAS.　　You are the king, and yet I am your equal
　　　in my right to speak. In that I too am Lord,

---

396 dog . . . verse: the Sphinx.

for I belong to Loxias,° not you.   415
I am not Creon's man. He's nothing to me.
Hear this, since you have thrown my blindness at me:
Your eyes can't see the evil to which you've come,
nor where you live, nor who is in your house.
Do you know your parents? Now knowing, you are   420
their enemy, in the underworld and here.
A mother's and a father's double-lashing
terrible-footed curse will soon drive you out.
Now you can see, then you will stare into darkness.
What place will not be harbor to your cry,   425
or what Cithaeron° not reverberate
when you have heard the bride-song in your palace
to which you sailed? Fair wind to evil harbor!
Nor do you see how many other woes
will level you to yourself and to your children.   430
So, at my message, and at Creon, too,
splatter muck! There will never be a man
ground into wretchedness as you will be.

OEDIPUS.   Am I to listen to such things from him!
May you be damned! Get out of here at once!   435
Go! Leave my palace! Turn around and go!

[*TIRESIAS begins to move away from OEDIPUS.*]

TIRESIAS.   I wouldn't have come had you not sent for me.
OEDIPUS.   I did not know you'd talk stupidity,
or I wouldn't have rushed to bring you to my house.
TIRESIAS.   Stupid I seem to you, yet to your parents   440
who gave you natural birth I seemed quite shrewd.
OEDIPUS.   Who? Wait! Who is the one who gave me birth?
TIRESIAS.   This day will give you birth,° and ruin too.
OEDIPUS.   What murky, riddling things you always say!
TIRESIAS.   Don't you surpass us all at finding out?   445
OEDIPUS.   You sneer at what you'll find has brought me greatness.
TIRESIAS.   And that's the very luck that ruined you.
OEDIPUS.   I wouldn't care, just so I saved the city.
TIRESIAS.   In that case I shall go. Boy, lead the way!
OEDIPUS.   Yes, let him lead you off. Here, underfoot,   450
you irk me. Gone, you'll cause no further pain.
TIRESIAS.   I'll go when I have said what I was sent for.
Your face won't scare me. You can't ruin me.
I say to you, the man whom you have looked for
as you pronounced your curses, your decrees   455
on the bloody death of Laius—he is here!
A seeming stranger, he shall be shown to be
a Theban born, though he'll take no delight

415 *Loxias:* Apollo.   426 *Cithaeron:* reference to the mountain on which Oedipus was to be exposed as an infant.   443 *give you birth:* that is, identify your parents.

in that solution. Blind, who once could see,
a beggar who was rich, through foreign lands   460
he'll go and point before him with a stick.
To his beloved children, he'll be shown
a father who is also brother; to the one
who bore him, son and husband; to his father,
his seed-fellow and killer. Go in   465
and think this out; and if you find I've lied,
say then I have no prophet's understanding!

[*Exit* TIRESIAS, *led by a* SERVANT. OEDIPUS *exits into the palace with his* ATTENDANTS.]

STASIMON 1

Strophe 1

CHORUS.   Who is the man of whom the inspired
        rock of Delphi° said
    he has committed the unspeakable
        with blood-stained hands?   470
    Time for him to ply a foot
    mightier than those of the horses
        of the storm in his escape;
    upon him mounts and plunges the weaponed
    son of Zeus,° with fire and thunderbolts,   475
    and in his train the dreaded goddesses
    of Death, who never miss.

Antistrophe 1

    The message has just blazed,
        gleaming from the snows   480
    of Mount Parnassus: we must track
        everywhere the unseen man.
    He wanders, hidden by wild
    forests, up through caves
        and rocks, like a bull,
    anxious, with an anxious foot, forlorn.   485
    He puts away from him the mantic° words come from earth's
    navel,° at its center, yet these live
    forever and still hover round him.

Strophe 2

    Terribly he troubles me,
        the skilled interpreter of birds!°   490
    I can't assent, nor speak against him.
        Both paths are closed to me.
    I hover on the wings of doubt,
        not seeing what is here nor what's to come.   495

---

469 *rock of Delphi:* Apollo's oracle at Delphi.   476 *son of Zeus:* Apollo.   487 *mantic:* prophetic.
487–488 *earth's navel:* Delphi.   491 *interpreter of birds:* Tiresias. The Chorus is troubled by his accusations.

What quarrel started in the house of Labdacus° *The lines of Laius*
or in the house of Polybus,°— *Oedipus foster father*
    either ever in the past
    or now, I never
heard, so that . . . with this fact for my touchstone   500
I could attack the public
    fame of Oedipus, by the side of the Labdaceans
an ally, against the dark assassination.

Antistrophe 2

    No, Zeus and Apollo
        understand and know things   505
mortal; but that another man
    can do more as a prophet than I can—
for that there is no certain test,
    though, skill to skill,
one man might overtake another.   510
No, never, not until
    I see the charges proved,
when someone blames him shall I nod assent. *Sphinx*
For once, as we all saw, the winged maiden° came
against him: he was seen then to be skilled,   515
    proved, by that touchstone, dear to the people. So,
never will my mind convict him of the evil.

EPISODE 2

[*Enter* CREON *from the right door of the skene and speaks to the* CHORUS.]

CREON.   Citizens, I hear that a fearful charge
    is made against me by King Oedipus!
    I had to come. If, in this crisis,   520
    he thinks that he has suffered injury
    from anything that I have said or done,
    I have no appetite for a long life—
    bearing a blame like that! It's no slight blow,
    the punishment I'd take from what he said: 525
    it's the ultimate hurt to be called traitor
    by the city, by you, by my own people!
CHORAGOS.   The thing that forced that accusation out
    could have been anger, not the power of thought.
CREON.   But who persuaded him that thoughts of mine   530
    had led the prophet into telling lies?
CHORAGOS.   I do not know the thought behind his words.
CREON.   But did he look straight at you? Was his mind right
    when he said that I was guilty of this charge?
CHORAGOS.   I have no eyes to see what rulers do.   535
    But here he comes himself out of the house.

---

496 *house of Labdacus:* the line of Laius. 497 *Polybus:* Oedipus's foster father. 514 *winged maiden:* the Sphinx.

[*Enter* OEDIPUS *from the palace.*]

OEDIPUS.   What? You here? And can you really have
    the face and daring to approach my house
    when you're exposed as its master's murderer
    and caught, too, as the robber of my kingship?   540
    Did you see cowardice in me, by the gods,
    or foolishness, when you began this plot?
    Did you suppose that I would not detect
    your stealthy moves, or that I'd not fight back?
    It's your attempt that's folly, isn't it—   545
    tracking without followers or connections,
    kingship which is caught with wealth and numbers?
CREON.   Now wait! Give me as long to answer back!
    Judge me for yourself when you have heard me!
OEDIPUS.   You're eloquent, but I'd be slow to learn   550
    from you, now that I've seen your malice toward me.
CREON.   That I deny. Hear what I have to say.
OEDIPUS.   Don't you deny it! You are the traitor here!
CREON.   If you consider mindless willfulness
    a prized possession, you are not thinking sense.   555
OEDIPUS.   If you think you can wrong a relative
    and get off free, you are not thinking sense.
CREON.   Perfectly just, I won't say no. And yet
    what is this injury you say I did you?
OEDIPUS.   Did you persuade me, yes or no, to send   560
    someone to bring that solemn prophet here?
CREON.   And I still hold to the advice I gave.
OEDIPUS.   How many years ago did your King Laius . . .
CREON.   Laius! Do what? Now I don't understand.
OEDIPUS.   Vanish—victim of a murderous violence?   565
CREON.   That is a long count back into the past.
OEDIPUS.   Well, was this seer then practicing his art?
CREON.   Yes, skilled and honored just as he is today.
OEDIPUS.   Did he, back then, ever refer to me?
CREON.   He did not do so in my presence ever.   570
OEDIPUS.   You did inquire into the murder then.
CREON.   We had to, surely, though we discovered nothing.
OEDIPUS.   But the "skilled" one did not say this then? Why not?
CREON.   I never talk when I am ignorant.
OEDIPUS.   But you're not ignorant of your own part.   575
CREON.   What do you mean? I'll tell you if I know.
OEDIPUS.   Just this: if he had not conferred with you
    he'd not have told about my murdering Laius.
CREON.   If he said that, you are the one who knows.
    But now it's fair that you should answer me.   580
OEDIPUS.   Ask on! You won't convict me as the killer.
CREON.   Well then, answer. My sister is your wife?
OEDIPUS.   Now there's a statement that I can't deny.
CREON.   You two have equal power in this country?
OEDIPUS.   She gets from me whatever she desires.   585

CREON.   And I'm a third? The three of us are equals?

OEDIPUS.   That's where you're treacherous to your kinship!

CREON.   But think about this rationally, as I do.

    First look at this: do you think anyone

    prefers the anxieties of being king   590

    to untroubled sleep—if he has equal power?

    I'm not the kind of man who falls in love

    with kingship. I am content with a king's power.

    And so would any man who's wise and prudent.

    I get all things from you, with no distress;   595

    as king I would have onerous duties, too.

    How could the kingship bring me more delight

    than this untroubled power and influence?

    I'm not misguided yet to such a point

    that profitable honors aren't enough.   600

    As it is, all wish me well and all salute;

    those begging you for something have me summoned,

    for their success depends on that alone.

    Why should I lose all this to become king?

    A prudent mind is never traitorous.   605

    Treason's a thought I'm not enamored of;

    nor could I join a man who acted so.

    In proof of this, first go yourself to Pytho°

    and ask if I brought back the true response.

    Then, if you find I plotted with that portent   610

    reader,° don't have me put to death by your vote

    only—I'll vote myself for my conviction.

    Don't let an unsupported thought convict me!

    It's not right mindlessly to take the bad

    for good or to suppose the good are traitors.   615

    Rejecting a relation who is loyal

    is like rejecting life, our greatest love.

    In time you'll know securely without stumbling,

    for time alone can prove a just man just,

    though you can know a bad man in a day   620

CHORAGOS.   Well said, to one who's anxious not to fall.

    Swift thinkers, Lord, are never safe from stumbling.

OEDIPUS.   But when a swift and secret plotter moves

    against me, I must make swift counterplot.

    If I lie quiet and await his move,   625

    he'll have achieved his aims and I'll have missed.

CREON.   You surely cannot mean you want me exiled!

OEDIPUS.   Not exiled, no. Your death is what I want!

CREON.   If you would first define what envy is . . .

OEDIPUS.   Are you still stubborn! Still disobedient?   630

CREON.   I see you cannot think!

OEDIPUS.   For me I can.

---

608 *Pytho:* Delphi.   **610–611** *portent reader:* Apollo's oracle or prophet.

CREON.   You should for me as well!

OEDIPUS.   But you're a traitor!

CREON.   What if you're wrong?

OEDIPUS.   Authority must be maintained.

CREON.   Not if the ruler's evil.

OEDIPUS.   Hear that, Thebes!

CREON.   It is my city too, not yours alone!   635

CHORAGOS.   Please don't, my Lords! Ah, just in time, I see
     Jocasta there, coming from the palace.
     With her help you must settle your quarrel.

[*Enter* JOCASTA *from the Palace.*]

JOCASTA.   Wretched men! What has provoked this ill-
     advised dispute? Have you no sense of shame,   640
     with Thebes so sick, to stir up private troubles?
     Now go inside! And Creon, you go home!
     Don't make a general anguish out of nothing!

CREON.   My sister, Oedipus your husband here
     sees fit to do one of two hideous things: 645
     to have me banished from the land—or killed!

OEDIPUS.   That's right: I caught him, Lady, plotting harm
     against my person—with a malignant science.

CREON.   May my life fail, may I die cursed, if I
     did any of the things you said I did!   650

JOCASTA.   Believe his words, for the god's sake, Oedipus,
     in deference above all to his oath
     to the gods. Also for me, and for these men!

KOMMOS°

Strophe 1

CHORUS.   Consent, with will and mind,
     my king, I beg of you!   655

OEDIPUS.   What do you wish me to surrender?

CHORUS.   Show deference to him who was not feeble in time past
     and is now great in the power of his oath!

OEDIPUS.   Do you know what you're asking?

CHORUS.   Yes.

OEDIPUS.   Tell me then.

CHORUS.   Never to cast into dishonored guilt, with an unproved   660
     assumption, a kinsman who has bound himself by curse.

OEDIPUS.   Now you must understand, when you ask this,
     you ask my death or banishment from the land.

Strophe 2

CHORUS.   No, by the god who is the foremost of all gods,
     the Sun! No! Godless,   665
       friendless, whatever death is worst of all,

---

653 *Kommos:* a dirge or lament sung by the Chorus and one or more of the chief characters.

let that be my destruction, if this
    thought ever moved me!
But my ill-fated soul
    this dying land
wears out—the more if to these older troubles   670
she adds new troubles from the two of you!
OEDIPUS.   Then let him go, though it must mean my death,
    or else disgrace and exile from the land.
    My pity is moved by your words, not by his—   675
    he'll only have my hate, wherever he goes.
CREON.   You're sullen as you yield; you'll be depressed
    when you've passed through this anger. Natures like yours
    are hardest on themselves. That's as it should be.
OEDIPUS.   Then won't you go and let me be?
CREON.   I'll go.   680
    Though you're unreasonable, they know I'm righteous.

                                           [Exit CREON.]

Antistrophe 1

CHORUS.   Why are you waiting, Lady?
    Conduct him back into the palace!
JOCASTA.   I will, when I have heard what chanced.
CHORUS.   Conjectures—words alone, and nothing based on thought.   685
    But even an injustice can devour a man.
JOCASTA.   Did the words come from both sides?
CHORUS.   Yes.
JOCASTA.   What was said?
CHORUS.   To me it seems enough! enough! the land already troubled,   690
    that this should rest where it has stopped.
OEDIPUS.   See what you've come to in your honest thought,
    in seeking to relax and blunt my heart?

Antistrophe 2

CHORUS.   I have not said this only once, my Lord.
    That I had lost my sanity,   695
        without a path in thinking—
be sure this would be clear
        if I put you away
who, when my cherished land
        wandered crazed   700
    with suffering, brought her back on course.
    Now, too, be a lucky helmsman!
JOCASTA.   Please, for the god's sake, Lord, explain to me
    the reason why you have conceived this wrath?
OEDIPUS.   I honor you, not them,° and I'll explain   705
    to you how Creon has conspired against me.
JOCASTA.   All right, if that will explain how the quarrel started.
OEDIPUS.   He says I am the murderer of Laius!

705 *them:* the Chorus.

JOCASTA.   Did he claim knowledge or that someone told him?

OEDIPUS.   Here's what he did: he sent that vicious seer   710
    so he could keep his own mouth innocent.

JOCASTA.   Ah then, absolve yourself of what he charges!
    Listen to this and you'll agree, no mortal
    is ever given skill in prophecy.
    I'll prove this quickly with one incident.   715
    It was foretold to Laius—I shall not say
    by Phoebus himself, but by his ministers—
    that when his fate arrived he would be killed
    by a son who would be born to him and me.
    And yet, so it is told, foreign robbers   720
    murdered him, at a place where three roads meet.
    As for the child I bore him, not three days passed
    before he yoked the ball-joints of its feet,°
    then cast it, by others' hands, on a trackless mountain.
    That time Apollo did not make our child   725
    a patricide, or bring about what Laius
    feared, that he be killed by his own son.
    That's how prophetic words determined things!
    Forget them. The things a god must track
    he will himself painlessly reveal.   730

OEDIPUS.   Just now, as I was listening to you, Lady,
    what a profound distraction seized my mind!

JOCASTA.   What made you turn around so anxiously?

OEDIPUS.   I thought you said that Laius was attacked
    and butchered at a place where three roads meet.   735

JOCASTA.   That is the story, and it is told so still.

OEDIPUS.   Where is the place where this was done to him?

JOCASTA.   The land's called Phocis, where a two-forked road
    comes in from Delphi and from Daulia.

OEDIPUS.   And how much time has passed since these events?   740

JOCASTA.   Just prior to your presentation here
    as king this news was published to the city.

OEDIPUS.   Oh, Zeus, what have you willed to do to me?

JOCASTA.   Oedipus, what makes your heart so heavy?

OEDIPUS.   No, tell me first of Laius' appearance,   745
    what peak of youthful vigor he had reached.

JOCASTA.   A tall man, showing his first growth of white.
    He had a figure not unlike your own.

OEDIPUS.   Alas! It seems that in my ignorance
    I laid those fearful curses on myself.   750

JOCASTA.   What is it, Lord? I flinch to see your face.

OEDIPUS.   I'm dreadfully afraid the prophet sees.
    But I'll know better with one more detail.

JOCASTA.   I'm frightened too. But ask: I'll answer you.

OEDIPUS.   Was his retinue small, or did he travel   755
    with a great troop, as would befit a prince?

723 ball-joints of its feet: the ankles.

JOCASTA. There were just five in all, one a herald.
　　There was a carriage, too, bearing Laius.
OEDIPUS. Alas! Now I see it! But who was it,
　　Lady, who told you what you know about this?　　　　　　　　　760
JOCASTA. A servant who alone was saved unharmed.
OEDIPUS. By chance, could he be now in the palace?
JOCASTA. No, he is not. When he returned and saw
　　you had the power of the murdered Laius,
　　he touched my hand and begged me formally　　　　　　　　765
　　to send him to the fields and to the pastures,
　　so he'd be out of sight, far from the city.
　　I did. Although a slave, he well deserved
　　to win this favor, and indeed far more.
OEDIPUS. Let's have him called back in immediately.　　　　　770
JOCASTA. That can be done, but why do you desire it?
OEDIPUS. I fear, Lady, I have already said
　　too much. That's why I wish to see him now.
JOCASTA. Then he shall come; but it is right somehow
　　that I, too, Lord, should know what troubles you.　　　　　775
OEDIPUS. I've gone so deep into the things I feared
　　I'll tell you everything. Who has a right
　　greater than yours, while I cross through this chance?
　　Polybus of Corinth was my father,
　　my mother was the Dorian Meropē.　　　　　　　　　　　780
　　I was first citizen, until this chance
　　attacked me—striking enough, to be sure,
　　but not worth all the gravity I gave it.
　　This: at a feast a man who'd drunk too much
　　denied, at the wine, I was my father's son.　　　　　　　785
　　I was depressed and all that day I barely
　　held it in. Next day I put the question
　　to my mother and father. They were enraged
　　at the man who'd let this fiction fly at me.
　　I was much cheered by them. And yet it kept　　　　　　790
　　grinding into me. His words kept coming back.
　　Without my mother's or my father's knowledge
　　I went to Pytho. But Phoebus sent me away
　　dishonoring my demand. Instead, other
　　wretched horrors he flashed forth in speech.　　　　　795
　　He said that I would be my mother's lover,
　　show offspring to mankind they could not look at,
　　and be his murderer whose seed I am.°
　　When I heard this, and ever since, I gauged
　　the way to Corinth by the stars alone,　　　　　　　　　800
　　running to a place where I would never see
　　the disgrace in the oracle's words come true.
　　But I soon came to the exact location
　　where, as you tell of it, the king was killed.

798 *be . . . am:* that is, murder my father.

Lady, here is the truth. As I went on,   805
when I was just approaching those three roads,
a herald and a man like him you spoke of
came on, riding a carriage drawn by colts.
Both the man out front and the old man himself°
tried violently to force me off the road.   810
The driver, when he tried to push me off,
I struck in anger. The old man saw this, watched
me approach, then leaned out and lunged down
with twin prongs° at the middle of my head!
He got more than he gave. Abruptly—struck   815
once by the staff in this my hand—he tumbled
out, head first, from the middle of the carriage.
And then I killed them all. But if there is
a kinship between Laius and this stranger,
who is more wretched than the man you see?   820
Who was there born more hated by the gods?
For neither citizen nor foreigner
may take me in his home or speak to me.
No, they must drive me off. And it is I
who have pronounced these curses on myself!   825
I stain the dead man's bed with these my hands,
by which he died. Is not my nature vile?
Unclean?—if I am banished and even
in exile I may not see my own parents,
or set foot in my homeland, or else be yoked   830
in marriage to my mother, and kill my father,
Polybus, who raised me and gave me birth?
If someone judged a cruel divinity
did this to me, would he not speak the truth?
You pure and awful gods, may I not ever   835
see that day, may I be swept away
from men before I see so great and so
calamitous a stain fixed on my person!
CHORAGOS.   These things seem fearful to us, Lord, and yet,
until you hear it from the witness, keep hope!   840
OEDIPUS.   That is the single hope that's left to me,
to wait for him, that herdsman—until he comes.
JOCASTA.   When he appears, what are you eager for?
OEDIPUS.   Just this: if his account agrees with yours
then I shall have escaped this misery.   845
JOCASTA.   But what was it that struck you in my story?
OEDIPUS.   You said he spoke of robbers as the ones
who killed him. Now: if he continues still
to speak of many, then I could not have killed him.
One man and many men just do not jibe.   850

---

809 *old man himself:* Laius.   813–814 *lunged . . . prongs:* Laius strikes Oedipus with a two-pronged
horse goad or whip.

But if he says one belted man, the doubt
is gone. The balance tips toward me. I did it.
JOCASTA.   No! He told it as I told you. Be certain.
He can't reject that and reverse himself.
The city heard these things, not I alone.   855
But even if he swerves from what he said,
he'll never show that Laius' murder, Lord,
occurred just as predicted. For Loxias
expressly said my son was doomed to kill him.
The boy—poor boy—he never had a chance   860
to cut him down, for he was cut down first.
Never again, just for some oracle
will I shoot frightened glances right and left.
OEDIPUS.   That's full of sense. Nonetheless, send a man
to bring that farm hand here. Will you do it?   865
JOCASTA.   I'll send one right away. But let's go in.
Would I do anything against your wishes?

[*Exit* OEDIPUS *and* JOCASTA *through the central door into the palace.*]

STASIMON 2

Strophe 1

CHORUS.   May there accompany me
    the fate to keep a reverential purity in what I say,
    in all I do, for which the laws have been set forth   870
    and walk on high, born to traverse the brightest,
    highest upper air; Olympus° only
    is their father, nor was it
    mortal nature
    that fathered them, and never will   875
    oblivion lull them into sleep;
    the god in them is great and never ages.

Antistrophe 1

    The will to violate, seed of the tyrant,
    if it has drunk mindlessly of wealth and power,
    without a sense of time or true advantage,   880
    mounts to a peak, then
    plunges to an abrupt . . . destiny,
    where the useful foot
    is of no use. But the kind
    of struggling that is good for the city   885
    I ask the god never to abolish.
    The god is my protector: never will I give that up.

Strophe 2

    But if a man proceeds disdainfully
       in deeds of hand or word

872 *Olympus:* Mount Olympus, home of the gods, treated as a god.

and has no fear of Justice
    or reverence for shrines of the divinities   890
(may a bad fate catch him
    for his luckless wantonness!),
if he'll not gain what he gains with justice
and deny himself what is unholy,   895
or if he clings, in foolishness, to the untouchable
(what man, finally, in such an action, will have strength
enough to fend off passion's arrows from his soul?),
if, I say, this kind of
    deed is held in honor—   900
why should I join the sacred dance?

Antistrophe 2

No longer shall I visit and revere
    Earth's navel° the untouchable,
nor visit Abae's° temple,
or Olympia,°   905
if the prophecies are not matched by events
    for all the world to point to.
No, you who hold the power, if you are rightly called
Zeus the king of all, let this matter not escape you
and your ever-deathless rule,   910
for the prophecies to Laius fade . . .
and men already disregard them;
nor is Apollo anywhere
    glorified with honors.
Religion slips away.   915

EPISODE 3

[*Enter* JOCASTA *from the palace carrying a branch wound with wool and a jar of incense. She is attended by two women.*]

JOCASTA.   Lords of the realm, the thought has come to me
to visit shrines of the divinities
with suppliant's branch in hand and fragrant smoke.
For Oedipus excites his soul too much
with alarms of all kinds. He will not judge   920
the present by the past, like a man of sense.
He's at the mercy of all terror-mongers.

[JOCASTA *approaches the altar on the right and kneels.*]

Since I can do no good by counseling,
Apollo the Lycēan!—you are the closest—
I come a suppliant, with these my vows,   925
for a cleansing that will not pollute him.
For when we see him shaken we are all
afraid, like people looking at their helmsman.

---

903 *Earth's navel:* Delphi.   904 *Abae:* a town in Phocis where there was another oracle of Apollo.
905 *Olympia:* site of the oracle of Zeus.

[*Enter a* MESSENGER *along one of the Parados. He sees* JOCASTA *at the altar and then addresses the* CHORUS.]

MESSENGER.   I would be pleased if you would help me, stranger.
    Where is the palace of King Oedipus?   930
    Or tell me where he is himself, if you know.
CHORUS.   This is his house, stranger. He is within.
    This is his wife and mother of his children.
MESSENGER.   May she and her family find prosperity,
    if, as you say, her marriage is fulfilled.   935
JOCASTA.   You also, stranger, for you deserve as much
    for your gracious words. But tell me why you've come.
    What do you wish? Or what have you to tell us?
MESSENGER.   Good news, my Lady, both for your house and
      husband.
JOCASTA.   What is your news? And who has sent you to us?   940
MESSENGER.   I come from Corinth. When you have heard my
      news
    you will rejoice, I'm sure—and grieve perhaps.
JOCASTA.   What is it? How can it have this double power?
MESSENGER.   They will establish him their king, so say
    the people of the land of Isthmia.°   945
JOCASTA.   But is old Polybus not still in power?
MESSENGER.   He's not, for death has clasped him in the tomb.
JOCASTA.   What's this? Has Oedipus' father died?
MESSENGER.   If I have lied then I deserve to die.
JOCASTA.   Attendant! Go quickly to your master,   950
    and tell him this.

                          [*Exit an* ATTENDANT *into the palace.*]

            Oracles of the gods!
    Where are you now? The man whom Oedipus
    fled long ago, for fear that he should kill him—
    he's been destroyed by chance and not by him!

[*Enter* OEDIPUS *from the palace.*]

OEDIPUS.   Darling Jocasta, my beloved wife,   955
    Why have you called me from the palace?
JOCASTA.   First hear what this man has to say. Then see
    what the god's grave oracle has come to now!
OEDIPUS.   Where is he from? What is this news he brings me?
JOCASTA.   From Corinth. He brings news about your father: 960
    that Polybus is no more! that he is dead!
OEDIPUS.   What's this, old man? I want to hear you say it.
MESSENGER.   If this is what must first be clarified,
    please be assured that he is dead and gone.
OEDIPUS.   By treachery or by the touch of sickness?   965
MESSENGER.   Light pressures tip agéd frames into their sleep.

945 *land of Isthmia:* Corinth, which is on an isthmus.

OEDIPUS.   You mean the poor man died of some disease.
MESSENGER.   And of the length of years that he had tallied.
OEDIPUS.   Aha! Then why should we look to Pytho's vapors,°
    or to the birds that scream above our heads?°   970
    If we could really take those things for guides,
    I would have killed my father. But he's dead!
    He is beneath the earth, and here am I,
    who never touched a spear. Unless he died
    of longing for me and I "killed" him that way!   975
    No, in this case, Polybus, by dying, took
    the worthless oracle to Hades with him.
JOCASTA.   And wasn't I telling you that just now?
OEDIPUS.   You were indeed. I was misled by fear.
JOCASTA.   You should not care about this anymore.   980
OEDIPUS.   I must care. I must stay clear of my mother's bed.
JOCASTA.   What's there for man to fear? The realm of chance
    prevails. True foresight isn't possible.
    His life is best who lives without a plan.
    This marriage with your mother—don't fear it.   985
    How many times have men in dreams, too, slept
    with their own mothers! Those who believe such things
    mean nothing endure their lives most easily.
OEDIPUS.   A fine, bold speech, and you are right, perhaps,
    except that my mother is still living,
    so I must fear her, however well you argue.   990
JOCASTA.   And yet your father's tomb is a great eye.
OEDIPUS.   Illuminating, yes. But I still fear the living.
MESSENGER.   Who is the woman who inspires this fear?
OEDIPUS.   Meropē, Polybus' wife, old man.   995
MESSENGER.   And what is there about her that alarms you?
OEDIPUS.   An oracle, god-sent and fearful, stranger.
MESSENGER.   Is it permitted that another know?
OEDIPUS.   It is. Loxias once said to me
    I must have intercourse with my own mother   1000
    and take my father's blood with these my hands.
    So I have long lived far away from Corinth.
    This has indeed brought much good luck, and yet,
    to see one's parents' eyes is happiest.
MESSENGER.   Was it for this that you have lived in exile?   1005
OEDIPUS.   So I'd not be my father's killer, sir.
MESSENGER.   Had I not better free you from this fear,
    my Lord? That's why I came—to do you service.
OEDIPUS.   Indeed, what a reward you'd get for that!
MESSENGER.   Indeed, this is the main point of my trip,   1010
    to be rewarded when you get back home.
OEDIPUS.   I'll never rejoin the givers of my seed!°

---

    969 *Pytho's vapors:* the prophecies of the oracle at Delphi.   970 *birds . . . heads:* the prophecies derived from interpreting the flights of birds.   1012 *givers of my seed:* that is, my parents. Oedipus still thinks Meropē and Polybus are his parents.

MESSENGER. My son, clearly you don't know what you're doing.

OEDIPUS. But how is that, old man? For the gods' sake, tell me!

MESSENGER. If it's because of them you won't go home.   1015

OEDIPUS. I fear that Phoebus will have told the truth.

MESSENGER. Pollution from the ones who gave you seed?

OEDIPUS. That is the thing, old man, I always fear.

MESSENGER. Your fear is groundless. Understand that.

OEDIPUS. Groundless? Not if I was born their son.   1020

MESSENGER. But Polybus is not related to you.

OEDIPUS. Do you mean Polybus was not my father?

MESSENGER. No more than I. We're both the same to you.

OEDIPUS. Same? One who begot me and one who didn't?

MESSENGER. He didn't beget you any more than I did.   1025

OEDIPUS. But then, why did he say I was his son?

MESSENGER. He got you as a gift from my own hands.

OEDIPUS. He loved me so, though from another's hands?

MESSENGER. His former childlessness persuaded him.

OEDIPUS. But had you bought me, or begotten me?   1030

MESSENGER. Found you. In the forest hallows of Cithaeron.

OEDIPUS. What were you doing traveling in that region?

MESSENGER. I was in charge of flocks which grazed those mountains.

OEDIPUS. A wanderer who worked the flocks for hire?

MESSENGER. Ah, but that day. I was your savior, son.   1035

OEDIPUS. From what? What was my trouble when you took me?

MESSENGER. The ball-joints of your feet might testify.

OEDIPUS. What's that? What makes you name that ancient trouble?

MESSENGER. Your feet were pierced and I am your rescuer.

OEDIPUS. A fearful rebuke those tokens left for me!   1040

MESSENGER. That was the chance that names you who you are.

OEDIPUS. By the gods, did my mother or my father do this?

MESSENGER. That I don't know. He might who gave you to me.

OEDIPUS. From someone else? You didn't chance on me?

MESSENGER. Another shepherd handed you to me.   1045

OEDIPUS. Who was he? Do you know? Will you explain!

MESSENGER. They called him one of the men of—was it Laius?

OEDIPUS. The one who once was king here long ago?

MESSENGER. That is the one! The man was shepherd to him.

OEDIPUS. And is he still alive so I can see him?   1050

MESSENGER. But you who live here ought to know that best.

OEDIPUS. Does any one of you now present know
    about the shepherd whom this man has named?
    Have you seen him in town or in the fields? Speak out!
    The time has come for the discovery!   1055

CHORAGOS. The man he speaks of, I believe, is the same
    as the field hand you have already asked to see.
    But it's Jocasta who would know this best.

OEDIPUS. Lady, do you remember the man we just
    now sent for—is that the man he speaks of?   1060

JOCASTA. What? The man he spoke of? Pay no attention!
    His words are not worth thinking about. It's nothing.

OEDIPUS.   With clues like this within my grasp, give up?
    Fail to solve the mystery of my birth?
JOCASTA.   For the love of the gods, and if you love your life,   1065
    give up this search! My sickness is enough.
OEDIPUS.   Come! Though my mothers for three generations
    were in slavery, you'd not be lowborn!
JOCASTA.   No, listen to me! Please! Don't do this thing!.
OEDIPUS.   I will not listen; I will search out the truth.   1070
JOCASTA.   My thinking is for you—it would be best.
OEDIPUS.   This "best" of yours is starting to annoy me.
JOCASTA.   Doomed man! Never find out who you are!
OEDIPUS.   Will someone go and bring that shepherd here?
    Leave her to glory in her wealthy birth!   1075
JOCASTA.   Man of misery! No other name
    shall I address you by, ever again.

                     [*Exit JOCASTA into the palace after a long pause.*]

CHORAGOS.   Why has your lady left, Oedipus,
    hurled by a savage grief? I am afraid
    disaster will come bursting from this silence.   1080
OEDIPUS.   Let it burst forth! However low this seed
    of mine may be, yet I desire to see it.
    She, perhaps—she has a woman's pride—
    is mortified by my base origins.
    But I who count myself the child of Chance,   1085
    the giver of good, shall never know dishonor.
    She is my mother,° and the months my brothers
    who first marked out my lowness, then my greatness.
    I shall not prove untrue to such a nature   *Climax–1168*
    by giving up the search for my own birth.   1090

STASIMON 3

Strophe

CHORUS.   If I have mantic power
    and excellence in thought,
    by Olympus,
        you shall not, Cithaeron, at tomorrow's
    full moon,   1095
    fail to hear us celebrate you as the countryman
    of Oedipus, his nurse and mother,
    or fail to be the subject of our dance,
        since you have given pleasure
    to our king.   1100
    Phoebus, whom we summon by "iē!,"
    may this be pleasing to you!

1087 *She . . . mother:* Chance is my mother.

Antistrophe

Who was your mother, son?
which of the long-lived nymphs
after lying with Pan,°   1105
    the mountain roaming . . . Or was it a bride
of Loxias?°
For dear to him are all the upland pastures.
Or was it Mount Cyllēnē's lord,°
or the Bacchic god,°   1110
    dweller of the mountain peaks,
who received you as a joyous find
from one of the nymphs of Helicon,
the favorite sharers of his sport?

EPISODE 4

OEDIPUS. If someone like myself, who never met him,   1115
    may calculate—elders, I think I see
    the very herdsman we've been waiting for.
    His many years would fit that man's age,
    and those who bring him on, if I am right,
    are my own men. And yet, in real knowledge,   1120
    you can outstrip me, surely: you've seen him.

[*Enter the old* HERDSMAN *escorted by two of Oedipus's* ATTENDANTS. *At first, the* HERDSMAN *will not look at* OEDIPUS.]

CHORAGOS. I know him, yes, a man of the house of Laius,
    a trusty herdsman if he ever had one.
OEDIPUS. I ask you first, the stranger come from Corinth:
    is this the man you spoke of?
MESSENGER.   That's he you see.   1125
OEDIPUS. Then you, old man. First look at me! Now answer:
    did you belong to Laius' household once?
HERDSMAN. I did. Not a purchased slave but raised in the palace.
OEDIPUS. How have you spent your life? What is your work?
HERDSMAN. Most of my life now I have tended sheep.   1130
OEDIPUS. Where is the usual place you stay with them?
HERDSMAN. On Mount Cithaeron. Or in that district.
OEDIPUS. Do you recall observing this man there?
HERDSMAN. Doing what? Which is the man you mean?
OEDIPUS. This man right here. Have you had dealings with him?   1135
HERDSMAN. I can't say right away. I don't remember.
MESSENGER. No wonder, master. I'll bring clear memory
    to his ignorance. I'm absolutely sure
    he can recall it, the district was Cithaeron,
    he with a double flock, and I, with one,   1140
    lived close to him, for three entire seasons,

1105 *Pan:* god of shepherds and woodlands, half man and half goat. See p. 947. **1107** *Loxias:* Apollo. **1109** *Mount Cyllēnē's lord:* Hermes, messenger of the gods. **1110** *Bacchic god:* Dionysus.

six months long, from spring right to Arcturus.°
Then for the winter I'd drive mine to my fold,
and he'd drive his to Laius' pen again.
Did any of the things I say take place?   1145
HERDSMAN.   You speak the truth, though it's from long ago.
MESSENGER.   Do you remember giving me, back then,
    a boy I was to care for as my own?
HERDSMAN.   What are you saying? Why do you ask me that?
MESSENGER.   There, sir, is the man who was that boy!   1150
HERDSMAN.   Damn you! Shut your mouth! Keep your silence!
OEDIPUS.   Stop! Don't you rebuke his words.
    Your words ask for rebuke far more than his.
HERDSMAN.   But what have I done wrong, most royal master?
OEDIPUS.   Not telling of the boy of whom he asked.   1155
HERDSMAN.   He's ignorant and blundering toward ruin.
OEDIPUS.   Tell it willingly—or under torture.
HERDSMAN.   Oh god! Don't—I am old—don't torture me!
OEDIPUS.   Here! Someone put his hands behind his back!
HERDSMAN.   But why? What else would you find out, poor man?   1160
OEDIPUS.   Did you give him the child he asks about?
HERDSMAN.   I did. I wish that I had died that day!
OEDIPUS.   You'll come to that if you don't speak the truth.
HERDSMAN.   It's if I speak that I shall be destroyed.
OEDIPUS.   I think this fellow struggles for delay.   1165
HERDSMAN.   No, no! I said already that I gave him.
OEDIPUS.   From your own home, or got from someone else?
HERDSMAN.   Not from my own. I got him from another.
OEDIPUS.   Which of these citizens? What sort of house?
HERDSMAN.   Don't—by the gods!—don't, master, ask me more!   1170
OEDIPUS.   It means your death if I must ask again.
HERDSMAN.   One of the children of the house of Laius.
OEDIPUS.   A slave—or born into the family?
HERDSMAN.   I have come to the dreaded thing, and I shall say it.
OEDIPUS.   And I to hearing it, but hear I must.   1175
HERDSMAN.   He was reported to have been—his son.
    Your lady in the house could tell you best.
OEDIPUS.   Because she gave him to you?
HERDSMAN.   Yes, my lord.
OEDIPUS.   What was her purpose?
HERDSMAN.   I was to kill the boy.
OEDIPUS.   The child she bore?
HERDSMAN.   She dreaded prophecies.   1180
OEDIPUS.   What were they?
HERDSMAN.   The word was that he'd kill his parents.
OEDIPUS.   Then why did you give him up to this old man?
HERDSMAN.   In pity, master—so he would take him home,
    to another land. But what he did was save him

    1142 *from spring right to Arcturus:* that is, from spring to early fall, when the summer star Arcturus (in the constellation Boötes) is no longer visible in the early evening sky. It does not rise at night again until the following spring.

for this supreme disaster. If you are the one   1185
  he speaks of—know your evil birth and fate!
OEDIPUS.   Ah! All of it was destined to be true!
  Oh light, now may I look my last upon you,
  shown monstrous in my birth, in marriage monstrous,
  a murderer monstrous in those I killed.   1190

[Exit OEDIPUS, *running into the palace.]*

STASIMON 4

Strophe 1
CHORUS.   Oh generations of mortal men,
    while you are living, I will
      appraise your lives at zero!
    What man
    comes closer to seizing lasting blessedness   1195
    than merely to seize its semblance,
    and after living in this semblance, to plunge?
    With your example before us,
    with your destiny, yours,
      suffering Oedipus, no mortal   1200
    can I judge fortunate.

Antistrophe 1
  For he,° outranging everybody,
  shot his arrow° and became the lord
    of wide prosperity and blessedness,
  oh Zeus, after destroying   1205
  the virgin with the crooked talons,°
  singer of oracles; and against death,
  in my land, he arose a tower of defense.
  From which time you were called my king
  and granted privileges supreme—in mighty   1210
  Thebes the ruling lord.

Strophe 2
  But now—whose story is more sorrowful than yours?
  Who is more intimate with fierce calamities,
  with labors, now that your life is altered?
  Alas, my Oedipus, whom all men know: 1215
  one great harbor—
  one alone sufficed for you,
  as son and father,
  when you tumbled,° plowman° of the woman's chamber.
  How, how could your paternal   1220
    furrows, wretched man,
  endure you silently so long.

    1202 *he:* Oedipus.   **1203** *shot his arrow:* took his chances; made a guess at the Sphinx's riddle.
1206 *virgin . . . talons:* the Sphinx.   **1216** *one great harbor:* metaphorical allusion to Jocasta's body.
1219 *tumbled:* were born and had sex.   *plowman:* Plowing is used here as a sexual metaphor.

Antistrophe 2

> Time, all-seeing, surprised you living an unwilled life
> and sits from of old in judgment on the marriage, not a marriage,
> where the begetter is the begot as well.   1225
> Ah, son of Laius . . .,
> would that—oh, would that
> I had never seen you!
> I wail, my scream climbing beyond itself
> from my whole power of voice. To say it straight: 1230
>   from you I got new breath—
> but I also lulled my eye to sleep.°

EXODOS

[*Enter the* SECOND MESSENGER *from the palace.*]

SECOND MESSENGER.   You who are first among the citizens,
>   what deeds you are about to hear and see!
>   What grief you'll carry, if, true to your birth,   1235
>   you still respect the house of Labdacus!
>   Neither the Ister nor the Phasis river
>   could purify this house, such suffering
>   does it conceal, or soon must bring to light—
>   willed this time, not unwilled. Griefs hurt worst   1240
>   which we perceive to be self-chosen ones.
CHORAGOS.   They were sufficient, the things we knew before,
>   to make us grieve. What can you add to those?
SECOND MESSENGER.   The thing that's quickest said and quickest heard:
>   our own, our royal one, Jocasta's dead.   1245
CHORAGOS.   Unhappy queen! What was responsible?
SECOND MESSENGER.   Herself. The bitterest of these events
>   is not for you, you were not there to see,
>   but yet, exactly as I can recall it,
>   you'll hear what happened to that wretched lady.   1250
>   She came in anger through the outer hall,
>   and then she ran straight to her marriage bed,
>   tearing her hair with the fingers of both hands.
>   Then, slamming shut the doors when she was in,
>   she called to Laius, dead so many years,   1255
>   remembering the ancient seed which caused
>   his death, leaving the mother to the son
>   to breed again an ill-born progeny.
>   She mourned the bed where she, alas, bred double—
>   husband by husband, children by her child.   1260
>   From this point on I don't know how she died,
>   for Oedipus then burst in with a cry,
>   and did not let us watch her final evil.
>   Our eyes were fixed on him. Wildly he ran
>   to each of us, asking for his spear   1265

1232 *I . . . sleep:* I failed to see the corruption you brought.

and for his wife—no wife: where he might find
the double mother-field, his and his children's.
He raved, and some divinity then showed him—
for none of us did so who stood close by.
With a dreadful shout—as if some guide were leading—   1270
he lunged through the double doors; he bent the hollow
bolts from the sockets, burst into the room,
and there we saw her, hanging from above,
entangled in some twisted hanging strands.
He saw, was stricken, and with a wild roar   1275
ripped down the dangling noose. When she, poor woman,
lay on the ground, there came a fearful sight:
he snatched the pins of worked gold from her dress,
with which her clothes were fastened: these he raised
and struck into the ball-joints of his eyes.°   1280
He shouted that they would no longer see
the evils he had suffered or had done,
see in the dark those he should not have seen,
and know no more those he once sought to know.
While chanting this, not once but many times   1285
he raised his hand and struck into his eyes.
Blood from his wounded eyes poured down his chin,
not freed in moistening drops, but all at once
a stormy rain of black blood burst like hail.
These evils, coupling them, making them one,   1290
have broken loose upon both man and wife.
The old prosperity that they had once
was true prosperity, and yet today,
mourning, ruin, death, disgrace, and every
evil you could name—not one is absent.   1295
CHORAGOS.   Has he allowed himself some peace from all this grief?
SECOND MESSENGER.   He shouts that someone slide the bolts and show
    to all the Cadmeians the patricide,
    his mother's—I can't say it, it's unholy—
    so he can cast himself out of the land,   1300
    not stay and curse his house by his own curse.
    He lacks the strength, though, and he needs a guide,
    for his is a sickness that's too great to bear.
    Now you yourself will see: the bolts of the doors
    are opening. You are about to see   1305
    a vision even one who hates must pity.

[*Enter the blinded* OEDIPUS *from the palace, led in by a household* SERVANT.]

CHORAGOS.   This suffering sends terror through men's eyes,
    terrible beyond any suffering
    my eyes have touched. Oh man of pain,
    what madness reached you? Which god from far off,   1310
    surpassing in range his longest spring,

1280 *ball-joints of his eyes:* his eyeballs. Oedipus blinds himself in both eyes at the same time.

struck hard against your god-abandoned fate?
Oh man of pain,
I cannot look upon you—though there's so much
I would ask you, so much to hear,   1315
so much that holds my eyes—
    so awesome the convulsions you send through me.
OEDIPUS.   Ah! Ah! I am a man of misery.
Where am I carried? Pity me! Where
is my voice scattered abroad on wings?   1320
    Divinity, where has your lunge transported me?
CHORAGOS.   To something horrible, not to be heard or seen.

KOMMOS

Strophe 1
OEDIPUS.   Oh, my cloud
of darkness, abominable, unspeakable as it attacks me,
not to be turned away, brought by an evil wind!   1325
Alas!
Again alas! Both enter me at once:
the sting of the prongs,° the memory of evils!
CHORUS.   I do not marvel that in these afflictions
you carry double griefs and double evils.   1330

Antistrophe 1
OEDIPUS.   Ah, friend,
so you at least are there, resolute servant!
Still with a heart to care for me, the blind man.
Oh! Oh!
I know that you are there. I recognize   1335
even inside my darkness, that voice of yours.
CHORUS.   Doer of horror, how did you bear to quench
your vision? What divinity raised your hand?

Strophe 2
OEDIPUS.   It was Apollo there, Apollo, friends,
who brought my sorrows, vile sorrows to their perfection,   1340
    these evils that were done to me.
But the one who struck them with his hand,
    that one was none but I, in wretchedness.
For why was I to see
when nothing I could see would bring me joy?   1345
CHORUS.   Yes, that is how it was.
OEDIPUS.   What could I see, indeed,
or what enjoy—what greeting
is there I could hear with pleasure, friends?
Conduct me out of the land   1350
    as quickly as you can!
Conduct me out, my friends,

    1328 *prongs:* refers to both the whip that Laius used and the two gold pins Oedipus used to blind
himself.

the man utterly ruined,
supremely cursed,
the man who is by gods
the most detested of all men!   1355

CHORUS.   Wretched in disaster and in knowledge:
oh, I could wish you'd never come to know!

Antistrophe 2

OEDIPUS.   May he be destroyed, whoever freed the savage shackles
from my feet when I'd been sent to the wild pasture,   1360
whoever rescued me from murder
and became my savior—
a bitter gift:
if I had died then,
I'd not have been such grief to self and kin.   1365

CHORUS.   I also would have had it so.

OEDIPUS.   I'd not have returned to be my father's
murderer; I'd not be called by men
my mother's bridegroom.
Now I'm without a god,   1370
child of a polluted parent,
fellow progenitor with him
who gave me birth in misery.
If there's an evil that
surpasses evils, that   1375
has fallen to the lot of Oedipus.

CHORAGOS.   How can I say that you have counseled well?
Better not to be than live a blind man.

OEDIPUS.   That this was not the best thing I could do—
don't tell me that, or advise me any more!   1380
Should I descend to Hades and endure
to see my father with these eyes? Or see
my poor unhappy mother? For I have done,
to both of these, things too great for hanging.
Or is the sight of children to be yearned for,   1385
to see new shoots that sprouted as these did?
Never, never with these eyes of mine!
Nor city, nor tower, nor holy images
of the divinities! For I, all-wretched,
most nobly raised—as no one else in Thebes—   1390
deprived myself of these when I ordained
that all expel the impious one—god-shown
to be polluted, and the dead king's son!°
Once I exposed this great stain upon me,
could I have looked on these with steady eyes?   1395
No! No! And if there were a way to block

1391–1393 *I . . . son:* Oedipus refers to his own curse against the murderer as well as his sins of patricide and incest.   1401 *Cithaeron:* the mountain on which the infant Oedipus was exposed.

the source of hearing in my ears, I'd gladly
have locked up my pitiable body,
so I'd be blind and deaf. Evils shut out—
that way my mind could live in sweetness.   1400
Alas, Cithaeron,° why did you receive me?
Or when you had me, not killed me instantly?
I'd not have had to show my birth to mankind.
Polybus, Corinth, halls—ancestral,
they told me—how beautiful was your ward,   1405
a scar that held back festering disease!
Evil my nature, evil my origin.
You, three roads, and you, secret ravine,
you oak grove, narrow place of those three paths
that drank my blood° from these my hands, from him   1410
who fathered me, do you remember still
the things I did to you? When I'd come here,
what I then did once more? Oh marriages! Marriages!
You gave us life and when you'd planted us
you sent the same seed up, and then revealed   1415
fathers, brothers, sons, and kinsman's blood,
and brides, and wives, and mothers, all the most
atrocious things that happen to mankind!
One should not name what never should have been.
Somewhere out there, then, quickly, by the gods,   1420
cover me up, or murder me, or throw me
to the ocean where you will never see me more!

[*Oedipus moves toward the* Chorus *and they back away from him.*]

Come! Don't shrink to touch this wretched man!
Believe me, do not be frightened! I alone
of all mankind can carry these afflictions.   1425

[*Enter* Creon *from the palace with* Attendants.]

Choragos.   Tell Creon what you wish for. Just when we need him
        he's here. He can act, he can advise you.
        He's now the land's sole guardian in your place.
Oedipus.   Ah! Are there words that I can speak to him?
        What ground for trust can I present? It's proved   1430
        that I was false to him in everything.
Creon.   I have not come to mock you, Oedipus,
        nor to reproach you for your former falseness.
        You men, if you have no respect for sons
        of mortals, let your awe for the all-feeding   1435
        flames of lordly Hēlius° prevent
        your showing unconcealed so great a stain,
        abhorred by earth and sacred rain and light.
        Escort him quickly back into the house!

1410 *my blood:* i.e., the blood of my father, Laius, and therefore my family's blood.   **1436** *Hēlius:*
the sun.

[handwritten margin notes: "Oedipus Daughters & Sons to have considered freaks"]

> If blood kin only see and hear their own   1440
> afflictions, we'll have no impious defilement.

OEDIPUS.   By the gods, you've freed me from one terrible fear,
> so nobly meeting my unworthiness:
> grant me something—not for me; for you!

CREON.   What do you want that you should beg me so?   1445

OEDIPUS.   To drive me from the land at once, to a place
> where there will be no man to speak to me!

CREON.   I would have done just that—had I not wished
> to ask first of the god what I should do.

OEDIPUS.   His answer was revealed in full—that I,   1450
> the patricide, unholy, be destroyed.

CREON.   He said that, but our need is so extreme,
> it's best to have sure knowledge what must be done.

OEDIPUS.   You'll ask about a wretched man like me?

CREON.   Is it not time you put your trust in the god?   1455

OEDIPUS.   But I bid you as well, and shall entreat you.
> Give her who is within what burial
> you will—you'll give your own her proper rites;
> but me—do not condemn my fathers' land
> to have me dwelling here while I'm alive,   1460
> but let me live on mountains—on Cithaeron
> famed as mine, for my mother and my father,
> while they yet lived, made it my destined tomb,
> and I'll be killed by those who wished my ruin!
> And yet I know: no sickness will destroy me,   1465
> nothing will: I'd never have been saved
> when left to die unless for some dread evil.
> Then let my fate continue where it will!
> As for my children, Creon, take no pains
> for my sons—they're men and they will never lack   1470
> the means to live, wherever they may be—
> but my two wretched, pitiable girls,
> who never ate but at my table, never
> were without me—everything that I
> would touch, they'd always have a share of it—   1475
> please care for them! Above all, let me touch
> them with my hands and weep aloud my woes!
> Please, my Lord!
> Please, noble heart! Touching with my hands,
> I'd think I held them as when I could see.   1480

[Enter ANTIGONE *and* ISMENE *from the palace with* ATTENDANTS.*]*

> What's this?
> Oh gods! Do I hear, somewhere, my two dear ones
> sobbing? Has Creon really pitied me
> and sent to me my dearest ones, my children?
> Is that it?   1485

CREON.   Yes, I prepared this for you, for I knew
> you'd feel this joy, as you have always done.

[handwritten margin notes: "Oedipus in an acts in an irrational behavior", "Ancient Greeks held fate", "Gods viewed differently than our God"]

OEDIPUS.   Good fortune, then, and, for your care, be guarded
    far better by divinity than I was!
    Where are you, children? Come to me! Come here   1490
    to these my hands, hands of your brother, hands
    of him who gave you seed, hands that made
    these once bright eyes to see now in this fashion.

[*OEDIPUS embraces his daughters.*]

    He, children, seeing nothing, knowing nothing,
    he fathered you where his own seed was plowed.   1495
    I weep for you as well, though I can't see you,
    imagining your bitter life to come,
    the life you will be forced by men to live.
    What gatherings of townsmen will you join,
    what festivals, without returning home   1500
    in tears instead of watching holy rites?
    And when you've reached the time for marrying,
    where, children, is the man who'll run the risk
    of taking on himself the infamy
    that will wound you as it did my parents?   1505
    What evil is not here? Your father killed
    his father, plowed the one who gave him birth,
    and from the place where he was sown, from there
    he got you, from the place he too was born.
    These are the wounds: then who will marry you?   1510
    No man, my children. No, it's clear that you
    must wither in dry barrenness, unmarried.

[*OEDIPUS addresses CREON.*]

    Son of Menoeceus! You are the only father
    left to them—we two who gave them seed
    are both destroyed: watch that they don't become   1515
    poor, wanderers, unmarried—they are your kin.
    Let not my ruin be their ruin, too!
    No, pity them! You see how young they are,
    bereft of everyone, except for you.
    Consent, kind heart, and touch me with your hand!   1520

[*CREON grasps OEDIPUS's right hand.*]

    You, children, if you had reached an age of sense,
    I would have counseled much. Now, pray you may live
    always where it's allowed, finding a life
    better than his was, who gave you seed.

CREON.   Stop this now. Quiet your weeping. Move away, into the house.   1525
OEDIPUS.   Bitter words, but I obey them.
CREON.   There's an end to all things.
OEDIPUS.   I have first this request.
CREON.   I will hear it.
OEDIPUS.   Banish me from my homeland.
CREON.   You must ask that of the god.

OEDIPUS.   But I am the gods' most hated man!
CREON.   Then you will soon get what you want.
OEDIPUS.   Do you consent?
CREON.   I never promise when, as now, I'm ignorant.
OEDIPUS.   Then lead me in.
CREON.   Come. But let your hold fall from your children.
OEDIPUS.   Do not take them from me, ever!
CREON.   Do not wish to keep all of the
   power. You had power, but that power did not follow you through life.

[*OEDIPUS's daughters are taken from him and led into the palace by* ATTENDANTS. OEDIPUS *is led into the palace by a* SERVANT. CREON *and the other* ATTENDANTS *follow. Only the* CHORUS *remains.*]

CHORUS.   People of Thebes, my country, see: here is that Oedipus—
   he who "knew" the famous riddle, and attained the highest power,
   whom all citizens admired, even envying his luck!
   See the billows of wild troubles which he has entered now!
   Here is the truth of each man's life: we must wait, and see his end,
   scrutinize his dying day, and refuse to call him happy
   till he has crossed the border of his life without pain.

[*Exit the* CHORUS *along each of the Parados.*]

QUESTIONS

1.   *Prologue and Parados.* What is the situation in Thebes as the play begins? Why does Oedipus want to discover the murderer of Laius?

2.   *Episode 1 and Stasimon 1.* When Tiresias refuses to speak, how is the reaction of Oedipus characteristic of him? What other examples of this behavior can you find?

3.   When Tiresias does speak, he speaks the truth. Why doesn't Oedipus accept the story that Tiresias tells?

4.   *Episode 2 and Stasimon 2.* Of what does Oedipus accuse Creon, and how does Creon defend himself? Why or why not is Creon convincing?

5.   What does Jocasta have to say about oracles and prophecy? Why do you think she expresses this attitude? How do her views differ from those of the Chorus?

6.   When does Oedipus begin to think that he himself is the murderer? What details lead him to this conclusion?

7.   *Episode 3 and Stasimon 3.* Why does the news from the Messenger from Corinth at first seem good? How is the situation reversed?

8.   *Episode 4 and Stasimon 4.* What do you make of the coincidences that the same Herdsman (a) saved the infant Oedipus from death, (b) was the lone survivor of the attack on Laius and also the sole witness to the attack, and (c) will provide testimony that will destroy Oedipus?

9.   What moral does the Chorus express about the life and downfall of Oedipus?

GENERAL QUESTIONS

1.   In *Oedipus the King,* the peripeteia, anagnorisis, and catastrophe all occur at the same moment. When is this moment? Who is most severely affected by it?

2. Sophocles describes Oedipus's life piecemeal, out of chronological order. Put the details into chronological order, and consider how you might dramatize them. Why does Sophocles's ordering of events make for an effective play? Be sure to emphasize some of the coincidences in the life and career of Oedipus.

3. What is the major conflict in the play? What other conflicts does Sophocles bring out? How is the complexity of the conflicts brought out by Sophocles?

4. In the light of your understanding of tragedy and the tragic hero, describe *Oedipus the King* as a tragedy.

5. Describe Sophocles's use of dramatic irony in the play.

6. Describe the functions of the Chorus and the Choragos. Explain the relationship of the choral odes to the play's actions.

RENAISSANCE DRAMA AND SHAKESPEARE'S THEATER

In the early years of the English Renaissance, there was a flourishing native tradition of theater that had developed first within the church and then with the cooperation of the church.[12] The bridge from religious drama to the drama of the Renaissance was created in a number of ways. Of great importance was the growth of traveling dramatic professional companies, who performed their plays in local innyards—square or quadrangular spaces surrounded by the rooms of the inn. In addition, plays were performed at court, in the great rooms of aristocratic houses, in the law courts, and at universities.

Aside from the performing tradition, the immediate influence on the creation of a new drama was the development of a taste for dramatic topics drawn from nonreligious sources. The earliest of such plays in the sixteenth century was the so-called **Tudor interlude,** named after the monarchs of the Tudor family who ruled England from 1485 to 1603. *Interlude* is a misnomer, for the plays were often quite long. The interludes, supported by the nobility, were tragedies, comedies, or historical plays that were performed by both professional actors and students. They sometimes featured abstract and allegorical characters and provided opportunities for both music and farcical action.

After the middle of the sixteenth century, the revival of ancient drama and culture came increasingly to the fore. The dominating influence was the Roman dramatist Seneca (4 b.c.e.–65 c.e.), eight of whose tragedies, derived from Greek tragedy, had survived from antiquity. A vital quality of the Senecan tragedies was that they were violent and bloody, and thus they gave a classical precedent for the revenge and murder that were to be featured in the Elizabethan drama. Seneca became important not so much because he had written great works but rather because he had written in Latin. He could therefore be readily understood by a generation of new dramatists who had been schooled in Roman history, culture, and literature.

---

[12]For an account of the medieval dramatic tradition, see Chapter 26, pp. 1176–78 and 1215–38.

Shakespeare Became a Theater Entrepreneur as well as a Writer

The first group of these Elizabethan playwrights included Christopher Marlowe, Thomas Kyd, Robert Greene, George Peele, Thomas Lodge, and John Lyly. These were the men whose plays William Shakespeare watched and acted in when he first arrived in London from Stratford-upon-Avon in the late 1580s. By 1594 he had joined the Lord Chamberlain's Men, the most popular of the London acting companies. He rose swiftly as both an actor and dramatist, and by 1599 he had become an active partner with the company (called the King's Men after the accession of James I in 1603) in a venture to construct a new theater, the Globe, within a stone's throw of the earlier theater, the Rose. It was for exclusive production at the Globe that Shakespeare wrote some of his greatest plays (including *Hamlet*) from 1599 to 1608, when the company began playing alternately at the outdoor Globe and the indoor Blackfriars (formerly a part of a monastery which had been adapted for theatrical presentations).

The Globe Was a Small But Versatile Theater That Strongly Influenced the Nature of Shakespeare's Plays

Compared with the massive Greek outdoor amphitheaters, the Globe was small. Some theater historians have calculated that it could have held an audience of as many as two to three thousand, although this estimate seems excessive, for half that number would have been extremely large. Moreover, we should not suppose that the theater was filled to the rafters for every performance.

THE GLOBE WAS A "RING"-TYPE THEATER OPEN TO THE SKY. Recent archaeological excavations of the site of the Globe, together with a complete reconstruction based on the knowledge newly gained, show that it was a twenty-sided building. For practical purposes it was round—as it is shown in a contemporary drawing—and its outer diameter was approximately a hundred feet. From above, it would have resembled a ring, or, as Shakespeare called the type in *Henry V*, a "wooden O." Its central yard was open to the sky, a detail that it had appropriated from the confined areas of the inns. The thrust stage, covered by a roof, was built thirty feet into the yard at the building's south side. Because of the uncertainty and capriciousness of English weather, the acting season extended from spring through fall. During the wettest and coldest months, the theater was dark.

THE GLOBE PROVIDED A NUMBER OF ACTING AREAS. This thrust stage was close to five feet high—probably lower in front (*downstage*) and higher in back (*upstage*). Actors could move anywhere on this stage to deliver their lines. On the second level above the stage was a gallery for spectators, musicians, and actors (as in the balcony scene in Shakespeare's *Romeo and Juliet*). Actors might enter this gallery to deliver lines, and then they might also descend from there to the main stage. The area below the stage was called the *hell.* At center stage there was a trapdoor to the hell that was used for the entrances and exits of devils, monsters, and ghosts such as the Ghost of Hamlet's father. Downstage, holding up the protective roof, there were two columns. The ceiling of this roof, called the *heavens*, was decorated with colorful paintings. A hut on the roof itself contained machinery for lowering and raising actors who took the roles of fairies, witches, and gods. Behind the upstage area, which could be curtained off for interior scenes, there was a small and cramped *tiring house* and storage area where actors changed their costumes and waited for their cues. Two or three doors opened out from the tiring house to the stage.

THERE WERE THREE LOCATIONS FOR THE AUDIENCE.　The admission price permitted spectators into the ground area. Those who remained there stood during the entire performance and crowded as close as they could to the stage. These people, who were patronizingly called the *groundlings*, often endured rain and cold in addition to the discomfort of their need to stand. For additional charges, spectators could get out of bad weather by sitting in one of the three seating levels within the roofed galleries (part of the "O"). Those who could afford it paid still another charge for seats directly on the stage—a custom that continued in English theaters until the time of David Garrick in the eighteenth century.

THE GLOBE, LIKE OTHER ELIZABETHAN THEATERS, MANDATED ITS OWN PRODUCTION AND STAGE CONVENTIONS.　Just as in the Athenian theater, there was no artificial lighting, and performances therefore took place in the afternoon. The plays were performed rapidly, without intermissions or indications of act and scene changes except for occasional rhymed couplets. With no curtain and no scenery, shifts in scene were indicated by the exits and entrances of the actors. This type of scene division produced swift changes in time and place and made for great fluidity and fast pacing.

The conditions of performance and the physical shape of the theater produced a number of theatrical conventions. The two columns supporting the stage roof, for example, were versatile. Sometimes they represented trees or the sides of buildings, and conventionally they were used as places of concealment and for eavesdropping. Time, place, and circumstances of weather were established through dialogue, as in the opening scene of *Hamlet* when Horatio speaks of "the morn, in russet mantle clad" (line 166), or in *As You Like It*, when Rosalind says, "This is the forest of Arden" (2.4.15).

The Globe's relatively small size and its thrust stage made for intimate performances. There was little separation of the audience and the actors, unlike the case with the *orchestra* in Greek theaters that widened the distance between actors and spectators, or with the proscenium and curtain of many modern theaters. Consequently, there was much interaction between actors and audience. The closeness of spectators to the stage led to two unique stage conventions. One of these, the **aside,** permits a character to make brief remarks directly to the audience or to another character without the rest of the characters' hearing the words. In the other, the **soliloquy,** a character alone onstage speaks his or her thoughts or plans directly to the audience. For example, in Hamlet's second soliloquy, he criticizes his emotional detachment from his father's murder and explains how he plans to test Claudius's guilt (2.2.524–580). We should realize that actors using these conventions spoke directly to members of the audience who were sitting next to the action. These spectators almost literally became additional members of the cast.

THE ACTORS FOLLOWED ESTABLISHED CONVENTIONS IN GESTURE AND COSTUME. The actors in Shakespeare's day were legally bound to the company of which they were members. Without the protection of the company, they were considered "rogues and vagabonds." In England the actors were always male, with adolescent boys performing the women's roles because women were excluded from the stage. The actors used no masks. Instead, they developed expressions and gestures that would seem to us, today, excessively stylized. The acting mannerisms sometimes seemed excessive to Shakespeare, too, as is indicated by Hamlet's instructions to the traveling actors. He tells them not to "saw the air too much with your hand" and not to "tear a passion to tatters, to very rags" (3.2.4–9).

The actors wore elaborate costumes to demonstrate the nature and status of the characters. Thus kings always wore robes and crowns, and they carried orbs and scepters. A fool (a type of comic and ironic commentator) wore a multicolored or *motley* costume, and clowns and "mechanicals" wore the common clothing of the humble classes. Ragged clothing indicated a reduction in circumstances, as in *King Lear*, and Ophelia's description of Hamlet's disordered clothing in the second act of *Hamlet* indicates the prince's disturbed mental condition (2.1.74–82). Whenever characters took on a disguise, as in *As You Like It*, this disguise was impenetrable to the other characters.

The New Globe Theater Has Been Built Near the Site of Shakespeare's Globe

Shakespeare's Globe burned in 1613, and the Globe that replaced it was torn down by the Puritans under Oliver Cromwell in 1644. From then on the location was variously occupied by tenements, breweries, other buildings, and a road. In the late 1980s, however, archaeological excavations took place at the sites of both the Globe and the nearby Rose theater, and the subsequent discoveries have provided exciting new information about theaters and theatergoing in Shakespeare's day. A reconstruction of the Globe was undertaken and is now complete—not at the original location but close by. The original site could not be used because it was preempted by a protected building and a vital street leading to Southwark Bridge. Theatergoers in London are now able to attend performances of Shakespeare's plays in this new theater under conditions almost identical to those that Shakespeare's audiences and acting company knew, including, for the "groundlings," rain, wind, cold, and the discomfort of standing (see the photograph of the reconstruction of the Globe stage, Insert III-3).[13]

---

[13]See J. R. Mulryne and Margaret Shewring, eds., *Shakespeare's Globe Rebuilt* (Cambridge: Cambridge UP, 1997). Further information about the Globe Theatre may be found at <shakespeare'sglobe>.

WILLIAM SHAKESPEARE, *HAMLET*

Shakespeare was born in 1564 in Stratford-upon-Avon, in western England. He attended the Stratford grammar school; he married in 1582, and he and his wife had three children. He left his family and moved to London sometime between 1585 and 1592. During this period he became a professional actor, and he also began writing plays and poems. Because the London theaters were closed during the plague years 1592–1594, he apparently worked at other jobs, about which we know nothing. By 1595, however, he was recognized as a major writer of comedies and tragedies. He soon became a member of the Lord Chamberlain's Men, the leading theatrical company, and, as we have seen, he became a shareholder in the new Globe Theatre in 1599. Because he realized good returns from the business venture and also from his plays, he became moderately wealthy. He stopped writing for the stage in 1611, having written a total of thirty-seven plays, of which eleven were tragedies. He also collaborated in writing a few other plays. During his retirement he lived in his native Stratford. He died in 1616 and is buried next to the altar of Stratford's Trinity Church, beneath a bust and an inscribed gravestone.

When the Lord Chamberlain's Men first staged *Hamlet* in 1602 at the Globe, it was not the first time the story had been dramatized on the London stage. There is evidence that a play based on the Hamlet story, now lost, had been performed before 1589. Therefore, at least some of the theatergoers might have known the story.

Even if none of them knew the story, however, they would have known the tradition of **revenge tragedy.** The Elizabethans had been introduced to the drama of vengeance through the English translations of Seneca's tragedies during the 1570s and early 1580s. Another important precedent was Thomas Kyd's *Spanish Tragedy* (ca. 1587), the first English play in the revenge tradition, which featured a hero who commits suicide. The major conventions of the genre were a ghost who calls for vengeance and a revenger who pretends to be insane at least part of the time. Above all, the tradition required that the revenger would also die, no matter how good a person he was or how just his cause might have been.

Although Elizabethan audiences were prepared for *Hamlet* by the revenge formula, they could have anticipated neither a protagonist of Hamlet's likeableness and complexity nor a play of such profundity. The earlier revengers were flat characters with a single fixation on getting even through personal vengeance. Hamlet, however, is acutely aware of the political and moral corruption of the Danish court, and he reflects on the fallen state of humanity. Experiencing despair and guilt, he even contemplates suicide. He learns from his experiences and meditations, discovering that he must look beyond reason and philosophy for ways of coping with the world. He also develops patience and learns to trust in Providence, the "divinity that shapes our ends" (5.2.10).

The play itself demonstrates the far-reaching effects of evil, which branches inexorably outward from Claudius's initial act of murder. The evil ensnares innocent and guilty alike. Hamlet, the avenger, becomes the direct and indirect cause of deaths, and as a result, he in turn also becomes an object of revenge. By the play's end, all the major and two of the minor characters are dead: Polonius, Ophelia, Rosencrantz, Guildenstern, Gertrude, Claudius, Laertes, and, finally, Hamlet himself. The play's crowning irony is that Hamlet does not complete his vengeance because of the murder of his father, King Hamlet. Rather, he kills Claudius immediately upon learning that the king has murdered Gertrude, his mother.

In the centuries since Shakespeare wrote *Hamlet*, the play has remained among the most popular, most moving, and most effective plays in the world. It has been translated into scores of languages. Major actors from Shakespeare's day to ours—including Richard Burbage as the first Hamlet, and Derek Jacoby, Kevin Kline, Mel Gibson, Ralph Fiennes, Kenneth Branagh, and Ethan Hawke—have starred in the role. Beyond the play's stage popularity, *Hamlet* has become one of the central documents of Western civilization. Somehow, most people know about Hamlet and are familiar with passages like "To be or not to be," "The play's the thing," and "The undiscovered country, from whose bourn / No traveler returns" even if they have never read the play or seen a live or filmed performance.

WILLIAM SHAKESPEARE (1564–1616)

The Tragedy of Hamlet, Prince of Denmark ~~~~~~ *ca. 1600*

Edited by Alice Griffin*

CHARACTERS

Claudius, *King of Denmark*
Hamlet, *Son to the former, and nephew to the present King*
Polonius, *Lord Chamberlain*
Horatio, *Friend to Hamlet*
Laertes, *Son to Polonius*
Valtemand ⎫
Cornelius ⎪
Rosencrantz ⎬ *Courtiers*
Guildenstern ⎪
Osric ⎭
A Gentleman
A Priest
Marcellus ⎫ *Officers*
Barnardo ⎭
Francisco, *a Soldier*
Reynaldo, *Servant to Polonius*
Players
Two Clowns, *gravediggers*
Fortinbras, *Prince of Norway*
A Norwegian Captain
English Ambassadors
Gertrude, *Queen of Denmark, mother to Hamlet*
Ophelia, *Daughter to Polonius*
Ghost of Hamlet's Father
Lords, Ladies, Officers, Soldiers, Sailors, Messengers, Attendants

*Professor Griffin's text for *Hamlet* was the Second Quarto (edition) published in 1604, with modifications based on the First Folio, published in 1623. Stage directions in those editions are printed here without brackets; added stage directions are printed within brackets. We have edited Griffin's notes for this text.

[SCENE: *Elsinore*]

ACT 1

Scene 1. [*A platform on the battlements of the castle*]

Enter BARNARDO *and* FRANCISCO, *two Sentinels.*

BARNARDO.	Who's there?	
FRANCISCO.	Nay, answer me. Stand and unfold° yourself.	
BARNARDO.	Long live the king.	
FRANCISCO.	Barnardo?	
BARNARDO.	He.	
FRANCISCO.	You come most carefully upon your hour.	5
BARNARDO.	'Tis now struck twelve, get thee to bed Francisco.	
FRANCISCO.	For this relief much thanks, 'tis bitter cold, And I am sick at heart.	
BARNARDO.	Have you had quiet guard?	
FRANCISCO.	Not a mouse stirring.	10
BARNARDO.	Well, good night:	

If you do meet Horatio and Marcellus,
The rival° of my watch, bid them make haste.

Enter HORATIO *and* MARCELLUS.

FRANCISCO.	I think I hear them. Stand ho, who is there?	
HORATIO.	Friends to this ground.	
MARCELLUS.	And liegemen° to the Dane°	15
FRANCISCO.	Give you good night.	
MARCELLUS.	O, farewell honest soldier,	

Who hath relieved you?

FRANCISCO.	Barnardo hath my place;	

Give you good night.   *Exit Francisco.*

MARCELLUS.	Holla, Barnardo!	
BARNARDO.	Say,	

What, is Horatio there?

HORATIO.	A piece of him.	
BARNARDO.	Welcome Horatio, welcome good Marcellus.	20
HORATIO.	What, has this thing appeared again tonight?	
BARNARDO.	I have seen nothing.	
MARCELLUS.	Horatio says 'tis but our fantasy,°	

And will not let belief take hold of him,
Touching this dreaded sight twice seen of us,   25
Therefore I have entreated him along
With us to watch the minutes of this night,
That if again this apparition come,
He may approve° our eyes and speak to it.

HORATIO.	Tush, tush, 'twill not appear.	
BARNARDO.	Sit down awhile,	30

And let us once again assail your ears,

---

2 *unfold:* reveal.   13 *rivals:* partners.   15 *liegemen:* subjects.   *Dane:* King of Denmark.
23 *fantasy:* imagination.   29 *approve:* prove reliable.

That are so fortified against our story,
What we have two nights seen.
HORATIO.   Well, sit we down,
And let us hear Barnardo speak of this,   35
BARNARDO.   Last night of all,
When yon same star that's westward from the pole°
Had made his course t'illume that part of heaven
Where now it burns, Marcellus and myself,
The bell then beating one—

Enter GHOST.

MARCELLUS.   Peace, break thee off, look where it comes again.   40
BARNARDO.   In the same figure like the king that's dead.
MARCELLUS.   Thou art a scholar, speak to it Horatio.
BARNARDO.   Looks a' not like the king? mark it Horatio.
HORATIO.   Most like, it harrows me with fear and wonder.
BARNARDO.   It would be spoke to.
MARCELLUS.   Question it Horatio.   45
HORATIO.   What art thou that usurp'st° this time of night,
Together with that fair and warlike form,
In which the majesty of buried Denmark°
Did sometimes° march? by heaven I charge thee speak.
MARCELLUS.   It is offended.
BARNARDO.   See, it stalks away.   50
HORATIO.   Stay, speak, speak, I charge thee speak.   *Exit* GHOST.
MARCELLUS.   'Tis gone and will not answer.
BARNARDO.   How now Horatio, you tremble and look pale,
Is not this something more than fantasy?
What think you on't?   55
HORATIO.   Before my God I might not this believe,
Without the sensible and true avouch°
Of mine own eyes.
MARCELLUS.   Is it not like the king?
HORATIO.   As thou art to thyself.
Such was the very armour he had on,   60
When he the ambitious Norway° combated:
So frowned he once, when in an angry parle°
He smote the sledded Polacks° on the ice.
'Tis strange.
MARCELLUS.   Thus twice before, and jump° at this dead hour,   65
With martial stalk hath he gone by our watch.
HORATIO.   In what particular thought to work, I know not,
But in the gross and scope° of mine opinion,   *general view*
This bodes some strange eruption to our state.

---

36 *pole:* North Star.   46 *usurp'st:* wrongfully occupy (both the time and the shape of the dead
king).   48 *buried Denmark:* the buried King of Denmark.   49 *Sometimes:* formerly.   57 *sensible . . .
avouch:* assurance of the truth of the senses.   61 *Norway:* King of Norway.   62 *Parle:* Parley, verbal battle.
63 *sledded Polacks:* Polish soldiers on sleds.   65 *jump:* just.   68 *gross and scope:* general view.

MARCELLUS.   Good now sit down, and tell me he that knows,   70
      Why this same strict and most observant watch
      So nightly toils the subject° of the land,   *Makes the subject toil*
      And why such daily cast of brazen cannon
      And foreign mart,° for implements of war,   *difficult*
      Why such impress° of shipwrights, whose sore° task   75
      Does not divide the Sunday from the week,
      What might be toward° that this sweaty haste
      Doth make the night joint-labourer with the day,
      Who is't that can inform me?
HORATIO.   That can I.
      At least the whisper goes so; our last king,   80
      Whose image even but now appeared to us,
      Was as you know by Fortinbras of Norway,
      Thereto pricked on by a most emulate° pride,
      Dared to the combat; in which our valiant Hamlet
      (For so this side of our known world esteemed him)   85
      Did slay this Fortinbras, who by a sealed compact,°
      Well ratified by law and heraldy,°
      Did forfeit (with his life) all those his lands
      Which he stood seized° of, to the conqueror:
      Against the which a moiety competent°   90
      Was gagèd° by our King, which had returned
      To the inheritance of Fortinbras,
      Had he been vanquisher; as by the same co-mart,°
      And carriage of the article designed,°
      His fell to Hamlet; now sir, young Fortinbras,   95
      Of unimprovèd mettle° hot and full,
      Hath in the skirts° of Norway here and there
      Sharked up° a list of lawless resolutes°
      For food and diet to some enterprise
      That hath a stomach° in't, which is no other,   100
      As it doth well appear unto our state,
      But to recover of us by strong hand
      And terms compulsatory, those foresaid lands
      So by his father lost; and this I take it,
      Is the main motive of our preparations,   105
      The source of this our watch, and the chief head°
      Of this post-haste and romage° in the land.
BARNARDO.   I think it be no other, but e'en so;
      Well may it sort° that this portentous figure
      Comes armèd through our watch so like the king   110
      That was and is the question of these wars.

Trade

---

72 *toils the subject:* makes the subjects toil.   74 *mart:* trade.   75 *impress:* conscription. *sore:* difficult.   77 *toward:* forthcoming.   83 *emulate:* rivaling 86 *compact:* treaty.   87 *law and heraldy:* heraldic
law regulating combats.   89 *seized:* possessed.   90 *moiety competent:* equal amount.   91 *gagèd:*
pledged.   93 *co-mart:* joint bargain.   94 *carriage . . . designed:* intent of the treaty drawn up.
96 *unimproved mettle:* untested (1) metal (2) spirit.   97 *skirts:* outskirts.   98 *Sharked up:* gathered up indiscriminately (as a shark preys).   *lawless resolutes:* determined outlaws.   100 *stomach:* show of courage.
106 *head:* fountainhead.   107 *romage:* bustle (rummage).   109 *sort:* turn out.

HORATIO.   A mote it is to trouble the mind's eye:
    In the most high and palmy° state of Rome, *Triumphant*
    A little ere the mightest Julius fell,
    The graves stood tenantless, and the sheeted dead   115
    Did squeak and gibber in the Roman Streets,
    As stars with trains of fire,° and dews of blood,
    Disasters° in the sun; and the moist star,°
    Upon whose influence Neptune's empire stands,
    Was sick almost to doomsday with eclipse.   120
    And even the like precurse° of feared events,
    As harbingers preceding still° the fates
    And prologue to the omen° coming on,
    Have heaven and earth together demonstrated
    Unto our climatures° and countrymen.   125

Enter GHOST.

    But soft, behold, lo where it comes again.
    I'll cross° it though it blast me: *Spreads his arms.*
                stay illusion,
    If thou hast any sound or use of voice,
    Speak to me.
    If there be any good thing to be done   130
    That may to thee do ease, and grace° to me,
    Speak to me.
    If thou art privy° to thy country's fate
    Which happily° foreknowing may avoid,
    O speak: 135
    Or if thou hast uphoarded in thy life
    Extorted treasure in the womb of earth,
    For which they say you spirits oft walk in death,

                                    The cock crows.

    Speak of it, stay and speak. Stop it Marcellus.
MARCELLUS.   Shall I strike as it with my partisan?°   140
HORATIO.   Do, if it will not stand
BARNARDO.   'Tis here.
HORATIO.   'Tis here.
MARCELLUS.   'Tis gone.   *Exit GHOST.*
    We do it wrong being so majestical,
    To offer it the show of violence,
    For it is as the air, invulnerable,   145
    And our vain blows malicious mockery.°

---

113 *palmy:* triumphant.   117 *stars . . . fire:* meteors.   118 *Disasters:* unfavorable portents.   *moist star:* moon.   121 *precurse:* portent.   122 *still:* always.   123 *omen:* disaster.   125 *climatures:* regions.   127 *cross:* (1) cross its path (2) spread my arms to make a cross of my body (to ward against evil).   131 *grace:* (1) honor (2) blessedness.   133 *art privy:* know secretly of.   134 *happily:* perhaps.   140 *partisan:* spear.   146 *malicious mockery:* mockery because they only imitate harm.

BARNARDO.   It was about to speak when the cock crew.°
HORATIO.   And then it started like a guilty thing,
    Upon a fearful summons; I have heard,
    The cock that is the trumpet to the morn,   150
    Doth with his lofty and shrill-sounding throat
    Awake the god of day, and at his warning
    Whether in sea or fire, in earth or air,°
    Th'extravagant and erring° spirit hies°
    To his confine, and of the truth herein   155
    This present object made probation.°
MARCELLUS.   If faded on the crowing of the cock.
    Some say that ever 'gainst° that season comes
    Wherein our Saviour's birth is celebrated
    This bird of dawning singeth all night long,   160
    And then they say no spirit dare stir abroad,
    The nights are wholesome,° then no planets strike,°
    No fairy takes,° nor witch hath power to charm,
    So hallowed, and so gracious is that time.
HORATIO.   So have I heard and do in part believe it.   165
    But look, the morn in russet° mantle clad
    Walks o'er the dew of yon high eastward hill:
    Break we our watch up and by my advice
    Let us impart what we have seen tonight
    Unto young Hamlet, for upon my life   170
    This spirit dumb to us, will speak to him:
    Do you consent we shall acquaint him with it,
    As needful in our loves,° fitting our duty?
MARCELLUS.   Let's do't I pray, and I this morning know
    Where we shall find him most convenient.   *Exeunt.*° 175

Scene 2. [A room of state in the castle]

Flourish.° *Enter* CLAUDIUS *Kings of Denmark,* GERTRUDE *the Queen,* [*members of the*] *Council: as*
POLONIUS; *and his son* LAERTES, HAMLET, [VALTEMAND *and* CORNELIUS] *cum aliis.*°

KING.   Though yet of Hamlet our dear brother's death
    The memory be green, and that it us befitted
    To bear our hearts in grief, and our whole kingdom
    To be contracted in one brow of woe,
    Yet so far hath discretion fought with nature,°   5
    That we° with wisest sorrow think on him
    Together with remembrance of ourselves:°

---

147 *cock crew:* (traditional signal for ghosts to return to their confines).   153 *sea . . . air:* the four elements (inhabited by spirits, each indigenous to a particular element).   154 *extravagant and erring:* going beyond its bounds (vagrant) and wandering.   *hies:* hastens.   156 *made probation:* gave proof. 158 *'gainst:* just before.   162 *wholesome:* healthy (night air was considered unhealthy).   *strike:* exert evil influence   163 *takes:* bewitches.   166 *russet:* reddish.   173 *needful . . . loves:* urged by our friendship. 175 S.D.: *Exeunt:* all exit.   0.1 S.D.: *Flourish:* fanfare or trumpets.   *cum aliis:* with others.   5 *nature:* natural impulse (of grief).   6 *we:* royal plural. The King speaks not only for himself, but for his entire government.   7 *remembrance of ourselves:* reminder of our duties.

Therefore our sometime° sister,° now our queen,
Th'imperial jointress° to this warlike state,
Have was as 'twere with a defeated joy,   10
With an auspicious, and a dropping eye,°
With mirth in funeral, and with dirge in marriage,
In equal scale weighing delight and dole,
Taken to wife: nor have we herein barred
Your better wisdoms,° which have freely gone   15
With this affair along—for all, our thanks.
Now follows that you know, young Fortinbras,
Holding a weak supposal of our worth°
Or thinking by our late dear brother's death
Our state to be disjoint and out of frame,°   20
Colleaguèd° with this dream of his advantage,°
He hath not failed to pester us with message
Importing the surrender of those lands
Lost by his father, with all bands° of law,
To our most valiant brother—so much for him: 25
Now for ourself, and for this time of meeting,
Thus much the business is. We have here writ
To Norway, uncle of young Fortinbras—
Who impotent and bed-rid scarcely hears
Of this his nephew's purpose—to suppress   30
His further gait° herein, in that the levies,
The lists, and full proportions are all made
Out of his subject.° and we here dispatch
You good Cornelius, and you Valtemand,
For bearers of this greeting to old Norway,   35
Giving to you no further personal power
To business with the king, more than the scope
Of these delated° articles allow:
Farewell, and let your haste commend your duty.°
CORNELIUS, VALTEMAND.   In that, and all things, will we show our duty.   40
KING.   We doubt it nothing, heartily farewell.

                              Exeunt VALTEMAND *and* CORNELIUS.

And now Laertes what's the news with you?
You told us to some suit, what is't Laertes?
You cannot speak of reason to the Dane
And lose your voice;° what wouldst thou beg, Laertes,   45
That shall not be my offer, not thy asking?°
The head is not more native° to the heart,

---

8 *sometime:* former. *sister:* sister-in-law. 9 *jointress:* widow who inherits the estate. 11 *auspic-ious . . . eye:* one eye happy, the other tearful. 14–15 *barred . . . wisdoms:* failed to seek and abide by your good advice. 18 *weak . . . worth:* low opinion of my ability in office. 20 *out of frame:* tottering. 21 *Colleaguèd:* supported. *advantage:* superiority. 24 *bands:* bonds. 31 *gait:* progress. 31–33 *levies . . . subject:* Taxes, conscriptions, and supplies are all obtained from his subjects. 38 *delated:* prescribed; de-fined. 39 *haste . . . duty:* prompt departure signify your respect. 45 *lose your voice:* speak in vain. 46 *offer . . . asking:* grant even before requested. 47 *native:* related.

The hand more instrumental to the mouth,
Than is the throne of Denmark to thy father.
What wouldst thou have, Laertes?

LAERTES.   My dread lord,   50
Your leave and favour° to return to France,
From whence, though willingly I came to Denmark,
To show my duty in your coronation,
Yet now I must confess, that duty done,
My thoughts and wishes bend again toward France,   55
And bow them to your gracious leave and pardon.°

KING.   Have you your father's leave? What says Polonius?

POLONIUS.   He hath my lord wrung from me my slow leave
By laboursome petition, and at last
Upon his will I sealed my hard consent.°   60
I do beseech you give him leave to go.

KING.   Take thy fair hour Laertes, time be thine,
And thy best graces spend it at thy will.
But now my cousin° Hamlet, and my son—

HAMLET.   [Aside.] A little more than kin,° and less than kind.°   65

KING.   How is it that the clouds still hang on you?

HAMLET.   Not so my lord, I am too much in the sun.°

QUEEN.   Good Hamlet cast thy nighted colour° off
And let thine eye look like a friend on Denmark,°
Do not for ever with thy vailèd° lids   70
Seek for thy noble father in the dust,
Thou know'st 'tis common, all that lives must die,
Passing through nature to eternity.

HAMLET.   Ay madam, it is common.°

QUEEN.   If it be,
Why seems it so particular with thee?   75

HAMLET.   Seems, madam? nay it is, I know not "seems."
'Tis not alone my inky cloak, good mother,
Nor customary suits of solemn black,
Nor windy suspiration of forced breath,
No, nor the fruitful river in the eye,°   80
Nor the dejected haviour° of the visage,
Together with all forms, moods, shapes of grief,
That can denote me truly: these indeed seem,
For they are actions that a man might play,°
But I have that within which passes show,   85
These but the trappings and the suits of woe.°

---

51 *leave and favour:* kind permission. 56 *pardon:* allowance. 60 *Upon . . . consent:* (1) At his request, I gave my grudging consent. (2) On the soft sealing wax of his (legal) will, I stamped my approval. 64 *cousin:* kinsman (used for relatives outside the immediate family). 65 *more than kin:* too much of a kinsman, being both uncle and stepfather. *less than kind:* (1) unkind because of being a kin (proverbial) and taking the throne from the former king's son (2) unnatural (as it was considered incest to marry the wife of one's dead brother). 67 *in the sun:* (1) in presence of the king (often associated metaphorically with the sun) (2) proverbial: "out of heaven's blessing into the warm sun" (3) of a "son." 68 *nighted colour:* black. 69 *Denmark:* the King of Denmark. 70 *vailèd:* downcast. 74 *common:* (1) general (2) vulgar. 79–80 *windy . . . eye:* (hyperbole used to describe exaggerated sighs and tears). 81 *haviour:* behavior. 84 *play:* act. 86 *trappings . . . woe:* outward, superficial costumes of mourning.

KING. 'Tis sweet and commendable in your nature Hamlet,
    To give these mourning duties to your father:
    But you must know your father lost a father,
    That father lost, lost his, and the survivor bound   90
    In filial obligation for some term
    To do obsequious sorrow:° but to persever
    In obstinate condolement,° is a course
    Of impious stubbornness, 'tis unmanly grief,
    It shows a will most incorrect to heaven,   95
    A heart unfortified, a mind impatient,
    An understanding simple and unschooled:
    For what we know must be, and is as common
    As any the most vulgar thing to sense,°
    Why should we in our peevish opposition   100
    Take it to heart? Fie, 'tis a fault to heaven,
    A fault against the dead, a fault to nature,
    To reason most absurd, whose common theme
    Is death of fathers, and who still° hath cried
    From the first corse,° till he that died today,   105
    "This must be so." We pray you throw to earth
    This unprevailing° woe, and think of us
    As of a father, for let the world take note
    You are the most immediate° to our throne,
    And with no less nobility of love   110
    Than that which dearest father bears his son,
    Do I impart toward you. For your intent
    In going back to school in Wittenberg,
    It is most retrograde° to our desire,
    And we beseech you, bend you° to remain   115
    Here in the cheer and comfort of our eye,
    Our chiefest courtier, cousin, and our son.
QUEEN.   Let not thy mother lose her prayers Hamlet,
    I pray thee stay with us, go not to Wittenberg.
HAMLET.   I shall in all my best obey you madam.   120
KING.   Why 'tis a loving and a fair reply,
    Be as ourself in Denmark. Madam come,
    This gentle and unforced accord of Hamlet
    Sits smiling to my heart, in grace whereof,
    No jocund health that Denmark drinks today,   125
    But the great cannon to the clouds shall tell,
    And the king's rouse° the heaven shall bruit° again,
    Re-speaking earthly thunder; come away.

Flourish: Exeunt all but HAMLET.

---

92 *do obsequious sorrow:* express sorrow befitting obsequies or funerals.   93 *condolement:* grief.
99 *As any . . . sense:* as the most ordinary thing the senses can perceive.   104 *still:* always.   105 *corse:*
corpse (of Abel, also, ironically, the first fratricide).   107 *unprevailing:* useless.   109 *most immediate:* next
in succession (though Danish kings were elected by the council, an Elizabethan audience might feel that
Hamlet, not Claudius, should be king).   114 *retrograde:* movement (of planets) in a reverse direction.
115 *beseech . . . you:* hope you will be inclined.   127 *rouse:* toast that empties the wine cup.   *bruit:* sound.

HAMLET.   O that this too too sullied° flesh would melt,
    Thaw and resolve itself into a dew,   130
    Or that the Everlasting had not fixed
    His canon° 'gainst self-slaughter. O God, God,
    How weary, stale, flat, and unprofitable
    Seem to me all the uses of this world!
    Fie on't, ah fie, 'tis an unweeded garden   135
    That grows to seed, things rank° and gross in nature
    Possess it merely.° That it should come to this,
    But two months dead, nay not so much, not two,
    So excellent a king, that was to this
    Hyperion° to a satyr,° so loving to my mother,   140
    That he might not beteem° the winds of heaven
    Visit her face too roughly—heaven and earth,
    Must I remember? why, she would hang on him
    As if increase of appetite had grown
    By what it fed on,° and yet within a month—   145
    Let me not think on't: Frailty, thy name is woman—
    A little month or ere those shoes were old
    With which she followed my poor father's body
    Like Niobe° all tears, why she, even she—
    O God, a beast that wants° discourse of reason   150
    Would have mourned longer—married with my uncle,
    My father's brother, but no more like my father
    Than I to Hercules: within a month,
    Ere yet the salt of most unrighteous° tears
    Had left the flushing° in her gallèd° eyes,   155
    She married. O most wicked speed, to post°
    With such dexterity to incestuous° sheets:
    It is not, nor it cannot come to good,
    But break my heart, for I must hold my tongue.

Enter HORATIO, MARCELLUS and BARNARDO.

HORATIO.   Hail to your lordship.
HAMLET.   I am glad to see you well;   160
    Horatio, or I do forget my self.
HORATIO.   The same my lord, and your poor servant ever.
HAMLET.   Sir my good friend, I'll change° that name with you:
    And what make you from Wittenberg, Horatio?
    Marcellus.   165
MARCELLUS.   My good lord.

---

      129 *sullied:* tainted.   **132** *canon:* divine edict.   **136** *rank:* (1) luxuriant, excessive (2) bad-smelling.
137 *merely:* entirely.   **140** *Hyperion:* god of the sun.   *satyr:* part-goat, part-man woodland deity (noted for lust).   **141** *beteem:* allow.   **144–145** *As if . . . on:* as if the more she fed, the more her appetite increased.   **149** *Niobe:* (who boasted of her children before Leto and was punished by their destruction; Zeus changed the weeping mother to a stone dropping continual tears).   **150** *wants:* lacks.   **154** *unrighteous:* (because untrue).   **155** *flushing:* redness.   *gallèd:* rubbed sore.   **156** *post:* rush.   **157** *incestuous:* (the church forbade marriage to one's brother's widow).   **163** *change:* exchange (and be called your friend).

HAMLET.   I am very glad to see you: good even, sir.
    But what in faith make you from Wittenberg?
HORATIO.   A truant disposition, good my lord.
HAMLET.   I would not hear your enemy say so,   170
    Nor shall you do mine ear that violence
    To make it truster of your own report
    Against yourself. I know you are no truant,
    But what is your affair in Elsinore?
    We'll teach you to drink deep ere you depart.   175
HORATIO.   My Lord, I came to see your father's funeral.
HAMLET.   I prithee do not mock me, fellow student,
    I think it was to see my mother's wedding.
HORATIO.   Indeed my lord it followed hard upon.
HAMLET.   Thrift, thrift, Horatio, the funeral baked meats°   180
    Did coldly° furnish forth the marriage tables.
    Would I had met my dearest° foe in heaven
    Or ever I had seen that day Horatio.
    My father, methinks I see my father.
HORATIO.   Where my lord?
HAMLET.   In my mind's eye Horatio.   185
HORATIO.   I saw him once, a' was a goodly° king.
HAMLET.   A' was a man, take him for all in all,
    I shall not look upon his like again.
HORATIO.   My lord, I think I saw him yesternight.
HAMLET.   Saw? Who?   190
HORATIO.   My lord, the king your father.
HAMLET.   The king my father?
HORATIO.   Season your admiration° for a while
    With an attent ear till I may deliver
    Upon the witness of these gentlemen
    This marvel to you.
HAMLET.   For God's love let me hear!   195
HORATIO.   Two nights together had these gentlemen,
    Marcellus and Barnardo, on their watch
    In the dead waste and middle of the night,
    Been thus encountered. A figure like your father
    Armed at point exactly, cap-a-pe,°   200
    Appears before them, and with solemn march,
    Goes slow and stately by them; thrice he walked
    By their oppressed° and fear-surprisèd eyes
    Within his truncheon's° length, whilst they distilled°
    Almost to jelly with the act of fear,   205
    Stand dumb and speak not to him; this to me
    In dreadful secrecy° impart they did,

---

    180 *funeral baked meats:* food prepared for the funeral.   181 *coldly:* when cold.   182 *dearest:* direst.   186 *goodly:* handsome.   192 *Season your admiration:* control your wonder.   200 *at point . . . cap-a-pe:* in every detail, head to foot.   203 *oppressed:* overcome by horror.   204 *truncheon:* staff (of office).   *distilled:* dissolved.   207 *in dreadful secrecy:* as a dread secret.

And I with them the third night kept the watch,
Where as they had delivered, both in time,
Form of the thing, each word made true and good,   210
The apparition comes: I knew your father,
These hands are not more like.

HAMLET.   But where was this?

MARCELLUS.   My lord upon the platform where we watch.

HAMLET.   Did you not speak to it?

HORATIO.   My lord I did,
But answer made it none, yet once methought   215
It lifted up it° head, and did address
Itself to motion° like as it would speak:
But even then the morning cock crew loud,
And at the sound it shrunk in haste away
And vanished from our sight.

HAMLET.   'Tis very strange.   220

HORATIO.   As I do live my honoured lord 'tis true,
And we did think it writ down in our duty
To let you know of it.

HAMLET.   Indeed indeed sirs, but this troubles me.
Hold you the watch tonight?

ALL.   We do my lord.   225

HAMLET.   Armed say you?

ALL.   Armed my lord.

HAMLET.   From top to toe?

ALL.   My lord from head to foot.

HAMLET.   Then saw you not his face.

HORATIO.   O yes my lord, he wore his beaver° up.   230

HAMLET.   What, looked he frowningly?

HORATIO.   A countenance more in sorrow than in anger.

HAMLET.   Pale, or red?

HORATIO.   Nay, very pale.

HAMLET.   And fixed his eyes upon you?

HORATIO.   Most constantly.

HAMLET.   I would I had been there.   235

HORATIO.   It would have much amazed you.

HAMLET.   Very like, very like, stayed it long?

HORATIO.   While one with moderate haste might tell° a hundred.

MARCELLUS, BARNARDO.   Longer, longer.

HORATIO.   Not when I saw't.

HAMLET.   His beard was grizzled,° no?   240

HORATIO.   It was as I have seen it in his life,
A sable silvered.°

HAMLET.   I will watch tonight;
Perchance 'twill walk again.

HORATIO.   I warr'nt it will.

---

216 *it*: its.   216–217 *address . . . motion*: start to move.   230 *beaver*: visor.   238 *tell*: count.
240 *grizzled*: grey.   242 *A sable silvered*: black flecked with gray.

HAMLET.   If it assume my noble father's person,
    I'll speak to it though hell itself should gape   245
    And bid me hold my peace;° I pray you all
    If you have hitherto concealed this sight
    Let it be tenable° in your silence still,
    And whatsoever else shall hap tonight,
    Give it an understanding but no tongue.   250
    I will requite your loves, so fare you well:
    Upon the platform 'twixt eleven and twelve
    I'll visit you.
ALL.   Our duty to your honour.
HAMLET.   Your loves, as mine to you:° farewell.   *Exeunt.* [*Hamlet remains.*]
    My father's spirit (in arms) all is not well,   255
    I doubt° some foul play, would the night were come;
    Till then sit still my soul. Foul deeds will rise,
    Though all the earth o'erwhelm them to men's eyes.   *Exit.*

Scene 3. [*Polonius's chambers*]

Enter LAERTES *and* OPHELIA *his sister.*

LAERTES.   My necessaries are embarked, farewell,
    And sister, as the winds give benefit
    And convoy° is assistant, do not sleep
    But let me hear from you.
OPHELIA.   Do you doubt that?
LAERTES.   For Hamlet, and the trifling of his favour,   5
    Hold it a fashion, and a toy in blood,°
    A violet in the youth of primy nature,°
    Forward,° not permanent, sweet, not lasting,
    The perfume and suppliance of° a minute,
    No more.
OPHELIA.   No more but so?
LAERTES.   Think it no more.   10
    For nature crescent° does not grow alone
    In thews and bulk,° but as this temple waxes°
    The inward service of the mind and soul
    Grows wide withal.° Perhaps he loves you now,
    And now no soil nor cautel° doth besmirch   15
    The virtue of his will:° but you must fear,
    His greatness weighed,° his will is not his own,
    For he himself is subject to his birth:
    He may not as unvalued persons° do,
    Carve° for himself, for on his choice depends   20

     245–246 *though hell . . . peace:* despite the risk of hell (for speaking to a demon) warning me to be silent.   **248** *tenable:* held, kept.   **254** *Your loves . . . you:* offer your friendship (rather than duty) in exchange for mine.   **256** *doubt:* fear.   **3** *convoy:* conveyance.   **6** *toy in blood:* whim of the passions. **7** *youth of primy nature:* early spring.   **8** *Forward:* premature.   **9** *suppliance of:* supplying diversion for. **11** *nature crescent:* man as he grows.   **12** *thews and bulk:* sinews and body.   *temple waxes:* body grows (1 Cor. 6:19).   **14** *withal:* at the same time.   **15** *cautel:* deceit.   **16** *will:* desire.   **17** *weighed:* considered. **19** *unvalued persons:* common people.   **20** *Carve:* choose (as does the one who carves the food).

The sanctity and health of this whole state,
And therefore must his choice be circumscribed
Unto the voice and yielding° of that body
Whereof he is the head. Then if he says he loves you,
It fits your wisdom so far to believe it   25
As he in his particular act and place
May give his saying deed,° which is no further
Than the main voice of Denmark goes withal.
Then weigh what loss your honour may sustain
If with too credent° ear you list° his songs,   30
Or lose your heart, or your chaste treasure open
To his unmast'red importunity.°
Fear it Ophelia, fear it my dear sister,
And keep you in the rear of your affection,
Out of the shot and danger of desire.   35
The chariest° maid is prodigal enough
If she unmask her beauty to the moon.
Virtue itself 'scapes not calumnious strokes.
The canker galls the infants° of the spring
Too oft before their buttons° be disclosed,   40
And in the morn and liquid dew of youth
Contagious blastments° are most imminent.
Be wary then, best safety lies in fear,
Youth to itself rebels,° though none else near.
OPHELIA.　I shall the effect° of this good lesson keep   45
As watchman to my heart: but good my brother,
Do not as some ungracious° pastors do,
Show me the steep and thorny way to heaven,
Whiles like a puffed and reckless libertine
Himself the primrose path of dalliance treads,   50
And recks not his own rede.°

Enter POLONIUS.

LAERTES.　　　　　　　　　O fear me not,°
I stay too long, but here my father comes:
A double blessing is a double grace,
Occasion smiles upon a second leave.°
POLONIUS.　Yet here Laertes? aboard, aboard for shame,   55
The wind sits in the shoulder of your sail,
And you are stayed for: there, my blessing with thee,
And these few precepts in thy memory
Look thou character.° Give thy thoughts no tongue,

---

23 *voice and yielding:* approving vote.　26–27 *in his . . . deed:* limited by personal responsibilities and rank, may perform what he promises.　30 *credent:* credulous.　*list:* listen to.　31–32 *your chaste . . . importunity:* lose your virginity to his uncontrolled persistence.　36 *chariest* most cautious.　39 *canker . . . infants:* cankerworm or caterpillar harms the young plants.　40 *buttons:* buds.　42 *blastments:* blights. 44 *to itself rebels:* lusts by nature.　45 *effect:* moral.　47 *ungracious:* lacking God's grace.　51 *recks . . . rede:* does not follow his own advice.　*fear me not:* Don't worry about me.　54 *Occasion . . . leave:* opportunity favors a second leave-taking.　59 *character:* write, impress, imprint.

Nor any unproportioned thought his act: 60
Be thou familiar, but by no means vulgar;°
Those friends thou hast, and their adoption tried,°
Grapple them unto thy soul with hoops of steel,
But do not dull° thy palm with entertainment
Of each new-hatched unfledged° comrade. Beware 65
Of entrance to a quarrel, but being in,
Bear't that th'opposèd may beware of thee.
Give every man thy ear, but few thy voice:
Take each man's censure,° but reserve thy judgment.
Costly thy habit° as thy purse can buy, 70
But not expressed in fancy,° rich, not gaudy,
For the apparel oft proclaims the man,
And they in France of the best rank and station,
Are of a most select and generous chief° in that:
Neither a borrower nor a lender be, 75
For loan oft loses both itself and friend,
And borrowing dulls the edge of husbandry;°
This above all, to thine own self be true
And it must follow as the night the day,
Thou canst not then be false to any man. 80
Farewell, my blessing season° this in thee.
LAERTES.   Most humbly do I take my leave my lord.
POLONIUS.   The time invites you, go, your servants tend.°
LAERTES.   Farewell Ophelia, and remember well
  What I have said to you.
OPHELIA.   'Tis in my memory locked, 85
  And you yourself shall keep the key of it.
LAERTES.   Farewell.   *Exit LAERTES.*
POLONIUS.   What is't Ophelia he hath said to you?
OPHELIA.   So please you, something touching the Lord Hamlet.
POLONIUS.   Marry,° well bethought: 90
  'Tis told me he hath very oft of late
  Given private time to you, and you yourself
  Have of your audience been most free and bounteous.
  If it be so, as so 'tis put on me,
  And that in way of caution, I must tell you, 95
  You do not understand yourself so clearly
  As it behooves my daughter, and your honour.
  What is between you? give me up the truth.
OPHELIA.   He hath my lord of late made many tenders°
  Of his affection to me. 100

---

61 *vulgar:* indiscriminately friendly.   62 *adoption tried:* loyalty proved.   64 *dull:* get calluses on.
65 *new-hatched unfledged:* new and untested.   69 *censure:* opinion.   70 *habit:* clothing.   71 *expressed
in fancy:* so fantastic as to be ridiculous.   74 *select . . . chief:* judicious and noble eminence.
77 *husbandry:* thrift.   81 *season:* bring to maturity.   83 *tend:* attend, wait.   90 *Marry:* (a mild oath, from
"By the Virgin Mary").   99 *tenders:* offers (see lines 106–109).

POLONIUS. Affection, puh, you speak like a green girl
    Unsifted° in such perilous circumstance.
    Do you believe his tenders as you call them?
OPHELIA.   I do not know my lord what I should think.
POLONIUS.   Marry, I will teach you; think yourself a baby   105
    That you have ta'en these tenders° for true pay
    Which are not sterling.° Tender yourself more dearly,°
    Or (not to crack the wind of the poor phrase,
    Running it thus°) you'll tender me a fool.°
OPHELIA.   My lord he hath importuned me with love   110
    In honourable fashion.
POLONIUS.   Ay, fashion you may call it, go to, go to.
OPHELIA.   And hath given countenance° to his speech, my lord,
    With almost all the holy vows of heaven.
POLONIUS.   Ay, springes° to catch woodcocks.° I do know   115
    When the blood burns, how prodigal the soul
    Lends the tongue vows: these blazes daughter,
    Giving more light than heat, extinct in both,
    Even in their promise, as it is a-making,°
    You must not take for fire. From this time   120
    Be something scanter of your maiden presence,
    Set your entreatments at a higher rate
    Than a command to parle;° for Lord Hamlet,
    Believe so much in him that he is young,
    And with a larger tether may he walk   125
    Than may be given you: in few° Ophelia,
    Do not believe his vows, for they are brokers°
    Not of that dye which their investments° show,
    But mere implorators° of unholy suits,
    Breathing° like sanctified and pious bonds,°   130
    The better to beguile. This is for all,
    I would not in plain terms from this time forth
    Have you so slander any moment leisure
    As to give words or talk with the Lord Hamlet.
    Look to't I charge you, come your ways.°   135
OPHELIA.   I shall obey, my lord.   [*Exeunt.*]

Scene 4. [*The platform on the battlements*]

Enter HAMLET, HORATIO *and* MARCELLUS.

HAMLET.   The air bites shrewdly,° it is very cold.
HORATIO.   It is a nipping and an eager° air.

---

   102 *Unsifted:* untested.   106 *tenders:* offers (of money).   107 *sterling:* genuine (currency). *Tender . . . dearly:* hold yourself at a higher value. 108–109 *crack . . . thus:* make the phrase lose its breath. 109 *tender . . . fool:* (1) make me look foolish (2) present me with a baby.   113 *countenance:* confirmation. 115 *springes:* snares. *woodcocks:* snipelike birds (believed to be stupid and therefore easily trapped). 118–119 *extinct . . . a-making:* losing both appearance, because of brevity, and substance, because of broken promises.   122–123 *Set . . . parle:* Don't rush to negotiate a surrender as soon as the besieger asks for a discussion of terms. 126 *few:* short. 127 *brokers:* (1) business agents (2) procurers. 128 *investments:* (1) business ventures (2) clothing. 129 *implorators:* solicitors. 130 *Breathing:* speaking softly. *bonds:* pledges. 135 *come your ways:* come along. 1 *shrewdly:* fiercely. 2 *eager:* sharp.

HAMLET.   What hour now?

HORATIO.   I think it lacks of twelve.

MARCELLUS.   No, it is struck.

HORATIO.   Indeed? I heard it not: it then draws near the season°   5
    Wherein the spirit held his wont to walk.

> *A flourish of trumpets, and two pieces [of ordnance] go off.*

    What does this mean my lord?

HAMLET.   The king doth wake° tonight and takes his rouse,°
    Keeps wassail° and the swagg'ring up-spring° reels:
    And as he drains his draughts of Rhenish° down,   10
    The kettle-drum and trumpet thus bray out
    The triumph of his pledge.°

HORATIO.   Is it a custom?

HAMLET.   Ay marry is't,
    But to my mind, though I am native here
    And to the manner born,° it is a custom   15
    More honoured in the breach than the observance.°
    This heavy-headed revel east and west
    Makes us traduced and taxed of° other nations:
    They clepe° us drunkards, and with swinish phrase
    Soil our addition,° and indeed it takes   20
    From our achievements, though performed at height,°
    The pith and marrow of our attribute.°
    So oft it chances in particular men,
    That for some vicious mole of nature° in them,
    As in their birth, wherein they are not guilty   25
    (Since nature cannot choose his origin),
    By the o'ergrowth of some complexion,°
    Oft breaking down the pales° and forts of reason,
    Or by some habit, that too much o'er-leavens°
    The form of plausive° manners—that these men,   30
    Carrying I say the stamp of one defect,
    Being nature's livery,° or fortune's star,°
    His virtues else be they as pure as grace,
    As infinite as man may undergo,
    Shall in the general censure° take corruption   35
    From that particular fault: the dram of evil
    Doth all the noble substance often doubt,
    To his own scandal.°

---

5 *season:* time, period.   8 *wake:* stay awake.   *rouse:* drinks that empty the cup.   9 *Keeps wassail:* holds drinking bouts.   *up-spring:* a vigorous German dance.   10 *Rhenish:* Rhine wine.   12 *triumph . . . pledge:* victory of emptying the cup with one draught.   15 *to . . . born:* accustomed to the practice since birth.   16 *More . . . observance:* better to break than to observe.   18 *traduced and taxed of:* defamed and taken to task by.   19 *clepe:* call.   19–20 *with swinish . . . addition:* blemish our reputation by comparing us to swine.   21 *at height:* to the maximum.   22 *attribute:* reputation.   24 *mole of nature:* natural blemish.   27 *o'er growth . . . complexion:* overbalance of one of the body's four humors or fluids believed to determine temperament.   28 *pales:* defensive enclosures.   29 *too much o'er-leavens:* excessively modifies (like too much leaven in bread).   30 *plausive:* pleasing.   32 *nature's livery:* marked by nature.   *fortune's star:* destined by chance.   35 *general censure:* public opinion.   36–38 *the dram . . . scandal:* the minute quantity of evil often casts doubt upon his noble nature, to his shame.

Enter GHOST.

HORATIO.	Look my lord, it comes.	
HAMLET.	Angels and ministers of grace defend us:	

    Be thou a spirit of health, or goblin damned,°   40
    Bring with thee airs from heaven, or blasts from hell,
    Be thy intents wicked, or charitable,
    Thou com'st in such a questionable° shape,
    That I will speak to thee. I'll call thee Hamlet,
    King, father, royal Dane. O answer me,   45
    Let me not burst in ignorance, but tell
    Why thy canonized° bones hearsèd° in death
    Have burst their cerements°? why the sepulchre,
    Wherein we saw thee quietly interred
    Hath oped his ponderous and marble jaws,   50
    To cast thee up again? What may this mean
    That thou, dead corse, again in complete steel
    Revisits thus the glimpses of the moon,
    Making night hideous, and we fools of nature°
    So horridly to shake our disposition   55
    With thoughts beyond the reaches of our souls,
    Say why is this? wherefore? what should we do?   *GHOST beckons* HAMLET.

HORATIO.   It beckons you to go away with it,
    As if it some impartment did desire°
    To you alone.

MARCELLUS.   Look with what courteous action   60
    It waves you to a more removèd ground,
    But do not go with it.

HORATIO.   No, by no means.

HAMLET.   It will not speak, then I will follow it.

HORATIO.   Do not my lord.

HAMLET.   Why what should be the fear?
    I do not set my life at a pin's fee,°   65
    And for my soul, what can it do to that
    Being a thing immortal as itself;
    It waves me forth again, I'll follow it.

HORATIO.   What if it tempt you toward the flood my lord,
    Or to the dreadful summit of the cliff   70
    That beetles o'er° his base into the sea,
    And there assume some other horrible form
    Which might deprive your sovereignty of reason,°
    And draw you into madness? think of it,
    The very place puts toys of desperation,°   75
    Without more motive, into every brain

---

40 *spirit . . . damned:* true ghost or demon from hell. **43** *questionable:* question-raising. **47** *canonized:* buried in accordance with church edict. *hearsèd:* entombed. **48** *cerements:* waxed cloth wrappings. **54** *fools of nature:* mocked by our natural limitations when faced with the supernatural. **59** *some . . . desire:* desired to impart something. **65** *fee:* value. **71** *beetles o'er:* overhangs. **73** *deprive . . . reason:* dethrone your reason from its sovereignty. **75** *toys of desperation:* desperate whims.

That looks so many fathoms to the sea
And hears it roar beneath.
HAMLET.   It waves me still:
   Go on, I'll follow thee.
MARCELLUS.   You shall not go my lord.
HAMLET.   Hold off your hands.   80
HORATIO.   Be ruled, you shall not go.
HAMLET.   My fate cries out,
   And makes each petty artire° in this body
   As hardy as the Nemean lion's° nerve;°
   Still am I called, unhand me gentlemen,
   By heaven I'll make a ghost of him that lets° me: 85
   I say away; go on, I'll follow thee.   *Exeunt Ghost and Hamlet.*
HORATIO.   He waxes desperate° with imagination.
MARCELLUS.   Let's follow, 'tis not fit thus to obey him.
HORATIO.   Have after—to what issue will this come?
MARCELLUS.   Something is rotten in the state of Denmark.   90
HORATIO.   Heaven will direct it.
MARCELLUS.   Nay, let's follow him.   *Exeunt.*

Scene 5. [*Another part of the platform*]

Enter GHOST and HAMLET.

HAMLET.   Whither wilt thou lead me? Speak, I'll go no further.
GHOST.   Mark me.
HAMLET.   I will.
GHOST.   My hour is almost come
   When I to sulphurous and tormenting flames
   Must render up myself.
HAMLET.   Alas poor ghost.
GHOST.   Pity me not, but lend thy serious hearing   5
   To what I shall unfold.
HAMLET.   Speak, I am bound° to hear.
GHOST.   So art thou to revenge, when thou shalt hear.
HAMLET.   What?
GHOST.   I am thy father's spirit,
   Doomed for a certain term to walk the night,   10
   And for the day confined to fast in fires,
   Till the foul crimes done in my days of nature°
   Are burnt and purged away: but that I am forbid
   To tell the secrets of my prison-house,
   I could a tale unfold whose lightest word   15
   Would harrow up thy soul, freeze thy young blood,
   Make thy two eyes like stars start from their spheres,°
   Thy knotted and combinèd locks to part,

---

82 *artire:* ligament.   83 *Nemean lion:* (killed by Hercules as one of his twelve labors).   *nerve:*
sinew.   85 *lets:* prevents.   87 *waxes desperate:* grows frantic.   6 *bound:* obliged by duty.   12 *crimes . . .
nature:* sins committed during my life on earth.   17 *spheres:* (1) orbits (according to Ptoleny, each planet
was confined to a sphere revolving around the earth) (2) sockets.

And each particular hair to stand an° end,
Like quills upon the fretful porpentine:°
But this eternal blazon° must not be
To ears of flesh and blood; list, list, O list:
If thou didst ever thy dear father love—   20

HAMLET. O God!

GHOST. Revenge his foul and most unnatural murder.   25

HAMLET. Murder?

GHOST. Murder most foul, as in the best it is,
But this most foul, strange and unnatural.

HAMLET. Haste me to know't, that I with wings as swift
As meditation or the thoughts of love,   30
May sweep to my revenge.

GHOST.   I find thee apt,°
And duller shouldst thou be than the fat° weed
That rots itself in ease on Lethe wharf,°
Wouldst thou not stir in this; now Hamlet hear,
'Tis given out, that sleeping in my orchard,°   35
A serpent stung me, so the whole ear of Denmark
Is by a forgèd process° of my death
Rankly abused:° but know thou noble youth,
The serpent that did sting thy father's life
Now wears his crown.

HAMLET.   O my prophetic soul!   40
My uncle?

GHOST. Ay, that incestuous, that adulterate° beast,
With witchcraft of his wit, with traitorous gifts,
O wicked wit and gifts, that have the power
So to seduce; won to his shameful lust   45
The will of my most seeming-virtuous queen;
O Hamlet, what a falling-off was there,
From me whose love was of that dignity
That it went hand in hand, even with the vow
I made to her in marriage, and to decline   50
Upon° a wretch whose natural gifts were poor
To° those of mine;
But virtue, as it never will be moved,
Though lewdness court it in a shape of heaven,°
So lust, though to a radiant angle linked,   55
Will sate itself in a celestial bed
And prey on garbage.
But soft, methinks I scent the morning air,
Brief let me be; sleeping within my orchard,

---

19 *an:* on. 20 *fretful porpentine:* angry porcupine. 21 *eternal blazon:* revelation about eternity.
31 *apt:* ready. 32 *fat:* slimy. 33 *Lethe wharf:* the banks of Lethe (river in Hades from which spirits drank to forget their past lives). 35 *orchard:* garden. 37 *process:* account. 38 *abused:* deceived.
42 *adulterate:* adulterous. 50–51 *decline Upon:* descend to. 52 *To:* compared to. 54 *shape of heaven:* angelic appearance.

My custom always of the afternoon,   60
Upon my secure° hour thy uncle stole
With juice of cursèd hebona° in a vial,
And in the porches of my ears did pour
The leperous° distilment, whose effect
Holds such an enmity with blood of man,   65
That swift as quicksilver it courses through
The natural gates and alleys of the body,
And with a sudden vigour it doth posset°
And curd, like eager° droppings into milk,
The thin and wholesome° blood; so did it mine,   70
And a most instant tetter° barked about°
Most lazar°-like with vile and loathsome crust
All my smooth body.
Thus was I sleeping by a brother's hand,
Of life, of crown, of queen at once dispatched,   75
Cut off even in the blossoms of my sin,
Unhouseled, disappointed, unaneled,°
No reck'ning° made, but sent to my account°
With all my imperfections on my head;
O horrible, O horrible, most horrible!   80
If thou hast nature in thee bear it not,
Let not the royal bed of Denmark be
A couch for luxury° and damnèd incest.
But howsoever thou pursues this act,
Taint not thy mind, nor let thy soul contrive   85
Against thy mother aught,° leave her to heaven,
And to those thorns that in her bosom lodge
To prick and sting her. Fare thee well at once,
The glow-worm shows the matin° to be near
And 'gins to pale this uneffectual fire:°   90
Adieu, adieu, adieu, remember me.   *Exit.*
HAMLET.   O all you host of heaven! O earth! what else?
And shall I couple° hell? O fie! Hold, hold my heart,
And you my sinews, grow not instant old,
But bear me stiffly up; remember thee?   95
Ay thou poor ghost, whiles memory holds a seat
In this distracted globe.° Remember thee?
Yea, from the table° of my memory
I'll wipe away all trivial fond° records,
All saws of books,° all forms, all pressures° past   100
That youth and observation copied there,

---

61 *secure:* unsuspecting.   62 *hebona:* poisonous sap of the ebony or henbane.   64 *leperous:* leprosy-causing.   68 *posset:* curdle.   69 *eager:* sour.   70 *wholesome:* healthy.   71 *tetter:* skin eruption. *barked about:* covered (like bark on a tree).   72 *lazar:* leper.   77 *Unhouseled . . . unaneled:* without final sacrament, unprepared (without confession) and lacking extreme unction (anointing).   78 *reck'ning:* (1) accounting (2) payment of my bill (3) confession and absolution. *account:* judgment.   83 *luxury:* lust. 86 *aught:* anything.   89 *matin:* dawn.   90 *'gins . . . fire:* his light becomes ineffective, made pale by day. 93 *couple:* engage in a contest against.   97 *distracted globe:* (his head).   98 *table:* tablet, "table-book." 99 *fond:* foolish.   100 *saws of books:* maxims (sayings) copied from books.

And thy commandment all alone shall live
Within the book and volume of my brain,
Unmixed with baser matter, yes by heaven:
O most pernicious woman!   105
O villain, villain, smiling damnèd villain!
My tables,° meet° it is I set it down
That one may smile, and smile, and be a villain,
At least I am sure it may be so in Denmark.
So uncle, there you are: now to my word,°   110
It is 'Adieu, adieu, remember me.'
I have sworn't.

Enter HORATIO and MARCELLUS.

HORATIO.   My lord, my lord!
MARCELLUS.   Lord Hamlet!
HORATIO.   Heaven secure° him.
HAMLET.   So be it.
MARCELLUS.   Illo, ho, ho, my lord!   115
HAMLET.   Hillo, ho, ho, boy, come° bird, come.
MARCELLUS.   How is't my noble lord?
HORATIO.   What news my lord?
HAMLET.   O, wonderful!
HORATIO.   Good my lord, tell it.
HAMLET.   No, you will reveal it.
HORATIO.   Not I my lord, by heaven.
MARCELLUS.   Nor I my lord.   120
HAMLET.   How say you then, would heart of man once think it?
    But you'll be secret?
BOTH.   Ay, by heaven, my lord.
HAMLET.   There's ne'er a villain dwelling in all Denmark
    But he's an arrant° knave.
HORATIO.   There needs no ghost my lord, come from the grave   125
    To tell us this.
HAMLET.   Why right, you are in the right,
    And so without more circumstance° at all
    I hold it fit that we shake hands and part,
    You, as your business and desire shall point you,
    For every man hath business and desire   130
    Such as it is, and for my own poor part,
    Look you, I will go pray.
HORATIO.   These are but wild and whirling words my lord.
HAMLET.   I am sorry they offend you, heartily,
    Yes faith, heartily.
HORATIO.   There's no offence my lord.   135

---

107 *tables:* tablet; notepad.   *meet:* fitting.   110 *word:* motto (to guide my actions).   113 *secure:* protect.   116 *Hillo . . . come:* falconer's cry with which Hamlet replies to their calls.   124 *arrant:* thoroughgoing.   127 *circumstance:* ceremony.

HAMLET.   Yes by Saint Patrick, but there is Horatio,
    And much offence too: touching this vision here,
    It is an honest° ghost, that let me tell you:
    For your desire to know what is between us,
    O'ermaster't as you may. And now good friends,   140
    As you are friends, scholars, and soldiers,
    Give me one poor request.
HORATIO.   What is't, my lord? we will.
HAMLET.   Never make known what you have seen tonight.
BOTH.   My lord we will not.
HAMLET.   Nay, but swear't.
HORATIO.   In faith   145
    My lord, not I.
MARCELLUS.   Nor I my lord, in faith.
HAMLET.   Upon my sword.
MARCELLUS.   We have sworn my lord already.
HAMLET.   Indeed, upon my sword,° indeed.
GHOST.   Swear.   *Ghost cries under the stage.*
HAMLET.   Ha, ha, boy, say'st thou so, art thou there, truepenny°?   150
    Come on, you hear this fellow in the cellarage,
    Consent to swear.
HORATIO.   Propose the oath my lord.
HAMLET.   Never to speak of this that you have seen.
    Swear by my sword.
GHOST.   [*Beneath.*] Swear.   155
HAMLET.   Hic et ubique?° then we'll shift our ground:
    Come hither gentlemen,
    And lay your hands again upon my sword,
    Swear by my sword
    Never to speak of this that you have heard.   160
GHOST.   [*Beneath.*] Swear by his sword.
HAMLET.   Well said old mole, canst work i'th' earth so fast?
    A worthy pioner°—once more remove;° good friends.
HORATIO.   O day and night, but this is wondrous strange.
HAMLET.   And therefore as a stranger give it welcome.   165
    There are more things in heaven and earth Horatio,
    Than are dreamt of in your philosophy.
    But come,
    Here as before, never so help you mercy,
    How strange or odd some'er I bear myself,   170
    (As I perchance hereafter shall think meet
    To put an antic disposition on°)
    That you at such times seeing me, never shall
    With arms encumbered° thus, or this head-shake,
    Or by pronouncing of some doubtful phrase,   175

---

138 *honest:* true (not a devil in disguise).   148 *sword:* (the cross-shaped hilt).   150 *truepenny:* old
pal.   156 *Hic et ubique:* here and everywhere.   163 *pioner:* digger (army trencher).   *remove:* move elsewhere.   172 *put . . . on:* assume a mad or grotesque behavior.   174 *encumbered:* folded.

As "Well, well, we know," or "We could and if we would,"
Or "If we list° to speak," or "There be and if they might,"
Or such ambiguous giving out, to note
That you know aught of me; this do swear,
So grace and mercy at your need help you.   180
GHOST.   [*Beneath.*] Swear. [*They swear.*]
HAMLET.   Rest, rest, perturbed spirit: so gentlemen,
With all my love I do commend me to you,°
And what so poor a man as Hamlet is,
May do t'express his love and friending to you   185
God willing shall not lack: let us go in together,
And still° your fingers on your lips I pray.
The time is out of joint: O cursèd spite,
That ever I was born to set it right.
Nay come, let's go together.   *Exeunt.*   190

ACT 2

Scene 1. [*Polonius's chambers*]

Enter old POLONIUS with his man REYNALDO.

POLONIUS.   Give him this money, and these notes Reynaldo.
REYNALDO.   I will my lord.
POLONIUS.   You shall do marvellous° wisely, good Reynaldo,
Before you visit him, to make inquire
Of his behaviour.
REYNALDO.   My lord, I did intend it.   5
POLONIUS.   Marry, well said, very well said; look you sir,
Inquire me first what Danskers° are in Paris,
And how, and who, what means, and where they keep,°
What company, at what expense, and finding
By this encompassment° and drift of question   10
That they do know my son, come you more nearer
Than your particular demands° will touch it,
Take you as 'twere some distant knowledge of him,
As thus, "I know his father, and his friends,
And in part him"—do you mark this, Reynaldo?   15
REYNALDO.   Ay, very well my lord.
POLONIUS.   'And in part him, but,' you may say, 'not well,
But if't be he I mean, he's very wild,
Addicted so and so;' and there put on him
What forgeries° you please, marry none so rank°   20
As may dishonour him, take heed of that,
But sir, such wanton, wild, and usual slips,
As are companions noted and most known
To youth and liberty.

---

177 *list:* please.   183 *commend . . . you:* put myself in your hands.   187 *still:* always.   3 *marvellous:*
wonderfully.   7 *Danskers:* Danes.   8 *keep:* lodge.   10 *encompassment:* roundabout way.   12 *particular
demands:* specific questions.   20 *forgeries:* inventions.   *rank:* excessive.

REYNALDO.   As gaming my lord.
POLONIUS.   Ay, or drinking, fencing, swearing,   25
    Quarrelling, drabbing°—you may go so far.
REYNALDO.   My lord, that would dishonour him.
POLONIUS.   Faith no, as you may season it in the charge.°
    You must not put another scandal on him,
    That he is open to incontinency,°   30
    That's not my meaning, but breathe his faults so quaintly°
    That they may seem the taints of° liberty,
    The flash and outbreak of a fiery mind,
    A savageness in unreclaimèd blood,°
    Of general assault.°
REYNALDO.   But my good lord—   35
POLONIUS.   Wherefore° should you do this?
REYNALDO.   Ay my lord,
    I would know that.
POLONIUS.   Marry sir, here's my drift,
    And I believe it is a fetch of warrant:°
    You laying these slight sullies on my son,
    As 'twere a thing a little soiled i'th' working,°   40
    Mark you, your party in converse, him you would sound,
    Having ever seen° in the prenominate crimes°
    The youth you breathe of guilty, be assured
    He closes with you in this consequence,°
    "Good sir," or so, or "friend," or "gentleman,"   45
    According to the phrase, or the addition°
    Of man and country.
REYNALDO.   Very good my lord.
POLONIUS.   And then sir, does a'° this, a' does, what was I
        about to say?
    By the mass I was about to say something,
    Where did I leave?
REYNALDO.   At "closes in the consequence,"   50
    At "friend, or so, and gentleman."
POLONIUS.   At "closes in the consequence," ay marry,
    He closes thus, "I know the gentleman,
    I saw him yesterday, or th'other day,
    Or then, or then, with such or such, and as you say,   55
    There was a' gaming, there o'ertook in's rouse,°
    There falling out at tennis," or perchance
    "I saw him enter such a house of sale,"
    Videlicet,° a brothel, or so forth. See you now,
    Your bait of falsehood takes this carp of truth,   60

---

26 *drabbing:* whoring.   28 *season . . . charge:* temper the charge as you make it.   30 *incontinency:*
uncontrolled lechery.   31 *quaintly:* delicately.   32 *taints of:* blemishes due to.   34 *unreclaimèd blood:* un-
bridled passion.   35 *general assault:* attacking all (young men).   36 *Wherefore:* why.   38 *fetch of warrant:* trick guaranteed to succeed.   40 *working:* handling.   42 *Having ever seen:* if he has ever seen.
prenominate crimes: aforenamed sins.   44 *closes . . . consequence:* comes to terms with you as follows.
46 *addition:* title, form of address.   48 *'a:* he.   56 *o'ertook in's rouse:* overcome by drunkenness.
59 *Videlicet:* namely.

And thus do we of wisdom, and of reach,°
With windlasses,° and with assays of bias,°
By indirections find directions out:
So by my former lecture and advice
Shall you my son; you have me, have you not?   65
REYNALDO.   My lord I have.
POLONIUS.   God bye ye, fare ye well.
REYNALDO.   Good my lord.
POLONIUS.   Observe his inclination in yourself.°
REYNALDO.   I shall my lord.
POLONIUS.   And let him ply° his music.
REYNALDO.   Well my lord.   70
POLONIUS.   Farewell.

                                                    Exit REYNALDO.

Enter OPHELIA.

                    How now Ophelia, what's the matter?
OPHELIA.   O my lord, my lord, I have been so affrighted.
POLONIUS.   With what, i'th'name of God?
OPHELIA.   My lord, as I was sewing in my closet,°
    Lord Hamlet with his doublet all unbraced,°   75
    No hat upon his head, his stockings fouled,
    Ungart'red, and down-gyvèd° to his ankle,
    Pale as his shirt, his knees knocking each other,
    And with a look so piteous in purport°
    As if he had been loosèd out of hell   80
    To speak of horrors, he comes before me.
POLONIUS.   Mad for thy love?
OPHELIA.   My lord I do not know,
    But truly I do fear it.
POLONIUS.   What said he?
OPHELIA.   He took me by the wrist, and held me hard,
    Then goes he to the length of all his arm,°   85
    And with his other hand thus o'er his brow,
    He falls to such perusal of my face
    As° a' would draw it; long stayed he so,
    At last, a little shaking of mine arm,
    And thrice his head thus waving up and down,   90
    He raised a sigh so piteous and profound
    As it did seem to shatter all his bulk,°
    And end his being; that done, he lets me go,
    And with his head over his shoulder turned
    He seemed to find his way without his eyes,
    For out adoors he went without their helps,   95
    And to the last bended their light on me.

    61 *reach:* far-reaching knowledge.   **62** *windlasses:* roundabout approaches.   *assays of bias:* indirect attempts.   **68** *in yourself:* personally.   **70** *ply:* practice.   **74** *closet:* private room.   **75** *doublet all unbraced:* jacket all unfastened.   **77** *down-gyvèd:* down around his ankles (like prisoners' fetters or gyves).   **79** *purport:* expression.   **85** *goes . . . arm:* holds me at arm's length.   **88** *As:* as if.   **92** *bulk:* body.

POLONIUS.   Come, go with me, I will go seek the king,
 This is the very ecstasy° of love,
 Whose violent property fordoes itself,°   100
 And leads the will to desperate undertakings
 As oft as any passion under heaven
 That does afflict our natures: I am sorry.
 What, have you given him any hard words of late?   105
OPHELIA.   No my good lord, but as you did command
 I did repel his letters, and denied
 His access to me.
POLONIUS.   That hath made him mad.
 I am sorry that with better heed and judgment
 I had not quoted° him. I feared he did but trifle
 And meant to wrack° thee, but beshrew my jealousy.°   110
 By heaven it is as proper to our age
 To cast beyond ourselves in our opinions,°
 As it is common for the younger sort
 To lack discretion; come, go we to the king,
 This must be known, which being kept close, might move 115
 More grief to hide, than hate to utter love.°   [*Exeunt.*]

Scene 2. [*A room in the castle*]

Flourish. Enter KING *and* QUEEN, ROSENCRANTZ *and* GUILDENSTERN, *cum aliis.*

KING.   Welcome dear Rosencrantz and Guildenstern.
 Moreover° that we much did long to see you,
 The need we have to use you did provoke
 Our hasty sending. Something have you heard
 Of Hamlet's transformation—so call it.   5
 Sith° nor th'exterior nor the inward man
 Resembles that it was. What it should be,
 More than his father's death, that thus hath put him
 So much from th'understanding of himself,
 I cannot dream of: I entreat you both,   10
 That being of so young days° brought up with him,
 And sith so neighboured to his youth and haviour,
 That you vouchsafe your rest° here in our court
 Some little time, so by your companies
 To draw him on to pleasures, and to gather   15
 So much as from occasion you may glean,
 Whether aught to us unknown afflicts him thus,
 That opened° lies within our remedy.

---

99 *ecstasy:* madness.   100 *Whose . . . itself:* that, by its violent nature, destroys the lover.
109 *quoted:* observed.   110 *wrack:* ruin.   *beshrew my jealousy:* curse my suspicion.   111–112 *proper . . .
opinions:* natural for old people to read more into something than is actually there.   115–116 *being kept
. . . love:* if kept secret, might cause more grief than if we risked the king's displeasure.   2 *Moreover:* in
addition to the fact.   6 *Sith:* since.   11 *of . . . days:* from your early days.   13 *vouchsafe your rest:* agree
to stay.   18 *opened:* discovered.

QUEEN.　Good gentlemen, he hath much talked of you,
　　And sure I am, two men there are not living　　　　　　　　　　20
　　To whom he more adheres. If it will please you
　　To show us so much gentry° and good will,
　　As to expend your time with us awhile,
　　For the supply and profit of our hope,
　　Your visitation shall receive such thanks　　　　　　　　　　25
　　As fits a king's remembrance.
ROSENCRANTZ.　　　　　　　　　　Both your majesties
　　Might by the sovereign power you have of us,
　　Put your dread pleasures more into command
　　Than to entreaty.
GUILDENSTERN.　　　　　But we both obey,
　　And here give up ourselves in the full bent,°　　　　　　　　30
　　To lay our service freely at your feet
　　To be commanded.
KING.　Thanks Rosencrantz, and gentle Guildenstern.
QUEEN.　Thanks Guildenstern, and gentle Rosencrantz.
　　And I beseech you instantly to visit　　　　　　　　　　35
　　My too much changèd son. Go some of you
　　And bring these gentlemen where Hamlet is.
GUILDENSTERN.　Heavens make our presence and our practices°
　　Pleasant and helpful to him.
QUEEN.　　　　　　　　　　Ay, amen.

　　　　　　　　　　　　Exeunt ROSENCRANTZ *and* GUILDENSTERN.

Enter POLONIUS.

POLONIUS.　Th'ambassadors from Norway my good lord,　　　　40
　　Are joyfully returned.
KING.　Thou still° hast been the father of good news.
POLONIUS.　Have I, my lord? Assure you, my good liege,
　　I hold my duty as I hold my soul,
　　Both to my God and to my gracious king;　　　　　　　　45
　　And I do think, or else this brain of mine
　　Hunts not the trail of policy° so sure
　　As it hath used to do, that I have found
　　The very cause of Hamlet's lunacy.
KING.　O speak of that, that do I long to hear.　　　　　　　50
POLONIUS.　Give first admittance to th'ambassadors,
　　My news shall be the fruit° to that great feast.
KING.　Thyself do grace to them, and bring them in.　　　[*Exit* POLONIUS.]
　　He tells me my dear Gertrude, he hath found
　　The head and source of all your son's distemper.　　　　　55
QUEEN.　I doubt° it is no other but the main,
　　His father's death and our o'erhasty marriage.
KING.　Well, we shall sift him.

---

22 *gentry:* courtesy.　30 *in the full bent:* to the utmost (in archery, bending the bow).　38 *practices:* (1) actions (2) plots.　42 *still:* always.　47 *policy:* (1) politics (2) plots.　52 *fruit:* dessert.　56 *doubt:* suspect.

Enter POLONIUS, VALTEMAND, *and* CORNELIUS.

                           Welcome, my good friends.
    Say Valtemand, what from our brother Norway?

VALTEMAND.   Most fair return of greetings and desires;   60
    Upon our first,° he sent out to suppress
    His nephew's levies, which to him appeared
    To be a preparation 'gainst the Polack,
    But better looked into, he truly found
    It was against your highness, whereat grieved   65
    That so his sickness, age, and impotence
    Was falsely borne in hand,° sends out arrests
    On Fortinbras, which he in brief obeys,
    Receives rebuke from Norway, and in fine,°
    Makes vow before his uncle never more   70
    To give th'assay° of arms against your majesty:
    Whereon old Norway, overcome with joy,
    Gives him threescore thousand crowns in annual fee,
    And his commission to employ those soldiers
    So levied (as before) against the Polack,   75
    With an entreaty herein further shown,
    That it might please you to give quiet pass°
    Through your dominions for this enterprise,
    On such regards of safety and allowance
    As therein are set down.   *[Giving a paper.]*
KING.   It likes° us well,   80
    And at our more considered time° we'll read,
    Answer, and think upon this business:
    Meantime, we thank you for your well-took labour,
    Go to your rest, at night we'll feast together.
    Most welcome home.   *Exeunt* AMBASSADORS.
POLONIUS.   This business is well ended.   85
    My liege and madam, to expostulate°
    What majesty should be, what duty is,
    Why day is day, night night, and time is time,
    Were nothing but to waste night, day, and time.
    Therefore since brevity is the soul of wit,°   90
    And tediousness the limbs and outward flourishes,°
    I will be brief. Your noble son is mad:
    Mad call I it, for to define true madness,
    What is't but to be nothing else but mad?
    But let that go.   95
QUEEN.   More matter, with less art.
POLONIUS.   Madam, I swear I use no art at all:
    That he is mad 'tis true: 'tis true, 'tis pity,
    And pity 'tis 'tis true: a foolish figure,°

---

61 *first:* first presentation.   67 *borne in hand:* deceived.   69 *fine:* finishing.   71 *assay:* test. 77 *pass:* passage.   80 *likes:* pleases.   81 *at . . . time:* when time is available for consideration.   86 *expostulate:* discuss.   90 *wit:* understanding.   91 *tediousness . . . flourishes:* embellishments and flourishes cause tedium.   98 *figure:* rhetorical figure.

But farewell it, for I will use no art.
Mad let us grant him then, and now remains   100
That we find out the cause of this effect,
Or rather say, the cause of this defect,
For this effect defective comes by cause:
Thus it remains, and the remainder thus.
Perpend.°   105
I have a daughter, have while she is mine,
Who in her duty and obedience, mark,
Hath given me this, now gather and surmise.
[*Reads.*] "To the celestial, and my soul's idol, the most
beautified° Ophelia,"—   110
That's an ill phrase, a vile phrase, "beautified" is a vile
phrase, but you shall hear. Thus: [*Reads.*]
    "In her excellent white bosom, these," &c.—
QUEEN.   Came this from Hamlet to her?
POLONIUS.   Good madam stay awhile, I will be faithful.   [*Reads.*] 115
        "Doubt thou the stars are fire,
            Doubt that the sun doth move,°
        Doubt° truth to be a liar,
            But never doubt I love.
O dear Ophelia, I am ill at these numbers, I have not   120
art to reckon° my groans, but that I love thee best, O
most best, believe it. Adieu.
        Thine evermore, most dear lady, whilst
        this machine° is to° him, Hamlet."
This in obedience hath my daughter shown me,   125
And more above hath his solicitings,
As they fell out by time, by means, and place,
All given to mine ear.
KING.   But how hath she
Received his love?
POLONIUS.   What do you think of me?
KING.   As of a man faithful and honourable.   130
POLONIUS.   I would fain prove so. But what might you think
When I had seen this hot love on the wing,
As I perceived it (I must tell you that)
Before my daughter told me, what might you,
Or my dear majesty your queen here think,   135
If I had played the desk or table-book,°
Or given my heart a winking° mute and dumb,
Or looked upon this love with idle° sight,
What might you think? No, I went round to work,
And my young mistress this I did bespeak,   140

---

105 *Perpend:* consider.   110 *beautified:* beautiful.   117 *move:* (as it was believed to do, around the earth).   118 *Doubt:* suspect.   121 *reckon:* express in meter.   124 *machine:* body.   *to:* attached to. 136 *played . . . book:* kept it concealed as in a desk or personal notebook.   137 *given . . . winking:* had my heart shut its eyes to the matter.   138 *idle:* unseeing.

"Lord Hamlet is a prince out of thy star,°
This must not be:" and then I prescripts° gave her
That she should lock herself from his resort,°
Admit no messengers, receive no tokens:
Which done, she took the fruits of my advice,   145
And he repellèd, a short tale to make,
Fell into a sadness, then into a fast,
Thence to a watch,° thence into a weakness,
Thence to a lightness,° and by this declension,
Into the madness wherein now he raves,   150
And all we mourn for.

KING.   Do you think 'tis this?
QUEEN.   It may be very like.
POLONIUS.   Hath there been such a time, I would fain know that,
  That I have positively said "'Tis so,"
  When it proved otherwise?
KING.   Not that I know.   155
POLONIUS.   Take this, from this, if this be otherwise;

[*Points to his head and shoulder.*]

  If circumstances lead me, I will find
  Where truth is hid, though it were hid indeed
  Within the center.
KING.   How may we try° it further?
POLONIUS.   You know sometimes he walks four hours together   160
  Here in the lobby.
QUEEN.   So he does indeed.
POLONIUS.   At such a time, I'll loose° my daughter to him.
  Be you and I behind an arras° then,
  Mark the encounter: if he love her not,
  And be not from his reason fall'n thereon,   165
  Let me be no assistant for a state,°
  But keep a farm and carters.
KING.   We will try it.

Enter HAMLET reading on a book.

QUEEN.   But look where sadly the poor wretch comes reading.
POLONIUS.   Away, I do beseech you both away,
  I'll board him presently,° O give me leave.   *Exeunt KING and QUEEN.*   170
  How does my good Lord Hamlet?
HAMLET.   Well, God-a-mercy.
POLONIUS.   Do you know me, my lord?
HAMLET.   Excellent well, you are a fishmonger.°
POLONIUS.   Not I my lord.   175

---

141 *out . . . star:* out of your sphere (above you in station).   142 *prescripts:* orders.   143 *resort:*
company.   148 *watch:* sleeplessness.   149 *lightness:* lightheadedness.   159 *try:* test.   162 *loose:* (1) release (2) turn loose.   163 *arras:* hanging tapestry.   166 *assistant . . . state:* state official.   170 *board him
presently:* approach him immediately.   174 *fishmonger:* (1) fish dealer (2) pimp.

HAMLET.   Then I would you were so honest a man.
POLONIUS.   Honest, my lord?
HAMLET.   Ay sir, to be honest as this world goes, is to be one
    man picked out of ten thousand.
POLONIUS.   That's very true, my lord.
HAMLET.   For if the sun breed maggots° in a dead dog, being a good   180
    kissing carrion°—have you a daughter?
POLONIUS.   I have my lord.
HAMLET.   Let her not walk i'th'sun:° conception° is a blessing, but as
    your daughter may conceive, friend look to'it.   185
POLONIUS.   [Aside.] How say you by that? Still harping on my daughter,
    yet he knew me not at first, a' said I was a fishmonger.
    A' is far gone, far gone, and truly in my youth, I suffered
    much extremity for love, very near this. I'll speak to him
    again. What do you read my lord?   190
HAMLET.   Words, words, words.
POLONIUS.   What is the matter my lord?
HAMLET.   Between who?
POLONIUS.   I mean the matter° that you read, my lord.
HAMLET.   Slanders sir; for the satirical rogue says here, that old men   195
    have grey beards, that their faces are wrinkled, their eyes
    purging thick amber and plum-tree gum,° and that they
    have a plentiful lack of wit, together with most weak
    hams. All which sir, though I most powerfully and
    potently believe, yet I hold it not honesty° to have it thus set   200
    down, for yourself sir shall grow old as I am: if like a crab
    you could go backward.
POLONIUS.   [Aside.] Though this be madness, yet there is method
    in't.
    Will you walk out of the air° my lord?   205
HAMLET.   Into my grave.
POLONIUS.   [Aside.] Indeed that's out of the air; how pregnant°
    sometimes his replies are, a happiness° that often
    madness hits on, which reason and sanity could not so
    prosperously° be delivered of. I will leave him, and   210
    suddenly contrive the means of meeting between him
    and my daughter. My honourable lord, I will most
    humbly take leave of you.
HAMLET.   You cannot sir take from me anything that I will more
    willingly part withal: except my life, except my life,   215
    except my life.
POLONIUS.   Fare you well my lord.
HAMLET.   These tedious old fools.

---

181 *breed maggots:* (in the belief that the rays of the sun caused maggots to breed in dead flesh).
182 *kissing carrion:* piece of flesh for kissing.   184 *Let . . . sun:* (1) (proverbial: "out of God's blessing, into
the warm sun") (2) because the sun is a breeder (3) don't let her go near me (with a pun on "sun" and
"son"). *conception:* (1) understanding (2) pregnancy.   194 *matter:* (1) content (Polonius's meaning)
(2) cause of a quarrel (Hamlet's interpretation).   197–198 *purging . . . gum:* exuding a viscous yellowish
discharge.   200 *honesty:* decency.   205 *out . . . air:* (in the belief that fresh air was bad for the sick).
207 *pregnant:* full of meaning.   208 *happiness:* aptness.   210 *prosperously:* successfully.

Enter ROSENCRANTZ and GUILDENSTERN.

POLONIUS.   You go to seek the Lord Hamlet, there he is.

ROSENCRANTZ.   [*To POLONIUS.*] God save you sir.   [*Exit POLONIUS.*]   220

GUILDENSTERN.   My honoured lord.

ROSENCRANTZ.   My most dear lord.

HAMLET.   My excellent good friends, how dost thou Guildenstern?
    Ah Rosencrantz, good lads, how do you both?

ROSENCRANTZ.   As the indifferent° children of the earth.   225

GUILDENSTERN.   Happy, in that we are not over-happy:
    On Fortune's cap we are not the very button.°

HAMLET.   Nor the soles of her shoe?

ROSENCRANTZ.   Neither my lord.

HAMLET.   Then you live about her waist, or in the middle of her   230
    favours?

GUILDENSTERN.   Faith, her privates° we.

HAMLET.   In the secret parts of Fortune? O most true, she is a
    strumpet.° What news?

ROSENCRANTZ.   None my lord, but that the world's grown honest.   235

HAMLET.   Then is doomsday near: but your news is not true. Let me
    question more in particular: what have you my good
    friends, deserved at the hands of Fortune, that she sends
    you to prison hither?

GUILDENSTERN.   Prison, my lord?   240

HAMLET.   Denmark's a prison.

ROSENCRANTZ.   Then is the world one.

HAMLET.   A goodly one, in which there are many confines, wards,°
    and dungeons; Denmark being one o'th'worst.

ROSENCRANTZ.   We think not so my lord.   245

HAMLET.   Why then 'tis none to you; for there is nothing either good
    or bad, but thinking makes it so: to me it is a prison.

ROSENCRANTZ.   Why then your ambition makes it one: 'tis too narrow for
    your mind.

HAMLET.   O God, I could be bounded in a nutshell, and count   250
    myself a king of infinite space; were it not that I have bad
    dreams.

GUILDENSTERN.   Which dreams indeed are ambition: for the very substance
    of the ambitious, is merely the shadow of a dream.

HAMLET.   A dream itself is but a shadow.   255

ROSENCRANTZ.   Truly, and I hold ambition of so airy and light a quality,
    that it is but a shadow's shadow.

HAMLET.   Then are our beggars bodies, and our monarchs and
    outstretched heroes the beggars' shadows:° shall we to th'
    court? for by my fay,° I cannot reason.   260

---

225 *indifferent:* ordinary.   227 *On Fortune's . . . button:* we are not at the height of our fortunes.
232 *privates:* (1) intimate friend (2) private parts.   234 *strumpet:* inconstant woman, giving favor to many.
243 *wards:* cells.   258–259 *Then are . . . shadows:* then beggars are the true substance and ambitious kings
and heroes the elongated shadows of beggars' bodies (for only a real substance can cast a shadow).
260 *fay:* faith.

BOTH.   We'll wait upon° you.

HAMLET.   No such matter. I will not sort° you with the rest of my
servants: for to speak to you like an honest man, I am most
dreadfully attended. But in the beaten way of friendship,
what make you at Elsinore?   265

ROSENCRANTZ.   To visit you my lord, no other occasion.

HAMLET.   Beggar that I am, I am even poor in thanks, but I thank
you, and sure dear friends, my thanks are too dear a
halfpenny:° were you not sent for? is it your own inclining?
is it a free° visitation? come, come, deal justly with me,   270
come, come, nay speak.

GUILDENSTERN.   What should we say my lord?

HAMLET.   Anything but to th'purpose: you were sent for, and there
is a kind of confession in your looks, which your modesties
have not craft enough to colour: I know the good king and   275
queen have sent for you.

ROSENCRANTZ.   To what end my lord?

HAMLET.   That you must teach me: but let me conjure° you, by the
rights of our fellowship, by the consonancy of our youth,°
by the obligation of our ever-preserved love, and by what   280
more dear a better proposer can charge you withal,° be
even and direct with me whether you were sent for or no.

ROSENCRANTZ.   [Aside to Guildenstern.] What say you?

HAMLET.   Nay then, I have an eye of° you: If you love me,
hold not off.   285

GUILDENSTERN.   My lord, we were sent for.

HAMLET.   I will tell you why, so shall my anticipation prevent° your
discovery,° and your secrecy to the king and queen moult
no feather.° I have of late, but wherefore I know not, lost all
my mirth, forgone all custom of exercises: and indeed it   290
goes so heavily with my disposition, that this goodly
frame the earth, seems to me a sterile promontory, this
most excellent canopy the air, look you, this brave°
o'erhanging firmament, this majestical roof fretted° with
golden fire,° why it appeareth nothing to me but a foul and   295
pestilent congregation of vapours.° What a piece of work is
a man! How noble in reason, how infinite in faculties,° in
form and moving, how express° and admirable in action,
how like an angel in apprehension, how like a god: the
beauty of the world; the paragon of animals; and yet to   300
me, what is this quintessence of dust? Man delights not
me, no, nor woman neither, though by your smiling, you
seem to say so.

---

261 *wait upon:* attend.   262 *sort:* class.   268–269 *too dear a halfpenny:* worth not even a halfpenny (as I have no influence).   270 *free:* voluntary.   278 *conjure:* appeal to.   279 *consonancy . . . youth:*
agreement in our ages.   281 *withal:* with.   284 *of:* on.   287 *prevent:* forestall.   288 *discovery:* disclosure.
288–289 *moult no feather:* change in no way.   293 *brave:* splendid.   294 *fretted:* ornamented with fret-
work.   295 *golden fire:* stars.   296 *pestilent . . . vapours:* (clouds were believed to carry contagion).   297
faculties: physical powers.   298 *express:* well framed.

ROSENCRANTZ.   My lord, there was no such stuff in my thoughts.

HAMLET.   Why did ye laugh then, when I said 'man delights not me'?   305

ROSENCRANTZ.   To think, my lord, if you delight not in man, what lenten
 entertainment° the players shall receive from you: we coted°
 them on the way, and hither are they coming to offer you
 service.

HAMLET.   He that plays the king shall be welcome, his majesty shall   310
 have tribute of me, the adventurous knight° shall use his
 foil and target,° the lover shall not sigh gratis,° the humorous
 man° shall end his part in peace,° the clown shall make
 those laugh whose lungs are tickle o'th'sere,° and the lady
 shall say her mind freely: or the blank verse shall halt° for't.   315
 What players are they?

ROSENCRANTZ.   Even those you were wont to take such delight in, the
 tragedians of the city.

HAMLET.   How chances it they travel? Their residence° both in
 reputation and profit was better both ways.   320

ROSENCRANTZ.   I think their inhibition comes by the means of the late
 innovation.°

HAMLET.   Do they hold the same estimation they did when I was in
 the city; are they so followed?

ROSENCRANTZ.   No indeed are they not.   325

HAMLET.   How comes it? Do they grow rusty?

ROSENCRANTZ.   Nay, their endeavour keeps in the wonted pace; but there
 is sir an aery° of children, like eyases,° that cry out on the
 top of question,° and are most tyrannically° clapped for't:
 these are now the fashion, and so berattle° the common   330
 stages° (so they call them) that many wearing rapiers° are
 afraid of goose-quills,° and dare scarce come thither.

HAMLET.   What, are they children? Who maintains 'em? How are
 they escoted°? Will they pursue the quality no longer than
 they can sing°? Will they not say afterwards if they should   335
 grow themselves to common players (as it is most like, if
 their means are not better) their writers do them wrong, to
 make them exclaim against their own succession°?

  306–307 *lenten entertainment:* meager treatment.   307 *coted:* passed.   311 *adventurous knight:*
knight errant (a popular stage character).   312 *foil and target:* sword blunted for stage fighting, and small
shield.   312 *gratis:* (without applause).   312–313 *humorous man:* eccentric character with a dominant
trait, caused by an excess of one of the four humors, or bodily fluids.   313 *in peace:* without interruption.
314 *tickle o'th'sere:* attuned to respond to laughter, as the finely adjusted gunlock responds to the touch
of the trigger (fr. hunting).   315 *halt:* limp (if she adds her own opinions and spoils the meter).   319 *residence:* i.e., in a city theatre.   321–322 *inhibition . . . innovation:* i.e., they were forced out of town by a
more popular theatrical fashion. The following speeches allude to the "War of the Theatres" (1601–1602)
between the child and adult acting companies.   328 *aery:* nest.   *eyases:* young hawks.   328–329 *that cry
. . . question:* whose shrill voices can be heard above all others.   329 *tyrannically:* strongly.   330 *berattle:*
berate.   330–331 *common stages:* public playhouses (the children's companies performed in private
theatres).   331 *wearing rapiers:* (worn by gentlemen).   332 *goose-quills:* pens (of satirical dramatists who
wrote for the children).   334 *escoted:* supported.   334–335 *pursue . . . sing:* continue acting only until
their voices change.   338 *succession:* inheritance.

ROSENCRANTZ.   Faith, there has been much to-do on both sides: and the
    nation holds it no sin to tarre° them to controversy. There   340
    was for a while, no money bid for argument,° unless the
    poet and the player went to cuffs in the question.°
HAMLET.   Is't possible?
GUILDENSTERN.   O there has been much throwing about of brains.
HAMLET.   Do the boys carry it away°?   345
ROSENCRANTZ.   Ay, that they do my lord, Hercules and his load too.°
HAMLET.   It is not very strange, for my uncle is king of Denmark,
    and those that would make mows° at him while my father
    lived, give twenty, forty, fifty, a hundred ducats apiece
    for his picture in little.° 'Sblood,° there is something in this   350
    more than natural, if philosophy° could find it out.

A flourish for the Players.

GUILDENSTERN.   There are the players.
HAMLET.   Gentlemen, you are welcome to Elsinore: your hands,
    come then, th'appurtenance° of welcome is fashion and
    ceremony; let me comply with you in this garb,° lest my   355
    extent° to the players, which I tell you must show fairly
    outwards, should more appear like entertainment than
    yours.° You are welcome: but my uncle-father, and aunt-mother,
    are deceived.
GUILDENSTERN.   In what my dear lord?   360
HAMLET.   I am but mad north-north-west; when the wind is southerly,
    I know a hawk from a handsaw.°

Enter POLONIUS.

POLONIUS.   Well be with you, gentlemen.
HAMLET.   Hark you Guildenstern, and you too, at each ear a hearer:
    that great baby you see there is not yet out of his swaddling   365
    clouts.°
ROSENCRANTZ.   Happily° he is the second time come to them, for they say
    an old man is twice a child.
HAMLET.   I will prophesy, he comes to tell me of the players, mark
    it.—You say right sir, a Monday morning, 'twas then   370
    indeed.
POLONIUS.   My lord, I have news to tell you.
HAMLET.   My lord, I have news to tell you. When Roscius° was an
    actor in Rome—

---

340 *tarre:* provoke.   341 *bid for argument:* paid for the plot of a proposed play.   342 *went . . .
question:* came to blows on the subject.   345 *carry it away:* carry off the prize.   346 *Hercules . . . too:*
(Shakespeare's own company at the Globe Theatre, whose sign was Hercules carrying the globe of the
world).   348 *mows:* mouths, grimaces.   350 *little:* a miniature. *'Sblood:* by God's blood.
351 *philosophy:* science.   354 *appurtenance:* accessory.   355 *comply . . . garb:* observe the formalities with
you in this style.   356 *extent:* i.e., of welcome.   357–358 *should . . . yours:* should appear more hospitable
than yours.   362 *I know . . . handsaw:* I can tell the difference between two things that are unlike ("hawk"
= [1] bird of prey [2] mattock, pickaxe; "handsaw" = [1] hernshaw or heron bird [2] small saw).
365–366 *swaddling clouts:* strips of cloth binding a newborn baby.   367 *Happily:* perhaps.   373 *Roscius:*
famous Roman actor.

POLONIUS.   The actors are come hither, my lord.   375

HAMLET.   Buz, buz.°

POLONIUS.   Upon my honour.

HAMLET.   Then came each actor on his ass—

POLONIUS.   The best actors in the world, either for tragedy, comedy,

   history, pastoral, pastoral-comical, historical-pastoral,   380

   tragical-historical, tragical-comical-historical-pastoral,

   scene individable,° or poem unlimited.° Seneca cannot be

   too heavy, nor Plautus° too light for the law of writ, and the

   liberty:° these are the only men.

HAMLET.   O Jephthah,° judge of Israel, what a treasure hadst thou.   385

POLONIUS.   What a treasure had he, my lord?

HAMLET.   Why

   'One fair daughter and no more,

      The which he lovèd passing° well.'

POLONIUS.   [*Aside.*] Still on my daughter.   390

HAMLET.   Am I not i'th' right, old Jephthah?

POLONIUS.   If you call me Jephthah my lord, I have a daughter that I

   love passing well.

HAMLET.   Nay, that follows not.

POLONIUS.   What follows then, my lord?   395

HAMLET.   Why

   "As by lot, God wot,"

  and then you know

    "It came to pass, as most like° it was:"

  the first row° of the pious chanson will show you more, for   400

  look where my abridgement° comes.

Enter four or five PLAYERS.

  You are welcome masters, welcome all. I am glad to see

  thee well: welcome, good friends. O my old friend, why

  thy face is valanced° since I saw thee last, com'st thou to

  beard me in Denmark? What, my young lady° and   405

  mistress? by'r lady, your ladyship is nearer to heaven than

  when I saw you last, by the altitude of a chopine.° Pray

  God your voice, like a piece of uncurrent° gold, be not

  cracked within the ring.° Masters, you are all welcome:

  we'll e'en to't like French falconers, fly at any thing we see:°   410

  we'll have a speech straight. Come give us a taste of your

  quality: come, a passionate speech.

---

    376 *Buz, buz:* (contemptuous).   **382** *scene individable:* play observing the unities (time, place, action). *poem unlimited:* play ignoring the unities. **382–383** *Seneca, Plautus:* Roman writers of tragedy and comedy, respectively. **383–384** *law . . . liberty:* "rules" regarding the unities and those exercising freedom from the unities. **385** *Jephthah:* (who was forced to sacrifice his only daughter because of a rash promise: Judges 11:29–39). **389** *passing:* surpassingly. **399** *like:* likely. **400** *row:* stanza. **401** *abridgement:* (the players who will cut short my song). **404** *valanced:* fringed with a beard. **405** *lady:* boy playing women's role. **407** *chopine:* thick-soled shoe. **408** *uncurrent:* not legal tender. **409** *ring:* (1) ring enclosing the design on a gold coin (to crack it within the ring [to steal the gold] made it "uncurrent") (2) sound. **410** *fly . . . see:* undertake any difficulty.

1. PLAYER. What speech, my good lord?

HAMLET. I heard thee speak me a speech once, but it was never
    acted, or if it was, not above once, for the play I remember   415
    pleased not the million, 'twas caviary to the general,° but it
    was (as I received it, and others, whose judgments in such
    matters cried in the top of mine°) an excellent play, well
    digested in the scenes, set down with as much modesty as
    cunning.° I remember one said there were no sallets.° In the   420
    lines, to make the matter savoury, nor no matter in the
    phrase that might indict the author of° affection, but called
    it an honest method, as wholesome as sweet, and by very
    much more handsome than fine:° one speech in't I chiefly
    loved, 'twas Aeneas' tale to Dido, and thereabout of it   425
    especially where he speaks of Priam's slaughter.° If it live in
    your memory begin at this line, let me see, let me see:
        "The rugged Pyrrhus,° like th'Hyrcanian beast'°—
    'tis not so: it begins with Pyrrhus—
        "The rugged Pyrrhus, he whose sable° arms,   430
    Black as his purpose, did the night resemble
    When he lay couched in th'ominous horse,°
    Hath now this dread and black complexion smeared
    With heraldy more dismal: head to foot
    Now is he total gules,° horridly tricked°   435
    With blood of fathers, mothers, daughters, sons,
    Baked and impasted° with the parching° streets,
    That lend a tyrannous and damnèd light
    To their lord's murder. Roasted in wrath and fire,
    And thus o'er-sizèd° with coagulate gore,   440
    With eyes like carbuncles,° the hellish Pyrrhus
    Old grandsire Priam seeks;"
    So proceed you.

POLONIUS. 'Fore God, my lord, well spoken, with good accent and
    good discretion.°   445

1. PLAYER. "Anon he finds him,
    Striking too short at Greeks, his antique° sword,
    Rebellious to his arm, lies where it falls,
    Repugnant to command,° unequal matched,
    Pyrrhus at Priam drives, in rage strikes wide,   450
    But with the whiff and wind of his fell° sword,
    Th'unnerved father falls: then senseless Ilium,°

---

416 *caviary . . . general:* like caviar, too rich for the general public.   418 *cried . . . mine:* spoke with
more authority than mine.   419–420 *modesty as cunning:* moderation as skill.   420 *sallets:* spicy bits.
422 *indict . . . of:* charge . . . with.   424 *handsome than fine:* dignified than finely wrought.   426 *Priam's
slaughter:* the murder of the King of Troy (as told in the Aeneid).   428 *Pyrrhus:* son of Achilles.   *Hyrcanian
beast:* tiger noted for fierceness.   430 *sable:* black.   432 *horse:* the hollow wooden horse used by the
Greeks to enter Troy.   435 *gules:* red.   *horridly tricked:* horribly decorated.   437 *impasted:* coagulated.
parching: (because the city was on fire).   440 *o'er-sizèd:* covered over.   441 *carbuncles:* red gems.   445
discretion: interpretation.   447 *antique:* ancient.   449 *Repugnant to command:* refusing to obey its commander.   451 *fell:* savage.   452 *senseless Ilium:* unfeeling Troy.

Seeming to feel this blow, with flaming top
Stoops to his base; and with a hideous crash
Takes prisoner Pyrrhus' ear. For lo, his sword   455
Which was declining on the milky head
Of reverend Priam, seemed i'th'air to stick;
So as a painted° tyrant Pyrrhus stood,
And like a neutral to his will and matter,°
Did nothing: 460
But as we often see, against° some storm,
A silence in the heavens, the rack° stand still,
The bold winds speechless, and the orb° below
As hush as death, anon the dreadful thunder
Doth rend the region, so after Pyrrhus' pause,   465
A rousèd vengeance sets him new awork,
And never did the Cyclops'° hammers fall
On Mars's armour, forged for proof eterne,°
With less remorse than Pyrrhus' bleeding sword
Now falls on Priam.   470
Out, out, thou strumpet Fortune: all you gods,
In general synod° take away her power,
Break all the spokes and fellies from her wheel,°
And bowl the round nave° down the hill of heaven
As low as to the fiends."°   475
POLONIUS.   This is too long.
HAMLET.   It shall to the barber's with your beard; prithee say on: he's
    for a jig, or a tale of bawdry, or he sleeps. Say on, come to
    Hecuba.
1. PLAYER.   "But who, ah woe, had seen the mobled° queen—"   480
HAMLET.   "The mobled queen"?
POLONIUS.   That's good, "mobled queen" is good.
1. PLAYER.   "Run barefoot up and down, threat'ning the flames
    With bissom rheum,° a clout° upon that head
    Where late the diadem stood, and for a robe,   485
    About her lank and all o'er-teemèd° loins,
    A blanket in the alarm of fear caught up—
    Who this had seen, with tongue in venom steeped,
    'Gainst Fortune's state° would treason have pronounced;
    But if the gods themselves did see her then,   490
    When she saw Pyrrhus make malicious sport
    In mincing with his sword her husband's limbs,
    The instant burst of clamour that she made,
    Unless things mortal move them not at all,
    Would have made milch° the burning eyes of heaven,   495
    And passion in the gods."

---

458 *painted:* pictured.   459 *like . . . matter:* unmoved by either his purpose or its achievement.
461 *against:* before.   462 *rack:* clouds.   463 *orb:* earth.   467 *Cyclops:* workmen of Vulcan, armorer of the
gods.   468 *for proof eterne:* to be eternally invincible.   472 *synod:* assembly.   473 *fellies . . . wheel:*
curved pieces of the rim of the wheel that fortune turns, representing a man's fortunes.   474 *nave:* hub.
475 *fiends:* i.e., of hell.   480 *mobled:* muffled in a scarf.   484 *bissom rheum:* binding tears. *clout:* cloth.
486 *o'er-teemed:* worn out by excessive childbearing.   489 *state:* reign.   495 *milch:* milky, moist.

POLONIUS.   Look where° he has not turned° his colour, and has tears in's
    eyes, prithee no more.
HAMLET.   'Tis well, I'll have thee speak out the rest of this soon.
    Good my lord, will you see the players well bestowed,° do   500
    you hear, let them be well used, for they are the abstract°
    and brief chronicles° of the time; after your death you were
    better have a bad epitaph than their ill report while you
    live.
POLONIUS.   My lord, I will use them according to their desert.°   505
HAMLET.   God's bodkin° man, much better. Use every man after° his
    desert, and who shall 'scape whipping? Use them after
    you own honour and dignity: the less they deserve, the
    more merit is in your bounty. Take them in.
POLONIUS.   Come sirs.   *Exeunt POLONIUS and PLAYERS.*   510
HAMLET.   Follow him friends, we'll hear a play tomorrow; [*Stops the
FIRST PLAYER.*] dost thou hear me, old friend, can you play
    The Murder of Gonzago?
1. PLAYER.   Ay my lord.
HAMLET.   We'll ha't tomorrow night. You could for a need° study a   515
    speech of some dozen or sixteen lines, which I would set
    down and insert in't, could you not?
1.   Player. Ay my lord.
HAMLET.   Very well, follow that lord, and look you mock him not.

                                                  [*Exit FIRST PLAYER.*]

    [*To Rosencrantz and Guildenstern.*] My good friends, I'll   520
    leave you till night, you are welcome to Elsinore.
ROSENCRANTZ.   Good my lord.   [*Exeunt ROSENCRANTZ and GUILDENSTERN.*]
HAMLET.   Ay so, God bye to you.—Now I am alone.
    O what a rogue and peasant slave am I.
    Is it not monstrous that this player here,   525
    But in a fiction, in a dream of passion,°
    Could force his soul so to his own conceit°
    That from her working all his visage wanned,°
    Tears in his eyes, distraction in his aspect,
    A broken voice, and his whole function° suiting   530
    With forms° to his conceit; and all for nothing,
    For Hecuba!
    What's Hecuba to him, or he to Hecuba,
    That he should weep for her? what would he do,
    Had he the motive and the cue for passion
    That I have? he would drown the stage with tears,   535
    And cleave the general ear° with horrid speech,

---

497 *where:* whether. *turned:* changed.   500 *bestowed:* lodged.   501 *abstract:* summary (noun).
502 *brief chronicles:* history in brief.   505 *desert:* merit.   506 *God's bodkin:* God's little body, the communion wafer (an oath).   *after:* according to.   515 *for a need:* if necessary.   526 *dream of passion:* portrayal of emotion.   527 *conceit:* imagination.   528 *wanned:* grew pale.   530 *function:* bearing.
531 *With forms:* in appearance.   537 *general ear:* ears of all in the audience.

Make mad the guilty and appal the free,°
Confound° the ignorant, and amaze indeed
The very faculties of eyes and ears; yet I,   540
A dull and muddy-mettled° rascal, peak°
Like John-a-dreams, unpregnant of° my cause,
And can say nothing; no, not for a king,
Upon whose property and most dear life,
A damned defeat was made: am I a coward?   545
Who calls me villain, breaks my pate° across,
Plucks off my beard° and blows it in my face,
Tweaks me by the nose, gives me the lie i'th'throat
As deep as to the lungs,° who does me this?
Ha, 'swounds,° I should take it; for it cannot be   550
But I am pigeon-livered,° and lack gall
To make oppression bitter, or ere this
I should ha' fatted all the region kites°
With this slave's offal: bloody, bawdy villain,
Remorseless, treacherous, lecherous, kindless° villain!   555
O vengeance!
Why what an ass am I, this is most brave,°
That I, the son of a dear father murdered,
Prompted to my revenge by heaven and hell,
Must like a whore unpack my heart with words,   560
And fall a-cursing like a very drab,°
A scullion,° fie upon't, foh.
About, my brains; hum, I have heard,
That guilty creatures sitting at a play,
Have by the very cunning of the scene   565
Been struck so to the soul, that presently°
They have proclaimed their malefactions:
For murder, though it have no tongue, will speak
With most miraculous organ: I'll have these players
Play something like the murder of my father   570
Before mine uncle, I'll observe his looks,
I'll tent° him to the quick, if a' do blench°
I know my course. The spirit that I have seen
May be a devil, and the devil hath power
T'assume a pleasing shape, yea, and perhaps   575
Out of my weakness, and my melancholy,
As he is very potent with such spirits,
Abuses me to damn me; I'll have grounds
More relative than this: the play's the thing
Wherein I'll catch the conscience of the king.   *Exit.*   580

---

538 *free:* innocent. **539** *Confound:* confuse. **541** *muddy-mettled:* dull-spirited. *peak:* pine, mope. **542** *John-a-dreams:* a daydreaming fellow. *unpregnant of:* unstirred by. **546** *pate:* head. **547** *Plucks . . . beard:* (a way of giving insult). **548–549** *gives . . . lungs:* insults me by calling me a liar of the worst kind (the lungs being deeper than the throat). **550** *'swounds:* God's wounds. **551** *pigeon-livered:* meek and uncouraged. **553** *region kites:* vultures of the upper air. **555** *kindless:* unnatural. **557** *brave:* fine. **561** *drab:* whore. **562** *scullion:* kitchen wench. **566** *presently:* immediately. **572** *tent:* probe. *blench:* flinch.

ACT 3

Scene 1. [A room in the castle]

Enter KING, QUEEN, POLONIUS, OPHELIA, ROSENCRANTZ, GUILDENSTERN, LORDS.

KING.   And can you by no drift of conference°
    Get from him why he puts on this confusion,°
    Grating so harshly all his days of quiet
    With turbulent and dangerous lunacy?
ROSENCRANTZ.   He does confess he feels himself distracted,   5
    But from what cause, a' will by no means speak.
GUILDENSTERN.   Nor do we find him forward to be sounded,°
    But with a crafty madness keeps aloof
    When we would bring him on to some confession
    Of his true state.
QUEEN.   Did he receive you well?   10
ROSENCRANTZ.   Most like a gentleman.
GUILDENSTERN.   But with much forcing of his disposition.°
ROSENCRANTZ.   Niggard of question,° but of our demands
    Most free in his reply.
QUEEN.   Did you assay° him
    To any pastime?   15
ROSENCRANTZ.   Madam, it so fell out that certain players
    We o'er-raught° on the way: of these we told him,
    And there did seem in him a kind of joy
    To hear of it: they are here about the court,
    And as I think, they have already order
    This night to play before him.   20
POLONIUS.   'Tis most true,
    And he beseeched me to entreat your majesties
    To hear and see the matter.°
KING.   With all my heart, and it doth much content me
    To hear him so inclined.   25
    Good gentlemen, give him a further edge,°
    And drive his purpose into these delights.
ROSENCRANTZ.   We shall my lord.   *Exeunt Rosencrantz and Guildenstern.*
KING.   Sweet Gertrude, leave us too,
    For we have closely° sent for Hamlet hither,
    That he, as 'twere by accident, may here   30
    Affront° Ophelia;
    Her father and myself, lawful espials,°
    Will so bestow° ourselves, that seeing unseen,
    We may of their encounter frankly° judge,

---

1 *drift of conference:* turn of conversation.   2 *puts . . . confusion:* seems so distracted ("puts on" indicates the king's private suspicion that Hamlet is playing mad).   7 *forward . . . sounded:* disposed to be sounded out.   12 *forcing . . . disposition:* forcing himself to be so.   13 *Niggard of question:* unwilling to talk.   14 *assay:* tempt.   17 *o'er-raught:* overtook.   23 *matter:* i.e., of the play.   26 *give . . . edge:* encourage his keen interest.   29 *closely:* secretly.   31 *Affront:* meet face to face with.   32 *espials:* spies.   33, 44 *bestow:* place.   34 *frankly:* freely.

And gather by him as he is behaved,   35
If't be th'affliction of his love or no
That thus he suffers for.

QUEEN.   I shall obey you.
   And for your part Ophelia, I do wish
   That your good beauties be the happy cause
   Of Hamlet's wildness, so shall I hope your virtues   40
   Will bring him to his wonted° way again,
   To both your honours.

OPHELIA.   Madam, I wish it may.   [*Exit* QUEEN.]

POLONIUS.   Ophelia, walk you here—Gracious,° so please you,
   We will bestow ourselves—read on this book,°
   That show of such an exercise° may colour°   45
   Your loneliness; we are oft to blame in this,
   'Tis too much proved,° that with devotion's visage
   And pious action, we do sugar o'er
   The devil himself.

KING.   [*Aside.*] O 'tis too true,°
   How smart a lash that speech doth give my conscience.   50
   The harlot's cheek, beautied with plast'ring art,
   Is not more ugly to° the thing that helps it,
   Than is my deed to my most painted word:°
   O heavy burden!

POLONIUS.   I hear him coming, let's withdraw my lord.   55

                                   Exeunt.

Enter HAMLET.

HAMLET.   To be, or not to be, that is the question,
   Whether 'tis nobler in the mind° to suffer
   The slings and arrows of outrageous fortune,
   Or to take arms against a sea of troubles,
   And by opposing, end them: to die, to sleep,   60
   No more; and by a sleep, to say we end
   The heart-ache, and the thousand natural shocks
   That flesh is heir to; 'tis a consummation
   Devoutly to be wished. To die, to sleep,
   To sleep, perchance to dream, ay there's the rub,°   65
   For in that sleep of death what dreams may come
   When we have shuffled off this mortal coil°
   Must give us pause—there's the respect°
   That makes calamity of so long life:°

---

41 *wanted:* customary.   43 *Gracious:* i.e., Your Grace.   44 *book:* (of prayer).   45 *exercise:* religious exercise.   *colour:* make plausible.   47 *'Tis . . . proved:* it is all too apparent.   49 *'tis too true:* (the king's first indication that he is guilty).   52 *to:* compared to.   51–53 *harlot's cheek . . . word:* just as the harlot's cheek is even uglier by contrast to the makeup that tries to beautify it, so my deed is uglier by contrast to the hypocritical words under which I hide it.   57 *nobler in the mind:* best, according to "sovereign" reason.   65 *rub:* obstacle.   67 *mortal coil:* (1) turmoil of mortal life (2) coil of flesh encircling the body.   68 *respect:* consideration.   69 *makes calamity of so long life:* makes living long a calamity.

> For who would bear the whips and scorns of time,   70
> Th'oppressor's wrong, the proud man's contumely,°
> The pangs of disprized love, the law's delay,°
> The insolence of office,° and the spurns
> That patient merit of th'unworthy takes,
> When he himself might his quietus° make   75
> With a bare bodkin;° who would fardels° bear,
> To grunt and sweat under a weary life,
> But that the dread of something after death,
> The undiscovered° country, from whose bourn°
> No traveller returns, puzzles the will,   80
> And makes us rather bear those ills we have,
> Than fly to others that we know not of.
> Thus conscience does make cowards of us all,
> And thus the native hue° of resolution
> Is sicklied o'er with the pale cast of thought,   85
> And enterprises of great pitch° and moment,°
> With this regard° their currents turn awry,°
> And lose the name of action. Soft you now,
> The fair Ophelia—Nymph, in thy orisons°
> Be all my sins remembered.

OPHELIA.   Good my lord,   90
> How does your honour for this many a day.°
HAMLET.   I humbly thank you: well, well, well.
OPHELIA.   My lord, I have remembrances of yours
> That I have longèd long to re-deliver,
> I pray you now receive them.
HAMLET.   No, not I,   95
> I never gave you aught.
OPHELIA.   My honoured lord, you know right well you did,
> And with them words of so sweet breath° composed
> As made the things more rich: their perfume lost,
> Take these again, for to the noble mind   100
> Rich gifts wax° poor when givers prove unkind.
> There my lord.
HAMLET.   Ha, ha, are you honest°?
OPHELIA.   My lord.
HAMLET.   Are you fair°?   105
OPHELIA.   What means your lordship?
HAMLET.   That if you be honest and fair, your honesty should admit
> no discourse to your beauty.°

---

71 *contumely:* contempt.   72 *law's delay:* longevity of lawsuits.   73 *office:* officials.   75 *quietus:* settlement of his debt.   76 *bare bodkin:* mere dagger.   *fardels:* burdens.   79 *undiscovered:* unknown, unexplored.   *bourn:* boundary.   84 *native hue:* natural complexion.   86 *pitch:* height, excellence. *moment:* importance.   87 *regard:* consideration.   *their currents turn awry:* change their course. 89 *orisons:* prayers (referring to her prayer book).   91 *this . . . day:* all these days.   98 *breath:* speech. 101 *wax:* grow.   103 *honest:* (1) chaste (2) truthful.   105 *fair:* (1) beautiful (2) honorable.   107–108 *admit . . . beauty:* (1) not allow communication with your beauty (2) not allow your beauty to be used as a trap (Hamlet may have overheard the Polonius–Claudius plot or spotted their movement behind the arras).

OPHELIA.   Could beauty my lord, have better commerce than with
     honesty?   110

HAMLET.   Ay truly, for the power of beauty will sooner transform
     honesty° from what it is to a bawd,° than the force of
     honesty can translate beauty into his likeness. This was
     sometime° a paradox, but now the time gives it proof. I did
     love you once.   115

OPHELIA.   Indeed my lord, you made me believe so.

HAMLET.   You should not have believed me, for virtue cannot so
     inoculate our old stock, but we shall relish of it.° I loved
     you not.

OPHELIA.   I was the more deceived.   120

HAMLET.   Get thee to a nunnery,° why wouldst thou be a breeder of
     sinners? I am myself indifferent honest,° but yet I could
     accuse me of such things, that it were better my mother
     had not borne me: I am very proud, revengeful, ambitious,
     with more offences at my beck,° than I have thoughts   125
     to put them in, imagination to give them shape, or time to
     act them in: what should such fellows as I do, crawling
     between earth and heaven? we are arrant° knaves all,
     believe none of us, go thy ways to a nunnery. Where's
     your father?   130

OPHELIA.   At home my lord.

HAMLET.   Let the doors be shut upon him, that he may play the fool
     nowhere but in's own house. Farewell.

OPHELIA.   O help him, you sweet heavens.

HAMLET.   If thou dost marry, I'll give thee this plague° for thy dowry: 135
     be thou as chaste as ice, as pure as snow, thou shalt not
     escape calumny; get thee to a nunnery, go, farewell. Or if
     thou wilt needs marry, marry a fool, for wise men know
     well enough what monsters° you make of them: to a nunnery
     go, and quickly too, farewell.   140

OPHELIA.   O heavenly powers, restore him.

HAMLET.   I have heard of your paintings too, well enough. God hath
     given you one face, and you make yourselves another: you
     jig,° you amble, and you lisp,° you nick-name God's
     creatures, and make your wantonness your ignorance,° go to,   145
     I'll no more on't, it hath made me mad. I say we will have
     no moe° marriage. Those that are married already, all but
     one shall live, the rest shall keep as they are: to a nunnery,
     go.   *Exit* HAMLET.

---

112 *honesty:* chastity. *bawd:* procurer, pimp.   114 *sometime:* once.   118 *inoculate . . . it:* change our sinful nature (as a tree is grafted to improve it) but we will keep our old taste (as will the fruit of the grafted tree).   121 *nunnery:* (1) cloister (2) slang for "brothel" (cf. "bawd" above).   122 *indifferent honest:* reasonably virtuous.   125 *beck:* beckoning.   128 *arrant:* absolute.   135 *plague:* curse.   139 *monsters:* horned cuckolds (men whose wives were unfaithful).   144 *jig:* walk in a mincing way.   *lisp:* put on affected speech.   145 *make your . . . ignorance:* excuse your caprices as being due to ignorance.   147 *moe:* more.

OPHELIA.   O what a noble mind is here o'erthrown!   150
    The courtier's, soldier's, scholar's, eye, tongue, sword,
    Th'expectancy and rose° of the fair state,
    The glass° of fashion, and the mould of form,°
    Th'observed of all observers, quite quite down,
    And I of ladies most deject and wretched,   155
    That sucked the honey of his music vows,
    Now see that noble and most sovereign° reason
    Like sweet bells jangled, out of tune and harsh,
    That unmatched form and feature° of blown° youth
    Blasted with ecstasy,° O woe is me,   160
    T'have seen what I have seen, see what I see.

Enter KING *and* POLONIUS.

KING.   Love? his affections° do not that way tend,
    Nor what he spake, though it lacked form a little,
    Was not like madness. There's something in his soul
    O'er which his melancholy sits on brood,   165
    And I do doubt,° the hatch and the disclose°
    Will be some danger; which for to prevent,
    I have in quick determination
    Thus set it down: he shall with speed to England,
    For the demand of our neglected° tribute: 170
    Haply° the seas, and countries different,
    With variable° objects, shall expel
    This something°-settled matter in his heart,
    Whereon his brains still beating puts him thus
    From fashion of himself.° What think you on't?   175
POLONIUS.   It shall do well. But yet do I believe
    The origin and commencement of his grief
    Sprung from neglected° love. How now Ophelia?
    You need not tell us what Lord Hamlet said,
    We heard it all. My lord, do as you please,   180
    But if you hold it fit, after the play,
    Let his queen-mother all alone entreat him
    To show his grief, let her be round° with him,
    And I'll be placed (so please you) in the ear
    Of° all their conference. If she find° him not,   185
    To England send him: or confine him where
    Your wisdom best shall think.
KING.   It shall be so,
    Madness in great ones must not unwatched go.   *Exeunt.*

---

      152 *expectancy and rose:* fair hope.   153 *glass:* mirror.   *mould of form:* model of manners.
157 *sovereign:* (because it should rule).   159 *feature:* external appearance.   159 *blown:* flowering.
160 *Blasted with ecstasy:* blighted by madness.   162 *affections:* emotions, afflictions.   166 *doubt:* fear.
165–166 *on brood . . . hatch . . . disclose:* (metaphor of a hen sitting on eggs).   170 *neglected:* (being un-
paid).   171 *Haply:* perhaps.   172 *variable:* varied.   173 *something:* somewhat-.   175 *fashion of himself:*
his usual self.   178 *neglected:* unrequited.   183 *round:* direct.   184–185 *in the ear Of:* so as to overhear.
185 *find:* find out.

Scene 2 [A hall in the castle]

Enter HAMLET and three of the PLAYERS.

HAMLET. Speak the speech° I pray you as I pronounced it to you,
   trippingly on the tongue, but if you mouth it° as many of
   your players do, I had as lief the town-crier spoke my
   lines. Nor do not saw the air too much with your hand
   thus, but use all gently, for in the very torrent, tempest,   5
   and as I may say, whirlwind of your passion, you must
   acquire and beget° a temperance that may give it smoothness.
   O it offends me to the soul, to hear a robustious°
   periwig-pated° fellow tear a passion to tatters, to very rags,
   to split the ears of the groundlings,° who for the most part   10
   are capable of° nothing but inexplicable dumb shows° and
   noise: I would have such a fellow whipped for o'erdoing
   Termagant.° It out-herods Herod,° pray you avoid it.
1. PLAYER. I warrant you honour.
HAMLET. Be not too tame neither, but let your own discretion be   15
   your tutor, suit the action to the word, the word to the
   action, with this special observance, that you o'erstep not
   the modesty° of nature: for any thing so o'erdone, is from°
   the purpose of playing, whose end both at the first, and
   now, was and is, to hold as 'twere the mirror up to nature,   20
   to show virtue her own feature, scorn° her own image, and
   the very age and body of the time his form and pressure.°
   Now this overdone, or come tardy off,° though it make the
   unskilful° laugh, cannot but make the judicious grieve, the
   censure of the which one,° must in your allowance°   25
   o'erweigh a whole theatre of others. O there be players
   that I have seen play, and heard others praise, and that
   highly (not to speak it profanely) that neither having
   th'accent of Christians, nor the gait of Christian, pagan,
   nor man, have so strutted and bellowed, that I have   30
   thought some of nature's journeymen° had made men, and
   not made them well, they imitated humanity so
   abominably.
1. PLAYER. I hope we have reformed that indifferently° with us, sir.
HAMLET. O reform it altogether, and let those that play your clowns   35
   speak no more than is set down for them,° for there be of
   them that will themselves laugh, to set on some quantity

---

   1 *the speech:* i.e., that Hamlet has inserted.   2 *mouth it:* deliver it slowly and overdramatically.
7 *acquire and beget:* achieve for yourself and instill in other actors.   8 *robustious:* boisterous.   9 *periwig-
pated:* wig-wearing.   10 *groundlings:* audience who paid least and stood on the ground floor.
11 *capable of:* able to understand.   *dumb shows:* pantomimed synopses of the action to follow (as below).
13 *Termagant:* violent, ranting character in the guild or mystery plays.   *out-herods Herod:* outdoes even
Herod, King of Judea, who commanded the slaughter of the Innocents and who was a ranting tyrant in
the Corpus Christi plays. See pp. 0000–0000.   18 *modesty:* moderation.   *from:* away from.   21 *scorn:* that
which should be scorned.   22 *age . . . pressure:* shape of the times in its accurate impression.   23 *come
tardy off:* understated, undercone.   24 *unskilful:* unsophisticated.   25 *one:* the judicious.   *allowance:* estimation.   31 *journeymen:* artisans working for others and not yet masters of their trades.
34 *indifferently:* reasonably well.   36 *speak no more . . . them:* stick to their lines.

of barren° spectators to laugh too, though in the meantime,
some necessary question° of the play be then to be considered:
that's villainous, and shows a most pitiful ambition   40
in the fool that uses it. Go make you ready.   *Exeunt PLAYERS.*

Enter POLONIUS, ROSENCRANTZ, and GUILDENSTERN.

How now my lord, will the king hear this piece of work?
POLONIUS.   And the queen too, and that presently.
HAMLET.   Bid the players make haste.   *Exit POLONIUS.*
Will you two help to hasten them?   45
ROSENCRANTZ.   Ay my lord.   *Exeunt they two.*
HAMLET.   What ho, Horatio!

Enter HORATIO.

HORATIO.   Here sweet lord, at your service.
HAMLET.   Horatio, thou art e'en as just° a man
As e'er my conversation coped withal.°   50
HORATIO.   O my dear lord.
HAMLET.   Nay, do not think I flatter,
For what advancement may I hope from thee,
That no revenue hast but thy good spirits
To feed and clothe thee? Why should the poor be flattered?
No, let the candied° tongue lick° absurd pomp,   55
And crook the pregnant° hinges of the knee
Where thrift may follow fawning.° Dost thou hear,
Since my dear soul was mistress of her choice,
And could of men distinguish her election,°
Sh'hath sealed° thee for herself, for thou hast been   60
As one in suff'ring all that suffers nothing,
A man that Fortune's buffets° and rewards
Hast ta'en with equal thanks; and blest are those
Whose blood° and judgment are so well co-mingled,
That they are not a pipe for Fortune's finger   65
To sound what stop° she please.° give me that man
That is not passion's slave, and I will wear him
In my heart's core, ay in my heart of heart,
As I do thee. Something too much of this.
There is a play tonight before the king,   70
One scene of it comes near the circumstance
Which I have told thee of my father's death.
I prithee when thou seest that act afoot,
Even with the very comment° of thy soul
Observe my uncle: if his occulted° guilt   75

---

38 *barren:* witless.   39 *question:* dialogue.   49 *just:* well balanced.   50 *coped withal:* had to do
with.   55–57 *candied . . . fawning:* (metaphor of a dog licking and fawning for candy).   55 *candied:*
flattering.   *lick* pay court to.   56–57 *crook . . . fawning:* obsequiously kneel when personal profit may
ensue.   56 *pregnant:* quick in motion.   59 *election:* choice.   60 *sealed:* confirmed.   62 *buffets:* blows.
64 *blood:* passions.   66 *sound . . . please:* play whatever tune she likes.   *stop:* finger hole in wind instrument for varying the sound.   74 *very comment:* acutest observation.   75 *occulted:* hidden.

Do not itself unkennel° in one speech,
It is a damnèd ghost° that we have seen,
And my imaginations are as foul
As Vulcan's stithy,° give him heedful note,
For I mine eyes will rivet to his face,   80
And after we will both our judgments join
In censure of his seeming.°

HORATIO.   Well my lord,
If a' steal aught the whilst this play is playing,
And 'scape detecting, I will pay° the theft.   *Sound a flourish.*   85

HAMLET.   They are coming to the play. I must be idle,°
Get you a place.

*Enter Trumpets and Kettledrums, KING, QUEEN, POLONIUS, OPHELIA, ROSENCRANTZ, GUILDENSTERN,
and other LORDS attendant, with his GUARD carrying torches. Danish March.*

KING.   How fares° our cousin Hamlet?
HAMLET.   Excellent i'faith, of the chameleon's dish: I eat the air,°
    promise-crammed, you cannot feed capons so.°
KING.   I have nothing with° this answer Hamlet, these words are   90
    not mine.°
HAMLET.   No, nor mine now. [*To Polonius.*] My lord, you played
    once i'th'university you say?
POLONIUS.   That did I my lord, and was accounted a good actor.
HAMLET.   What did you enact?   95
POLONIUS.   I did enact Julius Caesar, I was killed i'th'Capitol, Brutus
    killed me.
HAMLET.   It was a brute part of him to kill so capital a calf there. Be
    the players ready?
ROSENCRANTZ.   Ay my lord, they stay upon your patience.°   100
QUEEN.   Come hither my dear Hamlet, sit by me.
HAMLET.   No, good mother, here's metal more attractive.°
POLONIUS.   [*To the King.*] O ho, do you mark that?
HAMLET.   Lady, shall I lie in your lap?
OPHELIA.   No my lord.   105
HAMLET.   I mean, my head upon your lap?
OPHELIA.   Ay my lord.
HAMLET.   Do you think I meant country° matters?
OPHELIA.   I think nothing my lord.
HAMLET.   That's a fair thought to lie between maids' legs.   110
OPHELIA.   What is, my lord?

---

76 *unkennel:* force from hiding.   77 *damnèd ghost:* devil (not the ghost of my father).
79 *Vulcan's stithy:* the forge of the blacksmith of the gods.   82 *censure . . . seeming:* (1) judgment of his
appearance (2) disapproval of his pretending.   84 *pay:* i.e., for.   85 *be idle:* act mad.   87 *fares:* does, but
Hamlet takes it to mean "eats" or "dines."   88 *eat the air:* the chamelion supposedly ate air, but Hamlet
also puns on "heir."   89 *you cannot . . . so:* (1) even a capon cannot feed on air and your promises (2) like
a capon stuffed with food before being killed, I am stuffed (fed up) with your promises.   90 *nothing with:*
nothing to do with.   91 *not mine:* not in answer to my question.   100 *stay . . . patience:* await your
permission.   102 *metal more attractive:* (1) iron more magnetic (2) stuff ("mettle") more beautiful.
108 *country:* rustic, sexual (with a pun on a slang word for the female sexual organ).

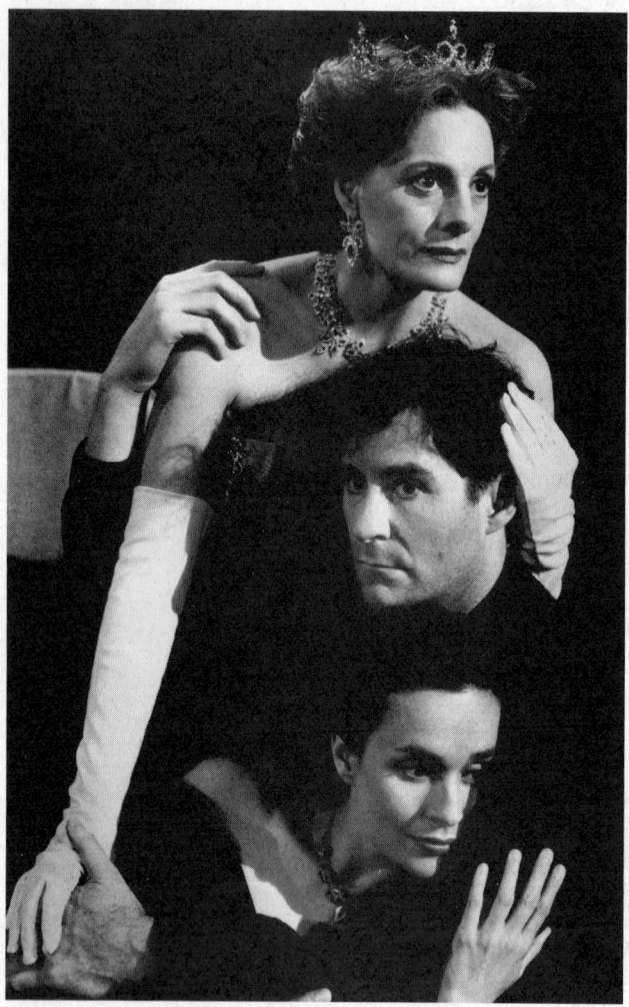

Hamlet (Kevin Kline), Queen Gertrude (Dana Ivy) and Ophelia (Diane Venora) contemplate their difficulties in the New York Shakespeare Festival production of *Hamlet* (1990), directed by Mr. Kline for the Public Broadcasting System.

HAMLET.   Nothing.
OPHELIA.   You are merry my lord.
HAMLET.   Who, I?
OPHELIA.   Ay my lord.   115
HAMLET.   O God, your only jig-maker: what should a man do but be
     merry, for look you how cheerfully my mother looks, and
     my father died within's two hours.
OPHELIA.   Nay, 'tis twice two months my lord.
HAMLET.   So long? Nay then let the devil wear black, for I'll have a   120
     suit of sables,° O heavens, die two months ago, and not

121 *sables:* (1) rich fur (2) black mourning garb.

forgotten yet? Then there's hope a great man's memory
may outlive his life half a year, but by'r lady° a' must build
churches then, or else shall a' suffer not thinking on,° with
the hobby-horse,° whose epitaph is "For O, for O, the   125
hobby-horse is forgot."

*The trumpets sound. The Dumb Show° follows. Enter a King and a Queen, very lovingly, the Queen
embracing him, and he her. She kneels and makes show of protestation unto him. He takes her up,
and declines his head upon her neck. He lies him down upon a bank of flowers; she seeing him asleep
leaves him: anon comes in another man, takes off his crown, kisses it, pours poison in the sleeper's
ears, and leaves him: the Queen returns, finds the King dead, and makes passionate action. The
poisoner with some three or four mutes° comes in again, seeming to condole with her. The dead body
is carried away. The poisoner wooes the Queen with gifts: she seems harsh and unwilling awhile, but
in the end accepts his love.*

                                                                    Exeunt.

OPHELIA.   What means this, my lord?
HAMLET.   Marry, this is miching mallecho,° it means mischief.
OPHELIA.   Belike this show imports the argument° of the play.

Enter PROLOGUE.

HAMLET.   We shall know by this fellow: the players cannot keep   130
   counsel,° they'll tell all.
OPHELIA.   Will a' tell us what this show meant?
HAMLET.   Ay, or any show that you will show him. Be not you
   ashamed to show, he'll not shame to tell you what it
   means.   135
OPHELIA.   You are naught,° you are naught, I'll mark the play.
PROLOGUE.   For us and for our tragedy,
   Here stooping to your clemency,
   We beg your hearing patiently.   *[Exit.]*
HAMLET.   Is this a prologue, or the posy° of a ring?   140
OPHELIA.   'Tis brief, my lord.
HAMLET.   As woman's love.

Enter PLAYER KING and QUEEN.

PLAYER KING.   Full thirty times hath Phoebus' cart° gone round
   Neptune's salt wash,° and Tellus' orbèd ground,°
   And thirty dozen moons with borrowed sheen   145
   About the world have times twelve thirties been,
   Since love our hearts, and Hymen° did our hands
   Unite commutual,° in most sacred bands.

---

123 *by'r lady:* by Our Lady (the Virgin Mary).   124 *not thinking on:* being forgotten.   125 *hobby-
horse:* (1) character in the May games (2) slang for "prostitute."   126 S.D.: *Dumb Show:* pantomimed synopsis of the action to follow.   126 S.D.: *mutes:* actors without speaking parts.   128 *miching mallecho:*
skulking mischief.   129 *imports the argument:* signifies the plot.   131 *counsel:* a secret.   136 *naught:*
naughty, lewd.   140 *posy:* motto (engraved in a ring).   143 *Phoebus' cart:* chariot of the sun.   144 *wash:*
sea. *Tellus . . . ground:* the earth (Tellus was a Roman earth goddess).   147 *Hymen:* Roman god of marriage.   148 *commutual:* mutually.

PLAYER QUEEN.   So many journeys may the sun and moon
    Make us again count o'er ere love be done,   150
    But woe is me, you are so sick of late,
    So far from cheer, and from your former state,
    That I distrust you:° yet though I distrust,
    Discomfort you, my lord, it nothing must.
    For women fear too much, even as they love,   155
    And women's fear and love hold quantity,°
    In neither aught, or in extremity:°
    Now what my love is, proof° hath made you know,
    And as my love is sized, my fear is so.
    Where love is great, the littlest doubts are fear,   160
    Where little fears grow great, great love grows there.
PLAYER KING.   Faith, I must leave thee love, and shortly too,
    My operant° powers their functions leave° to do,
    And thou shalt live in this fair world behind,
    Honoured, beloved, and haply° one as kind   165
    For husband shalt thou—
PLAYER QUEEN.   O confound the rest:
    Such love must needs be treason in my breast.
    In second husband let me be accurst,
    None wed the second, but who killed the first.
HAMLET.   [Aside.] That's wormwood,° wormwood.   170
PLAYER QUEEN.   The instances° that second marriage move°
    Are base respects of thrift,° but none of love.
    A second time I kill my husband dead,
    When second husband kisses me in bed.
PLAYER KING.   I do believe you think what now you speak,   175
    But what we do determine, oft we break:
    Purpose is but the slave to memory
    Of violent birth but poor validity.°
    Which now like fruit unripe sticks on the tree,
    But fall unshaken when they mellow be.   180
    Most necessary 'tis that we forget
    To pay ourselves what to ourselves is debt.°
    What to ourselves in passion we propose,
    The passion ending, doth the purpose lose.
    The violence of either grief or joy   185
    Their own enactures° with themselves destroy:
    Where joy most revels, grief doth most lament;
    Grief joys, joy grieves, on slender accident.
    This world is not for aye,° nor 'tis not strange
    That even our loves should with our fortunes change: 190
    For 'tis a question left us yet to prove,

---

153 *distrust you:* am worried about you.   156 *quantity:* proportion.   157 *In neither . . . extremity:* their love and fear are either absent or excessive.   158 *proof:* experience.   163 *operant:* vital.   *leave:* cease.   165 *haply:* perhaps.   170 *wormwood:* bitter (like the herb).   171 *instances:* causes.   *move:* motivate.   172 *respects of thrift:* consideration of profit.   178 *validity:* strength.   181–182 *Most . . . debt:* we are easy creditors to ourselves and forget our former promises (debts).   186 *enactures:* fulfillments. 189 *aye:* ever.

Whether love lead fortune, or else fortune love.°
The great man down, you mark his favourite flies,
The poor advanced, makes friends of enemies:
And hitherto doth love on fortune tend,   195
For who not needs, shall never lack a friend,
And who in want a hollow friend doth try,
Directly seasons him° his enemy.
But orderly to end where I begun,
Our wills and fates do so contrary run,   200
That our devices still° are overthrown,
Our thoughts are ours, their ends none of our own.
So think thou wilt no second husband wed,
But die thy thoughts when thy first lord is dead.

PLAYER QUEEN.   Nor earth to me give food, nor heaven light,   205
Sport and repose lock from me day and night,
To desperation turn my trust and hope,
An anchor's° cheer in prison be my scope,
Each opposite that blanks° the face of joy,
Meet what I would have well, and it destroy,   210
Both here and hence° pursue me lasting strife,
If once a widow, ever I be wife.

HAMLET.   If she should break it now.

PLAYER KING.   'Tis deeply sworn: sweet, leave me here awhile,
My spirits grow dull, and fain° I would beguile   215
The tedious day with sleep.   *Sleeps.*

PLAYER QUEEN.   Sleep rock thy brain.
And never come mischance between us twain.   *Exit.*

HAMLET.   Madam, how like you this play?

QUEEN.   The lady doth protest too much methinks.

HAMLET.   O but she'll keep her word.   220

KING.   Have you heard the argument°? Is there no offence in't?

HAMLET.   No, no, they do but jest, poison in jest, no offence
i'th'world.

KING.   What do you call the play?

HAMLET.   The Mouse-trap. Marry, how? Tropically:° this play is the   225
image of a murder done in Vienna: Gonzago is the duke's
name, his wife Baptista, you shall see anon, 'tis a knavish
piece of work, but what of that? Your majesty, and we
that have free° souls, it touches us not: let the galled jade
winch,° our withers are unwrung.°   230

Enter LUCIANUS.

This is one Lucianus, nephew to the king.

OPHELIA.   You are as good as a chorus,° my lord.

---

192 *fortune love:* fortune lead love.   198 *seasons him:* causes him to become.   201 *devices still:* plans always.   208 *anchor's:* hermit's.   209 *opposite that blanks:* contrary event that pales.   211 *here and hence:* in this world and the next.   215 *fain:* gladly.   221 *argument:* plot.   225 *Tropically:* figuratively.   229 *free:* innocent.   229–230 *galled jade winch:* chafed old horse wince (from its sores).   230 *withers are unwrung:* (1) shoulders are unchafed (2) consciences are clear.   232 *chorus:* actor who introduced the action.

HAMLET.   I could interpret between you and your love, if I could see
    the puppets dallying.
OPHELIA.   You are keen my lord, you are keen.°   235
HAMLET.   It would cost you a groaning to take off mine edge.
OPHELIA.   Still better and worse.°
HAMLET.   So you mistake° your husbands. Begin, murderer. Pox,°
    leave thy damnable faces° and begin. Come, the croaking
    raven doth bellow for revenge.   240
LUCIANUS.   Thoughts black, hands apt, drugs fit, and time agreeing,
    Confederate season, else no creature seeing,°
    Thou mixture rank, of midnight weeds collected,
    With Hecate's° ban° thrice blasted, thrice infected,
    Thy natural magic, and dire property,   245
    On wholesome° life usurps immediately.   *Pours the poison in his ears.*
HAMLET.   A' poisons him i'th'garden for's estate, his name's Gonzago,
    the story is extant, and written in very choice
    Italian, you shall see anon how the murderer gets the love
    of Gonzago's wife.   250
OPHELIA.   The king rises.
HAMLET.   What, frighted with false fire°?
QUEEN.   How fares my lord?
POLONIUS.   Give o'er the play.
KING.   Give me some light. Away!   255
ALL.   Lights, lights, lights!   *Exeunt all but* HAMLET *and* HORATIO.
HAMLET.   Why, let the stricken deer go weep,
        The hart ungallèd° play,°
    For some must watch while some must sleep,
        Thus runs the world away.   260
    Would not this° sir, and a forest of feathers,° if the rest of my
    fortunes turn Turk with° me, with two Provincial roses° on
    my razed° shoes, get me a fellowship° in a cry° of players?
HORATIO.   Half a share.°
HAMLET.   A whole one, I.   265
    For thou dost know, O Damon° dear,
        This realm dismantled was
    Of Jove° himself, and now reigns here
        A very very—pajock.°
HORATIO.   You might have rhymed.°   270

---

235 *keen:* (1) sharp (Ophelia's meaning) (2) sexually excited (Hamlet's interpretation).   237 *better and worse:* better wit but a worse meaning, with a pun on "better" and "bitter."   238 *mistake:* mis-take. *Pox:* a plague on it.   239 *faces:* exaggerated facial expressions.   242 *Confederate . . . seeing:* no one seeing me except time, my confederate.   244 *Hecate:* goddess of witchcraft. *ban:* evil spell. 246 *wholesome:* healthy.   252 *false fire:* discharge of blanks (not gunpowder).   257–258 *deer . . . play:* (the belief that a wounded deer wept, abandoned by the others).   258 *ungalled:* unhurt.   261 *this:* i.e., sample (of my theatrical talent). *feathers:* plumes (worn by actors).   262 *turn Turk with:* cruelly turn against. *Provincial roses:* rosettes named for Provins, France.   263 *razed:* slashed, decorated with cutouts. *fellowship:* partnership. *cry:* pack, troupe.   264 *share:* divisions of profits among members of a theatrical production company.   266 *Damon:* legendary ideal friend to Pythias.   268 *Jove:* (Hamlet's father).   269 *pajock:* peacock (associated with lechery).   270 *rhymed:* (used "ass" instead of "pajock").

HAMLET.   O good Horatio, I'll take the ghost's word for a thousand
    pound. Didst perceive?
HORATIO.   Very well my lord.
HAMLET.   Upon the talk of the poisoning?
HORATIO.   I did very well note him.   275

Enter ROSENCRANTZ and GUILDENSTERN.

HAMLET.   Ah ha, come, some music. Come, the recorders.°
    For if the king like not the comedy,
    Why then belike he likes it not, perdy.°
    Come, some music.
GUILDENSTERN.   Good my lord, vouchsafe me a word with you.   280
HAMLET.   Sir, a whole history.
GUILDENSTERN.   The king, sir—
HAMLET.   Ay sir, what of him?
GUILDENSTERN.   Is in his retirement, marvellous distempered.
HAMLET.   With drink sir?   285
GUILDENSTERN.   No my lord, with choler.°
HAMLET.   Your wisdom should show itself more richer to signify
    this to the doctor: for, for me to put him to his purgation,°
    would perhaps plunge him into more choler.
GUILDENSTERN.   Good my lord, put your discourse into some frame,° and   290
    start not so wildly from my affair.
HAMLET.   I am tame sir, pronounce.
GUILDENSTERN.   The queen your mother, in most great affliction of spirit,
    hath sent me to you.
HAMLET.   You are welcome.   295
GUILDENSTERN.   Nay good my lord, this courtesy is not of the right breed.°
    If it shall please you to make me a wholesome° answer, I
    will do your mother's commandment: if not, your pardon°
    and my return shall be the end of my business.
HAMLET.   Sir I cannot.   300
ROSENCRANTZ.   What, my lord?
HAMLET.   Make you a wholesome answer: my wit's diseased. But
    sir, such answer as I can make, you shall command, or
    rather as you say, my mother: therefore no more, but to
    the matter. My mother you say.   305
ROSENCRANTZ.   Then thus she says, your behaviour hath struck her into
    amazement and admiration.°
HAMLET.   O wonderful son that can so 'stonish a mother. But is there
    no sequel at the heels of this mother's admiration? Impart.
ROSENCRANTZ.   She desires to speak with you in her closet°   310
    ere you go to bed.
HAMLET.   We shall obey, were she ten times our mother. Have you
    any further trade with us?

---

    276 *recorders:* soft-toned woodwind instruments, similar to flutes.   278 *perdy:* by God (*pardieu*).
286 *choler:* anger.   288 *purgation:* (1) purging of excessive bile (2) judicial investigations (3) purgatory.
290 *frame:* order.   296 *breed:* (1) species (2) manners.   297 *wholesome:* reasonable.   298 *pardon:* permission to depart.   307 *admiration:* wonder.   310 *closet:* private room, bedroom.

ROSENCRANTZ.   My lord, you once did love me.

HAMLET.   And do still, by these pickers and stealers.°   315

ROSENCRANTZ.   Good my lord, what is your cause of distemper? You do
surely bar the door upon your own liberty, if you deny
your griefs to your friend.°

HAMLET.   Sir, I lack advancement.

ROSENCRANTZ.   How can that be, when you have the voice° of the king   320
himself for your succession in Denmark?

HAMLET.   Ay sir, but 'while the grass grows'°—the proverb is
something musty.°

Enter the PLAYERS with recorders.

O the recorders, let me see one. To withdraw° with you,
why do you go about to recover the wind of me,° as if you   325
would drive me into a toil°?

GUILDENSTERN.   O my lord, if my duty be too bold, my love is too
unmannerly.°

HAMLET.   I do not well understand that. Will you play
upon this pipe°?   330

GUILDENSTERN.   My lord I cannot.

HAMLET.   I pray you.

GUILDENSTERN.   Believe me. I cannot.

HAMLET.   I do beseech you.

GUILDENSTERN.   I know no touch of it° my lord.   335

HAMLET.   It is as easy as lying; govern these ventages° with your
fingers and thumb, give it breath with your mouth, and it
will discourse most eloquent music. Look you, these are
the stops.

GUILDENSTERN.   But these cannot I command to any utt'rance of harmony,   340
I have not the skill.

HAMLET.   Why look you now how unworthy a thing you make of
me: you would play upon me, you would seem to know
my stops, you would pluck out the heart of my mystery,
you would sound me from my lowest note to the top of my   345
compass.° and there is much music, excellent voice in this
little organ,° yet cannot you make it speak. 'Sblood, do you
think I am easier to be played on than a pipe? Call me what
instrument you will, though you can fret° me, you cannot
play upon me.   350

Enter POLONIUS.

God bless you sir.

---

315 *pickers and stealers:* hands (from the prayer, "Keep my hands from picking and stealing").
317–318 *deny . . . friend:* refuse to let your friend know the cause of your suffering.   320 *voice:* vote.
322 *while . . . grows:* (the proverb ends: "the horse starves").   323 *something musty:* somewhat too old
and trite (to finish).   324 *withdraw:* speak privately.   325 *recover . . . me:* drive me toward the wind, as
with a prey, to avoid its scenting the hunter.   326 *toil:* snare.   327–328 *is too unmannerly:* makes me forget my good manners.   330 *pipe:* recorder.   335 *know . . . it:* have no skill at fingering it.   336 *ventages:*
holes, stops.   346 *compass:* range.   347 *organ:* musical instrument.   349 *fret:* (1) irritate (2) play an instrument that has "frets" or bars to guide the fingering.

POLONIUS. My lord, the queen would speak with you, and presently.
HAMLET. Do you see yonder cloud that's almost in shape of a camel?
POLONIUS. By th'mass and 'tis, like a camel indeed.
HAMLET. Methinks it is like a weasel.   355
POLONIUS. It is backed like a weasel.
HAMLET. Or like a whale?
POLONIUS. Very like a whale.
HAMLET. Then I will come to my mother by and by.°
    [*Aside.*] They fool me to the top of my bent.°   360
    I will come by and by.
POLONIUS. I will say so. *Exit.*
HAMLET. "By and by" is easily said.
    Leave me, friends.   [*Exeunt all but* HAMLET.]
    'Tis now the very witching time of night.   365
    When churchyards yawn,° and hell itself breathes out
    Contagion° to this world: now could I drink hot blood,
    And do such bitter business as the day
    Would quake to look on: soft, now to my mother—
    O heart, lose not thy nature,° let not ever   370
    The soul of Nero° enter this firm bosom,
    Let me be cruel, not unnatural.
    I will speak daggers to her, but use none:
    My tongue and soul in this be hypocrites,°
    How in my words somever she be shent,°   375
    To give them seals,° never my soul consent. *Exit.*

Scene 3. [*A room in the castle*]

Enter KING, ROSENCRANTZ, *and* GUILDENSTERN.

KING. I like him not, nor stands it safe with us
    To let his madness range. Therefore prepare you,
    I your commission will forthwith dispatch,°
    And he to England shall along with you:
    The terms of our estate° may not endure   5
    Hazard so near's° as doth hourly grow
    Out of his brows.°
GUILDENSTERN.   We will ourselves provide:°
    Most holy and religious fear it is
    To keep those many many bodies safe
    That live and feed upon your majesty.   10
ROSENCRANTZ. The single and peculiar° life is bound
    With all the strength and armour of the mind
    To keep itself from noyance,° but much more

---

    359 *by and by:* very soon.   **360** *fool me . . . bent:* force me to play the fool to my utmost.
366 *churchyards yawn:* graves open.   **367** *Contagion:* (1) evil (2) diseases.   **370** *nature:* natural affection.
371 *Nero:* (who killed his mother).   **374** *My tongue . . . hypocrites:* I will speak cruelly but intend no harm.
375 *shent:* chastised.   **376** *give them seals:* confirm them with action (as a legal "deed" is confirmed with
a "seal").   **3** *forthwith dispatch:* immediately have prepared.   **5** *terms . . . estate:* circumstances of
my royal office.   **6** *near's:* near us.   **7** *brows:* effronteries. *provide:* prepare.   **11** *peculiar:* individual.
13 *noyance:* harm.

That spirit, upon whose weal° depends and rests
The lives of many; the cess° of majesty   15
Dies not alone, but like a gulf° doth draw
What's near it, with it. O 'tis a massy wheel
Fixed on the summit of the highest mount,
To whose huge spokes, ten thousand lesser things
Are mortised° and adjoined, which when it falls,   20
Each small annexment, petty consequence,
Attends° the boist'rous ruin. Never alone
Did the king sigh, but with a general groan.

KING.   Arm° you I pray you, to this speedy voyage,
For we will fetters put about this fear,   25
Which now goes too free-footed.

ROSENCRANTZ.   We will haste us.

Exeunt [ROSENCRANTZ *and* GUILDENSTERN.]

Enter POLONIUS.

POLONIUS.   My lord, he's going to his mother's closet:
Behind the arras I'll convey myself
To hear the process.° I'll warrant she'll tax him home,
And as you said, and wisely was it said,   30
'Tis meet° that some more audience than a mother,
Since nature makes them partial, should o'erhear
The speech of vantage,° fare you well my liege,°
I'll call upon you ere you go to bed,
And tell you what I know.

KING.   Thanks, dear my lord.   *Exit* [POLONIUS.]   35
O my offence is rank, it smells to heaven,
It hath the primal eldest curse° upon't,
A brother's murder. Pray can I not,
Though inclination be as sharp as will.°
My stronger guilt defeats my strong intent,   40
And like a man to double business bound,
I stand in pause where I shall first begin,
And both neglect; what if this cursèd hand
Were thicker than itself with brother's blood,
Is there not rain enough in the sweet heavens   45
To wash it white as snow? Whereto serves mercy
But to confront the visage of offence°?
And what's in prayer but this two-fold force,
To be forestallèd° ere we come to fall,
Or pardoned being down? Then I'll look up,   50
My fault is past. But O what form of prayer
Can serve my turn? "Forgive me my foul murder":

---

14 *weal:* well-being.   15 *cess:* cessation, death.   16 *gulf:* whirlpool.   20 *mortised:* securely fitted.
22 *Attends:* accompanies.   24 *Arm:* prepare.   29 *the process:* what proceeds.   31 *meet:* fitting.   33 *of
vantage:* from an advantageous position.   *liege:* lord.   37 *primal . . . curse:* curse of Cain.   39 *inclination
. . . will:* my desire to pray is as strong as my determination to do so.   47 *confront . . . offence:* plead in
man's behalf against sin (at the Last Judgment).   49 *forestallèd:* prevented.

That cannot be, since I am still possessed
Of those effects° for which I did the murder:
My crown, mine own ambition, and my queen.   55
May one be pardoned and retain th'offence?
In the corrupted currents of this world,
Offence's gilded hand may shove by justice,
And oft 'tis seen the wicked prize itself
Buys out the law;° but 'tis not so above,   60
There is no shuffling,° there the action lies
In his true nature,° and we ourselves compelled
Even to the teeth and forehead of our faults°
To give in evidence. What then? What rests°?
Try what repentance can. What can it not?   65
Yet what can it, when one can not repent?
O wretched state? O bosom black as death!
O limèd soul, that struggling to be free,
Art more engaged;° help, angels, make assay:°
Bow stubborn knees, and heart with strings of steel,   70
Be soft as sinews of the new-born babe,
All may be well.   [*He kneels.*]

Enter HAMLET.

HAMLET.   Now might I do it pat,° now a' is a-praying,
And now I'll do't, [*Draws his sword.*] and so a' goes to heaven,
And so am I revenged: that would be scanned:°   75
A villain kills my father, and for that,
I his sole son, do this same villain send
To heaven.
Why, this is hire and salary, not revenge.
A' took my father grossly,° full of bread,°   80
With all his crimes° broad blown,° as flush° as May,
And how his audit° stands who knows save heaven,
But in our circumstance and course of thought,
'Tis heavy° with him: and am I then revenged
To take him in the purging of his soul,   85
when he is fit and seasoned° for his passage?
No.   [*Sheathes his sword.*]
Up sword, and know thou a more horrid hent,°
When he is drunk asleep, or in his rage,
Or in th'incestuous pleasure of his bed,   90
At game, a-swearing, or about some act

---

54 *effects:* results.   59–60 *wicked . . . law:* fruits of the crime bribe the judge.   61 *shuffling:* evasion.   61–62 *action . . . nature.* (1) deed is seen in its true nature (2) legal action is sustained according to
the truth.   63 *to the teeth . . . faults:* meeting our sins face to face.   64 *rests:* remains.   68–69 *limèd . . .
engaged:* like a bird caught in lime (a sticky substance spread on twigs as a snare), the soul in its struggle
to clear itself only becomes more entangled.   69 *make assay:* I'll make an attempt.   73 *pat:* opportunely.
75 *would be scanned:* needs closer examination.   80 *grossly:* unpurified (by final rites).   *bread:* self-
indulgence.   81 *crimes:* sins.   *broad blown:* in full flower.   *flush:* lusty.   82 *audit:* account.   84 *heavy:*
grievous.   86 *seasoned:* ready (prepared).   88 *horrid hent:* horrible opportunity ("hint") for seizure
("hent") by me.

That has no relish° of salvation in't,
Then trip him that his heels may kick at heaven,
And that his soul may be as damned and black
As hell whereto it goes; my mother stays,   95
This physic° but prolongs thy sickly days   *Exit.*
KING.   [*Rises.*] My words fly up, my thoughts remain below,
Words without thoughts never to heaven go.   *Exit.*

Scene 4. [*The queen's closet*]

Enter QUEEN *and* POLONIUS.

POLONIUS.   A' will come straight, look you lay home° to him,
Tell him his pranks have been too broad° to bear with,
And that your grace hath screened and stood between
Much heat° and him. I'll silence me° even here:
Pray you be round with him.   5
HAMLET.   [*Within.*] Mother, mother, mother.
QUEEN.   I'll war'nt you,
Fear me not. Withdraw, I hear him coming. [POLONIUS *hides behind the arras.*]

Enter HAMLET.

HAMLET.   Now mother, what's the matter?
QUEEN.   Hamlet, thou hast thy father much offended.   10
HAMLET.   Mother, you have my father much offended.
QUEEN.   Come, come, you answer with an idle° tongue.
HAMLET.   Go, go, you question with a wicked tongue.
QUEEN.   Why, how now Hamlet?
HAMLET.   What's the matter now?
QUEEN.   Have you forgot me?
HAMLET.   No by the rood,° not so,
You are the queen, your husband's brother's wife,
And would it were not so, you are my mother.   15
QUEEN.   Nay, then I'll set those to you that can speak.°
HAMLET.   Come, come, and sit you down, you shall not budge,
You go not till I set you up a glass°
Where you may see the inmost part of you.   20
QUEEN.   What wilt thou do? Thou wilt not murder me?
Help, help, ho!
POLONIUS.   [*Behind the arras.*] What ho! help, help, help!
HAMLET.   How now, a rat? dead for a ducat,° dead.

Kills POLONIUS [*through the arras.*]

POLONIUS.   O I am slain!
QUEEN.   O me, what hast thou done?
HAMLET.   Nay I know not,   25
Is it the king?

92 *relish:* taste.   96 *physic:* (1) medicine (2) purgation of your soul by prayer.   1 *lay home:* thrust
home; speak sharply.   2 *broad:* unrestrained.   4 *heat:* anger.   *silence me:* hide in silence.   11 *idle:* foolish.   14 *rood:* cross.   17 *speak:* i.e., to you as you should be spoken to.   19 *glass:* looking glass.   23 *for a
ducat:* I wager a ducat (an Italian gold coin).

QUEEN.   O what a rash and bloody deed is this!
HAMLET.   A bloody deed, almost as bad, good mother,
    As kill a king, and marry with his brother.
QUEEN.   As kill a king?
HAMLET.   Ay lady, it was my word.   30
    [*To Polonius.*] Thou wretched, rash, intruding fool, farewell,
    I took thee for thy better,° take thy fortune,
    Thou find'st to be too busy is some danger.
    [*To the Queen.*] Leave wringing of your hands, peace, sit you down,
    And let me wring your heart, for so I shall   35
    If it be made of penetrable stuff,
    If damnèd custom° have not brazed° it so,
    That it be proof° and bulwark against sense.°
QUEEN.   What have I done, that thou dar'st wag thy tongue
    In noise so rude against me?
HAMLET.   Such an act   40
    That blurs the grace and blush of modesty,
    Calls virtue hypocrite, takes off the rose°
    From the fair forehead of an innocent love
    And sets a blister there,° makes marriage vows
    As false as dicers' oaths, O such a deed,   45
    As from the body of contraction° plucks
    The very soul and sweet religion makes
    A rhapsody° of words; heaven's face does glow,°
    Yea this solidity and compound mass°
    With heated visage, as against the doom,°   50
    Is thought-sick at the act.
QUEEN.   Ay me, what act,
    That roars so loud, and thunders in the index° ?
HAMLET.   Look here upon this picture, and on this,
    The counterfeit presentment° of two brothers:
    See what a grace was seated on this brow,   55
    Hyperion's curls, the front° of Jove himself,
    An eye like Mars, to threaten and command,
    A station° like the herald Mercury,
    New-lighted on a heaven-kissing hill,
    A combination and a form indeed,   60
    Where every god did seem to set his seal
    To give the world assurance of a man.
    This was your husband. Look you now what follows.
    Here is your husband, like a mildewed ear,°
    Blasting° his wholesome brother. Have you eyes?   65

---

32 *thy better:* the king.   **37** *custom:* habit.   *brazed:* brass-plated (brazened).   **38** *proof:* armor.
sense: sensibility.   **42** *rose:* (symbol of perfection and innocence).   **44** *blister there:* (whores were punished by being branded on the forehead).   **46** *body of contraction:* marriage contract.   **48** *rhapsody:*
(meaningless) mixture.   *glow:* blush.   **49** *solidity . . . mass:* solid earth, compounded of the four elements.
50 *against the doom:* expecting Judgment Day.   **52** *index:* (1) table of contents (2) prologue.
54 *counterfeit presentment:* painted likeness.   **56** *Hyperion:* Greek sun god.   *front:* forehead.
58 *station:* bearing.   **64** *ear:* i.e., of grain.   **65** *Blasting:* blighting.

Could you on this fair mountain leave to feed,°
And batten° on this moor? Ha! Have you eyes?
You cannot call it love, for at your age
The hey-day in the blood° is tame, it's humble,
And waits upon the judgment, and what judgment   70
Would step from this to this? Sense° sure you have
Else could you not have motion,° but sure that sense
Is apoplexed,° for madness would not err,
Nor sense to ecstasy was ne'er so thralled°
But it reserved some quantity of choice   75
To serve in such a difference.° What devil was't
That thus hath cozened you at hoodman-blind°?
Eyes without feeling, feeling without sight,
Ears without hands or eyes, smelling sans all,°
Or but a sickly part of one true sense   80
Could not so mope:° O shame, where is thy blush?
Rebellious hell,
If thou canst mutine° in a matron's bones,
To flaming youth let virtue be as wax
And melt in her own fire. Proclaim no shame   85
When the compulsive° ardour gives the charge,°
Since frost itself as actively doth burn,
And reason panders will.°

QUEEN.   O Hamlet, speak no more,
Thou turn'st my eyes into my very soul,
And there I see such black and grainèd° spots   90
As will not leave their tinct.°

HAMLET.   Nay, but to live
In the rank sweat of an enseamèd° bed,
Stewed in corruption, honeying, and making love
Over the nasty sty.

QUEEN.   O speak to me no more,
These words like daggers enter in mine ears,   95
No more, sweet Hamlet.

HAMLET.   A murderer and a villain,
A slave that is not twentieth part the tithe°
Of your precedent lord, a vice° of kings,
A cutpurse° of the empire and the rule,
That from a shelf the precious diadem stole   100
And put it in his pocket.

QUEEN.   No more.

HAMLET.   A king of shreds and patches—

---

66 *leave to feed:* leave off feeding.   67 *batten:* gorge yourself.   69 *hey-day in the blood:* youthful passion.   71 *Sense:* perception by the senses.   72 *motion:* impulse.   73 *apoplexed:* paralyzed.   74 *sense . . . thralled:* sensibility was never so enslaved by madness.   76 *in . . . difference:* where the difference was so great.   77 *cozened . . . blind:* cheated you at blindman's bluff.   79 *sans all:* without the other senses. 81 *so mope:* be so dull.   83 *mutine:* rebel, mutiny.   86 *compulsive:* compelling.   *gives the charge:* attacks. 88 *panders will:* pimps for lust.   90 *grained:* dyed in grain, unfading.   91 *leave their tinct:* lose their color. 92 *enseamèd:* greasy.   97 *tithe:* one-tenth part.   98 *vice:* buffoon (like the character of Vice in the morality plays).   99 *cutpurse:* pickpocket.

Enter the GHOST *in his night-gown.*°

    Save me and hover o'er me with your wings,
    You heavenly guards. What would your gracious figure?
QUEEN.   Alas, he's mad.   105
HAMLET.   Do you not come your tardy son to chide,
    That lapsed in time and passion° lets go by
    Th'important acting of your dread command?
    O say!
GHOST.   Do not forget: this visitation   110
    Is but to whet thy almost blunted purpose.
    But look, amazement on thy mother sits,
    O step between her and her fighting soul,
    Conceit° in weakest bodies strongest works,
    Speak to her Hamlet.
HAMLET.   How is it with you lady?   115
QUEEN.   Alas, how is't with you,
    That you do bend your eye on vacancy,°
    And with th'incorporal° air do hold discourse?
    Forth at your eyes your spirits° wildly peep,
    And as the sleeping soldiers in th'alarm,   120
    Your bedded° hairs, like life in excrements,°
    Start up and stand an° end. O gentle son,
    Upon the heat and flame of thy distemper
    sprinkle cool patience. Whereon do you look?
HAMLET.   On him, on him, look you how pale he glares,   125
    His form and cause conjoined, preaching to stones,
    Would make them capable.° Do not look upon me,
    Lest with this piteous action you convert
    My stern effects,° then what I have to do
    Will want° true colour,° tears perchance for blood.   130
QUEEN.   To whom do you speak this?
HAMLET.   Do you see nothing there?
QUEEN.   Nothing at all, yet all that is I see.
HAMLET.   Nor did you nothing hear?
QUEEN.   No, nothing but ourselves.
HAMLET.   Why look you there, look how it steals away,
    My father in his habit as he lived,°   135
    Look where he goes, even now out at the portal.   *Exit* [GHOST.]
QUEEN.   This is the very coinage of your brain,
    This bodiless creation ecstasy
    Is very cunning in.°
HAMLET.   Ecstasy?
    My pulse as yours doth temperately keep time,   140

      102.1 S.D.: *night-gown:* dressing gown.   107 *lapsed . . . passion:* having let time elapse and passion
cool.   114 *Conceit:* imagination.   117 *vacancy:* (she cannot see the ghost).   118 *incorporal:* bodiless.
119 *spirits:* vital forces.   121 *bedded:* lying flat.   *excrements:* outgrowths (of the body).   122 *an:* on.
127 *capable:* i.e., of feeling pity.   128–129 *convert . . . effects:* transform my outward signs of sternness.
130 *want:* lack.   *colour:* (1) complexion (2) motivation.   135 *habit . . . lived:* clothing he wore when
alive.   138–139 *bodiless . . . cunning in:* madness (ecstasy) is very skillful in causing an affected person to
hallucinate.

And makes as healthful music. It is not madness
That I have uttered; bring me to the test
And I the matter will re-word, which madness
Would gambol° from. Mother, for love of grace,
Lay not that flattering unction° to your soul,   145
That not your trespass but my madness speaks,
It will but skin and film the ulcerous place,
Whiles rank corruption mining° all within,
Infects unseen. Confess yourself to heaven,
Repent what's past, avoid what is to come,   150
And do not spread the compost° on the weeds
To make them ranker. Forgive me this my virtue,°
For in the fatness° of these pursy° times
Virtue itself of vice must pardon beg,
Yea curb and woo° for leave to do him° good.   155

QUEEN.   O Hamlet, thou hast cleft my heart in twain.

HAMLET.   O throw away the worser part of it,
And live the purer with the other half.
Good night, but go not to my uncle's bed,
Assume° a virtue if you have it not.   160
That monster custom, who all sense doth eat
Of habits evil,° is angel yet in this,
That to the use° of actions fair and good,
He likewise gives a frock or livery
That aptly° is put on. Refrain tonight,   165
And that shall lend a kind of easiness
To the next abstinence, the next more easy:
For use° almost can change the stamp° of nature,
And either . . . the° devil, or throw him out
With wondrous potency: once more good night,   170
And when you are desirous to be blessed,
I'll blessing beg of you. For this same lord,°
I do repent; but heaven hath pleased it so
To punish me with this, and this with me,
That I must be their scourge and minister.°   175
I will bestow° him and will answer well°
The death I gave him; so again good night.
I must be cruel only to be kind;
This bad begins, and worse remains behind.°
One word more, good lady.

QUEEN.   What shall I do?   180

---

144 *gambol:* leap.   145 *unction:* salve.   148 *mining:* undermining.   151 *compost:* manure.
152 *virtue:* sermon on virtue.   153 *fatness:* grossness.   *pursy:* flabby.   155 *curb and woo:* bow and plead.
him: vice.   160 *Assume:* put on the guise of.   161–162 *all sense . . . evil:* confuses the sense of right and
wrong in a habitué.   163 *use:* habit.   165 *aptly:* readily.   168 *use:* habit.   *stamp:* form.   169 *either . . . the:*
(word omitted, for which "tame," "curl," "lodge," and "quell" have been suggested).   172 *lord:* Polonius.
175 *their . . . minister:* heaven's punishment and agent of retribution.   176 *bestow:* stow away.   *answer
wea.* assume full responsibility for.   179 *bad . . . behind:* is a bad beginning to a worse end to come.

HAMLET.   Not this by no means that I bid you do:
    Let the bloat° king tempt you again to bed,
    Pinch wanton on your cheek, call you his mouse,
    And let him for a pair of reechy° kisses,
    Or paddling in your neck with his damned fingers,   185
    Make you to ravel° all this matter out
    That I essentially am not in madness,
    But mad in craft. 'Twere good you let him know,
    For who that's but a queen, fair, sober, wise,
    Would from a paddock, from a bat, a gib,°   190
    Such dear concernings hide? who would do so?
    No, in despite of sense and secrecy,
    Unpeg the basket on the house's top,
    Let the birds fly, and like the famous ape,
    To try conclusions° in the basket creep,   195
    And break your own neck down.°
QUEEN.   Be thou assured, if words be made of breath,
    And breath of life, I have no life to breathe
    What thou hast said to me.
HAMLET.   I must to England, you know that.
QUEEN.   Alack,   200
    I had forgot: 'tis so concluded on.
HAMLET.   There's letters sealed, and my two school-fellows,
    Whom I will trust as I will adders fanged,
    They bear the mandate, they must sweep my way
    And marshal me to knavery:° let it work,   205
    For 'tis the sport to have the enginer°
    Hoist with his own petar,° and't shall go hard
    But I will delve one yard below their mines,
    And blow them at the moon: O 'tis most sweet
    When in one line two crafts directly meet.°   210
    This man shall set me packing,°
    I'll lug the guts into the neighbour room;
    Mother good night indeed. This counsellor
    Is now most still, most secret, and most grave,
    Who was in life a foolish prating knave.   215
    Come sir, to draw toward an end with you.
    Good night mother.   *Exit HAMLET tugging in POLONIUS.*

---

182 *bloat:* bloated with dissipation.   184 *reechy:* filthy.   186 *ravel:* unravel.   190 *paddock, bat, gib:* toad, bat, tomcat ("familiars" or demons in animal shape that attend on witches).   193–196 *Unpeg . . . down:* (the story refers to an ape that climbs to the top of a house and opens a basket of birds; when the birds fly away, the ape crawls into the basket, tries to fly, and breaks his neck. The point is that if she gives away Hamlet's secret, she harms herself).   195 *try conclusions:* experiment.   204–205 *sweep . . . knavery:* (like the marshal who went before a royal procession, clearing the way, so Rosencrantz and Guildenstern clear Hamlet's path to some unknown evil).   206 *enginer:* maker of war engines.   207 *Hoist . . . betar:* blown up by his own bomb.   210 *in one . . . meet:* the digger of the mine and the digger of the countermine meet halfway in their tunnels.   211 *packing:* (1) i.e., my bags (2) rushing away (3) plotting.

ACT 4

Scene 1. [A room in the castle]

Enter KING and QUEEN with ROSENCRANTZ and GUILDENSTERN.

KING.   There's matter in these sighs, these profound heaves,
    You must translate, 'tis fit we understand them.
    Where is your son?
QUEEN.   Bestow this place on us° a little while.

                                               Exeunt ROSENCRANTZ and GUILDENSTERN.

    Ah mine own lord, what have I seen tonight!   5
KING.   What, Gertrude? How does Hamlet?
QUEEN.   Mad as the sea and wind when both contend
    Which is the mightier, in his lawless fit,
    Behind the arras hearing something stir,
    Whips out his rapier, cries "A rat, a rat,"   10
    And in this brainish apprehension° kills
    The unseen good old man.
KING.   O heavy deed!
    It had been so with us° had we been there:
    His liberty is full of threats to all,
    To you yourself, to us, to every one.   15
    Alas, how shall this bloody deed be answered?
    It will be laid to us,° whose providence°
    Should have kept short,° restrained, and out of haunt°
    This mad young man; but so much was our love,
    We would not understand what was most fit,   20
    But like the owner of a foul disease,
    To keep it from divulging,° let it feed
    Even on the pith of life: where is he gone?
QUEEN.   To draw apart the body he hath killed,
    O'er whom his very madness, like some ore   25
    Among a mineral of metals base,°
    Shows itself pure: a' weeps for what is done.
KING.   O Gertrude, come away:
    The sun no sooner shall the mountains touch,
    But we will ship him hence and this vile deed   30
    We must with all our majesty and skill
    Both countenance° and excuse. Ho Guildenstern!

Enter ROSENCRANTZ and GUILDENSTERN.

    Friends both, go join you with some further aid;
    Hamlet in madness hath Polonius slain,
    And from his mother's closet hath he dragged him.   35

---

4 *Bestow . . . us:* leave us.   11 *brainish apprehension:* insane delusion.   13 *us:* me (royal plural).
17 *laid to us:* blamed on me.   *providence:* foresight.   18 *short:* tethered by a short leash.   *out of haunt:*
away from others.   22 *divulging:* being divulged.   25–26 *ore . . . base:* pure ore (such as gold) in a mine of
base metal.   32 *countenance:* defend.

Go seek him out, speak fair, and bring the body
Into the chapel; I pray you haste in this.   [*Exeunt Gentlemen.*]
Come Gertrude, we'll call up our wisest friends,
And let them know both what we mean to do
And what's untimely done: [so haply slander,]   40
Whose whisper o'er the world's diameter,
As level° as the cannon to his blank°
Transports his° poisoned shot, may miss our name,
And hit the woundless° air. O come away,
My soul is full of discord and dismay.   *Exeunt.*   45

Scene 2. [*Another room in the castle*]

Enter HAMLET.

HAMLET.   Safely stowed.
   Gentlemen within: Hamlet, Lord Hamlet!
   But soft, what noise, who calls on Hamlet?
   O here they come.

Enter ROSENCRANTZ and GUILDENSTERN.

ROSENCRANTZ.   What have you done my lord with the dead body?
HAMLET.   Compounded it with dust whereto 'tis kin.   5
ROSENCRANTZ.   Tell us where 'tis that we may take it thence,
   And bear it to the chapel.
HAMLET.   Do not believe it.
ROSENCRANTZ.   Believe what?
HAMLET.   That I can keep your counsel° and not mine own.° Besides,   10
   to be demanded of° a sponge, what replication° should be
   made by the son of a king?
ROSENCRANTZ.   Take you me for a sponge, my lord?
HAMLET.   Ay sir, that soaks up the king's countenance,° his rewards,
   his authorities. But such officers do the king best service in   15
   the end; he keeps them like an apple in the corner of his
   jaw, first mouthed to be last swallowed: when he needs
   what you have gleaned, it is but squeezing you, and
   sponge, you shall be dry again.
ROSENCRANTZ.   I understand you not my lord.   20
HAMLET.   I am glad of it: a knavish speech sleeps in° a foolish ear.
ROSENCRANTZ.   My lord, you must tell us where the body is, and go with
   us to the king.
HAMLET.   The body is with the king, but the king° is not with the
   body. The king is a thing—   25
GUILDENSTERN.   A thing my lord?
HAMLET.   Of nothing, bring me to him. Hide fox, and all after.°   *Exeunt.*

---

42 *As level:* with a straight aim.   *blank:* while bull's-eye at the target's center.   43 *his:* slander's.
44 *woundless:* invulnerable.   10 *counsel:* (1) advice (2) secret.   *keep . . . own:* follow your advice and not
keep my own secret.   11 *demanded of:* questioned by.   *replication:* reply to a charge.   14 *countenance:*
favor.   21 *sleeps in:* means nothing to.   24 *king . . . king:* Hamlet's father . . . Claudius.   27 *Hide fox . . .*
after: (cry in a children's game, like hide-and-seek).

Scene 3. [*Another room in the castle*]

Enter KING *and two or three.*

KING.   I have sent to seek him, and to find the body:
　　How dangerous is it that this man goes loose,
　　Yet must not we put the strong law on him,
　　He's loved of the distracted multitude,°
　　Who like not in° their judgment, but their eyes,　　　　　　　　　　5
　　And where 'tis so, th'offender's scourge° is weighed
　　But never the offence: to bear all° smooth and even,
　　This sudden sending him away must seem
　　Deliberate pause° diseases desperate grown,
　　By desperate appliance° are relieved,　　　　　　　　　　　　　　10
　　Or not at all.

Enter ROSENCRANTZ *and all the rest.*

　　　　　　　　　How now, what hath befallen?
ROSENCRANTZ.   Where the dead body is bestowed my lord,
　　We cannot get from him.
KING.　　　　　　　　　　But where is he?
ROSENCRANTZ.   Without, my lord, guarded,° to know your pleasure.
KING.   Bring him before us.
ROSENCRANTZ.　　　　　　　　Ho, bring in the lord.　　　　　　　15

Enter HAMLET (*guarded*) *and* GUILDENSTERN.

KING.   Now Hamlet, where's Polonius?
HAMLET.   At supper.
KING.   At supper? where?
HAMLET.   Not where he eats, but where a' is eaten: a certain
　　convocation of politic° worms are e'en° at him. Your worm is your　　20
　　only emperor for diet, we fat all creatures else to fat us,
　　and we fat ourselves for maggots. Your fat king and your
　　lean beggar is but variable service,° two dishes but to one
　　table, that's the end.
KING.   Alas, alas.　　　　　　　　　　　　　　　　　　　　　　25
HAMLET.   A man may fish with the worm that hath eat of a king, and
　　eat of the fish that hath fed of that worm.
KING.   What dost thou mean by this?
HAMLET.   Nothing but to show you how a king may go a progress°
　　through the guts of a beggar.　　　　　　　　　　　　　　　　30
KING.   Where is Polonius?
HAMLET.   In heaven, send thither to see. If your messenger find him
　　not there, seek him i'th'other place yourself: but if indeed
　　you find him not within this month, you shall nose him as
　　you go up the stairs into the lobby.　　　　　　　　　　　　　35

　　4 *distracted multitude:* confused mob.　5 *in:* according to.　6 *scourge:* punishment.　7 *bear all:*
carry out everything.　9 *Deliberate pause:* considered delay.　10 *appliance:* remedy.　14 *guarded:* (Hamlet is under guard until he boards the ship).　20 *politic:* (1) statesmanlike (2) crafty.　*e'en:* even now.
23 *variable service:* different types of food.　29 *go a progress:* make a splendid royal journey from one
part of the country to another.

KING.   [*To ATTENDANTs.*] Go seek him there.
HAMLET.   A' will stay till you come.   [*Exeunt.*]
KING.   Hamlet, this deed, for thine especial safety—
    Which we do tender,° as we dearly grieve
    For that which thou hast done—must send thee hence   40
    With fiery quickness. Therefore prepare thyself,
    The bark is ready, and the wind at help,°
    Th'associates tend,° and every thing is bent
    For England.
HAMLET.   For England.
KING.   Ay Hamlet.
HAMLET.   Good.
KING.   So is it if thou knew'st our purposes.   45
HAMLET.   I see a cherub° that sees them: but come, for England.
    Farewell dear mother.
KING.   Thy loving father, Hamlet.
HAMLET.   My mother: father and mother is man and wife, man and
    wife is one flesh, and so my mother: come, for England.   *Exit.*   50
KING.   [*To ROSENCRANTZ and GUILDENSTERN.*]
    Follow him at foot,° tempt him with speed aboard,
    Delay it not, I'll have him hence tonight.
    Away, for every thing is sealed and done
    That else leans on° th'affair, pray you make haste.   [*Exeunt.*]
    And England,° if my love thou hold'st at aught°—   55
    As my great power thereof may give thee sense,
    Since yet thy cicatrice° looks raw and red
    After the Danish sword, and thy free awe
    Pays homage° to us—thou mayst not coldly set°
    Our sovereign process,° which imports at full   60
    By letters congruing° to that effect,
    The present° death of Hamlet. Do it England,
    For like the hectic° in my blood he rages,
    And thou must cure me; till I know 'tis done,
    Howe'er my haps,° my joys were ne'er begun.   *Exit.*   65

Scene 4. [*A plain in Denmark*]

Enter FORTINBRAS with his army over the stage.

FORTINBRAS.   Go captain, from me greet the Danish king,
    Tell him that by his license, Fortinbras
    Craves the conveyance° of a promised march
    Over his kingdom. You know the rendezvous:
    If that his majesty would aught with us,   5
    We shall express our duty in his eye,°
    And let him know so.

---

39 *tender:* cherish.   42 *at help:* helpful.   43 *tend:* wait.   46 *cherub:* (considered the watchmen of heaven).   51 *at foot:* at his heels.   54 *leans on:* relates to.   55 *England:* King of England.   *my love . . . aught:* you place any value on my favor.   57 *cicatrice:* scar.   58–59 *free . . . homage:* awe which you, though free, still show by paying homage.   59 *coldly set:* lightly estimate.   60 *process:* command.   61 *congruing:* agreeing.   62 *present:* immediate.   63 *hectic:* fever.   65 *haps:* fortunes.   3 *conveyance of:* escort for.   6 *in his eye:* face to face.

CAPTAIN.   I will do't, my lord.
FORTINBRAS.   Go softly° on.   *Exit.*

Enter HAMLET, ROSENCRANTZ, [GUILDENSTERN,] *etc.*

HAMLET.   Good sir whose powers° are these?
CAPTAIN.   They are of Norway sir.
HAMLET.   How purposed sir I pray you?   10
CAPTAIN.   Against some part of Poland.
HAMLET.   Who commands them sir?
CAPTAIN.   The nephew to old Norway, Fortinbras.
HAMLET.   Goes it against the main° of Poland sir,   15
     Or for some frontier?
CAPTAIN.   Truly to speak, and with no addition,
     We go to gain a little patch of ground
     That hath in it no profit but the name.°
     To pay five ducats, five, I would not farm it;   20
     Nor will it yield to Norway or the Pole
     A ranker° rate, should it be sold in fee.°
HAMLET.   Why then the Polack never will defend it.
CAPTAIN.   Yes, it is already garrisoned.
HAMLET.   Two thousand souls, and twenty thousand ducats   25
     Will not debate the question of° this straw:°
     This is th'imposthume of much wealth and peace,°
     That inward breaks, and shows no cause without
     Why the man dies. I humbly thank you sir.
CAPTAIN.   God bye you sir.   [*Exit.*]
ROSENCRANTZ.   Will't please you go my lord?   30
HAMLET.   I'll be with you straight, go a little before.

                               [*Exeunt all but* HAMLET.]

     How all occasions do inform against me,
     And spur my dull revenge. What is a man
     If his chief good and market° of his time
     Be but to sleep and feed? a beast, no more: 35
     Sure he that made us with such large discourse,°
     Looking before and after,° gave us not
     That capability and god-like reason
     To fust° in us unused. Now whether it be
     Bestial oblivion,° or some craven° scruple   40
     Of thinking too precisely on th'event°—
     A thought which quartered hath but one part wisdom,
     And ever three parts coward—I do not know
     Why yet I live to say "This thing's to do,"

---

8 *softly*: slowly.   9 *powers*: troops.   15 *main*: body.   19 *name*: glory.   22 *ranker*: higher (as annual interest on the total).   *in fee*: outright.   26 *debate . . . of*: settle the dispute over.   *straw*: triviality.   27 *imposthume . . . peace*: swelling discontent (inner abscess) resulting from too much wealth and peace.   34 *market*: profit.   36 *discourse*: power of reasoning.   37 *Looking . . . after*: seeing causes and effects.   39 *fust*: grow moldy.   40 *Bestial oblivion*: forgetfulness, as a beast forgets its parents.   *craven*: cowardly.   41 *event*: outcome.

Sith I have cause, and will, and strength, and means   45
To do't; examples gross° as earth exhort me:
Witness this army of such mass and charge,°
Led by a delicate and tender° prince,
Whose spirit with divine ambition puffed,
Makes mouths° at the invisible event,°   50
Exposing what is mortal, and unsure,
To all that fortune, death, and danger dare,
Even for an egg-shell. Rightly to be great,
Is not to stir without great argument,
But greatly to find quarrel in a straw   55
When honour's at the stake.° How stand I then
That have a father killed, a mother stained,
Excitements° of my reason, and my blood,
And let all sleep, while to my shame I see
The imminent death of twenty thousand men,   60
That for a fantasy and trick° of fame
Go to their graves like beds, fight for a plot
Whereon the numbers cannot try the cause,°
Which is not tomb enough and continent°
To hide the slain. O from this time forth,   65
My thoughts be bloody, or be nothing worth.   *Exit.*

Scene 5. [A room in the castle]

Enter QUEEN, HORATIO and a GENTLEMAN.

QUEEN.   I will not speak with her.
GENTLEMAN.   She is importunate, indeed distract,°
    Her mood will needs be° pitied.
QUEEN.   What would she have?
GENTLEMAN.   She speaks much of her father, says she hears
    There's tricks i'th'world, and hems,° and beats her heart,   5
    Spurns enviously at straws,° speaks things in doubt°
    That carry but half sense: her speech is nothing,
    Yet the unshapèd use of it doth move
    The hearers to collection;° they aim° at it,
    And botch° the words up fit to their own thoughts,   10
    Which as her winks, and nods, and gestures yield them,
    Indeed would make one think there might be thought,
    Though nothing sure, yet much unhappily.
HORATIO.   'Twere good she were spoken with, for she may strew
    Dangerous conjectures in ill-breeding minds.   15

---

46 *gross:* obvious. 47 *charge:* expense. 48 *delicate and tender:* gentle and young. 50 *mouths:* faces. *event:* outcome. 53–56 *Rightly . . . stake:* the truly great do not fight without just cause ("argument"), but it is nobly ("greatly") done to fight even for a trifle if honor is at stake. 58 *Excitements:* incentives. 61 *fantasy and trick:* illusion and trifle. 63 *Whereon . . . cause:* too small to accommodate all the troops fighting for it. 64 *continent:* container. 2 *distract:* insane. 3 *will needs be:* needs to be. 5 *hems:* coughs. 6 *Spurns . . . straws:* reacts maliciously to trifles. *in doubt:* ambiguous. 9 *collection:* inference. *arm:* guess. 10 *botch:* patch.

QUEEN.   Let her come in.   *Exit* GENTLEMAN.
    [*Aside.*] To my sick soul, as sin's true nature is;°
    Each toy° seems prologue to some great amiss,°
    So full of artless jealousy° is guilt,
    It spills itself, in fearing to be spilt.   20

Enter OPHELIA, *distracted.*°

OPHELIA.   Where is the beauteous majesty of Denmark?
QUEEN.   How now Ophelia?

OPHELIA.   [*Sings.*] How should I your true love know
                    From another one?
                    By his cockle hat and staff,°   25
                    And his sandal shoon.°

QUEEN.   Alas sweet lady, what imports this song?
OPHELIA.   Say you? nay, pray you mark.

        [*Sings.*] He is dead and gone, lady,
                    He is dead and gone,
                    At his head a grass-green turf,   30
                    At his heels a stone.
                O ho.
QUEEN.   Nay but Ophelia—
OPHELIA.   Pray you mark.

        [*Sings.*] White his shroud as the mountain snow—

Enter King.

QUEEN.   Alas, look here my lord,   35
OPHELIA.   [*Sings.*] Larded° all with sweet flowers,
                    Which bewept to the ground did not go,
                    With true-love showers.

KING.   How do you, pretty lady?
OPHELIA.   Well, God 'ild° you. They say the owl was a baker's
    daughter.° Lord, we know what we are, but know not what   40
    we may be. God be at your table.°
KING.   Conceit° upon her father.
OPHELIA.   Pray you let's have no words of this, but when they ask
    you what it means, say you this: 45

        [*Sings.*] Tomorrow is Saint Valentine's day,
                    All in the morning betime,°
                    And I a maid at your window
                    To be your Valentine.
                    Then up he rose, and donned his clo'es,   50

---

17 *as sin's . . . is:* as is natural for the guilty.   18 *toy:* trifle.   *amiss:* disaster.   19 *artless jealousy:* uncontrollable suspicion.   20 S.D.: *distracted:* insane.   25 *cockle hat and staff:* (marks of the pilgrim, the
cockle shell symbolizing his journey to the shrine of St. James; the pilgrim was a common metaphor for the
lover).   26 *shoon:* shoes.   36 *Larded:* trimmed.   40 *God 'ild:* God yield (reward).   40–41 *owl . . . daughter:* (in a medieval legend, a baker's daughter was turned into an owl because she gave Jesus short weight
on a loaf of bread).   42 *God . . . table:* (a blessing at dinner).   43 *Conceit:* thinking.   47 *betime:* early (because the first woman a man saw on Valentine's Day would be his true love).

And dupped° the chamber door,
Let in the maid, that out a maid,
   Never departed more.

KING.   Pretty Ophelia.

OPHELIA.   Indeed, la, without an oath I'll make an end on't.   55

[*Sings.*] By Gis° and by Saint Charity,
   Alack and fie for shame,
Young men will do't, if they come to't,
   By Cock° they are to blame.
Quoth she, Before you tumbled me,   60
   You promised me to wed.
He answers. So would I ha' done, by yonder sun,
   An° thou hadst not come to my bed.

KING.   How long hath she been thus?   65

OPHELIA.   I hope all will be well. We must be patient, but I cannot
choose but weep to think they would lay him i'th' cold
ground. My brother shall know of it, and so I thank you
for your good counsel. Come, my coach: good night
ladies, good night. Sweet ladies, good night, good night.   [*Exit OPHELIA.*]   70

KING.   Follow her close, give her good watch I pray you.   [*Exit HORATIO.*]
O this is the poison of deep grief, it springs
All from her father's death, and now behold:
O Gertrude, Gertrude,
When sorrows come, they come not single spies,   75
But in battalions: first her father slain,
Next, your son gone, and he most violent author
Of his own just remove, the people muddied,°
Thick and unwholesome in their thoughts and whispers
For good Polonius' death: and we have done but greenly°   80
In hugger-mugger° to inter him: poor Ophelia
Divided from herself and her fair judgment,
Without the which we are pictures or mere beasts,
Last, and as much containing° as all these,
Her brother is in secret come from France,   85
Feeds on his wonder,° keeps himself in clouds,°
And wants not buzzers° to infect his ear
With pestilent speeches of his father's death,
Wherein necessity, of matter beggared,
Will nothing stick our person to arraign°   90
In ear and ear:° O my dear Gertrude, this
Like to a murdering-piece° in many places
Gives me superfluous death.   *A noise within.*

QUEEN.   Alack, what noise is this?

---

51 *dupped:* opened.   **56** *Gis:* contraction of "Jesus."   **59** *Cock:* (vulgarization of "God" in oaths).
64 *An:* if.   **78** *muddied:* stirred up.   **80** *done but greenly:* acted like amateurs.   **81** *hugger-mugger:* secret
haste.   **84** *containing:* i.e., cause for sorrow.   **86** *Feeds . . . wonder:* sustains himself by wondering about
his father's death.   *clouds:* gloom, obscurity.   **87** *wants not buzzers:* lacks not whispering gossips.
89–90 *Wherein . . . arraign:* in which the tellers, lacking facts, will not hesitate to accuse me.   **91** *In ear and
ear:* whispering from one ear to another.   **92** *murdering-piece:* small cannon shooting shrapnel, to inflict
numerous wounds.

KING.   Attend!   *Enter a* MESSENGER.
    Where are my Switzers°. Let them guard the door.   95
    What is the matter?
MESSENGER.   Save yourself, my lord.
    The ocean, overpeering of his list,°
    Eats not the flats° with more impiteous haste
    Than young Laertes in a riotous head°
    O'erbears your officers: the rabble call him lord,   100
    And as the world were now but to begin,
    Antiquity forgot, custom not known,
    The ratifiers and props of every word,
    They cry "Choose we, Laertes shall be king!"
    Caps, hands, and tongues applaud it to the clouds,   105
    "Laertes shall be king, Laertes king!"   *A noise within.*
QUEEN.   How cheerfully on the false trail they cry.
    O this is counter,° you false Danish dogs.
KING.   The doors are broke.

Enter LAERTES *with others.*

LAERTES.   Where is this king? Sirs, stand you all without.°   110
DANES.   No, let's come in.
LAERTES.   I pray you give me leave.°
DANES.   We will, we will.   [*They retire.*]
LAERTES.   I thank you, keep the door. O thou vile king,
    Give me my father.
QUEEN.   Calmly, good Laertes.
LAERTES.   That drop of blood that's calm proclaims me bastard,   115
    Cries cuckold° to my father, brands° the harlot
    Even here between the chaste unsmirchèd brows
    Of my true mother.
KING.   What is the cause Laertes,
    That thy rebellion looks so giant-like?
    Let him go Gertrude, do not fear° our person,   120
    There's such divinity° doth hedge a king,
    That treason can but peep to° what it would,
    Acts little of his° will. Tell me Laertes,
    Why thou art this incensed. Let him go Gertrude.
    Speak man.   125
LAERTES.   Where is my father?
KING.   Dead.
QUEEN.   But not by him.
KING.   Let him demand his fill.

---

    95 *Switzers:* Swiss guards.   **97** *overpeering . . . list:* rising above its usual limits.   **98** *flats:* lowlands.
99 *head:* armed force.   **108** *counter:* following the scent backward.   **110** *without:* outside.   **111** *leave:*
i.e., to enter alone.   **116** *cuckold:* betrayed husband.   *brands:* (so harlots were punished).   **120** *fear:* i.e.,
for.   **121** *divinity:* divine protection.   **122** *peep to:* strain to see.   **123** *his:* treason's.

LAERTES.   How came he dead? I'll not be juggled with.
　　To hell allegiance, vows to the blackest devil,
　　Conscience and grace, to the profoundest pit.　　　　　　　　　　　130
　　I dare damnation: to this point I stand,
　　That both the worlds I give to negligence,°
　　Let come what comes, only I'll be revenged
　　Most throughly for my father.
KING.　　　　　　　　　　　Who shall stay you?
LAERTES.   My will, not all the world's:°　　　　　　　　　　　　　135
　　And for my means, I'll husband° them so well,
　　They shall go far with little.
KING.　　　　　　　　　　　Good Laertes,
　　If you desire to know the certainty
　　Of your dear father, is't writ in your revenge
　　That swoopstake,° you will draw both friend and foe,　　　　　　140
　　Winner and loser?
LAERTES.   None but his enemies.
KING.　　　　　　　　　　　Will you know them then?
LAERTES.   To his good friends thus wide I'll ope my arms,
　　And like the kind life-rend'ring pelican,°
　　Repast them with my blood.
KING.　　　　　　　　　　　Why now you speak　　　　　　　　145
　　Like a good child, and a true gentleman.
　　That I am guiltless of your father's death,
　　And am most sensibly° in grief for it,
　　It shall as level° to your judgment 'pear
　　As day does to your eye.　　　　　　　　　　　　　　　　　　150

　　[A noise within.]

　　[Crowd shouts.] Let her come in.
LAERTES.   How now, what noise is that?

Enter OPHELIA.

　　O heat, dry up my brains, tears seven time salt,
　　Burn out the sense and virtue° of mine eye!
　　By heaven, thy madness shall be paid with weight,°
　　Till our scale turn the beam,° O rose of May,　　　　　　　　　155
　　Dear maid, kind sister, sweet Ophelia:
　　O heavens, is't possible a young maid's wits
　　Should be as mortal as an old man's life?
　　Nature is fine in love, and where 'tis fine,
　　It sends some previous instance of itself　　　　　　　　　　　160
　　after the thing it loves.°

---

　　　132 *both . . . negligence:* I care nothing for this world or the next.　**135** *world's:* i.e., will.
136 *husband.* economize.　**140** *swoopstake:* sweeping in all the stakes in a game, both of winner and
loser.　**144** *pelican:* (the mother pelican was believed to nourish her young with blood pecked from her
own breast).　**148** *sensibly:* feelingly.　**149** *level:* plain.　**153** *sense and virtue:* feeling and power.
154 *with weight:* with equal weight.　**155** *turn the beam:* outweigh the other side.　**159–161** *Nature . . .*
loves: filial love that is so refined and pure sends some precious token (her wits) after the beloved dead.

OPHELIA. [*Sings.*] They bore him barefaced on the bier,
     Hey non nonny, nonny, hey nonny:
     And in his grave rained many a tear—

  Fare you well my dove.   165
LAERTES. Hadst thou thy wits, and didst persuade revenge,
 It could not move thus.
OPHELIA. You must sing "adown adown," and you call him adown-a.
 O how the wheel becomes it.° It is the false steward that
 stole his master's daughter.   170
LAERTES. This nothing's more than matter.°
OPHELIA. There's rosemary,° that's for remembrance, pray you love
 remember: and there is pansies, that's for thoughts.
LAERTES. A document° in madness, thoughts and remembrance
 fitted.°   175
OPHELIA. There's fennel for you, and columbines.° There's rue° for
 you, and here's some for me, we may call it herb of grace°
 o'Sundays: O, you must wear your rue with a difference.°
 There's daisy,° I would give you some violets,° but they
 withered all when my father died: they say a' made a good 180
 end;
  [*Sings.*] For bonny sweet Robin is all my joy.

LAERTES. Thought and affliction, passion, hell itself,
 She turns to favour and to prettiness.

OPHELIA. [*Sings.*] And will a' not come again,
     And will a' not come again?   185
      No, no, he is dead,
      Go to thy death-bed,
     He never will come again.

     His beard was as white as snow,
     All flaxen was his poll,°   190
      He is gone, he is gone,
      And we cast away moan,
     God ha' mercy on his soul.

 And of all Christian souls, I pray God. God bye you.   195

               Exit OPHELIA.

LAERTES. Do you see this, O God?
KING. Laertes, I must commune with your grief,
 Or you deny me right: go but apart,
 Make choice of whom your wisest friends you will,
 And they shall hear and judge 'twixt you and me;   200

   169 *wheel becomes it:* refrain ("adown") suits the subject (Polonius's fall). 171 *more than matter:* more eloquent than sane speech. 172 *There's rosemary:* (given to Laertes; she may be distributing imaginary or real flowers). 174 *document:* lesson. *thoughts . . . fitted:* thoughts of revenge matched with remembrance of Polonius. 176 *fennel columbines:* (given to the king, symbolizing flattery and ingratitude). *rue:* (given to the queen, symbolizing sorrow or repentance). 177 *herb of grace:* (because it symbolizes repentance). 178 *with a difference:* for a different reason (Ophelia's is for sorrow and the queen's for repentance). 179 *daisy:* (symbolizing dissembling). *violets:* (symbolizing faithfulness). 191 *flaxen . . . poll:* white was his head.

If by direct or by collateral° hand
They find us touched,° we will our kingdom give,
Our crown, our life, and all that we call ours
To you in satisfaction; but if not,
Be you content to lend your patience to us,   205
And we shall jointly labour with your soul
To give it due content.
LAERTES.   Let this be so.
His means of death, his obscure funeral,
No trophy,° sword, nor hatchment° o'er his bones,
No noble rite, nor formal ostentation,°   210
Cry° to be heard as 'twere from heaven to earth,
That I must call't in question.
KING.   So you shall,
And where th'offence is, let the great axe fall.
I pray you go with me.   [*Exeunt.*]

Scene 6. [*Another room in the castle*]

Enter HORATIO *and others.*

HORATIO.   What are they that would speak with me?
GENTLEMAN.   Seafaring men sir, they say they have letters for you.
HORATIO.   Let them come in.   [*Exit* ATTENDANT.]
          I do not know from what part of the world
          I should be greeted, if not from Lord Hamlet.   5

Enter SAILORS.

SAILOR.   God bless you sir.
HORATIO.   Let him bless thee too.
SAILOR.   A'shall sir, an't please him. There's a letter for you sir, it
          came from th'ambassador that was bound for England, if
          your name be Horatio, as I am let to know it is.   10
HORATIO.   [*Reads the letter.*] "Horatio, when thou shalt have
          overlooked° this, give these fellows some means to the king,
          they have letters for him. Ere we were two days old at sea,
          a pirate of very warlike appointment° gave us chase.
          Finding ourselves too slow of sail, we put on a compelled   15
          valour, and in the grapple° I boarded them. On the instant
          they got clear of our ship, so I alone became their prisoner.
          They have dealt with me like thieves of mercy,° but they
          knew what they did. I am to do a good turn for them. Let
          the king have the letters I have sent, and repair° thou to me   20
          with as much speed as thou wouldst fly death. I have
          words to speak in thine ear will make thee dumb, yet are

---

201 *collateral*: indirect.   202 *touched*: tainted with guilt.   209 *trophy*: memorial.   *hatchment*:
tablet displaying coat of arms.   210 *ostentation*: ceremony.   211 *Cry*: cry out.   12 *overlooked*: read over.
14 *appointment*: equipment.   16 *in the grapple*: when the pirate ship hooked onto ours.   18 *of mercy*:
merciful.   20 *repair*: come.

they much too light for the bore° of the matter. These good
fellows will bring thee where I am. Rosencrantz and
Guildenstern hold their course for England. Of them I   25
have much to tell thee. Farewell.

                        He that thou knowest thine, Hamlet."
Come, I will give you way° for these your letters,
And do't the speedier that you may direct me
To him from whom you brought them.   *Exeunt.*   30

Scene 7. [*Another room in the castle*]

Enter KING *and* LAERTES.

KING.   Now must your conscience my acquittance seal,°
        And you must put me in your heart for friend,
        Sith you have heard and with a knowing ear,
        That he which hath your noble father slain
        Pursued my life.
LAERTES.   It well appears: but tell me   5
        Why you proceeded not against these feats
        So crimeful and so capital in nature,
        As by your safety, greatness, wisdom, all things else,
        You mainly were stirred up.°
KING.   O for two special reasons,
        Which may to you perhaps seem much unsinewed,°   10
        But yet to me they're strong. The queen his mother
        Lives almost by his looks, and for myself,
        My virtue or my plague, be it either which,
        She's so conjunctive° to my life and soul,
        That as the star moves not but in his sphere,°   15
        I could not but by her. The other motive,
        Why to a public count° I might not go,
        Is the great love the general gender° bear him,
        Who dipping all his faults in their affection,
        Would like the spring that turneth wood to stone,°   20
        Convert his gyves to graces,° so that my arrows,
        Too slightly timbered° for so loud a wind,
        Would have reverted to my bow again,
        And not where I had aimed them.
LAERTES.   And so have I a noble father lost,   25
        A sister driven into desperate terms,°
        Whose worth, if praises may go back° again,

---

        23 *bore:* size, caliber.   28 *way:* access (to the king).   1 *my acquittance seal:* confirm my acquittal.
9 *mainly . . . up:* were strongly urged.   10 *much unsinewed:* very weak.   14 *conjunctive:* closely allied.
15 *in his sphere:* (referring to the Ptolemaic belief that each planet, fixed in its own sphere, revolved
around the earth).   17 *count:* accounting.   18 *general gender:* common people.   20 *the spring . . . stone:*
(the baths of King's Newnham in Warwickshire were described as being able to turn wood into stone because of their high concentrations of lime).   21 *Convert . . . graces:* regard his fetters (had he been imprisoned) as honors.   22 *slightly timbered:* light-shafted.   26 *desperate terms:* madness.   27 *go back:* i.e.,
before her madness.

Stood challenger on mount of all the age
For her perfections.° But my revenge will come.
KING.   Break not your sleeps for that, you must not think   30
    That we are made of stuff so flat and dull,
    That we can let our beard be shook with danger,
    And think it pastime. You shortly shall hear more,
    I loved your father, and we love ourself,
    And that I hope will teach you to imagine—   35

Enter a MESSENGER *with letters.*

    How now. What news?
MESSENGER.   Letters my lord, from Hamlet.
    These to your majesty, this to the queen.
KING.   From Hamlet? Who brought them?
MESSENGER.   Sailors my lord they say, I saw them not: 40
    They were given me by Claudio, he received them
    Of him that brought them.
KING.   Laertes you shall hear them:
    Leave us.   *Exit* [MESSENGER]
    [*Reads*] "High and mighty, you shall know I am set naked° on
    your kingdom. Tomorrow shall I beg leave to see your kingly
    eyes, when I shall, first asking your pardon° thereunto,   45
    recount the occasion of my sudden and more strange return.
                              Hamlet."
    What should this mean? Are all the rest come back?
    Or is it some abuse,° and no such thing?
LAERTES.   Know you the hand?
KING.   'Tis Hamlet's character.° "Naked,"   50
    And in a postscript here he says "alone."
    Can you devise° me?
LAERTES.   I am lost in it my lord, but let him come,
    It warms the very sickness in my heart
    That I shall live and tell him to his teeth,   55
    "Thus didest thou."
KING.   If it be so Laertes—
    As how should it be so? how otherwise?—
    Will you be ruled by me?
LAERTES.   Ay my lord,
    So you will not o'errule me to a peace.
KING.   To thine own peace: if he be now returned,   60
    As checking at° his voyage, and that he means
    No more to undertake it, I will work him
    To an exploit, now ripe in my device,°
    Under the which he shall not choose but fall:
    And for his death no wind of blame shall breathe,   65

    28–29 *challenger . . . perfections:* like a challenger on horseback, ready to defend against the world her claim to perfection.   **43** *naked:* without resources.   **45** *pardon:* permission.   **49** *abuse:* deception.   **50** *character:* handwriting.   **52** *devise me:* explain it.   **61** *checking at:* altering the course of (when the falcon forsakes one quarry for another).   **63** *ripe in my device:* already planned by me.

But even his mother shall uncharge the practice,°
   And call it accident.
LAERTES.   My lord, I will be ruled,
   The rather if you could devise it so
   That I might be the organ.°
KING.   It falls right.
   You have been talked of since your travel much,   70
   And that in Hamlet's hearing, for a quality
   Wherein they say you shine: your sum of parts°
   Did not together pluck such envy from him
   As did that one, and that in my regard
   Of the unworthiest siege.°
LAERTES.   What part is that my lord?   75
KING. A very riband° in the cap of youth,
   Yet needful too, for youth no less becomes°
   The light and careless livery° that it wears,
   Than settled age his sables° and his weeds°
   Importing health and graveness; two months since,°   80
   Here was a gentleman of Normandy—
   I have seen myself, and served against the French,
   And they can° well on horseback—but this gallant
   Had witchcraft in't, he grew unto his seat,
   And to such wondrous doing brought his horse,
   As had he been incorpsed and demi-natured°   85
   With the brave beast. So far he topped my thought,
   That I in forgery of° shapes and tricks
   Come short of what he did.
LAERTES.   A Norman was't?
KING. A Norman.
LAERTES. Upon my life, Lamord.°   90
KING.   The very same.
LAERTES. I know him well, he is the brooch° indeed
   And gem of all the nation.
KING. He made confession° of you,
   And gave you such a masterly report   95
   For art and exercise in your defence,
   And for your rapier most especial,
   That he cried out 'twould be a sight indeed
   If one could match you; the scrimers° of their nation
   He swore had neither motion, guard, nor eye,   100
   If you opposed them; sir this report of his
   Did Hamlet so envenom° with his envy,
   That he could nothing do but wish and beg

---

66 *uncharge the practice:* acquit the plot (of treachery).   69 *organ:* instrument.   72 *your sum of parts:* all your accomplishments.   75 *siege:* rank.   76 *riband:* decoration.   77 *becomes:* befits.   78 *livery:* clothing (denoting rank or occupation).   79 *sables:* fur-trimmed gowns.   *weeds:* garments.   80 *since:* ago. 83 *can:* can do.   86 *incorpsed . . . natured:* made into one body, sharing half its nature.   88 *in forgery of:* imagining.   91 *Lamord:* a name meaning "death" in French.   92 *brooch:* ornament.   94 *confession:* report.   99 *scrimers:* fencers.   102 *envenom:* poison.

Your sudden coming o'er to play with him.
Now out of this—

LAERTES.   What out of this, my lord?   105

KING. Laertes, was your father dear to you?
Or are you like the painting of a sorrow,
A face without a heart?

LAERTES.   Why ask you this?

KING. Not that I think you did not love your father,
But that I know love is begun by time,   110
And that I see in passages of proof,°
Time qualifies° the spark and fire of it:
There lives within the very flame of love
A kind of wick or snuff that will abate it,°
And nothing is at a like goodness still,°   115
For goodness growing to a plurisy,°
Dies in his own too-much. That we would do
We should do when we would: for this "would"° changes,
And hath abatements and delays as many
As there are tongues, are hands, are accidents,   120
And then this "should"° is like a spendthrift sigh,
That hurts by easing,° but to the quick° of th'ulcer:
Hamlet comes back, what would you undertake
To show yourself in deed your father's son
More than in words?

LAERTES.   To cut his throat i'th'church.   125

KING. No place indeed should murder sanctuarize,°
Revenge should have no bounds: but good Laertes,
Will you do this, keep close within your chamber:
Hamlet returned shall know you are come home,
We'll put on° those shall praise your excellence,   130
And set a double varnish on the fame
The Frenchman gave you, bring you in fine° together,
And wager on your heads; he being remiss,°
Most generous, and free from all contriving,
Will not peruse the foils, so that with ease,   135
Or with a little shuffling, you may choose
A sword unbated,° and in a pass of practice°
Requite him for your father.

LAERTES.   I will do't,
And for the purpose, I'll anoint my sword.
I bought an unction° of a mountebank°   140

---

111 *passages of proof*: examples drawn from experience. 112 *qualifies*: weakens. 114 *snuff . . . it*: charred end of the wick that will diminish the flame. 115 *still*: always. 116 *plurisy*: excess. 118 *"would"*: will to act. 121 *"should"*: reminder of one's duty. 121–122 *spendthrift . . . easing*: A sigh which, though giving temporary relief, wastes life, as each sigh draws a drop of blood away from the heart (a common Elizabethan belief). 122 *quick*: most sensitive spot. 126 *murder sanctuarize*: give sanctuary to murder. 130 *put on*: incite. 132 *in fine*: finally. 133 *remiss*: easy-going. 137 *unbated*: not blunted (the edges and points were blunted for fencing). *pass of practice*: (1) match for exercise (2) treacherous thrust. 140 *unction*: ointment. *mountebank*: quack doctor, medicine man.

So mortal,° that but dip a knife in it,
Where it draws blood, no cataplasm° so rare,
Collected from all simples° that have virtue°
Under the moon,° can save the thing from death
That is but scratched withal: I'll touch my point   145
With this contagion, that if I gall° him slightly,
It may be death.

KING.   Let's further think of this,
Weigh what convenience both of time and means
May fit us to our shape;° if this should fail,
And that our drift° look through° our bad performance,   150
'Twere better not assayed; therefore this project
Should have a back or second that might hold
If this did blast in proof,° soft, let me see,
We'll make a solemn wager on your cunning°—
I ha't: 155
When in your motion you are hot and dry,
As make your bouts more violent to that end,
And that he calls for drink, I'll have prepared him
A chalice for the nonce,° whereon but sipping,
If he by chance escape your venomed stuck,°   160
Our purpose may hold there; but stay, what noise?

Enter QUEEN.

How, sweet queen?
QUEEN.   One woe doth tread upon another's heel,
    So fast they follow; your sister's drowned, Laertes.
LAERTES.   Drowned! O where?   165
QUEEN.   There is a willow grows aslant a brook,
    That shows his hoar° leaves in the glassy stream,
    There with fantastic garlands did she make
    Of crow-flowers,° nettles, daisies, and long purples,°
    That liberal° shepherds give a grosser name,   170
    But our cold° maids do dead men's fingers call them.
    There on the pendent boughs her coronet weeds°
    Clamb'ring to hang, an envious sliver° broke,
    When down her weedy trophies and herself
    Fell in the weeping brook: her clothes spread wide,   175
    And mermaid-like awhile they bore her up,
    Which time she chanted snatches of old tunes,
    As one incapable of° her own distress,

---

141 *mortal:* deadly.   142 *cataplasm:* poultice.   143 *simples:* herbs.   *virtue:* power (of healing).
144 *Under the moon:* (when herbs were supposed to be collected to be most effective).   146 *gall:* scratch.
149 *shape:* plan.   150 *drift:* aim.   *look through:* be exposed by.   153 *blast in proof:* fail when tested (as a
bursting cannon).   154 *cunnings:* skills.   159 *nonce:* occasion.   160 *stuck:* thrust.   167 *hoar:* grey (on the
underside).   169 *crow-flowers:* buttercups.   *long purples:* spike-like early orchid.   170 *liberal:* libertine.
171 *cold:* chaste.   172 *coronet weeds:* garland of weeds.   173 *envious sliver:* malicious branch   178
incapable of: unable to understand.

Or like a creature native and induced
Unto° that element: but long it could not be   180
Till that her garments, heavy with their drink,
Pulled the poor wretch from her melodious lay
To muddy death.
LAERTES.   Alas, then she is drowned?
QUEEN.   Drowned, drowned.
LAERTES.   Too much of water hast thou, poor Ophelia,   185
And therefore I forbid my tears; but yet
It is our trick, nature her custom holds,
Let shame say what it will; when these° are gone,
The woman will be out.° Adieu my lord,
I have a speech o'fire that fain would blaze,   190
But that this folly douts it.°   *Exit.*
KING.   Let's follow, Gertrude,
How much I had to do to calm his rage;
Now fear I this will give it start again,
Therefore let's follow.   *Exeunt.*

ACT 5

Scene 1. [A churchyard]

Enter two CLOWNS°

1. CLOWN.   Is she to be buried in Christian burial,° when she wilfully
      seeks her own salvation?°
2. CLOWN.   I tell thee she is, therefore make her grave straight.° The
      crowner hath sat on her,° and finds it Christian burial.
1. CLOWN.   How can that be, unless she drowned herself in her own   5
      defence?°
2. CLOWN.   Why, 'tis found so.
1. CLOWN.   It must be "se offendendo,"° it cannot be else: for here lies
      the point: if I drown myself wittingly, it argues an act,
      and an act hath three branches, it is to act, to do, and to   10
      perform; argal,° she drowned herself wittingly.
2. CLOWN.   Nay, but hear you, goodman delver.
1. CLOWN.   Give me leave: here lies the water, good. Here stands the
      man, good. If the man go to this water and drown himself,
      it is, will he nill he,° he goes, mark you that. But if the   15
      water come to him, and drown him, he drowns not
      himself. Argal, he that is not guilty of his own death, shortens not his own
         life.

179–180 *indued Unto:* endowed by nature to exist in.   188 *these:* i.e., tears.   189 *woman . . . put:* womanly habits will be out of me.   191 *folly douts it:* tears put it out.   0.2 S.D.: *clowns:* rustics.
1 *Christian burial:* consecrated ground within a churchyard (where suicides were not allowed burial).
2 *salvation:* i.e., "damnation." The gravediggers make a number of such "mistakes," later termed "malapropisms." See p. 353.   3 *straight:* straightaway, at once.   4 *crowner . . . her:* coroner has ruled on her
case.   5–6 *her own defence:* (as self-defense justifies homicide, so may it justify suicide).   8 *"se offendendo".* (he means *"se defendendo,"* in self-defense).   11 *argal:* (corruption of "ergo" = therefore).   15 *will
he nill he:* will he or will he not (willy nilly).

2. CLOWN. But is this law?

1. CLOWN. Ay marry is't, crowner's quest° law.   20

2. CLOWN. Will you ha' the truth on't? If this had not been a
gentlewoman, she would have been buried out o'Christian
burial.

1. CLOWN. Why there thou say'st, and the more pity that great folk
should have countenance° in this world to drown or hang   25
themselves more than their even-Christen.° Come, my
spade; there is no ancient gentlemen but gardeners,
ditchers and grave-makers; they hold up Adam's profession.

2. CLOWN. Was he a gentleman?

1. CLOWN. A' was the first that ever bore arms.°   30

2. CLOWN. Why, he had none.

1. CLOWN. What, art a heathen? How dost thou understand the
Scripture? The Scripture says Adam digged; could he dig
without arms? I'll put another question to thee; if thou
answerest me not to the purpose, confess thyself—   35

2. CLOWN. Go to.

1. CLOWN. What is he that builds stronger than either the mason, the
shipwright, or the carpenter?

2. CLOWN. The gallows-maker, for that frame outlives a thousand
tenants.   40

1. CLOWN. I like thy wit well in good faith, the gallows does well, but
how does it well? It does well to those that do ill. Now
thou dost ill to say the gallows is built stronger than the
church. Argal, the gallows may do well to thee.° To't
again, come.   45

2. CLOWN. "Who builds stronger than a mason, a shipwright, or a
carpenter?"

1. CLOWN. Ay, tell me that, and unyoke.°

2. CLOWN. Marry, now I can tell.

1. CLOWN. To't.   50

2. CLOWN. Mass,° I cannot tell.

1. CLOWN. Cudgel thy brains no more about it, for your dull ass will
not mend his pace with beating, and when you are asked
this question next, say "a grave-maker:" the houses he
makes last till doomsday. Go get thee to Yaughan,° and   55
fetch me a stoup° of liquor.   [*Exit 2. CLOWN.*]

Enter HAMLET and HORATIO afar off.

1. CLOWN. [*Sings.*] In youth when I did love, did love,
         Methought it was very sweet,
         To contract oh the time for a° my behove,°
         O methought there a was nothing a meet.°   60

---

20 *quest:* inquest. 25 *countenance:* privilege. 26 *even-Christen:* fellow Christian. 30 *arms:* (with
a pun on "coat of arms"). 44 *to thee:* i.e., by hanging you. 48 *unyoke:* unharness (your wits, after this
exertion). 51 *Mass;* by the mass. 55 *Yaughan:* probably a local innkeeper. 56 *stoup:* stein, drinking
mug. 59 *oh, a:* (he grunts as he works). *behove:* benefit. 60 *meet:* suitable.

HAMLET.   Has this fellow no feeling of his business, that a'sings in
  grave-making?
HORATIO.   Custom hath made it in him a property of easiness.°
HAMLET.   'Tis e'en so, the hand of little employment hath the
  daintier sense.°   65
1. CLOWN.   [*Sings.*] But age with his stealing steps
                    Hath clawed me in his clutch,
                    And hath shipped me intil° the land,
                    As if I had never been such.   [*Throws up a skull.*]

HAMLET.   That skull had a tongue in it, and could sing once: how the   70
  knave jowls° it to the ground, as if'twere Cain's jaw-bone,°
  that did the first murder. This might be the pate of a
  politician, which this ass now o'erreaches;° one that
  would circumvent° God, might it not?
HORATIO.   It might my lord.   75
HAMLET.   Or of a courtier, which could say "Good morrow sweet
  lord, how dost thou good lord?" This might be my lord
  such-a-one, that praised my lord such-a-one's horse, when
  a'meant to beg it, might it not?
HORATIO.   It might my lord.   80
HAMLET.   Why e'en so, and now my Lady Worm's, chopless,° and
  knocked about the mazzard° with a sexton's spade; here's
  fine revolution an° we had the trick° to see't. Did these
  bones cost no more the breeding, but to play at loggets°
  with them? Mine ache to think on't.   85
1. CLOWN.   [*Sings.*] A pick-axe and a spade, a spade,
                    For and a shrouding sheet,
                    O a pit of clay for to be made
                    For such a guest is meet.°   [*Throws up another skull.*]

HAMLET.   There's another: why may not that be the skull of a   90
  lawyer? Where be his quiddities° now, his quillets,° his
  cases, his tenures,° and his tricks? Why does he suffer this
  rude knave now to knock him about the sconce° with a
  dirty shovel, and will not tell him of his action of battery?
  Hum, this fellow might be in's time a great buyer of land,   95
  with his statutes,° his recognizances,° his fines,° his double
  vouchers,° his recoveries:° is this the fine° of his fines, and
  the recovery° of his recoveries, to have his fine pate full of
  fine dirt? Will his vouchers vouch him no more of his
  purchases, and double ones too, than the length and   100

---

63 *Custom . . . easiness:* being accustomed to it has made him indifferent.   65 *daintier sense:* finer
sensibility (being uncalloused).   68 *intil:* into.   71 *jowls:* casts (with obvious pun).   *Cain's jaw-bone:* the
jawbone of an ass with which Cain murdered Abel.   73 *o'erreaches:* (1) reaches over (2) gets the better of.
74 *would circumvent:* tried to outwit.   81 *chopless:* lacking the lower jaw.   82 *mazzard:* head.   83 *an:* if.
trick: knack.   84 *loggets:* game in which small pieces of wood were thrown at fixed stakes.   89 *meet:* fitting.   91 *quiddities:* subtle definition.   *quillets:* minute distinctions.   92 *tenures:* property holdings.
93 *sconce:* head.   96 *statutes:* mortgages.   *recognizances:* promissory bonds.   96–97 *fines, recoveries:*
legal processes for transferring real estate.   97 *vouchers:* persons who vouched for a title to real estate.
fine: end.   98 *recovery:* attainment.

breadth of a pair of indentures?° The very conveyances° of
his lands will scarcely lie in this box,° and must th'inheritor°
himself have no more, ha?

HORATIO.   Not a jot more my lord.

HAMLET.   Is not parchment made of sheep-skins?   105

HORATIO.   Ay my lord, and of calves'-skins too.

HAMLET.   They are sheep and calves which seek out assurance° in
that. I will speak to this fellow. Whose grave's this, sirrah?

1. CLOWN.   Mine sir:

    [*Sings.*] O a pit of clay for to be made   110
           For such a guest is meet.

HAMLET.   I think it be thine indeed, for thou liest in't.

1. CLOWN.   You lie out on't° sir, and therefore 'tis not yours; for my
part I do not lie in't, and yet it is mine.

HAMLET.   Thou dost lie in't, to be in't and say it is thine: 'tis for the   115
dead, not for the quick,° therefore thou liest.

1. CLOWN.   'Tis a quick lie sir, 'twill away again from me to you.

HAMLET.   What man dost thou dig it for?

1. CLOWN.   For no man sir.

HAMLET.   What woman then?   120

1. CLOWN.   For none neither.

HAMLET.   Who is to be buried in't?

1. CLOWN.   One that was a woman sir, but rest her soul she's dead.

HAMLET.   How absolute° the knave is, we must speak by the card,° or
equivocation° will undo us. By the lord, Horatio, this   125
three years I have took note of it, the age is grown so
picked,° that the toe of the peasant comes so near the heel of
the courtier, he galls his kibe.° How long hast thou been
grave-maker?

1. CLOWN.   Of all the days i'th'year I came to't that day that our last   130
king Hamlet overcame Fortinbras.

HAMLET.   How long is that since?

1. CLOWN.   Cannot you tell that? Every fool can tell that. It was the very
day that young Hamlet was born: he that is mad and
sent into England.   135

HAMLET.   Ay marry, why was he sent into England?

1. CLOWN.   Why because a' was mad: a' shall recover his wits there, or
if a' do not, 'tis no great matter there.

HAMLET.   Why?

1. CLOWN.   'Twill not be seen in him there, there the men are as mad   140
as he.

HAMLET.   How came he mad?

1. CLOWN.   Very strangely they say.

HAMLET.   How strangely?

    100–101 *length . . . indentures:* contracts in duplicate, which spread out, would just cover his grave.
101 *conveyances:* deeds.   **102** *box:* the grave.   *inheritor:* owner.   **107** *assurance:* (1) security (2) transfer
of land.   **113** *on:* of.   **116** *quick:* living.   **124** *absolute:* precise.   *by the card:* exactly to the point (card on
which compass points are marked).   **125** *equivocation:* ambiguity.   **127** *picked:* fastidious ("picky").
128 *galls his kibe:* chafes the sore on the courtier's heel.

1. CLOWN. Faith, e'en with losing his wits. 145

HAMLET. Upon what ground?

1. CLOWN. Why here in Denmark: I have been sexton here man and
     boy thirty years.

HAMLET. How long will a man lie i'th'earth ere he rot?

1. CLOWN. Faith, if a' be not rotten before a' die, as we have many 150
     pocky° corses nowadays that will scarce hold the laying in,
     a' will last you some eight year, or nine year. A tanner will
     last you nine year.

HAMLET. Why he more than another?

1. CLOWN. Why sir, his hide is so tanned with his trade, that a' will 155
     keep out water a great while; and your water is a sore°
     decayer of your whoreson dead body. Here's a skull now:
     this skull hath lain you i'th'earth three-and-twenty years.

HAMLET. Whose was it?

1. CLOWN. A whoreson mad fellow's it was, whose do you think it 160
     was?

HAMLET. Nay, I know not.

1. CLOWN. A pestilence on him for a mad rogue, a' poured a flagon of
     Rhenish° on my head once; this same skull sir, was sir,
     Yorick's skull, the king's jester. 165

HAMLET. This?

1. CLOWN. E'en that.

HAMLET. Let me see. [*Takes the skull.*] Alas poor Yorick, I knew him
     Horatio, a fellow of infinite jest, of most excellent fancy,°
     he hath borne me on his back a thousand times: and now 170
     how abhorred in my imagination it is: my gorge rises at it.
     Here hung those lips that I have kissed I know not how
     oft. Where be your gibes now? your gambols, your songs,
     your flashes of merriment, that were wont to set the table
     on a roar?° not one now to mock your own grinning? quite 175
     chop-fallen?° Now get you to my lady's chamber, and tell
     her, let her paint an inch thick, to this favour° she must
     come. Make her laugh at that. Prithee Horatio, tell me one
     thing.

HORATIO. What's that, my lord? 180

HAMLET. Dost thou think Alexander looked o' this fashion
     i'th'earth?

HORATIO. E'en so.

HAMLET. And smelt so? pah.   [*Puts down the skull.*]

HORATIO. E'en so my lord. 185

HAMLET. To what base uses we may return, Horatio. Why may not
     imagination trace the noble dust of Alexander, til a'find it
     stopping a bung-hole?°

HORATIO. 'Twere to consider too curiously,° to consider so.

---

151 *pocky:* rotten (with venereal disease). 156 *sore:* grievous. 164 *Rhenish:* Rhine wine.
169 *fancy:* imagination. 175 *on a roar:* roaring with laughter. 176 *chop-fallen:* (a) lacking a lower jaw
(2) dejected, "down in the mouth." 177 *favour:* appearance. 188 *bung-hole:* hole in a cask.
189 *curiously:* minutely.

HAMLET.   No faith, not a jot, but to follow him thither with modesty°   190
    enough, and likelihood to lead it; as thus: Alexander died,
    Alexander was buried, Alexander returneth to dust, the
    dust is earth, of earth we make loam,° and why of that loam
    whereto he was converted, might they not stop a
    beer-barrel?   195
          Imperious Caesar, dead and turned to clay,
          Might stop a hole to keep the wind away.
          O that that earth which kept the world in awe,
          Should patch a wall t'expel the winter's flaw.°
    But soft, but soft awhile, here comes the king,   200
    The queen, the courtiers.

Enter KING, QUEEN, LAERTES, [*Doctor of Divinity*], *and a coffin, with Lords attendant.*

                Who is this they follow?
    And with such maimèd° rites? This doth betoken
    The corse they follow did with desp'rate hand
    Fordo it° own life; 'twas of some estate.°
    Couch° we awhile, and mark.   *[They retire.]*   205
HAMLET.   That is Laertes,
    A very noble youth: mark.
LAERTES.   What ceremony else?
DOCTOR.   Her obsequies have been as far enlarged
    As we have warranty: her death was doubtful,°   210
    And but that great command o'ersways the order,
    She should in ground unsanctified have lodged
    Til the last trumpet: for charitable prayers,
    Shards,° flints and pebbles should be thrown on her:
    Yet here she is allowed her virgin crants,°   215
    Her maiden strewments,° and the bringing home
    Of° bell and burial.
LAERTES.   Must there no more be done?
DOCTOR.   No more be done:
    We should profane the service of the dead,
    To sing sage requiem° and such rest to her   220
    As to peace-parted souls.
LAERTES.   Lay her i'th'earth,
    And from her fair and unpolluted flesh
    May violets spring: I tell thee churlish priest,
    A minist'ring angel shall my sister be,
    When thou liest howling.
HAMLET.   What, the fair Ophelia?   225
QUEEN.   [*Scattering flowers.*] Sweets to the sweet, farewell.
    I hoped thou shouldst have been my Hamlet's wife:
    I thought thy bride-bed to have decked, sweet maid,
    And not have strewed thy grave.

---

190 *modesty:* moderation.   193 *loam:* a clay mixture used as plaster.   199 *flaw:* windy gusts.
202 *maimèd:* abbreviated.   204 *Fordo it:* destroy its.   *estate:* social rank.   205 *Couch:* hide.   210 *doubtful:*
suspicious.   214 *Shards:* bits of broken pottery.   215 *crants:* garland.   216 *strewments:* flowers strewn on
the grave.   216–217 *bringing home Of:* laying to rest with.   220 *sage requiem:* solemn dirge.

LAERTES.   O treble woe
  Fall ten times treble on that cursèd head   230
  Whose wicked deed thy most ingenious sense°
  Deprived thee of. Hold off the earth awhile,
  Till I have caught her once more in mine arms;   *Leaps in the grave.*
  Now pile your dust upon the quick° and dead,
  Till of this flat a mountain you have made   235
  T'o'ertop old Pelion,° or the skyish head
  Of blue Olympus.
HAMLET.   [*Comes forward.*] What is he whose grief
  Bears such an emphasis? whose phrase of sorrow
  Conjures the wand'ring stars,° and makes them stand
  Like wonder-wounded hearers? This is I,   240
  Hamlet the Dane.   *HAMLET leaps in after LAERTES.*
LAERTES.   [*Grapples with him.*] The devil take thy soul.
HAMLET.   Thou pray'st not well,
  I prithee take thy fingers from my throat,
  For though I am not splenitive° and rash,
  Yet have I in me something dangerous,   245
  Which let thy wiseness fear; hold off thy hand.
KING.   Pluck them asunder.
QUEEN.   Hamlet, Hamlet!
ALL.   Gentlemen!
HORATIO.   Good my lord, be quiet.

        [*ATTENDANTS part them, and they come out of the grave.*]

HAMLET.   Why, I will fight with him upon this theme
  Until my eyelids will no longer wag.   250
QUEEN.   O my son, what theme?
HAMLET.   I loved Ophelia, forty thousand brothers
  Could not with all their quantity of love
  Make up my sum. What wilt thou do for her?
KING.   O he is mad, Laertes.   255
QUEEN.   For love of God, forbear° him.
HAMLET.   'Swounds,° show me what thou't do:
  Woo't° weep? woo't fight? woo't fast? woo't tear thyself?
  Woo't drink up eisel?° eat a crocodile?°
  I'll do't. Dost thou come here to whine?   260
  To outface me with leaping in her grave?
  Be buried quick with her, and so will I.
  And if thou prate of mountains, let them throw
  Millions of acres on us, till our ground,
  Singeing his pate against the burning zone,°   265

---

231 *sense:* mind.   234 *quick:* live.   236 *Pelion:* mountain (on which the Titans placed Mt. Ossa, to scale Mt. Olympus and reach the gods).   239 *Conjures . . . stars:* casts a spell over the planets. 244 *spenitive:* quick-tempered (anger was thought to originate in the spleen).   256 *forbear:* be patient with.   257 *'Swounds:* corruption of "God's wounds."   258 *Woo't:* wilt thou.   259 *eisel:* vinegar (thought to reduce anger and encourage melancholy).   *crocodile:* (associated with hypocritical tears). 265 *burning zone:* sun's sphere.

Make Ossa° like a wart. Nay, an thou'lt mouth,
I'll rant as well as thou.
QUEEN.   This is mere° madness,
And thus awhile the fit will work on him:
Anon as patient as the female dove
When that her golden couplets° are disclosed,   270
His silence will sit drooping.
HAMLET.   Hear you sir,
What is the reason that you use me thus?
I loved you ever; but it is no matter.
Let Hercules himself do what he may,
The cat will mew, and dog will have his day.   *Exit* HAMLET.   275
KING.   I pray thee good Horatio, wait upon him.   [HORATIO *follows*.]
[*Aside to Laertes*.] Strengthen your patience in our last night's speech,
We'll put the matter to the present push°—
Good Gertrude, set some watch over your son—
This grave shall have a living monument.°   280
An hour of quiet shortly shall we see,
Till then, in patience our proceeding be.   *Exeunt*.

Scene 2. [A hall in the castle]

Enter HAMLET *and* HORATIO.

HAMLET. So much for this sir, now shall you see the other;
     You do remember all the circumstance.
HORATIO.   Remember it my lord!
HAMLET.   Sir, in my heart there was a kind of fighting
     That would not let me sleep; methought I lay   5
     Worse than the mutines in the bilboes.° Rashly—
     And praised be rashness for it: let us know,
     Our indiscretion sometimes serves us well
     When our deep plots do pall,° and that should learn us
     There's a divinity that shapes our ends,
     Rough-hew them how we will—   10
HORATIO.   That is most certain.
HAMLET.   Up from my cabin,
     My sea-gown° scarfed about me, in the dark
     Groped I to find out them, had my desire,
     Fingered° their packet, and in fine° withdrew   15
     To mine own room again, making so bold,
     My fears forgetting manners, to unseal
     Their grand commission; where I found, Horatio—
     Ah royal knavery—an exact command,
     Larded° with many several sorts of reasons,
     Importing Denmark's health, and England's too,   20

---

266 *Ossa:* (see p. 1395, line 236 n.).   267 *mere:* absolute.   270 *golden couplets:* fuzzy yellow twin fledglings.   278 *present push:* immediate test.   280 *living monument:* (1) lasting tombstone (2) living sacrifice (Hamlet) to memorialize it.   6 *mutines* . . . *bilboes:* mutineers in shackles.   9 *pall:* fail.   13 *sea-gown:* short-sleeved knee-length gown worn by seamen.   15 *Fingered:* got my fingers on.   *in fine:* to finish.   20 *Larded:* embellished.

With ho, such bugs and goblins in my life,°
That on the supervise,° no leisure bated,°
No, not to stay° the grinding of the axe,
My head should be struck off.

HORATIO.   Is't possible?   25

HAMLET.   Here's the commission, read it at more leisure.
But wilt thou hear now how I did proceed?

HORATIO.   I beseech you.

HAMLET.   Being thus be-netted round with villainies,
Ere I could make a prologue to my brains,   30
They had begun the play.° I sat me down,
Devised a new commission, wrote it fair°—
I once did hold it, as our statists° do,
A baseness° to write fair, and laboured much
How to forget that learning, but sir now   35
It did me yeoman's° service: wilt thou know
Th'effect of what I wrote?

HORATIO.   Ay, good my lord.

HAMLET.   An earnest conjuration° from the king,
As England was his faithful tributary,
As love between them like the palm might flourish,   40
As peace should still her wheaten garland wear
And stand a comma° 'tween their amities,
And many such like "as'es"° of great charge,°
That on the view and know of these contents,
Without debatement further, more or less,   45
He should those bearers put to sudden death,
Not shriving° time allowed.

HORATIO.   How was this sealed?

HAMLET.   Why even in that was heaven ordinant,°
I had my father's signet° in my purse,
Which was the model° of that Danish seal: 50
Folded the writ up in the form of th'other,
Subscribed° it, gave't th'impression,° placed it safely,
The changeling° never known: now the next day
Was our sea-fight, and what to this was sequent
Thou knowest already.   55

HORATIO.   So Guildenstern and Rosencrantz go to't.

HAMLET.   Why man, they did make love to this employment,°
They are not near my conscience, their defeat

---

22 bugs . . . life: imaginary evils attributed to me, like imaginary goblins ("bugs") meant to frighten children.   23 supervise: looking over (the commission).   leisure bated: delay excepted.   24 stay: await. 30–31 Ere . . . play: Before I could outline the action in my mind, my brains started to play their part. 32 wrote it fair: wrote a finished (neat) copy, a "fair copy."   33 statists: statesmen.   34 baseness: mark of humble status.   36 yeoman's: (in the sense of "faithful").   38 conjuration: entreaty (he parodies the rhetoric of such documents).   42 comma: connection.   43 as'es: (1) the "as" clauses in the commission (2) asses.   charge: (1) weight (in the clauses) (2) burdens (on the asses).   47 shriving: confession and absolution.   48 was heaven ordinant: it was divinely ordained.   49 signet: seal.   50 model: replica.   52 Subscribed: signed.   impression: i.e., of the seal.   53 changeling: substitute (baby imp left when an infant was spirited away).   57 did . . . employment: asked for it.

Does by their own insinuation° grow:
'Tis dangerous when the baser nature comes   60
Between the pass° and fell° incensed points
Of mighty opposites.
HORATIO.   Why, what a king is this!
HAMLET. Does it not, think thee, stand me now upon°—
He that hath killed my king, and whored my mother,   65
Popped in between th'election° and my hopes,
Thrown out his angle° for my proper° life,
And with such cozenage°—is't not perfect conscience
To quit° him with this arm? And isn't not to be damned,
To let this canker of our nature° come
In further evil?   70
HORATIO. It must be shortly known to him from England
What is the issue of the business there.
HAMLET. It will be short, the interim is mine,
And a man's life's no more than to say "One."°
But I am very sorry good Horatio,   75
That to Laertes I forgot myself;
For by the image of my cause, I see
The portraiture of his;° I'll court his favours:
But sure the bravery° of his grief did put me
Into a towering passion.
HORATIO.   Peace, who comes here?   80

Enter young OSRIC.

OSRIC. Your lordship is right welcome back to Denmark.
HAMLET. I humbly thank you sir. [*Aside to Horatio.*] Dost know this
water-fly?
HORATIO. No my good lord.
HAMLET. Thy state is the more gracious,° for 'tis a vice to know him: 85
he hath much land, and fertile: let a beast be lord of beasts,
and his crib shall stand at the king's mess;° 'tis a chough,°
but as I say, spacious in the possession of dirt.
OSRIC. Sweet lord, if you lordship were at leisure, I should
impart a thing to you from his majesty.   90
HAMLET. I will receive it sir, with all diligence of spirit; put your
bonnet° to his right use, 'tis for the head.
OSRIC. I thank your lordship, it is very hot.
HAMLET. No, believe me 'tis very cold, the wind is northerly.
OSRIC. It is indifferent° cold my lord indeed.   95

---

59 *insinuation:* intrusion. 61 *pass:* thrust. *fell:* fierce. 63 *stand . . . upon:* become incumbent upon me now. 65 *election:* (the Danish king was so chosen). 66 *angle:* fishing hook. *proper:* very own. 67 *cozenage:* deception. 68 *quit:* repay, requite. 69 *canker of our nature:* cancer of humanity. 74 *to say "One":* to score one hit in fencing. 77–78 *by the image . . . his:* in the depiction of my situation, I see the reflection of his. 79 *bravery:* ostentation. 85 *gracious:* favorable. 86–87 *let a beast . . . mess:* An ass who owns enough property can eat with the king. 87 *chough:* chattering bird, jackdaw. 92 *bonnet:* hat. 95 *indifferent:* reasonably.

HAMLET.   But yet methinks it is very sultry and hot for my
   complexion.°

OSRIC.   Exceedingly, my lord, it is very sultry, as 'twere, I cannot
   tell how: but my lord, his majesty bade me signify to you
   that a' has laid a great wager on your head. Sir, this is the   100
   matter—

HAMLET.   [*Moves him to put on his hat.*] I beseech you remember—

OSRIC.   Nay good my lord, for mine ease,° in good faith. Sir, here
   is newly come to court Laertes, believe me, an absolute
   gentleman, full of most excellent differences,° of very soft   105
   society, and great showing: indeed to speak feelingly of
   him, he is the card° or calendar of gentry: for you shall find
   in him the continent of what part a gentleman would see.°

HAMLET.   Sir, his definement° suffers no perdition° in you, though I
   know to divide him inventorially would dozy°   110
   th'arithmetic of memory, and yet but yaw neither, in
   respect of his quick sail,° but in the verity of extolment,° I
   take him to be a soul of great article,° and his infusion° of
   such dearth and rareness, as to make true diction of him,
   his semblable° is his mirror, and who else would trace° him,   115
   his umbrage,° nothing more.°

OSRIC.   Your lordship speaks most infallibly of him.

HAMLET.   The concernancy° sir? why do we wrap the gentleman in
   our more rawer breath?°

OSRIC.   Sir?   120

HORATIO.   Is't not possible to understand in another tongue?° You
   will do't sir, really.

HAMLET.   What imports the nomination° of this gentleman?

OSRIC.   Of Laertes?

HORATIO.   His purse is empty already, all's golden words are spent.   125

HAMLET.   Of him, sir.

OSRIC.   I know you are not ignorant—

HAMLET.   I would you did sir, yet in faith if you did, it would not
   much approve me.° Well, sir.

OSRIC.   You are not ignorant of what excellence Laertes is—   130

HAMLET.   I dare not confess that, lest I should compare with him in
   excellence, but to know a man well were to know himself.°

---

   97 *complexion:* temperament.   103 *for mine ease:* for my own comfort.   105 *differences:* accomplishments.   107 *card:* shipman's compass card.   108 *continent . . . see:* (continuing the marine metaphor) (1) geographical continent (2) all the qualities a gentleman would look for.   109–116 *Sir . . . more:* (Hamlet outdoes Osric in affected speech).   109 *definement:* description.   *perdition:* loss.   110 *dozy:* dizzy. 111–112 *yaw . . . sail:* (1) moving in an unsteady course (as another boat would do, trying to catch up with Laertes "quick sail") (2) staggering to one trying to list his accomplishments.   112 *in . . . extolment:* to praise him truthfully.   113 *article:* scope.   *infusion:* essence.   114–116 *as to make . . . more:* to describe him truly I would have to employ his mirror to depict his only equal—himself, and who would follow him is only a shadow.   115 *semblable:* equal.   *trace:* (1) describe (2) follow.   116 *umbrage:* shadow. 118 *concernancy:* relevance.   119 *rawer breath:* crude speech.   121 *Is't not . . . tongue:* Cannot Osric understand his own way of speaking when used by another?   123 *nomination:* naming.   128–129 *if you did . . . me:* If you found me to be "not ignorant," it would prove little (as you are no judge of ignorance). 132 *to know . . . himself:* to know a man well, one must first know oneself.

OSRIC.   I mean sir for his weapon, but in the imputation° laid on
    him by them in his meed,° he's unfellowed.°

HAMLET.   What's his weapon?   135

OSRIC.   Rapier and dagger.

HAMLET.   That's two of his weapons—but well.

OSRIC.   The king sir, hath wagered with him six Barbary horses,
    against which he has impawned,° as I take it, six French
    rapiers and poniards,° with their assigns,° as girdle, hangers,°   140
    and so. Three of the carriages° in faith are very dear to
    fancy,° very responsive to the hilts, most delicate carriages,
    and of very liberal conceit.°

HAMLET.   What call you the carriages?

HORATIO.   I knew you must be edified by the margent° ere you had   145
    done.

OSRIC.   The carriages sir, are the hangers.

HAMLET.   The phrase would be more germane to the matter, if we
    could carry a cannon by our sides: I would it might be
    hangers till then, but on: six Barbary horses against six   150
    French swords, their assigns, and three liberal-conceited
    carriages—that's the French bet against the Danish. Why
    is this all "impawned" as you call it?

OSRIC.   The king sir, hath laid sir, that in a dozen passes between
    yourself and him, he shall not exceed you three hits°; he   155
    hath laid on twelve for nine, and it would come to
    immediate trial, if your lordship would vouchsafe the
    answer.°

HAMLET.   How if I answer no?

OSRIC.   I mean my lord, the opposition of your person in trial.   160

HAMLET.   Sir, I will walk here in the hall; if it please his majesty, it is
    the breathing time° of day with me; let the foils be brought,
    the gentleman willing, and the king hold his purpose, I
    will win for him an I can, if not, I will gain nothing but my
    shame and the odd hits.   165

OSRIC.   Shall I re-deliver you° e'en so?

HAMLET.   To this effect sir, after what flourish your nature will.°

OSRIC.   I commend° my duty to your lordship.

HAMLET.   Yours, yours.   [*Exit* OSRIC.]
    He does well to commend it himself, there are no tongues   170
    else for's turn.°

HORATIO.   This lapwing° runs away with the shell on his head.

HAMLET.   A' did comply° sir, with his dug° before a' sucked it: thus
    has he—and many more of the same bevy that I know the

---

    133 *imputation:* repute. **134** *meed:* worth. *unfellowed:* unequaled. **139** *impawned:* staked.
140 *poniards:* daggers. *assigns:* accessories. *girdle, hangers:* belt, straps attached thereto, from which
swords were hung. **141** *carriages:* hangers. **141–142** *dear to fancy:* rare in design. **143** *liberal conceit:*
elaborate conception. **145** *margent:* marginal note. **154–155** *laid . . . three hits:* wagered that in twelve
bouts Laertes must win three more than Hamlet. **158** *answer:* acceptance of the challenge (Hamlet interprets as "reply"). **163** *breathing time:* exercise period. **166** *re-deliver you:* take back your answer.
167 *after . . . will:* embellished as you wish. **168** *commend:* offer (Hamlet interprets as "praise").
170–171 *no tongues . . . turn:* no others who would. **172** *lapwing:* (reported to be so precocious that it
ran as soon as hatched). **173** *comply:* observe the formalities of courtesy. *dug:* mother's breast.

drossy° age dotes on—only got the tune of the time, and   175
out of an habit of encounter,° a kind of yeasty collection,°
which carries them through and through the most fond
and winnowed° opinions; and do but blow them to their
trial, and bubbles are out.°

Enter a LORD.

LORD.   My lord, his majesty commended him to you by young   180
    Osric, who brings back to him that you attend him in
    the hall. He sends to know if your pleasure hold to play
    with Laertes, or that you will take longer time.
HAMLET.   I am constant to my purposes, they follow the king's
    pleasure, if his fitness speaks,° mine is ready: now or   185
    whensoever, provided I be so able as now.
LORD.   The king, and queen, and all are coming down.
HAMLET.   In happy time.
LORD.   The queen desires you to use some gentle entertainment°
    to Laertes, before you fall to play.   190
HAMLET.   She well instructs me.   *[Exit LORD.]*
HORATIO.   You will lose this wager, my lord.
HAMLET.   I do not think so, since we went into France, I have been in
    continual practice, I shall win at the odds; but thou
    wouldst not think how ill all's here about my heart: but it   195
    is no matter.
HORATIO.   Nay good my lord—
HAMLET.   It is but a foolery, but it is such a kind of gaingiving° as
    would perhaps trouble a woman.
HORATIO.   If your mind dislike any thing, obey it. I will forestall their   200
    repair° hither, and say you are not fit.
HAMLET.   Not a whit, we defy augury;° there is a special providence
    in the fall of a sparrow.° If it be now, 'tis not to come:
    if it be not to come, it will be now; if it be not now,
    yet it will come—the readiness is all. Since no man has   205
    aught of what he leaves, what is't to leave betimes?° let
    be.

*A table prepared. Trumpets, Drums, and officers with cushions. Enter KING, Queen, and all the
state, [OSRIC], foils daggers, and LAERTES.*

KING.   Come Hamlet, come and take this hand from me.
    [Puts Laertes' hand into Hamlet's.]
HAMLET.   Give me your pardon sir, I have done you wrong,
    But pardon't as you are a gentleman.   210

---

175 *drossy:* frivolous.   176 *habit of encounter:* habitual association (with others as frivolous).
yeasty collection: frothy assortment of phrases.   177–178 *fond and winnowed:* trivial and considered.
178–179 *blow . . . out:* blow on them to test them and they are gone.   185 *his fitness speaks:* it agrees with
his convenience.   189 *gentle entertainment:* friendly treatment.   198 *gaingiving:* misgiving.   201 *repair:*
coming.   202 *augury:* omens.   202–203 *special . . . sparrow:* ("Are not two sparrows sold for a farthing?
and one of them shall not fall on the ground without your Father": Matthew 10:29).   206 *betimes:* early
(before one's time).

This presence knows, and you must needs have heard,
How I am punished with a sore distraction.°
What I have done
That might your nature, honour, and exception°
Roughly awake, I here proclaim was madness: 215
Was't Hamlet wronged Laertes? never Hamlet.
If Hamlet from himself be ta'en away,
And when he's not himself, does wrong Laertes,
Then Hamlet does it not, Hamlet denies it:
Who does it then? his madness. If't be so,   220
Hamlet is of the faction that is wronged,
His madness is poor Hamlet's enemy.
Sir, in this audience,
Let my disclaiming from a purposed evil,
Free me so far in your most generous thoughts,   225
That I have shot my arrow o'er the house
And hurt my brother.°

LAERTES.   I am satisfied in nature,
Whose motive in this case should stir me most
To my revenge, but in my terms of honour
I stand aloof, and will no reconcilement,   230
Till by some elder masters of known honour
I have a voice and precedent° of peace
To keep my name ungored:° but till that time,
I do receive your offered love, like love,
And will not wrong it.

HAMLET.   I embrace it freely,   235
And will this brother's wager frankly° play.
Give us the foils: come on.

LAERTES.   Come, one for me.

HAMLET.   I'll be your foil° Laertes, in mine ignorance
Your skill shall like a star i'th' darkest night
Stick fiery off° indeed.   240

LAERTES.   You mock me sir.

HAMLET.   No, by this hand.

KING.   Give them the foils young Osric. Cousin° Hamlet,
You know the wager.

HAMLET.   Very well my lord.
Your grace has laid the odds o'th'weaker side.

KING.   I do not fear it, I have seen you both,   245
But since he is bettered,° we have therefore odds.

LAERTES.   This is too heavy: let me see another.°

---

212 *sore distraction:* grievous madness.   214 *exception:* disapproval.   226–227 *That I have ... brother:* (that it was accidental).   232 *voice and precedent:* opinion based on precedent.   233 *name ungored:* reputation uninjured. Laertes says that he cannot accept Hamlet's apology formally until he is assured that his acceptance will not harm his honor or damage his reputation.   236 *frankly:* freely.   238 *foil:* (1) the blunted sword with which they fence (2) leaf of metal set under a jewel to make it shine more brilliantly.   240 *Stick fiery off:* show in shining contrast.   242 *Cousin:* kinsman.   246 *bettered:* either (a) judged to be better, or (b) better trained.   247 *another:* (the unbated and poisoned sword).

HAMLET.   This likes° me well, these foils have all a° length?
OSRIC.   Ay my good lord.   *Prepare to play.*
KING.   Set me the stoups° of wine upon that table: 250
    If Hamlet give the first or second hit,
    Or quit in answer of° the third exchange,
    Let all the battlements their ordnance fire.
    The king shall drink to Hamlet's better breath,
    And in the cup an union° shall he throw,   255
    Richer than that which four successive kings
    In Denmark's crown have worn: give me the cups,
    And let the kettle° to the trumpet speak,
    The trumpet to the cannoneer without,
    The cannons to the heavens, the heaven to earth,   260
    "Now the king drinks to Hamlet." Come begin.
    And you the judges bear a wary eye.   *Trumpets the while.*
HAMLET.   Come on sir.
LAERTES.   Come my lord.   *They play.*
HAMLET.   One.
LAERTES.   No.
HAMLET.   Judgment.
OSRIC.   A hit, a very palpable hit.

                       Flourish. Drum, trumpets and shot. A piece° goes off.

LAERTES.   Well, again.
KING.   Stay, give me drink. Hamlet, this pearl is thine.   265
    Here's to thy health: give him the cup.
HAMLET.   I'll play this bout first, set it by a while.
    Come.   *[They play.]*
        Another hit. What say you?
LAERTES.   A touch, a touch, I do confess't.
KING.   Our son shall win.
QUEEN.   He's fat° and scant of breath.   270
    Here Hamlet, take my napkin,° rub thy brows.   *[She takes HAMLET's cup.]*
    The queen carouses° to thy fortune, Hamlet.
HAMLET.   Good madam.
KING.   Gertrude, do not drink.
QUEEN.   I will my lord, I pray you pardon me.
KING.   [*Aside.*] It is the poisoned cup, it is too late.   275
HAMLET.   I dare not drink yet madam: by and by.
QUEEN.   Come, let me wipe thy face.
LAERTES.   [*To the King.*] My lord, I'll hit him now.
KING.   I do not think't.
LAERTES.   [*Aside.*] And yet 'tis almost 'gainst my conscience.
HAMLET.   Come for the third Laertes, you do but dally,   280
    I pray you pass° with your best violence,
    I am afeard you make a wanton of me.°

---

248 *likes:* pleases.   *all a:* all the same.   **250** *stoups:* goblets.   **252** *quit in answer of:* score a draw in.   **255** *union:* large pearl.   **258** *kettle:* kettledrum.   **264.1 S.D.:** *piece:* i.e., a cannon.   **270** *fat:* sweating (sweat was thought to be melted body fat).   **271** *napkin:* handkerchief.   **272** *carouses:* drinks.   **281** *pass:* thrust.   **282** *make a wanton of me:* are indulging me like a spoiled child.

LAERTES.   Say you so? Come on.   *Play.*
OSRIC.   Nothing neither way   [*They break off.*]
LAERTES.   Have at you now.°   [*Wounds Hamlet.*]

                                          In scuffling they change rapiers.

KING.   Part them, they are incensed.   285
HAMLET.   Nay, come again.   [*The QUEEN falls.*]
OSRIC.   Look to the queen there, ho!

                                                [*HAMLET wounds LAERTES.*]

HORATIO.   They bleed on both side. How is it, my lord?
OSRIC.   How is't, Laertes?
LAERTES.   Why as a woodcock° to my own springe,° Osric,
   I am justly killed with mine own treachery.   290
HAMLET.   How does the queen?
KING.   She sounds° to see them bleed.
QUEEN.   No, no, the drink, the drink, O my dear Hamlet,
   The drink, the drink, I am poisoned.   [*Dies.*]
HAMLET.   O villainy! ho! let the door be locked,
   Treachery, seek it out!   295
LAERTES.   It is here Hamlet. Hamlet, thou art slain,
   No medicine in the world can do thee good,
   In thee there is not half an hour of life,
   The treacherous instrument is in thy hand,
   Unbated° and envenomed. The foul practice°   300
   Hath turned itself on me, lo, here I lie
   Never to rise again: thy mother's poisoned:
   I can no more: the king, the king's to blame.
HAMLET.   The point envenomed too:
   Then venom, to thy work.   *Hurts the KING.*   305
ALL.   Treason! treason!
KING.   O yet defend me friends, I am but hurt.°
HAMLET.   Here, thou incestuous, murderous, damnèd Dane,
   Drink off this potion: is thy union here?
   Follow my mother.   *King dies.*   310
LAERTES.   He is justly served,
   It is a poison tempered° by himself:
   Exchange forgiveness with me, noble Hamlet,
   Mine and my father's death come not upon thee,°
   Nor thine on me.   *Dies.*
HAMLET.   Heaven make thee free° of it, I follow thee.   315
   I am dead, Horatio; wretched queen, adieu.
   You that look pale, and tremble at this chance,
   That are but mutes,° or audience to this act,
   Had I but time, as this fell sergeant° Death
   Is strict in his arrest, O I could tell you—   320

   285 *Have . . . now:* (the bout is over when Laertes attacks Hamlet and catches him off guard).
289 *woodcock:* snipe-like bird (believed to be foolish and therefore easily trapped).   *springe:* trap.
291 *sounds:* swoons.   300 *Unbated:* not blunted.   *practice:* plot.   307 *but hurt:* only wounded.
311 *tempered:* mixed.   313 *come . . . thee:* are not to be blamed on you.   315 *free:* guiltless.   318 *mutes:*
actors without speaking parts.   319 *fell sergeant:* cruel sheriff's officer.

But let it be; Horatio, I am dead,
Thou livest, report me and my cause aright
To the unsatisfied.°
HORATIO.   Never believe it;
I am more an antique Roman° than a Dane:
Here's yet some liquor left.
HAMLET.   As thou'rt a man,   325
Give me the cup, let go, by heaven I'll ha't.
O God, Horatio, what a wounded name,
Things standing thus unknown, shall live behind me.
If thou didst ever hold me in thy heart,
Absènt thee from felicity awhile,   330
And in this harsh world draw thy breath in pain
To tell my story.   *A march afar off, and shot within.*
                    What warlike noise is this?
OSRIC.   Young Fortinbras with conquest come from Poland,
To th'ambassadors of England gives
This warlike volley.
HAMLET.   O I die Horatio,   335
The potent poison quite o'er-crows° my spirit,
I cannot live to hear the news from England,
But I do prophesy th'election° lights
On Fortinbras, he has my dying voice,°
So tell him, with th'occurrents more and less°   340
Which have solicited°—the rest is silence.   *Dies.*
HORATIO.   Now cracks a noble heart: good night sweet prince,
And flights of angels sing thee to thy rest.
Why does the drum come hither?

Enter FORTINBRAS and English Ambassadors, with drum, colours, and attendants.

FORTINBRAS.   Where is this sight?
HORATIO.   What is it you would see?   345
If aught of woe, or wonder, cease your search.
FORTINBRAS.   This quarry cries on havoc.° O proud death,
What feast is toward° in thine eternal cell,
That thou so many princes at a shot
So bloodily hast struck?   350
AMBASSADOR.   The sight is dismal,
And our affairs from England come too late;
The ears° are senseless that should give us hearing,
To tell him his commandment is fulfilled,
That Rosencrantz and Guildenstern are dead:
Where should we have our thanks?

---

323 *unsatisfied:* uninformed.   324 *antique Roman:* ancient Roman (who considered suicide honorable).   336 *o'er-crows:* overpowers, conquers.   338 *election:* (for king of Denmark).   339 *voice:* vote.   340 *occurrents more and less:* events great and small.   341 *solicited:* incited me.   347 *quarry . . . havoc:* heap of dead bodies proclaims slaughter done here.   348 *toward:* in preparation.   352 *ears:* (of Claudius).

HORATIO.   Not from his mouth,   355
    Had it th'ability of life to thank you;
    He never gave commandment for their death;
    But since so jump° upon this bloody question,
    You from the Polack wars, and you from England
    Are here arrived, give order that these bodies   360
    High on a stage be placèd to the view,
    And let me speak to th'yet unknowing world
    How these things came about; so shall you hear
    Of carnal, bloody and unnatural acts,
    Of accidental judgments, casual° slaughters,   365
    Of deaths put on° by cunning and forced cause,°
    And in this upshot, purposes mistook,
    Fall'n on th'inventors' heads:° all this can I
    Truly deliver.
FORTINBRAS.   Let us haste to hear it,
    And call the noblest to the audience.   370
    For me, with sorrow I embrace my fortune;
    I have some rights of memory° in this kingdom,
    Which now to claim my vantage° doth invite me.
HORATIO.   Of that I shall have also cause to speak,
    And from his mouth whose voice will draw on more:°   375
    But let this same° be presently performed,
    Even while men's minds are wild,° lest more mischance
    On° plots and errors happen.
FORTINBRAS.   Let four captains
    Bear Hamlet like a soldier to the stage,
    For he was likely, had he been put on,°   380
    To have proved most royal; and for his passage,°
    The soldiers' music and the rite of war
    Speak loudly for him:
    Take up the bodies, such a sight as this,
    Becomes the field, but here shows much amiss.   385
    Go bid the soldiers shoot.

Exeunt marching: after the which a peal of ordnance are shot off.

QUESTIONS

1. *Act 1.* How do you learn in the first scene that something is wrong in Denmark?

2. In scene 2, how does Claudius appear? Does he seem rational? Good? A good administrator? A competent ruler? A loving husband and uncle?

3. What does Hamlet reveal about his own mental and psychological state in his first soliloquy?

---

358 *jump:* opportunely.   365 *casual:* unpremeditated.   366 *put on:* prompted by.   *forced cause:* being forced to act in self-defense.   367–368 *purposes . . . heads:* plots gone wrong and destroying their inventors.   372 *of memory:* remembered.   373 *vantage:* advantageous position.   375 *draw on more:* influence more (votes).   376 *this same:* this telling of the story.   377 *wild:* upset.   378 *On:* on top of.   380 *put on:* i.e., put on the throne.   381 *passage:* i.e., to the next world.

4. Why do both Laertes and Polonius caution Ophelia about Hamlet's interest in her?

5. What does the Ghost tell Hamlet to do and not to do? Why does Hamlet believe he needs independent proof about the validity of the Ghost?

6. *Act 2.* Who is Polonius? What is his analysis of Hamlet's "madness"? What do his speeches show us about him?

7. Describe Hamlet's self-accusation in the "O What a Rogue" soliloquy (1346, 2.2.524–80). To what degree is his accusation justified?

8. *Act 3.* How do you react to Hamlet's treatment of Ophelia in Act 3, Scene 1? What evidence suggests that he knows he is being watched by Claudius and Polonius?

9. What does Hamlet think of Claudius's reaction to "The Murder of Gonzago"? Why does Claudius not react to the dumb-show before the play-within-a-play?

10. Why does Hamlet not kill Claudius when the King is at prayer?

11. Describe Hamlet's treatment of Gertrude during their confrontation in her private room? Is Hamlet justified in his treatment? Why does the Ghost appear here?

12. *Act 4.* How are Laertes's wishes for revenge like Hamlet's wishes for revenge?

13. How does Claudius plan to use Laertes desire for vengeance against Hamlet? To what extent does Laertes allow himself to be used?

14. *Act 5.* Comic relief is a humorous episode designed to ease tension. How does the scene of the gravediggers qualify as comic relief? Why is comic relief appropriate at this point of the play? How does the scene broaden the play's themes?

15. Describe the lessons that Hamlet tells Horatio he has learned about life. How does this understanding show that Hamlet has changed? Why is it ironic?

16. How is Gertrude killed? Hamlet? Laertes? Claudius? Why does Hamlet insist that Horatio not commit suicide?

GENERAL QUESTIONS

1. Describe Claudius. Is he purely evil, or is he merely a flawed human being? Could the play also be called "The Tragedy of Claudius, King of Denmark"?

2. Characterize Horatio. Why does Hamlet trust and admire him? How is he different from Rosencrantz and Guildenstern? Are these characters round or flat? How can one justify Hamlet's arrangement for the deaths of R & G?

3. *Hamlet* is full of conflicts that oppose people to other people, to society, and to themselves. List all the conflicts you can find in the play. Decide which of these is the central conflict, and explain your choice.

4. What is the crisis of *Hamlet*? When does it occur? Whom does it affect? What is the catastrophe? The Resolution?

5. In Act 4, Claudius notes that "sorrows come . . . in battalions." By the end of the play these sorrows include the deaths of all the major characters except Horatio. To what degree can Claudius be held responsible for all the sorrows of the play? Which sorrows may be particularly traced to Hamlet?

6. How does Shakespeare demonstrate that *Hamlet* is a tragedy of the state as well as the individual? Is the condition of Denmark better or worse at the end of the play than at the beginning?

⟨⟩ TRAGEDY FROM SHAKESPEARE TO ARTHUR MILLER

Shakespeare's tragedies feature people of elevated station, such as kings, princes, dukes, and generals. When Shakespeare uses characters of a lower status, he often treats them as comic, as we see in the gravediggers in *Hamlet* and the "mechanicals" in *A Midsummer Night's Dream*. This distinction, traditional in literature, was based on the realistic acceptance of the fact that the political and social order rested on the lives and trials of the powerful and the elite. Their intellectual, political, and emotional journeys held more dramatic interest than the lives and concerns of people in lower social orders. The magnitude of their deeds—and errors—was a primary element giving tragedy its larger dimensions. Yet it was to people of the lesser orders that the future belonged. They were to become the heirs of developing democratic beliefs in the dignity not just of the few, but of the many.

As long as monarchy and despotism remained the principal political systems in Europe, however, most writers of tragedy continued to draw their subject matter from the lives of the nobility. But one can see anticipations of things to come. In the eighteenth century, an interesting experiment in tragedy—and also therefore a play looking toward the future—was *The London Merchant* (1731) by George Lillo (1693–1739), which forsook heroic characters altogether and instead dramatized the "history" of a young boy, apprentice George Barnwell, who makes an error in judgment that leads him to theft, murder, and finally the gallows. Lillo's aim was primarily moral and exemplary—the play was just as much a sermon as a drama. The impact of *The London Merchant* was not that the human spirit is elevated through adversity or that human beings should stand in awe before the tragic potential of their acts; rather it was that audiences should avoid mistakes such as those made by Lillo's gullible and misguided protagonist. It was clear that writers of tragedy would ultimately need to face the problem of reconciling the treatment of ordinary people with the tragic ideal of human dignity and nobility.

The late eighteenth century began with a number of political revolutions that continued into and throughout much of the twentieth. Most of these depended on the belief that human beings are perfectible, but the political beliefs of modern democracy did not add to the tradition of tragedy until the mid-twentieth century with the emergence of the talent of Arthur Miller. Miller's tragedy is drawn from the modern world as we know it. His characters are common people—those who live in modern cities and walk, drive, or take the bus to work; those who go to modern schools, succeed or fail there, and then go on to make a living either in business for themselves or by working for others for their livelihoods. These are the people we know and see every day, and Miller bases their stories on the language and experiences that we all see, hear, or otherwise learn about. It is such people who in his eyes are worthy subjects for tragedy.

ARTHUR MILLER, *DEATH OF A SALESMAN*

*Because of his large number of important dramas, Miller can just-
ly be considered a dominant modern American playwright. He was
born in New York in 1915 and educated at the University of
Michigan, where he won a prize for a play he had written as an undergraduate. After graduation he wrote with the Federal Theater
Project (part of President Roosevelt's New Deal). When that project
lost funding, he began writing radio plays, a novel, and, during
World War II, an account of military training. He then wrote a
play,* The Man Who Had All the Luck, *which met little success
on Broadway in 1944. After the war he quickly catapulted into fame as a dramatist with* All
My Sons *(1947);* Death of a Salesman *(1949);* An Enemy of the People *(1951, an
adaptation of Ibsen's play);* The Crucible *(1953); and* A View from the Bridge *(1955).
Many of these combine his interests in family relationships and sociopolitical issues. For instance,* All My Sons *explores the relationship between Joe Keller, an industrialist and war prof-
iteer who had allowed faulty engines to be installed in U.S. military aircraft, and his son Chris,
an army pilot returning home from World War II. The play investigates Joe Keller's guilt and
his emerging realization that the airmen who died because of his defective engines were "all" his
sons. Another of Miller's most important plays,* The Crucible, *reflects the suspicions and un-
founded accusations rampant in the McCarthy era early in the 1950s.*

Miller's later work includes the screenplay The Misfits *(1961), the last film in which Marilyn Monroe, who was then his wife, starred; and the plays* After the Fall *(1964),* Incident at
Vichy *(1964, made into a film in 1973 and done as a radio play in 2002),* The Price
(1968), Fame *(1970),* The Reason Why *(1972),* The Creation of the World and Other
Business *(1972),* The Archbishop's Ceiling *(1976),* The American Clock *(1980),
Playing for Time *(1985),* I Can't Remember Anything *(1987),* Clara *(1987), a film-
script titled* Everybody Wins *(1990),* The Ride Down Mount Morgan *(1991, London),
Broken Glass *(1994),* Some Kind of Love Story *(1998), and* Resurrection Blues *(2002,
Minneapolis). In 1996* The Crucible *was revised and presented as a successful film with
Daniel Day-Lewis and Winona Ryder.*

Death of a Salesman, which opened on Broadway on February 10, 1949, is similar to both
Oedipus the King and the traditional well-made play (see Chapter 31). Miller's play dramatizes the end of a much longer story. The stage action in the present (in Acts 1 and 2) covers
about twenty-four hours, from Monday evening to Tuesday evening. The story, however, covers much of Willy Loman's life, and his memories of past events constantly impose themselves
on the present. One of the play's central conflicts stems from a secret known only to Willy and
his son Biff, a secret that is concealed until near the play's end. Such secrets, having a profound significance in the action, are a feature of the traditional well-made play.

In writing a tragedy about the struggle and failure of Willy Loman, Miller effectively redefines the nature of tragedy in our modern period of democracy and belief in the
significance of common people. In a *New York Times* essay published shortly after the
Broadway opening, Miller argues that "the common man is as apt a subject for tragedy in
its highest sense as kings were."[14] He asserts that tragedy springs from the individual's
quest for a proper place in the world and from his or her readiness "to lay down . . . life,
if need be, to secure . . . [a] sense of personal dignity." Willy is flawed: He is self-deluded,
deceitful, unfaithful, and weak; he denies the truth when he is confronted with it. But
Miller links Willy's defects with the quest for dignity: "the flaw or crack in the character is
really . . . his inherent unwillingness to remain passive in the face of what he conceives to

---

[14]"Tragedy and the Common Man," *New York Times*, February 27, 1949, sec. 2, p. 1.

Stage set for *Death of a Salesman*.

be a challenge to his dignity, his image of his rightful status." It is with great justice that Linda asserts to her sons that attention must be paid to such a person. In this sense, Miller meets the challenge of creating a modern character worthy of tragic elevation.

Accordingly, *Death of a Salesman* is developed around the character of Willy Loman. At first, Miller wanted to call the play "The Inside of His Head," and his initial vision was of "an enormous face the height of the proscenium arch that would appear and open up, and we would see the inside of a man's head."[15] The play contains two types of time and action: real and remembered. Present events are enacted and described realistically, but such action often triggers Willy's memory of the past, which is always with him, shaping the way he reacts to the present. Sometimes past events can even occur simultaneously with present action, as in Act 1 when Willy speaks with his dead brother, whom he is remembering at the same time he is playing cards with Charley. At other times, past events take over the play completely although Willy continues to exist in the present.

Like the acting of past events, the setting of *Death of a Salesman* is symbolic and non-realistic (see Chapter 29). The play demonstrates the degree to which Miller relies on developments in the physical theater that took place between Shakespeare's day and our own. Miller adapts both the concepts of the picture-frame proscenium stage and the apron stage. Thus the Loman house—set on the proscenium stage—is a framework with three rooms (or acting areas) on three levels: the kitchen, the sons' bedroom, and Willy's bedroom. The forestage and apron are used for all scenes away from the house and for "memory" scenes. The house is hemmed in by apartment houses and lit with an "angry glow of orange," thus suggesting that Willy's present existence is urbanized and claustrophobic. When memory takes over, however, the apartment houses disappear (a technique of lighting), and the orange glow gives way to pastoral colors and the shadows of leaves—the setting for dreams about past times and hopes.

[15]Arthur Miller, "Introduction to the Collected Plays," *Arthur Miller's Collected Plays* (New York: Viking, 1957), p. 23.

Death of a Salesman is very much about dreams, illusions, and self-deception. Dreams pervade Willy's thoughts, conversation, family, and house, and the staging allows fluid transitions between current action and memory. Willy's central illusion is the American dream of success and wealth through the merchandizing of the self. This dream is embodied in a series of smaller dreams (illusions, lies) that Willy has created out of hope and then tried to bequeath to his sons. But reality destroys these dreams. Willy's expectation of a New York City job and a salary, for example, founders on the reality of his disastrous encounter with his preoccupied and unsympathetic boss. Only Linda escapes the tyranny of dreams. While she serves and supports Willy completely, she remains firmly planted in the reality of house payments, insurance premiums, and Willy's need for dignity and attention as his world falls apart.

At the end of the play, we are left with a number of questions about the degree to which Willy recognizes and understands the illusory nature of his dreams and his self-image. He does understand that he has run out of lies and has nothing left to sell. He also understands—according to Miller—his alienation from true values.

> Had Willy been unaware of his separation from values that endure he would have died contentedly while polishing his car. . . . But he was agonized by his awareness of being in a false position, so constantly haunted by the hollowness of all he had placed his faith in, so aware, in short, that he must somehow be filled with his spirit or fly apart, that he staked his life on the ultimate assertion.[16]

Yet at the end of the play, Willy is still in the grip of delusion. He imagines that his insurance money will make Biff "magnificent," and he dreams that his funeral will be massive. Both visions are delusions, for Biff has already abandoned the business world, and the funeral is attended by only five people. In the Requiem scene, Biff states that Willy's dreams were illusory: "He had all the wrong dreams. All, all wrong" (speech 16). Only the character ironically named Happy retains his own unreconstructed version of Willy's dream: "He had a good dream. It's the only dream you can have—to come out number-one man" (speech 25). Miller leaves it to the audience to evaluate the truth and validity of each character's assertions.

ARTHUR MILLER (b. 1915)

Death of a Salesman   ⤳⤳⤳   *1949*

CHARACTERS

> Willy Loman
> Linda, *his wife*
> Biff ⎫
> Happy ⎭ *his sons*
> Uncle Ben
> Charley
> Bernard
> The Woman
> Howard Wagner

---

[16]*Ibid.,* pp. 34–35.

Jenny
Stanley
Miss Forsythe
Letta

The action takes place in WILLY LOMAN's house and yard and in various places he visits in the New York and Boston of today.

ACT 1

A melody is heard, played upon a flute. It is small and fine, telling of grass and trees and the horizon. The curtain rises.

 Before us is the Salesman's house. We are aware of towering, angular shapes behind it, surrounding it on all sides. Only the blue light of the sky falls upon the house and forestage; the surrounding area shows an angry glow of orange. As more light appears, we see a solid vault of apartment houses around the small, fragile-seeming home. An air of the dream clings to the place, a dream rising out of reality. The kitchen at center seems actual enough, for there is a kitchen table with three chairs, and a refrigerator. But no other fixtures are seen. At the back of the kitchen there is a draped entrance, which leads to the living-room. To the right of the kitchen, on a level raised two feet, is a bedroom furnished only with a brass bedstead and a straight chair. On a shelf over the bed a silver athletic trophy stands. A window opens onto the apartment house at the side.

 Behind the kitchen, on a level raised six and a half feet, is the boys' bedroom, at present barely visible. Two beds are dimly seen, and at the back of the room a dormer window. (This bedroom is above the unseen living-room.) At the left a stairway curves up to it from the kitchen.

 The entire setting is wholly or, in some places, partially transparent. The roof-line of the house is one-dimensional; under and over it we see the apartment buildings. Before the house lies an apron, curving beyond the forestage into the orchestra. This forward area serves as the back yard as well as the locale of all Willy's imaginings and of his city scenes. Whenever the action is in the present the actors observe the imaginary wall-lines, entering the house only through its door at the left. But in the scenes of the past these boundaries are broken, and characters enter or leave a room by stepping "through" a wall onto the forestage.

[*From the right,* WILLY LOMAN, *the Salesman, enters, carrying two large sample cases. The flute plays on. He hears but is not aware of it. He is past sixty years of age, dressed quietly. Even as he crosses the stage to the doorway of the house, his exhaustion is apparent. He unlocks the door, comes into the kitchen, and thankfully lets his burden down, feeling the soreness of his palms. A word-sigh escapes his lips—it might be "Oh, boy, oh, boy." He closes the door, then carries his cases out into the living-room, through the draped kitchen doorway.*]

[LINDA, *his wife, has stirred in her bed at the right. She gets out and puts on a robe, listening. Most often jovial, she has developed an iron repression of her exceptions to* WILLY's *behavior—she more than loves him, she admires him, as though his mercurial nature, his temper, his massive dreams and little cruelties, served her only as sharp reminders of the turbulent longings within him, longings which she shares but lacks the temperament to utter and follow to their end.*]

LINDA. [*hearing* WILLY *outside the bedroom, calls with some trepidation*] Willy!
WILLY. It's all right. I came back.
LINDA. Why? What happened? [*slight pause*] Did something happen, Willy?
WILLY. No, nothing happened.

LINDA. You didn't smash the car, did you?   5

WILLY. [*with casual irritation*] I said nothing happened. Didn't you hear me?

LINDA. Don't you feel well?

WILLY. I'm tired to the death. [*The flute has faded away. He sits on the bed beside her, a little numb.*] I couldn't make it. I just couldn't make it, Linda.

LINDA. [*very carefully, delicately*] Where were you all day? You look terrible.

WILLY. I got as far as a little above Yonkers.° I stopped for a cup of coffee. Maybe   10 it was the coffee.

LINDA. What?

WILLY. [*after a pause*] I suddenly couldn't drive any more. The car kept going off onto the shoulder, y'know?

LINDA. [*helpfully*] Oh. Maybe it was the steering again. I don't think Angelo knows the Studebaker.

WILLY. No, it's me, it's me. Suddenly I realize I'm goin' sixty miles an hour and I don't remember the last five minutes. I'm—I can't seem to—keep my mind to it.

LINDA. Maybe it's your glasses. You never went for your new glasses.   15

WILLY. No, I see everything. I came back ten miles an hour. It took me nearly four hours from Yonkers.

LINDA. [*resigned*] Well, you'll just have to take a rest, Willy, you can't continue this way.

WILLY. I just got back from Florida.

LINDA. But you didn't rest your mind. Your mind is overactive, and the mind is what counts, dear.

WILLY. I'll start out in the morning. Maybe I'll feel better in the morning. [*She is*   20 *taking off his shoes.*] These goddam arch supports are killing me.

LINDA. Take an aspirin. Should I get you an aspirin? It'll soothe you.

WILLY. [*with wonder*] I was driving along, you understand? And I was fine. I was even observing the scenery. You can imagine, me looking at scenery, on the road every week of my life. But it's so beautiful up there, Linda, the trees are so thick, and the sun is warm. I opened the windshield and just let the warm air bathe over me. And then all of a sudden I'm goin' off the road! I'm tellin' ya, I absolutely forgot I was driving. If I'd've gone the other way over the white line I might've killed somebody. So I went on again— and five minutes later I'm dreamin' again, and I nearly—[*He presses two fingers against his eyes.*] I have such thoughts, I have such strange thoughts.

LINDA. Willy, dear. Talk to them again. There's no reason why you can't work in New York.

WILLY. They don't need me in New York. I'm the New England man. I'm vital in New England.

LINDA. But you're sixty years old. They can't expect you to keep traveling every   25 week.

WILLY. I'll have to send a wire to Portland. I'm supposed to see Brown and Morrison tomorrow morning at ten o'clock to show the line. Goddammit, I could sell them! [*He starts putting on his jacket.*]

LINDA. [*taking the jacket from him*] Why don't you go down to the place tomorrow and tell Howard you've simply got to work in New York? You're too accommodating, dear.

---

10 *Yonkers:* Yonkers is immediately north of New York City, touching the city limits of the Bronx. Because Willy lives in Brooklyn, to the south, he got no more than thirty or thirty-five miles from home.

WILLY.   If old man Wagner was alive I'd a been in charge of New York now! That man was a prince, he was a masterful man. But that boy of his, that Howard, he don't appreciate. When I went north the first time, the Wagner Company didn't know where New England was!

LINDA.   Why don't you tell those things to Howard, dear?

WILLY.   [*encouraged*] I will, I definitely will. Is there any cheese?   30

LINDA.   I'll make you a sandwich.

WILLY.   No, go to sleep. I'll take some milk. I'll be up right away. The boys in?

LINDA.   They're sleeping. Happy took Biff on a date tonight.

WILLY.   [*interested*] That so?

LINDA.   It was so nice to see them shaving together, one behind the other, in the   35
bathroom. And going out together. You notice? The whole house smells of shaving lotion.

WILLY.   Figure it out. Work a lifetime to pay off a house. You finally own it, and there's nobody to live in it.

LINDA.   Well, dear, life is a casting off. It's always that way.

WILLY.   No, no, some people—some people accomplish something. Did Biff say anything after I went this morning?

LINDA.   You shouldn't have criticized him, Willy, especially after he just got off the train. You mustn't lose your temper with him.

WILLY.   When the hell did I lose my temper? I simply asked him if he was making   40
any money. Is that a criticism?

LINDA.   But, dear, how could he make any money?

WILLY.   [*worried and angered*] There's such an undercurrent in him. He became a moody man. Did he apologize when I left this morning?

LINDA.   He was crestfallen, Willy. You know how he admires you. I think if he finds himself, then you'll both be happier and not fight any more.

WILLY.   How can he find himself on a farm? Is that a life? A farmhand? In the beginning, when he was young, I thought, well, a young man, it's good for him to tramp around, take a lot of different jobs. But it's more than ten years now and he has yet to make thirty-five dollars a week!

LINDA.   He's finding himself, Willy.   45

WILLY.   Not finding yourself at the age of thirty-four is a disgrace!

LINDA.   Shh!

WILLY.   The trouble is he's lazy, goddammit!

LINDA.   Willy, please!

WILLY.   Biff is a lazy bum!   50

LINDA.   They're sleeping. Get something to eat. Go on down.

WILLY.   Why did he come home? I would like to know what brought him home.

LINDA.   I don't know. I think he's still lost, Willy. I think he's very lost.

WILLY.   Biff Loman is lost. In the greatest country in the world a young man with such—personal attractiveness, gets lost. And such a hard worker. There's one thing about Biff—he's not lazy.

LINDA.   Never.   55

WILLY.   [*with pity and resolve*] I'll see him in the morning; I'll have a nice talk with him. I'll get him a job selling. He could be big in no time. My God! Remember how they used to follow him around in high school? When he smiled at one of them their faces lit up. When he walked down the street . . . [*He loses himself in reminiscences.*]

LINDA.   [*trying to bring him out of it*] Willy, dear, I got a new kind of American-type cheese today. It's whipped.

WILLY.   Why do you get American when I like Swiss?

LINDA.   I just thought you'd like a change—

WILLY.   I don't want a change! I want Swiss cheese. Why am I always being   60
contradicted?

LINDA.   [*with a covering laugh*] I thought it would be a surprise.

WILLY.   Why don't you open a window in here, for God's sake?

LINDA.   [*with infinite patience*] They're all open dear.

WILLY.   The way they boxed us in here. Bricks and windows, windows and bricks.

LINDA.   We should've bought the land next door.   65

WILLY.   The street is lined with cars. There's not a breath of fresh air in the neighborhood. The grass don't grow any more, you can't raise a carrot in the back yard. They
should've had a law against apartment houses. Remember those two beautiful elm trees
out there? When I and Biff hung the swing between them?

LINDA.   Yeah, like being a million miles from the city.

WILLY.   They should've arrested the builder for cutting those down. They massa-
cred the neighborhood. [*lost*] More and more I think of those days, Linda. This time of
year it was lilac and wisteria. And then the peonies would come out, and the daffodils.
What fragrance in this room!

LINDA.   Well, after all, people had to move somewhere.

WILLY.   No, there's more people now.   70

LINDA.   I don't think there's more people. I think—

WILLY.   There's more people! That's what's ruining this country! Population is
getting out of control. The competition is maddening! Smell the stink from that apartment house! And another one on the other side . . . How can they whip cheese?

[*On* WILLY'S *last line,* BIFF *and* HAPPY *raise themselves up in their beds, listening.*]

LINDA.   Go down, try it. And be quiet.

WILLY.   [*turning to* LINDA, *guiltily*] You're not worried about me, are you, sweetheart?

BIFF.   What's the matter?   75

HAPPY.   Listen!

LINDA.   You've got too much on the ball to worry about.

WILLY.   You're my foundation and my support, Linda.

LINDA.   Just try to relax, dear. You make mountains out of molehills.

WILLY.   I won't fight with him any more. If he wants to go back to Texas, let   80
him go.

LINDA.   He'll find his way.

WILLY.   Sure. Certain men just don't get started till later in life. Like Thomas Edison, I think. Or B. F. Goodrich.° One of them was deaf. [*He starts for the bedroom doorway.*]
I'll put my money on Biff.

LINDA.   And Willy—if it's warm Sunday we'll drive in the country. And we'll open
the windshield, and take lunch.

WILLY.   No, the windshields don't open on the new cars.

LINDA.   But you opened it today.   85

WILLY.   Me? I didn't. [*He stops.*] Now isn't that peculiar! Isn't that a remarkable—
[*He breaks off in amazement and fright as the flute is heard distantly.*]

---

82 *Thomas Edison, B. F. Goodrich:* Thomas A. Edison (1847–1931) was an American inventor who developed the electric light and the phonograph. Benjamin Franklin Goodrich (1841–1888) founded the B. F.
Goodrich Rubber and Tire Company. It was Edison who suffered from deafness.

LINDA.   What, darling?

WILLY.   That is the most remarkable thing.

LINDA.   What, dear?

WILLY.   I was thinking of the Chevvy. [*slight pause*] Nineteen twenty-eight . . . when   90
I had that red Chevvy—[*Breaks off.*] That funny? I coulda sworn I was driving that Chevvy
today.

LINDA.   Well, that's nothing. Something must've reminded you.

WILLY.   Remarkable. Ts. Remember those days? The way Biff used to simonize that
car? The dealer refused to believe there was eighty thousand miles on it. [*He shakes his
head.*] Heh! [*to LINDA*] Close your eyes, I'll be right up. [*He walks out of the bedroom.*]

HAPPY.   [*to BIFF*] Jesus, maybe he smashed up the car again!

LINDA.   [*calling after WILLY*] Be careful on the stairs, dear! The cheese is on the
middle shelf! [*She turns, goes over to the bed, takes his jacket, and goes out of the bedroom.*]

[*Light has risen on the boys' room. Unseen, WILLY is heard talking to himself, "Eighty thousand
miles," and a little laugh. BIFF gets out of bed, comes downstage a bit, and stands attentively. BIFF is
two years older than his brother HAPPY, well built, but in these days bears a worn air and seems less
self-assured. He has succeeded less, and his dreams are stronger and less acceptable than HAPPY's.
HAPPY is tall, powerfully made. Sexuality is like a visible color on him, or a scent that many women
have discovered. He, like his brother, is lost, but in a different way, for he has never allowed himself
to turn his face toward defeat and is thus more confused and hard-skinned, although seemingly more
content.*]

HAPPY.   [*getting out of bed*] He's going to get his license taken away if he keeps that   95
up. I'm getting nervous about him, y'know, Biff?

BIFF.   His eyes are going.

HAPPY.   No, I've driven with him. He sees all right. He just doesn't keep his mind
on it. I drove into the city with him last week. He stops at a green light and then it turns
red and he goes. [*He laughs.*]

BIFF.   Maybe he's color-blind.

HAPPY.   Pop? Why he's got the finest eye for color in the business. You know that.

BIFF.   [*sitting down on his bed*] I'm going to sleep.   100

HAPPY.   You're not still sour on Dad, are you, Biff?

BIFF.   He's all right, I guess.

WILLY.   [*underneath them, in the living-room*] Yes, sir, eighty thousand miles—eighty-
two thousand!

BIFF.   You smoking?

HAPPY.   [*holding out a pack of cigarettes*] Want one?   105

BIFF.   [*taking a cigarette*] I can never sleep when I smell it.

WILLY.   What a simonizing job, heh!

HAPPY.   [*with deep sentiment*] Funny, Biff y'know? Us sleeping in here again? The
old beds. [*He pats his bed affectionately.*] All the talk that went across those two beds, huh?
Our whole lives.

BIFF.   Yeah. Lotta dreams and plans.

HAPPY.   [*with a deep and masculine laugh*] About five hundred women would like to   110
know what was said in this room.

[*They share a soft laugh.*]

BIFF.   Remember that big Betsy something—what the hell was her name—over on
Bushwick Avenue?

HAPPY.   [*combing his hair*] With the collie dog!

BIFF. That's the one. I got you in there, remember?

HAPPY. Yeah, that was my first time—I think. Boy, there was a pig! [*They laugh, almost crudely.*] You taught me everything I know about women. Don't forget that.

BIFF. I bet you forgot how bashful you used to be. Especially with girls. 115

HAPPY. Oh, I still am, Biff.

BIFF. Oh, go on.

HAPPY. I just control it, that's all. I think I got less bashful and you got more so. What happened, Biff? Where's the old humor, the old confidence? [*He shakes* BIFF'S *knee.* BIFF *gets up and moves restlessly about the room.*] What's the matter?

BIFF. Why does Dad mock me all the time?

HAPPY. He's not mocking you, he— 120

BIFF. Everything I say there's a twist of mockery on his face. I can't get near him.

HAPPY. He just wants you to make good, that's all. I wanted to talk to you about Dad for a long time, Biff. Something's—happening to him. He—talks to himself.

BIFF. I noticed that this morning. But he always mumbled.

HAPPY. But not so noticeable. It got so embarrassing I sent him to Florida. And you know something? Most of the time he's talking to you.

BIFF. What's he say about me? 125

HAPPY. I can't make it out.

BIFF. What's he say about me?

HAPPY. I think the fact that you're not settled, that you're still kind of up in the air . . .

BIFF. There's one or two other things depressing him, Happy.

HAPPY. What do you mean? 130

BIFF. Never mind. Just don't lay it all to me.

HAPPY. But I think if you just got started—I mean—is there any future for you out there?

BIFF. I tell ya, Hap, I don't know what the future is. I don't know—what I'm supposed to want.

HAPPY. What do you mean?

BIFF. Well, I spent six or seven years after high school trying to work myself up. 135 Shipping clerk, salesman, business of one kind or another. And it's a measly manner of existence. To get on that subway on the hot mornings in summer. To devote your whole life to keeping stock, or making phone calls, or selling or buying. To suffer fifty weeks of the year for the sake of a two-week vacation, when all you really desire is to be outdoors, with your shirt off. And always to have to get ahead of the next fella. And still—that's how you build a future.

HAPPY. Well, you really enjoy it on a farm? Are you content out there?

BIFF. [*with rising agitation*] Hap, I've had twenty or thirty different kinds of jobs since I left home before the war, and it always turns out the same. I just realized it lately. In Nebraska when I herded cattle, and the Dakotas, and Arizona, and now in Texas. It's why I came home now, I guess, because I realized it. This farm I work on, it's spring there now, see? And they've got about fifteen new colts. There's nothing more inspiring or— beautiful than the sight of a mare and a new colt. And it's cool there now, see? Texas is cool now, and it's spring. And whenever spring comes to where I am, I suddenly get the feeling, my God, I'm not gettin' anywhere! What the hell am I doing, playing around with horses, twenty-eight dollars a week! I'm thirty-four years old, I oughta be makin' my future. That's when I come running home. And now, I get here, and I don't know what to do with myself. [*after a pause*] I've always made a point of not wasting my life, and everytime I come back here I know that all I've done is to waste my life.

HAPPY. You're a poet, you know that, Biff? You're a—you're an idealist!

BIFF.   No, I'm mixed up very bad. Maybe I oughta get married. Maybe I oughta get stuck into something. Maybe that's my trouble. I'm like a boy. I'm not married, I'm not in business, I just—I'm like a boy. Are you content, Hap? You're a success, aren't you? Are you content?

HAPPY.   Hell, no!   140

BIFF.   Why? You're making money, aren't you?

HAPPY.   [*moving about with energy, expressiveness*] All I can do now is wait for the merchandise manager to die. And suppose I get to be merchandise manager? He's a good friend of mine, and he just built a terrific estate on Long Island. And he lived there about two months and sold it, and now he's building another one. He can't enjoy it once it's finished. And I know that's just what I would do. I don't know what the hell I'm workin' for. Sometimes I sit in my apartment—all alone. And I think of the rent I'm paying. And it's crazy. But then, it's what I always wanted. My own apartment, a car, and plenty of women. And still, goddammit, I'm lonely.

BIFF.   [*with enthusiasm*] Listen, why don't you come out West with me?

HAPPY.   You and I, heh?

BIFF.   Sure, maybe we could buy a ranch. Raise cattle, use our muscles. Men built   145
like we are should be working out in the open.

HAPPY.   [*avidly*] The Loman Brothers, heh?

BIFF.   [*with vast affection*] Sure, we'd be known all over the counties!

HAPPY.   [*enthralled*] That's what I dream about, Biff. Sometimes I want to just rip my clothes off in the middle of the store and outbox that goddam merchandise manager. I mean I can outbox, outrun, and outlift anybody in that store, and I have to take orders from those common, petty sons-of-bitches till I can't stand it any more.

BIFF.   I'm tellin' you, kid, if you were with me I'd be happy out there.

HAPPY.   [*enthused*] See, Biff, everybody around me is so false that I'm constantly   150
lowering my ideals . . .

BIFF.   Baby, together we'd stand up for one another, we'd have someone to trust.

HAPPY.   If I were around you—

BIFF.   Hap, the trouble is we weren't brought up to grub for money. I don't know how to do it.

HAPPY.   Neither can I!

BIFF.   Then let's go!   155

HAPPY.   The only thing is—what can you make out there?

BIFF.   But look at your friend. Builds an estate and then hasn't the peace of mind to live in it.

HAPPY.   Yeah, but when he walks into the store the waves part in front of him. That's fifty-two thousand dollars a year coming through the revolving door, and I got more in my pinky finger than he's got in his head.

BIFF.   Yeah, but you just said—

HAPPY.   I gotta show some of those pompous, self-important executives over there   160
that Hap Loman can make the grade. I want to walk into the store the way he walks in. Then I'll go with you, Biff. We'll be together yet, I swear. But take those two we had tonight. Now weren't they gorgeous creatures?

BIFF.   Yeah, yeah, most gorgeous I've had in years.

HAPPY.   I get that any time I want, Biff. Whenever I feel disgusted. The only trouble is, it gets like bowling or something. I just keep knockin' them over and it doesn't mean anything. You still run around a lot?

BIFF.   Naa. I'd like to find a girl—steady, somebody with substance.

HAPPY.   That's what I long for.

BIFF.   Go on! You'd never come home.   165

HAPPY.   I would! Somebody with character, with resistance! Like Mom, y'know? You're gonna call me a bastard when I tell you this. That girl Charlotte I was with tonight is engaged to be married in five weeks. [*He tries on his new hat.*]

BIFF.   No kiddin'!

HAPPY.   Sure, the guy's in line for the vice-presidency of the store. I don't know what gets into me, maybe I just have an overdeveloped sense of competition or something, but I went and ruined her, and furthermore I can't get rid of her. And he's the third executive I've done that to. Isn't that a crummy characteristic? And to top it all, I go to their weddings! [*Indignantly, but laughing*] Like I'm not supposed to take bribes. Manufacturers offer me a hundred-dollar bill now and then to throw an order their way. You know how honest I am, but it's like this girl, see. I hate myself for it. Because I don't want the girl, and, still, I take it and—I love it!

BIFF.   Let's go to sleep.

HAPPY.   I guess we didn't settle anything, heh?   170

BIFF.   I just got one idea that I think I'm going to try.

HAPPY.   What's that?

BIFF.   Remember Bill Oliver?

HAPPY.   Sure, Oliver is very big now. You want to work for him again?

BIFF.   No, but when I quit he said something to me. He put his arm on my shoul-   175
der and he said, "Biff, if you ever need anything, come to me."

HAPPY.   I remember that. That sounds good.

BIFF.   I think I'll go to see him. If I could get ten thousand or even seven or eight thousand dollars I could buy a beautiful ranch.

HAPPY.   I bet he'd back you. 'Cause he thought highly of you, Biff. I mean, they all do. You're well liked, Biff. That's why I say to come back here, and we both have the apartment. And I'm tellin' you, Biff, any babe you want . . .

BIFF.   No, with a ranch I could do the work I like and still be something. I just wonder though. I wonder if Oliver still thinks I stole that carton of basketballs.

HAPPY.   Oh, he probably forgot that long ago. It's almost ten years. You're too sen-   180
sitive. Anyway, he didn't really fire you.

BIFF.   Well, I think he was going to. I think that's why I quit. I was never sure whether he knew or not. I know he thought the world of me, though. I was the only one he'd let lock up the place.

WILLY.   [*below*] You gonna wash the engine, Biff?

HAPPY.   Shh!

[*BIFF looks at HAPPY, who is gazing down, listening. WILLY is mumbling in the parlor.*]

HAPPY.   You hear that?

[*They listen. WILLY laughs warmly.*]

BIFF.   [*growing angry*] Doesn't he know Mom can hear that?   185

WILLY.   Don't get your sweater dirty, Biff!

[*A look of pain crosses BIFF's face.*]

HAPPY.   Isn't that terrible! Don't leave again, will you? You'll find a job here. You gotta stick around. I don't know what to do about him, it's getting embarrassing.

WILLY.   What a simonizing job!

BIFF.   Mom's hearing that!

WILLY.   No kiddin', Biff, you got a date? Wonderful!   190

HAPPY.   Go on to sleep. But talk to him in the morning, will you?
BIFF.   [*reluctantly getting into bed*] With her in the house. Brother!
HAPPY.   [*getting into bed*] I wish you'd have a good talk with him.

[*The light on their room begins to fade.*]

BIFF.   [*to himself in bed*] That selfish, stupid . . .
HAPPY.   Sh . . . Sleep, Biff.   195

[*Their light is out. Well before they have finished speaking, WILLY's form is dimly seen below in the darkened kitchen. He opens the refrigerator, searches in there, and takes out a bottle of milk. The apartment houses are fading out, and the entire house and surroundings become covered with leaves. Music insinuates itself as the leaves appear.*]

WILLY.   Just wanna be careful with those girls, Biff, that's all. Don't make any promises. No promises of any kind. Because a girl, y'know, they always believe what you tell 'em, and you're very young, Biff, you're too young to be talking seriously to girls.

[*Light rises on the kitchen. WILLY, talking, shuts the refrigerator door and comes downstage to the kitchen table. He pours milk into a glass. He is totally immersed in himself, smiling faintly.*]

WILLY.   Too young entirely, Biff. You want to watch your schooling first. Then when you're all set, there'll be plenty of girls for a boy like you. [*He smiles broadly at a kitchen chair.*] That so? The girls pay for you? [*He laughs.*] Boy, you must really be makin' a hit.

[*WILLY is gradually addressing—physically—a point offstage, speaking through the wall of the kitchen, and his voice has been rising in volume to that of a normal conversation.*]

WILLY.   I been wondering why you polish the car so careful. Ha! Don't leave the hubcaps, boys. Get the chamois to the hubcaps. Happy, use newspaper on the windows, it's the easiest thing. Show him how to do it, Biff! You see, Happy? Pad it up, use it like a pad. That's it, that's it, good work. You're doin' all right, Hap. [*He pauses, then nods in approbation for a few seconds, then looks upward.*] Biff, first thing we gotta do when we get time is clip that big branch over the house. Afraid it's gonna fall in a storm and hit the roof. Tell you what. We get a rope and sling her around, and then we climb up there with a couple of saws and take her down. Soon as you finish the car, boys, I wanna see ya. I got a surprise for you, boys.

BIFF.   [*offstage*] Whatta ya got, Dad?
WILLY.   No, you finish first. Never leave a job till you're finished—remember that.   200
[*looking toward the "big trees"*] Biff, up in Albany I saw a beautiful hammock. I think I'll buy it next trip, and we'll hang it right between those two elms. Wouldn't that be something? Just swingin' there under those branches. Boy, that would be . . .

[*YOUNG BIFF and YOUNG HAPPY appear from the direction WILLY was addressing. HAPPY carries rags and a pail of water. BIFF, wearing a sweater with a block "S," carries a football.*]

BIFF.   [*pointing in the direction of the car offstage*] How's that, Pop, professional?
WILLY.   Terrific. Terrific job, boys. Good work, Biff.
HAPPY.   Where's the surprise, Pop?
WILLY.   In the back seat of the car.
HAPPY.   Boy! [*He runs off.*]   205
BIFF.   What is it, Dad? Tell me, what'd you buy?
WILLY.   [*laughing, cuffs him*] Never mind, something I want you to have.
BIFF.   [*turns and starts off*] What is it, Hap?

HAPPY.   [*offstage*] It's a punching bag!

BIFF.   Oh, Pop!   210

WILLY.   It's got Gene Tunney's° signature on it!

[*HAPPY runs onstage with a punching bag.*]

BIFF.   Gee, how'd you know we wanted a punching bag?

WILLY.   Well, it's the finest thing for the timing.

HAPPY.   [*lies down on his back and pedals with his feet*] I'm losing weight, you notice, Pop?

WILLY.   [*to HAPPY*] Jumping rope is good too.   215

BIFF.   Did you see the new football I got?

WILLY.   [*examining the ball*] Where'd you get a new ball?

BIFF.   The coach told me to practice my passing.

WILLY.   That so? And he gave you the ball, heh?

BIFF.   Well, I borrowed it from the locker room. [*He laughs confidentially.*]   220

WILLY.   [*laughing with him at the theft*] I want you to return that.

HAPPY.   I told you he wouldn't like it!

BIFF.   [*angrily*] Well, I'm bringing it back!

WILLY.   [*stopping the incipient argument, to HAPPY*] Sure, he's gotta practice with a regulation ball, doesn't he? [*to BIFF*] Coach'll probably congratulate you on your initiative!

BIFF.   Oh, he keeps congratulating my initiative all the time, Pop.   225

WILLY.   That's because he likes you. If somebody else took that ball there'd be an uproar. So what's the report, boys, what's the report?

BIFF.   Where'd you go this time, Dad? Gee we were lonesome for you.

WILLY.   [*pleased, puts an arm around each boy and they come down to the apron*] Lonesome, heh?

BIFF.   Missed you every minute.

WILLY.   Don't say? Tell you a secret, boys. Don't breathe it to a soul. Someday I'll   230
have my own business, and I'll never have to leave home any more.

HAPPY.   Like Uncle Charley, heh?

WILLY.   Bigger than Uncle Charley! Because Charley is not—liked. He's liked, but he's not—well liked.

BIFF.   Where'd you go this time, Dad?

WILLY.   Well, I got on the road, and I went north to Providence. Met the Mayor.

BIFF.   The Mayor of Providence!   235

WILLY.   He was sitting in the hotel lobby.

BIFF.   What'd he say?

WILLY.   He said, "Morning!" And I said, "You got a fine city here, Mayor." And then he had coffee with me. And then I went to Waterbury. Waterbury is a fine city. Big clock city, the famous Waterbury clock. Sold a nice bill there. And then Boston—Boston is the cradle of the Revolution. A fine city. And a couple of other towns in Mass., and on to Portland and Bangor and straight home!

BIFF.   Gee, I'd love to go with you sometime, Dad.

WILLY.   Soon as summer comes.   240

HAPPY.   Promise?

---

211 *Gene Tunney:* James Joseph Tunney, a boxer who won the heavyweight championship from Jack Dempsey in 1926 and retired undefeated in 1928.

WILLY. You and Hap and I, and I'll show you all the towns. America is full of beautiful towns and fine, upstanding people. And they know me, boys, they know me up and down New England. The finest people. And when I bring you fellas up, there'll be open sesame for all of us, 'cause one thing, boys: I have friends. I can park my car in any street in New England, and the cops protect it like their own. This summer, heh?

BIFF AND HAPPY. [*together*] Yeah! You bet!

WILLY. We'll take our bathing suits.

HAPPY. We'll carry your bags, Pop!   245

WILLY. Oh, won't that be something! Me comin' into the Boston stores with you boys carryin' my bags. What a sensation!

[*BIFF is prancing around, practicing passing the ball.*]

WILLY. You nervous, Biff, about the game?

BIFF. Not if you're gonna be there.

WILLY. What do they say about you in school, now that they made you captain?

HAPPY. There's a crowd of girls behind him everytime the classes change.   250

BIFF. [*taking WILLY's hand*] This Saturday, Pop, this Saturday—just for you, I'm going to break through for a touchdown.

HAPPY. You're supposed to pass.

BIFF. I'm takin' one play for Pop. You watch me, Pop, and when I take off my helmet, that means I'm breakin' out. Then you watch me crash through that line!

WILLY. [*kisses BIFF*] Oh, wait'll I tell this in Boston!

[*BERNARD enters in knickers. He is younger than BIFF, earnest and loyal, a worried boy.*]

BERNARD. Biff, where are you? You're supposed to study with me today.   255

WILLY. Hey, looka Bernard. What're you lookin' so anemic about, Bernard?

BERNARD. He's gotta study, Uncle Willy. He's got Regents° next week.

HAPPY. [*tauntingly, spinning BERNARD around*] Let's box, Bernard!

BERNARD. Biff! [*He gets away from HAPPY.*] Listen, Biff, I heard Mr. Birnbaum say that if you don't start studyin' math he's gonna flunk you, and you won't graduate. I heard him!

WILLY. You better study with him, Biff. Go ahead now.   260

BERNARD. I heard him!

BIFF. Oh, Pop, you didn't see my sneakers! [*He holds up a foot for WILLY to look at.*]

WILLY. Hey, that's a beautiful job of printing!

BERNARD. [*wiping his glasses*] Just because he printed University of Virginia on his sneakers doesn't mean they've got to graduate him, Uncle Willy!

WILLY. [*angrily*] What're you talking about? With scholarships to three universi-   265
ties they're gonna flunk him?

BERNARD. But I heard Mr. Birnbaum say—

WILLY. Don't be a pest, Bernard! [*to his boys*] What an anemic!

BERNARD. Okay, I'm waiting for you in my house, Biff.

[*BERNARD goes off. The LOMANS laugh.*]

WILLY. Bernard is not well liked, is he?

BIFF. He's liked, but he's not well liked.   270

HAPPY. That's right, Pop.

257 *Regents:* a statewide high school proficiency examination administered in New York State.

WILLY.   That's just what I mean. Bernard can get the best marks in school, y'understand, but when he gets out in the business world, y'understand, you are going to be five times ahead of him. That's why I thank Almighty God you're both built like Adonises. Because the man who makes an appearance in the business world, the man who creates personal interest, is the man who gets ahead. Be liked and you will never want. You take me, for instance. I never have to wait in line to see a buyer. "Willy Loman is here!" That's all they have to know, and I go right through.

BIFF.   Did you knock them dead, Pop?

WILLY.   Knocked 'em cold in Providence, slaughtered 'em in Boston.

HAPPY.   [*on his back, pedaling again*] I'm losing weight, you notice, Pop?   275

[*LINDA enters, as of old, a ribbon in her hair, carrying a basket of washing.*]

LINDA.   [*with youthful energy*] Hello, dear!

WILLY.   Sweetheart!

LINDA.   How'd the Chevvy run?

WILLY.   Chevrolet, Linda, is the greatest car ever built. [*to the boys*] Since when do you let your mother carry wash up the stairs?

BIFF.   Grab hold there, boy!   280

HAPPY.   Where to, Mom?

LINDA.   Hang them up on the line. And you better go down to your friends, Biff. The cellar is full of boys. They don't know what to do with themselves.

BIFF.   Ah, when Pop comes home they can wait!

WILLY.   [*laughs appreciatively*] You better go down and tell them what to do, Biff.

BIFF.   I think I'll have them sweep out the furnace room.   285

WILLY.   Good work, Biff.

BIFF.   [*goes through wall-line of kitchen to doorway at back and calls down*] Fellas! Everybody sweep out the furnace room! I'll be right down!

VOICES.   All right! Okay, Biff.

BIFF.   George and Sam and Frank, come out back! We're hangin' up the wash! Come on, Hap, on the double! [*He and HAPPY carry out the basket.*]

LINDA.   The way they obey him!   290

WILLY.   Well, that's training, the training. I'm tellin' you, I was sellin' thousands and thousands, but I had to come home.

LINDA.   Oh, the whole block'll be at that game. Did you sell anything?

WILLY.   I did five hundred gross in Providence and seven hundred gross in Boston.

LINDA.   No! Wait a minute, I've got a pencil. [*She pulls pencil and paper out of her apron pocket.*] That makes your commission . . . Two hundred—my God! Two hundred and twelve dollars!

WILLY.   Well, I didn't figure it yet, but . . .   295

LINDA.   How much did you do?

WILLY.   Well, I—I did—about a hundred and eighty gross in Providence. Well, no—it came to—roughly two hundred gross on the whole trip.

LINDA.   [*without hesitation*] Two hundred gross. That's . . . [*She figures.*]

WILLY.   The trouble was that three of the stores were half closed for inventory in Boston. Otherwise I woulda broke records.

LINDA.   Well, it makes seventy dollars and some pennies. That's very good.   300

WILLY.   What do we owe?

LINDA.   Well, on the first there's sixteen dollars on the refrigerator—

WILLY.   Why sixteen?

LINDA.   Well, the fan belt broke, so it was a dollar eighty.
WILLY.   But it's brand new.   305
LINDA.   Well, the man said that's the way it is. Till they work themselves in, y'know.

[*They move through the wall-line into the kitchen.*]

WILLY.   I hope we didn't get stuck on that machine.
LINDA.   They got the biggest ads of any of them!
WILLY.   I know, it's a fine machine. What else?
LINDA.   Well, there's nine-sixty for the washing machine. And for the vacuum   310
cleaner there's three and a half due on the fifteenth. Then the roof, you got twenty-one
dollars remaining.
WILLY.   It don't leak, does it?
LINDA.   No, they did a wonderful job. Then you owe Frank for the carburetor.
WILLY.   I'm not going to pay that man! That goddam Chevrolet, they ought to pro-
hibit the manufacture of that car!
LINDA.   Well, you owe him three and a half. And odds and ends, comes to around
a hundred and twenty dollars by the fifteenth.
WILLY.   A hundred and twenty dollars! My God, if business don't pick up I don't   315
know what I'm gonna do!
LINDA.   Well, next week you'll do better.
WILLY.   Oh, I'll knock 'em dead next week. I'll go to Hartford. I'm very well liked
in Hartford. You know, the trouble is, Linda, people don't seem to take to me.

[*They move onto the forestage.*]

LINDA.   Oh, don't be foolish.
WILLY.   I know it when I walk in. They seem to laugh at me.
LINDA.   Why? Why would they laugh at you? Don't talk that way, Willy.   320

[*WILLY moves to the edge of the stage. LINDA goes into the kitchen and starts to darn stockings.*]

WILLY.   I don't know the reason for it, but they just pass me by. I'm not noticed.
LINDA.   But you're doing wonderful, dear. You're making seventy to a hundred
dollars a week.
WILLY.   But I gotta be at it ten, twelve hours a day. Other men—I don't know—
they do it easier. I don't know why—I can't stop myself—I talk too much. A man oughta
come in with a few words. One thing about Charley. He's a man of few words, and they respect him.
LINDA.   You don't talk too much, you're just lively.
WILLY.   [*smiling*] Well, I figure, what the hell, life is short, a couple of jokes. [*to*   325
himself] I joke too much! [*The smile goes.*]
LINDA.   Why? You're—
WILLY.   I'm fat. I'm very—foolish to look at, Linda. I didn't tell you, but Christmas
time I happened to be calling on F. H. Stewarts, and a salesman I know, as I was going in
to see the buyer I heard him say something about—walrus. And I—I cracked him right
across the face. I won't take that. I simply will not take that. But they do laugh at me. I
know that.
LINDA.   Darling . . .
WILLY.   I gotta overcome it. I know I gotta overcome it. I'm not dressing to advan-
tage, maybe.
LINDA.   Willy, darling, you're the handsomest man in the world—   330
WILLY.   Oh, no, Linda.

LINDA.   To me you are. [*slight pause*] The handsomest.

[*From the darkness is heard the laughter of a woman. WILLY doesn't turn to it, but it continues through LINDA's lines.*]

LINDA.   And the boys, Willy. Few men are idolized by their children the way you are.

[*Music is heard as behind a scrim, to the left of the house, The WOMAN, dimly seen, is dressing.*]

WILLY.   [*with great feeling*] You're the best there is, Linda, you're a pal, you know that? On the road—on the road I want to grab you sometimes and just kiss the life outa you.

[*The laughter is loud now, and he moves into a brightening area at the left, where THE WOMAN has come from behind the scrim and is standing, putting on her hat, looking into a "mirror" and laughing.*]

WILLY.   Cause I get so lonely—especially when business is bad and there's nobody   335
to talk to. I get the feeling that I'll never sell anything again, that I won't make a living for you, or a business, a business for the boys. [*He talks through THE WOMAN's subsiding laughter; THE WOMAN primps at the "mirror."*] There's so much I want to make for—

THE WOMAN.   Me? You didn't make me, Willy. I picked you.

WILLY.   [*pleased*] You picked me?

THE WOMAN.   [*who is quite proper-looking, WILLY's age*] I did. I've been sitting at that desk watching all the salesmen go by, day in, day out. But you've got such a sense of humor, and we do have such a good time together, don't we?

WILLY.   Sure, sure. [*He takes her in his arms.*] Why do you have to go now?

THE WOMAN.   It's two o'clock . . .   340

WILLY.   No, come on in! [*He pulls her.*]

THE WOMAN.   . . . my sisters'll be scandalized. When'll you be back?

WILLY.   Oh, two weeks about. Will you come up again?

THE WOMAN.   Sure thing. You do make me laugh. It's good for me. [*She squeezes his arm, kisses him.*] And I think you're a wonderful man.

WILLY.   You picked me, heh?   345

THE WOMAN.   Sure. Because you're so sweet. And such a kidder.

WILLY.   Well, I'll see you next time I'm in Boston.

THE WOMAN.   I'll put you right through to the buyers.

WILLY.   [*slapping her bottom*] Right. Well, bottoms up!

THE WOMAN.   [*slaps him gently and laughs*] You just kill me, Willy. [*He suddenly grabs*   350
her and kisses her roughly.] You kill me. And thanks for the stockings. I love a lot of stockings. Well, good night.

WILLY.   Good night. And keep your pores open!

THE WOMAN.   Oh, Willy!

[*THE WOMAN bursts out laughing, and LINDA's laughter blends in. THE WOMAN disappears into the dark. Now the area at the kitchen table brightens. LINDA is sitting where she was at the kitchen table, but now is mending a pair of her silk stockings.*]

LINDA.   You are, Willy. The handsomest man. You've got no reason to feel that—

WILLY.   [*coming out of THE WOMAN's dimming area and going over to LINDA*] I'll make it all up to you, Linda, I'll—

LINDA.   There's nothing to make up, dear. You're doing fine, better than—   355

WILLY.   [*noticing her mending*] What's that?

LINDA.   Just mending my stockings. They're so expensive—

WILLY.   [*angrily, taking them from her*] I won't have you mending stockings in this house! Now throw them out!

[*LINDA puts the stockings in her pocket.*]

BERNARD.   [*entering on the run*] Where is he? If he doesn't study!

WILLY.   [*moving to the forestage, with great agitation*] You'll give him the answers!   360

BERNARD   I do, but I can't on a Regents! That's state exam! They're liable to arrest me!

WILLY.   Where is he? I'll whip him, I'll whip him!

LINDA.   And he'd better give back that football, Willy, it's not nice.

WILLY.   Biff! Where is he? Why is he taking everything?

LINDA.   He's too rough with the girls, Willy. All the mothers are afraid of him!   365

WILLY.   I'll whip him!

BERNARD.   He's driving the car without a license!

[*THE WOMAN's laugh is heard.*]

WILLY.   Shut up!

LINDA.   All the mothers—

WILLY.   Shut up!   370

BERNARD.   [*backing quietly away and out*] Mr. Birnbaum says he's stuck up.

WILLY.   Get outa here!

BERNARD.   If he doesn't buckle down he'll flunk math! [*He goes off.*]

LINDA.   He's right, Willy, you've gotta—

WILLY.   [*exploding at her*] There's nothing the matter with him! You want him to be   375
a worm like Bernard? He's got spirit, personality . . .

[*As he speaks, LINDA, almost in tears, exits into the living-room. WILLY is alone in the kitchen, wilting and staring. The leaves are gone. It is night again, and the apartment houses look down from behind.*]

WILLY.   Loaded with it. Loaded! What is he stealing? He's giving it back, isn't he? Why is he stealing? What did I tell him? I never in my life told him anything but decent things.

[*HAPPY in pajamas has come down the stairs; WILLY suddenly becomes aware of HAPPY's presence.*]

HAPPY.   Let's go now, come on.

WILLY.   [*sitting down at the kitchen table*] Huh! Why did she have to wax the floors herself? Everytime she waxes the floors she keels over. She knows that!

HAPPY.   Shh! Take it easy. What brought you back tonight?

WILLY.   I got an awful scare. Nearly hit a kid in Yonkers. God! Why didn't I go to   380
Alaska with my brother Ben that time! Ben! That man was a genius, that man was success incarnate! What a mistake! He begged me to go.

HAPPY.   Well, there's no use in—

WILLY.   You guys! There was a man started with the clothes on his back and ended up with diamond mines!

HAPPY.   Boy, someday I'd like to know how he did it.

WILLY.   What's the mystery? The man knew what he wanted and went out and got it! Walked into a jungle, and comes out, the age of twenty-one, and he's rich! The world is an oyster, but you don't crack it open on a mattress!

HAPPY.   Pop, I told you I'm gonna retire you for life.   385

WILLY.   You'll retire me for life on seventy goddam dollars a week? And your women and your car and your apartment, and you'll retire me for life! Christ's sake, I couldn't get past Yonkers today! Where are you guys, where are you? The woods are burning! I can't drive a car!

[*CHARLEY has appeared in the doorway. He is a large man, slow of speech, laconic, immovable. In all he says, despite what he says, there is pity, and now, trepidation. He has a robe over pajamas, slippers on his feet. He enters the kitchen.*]

CHARLEY.   Everything all right?
HAPPY.   Yeah, Charley, everything's . . .
WILLY.   What's the matter?
CHARLEY.   I heard some noise. I thought something happened. Can't we do some-   390
thing about the walls? You sneeze in here, and in my house hats blow off.
HAPPY.   Let's go to bed, Dad. Come on.

[*CHARLEY signals to HAPPY to go.*]

WILLY.   You go ahead, I'm not tired at the moment.
HAPPY.   [*to WILLY*] Take it easy, huh? [*He exits.*]
WILLY.   What're you doin' up?
CHARLEY.   [*sitting down at the kitchen table opposite WILLY*] Couldn't sleep good. I had   395
a heartburn.
WILLY.   Well, you don't know how to eat.
CHARLEY.   I eat with my mouth.
WILLY.   No, you're ignorant. You gotta know about vitamins and things like that.
CHARLEY.   Come on, let's shoot. Tire you out a little.
WILLY.   [*hesitantly*] All right. You got cards?   400
CHARLEY.   [*taking a deck from his pocket*] Yeah, I got them. Someplace. What is it with those vitamins?
WILLY.   [*dealing*] They build up your bones. Chemistry.
CHARLEY.   Yeah, but there's no bones in a heartburn.
WILLY.   What are you talkin' about? Do you know the first thing about it?
CHARLEY.   Don't get insulted.   405
WILLY.   Don't talk about something you don't know anything about.

[*They are playing. Pause.*]

CHARLEY.   What're you doin' home?
WILLY.   A little trouble with the car.
CHARLEY.   Oh, [*Pause*] I'd like to take a trip to California.
WILLY.   Don't say.   410
CHARLEY.   You want a job?
WILLY.   I got a job, I told you that. [*after a slight pause*] What the hell are you offer-
ing me a job for?
CHARLEY.   Don't get insulted.
WILLY.   Don't insult me.
CHARLEY.   I don't see no sense in it. You don't have to go on this way.   415
WILLY.   I got a good job. [*slight pause*] What do you keep comin' in for?
CHARLEY.   You want me to go?
WILLY.   [*after a pause, withering*] I can't understand it. He's going back to Texas again. What the hell is that?
CHARLEY.   Let him go.

WILLY.   I got nothin' to give him, Charley, I'm clean, I'm clean.   420
CHARLEY.   He won't starve. None a them starve. Forget about him.
WILLY.   Then what have I got to remember?
CHARLEY.   You take it too hard. To hell with it. When a deposit bottle is broken you
don't get your nickel back.
WILLY.   That's easy enough for you to say.
CHARLEY.   That ain't easy for me to say.   425
WILLY.   Did you see the ceiling I put up in the living-room?
CHARLEY.   Yeah, that's a piece of work. To put up a ceiling is a mystery to me. How
do you do it?
WILLY.   What's the difference?
CHARLEY.   Well, talk about it.
WILLY.   You gonna put up a ceiling?   430
CHARLEY.   How could I put up a ceiling?
WILLY.   Then what the hell are you bothering me for?
CHARLEY.   You're insulted again.
WILLY.   A man who can't handle tools is not a man. You're disgusting.
CHARLEY.   Don't call me disgusting, Willy.   435

[*UNCLE BEN, carrying a valise and an umbrella, enters the forestage from around the right corner of
the house. He is a stolid man, in his sixties, with a mustache and an authoritative air. He is utterly
certain of his destiny, and there is an aura of far places about him. He enters exactly as* WILLY
speaks.]

WILLY.   I'm getting awfully tired, Ben.

[*BEN's music is heard.* BEN *looks around at everything.*]

CHARLEY.   Good, keep playing; you'll sleep better. Did you call me Ben?

[*BEN looks at his watch.*]

WILLY.   That's funny. For a second there you reminded me of my brother Ben.
BEN.   I only have a few minutes. [*He strolls, inspecting the place.* WILLY *and* CHARLEY
continue playing.]
CHARLEY.   You never heard from him again, heh? Since that time?   440
WILLY.   Didn't Linda tell you? Couple of weeks ago we got a letter from his wife in
Africa. He died.
CHARLEY.   That so.
BEN.   [*chuckling*] So this is Brooklyn, eh?
CHARLEY.   Maybe you're in for some of his money.
WILLY.   Naa, he had seven sons. There's just one opportunity I had with that   445
man . . .
BEN.   I must make a train, William. There are several properties I'm looking at in
Alaska.
WILLY.   Sure, sure! If I'd gone with him to Alaska that time, everything would've
been totally different.
CHARLEY.   Go on, you'd froze to death up there.
WILLY.   What're you talking about?
BEN.   Opportunity is tremendous in Alaska, William. Surprised you're not up   450
there.
WILLY.   Sure, tremendous.
CHARLEY.   Heh?

WILLY.   There was the only man I ever met who knew the answers.

CHARLEY.   Who?

BEN.   How are you all?   455

WILLY.   [*taking a pot, smiling*] Fine, fine.

CHARLEY.   Pretty sharp tonight.

BEN.   Is Mother living with you?

WILLY.   No, she died a long time ago.

CHARLEY.   Who?   460

BEN.   That's too bad. Fine specimen of a lady, Mother.

WILLY.   [*to CHARLEY*] Heh?

BEN.   I'd hoped to see the old girl.

CHARLEY.   Who died?

BEN.   Heard anything from Father, have you?   465

WILLY.   [*unnerved*] What do you mean, who died?

CHARLEY.   [*taking a pot*] What're you talkin' about?

BEN.   [*looking at his watch*] William, it's half-past eight!

WILLY.   [*As though to dispel his confusion he angrily stops CHARLEY's hand.*] That's my build!

CHARLEY.   I put the ace—   470

WILLY.   If you don't know how to play the game I'm not gonna throw my money away on you!

CHARLEY.   [*rising*] It was my ace, for God's sake!

WILLY.   I'm through, I'm through!

BEN.   When did Mother die?

WILLY.   Long ago. Since the beginning you never knew how to play cards.   475

CHARLEY.   [*picks up the cards and goes to the door*] All right! Next time I'll bring a deck with five aces.

WILLY.   I don't play that kind of game!

CHARLEY.   [*turning to him*] You ought to be ashamed of yourself!

WILLY.   Yeah?

CHARLEY.   Yeah! [*He goes out.*]   480

WILLY.   [*slamming the door after him*] Ignoramus!

BEN.   [*as WILLY comes toward him through the wall-line of the kitchen*] So you're William.

WILLY.   [*shaking BEN's hand*] Ben! I've been waiting for you so long! What's the answer? How did you do it?

BEN.   Oh, there's a story in that.

[*LINDA enters the forestage, as of old, carrying the wash basket.*]

LINDA.   Is this Ben?   485

BEN.   [*gallantly*] How do you do, my dear.

LINDA.   Where've you been all these years? Willy's always wondered why you—

WILLY.   [*pulling BEN away from her impatiently*] Where is Dad? Didn't you follow him? How did you get started?

BEN.   Well, I don't know how much you remember.

WILLY.   Well, I was just a baby, of course, only three or four years old—   490

BEN.   Three years and eleven months.

WILLY.   What a memory, Ben!

BEN.   I have many enterprises, William, and I have never kept books.

WILLY.   I remember I was sitting under the wagon in—was it Nebraska?

BEN.   It was South Dakota, and I gave you a bunch of wild flowers.   495

WILLY.   I remember you walking away down some open road.

BEN.   [*laughing*] I was going to find Father in Alaska.

WILLY.   Where is he?

BEN.   At that age I had a very faulty view of geography, William. I discovered after a few days that I was heading due south, so instead of Alaska, I ended up in Africa.

LINDA.   Africa!   500

WILLY.   The Gold Coast!

BEN.   Principally diamond mines.

LINDA.   Diamond mines!

BEN.   Yes, my dear. But I've only a few minutes—

WILLY.   No! Boys! Boys! [*YOUNG BIFF and HAPPY appear.*] Listen to this. This is your   505
Uncle Ben, a great man! Tell my boys, Ben!

BEN.   Why, boys, when I was seventeen I walked into the jungle, and when I was twenty-one I walked out. [*He laughs.*] And by God I was rich.

WILLY.   [*to the boys*] You see what I been talking about? The greatest things can happen!

BEN.   [*glancing at his watch*] I have an appointment in Ketchikan Tuesday week.

WILLY.   No, Ben. Please tell about Dad. I want my boys to hear. I want them to know the kind of stock they spring from. All I remember is a man with a big beard, and I was in Mamma's lap, sitting around a fire, and some kind of high music.

BEN.   His flute. He played the flute.   510

WILLY.   Sure, the flute, that's right!

[*New music is heard, a high, rollicking tune.*]

BEN.   Father was a very great and a very wild-hearted man. We would start in Boston, and he'd toss the whole family into the wagon, and then he'd drive the team right across the country; through Ohio, and Indiana, Michigan, Illinois, and all the Western states. And we'd stop in the towns and sell the flutes that he'd made on the way. Great inventor, Father. With one gadget he made more in a week than a man like you could make in a lifetime.

WILLY.   That's just the way I'm bringing them up, Ben—rugged, well liked, all-around.

BEN.   Yeah? [*to BIFF*] Hit that, boy—hard as you can. [*He pounds his stomach.*]

BIFF.   Oh, no, sir!   515

BEN.   [*taking boxing stance*] Come on, get to me! [*He laughs.*]

BIFF.   Okay! [*He cocks his fists and starts in.*]

WILLY.   Go to it, Biff! Go ahead, show him!

LINDA.   [*to WILLY*] Why must he fight, dear?

BEN.   [*sparring with BIFF*] Good boy! Good boy!   520

WILLY.   How's that, Ben, heh?

HAPPY.   Give him the left, Biff!

LINDA.   Why are you fighting?

BEN.   Good boy! [*suddenly comes in, trips BIFF, and stands over him, the point of his umbrella poised over BIFF's eye.*]

LINDA.   Look out, Biff!   525

BIFF.   Gee!

BEN.   [*patting BIFF's knee*] Never fight fair with a stranger, boy. You'll never get out of the jungle that way. [*taking LINDA's hand and bowing*] It was an honor and a pleasure to meet you, Linda.

LINDA.   [*withdrawing her hand coldly, frightened*] Have a nice—trip.

BEN.   [*to* WILLY] And good luck with your—what do you do?

WILLY.   Selling.   530

BEN.   Yes. Well . . . [*He raises his hand in farewell to all.*]

WILLY.   No, Ben, I don't want you to think . . . [*He takes* BEN's *arm to show him.*] It's Brooklyn, I know, but we hunt too.

BEN.   Really, now.

WILLY.   Oh, sure, there's snakes and rabbits and—that's why I moved out here. Why, Biff can fell any one of these trees in no time! Boys! Go right over to where they're building the apartment house and get some sand. We're gonna rebuild the entire front stoop right now! Watch this, Ben!

BIFF.   Yes, sir! On the double, Hap!   535

HAPPY.   [*as he and* BIFF *run off*] I lost weight, Pop, you notice?

[CHARLEY *enters in knickers, even before the boys are gone.*]

CHARLEY.   Listen, if they steal any more from that building the watchman'll put the cops on them!

LINDA.   [*to* WILLY] Don't let Biff . . .

[BEN *laughs lustily.*]

WILLY.   You shoulda seen the lumber they brought home last week. At least a dozen six-by-tens worth all kinds a money.

CHARLEY.   Listen, if that watchman—   540

WILLY.   I gave them hell, understand. But I got a couple of fearless characters there.

CHARLEY.   Willy, the jails are full of fearless characters.

BEN.   [*clapping* WILLY *on the back, with a laugh at* CHARLEY] And the stock exchange, friend!

WILLY.   [*joining in* BEN's *laughter*] Where are the rest of your pants?

CHARLEY.   My wife bought them.   545

WILLY.   Now all you need is a golf club and you can go upstairs and go to sleep. [*to* BEN] Great athlete! Between him and his son Bernard they can't hammer a nail!

BERNARD.   [*rushing in*] The watchman's chasing Biff!

WILLY.   [*angrily*] Shut up! He's not stealing anything!

LINDA.   [*alarmed, hurrying off left*] Where is he? Biff, dear! [*She exits.*]

WILLY.   [*moving toward the left, away from* BEN] There's nothing wrong. What's the   550
matter with you?

BEN.   Nervy boy. Good!

WILLY.   [*laughing*] Oh, nerves of iron, that Biff!

CHARLEY.   Don't know what it is. My New England man comes back and he's bleed-in', they murdered him up there.

WILLY.   It's contacts, Charley, I got important contacts!

CHARLEY.   [*sarcastically*] Glad to hear it, Willy. Come in later, we'll shoot a little   555
casino. I'll take some of your Portland money. [*He laughs at* WILLY *and exits.*]

WILLY.   [*turning to* BEN] Business is bad, it's murderous. But not for me, of course.

BEN.   I'll stop by on my way back to Africa.

WILLY.   [*longingly.*] Can't you stay a few days? You're just what I need, Ben, because I—I have a fine position here, but I—well, Dad left when I was such a baby and I never had a chance to talk to him and I still feel—kind of temporary about myself.

BEN.   I'll be late for my train.

[*They are at opposite ends of the stage.*]

WILLY.   Ben, my boys—can't we talk? They'd go into the jaws of hell for me, see,   560
but I—

BEN.   William, you're being first-rate with your boys. Outstanding, manly chaps!

WILLY.   [*hanging on to his words*] Oh, Ben, that's good to hear! Because sometimes
I'm afraid that I'm not teaching them the right kind of—Ben, how should I teach them?

BEN.   [*giving great weight to each word, and with a certain vicious audacity*] William,
when I walked into the jungle, I was seventeen. When I walked out I was twenty-one. And,
by God, I was rich! [*He goes off into darkness around the right corner of the house.*]

WILLY.   . . . was rich! That's just the spirit I want to imbue them with! To walk into
a jungle! I was right! I was right! I was right!

[*BEN is gone, but WILLY is still speaking to him as LINDA, in her nightgown and robe, enters the
kitchen, glances around for WILLY, then goes to the door of the house, looks out and sees him. Comes
down to his left. He looks at her.*]

LINDA.   Willy, dear? Willy?   565

WILLY.   I was right!

LINDA.   Did you have some cheese? [*He can't answer.*] It's very late, darling. Come
to bed, heh?

WILLY.   [*looking straight up*] Gotta break your neck to see a star in this yard.

LINDA.   You coming in?

WILLY.   Whatever happened to that diamond watch fob? Remember? When Ben   570
came from Africa that time? Didn't he give me a watch fob with a diamond in it?

LINDA.   You pawned it, dear. Twelve, thirteen years ago. For Biff's radio correspondence course.

WILLY.   Gee, that was a beautiful thing. I'll take a walk.

LINDA.   But you're in your slippers.

WILLY.   [*starting to go around the house at the left*] I was right! I was! [*Half to LINDA, as
he goes, shaking his head*] What a man! There was a man worth talking to. I was right!

LINDA.   [*calling after WILLY*] But in your slippers, Willy!   575

[*WILLY is almost gone when BIFF, in his pajamas, comes down the stairs and enters the kitchen.*]

BIFF.   What is he doing out there?

LINDA.   Sh!

BIFF.   God Almighty, Mom, how long has he been doing this?

LINDA.   Don't, he'll hear you.

BIFF.   What the hell is the matter with him?   580

LINDA.   It'll pass by morning.

BIFF.   Shouldn't we do anything?

LINDA.   Oh, my dear, you should do a lot of things, but there's nothing to do, so
go to sleep.

[*HAPPY comes down the stairs and sits on the steps.*]

HAPPY.   I never heard him so loud, Mom.

LINDA.   Well, come around more often; you'll hear him. [*She sits down at the table*   585
and mends the lining of WILLY's jacket.]

BIFF.   Why didn't you ever write me about this, Mom?

LINDA.   How would I write to you? For over three months you had no address.

BIFF.   I was on the move. But you know I thought of you all the time. You know
that, don't you, pal?

LINDA.   I know, dear, I know. But he likes to have a letter. Just to know that there's
still a possibility for better things.

BIFF.   He's not like this all the time, is he?   590

LINDA.   It's when you come home he's always the worst.

BIFF.   When I come home?

LINDA.   When you write you're coming, he's all smiles, and talks about the future, and—he's just wonderful. And then the closer you seem to come, the more shaky he gets, and then, by the time you get here, he's arguing, and he seems angry at you. I think it's just that maybe he can't bring himself to—to open up to you. Why are you so hateful to each other? Why is that?

BIFF.   [*evasively*] I'm not hateful, Mom.

LINDA.   But you no sooner come in the door than you're fighting!   595

BIFF.   I don't know why. I mean to change. I'm tryin', Mom, you understand?

LINDA.   Are you home to stay now?

BIFF.   I don't know. I want to look around, see what's doin'.

LINDA.   Biff, you can't look around all your life, can you?

BIFF.   I just can't take hold, Mom. I can't take hold of some kind of a life.   600

LINDA.   Biff, a man is not a bird, to come and go with the springtime.

BIFF.   Your hair . . . [*He touches her hair.*] Your hair got so gray.

LINDA.   Oh, it's been gray since you were in high school. I just stopped dyeing it, that's all.

BIFF.   Dye it again, will ya? I don't want my pal looking old. [*He smiles.*]

LINDA.   You're such a boy! You think you can go away for a year and . . . You've got   605
to get it into your head now that one day you'll knock on this door and there'll be strange people here—

BIFF.   What are you talking about? You're not even sixty, Mom.

LINDA.   But what about your father?

BIFF.   [*lamely*] Well, I meant him, too.

HAPPY.   He admires Pop.

LINDA.   Biff, dear, if you don't have any feeling for him, then you can't have any   610
feeling for me.

BIFF.   Sure I can, Mom.

LINDA.   No. You can't just come to see me, because I love him. [*with a threat, but only a threat, of tears*] He's the dearest man in the world to me, and I won't have anyone making him feel unwanted and low and blue. You've got to make up your mind now, dar-ling, there's no leeway any more. Either he's your father and you pay him that respect, or else you're not to come here. I know he's not easy to get along with—nobody knows that better than me—but . . .

WILLY.   [*from the left, with a laugh*] Hey, hey, Biffo!

BIFF.   [*starting to go out after WILLY*] What the hell is the matter with him? [*HAPPY stops him.*]

LINDA.   Don't—don't go near him!   615

BIFF.   Stop making excuses for him! He always, always wiped the floor with you. Never had an ounce of respect for you.

HAPPY.   He's always had respect for—

BIFF.   What the hell do you know about it?

HAPPY.   [*surlily*] Just don't call him crazy!

BIFF.   He's got no character—Charley wouldn't do this. Not in his own house—   620
spewing out that vomit from his mind.

HAPPY.   Charley never had to cope with what he's got to.

BIFF.   People are worse off than Willy Loman. Believe me, I've seen them!

LINDA.   Then make Charley your father, Biff. You can't do that, can you? I don't say he's a great man. Willy Loman never made a lot of money. His name was never in the paper. He's not the finest character that ever lived. But he's a human being, and a terrible thing is happening to him. So attention must be paid. He's not to be allowed to fall into his grave like an old dog. Attention, attention must be finally paid to such a person. You called him crazy—

BIFF.   I didn't mean—

LINDA.   No, a lot of people think he's lost his—balance. But you don't have to be   625
very smart to know what his trouble is. The man is exhausted.

HAPPY.   Sure!

LINDA.   A small man can be just as exhausted as a great man. He works for a company thirty-six years this March, opens up unheard-of territories to their trademark, and now in his old age they take his salary away.

HAPPY.   [*indignantly*] I didn't know that, Mom.

LINDA.   You never asked, my dear! Now that you get your spending money someplace else you don't trouble your mind with him.

HAPPY.   But I gave you money last—   630

LINDA.   Christmas time, fifty dollars! To fix the hot water it cost ninety-seven fifty! For five weeks he's been on straight commission,° like a beginner, an unknown!

BIFF.   Those ungrateful bastards!

LINDA.   Are they any worse than his sons? When he brought them business, when he was young, they were glad to see him. But now his old friends, the old buyers that loved him so and always found some order to hand him in a pinch—they're all dead, retired. He used to be able to make six, seven calls a day in Boston. Now he takes his valises out of the car and puts them back and takes them out again and he's exhausted. Instead of walking he talks now. He drives seven hundred miles, and when he gets there no one knows him any more, no one welcomes him. And what goes through a man's mind, driving seven hundred miles home without having earned a cent? Why shouldn't he talk to himself? Why? When he has to go to Charley and borrow fifty dollars a week and pretend to me that it's his pay? How long can that go on? How long? You see what I'm sitting here and waiting for? And you tell me he has no character? The man who never worked a day but for your benefit? When does he get the medal for that? Is this his reward—to turn around at the age of sixty-three and find his sons, who he loved better than his life, one a philandering bum—

HAPPY.   Mom!

LINDA.   That's all you are, my baby! [*To BIFF*] And you! What happened to the love   635
you had for him? You were such pals! How you used to talk to him on the phone every night! How lonely he was till he could come home to you!

BIFF.   All right, Mom. I'll live here in my room, and I'll get a job. I'll keep away from him, that's all.

LINDA.   No, Biff. You can't stay here and fight all the time.

BIFF.   He threw me out of this house, remember that.

LINDA.   Why did he do that? I never knew why.

BIFF.   Because I know he's a fake and he doesn't like anybody around who knows!   640

LINDA.   Why a fake? In what way? What do you mean?

BIFF.   Just don't lay it all at my feet. It's between me and him—that's all I have to say. I'll chip in from now on. He'll settle for half my pay check. He'll be all right. I'm going to bed. [*He starts for the stairs.*]

LINDA.   He won't be all right.

---

631 *straight commission:* refers to the fact that Willy is receiving no salary, only a commission (percentage) on the sales he makes.

BIFF.   [*turning on the stairs, furiously*] I hate this city and I'll stay here. Now what do you want?

LINDA.   He's dying, Biff.   645

[*HAPPY turns quickly to her, shocked.*]

BIFF.   [*after a pause*] Why is he dying?

LINDA.   He's been trying to kill himself.

BIFF.   [*with great horror*] How?

LINDA.   I live from day to day.

BIFF.   What're you talking about?   650

LINDA.   Remember I wrote you that he smashed up the car again? In February?

BIFF.   Well?

LINDA.   The insurance inspector came. He said that they have evidence. That all these accidents in the last year—weren't—weren't—accidents.

HAPPY.   How can they tell that? That's a lie.

LINDA.   It seems there's a woman . . . [*She takes a breath as*]   655

{ BIFF.   [*sharply but contained*] What woman?

  LINDA.   [*simultaneously*] . . . and this woman . . .

  LINDA.   What?

BIFF.   Nothing. Go ahead.

LINDA.   What did you say?   660

BIFF.   Nothing. I just said what woman?

HAPPY.   What about her?

LINDA.   Well, it seems she was walking down the road and saw his car. She says that he wasn't driving fast at all, and that he didn't skid. She says he came to that little bridge, and then deliberately smashed into the railing, and it was only the shallowness of the water that saved him.

BIFF.   Oh, no, he probably just fell asleep again.

LINDA.   I don't think he fell asleep.   665

BIFF.   Why not?

LINDA.   Last month . . . [*with great difficulty*] Oh, boys, it's so hard to say a thing like this! He's just a big stupid man to you, but I tell you there's more good in him than in many other people. [*She chokes, wipes her eyes.*] I was looking for a fuse. The lights blew out, and I went down the cellar. And behind the fuse box—it happened to fall out—was a length of rubber pipe—just short.

HAPPY.   No kidding?

LINDA.   There's a little attachment on the end of it. I knew right away. And sure enough, on the bottom of the water heater there's a new little nipple on the gas pipe.

HAPPY.   [*angrily*] That—jerk.   670

BIFF.   Did you have it taken off?

LINDA.   I'm—I'm ashamed to. How can I mention it to him? Every day I go down and take away that little rubber pipe. But, when he comes home, I put it back where it was. How can I insult him that way? I don't know what to do. I live from day to day, boys. I tell you, I know every thought in his mind. It sounds so old-fashioned and silly, but I tell you he put his whole life into you and you've turned your backs on him. [*She is bent over in the chair, weeping, her face in her hands.*] Biff, I swear to God! Biff, his life is in your hands!

HAPPY.   [*to BIFF*] How do you like that damned fool!

BIFF.   [*kissing her*] All right, pal, all right. It's all settled now. I've been remiss. I know that, Mom. But now I'll stay, and I swear to you, I'll apply myself. [*kneeling in front of her, in a fever of self-reproach*] It's just—you see, Mom, I don't fit in business. Not that I won't try. I'll try, and I'll make good.

HAPPY.   Sure you will. The trouble with you in business was you never tried to   675
please people.

BIFF.   I know, I—

HAPPY.   Like when you worked for Harrison's. Bob Harrison said you were tops,
and then you go and do some damn fool thing like whistling whole songs in the elevator
like a comedian.

BIFF.   [*against HAPPY*] So what? I like to whistle sometimes.

HAPPY.   You don't raise a guy to a responsible job who whistles in the elevator!

LINDA.   Well, don't argue about it now.   680

HAPPY.   Like when you'd go off and swim in the middle of the day instead of taking the line around.

BIFF.   [*his resentment rising*] Well, don't you run off? You take off sometimes, don't
you? On a nice summer day?

HAPPY.   Yeah, but I cover myself!

LINDA.   Boys!

HAPPY.   If I'm going to take a fade the boss can call any number where I'm sup-   685
posed to be and they'll swear to him that I just left. I'll tell you something that I hate to
say, Biff, but in the business world some of them think you're crazy.

BIFF.   [*angered*] Screw the business world!

HAPPY.   All right, screw it! Great, but cover yourself!

LINDA.   Hap, Hap!

BIFF.   I don't care what they think! They've laughed at Dad for years, and you
know why? Because we don't belong in this nuthouse of a city! We should be mixing cement on some open plain, or—or carpenters. A carpenter is allowed to whistle!

[*WILLY walks in from the entrance of the house, at left.*]

WILLY.   Even your grandfather was better than a carpenter. [*Pause. They watch*   690
him.] You never grew up. Bernard does not whistle in the elevator, I assure you.

BIFF.   [*as though to laugh WILLY out of it*] Yeah, but you do, Pop.

WILLY.   I never in my life whistled in an elevator! And who in the business world
thinks I'm crazy?

BIFF.   I didn't mean it like that, Pop. Now don't make a whole thing out of it,
will ya?

WILLY.   Go back to the West! Be a carpenter, a cowboy, enjoy yourself!

LINDA.   Willy, he was just saying—   695

WILLY.   I heard what he said!

HAPPY.   [*trying to quiet WILLY*] Hey, Pop, come on now . . .

WILLY.   [*continuing over HAPPY's line*] They laugh at me, heh? Go to Filene's, go to
the Hub, go to Slattery's,° Boston. Call out the name Willy Loman and see what happens!
Big shot!

BIFF.   All right, Pop.

WILLY.   Big!   700

BIFF.   All right!

WILLY.   Why do you always insult me?

BIFF.   I didn't say a word! [*to LINDA*] Did I say a word?

LINDA.   He didn't say anything, Willy.

WILLY.   [*going to the doorway of the living room*] All right, good night, good night.   705

LINDA.   Willy, dear, he just decided . . .

---

698 *Filene's, the Hub, Slattery's:* department stores in New England.

WILLY.   [*to BIFF*] If you get tired hanging around tomorrow, paint the ceiling I put up in the living-room.

BIFF.   I'm leaving early tomorrow.

HAPPY.   He's going to see Bill Oliver, Pop.

WILLY.   [*interestedly*] Oliver? For what?   710

BIFF.   [*with reserve, but trying, trying*] He always said he'd stake me. I'd like to go into business, so maybe I can take him up on it.

LINDA.   Isn't that wonderful?

WILLY.   Don't interrupt. What's wonderful about it? There's fifty men in the City of New York who'd stake him. [*to BIFF*] Sporting goods?

BIFF.   I guess so. I know something about it and—

WILLY.   He knows something about it! You know sporting goods better than Spald-   715
ing, for God's sake! How much is he giving you?

BIFF.   I don't know. I didn't even see him yet, but—

WILLY.   Then what're you talkin' about?

BIFF.   [*getting angry*] Well, all I said was I'm gonna see him, that's all!

WILLY.   [*turning away*] Ah, you're counting your chickens again.

BIFF.   [*starting left for the stairs*] Oh, Jesus, I'm going to sleep!   720

WILLY.   [*calling after him*] Don't curse in this house!

BIFF.   [*turning*] Since when did you get so clean?

HAPPY.   [*trying to stop them*] Wait a . . .

WILLY.   Don't use that language to me! I won't have it!

HAPPY.   [*grabbing BIFF, shouts*] Wait a minute! I got an idea. I got a feasible idea.   725
Come here, Biff, let's talk this over now, let's talk some sense here. When I was down in Florida last time, I thought of a great idea to sell sporting goods. It just came back to me. You and I, Biff—we have a line, the Loman Line. We train a couple of weeks, and put on a couple of exhibitions, see?

WILLY.   That's an idea!

HAPPY.   Wait! We form two basketball teams, see? Two waterpolo teams. We play each other. It's a million dollars' worth of publicity. Two brothers, see? The Loman Broth-ers. Displays in the Royal Palms—all the hotels. And banners over the ring and the bas-ketball court: "Loman Brothers." Baby, we could sell sporting goods!

WILLY.   That is a one-million-dollar idea!

LINDA.   Marvelous!

BIFF.   I'm in great shape as far as that's concerned.   730

HAPPY.   And the beauty of it is, Biff, it wouldn't be like a business. We'd be out playin' ball again . . .

BIFF.   [*enthused*] Yeah, that's . . .

WILLY.   Million-dollar . . .

HAPPY.   And you wouldn't get fed up with it, Biff. It'd be the family again. There'd be the old honor, and comradeship, and if you wanted to go off for a swim or some-thin'—well, you'd do it! Without some smart cooky gettin' up ahead of you!

WILLY.   Lick the world! You guys together could absolutely lick the civilized world.   735

BIFF.   I'll see Oliver tomorrow. Hap, if we could work that out . . .

LINDA.   Maybe things are beginning to—

WILLY.   [*wildly enthused, to LINDA*] Stop interrupting! [*to BIFF*] But don't wear sport jacket and slacks when you see Oliver.

BIFF.   No, I'll—

WILLY.   A business suit, and talk as little as possible, and don't crack any jokes.   740

BIFF.   He did like me. Always liked me.

LINDA.   He loved you!

WILLY.   [*to LINDA*] Will you stop! [*to BIFF*] Walk in very serious. You are not applying for a boy's job. Money is to pass. Be quiet, fine, and serious. Everybody likes a kidder, but nobody lends him money.

HAPPY.   I'll try to get some myself, Biff. I'm sure I can.

WILLY.   I see great things for you kids. I think your troubles are over. But remem-   745
ber, start big and you'll end big. Ask for fifteen. How much you gonna ask for?

BIFF.   Gee, I don't know—

WILLY.   And don't say "Gee." "Gee" is a boy's word. A man walking in for fifteen thousand dollars does not say "Gee!"

BIFF.   Ten, I think, would be top though.

WILLY.   Don't be so modest. You always started too low. Walk in with a big laugh. Don't look worried. Start off with a couple of your good stories to lighten things up. It's not what you say, it's how you say it—because personality always wins the day.

LINDA.   Oliver always thought the highest of him—   750

WILLY.   Will you let me talk?

BIFF.   Don't yell at her, Pop, will ya?

WILLY.   [*angrily*] I was talking, wasn't I?

BIFF.   I don't like you yelling at her all the time, and I'm tellin' you, that's all.

WILLY.   What're you, takin' over this house?   755

LINDA.   Willy—

WILLY.   [*turning on her*] Don't take his side all the time, godammit!

BIFF.   [*furiously*] Stop yelling at her!

WILLY.   [*suddenly pulling on his cheek, beaten down, guilt ridden*] Give my best to Bill Oliver—he may remember me.

[*He exits through the living-room doorway.*]

LINDA.   [*her voice subdued*] What'd you have to start that for? [*BIFF turns away.*] You   760
see how sweet he was as soon as you talked hopefully? [*She goes over to BIFF.*] Come up and say good night to him. Don't let him go to bed that way.

HAPPY.   Come on, Biff, let's buck him up.

LINDA.   Please, dear. Just say good night. It takes so little to make him happy. Come. [*She goes through the living-room doorway, calling upstairs from within the living-room.*] Your pajamas are hanging in the bathroom, Willy!

HAPPY.   [*looking toward where LINDA went out*] What a woman! They broke the mold when they made her. You know that, Biff?

BIFF.   He's off salary. My God, working on commission!

HAPPY.   Well, let's face it: he's no hot-shot selling man. Except that sometimes, you   765
have to admit, he's a sweet personality.

BIFF.   [*deciding*] Lend me ten bucks, will ya? I want to buy some new ties.

HAPPY.   I'll take you to a place I know. Beautiful stuff. Wear one of my striped shirts tomorrow.

BIFF.   She got gray. Mom got awful old. Gee, I'm gonna go in to Oliver tomorrow and knock him for a—

HAPPY.   Come on up. Tell that to Dad. Let's give him a whirl. Come on.

BIFF.   [*steamed up*] You know, with ten thousand bucks, boy!   770

HAPPY.   [*as they go into the living-room*] That's the talk, Biff, that's the first time I've heard the old confidence out of you! [*from within the living-room, fading off*] You're gonna live with me, kid, and any babe you want just say the word . . . [*The last lines are hardly heard. They are mounting the stairs to their parents' bedroom.*]

LINDA. [*entering her bedroom and addressing* WILLY, *who is in the bathroom. She is straightening the bed for him.*] Can you do anything about the shower? It drips.

WILLY. [*from the bathroom*] All of a sudden everything falls to pieces! Goddam plumbing, oughta be sued, those people. I hardly finished putting it in and the thing . . . [*His words rumble off.*]

LINDA. I'm just wondering if Oliver will remember him. You think he might?

WILLY. [*coming out of the bathroom in his pajamas*] Remember him? What's the mat-   775
ter with you, you crazy? If he'd've stayed with Oliver he'd be on top by now! Wait'll Oliver gets a look at him. You don't know the average caliber any more. The average young man today—[*He is getting into bed*]—is got a caliber of zero. Greatest thing in the world for him was to bum around.

[BIFF *and* HAPPY *enter the bedroom. Slight pause.*]

WILLY. [*stops short, looking at* BIFF] Glad to hear it, boy.

HAPPY. He wanted to say good night to you, sport.

WILLY. [*to* BIFF] Yeah. Knock him dead, boy. What'd you want to tell me?

BIFF. Just take it easy, Pop. Good night. [*He turns to go.*]

WILLY. [*unable to resist*] And if anything falls off the desk while you're talking to   780
him—like a package or something—don't you pick it up. They have office boys for that.

LINDA. I'll make a big breakfast—

WILLY. Will you let me finish? [*to* BIFF] Tell him you were in the business in the West. Not farm work.

BIFF. All right, Dad.

LINDA. I think everything—

WILLY. [*going right through her speech*] And don't undersell yourself. No less than   785
fifteen thousand dollars.

BIFF. [*unable to bear him*] Okay. Good night, Mom. [*He starts moving.*]

WILLY. Because you got a greatness in you, Biff, remember that. You got all kinds a greatness . . . [*He lies back, exhausted.*]

[BIFF *walks out.*]

LINDA. [*calling after* BIFF] Sleep well, darling!

HAPPY. I'm gonna get married, Mom. I wanted to tell you.

LINDA. Go to sleep, dear.   790

HAPPY. [*going*] I just wanted to tell you.

WILLY. Keep up the good work. [HAPPY *exits.*] God . . . remember that Ebbets Field° game? The championship of the city?

LINDA. Just rest. Should I sing to you?

WILLY. Yeah. Sing to me. [LINDA *hums a soft lullaby.*] When that team came out—he was the tallest, remember?

LINDA. Oh, yes. And in gold.   795

[BIFF *enters the darkened kitchen, takes a cigarette, and leaves the house. He comes downstage into a golden pool of light. He smokes, staring at the night.*]

WILLY. Like a young god. Hercules—something like that. And the sun, the sun all around him. Remember how he waved to me? Right up from the field, with the

---

792 *Ebbets Field:* the baseball stadium of the Brooklyn Dodgers before they moved to Los Angeles in 1958. Biff had played there in a city championship football game. See 2.210 (p. 1449).

representatives of three colleges standing by? And the buyers I brought, and the cheers when he came out—Loman, Loman, Loman! God Almighty, he'll be great yet. A star like that, magnificent, can never really fade away!

[*The light on WILLY is fading. The gas heater begins to glow through the kitchen wall, near the stairs, a blue flame beneath red coils.*]

    LINDA. [*timidly*] Willy dear, what has he got against you?
    WILLY. I'm so tired. Don't talk any more.

[*BIFF slowly returns to the kitchen. He stops, stares toward the heater.*]

    LINDA. Will you ask Howard to let you work in New York?
    WILLY. First thing in the morning. Everything'll be all right.   800

[*BIFF reaches behind the heater and draws out a length of rubber tubing. He is horrified and turns his head toward WILLY's room, still dimly lit, from which the strains of LINDA's desperate but monotonous humming rise.*]

    WILLY. [*staring through the window into the moonlight*] Gee, look at the moon moving between the buildings!

[*BIFF wraps the tubing around his hand and quickly goes up the stairs.*]

Act 2

[*Music is heard, gay and bright. The curtain rises as the music fades away. WILLY, in shirt sleeves, is sitting at the kitchen table, sipping coffee, his hat in his lap. LINDA is filling his cup when she can.*]

    WILLY. Wonderful coffee. Meal in itself.
    LINDA. Can I make you some eggs?
    WILLY. No. Take a breath.
    LINDA. You look so rested, dear.
    WILLY. I slept like a dead one. First time in months. Imagine, sleeping till ten on   5
a Tuesday morning. Boys left nice and early, heh?
    LINDA. They were out of here by eight o'clock.
    WILLY. Good work!
    LINDA. It was so thrilling to see them leaving together. I can't get over the shaving lotion in this house!
    WILLY. [*smiling*] Mmm—
    LINDA. Biff was very changed this morning. His whole attitude seemed to be   10
hopeful. He couldn't wait to get downtown to see Oliver.
    WILLY. He's heading for a change. There's no question, there simply are certain men that take longer to get—solidified. How did he dress?
    LINDA. His blue suit. He's so handsome in that suit. He could be a—anything in that suit!

[*WILLY gets up from the table. LINDA holds his jacket for him.*]

    WILLY. There's no question, no question at all. Gee, on the way home tonight I'd like to buy some seeds.
    LINDA. [*laughing*] That'd be wonderful. But not enough sun gets back there. Nothing'll grow any more.
    WILLY. You wait, kid, before it's all over we're gonna get a little place out in the   15
country, and I'll raise some vegetables, a couple of chickens . . .

Linda Loman (Mildred Dunnock) and Happy (Cameron Mitchell) restrain Biff (Arthur Kennedy) as he reproaches his father Willy (Lee J. Cobb) in the Morosco Theatre, New York City, original production of *Death of a Salesman,* staged by Elia Kazan.

LINDA.   You'll do it yet, dear.

[*WILLY walks out of his jacket, LINDA follows him.*]

WILLY.   And they'll get married, and come for a weekend. I'd build a little guest house. 'Cause I got so many fine tools, all I'd need would be a little lumber and some peace of mind.

LINDA.   [*joyfully*] I sewed the lining . . .

WILLY.   I could build two guest houses, so they'd both come. Did he decide how much he's going to ask Oliver for?

LINDA.   [*getting him into the jacket*] He didn't mention it, but I imagine ten or fifteen thousand. You going to talk to Howard today?   20

WILLY.   Yeah. I'll put it to him straight and simple. He'll just have to take me off the road.

LINDA.   And Willy, don't forget to ask for a little advance, because we've got the insurance premium. It's the grace period now.

WILLY.   That's a hundred . . . ?

LINDA.   A hundred and eight, sixty-eight. Because we're a little short again.

WILLY.   Why are we short?   25

LINDA.   Well, you had the motor job on the car . . .

WILLY.   That goddam Studebaker!

LINDA.   And you got one more payment on the refrigerator . . .

WILLY.   But it just broke again!

LINDA.   Well, it's old, dear.   30

WILLY.   I told you we should've bought a well-advertised machine. Charley bought a General Electric and it's twenty years old and it's still good, that son-of-a-bitch.

LINDA.   But, Willy—

WILLY.   Whoever heard of a Hastings refrigerator? Once in my life I would like to own something outright before it's broken! I'm always in a race with the junkyard! I just finished paying for the car and it's on its last legs. The refrigerator consumes belts like a goddam maniac. They time those things. They time them so when you finally paid for them, they're used up.

LINDA.   [*buttoning up his jacket as he unbuttons it*] All told, about two hundred dollars would carry us, dear. But that includes the last payment on the mortgage. After this payment, Willy, the house belongs to us.

WILLY.   It's twenty-five years!   35

LINDA.   Biff was nine years old when we bought it.

WILLY.   Well, that's a great thing. To weather a twenty-five year mortgage is—

LINDA.   It's an accomplishment.

WILLY.   All the cement, the lumber, the reconstruction I put in this house! There ain't a crack to be found in it any more.

LINDA.   Well, it served its purpose.   40

WILLY.   What purpose? Some stranger'll come along, move in, and that's that. If only Biff would take this house, and raise a family . . . [*He starts to go.*] Good-by, I'm late.

LINDA.   [*suddenly remembering*] Oh, I forgot! You're supposed to meet them for dinner.

WILLY.   Me?

LINDA.   At Frank's Chop House on Forty-eighth near Sixth Avenue.

WILLY.   Is that so! How about you?   45

LINDA.   No, just the three of you. They're gonna blow you to a big meal!

WILLY.   Don't say! Who thought of that?

LINDA.   Biff came to me this morning, Willy, and he said, "Tell Dad, we want to blow him to a big meal." Be there six o'clock. You and your two boys are going to have dinner.

WILLY.   Gee whiz! That's really somethin'. I'm gonna knock Howard for a loop, kid. I'll get an advance, and I'll come home with a New York job. Goddammit, now I'm gonna do it!

LINDA.   Oh, that's the spirit, Willy!   50

WILLY.   I will never get behind a wheel the rest of my life!

LINDA.   It's changing, Willy, I can feel it changing!

WILLY.   Beyond a question. G'by, I'm late. [*He starts to go again.*]

LINDA.   [*calling after him as she runs to the kitchen table for a handkerchief*] You got your glasses?

WILLY.   [*feels for them, then comes back in*] Yeah, yeah, got my glasses.   55

LINDA.   [*giving him the handkerchief*] And a handkerchief.

WILLY.   Yeah, handkerchief.

LINDA.   And your saccharine?

WILLY.   Yeah, my saccharine.

LINDA.   Be careful on the subway stairs.   60

[*She kisses him, and a silk stocking is seen hanging from her hand. WILLY notices it.*]

WILLY.   Will you stop mending stockings? At least while I'm in the house. It gets me nervous. I can't tell you. Please.

[*LINDA hides the stocking in her hand as she follows WILLY across the forestage in front of the house.*]

LINDA.   Remember, Frank's Chop House.

WILLY.   [*passing the apron*] Maybe beets would grow out there.

LINDA.   [*laughing*] But you tried so many times.

WILLY.   Yeah. Well, don't work hard today. [*He disappears around the right corner of*   65
the house.]

LINDA.   Be careful!

[*As WILLY vanishes, LINDA waves to him. Suddenly the phone rings. She runs across the stage and into the kitchen and lifts it.*]

LINDA.   Hello? Oh, Biff! I'm so glad you called, I just . . . Yes, sure, I just told him.
Yes, he'll be there for dinner at six o'clock, I didn't forget. Listen, I was just dying to tell
you. You know that little rubber pipe I told you about? That he connected to the gas
heater? I finally decided to go down the cellar this morning and take it away and destroy
it. But it's gone! Imagine? He took it away himself, it isn't there! [*She listens.*] When? Oh,
then you took it. Oh—nothing, it's just that I'd hoped he'd taken it away himself. Oh, I'm
not worried, darling, because this morning he left in such high spirits, it was like the old
days! I'm not afraid any more. Did Mr. Oliver see you? . . . Well, you wait there then. And
make a nice impression on him, darling. Just don't perspire too much before you see
him. And have a nice time with Dad. He may have big news too . . . That's right, a New
York job. And be sweet to him tonight, dear. Be loving to him. Because he's only a little
boat looking for a harbor. [*She is trembling with sorrow and joy.*] Oh, that's wonderful, Biff,
you'll save his life. Thanks, darling. Just put your arm around him when he comes into
the restaurant. Give him a smile. That's the boy . . . Good-by, dear . . . You got your comb?
. . . That's fine. Good-by, Biff dear.

[*In the middle of her speech, HOWARD WAGNER, thirty-six, wheels in a small typewriter table on which is a wire-recording machine and proceeds to plug it in. This is on the left forestage. Light slowly fades on LINDA as it rises on HOWARD. HOWARD is intent on threading the machine and only glances over his shoulder as WILLY appears.*]

WILLY.   Pst! Pst!

HOWARD.   Hello, Willy, come in.

WILLY.   Like to have a little talk with you, Howard.   70

HOWARD.   Sorry to keep you waiting. I'll be with you in a minute.

WILLY.   What's that, Howard?

HOWARD.   Didn't you ever see one of these? Wire recorder.

WILLY.   Oh. Can we talk a minute?

HOWARD.   Records things. Just got delivery yesterday. Been driving me crazy, the   75
most terrific machine I ever saw in my life. I was up all night with it.

WILLY.   What do you do with it?

HOWARD.   I bought it for dictation, but you can do anything with it. Listen to this.
I had it home last night. Listen to what I picked up. The first one is my daughter. Get this.
[*He flicks the switch and "Roll out the Barrel" is heard being whistled.*] Listen to that kid whistle.

WILLY.   That is lifelike, isn't it?

HOWARD.   Seven years old. Get that tone.

WILLY.   Ts, ts. Like to ask a little favor if you . . .   80

[*The whistling breaks off, and the voice of HOWARD's DAUGHTER is heard.*]

HIS DAUGHTER.   "Now you, Daddy."

HOWARD.   She's crazy for me! [*Again the same song is whistled.*] That's me! Ha! [*He winks.*]

WILLY.   You're very good!

[*The whistling breaks off again. The machine runs silent for a moment.*]

HOWARD.   Sh! Get this now, this is my son.

HIS SON.   "The capital of Alabama is Montgomery; the capital of Arizona is   85
Phoenix; the capital of Arkansas is Little Rock; the capital of California is Sacramento
..." [*and on, and on*]

HOWARD.   [*holding up five fingers*] Five years old, Willy!

WILLY.   He'll make an announcer some day!

HIS SON.   [*continuing*] "The capital ..."

HOWARD.   Get that—alphabetical order! [*The machine breaks off suddenly.*] Wait a
minute. The maid kicked the plug out.

WILLY.   It certainly is a—   90

HOWARD.   Sh, for God's sake!

HIS SON.   "It's nine o'clock, Bulova watch time. So I have to go to sleep."

WILLY.   That really is—

HOWARD.   Wait a minute! The next is my wife.

[*They wait.*]

HOWARD'S VOICE.   "Go on, say something." [*pause*] "Well, you gonna talk?"   95

HIS WIFE.   "I can't think of anything."

HOWARD'S VOICE.   "Well, talk—it's turning."

HIS WIFE.   [*shyly, beaten*] "Hello." [*Silence*] "Oh, Howard, I can't talk into this ..."

HOWARD.   [*snapping the machine off*] That was my wife.

WILLY.   That is a wonderful machine. Can we—   100

HOWARD.   I tell you, Willy, I'm gonna take my camera, and my bandsaw, and all my
hobbies, and out they go. This is the most fascinating relaxation I ever found.

WILLY.   I think I'll get one myself.

HOWARD.   Sure, they're only a hundred and a half. You can't do without it. Sup-
posing you wanna hear Jack Benny,° see? But you can't be at home at that hour. So you
tell the maid to turn the radio on when Jack Benny comes on, and this automatically goes
on with the radio ...

WILLY.   And when you come home you ...

HOWARD.   You can come home twelve o'clock, one o'clock, any time you like, and   105
you get yourself a Coke and sit yourself down, throw the switch, and there's Jack Benny's
program in the middle of the night!

WILLY.   I'm definitely going to get one. Because lots of time I'm on the road, and
I think to myself, what I must be missing on the radio!

HOWARD.   Don't you have a radio in the car?

WILLY.   Well, yeah, but who ever thinks of turning it on?

HOWARD.   Say, aren't you supposed to be in Boston?

WILLY.   That's what I want to talk to you about, Howard. You got a minute?   110

[*He draws a chair in from the wing.*]

HOWARD.   What happened? What're you doing here?

WILLY.   Well ...

---

103 *Jack Benny:* (1894–1974), vaudeville, radio, television, and movie comedian.

HOWARD.   You didn't crack up again, did you?

WILLY.   Oh, no. No . . .

HOWARD.   Geez, you had me worried there for a minute. What's the trouble?   115

WILLY.   Well, tell you the truth, Howard, I've come to the decision that I'd rather not travel any more.

HOWARD.   Not travel! Well, what'll you do?

WILLY.   Remember, Christmas time, when you had the party here? You said you'd try to think of some spot for me here in town.

HOWARD.   With us?

WILLY.   Well, sure.   120

HOWARD.   Oh, yeah, yeah. I remember. Well, I couldn't think of anything for you, Willy.

WILLY.   I tell ya, Howard. The kids are all grown up, y'know. I don't need much any more. If I could take home—well, sixty-five dollars a week, I could swing it.

HOWARD.   Yeah, but Willy, see I—

WILLY.   I tell ya why, Howard. Speaking frankly and between the two of us, y'-know—I'm just a little tired.

HOWARD.   Oh, I could understand that, Willy. But you're a road man, Willy, and   125
we do a road business. We've only got a half-dozen salesmen on the floor here.

WILLY.   God knows, Howard, I never asked a favor of any man. But I was with the firm when your father used to carry you up here in his arms.

HOWARD.   I know that, Willy, but—

WILLY.   Your father came to me the day you were born and asked me what I thought of the name of Howard, may he rest in peace.

HOWARD.   I appreciate that, Willy, but there just is no spot here for you. If I had a spot I'd slam you right in, but I just don't have a single solitary spot.

[*He looks for his lighter. WILLY has picked it up and gives it to him. Pause.*]

WILLY.   [*with increasing anger*] Howard, all I need to set my table is fifty dollars a   130
week.

HOWARD.   But where am I going to put you, kid?

WILLY.   Look, it isn't a question of whether I can sell merchandise, is it?

HOWARD.   No, but it's a business, kid, and everybody's gotta pull his own weight.

WILLY.   [*desperately*] Just let me tell you a story, Howard—

HOWARD.   'Cause you gotta admit, business is business.   135

WILLY.   [*angrily*] Business in definitely business, but just listen for a minute. You don't understand this. When I was a boy—eighteen, nineteen—I was already on the road. And there was a question in my mind as to whether selling had a future for me. Because in those days I had a yearning to go to Alaska. See, there were three gold strikes in one month in Alaska, and I felt like going out. Just for the ride, you might say.

HOWARD.   [*barely interested*] Don't say.

WILLY.   Oh, yeah, my father lived many years in Alaska. He was an adventurous man. We've got quite a little streak of self-reliance in our family. I thought I'd go out with my older brother and try to locate him, and maybe settle in the North with the old man. And I was almost decided to go, when I met a salesman in the Parker House.° His name was Dave Singleman. And he was eighty-four years old, and he'd drummed merchandise in thirty-one states. And old Dave, he'd go up to his room, y'understand, put on his green velvet slippers—I'll never forget—and pick up his phone and call the buyers, and without

138 *Parker House:* a hotel in Boston.

ever leaving his room, at the age of eighty-four, he made his living. And when I saw that, I realized that selling was the greatest career a man could want. 'Cause what could be more satisfying than to be able to go, at the age of eighty-four, into twenty or thirty different cities, and pick up a phone, and be remembered and loved and helped by so many different people? Do you know? when he died—and by the way he died the death of a salesman, in his green velvet slippers in the smoker of the New York, New Haven and Hartford, going into Boston—when he died, hundreds of salesmen and buyers were at his funeral. Things were sad on a lotta trains for months after that. [*He stands up. Howard has not looked at him.*] In those days there was personality in it, Howard. There was respect, and comradeship, and gratitude in it. Today, it's all cut and dried, and there's no chance for bringing friendship to bear—or personality. You see what I mean? They don't know me any more.

HOWARD. [*moving away, to the right*] That's just the thing, Willy.

WILLY. If I had forty dollars a week—that's all I'd need. Forty dollars, Howard. 140

HOWARD. Kid, I can't take blood from a stone, I—

WILLY. [*desperation is on him now*] Howard, the year Al Smith° was nominated, your father came to me and—

HOWARD. [*starting to go off*] I've got to see some people, kid.

WILLY. [*stopping him*] I'm talking about your father! There were promises made across this desk! You mustn't tell me you've got people to see—I put thirty-four years into this firm, Howard, and now I can't pay my insurance! You can't eat the orange and throw the peel away—a man is not a piece of fruit! [*after a pause*] Now pay attention. Your father—in 1928 I had a big year. I averaged a hundred and seventy dollars a week in commissions.

HOWARD. [*impatiently*] Now, Willy, you never averaged— 145

WILLY. [*banging his hand on the desk*] I averaged a hundred and seventy dollars a week in the year of 1928! And your father came to me—or rather, I was in the office here—it was right over this desk—and he put his hand on my shoulder—

HOWARD. [*getting up*] You'll have to excuse me, Willy, I gotta see some people. Pull yourself together. [*going out*] I'll be back in a little while.

[*On HOWARD's exit, the light on his chair grows very bright and strange.*]

WILLY. Pull myself together! What the hell did I say to him? My God, I was yelling at him! How could I! [*WILLY breaks off, staring at the light, which occupies the chair, animating it. He approaches this chair, standing across the desk from it.*] Frank, Frank, don't you remember what you told me that time? How you put your hand on my shoulder, and Frank . . . [*He leans on the desk and as he speaks the dead man's name he accidentally switches on the recorder, and instantly*]

HOWARD'S SON. ". . . of New York is Albany. The capital of Ohio is Cincinnati, the capital of Rhode Island is . . ." [*The recitation continues.*]

WILLY. [*leaping away with fright, shouting*] Ha! Howard! Howard! Howard! 150

HOWARD. [*rushing in*] What happened?

WILLY. [*pointing at the machine, which continues nasally, childishly, with the capital cities*] Shut it off! Shut it off!

HOWARD. [*pulling the plug out*] Look, Willy . . .

WILLY. [*pressing his hands to his eyes*] I gotta get myself some coffee. I'll get some coffee . . .

---

142 *Al Smith:* Alfred E. Smith was governor of New York State (1919–1921, 1923–1929) and the Democratic presidential candidate defeated by Herbert Hoover in 1928.

[*WILLY starts to walk out. HOWARD stops him.*]

HOWARD. [*rolling up the cord*] Willy, look . . .   155
WILLY. I'll go to Boston.
HOWARD. Willy, you can't go to Boston for us.
WILLY. Why can't I go?
HOWARD. I don't want you to represent us. I've been meaning to tell you for a long time now.
WILLY. Howard, are you firing me?   160
HOWARD. I think you need a good long rest, Willy.
WILLY. Howard—
HOWARD. And when you feel better, come back, and we'll see if we can work something out.
WILLY. But I gotta earn money, Howard. I'm in no position to—
HOWARD. Where are your sons? Why don't your sons give you a hand?   165
WILLY. They're working on a very big deal.
HOWARD. This is no time for false pride, Willy. You go to your sons and you tell them that you're tired. You've got two great boys, haven't you?
WILLY. Oh, no question, no question, but in the meantime . . .
HOWARD. Then that's that, heh?
WILLY. All right, I'll go to Boston tomorrow.   170
HOWARD. No, no.
WILLY. I can't throw myself on my sons. I'm not a cripple!
HOWARD. Look, kid, I'm busy this morning.
WILLY. [*grasping HOWARD's arm*] Howard, you've got to let me go to Boston!
HOWARD. [*hard, keeping himself under control*] I've got a line of people to see this   175
morning. Sit down, take five minutes, and pull yourself together, and then go home, will ya? I need the office, Willy [*He starts to go, turns, remembering the recorder, starts to push off the table holding the recorder.*] Oh, yeah. Whenever you can this week, stop by and drop off the samples. You'll feel better, Willy, and then come back and we'll talk. Pull yourself togeth-er, kid, there's people outside.

[*HOWARD exits, pushing the table off left. WILLY stares into space, exhausted. Now the music is heard—BEN's music—first distantly, then closer. As WILLY speaks, BEN enters from the right. He car-ries valise and umbrella.*]

WILLY. Oh, Ben, how did you do it? What is the answer? Did you wind up the Alaska deal already?
BEN. Doesn't take much time if you know what you're doing. Just a short business trip. Boarding ship in an hour. Wanted to say good-by.
WILLY. Ben, I've got to talk to you.
BEN. [*glancing at his watch*] Haven't much time, William.
WILLY. [*crossing the apron to BEN*] Ben, nothing's working out. I don't know what   180
to do.
BEN. Now, look here, William. I've bought timberland in Alaska and I need a man to look after things for me.
WILLY. God, timberland! Me and my boys in those grand outdoors!
BEN. You've a new continent at your doorstep, William. Get out of these cities, they're full of talk and time payments and courts of law. Screw on your fists and you can fight for a fortune up there.
WILLY. Yes, yes! Linda, Linda!

[LINDA *enters as of old, with the wash.*]

LINDA.   Oh, you're back?   185
BEN.   I haven't much time.
WILLY.   No, wait! Linda, he's got a proposition for me in Alaska.
LINDA.   But you've got—[*to BEN*] He's got a beautiful job here.
WILLY.   But in Alaska, kid, I could—
LINDA.   You're doing well enough, Willy!   190
BEN.   [*to LINDA*] Enough for what, my dear?
LINDA.   [*frightened of BEN and angry at him*] Don't say those things to him! Enough
to be happy right here, right now. [*to WILLY, while BEN laughs*] Why must everybody con-
quer the world? You're well liked, and the boys love you, and someday—[*to BEN*]—why
old man Wagner told him just the other day that if he keeps it up he'll be a member of
the firm, didn't he, Willy?
WILLY.   Sure, sure. I am building something with this firm, Ben, and if a man is
building something he must be on the right track, mustn't he?
BEN.   What are you building? Lay your hand on it. Where is it?
WILLY.   [*hesitantly*] That's true, Linda, there's nothing.   195
LINDA.   Why? [*to BEN*] There's a man eighty-four years old—
WILLY.   That's right, Ben, that's right. When I look at that man I say, what is there
to worry about?
BEN.   Bah!
WILLY.   It's true, Ben. All he has to do is go into any city, pick up the phone, and
he's making his living and you know why?
BEN.   [*picking up his valise*] I've got to go.   200
WILLY.   [*holding BEN back*] Look at this boy!

[BIFF, *in his high school sweater, enters carrying suitcase.* HAPPY *carries* BIFF's *shoulder guards, gold
helmet, and football pants.*]

WILLY.   Without a penny to his name, three great universities are begging for him,
and from there the sky's the limit, because it's not what you do, Ben. It's who you know
and the smile on your face! It's contacts, Ben, contacts! The whole wealth of Alaska passes over the lunch table at the Commodore Hotel,° and that's the wonder, the wonder of
this country, that a man can end with diamonds here on the basis of being liked! [*He
turns to* BIFF] And that's why when you get out on that field today it's important. Because
thousands of people will be rooting for you and loving you. [*to* BEN, *who has again begun to
leave*] And Ben! when he walks into a business office his name will sound out like a bell
and all the doors will open to him! I've seen it, Ben, I've seen it a thousand times! You
can't feel it with your hand like timber, but it's there!
BEN.   Good-by, William.
WILLY.   Ben, am I right? Don't you think I'm right? I value your advice.
BEN.   There's a new continent at your doorstep, William. You could walk out rich.   205
Rich! [*He is gone.*]
WILLY.   We'll do it here, Ben! You hear me? We're gonna do it here!

[YOUNG BERNARD *rushes in. The gay music of the Boys is heard.*]

BERNARD.   Oh, gee, I was afraid you left already!
WILLY.   Why? What time is it?

202 *Commodore Hotel:* a large hotel in New York City.

BERNARD.   It's half-past one!

WILLY.   Well, come on, everybody! Ebbets Field next stop! Where's the pennants?   210

[*He rushes through the wall-line of the kitchen and out into the dining-room.*]

LINDA.   [*to BIFF*] Did you pack fresh underwear?

BIFF.   [*who has been limbering up*] I want to go!

BERNARD.   Biff, I'm carrying your helmet, ain't I?

HAPPY.   No, I'm carrying the helmet.

BERNARD.   Oh, Biff, you promised me.   215

HAPPY.   I'm carrying the helmet.

BERNARD.   How am I going to get in the locker room?

LINDA.   Let him carry the shoulder guards. [*She puts her coat and hat on in the kitchen.*]

BERNARD.   Can I, Biff? 'Cause I told everybody I'm going to be in the locker room.

HAPPY.   In Ebbets Field it's the clubhouse.   220

BERNARD.   I meant the clubhouse. Biff!

HAPPY.   Biff!

BIFF.   [*grandly, after a slight pause.*] Let him carry the shoulder guards.

HAPPY.   [*as he gives BERNARD the shoulder guards*] Stay close to us now.

[*WILLY rushes in with the pennants.*]

WILLY.   [*handing them out*] Everybody wave when Biff comes out on the field.   225
[*HAPPY and BERNARD run off.*] You set now, boy?

[*The music has died away.*]

BIFF.   Ready to go, Pop. Every muscle is ready.

WILLY.   [*at the edge of the apron*] You realize what this means?

BIFF.   That's right, Pop.

WILLY.   [*feeling BIFF's muscles*] You're comin' home this afternoon captain of the All-Scholastic Championship Team of the City of New York.

BIFF.   I got it, Pop. And remember, pal, when I take off my helmet, that touch-   230
down is for you.

WILLY.   Let's go! [*He is starting out, with his arm around BIFF, when CHARLEY enters, as of old, in knickers.*] I got no room for you, Charley.

CHARLEY.   Room? For what?

WILLY.   In the car.

CHARLEY.   You goin' for a ride? I wanted to shoot some casino.

WILLY.   [*furiously*] Casino! [*incredulously*] Don't you realize what today is?   235

LINDA.   Oh, he knows, Willy. He's just kidding you.

WILLY.   That's nothing to kid about!

CHARLEY.   No, Linda, what's goin' on?

LINDA.   He's playing in Ebbets Field.

CHARLEY.   Baseball in this weather?   240

WILLY.   Don't talk to him. Come on, come on! [*He is pushing them out.*]

CHARLEY.   Wait a minute, didn't you hear the news?

WILLY.   What?

CHARLEY.   Don't you listen to the radio? Ebbets Field just blew up.

WILLY.   You go to hell! [*CHARLEY laughs. Pushing them out.*] Come on, come on!   245
We're late.

CHARLEY.   [*as they go*] Knock a homer, Biff, knock a homer!

WILLY.   [*the last to leave, turning to CHARLEY*] I don't think that was funny, Charley.
This is the greatest day of his life.

CHARLEY.   Willy, when are you going to grow up?

WILLY.   Yeah, heh? When this game is over, Charley, you'll be laughing out the other side of your face. They'll be calling him another Red Grange.° Twenty-five thousand a year.

CHARLEY.   [*kidding*] Is that so?   250

WILLY.   Yeah, that's so.

CHARLEY.   Well, then, I'm sorry, Willy. But tell me something.

WILLY.   What?

CHARLEY.   Who is Red Grange?

WILLY.   Put up your hands. Goddam you, put up your hands!   255

[*CHARLEY, chuckling, shakes his head and walks away, around the left corner of the stage. WILLY follows him. The music rises to a mocking frenzy.*]

WILLY.   Who the hell do you think you are, better than everybody else? You don't know everything, you big, ignorant, stupid. . . . Put up your hands!

[*Light rises, on the right side of the forestage, on a small table in the reception room of CHARLEY's office. Traffic sounds are heard. BERNARD, now mature, sits whistling to himself. A pair of tennis rackets and an overnight bag are on the floor beside him.*]

WILLY.   [*offstage*] What are you walking away for? Don't walk away! If you're going to say something say it to my face! I know you laugh at me behind my back. You'll laugh out of the other side of your goddam face after this game. Touchdown! Touchdown! Eighty thousand people! Touchdown. Right between the goal posts.

[*BERNARD is a quiet, earnest, but self-assured young man. WILLY's voice is coming from right upstage now. BERNARD lowers his feet off the table and listens. JENNY, his father's secretary, enters.*]

JENNY.   [*distressed*] Say, Bernard, will you go out in the hall?

BERNARD.   What is that noise? Who is it?

JENNY.   Mr. Loman. He just got off the elevator.   260

BERNARD.   [*getting up*] Who's he arguing with?

JENNY.   Nobody. There's nobody with him. I can't deal with him any more, and your father gets all upset everytime he comes. I've got a lot of typing to do, and your father's waiting to sign it. Will you see him?

WILLY.   [*entering*] Touchdown! Touch—[*He sees JENNY.*] Jenny, Jenny, good to see you. How're ya? Workin'? Or still honest?

JENNY.   Fine. How've you been feeling?

WILLY.   Not much any more, Jenny. Ha, ha! [*He is surprised to see the rackets.*]   265

BERNARD.   Hello, Uncle Willy.

WILLY.   [*almost shocked*] Bernard! Well, look who's here! [*He comes quickly, guiltily, to BERNARD and warmly shakes his hand.*]

BERNARD.   How are you? Good to see you.

WILLY.   What are you doing here?

BERNARD.   Oh, just stopped off to see Pop. Get off my feet till my train leaves. I'm   270
going to Washington in a few minutes.

WILLY.   Is he in?

BERNARD.   Yes, he's in his office with the accountants. Sit down.

---

249 *Red Grange:* Harold Edward Grange (1903–1991), all-America halfback (1923–1925) at the University of Illinois.

WILLY. [*sitting down*] What're you going to do in Washington?

BERNARD. Oh, just a case I've got there, Willy.

WILLY. That so? [*Indicating the rackets*] You going to play tennis there? 275

BERNARD. I'm staying with a friend who's got a court.

WILLY. Don't say. His own tennis court. Must be fine people, I bet.

BERNARD. They are, very nice. Dad tells me Biff's in town.

WILLY. [*with a big smile*] Yeah, Biff's in. Working on a very big deal, Bernard.

BERNARD. What's Biff doing? 280

WILLY. Well, he's been doing very big things in the West. But he decided to establish himself here. Very big. We're having dinner. Did I hear your wife had a boy?

BERNARD. That's right. Our second.

WILLY. Two boys! What do you know!

BERNARD. What kind of a deal has Biff got?

WILLY. Well, Bill Oliver—very big sporting-goods man—he wants Biff very badly. 285
Called him in from the West. Long distance, carte blanche, special deliveries. Your
friends have their own private tennis court?

BERNARD. You still with the old firm, Willy?

WILLY. [*after a pause*] I'm—I'm overjoyed to see how you made the grade,
Bernard, overjoyed. It's an encouraging thing to see a young man really—really—Looks
very good for Biff—very—[*He breaks off, then*] Bernard—[*He is so full of emotion, he breaks
off again.*]

BERNARD. What is it, Willy?

WILLY. [*small and alone*] What—what's the secret?

BERNARD. What secret? 290

WILLY. How—how did you? Why didn't he ever catch on?

BERNARD. I wouldn't know that, Willy.

WILLY. [*confidentially, desperately*] You were his friend, his boyhood friend. There's
something I don't understand about it. His life ended after that Ebbets Field game. From
the age of seventeen nothing good ever happened to him.

BERNARD. He never trained himself for anything.

WILLY. But he did, he did. After high school he took so many correspondence 295
courses. Radio mechanics; television; God knows what, and never made the slightest
mark.

BERNARD. [*taking off his glasses*] Willy, do you want to talk candidly?

WILLY. [*rising, faces BERNARD*] I regard you as a very brilliant man, Bernard. I value
your advice.

BERNARD. Oh, the hell with the advice, Willy. I couldn't advise you. There's just
one thing I've always wanted to ask you. When he was supposed to graduate, and the
math teacher flunked him—

WILLY. Oh, that son-of-a-bitch ruined his life.

BERNARD. Yeah, but, Willy, all he had to do was go to summer school and make up 300
that subject.

WILLY. That's right, that's right.

BERNARD. Did you tell him not to go to summer school?

WILLY. Me? I begged him to go. I ordered him to go!

BERNARD. Then why wouldn't he go?

WILLY. Why? Why! Bernard, that question has been trailing me like a ghost for 305
the last fifteen years. He flunked the subject, and laid down and died like a hammer
hit him!

BERNARD. Take it easy, kid.

WILLY. Let me talk to you—I got nobody to talk to. Bernard, Bernard, was it my fault? Y'see? It keeps going around in my mind, maybe I did something to him. I got nothing to give him.

BERNARD. Don't take it so hard.

WILLY. Why did he lay down? What is the story there? You were his friend!

BERNARD. Willy, I remember, it was June, and our grades came out. And he'd flunked math.   310

WILLY. That son-of-a-bitch!

BERNARD. No, it wasn't right then. Biff just got very angry, I remember, and he was ready to enroll in summer school.

WILLY. [surprised] He was?

BERNARD. He wasn't beaten by it at all. But then, Willy, he disappeared from the block for almost a month. And I got the idea that he'd gone up to New England to see you. Did he have a talk with you then?

[WILLY stares in silence.]

BERNARD. Willy?   315

WILLY. [with a strong edge of resentment in his voice] Yeah, he came to Boston. What about it?

BERNARD. Well, just that when he came back—I'll never forget this, it always mystifies me. Because I'd thought so well of Biff, even though he'd always taken advantage of me. I loved him, Willy, y'know? And he came back after that month and took his sneakers—remember the sneakers with "University of Virginia" printed on them? He was so proud of those, wore them every day. And he took them down in the cellar, and burned them up in the furnace. We had a fist fight. It lasted at least half an hour. Just the two of us, punching each other down the cellar, and crying right through it. I've often thought of how strange it was that I knew he'd given up his life. What happened in Boston, Willy?

[WILLY looks at him as at an intruder.]

BERNARD. I just bring it up because you asked me.

WILLY. [angrily] Nothing. What do you mean, "What happened?" What's that got to do with anything?

BERNARD. Well, don't get sore.   320

WILLY. What are you trying to do, blame it on me? If a boy lays down is that my fault?

BERNARD. Now, Willy, don't get—

WILLY. Well, don't—don't talk to me that way! What does that mean, "What happened?"

[CHARLEY enters. He is in his vest, and he carries a bottle of bourbon.]

CHARLEY. Hey, you're going to miss that train. [He waves the bottle.]

BERNARD. Yeah, I'm going. [He takes the bottle.] Thanks, Pop. [He picks up his   325
rackets and bag.] Good-by, Willy, and don't worry about it. You know, "If at first you don't succeed . . ."

WILLY. Yes, I believe in that.

BERNARD. But sometimes, Willy, it's better for a man just to walk away.

WILLY. Walk away?

BERNARD. That's right.

WILLY. But if you can't walk away?   330

BERNARD. [after a slight pause] I guess that's when it's tough. [extending his hand] Good-by, Willy.

WILLY.   [*shaking BERNARD's hand*] Good-by, boy.

CHARLEY.   [*an arm on BERNARD's shoulder*] How do you like this kid? Gonna argue a case in front of the Supreme Court.

BERNARD.   [*protesting*] Pop!

WILLY.   [*genuinely shocked, pained, and happy*] No! The Supreme Court!   335

BERNARD.   I gotta run. 'By, Dad!

CHARLEY.   Knock 'em dead, Bernard!

[*BERNARD goes off.*]

WILLY.   [*as CHARLEY takes out his wallet*] The Supreme Court! And he didn't even mention it!

CHARLEY.   [*counting out money on the desk*] He don't have to—he's gonna do it.

WILLY.   And you never told him what to do, did you? You never took any interest in   340
him.

CHARLEY.   My salvation is that I never took any interest in anything. There's some money—fifty dollars. I got an accountant inside.

WILLY.   Charley, look . . . [*with difficulty*] I got my insurance to pay. If you can manage it—I need a hundred and ten dollars.

[*CHARLEY doesn't reply for a moment; merely stops moving.*]

WILLY.   I'd draw it from my bank but Linda would know, and I . . .

CHARLEY.   Sit down, Willy.

WILLY.   [*moving toward the chair*] I'm keeping an account of everything, remember.   345
I'll pay every penny back. [*He sits.*]

CHARLEY.   Now listen to me, Willy . . .

WILLY.   I want you to know I appreciate . . .

CHARLEY.   [*sitting down on the table*] Willy, what're you doin'? What the hell is goin' on in your head?

WILLY.   Why? I'm simply . . .

CHARLEY.   I offered you a job. You can make fifty dollars a week. And I won't send   350
you on the road.

WILLY.   I've got a job.

CHARLEY.   Without pay? What kind of job is a job without pay? [*He rises.*] Now, look, kid, enough is enough. I'm no genius but I know when I'm being insulted.

WILLY.   Insulted!

CHARLEY.   Why don't you want to work for me?

WILLY.   What's the matter with you? I've got a job.   355

CHARLEY.   Then what're you walkin' in here every week for?

WILLY.   [*getting up*] Well, if you don't want me to walk in here—

CHARLEY.   I am offering you a job.

WILLY.   I don't want your goddam job!

CHARLEY.   When the hell are you going to grow up?   360

WILLY.   [*furiously*] You big ignoramus, if you say that to me again I'll rap you one! I don't care how big you are [*He's ready to fight.*]

[*Pause.*]

CHARLEY.   [*kindly, going to him*] How much do you need, Willy?

WILLY.   Charley, I'm strapped. I'm strapped. I don't know what to do. I was just fired.

CHARLEY.   Howard fired you?

WILLY.   That snotnose. Imagine that? I named him. I named him Howard.   365

CHARLEY.   Willy, when're you gonna realize that them things don't mean any-thing? You named him Howard, but you can't sell that. The only thing you got in this world is what you can sell. And the funny thing is that you're a salesman, and you don't know that.

WILLY.   I've tried to think otherwise, I guess. I always felt that if a man was impres-sive, and well liked, that nothing—

CHARLEY.   Why must everybody like you? Who liked J. P. Morgan?° Was he impres-sive? In a Turkish bath he'd look like a butcher. But with his pockets on he was very well liked. Now listen, Willy, I know you don't like me, and nobody can say I'm in love with you, but I'll give you a job because—just for the hell of it, put it that way. Now what do you say?

WILLY.   I—I just can't work for you, Charley.

CHARLEY.   What're you, jealous of me?   370

WILLY.   I can't work for you, that's all, don't ask me why.

CHARLEY.   [angered, takes out more bills] You been jealous of me all your life, you damned fool! Here, pay your insurance. [He puts the money in WILLY's hand.]

WILLY.   I'm keeping strict accounts.

CHARLEY.   I've got some work to do. Take care of yourself. And pay your insurance.

WILLY.   [moving to the right] Funny, y'know? After all the highways, and the trains,   375
and the appointments, and the years, you end up worth more dead than alive.

CHARLEY.   Willy, nobody's worth nothin' dead. [after a slight pause] Did you hear what I said?

[WILLY stands still, dreaming.]

CHARLEY.   Willy!

WILLY.   Apologize to Bernard for me when you see him. I didn't mean to argue with him. He's a fine boy. They're all fine boys, and they'll end up big—all of them. Someday they'll all play tennis together. Wish me luck, Charley. He saw Bill Oliver today.

CHARLEY.   Good luck.

WILLY.   [on the verge of tears] Charley, you're the only friend I got. Isn't that a re-   380
markable thing? [He goes out.]

CHARLEY.   Jesus!

[CHARLEY stares after him a moment and follows. All light blacks out. Suddenly raucous music is heard, and a red glow rises behind the screen at right. STANLEY, a young waiter, appears, carrying a table, followed by HAPPY, who is carrying two chairs.]

STANLEY.   [putting the table down] That's all right, Mr. Loman. I can handle it my-self. [He turns and takes the chairs from HAPPY and places them at the table.]

HAPPY.   [glancing around.] Oh, this is better.

STANLEY.   Sure, in the front there you're in the middle of all kinds a noise. When-ever you got a party, Mr. Loman, you just tell me and I'll put you back here. Y' know, there's a lotta people they don't like it private, because when they go out they like to see a lotta action around them because they're sick and tired to stay in the house by theirself. But I know you, you ain't from Hackensack.° You know what I mean?

---

368 *J. P. Morgan:* John Pierpont Morgan (1837–1913) was the founder of U.S. Steel and the head of a gigantic family fortune that was enlarged by his son, John Pierpont Morgan (1867–1943). Charley is prob-ably referring to the son.   384 *Hackensack:* a city in northeastern New Jersey; Stanley uses the name as a reference to unsophisticated visitors to New York City.

HAPPY.   [*sitting down*] So how's it coming, Stanley?   385

STANLEY.   Ah, it's a dog's life. I only wish during the war they'd a took me in the Army. I coulda been dead by now.

HAPPY.   My brother's back, Stanley.

STANLEY.   Oh, he come back, heh? From the Far West.

HAPPY.   Yeah, big cattle man, my brother, so treat him right. And my father's coming too.

STANLEY.   Oh, your father too!   390

HAPPY.   You got a couple of nice lobsters?

STANLEY.   Hundred per cent, big.

HAPPY.   I want them with claws.

STANLEY.   Don't worry. I don't give you no mice. [*HAPPY laughs.*] How about some wine? It'll put a head on the meal.

HAPPY.   No. You remember, Stanley, that recipe I brought you from overseas? With   395
the champagne in it?

STANLEY.   Oh, yeah, sure. I still got it tacked up yet in the kitchen. But that'll have to cost a buck apiece anyways.

HAPPY.   That's all right.

STANLEY.   What'd you, hit a number or somethin'?

HAPPY.   No, it's a little celebration. My brother is—I think he pulled off a big deal today. I think we're going into business together.

STANLEY.   Great! That's the best for you. Because a family business, you know what   400
I mean?—that's the best.

HAPPY.   That's what I think.

STANLEY.   'Cause what's the difference? Somebody steals? It's in the family. Know what I mean? [*sotto voce°*] Like this bartender here. The boss is goin' crazy what kinda leak he's got in the cash register. You put it in but it don't come out.

HAPPY.   [*raising his head*] Sh!

STANLEY.   What?

HAPPY.   You notice I wasn't lookin' right or left, was I?   405

STANLEY.   No.

HAPPY.   And my eyes are closed.

STANLEY.   So what's the—?

HAPPY.   Strudel's comin'.

STANLEY.   [*catching on, looks around*] Ah, no, there's no—   410

[*He breaks off as a furred, lavishly dressed Girl enters and sits at the next table. Both follow her with their eyes.*]

STANLEY.   Geez, how'd ya know?

HAPPY.   I got radar or something. [*staring directly at her profile*] Oooooooo . . . Stanley.

STANLEY.   I think that's for you, Mr. Loman.

HAPPY.   Look at that mouth. Oh God. And the binoculars.

STANLEY.   Geez, you got a life, Mr. Loman.   415

HAPPY.   Wait on her.

STANLEY.   [*going to the GIRL's table*] Would you like a menu, ma'am?

GIRL.   I'm expecting someone, but I'd like a—

---

402 *sotto voce:* spoken in an undertone or "stage" whisper.

HAPPY.   Why don't you bring her—excuse me, miss, do you mind? I sell champagne, and I'd like you to try my brand. Bring her a champagne, Stanley.

GIRL.   That's awfully nice of you.   420

HAPPY.   Don't mention it. It's all company money. [*He laughs.*]

GIRL.   That's a charming product to be selling, isn't it?

HAPPY.   Oh, gets to be like everything else. Selling is selling, y'know.

GIRL.   I suppose.

HAPPY.   You don't happen to sell, do you?   425

GIRL.   No, I don't sell.

HAPPY.   Would you object to a compliment from a stranger? You ought to be on a magazine cover.

GIRL.   [*looking at him a little archly*] I have been.

[*STANLEY comes in with a glass of champagne.*]

HAPPY.   What'd I say before, Stanley? You see? She's a cover girl.

STANLEY.   Oh, I could see, I could see.   430

HAPPY.   [*to the GIRL*] What magazine?

GIRL.   Oh, a lot of them [*She takes the drink.*] Thank you.

HAPPY.   You know what they say in France, don't you? "Champagne is the drink of the complexion"—Hya, Biff!

[*BIFF has entered and sits with HAPPY.*]

BIFF.   Hello, kid. Sorry I'm late.

HAPPY.   I just got here. Uh, Miss—?   435

GIRL.   Forsythe.

HAPPY.   Miss Forsythe, this is my brother.

BIFF.   Is Dad here?

HAPPY.   His name if Biff. You might've heard of him. Great football player.

GIRL.   Really? What team?   440

HAPPY.   Are you familiar with football?

GIRL.   No. I'm afraid I'm not.

HAPPY.   Biff is quarterback with the New York Giants.

GIRL.   Well, that is nice, isn't it? [*She drinks.*]

HAPPY.   Good health.   445

GIRL.   I'm happy to meet you.

HAPPY.   That's my name. Hap. It's really Harold, but at West Point they called me Happy.

GIRL.   [*now really impressed*] Oh, I see. How do you do? [*She turns her profile.*]

BIFF.   Isn't Dad coming?

HAPPY.   You want her?   450

BIFF.   Oh, I could never make that.

HAPPY.   I remember the time that idea would never come into your head. Where's the old confidence, Biff?

BIFF.   I just saw Oliver—

HAPPY.   Wait a minute. I've got to see that old confidence again. Do you want her? She's on call.

BIFF.   Oh, no. [*He turns to look at the GIRL.*]   455

HAPPY.   I'm telling you. Watch this. [*turning to the Girl*] Honey? [*She turns to him.*] Are you busy?

GIRL.   Well, I am . . . but I could make a phone call.

HAPPY.   Do that, will you, honey? And see if you can get a friend. We'll be here for a while. Biff is one of the greatest football players in the country.

GIRL.   [standing up] Well, I'm certainly happy to meet you.

HAPPY.   Come back soon.   460

GIRL.   I'll try.

HAPPY.   Don't try, honey, try hard.

[The GIRL exits. STANLEY follows, shaking his head in bewildered admiration.]

HAPPY.   Isn't that a shame now? A beautiful girl like that? That's why I can't get married. There's not a good woman in a thousand. New York is loaded with them, kid!

BIFF.   Hap, look—

HAPPY.   I told you she was on call!   465

BIFF.   [strangely unnerved] Cut it out, will ya? I want to say something to you.

HAPPY.   Did you see Oliver?

BIFF.   I saw him all right. Now look, I want to tell Dad a couple of things and I want you to help me.

HAPPY.   What? Is he going to back you?

BIFF.   Are you crazy? You're out of your goddam head, you know that?   470

HAPPY.   Why? What happened?

BIFF.   [breathlessly] I did a terrible thing today, Hap. It's been the strangest day I ever went through. I'm all numb, I swear.

HAPPY.   You mean he wouldn't see you?

BIFF.   Well, I waited six hours for him, see? All day. Kept sending my name in. Even tried to date his secretary so she'd get me to him, but no soap.

HAPPY.   Because you're not showin' the old confidence, Biff. He remembered you,   475 didn't he?

BIFF.   [stopping HAPPY with a gesture] Finally, about five o'clock, he comes out. Didn't remember who I was or anything. I felt like such an idiot, Hap.

HAPPY.   Did you tell him my Florida idea?

BIFF.   He walked away. I saw him for one minute. I got so mad I could've torn the walls down! How the hell did I ever get the idea I was a salesman there? I even believed myself that I'd been a salesman for him! And then he gave me one look and—I realized what a ridiculous lie my whole life has been! We've been talking in a dream for fifteen years. I was a shipping clerk.

HAPPY.   What'd you do?

BIFF.   [with great tension and wonder] Well, he left, see. And the secretary went out. I   480 was all alone in the waiting-room. I don't know what came over me, Hap. The next thing I know I'm in his office—paneled walls, everything. I can't explain it. I—Hap, I took his fountain pen.

HAPPY.   Geez, did he catch you?

BIFF.   I ran out. I ran down all eleven flights. I ran and ran and ran.

HAPPY.   That was an awful dumb—what'd you do that for?

BIFF.   [agonized] I don't know, I just—wanted to take something. I don't know. You gotta help me, Hap, I'm gonna tell Pop.

HAPPY.   You crazy? What for?   485

BIFF.   Hap, he's got to understand that I'm not the man somebody lends that kind of money to. He thinks I've been spiting him all these years and it's eating him up.

HAPPY.   That's just it. You tell him something nice.

BIFF.   I can't.

HAPPY.   Say you got a lunch date with Oliver tomorrow.

BIFF.   So what do I do tomorrow?   490

HAPPY.   You leave the house tomorrow and come back at night and say Oliver is thinking it over. And he thinks it over for a couple of weeks, and gradually it fades away and nobody's the worse.

BIFF.   But it'll go on forever!

HAPPY.   Dad is never so happy as when he's looking forward to something!

[*WILLY enters.*]

HAPPY.   Hello, scout!

WILLY.   Gee, I haven't been here in years!   495

[*STANLEY has followed WILLY in and sets a chair for him. STANLEY starts off but HAPPY stops him.*]

HAPPY.   Stanley!

[*STANLEY stands by, waiting for an order.*]

BIFF.   [*going to WILLY with guilt, as to an invalid*] Sit down, Pop. You want a drink?

WILLY.   Sure, I don't mind.

BIFF.   Let's get a load on.

WILLY.   You look worried.

BIFF.   N-no. [*to STANLEY*] Scotch all around. Make it doubles.   500

STANLEY.   Doubles, right. [*He goes.*]

WILLY.   You had a couple already, didn't you?

BIFF.   Just a couple, yeah.

WILLY.   Well, what happened, boy? [*nodding affirmatively, with a smile*] Everything   505
go all right?

BIFF.   [*takes a breath, then reaches out and grasps WILLY's hand*] Pal . . . [*He is smiling bravely, and WILLY is smiling too.*] I had an experience today.

HAPPY.   Terrific, Pop.

WILLY.   That so? What happened?

BIFF.   [*high, slightly alcoholic, above the earth*] I'm going to tell you everything from first to last. It's been a strange day. [*Silence. He looks around, composes himself as best he can, but his breath keeps breaking the rhythm of his voice.*] I had to wait quite a while for him, and—

WILLY.   Oliver?   510

BIFF.   Yeah, Oliver. All day, as a matter of cold fact. And a lot of—instances—facts, Pop, facts about my life came back to me. Who was it, Pop? Who ever said I was a salesman with Oliver?

WILLY.   Well, you were.

BIFF.   No, Dad, I was a shipping clerk.

WILLY.   But you were practically—

BIFF.   [*with determination*] Dad, I don't know who said it first, but I was never a   515
salesman for Bill Oliver.

WILLY.   What're you talking about?

BIFF.   Let's hold on to the facts tonight, Pop. We're not going to get anywhere bullin' around. I was a shipping clerk.

WILLY.   [*angrily*] All right, now listen to me—

BIFF.   Why don't you let me finish?

WILLY.   I'm not interested in stories about the past or any crap of that kind be-   520
cause the woods are burning, boys, you understand? There's a big blaze going on all around. I was fired today.

BIFF.   [*shocked*] How could you be?

WILLY.   I was fired, and I'm looking for a little good news to tell your mother, because the woman has waited and the woman has suffered. The gist of it is that I haven't got a story left in my head, Biff. So don't give me a lecture about facts and aspects. I am not interested. Now what've you got to say to me?

[STANLEY *enters with three drinks. They wait until he leaves.*]

WILLY.   Did you see Oliver?

BIFF.   Jesus, Dad!

WILLY.   You mean you didn't go up there?   525

HAPPY.   Sure he went up there.

BIFF.   I did. I—saw him. How could they fire you?

WILLY.   [*on the edge of his chair*] What kind of a welcome did he give you?

BIFF.   He won't even let you work on commission?

WILLY.   I'm out! [*driving*] So tell me, he gave you a warm welcome?   530

HAPPY.   Sure Pop, sure!

BIFF.   [*driven*] Well, it was kind of—

WILLY.   I was wondering if he'd remember you. [*to* HAPPY] Imagine, man doesn't see him for ten, twelve years and gives him that kind of a welcome!

HAPPY.   Damn right!

BIFF.   [*trying to return to the offensive*] Pop, look—   535

WILLY.   You know why he remembered you, don't you? Because you impressed him in those days.

BIFF.   Let's talk quietly and get this down to the facts, huh?

WILLY.   [*as though* BIFF *had been interrupting*] Well, what happened? It's great news, Biff. Did he take you into his office or'd you talk in the waiting-room?

BIFF.   Well, he came in, see, and—

WILLY.   [*with a big smile*] What'd he say? Betcha he threw his arm around you.   540

BIFF.   Well, he kinda—

WILLY.   He's a fine man. [*to* HAPPY] Very hard man to see, y'know.

HAPPY.   [*agreeing*] Oh, I know.

WILLY.   [*to* BIFF] Is that where you had the drinks?

BIFF.   Yeah, he gave me a couple of—no, no!   545

HAPPY.   [*cutting in*] He told him my Florida idea.

WILLY.   Don't interrupt. [*to* BIFF] How'd he react to the Florida idea?

BIFF.   Dad, will you give me a minute to explain?

WILLY.   I've been waiting for you to explain since I sat down here! What happened? He took you into his office and what?

BIFF.   Well—I talked. And—and he listened, see.   550

WILLY.   Famous for the way he listens, y'know. What was his answer?

BIFF.   His answer was—[*He breaks off, suddenly angry.*] Dad, you're not letting me tell you what I want to tell you!

WILLY.   [*accusing, angered*] You didn't see him, did you?

BIFF.   I did see him!

WILLY.   What'd you insult him or something? You insulted him, didn't you?   555

BIFF.   Listen, will you let me out of it, will you just let me out of it!

HAPPY.   What the hell!

WILLY.   Tell me what happened!

BIFF.   [*to* HAPPY] I can't talk to him!

[*A single trumpet note jars the ear. The light of green leaves stains the house, which holds the air of night and a dream.* YOUNG BERNARD *enters and knocks on the door of the house.*]

YOUNG BERNARD. [*frantically*] Mrs. Loman, Mrs. Loman!   560
HAPPY. Tell him what happened!
BIFF. [*to HAPPY*] Shut up and leave me alone!
WILLY. No, no! You had to go and flunk math!
BIFF. What math? What're you talking about?
YOUNG BERNARD. Mrs. Loman, Mrs. Loman!   565

[*LINDA appears in the house, as of old.*]

WILLY. [*wildly*] Math, math, math!
BIFF. Take it easy, Pop!
YOUNG BERNARD. Mrs. Loman!
WILLY. [*furiously*] If you hadn't flunked you'd've been set by now!
BIFF. Now, look, I'm gonna tell you what happened, and you're going to listen   570
to me.
YOUNG BERNARD. Mrs. Loman!
BIFF. I waited six hour—
HAPPY. What the hell are you saying?
BIFF. I kept sending in my name but he wouldn't see me. So finally he . . .

[*He continues unheard as light fades low on the restaurant.*]

YOUNG BERNARD. Biff flunked math!   575
LINDA. No!
YOUNG BERNARD. Birnbaum flunked him! They won't graduate him!
LINDA. But they have to. He's gotta go to the university. Where is he? Biff! Biff!
YOUNG BERNARD. No, he left. He went to Grand Central.
LINDA. Grand—You mean he went to Boston!   580
YOUNG BERNARD. Is Uncle Willy in Boston?
LINDA. Oh, maybe Willy can talk to the teacher. Oh, the poor, poor boy!

[*Light on house area snaps out.*]

BIFF. [*at the table, now audible, holding up a gold fountain pen*] . . . so I'm washed up
with Oliver, you understand? Are you listening to me?
WILLY. [*at a loss*] Yeah, sure. If you hadn't flunked—
BIFF. Flunked what? What're you talking about?   585
WILLY. Don't blame everything on me! I didn't flunk math—you did! What pen?
HAPPY. That was awful dumb, Biff, a pen like that is worth—
WILLY. [*seeing the pen for the first time*] You took Oliver's pen?
BIFF. [*weakening*] Dad, I just explained it to you.
WILLY. You stole Bill Oliver's fountain pen!   590
BIFF. I didn't exactly steal it! That's just what I've been explaining to you!
HAPPY. He had it in his hand and just then Oliver walked in, so he got nervous
and stuck it in his pocket!
WILLY. My God, Biff!
BIFF. I never intended to do it, Dad!
OPERATOR'S VOICE. Standish Arms, good evening!   595
WILLY. [*shouting*] I'm not in my room!
BIFF. [*frightened*] Dad, what's the matter? [*He and HAPPY stand up.*]
OPERATOR. Ringing Mr. Loman for you!
WILLY. I'm not there, stop it!
BIFF. [*horrified, gets down on one knee before WILLY*] Dad, I'll make good, I'll make   600
good. [*WILLY tries to get to his feet. BIFF holds him down.*] Sit down now.

WILLY.   No, you're no good, you're no good for anything.

BIFF.   I am, Dad, I'll find something else, you understand? Now don't worry about anything. [*He holds up* WILLY's *face.*] Talk to me, Dad.

OPERATOR.   Mr. Loman does not answer. Shall I page him?

WILLY.   [*attempting to stand, as though to rush and silence the Operator*] No, no, no!

HAPPY.   He'll strike something, Pop.   605

WILLY.   No, no . . .

BIFF.   [*desperately, standing over* WILLY] Pop, listen! Listen to me! I'm telling you something good. Oliver talked to his partner about the Florida idea. you listening? He—he talked to his partner, and he came to me . . . I'm going to be all right, you hear? Dad, listen to me, he said it was just a question of the amount!

WILLY.   Then you . . . got it?

HAPPY.   He's gonna be terrific, Pop!

WILLY.   [*trying to stand*] Then you got it, haven't you? You got it! You got it!   610

BIFF.   [*agonized, holds* WILLY *down*] No, no. Look, Pop. I'm supposed to have lunch with them tomorrow. I'm just telling you this so you'll know that I can still make an impression, Pop. And I'll make good somewhere, but I can't go tomorrow, see?

WILLY.   Why not? You simply—

BIFF.   But the pen, Pop!

WILLY.   You give it to him and tell him it was an oversight!

HAPPY.   Sure, have lunch tomorrow!   615

BIFF.   I can't say that—

WILLY.   You were doing a crossword puzzle and accidentally used his pen!

BIFF.   Listen, kid, I took those balls years ago, now I walk in with his fountain pen? That clinches it, don't you see? I can't face him like that! I'll try elsewhere.

PAGE'S VOICE.   Paging Mr. Loman!

WILLY.   Don't you want to be anything?   620

BIFF.   Pop, how can I go back?

WILLY.   You don't want to be anything, is that what's behind it?

BIFF.   [*now angry at* WILLY *for not crediting his sympathy*] Don't take it that way! You think it was easy walking into that office after what I'd done to him? A team of horses couldn't have dragged me back to Bill Oliver!

WILLY.   Then why'd you go?

BIFF.   Why did I go? Why did I go? Look at you! Look at what's become of you!   625

[*Off left,* THE WOMAN *laughs.*]

WILLY.   Biff, you're going to go to that lunch tomorrow, or—

BIFF.   I can't go. I've got no appointment!

HAPPY.   Biff, for . . . !

WILLY.   Are you spiting me?

BIFF.   Don't take it that way! Goddammit!   630

WILLY.   [*strikes* BIFF *and falters away from the table*] You rotten little louse! Are you spiting me?

THE WOMAN.   Someone's at the door, Willy!

BIFF.   I'm no good, can't you see what I am?

HAPPY.   [*separating them*] Hey, you're in a restaurant! Now cut it out, both of you! [*The girls enter.*] Hello, girls, sit down.

[THE WOMAN *laughs, off left.*]

MISS FORSYTHE.   I guess we might as well. This is Letta.   635

THE WOMAN. Willy, are you going to wake up?

BIFF. [*ignoring* WILLY] How're ya, miss, sit down. What do you drink?

MISS FORSYTHE. Letta might not be able to stay long.

LETTA. I gotta get up very early tomorrow. I got jury duty. I'm so excited! Were you fellows ever on a jury?

BIFF. No, but I been in front of them! [*The girls laugh.*] This is my father.   640

LETTA. Isn't he cute? Sit down with us, Pop.

HAPPY. Sit him down, Biff!

BIFF. [*going to him*] Come on, slugger, drink us under the table. To hell with it! Come on, sit down, pal.

[*On* BIFF'S *last insistence,* WILLY *is about to sit.*]

THE WOMAN. [*now urgently*] Willy, are you going to answer the door!

[THE WOMAN'S *call pulls* WILLY *back. He starts right, befuddled.*]

BIFF. Hey, where are you going?   645

WILLY. Open the door.

BIFF. The door?

WILLY. The washroom . . . the door . . . where's the door?

BIFF. [*leading* WILLY *to the left*] Just go straight down.

[WILLY *moves left.*]

THE WOMAN. Willy, Willy, are you going to get up, get up, get up, get up?   650

[WILLY *exits left.*]

LETTA. I think it's sweet you bring your daddy along.

MISS FORSYTHE. Oh, he isn't really your father!

BIFF. [*at left, turning to her resentfully*] Miss Forsythe, you've just seen a prince walk by. A fine, troubled prince. A hard-working, unappreciated prince. A pal, you understand? A good companion. Always for his boys.

LETTA. That's so sweet.

HAPPY. Well, girls, what's the program? We're wasting time. Come on, Biff. Gather round. Where would you like to go?   655

BIFF. Why don't you do something for him?

HAPPY. Me!

BIFF. Don't you give a damn for him, Hap?

HAPPY. What're you talking about? I'm the one who—

BIFF. I sense it, you don't give a good goddam about him. [*He takes the rolled-up*   660
hose from his pocket and puts it on the table in front of HAPPY.] Look what I found in the cellar, for Christ's sake. How can you bear to let it go on?

HAPPY. Me? Who goes away? Who runs off and—

BIFF. Yeah, but he doesn't mean anything to you. You could help him—I can't! Don't you understand what I'm talking about? He's going to kill himself, don't you know that?

HAPPY. Don't I know it! Me!

BIFF. Hap, help him! Jesus . . . help him . . . Help me, help me, I can't bear to look at his face! [*Ready to weep, he hurries out, up right.*]

HAPPY. [*staring after him*] Where are you going?   665

MISS FORSYTHE. What's he so mad about?

HAPPY. Come on, girls, we'll catch up with him.

MISS FORSYTHE.   [*as* HAPPY *pushes her out*] Say, I don't like that temper of his!

HAPPY.   He's just a little overstrung, he'll be all right!

WILLY.   [*off left, as* THE WOMAN *laughs*] Don't answer! Don't answer!   670

LETTA.   Don't you want to tell your father—

HAPPY.   No, that's not my father. He's just a guy. Come on, we'll catch Biff, and, honey, we're going to paint this town! Stanley, where's the check! Hey, Stanley!

[*They exit.* STANLEY *looks toward left.*]

STANLEY.   [*calling to* HAPPY *indignantly*] Mr. Loman! Mr. Loman!

[STANLEY *picks up a chair and follows them off. Knocking is heard off left.* THE WOMAN *enters, laughing.* WILLY *follows her. She is in a black slip; he is buttoning his shirt. Raw, sensuous music accompanies their speech.*]

WILLY.   Will you stop laughing? Will you stop?

THE WOMAN.   Aren't you going to answer the door? He'll wake the whole hotel.   675

WILLY.   I'm not expecting anybody.

THE WOMAN.   Whyn't you have another drink, honey, and stop being so damn self-centered?

WILLY.   I'm so lonely.

THE WOMAN.   You know you ruined me, Willy? From now on, whenever you come to the office, I'll see that you go right through to the buyers. No waiting at my desk any more, Willy. You ruined me.

WILLY.   That's nice of you to say that.   680

THE WOMAN.   Gee, you are self-centered! Why so sad? You are the saddest, self-centeredest soul I ever did see-saw. [*She laughs. He kisses her.*] Come on inside, drummer boy. It's silly to be dressing in the middle of the night. [*As knocking is heard*] Aren't you going to answer the door?

WILLY.   They're knocking on the wrong door.

THE WOMAN.   But I felt the knocking! And he heard us talking in here. Maybe the hotel's on fire!

WILLY.   [*his terror rising*] It's a mistake.

THE WOMAN.   Then tell him to go away!   685

WILLY.   There's nobody there.

THE WOMAN.   It's getting on my nerves, Willy. There's somebody standing out there and it's getting on my nerves!

WILLY.   [*pushing her away from him*] All right, stay in the bathroom here, and don't come out. I think there's a law in Massachusetts about it, so don't come out. It may be that new room clerk. He looked very mean. So don't come out. It's a mistake, there's no fire.

[*The knocking is heard again. He takes a few steps away from her, and she vanishes into the wing. The light follows him, and now he is facing* YOUNG BIFF, *who carries a suitcase.* BIFF *steps toward him. The music is gone.*]

BIFF.   Why didn't you answer?

WILLY.   Biff! What are you doing in Boston?   690

BIFF.   Why didn't you answer? I've been knocking for five minutes, I called you on the phone—

WILLY.   I just heard you. I was in the bathroom and had the door shut. Did anything happen home?

BIFF.   Dad—I let you down.

WILLY.   What do you mean?

BIFF.   Dad . . .   695

WILLY.   Biffo, what's this about? [*putting his arm around* BIFF] Come on, let's go downstairs and get you a malted.

BIFF.   Dad, I flunked math.

WILLY.   Not for the term?

BIFF.   The term. I haven't got enough credits to graduate.

WILLY.   You mean to say Bernard wouldn't give you the answers?   700

BIFF.   He did, he tried, but I only got a sixty-one.

WILLY.   And they wouldn't give you four points?

BIFF.   Birnbaum refused absolutely. I begged him, Pop, but he won't give me those points. You gotta talk to him before they close the school. Because if he saw the kind of man you are, and you just talked to him in your way, I'm sure he'd come through for me. The class came right before practice, see, and I didn't go enough. Would you talk to him? He'd like you, Pop. You know the way you could talk.

WILLY.   You're on. We'll drive right back.

BIFF.   Oh, Dad, good work! I'm sure he'll change it for you!   705

WILLY.   Go downstairs and tell the clerk I'm checkin' out. Go right down.

BIFF.   Yes, sir! See, the reason he hates me, Pop—one day he was late for class so I got up at the blackboard and imitated him. I crossed my eyes and talked with a lithp.

WILLY.   [*laughing*] You did? The kids like it?

BIFF.   They nearly died laughing!

WILLY.   Yeah? What'd you do?   710

BIFF.   The thquare root of thixthy twee is . . . [WILLY *bursts out laughing;* BIFF *joins him.*] And in the middle of it he walked in!

[WILLY *laughs and* THE WOMAN *joins in offstage.*]

WILLY.   [*without hesitation*] Hurry downstairs and—

BIFF.   Somebody in there?

WILLY.   No, that was next door.

[THE WOMAN. *laughs offstage.*]

BIFF.   Somebody got in your bathroom!   715

WILLY.   No, it's the next room, there's a party—

THE WOMAN.   [*enters, laughing. She lisps this.*] Can I come in? There's something in the bathtub, Willy, and it's moving!

[WILLY *looks at* BIFF, *who is staring open-mouthed and horrified at* THE WOMAN.]

WILLY.   Ah—you better go back to your room. They must be finished painting by now. They're painting her room so I let her take a shower here. Go back, go back . . . [*He pushes her.*]

THE WOMAN.   [*resisting*] But I've got to get dressed, Willy, I can't—

WILLY.   Get out of here! Go back, go back . . . [*suddenly striving for the ordinary*] This   720
is Miss Francis, Biff, she's a buyer. They're painting her room. Go back, Miss Francis, go back . . .

THE WOMAN.   But my clothes, I can't go out naked in the hall!

WILLY.   [*pushing her offstage*] Get outa here! Go back, go back!

[BIFF *slowly sits down on his suitcase as the argument continues offstage.*]

THE WOMAN.   Where's my stockings? You promised me stockings, Willy!

WILLY.   I have no stockings here!

THE WOMAN.   You had two boxes of size nine sheers for me, and I want them!   725

WILLY.   Here, for God's sake, will you get outa here!

THE WOMAN.   [*enters holding a box of stockings*] I just hope there's nobody in the hall. That's all I hope. [*To* BIFF] Are you football or baseball?

BIFF.   Football.

THE WOMAN.   [*angry, humiliated*] That's me too. G'night. [*She snatches her clothes from* WILLY, *and walks out.*]

WILLY.   [*after a pause*] Well, better get going. I want to get to the school first thing   730
in the morning. Get my suits out of the closet. I'll get my valise. [BIFF *doesn't move.*] What's the matter? [BIFF *remains motionless, tears falling*] She's a buyer. Buys for J. H. Simmons. She lives down the hall—they're painting. You don't imagine—[*He breaks off. After a pause*] Now listen, pal, she's just a buyer. She sees merchandise in her room and they have to keep it looking just so . . . [*Pause. Assuming command*] All right, get my suits. [BIFF *does-n't move.*] Now stop crying and do as I say. I gave you an order. Biff, I gave you an order! Is that what you do when I give you an order? How dare you cry! [*putting his arm around* BIFF] Now look, Biff, when you grow up you'll understand about these things. You must-n't—you mustn't overemphasize a thing like this. I'll see Birnbaum first thing in the morning.

BIFF.   Never mind.

WILLY.   [*getting down beside* BIFF] Never mind! He's going to give you those points. I'll see to it.

BIFF.   He wouldn't listen to you.

WILLY.   He certainly will listen to me. You need those points for the U. of Virginia.

BIFF.   I'm not going there.   735

WILLY.   Heh? If I can't get him to change that mark you'll make it up in summer school. You've got all summer to—

BIFF.   [*his weeping breaking from him*] Dad . . .

WILLY.   [*infected by it*] Oh, my boy . . .

BIFF.   Dad . . .

WILLY.   She's nothing to me, Biff. I was lonely, I was terribly lonely.   740

BIFF.   You—you gave her Mama's stockings! [*His tears break through and he rises to go.*]

WILLY.   [*grabbing for* BIFF] I gave you an order!

BIFF.   Don't touch me, you—liar!

WILLY.   Apologize for that!

BIFF.   You fake! You phony little fake! [*Overcome, he turns quickly and weeping fully*   745
goes out with his suitcase. WILLY *is left on the floor on his knees.*]

WILLY.   I gave you an order! Biff, come back here or I'll beat you! Come back here! I'll whip you!

[STANLEY *comes quickly in from the right and stands in front of* WILLY.]

WILLY.   [*shouts at* STANLEY] I gave you an order . . .

STANLEY.   Hey, let's pick it up, pick it up, Mr. Loman. [*He helps* WILLY *to his feet.*]
Your boys left with the chippies. They said they'll see you home.

[*A* SECOND WAITER *watches some distance away.*]

WILLY.   But we were supposed to have dinner together.

[*Music is heard,* WILLY's *theme.*]

STANLEY.   Can you make it?   750

WILLY.   I'll—sure, I can make it. [*suddenly concerned about his clothes*] Do I—I look all right?

STANLEY.   Sure, you look all right. [*He flicks a speck off WILLY's lapel.*]

WILLY.   Here—here's a dollar.

STANLEY.   Oh, your son paid me. It's all right.

WILLY.   [*putting it in STANLEY's hand*] No, take it. You're a good boy.   755

STANLEY.   Oh, no, you don't have to . . .

WILLY.   Here—here's some more, I don't need it any more. [*after a slight pause*] Tell me—is there a seed store in the neighborhood?

STANLEY.   Seeds? You mean like to plant?

[*As WILLY turns, STANLEY slips the money back into his jacket pocket.*]

WILLY.   Yes. Carrots, peas . . .

STANLEY.   Well, there's hardware stores on Sixth Avenue, but it may be too late   760
now.

WILLY.   [*anxiously*] Oh, I'd better hurry. I've got to get some seeds. [*He starts off to the right.*] I've got to get some seeds, right away. Nothing's planted. I don't have a thing in the ground.

[*WILLY hurries out as the light goes down. STANLEY moves over to the right after him, watches him off. The other waiter has been staring at WILLY.*]

STANLEY.   [*to the WAITER*] Well, whatta you looking at?

[*The WAITER picks up the chairs and moves off right. STANLEY takes the table and follows him. The light fades on this area. There is a long pause, the sound of the flute coming over. The light gradually rises on the kitchen, which is empty. HAPPY appears at the door of the house, followed by BIFF. HAPPY is carrying a large bunch of long-stemmed roses. He enters the kitchen, looks around for LINDA. Not seeing her, he turns to BIFF, who is just outside the house door, and makes a gesture with his hands, indicating "Not here, I guess." He looks into the living-room and freezes. Inside, LINDA, unseen, is seated, WILLY's coat on her lap. She rises ominously and quietly and moves toward HAPPY, who backs up into the kitchen, afraid.*]

HAPPY.   Hey, what're you doing up? [*LINDA says nothing but moves toward him implacably.*] Where's Pop? [*He keeps backing to the right, and now LINDA is in full view in the doorway to the living-room.*] Is he sleeping?

LINDA.   Where were you?

HAPPY.   [*trying to laugh it off*] We met two girls, Mom, very fine types. Here, we   765
brought you some flowers. [*offering them to her*] Put them in your room, Ma.

[*She knocks them to the floor at BIFF's feet. He has now come inside and closed the door behind him. She stares at BIFF, silent.*]

HAPPY.   Now what'd you do that for? Mom, I want you to have some flowers—

LINDA.   [*cutting HAPPY off, violently to BIFF*] Don't you care whether he lives or dies?

HAPPY.   [*going to the stairs*] Come upstairs, Biff.

BIFF.   [*with a flare of disgust, to HAPPY*] Go away from me! [*to LINDA*] What do you mean, lives or dies? Nobody's dying around here, pal.

LINDA.   Get out of my sight! Get out of here!   770

BIFF.   I wanna see the boss.

LINDA.   You're not going near him!

BIFF.   Where is he? [*He moves into the living-room and LINDA follows.*]

LINDA.   [*shouting after* BIFF] You invite him for dinner. He looks forward to it all day—[BIFF *appears in his parents' bedroom, looks around, and exists.*]—and then you desert him there. There's no stranger you'd do that to!

HAPPY.   Why? He had a swell time with us. Listen, when I—[LINDA *comes back into*   775
the kitchen.]—desert him I hope I don't outlive the day!

LINDA.   Get out of here!

HAPPY.   Now look, Mom . . .

LINDA.   Did you have to go to women tonight? You and your lousy rotten whores!

[BIFF *re-enters the kitchen.*]

HAPPY.   Mom, all we did was follow Biff around trying to cheer him up! [*to* BIFF]
Boy, what a night you gave me!

LINDA.   Get out of here, both of you, and don't come back! I don't want you tor-   780
menting him any more. Go on now, get your things together! [*to* BIFF] You can sleep in his apartment. [*She starts to pick up the flowers and stops herself.*] Pick up this stuff, I'm not your maid any more. Pick it up, you bum, you!

[HAPPY *turns his back to her in refusal.* BIFF *slowly moves over and gets down on his knees, picking up the flowers.*]

LINDA.   You're a pair of animals! Not one, not another living soul would have had the cruelty to walk out on that man in a restaurant!

BIFF.   [*not looking at her*] Is that what he said?

LINDA.   He didn't have to say anything. He was so humiliated he nearly limped when he came in.

HAPPY.   But, Mom, he had a great time with us—

BIFF.   [*cutting him off violently*] Shut up!   785

[*Without another word,* HAPPY *goes upstairs.*]

LINDA.   You! You didn't even go in to see if he was all right!

BIFF.   [*still on the floor in front of* LINDA, *the flowers in his hand; with self-loathing*] No. Didn't. Didn't do a damned thing. How do you like that, heh? Left him babbling in a toilet.

LINDA.   You louse. You . . .

BIFF.   Now you hit it on the nose! [*He gets up, throws the flowers in the wastebasket.*]
The scum of the earth, and you're looking at him!

LINDA.   Get out of here!   790

BIFF.   I gotta talk to the boss, Mom. Where is he?

LINDA.   You're not going near him. Get out of his house!

BIFF.   [*with absolute assurance, determination*] No. We're gonna have an abrupt conversation, him and me.

LINDA.   You're not talking to him!

[*Hammering is heard from outside the house, off right.* BIFF *turns toward the noise.*]

LINDA.   [*suddenly pleading*] Will you please leave him alone?   795

BIFF.   What's he doing out there?

LINDA.   He's planting the garden!

BIFF.   [*quietly*] Now? Oh, my God!

[BIFF *moves outside,* LINDA *following. The light dies down on them and comes up on the center of the apron as* WILLY *walks into it. He is carrying a flashlight, a hoe, and a handful of seed packets. He raps the top of the hoe sharply to fix it firmly, and then moves to the left, measuring off the distance with his foot. He holds the flashlight to look at the seed packets, reading off the instructions. He is in the blue of night.*]

WILLY.   Carrots . . . quarter-inch apart. Rows . . . one-foot rows. [*He measures it off.*] One foot. [*He puts down a package and measures off.*] Beets. [*He puts down another package and measures again.*] Lettuce. [*He reads the package, puts it down.*] One foot—[*He breaks off as BEN appears at the right and moves slowly down to him.*] What a proposition, ts, ts. Terrific, terrific. 'Cause she's suffered, Ben, the woman has suffered. You understand me? A man can't go out the way he came in, Ben, a man has got to add up to something. You can't, you can't—[*BEN moves toward him as though to interrupt.*] You gotta consider, now. Don't answer so quick. Remember, it's a guaranteed twenty-thousand-dollar proposition. Now look, Ben, I want you to go through the ins and outs of this thing with me. I've got nobody to talk to, Ben, and the woman has suffered, you hear me?

BEN.   [*standing still, considering*] What's the proposition?   800

WILLY.   It's twenty thousand dollars on the barrelhead. Guaranteed, gilt-edged, you understand?

BEN.   You don't want to make a fool of yourself. They might not honor the policy.

WILLY.   How can they dare refuse? Didn't I work like a coolie to meet every premium on the nose? And now they don't pay off? Impossible!

BEN.   It's called a cowardly thing, William.

WILLY.   Why? Does it take more guts to stand here the rest of my life ringing up   805
a zero?

BEN.   [*yielding*] That's a point, William. [*He moves, thinking, turns.*] And twenty thousand—that *is* something one can feel with the hand, it is there.

WILLY.   [*now assured, with rising power*] Oh, Ben, that's the whole beauty of it! I see it like a diamond, shining in the dark, hard and rough, that I can pick up and touch in my hand. Not like—like an appointment! This would not be another damned-fool appointment, Ben, and it changes all the aspects. Because he thinks I'm nothing, see, and so he spites me. But the funeral—[*straightening up*] Ben, that funeral will be massive! They'll come from Maine, Massachusetts, Vermont, New Hampshire! All the old-timers with the strange license plates—that boy will be thunder-struck. Ben, because he never realized—I am known! Rhode Island, New York, New Jersey—I am known, Ben, and he'll see it with his eyes once and for all. He'll see what I am, Ben! He's in for a shock, that boy!

BEN.   [*coming down to the edge of the garden*] He'll call you a coward.

WILLY.   [*suddenly fearful*] No, that would be terrible.

BEN.   Yes. And a damned fool.   810

WILLY.   No, no, he mustn't, I won't have that! [*He is broken and desperate.*]

BEN.   He'll hate you, William.

[*The gay music of the Boys is heard.*]

WILLY.   Oh, Ben, how do we get back to all the great times? Used to be so full of light, and comradeship, the sleigh-riding in winter, and the ruddiness on his cheeks. And always some kind of good news coming up, always something nice coming up ahead. And never even let me carry the valises in the house, and simonizing, simonizing that little red car! Why, why can't I give him something and not have him hate me?

BEN.   Let me think about it. [*He glances at his watch.*] I still have a little time. Remarkable proposition, but you've got to be sure you're not making a fool of yourself.

[*BEN drifts upstage and goes out of sight. BIFF comes down from the left.*]

WILLY. [*suddenly conscious of* BIFF, *turns and looks up at him, then begins picking up the*   815
packages of seeds in confusion] Where the hell is that seed? [*Indignantly*] You can't see nothing out here! They boxed in the whole goddam neighborhood!

BIFF.   There are people all around here. Don't you realize that?

WILLY.   I'm busy. Don't bother me.

BIFF.   [*taking the hoe from* WILLY] I'm saying good-by to you, Pop. [WILLY *looks at him,*
silent, unable to move.] I'm not coming back any more.

WILLY.   You're not going to see Oliver tomorrow?

BIFF.   I've got no appointment, Dad.   820

WILLY.   He put his arm around you, and you've got no appointment?

BIFF.   Pop, get this now, will you? Everytime I've left it's been a fight that sent me
out of here. Today I realized something about myself and I tried to explain it to you and
I—I think I'm just not smart enough to make any sense out of it for you. To hell with
whose fault it is or anything like that. [*He takes* WILLY's *arm.*] Let's just wrap it up, heh?
Come on in, we'll tell Mom. [*He gently tries to pull* WILLY *to left.*]

WILLY.   [*frozen, immobile, with guilt in his voice*] No, I don't want to see her.

BIFF.   Come on! [*He pulls again, and* WILLY *tries to pull away.*]

WILLY.   [*highly nervous*] No, no, I don't want to see her.   825

BIFF.   [*tries to look into* WILLY's *face, as if to find the answer there*] Why don't you want
to see her?

WILLY.   [*more harshly now*] Don't bother me, will you?

BIFF.   What do you mean, you don't want to see her? You don't want them calling
you yellow, do you? This isn't your fault; it's me, I'm a bum. Now come inside! [WILLY
strains to get away.] Did you hear what I said to you?

[WILLY *pulls away and quickly goes by himself into the house.* BIFF *follows.*]

LINDA.   [*to* WILLY] Did you plant, dear?

BIFF.   [*at the door, to* LINDA] All right, we had it out. I'm going and I'm not writing   830
any more.

LINDA.   [*going to* WILLY *in the kitchen*] I think that's the best way, dear. 'Cause there's
no use drawing it out, you'll just never get along.

[WILLY *doesn't respond.*]

BIFF.   People ask where I am and what I'm doing, you don't know, and you don't
care. That way it'll be off your mind and you can start brightening up again. All right?
That clears it, doesn't it? [WILLY *is silent, and* BIFF *goes to him.*] You gonna wish me luck,
scout? [*He extends his hand.*] What do you say?

LINDA.   Shake his hand, Willy.

WILLY.   [*turning to her, seething with hurt*] There's no necessity to mention the pen
at all, y'know.

BIFF.   [*gently*] I've got no appointment, Dad.   835

WILLY.   [*erupting fiercely*] He put his arm around . . .

BIFF.   Dad, you're never going to see what I am, so what's the use of arguing? If I
strike oil I'll send you a check. Meantime forget I'm alive.

WILLY.   [*to* LINDA] Spite, see?

BIFF.   Shake hands, Dad.

WILLY.   Not my hand.   840

BIFF.   I was hoping not to go this way.

WILLY.   Well, this is the way you're going. Good-by.

[BIFF *looks at him a moment, then turns sharply and goes to the stairs.*]

WILLY.   [*stops him with*] May you rot in hell if you leave this house!

BIFF.   [*turning*] Exactly what is it that you want from me?

WILLY.   I want you to know, on the train, in the mountains, in the valleys, wherev-   845
er you go, that you cut down your life for spite!

BIFF.   No, no.

WILLY.   Spite, spite, is the word of your undoing! And when you're down and out,
remember what did it. When you're rotting somewhere beside the railroad tracks, remember, and don't you dare blame it on me!

BIFF.   I'm not blaming it on you!

WILLY.   I won't take the rap for this, you hear?

[*HAPPY comes down the stairs and stands on the bottom step, watching.*]

BIFF.   That's just what I'm telling you!   850

WILLY.   [*sinking into a chair at the table, with full accusation*] You're trying to put a
knife in me—don't think I don't know what you're doing!

BIFF.   All right, phony! Then let's lay it on the line. [*He whips the rubber tube out of
his pocket and puts it on the table.*]

HAPPY.   You crazy—

LINDA.   Biff! [*She moves to grab the hose, but BIFF holds it down with his hand.*]

BIFF.   Leave it here! Don't move it!   855

WILLY.   [*not looking at it*] What is that?

BIFF.   You know goddam well what that is.

WILLY.   [*caged, wanting to escape*] I never saw that.

BIFF.   You saw it. The mice didn't bring it into the cellar! What is this supposed to
do, make a hero out of you? This supposed to make me sorry for you?

WILLY.   Never heard of it.   860

BIFF.   There'll be no pity for you, you hear it? No pity!

WILLY.   [*to LINDA*] You hear the spite!

BIFF.   No, you're going to hear the truth—what you are and what I am!

LINDA.   Stop it!

WILLY.   Spite!   865

HAPPY.   [*coming down toward BIFF*] You cut it now!

BIFF.   [*to HAPPY*] The man don't know who we are! The man is gonna know! [*to
WILLY*] We never told the truth for ten minutes in this house!

HAPPY   We always told the truth!

BIFF.   [*turning on him*] You big blow, are you the assistant buyer? You're one of the
two assistants to the assistant, aren't you?

HAPPY.   Well, I'm practically—   870

BIFF.   You're practically full of it! We all are! And I'm through with it. [*to WILLY*]
Now hear this, Willy, this is me.

WILLY.   I know you!

BIFF.   You know why I had no address for three months? I stole a suit in Kansas
City and I was in jail. [*to LINDA, who is sobbing*] Stop crying. I'm through with it.

[*LINDA turns from them, her hands covering her face.*]

WILLY.   I suppose that's my fault!

BIFF.   I stole myself out of every good job since high school!

WILLY.   And whose fault is that?   875

BIFF.   And I never got anywhere because you blew me so full of hot air I could
never stand taking orders from anybody! That's whose fault it is!

WILLY. I hear that!

LINDA. Don't, Biff!

BIFF. It's goddam time you heard that! I had to be boss big shot in two weeks, and   880
I'm through with it!

WILLY. Then hang yourself! For spite, hang yourself!

BIFF. No! Nobody's hanging himself, Willy! I ran down eleven flights with a pen in my hand today. And suddenly I stopped, you hear me? And in the middle of that office building, do you hear this? I stopped in the middle of that building and I saw—the sky. I saw the things that I love in this world. The work and the food and time to sit and smoke. And I looked at the pen and said to myself, what the hell am I grabbing this for? Why am I trying to become what I don't want to be? What am I doing in an office, making a contemptuous, begging fool of myself, when all I want is out there, waiting for me the minute I say I know who I am! Why can't I say that, Willy?

[*He tries to make* WILLY *face him, but* WILLY *pulls away and moves to the left.*]

WILLY. [*with hatred, threateningly.*] The door of your life is wide open!

BIFF. Pop! I'm a dime a dozen, and so are you!

WILLY. [*turning on him now in an uncontrolled outburst*] I am not a dime a dozen! I   885
am Willy Loman, and you are Biff Loman!

[BIFF *starts for* WILLY, *but is blocked by* HAPPY. *In his fury,* BIFF *seems on the verge of attacking his father.*]

BIFF. I am not a leader of men, Willy, and neither are you. You were never anything but a hard-working drummer who landed in the ash can like all the rest of them! I'm one dollar an hour, Willy! I tried seven states and couldn't raise it. A buck an hour! Do you gather my meaning? I'm not bringing home any prizes any more, and you're going to stop waiting for me to bring them home!

WILLY. [*directly to* BIFF] You vengeful, spiteful mutt!

[BIFF *breaks from* HAPPY. WILLY, *in fright, starts up the stairs.* BIFF *grabs him*]

BIFF. [*at the peak of his fury*] Pop I'm nothing! I'm nothing, Pop. Can't you understand that? There's no spite in it any more. I'm just what I am, that's all.

[BIFF'*s fury has spent itself, and he breaks down, sobbing, holding on to* WILLY, *who dumbly fumbles for* BIFF'*s face.*]

WILLY. [*astonished*] What're you doing? What're you doing? [*to* LINDA] Why is he crying?

BIFF. [*crying, broken*] Will you let me go, for Christ's sake? Will you take that phony   890
dream and burn it before something happens? [*Struggling to contain himself, he pulls away and moves to the stairs.*] I'll go in the morning. Put him—put him to bed. [*Exhausted,* BIFF *moves up the stairs to his room.*]

WILLY. [*after a long pause, astonished, elevated*] Isn't that—isn't that remarkable? Biff—he likes me!

LINDA. He loves you, Willy!

HAPPY. [*deeply moved*] Always did, Pop.

WILLY. Oh, Biff! [*staring wildly*] He cried! Cried to me. [*He is choking with his love, and now cries out his promise.*] That boy—that boy is going to be magnificent!

[BEN *appears in the light just outside the kitchen.*]

BEN. Yes, outstanding, with twenty thousand behind him.   895

LINDA. [*sensing the racing of his mind, fearfully, carefully*] Now come to bed, Willy. It's all settled now.

WILLY. [*finding it difficult not to rush out of the house*] Yes, we'll sleep. Come on. Go to sleep, Hap.

BEN. And it does take a great kind of a man to crack the jungle.

[*In accents of dread, BEN's idyllic music starts up.*]

HAPPY. [*his arm around LINDA*] I'm getting married, Pop, don't forget it. I'm changing everything. I'm gonna run that department before the year is up. You'll see, Mom. [*He kisses her.*]

BEN. The jungle is dark but full of diamonds, Willy.　　　900

[*WILLY turns, moves, listening to BEN.*]

LINDA. Be good. You're both good boys, just act that way, that's all.

HAPPY. 'Night, Pop. [*He goes upstairs.*]

LINDA. [*to WILLY*] Come, dear.

BEN. [*with greater force*] One must go in to fetch a diamond out.

WILLY. [*to LINDA, as he moves slowly along the edge of the kitchen, toward the door*] I just　　905
want to get settled down, Linda. Let me sit alone for a little.

LINDA. [*almost uttering her fear*] I want you upstairs.

WILLY. [*taking her in his arms*] In a few minutes, Linda. I couldn't sleep right now. Go on, you look awful tired. [*He kisses her.*]

BEN. Not like an appointment at all. A diamond is rough and hard to the touch.

WILLY. Go on now. I'll be right up.

LINDA. I think this is the only way, Willy.　　　910

WILLY. Sure, it's the best thing.

BEN. Best thing!

WILLY. The only way. Everything is gonna be—go on, kid, get to bed. You look so tired.

LINDA. Come right up.

WILLY. Two minutes.　　　915

[*LINDA goes into the living-room, then reappears in her bedroom. WILLY moves just outside the kitchen door.*]

WILLY. Loves me. [*wonderingly*] Always loved me. Isn't that a remarkable thing? Ben, he'll worship me for it!

BEN. [*with promise*] It's dark there, but full of diamonds.

WILLY. Can you imagine that magnificence with twenty thousand dollars in his pocket?

LINDA. [*calling from her room*] Willy! Come up!

WILLY. [*calling into the kitchen*] Yes! Yes. Coming! It's very smart, you realize that,　　920
don't you, sweetheart? Even Ben sees it. I gotta go, baby. 'By! 'By! [*going over to BEN, almost dancing*] Imagine? When the mail comes he'll be ahead of Bernard again!

BEN. A perfect proposition all around.

WILLY. Did you see how he cried to me? Oh, if I could kiss him, Ben!

BEN. Time, William, time!

WILLY. Oh, Ben, I always knew one way or another we were gonna make it, Biff and I!

BEN. [*looking at his watch*] The boat. We'll be late. [*He moves slowly off into the　　925
darkness.*]

WILLY. [*elegiacally, turning to the house*] Now when you kick off, boy, I want a seventy-yard boot, and get right down the field under the ball, and when you hit, hit low and hit hard, because it's important, boy. [*He swings around and faces the audience.*] There's all kinds of important people in the stands, and the first thing you know . . . [*suddenly realizing he is alone*] Ben! Ben, where do I . . . ? [*He makes a sudden movement of search.*] Ben, how do I . . . ?

LINDA. [*calling*] Willy, you coming up?

WILLY. [*uttering a gasp of fear, whirling about as if to quiet her*] Sh! [*He turns around as if to find his way; sounds, faces, voices, seem to be swarming in upon him and he flicks at them, crying*] Sh! Sh! [*Suddenly music, faint and high, stops him. It rises in intensity, almost to an unbearable scream. He goes up and down on his toes, and rushes off around the house.*] Shhh!

LINDA. Willy?

[*There is no answer. LINDA waits. BIFF gets up off his bed. He is still in his clothes. HAPPY sits up. BIFF stands listening.*]

LINDA. [*with real fear*] Willy, answer me! Willy!   930

[*There is the sound of a car starting and moving away at full speed.*]

LINDA. No!

BIFF. [*rushing down the stairs*] Pop!

[*As the car speeds off, the music crashes down in a frenzy of sound, which becomes the soft pulsation of a single cello string. BIFF slowly returns to his bedroom. He and HAPPY gravely don their jackets. LINDA slowly walks out of her room. The music has developed into a dead march. The leaves of day are appearing over everything. CHARLEY and BERNARD somberly dressed, appear and knock on the kitchen door. BIFF and HAPPY slowly descend the stairs to the kitchen as CHARLEY and BERNARD enter. All stop a moment when LINDA, in clothes of mourning, bearing a little bunch of roses, comes through the draped doorway into the kitchen. She goes to CHARLEY and takes his arm. Now all move toward the audience, through the wall-line of the kitchen. At the limit of the apron, LINDA lays down the flowers, kneels, and sits back on her heels. All stare down at the grave.*]

REQUIEM

CHARLEY. It's getting dark, Linda.

[*LINDA doesn't react. She stares at the grave.*]

BIFF. How about it, Mom? Better get some rest, heh? They'll be closing the gate soon.

[*LINDA makes no move. Pause.*]

HAPPY. [*deeply angered*] He had no right to do that. There was no necessity for it. We would've helped him.

CHARLEY. [*grunting*] Hmmm.

BIFF. Come along, Mom.   5

LINDA. Why didn't anybody come?

CHARLEY. It was a very nice funeral.

LINDA. But where are all the people he knew? Maybe they blame him.

CHARLEY. Naa. It's a rough world, Linda. They wouldn't blame him.

LINDA. I can't understand it. At this time especially. First time in thirty-five years   10
we were just about free and clear. He only needed a little salary. He was even finished with the dentist.

CHARLEY. No man only needs a little salary.

LINDA.   I can't understand it.

BIFF.   There were a lot of nice days. When he'd come home from a trip; or on Sundays, making the stoop; finishing the cellar; putting on the new porch; when he built the extra bathroom; and put up the garage. You know something, Charley, there's more of him in that front stoop than in all the sales he ever made.

CHARLEY.   Yeah. He was a happy man with a batch of cement.

LINDA.   He was so wonderful with his hands.   15

BIFF.   He had all the wrong dreams. All, all, wrong.

HAPPY.   [*almost ready to fight BIFF*] Don't say that!

BIFF.   He never knew who he was.

CHARLEY.   [*stopping HAPPY's movement and reply. To BIFF*] Nobody dast blame this man. You don't understand. Willy was a salesman. And for a salesman, there is no rock bottom to the life. He don't put a bolt to a nut, he don't tell you the law or give you medicine. He's a man way out there in the blue, riding on a smile and a shoeshine. And when they start not smiling back—that's an earthquake. And then you get yourself a couple of spots on your hat, and you're finished. Nobody dast blame this man. A salesman is got to dream, boy. It comes with the territory.

BIFF.   Charley, the man didn't know who he was.   20

HAPPY.   [*infuriated*] Don't say that!

BIFF.   Why don't you come with me, Happy?

HAPPY.   I'm not licked that easily. I'm staying right in this city, and I'm gonna beat this racket! [*He looks at BIFF, his chin set.*] The Loman Brothers!

BIFF.   I know who I am, kid.

HAPPY.   All right, boy. I'm gonna show you and everybody else that Willy Loman   25
did not die in vain. He had a good dream. It's the only dream you can have—to come out number-one man. He fought it out here, and this is where I'm gonna win it for him.

BIFF.   [*with a hopeless glance at HAPPY, bends toward his mother*] Let's go, Mom.

LINDA.   I'll be with you in a minute. Go on, Charley. [*He hesitates.*] I want to, just for a minute. I never had a chance to say good-by.

[*CHARLEY moves away, followed by HAPPY. BIFF remains a slight distance up and left of LINDA. She sits there, summoning herself. The flute begins, not far away, playing behind her speech.*]

LINDA.   Forgive me, dear. I can't cry. I don't know what it is, but I can't cry. I don't understand it. Why did you ever do that? Help me, Willy, I can't cry. It seems to me that you're just on another trip. I keep expecting you. Willy, dear, I can't cry. Why did you do it? I search and search and I search, and I can't understand it, Willy. I made the last payment on the house today. Today, dear. And there'll be nobody home. [*A sob rises in her throat.*] We're free and clear. [*sobbing more fully, released*] We're free. [*BIFF comes slowly toward her.*] We're free . . . We're free . . .

[*BIFF lifts her to her feet and moves out up right with her in his arms. LINDA sobs quietly. BERNARD and CHARLEY come together and follow them, followed by HAPPY. Only the music of the flute is left on the darkening stage as over the house the hard towers of the apartment buildings rise into sharp focus, and*

The curtain falls.]

QUESTIONS

Act 1

1.   What do you learn about Willy from the first stage direction?

2.   What instances of stealing are in the play? Why do Biff and Happy steal? Where did they learn about stealing? How is stealing related to salesmanship?

3. In Act 1 Willy claims that "I never in my life told him [Biff] anything but decent things." Is this assertion true? What does it show you about Willy?

Act 2 and Requiem

4. What does Willy's difficulty with machines—especially his car, the refrigerator, and Howard's tape recorder—suggest about him? To what extent are these machines symbolic?

5. When Willy sees Bernard in Charley's office, he asks, "What—what's the secret?" What secret is he asking about? Does such a secret exist?

6. In Act 2 Willy buys seeds and tries to plant a garden at night. Why is Willy so disturbed that "nothing's planted" and "I don't have a thing in the ground"? What do this garden and having "things in the ground" mean to Willy?

7. In Act 2, speech 867, Biff claims that "we never told the truth for ten minutes in this house!" What does he mean? To what extent is he right?

8. Linda's last line in the play—"We're free . . . we're free"—seems to refer to the house mortgage. In what other ways, however, might you take it?

GENERAL QUESTIONS

1. How does Miller use lighting, the set, blocking, and music to differentiate between action in the present and "memory" action?

2. The stage directions are full of information that cannot be played. In describing Happy, for example, Miller notes that "sexuality is like a color on him." What is the function of such stage directions?

3. How is Willy's suicide foreshadowed throughout the play? To what extent does this foreshadowing create tension?

4. Which characters are "real" and which are "hallucinations" that spring from Willy's memory? What are the major differences between these two groups?

5. Which characters are symbolic and what do they symbolize?

6. Describe the character of Willy Loman. What are his good qualities? In what ways does he have heroic stature? What are his bad qualities? To what extent is his "fall" the result of his flaws, and to what extent is it caused by circumstances beyond his control?

7. How is the relationship between Charley and Bernard different from the one between Willy and his sons? Why is this difference important?

8. Discuss Linda's character and role. In what ways is she supportive of Willy? In what ways does she encourage his deceptions and self-delusions?

9. What sort of person is Happy? What has he inherited from Willy? How is he a debasement of Willy? To what degree is he successful or happy?

10. Willy claims that success in business is based not on "what you do" but on "who you know and the smile on your face! It's contacts . . . a man can end up with diamonds on the basis of being well liked." How does the play support or reject this assertion?

11. Most of Willy's memories—Ben's visit, Boston, the football game—are from 1928. Why does Willy's memory return to 1928? Why is the contrast between 1928 and the present significant for Willy and for the play as a whole?

⚘ WRITING ABOUT TRAGEDY

As you plan and write an essay about tragedy, keep in mind all the elements of drama. A full discussion of traditional approaches to these elements—plot, character, point of view, setting, language, tone, symbol, and theme—is found in Chapter 26 (pp. 1240–43). Review this material before you begin your essay.

Although the basic elements remain consistent in tragedy, the form requires a few special considerations. In planning to write about plot and conflict, you might explore the crisis or climax—that point at which the downfall becomes inevitable. Similarly, you might consider the degree to which the conflicts shape or accelerate the tragic action. With character, pay special attention to the tragic protagonist and the major antagonists: What is the connection between the protagonist's strengths and weaknesses? To what extent does the protagonist bring on or cooperate with his or her own destruction? What key characteristics and behavior patterns ensure both the protagonist's heroic stature and fall? In dealing with tone, consider the degree to which the play is ironic. Do you know more about what is going on than the protagonist? Than most of the characters? If so, how does your knowledge affect your understanding of the play?

Along with these considerations, all the traditional elements of drama can provide fruitful essays about tragic drama. Here, however, we introduce an additional way of writing about literature: an examination of a problem. This approach can be employed to write about prose fiction, poetry, or any type of dramatic literature. Our discussion will naturally focus on tragedy—specifically *Hamlet*—and the plays in which problem solving can generate effective essays about tragic drama.

⚘ AN ESSAY ABOUT A PROBLEM

A **problem** is any question put before you that you cannot answer easily and correctly. The question "Who is the major character in *Hamlet*?" is not a problem, because the obvious answer is Hamlet. Let us, however, ask another question: "Why is it *correct* to say that Hamlet is the major character?" This question is not as easy as the first, and for this reason it creates a problem. It requires that we think about our answer, even though we do not need to search very far. Hamlet is the title character. He is involved in most of the actions of the play. He is so much the center of our liking and concern that his death causes sadness and regret. To "solve" this problem has required a set of responses, all of which provide answers to the question "Why?"

More complex, however, and more typical of most problems, are questions like these: "Why does Hamlet talk of suicide in his first soliloquy?" "Why does he treat Ophelia so coarsely in the 'nunnery' scene?" "Why does he delay in avenging his father's death?" Essays on a problem are normally concerned with such questions, because they require a good deal of thought, together with a number of interpretations knitted together into a whole essay. More broadly, dealing with problems is one of the major tasks of the intellectual, scientific, social, and political disciplines. Being able to advance and then explain solutions is therefore one of the most important techniques that you can acquire.

Strategies for Organizing Ideas

Your first purpose is to convince your reader that your solution is a good one. This you do by making sound conclusions from supporting evidence. In nonscientific subjects like literature, you rarely find absolute proofs, so your conclusions will not be *proved* in the way you prove triangles congruent in geometry. But your organization, your use of facts from the text, your interpretations, and your application of general or specific knowledge should all make your conclusions convincing. Thus your basic strategy is *persuasion*.

1. DEMONSTRATE THAT CONDITIONS FOR A SOLUTION ARE FULFILLED. This type of development is the most basic in writing—namely, illustration. You first explain that certain conditions need to exist for your solution to be plausible. Your central idea—really a brief answer to the question—is that the conditions do indeed exist. Your development is to show how the conditions can be found in the work.

Suppose that you are writing on the problem of why Hamlet delays revenge against Claudius. Suppose also that you make the point that Hamlet delays because he is never sure that Claudius is guilty. This is your "solution" to the problem. In your essay you support your answer by by challenging the credibility of the information Hamlet receives about the crime (i.e., the two visits from the Ghost and Claudius's distress at the play within the play). Once you have "attacked" these sources of data on the grounds that they are unreliable, you have succeeded because your solution is consistent with the details of the play.

2. ANALYZE WORDS IN THE PHRASING OF THE PROBLEM. Your object in this approach is to clarify important words in the statement of the problem, then to decide how applicable they are. This kind of attention to words, in fact, might give you enough material for all or part of your essay. Thus, an essay on the problem of Hamlet's delay might focus in part on a treatment of the word *delay:* What, really, does *delay* mean? For Hamlet, is there a difference between delay that is reasonable and delay that is unreasonable? Does Hamlet delay unreasonably? Is his delay the result of a psychological fault? Would speedy revenge be more or less reasonable than the delay? By the time you have answered such pointed questions, you will also have sufficient material for your full essay.

3. REFER TO LITERARY CONVENTIONS OR EXPECTATIONS. With this strategy, the argument is to establish that the problem can be solved by reference to the literary mode or conventions of a work, or to the limitations of the work itself. In other words, what appears to be a problem is really no more than a normal characteristic. A problem about the artificiality of the choruses in *Oedipus the King*, for example, might be resolved by reference to the fact that choruses were a normal feature of Greek drama. In a similar manner, the knowledge that delay is a convention of all revenge tragedy might provide a key to the problem of Hamlet's apparent procrastination.

4. ARGUE AGAINST POSSIBLE OBJECTIONS. With this strategy, you raise your own objections and then argue against them. Called **procatalepsis** or **anticipation,** this approach helps you sharpen your arguments, because *anticipating* and dealing with objections forces you to make analyses and use facts that you might otherwise overlook. Although procatalepsis can be used point by point throughout your essay, you may find it most useful at the end.

The situation to imagine is that someone is raising objections to your solution to the problem. It is then your task to show that the objections (1) are not accurate or valid, (2) are not strong or convincing, or (3) are based on unusual rather than usual conditions (on an exception and not the rule). Here are some examples of these approaches.

1. THE OBJECTION IS NOT ACCURATE OR VALID. You reject this objection by showing that either the interpretation or the conclusions are wrong and also by emphasizing that the evidence supports your solution.

> Although Hamlet's delay is reasonable, the claim might be made that his duty is to kill Claudius in revenge immediately after the Ghost's accusations. This claim is not persuasive because it assumes that Hamlet knows everything the audience knows. The audience accepts the Ghost's word that Claudius is guilty, but Hamlet has no certain reasons to believe the Ghost. Would it not seem insane for Hamlet to kill Claudius, who reigns legally, and then to claim he did it because of the Ghost's words? The argument for speedy revenge is not good because it is based on an incorrect view of Hamlet's situation.

2. THE OBJECTION IS NOT STRONG OR CONVINCING. You concede that the objection has some truth or validity, but you then try to show that it is weak and that your own solution is stronger.

> One might claim that Claudius's distress at the play within the play is evidence for his guilt and that therefore Hamlet should carry out his revenge right away. This argument has merit, and Hamlet's speech after Claudius has fled the scene ("I'll take the Ghost's word for a thousand pound") shows that the "conscience of the king" has been caught. But the king's guilty behavior is not a strong cause for killing him. Hamlet could justifiably ask for an investigation of his father's death on these grounds, but he could not justify a revenge killing. Claudius could not be convicted in any court on the testimony that he was disturbed at seeing *The Murder of Gonzago.* Even after the play within the play, the reasons for delay are stronger than for action.

3. THE OBJECTION DEPENDS ON UNUSUAL RATHER THAN USUAL CONDITIONS. You reject the objection on the grounds that it could be valid only if normal conditions were suspended. The objection depends on an exception, not a rule.

> The case for quick action is simple: Hamlet should kill Claudius right after seeing the Ghost (1.3) or else after seeing the King's reaction to the stage murder of Gonzago (3.2) or else after seeing the Ghost again (3.4). Redress under these circumstances, goes the argument, must be both personal and extralegal. This argument

wrongly assumes that due process does not exist in the Denmark of Hamlet and Claudius. Nothing in the play indicates that the Danes, even though they carouse a bit, do not value legality and the rules of evidence. Thus Hamlet cannot rush out to kill Claudius, because he knows that the king has not had anything close to due process. The argument for quick action is poor because it rests on an exception being made from civilized law.

Remember that writing an essay on a problem requires you to argue a position: Either there is a solution or there is not. To develop your position requires that you show the steps to your conclusion. Your general thematic form is thus (1) to describe the conditions that need to be met for the solution you propose, and then (2) to demonstrate that these conditions exist. If you assert that there is no solution, then your form would be the same for the first part, but your second part—the development—would show that these conditions have *not* been met.

In developing your response, use one or more of the strategies described in this chapter. These are, again, (1) to demonstrate that conditions for a solution are fulfilled, (2) to analyze the words in the phrasing of the problem, (3) to refer to literary conventions or expectations, and (4) to argue against possible objections. You might combine these. Thus, if we assume that your argument is that Hamlet's delay is reasonable, you might first consider the word *delay* (strategy 2). Then you might use strategy 1 to explain the reasons for Hamlet's delay. Finally, to answer objections to your argument, you might show that Hamlet acts promptly when he believes he is justified (strategy 4). Whatever your topic, the important thing is to use the method or methods that best help you make a good argument for your solution.

In your conclusion, try to affirm the validity of your solution in view of the supporting evidence. You might do this by reemphasizing your strongest points, or you might simply present a brief summary. Or you might think of your argument as still continuing and thus use the strategy of procatalepsis or anticipation to raise and answer possible objections to your solution, as in the last paragraph of the following demonstrative essay.

DEMONSTRATIVE STUDENT ESSAY

The Problem of Hamlet's Apparent Delay°

[1]   Many readers and spectators of Shakespeare's <u>Hamlet</u> have been puzzled by the prince's apparent failure to kill Claudius quickly. Early in the play, the Ghost calls on his son to "Revenge his foul and most unnatural murder" (1326, 1.5.25). Hamlet, however, delays his vengeance until the end of the play. The problem is why does he not act sooner. <u>The answer is that there is no unjustified delay and that in fact Hamlet acts as quickly as possible.</u>* This becomes evident when we

°See pp. 1307–1406 for this play.
*Central idea.

examine the conventions of revenge tragedy, the actual "call to revenge," and the steps that Hamlet takes to achieve vengeance.[†]

[2] Revenge tragedy conventionally requires that vengeance be delayed until the closing moments of the play. Given this limitation, Shakespeare must justify the wide gap of time between the call to revenge in Act 1 and the killing of Claudius in Act 5. We find such justification in the unreliability of the ghost's initial accusation, Hamlet's need for additional evidence, and the events that occur after this evidence is obtained.

The Ghost's accusations and demands are straightforward: he accuses his brother of murdering him and he calls on his son for vengeance. Shakespeare is careful, however, to establish that this testimony is doubtful. Horatio questions the Ghost's truthfulness and motives, and he warns Hamlet that the spirit might "assume some other horrible form / Which might deprive your sovereignty of reason, / And draw you into madness" (1324, 1.4.72-74). Hamlet himself expresses doubt about the ghost (1347, 2.2.573-79):

[3]
> The spirit that I have seen
> May be a devil, and the devil hath power
> T'assume a pleasing shape, yea, and perhaps
> Out of my weakness, and my melancholy,
> As he is very potent with such spirits,
> Abuses me to damn me; I'll have grounds
> More relative than this.

The prince thus cannot act on the unsupported word of the Ghost; he needs more evidence.

[4] There is no delay at this point in the play, because Hamlet quickly begins developing a plan of action. Immediately after speaking with the Ghost, he decides to cover himself under an "antic disposition" while he gathers information. He swears his companions to silence and warns them not to react knowingly if he should seem to behave strangely or insanely (1329, 1.5.169-79). His idea is that this pose will make him less suspicious and others less careful.

Once Hamlet has begun his plan, he takes advantage of every opportunity to carry out his vengeance. When the players come to Elsinore, he adroitly plans to test Claudius by making him publicly view a play, The Mousetrap, which shows a murder just like Claudius's murder of Hamlet's father. Hamlet states that Claudius's appearance will give him the clue he needs to confirm the Ghost's information (1347, 2.2.571-573).

[5]
> I'll observe his looks,
> I'll tent him to the quick, if a' do blench
> I know my course.

Once the king breaks up the performance in great agitation, which Hamlet correctly interprets as an admission of guilt, Hamlet declares confidence in the Ghost ("I'll take the ghost's word for a thousand pound" [1361, 3.2.271-272]). Moreover, he is psychologically ready to act against the king, for he asserts that he could "drink hot blood, / And do such bitter business as the day / Would quake to look

[†]Thesis sentence.

on" (1363, 3.2.367-369). Without doubt, Hamlet is only a prayer away from stabbing Claudius, for when he sees the king kneeling, his opportunity has merged with his desire and also with his promise to the Ghost. He tells the audience, "Now might I do it pat, now a' is a-praying, / And now I'll do't" (1365, 3.3.73-74).

But he does not "do't," and for this reason he is open to the claim that he cannot act. Again, however, Shakespeare carefully justifies this hesitation. The prince does not want to send Claudius's soul to heaven by killing him at prayer. This reason is not simply an excuse for delay. Rather, Hamlet wants his revenge to match Claudius's treacherous murder of old King Hamlet, who died without the chance to pray and repent (1365, 3.3.88-95):

[6]
> Up sword, and know thou a more horrid hent,
> When he is drunk asleep, or in his rage,
> Or in th'incestuous pleasure of his bed,
> At game, a-swearing, or about some act
> That has no relish of salvation in't,
> Then trip him that his heels may kick at heaven,
> And that his soul may be as damned and black
> As hell whereto it goes.

This deferral is in keeping with the code of personal blood vengeance, whereby the revenge must match or exceed the original crime. There is no question of Hamlet's incapacity to act, because his putting up his sword is reasonable and justifiable.

[7]
From this point on, Hamlet acts or reacts to every situation as the opportunity presents itself. After he kills Polonius, Claudius initiates a counterplot to send Hamlet off to England and execution. Clearly, Hamlet's chances to kill the king are thus reduced to zero. It is not until Act 5 that Hamlet gets back to Denmark, after having decisively thwarted Claudius's murderous instructions by turning them against Rosencrantz and Guildenstern. He makes it clear to Horatio, however, that he will take the earliest opportunity, and that "the readiness is all" (1401, 5.2.205). Once the rigged fencing match is under way, the opportunity finally comes. Claudius, Hamlet learns, has not only killed his father but has poisoned his mother, and he himself is about to die from Laertes's poisoned sword. Upon such certain information, Hamlet immediately kills Claudius. When the revenge is complete, the Ghost, who began the cry for vengeance is nowhere to be heard or seen, and four bodies lie on the stage.

[8]
Thus, we see that the problem of Hamlet's delay--and the vengeance does take four acts to carry out--is really not a problem. The prince acts in accordance with the code of revenge as quickly as circumstances permit. Although the text of the play supports this solution, critics might still argue that procrastination is an issue because Hamlet twice accuses himself of delay. This objection does not take into consideration that Hamlet's perception of time and action is distorted by his eagerness for vengeance. From Hamlet's subjective point of view, any break in activity is delay. From our objective viewpoint, however, delay is not a true issue.

WORK CITED

William Shakespeare. Hamlet. Literature: An Introduction to Reading and Writing, Ed. Edgar V. Roberts and Henry E. Jacobs. 7th ed. Upper Saddle River: Prentice Hall, 2004. 1307–1406.

Commentary on the Essay

The structure of the essay illustrates strategy 1 (p. 1477). Paragraph 2, however, makes brief use of strategy 3 in its reference to the conventions of revenge tragedy. In both paragraphs 6 and 8, the argument is carried on by use of pro-catalepsis, or strategy 4, whereby a counterargument is raised and then answered.

The introductory paragraph raises the problem of Hamlet's apparent delay and offers a brief statement of the solution (the central idea). This plan is developed in paragraphs 2–7 in exactly the same order in which the issues are raised in the introduction. Paragraph 2 deals with the conventions of revenge tragedy, and paragraph 3 takes up the issue of the Ghost's reliability. Paragraphs 4 and 5 deal with Hamlet's attempts to corroborate the Ghost's accusations, and paragraphs 6 and 7 consider the subsequent action. Note that each paragraph in the argument grows naturally out of the one that precedes it, just as all the paragraphs are linked to the introductory paragraph.

The concluding paragraph asserts that the original problem is solved; the paragraph then summarizes the steps of the solution. It also continues the argument by raising and then dealing with a possible objection.

Special Topics for Writing and Argument about Tragedy

1. Much has been made of the contrast in *Oedipus the King* between vision and blindness. Write an essay that considers this contrast as it is related to the character of Oedipus. How are blindness and seeing reversed, with regard to his understanding about the curse on the city, his attempts to ferret out the guilty ones, his awakening perceptions of his own responsibility and guilt, and his self-blinding? How can Tiresias be compared and contrasted with Oedipus?

2. Develop an argument for one of these assertions.
   a. Oedipus's fall is the result of fate, predestination, and the gods, and it would happen despite his character.
   b. Oedipus's fall is the result only of his character and has nothing to do with fate or the gods.

3. Write an essay considering the degree to which Gertrude and Ophelia in *Hamlet* justify Hamlet's assertion "Frailty, thy name is woman" (1316, 1.2.146). Questions you might take into account concern the status of these women, their power to exert their own individuality and to make their own decisions, Gertrude as a royal queen and Ophelia as an aristocratic daughter, their capacity to undergo the pain of bereavement, Hamlet's own feelings about the death of his father, and so on. To what degree should issues concerning these women be subjected to a feminist critical analysis? (See Chapter 33.)

4. Hamlet, Laertes, and Fortinbras are all young men whose fathers have been killed and who set out to avenge these deaths. Their courses of action, however, are different. In an essay, consider these three as typical or archetypal sons. What characteristics do they share? What, in turn, makes them individual and distinct? Compare and contrast how each character deals with his father's death. Which approach seems most reasonable to you? Most emotional? Most effective? For additional directions in handling comparison and contrast, consult Chapter 35.

5. *Death of a Salesman* was successfully produced in the People's Republic of China in 1983 and was revived on Broadway in 1984 with Dustin Hoffman and in 1999 with Brian Dennehy, and there were also successful television productions—by Lee J. Cobb in the 1950s and Dustin Hoffman in the 1980s. How do you account for the continuing interest in the play from the time it was first produced until the present moment, in other cultures as well as in contemporary America?

6. Write an essay discussing the ways in which *Death of a Salesman* comments on American life and values. What specific shortcomings of American life—social, economic, political, and personal—does Miller expose and attack? In what ways does Willy Loman represent these shortcomings? Conversely, how can he be seen as an innocent victim? To what degree might Willy's death be seen as redemptive and therefore as a defense of American life?

7. Considering *Oedipus the King, Hamlet,* and *Death of a Salesman,* write an essay defining and explaining tragedy. Include references to the nature of the tragic protagonists, the situations they face, their solutions to their problems, their responses to the consequences of their actions, and their worthiness of character. Be sure to compare and contrast the actions and speeches of the characters in the plays as evidence.

8. Use your library or the Internet to locate books on tragedy. Some general topics might be *ancient and modern tragedy, definitions, emotions, heroes, passions, problems,* and *questions.* You might also wish to locate specific books on Aristotle and tragedy or on *Oedipus the King, Hamlet,* and *Death of a Salesman.* Write a brief report on one of the books, being careful to consider topics such as the author's definitions of tragedy and the author's application of the topic to various specific plays. Try also to consider the completeness of the author's presentation of material and the persuasiveness of the author's arguments.

CHAPTER 28

The Comic Vision:
Restoring the Balance

Comedy as we know it arose in ancient Greece, just as tragedy did.[1] Comedy is therefore the fraternal twin of tragedy. Many comedies are filled with tragic potential, and many tragedies contain potentially comic plots. Indeed, tragedy can be seen as an abortive or incomplete comedy in which affairs go wrong, and comedy can be considered a tragedy in which the truth is discovered (or covered up), the hero saves the day, the villain is overcome, and equilibrium and balance are restored. The major differences are that tragedy moves toward despair or death, while comedy moves toward success, happiness, and marriage. Tragic diction is elevated and heroic. Comic diction can be elevated too, but often it is common or colloquial, and although it is frequently witty, it is also sometimes witless and bawdy. The primary difference is that the mask of tragedy grieves and weeps, but the mask of comedy smiles and laughs.

⚘ THE ORIGINS OF COMEDY

In the *Poetics*, Aristotle states that he knows less about the origin of Athenian comedy than of tragedy because at first comedy was not taken as seriously as tragedy (V.2, p. 21). He does say, however, that comedy, like tragedy, developed as an improvisatory form (IV.12, p. 19). Most comic improvisations were an outgrowth of "phallic songs," which were bacchanalian processions that took place during the **Lenaia,** the Athenian religious festival held in January–February each year in *Gamelion*, the month of weddings, just following the winter solstice.

The word *comedy* is consistent with this explanation, for as "a *komos* song" its Greek meaning is "a song of revels" or "a song sung by merrymakers." The revels, like the tragedies, were religious in ways that the Greeks considered meaningful but that seem secular

---

[1]For a more detailed discussion of how drama developed within the ancient Athenian religious festivals, see Chapter 27, pp. 1249–52.

to us today. During parades or processions at the Lenaia, the merrymakers expressed their joy boisterously, traded bawdy and obscene remarks with spectators, lampooned public persons, wore ceremonial phalluses, and dressed in paunchy costumes suggesting feasting, fatness, fertility, and fun. We may conclude that these *komos* processions were encouraged officially in the belief and hope that human ceremonies would encourage divine favor and bring about prosperity and happiness. As the form developing out of such processions, comedy began with many of these characteristics and has retained them to the present day. If one briefly may generalize about subsequent comedies—even those that are cold sober rather than boisterous—it is clear that love, marriage, and ritualized celebrations of a happy future are usually major concerns.

The Athenians Held Competitions for Comedy, Just as for Tragedy

Tragedy originated in Athens, but the same does not appear to be true of comedy. Rather, comedy coexisted in the areas surrounding Greece called *Magna Graecia* ("Greater Greece"). Aristotle himself admitted that it was "late" when comic performances were separated from the phallic songs (V.2, p.21); that is, comedy followed tragedy by many years. The earliest certain date for the existence of Athenian comedy is 486 B.C.E., when a state-sponsored comedy competition was won by a writer named Chionides. Although these earliest comedies apparently consisted of little more than loosely connected lampoons, they were highly enough regarded to justify regular competitions. Comedies were scheduled on each day of the festivals, following the tragedies and satyr plays.

According to Aristotle, the first writer to transform comedy by creating a thematic plot development was Crates, who won the first of his three prizes in about the mid–fifth century B.C.E. (V.3, p.21). It was at this time that comedies became popular enough to justify an additional state comedy competition, which was instituted in about 440 B.C.E. For the remainder of the century, writers of comedy as well as tragedy tried to win prizes for their new plays at both the Lenaia and the City Dionysia.

The Earliest Greek Comedy Is Called "Old Comedy"

The comedies of the fifth century B.C.E., called **Old Comedy** or **Old Attic Comedy** by later historians, followed intricate structural patterns and displayed complex poetic conventions. Nevertheless, they bore the marks of their origins in the bacchanalian *komos* processions. The actors (three or four men) and the members of the chorus (twenty-four men), each dressed in a distortingly padded costume, wore a character-defining mask and displayed a ceremonial phallus. The role of the chorus usually dictated the comedy's title (e.g., *The Frogs, The Wasps*). Customarily, the plot was fantastic and impossible, and the dialogue was farcical and bawdy. In the tradition of satires and tirades associated with the phallic songs and with early comedy, the comic dramatists freely lashed public persons (usually but not always without legal reprisal).

Although the most successful comedy writer of the fifth century B.C.E. was Magnes (flourished 475–450 B.C.E.), who won eleven times, the only writer whose works survive is Aristophanes (ca. 450–385 B.C.E.), who won four times. His work constitutes our principal firsthand knowledge of Greek Old Comedy. He wrote at least thirty-two comedies. Fortunately, eleven have survived, along with fragments of some of his other plays. His plots and actions are outrageous, his characters are funny, and his language is satirical, bawdy, and biting.

Middle Comedy Became Prominent after Aristophanes

Aristophanes lived into the next period of Greek comedy, called **Middle Comedy.** His plays *Ecclesiazusae* (ca. 391 B.C.E.) and *Plutus* (388 B.C.E.) presaged Middle Comedy. All the Middle Comedy plays by other authors are lost, although there are many extant fragments. Middle Comedy eliminated some of the complex patterns of Old Comedy and treated more broadly international and less narrowly Athenian topics. Political criticism was abandoned, and character types such as the braggart soldier were introduced. The role of the chorus was diminished or eliminated (as with tragedy), and the exaggerated costumes were eliminated.

New Comedy, a Type of Romantic Comedy, Flourished after Middle Comedy

By the end of the fourth century B.C.E., Middle Comedy was replaced by **New Comedy.** The most important of the New Comedy dramatists was Menander (342–292 B.C.E.), who was heralded in ancient times as the greatest comic writer of them all. Everyone knows quotations from Menander, such as "calling a spade a spade" and "The gods first make mad those they intend to destroy." St. Paul quotes him in 1 Corinthians 15:33 ("Bad company ruins good morals"), but after the fifth century C.E., copies of Menander's plays were no longer available and were presumed totally lost. In the last hundred years, however, many Menandrian manuscripts have been discovered, mostly in the sands of Egypt. We now have Menander's *Dyscolus* (*The Grouch*) in its entirety, and near-complete versions of some of his other comedies, together with numerous fragments and passages.[2] In total, the titles of close to one hundred of his plays are known. His comedies, which are romantic rather than satirical, employ such stock characters as young lovers, stubborn fathers, clever slaves, and long-separated relatives.

Roman Comedy Was Composed Largely in the Third and Second Centuries B.C.E.

After Menander, Greek power in the Mediterranean waned and was replaced by the might of Rome. In the third century B.C.E. Roman comedy began and flourished, largely through the translation and adaptation of Greek New Comedies. The significant Roman writers were Plautus (ca. 254–184 B.C.E.), with twenty surviving

---

[2]See David R. Slavitt and Palmer Bovie, eds., *Menander: The Grouch, Desperately Seeking Justice, Closely Cropped Locks, The Girl from Samos, The Shield* (Philadelphia: U of Pennsylvania P, 1998).

comedies, and Terence (ca. 186–159 B.C.E.), whose six comedies still exist. Briefly, the comedies of Plautus are brisk, while those of Terence are more restrained. The central issue in most of the Roman comedies is the overcoming of a **blocking agent,** or obstruction to true love, which could be almost anyone or anything—a rival lover, an angry father, a family feud, an old law, a previously arranged marriage, or differences in social class. The pattern of action, traditionally called the **plot of intrigue,** stems from the subterfuges that young lovers undertake to overcome the blocking agent, so that the outcome frequently heralds the victory of youth over age and the passing of control from one generation to the next.

❧ COMEDY FROM ROMAN TIMES TO THE RENAISSANCE

By the time the Roman Empire was established in 29 B.C.E., the writing of comedy had virtually disappeared because Roman dramatic creativity had been preempted by pantomime entertainments and public spectacles such as gladiatorial combat. Comedy thus accompanied tragedy into fifteen hundred years of obscurity—a period when the Roman Empire rose and fell, the Dark Ages descended, and the medieval period flourished. Although many comic and farcical scenes were included in the mystery cycles of late medieval times,[3] comedy as a form was not reestablished until the Renaissance.

Once reintroduced, comedy grew rapidly. By 1500 the six plays of Terence had been discovered and were achieving wide recognition, followed by the twenty surviving plays of Plautus. When English dramatists began writing comedies, they followed Roman conventions. The English plays of the mid-sixteenth century contained five acts and observed the unities of time, place, and action, thus following the rules and justifying the claim that they were "regular." Character types from the Roman comedies, such as the intriguing couple, the fussing father, and the bragging soldier, initially predominated. Soon, more specifically English types appeared, anticipating the roisterers in Shakespeare's *Henry IV* plays and the "mechanicals" in *A Midsummer Night's Dream*. By the end of the sixteenth century, when Shakespeare had completed many of his comedies, English comedy was in full bloom. It has often been observed that this comedy was Latin in structure but English in character.

When the sixteenth century began, the chief obstacle to a wide public assimilation of drama had been the absence of institutionalized theaters. London authorities, maintaining that playgoing was a sinful public nuisance, banned theaters within the city itself. Builders therefore had to construct theaters outside the London city limits. For example, the Rose and the Globe theaters, where Shakespeare saw his plays produced from the mid-1590s to 1611, were built in Southwark across the Thames. We should realize that many people in Shakespeare's audiences got to the theater by walking over London Bridge or by being ferried across the river, and that they returned home the same way.

---

[3]For a description of the medieval mystery or Corpus Christi plays, see Chapter 26, pp. 1178–79.

❦ THE PATTERNS, CHARACTERS, AND LANGUAGE OF COMEDY

Dictionaries sometimes give *funny* as a synonym for **comic,** but the two terms are not identical. Words like *funny, amusing, comical,* or *humorous* define our emotional conditioning to incidents, and our reactions always depend on context. We usually think it is funny or comical to see an actor in a slapstick routine falling down, being hit in the face with a cream pie, or being struck with a paddle. We laugh because we know that everything is staged and that no real harm is being done. But if we leave the theater and see some of the same things occurring on the streets, we are horrified to recognize that someone is enduring real harm and real pain. Street violence occurs randomly, with no apparent purpose, and there is nothing funny or comic about it. But onstage all actions occur as part of a governing pattern or plan leading to a satisfying outcome. It is the context that makes the difference.

Comedy Implies a Complete Narrative Pattern of Humorous Action

Comedy as a genre involves patterns of humorous or comic situations and actions that make up a complete and coherent story. Often the situations are simply ordinary; sometimes they are fantastic; sometimes they are even bizarre. But they are always resolvable and correctible (unless we are dealing with the special genre of problem comedy). The patterns grow out of character and situation, and they reach a resolution in a logical or at least an understandable pattern of development. In considering comic patterns, we perceive most dialogue and activity—even serious problems and dangerous situations—as amusing, entertaining, and usually instructive.

COMEDY INVOLVES A PATTERN OF EDUCATION AND CHANGE. In many comedies the principal characters benefit from learning about themselves and their commitments, about living well and loving deeply, about getting along with the people around them, and about finding their place in the world. This "education," which they receive in the play, enables them to improve, and the process of their learning reaches its height in crucial moments of illumination and change. The characters realize their past errors, are ready to amend them, and also are human and humble enough to ask forgiveness which, according to the comic pattern, is promptly granted. In many comedies, particularly those that touch on significant social and political problems, the audience is also educated, and the play's implication is that improvement should occur in the world just as it has occurred on the stage.

COMIC PROBLEMS FLOURISH AMID CHAOS AND POTENTIAL DISASTER. Before the moments of change leading to the comic conclusion, however, comedy must introduce many of the problems and complications that could, in real life, lead not to happiness but to unhappiness and even to calamity. These problems can be personal, social, political, economic, or military; in short, they may enter every arena of human affairs. A man wants to find love, but he also needs to find a place in the world and to gain his fortune. A woman needs to protect herself against someone who might take advantage of her, and thus she behaves defensively and strangely.

A group of people want to succeed in a business venture—or perhaps to fail in this venture. A politician is accused of corruption and thus needs help in exonerating himself. A man and woman in love become angry or disenchanted because they are fed lies and distortions about each other. Another man and woman need to overcome family hostility so that they may successfully begin their lives together with the approval of everyone around them. Still another man and woman, upon meeting for the first time, become so angry they threaten to murder each other. Failure, though it is to be always overcome in comedy, is never far away; it lurks over the horizon, around corners, in business rooms, and in malicious telephone calls, waiting to emerge and scatter uncertainty, indecisiveness, and distress.

All such situations, which might possibly lead to ruin, are the stuff of comedy. The worse things seem, and the more apparently chaotic, the better. In a good comic complication, the problems are constantly being fueled by misunderstanding, mistaken identity, misdirection, misinformed speech, errors in judgment, faults in intelligence, excessive or unreasonable behavior, and coincidences that stretch credulity.

THE COMIC CLIMAX IS THE PEAK OF CONFUSION.   Such complications lead ultimately to the comic climax, which is that moment or moments in the play when everything reaches the peak of confusion and when no good solution seems in sight. Misunderstanding is dominant, pressure is at a high point, and choices must be made even though solutions seem impossible. The catastrophe—the changing or turning point—is frequently launched by a sudden revelation in which a new fact, a misunderstood event, or a previously hidden identity is explained to characters and audience at the same time, and then things undergo a turnaround and start rushing toward improvement.

THE COMIC DÉNOUEMENT RESTORES SANITY AND CALM.   In most comedies, the events of the dénouement resolve the initial problems and allow for the comic resolution, which dramatizes how things are set right at every level of action. Errors are explained, personal lives are straightened out, people at odds with each other are reconciled, promises are made for the future, new families are formed through marriage, and a stable social order is reestablished.

Comic Characters Are More Limited Than Characters in Tragedy

Comic characters are relatively limited because they are almost necessarily common and representative rather than individual and heroic. Characters with breadth or individuality are therefore not typical of comedy. Instead, comedy gives us stock characters who represent classes, types, and generations. In Shakespeare's *A Midsummer Night's Dream* many of the characters are representative and stock figures. Egeus is a conventionally indignant and unreasonable father, and Hermia and Lysander are typical young lovers (along with Helena and Demetrius). In Kauffmann's *The More the Merrier* (Chapter 26) the two lovers, Emily and Raphael, are drawn from a world of high society, mutual acquaintances, and exclusive club life. Although Kauffmann's characters do succeed in confronting serious personal problems, it is difficult to imagine that they could ever reach the understanding and insight of majestic characters like Hamlet and Oedipus.

Comic Language Is a Vital Vehicle of Humor

As in other types of literature, comic dramatists use language to delineate character, to establish tone and mood, and to express ideas and feelings. In comedy, however, language is also one of the most important vehicles for humor. Some comedies are characterized by elegant and witty language, others by puns and bawdy jokes.

Characters in comedy tend either to be masters of language or to be mastered by it. Those who are skillful with language can use a witty phrase to satirize their foes and friends alike. Those who are unskilled with language, like Bottom in *A Midsummer Night's Dream,* bungle their speeches because they misuse words and stumble into inadvertent puns. Both types of characters are amusing; we smile a knowing smile with the wits and laugh aloud at the would-be wits and the bunglers.

❦ TYPES OF COMEDY

Differences in comic style, content, and intent that have evolved over the centuries make it possible to divide comedy into various types. The broadest of these divisions, based on both style and content, separates comic literature into *high comedy* and *low comedy.*

High Comedy Develops Mainly from Character

Ideally, **high comedy** (a term coined by George Meredith in 1877 in *The Idea of Comedy*) is witty, graceful, and sophisticated. The problems and complications are more closely related to character than to situation, even though, admittedly, they develop out of situations. The appeal of high comedy is to the intellect, for the comic resolution must come about because the characters learn enough to accept adjustments and changes in their lives. A simple change of situation alone will not do for high comedy.

1. ROMANTIC COMEDY FOCUSES ON PROBLEMS OF YOUTHFUL LOVE. One of the major kinds of high comedy is **romantic comedy,** which views action and character from the standpoint of earnest young lovers like Hermia and Lysander in *A Midsummer Night's Dream.* Ultimately derived from Roman comedy, this kind of play is built on a plot of intrigue featuring lovers who try to overcome opposition (such as Egeus) to achieve a successful union. The aim of such plays is amusement and entertainment rather than ridicule and reform. Although vice and folly may be exposed in romantic comedy, especially the follies of the antagonists blocking the young lovers, the dominant impulse is toleration and amused indulgence.

2. COMEDY OF MANNERS TESTS THE STRENGTH OF SOCIAL CUSTOMS AND ASSUMPTIONS. Related to romantic comedy is the **comedy of manners,** an important type from the seventeenth century to our own times. The comedy of manners examines and satirizes attitudes and customs in the light of high intellectual and moral standards. The dialogue is witty and sophisticated, and characters are often measured according to their linguistic and intellectual powers. The love plots are serious and real, even though they share with romantic comedy the need to create intrigues to overcome opposition and impediments. The realism

Theatre of Dionysus, fourth century B.C.E. Athens.

❧ *Exterior of the Globe Theatre.* Authentic reconstruction based on sixteenth-century drawings and archaeological research, opening 1996. London. (Photograph by April Roberts)

❧ *Interior of the Globe Theatre.* London. (Photograph by April Roberts)

Stage of the Globe Theater. London. (Photograph by April Roberts)

Pieter Brueghel the Elder (c. 1525-1569), *Landscape with the Fall of Icarus*, c. 1554-1555. Musées Royaux des Beaux-Arts, Brussels. (© Scala/Art Resource, New York)

and seriousness in some of the manners comedies written in Restoration England (1660–1700) in fact are so great that one might consider them not only as plays of manners but also as plays of social and personal problems.

3. SATIRIC COMEDY, LIKE ALL SATIRE, RIDICULES VICES AND FOLLIES. Midway between high and low comedy is **satiric comedy,** which is based in a comic attack on foolishness and/or viciousness. The playwright of satiric comedy assumes the perspective of a rational and moderate observer measuring human life against a moderate norm that is represented by high and serious characters. Members of the audience are invited to share this viewpoint as they, along with the dramatist, heap scorn upon the vicious and laugh loudly at the eccentric and the foolish.

Low Comedy Dwells Amid the Silly and the Bumbling

In **low comedy** emphasis is on funny remarks and outrageous circumstances; complications develop from situation and plot rather than from character. Plays of this type are by definition full of physical humor and stage business—a character rounds his forefinger and thumb to imitate a hole in a wall, through which other characters speak; an irascible man constantly breaks furniture; a character masquerading as a doctor takes the pulse of a father to determine the daughter's medical condition; characters who have just declared their love are visited by people to whom they formerly swore love.

The quintessential type of low comedy is **farce** (a word derived from the Latin word *farsus,* meaning "stuffed"), the aim of which, in the words of Henry Fielding, "is but to make you laugh." A farce is an outlandish physical comedy overflowing with silly characters, improbable happenings, wild clowning, pratfalls, extravagant language, and bawdy jokes.

Another type of farce is the ***commedia dell'arte,*** a prototypical comic drama that developed among traveling companies in Italy and France in the sixteenth and seventeenth centuries. The broadly humorous characters of *commedia dell'arte* recurred from play to play with consistent names and characteristics. The action usually involved a plot of intrigue. The lovers were the permanently youthful and glowing *Inamorato* and *Inamorata,* who were aided by Inamorata's clever servant, the *soubrette,* to overcome *Pantaloon,* the foolish and presuming old man. The servant characters were *Harlequin* (who was invisible) and *Columbine* (his sweetheart, also invisible), who were joined in high-jinks by *Pierrot* (a clown lover) and *Scaramouche* (the soldier). Other stock characters, most of whom were derived from Greek New Comedy by way of Roman comedy, have in turn become constant features of much subsequent comedy.

With characters of low comedy, of course, there is much tomfoolery and improvisation—the major qualities of the extreme form of farce, **slapstick,** which is named after the double paddles ("slap sticks") that made loud cracking noises when actors in the *commedia dell'arte* used them for striking each other. Slapstick depends heavily on exaggerated actions, poses, and facial expressions. In slapstick there is constant onstage business with objects such as paddles, pies, pails, paint, paste, or toilet paper, along with wild and improbable actions such as squirming, hiding, stumbling, tripping, tumbling, falling, and flopping.

Other Kinds of Comedy Emphasize Complexity and Absurdity

Other types of modern and contemporary comedy include **ironic comedy, realistic comedy,** and **comedy of the absurd.** All of these shun the happy endings of traditional comedy. Often, the blocking agents are successful, the protagonists are defeated, and the initial problem—either a realistic or an absurdist dilemma—remains unresolved. Such comedies, which began to appear in the late nineteenth century, illustrate the complexities and absurdities of modern life and the funny but futile efforts that people make when coming to grips with existence.

Many of the types of comedy just discussed still flourish. Romantic comedies, comedies of manners, and farces can be found on innumerable stages and movie screens. They revolve about a central situation that might be quite ordinary. (Will Hank get along with a visiting lodge member? Will Sue be accepted by schoolmates at her new school? Will Jim get a date for the prom?) Such situations find their ways into the huge numbers of **sitcoms** (situation comedies) that occupy prime-time television programs.

In view of the variety of comedy, it is most important to recognize that comedy is rarely a pure and discrete form. High comedies might include crude physical humor, especially with characters to be disapproved. Low comedies can sometimes contain wit and elegance. Satiric comedies might deal with successful young lovers. Romantic comedies can mock the vices and follies of weird and eccentric characters. Farce and slapstick can contain satire on social values and conventions.

PLAYS FOR STUDY

WILLIAM SHAKESPEARE, *A MIDSUMMER NIGHT'S DREAM*

For a brief biography, please see Chapter 27, p. 1306.

A Midsummer Night's Dream was written early in Shakespeare's career, in 1594 or 1595.[4] It is a romantic comedy dramatizing the idea that "the course of true love never did run smooth." This central line of action, which owes much to Roman comedy, involves blocked love, a journey of circumvention and education that takes the lovers from the world of laws and problems into an imaginary world of chaos and transformations, and an ultimate victory back in the world of daylight and order.

The subject of *A Midsummer Night's Dream* is love. Shakespeare skillfully interweaves this topic in the play's four separate plots, four groups of characters, and four styles of language. Each plot explores the nature of love, the madness of irrational love, and the harmony needed for regenerative love.

---

[4]See Chapter 27, pp. 1302–1306, for a description of Shakespeare's theater and career as a dramatist.

In the *overplot*—the action that establishes the time for the play—the relationship is between the rulers, Theseus and Hippolyta, who have undergone a change from irrational war to rational peace. As such, they represent the dynastic continuity of the state, the order of the daylight world of Athens, and the rigor of law. These characters are the rulers, and they speak predominantly in blank verse (unrhymed iambic pentameter; see p. 798).

The two connected *middle plots* concern the adventures of the four lovers and the actions of Oberon and Titania. The four lovers, embodying the most passionate and insistent phase of love, are from the middle class, and they speak mainly in rhymed couplets. During their long night of illusion in the woods, conjured by Oberon and his servant, Puck, their adventures drive them toward rationality, and they recognize and accept the need for faithfulness and constancy.

The parallel middle love plot involves the conflict between Oberon and Titania, the king and queen of the fairies, because of their mutually exclusive wishes to control a "changeling" child. Oberon is "jealous" and wants the child as an attendant, but Titania wants to keep him in her service because his mother had been Titania's attendant, friend, and confidante. With great power over Titania, Oberon humbles her, and she then reacknowledges his superiority—the proper attitude of a wife, according to Elizabethan males. Oberon and Titania, of course, are supernatural forces. Although they and the other fairies speak in both blank verse and rhymed couplets, the fairies are the only singing characters and also the only characters to speak in iambic tetrameter.

The examination of love in the *subplot* occurs partly in Titania's relationship with Bottom—the most hilarious instance of love madness in the play—and partly in the play-within-a-play about Pyramus and Thisby. This ridiculous tragedy echoes the central plot of *A Midsummer Night's Dream* and demonstrates, again, the pitfalls and unpredictability of love. It also emphasizes the happy and harmonious marriages and rapprochements that occur in both the overplot and the middle plots.

While *A Midsummer Night's Dream* is chiefly about love, it is equally concerned with the complicated relationship of perception, imagination, passion, art, and illusion. In Act 5 Theseus asserts that "The lunatic, the lover, and the poet" are alike because they all try to make reality conform with their own imaginations and desires ([1536] 5.1.7–22). It would seem that chaos would therefore be the normal state, but, as Hippolyta concludes in response to Theseus, order and certainty somehow prevail, "howsoever" extraordinary and almost miraculous this result may seem ([1536] 5.1.23–27). The movement of the play is governed by these ideas that, along with the brilliant language and comic actions, are directly attributable to the genius of Shakespeare.

WILLIAM SHAKESPEARE (1564–1616)

A Midsummer Night's Dream   1600 (ca. 1594)

Edited by Alice Griffin*

THE NAMES OF THE ACTORS

Theseus, *Duke of Athens*
Egeus, *father of Hermia*
Lysander, *beloved of Hermia*

*Professor Griffin's text for *A Midsummer Night's Dream* is the First Quarto (edition) published in 1600, with modifications based on the Quarto edition of 1619 and the First Folio, published in 1623. Stage directions in those editions are printed here without brackets; added stage directions are printed within brackets. We have edited Griffin's notes for this text.

Demetrius, *in love with Hermia, favoured by Egeus*
Philostrate, *Master of the Revels to Theseus*
Peter Quince, *a carpenter (Prologue)**
Nick Bottom, *a weaver (Pyramus)**
Francis Flute, *a bellows-mender (Thisby)**
Tom Snout, *a tinker (Wall)**
Snug, *a joiner (Lion)**
Robin Starveling, *a tailor (Moonshine)**
Hippolyta, *Queen of the Amazons, betrothed to Theseus*
Hermia, *daughter of Egeus, in love with Lysander*
Helena, *in love with Demetrius*
Oberon, *King of the Fairies*
Titania, *Queen of the Fairies*
Puck, *or Robin Goodfellow*
Peaseblossom ⎤
Cobweb ⎜
Moth ⎬ *Fairies*
Mustardseed ⎦

Other Fairies attending Oberon and Titania. Attendants on Theseus and Hippolyta.

SCENE. *Athens, and a wood nearby*

ACT 1

[Scene 1. Athens. The palace of Theseus]

Enter THESEUS, HIPPOLYTA,° [PHILOSTRATE,] *with others.*

THESEUS.   Now fair Hippolyta, our nuptial hour
    Draws on apace: four happy days bring in
    Another moon: but O, methinks how slow
    This old moon wanes! she lingers° my desires,
    Like to a stepdame or a dowager,°   5
    Long withering out° a young man's revenue.
HIPPOLYTA.   Four days will quickly steep themselves in night:
    Four nights will quickly dream away the time:
    And then the moon, like to a silver bow
    New-bent in heaven, shall behold the night   10
    Of our solemnities.
THESEUS.   Go Philostrate,
    Stir up the Athenian youth to merriments,
    Awake the pert° and nimble spirit of mirth,
    Turn melancholy forth to funerals:
    The pale companion° is not for our pomp.   [*Exit* PHILOSTRATE.]   15
    Hippolyta, I wooed thee with my sword,

---

*Characters who play in the interlude.   0.3 S.D.: *Theseus, Hippolyta:* In Greek legend, Theseus captured the Amazon Queen Hippolyta and brought her to Athens where they were married.   4 *lingers:* delays the fulfillment of.   5 *dowager:* a widow supported by her dead husband's heirs.   6 *withering out:* (1) depleting (2) growing withered.   13 *pert:* lively.   15 *companion:* fellow (contemptuous).

And won thy love doing thee injuries;
But I will wed thee in another key,
With pomp, with triumph,° and with revelling.

Enter EGEUS and his daughter HERMIA, LYSANDER and DEMETRIUS.

EGEUS.   Happy be Theseus, our renownèd duke.   20
THESEUS.   Thanks good Egeus:° what's the news with thee?
EGEUS.   Full of vexation come I, with complaint
    Against my child, my daughter Hermia.
    Stand forth Demetrius. My noble lord,
    This man hath my consent to marry her.   25
    Stand forth Lysander. And my gracious duke,
    This man hath bewitched the bosom of my child.
    Thou, thou Lysander, thou hast given her rhymes,
    And interchanged love tokens with my child:
    Thou hast by moonlight at her window sung,   30
    With feigning voice, verses of feigning° love,
    And stol'n the impression of her fantasy°
    With bracelets of thy hair, rings, gauds° conceits,°
    Knacks,° trifles, nosegays, sweetmeats—messengers
    Of strong prevailment in unhardened youth.   35
    With cunning hast thou filched my daughter's heart,
    Turned her obedience, which is due to me,
    To stubborn harshness. And my gracious duke,
    Be it so° she will not here before your grace
    Consent to marry with Demetrius,   40
    I beg the ancient privilege of Athens:
    As she is mine, I may dispose of her:
        Which shall be, either to this gentleman,
        Or to her death, according to our law
        Immediately° provided in that case.   45
THESEUS.   What say you, Hermia? Be advised, fair maid.
    To you your father should be as a god:
    One that composed your beauties: yea and one
    To whom you are but as a form in wax
    By him imprinted, and within his power   50
    To leave the figure, or disfigure it:
    Demetrius is a worthy gentleman.
HERMIA.   So is Lysander.
THESEUS   In himself he is:
    But in this kind, wanting your father's voice,°
    The other must be held the worthier.   55
HERMIA.   I would my father looked but with my eyes.
THESEUS.   Rather your eyes must with his judgment look.

---

19 *triumph:* public festival.   21 *Egeus:* (trisyllabic).   31 *feigning:* (1) deceptive (2) desirous ("fain-ing").   32 *stol'n . . . fantasy:* stealthily imprinted your image upon her fancy.   33 *gauds:* trinkets. *conceits:* either (a) love poetry, or (b) love tokens.   34 *Knacks:* knick-knacks.   39 *Be it so:* if it be that. 45 *Immediately:* precisely.   54 *in . . . voice:* in this respect, lacking your father's approval.

HERMIA.   I do entreat your grace to pardon me.
    I know not by what power I am made bold,
    Nor how it may concern my modesty,   60
    In such a presence, here to plead my thoughts:
    But I beseech your grace that I may know
    The worst that may befall me in this case,
    If I refuse to wed Demetrius.
THESEUS.   Either to die the death, or to abjure   65
    For ever the society of men.
    Therefore fair Hermia, question your desires,
    Know of your youth,° examine well your blood,°
    Whether, if you yield not to your father's choice,
    You can endure the livery° of a nun,   70
    For aye° to be in shady cloister mewed,°
    To live a barren sister all your life,
    Chanting faint hymns to the cold fruitless moon.°
    Thrice blessèd they that master so their blood,
    To undergo such maiden pilgrimage: 75
    But earthlier happy° is the rose distilled,°
    Than that which, withering on the virgin thorn,
    Grows, lives, and dies, in single blessedness.
HERMIA.   So will I grow, so live, so die my lord,
    Ere I will yield my virgin patent° up   80
    Unto his lordship, whose unwishèd yoke
    My soul consents not to give sovereignty.
THESEUS.   Take time to pause, and by the next moon,
    The sealing day betwixt my love and me,
    For everlasting bond of fellowship,   85
    Upon that day either prepare to die
    For disobedience to your father's will,
    Or else to wed Demetrius, as he would,
    Or on Diana's altar to protest°
    For aye, austerity and single life.   90
DEMETRIUS.   Relent, sweet Hermia, and Lysander, yield
    Thy crazèd° title to my certain right.
LYSANDER.   You have her father's love, Demetrius:
    Let me have Hermia's: do you marry him.
EGEUS.   Scornful Lysander, true, he hath my love: 95
    And what is mine, my love shall render him.
    And she is mine, and all my right of her
    I do estate° unto Demetrius.
LYSANDER.   I am, my lord, as well derived° as he,
    As well possessed;° my love is more than his: 100

---

    68 *Know . . . youth:* ask yourself as a young person.   68 *blood:* passions.   70 *livery:* habit.   71 *aye:* ever.   *mewed:* shut up.   73 *moon:* (the moon goddess Diana represented unmarried chastity). 76 *earthlier happy:* more happy on earth.   *distilled:* i.e., into perfume (thus its essence is passed on, as to a child).   80 *patent:* privilege.   89 *protest:* vow.   92 *crazèd:* flawed.   98 *estate:* transfer.   99 *well derived:* well born.   100 *well possessed:* wealthy.

My fortunes every way as fairly ranked
(If not with vantage) as° Demetrius':
And, which is more than all these boasts can be,
I am beloved of beauteous Hermia.
Why should not I then prosecute my right?   105
Demetrius, I'll avouch it to his head,°
Made love to Nedar's daughter, Helena,
And won her soul: and she, sweet lady, dotes,
Devoutly dotes, dotes in idolatry,
Upon this spotted° and inconstant man.   110
THESEUS.   I must confess that I have heard so much,
And with Demetrius thought to have spoke thereof:
But being over-full of self-affairs,
My mind did lose it. But Demetrius come,
And come Egeus, you shall go with me: 115
I have some private schooling for you both.
For you fair Hermia, look you arm yourself,
To fit your fancies to your father's will;
Or else the law of Athens yields you up
(Which by no means we may extenuate)   120
To death or to a vow of single life.
Come my Hippolyta, what cheer my love?
Demetrius and Egeus, go along:
I must employ you in some business
Against° our nuptial, and confer with you   125
Of something nearly° that concerns yourselves.
EGEUS.   With duty and desire we follow you.

Exeunt.° Manent° LYSANDER and HERMIA.

LYSANDER.   How now my love? Why is your cheek so pale?
How chance the roses there do fade so fast?
HERMIA.   Belike° for want of rain, which I could well   130
Beteem° them from the tempest of my eyes,
LYSANDER.   Ay me, for aught that I could ever read,
Could ever hear by tale or history,
The course of true love never did run smooth;
But either it was different in blood—   135
HERMIA.   O cross! too high° to be enthralled to low.°
LYSANDER.   Or else misgraffed° in respect of years—
HERMIA.   O spite! too old to be engaged to young.
LYSANDER.   Or else it stood upon the choice of friends—
HERMIA.   O hell! to choose love by another's eyes.   140
LYSANDER.   Or if there were a sympathy in choice,
War, death, or sickness did lay siege to it;
Making it momentany° as a sound,
Swift as a shadow, short as any dream,

---

102 *with vantage, as:* better, than.   106 *avouch . . . head:* prove it to his face.   110 *spotted:* stained
125 *Against:* in preparation for.   126 *nearly:* closely.   127 S.D.: *Exeunt:* they exit.   *Manent:* they remain.
130 *Belike:* likely.   131 *Beteem:* (1) pour out on (2) allow.   136 *high:* highborn.   *enthralled to low:* made
a slave to one of low birth.   137 *misgraffed:* badly joined.   143 *momentany:* momentary.

Brief as the lightning in the collied° night,   145
That, in a spleen,° unfolds both heaven and earth;
And ere a man hath power to say "Behold,"
The jaws of darkness do devour it up:
So quick bright things come to confusion.

HERMIA.   If then true lovers have been ever crossed,°   150
It stands as an edict in destiny:
Then let us teach our trial patience,°
Because it is a customary cross,
As due to love as thoughts and dreams and sighs,
Wishes and tears; poor Fancy's° followers.   155

LYSANDER.   A good persuasion: therefore hear me, Hermia:
I have a widow aunt, a dowager,
Of great revenue, and she hath no child:
From Athens is her house remote seven leagues,
And she respects° me as her only son: 160
There gentle Hermia, may I marry thee,
And to that place the sharp Athenian law
Cannot pursue us. If thou lov'st me then,
Steal forth thy father's house tomorrow night:
And in the wood, a league without the town,   165
Where I did meet thee once with Helena
To do observance to a morn of May,°
There will I stay° for thee.

HERMIA.   My good Lysander,
I swear to thee, by Cupid's strongest bow,
By his best arrow, with the golden head,°   170
By the simplicity of Venus' doves,
By that which knitteth souls and prospers loves,
And by that fire which burned the Carthage queen,
When the false Troyan° under sail was seen,
By all the vows that ever men have broke,   175
(In number more than ever women spoke)
In that same place thou has appointed me,
Tomorrow truly will I meet with thee.

LYSANDER.   Keep promise love: look, here comes Helena.

Enter HELENA.

HERMIA.   God speed fair Helena: whither away?   180
HELENA.   Call you me fair? That fair again unsay.
Demetrius loves your fair:° O happy fair!
Your eyes are lodestars,° and your tongue's sweet air°
More tuneable than lark to shepherd's ear,

---

145 *collied:* black as coal.   146 *in a spleen:* impulsively, in a sudden outburst.   150 *ever crossed:* evermore thwarted.   152 *teach . . . patience:* teach ourselves to be patient.   155 *Fancy:* love (sometimes infatuation).   160 *respects:* regards.   167 *do . . . May:* celebrate May Day.   168 *stay:* wait.   170 *golden head:* (The arrow with the gold Head causes love).   173–174 *Carthage Queen . . . false Troyan:* Dido, who burned herself to death on a funeral pyre when Frojan Aeneas deserted her.   182 *your fair:* i.e., beauty.   183 *lodestars:* guiding stars.   *air:* music.

When wheat is green, when hawthorn buds appear.   185
Sickness is catching: O were favour° so,
Yours would I catch, fair Hermia, ere I go,
My ear should catch your voice,° my eye your eye,°
My tongue should catch your tongue's sweet melody.
Were the world mine, Demetrius being bated,°   190
The rest I'd give to be to you translated.°
O teach me how you look, and with what art
You sway the motion of Demetrius' heart.

HERMIA.   I frown upon him; yet he loves me still.
HELENA.   O that your frowns would teach my smiles such skill.   195
HERMIA.   I give him curses; yet he gives me love.
HELENA.   O that my prayers could such affection move.
HERMIA.   The more I hate, the more he follows me.
HELENA.   The more I love, the more he hateth me.
HERMIA.   His folly, Helena, is no fault of mine.   200
HELENA.   None but your beauty; would that fault were mine.
HERMIA.   Take comfort: he no more shall see my face:
           Lysander and myself will fly this place.
           Before the time I did Lysander see,
           Seemed Athens as a paradise to me: 205
           O then, what graces in my love do dwell,
           That he hath turned a heaven unto a hell!
LYSANDER. Helen, to you our minds we will unfold:
           Tomorrow night, when Phoebe° doth behold
           Her silver visage in the wat'ry glass,°   210
           Decking with liquid pearl the bladed grass
           (A time that lovers' flights doth still° conceal)
           Through Athens gates have we devised to steal.
HERMIA.   And in the wood, where often you and I
           Upon faint primrose beds were wont to lie,   215
           Emptying our bosoms of their counsel° sweet,
           There my Lysander and myself shall meet,
           And thence from Athens turn away our eyes,
           To see new friends and stranger companies.°
           Farewell, sweet playfellow: pray thou for us: 220
           And good luck grant thee thy Demetrius.
           Keep word Lysander: we must starve our sight
           From lovers' food,° till morrow deep midnight.
LYSANDER. I will my Hermia.   *Exit* HERMIA.
           Helena adieu:
           As you on him, Demetrius dote on you.°   *Exit* LYSANDER.   225
HELENA.   How happy some, o'er other some, can be!
           Through Athens I am thought as fair as she.

---

186 *favour*: appearance.   188 *My ear . . . voice*: my ear should catch the tone of your voice.   *my eye your eye*: my eye should catch the way you glance.   190 *bated*: subtracted, excepted.   191 *translated*: transformed.   209 *Phoebe*: Diana, the moon.   210 *wat'ry glass*: mirror of the water.   212 *still*: always. 216 *counsel*: secrets.   219 *stranger companies*: the companionship of strangers.   223 *lovers' food*: the sight of the loved one.   225 *As . . . you*: As you dote on Demetrius, so may Demetrius also dote on you.

But what of that? Demetrius thinks not so:
He will not know what all but he do know.
And as he errs, doting on Hermia's eyes,   230
So I, admiring of his qualities.
Things base and vile, holding no quantity.°
Love can transpose to form and dignity.
Love looks not with the eyes, but with the mind:
And therefore is winged Cupid painted blind.   235
Nor hath Love's mind of any judgment taste:
Wings, and no eyes, figure° unheedy haste.
And therefore is Love said to be a child:
Because in choice he is so oft beguiled.
As waggish boys in game themselves forswear: 240
So the boy Love is perjured everywhere.
For ere Demetrius looked on Hermia's eyne,°
He hailed down oaths that he was only mine.
And when this hail some heat from Hermia felt,
So he dissolved, and show'rs of oaths did melt.   245
I will go tell him of fair Hermia's flight:
Then to the wood will he tomorrow night
Pursue her: and for this intelligence,°
If I have thanks, it is a dear expense.°
But herein mean I to enrich my pain,   250
To have his sight° thither and back again.   *Exit.*

[Scene 2. Quince's house]

Enter QUINCE *the Carpenter; and* SNUG *the Joiner; and* BOTTOM *the Weaver; and* FLUTE *the Bellows-mender; and* SNOUT *the Tinker; and* STARVELING *the Tailor.*°

QUINCE.   Is all our company here?
BOTTOM.   You were the best to call them generally,° man by man,
    according to the scrip.
QUINCE.   Here is the scroll of every man's name which is thought
    fit, through all Athens, to play in our interlude° before   5
    the duke and the duchess, on his wedding-day at night.
BOTTOM.   First good Peter Quince, say what the play treats on,
    then read the names of the actors: and so grow to a point.
QUINCE.   Marry,° our play is "The most lamentable comedy, and
    most cruel death of Pyramus and Thisby."   10
BOTTOM.   A very good piece of work I assure you, and a merry. Now
    good Peter Quince, call forth your actors by the scroll.
    Masters, spread yourselves.

---

    232 *holding no quantity:* out of proportion.   **237** *figure:* symbolize.   **242** *eyne:* eyes.
248 *intelligence:* information.   **249** *dear expense:* costly outlay (on Demetrius' part).   **250–251** *But . . .
sight:* but I will be rewarded just by the sight of him.   **0.2 S.D.:** the low characters' names describe their
work: *Quince:* quoins, wooden wedges used in building. *Snug:* fitting snugly, suiting a joiner of furniture.
Bottom: bobbin or core on which yarn is wound. *Flute:* mender of fluted church organs and bellows.
Snout: spout (of the kettles he mends).   *Starveling:* (tailors being traditionally thin).   **2** *generally:* Bottom
often uses the wrong word; here he means the opposite: "severally, one by one."   **5** *interlude:* short play.
9 *Marry:* indeed (mild oath, corruption of "by the Virgin Mary").

QUINCE.   Answer as I call you. Nick Bottom the weaver?
BOTTOM.   Ready: name what part I am for, and proceed.   15
QUINCE.   You, Nick Bottom, are set down for Pyramus.
BOTTOM.   What is Pyramus? A lover, or a tyrant?
QUINCE.   A lover that kills himself, most gallant, for love.
BOTTOM.   That will ask some tears in the true performing of it. If I
    do it, let the audience look to their eyes: I will move   20
    storms: I will condole° in some measure. To the rest—
    yet my chief humour° is for a tyrant. I could play Ercles°
    rarely, or a part to tear a cat in, to make all split.°
        The raging rocks
        And shivering shocks,   25
        Shall break the locks
          Of prison gates,
        And Phibbus' car°
        Shall shine from far,
        And make and mar   30
          The foolish Fates.
    This was lofty. Now name the rest of the players. This is
    Ercles' vein, a tyrant's vein: a lover is more condoling.
QUINCE.   Francis Flute, the bellows-mender?
FLUTE.   Here Peter Quince.   35
QUINCE.   Flute, you must take Thisby on you.
FLUTE.   What is Thisby? A wand'ring knight?
QUINCE.   It is the lady that Pyramus must love.
FLUTE.   Nay faith, let not me play a woman: I have a beard
    coming.   40
QUINCE.   That's all one:° you shall play it in a mask, and you may
    speak as small° as you will.
BOTTOM.   And° I may hide my face, let me play Thisby too: I'll speak
    in a monstrous little voice; "Thisne, Thisne," "Ah
    Pyramus, my lover dear, thy Thisby dear, and lady   45
    dear."
QUINCE.   No, no, you must play Pyramus: and Flute, you Thisby.
BOTTOM.   Well, proceed.
QUINCE.   Robin Starveling, the tailor?
STARVELING.   Here Peter Quince.   50
QUINCE.   Robin Starveling, you must play Thisby's mother. Tom
    Snout, the tinker?
SNOUT.   Here Peter Quince.
QUINCE.   You, Pyramus' father; myself, Thisby's father; Snug the
    joiner, you the lion's part: and I hope here is a play.   55
    fitted.°
SNUG.   Have you the lion's part written? Pray you, if it be, give
    it me: for I am slow of study.
QUINCE.   You may do it extempore: for it is nothing but roaring.

---

    21 *condole*: lament.   22 *humour*: inclination.   *Ercles*: Hercules (typified by ranting).   23 *tear* . . .
split: (terms for ranting and raging on the stage).   28 *Phibbus' car*: Phocbus Apollo's chariot.   41 *That's all
one*: never mind.   42 *small*: softly.   43 *And*: if.   56 *fitted*: cast.

BOTTOM.   Let me play the lion too. I will roar, that° I will do any   60
    man's heart good to hear me. I will roar, that I will make
    the duke say "Let him roar again: let him roar again."

QUINCE.   And you should do it too terribly, you would fright the
    duchess and the ladies, that they would shriek: and
    that were enough to hang us all.   65

ALL.   That would hang us, every mother's son.

BOTTOM.   I grant you, friends, if you should fright the ladies out of
    their wits, they would have no more discretion but to
    hang us: but I will aggravate° my voice so, that I will roar
    you as gently as any sucking dove: I will roar you and   70
    'twere° any nightingale.

QUINCE.   You can play no part but Pyramus: for Pyramus is a
    sweet-faced man; a proper° man as one shall see in a
    summer's day; a most lovely gentleman-like man: therefore
    you must needs play Pyramus.   75

BOTTOM.   Well: I will undertake it. What beard were I best to play
    it in?

QUINCE.   Why, what you will.

BOTTOM.   I will discharge it in either your straw-colour beard, your
    orange-tawny beard, your purple-in-grain° beard, or your   80
    French-crown-colour° beard, your perfit yellow.

QUINCE.   Some of your French crowns° have no hair at all; and
    then you will play barefaced. But masters here are your
    parts, and I am to entreat you, request you, and desire
    you, to con° them by tomorrow night: and meet me in the   85
    palace wood, a mile without the town, by moonlight;
    there will we rehearse: for if we meet in the city, we
    shall be dogged with company, and our devices° known.
    In the meantime, I will draw a bill of properties,° such
    as our play wants. I pray you fail me not.   90

BOTTOM.   We will meet, and there we may rehearse most obscenely°
    and courageously. Take pain, be perfit: adieu.

QUINCE.   At the duke's oak we meet.

BOTTOM.   Enough: hold, or cut bow-strings.°   *Exeunt.*

ACT 2

[Scene 1. A wood near Athens]

Enter a FAIRY at one door, and ROBIN GOODFELLOW [PUCK] at another.

PUCK.   How now spirit, whither wander you?

FAIRY.   Over hill, over dale,
    Thorough bush, thorough brier,

---

60 *that:* so that.   69 *aggravate:* (he means "moderate").   70–71 *and 'twere:* as if it were.
73 *proper:* handsome.   80 *purple-in-grain:* dyed permanently purple.   81 *French-crown-colour:* golden,
like French crowns (gold coins).   82 *French crowns:* bald heads believed to be caused by syphilis, the
"French" disease.   85 *con:* learn by heart.   88 *devices:* plans.   89 *bill of properties:* list of stage props.
91 *obscenely:* (he may mean "fittingly" or "obscurely").   94 *hold, or cut bow-strings:* (meaning uncertain,
but equivalent to "fish, or cut bait").

Over park, over pale,°
   Thorough flood, thorough fire: 5
I do wander everywhere,
Swifter than the moon's sphere:
And I serve the Fairy Queen,
To dew° her orbs° upon the green.
The cowslips° tall her pensioners° be,   10
In their gold coats, spots you see:
Those be rubies, fairy favours.°
In those freckles live their savours.°
I must go seek some dewdrops here,
And hang a pearl in every cowslip's ear.   15
Farewell thou lob° of spirits: I'll be gone,
Our queen and all her elves come here anon.

PUCK.   The king doth keep his revels here tonight.
Take heed the queen come not within his sight.
For Oberon is passing fell° and wrath,   20
Because that she, as her attendant, hath
A lovely boy, stol'n from an Indian king:
She never had so sweet a changeling.°
And jealous Oberon would have the child
Knight of his train, to trace° the forests wild.   25
But she, perforce,° withholds the lovèd boy,
Crowns him with flowers, and makes him all her joy.
And now, they never meet in grove or green,
By fountain clear, or spangled starlight sheen,
But they do square,° that all their elves for fear   30
Creep into acorn cups, and hide them there.

FAIRY.   Either I mistake your shape and making quite,
Or else you are that shrewd and knavish sprite
Called Robin Goodfellow. Are not you he
That frights the maidens of the villagery,   35
Skim milk,° and sometimes labour in the quern,°
And bootless° make the breathless housewife churn,
And sometime make the drink to bear no barm,°
Mislead night-wanderers, laughing at their harm?
Those that Hobgoblin call you, and sweet Puck,   40
You do their work, and they shall have good luck.
Are not you he?

PUCK.   Thou speakest aright;
I am that merry wanderer of the night.
I jest to Oberon, and make him smile,
When I a fat and bean-fed horse beguile,   45

---

4 *pale:* enclosure. **9** *dew:* bedew. *orbs:* fairy rings (circles of high grass). **10** *cowslips:* primroses.
pensioners: royal bodyguards. **12** *favours:* gifts. **13** *savours:* perfumes. **16** *lob:* lout, lubber. **20** *passing fell:* surpassingly fierce. **23** *changeling:* creature exchanged by fairies for a stolen baby (among the fairies, the stolen child). **25** *trace:* traverse. **26** *perforce:* by force. **30** *square:* quarrel. **36** *Skim milk:* steals the cream off the milk. *quern:* handmill for grinding grain. **37** *bootless:* without result. **38** *barm:* foamy head (therefore the drink was flat).

Neighing in likeness of a filly foal;
And sometime lurk I in a gossip's° bowl,
In very likeness of a roasted crab,°
And when she drinks, against her lips I bob,
And on her withered dewlap° pour the ale.　　　　　　　　　　　50
The wisest aunt, telling the saddest tale,
Sometime for three-foot stool mistaketh me:
Then slip I from her bum, down topples she,
And "tailor"° cries, and falls into a cough;
And then the whole quire° hold their hips and laugh,　　　　　55
And waxen° in their mirth, and neeze,° and swear
A merrier hour was never wasted° there.
But room° fairy: here comes Oberon.

FAIRY.　And here, my mistress. Would that he were gone.

Enter [OBERON] the King Of Fairies, at one door with his TRAIN, and the QUEEN [TITANIA], at another, with hers.

OBERON.　Ill met by moonlight, proud Titania.　　　　　　　　60
QUEEN.　What, jealous Oberon? Fairy, skip hence.
　　I have forsworn his bed and company.
OBERON.　Tarry, rash wanton,° Am not I thy lord?
QUEEN.　Then I must be thy lady; but I know
　　When thou hast stol'n away from fairyland,　　　　　　　　65
　　And in the shape of Corin° sat all day,
　　Playing on pipes of corn,° and versing love
　　To amorous Phillida.° Why art thou here
　　Come from the farthest steep of India?
　　But that, forsooth, the bouncing Amazon,°　　　　　　　　70
　　Your buskined° mistress and your warrior love,
　　To Theseus must be wedded; and you come,
　　To give their bed joy and prosperity.
OBERON.　How canst thou thus, for shame, Titania,
　　Glance at my credit with° Hippolyta,　　　　　　　　　　75
　　Knowing I know thy love to Theseus?
　　Didst thou not lead him through the glimmering night,
　　From Perigenia, whom he ravishèd?
　　And make him with fair Aegles break his faith,
　　With Ariadne, and Antiopa° ?　　　　　　　　　　　　　80
QUEEN.　These are the forgeries of jealousy:
　　And never, since the middle summer's spring,°
　　Met we on hill, in dale, forest, or mead,

---

47 *gossip's:* old woman's.　48 *crab:* crabapple (often put into ale).　50 *dewlap:* loose skin hanging about the throat.　54 *"tailor":* (variously explained: perhaps the squatting position of the tailor, or "tailard"—one with a tail).　55 *quire:* choir, group.　56 *waxen:* increase.　*neeze:* sneeze.　57 *wasted:* spent.　58 *room:* make room.　63 *Tarry, rash wanton:* wait, headstrong one.　66–68 *Corin, Phillida:* (traditional names in pastoral literature for a shepherd and his loved one, respectively).　67 *corn:* wheat straws.　70 *Amazon:* Hippolyta.　71 *buskined:* wearing boots.　75 *Glance . . . credit with:* hint at my favors from.　78–80 *Perigenia . . . Antiopa:* women that Theseus supposedly loved and deserted.　82 *middle . . . spring.* beginning of midsummer.

By pavèd° fountain, or by rushy brook,
Or in the beachèd margent° of the sea,   85
To dance our ringlets to the whistling wind,
But with thy brawls thou hast disturbed our sport.
Therefore° the winds, piping to us in vain,
As in revenge, have sucked up from the sea
Contagious° fogs: which falling in the land,   90
Hath every pelting° river made so proud,
That they have overborne their continents.°
The ox hath therefore stretched his yoke in vain,
The ploughman lost his sweat, and the green corn°
Hath rotted, ere his youth attained a beard:°   95
The fold° stands empty in the drownèd field,
And crows are fatted with the murrion° flock.
The nine men's morris° is filled up with mud;
And the quaint mazes° in the wanton green,°
For lack of tread, are undistinguishable.   100
The human mortals want° their winter here,
No night is now with hymn or carol blest;
Therefore the moon, the governess of floods,
Pale in her anger, washes all the air,
That rheumatic diseases do abound.   105
And thorough this distemperature,° we see
The seasons alter: hoary-headed frosts
Fall in the fresh lap of the crimson rose,
And on old Hiems'° thin and icy crown,
An odorous chaplet° of sweet summer buds   110
Is, as in mockery, set. The spring, the summer,
The childing° autumn, angry winter change
Their wonted liveries:° and the mazèd° world,
By their increase, now knows not which is which:
And this same progeny of evils comes   115
From our debate, from our dissension:
We are their parents and original.
OBERON.   Do you amend it then: it lies in you.
Why should Titania cross her Oberon?
I do but beg a little changeling boy,   120
To be my henchman.°
QUEEN.   Set your heart at rest.
The fairy land buys not the child of me.
His mother was a vot'ress° of my order:

---

84 *pavèd:* with a pebbly bottom.   85 *margent:* margin, shore.   88–117 *Therefore . . . original:* (the
disturbance in nature reflects the discord between Oberon and Titania).   90 *Contagious:* spreading pestilence.   91 *pelting:* paltry.   92 *overborne their continents:* overflown the banks which contain them.
94 *corn:* grain.   95 *beard:* the tassels on ripened grain.   96 *fold:* enclosure for livestock.   97 *murrion:*
dead from murrain, a cattle disease.   98 *nine men's morris:* game played on squares cut in the grass on
which stones or disks are moved.   99 *quaint mazes:* intricate paths.   *wanton green:* luxuriant grass.
101 *want:* lack.   106 *distemperature:* upset in nature.   109 *Hiems:* god of winter.   110 *odorous chaplet:*
sweet-smelling wreath.   112 *childing:* fruitful.   113 *wonted liveries:* accustomed dress.   *mazèd:* amazed.
121 *henchman:* attendant.   123 *vot'ress:* vowed and devoted follower.

And in the spicèd Indian air, by night,
Full often hath she gossiped by my side.   125
And sat with me on Neptune's yellow sands,
Marking th' embarkèd traders° on the flood:
When we have laughed to see the sails conceive,
And grow big-bellied with the wanton° wind;
Which she, with pretty and with swimming gait,   130
Following (her womb then rich with my young squire)
Would imitate, and sail upon the land,
To fetch me trifles, and return again,
As from a voyage, rich with merchandise.
But she, being mortal, of that boy did die,   135
And for her sake, do I rear up her boy:
And for her sake, I will not part with him.

OBERON.   How long within this wood intend you stay?
QUEEN.   Perchance till after Theseus' wedding day.
　　If you will patiently dance in our round,°   140
　　And see our moonlight revels, go with us:
　　If not, shun me, and I will spare° your haunts.
OBERON.   Give me that boy, and I will go with thee.
QUEEN.   Not for thy fairy kingdom. Fairies away
　　We shall chide downright, if I longer stay.   145

Exeunt [TITANIA *and her* TRAIN.]

OBERON.   Well, go thy way. Thou shalt not from this grove,
　　Till I torment thee for this injury.
　　My gentle Puck come hither: thou rem.emb'rest,
　　Since° once I sat upon a promontory,
　　And heard a mermaid, on a dolphin's back,   150
　　Uttering such dulcet and harmonious breath,
　　That the rude° sea grew civil° at her song,
　　And certain stars shot madly from their spheres,
　　To hear the sea-maid's music.
PUCK.   I remember.
OBERON.   That very time, I saw (but thou couldst not)   155
　　Flying between the cold moon and the earth,
　　Cupid, all armed: a certain aim he took
　　At a fair Vestal,° thronèd by the west,
　　And loosed his love-shaft smartly from his bow,
　　As it should pierce a hundred thousand hearts: 160
　　But I might see young Cupid's fiery shaft
　　Quenched in the chaste beams of the wat'ry moon:
　　And the imperial vot'ress° passèd on,
　　In maiden meditation, fancy-free.°
　　Yet marked I where the bolt° of Cupid fell.   165
　　It fell upon a little western flower;

127 *traders:* merchant ships.   129 *wanton:* sportive.   140 *round:* round dance.   142 *spare:* shun.
149 *Since:* when.   152 *rude:* rough.   *civil:* calm.   158 *Vestal:* virgin, probable reference to Queen
Elizabeth.   163 *imperial vot'ress:* royal devotee (Queen Elizabeth) of Diana.   164 *fancy-free:* free from
love.   165 *bolt:* arrow.

Before, milk-white; now purple with love's wound,
And maidens call it love-in-idleness.°
Fetch me that flow'r: the herb I showed thee once.
The juice of it, on sleeping eyelids laid,   170
Will make or man or woman madly dote
Upon the next live creature that it sees.
Fetch me this herb, and be thou here again
Ere the leviathan° can swim a league.

PUCK.   I'll put a girdle round about the earth,   175
    In forty minutes.   [*Exit.*]

OBERON.   Having once this juice,
    I'll watch Titania when she is asleep,
    And drop the liquor of it in her eyes:
    The next thing then she waking looks upon,
    (Be it on lion, bear, or wolf, or bull,   180
    On meddling monkey, or on busy° ape)
    She shall pursue it, with the soul of love.
    And ere I take this charm from off her sight
    (As I can take it with another herb)
    I'll make her render up her page to me.   185
    But who comes here? I am invisible,
    And I will overhear their conference.

Enter DEMETRIUS, HELENA *following him.*

DEMETRIUS.   I love thee not: therefore pursue me not.
    Where is Lysander and fair Hermia?
    The one I'll slay: the other slayeth me.   190
    Thou told'st me they were stol'n unto this wood:
    And here am I, and wood° within this wood:
    Because I cannot meet my Hermia.
    Hence, get thee gone, and follow me no more.

HELENA.   You draw me, you hard-hearted adamant:°   195
    But yet you draw not iron, for my heart
    Is true as steel. Leave you your power to draw,
    And I shall have no power to follow you.

DEMETRIUS.   Do I entice you? Do I speak you fair°?
    Or rather do I not in plainest truth   200
    Tell you I do not, nor I cannot love you?

HELENA.   And even for that, do I love you the more:
    I am your spaniel: and Demetrius,
    The more you beat me, I will fawn on you.
    Use me but as your spaniel: spurn me, strike me,   205
    Neglect me, lose me: only give me leave,
    Unworthy as I am, to follow you.
    What worser place can I beg in your love
    (And yet a place of high respect with me)
    Than to be usèd as you use your dog.   210

---

168 *love-in-idleness:* pansy.   174 *leviathan:* whale.   181 *busy:* mischievous.   192 *wood:* crazy.
195 *adamant:* (1) magnet (2) impenetrably hard lodestone.   199 *speak you fair:* speak to you in a kindly way.

DEMETRIUS.   Tempt not too much the hatred of my spirit,
    For I am sick, when I do look on thee.
HELENA.   And I am sick, when I look not on you.
DEMETRIUS.   You do impeach° your modesty too much,
    To leave the city and commit yourself   215
    Into the hands of one that loves you not,
    To trust the opportunity of night,
    And the ill counsel of a desert° place,
    With the rich worth of your virginity.
HELENA.   Your virtue is my privilege:° for that°.   220
    It is not night, when I do see your face,
    Therefore I think I am not in the night.
    Nor doth this wood lack worlds of company,
    For you, in my respect,° are all the world.
    Then how can it be said I am alone,   225
    When all the world is here to look on me?
DEMETRIUS.   I'll run from thee and hide me in the brakes,°
    And leave thee to the mercy of wild beasts.
HELENA.   The wildest hath not such a heart as you.
    Run when you will: the story shall be changed;   230
    Apollo flies, and Daphne° holds the chase:
    The dove pursues the griffin:° the mild hind°
    Makes speed to catch the tiger. Bootless° speed,
    When cowardice pursues, and valour flies.
DEMETRIUS.   I will not stay° thy questions. Let me go: 235
    Or if thou follow me, do not believe
    But I shall do thee mischief in the wood.   [*Exit* DEMETRIUS.]
HELENA.   Ay, in the temple, in the town, the field,
    You do me mischief. Fie Demetrius,
    Your wrongs do set a scandal on my sex: 240
    We cannot fight for love, as men may do:
    We should be wooed, and were not made to woo.
    I'll follow thee and make a heaven of hell,
    To die upon the hand I love so well.   *Exit.*
OBERON.   Fare thee well nymph. Ere he do leave this grove,   245
    Thou shalt fly him, and he shall seek thy love.

Enter PUCK.

    Hast thou the flower there? Welcome wanderer.
PUCK.   Ay, there it is.
OBERON.   I pray thee give it me.
    I know a bank where the wild thyme blows,
    Where oxlips and the nodding violet grows,   250
    Quite over-canopied with luscious woodbine,

---

214 *impeach:* discredit.   218 *desert:* deserted.   220 *Your . . . privilege:* your attraction is my excuse
(for coming).   *for that:* because.   224 *respect:* regard   227 *brakes:* thickets.   231 *Apollo . . . Daphine:* (in
Ovid, Apollo pursues Daphne, who turns into a laurel tree).   232 *griffin:* legendary beast with the head of
an eagle and the body of a lion.   *hind:* doe.   233 *Bootless:* useless.   235 *stay:* wait for.

With sweet musk-roses, and with eglantine:
There sleeps Titania, sometime of the night,
Lulled in these flowers, with dances and delight:
And there the snake throws° her enamelled skin,   255
Weed° wide enough to wrap a fairy in.
And with the juice of this, I'll streak her eyes,
And make her full of hateful fantasies.
Take thou some of it, and seek through this grove:
A sweet Athenian lady is in love   260
With a disdainful youth: anoint his eyes.
But do it when the next thing he espies
May be the lady. Thou shalt know the man
By the Athenian garments he hath on.
Effect it with some care, that he may prove   265
More fond° on her, than she upon her love:
And look thou meet me ere the first cock crow.
PUCK.   Fear not my lord: your servant shall do so.   *Exeunt.*

[Scene 2. Another part of the wood]

Enter TITANIA Queen of Fairies with her train.

QUEEN.   Come, now a roundel° and a fairy song:
Then, for the third part of a minute, hence—
Some to kill cankers in the musk-rose buds,
Some war with reremice° for their leathren wings,
To make my small elves coats, and some keep back   5
The clamorous owl, that nightly hoots and wonders
At our quaint° spirits. Sing me now asleep:
Then to your offices,° and let me rest.

Fairies sing.

You spotted snakes with double° tongue,
    Thorny hedgehogs be not seen,   10
Newts and blind-worms,° do no wrong,
    Come not near our Fairy Queen.
    Philomele,° with melody,
    Sing in our sweet lullaby,
Lulla, lulla, lullaby, lulla, lulla, lullaby.   15
    Never harm,
    Nor spell, nor charm,
Come our lovely lady nigh.
So good night, with lullaby.
1. FAIRY.   Weaving spiders come not here: 20
    Hence you long-legged spinners, hence:
Beetles black approach not near:
Worm nor snail do no offence.
Philomele, with melody, &c.   *She sleeps.*

---

255 *throws:* casts off.   256 *weed:* garment.   266 *fond:* doting, madly in love.   1 *roundel:* dance in a ring.   4 *reremice:* bats.   7 *quaint:* dainty.   8 *offices:* duties.   9 *double:* forked.   11 *blind-worms:* legless lizards.   13 *Philomele:* the nightingale.

2. FAIRY.   Hence away: now all is well: 25
        One aloof stand sentinel.   [*Exeunt fairies.*]

Enter OBERON [*and applies the flower juice to* TITANIA'S *eyelids.*]

OBERON.   What thou seest, when thou dost wake,
        Do it for thy true love take:
        Love and languish for his sake.
        Be it ounce,° or cat, or bear,   30
        Pard,° or boar with bristled hair,
        In thy eye that shall appear,
        When thou wak'st, it is thy dear:
        Wake when some vile thing is near.   [*Exit.*]

Enter LYSANDER *and* HERMIA.

LYSANDER.   Fair love, you faint with wand'ring in the wood: 35
        And to speak troth° I have forgot our way.
        We'll rest us Hermia, if you think it good,
        And tarry for the comfort of the day.
HERMIA.   Be't so Lysander: find you out a bed:
        For I upon this bank will rest my head.   40
LYSANDER.   One turf shall serve as pillow for us both,
        One heart, one bed, two bosoms, and one troth.°
HERMIA.   Nay good Lysander: for my sake, my dear,
        Lie further off yet; do not lie so near.
LYSANDER.   O take the sense, sweet, of my innocence.°   45
        Love takes the meaning in love's conference.°
        I mean that my heart unto yours is knit,
        So that but one heart we can make of it:
        Two bosoms interchainèd with an oath,
        So then two bosoms and a single troth.   50
        Then by your side no bed-room me deny:
        For lying so, Hermia, I do not lie.
HERMIA.   Lysander riddles very prettily.
        Now much beshrew° my manners and my pride,
        If Hermia meant to say Lysander lied.   55
        But gentle friend, for love and courtesy,
        Lie further off, in human modesty:
        Such separation as may well be said
        Becomes a virtuous bachelor and a maid,
        So far be distant, and good night sweet friend: 60
        Thy love ne'er alter till thy sweet life end.
LYSANDER.   Amen, amen, to that fair prayer say I,
        And then end life, when I end loyalty.
        Here is my bed: sleep give thee all his rest.
HERMIA.   With half that wish, the wisher's eyes be pressed.°   65
                                                                    They sleep.

---

    30 *ounce:* lynx.   31 *Pard:* leopard.   36 *troth:* truth.   42 *troth:* true love.   45 *take . . . innocence:*
understand the innocence of my remark.   46 *Love . . . conference:* Love enables lovers to understand each
other when they converse.   54 *beshrew:* curse.   65 *pressed:* i.e., by sleep.

Enter PUCK.

PUCK.   Through the forest have I gone,
    But Athenian found I none,
    On whose eyes I might approve°
    This flower's force in stirring love.
    Night and silence. Who is here?   70
    Weeds° of Athens he doth wear:
    This is he (my master said)
    Despisèd the Athenian maid:
    And here the maiden, sleeping sound,
    On the dank and dirty ground.   75
    Pretty soul, she durst not lie
    Near this lack-love, this kill-courtesy.
    Churl, upon thy eyes I throw
    All the power this charm doth owe.°
    When thou wak'st, let love forbid   80
    Sleep his seat on thy eyelid.°
    So awake when I am gone:
    For I must now to Oberon.   *Exit.*

Enter DEMETRIUS *and* HELENA *running.*

HELENA.   Stay, thou kill me, sweet Demetrius.
DEMETRIUS.   I charge thee hence, and do not haunt me thus.   85
HELENA.   O, wilt thou darkling° leave me? Do not so.
DEMETRIUS.   Stay on thy peril: I alone will go.   *Exit* DEMETRIUS.
HELENA.   O, I am out of breath in this fond° chase:
    The more my prayer, the lesser is my grace.°
    Happy is Hermia, wheresoe'er she lies: 90
    For she hath blessèd and attractive eyes.
    How came her eyes so bright? Not with salt tears:
    If so, my eyes are oft'ner washed than hers.
    No, no: I am as ugly as a bear:
    For beasts that meet me run away for fear.   95
    Therefore no marvel, though Demetrius
    Do as a monster, fly my presence thus.
    What wicked and dissembling glass° of mine,
    Made me compare with Hermia's sphery eyne° !
    But who is here? Lysander, on the ground?   100
    Dead, or asleep? I see no blood, no wound.
    Lysander, if you live, good sir awake.
LYSANDER.   [*Wakes.*] And run through fire, I will for thy sweet sake.
    Transparent° Helena, nature shows art,
    That through thy bosom, makes me see thy heart.   105
    Where is Demetrius? O how fit a word
    Is that vile name to perish on my sword!

---

68 *approve:* test   71 *Weeds:* garments.   79 *owe:* own.   80–81 *forbid . . . eyelid:* make you sleep-less (with love).   86 *darkling:* in the dark.   88 *fond:* foolishly doting.   89 *my grace:* favor shown to me. 98 *glass:* looking glass.   99 *sphery eyne:* starry eyes.   104 *Transparent:* radiant.

HELENA.   Do not say so, Lysander, say not so.
What though he love your Hermia? Lord, what though?
Yet Hermia still loves you: then be content.   110
LYSANDER.   Content with Hermia? No: I do repent
The tedious minutes I with her have spent.
Not Hermia, but Helena I love.
Who will not change a raven for a dove?
The will of man is by his reason swayed:°   115
And reason says you are the worthier maid.
Things growing are not ripe until their season:
So I, being young, till now ripe° not to reason.
And touching now the point° of human skill,°
Reason becomes the marshal to my will,   120
And leads me to your eyes; where I o'erlook
Love's stories, written in love's richest book.
HELENA.   Wherefore° was I to this keen mockery born?
When at your hands did I deserve this scorn?
Is't not enough, is't not enough, young man,   125
That I did never, no, nor never can,
Deserve a sweet look from Demetrius' eye,
But you must flout° my insufficiency?
Good troth you do me wrong, good sooth you do,
In such disdainful manner me to woo.   130
But fare you well: perforce I must confess,
I thought you lord of more true gentleness.°
O, that a lady, of one man refused,
Should of another, therefore be abused!   *Exit.*
LYSANDER.   She sees not Hermia. Hermia, sleep thou there,   135
And never mayst thou come Lysander near.
For, as a surfeit of the sweetest things
The deepest loathing to the stomach brings:
Or as the heresies that men do leave,
Are hated most of those they did deceive: 140
So thou, my surfeit and my heresy,
Of all be hated; but the most, of me:
And all my powers, address your love and might,
To honour Helen, and to be her knight.

                                                                                 Exit.

HERMIA.   [*Wakes.*] Help me Lysander, help me: do thy best   145
To pluck this crawling serpent from my breast.
Ay me, for pity. What a dream was here?
Lysander, look how I do quake with fear.
Methought a serpent eat my heart away,
And you sat smiling at his cruel prey.°   150
Lysander: what, removed? Lysander, lord!

---

115 *swayed:* ruled.   118 *ripe:* mature.   119 *point:* peak.   *skill:* knowledge.   123 *Wherefore:* why.
128 *flout:* mock.   132 *lord . . . gentleness:* more of a gentleman.   150 *prey:* preying.

What, out of hearing, gone? No sound, no word?
Alack, where are you? Speak, and if you hear:
Speak, of° all loves. I swoon almost with fear.
No? Then I well perceive you are not nigh: 155
Either death, or you, I'll find immediately.   *Exit.*

Act 3

[Scene 1. The wood]

Enter the Clowns *[*Quince, Snug, Bottom, Flute, Snout, *and* Starveling.*]*

Bottom.   Are we all met?
Quince.   Pat, pat: and here's a marvellous convenient place for
    our rehearsal. This green plot shall be our stage, this
    hawthorn brake° our tiring-house,° and we will do it in
    action, as we will do it before the duke.   5
Bottom.   Peter Quince?
Quince.   What sayest thou, bully° Bottom?
Bottom.   There are things in this Comedy of Pyramus and Thisby
    that will never please. First, Pyramus must draw a sword
    to kill himself; which the ladies cannot abide. How   10
    answer you that?
Snout.   By'r lakin,° a parlous° fear.
Starveling.   I believe we must leave the killing out, when all is done.
Bottom.   Not a whit: I have a device to make all well. Write me
    a prologue, and let the prologue seem to say, we will   15
    do no harm with our swords, and that Pyramus is not
    killed indeed: and for the more better assurance, tell
    them that I Pyramus am not Pyramus, but Bottom the
    weaver: this will put them out of fear.
Quince.   Well, we will have such a prologue, and it shall be   20
    written in eight and six.°
Bottom.   No, make it two more: let it be written in eight and
    eight.
Snout.   Will not the ladies be afeared of the lion?
Starveling.   I fear it, I promise you.   25
Bottom.   Masters, you ought to consider with yourselves, to bring
    in (God shield us) a lion among ladies, is a most dreadful
    thing. For there is not a more fearful wild-fowl than
    your lion living: and we ought to look to't.
Snout.   Therefore another prologue must tell he is not a lion.   30
Bottom.   Nay, you must name his name, and half his face must be
    seen through the lion's neck, and he himself must speak
    through, saying thus, or to the same defect:° "Ladies,"
    or "Fair ladies—I would wish you," or "I would request
    you," or "I would entreat you, not to fear,   35

---

    154 *of:* for the sake of.   **4** *brake:* thicket.   *tiring-house:* dressing room.   **7** *bully:* "old pal."
12 *By'r lakin:* mild oath, "by Our Lady."   *parlous:* awful, perilous.   **21** *eight and six:* alternate lines of
eight and six syllables (the ballad meter).   **33** *defect:* (he means "effect").

not to tremble: my life for yours. If you think I come
hither as a lion, it were pity of my life. No, I am no
such thing: I am a man as other men are." And there
indeed let him name his name, and tell them plainly he
is Snug the joiner.

QUINCE.   Well, it shall be so, but there is two hard things: that is,   40
to bring the moonlight into a chamber: for you know,
Pyramus and Thisby meet by moonlight.

SNOUT.   Doth the moon shine that night we play our play?

BOTTOM.   A calendar, a calendar: look in the almanac: find out   45
moonshine, find out moonshine.

QUINCE.   Yes, it doth shine that night.

BOTTOM.   Why then may you leave a casement of the great
chamber window, where we play, open; and the moon may
shine in at the casement.   50

QUINCE.   Ay, or else one must come in with a bush of thorns° and
a lantern, and say he comes to disfigure,° or to present,
the person of Moonshine. Then, there is another thing;
we must have a wall in the great chamber: for Pyramus
and Thisby, says the story, did talk through the chink   55
of a wall.

SNOUT.   You can never bring in a wall. What say you, Bottom?

BOTTOM.   Some man or other must present wall: and let him have
some plaster, or some loam, or some rough-cast° about
him, to signify wall; and let him hold his fingers thus: 60
and through that cranny, shall Pyramus and Thisby whisper.

QUINCE.   If that may be, then all is well. Come, sit down every
mother's son, and rehearse your parts. Pyramus, you
begin: when you have spoken your speech, enter into that
brake, and so every one according to his cue.   65

Enter PUCK.

PUCK.   What hempen homespuns° have we swagg'ring here,
So near the cradle of the Fairy Queen?
What, a play toward°? I'll be an auditor,
An actor too perhaps, if I see cause.

QUINCE.   Speak Pyramus. Thisby stand forth.   70

PYRAMUS.   Thisby, the flowers of odious savours sweet—

QUINCE.   "Odorous, odorous."

PYRAMUS.   —odours savours sweet,
So hath thy breath, my dearest Thisby dear.
But hark, a voice: stay thou but here awhile,   75
And by and by I will to thee appear.   *Exit* PYRAMUS.

PUCK.   A stranger Pyramus than e'er played here.   [*Exit.*]

THISBY.   Must I speak now?

---

51 *bush of thorns:* bundle of firewood (the man in the moon was supposed to have been placed
there as a punishment for gathering wood on Sundays).   52 *disfigure:* (he means "figure," symbolize).
59 *rough-cast:* coarse plaster of lime and gravel.   66 *hempen homespuns:* wearers of clothing spun at
home from hemp.   68 *toward:* in preparation.

QUINCE.   Ay marry must you. For you must understand he goes
    but to see a noise that he heard, and is to come again.   80
THISBY.   Most radiant Pyramus, most lily-white of hue,
    Of colour like the red rose, on triumphant brier,
    Most brisky juvenal,° and eke most lovely Jew,°
    As true as truest horse, that yet would never tire,
    I'll meet thee Pyramus, at Ninny's tomb.   85
QUINCE.   "Ninus' tomb,"° man: why, you must not speak that yet.
    That you answer to Pyramus. You speak all your part
    at once, cues and all. Pyramus, enter; your cue is past:
    it is "never tire."
THISBY.   O—As true as truest horse, that yet would never tire.   90

Enter PYRAMUS *with the ass-head* [*followed by* PUCK].

PYRAMUS.   If I were fair, Thisby, I were only thine.
QUINCE.   O monstrous! O strange! We are haunted. Pray masters,
    fly masters. Help!   *The clowns all exeunt.*
PUCK.   I'll follow you: I'll lead you about a round,°
    Through bog, through bush, through brake, through brier.   95
    Sometime a horse I'll be, sometime a hound,
    A hog, a headless bear, sometime a fire,
    And neigh, and bark, and grunt, and roar, and burn,
    Like horse, hound, hog, bear, fire, at every turn.   *Exit.*
BOTTOM.   Why do they run away? This is a knavery of them to   100
    make me afeared.

Enter SNOUT.

SNOUT.   O Bottom, thou art changed. What do I see on thee?
BOTTOM.   What do you see? You see an ass-head of your own, do
    you?   [*Exit* SNOUT.]

Enter QUINCE.

QUINCE.   Bless thee Bottom, bless thee. Thou art translated.°   *Exit.*   105
BOTTOM.   I see their knavery. This is to make an ass of me, to
    fright me if they could: but I will not stir from this
    place, do what they can. I will walk up and down here,
    and will sing that they shall hear I am not afraid.
      [*Sings.*] The woose° cock, so black of hue,   110
          With orange tawny bill,
          The throstle,° with his note so true,
          The wren, with little quill.°
TITANIA.   What angel wakes me from my flow'ry bed?

---

83 *brisky juvenal:* lively youth.   *Jew:* diminutive of either "juvenal" or "jewel."   86 *Ninus' tomb:*
(tomb of the founder of Nineveh, and meeting place of the lovers in Ovid's version of the Pyramus story).
94 *about a round:* in circles, like a round dance (round about).   105 *translated:* transformed.   110 *woosel:*
ousel, blackbird.   112 *throstle:* thrush.   113 *quill:* piping note.

BOTTOM.   [*Sings.*] The finch, the sparrow, and the lark,   115
          The plain-song° cuckoo gray:
      Whose note full many a man doth mark,
          And dares not answer, nay.

    For indeed, who would set his wit to° so foolish a bird?
    Who would give a bird the lie,° though he cry "cuckoo"°   120
    never so°?
TITANIA.   I pray thee, gentle mortal, sing again.
    Mine ear is much enamoured of thy note:
    So is mine eye enthrallèd to thy shape
    And thy fair virtue's force (perforce°) doth move me,   125
    On the first view to say, to swear, I love thee.
BOTTOM.   Methinks mistress, you should have little reason for
    that. And yet, to say the truth, reason and love keep
    little company together now-a-days. The more the pity,
    That some honest neighbours will not make them friends.   130
    Nay, I can gleek° upon occasion.
TITANIA.   Thou art as wise as thou art beautiful.
BOTTOM.   Not so neither: but if I had wit enough to get out of
    this wood, I have enough to serve mine own turn.
TITANIA.   Out of this wood do not desire to go: 135
    Thou shalt remain here, whether thou wilt or no.
    I am a spirit of no common rate:°
    The summer still doth tend upon my state,°
    And I do love thee: therefore go with me.
    I'll give thee fairies to attend on thee: 140
    And they shall fetch thee jewels from the deep,
    And sing, while thou on pressèd flowers dost sleep:
    And I will purge thy mortal grossness so,
    That thou shalt like an airy spirit go.
    Peaseblossom, Cobweb, Moth,° and Mustardseed!   145

Enter four FAIRIES.

PEASEBLOSSOM.   Ready.
COBWEB.   And I.
MOTH.   And I.
MUSTARDSEED.   And I.
ALL.   Where shall we go?
TITANIA.   Be kind and courteous to this gentleman,
    Hop in his walks and gambol° in his eyes,
    Feed him with apricocks° and dewberries,°   150

---

116 *plain-song:* sounding a simple unvaried note.   119 *set . . . to:* match his wit against.   120 *Who
. . . lie:* who could call a bird a liar.   "cuckoo": (which sounded like "cuckold" = a deceived husband).
121 *never so:* i.e., often.   125 *perforce:* by force.   131 *gleek:* joke satirically.   137 *rate:* rank, value
138 *still . . . state:* always serves as an attendant in my royal train.   145 *Moth:* mote (so pronounced), tiny
speck.   149 *gambol in:* caper before.   150 *apricocks:* apricots.   *dewberries:* blackberries.

With purple grapes, green figs, and mulberries.
The honey-bags steal from the humblebees,°
And for night-tapers, crop° their waxen thighs,
And light them at the fiery glow-worm's eyes,
To have my love to bed and to arise: 155
And pluck the wings from painted butterflies,
To fan the moonbeams from his sleeping eyes.
Nod to him elves, and do him courtesies.
PEASEBLOSSOM.   Hail, mortal.
COBWEB.   Hail.   160
MOTH.   Hail.
MUSTARDSEED.   Hail.
BOTTOM.   I cry your worships mercy,° heartily: I beseech your
    worship's name.
COBWEB.   Cobweb.   165
BOTTOM.   I shall desire you of more acquaintance, good Master
    Cobweb: if I cut my finger,° I shall make bold with you.
    Your name, honest gentleman?
PEASEBLOSSOM.   Peaseblossom.
BOTTOM.   I pray you commend me° to Mistress Squash,° your mother,   170
    and to Master Peascod,° your father. Good Master Peaseblossom,
    I shall desire you of more acquaintance, too.
    Your name I beseech you sir?
MUSTARDSEED.   Mustardseed.
BOTTOM.   Good Master Mustardseed, I know your patience well.   175
    That same cowardly giant-like ox beef hath devoured
    many a gentleman of your house. I promise you, your
    kindred hath made my eyes water ere now. I desire you
    of more acquaintance, good Master Mustardseed.
TITANIA.   Come wait upon him: lead him to my bower.   180
        The moon methinks looks with a wat'ry eye:
        And when she weeps, weeps every little flower,
            Lamenting some enforcèd° chastity.
            Tie up my lover's tongue, bring him silently.   *Exeunt.*

[Scene 2. Another part of the wood]

Enter [OBERON,] King of Fairies, solus.°

OBERON.   I wonder if Titania be awaked;
        Then what it was that next came in her eye,
        Which she must dote on in extremity.

Enter PUCK.

        Here comes my messenger. How now, mad spirit?
        What night-rule° now about this haunted grove?   5

---

152 *humblebees:* bumblebees.   153 *crop:* clip.   163 *I . . . mercy:* I respectfully beg your pardons.
167 *cut my finger:* (cobwebs were used to stop bleeding).   170 *commend me:* offer my respects.   *Squash:*
unripe peapod.   171 *Peascod:* ripe peapod.   183 *enforced:* violated.   S.D.: *solus:* alone.   5 *night-rule:*
diversion ("misrule") in the night.

PUCK. My mistress with a monster is in love.
    Near to her close and consecrated bower,
    While she was in her dull° and sleeping hour,
    A crew of patches,° rude mechanicals,°
    That work for bread upon Athenian stalls,°   10
    Were met together to rehearse a play,
    Intended for great Theseus' nuptial day:
    The shallowest thickskin of that barren sort,°
    Who Pyramus presented in their sport,
    Forsook his scene and entered in a brake: 15
    When I did him at this advantage take,
    An ass's nole° I fixèd on his head.
    Anon° his Thisby must be answerèd,
    And forth my mimic° comes. When they him spy,
    As wild geese, that the creeping fowler° eye,   20
    Or russet-pated choughs,° many in sort,°
    Rising and cawing at the gun's report,
    Sever themselves and madly sweep the sky,
    So at his sight away his fellows fly:
    And at our stamp, here o'er and o'er one falls: 25
    He murder cries, and help from Athens calls.
    Their sense thus weak, lost with their fears thus strong,
    Made senseless things begin to do them wrong.
    For briers and thorns at their apparel snatch:
    Some° sleeves, some hats; from yielders, all things catch°   30
    I led them on in this distracted° fear,
    And left sweet Pyramus translated there:
    When in that moment (so it came to pass)
    Titania waked, and straightway loved an ass.
OBERON. This falls out better than I could devise.   35
    But has thou yet latched° the Athenian's eyes
    With the love-juice, as I did bid thee do?
PUCK. I took him sleeping (that is finished too)
    And the Athenian woman by his side;
    That when he waked, of force° she must be eyed.   40

Enter DEMETRIUS and HERMIA.

OBERON. Stand close:° this is the same Athenian.
PUCK. This is the woman: but not this the man.
DEMETRIUS. O why rebuke you him that loves you so?
    Lay breath so bitter on your bitter foe.
HERMIA. Now I but chide: but I should use thee worse,   45
    For thou, I fear, hast given me cause to curse.

---

8 *dull:* drowsy. 9 *patches:* fools. *mechanicals:* workers. 10 *stalls:* shops. 13 *barren sort:* stupid crew. 17 *nole:* head, noodle. 18 *Anon:* presently. 19 *mimic:* actor. 20 *fowler:* hunter of fowl. 21 *russet-pated choughs:* grey-headed jackdaws. *sort:* a flock. 30 *Some:* ie., snatch. *from yielders . . . catch:* (everything joins in to harm the weak). 31 *distracted:* maddened. 36 *latched:* moistened. 40 *of force:* by necessity. 41 *close:* hidden.

If thou hast slain Lysander in his sleep,
Being o'er shoes in blood, plunge in the deep,
And kill me too.
The sun was not so true unto the day,   50
As he to me. Would he have stolen away
From sleeping Hermia? I'll believe as soon
This whole° earth may be bored,° and that the moon
May through the center creep, and so displease
Her brother's noontide with th' Antipodes.°   55
It cannot be but thou hast murdered him.
So should a murderer look; so dead,° so grim.

DEMETRIUS.   So should the murdered look, and so should I,
    Pierced through the heart with your stern cruelty.
    Yet you, the murderer, look as bright, as clear   60
    As yonder Venus in her glimmering sphere.°

HERMIA.   What's this to my Lysander? Where is he?
    Ah good Demetrius, wilt thou give him me?

DEMETRIUS.   I had rather give his carcass to my hounds.

HERMIA.   Out dog, out cur! Thou driv'st me past the bounds   65
    Of maiden's patience. Hast thou slain him then?
    Henceforth be never numbered among men.
    O, once tell true: tell true, even for my sake:
    Durst thou have looked upon him, being awake?
    And hast thou killed him sleeping? O brave touch°!   70
    Could not a worm,° an adder, do so much?
    An adder did it: for with doubler tongue°
    Than thine, thou serpent, never adder stung.

DEMETRIUS.   You spend your passion on a misprised mood°
    I am not guilty of Lysander's blood: 75
    Nor is he dead, for aught that I can tell.

HERMIA.   I pray thee, tell me then that he is well.

DEMETRIUS.   And if I could, what should I get therefore?

HERMIA.   A privilege never to see me more:
    And from thy hated presence part I so: 80
    See me no more, whether he be dead or no.   *Exit.*

DEMETRIUS.   There is no following her in this fierce vein.
    Here therefore for a while I will remain.
    So sorrow's heaviness doth heavier grow
    For debt that bankrout sleep doth sorrow owe:°   85
    Which now in some slight measure it will pay,
    If for his tender° here I make some stay.°   *Lies down.*

OBERON.   What hast thou done? Thou hast mistaken quite,
    And laid the love-juice on some true-love's sight.

---

53 *whole:* solid.   *be bored:* have a hole bored through it.   **55** *Her brother's . . . Antipodes:* the noon of her brother sun, by appearing among the Antipodes (the people on the other side of the earth). **57** *dead:* deadly.   **61** *sphere:* (in the Ptolemaic system, each planet moved in its own sphere around the earth).   **70** *brave touch:* splendid stroke (ironic).   **71** *worm:* snake.   **72** *doubler tongue:* (1) tongue more forked (2) more deceitful speech.   **74** *on . . . mood:* in mistaken anger.   **85** *For debt . . . owe:* because sleep cannot pay the debt of repose he owes the man who is kept awake by sorrow.   **87** *tender:* offer.   *stay:* pause.

    Of thy misprision° must perforce° ensue   90
    Some true love turned, and not a false turned true.
PUCK.   Then fate o'errules, that one man holding troth,
    A million fail, confounding° oath on oath.°
OBERON.   About the wood, go swifter than the wind,
    And Helena of Athens look thou find.   95
    All fancy-sick° she is, and pale of cheer,°
    With sighs of love, that costs the fresh blood dear.
    By some illusion see thou bring her here:
    I'll charm his eyes against she do appear.°
PUCK.   I go, I go, look how I go.   100
    Swifter than arrow from the Tartar's bow.°   *Exit.*
OBERON.   Flower of this purple dye,
    Hit with Cupid's archery,
    Sink in apple of his eye:
    When his love he doth espy,   105
    Let her shine as gloriously
    As the Venus of the sky.
    When thou wak'st, if she be by,
    Beg of her for remedy.

Enter PUCK.

PUCK.   Captain of our fairy band,
    Helena is here at hand,   110
    And the youth, mistook by me,
    Pleading for a lover's fee.°
    Shall we their fond pageant° see?
    Lord, what fools these mortals be!
OBERON.   Stand aside. The noise they make   115
    Will cause Demetrius to awake.
PUCK.   Then will two at once woo one:
    That must needs be sport alone.°
    And those things do best please me   120
    That befall prepost' rously.

Enter LYSANDER *and* HELENA.

LYSANDER.   Why should you think that I should woo in scorn?
    Scorn and derision never come in tears.
    Look when I vow, I weep: and vows so born,
    In their nativity all truth appears.°
    How can these things in me seem scorn to you,   125
    Bearing the badge° of faith to prove them true?
HELENA.   You do advance your cunning more and more.
    When truth kills truth,° O devilish-holy fray!

---

    90 *misprision:* mistake. *perforce:* of necessity. 93 *confounding:* destroying. *oath on oath:* one oath after another. 96 *fancy-sick:* lovesick. *cheer:* face. 99 *against . . . appear:* in preparation for her appearance. 101 *Tartar's bow:* (the Tartars, who used powerful Oriental bows, were famed as archers). 113 *fee:* reward. 114 *fond pageant:* foolish spectacle. 119 *alone:* unique. 124–125 *vows . . . appears:* vows born in weeping must be true ones. 127 *badge:* (1) outward signs (2) family crest. 129 *truth kills truth:* Former true love is killed by vows of present true love.

These vows are Hermia's. Will you give her o'er? 130
Weigh oath with oath, and you will nothing weigh.
Your vows to her and me, put in two scales,
Will even weigh: and both as light as tales.
LYSANDER.   I had no judgment, when to her I swore.
HELENA.   Nor none, in my mind, now you give her o'er. 135
LYSANDER.   Demetrius loves her: and he loves not you.
DEMETRIUS.   [*Awakes.*] O Helen, goddess, nymph, perfect, divine,
To what, my love, shall I compare thine eyne!
Crystal is muddy. O, how ripe in show,
Thy lips, those kissing cherries, tempting grow! 140
That pure congealèd white, high Taurus'° snow,
Fanned with the eastern wind, turns to a crow,
When thou hold'st up thy hand. O let me kiss
This princess of pure white,° this seal of bliss.
HELENA.   O spite! O hell! I see you all are bent 145
To set against me, for your merriment.
If you were civil,° and knew courtesy,
You would not do me thus much injury.
Can you not hate me, as I know you do,
But you must join in souls° to mock me too? 150
If you were men, as men you are in show,
You would not use a gentle lady so;
To vow, and swear, and superpraise my parts,°
When I am sure you hate me with your hearts.
You both are rivals, and love Hermia: 155
And now both rivals, to mock Helena.
A trim° exploit, a manly enterprise,
To conjure tears up in a poor maid's eyes
With your derision. None of noble sort
Would so offend a virgin, and extort° 160
A poor soul's patience, all to make you sport.
LYSANDER.   You are unkind, Demetrius: be not so.
For you love Hermia: this you know I know.
And here, with all good will, with all my heart,
In Hermia's love I yield you up my part: 165
And yours of Helena to be bequeath,
Whom I do love, and will do to my death.
HELENA.   Never did mockers waste more idle breath.
DEMETRIUS.   Lysander, keep thy Hermia: I will none,°
If e'er I loved her, all that love is gone. 170
My heart to her but as guest-wise sojourned:°
And now to Helen is it home returned,
There to remain.
LYSANDER.   Helen, it is not so.

---

141 *Taurus:* mountain range in Asia Minor.   144 *princess . . . white:* sovereign example of whiteness
(her hand).   147 *civil:* well behaved.   150 *join in souls:* agree in spirit.   153 *parts:* qualities.   157 *trim:*
fine (ironic).   160 *extort:* wring.   169 *none:* have none of her.   171 *to her . . . sojourned:* visited her only
as a guest.

DEMETRIUS.   Disparage not the faith thou dost not know,
    Lest to thy peril thou aby it dear.°
    Look where thy love comes: yonder is thy dear.   175

Enter HERMIA.

HERMIA.   Dark night, that from the eye his function takes,
    The ear more quick of apprehension makes.
    Wherein it doth impair the seeing sense,
    It pays the hearing double recompense.
    Thou art not by mine eye, Lysander, found: 180
    Mine ear, I thank it, brought me to thy sound.
    But why unkindly didst thou leave me so?
LYSANDER.   Why should he stay, whom love doth press to go?
HERMIA.   What love could press Lysander from my side?
LYSANDER.   Lysander's love, that would not let him bide—   185
    Fair Helena: who more engilds the night
    Than all your fiery oes and eyes of light.°
    Why seek'st thou me? Could not this make thee know,
    The hate I bare thee made me leave thee so?   190
HERMIA.   You speak not as you think: it cannot be.
HELENA.   Lo: She is one of this confederacy.
    Now I perceive they have conjoined all three,
    To fashion this false sport in spite of° me.
    Injurious° Hermia, most ungrateful maid,   195
    Have you conspired, have you with these contrived
    To bait° me with this foul derision?
    Is all the counsel° that we two have shared,
    The sisters' vows, the hours that we have spent,
    When we have chid the hasty-footed time   200
    For parting us; O, is all forgot?
    All schooldays' friendship, childhood innocence?
    We Hermia, like two artificial° gods,
    Have with our needles created both one flower,
    Both on one sampler,° sitting on one cushion,   205
    Both warbling of one song, both in one key;
    As if our hands, our sides, voices, and minds
    Had been incorporate.° So we grew together,
    Like to a double cherry, seeming parted,
    But yet an union in partition,   210
    Two lovely berries moulded on one stem:
    So with two seeming bodies, but one heart,
    Two of the first, like coats in heraldry,
    Due but to one, and crownèd with one crest.°
    And will you rent° our ancient love asunder,   215

---

    175 *aby it dear:* buy it at a high price.   188 *oes . . . light:* stars.   194 *in spite of:* to spite. 195 *Injurious:* insulting. 197 *bait:* attack. 198 *counsel:* secrets. 203 *artificial:* skilled in art. 205 *sampler:* work of embroidery. 208 *incorporate:* in one body. 213–214 *Two . . . crest:* (the two bodies being) like double coats of arms joined under one crest (with one heart). 215 *rent:* rend, tear.

Titania, Queen of the Fairies (Juliet Mills) is entranced by the ass's-eared Bottom (Paul Hard-wick) in the Royal Shakespeare Company production of *A Midsummer Night's Dream* (1959–62) at the Aldwych Theatre, London—director, Peter Hall.

> To join with men in scorning your poor friend?
> It is not friendly, 'tis not maidenly.
> Our sex, as well as I, may chide you for it;
> Though I alone do feel the injury.
> HERMIA.   I am amazèd at your passionate words: 220
>   I scorn you not. It seems that you scorn me.
> HELENA.   Have you not set Lysander, as in scorn,
>   To follow me, and praise my eyes and face?
>   And made your other love, Demetrius
>   (Who even but now did spurn° me with his foot)   225
>   To call me goddess, nymph, divine, and rare,
>   Precious, celestial? Wherefore speaks he this
>   To her he hates? And wherefore doth Lysander
>   Deny your love, so rich within his soul,
>   And tender° me (forsooth) affection,   230
>   But by your setting on, by your consent?
>   What though I be not so in grace° as you,
>   So hung upon with love, so fortunate,
>   But miserable most, to love unloved?
>   This you should pity, rather than despise.   235
> HERMIA.   I understand not what you mean by this.
> HELENA.   Ay, do. Persèver, counterfeit sad° looks:
>   Make mouths upon° me when I turn my back:

225 *spurn:* kick.   230 *tender:* offer.   232 *in grace:* favored.   237 *sad:* serious.   238 *mouths upon:* faces at.

Wink each at other, hold the sweet jest up.
This sport well carried, shall be chronicled.°   240
If you have any pity, grace, or manners,
You would not make me such an argument.°
But fare ye well: 'tis partly my own fault:
Which death or absence soon shall remedy.

LYSANDER.   Stay, gentle Helena: hear my excuse,   245
    My love, my life, my soul, fair Helena.

HELENA.   O excellent!

HERMIA.   Sweet, do not scorn her so.

DEMETRIUS.   If she cannot entreat,° I can compel.

LYSANDER.   Thou canst compel no more than she entreat.
    Thy threats have no more strength than her weak prayers.   250
    Helen, I love thee, by my life I do:
    I swear by that which I will lose for thee.
    To prove° him false that says I love thee not.

DEMETRIUS.   I say I love thee more than he can do.

LYSANDER.   If thou say so, withdraw, and prove° it too.   255

DEMETRIUS.   Quick, Come.

HERMIA.   Lysander, whereto tends all this?

LYSANDER.   Away, you Ethiope.°

DEMETRIUS.   No, no, sir,
    Seem to break loose: take on as you would follow;
    But yet come not.° You are a tame man, go.

LYSANDER.   Hang off,° thou cat, thou burr: vile thing, let loose;   260
    Or I will shake thee from me like a serpent.

HERMIA.   Why are you grown so rude? What change is this,
    Sweet love?

LYSANDER.   Thy love? Out, tawny Tartar, out;
    Out, loathèd med'cine: O hated potion, hence!

HERMIA.   Do you not jest?

HELENA.   Yes sooth: and so do you.   265

LYSANDER.   Demetrius, I will keep my word° with thee.

DEMETRIUS.   I would I had your bond.° For I perceive
    A weak bond holds you. I'll not trust your word.

LYSANDER.   What? Should I hurt her, strike her, kill her dead?
    Although I hate her, I'll not harm her so.   270

HERMIA.   What? Can you do me greater harm than hate?
    Hate me, wherefore°? O me, what news,° my love?
    Am not I Hermia? Are not you Lysander?
    I am as fair now, as I was erewhile.°
    Since night, you loved me; yet since night, you left me.   275

---

240 *chronicled:* written down in the history books.   242 *argument:* subject (of your mockery).
248 *entreat:* sway you by entreaty.   253, 255 *prove:* i.e., by a duel.   257 *Ethiope:* (because she is a
brunette).   258–259 *Seem . . . not:* You only seem to break loose from Hermia and pretend to follow
me to a duel, but you actually hold back.   260 *Hang off:* let go.   266 *keep my word:* i.e., to duel.
267 *bond:* written agreement.   272 *wherefore:* why.   *what news:* what's the matter.   274 *erewhile:* a
short while ago.

Why then, you left me—O, the gods forbid—
In earnest, shall I say?

LYSANDER.   Ay, by my life:
And never did desire to see thee more.
Therefore be out of hope, of question, of doubt:
Be certain: nothing truer: 'tis no jest   280
That I do hate thee, and love Helena.

HERMIA.   O me, you juggler,° you canker blossom,°
You thief of love: what, have you come by night,
And stol'n my love's heart from him?

HELENA.   Fine, i' faith.
Have you no modesty, no maiden shame,   285
No touch of bashfulness? What, will you tear
Impatient answers from my gentle tongue?
Fie, fie, you counterfeit, you puppet,° you.

HERMIA.   Puppet? Why so—ay, that way goes the game.
Now I perceive that she hath made compare   290
Between our statures, she hath urged her height,
And with her personage, her tall personage,
Her height (forsooth) she hath prevailed with him.
And are you grown so high in his esteem.
Because I am so dwarfish and so low?   295
How low am I, thou painted maypole? Speak:
How low am I? I am not yet so low,
But that my nails can reach unto thine eyes.

HELENA.   I pray you, though you mock me, gentlemen,
Let her not hurt me. I was never curst:°   300
I have no gift at all in shrewishness:
I am a right maid for my cowardice:°
Let her not strike me. You perhaps may think,
Because she is something lower than myself,
That I can match her.

HERMIA.   Lower? Hark again.   305

HELENA.   Good Hermia, do not be so bitter with me,
I evermore did love you Hermia.
Did ever keep your counsels, never wronged you;
Save that in love unto Demetrius,
I told him of your stealth unto this wood.   310
He followed you: for love I followed him.
But he hath chid me hence, and threatened me
To strike me, spurn me, nay to kill me too;
And now, so° you will let me quiet go,
To Athens will I bear my folly back,   315
And follow you no further. Let me go.
You see how simple and how fond° I am.

HERMIA.   Why, get you gone. Who is't that hinders you?

---

282 *juggler:* deceiver, *canker blossom:* worm that causes canker in blossoms.   288 *puppet:* (Hermia is short and Helena tall).   300 *curst:* bad-tempered.   302 *right . . . cowardice:* true woman in being cowardly.   314 *so:* if.   317 *fond:* foolish.

HELENA.   A foolish heart, that I leave here behind.

HERMIA.   What, with Lysander?

HELENA.   With Demetrius.   320

LYSANDER.   Be not afraid: she shall not harm thee Helena.

DEMETRIUS.   No sir: she shall not, though you take her part.

HELENA.   O when she's angry, she is keen and shrewd.°

    She was a vixen when she went to school:

    And though she be but little, she is fierce.   325

HERMIA.   "Little" again? Nothing but "low" and "little"?

    Why will you suffer her to flout° me thus?

    Let me come to her.

LYSANDER.   Get you gone, you dwarf;

    You minimus,° of hind'ring knot-grass° made;

    You bead, you acorn.

DEMETRIUS.   You are too officious   330

    In her behalf that scorns your services.

    Let her alone: speak not of Helena,

    Take not her part. For if thou dost intend°

    Never so little show of love to her,

    Thou shalt aby it.°

LYSANDER.   Now she holds me not: 335

    Now follow, if thou dar'st, to try whose right,

    Of thine or mine, is most in Helena.°

DEMETRIUS.   Follow? Nay, I'll go with thee, cheek by jowl.

                             Exeunt LYSANDER *and* DEMETRIUS.

HERMIA.   You, mistress, all this coil is long of° you.

    Nay, go not back.

HELENA.   I will not trust you, I,   340

    Nor longer stay in your curst company

    Your hands than mine are quicker for a fray:

    My legs are longer though, to run away.   [*Exit.*]

HERMIA.   I am amazed,° and know not what to say.   *Exit.*

OBERON.   This is thy negligence: still thou mistak'st,   345

    Or else commit'st thy knaveries wilfully.

PUCK.   Believe me, king of shadows, I mistook.

    Did not you tell me I should know the man

    By the Athenian garments he had on?

    And so far blameless proves my enterprise,   350

    That I have 'nointed an Athenian's eyes:

    And so far am I glad it so did sort,°

    As this their jangling I esteem a sport.

OBERON.   Thou seest these lovers seek a place to fight;

    Hie therefore Robin, overcast the night,   355

    The starry welkin° cover thou anon

---

    323 *keen and shrewd:* sharp and malicious.   **327** *flout:* mock.   **329** *minimus:* smallest of creatures. *knot-grass:* weed believed to stunt the growth if eaten.   **333** *intend:* extend.   **335** *aby it:* buy it dearly. **336–337** *try . . . Helena:* prove by fighting which of us has most right to Helena.   **339** *coil is long of:* turmoil is because of.   **344** *amazed:* confused.   **352** *sort:* turn out.   **356** *welkin:* sky.

With drooping fog as black as Acheron,°
And lead these testy° rivals so astray,
As° one come not within another's way.
Like to Lysander sometime frame thy tongue: 360
Then stir Demetrius up with bitter wrong:°
And sometime rail thou like Demetrius:
And from each other look thou lead them thus;
Till o'er their brows death-counterfeiting sleep
With leaden legs and batty wings doth creep: 365
Then crush this herb into Lysander's eye;
Whose liquor hath this virtuous° property,
To take from thence all error with his might,
And make his eyeballs roll with wonted° sight.
When they next wake, all this derision° 370
Shall seem a dream, and fruitless vision,
And back to Athens shall the lovers wend,
With league whose date° till death shall never end.
Whiles I in this affair do thee employ,
I'll to my queen and beg her Indian boy: 375
And then I will her charmèd eye release
From monster's view, and all things shall be peace.

PUCK.   My fairy lord, this must be done with haste,
For night's swift dragons cut the clouds full fast:
And yonder shines Aurora's harbinger,° 380
At whose approach, ghosts wand'ring here and there,
Troop home to churchyards: damnèd spirits all,
That in crossways° and floods° have burial,
Already to their wormy beds are gone:
For fear lest day should look their shames upon, 385
They wilfully themselves exile from light,
And must for aye consort° with black-browed night.

OBERON.   But we are spirits of another sort.
I with the morning's love have oft made sport,°
And like a forester, the groves may tread 390
Even till the eastern gate all fiery red,
Opening on Neptune, with fair blessèd beams,
Turns into yellow gold his salt green streams.
But notwithstanding, haste, make no delay:
We may effect this business yet ere day.   [Exit.] 395

PUCK.   Up and down, up and down,
I will lead them up and down.
I am feared in field and town.

---

357 *Acheron:* one of the four rivers in the underworld.   358 *testy:* irritable.   359 *As:* so that.
361 *wrong:* insult.   367 *virtuous:* potent.   369 *wonted:* (previously) accustomed.   370 *derision:* laughable
interlude.   373 *date:* term.   380 *Aurora's harbinger:* the morning star heralding Aurora, the dawn.
383 *crossways:* cross-roads, where suicides were buried.   *floods:* those who drowned.   387 *aye consort:*
ever associate.   389 *morning's . . . sport:* hunted with Cephalus (beloved of Aurora and himself devoted to
his wife Procris, whom he killed by accident; "sport" also = "amorous dalliance," and "love" = Aurora's
love for Oberon).

Goblin, lead them up and down.
Here comes one.   400

Enter LYSANDER.

LYSANDER.   Where art thou, proud Demetrius? Speak thou now.
PUCK.   Here villain, drawn° and ready. Where art thou?
LYSANDER.   I will be with thee straight.
PUCK.   Follow me then
    To plainer° ground.   [*Exit* LYSANDER.]

Enter DEMETRIUS.

DEMETRIUS.   Lysander, speak again.
    Thou runaway, thou coward, art thou fled?   405
    Speak: in some bush? Where dost thou hide thy head?
PUCK.   Thou coward, art thou bragging to the stars,
    Telling the bushes that thou look'st for wars,
    And wilt not come? Come recreant,° come thou child,
    I'll whip thee with a rod. He is defiled   410
    That draws a sword on thee.
DEMETRIUS.   Yea, art thou there?
PUCK.   Follow my voice: we'll try no manhood° here.   *Exeunt.*

[*Enter* LYSANDER.]

LYSANDER.   He goes before me and still dares me on:
    When I come where he calls, then he is gone
    The villain is much lighter-heeled than I;   415
    I followed fast: but faster he did fly,
    That fallen am I in dark uneven way,
    And here will rest me. [*Lie down.*] Come thou gentle day,
    For if but once thou show me thy grey light.
    I'll find Demetrius and revenge this spite.   [*Sleeps.*]   420

Enter PUCK *and* DEMETRIUS.

PUCK.   Ho, ho, ho! Coward, why com'st thou not?
DEMETRIUS.   Abide° me, if thou dar'st, for well I wot°
    Thou run'st before me, shifting every place,
    And dar'st not stand, nor look me in the face.
    Where art thou now?
PUCK.   Come hither: I am here.   425
DEMETRIUS.   Nay then thou mock'st me. Thou shalt buy this dear,°
    If ever I thy face by daylight see.
    Now go thy way. Faintness constraineth me
    To measure out my length on this cold bed.
    By day's approach look to be visited.   [*Lies down and sleeps.*]   430

Enter HELENA.

---

402 *drawn:* with sword drawn.   404 *plainer:* more level.   409 *recreant:* oath-breaker, coward.
412 *try no manhood:* test no valor.   422 *Abide:* wait for.   *wot:* know.   426 *buy this dear:* pay dearly
for this.

HELENA.   O weary night, O long and tedious night,
　　　　Abate° thy hours; shine comforts° from the east,
　　　　That I may back to Athens by daylight,
　　　　From these that my poor company detest:
　　　　And sleep, that sometimes shuts up sorrow's eye.　　　　　　　　435
　　　　Steal me awhile from mine own company.　　　　　　　　*Sleeps.*
PUCK.   Yet but three? Come one more,
　　　　Two of both kinds makes up four.
　　　　Here she comes, curst° and sad.
　　　　Cupid is a knavish lad,　　　　　　　　　　　　　　　　440
　　　　Thus to make poor females mad.

Enter HERMIA.

HERMIA.   Never so weary, never so in woe,
　　　　　Bedabbled with the dew, and torn with briers:
　　　　　I can no further crawl, no further go:
　　　　　My legs can keep no pace with my desires.　　　　　　　445
　　　　　Here will I rest me till the break of day.
　　　　　Heavens shield Lysander, if they mean a fray.　　　　*[Lies down and sleeps.]*
PUCK.   On the ground,
　　　　Sleep sound:
　　　　I'll apply　　　　　　　　　　　　　　　　　　　　450
　　　　To your eye,
　　　　Gentle lover, remedy.　　　　　*[Squeezes the love-juice on LYSANDER's eyelids.]*
　　　　When thou wak'st,
　　　　Thou tak'st
　　　　True delight　　　　　　　　　　　　　　　　　　455
　　　　In the sight
　　　　Of thy former lady's eye:
　　　　And the country proverb known,
　　　　That every man should take his own,
　　　　In your waking shall be shown.　　　　　　　　　　460
　　　　　Jack shall have Jill:
　　　　　Naught shall go ill:
　　　　The man shall have his mare again, and all shall be well.
　　　　　　　　　[Exit PUCK. The lovers remain asleep on stage.]

ACT 4

[Scene 1. The Wood]

Enter [TITANIA] QUEEN OF FAIRIES, and [BOTTOM] THE CLOWN, and FAIRIES, and the KING [OBERON] behind them [unseen].

TITANIA.   Come sit thee down upon this flow'ry bed,
　　　　　While I thy amiable° cheeks do coy,°
　　　　　And stick musk-roses in thy sleek smooth head,
　　　　　And kiss thy fair large ears, my gentle joy.

---

432 *Abate:* shorten. *shine comforts:* may strength, power shine. **439** *curst:* cross. **2** *amiable:* lovely. *coy:* caress.

BOTTOM. Where's Peaseblossom? 5

PEASEBLOSSOM. Ready.

BOTTOM. Scratch my head, Peaseblossom. Where's Mounsieur
Cobweb?

COBWEB. Ready.

BOTTOM. Mounsieur Cobweb, good mounsieur, get you your weapons 10
in your hand, and kill me a red-hipped humblebee on
the top of a thistle: and good mounsieur, bring me the
honey-bag. Do not fret yourself too much in the action,
mounsieur: and good mounsieur have a care the honey-
bag break not, I would be loath to have you overflowen 15
with a honey bag, signior. Where's Mounsieur
Mustardseed?

MUSTARDSEED. Ready.

BOTTOM. Give me your neaf,° Mounsieur Mustardseed. Pray you
leave your curtsy,° good mounsieur. 20

MUSTARDSEED. What's your will?

BOTTOM. Nothing, good mounsieur, but to help Cavalery° Cobweb
to scratch. I must to the barber's mounsieur, for
methinks I am marvellous hairy about the face. And I am
such a tender ass, if my hair do but tickle me, I must 25
scratch.

TITANIA. What, will thou hear some music, my sweet love?

BOTTOM. I have a reasonable good ear in music. Let's have the tongs°
and the bones.°

TITANIA. Or say, sweet love, what thou desirest to eat. 30

BOTTOM. Truly, a peck of provender. I could munch your good
dry oats. Methinks I have a great desire to a bottle° of hay.
Good hay, sweet hay, hath no fellow.

TITANIA. I have a venturous fairy that shall seek
The squirrel's hoard, and fetch thee new nuts. 35

BOTTOM. I had rather have a handful or two of dried pease. But
I pray you, let none of your people stir me: I have an
exposition of° sleep come upon me.

TITANIA. Sleep thou, and I will wind thee in my arms.
Fairies, be gone, and be all ways° away. [*Exeunt* FAIRIES.] 40
So doth the woodbine the sweet honeysuckle
Gently entwist: the female ivy so
Enrings the barky fingers of the elm.
O how I love thee! how I dote on thee! [*They sleep.*]

Enter ROBIN GOODFELLOW [PUCK.]

OBERON. [*Advances.*] Welcome good Robin. Seest thou this sweet sight? 45
Her dotage now I do begin to pity.
For meeting her of late behind the wood,

---

19 *neaf:* fist.   20 *leave your curtsy:* either (a) stop bowing, or (b) replace your hat.   22 *Cavalery:*
(he means "cavalier").   29 *tongs:* crude music made by striking tongs with a piece of metal.
bones: pieces of bone held between the fingers and clapped together rhythmically.   32 *bottle:* bundle.
38 *exposition of:* (he means "disposition to").   40 *all ways:* in every direction.

Seeking sweet favours° for this hateful fool,
I did upbraid her and fall out with her.
For she his hairy temples then had rounded   50
With coronet of fresh and fragrant flowers
And that same dew which sometime° on the buds
Was wont to° swell like round and orient° pearls,
Stood now within the pretty flowerets' eyes,
Like tears that did their own disgrace bewail.   55
When I had at my pleasure taunted her,
And she in mild terms begged my patience,
I then did ask of her her changeling child:
Which straight she gave me, and her fairy sent
To bear him to my bower in fairy land.   60
And now I have the boy, I will undo
This hateful imperfection of her eyes.
And gentle Puck, take this transformèd scalp
From off the head of this Athenian swain;
That he awaking when the other do,   65
May all to Athens back again repair,°
And think no more of this night's accidents,°
But as the fierce vexation of a dream.
But first I will release the Fairy Queen.
    Be as thou wast wont to be: 70
    See, as thou wast wont to see.
    Dian's bud o'er Cupid's flower°
    Hath such force and blessèd power.
Now my Titania, wake you, my sweet queen.
TITANIA. My Oberon, what visions have I seen!   75
    Methought I was enamoured of an ass.
OBERON. There lies your love.
TITANIA.   How came these things to pass?
    O, how mine eyes do loathe his visage now!
OBERON. Silence awhile Robin, take off this head:
    Titania, music call, and strike more dead   80
    Than common sleep of all these five the sense.°
TITANIA. Music, ho music! such as charmeth sleep.
PUCK. Now, when thou wak'st, with thine own fools' eyes peep.
OBERON. Sound music: *Music still.*°
    Come my queen, take hands with me,
    And rock the ground whereon these sleepers be.   [*Dance.*] 85
Now thou and I are new in amity,
And will tomorrow midnight solemnly
Dance in Duke Theseus' house triumphantly,°
And bless it to all fair prosperity.

48 *favours:* bouquets as love tokens. **52** *sometime:* formerly. **53** *Was wont to:* used to. *orient:* (where the most beautiful pearls came from). **66** *repair:* return. **67** *accidents:* incidents. **72** *Dian's bud . . . flower:* (Diana's bud counteracts the effects of love-in-idleness, the pansy). **80–81** *strike . . . sense:* Make these five (the lovers and Bottom) sleep more soundly. **84.1 S.D.:** *still:* continuously. **88** *triumphantly:* in celebration.

There shall the pairs of faithful lovers be　　　　　　　　　　90
　　　Wedded, with Theseus, all in jollity.
PUCK.　　Fairy King, attend and mark:
　　　I do hear the morning lark.
OBERON.　Then my queen, in silence sad,°
　　　Trip we after the night's shade:　　　　　　　　　　　95
　　　We the globe can compass soon,
　　　Swifter than the wand'ring moon.
TITANIA.　Come my lord, and in our flight,
　　　Tell me how it came this night,
　　　That I sleeping here was found,　　　　　　　　　　100
　　　With these mortals on the ground.　　　　　　*Exeunt.*

Wind° horns. Enter THESEUS, HIPPOLYTA, ECEUS *and all his train.*

THESEUS.　Go one of you, find out the forester:
　　　For now our observation° is performed.
　　　And since we have the vaward° of the day,
　　　My love shall hear the music of my hounds.　　　　　105
　　　Uncouple° in the western valley, let them go:
　　　Dispatch I say, and find the forester.　　　*[Exit an* ATTENDANT.*]*
　　　We will, fair queen, up to the mountain's top,
　　　And mark the musical confusion
　　　Of hounds and echo in conjunction.　　　　　　　　110
HIPPOLYTA.　I was with Hercules and Cadmus° once,
　　　When in a wood of Crete they bayed the bear,°
　　　With hounds of Sparta;° never did I hear
　　　Such gallant chiding. For besides the groves,
　　　The skies, the fountains, every region near　　　　　115
　　　Seemed all one mutual cry. I never heard
　　　So musical a discord, such sweet thunder.
THESEUS.　My hounds are bred out of the Spartan kind:
　　　So flewed, so sanded.° and their heads are hung
　　　With ears that sweep away the morning dew,　　　120
　　　Crook-kneed, and dewlapped° like Thessalian bulls:
　　　Slow in pursuit; but matched in mouth like bells,
　　　Each under each.° A cry° more tuneable
　　　Was never holloa'd to, nor cheered with horn,
　　　In Crete, in Sparta, nor in Thessaly.　　　　　　　125
　　　Judge when you hear. But soft.° What nymphs are these?
EGEUS.　My lord, this is my daughter here asleep,
　　　And this Lysander, this Demetrius is,
　　　This Helena, old Nedar's Helena.
　　　I wonder of their being here together.　　　　　　　130

---

94 *sad:* serious.　101.1 S.D.: *wind:* blow, sound.　103 *observation:* observance of the May Day rites. 104 *vaward:* vanguard, earliest part.　106 *Uncouple:* unleash (the dogs).　111 *Cadmus:* mythical builder of Thebes.　112 *bayed the bear:* brought the bear to bay, to its last stand.　113 *hounds of Sparta:* (a breed famous for their swiftness and quick scent).　119 *flewed, so sanded:* with hanging cheeks, so sand-colored.　121 *dewlapped:* with skin hanging from the chin.　122–123 *matched . . . each:* with each voice matched for harmony with the next in pitch, like bells in a chime.　123 *cry:* pack of dogs.　126 *soft:* wait.

THESEUS.　No doubt they rose up early to observe
　　The rite of May: and hearing our intent,
　　Came here in grace° of our solemnity.
　　But speak Egeus, is not this the day
　　That Hermia should give answer of her choice? 135
EGEUS.　It is, my lord.
THESEUS.　Go bid the huntsmen wake them with their horns.

Shout within: wind horns. They all start up.

　　Good morrow, friends. Saint Valentine is past.
　　Begin these wood-birds but to couple now?°
LYSANDER.　Pardon, my lord. 　　　　　　　　　　　　[*They kneel.*]
THESEUS.　　　　　　　　I pray you all, stand up. 140
　　I know you two are rival enemies.
　　How comes this gentle concord in the world,
　　That hatred is so far from jealousy,°
　　To sleep by hate° and fear no enmity?
LYSANDER.　My lord, I shall reply amazedly, 145
　　Half sleep, half waking. But as yet, I swear,
　　I cannot truly say how I came here.
　　But as I think—for truly would I speak,
　　And now I do bethink me, so it is—
　　I came with Hermia hither. Our intent 150
　　Was to be gone from Athens, where we might,
　　Without° the peril of the Athenian law—
EGEUS.　Enough, enough, my lord: you have enough.
　　I beg the law, the law upon his head:
　　They would have stol'n away, they would, Demetrius, 155
　　Thereby to have defeated you and me:
　　You of your wife, and me of my consent:
　　Of my consent that she should be your wife.
DEMETRIUS.　My lord, fair Helen told me of their stealth,
　　Of this their purpose hither, to this wood, 160
　　And I in fury hither followed them;
　　Fair Helena in fancy° following me.
　　But my good lord, I wot not by what power
　　(But by some power it is) my love to Hermia,
　　Melted as the snow, seems to me now 165
　　As the remembrance of an idle gaud,°
　　Which in my childhood I did dote upon:
　　And all the faith, the virtue of my heart,
　　The object and the pleasure of mine eye,
　　Is only Helena. To her, my lord, 170
　　Was I betrothed ere I saw Hermia:
　　But like a sickness,° did I loathe this food.

---

　　133 *grace:* honor.　**138–139** *Saint . . . now:* (birds traditionally chose their mates on St. Valentine's
Day).　**143** *jealousy:* suspicion.　**144** *hate:* one it hates.　**152** *Without:* beyond.　**162** *in fancy:* out of doting love.　**166** *idle gaud:* trifling toy.　**172** *sickness:* sick person.

But as in health, come° to my natural taste,
Now I do wish it, love it, long for it,
And will for evermore be true to it.

THESEUS.　Fair lovers, you are fortunately met. 175
Of this discourse we more will hear anon.
Egeus, I will overbear your will:
For in the temple, by and by,° with us,
These couples shall eternally be knit.
And for the morning now is something worn,° 180
Our purposed hunting shall be set aside.
Away with us to Athens. Three and three,
We'll hold a feast in great solemnity.
Come Hippolyta.

Exeunt DUKE [HIPPOLYTA, EGEUS] *and LORDS.* 185

DEMETRIUS.　These things seem small and undistinguishable,
Like far-off mountains turned into clouds.

HERMIA.　Methinks I see these things with parted° eye,
When everything seems double.

HELENA.　　　　　　　　So methinks:
And I have found Demetrius, like a jewel, 190
Mine own, and not mine own.°

DEMETRIUS.　　　　　　　Are you sure
That we are awake? It seems to me,
That yet we sleep, we dream. Do not you think
The duke was here, and bid us follow him?

HERMIA.　Yea, and my father.

HELENA.　　　　　　And Hippolyta. 195

LYSANDER.　And he did bid us follow to the temple.

DEMETRIUS.　Why then, we are awake: let's follow him,
And by the way let us recount our dreams.　*Exeunt Lovers.*

BOTTOM.　[*Wakes.*]　When my cue comes, call me, and I will answer.
My next is "Most fair Pyramus." Hey ho. Peter Quince? 200
Flute the bellows-mender? Snout the tinker? Starveling?
God's my life! Stol'n hence, and left me asleep? I have
had a most rare vision. I have had a dream, past the wit
of man to say what dream it was. Man is but an ass, if he
go about° to expound this dream. Methought I was— 205
there is no man can tell what. Methought I was, and
methought I had—but man is but a patched fool,° if he
will offer to say what methought I had. The eye of man
hath not heard, the ear of man hath not seen, man's hand is
not able to taste, his tongue to conceive, nor his 210
heart to report, what my dream was. I will get Peter
Quince to write a ballad of this dream: it shall be called
Bottom's Dream; because it hath no bottom: and I

---

173 *come:* i.e., back.　179 *by and by:* immediately.　181 *something worn:* somewhat worn on.
188 *parted:* divided (each eye seeing a separate image).　190–191 *like . . . own:* like a person who finds a
jewel: the finder is the owner, but insecurely so.　205 *go about:* attempt.　207 *patched fool:* fool dressed
in motley.

will sing it in the latter end of our play, before the duke.
Peradventure, to make it the more gracious, I shall sing   215
it at her° death.   *Exit.*

[Scene 2. Athens, Quince's house]

Enter QUINCE, FLUTE, SNOUT, and STARVELING.

QUINCE.   Have you sent to Bottom's house? Is he come home yet?
STARVELING.   He cannot be heard of. Out of doubt he is transported.°
FLUTE.   If he come not, then the play is marred. It goes not forward,
    doth it?
QUINCE.   It is not possible. You have not a man in all Athens able   5
    to discharge° Pyramus but he.
FLUTE.   No, he hath simply the best wit of any handicraft man in Athens.
QUINCE.   Yea, and the best person too, and he is a very paramour
    for a sweet voice.
FLUTE.   You must say "paragon." A paramour is (God bless us)   10
    a thing of naught.°

Enter SNUG THE JOINER.

SNUG.   Masters, the duke is coming from the temple, and there
    is two or three lords and ladies more married. If our
    sport had gone forward, we had all been made men.°
FLUTE.   O sweet bully Bottom. Thus hath he lost sixpence a day°   15
    during his life: he could not have 'scaped sixpence a day.
    And the duke had not given him sixpence a day for playing
    Pyramus, I'll be hanged. He would have deserved it.
    Sixpence a day in Pyramus, or nothing.

Enter BOTTOM.

BOTTOM.   Where are these lads? Where are these hearts?   20
QUINCE.   Bottom! O most courageous° day! O most happy hour!
BOTTOM.   Masters, I am to discourse wonders: but ask me not what.
    For if I tell you, I am not true Athenian. I will tell you
    everything, right as it fell out.
QUINCE.   Let us hear, sweet Bottom.   25
BOTTOM.   Not a word of me. All that I will tell you is, that the
    duke hath dined. Get your apparel together, good
    strings to your beards, new ribbands to your pumps, meet
    presently° at the palace, every man look o'er his part: for
    the short and the long is, our play is preferred.° In any   30
    case, let Thisby have clean linen: and let not him that
    plays the lion pare his nails, for they shall hang out for
    the lion's claws. And most dear actors, eat no onions nor
    garlic, for we are to utter sweet breath: and I do not
    doubt but to hear them say it is a sweet comedy. No more   35
    words: away, go away.   *Exeunt.*

---

    216 *her:* Thisby's.   **2** *transported:* carried away (by spirits).   **6** *discharge:* portray.   **11** *of naught:*
wicked, naughty.   **14** *made men:* men made rich.   **15** *sixpence a day:* i.e., as a pension   **21** *courageous:*
(he may mean "auspicious").   **29** *presently:* immediately.   **30** *preferred:* recommended (for presentation).

ACT 5

[Scene 1. The palace of Theseus]

Enter THESEUS, HIPPOLYTA, *and* PHILOSTRATE, *and his* LORDS.

HIPPOLYTA.   'Tis strange, my Theseus, that these lovers speak of.
THESEUS.   More strange than true. I never may believe
    These antick° fables, nor these fairy toys.°
    Lovers and madmen have such seething brains,
    Such shaping fantasies,° that apprehend   5
    More than cool reason ever comprehends.
    The lunatic, the lover, and the poet,
    Are of imagination all compact.°
    One sees more devils than vast hell can hold:
    That is the madman. The lover, all as frantic,   10
    Sees Helen's beauty in a brow of Egypt.°
    The poet's eye, in a fine frenzy rolling,
    Doth glance from heaven to earth, from earth to heaven.
    And as imagination bodies forth
    The forms of things unknown, the poet's pen   15
    Turns them to shapes, and gives to airy nothing,
    A local habitation and a name.
    Such tricks hath strong imagination,
    That if it would but apprehend some joy,
    It comprehends° some bringer of that joy.   20
    Or in the night, imagining some fear,
    How easy is a bush supposed a bear.
HIPPOLYTA.   But all the story of the night told over,
    And all their minds transfigured so together,
    More witnesseth than fancy's images,°   25
    And grows to something of great constancy:°
    But howsoever, strange and admirable.°

Enter LOVERS: LYSANDER, DEMETRIUS, HERMIA, *and* HELENA.

THESEUS.   Here come the lovers, full of joy and mirth.
    Joy, gentle friends, joy and fresh days of love
    Accompany your hearts.
LYSANDER.   More° than to us   30
    Wait in your royal walks, your board, your bed.
THESEUS.   Come now, what masques,° what dances shall we have,
    To wear away this long age of three hours
    Between our after-supper° and bed-time?
    Where is our usual manager of mirth?   35

---

     3 *antick:* fantastic. *fairy toys:* trivial fairy stories. 5 *fantasies:* imaginations. 8 *of . . . compact:* totally composed of imagination. 11 *a brow of Egypt:* the swarthy face of a gypsy (believed to come from Egypt). 20 *comprehends:* includes. 25 *More . . . images:* testifies that it is more than just imagination. 26 *constancy:* certainty. 27 *admirable:* to be wondered at. 30 *More:* even more (joy and love). 32, 40 *masques:* lavish courtly entertainments combining song and dance. 34 *after-supper:* late supper.

What revels are in hand? Is there no play,
To ease the anguish of a torturing hour?
Call Philostrate.
PHILOSTRATE.   Here, mighty Theseus.
THESEUS.   Say, what abridgment° have you for this evening?
What masque,° what music? How shall we beguile   40
The lazy time, if not with some delight?
PHILOSTRATE.   There is a brief° how many sports are ripe.°
Make choice of which your highness will see first.

[*Gives a paper.*]

THESEUS.   "The battle with the Centaurs, to be sung
By an Athenian eunuch to the harp."   45
We'll none of that. That have I told my love
In glory of my kinsman Hercules.
"The riot of the tipsy Bacchanals,
Tearing the Thracian singer in their rage."°
That is an old device: and it was played   50
When I from Thebes came last a conqueror.
"The thrice three Muses mourning for the death
Of Learning, late deceased in beggary."
That is some satire keen and critical,
Not sorting with° a nuptial ceremony.   55
"A tedious brief scene of young Pyramus
And his love Thisby; very tragical mirth."
Merry and tragical? Tedious and brief?
That is hot ice and wondrous strange snow.
How shall we find the concord of this discord?   60
PHILOSTRATE.   A play there is, my lord, some ten words long,
Which is as brief as I have known a play:
But by ten words, my lord, it is too long,
Which makes it tedious: for in all the play
There is not one word apt, one player fitted.°   65
And tragical, my noble lord, it is:
For Pyramus therein doth kill himself.
Which when I saw rehearsed, I must confess,
Made mine eyes water; but more merry tears
The passion of loud laughter never shed.   70
THESEUS.   What are they that do play it?
PHILOSTRATE.   Hard-handed men, that work in Athens here,
Which never laboured in their minds till now:
And now have toiled their unbreathed° memories
With this same play, against° your nuptial.   75

---

39 *abridgment:* either (a) diversion to make the hours seem shorter or (b) short entertainment.
40 *masque:* a light musical or non-musical drama, usually allegorical or mythological in subject, with many dances and panomime actions. Often the actors wore masks. 42 *brief:* list. *ripe:* ready. 48–49 *riot . . . rage:* (The singer Orpheus of Thrace was torn limb from limb by the Maenads, frenzied female priests of Bacchus). 55 *sorting with:* befitting. 65 *fitted:* (well) cast. 74 *unbreathed:* unpracticed, unexercised. 75 *against:* in preparation for.

THESEUS.   And we will hear it.
PHILOSTRATE.   No, my noble lord,
    It is not for you. I have heard it over,
    And it is nothing, nothing in the world;
    Unless you can find sport in their intents,
    Extremely stretched and conned° with cruel pain.   80
    To do your service.
THESEUS.   I will hear that play.
    For never anything can be amiss,
    When simpleness and duty tender° it.
    Go bring them in, and take your places, ladies.   [*Exit* PHILOSTRATE.]
HIPPOLYTA.   I love not to see wretchedness o'ercharged,°   85
    And duty in his service perishing.
THESEUS.   Why, gentle sweet, you shall see no such thing.
HIPPOLYTA.   He says they can do nothing in this kind.°
THESEUS.   The kinder we, to give them thanks for nothing.
    Our sport shall be to take what they mistake.   90
    And what poor duty cannot do, noble respect
    Takes it in might, not merit.°
    Where I have come, great clerks° have purposèd
    To greet me with premeditated welcomes;
    Where I have seen them shiver and look pale,   95
    Make periods in the midst of sentences,
    Throttle° their practised accent in their fears,
    And in conclusion dumbly have broke off,
    Not paying me a welcome. Trust me, sweet,
    Out of this silence yet I picked a welcome: 100
    And in the modesty of fearful duty°
    I read as much as from the rattling tongue
    Of saucy and audacious eloquence.
    Love, therefore, and tongue-tied simplicity,
    In° least, speak most, to my capacity.°   105

[*Enter* PHILOSTRATE.]

PHILOSTRATE.   So please your grace, the Prologue is addressed.°
THESEUS.   Let him approach.

Flourish trumpets. Enter the PROLOGUE [QUINCE].

PROLOGUE.   If we offend, it is with our good will.
    That you should think, we come not to offend,
    But with good will. To show our simple skill,   110
    That is the true beginning of our end.

---

80 *stretched and conned:* strained and memorized.   83 *tender:* offer.   85 *wretchedness
o'ercharged:* poor fellows taxing themselves too much.   88 *in this kind:* of this sort.   91–92 *noble . . .
merit:* a noble nature considers the sincerity of effort rather than the skill of execution.   93 *clerks:* scholars.   97 *Throttle:* choke on.   101 *fearful duty:* subjects whose devotions gave them stage fright.   105 *In:*
i.e., saying.   *capacity:* way of thinking.   106 *addressed:* ready.   108–117 *If . . . know:* (Quince's blunders in
punctuation exactly reverse the meaning).

Consider then, we come but in despite.°
We do not come, as minding to content you,
Our true intent is. All for your delight,
     We are not here. That you should here repent you,   115
The actors are at hand: and by their show,
You shall know all, that you are like to know.°
THESEUS.   This fellow doth not stand upon points.°
LYSANDER.   He hath rid his prologue like a rough colt: he knows
     not the stop.° A good moral my lord: it is not enough   120
     to speak; but to speak true.
HIPPOLYTA.   Indeed he hath played on his prologue like a child on a
     recorder:° a sound, but not in government.°
THESUS.   His speech was like a tangled chain: nothing impaired, but
     all disordered. Who is next?   125

Enter PYRAMUS and THISBY, WALL, MOONSHINE, and LION.

PROLOGUE.   Gentles, perchance you wonder at this show,
     But wonder on, till truth make all things plain.
This man is Pyramus, if you would know:
     This beauteous lady, Thisby is certain.
This man, with lime and rough-cast,° doth present   130
     Wall, that vile wall which did these lovers sunder:
And through Wall's chink, poor souls, they are content
     To whisper. At the which, let no man wonder.
This man, with lantern, dog, and bush of thorn,
     Presenteth Moonshine. For if you will know,   135
By moonshine did these lovers think no scorn
     To meet at Ninus' tomb, there, there to woo:
This grisly beast (which Lion hight° by name)
     The trusty Thisby, coming first by night,
Did scare away, or rather did affright: 140
     And as she fled, her mantle she did fall:°
Which Lion vile with bloody mouth did stain.
     Anon comes Pyramus, sweet youth and tall,°
And finds his trusty Thisby's mantle slain:
     Whereat, with blade, with bloody blameful blade,   145
He bravely broached° his boiling bloody breast.
     And Thisby, tarrying in mulberry shade,
His dagger drew, and died. For all the rest,
     Let Lion, Moonshine, Wall, and lovers twain.
At large° discourse, while here they do remain.   150
THESEUS.   I wonder if the lion be to speak.
DEMETRIUS.   No wonder, my lord: one lion may, when many asses do.
                    Exeunt [PROLOGUE, PYRAMUS,] LION, THISBY, MOONSHINE.

---

     112 *despite:* malice.   118 *stand upon points:* (1) pay attention to punctuation (2) bother about the
niceties (of expression).   120 *stop:* (1) halt (2) period.   123 *recorder:* flutelike wind instrument.   *in government:* well managed.   130 *rough-cast:* rough plaster made of lime and gravel.   138 *hight:* is called.
141 *fall:* let fall.   143 *tall:* brave.   146 *broached:* opened (Shakespeare parodies the overuse of alliteration
in the earlier bombastic Elizabethan plays).   150 *At large:* in full.

WALL.   In this same interlude° it doth befall
    That I, one Snout by name, present a wall:
    And such a wall, as I would have you think,   155
    That had in it a crannied hole or chink:
    Through which the lovers, Pyramus and Thisby,
    Did whisper often, very secretly.
    This loam, this rough-cast, and this stone doth show
    That I am that same wall: the truth is so.   160
    And this the cranny is, right and sinister,°
    Through which the fearful lovers are to whisper.
THESEUS.   Would you desire lime and hair to speak better?
DEMETRIUS.   It is the wittiest° partition° that ever I heard discourse,
    my lord.   165

Enter PYRAMUS.

THESEUS.   Pyramus draws near the wall: silence.
PYRAMUS.   O grim-looked night, O night with hue so black,
    O night, which ever art when day is not:
    O night, O night, alack, alack, alack,
    I fear my Thisby's promise is forgot.   170
    And thou O wall, O sweet, O lovely wall,
    That stand'st between her father's ground and mine,
    Thou wall, O wall, O sweet and lovely wall,
    Show me thy chink, to blink through with mine eyne.°
                      [*WALL holds up his fingers.*]
    Thanks, courteous wall. Jove shield thee well for this.   175
    But what see I? No Thisby do I see.
    O wicked wall, through whom I see no bliss,
    Cursed by thy stones for thus deceiving me.
THESEUS.   The wall methinks being sensible,° should curse again.°
PYRAMUS.   No in truth sir, he should not. "Deceiving me" is   180
    Thisby's cue: she is to enter now, and I am to spy her
    through the wall. You shall see it will fall pat° as I told you:
    yonder she comes.

Enter THISBY.

THISBY.   O wall, full often hast thou heard my moans,
    For parting my fair Pyramus and me.   185
    My cherry lips have often kissed thy stones;
    Thy stones with lime and hair knit up in thee.
PYRAMUS.   I see a voice: now will I to the chink,
    To spy and I can hear my Thisby's face.
    Thisby?   190

---

    153 *interlude:* short play.   **161** *right and sinister:* from right to left (he probably uses the fingers of his right and left hands to form the cranny).   **164** *wittiest:* most intelligent.   *partition:* (1) wall (2) section of a learned book or speech.   **174** *eyne:* eyes.   **179** *sensible:* capable of feelings and perception.   *again:* back.   **182** *pat:* exactly.

THISBY.   My love thou art, my love I think.
PYRAMUS.   Think what thou wilt, I am thy lover's grace:
          And, like Limander,° am I trusty still.
THISBY.   And I like Helen,° till the Fates me kill.
PYRAMUS.   Not Shafalus to Procrus,° was so true.   195
THISBY.   As Shafalus to Procrus, I to you.
PYRAMUS.   O kiss me through the hole of this vile wall.
THISBY.   I kiss the wall's hole, not your lips at all.
PYRAMUS.   Wilt thou at Ninny's° tomb meet me straightway?
THISBY.   Tide° life, tide death, I come without delay.   200

                                        [*Exeunt* PYRAMUS *and* THISBY.]

WALL.   Thus have I, Wall, my part dischargèd so;
         And being done, thus Wall away doth go.   *Exit.*
THESEUS.   Now is the mural° down between the two neighbours.
DEMETRIUS.   No remedy my lord, when walls are so wilful to hear
          without warning.°   205
HIPPOLYTA.   This is the silliest stuff that ever I heard.
THESEUS.   The best in this kind are but shadows.° and the worst are
          no worse, if imagination amend them.
HIPPOLYTA.   It must be your imagination then, and not theirs.
THESEUS.   If we imagine no worse of them than they of themselves,   210
          they may pass for excellent men. Here come two noble
          beasts in, a man and a lion.

Enter LION *and* MOONSHINE.

LION.   You ladies, you, whose gentle hearts do fear
         The smallest monstrous mouse that creeps on floor,
         May now perchance both quake and tremble here.   215
             When lion rough in wildest rage doth roar.
         Then know that I, as Snug the joiner am
         A lion fell,° nor else no lion's dam:°
         For if I should as lion come in strife
         Into this place, 'twere pity on my life.   220
THESEUS.   A very gentle beast, and of a good conscience.
DEMETRIUS.   The very best at a beast,° my lord, that e'er I saw.
LYSANDER.   This lion is a very fox for his valour.
THESEUS.   True: and a goose for his discretion.
DEMETRIUS.   Not so my lord: for his valour cannot carry his discretion,   225
          and the fox carries the goose.
THESEUS.   His discretion, I am sure, cannot carry his valour: for the
          goose carries not the fox. It is well: leave it to his discretion,
          and let us listen to the moon.
MOONSHINE.   This lanthorn° doth the hornèd moon present—   230

----

193 *Limander:* (he means "Leander").   194 *Helen:* (he means "Hero").   195 *Shafalus to Procrus:*
(he means "Cephalus" and "Procris" [see 3.2.389 n., p. 1527]).   199 *Ninny:* fool (he means "Ninus").
200 *Tide:* come, betide.   203 *mural:* wall.   205 *without warning:* either (a) without warning the parents
or (b) unexpectedly.   207 *in . . . shadows:* of this sort are only plays (or only actors).   218 *fell:* fierce.   *nor
. . . dam:* and not a lioness.   222 *best, beast:* (pronounced similarly).   230 *lanthorn:* lantern (once made
of horn).

DEMETRIUS.   He should have worn the horns on his head.°

THESEUS.   He is no crescent, and his horns are invisible within the circumference.

MOONSHINE.   This lanthorn doth the hornèd moon present,
Myself, the man i' th' moon do seem to be.   235

THESEUS.   This is the greatest error of all the rest; the man should be put into the lanthorn. How is it else the man i'th' moon?

DEMETRIUS.   He dares not come there for the candle; for you see, it is already in snuff.°   240

HIPPOLYTA.   I am aweary of this moon. Would he would change.

THESEUS.   It appears, by his small light of discretion, that he is in the wane: but yet in courtesy, in all reason, we must stay° the time.

LYSANDER.   Proceed, Moon.   245

MOONSHINE.   All that I have to say, is to tell you that the lanthorn is the moon, I the man i' th' moon, this thornbush my thornbush, and this dog my dog.

DEMETRIUS.   Why, all these should be in the lanthorn: for all these are in the moon. But silence: here comes Thisby.   250

Enter THISBY.

THISBY.   This is old Ninny's tomb. Where is my love?

LION.   Oh!   *The LION roars. THISBY runs off.*

DEMETRIUS.   Well roared, Lion.

THESEUS.   Well run, Thisby.

HIPPOLYTA.   Well shone, Moon. Truly, the moon shines with a good   255
grace.

[The LION shakes THISBY's mantle.]

THESEUS.   Well moused,° Lion.

DEMETRIUS.   And then came Pyramus.

Enter PYRAMUS. [Exit LION.]

LYSANDER.   And so the lion vanished.

PYRAMUS.   Sweet moon, I thank thee for thy sunny beams,   260
I thank thee, moon, for shining now so bright.
For by thy gracious, golden, glittering gleams,
I trust to take of truest Thisby sight.
But stay: O spite!
But mark, poor knight,   265
What dreadful dole° is here?
Eyes, do you see!
How can it be!
O dainty duck, O dear!
Thy mantle good,   270

230–231 *hornèd . . . head:* (referring to the cuckold or deceived husband, who supposedly grew horns).   240 *in snuff:* (1) in need of snuffing (having a long, burnt-out wick or snuff) (2) in a temper.   243 *stay:* await.   257 *moused:* shaken, as a cat shakes a mouse.   266 *dole:* grief.

What, stained with blood?
Approach, ye Furies° fell:
  O Fates!° come, come:
  Cut thread and thrum.°
  Quail,° crush, conclude, and quell.°   275
THESEUS. This passion, and the death of a dear friend, would go
  near to make a man look sad.
HIPPOLYTA. Beshrew° my heart, but I pity the man.
PYRAMUS. O wherefore Nature, didst thou lions frame?
  Since lion vile hath here deflowered my dear.   280
  Which is—no, no—which was the fairest dame
    That lived, that loved, that liked, that looked with cheer.
  Come tears, confound:
    Out sword, and wound
  The pap° of Pyramus: 285
    Ay, that left pap,
    Where heart doth hop. [*Stabs himself.*]
  Thus die, I, thus, thus, thus.
    Now am I dead,
    Now am I fled,   290
  My soul is in the sky.
  Tongue lose thy light,
    Moon° take thy flight,   [*Exit MOONSHINE.*]
  Now die, die, die, die, die.   [*Dies.*]
DEMETRIUS. No die,° but an ace° for him. For he is but one.   295
LYSANDER. Less than an ace, man. For he is dead, he is nothing.
THESEUS. With the help of a surgeon, he might yet recover, and
  prove an ass.
HIPPOLYTA. How chance Moonshine is gone before Thisby comes
  back and finds her lover?   300

Enter THISBY.

THESEUS. She will find him by starlight. Here she comes, and her
  passion ends the play.
HIPPOLYTA. Methinks she should not use a long one for such a
  Pyramus: I hope she will be brief.
DEMETRIUS. A mote will turn the balance, which Pyramus, which   305
  Thisby, is the better: he for a man. God warr'nt° us;
  she for a woman, God bless us.
LYSANDER. She hath spied him already with those sweet eyes.
DEMETRIUS. And thus she means,° videlicet°—
THISBY. Asleep my love?   310
    What, dead, my dove?

---

    272 *Furies:* classical spirits of the underworld who avenged murder. **273** *Fates:* three sisters who spun the thread of human destiny, which at will was cut with a shears. **274** *thrum:* fringelike end of the warp in weaving. **275** *Quail:* subdue. *quell:* kill. **278** *Beshrew:* curse (meant lightly). **285** *pap:* breast. **292–293** *Tongue . . . Moon:* (he reverses the two subjects). **295** *die:* (singular of "dice"). *ace:* a throw of one at dice. **306** *warr'nt:* warrant, protect. **309** *means:* laments. **309** *videlicet:* namely.

    O Pyramus, arise,
      Speak, speak. Quite dumb?
      Dead, dead? A tomb
    Must cover thy sweet eyes.   315
      These lily lips,
      This cherry nose,
    These yellow cowslip° cheeks,
      Are gone, are gone:
      Lovers, make moan: 320
    His eyes were green as leeks.
      O Sisters Three,°
      Come, come to me,
    With hands as pale as milk,
      Lay them in gore,   325
      Since you have shore
    With shears his thread of silk.
      Tongue, not a word:
      Come trusty sword,
    Come blade, my breast imbrue°   *[Stabs herself.]*   330
      And farewell friends:
      Thus Thisby ends:
    Adieu, adieu, adieu.   *[Dies.]*

THESEUS.   Moonshine and Lion are left to bury the dead.
DEMETRIUS.   Ay, and Wall too.   335
BOTTOM.   *[Starts up.]* No, I assure you, the wall is down that parted
    their fathers. Will it please you to see the Epilogue, or
    to hear a Bergomask° dance between two of our company?
THESEUS.   No epilogue, I pray you; for your play needs no excuse.
    Never excuse: for when the players are all dead, there   340
    need none to be blamed. Marry, if he that writ it had
    played Pyramus and hanged himself in Thisby's garter,
    it would have been a fine tragedy: and so it is truly, and
    very notably discharged. But come, your Bergomask:
    let your Epilogue alone.   *[A dance.]* 345
    The iron tongue° of midnight hath told° twelve.
    Lovers, to bed, 'tis almost fairy time.°
    I fear we shall outsleep the coming morn,
    As much as we this night have overwatched.
    This palpable gross° play hath well beguiled   350
    The heavy gait of night. Sweet friends, to bed.
    A fortnight hold we this solemnity,
    In nightly revels, and new jollity.   *Exeunt.*

Enter PUCK *[with a broom].*

---

   318 *cowslip:* yellow primrose.   **322** *Sisters Three:* the Fates.   **330** *imbrue:* stain with gore.
338 *Bergomask:* exaggerated country dance.   **346** *iron tongue:* i.e., of the bell.   **346** *told:* counted, tolled.
347 *fairy time:* (from midnight to daybreak).   **350** *palpable gross:* obvious and crude.

PUCK.   Now the hungry lion roars,
                And the wolf behowls the moon;   355
          Whilst the heavy° ploughman snores,
                All with weary task fordone.°
          Now the wasted brands° do glow,
          Whilst the screech-owl, screeching loud,
                Puts the wretch that lies in woe°   360
          In remembrance of a shroud.
                Now it is the time of night,
          That the graves, all gaping wide,
                Every one lets forth his sprite,°
          In the church-way paths to glide.   365
                And we fairies, that do run
          By the triple Hecate's° team,°
                From the presence of the sun,
          Following darkness like a dream,
                Now are frolic:° not a mouse   370
          Shall disturb this hallowed house.
          I am sent with broom before,
          To sweep the dust° behind° the door.

Enter KING and QUEEN OF FAIRIES, with all their train.

OBERON.   Through the house give glimmering light,
                By the dead and drowsy fire,   375
          Every elf and fairy sprite,
                Hop as light as bird from brier,
          And this ditty after me,
                Sing, and dance it trippingly.
TITANIA.   First rehearse your song by rote,   380
          To each word a warbling note.
          Hand in hand, with fairy grace,
          Will we sing and bless this place.   *[Song and dance.]*
OBERON.   Now, until the break of day,
          Through this house each fairy stray.   385
          To the best bride-bed will we,
          Which by us shall blessèd be:
          And the issue° there create,°
          Ever shall be fortunate:
          So shall all the couples three   390
          Ever true in loving be:
          And the blots of Nature's hand°
          Shall not in their issue° stand.
          Never mole, harelip, nor scar,

---

356 *heavy:* sleepy.   357 *fordone:* worn out, "done in."   358 *wasted brands:* burnt logs.
360 *wretch. . .woe:* sick person.   364 *sprite:* spirit, ghost.   367 *triple Hecate:* the moon goddess, identified
as Cynthia in heaven, Diana on earth, and Hecate in hell.   *team:* dragons that pull the chariot of the night
moon.   370 *frolic:* frolicsome.   373 *To sweep the dust:* (Puck often helped with household chores).
behind: from behind.   388, 393 *issue:* children.   388 *create:* created.   392 *blots . . . hand:* birth defects.

Nor mark prodigious,° such as are   395
Despisèd in nativity,
Shall upon their children be.
With this field-dew consecrate.
Every fairy take his gait,°
And each several° chamber bless,   400
Through this palace, with sweet peace;
And the owner of its blest,
Ever shall in safety rest.
Trip away: make no stay: *Exeunt* [*all but* PUCK].
Meet me all by break of day.   405

PUCK. If we shadows have offended,
Think but this, and all is mended,
That you have but slumbered here,
While these visions did appear.
And this weak and idle° theme,   410
No more yielding but° a dream,
Gentles, do not reprehend.
If you pardon, we will mend.°
And as I am an honest Puck,
If we have unearnèd luck,   415
Now to scape the serpent's tongue,°
We will make amends, ere long:
Else the Puck a liar call.
So, good night unto you all.
Give me your hands,° if we be friends;   420
And Robin shall restore amends.°   [*Exit.*]

QUESTIONS

Act 1

1. Describe the relationship between Theseus and Hippolyta. What does each of
    them represent? How does Shakespeare show us that they have different atti-
    tudes toward their marriage?

2. Characterize Hermia and Lysander. What blocks their relationship? How do they
    plan to circumvent these obstructions?

3. What are Helena's feelings about herself? About Hermia? About Demetrius?
    How might you account for her self-image?

4. Why have the mechanicals gathered at Quince's house? How does Shakespeare
    show us that Bottom is eager, ill-educated, energetic, and funny?

Act 2

5. What is Puck's job? What do you find out about his personality, habits, and pas-
    times in his first conversation?

---

395 *mark prodigious:* unnatural birthmark.   **399** *take his gait:* proceed.   **400** *several:* separate.
410 *idle:* foolish.   **411** *No . . . but:* yielding nothing more than.   **413** *mend:* improve.   **416** *serpent's tongue:* hissing of the audience.   **420** *hands:* applause.   **421** *restore amends:* do better in the future.

6. Why are Titania and Oberon fighting with each other, and what are the specific consequences of their conflict?

7. What does Oberon plan to do to Titania? Why? What is "love-in-idleness"? What power does it have? What does it symbolize?

8. Why are Demetrius and Helena in the woods? What does Oberon decide to do to them? What error occurs? What happens to Lysander when Helena awakens him?

Act 3

9. How and why does Puck change Bottom? How is this transformation appropriate? What happens when Bottom awakens Titania? Why?

10. What does Oberon decide to do when he realizes that Puck has made a mistake? What is Puck's attitude toward the confusion he has created?

11. What happens when Helena awakens Demetrius? How does this situation reverse the one that began the play? Explain Helena's reaction to the behavior of Demetrius and Lysander.

12. What real dangers (tragic potential) do the lovers face in Act 3? How do Oberon and Puck deal with these dangers? What is their plan? How successful is it?

Act 4

13. Why does Oberon cure Titania of her infatuation with Bottom? How does the relationship between Oberon and Titania change? How is this change symbolized? Why is it significant?

14. How are the relationships among the four lovers straightened out? How does each explain his or her feelings? What does Theseus decide about the couples? Why is this significant?

15. What momentous event occurs offstage and is briefly reported in Act 5, scene 2?

Act 5

16. Describe Pyramus and Thisby. What blocks their relationship? How do they plan to circumvent these obstructions? What happens to them?

17. What is the significance of the fairy masque (a combination of poetry, music, dance, and drama) that ends the play?

18. What does Puck's epilogue suggest about you as a reader or spectator? How does it reinforce the connections among dreaming, imagination, illusion, and drama?

GENERAL QUESTIONS

1. To what extent are the characters in this play conventional and representative types? What is the effect of Shakespeare's style of characterization?

2. Are any of the characters symbolic? If so, what do they symbolize? How does such symbolism reinforce the themes of the play?

3. How does Shakespeare employ language, imagery, and poetic form to define the characters in this play and differentiate among the various groups of characters?

4. To what extent do the two settings—city and woods—structure the play? Where does exposition occur? Complication and catastrophe? The comic resolution? How complete is the resolution? Why is the round-trip journey from one setting to the other necessary for the lovers? The rulers? The "hempen homespuns"?

5. What are the similarities or parallels in plot and theme between *A Midsummer Night's Dream* and "Pyramus and Thisby"? To what degree are they versions of the same play with different endings? Why do you think Shakespeare included the play-within-the-play in *A Midsummer Night's Dream*?

6. In the first soliloquy of the play, Helena discusses love. What kind of love is she talking about? What are its qualities and characteristics? How far do the relationships in the play bear out her ideas about love?

7. How well do the mechanicals understand the nature of dramatic illusion? What sorts of production problems concern them? How do they solve these?

8. What ideas about drama and the ways in which audiences respond to it does *A Midsummer Night's Dream* explore?

9. Compare the play-within-a-play in *A Midsummer Night's Dream* to the one in Act 3 of *Hamlet*. How are the internal plays and situations similar? Different? What parallels do you see in the connections between each play-within-a-play and the larger play in which each occurs?

THE THEATER OF MOLIÈRE

The seventeenth century was the golden age of French neoclassical theater (called *neo* or "new" because it marked the reintroduction of Greek and Latin models). The dominant political figure of the age was the "Sun King," Louis XIV, the absolute monarch of France. He and his court—a set of nobles, wits, would-be wits, and ladies- and gentlemen-in-waiting—dictated fashion to the world at large and made Paris the cultural center of Europe.

The members of this ruling class profoundly influenced the drama of the age because they were the theater's patrons and protectors. Writers of tragedy, the two most important of whom were Pierre Corneille (1606–1684) and Jean Racine (1639–1699), complimented the understanding and sympathy of the nobility by creating serious poetic dramas for them. More daring and risky was the role of the writers of comedy, who populated the stage with characters derived not so much from the nobility as from the middle classes, often mocking their appearance, customs, and tastes. The most important of the comic writers, the acknowledged master of comedy, was Molière, the pen name of Jean Baptiste Poquelin. While a young man, he joined a company of actors called the Illustrious Theater, who established themselves in a playhouse, produced a tragedy, and then went bankrupt. The acting company spent the next thirteen years touring the provinces of France, performing *commedia dell'arte* farces and short comic plays, many of them by Molière. These years gave him his real education in the theater. He soon developed into a superb actor, director, and—more important—writer.

Although the years in the provinces were not easy, the company was achieving recognition. The group returned to Paris in 1658 at the invitation of

Molière in the character of Sganarelle

King Louis XIV. The king was pleased with Molière's comedies and publicly provided support and protection. He also gave the company the authorization to use the *Théâtre de Petit Bourbon* at Versailles. In 1659, when the *Théâtre* was torn down, Louis provided a royal patent to use the *Palais Royale* in Paris. With the king's support, Molière spent the rest of his career at this theater as an actor, director, manager, and playwright.

Despite numerous adversities in his life, his creative output was great. He wrote twenty-nine plays, ranging from broad farce to satirical comedies of manners. He observed the theatrical conventions of his age, and he drew his plots from Roman comedy, Italian *commedia dell'arte,* and French farce, all of which schooled him in comic character, tempo, and situation. His inspirations were the manners, morals, and customs of the French gentry and middle class.

Molière was also innovative as a dramatist. He elevated comedy to the seriousness of tragedy, as in his satiric comedies *The Ridiculous Dilettantes (Les Précieuses Ridicules,* 1659), *The Misanthrope* (1666), *The Miser* (1668), and *Tartuffe* (1669). What is new in these serious comedies is Molière's thoughtful and detached perspective on vices and follies. His mainspring is character, and his norm is moderation in all forms of behavior. From this point of balance, his plots mock

and expose religious posturing, personal greed, social snobbery, and professional hypocrisy. In short, whatever is excessive is the subject of his satiric thrusts.

The *Théâtre Royale*, the Paris theater in which most of Molière's plays were
produced, was patterned on Italian theater design of the early seventeenth century—a design that by and large has dominated theater architecture up to the
present. The building was rectangular, with a proscenium stage at one end and
seating in the approximate shape of a horseshoe—orchestra and balcony—for
as many as six hundred spectators at the other end and both sides. Also at the
sides were galleries or private boxes. There may have been space in front of the
stage for special dances and ballets. A major innovation in design was the use of
footlights and large chandeliers, which were essential for indoor performances.
Either candles or oil lamps provided the light, and there was a constant need for
attentive stagehands and candle snuffers to forestall accidental fires.

The stage scenery could be lavish, but for economy much of it was probably used in the productions of many separate plays. Molière apparently favored
sparse sets and only minimal stage properties. The actors and actresses (women
were never excluded from the French stage) wore contemporary costumes. This
convention made Molière's satires all the more effective. Since his performers
were costumed like the social types being pictured and mocked, the comedies
became images of the social scenes inhabited by his audiences.

MOLIÈRE, *LOVE IS THE DOCTOR (L'AMOUR MÉDECIN)*

*Born in 1622, Molière received a Jesuit education and took up the study of law at Orléans. His
favorite reading, however, was not law, but rather the six surviving comedies of the Roman
dramatist Terence.[5] In 1643 he shocked his family by abandoning both the law and his father's
prosperous upholstering business and going into the theater, a career that was considered scandalous and sinful.*

*At the age of forty he began an unhappy marriage with Armande Béjart, the twenty-year-old
daughter (or sister) of his former mistress Madeleine Béjart (his enemies whispered that Armande was also his daughter). He endured constant ill health, but he was a fighter. He performed even on the day he died, collapsing onstage in 1673 while acting the lead role in his*
The Imaginary Invalid *and dying several hours later. Because of the suddenness of his death
he was not given last rites, and he was denied burial in consecrated ground.*

Love Is the Doctor (*L'Amour Médecin*) was first performed in 1665 at the palace of
Louis XIV at Versailles, where the king himself sometimes joined Molière's casts to indulge his own acting fantasies and to win applause from his courtiers. The play is typical of
Molière's comic farces, relying heavily on pantomime, dance, and music in the *commedia
dell'arte* tradition. The incidental music by Jean Baptiste Lully (1632–1687), who provided
music for many other Molière plays, has survived and is available in a modern recording.

The central character in *Love Is the Doctor*, Sganarelle, appears with the same name
in other Molière comedies, also in the tradition of the *commedia dell'arte*. Usually
Sganarelle tries to beat others, but as often as not he is beaten himself, and therefore he
is both the cause and the butt of laughter. His function in *Love Is the Doctor* is typical: He
is a wealthy businessman and a traditional paterfamilias, with the final word in family

---

[5]See pp. 1486–87 for a brief discussion of the Roman dramatists.

matters (like Egeus in *A Midsummer Night's Dream* and Polonius in *Hamlet*). He closely guards his daughter, Lucinda, from suitors to avoid having to pay a massive dowry to a son-in-law who, as he complains, might be a perfect stranger.

The plan by Lucinda and her suitor Clitander to marry despite Sganarelle's opposition is an example of the traditional intrigue plot, in which the father (or guardian), acting as blocking agent, chooses another man for the young woman, or, as in *Love Is the Doctor,* tries to prevent marriage entirely.[6] The *soubrette* in the play, who aids and abets the intrigue, is Lisette. Although in some intrigue plots the blocker is reconciled by the fact that the young man is independently rich, that does not happen in this play, for at the end Sganarelle is frustrated and outraged despite the surrounding merriment.

Molière's notable addition to the intrigue plot in *Love Is the Doctor* is his satiric treatment of doctors. Medical practice in the seventeenth century was based on the widely held theory that a healthy body contained a harmonious balance of the four bodily fluids or "humors"—blood, yellow bile, black bile, and phlegm. When one of the humors became excessive or "putrid," the imbalance made the patient sick. Illness, including mental illness, could also be caused by the *adust,* or burning, of a particular humor during a high fever. (The understanding of bacterial and viral causes of disease did not develop until two centuries after Molière.) When doctors made a diagnosis based on this system, their treatment was to purge the offending humor and its noxious pressures (as the doctors recommend for Lucinda many times in *Love Is the Doctor*). Depending on the humor, they employed one of four methods of purgation: (1) a lancing or "bleeding" to draw off blood, or "sanguine" (the most common purgation, but the patient, weakened by blood loss, would often die more speedily from the original disease); (2) an emetic to eliminate yellow bile, or "choler," through vomiting; (3) a laxative to purge black bile, or "melancholy"; and (4) various irritating (and sometimes poisonous) powders to eliminate "phlegm" through violent sneezing.

With such principles and treatments, doctors were open targets for satire, and *Love Is the Doctor* holds nothing back. Once Lisette reports Lucinda's illness, the play is invaded by Molière's cadre of funny physicians, who, like their real-life counterparts, were bearded men who dressed in black robes and hats. Molière satirizes his doctors on the grounds of cronyism, indifference to the condition of patients, pomposity, exploitation of gullibility, ignorance and indecision, resistance to innovation, and simple greed.

Despite the severity of his satire, however, Molière also presents the doctors in a comic-farcical light. Both when they are summoned and when they are paid, for example, they perform dances and pantomimes. Even the blatant self-exposure of Dr. Fillpocket (Filerin) can be construed as the excess one expects of farce, and therefore honest medical practitioners in Molière's day could have claimed that the doctors in *Love Is the Doctor* represented the exception, not the rule.

Although the following version of *L'Amour Médecin* follows Molière's text faithfully, I have taken latitude in a few instances to emphasize his sharp comic intentions. For example, his introduction of the quack elixir "Orviétan" in Act 2, scene 6, requires explanation, which I have included as part of the dramatic text in preference to creating an extensive footnote. Because the names of the doctors are not particularly meaningful, I have given them "tag names" that I hope will be readily appreciated by today's readers. Thus Drs. Tomès, De Fonandrès, Macroton, Bahays, and Filerin are, respectively, Slicer, De Pits, Gouger, Golfer, and Fillpocket. Generally, the medical recommendations of these doctors cannot be translated into modern terms. Readers will therefore need to rely on the brief description given here about medical practice in Molière's day. Alert

---

[6]The origin and nature of intrigue plots are more fully described on pp. 1487 and 1490–91.

readers may notice some anachronisms and inconsistencies, such as the use of the words *pathological* and *psychosomatic*; these are not inadvertent, but are made in the hope that they are consistent with the comic spirit of Molière.

MOLIÈRE (JEAN BAPTISTE POQUELIN) (1622–1673)

Love Is the Doctor (L'Amour Médecin) ⚬⚬⚬⚬ 1665

Translated by Edgar V. Roberts

CHARACTERS

> Sganarelle, *a wealthy Parisian merchant, father of* Lucinda
> Aminta, *his neighbor*
> Lucretia, *his niece*
> Mr. Williams, *his friend, a seller of tapestries*
> Mr. Josse, *another friend, a jeweller*
> Lucinda, *daughter of Sganarelle, in love with* Clitander
> Lisette, *maid to Lucinda, a soubrette*
> Champagne, *an assistant to Sganarelle, a dancer*
> Dr. Slicer [Tomès] ⎫
> Dr. De Pits [De Fonandrès] ⎪
> Dr. Gouger [Macroton] ⎬ *doctors*
> Dr. Golfer [Bahays] ⎪
> Dr. Fillpocket [Filerin] ⎭
> Clitander, *in love with Lucinda*
> A Justice
> A Mountebank, *a quack, seller of the cure-all "Orviétan"*
> Buffoons and Scaramouches, *assistants to the Mountebank*
> The Spirit of Comedy
> Musicians
> Singers
> Dancers
> Servants, etc.

The action takes place in Paris, in the house and drawing room of SGANARELLE [*and also on a street in Paris*].

ACT 1

Scene I

Enter SGANARELLE, AMINTA, LUCRETIA, MR. WILLIAMS, *and* MR. JOSSE.

SGANARELLE.   Life is strange. I agree with that great classical philosopher who said that those who have wealth also have woe,° and that misery breeds more misery. I've been married only once, and my wife is now dead.

MR. WILLIAMS.   How many wives would you have liked?

---

1 *woe:* Ecclesiastes 2:9–11.

SGANARELLE.   Don't mock, Mr. Williams; my loss is great, and I'm still sad when I think about her. I never liked her lifestyle, and we argued a great deal, but Death, as they say, settles everything. She's dead and I'm sorry, but if she were alive we would still be fighting. Of all the children that Heaven blessed us with, only my daughter has survived, but she is my greatest sorrow because she is sad beyond belief—in a deep depression I can't get her out of. Beyond that, she won't tell me what's wrong. I'm almost beside myself, and I need your good advice. You [*to LUCRETIA*] are my niece. You [*to AMINTA*] are my neighbor. You [*to MR. WILLIAMS and MR. JOSSE*] are my friends and equals. What should I do?

MR. JOSSE.   I believe that jewelry is what young women like best, and if I were you I would buy her some nice necklaces, brooches, or rings set with expensive diamonds, rubies, and emeralds.

MR. WILLIAMS.   If I were in your position, I'd get her an elegant tapestry showing a   5
landscape or historical scene. The sight of something like that in her room would pick up both her vision and her spirits.

AMINTA.   If you ask me, I wouldn't do anything of the sort. Rather, I'd get her married off as soon as possible—maybe to the man who, they say, asked you for her hand some time ago.

LUCRETIA.   I don't agree. She's not ready for marriage, and she's not strong enough to bear children. For her, having babies would be a quick way to go six feet under. She's too good for this world, and I think you should send her off to a convent, where she'll be able to do things to suit her special personality.

SGANARELLE.   I appreciate your thoughts, but they seem more to your interests than mine. You are a jeweler, Mr. Josse, and your advice would probably make you a handsome profit. You, Mr. Williams, have a tapestry shop, and I think you're trying to get rid of a little excess inventory. I've heard that your boyfriend, neighbor Aminta, is carrying a torch for my daughter, and you'd therefore like to have her married off and out of circulation. And as for you, my dear niece, you know that I have no plans to consent to a marriage for my daughter—I've got my reasons—but your advice to send her to religious orders suggests that you wouldn't mind becoming the only heir to all my money. So, ladies and gentlemen, your advice is perhaps the best in the world, but, if you please, I want none of it. Please go.

[*They leave, grumbling to themselves. SGANARELLE then speaks sarcastically to the audience.*]

There you have modern, up-to-date friends, who give their impersonal advice with no hope of gain whatever.

Act 1, Scene 2

He remains. Enter LUCINDA.

SGANARELLE.   [*Aside.*] That's my daughter taking a walk for exercise. She doesn't see me; she's sighing. Now she's raising her eyes to Heaven. [*To LUCINDA.*] Bless you, Lucinda. What's the matter? Why so sad and sorrowful? Why don't you tell me what's wrong? You can trust your dear old dad, so tell me what's on your mind. Don't worry. Give me a kiss, like a good little girl. [*Aside.*] I can't stand seeing her like this. [*To LUCINDA.*] Do you want me to die with unhappiness because of you? Won't you tell me what's troubling you? Tell me what's wrong and I'll do anything for you, I promise. Just tell me what's making you sad, because I swear on a stack of Bibles that there's nothing I won't do to make you happy. Tell me what you want. Are you jealous of any friends because they seem better dressed? I'll get you clothes that will make theirs seem like rags.—No? Does your room seem bare? I'll let you pick out the best furniture to be found anywhere.—No again? Well, maybe you want to learn music; I'll get you the best piano teacher there is.—Not that either? Maybe you're in love, and would like to be married. [*LUCINDA nods her head in agreement.*]

Act 1, Scene 3

They remain. Enter LISETTE.

LISETTE. Sir, you've just been chatting with your daughter. Did she tell you what's wrong?

SGANARELLE. No, she's being bitchy and it's making me mad.

LISETTE. Let me try; I'll sound her out a little.

SGANARELLE. It won't work. Since she's so stubborn, let her alone.

LISETTE. Just let me try. She may be more open with me than you. [*To LUCINDA.* 5 *During LISETTE'S speech, which SGANARELLE also overhears, he gets increasingly irritated with his daughter.*] Now, Madam, let us know what's wrong; don't keep on like this and upset everybody. It seems to me that something really mysterious is bothering you, and if you won't tell your father, maybe you'll tell me. Do you want anything from him? You know that he'll spare no expense for you. Do you want him to give you more freedom? More promenades in the park? More presents to tempt your fancy?—No? Maybe you're angry with someone, then.—No? Well then, maybe you have a secret wish to get married, and you'd like your father's consent. [*LUCINDA nods enthusiastically.*]—Ah, that's it; why all the secrecy? Sir, the mystery is solved, and—

SGANARELLE. [*Interrupting her.*] Get away, you ingrate; I won't talk to you any more. Be as stubborn as you like.

LUCINDA. Father, since you want me to tell you—

SGANARELLE. No, I'm finished with you.

LISETTE. Sir, her sadness—

SGANARELLE. She's a hussy, and enjoys hurting me. 10

LUCINDA. Father, I want—

SGANARELLE. Is this the gratitude I get for bringing you up so well?

LISETTE. But, sir—

SGANARELLE. No, I'm so mad I may have a stroke.

LUCINDA. But, Father— 15

SGANARELLE. I no longer have a speck of kindness for you.

LISETTE. But—

SGANARELLE. She's a cheap wench.

LISETTE. But—

SGANARELLE. An ungrateful slut. 20

LISETTE. But—

SGANARELLE. A trollop, who won't tell me what's wrong with her.

LISETTE. It's a husband that she wants!

SGANARELLE. [*Hearing but deliberately ignoring this piece of information.*] I'll turn her out of my house.

LISETTE. A husband! 25

SGANARELLE. I detest her.

LISETTE. [*Shouting increasingly more loudly.*] A husband!

SGANARELLE. And I disown her as my daughter.

LISETTE. A husband!

SGANARELLE. No, don't talk to me about it. 30

LISETTE. A husband!

SGANARELLE. Don't talk to me about it.

LISETTE. A husband!

SGANARELLE.   Don't talk to me about it.
LISETTE.   A husband, a husband, a husband!   35

[SGANARELLE stalks off.]

Act 1, Scene 4

LISETTE and LUCINDA remain.

LISETTE.   It's really true that none are so deaf as those who refuse to hear.
LUCINDA.   [*Ironically.*] Well, Lisette, you see how wrong I was to hide my feelings, and how all I had to do was to tell my father about everything I wanted.
LISETTE.   My God, he's a hard man. I swear, I'd enjoy playing some kind of trick on him to show him up. But why, Madam, did you hide your wishes from me?
LUCINDA.   Alas, what would I have gained? I might just as well have kept the secret for the rest of my life. Do you think I didn't foresee what he would do? I know his temper, and I'm in despair about the refusal he gave to the envoy sent to him to propose marriage to me. I've lost hope.
LISETTE.   [*As though recalling a forgotten incident.*] What's this? It's that stranger who   5
arranged for the proposal, the one for whom you—
LUCINDA.   Perhaps it's not right for me to speak so freely, but I confess, if I had the liberty to choose, he's the one I'd want. We've never spoken together; he's never been able to tell me he loves me. But, in all the places where he's seen me, his looks and gestures have indicated such tenderness, and his formal request for my hand has given me such a sense of his honor, that I can't help believing he loves me. No matter; you see how my father's reaction has hardened all this tenderness.
LISETTE.   Well, I have to say, I think you shouldn't have kept things secret from me, but I'll still help you. You need to be certain of your determination—
LUCINDA.   But what should I do against my father's authority?—And if he won't listen to my hopes—
LISETTE.   Come on now, you can't let yourself be led around like a sheep. As long as you don't offend his honor, you can free yourself at least a little from him. What does he want with you? You're of age, and you're not made of stone. I say again I'll help you in this affair. Your interests are mine, and, you'll see, I know a thing or two—But I see your father; let's go in. Leave everything to me.

[They hurry off.]

Act 1, Scene 5

Enter SGANARELLE.

SGANARELLE.   [*Laughing to himself.*] It's sometimes good to seem not to hear things you hear only too well. I was smart to sidestep that declaration of her hopes that I do not mean to satisfy. Is there anything more tyrannical than that custom by which marriage arrangements make paupers out of fathers?—Anything more futile and ridiculous than to spend your life grubbing and grabbing to get rich, and raising a daughter with care and love, only to be robbed of both of them at the hands of a total stranger, a nobody? No, no, I don't give a damn for that custom, and I'll keep my wealth and my daughter to myself.

Act 1, Scene 6

He remains. Enter LISETTE.

LISETTE.   [*Pretending not to see SGANARELLE.*]—Oh unhappiness! Oh disgrace! Oh, poor Mr. Sganarelle! Where can I find him?

SGANARELLE.   [*Aside.*] What's all this?

LISETTE.   Oh unhappy father, what will you do when you learn about this?

SGANARELLE.   [*Aside.*] What's going on?

LISETTE.   My poor mistress!   5

SGANARELLE.   [*Aside.*] I'm lost!

LISETTE.   —Oh!

SGANARELLE.   [*Running after LISETTE.*] Lisette!

LISETTE.   [*Pretending not to hear him, but making sure he hears her.*] What a misfortune!

SGANARELLE.   —Lisette!   10

LISETTE.   [*Still pretending.*] What bad luck!

SGANARELLE.   —Lisette!

LISETTE.   [*Pretending yet.*] How ghastly awful!

SGANARELLE.   —Lisette!

LISETTE.   [*Pretending just now to have noticed him.*] Ah, Sir.   15

SGANARELLE.   What's going on? What's wrong?

LISETTE.   Sir, your daughter—

SGANARELLE.   Oh, no!

LISETTE.   Sir, sir, don't cry like that. [*Aside.*] You'll make me laugh if you keep on.

SGANARELLE.   Tell me quickly.   20

LISETTE.   You daughter was hurt by your words and scared by your anger. [*Dramatizing and exaggerating her following descriptions to the utmost.*] She went to her room and, in despair, she opened the window facing the river—

SGANARELLE.   Oh, my God, no!

LISETTE.   Then, raising her head heavenward, she said, "No, it's impossible for me to live with the anger of my father, and since he is disowning me, I want to die!"

SGANARELLE.   She threw herself out?

LISETTE.   No sir. She sorrowfully closed the window, and threw herself on her bed,   25
where she wept bitterly. Suddenly, her face got pale, her eyes rolled in her head, her heart seemed to stop, and she fell into my arms!

SGANARELLE.   Oh, my poor daughter!

LISETTE.   By slapping her face and using smelling salts, I revived her. But she's getting worse, and I don't believe she can last the day.

SGANARELLE.   [*Calling to the offstage servant CHAMPAGNE.*] Champagne! Champagne! Champagne! [*Enter CHAMPAGNE.*] Quickly, go get the doctors, and as many as you can find! There can't be too many for this! Oh, my daughter, my poor daughter!

[*They leave quickly.*]

FIRST ENTR'ACTE

[*CHAMPAGNE, while dancing, knocks on the doors of four doctors, who begin dancing and then ceremoniously enter the house of the patient's father.*]

ACT 2

Scene 1

Enter SGANARELLE and LISETTE.

LISETTE.   Why do you need four doctors, Sir? Just one alone is enough to kill you.

SGANARELLE.   Be quiet. Four opinions are better than one.

LISETTE.   Can't your daughter die by herself, without the help of these gentlemen?

SGANARELLE.   Do you mean to say that it's the doctor who causes death, and not the disease?

LISETTE.   Absolutely. I know a man who proved beyond doubt that we should   5
never say, "This person died of a raging fever or a galloping consumption," but rather "That person was killed by the incompetence of two druggists and four doctors."

SGANARELLE.   Stop. You'll offend these gentlemen.

LISETTE.   Lord, Sir, our cat needed no drugs or treatment to recover from that jump she made from the rooftop to the street, and she didn't eat or move a muscle for three days. It's lucky for her there are no cat doctors, or they'd have wiped her out with their mindless purging and bleeding.

SGANARELLE.   Will you please keep your impertinent remarks to yourself? Here they are.

LISETTE.   Watch out. They'll tell you what you already know—that your daughter's sick. Only they'll bamboozle you by saying it in Latin!

Act 2, Scene 2

Enter DR. SLICER, DR. GOUGER, DR. DE PITS, *and* DR. GOLFER.

SGANARELLE.   Welcome, gentlemen!

DR. SLICER.   [*Pompously.*] We have made our diagnosis of your daughter, and she unquestionably has many impurities in her.

SGANARELLE.   My daughter is impure?

DR. SLICER.   You must understand that it is her body that is full of impurities— many corrupt and putrid humors.°

SGANARELLE.   Oh, thank you, I understand.   5

DR. SLICER.   But, we plan to consult about her.

SGANARELLE.   [*To attending servants.*] Come, bring chairs for the doctors.

LISETTE.   [*To* DR. SLICER.] Doctor, is that you?

SGANARELLE.   How do you know Dr. Slicer?

LISETTE.   From having seen him the other day at the home of a good friend of   10
your niece.

DR. SLICER.   How is her coachman?

LISETTE.   Fabulous; he's dead.

DR. SLICER.   Dead?

LISETTE.   Yes, dead.

DR. SLICER.   That cannot be!   15

LISETTE.   I don't know if it couldn't happen, but I do know that it did.

DR. SLICER.   And I tell you he can't be dead.

LISETTE.   And I tell you he's dead and buried.

DR. SLICER.   You've made a mistake.

LISETTE.   I saw it with my own eyes.   20

DR. SLICER.   It's impossible. Hippocrates° says that patients don't die of this disease until the end of the second or third week, and he was sick for only six days.

LISETTE.   Let Hippocrates talk all he wants; the coachman is dead.

SGANARELLE.   [*To* LISETTE.] Be quiet, chatterbox; we should leave. [*To the doctors.*] Gentlemen, we will leave you in peace for your consultation. I know it's not customary to pay in advance, but I'll pay you now, before I forget.

---

4 *corrupt and putrid humors:* internal illness of body fluids.   21 *Hippocrates:* ancient Greek physician, known as the father of medicine.

[He pays them, and each one, upon receiving the fee, makes a different show of thanks. SGANARELLE and LISETTE then leave.]

Act 2, Scene 3

DR. SLICER, DR. GOUGER, DR. DE PITS, and DR. GOLFER *remain.*

DR. DE PITS.   Paris is an incredibly large city, and a good medical practice requires long trips.

DR. SLICER.   I have an excellent mule for that; you won't believe the distances I make him go each day.

DR. DE PITS.   I have a marvelous horse; he never gets tired.

DR. SLICER.   Do you know the ground my mule has covered today? I was near the Arsenal first. Then I went to the suburb of St. Germain, from there to Le Marais, and then to St. Honoré Gate; after that to St. Jacques, to the Richelieu Gate, and finally here. When I leave, I'll go to the Place Royale.

DR. DE PITS.   My horse has gone to all those places today, and in addition I rode   5
him all the way to Ruel so I could see a patient.

DR. SLICER.   By the way, what position do you gentlemen take in the controversy between Doctors Theophrastus and Artemius? This is a matter that's dividing the whole profession.

DR. DE PITS.   I think Artemius is right.

DR. SLICER.   I do too. It's true that his treatment killed the patient, and that the recommendation of Theophrastus was infinitely better, but in the circumstances, Theophrastus was wrong. He should not have ignored the recommendation of Artemius, who was, we must recognize, the senior physician in the case. What do you say about it?

DR. DE PITS.   Proper procedure should always be respected. I think we would be lost without our strict order of authority.

DR. SLICER.   I agree; I'm as severe about this as the devil—unless it's among   10
friends. The other day three of us were consulting with an outside physician about a pa-tient. I stopped the whole business until we proceeded in absolute order. Meanwhile, the people of the house did their best as the illness reached a crisis, but I continued to insist on proper consultative procedure. Before we could end our conference, the patient died—may he rest in peace.

DR. DE PITS.   Insisting on our rights like that is the best way to keep lay people in their place, and show them that we're in control.

DR. SLICER.   A dead person is a dead person, and of no importance; but any neg-lect of standard operating procedures puts our whole profession in a bad light.

Act 2, Scene 4

They remain. Enter SGANARELLE.

SGANARELLE.   Gentlemen, my daughter's condition is becoming serious. Please tell me at once what you have decided.

DR. SLICER.   [*To DR. DE PITS.*] Sir, you speak.

DR. DE PITS.   No, Sir, you speak first.

DR. SLICER.   Please, Sir, don't be modest.

DR. DE PITS.   No, Sir, please, after you.   5

DR. SLICER.   Sir!

DR. DE PITS.   Sir!

SGANARELLE.   With all respect, gentlemen, forget your ceremony and remember our present urgency.

Sganarelle (Didier Rousselet), concerned about his health, consults with the battery of physicians (Patricia Buignet, Paola Durant, Mikael Manoukian, Celeste Morrow) in this French language production of *Love Is the Doctor* (*L'Amour Médecin*) at the LE NEON Theater in Arlington, Virginia, in February, 2003. Director: Didier Rousselet assisted by Dominique Montet. Simultaneous translations by Monica Neagoy. (Photo courtesy of LE NEON Theater, Arlington, VA)

[*All four doctors now speak together.*]

DR. SLICER.   The illness of your daughter—

DR. DE PITS.   The judgment of all these gentlemen together—   10

DR. GOUGER.   After our most exhaustive consultation—

DR. GOLFER.   To consider the case step by step, we—

SGANARELLE.   Gentlemen, please, speak one at a time.

DR. SLICER.   Sir, we have reached a diagnosis of your daughter's illness. My opinion is that it stems from a sanguinary superabundance—too much blood, to you. So my recommendation is blood letting; as soon as possible you should let as much blood from her as you can.

DR. DE PITS.   My best judgment is that her illness results from a putrefaction of   15
humors, caused by too much repletion. So my advice—listen carefully—is that she be given an emetic.

DR. SLICER.   I submit that an emetic will kill her.

DR. DE PITS.   And I believe that a bleeding is contra-indicated; it will bring about instant expiration—in other words, death.

DR. SLICER.   [*Huffily, to* DR. DE PITS.] You of course are a great authority.

DR. DE PITS.   [*Defensively, to* DR. SLICER] Yes, I am; I'll outshine you in any branch of medical knowledge.

DR. SLICER.   Do you recall that your wrongheaded treatment killed a man the   20
other day?

DR. DE PITS.   Do you recall that your bungling put a woman in her grave just three days ago?

DR. SLICER.   [*To SGANARELLE.*] I've given you my opinion.

DR. DE PITS.   [*To SGANARELLE.*] And I've informed you of my professional judgment.

DR. SLICER.   If you don't bleed your daughter immediately, she'll be a goner. [*He leaves.*]

DR. DE PITS.   And if you do bleed her, she'll die in a quarter of an hour.   25

[*He leaves.*]

Act 2, Scene 5

SGANARELLE, DR. GOUGER, and DR. GOLFER remain.

SGANARELLE.   Which of the two should I believe, and what should I do with such contrary advice? Gentlemen, I ask you to understand my predicament and tell me objectively what you believe would cure my daughter.

DR. GOUGER.   [*He speaks agonizingly slowly, drawing out his syllables and even stressing ordinarily silent letters.*] Sir, in these matters, we must proceed with circumspection, and, as they say, do nothing rashly, because the mistakes that we may make, according to our master, Hippocrates, may have dangerous consequences.

DR. GOLFER.   [*This one speaks at breakneck speed.*] He's right; we must be careful in what we do. This is not a child's game, and when we fail, it's not easy to repair the damage and restore the dead to life: *Experimentum periculosum:* in other words, medicine is a perilous experiment that we learn from as we go along. That's why we must reason carefully, weigh the alternatives, consider individual cases, examine all the possible causes of the illness, and see what remedies we may bring to the patient.

SGANARELLE.   [*Aside.*] One is as slow as a turtle, the other as fast as a jackrabbit.

DR. GOUGER.   [*He is the turtle.*] Therefore, Sir, to get down to the matter, I find that   5
your daughter is sick. She has a chronic sickness which will get worse unless it gets better, for her symptoms indicate a pathological and mordant—that is to say, bad—vapor which penetrates the membranes of the brain. Now this vapor, which is called *atmos* in Greek, is caused by putrid, tenacious, and glutinous humors which are contained in the lower bowel.

DR. GOLFER.   [*He is the jackrabbit.*] And, inasmuch as these humors were engendered there during an extended period, they have turned adust—that is, they have been overcooked, so to speak—and have produced the present pathology of the brain.

DR. GOUGER.   [*Still speaking slowly.*] Therefore, in order that we may draw out, detach, withdraw, expel, and evacuate these said humors, we must recommend an aggressive treatment of purgation. But first, I find, it would not be improper to prescribe anodynes of emollients° and cleansing solutions, together with refreshing medicinal juleps and syrups to be mixed with her herbal tea and her tonic.

DR. GOLFER.   After this, should come purging and bleeding, to be repeated as necessary.

DR. GOUGER.   This does not mean that your daughter won't die after all this, but at least you will have done your best, and may be consoled by the realization that she died in accordance with proper procedures.

DR. GOLFER.   It's much better to die by the rules than to recover in spite of them.   10

DR. GOUGER.   We are giving you our best professional advice.

DR. GOLFER.   And we have spoken to you as though you were our brother.

SGANARELLE.   [*To DR. GOUGER, drawing out his words.*] I thank you most humbly, Sir. [*To DR. GOLFER, as rapidly as possible.*] To you, Sir, I am infinitely obliged for the care that you have taken.

[*The doctors exit.*]

---

7 *anodynes of emollients:* soothing lotions.

Act 2, Scene 6

SGANARELLE, alone.

SGANARELLE.   Now I'm more uncertain than ever. What can I do? [*He ponders this question for a few moments.*] I've got an idea: I've heard about a medicine that can cure everything, which they make down in Orvieto, Italy. It's a marvelous new elixir called "Orviétan." The advertising says it's cured millions of people. I'll buy some for her. It's got to work.

[*He leaves.*]

Act 2, Scene 7

A Street. Enter SGANARELLE and MOUNTEBANK, accompanied by his BUFFOONS and SCARAMOUCHES.

SGANARELLE.   Hello, Sir. Please give me a bottle of your amazing new drug, Orviétan. How much does it cost?

MOUNTEBANK.   [*Singing.*]

> Would the gold in the richest of mines
> Be enough for this all-curing pill?
> By its magic it separates the ill
> From more ailments than forests have pines.
>> Agues and itches,
>> Fevers and twitches,
>> Plagues and neuroses,
>> Funks and psychoses,
>> Measles, congestions,
>> Strokes and depressions,
>> Organs that fail you,
>> All things that ail you—
> All can be cured by my Orviétan, my Orviétan,
> All can be cured by my Orviétan.

SGANARELLE.   Sir, I believe that all the gold in the world is not enough to pay you for your medicine. However, here's five hundred for you.

MOUNTEBANK.   [*Singing.*]

> Sing my praise, for these pills, I surmise—
> Such a bargain for such a small cost—
> Give new strength to those lives that are tossed
> By diseases the heavens devise.
>> Agues and itches,
>> Fevers and twitches,
>> Plagues and neuroses,
>> Funks and psychoses,
>> Measles, congestions,
>> Strokes and depressions,
>> Organs that fail you,
>> All things that ail you—
> All can be cured by my Orviétan, my Orviétan,
> All can be cured by my Orviétan.

[*Exit SGANARELLE.*]

A dance by the MOUNTEBANK'S BUFFOONS *and* SCARAMOUCHES.

ACT 3

Scene 1

Enter DR. FILLPOCKET, DR. SLICER, *and* DR. DE PITS.

DR. FILLPOCKET.   Gentlemen, as men of your experience you should be ashamed to have been so imprudent as to quarrel like young blockheads. Don't you see that such open arguments hurt us in the public eye? Isn't it enough that expert critics know all about the controversy and dissension among our authorities and ancient masters, without disclosing our humbug to the world by wrangling in front of spectators? I'm concerned that some members of our profession mismanage their public relations so badly, because lately we've been hurt, and if we're not careful we may ruin ourselves. I have nothing to lose in this, because I've already made my pile. Let it blow, rain, and hail, the dead are dead, and I'm rich enough not to fear the living. But in the long run, our squabbles and disputes don't advance the medical profession. Since Heaven has smiled on us and enabled us to hoodwink the public for centuries, let's not disabuse people by our excesses, but let us go on taking advantage of the gullible—and thereby go on making our bundles. You know we're not the only profession to prey on human vulnerability; it's the major study of half the world's population. Everyone wants to catch people in moments of weakness in order to cash in. Flatterers, for example, benefit from the human need for praise, and so they lay it on with a trowel; some people have made huge fortunes in this way. Alchemists benefit from people's greed by promising mountains of gold to fools stupid enough to invest in their phony technology about making gold out of lead. And people even pour money into those consummate fakers, the psychics, who manipulate the vanity and ambition of their victims by making rosy predictions about the future. But the greatest weakness of humanity is the love of life—yes, our instinct for self-preservation—and we, as doctors, all profit from it, even with our pompous nonsense. We reap gigantic rewards because of the worship and adoration that our profession gains from our patients' fear of death. Let us then preserve the high esteem that human fallibility has given us, and let us, in the eyes of that world of believers out there, agree to take the credit for our cures while we deceive people by convincing them to blame Nature for our blunders. Let's not go about, I say, stupidly destroying the happy continuation of this public misperception which puts bread on our tables; and from the dead, whom we put into the ground, let us raise up our boundless wealth.

DR. SLICER.   [*Spellbound.*] You are so right—so very right. But our dispute arose simply from hot blood, which we cannot always control.

DR. FILLPOCKET.   All right, then, gentlemen, put rancor aside, and make your apologies now.

DR. DE PITS.   I agree, if my emetic can be given to our present patient then Dr. Slicer can do as he pleases with the next patient.

DR. FILLPOCKET.   I couldn't say it better myself, and I'm glad to see good sense prevail.

DR. DE PITS.   It's done.

5

DR. FILLPOCKET.   Shake hands, then. [*DR. DE PITS and DR. SLICER shake hands.*] Goodbye. And next time, be more careful.

[*Exit DR. FILLPOCKET.*]

Act 3, Scene 2

DR. DE PITS and DR. SLICER remain. Enter LISETTE.

LISETTE.   Gentlemen, how can you stand there without seeking a way of getting even for the attack that has just been made against the practice of medicine?

DR. SLICER.   What do you mean?

LISETTE.   A brazen fellow has just had the nerve to practice your profession without a licence; he has just wiped out another fellow with a sword clean through the body.

DR. SLICER.   Listen, you can make fun of us now, but some day you'll be sick, and then we'll get you in our clutches.

LISETTE.   When I'm ready, then I'll give you permission to do me in.   5

[*Exit the doctors.*]

Act 3, Scene 3

LISETTE remains. Enter CLITANDER, dressed as a doctor.

CLITANDER.   Well, Lisette, what do you think of my outfit? Do you think I can fool our gentleman with it? Do I look the part of a doctor?

LISETTE.   You look fine, but you're late. It's good that Heaven has made me so good-natured. I can't see two lovers sighing for each other without feeling soft myself, and wishing to satisfy their longing. Hang the consequences, I've sworn to free Lucinda from her tyranny and give her to you. I liked you from the first. I'm an authority when it comes to men, and she couldn't have made a better choice than you. True love requires great risks, and we have devised a scheme that we hope will succeed. Our plans are already moving ahead. The man we're dealing with is not one of your brightest in the world, and if we fail now, we can find a thousand other ways to reach our goal. Wait for me alone over there; I'll be right back to get you.

[*CLITANDER leaves.*]

Act 3, Scene 4

LISETTE remains. Enter SGANARELLE.

LISETTE.   Sir, joy, joy!

SGANARELLE.   What's this?

LISETTE.   Rejoice.

SGANARELLE.   What for?

LISETTE.   And again, I say, rejoice!   5

SGANARELLE.   Tell me what's going on, and then I'll rejoice—maybe.

LISETTE.   No, I want you to rejoice in advance; I want you to sing and dance!

SGANARELLE.   Upon what?

LISETTE.   Upon my word.

SGANARELLE.   Okay, then. [*He sings and dances.*] La lera la la, la lera la. What the   10 devil!

LISETTE.   Sir, your daughter is cured!

SGANARELLE.   My daughter is cured?

LISETTE.   Yes. I am bringing you a doctor, but not just any doctor. He is the most important doctor on earth, who makes miraculous cures and puts all other doctors to shame.

SGANARELLE.   Where is he?

LISETTE.   I'll have him come in. [*She leaves.*]   15

SGANARELLE.   [*Alone.*] Let's see if this one will do better than the others.

Act 3, Scene 5

SGANARELLE remains. Enter LISETTE and CLITANDER in his doctor's robes.

LISETTE.   [*Leading CLITANDER.*] Here he is.

SGANARELLE.   This doctor has only a small growth of beard.

LISETTE.   Science is not measured by a beard, and he did not get his degrees because of his chin.

SGANARELLE.   Sir, I'm told that you have effective medications for regular bowel movements.

CLITANDER.   Sir, my remedies are entirely unique. Other doctors use emetics,   5
bleeding, medicines, and enemas, but I cure by words, sounds, letters, signs, and mystical rings.

LISETTE.   What did I tell you?

SGANARELLE.   Here is a great man!

LISETTE.   Sir, since your daughter is up and around, I'll get her over here.

SGANARELLE.   Please do. [*LISETTE leaves.*]

CLITANDER.   [*Taking SGANARELLE's pulse.*] Your daughter is indeed sick.   10

SGANARELLE.   You know that from taking *my* pulse?

CLITANDER.   Yes, because of the sympathetic vibrations passing between father and daughter.

Act 3, Scene 6

SGANARELLE and CLITANDER remain. Enter LUCINDA and LISETTE.

LISETTE.   [*To CLITANDER.*] Here, Sir, take this chair. [*To SGANARELLE.*] Let's go and leave them together.

SGANARELLE.   Why? I want to stay here.

LISETTE.   Are you kidding? We should go; a doctor has a hundred questions that it's not right for us to hear.

[*SGANARELLE and LISETTE move to a side of the stage.*]

CLITANDER.   [*Speaking to LUCINDA alone.*] Ah, Madam, I'm so overwhelmed with joy I hardly know how to begin speaking to you! When I could speak only with my eyes, I thought I had hundreds of things to say; but now that I have freedom to say what I want, I feel tongue-tied, and my happiness stifles my words.

LUCINDA.   I feel the same thing, and like you I sense movements of joy that catch   5
in my throat and prevent my speaking.

CLITANDER.   Ah, Madam, I would be so happy if you felt everything I feel, and if I could judge your heart by mine! But, Madam, may I believe that you were the one who thought of this happy stratagem that gives me such joy in your presence?

LUCINDA.   If you don't owe me the idea, at least you should know that I approved it eagerly.

SGANARELLE.   [*To LISETTE.*] He seems very close to her.

LISETTE.   [*To SGANARELLE.*] He's a doctor, and he's studying her facial features.

CLITANDER.   [*To LUCINDA.*] Will you be faithful, Madam, in the promises you make   10
to me?

LUCINDA.   And you, will you be firm in your present resolutions?

CLITANDER.   Ah, Madam, until death, and I'll demonstrate my love by what I'm now about to do.

SGANARELLE.   [*To CLITANDER.*] Well, our patient seems to be perking up.

CLITANDER.   That's because I've already tried one of the remedies of my great art on her. The mind has power over the body, and sickness often begins in the mind. My method is therefore to cure the spirit first before treating the body. Accordingly, I have studied her looks, her facial features, and the lines of her two hands; and by the science bestowed on me by Heaven, I have determined that her sickness is psychosomatic—she is sick in spirit. This disease comes entirely from her disordered imagination, which prompts her depraved wish to be married. My view is that there is nothing more extravagant or ridiculous than this wish for marriage.

SGANARELLE.   [*Aside.*] This is indeed a man of skill!   15

CLITANDER.   And all my life I have had, and will continue to have, an aversion for it.

SGANARELLE.   [*Aside.*] A great physician!

CLITANDER.   But, since it's necessary to flatter the imagination of patients, and because I see schizophrenic tendencies in her, and also because it would be perilous not to treat her quickly, I have taken advantage of her weakness and told her that I came here to ask you for her hand in marriage. When she heard that, her appearance changed for the better, her complexion brightened, and her eyes sparkled. I believe that if you keep her in this error for several days, you will see her recover completely.

SGANARELLE.   There's nothing I want more.

CLITANDER.   Afterwards we'll apply other remedies to cure her of this fantasy   20
entirely.

SGANARELLE.   That will be marvellous! [*To LUCINDA.*] Well, daughter, here is a gentleman who wishes to marry you, and I have told him he has my blessing!

LUCINDA.   Dear me, is this possible?

SGANARELLE.   Yes.

LUCINDA.   I'm not dreaming?

SGANARELLE.   No, you're not dreaming.   25

LUCINDA.   [*To CLITANDER.*] You really want to be my husband?

CLITANDER.   Yes, Madam.

LUCINDA.   And my father consents?

SGANARELLE.   Yes, daughter.

LUCINDA.   If this is true, I couldn't be happier!   30

CLITANDER.   Don't doubt it, Madam. It is not just today that I began loving you and longing to marry you. I came here only to ask for your hand, and, if you want to know the whole truth exactly as it is, this doctor's costume is nothing more than a false front. I pretended to be a doctor only to come close to you, the more easily to realize my goal of marrying you.

LUCINDA.   This all shows me the proofs of your tender love. I am deeply moved by them.

SGANARELLE.   [*Aside.*] Oh, the fool! the fool! the fool!

LUCINDA.   You approve of this gentleman as my husband, father, and do so willingly?

SGANARELLE.   Yes. Give me your hand, and you, Sir, give me yours, too, by way of   35
witness.

CLITANDER.   But, Sir—

SGANARELLE.   [*Stifling laughter.*] No, no, it's to—it's to ease her mind. Now, join hands. There, it's done.

CLITANDER.   Accept as a token of my faith this ring that I give you. [*Speaking low, to SGANARELLE.*] It's a special ring to cure her distracted mind.

LUCINDA.   Let us draw up the contract, so that everything will be complete.

CLITANDER.   Certainly; I would like that, Madam. [*To* SGANARELLE.] I'll show her the   40
man who writes my prescriptions, and make her believe he's a genuine Justice.

SGANARELLE.   Excellent!

CLITANDER.   [*Calling offstage.*] You there, send in the Justice I brought with me!

LUCINDA.   What, you brought along a Justice?

CLITANDER.   Yes, Madam.

LUCINDA.   I'm delighted!   45

SGANARELLE.   [*Chuckling.*] Oh, the fool! the fool!

Act 3, Scene 7

They all remain. Enter the JUSTICE, *appropriately robed.* CLITANDER *whispers to the* JUSTICE.

SGANARELLE.   [*To the* JUSTICE.] Welcome, Sir. I commission you to draft a contract
for these two young people. Please begin writing. [*While the* JUSTICE *is writing,* SGANARELLE
speaks to LUCINDA.] This will be a contract to end all contracts. [*To the* JUSTICE.] I give her
twenty million upon her marriage. Write that down!

LUCINDA.   I'm so overwhelmingly grateful to you, father.

JUSTICE.   Giving the contract to SGANARELLE.] There, it's done; you need only to
come and sign.

SGANARELLE.   How's that for a contract speedily finished?

CLITANDER.   [*To* SGANARELLE.] At least, Sir—

SGANARELLE.   No, no words of gratitude; say nothing, I beg you. [*Aside to*
CLITANDER.] Don't we both know what we're doing? [*To the* JUSTICE.] Come, give him the   5
pen. [*After* CLITANDER *signs,* SGANARELLE *gives the pen to* LUCINDA.] Come, come, sign it. Go
ahead; I'll sign too. [*He signs.*]

LUCINDA.   No, no. I want to hold the contract myself.

SGANARELLE.   All right, take it. [*After she has signed.*] Now, are you happy?

LUCINDA.   More than you can imagine!

SGANARELLE.   I'm please. I'm very pleased.

CLITANDER.   As for the rest, I not only took the trouble to bring a Justice along, but
to celebrate the occasion I brought singers and musicians too. Send them in! These are   10
the people I take with me every day on my rounds; I direct them, with their harmony, to
pacify the troubled minds of my patients.

Final Scene

All remain. Enter the SPIRIT OF COMEDY, DANCERS, *and* MUSICIANS.

> ALL THREE [COMEDY, DANCERS, *and* MUSICIANS].
> If you didn't have music and singing and dancing,
>   You'd spend your life with your mind in chains;
> For it's we, with our wonderful songs and our prancing,
>   Who win the fight against aches and pains.

> COMEDY

> Do you want to break free,
>   In the happiest way,
> From the mis'ry and grief
>   Of each long day?
>   Then sing your song

> The whole day long;
> Throw away your medicine,
> Along with the jar it's in,
> And join our throng
> As we sing along.

ALL THREE

> If you didn't have music and singing and dancing,
>   You'd spend your life with your mind in chains;
> For it's we, with our wonderful songs and our prancing,
>   Who win the fight against aches and pains.

[*While they are singing and dancing, and amidst all the Games, Smiles, and Pleasures,* CLITANDER *leads* LUCINDA *away.*]

SGANARELLE.   This is a marvelous way to cure someone! But where is my daughter, and where is the doctor?

LISETTE.   They left—to complete the rest of the marriage ritual.

SGANARELLE.   What are you saying? What—what marriage?

LISETTE.   In truth, Sir, the game has been bagged, and what you thought was a joke turns out to be the absolute truth!

SGANARELLE.   [*The* DANCERS *catch hold of him and bring him into the dance by force.*]   5
What's this? The devil! Let me go! Let me go, I tell you! Still more? A plague on everything!

[*Finis.*]

QUESTIONS

Act 1

1.   What does the opening scene indicate about Sganarelle's responses to other people? Describe his traits. What do you learn about his economic status? Why is this status important in the plot?

2.   Describe the father–daughter relationship that is brought out in scenes 2 and 3. Why is the relationship made to seem comic and not serious?

3.   Why is it important that we learn about a suitor whom Lucinda likes, and that there has been an "envoy" from him seeking to negotiate a marriage?

4.   Describe Lisette. Is she flat or round, representative or individualized? Why is she important? What is her relationship with Lucinda?

5.   Why does Sganarelle not want his daughter married? What do his reasons disclose about him? What effect does Sganarelle's behavior toward his daughter have on your attitude toward him at the play's conclusion?

Act 2

6.   Why is Sganarelle dramatized as a person with great faith in doctors? Why is Lisette skeptical about them?

7.   Study the dialogue between Lisette and Dr. Slicer (scene 2, paragraphs 8–22). Describe how character and speech here produce laughter.

8.   At the end of scene 2 a stage direction describes Sganarelle's payment to the doctors. Explain how pantomime and dance might be used here to augment Molière's satiric presentation of doctors. Be specific.

9. Though scene 3 is supposedly a medical "consultation" about the condition of Lucinda, the conversation has nothing to do with her. What does Molière achieve by introducing the topics the doctors actually discuss?

10. What treatments do the doctors prescribe for Lucinda? Though the doctors are contradictory, in what respects are some of them truthful? Why is their telling the truth comic?

11. Explain Sganarelle's role in the scenes with the doctors. What is the effect of these scenes on his seeking out the Mountebank, and also on his reception of Clitander in the next act when Clitander appears disguised as a doctor?

Act 3

12. Why does Dr. Fillpocket make such a long speech? How honest is he? Would he give this speech to anyone but fellow doctors? Is Molière's treatment of the speech comic? Serious? True? Partly true? Untrue?

13. What is the stratagem devised by Lisette and Clitander? How is it related to Sganarelle's already proven faith in doctors and medication?

14. Explain the irony of Clitander's confession to Lucinda and also of Sganarelle's responses beginning in scene 6, and extending to the revelation in the last scene. How does Molière keep the final scene light and comic?

15. How does Sganarelle react to the news that the marriage of Lucinda and Clitander is real? How is his reaction kept from seeming serious? If you were a director, what might you tell the actor playing Sganarelle to do during the concluding dance? Why?

GENERAL QUESTIONS

1. Who is the protagonist of *Love Is the Doctor*? What conflicts develop? Who and what are the antagonists? Which side is triumphant at the end?

2. A traditional topic for laughter is that the "biter gets bitten" and the "tables are turned." To what degree does Molière use this topic in the play? How successful is it as a means of developing humor?

3. The critic Harold C. Knutson has observed that in *Love Is the Doctor* we have "a particularly biting commentary on doctors and doctoring," and that one of the modes of satire is that the doctors "drop the mask and betray their callousness" and "contentiousness," and that their "concern" is not with their patients but rather with rules and formalities (*Molière: An Archetypal Approach* [Toronto: U of Toronto P, 1976], pp. 52–53). Do you agree or disagree with Professor Knutson's observations? Explain in detail.

4. Aside from the medical satire, describe the various doctors as characters. Which of the doctors is the most fully developed? Which are most amusing? Why?

❧ COMEDY FROM MOLIÈRE TO THE PRESENT

The subject of comedy in the centuries from Molière to the present is vast. In all the major European countries, and eventually in the United States, there were many comic dramatists. Some of them were successful in their time but are neglected today, such as Eugène Scribe in France, and some are known for works other than their comedies. In England in the seventeenth century, dramatists such as William Wycherley (1640–1716) and William Congreve (1670–1729) created a sophisticated type of drama, in the comedy of manners tradition, that is termed **Restoration comedy** because it developed after King Charles II was restored to the English throne in 1660. The Restoration comedies combined and contrasted elegant and boisterous manners, and they often dealt with serious social and sexual problems. In the first part of the eighteenth century dramatists created "sentimental" drama. Sentimental comedies showed individuals who verge on behavioral excesses but who eventually conform to morality because they are good at heart—hence the term *sentimental.*

The first half of the eighteenth century saw the popularity of other forms such as the musical play and the burlesque play. The musical play was first known as **ballad opera,** and later it was called **comic opera** and **musical comedy.** The characteristic of the musical play was the combination of spoken dialogue and brief songs. The first such play was *The Beggar's Opera* (1728) by John Gay (1685–1732).[7] *The Beggar's Opera* was also a burlesque that satirized the Italian operas so popular in the early eighteenth century. Henry Fielding (1707–1754), known for his later novels, wrote perhaps the best of the burlesques, *Tom Thumb, or The Tragedy of Tragedies* (1730, 1731), and, in addition, he wrote ballad operas in the manner of *The Beggar's Opera.* Also unique in Fielding's comic writing were a number of five-act plays dealing with serious social situations. The comic opera reached its high point in the nineteenth century with the Savoy Operas of William Gilbert (1836–1911) and Arthur Sullivan (1842–1900). The Gilbert and Sullivan operas, such as *H.M.S. Pinafore* (1878) and *The Mikado* (1885), are regularly performed today by both professionals and amateurs. In the United States during the twentieth century, the musical comedy form became a major force, as with the plays of Richard Rodgers (1902–1979) and Oscar Hammerstein II (1895–1960) and Alan Jay Lerner (1918–1986) and Frederick Loewe (1901–1987).

In the later nineteenth century, the major comic dramatists who were more or less in the pure comic tradition were Oscar Wilde (1854–1900) and George Bernard Shaw (1856–1950), two writers whose plays are still regularly revived and well attended. The twentieth century marked the appearance of important comic dramatists, including many, like Eugene O'Neill and Tennessee Williams, who are better known for more serious plays (see pp. 1208 and 1674). A number of writers divided their time between theater and film, as with George Kaufman (1889–1961), whose *The Man Who Came to Dinner* (1939) was successful both onstage and on the screen. For a time, Kaufman also wrote scripts for some of the early film comedies of the Marx Brothers. Many other comic playwrights experimented with comedy. Such a writer is Arthur Kopit (b. 1937), whose *Oh Dad, Poor Dad, Mamma's Hung You in the Closet and I'm Feelin' So Sad* (1961) created a great stir when it was first performed. Of particular note is the development

---

[7] See p. 732 for a song from *The Beggar's Opera.*

of the Theater of the Absurd. Some significant plays in this tradition are *Waiting for Godot* (1953) by Samuel Becket (1906–1989), *Rhinocéros* (1960) by Jean Genet (1910–1986), *The Sandbox* (1959) by Edward Albee (b. 1928), and *The Homecoming* (1960) by Harold Pinter (b. 1930).

It is fair to say that comedy today is characterized by great variety. All the types described earlier are being written (see pp. 1490–92). Serious plays may contain comic and farcical elements. Comic and farcical plays may introduce serious sequences and also may contain strong elements of satire. Satirical plays may contain songs to complement the onstage action and also to divert and entertain. It is clear that writers at the end of the twentieth century were combining the various comic forms that were brought into prominence by writers since the time of Moliére.

ANTON CHEKHOV, *THE BEAR*

Anton Chekhov was born in Taganrog in southern Russia in 1860, the son of a merchant and grandson of a serf. He entered medical school in Moscow in 1879, graduating in 1884. While a student he was also obligated to help support his family, and he turned to writing stories, jokes, and potboilers for pay under a variety of pen names, one of which was "The Doctor Without Patients." The Bear *belongs to the end of this early period, ten years before Chekhov's association with the Moscow Art Theater at the end of the century (see also p. 1604).*

Chekhov minimized The Bear, *referring to it as a "joke" and a "vaudeville"—both words suggesting a farcical work with little form or substance. Nevertheless the play was greatly acclaimed and financially successful, to the author's amazement and delight. Three months after its first performance in 1888, he likened* The Bear *to a "milk cow"("cash cow") because, to his happiness, it earned him a steady income.*

The Bear is a farce, a dramatic form designed preeminently to evoke laughter, and it therefore contains extravagant language and boisterous and sudden action. But there is also an underlying seriousness that sustains the humor. In their way, both Smirnov and Mrs. Popov have been failures; they could conceivably sink into lives of depression and futility, and both are walking a very fine wire as the play begins. Chekhov makes clear that Mrs. Popov is filled with resentment at her unfaithful and now dead husband, and also that she is chafing under her self-imposed resolution to lead a life of mourning and self-denial in his memory. Smirnov is having difficulty with creditors, and he admits that his relationships with the many women he has known have ended unhappily. He is therefore both cynical and angry.

The climax of the play is the improbable and preposterous challenge that Smirnov offers Mrs. Popov, resolved by the equally sudden and preposterous outcome. Despite the improbabilities of the play, however, the actions are not impossible because they manifest the true internal needs of the main characters. Chekhov's friend Leo Tolstoy, who criticized some of Chekhov's late plays, laughed heartily at *The Bear,* and countless audiences and readers since then have joined him in laughter.

ANTON CHEKHOV (1860–1904)

The Bear, A Joke in One Act   1900

CAST OF CHARACTERS

> Mrs. Popov. *A widow of seven months, Mrs. Popov is small and pretty, with dimples. She is a landowner. At the start of the play, she is pining away in memory of her dead husband.*
> Grigory Stepanovich Smirnov. *Easily angered and loud, Smirnov is older. He is a landowner, too, and a man of substance.*
> Luka. *Luka is Mrs. Popov's footman (a servant whose main tasks were to wait table and attend the carriages, in addition to general duties). He is old enough to feel secure in telling Mrs. Popov what he thinks.*
> Gardener, Coachman, Workmen, *who enter at the end.*

Scene. *The drawing room of* Mrs. Popov's *country home.*

[Mrs. Popov, *in deep mourning, does not remove her eyes from a photograph.*]

Luka. It isn't right, madam . . . you're only destroying yourself. . . . The chambermaid and the cook have gone off berry picking; every living being is rejoicing; even the cat knows how to be content, walking around the yard catching birds, and you sit in your room all day as if it were a convent, and you don't take pleasure in anything. Yes, really! Almost a year has passed since you've gone out of the house!

Mrs. Popov. And I shall never go out. . . . What for? My life is already ended. *He* lies in his grave; I have buried myself in these four walls . . . we are both dead.

Luka. There you go again! Your husband is dead, that's as it was meant to be, it's the will of God, may he rest in peace. . . . You've done your mourning and that will do. You can't go on weeping and mourning forever. My wife died when her time came, too. . . . Well? I grieved, I wept for a month, and that was enough for her; the old lady wasn't worth a second more. [*Sighs.*] You've forgotten all your neighbors. You don't go anywhere or accept any calls. We live, so to speak, like spiders. We never see the light. The mice have eaten my uniform. It isn't as if there weren't any nice neighbors—the district is full of them . . . there's a regiment stationed at Riblov, such officers—they're like candy— you'll never get your fill of them! And in the barracks, never a Friday goes by without a dance; and, if you please, the military band plays music every day. . . . Yes, madam, my dear lady: you're young, beautiful, in the full bloom of youth—if only you took a little pleasure in life . . . beauty doesn't last forever, you know! In ten years' time, you'll be wanting to wave your fanny in front of the officers—and it will be too late.

Mrs. Popov. [*Determined.*] I must ask you never to talk to me like that! You know that when Mr. Popov died, life lost all its salt for me. It may seem to you that I am alive, but that's only conjecture! I vowed to wear mourning to my grave and not to see the light of day. . . . Do you hear me? May his departed spirit see how much I love him. . . . Yes, I know, it's no mystery to you that he was often mean to me, cruel . . . and even unfaithful, but I shall remain true to the grave and show him I know how to love. There, beyond the grave, he will see me as I was before his death. . . .

Luka. Instead of talking like that, you should be taking a walk in the garden or have Toby or Giant harnessed and go visit some of the neighbors. . . .   5

Mrs. Popov. Ai! [*She weeps.*]

Luka. Madam! Dear lady! What's the matter with you! Christ be with you!

Mrs. Popov. Oh, how he loved Toby! He always used to ride on him to visit the Korchagins or the Vlasovs. How wonderfully he rode! How graceful he was when he pulled at the reins with all his strength! Do you remember? Toby, Toby! Tell them to give him an extra bag of oats today.

LUKA.   Yes, madam.

[*Sound of loud ringing.*]

MRS. POPOV.   [*Shudders.*] Who's that? Tell them I'm not at home!   10

LUKA.   Of course, madam. [*He exits.*]

MRS. POPOV.   [*Alone. Looks at the photograph.*] You will see, Nikolai, how much I can love and forgive . . . my love will die only when I do, when my poor heart stops beating. [*Laughing through her tears.*] Have you no shame? I'm a good girl, a virtuous little wife. I've locked myself in and I'll be true to you to the grave, and you . . . aren't you ashamed, you chubby cheeks? You deceived me, you made scenes, for weeks on end you left me alone . . .

LUKA.   [*Enters, alarmed.*] Madam, somebody is asking for you. He wants to see you. . . .

MRS. POPOV.   But didn't you tell them that since the death of my husband, I don't see anybody?

LUKA.   I did, but he didn't want to listen; he spoke about some very important   15
business.

MRS. POPOV.   I am *not at home!*

LUKA.   That's what I told him . . . but . . . the devil . . . he cursed and pushed past me right into the room . . . he's in the dining room right now.

MRS. POPOV.   [*Losing her temper.*] Very well, let him come in . . . such manners! [*LUKA goes out.*] How difficult these people are! What does he want from me? Why should he disturb my peace? [*Sighs.*] But it's obvious I'll have to go live in a convent. . . . [*Thoughtfully.*] Yes, a convent. . . .

SMIRNOV.   [*Enters while speaking to LUKA.*] You idiot, you talk too much. . . . Ass! [*Sees MRS. POPOV and changes to dignified speech.*] Madam, may I introduce myself: retired lieutenant of the artillery and landowner, Grigory Stepanovich Smirnov! I feel the necessity of troubling you about a highly important matter. . . .

MRS. POPOV.   [*Refusing her hand.*] What do you want?   20

SMIRNOV.   Your late husband, whom I had the pleasure of knowing, has remained in my debt for two twelve-hundred-ruble notes. Since I must pay the interest at the agricultural bank tomorrow, I have come to ask you, madam, to pay me the money today.

MRS. POPOV.   One thousand two hundred. . . . And why was my husband in debt to you?

SMIRNOV.   He used to buy oats from me.

MRS. POPOV.   [*Sighing, to LUKA.*] So, Luka, don't you forget to tell them to give Toby an extra bag of oats.

[*LUKA goes out.*]

[*To SMIRNOV.*] If Nikolai, my husband, was in debt to you, then it goes without saying that I'll pay; but please excuse me today. I haven't any spare cash. The day after tomorrow, my steward will be back from town and I will give him instructions to pay you what is owed; until then I cannot comply with your wishes. . . . Besides, today is the anniversary—exactly seven months ago my husband died, and I'm in such a mood that I'm not quite disposed to occupy myself with money matters.

SMIRNOV.   And I'm in such a mood that if I don't pay the interest tomorrow, I'll be   25
owing so much that my troubles will drown me. They'll take away my estate!

MRS. POPOV.   You'll receive your money the day after tomorrow.

SMIRNOV. I don't want the money the day after tomorrow. I want it today.

MRS. POPOV. You must excuse me. I can't pay you today.

SMIRNOV. And I can't wait until after tomorrow.

MRS. POPOV. What can I do, if I don't have it now? 30

SMIRNOV. You mean to say you can't pay?

MRS. POPOV. I can't pay. . . .

SMIRNOV. Hm! Is that your last word?

MRS. POPOV. That is my last word.

SMIRNOV. Positively the last? 35

MRS. POPOV. Positively.

SMIRNOV. Thank you very much. We'll make a note of that. [*Shrugs his shoulders.*] And people want me to be calm and collected! Just now, on the way here, I met a tax officer and he asked me: why are you always so angry, Grigory Stepanovich? Goodness' sake, how can I be anything but angry? I need money desperately . . . I rode out yesterday early in the morning, at daybreak, and went to see all my debtors; and if only one of them had paid his debt . . . I was dog-tired, spent the night God knows where—a Jewish tavern beside a barrel of vodka. . . . Finally I got here, fifty miles from home, hoping to be paid, and you treat me to a "mood." How can I help being angry?

MRS. POPOV. It seems to me that I clearly said: My steward will return from the country and then you will be paid.

SMIRNOV. I didn't come to your steward, but to you! What the hell, if you'll pardon the expression, would I do with your steward?

MRS. POPOV. Excuse me, my dear sir, I am not accustomed to such profane ex- 40 pressions nor to such a tone. I'm not listening to you any more. [*Goes out quickly.*]

SMIRNOV. [*Alone.*] Well, how do you like that? "A mood." . . . "Husband died seven months ago"! Must I pay the interest or mustn't I? I ask you: Must I pay, or must I not? So, your husband's dead, and you're in a mood and all that finicky stuff . . . and your steward's away somewhere; may he drop dead. What do you want me to do? Do you think I can fly away from my creditors in a balloon or something? Or should I run and bash my head against the wall? I go to Gruzdev—and he's not at home; Yaroshevich is hiding, with Kuritsin it's a quarrel to the death and I almost throw him out the window; Mazutov has diarrhea, and this one is in a "mood." Not one of these swine wants to pay me! And all because I'm too nice to them. I'm a sniveling idiot, I'm spineless, I'm an old lady! I'm too delicate with them! So, just you wait! You'll find out what I'm like! I won't let you play around with me, you devils! I'll stay and stick it out until she pays. Rrr! . . . How furious I am today, how furious! I'm shaking inside from rage and I can hardly catch my breath. . . . Damn it! My God, I even feel sick! [*He shouts.*] Hey, you!

LUKA. [*Enters.*] What do you want?

SMIRNOV. Give me some beer or some water! [*LUKA exits.*] What logic is there in this! A man needs money desperately, it's like a noose around his neck—and she won't pay because, you see, she's not disposed to occupy herself with money matters! . . . That's the logic of a woman! That's why I never did like and do not like to talk to women. I'd rather sit on a keg of gunpowder than talk to a woman. Brr! . . . I even have goose pimples, this broad has put me in such a rage! All I have to do is see one of those spoiled bitches from a distance, and I get so angry it gives me a cramp in the leg. I just want to shout for help.

LUKA. [*Entering with water.*] Madam is sick and won't see anyone.

SMIRNOV. Get out! [*LUKA goes.*] Sick and won't see anyone! No need to see me . . . 45 I'll stay and sit here until you give me the money. You can stay sick for a week, and I'll stay for a week . . . if you're sick for a year, I'll stay a year. . . . I'll get my own back, dear lady!

You can't impress me with your widow's weeds and your dimpled cheeks . . . we know all about those dimples! [*Shouts through the window.*] Semyon, unharness the horses! We're not going away quite yet! I'm staying here! Tell them in the stable to give the horses some oats! You brute, you let the horse on the left side get all tangled up in the reins again! [*Teasing.*] "Never mind" . . . I'll give you a never mind! [*Goes away from the window.*] Shit! The heat is unbearable and nobody pays up. I slept badly last night and on top of everything else this broad in mourning is "in a mood" . . . my head aches . . . [*Drinks, and grimaces.*] Shit! This is water! What I need is a drink! [*Shouts.*] Hey, you!

LUKA.   [*Enters.*] What is it?

SMIRNOV.   Give me a glass of vodka. [*LUKA goes out.*] Oaf! [*Sits down and examines himself.*] Nobody would say I was looking well! Dusty all over, boots dirty, unwashed, unkept, straw on my waistcoat. . . . The dear lady probably took me for a robber. [*Yawns.*] It's not very polite to present myself in a drawing room looking like this; oh well, who cares? . . . I'm not here as a visitor but as a creditor, and there's no official costume for creditors. . . .

LUKA.   [*Enters with vodka.*] You're taking liberties, my good man. . . .

SMIRNOV.   [*Angrily.*] What?

LUKA.   I . . . nothing . . . I only . . .   50

SMIRNOV.   Who are you talking to? Shut up!

LUKA.   [*Aside.*] The devil sent this leech. An ill wind brought him. . . . [*LUKA goes out.*]

SMIRNOV.   Oh how furious I am! I'm so mad I could crush the whole world into a powder! I even feel faint! [*Shouts.*] Hey, you!

MRS. POPOV.   [*Enters, eyes downcast.*] My dear sir, in my solitude, I have long ago grown unaccustomed to the masculine voice and I cannot bear shouting. I must request you not to disturb my peace and quiet!

SMIRNOV.   Pay me my money and I'll go.   55

MRS. POPOV.   I told you in plain language: I haven't any spare cash now; wait until the day after tomorrow.

SMIRNOV.   And I also told you respectfully, in plain language: I don't need the money the day after tomorrow, but today. If you don't pay me today, then tomorrow I'll have to hang myself.

MRS. POPOV.   But what can I do if I don't have the money? You're so strange!

SMIRNOV.   Then you won't pay me now? No?

MRS. POPOV.   I can't. . . .   60

SMIRNOV.   In that case, I can stay here and wait until you pay. . . . [*Sits down.*] You'll pay the day after tomorrow? Excellent! In that case I'll stay here until the day after tomorrow. I'll sit here all that time . . . [*Jumps up.*] I ask you: Have I got to pay the interest tomorrow, or not? Or do you think I'm joking?

MRS. POPOV.   My dear sir, I ask you not to shout! This isn't a stable!

SMIRNOV.   I wasn't asking you about a stable but about this: Do I have to pay the interest tomorrow or not?

MRS. POPOV.   You don't know how to behave in the company of a lady!

SMIRNOV.   No, I don't know how to behave in the company of a lady!   65

MRS. POPOV.   No, you don't! You are an ill-bred, rude man! Respectable people don't talk to a woman like that!

SMIRNOV.   Ach, it's astonishing! How would you like me to talk to you? In French, perhaps? [*Lisps in anger.*] Madame, je vous prie° . . . how happy I am that you're not paying

---

67 *Madame, je vous prie:* I beg you, Madam.

me the money. . . . Ah, pardon, I've made you uneasy! Such lovely weather we're having today! And you look so becoming in your mourning dress. [*Bows and scrapes.*]

MRS. POPOV.   That's rude and not very clever!

SMIRNOV.   [*Teasing.*] Rude and not very clever! I don't know how to behave in the company of ladies. Madam, in my time I've seen far more women than you've seen sparrows. Three times I've fought duels over women; I've jilted twelve women, nine have jilted me! Yes! There was a time when I played the fool; I became sentimental over women, used honeyed words, fawned on them, bowed and scraped. . . . I loved, suffered, sighed at the moon; I became limp, melted, shivered . . . I loved passionately, madly, every which way, devil take me, I chattered away like a magpie about the emancipation of women, ran through half my fortune as a result of my tender feelings; but now, if you will excuse me, I'm on to your ways! I've had enough! Dark eyes, passionate eyes, ruby lips, dimpled cheeks; the moon, whispers, bated breath—for all that I wouldn't give a good goddamn. Present company excepted, of course, but all women, young and old alike, are affected clowns, gossips, hateful, consummate liars to the marrow of their bones, vain, trivial, ruthless, outrageously illogical, and as far as this is concerned [*taps on his forehead.*], well, excuse my frankness, any sparrow could give pointers to a philosopher in petticoats! Look at one of those romantic creatures: muslin, ethereal demigoddess, a thousand raptures, and you look into her soul—a common crocodile! [*Grips the back of a chair; the chair cracks and breaks.*] But the most revolting part of it all is that this crocodile imagines that she has, above everything, her own privilege, a monopoly on tender feelings. The hell with it—you can hang me upside down by that nail if a woman is capable of loving anything besides a lapdog. All she can do when she's in love is slobber! While the man suffers and sacrifices, all her love is expressed in playing with her skirt and trying to lead him around firmly by the nose. You have the misfortune of being a woman, you know yourself what the nature of a woman is like. Tell me honestly: Have you ever in your life seen a woman who is sincere, faithful, and constant? You never have! Only old and ugly ladies are faithful and constant! You're more liable to meet a horned cat or a white woodcock than a faithful woman!

MRS. POPOV.   Pardon me, but in your opinion, who is faithful and constant in love?   70
The man?

SMIRNOV.   Yes, the man!

MRS. POPOV.   The man! [*Malicious laugh.*] Men are faithful and constant in love! That's news! [*Heatedly.*] What right have you to say that? Men are faithful and constant! For that matter, as far as I know, of all the men I have known and now know, my late husband was the best. . . . I loved him passionately, with all my being, as only a young intellectual woman can love; I gave him my youth, my happiness, my life, my fortune; he was my life's breath; I worshipped him as if I were a heathen, and . . . and, what good did it do—this best of men himself deceived me shamelessly at every step of the way. After his death, I found his desk full of love letters; and when he was alive—it's terrible to remember—he used to leave me alone for weeks at a time, and before my eyes he flirted with other women and deceived me. He squandered my money, made a mockery of my feelings . . . and, in spite of all that, I loved him and was true to him . . . and besides, now that he is dead, I am still faithful and constant. I have shut myself up in these four walls forever and I won't remove these widow's weeds until my dying day. . . .

SMIRNOV.   [*Laughs contemptuously.*] Widow's weeds . . . I don't know what you take me for! As if I didn't know why you wear that black outfit and bury yourself in these four walls! Well, well! It's no secret, so romantic! When some fool of a poet passes by this country house, he'll look up at your window and think: "Here lives the mysterious Tamara, who, for the love of her husband, buried herself in these four walls." We know these tricks!

MRS. POPOV. [*Flaring.*] What? How dare you say that to me?

SMIRNOV. You may have buried yourself alive, but you haven't forgotten to powder   75
yourself!

MRS. POPOV. How dare you use such expressions with me?

SMIRNOV. Please don't shout. I'm not your steward! You must allow me to call a
spade a spade. I'm not a woman and I'm used to saying what's on my mind! Don't you
shout at me!

MRS. POPOV. I'm not shouting, you are! Please leave me in peace!

SMIRNOV. Pay me my money and I'll go.

MRS. POPOV. I won't give you any money!   80

SMIRNOV. Yes, you will.

MRS. POPOV. To spite you, I won't pay you anything. You can leave me in peace!

SMIRNOV. I don't have the pleasure of being either your husband or your fiancé,
so please don't make scenes! [*Sits down.*] I don't like it.

MRS. POPOV. [*Choking with rage.*] You're sitting down?

SMIRNOV. Yes, I am.   85

MRS. POPOV. I ask you to get out!

SMIRNOV. Give me my money . . . [*Aside.*] Oh, I'm so furious! Furious!

MRS. POPOV. I don't want to talk to impudent people! Get out of here! [*Pause.*]
You're not going? No?

SMIRNOV. No.

MRS. POPOV. No?   90

SMIRNOV. No!

MRS. POPOV. We'll see about that. [*Rings.*]

[*LUKA enters.*]

Luka, show the gentleman out!

LUKA. [*Goes up to SMIRNOV.*] Sir, will you please leave, as you have been asked. You
mustn't . . .

SMIRNOV. [*Jumping up.*] Shut up! Who do you think you're talking to? I'll make
mincemeat out of you!

LUKA. [*His hand to his heart.*] Oh my God! Saints above! [*Falls into chair.*] Oh, I feel   95
ill! I can't catch my breath!

MRS. POPOV. Where's Dasha? Dasha! [*She shouts.*] Dasha! Pelagea! Dasha! [*She
rings.*]

LUKA. Oh! They've all gone berry picking . . . there's nobody at home . . . I'm ill!
Water!

MRS. POPOV. Will you please get out!

SMIRNOV. Will you please be more polite?

MRS. POPOV. [*Clenches her fist and stamps her feet.*] You're nothing but a crude bear!   100
A brute! A monster!

SMIRNOV. What? What did you say?

MRS. POPOV. I said that you were a bear, a monster!

SMIRNOV. [*Advancing toward her.*] Excuse me, but what right do you have to
insult me?

MRS. POPOV. Yes, I am insulting you . . . so what? Do you think I'm afraid of you?

SMIRNOV. And do you think just because you're one of those romantic creations,   105
that you have the right to insult me with impunity? Yes? I challenge you!

LUKA. Lord in Heaven! Saints above! . . . Water!

SMIRNOV. Pistols!

MRS. POPOV.   Do you think just because you have big fists and you can bellow like a bull, that I'm afraid of you? You're such a bully!

SMIRNOV.   I challenge you! I'm not going to let anybody insult me, and I don't care if you are a woman, a delicate creature!

MRS. POPOV.   [*Trying to get a word in edgewise.*] Bear! Bear! Bear!   110

SMIRNOV.   It's about time we got rid of the prejudice that only men must pay for their insults! Devil take it, if women want to be equal, they should behave as equals! Let's fight!

MRS. POPOV.   You want to fight! By all means!

SMIRNOV.   This minute!

MRS. POPOV.   This minute! My husband had some pistols . . . I'll go and get them right away. [*Goes out hurriedly and then returns.*] What pleasure I'll have putting a bullet through that thick head of yours! The hell with you! [*She goes out.*]

SMIRNOV.   I'll shoot her down like a chicken! I'm not a little boy or a sentimental   115
puppy. I don't care if she is delicate and fragile.

LUKA.   Kind sir! Holy father! [*kneels.*] Have pity on a poor old man and go away from here! You've frightened her to death and now you're going to shoot her?

SMIRNOV.   [*Not listening to him.*] If she fights, then it means she believes in equality of rights and emancipation of women. Here the sexes are equal! I'll shoot her like a chicken! But what a woman! [*Imitates her.*] "The hell with you! . . . I'll put a bullet through that thick head of yours! . . ." What a woman! How she blushed, her eyes shone . . . she accepted my challenge! To tell the truth, it was the first time in my life I've seen a woman like that. . . .

LUKA.   Dear sir, please go away! I'll pray to God on your behalf as long as I live!

SMIRNOV.   That's a woman for you! A woman like that I can understand! A real woman! Not a sour-faced nincompoop but fiery, gunpowder! Fireworks! I'm even sorry to have to kill her!

LUKA.   [*Weeps.*] Dear sir . . . go away!   120

SMIRNOV.   I positively like her! Positively! Even though she has dimpled cheeks, I like her! I'm almost ready to forget about the debt. . . . My fury has diminished. Wonderful woman!

MRS. POPOV.   [*Enters with pistols.*] Here they are, the pistols. Before we fight, you must show me how to fire. . . . I've never had a pistol in my hands before . . .

LUKA.   Oh dear Lord, for pity's sake. . . . I'll go and find the gardener and the coachman. . . . What did we do to deserve such trouble? [*Exit.*]

SMIRNOV.   [*Examining the pistols.*] You see, there are several sorts of pistols . . . there are special dueling pistols, the Mortimer with primers. Then there are Smith and Wesson revolvers, triple action with extractors . . . excellent pistols! . . . they cost a minimum of ninety rubles a pair. . . . You must hold the revolver like this . . . [*Aside.*] What eyes, what eyes! A woman to set you on fire!

MRS. POPOV.   Like this?   125

SMIRNOV.   Yes, like this . . . then you cock the pistol . . . take aim . . . put your head back a little . . . stretch your arm out all the way . . . that's right . . . then with this finger press on this little piece of goods . . . and that's all there is to do . . . but the most important thing is not to get excited and aim without hurrying . . . try to keep your arm from shaking.

MRS. POPOV.   Good . . . it's not comfortable to shoot indoors. Let's go into the garden.

SMIRNOV.   Let's go. But I'm giving you advance notice that I'm going to fire into the air.

MRS. POPOV.   That's the last straw! Why?   130

SMIRNOV.   Why? . . . Why . . . because it's my business, that's why.

MRS. POPOV.   Are you afraid? Yes? Aahhh! No, sir. You're not going to get out of it that easily! Be so good as to follow me! I will not rest until I've put a hole through your forehead . . . that forehead I hate so much! Are you afraid?

SMIRNOV.   Yes, I'm afraid.

MRS. POPOV.   You're lying! Why don't you want to fight?

SMIRNOV.   Because . . . because you . . . because I like you.

MRS. POPOV.   [*Laughs angrily.*] He likes me! He dares say that he likes me! [*Points*   135
to the door.] Out!

SMIRNOV.   [*Loads the revolver in silence, takes cap and goes; at the door, stops for half a minute while they look at each other in silence; then he approaches* MRS. POPOV *hesitantly.*] Listen. . . . Are you still angry? I'm extremely irritated, but, do you understand me, how can I express it . . . the fact is, that, you see, strictly speaking . . . [*He shouts.*] Is it my fault, really, for liking you? [*Grabs the back of a chair, which cracks and breaks.*] Why the hell do you have such fragile furniture! I like you! Do you understand? I . . . I'm almost in love with you!

MRS. POPOV.   Get away from me—I hate you!

SMIRNOV.   God, what a woman! I've never in my life seen anything like her! I'm lost! I'm done for! I'm caught like a mouse in a trap!

MRS. POPOV.   Stand back or I'll shoot!

SMIRNOV.   Shoot! You could never understand what happiness it would be to die   140
under the gaze of those wonderful eyes, to be shot by a revolver which was held by those little velvet hands. . . . I've gone out of my mind! Think about it and decide right away, because if I leave here, then we'll never see each other again! Decide . . . I'm a nobleman, a respectable gentleman, of good family. I have an income of ten thousand a year. . . . I can put a bullet through a coin tossed in the air . . . I have some fine horses. . . . Will you be my wife?

MRS. POPOV.   [*Indignantly brandishes her revolver.*] Let's fight! I challenge you!

SMIRNOV.   I'm out of my mind . . . I don't understand anything . . . [*Shouts.*] Hey, you, water!

MRS. POPOV.   [*Shouts.*] Let's fight!

SMIRNOV.   I've gone out of my mind. I'm in love like a boy, like an idiot! [*He grabs her hand, she screams with pain.*] I love you! [*Kneels.*] I love you as I've never loved before! I've jilted twelve women, nine women have jilted me, but I've never loved one of them as I love you. . . . I'm weak, I'm a limp rag. . . . I'm on my knees like a fool, offering you my hand. . . . Shame, shame! I haven't been in love for five years, I vowed I wouldn't; and suddenly I'm in love, like a fish out of water. I'm offering my hand in marriage. Yes or no? You don't want to? You don't need to! [*Gets up and quickly goes to the door.*]

MRS. POPOV.   Wait!

SMIRNOV.   [*Stops.*] Well?

MRS. POPOV.   Nothing . . . you can go . . . go away . . . wait. . . . No, get out, get out!   145
I hate you! But—don't go! Oh, if you only knew how furious I am, how angry! [*Throws revolver on table.*] My fingers are swollen from that nasty thing. . . . [*Tears her handkerchief furiously.*] What are you waiting for? Get out!

SMIRNOV.   Farewell!

MRS. POPOV.   Yes, yes, go away! [*Shouts.*] Where are you going? Stop. . . . Oh, go away! Oh, how furious I am! Don't come near me! Don't come near me!

SMIRNOV.   [*Approaching her.*] How angry I am with myself! I'm in love like a student. I've been on my knees. . . . It gives me the shivers. [*Rudely.*] I love you! A lot of good it will do me to fall in love with you! Tomorrow I've got to pay the interest, begin the mowing of the hay. [*Puts his arm around her waist.*] I'll never forgive myself for this. . . .

MRS. POPOV.   Get away from me! Get your hands away! I . . . hate you! I . . . challenge you!

[*Prolonged kiss, LUKA enters with an ax, the GARDENER with a rake, the COACHMAN with a pitchfork, and WORKMEN with cudgels.*]

LUKA.   [*Catches sight of the pair kissing.*] Lord in heaven! [*Pause.*]   150

MRS. POPOV.   [*Lowering her eyes.*] Luka, tell them in the stable not to give Toby any oats today.

CURTAIN

QUESTIONS

1. What was Mrs. Popov's life like with her late husband? What did she learn about him after his death? How has this knowledge affected her?

2. Who is Smirnov? What is he like, and how do you know? Why does he say what he does about women?

3. Why is Luka important? How do his responses highlight the emotions developing between Smirnov and Mrs. Popov?

4. What causes Mrs. Popov to call Smirnov a bear, a brute, a monster? What is his immediate response?

5. Why is Toby significant? How does he symbolize Mrs. Popov's shifting emotions?

GENERAL QUESTIONS

1. Where did you laugh in the play? Analyze those moments and try to determine the causes of your laughter.

2. From this play, what conclusions can you draw about farce as a dramatic form? Consider the breaking chairs, the shouting, the challenge, the attitude of Smirnov about being shot, the shifting of feelings, etc.

3. How does Chekhov's presentation of Smirnov and Mrs. Popov make their reversal of feelings seem normal and logical, although sudden, unexpected, and surprising?

4. What are the major ideas or themes in *The Bear*? Consider vows made by the living to the dead, the difficulty of keeping resolutions, the nature of powerful emotions, the need to maintain conventions and expectations, etc.

BETH HENLEY, *AM I BLUE*

Brought up in Mississippi, Beth Henley attended Southern Methodist University, where in her sophomore year she wrote Am I Blue, *which was first produced in December 1981. She attended acting school in Illinois and went to Hollywood to take up a career as a movie actress. However, at the same time she continued to work on new plays, and it is as a writer that she has been successful. Her most notable achievement is her "Southern Gothic" play* Crimes of the Heart (*first titled* Crimes of Passion), *for which she won the Great American Play contest in 1978 and the Pulitzer Prize for Drama in 1981. She also wrote* The Wake of Jamey Foster (*1983*), The Lucky Spot (*1987*), The Debutante Ball (*1991*), *and* Abundance (*1991*). *The year 1992 saw the publication of four collected plays* (Beth Henley: Four Plays), *including* The Miss Firecracker Contest, *a two-act play written in 1979 and first performed in 1984. Her recent play* Impossible Marriage *was produced off Broadway in 1998 at the Laura Pels Theater in New*

York. In addition, she has seen some of her shorter scripts produced as television plays. Crimes of the Heart *was made into a successful film in 1986, starring Diane Keaton, Jessica Lange, Sam Shepard, and Sissy Spacek.*

In many of her plays, Henley's comedic manner develops out of the eccentricity or "kookiness" of her main female characters. The comic *donnée* is that an unusual or even disturbed action is accepted as a normal event that begins a course of dramatic action. A character in one of Henley's television plays, for example, inadvertently sets a house on fire, but the outcome turns out to be fortunate because of a lucrative home insurance policy. In *Crimes of the Heart*, one of the characters, after a failed suicide attempt, explains herself by saying that she has been having "a bad day." Even in the serious play *Abundance*, the two main female characters begin their twenty-five-year friendship after they have come west in the 1860s to become mail-order brides of men they have never seen. Ashbe of *Am I Blue* is an early original in the pattern, with her liking for hot Kool-Aid and colored marshmallows, her habit of stealing ashtrays and then donating them to a fellow tenant, and her dabbling in voodoo.

Although *Am I Blue* is an amusing play, it deals with the difficulties of adjustment to adulthood, misconceptions about social roles, unfulfilled dreams, general aimlessness and indecisiveness, and the attempt to develop individuality. The larger political and historical context of the year of the supposed events of the play, 1968, is mentioned by neither Ashbe nor John Polk, but one might connect their difficulties with some of the disturbances of that year, particularly the assassinations of Robert Kennedy and Martin Luther King, Jr.; the frustrating and seemingly endless war in Vietnam; and the many antiwar demonstrations and riots, especially during the Democratic National Convention in Chicago in the summer. Henley is very specific in dating the action of *Am I Blue* on the night of November 11, 1968—in other words, after all these disturbing and destabilizing events had taken place, and also less than a week after the election that made Richard Nixon president. One might also note the irony that November 11 had before 1954 been called Armistice Day (now Veterans Day)—a holiday dedicated to peace and stability.

Am I Blue thus reflects the disturbances and disruptions of the late 1960s, even though it focuses on the individual concerns and problems of John Polk and Ashbe. Ashbe's father is an alcoholic who is absent when she needs him, and her mother has deserted the home entirely. John Polk is facing a difficult choice about his future career, and he is also trying to stay afloat in the swim of fraternity life. Unable to succeed in either situation, he seeks strength in rum instead of calling on his own inner resources. Nothing earthshaking is claimed for either John Polk or Ashbe at the play's end, but they both succeed in developing a degree of recognition—rejecting conventional behaviors and discovering their own capacities for friendship and dignity.

BETH HENLEY (b. 1952)

Am I Blue* ⸻ (1973) 1982

CHARACTERS

> John Polk Richards, *seventeen*
> Ashbe Williams, *sixteen*
> Hilda, *a waitress, thirty-five*
> *Street People:* Barker, Whore, Bum, Clareece

*The first New York City production was by the Circle Repertory Company.

[SCENE. *A bar, the street, the living room of a run-down apartment.*]

[TIME. *Fall 1968.*]

The scene opens on a street in the New Orleans French Quarter on a rainy, blue bourbon night. Various people—a WHORE, BUM, STREET BARKER, CLAREECE—appear and disappear along the street. The scene then focuses on a bar where a piano is heard from the back room playing softly and indistinctly "Am I Blue?" The lights go up on JOHN POLK, who sits alone at a table. He is seventeen, a bit overweight and awkward. He wears nice clothes, perhaps a navy sweater with large white monograms. His navy raincoat is slung over an empty chair. While drinking John Polk concentrates on the red and black card that he holds in his hand. As soon as the scene is established, ASHBE enters from the street. She is sixteen, wears a flowered plastic raincoat, a white plastic rain cap, red galoshes, a butterfly barrette, and jeweled cat-eye glasses. She is carrying a bag full of stolen goods. Her hair is very curly. Ashbe makes her way cautiously to John Polk's table. As he sees her coming, he puts the card into his pocket. She sits in the empty chair and pulls his raincoat over her head.

ASHBE.   Excuse me . . . do you mind if I sit here please?

JOHN POLK.   [*Looks up at her—then down into his glass.*] What are you doing hiding under my raincoat? You're getting it all wet.

ASHBE.   Well, I'm very sorry, but after all it is a raincoat. [*He tries to pull off coat.*] It was rude of me I know, but look I just don't want them to recognize me.

JOHN POLK.   [*Looking about.*] Who to recognize you?

ASHBE.   Well, I stole these two ashtrays from the Screw Inn, ya know right down   5
the street. [*She pulls out two glass commercial ashtrays from her white plastic bag.*] Anyway, I'm scared the manager saw me. They'll be after me I'm afraid.

JOHN POLK.   Well, they should be. Look, do you mind giving me back my raincoat? I don't want to be found protecting any thief.

ASHBE.   [*Coming out from under coat.*] Thief—would you call Robin Hood a thief?

JOHN POLK.   Christ.

ASHBE.   [*Back under coat.*] No, you wouldn't. He was valiant—all the time stealing from the rich and giving to the poor.

JOHN POLK.   But your case isn't exactly the same, is it? You're stealing from some   10
crummy little bar and keeping the ashtrays for yourself. Now give me back my coat.

ASHBE.   [*Throws coat at him.*] Sure, take your old coat. I suppose I should have explained—about Miss Marcey. [*Silence.*] Miss Marcey, this cute old lady with a little hump in her back. I always see her in her sun hat and blue print dress. Miss Marcey lives in the apartment building next to ours. I leave all the stolen goods, as gifts on her front steps.

JOHN POLK.   Are you one of those kleptomaniacs? [*He starts checking his wallet.*]

ASHBE.   You mean when people all the time steal and they can't help it?

JOHN POLK.   Yeah.

ASHBE.   Oh, no. I'm not a bit careless. Take my job tonight, my very first night job,   15
if you want to know. Anyway, I've been planning it for two months, trying to decipher which bar most deserved to be stolen from. I finally decided on the Screw Inn. Mainly because of the way they're so mean to Mr. Groves. He works at the magazine rack at Diver's Drugstore and is really very sweet, but he has a drinking problem. I don't think that's fair to be mean to people simply because they have a drinking problem—and, well, anyway, you see I'm not just stealing for personal gain. I mean, I don't even smoke.

JOHN POLK.   Yeah, well, most infants don't, but then again, most infants don't hang around bars.

ASHBE.   I don't see why not, Toulouse Lautrec did.

JOHN POLK.   They'd throw me out.

ASHBE.   Oh, they throw me out too, but I don't accept defeat. [*Slowly moves into him.*] Why it's the very same with my pickpocketing.

[*JOHN POLK sneers, turns away.*]

ASHBE.   It's a very hard act to master. Why every time I've done it, I've been   20
caught.

JOHN POLK.   That's all I need, is to have some slum kid tell me how good it is to
steal. Everyone knows it's not.

ASHBE.   [*About his drink.*] That looks good. What is it?

JOHN POLK.   Hey, would you mind leaving me alone—I just wanted to be alone.

ASHBE.   Okay, I'm sorry. How about if I'm quiet?

[*JOHN POLK shrugs. He sips drink, looks around, catches her eye, she smiles and sighs.*]

ASHBE.   I was just looking at your pin. What fraternity are you in?   25

JOHN POLK.   S.A.E.

ASHBE.   Is it a good fraternity?

JOHN POLK.   Sure, it's the greatest.

ASHBE.   I bet you have lots of friends.

JOHN POLK.   Tons.   30

ASHBE.   Are you being serious?

JOHN POLK.   Yes.

ASHBE.   Hmm. Do they have parties and all that?

JOHN POLK.   Yeah, lots of parties, booze, honking horns, it's exactly what you
would expect.

ASHBE.   I wouldn't expect anything. Why did you join?   35

JOHN POLK.   I don't know. Well, my brother . . . I guess it was my brother . . . he
told me how great it was, how the fraternity was supposed to get you dates, make you
study, solve all your problems.

ASHBE.   Gee, does it?

JOHN POLK.   Doesn't help you study.

ASHBE.   How about dates? Do they get you a lot of dates?

JOHN POLK.   Some.   40

ASHBE.   What were the girls like?

JOHN POLK.   I don't know—they were like girls.

ASHBE.   Did you have a good time?

JOHN POLK.   I had a pretty good time.

ASHBE.   Did you make love to any of them?   45

JOHN POLK.   [*To self.*] Oh, Christ . . .

ASHBE.   I'm sorry . . . I just figured that's why you had the appointment with the
whore . . . cause you didn't have anyone else . . . to make love to.

JOHN POLK.   How did you know I had the, ah, the appointment?

ASHBE.   I saw you put the red card in your pocket when I came up. Those red
cards are pretty familiar around here. The house is only about a block or so away. It's one
of the best though, really very plush. Only two murders and a knifing in its whole history.
Do you go there often?

JOHN POLK.   Yeah, I like to give myself a treat.   50

ASHBE.   Who do you have?

JOHN POLK.   What do you mean?

ASHBE.   I mean which girl. [*JOHN POLK gazes into his drink.*] Look, I just thought I might know her is all.

JOHN POLK.   Know her, ah, how would you know her?

ASHBE.   Well, some of the girls from my high school go there to work when they get out.   55

JOHN POLK.   G.G., her name is G.G.

ASHBE.   G.G. . . . Hmm, well, how does she look?

JOHN POLK.   I don't know.

ASHBE.   Oh, you've never been with her before?

JOHN POLK.   No.   60

ASHBE.   [*Confidentially.*] Are you one of those kinds that likes a lot of variety?

JOHN POLK.   Variety? Sure, I guess I like variety.

ASHBE.   Oh, yes, now I remember.

JOHN POLK.   What?

ASHBE.   G.G., that's just her working name. Her real name is Myrtle Reims, she's   65
Kay Reims' older sister. Kay is in my grade at school.

JOHN POLK.   Myrtle? Her name is Myrtle?

ASHBE.   I never liked the name either.

JOHN POLK.   Myrtle, oh, Christ. Is she pretty?

ASHBE.   [*Matter of fact.*] Pretty, no she's not real pretty.

JOHN POLK.   What does she look like?   70

ASHBE.   Let's see . . . she's, ah, well, Myrtle had acne and there are a few scars left. It's not bad. I think they sort of give her character. Her hair's red, only I don't think it's really red. It sort of fizzles out all over her head. She's got a pretty good figure . . . big top . . . but the rest of her is kind of skinny.

JOHN POLK.   I wonder if she has a good personality.

ASHBE.   Well, she was a senior when I was a freshman; so I never really knew her. I remember she used to paint her fingernails lots of different colors . . . pink, orange, purple. I don't know, but she kind of scares me. About the only time I ever saw her true personality was around a year ago. I was over at Kay's making a health poster for school. Anyway, Myrtle comes busting in, screaming about how she can't find her spangled bra anywhere. Kay and I just sat on the floor cutting pictures of food out of magazines while she was storming about slamming drawers and swearing. Finally, she found it. It was pretty garish—red with black and gold sequined G's on each cup. That's how I remember the name—G.G.

[*As ASHBE illustrates the placement of the G's she spots HILDA, the waitress, approaching. ASHBE pulls the raincoat over her head and hides on the floor. HILDA enters through the beaded curtains spilling her tray. HILDA is a woman of few words.*]

HILDA.   Shit, damn curtain. Nuther drink?

JOHN POLK.   Mam?   75

HILDA.   [*Points to drink.*] Vodka coke?

JOHN POLK.   No, thank you. I'm not quite finished yet.

HILDA.   Napkins clean.

[*ASHBE pulls her bag off the table. HILDA looks at ASHBE then to JOHN POLK. She walks around the table, as ASHBE is crawling along the floor to escape. ASHBE runs into HILDA's toes.*]

ASHBE.   Are those real gold?

HILDA.   You again. Out.   80

ASHBE.   She wants me to leave. Why should a paying customer leave? [*Back to HILDA.*] Now I'll have a mint julip and easy on the mint.

HILDA.   This pre-teen with you?

JOHN POLK.   Well, I . . . No . . . I . . .

HILDA.   I.D.'s.

ASHBE.   Certainly, I always try to cooperate with the management.   85

HILDA.   [*Looking at JOHN POLK'S I.D.*] I.D., 11-12-50. Date: 11-11-68.

JOHN POLK.   Yes, but . . . well, 11-12 is less than two hours away.

HILDA.   Back in two hours.

ASHBE.   I seem to have left my identification in my gold lamé bag.

HILDA.   Well, boo-hoo. [*Motions for ASHBE to leave with a minimum of effort. She goes   90
back to table.*] No tip.

ASHBE.   You didn't tip her?

JOHN POLK.   I figured the drinks were so expensive . . . I just didn't . . .

HILDA.   No tip!

JOHN POLK.   Look, Miss, I'm sorry. [*Going through his pockets.*] Here would you like
a . . . a nickel . . . wait, wait, here's a quarter.

HILDA.   Just move ass, sonny. You too, Barbie.   95

ASHBE.   Ugh, I hate public rudeness. I'm sure I'll refrain from ever coming here
again.

HILDA.   Think I'll go in the back room and cry.

[*ASHBE and JOHN POLK exit. HILDA picks up tray and exits through the curtain, tripping again.*]

HILDA.   Shit. Damn curtain.

[*ASHBE and JOHN POLK are now standing outside under the awning of the bar.*]

ASHBE.   Gee, I didn't know it was your birthday tomorrow. Happy birthday! Don't
be mad. I thought you were at least twenty or twenty-one, really.

JOHN POLK.   It's o.k. Forget it.   100

[*As they begin walking, various blues are heard coming from the nearby bars.*]

ASHBE.   It's raining.

JOHN POLK.   I know.

ASHBE.   Are you going over to the house now?

JOHN POLK.   No, not till twelve.

ASHBE.   Yeah, the red and black cards—they mean all night. Midnight till   105
morning.

[*At this point a street BARKER beckons the couple into his establishment. Perhaps he is accompanied
by a WHORE.*]

BARKER.   Hey mister, bring your baby on in, buy her a few drinks, maybe tonight ya
get lucky.

ASHBE.   Keep walking.

JOHN POLK.   What's wrong with the place?

ASHBE.   The drinks are watery rot gut, and the show girls are boys . . .

BARKER.   Up yours, punk!   110

JOHN POLK. [*Who has now sat down on a street bench.*] Look, just tell me where a cheap bar is. I've got to stay drunk, but I don't have much money left.

ASHBE. Yikes, there aren't too many cheap bars around here, and a lot of them check I.D.'s.

JOHN POLK. Well, do you know of any that don't?

ASHBE. No, not for sure.

JOHN POLK. Oh, God, I need to get drunk. 115

ASHBE. Aren't you?

JOHN POLK. Some, but I'm losing ground fast.

[*By this time a* BUM *who has been traveling drunkenly down the street falls near the couple and begins throwing up.*]

ASHBE. Oh, I know! You can come to my apartment. It's just down the block. We keep one bottle of rum around. I'll serve you a grand drink, three or four if you like.

JOHN POLK. [*Fretfully.*] No, thanks. 120

ASHBE. But look, we're getting all wet.

JOHN POLK. Sober too, wet and sober.

ASHBE. Oh, come on! Rain's blurring my glasses.

JOHN POLK. Well, how about your parents? What would they say?

ASHBE. Daddy's out of town and Mama lives in Atlanta; so I'm sure they won't mind. I think we have some cute little marshmallows. [*Pulling on him.*] Won't you really come?

JOHN POLK. You've probably got some gang of muggers waiting to kill me. Oh, all 125
right . . . what the hell, let's go.

ASHBE. Hurrah! Come on. It's this way. [*She starts across the stage, stops, and picks up an old hat.*] Hey, look at this hat. Isn't something! Here, wear it to keep off the rain.

JOHN POLK. [*Throwing hat back onto street.*] No, thanks, you don't know who's worn it before.

ASHBE. [*Picking hat back up.*] That makes it all the more exciting. Maybe it was a butcher's who slaughtered his wife or a silver pirate with a black bird on his throat. Who do you guess?

JOHN POLK. I don't know. Anyway what's the good of guessing? I mean you'll never really know.

ASHBE. [*Trying the hat on.*] Yeah, probably not. 130

[*At this point* ASHBE *and* JOHN POLK *reach the front door.*]

ASHBE. Here we are.

[ASHBE *begins fumbling for her key.* CLAREECE, *a teeny-bopper, walks up to* JOHN POLK.]

CLAREECE. Hey, man, got any spare change?

JOHN POLK. [*Looking through his pockets.*] Let me see . . . I . . .

ASHBE. [*Coming up between them, giving* CLAREECE *a shove.*] Beat it, Clareece. He's my company.

CLAREECE. [*Walks away and sneers.*] Oh, shove it, Frizzels. 135

ASHBE. A lot of jerks live around here. Come on in. [*She opens the door. Lights go up on the living room of a run-down apartment in a run-down apartment house. Besides being merely run-down the room is a malicious pig sty with colors, paper hats, paper dolls, masks, torn up stuffed animals, dead flowers and leaves, dress-up clothes, etc., thrown all about.*] My bones are cold. Do you want a towel to dry off?

JOHN POLK.   Yes, thank you.

ASHBE.   [*She picks up a towel off the floor and tosses it to him.*] Here. [*He begins drying off, as she takes off her rain things; then she begins raking things off the sofa.*] Please do sit down. [*He sits.*] I'm sorry the place is disheveled, but my father's been out of town. I always try to pick up and all before he gets in. Of course, he's pretty used to messes. My mother never was too good at keeping things clean.

JOHN POLK.   When's he coming back?

ASHBE.   Sunday, I believe. Oh, I've been meaning to say . . .   140

JOHN POLK.   What?

ASHBE.   My name's Ashbe Williams.

JOHN POLK.   Ashbe?

ASHBE.   Yeah, Ashbe.

JOHN POLK.   My name's John Polk Richards.   145

ASHBE.   John Polk? They call you John Polk?

JOHN POLK.   It's family.

ASHBE.   [*Putting on socks.*] These are my favorite socks, the red furry ones. Well, here's some books and magazines to look at while I fix you something to drink. What do you want in your rum?

JOHN POLK.   Coke's fine.

ASHBE.   I'll see if we have any. I think I'll take some hot Kool-Aid myself.   150
[She exits to the kitchen.]

JOHN POLK.   Hot Kool-Aid?

ASHBE.   It's just Kool-Aid that's been heated, like hot chocolate or hot tea.

JOHN POLK.   Sounds great.

ASHBE.   Well, I'm used to it. You get so much for your dime, it makes it worth your while. I don't buy presweetened, of course, it's better to sugar your own.

JOHN POLK.   I remember once I threw up a lot of grape Kool-Aid when I was a kid.   155
I've hated it ever since. Hey, would you check on the time?

ASHBE.   [*She enters carrying a tray with several bottles of food coloring, a bottle of rum, and a huge glass.*] I'm sorry we don't have Coke. I wonder if rum and Kool-Aid is good? Oh, we don't have a clock either.

[*She pours a large amount of rum into the large glass.*]

JOHN POLK.   I'll just have it with water then.

ASHBE.   [*She finds an almost empty glass of water somewhere in the room and dumps it in with the rum.*] Would you like food coloring in the water? It makes a drink all the more aesthetic. Of course, some people don't care for aesthetics.

JOHN POLK.   No, thank you, just plain water.

ASHBE.   Are you sure? The taste is entirely the same. I put it in all my water.   160

JOHN POLK.   Well . . .

ASHBE.   What color do you want?

JOHN POLK.   I don't know.

ASHBE.   What's your favorite color?

JOHN POLK.   Blue, I guess.   165

[*She puts a few blue drops into the glass. As she has nothing to stir with, she blows into the glass turning the water blue.*]

JOHN POLK.   Thanks.

ASHBE.   [*Exits. She screams from kitchen.*] Come on, say come on, cat, eat your fresh, good milk.

JOHN POLK.   You have a cat?

ASHBE.   [*off.*] No.

JOHN POLK.   Oh.   170

ASHBE.   [*She enters carrying a tray with a cup of hot Kool-Aid and Cheerios and colored marshmallows.*] Here are some Cheerios and some cute, little, colored marshmallows to eat with your drink.

JOHN POLK.   Thanks.

ASHBE.   I one time smashed all the big white marshmallows in the plastic bag at the grocery store.

JOHN POLK.   Why did you do that?

ASHBE.   I was angry. Do you like ceramics?   175

JOHN POLK.   Yes.

ASHBE.   My mother makes them. It's sort of her hobby. She is very talented.

JOHN POLK.   My mother never does anything. Well, I guess she can shuffle the bridge deck okay.

ASHBE.   Actually, my mother is a dancer. She teaches at a school in Atlanta. She's really very talented.

JOHN POLK.   [*Indicates ceramics.*] She must be to do all these.   180

ASHBE.   Well, Madeline, my older sister, did the blue one. Madeline gets to live with Mama.

JOHN POLK.   And you live with your father.

ASHBE.   Yeah, but I get to go visit them sometimes.

JOHN POLK.   You do ceramics too?

ASHBE.   No, I never learned . . . but I have this great potholder set. [*Gets up to show*   185
him.] See, I make lots of multicolored potholders and send them to Mama and Madeline. I also make paper hats. [*Gets material to show him.*] I guess they're more creative, but making potholders is more relaxing. Here, would you like to make a hat?

JOHN POLK.   I don't know, I'm a little drunk.

ASHBE.   It's not hard a bit. [*Hands him material.*] Just draw a real pretty design on the paper. It really doesn't have to be pretty, just whatever you want.

JOHN POLK.   It's kind of you to give my creative drives such freedom.

ASHBE.   Ha, ha, ha, I'll work on my potholder set a bit.

JOHN POLK.   What time is it? I've really got to check on the time.   190

ASHBE.   I know. I'll call the time operator.

[*She goes to the phone.*]

JOHN POLK.   How do you get along without a clock?

ASHBE.   Well, I've been late for school a lot. Daddy has a watch. It's 11:03.

JOHN POLK.   I've got a while yet. [*ASHBE twirls back to her chair, drops, and sighs.*] Are you a dancer, too?

ASHBE.   [*Delighted.*] I can't dance a bit, really. I practice a lot is all, at home in the   195
afternoon. I imagine you go to a lot of dances.

JOHN POLK.   Not really, I'm a terrible dancer. I usually get bored or drunk.

ASHBE.   You probably drink too much.

JOHN POLK.   No, it's just since I've come to college. All you do there is drink more beer and write more papers.

ASHBE.   What are you studying for to be?

In this first production of Henley's *Am I Blue* at the Margo Jones Experimental Theater of Southern Methodist University in Dallas, Texas, in 1973, Ashbe Williams (Marcie Glaser) enters the bar where she first meets John Polk (John Tillotson). The production was directed by Jill Christine Peters, with the set designed by John Gisondi.

JOHN POLK.   I don't know.   200
ASHBE.   Why don't you become a rancher?
JOHN POLK.   Dad wants me to help run his soybean farm.
ASHBE.   Soybean farm. Yikes, that's really something. Where is it?
JOHN POLK.   Well, I live in the Delta, Hollybluff, Mississippi. Anyway, Dad feels I should go to business school first; you know, so I'll become, well, management-minded. Pass the blue.
ASHBE.   Is that what you really want to do?   205
JOHN POLK.   I don't know. It would probably be as good as anything else I could do. Dad makes good money. He can take vacations whenever he wants. Sure it'll be a ball.
ASHBE.   I'd hate to have to be management-minded. [*JOHN POLK shrugs.*] I don't mean to hurt your feelings, but I would really hate to be a management mind. [*She starts*

walking on her knees, twisting her fists in front of her eyes, and making clicking sounds as a management mind would make.]

JOHN POLK.   Cut it out. Just forget it. The farm could burn down, and I wouldn't even have to think about it.

ASHBE.   [*After a pause.*] Well, what do you want to talk about?

JOHN POLK.   I don't know.   210

ASHBE.   When was the last dance you went to?

JOHN POLK.   Dances. That's great subject. Let's see, oh, I don't really remember—it was probably some blind date. God, I hate dates.

ASHBE.   Why?

JOHN POLK.   Well, they always say that they don't want popcorn, and they wind up eating all of yours.

ASHBE.   You mean, you hate dates just because they eat your popcorn? Don't you   215
think that's kind of stingy?

JOHN POLK.   It's the principle of the thing. Why can't they just say, yes, I'd like some popcorn when you ask them. But, no, they're always so damn coy.

ASHBE.   I'd tell my date if I wanted popcorn. I'm not that immature.

JOHN POLK.   Anyway, it's not only the popcorn. It's a lot of little things. I've finished coloring. What do I do now?

ASHBE.   Now you have to fold it. Here . . . like this. [*She explains the process with relish.*] Say, that's really something.

JOHN POLK.   It's kind of funny looking. [*Putting the hat on.*] Yeah, I like it, but you   220
could never wear it anywhere.

ASHBE.   Well, like what anyway?

JOHN POLK.   Huh?

ASHBE.   The things dates do to you that you don't like, the little things.

JOHN POLK.   Oh, well, just the way they wear those false eyelashes and put their hand on your knee when you're trying to parallel park, and keep on giggling and going off to the bathroom with their girl friends. It's obvious they don't want to go out with me. They just want to go out so that they can wear their new clothes and won't have to sit on their ass in the dormitory. They never want to go out with me. I can never even talk to them.

ASHBE.   Well, you can talk to me, and I'm a girl.   225

JOHN POLK.   Well, I'm really kind of drunk, and you're a stranger . . . well, I probably wouldn't be able to talk to you tomorrow. That makes a difference.

ASHBE.   Maybe it does. [*A bit of a pause and then extremely pleased by the idea she says.*] You know we're alike because I don't like dances either.

JOHN POLK.   I thought you said you practiced . . . in the afternoons.

ASHBE.   Well, I like dancing. I just don't like dances. At least not like . . . well, not like the one our school was having tonight . . . they're so corny.

JOHN POLK.   Yeah, most dances are.   230

ASHBE.   All they serve is potato chips and fruit punch, and then this stupid baby band plays and everybody dances around thinking they're so hot. I frankly wouldn't dance there. I would prefer to wait till I am invited to an exclusive ball. It doesn't really matter which ball, just one where they have huge, golden chandeliers and silver fountains, and serve delicacies of all sorts and bubble blue champagne. I'll arrive in a pink silk cape [*Laughing.*] I want to dance in pink!

JOHN POLK.   You're mixed up. You're probably one of those people that live in a fantasy world.

ASHBE.   I do not. I accept reality as well as anyone. Anyway, you can talk to me, remember. I know what you mean by the kind of girls it's hard to talk to. There are girls a

lot that way in the small clique at my school. Really tacky and mean. They expect everyone to be as stylish as they are, and they won't even speak to you in the hall. I don't mind
if they don't speak to me, but I really love the orphans, and it hurts my feelings when they
are so mean to them.

JOHN POLK.   What do you mean—they're mean to the "orpheens"? [*Giggles to himself at the wordplay.*]

ASHBE.   Oh, well, they sometimes snicker at the orphans' dresses. The orphans   235
usually have hand-me-down, drab, ugly dresses. Once Shelly Maxwell wouldn't let Glinda
borrow her pencil, even though she had two. It hurt her feelings.

JOHN POLK.   Are you best friends with these orphans?

ASHBE.   I hardly know them at all. They're really shy. I just like them a lot. They're
the reason I put spells on the girls in the clique.

JOHN POLK.   Spells, what do you mean, witch spells?

ASHBE.   Witch spells? Not really, mostly just voodoo.

JOHN POLK.   Are you kidding? Do you really do voodoo?   240

ASHBE.   Sure, here I'll show you my doll. [*Goes to get doll, comes back with straw
voodoo doll. Her air as she returns is one of frightening mystery.*] I know a lot about the subject.
Cora, she used to wash dishes in the Moonlight Cafe, told me all about voodoo. She's a
real expert on the subject, went to all the meetings and everything. Once she caused a
man's throat to rot away and turn almost totally black. She's moved to Chicago now.

JOHN POLK.   It doesn't really work. Does it?

ASHBE.   Well, not always. The thing about voodoo is that both parties have to believe in it for it to work.

JOHN POLK.   Do the girls in school believe in it?

ASHBE.   Not really, I don't think. That's where my main problem comes in. I have   245
to make the clique believe in it, yet I have to be very subtle. Mainly, I give reports in English class or Speech.

JOHN POLK.   Reports?

ASHBE.   On voodoo.

JOHN POLK.   That's really kind of sick, you know.

ASHBE.   Not really. I don't cast spells that'll do any real harm. Mainly, just the kind
of thing to make them think . . . to keep them on their toes. [*Blue-drink intoxication begins
to take over and JOHN POLK begins laughing.*] What's so funny?

JOHN POLK.   Nothing. I was just thinking what a mean little person you are.   250

ASHBE.   Mean! I'm not mean a bit.

JOHN POLK.   Yes, you are mean . . . [*Picking up color.*] . . . and green too.

ASHBE.   Green?

JOHN POLK.   Yes, green with envy of those other girls; so you play all those mean little tricks.

ASHBE.   Envious of those other girls, that stupid, close-minded little clique!   255

JOHN POLK.   Green as this marshmallow. [*Eats marshmallow.*]

ASHBE.   You think I want to be in some group . . . a sheep like you? A little sheep
like you that does everything when he's supposed to do it!

JOHN POLK.   Me a sheep . . . I do what I want!

ASHBE.   Ha! I've known you for an hour and already I see you for the sheep you are!

JOHN POLK.   Don't take your green meanness out on me.   260

ASHBE.   Not only are you a sheep, you are a NORMAL sheep. Give me back my
colors! [*Begins snatching colors away.*]

JOHN POLK.   [*Pushing colors at her.*] Green and mean! Green and mean! Green and
mean!

ASHBE. [*Throwing marshmallows at him.*] That's the reason you're in a fraternity and the reason you're going to manage your mind. And dates . . . you go out on dates merely because it's expected of you even though you have a terrible time. That's the reason you go to the whorehouse to prove you're a normal man. Well, you're much too normal for me.

JOHN POLK. Infant bitch. You think you're really cute.

ASHBE. That really wasn't food coloring in your drink, it was poison! [*She laughs,* 265
he picks up his coat to go, and she stops throwing marshmallows at him.] Are you going? I was only kidding. For Christ sake, it wasn't really poison. Come on, don't go. Can't you take a little friendly criticism?

JOHN POLK. Look, did you have to bother me tonight? I had enough problems without . . .

[*Phone rings. Both look at phone, it rings for the third time. He stands undecided.*]

ASHBE. Look, wait, we'll make it up. [*She goes to answer phone.*] Hello . . . Daddy. How are you? . . . I'm fine . . . Dad, you sound funny . . . What? . . . Come on, Daddy, you know she's not here. [*Pause.*] Look, I told you I wouldn't call anymore. You've got her number in Atlanta. [*Pause, as she sinks to the floor.*] Why have you started again? . . . Don't say that. I can tell it. I can. Hey, I have to go to bed now, I don't want to talk anymore, okay? [*Hangs up phone, then softly to self.*] Goddamnit.

JOHN POLK. [*He has heard the conversation and is taking off his coat.*] Hey, Ashbe . . . [*She looks at him blankly, her mind far away.*] You want to talk?

ASHBE. No, [*Slight pause.*] Why don't you look at my shell collection? I have this special shell collection. [*She shows him collection.*]

JOHN POLK. They're beautiful, I've never seen colors like this. [*ASHBE is silent, he* 270
continues to himself.] I used to go to Biloxi° a lot when I was a kid . . . One time my brother and I, we camped out on the beach. The sky was purple. I remember it was really purple. We ate pork and beans out of a can. I'd always kinda wanted to do that. Every night for about a week after I got home, I dreamt about these waves foaming over my head and face. It was funny. Did you find these shells or buy them?

ASHBE. Some I found, some I bought. I've been trying to decipher their meaning. Here, listen, do you hear that?

JOHN POLK. Yes.

ASHBE. That's the soul of the sea. [*She listens.*] I'm pretty sure it's the soul of the sea. Just imagine when I decipher the language. I'll know all the secrets of the world.

JOHN POLK. Yeah, probably you will. [*Looking into the shell.*] You know, you were right.

ASHBE. What do you mean? 275

JOHN POLK. About me, you were right. I am a sheep, a normal one. I've been trying to get out of it, but now I'm as big a sheep as ever.

ASHBE. Oh, it doesn't matter. You're company. It was rude of me to say.

JOHN POLK. No, because it was true. I really didn't want to go into a fraternity, I didn't even want to go to college, and I sure as hell don't want to go back to Hollybluff and work the soybean farm till I'm eighty.

ASHBE. I still say you could work on a ranch.

JOHN POLK. I don't know. I wanted to be a minister or something good, but I 280
don't even know if I believe in God.

270 *Biloxi:* city in southern Mississippi, on the Gulf of Mexico.

ASHBE. Yeah.

JOHN POLK. I never used to worry about being a failure. Now I think about it all the time. It's just I need to do something that's . . . fulfilling.

ASHBE. Fulfilling, yes, I see what you mean. Well, how about college? Isn't it fulfilling? I mean, you take all those wonderful classes, and you have all your very good friends.

JOHN POLK. Friends, yeah, I have some friends.

ASHBE. What do you mean?   285

JOHN POLK. Nothing . . . well, I do mean something. What the hell, let me try to explain. You see it was my "friends," the fraternity guys that set me up with G.G., excuse me, Myrtle, as a gift for my eighteenth birthday.

ASHBE. You mean, you didn't want the appointment?

JOHN POLK. No, I didn't want it. Hey, ah, where did my blue drink go?

ASHBE. [As she hands him the drink.] They probably thought you really wanted to go.

JOHN POLK. Yeah, I'm sure they gave a damn what I wanted. They never even   290
asked me. Hell, I would have told them a handkerchief, a pair of argyle socks, but, no, they have to get me a whore just because it's a cool-ass thing to do. They make me sick. I couldn't even stay at the party they gave. All the sweaty T-shirts, and moron sex stories . . . I just couldn't take it.

ASHBE. Is that why you were at the Blue Angel so early?

JOHN POLK. Yeah, I needed to get drunk, but not with them. They're such creeps.

ASHBE. Gosh, so you really don't want to go to Myrtle's?

JOHN POLK. No, I guess not.

ASHBE. Then are you going?   295

JOHN POLK. [Pause.] Yes.

ASHBE. That's wrong. You shouldn't go just to please them.

JOHN POLK. Oh, that's not the point anymore, maybe at first it was, but it's not anymore. Now I have go for myself . . . to prove to myself that I'm not afraid.

ASHBE. Afraid? [Slowly, as she begins to grasp his meaning.] You mean, you've never slept with a girl before?

JOHN POLK. Well, I've never been in love.   300

ASHBE. [In amazement.] You're a virgin?

JOHN POLK. Oh, God.

ASHBE. No, don't feel bad, I am too.

JOHN POLK. I thought I should be in love . . .

ASHBE. Well, you're certainly not in love with Myrtle. I mean, you haven't even   305
met her.

JOHN POLK. I know, but, God, I thought maybe I'd never fall in love. What then? You should experience everything . . . shouldn't you? Oh, what's it matter, everything's so screwed.

ASHBE. Screwed? Yeah, I guess it is. I mean, I always thought it would be fun to have a lot of friends who gave parties and go to dances all dressed up. Like the dance tonight . . . it might have been fun.

JOHN POLK. Well, why didn't you go?

ASHBE. I don't know. I'm not sure it would have been fun. Anyway, you can't go . . . alone.

JOHN POLK. Oh, you need a date?   310

ASHBE. Yeah, or something.

JOHN POLK. Say, Ashbe, ya wanna dance here?

ASHBE. No, I think we'd better discuss your dilemma.

JOHN POLK. What dilemma?

ASHBE. Myrtle. It doesn't seem right you should . . .   315

JOHN POLK. Let's forget Myrtle for now. I've got a while yet. Here have some more of this blue-moon drink.

ASHBE. You're only trying to escape through artificial means.

JOHN POLK. Yeah, you got it. Now come on. Would you like to dance? Hey, you said you liked to dance.

ASHBE. You're being ridiculous.

JOHN POLK. [*Winking at her.*] Dance?   320

ASHBE. John Polk, I just thought . . .

JOHN POLK. Hmm?

ASHBE. How to solve your problem . . .

JOHN POLK. Well . . .

ASHBE. Make love to me!   325

JOHN POLK. What?!

ASHBE. It all seems logical to me. It would prove you weren't scared, and you wouldn't be doing it just to impress others.

JOHN POLK. Look, I . . . I mean, I hardly know you . . .

ASHBE. But we've talked. It's better this way, really. I won't be so apt to point out your mistakes.

JOHN POLK. I'd feel great, stripping a twelve-year-old of her virginity.   330

ASHBE. I'm sixteen! Anyway, I'd be stripping you of yours just as well. I'll go put on some Tiger Claw perfume. [*She runs out.*]

JOHN POLK. Hey, come back! Tiger Claw perfume, Christ.

ASHBE. [*Entering.*] I think one should have different scents for different moods.

JOHN POLK. Hey, stop spraying that! You know I'm not going to . . . well, you'd get neurotic, or pregnant, or some damn thing. Stop spraying, will you!

ASHBE. Pregnant? You really think I could get pregnant?   335

JOHN POLK. Sure, it'd be a delightful possibility.

ASHBE. It really wouldn't be bad. Maybe I would get to go to Tokyo for an abortion. I've never been to the Orient.

JOHN POLK. Sure getting cut on is always a real treat.

ASHBE. Anyway, I might just want to have my dear baby. I could move to Atlanta with Mama and Madeline. It'd be wonderful fun. Why I could take him to the supermarket, put him in one of those little baby seats to stroll him about. I'd buy peach baby food and feed it to him with a tiny golden spoon. Why I could take colored pictures of him and send them to you through the mail. Come on . . . [*Starts putting pillows onto the couch.*] Well, I guess you should kiss me for a start. It's only etiquette, everyone begins with it.

JOHN POLK. I don't think I could even kiss you with a clear conscience. I mean,   340
you're so small with those little cat-eye glasses and curly hair . . . I couldn't even kiss you.

ASHBE. You couldn't even kiss me? I can't help it if I have to wear glasses. I got the prettiest ones I could find.

JOHN POLK. Your glasses are fine. Let's forget it, okay?

ASHBE. I know, my lips are too purple, but if I eat carrots, the dye'll come off and they'll be orange.

JOHN POLK. I didn't say anything about your lips being too purple.

ASHBE. Well, what is it? You're just plain chicken, I suppose . . .   345

JOHN POLK. Sure, right, I'm chicken, totally chicken. Let's forget it. I don't know how, but, somehow, this is probably all my fault.

ASHBE. You're darn right it's all your fault! I want to have my dear baby or at least get to Japan. I'm so sick of school I could smash every marshmallow in sight! [*She starts smashing.*] Go on to your skinny pimple whore. I hope the skinny whore laughs in your face, which she probably will because you have an easy face to laugh in.

JOHN POLK. You're absolutely right, she'll probably hoot and howl her damn fizzle red head off. Maybe you can wait outside the door and hear her, give you lots of pleasure, you sadistic little thief.

ASHBE. Thief! Was Robin Hood . . . Oh, what's wrong with this world? I just wasn't made for it, is all. I've probably been put in the wrong world, I can see that now.

JOHN POLK. You're fine in this world.   350

ASHBE. Sure, everyone just views me as an undesirable lump.

JOHN POLK. Who?

ASHBE. You, for one.

JOHN POLK. [*Pause.*] You mean because I wouldn't make love to you?

ASHBE. It seems clear to me.   355

JOHN POLK. But you're wrong, you know.

ASHBE. [*To self, softly.*] Don't pity me.

JOHN POLK. The reason I wouldn't wasn't that . . . it's just that . . . well, I like you too much to.

ASHBE. You like me?

JOHN POLK. Undesirable lump, Jesus. Your cheeks they're . . . they're . . .   360

ASHBE. My cheeks? They're what?

JOHN POLK. They're rosy.

ASHBE. My cheeks are rosy?

JOHN POLK. Yeah, your cheeks, they're really rosy.

ASHBE. Well, they're natural, you know. Say, would you like to dance?   365

JOHN POLK. Yes.

ASHBE. I'll turn on the radio. [*She turns on radio. Ethel Waters is heard singing "Honey in the Honeycomb." ASHBE begins snapping her fingers.*] Yikes, let's jazz it out.

[*They dance.*]

JOHN POLK. Hey, I'm not good or anything . . .

ASHBE. John Polk.

JOHN POLK. Yeah?   370

ASHBE. Baby, I think you dance fine!

[*They dance on, laughing, saying what they want till end of song. Then a radio announcer comes on and says the 12:00 news will be in five minutes. Billie Holiday, or Terry Pierce, begins singing, "Am I Blue?"*]

JOHN POLK. Dance?

ASHBE. News in five minutes.

JOHN POLK. Yeah.

ASHBE. That means five minutes till midnight.   375

JOHN POLK. Yeah, I know.

ASHBE. Then you're not . . .

JOHN POLK. Ashbe, I've never danced all night. Wouldn't it be something to . . . to dance all night and watch the rats come out of the gutter?

ASHBE. Rats?

JOHN POLK. Don't they come out at night? I hear New Orleans has lots of rats.   380

ASHBE. Yeah, yeah, it's got lots of rats.

JOHN POLK. Then let's dance all night and wait for them to come out.

ASHBE. All right . . . but, but how about our feet?

385

JOHN POLK. Feet?
ASHBE. They'll hurt.
JOHN POLK. Yeah.
ASHBE. [*Smiling.*] Okay, then let's dance.

[*He takes her hand, and they dance as lights black out and the music soars and continues to play.*]

End.

QUESTIONS

1. What do Ashbe's actions at the start tell you about her (such as hiding under the coat, stealing and giving the stolen things away, crawling away from the waitress)? What is disclosed by her speeches?

2. Describe the circumstances of Ashbe and her family. To what degree can her character and behavior be explained by these circumstances?

3. What is Ashbe's intention in her description of G.G., or Myrtle? What does her description tell you about her? What do you learn about her from her description of the only sort of dance she would like to go to (speech 231)?

4. What personal, occupational, and social difficulties is John Polk experiencing? Why is he trying to stay drunk before going to G.G.? What are his reactions to fraternity life and to the family business?

5. Explain the effects of the arguments between Ashbe and John Polk. How does their occasionally taunting each other influence their developing relationship?

6. Why does John Polk not take up Ashbe's invitation to make love? How does this refusal suggest the development of his character? Of Ashbe's character? What may be inferred by their concluding decision to dance the night away?

GENERAL QUESTIONS

1. What is the plot of *Am I Blue*? Who is the protagonist (or protagonists)? Who or what is the antagonist? How is the plot resolved?

2. Describe and analyze the verbal comedy of the play, such as the "two murders and a knifing" (speech 49), Ashbe's description of Myrtle (speeches 71–73), and the inquiry about what to mix with rum (speech 148).

3. What is appealing (or not appealing) about Ashbe and John Polk? To what extent are you to consider them as realistic persons? How might they be seen as symbols, and what might they symbolize?

4. What are the major themes or ideas of the play? To what extent does the comic mode obscure these ideas? To what extent does it bring them out?

5. What is the effect of the setting in the New Orleans French Quarter and the characters to be found there? What is shown about Ashbe and John Polk by their brief interactions with the characters in the bar, especially Hilda, and on the street?

🌿 WRITING ABOUT COMEDY

For an essay about comedy, you can choose most of the conventional topics, such as *plot, conflict, character, point of view, setting, style, tone, symbolism,* or *theme.* You might choose one of these, or two or more; for example, how language and action define character, how character and symbol convey meaning, or how set-ting may influence comic structure.

Planning and prewriting strategies for each of these conventional ele-ments are discussed at some length in Chapter 26 (pp. 1240–43) and in other chapters on prose fiction and poetry. As you develop your essay on comedy, you will find it helpful to look at these suggestions.

For the most part, planning and writing about specific features of comedy are much like addressing the same topics in other forms of drama, short stories, and poetry. However, a few areas of consideration—such as plot, character, and language—are especially significant in comic drama and can be handled in a distinctive fashion.

Questions for Discovering Ideas

PLOT, CONFLICT, STRUCTURE. What problems, adversities, or abnormal situations are in place at the comedy's opening? How is this initial situation complicated? Do the complications spring mainly from character or from situation? If from charac-ter, what aspects of behavior or personality create the problems? If from situation, what dilemmas or troubles plague the characters? What kinds of complications dominate—misunderstandings, disagreements, mistakes in identity, situational problems, or emotional entanglements? How important is coincidence?

What problems and complications occur early? Who is the comic protago-nist (or protagonists) and what is the protagonist's goal (money, success, mar-riage, land, freedom)? How is the protagonist blocked (fathers, rivals, laws, customs, his or her own personality)? How threatening is the obstruction? What plans are hatched to overcome the blocking agents? Are the plans sensible or silly? Who initiates and executes the plans? To what extent do plans succeed (or fail)—because of chance and good luck or because of skillful planning and manipulation?

Describe the conflicts. Which conflict is central, and whom do the con-flicts involve? Do they result from personality clashes or from situations? To what degree are they related to blocking activities? How does the action reach the cri-sis, and which characters are involved? What choices, decisions, plans, or con-clusions become necessary? What events or revelations (of character, emotion, background) produce the catastrophe, and how do these affect characters, cir-cumstances, and relationships?

In the comic resolution, to what extent are loose ends tied up and lives straightened out? Is reasonable order restored and regeneration assured or im-plied? Is the resolution satisfying? Disturbing? Does it leave you happy or thoughtful, or both? Are you amused by farce, pleased by romance, or disturbed by satire? If there is to be a marriage, whom will it bring together? What will the marriage settle, or whom will it divide? Most important, how can you account for your responses to the resolution and the play as a whole? How do they reflect the general aims of comedy?

CHARACTER. Which characters are realistic, conventional, round, flat, chang-ing, standing still? Who is the protagonist or lover, the antagonist or blocking agent? Which characters seem excessive, eccentric, or irrational? What is the nature of their excesses? To what extent do the excesses define the characters? How do you respond to the excessive or exaggerated characters? Does the comedy provide a "cure" for the excesses? In other words, do the characters learn and change? If so, why and how? If not, why not?

From what classes are the characters derived? What class characteristics do you find? Who are the stock or stereotyped characters, and what is their significance to the protagonist? How does the playwright invigorate the characters? Who is the choric figure or *raisonneur*, if there is one? Who is the confidant? Which character can be considered a foil (or foils)?

LANGUAGE.   Does the language consist of witty turns of phrase, confusions, puns, misunderstandings, or a mixture? Which characters are masters of language and which are mastered by it? Do characters use the same type of language and level of diction consistently? To what extent does language expose a character's self-interest or hypocrisy? If the language is witty and sparkling, what devices make it work effectively? If it is garbled and filled with misunderstandings, what types of errors does the playwright put into the characters' mouths? How does the language shape your response to characters, to ideas, and to the play as a whole?

Strategies for Organizing Ideas

To develop a central idea, isolate the feature you wish to explore and consider how it affects the shape and impact of the play. For *A Midsummer Night's Dream*, for example, you might focus on Puck's character and function. You might also develop a link between Puck's conventional role as a tricky servant with his love of mischief and the chaos he creates. Remember that it is difficult to develop essays from sentences like "Puck is a comic character" or "*Am I Blue* contains dramatic satire." A more focused assertion that also reveals your thematic development is necessary, such as "Puck, modeled on the tricky servant of Roman comedy, causes most of the play's confusion," or "*Am I Blue* attacks the general indifference of people with regard to the situations of others."

Organize your essay by grouping related types of details together (such as observations about characters, actions, direct statements, and specific words), and choose your own order of presentation. In writing about Puck as a tricky servant and creator of chaos, for example, you might present only one kind of detail—such as direct statements—and introduce these not in their order in the play but rather as they contribute to your analysis of Puck's character.

More often than not, your supporting details will represent a variety of types of evidence—dramatic dialogue and action, individual soliloquies, special properties (such as a love potion or a disguise), or the failure or development of various plans. For example, you might support an assertion about Puck by referring to his reputation, actions, and attitudes as though each of these is equally important. Other possible strategies are to demonstrate how the topics are related according to cause and effect, to build the topics from the least to the most significant, and to trace how a common idea or image provides unity. Whatever your method of development, be sure to validate your arguments with support-ing details.

A summary of key points will make your conclusion useful and effective. In addition, you can show how your conclusions in the body of the essay bear upon larger aspects of the play's meaning.

DEMONSTRATIVE STUDENT ESSAY

Setting as Symbol and Comic Structure in *A Midsummer Night's Dream*°

[1]   [Shakespeare's <u>A Midsummer Night's Dream</u> might superficially be consid-ered light and inconsequential. The changes of mind undergone by the two sets of lovers, the placing of an ass's head on one of the characters, the presence of un-realistic fairies, the acting of a silly sketch--all seem far-fetched. But the play is real. <u>It dramatizes the accidental and arbitrary origins of love, even though it considers this serious subject in the good-natured medium of comedy.</u>* To bring out both message and merriment, Shakespeare uses two settings--the city of Athens and the nearby forest. <u>The play's comic structure is governed by the movements between the order and the chaos that these two locations represent.</u>†

[2]   <u>At the play's beginning, Athens is presented as a world of daylight, order, and law.</u> In this setting, Duke Theseus has absolute authority, fathers are always right, and the law permits Egeus to "dispose" of Hermia "either to this gentleman [Demetrius], / Or to her death" ([1495] 1.1.43-44). The city is also the place for the exposition and the beginning of complications. Here, we meet the various groups of characters (except the fairies) and learn about the initial problem--namely, that the relationship between Hermia and Lysander is blocked by a raging father, a rival suitor, and an old law. In order to flee and then to overcome these obstruc-tions, Lysander asks Hermia to meet him in the woods. Her agreement begins a journey from Athens to the forest that ultimately includes everyone in the play--the four lovers, Egeus, the city rulers, and the "mechanicals."

[3]   The play's second setting, the woods outside Athens, is the kingdom of Oberon and Titania, the king and queen of the fairies. <u>It is a world of darkness, moonlight, chaos, madness, and dreams, a world that symbolizes the power of imagination and passion.</u> The disorder in this world has many sources, including Oberon's jealousy, Titania's infatuation, and Puck's delight in mischief. When the lovers and the mechanicals enter this setting, they also become disordered and chaotic.

The woods are the setting for complication, crisis, and catastrophe. <u>Confusion dominates the action here.</u> Puck disrupts the mechanicals' rehearsal and transforms Bottom into an ass-headed monster. More important, the pas-sions of the lovers are rearranged several times by Oberon and Puck through the

°See pp. 1493–1546 for this play.
*Central idea.
†Thesis sentence.

magic of "love-in-idleness," a flower that symbolizes love's irrational and overwhelming power. Although the first two adjustments of the lovers' feelings are done to help, each has the effect of raising the levels of complication and disorder.

[4] Puck gleefully observes that his actions are the cause of the play's confusions ([1520] 3.2.120-21):

> those things do best please me
> That befall prepost'rously.

Puck is right; his first application of love-in-idleness causes Lysander to fall wildly in love with Helena, and his second does the same to Demetrius.

The crisis and dénouement of the main plot also occur in the woods. A crisis occurs when the two lovers challenge each other and the women attack each other. At this point, complication is at a peak, and the fairies must develop a plan to resolve the threats. Puck therefore misleads the lovers to end their potential

[5] duel, and he adjusts their emotions one more time. The dénouement--the revelation of the newly restored emotions--occurs the next morning at the edge of the woods, in the presence of Egeus, Theseus, and Hippolyta. Thus, it ends the confusing relationships occurring in the forest and begins the regularity of relationships in the orderly world of city and society.

Resolution--the marriages and the mechanicals' production of Pyramus and Thisby--occurs in the first setting, the city, which represents law and order. But the journey to the second setting has had a significant effect on the urban world both for Theseus and for the lovers. The law has been softened, Egeus overruled; the

[6] young lovers have been allowed to marry as they like, and lives are set right. In the end, this second setting has also become the dream world of night and the supernatural, and the fairy dance and blessings closing the play only emphasize the harmony and the regenerative implications of the comic resolutions.

Setting, symbolism, and comic pattern thus combine in A Midsummer Night's Dream to produce an intricately plotted structure. Each element reinforces the others, bringing the play toward completion though time after time there seems to be no way out. The marvel of the play is that the two settings represent,

[7] realistically, two opposed states of being, and, dramatically, two distinct stages of comic structure. The journey out of Athens, into the woods, and then back to the city is also a journey from exposition and adversity, through complication, crisis, and catastrophe, to comic resolution.

WORK CITED

William Shakespeare, A Midsummer Night's Dream. Literature: An Introduction to Reading and Writing, 7th ed. Ed. Edgar V. Roberts and Henry E. Jacobs. Upper Saddle River: Prentice Hall, 2004. 1493–1546.

Commentary on the Essay

This essay deals with three elements of *A Midsummer Night's Dream*: setting, symbols, and comic structure. It demonstrates the way a number of different topics can be combined in a single essay. Consequently, the essay is organized to reflect the journey from the city to the woods and then back to the city.

The body of the essay takes up the settings, their symbolic meaning, and the relationship between setting and structure. Paragraph 2 deals with Athens both as a world of law and order and as the setting for exposition and the beginnings of complication. The supporting details include circumstance, actions, and dialogue.

Paragraphs 3–5 deal with the middle of the journey and of the play. Paragraph 3 discusses the symbolic implications of the forest setting, and paragraphs 4 and 5 take up the connection between the setting and comic structure, specifically, complication, crisis, and dénouement. Again, the supporting details in these paragraphs are a mixture of actions, circumstances, and direct quotations.

Paragraph 6 deals briefly with the return to the city, linking this setting with the play's comic resolution. The concluding paragraph returns to the idea about how *A Midsummer Night's Dream* connects setting, symbol, and comic pattern.

Special Topics for Writing and Argument about Comedy

1. Write an essay describing Shakespeare's comic technique in *A Midsummer Night's Dream*. Consider these questions: Is the basic situation serious? How does Shakespeare keep it comic? How does the boisterousness of the low characters influence your perceptions of the lovers and the courtly characters? Would the play be as interesting without Bottom and his crowd or without the fairies and their involvement? How does the comic outcome depend on the boisterousness and colorfulness provided by the players and the fairies? For research on Shakespeare as a comic dramatist, you might wish to consult Henry B. Charlton's classic study *Shakespeare's Comedies* (rpt. 1972) and/or a more recent book by Michael Mangan, *A Preface to Shakespeare's Comedies* (1996).

2. Although *Love Is the Doctor* is a farce, it deals with serious topic material, namely, a father trying to control his daughter's life, the exploitation of gullibility, and an illegal deception. How does Molière treat these topics and yet preserve the play's comic tone?

3. Write an essay that analyzes the relationship of situation to comedy in *Am I Blue*. How do the eccentricity of the characters and the improbability of their circumstances produce amusement? When you finish the play, do you believe that you have been seriously engaged? Simply entertained? Explain. For comparison with other Henley plays, you might wish to take out *Beth Henley: Four Plays* (1992) from your college library.

4. *The Bear* is one of Chekhov's most popular comedies. Read another Chekhov play (for example, *The Cherry Orchard, The Seagull, Three Sisters, Uncle Vanya*) and compare it to *The Bear* (characters with characters, dialogue with dialogue, situations with situations, and so on). As you make your comparison, attempt to explain the continued popularity of *The Bear*.

5. Write an essay about the nature of comedy, using *A Midsummer Night's Dream, Am I Blue, The Bear,* and *Love Is the Doctor* as material. Deal with issues like the following: How can comic material be defined? Does the happy outcome of a serious action qualify a play as a comedy, or should no action be serious? When is a comedy no longer comic but tragic? Are jokes necessary? Is farcical action necessary? Where are the edges between comedy and farce, on the one hand, and comedy

and tragedy on the other? For a research component for this topic, you might wish to introduce materials from books by Wylie Sypher (1956, rpt. 1982, an edition of two classic essays on the comic), G. S. Amur (1963), Robert Corrigan (1965), Robert B. Heilman (1978), T. G. A. Nelson (1990), Athene Seyler (1990), Frances Teague (1994), and Janet Suzman (1995).

6.   Treat the lovers in *A Midsummer Night's Dream* and *Love Is the Doctor* as types or archetypes (see Chapter 33). What is their situation? What problems block the fulfillment of their love? How serious are these problems? What actions and ruses do they plan to make things right? How are the pairs of lovers in the two plays similar? Different?

7.   Write a comic scene of your own between two people, perhaps a boy and a girl, as in *Am I Blue;* or a father and daughter, as in *Love Is the Doctor;* or two people who are at first angry with each other, as in *The Bear;* or a person under a spell and a person in normal touch with reality, as in *A Midsummer Night's Dream.* After you finish your scene, write a short essay explaining the principles on which you've written your scene, such as the reasons for your choice of material, your use of jokes (if any), straightforward dialogue, anger, outrage, amused responses, and so on.

Visions of Dramatic Reality and Nonreality: *Varying the Idea of Drama as Imitation*

A major dimension of drama is the relationship to reality that dramatists seek to create. From Aristotle's description of the origin of tragedy, we may conclude that drama was originally considered to be an "imitation of an action"; that is, each play represents a significant and discrete series of actions that make up a complete story in the lives of the major characters. The drama focuses on only those actions and speeches that are integral to the story, and the outcome of the action is the logically necessary consequence of the conflicts and issues raised in the play. To achieve such concentration, dramatists introduce restrictions and nonrealistic conventions that aid the presentation of the story. Thus there can be no absolutely realistic drama in the sense of the straightforward duplication of life. Rather, the issue is how far drama goes either toward or away from reality.

❦ REALISM AND NONREALISM IN DRAMA

The most important difference between realistic and nonrealistic drama concerns the play's relationships to the audience, the theater, and the world at large. In **realistic drama,** the playwright seeks to create an *illusion* of reality—**verisimilitude.** The situations, problems, characters, dialogue, and other elements are all those that might genuinely exist in the real world. The play presents a self-contained action in a world that professes to imitate reality. Ideally, the illusion of reality is never compromised; the actors never drop out of character, the audience is never addressed, and the play never acknowledges that it is a play.

In **nonrealistic drama,** even the pretense to achieve realism is abandoned, and the goal instead is to present essential features of character and society through techniques that *do not* try to mirror life. Nonrealistic drama employs whatever conventions the playwright finds useful. It can be full of devices that break through the illusion on the stage (or the page) and scream out that the play is a play—a work of art, a stylized imitation of something remotely connected to life.

Nonrealistic Drama Has Prevailed During Most of Dramatic History

From ancient Greek tragedy through Victorian melodrama, plays were artificial and conventionalized. The conventions of drama changed from age to age—choruses and masks in Greek tragedy, soliloquies and blank verse in Elizabethan plays, rhymed couplets in French and much English neoclassical drama. Although these conventions were nonrealistic, audiences and readers accepted them as normal features of dramatic presentation. The enduring eloquence and power of the nonrealistic tradition can be found in plays like Sophocles' *Oedipus the King*, Shakespeare's *Hamlet*, and Miller's *Death of a Salesman*.

By the nineteenth century, artificial and romantic drama dominated the stage. These plays featured lavish sets, gorgeous costumes, flamboyant acting, conventionalized plots, and happy endings. The characters were exaggerated and idealized—heroes saving the day, heroines swooning at every opportunity, and villains twirling their mustaches and leering at the audience as they plotted to steal the hero's sweetheart and swindle him out of his money.

Realistic Drama Developed in Opposition to Unrealistic Drama

In reaction to the unrealistic tradition, and as a likely development coincidental with democratic theories of society and government, a number of nineteenth-century dramatists created plays that presented realistic characters in realistic situations and that explored the real problems of contemporary society. The rebellion began slowly, and most of these writers were Europeans, among them Émile Zola (French), Henrik Ibsen (Norwegian), Maxim Gorki (Russian), and George Bernard Shaw (Irish-English). American realists, who came to this tradition somewhat later than the Europeans, included Eugene O'Neill, Langston Hughes, and Susan Glaspell (pp. 1208, 1608, and 1182).

DRAMATIC REALISM ATTEMPTS TO EXPLORE PEOPLE'S LIVES. In keeping with the goal of verisimilitude, realistic plays eliminate traditional but artificial dramatic conventions that do not occur in daily life, such as disguises, overheard conversations, asides, soliloquies, and verse. At its best, realistic drama is a close examination of character in conflict. The plots are straightforward and progress chronologically. The characters look, speak, and act as much as possible like real people. The settings are middle-class living rooms, the country houses of the wealthy, the squalid slums of the poor. Usually the plays explore ideas about the nature of humanity in conflict with social customs and prejudices.

REALISTIC THEATRICAL PRODUCTIONS EMPHASIZE LIFELIKE SETTINGS. The new realism called for equally new and realistic methods of production and action. Most theaters of the nineteenth century featured a darkened auditorium, a proscenium arch separating the audience from the players, and a picture-frame stage. The spectators watched the play as though the fourth wall of a room had been removed. The illusion was that the audience was eavesdropping on private conversations and events.

The settings and stage directions for realistic drama became as detailed and lifelike as possible. When the curtain went up, the audience saw a completely furnished room or office, much like the ones in which they themselves lived or worked. Ibsen's lengthy description of the setting for Acts 1 and 2 of *An Enemy of the People* (1882), for example, calls for the elaborate duplication of Norwegian middle-class living and dining rooms of the late nineteenth century (1882), complete with a sofa, a coffee table, a lighted lamp, a ceramic tile heating stove, a dining table at the end of a meal with all the china and utensils still on it, and a platter of roast beef. Lighting and costumes were equally realistic. Lighting was designed to duplicate the natural light at a particular time of day or the lamps burning in a room at night. Similarly, the lavish and beautiful costumes of nineteenth-century melodrama gave way to detailed realism in dress and makeup on the stage.

REALISTIC DRAMA REQUIRES ACTORS TO DUPLICATE THE SPEECH AND MANNERISMS OF LIVING PEOPLE. The most radical and permanent change caused by the new realism was in acting styles. In the Victorian theater, actors stood in one place, assumed a conventional stance, and declaimed their lines. In realistic drama, the acting became more natural and intimate. Actors began to combine movement with dialogue and to play "within the scene" to each other rather than to the spectators.

These changes were due, in large measure, to Konstantin Stanislavsky (1863–1938), one of the founders of the Moscow Art Theater (1898) and the inventor of what we now term **method acting.** Stanislavski argued that actors had to build characterizations on a lifelong study of inner truths and motivation. He taught actors to search inwardly, within the depths of their own imaginations, for the feelings, motivations, and behavior of the characters they portray.

A New Nonrealistic Drama Was Created in Opposition to Realism

No sooner had realism taken over the stage than a new nonrealistic drama began to emerge as a reaction against realism. Many playwrights in Europe and the United States decided that realism had gone too far and that the quest for minutely realistic details had sacrificed the essence of drama—character and universal truth. Playwrights began to explore every avenue of antirealistic drama.

A CONSEQUENCE OF NONREALISTIC DRAMA WAS EXPERIMENTAL STAGING. At the same time, new types of stages and theaters began to appear. The **thrust stage,** from Elizabethan theaters, was reintroduced. It projected into the audience, thus helping to destroy the fourth-wall principle of realistic drama. The **arena**

stage, or **theater-in-the-round,** was developed, which also called for new concepts in drama and production.[1]

Playwrights like Luigi Pirandello (Italian, 1867–1936) and Bertolt Brecht (German, 1898–1956) wrote plays that required only minimal sets or no sets at all. Using this same tradition, Thornton Wilder wrote plays (such as *Our Town*) in which the action occurs on a bare stage, with the backstage area in full view showing brick walls, heating pipes, ropes, pulleys, and other stage appurtenances. To a degree, both Miller's *Death of a Salesman* and Williams's *The Glass Menagerie* share in this tradition. Miller presents us with three rooms for his characters, together with a thrust stage in which dream sequences take place, while Williams utilizes projected images and claims that his scenes are "not realistic." Such characteristics remind us constantly that we are reading or watching a play—an illusion and an imitation—rather than real life.

✦ ELEMENTS OF REALISTIC AND NONREALISTIC DRAMA

THE TWO KINDS OF DRAMA IMPLY GREAT DIFFERENCES IN THEIR PRESENTATION OF NARRATIVE. Because realistic plays, like life, unfold chronologically, the *story* (as opposed to the *play*) is usually nearing conclusion when the stage action begins. In Glaspell's *Trifles*, for example, the story comprises incidents from Mrs. Wright's youth, her marital difficulties, and her reaction against her husband. All this, however, is presented in conversation; it all occurred *before* the play begins. Such events from the past have a profound impact on the present action in realistic drama, but the play itself presents only the last part of the story.

In nonrealistic drama, the structure of the plot is more fluid. Action shifts easily from the present to the past with little or no transition. Flashbacks are mixed with present action, and the entire play dramatizes the past through a present perspective. In Williams's *The Glass Menagerie*, recollected past action is revealed through the present memories of the narrator. Similarly, the action in Miller's *Death of a Salesman* constantly shifts between the present and memories of the past.

DRAMATIC CHARACTERS ARE SHAPED ACCORDING TO WHETHER THEY ARE CONCEIVED REALISTICALLY OR NONREALISTICALLY. The characters in realistic drama are as much as possible like living people. They can be representative, symbolic, or even stock characters, but they must sound and act like normal human beings, with backgrounds, emotions, motivations, and last names as well as first names. There must be reasons for their actions, words, conflicts, and relationships. Most important, they must be consistent. Their responses, decisions, and characteristics must be the same as in real life. Such fidelity to life is apparent in realistic plays like Glaspell's *Trifles* and Hughes's *Mulatto*.

---

[1]See pp. 1171–72 for an additional discussion of stages.

In modern nonrealistic drama, the characters can be nameless figures who have no background or motivation and who drop in and out of character, or who assume a number of different functions at different times, according to the dramatist's need. Tom is such a character in Williams's *The Glass Menagerie*. At various times he is a character in the action, a narrator who provides background and commentary, and a stage manager. As a character, he interacts with Laura and Amanda; as a narrator, he speaks directly to the audience; as a stage manager, he occasionally cues the technicians offstage about music and lighting.

These distinctions do not mean that realistic characters are always round and nonrealistic ones always flat. The way in which a playwright develops characters, realistically or nonrealistically, does not control the degree to which they are developed. Thus, true-to-life characters like Mr. Hale in *Trifles* or Jim O'-Connor in *The Glass Menagerie* are flat. By the same token, nonrealistic characters, like Tom in *The Glass Menagerie* or Willy Loman in *Death of a Salesman*, have enough depth and scope to be considered fully round.

LANGUAGE IS A SIGN OF THE DEGREES OF REALITY OR NONREALITY. In a realistic play, the language accurately represents the diction appropriate to the class or group of people portrayed. There is no poetry, no radical shift in style, and no direct address to the reader or speaker. In *Mulatto*, for instance, Cora and her uneducated children consistently use the vernacular speech patterns of African-Americans living in the South during the 1930s. Similarly, the characters in Glaspell's *Trifles* sound like Midwestern farmers and small-town residents.

Such verisimilitude is not required in nonrealistic drama. Playwrights employ any linguistic devices that suit their needs. Some characters therefore speak in verse, clichés, or even nonsense sounds. Others have two or three separate speeds of presentation, as Tom does in *The Glass Menagerie*. Dramatists are free to introduce snippets of poetry or song into the play, as in Wilder's *Our Town*, and some characters speak directly to the audience. Often the characters talk as though they are in a dream, or are living through their memories, or are so preoccupied with their concerns that the other characters are incidental to them.

THE STAGE ITSELF IS A GRAPHIC GUIDE TO THE LEVEL OF REALITY. Such differences in plot, characterization, and language are matched by differences in production techniques. Whereas the staging of a realistic drama must be as true to life as possible, as in *A Dollhouse*, nonrealistic drama is usually staged with few or no realistic effects. While the sets are based in reality, they are primarily symbolic and expressive of mood, employing lighting and a semitransparent painted cloth (called a **scrim**) to create the simultaneous effect of multiple places or times. Carefully controlled lighting indicates flashbacks, changes in mood, and shifts of location, and spotlights illuminate and emphasize objects and characters in ways that never happen in reality. In addition, the dramatist of a nonrealistic play is free to introduce music, special sound effects, words or images projected onto a wall or screen, action that flows off the stage into the auditorium, and speeches made directly to the spectators or the reader. All these and other devices break the illusion of reality and demand that we consider the play as an artistic construction. Such nonrealistic dramatic effects are described in the stage directions for both *Death of a Salesman* and *The Glass Menagerie.*

In this way, nonrealistic drama has moved progressively farther away from realism throughout the latter half of the twentieth century, and the beginning of the twenty-first. With the development of flexible theaters, in which the seats in certain locations are removed, with acting areas being set up throughout the house, the action of plays has moved offstage and into the space once occupied by the audience.

Paradoxically, as such drama becomes more nonrealistic, the theater itself, as a place for acting and performing, becomes the dominant reality. In the 1960s and 1970s, acting companies like the Living Theater in New York experimented with plays that began onstage, moved into the audience, and ended on the streets outside. Such productions represent the edge of drama. In the mid-1980s, the Old Vic Company in England produced *The Creation*—a series of medieval mystery plays—in which the actors mingled among the spectators, separating only when their parts were called for. Whenever new scenes were introduced, the standing spectators were (literally) swept aside to provide space, so that acting areas were being shaped by the shifting audience. A production that has remained popular into the year 2000 is *Tony n' Tina's Wedding*, which is the staging of a wedding and reception (in two different locations, one a church and the other a restaurant).[2] Because performers and audience interact, particularly at the reception, many members of the audience take on impromptu acting and speaking roles. Every performance is therefore spontaneous and unique. An argument might be made that such one-time performances represent superrealism, but in fact they blur the distinction between drama and the real world to the point where art almost ceases to be art, and all action everywhere—both real life and stage life—seems nothing but performance.

Most Plays Offer a Blend of Realism and Nonrealism

To this point we have been speaking as though realistic and nonrealistic drama were always at opposite extremes, but most plays are not purely realistic or nonrealistic. Rather, the terms represent the opposite ends of a continuum, and most plays fall somewhere between. Hughes's *Mulatto*, Glaspell's *Trifles*, and Ibsen's *A Dollhouse*, for example, are highly realistic, yet each modifies its realism through symbolism and selective emphasis. Conversely, the staging of *Our Town* is nonrealistic, yet the play's action is sufficiently realistic to justify the claim that it belongs at a midpoint between the two extremes. Both Miller's *Death of a Salesman* and Williams's *The Glass Menagerie* also fall near the middle of the continuum; they combine realistic language and characterization with nonrealistic settings, lighting, and structure.

---

[2]*Tony n' Tina's Wedding* has been running in New York for fourteen years and is so firmly fixed that it has created its own Web site at <www.tonylovestina.com>, a practice now common with many long-running plays. The play is now being performed in eleven other American cities.

PLAYS FOR STUDY

LANGSTON HUGHES, *MULATTO*

James Mercer Langston Hughes was born in Missouri in 1902 and reared in Kansas and Ohio. After living for a year in Mexico he attended Columbia University, but he left after one year. He received a B.A. from Lincoln University in Pennsylvania in 1929, and when he came to New York he soon became one of the leading figures in the Harlem Renaissance, an energetic burst of African-American literary creativity that also included Claude McKay (see p. 870). Over the next forty-five years, Hughes was to write in every major literary genre, including translations, regular columns for a weekly newspaper, and reports on the Spanish Civil War. His earliest works were poems that he published in the Crisis, *the official journal of the National Association for the Advancement of Colored People. Eventually he published fourteen books of poems and two novels, together with a number of short-story collections and many plays and texts for musical plays.*

The Great Depression, which began with the New York stock market crash in 1929, destroyed the economic underpinnings of the Harlem Renaissance. It was during the Depression that Hughes became radicalized. After visiting Haiti and Cuba he attacked what he considered U.S. imperialist interventions in those countries. He then spent a year in Soviet Russia, assisting in the preparation of a film on U.S. race relations. When he returned he published his first collection of stories, *The Ways of White Folks* (1934), in which he fictionalized his disaffection with the condition of both Southern and Northern African-Americans. One of the stories included in this collection was "Father and Son," a version of the material that he turned into the two-act play *Mulatto*, which was produced at the Vanderbilt Theater in New York in October 1935. The play had a run of 373 performances, the record at that time for a Broadway play by an African-American dramatist.

At that time, the growing African-American theater was dominated by two major themes, the first being the customs and problems of Southern blacks. The most pressing problem was the cruelty and injustice of lynching. Angelina Weld Grimke's *Rachael* (1920) and James Miller's *Never No More* (1932) openly condemned the practice. Dennis Donaghue's *Legal Murder* (1934) was an attack on the false conviction for rape of nine young black men from Scottsboro, Alabama, a topic that Hughes also treated in his early drama *Scottsboro Limited: Four Poems and a Play in Verse* (1932). The second major theme concerned the adjustments that blacks needed to make after they left the South and migrated to cities in the North. Frank Wilson's *Meek Mose* was perhaps the most optimistic of these plays, in which dispossessed blacks discover oil on their new property. More typical were Garland Anderson's *Appearances* (1925), about how a black bellhop overcomes false charges of rape, and Wallace Thurman's *Harlem* (1929), about the difficulties of a black Harlem family. This theme also dominates Lorraine Hansberry's *A Raisin in the Sun* (1959), the classic drama that marked the coming of age of post–World War II African-American playwrights.

Although Langston Hughes is not thought of principally as a dramatist, he wrote plays throughout his career. In addition to the plays already mentioned, he wrote *Little Ham* (1936) and *Soul Gone Home* (1937), a short fantasy play. As the first production for the radical Suitcase Theater, which he founded after returning as a correspondent from the Spanish Civil War, he wrote *Don't You Want to Be Free* (1938). He collaborated with Arna Bontemps in *When the Jack Hollers* (1936) and with Zora Neale Hurston in *Mule Bone* (reissued in 1991). In 1948 he wrote the lyrics for the Kurt Weill and Elmer Rice musical *Street Scene*, perhaps the best known of the plays in which he was involved. In 1951 he produced a libretto, *Just Around the Corner*, and in 1957 he wrote *Simply Heavenly*, a blues-musical play featuring the character Jesse Semple, whom he had created as a character in his weekly columns for the *Chicago Defender*. Although *Simply Heavenly* (which is a musical version of an earlier play, *Simple Takes a Wife*) concludes optimistically, one can find within it the serious theme of frustration resulting from the difficulties that African-Americans experience in seeking identity and recognition. Semple says, at one point:

> I'm broke, busted, and disgusted. And just spent mighty near my last nickel for a paper—and there ain't no news in it about colored folks. Unless we commit murder, robbery or rape, or are being chased by a mob, do we get on the front page, or hardly on the back. (Act 1, speech 5)

Hughes's interests in the last decades of his life were in the musical theater, particularly the introduction of gospel-related music and jazz. Three of his major efforts were *Black Nativity* (1961), *The Gospel Glory* (1962), and *Jericho-Jim Crow* (1964). His output as a dramatist was indeed great, even if it is overshadowed by his preeminence as a poet and fiction writer.

Hughes's *Mulatto* is one of his plays dealing with life in the South during the 1930s, a time when the system of white control over blacks was absolute and uncompromisingly harsh. Hughes's first conception of the play, as one dealing with father and son, is a perennial one. Colonel Tom Norwood and Robert Lewis, his mulatto son, recognize their relationship but also hate and reject each other. In *Mulatto* the realistic cause of conflict is the "color line"—the symbolic line that people of different races must cross in order to accept each other as human beings. Acceptance is an ideal goal, just as the color line is an insurmountable obstacle in the society that the play depicts. The lack of ability or will to cross the line governs the pattern of action and also the violent outcome. Colonel Norwood has lived in the same house with Cora Lewis for many years, and they do well together as long as he is not confronted with the issues of his paternity and his control over the plantation. There is no way he can recognize the four "yard blacks" on his plantation as his legitimate children, however, unless he is willing to forsake his identity as a white.

There are many other marks of dramatic realism, particularly the exploitation of black women (described in Act 1, speech 61), the front entrance of the Norwood house, Robert's complaints about Miss Gray, and his speeding with the Ford. All of his so-called "uppity" actions would not be unacceptable to white society if Robert were white, but because he is black they indicate a state of revolt. In addition, Robert's identity as half white, half black—he is called "yellow" by Colonel Tom—leaves him in an anomalous position, for he is not "white" enough to be equal or "black" enough to be subservient. The reality of his situation leads him to hate both whites and blacks alike, and the sudden eruption of his seething anger leads to his uncontrolled violence.

It is important to note that *Mulatto* reflects the reality of language in the South of the 1930s. Hughes's blacks, except for Robert and Sallie, use Southern black vernacular (called "darky talk" by Hughes). The introduction of such speech in literature was controversial at the time. Many black intellectuals who had also been a part of the Harlem Renaissance believed that dialect should be shunned, on the principle that it reinforced negative African-American stereotypes. However, Hughes believed that using the vernacular was above all truthful and realistic, enabling writers to demonstrate that blacks are not stereotypes, that they face human problems just like everyone else, and that they succeed and fail just like everyone else. Moreover, there were precedents for the realistic use of dialect that had been set by Mark Twain in *Tom Sawyer* and *Huckleberry Finn*, both of which are acknowledged classics of American literature.

Mulatto is one of Hughes's most important plays. In 1950 he refashioned it as a libretto, titled *The Barrier*, that was set to music by the composer Jan Meyerowitz. In addition, the play was translated into Spanish and published in South America in 1954.

LANGSTON HUGHES (1902–1967)

Mulatto 1935

CHARACTERS

Colonel Thomas Norwood. *Plantation owner, a still vigorous man of about sixty, nervous, refined, quick-tempered, and commanding; a widower who is the father of four living mulatto children by his Negro housekeeper.*

Cora Lewis. *A brown woman in her forties who has kept the house and been the mistress of Colonel Norwood for some thirty years.*

William Lewis. *The oldest son of Cora Lewis and the Colonel; a fat, easy-going, soft looking mulatto of twenty-eight; married.*

Sallie Lewis. *The seventeen-year-old daughter, very light with sandy hair and freckles, who could pass for white.*

Robert Lewis [Bert]. *Eighteen, the youngest boy; strong and well-built; a light mulatto with ivory-yellow skin and proud thin features like his father's; as tall as the Colonel, with the same gray-blue eyes, but with curly black hair instead of brown; of a fiery, impetuous temper—immature and willful—resenting his blood and the circumstances of his birth.*

Fred Higgins. *A close friend of Colonel Norwood; a county politician; fat and elderly, conventionally Southern.*

Sam. *An old Negro retainer, a personal servant of the Colonel.*

Billy. *The small son of William Lewis; a chubby brown kid about five.*

Talbot. *The overseer.*

Mose. *An elderly Negro, chauffeur for Mr. Higgins.*

A Storekeeper.

An Undertaker.

Undertaker's Helper. *Voice offstage only.*

The Mob.

Aст 1

TIME. *An afternoon in early fall.*

SETTING. *The same.*

ACTION. *The living room of the Big House on a plantation in Georgia. Rear center of the room, a vestibule with double doors leading to the porch; at each side of the doors, a large window with lace curtains and green shades; at left a broad flight of stairs leading to the second floor; near the stairs, downstage, a doorway leading to the dining room and kitchen; opposite at right of stage, a door to the library. The room is furnished in the long outdated horsehair and walnut style of the nineties; a crystal chandelier, a large old-fashioned rug, a marble-topped table, upholstered chairs. At the right there is a small cabinet. It is a very clean, but somewhat shabby and rather depressing room, dominated by a large oil painting of* NORWOOD's *wife of his youth on the center wall. The windows are raised. The afternoon sunlight streams in.*

ACTION. *As the curtain rises, the stage is empty. The door at the right opens and* COLONEL NORWOOD *enters, crossing the stage toward the stairs, his watch in his hand. Looking up, he shouts:.*

NORWOOD.   Cora! Oh Cora!

CORA.   [*Heard above*] Yes, sir, Colonel Tom.

NORWOOD.   I want to know if that child of yours means to leave here this afternoon?

CORA.   [*At head of steps now*] Yes, sir, she's goin' directly. I's gettin' her ready now, packin' up an' all. 'Course, she wants to tell you goodbye 'fore she leaves.

NORWOOD.   Well, send her down here. Who's going to drive her to the railroad?   5
The train leaves at three—and it's after two now. You ought to know you can't drive ten miles in no time.

CORA.   [*Above*] Her brother's gonna drive her. Bert. He ought to be back here most any time now with the Ford.

NORWOOD.   [*Stopping on his way back to the library*] Ought to be *back* here? Where's he gone?

CORA.   [*Coming downstairs nervously*] Why, he driv in town 'fore noon, Colonel Tom. Said he were lookin' for some tubes or somethin' 'nother by de mornin' mail for de radio he's been riggin' up out in de shed.

NORWOOD.   Who gave him permission to be driving off in the middle of the morning? I bought that Ford to be used when I gave orders for it to be used, not . . .

CORA.   Yes, sir, Colonel Tom, but . . .   10

NORWOOD.   But what? [*Pausing. Then deliberately*] Cora, if you want that hardheaded yellow son of yours to get along around here, he'd better listen to me. He's no more than any other black buck on this plantation—due to work like the rest of 'em. I don't take such a performance from nobody under me—driving off in the middle of the day to town, after I've told him to bend his back in that cotton. How's Talbot going to keep the rest of those darkies working right if that boy's allowed to set that kind of an example? Just because Bert's your son, and I've been damn fool enough to send him off to school for five or six years, he thinks he has a right to privileges, acting as if he owned this place since he's been back here this summer.

CORA.   But, Colonel Tom . . .

NORWOOD.   Yes, I know what you're going to say. I don't give a damn about him! There's no nigger-child of mine, yours, ours—no darkie—going to disobey me. I put him in that field to work, and he'll stay on this plantation till I get ready to let him go. I'll tell Talbot to use the whip on him, too, if he needs it. If it hadn't been that he's yours, he'd-a had a taste of it the other day. Talbot's a damn good overseer, and no saucy, lazy Nigras stay on this plantation and get away with it. [*To* CORA] Go on back upstairs and see about getting Sallie out of here. Another word from you and I won't send your [*Sarcastically*] pretty little half-white daughter anywhere, either. Schools for darkies! Huh! If you take that boy of yours for an example, they do 'em more harm than good. He's learned nothing in college but impudence, and he'll stay here on this place and work for me awhile before he gets back to any more schools. [*He starts across the room.*]

CORA.   Yes, sir, Colonel Tom. [*Hesitating*] But he's just young, sir. And he was mighty broke up when you said last week he couldn't go back to de campus. [*COLONEL NORWOOD turns and looks at CORA commandingly. Understanding, she murmurs*] Yes, sir. [*She starts upstairs, but turns back.*] Can't I run and fix you a cool drink, Colonel Tom?

NORWOOD.   No, damn you! Sam'll do it.   15

CORA.   [*Sweetly*] Go set down in de cool, then, Colonel. 'Taint good for you to be going' on this way in de heat. I'll talk to Robert maself soon's he comes in. He don't mean nothing—just smart and young and kinder careless, Colonel Tom, like ma mother said you used to be when you was eighteen.

NORWOOD.   Get on upstairs, Cora. Do I have to speak again? Get on! [*He pulls the cord of the servants' bell.*]

CORA.   [*On the steps*] Does you still be in the mind to tell Sallie good-bye?

NORWOOD.   Send her down here as I told you. [*Impatiently*] Where's Sam? Send him here first. [*Fuming*] Looks like he takes his time to answer that bell. You colored folks are running the house to suit yourself nowadays.

CORA.   [*Coming downstairs again and going toward the door under the steps*] I'll get Sam   20
for you.

[*CORA exits left. NORWOOD paces nervously across the floor. Goes to the window and looks out down the road. Takes a cigar from his pocket, sits in a chair with it unlighted, scowling. Rises, goes toward servants' bell and rings it again violently as SAM enters, out of breath.*]

NORWOOD.   What the hell kind of a tortoise race is this? I suppose you were out in the sun somewhere sleeping?

SAM.   No, sah, Colonel Norwood. Just tryin' to get Miss Sallie's valises down to de yard so's we can put 'em in de Ford, sah.

NORWOOD.   [*Out of patience*] Huh! Darkies waiting on darkies! I can't get service in my own house. Very well. [*Loudly*] Bring me some whiskey and soda, and ice in a glass. Is that damn Frigidaire working right? Or is Livonia still too thickheaded to know how to run it? Any ice cubes in the thing?

SAM.   Yes, sah, Colonel, yes, sah. [*Backing toward door left*] 'Scuse me, please sah, but [*As NORWOOD turns toward library*] Cora say for me to ask you is it all right to bring that big old trunk what you give Sallie down by de front steps. We ain't been able to tote it down them narrer little back steps, sah. Cora, say, can we bring it down de front way through here?

NORWOOD.   No other way? [*SAM shakes his head*] Then pack it on through the back,   25
quick. Don't let me catch you carrying any of Sallie's baggage out of that front door here. You-all'll be wanting to go in and out the front way next. [*Turning away, complaining to himself*] Darkies have been getting mighty fresh in this part of the country since the war. The damn Germans should've . . . [*To SAM*] Don't take that trunk out that front door.

SAM.   [*Evilly, in a cunning voice*] I's seen Robert usin' de front door—when you ain't here, and he comes up from de cabin to see his mammy. [*SALLIE, the daughter, appears at the top of the stairs, but hesitates about coming down.*]

NORWOOD.   Oh, you have, have you? Let me catch him and I'll break his young neck for him. [*Yelling at SAM*] Didn't I tell you some whiskey and soda an hour ago?

[*SAM exits left. SALLIE comes shyly down the stairs and approaches her father. She is dressed in a little country-style coat-suit ready for traveling. Her features are Negroid, although her skin is very fair. COLONEL NORWOOD gazes down at her without saying a word as she comes meekly toward him, half-frightened.*]

SALLIE.   I just wanted to tell you goodbye, Colonel Norwood, and thank you for letting me go back to school another year, and for letting me work here in the house all summer where mama is. [*NORWOOD says nothing. The girl continues in a strained voice as if making a speech*] You mighty nice to us colored folks certainly, and mama says you the best white man in Georgia. [*Still NORWOOD says nothing. The girl continues.*] You been mighty nice to your—I mean to us colored children, letting my sister and me go off to school. The principal says I'm doing pretty well and next year I can go to Normal and learn to be a teacher. [*Raising her eyes*] You reckon I can, Colonel Tom?

NORWOOD.   Stand up straight and let me see how you look. [*Backing away*] Humm-m! Getting kinder grown, ain't you? Do they teach you in that school to have good manners, and not be afraid of work, *and to respect white folks?*

SALLIE.   Yes, sir, I been taking up cooking and sewing, too.   30

NORWOOD.   Well, that's good. As I recall it, that school turned your sister out a right smart cook. Cora tells me she's got a good job in some big hotel in Chicago. I'm thinking about you going on up North there with her in a year or two. You're getting too old to be around here, and too womanish. [*He puts his hands on her arms as if feeling her flesh*]

SALLIE.   [*Drawing back slightly*] But I want to live down here with mama. I want to teach school in that there empty school house by the Cross Roads what hasn't had a teacher for five years.

[*SAM has been standing with the door cracked, overhearing the conversation. He enters with the drink and places it on the table, right. NORWOOD sits down, leaving the girl standing, as SAM pours out a drink.*]

NORWOOD.   Don't get that into your head, now. There's been no teacher there for years—and there won't be any teacher there, either. Cotton teaches these pickaninnies enough around here. Some of 'em's too smart as it is. The only reason I did have a teacher there once was to get you young ones o' Cora's educated. I gave you all a chance and I hope you appreciate it. [*He takes a long drink.*] Don't know why I did it. No other white man in these parts ever did it, as I know of. [*To SAM*] Get out of here! [*SAM exits left*] Guess I couldn't stand to see Cora's kids working around here dumb as the rest of these no-good darkies—need a dozen of 'em to chop one row of cotton, or to keep a house clean. Or maybe I didn't want Talbot eyeing you gals. [*Taking another drink*] Anyhow, I'm glad you and Bertha turned out right well. Yes, hum-m-m! [*Straightening up*] You know I tried to do something for those brothers of yours, too, but William's stupid as an ox—good for work, though—and that Robert's just an impudent, hardheaded, yellow young fool. I'm gonna break his damn neck for him if he don't watch out. Or else put Talbot on him.

SALLIE.   [*Suddenly frightened*] Please, sir, don't put the overseer on Bert, Colonel Tom. He was the smartest boy at school, Bert was. On the football team, too. Please, sir, Colonel Tom. Let brother work here in the house, or somewhere else where Talbot can't mistreat him. He ain't used . . .

NORWOOD.   [*Rising*] Telling me what to do, heh? [*Staring at her sternly*] I'll use the   35
back of my hand across your face if you don't hush. [*He takes another drink. The noise of a Ford is heard outside.*] That's Bert now, I reckon. He's to take you to the railroad line, and while you're riding with him, you better put some sense into his head. And tell him I want to see him as soon as he gets back here. [*CORA enters left with a bundle and an umbrella. SAM and WILLIAM come downstairs with a big square trunk, and exit hurriedly, left.*]

SALLIE.   Yes, sir, I'll tell him.

CORA.   Colonel Tom, Sallie ain't got much time now. [*To the girl*] Come on, chile. Bert's here. Yo' big brother and Sam and Livonia and everybody's all waiting at de back door to say goodbye. And your baggage is being packed in. [*Noise of another car is heard outside.*] Who else is that there coming up de drive? [*CORA looks out the window.*] Mr. Higgins' car, Colonel Tom. Reckon he's coming to see you . . . Hurry up out o' this front room, Sallie. Here, take these things of your'n [*Hands her the bundle and parasol*] while I opens de door for Mr. Higgins. [*In a whisper*] Hurry up, chile! Get out! [*NORWOOD turns toward the front door as CORA goes to open it*]

SALLIE. [*Shyly to her father*] Goodbye, Colonel Tom.

NORWOOD. [*His eyes on the front door, scarcely noticing the departing SALLIE, he motions.*] Yes, yes goodbye! Get on now! [*CORA opens the front door as her daughter exits left.*] Well, well! Howdy do, Fred. Come in, come in! [*CORA holds the outer door of the vestibule wide as FRED HIGGINS enters with rheumatic dignity, supported on the arm of his chauffeur, MOSE, a very black Negro in a slouchy uniform. CORA closes the door and exits left hurriedly, following SALLIE.*]

NORWOOD. [*Smiling*] How's the rheumatiz today? Women or licker or heat   40
must've made it worse—from the looks of your speed!

HIGGINS [*Testily, sitting down puffing and blowing in a big chair*] I'm in no mood for fooling, Tom, not now. [*To MOSE*] All right. [*The CHAUFFEUR exits front. HIGGINS continues angrily.*] Norwood, that damned yellow nigger buck of yours that drives that new Ford tried his best just now to push my car off the road, then got in front of me and blew dust in my face for the last mile coming down to your gate, trying to beat me in here—which he did. Such a deliberate piece of impudence I don't know if I've ever seen out of a nigger before in all the sixty years I've lived in this country. [*The noise of the Ford is heard going out the drive, and the cries of the NEGROES shouting farewells to SALLIE. HIGGINS listens indignantly.*] What kind of crazy coons have you got on your place, anyhow? Sounds like a black Baptist picnic to me. [*Pointing to the window with his cane*] Tom, listen to that.

NORWOOD. [*Flushing*] I apologize to you, Fred, for each and every one of my darkies. [*SAM enters with more ice and another glass.*] Permit me to offer you a drink. I realize I've got to tighten down here.

HIGGINS. Mose tells me that was Cora's boy in that Ford—and that young black fool is what I was coming here to talk to you about today. That boy! He's not gonna be around here long—not the way he's acting. The white folks in town'll see to that. Knowing he's one of your yard niggers, Norwood, I thought I ought to come and tell you. The white folks at the Junction aren't intending to put up with him much longer. And I don't know what good the jail would do him once he got in there.

NORWOOD. [*Tensely*] What do you mean, Fred—jail? Don't I always take care of the folks on my plantation without any help from the Junction's police force? Talbot can do more with an unruly black buck than your marshal.

HIGGINS. Warn't lookin' at it that way, Tom. I was thinking how weak the doors to   45
that jail is. They've broke 'em down and lynched four niggers to my memory since it's been built. After what happened this morning, you better keep that yellow young fool out o' town from now on. It might not be safe for him around there—today, or no other time.

NORWOOD. What the hell? [*Perturbed*] He went in just now to take his sister to the depot. Damn it, I hope no ruffians'll break up my new Ford. What was it, Fred, about this morning?

HIGGINS. You haven't heard? Why, it's all over town already. He sassed out Miss Gray in the post office over a box of radio tubes that come by mail.

NORWOOD. He did, heh?

HIGGINS. Seems like the stuff was sent C.O.D. and got here all smashed up, so he wouldn't take it. Paid his money first before he saw the box was broke. Then wanted the money order back. Seems like the post office can't give money orders back—rule against it. Your nigger started to argue, and the girl at the window—Miss Gray—got scared and yelled for some of the mail clerks. They threw Bert out of the office, that's all. But that's enough. Lucky nothing more didn't happen. [*Indignantly*] That Bert needs a damn good beating—talking back to a white woman—and I'd like to give it to him myself, the way he kicked the dust up in my eyes all the way down the road coming out here. He was mad, I reckon. That's one yellow buck don't know his place, Tom, and it's your fault he don't—sending 'em off to be educated.

NORWOOD.   Well, by God, I'll show him. I wish I'd have known it before he left 50 here just now.

HIGGINS.   Well, he's sure got mighty aggravating ways for a buck his color to have. Drives down the main street and don't stop for nobody, white or black. Comes in my store and if he ain't waited on as quick as the white folks are, he walks out and tells the clerk his money's as good as a white man's any day. Said last week standing out on my store front that he wasn't *all* nigger no how; said his name was Norwood—not Lewis, like the rest of his family—and part of your plantation here would be his when you passed out—and all that kind of stuff, boasting to the walleyed coons listening to him.

NORWOOD.   [*Astounded*] Well, I'll be damned!

HIGGINS.   Now, Tom, you know that don't go 'round these parts 'o Georgia, nor nowhere else in the South. A darkie's got to keep in his place down here. Ruinous to other niggers hearing that talk, too. All this postwar propaganda on the radio about freedom and democracy—why the niggers think it's meant for them! And that Eleanor Roosevelt,° she ought to been muzzled. She's driving our niggers crazy—your boy included! Crazy! Talking about civil rights. Ain't been no race trouble in our country for three years—since the Deekin's lynching—but I'm telling you, Norwood, you better see that that buck of yours goes away from here. I'm speaking on the quiet, but I can see ahead. And what happened this morning about them radio tubes wasn't none too good.

NORWOOD.   [*Beside himself with rage*] A black ape! I—I . . .

HIGGINS.   You been too decent to your darkies, Norwood. That's what's the matter 55 with you. And then the whole country suffers from a lot of impudent bucks who take lessons from your crowd. Folks been kicking about that, too. Guess you know it. Maybe that's the reason you didn't get that nomination for committeeman a few years back.

NORWOOD.   Maybe 'tis, Higgins. [*Rising and pacing the room*] God damn niggers! [*Furiously*] Everything turns on niggers, niggers, niggers! No wonder Yankees call this the Black Belt! [*He pours a large drink of whiskey.*]

HIGGINS.   [*Soothingly*] Well, let's change the subject. Hand me my glass, there, too.

NORWOOD.   Pardon me, Fred. [*He puts ice in his friend's glass and passes him the bottle.*]

HIGGINS.   Tom, you get excited too easy for warm weather . . . Don't ever show black folks they got you going, though. I think sometimes that's where you make your mistake. Keep calm, keep calm—and then you command. Best plantation manager I ever had never raised his voice to a nigger—and they were scared to death of him.

NORWOOD.   Have a smoke. [*Pushes cigars toward HIGGINS*] 60

HIGGINS.   You ought've married again, Tom—brought a white woman out here on this damn place o' yours. A woman could help you run things. Women have soft ways, but they can keep things humming. Nothing but blacks in the house—a man gets soft like niggers are inside. [*Puffing at cigar*] And living with a colored woman! Of course, I know we all have 'em—I didn't know you could make use of a white girl till I was past twenty.

53 *Eleanor Roosevelt:* Eleanor Roosevelt (1884–1962), the wife of President Franklin D. Roosevelt, was an outspoken champion of minority causes.

Thought too much o' white women for that—but I've given many a yellow gal a baby in my time. [*Long puff at cigar*] But for a man's own house you need a wife, not a black woman.

NORWOOD.　Reckon you're right, Fred, but it's too late to marry again now. [*Shrugging his shoulders*] Let's get off of darkies and women for awhile. How's crops? [*Sitting down*] How's politics going?

HIGGINS.　Well, I guess you know the Republicans is trying to stir up trouble for us in Washington. I wish the South had more men like Bilbo and Rankin° there. But, say, by the way, Lawyer Hotchkiss wants to see us both about that budget money next week. He's got some real Canadian stuff at his office, in his filing case, too—brought back from his vacation last summer. Taste better'n this old mountain juice we get around here. Not meaning to insult your drinks, Tom, but just remarking. I serve the same as you myself, label and all.

NORWOOD.　[*Laughing*] I'll have you know, sir, that this is prewar licker, sir!

HIGGINS.　Hum-m-m! Well, it's got me feelin' better'n I did when I come in here—　65 whatever it is. [*Puffs at his cigar*] Say, how's your cotton this year?

NORWOOD.　Doin' right well, specially down in the south field. Why not drive out that road when you leave and take a look at it? I'll ride down with you. I want to see Talbot, anyhow.

HIGGINS.　Well, let's be starting. I got to be back at the Junction by four o'clock. Promised to let that boy of mine have the car to drive over to Thomasville for a dance tonight.

NORWOOD.　One more shot before we go. [*He pours out drinks.*] The young ones must have their fling, I reckon. When you and I grew up down here it used to be a carriage and the best pair of black horses when you took the ladies out—now it's an automobile. That's a good lookin' new car of yours, too.

HIGGINS.　Right nice.

NORWOOD.　Been thinking about getting a new one myself, but money's been　70 kinder tight this year, and conditions are none too good yet, either. Reckon that's why everybody's so restless. [*He walks toward stairs calling.*] Cora! Oh, Cora! . . . If I didn't have a few thousand put away, I'd feel the pinch myself. [*As* CORA *appears on the stairs.*] Bring me my glasses up there by the side of my bed . . . Better whistle for Mose, hadn't I, Higgins? He's probably 'round back with some of his women. [*Winking*] You know I got some nice black women in this yard.

HIGGINS.　Oh, no, not Mose. I got my servants trained to stay in their places—right where I want 'em—while they're working for me. Just open the door and tell him to come in here and help me out. [NORWOOD *goes to the door and calls the* CHAUFFEUR. *MOSE enters and assists his master out to the car.* CORA *appears with the glasses, goes to the vestibule and gets the* COLONEL'S *hat and cane which she hands him.*]

NORWOOD.　[*To* CORA] I want to see that boy o' yours soon as I get back. That won't be long, either. And tell him to put up that Ford of mine and don't touch it again.

CORA.　Yes, sir, I'll have him waiting here. [*In a whisper*] It's hot weather, Colonel Tom. Too much of this licker makes your heart upset. It ain't good for you, you know. [NORWOOD *pays her no attention as he exits toward the car. The noise of the departing motor is heard. Cora begins to tidy up the room. She takes a glass from a side table. She picks up a doily that*

---

63 *Bilbo, Rankin:* Theodore Bilbo (1877–1947), senator from Mississippi from 1935 to 1947, and John Eliot Rankin (1882–1960), Mississippi Representative to the House from 1921 to 1953, were both noted advocates of white supremacy.

was beneath the glass and looks at it long and lovingly. Suddenly she goes to the door left and calls toward the kitchen.] William, you William! Com'ere, I want to show you something. Make haste, son. [*As* CORA *goes back toward the table, her eldest son,* WILLIAM *enters carrying a five-year-old boy.*] Look here at this purty doily yo' sister made this summer while she been here. She done learned all about sewing and making purty things at school. Ain't it nice, son?

WILLIAM.   Sho' is. Sallie takes after you, I reckon. She's a smart little crittur, ma. [*Sighs*] De Lawd knows, I was dumb at school. [*To his child*] Get down, Billy, you's too heavy. [*He puts the boy on the floor*] This here sewin's really fine.

BILLY.   [*Running toward the big upholstered chair and jumping up and down on the spring seat*] Gityap! I's a mule driver. Haw! Gee!   75

CORA.   You Billy, get out of that chair 'fore I skins you alive. Get on into de kitchen, sah.

BILLY.   I'm playin' horsie, grandma. [*Jumps up in the chair*] Horsie! Horsie!

CORA.   Get! That's de Colonel's favorite chair. If he knows any little darkie's been jumpin' on it, he raise sand. Get on, now.

BILLY.   Ole Colonel's ma grandpa, ain't he? Ain' he ma white grandpa?

WILLIAM.   [*Snatching the child out of the chair*] Boy, I'm gonna fan your hide if you   80
don't hush!

CORA.   Shs-ss-s! You Billy, hush yo' mouth! Chile, where you hear that? [*To her son*] Some o' you all been talking too much in front o' this chile. [*To the boy*] Honey, go on in de kitchen till yo' daddy come. Get a cookie from 'Vonia and set down on de back porch. [*Little* BILLY *exits left*]

WILLIAM.   Ma, you know it 'twarn't me told him. Bert's the one been goin' all over de plantation since he come back from Atlanta remindin' folks right out we's Colonel Norwood's chilluns.

CORA.   [*Catching her breath*] Huh!

WILLIAM.   He comes down to my shack tellin' Billy and Marybell they got a white man for grandpa. He's gonna get my chilluns in trouble sho'—like he got himself in trouble when Colonel Tom whipped him.

CORA.   Ten or 'leven years ago, warn't it?   85

WILLIAM.   And Bert's *sho'* in trouble now. Can't go back to that college like he could-a if he'd-a had any sense. You can't fool with white folks—an de Colonel ain't never really liked Bert since that there first time he beat him, either.

CORA.   No, he ain't. Leastwise, he ain't understood him. [*Musing sadly in a low voice*] Time Bert was 'bout seven, warn't it? Just a little bigger'n yo' Billy.

WILLIAM.   Yes.

CORA.   Went runnin' up to Colonel Tom out in de horse stables when de Colonel was showin' off his horses—I 'members so well—to fine white company from town. Lawd, that boy's always been foolish! He went runnin' up and grabbed a-holt de Colonel and yelled right in front o' de white folks' faces, "O, papa, Cora say de dinner's ready, papa!" Ain't never called him papa before, and I don't know where he got it from. And Colonel Tom knocked him right backwards under de horse's feet.

WILLIAM.   And when de company were gone, he beat that boy unmerciful.   90

CORA.   I thought sho' he were gonna kill ma chile that day. And he were mad at me, too, for months. Said I was teaching you chilluns who they pappy were. Up till then Bert had been his favorite little colored child round here.

WILLIAM.   Sho' had.

CORA.   But he never like him no more. That's why he sent him off to school so soon to stay, winter and summer, all these years. I had to beg and plead to have him home this summer—but I's sorry now I ever got that boy back here again.

WILLIAM.   He's sho' growed more like de Colonel all de time, ain't he? Bert thinks he's a real white man hisself now. Look at de first thing he did when he come home, he ain't seen de Colonel in six years—and Bert sticks out his hand fo' to shake hands with him!

CORA.   Lawd! That chile!   95

WILLIAM.   Just like white folks! And de Colonel turns his back and walks off. Can't blame him. He ain't used to such doings from colored folks. God knows what's got into Bert since he come back. He's acting like a fool—just like he was a boss man round here. Won't even say "Yes, sir" and "No, sir" no more to de white folks. Talbot asked him warn't he gonna work in de field this mornin'. Bert say "No!" and turn and walk away. White man so mad, I could see him nearly foam at de mouth. If he warn't yo' chile, ma, he'd been knocked in de head fo' now.

CORA.   You's right.

WILLIAM.   And you can't talk to him. I tried to tell him something the other day, but he just laughed at me, and said we's all just scared niggers on this plantation. Says he ain't no nigger, no how. He's a Norwood. He's half-white, and he's gonna act like it. [*In amazement at his brother's daring*] And this is Georgia, too!

CORA.   I's scared to death for de boy, William. I don't know what to do. De Colonel says he won't send him off to school no mo'. Says he's mo' sassy and impudent now than any nigger he ever seed. Bert never has been like you was, and de girls, quiet and sensible like you knowed you had to be. [*She sits down*] De Colonel say he's gonna make Bert stay here now and work on this plantation like de rest of his niggers. He's gonna show him what color he is. Like that time when he beat him for callin' him "papa." He say he's gwine to teach him his place and make de boy know where he belongs. Seems like me or you can't show him. Colonel Tom has to take him in hand, or these white folks'll kill him around here and then—oh, My God!

WILLIAM.   A nigger's just got to know his place in de South, that's all, ain't he, ma?   100

CORA.   Yes, son. That's all, I reckon.

WILLIAM.   And ma brother's one damn fool nigger. Don't seems like he knows nothin'. He's gonna ruin us all round here. Makin' it bad for everybody.

CORA.   Oh, Lawd, have mercy! [*Beginning to cry*] I don't know what to do. De way he's acting up can't go on. Way he's acting to de Colonel can't last. Somethin's gonna happen to ma chile. I had a bad dream last night, too, and I looked out and seed de moon all red with blood. I seed a path o' living blood across this house, I tell you, in my sleep. Oh, Lawd, have mercy! [*Sobbing*] Oh, Lawd, help me in ma troubles. [*The noise of the returning Ford is heard outside. CORA looks up, rises, and goes to the window.*] There's de chile now, William. Run out to de back door and tell him I wants to see him. Bring him in here where Sam and Livonia and de rest of 'em won't hear ever'thing we's sayin'. I got to talk to ma boy. He's ma baby boy, and he don't know de way.

[*Exit WILLIAM through the door left. CORA is wiping her eyes and pulling herself together when the front door is flung open with a bang and ROBERT enters.*]

ROBERT.   [*Running to his mother and hugging her teasingly*] Hello, ma! Your daughter got off, and I've come back to keep you company in the parlor! Bring out the cookies and lemonade. *Mister* Norwood's here!

CORA.   [*Beginning to sob anew*] Take yo' hands off me, boy! Why don't you mind?   105
Why don't you mind me?

ROBERT.   [*Suddenly serious, backing away*] Why, mamma, what's the matter? Did I scare you? Your eyes are all wet! Has somebody been telling you 'bout this morning?

CORA.   [*Not heeding his words*] Why don't you mind me, son? Ain't I told you and told you not to come in that front door, never? [*Suddenly angry*] Will somebody have to beat it into you? What's got wrong with you when you was away at that school? What am I gonna do?

ROBERT. [*Carelessly*] Oh, I knew that the Colonel wasn't here. I passed him and old man Higgins on the road down by the south patch. He wouldn't even look at me when I waved at him. [*Half playfully*] Anyhow, isn't this my old man's house? Ain't I his son and heir? [*Grandly, strutting around*] Am I not Mr. Norwood, Junior?

CORA. [*Utterly serious*] I believe you goin' crazy, Bert. I believes you wants to get us all killed or run away or something awful like that. I believes . . . [*WILLIAM enters left*]

WILLIAM.   Where's Bert? He ain't come round back—[*Seeing his brother in the room*]   110
How'd you get in here?

ROBERT. [*Grinning*] Houses have front doors.

WILLIAM.   Oh, usin' de front door like de white folks, heh? You gwine do that once too much.

ROBERT.   Yes, like de white folks. What's a front door for, you rabbit-hearted coon?

WILLIAM.   Rabbit-hearted coon's better'n a dead coon any day.

ROBERT.   I wouldn't say so. Besides you and me's only half-coons, anyhow, big boy.   115
And I'm gonna act like my white half, not my black half. Get me, kid?

WILLIAM.   Well, you ain't gonna act like it long here in de middle o' Georgy. And you ain't gonna act like it when de Colonel's around, either.

ROBERT.   Oh, no? My stay down here'll be short and sweet, boy, short and sweet. The old man won't send me away to college no more—so you think I'm gonna stick around and work in the fields? Like fun! I might stay here awhile and teach some o' you darkies to think like men, maybe—till it gets too much for the old Colonel—but no more bowing down to white folks for me—not Robert Norwood.

CORA. Hush, son!

Robert.   Certainly not right on my own old man's plantation—Georgia or no Georgia.

WILLIAM.   [*Scornfully*] I hears you.   120

ROBERT.   *You* can do it if you want to, but I'm ashamed of you. I've been away from here six years. [*Boasting*] I've learned something, seen people in Atlanta, and Richmond, and Washington where the football team went—real colored people who don't have to take off their hats to white folks or let 'em go to bed with their sisters—like that young Higgins boy, asking me what night Sallie was comin' to town. A damn cracker! [*To CORA*] 'Scuse me, ma. [*Continuing*] Back here in these woods maybe Sam and Livonia and you and mama and everybody's got their places fixed for 'em, but not me. [*Seriously*] Nobody's gonna fix a place for me. I'm old man Norwood's son. Nobody fixed a place for him. [*Playfully again*] Look at me. I'm a 'fay boy. [*Pretends to shake his hair back*] See these gray eyes? I got the right to everything everybody else has. [*Punching his brother in the belly*], Don't talk to me, old slavery-time Uncle Tom.

WILLIAM.   [*Resentfully*] I ain't playin', boy. [*Pushes younger brother back with some force*] I ain't playin' a-tall.

CORA.   All right, chilluns, stop. Stop! And William, you take Billy and go on home. 'Vonia's got to get supper and she don't like no young-uns under her feet in de kitchen. I wants to talk to Bert in here now 'fore Colonel Tom gets back. [*Exit WILLIAM left. CORA continues to BERT*] Sit down, child, right here a minute and listen.

ROBERT.   [*Sitting down*] All right, ma.

CORA.   Hard as I's worked and begged and humbled maself to get de Colonel to   125
keep you chilluns in school, you comes home wid yo' head full o' stubbornness and yo' mouth full o' sass for me an' de white folks an' everybody. You know can't no colored boy here talk like you's been doin' to no white folks, let alone to de Colonel and that old devil of a Talbot. They ain't gonna stand fo' yo' sass. Not only you, but I 'spects we's all gwine

to pay fo' it, every colored soul on this place. I was scared to death today fo' yo' sister, Sallie, scared de Colonel warn't gwine to let her go back to school, neither, 'count o' yo' doins, but he did, thank Gawd—and then you come near makin' her miss de train. Did she have time to get her ticket and all?

ROBERT.   Sure! Had to drive like sin to get there with her, though. I didn't mean to be late getting back here for her, ma, but I had a little run-in about them radio tubes in town.

CORA.   [*Worried*] What's that?

ROBERT.   The tubes was smashed when I got 'em, and I had already made out my money order, so the woman in the post office wouldn't give the three dollars back to me. All I did was explain to her that we could send the tubes back—but she got hot because there were two or three white folks waiting behind me to get stamps, I guess. So she yells at me to move on and not give her any of my "educated nigger talk." So I said, "I'm going to finish showing you these tubes before I move on"—and then she screamed and called the mail clerk working in the back, and told him to throw me out. [*Boasting*] He didn't do it by himself, though. Had to call all the white loafers out in the square to get me through that door.

CORA.   [*Fearfully*] Lawd have mercy!

ROBERT.   Guess if I hadn't-a had the Ford then, they'd've beat me half-to-death,   130
but when I saw how many crackers there was, I jumped in the car and beat it on away.

CORA.   Thank God for that!

ROBERT.   Not even a football man [*Half-boasting*] like me could tackle the whole junction. 'Bout a dozen colored guys standing around, too, and not one of 'em would help me—the dumb jiggaboos! They been telling me ever since I been here, [*Imitating darky talk*] "You can't argue wid whut folks, man. You better stay out o' this Junction. You must ain't got no sense, nigger! You's a fool" . . . Maybe I am a fool, ma—but I didn't want to come back here nohow.

CORA.   I's sorry I sent for you.

ROBERT.   Besides you, there ain't nobody in this country but a lot of evil white folks and cowardly niggers. [*Earnstly*] I'm no nigger, anyhow, am I, ma? I'm half-white. The Colonel's my father—the richest man in the county—and I'm not going to take a lot of stuff from nobody if I do have to stay here, not from the old man either. He thinks I ought to be out there in the sun working, with Talbot standing over me like I belonged in the chain gang. Well, he's got another thought coming! [*Stubbornly*] I'm a Norwood—not a field-hand nigger.

CORA.   You means you ain't workin' no mo'?   135

ROBERT.   [*Flaring*] No, I'm not going to work in the fields. What did he send me away to school for—just to come back here and be his servant, or pick his hills of cotton?

CORA.   He sent you away to de school because *I* asked him and begged him, and got down on my knees to him, that's why. [*Quietly*] And now I just wants to make you see some sense, if you can. I knows, honey, you reads in de books and de papers, and you knows a lot more'n I do. But, chile, you's in Georgy—and I don't see how it is you don't know where you's at. This ain't up North—and even up yonder where we hears it's so fine, yo' sister has to pass for white to get along good.

ROBERT.   [*Bitterly*] I know it.

CORA.   She ain't workin' in no hotel kitchen like de Colonel thinks. She's in a office typewriting. And Sallie's studyin' de typewriter, too, at de school, but yo' pappy don't know it. I knows we ain't s'posed to study nothin' but cookin' and hard workin' here in Georgy. That's all I ever done, or knowed about. I been workin' on this very place all ma life—even 'fore I come to live in this Big House. When de Colonel's wife died, I come

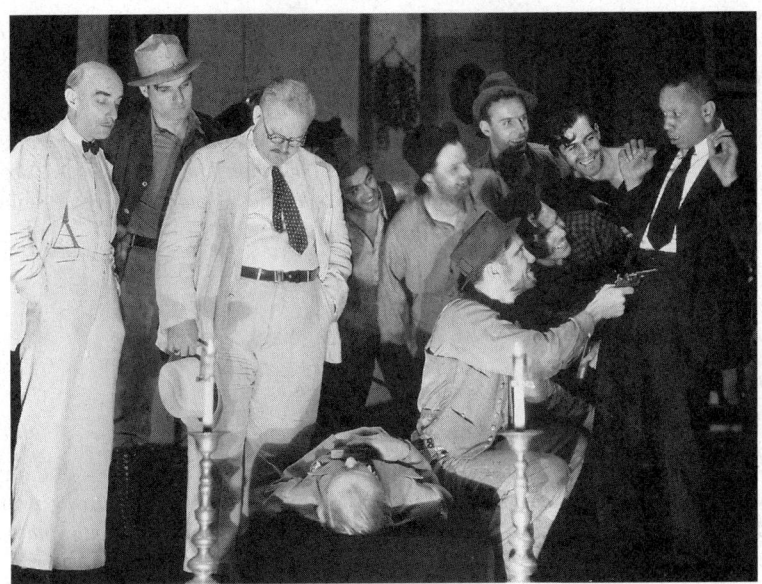

Robert, who has been apprehended here, is confronted and taunted by members of the Mob as Higgins, Talbot, and the Undertaker stand beside the body of Colonel Thomas Norwood, in the original production of Hughes's *Mulatto* at the Vanderbilt Theater in New York, October, 1935, produced and directed by Martin Jones. The actors are unidentified.

here, and borned you chilluns. And de Colonel's been real good to me in his way. Let you all sleep in this house with me when you was little, and sent you all off to school when you growed up. Ain't no white man in this county done that with his cullud chilluns before, far as I can know. But you—Robert, be awful, awful careful! When de Colonel comes back, in a few minutes, he wants to talk to you. Talk right to him, boy. Talk like you was colored, 'cause you ain't white.

ROBERT.   [*Angrily*] And I'm not black either. Look at me, mama. [*Rising and throwing up his arms*] Don't I look like my father? Ain't I as light as he is? Ain't my eyes gray like his eyes are? [*The noise of a car is heard outside*] Ain't this our house?   140

CORA.   That's him now. [*Agitated*] Hurry, chile, and let's get out of this room. Come on through yonder to the kitchen. [*She starts toward the door left.*] And I'll tell him you're here.

ROBERT.   I don't want to run into the kitchen. Isn't this our house? [*As CORA crosses hurriedly left, ROBERT goes toward the front door*] The Ford is parked out in front, anyway.

CORA.   [*At the door left to the rear of the house*] Robert! Robert! [*As ROBERT nears the front door, COLONEL NORWOOD enters, almost runs into the boy, stops at the threshold and stares unbelievingly at his son. CORA backs up against the door left.*]

NORWOOD.   Get out of here! [*He points toward the door to rear of the house where CORA is standing*].

ROBERT.   [*Half-smiling*] Didn't you want to talk to me?   145

NORWOOD.   Get out of here!

ROBERT.   Not that way. [*The COLONEL raises his cane to strike the boy. CORA screams. BERT draws himself up to his full height, taller than the old man and looking very much like him, pale and proud. The man and the boy face each other. NORWOOD does not strike.*]

NORWOOD.   [*In a hoarse whisper*] Get out of here. [*His hand is trembling as he points.*]

CORA.   Robert! Come on, son, come on! Oh, my God, come on. [*Opening the door left*]

ROBERT.   Not that way, ma. [*ROBERT walks proudly out the front door. NORWOOD, in an   150
impotent rage, crosses the room to a small cabinet right, opens it nervously with a key from his pocket,
takes out a pistol, and starts toward the front door. CORA overtakes him, seizes his arm, stops him.*]

CORA.   He's our son, Tom. [*She sinks slowly to her knees, holding his body.*] Remember,
he's our son.

Curtain

ACT 2

Scene 1

TIME. *After supper. Sunset.*

SETTING. *The same.*

ACTION. *As the curtain rises, the stage is empty. Through the windows the late afternoon sun makes
two bright paths toward the footlights. SAM, carrying a tray bearing a whiskey bottle and a bowl of
ice, enters left and crosses toward the library. He stoops at the door right, listens a moment, knocks,
then opens the door and goes in. In a moment SAM returns. As he leaves the library, he is heard replying to a request of NORWOOD's.*

SAM.   Yes, sah, Colonel! Sho' will, sah! Right away, sah! Yes, sah, I'll tell him. [*He
closes the door and crosses the stage muttering to himself.*] Six o'clock. Most nigh that now. Better tell Cora to get that boy right in here. Can't nobody else do notin' with that fool Bert
but Cora. [*He exits left. Can be heard calling*] Cora! You, Cora . . .

[*Again the stage is empty. Off stage, outside, the bark of a dog is heard, the sound of Negroes singing
down the road, the cry of a child. The breeze moves the shadows of leaves and tree limbs across the
sunlit paths from the windows. The door left opens and CORA enters, followed by ROBERT.*]

CORA.   [*Softly to ROBERT behind her in the dining room*] It's all right, son. He ain't
come out yet, but it's nearly six, and that's when he said he wanted you, but I was afraid
maybe you was gonna be late. I sent for you to come up here to de house and eat supper
with me in de kitchen. Where'd you eat yo' vittals at, chile?

ROBERT.   Down at Willie's house, ma. After the old man tried to hit me you still
want me to hang around and eat up here?

CORA.   I wanted you to be here on time, honey, that's all. [*She is very nervous.*] I
kinder likes to have you eat with me sometimes, too, but you ain't et up here more'n
once this summer. But this evenin' I just wanted you to be here when de Colonel sent
word for you, 'cause we's done had enough trouble today.

ROBERT.   He's not here on time, himself, is he?   5

CORA.   He's in de library. Sam couldn't get him to eat no supper tonight, and I
ain't seen him a-tall.

ROBERT.   Maybe he wants to see me in the library, then.

CORA.   You know he don't 'low no colored folks in there 'mongst his books and
things 'cept Sam. Some o' his white friends goes in there, but none o' us.

ROBERT.   Maybe he wants to see *me* in there, though.

CORA.   Can't you never talk sense, Robert? This ain't no time for foolin' and   10
jokin'. Nearly thirty years in this house and I ain't never been in there myself, not once,
'mongst de Colonel's papers. [*The clock strikes six.*] Stand over yonder and wait till he
comes out. I's gwine on upstairs now, so's he can talk to you. And don't aggravate him no

mo' for' God's sake. Agree to whatever he say. I's scared fo' you, chile, de way you been actin', and de fool tricks you done today, and de trouble about de post office besides. Don't aggravate him. Fo' yo' sake, honey, 'cause I loves you—and fo' all de po' colored folks on this place what has such a hard time when his humors get on him—agree to whatever he say, will you Bert?

ROBERT.   All right, ma. [*Voice rising*] But he better not start to hit me again.

CORA.   Shs-ss-s! He'll hear you. He's right in there.

ROBERT.   [*Sullenly*] This was the day I ought to have started back to school—like my sister. I stayed my summer out here, didn't I? Why didn't he keep his promise to me? You said if I came home I could go back to college again.

CORA.   Shs-ss-s! He'll be here now. Don't say nothin', chile, I's done all I could.

ROBERT.   All right, ma.

CORA.   [*Approaching the stairs*] I'll be in ma room, honey, where I can hear you when you goes out. I'll come down to de back door and see you 'fore you goes back to de shack. Don't aggravate him, chile.

[*She ascends the stairs. The boy sits down sullenly, left, and stares at the door opposite from which his father must enter. The clock strikes the quarter after six. The shadows of the window curtains have lengthened on the carpet. The sunshine has deepened to a pale orange, and the light paths grow less distinct across the floor. The boy sits up straight in his chair. He looks at the library door. It opens. NORWOOD enters. He is bent and pale. He looks across the room and sees the boy. Suddenly he straightens up. The old commanding look comes into his face. He strides directly across the room toward his son. The boy, half afraid, half defiant, yet sure of himself, rises. Now that ROBERT is standing, the white man turns, goes back to a chair near the table, right, and seats himself. He takes out a cigar, cuts off the end and lights it, and in a voice of mixed condescension and contempt, he speaks to his son. ROBERT remains standing near the chair.*]

NORWOOD.   I don't want to have to beat you another time as I did when you were a child. The next time I might not be able to control myself. I might kill you if I touched you again. I been runnin' this plantation for thirty-five years, and I never had to beat a Nigra as old as you are. I never had to beat one of Cora's children either—but you. The rest of 'em had sense 'nough to keep out of my sight, and to speak to me like they should . . . I don't have any trouble with my colored folks. Never have trouble. They do what I say, or what Mr. Talbot says, and that's all there is to it, I give 'em a chance. If they turn in their crops they get paid. If they're workin' for wages, they get paid. If they want to spend their money on licker, or buy an old car, or fix up their cabins, they can. Do what they choose long as they know their places and it don't hinder their work. And to Cora's young ones I give all the chances any colored folks ever had in these parts. More'n many a white child's had. I sent you all off to school. Let Bertha go on up North when she got grown and educated. Intend to let Sallie do the same. Gave your brother William that house he's living in when he got married, pay him for his work, help him out if he needs it. None of my darkies suffer. Sent you to college. Would have kept on, would have sent you back today, but I don't intend to pay for no darky, or white boy either if I had one, that acts the way you've been acting. And certainly for no black fool. Now I want to know what's wrong with you? I don't usually talk about what I'm going to do with anybody on this place. It's my habit to tell people *what to do*, not to discuss it with 'em. But I want to know what's the matter with you—whether you're crazy or not. In that case, you'll have to be locked up. And if you aren't, you'll have to change your ways a damn sight or it won't be safe for you here, and you know it—venting your impudence on white women, parking the car in front of my door, driving like mad through the Junction, and going, everywhere, just as you please. Now, I'm going to let you talk to me, but I want you to talk right.

15

ROBERT.   [*Still standing*] What do you mean, "talk right"?

NORWOOD.   I mean talk like a nigger should to a white man.

ROBERT.   Oh! But I'm not a nigger, Colonel Tom. I'm your son.   20

NORWOOD.   [*Testily*] You're Cora's boy.

ROBERT.   Women don't have children by themselves.

NORWOOD.   Nigger women don't know the fathers. You're a bastard.

[*ROBERT clenches his fist. NORWOOD turns toward the drawer where the pistol is, takes it out, and lays it on the table. The wind blows the lace curtains at the windows, and sweeps the shadows of falling leaves across the paths of sunlight on the floor.*]

ROBERT.   I've heard that before. I've heard it from Negroes, and I've heard it from white folks. Now I hear it from you. [*Slowly*] You're talking about my mother.

NORWOOD.   I'm talking about Cora, yes. Her children are bastards.   25

ROBERT.   [*Quickly*] And you're their father. [*Angrily*] How come I look like you, if you're not my father?

NORWOOD.   Don't shout at me, boy. I can hear you. [*Half-smiling*] How come your skin is yellow and your elbows rusty? How come they threw you out of the post office today for talking to a white woman? How come you're the crazy young buck you are?

ROBERT.   They had no right to throw me out. I asked for my money back when I saw the broken tubes. Just as you had no right to raise that cane today when I was standing at the door of this house where *you* live, while *I* have to sleep in a shack down the road with the field hands. [*Slowly*] But my mother sleeps with you.

NORWOOD.   You don't like it?

ROBERT.   No, I don't like it.   30

NORWOOD.   What can you do about it?

ROBERT.   [*After a pause*] I'd like to kill all the white men in the world.

NORWOOD.   [*Starting*] Niggers like you are hung to trees.

ROBERT.   I'm not a nigger.

NORWOOD.   You don't like your own race? [*ROBERT is silent*] Yet you don't like white   35
folks either?

ROBERT.   [*Defiantly*] You think I ought to?

NORWOOD.   You evidently don't like me.

ROBERT.   [*Boyishly*] I used to like you, when I first knew you were my father, when I was a little kid, before that time you beat me under the feet of your horses. [*Slowly*] I liked you until then.

NORWOOD.   [*A little pleased*] So you did, heh? [*Fingering his pistol*] A pickaninny calling me "papa." I should've broken your young neck for that first time. I should've broken your head for you today, too—since I didn't then.

ROBERT.   [*Laughing scornfully*] You should've broken my head?   40

NORWOOD.   Should've gotten rid of you before this. But you was Cora's child. I tried to help you. [*Aggrieved*] I treated you decent, schooled you. Paid for it. But tonight you'll get the hell off this place and stay off. Get the hell out of this county. [*Suddenly furious*] Get out of this state. Don't let me lay eyes on you again. Get out of here now. Talbot and the storekeeper are coming up here this evening to talk cotton with me. I'll tell Talbot to *see* that you go. That's all. [*NORWOOD motions toward the door, left.*] Tell Sam to come in here when you go out. Tell him to make a light here.

ROBERT.   [*Impudently*] Ring for Sam—I'm not going through the kitchen. [*He starts toward the front door*] I'm not your servant. You're not going to tell me what to do. You're not going to have Talbot run me off the place like a field hand you don't want to use any more.

NORWOOD.   [*Springing between his son and the front door, pistol in hand*] You black bastard! [*ROBERT goes toward him calmly, grasps his father's arm and twists it until the gun falls to the floor. The older man bends backward in startled fury and pain.*] Don't you dare put your . . .

ROBERT.   [*Laughing*] Why don't you shoot, papa? [*Louder*] Why don't you shoot?

NORWOOD.   [*Gasping as he struggles, fighting back*] . . . black . . . hands . . . on . . .   45
you . . .

ROBERT.   [*Hysterically, as he takes his father by the throat*] Why don't you shoot, papa? [*NORWOOD's hands claw the air helplessly. ROBERT chokes the struggling white man until his body grows limp*] Why don't you shoot! [*Laughing*] Why don't you shoot? Huh? Why?

[*CORA appears at the top of the stairs, hearing the commotion. She screams.*]

CORA.   Oh, my God! [*She rushes down. ROBERT drops the body of his father at her feet in a path of flame from the setting sun. CORA starts and stares in horror.*]

ROBERT.   [*Wildly*] Why didn't he shoot, mama? He didn't want *me* to live. Why didn't he shoot? [*Laughing*] He was the boss. Telling me what to do. Why didn't he shoot, then? He was the white man.

CORA.   [*Falling on the body*] Colonel Tom! Colonel Tom! Tom! Tom! [*Gazes across the corpse at her son*] He's yo' father, Bert.

ROBERT.   He's dead. The white man's dead. My father's dead. [*Laughing*] I'm   50
living.

CORA.   Tom! Tom! Tom!

ROBERT.   Niggers are living. He's dead. [*Picks up the pistol*] This is what he wanted to kill me with, but he's dead. I can use it now. Use it on all the white men in the world, because they'll be coming looking for me now. [*Stuffs the pistol into his shirt*] They'll want me now.

CORA.   [*Rising and running toward her boy*] Quick, chile, out that way, [*Pointing toward the front door*] so they won't see you in de kitchen. Make for de swamp, honey. Cross de fields fo' de swamp. Go de crick way. In runnin' water, dogs can't smell no tracks. Hurry, chile!

ROBERT.   Yes, mama. I can go out the front way now, easy. But if I see they gonna get me before I can reach the swamp, I'm coming back here, mama, and [*Proudly*] let them take me out of my father's house—if they can. [*Pats the gun under his shirt*] They're not going to string me up to some roadside tree for the crackers to laugh at.

CORA.   [*Moaning aloud*] Oh, O-o-o! Hurry! Hurry, chile!   55

ROBERT.   I'm going, ma. [*He opens the door. The sunset streams in like a river of blood.*]

CORA.   Run, chile!

ROBERT.   Not out of my father's house. [*He exits slowly, tall and straight against the sun.*]

CORA.   Fo' God's sake, hurry, chile! [*Glancing down the road*] Lawd have mercy! There's Talbot and de storekeeper in de drive. They sees my boy! [*Moaning*] They sees ma boy. [*Relieved*] But thank God, they's passin' him! [*CORA backs up against the wall in the vestibule. She stands as if petrified as TALBOT and the STOREKEEPER enter.*]

TALBOT.   Hello, Cora. What's the matter with you? Where's that damn fool boy o'   60
your'n goin', coming out the front door like he owned the house? What's the matter with you, woman? Can't you talk? Can't you talk? Where's Norwood? Let's have some light in this dark place. [*He reaches behind the door and turns on the lights. CORA remains backed up against the wall, looking out into the twilight, watching ROBERT as he goes across the field.*] Good God, Jim! Look at this! [*The TWO WHITE MEN stop in horror before the sight of NORWOOD's body on the floor.*]

STOREKEEPER.   He's blue in the face. [*Bends over the body*] That nigger we saw walking out the door! [*Rising excitedly*] That nigger bastard of Cora's . . . [*Stooping over the body again*] Why the Colonel's dead!

TALBOT.   That nigger! [*Rushes toward the door*] He's running toward the swamp now . . . We'll get him . . . Telephone town—there, in the library. Telephone the sheriff. Get men, white men, after that nigger.

[*The* STOREKEEPER *rushes into the library. He can be heard talking excitedly on the phone.*]

STOREKEEPER.   Sheriff! Sheriff! Is this the sheriff? I'm calling from Norwood's plantation. That nigger, Bert, has just killed Norwood—and run, headed for the swamp. Notify the gas station at the crossroads! Tell the boys at the sawmill to head him off at the creek. Warn everybody to be on the lookout. Call your deputies! Yes! Spread a dragnet. Get out the dogs. Meanwhile we'll start after him. [*He slams the phone down and comes back into the room.*] Cora, where's Norwood's car? In the barn? [CORA *does not answer.*]

TALBOT.   Talk, you black bitch!

[*She remains silent.* TALBOT *runs, yelling and talking, out into the yard, followed by the* STOREKEEPER. *Sounds of excited shouting outside, and the roar of a motor rushing down the drive. In the sky the twilight deepens into early night.* CORA *stands looking into the darkness.*]

CORA.   My boy can't get to de swamp now. They's telephoned the white folks down that way. So he'll come back home now. Maybe he'll turn into de crick and follow de branch home directly. [*Protectively*] But they shan't get him. I'll make a place for to hide him. I'll make a place upstairs down under de floor, under ma bed. In a minute ma boy'll be runnin' from de white folks with their hounds and their ropes and their guns and everything they uses to kill po' colored folks with. [*Distressed*] Ma boy'll be out there runnin. [*Turning to the body on the floor*] Colonel Tom, you hear me? Our boy, out there runnin'. [*Fiercely*] *You* said he was ma boy—*ma* bastard boy. I heard you . . . but he's yours too . . . but yonder in de dark runnin'—runnin' from yo' people, from white people. [*Pleadingly*] Why don't you get up and stop 'em? He's *your* boy. His eyes is gray—like your eyes. He's tall like you's tall. He's proud like you's proud. And he's runnin'—runnin' from po' white trash what ain't worth de little finger o' nobody what's got your blood in 'em, Tom. [*Demandingly*] Why don't you get up from there and stop 'em, Colonel Tom? What's that you say? He ain't your chile? He's ma bastard chile? My yellow bastard chile? [*Proudly*] Yes, he's mine. But don't call him that. Don't you touch him. Don't you put your white hands on him. You's beat him enough, and cussed him enough. Don't you touch him now. He *is* ma boy and no white folks gonna touch him now. That's finished. I'm gonna make a place for him upstairs under ma bed. [*Backs away from the body toward the stairs*] He's ma chile. Don't you come in ma bedroom while he's up there. Don't you come to my bed no mo'. I calls you to help me now, and you just lays there. I calls you for to wake up, and you just lays there. Whenever you called me, in de night, I woke up. When you called for me to love, I always reached out ma arms fo' you. I borned you five chilluns and now one of 'em is out yonder in de dark runnin' from yo' people. Our youngest boy out yonder in de dark runnin'. [*Accusingly*] He's runnin' from you, too. You said he warn't your'n—he's just Cora's po' little yellow bastard. But he *is* your'n, Colonel Tom. [*Sadly*] And he's runnin' from you. You are out yonder in de dark, [*Points toward the door*] runnin' our chile, with de hounds and de gun in yo' hand, and Talbot's followin' 'hind you with a rope to hang Robert with. [*Confidently*] I been sleepin' with you too long, Colonel Tom, not to know that this ain't you layin' down there with yo' eyes shut on de floor. You can't fool me—you ain't never been so still like this before—you's out yonder runnin' ma boy through de fields in de dark, runnin' ma poor little helpless Bert

65

through de fields in de dark to lynch him . . . Damn you, Colonel Norwood! [*Backing slowly up the stairs, staring at the rigid body below her*] Damn you, Thomas Norwood! God damn you!

Curtain

Scene 2

TIME. *One hour later. Night.*

SETTING. *The same.*

ACTION. *As the curtain rises, the* UNDERTAKER *is talking to* SAM *at the outer door. All through this act the approaching cries of the man hunt are heard.*

UNDERTAKER.   Reckon there won't be no orders to bring his corpse back out here, Sam. None of us ain't seen Talbot or Mr. Higgins, but I'm sure they'll be having the funeral in town. The coroner told us to bring the body into the Junction. Ain't nothing' but niggers left out here now.

SAM.   [*Very frightened*] Yes, sah! Yes, sah! You's right, sah! Nothin' but us niggers, sah!

UNDERTAKER.   The Colonel didn't have no relatives far as you know, did he, Sam?

SAM.   No, sah. Ain't had none. No, sah! You's right, sah!

UNDERTAKER.   Well, you got everything o' his locked up around here, ain't you?   5
Too bad there ain't no white folks about to look after the Colonel's stuff, but every white man that's able to walk's out with the posse. They'll have that young nigger swingin' before ten.

SAM.   [*Trembling*] Yes, sah, yes, sah! I 'spects so. Yes, sah!

UNDERTAKER.   Say, where's that woman the Colonel's been living with—where's that black housekeeper, Cora, that murderin's bastard's mother?

SAM.   She here, sah! She's up in her room.

UNDERTAKER.   [*Curiously*] I'd like to see how she looks. Get her down here. Say, how about a little drink before we start that ride back to town, for me and my partner out there with the body?

SAM.   Cora got de keys to all de licker, sah!   10

UNDERTAKER.   Well, get her down here then, double quick! [SAM *goes up the stairs. The* UNDERTAKER *leans in the front doorway talking to his partner outside in the wagon*] Bad business, a white man having saucy nigger children on his hands, and his black woman living in his own house.

VOICE OUTSIDE.   Damn right, Charlie.

UNDERTAKER.   Norwood didn't have a gang o' yellow gals, though, like Higgins and some o' these other big bugs. Just this one bitch far's I know, livin' with him damn near like a wife. Didn't even have much company out here. And they tell me ain't been a white woman stayed here overnight since his wife died when I was a baby. [SAM's *shuffle is heard on the stairs*] Here comes a drink, I reckon, boy. You needn't get down off the ambulance. I'll have Sam bring it out there to you. [SAM *descends followed by* CORA *who comes down the stairs. She says nothing. The* UNDERTAKER *looks up grinning at* CORA] Well, so you're the Cora that's got these educated nigger children? Hum-m! Well, I guess you'll see one of 'em swinging full of bullet holes when you wake up in the morning. They'll probably hang him to that tree down here by the Colonel's gate—'cause they tell me he strutted right out the front gate past that tree after the murder. Or maybe they'll burn him. How'd you like to see him swinging there roasted in the morning when you wake up, girlie?

CORA. [*Calmly*] Is that all you wanted to say to me?

UNDERTAKER. Don't get smart! Maybe you think there's nobody to boss you now. 15
We gonna have a little drink before we go. Get out a bottle of rye.

CORA. I takes ma orders from Colonel Norwood, sir.

UNDERTAKER. Well, you'll take no more orders from him. He's dead out there in
my wagon—so get along and get the bottle.

CORA. He's out yonder with de mob, not in your wagon.

UNDERTAKER. I tell you he's in my wagon!

CORA. He's out there with de mob. 20

UNDERTAKER. God damn! [*To his partner outside*] I believe this black woman's gone
crazy in here. [*To* CORA] Get the keys out for that licker, and be quick about it! [*CORA does
not move.* SAM *looks from one to the other, frightened.*]

VOICE OUTSIDE. Aw, to hell with the licker, Charlie. Come on, let's start back to
town. We want to get in on some of that excitement, too. They should've found that nigger by now—and I want to see 'em drag him out here.

UNDERTAKER. All right, Jim. [*To* CORA *and* SAM] Don't you all go to bed until you
see that bonfire. You niggers are getting besides yourselves around Polk County. We'll
burn a few more of you if you don't be careful. [*He exits, and the noise of the dead-wagon
going down the road is heard.*]

SAM. Oh, Lawd, hab mercy on me! I prays, Lawd hab mercy! O, ma Lawd, ma
Lawd, ma Lawd! Cora, is you a fool? *Is* you a fool? Why didn't you give de mens de licker,
riled as these white folks is? In ma old age is I gonna be burnt by de crackers? Lawd, is I
sinned? Lawd, what has I done? [*Suddenly stops moaning and becomes schemingly calm*] I
don't have to stay here tonight, does I? I done locked up de Colonel's library, and he
can't be wantin' nothin'. No, ma Lawd, he won't want nothin' now. He's with Jesus—or
with de devil, one. [*To* CORA] I's gwine on away from here. Sam's gwine in town to his
chilluns' house, and I ain't gwine by no road either. I gwine through de holler where I
don't have to pass no white folks.

CORA. Yes, Samuel, you go on. De Colonel can get his own drinks when he comes 25
back tonight.

SAM. [*Bucking his eyes in astonishment at* CORA] Lawd God Jesus!

[*He bolts out of the room as fast as his old legs will carry him.* CORA *comes down stairs, looks for a
long moment out into the darkness, then closes the front door and draws the blinds. She looks down
at the spot where the* COLONEL*'s body lay.*]

CORA. All de colored folks are runnin' from you tonight. Po' Colonel Tom, you
too old now to be out with de mob. You got no business goin', but you had to go, I reckon. I 'members that time they hung Luke Jordan, you sent yo' dogs out to hunt him. The
next day you killed all de dogs. You were kinder softhearted. Said you didn't like that
kind of sport. Told me in bed one night you could hear them dogs howlin' in yo' sleep.
But de time they burnt de courthouse when that po' little cullud boy was locked up in it
cause they said he hugged a white girl, you was with 'em again. Said you had to go help
'em. Now you's out chasin' ma boy. [*As she stands at the window, she sees a passing figure.*]
There goes yo' other woman, Colonel Tom, Livonia is runnin' from you too, now. She
would've wanted you last night. Been wantin' you again ever since she got old and fat and
you stopped layin' with her and put her in the kitchen to cook. Don't think I don't know,
Colonel Tom. Don't think I don't remember them nights when you used to sleep in that
cabin down by de spring. I knew 'Vonia was there with you. I ain't no fool, Colonel Tom.
But she ain't bore you no chilluns. I'm de one that bore 'em. [*Musing*] White mens, and
colored womens, and little bastard chilluns—that's de old way of de South—but it's ending now. Three of your yellow brothers yo' father had by Aunt Sallie Deal—what had to

come and do your laundry to make her livin'—you got colored relatives scattered all over this county. Them de ways o' de South—mixtries, mixtries. [*WILLIAM enters left, silently, as his mother talks. She is sitting in a chair now. Without looking up*] Is that you, William?

WILLIAM. Yes, ma, it's me.

CORA. Is you runnin' from him, too?

WILLIAM. [*Hesitatingly*] Well, ma, you see . . . don't you think kinder . . . well, I   30
reckon I ought to take Libby and ma babies on down to de church house with Reverend Martin and them, or else get 'long to town if I can hitch up them mules. They's scared to be out here, my wife and her ma. All de folks done gone from de houses down yonder by de branch, and you can hear de hounds a bayin' off yonder by de swamp, and cars is tearin' up that road, and de white folks is yellin' and hollerin' and carryin' on somethin' terrible over toward de brook. I done told Robert 'bout his foolishness. They's gonna hang him sure. Don't you think you better be comin' with us, ma. That is, do you want to? 'Course we can go by ourselves, and maybe you wants to stay here and take care o' de big house. I don't want to leave you, ma, but I . . . I . . .

CORA. Yo' brother'll be back, son, then I won't be by myself.

WILLIAM. [*Bewildered by his mother's sureness*] I thought Bert went . . . I thought he run . . . I thought . . .

CORA. No, honey. He went, but they ain't gonna get him out there. I sees him comin' back here now, to be with me. I's gwine to guard him 'till he can get away.

WILLIAM. Then de white folks'll come here, too.

CORA. Yes, de Colonel'll come back here sure. [*The deep baying of the hounds is   35 heard at a distance through the night.*] Colonel Tom will come after his son.

WILLIAM. My God, ma! Come with us to town.

CORA. Go on, William, go on! Don't wait for them to get back. You never was much like neither one o' them—neither de Colonel or Bert—you's mo' like de field hands. Too much o' ma blood in you, I guess. You never liked Bert much, neither, and you always was afraid of de Colonel. Go on, son, and hide yo' wife and her ma and your chilluns. Ain't nothin' gonna hurt you. You never did go against nobody. Neither did I, till tonight. Tried to live right and not hurt a soul, white or colored. [*Addressing space*] I tried to live right, Lord. [*Angrily*] Tried to live right, Lord. [*Throws out her arms resentfully as if to say, "and this is what you give me."*] What's de matter, Lawd, you ain't with me?

[*The hounds are heard howling again.*]

WILLIAM. I'm gone, ma. [*He exits fearfully as his mother talks.*]

Cora. [*Bending over the spot on the floor where the COLONEL has lain. She calls.*] Colonel Tom! Colonel Tom! Colonel Tom! Look! Bertha and Sallie and William and Bert, all your chilluns, runnin' from you, and you layin' on de floor there, dead! [*Pointing*] Out yonder with the mob, dead. And when you come home, upstairs in my bed on top of my body, dead. [*Goes to the window, returns, sits down, and begins to speak as if remembering a far-off dream.*] Colonel Thomas Norwood! I'm just poor Cora Lewis, Colonel Norwood. Little black Cora Lewis, Colonel Norwood. I'm just fifteen years old. Thirty years ago, you put your hands on me to feel my breasts, and you say, "You a pretty little piece of flesh, ain't you? Black and sweet, ain't you?" And I lift up ma face, and you pull me to you, and we laid down under the trees that night, and I wonder if your wife'll know when you go back up the road into the big house. And I wonder if my mama'll know it, when I go back to our cabin. Mama said she nursed you when you was a baby, just like she nursed me. And I loved you in the dark, down there under that tree by de gate, afraid of you and proud of you, feelin' your gray eyes lookin' at me in de dark. Then I cried and cried and told ma mother about it, but she didn't take it hard like I thought she'd take it. She said fine white mens like de young Colonel always took good care o' their colored womens. She said it was better than marryin' some black field hand and workin' all your life in de cotton and cane. Better even than havin' a job like ma had, takin' care o' de white chilluns. Takin' care o' you, Colonel Tom. [*As* CORA *speaks the sound of the approaching mob gradually grows louder and louder. Auto horns, the howling of dogs, the far-off shouts of men, full of malignant force and power, increase in volume.*] And I was happy because I liked you, 'cause you was tall and proud, 'cause you said I was sweet to you and called me purty. And when yo' wife died—de Mrs. Norwood [*Scornfully*] that never bore you any chilluns, the pale beautiful Mrs. Norwood that was like a slender pine tree in de winter frost . . . I knowed you wanted me. I was full with child by you then—William, it was—our first boy. And ma mammy said, go up there and keep de house for Colonel Tom, sweep de floors and make de beds, and by and by, you won't have to sweep de floors and make no beds. And what ma mammy said was right. It all come true. Sam and Rusus and 'Vonia and Lucy did de waitin' on you and me, and de washin' and de cleanin' and de cookin'. And all I did was a little sewin' now and then, and a little preservin' in de summer and a little makin' of pies and sweet cakes and things you like to eat on Christmas. And de years went by. And I was always ready for you when you come to me in de night. And we had them chilluns, your chilluns and mine, Tom Norwood, all of 'em! William, born dark like me, dumb like me, and then Baby John what died; then Bertha, white and smart like you; and then Bert with your eyes and your ways and your temper, and mighty nigh your color; then Sallie, nearly white, too, and smart, and purty. But Bert was yo' chile! He was always yo' child . . . Good-looking, and kind, and headstrong, and strange, and stubborn, and proud like you, and de one I could love most 'cause he needed de most lovin'. And he wanted to call you "papa," and I tried to teach him no, but he did it anyhow and [*Sternly*] you beat him, Colonel Thomas Norwood. And he growed up with de beatin' in his heart and your eyes in his head, and your ways, and your pride. And this summer he looked like you that time I first knowed you down by de road under them trees, young and fiery and proud. There was no touchin' Bert, just like there was no touchin' you. I could only love him, like I loved you. I could only love him. But I couldn't talk to him, because he hated you. He had your ways—and you beat him! After you beat that chile, then you died, Colonel Norwood. You died here in this house, and you been living dead a long time. You lived dead. [*Her voice rises above the nearing sounds of the mob.*] And when I said this evenin', "Get up! Why don't you help me?" You'd done been dead a long time—a long time before you laid down on this floor, here, with the breath choked out o' you—and Bert standin' over you living, living, living. That's why you hated him. And you want to kill him. Always, you wanted to kill him. Out there with de hounds and de torches and de cars and de guns, you want to kill ma boy. But you won't kill him! He's comin' home first. He's comin' home to me. He's comin' home! [*Outside the noise is tremendous now, the lights of autos flash on the window curtains, there are shouts and cries.* CORA *sits, tense, in the middle of the room.*] He's comin' home!

A MAN'S VOICE. [*Outside*] He's somewhere on this lot.

ANOTHER VOICE. Don't shoot, men. We want to get him alive.

VOICE. Close in on him. He must be in them bushes by the house.

FIRST VOICE. Porch! Porch! Porch! There he is yonder—running to the door!

[*Suddenly shots are heard. The door bursts open and* ROBERT *enters, firing back into the darkness. The shots are returned by the mob, breaking the windows. Flares, lights, voices, curses, screams.*]

VOICES. Nigger! Nigger! Nigger! Get the nigger!

[CORA *rushes toward the door and bolts it after her son's entrance.*]

40

CORA. [*Leaning against the door*] I was waiting for you, honey. Yo' hiding place is all   45
ready, upstairs, under ma bed, under de floor. I sawed a place there fo' you. They can't
find you there. Hurry—before yo' father comes.

ROBERT. [*Panting*] No time to hide, ma. They're at the door now. They'll be coming up the back way, too. [*Sounds of knocking and the breaking of glass*] They'll be coming in
the windows. They'll be coming in everywhere. And only one bullet left, ma. It's for me.

CORA. Yes, it's fo' you, chile. Save it. Go upstairs in mama's room. Lay on ma bed
and rest.

ROBERT. [*Going slowly toward the stairs with the pistol in his hand*] Goodnight, ma.
I'm awful tired of running, ma. They been chasing me for hours.

CORA. Goodnight, son.

[*CORA follows him to the foot of the steps. The door begins to give at the forcing of the mob. As
ROBERT disappears above, it bursts open. A great crowd of white men pour into the room with guns,
ropes, clubs, flashlights, and knives. CORA turns on the stairs, facing them quietly. TALBOT, the
leader of the mob, stops.*]

TALBOT. Be careful, men. He's armed. [*To CORA*] Where is that yellow bastard of   50
yours—upstairs?

CORA. Yes, he's going to sleep. Be quiet, you all. Wait. [*She bars the way with outspread arms.*]

TALBOT. [*Harshly*] Wait, hell! Come on, boys, let's go. [*A single shot is heard upstairs.*] What's that?

CORA. [*Calmly*] My boy . . . is gone . . . to sleep!

[*TALBOT and some of the men rush up the stairway, CORA makes a final gesture of love toward the
room above. Yelling and shouting, through all the doors and windows, a great crowd pours into the
room. The roar of the mob fills the house, the whole night, the whole world. Suddenly TALBOT returns
at the top of the steps and a hush falls over the crowd.*]

TALBOT. Too late, men. We're just a little too late.

[*A sigh of disappointment rises from the mob. TALBOT comes down the stairs, walks up to CORA and
slaps her once across the face. She does not move. It is as though no human hand can touch her
again.*]

Curtain

QUESTIONS

Act 1

1. Throughout the act—and the play—why are the children of Colonel Norwood
   and Cora referred to as just Cora's children?

2. Why does the Colonel deny permission for Sallie's bags to be carried through
   the front door?

3. Throughout the act, what do we learn about Robert's attitudes toward his circumstances on the plantation? What do the Colonel and Higgins say about his
   attitude? Once Robert appears, what does he himself say about his situation?

4. What does the Colonel say about Sallie's ambition to reopen a nearby school?
   What does he advise her to do instead?

5. Who is Talbot? What does he represent? Why does he not appear until late in the
   second act?

6.   What does Higgins report about how Robert has behaved in town? What does he tell Colonel Norwood to do about it?

7.   As expressed in speech 61, what is Higgins's attitude toward black women? What does this attitude disclose about his character?

8.   Describe the effect on both Robert and Colonel Norwood of the childhood incident when Robert called the Colonel "papa."

9.   What has the Colonel decided to do about Robert? What are Cora's fears not only for Robert but for others?

Act 2, Scene 1

10.   What are the issues in the confrontation between Robert and Colonel Norwood?

11.   What is Robert's dilemma (speech 35)? What has the Colonel now determined to do about Robert?

12.   What is Robert's response to the Colonel's display of the gun, and his threat to use it?

13.   What do Talbot and the storekeeper do once they learn that Colonel Norwood is dead? What chance does Robert have to escape?

14.   Why does Cora speak so extensively over the Colonel's body?

Act 2, Scene 2

15.   Why are the undertaker and his companion introduced at this point? What are they like?

16.   According to Cora (speech 27), what was the nature of the old "ways" of the south?

17.   What is the purpose of Cora's second extensive monologue (speech 39)?

18.   What finally happens to Robert? Why does Talbot slap Cora at the end?

GENERAL QUESTIONS

1.   Describe *Mulatto* as a realistic play. Why is it important that the play contain many details about the plantation and the customs of the country?

2.   What is the symbolism of the front door? The incident at the post office in town? Driving the Ford fast?

3.   Describe Colonel Norwood. What characteristics of a Southern plantation owner does he exhibit? What is shown about him by his having sent Robert and his sisters away to school? What does Cora say about him before and after he is dead?

4.   Describe the character of Robert. What are his dominant traits? How politic is he in dealing with his circumstances? To what extent does he bring about his own destruction?

5.   Describe Cora. What has her life been like? To what degree has she sacrificed her individuality to stay with Colonel Norwood? How does she try to protect her children? In her two major lengthy speeches, what seems to be happening to her?

6.   In light of the historical time when the play was written and produced, could there have been any other outcome?

THORNTON WILDER, *OUR TOWN*

Thornton Wilder was born in Wisconsin in 1897 but had an international education. His father served as American consul in Hong Kong, and Wilder was therefore educated partly in China and partly in the United States. He received his higher education at Oberlin, Yale, and Princeton and became deeply read in the classics. After graduation he seems at first to have had indeterminate career goals, though as an undergraduate he worked in the theater departments and wrote short plays which he was able to see produced. He spent time as an archaeologist in Italy, taught French at an exclusive school in New Jersey, and with the aid of his friend Robert Hutchins, president of the University of Chicago, taught creative writing at Chicago for six years in the 1930s.

At some point in his early twenties, however, he had made his decision to become a writer. His first work was a novel, Cabala, which was not particularly successful, but the major novel he wrote before he was thirty, The Bridge of San Luis Rey, received the Pulitzer Prize for Fiction in 1927. He steadily pursued his aspirations to become a dramatist and created a play, The Woman of Andros (1930), which he adapted from the Roman playwright Terence. He also published a number of short plays in 1931. He developed a friendship with Gertrude Stein, and in conversations and correspondence with her he became interested in experimental theater and also in the concept that real drama was to grow out of the concerns of ordinary people, not out of issues of peace or war among individuals in the nation's power structure. The major dramatic outgrowth of this interest was Our Town, which was first produced in 1938 and which earned him his second Pulitzer Prize. He was the first writer to have received the prize for both fiction and drama.

He won another Pulitzer Prize for Drama in 1943 for his play The Skin of Our Teeth (1942), but by this time America was at war and Wilder was in the service. He was not simply a literary figurehead who was brought in for publicity; he enlisted in the Army Air Force and served as an intelligence officer in Italy. He planned air assaults, which were actually carried out, and was invaluable in developing the strategy that helped defeat the Nazi forces in Italy prior to the American landings in France in 1944. He received a Bronze Star for this important work, and he also received awards from both the French and the English governments. These were not his only distinctions during his lifetime. He was the first recipient of the National Medal for Literature in 1965, and by the end of his career he had been given a plethora of awards and distinctions. There were not many people of the theater in both America and England who did not know him and respect him.

After the war the most notably popular of his many works was an adaptation of an earlier play, The Merchant of Yonkers, which he had originally published in 1938. He revised this as The Matchmaker in 1957, and it was this play that in 1963 became the popular Hello Dolly! as adapted and set to music by Michael Stewart and Jerry Herman. Songs from Hello Dolly! went to the top of the charts, and it was from his rights to this production that Wilder realized his greatest financial success. Of particular note in the latter part of his career was his collaboration in 1961 with the composer Paul Hindemith (1895–1963), for whom he created an opera libretto of his earlier short play The Long Christmas Dinner (1931). Wilder died in 1975, and his extensive collection of letters, notes, drafts, and correspondence were collected and now are deposited in the Beinecke Library at Yale University, from which he had received his bachelor's degree.

Our Town is the best known of Wilder's plays. It has been defined as realistic, but its staging is anything but that. When the play was first performed in Boston in 1938, with scenery, it received unfavorable reviews and closed within a week. Things looked bleak for the play. Ironically, however, it was then that Wilder ordered the removal of all the scenery and most of the properties. After that the play was praised for its realism, and it has gone on to great acclaim as one of the most popular dramas in the modern American theater. It is no exaggeration to say that the play contains strong elements of realism within an unrealistic framework. The setting for *Our Town* is kept to an absolute minimum. Wilder's opening directions are "No curtain. / No scenery."

As the play progresses we see that virtually everything is left to the abilities of the actors and the imaginations of the audience. Wilder's stage is empty, showing only the rear walls and the accoutrements that might be expected on a bare stage. There are no more props and scenery than a table, some chairs, ladders, and a bench. In the second and third acts we view three rows of chairs, which are at first to be considered as church pews and then as the graves of a number of deceased citizens of Grover's Corners. Wilder leaves it up to the characters themselves to bring the scenes and activities before our eyes, but he includes many stage directions—many more than in most plays—and his actors in this respect engage in a good deal of pantomime. For instance, in Act 1 Howie Newsome walks beside an imaginary horse and distributes imaginary bottles of milk; in Act 2 Emily and George show us how to sip make-believe sodas through make-believe straws (this is actually kind of fun); and in Act 3 Mrs. Webb shivers from the cold air coming through a nonexistent door. Through such imaginative techniques Wilder calls our attention to the play's theatricality and to the nature of drama as a fictional representation of life.

Our Town also exemplifies Wilder's careful construction of plot and character. At one level, the plot is simple. As shown in Wilder's dramatization of the Webb and Gibbs families, the play is a celebration of everyday American life, with an emphasis on familial relationships and personal stability, but it also demonstrates the anguish and poignancy of a young woman's death in childbirth. In a general way, these three actions progress through exposition, complication, crisis, and dénouement or resolution. The topic of death and bereavement is of course brought into focus in Act 3. Here we find both crisis and resolution as Emily at first denies and regrets death but finally deals with it by her pronouncements that people should live to the fullest as long as they live and should devote their care, faith, love, and attention to their loved ones. As Wilder says in a preface to the play, *Our Town* "is an attempt to find a value above all price for the smallest events of daily life." This is a pearl of great price indeed.

Although on the surface everything seems placid within the Webb and Gibbs families and among their neighbors in Grover's Corners, there are hints and suggestions of the less savory social and political realities that are never far from the surface within the nation as a whole. In Act 1 a number of putative members of the audience raise issues such as "social injustice and industrial inequality" and "much drinking," and we learn that "there ain't much" culture or love of beauty in Grover's Corners. The choir director, we discover, is an alcoholic, and in Act 3 we learn that he has carried his bitterness about life even into the grave. George's cronies, the baseball players, attend the wedding in Act 2, and with their embarrassing heckling they demonstrate their emotional immaturity and also their ignorance of human relationships and married love.

A vital additional dimension of the play results from its comprehensive geographical and cultural references, from the past to the future. As the play begins we learn about the latitude and longitude of Grover's Corners, a detail that is, to say the least, unexpected and unique. We also learn that the town has a number of Protestant churches and a Catholic church, that it has a jail, that there is an ethnic section of the town, that William Jennings Bryan once made a speech there, and that the town's major business is the manufacture of blankets. From the Stage Manager, who is constantly on the stage, we hear references to ancient Babylon, the Roman Empire, World War I, the first flight across the Atlantic, and the anticipation of people living a thousand years in the future who will learn from a copy of the play about "the way we were: in our growing up and in our marrying and in our living and in our dying" (Act 1, speech 187). The regular background performances of well-known hymns give a taste of the music the people in Grover's

Corners regularly heard, and the performances of the "Largo" from Handel's opera *Xerxes,* the wedding music from Wagner's *Lohengrin,* and Mendelssohn's "Wedding March" from his music for *A Midsummer Night's Dream* are familiar to virtually all Americans regardless of their individual tastes in music. At the play's conclusion, Wilder reminds us of the cosmic context of the play, for the final references are to stars that are millions of light-years from the earth. The implication is that the story of the Gibbs and Webb families is not just for a time but for all time, and not just for our earth but for all the unknown earths that have existed, might exist, or might yet exist throughout the universe.

THORNTON WILDER (1897–1975)

Our Town ⤙⤙⤙ 1938

CHARACTERS (IN THE ORDER OF THEIR APPEARANCE)

> Stage Manager
> Dr. Gibbs
> Joe Crowell, Jr.
> Howie Newsome
> Mrs. Gibbs
> Mrs. Webb
> George Gibbs
> Rebecca Gibbs
> Wally Webb
> Emily Webb
> Professor Willard
> Mr. Webb
> Woman in the Balcony
> Man in the Auditorium
> Lady in a Box
> Simon Stimson
> Mrs. Soames
> Constable Warren
> Si Crowell
> Three Baseball Players
> Sam Craig
> Joe Stoddard
> Woman among the Dead
> Man among the Dead

The entire play takes place in Grover's Corners, New Hampshire.

ACT 1

> No curtain.
> No scenery.
> The audience, arriving, sees an empty stage in half-light.
> Presently the STAGE MANAGER, hat on and pipe in mouth, enters and begins placing a table and three chairs downstage left, and a table and three chairs downstage right. He also places a low bench at the corner of what will be the Webb house, left.
> "Left" and "right" are from the point of view of the actor facing the audience. "Up" is toward the back wall.

As the house lights go down he has finished setting the stage and leaning against the right proscenium pillar watches the late arrivals in the audience.

When the auditorium is in complete darkness he speaks.

STAGE MANAGER. This play is called "Our Town." It was written by Thornton Wilder; produced and directed by A . . . (or: produced by A . . . ; directed by B . . .). In it you will see Miss C . . . ; Miss D . . . ; Miss E . . . ; and Mr. F . . . ; Mr. G . . . ; Mr. H . . . ; and many others. The name of the town is Grover's Corners, New Hampshire—just across the Massachusetts line: latitude 42 degrees 40 minutes; longitude 70 degrees 37 minutes. The First Act shows a day in our town. The day is May 7, 1901. The time is just before dawn.

[*A rooster crows.*]

The sky is beginning to show some streaks of light over in the East there, behind our mount'in. The morning star always gets wonderful bright the minute before it has to go,—doesn't it?

[*He stares at it for a moment, then goes upstage.*]

Well, I'd better show you how our town lies. Up here

[*That is: parallel with the back wall.*]

is Main Street. Way back there is the railway station; tracks go that way. Polish Town's across the tracks, and some Canuck families.

[*Toward the left.*]

Over there is the Congregational Church; across the street's the Presbyterian. Methodist and Unitarian are over there. Baptist is down in the holla' by the river. Catholic Church is over beyond the tracks. Here's the Town Hall and Post Office combined; jail's in the basement. Bryan once made a speech from these very steps here. Along here's a row of stores. Hitching posts and horse blocks in front of them. First automobile's going to come along in about five years—belonged to Banker Cartwright, our richest citizen . . . lives in the big white house up on the hill. Here's the grocery store and here's Mr. Morgan's drugstore. Most everybody in town manages to look into those two stores once a day. Public School's over yonder. High School's still farther over. Quarter of nine mornings, noontimes, and three o'clock afternoons, the hull town can hear the yelling and screaming from those schoolyards.

[*He approaches the table and chairs downstage right.*]

This is our doctor's house,—Doc Gibbs. This is the back door.

[*Two arched trellises, covered with vines and flowers, are pushed out, one by each proscenium pillar.*]

There's some scenery for those who think they have to have scenery. This is Mrs. Gibbs' garden. Corn . . . peas . . . beans . . . hollyhocks . . . heliotrope . . . and a lot of burdock.

[*Crosses the stage.*]

In those days our newspaper come out twice a week—the Grover's Corners *Sentinel*—and this is Editor Webb's house. And this is Mrs. Webb's garden. Just like Mrs. Gibbs', only it's got a lot of sunflowers, too.

[*He looks upward, center stage.*]

Right here . . . 's a big butternut tree.

[*He returns to his place by the right proscenium pillar and looks at the audience for a minute.*]

Nice town, y'know what I mean? Nobody very remarkable ever comes of it, s'far as we know. The earliest tombstones in the cemetery up there on the mountain say 1670–1680—they're Grovers and Cartwrights and Gibbses and Herseys—same names as are around here now.

Well, as I said: it's about dawn. The only lights on in town are in a cottage over by the tracks where a Polish mother's just had twins. And in the Joe Crowell house, where Joe Junior's getting up so as to deliver the paper. And in the depot, where Shorty Hawkins is gettin' ready to flag the 5:45 for Boston.

[*A train whistle is heard. The STAGE MANAGER takes out his watch and nods.*]

Naturally, out in the country—all around—there've been lights on for some time, what with milkin's and so on. But town people sleep late. So—another day's begun. There's Doc Gibbs comin' down Main Street now, comin' back from that baby case. And here's his wife comin' downstairs to get breakfast.

[*MRS. GIBBS, a plump, pleasant woman in the middle thirties, comes "downstairs" right. She pulls up an imaginary window shade in her kitchen and starts to make a fire in her stove.*]

Doc Gibbs died in 1930. The new hospital's named after him. Mrs. Gibbs died first—long time ago, in fact. She went out to visit her daughter, Rebecca, who married an insurance man in Canton, Ohio, and died there—pneumonia—but her body was brought back here. She's up in the cemetery there now—in with a whole mess of Gibbses and Herseys—she was Julia Hersey 'fore she married Doc Gibbs in the Congregational Church over there. In our town we like to know the facts about everybody.

There's Mrs. Webb, coming downstairs to get her breakfast, too.—That's Doc Gibbs. Got that call at half past one this morning. And there comes Joe Crowell, Jr., delivering Mr. Webb's Sentinel.

[*DR. GIBBS has been coming along Main Street from the left. At the point where he would turn to approach his house, he stops, sets down his—imaginary—black bag, takes off his hat, and rubs his face with fatigue, using an enormous handkerchief. MRS. WEBB, a thin, serious, crisp woman, has entered her kitchen, left, tying on an apron. She goes through the motions of putting wood into a stove, lighting it, and preparing breakfast. Suddenly JOE CROWELL, JR., eleven, starts down Main Street from the right, hurling imaginary newspapers into doorways.*]

JOE CROWELL, JR.   Morning, Doc Gibbs.

DR. GIBBS.   Morning, Joe.

JOE CROWELL, JR.   Somebody been sick, Doc?

DR. GIBBS.   No. Just some twins born over in Polish Town.   5

JOE CROWELL, JR.   Do you want your paper now?

DR. GIBBS.   Yes, I'll take it—Anything serious goin' on in the world since Wednesday?

JOE CROWELL, JR.   Yessir. My schoolteacher, Miss Foster's getting married to a fella over in Concord.

DR. GIBBS.   I declare—How do you boys feel about that?

JOE CROWELL, JR.   Well, of course, it's none of my business—but I think if a person   10 starts out to be a teacher, she ought to stay one.

DR. GIBBS.   How's your knee, Joe?

JOE CROWELL, JR.   Fine, Doc, I never think about it at all. Only like you said, it always tells me when it's going to rain.

DR. GIBBS.   What's it telling you today? Goin' to rain?

JOE CROWELL, JR.   No, sir.
DR. GIBBS.   Sure?   15
JOE CROWELL, JR.   Yessir.
DR. GIBBS.   Knee ever make a mistake?
JOE CROWELL, JR.   No, sir.

[*JOE goes off. DR. GIBBS stands reading his paper.*]

STAGE MANAGER.   Want to tell you something about that boy Joe Crowell there. Joe was awful bright—graduated from high school here, head of his class. So he got a scholarship to Massachusetts Tech. Graduated head of his class there, too. It was all wrote up in the Boston paper at the time. Goin' to be a great engineer, Joe was. But the war broke out and he died in France—All that education for nothing.

HOWIE NEWSOME.   [*Off left.*] Giddap, Bessie! What's the matter with you today?   20
STAGE MANAGER.   Here comes Howie Newsome, deliverin' the milk.

[*HOWIE NEWSOME, about thirty, in overalls, comes along Main Street from the left, walking beside an invisible horse and wagon and carrying an imaginary rack with milk bottles. The sound of clinking milk bottles is heard. He leaves some bottles at MRS. WEBB's trellis, then, crossing the stage to MRS. GIBBS', he stops center to talk to DR. GIBBS.*]

HOWIE NEWSOME.   Morning, Doc.
DR. GIBBS.   Morning, Howie.
HOWIE NEWSOME.   Somebody sick?
DR. GIBBS.   Pair of twins over to Mrs. Goruslawski's.   25
HOWIE NEWSOME.   Twins, eh? This town's gettin' bigger every year.
DR. GIBBS.   Goin' to rain, Howie?
HOWIE NEWSOME.   No, no. Fine day—that'll burn through. Come on, Bessie.
DR. GIBBS.   Hello Bessie. [*He strokes the horse, which has remained up center.*] How old is she, Howie?

HOWIE NEWSOME.   Going on seventeen. Bessie's all mixed up about the route ever   30
since the Lockharts stopped takin' their quart of milk every day. She wants to leave 'em a quart just the same—keeps scolding me the hull trip.

[*He reaches MRS. GIBBS' back door. She is waiting for him.*]

MRS. GIBBS.   Good morning, Howie.
HOWIE NEWSOME.   Morning, Mrs. Gibbs. Doc's just comin' down the street.
MRS. GIBBS.   Is he? Seems like you're late today.
HOWIE NEWSOME.   Yes. Somep'n went wrong with the separator.° Don't know what
'twas. [*He passes DR. GIBBS up center.*] Doc!
DR. GIBBS.   Howie!   35
MRS. GIBBS.   [*Calling upstairs.*] Children! Children! Time to get up.
HOWIE NEWSOME.   Come on, Bessie!

[*He goes off right.*]

MRS. GIBBS.   George! Rebecca!

[*DR. GIBBS arrives at his back door and passes through the trellis into his house.*]

MRS. GIBBS.   Everything all right, Frank?

---

34 A separator is a machine that separates whole milk into cream and skim milk.

DR. GIBBS.   Yes. I declare—easy as kittens.   40

MRS. GIBBS.   Bacon'll be ready in a minute. Set down and drink your coffee. You can catch a couple hours' sleep this morning, can't you?

DR. GIBBS.   Hm! . . . Mrs. Wentworth's coming at eleven. Guess I know what's it's about, too. Her stummick ain't what it ought to be.

MRS. GIBBS.   All told, you won't get more'n three hours' sleep. Frank Gibbs, I don't know what's goin' to become of you. I do wish I could get you to go away someplace and take a rest. I think it would do you good.

MRS. WEBB.   Emileeee! Time to get up! Wally! Seven o'clock!

MRS. GIBBS.   I declare, you got to speak to George. Seems like something's come   45
over him lately. He's no help to me at all. I can't even get him to cut me some wood.

DR. GIBBS.   [*Washing and drying his hands at the sink.* MRS. GIBBS *is busy at the stove.*] *Is* he sassy to you?

MRS. GIBBS.   No. He just whines! All he thinks about is that baseball—George! Rebecca! You'll be late for school.

DR. GIBBS.   M-m-m . . .

MRS. GIBBS.   George!

DR. GIBBS.   George, look sharp!   50

GEORGE'S VOICE.   Yes, Pa!

DR. GIBBS.   [*As he goes off the stage.*] Don't you hear your mother calling you? I guess I'll go upstairs and get forty winks.

MRS. WEBB.   Walleee! Emileee! You'll be late for school! Walleee! You wash yourself good or I'll come up and do it myself.

REBECCA GIBBS' VOICE.   Ma! What dress shall I wear?

MRS. GIBBS.   Don't make a noise. Your father's been out all night and needs his   55
sleep. I washed and ironed the blue gingham for you special.

REBECCA.   Ma, I hate that dress.

MRS. GIBBS.   Oh, hush—up—with—you.

REBECCA.   Every day I go to school dressed like a sick turkey.

MRS. GIBBS.   Now, Rebecca, you always look *very* nice.

REBECCA.   Mama, George's throwing soap at me.   60

MRS. GIBBS.   I'll come and slap the both of you,—that's what I'll do.

[*A factory whistle sounds. The* CHILDREN *dash in and take their places at the tables. Right,* GEORGE, *about sixteen, and* REBECCA, *eleven. Left,* EMILY *and* WALLY, *same ages. They carry strapped schoolbooks.*]

STAGE MANAGER.   We've got a factory in our town too—hear it? Makes blankets. Cartwrights own it and it brung 'em a fortune.

MRS. WEBB.   Children! Now I won't have it. Breakfast is just as good as any other meal and I won't have you gobbling like wolves. It'll stunt your growth,—that's a fact. Put away your book, Wally.

WALLY.   Aw, Ma! By ten o'clock I got to know all about Canada.

MRS. WEBB.   You know the rule's well as I do—no books at table. As for me, I'd   65
rather have my children healthy than bright.

EMILY.   I'm both, Mama: you know I am. I'm the brightest girl in school for my age. I have a wonderful memory.

MRS. WEBB.   Eat your breakfast.

WALLY.   I'm bright, too, when I'm looking at my stamp collection.

MRS. GIBBS.   I'll speak to your father about it when he's rested. Seems to me twenty-five cents a week's enough for a boy your age. I declare I don't know how you spend it all.

GEORGE.   Aw, Ma,—I gotta lotta things to buy.   70

MRS. GIBBS.   Strawberry phosphates—that's what you spend it on.

GEORGE.   I don't see how Rebecca comes to have so much money. She has more'n a dollar.

REBECCA.   [*Spoon in mouth, dreamily*] I've been saving it up gradual.

MRS. GIBBS.   Well, dear, I think it's a good thing to spend some every now and then.

REBECCA.   Mama, do you know what I love most in the world—do you?—Money   75

MRS. GIBBS.   Eat your breakfast.

THE CHILDREN.   Mama, there's first bell.—I gotta hurry.—I don't want any more—I gotta hurry.

[*The CHILDREN rise, seize their books and dash out through the trellises. They meet, down center, and chattering, walk to Main Street, then turn left. The STAGE MANAGER goes off, unobtrusively, right.*]

MRS. WEBB.   Walk fast, but you don't have to run. Wally, pull up your pants at the knee. Stand up straight, Emily.

MRS. GIBBS.   Tell Miss Foster I send her my best congratulations—can you remember that?

REBECCA.   Yes, Ma.   80

MRS. GIBBS.   You look real nice, Rebecca. Pick up your feet.

ALL.   Good-bye.

[*MRS. GIBBS fills her apron with food for the chickens and comes down to the footlights.*]

MRS. GIBBS.   Here, chick, chick, chick. No, go away, you. Go away. Here, chick, chick, chick. What's the matter with you? Fight, fight, fight,—that's all you do. Hm . . . you don't belong to me. Where'd you come from? [*She shakes her apron.*] Oh, don't be so scared. Nobody's going to hurt you.

[*MRS. WEBB is sitting on the bench by her trellis, stringing beans.*]

Good morning, Myrtle. How's your cold?

MRS. WEBB.   Well, I still get that tickling feeling in my throat. I told Charles I didn't know as I'd go to choir practice tonight. Wouldn't be any use.

MRS. GIBBS.   Have you tried singing over your voice?   85

MRS. WEBB.   Yes, but somehow I can't do that and stay on the key. While I'm resting myself I thought I'd string some of these beans.

MRS. GIBBS.   [*Rolling up her sleeves as she crosses the stage for a chat*] Let me help you. Beans have been good this year.

MRS. WEBB.   I've decided to put up forty quarts if it kills me. The children say they hate 'em, but I notice they're able to get 'em down all winter.

[*Pause. Brief sound of chickens cackling.*]

MRS. GIBBS.   Now, Myrtle. I've got to tell you something, because if I don't tell somebody I'll burst.

MRS. WEBB.   Why, Julia Gibbs!   90

MRS. GIBBS.   Here, give me some more of those beans. Myrtle, did one of those secondhand-furniture men from Boston come to see you last Friday?

MRS. WEBB.   No-o.

MRS. GIBBS.   Well, he called on me. First I thought he was a patient wantin' to see Dr. Gibbs. 'N he wormed his way into my parlor, and, Myrtle Webb, he offered me three hundred and fifty dollars for Grandmother Wentworth's highboy, as I'm sitting here!

MRS. WEBB.   Why, Julia Gibbs!

MRS. GIBBS.   He did! That old thing! Why, it was so big I didn't know where to put   95
it and I almost give it to Cousin Hester Wilcox.

MRS. WEBB.   Well, you're going to take it, aren't you?

MRS. GIBBS.   I don't know.

MRS. WEBB.   You don't know—three hundred and fifty dollars! What's come over
you?

MRS. GIBBS.   Well, if I could get the Doctor to take the money and go away someplace on a real trip, I'd sell it like that.—Y'know, Myrtle, it's been the dream of my life to
see Paris, France—Oh, I don't know. It sounds crazy, I suppose, but for years I've been
promising myself that if we ever had the chance—

MRS. WEBB.   How does the doctor feel about it?   100

MRS. GIBBS.   Well, I did beat about the bush a little and said that if I got a legacy—
that's the way I put it—I'd make him take me somewhere.

MRS. WEBB.   M-m-m . . . What did he say?

MRS. GIBBS.   You know how he is. I haven't heard a serious word out of him since
I've known him. No, he said, it might make him discontented with Grover's Corners to go
traipsin' about Europe; better let well enough alone, he says. Every two years he makes a
trip to the battlefields of the Civil War and that's enough treat for anybody, he says.

MRS. WEBB.   Well, Mr. Webb just *admires* the way Dr. Gibbs knows everything about
the Civil War. Mr. Webb's a good mind to give up Napoleon and move over to the Civil
War, only Dr. Gibbs being one of the greatest experts in the country just makes him
despair.

MRS. GIBBS.   It's a fact! Dr. Gibbs is never so happy as when he's at Antietam or   105
Gettysburg. The times I've walked over those hills, Myrtle, stopping at every bush and
pacing it all out, like we were going to buy it.

MRS. WEBB.   Well, if that secondhand man's really serious about buyin' it, Julia,
you sell it. And then you'll get to see Paris, all right. Just keep droppin' hints from time to
time—that's how I got to see the Atlantic Ocean, y'know.

MRS. GIBBS.   Oh, I'm sorry I mentioned it. Only it seems to me that once in your
life before you die you ought to see a country where they don't talk in English and don't
even want to.

[*The* STAGE MANAGER *enters briskly from the right. He tips his hat to the ladies, who nod their
heads.*]

STAGE MANAGER.   Thank you, ladies. Thank you very much.

[*MRS. GIBBS and MRS. WEBB gather up their things, return into their homes and disappear*].

Now we're going to skip a few hours. But first we want a little more information about the
town, kind of a scientific account, you might say. So I've asked Professor Willard of our
State University to sketch in a few details of our past history here. Is Professor Willard
here?

[*PROFESSOR WILLARD, a rural savant, pince-nez on a wide satin ribbon, enters from the right with
some notes in his hand.*]

May I introduce Professor Willard of our State University. A few brief notes, thank you,
Professor,—unfortunately our time is limited.

PROFESSOR WILLARD.   Grover's Corners . . . let me see . . . Grover's Corners lies on
the old Pleistocene granite of the Appalachian range. I may say it's some of the oldest
land in the world. We're very proud of that. A shelf of Devonian basalt crosses it with vestiges of Mesozoic shale, and some sandstone outcroppings; but that's all more recent: two

hundred, three hundred million years old. Some highly interesting fossils have been found . . . I may say: unique fossils . . . two miles out of town, in Silas Peckham's cow pasture. They can be seen at the museum in our University at any time—that is, at any reasonable time. Shall I read some of Professor Gruber's notes on the meteorological situation—mean precipitation, et cetera?

STAGE MANAGER. Afraid we won't have time for that, Professor. We might have a   110
few words on the history of man here.

PROFESSOR WILLARD. Yes . . . anthropological data: Early Amerindian stock. Cotahatchee tribes . . . no evidence before the tenth century of this era . . . hm . . . now entirely disappeared . . . possible traces in three families. Migration toward the end of the seventeenth century of English brachiocephalic blue-eyed stock . . . for the most part. Since then some Slav and Mediterranean.

STAGE MANAGER. And the population, Professor Willard?

PROFESSOR WILLARD. Within the town limits: 2,640.

STAGE MANAGER. Just a moment, Professor.

[*He whispers into the professor's ear.*]

PROFESSOR WILLARD. Oh, yes, indeed?—The population, *at the moment*, is 2,642.   115
The Postal District brings in 507 more, making a total of 3,149.—Mortality and birth rates: constant—by MacPherson's gauge: 6.032.

STAGE MANAGER. Thank you very much, Professor. We're all very much obliged to you, I'm sure.

PROFESSOR WILLARD. Not at all, sir; not at all.

STAGE MANAGER. This way, Professor, and thank you again.

[*Exit PROFESSOR WILLARD.*]

Now the political and social report: Editor Webb—Oh, Mr. Webb?

[*MRS. WEBB appears at her back door.*]

MRS. WEBB. He'll be here in a minute. . . . He just cut his hand while he was eatin' an apple.

STAGE MANAGER. Thank you, Mrs. Webb.   120

MRS. WEBB. Charles! Everybody's waitin'.

[*Exit MRS. WEBB.*]

STAGE MANAGER. Mr. Webb is Publisher and Editor of the Grover's Corners *Sentinel*. That's our local paper, y'know.

[*MR. WEBB enters from his house, pulling on his coat. His finger is bound in a handkerchief.*]

MR. WEBB. Well . . . I don't have to tell you that we're run here by a Board of Selectmen—All males vote at the age of twenty-one. Women vote indirect. We're lower middle class: sprinkling of professional men . . . ten per cent illiterate laborers. Politically, we're eighty-six per cent Republicans; six per cent Democrats; four per cent Socialists; rest, indifferent. Religiously, we're eighty-five per cent Protestants; twelve per cent Catholics; rest, indifferent.

STAGE MANAGER. Have you any comments, Mr. Webb?

MR. WEBB. Very ordinary town, if you ask me. Little better behaved than most.   125
Probably a lot duller. But our young people here seem to like it well enough. Ninety per cent of 'em graduating from high school settle down right here to live even when they've been away to college.

STAGE MANAGER.   Now, is there anyone in the audience who would like to ask Editor Webb anything about the town?

WOMAN IN THE BALCONY.   Is there much drinking in Grover's Corners?

MR. WEBB.   Well, ma'am, I wouldn't know what you'd call *much*. Satiddy nights the farmhands meet down in Ellery Greenough's stable and holler some. We've got one or two town drunks, but they're always having remorses every time an evangelist comes to town. No, ma'am, I'd say likker ain't a regular thing in the home here, except in the medicine chest. Right good for snake bite, y'know—always was.

BELLIGERENT MAN AT BACK OF AUDITORIUM.   Is there no one in town aware of—

STAGE MANAGER.   Come forward, will you, where we can all hear you—What were   130
you saying?

BELLIGERENT MAN.   Is there no one in town aware of social injustice and industrial inequality?

MR. WEBB.   Oh, yes, everybody is—somethin' terrible. Seems like they spend most of their time talking about who's rich and who's poor.

BELLIGERENT MAN.   Then why don't they do something about it?

[*He withdraws without waiting for an answer.*]

MR. WEBB.   Well, I dunno . . . I guess we're all hunting like everybody else for a way the diligent and sensible can rise to the top and the lazy and quarrelsome can sink to the bottom. But it ain't easy to find. Meanwhile, we do all we can to help those that can't help themselves and those that can we leave alone—Are there any other questions?

LADY IN A BOX.   Oh, Mr. Webb? Mr. Webb, is there any culture or love of beauty in   135
Grover's Corners?

MR. WEBB.   Well, ma'am, there ain't much—not in the sense you mean. Come to think of it, there's some girls that play the piano at High School Commencement; but they ain't happy about it. No, ma'am, there isn't much culture; but maybe this is the place to tell you that we've got a lot of pleasures of a kind here: we like the sun comin' up over the mountain in the morning, and we all notice a good deal about the birds. We pay a lot of attention to them. And we watch the change of the seasons; yes, everybody knows about them. But those other things—you're right, ma'am—there ain't *much—Robinson Crusoe* and the Bible; and Handel's "Largo," we all know that; and Whistler's "Mother"—those are just about as far as we go.

LADY IN A BOX.   So I thought. Thank you, Mr. Webb.

STAGE MANAGER.   Thank you, Mr. Webb.

[*MR. WEBB retires.*]

Now, we'll go back to the town. It's early afternoon. All 2,642 have had their dinners and all the dishes have been washed.

[*MR. WEBB, having removed his coat, returns and starts pushing a lawn mower to and fro beside his house.*]

There's an early-afternoon calm in our town: a buzzin' and a hummin' from the school buildings; only a few buggies on Main Street—the horses dozing at the hitching posts; you all remember what it's like. Doc Gibbs is in his office, tapping people and making them say "ah." Mr. Webb's cuttin' his lawn over there; one man in ten thinks it's a privilege to push his own lawn mower. No, sir. It's later than I thought. There are the children coming home from school already.

[*Shrill girls' voices are heard, off left. EMILY comes along Main Street, carrying some books. There are some signs that she is imagining herself to be a lady of startling elegance.*]

EMILY.   I *can't*, Lois. I've go to go home and help my mother. I *promised.*

MR. WEBB.   Emily, walk simply. Who do you think you are today?   140

EMILY.   Papa, you're terrible. One minute you tell me to stand up straight and the next minute you call me names. I just don't listen to you.

[*She gives him an abrupt kiss.*]

MR. WEBB.   Golly, I never got a kiss from such a great lady before.

[*He goes out of sight.* EMILY *leans over and picks some flowers by the gate of her house.* GEORGE GIBBS *comes careening down Main Street. He is throwing a ball up to dizzying heights, and waiting to catch it again. This sometimes requires his taking six steps backward. He bumps into an* OLD LADY *invisible to us.*]

GEORGE.   Excuse me, Mrs. Forrest.

STAGE MANAGER [*as* MRS. FORREST].   Go out and play in the fields, young man. You got no business playing baseball on Main Street.

GEORGE.   Awfully sorry, Mrs. Forrest—Hello, Emily.   145

EMILY.   H'lo.

GEORGE.   You made a fine speech in class.

EMILY.   Well . . . I was really ready to make a speech about the Monroe Doctrine, but at the last minute Miss Corcoran made me talk about the Louisiana Purchase instead. I worked an awful long time on both of them.

GEORGE.   Gee, it's funny, Emily. From my window up there I can just see your head nights when you're doing your homework over in your room.

EMILY.   Why, can you?   150

GEORGE.   You certainly do stick to it, Emily. I don't see how you can sit still that long. I guess you like school.

EMILY.   Well, I always feel it's something you have to go through.

GEORGE.   Yeah.

EMILY.   I don't mind it really. It passes the time.

GEORGE.   Yeah—Emily, what do you think? We might work out a kinda telegraph   155
from your window to mine; and once in a while you could give me a kinda hint or two about one of those algebra problems. I don't mean the answers, Emily, of course not . . . just some little hint.

EMILY.   Oh, I think *hints* are allowed.—So—ah—if you get stuck, George, you whistle to me; and I'll give you some hints.

GEORGE.   Emily, you're just naturally bright, I guess.

EMILY.   I figure that it's just the way a person's born.

GEORGE.   Yeah. But, you see, I want to be a farmer, and my Uncle Luke says whenever I'm ready I can come over and work on his farm and if I'm any good I can just gradually have it.

EMILY.   You mean the house and everything?   160

[*Enter* MRS. WEBB *with a large bowl and sits on the bench, by her trellis.*]

GEORGE.   Yeah. Well, thanks . . . I better be getting out to the baseball field. Thanks for the talk, Emily. Good afternoon, Mrs. Webb.

MRS. WEBB.   Good afternoon, George.

GEORGE.   So long, Emily.

EMILY.   So long, George.

MRS. WEBB.   Emily, come and help me string these beans for the winter. George   165
Gibbs let himself have a real conversation, didn't he? Why, he's growing up. How old would George be?

EMILY.   I don't know.

MRS. WEBB.   Let's see. He must be almost sixteen.

EMILY.   Mama, I made a speech in class today and I was very good.

MRS. WEBB.   You must recite it to your father at supper. What was it about?

EMILY.   The Louisiana Purchase. It was like silk off a spool. I'm going to make   170
speeches all my life. Mama, are these big enough?

MRS. WEBB.   Try and get them a little bigger if you can.

EMILY.   Mama, will you answer me a question, serious?

MRS. WEBB.   Seriously, dear—not serious.

EMILY.   Seriously,—will you?

MRS. WEBB.   Of course, I will.   175

EMILY.   Mama, am I good looking?

MRS. WEBB.   Yes, of course you are. All my children have got good features; I'd be
ashamed if they hadn't.

EMILY.   Oh, Mama, that's not what I mean. What I mean is: am I *pretty?*

MRS. WEBB.   I've already told you, yes. Now that's enough of that. You have a nice
young pretty face. I never heard of such foolishness.

EMILY.   Oh, Mama, you never tell us the truth about anything.   180

MRS. WEBB.   I *am* telling you the truth.

EMILY.   Mama, were you pretty?

MRS. WEBB.   Yes, I was, if I do say it. I was the prettiest girl in town next to Mamie
Cartwright.

EMILY.   But, Mama, you've got to say something about me. Am I pretty enough . . .
to get anybody . . . to get people interested in me?

MRS. WEBB.   Emily, you make me tired. Now stop it. You're pretty enough for all   185
normal purposes. Come along now and bring that bowl with you.

EMILY.   Oh, Mama, you're no help at all.

STAGE MANAGER.   Thank you. Thank you! That'll do. We'll have to interrupt again
here. Thank you, Mrs. Webb; thank you, Emily.

[*MRS. WEBB and EMILY withdraw.*]

There are some more things we want to explore about this town.

[*He comes to the center of the stage. During the following speech the lights gradually dim to darkness,
leaving only a spot on him.*]

I think this is a good time to tell you that the Cartwright interests have just begun
building a new bank in Grover's Corners—had to go to Vermont for the marble, sorry to
say. And they've asked a friend of mine what they should put in the cornerstone for people to dig up . . . a thousand years from now. . . . Of course, they've put in a copy of the
New York Times and a copy of Mr. Webb's *Sentinel*. . . . We're kind of interested in this because some scientific fellas have found a way of painting all that reading matter with a
glue—silicate glue—that'll make it keep a thousand—two thousand years. We're putting
in a Bible . . . and the Constitution of the United States—and a copy of William Shakespeare's plays. What do you say, folks? What do you think? Y'know—Babylon once had
two million people in it, and all we know about 'em is the names of the kings and some
copies of wheat contracts . . . and contracts for the sale of slaves. Yet every night all those
families sat down to supper, and the father came home from his work, and the smoke
went up the chimney,—same as here. And even in Greece and Rome, all we know about
the *real* life of the people is what we can piece together out of the joking poems and the
comedies they wrote for the theatre back then.

So I'm going to have a copy of this play put in the cornerstone and the people a thousand years from now'll know a few simple facts about us—more than the Treaty of Versailles and the Lindbergh flight.

See what I mean?

So—people a thousand years from now—this is the way we were in the provinces north of New York at the beginning of the twentieth century. This is the way we were: in our growing up and in our marrying and in our living and in our dying.

[*A choir partially concealed in the orchestra pit has begun singing "Blessed Be the Tie That Binds."* SIMON STIMSON *stands directing them. Two ladders have been pushed onto the stage; they serve as indication of the second story in the* GIBBS *and* WEBB *houses.* GEORGE *and* EMILY *mount them, and apply themselves to their schoolwork.* DR. GIBBS *has entered and is seated in his kitchen reading.*]

Well!—good deal of time's gone by. It's evening. You can hear choir practice going on in the Congregational Church. The children are at home doing their schoolwork. The day's running down like a tired clock.

SIMON STIMSON.   Now look here, everybody. Music come into the world to give pleasure—Softer! Softer! Get it out of your heads that music's only good when it's loud. You leave loudness to the Methodists. You couldn't beat 'em, even if you wanted to. Now again. Tenors!

GEORGE.   Hssst! Emily!

EMILY.   Hello.

GEORGE.   Hello!   190

EMILY.   I can't work at all. The moonlight's so *terrible.*

GEORGE.   Emily, did you get the third problem?

EMILY.   Which?

GEORGE.   The *third?*   195

EMILY.   Why, yes, George—that's the easiest of them all.

GEORGE.   I don't see it. Emily, can you give me a hint?

EMILY.   I'll tell you one thing: the answer's in yards.

GEORGE.   !!! In yards? How do you mean?

EMILY.   In *square* yards.   200

GEORGE.   Oh . . . in square yards.

EMILY.   Yes, George, don't you see?

GEORGE.   Yeah.

EMILY.   In square yards of *wallpaper.*

GEORGE.   Wallpaper,—oh, I see. Thanks a lot, Emily.   205

EMILY.   You're welcome. My, isn't the moonlight *terrible?* And choir practice going on—I think if you hold your breath you can hear the train all the way to Contoocook. Hear it?

GEORGE.   M-m-m—What do you know!

EMILY.   Well, I guess I better go back and try to work.

GEORGE.   Good night, Emily. And thanks.

EMILY.   Good night, George.   210

SIMON STIMSON.   Before I forget it: how many of you will be able to come in Tuesday afternoon and sing at Fred Hersey's wedding?—show your hands. That'll be fine; that'll be right nice. We'll do the same music we did for Jane Trowbridge's last month.— Now we'll do: "Art Thou Weary; Art Thou Languid?" It's a question, ladies and gentlemen, make it talk. Ready.

DR. GIBBS.   Oh, George, can you come down a minute?

GEORGE.   Yes, Pa.

[*He descends the ladder.*]

DR. GIBBS.   Make yourself comfortable, George; I'll only keep you a minute. George, how old are you?

GEORGE.   I? I'm sixteen, almost seventeen.   215

DR. GIBBS.   What do you want to do after school's over?

GEORGE.   Why, you know, Pa. I want to be a farmer on Uncle Luke's farm.

DR. GIBBS.   You'll be willing, will you, to get up early and milk and feed the stock . . . and you'll be able to hoe and hay all day?

GEORGE.   Sure, I will. What are you . . . what do you mean, Pa?

DR. GIBBS.   Well, George, while I was in my office today I heard a funny sound . . .   220
and what do you think it was? It was your mother chopping wood. There you see your mother—getting up early; cooking meals all day long; washing and ironing;—and still she has to go out in the back yard and chop wood. I suppose she just got tired of asking you. She just gave up and decided it was easier to do it herself. And you eat her meals, and put on the clothes she keeps nice for you, and you run off and play baseball,—like she's some hired girl we keep around the house but that we don't like very much. Well, I knew all I had to do was call your attention to it. Here's a handkerchief, son. George, I've decided to raise your spending money twenty-five cents a week. Not, of course, for chopping wood for your mother, because that's a present you give her, but because you're getting older—and I imagine there are lots of things you must find to do with it.

GEORGE.   Thanks, Pa.

DR. GIBBS.   Let's see—tomorrow's your payday. You can count on it—Hmm. Probably Rebecca'll feel she ought to have some more too. Wonder what could have happened to your mother. Choir practice never was as late as this before.

GEORGE.   It's only half past eight, Pa.

DR. GIBBS.   I don't know why she's in that old choir. She hasn't any more voice than an old crow. . . . Traipsin' around the streets at this hour of the night. . . . Just about time you retired, don't you think?

GEORGE.   Yes, Pa.   225

[*GEORGE mounts to his place on the ladder. Laughter and good nights can be heard on stage left and presently MRS. GIBBS, MRS. SOAMES and MRS. WEBB come down Main Street. When they arrive at the corner of the stage they stop.*]

MRS. SOAMES.   Good night, Martha. Good night, Mr. Foster.

MRS. WEBB.   I'll tell Mr. Webb; I *know* he'll want to put it in the paper.

MRS. GIBBS.   My, it's late!

MRS. SOAMES.   Good night, Irma.

MRS. GIBBS.   Real nice choir practice, wa'n't it? Myrtle Webb! Look at that moon,   230
will you! Tsk—tsk—tsk. Potato weather, for sure.

[*They are silent a moment, gazing up at the moon.*]

MRS. SOAMES.   Naturally I didn't want to say a word about it in front of those others, but now we're alone—really, it's the worst scandal that ever was in this town!

MRS. GIBBS.   What?

MRS. SOAMES.   Simon Stimson!

MRS. GIBBS.   Now, Louella!

MRS. SOAMES.   But, Julia! To have the organist of a church *drink* and *drunk* year   235
after year. You know he was drunk tonight.

MRS. GIBBS.   Now, Louella! We all know about Mr. Stimson, and we all know about the troubles he's been through, and Dr. Ferguson knows too, and if Dr. Ferguson keeps him on there in his job the only thing the rest of us can do is just not to notice it.

MRS. SOAMES.   *Not to notice it!* But it's getting worse.

MRS. WEBB.   No, it isn't, Louella. It's getting better. I've been in that choir twice as long as you have. It doesn't happen anywhere near so often. . . . My, I hate to go to bed on a night like this—I better hurry. Those children'll be sitting up till all hours. Good night, Louella.

[*They all exchange good nights. She hurries downstage, enters her house and disappears.*]

MRS. GIBBS.   Can you get home safe, Louella?

MRS. SOAMES.   It's as bright as day. I can see Mr. Soames scowling at the window   240
now. You'd think we'd been to a dance the way the menfolk carry on.

[*More good nights. MRS. GIBBS arrives at her home and passes through the trellis into the kitchen.*]

MRS. GIBBS.   Well, we had a real good time.

DR. GIBBS.   You're late enough.

MRS. GIBBS.   Why, Frank, it ain't any later 'n usual.

DR. GIBBS.   And you stopping at the corner to gossip with a lot of hens.

MRS. GIBBS.   Now, Frank, don't be grouchy. Come out and smell the heliotrope in   245
the moonlight.

[*They stroll out arm in arm along the footlights.*]

Isn't that wonderful? What did you do all the time I was away?

DR. GIBBS.   Oh, I read—as usual. What were the girls gossiping about tonight?

MRS. GIBBS.   Well, believe me, Frank—there is something to gossip about.

DR. GIBBS.   Hmm! Simon Stimson far gone, was he?

MRS. GIBBS.   Worst I've ever seen him. How'll that end, Frank? Dr. Ferguson can't forgive him forever.

DR. GIBBS.   I guess I know more about Simon Stimson's affairs than anybody in   250
this town. Some people ain't made for small-town life. I don't know how that'll end; but there's nothing we can do but just leave it alone. Come, get in.

MRS. GIBBS.   No, not yet . . . Frank, I'm worried about you.

DR. GIBBS.   What are you worried about?

MRS. GIBBS.   I think it's my duty to make plans for you to get a real rest and change. And if I get that legacy, well, I'm going to insist on it.

DR. GIBBS.   Now, Julia, there's no sense in going over that again.

MRS. GIBBS.   Frank, you're just *unreasonable!*   255

DR. GIBBS.   [*Starting into the house.*] Come on, Julia, it's getting late. First thing you know you'll catch cold. I gave George a piece of my mind tonight. I reckon you'll have your wood chopped for a while anyway. No, no, start getting upstairs.

MRS. GIBBS.   Oh, dear. There's always so many things to pick up, seems like. You know, Frank, Mrs. Fairchild always locks her front door every night. All those people up that part of town do.

DR. GIBBS.   [*Blowing out the lamp.*] They're all getting citified, that's the trouble with them. They haven't got nothing fit to burgle and everybody knows it.

[*They disappear. REBECCA climbs up the ladder beside GEORGE.*]

GEORGE.   Get out, Rebecca. There's only room for one at this window. You're always spoiling everything.

REBECCA.   Well, let me look just a minute.   260

GEORGE.   Use your own window.

REBECCA.   I did, but there's no moon there. . . . George, do you know what I think, do you? I think maybe the moon's getting nearer and nearer and there'll be a big 'splosion.

GEORGE.   Rebecca, you don't know anything. If the moon were getting nearer, the guys that sit up all night with telescopes would see it first and they'd tell about it, and it'd be in all the newspapers.

REBECCA.   George, is the moon shining on South America, Canada and half the whole world?

GEORGE.   Well—prob'ly is.   265

[*The STAGE MANAGER strolls on. Pause. The sound of crickets is heard.*]

STAGE MANAGER.   Nine thirty. Most of the lights are out. No, there's Constable Warren trying a few doors on Main Street. And here comes Editor Webb, after putting his newspaper to bed.

[*MR. WARREN, an elderly policeman, comes along Main Street from the right, MR. WEBB from the left.*]

MR. WEBB.   Good evening, Bill.

CONSTABLE WARREN.   Evenin', Mr. Webb.

MR. WEBB.   Quite a moon!

CONSTABLE WARREN.   Yepp.   270

MR. WEBB.   All quiet tonight?

CONSTABLE WARREN.   Simon Stimson is rolling around a little. Just saw his wife movin' out to hunt for him so I looked the other way—there he is now.

[*SIMON STIMSON comes down Main Street from the left, only a trace of unsteadiness in his walk.*]

MR. WEBB.   Good evening, Simon . . . Town seems to have settled down for the night pretty well . . .

[*SIMON STIMSON comes up to him and pauses a moment and stares at him, swaying slightly.*]

Good evening . . . Yes, most of the town's settled down for the night, Simon . . . I guess we better do the same. Can I walk along a ways with you?

[*SIMON STIMSON continues on his way without a word and disappears at the right.*]

Good night.

CONSTABLE WARREN.   I don't know how that's goin' to end, Mr. Webb.

MR. WEBB.   Well, he's seen a peck of trouble, one thing after another . . . Oh, Bill   275
. . . if you see my boy smoking cigarettes, just give him a word, will you? He thinks a lot of you, Bill.

CONSTABLE WARREN.   I don't think he smokes no cigarettes, Mr. Webb. Leastways, not more'n two or three a year.

MR. WEBB.   Hm . . . I hope not—Well, good night, Bill.

CONSTABLE WARREN.   Good night, Mr. Webb.

[*Exit.*]

MR. WEBB.   Who's that up there? Is that you, Myrtle?

EMILY.   No, it's me, Papa.   280

MR. WEBB.   Why aren't you in bed?

EMILY.   I don't know. I just can't sleep yet, Papa. The moonlight's so *won*-derful. And the smell of Mrs. Gibbs' heliotrope. Can you smell it?

MR. WEBB.   Hm . . . Yes. Haven't any troubles on your mind, have you, Emily?

EMILY.   *Troubles*, Papa? No.

MR. WEBB.   Well, enjoy yourself, but don't let your mother catch you. Good night,   285
Emily.

EMILY.   Good night, Papa.

[*MR. WEBB crosses into the house, whistling "Blessed Be the Tie That Binds" and disappears.*]

REBECCA.   I never told you about that letter Jane Crofut got from her minister
when she was sick. He wrote Jane a letter and on the envelope the address was like this: It
said: Jane Crofut; The Crofut Farm; Grover's Corners; Sutton County; New Hampshire;
United States of America.

GEORGE.   What's funny about that?

REBECCA.   But listen, it's not finished: the United States of America; Continent of
North America; Western Hemisphere; the Earth; the Solar System; the Universe; the
Mind of God—that's what it said on the envelope.

GEORGE.   What do you know!   290

REBECCA.   And the postman brought it just the same.

GEORGE.   What do you know!

STAGE MANAGER.   That's the end of the First Act, friends. You can go and smoke
now, those that smoke.

ACT 2

The tables and chairs of the two kitchens are still on the stage.

The ladders and the small bench have been withdrawn.

The STAGE MANAGER has been at his accustomed place watching the audience return to
its seats.

STAGE MANAGER.   Three years have gone by. Yes, the sun's come up over a thousand times. Summers and winters have cracked the mountains a little bit more and the
rains have brought down some of the dirt.

Some babies that weren't even born before have begun talking regular sentences
already; and a number of people who thought they were right young and spry have noticed that they can't bound up a flight of stairs like they used to, without their heart fluttering a little.

All that can happen in a thousand days.

Nature's been pushing and contriving in other ways, too: a number of young people fell in love and got married.

Yes, the mountain got bit away a few fractions of an inch; millions of gallons of
water went by the mill; and here and there a new home was set up under a roof. Almost
everybody in the world gets married, you know what I mean? In our town there aren't
hardly any exceptions. Most everybody in the world climbs into their graves married. The
First Act was called the Daily Life. This act is called Love and Marriage. There's another
act coming after this: I reckon you can guess what that's about.

So: It's three years later. It's 1904. It's July 7th, just after High School Commencement. That's the time most of our young people jump up and get married. Soon as
they've passed their last examinations in solid geometry and Cicero's Orations, looks like
they suddenly feel themselves fit to be married.

It's early morning. Only this time it's been raining. It's been pouring and thundering. Mrs. Gibbs' garden, and Mrs. Webb's here: drenched. All those bean poles and pea

vines: drenched. All yesterday over there on Main Street, the rain looked like curtains being blown along.

Hm . . . it may begin again any minute. There! You can hear the 5:45 for Boston.

[*MRS. GIBBS and MRS. WEBB enter their kitchen and start the day as in the First Act.*]

And there's Mrs. Gibbs and Mrs. Webb come down to make breakfast, just as though it were an ordinary day. I don't have to point out to the women in my audience that those ladies they see before them, both of those ladies cooked three meals a day—one of 'em for twenty years, the other for forty—and no summer vacation. They brought up two children apiece, washed, cleaned the house,—and *never a nervous breakdown.*

It's like what one of those Middle West poets said: You've got to love life to have life, and you've got to have life to love life . . . It's what they call a vicious circle.

HOWIE NEWSOME.   [*Offstage left.*] Giddap, Bessie!

STAGE MANAGER.   Here comes Howie Newsome delivering the milk. And there's Si Crowell delivering the papers like his brother before him.

[*SI CROWELL has entered hurling imaginary newspapers into doorways; HOWIE NEWSOME has come along Main Street with Bessie.*]

SI CROWELL.   Morning, Howie.

HOWIE NEWSOME.   Morning, Si—Anything in the papers I ought to know?   5

SI CROWELL.   Nothing much, except we're losing about the best baseball pitcher Grover's Corners ever had—George Gibbs.

HOWIE NEWSOME.   Reckon he is.

SI CROWELL.   He could hit and run bases, too.

HOWIE NEWSOME.   Yep. Mighty fine ball player. Whoa! Bessie! I guess I can stop and talk if I've a mind to!

SI CROWELL.   I don't see how he could give up a thing like that just to get married.   10
Would you, Howie?

HOWIE NEWSOME.   Can't tell, Si. Never had no talent that way.

[*CONSTABLE WARREN enters. They exchange good mornings.*]

You're up early, Bill.

CONSTABLE WARREN.   Seein' if there's anything I can do to prevent a flood. River's been risin' all night.

HOWIE NEWSOME.   Si Crowell's all worked up here about George Gibbs' retiring from baseball.

CONSTABLE WARREN.   Yes, sir; that's the way it goes. Back in '84 we had a player, Si—even George Gibbs couldn't touch him. Name of Hank Todd. Went down to Maine and become a parson. Wonderful ball player.—Howie, how does the weather look to you?

HOWIE NEWSOME.   Oh, 'tain't bad. Think maybe it'll clear up for good.   15

[*CONSTABLE WARREN and SI CROWELL continue on their way. HOWIE NEWSOME brings the milk first to MRS. GIBBS' house. She meets him by the trellis.*]

MRS. GIBBS.   Good morning, Howie. Do you think it's going to rain again?

HOWIE NEWSOME.   Morning, Mrs. Gibbs. It rained so heavy, I think maybe it'll clear up.

MRS. GIBBS.   Certainly hope it will.

HOWIE NEWSOME.   How much did you want today?

MRS. GIBBS.   I'm going to have a houseful of relations, Howie. Looks to me like I'll   20
need three-a-milk and two-a-cream.

HOWIE NEWSOME.   My wife says to tell you we both hope they'll be very happy, Mrs. Gibbs. Know they will.

MRS. GIBBS.   Thanks a lot, Howie. Tell your wife I hope she gits there to the wedding.

HOWIE NEWSOME.   Yes, she'll be there; she'll be there if she kin.

[*HOWIE NEWSOME crosses to MRS. WEBB's house.*]

Morning, Mrs. Webb.

MRS. WEBB.   Oh, good morning, Mr. Newsome. I told you four quarts of milk, but I hope you can spare me another.

HOWIE NEWSOME.   Yes'm . . . and the two of cream.

MRS. WEBB.   Will it start raining again, Mr. Newsome?   25

HOWIE NEWSOME.   Well. Just sayin' to Mrs. Gibbs as how it may lighten up. Mrs. Newsome told me to tell you as how we hope they'll both be very happy, Mrs. Webb. Know they will.

MRS. WEBB.   Thank you, and thank Mrs. Newsome and we're counting on seeing you at the wedding.

HOWIE NEWSOME.   Yes, Mrs. Webb. We hope to git there. Couldn't miss that. Come on, Bessie.

[*Exit HOWIE NEWSOME. DR. GIBBS descends in shirt sleeves, and sits down at his breakfast table.*]

DR. GIBBS.   Well, Ma, the day has come. You're losin' one of your chicks.   30

MRS. GIBBS.   Frank Gibbs, don't you say another word. I feel like crying every minute. Sit down and drink your coffee.

DR. GIBBS.   The groom's up shaving himself—only there ain't an awful lot to shave. Whistling and singing, like he's glad to leave us—Every now and then he says "I do" to the mirror, but it don't sound convincing to me.

MRS. GIBBS.   I declare, Frank, I don't know how he'll get along. I've arranged his clothes and seen to it he's put warm things on,—Frank! they're too *young*. Emily won't think of such things. He'll catch his death of cold within a week.

DR. GIBBS.   I was remembering my wedding morning, Julia.

MRS. GIBBS.   Now don't start that, Frank Gibbs.   35

DR. GIBBS.   I was the scaredest young fella in the State of New Hampshire. I thought I'd make a mistake for sure. And when I saw you comin' down that aisle I thought you were the prettiest girl I'd ever seen, but the only trouble was that I'd never seen you before. There I was in the Congregational Church marryin' a total stranger.

MRS. GIBBS.   And how do you think I felt!—Frank, weddings are perfectly awful things. Farces, that's what they are! [*She puts a plate before him.*] Here, I've made something for you.

DR. GIBBS.   Why, Julia Hersey—French toast!

MRS. GIBBS.   'Tain't hard to make and I had to do something.

[*Pause. DR. GIBBS pours on the syrup.*]

DR. GIBBS.   How'd you sleep last night, Julia?   40

MRS. GIBBS.   Well, I heard a lot of the hours struck off.

DR. GIBBS.   Ye-e-s! I get a shock every time I think of George setting out to be a family man—that great gangling thing!—I tell you Julia, there's nothing so terrifying in the world as a *son*. The relation of father and son is the darndest, awkwardest—

MRS. GIBBS.   Well, mother and daughter's no picnic, let me tell you.

DR. GIBBS.   They'll have a lot of troubles, I suppose, but that's none of our business. Everybody has a right to their own troubles.

The Stage Manager (Spalding Gray), acting as a minister, performs the marriage of George (Eric Stolz) and Emily (Penelope Ann Miller) in the PBS Masterpiece Theater version of the 1989 Lincoln Center (New York) production of *Our Town*, directed by Gregory Mosher.

MRS. GIBBS.   [*At the table, drinking her coffee, meditatively.*] Yes . . . people are meant   45
to go through life two by two. 'Tain't natural to be lonesome.

[*Pause. DR. GIBBS starts laughing.*]

DR. GIBBS.   Julia, do you know one of the things I was scared of when I married you?
MRS. GIBBS.   Oh, go along with you!
DR. GIBBS.   I was afraid we wouldn't have material for conversation more'n'd last us a few weeks.

[*Both laugh.*]

I was afraid we'd run out and eat our meals in silence, that's a fact.—Well, you and I been conversing for twenty years now without any noticeable barren spells.
MRS. GIBBS.   Well,—good weather, bad weather'tain't very choice, but I always find something to say. [*She goes to the foot of the stairs.*] Did you hear Rebecca stirring around upstairs?

DR. GIBBS.   No. Only day of the year Rebecca hasn't been managing everybody's   50
business up there. She's hiding in her room—I got the impression she's crying.

MRS. GIBBS.   Lord's sakes!—This has got to stop. Rebecca! Rebecca! Come and get
your breakfast.

[*GEORGE comes rattling down the stairs, very brisk.*]

GEORGE.   Good morning, everybody. Only five more hours to live.

[*Makes the gesture of cutting his throat, and a loud "k-k-k," and starts through the trellis.*]

MRS. GIBBS.   George Gibbs, where are you going?

GEORGE.   Just stepping across the grass to see my girl.

MRS. GIBBS.   Now, George! You put on your overshoes. It's raining torrents. You   55
don't go out of this house without you're prepared for it.

GEORGE.   Aw, Ma. It's just a *step!*

MRS. GIBBS.   George! You'll catch your death of cold and cough all through the
service.

DR. GIBBS.   George, do as your mother tells you!

[*DR. GIBBS goes upstairs. GEORGE returns reluctantly to the kitchen and pantomimes putting on
overshoes.*]

MRS. GIBBS.   From tomorrow on you can kill yourself in all weathers, but while
you're in my house you'll live wisely, thank you.—Maybe Mrs. Webb isn't used to callers at
seven in the morning. Here, take a cup of coffee first.

GEORGE.   Be back in a minute. [*He crosses the stage, leaping over the puddles.*] Good   60
morning, Mother Webb.

MRS. WEBB.   Goodness! You frightened me!—Now, George, you can come in a
minute out of the wet, but you know I can't ask you in.

GEORGE.   Why not—?

MRS. WEBB.   George, you know's well as I do: the groom can't see his bride on his
wedding day, not until he sees her in church.

GEORGE.   Aw!—that's just a superstition—Good morning, Mr. Webb.

[*Enter MR. WEBB.*]

MR. WEBB.   Good morning, George.   65

GEORGE.   Mr. Webb, you don't believe in that superstition, do you?

MR. WEBB.   There's a lot of common sense in some superstitions, George.

[*He sits at the table, facing right.*]

MRS. WEBB.   Millions have folla'd it, George, and you don't want to be the first to
fly in the face of custom.

GEORGE.   How is Emily?

MRS. WEBB.   She hasn't waked up yet. I haven't heard a sound out of her.   70

GEORGE.   Emily's *asleep!!!*

MRS. WEBB.   No wonder! We were up 'til all hours, sewing and packing. Now I'll
tell you what I'll do; you set down here a minute with Mr. Webb and drink this cup of coffee; and I'll go upstairs and see she doesn't come down and surprise you. There's some
bacon too; but don't be long about it.

[*Exit MRS. WEBB. Embarrassed silence. MR. WEBB dunks doughnuts in his coffee. More silence.*]

MR. WEBB.   [*Suddenly and loudly.*] Well George, how are *you?*

GEORGE. [*Startled, choking over his coffee.*] Oh, fine, I'm fine. [*Pause.*] Mr. Webb, what sense could there be in a superstition like that?

MR. WEBB. Well, you see,—on her wedding morning a girl's head's apt to be full   75
of . . . clothes and one thing and another. Don't you think that's probably it?

GEORGE. Ye-e-s. I never thought of that.

MR. WEBB. A girl's apt to be a mite nervous on her wedding day.

[*Pause.*]

GEORGE. I wish a fellow could get married without all that marching up and down.

MR. WEBB. Every man that's ever lived has felt that way about it, George; but it hasn't been any use. It's the womenfolk who've built up weddings, my boy. For a while now the women have it all their own. A man looks pretty small at a wedding, George. All those good women standing shoulder to shoulder making sure that the knot's tied in a mighty public way.

GEORGE. But . . . *you believe* in it, don't you, Mr. Webb?   80

MR. WEBB. [*With alacrity.*] Oh; yes; oh, yes. Don't you misunderstand me, my boy. Marriage is a wonderful thing,—wonderful thing. And don't you forget that, George.

GEORGE. No, sir.—Mr. Webb, how old were you when you got married?

MR. WEBB. Well, you see: I'd been to college and I'd taken a little time to get settled. But Mrs. Webb—she wasn't much older than what Emily is. Oh, age hasn't much to do with it, George,—not compared with . . . uh . . . other things.

GEORGE. What were you going to say, Mr. Webb?

MR. WEBB. Oh, I don't know—Was I going to say something?   85

[*Pause.*]

George, I was thinking the other night of some advice my father gave me when I got married. Charles, he said, Charles, start out early showing who's boss, he said. Best thing to do is to give an order, even if it don't make sense; just so she'll learn to obey. And he said: if anything about your wife irritates you—her conversation, or anything—just get up and leave the house. That'll make it clear to her, he said. And, oh, yes! he said, never, *never let your wife know how much money you have, never.*

GEORGE. Well, Mr. Webb . . . I don't think I could . . .

MR. WEBB. So I took the opposite of my father's advice and I've been happy ever since. And let that be a lesson to you, George, never to ask advice on personal matters.— George, are you going to raise chickens on your farm?

GEORGE. What?

MR. WEBB. Are you going to raise chickens on your farm?

GEORGE. Uncle Luke's never been much interested, but I thought—   90

MR. WEBB. A book came into my office the other day, George, on the Philo System of raising chickens. I want you to read it. I'm thinking of beginning in a small way in the back yard, and I'm going to put an incubator in the cellar—

[*Enter MRS. WEBB.*]

MRS. WEBB. Charles, are you talking about that old incubator again? I thought you two'd be talking about things worth while.

MR. WEBB. [*Bitingly.*] Well, Myrtle, if you want to give the boy some good advice, I'll go upstairs and leave you alone with him.

MRS. WEBB. [*Pulling GEORGE up.*] George, Emily's got to come downstairs and eat her breakfast. She sends you her love but she doesn't want to lay eyes on you. Good-by.

GEORGE. Good-by.   95

[*GEORGE crosses the stage to his own home, bewildered and crestfallen. He slowly dodges a puddle and disappears into his house.*]

MR. WEBB.   Myrtle, I guess you don't know about that older superstition.
MRS. WEBB.   What do you mean, Charles?
MR. WEBB.   Since the cave men: no bridegroom should see his father-in-law on the day of the wedding, or near it. Now remember that.

[*Both leave the stage.*]

STAGE MANAGER.   Thank you very much, Mr. and Mrs. Webb.—Now I have to interrupt again here. You see, we want to know how all this began—this wedding, this plan to spend a lifetime together. I'm awfully interested in how big things like that begin.

You know how it is: you're twenty-one or twenty-two and you make some decisions; then whisssh! you're seventy: you've been a lawyer for fifty years, and that white-haired lady at your side has eaten over fifty thousand meals with you.

How do such things begin?

George and Emily are going to show you now the conversation they had when they first knew that . . . that . . . as the saying goes . . . they were meant for one another. But before they do it I want you to try and remember what it was like to have been very young. And particularly the days when you were first in love; when you were like a person sleepwalking, and you didn't quite see the street you were in, and didn't quite hear everything that was said to you. You're just a little bit crazy. Will you remember that please?

Now they'll be coming out of high school at three o'clock. George has just been elected President of the Junior Class, and as it's June, that means he'll be President of the Senior Class all next year. And Emily's just been elected Secretary and Treasurer. I don't have to tell you how important that is.

[*He places a board across the backs of two chairs, which he takes from those at the GIBBS family's table. He brings two high stools from the wings and places them behind the board. Persons sitting on the stools will be facing the audience. This is the counter of MR. MORGAN'S drugstore. The sounds of young people's voices are heard off left.*]

Yepp,—there they are coming down Main Street now.

[*EMILY, carrying an armful of—imaginary—schoolbooks, comes along Main Street from the left.*]

EMILY.   I can't, Louise. I've go to go home. Good—by. Oh, Ernestine! Ernestine!   100
Can you come over tonight and do Latin? Isn't that Cicero the worst thing—! Tell your mother you *have* to. G'by. G'by, Helen. G'by, Fred.

[*GEORGE, also carrying books, catches up with her.*]

GEORGE.   Can I carry your books home for you, Emily?
EMILY.   [*Coolly.*] Why . . . uh . . . Thank you. It isn't far.

[*She gives them to him.*]

GEORGE.   Excuse me a minute, Emily—Say, Bob, if I'm a little late, start practice anyway. And give Herb some long high ones.
EMILY.   Good-by, Lizzy.
GEORGE.   Good-by, Lizzy.—I'm awfully glad you were elected, too, Emily.   105
EMILY.   Thank you.

[*They have been standing on Main Street, almost against the back wall. They take the first steps toward the audience when* GEORGE *stops and says:*]

GEORGE.   Emily, why are you mad at me?

EMILY.   I'm not mad at you.

GEORGE.   You've been treating me so funny lately.

EMILY.   Well, since you ask me, I might as well say it right out, George,   110

[*She catches sight of a teacher passing.*]

Good-by, Miss Corcoran.

GEORGE.   Good-by, Miss Corcoran.—Wha—what is it?

EMILY.   [*Not scoldingly; finding it difficult to say.*] I don't like the whole change that's come over you in the last year. I'm sorry if that hurts your feelings, but I've got to—tell the truth and shame the devil.

GEORGE.   A *change?*—Wha—*what do* you mean?

EMILY.   Well, up to a year ago I used to like you a lot. And I used to watch you as you did everything . . . because we'd been friends so long . . . and then you began spending all your time at *baseball* . . . and you never stopped to speak to anybody any more. Not even to your own family you didn't . . . and, George, it's a fact, you've got awful conceited and stuck-up, and all the girls say so. They may not say so to your face, but that's what they say about you behind your back, and it hurts me to hear them say it, but I've got to agree with them a little. I'm sorry if it hurts your feelings . . . but I can't be sorry I said it.

GEORGE.   I . . . I'm glad you said it, Emily. I never thought that such a thing was   115 happening to me. I guess it's hard for a fella not to have faults creep into his character.

[*They take a step or two in silence, then stand still in misery.*]

EMILY.   I always expect a man to be perfect and I think he should be.

GEORGE.   Oh . . . I don't think it's possible to be perfect, Emily.

EMILY.   Well, my *father is*, and as far as I can see *your* father is. There's no reason on earth why you shouldn't be, too.

GEORGE.   Well, I feel it's the other way round. That men aren't naturally good; but girls are.

EMILY.   Well, you might as well know right now that I'm not perfect. It's not as easy   120 for a girl to be perfect as a man, because we girls are more—more nervous.—Now I'm sorry I said all that about you. I don't know what made me say it.

GEORGE.   Emily,

EMILY.   Now I can see it's not the truth at all. And I suddenly feel that it isn't important, anyway.

GEORGE.   Emily . . . would you like an ice-cream soda, or something, before you go home?

EMILY.   Well, thank you . . . I would.

[*They advance toward the audience and make an abrupt right turn, opening the door of* MORGAN'S *drugstore.*]

Under strong emotion, EMILY *keeps her face down.*

GEORGE *speaks to some passers-by.*]

GEORGE.   Hello, Stew,—how are you?—Good afternoon, Mrs. Slocum.   125

[*The* STAGE MANAGER, *wearing spectacles and assuming the role of* MR. MORGAN, *enters abruptly from the right and stands between the audience and the counter of his soda fountain.*]

STAGE MANAGER.   Hello, George. Hello, Emily. What'll you have?—Why, Emily Webb,—what you been crying about?

GEORGE.   [*He gropes for an explanation.*] She . . . she just got an awful scare, Mr. Morgan. She almost got run over by that hardware-store wagon. Everybody says that Tom Huckins drives like a crazy man.

STAGE MANAGER.   [*Drawing a drink of water.*] Well, now! You take a drink of water, Emily. You look all shook up. I tell you, you've got to look both ways before you cross Main Street these days. Gets worse every year.—What'll you have?

EMILY.   I'll have a strawberry phosphate, thank you, Mr. Morgan.

GEORGE.   No, no, Emily. Have an ice-cream soda with me. Two strawberry ice-cream sodas, Mr. Morgan.   130

STAGE MANAGER.   [*Working the faucets.*] *Two* strawberry ice-cream sodas, yes sir. Yes, sir. There are a hundred and twenty-five horses in Grover's Corners this minute I'm talking to you. State Inspector was in here yesterday. And now they're bringing in these automo-biles, the best thing to do is to just stay home. Why, I can remember when a dog could go to sleep all day in the middle of Main Street and nothing come along to disturb him. [*He sets the imaginary glasses before them.*] There they are. Enjoy 'em. [*He sees a customer, right.*] Yes, Mrs. Ellis. What can I do for you? [*He goes out right.*]

EMILY.   They're so expensive.

GEORGE.   No, no,—don't you think of that. We're celebrating our election. And then do you know what else I'm celebrating?

EMILY.   N-no.

GEORGE.   I'm celebrating because I've got a friend who tells me all the things that ought to be told me.   135

EMILY.   George, *please* don't think of that. I don't know why I said it. It's not true. You're—

GEORGE.   No, Emily, you stick to it. I'm glad you spoke to me like you did. But you'll *see:* I'm going to change so quick—you bet I'm going to change. And, Emily, I want to ask you a favor.

EMILY.   What?

GEORGE.   Emily, if I go away to State Agriculture College next year, will you write me a letter once in a while?

EMILY.   I certainly will. I certainly will, George . . .   140

[*Pause. They start sipping the sodas through the straws.*]

It certainly seems like being away three years you'd get out of touch with things. Maybe letters from Grover's Corners wouldn't be so interesting after a while. Grover's Corners isn't a very important place when you think of all—New Hampshire; but I think it's a very nice town.

GEORGE.   The day wouldn't come when I wouldn't want to know everything that's happening here. I *know that's* true, Emily.

EMILY.   Well, I'll try to make my letters interesting.

[*Pause.*]

GEORGE.   Y'know. Emily, whenever I meet a farmer I ask him if he thinks it's important to go to Agriculture School to be a good farmer.

EMILY.   Why, George—

GEORGE.   Yeah, and some of them say that it's even a waste of time. You can get all those things, anyway, out of the pamphlets the government sends out. And Uncle Luke's getting old,—he's about ready for me to start in taking over his farm tomorrow, if I could.   145

EMILY.   My!

GEORGE.   And, like you say, being gone all that time . . . in other places and meeting other people . . . Gosh, if anything like that can happen I don't want to go away. I guess new people aren't any better than old ones. I'll bet they almost never are. Emily . . . I feel that you're as good a friend as I've got. I don't need to go and meet the people in other towns.

EMILY.   But, George, maybe it's very important for you to go, and learn all that about—cattle judging and soils and those things. . . . Of course, I don't know.

GEORGE.   [*After a pause, very seriously.*] Emily, I'm going to make up my mind right now. I won't go. I'll tell Pa about it tonight.

EMILY.   Why, George, I don't see why you have to decide right now. It's a whole   150
year away.

GEORGE.   Emily, I'm glad you spoke to me about that . . . that fault in my character. What you said was right; but there was *one* thing wrong in it, and that was when you said that for a year I wasn't noticing people, and . . . you, for instance. Why, you say you were watching me when I did everything . . . I was doing the same about you all the time. Why, sure,—I always thought about you as one of the chief people I thought about. I always made sure where you were sitting on the bleachers, and who you were with, and for three days now I've been trying to walk home with you; but something's always got in the way. Yesterday I was standing over against the wall waiting for you, and you walked home with Miss Corcoran.

EMILY.   George! . . . Life's awful funny! How could I have known that? Why, I thought—

GEORGE.   Listen, Emily, I'm going to tell you why I'm not going to Agriculture School. I think that once you've found a person that you're very fond of . . . I mean a person who's fond of you, too, and likes you enough to be interested in your character . . . Well, I think that's just as important as college is, and even more so. That's what I think.

EMILY.   I think it's awfully important, too.

GEORGE.   Emily.   155

EMILY.   Y-yes, George.

GEORGE.   Emily, if I do improve and make a big change would you be . . . I mean:
could you be . . .

EMILY.   I . . . I am now; I always have been.

GEORGE.   [*Pause.*] So I guess this is an important talk we've been having.

EMILY.   Yes . . . Yes.   160

GEORGE.   [*Takes a deep breath and straightens his back.*] Wait just a minute and I'll
walk you home.

[*With mounting alarm he digs into his pockets for the money. The* STAGE MANAGER *enters, right.*
GEORGE, *deeply embarrassed, but direct, says to him:*]

Mr. Morgan, I'll have to go home and get the money to pay you for this. It'll only take me
a minute.

STAGE MANAGER.   [*Pretending to be affronted.*] What's that? George Gibbs, do you
mean to tell me—!

GEORGE.   Yes, but I had reasons, Mr. Morgan—Look, here's my gold watch to keep
until I come back with the money.

STAGE MANAGER.   That's all right. Keep your watch. I'll trust you.

GEORGE.   I'll be back in five minutes.   165

STAGE MANAGER.   I'll trust you ten years, George,—not a day over—Got all over
your shock, Emily?

EMILY.　Yes, thank you, Mr. Morgan. It was nothing.

GEORGE.　[*Taking up the books from the counter.*] I'm ready.

[*They walk in grave silence across the stage and pass through the trellis at the Webbs' back door and disappear. The* STAGE MANAGER *watches them go out, then turns to the audience, removing his spectacles.*]

STAGE MANAGER.　Well,

[*He claps his hands as a signal.*]

Now we're ready to get on with the wedding.

[*He stands waiting while the set is prepared for the next scene.* STAGEHANDS *remove the chairs, tables and trellises from the Gibbs and Webb houses. They arrange the pews for the church in the center of the stage. The congregation will sit facing the back wall. The aisle of the church starts at the center of the back wall and comes toward the audience. A small platform is placed against the back wall on which the* STAGE MANAGER *will stand later, playing the minister. The image of a stained-glass window is cast from a lantern slide upon the back wall. When all is ready the* STAGE MANAGER *strolls to the center of the stage, down front, and, musingly, addresses the audience.*]

There are a lot of things to be said about a wedding; there are a lot of thoughts that go on during a wedding. We can't get them all into one wedding, naturally, and especially not into a wedding at Grover's Corners, where they're awfully plain and short.

In this wedding I play the minister. That gives me the right to say a few more things about it. For a while now, the play gets pretty serious. Y'see, some churches say that marriage is a sacrament. I don't quite know what that means, but I can guess. Like Mrs. Gibbs said a few minutes ago: People were made to live two-by-two.

This is a good wedding, but people are so put together that even at a good wedding there's a lot of confusion way down deep in people's minds and we thought that that ought to be in our play, too.

The real hero of this scene isn't on the stage at all, and you know who that is. It's like what one of those European fellas said: every child born into the world is nature's attempt to make a perfect human being. Well, we've seen nature pushing and contriving for some time now. We all know that nature's interested in quantity; but I think she's interested in quality, too,—that's why I'm in the ministry.

And don't forget all the other witnesses at this wedding,—the ancestors. Millions of them. Most of them set out to live two-by-two, also. Millions of them. Well, that's all my sermon. 'Twan't very long, anyway.

[*The organ starts playing Handel's "Largo." The congregation streams into the church and sits in silence. Church bells are heard.* MRS. GIBBS *sits in the front row, the first seat on the aisle, the right section; next to her are* REBECCA *and* DR. GIBBS. *Across the aisle* MRS. WEBB, WALLY, *and* MR. WEBB. *A small choir takes its place, facing the audience under the stained-glass window.* MRS. WEBB, *on the way to her place, turns back and speaks to the audience.*]

MRS. WEBB.　I don't know why on earth I should be crying. I suppose there's nothing to cry about. It came over me at breakfast this morning; there was Emily eating her breakfast as she's done for seventeen years and now she's going off to eat it in someone else's house. I suppose that's it. 170

And Emily! She suddenly said: I can't eat another mouthful, and she put her head down on the table and *she* cried. [*She starts toward her seat in the church, but turns back and adds:*] Oh, I've got to say it: you know, there's something downright cruel about sending our girls out into marriage this way.

I hope some of her girl friends have told her a thing or two. It's cruel, I know, but I couldn't bring myself to say anything. I went into it blind as a bat myself. [*In half-amused exasperation.*] The whole world's wrong, that's what's the matter. There they come.

[*She hurries to her place in the pew.* GEORGE *starts to come down the right aisle of the theatre, through the audience. Suddenly* THREE MEMBERS *of his baseball team appear by the right proscenium pillar and start whistling and catcalling to him. They are dressed for the ball field.*]

THE BASEBALL PLAYERS.   Eh, George, George! Hast—yaow! Look at him, fellas—he looks scared to death. Yaow! George, don't look so innocent, you old geezer. We know what you're thinking. Don't disgrace the team, big boy. Whoo-oo-oo.

STAGE MANAGER.   All right! All right! That'll do. That's enough of that.

[*Smiling, he pushes them off the stage. They lean back to shout a few more catcalls.*]

There used to be an awful lot of that kind of thing at weddings in the old days,—Rome, and later. We're more civilized now,—so they say.

[*The choir starts singing "Love Divine, All Love Excelling—." * GEORGE *has reached the stage. He stares at the congregation a moment, then takes a few steps of withdrawal, toward the right proscenium pillar. His mother, from the front row, seems to have felt his confusion. She leaves her seat and comes down the aisle quickly to him.*]

MRS. GIBBS.   George! George! What's the matter?
GEORGE.   Ma, I don't want to grow old. Why's everybody pushing me so?
MRS. GIBBS.   Why, George . . . you wanted it.   175
GEORGE.   No, Ma, listen to me—
MRS. GIBBS.   No, no, George,—you're a man now.
GEORGE.   Listen, Ma,—for the last time I ask you . . . All I want to do is be a fella—
MRS. GIBBS.   George! If anyone should hear you! Now stop. Why, I'm ashamed of you!
GEORGE.   [*He comes to himself and looks over the scene.*] What? Where's Emily!   180
MRS. GIBBS.   [*Relieved.*] George! You gave me such a turn.
GEORGE.   Cheer up, Ma. I'm getting married.
MRS. GIBBS.   Let me catch my breath a minute.
GEORGE.   [*Comforting her.*] Now, Ma, you save Thursday nights. Emily and I are coming over to dinner every Thursday night . . . you'll see. Ma, what are you crying for? Come on; we've got to get ready for this.

[*MRS. GIBBS, mastering her emotion, fixes his tie and whispers to him. In the meantime,* EMILY, *in white and wearing her wedding veil, has come through the audience and mounted onto the stage. She too draws back, frightened, when she sees the congregation in the church. The choir begins: "Blessed Be the Tie That Binds."*]

EMILY.   I never felt so alone in my whole life. And George over there, looking   185
so . . . ! I *hate* him. I wish I were dead. Papa! Papa!
MR. WEBB.   [*Leaves his seat in the pews and comes toward her anxiously.*] Emily! Emily! Now don't get upset.
EMILY.   But, Papa,—I don't want to get married.
MR. WEBB.   Sh-sh-Emily. Everything's all right.
EMILY.   Why can't I stay for a while just as I am? Let's go away,—
MR. WEBB.   No, no, Emily. Now stop and think a minute.   190
EMILY.   Don't you remember that you used to say,—all the time you used to say—all the time: that I was *your* girl! There must be lots of places we can go to. I'll work for you. I could keep house.

MR. WEBB.   Sh . . . You mustn't think of such things. You're just nervous, Emily. [*He turns and calls:*] George! George! Will you come here a minute? [*He leads her toward* GEORGE.] Why you're marrying the best young fellow in the world. George is a fine fellow.

EMILY.   But Papa,—

[*MRS. GIBBS returns unobtrusively to her seat. MR. WEBB has one arm around his daughter. He places his hand on GEORGE'S shoulder.*]

MR. WEBB.   I'm giving away my daughter, George. Do you think you can take care of her?

GEORGE.   Mr. Webb, I want to . . . I want to try. Emily, I'm going to do my best. I   195
love you, Emily. I need you.

EMILY.   Well, if you love me, help me. All I want is someone to love me.

GEORGE.   I will, Emily. Emily, I'll try.

EMILY.   And I mean for *ever*. Do you hear? For ever and ever.

[*They fall into each other's arms. The March from* Lohengrin *is heard. The STAGE MANAGER, as* CLERGYMAN, *stands on the box, up center.*]

MR. WEBB.   Come, they're waiting for us. Now you know it'll be all right. Come, quick.

[*GEORGE slips away and takes his place beside the STAGE MANAGER–CLERGYMAN. EMILY proceeds up the aisle on her father's arm.*]

STAGE MANAGER.   Do you, George, take this woman, Emily, to be your wedded wife,   200
to have . . .

[*MRS. SOAMES has been sitting in the last row of the congregation. She now turns to her neighbors and speaks in a shrill voice. Her chatter drowns out the rest of the clergyman's words.*]

MRS. SOAMES.   Perfectly lovely wedding! Loveliest wedding I ever saw. Oh, I do love a good wedding, don't you? Doesn't she make a lovely bride?

GEORGE.   I do.

STAGE MANAGER.   Do you, Emily, take this man, George, to be your wedded husband,—

[*Again his further words are covered by those of MRS. SOAMES.*]

MRS. SOAMES.   Don't know *when* I've seen such a lovely wedding. But I always cry. Don't know why it is, but I always cry. I just like to see young people happy, don't you? Oh, I think it's lovely.

[*The ring. The kiss. The stage is suddenly arrested into silent tableau. The STAGE MANAGER, his eyes on the distance, as though to himself.*]

STAGE MANAGER.   I've married over two hundred couples in my day. Do I believe in   205
it? I don't know. M . . . marries N . . . millions of them. The cottage, the go-cart, the Sunday-afternoon drives in the Ford, the first rheumatism, the grandchildren, the second rheumatism, the deathbed, the reading of the will,—

[*He now looks at the audience for the first time, with a warm smile that removes any sense of cynicism from the next line.*]

Once in a thousand times it's interesting.

—Well, let's have Mendelssohn's "Wedding March"!

[*The organ picks up the March. The BRIDE and GROOM come down the aisle, radiant, but trying to be very dignified.*]

MRS. SOAMES.   Aren't they a lovely couple? Oh, I've never been to such a nice wedding. I'm sure they'll be happy. I always say: *happiness*, that's the great thing! The important thing is to be happy.

[*The BRIDE and GROOM reach the steps leading into the audience. A bright light is thrown upon them. They descend into the auditorium and run up the aisle joyously.*]

STAGE MANAGER.   That's all the Second Act, folks. Ten minutes' intermission.

Curtain

ACT 3

[*During the intermission the audience has seen the STAGEHANDS arranging the stage. On the right-hand side, a little right of the center, ten or twelve ordinary chairs have been placed in three openly spaced rows facing the audience. These are graves in the cemetery. Toward the end of the intermission the ACTORS enter and take their places. The front row contains: toward the center of the stage, an empty chair; then MRS. GIBBS; SIMON STIMSON. The second row contains, among others, MRS. SOAMES. The third row has WALLY WEBB. The dead do not turn their heads or their eyes to right or left, but they sit in a quiet without stiffness. When they speak their tone is matter-of-fact, without sentimentality and, above all, without lugubriousness. The STAGE MANAGER takes his accustomed place and waits for the house lights to go down.*]

STAGE MANAGER.   This time nine years have gone by, friends—summer, 1913. Gradual changes in Grover's Corners. Horses are getting rarer. Farmers coming into town in Fords. Everybody locks their house doors now at night. Ain't been any burglars in town yet, but everybody's heard about 'em. You'd be surprised, though—on the whole, things don't change much around here.

This is certainly an important part of Grover's Corners. It's on a hilltop—a windy hilltop—lots of sky, lots of clouds,—often lots of sun and moon and stars. You come up here, on a fine afternoon and you can see range on range of hills—awful blue they are—up there by Lake Sunapee and Lake Winnipesaukee . . . and way up, if you've got a glass, you can see the White Mountains and Mt. Washington—where North Conway and Conway is. And, of course, our favorite mountain, Mt. Monadnock's right here—and all these towns that lie around it: Jaffrey, 'n East Jaffrey, 'n Peterborough, 'n Dublin; and

[*Then pointing down in the audience.*]

there, quite a ways down, is Grover's Corners. Yes, beautiful spot up here. Mountain laurel and li-lacks. I often wonder why people like to be buried in Woodlawn and Brooklyn when they might pass the same time up here in New Hampshire. Over there

[*Pointing to stage left.*]

are the old stones,—1670, 1680. Strong-minded people that come a long way to be independent. Summer people walk around there laughing at the funny words on the tombstones . . . it don't do any harm. And genealogists come up from Boston get paid by city people for looking up their ancestors. They want to make sure they're Daughters of the American Revolution and of the *Mayflower*. Well, I guess that don't do any harm, either. Wherever you come near the human race, there's layers and layers of nonsense . . .

Over there are some Civil War veterans. Iron flags on their graves . . . New Hampshire boys . . . had a notion that the Union ought to be kept together, though they'd never seen more than fifty miles of it themselves. All they knew was the name, friends—the United States of America. The United States of America. And they went and died about it.

This here is the new part of the cemetery. Here's your friend Mrs. Gibbs. 'N let me see—Here's Mr. Stimson, organist at the Congregational Church. And Mrs. Soames who enjoyed the wedding so—you remember? Oh, and a lot of others. And Editor Webb's boy, Wallace, whose appendix burst while he was on a Boy Scout trip to Crawford Notch.

Yes, an awful lot of sorrow has sort of quieted down up here. People just wild with grief have brought their relatives up to this hill. We all know how it is . . . and then time . . . and sunny days . . . and rainy days . . . 'n snow . . . We're all glad they're in a beautiful place and we're coming up here ourselves when our fit's over.

Now there are some things we all know, but we don't take'-m out and look at'm very often. We all know that *something is* eternal. And it ain't houses and it ain't names, and it ain't earth, and it ain't even the stars . . . everybody knows in their bones that *something is* eternal, and that something has to do with human beings. All the greatest people ever lived have been telling us that for five thousand years and yet you'd be surprised how people are always losing hold of it. There's something way down deep that's eternal about every human being.

[*Pause.*]

You know as well as I do that the dead don't stay interested in us living people for very long. Gradually, gradually, they lose hold of the earth . . . and the ambitions they had . . . and the pleasures they had . . . and the things they suffered . . . and the people they loved. They get weaned away from earth—that's the way I put it,—weaned away.

And they stay here while the earth part of em burns away, burns out; and all that time they slowly get indifferent to what's goin' on in Grover's Corners.

They're waitin'. They're waitin' for something that they feel is comin'. Something important, and great. Aren't they waitin' for the eternal part in them to come out clear? Some of the things they're going to say maybe'll hurt your feelings—but that's the way it is: mother'n daughter . . . husband 'n wife . . . enemy 'n enemy . . . money 'n miser . . . all those terribly important things kind of grow pale around here. And what's left when memory's gone, and your identity, Mrs. Smith?

[*He looks at the audience a minute, then turns to the stage.*]

Well! There are some *living* people. There's Joe Stoddard, our undertaker, supervising a new-made grave. And here comes a Grover's Corners boy, that left town to go out West.

[JOE STODDARD *has hovered about in the background.* SAM CRAIG *enters left, wiping his forehead from the exertion. He carries an umbrella and strolls front.*]

SAM CRAIG.   Good afternoon, Joe Stoddard.
JOE STODDARD.   Good afternoon, good afternoon. Let me see now: do I know you?
SAM CRAIG.   I'm Sam Craig.
JOE STODDARD.   Gracious sakes' alive! Of all people! I should'a knowed you'd be back for the funeral. You've been away a long time, Sam.
SAM CRAIG.   Yes, I've been away over twelve years. I'm in business out in Buffalo now, Joe. But I was in the East when I got news of my cousin's death, so I thought I'd combine things a little and come and see the old home. You look well.
JOE STODDARD.   Yes, yes, can't complain. Very sad, our journey today, Samuel.
SAM CRAIG.   Yes.

5

JOE STODDARD. Yes, yes. I always hate to supervise when a young person is taken. They'll be here in a few minutes now. I had to come here early today—my son's supervisin' at the home.

SAM CRAIG. [*Reading stones.*] Old Farmer McCarty, I used to do chores for him— after school. He had the lumbago.

JOE STODDARD. Yes, we brought Farmer McCarty here a number of years ago now.

SAM CRAIG. [*Staring at MRS. GIBBS's knees.*] Why, this is my Aunt Julia . . . I'd forgotten that she'd . . . of course, of course.

JOE STODDARD. Yes, Doc Gibbs lost his wife two—three years ago . . . about this time. And today's another pretty bad blow for him, too.

MRS. GIBBS. [*To SIMON STIMSON: in an even voice.*] That's my sister Carey's boy, Sam . . . Sam Craig.

SIMON STIMSON. I'm always uncomfortable when *they're* around.

MRS. GIBBS. Simon.

SAM CRAIG. Do they choose their own verses much, Joe?

JOE STODDARD. No . . . not usual. Mostly the bereaved pick a verse.

SAM CRAIG. Doesn't sound like Aunt Julia. There aren't many of those Hersey sisters left now. Let me see: where are . . . I wanted to look at my father's and mother's . . .

JOE STODDARD. Over there with the Craigs . . . Avenue F.

SAM CRAIG. [*Reading SIMON STIMSON's epitaph.*] He was organist at church, wasn't he?—Hm, drank a lot, we used to say.

JOE STODDARD. Nobody was supposed to know about it. He'd seen a peck of trouble. [*Behind his hand.*] Took his own life, y' know?

SAM CRAIG. Oh, did he?

JOE STODDARD. Hung himself in the attic. They tried to hush it up, but of course it got around. He chose his own epy-taph. You can see it there. It ain't a verse exactly.

SAM CRAIG. Why, it's just some notes of music—what is it?

JOE STODDARD. Oh, I wouldn't know. It was wrote up in the Boston papers at the time.

SAM CRAIG. Joe, what did she die of?

JOE STODDARD. Who?

SAM CRAIG. My cousin.

JOE STODDARD. Oh, didn't you know? Had some trouble bringing a baby into the world. 'Twas her second, though. There's a little boy 'bout four years old.

SAM CRAIG. [*Opening his umbrella.*] The grave's going to be over there?

JOE STODDARD. Yes, there ain't much more room over here among the Gibbses, so they're opening up a whole new Gibbs section over by Avenue B. You'll excuse me now. I see they're comin'.

[*From left to center, at the back of the stage, comes a procession. FOUR MEN carry a casket, invisible to us. All the rest are under umbrellas. One can vaguely see: DR. GIBBS, GEORGE, the WEBBS, etc. They gather about a grave in the back center of the stage, a little to the left of center.*]

MRS. SOAMES. Who is it, Julia?

MRS. GIBBS. [*Without raising her eyes.*] My daughter-in-law, Emily Webb.

MRS. SOAMES. [*A little surprised, but no emotion.*] Well, I declare! The road up here must have been awful muddy. What did she die of, Julia?

MRS. GIBBS. In childbirth.

MRS. SOAMES. Childbirth. [*Almost with a laugh.*] I'd forgotten all about that. My, wasn't life awful—[*With a sigh.*] and wonderful.

SIMON STIMSON. [*With a sideways glance.*] Wonderful, was it?

MRS. GIBBS.   Simon! Now, remember!

MRS. SOAMES.   I remember Emily's wedding. Wasn't it a lovely wedding! And I re-   40
member her reading the class poem at Graduation Exercises. Emily was one of the
brightest girls ever graduated from High School. I've heard Principal Wilkins say so time
after time. I called on them at their new farm, just before I died. Perfectly beautiful farm.

A WOMAN AMONG THE DEAD.   It's on the same road we lived on.

A MAN AMONG THE DEAD.   Yepp, right smart farm.

[*They subside. The group by the grave starts singing "Blessed Be the Tie That Binds."*]

A WOMAN AMONG THE DEAD.   I always liked that hymn. I was hopin' they'd sing
a hymn.

[*Pause. Suddenly EMILY appears from among the umbrellas. She is wearing a white dress. Her hair
is down her back and tied by a white ribbon like a little girl. She comes slowly, gazing wonderingly at
the dead, a little dazed. She stops halfway and smiles faintly. After looking at the mourners for a moment, she walks slowly to the vacant chair beside MRS. GIBBS and sits down.*]

EMILY.   [*To them all, quietly, smiling.*] Hello.

MRS. SOAMES.   Hello, Emily.   45

A MAN AMONG THE DEAD.   Hello, M's Gibbs.

EMILY.   [*Warmly.*] Hello, Mother Gibbs.

MRS. GIBBS.   Emily.

EMILY.   Hello. [*With surprise.*] It's raining.

[*Her eyes drift back to the funeral company.*]

MRS. GIBBS.   Yes . . . They'll be gone soon, dear. Just rest yourself.   50

EMILY.   It seems thousands and thousands of years since I . . . Papa remembered
that that was my favorite hymn.

Oh, I wish I'd been here a long time. I don't like being new here.—How do you do.
Mr. Stimson?

SIMON STIMSON.   How do you do, Emily.

[*EMILY continues to look about her with a wondering smile; as though to shut out from her mind the
thought of the funeral company she starts speaking to MRS. GIBBS with a touch of nervousness.*]

EMILY.   Mother Gibbs, George and I have made that farm into just the best place
you ever saw. We thought of you all the time. We wanted to show you the new barn and a
great long ce-ment drinking fountain for the stock. We bought that out of the money you
left us.

MRS. GIBBS.   I did?

EMILY.   Don't you remember, Mother Gibbs—the legacy you left us? Why, it was   55
over three hundred and fifty dollars.

MRS. GIBBS.   Yes, yes, Emily.

EMILY.   Well, there's a patent device on the drinking fountain so that it never overflows, Mother Gibbs, and it never sinks below a certain mark they have there. It's fine.
[*Her voice tails off and her eyes return to the funeral group.*]
It won't be the same to George without me, but it's a lovely farm. [*Suddenly she looks directly at MRS. GIBBS.*] Live people don't understand, do they?

MRS. GIBBS.   No, dear—not very much.

EMILY.   They're sort of shut up in little boxes, aren't they? I feel as though I knew
them last a thousand years ago . . . My boy is spending the day at Mrs. Carter's. [*She sees*

MR. CARTER *among the dead.*] Oh, Mr. Carter, my little boy is spending the day at your house.

MR. CARTER.   Is he?   60

EMILY.   Yes, he loves it there—Mother Gibbs, we have a Ford, too. Never gives any trouble. I don't drive, though. Mother Gibbs, when does this feeling go away?—Of being . . . one of *them?* How long does it . . . ?

MRS. GIBBS.   Sh! dear. Just wait and be patient.

EMILY.   [*With a sigh.*] I know—Look they're finished. They're going.

MRS. GIBBS.   Sh—.

[*The umbrellas leave the stage.* DR. GIBBS *has come over to his wife's grave and stands before it a moment.* EMILY *looks up at his face.* MRS. GIBBS *does not raise her eyes.*]

EMILY.   Look! Father Gibbs is bringing some of my flowers to you. He looks just   65
like George, doesn't he? Oh, Mother Gibbs, I never realized before how troubled and how . . . how in the dark live persons are. Look at him. I loved him so. From morning till night, that's all they are troubled.

[DR. GIBBS *goes off.*]

THE DEAD.   Little cooler than it was—Yes, that rain's cooled it off a little. Those northeast winds always do the same thing, don't they? If it isn't a rain, it's a three-day blow.

[*A patient calm falls on the stage. The* STAGE MANAGER *appears at his proscenium pillar, smoking.* EMILY *sits up abruptly with an idea.*]

EMILY.   But, Mother Gibbs, one can go back; one can go back there again . . . into living. I feel it. I know it. Why just then for a moment I was thinking about . . . about the farm . . . and for a minute I *was* there, and my baby was on my lap as plain as day.

MRS. GIBBS.   Yes, of course you can.

EMILY.   I can go back there and live all those days over again . . . why not?

MRS. GIBBS.   All I can say is, Emily, don't.   70

EMILY.   [*She appeals urgently to the* STAGE MANAGER.] But it's true, isn't it? I can go and live . . . back there . . . again.

STAGE MANAGER.   Yes, some have tried—but they soon come back here.

MRS. GIBBS.   Don't do it, Emily.

MRS. SOAMES.   Emily, don't. It's not what you think it'd be.

EMILY.   But I won't live over a sad day. I'll choose a happy one—I'll choose the day   75
I first knew that I loved George. Why should that be painful?

[THEY *are silent. Her question turns to the* STAGE MANAGER.]

STAGE MANAGER.   You not only live it; but you watch yourself living it.

EMILY.   Yes?

STAGE MANAGER.   And as you watch it, you see the thing that they—down there—never know. You see the future. You know what's going to happen afterwards.

EMILY.   But is that—painful? Why?

MRS. GIBBS.   That's not the only reason why you shouldn't do it, Emily. When   80
you've been here longer you'll see that our life here is to forget all that, and think only of what's ahead, and be ready for what's ahead. When you've been here longer you'll understand.

EMILY.   [*Softly.*] But, Mother Gibbs, how can I *ever* forget that life? It's all I know. It's all I had.

MRS. SOAMES.   Oh, Emily. It isn't wise. Really, it isn't.

EMILY.   But it's a thing I must know for myself. I'll choose a happy day, anyway.

MRS. GIBBS.   No!—At least, choose an unimportant day. Choose the least important day in your life. It will be important enough.

EMILY.   [*To herself*] Then it can't be since I was married; or since the baby was born. [*To the STAGE MANAGER, eagerly*] I can choose a birthday at least, can't I?—I choose my twelfth birthday. 85

STAGE MANAGER.   All right. February 11th, 1899. A Tuesday.—Do you want any special time of day?

EMILY.   Oh, I want the whole day.

STAGE MANAGER.   We'll begin at dawn. You remember it had been snowing for several days; but it had stopped the night before, and they had begun clearing the roads. The sun's coming up.

EMILY.   [*With a cry; rising.*] There's Main Street . . . why, that's Mr. Morgan's drugstore before he changed it! . . . And there's the livery stable.

[*The stage at no time in this act has been very dark; but now the left half of the stage gradually becomes very bright—the brightness of a crisp winter morning. EMILY walks toward Main Street.*]

STAGE MANAGER.   Yes, it's 1899. This is fourteen years ago. 90

EMILY.   Oh, that's the town I knew as a little girl. And, look, there's the old white fence that used to be around our house. Oh, I'd forgotten that! Oh, I love it so! Are they inside?

STAGE MANAGER.   Yes, your mother'll be coming downstairs in a minute to make breakfast.

EMILY.   [*Softly.*] Will she?

STAGE MANAGER.   And you remember: your father had been away for several days; he came back on the early-morning train.

EMILY.   No . . .? 95

STAGE MANAGER.   He'd been back to his college to make a speech—in western New York, at Clinton.

EMILY.   Look! There's Howie Newsome. There's our policeman. But he's *dead*; he *died*.

[*The voices of HOWIE NEWSOME, CONSTABLE WARREN and JOE CROWELL, JR., are heard at the left of the stage. EMILY listens in delight.*]

HOWIE NEWSOME.   Whoa, Bessie!—Bessie! 'Morning, Bill.

CONSTABLE WARREN.   Morning, Howie.

HOWIE NEWSOME.   You're up early. 100

CONSTABLE WARREN.   Been rescuin' a party; darn near froze to death, down by Polish Town thar. Got drunk and lay out in the snowdrifts. Thought he was in bed when I shook'm.

EMILY.   Why, there's Joe Crowell . . .

JOE CROWELL.   Good morning, Mr. Warren. 'Morning, Howie.

[*MRS. WEBB has appeared in her kitchen, but EMILY does not see her until she calls.*]

MRS. WEBB.   Chil-*dren!* Wally! Emily! . . . Time to get up!

EMILY.   Mama, I'm here! Oh! how young Mama looks! I didn't know Mama was ever that young. 105

MRS. WEBB.   You can come and dress by the kitchen fire, if you like; but hurry.

[*HOWIE NEWSOME has entered along Main Street and brings the milk to MRS. WEBB's door.*]

Good morning, Mr. Newsome. Whhhh—it's cold.

    HOWIE NEWSOME.   Ten below by my barn, Mrs. Webb.

    MRS. WEBB.   Think of it! Keep yourself wrapped up.

[*She takes her bottles in, shuddering.*]

    EMILY.   [*With an effort.*] Mama, I can't find my blue hair ribbon anywhere.

    MRS. WEBB.   Just open your eyes, dear, that's all. I laid it out for you special—on   110
the dresser, there. If it were a snake it would bite you.

    EMILY.   Yes, yes . . .

[*She puts her hand on her heart. MR. WEBB comes along Main Street, where he meets CONSTABLE
WARREN. Their movements and voices are increasingly lively in the sharp air.*]

    MR. WEBB.   Good morning, Bill.

    CONSTABLE WARREN.   Good morning, Mr. Webb. You're up early.

    MR. WEBB.   Yes, just been back to my old college in New York State. Been any trou-
ble here?

    CONSTABLE WARREN.   Well, I was called up this mornin' to rescue a Polish fella—   115
darn near froze to death he was.

    MR. WEBB.   We must get it in the paper.

    CONSTABLE WARREN.   'Twan't much.

    EMILY.   [*Whispers.*] Papa.

[*MR. WEBB shakes the snow off his feet and enters his house. CONSTABLE WARREN goes off, right.*]

    MR. WEBB.   Good morning, Mother.

    MRS. WEBB.   How did it go, Charles?   120

    MR. WEBB.   Oh, fine, I guess. I told'm a few things. Everything all right here?

    MRS. WEBB.   Yes—can't think of anything that's happened, special. Been right
cold. Howie Newsome says it's ten below over to his barn.

    MR. WEBB.   Yes, well, it's colder than that at Hamilton College. Students' ears are
falling off. It ain't Christian.—Paper have any mistakes in it?

    MRS. WEBB.   None that I noticed. Coffee's ready when you want it. [*He starts
upstairs.*] Charles! Don't forget; it's Emily's birthday. Did you remember to get her
something?

    MR. WEBB.   [*Patting his pocket.*] Yes, I've got something here. [*Calling up the stairs.*]   125
Where's my girl? Where's my birthday girl?

[*He goes off left.*]

    MRS. WEBB.   Don't interrupt her now, Charles. You can see her at breakfast. She's
slow enough as it is. Hurry up, children! It's seven o'clock. Now, I don't want to call you
again.

    EMILY.   [*Softly, more in wonder than in grief.*] I can't bear it. They're so young and
beautiful. Why did they ever have to get old? Mama, I'm here. I'm grown up. I love you
all, everything.—I can't look at everything hard enough.

[*She looks questioningly at the STAGE MANAGER, saying or suggesting: "Can I go in?" He nods
briefly. She crosses to the inner door to the kitchen, left of her mother, and as though entering the room,
says, suggesting the voice of a girl of twelve:*]

Good morning, Mama.

    MRS. WEBB.   [*Crossing to embrace and kiss her; in her characteristic matter-of-fact
manner.*] Well, now, dear, a very happy birthday to my girl and many happy returns. There
are some surprises waiting for you on the kitchen table.

EMILY.   Oh, Mama, you shouldn't have. [*She throws an anguished glance at the* STAGE
MANAGER.] I can't—I can't.

MRS. WEBB.   [*Facing the audience, over her stove.*] But birthday or no birthday, I want   130
you to eat your breakfast good and slow. I want you to grow up and be a good strong girl.

That in the blue paper is from your Aunt Carrie; and I reckon you can guess who
brought the postcard album. I found it on the doorstep when I brought in the milk—
George Gibbs . . . must have come over in the cold pretty early . . . right nice of him.

EMILY.   [*To herself.*] Oh, George! I'd forgotten that. . . .

MRS. WEBB.   Chew that bacon good and slow. It'll help keep you warm on a
cold day.

EMILY.   [*With mounting urgency.*] Oh, Mama, just look at me one minute as though
you really saw me. Mama, fourteen years have gone by. I'm dead. You're a grandmother,
Mama. I married George Gibbs, Mama. Wally's dead, too. Mama, his appendix burst on a
camping trip to North Conway. We felt just terrible about it—don't you remember? But,
just for a moment now we're all together. Mama, just for a moment we're happy. *Let's look
at one another.*

MRS. WEBB.   That in the yellow paper is something I found in the attic among your
grandmother's things. You're old enough to wear it now, and I thought you'd like it.

EMILY.   And this is from you. Why, Mama, it's just lovely and it's just what I wanted.   135
It's beautiful!

[*She flings her arms around her mother's neck. Her* MOTHER *goes on with her cooking, but is
pleased.*]

MRS. WEBB.   Well, I hoped you'd like it. Hunted all over. Your Aunt Norah
couldn't find one in Concord, so I had to send all the way to Boston. [*Laughing.*] Wally
has something for you, too. He made it at manual-training class and he's very proud of it.
Be sure you make a big fuss about it—Your father has a surprise for you, too; don't know
what it is myself. Sh—here he comes.

MR. WEBB.   [*Offstage.*] Where's my girl? Where's my birthday girl?

EMILY.   [*In a loud voice to the* STAGE MANAGER.] I can't. I can't go on. It goes so fast.
We don't have time to look at one another.

[*She breaks down sobbing. The lights dim on the left half of the stage.* MRS. WEBB *disappears.*]

I didn't realize. So all that was going on and we never noticed. Take me back—up
the hill—to my grave. But first: Wait! One more look.

Good-by, Good-by, world. Good-by, Grover's Corners . . . Mama and Papa. Good-by
to clocks ticking . . . and Mama's sunflowers. And food and coffee. And new-ironed dresses and hot baths . . . and sleeping and waking up. Oh, earth, you're too wonderful for
anybody to realize you.

[*She looks toward the* STAGE MANAGER *and asks abruptly, through her tears:*]

Do any human beings ever realize life while they live it—every, every minute?

STAGE MANAGER.   No. [*Pause.*] The saints and poets, maybe—they do some.

EMILY.   I'm ready to go back.   140

[*She returns to her chair beside* MRS. GIBBS. *Pause.*]

MRS. GIBBS.   Were you happy?

EMILY.   No . . . I should have listened to you. That's all human beings are! Just
blind people.

MRS. GIBBS.   Look, it's clearing up. The starts are coming out.

EMILY.   Oh, Mr. Stimson, I should have listened to them.

SIMON STIMSON.   [*With mounting violence; bitingly.*] Yes, now you know. Now you   145
know! That's what it was to be alive. To move about in a cloud of ignorance; to go up and
down trampling on the feelings of those . . . of those about you. To spend and waste time
as though you had a million years. To be always at the mercy of one self-centered passion,
or another. Now you know—that's the happy existence you wanted to go back to. Ignorance and blindness.

MRS. GIBBS.   [*Spiritedly.*] Simon Stimson, that ain't the whole truth and you know
it. Emily, look at that star. I forget its name.

A MAN AMONG THE DEAD.   My boy Joel was a sailor, knew 'em all. He'd set on the
porch evenings and tell 'em all by name. Yes, sir, wonderful!

ANOTHER MAN AMONG THE DEAD.   A star's mighty good company.

A WOMAN AMONG THE DEAD.   Yes. Yes, 'tis.

SIMON STIMSON.   Here's one of *them* coming.   150

THE DEAD.   That's funny. 'Tain't no time for one of them to be here.—Goodness
sakes.

EMILY.   Mother Gibbs, it's George.

MRS. GIBBS.   Sh, dear. Just rest yourself.

EMILY.   It's George.

[*GEORGE enters from the left, and slowly comes toward them.*]

A MAN FROM AMONG THE DEAD.   And my boy, Joel, who knew the stars—he used to   155
say it took millions of years for that speck o'light to git to the earth. Don't seem like a
body could believe it, but that's what he used to say—millions of years.

[*GEORGE sinks to his knees then falls full length at EMILY's feet.*]

A WOMAN AMONG THE DEAD.   Goodness! That ain't no way to behave!

MRS. SOAMES.   He ought to be home.

EMILY.   Mother Gibbs?

MRS. GIBBS.   Yes, Emily?

EMILY.   They don't understand, do they?   160

MRS. GIBBS.   No, dear. They don't understand.

[*The STAGE MANAGER appears at the right, one hand on a dark curtain which he slowly draws
across the scene. In the distance a clock is heard striking the hour very faintly.*]

STAGE MANAGER.   Most everybody's asleep in Grover's Corners. There are a few
lights on: Shorty Hawkins, down at the depot, has just watched the Albany train go by.
And at the livery stable somebody's setting up late and talking—Yes, it's clearing up.
There are the stars—doing their old, old crisscross journeys in the sky. Scholars haven't
settled the matter yet, but they seem to think there are no living beings up there. Just
chalk . . . or fire. Only this one is straining away, straining away all the time to make something of itself. The strain's so bad that every sixteen hours everybody lies down and gets a
rest. [*He winds his watch.*] Hm . . . Eleven o'clock in Grover's Corners—You get a good
rest, too. Good night.

The End

QUESTIONS

Act 1

1. What expositional details are found in the Stage Manager's extensive opening speech? Why does the Stage Manager tell us about the death of Dr. Gibbs, even before we see him on stage? What sort of person is the Stage Manager designed to be? How many roles does he take on in the course of the play?

2. Who is Joe Crowell, Jr.? Why do we learn about him and see him before the major characters appear on stage? Who is Howie Newsome? What does he do? Why do we see him at various later points in the play?

3. Is anything unusual happening in the Gibbs home when Dr. Gibbs enters? How do Julia Gibbs and Myrtle Webb get together to speak with each other? What kind of people are the Gibbses and the Webbs? Why are their names so close to each other in spelling and pronunciation?

4. What is the significance of the highboy owned by Mrs. Gibbs?

5. Why does the Stage Manager introduce Professor Willard and Mr. Webb to explain details about the town? What particular competence does Mr. Webb have to deal with the nature of Grover's Corners and statistical information about it?

6. What is accomplished by the brief question session of Act 1, speeches 126–138? Why do the actors in the audience raise apparently negative questions?

7. When Emily and George first meet on stage, what do we learn about them? Why does Emily talk immediately to her mother after George leaves? Why do they leave the stage when Act 1, speech 187 begins?

8. What is the purpose of the Stage Manager's discussion in Act 1, speech 187?

9. Why is there so much discussion about Simon Stimson, the choir director?

10. What is the significance of Rebecca's discussion of the address in Act 1, speeches 287–291? How is this address related to the play's third-act conclusion?

Act 2

11. Why does the Stage Manager discuss the importance of marriage?

12. What may be inferred from the report that George Gibbs is thinking of giving up baseball? From Act 2, speech 30, what do we learn is about to happen on this day, July 7, 1904? Why does "Mother Webb" not ask George to come into the Webb house?

13. What is funny about Mr. Webb's advice to George? What is the serious purpose of the humor?

14. Why does the Stage Manager stop the action of the day and go back a year in time? How do Emily and George discover that they are going to marry each other?

15. What does George's offer to give Mr. Morgan his gold watch show about him?

16. What is significant about the fact that both George and Emily are hesitant about their marriage just before the ceremony begins?

17. Why are the sounds of the marriage vows drowned out by the talking of Mrs. Soames?

18. Why does the Stage Manager, as the minister, discuss weddings and say, "Once in a thousand times it's interesting"?

Act 3

19. Describe the scene at the beginning of Act 3. How do the stage directions indicate that we are to know that the characters are dead? Why does the Stage Manager describe the location of the local cemetery? Why does he point out who is buried in the cemetery?

20. What does the Stage Manager mean by saying (Act 3, speech 1) that "we're coming up here ourselves when our fit's over"?

21. Why are Joe Stoddard and Sam Craig present in these early parts of Act 3? From what locations have they come?

22. How do we learn about the death of Emily (Act 3, speech 36)? What is Emily's main concern when she first talks to Mrs. Gibbs? What has happened as a result of the bequest from the sale of Mrs. Gibbs's highboy?

23. How does Emily conclude that "one can go back; one can go back there again"? Why does Mrs. Gibbs attempt to dissuade her from going back?

24. Why does Emily choose to go back to the day of her twelfth birthday? Whose voices does she first hear? What is unusual, or usual, about what happens to her on this day of return? Explain.

25. Why is Emily's urgent speech (Act 3, speech 133) ignored by her mother? What is the situation of Emily's return? Why does she say that she is ready to go back?

26. What does Emily conclude about her visit to the past? What is the meaning of her question to the Stage Manager (Act 3, speech 138)? What purpose is served by Simon Stimson's speech (Act 3, speech 145)?

27. Just before the play's end, why does "A Man from among the Dead" present information he acquired from his boy Joel (Act 3, speech 155)?

GENERAL QUESTIONS

1. What particular advantages accrue to the play because of the many various tasks performed by the Stage Manager, such as exposition, explanation and commentary, participation in the action, taking the role of a moderator or master of ceremonies, and so on? Why does the Stage Manager remain on stage even when he is not in a specific role? What do you think he does when other characters are holding the stage?

2. How closely does this play follow the structural pattern of exposition, complication, crisis, and resolution? Where is the crisis? The dénouement? How are the issues of the play resolved?

3. Who, if anyone, is the protagonist in *Our Town*? Who or what are the antagonists? What are the conflicts?

4. Some critics have decided that the play is not so much a play of realism but is rather an idealized pageant devoted to a view of American society that no longer exists, if it ever existed. To what degree is this view of the play accurate?

5. To what extent does *Our Town* rely on stereotypical or stock characters? If some of the characters are stereotypical, should that be counted as a defect? What evidence of the depth and variety of characters does Wilder present? What negative quality or qualities does he present?

6. Discuss the following quotation by Arthur Miller about the play's "informing principle," which, he states, is "the indestructibility, the everlastingness, of the

family and the community, its rhythm of life, its rootedness in the essentially safe cosmos despite troubles, wracks, and seemingly disastrous, but essentially temporary, dislocations."

7. Describe the language of the play as indicated by the many conversational suggestions for pronunciation and also by the many conversational idioms, such as "gotta lotta," "the hull town" rather than "the whole town," "y'know," "s'far," "awful bright," and "gettin" rather than "getting," and so on throughout the text.

TENNESSEE WILLIAMS, *THE GLASS MENAGERIE*

Tennessee Williams (1911–1983) grew up in Mississippi and Missouri, and many of his plays reflect the attitudes and customs that he encountered in his early years. Until he was eight, his family lived in genteel poverty, mostly in Columbus, Mississippi. In 1919 the family moved to a lower-class neighborhood in St. Louis. Williams, who was sickly and bookish, tried to escape from poverty and family conflicts by writing and going to the movies. One of his few companions during those years was his shy and withdrawn sister, Rose.

He entered the University of Missouri in 1931, but the Depression and family poverty forced him to drop out and go to work in a shoe warehouse. After two years of this work, he suffered a nervous collapse, but he finally finished college at the University of Iowa. He then began wandering the country, doing odd jobs and also writing. His first full-length play, Battle of Angels, *was produced in 1940 but was unsuccessful. He continued to write, however, and was able to get* The Glass Menagerie *staged in 1945. The critical and popular success of this play marked the beginning of many good years in the theater. Along with Arthur Miller, during the 1940s and 1950s Williams dominated the American stage, going on to write many one-act plays and more than fifteen full-length dramas (many of which became successful films), including* A Streetcar Named Desire *(1947, Pulitzer Prize),* The Rose Tattoo *(1951),* Cat on a Hot Tin Roof *(1955, Pulitzer Prize),* Suddenly Last Summer *(1958), and* The Night of the Iguana *(1961).*

The Glass Menagerie, written in 1944 and produced with favorable reviews in Chicago and New York in 1945, is a largely autobiographical play that explores the family dynamics, delusions, and personalities of the Wingfields. Williams originally developed his ideas for the play in a short story called "Portrait of a Girl in Glass" and then in a screenplay for Metro-Goldwyn-Mayer titled *The Gentleman Caller.* In these treatments as well as in *The Glass Menagerie,* Laura Wingfield is modeled after his sister, Rose Williams. The least competent member of the family, she is crippled by her own insecurity and her mother's expectations. At every opportunity, Laura withdraws into a world of glass figurines and old phonograph records left by her father when he abandoned the family. Amanda Wingfield is patterned after Williams's mother. She valiantly tries to hold the family together and provide for Laura's future, but her perspectives are skewed by her romanticized memories of a gracious Southern past of plantations, formal dances, and "gentleman callers." Tom, a figure based on the playwright himself, is desperate to escape the trap of his impoverished family. He seeks to emulate the long-missing father and move out of the drab Wingfield apartment into adventure and experience.

The play offers a fascinating mixture of realistic and nonrealistic dramatic techniques. The realistic elements are the characters (excluding Tom when he narrates) and the language. This is especially true of Amanda's language, in which Williams skillfully recreates the diction and cadences characteristic of the Deep South. As he points out in his production notes and stage directions, the play's structure and staging are nonrealistic. Williams employs various devices nonrealistically, including the narrator, music, lighting, and screen projections, to underscore the emotions of his characters and to explore ideas about family and personality.

One of Williams's most effective nonrealistic techniques in *The Glass Menagerie* is its structure as "a memory play," and therefore its illustration of how a first-person narrator can be used in a drama. The characters and the action are not real and they do not exist in the present. Rather, they represent Tom's memories and feelings about events that occurred approximately five years earlier, when America was in the grip of the Great Depression, when the Spanish Civil War had resulted in the imposition of a fascist dictatorship in Spain, and when World War II was beginning in Europe. As the narrator, Tom exists at the time of the action (1944), but the events he introduces are occurring in about 1939. When Tom becomes a character in the Wingfield household, he is the Tom of this earlier period, quite distinct from his identity as the present narrator. Thus, the action in the apartment is not strictly a realistic recreation of life. Instead, even though the actions and characters seem realistic, they are exaggerated and reshaped as Tom remembers them and regrets them.

TENNESSEE WILLIAMS (1911–1983)

The Glass Menagerie   1945

THE CHARACTERS

Amanda Wingfield (*the mother*)
A little woman of great but confused vitality clinging frantically to another time and place. Her characterization must be carefully created, not copied from type. She is not paranoiac, but her life is paranoia. There is much to admire in Amanda, and as much to love and pity as there is to laugh at. Certainly she has endurance and a kind of heroism, and though her foolishness makes her unwittingly cruel at times, there is tenderness in her slight person.

Laura Wingfield (*her daughter*)
Amanda, having failed to establish contact with reality, continues to live vitally in her illusions, but Laura's situation is even graver. A childhood illness has left her crippled, one leg slightly shorter than the other, and held in a brace. This defect need not be more than suggested on the stage. Stemming from this, Laura's separation increases till she is like a piece of her own glass collection, too exquisitely fragile to move from the shelf.

Tom Wingfield (*her son*)
And the narrator of the play. A poet with a job in a warehouse. His nature is not remorseless, but to escape from a trap he has to act without pity.

Jim O'Connor (*the gentleman caller*)
A nice, ordinary, young man.

PRODUCTION NOTES

Being a "memory play," *The Glass Menagerie* can be presented with unusual freedom of convention. Because of its considerably delicate or tenuous material, atmospheric touches and subtleties of direction play a particularly important part. Expressionism and all other unconventional techniques in drama have only one valid aim, and that is a closer approach to truth. When a play employs unconventional techniques, it is not, or certainly shouldn't be, trying to escape its responsibility of dealing with reality, or interpreting experience, but is actually or should be attempting to find a closer approach, a more penetrating and vivid expression of things as they are. The straight realistic play with its genuine Frigidaire and authentic ice-cubes, its characters who speak exactly as its audience speaks, corresponds to the academic landscape and has the same virtue of a photographic likeness. Everyone should know nowadays the unimportance of the photographic in art: that truth, life, or reality is an organic thing which the poetic imagination can represent or suggest, in essence, only through transformation, through changing into other forms than those which were merely present in appearance.

These remarks are not meant as a preface only to this particular play. They have to do with a conception of a new, plastic theatre which must take the place of the exhausted theatre of realistic conventions if the theatre is to resume vitality as a part of our culture.

THE SCREEN DEVICE: There is *only one important difference between the original and the acting version of the play* and that is the *omission* in the latter of the device that I tentatively included in my *original* script. This device was the use of a screen on which were projected magic-lantern slides bearing images or titles. I do not regret the omission of this device from the original Broadway production. The extraordinary power of Miss Taylor's° performance made it suitable to have the utmost simplicity in the physical production. But I think it may be interesting to some readers to see how this device was conceived. So I am putting it into the published manuscript. These images and legends, projected from behind, were cast on a section of wall between the front-room and dining-room areas, which should be indistinguishable from the rest when not in use.

The purpose of this will probably be apparent. It is to give accent to certain values in each scene. Each scene contains a particular point (or several) which is structurally the most important. In an episodic play, such as this, the basic structure or narrative line may be obscured from the audience; the effect may seem fragmentary rather than architectural. This may not be the fault of the play so much as a lack of attention in the audience. The legend or image upon the screen will strengthen the effect of what is merely allusion in the writing and allow the primary point to be made more simply and lightly than if the entire responsibility were on the spoken lines. Aside from this structural value, I think the screen will have a definite emotional appeal, less definable but just as important. An imaginative producer or director may invent many other uses for this device than those indicated in the present script. In fact the possibilities of the device seem much larger to me than the instance of this play can possibly utilize.

THE MUSIC: Another extra-literary accent in this play is provided by the use of music. A single recurring tune, "The Glass Menagerie,"° is used to give emotional emphasis to suitable passages. This tune is like circus music, not when you are on the grounds or in the immediate vicinity of the parade, but when you are at some distance and very likely thinking of something else. It seems under those circumstances to continue almost interminably and it weaves in and out of your preoccupied consciousness; then it is the lightest, most delicate music in the world and perhaps the saddest. It expresses the surface vivacity of life with the underlying strain of immutable and inexpressible sorrow. When you look at a piece of delicately spun glass you think of two things: how beautiful it

Miss Taylor's: The role of Amanda was first played by the American actress Laurette Taylor (1884–1946). *"The Glass Menagerie":* Original music, including this recurrent theme, was composed for the play by Paul Bowles.

is and how easily it can be broken. Both of those ideas should be woven into the recurring tune, which dips in and out of the play as if it were carried on a wind that changes. It serves as a thread of connection and allusion between the narrator with his separate point in time and space and the subject of his story. Between each episode it returns as reference to the emotion, nostalgia, which is the first condition of the play. It is primarily Laura's music and therefore comes out most clearly when the play focuses upon her and the lovely fragility of glass which is her image.

THE LIGHTING: The lighting in the play is not realistic. In keeping with the atmosphere of memory, the stage is dim. Shafts of light are focused on selected areas or actors, sometimes in contradistinction to what is the apparent center. For instance, in the quarrel scene between Tom and Amanda, in which Laura has no active part, the clearest pool of light is on her figure. This is also true of the supper scene, when her silent figure on the sofa should remain the visual center. The light upon Laura should be distinct from the others, having a peculiar pristine clarity such as light used in early religious portraits of female saints or madonnas. A certain correspondence to light in religious paintings, such as El Greco's,° where the figures are radiant in atmosphere that is relatively dusky, could be effectively used throughout the play. (It will also permit a more effective use of the screen.) A free, imaginative use of light can be of enormous value in giving a mobile, plastic quality to plays of a more or less static nature.

Tennessee Williams

SCENE 1

The Wingfield apartment is in the rear of the building, one of those vast hive-like conglomerations of cellular living-units that flower as warty growths in overcrowded urban centers of lower middle-class population and are symptomatic of the impulse of this largest and fundamentally enslaved section of American society to avoid fluidity and differentiation and to exist and function as one interfused mass of automatism.

The apartment faces an alley and is entered by a fire escape, a structure whose name is a touch of accidental poetic truth, for all of these huge buildings are always burning with the slow and implacable fires of human desperation. The fire escape is part of what we see—that is, the landing of it and steps descending from it.

The scene is memory and is therefore nonrealistic. Memory takes a lot of poetic license. It omits some details; others are exaggerated, according to the emotional value of the articles it touches, for memory is seated predominantly in the heart. The interior is therefore rather dim and poetic.

At the rise of the curtain, the audience is faced with the dark, grim rear wall of the Wingfield tenement. This building is flanked on both sides by dark, narrow alleys which run into murky canyons of tangled clotheslines, garbage cans, and the sinister latticework of neighboring fire escapes. It is up and down these side alleys that exterior entrances and exits are made during the play. At the end of TOM's opening commentary, the dark tenement wall slowly becomes transparent° and reveals the interior of the ground-floor Wingfield apartment.

Nearest the audience is the living room, which also serves as a sleeping room for LAURA, the sofa unfolding to make her bed. Just beyond, separated from the living room by a wide arch or second

---

El Greco: Greek painter (ca. 1548–1614) who lived in Spain; typical paintings have elongated and distorted figures and extremely vivid foreground lighting set against a murky background.   *transparent:* The wall is painted on a scrim, a transparent curtain that is opaque when lit from the front and transparent when lit from behind.

proscenium with transparent faded portieres° (or second curtain), is the dining room. In an old-fashioned whatnot° in the living room are seen scores of transparent glass animals. A blown-up photograph of the father hangs on the wall of the living room, to the left of the archway. It is the face of a very handsome young man in a doughboy's° First World War cap. He is gallantly smiling, ineluctably smiling, as if to say "I will be smiling forever."

Also hanging on the wall, near the photograph, are a typewriter keyboard chart and a Gregg shorthand diagram. An upright typewriter on a small table stands beneath the charts.

The audience hears and sees the opening scene in the dining room through both the transparent fourth wall of the building and the transparent gauze portieres of the dining-room arch. It is during this revealing scene that the fourth wall slowly ascends, out of sight. This transparent exterior wall is not brought down again until the very end of the play, during TOM's final speech.

The narrator is an undisguised convention of the play. He takes whatever license with dramatic convention is convenient to his purposes.

TOM enters, dressed as a merchant sailor, and strolls across to the fire escape. There he stops and lights a cigarette. He addresses the audience.

TOM.   Yes, I have tricks in my pocket, I have things up my sleeve. But I am the opposite of a stage magician. He gives you illusion that has the appearance of truth. I give you truth in the pleasant disguise of illusion.

To begin with, I turn back time. I reverse it to that quaint period, the thirties, when the huge middle class of America was matriculating in a school for the blind. Their eyes had failed them, or they had failed their eyes, and so they were having their fingers pressed forcibly down on the fiery Braille alphabet of a dissolving economy.

In Spain there was revolution. Here there was only shouting and confusion. In Spain there was Guernica.° Here there were disturbances of labor, sometimes pretty violent, in otherwise peaceful cities such as Chicago, Cleveland, Saint Louis. . . . This is the social background of the play.

[Music begins to play.]

The play is memory. Being a memory play, it is dimly lighted, it is sentimental, it is not realistic. In memory everything seems to happen to music. That explains the fiddle in the wings.

I am the narrator of the play, and also a character in it. The other characters are my mother, Amanda, my sister, Laura, and a gentleman caller who appears in the final scenes. He is the most realistic character in the play, being an emissary from a world of reality that we were somehow set apart from. But since I have a poet's weakness for symbols, I am using this character also as a symbol; he is the long-delayed but always expected something that we live for.

There is a fifth character in the play who doesn't appear except in this larger-than-life-size photograph over the mantel. This is our father who left us a long time ago. He was a telephone man who fell in love with long distances; he gave up his job with the telephone company and skipped the light fantastic out of town . . . .

---

portieres: curtains hung in a doorway; in production, these may also be painted on a scrim. whatnot: a small set of shelves for ornaments. doughboy: popular name for an American infantryman during World War I. Guernica: a Basque town that was destroyed in 1937 by German planes fighting on General Franco's side during the Spanish Civil War. The huge mural Guernica, painted by Pablo Picasso, depicts the horror of that bombardment. For a reproduction see Insert I-5.

Amanda—Past

The last we heard of him was a picture postcard from Mazatlan, on the Pacific coast of Mexico, containing a message of two words: "Hello—Goodbye!" and no address.

I think the rest of the play will explain itself. . . .

[*Amanda's voice becomes audible through the portieres.*]

[*Legend on screen: "Où sont les neiges."*] *— Where are the snows of yesteryear*

[*TOM divides the portieres and enters the dining room. AMANDA and LAURA are seated at a drop-leaf table. Eating is indicated by gestures without food or utensils. AMANDA faces the audience. TOM and LAURA are seated profile. The interior has lit up softly and through the scrim we see AMANDA and LAURA seated at the table.*]

AMANDA. [*calling*] Tom?
TOM. Yes, Mother.
AMANDA. We can't say grace until you come to the table!
TOM. Coming, Mother. [*He bows slightly and withdraws, reappearing a few moments later in his place at the table.*]   5
AMANDA. [*to her son*] Honey, don't *push* with your *fingers*. If you have to push with something, the thing to push with is a crust of bread. And chew—chew! Animals have secretions in their stomachs which enable them to digest food without mastication, but human beings are supposed to chew their food before they swallow it down. Eat food leisurely, son, and really enjoy it. A well-cooked meal has lots of delicate flavors that have to be held in the mouth for appreciation. So chew your food and give your salivary glands a chance to function!

[*Tom deliberately lays his imaginary fork down and pushes his chair back from the table.*]

TOM. I haven't enjoyed one bite of this dinner because of your constant directions on how to eat it. It's you that make me rush through meals with your hawklike attention to every bite I take. Sickening—spoils my appetite—all this discussion of—animals' secretion—salivary glands—mastication! *Chew*
AMANDA. [*lightly*] Temperament like a Metropolitan star.°

[*TOM rises and walks toward the living room.*]

You're not excused from the table.
TOM. I'm getting a cigarette.
AMANDA. You smoke too much.   10

[*LAURA rises.*]

LAURA. I'll bring in the blanc mange.°

[*TOM remains standing with his cigarette by the portieres.*] *Foot Note*

AMANDA. [*rising*] No, sister, no, sister°—you be the lady this time and I'll be the darky. *diction*
LAURA. I'm already up.

1.11 S.D.: *"Où sont les neiges":* "Where are the snows (of yesteryear)," refrain from "The Ballade of Dead Ladies" by the French poet François Villon (ca. 1431–1463).   8 *Metropolitan star:* the Metropolitan Opera in New York City; opera stars are traditionally considered to be highly temperamental.   11 *blanc mange:* a bland molded pudding or custard.   12 *sister:* In the South of Amanda's youth, the oldest daughter in a family was frequently called "sister" by her parents and siblings.

AMANDA.   Resume your seat, little sister—I want you to stay fresh and pretty—for gentlemen callers!

LAURA.   [*sitting down*] I'm not expecting any gentlemen callers.   15

AMANDA.   [*crossing out to the kitchenette, airily*] Sometimes they come when they are least expected! Why, I remember one Sunday afternoon in Blue Mountain°—

[*She enters the kitchenette.*]

TOM.   I know what's coming!

LAURA.   Yes. But let her tell it.

TOM.   Again?

LAURA.   She loves to tell it.   20

[*AMANDA returns with a bowl of dessert.*]

AMANDA.   One Sunday afternoon in Blue Mountain—your mother received—*seventeen!*—gentlemen callers! Why, sometimes there weren't chairs enough to accommodate them all. We had to send the nigger over to bring in folding chairs from the parish house.

TOM.   [*remaining at the portieres*] How did you entertain those gentlemen callers?

AMANDA.   I understood the art of conversation!

TOM.   I bet you could talk.

AMANDA.   Girls in those days *knew* how to talk, I can tell you.   25

TOM.   Yes?

[*Image on screen: AMANDA as a girl on a porch, greeting callers.*]

AMANDA.   They knew how to entertain their gentlemen callers. It wasn't enough for a girl to be possessed of a pretty face and a graceful figure—although I wasn't slighted in either respect. She also needed to have a nimble wit and a tongue to meet all occasions.

TOM.   What did you talk about?

AMANDA.   Things of importance going on in the world! Never anything coarse or common or vulgar.

[*She addresses TOM as though he were seated in the vacant chair at the table though he remains by the portieres. He plays this scene as though reading from a script.*°]

My callers were gentleman—all! Among my callers were some of the most prominent young planters of the Mississippi Delta—planters and sons of planters!

[*TOM motions for music and a spot of light on AMANDA. Her eyes lift, her face glows, her voice becomes rich and elegiac.*] expressing quiet nostalgia for past

[*Screen legend: "Où sont les neiges d'antan?"*°] Where are the snows of yesterday?

There was young Champ Laughlin who later became vice-president of the Delta Planters Bank. Hadley Stevenson who was drowned in Moon Lake and left his widow one hundred and fifty thousand in Government bonds. There were the Cutrere brothers, Wesley and Bates. Bates was one of my bright particular beaux! He got in a quarrel with

---

16 *Blue Mountain:* an imaginary town in northwest Mississippi modeled after Clarksville, where Williams spent much of his youth. Blue Mountain (Clarksville) is at the northern edge of the Mississippi Delta, a large fertile plain that supports numerous plantations. This is the recollected world of Amanda's youth—plantations, wealth, black servants, and gentlemen callers who were the sons of cotton planters. 29.1 S.D. *script:* Here Tom becomes both a character in the play and the stage manager. 29.2 S.D. *"Où sont les neiges d'antan?":* Where are the snows of yesteryear? See the note on p. 1679.

dead ladies of the past

that wild Wainwright boy. They shot it out on the floor of Moon Lake Casino. Bates was shot through the stomach. Died in the ambulance on his way to Memphis. His widow was also well provided-for, came into eight or ten thousand acres, that's all. She married him on the rebound—never loved her—carried my picture on him the night he died! And there was that boy that every girl in the Delta had set her cap for! That beautiful, brilliant young Fitzhugh boy from Greene County!

TOM.   What did he leave his widow?   30

AMANDA.   He never married! Gracious, you talk as though all of my old admirers had turned up their toes to the daisies!

TOM.   Isn't this the first you've mentioned that still survives?

AMANDA.   That Fitzhugh boy went North and made a fortune—came to be known as the Wolf of Wall Street! He had the Midas touch,° whatever he touched turned to gold! And I could have been Mrs. Duncan J. Fitzhugh, mind you! But—I picked your *father!*

LAURA.   [*rising*] Mother, let me clear the table.

AMANDA.   No, dear, you go in front and study your typewriter chart. Or practice   35
your shorthand a little. Stay fresh and pretty!—It's almost time for our gentlemen callers to start arriving. [*She flounces girlishly toward the kitchenette.*] How many do you suppose we're going to entertain this afternoon?

[*TOM throws down the paper and jumps up with a groan.*]

LAURA.   [*alone in the dining room*] I don't believe we're going to receive any, Mother.

AMANDA.   [*reappearing airily*] What? No one?—not one? You must be joking!

[*LAURA nervously echoes her laugh. She slips in a fugitive manner through the half-open portieres and draws them gently behind her. A shaft of very clear light is thrown on her face against the faded tapestry of the curtains. Faintly the music of "The Glass Menagerie" is heard as she continues lightly:*]

Not one gentleman caller? It can't be true! There must be a flood, there must have been a tornado!

LAURA.   It isn't a flood, it's not a tornado, Mother. I'm just not popular like you were in Blue Mountain. . . .

[*TOM utters another groan. LAURA glances at him with a faint, apologetic smile. Her voice catches a little:*]   *language of expression*

Mother's afraid I'm going to be an old maid.

[*The scene dims out with the "Glass Menagerie" music.*]

SCENE 2

On the dark stage the screen is lighted with the image of blue roses. Gradually LAURA's figure becomes apparent and the screen goes out. The music subsides.

LAURA is seated in the delicate ivory chair at the small clawfoot table. She wears a dress of soft violet material for a kimono—her hair is tied back from her forehead with a ribbon. She is washing and polishing her collection of glass. AMANDA appears on the fire escape steps. At the sound of her ascent, LAURA catches her breath, thrusts the bowl of ornaments away, and seats herself stiffly before the diagram of the typewriter keyboard as though it held her spellbound. Something has happened to AMANDA. It is written in her face as she climbs to the landing: a look that is grim and hopeless and

---

33 *Midas touch:* In Greek mythology, King Midas was given the power to turn everything he touched into gold.

a little absurd. She has on one of those cheap or imitation velvety-looking cloth coats with imitation fur collar. Her hat is five or six years old, one of those dreadful cloche hats that were worn in the late Twenties, and she is clutching an enormous black patent-leather pocketbook with nickel clasps and initials. This is her full-dress outfit, the one she usually wears to the D.A.R.° Before entering she looks through the door. She purses her lips, opens her eyes very wide, rolls them upward and shakes her head. Then she slowly lets herself in the door. Seeing her mother's expression, LAURA touches her lips with a nervous gesture.

LAURA.   Hello, Mother, I was—[*She makes a nervous gesture toward the chart on the wall. AMANDA leans against the shut door and stares at LAURA with a martyred look.*]

AMANDA.   Deception? Deception? [*She slowly removes her hat and gloves, continuing the sweet suffering stare. She lets the hat and gloves fall on the floor—a bit of acting.*]

LAURA.   [*shakily*] How was the D.A.R. meeting?

[*AMANDA slowly opens her purse and removes a dainty white handkerchief which she shakes out delicately and delicately touches to her lips and nostrils.*]

Didn't you go to the D.A.R. meeting, Mother?

AMANDA.   [*faintly, almost inaudibly*]—No.—No. [*then more forcibly:*] I did not have the strength—to go to the D.A.R. In fact, I did not have the courage! I wanted to find a hole in the ground and hide myself in it forever! [*She crosses slowly to the wall and removes the diagram of the typewriter keyboard. She holds it in front of her for a second, staring at it sweetly and sorrowfully—then bites her lips and tears it in two pieces.*]

LAURA.   [*faintly*] Why did you do that, Mother?   5

[*AMANDA repeats the same procedure with the chart of the Gregg Alphabet.*]

Why are you—

AMANDA.   Why? Why? How old are you, Laura?

LAURA.   Mother, you know my age.

AMANDA.   I thought you were an adult; it seems that I was mistaken. [*She crosses slowly to the sofa and sinks down and stares at LAURA.*]

LAURA.   Please don't stare at me, Mother.

[*AMANDA closes her eyes and lowers her head. There is a ten-second pause.*]

AMANDA.   What are we going to do, what is going to become of us, what is the   10
future?

[*There is another pause.*]

LAURA.   Has something happened, Mother?

[*AMANDA draws a long breath, takes out the handkerchief again, goes through the dabbing process.*]

Mother, has—something happened?

AMANDA.   I'll be all right in a minute, I'm just bewildered—[*She hesitates.*]—by life. . . .

LAURA.   Mother, I wish that you would tell me what's happened!

AMANDA.   As you know, I was supposed to be inducted into my office at the D.A.R. this afternoon.

[*Screen image: A swarm of typewriters.*]

0.2 *D.A.R.:* Daughters of the American Revolution, a patriotic women's organization (founded in 1890) open only to women whose ancestors aided the American Revolution.

But I stopped off at Rubicam's Business College to speak to your teachers about your having a cold and ask them what progress they thought you were making down there.

LAURA. Oh. . . .

AMANDA. I went to the typing instructor and introduced myself as your mother. She didn't know who you were.

"Wingfield," she said, "We don't have any such student enrolled at the school!"

I assured her she did, that you had been going to classes since early in January.

"I wonder," she said, "if you could be talking about that terribly shy little girl who dropped out of school after only a few days' attendance?"

"No," I said, "Laura, my daughter, has been going to school every day for the past six weeks!"

"Excuse me," she said. She took the attendance book out and there was your name, unmistakably printed, and all the dates you were absent until they decided that you had dropped out of school.

I still said, "No, there must have been some mistake! There must have been some mix-up in the records!"

And she said, "No—I remember her perfectly now. Her hands shook so that she couldn't hit the right keys! The first time we gave a speed test, she broke down completely—was sick at the stomach and almost had to be carried into the wash room! After that morning she never showed up any more. We phoned the house but never got any answer"—While I was working at Famous-Barr,° I suppose, demonstrating those—

[*She indicates a brassiere with her hands.*]

Oh! I felt so weak I could barely keep on my feet! I had to sit down while they got me a glass of water! Fifty dollars' tuition, all of our plans—my hopes and ambitions for you—just gone up the spout, just gone up the spout like that.

[*LAURA draws a long breath and gets awkwardly to her feet. She crosses to the Victrola and winds it up.*°] *no electrically*

What are you doing?

LAURA. Oh! [*She releases the handle and returns to her seat.*]

AMANDA. Laura, where have you been going when you've gone out pretending that you were going to business college?

LAURA. I've just been going out walking.

AMANDA. That's not true.

LAURA. It is. I just went walking.

AMANDA. Walking? Walking? In winter? Deliberately courting pneumonia in that light coat? Where did you walk to, Laura?

LAURA. All sorts of places—mostly in the park.

AMANDA. Even after you'd started catching that cold?

LAURA. It was the lesser of two evils, Mother.

[*Screen image: Winter scene in a park.*]

I couldn't go back there. I—threw up—on the floor!

15

20

25

16.8 *Famous-Barr:* a department store in St. Louis. 16.11 S.D. *winds it up:* Laura is using a spring-powered (rather than electric) phonograph that has to be rewound frequently. See the note on p. 283.

AMANDA.   From half past seven till after five every day you mean to tell me you walked around the park, because you wanted to make me think that you were still going to Rubicam's Business College?

LAURA.   It wasn't as bad as it sounds. I went inside places to get warmed up.

AMANDA.   Inside where?

LAURA.   I went in the art museum and the bird houses at the Zoo. I visited the penguins every day! Sometimes I did without lunch and went to the movies. Lately I've been spending most of my afternoons in the Jewel Box, that big glass house where they raise the tropical flowers.

AMANDA.   You did all this to deceive me, just for deception? [*LAURA looks down.*]   30
Why?

LAURA.   Mother, when you're disappointed, you get that awful suffering look on your face, like the picture of Jesus' mother in the museum!

AMANDA.   Hush!

LAURA.   I couldn't face it.

[*There is a pause. A whisper of strings is heard. Legend on screen: "The Crust of Humility."*]

AMANDA.   [*hopelessly fingering the huge pocketbook*] So what are we going to do the rest of our lives? Stay home and watch the parades go by? Amuse ourselves with the glass menagerie, darling? Eternally play those worn-out phonograph records your father left as a painful reminder of him? We won't have a business career—we've given that up because it gave us nervous indigestion! [*She laughs wearily.*] What is there left but dependency all our lives? I know so well what becomes of unmarried women who aren't prepared to occupy a position. I've seen such pitiful cases in the South—barely tolerated spinsters living upon the grudging patronage of sister's husband or brother's wife!— stuck away in some little mousetrap of a room—encouraged by one in-law to visit another—little birdlike women without any nest—eating the crust of humility all their life!

Is that the future that we've mapped out for ourselves? I swear it's the only alternative I can think of! [*She pauses.*] It isn't a very pleasant alternative, is it? [*She pauses again.*] Of course—some girls *do* marry.

[*LAURA twists her hands nervously.*]

Haven't you ever liked some boy?

LAURA.   Yes. I liked one once. [*She rises.*] I came across his picture a while ago.   35

AMANDA.   [*with some interest*] He gave you his picture?

LAURA.   No, it's in the yearbook.

AMANDA.   [*disappointed*] Oh—a high school boy.

[*Screen image: JIM as the high school hero bearing a silver cup.*]

LAURA.   Yes. His name was Jim. [*She lifts the heavy annual from the claw-foot table.*] Here he is in *The Pirates of Penzance.*°

AMANDA.   [*absently*] The what?   40

LAURA.   The operetta the senior class put on. He had a wonderful voice and we sat across the aisle from each other Mondays, Wednesdays and Fridays in the Aud. Here he is with the silver cup for debating! See his grin?

AMANDA.   [*absently*] He must have had a jolly disposition.

LAURA.   He used to call me—Blue Roses.

---

39 *The Pirates of Penzance:* a comic light opera (1879) by W. S. Gilbert and Arthur Sullivan.

[*Screen image: Blue roses.*]

AMANDA.   Why did he call you such a name as that?

LAURA.   When I had that attack of pleurosis—he asked me what was the matter   45
when I came back. I said pleurosis—he thought that I said Blue Roses! So that's what he
always called me after that. Whenever he saw me, he'd holler, "Hello, Blue Roses!"I did-
n't care for the girl that he went out with. Emily Meisenbach. Emily was the best-dressed
girl at Soldan. She never struck me, though, as being sincere. . . . It says in the Personal
Section—they're engaged. That's—six years ago! They must be married by now.

AMANDA.   Girls that aren't cut out for business careers usually wind up married to
some nice man. [*She gets up with a spark of revival.*] Sister, that's what you'll do!

[*LAURA utters a startled, doubtful laugh. She reaches quickly for a piece of glass.*]

LAURA.   But, Mother—

AMANDA.   Yes? [*She goes over to the photograph.*]

LAURA.   [*in a tone of frightened apology*] I'm—crippled!

AMANDA.   Nonsense! Laura, I've told you never, never to use that word.   50
Why, you're not crippled, you just have a little defect—hardly noticeable, even!
When people have some slight disadvantage like that, they cultivate other things to make
up for it—develop charm—and vivacity—and—*charm*! That's all you have to do! [*She
turns again to the photograph.*] One thing your father had *plenty of*—was *charm*!

[*The scene fades out with music.*]

SCENE 3

[*Legend on screen: "After the fiasco—"*]

TOM speaks from the fire escape landing.]

TOM.   After the fiasco at Rubicam's Business College, the idea of getting a gentleman caller for Laura began to play a more and more important part in Mother's calculations. It became an obsession. Like some archetype of the universal unconscious, the
image of the gentleman caller haunted our small apartment. . . .

[*Screen image: A young man at the door of a house with flowers.*]

An evening at home rarely passed without some allusion to this image, this specter, this
hope. . . . Even when he wasn't mentioned, his presence hung in Mother's preoccupied
look and in my sister's frightened, apologetic manner—hung like a sentence passed
upon the Wingfields!

Mother was a woman of action as well as words. She began to take logical steps in
the planned direction. Late that winter and in the early spring—realizing that extra
money would be needed to properly feather the nest and plume the bird—she conducted a vigorous campaign on the telephone, roping in subscribers to one of those magazines for matrons called *The Homemaker's Companion,* the type of journal that features the
serialized sublimations of ladies of letters who think in terms of delicate cuplike breasts,
slim, tapering waists, rich, creamy thighs, eyes like wood smoke in autumn, fingers that
soothe and caress like strains of music, bodies as powerful as Etruscan sculpture.

[*Screen image: The cover of a glamor magazine.*

AMANDA enters with the telephone on a long extension cord. She is spotlighted in the dim stage.]

AMANDA.   Ida Scott? This is Amanda Wingfield! We *missed* you at the D.A.R. last
Monday! I said to myself: She's probably suffering with that sinus condition! How is that
sinus condition?

Horrors! Heaven have mercy!—You're a Christian martyr, yes, that's what you are,
a Christian martyr!

Well, I just now happened to notice that your subscription to the *Companion's* about
to expire! Yes, it expires with the next issue, honey!—just when that wonderful new serial
by Bessie Mae Hopper is getting off to such an exciting start. Oh, honey, it's something
that you can't miss! You remember how *Gone with the Wind*° took everybody by storm? You
simply couldn't go out if you hadn't read it. All everybody *talked* was Scarlett O'Hara.
Well, this is a book that critics already compare to *Gone with the Wind*. It's the *Gone with the
Wind* of the post-World-War generation!—What?—Burning?—Oh, honey, don't let them
burn, go take a look in the oven and I'll hold the wire! Heavens—I think she's hung up!

[*The scene dims out.*]

[*Legend on screen: "You think I'm in love with Continental Shoemakers?"*]

[*Before the lights come up again, the violent voices of* TOM *and* AMANDA *are heard. They are quarreling behind the portieres. In front of them stands* LAURA *with clenched hands and panicky expression. A clear pool of light is on her figure throughout this scene.*]

TOM.   What in Christ's name am I—
AMANDA.   [*shrilly*] Don't you use that—
TOM.   —supposed to do!
AMANDA.   —expression! Not in my—   5
TOM.   Ohhh!
AMANDA.   —presence! Have you gone out of your senses?
TOM.   I have, that's true, *driven* out!
AMANDA.   What is the matter with you, you—big—big—IDIOT!   10
TOM.   Look!—I've got *no thing*, no single thing—
AMANDA.   Lower your voice!
TOM.   —in my life here that I can call my OWN! Everything is—
AMANDA.   Stop that shouting!
Tom.   Yesterday you confiscated my books! You had the nerve to—   15
AMANDA.   I took that horrible novel back to the library—yes! That hideous book
by that insane Mr. Lawrence.°

[*TOM laughs wildly.*]

I cannot control the output of diseased minds or people who cater to them—

[*TOM laughs still more wildly.*]

BUT I WON'T ALLOW SUCH FILTH BROUGHT INTO MY HOUSE! No, no, no, no, no!
TOM.   House, house! Who pays rent on it, who makes a slave of himself to—
AMANDA.   [*fairly screeching*] Don't you DARE to—
TOM.   No, no, *I* mustn't say things! *I've* got to just—
AMANDA.   Let me tell you—   20

2.3 *Gone with the Wind:* popular novel (1936) by Margaret Mitchell (1900–1949), set in the South
before, during, and after the Civil War. Scarlett O'Hara was the heroine. See p. 1737.   16 *Lawrence:* D. H.
Lawrence (1885–1930), English poet and fiction writer, popularly known as an advocate of passion and sexuality. See "The Horse Dealer's Daughter," pp. 478–89.

TOM.   I don't want to hear any more!

[*He tears the portieres open. The dining-room area is lit with turgid smoky red glow. Now we see* AMANDA; *her hair is in metal curlers and she is wearing a very old bathrobe, much too large for her slight figure, a relic of the faithless Mr. Wingfield. The upright typewriter now stands on the drop-leaf table, along with a wild disarray of manuscripts. The quarrel was probably precipitated by* AMANDA'*s interruption of* TOM'*s creative labor. A chair lies overthrown on the floor. Their gesticulating shadows are cast on the ceiling by the fiery glow.*]

AMANDA.   You *will* hear more, you—

TOM.   No, I won't hear more, I'm going out!

AMANDA.   You come right back in—

TOM.   Out, out, out! Because I'm—   25

AMANDA.   Come back here, Tom Wingfield! I'm not through talking to you!

TOM.   Oh, go—

LAURA.   [*desperately*]—Tom!

AMANDA.   You're going to listen, and no more insolence from you! I'm at the end of my patience!

[*He comes back toward her.*]

Tom.   What do you think I'm at? Aren't I supposed to have any patience to reach   30
the end of, Mother? I know, I know. It seems unimportant to you, what I'm *doing*—what I *want* to do—having a little *difference* between them! You don't think that—

AMANDA.   I think you've been doing things that you're ashamed of. That's why you act like this. I don't believe that you go every night to the movies. Nobody goes to the movies night after night. Nobody in their right minds goes to the movies as often as you pretend to. People don't go to the movies at nearly midnight, and movies don't let out at two A.M. Come in stumbling. Muttering to yourself like a maniac! You get three hours' sleep and then go to work. Oh, I can picture the way you're doing down there. Moping, doping, because you're in no condition.

TOM.   [*wildly*] No, I'm in no condition!

AMANDA.   What right have you got to jeopardize your job? Jeopardize the security of us all? How do you think we'd manage if you were—

TOM.   Listen! You think I'm crazy about the *warehouse*? [*He bends fiercely toward her slight figure.*] You think I'm in love with the Continental Shoemakers? You think I want to spend fifty-five *years* down there in that—*celotex interior!* with—*fluorescent—tubes!* Look! I'd rather somebody picked up a crowbar and battered out my brains—than go back mornings! I *go!* Every time you come in yelling that God damn *"Rise and Shine!"* *"Rise and Shine!"* I say to myself, "How *lucky dead* people are!" But I get up. I *go!* For sixty-five dollars a month I give up all that I dream of doing and being *ever!* And you say self—*self's* all I ever think of. Why, listen, if self is what I thought of, Mother, I'd be where he is—GONE! [*He points to his father's picture.*] As far as the system of transportation reaches! [*He starts past her. She grabs his arm.*] Don't grab at me, Mother!

AMANDA.   Where are you going?   35

TOM.   I'm going to the *movies!*

AMANDA.   I don't believe that lie!

[TOM *crouches toward her, overtowering her tiny figure. She backs away, gasping.*]

TOM.   I'm going to opium dens! Yes, opium dens, dens of vice and criminals' hangouts, Mother. I've joined the Hogan Gang,° I'm a hired assassin, I carry a tommy

---

38 *Hogan Gang:* one of the major criminal organizations in St. Louis in the 1930s.

gun in a violin case! I run a string of cat houses in the Valley! They call me Killer, Killer Wingfield, I'm leading a double life, a simple, honest warehouse worker by day, by night a dynamic *czar* of the *underworld, Mother.* I go to gambling casinos, I spin away fortunes on the roulette table! I wear a patch over one eye and a false mustache, sometimes I put on green whiskers. On those occasions they call me—*El Diablo!*° Oh, I could tell you many things to make you sleepless! My enemies plan to dynamite this place. They're going to blow us all sky-high some night! I'll be glad, very happy, and so will you! You'll go up, up on a broomstick, over Blue Mountain with seventeen gentlemen callers! You ugly—babbling old—*witch.* . . .

[*He goes through a series of violent, clumsy movements, seizing his overcoat, lunging to the door, pulling it fiercely open. The women watch him, aghast. His arm catches in the sleeve of the coat as he struggles to pull it on. For a moment he is pinioned by the bulky garment. With an outraged groan he tears the coat off again, splitting the shoulder of it, and hurls it across the room. It strikes against the shelf of LAURA's glass collection, and there is a tinkle of shattering glass. LAURA cries out as if wounded.*

Music.

Screen legend: "The Glass Menagerie."]

LAURA.   [*shrilly*] My glass!—menagerie. . . . [*She covers her face and turns away.*]

[*But AMANDA is still stunned and stupefied by the "ugly witch" so that she barely notices this occurrence. Now she recovers her speech.*]

AMANDA.   [*in an awful voice*] I won't speak to you—until you apologize!   40

[*She crosses through the portieres and draws them together behind her. TOM is left with LAURA. LAURA clings weakly to the mantel with her face averted. TOM stares at her stupidly for a moment. Then he crosses to the shelf. He drops awkwardly on his knees to collect the fallen glass, glancing at LAURA as if he would speak but couldn't.*

"The Glass Menagerie" music steals in as the scene dims out.]

SCENE 4

The interior of the apartment is dark. There is a faint light in the alley. A deep-voiced bell in a church is tolling the hour of five.

TOM appears at the top of the alley. After each solemn boom of the bell in the tower, he shakes a little noisemaker or rattle as if to express the tiny spasm of man in contrast to the sustained power and dignity of the Almighty. This and the unsteadiness of his advance make it evident that he has been drinking. As he climbs the few steps to the fire escape landing light steals up inside. LAURA appears in the front room in a nightdress. She notices that TOM's bed is empty. TOM fishes in his pockets for his door key, removing a motley assortment of articles in the search, including a shower of movie ticket stubs and an empty bottle. At last he finds the key, but just as he is about to insert it, it slips from his fingers. He strikes a match and crouches below the door.

TOM.   [*bitterly*] One crack—and it falls through!

[*LAURA opens the door.*]

LAURA.   Tom! Tom, what are you doing?
TOM.   Looking for a door key.

38 *El Diablo:* the devil.

LAURA.   Where have you been all this time?

TOM.   I have been to the movies.   5

LAURA.   All this time at the movies?

TOM.   There was a very long program. There was a Garbo° picture and a Mickey Mouse and a travelogue and a newsreel and a preview of coming attractions. And there was an organ solo and a collection for the Milk Fund—simultaneously—which ended up in a terrible fight between a fat lady and an usher!

LAURA.   [innocently] Did you have to stay through everything?

TOM.   Of course! And, oh I forgot! There was a big stage show! The headliner on this stage show was Malvolio° the Magician. He performed wonderful tricks, many of them, such as pouring water back and forth between pitchers. First it turned to wine and then it turned to beer and then it turned to whisky. I know it was whisky it finally turned into because he needed somebody to come up out of the audience to help him, and I came up—both shows! It was Kentucky Straight Bourbon. A very generous fellow, he gave souvenirs. [He pulls from his back pocket a shimmering rainbow-colored scarf.] He gave me this. This is his magic scarf. You can have it, Laura. You wave it over a canary cage and you get a bowl of goldfish. You wave it over the goldfish bowl and they fly away canaries. . . . But the wonderfullest trick of all was the coffin trick. We nailed him into a coffin and he got out of the coffin without removing one nail. [He has come inside.] There is a trick that would come in handy for me—get me out of this two-by-four situation! [He flops onto the bed and starts removing his shoes.]

LAURA.   Tom—shhh!   10

TOM.   What're you shushing me for?

LAURA.   You'll wake up Mother.

TOM.   Goody, goody! Pay 'er back for all those "Rise an' Shines." [He lies down, groaning.] You know it don't take much intelligence to get yourself into a nailed-up coffin, Laura. But who in hell ever got himself out of one without removing one nail?

[As if in answer, the father's grinning photograph lights up. The scene dims out.]

[Immediately following, the church bell is heard striking six. At the sixth stroke the alarm clock goes off in AMANDA's room, and after a few moments we hear her calling: "Rise and Shine! Rise and Shine! Laura, go tell your brother to rise and shine!"]

TOM.   [sitting up slowly] I'll rise—but I won't shine.

[The light increases.]

AMANDA.   Laura, tell your brother his coffee is ready.   15

[LAURA slips into the front room.]

LAURA.   Tom!—It's nearly seven. Don't make Mother nervous.

[He stares at her stupidly.]

[Beseechingly.] Tom, speak to Mother this morning. Make up with her, apologize, speak to her!

TOM.   She won't to me. It's her that started not speaking.

---

7 *Garbo:* Greta Garbo (1905–1990), Swedish star of American silent and early sound films. 9 *Malvolio:* the name, borrowed from a puritanical character in Shakespeare's *Twelfth Night*, means "malevolence" or "ill-will."

LAURA.   If you just say you're sorry she'll start speaking.

TOM.   Her not speaking—is that such a tragedy?

LAURA.   Please—please!   20

AMANDA.   [*calling from the kitchenette*] Laura, are you going to do what I asked you to do, or do I have to get dressed and go out myself?

LAURA.   Going, going—soon as I get on my coat!

[*She pulls on a shapeless felt hat with a nervous, jerky movement, pleadingly glancing at* TOM. *She rushes awkwardly for her coat. The coat is one of* AMANDA'S, *inaccurately made-over, the sleeves too short for* LAURA.]

Butter and what else?

AMANDA.   [*entering from the kitchenette*] Just butter. Tell them to charge it.

LAURA.   Mother, they make such faces when I do that.

AMANDA.   Sticks and stones can break our bones, but the expression on   25
Mr. Garfinkel's face won't harm us! Tell your brother his coffee is getting cold.

LAURA.   [*at the door*] Do what I asked you, will you, will you, Tom?

[*He looks sullenly away.*]

AMANDA.   Laura, go now or just don't go at all!

LAURA.   [*rushing out*] Going—going!

[*A second later she cries out.* TOM *springs up and crosses to the door.* TOM *opens the door.*]

TOM.   Laura?

LAURA.   I'm all right. I slipped, but I'm all right.   30

AMANDA.   [*peering anxiously after her*] If anyone breaks a leg on those fire-escape steps, the landlord ought to be sued for every cent he possesses! [*She shuts the door. Now she remembers she isn't speaking to* TOM *and returns to the other room.*]

[*As* TOM *comes listlessly for his coffee, she turns her back to him and stands rigidly facing the window on the gloomy gray vault of the areaway. Its light on her face with its aged but childish features is cruelly sharp, satirical as a Daumier print.*°
The music of "Ave Maria"° is heard softly.

TOM *glances sheepishly but sullenly at her averted figure and slumps at the table. The coffee is scalding hot; he sips it and gasps and spits it back in the cup. At his gasp,* AMANDA *catches her breath and half turns. Then she catches herself and turns back to the window.* TOM *blows on his coffee, glancing sidewise at his mother. She clears her throat.* TOM *clears his. He starts to rise, sinks back down again, scratches his head, clears his throat again.* AMANDA *coughs.* TOM *raises his cup in both hands to blow on it, his eyes staring over the rim of it at his mother for several moments. Then he slowly sets the cup down and awkwardly and hesitantly rises from the chair.*]

TOM.   [*hoarsely*] Mother. I—I apologize, Mother.

[AMANDA *draws a quick, shuddering breath. Her face works grotesquely. She breaks into childlike tears.*]

I'm sorry for what I said, for everything that I said, I didn't mean it.

31.2 S. D. *Daumier print:* Honoré Daumier (1808–1879), French painter and engraver whose prints frequently satirized his society.   31.3 S. D. *"Ave Maria":* a Roman Catholic prayer to the Virgin Mary; the musical setting called for here is by Franz Schubert (1797–1828).

AMANDA. [*sobbingly*] My devotion has made me a witch and so I make myself hateful to my children!

TOM. *No, you don't.*

AMANDA. I worry so much, don't sleep, it makes me nervous! 35

TOM. [*gently*] I understand that.

AMANDA. I've had to put up a solitary battle all these years. But you're my right-hand bower!° Don't fall down, don't fail!

TOM. [*gently*] I try, Mother.

AMANDA. [*with great enthusiasm*] Try and you will *succeed!* [*The notion makes her breathless.*] Why, you—you're just *full* of natural endowments! Both of my children—they're *unusual* children! Don't you think I know it? I'm so—*proud!* Happy and—feel I've—so much to be thankful for but—promise me one thing, son!

TOM. What, Mother? 40

AMANDA. Promise, son, you'll—never be a drunkard!

TOM. [*turns to her grinning*] I will never be a drunkard, Mother.

AMANDA. That's what frightened me so, that you'd be drinking! Eat a bowl of Purina!

TOM. Just coffee, Mother.

AMANDA. Shredded wheat biscuit? 45

TOM. No. No, Mother, just coffee.

AMANDA. You can't put in a day's work on an empty stomach. You've got ten minutes—don't gulp! Drinking too-hot liquids makes cancer of the stomach. . . . Put cream in.

TOM. No, thank you.

AMANDA. To cool it.

TOM. No! No, thank you, I want it black. 50

AMANDA. I know, but it's not good for you. We have to do all that we can to build ourselves up. In these trying times we live in, all that we have to cling to is—each other. . . . That's why it's so important to—Tom, I—I sent out your sister so I could discuss something with you. If you hadn't spoken I would have spoken to you. [*She sits down.*]

Tom. [*gently*] What is it, Mother, that you want to discuss?

AMANDA. *Laura!*

[*TOM puts his cup down slowly.*]

[*Legend on screen "Laura." Music: "The Glass Menagerie."*]

TOM. —Oh.—Laura . . .

AMANDA. [*touching his sleeve*] You know how Laura is. So quiet but—still water runs 55 deep! She notices things and I think she—broods about them.

[*TOM looks up.*]

A few days ago I came in and she was crying.

TOM. What about?

AMANDA. You.

TOM. Me?

AMANDA. She has an idea that you're not happy here.

TOM. What gave her that idea? 60

***

37 right-hand bower or **rightbower:** the Jack of trump in the card game *500*, the second-highest card (below the joker).

AMANDA.   What gives her any idea? However, you do act strangely.—I'm not criticizing, understand *that!* I know your ambitions do not lie in the warehouse, that like everybody in the whole wide world—you've had to—make sacrifices, but—Tom—Tom—life's not easy, it calls for—Spartan endurance! There's so many things in my heart that I cannot describe to you! I've never told you but I—*loved* your father. . . .

TOM.   [*gently*] I know that, Mother.

AMANDA.   And you—when I see you taking after his ways! Staying out late—and—well, you *had* been drinking the night you were in that—terrifying condition! Laura says that you hate the apartment and that you go out nights to get away from it! Is that true, Tom?

TOM.   No. You say there's so much in your heart that you can't describe to me. That's true of me, too. There's so much in my heart that I can't describe to *you!* So let's respect each other's—

AMANDA.   But, why—*why*, Tom—are you always so *restless?* Where do you *go* to,   65
nights?

TOM.   I—go to the movies.

AMANDA.   Why do you go to the movies so much, Tom?

TOM.   I go to the movies because—I like adventure. Adventure is something I don't have much of at work, so I go to the movies.

AMANDA.   But, Tom, you go to the movies *entirely* too *much!*

TOM.   I like a lot of adventure.   70

[*AMANDA looks baffled, then hurt. As the familiar inquisition resumes, TOM becomes hard and impatient again. Amanda slips back into her querulous attitude toward him.*

Image on screen: A sailing vessel with Jolly Roger.°]

AMANDA.   Most young men find adventure in their careers.

TOM.   Then most young men are not employed in a warehouse.

AMANDA.   The world is full of young men employed in warehouses and offices and factories.

TOM.   Do all of them find adventure in their careers?

AMANDA.   They do or they do without it! Not everybody has a craze for adventure.   75

TOM.   Man is by instinct a lover, a hunter, a fighter, and none of those instincts are given much play at the warehouse!

AMANDA.   Man is by instinct! Don't quote instinct to me! Instinct is something that people have got away from! It belongs to animals! Christian adults don't want it!

TOM.   What do Christian adults want, then, Mother?

AMANDA.   Superior things! Things of the mind and the spirit! Only animals have to satisfy instincts! Surely your aims are somewhat higher than theirs! Than monkeys—pigs—

TOM.   I reckon they're not.   80

AMANDA.   You're joking. However, that isn't what I wanted to discuss.

TOM.   [*rising*] I haven't much time.

AMANDA.   [*pushing his shoulders*] Sit down.

TOM.   You want me to punch in red° at the warehouse, Mother?

AMANDA.   You have five minutes. I want to talk about Laura.   85

70.3 S. D. *Jolly Roger*: the traditional flag of a pirate ship—a skull and crossbones on a field of black.   84 *punch in red*: arrive late for work; the time clock stamps late arrival times in red on the time card.

[*Screen legend: "Plans and Provisions."*]

TOM.   All right! What about Laura?

AMANDA.   We have to be making some plans and provisions for her. She's older than you, two years, and nothing has happened. She just drifts along doing nothing. It frightens me terribly how she just drifts along.

TOM.   I guess she's the type that people call home girls.

AMANDA.   There's no such type, and if there is, it's a pity! That is unless the home is hers, with a husband!

TOM.   What?   90

AMANDA.   Oh, I can see the handwriting on the wall as plain as I see the nose in front of my face! It's terrifying! More and more you remind me of your father! He was out all hours without explanation!—Then *left! Goodbye!* And me with the bag to hold. I saw that letter you got from the Merchant Marine. I know what you're dreaming of. I'm not standing here blindfolded. [*She pauses.*] Very well, then. Then *do* it! But not till there's somebody to take your place.

TOM.   What do you mean?

AMANDA.   I mean that as soon as Laura has got somebody to take care of her, married, a home of her own, independent—why, then you'll be free to go wherever you please, on land, on sea, whichever way the wind blows you! But until that time you've got to look out for your sister. I don't say me because I'm old and don't matter! I say for your sister because she's young and dependent.

I put her in business college—a dismal failure! Frightened her so it made her sick at the stomach. I took her over to the Young People's League at the church. Another fiasco. She spoke to nobody, nobody spoke to her. Now all she does is fool with those pieces of glass and play those worn-out records. What kind of a life is that for a girl to lead?

TOM.   What can I do about it?

AMANDA.   Overcome selfishness! Self, self, self is all that you ever think of!   95

[*TOM springs up and crosses to get his coat. It is ugly and bulky. He pulls on a cap with earmuffs.*]

Where is your muffler? Put your wool muffler on!

[*He snatches it angrily from the closet, tosses it around his neck and pulls both ends tight.*]

Tom! I haven't said what I had in mind to ask you.

TOM.   I'm too late to—

AMANDA.   [*catching his arm—very importunately; then shyly*] Down at the warehouse, aren't there some—nice young men?

TOM.   No!

AMANDA.   There *must* be—*some* . . .

TOM.   Mother—[*He gestures.*]   100

AMANDA.   Find out one that's clean-living—doesn't drink and ask him out for sister!

TOM.   What?

AMANDA.   For *sister!* To *meet!* Get *acquainted!*

TOM.   [*stamping to the door*] Oh, my *go-osh!*

AMANDA.   Will you? [*He opens the door. She says, imploringly:*] Will you?   105

[*He starts down the fire escape.*]

Will you? *Will* you, dear?

TOM.   [*calling back*] Yes!

[AMANDA *closes the door hesitantly and with a troubled but faintly hopeful expression.*

Screen image: The cover of a glamor magazine.

The spotlight picks up AMANDA *on the phone.*]

> AMANDA.   Ella Cartwright? This is Amanda Wingfield! How are you honey? How is
> that kidney condition?

[*There is a five-second pause.*]

Horrors!

[*There is another pause.*]

> You're a Christian martyr, yes, honey, that's what you are, a Christian martyr! Well,
> I just now happened to notice in my little red book that your subscription to the
> *Companion* has just run out! I knew that you wouldn't want to miss out on the wonderful
> serial starting in this new issue. It's by Bessie Mae Hopper, the first thing she's written
> since *Honeymoon for Three.* Wasn't that a strange and interesting story? Well, this one is
> even lovelier, I believe. It has a sophisticated, society background. It's all about the horsey
> set on Long Island!

[*The light fades out.*]

SCENE 5

[*Legend on the screen: "Annunciation."*

Music is heard as the light slowly comes on.

It is early dusk of a spring evening. Supper has just been finished in the Wingfield apartment.
AMANDA *and* LAURA, *in light-colored dresses, are removing dishes from the table in the dining room,
which is shadowy, their movements formalized almost as a dance or ritual, their moving forms as
pale and silent as moths.* TOM, *in white shirt and trousers, rises from the table and crosses toward the
fire escape.*]

> AMANDA.   [*as he passes her*] Son, will you do me a favor?
> TOM.   What?
> AMANDA.   Comb your hair! You look so pretty when your hair is combed!

[*Tom slouches on the sofa with the evening paper. Its enormous headline reads: "Franco
Triumphs."*°]

There is only one respect in which I would like you to emulate your father.

> TOM.   What respect is that?
> AMANDA.   The care he always took of his appearance. He never allowed himself to   5
> look untidy.

[*He throws down the paper and crosses to the fire escape.*]

Where are you going?

> TOM.   I'm going out to smoke.
> AMANDA.   You smoke too much. A pack a day at fifteen cents a pack. How much
> would that amount to in a month? Thirty times fifteen is how much, Tom? Figure it out

---

3.2 S. D. *"Franco Triumphs"*: Francisco Franco (1892–1975), dictator of Spain from 1939 until his
death, was the general of the victorious Falangist armies in the Spanish Civil War (1936–1939).

and you will be astounded at what you could save. Enough to give you a night-school course in accounting at Washington U.° ! Just think what a wonderful thing that would be for you, son!

[*Tom is unmoved by the thought.*]

> TOM.   I'd rather smoke. [*He steps out on the landing, letting the screen door slam.*]
> AMANDA.   [*sharply*] I know! That's the tragedy of it. . . . [*Alone, she turns to look at her husband's picture.*]

[*Dance music: "The World Is Waiting for the Sunrise!"°*]

> TOM.   [*to the audience*] Across the alley from us was the Paradise Dance Hall. On   10
> evenings in spring the windows and doors were open and the music came outdoors. Sometimes the lights were turned out except for a large glass sphere that hung from the ceiling. It would turn slowly about and filter the dusk with delicate rainbow colors. Then the orchestra played a waltz or a tango, something that had a slow and sensuous rhythm. Couples would come outside, to the relative privacy of the alley. You could see them kissing behind ash pits and telephone poles. This was the compensation for lives that passed like mine, without any change or adventure. Adventure and change were imminent in this year. They were waiting around the corner for all these kids. Suspended in the mist over Berchtesgaden,° caught in the folds of Chamberlain's umbrella. In Spain there was Guernica! But here there was only hot swing music and liquor, dance halls, bars, and movies, and sex that hung in the gloom like a chandelier and flooded the world with brief, deceptive rainbows. . . . All the world was waiting for bombardments!

[*AMANDA turns from the picture and comes outside.*]

> AMANDA.   [*sighing*] A fire escape landing's a poor excuse for a porch. [*She spreads a newspaper on a step and sits down, gracefully and demurely as if she were settling into a swing on a Mississippi veranda.*] What are you looking at?
> TOM.   The moon.
> AMANDA.   Is there a moon this evening?
> TOM.   It's rising over Garfinkel's Delicatessen.
> AMANDA.   So it is! A little silver slipper of a moon. Have you made a wish on it yet?   15
> TOM.   Um-hum.
> AMANDA.   What did you wish for?
> TOM.   That's a secret.
> AMANDA.   A secret, huh? Well, I won't tell mine either. I will be just as mysterious as you.
> TOM.   I bet I can guess what yours is.   20
> AMANDA.   Is my head so transparent?

---

7 *Washington U:* Washington University, a highly competitive liberal arts school in St. Louis. 9.1 S. D. *"The World . . . Sunrise":* popular song written in 1919 by Eugene Lockhart and Ernest Seitz. 10 *Berchtesgaden . . . Guernica:* The three names mentioned are all foreshadowings of World War II. Berchtesgaden, a resort in the Bavarian Alps, was Adolf Hitler's favorite residence. Neville Chamberlain was the British prime minister who signed the Munich Pact with Hitler in 1938, allowing Nazi Germany to occupy parts of Czechoslovakia. Chamberlain, who always carried an umbrella, declared that he had ensured "peace in our time." The bombardment of Guernica during the Spanish Civil War made the name of the town synonymous with the horrors of war, and especially the killing of civilian women and children. (See p. 1678 and Insert I-5.)

Tom. You're not a sphinx.°

Amanda. No, I don't have secrets. I'll tell you what I wished for on the moon. Success and happiness for my precious children! I wish for that whenever there's a moon, and when there isn't a moon, I wish for it, too.

Tom. I thought perhaps you wished for a gentleman caller.

Amanda. Why do you say that? 25

Tom. Don't you remember asking me to fetch one?

Amanda. I remember suggesting that it would be nice for your sister if you brought home some nice young man from the warehouse. I think that I've made that suggestion more than once.

Tom. Yes, you have made it repeatedly.

Amanda. Well?

Tom. We are going to have one. 30

Amanda. *What?*

Tom. A gentleman caller!

[*The annunciation is celebrated with music.*

Amanda *rises.*

Image on screen: *A caller with a bouquet.*]

Amanda. You mean you have asked some nice young man to come over?

Tom. Yep. I've asked him to dinner.

Amanda. You really did? 35

Tom. I did!

Amanda. You did, and did he—*accept?*

Tom. He did!

Amanda. Well, well—well, well! That's—lovely!

Tom. I thought that you would be pleased. 40

Amanda. It's definite then?

Tom. Very definite.

Amanda. Soon?

Tom. Very soon.

Amanda. For heaven's sake, stop putting on and tell me some things, will you? 45

Tom. What things do you want me to tell you?

Amanda. *Naturally* I would like to know when he's *coming!*

Tom. He's coming tomorrow.

Amanda. *Tomorrow?*

Tom. Yep. Tomorrow. 50

Amanda. But, Tom!

Tom. Yes, Mother?

Amanda. Tomorrow gives me no time!

Tom. Time for what?

Amanda. Preparations! Why didn't you phone me at once, as soon as you asked 55
him, the minute that he accepted? Then, don't you see, I could have been getting ready!

Tom. You don't have to make any fuss.

---

22 *sphinx*: a mythological monster with the head of a woman and body of a lion, famous for her
riddles. See p. 945 and Chapter 27, pp. 1264 ff.

Amanda (Jessica Tandy) tries to charm the Gentleman Caller (John Heard) on behalf of her indifferent daugher Laura (Amanda Plummer) in the Eugene O'Neill Theater production of *The Glass Menagerie*, directed by John Dexter (1983–84).

AMANDA.   Oh, Tom, Tom, Tom, of course I have to make a fuss! I want things nice, not sloppy! Not thrown together. I'll certainly have to do some fast thinking, won't I?

TOM.   I don't see why you have to think at all.

AMANDA.   You just don't know. We can't have a gentleman caller in a pigsty! All my wedding silver has to be polished, the monogrammed table linen ought to be laundered! The windows have to be washed and fresh curtains put up. And how about clothes? We have to *wear* something, don't we?

TOM.   Mother, this boy is no one to make a fuss over!

AMANDA.   Do you realize he's the first young man we've introduced to your sister? It's terrible, disgraceful that poor little sister has never received a single gentleman caller! Tom, come inside! [*She opens the screen door.*]

TOM.   What for?

60

AMANDA.   I want to ask you some things.

TOM.   If you're going to make such a fuss, I'll call it off, I'll tell him not to come!

AMANDA.   You certainly won't do anything of the kind. Nothing offends people 65
worse than broken engagements. It simply means I'll have to work like a Turk! We won't
be brilliant, but we will pass inspection. Come on inside.

[*Tom follows her inside, groaning.*]

Sit down.

TOM.   Any particular place you would like me to sit?

AMANDA.   Thank heavens I've got that new sofa! I'm also making payments on a
floor lamp I'll have sent out! And put the chintz covers on, they'll brighten things up! Of
course I'd hoped to have these walls re-papered. . . . What is the young man's name?

Tom.   His name is O'Connor.

AMANDA.   That, of course, means fish°—tomorrow is Friday! I'll have that salmon
loaf—with Durkee's dressing! What does he do? He works at the warehouse?

TOM.   Of course! How else would I— 70

AMANDA.   Tom, he—doesn't drink?

TOM.   Why do you ask me that?

AMANDA.   Your father *did!*

TOM.   Don't get started on that!

AMANDA.   He *does* drink, then? 75

TOM.   Not that I know of!

AMANDA.   Make sure, be certain! The last thing I want for my daughter's a boy who
drinks!

TOM.   Aren't you being a little bit premature? Mr. O'Connor has not yet appeared
on the scene!

AMANDA.   But will tomorrow. To meet your sister, and what do I know about his
character? Nothing! Old maids are better off than wives of drunkards!

TOM.   Oh, my God! 80

AMANDA.   Be still!

TOM.   [*leaning forward to whisper*] Lots of fellows meet girls whom they don't marry!

AMANDA.   Oh, talk sensibly, Tom—and don't be sarcastic! [*She has gotten a
hairbrush.*]

TOM.   What are you doing?

A*manda.*   I'm brushing that cowlick down! [*She attacks his hair with the brush.*] What 85
is this young man's position at the warehouse?

TOM.   [*submitting grimly to the brush and the interrogation*] This young man's position
is that of a shipping clerk, Mother.

AMANDA.   Sounds to me like a fairly responsible job, the sort of job *you* would be in
if you just had more *get-up.* What is his salary? Have you any idea?

TOM.   I would judge it to be approximately eighty-five dollars a month.

AMANDA.   Well—not princely, but—

TOM.   Twenty more than I make. 90

AMANDA.   Yes, how well I know! But for a family man, eighty-five dollars a month is
not much more than you can just get by on. . . .

TOM.   Yes, but Mr. O'Connor is not a family man.

AMANDA.   He might be, mightn't he? Some time in the future?

---

69 *fish*: Amanda assumes that O'Connor is Catholic. Until the 1960s, Roman Catholics were required
by the church to abstain from meat on Fridays.

limited Vision

relationship or *Truth*

TOM.   I see. Plans and provisions.

AMANDA.   You are the only young man that I know of who ignores the fact that the   95
future becomes the present, the present the past, and the past turns into everlasting regret if you don't plan for it!

TOM.   I will think that over and see what I can make of it.

AMANDA.   Don't be supercilious with your mother! Tell me some more about
this—what do you call him?

TOM.   James D. O'Connor. The D. is for Delaney.

AMANDA.   Irish on *both* sides! *Gracious!* And he doesn't drink?

TOM.   Shall I call him up and ask him right this minute?   100

AMANDA.   The only way to find out about those things is to make discreet inquiries
at the proper moment. When I was a girl in Blue Mountain and it was suspected that a
young man drank, the girl whose attentions he had been receiving, if any girl *was*, would
sometimes speak to the minister of his church, or rather her father would if her father
was living, and sort of feel him out on the young man's character. That is the way such
things are discreetly handled to keep a young woman from making a tragic mistake!

TOM.   Then how did you happen to make a tragic mistake?

AMANDA.   That innocent look of your father's had everyone fooled! He *smiled*—
the world was *enchanted!* No girl can do worse than put herself at the mercy of a handsome appearance! I hope that Mr. O'Connor is not too good-looking.

TOM.   No, he's not too good-looking. He's covered with freckles and hasn't too
much of a nose.

AMANDA.   He's not right-down homely, though?   105

TOM.   Not right-down homely. Just medium homely, I'd say.

AMANDA.   Character's what to look for in a man.

TOM.   That's what I've always said, Mother.

AMANDA.   You've never said anything of the kind and I suspect you would never
give it a thought.

TOM.   Don't be so suspicious of me.   110

AMANDA.   At least I hope he's the type that's up and coming.

TOM.   I think he really goes in for self-improvement.

AMANDA.   What reason have you to think so?

TOM.   He goes to night school.

AMANDA.   [*beaming*] Splendid! What does he do, I mean study?   115

TOM.   Radio engineering and public speaking!

AMANDA.   Then he has visions of being advanced in the world! Any young man
who studies public speaking is aiming to have an executive job some day! And radio engineering? A thing for the future! Both of these facts are very illuminating. Those are the
sort of things that a mother should know concerning any young man who comes to call
on her daughter. Seriously or—not.

TOM.   One little warning. He doesn't know about Laura. I didn't let on that we
had dark ulterior motives. I just said, why don't you come and have dinner with us? He
said okay and that was the whole conversation.

AMANDA.   I bet it was! You're eloquent as an oyster. However, he'll know about
Laura when he gets here. When he sees how lovely and sweet and pretty she is, he'll
thank his lucky stars he was asked to dinner.

TOM.   Mother, you mustn't expect too much of Laura.   120

AMANDA.   What do you mean?

TOM.   Laura seems all those things to you and me because she's ours and we love
her. We don't even notice she's crippled any more.

AMANDA.   Don't say crippled! You know that I never allow that word to be used!

TOM.   But face facts, Mother. She is and—that's not all—

AMANDA.   What do you mean "not all"?   125

TOM.   Laura is very different from other girls.

AMANDA.   I think the difference is all to her advantage.

TOM.   Not quite all—in the eyes of others—strangers—she's terribly shy and lives in a world of her own and those things make her seem a little peculiar to people outside the house.

AMANDA.   Don't say peculiar.

TOM.   Face the facts. She is.   130

[*The dance hall music changes to a tango that has a minor and somewhat ominous tone.*]

AMANDA.   In what way is she peculiar—may I ask?

TOM.   [*gently*] She lives in a world of her own—a world of little glass ornaments, Mother. . . .

[*He gets up. AMANDA remains holding the brush, looking at him, troubled.*]

She plays old phonograph records and—that's about all—[*He glances at himself in the mirror and crosses to the door.*]

AMANDA.   [*sharply*] Where are you going?

TOM.   I'm going to the movies. [*He goes out the screen door.*]

AMANDA.   Not to the movies, every night to the movies! [*She follows quickly to the   135
screen door.*] I don't believe you always go to the movies!

[*He is gone. AMANDA looks worriedly after him for a moment. Then vitality and optimism return and she turns from the door, crossing to the portieres.*]

Laura! Laura!

[*LAURA answers from the kitchenette.*]

LAURA.   Yes, Mother.

AMANDA.   Let those dishes go and come in front!

[*LAURA appears with a dish towel. AMANDA speaks to her gaily.*]

Laura, come here and make a wish on the moon!

[*Screen image: The Moon.*]

LAURA.   [*entering*] Moon—moon?

AMANDA.   A little silver slipper of a moon. Look over your left shoulder, Laura, and make a wish!

[*LAURA looks faintly puzzled as if called out of sleep. AMANDA seizes her shoulders and turns her at an angle by the door.*]

Now! Now, darling, *wish!*

LAURA.   What shall I wish for, Mother?   140

AMANDA.   [*her voice trembling and her eyes suddenly filling with tears*] Happiness! Good fortune!

[*The sound of the violin rises and the stage dims out.*]

SCENE 6

[*The light comes up on the fire escape landing. Tom is leaning against the grill, smoking. Screen image: The high school hero.*]

TOM. And so the following evening I brought Jim home to dinner. I had known Jim slightly in high school. In high school Jim was a hero. He had tremendous Irish good nature and vitality with the scrubbed and polished look of white chinaware. He seemed to move in a continual spotlight. He was a star in basketball, captain of the debating club, president of the senior class and the glee club and he sang the male lead in the annual light operas. He was always running or bounding, never just walking. He seemed always at the point of defeating the law of gravity. He was shooting with such velocity through his adolescence that you would logically expect him to arrive at nothing short of the White House by the time he was thirty. But Jim apparently ran into more interference after his graduation from Soldan. His speed had definitely slowed. Six years after he left high school he was holding a job that wasn't much better than mine.

[*Screen image: The Clerk.*]

He was the only one at the warehouse with whom I was on friendly terms. I was valuable to him as someone who could remember his former glory, who had seen him win basketball games and the silver cup in debating. He knew of my secret practice of retiring to a cabinet of the washroom to work on poems when business was slack in the warehouse. He called me Shakespeare. And while the other boys in the warehouse regarded me with suspicious hostility, Jim took a humorous attitude toward me. Gradually his attitude affected the others, their hostility wore off and they also began to smile at me as people smile at an oddly fashioned dog who trots across their path at some distance.

I knew that Jim and Laura had known each other at Soldan, and I had heard Laura speak admiringly of his voice. I didn't know if Jim remembered her or not. In high school Laura had been as unobtrusive as Jim had been astonishing. If he did remember Laura, it was not as my sister, for when I asked him to dinner, he grinned and said, "You know, Shakespeare, I never thought of you as having folks!"

He was about to discover that I did. . . .

[*Legend on screen: "The accent of a coming foot."*]

[*The light dims out on Tom and comes up in the Wingfield living room—a delicate lemony light. It is about five on a Friday evening of late spring which comes "scattering poems in the sky."*

AMANDA has worked like a Turk in preparation for the gentleman caller. The results are astonishing. The new floor lamp with its rose silk shade is in place, a colored paper lantern conceals the broken light fixture in the ceiling, new billowing white curtains are at the windows, chintz covers are on the chairs and sofa, a pair of new sofa pillows make their initial appearance. Open boxes and tissue paper are scattered on the floor.

LAURA stands in the middle of the room with lifted arms while AMANDA crouches before her, adjusting the hem of a new dress, devout and ritualistic. The dress is colored and designed by memory. The arrangement of LAURA's hair is changed; it is softer and more becoming. A fragile, unearthly prettiness has come out in LAURA: she is like a piece of translucent glass touched by light, given a momentary radiance, not actual, not lasting.]

AMANDA. [*impatiently*] Why are you trembling?
LAURA. Mother, you've made me so nervous!
AMANDA. How have I made you nervous?

LAURA.   By all this fuss! You make it seem so important!   5
AMANDA.   I don't understand you, Laura. You couldn't be satisfied with just sitting home, and yet whenever I try to arrange something for you, you seem to resist it. [*She gets up.*] Now take a look at yourself. No, wait! Wait just a moment—I have an idea!
LAURA.   What is it now?

[*AMANDA produces two powder puffs which she wraps in handkerchiefs and stuffs in LAURA's bosom.*]

LAURA.   Mother, what are you doing?
AMANDA.   They call them "Gay Deceivers"!
LAURA.   I won't wear them!   10
AMANDA.   You will!
LAURA.   Why should I?
AMANDA.   Because, to be painfully honest, your chest is flat.
LAURA.   You make it seem like we were setting a trap.
AMANDA.   All pretty girls are a trap, a pretty trap, and men expect them to be.   15

[*Legend on screen: "A pretty trap."*]

Now look at yourself, young lady. This is the prettiest you will ever be! [*She stands back to admire LAURA.*] I've got to fix myself now! You're going to be surprised by your mother's appearance!

[*AMANDA crosses through the portieres, humming gaily. LAURA moves slowly to the long mirror and stares solemnly at herself. A wind blows the white curtains inward in a slow, graceful motion and with a faint, sorrowful sighing.*]

AMANDA.   [*from somewhere behind the portieres*] It isn't dark enough yet.

[*LAURA turns slowly before the mirror with a troubled look.*

Legend on screen: "This is my sister: Celebrate her with strings!" Music plays.]

AMANDA.   [*laughing, still not visible*] I'm going to show you something. I'm going to make a spectacular appearance!
LAURA.   What is it, Mother?
AMANDA.   Possess your soul in patience—you will see! Something I've resurrected from that old trunk! Styles haven't changed so terribly much after all. . . . [*She parts the portieres.*] Now just look at your mother! [*She wears a girlish frock of yellowed voile with a blue silk sash. She carries a bunch of jonquils—the legend of her youth is nearly revived. Now she speaks feverishly:*] This is the dress in which I led the cotillion. Won the cakewalk twice at Sunset Hill, wore one Spring to the Governor's Ball in Jackson!° See how I sashayed around the ballroom, Laura? [*She raises her skirt and does a mincing step around the room.*] I wore it on Sundays for my gentlemen callers! I had it on the day I met your father. . . . I had malaria fever all that Spring. The change of climate from East Tennessee to the Delta—weakened resistance. I had a little temperature all the time—not enough to be serious—just enough to make me restless and giddy! Invitations poured in—parties all over the Delta! "Stay in bed," said Mother, "you have a fever!"—but I just wouldn't. I took quinine° but kept on going, going! Evenings, dances! Afternoons, long, long rides! Picnics—lovely! So

19 *Jackson:* capital of Mississippi. Amanda refers to the social events of her youth. A cotillion is a formal ball, often given for debutantes. The cakewalk is a strutting dance step.   *quinine:* long used as a standard drug to control malaria.

lovely, that country in May—all lacy with dogwood, literally flooded with jonquils! That was the spring I had the craze for jonquils. Jonquils became an absolute obsession. Mother said, "Honey, there's no more room for jonquils." And still I kept on bringing in more jonquils. Whenever, wherever I saw them, I'd say, "Stop! Stop! I see jonquils!" I made the young men help me gather the jonquils! It was a joke, Amanda and her jonquils. Finally there were no more vases to hold them, every available space was filled with jonquils. No vases to hold them? All right, I'll hold them myself! And then I—[*She stops in front of the picture. Music plays.*] met your father! Malaria fever and jonquils and then—this—boy. . . . [*She switches on the rose-colored lamp.*] I hope they get here before it starts to rain. [*She crosses the room and places the jonquils in a bowl on the table.*] I gave your brother a little extra change so he and Mr. O'Connor could take the service car home.

> LAURA.   [*with an altered look*] What did you say his name was?   20
> AMANDA.   O'Connor.
> LAURA.   What is his first name?
> AMANDA.   I don't remember. Oh, yes, I do. It was—Jim.

[*LAURA sways slightly and catches hold of a chair.*

Legend on screen: "Not Jim!"]

> LAURA.   [*faintly*] Not—Jim!
> AMANDA.   Yes, that was it, it was Jim! I've never known a Jim that wasn't nice!   25

[*The music becomes ominous.*]

> LAURA.   Are you sure his name is Jim O'Connor?
> AMANDA.   Yes. Why?
> LAURA.   Is he the one that Tom used to know in high school?
> AMANDA.   He didn't say so. I think he just got to know him at the warehouse.
> LAURA.   There was a Jim O'Connor we both knew in high school—[*Then, with*   30
> *effort.*] If that is the one that Tom is bringing to dinner—you'll have to excuse me, I won't come to the table.
> AMANDA.   What sort of nonsense is this?
> LAURA.   You asked me once if I'd ever liked a boy. Don't you remember I showed you this boy's picture?
> AMANDA.   You mean the boy you showed me in the yearbook?
> LAURA.   Yes, that boy.
> AMANDA.   Laura, Laura, were you in love with that boy?   35
> LAURA.   I don't know, Mother. All I know is I couldn't sit at the table if it was him!
> AMANDA.   It won't be him! It isn't the least bit likely. But whether it is or not, you will come to the table. You will not be excused.
> LAURA.   I'll have to be, Mother.
> AMANDA.   I don't intend to humor your silliness, Laura. I've had too much from you and your brother, both! So just sit down and compose yourself till they come. Tom has forgotten his key so you'll have to let them in, when they arrive.
> LAURA.   [*panicky*] Oh, Mother—*you* answer the door!   40
> AMANDA.   [*lightly*] I'll be in the kitchen—busy!
> LAURA.   Oh, Mother, please answer the door, don't make me do it!
> AMANDA.   [*crossing into the kitchenette*] I've got to fix the dressing for the salmon. Fuss, fuss—silliness!—over a gentleman caller!

[*The door swings shut, LAURA is left alone.*

Legend on screen: "Terror!"

She utters a low moan and turns off the lamp—sits stiffly on the edge of the sofa, knotting her fingers together.

Legend on screen: "The Opening of a Door!"

Tom *and* Jim *appear on the fire escape steps and climb to the landing. Hearing their approach,* Laura *rises with a panicky gesture. She retreats to the portieres. The doorbell rings.* Laura *catches her breath and touches her throat. Low drums sound.*]

> AMANDA.   [*calling*] Laura, sweetheart! The door!

[Laura *stares at it without moving.*]

> JIM.   I think we just beat the rain.   45
> TOM.   Uh-huh. [*He rings again, nervously.* Jim *whistles and fishes for a cigarette.*]
> AMANDA.   [*very, very gaily*] Laura, that is your brother and Mr. O'Connor! Will you let them in, darling?

[Laura *crosses toward the kitchenette door.*]

> LAURA.   [*breathlessly*] Mother—you go to the door!

[Amanda *steps out of the kitchenette and stares furiously at* Laura. *She points imperiously at the door.*]

> LAURA.   Please, please!
> AMANDA.   [*in a fierce whisper*] What is the matter with you, you silly thing?   50
> LAURA.   [*desperately*] Please, you answer it, *please!*
> AMANDA.   I told you I wasn't going to humor you, Laura. Why have you chosen this moment to lose your mind?
> LAURA.   Please, please, please, you go!
> AMANDA.   You'll have to go to the door because I can't.
> LAURA.   [*despairingly*] I can't either!   55
> AMANDA.   *Why?*
> LAURA.   I'm *sick!*
> AMANDA.   I'm sick, too—of your nonsense! Why can't you and your brother be normal people? Fantastic whims and behavior!

[Tom *gives a long ring.*]

Preposterous goings on! Can you give me one reason—[*She calls out lyrically.*] *Coming!* Just one second!—why you should be afraid to open a door? Now you answer it, Laura!

> LAURA.   Oh, oh, oh . . . [*She returns through the portieres, darts to the Victrola, winds it frantically and turns it on.*]
> AMANDA.   Laura Wingfield, you march right to that door!   60
> LAURA.   *Yes—yes, Mother!*

[*A faraway, scratchy rendition of "Dardanella"° softens the air and gives her strength to move through it. She slips to the door and draws it cautiously open.* Tom *enters with the caller,* Jim O'Connor.]

> TOM.   Laura, this is Jim. Jim, this is my sister, Laura.
> JIM.   [*stepping inside*] I didn't know that Shakespeare had a sister!

---

61 S.D. *"Dardanella":* a popular song and dance tune written in 1919 by Fred Fisher, Felix Bernard, and Johnny S. Black.

LAURA.   [*retreating, stiff and trembling, from the door*] How—how do you do?

JIM.   [*heartily, extending his hand*] Okay!   65

[*LAURA touches it hesitantly with hers.*]

JIM.   Your hand's *cold*, Laura!

LAURA.   Yes, well—I've been playing the Victrola. . . .

JIM.   Must have been playing classical music on it! You ought to play a little hot swing music to warm you up!

LAURA.   Excuse me—I haven't finished playing the Victrola. . . . [*She turns awkwardly and hurries into the front room. She pauses a second by the Victrola. Then she catches her breath and darts through the portieres like a frightened deer.*]

JIM.   [*grinning*] What was the matter?   70

TOM.   Oh—with Laura? Laura is—terribly shy.

JIM.   Shy, huh? It's unusual to meet a shy girl nowadays. I don't believe you ever mentioned you had a sister.

TOM.   Well, now you know. I have one. Here is the *Post Dispatch.°* You want a piece of it?

JIM.   Uh-huh.

TOM.   What piece? The comics?   75

JIM.   Sports! [*He glances at it.*] Ole Dizzy Dean° is on his bad behavior.

TOM.   [*uninterested*] Yeah? [*He lights a cigarette and goes over to the fire-escape door.*]

JIM.   Where are *you* going?

TOM.   I'm going out on the terrace.

JIM.   [*going after him*] You know, Shakespeare—I'm going to sell you a bill of goods!   80

TOM.   What goods?

JIM.   A course I'm taking.

TOM.   Huh?

JIM.   In public speaking! You and me, we're not the warehouse type.

TOM.   Thanks—that's good news. But what has public speaking got to do with it?   85

JIM.   It fits you for—executive positions!

TOM.   Awww.

JIM.   I tell you it's done a helluva lot for me.

[*Image on screen: Executive at his desk.*]

TOM.   In what respect?

JIM.   In every! Ask yourself what is the difference between you an' me and men in   90
the office down front? Brains?—No!—Ability?—No! Then what? Just one little thing—

TOM.   What is that one little thing?

JIM.   Primarily it amounts to—social poise! Being able to square up to people and hold your own on any social level!

AMANDA.   [*from the kitchenette*] Tom?

TOM.   Yes, Mother?

AMANDA.   Is that you and Mr. O'Connor?   95

TOM.   Yes, Mother.

AMANDA.   Well, you just make yourselves comfortable in there.

TOM.   Yes, Mother.

---

73 *Post Dispatch:* the *St. Louis Post Dispatch*, a newspaper.   **76** *Dizzy Dean:* Jerome Herman (or Jay Hanna) Dean (1911–1974), outstanding pitcher with the St. Louis Cardinals during the 1930s.

AMANDA.   Ask Mr. O'Connor if he would like to wash his hands.

JIM.   Aw, no—no—thank you—I took care of that at the warehouse. Tom—   100

TOM.   Yes?

JIM.   Mr. Mendoza was speaking to me about you.

TOM.   Favorably?

JIM.   What do you think?

TOM.   Well—   105

JIM.   You're going to be out of a job if you don't wake up.

TOM.   I am waking up—

JIM.   You show no signs.

TOM.   The signs are interior.

[*Image on screen: The sailing vessel with the Jolly Roger again.*]

TOM.   I'm planning to change. [*He leans over the fire escape rail, speaking with quiet ex-*   110
hilaration. The incandescent marquees and signs of the first-run movie houses light his face from
across the alley. He looks like a voyager.] I'm right at the point of committing myself to a future that doesn't include the warehouse and Mr. Mendoza or even a night-school course
in public speaking.

JIM.   What are you gassing about?

TOM.   I'm tired of the movies.

JIM.   Movies!

TOM.   Yes, movies! Look at them—[*a wave toward the marvels of Grand Avenue*] All
of those glamorous people—having adventures—hogging it all, gobbling the whole
thing up! You know what happens? People go to the *movies* instead of *moving!* Hollywood
characters are supposed to have all the adventures for everybody in America, while everybody in America sits in a dark room and watches them have them! Yes, until there's a war.
That's when adventure becomes available to the masses! *Everyone's* dish, not only
Gable's!° Then the people in the dark room come out of the dark room to have some adventures themselves—goody, goody! It's our turn now, to go to the South Sea Island—to
make a safari—to be exotic, far-off! But I'm not patient. I don't want to wait till then. I'm
tired of the *movies* and I am *about to move!*

JIM.   [*incredulously*] Move?   115

TOM.   Yes.

JIM.   When?

TOM.   Soon!

JIM.   Where? Where?

[*The music seems to answer the question, while TOM thinks it over. He searches in his pockets.*]

TOM.   I'm starting to boil inside. I know I seem dreamy, but inside—well, I'm boil-   120
ing! Whenever I pick up a shoe, I shudder a little thinking how short life is and what I am
doing! Whatever that means, I know it doesn't mean shoes—except as something to wear
on a traveler's feet! [*He finds what he has been searching for in his pockets and holds out a paper*
to JIM.] Look—

JIM.   What?

TOM.   I'm a member.

JIM.   [*reading*] The Union of Merchant Seamen.

TOM.   I paid my dues this month, instead of the light bill.

---

114 *Gable:* Clark Gable (1901–1960), popular American screen actor and matinee idol from the
1930s to his death.

JIM.   You will regret it when they turn off the lights.   125
TOM.   I won't be here.
JIM.   How about your mother?
TOM.   I'm like my father. The bastard son of a bastard! Did you notice how he's
grinning in his picture in there? And he's been absent going on sixteen years!
JIM.   You're just talking, you drip. How does your mother feel about it?
TOM.   Shhh! Here comes Mother! Mother is not acquainted with my plans!   130
AMANDA.   [*coming through the portieres*] Where are you all?
TOM.   On the terrace, Mother.

[*They start inside. She advances to them. TOM is distinctly shocked at her appearance. Even JIM
blinks a little. He is making his first contact with the girlish Southern vivacity and in spite of the
night-school course in public speaking is somewhat thrown off the beam by the unexpected outlay of
social charm. Certain responses are attempted by JIM but are swept aside by AMANDA's gay laughter
and chatter. TOM is embarrassed but after the first shock JIM reacts very warmly. He grins and chuckles, is altogether won over.*

Image on screen: AMANDA as a girl.]

AMANDA.   [*coyly smiling, shaking her girlish ringlets*] Well, well, well, so this is
Mr. O'Connor. Introductions entirely unnecessary. I've heard so much about you from
my boy. I finally said to him, Tom—good gracious!—why don't you bring this paragon to
supper? I'd like to meet this nice young man at the warehouse!—instead of just hearing
him sing your praises so much! I don't know why my son is so stand-offish—that's not
Southern behavior!
       Let's sit down and—I think we could stand a little more air in here! Tom, leave the
door open. I felt a nice fresh breeze a moment ago. Where has it gone to? Mmm, so warm
already! And not quite summer, even. We're going to burn up when summer really gets
started. However, we're having—we're having a very light supper. I think light things are
better fo' this time of year. The same as light clothes are. Light clothes an' light food are
what warm weather calls fo'. You know our blood gets so thick during th' winter—it takes
a while fo' us to *adjust* ourselves!—when the season changes. . . . It's come so quick this
year. I wasn't prepared. All of sudden—heavens! Already summer! I ran to the trunk an'
pulled out this light dress—terribly old! Historical almost! But feels so good—so good
an' co-ol, y'know. . . .
       TOM.   Mother—
       AMANDA.   Yes, honey?   135
       TOM.   How about—supper?
       AMANDA.   Honey, you go ask Sister if supper is ready! You know that Sister is in full
charge of supper! Tell her you hungry boys are waiting for it. [*To JIM.*] Have you met
Laura?
       JIM.   She—
       AMANDA.   Let you in? Oh, good, you've met already! It's rare for a girl as sweet an'
pretty as Laura to be domestic! But Laura is, thank heavens, not only pretty but also very
domestic. I'm not at all. I never was a bit. I never could make a thing but angel-food cake.
Well, in the South we had so many servants. Gone, gone, gone. All vestige of gracious living! Gone completely! I wasn't prepared for what the future brought me. All of my gentlemen callers were sons of planters and so of course I assumed that I would be married
to one and raise my family on a large piece of land with plenty of servants. But man proposes—and woman accepts the proposal! to vary that old, old saying a little but—I married no planter! I married a man who worked for the telephone company! That gallantly
smiling gentleman over there! [*She points to the picture.*] A telephone man who—fell in

love with long-distance! Now he travels and I don't even know where! But what am I going on for about my—tribulations? Tell me yours—I hope you don't have any! Tom?

TOM.   [*returning*] Yes, Mother?   140

AMANDA.   Is supper nearly ready?

TOM.   It looks to me like supper is on the table.

AMANDA.   Let me look—[*She rises prettily and looks through the portieres.*] Oh lovely! But where is Sister?

TOM.   Laura is not feeling well and she says that she thinks she'd better not come to the table.

AMANDA.   What? Nonsense! Laura? Oh, Laura!   145

LAURA.   [*from the kitchenette, faintly*] Yes, Mother.

AMANDA.   You really must come to the table. We won't be seated until you come to the table! Come in, Mr. O'Connor. You sit over there and I'll. . . . Laura? Laura Wingfield! You're keeping us waiting, honey! We can't say grace until you come to the table!

[*The kitchenette door is pushed weakly open and LAURA comes in. She is obviously quite faint, her lips trembling, her eyes wide and staring. She moves unsteadily toward the table.*]

Screen legend: "Terror!"

Outside a summer storm is coming on abruptly. The white curtains billow inward at the windows and there is a sorrowful murmur from the deep blue dusk.

LAURA suddenly stumbles; she catches at a chair with a faint moan.]

TOM.   Laura!

AMANDA.   Laura!

[*There is a clap of thunder.*

Screen legend: "Ah!"]

[*despairingly*] Why, Laura, you are ill, darling! Tom, help your sister into the living room, dear! Sit in the living room, Laura—rest on the sofa. Well! [*To JIM as TOM helps his sister to the sofa in the living room.*] Standing over the hot stove made her ill! I told her that it was just too warm this evening, but—

[*TOM comes back to the table.*]

Is Laura all right now?

TOM.   Yes.   150

AMANDA.   What is that? Rain? A nice cool rain has come up! [*She gives JIM a frightened look.*] I think we may—have grace—now . . . [*TOM looks at her stupidly.*] Tom, honey— you say grace!

TOM.   Oh . . . "For these and all thy mercies—"

[*They bow their heads, AMANDA stealing a nervous glance at JIM. In the living room LAURA, stretched on the sofa, clenches her hand to her lips, to hold back a shuddering sob.*]

God's Holy Name be praised—

[*The scene dims out.*]

SCENE 7

[*It is half an hour later. Dinner is just being finished in the dining room. LAURA is still huddled upon the sofa, her feet drawn under her, her head resting on a pale blue pillow, her eyes wide and mysteriously watchful. The new floor lamp with its shade of rose-colored silk gives a soft, becoming light to her face, bringing out the fragile, unearthly prettiness which usually escapes attention. From outside there is a steady murmur of rain, but it is slackening and soon stops; the air outside becomes pale and luminous as the moon breaks through the clouds. A moment after the curtain rises, the lights in both rooms flicker and go out.]*

JIM.   Hey, there, Mr. Light Bulb!

[*AMANDA laughs nervously.*

Legend on screen: "Suspension of a public service."]

AMANDA.   Where was Moses when the lights went out? Ha-ha. Do you know the answer to that one, Mr. O'Connor?
JIM.   No, Ma'am, what's the answer?
AMANDA.   In the dark!

[*JIM laughs appreciatively.*]

Everybody sit still. I'll light the candles. Isn't it lucky we have them on the table? Where's a match? Which of you gentlemen can provide a match?
JIM.   Here.   5
AMANDA.   Thank you, Sir.
JIM.   Not at all, Ma'am!
AMANDA.   [*as she lights the candles*] I guess the fuse has burnt out. Mr. O'Connor, can you tell a burnt-out fuse? I know I can't and Tom is a total loss when it comes to mechanics. [*They rise from the table and go into the kitchenette, from where their voices are heard.*] Oh, be careful you don't bump into something. We don't want our gentleman caller to break his neck. Now wouldn't that be a fine howdy-do?
JIM.   Ha-ha! Where is the fuse-box?
AMANDA.   Right here next to the stove. Can you see anything?   10
JIM.   Just a minute.
AMANDA.   Isn't electricity a mysterious thing? Wasn't it Benjamin Franklin who tied a key to a kite? We live in such a mysterious universe, don't we? Some people say that science clears up all the mysteries for us. In my opinion it only creates more! Have you found it yet?
JIM.   No, Ma'am. All these fuses look okay to me.
AMANDA.   Tom!
TOM.   Yes, Mother?   15
AMANDA.   That light bill I gave you several days ago. That one I told you we got the notices about?

[*Legend on screen: "Ha!"*]

TOM.   Oh—yeah.
AMANDA.   You didn't neglect to pay it by any chance?
TOM.   Why, I—
AMANDA.   Didn't! I might have known it!   20
JIM.   Shakespeare probably wrote a poem on that light bill, Mrs. Wingfield.
AMANDA.   I might have known better than to trust him with it! There's such a high price for negligence in this world!
JIM.   Maybe the poem will win a ten-dollar prize.

AMANDA.   We'll just have to spend the remainder of the evening in the nineteenth century, before Mr. Edison made the Mazda lamp!°

JIM.   Candlelight is my favorite kind of light.   25

AMANDA.   That shows you're romantic! But that's no excuse for Tom. Well, we got through dinner. Very considerate of them to let us get through dinner before they plunged us into everlasting darkness, wasn't it, Mr. O'Connor?

JIM.   Ha-ha!

AMANDA.   Tom, as a penalty for your carelessness you can help me with the dishes.

JIM.   Let me give you a hand.

AMANDA.   Indeed you will not!   30

JIM.   I ought to be good for something.

AMANDA.   Good for something? [Her tone is rhapsodic.] You? Why, Mr. O'Connor, nobody, nobody's given me this much entertainment in years—as you have!

JIM.   Aw, now, Mrs. Wingfield!

AMANDA.   I'm not exaggerating, not one bit! But Sister is all by her lonesome. You go keep her company in the parlor! I'll give you this lovely old candelabrum that used to be on the altar at the Church of the Heavenly Rest. It was melted a little out of shape when the church burnt down. Lightning struck it one spring. Gypsy Jones was holding a revival at the time and he intimated that the church was destroyed because the Episcopalians gave card parties.

JIM.   Ha-ha.   35

AMANDA.   And how about you coaxing Sister to drink a little wine? I think it would be good for her! Can you carry both at once?

JIM.   Sure. I'm Superman!

AMANDA.   Now, Thomas, get into this apron!

[JIM comes into the dining room, carrying the candelabrum, its candles lighted, in one hand and a glass of wine in the other. The door of the kitchenette swings closed on AMANDA's gay laughter; the flickering light approaches the portieres. LAURA sits up nervously as JIM enters. She can hardly speak from the almost intolerable strain of being alone with a stranger.

Screen legend: "I don't suppose you remember me at all!"

At first, before JIM's warmth overcomes her paralyzing shyness, LAURA's voice is thin and breathless, as though she had just run up a steep flight of stairs. JIM's attitude is gently humorous. While the incident is apparently unimportant, it is to LAURA the climax of her secret life.]

JIM.   Hello there, Laura.

LAURA.   [faintly] Hello.   40

[She clears her throat.]

Jim.   How are you feeling now? Better?

LAURA.   Yes. Yes, thank you.

JIM.   This is for you. A little dandelion wine. [He extends the glass toward her with extravagant gallantry.]

LAURA.   Thank you.

JIM.   Drink it—but don't get drunk!   45

[He laughs heartily. LAURA takes the glass uncertainly; she laughs shyly.]

---

24 Mazda lamp: Thomas A. Edison (1847–1931) developed the first practical incandescent lamp in 1879.

Where shall I set the candles?

> LAURA. Oh—oh, anywhere . . .
>
> JIM. How about here on the floor? Any objections?
>
> LAURA. No.
>
> JIM. I'll spread a newspaper under to catch the drippings. I like to sit on the floor.

Mind if I do?

> LAURA. Oh, no.   50
>
> JIM. Give me a pillow?
>
> LAURA. What?
>
> JIM. A pillow!
>
> LAURA. Oh . . . [*She hands him one quickly.*]
>
> JIM. How about you? Don't you like to sit on the floor?   55
>
> LAURA. Oh—yes.
>
> JIM. Why don't you, then?
>
> LAURA. I—will.
>
> JIM. Take a pillow!

[*Laura does. She sits on the floor on the other side of the candelabrum. JIM crosses his legs and smiles engagingly at her.*] I can't hardly see you sitting way over there.

> LAURA. I can—see you. *= Shadow*   60
>
> JIM. I know, but that's not fair, I'm in the limelight.

[*LAURA moves her pillow closer.*]

Good! Now I can see you! Comfortable?

> LAURA. Yes.
>
> JIM. So am I. Comfortable as a cow! Will you have some gum?
>
> LAURA. No, thank you.
>
> JIM. I think that I will indulge, with your permission. [*He musingly unwraps a stick*   65
> *of gum and holds it up.*] Think of the fortune made by the guy that invented the first piece
> of chewing gum. Amazing, huh? The Wrigley Building° is one of the sights of Chicago—
> I saw it when I went up to the Century of Progress.° Did you take in the Century of
> Progress?
>
> LAURA. No, I didn't. *Past - present - future*
>
> JIM. Well, it was quite a wonderful exposition. What impressed me most was the
> Hall of Science. Gives you an idea of what the future will be in America, even more won-
> derful than the present time is! [*There is a pause. JIM smiles at her.*] Your brother tells me
> you're shy. Is that right—Laura?
>
> LAURA. I—don't know.
>
> JIM. I judge you to be an old-fashioned type of girl. Well, I think that's a pretty
> good type to be. Hope you don't think I'm being too personal—do you?
>
> LAURA. [*Hastily, out of embarrassment*] I believe I *will* take a piece of gum, if you—   70
> don't mind. [*clearing her throat*] Mr. O'Connor, have you—kept up with your singing?
>
> JIM. Singing? Me?
>
> LAURA. Yes. I remember what a beautiful voice you had.
>
> JIM. When did you hear me sing?

[*LAURA does not answer, and in the long pause which follows a man's voice is heard singing offstage.*]

---

65 *Wrigley Building:* Finished in 1924, this was one of the first skyscrapers in the United States. *Century of Progress:* a world's fair held in Chicago (1933–1934) to celebrate the city's centennial.

VOICE:

> O blow, ye winds, heigh-ho,
> A-roving I will go!
>   I'm off to my love
>   With a boxing glove—
> Ten thousand miles away!°

JIM.   You say you've heard me sing?   75

LAURA.   Oh, Yes! Yes, very often . . . I—don't suppose—you remember me—at all?

JIM.   [*smiling doubtfully*] You know I have an idea I've seen you before. I had that idea soon as you opened the door. It seemed almost like I was about to remember your name. But the name that I started to call you—wasn't a name! And so I stopped myself before I said it.

LAURA.   Wasn't it—Blue Roses?

JIM.   [*springing up, grinning*] Blue Roses! My gosh, yes—Blue Roses! That's what I had on my tongue when you opened the door! Isn't it funny what tricks your memory plays? I didn't connect you with high school somehow or other. But that's where it was; it was high school. I didn't even know you were Shakespeare's sister! Gosh, I'm sorry.

LAURA.   I didn't expect you to. You—barely knew me!   80

JIM.   But we did have a speaking acquaintance, huh?

LAURA.   Yes, we—spoke to each other.

JIM.   When did you recognize me?

LAURA.   Oh, right away!

JIM.   Soon as I came in the door?   85

LAURA.   When I heard your name I thought it was probably you. I knew that Tom used to know you a little in high school. So when you came in the door—well, then I was—sure.

JIM.   Why didn't you *say* something, then?

LAURA.   [*breathlessly*] I didn't know what to say, I was—too surprised!

JIM.   For goodness' sakes! You know, this sure is funny!

LAURA.   Yes! Yes, isn't it, though . . .   90

JIM.   Didn't we have a class in something together?

LAURA.   Yes, we did.

JIM.   What class was that?

LAURA.   It was—singing—chorus!

JIM.   Aw!   95

LAURA.   I sat across the aisle from you in the Aud.

JIM.   Aw!

LAURA.   Mondays, Wednesdays, and Fridays.

JIM.   Now I remember—you always came in late.

LAURA.   Yes, it was so hard for me, getting upstairs. I had that brace on my leg—it   100
clumped so loud!

JIM.   I never heard any clumping.

LAURA.   [*wincing at the recollection*] To me it sounded like—thunder!

JIM.   Well, well, well, I never even noticed.

LAURA.   And everybody was seated before I came in. I had to walk in front of all those people. My seat was in the back row. I had to go clumping all the way up the aisle with everyone watching!

---

74 *O blow . . . :* This is a simplified version of the refrain of "A Capital Ship" (1885), a song that Charles E. Carryl (1841–1920) wrote for the music of the early-nineteenth-century Irish sea shanty "Ten Thousand Miles Away."

JIM.   You shouldn't have been self-conscious.   105

LAURA.   I know, but I was. It was always such a relief when the singing started.

JIM.   Aw, yes, I've placed you now! I used to call you Blue Roses. How was it that I got started calling you that?

LAURA.   I was out of school a little while with pleurosis. When I came back you asked me what was the matter. I said I had pleurosis—you thought that I said *Blue Roses.* That's what you always called me after that!

JIM.   I hope you didn't mind.

LAURA.   Oh, no—I liked it. You see, I wasn't acquainted with many—people. . . .   110

JIM.   As I remember you sort of stuck by yourself.

LAURA.   I—I—never have had much luck at—making friends.

JIM.   I don't see why you wouldn't.

LAURA.   Well, I—started out badly.

JIM.   You mean being—   115

LAURA.   Yes, it sort of—stood between me—

JIM.   You shouldn't have let it!

LAURA.   I know, but it did, and—

JIM.   You were shy with people!

LAURA.   I tried not to be but never could—   120

JIM.   Overcome it?

LAURA.   No, I—I never could!

JIM.   I guess being shy is something you have to work out of kind of gradually.

LAURA.   [*sorrowfully*] Yes—I guess it—

JIM.   Takes time!   125

LAURA.   Yes—

JIM.   People are not so dreadful when you know them. That's what you have to remember! And everybody has problems, not just you, but practically everybody has got some problems. You think of yourself as having the only problems, as being the only one who is disappointed. But just look around you and you will see lots of people as disappointed as you are. For instance, I hoped when I was going to high school that I would be further along at this time, six years later, than I am now. You remember that wonderful write-up I had in *The Torch?*

LAURA.   Yes! [*She rises and crosses to the table.*]

JIM.   It said I was bound to succeed in anything I went into!

[*LAURA returns with the high school yearbook.*]

Holy Jeez! *The Torch!*

[*He accepts it reverently. They smile across the book with mutual wonder. LAURA crouches beside him and they begin to turn the pages. LAURA's shyness is dissolving in his warmth.*]

LAURA.   Here you are in *The Pirates of Penzance!*   130

JIM.   [*wistfully*] I sang the baritone lead in that operetta.

LAURA.   [*raptly*] So—beautifully!

JIM.   [*protesting*] Aw—

LAURA.   Yes, yes—beautifully—beautifully!

JIM.   You heard me?   135

LAURA.   All three times!

JIM.   No!

LAURA.   Yes!

JIM.   All three performances?

LAURA.   [*looking down*] Yes.   140

JIM.   Why?

LAURA.   I—wanted to ask you to—autograph my program. [*She takes the program from the back of the yearbook and shows it to him.*]

JIM.   Why didn't you ask me to?

LAURA.   You were always surrounded by your own friends so much that I never had a chance to.

JIM.   You should have just—   145

LAURA.   Well, I—thought you might think I was—

JIM.   Thought I might think you was—what?

LAURA.   Oh—

JIM.   [*with reflective relish*] I was beleaguered by females in those days.

LAURA.   You were terribly popular!   150

JIM.   Yeah—

LAURA.   You had such a—friendly way—

JIM.   I was spoiled in high school.

LAURA.   Everybody—liked you!

JIM.   Including you?   155

LAURA.   I—yes, I—did, too—[*She gently closes the book in her lap.*]

JIM.   Well, well, well! Give me that program, Laura.

[*She hands it to him. He signs it with a flourish.*]

There you are—better late than never!

LAURA.   Oh, I—what a—surprise!

JIM.   My signature isn't worth very much right now. But some day—maybe—it will increase in value! Being disappointed is one thing and being discouraged is something else. I am disappointed but I am not discouraged. I'm twenty-three years old. How old are you?

LAURA.   I'll be twenty-four in June.   160

JIM.   That's not old age!

LAURA.   No, but—

JIM.   You finished high school?

LAURA.   [*with difficulty*] I didn't go back.   *Present difficulties*

JIM.   You mean you dropped out?   165

LAURA.   I made bad grades in my final examinations. [*She rises and replaces the book and the program on the table. Her voice is strained.*] How is—Emily Meisenbach getting along?

JIM.   Oh, that kraut-head!

LAURA.   Why do you call her that?

JIM.   That's what she was.

LAURA.   You're not still—going with her?   170

JIM.   I never see her.

LAURA.   It was in the "Personal" section that you were—engaged!

JIM.   I know, but I wasn't impressed by that—propaganda!

LAURA.   It wasn't—the truth?

JIM.   Only in Emily's optimistic opinion!   175

LAURA.   Oh—

[*Legend: "What have you done since high school?"*]

JIM *lights a cigarette and leans indolently back on his elbows smiling at* LAURA *with a warmth and charm which lights her inwardly with altar candles. She remains by the table, picks up a piece from the glass menagerie collection, and turns it in her hands to cover her tumult.*]

JIM. [*after several reflective puffs on his cigarette*] What have you done since high school?

[*She seems not to hear him.*]

Huh?

[*LAURA looks up.*]

I said what have you done since high school, Laura?

    LAURA. Nothing much.

    JIM. You must have been doing something these six long years.

    LAURA. Yes.   180

    JIM. Well, then, such as what?

    LAURA. I took a business course at business college—

    JIM. How did that work out?

    LAURA. Well, not very—well—I had to drop out, it gave me—indigestion—

[*JIM laughs gently.*]

    JIM. What are you doing now?   185

    LAURA. I don't do anything—much. Oh, please don't think I sit around doing nothing! My glass collection takes up a good deal of time. Glass is something you have to take good care of.

    JIM. What did you say—about glass?

    LAURA. Collection I said—I have one—[*She clears her throat and turns away again, acutely shy.*]

    JIM. [*abruptly*] You know what I judge to be the trouble with you? Inferiority complex! Know what that is? That's what they call it when someone low-rates himself! I understand it because I had it too. Although my case was not so aggravated as yours seems to be. I had it until I took up public speaking, developed my voice, and learned that I had an aptitude for science. Before that time I never thought of myself as being outstanding in any way whatsoever! Now I've never made a regular study of it, but I have a friend who says I can analyze people better than doctors that make a profession of it. I don't claim that to be necessarily true, but I can sure guess a person's psychology. Laura! [*He takes out his gum.*] Excuse me, Laura. I always take it out when the flavor is gone. I'll use this scrap of paper to wrap it in. I know how it is to get it stuck on a shoe. [*He wraps the gum in paper and puts it in his pocket.*] Yep—that's what I judge to be your principal trouble. A lack of confidence in yourself as a person. You don't have the proper amount of faith in yourself. I'm basing that fact on a number of your remarks and also on certain observations I've made. For instance that clumping you thought was so awful in high school. You say that you even dreaded to walk into class. You see what you did? You dropped out of school, you gave up an education because of a clump, which as far as I know was practically nonexistent! A little physical defect is what you have. Hardly noticeable even! Magnified thousands of times by imagination! You know what my strong advice to you is? Think of yourself as *superior* in some way!

    LAURA. In what way would I think?   190

    JIM. Why, man alive, Laura! Just look about you a little. What do you see? A world full of common people! All of 'em born and all of 'em going to die! Which of them has one-tenth of your good points! Or mine! Or anyone else's, as far as that goes—gosh! Everybody excels in some one thing. Some in many! [*He unconsciously glances at himself in the mirror.*] All you've got to do is discover in *what!* Take me, for instance. [*He adjusts his tie at the mirror.*] My interest happens to lie in electro-dynamics. I'm taking a course in radio engineering at night school, Laura, on top of a fairly responsible job at the warehouse. I'm taking that course and studying public speaking.

LAURA.   Ohhhh.

JIM.   Because I believe in the future of television! [*turning his back to her*] I wish to be ready to go up right along with it. Therefore I'm planning to get in on the ground floor. In fact I've already made the right connections and all that remains is for the industry itself to get under way! Full steam—[*His eyes are starry.*] Knowledge—Zzzzzp! Money—Zzzzzp!—Power! That's the cycle democracy is built on!

[*His attitude is convincingly dynamic. LAURA stares at him, even her shyness eclipsed in her absolute wonder. He suddenly grins.*]

I guess you think I think a lot of myself!

LAURA.   No—o-o-o, I—

JIM.   Now how about you? Isn't there something you take more interest in than   195
anything else?

LAURA.   Well, I do—as I said—have my—glass collection—

[*A peal of girlish laughter rings from the kitchenette.*]

JIM.   I'm not right sure I know what you're talking about. What kind of glass is it?

LAURA.   Little articles of it, they're ornaments mostly! Most of them are little animals made out of glass, the tiniest little animals in the world. Mother calls them a glass menagerie! Here's an example of one, if you'd like to see it! This one is one of the oldest. It's nearly thirteen.

[*Music: "The Glass Menagerie."*

He stretches out his hand.]

Oh, be careful—if you breathe, it breaks!

JIM.   I'd better not take it. I'm pretty clumsy with things.

LAURA.   Go, on, I trust you with him! [*She places the piece in his palm.*] There now—   200
you're holding him gently! Hold him over the light, he loves the light! You see how the light shines through him?

JIM.   It sure does shine!

LAURA.   I shouldn't be partial, but he is my favorite one.

JIM.   What kind of a thing is this one supposed to be?

LAURA.   Haven't you noticed the single horn on his forehead?

JIM.   A unicorn, huh?   205

LAURA.   Mmmm-hmmm!

JIM.   Unicorns—aren't they extinct in the modern world?

LAURA.   I know!

JIM.   Poor little fellow, he must feel sort of lonesome.

LAURA.   [*smiling*] Well, if he does, he doesn't complain about it. He stays on a shelf   210
with some horses that don't have horns and all of them seem to get along nicely together.

JIM.   How do you know?

LAURA.   [*lightly*] I haven't heard any arguments among them!

JIM.   [*grinning*] No arguments, huh? Well, that's a pretty good sign! Where shall I set him?

LAURA.   Put him on the table. They all like a change of scenery once in a while!

JIM.   Well, well, well, well—[*He places the glass piece on the table, then raises his arms*   215
and stretches.] Look how big my shadow is when I stretch!

LAURA.   Oh, oh, yes—it stretches across the ceiling!

Know when to hold them —
When to walk away —
When to fight —

Williams ~ The Glass Menagerie, Scene 7   1717

JIM.   [*crossing to the door*] I think it's stopped raining. [*He opens the fire-escape door and the background music changes to a dance tune.*] Where does the music come from?

LAURA.   From the Paradise Dance Hall across the alley.

JIM.   How about cutting the rug a little, Miss Wingfield?

LAURA.   Oh, I—   220

JIM.   Or is your program filled up? Let me have a look at it. [*He grasps an imaginary card.*] Why, every dance is taken! I'll just have to scratch some out.

[*Waltz music: "La Golondrina"°*]

Ahh, a waltz! [*He executes some sweeping turns by himself, then holds his arms toward* LAURA.]

LAURA.   [*breathlessly*] I—can't dance.

JIM.   There you go, that inferiority stuff!

LAURA.   I've never danced in my life!

JIM.   Come on, try!   225

LAURA.   Oh, but I'd step on you!

JIM.   I'm not made out of glass.

LAURA.   How—how—how do we start?

JIM.   Just leave it to me. You hold your arms out a little.

LAURA.   Like this?   230

JIM.   [*taking her in his arms*] A little bit higher. Right. Now don't tighten up, that's the main thing about it—relax.

LAURA.   [*laughing breathlessly*] It's hard not to.

JIM.   Okay.

LAURA.   I'm afraid you can't budge me.

JIM.   What do you bet I can't? [*He swings her into motion.*]   235

LAURA.   Goodness, yes, you can!

JIM.   Let yourself go, now, Laura, just let yourself go.

LAURA.   I'm—

JIM.   Come on!

LAURA.   —trying!   240

JIM.   Not so stiff—easy does it!

LAURA.   I know but I'm—

JIM.   Loosen th' backbone! There now, that's a lot better.

LAURA.   Am I?

JIM.   Lots, lots better! [*He moves her about the room in a clumsy waltz.*]   245

LAURA.   Oh, my!

JIM.   Ha-ha!

LAURA.   Oh, my goodness!

JIM.   Ha-ha-ha!

[*They suddenly bump into the table, and the glass piece on it falls to the floor. Jim stops the dance.*]

What did we hit?

LAURA.   Table.   250

JIM.   Did something fall off it? I think—

LAURA.   Yes.

JIM.   I hope that it wasn't the little glass horse with the horn!

LAURA.   Yes. [*She stoops to pick it up.*]

220 S. D. *"La Golondrina"*: a popular Mexican song (1883) written by Narciso Seradell (1843–1910).

JIM.   Aw, aw, aw. Is it broken?   255

LAURA.   Now it is just like all the other horses.

JIM.   It's lost its—

LAURA.   Horn! It doesn't matter. Maybe it's a blessing in disguise.

JIM.   You'll never forgive me. I bet that that was your favorite piece of glass.

LAURA.   I don't have favorites much. It's no tragedy, Freckles. Glass breaks so easi-   260
ly. No matter how careful you are. The traffic jars the shelves and things fall off them.

JIM.   Still I'm awfully sorry that I was the cause.

LAURA.   [*smiling*] I'll just imagine he had an operation. The horn was removed to
make him feel less—freakish!

[*They both laugh.*]

Now he will feel more at home with the other horses, the ones that don't have
horns. . . .

JIM.   Ha-ha, that's very funny! [*Suddenly he is serious.*] I'm glad to see that you have
a sense of humor. You know—you're—well—very different! Surprisingly different from
anyone else I know! [*His voice becomes soft and hesitant with a genuine feeling.*] Do you mind
me telling you that?

[*LAURA is abashed beyond speech.*]

I mean it in a nice way—

[*LAURA nods shyly, looking away.*]

You make me feel sort of—I don't know how to put it! I'm usually pretty good at expressing things, but—this is something that I don't know how to say!

[*LAURA touches her throat and clears it—turns the broken unicorn in her hands. His voice becomes
softer.*]

Has anyone ever told you that you were pretty?

[*There is a pause, and the music rises slightly. LAURA looks up slowly, with wonder, and shakes her
head.*]

Well, you are! In a very different way from anyone else. And all the nicer because of
the difference, too.

[*His voice becomes low and husky. LAURA turns away, nearly faint with the novelty of her emotions.*]

I wish that you were my sister. I'd teach you to have some confidence in yourself.
The different people are not like other people, but being different is nothing to be
ashamed of. Because other people are not such wonderful people. They're one hundred
times one thousand. You're one times one! They walk all over the earth. You just stay
here. They're common as—weeds, but—you—well, you're—*Blue Roses*!

[*Image on screen: Blue Roses.*]

The music changes.]

LAURA.   But blue is wrong for—roses. . . .

JIM.   It's right for you! You're—pretty!   265

LAURA.   In what respect am I pretty?

JIM.   In all respects—believe me! Your eyes—your hair—are pretty! Your hands
are pretty! [*He catches hold of her hand.*] You think I'm making this up because I'm invited

to dinner and have to be nice. Oh, I could do that! I could put on an act for you, Laura, and say lots of things without being very sincere. But this time I am. I'm talking to you sincerely. I happened to notice you had this inferiority complex that keeps you from feeling comfortable with people. Somebody needs to build your confidence up and make you proud instead of shy and turning away and—blushing. Somebody—ought to—*kiss* you, Laura!

[*His hand slips slowly up her arm to her shoulder as the music swells tumultuously. He suddenly turns about and kisses her on the lips. When he releases her, LAURA sinks on the sofa with a bright, dazed look. Jim backs away and fishes in his pocket for a cigarette.*

Legend on screen: "A souvenir."]

Stumblejohn!

[*He lights the cigarette, avoiding her look. There is a peal of girlish laughter from AMANDA in the kitchenette. LAURA slowly raises and opens her hand. It still contains the little broken glass animal. She looks at it with a tender, bewildered expression.*]

Stumblejohn! I shouldn't have done that—that was way off the beam. You don't smoke, do you?

[*She looks up, smiling, not hearing the question. He sits beside her rather gingerly. She looks at him speechlessly—waiting. He coughs decorously and moves a little further aside as he considers the situation and senses her feelings, dimly, with perturbation. He speaks gently.*]

Would you—care for a mint?

[*She doesn't seem to hear him but her look grows brighter even.*]

Peppermint? Life Saver? My pocket's a regular drugstore—wherever I go. . . . [*He pops a mint in his mouth. Then he gulps and decides to make a clean breast of it. He speaks slowly and gingerly.*] Laura, you know, if I had a sister like you, I'd do the same thing as Tom. I'd bring out fellows and—introduce her to them. The right type of boys—of a type to—appreciate her. Only—well—he made a mistake about me. Maybe I've got no call to be saying this. That may not have been the idea in having me over. But what if it was? There's nothing wrong about that. The only trouble is that in my case—I'm not in a situation to—do the right thing. I can't take down your number and say I'll phone. I can't call up next week and—ask for a date. I thought I had better explain the situation in case you—misunderstood it and—I hurt your feelings. . . .

[*There is a pause. Slowly, very slowly, LAURA's look changes, her eyes returning slowly from his to the glass figure in her palm. AMANDA utters another gay laugh in the kitchenette.*]

LAURA.   [*faintly*] You—won't—call again?

JIM.   No, Laura, I can't. [*He rises from the sofa.*] As I was just explaining, I've—got strings on me, Laura, I've—been going steady! I go out all the time with a girl named Betty. She's a home-girl like you, and Catholic, and Irish, and in a great many ways we—get along fine. I met her last summer on a moonlight boat trip up the river to Alton,° on the *Majestic*. Well—right away from the start it was—love!

[*Legend: Love!*]

LAURA *sways slightly forward and grips the arm of the sofa. He fails to notice, now enrapt in his own comfortable being.*]

269.1 *Alton:* a city in Illinois about twenty miles north of St. Louis on the Mississippi River.

Being in love has made a new man of me!

[*Leaning stiffly forward, clutching the arm of the sofa,* LAURA *struggles visibly with her storm. But* JIM *is oblivious; she is a long way off.*]

The power of love is really pretty tremendous! Love is something that—changes the whole world, Laura!

[*The storm abates a little and* LAURA *leans back. He notices her again.*]

It happened that Betty's aunt took sick, she got a wire and had to go to Centralia.° So Tom—when he asked me to dinner—I naturally just accepted the invitation, not knowing that you—that he—that I—[*He stops awkwardly.*] Huh—I'm a stumblejohn!

[*He flops back on the sofa. The holy candles on the altar of* LAURA'*s face have been snuffed out. There is a look of almost infinite desolation.* JIM *glances at her uneasily.*]

I wish that you would—say something.

[*She bites her lip which was trembling and then bravely smiles. She opens her hand again on the broken glass figure. Then she gently takes his hand and raises it level with her own. She carefully places the unicorn in the palm of his hand, then pushes his fingers closed upon it.*]

What are you—doing that for? You want me to have him? Laura?

[*She nods.*]

What for?

     LAURA.   A—souvenir. . .   270

[*She rises unsteadily and crouches beside the Victrola to wind it up.*

Legend on screen: "Things have a way of turning out so badly!" Or image: "Gentleman caller waving goodbye—gaily."

At this moment AMANDA *rushes brightly back into the living room. She bears a pitcher of fruit punch in an old-fashioned cut-glass pitcher, and a plate of macaroons. The plate has a gold border and poppies painted on it.*]

     AMANDA.   Well, well, well! Isn't the air delightful after the shower? I've made you children a little liquid refreshment. [*She turns gaily to* JIM.] Jim, do you know that song about lemonade?

          "Lemonade, lemonade

          Made in the shade and stirred with a spade—

          Good enough for any old maid!"

     JIM.   [*uneasily*] Ha-ha! No—I never heard it.

     AMANDA.   Why, Laura! You look so serious!

     JIM.   We were having a serious conversation.

     AMANDA.   Good! Now you're better acquainted!   275

     JIM.   [*uncertainly*] Ha-ha! Yes.

     AMANDA.   You modern young people are much more serious-minded than my generation. I was so gay as a girl!

     JIM.   You haven't changed, Mrs. Wingfield.

     AMANDA.   Tonight I'm rejuvenated! The gaiety of the occasion, Mr. O'Connor! [*She tosses her head with a peal of laughter, spilling some lemonade.*] Oooo! I'm baptizing myself!

     269.8 *Centralia:* a city in Illinois about sixty miles east of St. Louis.

JIM.   Here—let me—   280
AMANDA.   [*setting the pitcher down*] There now. I discovered we had some maraschi-
no cherries. I dumped them in, juice and all!
JIM.   You shouldn't have gone to that trouble, Mrs. Wingfield.
AMANDA.   Trouble, trouble? Why, it was loads of fun! Didn't you hear me cutting up
in the kitchen? I bet your ears were burning! I told Tom how outdone with him I was for
keeping you to himself so long a time! He should have brought you over much, much
sooner! Well, now that you've found your way, I want you to be a very frequent caller! Not
just occasional but all the time. Oh, we're going to have a lot of gay times together! I see
them coming! Mmm, just breathe that air! So fresh, and the moon's so pretty! I'll skip
back out—I know where my place is when young folks are having a—serious conversation!
JIM.   Oh, don't go out, Mrs. Wingfield. The fact of the matter is I've got to be
going.
AMANDA.   Going, now? You're joking! Why, it's only the shank of the evening,°   285
Mr. O'Connor!
JIM.   Well, you know how it is.
Amanda.   You mean you're a young workingman and have to keep workingmen's
hours. We'll let you off early tonight. But only on the condition that next time you stay later.
What's the best night for you? Isn't Saturday night the best night for you workingmen?
JIM.   I have a couple of time-clocks to punch, Mrs. Wingfield. One at morning, an-
other one at night!
AMANDA.   My, but you *are* ambitious! You work at night, too?
JIM.   No, Ma'am, not work but—Betty!   290

[*He crosses deliberately to pick up his hat. The band at the Paradise Dance Hall goes into a tender
waltz.*]

AMANDA.   Betty? Betty? Who's—Betty!

[*There is an ominous cracking sound in the sky.*]

JIM.   Oh, just a girl. The girl I go steady with!

[*He smiles charmingly. The sky falls.*]

Legend: "The Sky Falls."]

AMANDA.   [*a long-drawn exhalation*] Ohhh . . . Is it a serious romance,
Mr. O'Connor?
JIM.   We're going to be married the second Sunday in June.
AMANDA.   Ohhh—how nice! Tom didn't mention that you were engaged to be   295
married.
JIM.   The cat's not out of the bag at the warehouse yet. You know how they are.
They call you Romeo and stuff like that. [*He stops at the oval mirror to put on his hat. He care-
fully shapes the brim and the crown to give a discreetly dashing effect.*] It's been a wonderful
evening, Mrs. Wingfield. I guess this is what they mean by Southern hospitality.
AMANDA.   It really wasn't anything at all.
JIM.   I hope it don't seem like I'm rushing off. But I promised Betty I'd pick her up
at the Wabash depot, an' by the time I get my jalopy down there her train'll be in. Some
women are pretty upset if you keep 'em waiting.

---

285 *shank of the evening:* still early, the best part of the evening.

AMANDA.　Yes, I know—the tyranny of women! [*She extends her hand.*] Goodbye, Mr. O'Connor. I wish you luck—and happiness—and success! All three of them, and so does Laura! Don't you, Laura?

LAURA.　Yes!　　　　　　　　　　　　　　　　　　　　　　　　　300

JIM.　[*taking LAURA's hand*] Goodbye, Laura. I'm certainly going to treasure that souvenir. And don't you forget the good advice I gave you. [*He raises his voice to a cheery shout.*] So long, Shakespeare! Thanks again, ladies. Good night!

[*He grins and ducks jauntily out. Still bravely grimacing, Amanda closes the door on the gentleman caller. Then she turns back to the room with a puzzled expression. She and LAURA don't dare to face each other. LAURA crouches beside the Victrola to wind it.*]

AMANDA.　[*faintly*] Things have a way of turning out so badly. I don't believe that I would play the Victrola. Well, well—well! Our gentleman caller was engaged to be married? [*She raises her voice.*] Tom!

TOM.　[*from the kitchenette*] Yes, Mother?

AMANDA.　Come in here a minute. I want to tell you something awfully funny.

TOM.　[*entering with a macaroon and a glass of the lemonade*] Has the gentleman caller　　305
gotten away already?

AMANDA.　The gentleman caller has made an early departure. What a wonderful joke you played on us!

TOM.　How do you mean?

AMANDA.　You didn't mention that he was engaged to be married.

TOM.　Jim? Engaged?

AMANDA.　That's what he just informed us.　　　　　　　　　　　310

TOM.　I'll be jiggered! I didn't know about that.

AMANDA.　That seems very peculiar.

TOM.　What's peculiar about it?

AMANDA.　Didn't you call him your best friend down at the warehouse?

TOM.　He is, but how did I know?　　　　　　　　　　　　　315

AMANDA.　It seems extremely peculiar that you wouldn't know your best friend was going to be married!

TOM.　The warehouse is where I work, not where I know things about people!

AMANDA.　You don't know things anywhere! You live in a dream; you manufacture illusions! Misleading visual images

[*He crosses to the door.*]

Where are you going?

TOM.　I'm going to the movies.

AMANDA.　That's right, now that you've had us make such fools of ourselves. The　　320
effort, the preparations, all the expense! The new floor lamp, the rug, the clothes for Laura! All for what? To entertain some other girl's fiancé! Go to the movies, go! Don't think about us, a mother deserted, an unmarried sister who's crippled and has no job! Don't let anything interfere with your selfish pleasure! Just go, go, go—to the movies!

TOM.　All right, I will! The more you shout about my selfishness to me the quicker I'll go, and I won't go to the movies!

AMANDA.　Go, then! Go to the moon—you selfish dreamer!

[*TOM smashes his glass on the floor. He plunges out on the fire escape, slamming the door. LAURA screams in fright. The dance-hall music becomes louder. Tom stands on the fire escape, gripping the rail. The moon breaks through the storm clouds, illuminating his face.*]

Legend on screen: "And so goodbye . . ."

TOM's *closing speech is timed with what is happening inside the house. We see, as though through soundproof glass, that* AMANDA *appears to be making a comforting speech to* LAURA, *who is huddled upon the sofa. Now that we cannot hear the mother's speech, her silliness is gone and she has dignity and tragic beauty.* LAURA's *hair hides her face until, at the end of the speech, she lifts her head to smile at her mother.* AMANDA's *gestures are slow and graceful, almost dancelike, as she comforts her daughter. At the end of her speech she glances a moment at the father's picture—then withdraws through the portieres. At the close of* TOM's *speech,* LAURA *blows out the candles, ending the play.*]

TOM.   I didn't go to the moon, I went much further—for time is the longest distance between two places. Not long after that I was fired for writing a poem on the lid of a shoe-box. I left Saint Louis. I descended the steps of this fire escape for a last time and followed, from then on, in my father's footsteps, attempting to find in motion what was lost in space. I traveled around a great deal. The cities swept about me like dead leaves, leaves that were brightly colored but torn away from the branches. I would have stopped, but I was pursued by something. It always came upon me unawares, taking me altogether by surprise. Perhaps it was a familiar bit of music. Perhaps it was only a piece of transparent glass. Perhaps I am walking along a street at night, in some strange city, before I have found companions. I pass the lighted window of a shop where perfume is sold. The window is filled with pieces of colored glass, tiny transparent bottles in delicate colors, like bits of a shattered rainbow. Then all at once my sister touches my shoulder. I turn around and look into her eyes. Oh, Laura, Laura, I tried to leave you behind me, but I am more faithful than I intended to be! I reach for a cigarette, I cross the street, I run into the movies or a bar, I buy a drink, I speak to the nearest stranger—anything that can blow your candles out!

[LAURA *bends over the candles.*]

For nowadays the world is lit by lightning! Blow out your candles, Laura—and so goodbye. . . .

[*She blows the candles out.*]

QUESTIONS

1.   What does the setting described in the opening stage direction tell you about the Wingfields? Consider especially the adjectives and the symbolism of the alley and the fire escape.

2.   Who is the "fifth character" in the play, and how is his presence established? In what ways is Tom a parallel to this character?

3.   What does Amanda reveal about her past in scene 1? How does Williams reveal that Amanda often dwells in the past?

4.   What happened to Laura at Rubicam's Business College? How can you account for her behavior? What plan of Amanda's did she upset?

5.   What new plan for Laura's future does Amanda begin to develop in scene 2? Why is the plan impracticable? Why is the image of Jim introduced here?

6.   Summarize the argument between Tom and Amanda in scene 3. What does Amanda assert about Tom? What does he claim about his life? Why is Laura spotlighted throughout the argument?

7.   What sort of agreement does Amanda try to reach with Tom about Laura in scene 4?

broken dream

8.　How do Amanda and Laura react to the news of a gentleman caller? Describe Laura's feelings toward Jim during the conversation and the dancing in scene 7. Describe how he changes after the kiss.

9.　Explain the symbolism of the unicorn (both whole and broken). Why does Laura give it to Jim as a souvenir?

10.　What is Tom's situation at the end? To what degree has he achieved his dreams of escape and adventure?

11.　Describe Amanda's and Laura's concluding situations. Why does Laura blow out the candles? What is the future for these women?

GENERAL QUESTIONS

1.　Explain the most striking nonrealistic aspects of the play. What do these contribute to the play's meaning and impact? Which aspect is the most effective? Why?

2.　Which characters in the play change significantly? To what extent do the characters succeed or fail? How do they try to escape the realities they face?

3.　Consider Tom as character and narrator. Explain why his language changes as he shifts between narrator and character. What does the character dream about and strive for? What does the narrator learn about these dreams and strivings?

4.　Explain why Laura cannot deal with reality. What does her glass menagerie symbolize?

5.　Williams says that there is much to admire, pity, and laugh at in Amanda. What aspects of her character are admirable? Pitiable? Laughable? Which reaction is dominant for you at the close of the play? Why?

6.　Tom calls Jim the play's "most realistic character." In what ways is Jim realistic? How are his dreams and goals more (or less) realistic than Tom's?

7.　At the opening, Tom (as narrator) mentions the "social background," and he remarks on it throughout. Discuss how this background relates to the play, especially the events occurring in Europe.

8.　Discuss the play's religious allusion and imagery, especially Malvolio the Magician, the "Ave Maria," the "Annunciation," the Paradise Dance Hall, and Laura's candles. How do these references affect the play's level of reality?

WRITING ABOUT REALISTIC AND NONREALISTIC DRAMA

Your essay should take into account the traditional elements of drama—plot, character, language, setting, symbol, and theme. Conventional approaches to these elements are discussed in Chapter 26 (pp. 1240–43), and you may want to review this material. As you plan your essay, your overall concern should be to determine the relative degrees of realism or nonrealism with which the elements are presented and developed. Your discoveries here will enable you to describe the ways in which the play establishes its views and ideas about life and the world. In short, how do conventional aspects of dramatic structure, together with the degree of realism or nonrealism, create a perspective that is the unique property of the play?

Questions for Discovering Ideas

PLOT. Does the play unfold in a chronological order that imitates reality, or does it mix past and present action? Is the action true to life or stylized? Are the conflicts resolved realistically, or does the playwright employ a conventional and perhaps improbable happy (or sad) ending? How does the realistic or nonrealistic development of these aspects affect the play's meaning and impact?

CHARACTER. Are the characters realistic or symbolic, representative, or stereotyped? Are they round or flat? Are they motivated by lifelike considerations, like Amanda in *The Glass Menagerie,* who lives only in the past? Or are they motivated by the play's requirements, like the narrator, who has the artificial role of speaking directly to the audience? Are the characters consistent, or do they drop in and out of character? Is their clothing and makeup (as described in the stage directions) an imitation of real life, or is it theatrical and nonrealistic? Are all the characters developed in the same manner, or are there differences in the degree of realism you find in each? Is one character more or less realistic than any of the others? If so, why? Of what importance is this character to the play as a whole?

LANGUAGE. Look carefully at the diction, style, and patterns of the dialogue. In realistic drama, what is the nature of the speeches? Is the language colloquial, formal, low? Is it appropriate for the characters? Is the dialogue normal or natural, granted the situation? Do the characters speak loudly? Do they whisper? Shout? Why? What pattern or consistency can you discover by studying how the characters speak? Within the confines of realistic drama, what normal or realistic variations occur? (For example, a letter is read aloud, a phone conversation occurs, a character is alone onstage and speaks to characters offstage as in O'Neill's *Before Breakfast* [p. 1209], or a character speaks to characters who do not hear.) What proportion of the dialogue is ordinary two- or three-way conversation? How much variation occurs, and what kind is it? Why do you think the dramatists have varied the normal dialogue, and how do these variations shape your perception of the play?

In nonrealistic drama, some dialogue will be realistically normal or appear so, but much of it will be shaped by the play's nonrealistic premise. How do you identify nonrealistic speech? Do you find nonrealistic devices such as verse, song, or unnatural and patterned repetition? Does any character seem to be speaking in different voices? If so, why? Which characters seem to ignore other characters and speak instead to the air or to the audience? How extensive is such direct address? Does a single character do most of this talking? If so, what is he or she like? What does the character tell you about himself or herself? About the other characters in the play? The background? Plot? Action? Setting? Staging? How accurate and objective is this character? How does this direct address shape and control your responses?

In sum, how do all aspects of language determine the extent to which the play effectively communicates ideas and emotions to you? As you deal with language, also consider the significance of other aspects of sound indicated in the stage directions, such as sound effects or music.

SETTING.   To what degree do the stage directions present the setting as realistic or nonrealistic? Do the directions call for the reproduction of an actual room or place? How much specific detail is included? If less than a fully realistic setting is described, how far does the playwright go in reducing the setting to the bare stage? How much of the physical theater (brick walls, pipes, wires, lights, back-stage ropes) does the playwright indicate that he or she wants you to see or imagine? To what extent do you find symbolic, impressionistic, and nonrealistic devices such as transparent walls? How do the stage directions describe lighting? Is the lighting used realistically, to recreate natural illumination, or nonrealisti-cally, to isolate and emphasize specific places, objects, characters, or actions? Most important, how do the setting and its degree of realism (or nonrealism) contribute to the impact and meaning of the play?

SYMBOLISM.   Because symbols operate in life as they do in art, there is symbol-ism both in the realistic plays of Glaspell and Ibsen and in the relatively nonre-alistic dramas of Miller and Williams. Are symbols introduced through realistic or logical techniques, or do they appear illogically and nonrealistically? You can focus your exploration directly on the symbol and its meaning (the water pollu-tion in *An Enemy of the People*) or the nonrealistic methods through which it is es-tablished (the blue roses in *The Glass Menagerie*).

THEME.   What are the important concepts in the play, and how are they con-veyed? Be sure to give special consideration to significantly realistic or nonreal-istic techniques. In considering realistic plays like *Trifles* or *Mulatto,* explore the ways in which realism in character, action, and setting contribute to the plays' ideas. Conversely, consider how Williams employs a strikingly nonrealistic de-vice, such as the music or the screen projections, to convey and emphasize the themes of *The Glass Menagerie.*

Strategies for Organizing Ideas

Your central idea should show how realistic or nonrealistic elements affect part or all of the play. Try to connect the topic with its effect. For example, begin with sen-tences such as these: (1) "Tom as a nonrealistic narrator and realistic character unifies *The Glass Menagerie* and gives the play a coherent and subjective point of view." (2) "In *An Enemy of the People* [Chapter 31], the Mayor's threats of real-life economic reprisal bring out Dr. Stockmann's combativeness and moral strength."

The supporting details can be organized in any way that produces a logical and convincing essay. If you are writing about the ways in which nonrealistic de-vices emphasize meaning in *The Glass Menagerie,* for example, you might organ-ize your essay around the setting, the lighting, and the screen device. When your essay focuses on only one element, you can organize your supporting details to reflect the order in which they occur in the play.

In your conclusion you might raise larger issues than you have already raised, or you might make broader connections not only about your topic but also about the play as a whole. You might also reconsider the significance of the play's general level of realistic or nonrealistic techniques.

DEMONSTRATIVE STUDENT ESSAY

Realism and Nonrealism in Tom's Triple Role in *The Glass Menagerie*°

[1]
In <u>The Glass Menagerie</u>, Tennessee Williams combines realistic and nonrealistic elements to explore the personalities and conflicts of the Wingfield family. <u>One of his most effective nonrealistic elements in the play is his use of Tom in three different roles.</u>* <u>As a realistic character within the action, a nonrealistic stage manager of the action, and a nonrealistic narrator of the entire play, Tom combines three functions that significantly shape our perceptions.</u>†

[2]
<u>As a realistic character involved in the recollected action of the play, Tom is ensnared by the economic and emotional demands of his family and his job.</u> In the opening description of the characters, Williams explains Tom's plight: "to escape from a trap he [Tom] has to act without pity." In addition, Tom himself dramatically expresses his need to escape from his stifling life at home. He discusses this need with his mother in Scene 3, with Laura in Scene 4, and, above all, with Jim in Scene 6. Here, we see that Tom craves not only escape but also adventure. He tells Jim, "I'm planning a change." And he clearly expresses his desire to move out of the prison house of the family:

> It's our turn now, to go the South Sea Island—to make a safari—to be exotic, far off! But I'm not patient. I don't want to wait till then, I'm tired of the <u>movies</u> and I am <u>about</u> to <u>move</u>! (1706, Scene 6, speech 114)

> I'm starting to boil inside. I know I seem dreamy, but inside—well, I'm boiling. (1706, Scene 6, speech 120)

These expressions of his need to escape define a major line of the realistic thought and action in <u>The Glass Menagerie</u>.

[3]
<u>Tom's realism as a character is undercut by his momentary role as a stage manager in Scene 1.</u> Here, he speaks with Amanda <u>"as though reading from a script."</u> In this same scene, "Tom <u>motions for music and a spot of light on</u> Amanda." Although this device is abandoned, the image of Tom holding an imaginary script and giving cues to the musicians and the lighting technicians breaks any possible illusions that the play is imitating real life. The role as manager emphasizes the fact that <u>The Glass Menagerie</u> is a play designed for the stage and for live actors carrying out conventional stage roles.

[4]
<u>Tom's part in shaping and unifying the play is most apparent in his nonrealistic function as narrator.</u> In this role, he stands aside from the action occurring in the Wingfield apartment, and he also speaks directly to us. He introduces the characters, provides background, and supplies an ongoing commentary. In addition, he presents his own subjective views and also personifies the play's theme of escape. As the past character, the one actually involved in the play's action, he represents a yearning for freedom and adventure. As the present narrator, he

---

°See pp. 1675–1723 for this play.
*Central idea.
†Thesis sentence.

speaks truths that his character in its past role has not yet learned, and he thus recognizes that escape from the past is impossible. When the play closes, he tells us that he remains trapped (1723, Scene 7, speech 323), and thus he provides a final perspective on the central theme of escape.

[5] The second striking aspect of Tom's function as narrator concerns his complete control of the play. Because he is the narrator, the action in The Glass Menagerie represents Tom's memories of events, rather than the events themselves. In the first speech of Scene 1, he tells us, "The play is memory. Being a memory play, it is dimly lighted, it is sentimental, it is not realistic." Since the events from the past that occur onstage emerge from Tom's memory, it is he who provides an overriding unity and perspective. We see everything through his mind and from his point of view. As a nonrealistic narrator, he holds the stage action together and totally controls our responses.

[6] Williams thus uses Tom in three distinct ways to create unity and perspective. As a realistic character aching to leave the confines of home, Tom embodies the theme of escape. As a nonrealistic stage manager, he illustrates the artificiality of the dramatic literary form and stresses the legendary nature of the action. As the play's narrator, he imposes a subjective but coherent control over the action and offers thematic resolution. The nonrealistic aspects of his roles mesh perfectly with other devices that Williams employs nonrealistically, especially the slides, music, and lighting.

[7] Whether realistic or unrealistic, however, The Glass Menagerie is about life—its desires, its dreams, its need for independent action, its disappointments, and its poignancy. If Williams did not dramatize these issues, the technique alone would not make a great play. But he does dramatize them, and as a result the freedom of action and character he achieves through the combination of roles for Tom enables him to achieve a remarkable unity of topic, merging past with present and reality with unreality. Williams's use of Tom, then, is a major reason The Glass Menagerie is a great modern drama.

WORK CITED

Tennessee Williams, The Glass Menagerie. Literature: An Introduction to Reading and Writing. 7th ed. Ed. Edgar V. Roberts and Henry E. Jacobs. Upper Saddle River: Prentice Hall, 2004. 1675–1723.

Commentary on the Essay

This essay shows how Williams's manipulation of Tom creates artistic and thematic unity in *The Glass Menagerie*. The primary focus is on character, but a number of distinct topics are taken up in connection with this element because the essay concerns Tom as a character, stage director, and narrator.

The body of the essay (paragraphs 2–5) takes up these three roles in the order listed in the introduction. Notice that this order does not reflect the sequence in which these roles occur in the play. Rather, they are organized to reflect a progression from the most realistic to the most nonrealistic aspects of

Tom's three different functions. Thus, paragraph 2 discusses Tom as a realistic character and connects him to one of the play's central themes—entrapment and the desire to escape. Paragraphs 3, 4, and 5 shift to a consideration of Tom first as stage manager and second as narrator. These paragraphs explain the nonrealistic nature of these roles and explore the effects of Tom as the nonrealistic figure.

The concluding two paragraphs (6 and 7) provide a review and summary of the three roles Tom plays and the effects each produces in connection with theme and unity. In addition, they suggest a connection between the nonrealistic aspects of Tom's roles and the play's great power.

Throughout the body, direct quotation of dialogue or action as indicated in the stage directions is employed as supporting evidence. Quotations are used to validate specific points and are documented either within parentheses or in the body of discourse itself.

Special Topics for Writing and Argument about Dramatic Reality and Nonreality

1. Compare the families of the Wingfields in *The Glass Menagerie*, the Gibbses and Webbs in *Our Town*, and Colonel Norwood in *Mulatto* (to which you might wish to add the Helmers in *A Dollhouse* and the Wrights in *Trifles*). What concept of family do these plays present? What good and bad effects do the families create? Which type of effect predominates? How realistic is the internal family dissension? How serious? How essential to the various plots? What is unusual or illogical about the dissentions? How? Why?

2. Compare the sets of *Our Town* and *The Glass Menagerie*. What elements of realism or nonrealism are common to both? How? Why? What effects would the sets have on the audience? Why?

3. The screen device described in Williams's Production Notes (p. 1676) is omitted from most productions of *The Glass Menagerie*. Why? Consider the advantages or disadvantages of referring to this device in the printed text. How do the screen images affect your reading?

4. Describe Hughes's symbolism in *Mulatto*. How does the symbolism bring out the black–white differences in the play? Which locations, objects, and actions are symbolic, and what do they symbolize? In what ways are the symbols realistic? If they were not realistic, would they be successful as symbols?

5. Consider any of the plays in this chapter, using a feminist approach (see Chapter 33 for a discussion of this approach). What elements of realism or nonrealism are relevant to such a discussion? To aid your discussion, you might use a study by Patricia R. Schroeder, *The Feminist Possibilities of Dramatic Realism* (Madison, NJ: Fairleigh Dickinson UP, 1996).

6. Write a research essay on the concept and practice of literary realism. To begin your research, you might wish to use books like these: Hugh S. Davies, *Realism in the Drama* (Cambridge, Cambridge UP, 1934); John B. Moore, *The Comic and the Realistic in English Drama* (New York: Russell & Russell, 1965); Harold H. Kolb, *The Illusion of Life: American Realism as a Literary Form* (Charlottesville: U of Virginia P, 1969); and Joseph P. Stern, *On Realism* (Boston: Routledge, 1973).

7.   Write two separate versions of a scene of your own. (Some possible topics: a woman confronts her boyfriend upon learning that he has been seeing someone else; a man has an interview with his boss and learns that he is being fired; an army lieutenant tells his platoon that they are about to be attacked; a woman realizes that she is the best salesperson in the firm.) In the first, aim for total reality; in the second, for total unreality. What differences do you think your intentions in each case require of you as a practicing dramatist? What different requirements are made on your dialogue, on your action, on your setting, and on your costuming and suggested makeup for your actors? What elements do you think are the most unrealistic in your unrealistic version, and why do you believe you make them so unrealistic? Does the lack of realism, in your judgment, make your scene either more or less dramatic? Write an introductory essay to your two versions explaining these and other principles of your dramatic composition.

Dramatic Vision and the Motion Picture Camera: *Drama on the Silver Screen, Television Set, and Computer Monitor*

Film is the word most often used for motion pictures, although other common words are *cinema, movies,* and sometimes *pics.* It is a specialized type of drama, utilizing, like drama, the techniques of dialogue, monologue, and action. Also like drama, it employs movement and spectacle. For these reasons, film can be studied for aspects such as character, plot, structure, tone, and symbolism. Unlike drama, however, film embodies techniques from photography, film chemistry, electronic technology, sound, and editing. These techniques are extremely specialized, and for this reason they require special consideration.

A THUMBNAIL HISTORY OF FILM

Film arose out of technologies developed in the late nineteenth century. The first of these was the creation of a flexible substance—celluloid—that could accept the chemical emulsions that in the early years of photography could be applied only to glass. Other significant inventions were the motion picture camera and projector, together with screens coated with reflective silver iodide and on which the pictures were projected. Once these were in place, and once producers and directors decided to use the medium for full-length dramas, movies as we know them came into existence.

Although the earliest filmmakers thought of motion pictures as private entertainment, they soon recognized that the development of large filmmaking studios, national distribution, and a system of local movie theaters could become extremely lucrative. The history of film is hence just as much a history of the film business as of the art and development of film dramas and film acting. The enormous potential of the movie business was first realized with the production in 1915 of D. W. Griffith's landmark but still controversial film *Birth of a Nation*, which reaped an enormous profit on a small investment.

The first motion pictures were black and white and were silent. Producers realized that large profits required easily recognized actors with "big names," and so the "star system" made national figures out of actors such as Mary Pickford, Charlie Chaplin, and Rudolph Valentino. In 1928 the first talking picture, *Lights of New York*, was made. Film as we know it today was substantially established in 1933 with the first technicolor film, *La Cucaracha*, a "short subject," and in 1935 with *Becky Sharp*, a feature film. Since then the use of color in films has undergone great refinement and improvement.

For a time after the end of World War II, the growth of television inhibited the power of the large studios. Soon, however, many films were developed specifically for television viewing, and popular pictures were released for television use. In the last decade or two, with the advent of videotape and then DVD technology, home viewing of films has become a normal feature of American life. Today, movie rental outlets can be found in shopping districts everywhere, with the result that most of the movies ever made are within the reach of anyone with a television set and the proper playing equipment. Early dramatists dreamed of filling their theaters for a number of consecutive performances, thus reaching perhaps several thousand persons. Film writers today, however, reach millions in first-run movie houses and many millions more on television reruns, videocassettes, and DVD.

DVD TECHNOLOGY AND FILM STUDY

DVD technology (*digital video disc* or *digital versatile disc*), now widely available, promises a flourishing future for students of film. The video resolution of DVD is superior to that of videotape. DVDs also often contain many extra features that provide interesting background and sidelights for film study. The DVD for Jonathan Demme's *The Silence of the Lambs* (1990) is exemplary. It includes the entire film itself, together with a wide variety of additional material. The disk contains an index that can be easily set up on a TV screen, and the various parts (chapters) of the film can be selected, played, stopped, slowed, reversed, and enlarged as the viewer wishes. There are voiceovers by the principal actors, who comment on various scenes in which they figure prominently. There is also frequent voiceover commentary by the director, the screenwriter, and an FBI consultant. Additional features for study are selected scenes that were reduced or omitted in the final editing, together with reports of research into abnormal psychology that were used in the creation of the film's diabolical villain.

Of comparable interest is the recent DVD remastered edition of Welles's *Citizen Kane*, which contains voiceover running analyses of the entire movie by both Roger Ebert and Peter Bogdanovich. (Turner Home Video © 2001). In addition, many DVDs offer materials unobtainable in other formats. The 1964 Richard Burton production of *Hamlet*, for example, is available only on DVD (in black and white). The DVD of Terry Gilliam's *Brazil* (1985) includes instructive interviews about the problems and controversies that preceded and followed the film's release.

❦ STAGE PLAYS AND FILM

Although film is a form of drama, there are a number of important differences between film and stage productions. Plays can be produced many times, in many different places, with many different people. In bringing a play to life, the producer and director use not only actors but also artists, scene designers, carpenters, painters, lighting technicians, costume makers, choreographers, music directors, and musicians. For the actual performance of a play, however, the stage itself limits what can be done. In each theater production, the actors, setting, and effects are all physically confined to the stage.

The stage for makers of film, however, is virtually infinite, and the absence of restrictions permits the inclusion of any details whatever—car chases, underwater adventures, flying geese following an airplane, wartime combat, legislative debates, executive discussions; scenes in living rooms, courtrooms, boxing rings, hotel rooms, football stadiums, and kitchens; and locations in cities and countrysides anywhere—domestic or foreign, modern or ancient. If the setting is a desert island, the filmmaker can travel to such an island and film it in all its reality, complete with beach, palm trees, huts, and authentic natives-turned-actors, and if additional scenery is desired, technicians can dub it in by computer enhancement, as in *Cast Away* (2000) by Robert Zemeckis. If the scene is a distant planet, the filmmaker can create an exotic planet location in the studio, with appropriate scenery, props, effects, lighting, and costumes for the space travelers. Additional special effects, in which filmmakers often indulge too freely, are created by computers, which permit film scenes that were unimaginable for the greatest part of theater history. The freedom enjoyed by the filmmaker, in short, almost limitlessly exceeds the freedom of the play producer. Nothing is left to the audience's imagination.

The two types of dramatic productions—drama and film—are therefore greatly different. Each new production of a play is unlike every other production, because not only the actors but also the appurtenances of the staging are unique. Shakespeare's play *Hamlet*, for example, has been produced innumerable times since Shakespeare's actors at London's Globe Theatre first performed it at the beginning of the seventeenth century, and each subsequent production, including the various filmed versions, has been different from all the rest.

Paradoxically, this same variety cannot occur with film. Although the filmmaker has great freedom in producing each individual movie, this freedom also imposes its own limitations. Because of high production costs and also because films reach a mass audience through wide distribution, films are generally released in only one version, perhaps with "remakes" and dubbed versions for foreign audiences. Thus Orson Welles's *Citizen Kane* (1941) is in only one form, and although it was restored and reedited in 1991, and received additional changes and restorations for DVD in 2001, it remains in this form even though it is frequently shown and seen. Interestingly, no person can ever claim to have seen all the productions of plays like *Hamlet*, but everyone who sees a film like *Citizen Kane* can claim to have seen it in its entirety.

THE AESTHETICS OF FILM

To the degree that film is confined to a screen, it can be compared visually with the art of the painter and the still photographer. It uses the language of visual art. One object in a painting can take on special relationships to others as the artist directs the eyes of the observer. A color used in one part can be balanced with the same color, or its complement, in another part. Painters and photographers can introduce certain colors and details as symbols and can suggest allegorical interpretations through the inclusion of mythical figures or universally recognized objects. Particular effects can be achieved with the use of the textures of paint or with control over shutter speed, focus, and various techniques of development. The techniques and effects are extensive.

The filmmaker is able to utilize most of the resources of the still photographer and many of those of the painter and can augment these with special effects. Artistically, the most confining aspect of film is the rectangular screen, but aside from that, film is unrestricted. Based in a dramatic text called a film script or shooting script, the film uses words and their effects, but it also employs the language of visual art and especially the particular vividness and power of moving pictures. When considering film, then, you should realize that film communicates not only with words but also by using various visual techniques. The visual presentation is inseparable from the medium of film itself.

THE TECHNIQUES OF FILM

There are many techniques of film, and a full description and documentation of them can be—and has become—extensive.[1] In evaluating film, however, you need to familiarize yourself only with those aspects of technique that have an immediate bearing on your responses and interpretations.

Editing or Montage Is the Assembling of a Film out of Separate Parts

A finished film is a composite, not a continuous work filmed from start to end. The putting together of the film is the process of editing, or **montage** (assemblage, mounting, construction), which at one time involved cutting and gluing,

---

[1]See, for example, David Bleiler, *TLA Film, Video, and DVD Guide 2002–2003: The Discerning Film Lover's Guide* (2001), Roger Ebert, *Roger Ebert's Movie Yearbook 2003* (2002); Roger Ebert, *The Great Movies* (2002); Louis D. Giannetti, *Understanding Movies*, 9th ed. (2001); Leslie Halliwell, *Halliwell's Film and Video Guide 2003*, John Walker ed. (2002); Ephraim Katz, *The Film Encyclopedia*, 4th ed., revised by Fred Klein and Ronald Dean Nolan (2001); James Monaco, *How to Read a Film: The World of Movies, Media, and Multimedia: Language, History, Theory*, 3rd ed. (2000); Richard Beck Peacock, *The Art of Movie Making: Script to Screen* (2000); John Pym, *Time Out Film Guide 2002*, 11th ed. (2002); Robert Sklar, *A World History of Film* (2002); and David Thomson, *The New Biographical Dictionary of Film* (2002).   See also the Internet Movie Data Base for complete data on films of all periods, at <www.imdb.com>.

but which now takes place on computers. Depending on the flexibility of the film script, the various scenes of the film are planned before shooting begins, but the major task of montage is accomplished in a studio by editing specialists.

If we again compare film with a stage play, we note that a theatrical production moves continuously, with pauses only for intermissions and scene changes. Your perception of the action is caused by your distance from the stage (perhaps aided by opera glasses or binoculars). Also, even as you move your eyes from one character to another, you still perceive the entire stage. In a film, however, the directors and editors *create* these continuous perceptions for you by piecing together different parts. The editors begin with many "takes" (separately photographed scenes, including many versions of the same scenes). What they select, or "mount," will be the film, and we never see the discarded scenes (unless they appear on a special DVD). Thus, it is editing that puts everything together.

MONTAGE CREATES NARRATIVE CONTINUITY.   The first use of montage, already suggested, is narrative continuity. For example, a climb up a steep cliff can be shown at the bottom, middle, and top (with backward slips and falls to show the danger of the climb and to make viewers catch their breath). All such narrative sequences result from the assembling of individual pieces, each one representing phases of the activity. A classic example of a large number of separate parts forming a narrative unit is the well-known shower murder in Alfred Hitchcock's *Psycho* (1959), where a forty-five-second sequence is made up of seventy-eight different shots (the woman in the shower, the murderer behind the curtain, the attack, the slumping figure, the running water, the dead woman's eye, the bathtub drain, etc.).

MONTAGE PROVIDES EXPLANATION OF CHARACTER AND MOTIVATION.   Montage is used in flashbacks to explain present, ongoing actions or characteristics, or in illustration of a character's thoughts and memories; or in brief examples from the unremembered past of a character suffering from amnesia. It also supplies direct visual explanation of character. A famous example occurs in Welles's *Citizen Kane* (the subject of the demonstrative essay on page 1749). The concluding scene shows overhead views of Kane's vast collection of statuary and mementos. At the very end, the camera focuses on a raging furnace, into which workmen have thrown his boyhood sled, which bears the brand name "Rosebud" (we have fleetingly seen Kane playing with the sled as a boy). Because "Rosebud" is Kane's last word, and everyone in the film is trying to decipher its meaning, this final scene reveals that Kane's dying thoughts were of his lost boyhood, before he was taken away from his parents, and that his unhappy life has resulted from his early rejection and personal pain.

MONTAGE FACILITATES DIRECTORIAL COMMENTARY.   Montage is also used symbolically as commentary, as in an early sequence in Charlie Chaplin's *Modern Times* (1936) that shows a large group of workers rushing to their factory jobs. Immediately following this scene is a view of a large, milling herd of sheep. By this symbolic montage, Chaplin suggests that the men are being herded and dehumanized by modern industry. Thus, montage and editorial statement go hand in hand.

MONTAGE IS USED IN MANY OTHER WAYS.   Montage can also produce other characteristics through camera work, development, and special effects. For example, filmmakers can reverse an action to emphasize its illogicality or ridiculousness. Editing can also speed up action (which makes even the most serious things funny) or slow things down. It can also blend one scene with another or juxtapose two or more actions in quick succession to show what people are doing while they are separated. The possibilities for creativity and innovation are extensive.

Film Utilizes Special Visual Techniques

THE CAMERA IS THE BASIC TOOL OF FILM.   Whereas editing or montage is a finishing technique, the work of film begins with the camera, which permits great freedom in the presentation of characters and actions. In a film, the visual viewpoint can shift. Thus, a film can begin with a distant shot of the actors—a "long shot"—much like the view of actors onstage. Then the camera can zoom in to show a close-up or zoom out to present a wide and complete panorama. Usually a speaking actor will be the subject of a close-up, but the camera can also capture other actors' reactions in close-up. You must interpret the effects of close-ups and long shots yourself, but it should be plain that the frequent use of either—or of middle-distance views—is a means by which film directors control the perceptions of their characters and situations.

The camera can also move from character to character or from character to object. In this way, film can mark a series of reactions, concentrate your attention on a character's attitude, or comment visually on a character's actions. If a man and woman are in love, for example, the camera can shift, either directly or through montage, from the couple to flowers and trees, thus associating their love visually with objects of beauty and growth. Should the flowers be wilted and the trees leafless, however, the visual commentary might be that their love is doomed and hopeless.

The camera can also be used in the creation of unique effects. A common technique is slow motion, which can be used to emphasize a certain aspect of a person's character. The concentrated focus on a child running happily in a meadow (as in *The Color Purple* [1985] by Steven Spielberg) suggests the joy inherent in such movement. Surprisingly, speed is sometimes indicated by slow motion, which emphasizes strong muscular effort (as in the running scenes in Hugh Hudson's *Chariots of Fire* [1981]).

Many other camera techniques bear on action and character. The focus can be sharp at one point, indistinct at another. Moving a speaking character out of focus can suggest that listeners are bored. Sharp or blurred focus can also show that a character has seen things exactly or inexactly. In action sequences, the camera can be mounted in a moving vehicle to "track" or follow running human beings or horses, speeding bicycles and cars (as in Woody Allen's *Annie*

Hall [1977]), or moving sailboats, canoes, speedboats, or rowboats. A camera operator on foot can also be the tracker, or the camera may track ground movement from an aircraft. Movement can also be captured by a rotating camera that follows a moving object or character. Alternatively, the camera can be fixed while a character or object moves from one side to the other.

THE PICTURES IN FILM INVOLVE LIGHT, SHADOW, AND COLOR. As in the theater, the filmmaker uses light, shadow, and color to reinforce ideas and to create realistic and symbolic effects. Characters in bright light are presumably open and frank, whereas characters in shadow may be hiding something, particularly in black-and-white films. Flashing or strobe lights might indicate a changeable or sinister character or situation. A scene in sunshine, which brings out colors, and the same scene in rain and clouds or in twilight, all of which mute colors, create different moods. An example of such contrasts is the film *From Hell* (2001), directed by Albert and Allen Hughes, in which virtually the entire action takes place in darkness, and only the final scene is filmed in full light.

Colors, of course, have much the same meaning that they have in any other artistic medium. Blue sky and clear light suggest happiness, while greenish light can indicate something ghoulish. A memorable control of color occurs midway through David O. Selznick's *Gone with the Wind* (1939) when Scarlett O'Hara reflects upon the devastation of her plantation home, Tara. She resolves never to be hungry again, and as she speaks she is silhouetted against a darkened orange sky—a background that suggests how totally the way of life she knew as a young woman has been burned away. As in this example, you may expect colors to complement the story of the film. Thus, lovers may wear clothing with the same or complementary colors, whereas people who are not "right" for each other may wear clashing colors.

Action Is the Essence of Film

The strength of film is direct action. Actions of all sorts—running, swimming, driving a car, fighting, embracing and kissing, or even just sitting; chases, trick effects, ambushes—all these and more create a sense of immediate reality, and all are tied (or should be) to narrative development. Scenes of action can run on for several minutes, with little or no accompanying dialogue, to carry on the story or to convey ideas about the interests and abilities of the characters.

Camera Angles and Views of the Heads, Bodies, and Movements of Actors Are Related to a Film's Content

Closely related to the portrayal of action is the way in which film shows the human body (and animal bodies) together with bodily motion and gesture (or body language). The view or perspective that the filmmaker presents is particularly important. A torso shot of a character may stress no more than the content of that character's speech. A close-up shot, however, with the character's head filling the screen, may emphasize motives as well as content. The camera can also distort ordinary expectations of reality. Using wide-angle lenses and close-ups, for example, human subjects can be made to seem bizarre or grotesque, as are the faces in the crowd in Woody Allen's *Stardust Memories* (1980). Sometimes the camera creates other bodily distortions—for example, enlarging the limbs of the forest dweller in Ingmar Bergman's *The Virgin Spring* (1959) or throwing into unnatural prominence a scolding mouth or a suspicious eye. Distortion invites interpretation: The filmmaker may be asserting that certain human beings, even supposedly normal ones, are odd, sinister, intimidating, or psychopathic.

Sound Is Integral to the Presentation and Content of a Film

DIALOGUE AND MUSIC COMPLEMENT FILM DRAMATIZATIONS.   The first business of the sound track is the spoken dialogue, which is "mixed" in editing to be synchronized with the action. There are also many other elements in the sound track. Music, the most important, creates and augments moods. A melody in a major or minor key, or in a slow or fast tempo, can affect our perception of actions. If a character is thinking deeply, a complementary sound may be muted strings. But if the character is going insane, the music may become discordant and percussive.

Sometimes, music gives a film a special identity. Hudson's *Chariots of Fire* (1981), for example, includes music by Vangelis Papathanassiou. Although this music is independently well known, it is always associated with the film. In addition, musical accompaniments can directly render dramatic statement, without dialogue. An example occurs in Welles's *Citizen Kane* (1941). Beginning that portion of the narrative derived from the autobiography of a character who is now dead (the scene first focuses on his statue), the musical sound track by Bernard Herrmann quotes the *Dies Irae* theme from the Catholic mass for the dead. The instrumentation, however, makes the music funny, and we smile rather than grieve. Herrmann, incidentally, varies this theme elsewhere in the film, usually for comic effect.

FILM USES SPECIAL AND OFTEN INGENIOUS SOUND EFFECTS.   Special sound effects can also augment a film's action. The sound of a blow can be enhanced electronically to cause an impact similar to the force of the blow itself (as in the boxing scenes from the many *Rocky* films). At times some sounds, such as the noises of wailing people, squeaking or slamming doors, marching feet, or moving vehicles, are filtered electronically to create weird or ghostly effects. Often a character's words echo rapidly and sickeningly to show dismay or anguish.

TWO FILM SCENES FOR STUDY

ORSON WELLES AND HERMAN J. MANKIEWICZ, *SHOT 71*
FROM THE SHOOTING SCRIPT OF CITIZEN KANE

Orson Welles (1915–1985) developed an early interest in the theater. As a youth he traveled extensively, even spending some time in Spain as a bullfighter. In 1937 he co-founded the Mercury Theater, specializing in hour-long Sunday evening radio dramatizations. In October 1938 he achieved early immortality by acting in and directing a version of H. G. Wells's The War of the Worlds. *This production created a near panic in the nation among listeners who did not understand they were hearing a dramatic production, not a real news broadcast about invaders from the planet Mars.*

Within a few years Welles, along with Herman J. Mankiewicz, planned a film on a larger-than-life American figure. Their model was the newspaper magnate William Randolph Hearst. Mankiewicz produced a lengthy draft of the script, which was titled first American *and then, a little later,* John Citizen, USA. *Welles changed the plot, rewrote many sections, and edited and shortened much of the original material. It was during this process of rewriting and editing that the title* Citizen Kane *was proposed and accepted. Soon, Welles began production with many of the actors of the Mercury Theater. Hearst, who quickly learned about the forthcoming film, sought a legal restraint on it, but* Citizen Kane *was successfully completed despite his efforts. The film reached the movie theaters with massive critical acclaim.*

In 1958 a poll of international critics listed *Citizen Kane* as one of the twelve best films ever made. Its use of a format similar to *The March of Time* (a popular news feature series that ran regularly as a "selected short subject" in movie theaters), deep-focus camera work, unusual camera angles, contrasts of light and shadow, and its employment of four distinct points of view, together with its relentless insights into the major figure, all combined to make it a pioneering work in the history of film. Today, it is one of the touchstones in any discussion of movies, and its continued recognition justifies the claim that Welles was one of the great directors. After *Citizen Kane*, however, Welles struggled with personal and financial difficulties on each of his films, and he never again reached the heights of his first attempt.

The scene included here occurs about two-thirds of the way through the film. It is vital because it is a major indicator of Kane's personal decline. At first imbued with ideals for informing and reforming society, Kane (played by Welles) becomes publisher of a newspaper he has inherited, and he advances public-minded editorial policies. A high point in his career is his running for governor of the state, but he loses the election after his secret love affair is made public. The scene occurs right after the election loss. His most loyal supporter and coworker, Jedediah "Jed" Leland (Joseph Cotten), confronts him and asks for a transfer to Chicago. The unspoken issue in the scene is that both men know that their friendship has been lost not because of the election but because of Kane's misperceptions of people and his desertion of his earlier ideals.

The scene is taken from the so-called shooting script, which in film most closely corresponds to a dramatic text; it is the full version, with copious directions for the actors. A comparison of this "shot," or scene, with the filmed version will show that some of the dialogue was trimmed for purposes of pacing and speed. The shortening indicates a major characteristic of film (and the production of plays), namely, to reduce speeches to no more than the essentials in order to keep the action moving and hold the audience's attention.

ORSON WELLES (1915–1985)
AND HERMAN J. MANKIEWICZ (1897–1953)

Shot 71 from the Shooting Script of Citizen Kane* *(1941)*

RKO Radio Pictures. A Mercury Production. Producer and Director, Orson Welles. Photographer, Gregg Toland. Editor, Robert Wise. Art Director, Van Nest Polglase. Music, Bernard Herrmann. Special Effects, Vernon L. Walker.

Dissolve in.

71 Int. Kane's Office—"Inquirer"—Night—1916

[*KANE looks up from his desk as there is a knock on the door.*]

    KANE.   Come in.

[*LELAND enters.*]

    KANE.   [*Surprised*] I thought I heard somebody knock.
    LELAND.   [*A bit drunk*] I knocked. [*He looks at him defiantly*]
    KANE.   [*Trying to laugh it off*] Oh! An official visit of state, eh? [*Waves his hand*] Sit down, Jedediah.
    LELAND.   [*Sitting down angrily*] I'm drunk.   5
    KANE.   Good! It's high time—
    LELAND.   You don't have to be amusing.
    KANE.   All right. Tell you what I'll do. I'll get drunk, too.
    LELAND.   [*Thinks this over*] No. That wouldn't help. Besides, you never get drunk. [*Pauses*] I want to talk to you—about—about—[*He can't get it out*]
    KANE.   [*Looks at him sharply a moment*] If you've got yourself drunk to talk to me   10
about Susan Alexander—I'm not interested.
    LELAND.   She's not important. What's much more important—[*He keeps glaring at KANE*]
    KANE.   [*As if genuinely surprised*] Oh! [*He gets up*] I frankly didn't think I'd have to listen to that lecture from you. [*Pauses*] I've betrayed the sacred cause of reform, is that it? I've set back the sacred cause of reform in this state twenty years. Don't tell me, Jed, *you*—

[*Despite his load,° LELAND manages to achieve a dignity about the silent contempt with which he looks at KANE.*]

    KANE.   [*An outburst*] What makes the sacred cause of reform so sacred? Why does the sacred cause of reform have to be exempt from all the other facts of life? Why do the laws of this state have to be executed by a man on a white charger?

[*LELAND lets the storm ride over his head.*]

    KANE.   [*Cont'd*] [*Calming down*] But, if that's the way they want it—they've made their choice. The people of this state obviously prefer Mr. Rogers to me. [*His lips tighten*] So be it.
    LELAND.   You talk about the people as though they belong to you. As long as I can   15
remember you've talked about giving the people their rights as though you could make

---

*The scene is gratefully reprinted from *The Citizen Kane Book* (Boston: Little, Brown & Co., 1971), pp. 228–231.   13 S. D.: *load:* i.e., a heavy amount of liquor.

Still from *Citizen Kane.*

them a present of liberty—in reward for services rendered. You remember the working-man? You used to write an awful lot about the workingman. Well, he's turning into some-thing called organized labor, and you're not going to like that a bit when you find out it means that he thinks he's entitled to something as his right and not your gift. [*He pauses*] And listen, Charles. When your precious underprivileged really do get together—that's going to add up to something bigger—than your privilege—and then I don't know what you'll do. Sail away to a desert island, probably, and lord it over the monkeys.

KANE.   Don't worry about it too much, Jed. There's sure to be a few of them there to tell me where I'm wrong.

LELAND.   You may not always be that lucky. [*Pauses*] Charlie, why can't you get to look at things less personally? Everything doesn't have to be between you and—the per-sonal note doesn't always—

KANE.   [*Violently*] The personal note is all there is to it. It's all there ever is to it. It's all there ever is to anything! Stupidity in our government—crookedness—even just com-placency and self-satisfaction and an unwillingness to believe that anything done by a cer-tain class of people can be wrong—you can't fight those things impersonally. They're not impersonal crimes against the people. They're being done by actual persons—with actu-al names and positions and—the right of the American people to their own country is not an academic issue, Jed, that you debate—and then the judges retire to return a ver-dict—and the winners give a dinner for the losers.

LELAND.   You almost convince me, almost. The truth is, Charlie, you just don't care about anything except you. You just want to convince people that you love them so much that they should love you back. Only you want love on your own terms. It's some-thing to be played your way—according to your rules. And if anything goes wrong and you're hurt—then the game stops, and you've got to be soothed and nursed, no matter what else is happening—and no matter who else is hurt!

[*They look at each other.*]

    KANE.   [*Trying to kid him into a better humor*] Hey, Jedediah!   20

[*LELAND is not to be seduced.*]

    LELAND.   Charlie, I wish you'd let me work on the Chicago paper—you said your-self you were looking for someone to do dramatic criticism there—
    KANE.   You're more valuable here.

[*There is silence.*]

    LELAND.   Well, Charlie, then I'm afraid there's nothing I can do but to ask you to accept—
    KANE.   [*Harshly*] All right. You can go to Chicago.
    LELAND.   Thank you.   25

[*There is an awkward pause. KANE opens a drawer of his desk and takes out a bottle and two glasses.*]

    KANE.   I guess I'd better *try* to get drunk, anyway.

[*KANE hands JED a glass, which he makes no move to take.*]

    KANE.   [*Cont'd*] But I warn you, Jedediah, you're not going to like it in Chicago. The wind comes howling in off the lake, and the Lord only knows if they've ever heard of lobster Newburg.
    LELAND.   Will a week from Saturday be all right?
    KANE.   [*Wearily*] Anytime you say.
    LELAND.   Thank you.   30

[*KANE looks at him intently and lifts the glass.*]

    KANE.   A toast, Jedediah—to love on *my* terms. Those are the only terms anybody knows—his own.

                                                    Dissolve

QUESTIONS

1.   What do you learn about the past and present relationship of Kane and Leland in this scene? What do Leland's speeches indicate about Kane's attitudes toward people? About Kane's shortcomings?

2.   Basing your conclusions on this scene, why do you think the film is named *Citizen Kane,* and not something like *The Life of an American Tycoon* or *The Perils of Wealth*?

3.   This scene is one of the revolutionary ones in the film because Welles and Toland (the principal photographer) shot it from floor height, emphasizing the distance from the camera to the heads of the characters. What effect do you think this vantage point has on viewers of the film? If you have seen the film, what do you think the camera angles and the lighting contribute to your per-ception of the characters?

ARTHUR LAURENTS, A SCENE FROM *THE TURNING POINT*

Arthur Laurents is one of the most successful dramatists and screenplay writers of the postwar period. Among his achievements in film are The Snake Pit *(1948),* Anastasia *(1956), and* The Way We Were *(1973). His plays* West Side Story *(1957) and* Gypsy *(1959) had successful Broadway runs as musicals and also became successful films. His very first play,* Home of the Brave *(1946), was revived in 1999, and his* Time of the Cuckoo *(1952) was revived at Lincoln Center in New York in 2000. A recent work,* The Radical Mystique, *was produced in 1995 at the City Center. The* Turning Point *(1977), which Laurents also published as a novel, received the Golden Globe Award, the National Board of Review Best Picture, and the Writers Guild of America Award as the best film of the year.*

The Turning Point takes place against the background of ballet and the life of professional dancers. Deedee Rodgers (Shirley MacLaine) and Emma Jacklin (Anne Bancroft) had been close friends and rivals as young dancers with the American Ballet Theater. Deedee became pregnant and married before she had a chance to become a star, and after the birth of her daughter, Emilia, she left the stage entirely for family life. With her husband Wayne (Tom Skerrit), who had also earlier been a dancer, she moved to Oklahoma, had two more children, and established a successful ballet school.

During the following seventeen years, Deedee has believed she could have gained stardom if she had not become a mother. She has also carried a grudge against Emma for having urged her to have the baby. In this way, Deedee believes, Emma pushed her aside when the two women had competed for the once-in-a-lifetime opportunity to dance in a new ballet. Emma, who won the role, went on to become famous as the company's prima ballerina. However, she has lived her life alone, her principal companions being the three dogs she keeps in her elegant apartment.

As the film opens, the ballet company comes to perform in Oklahoma City. Deedee's first daughter, Emilia (Leslie Browne), is now a promising dancer, and with Emma's help and support she becomes a star with the company during the following summer in New York. The scene included here occurs after a gala performance by the company, in which Emilia has brilliantly performed her first major solo dance, and in which Emma has been featured in a solo from *Anna Karenina*, perhaps for the last time.

At the reception after the gala, Emma makes a show of acknowledging Emilia, a gesture that angers Deedee and leads her to conclude that for a number of months Emma has been trying to gain undue influence over Emilia. Shortly after this, the company's director, Adelaide (Martha Scott) asks Emma to create a new production of Tchaikowsky's *Sleeping Beauty* ballet, but *not* to dance in it. This request hits Emma with full force, for she now recognizes that she is getting old and is about to be pushed aside by dancers who, like Emilia, are young and strong. She rushes out and stops at the nearby bar, where she encounters Deedee. The scene, which is virtually a short play all by itself, then develops, as the long-pent-up frustration, apprehension, and guilt of both women emerge.

ARTHUR LAURENTS (b. 1918)

A Scene from *The Turning Point* ⤙⤚ 1977

Twentieth Century Fox. Producers, Herbert Ross and Arthur Laurents. Executive Producer, Nora Kaye. Photography, Robert Surtees. Film editor, William Reynolds. Music adapter, John Lanchbery. Director, Herbert Ross.

[SCENE] *Interior Bar—Rainbow Room*

[DEEDEE *is alone at the bar, drinking champagne. As* EMMA, *on her way to the Ladies' room, comes toward her,* DEEDEE *smiles and does a half-curtsy.* EMMA *stops and smiles back. Then she tosses her evening bag onto the bar.*]

EMMA. [*to the bartender*]. Champagne, please.

[*Declaration of war accepted. During the following, they both get refills, but they do not guzzle; there is no need for them to get drunk. Emotionally, each is ready to burst anyway. They (and we) are unaware of the bartender and he is unaware of them. For despite the lines, despite what each feels underneath, they are totally charming: two smiling, lovely, delightful friends having a chat.*]

DEEDEE. Remember the fairy tales we used to take turns reading to Emilia? Like the one about the two princesses? Every time one opened her mouth, out came diamonds and rubies. Every time the other opened her mouth, out came newts and hoptoads. Newts and hoptoads—[*taps her chest*]—coming out.

EMMA. One of those little toads has already made an appearance.

DEEDEE. Really! When?

EMMA. In my dressing room. When you said I shouldn't have bought Emilia that   5
dress. Twice, you said it. Just before a performance. . . . I danced better tonight than I have in years.

DEEDEE. So I heard.

EMMA. Oh, another little toad! You've kept quite a few bottled up all these years, haven't you?

DEEDEE. Ohhh—embalmed, really.

EMMA. I think not. Why don't you let them out? I don't have a performance tomorrow.

[DEEDEE *looks at her, then accepts the challenge. She puts her glass down on the bar and holds out her hands with her fists clenched.*]

DEEDEE. Okay. Pick.   10

[EMMA *puts her glass down and points to a fist.* DEEDEE *opens it.*]

DEEDEE. Ah, a tiny one. I'd practically forgotten him. [*Looks up now.*] Why'd you make your best pal doubt herself and her hubby, Emma? Why'd you take the chance of lousing up her marriage? Why'd you say: "You better have that baby. It's the only way you can hold on to Wayne." I'm just curious now.

EMMA. You have a curious memory, but don't we all? As I remember, I said if you had an abortion, you might lose Wayne.

DEEDEE. Sweet, but inaccurate. I've remembered your exact words for lo, these too many moons. I eventually figured out why you said 'em. Because you also said: "Forget Michael's ballet, there'll be others." You clever little twinkletoes! You knew a ballet like that comes once in a career. You wanted it real bad, so you lied to make sure you got what you wanted.

EMMA. I've never had to lie to get what I wanted, Deedee. I'm too good.

DEEDEE. Really?   15

EMMA. Oh, yes.

DEEDEE. Well, I suppose if you said "bullshit," you'd say it in French.

[*Close shot.*]

EMMA. If that word came as naturally to me as it does to you, I'd have used it several times by now. In English. I think it's more appropriate that you say it—to yourself.

For trying to blame *me* for what you did, for example. The choice was yours. It's much too late to regret it now, Deedee.

DEEDEE.   And the same to you, Emma me darlin'.

EMMA.   I certainly don't regret mine.   20

DEEDEE.   Then why are you trying to become a mother at your age?

EMMA.   Ooh, that's not a little toad. That's a rather large bullfrog. I don't want to be anybody's mother. I think of Emilia as a friend. And one reason I tried to help—stupid me—I thought it would make you happy if your daughter became what you wanted to be and couldn't be.

DEEDEE.   Meaning you. It's so lovely to be you.

EMMA.   Obviously, you think so.

DEEDEE.   Oh, no no no no no no!   25

EMMA.   No no no no?

DEEDEE.   No; alas. And I doubt if Emilia could become you. Oh, she's as talented. She works as hard. But there's one thing, dearest friend, that you are that she, poor darling, is not.

EMMA.   And what, pray tell, is that?

DEEDEE.   A killer. You'll walk over anybody and still get a good night's sleep. That's what got you where you are, Emma.

[*She is smiling adorably.* EMMA *smiles back, finishes her drink, pushes the glass to the bartender, keeps smiling until it is refilled, then picks it up. They are both smiling, almost laughing as* EMMA *looks at her drink, looks at* DEEDEE, *then throws the champagne in* DEEDEE's *face. A moment. Then* DEEDEE *sets down her glass.*]

DEEDEE.   Good girl.   30

[*She picks up her evening bag and starts out of the bar toward the exit and the elevators. The cool reaction infuriates* EMMA. *She puts down her glass and starts after* DEEDEE.]

Interior Corridor Outside Rainbow Room

[EMMA *comes through the entrance to the Rainbow Room just as* DEEDEE *steps into an elevator.*]

EMMA.   Deedee!

[*She runs for the elevator and just gets in as the doors are closing.*]

Interior Elevator—Rockefeller Center

EMMA.   I'm sick to death of your jealousy and resentment!

DEEDEE.   So am I.

EMMA.   Then stop blaming your goddamn life on me! You picked it!

DEEDEE.   You did. You took away the choice, you didn't give me the chance to find   35
out if I was good enough.

EMMA.   I can tell you now: you weren't.

[*The elevator doors open and* DEEDEE *strides out,* EMMA *after her.*]

Exterior Rockefeller Plaza—Night

[EMMA *is fast after* DEEDEE, *their heels clicking on the stone.*]

EMMA.   You knew it yourself. That's why you married Wayne!

DEEDEE.   [*whirls around*] I loved him!

EMMA.   So much that you said to hell with your career!

DEEDEE.   Yes!   40

EMMA.   And got pregnant to prove you meant it!

DEEDEE.   Yes!

EMMA.   Lie to yourself, not to me. You got married because you knew you were second-rate; you got pregnant because Wayne was a ballet dancer, and that meant queer!

DEEDEE.   *He wasn't!*

EMMA.   Still afraid someone will think he is? You were terrified then! You had to   45
prove he was a man! *That's* why you had a baby!

DEEDEE.   That's a goddamn lie!

EMMA.   It's the goddamn truth! You saddled him with a baby and blew his career!
And now she's grown up and better than you ever were and you're jealous!

DEEDEE.   You're certifiable! You'll use anything for an excuse.

EMMA.   What's that an excuse for?

DEEDEE.   Trying to take away my child!   50

EMMA.   I return the compliment: you're a liar!

DEEDEE.   And you're a user. You have been your whole life! Me, Michael—pretending to love him!—Adelaide and now Emilia!

EMMA.   How Emilia?!

DEEDEE.   "How Emilia." That display five minutes ago: Curtsy! Applause! Embrace! For *you*, not her! You were using her so everyone'd say: "Emma's so gracious,
Emma's so wonderful!"

EMMA.   Untrue!   55

DEEDEE.   You *are* wonderful! You're amazing! It's incredible how you keep going
on. You're over the hill; you know it and *you're* terrified. All you've got are your scrapbooks and your old toe shoes and those stupid, ridiculous dogs! What are you going to fill
in with, Emma? Not my daughter. You keep your goddam hands off!

EMMA.   I'm better for her than you are.

DEEDEE.   Like hell!

EMMA.   She came to me because her mother wasn't there. Her mother was too
busy screwing her head off!

DEEDEE.   You bitch!   60

[*She whacks* EMMA *with her evening bag. For a moment,* EMMA *is too startled to move. But as*
DEEDEE *lifts her bag again,* EMMA *blocks it with one hand and with the other whacks* DEEDEE *with
her evening bag. They both go at it: rarely hitting, ducking blows, slamming out blindly with their
evening bags.*]

Exterior Rockefeller Center—Night

[*There they are, these two ladies in their evening gowns, each making a last pass, a last weak attempt to hit the other, and missing. They are panting, exhausted, and at last, they stop and just
stand there, breathing hard.*]

[*Close shot—Their breath is coming back.* DEEDEE *smiles.*]

DEEDEE.   If there'd been a photographer handy, you'd have a whole new career.

EMMA.   I must look awful.

DEEDEE.   No: beautiful. I don't know how you do it.

[EMMA *has taken out a mirror and is looking in it.*]

EMMA.   If I can borrow your comb, I'll show you. Oh, I lost an earring.

DEEDEE.   [*handing her a comb*] I'm sorry.   65
EMMA.   I'm not.
DEEDEE.   Really?
EMMA.   Yes.

[*She returns the comb, and they start walking, looking for the lost earring. The following is very quiet:*]

DEEDEE.   Jealousy is poison. Makes you a monster.
EMMA.   Well, it does make one unfair. [*Smiles.*] Two.   70
DEEDEE.   Two?
EMMA.   Me, too.
DEEDEE.   [*a second, then laughs*] Emma, you made a good joke!
EMMA.   Yes, I did. . . . I'm really not so humorless.
DEEDEE.   Listen, you got off some really good ones before. Oh, look!   75

[*She picks up the earring and gives it to EMMA.*]

EMMA.   How did it get over here? Thank you.
DEEDEE.   You also hit a couple of bull's-eyes before.
EMMA.   So did you.
DEEDEE.   Sit?
EMMA.   Oh, please.   80

[*They sit on the rim of the fountain.*]

EMMA.   I don't really remember what I said about having the baby. But I do know I would have said anything to make sure I got that ballet. . . . I had to have it, Deedee. I just had to.
DEEDEE.   My God. Oh Emma. Emma, I didn't know how much all I wanted was for you to say just that. . . . Let's have a drink!
EMMA.   Absolutely!

[*They get up. EMMA links her arm through DEEDEE's as they start walking.*]

EMMA.   It's good.
DEEDEE.   You bet.   85
EMMA.   I'm glad Wayne's coming.
DEEDEE.   Me, too. . . . How's with Carter?
EMMA.   Ça va. . . . *That's bullshit in French.*

[*DEEDEE laughs and walks toward the street, to a taxi. But EMMA has stopped, turned toward the entrance to the party.*]

DEEDEE.   Not back to the party?
EMMA.   I have to.   90
DEEDEE.   [*nods, understands*] Call me when you wake up.
EMMA.   If not before.

[*They smile—and walk in opposite directions.*]

QUESTIONS

1.   Despite the fact that the two women carry their anger so far as to strike each other, what does the scene show about the nature of friendship? What key admissions do the women make to effect their reconciliation?

2.   The film omits the last ten speeches of the script (concluding with "to say just that" in speech 82). Justify eliminating these last speeches.

3.   What is the effect of the fact that the locations of this scene move from the interior bar to the exterior plaza? Granted the actions of the two women, why can the scene not be in a single location (as it would necessarily be if written for the theater)? On the basis of your answers, what conclusions can you draw about the comparative freedoms and limitations of film and theater?

4.   View the film *The Turning Point*, and compare the details of the script with the final filmed version of the scene. Explain the purpose and nature of the changes in the film. If you had the freedom of a film director, what other liberties might you take in the performance? Why?

WRITING ABOUT FILM

Obviously the first requirement is to see the film, either in a theater, on videocassette, or on DVD. No matter how you see it, you should go through it at least twice, making notes, because your discussion takes on value the more thoroughly you know the material. Include the names of the scriptwriter, director, composer, special effects editor, chief photographer, and major actresses and actors. If particular speeches are worth quoting, remember the general circumstances of the quotation and also, if possible, key words. Take notes on costume and color or (if the film is in black and white) on light and shade. You may need to rely on memory, but if you have a videotape or a DVD, you can easily replay important sections of the film and can verify important details.

Questions for Discovering Ideas

Action

- How important is action? Is there much repetition of action, say, in slow motion, or from different angles? Are actors (or animals) viewed closely or distantly? Why?

- What actions are stressed (chases, concealment, gun battles, lovemaking, etc.)? What does the type of action contribute to the film?

- What do close-ups (smiles and laughter, frowns, leers, anxious looks, etc.) show about character and motivation?

- What actions indicate seasonal conditions (e.g., cold by a character's stamping of feet, warmth by the character's removing a coat or shirt)? What connection do these actions have to the film's general ideas?

- Does the action show any changing of mood, say, from sadness to happiness or from indecision to decision?

Cinematographic Techniques

- What notable techniques are used (colors, lighting, etc.)? What is their relationship to the film's characterizations and themes?

- What characterizes the use of the camera (tracking, close-ups, distant shots, camera angles, etc.)? How do the camera perspectives reinforce or detract from the film's theme and plot?

- How does the editing (the sequencing of scenes) reinforce or detract from story and theme?
- What scene or scenes best exemplify how the cinematographic techniques interact with the theme, plot, characters, setting, and so on? Why?

Acting

- How well do the actors adapt to the medium of film? How well do they deliver their lines? How convincing are their performances?
- How well do the actors control their facial expressions and body movement? Are they graceful? Awkward?
- What does their appearance lend to your understanding of their characters?
- Does it seem that the actors are genuinely creating their roles, or are they just reading through the parts?

Strategies for Organizing Ideas

State your central idea and thesis sentence. You should include the background necessary to support points you make in the body of the essay and should also name the major creative and performing persons of the film.

Any of the organizing strategies discussed in this book's previous chapters, such as plot, structure, character, ideas, or setting, are equally valid for an essay on a film that you will need to consider them in a visual context. For example, if you choose to discuss the effects of a character on the plot, you need to develop your argument using the evidence of camera techniques, montage, sound effects, and the like.

When discussing film techniques, be sure to have good notes so that your supporting details are accurate. A good method is to concentrate on technique in only a few scenes. If you analyze the effects of montage, for example, you can use a videocassette or DVD so you can replay the scene a number of times.

In the conclusion of your essay, you might evaluate the effectiveness of the cinematic form to story and idea. Are all the devices of film used in the best possible way? Is anything overdone? Is anything underplayed? Is the film good, bad, or indifferent up to a point, and then does it change? How? Why?

DEMONSTRATIVE STUDENT ESSAY

Welles's *Citizen Kane*°: Whittling a Giant Down to Size

<u>Citizen Kane</u> (1941) is a superbly crafted film in black and white. The script is by Herman Mankiewicz and Orson Welles, with photography by Gregg Toland, music by Bernard Herrmann, direction and production by Welles, and the leading role by Welles. It is the story of a wealthy and powerful man, Charles Foster Kane,

°See pp. 1740–42 for a scene from *Citizen Kane*.

[1] who exemplifies the American Dream of economic self-sufficiency, self-determination, and self, period. <u>The film does not explore the "greatness" of the hero, however, but rather exposes him as a misguided, unhappy person who tries to buy love and remake reality.</u>* <u>All aspects of the picture--characterization, structure, and technique--are focused on this goal.</u>[†]

[2] <u>At the film's heart is the deterioration of Kane, the newly deceased newspaper magnate and millionaire.</u> He is not all bad, for he begins well before going tragically downward. For example, the view we see of him as a child, being taken away from home, invites sympathy. When we next see him as a young man, he idealistically takes over a daily newspaper, the Inquirer. This idealism makes him admirable but also makes his deterioration tragic. As he says to Thatcher in a moment of insight, he could have been a great person if he had not been wealthy. His corruption begins when he tries to alter the world to suit himself, as in his demented attempt to make an opera star out of his second wife, Susan, and his related attempt to shape critical praise for her. Even though he builds an opera house for her and also sponsors many performances, he cannot change reality. This tampering with truth indicates how completely he loses his youthful integrity.

[3] <u>The structure is progressively arranged to bring out such weaknesses.</u> The film flows out of the opening obituary newsreel, from which we learn that Kane's dying word was the name "Rosebud" (the brand name of his boyhood sled, which is spoken at the beginning by a person [Kane] whose mouth is shown in close-up). The newsreel director, wanting to get the inside story, assigns a reporter named Thompson to learn about "Rosebud." Thompson's search unifies the rest of the film; he goes from place to place and person to person to collect materials and conduct interviews that disclose Kane's increasing strangeness and alienation. At the end, although the camera abandons Thompson and focuses on the burning sled, he has been successful in uncovering the story of Kane's deterioration (even though he himself never learns what "Rosebud" means). Both the sled and the reporter therefore tie together the many aspects of the film.

[4] <u>It is through Thompson's searches that the film presents the flashback accounts of Kane's deterioration.</u> The separate people being interviewed (including Thatcher's handwritten account) each contribute something different to the narrative because their experiences with Kane have all been unique. As a result of these individual points of view, the story is intricate. For example, we learn in the Bernstein section that Jedediah proudly saves a copy of Kane's declaration about truth in reporting. We do not learn in Jedediah's interview, however, that he, Jedediah (Joseph Cotten), sends the copy back to Kane as an indictment of Kane's betrayal of principle. Rather, it is in <u>Susan's</u> account that we learn about the return, even though she herself understands nothing about it. This subtlety, so typical of the film, marks the ways in which the biography of Kane is progressively revealed.

<u>Thus, the major importance of these narrating characters is to reveal and reflect Kane's disintegration.</u> Jedediah is a man of principle who works closely with Kane, but after the lost election he rebels when he understands the falseness of Kane's personal life. He becomes alienated after Kane completes the unfinished attack on Susan's performance. Jedediah's change, or perhaps his assertion of principle, thus reveals Kane's increasing corruption. Susan, Kane's second

*Central idea.
[†]Thesis sentence.

[5]   wife (Dorothy Comingore), is naive, sincere, and warm, but her drinking, her attempted suicide, and her final separation show the harm of Kane's warped visions. Bernstein (Everett Sloane), the first person Thompson interviews, is a
solitary figure who is uncritical of Kane, but it is he who first touches the theme
about the mystery of Kane's motivations. Bernstein also takes on life when he
speaks of his forty-five year memory of the girl in white. Even though this revelation is brief, it suggests layers of feeling and longing.

In addition to these perceptive structural characterizations, Citizen Kane is
a masterpiece of film technique. The camera images are sharp, with clear depth
of field. In keeping with Kane's disintegration and mysteriousness, the screen is
rarely bright. Instead, the film makes strong use of darkness and contrasts, almost to the point at times of blurring distinctions between people. Unique in Gregg
[6]   Toland's camera work are the many shots taken from waist height or below, dis-
torting the bodies of the characters by distancing their heads--suggesting that the
characters are preoccupied with their own concerns and oblivious to normal perspectives. Nowhere is this distortion better exemplified than in the scene between
Kane and Jedediah in the empty rooms after the lost election, when Jedediah
asks permission to leave for Chicago.

As might be expected in a film so dominated by its central figure, the many
symbols create strong statements about character. The most obvious is the sled,
"Rosebud," the dominating symbol of the need for love and acceptance in childhood. Another notable symbol is glass and, in one scene, ice. In the party scene,
two ice statues are in the foreground of the employees of the Inquirer. In another
scene, a bottle looms large in front of Jedediah, who is drunk. In another, a pill
bottle and drinking glass are in front of Susan, who has just used them in her sui-
[7]   cide attempt. The suggestion of these carefully photographed symbols is that life
is brittle and temporary. Particularly symbolic is the bizarre entertainment in the
party scene. Because Kane joins the dancing and singing, the action suggests
that he is doing no more than taking a role in life, never being himself or knowing
himself. Symbols that frame the film are the wire fence and the "No Trespassing"
sign at both beginning and end. These symbols suggest that even if we understand a little about Kane, or anyone else, there are boundaries we cannot pass,
depths we can never reach.

There are also amusing symbols that suggest the diminution not only of
Kane but also of the other characters. An example is Bernstein's high-backed
chair, which makes him look like a small child. Similarly, the gigantic fireplace at
Xanadu makes both Kane and Susan seem like pygmies--a symbol that great
wealth dwarfs and dehumanizes people. Especially comic is Kane's picnic at
Xanadu. In going into the country, Kane and his friends do not walk but ride in a
[8]   long line of cars--more like a funeral procession than a picnic--and they stay
overnight in a massive tent. Quite funny is the increasing distance between Kane
and Emily, his first wife, in the rapid-fire shots that portray their developing separation. Even more comic is the vast distance at Xanadu between Kane and Susan
when they discuss their life together. They are so far apart that they must shout to
be heard. Amusing as these symbols of diminution and alienation are, however,
they are also pathetic, because at first Kane finds closeness with both his wives.

In all respects, Citizen Kane is a superb film. This is not to say that the characters are likable or that the amusing parts make it a comedy. Instead, the film
pursues truth, suggesting that greatness and wealth cannot give happiness. It is
relentless in whittling away at its major figure. Kane is likable at times, and he is

[9]   enormously generous (as shown when he sends Jedediah $25,000 in severance pay). But these high moments show the contrasting depths to which Kane falls, with the general point being that people who are powerful and great may deteriorate even at their height. The goal of the newsreel director at the beginning is to get at the "real story" behind the public man. There is more to any person than a two-hour film can reveal, but within its limits, <u>Citizen Kane</u> gets at the real story, and the real story is both sad and disturbing.

WORK CITED

<u>Citizen Kane</u>. By Orson Welles and Herman R. Mankiewicz. Dir. Orson Wells. Perf. Orson Welles et al. 1941. DVD. Turner Entertainment Co. and Warner Home Video, © 2001.

Commentary on the Essay

The major point of this essay is that the film diminishes the major figure, Kane. In this respect the essay illustrates the analysis of *character* (Chapter 4), and it therefore emphasizes how film can be considered as a form of literature. Also shown in the essay are other methods of literary analysis: *structure* (Chapter 3) and *symbolism* (Chapter 9). Of these topics, only the use of symbols, because they are visually presented in the film, is unique to the medium of film as opposed to the medium of words.

Any one of the topics might be developed as a separate essay. There is more than enough about the character of Susan, for example, to sustain a complete essay, and the film's structure could be extensively explored. *Citizen Kane* itself as a repository of film techniques is rich enough for an exhaustive, book-length account.

Because the essay is about a film, the unique aspect of paragraph 1 is the opening brief description (stressing the medium of black and white) and the credits to the scriptwriters, principal photographer, composer, and director. Unlike works written by a single author, film is a collaborative medium, and therefore it is appropriate to recognize the separate efforts of the principal contributors.

Paragraph 2 begins the body and carries out a brief analysis of the major character. Paragraphs 3 to 5 discuss various aspects of the film's structure (the second topic announced in the thesis sentence) as they bear on Kane. Paragraph 3 explains the unifying importance of the sled and the reporter, Thompson. Paragraph 4 focuses on the film's use of flashback as a structural technique, while paragraph 5 discusses three of the flashback characters as they either intentionally or unintentionally reveal Kane's flaws. In paragraphs 6 to 8, the topic is film technique, the third and last topic of the thesis sentence. Paragraph 6 focuses on light, camera angles, and distortion; paragraph 7 treats visual symbols; paragraph 8 continues the topic of symbols but extends it to amusing ones. The final paragraph restates the central idea and also relates the theme of deterioration to the larger issue of how great wealth and power affect character. Thus, as a conclusion, this paragraph not only presents a summary but also notes the film's general ideas.

Special Topics for Writing and Argument about Film

1. Select a single film technique, such as the use of color, the control of light, or the photographing of action, and write an essay describing how it is used in a film. For best results, use a DVD or a videocassette for your study. As much as possible, try to explain how the technique is used throughout the film. Determine constant and contrasting features, the relationship of the technique to the development of story and character, and so on.

2. Write an essay explaining how all the film techniques of a particular part or section are employed (e.g., camera angles, close-ups or long shots, tracking, on-camera and off-camera speeches, lighting, depth of field). For your study, you will have to rerun the section a number of times, trying to notice elements for the first time and also reinforcing your first observations. To add a research element to this question, you might consult the works by Bleiler, Ebert, Giannetti, Halliwell, Katz, Monaco, Peacock, Sklar, and Thomson listed in the footnote on page 1734.

3. Pick out a news story and write a dramatic scene about it. Next, consider how to write the scene for a film, providing directions for actors and camera operators (e.g., "As Character A speaks, his face shows that he is lying; the camera zooms slowly in on his face, with a loss of focus," or "As Character A speaks, the camera focuses on Character B exchanging looks with Character C"). When you are done, write an explanation of how you intend your directions to bring out details about your story and characters.

A Career in Drama:
Two Major Plays of Henrik Ibsen

The Norwegian playwright Henrik Johan Ibsen (1828–1906) is the acknowledged originator—the "father"—of modern drama. He deserves this recognition because of his pioneering selections of challenging and sometime shocking private and public issues. Today there are few restrictions on dramatists except success at the box office. Plays may range freely on almost any subject, such as the drug culture, sexual perversity, the right to commit suicide, the problems of real-estate dealers, the life of a go-go dancer, violence, family dissension, homosexuality, and the Vietnam war. If one includes film as drama, there is virtually no limit to the topics that dramatists can explore. It is well to stress that dramatists have not always been this free and that Ibsen was in the forefront of the struggle for free dramatic expression. A brief consideration of some of his major dramatic topics shows his originality and daring: the blinding and crippling effects of congenital syphilis, a woman's renunciation of a traditional protective marriage, suicide, the manipulations of people seeking personal benefits, the sacrifices of pursuing truth, the rejection of a child by a parent, and the abandonment of personal happiness in favor of professional interests.

⚘ IBSEN'S LIFE AND EARLY WORK

Ibsen was born in Skien (*shee-en*), Norway, a small town just seventy miles southwest of the capital, Christiania (now Oslo). Although his parents had been prosperous, they went bankrupt when he was only seven, and afterward the family struggled against poverty. When Ibsen was fifteen he was apprenticed to

a pharmacist, and he seemed headed for a career in this profession even though he hated it. By 1849, however, when he wrote *Catiline*, his first play in verse, it was clear that the theater was to be his life. Largely through the efforts of the famous violinist Ole Bull, a new National Theater had been established in Bergen, and Ibsen was appointed its director. He stayed in Bergen for six years and then went to Christiania, where for the next five years he tried to fashion a genuine Norwegian national theater. His attempts proved fruitless, for the theater went bankrupt in 1862. After writing *The Pretenders* in 1864, he secured enough governmental travel money to enable him to leave Norway. For the next twenty-seven years he lived in Germany and Italy in what has been called a "self-imposed" exile.

Although this first part of Ibsen's theatrical career was devoted to many practical matters—production, management, directing, and finances—he was also constantly writing. His early plays were in verse and were mainly nationalist and romantic, as a few representative titles suggest: *Lady Inger of Oestraat* (1855), *The Feast of Solhaug* (1856), *Olaf Liljekrans* (1857). In his first ten years in Germany and Italy he finished four plays. The best known of these is *Peer Gynt* (1867), a fantasy play about a historical Norwegian hero, Peer Gynt, who is saved from spiritual emptiness by the love of the patient heroine Solveig. Today, *Peer Gynt* is best known because of the incidental music written for it by Norway's major composer, Edvard Grieg (1843–1907). Ibsen asked Grieg to compose the music for the initial performances in 1876. Grieg's response was enthusiastic and creative, and the result is enjoyed today by millions. Ibsen also supplied the poem for which Grieg composed one of his loveliest songs, "A Swan."

❦ IBSEN'S MAJOR PROSE PLAYS

During the years when Ibsen was fighting poverty and establishing his career in the theater, Europe was undergoing great political and intellectual changes. Throughout the nineteenth century, Ibsen's home country, Norway, was trying to release itself from the domination of neighboring Sweden and to establish its own territorial and national integrity. In Ibsen's twentieth year, 1848, the "February Uprising" in Paris resulted in the deposition of the French king and the establishment of a new French republic. This same year also saw the publication of the *Communist Manifesto* of Karl Marx (1818–1883). In 1864, the year Ibsen left Norway, Marx's first socialist International was held in London. In addition, during the time Ibsen lived in Italy and Germany, both countries were going through the tenuous political processes of becoming true nation-states. In short, change was everywhere.

Ibsen also was changing and growing as a thinker and dramatist, driven by the idea that a forward and creative drama could bring about deeper and more permanent changes than could be effected by soldiers and politicians. Toward this end he developed the realistic **problem play.** Such a play posited a major personal, social, professional, or political problem that occasioned the play's dramatic conflicts and tensions. Each problem was timely, topical, and realistic, as were the characters, places, situations, and outcomes. In this vein Ibsen wrote the twelve major prose plays on which his reputation rests: *The Pillars of Society* (1877), *A Dollhouse* (1879), *Ghosts* (1881), *An Enemy of the People* (1882), *The Wild Duck* (1884), *Rosmersholm* (1886), *The Lady from the Sea* (1888), *Hedda Gabler* (1890), *The Master Builder* (1892), *Little Eyolf* (1894), *John Gabriel Borkman* (1896), and *When We Dead Awaken* (1899). He finished the first eight of these plays while living in Germany and Italy, the last four after returning to Norway in 1891.

In these major plays Ibsen dramatizes human beings breaking free from restrictions and inhibitions and trying to establish their individuality and freedom—freedom of self, inquiry, pursuit of truth, artistic dedication, and, above all, the freedom of love. In attempting to achieve these goals, Ibsen's dramatic characters find internal opposition in self-interest, self-indulgence, and self-denial, and external opposition in the personal and political influences and manipulations of others. Because the plays are designed to be realistic, Ibsen's characters fall short of their goals. At best they achieve a respite in their combat, as in *An Enemy of the People*, or begin a quest in new directions, as in *A Dollhouse*. They always make great sacrifices, sometimes losing life itself, as in *Hedda Gabler* and *John Gabriel Borkman*.

❧ TWO MAJOR REALISTIC PLAYS

A Dollhouse (*Et Dukkehjem*, 1879)[1] and *An Enemy of the People* (*En Folkefiende*, 1882) are representative of Ibsen's major drama. They present believable people confronting virtually insoluble personal, marital, economic, and political problems. To make the problems seem real, Ibsen also specifies realistic locations: The setting for all three acts of *A Dollhouse* is the living room of the Helmer house, including piano, Christmas tree, carpeting, and wall engravings. In *An Enemy of the People* the settings are equally realistic, though more varied, changing from the Stockmann household to the print shop and the large home of Captain Horster. Ibsen is so scrupulous about stage realism in *An Enemy of the People* that a comparison of the Stockmann living room (Acts 1 and 2) and the study (Act 5) shows that the room arrangements and the placements of the doors correspond exactly, as though he had drawn a floor plan before he created his set directions.

---

[1]Ibsen's title *Et Dukkehjem* literally means the home (*hjem*) of a doll or puppet (*dukke*). *A Doll's House*, the traditional and most common English title of the play, is not an accurate rendering of *dukkehjem*, and, in addition, it is misleading because of some of the connotations of our word *doll*. Recent translators have used *A Doll House* as the title, but this form is not in regular use. Our English word for a toy house for dolls is listed in collegiate dictionaries as *dollhouse*, a one-word compound. *A Dollhouse* is therefore preferable to the other two titles because it accurately renders *Et Dukkehjem*, and it is also the form accepted in current dictionaries.

IBSEN'S PROBLEM PLAYS ARE INTEGRATED WITH EVENTS THAT HAVE HAPPENED BEFORE THE PLAYS BEGIN. In addition to the realistic staging, Ibsen's realism includes the technique of presentation, particularly the exposition about the root causes of the problems that come to a head in the plays themselves. As *A Dollhouse* unfolds, we learn that years earlier, Nora Helmer had extended herself beyond her means to save Torvald from a near-fatal illness. We also learn that there had been an earlier relationship between Krogstad and Christine Linde. Similarly, in *An Enemy of the People*, we learn about Dr. Stockmann's earlier investigations into the problems of the water contamination, his indebtedness to his brother for his job, and the dangerous and criminal cutting of corners that occurred when the town's therapeutic spa was built. These details are logically and chronologically essential for our understanding of the problems and conflicts within both plays.

IBSEN'S PLAYS ARE HIGHLY SYMBOLIC. Both *A Dollhouse* and *An Enemy of the People* are realistic, and they, like all the major plays, are replete with contextual symbolism. One of the later plays, for example, *John Gabriel Borkman*, dramatizes the freezing to death of the major character, an occurrence symbolizing what Borkman had done to himself much earlier by denying love. In *A Dollhouse*, one of the earliest of the great plays, the title itself symbolizes the dependent and dehumanized role of the wife within traditional middle-class marriages. In addition, the entire nation of Norway (cold, legal, male) is contrasted symbolically with Italy (warm, emotional, female). Ironically, the break in the Helmers's marriage is symbolically aligned with events that occur or have occurred in both locations. Other symbols in *A Dollhouse* are the Christmas tree, the children's presents, the death of Dr. Rank, and the mailbox. In *An Enemy of the People* the symbols are the town spa, the toxic wastes from the nearby tanneries, and the concepts of public opinion and the popular majority. Additional symbols are the Mayor's hat and stick, Evensen's horn, and the spring weather at the play's end. Perhaps the major symbol is the intrafamily antagonism of Dr. Thomas Stockmann and Mayor Peter Stockmann, for all the other conflicts stem from their personal alienation.

❦ IBSEN AND THE "WELL-MADE PLAY"

The plot and structure of both *A Dollhouse* and *An Enemy of the People* show Ibsen's use of the conventions of the **well-made play** (*la pièce bien faite*), a form developed and popularized in nineteenth-century France by Eugène Scribe (1791–1861) and Victorien Sardou (1831–1908). Ibsen was familiar with well-made plays, having directed many of them himself at Bergen and Christiania (Oslo). The well-made play follows a rigid and efficient structure in which the drama begins at the story's climax. Usually the plot is built on a secret known by the audience and perhaps one or two of the characters. The well-made play thus begins in suspense and offers a pattern of increasing tension produced through exposition and the timely arrivals of new characters (like Krogstad and Vik) and threatening news or props like the Mayor's information about the last will and testament of Morten Kiil. In the course of action of the well-made play, the fortunes of the protagonist go from a low point, through a *peripeteia* or reversal (Aristotle's concept), to a high point at which the protagonist confronts and defeats the villain.

Although Ibsen makes use of many of the structural elements of the well-made play, he varies and departs from the pattern to suit his realistic purposes. Thus in *An Enemy of the People* his principal variations are his emphasis on the characterizations of the Stockmann brothers and also his introduction of *three* sets of villains confronting Dr. Stockmann in the fifth act (the Mayor, Morten Kiil, and Hovstad and Billing). In addition, because *An Enemy of the People* is a play about ideas and principles, Ibsen concludes the play on the new note of Dr. Stockmann's dedication to growth and the future. In *A Dollhouse* his variation is that Nora's confrontation with Krogstad, who is the apparent villain, does not lead to a satisfactory resolution but rather precipitates the more significant albeit intractable confrontation with her husband. In *A Dollhouse* and also in *An Enemy of the People* there is not a traditionally well-made victorious outcome; rather there are provisional outcomes—adjustments—in keeping with the realistic concept that as life goes on, problems continue.

✤ IBSEN'S TIMELINESS AND DRAMATIC POWER

Ibsen's focus on real-life issues has given his plays continued timeliness and strength. *A Dollhouse*, for example, vividly portrays the totally dependent position of married women in the nineteenth century. Most notably, a woman could not borrow funds without a man's cosignature, and Nora had to violate the law to obtain the money to restore her husband's health. The mailbox, to which Torvald has the only key, symbolizes this limitation, and the ultimate disclosure of the box's contents, rather than freeing Nora and Torvald, highlights her dependency. Today's feminism has stressed the issues of female freedom and equality, together with many other issues vital to women, but the need for feminine individuality and independence has not been more originally and forcefully dramatized than in *A Dollhouse*.

In a remarkably prophetic vein, *An Enemy of the People* deals powerfully with the effects of pollution and the conflicts between preservers of the environment and proponents of business as usual. This issue emerges early in the play as soon as Dr. Stockmann learns about the toxic wastes contaminating the water of the town spa, on which the economic livelihood of the entire town depends.

At first the conflict resulting from Dr. Stockmann's discovery seems minor because his facts are so unassailable. But the issue is raised to a political level with the entry of the local newspaper editor and his publisher. Once Mayor Stockmann convinces these men that Dr. Stockmann is using his discoveries to suit his own political goals, the play enlarges into the opposition between the individual and society at large. As these conflicts develop, Ibsen creates two of the great moments in the history of drama—those scenes in Acts 2 and 3 in which Dr. Stockmann and his brother the Mayor argue over the issue of truth and individuality versus interest and collective public opinion. Their conflict comes to a head in Act 4, in which Ibsen, through Dr. Stockmann, establishes an individual's need and absolute right to pursue truth, wherever it may lead. The dramatic force of the emptied stage at the end of this act, with the cries and jeers of the angry mob reverberating loudly backstage, has not been equaled.

BIBLIOGRAPHIC STUDIES

Because of Ibsen's importance, there have been many translations and editions of his plays. The Modern Library Giant edition of Farquharson-Sharp's translations of *Eleven Plays by Henrik Ibsen* (introduction by H. L. Mencken) has been a mainstay for many decades. Rolf Fjelde published paperback translations in 1970 and followed these up with *The Complete Major Prose Plays* in 1978 (twelve plays). Michael Meyer's translations (sixteen plays in four paperback volumes, 1986) are of major significance. Other individual and collected plays have been translated by Peter Watts, Una Ellis-Fermor, James McFarlane, Christopher Hampton, Inger Lignell, Nicholas Rudall, William Archer, Christopher Fry, and Kenneth McLeish. These names by no means constitute a complete list. A short edition of Ibsen's poetry has been translated by Michael Feingold (1987).

The major biography of Ibsen is Halvdan Hoht, *Life of Ibsen,* translated and edited by Einar Haugen and A. E. Santaniello (New York: Blom, 1971). Significant critical and biographical studies include George Bernard Shaw, *The Quintessence of Ibsenism* (1891; rpt. 1957), the pioneering work of Ibsen criticism; Rolf Fjelde, *Ibsen: A Collection of Critical Essays* (Englewood Cliffs: Prentice Hall, 1965); Michael Meyer, *Henrik Ibsen: The Farewell to Poetry 1864–1882* (London: Hart-Davis, 1971); James Hurt, *Catiline's Dream: An Essay on Ibsen's Plays* (Urbana: U of Illinois P, 1972); Clela Allphin, *Women in the Plays of Henrik Ibsen* (New York: Revisionist, 1975); Harold Clurman, *Ibsen* (New York: Macmillan, 1977); Einar Haugen, *Ibsen's Drama: Author to Audience* (Minneapolis: U of Minnesota P, 1979); David Thomas, *Henrik Ibsen* (London, Macmillan, 1983); Yvonne Shafer, ed., *Approaches to Teaching Ibsen's* A Doll House (New York: MLA, 1985); Charles R. Lyons, ed., *Critical Essays on Henrik Ibsen* (Boston: Hall, 1987); Frederick Marker and Lise-Lone Marker, *Ibsen's Lively Art* (New York: Cambridge UP, 1989); Joan Templeton, "The *Doll House* Backlash: Criticism, Feminism, and Ibsen," *PMLA* 104 (1989): 28–40; Naomi Lebowitz, *Ibsen and the Great World* (Baton Rouge: Louisiana UP, 1990); Errol Durbach, A Doll's House: *Ibsen's Myth of Transformation* (Boston: Twayne, 1991); Brian Johnston, *The Ibsen Cycle: The Design of the Plays from* Pillars of Society *to* When We Dead Awaken (University Park: Pennsylvania State UP, 1992); and James McFarlane, ed., *The Cambridge Companion to Ibsen* (Cambridge: Cambridge UP, 1994).

HENRIK IBSEN (1828–1906)

A Dollhouse (Et Dukkehjem) 1879

Translated by R. Farquharson Sharp

CHARACTERS

> Torvald Helmer, *a lawyer and bank manager*
> Nora, *his wife*
> Doctor Rank
> Mrs. Christine Linde
> Nils Krogstad, *a lawyer and bank clerk*
> Ivar, Bob, *and* Emmy, the Helmers' *three young children*
> Anne, *their nurse*
> Helen, *a housemaid*
> A Porter

The action takes place in HELMER's apartment.

ACT 1

SCENE. *A room furnished comfortably and tastefully, but not extravagantly. At the back, a door to the right leads to the entrance hall, another to the left leads to HELMER's study. Between the doors stands a piano. In the middle of the left-hand wall is a door, and beyond it a window. Near the window are a round table, armchairs and a small sofa. In the right-hand wall, at the farther end, another door; and on the same side, nearer the footlights, a stove, two easy chairs and a rocking-chair; between the stove and the door, a small table. Engravings on the walls; a cabinet with china and other small objects; a small book-case with well-bound books. The floors are carpeted, and a fire burns in the stove. It is winter.*

A bell rings in the hall; shortly afterwards the door is heard to open. Enter NORA, humming a tune and in high spirits. She is in outdoor dress and carries a number of parcels; these she lays on the table to the right. She leaves the outer door open after her, and through it is seen a PORTER who is carrying a Christmas Tree and a basket, which he gives to the MAID who has opened the door.

NORA.   Hide the Christmas Tree carefully, Helen. Be sure the children do not see it till this evening, when it is dressed. [*to the PORTER, taking out her purse.*] How much?

PORTER.   Sixpence.

NORA.   There is a shilling. No, keep the change. [*The PORTER thanks her, and goes out. NORA shuts the door. She is laughing to herself, as she takes off her hat and coat. She takes a packet of macaroons from her pocket and eats one or two; then goes cautiously to her husband's door and listens.*] Yes, he is in.

Animals were all caged

[*Still humming, she goes to the table on the right.*]

HELMER. [*calls out from his room*] Is that my little lark twittering out there?

NORA. [*busy opening some of the parcels*] Yes, it is!   5

HELMER. Is my little squirrel bustling about?

NORA. Yes!

HELMER. When did my squirrel come home?

NORA. Just now. [*puts the bag of macaroons into her pocket and wipes her mouth.*] Come in here, Torvald, and see what I have bought.

HELMER. Don't disturb me. [*A little later, he opens the door and looks into the room, pen   10
in hand.*] Bought, did you say? All these things? Has my little spendthrift been wasting money again?

NORA. Yes, but, Torvald, this year we really can let ourselves go a little. This is the first Christmas that we have not needed to economise.

HELMER. Still, you know, we can't spend money recklessly.

NORA. Yes, Torvald, we may be a wee bit more reckless now, mayn't we? Just a tiny wee bit! You are going to have a big salary and earn lots and lots of money.

HELMER. Yes, after the New Year; but then it will be a whole quarter before the salary is due.

NORA. Pooh! we can borrow till then.   15

HELMER. Nora! [*goes up to her and takes her playfully by the ear.*] The same little featherhead! Suppose, now, that I borrowed fifty pounds to-day, and you spent it all in the Christmas week, and then on New Year's Eve a slate fell on my head and killed me, and—

NORA. [*putting her hands over his mouth*] Oh! don't say such horrid things.

HELMER. Still, suppose that happened—what then?

NORA. If that were to happen, I don't suppose I should care whether I owed money or not.

HELMER. Yes, but what about the people who had lent it?   20

NORA. They? Who would bother about them? I should not know who they were.

HELMER. That is like a woman! But seriously, Nora, you know what I think about that. No debt, no borrowing. There can be no freedom or beauty about a home life that depends on borrowing and debt. We two have kept bravely on the straight road so far, and we will go on the same way for the short time longer that there need be any struggle.

NORA. [*moving towards the stove*] As you please, Torvald.

HELMER. [*following her*] Come, come, my little skylark must not droop her wings. What is this! Is my little squirrel out of temper? [*taking out his purse.*] Nora, what do you think I have got here?

NORA. [*turning around quickly*] Money!   25

HELMER. There you are. [*gives her some money*] Do you think I don't know what a lot is wanted for housekeeping at Christmas-time?

NORA. [*counting*] Ten shillings—a pound—two pounds! Thank you, thank you, Torvald; that will keep me going for a long time.

HELMER. Indeed it must.

NORA. Yes, yes, it will. But come here and let me show you what I have bought. And all so cheap! Look, here is a new suit for Ivar, and a sword; and a horse and a trumpet for Bob; and a doll and dolly's bedstead for Emmy—they are very plain, but anyway she will soon break them in pieces. And here are dress-lengths and handkerchiefs for the maids; old Anne ought really to have something better.

HELMER. And what is in this parcel?   30

NORA. [*crying out*] No, no! you mustn't see that till this evening.

HELMER.   Very well. But now tell me, you extravagant little person, what would you like for yourself?

NORA.   For myself? Oh, I am sure I don't want anything.

HELMER.   Yes, but you must. Tell me something reasonable that you would particularly like to have.

NORA.   No, I really can't think of anything—unless, Torvald— 35

HELMER.   Well?

NORA.   [*playing with his coat buttons, and without raising her eyes to his*] If you really want to give me something, you might—you might—

HELMER.   Well, out with it!

NORA.   [*speaking quickly*] You might give me money, Torvald. Only just as much as you can afford; and then one of these days I will buy something with it.

HELMER.   But, Nora— 40

NORA.   Oh, do! dear Torvald; please, please do! Then I will wrap it up in beautiful gilt paper and hang it on the Christmas Tree. Wouldn't that be fun?

HELMER.   What are little people called that are always wasting money?

NORA.   Spendthrifts—I know. Let us do as you suggest, Torvald, and then I shall have time to think what I am most in want of. That is a very sensible plan, isn't it?

HELMER.   [*smiling*] Indeed it is—that is to say, if you were really to save out of the money I give you, and then really buy something for yourself. But if you spend it all on the housekeeping and any number of unnecessary things, then I merely have to pay up again.

NORA.   Oh but, Torvald— 45

HELMER.   You can't deny it, my dear little Nora. [*puts his arm round her waist*] It's a sweet little spendthrift, but she uses up a deal of money. One would hardly believe how expensive such little persons are!

NORA.   It's a shame to say that. I do really save all I can.

HELMER.   [*laughing*] That's very true—all you can. But you can't save anything!

NORA.   [*smiling quietly and happily*] You haven't any idea how many expenses we skylarks and squirrels have, Torvald.

HELMER.   You are an odd little soul. Very like your father. You always find some 50 new way of wheedling money out of me, and, as soon as you have got it, it seems to melt in your hands. You never know where it has gone. Still, one must take you as you are. It is in the blood; for indeed it is true that you can inherit these things, Nora.

NORA.   Ah, I wish I had inherited many of papa's qualities.

HELMER.   And I would not wish you to be anything but just what you are, my sweet little skylark. But, do you know, it strikes me that you are looking rather—what shall I say—rather uneasy to-day?

NORA.   Do I?

HELMER.   You do, really. Look straight at me. 55

NORA.   [*looks at him*] Well?

HELMER.   [*wagging his finger at her*] Hasn't Miss Sweet-Tooth been breaking rules in town to-day?

NORA.   No; what makes you think that?

HELMER.   Hasn't she paid a visit to the confectioner's?

NORA.   No, I assure you, Torvald— 60

HELMER.   Not been nibbling sweets?

NORA.   No, certainly not.

HELMER.   Not even taken a bite at a macaroon or two?

NORA.   No, Torvald, I assure you really—

HELMER.   There, there, of course I was only joking.   65

NORA.   [*going to the table on the right*] I should not think of going against your wishes.

HELMER.   No, I am sure of that! besides, you gave me your word—[*going up to her*] Keep your little Christmas secrets to yourself, my darling. They will all be revealed to-night when the Christmas Tree is lit, no doubt.

NORA.   Did you remember to invite Doctor Rank?

HELMER.   No. But there is no need; as a matter of course he will come to dinner with us. However, I will ask him when he comes in this morning. I have ordered some good wine. Nora, you can't think how I am looking forward to this evening.

NORA.   So am I! And how the children will enjoy themselves, Torvald!   70

HELMER.   It is splendid to feel that one has a perfectly safe appointment, and a big enough income. It's delightful to think of, isn't it?

NORA.   It's wonderful!

HELMER.   Do you remember last Christmas? For a full three weeks beforehand you shut yourself up every evening till long after midnight, making ornaments for the Christmas Tree and all the other fine things that were to be a surprise to us. It was the dullest three weeks I ever spent!

NORA.   I didn't find it dull.

HELMER.   [*smiling*] But there was precious little result, Nora.   75

NORA.   Oh, you shouldn't tease me about that again. How could I help the cat's going in and tearing everything to pieces?

HELMER.   Of course you couldn't, poor little girl. You had the best of intentions to please us all, and that's the main thing. But it is a good thing that our hard times are over.

NORA.   Yes, it is really wonderful.

HELMER.   This time I needn't sit here and be dull all alone, and you needn't ruin your dear eyes and your pretty little hands—

NORA.   [*clapping her hands*] No, Torvald, I needn't any longer, need I! It's wonderfully lovely to hear you say so! [*taking his arm*] Now I will tell you how I have been thinking   80
we ought to arrange things, Torvald. As soon as Christmas is over—[*A bell rings in the hall.*] There's the bell. [*She tidies the room a little.*] There's someone at the door. What a nuisance!

HELMER.   If it is a caller, remember I am not at home.

MAID.   [*in the doorway*] A lady to see you, ma'am—a stranger.

NORA.   Ask her to come in.

MAID.   [*to HELMER*] The doctor came at the same time, sir.

HELMER.   Did he go straight into my room?   85

MAID.   Yes sir.

[*HELMER goes into his room. The MAID ushers in MRS. LINDE, who is in travelling dress, and shuts the door.*]

MRS. LINDE.   [*in a dejected and timid voice*] How do you do, Nora?

NORA.   [*doubtfully*] How do you do—

MRS. LINDE.   You don't recognise me, I suppose.

NORA.   No, I don't know—yes, to be sure, I seem to—[*suddenly*] Yes! Christine! Is   90
it really you?

MRS. LINDE.   Yes, it is I.

NORA.   Christine! To think of my not recognising you! And yet how could I—[*in a gentle voice*] How you have altered, Christine!

MRS. LINDE.   Yes, I have indeed. In nine, ten long years—

NORA.   Is it so long since we met? I suppose it is. The last eight years have been a happy time for me, I can tell you. And so now you have come into the town, and have taken this long journey in winter—that was plucky of you.

MRS. LINDE.   I arrived by steamer this morning.   95

NORA.   To have some fun at Christmas-time, of course. How delightful! We will have such fun together! But take off your things. You are not cold, I hope. [*helps her*] Now we will sit down by the stove, and be cosy. No, take this arm-chair; I will sit here in the rocking-chair. [*takes her hands*] Now you look like your old self again; it was only the first moment—You are a little paler, Christine, and perhaps a little thinner.

MRS. LINDE.   And much, much older, Nora.

NORA.   Perhaps a little older; very, very little; certainly not much. [*stops suddenly and speaks seriously*] What a thoughtless creature I am, chattering away like this. My poor, dear Christine, do forgive me.

MRS. LINDE.   What do you mean, Nora?

NORA.   [*gently*] Poor Christine, you are a widow.   100

MRS. LINDE.   Yes; it is three years ago now.

NORA.   Yes, I knew; I saw it in the papers. I assure you, Christine, I meant ever so often to write to you at the time, but I always put it off and something always prevented me.

MRS. LINDE.   I quite understand, dear.

NORA.   It was very bad of me, Christine. Poor thing, how you must have suffered. And he left you nothing?

MRS. LINDE.   No.   105

NORA.   And no children?

MRS. LINDE.   No.

NORA.   Nothing at all, then?

MRS. LINDE.   Not even any sorrow or grief to live upon.

NORA.   [*looking incredulously at her*] But, Christine, is that possible?   110

MRS. LINDE.   [*smiles sadly and strokes her hair*] It sometimes happens, Nora.

NORA.   So you are quite alone. How dreadfully sad that must be. I have three love-ly children. You can't see them just now, for they are out with their nurse. But now you must tell me all about it.

MRS. LINDE.   No, no; I want to hear you.

NORA.   No, you must begin. I mustn't be selfish to-day; to-day I must only think of your affairs. But there is one thing I must tell you. Do you know we have just had a great piece of good luck?

MRS. LINDE.   No, what is it?   115

NORA.   Just fancy, my husband has been made manager of the Bank!

MRS. LINDE.   Your husband? What good luck!

NORA.   Yes, tremendous! A barrister's profession is such an uncertain thing, espe-cially if he won't undertake unsavoury cases; and naturally Torvald has never been willing to do that, and I quite agree with him. You may imagine how pleased we are! He is to take up his work in the Bank at the New Year, and then he will have a big salary and lots of commissions. For the future we can live quite differently—we can do just as we like. I feel so relieved and so happy, Christine! It will be splendid to have heaps of money and not need to have any anxiety, won't it?

MRS. LINDE.   Yes, anyhow I think it would be delightful to have what one needs.

NORA.   No, not only what one needs, but heaps and heaps of money.   120

MRS. LINDE.   [*smiling*] Nora, Nora haven't you learnt sense yet? In our schooldays you were a great spendthrift.

NORA.   [*laughing*] Yes, that is what Torvald says now. [*wags her finger at her*] But "Nora, Nora" is not so silly as you think. We have not been in a position for me to waste money. We have both had to work.

MRS. LINDE.   You too?

NORA.   Yes; odds and ends, needlework, crochet-work, embroidery, and that kind of thing. [*dropping her voice*] And other things as well. You know Torvald left his office when we were married? There was no prospect of promotion there, and he had to try and earn more than before. But during the first year he overworked himself dreadfully. You see, he had to make money every way he could, and he worked early and late; but he couldn't stand it, and fell dreadfully ill, and the doctors said it was necessary for him to go south.

MRS. LINDE.   You spent a whole year in Italy didn't you?   125

NORA.   Yes. It was no easy matter to get away, I can tell you. It was just ar Ivar was born; but naturally we had to go. It was a wonderfully beautiful journey, and it saved Torvald's life. But it cost a tremendous lot of money, Christine.

MRS. LINDE.   So I should think.

NORA.   It cost about two hundred and fifty pounds. That's a lot, isn't it?

MRS. LINDE.   Yes, and in emergencies like that it is lucky to have the money.

NORA.   I ought to tell you that we had it from papa.   130

MRS. LINDE.   Oh, I see. It was just about that time that he died, wasn't it?

NORA.   Yes; and, just think of it, I couldn't go and nurse him. I was expecting little Ivar's birth every day and I had my poor sick Torvald to look after. My dear, kind father—I never saw him again, Christine. That was the saddest time I have known since our marriage.

MRS. LINDE.   I know how fond you were of him. And then you went off to Italy?

NORA.   Yes; you see we had money then, and the doctors insisted on our going, so we started a month later.

MRS. LINDE.   And your husband came back quite well?   135

NORA.   As sound as a bell!

MRS. LINDE.   But—the doctor?

NORA.   What doctor?

MRS. LINDE.   I thought your maid said the gentleman who arrived here just as I did was the doctor?

NORA.   Yes, that was Doctor Rank, but he doesn't come here professionally. He is   140 our greatest friend, and comes in at least once every day. No, Torvald has not had an hour's illness since then, and our children are strong and healthy and so am I. [*jumps up and claps her hands*] Christine! Christine! it's good to be alive and happy!—But how horrid of me; I am talking of nothing but my own affairs. [*sits on a stool near her, and rests her arms on her knees*] You mustn't be angry with me. Tell me, is it really true that you did not love your husband? Why did you marry him?

MRS. LINDE.   My mother was alive then, and was bedridden and helpless, and I had to provide for my two younger brothers; so I did not think I was justified in refusing his offer.

NORA.   No, perhaps you were quite right. He was rich at that time, then?

MRS. LINDE.   I believe he was quite well off. But his business was a precarious one; and, when he died, it all went to pieces and there was nothing left.

NORA.   And then?—

MRS. LINDE.   Well, I had to turn my hand to anything I could find—first a small   145 shop, then a small school, and so on. The last three years have seemed like one long working-day, with no rest. Now it is at an end, Nora. My poor mother needs me no more, for she is gone; and the boys do not need me either; they have got situations and can shift for themselves.

NORA.   What a relief you must feel it—

MRS. LINDE.   No, indeed; I only feel my life unspeakably empty. No one to live for any more. [*gets up restlessly*] That was why I could not stand the life in my little backwater any longer. I hope it may be easier here to find something which will busy me and occupy my thoughts. If only I could have the good luck to get some regular work—office work of some kind—

NORA.   But, Christine, that is so frightfully tiring, and you look tired out now. You had far better go away to some watering-place.

MRS. LINDE.   [*walking to the window*] I have no father to give me money for a journey, Nora.

NORA.   [*rising*] Oh, don't be angry with me.   150

MRS. LINDE.   [*going up to her*] It is you that must not be angry with me, dear. The worst of a position like mine is that it makes one so bitter. No one to work for, and yet obliged to be always on the look-out for chances. One must live, and so one becomes selfish. When you told me of the happy turn your fortunes have taken—you will hardly believe it—I was delighted not so much on your account as on my own.

NORA.   How do you mean?—Oh, I understand. You mean that perhaps Torvald could get you something to do.

MRS. LINDE.   Yes, that was what I was thinking of.

NORA.   He must, Christine. Just leave it to me; I will broach the subject very cleverly—I will think of something that will please him very much. It will make me so happy to be of some use to you.

MRS. LINDE.   How kind you are, Nora, to be so anxious to help me! It is doubly   155
kind in you, for you know so little of the burdens and troubles of life.

NORA.   I—? I know so little of them?

MRS. LINDE.   [*smiling*] My dear! Small household cares and that sort of thing!—
You are a child, Nora.

NORA.   [*tosses her head and crosses the stage*] You ought not to be so superior.

MRS. LINDE.   No?

NORA.   You are just like the others. They all think that I am incapable of anything   160
really serious—

MRS. LINDE.   Come, come—

NORA.   —that I have gone through nothing in this world of cares.

MRS. LINDE.   But, my dear Nora, you have just told me all your troubles.

NORA.   Pooh!—those were trifles. [*lowering her voice*] I have not told you the important thing.

MRS. LINDE.   The important thing? What do you mean?   165

NORA.   You look down upon me altogether, Christine—but you ought not to. You are proud, aren't you, of having worked so hard and so long for your mother?

MRS. LINDE.   Indeed, I don't look down on any one. But it is true that I am both proud and glad to think that I was privileged to make the end of my mother's life almost free from care.

NORA.   And you are proud to think of what you have done for your brothers.

MRS. LINDE.   I think I have the right to be.

NORA.   I think so, too. But now, listen to this; I too have something to be proud of   170
and glad of.

MRS. LINDE.   I have no doubt you have. But what do you refer to?

NORA.   Speak low. Suppose Torvald were to hear! He mustn't on any account—no one in the world must know, Christine, except you.

MRS. LINDE.   But what is it?

NORA.   Come here. [*pulls her down on the sofa beside her*] Now I will show you that I too have something to be proud and glad of. It was I who saved Torvald's life.

MRS. LINDE.   "Saved"? How?   175

NORA.   I told you about our trip to Italy. Torvald would never have recovered if he had not gone there—

MRS. LINDE.   Yes, but your father gave you the necessary funds.

NORA.   [*smiling*] Yes, that is what Torvald and all the others think, but—

MRS. LINDE.   But—

NORA.   Papa didn't give us a shilling. It was I who procured the money.   180

MR. LINDE.   You? All that large sum?

NORA.   Two hundred and fifty pounds. What do you think of that?

MRS. LINDE.   But, Nora, how could you possibly do it? Did you win a prize in the Lottery?

NORA.   [*contemptuously*] In the Lottery? There would have been no credit in that.

MRS. LINDE.   But where did you get it from, then?   185

NORA.   [*humming and smiling with an air of mystery*] Hm, hm! Aha!

MRS. LINDE.   Because you couldn't have borrowed it.

NORA.   Couldn't I? Why not?

MRS. LINDE.   No, a wife cannot borrow without her husband's consent.

NORA.   [*tossing her head*] Oh, if it is a wife who has any head for business—a wife   190
who has the wit to be a little bit clever—

MRS. LINDE.   I don't understand it at all, Nora.

NORA.   There is no need you should. I never said I had borrowed the money. I may have got it some other way. [*lies back on the sofa*] Perhaps I got it from some other admirer. When anyone is as attractive as I am—

MRS. LINDE.   You are a mad creature.

NORA.   Now, you know you're full of curiosity, Christine.

MRS. LINDE.   Listen to me, Nora dear. Haven't you been a little bit imprudent?   195

NORA.   [*sits up straight*] Is it imprudent to save your husband's life?

MRS. LINDE.   It seems to me imprudent, without his knowledge, to—

NORA.   But it was absolutely necessary that he should not know! My goodness, can't you understand that? It was necessary he should have no idea what a dangerous condition he was in. It was to me that the doctors came and said that his life was in danger, and that the only thing to save him was to live in the south. Do you suppose I didn't try, first of all, to get what I wanted as if it were for myself? I told him how much I should love to travel abroad like other young wives; I tried tears and entreaties with him; I told him that he ought to remember the condition I was in, and that he ought to be kind and indulgent to me; I even hinted that he might raise a loan. That nearly made him angry, Christine. He said I was thoughtless, and that it was his duty as my husband not to indulge me in my whims and caprices—as I believe he called them. Very well I thought, you must be saved—and that was how I came to devise a way out of the difficulty—

MRS. LINDE.   And did your husband never get to know from your father that the money had not come from him?

NORA.   No, never. Papa died just at that time. I had meant to let him into the se-   200
cret and beg him never to reveal it. But he was so ill then—alas, there never was any need to tell him.

MRS. LINDE.   And since then have you never told your secret to your husband?

NORA.   Good Heavens, no! How could you think so? A man who has such strong opinions about these things! And besides, how painful and humiliating it would be for Torvald, with his manly independence, to know that he owed me anything! It would upset our mutual relations altogether; our beautiful happy home would no longer be what it is now.

MRS. LINDE.   Do you mean never to tell him about it?

NORA.   [*meditatively, and with a half smile*] Yes—some day, perhaps, after many years, when I am no longer as nice-looking as I am now. Don't laugh at me! I mean of course, when Torvald is no longer as devoted to me as he is now; when my dancing and dressing-up and reciting have palled on him; then it may be a good thing to have something in reserve—[*breaking off*] What nonsense! That time will never come. Now, what do you think of my great secret, Christine? Do you still think I am of no use? I can tell you, too, that this affair has caused me a lot of worry. It has been by no means easy for me to meet my engagements punctually. I may tell you that there is something that is called, in business, quarterly interest, and another thing called payment in instalments, and it is always so dreadfully difficult to manage them. I have had to save a little here and there, where I could, you understand. I have not been able to put aside much from my housekeeping money, for Torvald must have a good table. I couldn't let my children be shabbily dressed; I have felt obliged to use up all he gave me for them, the sweet little darlings!

MRS. LINDE.   So it has all had to come out of your own necessaries of life, poor Nora?   205

NORA.   Of course. Besides, I was the one responsible for it. Whenever Torvald has given me the money for new dresses and such things, I have never spent more than half of it; I have always bought the simplest and cheapest things. Thank Heaven, any clothes look well on me, and so Torvald has never noticed it. But it was often very hard on me, Christine—because it is delightful to be really well dressed, isn't it?

MRS. LINDE.   Quite so.

NORA.   Well, then I have found other ways of earning money. Last winter I was lucky enough to get a lot of copying to do; so I locked myself up and sat writing every evening until quite late at night. Many a time I was desperately tired; but all the same it was a tremendous pleasure to sit there working and earning money. It was like being a man.

MRS. LINDE.   How much have you been able to pay off in that way?

NORA.   I can't tell you exactly. You see, it is very difficult to keep an account of a business matter of that kind. I only know that I have paid every penny that I could scrape together. Many a time I was at my wits' end. [*smiles*] Then I used to sit here and imagine that a rich old gentleman had fallen in love with me—   210

MRS. LINDE.   What! Who was it?

NORA.   Be quiet!—that he had died; and that when his will was opened it contained, written in big letters, the instruction: "The lovely Mrs. Nora Helmer is to have all I possess paid over to her at once in cash."

MRS. LINDE.   But, my dear Nora—who could the man be?

NORA.   Good gracious, can't you understand? There was no old gentleman at all; it was only something that I used to sit here and imagine, when I couldn't think of any way of procuring money. But it's all the same now; the tiresome old person can stay where he is, as far as I am concerned; I don't care about him or his will either, for I am free from care now. [*jumps up*] My goodness, it's delightful to think of, Christine! Free from care! To be able to be free from care, quite free from care; to be able to play and romp with the children; to be able to keep the house beautifully and have everything just as Torvald likes it! And, think of it, soon the spring will come and the big blue sky! Perhaps we shall be able to take a little trip—perhaps I shall see the sea again! Oh, it's a wonderful thing to be alive and be happy. [*A bell is heard in the hall.*]

MRS. LINDE.   [*rising*] There is the bell; perhaps I had better go.   215

NORA.   No, don't go; no one will come in here; it is sure to be for Torvald.

SERVANT.   [*at the hall door*] Excuse me, ma'am—there is a gentleman to see the master, and as the doctor is with him—

NORA.   Who is it?

KROGSTAD.   [*at the door*] It is I, Mrs. Helmer. [*Mrs. Linde starts, trembles, and turns to the window.*]

NORA.   [*takes a step towards him, and speaks in a strained, low voice*] You? What is it?   220 What do you want to see my husband about?

KROGSTAD.   Bank business—in a way. I have a small post in the Bank, and I hear your husband is to be our chief now—

NORA.   Then it is—

KROGSTAD.   Nothing but dry business matters, Mrs. Helmer; absolutely nothing else.

NORA.   Be so good as to go into the study, then. [*She bows indifferently to him and shuts the door into the hall; then comes back and makes up the fire in the stove.*]

MRS. LINDE.   Nora—who was that man?   225

NORA.   A lawyer, of the name of Krogstad.

MRS. LINDE.   Then it really was he.

NORA.   Do you know the man?

MRS. LINDE.   I used to—many years ago. At one time he was a solicitor's clerk in our town.

NORA.   Yes, he was.   230

MRS. LINDE.   He is greatly altered.

NORA.   He made a very unhappy marriage.

MRS. LINDE.   He is a widower now, isn't he?

NORA.   With several children. There now, it is burning up.

[*Shuts the door of the stove and moves the rocking-chair aside.*]

MRS. LINDE.   They say he carries on various kinds of business.   235

NORA.   Really! Perhaps he does; I don't know anything about it. But don't let us think of business; it is so tiresome.

DOCTOR RANK.   [*comes out of HELMER'S study. Before he shuts the door he calls to him.*] No, my dear fellow, I won't disturb you; I would rather go in to your wife for a little while. [*shuts the door and sees MRS. LINDE*] I beg your pardon; I am afraid I am disturbing you too.

NORA.   No, not at all. [*introducing him*] Doctor Rank, Mrs. Linde.

RANK.   I have often heard Mrs. Linde's name mentioned here. I think I passed you on the stairs when I arrived, Mrs. Linde?

MRS. LINDE.   Yes, I go up very slowly; I can't manage stairs well.   240

RANK.   Ah! some slight internal weakness?

MRS. LINDE.   No, the fact is I have been overworking myself.

RANK.   Nothing more than that? Then I suppose you have come to town to amuse yourself with our entertainments?

MRS. LINDE.   I have come to look for work.

RANK.   Is that a good cure for overwork?   245

MRS. LINDE.   One must live, Doctor Rank.

RANK.   Yes, the general opinion seems to be that it is necessary.

NORA.   Look here, Doctor Rank—you know you want to live.

RANK.   Certainly. However wretched I may feel, I want to prolong the agony as long as possible. All my patients are like that. And so are those who are morally diseased; one of them, and a bad case too, is at this very moment with Helmer—

MRS. LINDE.   [*sadly*] Ah!   250

NORA.   Whom do you mean?

RANK.   A lawyer of the name of Krogstad, a fellow you don't know at all. He suffers from a diseased moral character, Mrs. Helmer; but even he began talking of its being highly important that he should live.

NORA.   Did he? What did he want to speak to Torvald about?

RANK.   I have no idea; I only heard that it was something about the Bank.

NORA.   I didn't know this—what's his name—Krogstad had anything to do with   255
the Bank.

RANK.   Yes, he has some sort of appointment there. [*to MRS. LINDE*] I don't know whether you find also in your part of the world that there are certain people who go zealously snuffing about to smell out moral corruption, and, as soon as they have found some, put the person concerned into some lucrative position where they can keep their eye on him. Healthy natures are left out in the cold.

MRS. LINDE.   Still I think the sick are those who most need taking care of.

RANK.   [*shrugging his shoulders*] Yes, there you are. That is the sentiment that is turning Society into a sickhouse.

[*NORA, who has been absorbed in her thoughts, breaks out into smothered laughter and claps her hands.*]

RANK.   Why do you laugh at that? Have you any notion what Society really is?

NORA.   What do I care about tiresome Society? I am laughing at something quite   260
different, something extremely amusing. Tell me, Doctor Rank, are all the people who are employed in the Bank dependent on Torvald now?

RANK.   Is that what you find so extremely amusing?

NORA.   [*smiling and humming*] That's my affair! [*walking about the room*] It's perfectly glorious to think that we have—that Torvald has so much power over so many people. [*takes the packet from her pocket*] Doctor Rank, what do you say to a macaroon?

RANK.   What, macaroons? I thought they were forbidden here.

NORA.   Yes, but these are some Christine gave me.

MRS. LINDE.   What! I?—   265

NORA.   Oh, well, don't be alarmed! You couldn't know that Torvald had forbidden them. I must tell you that he is afraid they will spoil my teeth. But, bah!—once in a way— That's so, isn't it, Doctor Rank? By your leave? [*puts a macaroon into his mouth*] You must have one too, Christine. And I shall have one, just a little one—or at most two. [*walking about*] I am tremendously happy. There is just one thing in the world now that I should dearly love to do.

RANK.   Well, what is that?

NORA.   It's something I should dearly love to say, if Torvald could hear me.

RANK.   Well, why can't you say it?

NORA.   No, I daren't; it's so shocking.   270

MRS. LINDE.   Shocking?

RANK.   Well, I should not advise you to say it. Still, with us you might. What is it you would so much like to say if Torvald could hear you?

NORA.   I should just love to say—Well, I'm damned!

RANK.   Are you mad?

MRS. LINDE.   Nora, dear—!   275

RANK. Say it, here he is!
NORA. [*hiding the packet*] Hush! Hush! Hush!

[*HELMER comes out of his room, with his coat over his arm and his hat in his hands.*]

NORA. Well, Torvald dear, have you got rid of him?
HELMER. Yes, he has just gone.
NORA. Let me introduce you—this is Christine, who has come to town.   280
HELMER. Christine—? Excuse me, but I don't know—
NORA. Mrs. Linde, dear; Christine Linde.
HELMER. Of course. A school friend of my wife's, I presume?
MRS. LINDE. Yes, we have known each other since then.
NORA. And just think, she has taken a long journey in order to see you.   285
HELMER. What do you mean?
MRS. LINDE. No, really, I—
NORA. Christine is tremendously clever at book-keeping, and she is frightfully anxious to work under some clever man, so as to perfect herself—
HELMER. Very sensible, Mrs. Linde.
NORA. And when she heard you had been appointed manager of the Bank—the   290
news was telegraphed, you know—she travelled here as quick as she could. Torvald, I am sure you will be able to do something for Christine, for my sake, won't you?
HELMER. Well, it is not altogether impossible. I presume you are a widow, Mrs. Linde?
MRS. LINDE. Yes.
HELMER. And have had some experience of book-keeping?
MRS. LINDE. Yes, a fair amount.
HELMER. Ah! well, it's very likely I may be able to find something for you—   295
NORA. [*clapping her hands*] What did I tell you? What did I tell you?
HELMER. You have just come at a fortunate moment, Mrs. Linde.
MRS. LINDE. How am I to thank you?
HELMER. There is no need. [*puts on his coat*] But to-day you must excuse me—
RANK. Wait a minute; I will come with you.   300

[*Brings his fur coat from the hall and warms it at the fire.*]

NORA. Don't be long away, Torvald dear.
HELMER. About an hour, not more.
NORA. Are you going too, Christine?
MRS. LINDE. [*putting on her cloak*] Yes, I must go and look for a room.
HELMER. Oh, well then, we can walk down the street together.   305
NORA. [*helping her*] What a pity it is we are so short of space here: I am afraid it is impossible for us—
MRS. LINDE. Please don't think of it! Good-bye, Nora dear, and many thanks.
NORA. Good-bye for the present. Of course you will come back this evening. And you too, Dr. Rank. What do you say? If you are well enough? Oh, you must be! Wrap yourself up well.

[*They go to the door all talking together. Children's voices are heard on the staircase.*]

NORA. There they are. There they are! [*She runs to open the door. The NURSE comes in with the children.*] Come in! Come in! [*stoops and kisses them*] Oh, you sweet blessings! Look at them, Christine! Aren't they darlings?

RANK. Don't let us stand here in the draught.   310
HELMER. Come along, Mrs. Linde; the place will only be bearable for a mother now!

[*RANK, HELMER and MRS. LINDE go downstairs. The NURSE comes forward with the children; NORA shuts the hall door.*]

NORA. How fresh and well you look! Such red cheeks!—like apples and roses. [*The children all talk at once while she speaks to them.*] Have you had great fun? That's splendid! What, you pulled both Emmy and Bob along on the sledge?—both at once?—that *was* good. You are a clever boy, Ivar. Let me take her for a little, Anne. My sweet little baby doll! [*takes the baby from the MAID and dances it up and down*] Yes, yes, mother will dance with Bob too. What! Have you been snowballing? I wish I had been there too! No, no, I will take their things off, Anne; please let me do it, it is such fun. Go in now, you look half frozen. There is some coffee for you on the stove.

[*The NURSE goes into the room on the left. NORA takes off the children's things and throws them about, while they all talk to her at once.*]

NORA. Really! Did a big dog run after you? But it didn't bite you? No, dogs don't bite nice little dolly children. You mustn't look at the parcels, Ivar. What are they? Ah, I daresay you would like to know. No, no—it's something nasty! Come, let us have a game! What shall we play at? Hide and Seek? Yes, we'll play Hide and Seek. Bob shall hide first. Must I hide? Very well, I'll hide first.

[*She and the children laugh and shout, and romp in and out of the room; at last NORA hides under the table, the children rush in and look for her, but do not see her; they hear her smothered laughter, run to the table, lift up the cloth and find her. Shouts of laughter. She crawls forward and pretends to frighten them. Fresh laughter. Meanwhile there has been a knock at the hall door, but none of them has noticed it. The door is half opened, and KROGSTAD appears. He waits a little; the game goes on.*]

KROGSTAD. Excuse me, Mrs. Helmer.
NORA. [*with a stifled cry, turns round and gets up on to her knees*] Ah! what do you   315
want?
KROGSTAD. Excuse me, the outer door was ajar; I suppose someone forgot to shut it.
NORA. [*rising*] My husband is out, Mr. Krogstad.
KROGSTAD. I know that.
NORA. What do you want here, then?
KROGSTAD. A word with you.   320
NORA. With me?—[*to the children, gently*] Go in to nurse. What? No, the strange man won't do mother any harm. When he has gone we will have another game. [*She takes the children into the room on the left, and shuts the door after them.*] You want to speak to me?
KROGSTAD. Yes, I do.
NORA. To-day? It is not the first of the month yet.
KROGSTAD. No, it is Christmas Eve, and it will depend on yourself what sort of a Christmas you will spend.
NORA. What do you want? To-day it is absolutely impossible for me—   325
KROGSTAD. We won't talk about that till later on. This is something different. I presume you can give me a moment?
NORA. Yes—yes, I can—although—
KROGSTAD. Good. I was in Olsen's Restaurant and saw your husband going down the street—

NORA. Yes?

KROGSTAD With a lady.

NORA. What then?

KROGSTAD. May I make so bold as to ask if it was a Mrs. Linde?

NORA. It was.

KROGSTAD. Just arrived in town?

NORA. Yes, to-day.

KROGSTAD. She is a great friend of yours, isn't she?

NORA. She is. But I don't see—

KROGSTAD. I knew her too, once upon a time.

NORA. I am aware of that.

KROGSTAD. Are you? So you know all about it; I thought as much. Then I can ask you, without beating about the bush—is Mrs. Linde to have an appointment in the Bank?

NORA. What right have you to question me, Mr. Krogstad?—You, one of my husband's subordinates! But since you ask, you shall know. Yes, Mrs. Linde *is* to have an appointment. And it was I who pleaded her cause, Mr. Krogstad, let me tell you that.

KROGSTAD. I was right in what I thought, then.

NORA. [*walking up and down the stage*] Sometimes one has a tiny little bit of influence, I should hope. Because one is a woman, it does not necessarily follow that—. When anyone is in a subordinate position, Mr. Krogstad, they should really be careful to avoid offending anyone who—who—

KROGSTAD. Who has influence?

NORA. Exactly.

KROGSTAD. [*changing his tone*] Mrs. Helmer, you will be so good as to use your influence on my behalf.

NORA. What? What do you mean?

KROGSTAD. You will be so kind as to see that I am allowed to keep my subordinate position in the Bank.

NORA. What do you mean by that? Who proposes to take your post away from you?

KROGSTAD. Oh, there is no necessity to keep up the pretence of ignorance. I can quite understand that your friend is not very anxious to expose herself to the chance of rubbing shoulders with me; and I quite understand, too, whom I have to thank for being turned out.

NORA. But I assure you—

KROGSTAD. Very likely; but, to come to the point, the time has come when I should advise you to use your influence to prevent that.

NORA. But, Mr. Krogstad, I *have* no influence.

KROGSTAD. Haven't you? I thought you said yourself just now—

NORA. Naturally I did not mean you to put that construction on it. I! What should make you think I have any influence of that kind with my husband?

KROGSTAD. Oh, I have known your husband from our student days. I don't suppose he is any more unassailable than other husbands.

NORA. If you speak slightingly of my husband, I shall turn you out of the house.

KROGSTAD. You are bold, Mrs. Helmer.

NORA. I am not afraid of you any longer. As soon as the New Year comes, I shall in a very short time be free of the whole thing.

KROGSTAD. [*controlling himself*] Listen to me, Mrs. Helmer. If necessary, I am prepared to fight for my small post in the Bank as if I were fighting for my life.

NORA. So it seems.

KROGSTAD.   It is not only for the sake of the money; indeed, that weighs least with me in the matter. There is another reason—well, I may as well tell you. My position is this. I daresay you know, like everybody else, that once, many years ago, I was guilty of an indiscretion.

NORA.   I think I have heard something of the kind.

KROGSTAD.   The matter never came into court; but every way seemed to be closed to me after that. So I took to the business that you know of. I had to do something; and, honestly, I don't think I've been one of the worst. But now I must cut myself free from all that. My sons are growing up; for their sake I must try and win back as much respect as I can in the town. This post in the Bank was like the first step up for me—and now your husband is going to kick me downstairs again into the mud.

NORA.   But you must believe me, Mr. Krogstad; it is not in my power to help you   365
at all.

KROGSTAD.   Then it is because you haven't the will; but I have means to compel you.

NORA.   You don't mean that you will tell my husband that I owe you money?

KROGSTAD.   Hm!—suppose I were to tell him?

NORA.   It would be perfectly infamous of you. [sobbing] To think of his learning my secret, which has been my joy and pride, in such an ugly, clumsy way—that he should learn it from you! And it would put me in a horribly disagreeable position—

KROGSTAD.   Only disagreeable?   370

NORA.   [impetuously] Well, do it, then!—and it will be the worse for you. My husband will see for himself what a blackguard you are, and you certainly won't keep your post then.

KROGSTAD.   I asked you if it was only a disagreeable scene at home that you were afraid of?

NORA.   If my husband does get to know of it, of course he will at once pay you what is still owing, and we shall have nothing more to do with you.

KROGSTAD.   [coming a step nearer] Listen to me, Mrs. Helmer. Either you have a very bad memory or you know very little of business. I shall be obliged to remind you of a few details.

NORA.   What do you mean?   375

KROGSTAD.   When your husband was ill, you came to me to borrow two hundred and fifty pounds.

NORA.   I didn't know any one else to go to.

KROGSTAD.   I promised to get you that amount—

NORA.   Yes, and you did so.

KROGSTAD.   I promised to get you that amount, on certain conditions. Your mind   380
was so taken up with your husband's illness, and you were so anxious to get the money for your journey, that you seem to have paid no attention to the conditions of our bargain. Therefore it will not be amiss if I remind you of them. Now, I promised to get the money on the security of a bond which I drew up.

NORA.   Yes, and which I signed.

KROGSTAD.   Good. But below your signature there were a few lines constituting your father a surety for the money; those lines your father should have signed.

NORA.   Should? He did sign them.

KROGSTAD.   I had left the date blank; that is to say your father should himself have inserted the date on which he signed the paper. Do you remember that?

NORA.   Yes, I think I remember—   385

KROGSTAD.   Then I gave you the bond to send by post to your father. Is that not so?

NORA.   Yes.

KROGSTAD.   And you naturally did so at once, because five or six days afterwards you brought me the bond with your father's signature. And then I gave you the money.

NORA.   Well, haven't I been paying it off regularly?

KROGSTAD.   Fairly so, yes. But—to come back to the matter in hand—that must have been a very trying time for your, Mrs. Helmer?   390

NORA.   It was, indeed.

KROGSTAD.   Your father was very ill, wasn't he?

NORA.   He was very near his end.

KROGSTAD.   And died soon afterwards?

NORA.   Yes.   395

KROGSTAD.   Tell me, Mrs. Helmer, can you by any chance remember what day your father died?—on what day of the month, I mean.

NORA.   Papa died on the 29th of September.

KROGSTAD.   That is correct; I have ascertained it for myself. And, as that is so, there is a discrepancy [*taking a paper from his pocket*] which I cannot account for.

NORA.   What discrepancy? I don't know—

KROGSTAD.   The discrepancy consists, Mrs. Helmer, in the fact that your father   400
signed this bond three days after his death.

NORA.   What do you mean? I don't understand—

KROGSTAD.   Your father died on the 29th of September. But, look here; your father has dated his signature the 2nd of October. It is a discrepancy, isn't it? [*NORA is silent.*] Can you explain it to me? [*NORA is still silent.*] It is a remarkable thing, too, that the words "2nd of October," as well as the year, are not written in your father's handwriting but in one that I think I know. Well, of course it can be explained; your father may have forgotten to date his signature, and someone else may have dated it haphazard before they knew of his death. There is no harm in that. It all depends on the signature of the name; and *that* is genuine, I suppose, Mrs. Helmer? It was your father himself who signed his name here?

NORA.   [*after a short pause, throws her head up and looks defiantly at him*] No, it was not. It was I that wrote papa's name.

KROGSTAD.   Are you aware that is a dangerous confession?

NORA.   In what way? You shall have your money soon.   405

KROGSTAD.   Let me ask you a question; why did you not send the paper to your father?

NORA.   It was impossible; papa was so ill. If I had asked him for his signature, I should have had to tell him what the money was to be used for; and when he was so ill himself I couldn't tell him that my husband's life was in danger—it was impossible.

KROGSTAD.   It would have been better for you if you had given up your trip abroad.

NORA.   No, that was impossible. That trip was to save my husband's life; I couldn't give that up.

KROGSTAD.   But did it never occur to you that you were committing a fraud on me?   410

NORA.   I couldn't take that into account; I didn't trouble myself about you at all. I couldn't bear you, because you put so many heartless difficulties in my way, although you knew what a dangerous condition my husband was in.

KROGSTAD.   Mrs. Helmer, you evidently do not realise clearly what it is that you have been guilty of. But I can assure you that my one false step, which lost me all my reputation, was nothing more or nothing worse than what you have done.

NORA.   You? Do you ask me to believe that you were brave enough to run a risk to save your wife's life?

KROGSTAD.   The law cares nothing about motives.

NORA. Then it must be a very foolish law. 415

KROGSTAD. Foolish or not, it is the law by which you will be judged, if I produce this paper in court.

NORA. I don't believe it. Is a daughter not to be allowed to spare her dying father anxiety and care? Is a wife not to be allowed to save her husband's life? I don't know much about law; but I am certain that there must be laws permitting such things as that. Have you no knowledge of such laws—you who are a lawyer? You must be a very poor lawyer, Mr. Krogstad.

KROGSTAD. Maybe. But matters of business—such business as you and I have had together—do you think I don't understand that? Very well. Do as you please. But let me tell you this—if I lose my position a second time, you shall lose yours with me.

[*He bows, and goes out through the hall.*]

NORA. [*appears buried in thought for a short time, then tosses her head*] Nonsense! Trying to frighten me like that!—I am not so silly as he thinks. [*begins to busy herself putting the children's things in order*] And yet—? No, it's impossible! I did it for love's sake.

THE CHILDREN. [*in the doorway on the left*] Mother, the stranger man has gone out 420 through the gate.

NORA. Yes, dears, I know. But, don't tell anyone about the stranger man. Do you hear? Not even papa.

CHILDREN. No, mother; but will you come and play again?

NORA. No, no—not now.

CHILDREN. But, mother, you promised us.

NORA. Yes, but I can't now. Run away in; I have such a lot to do. Run away in, my 425 sweet little darlings. [*She gets them into the room by degrees and shuts the door on them; then sits down on the sofa, takes up a piece of needlework and sews a few stitches, but soon stops.*] No! [*throws down the work, gets up, goes to the hall door and calls out*] Helen! bring the Tree in. [*goes to the table on the left, opens a drawer, and stops again*] No, no! it is quite impossible!

MAID. [*coming in with the Tree*] Where shall I put it, ma'am?

NORA. Here, in the middle of the floor.

MAID. Shall I get you anything else?

NORA. No, thank you. I have all I want.

[*Exit MAID.*]

NORA. [*begins dressing the tree*] A candle here—and flowers here—. The horrible 430 man! It's all nonsense—there's nothing wrong. The Tree shall be splendid! I will do everything I can think of to please you, Torvald!—I will sing for you, dance for you— [*HELMER comes in with some papers under his arm*] Oh! are you back already?

HELMER. Yes. Has anyone been here?

NORA. Here? No.

HELMER. That is strange. I saw Krogstad going out of the gate.

NORA. Did you? Oh yes, I forgot, Krogstad was here for a moment.

HELMER. Nora, I can see from your manner that he has been here begging you to 435 say a good word for him.

NORA. Yes.

HELMER. And you were to appear to do it of your own accord; you were to conceal from me the fact of his having been here; didn't he beg that of you too?

NORA. Yes, Torvald, but—

HELMER. Nora, Nora, and you would be a party to that sort of thing? To have any talk with a man like that, and give him any sort of promise? And to tell me a lie into the bargain?

NORA.   A lie—?   440

HELMER.   Didn't you tell me no one had been here? [*shakes his finger at her*] My little song-bird must never do that again. A song-bird must have a clean beak to chirp
with—no false notes! [*puts his arm round her waist*] That is so, isn't it? Yes, I am sure it
is. [*lets her go*] We will say no more about it. [*sits down by the stove*] How warm and snug it
is here!

[*Turns over his papers.*]

NORA.   [*after a short pause, during which she busies herself with the Christmas Tree*]
Torvald!

HELMER.   Yes.

NORA.   I am looking forward tremendously to the fancy dress ball at the Stenborgs' the day after to-morrow.

HELMER.   And I am tremendously curious to see what you are going to surprise me   445
with.

NORA.   It was very silly of me to want to do that.

HELMER.   What do you mean?

NORA.   I can't hit upon anything that will do; everything I think of seems so silly
and insignificant.

HELMER.   Does my little Nora acknowledge that at last?

NORA.   [*standing behind his chair with her arms on the back of it*] Are you very busy,   450
Torvald?

HELMER.   Well—

NORA.   What are all those papers?

HELMER.   Bank business.

NORA.   Already?

HELMER.   I have got authority from the retiring manager to undertake the neces-   455
sary changes in the staff and in the rearrangement of the work; and I must make use of
the Christmas week for that, so as to have everything in order for the new year.

NORA.   Then that was why this poor Krogstad—

HELMER.   Hm!

NORA.   [*leans against the back of his chair and strokes his hair*] If you hadn't been so
busy I should have asked you a tremendously big favour, Torvald.

HELMER.   What is that? Tell me.

NORA.   There is no one has such good taste as you. And I do so want to look nice   460
at the fancy-dress ball. Torvald, couldn't you take me in hand and decide what I shall go
as, and what sort of a dress I shall wear?

HELMER.   Aha! so my obstinate little woman is obliged to get someone to come to
her rescue?

NORA.   Yes, Torvald, I can't get along a bit without your help.

HELMER.   Very well, I will think it over, we shall manage to hit upon something.

NORA.   That *is* nice of you. [*Goes to the Christmas Tree. A short pause.*] How pretty the
red flowers look—. But, tell me, was it really something very bad that this Krogstad was
guilty of?

HELMER.   He forged someone's name. Have you any idea what that means?   465

NORA.   Isn't it possible that he was driven to do it by necessity?

HELMER.   Yes; or, as in so many cases, by imprudence. I am not so heartless as to
condemn a man altogether because of a single false step of that kind.

NORA.   No you wouldn't, would you, Torvald?

HELMER.   Many a man has been able to retrieve his character, if he has openly confessed his fault and taken his punishment.

NORA.   Punishment—?   470

HELMER.   But Krogstad did nothing of that sort; he got himself out of it by a cunning trick, and that is why he has gone under altogether.

NORA.   But do you think it would—?

HELMER.   Just think how a guilty man like that has to lie and play the hypocrite with everyone, how he has to wear a mask in the presence of those near and dear to him, even before his own wife and children. And about the children—that is the most terrible part of it all, Nora.

NORA.   How?

HELMER.   Because such an atmosphere of lies infects and poisons the whole life of   475
a home. Each breath the children take in such a house is full of the germs of evil.

NORA.   [coming nearer him] Are you sure of that?

HELMER.   My dear, I have often seen it in the course of my life as a lawyer. Almost everyone who has gone to the bad early in life has had a deceitful mother.

NORA.   Why do you only say—mother?

HELMER.   It seems most commonly to be the mother's influence, though naturally a bad father's would have the same result. Every lawyer is familiar with the fact. This Krogstad, now, has been persistently poisoning his own children with lies and dissimulation; that is why I say he has lost all moral character. [holds out his hands to her] That is why my sweet little Nora must promise me not to plead his cause. Give me your hand on it. Come, come, what is this? Give me your hand. There now, that's settled. I assure you it would be quite impossible for me to work with him; I literally feel physically ill when I am in the company of such people.

NORA.   [takes her hand out of his and goes to the opposite side of the Christmas Tree] How   480
hot it is in here; and I have such a lot to do.

HELMER.   [getting up and putting his papers in order] Yes, and I must try and read through some of these before dinner; and I must think about your costume, too. And it is just possible I may have something ready in gold paper to hang up on the Tree. [Puts his hand on her head.] My precious little singing-bird!

[He goes into his room and shuts the door after him.]

NORA.   [after a pause, whispers] No, no—it isn't true. It's impossible; it must be impossible.

[The NURSE opens the door on the left.]

NURSE.   The little ones are begging so hard to be allowed to come in to mamma.

NORA.   No, no, no! Don't let them come in to me! You stay with them, Anne.

NURSE.   Very well, ma'am.   485

[Shuts the door.]

NORA.   [pale with terror] Deprave my little children? Poison my home? [a short pause. Then she tosses her head.] It's not true. It can't possibly be true.

ACT 2

THE SAME SCENE. The Christmas Tree is in the corner by the piano, stripped of its ornaments and with burnt-down candle-ends on its dishevelled branches. NORA's cloak and hat are lying on the sofa. She is alone in the room, walking about uneasily. She stops by the sofa and takes up her cloak.

NORA.   [drops the cloak] Someone is coming now! [goes to the door and listens] No—it is no one. Of course, no one will come to-day, Christmas Day—nor tomorrow either. But, perhaps—[opens the door and looks out] No, nothing in the letter-box; it is quite empty.

[*comes forward*] What rubbish! of course he can't be in earnest about it. Such a thing couldn't happen; it is impossible—I have three little children.

[*Enter the* NURSE *from the room on the left, carrying a big cardboard box.*]

NURSE.   At last I have found the box with the fancy dress.

NORA.   Thanks; put it on the table.

NURSE.   [*doing so*] But it is very much in want of mending.

NORA.   I should like to tear it into a hundred thousand pieces.   5

NURSE.   What an idea! It can easily be put in order—just a little patience.

NORA.   Yes, I will go and get Mrs. Linde to come and help me with it.

NURSE.   What, out again? In this horrible weather? You will catch cold, ma'am, and make yourself ill.

NORA.   Well, worse than that might happen. How are the children?

NURSE.   The poor little souls are playing with their Christmas presents, but—   10

NORA.   Do they ask much for me?

NURSE.   You see, they are so accustomed to have their mamma with them.

NORA.   Yes, but, nurse, I shall not be able to be so much with them now as I was before.

NURSE.   Oh well, young children easily get accustomed to anything.

NORA.   Do you think so? Do you think they would forget their mother if she went   15
away altogether?

NURSE.   Good heavens!—went away altogether?

NORA.   Nurse, I want you to tell me something I have often wondered about—how could you have the heart to put your own child out among strangers?

NURSE.   I was obliged to, if I wanted to be little Nora's nurse.

NORA.   Yes, but how could you be willing to do it?

NURSE.   What, when I was going to get such a good place by it? A poor girl who has   20
got into trouble should be glad to. Besides, that wicked man didn't do a single thing for me.

NORA.   But I suppose your daughter has quite forgotten you.

NURSE.   No, indeed she hasn't. She wrote to me when she was confirmed, and when she was married.

NORA.   [*putting her arms round her neck*] Dear old Anne, you were a good mother to me when I was little.

NURSE.   Little Nora, poor dear, had no other mother but me.

NORA.   And if my little ones had no other mother, I am sure you would—What   25
nonsense I am talking! [*opens the box*] Go in to them. Now I must—. You will see tomorrow how charming I shall look.

NURSE.   I am sure there will be no one at the ball so charming as you, ma'am.

[*Goes into the room on the left.*]

NORA.   [*begins to unpack the box, but soon pushes it away from her*] If only I dared go out. If only no one would come. If only I could be sure nothing would happen here in the meantime. Stuff and nonsense! No one will come. Only I mustn't think about it. I will brush my muff. What, lovely gloves! Out of my thoughts, out of my thoughts! One, two, three, four, five, six—[*Screams.*] Ah! there is someone coming—

[*Makes a movement towards the door, but stands irresolute.*]

[*Enter* MRS. LINDE *from the hall, where she has taken off her cloak and hat.*]

NORA.   Oh, it's you, Christine. There is no one else out there, is there? How good of you to come!

MRS. LINDE.   I heard you were up asking for me.

NORA.   Yes, I was passing by. As a matter of fact, it is something you could help me   30
with. Let us sit down here on the sofa. Look here. To-morrow evening there is to be a
fancy-dress ball at the Stenborgs', who live about us; and Torvald wants me to go as a
Neapolitan fisher-girl, and dance the Tarantella that I learnt at Capri.

MRS. LINDE.   I see; you are going to keep up the character.

NORA.   Yes, Torvald wants me to. Look, here is the dress; Torvald had it made for
me there, but now it is all so torn, and I haven't any idea—

MRS. LINDE.   We will easily put that right. It is only some of the trimming come un-
sewn here and there. Needle and thread? Now then, that's all we want.

NORA.   It *is* nice of you.

MRS. LINDE.   [*sewing*] So you are going to be dressed up to-morrow, Nora. I will tell   35
you what—I shall come in for a moment and see you in your fine feathers. But I have
completely forgotten to thank you for a delightful evening yesterday.

NORA.   [*gets up, and crosses the stages*] Well I don't think yesterday was a pleasant as
usual. You ought to have come to town a little earlier, Christine. Certainly Torvald does
understand how to make a house dainty and attractive.

MRS. LINDE.   And so do you, it seems to me; you are not your father's daughter for
nothing. But tell me, is Doctor Rank always as depressed as he was yesterday?

NORA.   No; yesterday it was very noticeable. I must tell you that he suffers from a
very dangerous disease. He has consumption of the spine, poor creature. His father was
a horrible man who committed all sorts of excesses; and that is why his son was sickly
from childhood, do you understand?

MRS. LINDE.   [*dropping her sewing*] But, my dearest Nora, how do you know anything about such things?

NORA.   [*walking about*] Pooh! When you have three children, you get visits now   40
and then from—from married women, who know something of medical matters, and
they talk about one thing and another.

MRS. LINDE.   [*goes on sewing. A short silence*] Does Doctor Rank come here every
day?

NORA.   Every day regularly. He is Torvald's most intimate friend, and a great
friend of mine too. He is just like one of the family.

MRS. LINDE.   But tell me this—is he perfectly sincere? I mean, isn't he the kind of
man that is very anxious to make himself agreeable?

NORA.   Not in the least. What makes you think that?

MRS. LINDE.   When you introduced him to me yesterday, he declared he had often   45
heard my name mentioned in this house; but afterwards I noticed that your husband
hadn't the slightest idea who I was. So how could Doctor Rank—?

NORA.   That is quite right, Christine. Torvald is so absurdly fond of me that he
wants me absolutely to himself, as he says. At first he used to seem almost jealous if I mentioned any of the dear folk at home, so naturally I gave up doing so. But I often talk about
such things with Doctor Rank, because he likes hearing about them.

MRS. LINDE.   Listen to me, Nora. You are still very like a child in many things, and
I am older than you in many ways and have a little more experience. Let me tell you
this—you ought to make an end of it with Doctor Rank.

NORA.   What ought I to make an end of?

MRS. LINDE.   Of two things, I think. Yesterday you talked some nonsense about a
rich admirer who was to leave you money—

NORA.   An admirer who doesn't exist, unfortunately! But what then?   50

MRS. LINDE.   Is Doctor Rank a man of means?

NORA. Yes, he is.

MRS. LINDE. And has no one to provide for?

NORA. No, no one; but—

MRS. LINDE. And comes here every day?   55

NORA. Yes, I told you so.

MRS. LINDE. But how can this well-bred man be so tactless?

NORA. I don't understand you at all.

MRS. LINDE. Don't prevaricate, Nora. Do you suppose I don't guess who lent you the two hundred and fifty pounds?

NORA. Are you out of your senses? How can you think of such a thing! A friend of   60 ours, who comes here every day! Do you realise what a horribly painful position that would be?

MRS. LINDE. Then it really isn't he?

NORA. No, certainly not. It would never have entered into my head for a moment. Besides, he had no money to lend then; he came into his money afterwards.

MRS. LINDE. Well, I think that was lucky for you, my dear Nora.

NORA. No, it would never have come into my head to ask Doctor Rank. Although I am quite sure that if I had asked him—

MRS. LINDE. But of course you won't.   65

NORA. Of course not. I have no reason to think it could possibly be necessary. But I am quite sure that if I told Doctor Rank—

MRS. LINDE. Behind your husband's back?

NORA. I must make an end of it with the other one, and that will be behind his back too. I *must* make an end of it with him.

MRS. LINDE. Yes, that is what I told you yesterday, but—

NORA. [*walking up and down*] A man can put a thing like that straight much easier   70 than a woman—

MRS. LINDE. One's husband, yes.

NORA. Nonsense! [*standing still*] When you pay off a debt you get your bond back, don't you?

MRS. LINDE. Yes, as a matter of course.

NORA. And can tear it into a hundred thousand pieces, and burn it up—the nasty dirty paper!

MRS. LINDE. [*looks hard at her, lays down her sewing and gets up slowly*] Nora, you are   75 concealing something from me.

NORA. Do I look as if I were?

MRS. LINDE. Something has happened to you since yesterday morning. Nora, what is it?

NORA. [*going nearer to her*] Christine! [*listens*] Hush! there's Torvald come home. Do you mind going in to the children for the present? Torvald can't bear to see dressmaking going on. Let Anne help you.

MRS. LINDE. [*gathering some of the things together*] Certainly—but I am not going away from here till we have had it out with one another.

[*She goes into the room on the left, as HELMER comes in from the hall.*]

NORA. [*going up to HELMER*] I have wanted you so much, Torvald dear.   80

HELMER. Was that the dressmaker?

NORA. No, it was Christine; she is helping me to put my dress in order. You will see I shall look quite smart.

HELMER. Wasn't that a happy thought of mine, now?

NORA.   Splendid! But don't you think it is nice of me, too, to do as you wish?

HELMER.   Nice?—because you do as your husband wishes? Well, well, you little   85
rogue, I am sure you did not mean it in that way. But I am not going to disturb you; you
will want to be trying on your dress, I expect.

NORA.   I suppose you are going to work.

HELMER.   Yes. [*shows her a bundle of papers*] Look at that. I have just been into the
bank. [*Turns to go into his room.*]

NORA.   Torvald.

HELMER.   Yes.

NORA.   If your little squirrel were to ask you for something very, very prettily—?   90

HELMER.   What then?

NORA.   Would you do it?

HELMER.   I should like to hear what it is, first.

NORA.   Your squirrel would run about and do all her tricks if you would be nice,
and do what she wants.

HELMER.   Speak plainly.   95

NORA.   Your skylark would chirp about in every room, with her song rising and
falling—

HELMER.   Well, my skylark does that anyhow.

NORA.   I would play the fairy and dance for you in the moonlight, Torvald.

HELMER.   Nora—you surely don't mean that request you made of me this
morning?

NORA.   [*going near him*] Yes, Torvald, I beg you so earnestly—   100

HELMER.   Have you really the courage to open up that question again?

NORA.   Yes, dear, you *must* do as I ask; you *must* let Krogstad keep his post in the
Bank.

HELMER.   My dear Nora, it is his post that I have arranged Mrs. Linde shall have.

NORA.   Yes, you have been awfully kind about that; but you could just as well dismiss some other clerk instead of Krogstad.

HELMER.   This is simply incredible obstinacy! Because you chose to give him a   105
thoughtless promise that you would speak for him, I am expected to—

NORA.   That isn't the reason, Torvald. It is for your own sake. This fellow writes in
the most scurrilous newspapers; you have told me so yourself. He can do you an unspeakable amount of harm. I am frightened to death of him—

HELMER.   Ah, I understand; it is recollections of the past that scare you.

NORA.   What do you mean?

HELMER.   Naturally you are thinking of your father.

NORA.   Yes—yes, of course. Just recall to your mind what these malicious creatures   110
wrote in the papers about papa, and how horribly they slandered him. I believe they
would have procured his dismissal if the Department had not sent you over to inquire
into it, and if you had not been so kindly disposed and helpful to him.

HELMER.   My little Nora, there is an important difference between your father and
me. Your father's reputation as a public official was not above suspicion. Mine is, and I
hope it will continue to be so, as long as I hold my office.

NORA.   You never can tell what mischief these men may contrive. We ought to be
so well off, so snug and happy here in our peaceful home, and have no cares—you and I
and the children, Torvald! That is why I beg you so earnestly—

HELMER.   And it is just by interceding for him that you make it impossible for me
to keep him. It is already known at the Bank that I mean to dismiss Krogstad. Is it to get
about now that the new manager has changed his mind at his wife's bidding—

NORA.   And what if it did?

HELMER.   Of course!—if only this obstinate little person can get her way! Do you   115
suppose I am going to make myself ridiculous before my whole staff, to let people think
that I am a man to be swayed by all sorts of outside influence? I should very soon feel the
consequences of it, I can tell you! And besides, there is one thing that makes it quite impossible for me to have Krogstad in the Bank as long as I am manager.

NORA.   Whatever is that?

HELMER.   His moral failings I might perhaps have overlooked, if necessary—

NORA.   Yes, you could—couldn't you?

HELMER.   And I hear he is a good worker, too. But I knew him when we were boys.
It was one of those rash friendships that so often prove an incubus in after life. I may as
well tell you plainly, we were once on very intimate terms with one another. But this tactless fellow lays no restraint on himself when other people are present. On the contrary,
he thinks it gives him the right to adopt a familiar tone with me, and every minute it is "I
say, Helmer, old fellow!" and that sort of thing. I assure you it is extremely painful for me.
He would make my position in the Bank intolerable.

NORA.   Torvald, I don't believe you mean that.   120

HELMER.   Don't you? Why not?

NORA.   Because it is such a narrow-minded way of looking at things.

HELMER.   What are you saying? Narrow-minded? Do you think I am narrow-minded?

NORA.   No, just the opposite, dear—and it is exactly for that reason.

HELMER.   It's the same thing. You say my point of view is narrow-minded, so I must   125
be so too. Narrow-minded! Very well—I must put an end to this. [*Goes to the hall-door and
calls.*] Helen!

NORA.   What are you going to do?

HELMER.   [*looking among his papers*] Settle it. [*Enter* MAID.] Look here; take this letter and go downstairs with it at once. Find a messenger and tell him to deliver it, and be
quick. The address is on it, and here is the money.

MAID.   Very well, sir.

[*Exits with the letter.*]

HELMER.   [*putting his papers together*] Now then, little Miss Obstinate.

NORA.   [*breathlessly*] Torvald—what was that letter?   130

HELMER.   Krogstad's dismissal.

NORA.   Call her back, Torvald! There is still time. Oh Torvald, call her back! Do it
for my sake—for your own sake—for the children's sake! Do you hear me, Torvald? Call
her back!! You don't know what that letter can bring upon us.

HELMER.   It's too late.

NORA.   Yes, it's too late.

HELMER.   My dear Nora, I can forgive the anxiety you are in, although really it is   135
an insult to me. It is, indeed. Isn't it an insult to think that I should be afraid of a starving quill-driver's vengeance? But I forgive you nevertheless, because it is such eloquent
witness to your great love for me. [*takes her in his arms*] And that is as it should be, my
own darling Nora. Come what will, you may be sure I shall have both courage
and strength if they be needed. You will see I am man enough to take everything upon
myself.

NORA.   [*in a horror-stricken voice*] What do you mean by that?

HELMER.   Everything, I say—

NORA.   [*recovering herself*] You will never have to do that.

HELMER.   That's right. Well, we will share it, Nora, as man and wife should. That is
how it shall be. [*caressing her*] Are you content now? There! there!—not these frightened

dove's eyes! The whole thing is only the wildest fancy!—Now, you must go and play through the Tarantella and practise with your tambourine. I shall go into the inner office and shut the door, and I shall hear nothing; you can make as much noise as you please. [*turns back at the door*] And when Rank comes, tell him where he will find me.

[*Nods to her, takes his papers and goes into his room, and shuts the door after him*]

NORA.　[*bewildered with anxiety, stands as if rooted to the spot, and whispers*] He is capa-　140
ble of doing it. He will do it. He will do it in spite of everything.—No, not that! Never, never! Anything rather than that! Oh, for some help, some way out of it! [*The door-bell rings.*] Doctor Rank! Anything rather than that—anything, whatever it is!

[*She puts her hands over her face, pulls herself together, goes to the door and opens it. RANK is stand-ing without, hanging up his coat. During the following dialogue it begins to grow dark.*]

NORA.　Good-day, Doctor Rank. I knew your ring. But you mustn't go in to Torvald now; I think he is busy with something.
RANK.　And you?
NORA.　[*brings him in and shuts the door after him*] Oh, you know very well I always have time for you.
RANK.　Thank you. I shall make use of as much of it as I can.
NORA.　What do you mean by that? As much of it as you can?　145
RANK.　Well, does that alarm you?
NORA.　It was such a strange way of putting it. Is anything likely to happen?
RANK.　Nothing but what I have long been prepared for. But I certainly didn't ex-pect it to happen so soon.
NORA.　[*gripping him by the arm*] What have you found out? Doctor Rank, you must tell me.
RANK.　[*sitting down by the stove*] It is all up with me. And it can't be helped.　150
NORA.　[*with a sigh of relief*] Is it about yourself?
RANK.　Who else? It is no use lying to one's self. I am the most wretched of all my patients, Mrs. Helmer. Lately I have been taking stock of my internal economy. Bankrupt! Probably within a month I shall lie rotting in the churchyard.
NORA.　What an ugly thing to say!
RANK.　The thing itself is cursedly ugly, and the worst of it is that I shall have to face so much more that is ugly before that. I shall only make one more examination of myself; when I have done that, I shall know pretty certainly when it will be that the hor-rors of dissolution will begin. There is something I want to tell you. Helmer's refined na-ture gives him an unconquerable disgust at everything that is ugly; I won't have him in my sick-room.
NORA.　Oh, but, Doctor Rank—　155
RANK.　I won't have him there. Not on any account. I bar my door to him. As soon as I am quite certain that the worst has come, I shall send you my card with a black cross on it, and then you will know that the loathsome end has begun.
NORA.　You are quite absurd to-day. And I wanted you so much to be in a really good humour.
RANK.　With death stalking beside me?—To have to pay this penalty for another man's sin! Is there any justice in that? And in every single family, in one way or another, some such inexorable retribution is being exacted—
NORA.　[*putting her hands over her ears*] Rubbish! Do talk of something cheerful.

Torvald Helmer (Sam Waterston) begs Nora (Liv Ullmann) to reconsider her decision to leave home in the Joseph Papp New York Shakespeare Festival production
(1995) of *A Dollhouse* (director, Tormod Skagestad).

RANK. Oh, it's a mere laughing matter, the whole thing. My poor innocent spine   160
has to suffer for my father's youthful amusements.

NORA. [*sitting at the table on the left*] I suppose you mean that he was too partial to
asparagus and pâté de foie gras, don't you.

RANK. Yes, and to truffles.

NORA. Truffles, yes. And oysters too, I suppose?

RANK. Oysters, of course, that goes without saying.

NORA. And heaps of port and champagne. It is sad that all these nice things   165
should take their revenge on our bones.

RANK. Especially that they should revenge themselves on the unlucky bones of
those who have not had the satisfaction of enjoying them.

NORA. Yes, that's the saddest part of it all.

RANK. [*with a searching look at her*] Hm!—

NORA. [*after a short pause*] Why did you smile?

RANK. No, it was you that laughed. 170

NORA. No, it was you that smiled, Doctor Rank!

RANK. [*rising*] You are a greater rascal than I thought.

NORA. I am in a silly mood to-day.

RANK. So it seems.

NORA. [*putting her hands on his shoulders*] Dear, dear Doctor Rank, death mustn't 175 take you away from Torvald and me.

RANK. It is a loss you would easily recover from. Those who are gone are soon forgotten.

NORA. [*looking at him anxiously*] Do you believe that?

RANK. People form new ties, and then—

NORA. Who will form new ties?

RANK. Both you and Helmer, when I am gone. You yourself are already on the 180 high road to it, I think. What did that Mrs. Linde want here last night?

NORA. Oho!—you don't mean to say you are jealous of poor Christine?

RANK. Yes, I am. She will be my successor in this house. When I am done for, this woman will—

NORA. Hush! don't speak so loud. She is in that room.

RANK. To-day again. There, you see.

NORA. She has only come to sew my dress for me. Bless my soul, how unreason- 185 able you are! [*sits down on the sofa*] Be nice now, Doctor Rank, and tomorrow you will see how beautifully I shall dance, and you can imagine I am doing it all for you—and for Torvald too, of course. [*takes various things out of the box*] Doctor Rank, come and sit down here, and I will show you something.

RANK. [*sitting down*] What is it?

NORA. Just look at those!

RANK. Silk stockings.

NORA. Flesh-coloured. Aren't they lovely? It is so dark here now, but to-morrow—. No, no, no! you must only look at the feet. Oh well, you may have leave to look at the legs too.

RANK. Hm!— 190

NORA. Why are you looking so critical? Don't you think they will fit me?

RANK. I have no means of forming an opinion about that.

NORA. [*looks at him for a moment*] For shame! [*hits him lightly on the ear with the stockings*] That's to punish you. [*folds them up again*]

RANK. And what other nice things am I to be allowed to see?

NORA. Not a single thing more, for being so naughty. [*She looks among the things,* 195 *humming to herself.*]

RANK. [*after a short silence*] When I am sitting here, talking to you as intimately as this, I cannot imagine for a moment what would have become of me if I had never come into this house.

NORA. [*smiling*] I believe you do feel thoroughly at home with us.

RANK. [*in a lower voice, looking straight in front of him*] And to be obliged to leave it all—

NORA. Nonsense, you are not going to leave it.

RANK. [*as before*] And not be able to leave behind one the slightest token of one's 200 gratitude, scarcely even a fleeting regret—nothing but an empty place which the first comer can fill as well as any other.

NORA. And if I asked you now for a—? No!

RANK.   For what?

NORA.   For a big proof of your friendship—

RANK.   Yes, yes!

NORA.   I mean a tremendously big favour—   205

RANK.   Would you really make me so happy for once?

NORA.   Ah, but you don't know what it is yet.

RANK.   No—but tell me.

NORA.   I really can't, Doctor Rank. It is something out of all reason; it means advice, and help, and a favour—

RANK.   The bigger a thing it is the better. I can't conceive what it is you mean. Do   210
tell me. Haven't I your confidence?

NORA.   More than anyone else. I know you are my truest and best friend, and so I
will tell you what it is. Well, Doctor Rank, it is something you must help me to prevent.
You know how devotedly, how inexpressibly deeply Torvald loves me; he would never for
a moment hesitate to give his life for me.

RANK.   [*leaning towards her*] Nora—do you think he is the only one—?

NORA.   [*with a slight start*] The only one—?

RANK.   The only one who would gladly give his life for your sake.

NORA.   [*sadly*] Is that it?   215

RANK.   I was determined you should know it before I went away, and there will
never be a better opportunity than this. Now you know it, Nora. And now you know, too,
that you can trust me as you would trust no one else.

NORA.   [*rises, deliberately and quietly*] Let me pass.

RANK.   [*makes room for her to pass him, but sits still*] Nora!

NORA.   [*at the hall door*] Helen, bring in the lamp. [*goes over to the stove*] Dear Doctor Rank, that was really horrid of you.

RANK.   To have loved you as much as anyone else does? Was that horrid?   220

NORA.   No, but to go and tell me so. There was really no need—

RANK.   What do you mean? Did you know—? [*MAID enters with lamp, puts it down on
the table, and goes out.*] Nora—Mrs. Helmer—tell me, had you any idea of this?

NORA.   Oh, how do I know whether I had or whether I hadn't? I really can't tell
you—To think you could be so clumsy, Doctor Rank! We were getting on so nicely.

RANK.   Well, at all events you know now that you can command me, body and soul.
So won't you speak out?

NORA.   [*looking at him*] After what happened?   225

RANK.   I beg you to let me know what it is.

NORA.   I can't tell you anything now.

RANK.   Yes, yes. You mustn't punish me in that way. Let me have permission to do
for you whatever a man may do.

NORA.   You can do nothing for me now. Besides, I really don't need any help at all.
You will find that the whole thing is merely fancy on my part. It really is so—of course it
is! [*Sits down in the rocking-chair, and looks at him with a smile*] You are a nice sort of man,
Doctor Rank!—don't you feel ashamed of yourself, now the lamp has come?

RANK.   Not a bit. But perhaps I had better go—for ever?   230

NORA.   No, indeed, you shall not. Of course you must come here just as before.
You know very well Torvald can't do without you.

RANK.   Yes, but you?

NORA.   Oh, I am always tremendously pleased when you come.

RANK.   It is just that, that put me on the wrong track. You are a riddle to me. I have
often thought that you would almost as soon be in my company as in Helmer's.

NORA.   Yes—you see there are some people one loves best, and others whom one   235
would almost always rather have as companions.

RANK.   Yes, there is something in that.

NORA.   When I was at home, of course I loved papa best. But I always thought it
tremendous fun if I could steal down into the maid's room, because they never moralised
at all, and talked to each other about such entertaining things.

RANK.   I see—it is *their* place I have taken.

NORA.   [*jumping up and going to him*] Oh, dear, nice Doctor Rank, I never meant
that at all. But surely you can understand that being with Torvald is a little like being with
papa—

[*Enter MAID from the hall*]

MAID.   If you please, ma'am. [*whispers and hands her a card*]   240

NORA.   [*glancing at the card*] Oh! [*puts it in her pocket*]

RANK.   Is there anything wrong?

NORA.   No, no, not in the least. It is only something—it is my new dress—

RANK.   What? Your dress is lying there.

NORA.   Oh, yes, that one; but this is another. I ordered it. Torvald mustn't know   245
about it—

RANK.   Oho! Then that was the great secret.

NORA.   Of course. Just go in to him; he is sitting in the inner room. Keep him as
long as—

RANK.   Make your mind easy; I won't let him escape. [*goes into HELMER'S room*]

NORA.   [*to the MAID*] And he is standing waiting in the kitchen?

MAID.   Yes; he came up the back stairs.   250

NORA.   But didn't you tell him no one was in?

MAID.   Yes, but it was no good.

NORA.   He won't go away?

MAID.   No; he says he won't until he has seen you, ma'am.

NORA.   Well, let him come in—but quietly. Helen, you mustn't say anything about   255
it to anyone. It is a surprise for my husband.

MAID.   Yes, ma'am, I quite understand.   [*Exit.*]

NORA.   This dreadful thing is going to happen! It will happen in spite of me! No,
no, no, it can't happen—it shan't happen!

[*She bolts the door of HELMER'S room. The MAID opens the hall door for KROGSTAD and shuts it after
him. He is wearing a fur coat, high boots and a fur cap.*]

NORA.   [*advancing towards him*] Speak low—my husband is at home.

KROGSTAD.   No matter about that.

NORA.   What do you want of me?   260

KROGSTAD.   An explanation of something.

NORA.   Make haste then. What is it?

KROGSTAD.   You know, I suppose, that I have got my dismissal.

NORA.   I couldn't prevent it, Mr. Krogstad. I fought as hard as I could on your side,
but it was no good.

KROGSTAD.   Does your husband love you so little, then? He knows that what I can   265
expose you to, and yet he ventures—

NORA.   How can you suppose that he has any knowledge of the sort?

KROGSTAD.   I didn't suppose so at all. It would not be the least like our dear Torvald Helmer to show so much courage—

NORA.   Mr. Krogstad, a little respect for my husband, please.

KROGSTAD.   Certainly—all the respect he deserves. But since you have kept the matter so carefully to yourself, I make bold to suppose that you have a little clearer idea, than you had yesterday, of what it actually is that you have done?

NORA.   More than you could ever teach me.   270

KROGSTAD.   Yes, such a bad lawyer as I am.

NORA.   What is it you want of me?

KROGSTAD.   Only to see how you were, Mrs. Helmer. I have been thinking about you all day long. A mere cashier, a quill-driver, a—well, a man like me—even he has a little of what is called feeling, you know.

NORA.   Show it, then; think of my little children.

KROGSTAD.   Have you and your husband thought of mine? But never mind about   275 that. I only wanted to tell you that you need not take this matter too seriously. In the first place there will be no accusation made on my part.

NORA.   No, of course not; I was sure of that.

KROGSTAD.   The whole thing can be arranged amicably; there is no reason why anyone should know anything about it. It will remain a secret between us three.

NORA.   My husband must never get to know anything about it.

KROGSTAD.   How will you be able to prevent it? Am I to understand that you can pay the balance that is owing?

NORA.   No, not just at present.   280

KROGSTAD.   Or perhaps that you have some expedient for raising the money soon?

NORA.   No expedient that I mean to make use of.

KROGSTAD.   Well, in any case, it would have been of no use to you now. If you stood there with ever so much money in your hand, I would never part with your bond.

NORA.   Tell me what purpose you mean to put it to.

KROGSTAD.   I shall only preserve it—keep it in my possession. No one who is not   285 concerned in the matter shall have the slightest hint of it. So that if the thought of it has driven you to any desperate resolution—

NORA.   It has.

KROGSTAD.   If you had it in your mind to run away from your home—

NORA.   I had.

KROGSTAD.   Or even something worse—

NORA.   How could you know that?   290

KROGSTAD.   Give up the idea.

NORA.   How did you know I had thought of *that?*

KROGSTAD.   Most of us think of that at first. I did, too—but I hadn't the courage.

NORA.   [*faintly*] No more had I.

KROGSTAD.   [*in a tone of relief*] No, that's it, isn't it—you hadn't the courage either?   295

NORA.   No, I haven't—I haven't.

KROGSTAD.   Besides, it would have been a great piece of folly. Once the first storm at home is over—. I have a letter for your husband in my pocket.

NORA.   Telling him everything?

KROGSTAD.   In as lenient a manner as I possibly could.

NORA.   [*quickly*] He mustn't get the letter. Tear it up. I will find some means of get-   300 ting money.

KROGSTAD.   Excuse me, Mrs. Helmer, but I think I told you just now—

NORA.   I am not speaking of what I owe you. Tell me what sum you are asking my husband for, and I will get the money.

KROGSTAD.   I am not asking your husband for a penny.

NORA.   What do you want, then?

KROGSTAD.   I will tell you. I want to rehabilitate myself, Mrs. Helmer; I want to get   305
on; and in that your husband must help me. For the last year and a half I have not had a
hand in anything dishonourable, and all that time I have been struggling in most restricted circumstances. I was content to work my way up step by step. Now I am turned
out, and I am not going to be satisfied with merely being taken into favour again. I want
to get on, I tell you. I want to get into the Bank again, in a higher position. Your husband
must make a place for me—

NORA.   That he will never do!

KROGSTAD.   He will; I know him; he dare not protest. And as soon as I am in there
again with him, then you will see! Within a year I shall be the manager's right hand. It will
be Nils Krogstad and not Torvald Helmer who manages the Bank.

NORA.   That's a thing you will never see!

KROGSTAD.   Do you mean that you will—?

NORA.   I have courage enough for it now.   310

KROGSTAD.   Oh, you can't frighten me. A fine, spoilt lady like you—

NORA.   You will see, you will see.

KROGSTAD.   Under the ice, perhaps? Down into the cold, coal-black water? And
then, in the spring, to float up to the surface, all horrible and unrecognisable, with your
hair fallen out—

NORA.   You can't frighten me.

KROGSTAD.   Nor you me. People don't do such things, Mrs. Helmer. Besides, what   315
use would it be? I should have him completely in my power all the same.

NORA.   Afterwards? When I am no longer—

KROGSTAD.   Have you forgotten that it is I who have the keeping of your reputation? [*NORA stands speechlessly looking at him.*] Well, now, I have warned you. Do not do anything foolish. When Helmer has had my letter, I shall expect a message from him. And be
sure you remember that it is your husband himself who has forced me into such ways as
this again. I will never forgive him for that. Good-bye, Mrs. Helmer.

[*Exit through the hall*]

NORA.   [*goes to the hall door, opens it slightly and listens*] He is going. He is not putting
the letter in the box. Oh no, no! that's impossible! [*opens the door by degrees*] What is that?
He is standing outside. He is not going downstairs. Is he hesitating? Can he—

[*A letter drops into the box; then KROGSTAD'S footsteps are heard, till they die away as he goes downstairs. NORA utters a stifled cry and runs across the room to the table by the sofa. A short pause.*]

NORA.   In the letter-box. [*steals across to the hall door*] There it lies—Torvald,
Torvald, there is no hope for us now!

[*MRS. LINDE comes in from the room on the left, carrying the dress.*]

MRS. LINDE.   There, I can't see anything more to mend now. Would you like to try   320
it on—?

NORA.   [*in a hoarse whisper*] Christine, come here.

MRS. LINDE.   [*throwing the dress down on the sofa*] What is the matter with you? You
look so agitated!

NORA.   Come here. Do you see that letter? There, look—you can see it through
the glass in the letter-box.

MRS. LINDE.   Yes, I see it.

NORA.   That letter is from Krogstad.   325

MRS. LINDE.   Nora—it was Krogstad who lent you the money!

NORA.   Yes, and now Torvald will know all about it.

MRS. LINDE.   Believe me, Nora, that's the best thing for both of you.

NORA.   You don't know all. I forged a name.

MRS. LINDE.   Good heavens—!   330

NORA.   I only want to say this to you, Christine—you must be my witness.

MRS. LINDE.   Your witness? What do you mean? What am I to—?

NORA.   If I should go out of my mind—and it might easily happen—

MRS. LINDE.   Nora!

NORA.   Or if anything else should happen to me—anything, for instance, that   335
might prevent my being here—

MRS. LINDE.   Nora! Nora! you are quite out of your mind.

NORA.   And if it should happen that there were someone who wanted to take all
the responsibility, all the blame, you understand—

MRS. LINDE.   Yes, yes—but how can you suppose—?

NORA.   Then you must be my witness, that it is not true, Christine. I am not out of
my mind at all; I am in my right senses now, and I tell you no one else has known anything about it; I, and I alone, did the whole thing. Remember that.

MRS. LINDE.   I will, indeed. But I don't understand all this.   340

NORA.   How should you understand it? A wonderful thing is going to happen.

MRS. LINDE.   A wonderful thing?

NORA.   Yes, a wonderful thing!—But it is so terrible, Christine; it *mustn't* happen,
not for all the world.

MRS. LINDE.   I will go at once and see Krogstad.

NORA.   Don't go to him; he will do you some harm.   345

MRS. LINDE.   There was a time when he would gladly do anything for my sake.

NORA.   He?

MRS. LINDE.   Where does he live?

NORA.   How should I know—? Yes [*feeling in her pocket*] here is his card. But the letter, the letter—!

HELMER.   [*calls from his room, knocking at the door*] Nora!   350

NORA.   [*cries out anxiously*] Oh, what's that? What do you want?

HELMER.   Don't be so frightened. We are not coming in; you have locked the door.
Are you trying on your dress?

NORA.   Yes, that's it. I look so nice, Torvald.

MRS. LINDE.   [*who has read the card*] I see he lives at the corner here.

NORA.   Yes, but it's no use. It is hopeless. The letter is lying there in the box.   355

MRS. LINDE.   And your husband keeps the key?

NORA.   Yes, always.

MRS. LINDE.   Krogstad must ask for his letter back unread, he must find some
pretence—

NORA.   But it is just at this time that Torvald generally—

MRS. LINDE.   You must delay him. Go in to him in the meantime. I will come back   360
as soon as I can.

[*She goes out hurriedly through the hall door.*]

NORA.   [*goes to* HELMER'S *door, opens it and peeps in*] Torvald!

HELMER.   [*from the inner room*] Well? May I venture at last to come into my own
room again? Come along, Rank, now you will see—[*halting in the doorway*] But what is
this?

NORA.   What is what, dear?

HELMER.   Rank led me to expect a splendid transformation.

RANK.   [*in the doorway*] I understood so, but evidently I was mistaken.   365

NORA.   Yes, nobody is to have the chance of admiring me in my dress until tomorrow.

HELMER.   But, my dear Nora, you look so worn out. Have you been practising too much?

NORA.   No, I have not practised at all.

HELMER.   But you will need to—

NORA.   Yes, indeed I shall, Torvald. But I can't get on a bit without you to help me;   370
I have absolutely forgotten the whole thing.

HELMER.   Oh, we will soon work it up again.

NORA.   Yes, help me, Torvald. Promise that you will! I am so nervous about it—all
the people—. You must give yourself up to me entirely this evening. Not the tiniest bit of
business—you mustn't even take a pen in your hand. Will you promise, Torvald dear?

HELMER.   I promise. This evening I will be wholly and absolutely at your service,
you helpless little mortal. Ah, by the way, first of all I will just—

[*Goes towards the hall door*]

NORA.   What are you going to do there?

HELMER.   Only see if any letters have come.   375

NORA.   No, no! don't do that, Torvald!

HELMER.   Why not?

NORA.   Torvald, please don't. There is nothing there.

HELMER.   Well, let me look. [*Turns to go to the letter-box.* NORA, *at the piano, plays the
first bars of the Tarantella.* HELMER *stops in the doorway.*] Aha!

NORA.   I can't dance to-morrow if I don't practise with you.   380

HELMER.   [*going up to her*] Are you really so afraid of it, dear.

NORA.   Yes, so dreadfully afraid of it. Let me practise at once; there is time now,
before we go to dinner. Sit down and play for me, Torvald dear; criticise me, and correct
me as you play.

HELMER.   With great pleasure, if you wish me to.

[*Sits down at the piano.*]

NORA.   [*takes out of the box a tambourine and a long variegated shawl. She hastily drapes
the shawl round her. Then she springs to the front of the stage and calls out.*] Now play for me! I
am going to dance!

[HELMER *plays and* NORA *dances.* RANK *stands by the piano behind* HELMER *and looks on.*]

HELMER.   [*as he plays*] Slower, slower!   385

NORA.   I can't do it any other way.

HELMER.   Not so violently, Nora!

NORA.   This is the way.

HELMER.   [*stops playing*] No, no—that is not a bit right.

NORA.   [*laughing and swinging the tambourine*] Didn't I tell you so?   390

RANK.   Let me play for her.

HELMER.   [*getting up*] Yes, do. I can correct her better then.

[RANK *sits down at the piano and plays.* NORA *dances more and more wildly.* HELMER *has taken up
a position beside the stove, and during her dance gives her frequent instructions. She does not seem
to hear him; her hair comes down and falls over her shoulders; she pays no attention to it, but goes
on dancing. Enter* MRS. LINDE.]

MRS. LINDE.   [*standing as if spell-bound in the doorway*] Oh!—

NORA.   [*as she dances*] Such fun, Christine!

HELMER.   My dear darling Nora, you are dancing as if your life depended on it.   395

NORA.   So it does.

HELMER.   Stop, Rank; this is sheer madness. Stop, I tell you! [*RANK stops playing, and NORA suddenly stands still. HELMER goes up to her.*] I could never have believed it. You have forgotten everything I taught you.

NORA.   [*throwing away the tambourine*] There, you see.

HELMER.   You will want a lot of coaching.

NORA.   Yes, you see how much I need it. You must coach me up to the last minute.   400
Promise me that, Torvald!

HELMER.   You can depend on me.

NORA.   You must not think of anything but me, either to-day or to-morrow; you mustn't open a single letter—not even open the letter-box—

HELMER.   Ah, you are still afraid of that fellow—

NORA.   Yes, indeed I am.

HELMER.   Nora, I can tell from your looks that there is a letter from him lying   405
there.

NORA.   I don't know; I think there is; but you must not read anything of that kind now. Nothing horrid must come between us till this is all over.

RANK.   [*whispers to HELMER*] You mustn't contradict her.

HELMER.   [*taking her in his arms*] The child shall have her way. But to-morrow night, after you have danced—

NORA.   Then you will be free.

[*MAID appears in the doorway to the right.*]

MAID.   Dinner is served, ma'am.   410

NORA.   We will have champagne, Helen.

MAID.   Very good, ma'am.   [*Exit.*]

HELMER.   Hullo!—are we going to have a banquet?

NORA.   Yes, a champagne banquet till the small hours. [*calls out*] And a few maca-roons, Helen—lots, just for once!

HELMER.   Come, come, don't be so wild and nervous. Be my own little skylark, as   415
you used.

NORA.   Yes, dear, I will. But go in now and you too, Doctor Rank. Christine, you must help me to do up my hair.

RANK.   [*whispers to HELMER as they go out*] I suppose there is nothing—she is not ex-pecting anything?

HELMER.   Far from it, my dear fellow; it is simply nothing more than this childish nervousness I was telling you of.

[*They go into the right-hand room.*]

NORA.   Well!

MRS. LINDE.   Gone out of town.   420

NORA.   I could tell from your face.

MRS. LINDE.   He is coming home to-morrow evening. I wrote a note for him.

NORA.   You should have let it alone; you must prevent nothing. After all, it is splendid to be waiting for a wonderful thing to happen.

MRS. LINDE.   What is it that you are waiting for?

NORA.   Oh, you wouldn't understand. Go in to them, I will come in a moment.   425

[*MRS. LINDE goes into the dining-room. NORA stands still for a little while, as if to compose herself.*

Then she looks at her watch.] Five o'clock. Seven hours till midnight; and then four-and-twenty hours till the next midnight. Then the Tarantella will be over. Twenty-four and seven? Thirty-one hours to live.

HELMER. [*from the doorway on the right*] Where's my little skylark?

NORA. [*going to him with her arms outstretched*] Here she is!

ACT 3

THE SAME SCENE. *The table has been placed in the middle of the stage, with chairs round it. A lamp is burning on the table. The door into the hall stands open. Dance music is heard in the room above. MRS. LINDE is sitting at the table idly turning over the leaves of a book; she tries to read, but does not seem able to collect her thoughts. Every now and then she listens intently for a sound at the outer door.*

MRS. LINDE. [*looking at her watch*] Not yet—and the time is nearly up. If only he does not—. [*listens again*] Ah, there he is. [*Goes into the hall and opens the outer door carefully. Light footsteps are heard on the stairs. She whispers.*] Come in. There is no one here.

KROGSTAD. [*in the doorway*] I found a note from you at home. What does this mean?

MRS. LINDE. It is absolutely necessary that I should have a talk with you.

KROGSTAD. Really? And is it absolutely necessary that it should be here?

MRS. LINDE. It is impossible where I live; there is no private entrance to my   5
rooms. Come in; we are quite alone. The maid is asleep, and the Helmers are at the dance upstairs.

KROGSTAD. [*coming into the room*] Are the Helmers really at a dance to-night?

MRS. LINDE. Yes, why not?

KROGSTAD. Certainly—why not?

MRS. LINDE. Now, Nils, let us have a talk.

KROGSTAD. Can we two have anything to talk about?   10

MRS. LINDE. We have a great deal to talk about.

KROGSTAD. I shouldn't have thought so.

MRS. LINDE. No, you have never properly understood me.

KROGSTAD. Was there anything else to understand except what was obvious to all the world—a heartless woman jilts a man when a more lucrative chance turns up?

MRS. LINDE. Do you believe I am as absolutely heartless as all that? And do you be-   15
lieve that I did it with a light heart?

KROGSTAD. Didn't you?

MRS. LINDE. Nils, did you really think that?

KROGSTAD. If it were as you say, why did you write to me as you did at the time?

MRS. LINDE. I could do nothing else. As I had to break with you, it was my duty also to put an end to all that you felt for me.

KROGSTAD. [*wringing his hands*] So that was it. and all this—only for the sake of   20
money!

MRS. LINDE. You must not forget that I had a helpless mother and two little brothers. We couldn't wait for you, Nils; your prospects seemed hopeless then.

KROGSTAD. That may be so, but you had no right to throw me over for any one else's sake.

MRS. LINDE. Indeed I don't know. Many a time did I ask myself if I had the right to do it.

KROGSTAD. [*more gently*] When I lost you, it was as if all the solid ground went from under my feet. Look at me now—I am a shipwrecked man clinging to a bit of wreckage.

MRS. LINDE. But help may be near.   25

KROGSTAD. It *was* near; but then you came and stood in my way.

MRS. LINDE. Unintentionally, Nils. It was only to-day that I learnt it was your place I was going to take in the Bank.

KROGSTAD. I believe you, if you say so. But now that you know it, are you not going to give it up to me?

MRS. LINDE. No, because that would not benefit you in the least.

KROGSTAD. Oh, benefit, benefit—I would have done it whether or no.   30

MRS. LINDE. I have learnt to act prudently. Life, and hard, bitter necessity have taught me that.

KROGSTAD. And life has taught me not to believe in fine speeches.

MRS. LINDE. Then life has taught you something very reasonable. But deeds you must believe in?

KROGSTAD. What do you mean by that?

MRS. LINDE. You said you were like a shipwrecked man clinging to some   35
wreckage.

KROGSTAD. I had good reason to say so.

MRS. LINDE. Well, I am like a shipwrecked woman clinging to some wreckage—no one to mourn for, no one to care for.

KROGSTAD. It was your own choice.

MRS. LINDE. There was no other choice—then.

KROGSTAD. Well, what now?   40

MRS. LINDE. Nils, how would it be if we two shipwrecked people could join forces?

KROGSTAD. What are you saying?

MRS. LINDE. Two on the same piece of wreckage would stand a better chance than each on their own.

KROGSTAD. Christine!

MRS. LINDE. What do you suppose brought me to town?   45

KROGSTAD. Do you mean that you gave me a thought?

MRS. LINDE. I could not endure life without work. All my life, as long as I can remember, I have worked, and it has been my greatest and only pleasure. But now I am quite alone in the world—my life is so dreadfully empty and I feel so forsaken. There is not the least pleasure in working for one's self. Nils, give me someone and something to work for.

KROGSTAD. I don't trust that. It is nothing but a woman's overstrained sense of generosity that prompts you to make such an offer of yourself.

MRS. LINDE. Have you ever noticed anything of the sort in me?

KROGSTAD. Could you really do it? Tell me—do you know all about my past life?   50

MRS. LINDE. Yes.

KROGSTAD. And do you know what they think of me here?

MRS. LINDE. You seemed to me to imply that with me you might have been quite another man.

KROGSTAD. I am certain of it.

MRS. LINDE. Is it too late now?   55

KROGSTAD. Christine, are you saying this deliberately? Yes, I am sure you are. I see it in your face. Have you really the courage, then—?

MRS. LINDE. I want to be a mother to someone, and your children need a mother. We two need each other. Nils, I have faith in your real character—I can dare anything together with you.

KROGSTAD. [*grasps her hands*] Thanks, thanks, Christine! Now I shall find a way to clear myself in the eyes of the world. Ah, but I forgot—

MRS. LINDE. [*listening*] Hush! The Tarantella! Go, go!

KROGSTAD.   Why? What is it? 60

MRS. LINDE.   Do you hear them up there? When that is over, we may expect them back.

KROGSTAD.   Yes, yes—I will go. But it is all no use. Of course you are not aware what steps I have taken in the matter of the Helmers.

MRS. LINDE.   Yes. I know all about that.

KROGSTAD.   And in spite of that have you the courage to—?

MRS. LINDE.   I understand very well to what lengths a man like you might be driv- 65 en by despair.

KROGSTAD.   If I could only undo what I have done!

MRS. LINDE.   You can. Your letter is lying in the letter-box now.

KROGSTAD.   Are you sure of that?

MRS. LINDE.   Quite sure, but—

KROGSTAD.   [*with a searching look at her*] Is that what it all means?—that you want to 70 save your friend at any cost? Tell me frankly. Is that it?

MRS. LINDE.   Nils, a woman who has once sold herself for another's sake, doesn't do it a second time.

KROGSTAD.   I will ask for my letter back.

MRS. LINDE.   No, no.

KROGSTAD.   Yes, of course I will. I will wait here till Helmer comes; I will tell him he must give me my letter back—that it only concerns my dismissal—that he is not to read it—

MRS. LINDE.   No, Nils, you must not recall your letter. 75

KROGSTAD.   But, tell me, wasn't it for that very purpose that you asked me to meet you here?

MRS. LINDE.   In my first moment of fright, it was. But twenty-four hours have elapsed since then, and in that time I have witnessed incredible things in this house. Helmer must know all about it. This unhappy secret must be disclosed; they must have a complete understanding between them, which is impossible with all this concealment and falsehood going on.

KROGSTAD.   Very well, if you will take the responsibility. But there is one thing I can do in any case, and I shall do it at once.

MRS. LINDE.   [*listening*] You must be quick and go! The dance is over; we are not safe a moment longer.

KROGSTAD.   I will wait for you below. 80

MRS. LINDE.   Yes, do. You must see me back to my door.

KROGSTAD.   I have never had such an amazing piece of good fortune in my life.

[*Goes out through the outer door. The door between the room and the hall remains open.*]

MRS. LINDE.   [*tidying up the room and laying her hat and cloak ready*] What a differ- ence! what a difference! Someone to work for and live for—a home to bring comfort into. That I will do, indeed. I wish they would be quick and come—[*listens*] Ah, there they are now. I must put on my things.

[*Takes up her hat and cloak. HELMER'S and NORA'S voices are heard outside; a key is turned, and HELMER brings NORA almost by force into the hall. She is in an Italian costume with a large black shawl round her; he is in evening dress and a black domino which is flying open.*]

NORA.   [*hanging back in the doorway, and struggling with him*] No, no, no!—don't take me in. I want to go upstairs again; I don't want to leave so early.

HELMER.   But, my dearest Nora— 85

NORA.   Please, Torvald dear—please, *please*—only an hour more.

HELMER.   Not a single minute, my sweet Nora. You know that was our agreement. Come along into the room; you are catching cold standing there.

[*He brings her gently into the room, in spite of her resistance.*]

MRS. LINDE.   Good evening.

NORA.   Christine!

HELMER.   You here, so late, Mrs. Linde?   90

MRS. LINDE.   Yes, you must excuse me; I was so anxious to see Nora in her dress.

NORA.   Have you been sitting here waiting for me?

MRS. LINDE.   Yes, unfortunately I came too late, you had already gone upstairs; and I thought I couldn't go away without having seen you.

HELMER.   [*taking off NORA's shawl*] Yes, take a good look at her. I think she is worth looking at. Isn't she charming, Mrs. Linde?

MRS. LINDE.   Yes, indeed she is.   95

HELMER.   Doesn't she look remarkably pretty? Everyone thought so at the dance. But she is terribly self-willed, this sweet little person. What are we to do with her? You will hardly believe that I had almost to bring her away by force.

NORA.   Torvald, you will repent not having let me stay, even if it were only for half an hour.

HELMER.   Listen to her, Mrs. Linde! She had danced her Tarantella, and it had been a tremendous success, as it deserved—although possibly the performance was a trifle too realistic—a little more so, I mean, than was strictly compatible with the limitations of art. But never mind about that! The chief thing is, she had made a success—she had made a tremendous success. Do you think I was going to let her remain there after that, and spoil the effect? No indeed! I took my charming little Capri maiden—my capricious little Capri maiden, I should say—on my arm; took one quick turn round the room; a curtsey on either side, and, as they say in novels, the beautiful apparition disappeared. An exit ought always to be effective, Mrs. Linde; but that is what I cannot make Nora understand. Pooh! this room is hot. [*throws his domino on a chair and opens the door of his room*] Hullo! it's all dark in here. Oh, of course—excuse me—.

[*He goes in and lights some candles.*]

NORA.   [*in a hurried and breathless whisper*] Well?

MRS. LINDE.   [*in a low voice*] I have had a talk with him.   100

NORA.   Yes, and—

MRS. LINDE.   Nora, you must tell your husband all about it.

NORA.   [*in an expressionless voice*] I knew it.

MRS. LINDE.   You have nothing to be afraid of as far as Krogstad is concerned; but you must tell him.

NORA.   I won't tell him.   105

MRS. LINDE.   Then the letter will.

NORA.   Thank you, Christine. Now I know what I must do. Hush—!

HELMER.   [*coming in again*] Well, Mrs. Linde, have you admired her?

MRS. LINDE.   Yes, and now I will say good-night.

HELMER.   What already? Is this yours, this knitting?   110

MRS. LINDE.   [*taking it*] Yes, thank you, I had very nearly forgotten it.

HELMER.   So you knit?

MRS. LINDE.   Of course.

HELMER.   Do you know, you ought to embroider.

MRS. LINDE.   Really? Why?   115

HELMER.   Yes, it's far more becoming. Let me show you. You hold the embroidery thus in your left hand, and use the needle with the right—like this—with a long, easy sweep. Do you see?

MRS. LINDE.   Yes, perhaps—

HELMER.   But in the case of knitting—that can never be anything but ungraceful; look here—the arms close together, the knitting-needles going up and down—it has a sort of Chinese effect—. That was really excellent champagne they gave us.

MRS. LINDE.   Well,—good-night, Nora, and don't be self-willed any more.

HELMER.   That's right, Mrs. Linde.   120

MRS. LINDE.   Good-night, Mr. Helmer.

HELMER.   [accompanying her to the door] Good-night, good-night. I hope you will get home all right. I should be very happy to—but you haven't any great distance to go. Good-night, good-night. [She goes out; he shuts the door after her, and comes in again.] Ah!— at last we have got rid of her. She is a frightful bore, that woman.

NORA.   Aren't you very tired, Torvald?

HELMER.   No, not in the least.

NORA.   Nor sleepy?   125

HELMER.   Not a bit. On the contrary, I feel extraordinarily lively. And you?—you really look both tired and sleepy.

NORA.   Yes, I am very tired. I want to go to sleep at once.

HELMER.   There, you see it was quite right of me not to let you stay there any longer.

NORA.   Everything you do is quite right, Torvald.

HELMER.   [kissing her on the forehead] Now my little skylark is speaking reasonably.   130
Did you notice what good spirits Rank was in this evening?

NORA.   Really? Was he? I didn't speak to him at all.

HELMER.   And I very little, but I have not for a long time seen him in such good form. [looks for a while at her and then goes nearer to her] It is delightful to be at home by our- selves again, to be all alone with you—you fascinating, charming little darling!

NORA.   Don't look at me like that, Torvald.

HELMER.   Why shouldn't I look at my dearest treasure?—at all the beauty that is mine, all my very own?

NORA.   [going to the other side of the table] You mustn't say things like that to me   135
to-night.

HELMER.   [following her] You have still got the Tarantella in your blood, I see. And it makes you more captivating than ever. Listen—the guests are beginning to go now. [in a lower voice] Nora—soon the whole house will be quiet.

NORA.   Yes, I hope so.

HELMER.   Yes, my own darling Nora. Do you know, when I am out at a party with you like this, why I speak so little to you, keep away from you, and only send a stolen glance in your direction now and then?—do you know why I do that? It is because I make believe to myself that we are secretly in love, and you are my secretly promised bride, and that no one suspects there is anything between us.

NORA.   Yes, yes—I know very well your thoughts are with me all the time.

HELMER.   And when we are leaving, and I am putting the shawl over your beautiful   140
young shoulders—on your lovely neck—then I imagine that you are my young bride and that we have just come from the wedding, and I am bringing you for the first time into our home—to be alone with you for the first time—quite alone with my shy little darling! All this evening I have longed for nothing but you. When I watched the seductive figures

of the Tarantella, my blood was on fire; I could endure it no longer, and that was why I brought you down so early—

NORA.   Go away, Torvald! You must let me go. I won't—

HELMER.   What's that? You're joking, my little Nora! You won't—you won't? Am I not your husband—?

[*A knock is heard at the outer door.*]

NORA.   [*starting*] Did you hear—?

HELMER.   [*going into the hall*] Who is it?

RANK.   [*outside*] It is I. May I come in for a moment?   145

HELMER.   [*in a fretful whisper*] Oh, what does he want now? [*aloud*] Wait a minute! [*unlocks the door*] Come, that's kind of you not to pass by our door.

RANK.   I thought I heard your voice, and felt as if I should like to look in. [*with a swift glance round*] Ah, yes!—these dear familiar rooms. You are very happy and cosy in here, you two.

HELMER.   It seems to me that you looked after yourself pretty well upstairs too.

RANK.   Excellently. Why shouldn't I? Why shouldn't one enjoy everything in this world?—at any rate as much as one can, and as long as one can. The wine was capital—

HELMER.   Especially the champagne.   150

RANK.   So you noticed that too? It is almost incredible how much I managed to put away!

NORA.   Torvald drank a great deal of champagne tonight, too.

RANK.   Did he?

NORA.   Yes, and he is always in such good spirits afterwards.

RANK.   Well, why should one not enjoy a merry evening after a well-spent day?   155

HELMER.   Well spent? I am afraid I can't take credit for that.

RANK.   [*clapping him on the back*] But I can, you know!

NORA.   Doctor Rank, you must have been occupied with some scientific investigation to-day.

RANK.   Exactly.

HELMER.   Just listen!—little Nora talking about scientific investigations!   160

NORA.   And may I congratulate you on the result?

RANK.   Indeed you may.

NORA.   Was it favourable, then?

RANK.   The best possible, for both doctor and patient—certainty.

NORA.   [*quickly and searchingly*] Certainty?   165

RANK.   Absolute certainty. So wasn't I entitled to make a merry evening of it after that?

NORA.   Yes, you certainly were, Doctor Rank.

HELMER.   I think so too, so long as you don't have to pay for it in the morning.

RANK.   Oh well, one can't have anything in this life without paying for it.

NORA.   Doctor Rank—are you fond of fancy-dress balls?   170

RANK.   Yes, if there is a fine lot of pretty costumes.

NORA.   Tell me—what shall we two wear at the next?

HELMER.   Little featherbrain!—are you thinking of the next already?

RANK.   We two? Yes, I can tell you. You shall go as a good fairy—

HELMER.   Yes, but what do you suggest as an appropriate costume for that?   175

RANK.   Let your wife go dressed just as she is in everyday life.

HELMER.   That was really very prettily turned. But can't you tell us what you will be?

RANK. Yes, my dear friend, I have quite made up my mind about that.

HELMER. Well?

RANK. At the next fancy dress ball I shall be invisible. 180

HELMER. That's a good joke!

RANK. There is a big black hat—have you never heard of hats that make you invisible? If you put one on, no one can see you.

HELMER. [*suppressing a smile*] Yes, you are quite right.

RANK. But I am clean forgetting what I came for. Helmer, give me a cigar—one of the dark Havanas.

HELMER. With the greatest pleasure. [*offers him his case*] 185

RANK. [*takes a cigar and cuts off the end*] Thanks.

NORA. [*striking a match*] Let me give you a light.

RANK. Thank you. [*She holds the match for him to light his cigar.*] And now good-bye!

HELMER. Good-bye, good-bye, dear old man!

NORA. Sleep well, Doctor Rank. 190

RANK. Thank you for that wish.

NORA. Wish me the same.

RANK. You? Well, if you want me to sleep well! And thanks for the light.

[*He nods to them both and goes out.*]

HELMER. [*in a subdued voice*] He has drunk more than he ought.

NORA. [*absently*] Maybe. [*HELMER takes a bunch of keys out of his pocket and goes into* 195 *the hall.*] Torvald! what are you going to do there?

HELMER. Empty the letter-box; it is quite full; there will be no room to put the newspaper in to-morrow morning.

NORA. Are you going to work to-night?

HELMER. You know quite well I'm not. What is this? Some one has been at the lock.

NORA. At the lock—?

HELMER. Yes, someone has. What can it mean? I should never have thought the 200 maid—. Here is a broken hairpin. Nora, it is one of yours.

NORA. [*quickly*] Then it must have been the children—

HELMER. Then you must get them out of those ways. There, at last I have got it open. [*Takes out the contents of the letter-box, and calls to the kitchen.*] Helen!—Helen, put out the light over the front door. [*Goes back into the room and shuts the door into the hall. He holds out his hand full of letters.*] Look at that—look what a heap of them there are. [*turning them over*] What on earth is that?

NORA. [*at the window*] The letter—No! Torvald, no!

HELMER. Two cards—of Rank's.

NORA. Of Doctor Rank's? 205

HELMER. [*looking at them*] Doctor Rank. They were on the top. He must have put them in when he went out.

NORA. Is there anything written on them?

HELMER. There is a black cross over the name. Look there—what an uncomfortable idea! It looks as if he were announcing his own death.

NORA. It is just what he is doing.

HELMER. What? Do you know anything about it? Has he said anything to you? 210

NORA. Yes. He told me that when the cards came it would be his leave-taking from us. He means to shut himself up and die.

HELMER. My poor old friend. Certainly I knew we should not have him very long with us. But so soon! And so he hides himself away like a wounded animal.

NORA.   If it has to happen, it is best it should be without a word—don't you think so, Torvald?

HELMER.   [*walking up and down*] He had so grown into our lives. I can't think of him as having gone out of them. He, with his sufferings and his loneliness, was like a cloudy background to our sunlit happiness. Well, perhaps it is best so. For him, anyway. [*standing still*] And perhaps for us too, Nora. We two are thrown quite upon each other now. [*puts his arms round her*] My darling wife, I don't feel as if I could hold you tight enough. Do you know, Nora, I have often wished that you might be threatened by some great danger, so that I might risk my life's blood, and everything, for your sake.

NORA.   [*disengages herself, and says firmly and decidedly*] Now you must read your   215
letters, Torvald.

HELMER.   No, no; not to-night. I want to be with you, my darling wife.

NORA.   With the thought of your friend's death—

HELMER.   You are right, it has affected us both. Something ugly has come between us—the thought of the horrors of death. We must try and rid our minds of that. Until then—we will each go to our own room.

NORA.   [*hanging on his neck*] Good-night, Torvald—Good-night!

HELMER.   [*kissing her on the forehead*]. Good-night, my little singing-bird. Sleep   220
sound, Nora. Now I will read my letters through.

[*He takes his letters and goes into his room, shutting the door after him.*]

NORA.   [*gropes distractedly about, seizes HELMER's domino, throws it round her, while she says in quick, hoarse, spasmodic whispers*] Never to see him again. Never! Never! [*puts her shawl over her head*] Never to see my children again either—never again. Never! Never!— Ah! the icy, black water—the unfathomable depths—If only it were over! He has got it now—now he is reading it. Good-by, Torvald and my children!

[*She is about to rush out through the hall, when HELMER opens his door hurriedly and stands with an open letter in his hand.*]

HELMER.   Nora!

NORA.   Ah!—

HELMER.   What is this? Do you know what is in this letter?

NORA.   Yes, I know. Let me go! Let me get out!   225

HELMER.   [*holding her back*] Where are you going?

NORA.   [*trying to get free*] You shan't save me, Torvald!

HELMER.   [*reeling*] True? Is this true, that I read here? Horrible! No, no—it is impossible that it can be true.

NORA.   It is true. I have loved you above everything else in the world.

HELMER.   Oh, don't let us have any silly excuses.   230

NORA.   [*taking a step towards him*] Torvald—!

HELMER.   Miserable creature—what have you done?

NORA.   Let me go. You shall not suffer for my sake. You shall not take it upon yourself.

HELMER.   No tragedy airs, please. [*locks the hall door*] Here you shall stay and give me an explanation. Do you understand what you have done? Answer me? Do you understand what you have done?

NORA.   [*looks steadily at him and says with a growing look of coldness in her face*] Yes,   235
now I am beginning to understand thoroughly.

HELMER.   [*walking about the room*] What a horrible awakening! All these eight years—she who was my joy and pride—a hypocrite, a liar—worse, worse—a criminal! The unutterable ugliness of it all! For shame! For shame! [*NORA is silent and looks steadily at him. He stops in front of her.*] I ought to have suspected that something of the sort would happen. I ought to have foreseen it. All your father's want of principle—be silent!—all your father's want of principle has come out in you. No religion, no morality, no sense of duty—. How I am punished for having winked at what he did! I did it for your sake, and this is how you repay me.

NORA. Yes, that's just it.

HELMER. Now you have destroyed all my happiness. You have ruined all my future. It is horrible to think of! I am in the power of an unscrupulous man; he can do what he likes with me, ask anything he likes of me, give me any orders he pleases—I dare not refuse. And I must sink to such miserable depths because of a thoughtless woman!

NORA. When I am out of the way, you will be free.

HELMER. No fine speeches, please. Your father had always plenty of those ready, too. What good would it be to me if you were out of the way, as you say? Not the slightest. He can make the affair known everywhere; and if he does, I may be falsely suspected of having been a party to your criminal action. Very likely people will think I was behind it all—that it was I who prompted you! And I have to thank you for all this—you whom I have cherished during the whole of our married life. Do you understand now what it is you have done for me?   240

NORA. [*coldly and quietly*] Yes.

HELMER. It is so incredible that I can't take it in. But we must come to some understanding. Take off that shawl. Take it off, I tell you. I must try and appease him some way or another. The matter must be hushed up at any cost. And as for you and me, it must appear as if everything between us were just as before—but naturally only in the eyes of the world. You will still remain in my house, that is a matter of course. But I shall not allow you to bring up the children; I dare not trust them to you. To think that I should be obliged to say so to one whom I have loved so dearly, and whom I still—. No, that is all over. From this moment happiness is not the question; all that concerns us is to save the remains, the fragments, the appearance—

[*A ring is heard at the front-door bell.*]

HELMER. [*with a start*] What is that? So late! Can the worst—? Can he—? Hide yourself, Nora. Say you are ill.

[*NORA stands motionless. HELMER goes and unlocks the hall door.*]

MAID. [*half-dressed, comes to the door*] A letter for the mistress.

HELMER. Give it to me. [*takes the letter, and shuts the door*] Yes, it is from him. You shall not have it; I will read it myself.   245

NORA. Yes, read it.

HELMER. [*standing by the lamp*] I scarcely have the courage to do it. It may mean ruin for both of us. No, I must know. [*tears open the letter, runs his eye over a few lines, looks at a paper enclosed and gives a shout of joy*] Nora! [*She looks at him questioningly.*] Nora!—No, I must read it once again—. Yes, it is true! I am saved! Nora, I am saved!

NORA. And I?

HELMER. You too, of course; we are both saved, both you and I. Look, he sends you your bond back. He says he regrets and repents—that a happy change in his life— never mind what he says! We are saved, Nora! No one can do anything to you. Oh, Nora, Nora!—no, first I must destroy these hateful things. Let me see—. [*takes a look at the bond*] No, no, I won't look at it. The whole thing shall be nothing but a bad dream to me. [*tears up the bond and both letters, throws them all into the stove, and watches them burn*] There—now it doesn't exist any longer. He says that since Christmas Eve you—. These must have been three dreadful days for you, Nora.

NORA.   I have fought a hard fight these three days.   250

HELMER.   And suffered agonies, and seen no way out but—. No, we won't call any of the horrors to mind. We will only shout with joy, and keep saying "It's all over! It's all over!" Listen to me, Nora. You don't seem to realise that it is all over. What is this?—such a cold, set face! My poor little Nora, I quite understand; you don't feel as if you could believe that I have forgiven you. But it is true, Nora, I swear it; I have forgiven you everything. I know that what you did, you did out of love for me.

NORA.   That is true.

HELMER.   You have loved me as a wife ought to love her husband. Only you had not sufficient knowledge to judge of the means you used. But do you suppose you are any the less dear to me, because you don't understand how to act on your own responsibility? No, no; only lean on me; I will advise you and direct you. I should not be a man if this womanly helplessness did not just give you a double attractiveness in my eyes. You must not think any more about the hard things I said in my first moment of consternation, when I thought everything was going to overwhelm me. I have forgiven you, Nora; I swear to you I have forgiven you.

NORA.   Thank you for your forgiveness.

[She goes out through the door to the right.]

HELMER.   No, don't go—. [looks in] What are you doing in there?   255

NORA.   [from within] Taking off my fancy dress.

HELMER.   [standing at the open door] Yes, do. Try and calm yourself, and make your mind easy again, my frightened little singing-bird. Be at rest, and feel secure; I have broad wings to shelter you under. [walks up and down by the door] How warm and cosy our home is, Nora. Here is shelter for you; here I will protect you like a hunted dove that I have saved from a hawk's claws. I will bring peace to your poor beating heart. It will come, little by little, Nora, believe me. Tomorrow morning you will look upon it all quite differently; soon everything will be just as it was before. Very soon you won't need me to assure you that I have forgiven you; you will yourself feel the certainty that I have done so. Can you suppose I should ever think of such a thing as repudiating you, or even reproaching you? You have no idea what a true man's heart is like, Nora. There is something so indescribably sweet and satisfying, to a man, in the knowledge that he has forgiven his wife— forgiven her freely, and with all his heart. It seems as if that had made her, as it were, doubly his own; he has given her a new life, so to speak; and she has in a way become both wife and child to him. So you shall be for me after this, my little scared, helpless darling. Have no anxiety about anything, Nora; only be frank and open with me, and I will serve as will and conscience both to you—. What is this? Not gone to bed? Have you changed your things?

NORA.   [in everyday dress] Yes, Torvald, I have changed my things now.

HELMER.   But what for?—so late as this.

NORA.   I shall not sleep to-night.   260

HELMER.   But, my dear Nora—

NORA.   [looking at her watch] It is not so very late. Sit down here, Torvald. You and I have much to say to one another.

[She sits down at one side of the table.]

HELMER.   Nora—what is this?—this cold, set face?

NORA.   Sit down. it will take some time; I have a lot to talk over with you.

HELMER. [*sits down at the opposite side of the table*] You alarm me, Nora!—and I don't   265
understand you.

NORA. No, that is just it. You don't understand me, and I have never understood
you either—before to-night. No, you mustn't interrupt me. You must simply listen to
what I say. Torvald, this is a settling of accounts.

HELMER. What do you mean by that?

NORA. [*after a short silence*] Isn't there one thing that strikes you as strange in our
sitting here like this?

HELMER. What is that?

NORA. We have been married now eight years. Does it not occur to you that this is   270
the first time we two, you and I, husband and wife, have had a serious conversation?

HELMER. What do you mean by serious?

NORA. In all these eight years—longer than that—from the very beginning of our
acquaintance, we have never exchanged a word on any serious subject.

HELMER. Was it likely that I would be continually and for ever telling you about
worries that you could not help me to bear?

NORA. I am not speaking about business matters. I say that we have never sat
down in earnest together to try and get at the bottom of anything.

HELMER. But, dearest Nora, would it have been any good to you?   275

NORA. That is just it; you have never understood me. I have been greatly
wronged, Torvald—first by papa and then by you.

HELMER. What! By us two—by us two, who have loved you better than anyone else
in the world?

NORA. [*shaking her head*] You have never loved me. You have only thought it pleasant to be in love with me.

HELMER. Nora, what do I hear you saying?

NORA. It is perfectly true, Torvald. When I was at home with papa, he told me his   280
opinion about everything, and so I had the same opinions; and if I differed from him I
concealed the fact, because he would not have liked it. He called me his doll-child, and
he played with me just as I used to play with my dolls. And when I came to live with you—

HELMER. What sort of an expression is that to use about our marriage?

NORA. [*undisturbed*] I mean that I was simply transferred from papa's hands into
yours. You arranged everything according to your own taste, and so I got the same tastes
as you—or else I pretended to, I am really not quite sure which—I think sometimes the
one and sometimes the other. When I look back on it, it seems to me as if I had been living here like a poor woman—just from hand to mouth. I have existed merely to perform
tricks for you, Torvald. But you would have it so. You and papa have committed a great
sin against me. It is your fault that I have made nothing of my life.

HELMER. How unreasonable and how ungrateful you are, Nora! Have you not
been happy here?

NORA. No, I have never been happy. I thought I was, but it has never really been so.

HELMER. Not—not happy!   285

NORA. No, only merry. And you have always been so kind to me. But our home
has been nothing but a playroom. I have been your doll-wife, just as at home I was papa's
doll-child; and here the children have been my dolls. I thought it great fun when you
played with me, just as they thought it great fun when I played with them. That is what
our marriage has been, Torvald.

HELMER. There is some truth in what you say—exaggerated and strained as your
view of it is. But for the future it shall be different. Playtime shall be over, and lesson-time
shall begin.

NORA.   Whose lessons? Mine, or the children's?

HELMER.   Both yours and the children's, my darling Nora.

NORA.   Alas, Torvald, you are not the man to educate me into being a proper wife   290
for you.

HELMER.   And you can say that!

NORA.   And I—how am I fitted to bring up the children?

HELMER.   Nora!

NORA.   Didn't you say so yourself a little while ago—that you dare not trust me to
bring them up?

HELMER.   In a moment of anger! Why do you pay any heed to that?   295

NORA.   Indeed, you were perfectly right. I am not fit for the task. There is another
task I must undertake first. I must try and educate myself—you are not the man to help
me in that. I must do that for myself. And that is why I am going to leave you now.

HELMER.   [springing up] What do you say?

NORA.   I must stand quite alone, if I am to understand myself and everything
about me. It is for that reason that I cannot remain with you any longer.

HELMER.   Nora! Nora!

NORA.   I am going away from here now, at once. I am sure Christine will take me   300
in for the night—

HELMER.   You are out of your mind! I won't allow it! I forbid you!

NORA.   It is no use forbidding me anything any longer. I will take with me what belongs to myself. I will take nothing from you, either now or later.

HELMER.   What sort of madness is this!

NORA.   To-morrow I shall go home—I mean, to my old home. It will be easiest for
me to find something to do there.

HELMER.   You blind, foolish woman!   305

NORA.   I must try and get some sense, Torvald.

HELMER.   To desert your home, your husband and your children! And you don't
consider what people will say!

NORA.   I cannot consider that at all. I only know that it is necessary for me.

HELMER.   It's shocking. This is how you would neglect your most sacred duties.

NORA.   What do you consider my most sacred duties?   310

HELMER.   Do I need to tell you that? Are they not your duties to your husband and
your children?

NORA.   I have other duties just as sacred.

HELMER.   That you have not. What duties could those be?

NORA.   Duties to myself.

HELMER.   Before all else, you are a wife and a mother.   315

NORA.   I don't believe that any longer. I believe that before all else I am a reasonable human being, just as you are—or, at all events, that I must try and become one. I
know quite well, Torvald, that most people would think you right, and that views of that
kind are to be found in books; but I can no longer content myself with what most people
say, or with what is found in books. I must think over things for myself and get to understand them.

HELMER.   Can you not understand your place in your own home? Have you not a
reliable guide in such matters as that?—have you no religion?

NORA.   I am afraid, Torvald, I do not exactly know what religion is.

HELMER.   What are you saying?

NORA.   I know nothing but what the clergyman said when I went to be confirmed.   320
He told us that religion was this, and that, and the other. When I am away from all this,

and am alone, I will look into that matter too. I will see if what the clergyman said is true, or at all events if it is true for me.

HELMER. This is unheard of in a girl of your age! But if religion cannot lead you aright, let me try and awaken your conscience. I suppose you have some moral sense? Or—answer me—am I to think you have none?

NORA. I assure you, Torvald, that is not an easy question to answer. I really don't know. The thing perplexes me altogether. I only know that you and I look at it in quite a different light. I am learning, too, that the law is quite another thing from what I supposed; but I find it impossible to convince myself that the law is right. According to it a woman has no right to spare her old dying father, or to save her husband's life. I can't believe that.

HELMER. You talk like a child. You don't understand the conditions of the world in which you live.

NORA. No, I don't. But now I am going to try. I am going to see if I can make out who is right, the world or I.

HELMER. You are ill, Nora; you are delirious; I almost think you are out of your mind.   325

NORA. I have never felt my mind so clear and certain as to-night.

HELMER. And is it with a clear and certain mind that you forsake your husband and your children?

NORA. Yes, it is.

HELMER. Then there is only one possible explanation.

NORA. What is that?   330

HELMER. You do not love me any more.

NORA. No, that is just it.

HELMER. Nora!—and you can say that?

NORA. It gives me great pain, Torvald, for you have always been so kind to me, but I cannot help it. I do not love you any more.

HELMER. [regaining his composure] Is that a clear and certain conviction too?   335

NORA. Yes, absolutely clear and certain. That is the reason why I will not stay here any longer.

HELMER. And can you tell me what I have done to forfeit your love?

NORA. Yes, indeed I can. It was to-night, when the wonderful thing did not happen; then I saw you were not the man I had thought you.

HELMER. Explain yourself better—I don't understand you.

NORA. I have waited so patiently for eight years; for, goodness knows, I knew very   340
well that wonderful things don't happen every day. Then this horrible misfortune came upon me; and then I felt quite certain that the wonderful thing was going to happen at last. When Krogstad's letter was lying out there, never for a moment did I imagine that you would consent to accept this man's conditions. I was so absolutely certain that you would say to him: Publish the thing to the whole world. And when that was done—

HELMER. Yes, what then?—when I had exposed my wife to shame and disgrace?

NORA. When that was done, I was so absolutely certain, you would come forward and take everything upon yourself, and say: I am the guilty one.

HELMER. Nora—!

NORA. You mean that I would never have accepted such a sacrifice on your part? No, of course not. But what would my assurances have been worth against yours? That was the wonderful thing which I hoped for and feared; and it was to prevent that, that I wanted to kill myself.

HELMER. I would gladly work night and day for you, Nora—bear sorrow and want   345
for your sake. But no man would sacrifice his honour for the one he loves.

NORA.   It is a thing hundreds of thousands of women have done.

HELMER.   Oh, you think and talk like a heedless child.

NORA.   Maybe. But you neither think nor talk like the man I could bind myself to. As soon as your fear was over—and it was not fear for what threatened me, but for what might happen to you—when the whole thing was past, as far as you were concerned it was exactly as if nothing at all had happened. Exactly as before, I was your little skylark, your doll, which you would in future treat with doubly gentle care, because it was so brittle and fragile. [*getting up*] Torvald—it was then it dawned upon me that for eight years I had been living here with a strange man, and had borne him three children—. Oh, I can't bear to think of it! I could tear myself into little bits!

HELMER.   [*sadly*] I see, I see. An Abyss has opened between us—there is no denying it. But, Nora, would it not be possible to fill it up?

NORA.   As I am now, I am no wife for you.   350

HELMER.   I have it in me to become a different man.

NORA.   Perhaps—if your doll is taken away from you.

HELMER.   But to part!—to part from you! No, no, Nora, I can't understand that idea.

NORA.   [*going out to the right*] That makes it all the more certain that it must be done.

[*She comes back with her cloak and hat and a small bag which she puts on a chair by the table.*]

HELMER.   Nora, Nora, not now! Wait till to-morrow.   355

NORA.   [*putting on her cloak*] I cannot spend the night in a strange man's room.

HELMER.   But can't we live here like brother and sister—?

NORA.   [*putting on her hat*] You know very well that would not last long. [*puts the shawl round her*] Good-bye, Torvald. I won't see the little ones. I know they are in better hands than mine. As I am now, I can be of no use to them.

HELMER.   But some day, Nora—some day?

NORA.   How can I tell? I have no idea what is going to become of me.   360

HELMER.   But you are my wife, whatever becomes of you.

NORA.   Listen, Torvald. I have heard that when a wife deserts her husband's house, as I am doing now, he is legally freed from all obligations towards her. In any case I set you free from all your obligations. You are not to feel yourself bound in the slightest way, any more than I shall. There must be perfect freedom on both sides. See here is your ring back. Give me mine.

HELMER.   That too?

NORA.   That too.

HELMER.   Here it is.   365

NORA.   That's right. Now it is all over. I have put the keys here. The maids know all about everything in the house—better than I do. To-morrow, after I have left her, Christine will come here and pack up my own things that I brought with me from home. I will have them sent after me.

HELMER.   All over! All over!—Nora, shall you never think of me again?

NORA.   I know I shall often think of you and the children and this house.

HELMER.   May I write to you, Nora?

NORA.   No—never. You must not do that.   370

HELMER.   But at least let me send you—

NORA.   Nothing—nothing—

HELMER.   Let me help you if you are in want.

NORA.   No. I can receive nothing from a stranger.

HELMER.   Nora—can I never be anything more than a stranger to you?   375

NORA. [*taking her bag*] Ah, Torvald, the most wonderful thing of all would have to happen.

HELMER. Tell me what that would be!

NORA. Both you and I would have to be so changed that—. Oh, Torvald, I don't believe any longer in wonderful things happening.

HELMER. But I will believe in it. Tell me? So changed that—?

NORA. That our life together would be a real wedlock. Good-bye.   380

[*She goes out through the hall.*]

HELMER. [*sinks down on a chair at the door and buries his face in his hands*] Nora! Nora! [*looks round, and rises*] Empty. She is gone. [*A hope flashes across his mind.*] The most wonderful thing of all—?

[*The sound of a door slamming is heard from below.*]

QUESTIONS

Act 1

1. What does the opening stage direction reveal about the Helmer family? About the time of year?

2. Explain the ways Nora and Torvald behave toward each other.

3. What does Torvald's refusal to consider borrowing and debt tell you about him (speech 22)? Where else in the play are these characteristics important?

4. What have the Helmer finances been like in the past? How is their situation about to change?

5. How are Mrs. Linde and Nora alike? Different? Why is it ironic that Nora helps Christine get a job at the bank? How will this affect Krogstad? Nora?

6. How does Ibsen show that Krogstad is a threat when he first appears?

7. Why should Nora's scene with her children in Act 1 not be cut in production? What does it show about Nora and the household?

8. What is Nora's secret "crime"? What is the explanation and justification for it? At the end of the act, what new problems does she face?

Act 2

9. What is symbolized by the stripped Christmas tree?

10. What is implied about Nora's self-perceptions when she calls herself "your little squirrel" and "your skylark"?

11. After sending Krogstad's dismissal, Torvald tells Nora that "You will see I am man enough to take everything upon myself" (speech 135). How does this speech conform to Nora's hopes? How is it ironic?

12. Why does Nora flirt with Dr. Rank? How and why does he distress her?

13. Why does Nora dance the Tarantella so wildly?

14. What is the "wonderful thing" that Nora is waiting for?

Act 3

15. Explain Christine's past rejection of Krogstad. Why will she accept him now? How will their union differ from the Helmers' marriage?

16. What does Christine decide to do about Krogstad's letter? Why?

17. Explain the reactions of Torvald and Nora to the death of Dr. Rank.

18. Describe Torvald's reaction to Krogstad's first letter. How does Nora respond to Torvald? How do you respond to him? Why?

19. Explain what Nora learns about Torvald, herself, her marriage, and her identity as a woman as a result of Torvald's responses. Why does she decide to leave?

GENERAL QUESTIONS

1. Which elements and aspects of *A Dollhouse* are most and least realistic? Explain.

2. Consider Ibsen's symbolism, with reference to Dr. Rank, macaroons, the Christmas tree, the presents, the locked mailbox, the dance, Nora's black shawl, her change of clothing in Act 3, and the door slam at the play's close.

3. Is Nora a victim of circumstances or a villain who brings about problems? What is Ibsen's view? What is yours? Why?

4. Describe the "role-playing" in the Helmer marriage. Does any evidence suggest that Nora knows she is playing a role? What degree of self-awareness, if any, characterizes Torvald's role-playing?

5. When Nora asks Torvald to restore Krogstad's job, Torvald refuses on the ground that he should not give in to his wife's pressure (Act 2, speech 113). Later, he claims that their marriage is destroyed, but that they should keep up the appearance of marital stability (Act 3, speech 242). In the light of such statements, describe Torvald's character. What concerns him most about life and marriage?

6. A major theme in the play is that weakness and corruption are passed from generation to generation. Examine this theme in connection with Krogstad and his sons, Nora and her children, Nora and her father, and Dr. Rank.

7. Discuss the ideas about individual growth, marriage, and social convention in the play. How are these ideas developed and related? Which character most closely embodies Ibsen's ideas?

8. Write an essay about any or all of the following questions:
    a. Is *A Dollhouse* a comedy, a tragedy, or something in between?
    b. How do the play's characters change for the better (or worse)?
    c. How negative, or affirmative, is the conclusion? Why?

HENRIK IBSEN (1828–1906)

An Enemy of the People (En Folkefiende)   1882

Translated by Edgar V. Roberts

CHARACTERS

> Dr. Thomas Stockmann, *a physician, and Chief Medical Officer of the town's Therapeutic Spa*
> Mrs. Katrina Stockmann, *his wife*
> Petra Stockmann, *their daughter, a young woman; a teacher*
> Eilif Stockmann, *their thirteen-year-old son*
> Morten Stockmann, *their ten-year-old son*

Peter Stockmann (The Mayor), *Dr. Stockmann's older brother, Principal Executive and Chief Constable of the local government, Chief Executive Officer of the Governing Board of the Spa, etc., etc.*

Morten Kiil, *owner of the tannery at the nearby town of Mølledal, and Mrs. Stockmann's stepfather*

Captain Horster, *a ship's captain, friendly to Dr. Stockmann and his family*

Hovstad, *editor-in-chief of* The People's Messenger

Billing, *assistant editor of the* Messenger

Aslaksen, *owner of a printing business, publisher of the* Messenger, *chair of the local Homeowners Association, and Secretary of the Temperance Union*

Vik, *a stout citizen; a shipowner, and Captain Horster's employer*

Workers, *seen in Aslaksen's print shop in Act 3*

Local Townspeople, *men, women, and children—of all classes—who attend the meeting in Act 4. Three of these are named: Lamstad (2 Citizen); Pettersen, a drunken man; and Skipper Evensen, whose main task is to blow a horn. A number of the other citizens and workers have speaking lines. All react, demonstrate, and shout as a group.*

The location of the play is an unnamed town on the southern coast of Norway. The time and circumstances are those of 1882, the date of the play.

Act 1

SCENE. *Evening in the living room of DR. and MRS. STOCKMANN. The room is plainly but neatly furnished. At stage right are two doors, the upstage one leading to a hallway, the downstage one to DR. STOCKMANN's study. At upstage left, a door leads to the other family rooms. In the middle of the stage-left wall is a ceramic tile heating stove, and, farther downstage, a sofa with a mirror above and an oval coffee table in front. A lamp with a prominent lampshade is burning on the table. An open door in the back wall shows the dining room. BILLING is alone at the dining table, which also holds a lighted lamp. A napkin is tucked into his collar, and MRS. STOCKMANN is serving him from a platter of roast beef. The other chairs are empty, but the table has not yet been cleared of the plates, etc., of the diners who have left the table.*

MRS. STOCKMANN.   You see, Mr. Billing, if you come late, you have to settle for cold food.

BILLING.   [*Speaks while eating.*] This is good, thank you, really fine.

MRS. STOCKMANN.   My husband is very punctual about his meals, you know—

BILLING.   That's all right with me. In fact, I think I enjoy eating more when I'm alone.

MRS. STOCKMANN.   Well, since you feel that way—[*Turns toward sounds at the hallway door.*] That's probably Mr. Hovstad.   5

BILLING.   You're right.

[*MAYOR PETER STOCKMANN enters, wearing an overcoat and his official hat and carrying a walking-stick.*]

THE MAYOR.   Good evening, Katrina.

MRS. STOCKMANN.   [*Enters the living room.*] Good evening. How are you? How nice of you to come over!

THE MAYOR.   I was just passing by, and so—[*Looks into the dining room.*] But I see you have another guest.

MRS. STOCKMANN.   [*somewhat embarrassed*] Oh, no, he came by quite by chance.   10
[*Speaks rapidly.*] Won't you have something to eat, too?

THE MAYOR.   Me? No, thank you. With my digestion, I can't eat hot meals at night.

MRS. STOCKMANN.   Not even just this once?

THE MAYOR.   No, my dear, no. I stick to my tea, bread, and butter, which is healthier for me—and cheaper, too.

MRS. STOCKMANN.   [*Smiles.*] Now, you can't say that Thomas and I are spendthrifts.

THE MAYOR.   No, not you, I'd never say that about *you.* [*Points to the doctor's study.*]   15
Is he in there?

MRS. STOCKMANN.   No, he went walking with the boys after dinner.

THE MAYOR.   I don't think that's a good idea. [*Listens.*] He may be coming now.

MRS. STOCKMANN.   No, not yet. [*A knock at the door.*] Come in! [*EDITOR HOVSTAD enters from the hallway.*] Oh, it's Mr. Hovstad!

HOVSTAD.   Yes. Please excuse me. I was delayed at the printer's. Mr. Mayor, good evening.

THE MAYOR.   [*Bows formally.*] Good evening. I suppose you're here on business?   20

HOVSTAD.   Yes, partly. It's about an article for the paper.

THE MAYOR.   As I thought. I understand my brother is a regular contributor to *The People's Messenger.*

HOVSTAD.   Yes, he writes for the *Messenger* on local matters.

MRS. STOCKMANN.   [*to HOVSTAD*] Would you like—[*Points to the dining room.*]

THE MAYOR.   Yes indeed. I'm sure *I* don't blame him for writing for a sympathetic   25
audience. Besides that, Mr. Hovstad, I have nothing against your paper.

HOVSTAD.   No, I shouldn't think you did.

THE MAYOR.   On the whole, there's a beautiful sense of toleration in the town—
genuine public spirit. And it all comes from our mutual interest—an interest that concerns to the highest degree all upright citizens—

HOVSTAD.   The Town Spa, yes.

THE MAYOR.   Precisely—our superb new Therapeutic Baths. Remember this, Mr.
Hovstad, the Spa will bring us together. No question about it.

HOVSTAD.   Thomas says the same thing.   30

THE MAYOR.   Think of how the town has been reviving in the last year! People now
have more money! There's life, and activity! Land and property values are soaring!

HOVSTAD.   Unemployment is going down.

THE MAYOR.   Yes, you're right. Tax rates for maintaining the poor are being lifted,
and the middle class is relieved. Moreover, their relief will be greater if we have a good
summer—huge crowds of visitors—and especially flocks of sick people, who will bring
fame to our institution.

HOVSTAD.   I hear that the long-range weather forecasts are good.

THE MAYOR.   Things look favorable. We're getting inquiries and reservations for   35
apartments every day.

HOVSTAD.   Well, the Doctor's article will be timely and relevant.

THE MAYOR.   Oh, he's written something new?

HOVSTAD.   This is something he wrote last winter—a commendation of the Spa
and a description of its healthful benefits. But I held it for publication until now.

THE MAYOR.   Oh, was there some sort of problem?

HOVSTAD.   No, not that. I thought it better to hold it till now, in the spring, be-   40
cause it's now that people make their summer plans.

THE MAYOR.   Indeed, you're quite right, Mr. Hovstad.

MRS. STOCKMANN.   Yes, Thomas is a tireless booster of the Spa.

THE MAYOR.   Well, he's also one of the staff.

HOVSTAD.   Yes, and more, he was the first to create the idea of the Spa.

THE MAYOR.   Oh he did, did he? I hear that certain people think this, but never-   45
theless it seems to me that *I* also had a modest role in the undertaking.

MRS. STOCKMANN.   Yes, Thomas always says that.

HOVSTAD.   No one denies your share, Mr. Mayor. You got things going and made
the Spa a reality. We all know that. I meant only that the Doctor got the idea first.

THE MAYOR.   Oh, yes, the *idea*. My brother has had lots of ideas—unfortunately.
But when things get practical, you need different sorts of people, Mr. Hovstad. And I
might have expected that here, in this house—

MRS. STOCKMANN.   But dear Brother—

HOVSTAD.   How could the Mayor—   50

MRS. STOCKMANN.   Please go in and have something to eat, Mr. Hovstad. My husband will be back soon.

HOVSTAD.   Perhaps just a little something, thank you. [*Goes to the dining room.*]

THE MAYOR.   [*Lowers his voice.*] Have you ever noticed that these country louts
never have any manners?

MRS. STOCKMANN.   Now why should you bother yourself about that? Can't you and
Thomas, as brothers, share the recognition?

THE MAYOR.   I would have thought so, but apparently not everyone seems satisfied   55
with only a share.

MRS. STOCKMANN.   Come now—you and Thomas get along so well together.
[*Listens to noises in the hallway.*] Here he comes now, I think. [*Goes to the hallway door and
opens it.*]

DR. STOCKMANN.   [*Speaks to various persons while entering amid general noise and laughter.*] Katrina, I've brought another guest. Isn't it great? Now then, Captain Horster, hang
your coat on this rack. Oh, you're not wearing an overcoat? Katrina, just think, I met him
on our walk and he almost didn't want to come along. [*CAPTAIN HORSTER, followed by DR.
STOCKMANN, enters the room and greets MRS. STOCKMANN.*] In with you, boys. [*EILIF and MORTEN
enter.*] The walk gave them a new appetite. Join us, Captain Horster, and have some roast
beef.

[*He escorts HORSTER into the dining room. The boys follow them.*]

MRS. STOCKMANN.   But Thomas, do you see—

DR. STOCKMANN.   [*Turns in the doorway.*] Oh, Peter, it's you. [*Shakes hands with the
MAYOR.*] This is really great!

THE MAYOR.   I was just leaving—   60

DR. STOCKMANN.   Nonsense. Stay for some hot toddy. You didn't forget the toddy,
did you Katrina?

MRS. STOCKMANN.   Of course not. The water's just boiling.

[*She goes into the dining room.*]

THE MAYOR.   Hot toddy, too—!

DR. STOCKMANN.   Yes, have a seat so we can have it in comfort.

THE MAYOR.   No, thanks, I never stay at a drinking party.   65

DR. STOCKMANN.   But this isn't a party.

THE MAYOR.   It seems to me—[*Looks toward the dining room.*] It's amazing how they
eat that much food.

DR. STOCKMANN.   [*Rubs his hands.*] Yes, it's great to see young people eat. They
never get filled up, and that's as it should be. They need the food to get strong, Peter, because they're the ones who'll be stirring things up in the future.

THE MAYOR.   And just what, as you put it, is going to need "stirring up"?

DR. STOCKMANN.   You'll have to ask the young people that—when the time comes.   70
But then, of course, old fogies like you and me won't be around to see it.

THE MAYOR.   Really! I'm not sure I like that expression.

DR. STOCKMANN.   Don't be so literal, Peter. You know that I'm quite happy. I'm
glad to be alive here and now, and to be at the cutting edge. Everything is growing and
coming to fruition, and it seems that an entire new world is emerging around me.

THE MAYOR.   You really think so?

DR. STOCKMANN.   Yes, but you can't see it the way I do. You've lived here all your
life, and you're too used to things. But I was buried all those years up north; I never saw
anyone with any new ideas. Well, to me, being here is the same as having flown into the
middle of a bustling metropolitan center.

THE MAYOR.   A metropolitan center?   75

DR. STOCKMANN.   I know what you mean. Ours is a small town. But there's also life
here—promise, and countless things to work and struggle for. That's the main thing.
[*Calls.*] Katrina, did the mailman come today?

MRS. STOCKMANN.   [*in the dining room*] No, he didn't.

DR. STOCKMANN.   And then, Peter, to be well off! When you've lived at just a subsistence level, as we did, you value that.

THE MAYOR.   God forbid—

DR. STOCKMANN.   It's true. Up there we often lived close to the line. But now, we   80
live like kings! We had roast beef today not only for dinner, but also for supper. Come
and have some, or at least let me show it to you. Come here—

THE MAYOR.   No, no, it's unnecessary.

DR. STOCKMANN.   Well, come here, then. Do you see our new tablecloth?

THE MAYOR.   Yes, I noticed.

DR. STOCKMANN.   And we bought a lampshade. Do you see? Katrina had saved the
money for it. It makes the room so cosy. Stand here—no, no, right here—yes, here. Do
you see the way it focuses the light downward? I really think that's elegant. Right?

THE MAYOR.   Yes, if people can permit such luxury.   85

DR. STOCKMANN.   Oh yes, I can afford it. Katrina says I now make almost as much
as we spend!

THE MAYOR.   Of course, almost!

DR. STOCKMANN.   Scientists like me are entitled to a better life, but even then I'm
sure that most civil servants live better than I do.

THE MAYOR.   Well, yes, a chief officer, a superior court judge—

DR. STOCKMANN.   Well then, most businessmen, who spend two or three times   90
more—

THE MAYOR.   Their circumstances are not the same as yours.

DR. STOCKMANN.   At any rate, I don't waste money. But I can't deny my need to entertain my friends. I was away from everything for so long, and I'm hungry for young,
vital, ambitious associates with inquiring and active minds. That description fits everyone
enjoying supper in there. You should really get to know Hovstad.

THE MAYOR.   By the way, Hovstad told me he was publishing one of your articles.

DR. STOCKMANN.   One of my articles?

THE MAYOR.   Yes, the one you wrote last winter about the Spa.   95

DR. STOCKMANN.   Oh yes, but I don't want that one printed just yet.

THE MAYOR.   Not yet? This seems to be a good time.

DR. STOCKMANN.   Well, yes, under normal circumstances. [*Paces.*]

THE MAYOR.   [*Looks at him closely.*] Is something wrong with the present
circumstances?

DR. STOCKMANN.   [*Stops.*] To be frank, Peter, I can't say right now. There really   100
could be some problems—but it's possible that there's no problem at all. It may be no
more than my imagination.

THE MAYOR.   You're being very mysterious. Is something going on that I don't
know about? You should know that I, as Chief Executive Officer of the Governing Board
of the Baths—

DR. STOCKMANN.   And you should know that I—. But let's not lash out at each
other, Peter.

THE MAYOR.   Of course not. I don't "lash out" at people, as you put it. But I must
insist on orderly procedure, and that only the properly designated officials treat problems that may arise. I can't tolerate anyone going behind our backs.

DR. STOCKMANN.   Did I ever try to go behind anyone's back?

THE MAYOR.   Let's just say that you tend to do things in your own way, and that's   105
not very different. Individuals must subordinate their own interests to those of the community—or, to be more accurate, to the authorities who hold the community interest in
trust.

DR. STOCKMANN.   I'm sure. But what in hell does this have to do with me?

THE MAYOR.   My good Thomas, this is what you never seem willing to learn. But
look out, because some day, sooner or later, you'll have to pay for it. Now I've told you.
Good-bye.

DR. STOCKMANN.   Are you crazy? You're on the wrong track!

THE MAYOR.   I'm usually not. Please excuse me now. [*Bows toward the dining room*].
Good night, Katrina. Good night, gentlemen. [*Leaves.*]

MRS. STOCKMANN.   [*Enters from the dining room.*] He's gone?   110

DR. STOCKMANN.   Yes, and in a foul mood.

MRS. STOCKMANN.   But dear Thomas, did you provoke him again?

DR. STOCKMANN.   No, not at all. And he can't make me give him any report before
I'm ready.

MRS. STOCKMANN.   What are you making a report about?

DR. STOCKMANN.   Don't ask, Katrina.—But why hasn't the mailman come yet?   115

[*HOVSTAD, BILLING, and HORSTER enter from the dining room, followed by EILIF and MORTEN.*]

BILLING.   [*Stretches.*] Ah! A meal like that makes me feel like a new man, damn it.

HOVSTAD.   The mayor was not his usual sweet self, then?

DR. STOCKMANN.   It's just his bad digestion.

HOVSTAD.   I think that he couldn't stomach the two of us from the *Messenger.*

MRS. STOCKMANN.   I thought that you both carried it off well.   120

HOVSTAD.   Well, I think we have more of a truce than a peace.

BILLING.   Yes, that's the right word for it.

DR. STOCKMANN.   Let's not forget that Peter is all alone. He has no life, nothing
but his job. And then think of the awful tea that he's always pouring into himself—! But
now then, boys, sit down at the table. Can we have that hot toddy now, Katrina?

MRS. STOCKMANN.   [*Goes to the dining room.*] I'll have it right away!

DR. STOCKMANN.   Sit next to me, Captain Horster. We haven't seen you for a long   125
time—. Please sit down, friends.

[*They sit at the table. MRS. STOCKMANN carries in a tray with the appropriate glasses, bottles, etc.*]

MRS. STOCKMANN.   Here you are, gentlemen. This is arrack. This is rum. This is
cognac. Just serve yourselves.

DR. STOCKMANN.   [*Takes a glass.*] Thank you, we will. [*They all pour drinks for themselves.*] And let's have cigars. Eilif, you know where they are. And Morten, bring me my

pipe. [*The boys leave for the room on the right.*] I think Eilif takes a cigar once in a while, but I ignore it. [*Calls out.*] Morten, get my smoking-cap, too. Tell him where it is, Katrina. Ah, he has it. [*The boys bring the things.*] Now, friends. I'll stick with my pipe, you know. This one has seen many a day with me up north. [*They all touch glasses; cries of "Skoal," etc.*] Good health! Skoal! Ah, it's good to be warm and comfortable.

MRS. STOCKMANN.   [*Sits down and begins knitting.*] Do you sail soon, Captain Horster?

HORSTER.   Yes, I expect as early as next week,

MRS. STOCKMANN.   To America, I suppose?   130

HORSTER.   Yes, that's the schedule.

MRS. STOCKMANN.   Then you can't vote in the next election?

HORSTER.   Is there an election?

MRS. STOCKMANN.   You didn't know?

HORSTER.   No, I usually don't get involved.   135

MRS. STOCKMANN.   You aren't concerned about public affairs?

HORSTER.   No, I don't follow politics.

BILLING.   Even so, people should vote.

HORSTER.   Even if they don't know the issues?

BILLING.   Don't know? What do you mean? Every community is like a large ship;   140
everyone should be ready to be a pilot.

HORSTER.   That may be true on shore, but it won't work on a ship.

HOVSTAD.   It's amazing that sailors have such small concern about what happens on land.

BILLING.   Yes, amazing.

DR. STOCKMANN.   Sailors are like migratory birds, Hovstad; they find their homes anywhere, north or south. And that's one more reason for our own vigilance. Mr. Hovstad, is there anything of local interest in tomorrow's *Messenger*?

HOVSTAD.   No, but I was planning to publish your article the day after tomorrow. 145

DR. STOCKMANN.   My article, damn it all!—Listen, you'll have to hold that a bit longer.

HOVSTAD.   Really? We have the space, and it's just the right time—

DR. STOCKMANN.   Yes, I understand, but wait just the same.

[*PETRA enters from the hallway, wearing a hat and coat, and carrying a stack of notebooks.*]

PETRA.   Good evening.

DR. STOCKMANN.   Good evening, Petra.   150

[*She greets everyone and removes her things and puts them on a chair near the door.*]

PETRA.   I see that you've been having a good time while I've been working like a slave.

DR. STOCKMANN.   Well then, now it's your turn to enjoy.

BILLING.   Can I get you a drink?

PETRA.   [*Goes to the table.*] Thanks, I'll do it myself; you always make it too strong. Oh, by the way, Father, I have a letter for you.

[*Goes to her things on the chair and removes a letter from her coat pocket.*]

DR. STOCKMANN.   A letter? Who sent it?   155

PETRA.   The mailman delivered it just as I was leaving—

DR. STOCKMANN.   [*Gets up and goes to her.*] And you give it to me only now?

PETRA.   I had no time to run upstairs again. Here you are.

DR. STOCKMANN.   [*Grabs the letter and looks eagerly at it.*] Let's see, let's see. Yes, this is it—!

MRS. STOCKMANN.   Is this the one you've been expecting, Thomas?   160

DR. STOCKMANN.   Yes. I have to go to go in.—Where's the lamp, Katrina? Is there no light in my room again?

MRS. STOCKMANN.   Yes, it's lit and it's on your writing desk.

DR. STOCKMANN.   Good, good. Excuse me—just a few minutes—[*Goes into his study at the right.*]

PETRA.   What's this all about, Mother?

MRS. STOCKMANN.   I don't know. He's been asking about the mailman for the last   165
few days.

BILLING.   Probably a report about an out-of-town patient.

PETRA.   Poor Dad, he may be working too hard. [*Mixes herself a drink.*] This looks so good!

HOVSTAD.   Were you teaching in the evening school too?

PETRA.   [*Speaks while holding the glass and drinking.*] Two hours.

BILLING.   And also four hours this morning?   170

PETRA.   Five hours.

MRS. STOCKMANN.   And you still have papers to grade?

PETRA.   A stack, yes.

HORSTER.   You seem overwhelmed with work.

PETRA.   Yes, but that's all right. I feel healthfully tired because of it.   175

BILLING.   You like that?

PETRA.   Yes, because I sleep so well.

MORTEN.   You must be really a bad person, Petra.

PETRA.   Bad?

MORTEN.   Yes, because you work so hard. Mr. Rørlund says work is punishment for   180
our sins.

EILIF.   Pooh! What a dumbbell, to swallow garbage like that.

MRS. STOCKMANN.   Now then, Eilif!

BILLING.   [*Laughing.*] Kids, anyway!

HOVSTAD.   Don't you like working, Morten?

MORTEN.   Not on your life!   185

HOVSTAD.   Then what would you like to be?

MORTEN.   I'd like to be a Viking.

EILIF.   You'd have to be a heathen, then.

MORTEN.   Well, I could join the heathen church, couldn't I?

BILLING.   That's it, Morten. I agree completely.   190

MRS. STOCKMANN.   [*Signals negatively to* BILLING.] Now, Mr. Billing, you don't believe that.

BILLING.   Yes, damn it! I'm proud to be a heathen. We'll all be heathens before long.

MORTEN.   And then we'll be able to do anything we want?

BILLING.   Well, you see, Morten—

MRS. STOCKMANN.   Boys, you'll have to go to your rooms. You have studying to do   195
for tomorrow.

EILIF.   But I want to stay here—

MRS. STOCKMANN.   No, no, off you go now.

[*The boys say good-night and leave through the doorway on the left.*]

HOVSTAD.   Do you think there's any harm in what I was saying?

MRS. STOCKMANN.   I'm not sure, but I don't like it.

PETRA.   But Mother, you're being foolish about this.   200

MRS. STOCKMANN.   You might be right, but I don't like it—not in our own house.

PETRA.   There's such great hypocrisy, both at home and at school. At home we can't speak, and at school we have to tell lies to the children.

HORSTER.   You tell lies?

PETRA.   Yes, don't you realize we have to teach all sorts of things we don't believe?

BILLING.   You're quite right.   205

PETRA.   If I had enough money I'd start my own school, where things would go differently.

BILLING.   Oh, just money—

HORSTER.   If you have ideas about a new school, Miss Stockmann, I'd be happy to offer you rooms. The house my father left me is empty, and there's a huge dining room downstairs.

PETRA.   [Laughs.] Why thank you, but nothing is likely to happen.

HOVSTAD.   No, I think Miss Petra is more likely to go into journalism. By the way,   210
have you been able to finish translating that English story you promised for us?

PETRA.   No, not yet, but soon, I hope.

[DR. STOCKMANN enters from his study, with the open letter in hand.]

DR. STOCKMANN.   [Waves the letter.] Well, the town is about to get some real news!

BILLING.   Real news?

MRS. STOCKMANN.   What do you mean?

DR. STOCKMANN.   A major discovery, Katrina.   215

HOVSTAD.   Truly?

MRS. STOCKMANN.   Your own discovery?

DR. STOCKMANN.   Yes, my own. [Paces.] Just let them accuse me of imagining things. [Laughs.] They'll have to be careful now about what they say.

PETRA.   Father, what is it?

DR. STOCKMANN.   All in due time. If only Peter were here now! It all shows how   220
human beings can go around and make judgments no better than the blindest of moles—

HOVSTAD.   Doctor, what are you saying?

DR. STOCKMANN.   [Stands at the table.] I ask, is it or is it not accepted opinion that our town is a healthy place?

HOVSTAD.   It is, yes.

DR. STOCKMANN.   A model for good health, in fact—a center to be accepted enthusiastically for those who are either ill or well?

MRS. STOCKMANN.   Yes, but Thomas, dear—   225

DR. STOCKMANN.   And we've touted it highly. I myself have written pamphlets and articles for the Messenger?

HOVSTAD.   Yes, and so?

DR. STOCKMANN.   And we've called our Spa "the artery of our town's blood" and "the center of the town's nervous system," and who the devil knows what other silly phrases—

BILLING.   In an extreme moment, I once said "the town's throbbing heart."

DR. STOCKMANN.   Right. Well, do you know the truth about these curative baths, so   230
marvellous, so magnificent, so highly eulogized—and so expensive? Do you know?

HOVSTAD.   No, but tell us.

MRS. STOCKMANN.   What are they?

DR. STOCKMANN.   The whole thing's a sewer!

PETRA.   The Spa, Father?

MRS. STOCKMANN.   [*At the same time.*] Our baths?   235

HOVSTAD.   But—

BILLING.   Unbelievable!

DR. STOCKMANN.   All the Spa buildings constitute a whited, polluted sepulcher—a threat to public health! All that poisoned runoff up at Mølledal, all that filth, is contaminating the water going to our reservoir! And the same damned, deadly effluent is also filtering out on our shore!

HORSTER.   Do you mean at our Spa buildings, where our visitors take their treatments?

DR. STOCKMANN.   Yes, right there.   240

HOVSTAD.   But Doctor, how do you know all this?

DR. STOCKMANN.   I've suspected something for quite a while, because last year some of the patients had unusual symptoms—typhoid, and gastrointestinal flu. Now I've studied things thoroughly.

MRS. STOCKMANN.   You're right about those illnesses.

DR. STOCKMANN.   At first we concluded that people were infected before they came here. But this winter I started thinking differently, and began analyzing our water.

MRS. STOCKMANN.   So this is why you've been so busy.   245

DR. STOCKMANN.   Yes, Katrina, I've been busy. But here we don't have much laboratory equipment, so I sent samples of the seawater and drinking water to the university for an exact chemical analysis.

HOVSTAD.   Did they send you a report?

DR. STOCKMAN.   [*Shows the letter.*] This is it. It shows conclusively that our water contains dangerously high levels of bacteria, both for drinking and bathing.

MRS. STOCKMANN.   Thank heaven you found out now, before the summer season.

DR. STOCKMANN.   Let's all be thankful.   250

HOVSTAD.   What are you planning to do now, Doctor?

DR. STOCKMANN.   Obviously, to make things right.

HOVSTAD.   Is that possible?

DR. STOCKMANN.   It must be possible, or else our Spa will be useless. But I have a plan.

MRS. STOCKMANN.   But, dear Thomas, why did you keep this so quiet?   255

DR. STOCKMANN.   Should I have chattered about it around town without conclusive evidence? I'm not that kind of idiot.

PETRA.   But you could have told us.

DR. STOCKMANN.   Not to you, not to anyone. But tomorrow you may go and tell the old Badger—

MRS. STOCKMANN.   Now Thomas!

DR. STOCKMANN.   All right, your stepfather. This will surprise him. He, along with others, thinks I'm crazy, but now they'll see! [*Paces, rubbing his hands.*] This will really get the town stirred up, Katrina. Completely new water lines will have to be installed.   260

HOVSTAD.   [*Rises.*] All the water lines—?

DR. STOCKMANN.   Certainly. The intakes are too low; they'll need to be put on higher ground.

PETRA.   So you were right all the time.

DR. STOCKMANN.   You remember that, Petra? I wrote against the final plans before work was started. They paid no attention to me then, but they'll pay attention now! I've had a report ready for the Governing Board for the last week, and was only waiting for this. [*Waves the letter.*] I'll send it right away. [*Goes to his office, returning with papers.*] See here, all four sheets, along with an explanatory letter. A newspaper, Katrina, something for wrapping. That's fine. Now give it to—to—[*stamps his foot*]—what's her name? The maid, and tell her to take it to the Mayor.

[MRS. STOCKMANN *takes the package and leaves through the dining room.*]

PETRA.   Father, what will Uncle Peter say about this?   265
DR. STOCKMANN.   What can he say? He should be glad that such important facts have been discovered.
HOVSTAD.   Would you consent to my publishing an article about this in the *Messenger?*
DR. STOCKMANN.   That would be excellent.
HOVSTAD.   The public should know, and the sooner the better.
DR. STOCKMANN.   Certainly.   270
MRS. STOCKMANN.   [*Returns.*] She's just gone off with it.
BILLING.   Doctor, you're the most important man in town.
DR. STOCKMANN.   [*Paces happily.*] Oh, come now! I've just been doing my civic duty. I was lucky enough to find the treasure. But just the same—
BILLING.   Hovstad, shouldn't the town give Dr. Stockmann some token of gratitude?
HOVSTAD.   Well, I'll certainly suggest one.   275
BILLING.   And I'll take up the matter with Aslaksen.
DR. STOCKMANN.   Dear friends, no nonsense. I won't hear of any ceremonies. And if the Governing Board should recommend a raise, I won't accept it. Katrina, I tell you, I'll turn it down.
MRS. STOCKMANN.   Thomas, you're right.
PETRA.   [*Raises her glass.*] Father, your health!
HOVSTAD AND BILLING.   Skoal, Doctor! Cheers!   280
HORSTER.   [*Clinks glasses with* DR. STOCKMANN.] I hope this affair brings you endless good luck!
DR. STOCKMANN.   Thank you, dear friends, thank you. I'm so overwhelmingly glad! Oh what a blessing it is to realize that you've been able to serve your home town and fellow citizens. Hurrah, Katrina!

[*He embraces her and they do a whirling dance, with* MRS. STOCKMANN *laughingly protesting. Laughter, applause, and cheers for the* DOCTOR. *The boys poke their heads in at the door.*]

End of the First Act

ACT 2

SCENE. *The same, the next morning.* MRS. STOCKMANN, *holding a letter, enters from the closed dining-room door. She calls toward the door of the* DOCTOR's *study to announce herself.*

MRS. STOCKMANN.   Are you in there, Thomas?
DR. STOCKMANN.   [*Answers from within.*] Yes, I just came in. [*Enters.*] What have you got there?
MRS. STOCKMANN.   A letter from your brother. [*Gives it to him.*]
DR. STOCKMANN.   Ah, let's see. [*Opens the letter and reads.*] "Find enclosed the materials you sent me"—[*Reads on and mutters.*] Hmm!
MRS. STOCKMANN.   Well, what does he say?   5

DR. STOCKMANN. [*Puts the papers in a pocket.*] Nothing more than that he will stop by to see us at about noon.

MRS. STOCKMANN. Well then, be sure to be at home.

DR. STOCKMANN. I will. I've already done my morning rounds.

MRS. STOCKMANN. I wonder what he's going to say.

DR. STOCKMANN. Most probably he'll be unhappy because he didn't discover the problem before I did.

MRS. STOCKMANN. Doesn't that make you nervous?

DR. STOCKMANN. No, he'll probably be broad-minded about things, but you know he gets damned anxious about anyone else invading his turf to do something good for the town.

MRS. STOCKMANN. Well, I think you ought to share this with him. Why not let it be known that he was the one who got you going?

DR. STOCKMANN. Fine. It's okay with me. I just want to put things right.

[*MORTEN KIIL peeks in from the hallway, looks around inquiringly, and chuckles.*]

MORTEN KIIL. Is it—is it true?

MRS. STOCKMANN. Father, how nice.

DR. STOCKMANN. Father Kiil, good morning.

MRS. STOCKMANN. Please come in.

MORTEN KIIL. I'll come in if it's true, but I'm going if it's not.

DR. STOCKMANN. If what is true?

MORTEN KIIL. The crazy story about the water supply. Is it true?

DR. STOCKMANN. It's true, but how did you hear about it?

MORTEN KIIL. [*Enters.*] Petra flew by on her way to school.

DR. STOCKMANN. Oh she did?

MORTEN KIIL. Yes, and she says—. I thought she was kidding, but she wouldn't joke about a thing like that.

DR. STOCKMANN. Certainly not; it's unthinkable.

MORTEN KIIL. Well, if you believe everything people tell you, they'll make you a laughingstock before you know it. But it's true, then?

DR. STOCKMANN. Absolutely true. But please sit down, Father. [*KIIL sits on the sofa.*] I think the town has been lucky—

MORTEN KIIL. [*Stifles laughter.*] Luck for the town?

DR. STOCKMANN. Yes, because my discovery was just in time.

MORTEN KIIL. [*Still amused.*] Sure, sure, sure.—But I never would have believed that you'd play such hocus-pocus on your own brother.

DR. STOCKMANN. Hocus-pocus?

MRS. STOCKMANN. Now really, Father.

MORTEN KIIL. [*Puts his hands and chin on the handle of his walking-cane, and winks at DR. STOCKMANN.*] Now, what's the story again? Some pernicious monsters have invaded the water intakes, right?

DR. STOCKMANN. Right, infectious bacteria.

MORTEN KIIL. And, as Petra says, there are hordes of these—huge hordes—right?

DR. STOCKMANN. Right, millions and billions, in fact.

MORTEN KIIL. But they're invisible, right?

DR. STOCKMANN. Right.

MORTEN KIIL. [*Laughs.*] Damn it all, I never heard anything better than this!

DR. STOCKMANN. What are you saying?

MORTEN KIIL. But Mayor Stockmann will never believe it.

DR. STOCKMANN.   We'll see about that.

MORTEN KIIL.   Do you think he's that big a fool—

DR. STOCKMANN.   My hope is that everyone in town will be such "fools," as you say.   45

MORTEN KIIL.   Everyone in town. It'd serve them right, too. They pressured me out of town government, they did. They think they know so much, but now they'll pay. Keep your magic spells going, Stockmann.

DR. STOCKMANN.   Now Mr. Kiil, really—

MORTEN KIIL.   Keep fooling them. [*Gets up.*] If you make the Mayor and his henchmen believe this, I'll give ten thousand to the poor—just like that.

DR. STOCKMANN.   Now this is very generous.

MORTEN KIIL.   Yes, I'm not wealthy, mind you, but if you pull this off, I'll remem-   50
ber the poor with five thousand—this next Christmas.

[*EDITOR HOVSTAD enters through the hallway door.*]

HOVSTAD.   Good morning. [*Sees MORTEN KIIL.*] Oh, I'm sorry.

DR. STOCKMANN.   Don't be. Come in.

MORTEN KIIL.   [*Chuckles.*] Aha! He's in on it too?

HOVSTAD.   What do you mean?

DR. STOCKMANN.   Yes, he knows everything.   55

MORTEN KIIL.   I'm not surprised. Get plenty of coverage about this in the papers. Make it big. I'll leave you to your work.

DR. STOCKMANN.   Can't you stay?

MORTEN KIIL.   No, I've got to go. Keep pushing this hocus-pocus, and, damn it all, you'll never be sorry, I promise you.

[*MORTEN KIIL leaves. MRS. STOCKMANN follows him out.*]

DR. STOCKMANN.   [*Laughs.*] Can you believe it? The old fellow doesn't believe the news about the water lines.

HOVSTAD.   Oh, so that's what all this was about.   60

DR. STOCKMANN.   Yes. Are you here about the same thing?

HOVSTAD.   I am. Can you spare me a few moments, Doctor?

DR. STOCKMANN.   Certainly, friend.

HOVSTAD.   Has the Mayor contacted you yet?

DR. STOCKMANN.   No, but he'll be coming by later.   65

HOVSTAD.   I've been thinking a lot about this.

DR. STOCKMANN.   And?

HOVSTAD.   Well you, as a doctor, see only one side of this, but there are lots of other considerations.

DR. STOCKMANN.   What do you mean? Let's sit. No, take the sofa. [*They sit, HOVSTAD on the sofa, DR. STOCKMANN on a chair next to the oval table.*] Now, you were telling me—

HOVSTAD.   Yesterday you said that the polluted water came from foul seepage   70
through the ground.

DR. STOCKMANN.   Absolutely—toxic seepage from the putrid swamp up at Mølledal.

HOVSTAD.   With your leave, Doctor, I believe it's another kind of swamp.

DR. STOCKMANN.   What do you mean? What kind of swamp?

HOVSTAD.   The swamp on which our whole communal life stands and decays.

DR. STOCKMANN.   In the devil's name, Mr. Hovstad, what sort of talk is this?   75

HOVSTAD.   Piece by piece, the town has been taken over by a small clique of bureaucrats.

DR. STOCKMANN.   Come now, the government is not large.

HOVSTAD.   No, the government is just the tip of the iceberg. It's the town bigwigs, the ones with money, that have us in their clutches.

DR. STOCKMANN.   Yes, but these are people with brains and dedication.

HOVSTAD.   Where were their brains and dedication when the water lines were put   80
where they now lie?

DR. STOCKMANN.   Well, I grant the stupidity of that, but things will soon be corrected.

HOVSTAD.   Do you think this will be easy?

DR. STOCKMANN.   At any rate, easy or not, it'll happen.

HOVSTAD.   Yes, but only with the support of the press.

DR. STOCKMANN.   But, friend, it won't be needed. I'm sure my brother—   85

HOVSTAD.   Pardon me, Doctor. I have to tell you that I'm planning a series of editorials.

DR. STOCKMANN.   In the paper?

HOVSTAD.   Yes. When I first took over the *Messenger* my idea was to break up the ring of old bootlickers with all the power.

DR. STOCKMANN.   Yes, but you told me you came close to bankruptcy because of this policy.

HOVSTAD.   You're right; I admit it. It was inopportune to undermine public confi-   90
dence in those men then, because the whole Spa project depended on them. But now things are going well, and we can kiss these pompous crown princes goodbye.

DR. STOCKMANN.   Even if they're replaced, they've done the town excellent service.

HOVSTAD.   We'll give them their due. But a writer like me, with the advancement of the people as an objective, can't let this chance slide away to destroy the public's fairy-tale illusions of aristocratic infallibility.

DR. STOCKMANN.   I agree with you there. Fairy tales must go.

HOVSTAD.   I hesitate because the Mayor is your brother, but I'm sure that your pri-ority is to the truth.

DR. STOCKMANN.   That's self-evident. [*Bursts out.*] Yes, but—   95

HOVSTAD.   You must realize that I see nothing to gain for myself in all this.

DR. STOCKMANN.   My friend, who would ever think otherwise?

HOVSTAD.   I was born poor, and that has enabled me to see what the lower classes need. And this is that the people themselves should have a role to play in government, be-cause this, and only this, will bring out their abilities and intelligence and self-esteem—

DR. STOCKMANN.   I understand your point.

HOVSTAD.   You realize that dedicated journalists must take every opportunity in   100
the effort to liberate the masses, even though they might be called agitators or rabble rousers. For me, I'm willing to risk these accusations as long as my conscience is clear—

DR. STOCKMANN.   Just that, yes! Just that, My dear Mr. Hovstad, but all the same—
[*A knocking at the door.*] The devil! Come in!

[*ASLAKSEN the printer enters, in a well-worn black suit and a wrinkled white scarf. He holds his hat and his gloves in his hands.*]

ASLAKSEN.   [*Bows.*] Doctor, please excuse my intrusion—

DR. STOCKMANN.   [*Rises.*] Well, hello! It's Mr. Aslaksen, the printer.

ASLAKSEN.   Yes, Doctor, you're right.

HOVSTAD.   [*Stands.*] Do you want me, Aslaksen?   105

ASLAKSEN.   No, I didn't know you'd be here. I came to see the Doctor.

DR. STOCKMANN.   Well, then, what can I do for you?

ASLAKSEN.   Did I hear things right from Mr. Billing, that you plan to clean up our water systems?

DR. STOCKMANN.   That's right, the ones for the Spa.

ASLAKSEN.   Yes, I understand. Well, I want to give you my support on this.   110

HOVSTAD.   [to DR. STOCKMANN] You see my point.

DR. STOCKMANN.   This is very kind of you, but—

ASLAKSEN.   It would be good to have us local tradesmen behind you. Together we make a solid majority in town, and it's always good to have the majority with you, Doctor.

DR. STOCKMANN.   You're certainly right, but this matter is so noncontroversial that it could never become a political issue—

ASLAKSEN.   Even so, support would be helpful. Our local politicians never like to   115 do anything that someone else originates. That's why I think we might demonstrate a bit.

HOVSTAD.   He has a good point.

DR. STOCKMANN.   Demonstrate, you say? But how would you demonstrate?

ASLAKSEN.   Naturally, with great moderation, Doctor. I always do things moderately, for to me, moderation is a citizen's first obligation.

DR. STOCKMANN.   You are indeed well known for your moderation, Mr. Aslaksen.

ASLAKSEN.   I take pride in this. And this water-contamination business is impor-   120 tant. The Spa can put the town on the map, and those of us in the trades, and those with rental property, can become rich. This is why we support you. You understand that I speak as Chair of the Homeowners Association—

DR. STOCKMANN.   Yes—?

ASLAKSEN.   And also as Secretary of the Temperance Union. You knew that this is one of my causes?

DR. STOCKMANN.   Oh yes, yes.

ASLAKSEN.   Well, you can see that I have many contacts, and with my reputation for moderation I have no small influence in town. You might say, in fact, that I have a certain degree of power.

DR. STOCKMANN.   Yes, Mr. Aslaksen, I know.   125

ASLAKSEN.   So it would be relatively easy for me to initiate a testimonial.

DR. STOCKMANN.   A testimonial?

ASLAKSEN.   Yes, public recognition of your importance in an affair of such vital concern to the town. We would need, of course, a statement that would be judicious and moderate—something that would not be disagreeable to our local authorities. With care, I believe that we would not offend anyone.

HOVSTAD.   But even if someone were offended—

ASLAKSEN.   No, no, Mr. Hovstad, you don't get anywhere by insulting those who   130 have power over you. I once learned that the hard way. But no one can be put off by citizens expressing their views openly and moderately.

DR. STOCKMANN.   [Shakes ASLAKSEN's hand.] Your support is most gratifying, Mr. Aslaksen. May I pour you some sherry?

ASLAKSEN.   No thanks, I never touch hard liquor.

DR. STOCKMANN.   Well, then, a glass of beer?

ASLAKSEN.   Nothing even like that so early in the day. I'm off now to see a few landlords, to get things in motion.

DR. STOCKMANN.   This is quite kind of you, Mr. Aslaksen. But are all these cautious   135 steps necessary? Things seem so self-evident.

ASLAKSEN.   It's hard to get the authorities moving, Doctor, though sometimes I understand their slowness—

HOVSTAD.   We're planning to stir things up in tomorrow's *Messenger*, Aslaksen.

ASLAKSEN.   But not too much, Mr. Hovstad. Without moderation, you'll get nowhere; believe me, I've learned that. Well, thank you, Doctor. Be assured that we smallbusiness people stand behind you like a wall. The solid majority is with you, Doctor.

DR. STOCKMANN.   [*Shakes ASLAKSEN's hand.*] Good Mr. Aslaksen, I'm deeply grateful to you for this. Thank you. Goodbye.

ASLAKSEN.   [*to HOVSTAD*] I'm going to the print shop. Can you join me, Mr. Hovstad?   140

HOVSTAD.   Later; I need to stay here a little while longer.

ASLAKSEN.   Good, I'll see you soon, then.

[*ASLAKSEN bows and leaves. DR. STOCKMANN accompanies him into the hallway, and then returns.*]

HOVSTAD.   Well, Doctor, what do you think? Isn't it time to put a little courage into such spineless fence-sitters?

DR. STOCKMANN.   You mean Aslaksen?

HOVSTAD.   Yes, I do. He's a fine enough fellow, but he can't take a decisive step,   145
and there are many just like him. They bend in the wind, this way and that way, and finally they never accomplish anything.

DR. STOCKMANN.   Well, Aslaksen's heart seems in the right place.

HOVSTAD.   Yes, but if he were more decisive he'd be better.

DR. STOCKMANN.   I have to agree with you there.

HOVSTAD.   That's why the time is now so ripe. Public worship of authority must end, and this official blunder with the water contamination must be brought home to the voters.

DR. STOCKMANN.   Well, all right. The common good should be foremost. But be-   150
fore more is done, I'll have to talk to my brother.

HOVSTAD.   In any event, I'll put together a feature article, and if the Mayor won't listen to you—

DR. STOCKMANN.   You don't believe he won't listen?

HOVSTAD.   Anything is possible, and if it happens—

DR. STOCKMANN.   If it happens—if—you can publish my entire report—every last word.

HOVSTAD.   Do I have your promise on that?   155

DR. STOCKMANN.   [*Gives HOVSTAD the report.*] Here, take it; there's no harm in your reading it. You can return it later.

HOVSTAD.   Good; I will. Thank you, Doctor, and goodbye.

DR. STOCKMANN.   Goodbye. Everything is going to come out right, Mr. Hovstad, perfectly right.

HOVSTAD.   [*Bows and leaves.*] We'll see, we'll see.

DR. STOCKMANN.   [*Opens the dining-room door and calls.*] Katrina! Oh it's you, Petra.   160

PETRA.   [*Enters.*] Yes, I just got home from school.

MRS. STOCKMANN.   [*Enters.*] Didn't Peter come yet?

DR. STOCKMANN.   No, but I've been talking to Hovstad about the broader significance of the water situation. He's quite excited, and has given me the freedom to publish about it in the *Messenger* whenever it's necessary.

MRS. STOCKMANN.   Will it be necessary?

DR. STOCKMANN.   No, not at all, but it's still gratifying to have support from the   165
open-minded and independent press. Not only this, Katrina, but the Chair of the Home-owners Association has come to see me.

MRS. STOCKMANN.   Well, what was on his mind?

DR. STOCKMANN.   He promised his support, too, and everyone will support me if necessary. Katrina, do you know the support I have in back of me?

MRS. STOCKMANN.   No. What is it?

DR. STOCKMANN.   The solid majority.

MRS. STOCKMANN.   Is that really a good thing for you, Thomas?   170

DR. STOCKMANN.   Yes, I believe so. [*Paces while rubbing his hands.*] Good Lord, how lucky it is to stand this way, as part of a family with one's fellow citizens!

PETRA.   And to be so right about things, father.

DR. STOCKMANN.   Beyond that, to do it for one's own hometown!

[*A doorbell rings.*]

MRS. STOCKMANN.   That was the doorbell.

DR. STOCKMANN.   It's him, then. [*A knock is heard at the door.*] Come in!   175

THE MAYOR.   [*Enters from the hallway.*] Good morning.

DR. STOCKMANN.   Peter, I'm delighted to see you.

MRS. STOCKMANN.   How are you today, Peter?

THE MAYOR.   All right, thank you. [*To DR. STOCKMANN.*] Yesterday evening I received your report about the water condition at the Spa.

DR. STOCKMANN.   Did you finish it?   180

THE MAYOR.   Yes, I did.

DR. STOCKMANN.   Well, what's your response to it?

THE MAYOR.   [*Looks at the women.*] Well—

MRS. STOCKMANN.   Come, Petra.

[*The women leave through the door at the left.*]

THE MAYOR.   [*Pauses briefly before he speaks.*] Did you really need to do your studies   185
behind my back?

DR. STOCKMANN.   Yes, because I had to be sure—

THE MAYOR.   Then you're sure now?

DR. STOCKMANN.   You must realize that I am.

THE MAYOR.   Do you plan to submit your study as an official report to the Governing Board of the Spa?

DR. STOCKMANN.   Yes. Something should be done right away.   190

THE MAYOR.   In your usual manner, you make exaggerations in your report. I cite your claim that patients at our Baths are receiving perpetual poison.

DR. STOCKMANN.   Can you say it any other way, Peter? Our water, which we provide to the trusting souls who pay us huge fees to restore them to health, is poison for both drinking and bathing.

THE MAYOR.   And then you conclude that we must build diversionary drains for these so-called poisons from Mølledal, and also lay new intake mains?

DR. STOCKMANN.   Yes. Can you think of anything else? I can't.

THE MAYOR.   This morning I consulted with our Chief Engineer, and, in jest, as a   195
trial balloon, I asked him about possible costs for such proposals, just in the remote case they might be needed at some future time.

DR. STOCKMANN.   At some future time?

THE MAYOR.   Believe me, he was amused even at the suggestion. Do you have any idea what the new work would cost? His estimate is that the range could be anywhere from twenty-five to thirty million.

DR. STOCKMANN.   That much?

THE MAYOR.   Yes, and worse, the planning and construction would drag out for two years or more.

DR. STOCKMANN.   That long? Two whole years?   200

THE MAYOR.   Or more. And what could we do with the Spa facilities during this time? We'd need to close them. And even after the repairs, do you think anyone would come near them again, with the reputation that they'd been health hazards?

DR. STOCKMANN.   But Peter, they *are* hazardous.

THE MAYOR.   And all this is happening just as we're getting started. Nearby coastal towns have the same potential for therapeutic baths as ours. Don't you think their public relations people would work overtime to take our clientele? Where would that put us? We'd probably have to declare the whole extravagant thing a total loss, and then, Thomas, you would have brought your hometown to ruin.

DR. STOCKMANN.   Me? Ruin?

THE MAYOR.   The only viable future for this town is the Spa. You know that as well   205
as I do.

DR. STOCKMANN.   Well, what's your solution, then?

THE MAYOR.   I'm not persuaded by your report that the water is as bad as you make it seem.

DR. STOCKMANN.   Peter, it's worse, or at any rate it will be worse once the summer heat sets in.

THE MAYOR.   I told you that you exaggerate the danger. Surely a competent doctor can control noxious elements in the water, or neutralize them if they grow too plentiful.

DR. STOCKMANN.   And so? What else?   210

THE MAYOR.   We must acknowledge that current procedures for securing water cannot be substantially changed. But I believe that the Governing Board, if funding is available, might not be unwilling to institute certain improvements.

DR. STOCKMANN.   Do you believe that I can consent to this kind of underhanded scheme?

THE MAYOR.   An underhanded scheme?

DR. STOCKMANN.   Yes, an underhanded scheme, a lie, an outright crime against the town!

THE MAYOR.   As I've remarked, I've seen no persuasive evidence that the commu-   215
nity is in any sort of danger.

DR. STOCKMANN.   Yes you have! There's no choice. You know my report is absolutely truthful, though you won't admit it. You're the one who insisted on the present locations of the intake mains and the Spa buildings, and it's this—your own damned blunder—that you won't admit. Bah! Do you imagine I don't see through you?

THE MAYOR.   Well, let's suppose, then, that you're right. I have the town's interests at heart, and without my present credibility I'm powerless to work for community betterment. For these reasons you must not submit your report. You must hold it back in the public interest. Then later, privately and quietly, we'll exert our best efforts. But for now, nothing—not a word—can be made public about this fatal affair.

DR. STOCKMANN.   My dear Peter, you may not be able to keep it quiet.

THE MAYOR.   It must be, and shall be.

DR. STOCKMANN.   You can't do it. Too many people already know.   220

THE MAYOR.   Know? Who? You can't mean that crew from the *Messenger*?

DR. STOCKMANN.   Yes, the open-minded and independent press will let you know your duty.

THE MAYOR.   [*Pauses before speaking.*] Thomas, you're a thoughtless and impetuous man. Have you considered what might happen to you because of all this?

DR. STOCKMANN.   To me?

THE MAYOR.   Yes, to you—and to your family.   225

DR. STOCKMANN.   What in the devil's name do you mean?

THE MAYOR.   As your older brother, have I not always been helpful to you?

DR. STOCKMANN.   Yes, and I'm thankful to you.

THE MAYOR.   Well, to a degree my own interests have coincided with yours. My hope has been that helping you better yourself financially would give me the power to hold you back on occasions.

DR. STOCKMANN.   You mean you did this for yourself?   230

THE MAYOR.   Yes, but only to a degree. Any public official is distressed when clos-est relatives do compromising things again and again.

DR. STOCKMANN.   You think I do compromising things?

THE MAYOR.   Yes, unfortunately, even when you don't mean to. You're naturally combative, Thomas, and you keep none of your thoughts private, whether they're plausi-ble or implausible, but you publish them as soon as you get them either in short articles or whole pamphlets.

DR. STOCKMANN.   But isn't a citizen obligated to share new ideas with the public?

THE MAYOR.   The public has no need for new ideas. The public is best served by   235
the good, old, recognized ideas they already have.

DR. STOCKMANN.   You really believe this?

THE MAYOR.   Yes, I do. And now I must speak frankly to you, which I have always avoided because you can be so irritable. The truth is, Thomas, you have no idea of how you hurt yourself by your thoughtless manner. You tear down politicians, and you de-nounce the government, by claiming that you are ignored or that you are victimized. But with such obstinacy, what else can you expect?

DR. STOCKMANN.   So, I'm obstinate, am I?

THE MAYOR.   Yes, you're an impossibly obstinate man to work with; I know. You place yourself above all consideration for others, and you have forgotten totally that I am the one you can thank for your position as Chief Medical Officer of the Spa—

DR. STOCKMANN.   But I was the natural one for this position—I and no one else! I   240
originated the idea that the town could become a thriving center for therapeutic baths, and for many years, despite obstructions, I was the one who wrote vigorously to make the Baths a reality.

THE MAYOR.   No doubt, but you were too early. Things were not yet right, but you didn't think of that because you were locked away up north. It's a fact, however, that as soon as things came together, I, along with others, took over, and—

DR. STOCKMANN.   And created the mess we have now. You fellows certainly did things right!

THE MAYOR.   As far as I can see, this whole matter is just another of your habitual ways of attacking people in authority. To you, rebelliousness is a personal way of life. But I've told you, Thomas, that the very existence of the town is now the issue—not to men-tion my own reputation. And therefore I tell you, Thomas, that I'll be absolute about the demand I'm going to make on you.

DR. STOCKMANN.   What's this?

THE MAYOR.   Now that you've spoken out when you should have kept quiet, the   245
matter can no longer be hushed up. Rumors will fly, and they'll be used against us. The only thing to do is for you to issue a public denial.

DR. STOCKMANN.   Me? But how can I do that?

THE MAYOR.   We'll expect that further studies have shown you that things are not as serious or dangerous as your first thoughts had led you to conclude.

DR. STOCKMANN.   You expect me to say this?

THE MAYOR.   Moreover, you must publicly express your confidence in the integri-ty of the Governing Board of the Spa, and in their willingness to remedy any possible problems whatever.

DR. STOCKMANN.   But you can't set things right now just by cutting and pasting.   250
Peter, I'm giving you my professional judgment.

THE MAYOR.   Because you serve the Governing Board, you have no right to an in-dependent professional judgment.

DR. STOCKMANN.   [Exclaims incredulously.] No right?

THE MAYOR.   Privately, of course, you may think what you wish. But as an official who must report to the Governing Board, you cannot make a public announcement contrary to Board policy.

DR. STOCKMANN.   I've never—. As a doctor, as a scientist, I have no right—?

THE MAYOR.   This is not just a matter of science. It's complex, and there are fiscal implications.   255

DR. STOCKMANN.   Complexity and fiscal implications can go to hell! I'm free to speak out on any subject on earth!

THE MAYOR.   Be my guest! But not about the Spa. We forbid you that.

DR. STOCKMANN.   You forbid me? You? You pack of—

THE MAYOR.   I forbid you—I—the Chief Executive Officer of the Governing Board. And when I forbid you, you *must* obey!

DR. STOCKMANN.   [*Suppresses rage.*] Peter, if we weren't brothers—   260

PETRA.   [*Enters.*] Father, he can't speak to you like this!

MRS. STOCKMANN.   [*Enters, trying to restrain* PETRA.] Petra, Petra—

THE MAYOR.   So you've been listening!

MRS. STOCKMANN.   You were so loud, we couldn't help hearing.

PETRA.   Yes, I listened!   265

THE MAYOR.   Well, actually, I'm glad—

DR. STOCKMANN.   You were talking about forbidding and obeying?

THE MAYOR.   Your insolence forced me to speak like that to you.

DR. STOCKMANN.   So I am to issue a lie publicly?

THE MAYOR.   You must make a statement—something like the one we spoke of.   270

DR. STOCKMANN.   And if I don't—obey?

THE MAYOR.   Then we ourselves will issue a statement of reassurance for the public.

DR. STOCKMANN.   If you do, I'll have to write against your position. I'll stand behind my conclusions. I'll prove you're wrong and I'm right. What will you do then?

THE MAYOR.   Then I won't be able to prevent your dismissal.

DR. STOCKMANN.   What—?   275

PETRA.   Father—dismissed!

MRS. STOCKMANN.   Fired!

THE MAYOR.   Dismissed as Chief Medical Officer of the Spa. I'll find myself in the position of giving you instant notice, and suspending you from your duties at the Spa.

DR. STOCKMANN.   You'd risk that!

THE MAYOR.   You're the one running the risks!   280

PETRA.   Uncle, this is shocking conduct toward a man like father!

MRS. STOCKMANN.   Petra, will you hold your tongue!

THE MAYOR.   [*To* PETRA.] Oh, so we already speak out with no restraint. I might have expected it. [*To* MRS. STOCKMANN.] My dear sister-in-law, you're the least impulsive person here. Use your influence over your husband to persuade him of the dangers he's running for the family and—

DR. STOCKMANN.   Family concerns are mine, and mine only!

THE MAYOR.   —for the family, I was saying, and for the town he lives in.   285

DR. STOCKMANN.   I'm the one who holds the good of the town foremost by trying to disclose the real dangers that face us. I'll show you who loves the town.

THE MAYOR.   You, who in blind defiance goes ahead to cut off the town's most important nourishment?

DR. STOCKMANN.   But what gives us our living gives poison to others! Are you insane? We live here by dealing in filth and corruption! Our thriving business life is nourished on lies!

THE MAYOR.   A fairy tale, or worse! Any person who can say such damaging things about his own hometown must be an enemy of society!

DR. STOCKMANN.   [*Confronts him.*] You dare—   290

MRS. STOCKMANN.   [*Stands between them to restrain them.*] Thomas!

PETRA.   [*Takes her father's arm.*] Father, control yourself!

THE MAYOR.   I will not be a party to violence! You've been warned; consider yourself—and your family! Goodbye! [*Leaves alone through the hallway.*]

DR. STOCKMANN.   [*Paces.*] Must I put up with this, Katrina, and in my own home?

MRS. STOCKMANN.   It's been both shameful and humiliating!   295

PETRA.   I'd like to tell him a thing or two—

DR. STOCKMANN.   I'm at fault for not baring my teeth at him sooner—and biting him. He suggested that I'm an enemy of the town! Me! I'm not going to take this!

MRS. STOCKMANN.   But dear Thomas, your brother has the power—

DR. STOCKMANN.   Yes, but I have the right.

MRS. STOCKMANN.   Yes, right, right. But what good is right without might?   300

PETRA.   Mother, how can you say that?

DR. STOCKMANN.   Don't be absurd, Katrina. When people are free, rightness always implies power. Besides, I have the open-minded and independent press in front of me, and the solid majority behind me. There's a good deal of power here, believe me.

MRS. STOCKMANN.   But God in heaven, Thomas, you don't plan to—

DR. STOCKMANN.   Don't plan to what?

MRS. STOCKMANN.   To set yourself against your brother?   305

DR. STOCKMANN.   What the hell else should I do? Shouldn't I follow what's true and right?

PETRA.   Just what I wanted to say.

MRS. STOCKMANN.   You won't get anywhere. If they oppose you, they'll stop you from doing anything.

DR. STOCKMANN.   Katrina, just wait, and you'll see that I'll take the war to them.

MRS. STOCKMANN.   Yes, you'll drive yourself into your dismissal—that you'll do.   310

DR. STOCKMANN.   Whatever happens, I'll have fulfilled my obligations to the public—and I have been called the enemy of society!

MRS. STOCKMANN.   But think of your family, Thomas—your home—those who depend on you.

PETRA.   Oh Mother, you always think of us first.

MRS. STOCKMANN.   Well, you may talk, but you could take care of yourself, if you had to. But think of the boys, Thomas, and of your own needs, and of me—

DR. STOCKMANN.   Katrina, you're talking nonsense. Do you think I could ever live   315
with myself again if I had to go crawling—like a beaten coward—to Peter and his damned bootlickers?

MRS. STOCKMANN.   I don't know about that, but God help us from the sort of luck we'll all have if you keep up your defiance. You'll be back at zero, with no job and no secure income. We've had our fill of that, Thomas. Think about it, and think of what can happen.

DR. STOCKMANN.   [*Squirms and clenches his fists.*] So much for being free but without power. Katrina, it's horrible.

MRS. STOCKMANN.   Yes, they're being horrible to you. it's true. But, God in heaven, there's so much unfairness that people have to endure in the world. [*EILIF and MORTEN, schoolbooks in their hands, enter while she is speaking.*] Think of our boys, Thomas, and what may happen to them. Surely you'd never—

DR. STOCKMANN.   [*Appears deeply moved.*] The boys—. [*With an effort, he becomes resolute.*] No, I'll never knuckle under, even if the world falls apart! [*Strides toward his office.*]

MRS. STOCKMANN.   [*Follows him.*] Thomas, what are you doing?   320
DR. STOCKMANN.   [*Turns at the door.*] I want the right to look my own boys in the eyes when they're grown up and free! [*Leaves.*]
MRS. STOCKMANN.   [*Begins crying.*] God help and preserve us!
PETRA.   Father is marvelous! He'll never give in!

[*The boys are dumfounded, while PETRA cautions them to say nothing.*]

End of the Second Act

ACT 3

SCENE. *Afternoon. The editorial office of* THE PEOPLE'S MESSENGER. *On the rear wall, stage left, is the main outside door. At stage right, the rear wall contains the print-shop door, with glass windows through which the print shop can be seen. Several compositors are setting type, and one worker is operating a handpress. In the stage-right wall is another door. A long table in the middle of the room is spread out with papers, books, etc. There is a downstage window in the stage-left wall, in front of which there is a desk and a high stool where HOVSTAD is sitting and writing. Other chairs are at the table and along the walls. The office is generally drab and threadbare; all the furniture is old, nicked, stained, torn, and worn out. BILLING enters from the right, holding DR. STOCKMANN's manuscript.*

BILLING.   Now this is something!
HOVSTAD.   Did you finish reading it?
BILLING.   [*Puts the manuscript on the desk.*] I certainly did.
HOVSTAD.   The Doctor doesn't pull any punches.
BILLING.   None at all. His words are sledgehammer blows!   5
HOVSTAD.   You're right, but these people won't throw in the towel at the first hard punch.
BILLING.   I agree, and for this reason we have to keep slugging away, blow after blow, until we knock out the whole establishment. As I was reading this I could see a dawning revolution.
HOVSTAD.   [*Turns toward the print shop.*] Shhh! Don't let Aslaksen hear you.
BILLING.   [*Lowers his voice.*] Aslaksen is scared of his own shadow. But you're the one in charge, right? You're printing the Doctor's article?
HOVSTAD.   Yes. Let's hope the mayor doesn't agree to go along with things first.   10
BILLING.   That would be damned awkward.
HOVSTAD.   Well, either way we come out ahead. If the Mayor doesn't get on board with the Doctor's suggestions, all the tradespeople and the Homeowners Association will be on his neck. And if he does get on board, he'll alienate most of the shareholders of the Baths, who up to now have been his prime supporters.
BILLING.   Yes, because they'll have to pay through the nose—
HOVSTAD.   You can bet on it. And then the ring will be broken. From then on, in paper after paper, we'll expose the incompetence of the Mayor on one thing or another, and make clear that the town's elective positions—all of them—should be taken over by people with fresh ideas.
BILLING.   You've pictured it! I see it! Damn it, we're at the beginning of a   15
revolution!

[*A knock at the outside door.*]

HOVSTAD.   Shh! [*Calls.*] Come in! [*DR. STOCKMANN enters; HOVSTAD rises to greet him.*] Ah, Doctor, welcome!
DR. STOCKMANN.   Go ahead and print, Mr. Hovstad.

HOVSTAD.   You're sure.

BILLING.   Hurrah!

DR. STOCKMANN.   Print away. Yes, I'm sure. They'll have to take it. This town is   20
going to see a knock-down, drag-out fight!

BILLING.   I hope we'll slit their throats, Doctor.

DR. STOCKMANN.   This article is only the start. I have ideas for four or five more already. Where is Aslaksen?

BILLING.   [*Goes to the print-shop door and calls.*] Aslaksen, please come in for a moment.

HOVSTAD.   Did you say four or five articles, all about this?

DR. STOCKMANN.   No, not all on the same topic, but all of them stem out of the   25
water-pollution issue. Things follow each other, just like fixing up an old house. It's just
like that.

BILLING.   That's true, damn it. Once you start, you can't stop until you tear down
the whole rickety structure.

ASLAKSEN.   [*Enters.*] Tear down! The Doctor doesn't think the Bath Houses should
be torn down?

HOVSTAD.   Not at all; don't worry.

DR. STOCKMANN.   We have something else in mind. Well, Mr. Hovstad, what's your
response to my article?

HOVSTAD.   It's a masterpiece.   30

DR. STOCKMANN.   Honestly now? I'm very pleased.

HOVSTAD.   It's clear and to the point. It requires no special vocabulary or expertise. You'll rally all intelligent people.

ASLAKSEN.   And all prudent people, too?

BILLING.   Prudent, imprudent—the whole town.

ASLAKSEN.   Why then, we could certainly risk printing it.   35

DR. STOCKMANN.   Absolutely!

HOVSTAD.   Tomorrow's morning issue will have it.

DR. STOCKMANN.   Yes, in God's name, we shouldn't lose a single day. Mr. Aslaksen,
would you please see to it personally that the printing goes right?

ASLAKSEN.   I'll do it gladly.

DR. STOCKMANN.   Treasure it carefully, as if it were gold—no typographic errors.   40
I'll come in later to read proof. I can't tell you how anxious I am to see the thing printed,
and striking—

BILLING.   Striking—yes, like a flash of lightning—

DR. STOCKMANN.   —and meeting the approval of intelligent citizens. You won't believe what I've been through since morning. I've been insulted and menaced, and
they've even threatened my basic human rights—

BILLING.   Your basic rights?

DR. STOCKMANN.   —they've tried to humiliate me, make me a coward, and set personal gain above my deepest, holiest convictions.

BILLING.   Damn it, this is unspeakable!   45

HOVSTAD.   Well, you can't expect anything else from this bunch.

DR. STOCKMANN.   But they haven't seen the end of me. With the *Messenger* as my
power base, I'll put things in black and white, and every day I'll fire off one explosive article after another—

ASLAKSEN.   But, listen—

BILLING.   Hurrah! It's war! It's war!

DR. STOCKMANN.   I'll bring them to the ground! I'll crush them! I'll destroy their   50
fortress in the eyes of all right-thinking people!

ASLAKSEN.   But be moderate, good Doctor. Shoot, but with caution—

BILLING.   No, no, don't spare the dynamite!

DR. STOCKMANN.   [*Goes on calmly.*] The issue is no longer just water pipes and sewers—No, our entire social structure needs cleansing and disinfecting—

BILLING.   Words of prophecy!

DR. STOCKMANN.   Everywhere, the bumbling incompetents should be put to pasture, and that means *all.* Today I've gotten a sense of a more perfect future—it's not clear yet, but it's taking shape in my mind. We need new standard-bearers, my friends, and new commanding officers at all our outposts.   55

BILLING.   Hear, hear!

DR. STOCKMANN.   To make it possible, we must all pull together. With unity, the revolution can be like a ship gliding smoothly from harbor. Am I right?

HOVSTAD.   My view is that we're close to getting municipal government into the right hands.

ASLAKSEN.   And there'll be no risk as long as we're moderate.

DR. STOCKMANN.   To hell with the risk! Everything I do, I do in the name of truth   60
and because of my conscience.

HOVSTAD.   Doctor, you've earned our support.

ASLAKSEN.   Yes, our support. The Doctor is a true friend—a true benefactor of society.

BILLING.   Damn it, Aslaksen, Dr. Stockmann is a friend of the people!

ASLAKSEN.   I think the Homeowners Association will soon make use of that expression.

DR. STOCKMANN.   [*Is moved, and shakes their hands.*] Thank you, thank you, dear   65
friends. This phrase is so stirring; my own brother used a different one, but he'll regret it. I have to go and see a poor devil of a patient now, but I'll come back soon, as I said. Mr. Aslaksen, take care of the manuscript, and set the type carefully. Don't take out any exclamation points. You can add some, if you want. Good, good. For the moment, goodbye, goodbye!

[*They escort him to the main door, shaking hands, etc. He leaves.*]

HOVSTAD.   This man will be immensely useful.

ASLAKSEN.   Yes, but only with regard to the Spa. To follow him in other things might not be politic.

HOVSTAD.   Well, that depends—

BILLING.   You're always so damned afraid, Aslaksen.

ASLAKSEN.   Afraid? On local matters, Mr. Billing, I've learned to be cautious. I've   70
learned this in the game of life. But put me in the area of national politics, even against the Government itself, and see how afraid I am.

BILLING.   You're right, I grant. But isn't this contradictory?

ASLAKSEN.   No, because I'm a man of conscience. Criticizing the national government is harmless, because the fellows up there don't notice, and they just stay put. But local politicians can be thrown out, and if you *do* get them out you might wind up with a bunch of incompetents—and really hurt not only the Homeowners but everyone.

HOVSTAD.   But don't you believe that the improved education of the populace is a necessary consequence of self-government?

ASLAKSEN.   Mr. Hovstad, when one's self-interests are at stake, other considerations are not as significant.

HOVSTAD.   I hope I'll never hold self-interest first!   75

BILLING.   Hear, hear!

ASLAKSEN.   [*Smiles, and points to* HOVSTAD'S *desk.*] Mr. Sheriff Stensgaard preceded you at that desk.

BILLING.   [*Spits.*] He was a renegade!

HOVSTAD.   I'm not a turncoat, and I hope I never will be.

ASLAKSEN.   A politician should never say "never," Mr. Hovstad. And you, Mr.   80
Billing, you may need to pull in your sails a bit, since you've submitted your application for the Secretaryship of the Judicial Bench.

BILLING.   I—

HOVSTAD.   Is this true, Billing?

BILLING.   Well, yes, damn it, but you can understand my aim is to be a gadfly to the establishment.

ASLAKSEN.   This isn't my business. But if you imply that I'm afraid or contradictory, I remind you that the record of Aslaksen the printer is open. I've always been consistent, except for becoming more moderate. My heart is always with the people, but I won't deny that my mind goes with the authorities—the local ones, that is. [*Leaves through the print-shop door.*]

BILLING.   Hovstad, we've got to get him out.   85

HOVSTAD.   Have you got anyone else in mind to finance our paper and printing costs?

BILLING.   Damn it all that we don't have financial security.

HOVSTAD.   [*Sits at his desk.*] Yes, that would help—

BILLING.   Do you think that Dr. Stockmann—

HOVSTAD.   What's the use? He hasn't got anything.   90

BILLING.   No, but he may be close to a hot prospect. You know—old Morten Kiil, the one they call the "Badger."

HOVSTAD.   [*Speaks while writing.*] Do you know for sure that he's well fixed?

BILLING.   Yes, damn it! And the Stockmanns stand to inherit. At least the Stockmann children will get something.

HOVSTAD.   [*Faces* BILLING *directly.*] Are you counting on this?

BILLING.   Counting on it? Naturally, I never count on anything.   95

HOVSTAD.   You're right, and don't plan on the Secretaryship either. You're not on the final list.

BILLING.   You think I don't know that? Nothing could please me more. Losing the job will put me in fighting trim, and you need that here in the boondocks, where nothing ever happens to egg you on.

HOVSTAD.   [*Continues to write.*] Of course, of course.

BILLING.   But I'll make a mark yet!—Excuse me; I'm going to write the appeal to the Homeowners Association now. [*Leaves through the door on the right.*]

HOVSTAD.   [*Stays at his desk, chews the end of his pen, and talks slowly to himself.*] So,   100
this is how it is. [*A knock at the entrance door.*] Come in! [PETRA *enters.* HOVSTAD *rises.*] It's you, here? Why did you come?

PETRA.   Yes. Please excuse me—

HOVSTAD.   [*Offers her a chair.*] Please sit down.

PETRA.   No, thank you, I have to go right away.

HOVSTAD.   You have a word from your father, perhaps?

PETRA.   No, I'm here on my own. [*Takes a book out of her coat.*] This is the English   105
story.

HOVSTAD.   Why are you bringing it back?

PETRA.   I won't translate it.

HOVSTAD.   But you gave me your word—

PETRA. I did, but then I hadn't read it. You haven't read it either?

HOVSTAD. You know I don't read English, but— 110

PETRA. Well, this is why you need something else. [*Puts the book on the table.*] You can't run this in the *Messenger*.

HOVSTAD. Why not?

PETRA. It contradicts everything you stand for.

HOVSTAD. Well, but then—

PETRA. You don't understand. The story's main theme is that a supernatural 115 power protects the so-called good people in the world and makes everything best for them in the end—and that all the so-called evil people get their punishment.

HOVSTAD. But that's all right. It's what our readers demand.

PETRA. Are you the one to give it to them? You know every single word is a fairy tale; things aren't like that in the real world.

HOVSTAD. You're right. But realize that an editor is not totally free. If I want to lead my readers on the important political objectives of liberation and progress, I can't scare them off. A moral story like this one, on the back page, promotes their willingness to accept my editorial opinions on the front page; it makes them more confident.

PETRA. Come now! You set such a web for your readers. You're not a spider!

HOVSTAD. [*Smiles.*] No. I thank you for including me in your elevated simile, but 120 the strategy was really Billing's, not mine.

PETRA. Billing's?

HOVSTAD. Yes. In any event, he explained the idea the other day. It's Billing who wants the story. I don't know it myself.

PETRA. But how can Billing, with his emancipated outlook—

HOVSTAD. Well, Billing is many things to many people. I'm told he's also looking for a job in the magistrate's office.

PETRA. I don't believe it. How could he make himself such a conformist? 125

HOVSTAD. Ask him.

PETRA. I would never have thought this of Billing.

HOVSTAD. [*Looks at her intently.*] No? Is this so unexpected?

PETRA. Yes. But maybe not. I'm really not sure—

HOVSTAD. We journalists are not heroes, Miss. 130

PETRA. You mean that?

HOVSTAD. Sometimes I think so.

PETRA. I can understand this about ordinary, everyday circumstances. But now, when you've taken a hand in this great cause—

HOVSTAD. You mean this business with your father?

PETRA. Yes. It seems to me that you must think of yourself as a person above most 135 others.

HOVSTAD. Yes, I rather do feel that way today.

PETRA. Of course you do. Why shouldn't you? You've really chosen a noble call-ing—to prepare the way for unrecognized truths and bold new ways of seeing—or even just to stand up without fear to support an injured man—

HOVSTAD. Yes, especially when the injured man is—how should I say it—

PETRA. You mean when he's so upright and honest?

HOVSTAD. [*Softens his tone.*] Rather I mean when that man is your father. 140

PETRA. [*Is suddenly struck.*] That?

HOVSTAD. Yes, Miss Petra—Petra.

PETRA. Is this what's first and foremost to you? Not principle, not truth, not the warmth of my father's great heart?

HOVSTAD.   Yes, of course, all that, too.

PETRA.   No, thanks, Hovstad. You're being dishonest, and I can't believe you any   145
more in anything.

HOVSTAD.   Can you be so angry at me when it's because of you—

PETRA.   I'm angry because you haven't been honest with Father. You talked to him
as though truth and the common good were uppermost in your mind. You've made fools
of both Father and me. You're not what you seem, and I'll never forgive you for that—
never!

HOVSTAD.   You shouldn't be so spiteful, Miss Petra, not now, especially.

PETRA.   Why not now?

HOVSTAD.   Your father can't get anywhere without my help.   150

PETRA.   [*Stares at him in disgust.*] So you're also like that! Shame!

HOVSTAD.   No, I'm sorry. I just blurted that out. Don't believe what I said!

PETRA.   I know what to believe. Goodbye!

ASLAKSEN.   [*Hurries in from the print shop, trying to be secret.*] Hellfire and damnation,
Mr. Hovstad!—[*Sees PETRA.*] This is bad—

PETRA.   [*Points to the book on the desk, and walks toward the main door.*] That's the   155
book. Get someone else to translate it.

HOVSTAD.   [*Follows her.*] But Miss—

PETRA.   Goodbye! [*She leaves.*]

ASLAKSEN.   Listen, Mr. Hovstad—

HOVSTAD.   Yes, yes, what is it?

ASLAKSEN.   The Mayor is in the print shop.   160

HOVSTAD.   You say the Mayor?

ASLAKSEN.   Yes. He wants to talk with you. He came in the back way—I guess he
didn't want to be seen.

HOVSTAD.   What's this about? No, wait, I'll go myself. [*Goes to the print-shop door and
invites the MAYOR in. The MAYOR enters.*] Aslaksen, please see that no one—

ASLAKSEN.   I understand. [*Goes into the print room.*]

THE MAYOR.   You were not expecting me, Mr. Hovstad?   165

HOVSTAD.   I certainly wasn't.

THE MAYOR.   [*Looks around the room.*] You've made things cosy here. Quite nice.

HOVSTAD.   Well—

THE MAYOR.   And now I come here without an appointment to make a greater demand on your time.

HOVSTAD.   My pleasure, Mr. Mayor. I'm at your service. But let me take your   170
things. [*Puts the MAYOR's hat and walking-stick on a stool.*] Won't you sit down?

THE MAYOR.   [*Sits beside the table.*] Thank you. [*HOVSTAD also sits at the table.*] Today,
Mr. Hovstad, I've had a—an extremely distressing experience.

HOVSTAD.   Yes, with all the many duties of the Mayor's office—

THE MAYOR.   The one today concerns the Chief Medical Officer of the Spa.

HOVSTAD.   The Doctor?

THE MAYOR.   He has written a sort of report to the Governing Board, claiming that   175
there are supposed shortcomings at the Spa.

HOVSTAD.   No, he said this?

THE MAYOR.   Didn't he tell you? I understood him to say—

HOVSTAD.   Well, yes, it's true he let something drop about—

ASLAKSEN.   [*Enters from the print shop.*] I'll need that manuscript—

HOVSTAD.   [*Speaks brusquely.*] There—it's on the desk.   180

ASLAKSEN.   [*Finds it.*] Good.

THE MAYOR.   But see, that's it!

ASLAKSEN.   Yes, Mr. Mayor, this is the Doctor's article.

HOVSTAD.   Oh, is this the one you mean?

THE MAYOR.   The same. What do you think of it?   185

HOVSTAD.   Well, I'm not an expert, and I've only looked it over briefly.

THE MAYOR.   But you're still going to print it?

HOVSTAD.   I can't say no to a man with such impressive credentials—

ASLAKSEN.   Mr. Mayor, I have no say in the paper's policies.

THE MAYOR.   Certainly.   190

ASLAKSEN.   I only print the copy put in my hands.

THE MAYOR.   As well you should.

ASLAKSEN.   [*Walks toward the print shop.*] And therefore I must—

THE MAYOR.   But stay a moment, Mr. Aslaksen. [*ASLAKSEN remains.*] With your permission, Mr. Hovstad?

HOVSTAD.   By all means, Mr. Mayor.   195

THE MAYOR.   Mr. Aslaksen, you're a sober and deliberate man.

ASLAKSEN.   Your good opinion pleases me, sir.

THE MAYOR.   And a man with influence in many circles.

ASLAKSEN.   Well, it's mostly among the little people.

THE MAYOR.   The small taxpayers are the great majority—here and elsewhere.   200

ASLAKSEN.   Right.

THE MAYOR.   And I don't question that you know the common feelings of most of them. You follow me?

ASLAKSEN.   Yes, Mr. Mayor, I think I may safely say I do know them.

THE MAYOR.   Yes, and if there's such an admirable spirit of self-sacrifice among citizens of smaller means in our town, then—

ASLAKSEN.   What's this?   205

HOVSTAD.   Self-sacrifice?

THE MAYOR.   This is a beautiful token of public spirit—an overwhelmingly beautiful token. I almost said I didn't expect it. But you know these feelings more thoroughly than I do.

ASLAKSEN.   Yes, but Mr. Mayor—

THE MAYOR.   And the sacrifice the town will need to make will not be small.

HOVSTAD.   The town?   210

ASLAKSEN.   But I don't understand—It's the Spa—

THE MAYOR.   The first estimate for the changes recommended by the Chief Medical Officer are close to thirty million.

ASLAKSEN.   That's a huge sum, but—

THE MAYOR.   Naturally we'll need to float municipal bonds.

HOVSTAD.   [*Rises.*] This could never mean that the townspeople—   215

ASLAKSEN.   This can't come out of the town's property taxes—out of the empty pockets of the small taxpayers.

THE MAYOR.   Yes, my good Mr. Aslaksen, where else can we raise the money?

ASLAKSEN.   The people who own the Spa can do it.

THE MAYOR.   The shareholders can't extend themselves beyond where they've already gone.

ASLAKSEN.   Mr. Mayor, is this completely certain?   220

THE MAYOR.   I've assured myself of it. If we want these extensive changes, the town itself must pay for them.

ASLAKSEN.   But God damn it to hell—! I'm sorry, your Honor—this is something else!

Dr. Thomas Stockmann (Fredric March) and his family (Florence Eldridge, Richard Trask, Anna Minot, and Ralph Robertson) are deeply fearful when they hear the angry crowd outside their home, in the Broadhurst Theatre, New York City production of *An Enemy of the People* (1950–51), directed by Robert Lewis.

HOVSTAD.   It certainly is!

THE MAYOR.   The worst part is that, for at least a couple of years, we'll have to close the Spa entirely.

HOVSTAD.   Closed? Entirely closed?

ASLAKSEN.   For two years?

THE MAYOR.   Yes, the work will take two years—at least.

ASLAKSEN.   But damn it all, Mr. Mayor, we can never put up with that! How can the Homeowners live?

THE MAYOR.   There's no easy answer, Mr. Aslaksen. But what can we do? Do you believe we'll get a single guest if someone goes around and paints the picture that our water is poisoned, that we live in a sewer, that the whole town—

ASLAKSEN.   And this is all just imagination?

THE MAYOR.   With all my best will, I've been able to reach no other conclusion about it.

ASLAKSEN.   Well, then, it's totally inexcusable of Dr. Stockmann—I beg your pardon, Mr. Mayor, but—

THE MAYOR.   What you're implying is regrettably true, Mr. Aslaksen. My brother
has always been an impetuous man.

ASLAKSEN.   Mr. Hovstad, can you still support him after this?

HOVSTAD.   But who would have believed that—?   235

THE MAYOR.   I've prepared an impartial brief reviewing the conditions, and in it
I've shown that any possible shortcomings may be addressed without shattering the current budget for the Spa.

HOVSTAD.   Do you have a copy, Mr. Mayor?

THE MAYOR.   [*Reaches into a pocket.*] I do. I brought it along in case—

ASLAKSEN.   Oh my God, here he is!

THE MAYOR.   Who? My brother?   240

HOVSTAD.   Where? Where?

ASLAKSEN.   He's coming through the print shop!

THE MAYOR.   Unfortunate. I don't want a confrontation here, but I still have a few
more things to tell you.

HOVSTAD.   [*Directs him to the door on the right.*] Go in here for a time.

THE MAYOR.   But—?   245

HOVSTAD.   No one but Billing is there.

ASLAKSEN.   Quickly, Your Honor, he's here now!

THE MAYOR.   All right then, but be quick with him. [*Leaves through the door on the
right.* ASLAKSEN *opens it and closes it for him.*]

HOVSTAD.   Make as though you're busy, Aslaksen.

[HOVSTAD *sits at his table and writes.* ASLAKSEN *works with papers on a chair at the right.*]

DR. STOCKMANN.   [*Enters from the print shop.*] Here I am again. [*Puts down his hat*   250
and walking-stick.]

HOVSTAD.   [*Concentrates on his writing.*] Already, Doctor? Aslaksen, hurry up with
the copy we spoke of. Time's getting tight for us.

DR. STOCKMANN.   [*To* ASLAKSEN.] I conclude the proofs aren't ready yet.

ASLAKSEN.   [*Does not look up.*] No, the Doctor shouldn't expect them so soon.

DR. STOCKMANN.   No, but I'm naturally impatient. I won't rest for a minute until I
see everything in print.

HOVSTAD.   Well, it'll take at least another hour. That's right, isn't it, Aslaksen?   255

ASLAKSEN.   I'm afraid so.

DR. STOCKMANN.   All right, dear friends. I'll come back again and again if I need
to. When something so important as the welfare of the whole town is at stake, it's no time
to be lazy. [*Begins to leave, but stops and comes back.*] Just one more thing—

HOVSTAD.   Excuse me, but could we do it another time?

DR. STOCKMANN.   I'll be done in a jiffy. It's just this: When people read my
article tomorrow they'll also realize I've spent the whole winter working in the town's best
interest—

HOVSTAD.   Yes, but Doctor—   260

DR. STOCKMANN.   I know what you'll say, that it was only my duty. Damn it all, any
citizen would do the same. And I agree with you, but my fellow citizens out there—. God
in heaven, think of their high opinion of me—!

ASLAKSEN.   Yes, Doctor, the people have thought highly of you, up till now.

DR. STOCKMANN.   And that's why I'm afraid that—. This is what I want to say: If my
article creates an incentive, especially for the poor, to take a future share of town government into their own hands—

HOVSTAD.   [*Rises, clears throat.*] Doctor, I won't hide this from you—

DR. STOCKMANN.   Just as I thought; I knew it. But I won't have it. If anyone is set-   265
ting something up—

HOVSTAD.   Like what?

DR. STOCKMANN.   Well, whatever—a demonstration, a testimonial dinner, a solici-
tation for a gift—then by all that's sacred, promise me to nip it in the bud. And you too,
Mr. Aslaksen. Am I clear?

HOVSTAD.   Doctor, pardon me, but we've got to tell you the plain truth.

[*MRS. STOCKMANN, in hat and coat, enters from the main outside door.*]

MRS. STOCKMANN.   [*Sees the DOCTOR.*] I was right!

HOVSTAD.   [*Walks toward her.*] You also, Mrs. Stockmann?   270

DR. STOCKMANN.   Katrina, what the hell are you doing here?

MRS. STOCKMANN.   You know what I'm doing.

HOVSTAD.   Please sit down. Or perhaps—

MRS. STOCKMANN.   Please, no thank you. And please don't mind my coming here
for Stockmann, because, I want you to know, I'm the mother of three children.

DR. STOCKMANN.   Claptrap! They know all that!   275

MRS. STOCKMANN.   Well, it seems that you haven't been thinking of your wife and
children lately, or else you wouldn't go on like this, leading us into disaster.

DR. STOCKMANN.   But Katrina, this is insane! Does having a wife and children
stop a man from proclaiming the truth—from being a good citizen—from serving his
hometown?

MRS. STOCKMANN.   All these things, Thomas, but moderately.

ASLAKSEN.   I say that, too. Moderation in everything.

MRS. STOCKMANN.   And because of this, Mr. Hovstad, you are hurting us when you   280
coax my husband away from house and home and make him a dupe in all this.

HOVSTAD.   I'm not making anyone a dupe—

DR. STOCKMANN.   Dupe? Do you think I'm letting myself be used?

MRS. STOCKMANN.   You are. You're the most intelligent man in town, but, Thomas,
you're so easy to deceive. [*To HOVSTAD.*] And just think that he loses his position at the
Spa as soon as you publish his article—

ASLAKSEN.   What?

HOVSTAD.   Doctor, now see—   285

DR. STOCKMANN.   [*Laughs.*] Just let them try! They'll regret it, because the solid
majority is backing me!

MRS. STOCKMANN.   Yes, that's the problem, to have something as terrible as that
backing you!

DR. STOCKMANN.   Nonsense, Katrina! Go home and look after the house, and
leave the community to me. Why are you so afraid when I'm so confident and cheerful?
[*Paces, rubbing his hands.*] The people and the truth will be victorious, you can bet on it. I
can see it—all the open-minded middle classes forming a triumphant army—! [*Stops at
the chair where the MAYOR put his hat and stick.*] Now what the hell is this?

ASLAKSEN.   [*Sees the things.*] Oh, my God!

HOVSTAD.   [*Likewise.*] Ahem!   290

DR. STOCKMANN.   Here you see the highest authority!

[*Mockingly holds the MAYOR's hat high in the air.*]

MRS. STOCKMANN.   The Mayor's hat!

DR. STOCKMANN.   And here's the crook of power, too. [*Displays the MAYOR's walking
stick.*] How by all the fiends of hell did—

HOVSTAD.   Now, well—

DR. STOCKMANN.   Ah, I understand. He came here to harangue you. [*Laughs.*] He   295
sure came to the right place! And then he saw me in the print shop—. [*Bursts out laughing.*] Did he run, Mr. Aslaksen?

ASLAKSEN.   [*Speaks rapidly.*] Oh yes, he ran, Doctor.

DR. STOCKMANN.   Ran away from both his stick and—. Ran away, my foot! Peter
doesn't run away from anything. But where the devil did you put him? Aha! In here, naturally. Now you'll see, Katrina!

MRS. STOCKMANN.   Thomas, please—

ASLAKSEN.   Be careful, Doctor.

[*Still holding the stick, DR. STOCKMANN puts on the MAYOR's hat. He goes to the door at the right,
opens it, and salutes as THE MAYOR enters in a rage. BILLING follows.*]

THE MAYOR.   What do you mean by this clowning?   300

DR. STOCKMANN.   [*Paces.*] Have respect, dear Peter. I'm the town's chief authority now!

MRS. STOCKMANN.   [*On the verge of tears.*] Thomas, don't—

THE MAYOR.   [*Follows him.*] Give me my hat and stick!

DR. STOCKMANN.   [*As before.*] *You* are only the constable, while *I* am the Mayor—*I*
am master of the whole town!

THE MAYOR.   Take off that hat! Remember, it's part of an official uniform!   305

DR. STOCKMANN.   Piffle! Do you think the people, waking up like a lion, are scared
of uniforms? There'll be a revolution in town tomorrow; you'd better know that. You
thought you could dismiss me, but I'll dismiss you—from all your posts. You think I can't?
Well, listen: I've got the power of the people with me. Hovstad and Billing will thunder in
the *People's Messenger,* and Aslaksen the Printer will lead the charge of the entire Homeowners Association—

ASLAKSEN.   I won't do it, Doctor.

DR. STOCKMANN.   But of course you will—

THE MAYOR.   Aha! Mr. Hovstad has perhaps decided to be part of this insurrection, then?

HOVSTAD.   No, Mr. Mayor.   310

ASLAKSEN.   No, Mr. Hovstad isn't such a fool as to wreck himself and his paper for
no more than an insane idea!

DR. STOCKMANN.   [*Looks around the room.*] What does all this mean?

HOVSTAD.   You've put things in a false light, Doctor, and I can't support you any
longer.

BILLING.   And in light of what the Mayor has just been telling me—

DR. STOCKMANN.   False? Let me worry about that. Just print the article, and I'll jus-   315
tify it.

HOVSTAD.   I won't print it. I cannot, I will not, and I dare not print it!

DR. STOCKMANN.   Dare not? What talk is this? You're the editor, and it's the editors
who make editorial decisions, I hope.

HOVSTAD.   No, it's the subscribers, Doctor.

THE MAYOR.   A good thing, too.

ASLAKSEN.   Public opinion—enlightened people—homeowners and such peo-   320
ple—they rule the papers.

DR. STOCKMANN.   [*Speaks calmly.*] And all this is now against me?

ASLAKSEN.   Yes, it is. Printing your article would ruin the community completely.

THE MAYOR.   My hat and stick, please. [*DR. STOCKMANN lays the things on the table.*
THE MAYOR takes them.] Your tenure as the town's chief authority has ended abruptly.

DR. STOCKMANN.   No, it's not over yet. [*To HOVSTAD.*] Then it's quite impossible to publish my article in the *Messenger?*

HOVSTAD.   Quite impossible, and also because of your family.   325

MRS. STOCKMANN.   You needn't bother about the family, Mr. Hovstad.

THE MAYOR.   [*Takes a sheet of paper from his pocket, and offers it to HOVSTAD.*] If you put this in, it will be sufficient for the guidance of the public. It's an official explanation. Mr. Hovstad, would you please?

HOVSTAD.   [*Accepts the paper.*] Good. We'll print it right away.

DR. STOCKMANN.   But not mine! But you'll find that you can't suppress the truth so easily. Mr. Aslaksen, please publish my manuscript as a pamphlet—at my expense, and under my name. I'll have four hundred copies—no, five hundred! Make it six!

ASLAKSEN.   If you paid me its weight in gold, Doctor, I couldn't use my press for a   330
thing like this. I wouldn't dare, in the light of public opinion. No one in the whole town will print it!

DR. STOCKMANN.   Then give it back to me.

HOVSTAD.   [*Gives him the manuscript.*] Here you are.

DR. STOCKMANN.   [*Picks up his hat and stick.*] I'll make it public anyway. I'll call an open meeting, and all my fellow townspeople will come to hear me read the truth!

THE MAYOR.   No organization in town would let you rent their hall for this purpose.

ASLAKSEN.   Not a single one. I'm sure of it.   335

BILLING.   No, damn it, not one!

MRS. STOCKMANN.   This is a disgrace. Why is everyone turning against you?

DR. STOCKMANN.   [*Speaks in anger.*] I'll tell you why. All the men in this town are no better than old women—like you. They all think only of their families, and not of the community.

MRS. STOCKMANN.   [*Takes his arm.*] Then I'll show them an—old woman—acting for once as men of power should act. I'll stand with you, Thomas.

DR. STOCKMANN.   Bravely said, Katrina! On my soul, I'll make things public. If I   340
can't rent a hall, I'll hire a drummer to follow me all over town, and I'll shout out the truth at every corner!

THE MAYOR.   Certainly you're not such a prize idiot as all that!

DR. STOCKMANN.   Oh yes I am!

ASLAKSEN.   You won't find a single voter to back you up.

BILLING.   No, damn it, you won't!

MRS. STOCKMANN.   Don't give in, Thomas. I'll send the boys with you.   345

DR. STOCKMANN.   That's an inspired idea!

MRS. STOCKMANN.   Morten will love it, and Eilif will go along.

DR. STOCKMANN.   Yes, and Petra, and you too, Katrina.

MRS. STOCKMANN.   No, no, that's not for me. But I'll watch at the window and support you. That I can do.

DR. STOCKMANN.   [*Embraces her and kisses her.*] Thanks for this. Now, my good gen-   350
tlemen, we'll have a trial by combat! We'll see whether a pack of cowards can squelch a patriot trying to make the world a cleaner place!

[*He and MRS. STOCKMANN leave by the main door.*]

THE MAYOR.   [*Shakes his head reflectively.*] Now he's made her go crazy too!

End of the Third Act

ACT 4

SCENE. *The following night. A large room in the home of* CAPTAIN HORSTER. *An anteroom at the back can be seen through opened folding doors. The entrance door is at the extreme rear. Three windows are in the wall at stage left, and lighted lamps at these windows illuminate the room. Downstage from these windows is a table, with candles and a chair. A small podium, on which there is a table with chair, candles, bell, water, and glass, is set at the middle of the stage-right wall. There is a door in this wall downstage from the podium, and some chairs are near it. The room is almost filled with an assortment of townspeople, including a few women and children, and at the curtain the townsfolk continue entering from the anteroom.*

> 1 CITIZEN.   [*Speaks to another citizen.*] Hello, Lamstad! You here too?
> 2 CITIZEN.   I always come to public meetings.
> 3 CITIZEN.   D'you have your whistle?
> 2 CITIZEN.   You bet. Got yours?
> 3 CITIZEN.   Right here! And old Skipper Evensen's bringin' a cow-horn!   5
> 2 CITIZEN.   He's a real joker, that Evensen!

[*General laughter and noise from the crowd.*]

> 4 CITIZEN.   [*Meets the three citizens.*] What's going on here tonight?
> 2 CITIZEN.   Dr. Stockmann is speaking against the Mayor.
> 4 CITIZEN.   But my God, they're brothers!
> 1 CITIZEN.   So what? Dr. Stockmann ain't scared.   10
> 3 CITIZEN.   But he goofed up; I read that in the *Messenger*.
> 2 CITIZEN.   He's on the wrong side this time, because he couldn't rent the halls of the Homeowners Association or the Downtown Civic Club.
> 1 CITIZEN.   He couldn't even get the one at the Spa.
> 2 CITIZEN.   Not on your life, man.
> 5 CITIZEN.   Whose side are we on here?   15
> 6 CITIZEN.   Just watch Aslaksen, and follow his lead.
> BILLING.   [*Comes through the crowd, carrying a writing case.*] Excuse me please. Please let me through. I'm a reporter for the *Messenger*. [*Sits at the table on the left.*]
> 1 LABORER.   Who's that?
> 2 LABORER.   Oh, that's Billing. He works at Aslaksen's paper.

[*MRS. STOCKMANN and PETRA enter from the door at the right, escorted by* CAPTAIN HORSTER. EILIF *and* MORTEN *follow them.*]

> HORSTER.   [*Points to the chairs.*] Please sit here. Then, if things get out of hand, you   20
> can leave easily.
> MRS. STOCKMANN.   You're not expecting any trouble?
> HORSTER.   With a crowd like this you can't tell. But just sit tight here. You'll be fine!
> MRS. STOCKMANN.   [*Sits, along with* PETRA.] Letting my husband use the room was so kind.
> HORSTER.   Well, since he couldn't get one elsewhere—
> PETRA.   It was brave of you, Captain Horster.   25
> HORSTER.   Oh, it was nothing.

[*HOVSTAD and ASLAKSEN enter amid the crowd: "Excuse me!" "Please!" etc.*]

> ASLAKSEN.   [*Goes to* HORSTER.] Is the Doctor here yet?
> HORSTER.   He's in the next room.

[*Noise from the crowd at the anteroom door.*]

HOVSTAD.   Here's the Mayor!

BILLING.   Well I'll be damned, he's here after all!   30

[*THE MAYOR enters through the crowd, which parts for him. He bows and greets people as he goes, and takes a stand near the left wall. DR. STOCKMANN then enters from the door at the right, wearing a black frock coat and a white tie. A few townspeople applaud, but they are quickly restrained. Then perfect silence.*]

DR. STOCKMANN.   [*Speaks quietly to MRS. STOCKMANN.*] Are you all right?

MRS. STOCKMANN.   Just fine, thanks. [*Lowers voice.*] Thomas, please don't lose your temper.

DR. STOCKMANN.   No, I'll control myself. [*Takes out his watch and looks at it. Steps to the podium and bows.*] It's quarter past—time to start. [*Takes his manuscript from his pocket.*]

ASLAKSEN.   [*Speaks loudly.*] First we should elect someone as Chair!

DR. STOCKMANN.   That won't be necessary.   35

VARIOUS VOICES IN THE CROWD.   Yes! Hear, hear! Elect a Chair! etc.

THE MAYOR.   I too think we should have a Chair!

DR. STOCKMANN.   But I called this meeting to give a lecture, Peter.

THE MAYOR.   [*Speaks to the crowd.*] This lecture may lead to controversy, however, and for that we need someone to chair.

VARIOUS VOICES.   A Chair! Elect someone! etc.   40

HOVSTAD.   It seems there is a consensus to elect a Chair!

DR. STOCKMANN.   [*Speaks resignedly.*] All right—let the majority rule.

ASLAKSEN.   Will the Mayor consent to serve? [*Various townspeople applaud. Shouts of "Yes, Mr. Mayor!" "He should chair!" etc.*]

THE MAYOR.   You will all understand why I must ask to be excused from serving you. But we do have an acceptable candidate. I recommend to you the President of the Homeowner's Association, Mr. Aslaksen!

VARIOUS VOICES.   Yay, Aslaksen! Yes! Hurrah for Aslaksen! etc.   45

[*DR. STOCKMANN picks up his manuscript and leaves the podium.*]

ASLAKSEN.   As my fellow citizens have such confidence in me, I am not unwilling to accept—

[*Applause. Cheers. Whistles. etc. ASLAKSEN mounts the podium.*]

BILLING.   [*Writes.*] "Mr. Aslaksen was elected by acclamation."

ASLAKSEN.   As your newly elected Chair, permit me a few short words. You all know me as a peaceful and quiet person. I believe in sober moderation, and in—and in moderate sobriety!

VARIOUS TOWNSPEOPLE.   Yes, we know! *Bravo!* etc. [*Light applause.*]

ASLAKSEN.   I am a graduate of the school of hard knocks, and I've learned that the   50
most important virtue of a citizen is moderation—

THE MAYOR.   Hear, hear!

ASLAKSEN.   And furthermore, that discretion and moderation are essential to public service. Therefore I suggest to the distinguished man who has called this meeting that he exert all efforts to keep within the limits of moderation.

7 CITIZEN.   [*Stands near the door stage right.*] Let's hear it for the Moderation Party!

VARIOUS VOICES.   Be quiet! Shut your damn mouth! Shh! etc.

ASLAKSEN.   No demonstrations! Please keep order! Is there anyone who wishes to   55
speak?

THE MAYOR. Mr. Chairman.

ASLAKSEN. The Honorable Mayor Stockmann has the floor.

THE MAYOR. Because I am the closest relative of the Chief Medical Officer of the Spa, you will understand my reticence in speaking. But out of my duty as the Chief Executive Officer, and out of my concern for the town, I must present a motion. I believe that no one here considers it in the town's interest to publicize unsubstantiated and dubious reports concerning the sanitary condition of our water supplies.

VARIOUS VOICES. Absolutely not! No, no! No such reports! etc.

THE MAYOR. Therefore I move that this assembly refuse to permit the Chief Medical Officer to give his lecture or discuss it. [*Voice of "Second the motion."*]   60

DR. STOCKMANN. [*Angrily.*] Refuse permission?—What's all this?—

MRS. STOCKMANN. [*Coughs.*] Ahem!

DR. STOCKMANN. [*Collects himself.*] Well, all right for now. Go ahead.

THE MAYOR. In my report printed in the *Messenger*, I laid out the facts so that all impartial citizens might draw their own conclusions. In it you have seen that the Chief Medical Officer's recommendations—in addition to being a direct vote of no confidence in the town's principal citizens—would require unacceptable tax increases for the town, to the extent of many millions.

[*Cries of indignation and many whistles and catcalls.*]

ASLAKSEN. [*Rings bell.*] Order, gentlemen. [*Stands.*] I rise to support the motion of   65
the Mayor. He's right that there's more to the Doctor's actions than meets the eye. He begins with the Spa, but his real motive is revolution—to get control of the town government. The Doctor of course is honest—no question of that. I too believe in self-government, with the proviso that it does not raise taxes. But higher taxes would result here, and therefore I'll see Dr. Stockmann in hell before I support him on this! Excuse my language, but some things have too high a cost. [*Vigorous approval from all sides.*]

HOVSTAD. My position also needs clarification. Dr. Stockmann's analysis at first seemed reasonable, and I judged him worthy of support. But we soon found cause to believe that we had been led astray by false conclusions—

DR. STOCKMANN. False—?

HOVSTAD. Well, not totally reliable conclusions, if you will. The Mayor's statement has established that. I think no one here doubts my devotion to freedom. The record of the *Messenger* on such important political issues is widely recognized. But from wiser and more experienced men I have learned that the paper should take cautious and prudent stands on local issues.

ASLAKSEN. I agree completely with the speaker.

HOVSTAD. And on this current issue, it's certain that there's now a consensus   70
against Dr. Stockmann. Is it not then, gentlemen, an editor's duty to work in tandem with popular sentiment? Is not an editor obligated to work diligently on behalf of the readers whose causes he accepts and reflects? Am I wrong in this?

VARIOUS VOICES. No! You're right! Well said! etc.

HOVSTAD. Personally, this public disagreement with Dr. Stockmann, in whose home I have been a guest, has caused me great agony. Till now he has deserved the unconditional respect of his fellow citizens. With so much virtue, his only flaw is his tendency to be ruled by his feelings rather than his judgment.

A SMALL NUMBER OF VOICES. True! Stockmann is okay! etc.

HOVSTAD. Nevertheless, my overriding concern for the public has directed me to make this break. In addition, there's another reason for which he should be deterred from his present course, and that is concern for his family—

DR. STOCKMANN.   Just stick to water intakes and sewers!   75

HOVSTAD.   —Concern for his wife and children, for whom he has made no security.

MORTEN.   Does he mean us, Mother?

MRS. STOCKMANN.   Shh!

ASLAKSEN.   Gentlemen, are you ready to vote on the Mayor's motion?

DR. STOCKMANN.   There's no need. This evening I don't wish to speak about the   80
filthiness of the Spa. No, you'll hear something different.

THE MAYOR.   [*Aside.*] What's next?

PETTERSEN.   [*He is drunk, and stands near the back door.*] I pay taxes, and I want to
talk! My insolent—absolute—unacceptable comment is—

VARIOUS VOICES.   He's plastered! Shut him up! Put that lush out! What an idiot!
Pipe down! etc. [*PETTERSEN is ejected.*]

DR. STOCKMANN.   May I speak?

ASLAKSEN.   [*Rings the bell.*] Dr. Stockmann has the floor.   85

DR. STOCKMANN.   Thank you. A few days ago, I would have allowed no one to silence me as has been done tonight. Like a lion, I would have defended my sacred right to
speak. But now this doesn't matter to me, because I have more important things to say.
[*The crowd, one of whom is MORTEN KIIL, moves closer to him.*] In the last few days I've been
thinking things over a good deal, so much that my head was almost spinning—

THE MAYOR.   [*Coughs.*] Ahem!

DR. STOCKMANN.   —but I have put things in order, and that's why I'm in front of
you this evening. I have a unique discovery to tell you about, my fellow citizens, a revelation far more significant than the pollution of our water and the contaminated ground at
our Therapeutic Spa.

VARIOUS VOICES.   [*Shout.*] Not that! Out of order! Not about the Spa! We won't listen! etc.

DR. STOCKMANN.   No, my topic tonight is my great discovery of the last few days—   90
that it is our moral life that is polluted and that it is our communal assumptions that are
built on contaminated ground.

VARIOUS VOICES.   [*Hushed.*] What's this about? What's he mean? etc.

THE MAYOR.   What kind of insinuation—!

ASLAKSEN.   [*Rings his bell.*] The speaker is cautioned to be moderate.

DR. STOCKMANN.   I was brought up in this town, and I have always loved it. When I
had to leave it I was still not old, and in my exile I thought of it fondly almost as a place
inhabited by angels. [*Brief applause in the crowd.*] In the depressing hell-hole up north
where I practiced for so many years, the people lived far apart, here and there, among
the rocks, and I sometimes thought that that they didn't need a physician like myself but
rather a veterinarian.

BILLING.   [*Puts down his pen.*] Well, damn it, I never heard—   95

HOVSTAD.   You're insulting the common people!

DR. STOCKMANN.   Now wait! From what I've said, you'll agree that up north I didn't
forget you. I was more like a brooding hen, and what I hatched was—the plan for our
Therapeutic Spa! [*Applause and objections.*] When I was fortunate enough to return home
I thought my life had reached fulfillment. But I had an ardent, relentless, burning wish,
and that was to serve you and to be an asset to you.

THE MAYOR.   [*Looks at the ceiling.*] This is a strange way of doing it!

DR. STOCKMANN.   And so, blinded to reality, I was in bliss. However, yesterday
morning—no, really the evening before—my blind eyes were opened, and the first thing
I saw was the incredible stupidity of our authorities—

[*Consternation, objections, laughter. MRS. STOCKMANN coughs strongly.*]

THE MAYOR. Mr. Chairman!   100

ASLAKSEN. [*Rings his bell.*] The chair has authority to rule—

DR. STOCKMANN. Let's not quibble about a word, Mr. Aslaksen. I only mean that I began to realize how bull-headed the town leaders had been about the Spa. Generally, I find official types unbearable. They inhibit freedom at every turn. They're no better than goats among newly sprouted trees; they destroy everything. They frustrate a free person at every turn, and I don't see why they shouldn't be exterminated like any pest—

[*Uproar in the room.*]

THE MAYOR. Mr. Chairman, can this be allowed?

ASLAKSEN. [*Rings his bell.*] Doctor—!

DR. STOCKMANN. I don't know why I didn't see the nature of the official types   105
before—when each day I could see such a shining example right here in town—my brother Peter—dull in wit, inflexible in prejudice—

[*Laughter, uproar, whistles.* MRS. STOCKMANN *coughs continuously.* ASLAKSEN *rings his bell loudly, etc.*]

PETTERSEN. [*Who has returned.*] Hey, is he talking about me? My name's Pettersen, but damn it to hell if I—

VARIOUS VOICES. [*Shout in anger.*] Throw the drunk out! Through the door with 'im! etc. [*PETTERSEN is thrown out again.*]

THE MAYOR. Who was that—individual?

1 CITIZEN. I don't know, Mr. Mayor.

2 CITIZEN. He has no business here.   110

3 CITIZEN. He's probably a lumberman over at—[*The rest cannot be heard.*]

ASLAKSEN. Obviously that man's brain is drowned in beer! [*Laughter.*] Continue, Doctor, but be moderate.

DR. STOCKMANN. So then, neighbors, I will say nothing more about our leading citizens. No one should claim that my main objective is to criticize them, for I take comfort that such parasites—living fossils of a passing age—are racing toward their own extinction. They don't need a doctor's help to hurry them along! No, *they're* not the danger; *they're* not the ones most active in poisoning our moral life and polluting the ground under us. No, *they're* not the worst enemies of truth and freedom.

VARIOUS VOICES. [*Speaking from all sides.*] Who then? Who is it? Name them! etc.

DR. STOCKMANN. Don't worry! I'll name them! This is the great discovery I made   115
yesterday. [*Raises his voice.*] The most dangerous enemy of truth and freedom among us is the solid majority. Yes, the damned, solid, popular majority! That's it! Now you know!

[*Tremendous uproar in the room. Most people are shouting, stamping their feet, whistling, booing, hissing, etc. A few older people look slyly at each other and appear to be enjoying themselves.* MRS. STOCKMANN *stands anxiously.* EILIF *and* MORTEN *begin quarrelling with some other boys who are demonstrating.* ASLAKSEN *rings his bell and pleads for order.* HOVSTAD *and* BILLING *try to speak, but are drowned out. Finally, things quiet down.*]

ASLAKSEN. As Chair, I ask the speaker to withdraw his immoderate language and apologize to the body.

DR. STOCKMANN. Not for the world, Mr. Aslaksen! It's the majority in our town who are denying me my free right to speak the truth.

HOVSTAD. The majority always has right on its side.

BILLING. And, damn it, it always has truth, too!

DR. STOCKMANN.   The majority is never right—never, I say! Majority rule is nothing   120
more than a fairy tale that all thinking people must oppose. Who forms the majority—
the intelligent or the stupid? Is there any doubt that the stupid make up the landslide
majority everywhere on earth? But you can throw me in hell if it's ever been part of an
eternal plan for the stupid to control the intelligent! [*Outcries, catcalls, disturbance.*] All
right, you can shout me down, but you can't answer me. The majority does have *might*—
more's the pity—but not *right*. *I* am right, along with a small number of others. It's the
minority that's always right! [*More outcries, demonstrations, etc.*]

HOVSTAD.   [*Laughs.*] So in the last few days Dr. Stockmann has become an
aristocrat!

DR. STOCKMANN.   I've said that I won't waste words on people like that shipwrecked crew of officials behind us. They're no longer even relevant. My thoughts are
rather on the few who are creating new and exciting ideas. Such people are in the front
ranks, beyond the shortsighted vision of the solid majority. *They* are leading the fight for
ideas that are so new and rare that as yet they haven't recruited great numbers to their
cause.

HOVSTAD.   Oh, so now the Doctor's a revolutionary!

DR. STOCKMANN.   Yes, in God's name, I am, Mr. Hovstad! I want to revolt against
the fairy tale that truth belongs to the majority alone. What are the truths the majority
usually flocks around? Old, worn-out, and disintegrating truths. And when a truth gets
too old, gentlemen, it's close to being a lie. [*Laughter and scorn at him.*] Yes, believe as you
wish, but truths don't live for 969 years, like Methuselah. An average truth can live no
more than seventeen or eighteen, or at best twenty years. In fact, truths this old are fading and dying, but it's only then that the majority harvests them for the food of their
moral life. As a doctor, I assure you that there's only moral starvation there. All these
dead popular beliefs, which are no better than salted meat that's gone rotten, are the
cause of our present epidemic of moral scurvy.

ASLAKSEN.   It seems to me that the speaker has wandered away from his text.   125

THE MAYOR.   I'm in agreement with the Chair.

DR. STOCKMANN.   Peter, you're crazy! I *am* staying on my subject, which is exactly
this: It's the mass, the majority—the fiendish, solid majority—that's poisoning the
sources of our moral life and passing its waste on the very ground we stand on.

HOVSTAD.   And the great open-minded majority does all this because they're reasonable enough to recognize only secure and sanctioned truths?

DR. STOCKMANN.   Ah, my good Mr. Hovstad, don't pretend to speak about truths!
The truths that the mass accepts today are the truths secured by the advance guard at the
time of our grandparents. Today's forward thinkers have gone far beyond them. I believe
there's only one essential truth, and that is that no society can be healthy if it lives on out-
moded, marrowless truths.

HOVSTAD.   Well, instead of standing there with your mind in the blue, why not   130
make it interesting and tell us what you mean by these "marrowless truths" we live on.

[*Support from various parts of the crowd.*]

DR. STOCKMANN.   Well, I could go on forever, but I might begin with one which is
really an outrageous lie but which all the same feeds the *Messenger* and the *Messenger's*
readers.

HOVSTAD.   And that is—?

DR. STOCKMANN.   It's the idea given to you from the past and which you transmit
mindlessly at every opportunity. It's the falsehood that the crowd, the mass, the majority,
form the kernel of the people—in fact, that they are the people—and that the common

people, the most apathetic and worst prepared in society, have the same right to condemn and approve, to manage and advise, as those few people who are truly enlightened.

BILLING. I hear this, damn it, but—

HOVSTAD. [*Shouts at the same time.*] Citizens, remember this!   135

VARIOUS VOICES. Aren't we the people! So only the aristocrats run things? etc.

1 LABORER. Down with him for talking like this!

2 LABORER. Yeah, throw 'im out!

3 CITIZEN. [*Shouts.*] Toot your horn, Evensen!

[*Sounds of a loud horn. Whistles and tremendous uproar in the room.*]

DR. STOCKMANN. [*Speaks when the noise subsides.*] Gentlemen, please listen. Can't   140
you hear the truth for a change? I never expected that you'd all agree with me, but I
thought that Mr. Hovstad might, at least after a while. He claims to be a freethinker—

VARIOUS VOICES. [*In startled but hushed tones.*] He's a freethinker? What? Is Editor
Hovstad a freethinker?

HOVSTAD. [*Shouts.*] Prove this, Dr. Stockmann! When did I say this in print?

DR. STOCKMANN. [*Pauses briefly.*] No, damn it, you're right—you've never been
that honest. Well, I won't leave you dangling in the wind, Mr. Hovstad. [*To the crowd.*] Let
me be the freethinker then. I'm going to persuade you logically that the *People's Messenger*
misleads you shamelessly by telling you that you—the common folk, the masses—form
what is called "The People." This is a lie, for common folk are only the raw material of the
people. [*Grumbling, laughter, and commotion in the room.*] Well, consider the differences between thoroughbred and street animals. For instance, a farmyard hen is too scrawny for
good eating. And its eggs? A common crow or raven does just as well. But with thoroughbred Spanish or Japanese hens, or well-nourished pheasants or turkeys, the story is different. As further evidence, consider the lives of dogs, which we human beings so closely
resemble. Compare an ordinary street mongrel with a registered collie or setter which
has been bred for many generations. Don't you think these thoroughbred dogs have better brains than the curs? You know the answer. The pups of the well-bred dogs take to
training naturally, and do things that common mongrels could never learn. [*Uproar and
disapproval all around.*]

9 CITIZEN. [*Shouts.*] So you think we're dogs?

10 CITIZEN. We're not animals, *Sir* Doctor!   145

DR. STOCKMANN. Yes, my friend, we really *are*, believe me—the highest animals on
earth—but even among us there are just a few really good ones. Among people, there are
wide differences between thoroughbreds and mongrels. And the funny thing is that Editor Hovstad totally agrees with me as long as the subject is four-footed creatures—

HOVSTAD. Yes, but they're in a different category.

DR. STOCKMANN. You see! When I apply the principle to us two-legged animals, he
refuses the logic. He won't follow his ideas to their necessary conclusion, but rather turns
everything upside down, and pontificates in the *Messenger* about the farmyard hens and
mongrel curs being the best of the human menagerie! But it's always that way as long as
popular bromides control the soul, and people don't free themselves to reach their own
highest mental and spiritual distinction.

HOVSTAD. I don't claim distinction of any sort. I come from simple peasants, and
I'm proud of my deep roots in the common people he's now insulting.

VARIOUS VOICES. Hurrah for Hovstad! Well said! etc.   150

DR. STOCKMANN. You recognize that common people are not confined to the
lower economic levels. They yelp at our heels wherever we go, even in the highest circles
and professions. I cite as an example His Honor, the Mayor. My brother Peter is just as
common as anyone in two shoes—

[*Laughter and hisses.*]

THE MAYOR.　I protest these personal slurs!

DR. STOCKMANN.　[*Undisturbed.*] And he's common not because he is—as I am—a descendant of an old Pomeranian pirate. This is, I confess, our common origin—

THE MAYOR.　That family legend is not true!

DR. STOCKMANN.　But he is low because he uncritically accepts the opinions of his　155
superiors as his own. People like that are intellectual rabble, and this is why my states-manlike brother Peter is so undistinguished and narrow-minded.

THE MAYOR.　Mr. Chairman—!

HOVSTAD.　So in this country people can be open-minded only if they're distinguished! This is certainly news!

DR. STOCKMANN.　Yes, that's *one* of my discoveries. Another is that open-mindedness is virtually the same as morality. This is why it's so indefensible for the *Messenger* to preach day in and day out that the people, the masses, the solid majority, are the guardians of understanding and morality, and that social and political evils are a residue of culture, just as the pollution of our Spa is a residue of the tannery wastes up at Mølledal. [*Uproar and interruptions. Unaffected, he laughs in his exhilaration.*] And yet the *Messenger* preaches on about elevating the masses to their higher destiny! But damn it all, if the *Messenger's* doctrines were right, then elevating the masses would do no more than drive them straight into the devil's hands! But fortunately this theory is only folklore. No, it's stupidity, poverty, and ugliness that make Old Nick prosper. A house that is not well cleaned and ventilated will soon make its inhabitants lose their moral judgment. Without the oxygen gained from constant cleansing, we lose our conscience. And I conclude that oxygen is lacking in many households here in town, because the popular majority have desensitized their consciences and are willing to build the town's wealth on a cesspool of lies and deceit.

ASLAKSEN.　Accusations like this, against the entire town, are outrageous!

10 CITIZEN.　I move that the Chair rule the speaker out of order.　160

VARIOUS VOICES.　Second! Hear, hear! Out of order! etc.

DR. STOCKMANN.　[*Becomes angry.*] If I can't speak here, I'll declare the truth in the streets! I'll write for papers in other towns! The entire country will see what's going on here!

HOVSTAD.　It seems that Dr. Stockmann is bent on ruining the town.

DR. STOCKMANN.　Yes, I love my hometown so much that I prefer its ruin to its living on lies.

ASLAKSEN.　Now you've *really* said it!　165

[*Uproar, shouts, catcalls, etc.* MRS. STOCKMANN *coughs, but* DR. STOCKMANN *no longer listens to her.*]

HOVSTAD.　[*Shouts over the noise.*] Any person aiming to destroy the community is a public enemy!

DR. STOCKMANN.　[*With rising anger.*] If the community lives on lies, what does its destruction matter? It ought to be pounded to rubble, or its pollution will infect other towns, and, finally, the entire country! And I say, with every fiber of my being, that if things go that far, may the country itself die, and may all its people be eliminated!

11 CITIZEN.　This is the talk of a real enemy of the people!

BILLING.　That voice—God damn it—that voice is the People's voice!

THE ENTIRE CROWD.　[*Shouts.*] He's an enemy of the people! He hates his country!　170
He hates all the people! etc.

ASLAKSEN.　I'm deeply disturbed, both publicly and personally, at what we've heard. Dr. Stockmann has revealed an unfortunate part of himself I would never have dreamed possible. But the expression just voiced by one of you conveys the sense of this meeting, and hence I would entertain the following resolution of censure: "This assembly declares that Dr. Thomas Stockmann, Chief Medical Officer of the Spa, is an enemy of the people."

[*Cry of "So move" and "Second the motion." Tremendous applause and cheers, stamping of feet, etc. A few men surround* DR. STOCKMANN *and hiss and menace him.* MRS. STOCKMANN *and* PETRA *stand up.* MORTEN *and* EILIF *begin fighting other boys who have joined the hissing, but they are separated by nearby adults.*]

DR. STOCKMANN. [*To those menacing him.*] You fools! I tell you—

ASLAKSEN. [*Rings his bell.*] You no longer have the floor, Doctor. We'll take a vote, but as a personal privilege for the Doctor, we'll do it by ballot and not by voice or hand. Mr. Billing, do you have any paper?

BILLING. Yes I do, both blue and white.

ASLAKSEN. [*Walks to him.*] That's good, it will make the process easier. Cut it up;   175
yes, like that. [*To the crowd.*] Take blue for no; white for yes. I myself will collect your votes.

[*THE MAYOR leaves while* ASLAKSEN *and a few others put the ballots in their hats and distribute them.*]

1 CITIZEN. [*To* HOVSTAD.] What should we think about the Doctor? Has he gone off his rocker?

HOVSTAD. You know he's always been headstrong.

2 CITIZEN. [*To* BILLING.] Billing, you've been at the house. Did you ever see him drinking?

BILLING. Well, I can't be sure, but there's always liquor on his table.

3 CITIZEN. I think he goes around the bend at times.   180

1 CITIZEN. Has there been any madness in the family?

BILLING. I wouldn't be surprised.

4 CITIZEN. No, it looks like pure spite to me; I think he's out to get someone.

BILLING. Well, he did get turned down on his request for a raise.

THE FOUR CITIZENS. [*Agree among themselves.*] Ah, we see it all now!   185

PETTERSEN. [*Who has returned again.*] Gimme a blue one! And a white one too!

ANGRY VOICES. There's that lush again! Out with him! etc.

MORTEN KIIL. [*Speaks to* DR. STOCKMANN.] Well, Stockmann, do you see what your hocus-pocus has done for you?

DR. STOCKMANN. I've done my duty as I saw it.

MORTEN KIIL. What did you say about the tanneries at Mølledal?   190

DR. STOCKMANN. You understood me—that they're the source of the toxic waste.

MORTEN KIIL. Including my tannery?

DR. STOCKMANN. Yes, I'm sorry, but yours is the worst.

MORTEN KIIL. Are you going to put this in the paper?

DR. STOCKMANN. I won't hold anything back.   195

MORTEN KIIL. That may cost you plenty, Stockmann. [*Leaves.*]

VIK. [*Goes to* HORSTER, *ignoring the women.*] So, Captain, you permit your house to be used by an enemy of the people.

HORSTER. Mr. Vik, I have a right to do as I wish with my own property.

VIK. Well, then, you can't object if I exercise the same right with mine.

HORSTER. Sir, what are you saying?   200

VIK. You'll understand in the morning. [*Turns and walks away.*]

PETRA. Captain Horster, wasn't he your shipowner?

HORSTER.   Yes, that was Mr. Vik.

ASLAKSEN.   [*Ballots in hand, he steps on the podium and rings his bell.*] Order, please! Gentlemen, here are the results. All of you have voted but one—

12 CITIZEN.   [*A young man.*] Yeah, that was the drunk!   205

ASLAKSEN.   And by a unanimous vote—except for a drunken man—this body of citizens declares that Dr. Thomas Stockmann, Chief Medical Officer of the Spa, is an enemy of the people! [*Applause, outcries.*] Let's have three cheers for our ancient and noble community! [*Cheers.*] Let's also have three cheers for our honorable Mayor, who has put our town above duty to family! [*More cheers.*] Our business is ended. Do I hear a motion to adjourn? [*Cries of "So move," "Second."*] The meeting is now adjourned! [*Steps down.*]

BILLING.   Long live our Chair!

THE ENTIRE CROWD.   Hurray for Aslaksen the Printer! etc.

DR. STOCKMANN.   Petra, my coat and hat. Captain, do you have space for passengers to the New World?

HORSTER.   Yes, Doctor, for you and yours I'll make room.   210

DR. STOCKMANN.   [*As PETRA helps him with his coat.*] Katrina, boys, let's go. [*He takes his wife's arm.*]

MRS. STOCKMANN.   [*Lowers her voice.*] Thomas, the back way.

DR. STOCKMANN.   There's no back way for me, Katrina. [*Raises his voice.*] You'll be hearing from this enemy of the people again before he shakes the dust of this town from his feet.° I cannot be as charitable as the person who said, "Forgive them, for they know not what they do!"°

ASLAKSEN.   Dr. Stockmann, that's blasphemy!

BILLING.   Well, God d—. This is too much for a believing person!   215

13 CITIZEN.   [*Coarsely.*] So he's threatening us, is he?

ANGRY VOICES.   Smash his windows! Toss him in the fjord! etc.

3 CITIZEN.   [*Shouts.*] Blow your horn, Evensen! Toot, toot!

[*Loud horn calls, whistles, shouts, general turmoil. HORSTER leads DR. STOCKMANN and his family toward the door at the rear.*]

THE WHOLE CROWD.   [*Howls, etc. at them.*] Enemy of the people! Enemy of the people! Enemy of the people!

BILLING.   [*Gathers his notes.*] Well, damned if I'd go over and have a toddy with the   220
Stockmanns tonight!

[*The crowd pushes out the rear door. Their noise continues outside. From the street the receding shouts continue: "Enemy of the people," "Enemy of the People!"*]

End of the Fourth Act

ACT 5

SCENE. DR. STOCKMANN's *study, the next morning. The room is in general disorder. At the walls are bookcases, along with cabinets containing various specimens. At the rear, a center door leads to the hallway. Downstage in the stage-left wall there is a door to the living room. The two windows in the stage-right wall are completely broken. In the middle of the room is the Doctor's desk, strewn with books, papers, etc. DR. STOCKMANN, in dressing gown, slippers, and smoking cap, is using an umbrella to scrape out broken glass and other debris from under a cabinet. Shortly after the curtain he produces a large stone.*

213 *he shakes . . . from his feet:* Mark 6:11.   *Forgive them . . . what they do:* Luke 23:34.

DR. STOCKMANN.   [*Calls through the living-room door.*] Here's another one, Katrina.

MRS. STOCKMANN.   [*Offstage.*] I'm sure you'll find more.

DR. STOCKMANN.   [*Adds the stone to a pile on the desk.*] These stones will be keep-sakes. Eilif and Morten will see them every day, and will inherit them when they grow up. [*Rakes under another bookcase.*] Did what's-her-name get the glazier yet?

MRS. STOCKMANN.   [*Enters.*] Yes, but he wasn't sure he could make it today.

DR. STOCKMANN.   You'll soon see that he won't dare to come.   5

MRS. STOCKMANN.   Randina—the maid—thought the same. He's afraid because of the neighbors. [*Looks toward the door on the left, and calls.*] What is it, Randina? Yes, I'll take it. [*Leaves and returns immediately .*] It's a letter for you, Thomas.

DR. STOCKMANN.   Thank you. [*Takes the letter, opens it, and reads it quickly.*] Ah, as I expected.

MRS. STOCKMANN.   Who's it from?

DR. STOCKMANN.   Our landlord. It's a notice to leave.

MRS. STOCKMANN.   Can it be? He's such a nice man—   10

DR. STOCKMANN.   [*Looks at the letter.*] Says he doesn't dare do anything else. His fellow-citizens—public sentiment—dependent on others—can't offend superiors—no choice. You get the picture.

MRS. STOCKMANN.   But you see his reasons, Thomas.

DR. STOCKMANN.   Yes, I see. I see that the whole town is made up of cowards; they're all afraid of each other. [*Tosses the letter on the desk.*] But, Katrina, it's no matter. We'll sail to America, and then—

MRS. STOCKMANN.   Is this the best thing to do, Thomas?

DR. STOCKMANN.   Do you think we should stay here, where they've branded me as   15
an enemy of the people, threatened me, and smashed my windows? And look, they've ripped my black trousers!

MRS. STOCKMANN.   Oh, dear! That's your best pair.

DR. STOCKMANN.   You should never battle for truth and freedom in your Sunday best! It isn't the trousers; you can sew them up again. It's rather the injustice that these scum dared to attack me as though they were my equals. I can never accept that.

MRS. STOCKMANN.   Certainly they treated you shabbily, Thomas, but does that jus-tify leaving our own country permanently?

DR. STOCKMANN.   Don't you suppose the common mongrels are just as spiteful in other Norwegian towns we could live in? There's not much to choose from. But crap, their snapping at heels isn't the worst! The worst is that everyone in this country is a slave to party—though for that matter it's probably no different anywhere else. In the West, I'm sure, they have the same popular majority, the same pseudo-liberal public opinion, and all that devil's garbage. But, you see, things there are on a huge scale. They may *kill* you, but they don't *torture* you with a thousand cuts, as they do here; they don't put your soul in a vise and squeeze the life out of you. If you need to, though, you can get away there. [*Paces.*] If only I knew of a bargain on an unexplored forest, or a tiny island in the South Seas—

MRS. STOCKMANN.   But what of the boys, Thomas?   20

DR. STOCKMANN.   [*Stops.*] You're so strange, Katrina! Do you want the boys to grow up in a society like ours? Last night you saw that half the people are crazy enough to be in straightjackets, and if the other half haven't lost their minds, it's because they're such blockheads they have nothing to lose.

MRS. STOCKMANN.   No, but Thomas, you speak so imprudently.

DR. STOCKMANN.   Well, isn't what I'm saying right? Don't they turn everything up-side down? Don't they mix up right and wrong? Don't they call everything a lie that I know is the truth? But the most insane thing is that these grown people, who profess to support freedom, go around as a party and try to fool themselves and others into thinking that they're broad-minded and independent. Katrina, have you ever heard the like?

MRS. STOCKMANN.   Yes, it's wrong, but—[PETRA *enters from the living room.*] What, already back from school?

PETRA.   Yes. I've been dismissed.   25

MRS. STOCKMANN.   Dismissed?

DR. STOCKMANN.   You too, Petra?

PETRA.   Mrs. Busk gave me my walking papers, and I thought it best to go right away.

DR. STOCKMANN.   You did right.

MRS. STOCKMANN.   Who would have expected that Mrs. Busk was that sort of   30 person?

PETRA.   She isn't that sort, Mother. I could see how it hurt her. But she didn't dare do anything else, she said, and so I got fired.

DR. STOCKMANN.   [*Laughs and rubs his hands.*] She didn't dare either. How marvellous!

MRS. STOCKMANN.   Well, after the horrible scene last night—

PETRA.   That wasn't all. Father, just listen!

DR. STOCKMANN.   Well?   35

PETRA.   She showed me three letters she had got only this morning.

DR. STOCKMANN.   With no signatures, I assume?

PETRA.   Yes.

DR. STOCKMANN.   Because they didn't *dare* sign their names, Katrina.

PETRA.   And two of them reported that a man who had been a guest in our home   40 declared at the Club that I held dangerously liberated views on a number of things—

DR. STOCKMANN.   You didn't disavow them, I hope?

PETRA.   You know I didn't. Mrs. Busk herself, in private anyway, has liberated views, but because this is coming out about me, she didn't dare keep me.

MRS. STOCKMANN.   And one of our guests! That's what you get for your hospitality, Thomas!

DR. STOCKMANN.   We can't stay in this pig sty any longer. Pack our things right away, Katrina. The sooner we leave, the better.

MRS. STOCKMANN.   Shh! There's someone in the hall. Go see who it is, Petra.   45

PETRA.   [*Opens the living-room door.*] Oh, it's you, Captain Horster! Please come in.

HORSTER.   [*Enters.*] Good morning. I wanted to see how you're doing.

DR. STOCKMANN.   [*Shakes his hand.*] Thank you. You're so kind.

MRS. STOCKMANN.   And thank you again for protecting us from the mob, Captain Horster.

PETRA.   But how were you able to get back home again?   50

HORSTER.   Oh, I managed. I can take care of myself, and that crowd has more bark than bite.

DR. STOCKMANN.   Isn't their hangdog cowardice amazing? [*Shows the stones on the desk.*] Look, here are the stones they used to break our windows. Just look! No more than two in this pile have any class as rocks at all; the rest are gravel—just pebbles! And the crowd stood out there milling around, threatening to beat me to a pulp! But for action—action—you just don't see that in this town!

HORSTER.   This time, though, it was best for you, Doctor.

DR. STOCKMANN.   Your're right. But it still makes you mad, because if the country ever gets into a serious all-out fight, you'll see that public opinion will be to run away,

Captain Horster, and the solid majority will be scared off like sheep. It's enough to make you sick. But hell, it's stupid to go on like this. They've called me the people's enemy, and so I'll *be* the people's enemy.

MRS. STOCKMANN.   You can never be that, Thomas.   55

DR. STOCKMANN.   Don't be too sure, Katrina. Being called such an ugly name is the same as being stabbed in the lung. That ghastly name is sitting in my stomach and gnawing at me like a cancer. No medicine can help this.

PETRA.   No, Father, you should just laugh at them.

HORSTER.   Doctor, one day they'll see things your way.

MRS. STOCKMANN.   Yes, as sure as you're standing here.

DR. STOCKMANN.   Sure, when it's too late. Well, they deserve it. Let them roll in   60
their own filth and regret that they once drove a patriot into exile. When do you sail, Captain Horster?

HORSTER.   Well, I came here to tell you—

DR. STOCKMANN.   Is something wrong with the ship?

HORSTER.   No, but what happened is that *I'm* not going along.

PETRA.   You haven't gotten your notice?

HORSTER.   [*Smiles.*] Yes, that's it.   65

PETRA.   You too!

MRS. STOCKMANN.   Thomas, do you see?

DR. STOCKMANN.   And all for the sake of truth! If I'd thought for one minute—

HORSTER.   Don't worry. I'll get a post from some shipping line or other out of town.

DR. STOCKMANN.   And here we have the estimable Mr. Vik—a man of wealth and   70
independence. What a God-damned farce!

HORSTER.   Oh, he's right-minded otherwise. He said he would've kept me, if he dared—

DR. STOCKMANN.   But he didn't dare? No, that goes without saying.

HORSTER.   He says it's not easy, being a party man and all—

DR. STOCKMANN.   Now here's a truth from on high! A party is like a meat grinder. It grinds everyone's brains together into a dead-level mash—fatheads and meatheads, all together.

MRS. STOCKMANN.   Thomas, really now!   75

PETRA.   [*To HORSTER.*] If you hadn't taken us home, things might have been different for you.

HORSTER.   I have no regrets.

PETRA.   [*Extends her hand.*] Thank you for that!

HORSTER.   [*To DR. STOCKMANN.*] What I came to tell you is that I've another idea, if you're really resolved to leave—

DR. STOCKMANN.   Excellent! The sooner the better—   80

[*A knock is heard offstage.*]

MRS. STOCKMANN.   Shh! Someone's knocking.

PETRA.   It must be Uncle.

DR. STOCKMANN.   Ah! [*Calls.*] Come in!

MRS. STOCKMANN.   Dear Thomas, please promise me—

[*The MAYOR enters from the hallway door.*]

THE MAYOR.   You're busy. I can come back later—   85

DR. STOCKMANN.   Not at all. Come in.

THE MAYOR.   But I'd like to talk to you—just the two of us.

MRS. STOCKMANN.   We'll go to the living room.

HORSTER.   And I'll come back later.

DR. STOCKMANN.   No, please, Captain, stay with them. I'd like to hear more—   90

HORSTER.   I'll be glad to wait.

[*He follows* MRS. STOCKMANN *and* PETRA *into the living-room. The* MAYOR *says nothing but looks at the windows.*]

DR. STOCKMANN.   You may find quite a draft here today. Why don't you put on your hat?

THE MAYOR.   Thank you. [*Does so.*] I think I caught a cold last night. I stood and froze—

DR. STOCKMANN.   You did? I thought it was rather warm.

THE MAYOR.   I'm sorry I had no power to stop last night's excesses.   95

DR. STOCKMANN.   Do you have anything else in particular to tell me?

THE MAYOR.   [*Takes out a large envelope.*] This letter, from the Governing Board of the Spa.

DR. STOCKMANN.   My notice?

THE MAYOR.   Yes, bearing today's date. [*Puts the envelope on the desk.*] This is painful, but considering public opinion, we didn't dare do anything else.

DR. STOCKMANN.   [*Smiles.*] Didn't dare? I keep hearing echoes today!   100

THE MAYOR.   It's important for you to understand your present position. You can plan on no future medical practice here in town.

DR. STOCKMANN.   The practice be damned to hell! But why are you so sure?

THE MAYOR.   The Homeowners Association is circulating a petition from house to house recommending that responsible citizens stop using your services. I assure you that not a single family head will refuse to sign. Quite simply, no one will dare to refuse.

DR. STOCKMANN.   I don't doubt you. But what then?

THE MAYOR.   My advice is that you'd best leave town for a period.   105

DR. STOCKMANN.   Yes, I've been thinking about that.

THE MAYOR.   Good. And then after you've thought things out for a time—say half a year—after mature consideration you might find it fitting to write a brief apology admitting your mistake—

DR. STOCKMANN.   You mean that I might get my post back?

THE MAYOR.   Perhaps. It's not impossible.

DR. STOCKMANN.   But what about public opinion? You wouldn't dare go against   110
public opinion.

THE MAYOR.   Public opinion is variable. And, frankly, it's especially important to us to have some sort of written apology from you.

DR. STOCKMANN.   Oh, you're licking your chops for that! But for Christ's sake, don't you recall what I told you about such dirty tricks?

THE MAYOR.   Things were different then. You believed the whole town was behind you—

DR. STOCKMANN.   Yes, and now I believe the whole town's on my neck. [*Flares up.*] But even if the devil and his great-grandmother were on my neck—! Never! I say never!

THE MAYOR.   Thomas, a family man can't behave as you do. You have no right,   115
Thomas!

DR. STOCKMANN.   No right? There's only one thing in the world that free persons have no right to do, and do you know what that is?

THE MAYOR.   No.

DR. STOCKMANN. Naturally, but I'll tell you. Free persons have no right to get down and roll in filth—no right to lower themselves to the point where they're spitting in their own faces.

THE MAYOR. This has a jingle of plausibility, and it would explain your stubbornness if there were nothing else—. But there is—something else.

DR. STOCKMANN. What are you talking about? 120

THE MAYOR. You understand me very well. But as your brother, and as a man of perception, I advise you not to be too confident about prospects and hopes that may so easily fall through.

DR. STOCKMANN. Just what are you getting at?

THE MAYOR. Do you expect me to believe you know nothing about Mr. Kiil's will?

DR. STOCKMANN. Well, I know that his small estate will go to a foundation for old working people. But what does that have to do with me?

THE MAYOR. Well, first, the estate is not small. Mr. Tannerymaster Kiil is a rather 125
wealthy man.

DR. STOCKMANN. I never had any idea!

THE MAYOR. Oh—truly? None? You also had no idea that a not insignificant amount of his wealth will go to your children, and that you and your wife will enjoy the interest for life? Didn't he ever tell you?

DR. STOCKMANN. No, never a blessed word! Rather the reverse. He always blasts away interminably about ridiculously high taxes. But you're sure of all this, Peter?

THE MAYOR. I have it on the best authority.

DR. STOCKMANN. Then, praise God, Katrina's secure—and the children too! I'll 130
tell her right away. [Calls.] Katrina! Katrina!

THE MAYOR. [Holds him back.] Shh! Not a word yet!

MRS. STOCKMANN. [Opens the door.] What is it, Thomas?

DR. STOCKMANN. Not a thing. Wait inside a bit more. [She closes the door. He begins pacing.] Secure! And think—they're all secure, and for life. What a blessed feeling—to know you're secure!

THE MAYOR. Yes, but you're really not. Mr. Kiil the tanner can change his will whenever he wants.

DR. STOCKMANN. But, my good Peter, he won't. The old Badger is dancing for joy 135
at the way I went after you and your precious cohorts.

THE MAYOR. [Starts, and looks intently at him.] This puts things in a new light.

DR. STOCKMANN. What things?

THE MAYOR. This whole business was a coordinated maneuver. These wild and reckless slurs that you—in the name of truth—have aimed at our municipal leaders—

DR. STOCKMANN. Were what?

THE MAYOR. They were no more than an exchange for being named in that re- 140
vengeful old man's will.

DR. STOCKMANN. [Almost speechless.] Peter, you're the most nauseating scum I've ever known!

THE MAYOR. This is the end between us. Your dismissal is final, because we now have a weapon against you. [Leaves.]

DR. STOCKMANN. Oh, my God! [Calls toward the living room.] Katrina, scrub the floor after him! Have her bring a pail—God damn it—what's-her-name, with the sooty nose—

MRS. STOCKMANN. [At the living-room door.] Thomas, hush, hush!

PETRA. [Also at the door.] Father, Grandpa is here, and wants to speak with you 145
alone.

DR. STOCKMANN.   Why not? [*Goes to the door. PETRA and MRS. STOCKMANN leave. MORTEN KIIL enters and DR. STOCKMANN closes the door.*] Come in, Father. What is it? Please sit down.

MORTEN KIIL.   No, thank you. [*Looks around.*] You've made it look cosy here today, Stockmann.

DR. STOCKMANN.   Yes, doesn't it look that way?

MORTEN KIIL.   Really fine, and lots of fresh air. Today you have plenty of that oxeegin you talked about yesterday. You have a clear conscience today, I suppose.

DR. STOCKMANN.   Yes, I have.   150

MORTEN KIIL.   I believe it. [*Pats his coat pocket.*] Do you know what I've got here?

DR. STOCKMANN.   A clear conscience too, I hope.

MORTEN KIIL.   Bah! Better than that. [*Takes out a leather folder, opens it, and shows a sheaf of papers.*]

DR. STOCKMANN.   [*Looks at him in surprise.*] Shares in the Spa?

MORTEN KIIL.   It wasn't hard to buy 'em today.   155

DR. STOCKMANN.   And you've been out snapping them up—

MORTEN KIIL.   All I could afford.

DR. STOCKMANN.   But, my good Father, the Spa is in such desperate condition!

MORTEN KIIL.   If only you return to sanity, you can put it back in tune soon enough.

DR. STOCKMANN.   Well, you yourself can see I'm doing all I can. But—everyone in   160
town is crazy.

MORTEN KIIL.   You said yesterday that the worst pollution came from my tannery. If that's true, then my grandfather and my father before me and I myself have all been poisoning the town for many years, like three angels of death. Do you believe I can live with that kind of shame?

DR. STOCKMANN.   Well, you'll have to get used to it.

MORTEN KIIL.   No, thanks. I prize my good name and reputation. I hear that people call me "the Badger," which is a sort of pig. But there's no way on earth they'll be right about this. I'm going to live and die with a clean reputation.

DR. STOCKMANN.   How do you plan to do that?

MORTEN KIIL.   You're going to make me clean, Stockmann.   165

DR. STOCKMANN.   Me?

MORTEN KIIL.   Do you know what money I used for the shares? No, you don't, but I'll tell you. It's the money that Katrina, Petra, and the boys will have when I'm gone. Yes, you see, I've been able to salt a little away, despite everything.

DR. STOCKMANN.   [*With rising anger.*] You've used Katrina's inheritance for that!

MORTEN KIIL.   Yes. Everything is now sunk in the Spa. And now I'll find out, Stockmann, if you're a total lunatic! If you still say that tiny monsters and other such things come from my tannery, it's as though you're cutting wide strips of skin from the bodies of Katrina, and Petra, and the boys. A decent family man couldn't do that—unless he's totally crazy.

DR. STOCKMANN.   [*Paces.*] But I am totally crazy—totally!   170

MORTEN KIIL.   You can't be so raving, foaming crazy that you'd destroy your wife and children.

DR. STOCKMANN.   [*Stands in front of him.*] Why didn't you ask me before you bought all this trash?

MORTEN KIIL.   Once something's done, it's best to finish it.

DR. STOCKMANN.   [*Paces uneasily.*] If only I weren't so sure—. But I *am* sure! I'm absolutely positive!

MORTEN KIIL.   [*Weighs the folder in his hand.*] If you hang on to your insane ideas,   175
these will be worthless, you know. [*Returns the folder to his pocket.*]

DR. STOCKMANN.   God damn it all! Researchers should be able to unearth a coun-
teragent, some sort of antidote—

MORTEN KIIL.   To kill the tiny monsters?

DR. STOCKMANN.   Yes, or to make them harmless.

MORTEN KIIL.   Couldn't you try rat poison?

DR. STOCKMANN.   Don't be foolish.—But everyone says it's only my imagination.   180
Well, let's have it their way—it's imagination. Didn't the short-sighted curs censure me as
an enemy of the people—and weren't they howling to claw my clothes off, too?

MORTEN KIIL.   And all the windows they smashed for you!

DR. STOCKMANN.   And then there's my family responsibility. I'll take it up with
Katrina. She's superb on these things.

MORTEN KIIL.   Right, she's a sensible woman; listen to her.

DR. STOCKMANN.   [*Turns toward him.*] But you, how could you mess things up so totally? To gamble with Katrina's inheritance, and leave me in such a painful bind? When I
look at you, I think I'm seeing the devil himself.

MORTEN KIIL.   I can see it's time to go. But I want an answer before two o'clock. *Yes*   185
or *no.* With a "no," I'll will everything to my foundation before the day is over.

DR. STOCKMANN.   And what does Katrina get then?

MORTEN KIIL.   Not even a pinch of snuff.

[*The hall door opens, showing* HOVSTAD *and* ASLAKSEN *waiting to enter.*]

MORTEN KIIL.   Well, look at this pair!

DR. STOCKMANN.   [*Glares at them.*] What—? You dare come to see me?

HOVSTAD.   Yes, of course.   190

ASLAKSEN.   We've come to talk to you.

MORTEN KIIL.   [*Whispers to DR. STOCKMANN.*] "Yes" or "no," before two o'clock.

[*Leaves through the hallway door as* HOVSTAD *and* ASLAKSEN *enter.*]

ASLAKSEN.   [*Glances at* HOVSTAD.] Oho!

DR. STOCKMANN.   Well, what is it? And be quick!

HOVSTAD.   I understand how you feel about our stand toward you last night—   195

DR. STOCKMANN.   Oh, by all the devils in hell, you took a fine stand. You were as
upright as a bent-over crone. "Spineless" is the right word to describe you.

HOVSTAD.   Whatever you call it, we couldn't do anything else.

DR. STOCKMANN.   You mean you didn't *dare* do anything else. Is that more like it?

HOVSTAD.   Okay, say it your way.

ASLAKSEN.   But why didn't you tell us in advance, just a small hint to Mr. Hovstad   200
or me?

DR. STOCKMANN.   A hint? About what?

ASLAKSEN.   About the idea behind it.

DR. STOCKMANN.   I don't follow you.

ASLAKSEN.   [*Nods confidentially.*] Oh I'm sure you do, Dr. Stockmann.

HOVSTAD.   There's no reason to conceal things any longer.   205

DR. STOCKMANN.   [*Stares from one to the other.*] What in the God-damn hell—?

ASLAKSEN.   May I ask, isn't your father-in-law buying up shares in the Spa all over
town?

DR. STOCKMANN.   Yes, he's been buying shares today, but—?

ASLAKSEN.   It would have been wiser to have someone else do it—someone not so
closely related.

HOVSTAD.   And you shouldn't have used your own name. No one needed to know   210
where the criticism about the Spa came from. You should have taken me in with you, Dr.
Stockmann.

DR. STOCKMANN.   [*Stares ahead blankly; a light seems to dawn for him, and he speaks as
though struck from on high.*] Can this be possible? Can such things happen?

ASLAKSEN.   [*Smiles.*] They can indeed. But only if you have a little—strategy—if
you get my meaning.

HOVSTAD.   And you should bring in others, because there's less risk for the individual when others are with you.

DR. STOCKMANN.   [*Now composed.*] All right, gentlemen. What is it you want?

ASLAKSEN.   Mr. Hovstad should—   215

HOVSTAD.   No, *you* should explain, Aslaksen.

ASLAKSEN.   Well, now that we understand how things are fitting together, we
thought we could make the *Messenger* available to you.

DR. STOCKMANN.   Would you dare that now? What of public opinion? Aren't you
afraid of a storm of criticism?

HOVSTAD.   We'll ride that out.

ASLAKSEN.   And the Doctor must be ready to reverse positions quickly. As soon as   220
your attack has had its effect—

DR. STOCKMANN.   As soon as Mr. Kiil and I have bought all the shares at panic
prices, you mean—?

HOVSTAD.   I presume that you have a—scientific purpose?—in wishing to control
the Spa?

DR. STOCKMANN.   Oh yes. It was for a *scientific purpose* that I brought the Old Badger in with me. And so we'll fiddle a bit with the intake pipes, and look professional while
digging samples at the beach, and the town won't be out half a dollar. Doesn't that sound
good?

HOVSTAD.   I agree—particularly if you have the *Messenger* with you.

ASLAKSEN.   In a free society the Press is powerful, Doctor.   225

DR. STOCKMANN.   Definitely, and so is public opinion. And you, Mr. Aslaksen, you
will act as the conscience of the Homeowners Association?

ASLAKSEN.   Of both the Homeowners Association *and* the Temperance Society.
Bank on it.

DR. STOCKMANN.   But gentlemen—I'm ashamed to ask about it, but what consideration for you—?

HOVSTAD.   You understand that we'd prefer to help you for nothing. But *The
People's Messenger* is on wobbly legs. Things are not right, and I really don't want to close
the paper now, when there's so much to work for in the larger political scene.

DR. STOCKMANN.   I agree. That would be hard for a *friend* of the people like you.   230
[*Flares up.*] But I'm an *enemy* of the people! [*Searches around.*] Where did I put my stick?
Where the hell's the stick?

HOVSTAD.   What's all this?

ASLAKSEN.   You'd never—?

DR. STOCKMANN.   [*Stands.*] Well, suppose I don't give you a dime's worth of my
shares. Don't forget that the rich stay rich by hanging onto their money!

HOVSTAD.   Well, don't forget that your manipulation of shares can be reported in
more than one way!

DR. STOCKMANN.   And you have just the talent for it! If I don't help the *Messenger*,   235
you'll put a sinister turn on everything. You'll come howling after me and try to choke me
the way a hound chokes a rabbit.

HOVSTAD.   That's nature's way; the strongest animals survive.

ASLAKSEN.   And take the nearest food, too.

DR. STOCKMANN.   [*While searching around.*] Then go find yours in a gutter, damn it, because we're about to see which of the three of us is the strongest animal! [*Finds his umbrella and waves it.*] Here you go!

HOVSTAD.   You can't be violent!

ASLAKSEN.   Be careful with that umbrella!   240

DR. STOCKMANN.   Out the window with you, Mr. Hovstad!

HOVSTAD.   [*At the hallway door.*] You're mad!

DR. STOCKMANN.   Out the window, Mr. Aslaksen! I tell you, jump! Distinguish yourself by being first for once!

ASLAKSEN.   [*Dodges him at the desk.*] Moderation, Doctor! I'm not strong! I can't do this! [*Shouts.*] Help! Help!

[*MRS. STOCKMANN, PETRA, and HORSTER from the living room.*]

MRS. STOCKMANN.   For the love of God! Thomas, what's going on here?   245

DR. STOCKMANN.   [*Swings the umbrella.*] Jump, I tell you! Into the gutter!

HOVSTAD.   This is an unprovoked attack! I call you as a witness, Captain Horster! [*Rushes out down the hall.*]

ASLAKSEN.   [*In confusion.*] If only I knew the way out—[*Slips out through the living-room door.*]

MRS. STOCKMANN.   [*Restrains DR. STOCKMANN.*] Thomas, control yourself!

DR. STOCKMANN.   [*Throws down the umbrella.*] Damn, they got away after all!   250

MRS. STOCKMANN.   But what was it they wanted with you?

DR. STOCKMANN.   I'll tell you later; I've got to do something else right now. [*Goes to the desk and writes on a card.*] Katrina, what's written here?

MRS. STOCKMANN.   "No! No! No!" What does it mean?

DR. STOCKMANN.   I'll explain that later, too. [*Holds out the card.*] Petra, tell Soot-face to run this over to the Badger as fast as she can. Hurry! [*PETRA takes the card and leaves through the hallway door.*] Today I've been hounded by all the devils of hell! But now I'll use my pen to stab them! My ink will be venom and gall to poison them! My inkpot will crack their skulls!

MRS. STOCKMANN.   Yes, but we're leaving the country, Thomas.   255

[*PETRA returns.*]

DR. STOCKMANN.   Well?

PETRA.   She took it.

DR. STOCKMANN.   Great!—Leaving, you say? No, I'll be damned if we leave! We're staying where we are, Katrina.

PETRA.   We're staying?

MRS. STOCKMANN.   Here, in town?   260

DR. STOCKMANN.   Yes, here, absolutely. The battlefield is here; the fight will be here; and I'll win here! But we've got to have a roof over our heads. Once you stitch up my trousers, I'll go out to find another house.

HORSTER.   But you can share my house.

DR. STOCKMANN.   I can?

HORSTER.   Absolutely. I've got plenty of room, and I'm almost never home.

MRS. STOCKMANN.   Captain Horster, you're so sweet!   265

PETRA.   Thank you!

DR. STOCKMANN.   [*Shakes his hand.*] Thank you, thank you. Well, with that trouble past I can begin things in earnest. There are hundreds of things to look into, Katrina, and I'll be able to do it almost full-time—I meant to tell you earlier—because I've been sacked at the Spa.

MRS. STOCKMANN.   [*Sighs.*] I expected that.

DR. STOCKMANN.   And they're taking away my practice, too. Well, so what? I still have all the poor people, the ones who can't pay, and, God in Heaven, they're the ones who need me most. Well, damn it, those little tyrants will have to listen to me! I'll preach to them both in season and out of season, as it's written somewhere!

MRS. STOCKMANN.   But dearest Thomas, I think you've seen what comes from   270
preaching.

DR. STOCKMANN.   Katrina, don't be absurd! Should I let myself be destroyed by public opinion and the solid majority and all that devilish drivel? No thanks! What I want is plain and clear and simple. I only want to pound it into the skulls of these mongrels that the so-called progressive thinkers are the most treacherous enemies of freedom, that party policies wring the neck of every young and promising truth, that political expediency turns morality and justice upside down, and that the result of all this is that they're making life here a total nightmare. Don't you think, Captain Horster, I can make people understand this?

HORSTER.   I'm sure you can. I don't know much about such things.

DR. STOCKMANN.   Well, you see; listen. The ones to be exterminated are the party bigwigs. A party leader is like the dominant wolf in a pack. To stay on top, he has to keep cutting down his rivals, or otherwise he's finished. Take Hovstad and Aslaksen, for example. How many rivals have they sent howling—or in any event clawed and bitten until they can do nothing more than join the Homeowners Association or subscribe to *The People's Messenger*? [*Sits at the edge of the desk.*] Come here, Katrina—. See the lovely sunlight streaming in. And breathe in that wonderfully fresh springtime air!

MRS. STOCKMANN.   If only we could live on sunshine and fresh air, Thomas!

DR. STOCKMANN.   I know, you'll have to pinch pennies for a while, but that's   275
minor; things will be all right. What worries me is that there's no one around with the dedication to *real* freedom of thought to take up my work after me.

PETRA.   Father, don't talk like that. You've lots of time. [*EILIF and MORTEN enter from the living room.*] Well hello, here come the boys already.

MRS. STOCKMANN.   Did you get a holiday?

MORTEN.   No. We had a fight with some other boys at recess.

EILIF.   They were the ones who started it!

MORTEN.   Right, and so Mr. Rørlund sent us home for a couple of days.   280

DR. STOCKMANN.   [*Snaps his fingers and jumps off the desk.*] That's it! By God, I've got it! You'll never set foot in school again!

BOTH BOYS.   Yay! No more school!

MRS. STOCKMANN.   But Thomas!

DR. STOCKMANN.   I said never! I'll be your teacher. I mean you'll never learn anything in God's creation—

MORTEN.   Hooray!   285

DR. STOCKMANN.   —if I don't turn you into men of distinction and independent minds. Petra, you'll have to help me with this.

PETRA.   Father, count on me.

DR. STOCKMANN.   And I'll hold classes in the very room where they vilified me as an enemy of the people. But we need more; I'll need at least a dozen children to begin with.

MRS. STOCKMANN.   You won't get that kind in this town.

DR. STOCKMANN.   We can. [*To the boys.*] You must know some street kids—society's   290
real castaways?

MORTEN. Sure thing, Father, I know loads of 'em!

DR. STOCKMANN. Fine! Bring a few of them to me. This time I'm going to experiment with the mongrels themselves. There may be some remarkable minds there.

MORTEN. And what will we do once we grow to be men of distinction and independent minds?

DR. STOCKMANN. Boys, you'll drive all the wolves back into the wilderness!

[EILIF *looks skeptical;* MORTEN *jumps and cheers.*]

MRS. STOCKMANN. Let's hope it's not the wolves who drive *you* away, Thomas.   295

DR. STOCKMANN. Don't be foolish, Katrina! Drive me out?—Now, when I'm the strongest man in town?

MRS. STOCKMANN. The strongest—now?

DR. STOCKMANN. Yes, and I'll go so far to say that now I'm one of the strongest men in the whole world!

MORTEN. Right on!

DR. STOCKMANN. [*Lowers his voice.*] Shh! Don't say anything yet, but I've made an-   300
other great discovery.

MRS. STOCKMANN. Another one?

DR. STOCKMANN. Yes, certainly, certainly. [*Gathers them around him, and speaks fervently.*] My discovery, you see, is that the strongest person in the world is the one who stands most alone.

MRS. STOCKMANN. [*Smiles and shakes her head.*] Oh, Thomas!

PETRA. [*Confidently takes his hands.*] Father!

End of the Play

QUESTIONS

Act 1

1. Why does Ibsen introduce the Mayor before Dr. Stockmann?
2. What traits does the Mayor show in his conversations with Hovstad and Dr. Stockmann? In what ways are these traits important?
3. Why does Dr. Stockmann wish at first to hold back the publication of the paper he had written the previous winter?
4. Why does Ibsen include the casual conversation scenes before Petra's first entrance and after Dr. Stockmann leaves for his study? What do we learn about the various characters in these scenes?
5. What is Dr. Stockmann's discovery about the town spa? What is his view of the situation? To what degree is he naive about the effects of his discovery?

Act 2

6. Describe Morten Kiil. What is his relationship with Dr. Stockmann? What does he know about science? What is ironic and comic about his promise to benefit the poor?
7. During his discussion with Dr. Stockmann, how does Hovstad escalate the issue of the water pollution? Why are these conversations important?
8. Who is Aslaksen? What does he represent? Why is he interesting? In what ways does he seem to be a flat character? Why does he refer to "moderation" here and throughout the play?

9. Describe the development of the scene between Dr. Stockmann and the Mayor. What are the Mayor's responses to Dr. Stockmann's discovery? How valid is the Mayor's position? If *you* lived in the town, what would you think about Dr. Stockmann's discovery?

10. Assume that speeches 200–225 represent a point when genuinely creative discussion and compromise might occur. In light of the characters of the brothers, why does the situation between them deteriorate, bringing about anger rather than understanding?

Act 3

11. How do the opening references to boxing and military ordnance provide a theme for this act?

12. How are Dr. Stockmann's new views of the spa situation different from those he had in Act 1? How has his conversation with the Mayor influenced his attitude?

13. What attitudes toward Dr. Stockmann are brought out in the conversations of Billing, Hovstad, and Aslaksen? What character traits of these men does Ibsen bring out?

14. Why does Petra return the English story to Hovstad? What is the meaning of the scene between them?

15. Describe the process by which the Mayor undermines Dr. Stockmann's report. Why does the Mayor attack Dr. Stockmann's character?

16. What is the effect on Dr. Stockmann of the entry of his wife? Characterize the relationship between them.

17. Explain the tension between Dr. Stockmann and the Mayor. How does the changing allegiance of Hovstad and Aslaksen contribute to this tension? How does Dr. Stockmann feel at the end of the act?

Act 4

18. Why does Horster offer Dr. Stockmann his home for the meeting and, later, for living and teaching (and earlier had offered the home to Petra for teaching)?

19. How does the Mayor, with Aslaksen, take over the meeting? How does this action contribute to the play's theme against the popular majority?

20. How do the Mayor and Aslaksen attack Dr. Stockmann's integrity? How does Dr. Stockmann overcome their maneuvers?

21. Describe Dr. Stockmann's speeches against the popular majority. What is the basis of his criticism? How are his ideas connected with Hovstad's ideas in Act II? What ideas are new (e.g., the majority–minority polarity, the analogy with animals, the need for exterminating corrupt societies)? Why does he include the Mayor in his attack?

22. Why are the appearances of Pettersen, the drunk, important? Why are the crowd responses important?

23. Explain Dr. Stockmann's assertions that truths can live for no more than eighteen to twenty years (speech 124).

24. What is the effect of Dr. Stockmann's quotations of the New Testament passages at the end of the act?

Act 5

25. What is the physical state of Dr. Stockmann's study? Why is it in this condition?

26. Describe the effect of the verbal pattern "didn't dare not to" in the course of the act. Connect this pattern to the theme about public opinion and the popular majority.

27. Why does the Mayor describe the last will and testament of Morten Kiil? How does this news precipitate the final break between the two brothers?

28. Describe the attitudes of Hovstad and Aslaksen in this act. How have they changed? How are their speeches hypocritical? Why does Dr. Stockmann threaten them?

29. What choice does Morten Kiil offer Dr. Stockmann? How might this choice be taken as the crisis and climax of the play? How does his choice parallel the development of his attitudes in Act 3?

30. Why does the play end on the news of Dr. Stockmann's latest discovery? How does this discovery reflect what has happened to him?

GENERAL QUESTIONS

1. Consider *An Enemy of the People* as a realistic drama. What particularly realistic devices does Ibsen utilize (e.g., time, place, the positions and relationships of scenery and properties, motivation)? How heavily does Ibsen rely upon sudden changes and unforeseen developments? What is the effect of such theatrical changes?

2. Trace the theme of the *friend/enemy of the people* in the course of the play. How does the term fit Dr. Stockmann, first as a friend, then as an enemy? How might the term be explained as ironic? What role is he playing at the play's end?

3. Characterize Dr. Stockmann. Consider things such as his idealism, pride, bravery, individuality, temper, political awareness, degree of cooperativeness, attitude toward his wife, general attitude toward his family, and the attitude of others toward him. How correct are the Mayor's opinions about him?

4. Defend the proposition that Dr. Stockmann's attack against the popular majority is more accurately explained as an attack against the *political and hypocritical manipulation* of the popular majority.

5. Explain the opposition in the play of minority versus majority rights. What is the connection between individual rights and Dr. Stockmann's insistence on, first, drawing, proclaiming, and publishing his own professional discoveries and opinions, and, later, educating young children to have "independent minds"? You might also consider the recurring references to public opinion and Dr. Stockmann's attack against political parties in Act 5.

6. Explain the symbolic value of the Mølledal tanneries. What is the realistic meaning of the tanneries? How important are the tanneries in the play's development? Explain the use and meaning of other symbols in the play.

7. Describe the shortcomings and limitations of Dr. Stockmann's arguments in Act 4. Why do some of his ideas seem incorrect and even naïve?

8. What do you find in the play that is comic? Why do you think Ibsen included humor?

9. Write a character study of any of the major or minor characters in *An Enemy of the People*.

Special Topics for Writing and Argument about Ibsen

1. Ibsen's realism: places, situations, characters, conflicts, outcomes.
2. The permanence and importance of Ibsen's subject material: accuracy, comprehensiveness, insightfulness, and relevance then and now.
3. Organizational patterns in Ibsen's plays.
4. Ibsen's major characters: their natures, excellences, shortcomings.
5. The major antagonists in Ibsen: their interests, characteristics, and actions.
6. Ibsen's use of minor characters: their qualities, roundness or flatness, effects on major characters, and rewards or punishments.
7. The predicaments and dilemmas faced by Ibsen's major characters.
8. Ibsen's treatment of women: their nature, their relationships with men, their interests, their attempts to find identity and security.
9. Morality, ethics, and personal integrity in the makeup of Ibsen's characters and in the problems put forth in the plays.
10. The formal structures of Ibsen's plays.
11. Ibsen's use of symbols.
12. Ibsen's dialogue: the shorter speeches and their use; the situations in which he uses longer speeches, and their dramatic and ideological purposes.
13. Ibsen's use of humor and irony.
14. Law and legality as a force in the plays, whether for good or bad, reward or threat.
15. Ibsen's exposure of subterfuge and hypocrisy.
16. Problems in the staging of Ibsen's plays.

❧ EDITED SELECTIONS FROM CRITICISM OF IBSEN'S DRAMA

The following selected criticism is intended to supply details and ideas for essays on Ibsen's plays, particularly *A Dollhouse* and *An Enemy of the People*. For a more detailed bibliography, consult the "Bibliographic Sources" section (p. 1759), which may be augmented with your college library catalogue and the most recent volumes of the *MLA International Bibliography* available in your library's reference room. The bracketed page numbers refer to the original pagination of the sources included here. Footnotes, original Norwegian passages, and unnecessary references have been deleted here.

Freedom, Truth, and Society—Rhetoric and Reality*

During the night of 9 January 1871, a young Dane lay awake in his hospital bed in Rome [68] writing. He was committing to paper a poem to which he had given the title 'To Henrik Ibsen'. He had recently received a letter from Ibsen—a letter carrying a powerful appeal

---

*From Bjorn Hemmer, "Ibsen and the Realistic Problem Drama," in James McFarlane, ed., *The Cambridge Companion to Ibsen* (Cambridge: Cambridge UP, 1994).

to him to put himself at the head of the 'revolution of the human spirit' which the age cried out for. In the poem which formed his enthusiastic response, the young Dane—the critic Georg Brandes (1842–1927)—described how all those mendacious and authoritarian forces of the contemporary age would be brought low when 'the intellectuals' made their revolt. And he raised the banner of freedom and progress with the words: 'Truth and Freedom are one and the same.'

Time after time in the years that followed, Ibsen was himself to raise this same revolutionary banner—with truth and freedom as the central watchwords. In later years these concepts could sound both abstract and ambiguous; nevertheless, within their historical context, they served as a battle cry in the struggle against the prevailing situation. 'Truth' alone—that truth of the new age such as a Brandes and an Ibsen saw it—could achieve liberation. Without truth there could be no change, no genuine 'freedom'. This was the ideological basis for that quartet of realistic social plays which Ibsen published in the years between 1877 and 1882: *Pillars of Society, A Doll's House, Ghosts* and *An Enemy of the People.* In both the first and the last of these plays the double-barrelled phrase 'truth and freedom' is used as a rallying cry and as a definition of what in the final instance the problematic reality of the day—'society'—lacked. This was the battle-ground on which Ibsen and Brandes found each other and where they could make common cause. However unlike they may have been, one thing they were agreed on: that *they* were conducting the case for progress and the future. They did nor stand alone, but they must be counted as the indisputable leaders in the campaign for a modern, radical and realistic literature in the cultural life of Scandinavia of this age. It was these two who most power- [69] fully challenged the values of the existing middle-class society and who formulated the basic rights and liberties of the individual.

In November of the same year in which he wrote his poem to Ibsen, Brandes began a series of public lectures in Copenhagen on the literature of nineteenth-century Europe. These lectures provoked great attention and controversy, precisely because in them Brandes called upon writers to revolt. He did it in the light of an ideology of liberation which he himself linked directly to the ideas of freedom which underlay the French Revolution of 1789.

His main concern, Brandes declared, was not *political* opposition, for political liberty had very largely been assured. What was at stake was 'liberty of the spirit', 'liberty of thought and of the human condition'. The entire range of 'social values' would have to be changed radically by the younger generation before a new and vigorous literature could begin any new growth. But in Brandes's view it was surely the writers themselves who ought to take the lead in this work on behalf of progress.

What Brandes directs his criticism against is a conservative, stagnant society which 'under the mask of liberty has all the features of tyranny'. His target is Victorian society with its facade of false morality and its manipulation of public opinion. It is this same kind of society that Ibsen turns the searchlight on in his first realistic dramas. The people who live in such a society know the weight of 'public opinion' and of all those agencies which keep watch over society's 'law and order': the norms, the conventions and the traditions which in essence belong to the past but which continue into the present and there thwart individual liberty in a variety of ways. Not all see this as a problem. Consul Bernick, the bank manager Torvald Helmer and Pastor Manders have all accepted the premises for this kind of bourgeois living and have adapted to society's demands—without any awareness of the cost in human terms. In their own estimation, their task is to confirm the existing social structure—'pillars of society'.

The point that Ibsen and Brandes were making was that this kind of society could not satisfy the natural need of the individual for freedom. It all had to do with power,

with status and with the role of the sexes. The repressive attitude of bourgeois society to-   [70]
wards everything that threatened its own position of power demonstrated only too clearly how far it had moved from the standpoint of the revolutionary citizens of 1789. The
question of political and spiritual liberty had been thrust into the background by what
had constantly been the motivating force in the life of the individual: economic freedom.
Capital gave a position of power in society; and once those positions had been won, the
bourgeois individual had acquired something which had to be defended. In this way, the
bourgeois individual became a defender of the status quo and a traitor to his own officially expressed values. Official rhetoric was one thing; the realities on the other hand
were something else.

It is this which forms the background to Ibsen's and Brandes's criticism of contemporary society. They found in their age a clear dichotomy between ideology and practice,
a contradiction between the official and the private life of the bourgeois individual. Behind the splendour of the Victorian family facade there was to be found a much murkier
reality. It was precisely these contradictions, this problematical element, in the bourgeois
world that Ibsen made his special field as a realistic commentator on contemporary life.
Both Ibsen and Brandes wanted to make the individual the sustaining element in society
and thereby dethrone the bourgeois family as the central institution of society. From the
perspective of the bourgeois individual the family is a micro-society which mirrors the nature of the macro-society and which is to bear witness to its health. In *Pillars of Society* the
scoundrelly Consul Bernick is praised by the young teacher Rørlund for his 'exemplary
family life'; and the consul's fellow-conspirator, the businessman Rummel, delivers himself of the following pronouncement: 'A man's home ought to be like a showcase'. But he
himself recommends an *arranged* family tableau behind the glass walls.

In the spirit of liberalism, Ibsen lets the individual's status in the family stand as an
illustration of his position in the wider society. The power structure within the walls of the
domestic home reflects the hierarchical power structures which prevail in the wider
world. But those who participate in public life also encounter other repressive forces.
Consul Bernick eventually admits that he feels like an isolated tool of an uncomprehending and crippled society, controlled in all his actions.

The main social perspective in Ibsen's first realistic plays coincides with the perspective of Brandes's lecture series on 'Main Currents in Nineteenth Century Literature'.
Here Brandes had presented a well-formulated programme for a new 'modern' literature. His challenge to his fellow authors was primarily that they should enter into their   [71]
own times and make contemporary concrete reality the subject of their writing: 'What
shows a literature in our own day to be a living thing is the fact of its subjecting problems
to debate. . . For a literature to submit nothing to debate is tantamount to its being in the
process of losing all significance.

What sort of 'problems' he had in mind is illustrated by the examples he immediately adduces: marriage, religion, property rights, the relationships between the sexes,
and social conditions. The objectives of his programme seem to have been both social
and aesthetic. Brandes's idea was not that literature should become an instrument of abstract debate about prevailing social problems; his intention was to point out that if literature was to have any useful function at all, it had to come to grips with those conditions
which invade and determine the concrete existence of the individual. Literature—as he
put it—was to deal with 'our life', not with 'our dreams'.

If Ibsen's dramas in the period 1877 to 1882 have come to be designated as realistic *problem* plays, this has to be seen against the background of Brandes's formula-like
statement. Some Ibsen scholars prefer the rubric 'critical realism'; others again have chosen to apply the term 'modern contemporary drama' to the whole series of works after

1877. Each of these different designations nevertheless has a bearing on one or other of the central elements in the kind of literary realism which Ibsen practised: on social problems, on critical perspective and contemporaneity. Indeed this last is often accepted as one of the defining characteristics of realism: '*Il faut être de temps.*'

Within the framework of these dramas, Ibsen concentrates on some phase in the contemporary situation where a latent crisis suddenly becomes visible. In this way he was able to embody contemporary social problems through the medium of an individual's destiny. This is another of realism's main tenets in the matter of individual characterization: the particular is to throw light on the general, and from one's response to a particular individual one should be able to glimpse the socially representative type. This, according to René Wellek, is an almost universal demand in theories of realism. It marks not only a polemical break with romantic characterization, but is also linked to realism's demand for objective reality and to its implicit didactic tendency. 'Truth' and 'sincerity' are concepts central to Linda Nochlin's account of the realists' own definition of where they stand. It may sound paradoxical to say that the realists combined on the one hand a wish for the objective presentation of reality with a didactic purpose on the other; but the paradox is illusory. A work of realism aspires to convey a moral message of general validity, and this is why the realist has need of the socially representative type. In Ibsen this [72] sometimes leads to a difficult balancing act between over-explicitness and caricatured characterization on the one hand, and on the other an objective evocation of plausible human types, where the author's presence is less evident. Viewed from a later standpoint in time, there are some things—particularly his treatment of selected male characters— that might prompt one to set a question mark against his 'realism'.

* * *

In his poetic practice, Ibsen demonstrates time after time that he conceives of truth as something individual and subjective. It is always the minority which is right. This [73] is why he lets Nora go out into the world alone both to find out who she really is and to be able to re-assess values and concepts. Ibsen has her sweep aside any doubts about what the problem is: 'I must try to discover who is right, society or me'. She admits her husband is right when he says she no longer understands the society they live in. As a dramatist, Ibsen must make it evident to his audience that Nora, as the drama moves towards its close, is truer and freer than before—and that her path is one of general validity. Helmer has mobilized the rhetoric of established society to keep Nora within the framework of the community and of the family. The reaction of the public was—and possibly still is— dependent on whether Nora's (and Ibsen's) use of an alternative rhetoric carries greater weight and conviction.

Nora's situation illustrates the pattern central to Ibsen's realistic problem dramas: the individual in opposition to a hostile society. The structure of the conflict is simple— and nobody can be in any doubt as to where the author's sympathies lie. Collective aberration about which ideals or values are true and which are false means that Ibsen sets in motion a process whereby concepts which are central to the bourgeois world are subject to re-definition. It is a striking feature of, for example, *Ghosts* that the reactionary Manders and the radical Helene Alving both make use of the concept of 'the ideal', despite their having totally contradictory views of the meaning of 'truth' and of individual 'freedom' in life. Ibsen clearly saw that the concepts of established bourgeois society needed a new content—something which he himself drew attention to in a letter to Brandes. In this same letter he writes of the need for 'a revolution of the human spirit', and claimed that the 1789 rallying-cry of 'Liberty, equality, fraternity' needed filling with new meaning.

Perhaps the battle-lines between the conservative bourgeoisie and the radical intelligentsia in Scandinavia in this age of Ibsen and Brandes were not as clearly drawn as all this might suggest. The literary history of Northern Europe has very largely been based on the premises of radicalism. The perspective may not entirely falsify history, but it does somewhat oversimplify it. There are distinctly conservative elements to be found in Ibsen's works of social criticism; and he gave clear acknowledgement of the part he played within the society he was attacking: 'One never stands totally without some share of responsibility or guilt in the society to which one belongs'. This is why he defines, in one and the same breath, the writing of poetry as the passing of judgement upon one's own self. Some of the phenomena he criticized were things he well knew from his own inner life. Honest introspection—what he was inclined to call 'self-anatomy'—had made   [74] it clear to him that he too bore the stamp of the Victorian society of the day. Life and learning were not always the same, as he admitted in a speech to Norwegian students in Christiania in 1874. The irony directed at those who histrionically held high the banner of the ideal at no great cost to themselves lost none of its point when applied to himself and to fellow writers.

Nevertheless he stood distanced, an outsider, from the society he was criticizing. Like Brandes, he was marginalized in respect of the collective life of his own people—not least by the concrete fact of his own twenty-seven years in exile. It was a stance which gave Ibsen both a personal freedom as an artist and also the clarifying perspective of distance—something he always claimed as a necessity for himself as a writer.

It is something of a paradox that, in this socially critical phase of his authorship, he was able to create a large and broadly based market among the wider European public for his art. What he had to offer to this bourgeois public was a successive chronicling of their own vices and lies. Granted the setting of his works was Norwegian, but the perspective on Victorian morality was international enough when he allowed it to reveal its defects.

It is not to be wondered at that Ibsen's dramas provoked scandal and outrage. Yet at the same time he won a large following, including many of those whom he had attacked. Even a proportion of 'the pillars of society' found it worthwhile to listen to what this author had to say. This could well imply that bourgeois society had not entirely lost its sense of its past and of its own lost ideals. Even bourgeois society was ready to acknowledge that contemporary reality might have its problems—with socially destabilizing phenomena like industrialization, positivism, liberalism, secularization, political polarization and the like. Society in the 1870s was becoming increasingly fluid. Only the most conservative forces wished to defend its 'law and order' by neutralizing such 'enemies of the people' as Ibsen and Brandes. But strong resistance could be found—and this gave Ibsen an adversary and the stuff of conflict for his dramas. The opposition consisted of all those who wished to withdraw within the circle of their own little community, their small township or their family—there to defend their world against the threat from the new or larger world 'out there'. Ibsen himself in these years was a resident of this wider and freer European cultural scene. And he wrote about Norwegian provincial life. When for his first realistic problem drama he chose as its setting 'a small, Norwegian coastal town', this was clearly connected to its being a milieu he was greatly familiar with from his childhood and early years. As an observant outsider he had lived in a small community of this kind—in Grimstad in the 1840s—and it was here he had first begun his career as a writer. Patterns and tensions—social, economic and psychological—present themselves much   [75] more clearly in a small and easily surveyable community of this kind than in a larger and more pluralist society. For a dramatist, a society of this sort could nicely function as a social laboratory.

The Story Behind *An Enemy of the People**

The plot of *An Enemy of the People* had its origin in two actual incidents. Alfred Meisner, a young German poet whom Ibsen knew in Munich, had told him how, when his father had been medical officer at the spa of Teiplitz in the eighteen-thirties, there had occurred an outbreak of cholera which the Doctor felt it his duty to make known publicly. As a result the season was ruined and the citizens of Teiplitz became so enraged that they stoned the Doctor's house and forced him to flee the town.

Then there had been the case in Norway of a chemist named Harald Thaulow. For nearly ten years Thaulow had furiously attacked the Christiania Steam Kitchens for neglecting their duty towards the city's poor. He had delivered a violent speech on the subject in 1874, during Ibsen's visit to Norway; and on 23 February 1881, only a fortnight before he died, Thaulow had attempted to read a prepared speech at the annual general meeting of the Steam Kitchens. The chairman of the meeting tried to prevent him from speaking, and eventually the public forced him, amid commotion, to withdraw. Ibsen read a report of this meeting in *Aftenposten*, just at the time when his indignation at the reception of *Ghosts* was reaching its climax, and he must have recognised in the eccentric old chemist a spirit very kindred to its own. . . .

As with *The Pillars of Society*, an English Member of Parliament may also have con- [312] tributed something to the play. Charles Bradlaugh, having narrowly escaped imprisonment for his part in a pamphlet advocating birth control (he had actually been sentenced, but had escaped on appeal) had, been elected Radical M.P. for Northhampton in 1880, but had been barred from taking his seat on the ground that, since he was a confessed free-thinker, the oath would not bind him. New elections were held in Northampton, and he was returned each time, but was still excluded; in 1881, he was forcibly removed from the house by ten policemen. It was not until 1886 that a new Speaker granted him the right to take the oath and sit. 'You should hear Ibsen on Bradlaugh—he has the most vivid sympathy for him', wrote William Archer to his brother Charles on 14 March 1882, when Ibsen was about to start writing *An Enemy of the People;* and Bradlaugh has an obvious deal in common with Dr. Stockmann. . . . But, as Ibsen stated in his letter to Hegel of 9 September 1882, he himself was probably the chief model for the characters, at any rate in Act Four; and it is worth remembering that the house in Skien in which Ibsen had been born had been called Stockmannsgården. . . .

An Enemy of the People was published on 28 November 1882, in an edition (despite [314] the calamitous sales of *Ghosts*) of ten thousand copies. Its reception was mixed. Not surprisingly, Dr. Stockmann's hard remarks about political parties offended all the reviewers who belonged to either; a contemporary cartoon showed Ibsen chastising first the Liberals to the delight of the Tories, then the Tories to the delight of the Liberals, and finally, in the person of Dr. Stockmann, both together. Henrik Jæger, fresh from lecturing against *Ghosts* round the country, declared in *Afterposten* that *An Enemy of the People* was 'personally the most likeable, psychologically the most interesting, and aesthetically the weakest of Ibsen's plays'. Arne Garborg, in *Nyt Tidsskrift* praised its technique but complained that 'there is a great deal of violent swearing', and that the public meeting in Act Four, which evidently nettled him, was 'rather detached and distant, almost as though portrayed from some other age but in a modern setting'. Erik Vullum in *Dagbladet* objected that, just as Bjørnson had been going round the country 'and even in America', holding meetings to proclaim his convictions about truth and justice, so 'now Ibsen

*From Michael Meyer, *Henrik Ibsen: The Farewell to Poetry 1864–1882* (London: Hart-Davis, 1971).

comes and does exactly the same; he holds public meetings from town to town, and the public has to pay to attend them'. . . .

The theatres seized eagerly upon the play. The Christiania Theatre and the Royal Theatres of Copenhagen and Stockholm, all of which had rejected *Ghosts* as unfit for public presentation, immediately acquired production rights of *An Enemy of the People*, apparently unembarrassed by the fact that its theme was the unworthiness of those who 'do not dare'. Hans Schrøder, the director of the Christiania Theatre, telegraphed Ibsen for permission to give the first public performance of the play, and Ibsen agreed, stinging them for a lump payment of 4,000 crowns (£ 222); he had let them have *A Doll's House* for 2,500 crowns (£ 139). During December he wrote Schrøder three letters which have only recently come to light, and which are indispensable reading to any director attempting to stage the play:

[315]
[316]

Rome, 14 December 1882

Permit me to address to you a few lines concerning the forthcoming production of *An Enemy of the People*. It is not my intention or wish to attempt to influence *in absentio* either the staging or the casting; but the expression of certain feelings which I hold regarding various aspects of the play can do no harm.

I trust I may assume that Mrs. Wolf will play Mrs Stockmann. . . . If for the role of Hovstad you have an otherwise suitable actor of not too heroic build, that is the kind of man you should choose. Hovstad is the son of poor people, has grown up in a dirty home on wretched and inadequate food, has frozen and toiled horribly throughout his childhood, and subsequently, as a poverty-stricken young man, has had to undergo considerable privation. Such living conditions leave their mark not only on a man's spirit but also on his outward appearance. Men of heroic exterior are an exception among the plebs. Whatever the circumstances Hovstad must always wear a depressed appearance, somewhat shrunken and stooping, and uncertain in his movements; all, of course, portrayed with complete naturalism.

Billing's lines are so worded that they require an east-coast and not e.g. a Bergen dialect. He is, essentially, an east-coast character.

Captain Horster has been ridiculously misunderstood by a Danish critic. He characterises Horster as an old man, Dr. Stockmann's old friend, etc. This is, of course, utterly wrong. Horster is a young man, one of the young people whose healthy appetite delights the Doctor, though he is an infrequent visitor at the house because he dislikes the company of Hovstad and Billing. Already in Act One, Horster's interest in Petra must subtly and delicately be indicated, and during the brief exchanges between him and her in Act Five we must sense that they stand at the threshold of a deep and passionate relationship.

Both the boys must be carefully instructed so that the difference in their characters is clearly established. And I must beg that in Act Four every possible actor at your disposal be used. The stage director must here enjoin the greatest possible naturalism and strictly forbid any caricaturing or exaggeration. The more realistic characters you can work into the crowd the better.

[317]

Throughout the play the stage director must inexorably insist that none of the players alters his or her lines. They must be spoken exactly as they stand in the text. A lively tempo is desirable. When I was last at the Christiania Theatre the speech seemed to me to be very slow.

But above all, truthfulness to nature—the illusion that everything is real and that one is sitting and watching something that is actually taking place in real life. *An Enemy of the People* is not easy to stage. It demands exceptionally well-drilled ensemble playing, i.e. protracted and meticulously supervised rehearsals. But I rely upon the good-will of all concerned . . .

On 31 December Ibsen wrote again:

I fear I must once again trouble you with a few lines. From your kind letter which reached me yesterday I gather it is intended to have both the boys in my play acted by girls. This has somewhat disturbed me, since it seems to imply that sufficient attention has not been paid to the spirit in which this play was written and in which it requires to be staged. To allow boys' parts to be taken by women may sometimes be excusable in operetta, vaudeville, or the so-called romantic drama; for in these the prime requirement is unqualified illusion; every member of the audience is fully conscious throughout the evening that he is merely sitting in a theatre and watching a theatrical performance. But this should not be the case when *An Enemy of the People* is being acted. The spectator must feel as though he were invisibly present in Dr. Stockmann's living-room; everything here must seem real; the two boys included. Consequently they cannot be played by actresses dressed up in wigs and stays; their feminine figures will not be able to be concealed by their costume of shirt and trousers, and they will never make any spectator believe that he is [318] looking at real schoolboys from some small town. How in any case can a grown woman make herself look like a ten year old child? Both parts must therefore be played by children, at worst by a couple of small girls whose figures are not yet fully developed; and then damn the corsets and let them have big boys' boots on their legs. They must also, of course, be taught the way boys behave.

It is stated in the play that at the public meeting Dr. Stockmann is to be dressed in black; but his clothes must not be new or elegant, and his white cravat should sit a little crooked. . . .

An Enemy of the People is less frequently performed today than most of Ibsen's mature plays, for two principal reasons. One is, simply, the size of the cast. A crowd costs money, and without a crowd the great fourth act loses much of its impact (and a small crowd is almost worse than no crowd at all). The other problem is ideological. Some of the opinions expressed by Dr. Stockmann, especially his demand for 'aristocrats', contempt for the masses, and assertion that 'the minority is always right' strike an illiberal note in modern ears. On these points Ibsen was in fact expressing a commonly shared attitude; Mill, Tocqueville, Dickens and most liberal thinkers of the time distrusted the [319] tyranny of the commonplace majority. 'Those whose opinions go by the name of public opinion . . . are always a mass, that is to say, collective mediocrity', wrote Mill in his great essay *On Liberty*. 'No government by a democracy or a numerous aristocracy, either in its political acts or in the opinions, qualities, and tone of mind which it fosters, ever did or could rise above mediocrity, except in so far as the sovereign Many have let themselves be guided (which in their best times they always have done) by the counsels and influence of a more highly gifted and instructed One or Few. The initiation of all wise or noble things comes and must come from individuals; generally at first from some one individual.' That is precisely Dr. Stockmann's message. But it is an unfashionable viewpoint to put forward in an age of universal suffrage.

The play has, too, suffered worse than most from the dead hand of academic criticism. The kind of commentator that dismisses *Emperor and Galilean* as 'stone-cold', *Brand* as 'ambiguous' and *Little Eyolf* as 'a falling-off' (to quote from a recent and embarrassing

English book intended as a vindication of Ibsen) has tended to reject *An Enemy of the People* as 'thin'. It lacks, indeed, the extra density and overtones of Ibsen's later works; but there are precious few other plays outside the Greeks, Shakespeare and Chekhov with which it need fear comparison. The truths it expresses have not dated, and are not likely to as long as there are town councils and politicians. Even adequately performed, it is one of the most accessible and compulsive of Ibsen's plays; and Dr. Stockmann is one of the half-dozen greatest male parts he wrote. . . .

        . . . The historical importance of *An Enemy of the People* lies, as Erik Bøgh realised, in   [321] that it is, except for *Danton's Death,* which no-one then knew about, the first political debate which succeeds in remaining a great play. It possesses, too, a wit and lightness which people do not usually associate with Ibsen, though he had both qualities at his command, as *Peer Gynt* and *The League of Youth* bear witness. It is the most Shavian of Ibsen's plays; and the last act is one of his finest. What, one might ask on finishing Act Four, *can* he write that will not seem an anti-climax after this? Yet when one has read or seen that final act, one wonders how else one could possibly have supposed that he would end the play—the surest test of dramatic inevitability.

        Some months after the publication of *An Enemy of the People* Georg Brandes wrote to Ibsen apparently (the letter is lost) rebuking him for isolationism and not putting his shoulder to the progressive wheel. Ibsen replied (12 June 1883): 'You are of course right when you say that we must all try to spread our opinions. But I firmly believe that an intellectual pioneer can never gather a majority around him. In ten years the majority may have reached the point where Dr. Stockmann stood when the people held their meeting. But during those ten years the Doctor has not stood stationary; he is still at least ten years ahead of the others. The majority, the masses, the mob, will never catch him up; he can never rally them behind him. I myself feel a similarly unrelenting compulsion to keep pressing forward. A crowd now stands where I stood when I wrote my earlier books. But I myself am there no longer, I am somewhere else—far ahead of them—or so I hope.'

        To the end of his literary career, which spanned fifty years, Ibsen was to keep moving relentlessly forward, never repeating the pattern of an earlier success. Just as, fifteen years previously, he had abandoned the epic form of poetic drama which had established him, so now he was to abandon the type of (to use a loose term) sociological drama which was to spread his fame throughout the western world, and with which his name is still principally and misleadingly linked. Having exposed the hollowness of a certain kind of left-wing politician in *The League of Youth,* he had gone on to expose the equal hollowness of their right-wing counterparts in *The Pillars of Society;* having questioned the sanctity of marriage in *A Doll's House,* he had questioned it yet further, together with several other equally sacred cows, in *Ghosts.* Then he had returned to the field of politics, broad-   [322] ening his sights so as to include the ordinary voter in his line of fire. *An Enemy of the People* is an attack, not merely on those who lead people by the nose, but on those who allow themselves to be thus led. These four plays, for all their differences, shared one theme in common: the necessity of discovering who one really is and of trying to become that person. In his next play, he was to question even this belief.

Ibsen's Feminist Characters*

Anyone who claims that Ibsen thought of Nora as a silly, hysterical, or selfish woman is ei-   [34] ther ignoring or misrepresenting the plain truth, present from the earliest to the most recent biographies, that Ibsen admired, even adored, Nora Helmer. Among all his

*From Joan Templeton, "The *Doll House* Backlash: Criticism, Feminism, and Ibsen." *PMLA* 104 (1989): 28–40.

characters, she was the one he liked best and found most real. While working on *A Doll House*, he announced to Suzannah Ibsen, his wife, "I've just seen Nora. She came right over to me and put her hand on my shoulder." The quick-witted Suzannah replied at once, "What was she wearing?" In a perfectly serious tone, Ibsen answered, "A simple blue woolen dress."

After *A Doll House* had made him famous, Ibsen was fond of explaining that his [35] heroine's "real" name was "Eleanora" but that she had been called "Nora" from childhood. Bergliot Bjornson Ibsen, the playwright's daughter-in-law, tells the story of how she and her husband, Sigurd, on one of the last occasions on which they saw Ibsen out of bed in the year he died, asked permission to name their newborn daughter "Eleanora." Ibsen was greatly moved. "God bless you, Bergliot," he said to her. He had, in fact, christened his own Nora with a precious gift, for both "Nora" and "Eleanora" were names given to the sister of Ole Schulerud, one of the few close friends of Ibsen's life, who in the early years of grinding poverty believed in Ibsen's genius and tirelessly hawked his first play to bookseller after bookseller, finally spending his small inheritance to pay for its publication.

Ibsen was inspired to write *A Doll House* by the terrible events in the life of his protégé Laura Petersen Kieler, a Norwegian journalist of whom he was extremely fond. Married to a man with a phobia about debt, she had secretly borrowed money to finance an Italian journey necessary for her husband's recovery from tuberculosis. She worked frantically to reimburse the loan, exhausting herself in turning out hackwork, and when her earnings proved insufficient, in desperation she forged a check. On discovering the crime, her husband demanded a legal separation on the grounds that she was an unfit mother and had her placed in an asylum, where she was put in the insane ward. Throughout the affair, Ibsen, her confidant and adviser, was greatly disturbed; he brooded on the wife, "forced to spill her heart's blood," as he wrote in a letter to her, and on the oblivious husband, allowing his wife to slave away on unworthy jobs, concerned neither about her physical welfare nor her work. Having done all for love, Laura Kieler was treated monstrously for her efforts by a husband obsessed with his standing in the eyes of the world. In Ibsen's working notes for *A Doll House* we find:

> She has committed forgery, and is proud of it; for she has done it out of love for her husband, to save his life. But this husband of hers takes his standpoint, conventionally honorable, on the side of the law, and sees the situation with male eyes.

The conflict between love and law, between heart and head, between feminine and masculine, is the moral center of *A Doll House*. But Ibsen would sharpen life's blurred edges to meet art's demand for plausibility. The heroine would be a housewife, not a writer, and the hackwork not bad novels but copying; her antagonist, the husband, would not be a cruel brute but a kind guardian: rather than put her into an asylum, he would merely denounce her as an unfit wife and mother, permitting her to receive bed and board, and then, once his reputation was safe, would offer to forgive her and take her back on the spot. The Helmers, in other words, would be "normal." And this normality would transform a sensational *fait divers* into a devastating picture of the ordinary relations between wife and husband and allow Ibsen to treat what he called, in a letter to Edmund Gosse, "the problems of married life." Moreover, he would reverse the ending: the original Nora, the career journalist, had begged to be taken back; his housewife would sadly, emphatically refuse to stay.

A year after *A Doll House* appeared, when Ibsen was living in Rome, a Scandinavian woman arrived there, who had left her husband and small daughter to run away with her lover. The Norwegian exile community considered her behavior unnatural and asked Ibsen what he thought. "It is not unnatural, only it is unusual" was Ibsen's opinion. The woman made it a point to speak with Ibsen, but to her surprise he treated her offhand-edly. "Well, I did the same thing your Nora did," she said, offended. Ibsen replied quiet-ly, "My Nora went alone."

A favorite piece of evidence in the argument that Ibsen was not interested in women's rights is his aversion to John Stuart Mill. It is popular to quote Ibsen's remark to Georg Brandes about Mill's declaration that he owed the best things in his writing to his wife, Harriet Taylor: " 'Fancy!' [Ibsen] said smiling, 'if you had to read Hegel or Krause with the thought that you did not know for certain whether it was Mr. or Mrs. Hegel, Mr. or Mrs. Krause you had before you!' " But in fact, Brandes, one of Ibsen's closest associ-ates and probably the critic who understood him best, reports this mot in a discussion of Ibsen's wholehearted support of the women's movement. He notes that Mill's assertion "seemed especially ridiculous to Ibsen, with his marked individualism," and explains that although Ibsen had at first little sympathy for feminism—perhaps, Brandes guesses, be-cause of "irritation at some of the ridiculous forms the movement assumed"—this initial response gave way "to a sympathy all the more enthusiastic" when he saw that it was "one of the great rallying points in the battle of progress." [34]

A well-known, perhaps embarrassing fact about Ibsen, never brought up in discus-sions disclaiming his interest in women's rights, is that when he made the banquet speech denying that he had consciously worked for the movement, he was primarily in-terested in young women and annoyed by the elderly feminists who surrounded him. During the seventieth-birthday celebrations, Ibsen constantly exhibited his marked and, as Michael Meyer has it, "rather pathetic longing for young girls." He had already had several romantic friendships, including one that had caused a family scandal and threat-ened to wreck his marriage. In the light of this fully documented biographical informa-tion about the aging playwright, is his intention in *A Doll House* more likely to be revealed by what he said in irritation at a banquet or by what he wrote twenty years earlier in sketching out his play?

> A woman cannot be herself in the society of today, which is exclusively a masculine society, with laws written by men, and with accusers and judges who judge feminine conduct from the masculine standpoint.

A Doll House is not about Everybody's struggle to find him- or herself but, according to its author, about Everywoman's struggle against Everyman.

A Doll House is a natural development of the play Ibsen had just written, the un-abashedly feminist *Pillars of Society;* both plays reflect Ibsen's extremely privileged femi-nist education, which he shared with few other nineteenth-century male authors and which he owed to a trio of extraordinary women: Suzannah Thoresen Ibsen, his wife; Magdalen Thoresen, his colleague at the Norwegian National Theatre in Bergen, who was Suzannah's stepmother and former governess; and Camilla Wergeland Collett, Ibsen's literary colleague, valued friend, and the founder of Norwegian feminism.

Magdalen Thoresen wrote novels and plays and translated the French plays Ibsen put on as a young stage manager at the Bergen theater. She was probably the first "New Woman" he had ever met. She pitied the insolvent young writer, took him under her wing, and brought him home. She had passed her strong feminist principles on to her charge, the outspoken and irrepressible Suzannah, who adored her strong-minded step-mother and whose favorite author was George Sand. The second time Ibsen met Suzan-nah he asked her to marry him. Hjordis, the fierce shield-maiden of *The Vikings at*

Helgeland, the play of their engagement, and Svanhild, the strong-willed heroine of *Love's Comedy,* the play that followed, owe much to Suzannah Thoresen Ibsen. Later, Nora's way of speaking would remind people of Suzannah's.

The third and perhaps most important feminist in Ibsen's life was his friend Camilla Collett, one of the most active feminists in nineteenth-century Europe and founder of the modern Norwegian novel. Fifteen years before Mill's *Subjection of Women,* Collett wrote *Amtmandens Døtre (The Governor's Daughters).* Faced with the choice of a masculine nom de plume or no name at all on the title page, Collett brought out her novel anonymously in two parts in 1854 and 1855, but she nonetheless became widely known as the author. Its main argument, based on the general feminist claim that women's feelings matter, is that women should have the right to educate themselves and to marry whom they please. In the world of the governor's daughters, it is masculine success that matters. Brought up to be ornaments and mothers, women marry suitable men and devote their lives to their husbands' careers and to their children. The novel, a cause célèbre, made Collett famous overnight.

Collett regularly visited the Ibsens in their years of exile in Germany, and she and Suzannah took every occasion to urge Ibsen to take up the feminist cause. They had long, lively discussions in the years preceding *A Doll House,* when feminism had become a strong movement and the topic of the day in Scandinavia. Collett was in Munich in 1877, when Ibsen was hard at work on *Pillars of Society,* and Ibsen's biographer Koht speculates that Ibsen may have deliberately prodded her to talk about the women's movement in order to get material for his dialogue. In any case, the play undoubtedly owes much to the conversations in the Ibsen household, as well as to the Norwegian suffragette Aasta Hansteen, the most notorious woman in the country. Deliberately provocative, Hansteen took to the platform wearing men's boots and carrying a whip to protect herself against the oppressor. A popular news item during the Ibsens' visit to Norway in 1874, Hansteen became the model for Lona Hessel, the shocking *raisonneuse* of *Pillars of Society.*

The play opens with a striking image of woman's place in the world: eight ladies participating in what has been, since antiquity, the most quintessentially female activity in literature—they are "busy sewing"—as they listen to the town schoolmaster read aloud from *Woman as the Servant of Society.* Lona Hessel bursts in, and when the ladies ask her how she can aid their "Society for the Morally Disabled," she suggests, "I can air it out." Returning from America, where she is rumored to have sung in saloons (even for money!), lectured, and written a book, Lona is the New Woman with a vengeance who teaches the others the truth. Lona had loved Bernick, but she packed her bags when he rejected her to marry for money. Bernick turns out not to have been much of a loss, however; he has reduced his wife, Betty, to an obedient cipher and made a personal servant of his sister, Martha, a paradigm of the nineteenth-century spinster who devotes her life to a male relative. Martha's story may have had its source in *The Governor's Daughters.* Like Collett's Margarethe, Martha had once loved a young man but, too modest to declare her feelings, suffered in silence. She now lives for her brother, who is insufferable when he speaks of her; she is a "nonentity," he explains, "who'll take on whatever comes along." It is in explaining Martha's exemplary function in life that Bernick speaks the line, "People shouldn't always be thinking of themselves first, especially women." Dina Dorf, Bernick's ward, disregards this happy maxim, and though she agrees to marry, she tells her husband-to-be, "But first I want to work, become something the way you have. I don't want to be a thing that's just taken along." Dina knows beforehand what Nora learns after eight years of marriage: "I have to try to educate myself. . . . I've got to do it alone."

Pillars of Society, little known and played outside Scandinavia and Germany, is one of the most radically feminist works of nineteenth-century literature. Ibsen took the old

[37]

maid, the butt of society's ridicule, a figure of pity and contempt, and made her a hero-ine. Rejected as unfit to be a wife, Lona Hessel refuses to sacrifice herself to a surrogate family and escapes to the New World, where she leads an independent, authentic life. As *raisonneuse*, she summarizes his point of view for Bernick and the rest: "This society of yours is a bachelors' club. You don't see women."

It is simply not true, then, that Ibsen was not interested in feminism. It is also not true that "there is no indication that Ibsen was thinking of writing a feminist play when he first began to work seriously on *A Doll House* in the summer of 1879." In the spring of that year, while Ibsen was planning his play, a scandalous incident, easily available in the biographies, took place that proves not only Ibsen's interest in women's rights but his passionate support for the movement. Ibsen had made two proposals to the Scandina-vian Club in Rome, where he was living: that the post of librarian be opened to women candidates and that women be allowed to vote in club meetings. In the debate on the proposal, he made a long, occasionally eloquent speech, part of which follows:

> Is there anyone in this gathering who dares assert that our ladies are inferior to us in culture, or intelligence, or knowledge, or artistic talent? I don't think many men would dare suggest that. Then what is it men fear? I hear there is a tradition here that women are cunning intriguers, and that therefore we don't want them. Well, I have encountered a good deal of male intrigue in my time.

Ibsen's first proposal was accepted, the second not, failing by one vote. He left the club in a cold rage. A few days later, he astonished his compatriots by appearing at a gala evening. People thought he was penitent. But he was planning a surprise: facing the ball-room and its dancing couples, he interrupted the music to make a terrible scene, ha-ranguing the celebrants with a furious tirade. He had tried to bring them progress, he shouted, but their cowardly resistance had refused it. The women were especially con-temptible, for it was for them he had tried to fight. A Danish countess fainted and had to be removed, but Ibsen continued, growing more and more violent. Gunnar Heiberg, who was present, later gave this account of the event:

> As his voice thundered it was as though he were clarifying his own thoughts, as his tongue chastised it was as though his spirit were scouring the darkness in search of his present spiritual goal—his poem [*A Doll House*]—as though he were personally bringing out his theories, incarnating his characters. And when he was done, he went out into the hall, took his overcoat and walked home. [38]

In 1884, five years after *A Doll House* had made Ibsen a recognized champion of the feminist cause, he joined with H. E. Berner, president of the Norwegian Women's Rights League, and with his fellow Norwegian writers Bjornson, Lie, and Kielland, in signing a petition to the Storting, the Norwegian parliament, urging the passage of a bill establish-ing separate property rights for married women. When he returned the petition to Bjornson, Ibsen wryly commented that the Storting should not be interested in men's opinions: "To consult men in such a matter is like asking wolves if they desire better pro-tection for the sheep." He also spoke of his fears that the current campaign for universal suffrage would come to nothing. The solution, which he despaired of seeing, would be the formation of a "strong, resolute progressive party" that would include in its goals "the statutory improvement of the position of woman."

It is foolish to apply the formalist notion that art is never sullied by argument to Ibsen's middle-period plays, written at a time when he was an outspoken and direct fight-er in what he called the "mortal combat between two epochs." Ibsen was fiercely his own man, refusing all his life to be claimed by organizations or campaigns of many sorts, including the Women's Rights League and the movement to remove the mark of Sweden from the Norwegian flag. And he had a deeply conservative streak where manners were concerned (except when he lost his temper), for he was acutely suspicious of show. Temperamentally, Ibsen was a loner. But he was also, as Georg Brandes declared, "a born polemist." While it is true that Ibsen never reduced life to "ideas," it is equally true that he was passionately interested in the events and ideas of his day. He was as deeply anchored in his time as any writer has been before or since. Writing to his German translator a year after the publication of *A Doll House*, Ibsen offered one of the truest self-appraisals a writer has ever made:

> Everything that I have written is intimately connected with what I have lived through, even if I have not lived it myself. Every new work has served me as emancipation and catharsis; for none of us can escape the responsibility and the guilt of the society to which we belong.

A Marxist Approach to *A Doll House**

Theatrical production is a process that illuminates the dramatic text, and criticism is the [76] tool that enables theater artists to make the most effective choices. This is the central premise of Drama 102 (Play Analysis), in which we discuss eight or so plays from a variety of critical viewpoints. Although some of the plays lend themselves more readily to a particular kind of analysis (such as a Jungian reading of *The Emperor Jones*), we point out that this affinity should not exclude additional insights that can be gained from a structuralist or feminist reading. We stress that criticism is a preamble to production and that plays are complex and multifaceted. Moreover, we discourage the theatrical sleight of hand that frequently reduces plays to a single metaphor, and we encourage our students to view drama through the lenses of differing approaches.

In teaching *A Doll House* we first examine the text from a traditional point of view stressing historical and biographical considerations. We review Ibsen's commitment to women's rights and his interest in the career of Laura Kieler, who some critics believe was the model for Nora. Indeed, F. L. Lucas has stated that "one cannot fully understand Nora without knowing something of the strange, yet true story of Laura Kieler." By comparing the two women it is possible to watch Ibsen's heroine emerge from the despair and pain that characterized much of Kieler's life.

Still, the historical and biographical approach is limiting, and our next step is to explore the play through another lens. (The metaphor of the "lens" we have found to be particularly effective since it implies that there are no right or wrong interpretations but rather discoveries that can be made by studying a play from more than one vantage point.) The critical method that has stimulated many of our recent students—and that concerns us here—is a Marxist reading of the play. Marxist criticism is a complex topic, and, as the recent work of Fredric Jameson, Henri Arvon, and Raymond Williams exemplifies, critical methodologies vary widely. Moreover, many American students come to Marxist aesthetics with reluctance, conditioned partly by a distrust of all things Russian. Thus we try to emphasize specific issues on which critics agree, and we assign short readings from Terry Eagleton's *Marxism and Literary Criticism* as a point of departure.

It is important, of course, to review Marx's early writings with their humanistic focus and analysis of class structure. Notions of the dialectic and of human alienation are

*From Barry Witham and John Lutterbie, "A Marxist Approach to *A Doll House*," in Yvonne Shafer, ed., *Approaches to Teaching Ibsen's* A Doll House (New York: MLA, 1985).

productive ways of introducing students to Marx since alienation seems to be a concept with which they can identify. This approach has the added value of breaking down some initial prejudices toward the subject matter. By stressing the human side of Marx's work, we can reduce student resistance and encourage a more objective view of the social analy-   [77]
sis that follows.

We then talk about the text of the play as an objectification of the author's idea, a process that is a creative act but that in dialectical terms is imperfect because it can never completely express Ibsen's vision or totally repress unconscious ideas that shape the text. Drawing on both Terry Eagleton and Louis Althusser (*Lenin and Philosophy*), we define ideology as a false consciousness, a system of beliefs and ideas that functions to disguise the inequities of a class-based society. Using this definition to examine the play, we stress the concept that ideology is shaped by both what is in the text (Torvald's domination of Nora) and by what is "absent" (Nora's relationship with her mother). One of the primary goals of any Marxist analysis is the investigation of ideological content, and the existence of this content allows Marxist critics to argue that all works of art are political. This is a highly controversial point with many students, and the discussions often become heated as we examine its implications.

We then focus on the economic realities of Ibsen's world. *A Doll House* is especially suited to this type of examination because the bank—an obvious and blatant symbol for money—stands at the center of the play. Torvald has just been appointed manager. Mrs. Linde wants to work there, as does Krogstad. And Nora's jubilance at the beginning of the play is directly related to the financial security ensured by Torvald's new job. More-over, an economic analysis quickly reveals how the consciousness of the characters is shaped and determined by their class and status. Even though Downs has argued that "except for three virtual supernumeraries, all the persons of the play belong to the edu-cated middle class," it is clear that class differences do exist. Torvald stands for the mon-eyed elite—in this case the bank owners—while Mrs. Linde and Krogstad function as workers struggling to maintain a subsistence income.

A principal tenet of Marxist criticism is that human consciousness is a product of social conditions and that human relationships are often subverted by and through eco-nomic considerations. Mrs. Linde has sacrificed a genuine love to provide for her broth-ers, and Krogstad has committed a crime to support his children. Anne-Marie, the maid, has also been the victim of her economic background. Because she's "a girl who's poor and gotten in trouble," her relationship with her child has been interrupted and virtual-ly destroyed. In each instance the need for money is linked with the ability to exist. But while the characters accept the social realities of their misfortunes, they do not appear to question how their human attitudes have been thoroughly shaped by socioeconomic considerations.

Once students begin to perceive how consciousness is affected by economics, a Marxist reading of Ibsen's play can illuminate a number of areas. Krogstad, for example, becomes less of a traditional villain when we realize that he is fighting for his job at the bank "as if it were life itself." And his realization of the senselessness of their lives is   [78]
poignantly revealed when he reflects on Mrs. Linde's past, "all this simply for money." Even Dr. Rank speaks about his failing health and imminent death in entirely financial terms. "These past few days I've been auditing my internal accounts. Bankrupt! Within a month I'll probably be laid out and rotting in the churchyard."

All these characters, however, serve as foils for the central struggle between Nora and Torvald and highlight the pilgrimage that Nora makes in the play. At the outset two things are clear: (1) Nora is enslaved by Torvald in economic terms, and (2) she equates personal freedom with the acquisition of wealth. The play begins joyfully not only be-cause it is the holiday season but also because Torvald's promotion to bank manager will ensure "a safe, secure job with a comfortable salary." Nora is happy because she sees the future in wholly economic terms. "Won't it be lovely to have stacks of money and not a care in the world?"

What she learns, however, is that financial enslavement is symptomatic of other forms of enslavement—master–slave, male–female, sexual objectification, all of which characterize her relationship with Torvald—and that money is no guarantee of happiness. At the end of the play she renounces not only her marital vows but also her financial dependence because she has discovered that personal and human freedom are not measured in economic terms.

This discovery also prompts her to reexamine the society of which she is a part and leads us into a consideration of the ideology in the play. In what sense has Nora committed a criminal offense in forging her father's name? Is it indeed just that she should be punished for an altruistic act, one that cost her dearly both in terms of self-denial and the destruction of her family? Ibsen's defense of Nora is clear, of course, and his implicit indictment of a society that encourages this kind of injustice stimulates a discussion of the assumptions that created the law.

One of the striking things about *A Doll House* is how Anne-Marie accepts her alienation from her child as if it were natural, given the circumstances of class and money. It does not occur to her that laws were framed by other people and thus are capable of imperfection and susceptible to change. Nora broke a law that not only tries to stop thievery (the appropriation of capital) by outlawing forgery but also discriminates against anyone deemed a bad risk. Question leads to question as the class investigates why women were bad risks and why they had difficulty finding employment. It becomes obvious that the function of women in this society was not "natural" but artificial, a role created by their relationship to the family and by their subservience to men. In the marketplace they were a labor force expecting subsistence wages and providing an income to supplement that earned by their husbands or fathers. . . .   [79]

Viewing the play through the lens of Marxist aesthetics does make one thing clear. Nora's departure had ramifications for her society that went beyond the marriage bed. By studying the play within the context of its socioeconomic structure, we can see how the ideology in the text affects the characters and how they perpetuate the ideology. The conclusion of *A Doll House* was a challenge to the economic superstructures that had controlled and excluded the Noras of the world by manipulating their economic status and, by extension, their conscious estimation of themselves and their place in society.

The Character of Dr. Stockmann in *An Enemy of the People**

An Enemy of the People is at once the most high-spirited and the most overtly didactic of   [115]
Ibsen's major plays. Dr. Stockmann is a major comic creation, a courageous spokesman for Ibsen's ideas, which are presented explicitly by means of the public speech in Act IV. He is made even more attractive by his minor failings—his naiveté, his impetuousness, and his touches of vanity and self-indulgence. Ranged around him is a rogues' gallery of caricatures of Norwegian small-town types, from the tea-drinking Mayor down through representatives of the "free press" and the "compact majority" to the timid proletarian radical, Hovstad.

Ibsen wrote *An Enemy of the People* very quickly; he began it in March of 1882, at the height of the controversy over *Ghosts*, and completed it in June, less than three months later. It is true that he had been planning the play two years earlier and had laid his plans

---

*From James Hurt, *Catiline's Dream: An Essay on Ibsen's Plays* (Urbana: U of Illinois P, 1972).

aside to write *Ghosts*. Nevertheless, the final version of the play seems to have been influenced by the reception of *Ghosts*, especially the attacks from the liberal press in Norway, which particularly infuriated Ibsen. In January, just before beginning the play, for example, he had written to Brandes, using language very much like Stockmann's: [116]

> And what can be said of the attitude assumed by the so-called liberal press—of those leaders of the people who speak and write of freedom of action and thought but who at the same time make themselves the slaves of the supposed opinions of their subscribers? I receive more and more proof that there is something demoralizing in engaging in politics and in joining parties. It will never, in any case, be possible to me to join a party that has the majority on its side. Bjoernson says, "The majority is always right." And as a practical politician he is bound, I suppose, to say so. I, on the contrary, must of necessity say, "The minority is always right." Naturally I am not thinking of that minority of standpatters who are left behind by the great middle party that we call liberal; I mean that minority which leads the van and pushes on to points the majority has not yet reached. I mean: that man is right who has allied himself most closely with the future.

These sentiments, and a number of similar ones from the letters written about this time, are repeated almost verbatim by Stockmann in his Act IV speech to the public meeting. Stockmann, like Ibsen, is anything but a democrat; he is a thoroughgoing aristocrat, though the aristocracy he calls for is one of the mind and spirit. Audiences, probably rightly, have generally chosen to emphasize less Stockmann's radical individualism than his courageous defiance of established authority, and have made *An Enemy of the People* into a "revolutionary" play in ways very far from Ibsen's intention.

Despite the similarity of Ibsen's and Stockmann's views, however, the doctor is much more than a mouthpiece for Ibsen, a portrait of the artist as a village radical. The comic irony with which Ibsen portrayed Stockmann is suggested in his comments in the letter he sent to his publisher along with the manuscript:

> I have the pleasure of sending you herewith the remainder of the manuscript of my new play. I have enjoyed writing this play, and I feel quite lost and lonely now that it is out of my hands. Dr. Stockmann and I got on so very well together; we agree on [117] so many subjects. But the doctor is more muddle-headed than I am; and moreover he has other peculiarities that permit him to say things which would not be taken so well if I myself said them. I think you will agree with me when you have read the manuscript.

There is something of Hjalmar Ekdal as well as of Gregers Werle in Dr. Stockmann's character. Like Hjalmar, he leaves the household to his quiet, competent wife, whom he often dismays with his habit of having guests in for meals they can ill afford. "Catherine says I earn almost as much as we spend," he proudly tells his brother. And like Hjalmar with his bread and butter, Stockmann is an inveterate snacker although, unlike Hjalmar, Stockmann enjoys seeing others eat, too. He is incredibly naive; as late as Act III he is still convinced that his discovery that the Baths are polluted will earn him the love and gratitude of his fellow citizens, and he modestly tells Hovstad that he must discourage any proposals for "a torchlight procession or a banquet or—a subscription for some little token of thanks." A comic irony envelops even the final tableau. "I've made a great discovery," he announces. "The strongest man in the world is he who stands most alone."

But as he speaks, he is standing in the middle of an admiring group made up of his wife, his daughter, his two sons, and Captain Horster, who has donated his house to Stockmann. The actual last lines of the play are Mrs. Stockmann's loving, "Oh, Thomas—!" and Petra's "Father!" as she "warmly clasps his hands."

Much of the richness and complexity of character that make Stockmann more than a two-dimensional mouthpiece comes from the presence in the play of Ibsen's myth of the self. Stockmann—gregarious, outgoing, and impulsive—seems at the opposite pole from such lonely, introspective, and self-conscious characters as Brand and Mrs. Alving. And yet his inner experiences and his spiritual development have much in common with theirs. This psychological background also helps to account for the strange combination of traits in his character: his gullibility, his quick temper, his fierce individualism, his egotism, and his obstinacy. It helps to explain the psychological roots of his final slogan: "The strongest man in the world is he who stands most alone."

The original plan for the Baths came from Dr. Stockmann himself, although his [118] brother Peter tries to claim equal credit for it. He has thought of the plan while working as a rural doctor in the north. He describes the circumstances in his fourth-act speech:

> DR. STOCKMANN.   For years I lived far up in the north. As I wandered among those people who lived scattered over the mountains, I often thought it would have been better for those poor degraded creatures if they'd had a vet instead of a man like me! . . . I sat there brooding like a duck on an egg; and the chick I hatched was— the plan for these Baths.

Once conceived, the idea has possessed Stockmann. At first it has met with indifference in the town, but he has persisted. "For years I fought alone for this idea! I wrote, and wrote—" he reminds his brother.

The plan for the Baths thus takes on the character of an obsessive project of the will, and the setting in which it is conceived is appropriate for such a project. Although the dominant settings for the myth of the self are "the valley," "the heights," and "the peaks," the cardinal compass points are sometimes subsumed into the pattern. The north is associated with the will and with projects of the will. Brand is a northerner, and he tells Ejnar that he was never "at home among you southerners." Gregers Werle, Rebecca West, and Ellida Wangel all conceive projects of the will in the isolated north. The south is associated with wholeness and the "joy of life." Nora has had a glimpse of these qualities on her trip to Italy and Oswald yearns for the sunlight and joy of Paris. Erhart Borkman's flight from the externally imposed duties of his northern home is toward the sunlight of Italy. The west, more rarely, is associated with freedom, as in *The Pillars of Society*, and the east, because the sun rises there, sometimes symbolizes transcendence and integration, as in *Emperor and Galilean*.

The plan for the Baths, desirable as it is for its own sake, is sufficiently ambiguous in its psychological meaning for Stockmann to explain his otherwise incredible blindness to reality at the beginning of the play. Obsessed by his project, he has built up a ludicrously idealistic conception of his fellow citizens. He believes that his self-centered and cynical brother will only regret that he was not the one to discover the pollution of the [119] Baths, he takes the representatives of the "free press" and the "compact majority" at their own evaluation, and he believes that the mass of his fellow townspeople will spontaneously offer him a torchlight procession for having revealed the truth, even though it is against their own interests. Most telling of all, he has a naive conception of his own motivations; he does not realize until the last scene how much of his own courage has been based on his presumed financial security.

Stockmann's project of the will, like all projects of the will in Ibsen, has led its creator into a position farther and farther removed from reality. The action of the play covers its gradual collapse, as one support after another is taken away from Stockmann: first his idealistic conception of his brother, then his illusions about the free press, the property owners, and the mass of citizens, and finally his illusions about his own motivations.

Stockmann's reaction to the loss of his defensive project is psychologically consistent with this interpretation of the project itself. Many of his attitudes and actions seem like distant echoes of Brand's lonely withdrawal into an inner world. Stockmann's ebullient self-confidence sometimes verges on messianism, as when he compares himself to Christ after the disastrous public meeting ("I'm not so forgiving as a certain person. I don't say, 'I forgive ye, for ye know not what ye do!'") and when he chooses twelve for the number of his pupil-disciples at the end of the play. His exaggerated respect for scientific facts to the neglect of any sympathetic understanding of their implications for his fellow citizens also indicates something of a defensive withdrawal into the world of his own mind. And most telling of all, the doctrine he enunciates at the public meeting can be read not only as a heroic battle-cry of individualism but also, in its celebration of the lonely, self-sufficient individual and its savage contempt for the "masses," as a defensive, schizoid "rising above" the threat of other people. There is a certain hysterical quality in Dr. Stockmann's cry for the whole town to be wiped out—"Let the whole land be laid waste! Let the whole people be exterminated!"—and in his scathing attacks on the "majority" as vermin," "short-winded sheep," and "filthy, ragged, common curs."

This ambiguous undercurrent in the public meeting scene continues through the last act of the play, which is full of muted suggestions of the kind of mystic integration and rebirth associated with an "ascent to the peaks." When the act begins it appears that Stockmann has reached the lowest point in his fortunes. It is the morning after the tumultuous public meeting at which he was branded an "enemy of the people," Captain Horster has had to escort him and his family home in order to prevent their being physically assaulted, and the mob has broken out all the windows in the house. Stockmann has decided to emigrate to America with his family. A series of visitors—"the Devil's messengers"—however, disillusion him even more. First he learns that Horster has been fired by his shipowner. Then the Mayor arrives to deliver Stockmann's own letter of dismissal, tells him that his father-in-law's will leaves all his money to Stockmann, and accuses him of creating a scandal merely to please his embittered father-in-law. The father-in-law himself, Morten Kiil, is next; his pride has been hurt by the suggestion that his tanneries have poisoned the Baths, he has bought up most of the shares in the Baths, and he tells Stockmann that his wife will lose her inheritance if he does not recant. At this temptation, Stockmann wavers: "I must talk to Catherine. She knows about these things." [120]

When Kiil leaves, Hovstad and Aslaksen arrive. They have heard of Morten Kiil's purchases of stock and assume that Stockmann has merely been trying to drive down the value of the stocks for personal profit. They threaten to expose him if he does not share his profits with them.

At this final straw, Stockmann loses his last illusion about his fellow townspeople that survived from his project of the will. He chases Hovstad and Aslaksen off with an umbrella and sends a note to Kiil refusing to recant. In a scene reminiscent of Brand's decision to "march under his own flag," he decides to remain in the town and start a school to build a new society of "free men and aristocrats." A hint of the mythic mountain peaks survives in the "glorious fresh spring air" blowing in through the shattered windows of Stockmann's study, as he gathers his family and friends around him and announces the birth of the new Stockmann—the "strongest man in the world" because he "stands alone."

Special Writing Topics

about

LITERATURE

Writing and Documenting the Research Essay

Broadly, **research** is the act of systematic investigation, examination, and experimentation. It is the basic tool of intellectual inquiry for anyone engaged in any discipline—physics, chemistry, biology, psychology, anthropology, history, and literature, to name just a few disciplines. With research, our understanding and our civilization grow; without it, they die.

The beginning assumption of doing research is that the researcher is exploring new areas of knowledge. With each assignment the researcher acquires not only the knowledge gained from the particular task but also the skills needed to undertake further research and thereby to gain further knowledge. Some research tasks are elementary, such as using a dictionary to discover the meaning of a word and thereby aiding the understanding of an important passage. More involved research uses an array of resources: encyclopedias, biographies, introductions, critical studies, bibliographies, and histories. When you begin a research task you usually have little or no knowledge about your topic, but with such resources it is possible to acquire expert knowledge in a relatively short time.

While research is the animating spark of all disciplines, our topic here is **literary research**—the systematic use of primary and secondary sources in studying a literary problem. In doing literary research, you consult not only individual works themselves (*primary sources*) but many other works that shed light on them and interpret them (*secondary sources*). Typical research tasks are to learn important facts about a work and about the period in which it was written; to learn about the lives, careers, and other works of authors; to discover and apply the comments and judgments of modern or earlier critics; to learn details that help explain the meaning of works; and to learn about critical and artistic taste.

SELECTING A TOPIC

In most instances, your instructor assigns a research essay on a specific topic. Sometimes, however, the choice of a topic is left entirely up to you. For such assignments, it is helpful to know the types of research essays you might find most congenial. Here are some possibilities.

1. *A particular work.* You might treat character (for example, "The Character of Bottom in Shakespeare's *A Midsummer Night's Dream*" or "The Question of Whether Willie Loman Is a Hero or an Antihero in Miller's *Death of a Salesman*") or tone, ideas, structure, form, and the like. A research paper on a single work is similar to an essay on the same work, except that the research paper takes into account more views and facts than those you are likely to have without the research.

2. *A particular author.* A project might focus on an idea or some facet of style, imagery, setting, or tone of the author, tracing the origins and development of the topic through a number of different stories, poems, or plays. An example is "The Idea of the True Self as Developed by Frost in His Poetry before 1920." This type of essay is suitable if you are writing on a poet whose works are short, though a topic like "Shakespeare's Idea of the Relationships between Men and Women as Dramatized in *A Midsummer Night's Dream* and *Hamlet*" is also possible.

3. Comparison and contrast (see Chapter 35). There are two types.
   a. *An idea or quality common to two or more authors.* Here you show points of similarity or contrast, or else you show how one author's work can be taken to criticize another's. A possible subject is "The Theme of Ineffectuality in Joyce Carol Oates, John Steinbeck, and Mark Twain" or "Langston Hughes's Antidiscrimination Poems in the Context of Twentieth-Century Race Relations."
   b. *Different critical views of a particular work or body of works.* Sometimes much is to be gained from an examination of differing critical opinions on topics like "The Meaning of Shirley Jackson's 'The Lottery,'" "Various Interpretations of Emily Dickinson's Poems about Death," or "The Question of Hamlet's Hesitation." Such a study would attempt to determine the critical opinion and taste to which a work did or did not appeal, and it might also aim at conclusions about whether the work was in the advance or rear guard of its time.

4. *The influence of an idea, author, philosophy, political situation, or artistic movement on specific works of an author or authors.* An essay on influences can be specific and to the point, as in "Details of 1960s Military Life in Vietnam in Tim O'Brien's 'The Things They Carried,'" or else it can be more abstract and critical, as in "The Influence of Attitudes toward the Vietnam War on the Narration of Tim O'Brien's 'The Things They Carried.'"

5. *The origin of a particular work or type of work.* Such an essay might examine an author's biography to discover the germination and development of a work—for example, "Details in a Number of Frost's Early Poems and Their Relationship to His Early Years as a Practicing Farmer." Another way of discovering origins might be to relate a work to a particular type or tradition: "*Hamlet* as Revenge Tragedy" or "Sophocles's *Oedipus the King* and Its Origins in the Conventions of Ancient Athenian Drama."

If you consider these types, an idea of what to write may come to you. Perhaps you have particularly liked one author or several authors. If so, you might start to think along the lines of types 1, 2, and 3. If you are interested in influences or origins, then type 4 or 5 may suit you better.

If you still cannot decide on a topic after rereading the works you have liked, then you should carry your search for a topic into your school library. Look up your author or authors in the computer or card catalogue. Your first goal should be to find a relatively recent book-length critical study published by a university press. Look for a title indicating that the book is a general one dealing with the author's major works rather than just one work. Study those chapters relevant to the work or works you have chosen. Most writers of critical studies describe their purpose and plan in their introductions or first chapters, so begin with the first part of the book. If there is no separate chapter on the primary text, use the index as your guide to the relevant pages. Reading in this way will give you enough knowledge about the issues and ideas raised by the work to enable you to select a promising topic. Once you make your decision, you are ready to develop a working bibliography.

❦ SETTING UP A BIBLIOGRAPHY

The best way to develop a working bibliography of books and articles is to begin with major critical studies of the writer or writers. Again, go to the computer or card catalogue and find books that have been published by university presses. These books always contain comprehensive bibliographies. Be careful to read the chapters on your primary work or works and to look for the footnotes or endnotes, for often you can save time if you record the names of books and articles listed in these notes. Then refer to the bibliographies included at the ends of the books, and select likely looking titles. Now, look at the dates of publication of the scholarly books. Let us suppose that you have been looking at three, published in 1989, 1998, and 2002. Unless you are planning an extensive research assignment, you can safely assume that the writers of critical works will have done the selecting for you of important works published before the date of publication. These bibliographies will be reliable, and you can use them with confidence. Thus, the bibliography in a book published in 2002 will be complete up through about 2000–2001, for the writer will have finished the manuscript a year or two before the book was published. But such bibliographies will not go up to the present. For that, you will need to search for works published after the most recent of the books.

Consult Bibliographical Guides

Fortunately for students doing literary research, the Modern Language Association (MLA) of America has been providing a complete bibliography of literary studies for years, not only in English and American literatures but in the literatures of many foreign languages. This is the *MLA International Bibliography of Books and Articles on the Modern Languages and Literatures* (*MLA Bibliography*). The *MLA Bibliography* started achieving completeness in the late 1950s. By 1969 the project had grown so large that it was published in many parts, which are bound together in library editions. University and college libraries have sets of this bibliography on open shelves or tables. The *MLA Bibliography* is also published on CD-ROM and on the Internet, formats accessible to you through your college library facilities.

There are many other bibliographies useful for students doing literary research, such as the *Essay and General Literature Index*, the *International Index*, the *Reader's Guide to Periodical Literature*, *A Bibliography of Literary Theory and Criticism* (available on the Internet at <http://fyl.unizar.es/filologia_inglesa/bibliography.html>), and various specific indexes. The *MLA Bibliography* is more than adequate, however, for most purposes. Remember that as you progress in your reading, the notes and bibliographies in the works you consult will also constitute an unfolding selective bibliography. For the demonstrative student research essay in this chapter, a number of entries were discovered not from bibliographies like those just listed but from the reference lists in critical books.

The *MLA Bibliography*, in the traditional book format, is conveniently organized by period and author. Should you be doing research about Gwendolyn Brooks, look her up in *Volume I: British and Irish, Commonwealth, English, Caribbean, and American Literatures*, where you will also find references to most other authors of works in English, such as Shakespeare, Wordsworth, and Kincaid. You will find most books and articles listed under the author's last name. In the *MLA Bibliography*, journal references are abbreviated, but a lengthy list explaining abbreviations appears at the beginning of the volume. Using the *MLA Bibliography* in the book format, begin with the most recent one and then go backward to your stopping point. If your library has machines dedicated to the electronic versions of the bibliography, you can do your searching by typing in the name of your author or subject. By whatever means you gain access to the bibliography, be sure to get the complete information, especially volume numbers and years of publication, for each article and book. You are now ready to find your sources and to take notes.

❧ ONLINE LIBRARY SERVICES

Today, virtually all libraries have their own computerized catalogues. In addition, many libraries are connected with a vast array of local, national, and even international libraries, so that by using various online services, you can extend your research far beyond the capacities of your own library. You can even use a personal computer to gain access to the catalogues of large research libraries, provided that you punch in the correct entry information, are able and willing to follow the program codes, and are also patient and persistent. By using search engines to gain access to sites on the World Wide Web, you can also discover special topics directly related to your subject—organizations devoted to making awards, for example, or clubs or other organizations that have been established in the home cities of particular authors, or works on topics inspired by various authors.

The ease with which you can gain access to many libraries through a computer search is variable. Some library catalogues are friendly while others require a certain amount of trial and error.[1] In many cases you will need several tries to learn how to find what you are looking for, because the words some libraries use to categorize holdings are not immediately apparent. In all cases, practice with the various systems is essential, for you cannot expect to get the most out of an electronic search the first time you try.

After you have gained access, you can look up books by specific authors, or can select books about particular topics. If your author is Shakespeare, for example, you can ask for specific titles of his works or for books about him. A recent search for critical and interpretive works about Shakespeare in a major university library produced a list of 3,722 titles (not just in English but also in other languages). The same library listed 600 works (including videos) specifically about *Hamlet*. Another major university library produced 6,842 titles on Shakespeare biography and interpretation, and 411 titles exclusively on *Hamlet*. Obviously these numbers are too massive for ordinary classroom purposes, and your principal task in the face of such numbers is to be selective. Narrow your search. Look through a number of the titles, and pick out only those that you think will be most useful to you.

IMPORTANT CONSIDERATIONS ABOUT COMPUTER-AIDED RESEARCH

You must always keep in mind that online catalogues can give you only what has been entered into them. If one library classifies a work under "criticism and interpretation" and another classifies it under "characters," a search of "criticism and interpretation" at the first library will find the work but the same search at the second will not. Sometimes the inclusion of an author's life dates immediately following the name will throw off your search. Typographic errors in the system will cause additional search problems, although many programs try to forestall such difficulties by providing "nearby" entries to enable you to determine whether incorrectly entered topics may prove helpful to you. Also, if you use online services, be careful to determine the year when the computerization began. Many libraries have a recent commencement date—1978, for example, or 1985. For completeness, therefore, you would need assistance in finding catalogue entries for items published before these years.

Just a few years ago, the broadness of scope that electronic searches provide for most undergraduate students doing research assignments was not possible; today, it is commonplace. Even with the astounding possibilities of electronic resources, however, it is still necessary to take out actual books and articles—and read them and take notes on them—before you can begin and complete a research essay. The electronic services can help you locate materials, but they cannot do your reading, note taking, and writing. All that is still up to you, as it always has been.

---

[1]Libraries generally encourage access to their resources, so proper entry instructions are often attached to computer terminals, particularly for internal use. When you are hooked into catalogues of distant libraries, you will find that the computer screen itself contains instructions about what you need to do to continue your search.

Your list will make up a fairly comprehensive search bibliography, which you can use when you physically enter the library to begin collecting and using materials. A major convenience is that many associated libraries, such as state colleges and urban public libraries, have pooled their resources. Thus, if you use the services of a network of nearby county libraries, you can go to another library to use materials that are not accessible at your own college or branch. If distances are great, however, and your own library does not have a book that you think is important to your project, you can ask a librarian to get the book for you through the Interlibrary Loan Service. Usually, given time, the libraries will accommodate as many of your needs as they can.

TAKING NOTES AND PARAPHRASING MATERIAL

There are many ways of taking notes, but the consensus is that the best method is to use note cards. If you have never used cards before, you might profit from consulting any one of a number of handbooks and special workbooks on research.[2] The principal advantage of cards is that they can be classified; numbered and renumbered; shuffled; tried out in one place, rejected, and then used in another place (or thrown away); and arranged in order when you start to write.

Take Complete and Accurate Notes

WRITE THE SOURCE ON EACH CARD.　As you take notes, write the source of your information on each card. This may seem bothersome, but it is easier than going back to the library to locate the correct source after you have begun your essay. You can save time if you take the complete data on one card—a "master card" for that source—and then create an abbreviation for the separate note cards you take from the source. Here is an example, which also includes the location where the reference was originally found (e.g., card catalogue, computer search, bibliography in a book, the *MLA Bibliography*, etc.). Observe that the author's last name goes first.

Donovan, Josephine, ed.　　　　　　　　　　　PN
　　<u>Feminist Literary Criticism: Explorations</u>　　98
　　<u>in Theory</u>. 2nd ed. Lexington:　　　　　　W64
　　UP of Kentucky, 1989.　　　　　　　　　　　F4

DONOVAN

Card Catalogue, "Women"

---

[2]See, for example, Melinda G. Kramer, Glenn Leggett, and C. David Mead, *Prentice Hall Handbook for Writers*, 12th ed. (Englewood Cliffs: Prentice Hall, 1995), 501–05.

If you take many notes from this book, the name *Donovan* will serve as identification. Be sure not to lose your master cards because you will need them when you prepare your list of works cited. If possible, record the complete bibliographical data in a computer file.

RECORD THE PAGE NUMBER FOR EACH NOTE. It would be hard to guess how much exasperation has been caused by the failure to record page numbers in notes. Be sure to write the page number down first, *before* you begin to take your note, and, to be doubly sure, write the page number again at the end of your note. If the detail goes from one page to the next in your source, record the exact spot where the page changes, as in this example.

Heilbrun and Stimson, in DONOVAN, pp. 63–64

⁶³ After the raising of the feminist consciousness it is necessary to develop / ⁶⁴ "the growth of moral perception" through anger and the "amelioration of social inequities."

The reason for such care is that you may wish to use only a part of a note you have taken, and when there are two pages you will need to be accurate in locating what goes where.

RECORD ONLY ONE FACT OR OPINION ON A CARD. Record only one major element on each card—one quotation, one paraphrase, one observation—*never two or more.* You might be tempted to fill up the entire card with many separate but unrelated details, but such a try at economy often gets you in trouble because you might want to use some of the details in other places. If you have only one entry per card, you will avoid such problems and also retain the freedom you need.

USE QUOTATION MARKS FOR ALL QUOTED MATERIAL. In taking notes it is extremely important—vitally important—to distinguish copied material from your own words. *Always put quotation marks around every direct quotation you copy verbatim from a source.* Make the quotation marks *immediately, before you forget,* so that you will always know that the words of your notes within quotation marks are the words of another writer.

Often, as you take a note, you may use some of your own words and some of the words from your source. In cases like this you should be even more cautious. Put quotation marks around *every word* that you take directly from the source, even if your note looks like a picket fence. Later, when you begin writing your essay, your memory of what is yours and not yours will be dim, and if you use another's words in your own essay without proper acknowledgment, you are risking the charge of plagiarism. Much of the time, plagiarism is caused not by deliberate deception but rather by sloppy note taking.

If Your Source Is Long, Make a Brief and Accurate Paraphrase

When you take notes, it is best to paraphrase the sources. A paraphrase is a restatement in your own words, and because of this it is actually a first step in the writing of your essay. In Chapter 13 (p. 628) you will find a discussion of how to write a paraphrase of a poem. If you practice the directions you find there, for whatever genre of literature you are discussing, you will be well prepared to write paraphrases when doing your research.

A big problem in paraphrasing is to capture the idea in the source without duplicating the words. The best way is to read and reread the passage you are noting. Turn over the book or journal—or put your computer screen to sleep— and write out the idea *in your own words* as accurately as you can. Once you have completed this note, compare it with the original and make corrections to improve your thought and emphasis. Add a short quotation if you believe it is needed, but be sure to use quotation marks. If your paraphrase is too close to the original, *throw out the note and write another one.* This effort may have its own reward because often you may be able to transfer some or even all of your note, word for word, directly to the appropriate place in your research essay.

To see the problems of paraphrasing, let us look at a paragraph of criticism and then see how a student doing research might take notes on it. The paragraph is by Maynard Mack, from an essay titled "The World of Hamlet," originally published in *The Yale Review* 41 (1952) and reprinted in *Twentieth Century Interpretations of Hamlet*, ed. David Bevington (Englewood Cliffs: Prentice Hall, 1968), p. 57.

> The powerful sense of mortality in Hamlet is conveyed to us, I think, in three ways. First, there is the play's emphasis on human weakness, the instability of human purpose, the subjection of humanity to fortune—all that we might call the aspect of failure in man. Hamlet opens this theme in Act I, when he describes how from that single blemish, perhaps not even the victim's fault, a man's whole character may take corruption. Claudius dwells on it again, to an extent that goes far beyond the needs of the occasion, while engaged in seducing Laertes to step behind the arras of a seemer's world and dispose of Hamlet by a trick. Time qualifies everything, Claudius says, including love, including purpose. As for love—it has a "plurisy" in it and dies of its own too much. As for purpose—"That we would do, We should do when we would, for the 'would' changes. And hath abatements and delays as many As there are tongues, are hands, are accidents; And then this 'should' is like a spendthrift's sigh, That hurts by easing." The player-king, in his long speeches to his queen in the play within the play, sets the matter in a still darker light. She means these protestations of undying love, he knows, but our purposes depend on our memory, and our memory fades fast. Or else, he suggests, we propose something to ourselves in a condition of strong feeling, but then the feeling goes, and with it the resolve. Or else our fortunes change, he adds, and with these our loves: "The great man down, you mark his favorite flies." The subjection of human aims to fortune is a reiterated theme in *Hamlet*, as subsequently in *Lear*. Fortune is the harlot goddess in whose secret parts men like Rosencrantz and Guildenstern live and thrive; the strumpet who threw down Troy and Hecuba and Priam; the outrageous foe whose slings and arrows a man of principle must suffer or seek release in suicide. Horatio suffers them with composure: he is one of the

blessed few "Whose blood and judgment are so well co-mingled / That there are not a pipe for fortune's finger / To sound what stop she please." For Hamlet the task is of a greater difficulty.

Because taking notes forces a shortening of this or any criticism, it also requires you to discriminate, judge, interpret, and select; good note taking is not easy. There are some things to guide you, however, when you go through the many sources you uncover.

THINK ABOUT THE PURPOSE OF YOUR RESEARCH. You may not know exactly what you are "fishing for" when you start to take notes, for you cannot prejudge what your essay will contain. Research is a form of discovery. But soon you will notice subjects and issues that your sources constantly explore. If you can accept one of these as your major topic, or focus of interest, you can use that as your guide in all further note taking.

For example, suppose you are taking notes on critical works about *Hamlet,* and after a certain amount of reading you have decided to focus on "Shakespeare's Tragic Views in *Hamlet.*" This decision would prompt you to take a note when you come to Mack's thought about mortality and death in the passage quoted above. In this instance, the following note would suffice.

Mack, in Bevington, 57   Death and
                                                               Mortality

Mack cites three ways in which <u>Hamlet</u> stresses death and mortality. The
first (57) is an emphasis on human shortcomings and "weakness." Corruption,
loss of memory and enthusiasm, bad luck, misery--all suit the sense of the
closeness of death to life.   57

Let us now suppose that you want a fuller note, in the expectation that you do not need just the topic alone but also some of Mack's detail. Here is such a note.

Mack, in Bevington, 57   Death and
                                                               Mortality

The first of Mack's "three ways" in which a "powerful sense of mortality" is
shown in <u>Hamlet</u> is the illustration of human "weakness," "instability," and
helplessness before fate. In support, Mack refers to Hamlet's early speech on a
single fault leading to "corruption," also to Claudius's speech (in the scene
persuading Laertes to trick Hamlet). The player-king also talks about his
queen's forgetfulness and therefore inconstancy by default. As slaves to
fortune, Rosencrantz and Guildenstern are examples. Horatio is not a slave,
however. Hamlet's case is by far the worst of all.   57

In an actual essay, any part of this note would be useful. The words are almost all the note taker's own, and the few quotations are within quotation marks. Note that Mack, the critic, is properly recognized as the source of the criticism, so that you could adapt the note easily when you are doing your writing. The key here is that your taking of notes should be guided by your developing plan for your essay.

Note taking is part of your thinking and composing process. You cannot predict whether you will be able to use each of your notes, and you will therefore exclude many notes when you write your essay. You will always find, however, that taking notes is easier once you have determined your purpose.

PROVIDE A TITLE FOR EACH NOTE. To help plan and develop the various parts of your essay, write a title for each of your notes in the upper right corner of the card, as in the examples in this chapter. *This practice is a form of outlining that will help you immeasurably when you write your essay.* Let us assume that you have chosen to study the importance of the Ghost in the play (the topic of the demonstrative student essay on p. 1906). As you delve into your sources, you discover that there are conflicting views about how the Ghost should be understood. Here is a note about one of the questionable qualities of this character.

Negative, Devilish

Eleanor Prosser. <u>Hamlet and Revenge</u>. 2nd ed. Stanford: Stanford UP, 1971

[133] When describing his pain and suffering as a dead spirit, the Ghost is not specific but emphasizes the horror. He should, if a good spirit, try to use his suffering to urge repentance and salvation for Hamlet. [134] This emphasis is a sign that he is closer in nature to a devil than to a soul earning its way to redemption.

Notice that the title classifies the topic of the note. If you use such classifications while taking notes, a number of like-titled cards could form the substance of a section in your essay about the negative qualities of the Ghost in *Hamlet*. In addition, once you decide that "Negative, Devilish" is one of the topics you plan to explore, the topic itself will guide you in further study and note taking.

WRITE DOWN YOUR OWN ORIGINAL THOUGHTS, AND BE SURE TO MARK THEM AS YOUR OWN. As you take notes, you will be developing a number of your own observations and thoughts. Do not push these aside in your mind, on the chance of remembering them later, but write them down immediately. Often you may notice a detail that your source does not mention, or you may get a hint for an idea that the critic does not develop. Often, too, you may get thoughts that can serve as "bridges" between details in your notes or as introductions or concluding observations. Be sure to title your comments and also to mark them as your own thought. Here is such a note, which is related to the importance of the Ghost in the structure of *Hamlet*.

> **My Own**   **Structure**
>
> Shakespeare does an excellent job in creating and developing the Ghost. The Ghost shows many characteristics of a living human being, and he is fully integrated in the play's structure.

Observe that some of the ideas and language from this note are used in paragraphs 9 and 10 of the demonstrative essay (p. 1909).

SORT YOUR CARDS INTO GROUPS.   If you do a careful and thorough job of taking notes, your essay will already have been forming in your mind. The titles of your cards will suggest areas to be developed as you do your planning and initial drafting. Once you have assembled a stack of note cards derived from a reasonable number of sources (your instructor may have assigned an approximate number or a minimum number), you can sort them into groups according to the topics and titles. For the demonstrative research essay, after some shuffling and retitling, the cards were assembled in the following groups.

1. Importance in the play's action.
2. Importance in the play's themes.
3. Condition as a spirit
   a. Good signs.
   b. Negative, devilish signs.
4. Human traits.
5. Importance in the play's structure.
6. Effect on other characters.

If you look at the major sections of the demonstrative student essay (pp. 1906–1912), you will see that the topics are closely adapted from these groups of cards. In other words, *the arrangement of the cards is an effective means of organizing and developing a research essay.*

ARRANGE THE CARDS IN EACH GROUP ACCORDING TO TOPICS AND IDEAS.   There is still much to do with each group of cards. You cannot use the details as they fall randomly in your stack. You need to decide which notes are relevant. You might also need to retitle some cards and use them elsewhere. Those that remain will have to be arranged in a clear and logical order to be used in the essay.

Once you have your cards in order, you can write whatever comments or transitions are needed to move from detail to detail. Write this material directly on the cards, and be sure to use pencils or inks of different color, so that you can distinguish later between the original note and what you add now. Here is an example of such a "developed" note card.

Campbell, 127　　　　　　　　　　　　　　　　　　　**Negative, Devilish**

Shakespeare's Ghost reflects the general uncertainty at the time about how ghosts were to be interpreted. **127**

This general uncertainty may be the best way to answer the question about the Ghost's ambiguous nature. Moreover, Shakespeare may have been trying to make his own Ghost more lifelike than consistent.

By adding such commentary to your note cards, you will facilitate the actual writing of your first draft. In many instances, the note and the comment can be moved directly into the paper with only minor revision (material from this note and comment appears in paragraph 6 of the demonstrative student essay).

BE CREATIVE AND ORIGINAL EVEN THOUGH YOU ARE DOING RESEARCH.　You will not always transfer your notes directly into your essay. The major trap to avoid in a research paper is that your use of sources can become an end in itself and therefore a shortcut for your own thinking and writing. Often, students make the mistake of introducing details the way a master of ceremonies introduces performers in a variety show. This is unfortunate because it is the *student* whose essay will be judged, even though the sources, like the performers, do all the work. Thus, it is important to be creative and original in a research essay and to do your own thinking and writing, even though you are relying heavily on your sources. Here are four ways in which research essays may be original.

1. SELECTION.　In each major part of your essay you will include many details from your sources. To be creative you should select different but related details and avoid overlapping or repetition. Your completed essay will be judged on the basis of the thoroughness with which you make your points with different details (which in turn will represent the completeness of your research). Even though you are relying on published materials and cannot be original on that score, your selection can be original because you bring these materials together for the first time, and because you emphasize some details and minimize others. Inevitably, your assemblage of details from your sources will be unique and therefore original.

2. DEVELOPMENT.　Your arrangement of your various points is an obvious area of originality: One detail seems naturally to precede another, and certain conclusions develop out of certain details. As you present the details, conclusions, and arguments from your sources, you can also add an original stamp by introducing supporting details different from those in the source material. You can also add your own emphasis to particular points—an emphasis that you do not find in your sources.

Naturally, the words that you use will be original because they are yours. Your topic sentences, for example, will all be your own. As you introduce details and conclusions, you will need to write "bridges" to get yourself from point to point. These can be introductory remarks or transitions. In other words, as you write, you are not just stringing your notes together, but rather you are actively tying thoughts together in a variety of creative and unique ways.

3. EXPLANATION OF CONTROVERSIAL VIEWS.   Closely related to your selection is that in your research you may have found conflicting or differing views on a topic. If you make a point to describe and distinguish these views, and explain the reasons for the differences, you are presenting material originally. To see how differing views can be handled, see paragraphs 4 and 5 of the demonstrative student essay on page 1907.

4. CREATION OF YOUR OWN INSIGHTS AND POSITIONS.   There are three possibilities here, all related to how well you have learned the primary texts on which your research in secondary sources is based.

a.   **Your own interpretations and ideas.**   An important part of taking notes is to make your own points *precisely when they occur to you*. Often you can expand these as truly original parts of your essay. Your originality does not need to be extensive; it may consist of no more than a single insight. Here is such a card, which was written during research on the Ghost in *Hamlet*.

My Own   **For the Introduction**

The Ghost is minor in the action but major in the play. He is seen twice in scene 1, but this scene is really all about him. (Also about his appearances before the play opens.) In scene 4 of Act 1 he comes again and leads Hamlet off to scene 5--the biggest for him as an acting and speaking character. He speaks after this only from under the stage, and then a small appearance (but important) in Act 3, scene 4, and that's all. He is dominant because he sets everything in motion and therefore his presence is felt everywhere in the play.

The originality here is built around the idea of the small role but dominant importance of the Ghost. The discovery is not unusual or startling, but it nevertheless represents original thought about *Hamlet*. When modified and adapted (and put into full sentences with proper punctuation), the material of the card supplies much of the opening paragraph of the demonstrative student essay. You can see that your development of a "My Own" note card is important for your research essay.

b.   **Gaps in the sources.**   As you read your secondary sources, you may realize that an obvious conclusion is not made or that a certain detail is not stressed. Here is an area for you to develop on your own. Your conclusion can involve a particular interpretation or major point of comparison, or it can rest on a particularly important but underemphasized word or fact. In the demonstrative essay, for example, the writer discusses the idea that the Ghost's commands make it impossible for Hamlet to solve problems through negotiation—the way he might have chosen as prince and student—but instead force him into a plan requiring murder. Most critics observe that Hamlet's life is changed because of the Ghost, but they have not stressed this aspect of the change. Given such a critical "vacuum" (assuming that you cannot read all the articles about some of your topics, where your discovery may already have been dealt with a number of times), it is right to begin filling it with your own insights. A great deal of scholarship is created in this way.

c. **Disputes with the sources.** Your sources may present certain arguments with which you want to disagree. As you develop your disagreement, you will be arguing originally, for the use you make of detail will be different from the use made by the critic or critics whom you are disputing. Also, your conclusions will be your own. This area of originality is similar to the laying out of controversial critical views, except that you furnish one of the opposing views yourself. The approach is limited because it is difficult to find many substantive points of interpretation on which there are not already clearly delineated opposing views. Paragraphs 5 and 6 of the demonstrative student essay show a small point of disagreement (about whether Shakespeare was concerned with consistency in presenting the Ghost's spirit nature) but one that is nevertheless original.

DOCUMENTING YOUR WORK

It is essential to acknowledge—to *document*—all sources from which you have quoted or paraphrased factual and interpretive information.[3] If you do not give due acknowledgment, you run the risk of being challenged for presenting other people's work as your own. This is plagiarism, and it is a serious academic offense that can get you into trouble. As the means of documentation, various reference systems use parenthetical references, footnotes, or endnotes. Whatever system is used, documentation almost always includes a carefully prepared bibliography, or list of works cited.

We will first discuss the list of works cited and then review the two major reference systems for use in a research paper. Parenthetical references, preferred by the Modern Language Association (MLA) since 1984, are described in Joseph Gibaldi, *MLA Handbook for Writers of Research Papers*, 6th ed. (New York: MLA, 2003). Footnotes or endnotes, recommended by the MLA before 1984, are still required by many instructors.

---

[3]For the documentation materials you get online and on the Internet, see Appendix I, "MLA Recommendations for Documenting Electronic Sources," pp. 1953–56.

A List of Works Cited (Bibliography) Is a List of the Works You Have Used

The key to any reference system is a carefully prepared list of works cited that is included at the end of the essay. "Works cited" means exactly that; the list should include just those books and articles you have actually *used* in your essay. If, however, your instructor requires that you use footnotes or endnotes, you can extend your concluding list to be a complete bibliography both of works cited and also of works consulted but not actually used. *Always, always, always follow your instructor's directions.*

The list of works cited should include the following information, in each entry, in the form indicated. If you are using a word processor with the capacity to print italics, you can italicize book and article titles rather than underline them, but be sure to notify your instructor in advance.

FOR A BOOK

1. The author's name, last name first, followed by first name and middle name or initial. Period.
2. The title, italicized or underlined. Period.
3. The city of publication (not state or nation), colon; publisher (easily recognized abbreviations or key words can be used unless they seem awkward or strange; see the *MLA Handbook*), comma; year of publication. Period.

FOR AN ARTICLE

1. The author's name, last name first, followed by first name and middle name or initial. Period.
2. The title of the article in quotation marks. Period.
3. The title of the journal or periodical, italicized or underlined, followed by the volume number in Arabic (*not* Roman) numbers with no punctuation, then the year of publication within parentheses. Colon. For a daily paper or weekly magazine, omit the parentheses and cite the date in the British style followed by a colon (day, month, year, as in *29 Dec. 2002:*). Inclusive page numbers. Period (without any preceding *p.* or *pp.*).

The works cited should be listed alphabetically according to the last names of authors, with unsigned articles included in the list alphabetically by titles. Bibliographical lists are begun at the left margin, with subsequent lines in hanging indentation, so that the key locating word—the author's last name or the first title word of an unsigned article—can be easily seen. Many unpredictable and complex combinations, including ways to describe works of art, musical or other performances, and films, are detailed extensively in the *MLA Handbook.* Here are two model entries.

Book

- Alpers, Antony. *The Life of Katherine Mansfield.* New York: Viking, 1980.

Article

- Hankin, Cheryl. "Fantasy and the Sense of an Ending in the Work of Katherine Mansfield." *Modern Fiction Studies* 24 (1978): 465–74.

Refer to Works Parenthetically as You Draw Details from Them

Within the text of your research essay, use parentheses in referring to works from which you are using facts and conclusions. This parenthetical citation system is recommended in the *MLA Handbook,* and its principle is to provide documentation without asking readers to interrupt their reading to find footnotes or endnotes. Readers wanting to see the complete reference can easily find it in your list of works cited. With this system, you incorporate the author's last name and the relevant page number or numbers directly, whenever possible, into the body of your essay. If the author's name is mentioned in your discussion, you need to give only the page number or numbers in parentheses. Here are two examples.

> Alexander Pope believed in the idea that the universe is a whole, a totally unified body, which provides a "viable benevolent system for the salvation of everyone who does good" (Kallich 24).

> Martin Kallich draws attention to Alexander Pope's belief in the idea that the universe is a whole, a totally unified body, which provides a "viable benevolent system for the salvation of everyone who does good" (24).

Footnotes and Endnotes Are Formal and Traditional Reference Formats

The most formal system of documentation still widely used is that of *footnotes* (references at the bottom of each page) or *endnotes* (references listed numerically at the end of the essay). If your instructor wants you to use one of these formats, do the following: Make a note the first time you quote or refer to a source, with the details ordered as outlined below.

FOR A BOOK

1. The author's name, first name or initials first, followed by middle name or initial, then last name. Comma.

2. The title, underlined or italicized for a book, no punctuation. If you are referring to a work in a collection (article, story, poem) use quotation marks for that, but italicize or underline the title of the book. No punctuation, but use a comma after the title if an editor, translator, or edition number follows.

3. The name of the editor or translator, if relevant. Abbreviate "editor" or "edited by" as *ed.,* "editors" as *eds.* Use *trans.* for "translator" or "translated by." No punctuation, but use a comma if an edition number follows.

4. The edition (if indicated), abbreviated thus: *2nd ed., 3rd ed.,* and so on. No punctuation.

5. The publication facts, in parentheses, without any preceding or following punctuation, in the following order.

   a. City (but not the state or nation) of publication, colon.

   b. Publisher (clear abbreviations are acceptable and desirable), comma.

   c. Year of publication.

6. The page number(s) with no *p.* or *pp.,* for example, 65, 6–10, 15–19, 295–307, 311–16. Period. If you are referring to longer works, such as novels or longer

stories with division or chapter numbers, include these numbers for readers who may be using an edition different from yours.

FOR A JOURNAL OR MAGAZINE ARTICLE

1. The author, first name or initials first, followed by middle name or initial, then last name. Comma.
2. The title of the article, in quotation marks. Comma.
3. The name of the journal, italicized or underlined. No punctuation.
4. The volume number, in Arabic numerals. No punctuation.
5. The year of publication within parentheses. Colon. For newspaper and journal articles, omit the parentheses, and include day, month, and year (in the British style: *21 May 2001*). Colon.
6. The page number(s) with no *p.* or *pp.:* 65, 6–10, 34–36, 98–102, 345–47. Period.

For later notes to the same work, use the last name of the author as the reference unless you are referring to two or more works by the same author. Thus, if you refer to only one work by, say, Langston Hughes, the name *Hughes* will be enough for all later references. Should you be referring to other works by Hughes, however, you will also need to make a short reference to the specific works to distinguish them, such as *Hughes, "Mulatto,"* and *Hughes, "Theme for English B."*

Footnotes are placed at the bottom of each page, and endnotes are included on a separate page, or pages, at the end of your essay. The first lines of both footnotes and endnotes should be paragraph indented, and continuing lines should be flush with the left margin. Both endnote and footnote numbers are positioned slightly above the line (as superior numbers) like this:[12]. You can single-space footnotes and endnotes and leave a line of space between them. Additionally, today's computer programs have specially designed and consecutively numbered footnote formats. These are generally acceptable, but be sure to consult your instructor. (For more detailed coverage of footnoting practices, see the *MLA Handbook*.)

SAMPLE FOOTNOTES. In the examples below, book titles and periodicals are shown *italicized*, as they would be in an essay prepared on the computer. If the essay is typewritten or handwritten, these titles should be underlined.

[1]Blanche H. Gelfant, *Women Writing in America: Voices in Collage* (Hanover: UP of New England, for Dartmouth College, 1984) 110.

[2]Günter Grass, "Losses," *Granta* 42 (Winter 1992): 99.

[3]John O'Meara, "*Hamlet* and the Fortunes of Sorrowful Imagination: A Re-examination of the Genesis and Fate of the Ghost," *Cahiers Elisabéthains* 35 (1989): 21.

[4]Grass 104.

[5]Gelfant 141.

[6]O'Meara 17.

As a principle, you do not need to repeat in a footnote or endnote any material you have already mentioned in your own discourse. For example, if you recognize the author and title of your source, then the footnote or endnote should give no more than the data about publication. Here is an example.

> In *The Fiction of Katherine Mansfield,* Marvin Magalaner points out that Mansfield was as skillful in the development of epiphanies (that is, the use of highly significant though perhaps unobtrusive actions or statements to reveal the depths of a particular character) as James Joyce himself, the "inventor" of the technique.[9]

---

[9](Carbondale: Southern Illinois UP, 1971) 130.

Many Academic Disciplines Set Their Own Requirements for Documentation

Other reference systems and style manuals have been adopted by various disciplines (e.g., mathematics, medicine, psychology) to serve their own special needs. If you receive no instructions from your instructors in other courses, you can adapt the systems described here. If you need to use the documentation methods of other fields, however, use the *MLA Handbook* for guidance about what style manual to select.

Final Advice: When in Doubt, Consult Your Instructor

As long as all you want from a reference is the page number of a quotation or paraphrase, the parenthetical system described briefly here—and detailed fully in the *MLA Handbook*—is the most suitable and convenient one you can use. However, you may wish to use footnotes or endnotes if you need to add more details, provide additional explanations, or refer your readers to other materials that you are not using.

Whatever method you follow, *you must always acknowledge sources properly.* Remember that whenever you begin to write and make references, you might forget a number of specific details about documentation, and you will certainly discover that you have many questions. Be sure, then, to ask your instructor, who is your final authority.

STRATEGIES FOR ORGANIZING IDEAS IN YOUR RESEARCH ESSAY

In your research essay you may wish to expand your introduction more than usual because of the need to relate the problem of research to your topic. You may wish to bring in relevant historical or biographical information (see, for example, the introduction of the demonstrative student research essay on pp. 1906–1912). You may also wish to summarize critical opinion or describe critical problems about your topic. The idea is to lead your reader into your topic by providing interesting and significant materials that you have found.

Because of the length of most research essays, some instructors require a topic outline, which is in effect a brief table of contents. This pattern is observed in the demonstrative student research essay. *Because the inclusion of an outline is a matter of the instructor's choice, be sure to learn whether your instructor requires it.*

As you write the body and conclusion of your research essay, your development will be governed by your choice of topic. Consult the relevant chapters in this book about what to include for whatever approach or approaches you select (setting, ideas, point of view, character, tone, or any other).

In length, the research essay can be anywhere from five to fifteen or more pages, depending on your instructor's assignment. Obviously, an essay on a single work will be shorter than one based on several. If you narrow the scope of your topic, as suggested in the approaches described at the beginning of this chapter, you can readily keep your essay within the assigned length. The following demonstrative student research essay, for example, illustrates approach 1 (p. 1888) by being limited to only one character in one play. Were you to write on characters in a number of other plays by Shakespeare (approach 2), you could limit your total number of pages by stressing comparative treatments and by avoiding excessive detail about problems pertaining to only one work.

Although you limit your topic yourself in consultation with your instructor, you may encounter problems because you will deal not with one source alone but with many. Naturally the sources will provide you with details and also with many of your ideas. The problem is to handle the many strands without piling on too many details, and also without being led into digressions. It is important therefore to keep your central idea foremost; the constant stressing of your central idea will help you both to select relevant materials and to reject irrelevant ones.

It bears reemphasis that you need to distinguish between *your own work* and the *sources* you are using. Your readers will assume that everything you write is your own unless you indicate otherwise. Therefore, when blending your words with the ideas from sources, be clear about proper acknowledgments. Most commonly, if you are simply presenting details and facts, you can write straightforwardly and let parenthetical references suffice as your authority, as in the following sentence from the demonstrative student research essay.

> Thus he is most emphatic that Hamlet should not kill her along with Claudius (Fisch 80), and he also voices concern about the reputation and future of Denmark (Gottschalk, "Scanning" 165).

Although the words belong to the writer of the essay, the parenthetical references clearly indicate that the ideas for the sentence are derived from the two sources.

If you use an interpretation unique to a particular writer, or if you rely on a significant quotation from your source, you should make your acknowledgment an essential part of your discussion, as in this sentence.

> A. C. Bradley (126) suggests that these speeches indicate Shakespeare's master touch in the development of the Ghost's character.

Here the idea of the critic is singled out for special acknowledgment. If you indicate your sources in this way, no confusion can arise about how you have used them.

DEMONSTRATIVE STUDENT RESEARCH ESSAY

The Ghost in *Hamlet*°

OUTLINE

I.   Introduction
    A.   The Importance of the Ghost in <u>Hamlet</u>
    B.   The Ghost's Influence on the Play's Themes
II.   The Ghost's Status as a Spirit
III.   The Ghost's Character
IV.   The Ghost's Importance in the Structure of the Play
V.   The Ghost's Effect
VI.   Conclusion

I. INTRODUCTION

A. The Importance of the Ghost in <u>Hamlet</u>

[1]   <u>Even though the Ghost of Hamlet's father is present in only a few scenes of Hamlet, he is a dominating presence.</u>* He appears twice in the first scene, and this entire scene itself is about the meaning of these and earlier appearances. He enters again in the fourth scene of Act 1, when he beckons to Hamlet and leads him offstage, in this way providing an early illustration of Hamlet's courage (Edgar 257). In the fifth scene of Act 1 he speaks for the first time, explaining how his brother Claudius murdered him, and exhorting his son, Hamlet, to kill Claudius in retribution. Because this cry for revenge directly or indirectly causes the rest of the play's action, it is clear, as Marjorie Garber puts it, that "the dead man turned Ghost is more powerful than he was when living" (304). After some words which the Ghost speaks from underground (i.e., under the stage), he does not enter again until the fourth scene of Act 3, in the queen's closet or bedroom, when he reveals himself to Hamlet--but not to Gertrude--to reproach the Prince for not yet having killed Claudius. The Ghost is not present at the play's end, but the actions he sets in motion are concluded there, and hence his effect remains dominant.

B. The Ghost's Influence on the Play's Themes

[2]   <u>Not only is the Ghost dominant over actions, but he is also directly linked to many of the play's themes.</u> William Kerrigan calls the Ghost a "nightmind" who introduces the mental darkness of evil that pervades the play (42). In addition, the Ghost intensifies the play's "interior suffering" (Paris 85). This suffering is brought out in Hamlet's anguished soliloquies and also in the pain of Ophelia, Laertes, and even Claudius himself. Another theme is shown by the Ghost's commands to Hamlet--that of responsibility, whether personal, political, or conjugal (McFarland 15). Hamlet of course does not rush right out to kill Claudius, despite the Ghost's urgings, and hence the Ghost is indirectly responsible for the theme of

°See pp. 1306–1406 for this play.
*Central idea.

hesitation--this great "Sphinx of modern Literature"--which has become one of the weaknesses cited most frequently about Hamlet's character (Jones 22). The Ghost's scary presence also poses questions about the power of superstition, terror, and fear (Campbell 211). Beyond these, deeply within the psychological realm, the Ghost has been cited as a "confirmation" of the influence of "psychic residues in governing and shaping human life" (McFarland 34), not to mention the significance of the Oedipus complex in the development of Hamlet's character.

[3]   Because the Ghost is so important, one hardly needs to justify studying him. <u>His importance can be traced in his spirit nature, his influence on the play's structure, and his effect on Hamlet and therefore indirectly on all the major characters.</u>[†]

II. THE GHOST'S STATUS AS A SPIRIT

<u>The Ghost is shown as an apparition of questionable and vague status.</u> When Hamlet first sees the Ghost, he asks whether he sees "a spirit of health, or goblin damned" (1.4.40). Horatio adds that Hamlet is "desperate with imagination" (1.4.87), thus throwing doubt on the Ghost's reality even though the vision is seen by everyone onstage. When speaking with Hamlet, the Ghost is vague about his out-of-earth location, complaining that he is suffering hellish fires but intimating that he will be compelled to do so only until his earthly sins are purged away. Although this description, according to Anthony Holden, indicates that "the Ghost . . . occupies an authentically Catholic version of Purgatory" (28), and Dobson and Wells state that "the Ghost seems to belong to a Catholic theology rather than a

[4] Protestant one" (182), Shakespeare's treatment is not an unambiguous rendering of Catholic doctrine. Thus the Ghost says that he is allowed to walk the earth for a certain time, presumably, according to the first-act treatment, only at night. But then, in Act 3, scene 4, the Ghost appears in the Queen's private room. Does this visit take place at night or during the day? This inconsistency about where and when the Ghost spends his time may have been deliberate on Shakespeare's part, for showing a ghost straight out of purgatory might have seemed dangerously close to Catholic doctrine. It was apparently safest for writers in a dominant Protestant culture to show the ghost only of a person who was "freshly dead or on the point of death" (O'Meara 15), and also to make the details vague and ambiguous.

<u>The status and existence of Shakespeare's Ghost therefore reflects uncertainties during the Elizabethan period.</u> Lily Campbell offers a number of ways in which Elizabethans dealt with these uncertainties. First, James I of England (when still James VI of Scotland), in writing about departed spirits, emphasized that the devil himself could choose the shape of loved ones to deceive and corrupt living persons. It is this danger that Hamlet specifically describes. Second, as already

[5] mentioned, some Elizabethan religious thinkers held it possible for souls in purgatory to return to earth for a time and speak to the living. Third, scientifically oriented thinkers interpreted ghostly appearances as a sign of madness or deep melancholia (Campbell 121), or what O'Meara calls "sorrowful imagination" (19). There were apparently a number of "tests" that might have enabled people to determine the authenticity of ghosts. Most of these required that the spirit should show goodness of character and give comfort to the living (Campbell 123).

<u>The Ghost of King Hamlet both passes and fails these tests.</u> He is not totally bad (Campbell 126), but he urges Hamlet to commit murder, something

[†]Thesis sentence.

that no ghost trying to reach heaven would possibly do (McFarland 36). Although the Ghost describes the pain of a soul in purgatory, he does so to create fear, not to urge Hamlet to seek salvation. Thus he is more like the devil than a spirit on the way to redemption (Prosser 133-34; Frye 22). Another sign suggesting the Ghost's devilishness is that he withholds his appearance from Gertrude when he shows himself to Hamlet in Act 3, scene 4 (Campbell 124).

[6]   Hamlet creates his own test of the Ghost by getting the touring actors to perform The Murder of Gonzago. Once he sees the King's disturbance at the play, Hamlet concludes that the Ghost is real and not just a "figment of his melancholy imagination" (Harrison 883). Perhaps the best answer to the conflicting views of the Ghost is given by Lily Campbell, who suggests that the ambiguity indicates the general uncertainty about ghosts among Shakespeare's contemporaries (127). In other words, there was no unanimity about the nature and purposes of ghosts, and Shakespeare's Ghost reflected common Elizabethan understanding and attitudes.

III. THE GHOST'S CHARACTER

Uncertainty and theology aside, the Ghost is probably Shakespeare's rendering of what he thought a ghost would be like. Shakespeare inherited a tradition of noisy, bloodthirsty ghosts from his sources--what Harold Fisch calls a "Senecan ghost" (91). There was also a tradition of "hungry ghosts," who were spirits prowling about the earth "searching for the life they were deprived of"

[7]   (Austin 93). In this tradition, Shakespeare's Ghost is bloodthirsty, although ironically not as bloodthirsty as Hamlet himself becomes during the play (Gottschalk 166). The Ghost is surrounded by awe and horror (DeLuca 147) and is frightening, both to the soldiers at the beginning of the play and also to Hamlet in Act 3, scene 4 (Charney, Style 167–68). It seems that horror is the main effect that Shakespeare wanted as accompaniment to the Ghost.

Although the Ghost is bloodthirsty and horrible, he has redeeming qualities (Alexander 30). He is toned down from a ghost in an anonymous and lost earlier play, perhaps a first version of Hamlet by Shakespeare himself (Bloom 383), which was described by Shakespeare's contemporary Thomas Lodge (1558–1625). Lodge talked about "ye ghost which cried so miserally [pitifully, sorrowfully] at ye theator . . . Hamlet, reuenge" [sic]. Shakespeare's Ghost also cries

[8]   out for vengeance, but as a former loving husband he is still concerned for the welfare of Hamlet's mother, Gertrude, directing his son to treat her kindly and help her (Kerrigan 54). Also, as a former king, he voices concern about the reputation and future of Denmark (Gottschalk 165). Paul Gottschalk points to these redeeming qualities to indicate that the Ghost is concerned with "restoration" as well as "retaliation" (166)--a view not shared by Norman Austin, who calls the Ghost "the spirit of ruin" (105).

Indeed, the Ghost has many qualities of a living human being. For example, he is witty, as Maurice Charney observes about the following interchange between the Ghost and Hamlet just at the beginning of the revelation speeches in Act 1, scene 5, lines 6–7:

HAMLET.   Speak, I am bound to hear.

GHOST.   So art thou to revenge, when thou shalt hear.

[9]   In other words, even though the Ghost may have come "with . . . airs from heaven, or blasts from hell" (1.4. 41), he is still mentally alert enough to make a pun out of Hamlet's word "bound" (Charney, <u>Style</u> 118). To this quickness can be added his shrewd ability to judge his son's character. He knows that Hamlet may neglect duty, and hence his last words in Act 1, scene 5, are "remember me," and his first words in Act 3, scene 4 are "Do not forget." A. C. Bradley suggests that these speeches indicate Shakespeare's master touch in the development of the Ghost's character (126).

        <u>The Ghost also shows other human traits</u>. He feels strong remorse about his lifelong crimes and "imperfections" for which his sudden death did not give him time to atone. It is this awareness that has made him bitter and vengeful. Also, he has a sense of appropriateness that extends to what he wears. Thus, at the beginning he appears on the parapets dressed in full armor. This battle uni-

[10]   form is in keeping with the location and also with his vengeful mission (Aldus 54). The armor is intimidating, a means of enforcing the idea that the Ghost in death has become a "spirit of hatred" (Austin 99). By contrast, in the closet scene he wears a dressing gown ["in his habit as he lived," 3.4.135], as though he is prepared for ordinary palace activities of both business and leisure (Charney, <u>Style</u> 26).

IV. THE GHOST'S IMPORTANCE IN THE STRUCTURE OF THE PLAY

        <u>Shakespeare's great strength as a dramatist is shown not only in his giving the Ghost such a round, full character but also in his integrating the Ghost fully within the play's structure</u>. According to Peter Alexander, the Ghost is "indispensable" in the plot as the source of communication to set things in motion (29). The Ghost is also a director and organizer as well as an informer--a figure who keeps

[11]   the action moving until there is no stopping it (Aldus 100). A careful study of his speeches shows that he is a manipulator, playing on his son's emotions to make him hurry to kill the king. In addition, the Ghost is persistent, because his return to Hamlet in Act 3, scene 4, to "whet thy almost blunted purpose" (line 111) is the mark of a manager who nervously intervenes when his directions are being neglected or delayed.

        <u>The Ghost is also significant in a major structure of the play</u>. During the imagined period when the events at Elsinore are taking place, Denmark is undergoing a national mobilization in preparation for war against Norway (Alexander 34). Structurally, the beginning and ending of <u>Hamlet</u> are marked by the fear of war and the political takeover by "Young Fortinbras" of Norway, who is like Hamlet because King Hamlet, now the Ghost, had killed Old Fortinbras in single

[12]   combat. Young Fortinbras is therefore as much an avenger as Hamlet (Honan 283), and the cause is King Hamlet, who now as a Ghost pushes Hamlet to vengeance. So strong is the Ghost's anger against Claudius that he insists on revenge even if it means the defeat of his country in the face of impending war. Ironically, the Ghost in death brings about the passing of the kingdom he courageously defended in life.

        <u>An additional major structure involves the Ghost</u>. Maurice Charney observes that the Ghost is significant in the "symmetrical" poison plots in the play (<u>Style</u> 39). The first of these plots, the poisoning of King Hamlet, is described by the Ghost himself in Act 1, scene 5. The poisoning of the player king in Act 3,

[13]   scene 2, is a reenactment of the first murder, and it occurs in approximately the middle of the action. The final poisonings--of Gertrude, Laertes, Claudius, and finally Hamlet himself--occur in Act 5, scene 2, the play's last scene. These actions have value as symbolic frames that measure the deterioration of the play's major characters.

V. THE GHOST'S EFFECT

Beyond the Ghost's practical and structural importance in the action, he has profound psychological influence, mainly negative, on the characters. Roy Walker describes him as a "prologue" to the "omen" of Hamlet himself, who is the agent of the "dread purpose" of vengeance (220). Because Hamlet is already suffering depression and melancholia, this murderous mission opens the wounds of his vulnerability (Campbell 127–28). Literally, Hamlet must give up

[14]   everything he has ever learned, even "the movement of existence itself," so that he can carry out the Ghost's commandment (McFarland 32–33). In Harold Bloom's words, "everything in the play depends upon Hamlet's response to the Ghost" (387). Because of this malignant ghostly influence, Hamlet is gripped by a melancholy that undermines his love for Ophelia, his possible friendship with Laertes, and his relationship with his mother (Kirsch 31; Kott 49). The effects are like waves radiating outwardly, with the Ghost at the center as a relentless, destructive force. No one escapes.

This overwhelming ghostly force possesses Hamlet once the first encounter has occurred. This possession is shown both literally and figuratively when the Ghost goes underground in Act 1, scene 5, and hears Hamlet's conversation with Horatio and the guards. The Ghost thus represents "dimensions of reality" beyond what we see on the stage, a mysterious world "elsewhere" that dominates the very souls of living persons (Charney, "Asides" 127). As a result of

[15]   this ever-present force, which as far as Hamlet is concerned might become visible at any moment, Hamlet is denied the healing that might normally occur after the death of a parent (Kirsch 26). The steady pressure to kill Claudius disrupts any movement to mental health and creates what Kirsch calls a "pathology of depression" (26) that inhibits Hamlet's actions (Bradley 123), causes his Oedipal preoccupation with the sexuality of his parents (Kirsch 22), and brings about his desire for the oblivion of suicide (Kirsch 27).

It is, finally, this power over his son that gives the Ghost the greatest influence in the play. Once the Ghost has appeared, Hamlet is not and never can be the same. He loses the dignity and composure that he has assumed as his right as a prince of Denmark and as a student in quest of knowledge (McFarland 38). The Ghost's commands make it impossible for Hamlet to solve problems through negotiation--the way he might have chosen as prince and

[16]   student. The commands force him instead into a plan requiring murder. What could be more normal than hesitation under such circumstances? Despite all Hamlet's reflections, however, the web of vengeance woven by the Ghost finally closes in on all those caught in it, both the deserving and undeserving. There is no solution but the final one--real death, which is the literal conclusion of the symbolic death represented by the Ghost when he first appears on the Elsinore battlements.

VI. CONCLUSION

The Ghost is real in terms of the play's action and structure. He is seen by the characters on the stage, and when he speaks we hear him. He is made round and full by Shakespeare, and his motivation is direct and clear, even though the signs of his status as a spirit are presented ambiguously. But the Ghost is more. He has been made a Ghost by the greed and envy of Claudius, and for this rea-

[17] son he becomes in the play either a conscious or an unwitting agent of the "unseen Fates or forces" of his own doom (Walker 220). What he brings is the horror that lurks within the depths of good, moral people, waiting to overwhelm them and destroy them. Once the forces are released, there is no holding them and there is no way to rescue those that are hurt, and the tragedy of it all is that there is no way to win against these odds.

WORKS CITED

Aldus, P. J. Mousetrap: Structure and Meaning in Hamlet. Toronto: U of Toronto P, 1977.

Alexander, Peter. Hamlet: Father and Son. Oxford: Clarendon, 1955.

Austin, Norman. "Hamlet's Hungry Ghost." Shenandoah 37.1 (1987): 78–105.

Bloom, Harold. Shakespeare: The Invention of the Human. New York: Riverhead, 1998.

Bradley, A. C. Shakespearean Tragedy. 1904. London: Macmillan, 1950.

Campbell, Lily B. Shakespeare's Tragic Heroes: Slaves of Passion. New York: Barnes, 1959.

Charney, Maurice. "Asides, Soliloquies, and Offstage Speech in Hamlet." Shakespeare and the Sense of Performance: Essays in the Tradition of Performance Criticism in Honor of Bernard Beckerman. Ed. Marvin and Ruth Thompson. Newark: U of Delaware P, 1989. 116–31.

---. Style in Hamlet. Princeton: Princeton UP, 1969.

DeLuca, Diana Macintyre. "The Movements of the Ghost in Hamlet." Shakespeare Quarterly 24 (1973): 147–54.

Dobson, Michael, and Stanley Wells. The Oxford Companion to Shakespeare. Oxford: Oxford UP, 2001.

Edgar, Irving I. Shakespeare, Medicine, and Psychiatry. New York: Philosophical Library, 1970.

Fisch, Harold. Hamlet and the Word. New York: Ungar, 1971.

Frye, Roland Mushat. The Renaissance Hamlet: Issues and Responses in 1600. Princeton: Princeton UP, 1984.

Garber, Marjorie. "Hamlet: Giving Up the Ghost." William Shakespeare: Hamlet. Ed. Suzanne L. Wofford. Boston: Bedford, 1994. 297–331.

Gottschalk, Paul. "Hamlet and the Scanning of Revenge." Shakespeare Quarterly 24 (1973): 155–70.

Harrison, G. B., ed. Shakespeare: The Complete Works. New York: Harcourt, 1948.

Holden, Anthony. William Shakespeare: The Man behind the Genius: A Biography. Boston: 1968. Little, 1999.

Honan, Park. <u>Shakespeare: A Life</u>. Oxford: Oxford UP, 1998.

Jones, Ernest. <u>Hamlet and Oedipus</u>. 1949. New York: Doubleday, 1954.

Kerrigan, William. <u>Hamlet's Perfection</u>. Baltimore: Johns Hopkins UP, 1994.

Kirsch, Arthur. "Hamlet's Grief." <u>ELH</u> 48 (1981): 17–36.

Kott, Jan. <u>Shakespeare, Our Contemporary</u>. Trans. Boleslaw Taborski. 1967. London: Methuen, 1970.

McFarland, Thomas. <u>Tragic Meanings in Shakespeare</u>. New York: Random, 1966.

O'Meara, John. "<u>Hamlet</u> and the Fortunes of Sorrowful Imagination: A Re-exami- nation of the Genesis and Fate of the Ghost." <u>Cahiers Elisabéthains</u> 35 (1989): 15–25.

Paris, Jean. <u>Shakespeare</u>. Trans. Richard Seaver. New York: Grove, 1960.

Prosser, Eleanor. <u>Hamlet and Revenge</u>. 2nd ed. Stanford: Stanford UP, 1971.

Walker, Roy. "Hamlet: The Opening Scene." <u>Shakespeare: Modern Essays in Crit- icism</u>. Ed. Leonard F. Dean. New York: Oxford UP, 1961.

Commentary on the Essay

This essay illustrates an assignment requiring about twenty-five sources and about 2,500 words (there are actually 27 sources). The sources were located through an examination of library catalogues, the *MLA Bibliography,* library bookshelves, the Internet, and the bibliographies in some of the listed books. They represent the range of materials available in a college library with a selective, not exhaustive, set of holdings. Two of the sources (Austin and O'Meara) were obtained through Interlibrary Loan.

The writing itself is developed from the sources listed. Originality (see p. 1898) is provided by the structure and development of the essay, additional observations not existing in the sources, and transitions. The topic outline is placed appropriately at the beginning—a pattern you can follow unless your instructor asks for a more detailed outline, or, perhaps, for no outline at all.

Because the essay is concerned with only one work—and one subject about that work—it demonstrates approach 1 (p. 1888). The essay is eclectic, introducing discussions of ideas, character, style, and structure. These four topics fulfill the goal of covering the ground thoroughly within the confines of the assignment. A shorter research assignment might deal with no more than, say, the Ghost's character, ignoring other topics. A longer essay might deal further with the philosophical and theological meanings of ghosts during the Elizabethan period, or a more detailed study of all the traits of the Ghost's character, and so on.

The central idea of the essay is stressed in paragraph 1, along with an assertion that the Ghost is a major influence in the play, together with a concession that the Ghost is only a minor character in the action. The research for this paragraph is derived primarily from a reading of the play itself. Paragraph 2, continuing the exploration of the central idea, demonstrates that the Ghost figures in the major themes of *Hamlet.* Paragraph 3 is mainly functional, being used as the location of the thesis sentence.

Part II, containing paragraphs 4–6, deals with the Ghost's status as a spirit. Part III, with paragraphs 7–10 is concerned with the Ghost's human rather than spiritual characteristics. Part IV, with paragraphs 11–13, deals with the significance of the Ghost in the major structures that dominate the play. Part V, with three paragraphs, considers the Ghost's negative and overwhelming influence over the major figures of *Hamlet,* the emphasis being the character of Hamlet as the transferring agent of the Ghost's destructive revenge. The concluding paragraph (17) sums up the essay with the final idea of how the Ghost affects the tragic nature of *Hamlet.*

The list of works cited is the basis of all parenthetical references in the essay, in accordance with the *MLA Handbook for Writers of Research Papers,* 6th ed. Using these references, an interested reader can consult the sources for a more detailed development of the ideas in the demonstrative essay. The works cited can also serve as a springboard for expanded research.

Critical Approaches Important in the Study of Literature

A number of critical theories or approaches for understanding and interpreting literature are available to critics and students alike.[1] Many of these were developed during the twentieth century to create a discipline of literary studies comparable with disciplines in the natural and social sciences. Literary critics have often borrowed liberally from other disciplines (e.g., history, psychology, politics, anthropology) but have primarily aimed at developing literature as a study in its own right.

At the heart of the various critical approaches are many fundamental questions: What is literature? What does it do? Is its concern only to tell stories, to entertain, or is it to express emotions? To what degree is literature an art, as opposed to an instrument for imparting knowledge? How does it get its ideas across? What more does it do than express ideas? How valuable was literature in the past, and how valuable is it now? What can it contribute to intellectual, artistic, political, and social thought and history? How is literature used, and how and why is it misused? Is it private? Public? What theoretical and technical expertise may be invoked to enhance literary studies?

Questions such as these indicate that criticism is concerned not only with reading and interpreting stories, poems, and plays but also with establishing theoretical understanding. Because of such extensive aims, you will understand that a full explanation and illustration of the approaches would fill the pages of a long book. The following descriptions are therefore intended as no more than brief introductions. Bear in mind that in the hands of skilled critics, the approaches are so subtle, sophisticated, and complex that they are not only critical stances but also philosophies.

---

[1]Some of the approaches described in this chapter are presented more simply in Chapter 1 as basic study techniques for writing about literary works.

Although the various approaches provide widely divergent ways to study literature and literary problems, they reflect major tendencies rather than absolute straitjacketing. Not every approach is appropriate for every work, nor are the approaches always mutually exclusive. Even the most devoted practitioners of the methods do not pursue them rigidly. In addition, some of the approaches are more "user friendly" than others for certain types of discovery. To a degree at least, most critics therefore take a particular approach but utilize methods that technically belong to one or more of the other approaches. A critic stressing the topical/historical approach, for example, might introduce the close study of a work that is associated with the method of the New Criticism. Similarly, a psychoanalytical critic might include details about archetypes. In short, a great deal of criticism is *pragmatic* or *eclectic* rather than rigid.

The approaches to be considered here are these: moral/intellectual, topical/historical, New Critical/formalist, structuralist, feminist, economic determinist/Marxist, psychological/psychoanalytic, archetypal/symbolic/mythic, deconstructionist, and reader-response.

The object of learning about these approaches, like everything else in this book, is to help you develop your own capacities as a reader and writer. Accordingly, following each of the descriptions is a brief paragraph showing how Hawthorne's story "Young Goodman Brown" (Chapter 9) might be considered in the light of the particular approach. The illustrative paragraph following the discussion of structuralism, for example, shows an application of the structuralist approach to Goodman Brown and his story, and so also with the feminist approach, the economic determinist approach, and the others. Whenever you are doing your own writing about literature, you are free to use the various approaches as part or all of your assignment, if you believe the approach may help you.

MORAL/INTELLECTUAL

The **moral/intellectual critical approach** is concerned with content and values (see also Chapters 10, 23). The approach is as old as literature itself, for literature is a traditional mode of imparting morality, philosophy, and religion. The concern in moral/intellectual criticism is not only to discover meaning but also to determine whether works of literature are both *true* and *significant*.

To study literature from the moral/intellectual perspective is therefore to determine whether a work conveys a lesson or a message and whether it can help readers lead better lives and improve their understanding of the world: What ideas does the work contain? How strongly does the work bring forth its ideas? What application do the ideas have to the work's characters and situations? How may the ideas be evaluated intellectually? Morally? Discussions based on such questions do not imply that literature is primarily a medium of moral and intellectual exhortation. Ideally, moral/intellectual criticism should differ from sermonizing to the degree that readers should always be left with their own decisions about whether to assimilate the ideas of a work and about whether the ideas—and values—are personally or morally acceptable.

Sophisticated critics have sometimes demeaned the moral/intellectual approach on the grounds that "message hunting" reduces a work's artistic value by treating it like a sermon or political speech; but the approach will be valuable as long as readers expect literature to be applicable to their own lives.

EXAMPLE

"Young Goodman Brown" raises the issue of how an institution designed for human elevation, such as the religious system of colonial Salem, can be so ruinous. Does the failure result from the system itself or from the people who misunderstand it? Is what is true of religion as practiced by Brown also true of social and political institutions? Should any religious or political philosophy be given greater significance than good will and mutual trust? One of the major virtues of "Young Goodman Brown" is that it provokes questions like these but at the same time provides a number of satisfying answers. A particularly important one is that religious and moral beliefs should not be used to justify the condemnation of others. Another important answer is that attacks made from the refuge of a religion or group, such as Brown's Puritanism, are dangerous because the judge may condemn without thought and without personal responsibility.

TOPICAL/HISTORICAL

The **topical/historical critical approach** stresses the relationship of literature to its historical period, and for this reason it has had a long life. Although much literature may be applicable to many places and times, much of it also directly reflects the intellectual and social worlds of the authors. When was the work written? What were the circumstances that produced it? What major issues does it deal with? How does it fit into the author's career? Keats's poem "On First Looking into Chapman's Homer" (p. 728), for example, is his excited response to his reading of one of the major literary works of Western civilization. Hardy's "Channel Firing" (p. 710) is an acerbic response to continued armament and preparation for war during the twentieth century.

The topical/historical approach investigates relationships of this sort, including the elucidation of words and concepts that today's readers may not immediately understand. Obviously, the approach requires the assistance of footnotes, dictionaries, library catalogues, histories, and handbooks.

A common criticism of the topical/historical approach is that in the extreme, it deals with background knowledge rather than with literature itself. It is possible, for example, for a topical/historical critic to describe a writer's life, the period of the writer's work, and the social and intellectual ideas of the time—all without ever considering the meaning, importance, and value of the work itself.

A reaction against such an unconnected use of historical details is the so-called **New Historicism.** This approach justifies the introduction of historical knowledge by integrating it with the understanding of particular texts. Readers of Arnold's "Dover Beach" (p. 671), for example, sometimes find it difficult to follow the meaning of Arnold's statement "The Sea of Faith/Was once, too, at the full." Historical background has a definite role to play here. In Arnold's time there developed a method of treating the Bible as a historical document rather than divinely inspired revelation. This approach has been called the Higher Criticism of the Bible, and to many thoughtful people of the time it undermined the concept that the Bible was divine, infallible, and inerrant. Therefore the "Sea of Faith" was thought to be not at full but rather at ebb tide. Because the introduction of such historical material is designed to facilitate the reading of the poem—and also the reading of other literature of the period—the New Historicism represents an integration of knowledge and interpretation. As a principle, New Historicism entails the acquisition of as much historical information as possible, because our knowledge of the relationship of literature to its historical period can never be complete. The practitioner of the historical criticism must always seek new information on the grounds that it may prove relevant to the understanding of literature.

EXAMPLE

"Young Goodman Brown" is an allegorical story by Nathaniel Hawthorne (1804–1864), the major New England writer who probed deeply into the relationship between religion and guilt. His ancestors had been involved in religious persecutions, including the Salem witch trials, and he, living 150 years afterward, wanted to analyze the weaknesses and uncertainties of the sin-dominated religion of the earlier period, a tradition of which he was a resentful heir. Not surprisingly, therefore, "Young Goodman Brown" takes place in Salem during Puritan times, and Hawthorne's implied judgments are those of a severe critic of how the harsh old religion destroyed personal and family relationships. Although the immediate concerns of the story belong to a vanished age, Hawthorne's treatment is still valuable because it is still timely.

NEW CRITICAL/FORMALIST

New Criticism has been a dominant force in contemporary literary studies. It focuses on literary texts as formal works of art, and for this reason it can be seen as a reaction against the topical/historical approach. The objection raised by New Critics is that as topical/historical critics consider literary history, they evade direct contact with actual texts.

The inspiration for the **New Critical/formalist critical** approach was the French practice of *explication de texte,* a method that emphasizes detailed examination and explanation. (See "Writing an Explication of a Poem," p. 629.) The New Criticism is at its most brilliant in the formal analysis of smaller units such as entire poems and short passages. For the analysis of larger structures, the New Criticism also utilizes a number of techniques that have been selected as the basis of chapters in this book. Discussions of point of view, tone, plot, character, and structure, for example, are formal ways of looking at literature that are derived from the New Criticism.

The aim of the formalist study of literature is to provide readers not only with the means of explaining the content of works (what, specifically, does a work say?) but also with the insights needed for evaluating the artistic quality of individual works and writers (how well is it said?). A major aspect of New Critical thought is that content and form—including all ideas, ambiguities, subtleties, and even apparent contradictions—were originally within the conscious or subconscious control of the author. There are no accidents. It does not necessarily follow, however, that today's critic is able to define the author's intentions exactly, for such intentions require knowledge of biographical details that are irretrievably lost. Each literary work therefore takes on its own existence and identity, and the critic's work is to discover a reading or readings that explain the facts of the text. Note that the New Critic does not claim infallible interpretations and does not exclude the validity of multiple readings of the same work.

Dissenters from the New Criticism have noted a tendency by New Critics to ignore relevant knowledge that history and biography can bring to literary studies. In addition, the approach has been subject to the charge that stressing the explication of texts alone fails to deal with literary value and appreciation. In other words, the formalist critic, in explaining the meaning of literature, sometimes neglects the reasons for which readers find literature stimulating and valuable.

EXAMPLE

A major aspect of Hawthorne's "Young Goodman Brown" is that the details are so vague and dreamlike that many readers are uncertain about what is happening. The action is a nighttime walk by the protagonist, Young Goodman Brown, into a deep forest where he encounters a mysterious satanic ritual that leaves him bitter and misanthropic. This much seems clear, but the precise nature of Brown's experience is not clear, nor is the identity of the stranger (father, village elder, devil) who accompanies Brown as he begins his walk. At the story's end Hawthorne's narrator states that the whole episode may have been no more than a dream or nightmare. Yet when morning comes, Brown walks back into town as though returning from an overnight trip, and he recoils in horror from his fellow villagers, including his wife Faith (paragraph 70). Could his attitude result from nothing more than a nightmare?

Even at the story's end these uncertainties remain. For this reason one may conclude that Hawthorne deliberately creates the uncertainties to reveal how people like Brown build defensive walls of judgment around themselves. The story thus implies that the real source of Brown's anger is as vague as his nocturnal walk, but he doesn't understand it in this way. Because Brown's vision and judgment are absolute, he rejects everyone around him, even if the cost is a life of bitter suspicion and spiritual isolation.

STRUCTURALIST

The principle of structuralism stems from the attempt to find relationships and connections among elements that appear to be separate and discrete. Just as physical science reveals unifying universal principles of matter such as gravity and the forces of electromagnetism (and is constantly searching for a "unified field theory"), the **structuralist critical approach** attempts to discover the forms unifying all literature. Thus a structural description of Maupassant's "The Necklace" (pp. 4–11) stresses that the main character, Mathilde, is an *active* protagonist who undergoes a *test* (or series of tests) and emerges with a victory, though not the kind she had originally hoped for. The same might be said of Mrs. Popov and Smirnov in Chekhov's *The Bear* (pp. 1570–79). If this same kind of structural view is applied to Bierce's "An Occurrence at Owl Creek Bridge" (pp. 234–40), the protagonist is defeated in the test. Generally, the structural approach applies such patterns to other works of literature to determine that certain protagonists are active or submissive, that they pass or fail their tests, or that they succeed or fail at other encounters. The key is that many apparently unrelated works reveal many common patterns or contain similar structures with important variations.

The structural approach is important because it enables critics to discuss works from widely separate cultures and historical periods. In this respect, critics have followed the leads of modern anthropologists, most notably Claude Lévi-Strauss (1908–1990). Along such lines, critics have undertaken the serious examination of folk and fairy tales. Some of the groundbreaking structuralist criticism, for example, was devoted to the structural principles underlying folktales of Russia. The method also bridges popular and serious literature, making little distinction between the two insofar as the description of the structures is concerned. Indeed, structuralism furnishes an ideal approach for comparative literature, and the method also enables critics to consolidate genres such as modern romances, detective tales, soap operas, situation comedies, and film.

Like the New Criticism, structuralism aims at comprehensiveness of description, and many critics would insist that the two are complementary and not separate. A distinction is that the New Criticism is at its best in dealing with smaller units of literature, whereas structuralism is best in the analysis of narratives and therefore larger units such as novels, myths, stories, plays, and films. Because structuralism shows how fiction is organized into various typical situations, the approach merges with the *archetypal* approach (see below, p. 1923), and at times it is difficult to find any distinctions between structural and archetypal criticism.

Structuralism, however, deals not just with narrative structures but also with structures of any type, wherever they occur. For example, structuralism makes great use of linguistics. Modern linguistic scholars have determined that there is a difference between "deep structures" and "surface structures" in language. A structuralist analysis of style, therefore, emphasizes how writers utilize such structures. The structuralist interpretation of language also perceives distinguishing types or "grammars" of language that are recurrent in various types of literature. Suppose, for example, that you encounter opening passages like the following:

1

Once upon a time a young prince fell in love with a young princess. He decided to tell her of his love, and early one morning he left his castle on his white charger, riding toward her castle home high in the mountains.

2

Early that morning, Alan had found himself thinking about Anne. He had believed her when she said she loved him, but his feelings about her were not certain, and his thinking had left him still unsure.

The words of these two passages create different and distinct frames of reference. One is a fairy tale of the past, the other a modern internalized reflection of feeling. The passages therefore demonstrate how language itself fits into predetermined patterns or structures. Similar uses of language structures can be associated with other types of literature.

EXAMPLE

Young Goodman Brown is a hero who is passive, not active. He is a *witness*, a *receiver* rather than a *doer*. His only action—taking his trip in the forest—occurs at the story's beginning. After that point, he no longer acts but instead is acted upon, and his reactions to what he sees around him put his life's beliefs to a test. Of course, many protagonists undergo similar testing (such as rescuing victims and overcoming particularly terrible dragons), and they emerge as heroes or conquerors. Not so with Goodman Brown. He is a responder who allows himself to be victimized by his own perceptions—or misperceptions. Despite all his previous experiences with his wife and with the good people of his village, he generalizes too hastily. He lets the single disillusioning experience of his nightmare govern his entire outlook on others, and thus he fails his test and turns his entire life into darkness.

❧ FEMINIST

The **feminist critical approach** holds that most of our literature presents a masculine–patriarchal view in which the role of women is negated or at best minimized. As an adjunct of the feminist movement in politics, the feminist critique of literature seeks to raise consciousness about the importance and unique nature of women in literature.

Specifically, the feminist view attempts (1) to show that writers of traditional literature have ignored women and have also transmitted misguided and prejudiced views of them, (2) to stimulate the creation of a critical milieu that reflects a balanced view of the nature and value of women, (3) to recover the works of women writers of past times and to encourage the publication of present women writers so that the literary canon can be expanded to recognize women as thinkers and artists, and (4) to urge transformations in the language so as to eliminate inequities and inequalities that have resulted from centuries of linguistic inertia and antifeminist sensitivity.

In form, the feminist perspective requires the evaluation of literary works from the standpoint of the presentation of women. For works such as "The Necklace" (story, p. 4), "Patterns" (poem, p. 1115), and *The Bear* (play, p. 1570), a feminist critique focuses on how such works treat women and also on either the shortcomings or enlightenment of the author as a result of this treatment: How important are the female characters, how individual in their own right?

Are they credited with their own existence and their own character? In their relationships with men, how are they treated? Are they given equal status? Ignored? Patronized? Demeaned? Pedestalized? How much interest do the male characters exhibit about women's concerns?

EXAMPLE

At the beginning of "Young Goodman Brown," Brown's wife, Faith, is only peripheral. In the traditional patriarchal spirit of wife-as-adjunct, she asks her husband to stay at home and take his journey at another time. Hawthorne does not give her the intelligence or dignity, however, to let her explain her concern (or might he not have been interested in what she had to say?) and she therefore remains in the background with her pink hair ribbon as her distinguishing symbol of submissive inferiority. During the mid-forest satanic ritual she appears again and is given power, but only the power to cause her husband to go astray. Once she is led in as a novice in the practice of demonism, her husband falls right in step. Unfortunately, by following her, Brown can conveniently excuse himself from guilt by claiming that "she" had made him do it, just as Eve, in some traditional views of the fall of humankind, compelled Adam to eat the apple (Genesis 3:16-17). Hawthorne's attention to the male protagonist, in other words, permits him to neglect the possibility of a female protagonist.

ECONOMIC DETERMINIST/MARXIST

The concept of cultural and economic determinism is one of the major political ideas of the nineteenth century. Karl Marx (1818–1883) emphasized that the primary influence on life was economic, and he saw society as an opposition between the capitalist and working classes. The literature that emerged from this kind of analysis features individuals in the grips of the struggle. Often called proletarian literature, it emphasizes the lower class—the poor and oppressed who spend their lives in endless drudgery and misery, and whose attempts to rise above their disadvantages usually result in renewed suppression (see pp. 1878–80).

Marx's political ideas were never widely accepted in the United States and have faded still more after the political breakup of the Soviet Union, but the idea of economic determinism (and the related term *Social Darwinism*) is still credible. As a result, much literature can be judged from an economic perspective even though the economic critics may not be Marxian: What is the economic status of the characters? What happens to them as a result of this status? How do they fare against economic and political odds? What other conditions stemming from their class does the writer emphasize (e.g., poor education, poor nutrition, poor health care, inadequate opportunity)? To what extent does the work fail by overlooking the economic, social, and political implications of its material? In what other ways does economic determinism affect the work? How should readers consider the story in today's developed or underdeveloped world? Seemingly, Hawthorne's story "Young Goodman Brown," which we have used for analysis in these discussions, has no major economic implications, but an **economic determinist/Marxist critical approach** might take the following turns:

EXAMPLE

"Young Goodman Brown" is a fine story just as it is. It deals with the false values instilled by the skewed acceptance of sin-dominated religion, but it overlooks the economic implications of this situation. One suspects that the real story in the little world of Goodman Brown's Salem should be about survival and the disruption that an alienated member of society can produce. After Brown's condemnation and distrust of others forces him into his own shell of sick imagination, Hawthorne does not consider how such a disaffected character would injure the economic and public life of the town. Consider this, just for a moment: Why would the people from whom Brown recoils in disgust want to deal with him in business or personal matters? In town meetings, would they want to follow his opinions on crucial issues of public concern and investment? Would his preoccupation with sin and damnation make him anything more than a horror in his domestic life? Would his wife, Faith, be able to discuss household management with him, or how to take care of the children? All these questions of course are pointed toward another story—a story that Hawthorne did not write. They also indicate the shortcomings of Hawthorne's approach, because it is clear that the major result of Young Goodman Brown's selfish preoccupation with evil would be a serious disruption of the economic and political affairs of his small community.

PSYCHOLOGICAL/PSYCHOANALYTIC

The scientific study of the mind is a product of psychodynamic theory as established by Sigmund Freud (1856–1939) and of the psychoanalytic method practiced by his followers. Psychoanalysis provided a new key to the understanding of character by claiming that behavior is caused by hidden and unconscious motives. It was greeted as a revelation with far-reaching implications for all intellectual pursuits. Not surprisingly it had a profound and continuing effect on post-Freudian literature.

In addition, its popularity produced a **psychological/psychoanalytic approach** to criticism.[2] Some critics use the approach to explain fictional characters, as in the landmark interpretation by Freud and Ernest Jones that Shakespeare's Hamlet suffers from an Oedipus complex. Still other critics use it as a way of analyzing authors and the artistic process. For example, John Livingston Lowes's study *The Road to Xanadu* presents a detailed examination of the mind, reading, and neuroses of Coleridge, the author of "Kubla Khan" (p. 705).

Critics using the psychoanalytic approach treat literature somewhat like information about patients in therapy. In the work itself, what are the obvious and hidden motives that cause a character's behavior and speech? How much background (e.g., repressed childhood trauma, adolescent memories) does the author reveal about a character? How purposeful is this information with regard to the character's psychological condition? How much is important in the analysis and understanding of the character?

[2]See also Chapter 4, "Characters: The People in Fiction."

In the consideration of authors, critics utilizing the psychoanalytic model consider questions like these: What particular life experiences explain characteristic subjects or preoccupations? Was the author's life happy? Miserable? Upsetting? Solitary? Social? Can the death of someone in the author's family be associated with melancholy situations in that author's work? All eleven brothers and sisters of the English poet Thomas Gray, for example, died before reaching adulthood. Gray was the only one to survive. In his poetry, Gray often deals with death, and he is therefore considered one of the "Graveyard School" of eighteenth-century poets. A psychoanalytical critic might make much of this connection.

EXAMPLE

> At the end of "Young Goodman Brown," Hawthorne's major character is no longer capable of normal existence. His nightmare should be read as a symbol of what in reality would have been lifelong mental subjection to the type of puritanical religion that emphasizes sin and guilt. Such preoccupation with sin is no hindrance to psychological health if the preoccupied people are convinced that God forgives them and grants them mercy. In their dealings with others, they remain healthy as long as they believe that other people have the same sincere trust in divine forgiveness. If their own faith is weak and uncertain, however, and if they cannot believe in forgiveness, then they are likely to transfer their own guilt—really a form of personal terror—to others. They remain conscious of their own sins, but they find it easy to claim that others are sinful—even those who are spiritually spotless, and even their own family, who should be dearest to them. When this process of projection or transference occurs, such people have created the rationale of condemning others because of their own guilt. The price that they pay is a life of gloom, a fate that Hawthorne designates for Goodman Brown after his nightmare about demons in human form.

ARCHETYPAL/SYMBOLIC/MYTHIC

The **archetypal/symbolic/mythic critical approach,** derived from the work of the Swiss psychoanalyst Carl Jung (1875–1961), presupposes that human life is built up out of patterns, or *archetypes* ("first molds" or "first patterns") that are similar throughout various cultures and historical times.[3] The approach is similar to the structuralist analysis of literature, for both approaches stress the connections that may be discovered in literature written in different times and in vastly different locations in the world.

In literary evaluation, the archetypal approach is used to support the claim that the very best literature is grounded in archetypal patterns. The archetypal critic therefore looks for archetypes such as God's creation of human beings, the sacrifice of a hero, or the search for paradise. How does an individual story, poem, or play fit into any of the archetypal patterns? What truths does this correlation provide (particularly truths that cross historical, national, and cultural

---

[3]Symbolism is also considered in Chapters 9 and 21.

lines)? How closely does the work fit the archetype? What variations can be seen? What meaning or meanings do the connections have?

The most tenuous aspect of archetypal criticism is Jung's assertion that the recurring patterns provide evidence for a "universal human consciousness" that all of us, by virtue of our humanity, still retain in our minds and in our very blood.

Not all critics accept the hypothesis of a universal human consciousness, but they nevertheless consider the approach important for comparisons and contrasts (see Chapter 35). Many human situations, such as adolescence, dawning love, the search for success, the reconciliation with one's mother and father, and the encroachment of age and death, are similar in structure and can be analyzed as archetypes. For example, the following situations can be seen as a pattern or archetype of initiation: A young man discovers the power of literature and understanding (Keats's "On First Looking into Chapman's Homer"); a man determines the importance of truth and fidelity amidst uncertainty (Arnold's "Dover Beach"); a man and woman fall in love despite their wishes to remain independent (Chekhov's *The Bear*); a woman gains strength and integrity because of previously unrealized inner resources (Maupassant's "The Necklace"). The archetypal approach encourages the analysis of variations on the same theme, as in Glaspell's "A Jury of Her Peers" (p. 188) and Faulkner's "A Rose for Emily" (p. 130) when characters choose to ignore the existence of a crime (one sort of initiation) and also, as a result, assert their own individuality and freedom (another sort of initiation).

EXAMPLE

In the sense that Young Goodman Brown undergoes a change from psychological normality to rigidity, the story is a reverse archetype of the initiation ritual. According to the archetype of successful initiation, initiates seek to demonstrate their worthiness to become full-fledged members of society. Telemachus in Homer's *Odyssey*, for example, is a young man who in the course of the epic goes through the initiation rituals of travel, discussion, and battle. But in "Young Goodman Brown" we see initiation in reverse, for just as there is an archetype of successful initiation, Brown's initiation leads him into failure. In the private areas of life on which happiness depends, he falls short. He sees evil in his fellow villagers, condemns his minister, and shrinks even from his own family. His life therefore becomes filled with despair and gloom. His suspicions are those of a Puritan of long ago, but the timeliness of Hawthorne's story is that the archetype of misunderstanding and condemnation has not changed. Today's headlines of misery and war are produced by the same kind of intolerance that is exhibited by Goodman Brown.

DECONSTRUCTIONIST

The **deconstructionist critical approach**—which deconstructionists explain not as an approach but rather as a performance or as a strategy of reading—was developed by the French critic Jacques Derrida (b. 1930). In the 1970s and

1980s it became a major but also controversial mode of criticism. As a literary theory, deconstructionism produces a type of analysis that stresses ambiguity and contradiction.

A major principle of deconstructionism is a criticism of the so-called *logocentrism* of Western thought; that is, Western philosophers have based their ideas on the assumption that central truth is knowable and entire; this view is incorrect, according to a deconstructionist. The deconstructionist position is instead that there is no central truth because circumstances and time, which are changeable and sometimes arbitrary, govern the world of the intellect. This analysis leads to the declaration "All interpretation is misinterpretation." That is, literary works cannot be encapsulated as organically unified entireties, and therefore there is not *one correct interpretation* but only *interpretations*, each one possessing its own validity. Another way to put this idea is that there cannot be a single reading of texts, but only readings, which alter according to time and intellectual circumstances.

In "deconstructing" a work, therefore, the deconstructionist critic raises questions about what other critics have claimed about the work: Is a poem accepted as a model of classicism? Then it also exhibits qualities of romanticism. Is a story about a young Native American's flight from school commonly taken as a criticism of modern urban life? Then it may also be taken as a story of the failure of youth. In carrying out such criticism, deconstructionist critics place heavy emphasis on the ideas contained in terms such as *ambivalence, discrepancy, enigma, uncertainty, delusion, indecision,* and *lack of resolution,* among others. These words, incidentally, are all located in an essay written by a critic espousing the deconstructionist approach.

The deconstructionist attack on "correct," "privileged," or "accepted" readings is also related to the principle that language, and therefore literature, is unstable. "Linguistic instability" means that the understanding of words can never be exact or comprehensive because there is a never-ending *play* between the words in a text and their many shades of meaning, including possible future meanings. That is, the words do not remain constant and produce a definite meaning, but instead call forth the possibility of "infinite substitutions" of meaning. This is the deconstructionist principle of *undecidability.* On this principle each work of literature is ambiguous and uncertain because its full meaning is constantly being *deferred.* Such infinite play—or semantic tension—renders language unstable and makes correct or accepted readings impossible.

A number of critics have found the deconstructionist position elusive and vague. They grant that literary works are often ambiguous, uncertain, and apparently contradictory, but they explain that the cause of these conditions is not linguistic instability but rather authorial intention. They also point out that the deconstructionist linguistic analysis is derivative, unoriginal, and incorrect. In addition, critics claim that the deconstructionist linguistic position does not support deconstructionist assertions about linguistic instability. Critics also draw attention to the contradiction that deconstructionism cannot follow its major premise about there being no "privileged readings" because it must recognize the privileged readings in order to invalidate or "subvert" them.

EXAMPLE

There are many uncertainties in the details of "Young Goodman Brown." If one starts with the stranger on the path, one might conclude that he could be Brown's father, because he recognizes Brown immediately and speaks to him jovially. On the other hand, the stranger could be the devil (he is recognized as such by Goody Cloyse) because of his wriggling walking stick. After disappearing, the stranger also takes on the characteristics of an omniscient cult leader and seer, because at the satanic celebration he knows all the secret sins committed by Brown's neighbors and the community of greater New England. Additionally, he might represent a perverted conscience whose aim is to mislead and befuddle people by steering them into the holier-than-thou judgmental attitude that Brown adopts. This method would be truly diabolical—to use religion in order to bring people to their own damnation. That the stranger is an evil force is therefore clear, but the pathways of his evil are not as clear. He seems to work his mission of damnation by reaching the souls of persons like Goodman Brown through means ordinarily attributed to conscience. If the stranger represents a satanic conscience, what are we to suppose that Hawthorne is asserting about what is considered real conscience?

ⱳ READER-RESPONSE

The **reader-response critical approach** is rooted in *phenomenology*, a branch of philosophy that deals with the understanding of how things appear. The phenomenological idea of knowledge is that reality is to be found not in the external world itself but rather in our mental *perception* of externals. That is, all that we human beings can know—actual *knowledge*—is our collective and personal understanding of the world and our conclusions about it.

As a consequence of the phenomenological concept, reader-response theory holds that the reader is a necessary third party in the author-text-reader relationship that constitutes the literary work. The work, in other words, is not fully created until readers make a *transaction* with it by assimilating it and *actualizing* it in the light of their own knowledge and experience. The representative questions of the theory are these: What does this work mean to me, in my present intellectual and moral makeup? How can the work improve my understanding and widen my insights? How can my increasing understanding help me understand the work more deeply? The theory is that the free interchange or transaction that such questions bring about leads toward interest and growth so that readers can assimilate literary works and accept them as part of their lives and as part of the civilization in which they live.

As an initial way of reading, the reader-response method may be personal and anecdotal. In addition, by stressing response rather than interpretation, one of the leading exponents of the method (Stanley Fish) has raised the extreme question about whether texts, by themselves, have objective identity. These aspects have been cited as both a shortcoming and an inconsequentiality of the method.

It is therefore important to stress that the reader-response theory is *open*. It permits beginning readers to bring their own personal reactions to literature, but it also aims to increase their discipline and skill. The more that readers bring to literature through their interests and disciplined studies, the more "competent" and comprehensive their transactions will be. It is possible, for example, to explain the structure of a work not according to commonly recognized categories such as exposition and climax, but rather according to the personal reactions of representative readers. The contention is that structure, like other avenues of literary study such as tone or the comprehension of figurative language, refers to clearly definable responses that readers experience when reading and transacting with works. By such means, literature is subject not only to outward and objective analysis, but also to inward and psychological response. The reader-response approach thus lends an additional dimension to the critical awareness of literature. Should literary works ask that readers possess special knowledge in fields such as art, politics, science, philosophy, religion, or morality, then competent readers will seek out such knowledge and utilize it in developing their responses. Also, because students experience many similar intellectual and cultural disciplines, it is logical to conclude that responses will tend not to diverge but rather to coalesce; agreements result not from personal but from cultural similarities. The reader-response theory, then, can and should be an avenue toward informed and detailed understanding of literature, but the initial emphasis is the *transaction* that readers make with literary works.

EXAMPLE

"Young Goodman Brown" is worrisome because it shows so disturbingly that good intentions may cause harmful results. I think that a person with too high a set of expectations is ripe for disillusionment, just as Goodman Brown is. When people don't measure up to this person's standard of perfection, they can be thrown aside as though they are worthless. They may be good people, but whatever past mistakes they have made make it impossible for the person with high expectations to endure them. Goodman Brown makes the same kind of misjudgment, expecting perfection and turning sour when he learns about flaws. It is not that he is not a good man, because he is shown at the start as a person of belief and stability. He uncritically accepts his nightmare revelation that everyone else is evil, however (including his parents), and he finally distrusts everyone because of this baseless suspicion. He cannot look at his neighbors without avoiding them like an "anathema," and he turns away from his own wife "without a greeting" (paragraph 70). Brown's problem is that he equates being human with being unworthy. By such a distorted standard of judgment, all of us fail, and that is what makes the story so disturbing.

Taking Examinations on Literature

Succeeding on a literature examination is largely a result of intelligent and skillful preparation. Preparing means (1) studying the material assigned, in conjunction with the comments made in class by your instructor and by fellow students in discussion; (2) developing and reinforcing your own thoughts; (3) anticipating exam questions by creating and answering your own practice questions; and (4) understanding the precise function of the test in your education.

First, realize that the test is not designed either to trap you or to hold down your grade. The grade you receive is a reflection of your achievement in the course. If your grades are low, you can improve them through diligent and systematic study. Those students who can easily do satisfactory work might do superior work if they improved their habits of study and preparation. From whatever level you begin, you can increase your achievement by improving your study methods.

Your instructor has three major concerns in evaluating your tests (assuming the correct use of English): (1) to assess the extent of your command over the subject material of the course (How good is your retention?); (2) to assess how well you respond to a question or deal with an issue (How well do you separate the important from the unimportant?); and (3) to assess how well you draw conclusions about the material (How well are you educating yourself?).

ANSWER THE QUESTIONS THAT ARE ASKED

Many elements go into writing good answers on tests, but *responsiveness* is the most important. A major cause of low exam grades is that students often do not *answer* the questions asked. Does that failure seem surprising? The problem is that some students do no more than retell a story or restate an argument, but they do not lock on to the issues in the question. This is not an uncommon problem. There-fore, if you are asked, "Why does . . . ?" be sure to emphasize the *why* and use the *does* only to exemplify the *why*. If the question is about *organization*, focus on organization. If the question is about the *interpretation* of an idea, deal with the interpretation of the idea. In short, always respond directly to the question or instruction. Answer what is asked. Compare the following two answers to the same question.

Question: How is the setting of Ambrose Bierce's "An Occurrence at Owl Creek Bridge" (Chapter 5) important in the story's development?

ANSWER A

The setting of Bierce's "An Occurrence at Owl Creek Bridge" is a major element in the story's development. The first scene is on a railroad bridge in northern Alabama, and the action is that a man, Peyton Farquhar, is about to be hanged. He is a Southerner who has been sur-rounded and captured by Union soldiers. They are ready to string him up and they have the guns and power, so he cannot escape. He is so scared that his own watch seems to sound loudly and slowly, like a cannon. He also thinks about how he might escape, once he is hanged, by free-ing his hands and throwing off the noose that will soon be choking and killing him. The scene shifts to the week before, at Farquhar's plantation. A Union spy de-ceives Farquhar, thereby tempting him to try to sabotage the Union efforts to keep the railroad open. Because the spy tells Farquhar about the punishment, the reader assumes that Farquhar had tried to sabotage the bridge, was caught, and now is going to be hanged. The third scene is also at the bridge, but it is about what Farquhar sees and thinks in his own mind: He imagines that he has been hanged and then escapes. He thinks he falls into the creek, frees himself from the ropes, and makes it to shore, from which he makes the long walk home. His final vision is of his wife coming out of the house to meet him, with everything look-ing beautiful in the morning sunshine. Then we find out that all this was just in his mind, because we are back on the bridge, from which Farquhar is swinging, hanged, dead, with a broken neck.

ANSWER B

The setting of Bierce's "An Occurrence at Owl Creek Bridge" is a major element in the story's development. The railroad bridge in northern Alabama, from which the doomed Peyton Farquhar will be hanged, is a frame for the story. The bridge, which begins as a real-life bridge in the first scene, becomes the bridge that the dying man imagines in the third. In between there is a brief scene at Farquhar's home, which took place a week before. The setting thus marks the progression of Farquhar's dying vision. He begins to distort and slow down reali-ty—at the real bridge—when he realizes that there is no escape. The first indica-tion of this distortion is that his watch seems to be ticking as slowly as a black-smith's hammer. Once he is dropped from the bridge to be hanged, his per-ceptions slow down time so much that he imagines his complete escape before his death: falling into the water, freeing him-self, being shot at, getting to shore, walk-ing through a darkening forest, and returning home in beautiful morning sunshine. The final sentence of the story brutally restores the real situation at the railroad bridge and makes clear that Farquhar is hanging from it and is actual-ly dead despite his imaginings. In all re-spects, therefore, the setting is essential to the story's development.

Answer A begins well and introduces important details of the story's setting, but it does not answer the question because it does not show how the details figure into the story's development. On the other hand, answer B focuses directly on the connection between the locations and the changes in the protagonist's perceptions. Because of this emphasis, B answers the question and is also shorter than A; with the focus directly on the issue, there is no need for irrelevant narrative details. Thus, A is unresponsive and unnecessarily long, whereas B is responsive and includes details only if they exemplify the major points.

⁄⁄ SYSTEMATIC PREPARATION

Your challenge is how best to prepare yourself to have a knowledgeable and ready mind at examination time. If you simply cram facts into your head for the test in the hope that you can adjust to the questions, you will likely flounder. You need a systematic approach.

Read and Reread the Material on Which You Are to Be Examined

Above all, recognize that your preparation should begin as soon as the course begins, not on the night before the exam. Complete each assignment by the date it is due, for you will understand the classroom discussion only if you know the material (see also the guides for study in Chapter 1, pp. 11–12). Then, about a week before the exam, review each assignment, preferably rereading everything completely. With this preparation, your study on the night before the exam will be fruitful and might be viewed as a climax of preparation, not the entire preparation.

Construct Your Own Questions: Go on the Attack

To prepare yourself well for an exam, read *actively*, not passively. Read with a goal, and *go on the attack* by anticipating test conditions—creating and answering your own practice questions. Don't waste time trying to guess the questions you think your instructor might ask. Guessing correctly might happen (and wouldn't you be happy if it did?) but do not turn your study into a game of chance. Instead, arrange the subject matter by asking yourself questions that help you get things straight.

How can you construct your own questions? It is not as hard as you might think. Your instructor may have announced certain topics or ideas to be tested on the exam, and you might develop questions from these, or you might apply general questions to the specifics of your assignments, as in the following examples.

1. *Ideas about a character and the interactions of characters* (see also Chapter 4). What is *A* like? How does *A* grow or change in the work? What does *A* learn or not learn that brings about the conclusion? To what degree does *A* represent a type or an idea? How does *B* influence *A*? Does a change in *C* bring about any corresponding change in *A*?

2. *Ideas about technical and structural questions.* These can be broad, covering every-thing from point of view (Chapter 5) to poetic form (Chapter 20). The best guide here is to study those technical aspects that have been discussed in class, for it is unlikely that you will be asked to go beyond the levels considered in classroom discussion.

3. *Ideas about events or situations.* What relationship does episode *A* have to situation *B*? Does *C's* thinking about situation *D* have any influence on the outcome of event *E*?

4. *Ideas about a problem* (see also Chapter 27, pp. 1476–82). Why is character *A* or situation *X* this way and not that way? Is the conclusion justified by the ideas and events leading up to it?

Rephrase Your Notes as Questions

Because your classroom notes are the fullest record you have about your in-structor's views, one of the best ways to construct questions is to develop them from these notes. As you select topics and phrase questions, refer to passages from the texts that were studied by the class and stressed by your instructor. If there is time, memorize as many important phrases or lines as you can from the studied works. Plan to incorporate these into your answers as evidence to sup-port the points you make. Remember that it is useful to work not only with main ideas from your notes but also with matters such as character, setting, imagery, symbolism, ideas, and organization.

Obviously, you cannot make questions from all your notes, and you will therefore need to select from those that seem most important. As an example, here is a short note written by a student during a classroom discussion of Shake-speare's *Hamlet*: "In a major respect, a study in how private problems get public, how a court conspiracy can produce disastrous national and even international consequences." Notice that you can devise practice questions from this note.

1. In what ways is *Hamlet* not only about private problems but also about public ones?

2. Why should the consequences of Claudius's murder of Hamlet's father be consid-ered disastrous?

The principle here is that most exam questions do not ask just about *what,* but rather get into the issues of *why.* Observe that the first question therefore in-troduces the words *in what ways* to the phrasing of the note. For the second, the word *why* has been used. Either question creates the need for you to study point-edly, and neither asks you merely to describe events from the play. Question 1 requires you to consider the wider political effects of Hamlet's hostility toward Claudius, including Hamlet's murder of Polonius and the subsequent madness of Ophelia. Question 2, with its emphasis on disaster, leads you to consider not only the ruination of the hopes and lives of those in the play but also the impor-tance of young Fortinbras and the eventual establishment of Norwegian control over Denmark after Claudius and Hamlet are gone. If you were to spend fifteen or twenty minutes writing practice answers to these questions, you could be con-fident in taking an examination on the material, for you could likely adapt, or even partially duplicate, your study answers to any exam question about the personal and political implications of Claudius's murder of his brother.

Practice Creating Your Own Questions Even When Time Is Short

Whatever your subject, spend as much study time as possible making and answering your own questions. *Writing practice answers is one of the most important things you can do in preparing for your exam.* Remember also to work with your own remarks and the ideas you develop in the notebook or journal entries that you make when doing your regular assignments (see Chapter 1, pp. 13–14). Many of these will give you additional ideas for your own questions, which you can practice along with the questions you develop from your classroom notes.

Obviously, with limited study time, you will not be able to create your own questions and answers indefinitely. Even so, don't neglect asking and answering your own questions. If time is too short for full practice answers, write out the main heads, or topics, of an answer. When the press of time (or the need for sleep) no longer permits you to make even such a brief outline answer, keep thinking of questions and their answers on the way to the exam. *Never read passively or unresponsively; always read with a creative, question-and-answer goal.* Think of studying as a preliminary step leading to writing.

The time you spend in this way will be valuable, for as you practice, you will develop control and therefore confidence. Often those who have difficulty with tests, or claim a phobia about them, prepare passively rather than actively. Your instructor's test questions compel responsiveness, organization, thought, and insight. But a passively prepared student is not ready for this challenge and therefore writes answers that are unresponsive and filled with summary. The grade for such a performance is low, and the student's fear of tests is reinforced. The best way to break such long-standing patterns of fear or uncertainty is to study actively and creatively.

Study with a Classmate

Often the thoughts of another person can help you understand the material to be tested. Find a fellow student with whom you can work comfortably but also productively, for both of you together can help each other individually. In view of the need for steady preparation throughout a course, regular discussions about the material are a good idea. You might also make your joint study systematic by setting aside a specific evening or afternoon for work sessions. Many students have said that they encounter problems in taking examinations because they are unfamiliar with the ways in which questions are phrased. Consequently, they waste time in understanding and interpreting the questions before they begin their answers, and sometimes they lose all their time because they misunderstand the questions entirely. If you work with a fellow student, however, and trade questions, you will be gaining experience (and confidence) in dealing with this basic difficulty about exams. Working with someone else can be extremely rewarding, just as it can also be stimulating and instructive. Make the effort, and you'll never regret it.

TWO BASIC TYPES OF QUESTIONS ABOUT LITERATURE

Generally, there are two types of questions on literature exams. Keep them in mind as you prepare. The first type is *factual*, or *mainly objective*; and the second is *general, comprehensive, broad,* or *mainly subjective*. Except for multiple-choice questions, very few questions are purely objective in a literature course.

Anticipate the Kinds of Factual Questions That Might Be Asked

MULTIPLE-CHOICE QUESTIONS ASK YOU TO PICK THE MOST ACCURATE AND LIKELY ANSWERS. Multiple-choice questions are almost necessarily factual. Your instructor will most likely use them for short quizzes, usually on days when an assignment is due, to make sure that you are keeping up with the reading. Multiple-choice questions test your knowledge of facts and your ingenuity in perceiving subtleties of phrasing. On literature exams, however, this type of question is rare.

IDENTIFICATION QUESTIONS ASK FOR ACCURACY, EXPLANATION, AND A CERTAIN AMOUNT OF INTERPRETATION. Identification questions are interesting and challenging because they require you both to know details and also to develop thoughts about them. This type of question is frequently used as a check on the depth and scope of your reading. In fact, an entire exam could be composed of only identification questions, each demanding perhaps five minutes for you to answer. Here are some typical examples of what you might be asked to identify.

1. *A character.* To identify a character, it is necessary to describe briefly the character's position, main activity, and significance. Let us assume that "Prince Prospero" is the character to be identified. Our answer should state that he is the prince (position) who invites a thousand followers to his castle to enjoy themselves while keeping out the plague of the Red Death in Edgar Allan Poe's "The Masque of the Red Death" (main activity). Prospero's egotism and arrogance are the major causes of the action, and he embodies the story's theme that pride is vain and that death is inescapable (significance). Under the category of "significance," of course, you might develop as many ideas as you have time for, but the short example here is a general model for most identification questions.

2. *Incidents or situations.* In identifying an incident or a situation (for example, "A woman mourns the death of her husband"), first describe the circumstances and the principal character involved in them (Mrs. Popov's reaction to her widowhood in Anton Chekhov's play *The Bear*, or the Widow's reaction to her husband's death in "The Widow of Ephesus" by Petronius). Then, describe the importance of this incident or situation in the work. For example, in *The Bear*, Mrs. Popov is mourning the death of her husband, and in the course of the play Chekhov uses her feelings to show amusingly that life and love with real emotion are stronger than allegiance to the dead. Very much the same applies to "The Widow of Ephesus."

3. *Things, places, and dates.* Your instructor may ask you to identify a hair ribbon (Nathaniel Hawthorne's "Young Goodman Brown") or a beach (Matthew Arnold's "Dover Beach" or Amy Clampitt's "Beach Glass"), or the date of Amy Lowell's "Patterns" (1916). For dates, you may be given a leeway of five or ten years. What is important about a date is not so much exactness as historical and intellectual perspective. The date of "Patterns," for example, was the third year of World War I, and the poem consequently reflects a reaction against the protracted and senseless loss of life in war (even though details of the poem itself suggest an eighteenth-century war). To claim "World War I" as the date of the poem would be acceptable as an answer if it happens that you cannot remember the exact date.

4. *Quotations.* You should remember enough of the text to identify a passage taken from it, or at least to make an informed guess. Generally, you should (1) locate the quotation, if you remember it, or else describe the probable location; (2) show the ways in which the quotation is typical of the content and style of the work you have read; and (3) describe the importance of the passage. If you suffer a momentary lapse of memory, write a reasoned and careful explanation of your guess. Even if your guess is wrong, the knowledge and cogency of your explanation should give you points.

TECHNICAL AND ANALYTICAL QUESTIONS AND PROBLEMS REQUIRE YOU TO RELATE KNOWLEDGE AND TECHNICAL UNDERSTANDING TO THE ISSUE. In a scale of ascending importance, the third and most difficult type of factual question relates to those matters of writing with which much of this book is concerned: technique and analysis. You might be asked to discuss the *setting, images, point of view,* or *important idea* of a work; you might be asked about the *tone and style* of a story or poem; or you might be asked to *explicate* a poem that may or may not be duplicated for your benefit (if it is not duplicated, woe to students who have not studied their assignments). Questions like these assume that you have technical knowledge, and they also ask you to examine the text within the limitations imposed by the directions.

Obviously, technical questions occur more frequently in advanced courses than in elementary ones, and the questions become more subtle as the courses become more advanced. Instructors of introductory courses may ask about ideas and problems but will likely not use many of the others unless they state their intentions to do so in advance or unless technical terms have been studied in class.

Questions of this type are fairly long, perhaps allowing from fifteen to twenty-five minutes for each one. If you have two or more of these questions, try to space your time sensibly; do not devote eighty percent of your time to one question and leave only twenty percent for the rest.

Understand How Your Responses Will Be Judged and Graded

IDENTIFICATION QUESTIONS PROBE YOUR UNDERSTANDING AND APPLICATION OF FACTS. In all factual questions, your instructor is testing (1) your factual command and (2) your quickness in relating a part to the whole. Thus, suppose you are identifying the incident "A man kills a canary." It is correct to say that Susan Glaspell's story "A Jury of Her Peers" (or her play *Trifles*) is the location of the incident, that the murdered farmer John Wright is the killer, and that the canary belonged to his wife, Minnie. Knowledge of these details clearly establishes that you know the facts. But a strong answer must go further. Even in the brief time you have for short answers, you should always connect the facts (1) to major causation in the work, (2) to an important idea or ideas, (3) to the development of the work, and (4) for a quotation, to the style. Time is short and you must be selective, but if you can make your answer move from facts to significance, you will always fashion superior responses. Along these lines, let us look at an answer identifying the action from "A Jury of Her Peers."

> The action is from Glaspell's "A Jury of Her Peers." The man who kills the bird is John Wright, the dead man, and the owner is his wife, Minnie, who has been jailed on suspicion of murder. The wringing of the little bird's neck is important because it is shown as an excruciating indignity and outrage in Minnie Wright's desperate life, and it obviously has made her angry enough to put a rope around Wright's head and strangle him in his sleep. It is thus the cause not only of the murder but also of the investigation bringing the two lawmen and their wives to the Wright kitchen. In fact, the killing of the bird makes the story possible inasmuch as it is the two women who discover the dead bird's remains, and this discovery is the means by which Glaspell highlights them as the major characters of the action. Because the husband's brutal act shows how bleak the life of Minnie Wright actually was, it dramatizes the lonely and victimized plight of women in a male-dominated way of life like that on the Wright farm. The discovery also raises the issue of legality and morality, because the women decide to conceal the evidence, therefore protecting Minnie Wright from conviction and punishment.

Any of the points in this answer could be developed as a separate essay, but the paragraph is successful as a short answer because it goes beyond fact to deal with significance. Clearly, such answers are possible at the time of an exam only if you have devoted considerable thought beforehand to the works on which you are tested. The more thinking and practicing you do before an exam, the better your answers will be. Remember this advice as an axiom: *You cannot write superior answers if you do not think extensively before the exam.* By ambitious advance study, you will be able to reduce surprise to a minimum.

LONGER FACTUAL QUESTIONS PROBE YOUR KNOWLEDGE AND YOUR ABILITY TO ORGANIZE YOUR THOUGHTS. More extended factual questions also require more thoroughly developed organization. Remember that for these questions your skills in writing essays are important, because the quality of your composition will determine a major share of your instructor's evaluation of your answers. It is therefore best to take several minutes to gather your thoughts before you begin to write. Remember, *a ten-minute planned answer is preferable to a twenty-five-minute unplanned answer.* You do not need to write every possible fact on each particular question. Of greater importance is the use to which you put the facts that you know and the organization and development of your answer. Use a sheet of scratch paper to jot down important facts and your ideas about them in relation to the question. Then put them together, phrase a thesis sentence, and use your facts to exemplify and support your thesis.

It is always necessary to begin your answer pointedly, using key words or phrases from the question or direction if possible, so that your answer will have thematic shape. You should *never* begin an answer with "Because" and then go on from there without referring again to the question. To be most responsive during the short time available for an exam, you should use the question as your guide for your answer. Let us suppose that you have the following question on your test: "How does Glaspell use details in 'A Jury of Her Peers' to reveal the character of Minnie Wright?" The most common way to go astray on such a question—and the easiest thing to do also—is to concentrate on Mrs. Wright's character rather than on how Glaspell uses detail to bring out her character. The word *how* makes a vast difference in the nature of the final answer, and hence a good method on the exam is to duplicate key phrases in the question to ensure that you make your major points clear. Here is an opening sentence that uses the key words and phrases (italicized here) from the question to organize thought and provide focus.

> Glaspell *uses details* of setting, marital relationships, and personal habits *to reveal the character of Minnie Wright* as a person of great but unfulfilled potential whom anger has finally overcome.

Because this sentence repeats the key phrases from the question and also because it promises to show *how* the details are to be focused on the character, it suggests that the answer to follow will be responsive.

General or Comprehensive Questions Require You to Connect a Number of Works to Broader Matters of Idea and Technique

General or comprehensive questions are particularly important on final examinations, when your instructor is testing your total comprehension of the course material. Considerable time is usually allowed for answering this type of question, which can be phrased in a number of ways.

1. A *direct question* asking about philosophy, underlying attitudes, main ideas, characteristics of style, backgrounds, and so on. Here are some possible questions in this category.

   What use do _____, _____, and _____ make of the topic of _____?

   Define and characterize the short story as a genre of literature.

   Explain the use of dialogue by Hawthorne, Oates, and Walker.

   Contrast the technique of point of view as used by _____, _____, and _____.

2. A *"comment" question*, often based on an extensive quotation, borrowed from a critic or written by your instructor for the occasion, asking about a broad class of writers, a literary movement, or the like. Your instructor may ask you to treat this question broadly (taking in many writers) or else to apply the quotation to a specific writer.

3. A *"suppose" question*, such as "What advice might Minnie Wright of Glaspell's 'A Jury of Her Peers' give the speakers of Elizabeth Barrett Browning's 'How Do I Love Thee' and Keats's 'Bright Star'?" or "What might the speaker of Lowell's

poem 'Patterns' say if she were told that her dead lover was actually a person like Goodman Brown of Hawthorne's 'Young Goodman Brown'?" Although "suppose" questions seem whimsical at first sight, they have a serious design and should prompt original and radical thinking. The first question, for example, might cause a test writer to bring out, from Minnie Wright's perspective, that the love expressed by both speakers overlooks the possibilities of changes in character over a long period. She would likely sympathize with the speaker of "How Do I Love Thee," a woman, but she might also say that the speaker's enthusiasm would need to be augmented by the constant exertion of kindness and mutual understanding. For the speaker of "Bright Star," a man, Mrs. Wright might say that the steadfast love he seeks should be linked to thoughtfulness and constant communication as well as passion.

Although "suppose" questions (and answers) are speculative, the need to respond to them requires a detailed consideration of the works involved, and in this respect the "suppose" question is a salutary means of learning. It is of course difficult to prepare for a "suppose" question, which you can therefore regard as a test not only of your knowledge but also of your inventiveness and ingenuity.

Understand How Your Responses to General and Comprehensive Questions Will Be Judged and Graded

When answering broad, general questions, you are dealing with an unstructured situation, and not only must you supply an *answer* but—equally important—you also must create a *structure* within which your answer can have meaning. You might say that you make up your own specific question out of the original general question. If you were asked to consider the role of women as seen in works by Lowell, Maupassant, and Glaspell, for example, you would structure the question by focusing a number of clearly defined topics. A possible way to begin answering such a question might be this.

> Lowell, Maupassant, and Glaspell present a view of female resilience by demonstrating the inner control, endurance, and power of adaptation of their major characters.

With this sort of focus, you would be able to proceed point by point, introducing supporting data as you form your answer.

As a general rule, the best method for answering a comprehensive question is comparison-contrast (see also Chapter 35). The reason is that in dealing with, say, a general question on Butler, Chekhov, and Keats, it is too easy to write *three* separate essays rather than *one*. Thus, you should try to create a topic such as "the treatment of real or idealized love" or "the difficulties in male–female relationships" and then develop your answer point by point rather than writer by writer. By creating your answer in this way, you can bring in references to each or all of the writers as they become relevant. If you were to treat each writer separately, your comprehensive answer would lose focus and effectiveness, and it would also be repetitive.

Remember that in judging your response to a general question, your instructor is interested in seeing (1) how effectively you perceive and explain the significant issues in the question, (2) how intelligently and clearly you organize your answer, and (3) how persuasively you link your answer to materials from the work as supporting evidence.

Bear in mind that in answering comprehensive questions, you do not have the freedom to write about anything at all. You must stick to the questions. The freedom you do have, however, is the freedom to create your own organization and development in response to the questions your instructor has presented to you. The underlying idea of the comprehensive, general question is that you possess special knowledge and insights that cannot be discovered by more factual questions. You must therefore formulate your own responses to the material and introduce evidence that reflects your own insights and command of information.

Two final words: Good luck.

Comparison-Contrast and Extended Comparison-Contrast: *Learning by Seeing Literary Works Together*

Comparison-contrast analysis is the act of putting things side by side—juxtaposing them, looking at them together—for a variety of purposes such as description, enhanced understanding, evaluation, and decision making. The technique underlies other important techniques, specifically (1) the analysis of causes and effects, and (2) the scientific method of constant-and-variable analysis. Significant questions of all these methods are, How is *A* both like and unlike *B*? What are the causes of *A*? How does a change in *A* affect *B*? These are all questions that call into play the technique of comparison and contrast.

The educational significance of the technique is to encourage you to make connections—one of the major aspects of productive thought. As long as things *seem* different and disconnected they in fact *are* different and disconnected. In practice, they are two separate and distinct entities. But when you can discover that they have similarities and connections, then you can make relationships clear. You are in a position both to stress points of likeness and also to demonstrate just what makes things distinct and unique. For all these reasons, it is vital for you to find similarities and differences through the technique of comparison and contrast.

The immediate goals of a comparison-contrast essay on literary works is to compare and contrast different authors; two or more works by the same author; different drafts of the same work; or characters, incidents, techniques, and ideas in the same work or in a number of separate works. Developing a comparison-contrast analysis enables you to study works in perspective. No matter what works you consider together, the method helps you get at the essence of a work or writer. Similarities are brought out by comparison; differences, by contrast. In other words, you can enhance your understanding of what a thing *is* by using comparison-contrast to determine what it *is not*.

For example, our understanding of Shakespeare's Sonnet 30, "When to the Sessions of Sweet Silent Thought" (Chapter 17) can be augmented if we compare it with Denise Levertov's poem "A Time Past" (Chapter 13). Both poems treat recollections of past experiences told by a speaker to a listener, and we as readers become, as it were, witnesses to the poems. Both poems refer to persons, dead or absent, with whom the speakers were closely involved. In these respects, the poems are comparable.

In addition to these similarities, there are significant differences. Shakespeare's speaker numbers the dead persons as friends whom he laments generally. Levertov's speaker refers to a number of vanished people, but her major focus is on one person with whom she had been in love—her husband—whose sight at one time made her joyful and happy. Levertov's topics are the sorrow of past memory and lost love, the inexorable power of change, and the causes of isolation and regret. Shakespeare refers to dead friends as a way of accounting for present sorrows, but then his speaker turns to the present and asserts that thinking about the "dear friend" being addressed enables him to restore past "losses" and end all "sorrows." In Levertov's poem, there is recognition of both past and present, but no reconciliation. Instead the speaker focuses on the unpleasantness and distastefulness of the changes that time has wrought. Both poems are similarly retrospective, but they differ widely in their conclusions of how the present has been altered by the past.

❧ GUIDELINES FOR THE COMPARISON-CONTRAST METHOD

The preceding example, although brief, shows how the comparison-contrast method makes it possible to identify leading similarities and distinguishing differences in two works. Frequently you can overcome difficulty in understanding one work by comparing and contrasting it with another work on a comparable subject. A few guidelines will help direct your efforts in writing comparison-contrast essays.

Clarify Your Intention

When planning a comparison-contrast essay, first decide on your goal, for you can use the method in a number of ways. One objective is the equal and mutual illumination of two (or more) works. For example, an essay comparing Welty's "A Worn Path" (p. 138) with Hawthorne's "Young Goodman Brown" (p. 403) might be designed to (1) compare ideas, characters, or methods in these stories equally, without stressing or favoring either. You might also (2) emphasize "Young Goodman Brown," and therefore you would use "A Worn Path" as material for highlighting Hawthorne's story. Or, instead, you could (3) show your liking of one story at the expense of another, or (4) emphasize a method or idea that you think is especially noteworthy or appropriate.

A first task, therefore, is to decide what to emphasize. The demonstrative student essay on pages 1945–47 gives "equal time" to both works being considered, without claiming the superiority of either. Unless you have a different rhetorical goal, this essay provides a suitable guide for most comparisons.

Find Common Grounds for Comparison

The second stage in preparing a comparison-contrast essay is to select and articulate a common ground for discussion. It is pointless to compare dissimilar things, for the resulting conclusions will not have much value. Instead, compare like with like: idea with idea, characterization with characterization, setting with setting, point of view with point of view, tone with tone. Nothing much can be learned from a comparison of Wilder's view of individuality and Chekhov's view of love; but a comparison of the relationship of individuality with identity and character in Wilder and Chekhov suggests common ground, with the promise of significant ideas to be developed through the examination of similarities and differences.

In seeking common ground, you will need to be inventive and creative. For instance, if you compare Maupassant's "The Necklace" (p. 4) and Chekhov's *The Bear* (p. 1570), these two works at first may seem dissimilar. Yet common ground can be discovered, such as the treatment of self-deceit, the effects of chance on human affairs, and the authors' views of women. Although other works may seem even more dissimilar than these, it is usually possible to find a common ground for comparison and contrast. Much of your success in an essay of this type depends on your finding a workable basis—a common denominator—for comparison.

Integrate the Bases of Comparison

Let us assume that you have decided on your rhetorical purpose and on the basis or bases of your comparison. You have done your reading and taken notes, and you have a rough idea of what to say. The remaining problem is the treatment of your material.

One method is to make your points first about one work and then about the other. Unfortunately, such a comparison makes your paper seem like two separate lumps. ("Work 1" takes up one half of your paper, and "Work 2" takes up the other half.) Also, the method involves repetition because you must repeat many points when you treat the second subject.

Therefore, a better method is to treat the major aspects of your main idea and to refer to the two (or more) works as they support your arguments. Thus you refer constantly to *both* works, sometimes within the same sentence, and remind your reader of the point of your discussion. There are reasons for the superiority of this method: (1) You do not repeat your points needlessly, for you develop them as you raise them. (2) By constantly referring to the two works, you make your points without requiring a reader with a poor memory to reread previous sections.

As a model, here is a paragraph on "Natural References as a Basis of Comparison in Frost's 'Desert Places' and Shakespeare's Sonnet 73: 'That Time of Year Thou May'st in Me Behold' " (the poems are both in Chapter 20). The virtue of the paragraph is that it uses material from both poems simultaneously, as nearly as the time sequence of sentences allows, as the substance for the development of the ideas.

> (1) Both writers link their ideas to events occurring in the natural world. (2) Night as a parallel with death is common to both poems, with Frost speaking about it in his first line and Shakespeare introducing it in his seventh. (3) Along with night, Frost emphasizes the onset of winter and snow as a time of death and desolation. (4) With this natural description, Frost also symbolically refers to empty, secret, dead places in the inner spirit—crannies of the soul where bleak winter snowfalls correspond to selfishness and indifference. (5) By contrast, Shakespeare uses the fall season, with the yellowing and dropping of leaves and the migrations of birds, to stress the closeness of real death and therefore the need to love fully during the time remaining. (6) Both poems thus share a sense of gloom because both present death as inevitable and final, just like the emptiness of winter. (7) Because Shakespeare's sonnet is addressed to a listener who is also a loved one, however, it is more outgoing than the more introspective poem of Frost. (8) Frost turns the snow, the night, and the emptiness of the universe inward in order to show the speaker's inner bleakness, and by extension, the bleakness of many human spirits. (9) Shakespeare instead uses the bleakness of seasons, night, and dying fires to state the need for loving "well." (10) The poems thus use common and similar references for different purposes and effects.

This paragraph links Shakespeare's references to nature to those of Frost. Five sentences speak of both authors together; three speak of Frost alone and two of Shakespeare alone, but all the sentences are unified topically. This interweaving of references indicates that the writer has learned both poems well enough to consider them together, and it also enables the writing to be more pointed and succinct than if the works were separately treated.

You can learn from this example: If you develop your essay by putting your two subjects constantly together, you will write economically and pointedly (not only for essays but also for tests). Beyond that, if you digest the material as successfully as this method indicates, you demonstrate that you are fulfilling a major educational goal—the assimilation and *use* of material. Too often, because you learn things separately (in separate works and courses, at separate times), you tend also to compartmentalize them. Instead, you should always try to relate them, to *synthesize* them. Comparison and contrast help in this process of putting together, of seeing things not as fragments but as parts of wholes.

Avoid the Tennis-Ball Method

As you make your comparison, do not confuse an interlocking method with a "tennis-ball" method, in which you bounce your subject back and forth constantly and repetitively, almost as though you were hitting observations back and forth over a net. The tennis-ball method is shown in the following example from a comparison of the characters Mathilde (Maupassant's "The Necklace") and Mrs. Popov (Chekhov's *The Bear*).

Mathilde is a young married woman; Mrs. Popov is also young but a widow. Mathilde has a social life, but she doesn't have more than one friend; Mrs. Popov chooses to lead a life of solitude. Mathilde's daydreams about wealth are responsible for her misfortune, and Mrs. Popov's dedication to the memory of her husband is capable of ruining her life. Mathilde is made unhappy because of her shortcomings, but Mrs. Popov is rescued despite her shortcomings. In Mathilde's case the focus is on adversity not only causing trouble but also strengthening character. Similarly, in Mrs. Popov's case the focus is on a strong person realizing her strength regardless of her conscious decision to weaken herself.

Imagine the effect of an entire essay written in this boring 1, 2, 1, 2, 1, 2 order. Aside from the repetition and unvaried patterning of subjects, the tennis-ball method does not permit much illustrative development. You should not feel so constrained that you cannot take two or more sentences to develop a point about one writer or subject before you include comparative references to another. If you remember to interlock the two subjects of comparison, however, as in the paragraph about Frost and Shakespeare, your method will give you the freedom to develop your topics fully.

❦ THE EXTENDED COMPARISON-CONTRAST ESSAY

For a longer essay about a number of works—such as a limited research paper, comprehensive exam questions, and the sort of extended essay required at the end of a semester—comparison-contrast is an essential method. You may wish to compare the works on the basis of elements such as ideas, plot, structure, character, metaphor, point of view, or setting. Because of the larger number of works, however, you will need to modify the way in which you employ comparison-contrast. Suppose you are dealing with not just two works but with six, seven, or more. You need first to find a common ground to use as your central, unifying idea, just as you do for a comparison of only two works. Once you establish the common ground, you can classify or group your works on the basis of the similarities and differences they exemplify with regard to the topic. The idea is to get two *groups* for comparison, not just two works.

Let us assume that three or four works treat a topic in one way but that two or three do it in another (e.g., either criticism or praise of wealth and trade, the joys or sorrows of love, the enthusiasm of youth, gratitude for life, or the disillusionment of age). In writing about these works, you might treat the topic itself in a straightforward comparison-contrast method but use details from the works within the groupings as the material that you use for illustration and argument.

To make your essay as specific as possible, it is best to stress only a small number of works with each of your subpoints. Once you have established these points, there is no need to go into abundant detail with all the other works you are studying. Instead, you need to make no more than brief references to the other works, for your purpose should be to strengthen your points without creating more and more examples. Once you go to another subpoint, you use different works for illustration, so that by the end of your essay, you will have given due attention to each work in your assignment. In this way—by treating many works in small comparative groups—you can keep your essay reasonably brief, for there is no need to go into unproductive detail.

For illustration, the demonstrative student essay on pages 1948–50 shows how this grouping may be done. In the first part of the body of this essay, six works are used comparatively to show how private needs conflict with social, public demands. The next part shows how three works can be compared and contrasted on the basis of how they treat the topic of public concerns as expressed through law.

CITING REFERENCES IN A LONGER COMPARISON-CONTRAST ESSAY

For the longer comparison-contrast essay, you may find a problem in making references to many different works. Generally you do not need to repeat references. For example, if you refer to Louise of Chopin's "The Story of an Hour" or to Prospero of Poe's "The Masque of the Red Death," you should make the full references only once and then refer later just to the character, story, or author, according to your needs.

When you quote lines or passages or when you cite actions or characters in special ways, you should use parenthetical line, speech, or paragraph references, as in the demonstrative essay on pages 1948–50. Be guided by the following principle: If you make a specific reference that you think your reader might want to examine in more detail, supply the line, speech, or paragraph number. If you refer to minor details that might easily be unnoticed or forgotten, also supply the appropriate number. Your principle should be to include the appropriate locating numbers whenever you are in doubt about references.

WRITING A COMPARISON-CONTRAST ESSAY

In planning your essay, you should first narrow and simplify your topic so that you can handle it conveniently. If your subject is a comparison of two poets (as in the comparison-contrast of Lowell and Owen on pp. 1945–47), choose one or two of each poet's poems on the same or a similar topic, and write your essay about these.

Once you have found an organizing principle, along with the relevant works, begin to refine and to focus the direction of your essay. As you study each work, note common or contrasting elements and use these to form your central idea. At the same time, you can select the most illustrative works and classify them according to your topic, such as war, love, work, faithfulness, or self-analysis.

Strategies for Organizing Ideas

Begin by stating the works, authors, characters, or ideas that you are considering; then show how you have narrowed the topic. Your central idea should briefly highlight the principal grounds of comparison and contrast, such as that both works treat a common topic, exhibit a similar idea, use a similar form, or develop an identical attitude, and also that major or minor differences help make the works unique. You may also assert that one work is superior to the other, if you wish to make this judgment and defend it.

The body of your essay is governed by the works and your basis of comparison (presentations of ideas, depictions of character, uses of setting, qualities of style and tone, uses of poetic form, uses of comparable imagery or symbols, uses of point of view, and so on). For a comparison-contrast treatment on such a basis, your goal should be to shed light on both (or all) of the works you are treating. For example, you might examine stories written in the first-person point of view (see Chapter 5). An essay on this topic might compare the ways in which each author uses point of view to achieve similar or distinct effects; or it might compare poems that employ similar images, symbols, or ironic methods. Sometimes, the process can be as simple as identifying female or male protagonists and comparing the ways in which their characters are developed. Another obvious approach is to compare the *subjects*, as opposed to the *idea*. You might identify works dealing with general subjects such as love, death, youth, race, or war. Such groupings provide a basis for excellent comparisons and contrasts.

As you develop your essay, remember to keep comparison-contrast foremost. That is, your discussions of point of view, figurative language, or whatever should not so much explain these topics *as topics* but rather should explore *similarities and differences* of the works you are comparing. If your topic is an idea, for example, you need to explain the idea, but just enough to establish points of similarity or difference. As you develop such an essay, you might illustrate your arguments by referring to related uses of elements such as setting, characterization, symbolism, point of view, or metaphor. When you introduce these new subjects, you will be on target as long as you use them comparatively.

In concluding, you might reflect on other ideas or techniques in the works you have compared, make observations about similar qualities, or summarize briefly the grounds of your comparison. If there is a point you have considered especially important, you might stress that point again in your conclusion. Also, your comparison might have led you to conclude that one work—or group of works—is superior to another. Stressing that point again would make an effective conclusion.

DEMONSTRATIVE STUDENT ESSAY (TWO WORKS)

The Treatment of Responses to War in Amy Lowell's "Patterns" and Wilfred Owen's "Anthem for Doomed Youth"°

[1]   <u>Lowell's "Patterns" and Owen's "Anthem for Doomed Youth" are both powerful and unique condemnations of war.</u>* Owen's short poem speaks broadly and generally about the ugliness of war and also about large groups of sorrowful people. Lowell's longer poem focuses on the personal grief of just one person. In a

°See pp. 1115 and 698 for these poems.
*Central idea.

sense, Lowell's poem begins where Owen's ends, a fact that accounts for both the similarities and the differences between the two works. The antiwar themes can be compared on the basis of their subjects, their lengths, their concreteness, and their use of a common metaphor.[†]

"Anthem for Doomed Youth" attacks war more directly than "Patterns." Owen's opening line, "What passing-bells for those who die as cattle?" suggests that in war human beings are depersonalized before they are slaughtered, like so much meat, and his observations about the "monstrous" guns and the "shrill, demented" shells unambiguously condemn the horrors of war. By contrast, in "Patterns," warfare is far away, on another continent, intruding only when the [2] messenger delivers the letter stating that the speaker's fiancé has been killed (lines 63–64). A comparable situation governs the last six lines of Owen's poem, quietly describing how those at home respond to the news that their loved ones have died in war. Thus the antiwar focus in "Patterns" is the contrast between the calm, peaceful life of the speaker's garden and the anguish of her responses. In "Anthem for Doomed Youth," the stress is more on the external horrors of war that bring about the need for ceremonies honoring the dead.

Another major difference between the poems is their wide discrepancy in length. "Patterns" is an interior monologue or meditation of 107 lines, but it could not be shorter and still be convincing. In the poem the speaker thinks of the past and contemplates her future loneliness. Her final outburst, "Christ! What are patterns for?" could make no sense if she did not explain her situation as extensively as she does. "Anthem for Doomed Youth," however, is brief--a fourteen-line sonnet--because it is more general and less personal than "Patterns." Although [3] Owen's speaker shows great sympathy, he or she views the sorrows of others distantly, unlike Lowell, who goes right into the mind and spirit of the grieving woman. Owen's use, in his last six lines, of phrases such as "tenderness of patient minds" and "drawing down of blinds" is a powerful representation of deep grief. He gives no further details even though thousands of individual stories might be told. In contrast, Lowell tells just one of these stories as she focuses on her solitary speaker's lost hopes and dreams. Thus the contrasting lengths of the poems are determined by each poet's treatment of the topic.

Despite these differences of approach and length, both poems are similarly concrete and real. Owen moves from the real scenes and sounds of far-off battlefields to the homes of the many soldiers who have been killed in battle, but Lowell's scene is a single place--the garden of her speaker's estate. The speaker walks on real gravel along garden paths that contain daffodils, squills, a fountain, [4] and a lime tree. She thinks of her clothing and her ribboned shoes, and also of her fiancé's boots, sword hilts, and buttons. The images in Owen's poem are equally real but are not associated with individuals as in "Patterns." Thus Owen's images are those of cattle, bells, rifle shots, shells, bugles, candles, and window blinds. Although both poems reflect reality, Owen's details are more general and public; Lowell's are more personal and intimate.

Along with this concreteness, the poems share a major metaphor: that cultural patterns both control and frustrate human wishes and hopes. In "Patterns," this metaphor is shown in warfare itself (line 106), which is the pinnacle of organized human patterns of destruction. Further examples of the metaphor are found in details about clothing (particularly the speaker's stiff, confining gown in lines 5,

[†]Thesis sentence.

[5] 18, 21, 73, and 101, and also the lover's military boots in lines 46 and 49); the orderly, formal garden paths in which the speaker is walking (lines 1 and 93); her restraint at hearing about her lover's death; and her courtesy, despite her grief, in ordering refreshment for the messenger (line 69). Within such rigid patterns, her hopes for happiness have vanished, along with the sensuous spontaneity symbolized by her lover's hope to make love to her on a "shady seat" in the garden (lines 85–89). The metaphor of the constricting pattern is also seen in "Anthem for Doomed Youth," except that in this poem, the pattern is the funeral, not love or marriage. Owen's speaker contrasts the calm, peaceful tolling of "passing-bells" (line 1) to the frightening sounds of war represented by the "monstrous anger of the guns," "the stuttering rifles' rapid rattle," and "the demented choirs of wailing shells" (lines 2-8). Thus, while Lowell uses the metaphor to reveal the irony of hope and desire being destroyed by war, Owen uses it to reveal the irony of war's negation of peaceful ceremonies.

[6] <u>Though in these ways the poems share topics and some aspects of treatment, they are distinct and individual.</u> "Patterns" includes many references to visible things, whereas "Anthem for Doomed Youth" emphasizes sound (and silence). Both poems conclude on powerfully emotional although different notes. Owen's poem dwells on the pathos and sadness that war brings to many unnamed people, and Lowell's expresses the most intimate thoughts of a woman who is alone in the first agony of her grief. Although neither poem attacks the usual platitudes and justifications for war (the needs to mobilize, to sacrifice, to achieve peace through fighting, and so on), the attack is there by implication, for both poems make their appeal by stressing how war destroys the relationships that make life worth living. For this reason, despite their differences, both "Patterns" and "Anthem for Doomed Youth" are parallel antiwar poems, and both are strong expressions of feeling.

WORKS CITED

Amy Lowell, "Patterns." <u>Literature: An Introduction to Reading and Writing</u>. 7th ed. Ed. Edgar V. Roberts and Henry F. Jacobs. Upper Saddle River: Prentice Hall, 2004. 1115.

Wilfred Owen, "Anthem for Doomed Youth." Roberts and Jacobs, 698.

Commentary on the Essay

This essay shows how approximately equal attention can be given to the two works being studied. Words stressing similarity are *common, share, equally, parallel, both, similar,* and *also.* Contrasts are stressed by *while, whereas, different, dissimilar, contrast, although,* and *except.* Transitions from paragraph to paragraph are not different in this type of essay from those in other essays. Thus, the phrases *despite, along with this,* and *in these ways,* which are used here, could be used anywhere for the same transitional purpose.

The central idea—that the poems mutually condemn war—is brought out in paragraph 1, together with the supporting idea that the poems blend into each other because both show responses to news of battle casualties.

Paragraph 2, the first in the body, discusses how each poem brings out its attack on warfare. Paragraph 3 explains the differing lengths of the poems as a function of differences in perspective. Because Owen's sonnet views war and its effects at a distance, it is brief; but because Lowell's interior monologue views death intimately, it needs more detail and greater length.

Paragraph 4, on the topic of concreteness and reality, shows that the two works can receive equal attention without the bouncing back and forth of the tennis-ball method. Three of the sentences in this paragraph (3, 4, and 6) are devoted exclusively to details in one poem or the other; but sentences 1, 2, 5, and 7 refer to both works, stressing points of broad or specific comparison. The scheme demonstrates that the two works are, in effect, interlocked within the paragraph.

Paragraph 5, the last in the body, considers the similar and dissimilar ways in which the poems treat the common metaphor of cultural patterns.

The conclusion, paragraph 6, summarizes the central idea, and it also stresses the ways in which the two poems, although similar, are distinct and unique.

DEMONSTRATIVE STUDENT ESSAY (EXTENDED COMPARISON-CONTRAST)

Literary Treatments of the Conflicts between Private and Public Life

[1]   <u>The conflict between private or personal life, on the one hand, and public or civic and national life, on the other, is a topic common to many literary works.</u>° Authors show that individuals try to maintain their personal lives and commitments even though they are tested and stressed by public and external forces. Ideally, individuals should have the freedom to follow their own wishes independently of the outside world. It is a fact, however, that living itself causes people to venture into the public world and therefore to encounter conflicts. Getting married, following a profession, observing the natural world, looking at a person's possessions, taking a walk--all these draw people into the public world in which rules, regulations, and laws override private wishes. To greater and lesser degrees, such conflicts are found in Matthew Arnold's "Dover Beach," Ambrose Bierce's "An Occurrence at Owl Creek Bridge," Anton Chekhov's <u>The Bear</u>, Susan Glaspell's "A Jury of Her Peers," Kate Chopin's "The Story of an Hour," Thomas Hardy's "Channel Firing," Nathaniel Hawthorne's "Young Goodman Brown," John Keats's "Bright Star," Irving Layton's "Rhine Boat Trip," Amy Lowell's "Patterns," William Shakespeare's Sonnet 73: "That Time of Year Thou May'st in Me Behold," and William Wordsworth's "Lines Written in Early Spring."* <u>In these works, conflicts are shown between interests of individuals and those of the social, legal, and military public.</u>†

°Central idea.
*See pp. 671, 234, 1570, 188, 362, 710, 403, 730, 1111, 1115, 873, and 1001 for these works.
†Thesis sentence.

[2]   One of the major private-public conflicts is created by the way in which characters respond to social conventions and expectations. In Chekhov's The Bear, for example, Mrs. Popov has given up her personal life to memorialize her dead husband. She wears black, stays in her house for a whole year, and swears eternal fidelity; and she does all this to fulfill what she considers her public role as a grieving widow. Fortunately for her, Smirnov arrives on the scene and arouses her enough to make her give up this deadly pose. Not as fortunate is Hawthorne's Goodman Brown in "Young Goodman Brown." Brown's obligation is much less public and also more philosophical than Mrs. Popov's because his religiously inspired vision of evil creates a lifelong gloom in him. Although Mrs. Popov is easily moved from her position by the prospect of immediate life and vitality, Brown's fidelity to his vision of distrust locks him into a fear of evil from which not even his own faithful wife can shake him. The two characters therefore go in entirely different directions--one toward personal fulfillment, the other toward personal destruction.

[3]   Of particular importance is that philosophical or religious difficulties such as those of Goodman Brown force a crisis in an individual life. In Arnold's "Dover Beach," for example, the speaker expresses regret about uncertainty and the loss of religious faith that wear away civilization just like surf beating on the stones of Dover Beach. This situation might make a person dreary and depressed, just like Goodman Brown. Arnold's speaker, however, in the lines "Ah, love, let us be true / To one another," finds power in personal fidelity and commitment (lines 29-30). In other words, the public world of "human misery" and the diminishing "Sea of Faith" is beyond control, and therefore all that is left is personal commitment. This is not to say that "Young Goodman Brown," as a story, is negative, for Hawthorne implies that a positive personal life lies in the denial of choices like those made by Brown and in the acceptance of choices like those made by Mrs. Popov and Arnold's speaker.

[4]   To deny or to ignore the public world is a possible option that, under some circumstances, can be chosen. For example, "Dover Beach" reflects a conscious decision to ignore the philosophic and religious uncertainty that the speaker finds in the intellectual and public world. Even more independent of such a public world, Shakespeare's "That Time of Year" and Keats's "Bright Star" bring out their ideas as reflections on purely personal situations. Shakespeare's speaker deals with the love between himself and the listener, whereas Keats's speaker, addressing a distant star, considers his need for steadfastness in his relationship with his "fair love." Louise in Chopin's "The Story of an Hour" embodies an interesting variation on the personal matters brought up in these two sonnets. At first, Louise is crushed by the news coming from the public world that her husband has been killed. Her first vision of herself is that of a grieving, private widow. As she thinks about things, however, she quickly begins to anticipate the liberation and freedom--to become free to explore the public world--which widowhood will give her. Ironically, it is the reappearance of her husband, who moves freely in the public world, that causes her sudden heart failure. What she looked forward to as the possibility of free choice to do and go where she wishes has suddenly been withdrawn from her by her renewed status within the publicly sanctioned system of marriage, and it is the abrupt loss of this possibility that ends her life.

The complexity of the conflicts between private and public life is brought out in the way in which structures secure their power through law and legality. With immense power, the law often acts as an arbitrary form of public judgment that disregards personal needs and circumstances. This idea is brought out on the most personal level in Glaspell's "A Jury of Her Peers," in which the two major characters, both women, are faced urgently with the conflict between their personal identification with the accused woman, Minnie, and their public obligation to the law. One of the women, Mrs. Peters, is reminded that she is "married to the law," but she and Mrs. Hale suppress the evidence that they know would condemn Minnie, even though technically--by law, that is--their knowledge is public property. Their way of resolving the conflict therefore involves their rejection of public demands in favor of personal concerns.

[5]

The legal conflict can also be treated more generally and philosophically. For example, Wordsworth deals with the morality--or immorality--of the conflict in "Lines Written in Early Spring," when he says, "Have I not reason to lament / What man has made of man" (lines 15–16). "What man has made of man" in its most extreme form is legalized suppression and persecution, but Wordsworth does little more with the topic than to say that he laments it. Layton, however, in "Rhine Boat Trip," deals with the extremity of human cruelty. In this poem, Layton condemns the Nazi exterminations of "Jewish mothers" and "murdered rabbis" during the Holocaust of World War II. Ironically, the exterminations were carried out legally, for it has commonly been observed that the Nazis created laws to justify all their atrocities.

[6]

It is works about warfare that especially highlight how irreconcilable the conflicts between personal and public concerns can become. A comic but nevertheless real instance is dramatized by Hardy in "Channel Firing." In this poem, set in a church graveyard, the skeleton of "Parson Thirdly" views "gunnery practice out at sea" (line 10) as evidence that his "forty year" dedication to serving his church was a waste of time. His conclusion is that he would have been better off ignoring his public role and instead sticking "to pipes and beer." Although Thirdly is disillusioned, he has not been as deeply affected personally by warfare as the speaker of Lowell's "Patterns." Her fiancé, she learns, has been killed fighting abroad; and his death leads her to question--and by implication to doubt--the external "patterns" that destroy one's personal plans for life (line 107). Unlike both these characters, who are deeply touched by the effects of warfare, Peyton Farquhar, the main character in Bierce's "An Occurrence at Owl Creek Bridge," is actually killed by his commitment to a public concern--that of the Southern forces in the Civil War. As in "Channel Firing" and "Patterns," Farquhar's situation shows the absolute power of the public world over the private.

[7]

The works examined here are in general agreement that, under ideal conditions, the private world should be supreme over the public. They also demonstrate that in many ways, the public world invades the private world with a wide range of effects, from making people behave foolishly to destroying them utterly. Naturally, the tone of the works is shaped by the degree of seriousness of the conflict. Chekhov's The Bear is good-humored and farcical because the characters overcome the social roles in which they are cast. More sober are works such as "Dover Beach" and "Young Goodman Brown," in which characters either are overcome by public commitments or deliberately turn their backs on them. In the highest range of seriousness are works such as "Rhine Boat Trip," "Patterns," and "An Occurrence at Owl Creek Bridge," in which the individual is crushed by irresistible public forces. The works compared and contrasted here show varied and powerful conflicts between personal interests and public demands.

[8]

Commentary on the Essay

This essay, combining for discussion all three genres of fiction, poetry, and drama, is visualized as an assignment at the end of a unit of study. The expectation prompting the assignment is that a fairly large number of literary works can be profitably compared on the basis of a unifying subject, idea, or technique. For this essay, the works—seven poems, four stories, and a short play—are compared and contrasted on the common topic of private–public conflicts. It is obviously impossible to discuss all the works in detail in every paragraph. The essay therefore demonstrates that a writer may introduce a large number of works in a straightforward comparison-contrast method without a need for detailed comparison of each work with every other work on each of the major subtopics (social, legal, military).

Thus, the first section, consisting of paragraphs 2–4, treats six of the works. In paragraph 2, however, only two works are discussed, and in paragraph 3 one of these works is carried over for comparison with only one additional work. The fourth paragraph springs out of the second, utilizing one of the works discussed there and then bringing out comparisons with three additional works.

The same technique is used in the rest of the essay. Paragraph 5 introduces only one work; paragraph 6 introduces two additional works; and paragraph 7 introduces three works for comparison and contrast. Each of the twelve works is then eventually discussed at least once in terms of how it contributes to the major topic. One might note that the essay concentrates on a relatively small number of the works, such as Chekhov's *The Bear* and Hawthorne's "Young Goodman Brown," but that as newer topics are introduced, the essay goes on to works that are more closely connected to these topics.

The technique of extended comparison-contrast used in this way shows how the various works can be defined and distinguished in relation to the common idea. The concluding paragraph summarizes these distinctions by suggesting a continuous line along which each of the works may be placed.

Even so, the treatment of so many texts might easily cause crowding and confusion. The division of the major topic into subtopics, as noted, is a major means of trying to make the essay easy to follow. An additional means is the introduction of transitional words and phrases such as *also, choose*, and *one of the major conflicts*.

An extended comparison-contrast essay cannot present a full treatment of each of the works. The works are unique, and there are many elements that do not yield to the comparison-contrast method. Ideas that are particularly important in Hardy's "Channel Firing," for example, are (1) that human beings need eternal rest and not eternal life, (2) that God is amused by—or indifferent to—human affairs, (3) that religious callings or vocations may be futile, and (4) that war itself is the supreme form of cruelty. All these topics could be treated in another essay, but they are not germane to the subject of this essay. A topic compatible with the general private–public topic is needed, and the connection is readily made (paragraph 7) through the character of Hardy's Parson Thirdly. Because the essay deals with the conflicts brought out by Thirdly's comments,

Hardy's poem is linked to all the other works for comparative purposes. So it is with the other works, each of which could also be the subject of analysis from many standpoints other than comparison-contrast. The effect of the comparison of all the works collectively, however, is the enhanced understanding of each of the works separately. To achieve such an understanding and to explain it are the major goals of the extended comparison-contrast method.

Special Topics for Writing and Argument about Comparison and Contrast

1. The use of the speaker in Arnold's "Dover Beach" (p. 671) and Wordsworth's "Lines Written in Early Spring" (p. 1001).

2. The description of fidelity to love in Keats's "Bright Star" (p. 730) and Shakespeare's Sonnet 73: "That Time of Year Thou May'st in Me Behold" (p. 873), Arnold's "Dover Beach" (p. 671), or Lowell's "Patterns" (p. 1115).

3. The view of women in Chekhov's *The Bear* (p. 1570) and Maupassant's "The Necklace" (p. 4) or in Glaspell's "A Jury of Her Peers" (p. 188) and O'Neill's "Before Breakfast" (p. 1209).

4. The use of descriptive scenery in Hawthorne's "Young Goodman Brown" (p. 403) and Lowell's "Patterns" (p. 1115) or in Poe's "The Masque of the Red Death" (p. 302) and Bierce's "An Occurrence at Owl Creek Bridge" (p. 234).

5. Symbols of disapproval in Hardy's "Channel Firing" (p. 710) and Frost's "Desert Places" (p. 861).

6. The treatment of loss in Yeats's "The Wild Swans at Coole" (p. 1159) and Wagner's "The Boxes" (p. 1151).

7. Treatments of religion in "God's Grandeur" by Hopkins (p. 818) and "Batter My Heart" by Donne (p. 648).

8. Any of the foregoing topics applied to a number of separate works. Please consult the Topical and Thematic Table of Contents for possible additional subjects.

Appendix 1

MLA Recommendations for Documenting Electronic Sources

Both students and instructors can now take advantage of the technology available to assist in research. While many libraries offer varied databases that enable researchers to locate information easily, the main thrust of technology is now the exploration of the World Wide Web. Through the use of various search engines, you simply need to enter the name of an author, a title, or a topic, upon which you will be linked to a host of resources from all over the world—home pages of specific authors, literary organizations, and works on various topics by contemporary writers. You'll find a good deal of what you're searching for in only a few minutes. An important caveat is that many sources still remain in printed journals and magazines which may or may not be on the Web. To make your searches thorough, therefore, *you must never neglect to search for printed information.*

This appendix provides general guidelines for making electronic source citations, and therefore is intended to augment the section titled "Documenting Your Work" in Chapter 32. For general information on citation recommendations by the Modern Language Association (MLA), see Joseph Gibaldi, *MLA Handbook for Writers of Research Papers,* 6th ed. (New York: MLA, 2003).

Because the available methods of obtaining electronic information are developing so rapidly, the printed style manuals have had difficulty keeping up with the changes. If you do a Web search looking for information on these styles, chances are that the information you discover will vary from site to site. Therefore, you need to know the basics that are required for the citation of your sources.

When recovering electronic sources, it is vital to type every letter, number, symbol, dot, underline, and space accurately. Recovery systems are unforgiving, and mistakes or omissions of any sort will make it impossible for you to retrieve your source. The sources are often transitory because someone, somewhere, must maintain them (through the updating of information and the paying of fees). The sources are therefore not always reliable, so printing a copy of sources you plan to cite will make your citations both definite and accurate. If the uniform resource locator (URL) you have used does not turn up the material for which you are searching, you may be able to locate it simply by typing in the name of the author or the name of the article. You may often rely on your search engine to turn up the material for you.

By the same token, it is essential for you, when you are compiling your own list of works cited, to be absolutely accurate in reproducing the URL of your sources. You must assume that someone reading your essay and using your list will want to check out the sources themselves, and any errors in your transcription will create only confusion.

The style generally accepted in the "cyber" world, and the one recommended by the MLA, places angle brackets (< >) before and after Internet addresses and URLs. If you see brackets around an address you want to use, do not use them as part of the address when you are seeking retrieval. Also, since a number of word-processing programs now support the use of italics, you can use italics as a regular practice. Some researchers, however, still prefer underlines, and if your programs (or typewriter) cannot produce italics, of course use underlines. If in doubt about which to use, consult your instructor.

⫲ MLA STYLE GUIDELINES

Many of the guidelines the MLA has authorized for the citation of electronic sources overlap with the MLA recommendations for printed sources, but to avoid ambiguity a number of recommendations bear repetition. Electronic materials are to be documented in basically the same style as printed sources. According to the sixth edition of the *MLA Handbook*, which illustrates virtually all the situations you will ever encounter, the following items need to be included if they are available.

1. The name of the author, editor, compiler, or translator of the source (if available and relevant), last name first, followed by an abbreviation, such as *ed.*, if appropriate.

2. If there is no author listed in the source, you should list the title first: the title of a poem, short story, article, or similar short work within a scholarly project, database, or periodical (in quotation marks); or the title of a posting to a discussion list or forum (taken from the subject line and enclosed by quotation marks), concluded by the phrase "Online posting."

3. The title of a book, underlined or italicized.

4. The name of the editor, compiler, or translator of the text (if relevant and if not cited earlier), preceded by (not followed by) any necessary abbreviations, such as *Ed.*

5. Publication information for any printed version of the source.

6. The title of the scholarly project, database, periodical, or professional or personal site, underlined or italicized; or, for a professional or personal site with no title, a description such as "Home page."

7. The name of the editor of the scholarly project or database (if available).

8. The version number of the source (if not part of the title), or, for a journal, the volume number, issue number, or other identifying number. All numbers should be in Arabic, not Roman numerals.

9. The date of publication or posting that you find in your source. Sometimes the original date is no longer available because it has been replaced with an update; if so, cite that. Dates should be arranged by (a) day of the month, (b) month (the names of longer months may be abbreviated), and (c) year.

10. For a work from a subscription service, the name of the service (and name, city, and state abbreviation if the subscriber is a library).

11. For a posting to a discussion list or forum, the name of the list or forum.

12. The number range or total number of pages, paragraphs, or other sections, if they are numbered. If you do your own numbering, include your numbers within square brackets [ ], and be sure to indicate what you have numbered.

13. The name of any institution or organization sponsoring or associated with the Web site.

14. The date when you consulted the source. If you have looked at the site a number of times, include the most recent date of use. The principle here is that the date immediately before the uniform resource locator (URL) will mark the last time you used the source.

15. The electronic address or URL of the source in angle brackets < >. Many programs now automatically include the angle brackets. If the URL is too long to fit on one line, it should be divided at a slash (/) if possible—do not introduce hypenations into the URL as these may be mistaken for actual significant characters in that address.

The following examples show the formats you are likely to use most often.

For a Book

> Shaw, Bernard. <u>Pygmalion</u>. 1916, 1999. Bartleby
>   Archive. 1 Mar. 2003 <http://www.bartleby.com/
>   138/index.html>.

For a Poem

> Carroll, Lewis. <u>The Hunting of the Snark</u>. 1876.
>   2 Jan. 2003 <http://www.everypoet.com/archive/
>   poetry/Lewis_Carroll/lewis_carroll_the_hunting_
>   of_the_snark.htm>.

For a Journal Article

> Charles, Cristie Cowles. "Why We Need More Assessment
>   of Online Composition Courses: A Brief Histo-
>   ry." <u>Kairos</u> 7.3 (Fall 2002). Multiple sections.
>   3 Jan. 2002 <http://english.ttu.edu/kairos/7.3/
>   binder2.html?coverweb/charles/index.html>.

For a Magazine Article

> Tallmer, Jerry. "An Uncivil War: Legendary Literary
>   Figures Lillian Hellman and Mary McCarthy bat-
>   tle in Nora Ephron's <u>Imaginary Friends</u> at the
>   Ethel Barrymore Theatre." <u>Playbill</u> 19 Dec.

```
2002. 1 Mar. 2003. <http://www.playbill.com/
features/article/76959.html>.
```

Posting to a Discussion List

```
Webb, David L. "Re: Problems of Crowlianism & His
    Singular Theorizing." Online posting. Google
    Groups. 25 Dec. 2002. 1 Mar. 2003.
    <http://groups.google.com/groups?q=
    Crowlianism&hl=en&lr=&ie=UTF-8&selm=
    aubdu2%241ea4e%241%40hades.csu.net&rnum=1>.
```

For a Scholarly Project

```
Voice of the Shuttle: Web Page for Humanities
    Research. Ed. Alan Liu. 6 Sept. 2001. U of
    California Santa Barbara. 4 Jan. 2003
    <http://vos.ucsb.edu/>.
```

For a Professional Site

```
Nobel e-Museum. The Nobel Foundation. 14 Jan. 2003.
    2 Mar. 2003 <http://www.nobel.se/>.
```

For a Personal Site

```
Barrett, Dan. The Gentle Giant Home Page. 21 Feb.
    2003. 3 Mar. 2003. <http://www.blazemonger.com/
    GG/index.html>.
```

For Synchronous Communications (Such as MOOs, MUDs, and IRCs)

```
DU Educational Technology Services, Inc. Group
    Discussion. 22 Nov. 1999. 3 Jan. 2003
    <moo.du.org>.
```

Appendix II

Brief Biographies
of the Poets in Part II

JACK AGÜEROS (B. 1934) • Agüeros, a native of New York, is a well known Latino writer. He earned a B.A. from Brooklyn College and an M.A. from Occidental College. Not only has he written poetry, but he has also done plays, stories, and film scripts. His stories are contained in *Dominoes and Other Stories* (1993), and his poetry collections are *Correspondence Between the Stonehaulers* (1991) and *Sonnets from the Puerto Rican* (1996). "Sonnet for You, Familiar Famine" is from *Sonnets from the Puerto Rican.*

BRIAN W. ALDISS (B. 1925) • Aldiss is best known as a writer of science fiction, but he has also written novels, dramas, reviews, and considerable poetry. He was educated in English private schools, and during World War II he served in the Far East (Burma, Sumatra). After the war he worked for a time as a bookseller in Oxford, when he also began writing. His first published work was *The Brightfount Diaries* (1955), after which his output flourished. Among his many works are the companion novels *Frankenstein Unbound* (1973) and *Dracula Unbound* (1991). One of his poetry collections is *Homelife with Cats* (1992). Recent novels are *Somewhere East of Life* (1994) and *White Mars* (2000). He was the recipient of the British Science Fiction Award in 1972 and is a founding trustee of World Science Fiction (1982). Also, his novel *A.I. [Artificial Intelligence]* was adapted as a film that was released in 2001.

A. R. AMMONS (ARCHIE RANDOLPH AMMONS, 1926–2001) • Ammons was educated in North Carolina and California. He began teaching at Cornell University in 1964, the year in which his second poetry collection was published. Among his honors were the Bollingen Prize (1973–74), a MacArthur Fellowship, and the Robert Frost medal from the Poetry Society of America. Some of his collections of poetry are *The Selected Poems: Expanded Edition* (1986), *Sumerian Vistas* (1987), *Garbage* (1993), and *Brink Road* (1996). He published a long poem, *Glare*, in 1997. "80-Proof" was included in *Diversifications* (1975).

MAYA ANGELOU (B. 1928) • Born in St. Louis, Angelou acted and sang before becoming a writer. She is known as much for her fiction as for her poetry, and she has also written plays. She achieved recognition with *I Know Why the Caged Bird Sings* (1970). *Just Give Me a Cool Drink of Water 'fore I Diiie* appeared in 1971, and she has published regularly since. Her national importance was recognized when she was chosen to read her poetry at the inauguration of President Clinton in January 1993. Her collection of essays *Even the Stars Look Lonesome* appeared in 1997. Her collected work is *The Complete Collected Poems of Maya Angelou* (1994). In recent years she has spoken and sung on a number of public television productions.

MATTHEW ARNOLD (1822–1888) • One of the major Victorian poets, Arnold was brought up among books and learning, and eventually (1857) became a professor of poetry at Oxford. In his Oxford lectures he described a loss of security and religious faith, and hence he stressed the need to recover absolutes—which to him was the major "function of criticism at the present time." "Dover Beach" is, along with "The Scholar Gypsy" and "Stanzas from the Grande Chartreuse," among his best-known poems.

MARGARET ATWOOD (B. 1939) • Atwood is one of Canada's premier and most prolific writers, having published many books of poetry, a number of novels and stories, and much criticism. In addition, she is editor of *The Oxford Book of Canadian Verse* (1982). One of her most widely recognized works is the anti-utopian novel *The Handmaid's Tale* (1986), which describes a futuristic nightmare society of fear and repression for women. This story was adapted as a movie in 1990. The stories in her collection *Wilderness Tips* (1992) reflect regret and diminished hopes, unlike the more comic topic of the poem "Siren Song." The scope of her work may be inferred from some of her later publications: *Poems* (1994), *Princess Prunella and the Purple Peanut* (1995), *Morning in the Burned House* (1995), *The Edible Woman* (1998), *Dancing Girls: And Other Stories* (1998), *Lady Oracle* (1998), and *The Blind Assassin* (2000, 2001).

W. H. AUDEN (WYSTAN HUGH AUDEN, 1907–1973) • Auden was born in England but became a permanent resident of the United States after the Spanish Civil War. A Marxist in his youth, he became a devout Christian in later years. He wrote prolifically, including collaborations with the dramatist Christopher Isherwood and the poet Louis MacNeice. Another notable collaboration is the libretto for Igor Stravinsky's opera *The Rake's Progress* (1951). He edited *The Oxford Book of Light Verse* (1938).

WENDELL BERRY (B. 1934) • One of the most popular poets in the United States, Berry is a resident of Kentucky, where he was brought up and educated, and where he taught for many years. His output as a poet, essayist, and novelist has been voluminous. He has published many separate volumes of poetry, including *The Broken Ground* (1964), *Clearing* (1977), *The Wheel* (1982), *Entries* (1997), and *A Timbered Choir: The Sabbath Poems, 1979–1997* (1998). Readers can find some of his short fiction in *Fidelity: Five Stories* (1993). His *The Memory of Old Jack* (1999) is a recent novel. An early edition of his collected verse is *Collected Poems, 1957–1982* (1985).

EARLE BIRNEY (ALFRED EARLE BIRNEY, 1904–1995) • One of the major modern Canadian writers, Birney was born in Calgary, Alberta, and received his higher education at the University of British Columbia. He was editor of *Twentieth Century Canadian Poetry* (1953). In 1975 McClelland and Stewart of Canada issued his collected poetry. By 1985 he had published more than a dozen collections of poetry in addition to numerous stories and plays.

ELIZABETH BISHOP (1911–1979) • Bishop was brought up by an aunt in Worcester, Massachusetts. She attended private schools and Vassar College. During much of her life she lived in Brazil. She taught for a time at the University of Washington and then at Harvard. Her first collection of poems was *North and South* (1946), which she expanded in 1955 as *North and South—A Cold Spring*, for which she received the Pulitzer Prize in Poetry in 1956.

WILLIAM BLAKE (1757–1827) • Blake was apprenticed to an engraver in London at the age of fourteen. Throughout his career he published his poems with his own engravings, and these original editions are now valuable collector's items. Blake was a revolutionary at heart who thought that humanity would flower if institutions were eliminated or at least redirected. *Songs of Experience*, from which "London" is taken, is a collection of poems on this theme, published in 1794, five years after the outbreak of the French Revolution. In this same year he published *Songs of Innocence*, from which "The Lamb" is taken.

LOUISE BOGAN (1897–1970) • Born in Maine, Bogan spent most of her life in New York, writing regular reviews for *The New Yorker*. Her first volume of poems was *Body of This Death* (1923), in which "Women" appeared. Her *Collected Poems* (1954) was awarded the

Bollingen Prize. Her major critical work was *Achievement in American Poetry, 1900–1950* (1951). *Journey Around My Room* (1980) is an autobiographical work that was published posthumously.

ARNA BONTEMPS (1902–1973) • Born in Louisiana, Bontemps by profession was a librarian (at Fisk University). In addition to poetry, he published a number of novels and works of children's fiction. *One Hundred Years of Negro Freedom* (1961) is a widely heralded historical work.

ANNE BRADSTREET (1612–1672) • Bradstreet was born in England. She married early and came to the American colonies when she was eighteen. Her career was that of wife and mother, and she bore eight children. Nevertheless she managed to write poems regularly and kept them together in manuscript. In 1650 her brother-in-law had them published in London without her knowledge, and she was therefore unable to make corrections. The volume, titled *The Tenth Muse,* was the first poetic publication in England by anyone living in colonial America. A second and corrected edition was considered about 1666, but the new edition did not appear until six years after her death.

EMILY BRONTË (1818–1848) • The middle child of the Brontë sisters, Emily received no more than a minimum of formal education and was largely home taught and self taught, although she spent a brief time in Belgium studying music and languages. Generally, her brief life was characterized by poverty and deprivation. She was deeply affected by the landscape on the moors near Haworth, the family home in Yorkshire in the Northern part of England, and her almost mystical identification of land and character pervades her best known work, the novel *Wuthering Heights* (1847). She and her sisters published a joint collection of verse in 1846, *Poems, by Currer, Ellis, and Acton Bell* (i.e., Charlotte, Emily, and Anne). "No Coward Soul Is Mine" is considered one of her best poems, along with "The Night Is Darkening Round Me" and "Remembrance."

GWENDOLYN BROOKS (1917–2000) • Brooks was born in Chicago, where she spent most of her life. Winner of the Pulitzer Prize for Poetry in 1950 (for *Annie Allen,* 1949), she was concerned with race in both her fictional and poetic works. "We Real Cool" exemplified this emphasis. In 1967 she began directing her work toward African-American readers, and she published a number of her poems in pamphlet form, of which *Primer for Blacks* (1980) is one. Her last published works are *Blacks* (1991), *Maud Martha* (1993), and *Selected Poems* (1999).

ELIZABETH BARRETT BROWNING (1806–1861) • English born, Elizabeth Barrett suffered a crippling spinal injury when still a girl. Despite this adversity she had become a widely recognized poet when she married Robert Browning in 1846. Because of her condition and the English climate, the Brownings moved to Italy, where they remained until Elizabeth's death. During her lifetime, her reputation as a poet eclipsed Robert's. Her *Cry of the Children* (1843) was an early poetic protest against the unjust industrial exploitation of underage children as workers. In 1850 she published *Sonnets from the Portuguese,* which she presented as a gift to her husband.

ROBERT BROWNING (1812–1889) • In his twenties and early thirties, Browning wrote a number of versified plays for the stage, but these were unsuccessful, and he did not achieve fame in his native England until he was well into his fifties. Because of his experience with drama, he found his poetic voice within the medium of the dramatic monologue, which he perfected to a high degree. "My Last Duchess," "Soliloquy of the Spanish Cloister," and "Porphyria's Lover" appeared in his *Dramatic Lyrics* of 1842, exactly during the time when he was also writing his plays.

WILLIAM CULLEN BRYANT (1794–1878) • Bryant was born in Massachusetts and spent his adult life in New York. Early in his career he practiced law, which he disliked, and after ten years of that he was pleased to take up literature and editorial work. He was a newspaper editor and owner for fifty years and at the time of his death he was one of the most beloved writers in the United States. His best known work was *Thanatopsis*, which he wrote when still a boy and published at the age of seventeen. He published many collections of poems and also did successful translations of Homer's *Iliad* and *Odyssey*. Quotations from his poem "Song of Marion's Men" (1832) may be found on pp. 383–86.

ROBERT BURNS (1759–1796) • The best-known and most loved poet of Scotland, Burns gave up farming and taught himself to read and write English, French, and Latin. He published his first volume, *Scots Poems Chiefly in the Scottish Dialect*, in 1786. His use of the down-to-earth idiom of Scots peasants, together with joyous irreverence and frank lustiness, made him instantly famous.

GEORGE GORDON, LORD BYRON (1788–1824) • One of the major English Romantic poets, Byron created the so-called Byronic hero, a driven and solitary figure who is misunderstood by his fellow human beings. He published his semiautobiographical poem "Childe Harolde's Pilgrimage" in 1811. In 1815 he published *Hebrew Melodies* (1815), in which "The Destruction of Sennacherib" appeared. That year, he left England and never returned. He continued writing poetry as he traveled, including the 16,000-line unfinished poem *Don Juan*. He died at Missolonghi, in Greece, while fighting for Greek independence.

THOMAS CAMPION (1567–1620) • English-born Campion was known in his day not only as a poet but also as a composer. He set many of his poems to music, including "Cherry Ripe." Two of his collections are *A Book of Airs* (1601) and *The Third and Fourth Books of Airs* (ca. 1617). His interest in the relationship of music and poetry prompted him to write a discourse on English metrics, *Observation in the Art of English Poesy* (1602).

LEWIS CARROLL (1832–1898) • Carroll is the pen name of the English writer Charles L. Dodgson, who is famous for *Alice's Adventures in Wonderland* and *Through the Looking-Glass*. Carroll was also a mathematician, lecturer, logician, and photographer. "Jabberwocky," from *Through the Looking-Glass*, stems out of his interest in words. The word *chortle*, which he created in this poem (a blending of *chuckle* and *snort*), is now standard English.

HAYDEN CARRUTH (B. 1921) • Carruth was a native of Connecticut and received degrees at the Universities of North Carolina and Chicago. In World War II he served for two years in Italy. After the war he worked for a time as an editor and taught, among other schools, at Syracuse and Bucknell. He is the author of more than two dozen poetry collections, the most recent being *Doctor Jazz: Poems, 1996–2000* (2001). Among his many distinctions he has received the Harriet Monroe Poetry Prize, a Guggenheim Fellowship, an NEA grant, and the National Book Award of 1996 for his collection *Scrambled Eggs and Whisky: Poems: 1991–1995* (1996).

JIMMY CARTER (B. 1924) • James Earl Carter was born in Plains, Georgia, which is still his home. He graduated from the U.S. Naval Academy (1946), served in the Navy, became a peanut farmer, was governor of Georgia (1971–1975), and was elected thirty-ninth president of the United States (1977–1981). Since his presidency he has distinguished himself in many national and international causes, such as creating the Carter Foundation, serving with the International Negotiation Network, and working closely with Habitat for Humanity. He has been the recipient of devoted recognition and many honorary degrees, but despite his national and international standing he has frequently been seen on TV house-building programs serving as a worker, along with other workers, on Habitat projects. His continued work for peace was recognized in 2002, when he received the Nobel Peace Prize. His varied list of published works is extensive, and he has even cowritten, with his daughter Amy, a children's book. In 1995 he published *Always a Reckoning and Other Poems*, from which "I Wanted to Share My Father's World" is selected.

AMY CLAMPITT (1920–1994) • Clampitt was a native of Iowa, receiving her education at Grinnell College and later at Columbia University. For many years she worked in the publishing field and also for the National Audubon Society. Although she wrote poetry during most of her lifetime, she was not published until she was in her sixties, her first volume being *The Kingfisher* (1983). During the remainder of her life she published regular volumes of poems, completing *What the Light Was Like* (1985), *Archaic Figure* (1987), and *Westward* (1990). In 1994, the last year of her life, she published her final collection, *A Silence Opens.*

LUCILLE CLIFTON (B. 1936) • Clifton was born and educated in New York. Her productivity as a writer began in the 1970s and has been strong ever since. One of her earliest poetry collections was *An Ordinary Woman* (1974). Later she published *Next: New Poems* (1987) and *Good Woman: Poems and a Memoir, 1969–1980* (1987). In addition to her poetry, she has written a number of stories and poems for children, such as *All Us Come Cross the Water* (1973), *The Book of Light* (1993), *Everett Anderson's Christmas Coming* (1993), and *The Lucky Stone* (1999). A collection of her poems is *Blessing the Boats: New and Selected Poems, 1988–2000* (2000).

ARTHUR HUGH CLOUGH (1819–1861) • Clough's father was a businessman who often worked in the United States, and for a period of five years as a boy Arthur lived with the family in South Carolina. Returning to England, he attended Rugby, a famous public (i.e., private) school, and became a favorite in the household of Dr. Thomas Arnold, the headmaster. Though Clough had a good deal of academic promise, his achievement did not measure up, and he felt that he had failed in his academic goals. He was fond of giving his poems titles in foreign languages, such as "Qua Cursum Ventus" (The Wind Creates the Course [of the ship]), "Wen Gott Betrügt, Ist Wohl Betrogen" ([The Person] Whom God Deceives Is Well Deceived), "Sehnsucht" (Longing), and "Tò Kalón" (The Beautiful). His "Say Not the Struggle Nought Availeth" is one of his famous poems, together with the satiric "The Latest Decalogue." After Clough died in Florence in 1861, his good friend Matthew Arnold commemorated his life in the monody "Thyrsis" (1866), one of the best-known elegies in the English language.

LEONARD COHEN (B. 1934) • Cohen is a native of Montreal, and he received his education at McGill University and also at Columbia. He traveled widely, spending years in Greece, England, New York, and California. He began writing poetry early. His first collections were *Let Us Compare Mythologies* (1956) and *The Spice Box of Earth* (1961). He also published two successful novels, *The Favorite Game* (1963) and *Beautiful Losers* (1966). Today he is best known for his featured television concerts and also for the many record albums and compact disc collections of his songs and music. Among the most recent of these are *The Future* (1992) and *Cohen Live* (1994). An anthology of his work is *The Concise Leonard Cohen* (1999).

SAMUEL TAYLOR COLERIDGE (1772–1834) • Coleridge was born in Devon, in southern England, and studied at Cambridge University but did not earn a degree. After a short stint as a soldier he fell into dire financial straits, from which he was rescued by the Wedgwood brothers (of ceramic fame), who provided him with an annuity so that he could devote himself to poetry. Wordsworth and he together published the *Lyrical Ballads* of 1798, a collection that is the benchmark of the English Romantic movement. Coleridge contributed "The Rime of the Ancient Mariner," his most famous poem, and also "Kubla Khan." After 1802 he wrote little poetry, but his *Biographia Literaria* of 1817 is one of the major works of literary criticism of the early nineteenth century.

BILLY COLLINS (B. 1941) • A native of New York, Collins received degrees at Holy Cross and the University of California at Riverside. He lives in New York and is a Distinguished Professor of English at Lehman College. Among his collections of poetry are *The Apple That Astonished Paris* (1989), which includes "Schoolsville"; *Questions about Angels* (1991), a winner in the National Poetry Series competition; *The Art of Drowning* (1996); *Picnic, Lightning*

(1998); and *Sailing Around the Room: New and Selected Poems* (2001). In 2001 he was named American Poet Laureate for 2001–2002, and the next year he was reappointed.

FRANCES CORNFORD (1886–1960) • Cornford, a granddaughter of Charles Darwin, lived most of her life in Cambridge, England. She published only a few volumes of verse, and her *Collected Poems* was published in 1954.

WILLIAM COWPER (1731–1800) • Cowper is universally recognized because of his lines "God moves in a mysterious way / His wonders to perform." He received his education at an English private ("public") school, an institution that he attacked in his *Tirocinium* in 1785. He was qualified to practice law but never made a career of it. Although throughout his life he was troubled with depression and he made at least two suicide attempts, he wrote a considerable amount of prose and much poetry. His most widely recognized long poem is *The Task* (1785), and his best lyric poems are found in the *Olney Hymns* (1775), which contain "God Moves in a Mysterious Way" and "Oh, for a Closer Walk with God."

STEPHEN CRANE (1871–1900) • For a brief biography, see p. 112.

ROBERT CREELEY (B. 1926) • A native of Massachusetts, Robert Creeley received his master's degree from the University of New Mexico. He has received wide recognition and many honors, including a Bollingen Prize and the appointment as New York State Poet for 1989–1991. He is closely associated with the "Black Mountain Poets," a group that in the immediate post–World War II years was connected with Black Mountain College in North Carolina. This group advocated a minimalist approach to expression and believed that poetic form should follow the content. On this principle, poetry has no preconceptions, but it evolves freely and spontaneously as the poet writes it. Creeley has authored numerous books of poetry, together with short stories, correspondence, and essays. Some of his recent collections are *Thinking* (2000), *For Friends* (2000), and *Just in Time: Poems, 1984–1994* (2001). "Do You Think . . ." (1972) is drawn from his *Selected Poems* of 1991.

E. E. CUMMINGS (1894–1962) • Cummings studied at Harvard, receiving a master's degree there. During World War I, he served in the Ambulance Corps in France and, as a result of false charges of treason, was imprisoned—an experience he wrote about in his first work, *The Enormous Room* (1922). He began publishing poetry shortly thereafter and continued doing so throughout his life. His collected poetry, consisting of more than a thousand poems, was published in 1992.

PETER DAVISON (B. 1928) • Davison was born in New York City but grew up in Colorado. He received degrees at Harvard and Cambridge and has served as a lecturer and also as an editor with a number of leading publishers. His first poetry collection was *The Breaking of the Day and Other Poems* (1964). Among his numerous collections since then are *Praying Wrong: New and Selected Poems* (1985), *The Poems of Peter Davison, 1957–1995* (1995), and *Breathing Room: New Poems* (2000). "Delphi" is selected from *The Breaking of the Day and Other Poems.*

CARL DENNIS (B. 1939) • Dennis is a native of St. Louis, and received degrees from the University of Minnesota and the University of California, Berkeley. He has taught for many years at the University of Buffalo. A few of his many poetry collections are *A House of My Own* (1974), *Signs and Wonders,* (1979), and *Practical Gods* (2001). "The God Who Loves You" is from *Practical Gods,* the collection for which Dennis was awarded the Pulitzer Prize in Poetry in 2002.

JAMES DICKEY (1923–1997) • Dickey was a native of Georgia. He served in World War II and afterwards spent a number of years writing advertising copy. After 1969 he became a full-time writer and teacher. During the 1980s he published three volumes of poetry. Usually his poems are narratives that touch on violence and tragedy. "The Performance," for example, demonstrates, on the one hand, the violence that characterizes Dickey's well-received novel *Deliverance* (1970) and, on the other, the courageousness of a man insisting on his individuality and rights even against the greatest odds. One of his late novels was *To the White Sea*, published in 1993. A number of his works have been published posthumously in *The James Dickey Reader* (1999). His letters are included in *Crux: The Letters of James Dickey* (1999), and his poetry is collected in *James Dickey: The Selected Poems* (1998).

EMILY DICKINSON (1830–1886) • For a detailed biography, see pp. 1011–18.

JOHN DONNE (CA. 1572–1631) • Donne was born into a Roman Catholic family at a time when the Protestant reign of Elizabeth I was firmly established. In 1591 he enrolled at Lincoln's Inn in London to study science, philosophy, law, languages, and literature. In order to rise in English aristocratic circles, he changed his religion to Anglicanism. His hopes were ended in 1601, however, because of his elopement with Ann More, whose uncle accused him of a clandestine marriage (then a crime if the woman was an heiress) and had him jailed. Although the marriage was recognized in 1602, Donne could not regain political favor, and he and Ann struggled until he took a doctorate of divinity in 1616 (Ann died in 1617). He found favor and rose quickly to become Dean of St. Paul's Cathedral in London, where his sermons were well attended by the "nobility and gentry." He became widely known, publishing more than 130 of the sermons he delivered during his decade as dean. His poems, both religious and love poems, were not published during his lifetime but were circulated only privately in manuscript. They were first published two years after his death. For two centuries he was neglected, but in the twentieth century he has earned recognition as one of the greatest of English poets.

MICHAEL DRAYTON (1563–1631) • Like his friend Shakespeare, Drayton was a native of Warwickshire. He became educated while serving in an aristocratic household. He was a versatile poet, writing not only sonnets but also topographic poetry (*England's Heroical Epistles*, 1599), epic (*Nymphidia*, 1627), and satire (*The Owl*, 1604), in addition to popular ballads, myths, and scriptural paraphrases. "Since There's No Help" appeared in his sonnet sequence *Idea, the Shepheards Garland* (1593).

JOHN DRYDEN (1631–1700) • Poet Laureate from 1668 to 1688, Dryden was one of the foremost English poets and dramatists of the seventeenth century. Dr. Johnson considered him the father of English literary criticism. Dryden's major poetic achievement was to fine-tune the heroic or neoclassic couplet, which he used for "To the Memory of Mr. Oldham." He is best known for his verse satires *Mac Flecknoe* (1676, 1682) and *Absalom and Achitophel* (1681), both in rhymed couplets. Nevertheless, he used blank verse for his best play, *All for Love* (1677), which deals with the same material as Acts 4 and 5 of Shakespeare's *Antony and Cleopatra*. In 1688 he lost his official positions because he had been a supporter of King James II, who had been deposed. During the last twelve years of his life, therefore, Dryden was forced to support himself mainly with poetic translations, providing his contemporaries with versions of Virgil, Ovid, Juvenal, and Chaucer.

PAUL LAURENCE DUNBAR (1872–1906) • Dunbar was born in Ohio, the son of former slaves. During his brief life he rose to prominence as a poet, dramatist, and novelist. His first two collections of poems, *Oak and Ivy* (1893) and *Majors and Minors* (1895), in which "Sympathy" appeared, were favorably reviewed by William Dean Howells. His collected poems were published posthumously in 1913.

STEPHEN DUNN (B. 1939) • Born in New York, Dunn received a master's degree from Syracuse in 1960. He is perhaps the only Pulitzer Prize winner in Poetry to have played professional basketball. He has taught at a number of schools, including the University of Michigan and Stockton State College in New Jersey. Some of his collections are *Five Impersonations* (1971), *Looking for Holes in the Ceiling* (1974), *Between Angels* (1989), and *Loosestrife* (1996). It was for *Different Hours* (2000) that he received the Pulitzer Prize. "Hawk" is taken from *Between Angels*.

RAY DUREM (1915–1963) • Selected poems by Durem were printed in Dudley Randall's *The Black Poets: A New Anthology* (1971). Durem's collected verse appeared in *Take No Prisoners* (1962, 1971).

RICHARD GHORMLEY EBERHART (B. 1904) • Eberhart is a man of incredible longevity. The recipient of many awards, including the Pulitzer Prize in Poetry in 1966, he was born in Minnesota and received his higher education at Dartmouth and Cambridge. His many works include *Maine Poems* (1988) and *Collected Poems* of 1930, 1976, and 1988. In addition, *Long Reach: Uncollected Poems, 1948–1983* appeared in 1984; *New and Selected Poems: 1930–1990*, in 1990; and *Collected Poems 1930–1976: Including 43 New Poems* in 2001. In 1982 the governor of New Hampshire, Eberhart's home state, proclaimed a Richard Eberhart Day in his honor.

BART EDELMAN (B. 1951) • Edelman is a native of New Jersey. He received degrees at Hofstra University and now teaches at Glendale College. In addition to his collections of poetry (*Crossing the Hackensack* [1993], *Under Damaris' Dress* [1996], and *The Alphabet of Love* [1999], *The Gentle Man* [2001]), he has served as the editor of *Eclipse*, has been awarded a number of significant grants and fellowships, and has done considerable research abroad.

T. S. ELIOT (1888–1965) • Born in Missouri, Thomas Stearns Eliot moved to England in 1914 and became a British citizen in 1927. With *The Waste Land* in 1922, he electrified the literary world because of his poetic use of colloquial speech and frank subject matter. Though he is considered a hyper-serious poet, his lighter side is shown in *Old Possum's Book of Practical Cats* (1939). These poems achieved popular fame in 1981 in the Broadway musical *Cats*, which then began a record run of nineteen consecutive years, not closing until 2000.

ELIZABETH TUDOR, QUEEN ELIZABETH I (1533–1603) • Queen of England from 1558 to 1603, Elizabeth was famed for her eloquence and wit. She is perhaps best remembered for the support she gave to Shakespeare and the acting company at the Globe Theater. She wrote a number of translations and left a small number of poems. Some other poems attributed to her are of doubtful authorship. Her works were edited and published in 1964.

JAMES EMANUEL (B. 1921) • Emanuel was born in Nebraska and attended Howard University. He earned his Ph.D. at Columbia in 1962 and joined the faculty of English at the City College of New York. Throughout his career, he has regularly written poetry, publishing poems in journals such as *Phylon* and *Negro Digest*. An early collection of his poems is *Panther Man* (1970). Other collections are *Black Man Abroad: The Toulouse Poems* (1978), *A Chisel in the Dark* (1980), *The Broken Bowl* (1983), *Deadly James and Other Poems* (1987), and *Jazz: From the Haiku King* (1999). In 1967 he published a biography of Langston Hughes for the Twayne Series of American Authors.

LYNN EMANUEL (B. 1949) • Emanuel is a native of New York and currently is director of the University of Pittsburgh's writing program. Her first two collections of poetry are *Hotel Fiesta* and *The Dig*, which have been reprinted together by the University of Illinois Press. A recent poetry collection is *Then, Suddenly* (1999).

RALPH WALDO EMERSON (1803–1882) • Emerson, known in his time as the Sage of Concord, was born in Massachusetts and studied to be a minister. His first profession was indeed the ministry, but conscientiously he could not continue when he found it impossible to maintain the orthodoxy that was demanded of the Unitarian faith. Increasingly he turned to philosophy and became the acknowledged leader of the Transcendental movement, the ideas of which he enunciated in his seminal book "Nature" (1836). His belief in the power of the human mind led him naturally into his involvement with the equal rights of women and also with the abolitionist movement prior to the Civil War. His literary output was enormous. "The American Scholar" (1837) is one of his major essays, as is "Self Reliance" (1841). His reputation as a poet was established by *Poems* in

1846 and *May-Day* in 1867. He has been called one of the most significant of all American thinkers.

ABBIE HUSTON EVANS (1881–1983) • Evans was perhaps the longest-lived of all American or British poets, dying in 1983 at the age of 102. She began receiving recognition in the 1930s and was granted an honorary Litt.D. degree from Bowdoin College in 1961. Her collections of poems are *Outcrop* (1928), *The Bright North* (1938), and *Fact of Crystal* (1961). The University of Pittsburgh Press published her *Collected Poems* in 1970. "The Iceberg Seven-eighths Under" was first published in *Fact of Crystal.*

MARI EVANS • Evans has written fiction and criticism in addition to a major collection of poems, *I Am a Black Woman* (1970). *JD* (1975) is a collection of four stories about a young boy living in an urban housing project. Her *Black Women Writers (1950–1980): A Critical Evaluation* appeared in 1984, and *A Dark and Splendid Mass* was published in 1992. Interest in social matters prompted *Dear Corinne: Tell Somebody,* a children's book about child abuse (1999). A book of alternative nursery rhymes is entitled *Singing Black Children* (1976; 1996 20th anniversary edition).

JOHN CHIPMAN FARRAR (1896–1974) • Farrar was a native of Vermont. He began studies at Yale but his education was interrupted by his service in World War I. After returning from the war he completed his degree in 1919. He became the author of a number of books but he is best known as a publisher, one of the founding partners of the still flourishing house of Farrar, Straus & Giroux. Another of his achievements was his involvement in the beginning of the Breadloaf Writer's Conference. The poem "Song for a Forgotten Shrine to Pan" was published in 1919 and was included in the *Yale Younger Poets Anthology* (1998).

EDWARD FIELD (B. 1924) • A native of Brooklyn, Field studied at New York University and also, for a time, studied method acting at the Moscow Art Theatre. "Icarus" is taken from his first collection of poems, *Stand Up, Friend, with Me* (1963). Another of his collections is *Stars in My Eyes* (1979). In 1990 he edited *Head of a Sad Angel,* stories by Alfred Chester, with an introduction by Gore Vidal.

CAROLYN FORCHÉ (B. 1950) • Forché is a native of Detroit. After her first volume of poems in the Yale Younger Poets series (*Gathering the Tribes* [1976]) she spent two years in El Salvador as a journalist for Amnesty International. In 1982 she translated Claribel Alegria's *Flowers for the Volcano* in an English–Spanish edition. Her next volume of poetry was *The Country Between Us* in 1982. The section of this collection titled "In Salvador, 1978–80" contains "The Colonel." In 1993 she published *Against Forgetting: Twentieth-Century Poetry of Witness,* an anthology of poems protesting against repression and genocide. In 1995 she published a long poem, *The Angel of History,* followed in 2003 by her poetry collection *Blue Hour.*

ROBERT CHURCHILL FRANCIS (1901–1987) • Francis received his higher education at Harvard and lived most of his life in Amherst, Massachusetts, not far from the home of Emily Dickinson. Some of his collections are *The Orb Weaver* (1980), *Come Out into the Sun* (1965), *Like Ghosts of Eagles* (1974), and *Butter Hill and Other Poems* (1984). His collected verse appeared in *Collected Poems 1936–1976* (1976). He received a number of distinctions, among them the Brandeis University Creative Arts Award in 1974.

ROBERT FROST (1874–1963) • For a detailed biography, see pp. 1048–53.

ISABELLA GARDNER (1915–1981) • Isabella Gardner was born in Massachusetts. During her lifetime, she acted, edited *Poetry* magazine (1952–1956), taught, published four volumes of poems, and gave frequent poetry readings. She declared herself "a poet who is woman first and poet second." Two years before her death, she published much of her poetry in *Isabella Gardner: The Collected Poems.*

JOHN GAY (1685–1732) • English poet and playwright John Gay was born and educated in Devon. As a young boy he was apprenticed to a silk mercer but freed himself to become a writer in London. For a time in the late 1720s, he was a gentleman-in-waiting to the young Duke of Cumberland, for whom he wrote his *Fables,* which were among the most popular poems in the eighteenth century. His most famous play is *The Beggar's Opera* (1728), which at a stroke created ballad opera—a form featuring spoken dialogue and songs sung to popular music. "Let Us Take the Road" is from this play, and the music is the "March" in the opera *Rinaldo* (1711) by Georg Friderich Handel.

CHIEF DAN GEORGE (1899–1981) • In the early part of his life, Chief Dan George took many jobs unrelated to writing. In 1947 he became chief of the Tse-lal-Watt Sioux tribe, holding this post until 1959. In the 1960s he launched himself on an acting and writing career. His greatest success as an actor was in the film *Little Big Man* (1970), for which he received an Oscar nomination as best supporting actor. After this time he appeared in a number of films and television shows, and he spent much time campaigning for more Native American involvement in the film industry. His autobiography *You Call Me Chief* appeared in 1981, the last year of his life. His poem "My Heart Soars" is from *Sannichtoni* (1974).

ALLEN GINSBERG (1926–1997) • One of the major voices of the "beat generation" of the 1950s and 1960s, Ginsberg was born in New Jersey and lived in San Francisco for a time. For many years he was Distinguished Professor of English at Brooklyn College. His landmark poetry collection was *Howl and Other Poems* (1956), which occasioned a court case when certain persons sued, unsuccessfully, to suppress it on the grounds of obscenity. Ironically, his collection of 1973, *The Fall of America: Poems of These States,* received a National Book Award. Among his later publications were *Cosmopolitan Greetings: Poems 1986–1992* (1994) and a four-CD/cassette box set titled *Holy Soul Jelly Roll: Poems and Songs 1949–1993* (available from Rhino Word Beat).

NIKKI GIOVANNI (YOLANDE CORNELIA GIOVANNI, JR., B. 1943) • Giovanni, a poet whose reputation has coincided with the development of African-American consciousness and pride, was born in Tennessee. She has written poems for children and has also published interviews with James Baldwin and Alice Walker. Among her early collections of poetry are *Black Feeling, Black Talk* (1968), *Black Judgment* (1968), and *Cotton Candy on a Rainy Day* (1978). More recent works are *Those Who Ride the Night Winds* (1983), *Sacred Cows—and Other Edibles* (1988), *The Selected Poems of Nikki Giovanni* (1996), *Love Poems* (1997), *Blues: For All the Changes: New Poems* (1999), and *Quilting the Black-Eyed Pea: Poems and Not Quite Poems* (2002).

LOUISE GLÜCK (B. 1943) • A native of New York, Glück took her higher education at Sarah Lawrence and Columbia. She currently lives in Vermont and teaches at Williams College. Recent poetry collections are *Ararat* (1990), *The Wild Iris* (1992), *Meadowlands* (1996), *Vita Nova: Poems* (1999), and *The Seven Ages* (2001). In 1985 she received the National Book Critics Circle Award.

JORIE GRAHAM (B. 1951) • Graham is a person of international credentials. She is a native of New York but was brought up in Italy and studied in Paris. She received a degree in film from New York University. Later she studied writing at the University of Iowa, where she is a faculty member; she is also on the faculty of Harvard University. Her poetry is thoughtful—a number of critics have said difficult—as well as reflective and challenging. Among her collections are *The End of Beauty* (1987), *Region of Unlikeness* (1991), *Materialism* (1993, 1998), *The Dream of the Unified Field* (1995), *The End of Beauty* (1998), and *Swarm* (2000).

ROBERT GRAVES (1895–1985) • Graves fought in the British army in World War I and was badly wounded. His early autobiographical memoir, *Good-Bye to All That* (1929), deals in part with his war experiences. He became famous in the 1970s, when the BBC and PBS dramatized his historical novels about the life and times of the Roman Emperor Claudius. His studies of mythology, *The White Goddess* (1947) and *The Greek Myths* (1955), have explained the meaning of ancient religion to a generation of students.

THOMAS GRAY (1716–1771) • Gray was professor of history at Cambridge University. His poetic output was small, but nevertheless in 1757 he was offered the honor of the Poet Laureateship, which he refused. The "Elegy Written in a Country Churchyard" has been called one of the most often quoted poems of the English language. Another of Gray's frequently quoted poems is the "Ode on a Distant Prospect of Eton College," which concludes with the familiar lines "Where ignorance is bliss / 'Tis folly to be wise."

SUSAN GRIFFIN (B. 1943) • Susan Griffin is a native of California and received her B.A. and M.A. degrees from San Francisco State. During her career she has served as an editor, teacher, playwright, and writer, and she is a leading feminist critic. She received a number of grants and distinctions and holds an honorary Ph.D. Among her poetry volumes are *Dear Sky* (1971), *Like the Iris of an Eye* (1976), *Unremembered Country: Poems* (1987), and *Bending Home: Selected and New Poems, 1967–1998* (1998). She is also the author of many volumes of nonfiction.

MARILYN HACKER (B. 1942) • Hacker, a native of New York City, has been the recipient of a National Book Award (1975) and a Guggenheim Fellowship. Her collections of poems include *Presentation Piece* (1974); *Separations* (1976); *Taking Notice* (1980), which includes "Sonnet Ending with a Film Subtitle"; and *Selected Poems* (1994). The year 1990 saw the publication of the collection *Going Back to the River*, and in the same year she included new and selected poems in *The Hang-Glider's Daughter*. Other collections are *Selected Poems: 1965–1990* (1995) and *Love, Death, and the Changing of the Seasons* (1995). *Squares and Courtyards* (2000) is a recent collection. In 1989 the composer Dennis Riley set five of her poems to music for soprano and chamber ensemble. In 1995 she was awarded the Lenore Marshall Poetry Prize for her eighth book of poems, *Winter Numbers* (1994).

JOHN HAINES (B. 1936) • Born in Virginia, Haines served in the Navy during World War II, receiving a number of battle stars. He lives in Alaska, where at various times he has supported himself by working as a hunter, gardener, fisherman, and trapper, in addition to writing. If any modern American writer can lay claim to being a poet of Nature and the frontier, it is Haines. He has published a number of collections, including *News from the Glacier: Selected Poems* (1982), *New Poems 1980–88* (1990), *The Owl in the Mask of the Dreamer: Collected Poems* (1996), *At the End of this Summer: Poems 1948–1954* (1997), *The Stars, the Snow, the Fire* (2000), and *From the Century's End: Poems: 1990–1999* (2001).

DANIEL HALPERN (B. 1945) • Halpern was born and raised in New York and is a professor in the graduate writing program of Columbia University. He has lived on both the East and West Coasts and also has a residence in Morocco. He has produced a number of poetry volumes, including *Traveling on Credit* (1972), *Seasonal Rights* (1982), *Foreign Neon* (1991), *Selected Poems* (1994), and *Something Shining: Poems* (1999). He has also done work in editing and translating and is editor of *The Art of the Story: An International Anthology of Contemporary Short Stories* (2000). Uniquely interesting about him is that he has coauthored a cookbook, *The Good Food: Soups, Stews, and Pastas* (1985). He has also written a tourist's guide, *Guide to the Essential Restaurants of Italy* (1990).

H. S. HAMOD (B. 1936) • Sam Hamod is a Lebanese American who was born in Indiana. He received a Ph.D. from the Writer's Workshop of the University of Iowa and has served as director of the National Communications Institute in Washington, D.C. He has published a large number of poetic volumes, including *Dying with the Wrong Name* (1980), from which "Leaves" is selected.

THOMAS HARDY (1840–1928) • Hardy was born in Dorsetshire, in southwest England, which he called "Wessex" in his novels and poems. He began a career as an architect but gave it up to become a novelist. In 1898, after he had published more than a dozen novels, including *Tess of the D'Urbervilles*, *The Return of the Native*, and *Jude the Obscure*, he gave up novels and devoted himself to poetry. Before his death in 1928, he had published eight volumes of verse, which were collected and published posthumously in 1931.

JOY HARJO (B. 1951) • Harjo, who is Creek, Cherokee, and French, was born in Oklahoma. She received her B.A. from the University of New Mexico and her M.F.A. at the University of Iowa and has taught at a number of schools, including Arizona State University. In 1990 she received the American Indian Distinguished Achievement Award, and in 1991 she received the Josephine Miles Award for excellence in literature. She enjoys playing the saxophone and has done some musical recordings. Her poetry collections are *The Last Song* (1975), *What Moon Drove Me to This?* (1980), *She Had Some Horses* (1983), *Secrets from the Center of the World* (1989), *In Mad Love and War* (1990), *The Woman Who Fell from the Sky* (1996, 1998), *A Map to the Next World: Poems and Tales* (2000), and *How We Became Human: New And Selected Poems* (2002). She was a coeditor of *Reinventing the Enemy's Language: North American Native Women's Writing* (1997).

FRANCES E. W. HARPER (1825–1911) • Although Harper was a native of Maryland, a slave state in 1825, she was born free. She ensured her continued freedom by eventually moving to the free state of Pennsylvania. Before the Civil War she lectured extensively against slavery and supported the Underground Railroad. Early collections of her work were *Forest Leaves* (1845), *Eventide* (1854), and *Poems on Miscellaneous Subjects* (1854), the last containing a preface by William Lloyd Garrison. Her novel, *Iola Leroy, or Shadows Uplifted* (1892), was well received and was included as part of a collection of fiction by African-American writers. One of her better-known poetry collections is *Atlanta Offering: Poems* (1895). In 1970 and 1988 her reputation as a poet was permanently secured with the publication of complete editions of her poems.

MICHAEL S. HARPER (B. 1938) • Born in Brooklyn, the American poet Michael S. Harper should not be confused with the English writer Michael Harper. Harper has held distinguished visiting professorships at Carlton College and at Colgate and has received both a Guggenheim Fellowship and a National Endowment for the Arts Creative Writing Award. He currently teaches at Brown University. Some of his collections of poems are *Dear John, Dear Coltrane* (1970, 1985), *Images of Kin* (1977), *Nightmare Begins Responsibility* (1975), *Healing Song for the Inner Ear* (1984), and *Honorable Amendments* (1995). "Called" is from *Nightmare Begins Responsibility*.

ROBERT HASS (B. 1941) • A native of California, Hass is one of America's most distinguished poets. He was educated at Stanford. He taught at St. Mary's College and then became poet resident at the University of California at Berkeley. His first collection of poems, *Field Guide* (1973), received the Yale Series of Younger Poets Award. Among his many later collections are *Praise* (1979), *Twentieth Century Pleasures* (1984), *Human Wishes* (1989), and *Sun Under Wood* (1996). He has recently published a number of translations of the work of Czeslaw Milosz. In 1995 he was made United States Poet Laureate.

ROBERT HAYDEN (1913–1980) • Born in Detroit and educated at the University of Michigan, Hayden became a professor of English at both Fisk and Michigan. His earliest collection of poems was *Heart-Shape in the Dust* (1940). He received a special prize for *A Ballad of Remembrance* at the World Festival of Negro Arts held in Senegal in 1962. His *Words in the Mourning Time* (1970) included laments for the assassinated leaders Martin Luther King and Robert Kennedy, together with poems opposing the Vietnam War.

SEAMUS HEANEY (B. 1939) • Heaney lives in Northern Ireland, which for many decades has been beset with Protestant–Catholic strife. Although the tensions of this situation have permeated some of his work, he has written broadly on many topics. Among Heaney's collections of verse are *Wintering Out* (1972), *Field Work* (1979), *Seamus Heaney: Selected Poems, 1966–1987* (1990), *The Spirit Level* (1996) and *Opened Ground: Selected Poems 1966–1996* (1999). His verse translation (1999) of the Old English poem *Beowulf* was well accepted both critically and commercially. His *Finders Keepers: Selected Prose 1971–2001* was published in 2002. The highlight of his many awards and distinctions is the Nobel Prize in Literature in 1995.

GEORGE HERBERT (1593–1633) • Herbert, whose brother was an English lord, became a priest in 1630 after a career in government service. He died in 1633, leaving his poems to a friend, Nicholas Ferrar, who had them printed in 1633 as *The Temple*. The intricacy of Herbert's thought, illustrated in poems like "The Pulley" and "The Collar," has caused later critics to classify him as a "metaphysical" poet. In the twentieth century a large number of church-music composers have set many of his lyrics as choral anthems.

ROBERT HERRICK (1591–1674) • Herrick attended Cambridge and became an Anglican priest in 1627. During the English Civil War he remained loyal to King Charles I, for which he was removed from service in 1647, but he resumed his duties after the Restoration of Charles II in 1660. His major collection of poems was *Hesperides*, published in 1648. A number of people expressed disapproval because of his frank subject matter, but, as he said, though his muse was jocund, his spirit was chaste. "To the Virgins, to Make Much of Time" is one of the better-known poems in the *carpe diem* tradition.

WILLIAM HEYEN (B. 1940) • Heyen's father came to the United States from Germany in 1928. Two uncles who remained in Germany joined the Nazi party and were killed in combat when serving in the German army in World War II. Heyen's concern with the Holocaust is thus a complex product of his ethnic ties and his anguish over Nazi atrocities. "The Hair: Jacob Korman's Story" was published in *Erika: Poems of the Holocaust* (1984). Among his volumes of poems are *The City Parables* (1980), *Pterodactyl Rose: Poems of Ecology*, and *Ribbons: The Gulf War*. A collection of his poems titled *The Host: Selected Poems, 1965–1990* was published in 1994. This collection is also available in cassette form. A more recent collection is *Crazy Horse in Stillness: Poems* (1996). In 2002 he was the editor of *September 11, 2001: American Writers Respond*, a collection of works on the topic of the Al Qaeda attacks against the United States.

JOHN HOLLANDER (B. 1929) • Hollander was born in New York, received his Ph.D. from the University of Indiana, and has taught at Hunter College and Yale University. He is a remarkably energetic and diversified poet, writing shaped verse (such as "Swan and Shadow"), children's verse, and nonsense verse. His musical-critical study *The Untuning of the Sky: Ideas of Music in English Poetry, 1500–1700* appeared in 1961. In 1967 he published *Jiggery-Pokery: A Compendium of Double Dactyls*, in collaboration with Anthony Hecht. His *Rhyme's Reason* (1981) is a guide to the various forms of English verse, which he illustrates with his own examples. *Figurehead and Other Poems*, a recent collection, was published in 1999.

A. D. HOPE (ALEC DERWENT HOPE, 1907–2000) • Hope was an Australian whose lyrics were praised for their traditionalism, their clarity and directness, their satire, and their search for redemption in love, literature, and art. Collections are *Collected Poems* (1966), *Collected Poems, 1930–1970* (1972), *Antechinus: Poems 1975–1980* (1981), and *Selected Poems* (1992). A play, *Ladies from the Sea*, appeared in 1987. The Australian National University recognized Hope by granting him an honorary Litt.D. degree in 1972. *A. D. Hope*, a study of Hope by Robert Darling, was published in 1997 in the Twayne's English Authors Series.

GERARD MANLEY HOPKINS (1844–1889) • Hopkins was an English poet gifted not only in poetry but also in music and art. At the age of twenty-two he converted to Roman Catholicism and became a Jesuit priest. Although he published the long poem *The Wreck of the Deutschland* in 1875, the poems linking his devotion to Nature, on which his reputation now rests, were not published until early in the twentieth century. Hopkins used the term "sprung rhythm" for his metrical system (see the Glossary of Literary Terms).

CAROLINA HOSPITAL (B. 1957) • Hospital was born in Cuba in 1957 and was brought to the United States as a child of four, two years after the Castro revolution. She thus received an American education, and she earned an M.A. from the University of Florida in 1984. She included "Dear Tia" in her collection *Cuban American Writers: Los Atrevidos* (1988).

A. E. HOUSMAN (1859–1936) • Housman was a professor of classics at Cambridge University. He created one major book of verse, *A Shropshire Lad* (1896), a collection of poems stressing the brevity and fragility of youth and love. His major scholarly pursuit was a study of the ancient Latin writer Manilius, whose works he edited. His *More Poems* was published posthumously, and his *Complete Poems* was published in 1956.

JULIA WARD HOWE (1819–1910) • Julia Ward married Samuel Howe, and with him edited the Boston *Commonwealth*, a journal devoted to humanitarian causes. She became an activist for women's liberation, world peace, and the abolition of slavery, and she was the first woman elected to the American Academy of Arts and Letters. According to tradition, she wrote the "Battle Hymn of the Republic" after watching troops marching to battle. The poem was immediately popular among Union soldiers, and since that time it has remained her most popular poem and one of America's representative patriotic songs (sung to the music of "John Brown's Body").

LANGSTON HUGHES (1902–1967) • For a brief biography, see pp. 1608–1610.

JOHN HALL INGHAM (1860–CA. 1925) • Ingham's major work of poetry was *Pompeii of the West and Other Poems* (1903). In *An American Anthology* (1900), Clarence Steadman published "George Washington," together with two other Ingham poems, "A Summer Sanctuary" and "Genesis." In 1919, the composer Frances McCollin set his poem "The Midnight Sea" to voice for accompanying piano.

JOSEPHINE JACOBSEN (B. 1908) • Jacobsen, a Canadian by birth, received no higher education because her parents believed that she, as a young woman, would receive no benefit from it. However, she began writing poetry in 1940 with *Let Each Man Remember*, and she has continued to write voluminously since then. Now in her nineties, her works make up an extended list. Her *The Shade-Seller: New and Selected Poems* appeared in 1974, and *In the Crevice of Time* was published in 1995. Among her many honors are a Consultantship in Poetry to the Library of Congress and an award from the American Academy of Arts and Letters.

RANDALL JARRELL (1914–1965) • Jarrell was born in Tennessee. He received his B.A. and M.A. degrees from Vanderbilt University. He wrote poetry, criticism, a novel, and children's fiction. His 1945 collection of poems, *Little Friend, Little Friend*, which includes "The Death of the Ball Turret Gunner," resulted from his service in the Army Air Corps during World War II. He published a number of other verse collections, including *Selected Poems* (1955) and *The Woman at the Washington Zoo* (1960).

ROBINSON JEFFERS (1887–1962) • Jeffers was born in Pittsburgh and spent most of his life in California. He used negative and often brutal subject matter in his poetry, for example, fratricide in *Give Your Heart to the Hawks* (1933), betrayal in *Dear Judas, and Other Poems* (1929), and infidelity in *Thurso's Landing, and Other Poems* (1932). His adaptation of Euripides' *Medea* (1947), starring Judith Anderson in the title role, won him wide national recognition. "The Answer" and "The Purse-Seine" appeared in his *Selected Poetry* (1938).

BEN JONSON (1573–1637) • Jonson was raised in the household of his stepfather, a bricklayer, and young Ben began his working life in that trade. He was able to free himself to attend the Westminster School, where he began acquiring his immense store of knowledge. After brief service as a soldier, he embarked on a career as poet and playwright. After Shakespeare retired in 1611, Jonson was, in effect, the major practicing dramatist in England. In 1616 he published his nondramatic poems, *Epigrams* and *The Forrest*. He became England's first Poet Laureate in 1619.

DONALD JUSTICE (B. 1925) • Born in Florida, Justice received his B.A. from the University of Miami (1945). He received his Ph.D. from the University of Iowa and became a member of the faculty there. His collections of poetry include *The Summer Anniversaries* (1959); *Departures* (1973); *Selected Poems* (1979), for which he was awarded the Pulitzer

Prize in 1980; *The Sunset Maker* (1987); and *New and Selected Poems* (1995). A generous selection of his work has been included in *A Donald Justice Reader* (1991).

JOHN KEATS (1795–1821) • Keats is one of the major English Romantic poets. Both his parents died when he was still a child, and at the age of fifteen he was apprenticed to an apothecary-surgeon. In 1816 he received his license to practice medicine, but almost immediately he gave up that career in order to become a full-time poet. In the following five years he created a magnificent body of poetry. Mortally afflicted with tuberculosis, he went to Rome, where he took rooms in the building adjoining the Spanish Steps. He died in Rome at the age of twenty-six and is buried in the English Cemetery in Rome near the Pyramid of Sestus Sextus.

X. J. KENNEDY (JOSEPH CHARLES KENNEDY, B. 1929) • Kennedy is a New Jersey native. He received an M.A. from Columbia University and a *Certificat* from the University of Paris (1956). His first book of verse was *Nude Descending a Staircase* (1961), which has been followed by many other major poetry collections. "Old Men Pitching Horseshoes" is from *Cross Ties* (1985), which received the *Los Angeles Times* Book Award for Poetry in 1985. Recently Kennedy, with Dorothy Kennedy and Jane Dyer, has published an anthology of poems for children, *Talking Like the Rain: A Read-To-Me-Book of Poems* (2002), and with Joy Allen he has published *Exploding Gravy: Poems to Make You Laugh* (2002). "John While Swimming" is selected from his 1986 "juvenile" collection titled *Brats*.

HENRY KING (1592–1669) • King became Bishop of Chichester in 1642 and held this position for the rest of his life. He had been a friend of John Donne and was likely one of Donne's early editors. During his lifetime he published two volumes of his own verse, one a poetic rendering of the Psalms and the other an edition of *Poems, Elegies, Paradoxes, and Sonnets* (1657). His collected poems were published in 1965.

GALWAY KINNELL (B. 1927) • Kinnell was born in Rhode Island and received degrees from Princeton and the University of Rochester. During his career he has taught at many schools, including the Universities of Grenoble in France, Teheran in Iran (on a Fulbright Fellowship), and Hawaii. Among his many distinctions, he was awarded the National Book Award for Poetry and the Pulitzer Prize in Poetry, both in 1983, for *Selected Poems* (1982). He was also the recipient of the prestigious MacArthur Fellowship. He has published a great number of poetry collections, such as *What a Kingdom It Was* (1960) and *New Selected Poems* (2000). "After Making Love We Hear Footsteps" was included in *Mortal Acts, Mortal Words* (1980).

CAROLYN KIZER (B. 1925) • Born in Spokane, Washington, Kizer studied at the University of Washington with Theodore Roethke. During much of her life she has lived in California. One of her specialties is the adaptation of poems from China and Japan. "Night Sounds," from *Mermaids in the Basement* (1984), is an example. Since 1959 she has regularly published poetry collections, some of which are *Knock Upon Silence* (1965), *Midnight Was My Cry* (1971), *The Nearness of You* (1986), and *Harping On: Poems 1985–1995* (1996). In 1985 her collection of poems *Yin* (1984) received the Pulitzer Prize in Poetry.

MAXINE WINOKUR KUMIN (B. 1925) • Kumin was born in Philadelphia and received B.A. and M.A. degrees at Radcliffe. She has lived on a horse farm in New Hampshire for many years and has been named the poet laureate of that state. In addition to her dozen volumes of poetry she has written novels, stories, children's books (two in collaboration with Anne Sexton), and essays. Her fourth collection of poetry, *Up Country: Poems of New England* (1972), received the 1973 Pulitzer Prize. *Our Ground Time Here Will Be Brief* appeared in 1982. A recent collection is *Connecting the Dots* (1996). In 2001 she published a new collection, *The Long Marriage: Poems.*

PHILIP LARKIN (1922–1985) • A novelist, editor, and reviewer as well as a poet, Larkin was born in northern England and attended Oxford. His first collection of verse was

The North Ship (1946), followed nine years later by *The Less Deceived*, in which "Next Please" was printed. In 1964 he published *The Whitsun Weddings*, and in 1974 *High Windows*.

IRVING PETER LAYTON (B. 1912) • Although he was born in Romania, Layton has become one of Canada's major poets, publishing more than fifty poetry collections, including selected poetry in 1966, 1972, and 1986. A comprehensive selection of his poems, *A Wild Peculiar Joy: Selected Poems 1945–1982*, was published in 1983. *The Love Poems of Irving Layton* and *Dance with Desire: Love Poems* were published in 1984 and 1986. A new edition of *The Love Poems of Irving Layton* appeared in 2003. In 1982 and 1983 he was a nominee for the Nobel Prize in Literature.

LI-YOUNG LEE (B. 1957) • Lee is a native of Indonesia and is acknowledged as a powerful voice among Asian-Americans. He was the recipient of grants from the National Endowment for the Arts and from the Guggenheim Foundation. His major collections thus far are *Rose Poems* (1986) and *The City in Which I Love You* (1990), which was the Lamont Poetry Selection for 1990. His *Book of My Nights: Poems* appeared in 2001. In 1995 he published *The Winged Seed: A Remembrance*, an autobiographical memoir.

DENISE LEVERTOV (1923–1997) • Levertov was a native of England whose parents were Welsh and Jewish. She was educated at home and served as a nurse in World War II. After the war she married an American and left England to live in the United States. She began publishing poems in her twenties. Since her first poetry collection, *The Double Image*, which appeared in 1946, she published at least two collections each decade. In the 1970s she published four. Her collections ranged from personal topics to deeply political ones, particularly *Light Up the Cave* (1981), which contains a number of poems on the Vietnam War. Some of her last poetry collections were *The Double Image* (1991), *Evening Train* (1992), and *Sands of the Well* (1996). In 1995 the Academy of American Poets awarded her an Academy Fellowship. A posthumous collection of her poetry is *The Great Unknowing: Last Poems* (1999).

PHILIP LEVINE (B. 1928) • Levine's parents were Russian Jewish immigrants who settled in Detroit. He was educated there, and for higher education he went to Wayne University (now Wayne State University) and also the University of Iowa. For a long time he took industrial jobs, living in a number of cities before he became a professor at Fresno State in California. He is noted for his use of plain language and straightforward, simple syntax, in keeping with his pronounced sympathies for ordinary, working-class people. He has published many collections of poetry, including *They Feed, They Lion* (1972) and *The Names of the Lost* (1976), which were reprinted together in 1999. Other collections are *One for the Rose* (1981), *A Walk with Tom Jefferson* (1988), *What Work Is Like* (1991), *The Simple Truth* (1994), and *New Selected Poems* (1995). He has been honored with the American Book Award, the National Book Award, and the Pulitzer Prize for *The Simple Truth*.

ALAN P. LIGHTMAN (B. 1948) • Lightman, a faculty member of the Massachusetts Institute of Technology, is a native of Tennessee. He received degrees from Princeton and the California Institute of Technology. He is well known for his scientific writings, such as *Great Ideas in Physics* and *Time for the Stars*. More recently he has written *The Inflationary Universe: The Quest for a New Theory of Cosmic Origins* (1998). He has also written fiction. His novel *Good Benito* (1994), for example, describes the life and tribulations of a young scientist. A recent novel is *The Diagnosis* (2002).

ABRAHAM LINCOLN (1809–1865) • Abraham Lincoln was the sixteenth president of the United States. He was born in Kentucky in 1809 and with his family moved to southwestern Indiana in 1816. Because the area was still wild, Lincoln, though still a child, was needed in helping his father clear the land and in performing the many duties needed for a frontier life of poverty. There was virtually no time for him to attend school. Eventually he rose to be the partner in a successful law firm in Illinois, and then he went into state politics. In 1844, before he stood for any national office and when he was campaigning for Henry Clay (1777–1852) for the presidency, he returned to Indiana, and it was then that he wrote "My Childhood's Home," one of his three surviving poems. He is perhaps the most often quoted of American presidents, and it is for his many memorable speeches, such as the Gettysburg Address, that he is best known.

LIZ LOCHHEAD (B. 1947) • In addition to her poetry, Lochhead writes plays, translations, and television scripts. She is a native of Scotland and has taught at the Glasgow School of Art and the University of Glasgow. Her poetry collection *Memo for Spring* (1972) earned her a fellowship award from the Scottish Arts Council (1973). Some of her other poetry collections are *The Grimm Sisters* (1981), *Dreaming Frankenstein and Collected Poems* (1984), and *Bagpipe Muzak* (1991). She is a featured poet in the collection *Three Scottish Poets* of 1992 and in another collection, *Four Women Poets* (1996). Later works are *Perfect Days*, a play (2000); *Medea*, a translation/version of the *Medea* of Euripides (2001); and *Miseryguts/Taruffe*, translations of two Molière plays (2002).

WILLIAM WADSWORTH LONGFELLOW (1807–1882) • Longfellow was acknowledged in his own time as one of the great U.S. poets. He was so popular, and his poetry sold so well, that he was able to live on the proceeds of his writing. After graduating from Bowdoin College in 1825 he began mastering Spanish, French, Italian, German, and the Scandinavian languages. This mastery equipped him to accept a professorship in languages at Harvard in 1836. His translation of Dante's *Divine Comedy* appeared in 1867, and at this same time he composed a number of sonnets that he published in 1867 and 1875. Some of his best-known works are *Ballads and Other Poems* (1842), *Evangeline* (1847), *The Song of Hiawatha* (1855), *The Children's Hour* (1860), and *Paul Revere's Ride* (1863).

AUDRE LORDE (1934–1992) • Lorde was a New Yorker whose parents were immigrants from Jamaica. She was educated at the National University of Mexico, Hunter College, and Columbia. Some of her poetry collections are *Chosen Poems Old and New* (1982), *Our Dead Behind Us* (1986), and *Undersong* (1992). *The Marvelous Arithmetics of Distance: Poems 1987–1992* (1993) was a posthumous collection.

AMY LOWELL (1874–1925) • Lowell was a proponent of the Imagist school of poetry early in the twentieth century. Her earliest collection of poems was *A Dome of Many-Colored Glass* (1912). Later collections were *Sword Blades and Poppy Seed* (1914) and *Legends* (1921). "Patterns" appeared in her collection *Men, Women, and Ghosts* (1916).

THOMAS LUX (B. 1946) • A winner of the Kingsley Tufts Poetry Award, Lux was educated at the University of Iowa and has taught at Sarah Lawrence College for many years. His poetry has been characterized as an "ironic mingling of humor and sincerity." Some of his collections are *The Land Sighted* (1970), *The Drowned River: New Poems* (1990), *Pecked to Death by Swans* (1993), *Split Horizon* (1994), *The Blind Swimmer: Selected Early Poems, 1970–1975* (1996), *New and Selected Poems 1975–1995* (1997), and *The Street of Clocks* (2001).

GWENDOLYN MAC EWAN (1941–1987) • A major Canadian voice in poetry as well as the short story and the novel, MacEwan treats subjects such as birth, the passing of time, death, and the importance of spirituality. From her first collection of poems in 1963 (*The Rising Sun*), she published regularly until her death in 1987. Some of her later collections are *Magic Animals* (1974), *The T. E. Lawrence Poems* (1982), *Earthlight* (1982), and *After Worlds* (1985).

ARCHIBALD MACLEISH (1892–1982) • A native of Illinois, MacLeish graduated from Yale and had a varied public career during the years when he was also writing poetry. He received a Pulitzer Prize three times, twice for his poetry (in 1932, for *Conquistador*, and 1952, for *Collected Poems, 1917–1952*). In 1944 and 1945 he served President Franklin D. Roosevelt as an Assistant Secretary of State. Among his many poetry collections are *Songs for a Summer Day* (1915), *Songs for Eve* (1954), and *New and Collected Poems 1917–1976* (1976). "Ars Poetica" appeared in *Streets of the Moon* (1926).

CHRISTOPHER MARLOWE (1564–1593) • Marlowe is known as the major English dramatist before Shakespeare (*Tamberlaine the Great, Dr. Faustus, The Jew of Malta,* and *Edward II*), and he may have collaborated in some of Shakespeare's earliest plays. Marlowe's unfinished poem *Hero and Leander* was completed by George Chapman and published in 1598. "Come Live with Me and Be My Love" was first published in 1599 in *The Passionate Pilgrim* and was republished with Sir Walter Raleigh's accompanying poem in *England's Helicon* in 1600. A definitive edition of Marlowe's poems appeared in 1968.

ANDREW MARVELL (1621–1678) • Marvell, one of the major metaphysical poets of the seventeenth century, was active during the unsettled period of the English Civil Wars of 1642–1649, the Commonwealth, and the Protectorate of Oliver Cromwell. The Restoration of King Charles II (1660) ushered in a period of relative calm in Marvell's life. During his long career, which he began as a tutor in an aristocratic household, he assisted Milton (who served as Latin Secretary for the English Commonwealth), and he also was a Member of Parliament. His poems were not published until three years after his death. A modern edition of his *Poems and Letters* was published in 1971.

JOHN MASEFIELD (1878–1967) • The English poet John Masefield, though not an academic, was a compulsive reader and writer. In his youth he was a merchant seaman and worker at odd jobs in the United States. Eventually he published fifty volumes of poems, together with many plays and novels, and he became Poet Laureate of England in 1930. His two best-known poems are "I Must Go Down to the Sea Again," included in *Salt-Water Ballads* (1902), and "Cargoes," which appeared in *Ballads and Poems* (1910).

HEATHER MCHUGH (B. 1948) • McHugh is a native Californian who has taught in Washington, North Carolina, and Iowa, and lived in Maine. Her B.A. is from Radcliffe, her M.A. from Denver University. Her poetry was first collected in *Dangers* (1977) and *A World of Difference* (1981). Recent collections are *Broken English: Poetry and Partiality* (1993), *Hinge & Sign: Poems, 1968–1993* (1994), and *The Father of the Predicaments* (1999, 2001).

CLAUDE MCKAY (1890–1948) • McKay, one of the important voices in the Harlem Renaissance of the 1920s, was born in Jamaica, immigrated to the United States in 1912, and settled in Harlem in 1914. He wrote a number of novels, including *Home to Harlem* (1928), and short stories, published in *Gingertown* (1932). His poems were collected in *Songs of Jamaica* (1911), *Spring in New Hampshire and other Poems* (1920), and *Harlem Shadows* (1922), where we find "In Bondage" and "The White City."

HERMAN MELVILLE (1819–1891) • Melville is best known as the author of *Moby-Dick* (1851), which has been called the greatest of all American novels. He was born in New York. At the age of fifteen he left school to take up clerical work, to which he refers in his famous and long story "Bartleby the Scrivener" (1856). He spent a number of years as a seaman, which gave him the experience to write *Typee* (1846), *Omoo* (1847), *Mardi* (1849), *Redburn* (1849), *White-Jacket* (1850), and *Billy Budd* (1888, 1924), in addition to *Moby-Dick*. He wrote an extensive poem based on his visit to the Near East, *Clarel* (1876), and collected his poems in *Battle-Pieces and Aspects of the War* (1866, containing "Shiloh"), *John Marr and Other Sailors* (1888), *Timoleon* (1891), and the posthumous *Weeds and Wildings, with a Rose or Two* (1924).

EVE MERRIAM (1916–1992) • Merriam was a Pennsylvanian who received her B.A. from the University of Pennsylvania and who also studied at the University of Wisconsin and Columbia University. In the late thirties and early forties she wrote for radio and also was a copyeditor for radio shows. She is known as a superb and prolific writer of children's poetry, but she also wrote nine volumes of adult poetry, in addition to her plays and biographies. Some of her poetry collections are *The Trouble with Love* (1960), *The Inner City Mother Goose* (1969/1996), and *Embracing the Dark: New Poems* (1995), a posthumous collection. "Reply to the Question" is from *Rainbow Writing* (1976).

W. S. MERWIN (WILLIAM STANLEY MERWIN, B. 1927) • Merwin was born in New York and raised in New Jersey and Pennsylvania. He currently lives in Hawaii. He published *Selected Translations 1948–1968* in 1968 and was distinguished by a PEN translation prize for this work. In 1988 he published two collections of poems: *The Rain in the Trees* and *Selected Poems*. In 1996 he published *The Vixen*, a collection of poems about people and life in the southern part of France. Also in 1996 he published *Flower & Hand: Poems 1977–1983*. Three long poems make up his *The River Sound* (1999). In 2001 he published *The Pupil: Poems*. He was awarded the Pulitzer Prize in Poetry for *The Carriers of Ladders* (1970). "Odysseus" appeared in one of his early collections, *The Drunk in the Furnace* (1960).

EDNA ST. VINCENT MILLAY (1892–1950) • Known as a free spirit at Vassar, Millay matured quickly, receiving the Pulitzer Prize for Poetry—the first woman to do so—for *The Harp Weaver and Other Poems* (1923), which contained "What Lips My Lips Have Kissed." Her maturing concerns were reflected in *Make Bright the Arrows* (1940) and especially *The Murder of Lidice* (1942), which she wrote for radio presentation after the Nazi extermination of that Czech village. She published her *Collected Sonnets* in 1941. *Edna St. Vincent Millay: Collected Poems*, a centenary edition, was published in 1993.

JOHN MILTON (1608–1674) • Milton is acknowledged as one of the greatest English poets. His fame rests largely on the epic poem *Paradise Lost*, which he wrote in 1667, long after he became blind. He led a varied career and wrote extensively in both verse and prose, including many Latin poems. His most important political position was as Latin Secretary to Oliver Cromwell during the Interregnum (1649–1660). Latin at that time was the language of diplomacy, and a good Latinist like Milton was essential to the government. Milton's *Poems* was published in 1645, and he issued a second edition in 1673.

JUDITH MINTY (B. 1937) • Minty is of Finnish, Irish, and Mohawk descent. She has done a variety of things in addition to writing poetry, including working as a speech therapist, selling cosmetics, and introducing poetry to prisoners. She resides in Arcata, California, and has taught at Humboldt State University and the University of California at Santa Cruz. Among her poetry collections are *Lake Songs and Other Fears* (1974), *In the Presence of Mothers* (1981), *Counting the Losses* (1986), and *Dancing the Fault* (1991). A recent poetry collection is *Walking with the Bear* (2000).

N. SCOTT MOMADAY (B. 1934) • A member of the Kiowa tribe, Momaday was educated at the University of New Mexico and Stanford University. He has taught at Stanford and the University of Arizona. His reputation as a writer was gained by his *House Made of Dawn* (1968) and *The Way to Rainy Mountain* (1969). Despite his success as a novelist, he considers himself a poet. Some of his collections are *Angle of Geese and Other Poems* (1974), *The Gourd Dancer* (1976), and *In the Presence of the Sun: Stories and Poems 1961–1991* (1992).

LISEL MUELLER (B. 1924) • Lisel Neumann Mueller came to this country from Germany in 1939, just as World War II was intensifying in Europe. She studied at the University of Indiana and has taught at Goddard College. Even though English is not her first language, she has mastered the craft of English poetry and has made English translations of works by Marie Luise Kaschnitz. Her poetry volumes are *Dependencies* (1965, rpt. 1998), *The Private Life* (1976), *The Need to Hold Still* (1980), *Second Language: Poems* (1986), and *Waving from Shore: Poems* (1989). Her Pulitzer Prize–winning *Alive Together: New and Selected Poems* (1996) includes poems from each of these collections and adds a number of new poems. "Hope" was originally published in *The Private Life*.

OGDEN NASH (1902–1971) • Nash is most closely associated with *The New Yorker*, which he served as an editor for many years. Wit, humor, and satire characterize his verse, with an emphasis on original and funny rhymes and rhythms. Students of music may remember his voice on a 1950s recording of Camille Saint-Saëns's *Carnival of the Animals*. His many poetry collections include *Free Wheeling* (1931), *The Bad Parents' Garden of Verse* (1936), *You Can't Get There from Here* (1957), *Everyone But Thee and Me* (1962), and *Bed Riddance* (1970).

HOWARD NEMEROV (1920–1991) • Nemerov graduated from Harvard and served in World War II. After the war he taught at a number of colleges and began publishing his many essays, stories, plays, and poems. His poetry collections include *The Image and the Law* (1947), *The Western Approaches: Poems 1973–1975* (1975), and *Inside the Onion* (1985). The Library of Congress honored him as Poet Laureate from 1986 to 1988.

JIM NORTHRUP (B. 1943) • Northrup is a Chippewa Indian and lives with his family on the Fond du Lac Reservation in Minnesota. He has published a number of stories, and his poems have been published mainly in magazines and journals. His major poetry collection, which also contains stories, is *Walking the Rez Road* (1993). His *The Rez Road Follies* was published in 1997. More recently he has published poems in *Nitaawichige: Selected Poetry and Prose by Four Anishinaabe Writers* (2002). He writes a syndicated column and also works as an artist.

NAOMI SHIHAB NYE (B. 1952) • Nye, a Palestinian-American, is a native of Missouri but has lived for a time in Jerusalem. She is not only a poet but also a writer of children's books and, interestingly, a folk singer (with recordings to her credit). In her work as a teacher she has taught at the University of Hawaii and the University of Texas at Austin. She has published her poetry in a number of collections, including *Tattooed Feet* (1977), *Different Ways to Pray* (1980), *Hugging the Jukebox* (1982), *Yellow Glove* (1986), *Texas Poets in Concert: A Quartet* (1990, as one of four poets), *Red Suitcase* (1994), *The Words Under the Words: Selected Poems* (1995), *Fuel* (1998), *Come With Me: Poems for a Journey* (2000), and *19 Varieties of Gazelle: Poems of the Middle East* (2002). A collection of her essays, *Never in a Hurry*, was published in 1996. She recently published *The Space between Our Footsteps: Poems and Paintings from the Middle East* (1998). *Habibi* (1997, 1999) is an autobiographical novel for young people.

JOYCE CAROL OATES (B. 1938) • For a brief biography, see p. 201.

SHARON OLDS (B. 1942) • Born in San Francisco, Olds received her Ph.D. from Columbia in 1972 and has taught at New York University, Sarah Lawrence, Brandeis, and Columbia. In 1998 she was named New York State Poet. Her early poetry collections are *Satan Says* (1980) and *The Dead and the Living* (1984), which contains "35/10." Recent collections are *The Gold Cell* (1987), *The Father* (1992), *The Wellspring* (1996), *Blood, Tin, Straw* (1999), and *The Unswept Room* (2002). Although her poems are often physical and deeply personal, she remains, at heart, a private person. In a recent informal survey, members of the Academy of American Poets most often named her as their favorite contemporary American poet.

MARY OLIVER (B. 1935) • A native of Cleveland, Oliver took her higher education at Ohio State University and Vassar College. She is a longtime resident of Provincetown, Massachusetts, and is on the faculty of Bennington College. Her poetry collections have been regular and numerous, including *No Voyage and Other Poems* (1963), *Sleeping in the Forest* (1978), *American Primitive* (1983), *New and Selected Poems* (1992), *White Pine: Poems and Prose Poems* (1994), *Blue Pastures* (1995), *West Wind* (1997), and *Winter Hours: Poetry, Prose, and Essays* (1999). She is also the author of *A Poetry Handbook* (1994) and *Rules for the Dance: A Handbook for Writing and Reading Metrical Verse* (1998). She received the National Book Award and the Shelley Memorial Award, and in 1984 she was honored with the Pulitzer Prize in Poetry for *American Primitive*.

MICHAEL ONDAATJE (B. 1943) • Ondaatje was born in Ceylon (now Sri Lanka) and was educated in Ceylon, England, and Canada. He lives in Toronto, where he teaches and also pursues his hobby of raising and breeding dogs. He is best known for his widely acclaimed novel *The English Patient* (1992), which was made into a movie (1996) that received a number of best-picture awards and also won nine Oscars at the 1997 Academy Awards ceremony. Before this commercial success, Ondaatje had written plays and had also directed films. The interest he has in film is also shown in "Late Movies with Skyler."

Among his ten volumes of poetry are *There's a Trick with a Knife I'm Learning to Do* (1979), *The Cinnamon Peeler* (1991), and *Handwriting: Poems* (1999). In 2000 he published *Anil's Ghost*, a novel about the horrors of the internecine wars in Sri Lanka.

SIMON ORTIZ (B. 1941) • Ortiz, of the Acoma Pueblo Indian Nation, was born in New Mexico. He attended the Universities of New Mexico and Iowa. His first volume of poetry was *Naked in the Wind* (1971). In 1991 he published the collection *After and Before the Lightning. Woven Stone*, a three-in-one volume of poems containing a memoir, appeared in 1992. His best-known collection of stories is *Howbah Indians* (1978). A recent collection of stories is *Men on the Moon: Collected Short Stories* (1999).

MICHEAL O'SIADHAIL (B. 1941) • Micheal O'Siadhail (pronounced "mehall ohsheel") is Irish. He was born in Dublin and attended the Clongowes Wood School, the same school James Joyce had attended many years before. He received degrees from Trinity College, Dublin, and attended the University of Oslo in Norway. A noteworthy distinction is that he has performed various governmental services, one of which was his membership on the Arts Council of the Republic of Ireland. He is the author of nine collections of poetry, among which are *The Leap Year* (1978), *Springnight* (1983), *Hail! Madam Jazz: New and Selected Poems* (1992), and *The Gossamer Wall* (2002). "Abundance" is from *Poems: 1975–1995* (1999).

WILFRED OWEN (1893–1918) • A native of Shropshire, England, Owen became a British Army officer and was killed in France in 1918, just a week before the Armistice. He published only four poems in his lifetime, but after his death Siegfried Sassoon issued a collection of twenty-four poems (1920). Benjamin Britten used a number of Owen's poems, including "Anthem for Doomed Youth," as texts for his *War Requiem* (1962). The popular band 10,000 Maniacs recorded a version of both "Anthem for Doomed Youth" and "Dulce et Decorum Est" on their album *Hope Chest* (Elektra 9-60962-2).

P. K. PAGE (PATRICIA KATHLEEN PAGE IRWIN, B. 1916) • Versatile as artist, fiction writer, and poet, Page was born in England and came to Canada with her parents in 1919. After completing school she did work in business, research, and radio. She married a diplomat, W. A. Irwin, who at various times served as Canadian ambassador to Australia, Brazil, and Mexico. One of her earliest works, a novel titled *The Sun and the Moon* (1944), was published under the pen name Judith Cape. Her earliest collection of poetry was *As Ten as Twenty* (1946). Among her many later collections are *The Metal and the Flower* (1954), *Evening Dance of the Grey Flies* (1981), *The Glass Air* (1985), *A Flask of Sea Water* (1989), and *The Hidden Room: Collected Poems* (1997, rpt. 2003).

DOROTHY PARKER (1893–1967) • Parker became legendary because of her many witty "one-liners" and also because of her often caustic book and drama reviews for *The New Yorker* in the period between the World Wars. Her first volume of poetry was *Enough Rope* (1926), which included "Résumé." "Penelope" was included in her comprehensive collection *Not So Deep as a Well* (1936). She wrote many short stories and served as a correspondent during the Spanish Civil War in the late 1930s.

LINDA PASTAN (B. 1932) • Pastan was born in New York. She received a B.A. from Radcliffe and an M.A. from Brandeis. Among her many volumes of verse are *A Perfect Circle of Sun* (1971), *Setting the Table* (1980), *Waiting for My Life* (1981), *PM/AM: New and Selected Poems* (1983), *A Fraction of Darkness* (1985), *An Early Afterlife* (1996), *Carnival Evening: New and Selected Poems 1968–1998* (1998), and *The Last Uncle* (2002).

MOLLY PEACOCK (B. 1947) • Peacock was born in Buffalo, New York, and received a master's degree with honors from Johns Hopkins University. The first of her many collections of poetry was *And Live Apart* (1980), and recently she has published *Paradise, Piece by Piece* (1998). "Desire" is selected from *Raw Heaven* (1984). She is known as a poet who deals with the "pain and joy of living," and she has been praised for her fearless and uninhibited treatment of subjects that many consider taboo, even for personal and confessional poets.

MARGE PIERCY (B. 1936) • A native of Detroit, Piercy received her B.A. from the University of Michigan (1957) and M.A. from Northwestern (1958). She now lives in Cape Cod. Among her novels are *Braided Lives* (1980) and *Fly Away Home* (1984). The first of her many poetry collections was *Breaking Camp* (1968). Others are *The Moon Is Always Female* (1980); *Circles on the Water: Selected Poems* (1982), including "A Work of Artifice" and "The Secretary Chant"; and *Available Light* (1988). Her most recent poetic volumes are *What Are Big Girls Made Of?* (1996), *Early Grrrl: The Early Poems of Marge Piercy* (1999), and *The Art of Blessing the Day: Poems with a Jewish Theme* (1999).

ROBERT PINSKY (B. 1940) • Poet, scholar, and translator, Pinsky was educated in his home state of New Jersey and also at Stanford. He has taught at the University of California, Boston University, and Harvard. Some of his poetry collections are *Sadness and Happiness* (1975), *An Explanation of America* (1979), *The Want Bone* (1990), and *The Figured Wheel: New and Collected Poems 1966–1996* (1996, 1997). His *Explanation of America* (1979) is a book-length poem. For a time he was poetry editor of *The New Republic*. In the 1990s he became Poet Laureate of the United States for three successive terms, the only person to be so honored. He has used the prestige of his position advantageously. He brought out a short book (*The Sounds of Poetry: A Brief Guide* [1998]), and he also has done much to put poetry before the public eye, appearing regularly on national television to read poems and to comment extensively on poetry. In this capacity he has become the most widely recognized person to serve as United States Poet Laureate. One of his important efforts for poetry has been the development of the Favorite Poem Project. The result, on which he worked in collaboration with many people from all walks of life, is *Americans' Favorite Poems* (1999). With Maggie Dietz, he published *Poems to Read* in 2002. "Dying" is taken from his collection *History of My Heart* (1984, 1998).

SYLVIA PLATH (1932–1963) • One of the most confessional of poets, Plath was born in Massachusetts. After graduating from Smith College in 1955, she received a Fulbright Scholarship to England. She spent 1955–1956 in Cambridge, where she married Ted Hughes (1930–1999), who later became English Poet Laureate. The following years brought overpowering emotional distress, and she took her own life in 1963. Her poetry during these final years reflects the personal anguish that led to her suicide. Plath's *The Collected Poems* (1981) was awarded the 1982 Pulitzer Prize in Poetry.

EDGAR ALLAN POE (1809–1849) • For a brief biography, see p. 302.

KATHA POLLITT (B. 1949) • A native of New York, Pollitt received her B.A. at Radcliffe. She has worked as an editor for the weekly magazine *The Nation* for many years and is an associate faculty member of the Bennington Writing Seminars Program. She has also achieved wide recognition as an essayist. Her first book of poems was *Antarctic Traveler* (1982). An important recent work is *Reasonable Creatures: Essays on Women and Feminism* (1995).

ALEXANDER POPE (1688–1744) • Pope is the eminent eighteenth-century English poet, the acknowledged master of the neoclassic couplet. A childhood accident deformed his spine and retarded his physical growth, but it did not hinder his poetic gifts. Because his family was Roman Catholic, he was not sent to school but was educated at home. By age 23 he had completed *An Essay on Criticism* (1711), the leading English work of criticism in poetic form. After 1725 he devoted himself principally to writing satire, producing *The Dunciad* (1728, rev. 1743), the *Moral Essays* (1731–35), *An Epistle to Dr. Arbuthnot* (1735), and other satiric works, including the *Epilogues to the Satires* in dialogue form (1738). One of his life's plans was to publish a major philosophic work in poetry, but the only part he completed was *An Essay on Man* (1734).

EZRA POUND (1885–1972) • A native of Idaho, Pound was educated at the University of Pennsylvania and spent most of his life in Europe. He was the leading exponent of poetic imagism (see also Amy Lowell). During World War II he broadcast pro-Axis propaganda from Rome. After the war he was prosecuted for this but was exonerated on the grounds of insanity. Pound is as much known for his influence on other poets as for his own poetry (T. S. Eliot acknowledged him as "the better maker" in the dedication to *The Waste Land*). He published many poetry collections, such as *Exultations* (1909), *Canzoni* (1911), and *Cathay* (1915), which contained his versions of Chinese poems (see p. 1128). His major work was the *Cantos*, which he worked on throughout his life after publishing the first portion in 1925.

AL PURDY (ALFRED WELLINGTON PURDY, 1918–2000) • Purdy was born in Ontario and spent considerable time as a factory worker, not coming to poetry until he was in his forties with his first collection, *Poems for all the Annettes* (1962, 1968). After this time he published collections regularly, including *The Cariboo Horses* (1965), *Selected Poems* (1972), *The Stone Bird* (1981), *Piling Blood* (1984), *Collected Poems* (1986), *Rooms for Rent in the Outer Planets: Selected Poems 1962–1996* (1996), and *To Paris Never Again: New Poems* (1997).

SALVATORE QUASÍMODO (1901–1968) • A native of Italy, Quasímodo's early work was part of the so-called Italian "hermetic" period prior to World War II. That is, his poetry was highly imagistic, personal, and nonpolitical. During the war he became militantly antifascist, and for this reason Mussolini sent him to prison. After the war he became deeply concerned with the conditions of common people. In addition, he translated many works into Italian. He was the recipient of the Nobel Prize in Literature in 1959. His *Complete Poems* was published in 1984.

SIR WALTER RALEIGH (CA. 1552–1618) • Raleigh was a courtier, explorer, and adventurer who alternately pleased and displeased Queen Elizabeth I. During the reign of James I he was imprisoned for thirteen years in the Tower of London. He was released to go on an expedition to South America, which proved disastrous. In 1618 he was executed for treason. Like many aristocrats he wrote extensively but circulated his poetry mostly in manuscript, with rare exceptions such as "The Nymph's Reply to the Shepherd." His collected poems were edited and published in 1951.

DUDLEY RANDALL (1914–2000) • A native of Washington, D.C., Randall spent five years working in the foundry at the Ford River Rouge plant in Michigan. He became a librarian after that and went on to the position of head librarian. In 1965 he founded the Broadside Press, an important and valuable publisher for African-American writers. One of the first poems from the press was "Ballad of Birmingham," which had earlier (1963) been set to music and made popular by the folk singer Jerry Moore. Randall's major poetry collections are *More to Remember: Poems of Four Decades* (1971) and *A Litany of Friends: New and Selected Poems* (1981, 1983).

JOHN CROWE RANSOM (1888–1974) • Along with Robert Penn Warren, Alan Tate, and Cleanth Brooks, Ransom was one of the important exponents of the New Criticism (see Chapter 33, p. 1917). He founded the *Kenyon Review* and edited it for twenty years. His major poetry collections are *Chills and Fever* (1924), *Two Gentlemen in Bonds* (1927), and *Selected Poems* (1945, revised in 1963 and 1969).

JOHN RAVEN (B. 1936) • Raven's poems figured importantly in Dudley Randall's collection *The Black Poets: A New Anthology* (1971). His major collection of poems is *Blues for Momma* (1970).

ANNE BARBARA RIDLER (1912–2001) • Ridler was a writer not only of poems but also of plays, film plays, songs, and translations. She was an editor at the Oxford University Press, which published some of her poems, and also at Faber and Faber, where T. S. Eliot was an editor. She published her first collection of poems, *Poems*, in 1939. Following collections were *A Dream Observed and Other Poems* (1941), *The Golden Bird and Other Poems* (1951), *Selected Poems* (1961), *Some Time After and Other Poems* (1972), *New and Selected Poems* (1988), *Collected Poems* (1994), and *Anne Ridler: Collected Poems* (1997). She edited many collections, including an anthology of ghost stories. Most notable among her many other writings are English translations of the libretti of Mozart's operas *The Marriage of Figaro* and *Cosi fan Tutte*.

EDWIN ARLINGTON ROBINSON (1869–1935) • Robinson began his career inauspiciously with various jobs in New York City. The publication of *The Children of the Night* (1897) and *Captain Craig* (1902) impressed President Theodore Roosevelt, who arranged a position for him as clerk in the New York Customs House. After publication of *The Town Down the River* in 1910, he was able to support himself with his poetry. "Tilbury Town," where many of his poetic characters reside, is modeled on Gardiner, Maine, the town where he grew up. He is particularly notable because he received the first Pulitzer Prize in Poetry ever to be awarded (1922). He received the prize twice more, in 1924 and 1928.

THEODORE ROETHKE (1908–1963) • Roethke was born in Saginaw, Michigan, where his father operated a successful greenhouse. After graduating from the University of Michigan he taught at a number of schools, primarily at the University of Washington. His first book was *Open House* (1941), and his second was *The Lost Son and Other Poems* (1948), which included "My Papa's Waltz." His collection *The Waking* (1953) received the Pulitzer Prize in Poetry for 1954. His *Collected Poems* was published posthumously in 1966. When he died in 1963 he had achieved wide recognition and acclaim. In addition to distinguishing himself, he also taught other poets, numbering James Wright among his students at the University of Washington.

CHRISTINA ROSSETTI (1830–1894) • English-born Christina Rossetti's religious lyrics and ballads have made her a favorite with composers such as Gustav Holst and John Rutter. Painters of the Pre-Raphaelite Brotherhood, of whom her brother Dante Gabriel Rossetti was a leading figure, frequently called upon her to pose for their paintings. Ill health forced her to forsake a career as a governess, and after 1874 she became a virtual invalid. Some of her poetry collections are *Goblin Market and Other Poems* (1862), *The Prince's Progress and Other Poems* (1866), and *A Pageant and Other Poems* (1872). A modern edition of her *Complete Poems* was published in 1979.

FRIEDRICH RÜCKERT (1788–1866) • A younger contemporary of Goethe, Rückert became recognized in Germany as a poet who translated and popularized literature of the Orient. Some of his works are *Harnessed Sonnets* (1814), *The Wisdom of the Brahman* (1836), and the posthumous *Songs on the Death of Children* (1872). Today Rückert is known best because of the music that Gustav Mahler (1860–1911) composed for *Five Rückert Songs* (1901–1902) and *Songs on the Death of Children* (1902–1904).

MURIEL RUKEYSER (1913–1980) • A *poète engagée*, Rukeyser was arrested in Alabama in the 1930s for demonstrating in favor of the Scottsboro Nine (see also Chapter 29, p. 1608). Later, she wrote on behalf of an imprisoned Korean poet in *The Gates* (1976). She published many collections, including *Theory of Flight* (1935), *Beast in View* (1944), *Body of Waking* (1958), and *Collected Poems* (1979).

LUIS OMAR SALINAS (B. 1937) • Salinas was born in Texas. He attended Fresno State University from 1967 to 1972 and made his home in California. His first volume of poems was *Crazy Gypsy* (1970). In 1973 he edited *From the Barrio: A Chicano Anthology*, and in 1975 he was one of four poets included (along with Gary Soto) in *Entrance: Four Chicano Poets*. Since then he has been regularly productive. One of his major volumes was *The Sadness of Days: Selected and New Poems*, which appeared in 1987.

SONIA SANCHEZ (B. 1934) • Sanchez was born in Alabama. She received a B.A. from Hunter College in 1955, and for a time after that she worked for the Congress of Racial Equality. Her major teaching position was at Temple University. Early volumes of poetry were *Homecoming* (1969) and *We a BaddDDD People* (1970). Later she published *homegirls & handgrenades* (1984) and *Under a Soprano Sky* (1987), and more recently *Does Your House Have Lions* (1997), *Wounded in the House of a Friend* (1997), *Like the Singing Coming Off the Drums: Love Poems* (1998), and *Shake Loose My Skin: New and Selected Poems* (1999, 2000).

CARL SANDBURG (1878–1967) • It is fair to say that Sandburg "knocked around" a good deal in his youth before working his way through Knox (then Lombard) College in

Galesburg, Illinois, his hometown. He published a volume of poetry in 1904 but did not gain recognition until 1914, when *Poetry* printed some of his poems. Later he published *Chicago Poems* (1916), *Smoke and Steel* (1920), *Selected Poems* (1926), and *Good Morning, America* (1928). He received the Pulitzer Prize in History (1939) for his biography of Abraham Lincoln and the Pulitzer Prize in Poetry (1951) for his *Complete Poems* of 1950.

MAY SARTON (ELEANOR MAY SARTON, 1912–1995) • Sarton was born in Belgium and at the age of four came to the United States with her parents. Eventually she taught at both Harvard University and Wellesley College. Her first poetry volume, *Encounter in April*, appeared in 1937, and she published regularly after that, her final volume (*Coming into Eighty*) appearing in 1994, the year before her death. Her *Collected Poems, 1930–1970*, was published in 1974. An anthology of her work in all literary genres was edited by Bradford Daziel and published in 1991 as *Sarton Selected*.

SIEGFRIED SASSOON (1886–1967) • Sassoon served as an officer in World War I, was wounded twice, and was awarded two medals for bravery (one of which he threw away). He is most widely recognized for his antiwar collections *The Old Huntsman* (1917) and *Counter-Attack and Other Poems* (1918), which contains "Dreamers." Neither of these books was well received. Later, Sassoon turned to spiritual subjects, as shown in *Vigils* (1935) and *Sequences* (1956). His *Collected Poems* was published in 1961.

GJERTRUD CECILIA SCHNACKENBERG (B. 1953) • Originally from Washington State, Schnackenberg now lives in Boston. She achieved great critical acclaim with the publication of her first volume of poems, *Portraits and Elegies* (1982, rev. ed. 1986). She later published *The Lamplit Answer* (1985), *A Gilded Lapse of Time* (1992, 1994), and *Supernatural Love: Poems 1978–1992* (2000). She won the Rome Prize in literature for 1983–1984 and received an honorary doctorate from Mount Holyoke College, her alma mater, in 1985.

VIRGINIA SCOTT (B. 1937) • Canadian born, Scott received her degrees at Boston University and Wisconsin. She created, edited, and managed the Sunbury Press, a small press, and received a national award for this work in 1980. She has published poetry widely in journals. Her collected poems appear in *The Witness Box* (1985) and *Toward Appomattox* (1992). She taught at Lehman College for many years.

ALAN SEEGER (1886–1916) • Seeger was born in New York and was educated at Harvard. When World War I began he joined the French Foreign Legion, and he was killed in combat during the Battle of the Somme in 1916. His war poems were published in the posthumous *Poems* (1916).

BRENDA SEROTTE (B. 1946) • Serotte was born and educated in New York; she currently lives in Florida. For many years she worked as a secretary, and she received a bachelor's degree from Lehman College. For a time she taught in a junior high school, and her experiences there have inspired many of her poems. Her background is that of Sephardic Jewry, her immediate forbears having left Turkey in 1918 to come to the United States. She describes life among Sephardic immigrants in "Turkish Days," published in the journal *Hopscotch* in 1999. Her poem "The Moor's Ring" won both the Edmond Jabès Prize and the Boas Prize. Currently she is completing a biographical memoir, *Turkish Delights, and Other Fattening Recollections*.

ANNE SEXTON (1928–1974) • Massachusetts born, Sexton is one of the more personal confessional poets. *To Bedlam and Part Way Back* (1960), for example, developed out of a nervous breakdown, and her posthumous *The Awful Rowing Toward God* (1975) describes some of the feelings leading to her suicide in 1974. Her collection *Live or Die* (1966) was awarded the Pulitzer Prize in Poetry for 1967.

WILLIAM SHAKESPEARE (1564–1616) • For a brief biography, see pp. 1306–1307.

KARL SHAPIRO (1913–2000) • Baltimore born, Shapiro lived in Nebraska and California. He was recognized early in his distinguished career as a poet and critic—his *V-Letter and Other Poems* (1944) receiving the 1945 Pulitzer Prize. Among his many poetry collections are *Essay on Rime* (1945), *Poems of a Jew* (1958), *Selected Poems* (1968), *Selected Poems: 1940–1977* (1978), and *The Wild Card: Selected Poems Early and Late* (1998). He edited *Poetry* magazine for five years, *Prairie Schooner* for ten.

PERCY BYSSHE SHELLEY (1792–1822) • Shelley is one of the major English Romantic poets. He was a quintessential revolutionary and suffered expulsion from Oxford as a result of an early pamphlet titled *The Necessity of Atheism*. He married before he was twenty but within three years left his wife and went to Italy with Mary Godwin (1797–1851), the author of *Frankenstein*. The two were married in 1816. Throughout these years Shelley was writing his best-known short poems. He was working on his long philosophic poem *The Triumph of Life* in 1822 when he was drowned during a storm at sea. There are many excellent modern editions of his works, including the Houghton-Mifflin Cambridge edition and the Oxford edition.

JANE SHORE (B. 1947) • Shore was born in New Jersey and took her M.A. at the University of Iowa in 1971. Her poems have been widely circulated in journals and magazines, and the general merit of her work is shown by frequent prizes and awards, including a grant from the National Endowment for the Arts. Her poetry collections are *Lying Down in the Olive Press* (1969), *Eye Level* (1977), *The Minute Hand* (1987), *This Time, for Always* (1990), *Music Minus One: Poems* (1996, 1997), and *Happy Family* (1999, 2000).

LESLIE MARMON SILKO (B. 1948) • A Native American, Silko was brought up in Laguna Pueblo, New Mexico. She has taught at the University of Arizona and also at the University of New Mexico, and she has been honored with a MacArthur Foundation Fellowship. The topic in most of her works is the tradition of the Navajo people, which she treats with great love and understanding, as in "Where Mountain Lion Lay Down with Deer" (p. 1139), which connects the individual with the past, the land, and Nature. A recent novel is *Gardens in the Dunes* (1999, 2000).

DAVE SMITH (B. 1942) • Smith, a native of Virginia, earned his B.A. from the University of Virginia in 1965 and for a time taught high school, including the coaching of football. He received his Ph.D. at Ohio University in 1976. He then taught at the University of Utah in Salt Lake City. Some of his collections are *Bull Island*(1970), *Goshawk, Antelope* (1979), *The Roundhouse Voice: Poems 1970–1985* (1985), *Fate's Kite: Poems 1991–1995* (1995), *Floating on Solitude: Three Volumes of Poetry* (1996), and *The Wick of Memory: New and Selected Poems 1970–2000* (2000). "Bluejays" is from *Homage to Edgar Allan Poe* (1981).

STEVIE SMITH (FLORENCE MARGARET SMITH, 1902–1971) • Smith was a native of Hull, in Yorkshire. During her life she worked in publishing, and in addition she became well known as a radio personality because of her many poetry readings for the BBC. Some of her poetry collections were *A Good Time Was Had by All* (1937) and *Not Waving But Drowning* (1957). Posthumous collections of her work are *Scorpion and Other Poems* (1972) and *Collected Poems* (1975).

W. D. SNODGRASS (B. 1926) • Snodgrass is a native of Pennsylvania. He received his B.A. from the University of Iowa and also did graduate study there. He taught at Wayne State University in Detroit (1959–1967) and was there when he published *Heart's Needle*, for which he received the 1960 Pulitzer Prize in Poetry. Among his other collections are *Gallows Songs of Christian Morgenstern* (1967), *After Experience* (1968), *If Birds Build with Your Hair* (1979), *Each in His Season* (1993), and *The Fuehrer Bunker: The Complete Cycle* (1995). *After Images: Autobiographical Sketches* (1999) is a collection of his essays. His *De/Compositions: 101 Good Poems Gone Wrong*, a unique anthology of poems together with facing-page versions of the poems by Snodgrass, was published in 2001.

GARY SOTO (B. 1952) • Soto is a native of Fresno, California, and was educated in California. Since 1980 he has taught at Berkeley. Because of his native city he has sometimes been grouped with a "Fresno" school of poets. His first poetry collection was *The Elements of San Joaquin* (1977). Later collections are *The Tale of Sunlight* (1978), *Where Sparrows Work Hard* (1981), *Black Hair* (1985), *New and Selected Poems* (1995), *Junior College: Poems* (1997), and *A Natural Man* (1999). Soto is a prolific writer with many different interests, including works for young people. His book *Baseball in April* (1990), for example, was named a Best Book for Young Adults in 1990.

STEPHEN SPENDER (1909–1995) • Sir Stephen Spender, along with W. H. Auden, Christopher Isherwood, and Louis MacNeice, was one of the poets known as the Oxford Poets during the late 1920s and early 1930s. After leaving Oxford, Spender lived for a time in Germany. He believed firmly in the need for poets to be politically engaged, and he joined the Communist Party for a few weeks in the 1930s, although he later renounced this affiliation (in *The God That Failed* [1950]). Along with editing journals and writing many prose works, he, with John Lehmann, wrote a five-act poetic play *Trial of a Judge*, based on circumstances in Germany at the time of Hitler. Spender's first poems were collected in a small book titled *Twenty Poems* in 1930. Later collections were *Poems of Dedication* (1947), *Edge of Being: Poems* (1949), and *Collected Poems 1928–1953* (1955). He was knighted in 1962.

WILLIAM E. STAFFORD (1914–1993) • Stafford, who published more than two dozen volumes of verse, was born in Kansas. He received his Ph.D. from Iowa State in 1955. In 1975 he was named Poet Laureate of Oregon, and at his death in 1993 he was a professor emeritus at Lewis and Clark College. For *Traveling through the Dark* (1962), his second volume of poetry, he won the National Book Award for Poetry in 1963. Among his many poetry collections are *Wyoming* (1985) and *An Oregon Message* (1987). With Marvin Bell, he published *Segues* in 1983. *Down in My Heart* (1994) is his autobiography of the years he spent in an internment camp for conscientious objectors in World War II.

MAURA STANTON (B. 1946) • Stanton was born in Illinois. She took her B.A. at the University of Minnesota (1969) and her M.F.A. at the University of Iowa (1971). Since 1982 she has taught at the University of Indiana. Her major collections of poems are *Snow on Snow* (1975), which includes "The Conjurer"; *Cries of Swimmers* (1984); *The Country I Come From* (1988); and *Life among the Trolls* (1998). Her major novel is *Molly Companion* (1977).

GERALD STERN (B. 1925) • Stern was born in Pittsburgh and became a faculty member of the University of Iowa's Writer's Workshop. He was honored by three grants from the National Endowment for the Arts and by a Guggenheim Fellowship. His *Lucky Life* (1977), which contains "Burying an Animal," received the Lamont Prize in Poetry in 1977. Most recently he published *Leaving Another Kingdom: Selected Poems* (1990), *Bread Without Sugar* (1992), *Odd Mercy* (1995), *This Time* (1998), and *Last Blue* (2000).

WALLACE STEVENS (1879–1955) • Stevens spent his professional life in business rather than academia. He wrote most of his poems after the age of fifty, but he included "The Emperor of Ice-Cream" and "Disillusionment of Ten O'clock," both earlier poems, in the first edition of *Harmonium* in 1923. Some of his poetic collections are a second version of *Harmonium* (1931) and also *The Auroras of Autumn* (1950) and *Collected Poems* (1954).

ANNE STEVENSON (B. 1933) • Anne Stevenson, a dual citizen of the United States and England, has been living mainly in England since 1962. She received degrees from the University of Michigan in 1954 and 1962. One of her many talents is that she is an accomplished cellist and has taught cello. She is the writer of a successful biography of Sylvia Plath and has published many reviews, essays, and poetry collections. In 1996 she published *The Collected Poems of Anne Stevenson*. "The Spirit Is too Blunt an Instrument" is taken from *Selected Poems 1956–1986* (1987).

MARK STRAND (B. 1934) • Strand was born in Prince Edward Island, Canada. He studied at Antioch, Yale, and the University of Iowa and taught at the University of Utah. He has received many honors, including a particularly prized MacArthur Foundation Fellowship. In 1990 he was named United States Poet Laureate. Some of his collections are

Selected Poems (1990), *The Continuous Life* (1990, 1992), and *Blizzard of One* (1999, 2000), for which he was awarded the Pulitzer Prize in Poetry.

MAY SWENSON (1919–1989) • Swenson was born in Utah and was of Swedish ancestry. She experimented constantly in her poetry, not only in content but also in form, as is shown in her work with shaped verse. Her *Iconographs* (1970) was a collection of formed poetry. The formed poem "Women" was included in her collection *New and Selected Things Taking Place* (1978). She also did translations from Swedish, as represented by *Windows and Stones* (1972).

JONATHAN SWIFT (1667–1745) • Swift was born in Ireland. He became Dean of St. Patrick's Cathedral in Dublin, a position in which he served for thirty-one years. His most famous prose works are *A Tale of a Tub* (1704), *Gulliver's Travels* (1726), and *A Modest Proposal* (1729). Throughout his life, however, he constantly wrote poetry, and he devoted himself almost exclusively to poetry after 1730. His poems were edited by Harold Williams and published in three volumes in 1937.

JAMES TATE (B. 1943) • Tate was born in Kansas City, earning degrees from the Universities of Kansas and Iowa. He taught English at the University of Massachusetts. Since his first collection, *The Lost Pilot,* published when he was only twenty-three, he has published a dozen volumes of verse. More recent works include *Viper Jazz* (1976); *Riven Doggeries* (1979); *Reckoner* (1986); *Distance from Loved Ones* (1990); *Selected Poems* (1991), for which he received the Pulitzer Prize for Poetry in 1992; *Shroud of the Gnome* (1997, 1999); and *Memoir of the Hawk: Poems* (2001). In 1994 he received the National Book Award for his collection *Worshipful Company of Fletchers,* and in 1995 he was awarded the Tanning Prize—the largest annual literary prize in the United States—for his achievement as a poet. He was selected to edit *The Best American Poetry, 1997* (1997). "The Blue Booby" is from *The Oblivion Ha-Ha* (1970), his second major collection.

ALFRED, LORD TENNYSON (1809–1892) • One of the most popular of the Victorian poets, Tennyson became Poet Laureate in 1850. His earliest verse was published in collaboration with his brother Charles in *Poems by Two Brothers* (1727). Some of his other collections were *Poems* (1842), *Locksley Hall* (1842), *The Princess* (1847), *Maud, and Other Poems* (1855), and *Idylls of the King* (1857–1891). He wrote *In Memoriam,* in which the well-known phrase "nature red in tooth and claw" appears, from 1833 to 1850. A new collected and annotated edition of his poetry was published in 1969, but there are also many other useful editions.

ELAINE TERRANOVA (B. 1939) • Terranova was born in Pennsylvania and received an MFA degree from Goddard College in 1977. Among her distinctions is an NEA fellowship in poetry. She has printed poems in many significant journals. Among her collections are *The Cult of the Right Hand* (1991) and *Damages* (1995, 1996), from which "Rush Hour" is selected.

DYLAN THOMAS (1914–1953) • A native of Wales, Thomas published his first collection, *Eighteen Poems,* in 1934. After World War II he became immensely popular in America as a speaker and lecturer because of the incantatory power with which he read his own poems. Fortunately, many of his readings survive on records available in college libraries. Thomas's *Collected Poems 1934–1952* was published in 1952 and was a commercial success. *The Poems of Dylan Thomas,* a definitive edition, was published in 1971. In the 1980s, the musician John Cale set "Do Not Go Gentle" to music as part of his *Falklands Suite* (found on Cale's *Words for the Dying,* Opal/Warner Bros. 9-26024-2).

JEAN TOOMER (1894–1967) • Toomer was born in Washington, D.C., studied at five colleges, and eventually settled in the African-American community in Sparta, Georgia. An important voice in the Harlem Renaissance, Toomer published his only book, *Cane,* a grouping of stories, poems, and a play, in 1923. A collection of his works is found in *The Wayward and the Seeking* (1980).

CHASE TWICHELL (B. 1950) • Twichell, born in Connecticut, received her B.A. from Trinity College in Hartford and her M.A. from the University of Iowa. For a time she did editorial work, and she now teaches at Princeton University. She has also taught at both the University of Alabama and Hampshire College. She has received a Guggenheim Fellowship and also a grant from the National Endowment for the Arts. Among her poetry collections are *Northern Spy* (1981), *The Odds* (1986), *Perdido* (1991), *The Ghost of Eden* (1995, 1998), and *The Snow Watcher* (1998).

PETER ULISSE (B. 1944) • Ulisse lives in Connecticut, where he chairs the Humanities Department of Housatonic Community Technical College. He has written many poetry reviews for *Small Pond of Literature* and has served as editor of the *Connecticut River Review*. His first major poetry collection was *Vietnam Voices* (1990). In 1995 he published *Memory Is an Illusive State*, which includes "Odyssey: 20 Years Later."

JOHN UPDIKE (B. 1932) • For a brief biography, see p. 339.

MONA VAN DUYN (B. 1921) • Van Duyn is a native of Iowa and received her college degrees there. She taught for a time at the University of Washington and has been considered a "Northwest" poet for this reason. Among her poetry collections are *Valentines to the Wide World* (1959), *Merciful Disguises* (1973), *Near Changes* (1990, 1992), *Firefall* (1994), and *Selected Poems* (2002).

JUDITH VIORST (B. 1931) • Viorst is a native of New Jersey and received her degrees from Rutgers and the Washington Psychoanalytic Institute. She is known for her wry humor. Her first major volume was *It's Hard to Be Hip over Thirty and Other Tragedies of Married Life* in 1968. Among later works are *Necessary Losses* (1986), *Forever Fifty and Other Negotiations* (1989, 1996), and *Suddenly Sixty, and Other Shocks of Later Life* (2000). She also has written a considerable amount of fiction for young people.

SHELLY WAGNER (B. CA. 1948) • A resident of Virginia, Wagner received her B.A. from Old Dominion University, after which she worked as an interior designer and social worker. Her younger son Andrew drowned in 1984, and it was five years later that she began her cycle of elegiac poems, *The Andrew Poems*, including "Boxes," which was published in 1994. Before this she had published poetry in publications such as *American Poetry Review* and *Poetry East*.

DAVID WAGONER (B. 1926) • Wagoner was born in Ohio and studied at Pennsylvania State University and the University of Indiana. In 1954 he began teaching at the University of Washington, where he was a colleague, and later an editor, of Theodore Roethke. He has been extremely productive both as poet and novelist. A few of his many poetry collections are *Dry Sun, Dry Wind* (1953), *Staying Alive* (1966), *Collected Poems* (1976), *Landfall* (1981), *Through the Forest: New and Selected Poems* (1987), and *Walt Whitman Bathing* (1996).

ALICE WALKER (B. 1944) • For a brief biography, see p. 86.

EDMUND WALLER (1606–1687) • Waller, whom Dryden constantly praised for the quality and originality of his poetic couplets, was a Royalist during the English Civil Wars of 1642–1649, and for his efforts he was forced into exile. He returned in 1651 after swearing loyalty to Oliver Cromwell. After the Restoration, he supported King Charles II. His major collections of poetry were *Poems* (1645) and *Divine Poems* (1685).

ROBERT PENN WARREN (1905–1989) • Three-time winner of the Pulitzer Prize (1947, 1957, 1978) and the first United States Poet Laureate (1985), Warren was one of the leaders of the New Criticism (see Chapter 33) and was also a leading exponent of Southern literature and culture. With Cleanth Brooks, he wrote the *Understanding Poetry, Understanding Drama,* and *Understanding Fiction* series of textbooks that taught the techniques of New Criticism to a generation of graduate and undergraduate students His novel *All the King's Men* (1946) was made into a prize-winning motion picture in 1950. During his teaching career he taught at the University of Minnesota and then at Yale. Some of his poetry collections are *Thirty-Six Poems* (1935), *Promises* (1957), and *New and Selected Poems* (1985).

CHARLES HARPER WEBB (B. 1952) • Webb is a native of Pennsylvania but grew up in Texas. He received degrees at Rice University, the University of Washington, and the University of Southern California. He teaches at California State University at Long Beach. Some of his books are *Everyday Outrages* (1989), *Poetry That Heals* (1991), and *A Webb for All Seasons* (1992). He has also published a novel, *The Wilderness Effect* (1982). Interestingly, before he took up teaching as a profession he had spent a decade as a rock guitarist and singer.

PHYLLIS WEBB (B. 1927) • Webb is a native of British Columbia. She was educated at the University of British Columbia and also at McGill University. During her career she worked with the Canadian Broadcasting Company both as a program planner and a producer; she has also taught in various Canadian colleges and universities as a guest lecturer and professor. A major concern in her poetry has been the problem of maintaining personal integrity amid a world of "hate and broken things," to quote from one of her poems in *Trio* (1954). One of her interests has been to experiment with a form of Persian poetry, the *ghazal*, which consists of five couplets. Among her poetry collections are *Wilson's Bowl* (1980), *The Vision Tree* (1982), *Selected Poems* (1982), *Water and Light: Ghazals and Anti Ghazals* (1984), and *Hanging Fire* (1990).

BRUCE WEIGL (B. 1949) • Weigl, who teaches at Penn State, was born in Ohio. He took his B.A. at Oberlin (1974) and his Ph.D. at the University of Utah (1979). His poetry collections include *Like a Sack Full of Old Quarrels* (1976), *Executioner* (1977), *A Romance* (1979), *The Monkey Wars* (1984), *Song of Napalm* (1988), *What Saves Us* (1992), and *Sweet Lorain* (1996). His most recent collections are *Archaeology of the Circle: New and Selected Poems* (1998, 1999), *After the Others* (1999), and *The Unraveling Strangeness* (2002).

PHILLIS WHEATLEY (CA. 1753–1784) • Wheatley was born in Africa. She was captured by slave traders and sold to John Wheatley, a Boston merchant, who treated her virtually as a daughter and saw to it that she was educated. When she published her *Poems on Various Subjects, Religious and Moral* (1773), however, the temper of the times made it necessary to include prefaces by Massachusetts men verifying that she was qualified to write poetry and that she had indeed written the poems in the collection. Although she wrote a second volume of poetry, she could not find a publisher for it during her lifetime. Her collected works were published in 1988.

WALT WHITMAN (1819–1892) • Whitman, who became a legend during his lifetime, is one of America's major poets. He was born in New York and lived with his family in both Long Island and Brooklyn. At various times he worked as a printer, teacher, reporter, and government bureaucrat. In addition, he served as a nurse during the Civil War. His major work was *Leaves of Grass*, which he first published as a collection of twelve poems in 1855, and to which he added as time went on. Many editions were published in his lifetime, the last one in 1892. *Drum Taps*, poems based on his Civil War experiences, was published in 1865; a second edition contained "When Lilacs Last in the Dooryard Bloom'd," his poem on the death of Lincoln.

JOHN GREENLEAF WHITTIER (1807–1892) • Whittier was born in Massachusetts of Quaker stock. He was not formally educated and was trained to be a shoemaker. However, he was a compulsive reader and at the age of nineteen he wrote a poem that was accepted by William Lloyd Garrison for publication in the Newburyport *Press*. From that point Whittier went on to become one of America's best known poets and writers. Joining the abolitionist movement, he worked diligently in that cause, and for a brief period he served in the Massachusetts Legislature. The best way to describe his poetic output is that it was voluminous, and with his publication of *Snow-Bound* in 1866 and *Poetical Works* in 1869 he became financially secure. A particularly notable achievement was his being part of the group that founded the *Atlantic Monthly* in 1857.

CORNELIUS WHUR (1782–1853) • Whur was a Methodist minister in Suffolk, England. In 1837 he published a poetry collection, *Village Musings on Moral and Religious Subjects*, which included "The First-Rate Wife." In his obituary notice he was recognized not only as a "distinguished" poet but also as a gardener.

RICHARD WILBUR (B. 1921) • Wilbur was born in New York. He has published a number of poetry collections, including *New and Collected Poems* (1988, 1989), for which he was awarded the Pulitzer Prize in Poetry. He has also made a number of well-received translations of French drama and has published collections for children, such as *The Pig in the Spigot* (2000). In 1988 he was distinguished as the second United States Poet Laureate (the first being Robert Penn Warren). His most recent collection is *Mayflies: New Poems and Translations* (2000).

C. K. WILLIAMS (CHARLES KENNETH WILLIAMS, B. 1936) • Williams is a native of New Jersey who graduated from Bucknell and the University of Pennsylvania. He taught at a number of schools and colleges and has become a permanent resident of France. He is known for his discursively long lines in the manner of Walt Whitman. Among his many volumes of poems are *Tar* (1983); *Flesh and Blood* (1987), for which he was awarded the 1987 National Book Critics Circle Award; *Poems, 1963–1983* (1988); *A Dream of the Mind* (1992); and *Repair* (1999). Recently he has undertaken translations of Greek drama. "Dimensions" is taken from *Lies*, his collection of 1969.

WILLIAM CARLOS WILLIAMS (1883–1963) • Williams spent his career as a practicing pediatrician, but he early became friendly with the poets Ezra Pound and Hilda Doolittle (H. D.). He developed a second career as a writer, producing poems, plays, stories, novels, and essays. At the age of thirty he began publishing poems, beginning with *Poems* (1913) and *Tempers* (1913) and ending with *Pictures from Brueghel* (1963), for which he was posthumously awarded the Pulitzer Prize.

WILLIAM WORDSWORTH (1770–1850) • For a brief biography, see pp. 985–92.

JAMES WRIGHT (1927–1980) • Wright was born in Martins Ferry, Ohio, and received his Ph.D. at the University of Washington, where he was a student of Theodore Roethke. In 1966 he began teaching at Hunter College, and he remained there until his death in 1980. His first poetry collection, *The Green Wall*, appeared in 1957, and after that he published collections regularly, receiving the 1972 Pulitzer Prize in Poetry for his *Collected Poems* (1971). *This Journey* was published posthumously in 1982, and *Above the River: The Complete Poems* appeared in 1990.

SIR THOMAS WYATT (CA. 1503–1542) • Wyatt was a courtier in the service of King Henry VIII. He is credited with introducing the sonnet form into English as a result of his translations of the sonnets of the Italian sonneteer Petrarch. He circulated his poems in manuscript, although a number of them were anthologized after his death in *The Court of Venus* (1542) and *Seven Penitential Psalms* (1549). Modern editions of his poems were published in 1969, 1975, and 1978.

WILLIAM BUTLER YEATS (1865–1939) • The foremost Irish poet of the twentieth century, Yeats was instrumental in the founding of the Abbey Theatre in Dublin in 1899. An unorthodox thinker, he developed his poems out of his vast reading and his special interest in spiritualism. He published many volumes of poems, including *The Green Helmet* (1910), *The Wild Swans at Coole* (1917), *The Winding Stair* (1929), and *The Collected Poems* (1932). He was awarded the Nobel Prize for Literature in 1923.

PAUL ZIMMER (B. 1934) • Zimmer, whose sister was the science-fiction writer Marion Zimmer Bradley (1930–1999), was born in Canton, Ohio, and received his B.A. from Kent State University. He has managed bookstores and university presses, including the University of Iowa Press. Among his many volumes of poems are *A Seed on the Wind* (1960), *The Ribs of Death* (1967), *Family Reunion* (1983), and *Big Blue Train* (1993). His "Zimmer" poems are collected in *The Zimmer Poems* (1976), *Earthbound Zimmer* (1983), *The American Zimmer* (1984), *The Great Bird of Love* (1989), and *Crossing to Sunlight: Selected Poems* (1996).

Glossary
of Literary Terms

This glossary presents brief definitions of terms and concepts that are boldfaced in the text. Page references indicate where readers may find additional detail and illustration, together with discussions about how the concepts can be utilized in studying and writing about literature. Words italicized as a part of various definitions are also separately and fully glossed in their own right.

Abstract diction   Language describing qualities that are rarefied and theoretical (e.g., "good," "interesting," "neat," and so on); distinguished from *concrete diction*. 314, 636

Absurd   See *comedy of the absurd*.

Accent   See *beat*.

Accented syllable   The syllable on which a heavy accent is placed. 797

Accentual rhythm   See *sprung rhythm*.

Actions or **incidents**   The events or occurrences in a work. 3, 52, 58, 107, 1166

Actors   Persons who perform as characters in a drama. 1170–71

Allegory   A complete *narrative* that can also be applied to a parallel set of situations that may be political, moral, religious, or philosophical. 57, 58; Ch. 9: 393–438; 396–97; 1170

Alliteration   The repetition of identical consonant sounds (most often the sounds beginning words) in close proximity (e.g., "pensive poets," "grown grey," "brazen brainless brothers"). 796, 805

Allusion   Unacknowledged references and quotations which authors make while assuming that readers will recognize the original sources and relate their meanings to the new context. Allusions are hence compliments that the author pays to readers for their perceptiveness, knowledge, and awareness. 398, 890–92

Amphibrach   A three-syllable poetic *foot* consisting of a light, heavy, and light stress. 801

Amphimacer or **Cretic**   A three-syllable *foot* consisting of a heavy, light, and heavy stress. 801

Anagnorisis or **recognition**   Aristotle's term describing the point in a play, usually the *climax*, when a character experiences understanding. 1255

Analysis   See *commentary*.

Analytical sentence outline   A scheme or plan for an essay, arranged according to topics (A, B, C, etc.) and with the topics expressed in sentences. 30

Analyzed rhyme   See *inexact rhyme*.

Anapest   A three-syllable *foot* consisting of two light stresses climaxed by a heavy stress. 800

Anaphora ("to carry again or repeat") The repetition of the same word or phrase throughout a work or a section of a work. The effect is to lend weight and emphasis. 729

Ancillary characters Characters who set off or highlight the protagonist and who provide insight into the action. The *foil, choric figure,* and *raisonneur* are all ancillary characters. 1165

Antagonist The person, idea, force, or general set of circumstances opposing the *protagonist,* an essential element of *plot.* 52, 162, 1165

Anticipation See *procatalepsis.*

Antimetabole See *chiasmus.*

Antithesis A rhetorical device of opposition or contrast, in which one idea or word is established, and then the opposite idea or word is expressed, as in "I *burn* and *freeze*" and "I *love* and *hate.*" 640, 847

Apostrophe The addressing of a discourse to a real or imagined person who is not present; also, a speech to an abstraction. 730

Apron or **thrust stage** A stage that projects into the auditorium area, thus increasing the space for action; a characteristic feature of Elizabethan theaters and many recent ones. 1171, 1303, 1604

Archetypal/Symbolic/Mythic critical approach An interpretive approach explaining literature in terms of archetypal patterns (e.g., God's creation of human beings, the sacrifice of a hero, or the search for paradise). 1923

Archetype A character, action, or situation that is a prototype or pattern of human life generally; a situation that occurs over and over again in literature, such as a quest, an initiation, or an attempt to overcome evil. Many *myths* are archetypes. 924

Archon, Eponymous In ancient Athens, the Eponymous Archon, or Archon Eponymous, was a leading magistrate, after whom the year was named. He made arrangements for the tragedies and comedies to be performed at the yearly festivals in honor of the god Dionysus. 1250

Arena stage or **theater-in-the-round** A theater arrangement, often outdoors, in which the audience totally surrounds a *platform stage,* with all actors entering and exiting along the same aisles used by the audience. 1171

Argument The development of an idea, including the introduction of a hypothesis or major idea, supporting details, and logical conclusions. 19, 439

Aside A speech, usually short, delivered by a character to another character or to the audience, the convention being that the other characters on stage cannot hear it; the speaker usually reveals his or her thoughts or plans. 1304

Assertion A sentence putting an *idea* (the subject) into operation (the predicate); necessary for both developing and understanding the idea. 439

Assonance The repetition of identical vowel sounds in different words in close proximity, as in the d*ee*p gr*ee*n s*ea.* 796, 804

Atmosphere or **mood** The emotional aura invoked by a work. 56, 278

Audience or **intended reader** (1) The people attending a theatrical production. (2) The intended group of readers for whom a writer writes. 1173

Auditory images Descriptions of sounds. 698

Authorial symbols See *contextual symbols.*

Authorial voice The *voice* or *speaker* used by authors when seemingly speaking for themselves. The use of the term makes it possible to discuss a narration or presentation without identifying the ideas absolutely with those of the author. See also *speaker, point of view,* and *third-person point of view.* 54, 231

Bacchius or **Bacchic** A three-syllable *foot* consisting of a light stress followed by two heavy stresses, as in "a new song." 801

Ballad, ballad measure   A narrative poem composed of *quatrains* in which lines of iambic tetrameter alternate with iambic trimeter, rhyming *x a x a*. 3, 618, 810, 850

Ballad opera   An eighteenth-century comic drama, originated by John Gay's *The Beggar's Opera* in 1728, featuring lyrics set to existing tunes. See also *comic opera*. 1569

Beast fable   A fable featuring animals with human characteristics. 397

Beat or **accent**   A heavy stress or accent in a line of poetry. The number of beats in a line usually dictates the meter of the line (five beats in a *pentameter* line, etc.). 797

Blank verse   Unrhymed *iambic pentameter*. 3, 846

Blocking   In the performance of a play, the grouping and movement of characters on stage. 1171

Blocking agent   A person, circumstance, or attitude that obstructs the union of lovers. 1487

Box set   In the modern theater, a realistic setting of a single room from which the "fourth wall" is missing, so that the stage resembles a three-dimensional picture. 1171–72

Brainstorming   The exploration, discovery, and development of details to be used in a composition. 17

Breve   A mark in the shape of a bowl-like half circle (˘) to indicate a light stress or unaccented syllable. See *schwa*. 798

Business or **stage business**   The gestures, expressions, and general activity (beyond *blocking*) of actors onstage. Usually, business is designed to create laughter. It is often spontaneous. 1171

Buskins   Elegantly laced boots (*kothorni* or *cothurni*) worn by the actors in ancient Greek tragedy. Eventually the buskins became elevator shoes to stress the royal status of actors by making them tall. 1261

Cacophony   Meaning "bad sound," the term *cacophony* refers to words combining sharp or harsh sounds; opposite of *euphony*. 805

Cadence group   A coherent word group spoken as a single rhythmical unit, such as a noun phrase ("our sacred honor") or prepositional phrase ("of parting day")— of major importance in the rhythms of *open form poetry*. 803

Caesura, caesurae   The pause(s) separating phrases within lines of poetry, an important aspect of poetic *rhythm*. 801, 803

Catastrophe   The "overturning" of the dramatic *plot*, the fourth stage in the structure after the *climax*. The *dénouement* of a play, in which things are explained and put into place. 1168

Catharsis (purgation)   Aristotle's concept that tragedy, by arousing pity and fear (*eleos* and *phobos*), regularizes and shapes the emotions, and that therefore tragedy is essential in civilized society. 1253–54

Central idea or **central argument**   (1) The thesis or main idea of an essay. 25 (2) The *theme* of a literary work. 58

Character   An extended verbal representation of a human being, the inner self that determines thought, speech, and behavior. 3, 51, 58; Ch. 4: 157–224; 1164–66

Chiasmus or **antimetabole**   A rhetorical pattern in which words and ideas are repeated in the sequence *a b b a*, as in "I *lead* the life I *love*; I *love* the life I *lead*." 641

Choragos or **choregus**   The sponsor or financial backer of a classical Greek dramatic production. Often the *choragos* was honored by serving as the leader (*koryphaios*) of the chorus. 1258

Choree   See *trochee*.

Choric figure   A character who remains detached from the action and who provides commentary. See also *raisonneur*. 1165

Chorus   In ancient Athenian drama, the chorus was composed of fifteen young men in tragedies, and twenty-four in comedies, who chanted in unison and performed dance movements to a flute accompaniment. 1249

Chronology ("logic of time") The sequence of events in a work, with emphasis on the complex intertwining of cause and effect. 52, 1166

City Dionysia See *Dionysia*.

Clerihew A humorous closed-form poem in four lines, rhyming *a b a b*, usually about a famous real or literary person. 852

Cliché rhymes Trite and widely used rhymes, such as *moon* and *June* or *trees* and *breeze*. 806

Climax (Greek for "ladder") The high point of *conflict* and tension preceding the resolution or *dénouement* of a drama or story; the point of decision, of inevitability and no return. The climax is sometimes merged with the *crisis* in the consideration of dramatic and narrative structure. 110, 1167

Closed-form poetry Poetry written in specific and traditional patterns produced through control of *rhyme, meter,* line-length, and line groupings. 845–53

Comedy A literary genre which, like *tragedy*, originated in the *Dionysia* festivals of ancient Athens. Derived from the Greek *komos* songs or "songs of merrymakers," the first comedies were wildly boisterous. Subsequently comedies became more subdued and realistic. In typical comedies today, confusions and doubts are resolved satisfactorily if not happily, and usually comedies are characterized by smiles and laughter. Ch. 28: 1484–1602

Comedy of the absurd A modern form of comedy dramatizing the apparent pointlessness, ambiguity, uncertainty, and absurdity of existence. 1492, 1570

Comedy of manners A form of comedy, usually *regular* (five acts or three acts), in which attitudes and customs are examined and satirized in the light of high intellectual and moral standards. The *dialogue* is witty and sophisticated, and characters are often measured according to their linguistic and intellectual powers. 1490

Comic A pattern of action, including funny situations and language, that is solvable and correctible, and therefore satisfying. 1489

Comic opera An outgrowth of eighteenth-century *ballad operas*, but different from them in having music specially composed for the lyrics. 1569

Commedia dell'arte Broadly humorous farce developed in sixteenth-century Italy, featuring stock characters, stock situations, and much improvised *dialogue*. 1491

Commentary, analysis, or **interpretation** Passages of explanation and reflection about the meaning of actions, thoughts, dialogue, historical movements, and so on. 57

Commentator See *raisonneur*.

Common ground of assent Those interests, concerns, and assumptions that the writer assumes in common with readers so that an effective and persuasive *tone* may be maintained. 762

Common measure A closed poetic quatrain, rhyming *a b a b*, in which lines of iambic tetrameter alternate with iambic trimeter. See also *ballad measure* and *hymnal measure*. 851

Comparison-contrast A technique of analyzing two or more works in order to determine similarities and differences in topic, treatment, and quality. Ch. 35: 1939–52

Complete, completeness The second aspect of Aristotle's definition of *tragedy*, emphasizing the logic and wholeness of the play. 1255

Complex sentence A sentence consisting of an independent clause together with a subordinate or dependent clause. 317

Complication A stage of narrative and dramatic structure in which the major *conflicts* are brought out; the *rising action* of a *drama*. 110, 1167

Compound sentence A sentence consisting of two simple sentences joined by a conjunction. 317

Concrete diction Words that describe exact and particular conditions or qualities, such as *cold, sweet,* and *creamy* in reference to an ice-cream sundae. These words are *concrete,* while the application of *good* or *neat* to the sundae is *abstract.* See also *abstract diction.* 54, 314, 636

Concrete poetry See *visual poetry.*

Conflict The opposition between two characters, between large groups of people, or between *protagonists* and larger forces such as natural objects, ideas, modes of behavior, public opinion, and the like. Conflict may also be internal and psychological, involving choices facing a *protagonist.* It is the essence of *plot.* 52, 107, 1166

Connotation The meanings that words suggest beyond their bare dictionary definitions. 315, 642

Consonants or **consonant segments** Consonant sounds; sounds produced as a result of the touching or close proximity of the tongue or the lips in relation to the teeth or palate (e.g., *m, n, p, f, sh, ch*); contrasted with *vowel segments.* 795–96

Contextual symbol A symbol that is derived not from common historical, cultural, or religious materials, but that is rather developed within the context of an individual work. See also *cultural symbol.* 57, 395, 886, 1169

Convention An accepted feature of a genre, such as the *point of view* in a story, the *form* of a poem (e.g., sonnet, ode), the competence or brilliance of the detective in detective fiction, the impenetrability of disguise and concealment in a Shakespearean play, or the *chorus* in Greek drama. 24

Corpus Christi play A type of medieval drama that enacts events from the Bible, such as the killing of Abel by Cain, the problems of Noah, the anger of Herod, and so on. The word is derived from the religious festival of Corpus Christi ("Christ's body"), held in the spring of each year. Also called *mystery plays.* See also *cycle.* 1178, 1217–38

Cosmic irony (irony of fate) *Situational irony* that is connected to a pessimistic or fatalistic view of life. 355

Costumes The clothes worn by actors, designed to indicate historical periods, social status, economic levels, etc. 1173

Cothurni See *buskins.*

Couplet Two lines which may be unified by rhyme or, in Biblical poetry, by content. 3, 846

Creative non-fiction A type of literature that is technically nonfiction, such as diaries and journals, but which nevertheless involves a degree of imagination. 3

Cretic See *amphimacer.*

Crisis The point of uncertainty and tension—the *turning point*—that results from the *conflicts* and difficulties brought about through the complications of the *plot.* The crisis leads to the *climax*—that is, to the decision made by the *protagonist* to resolve the *conflict.* Sometimes the *crisis* and the *climax* are considered as two elements of the same stage of *plot* development. 110, 1167

Cultural (universal) symbol A symbol recognized and shared as a result of a common social and cultural heritage. See also *contextual symbol.* 57, 394, 886, 1169

Cycle (1) A group of closely related works. (2) In medieval religious drama, the complete set of plays performed during the Corpus Christi festival, from the creation of the world to the resurrection. As many as forty plays could make up the cycle. See also *Corpus Christi plays.* 1178

Dactyl A three-syllable *foot* consisting of a heavy *stress* followed by two lights, as in *notable, parable,* and *terrible.* 800

Dactylic rhyme Rhyming dactyls, such as *spillable* and *syllable* or *mortify* and *fortify.* 808

Deconstructionist critical approach An interpretive literary approach that rejects absolute interpretations and stresses ambiguities and contradictions. 1924

Decorum The convention or expectation that words and subjects should be exactly appropriate—*high* or *formal* words for serious subjects (e.g., *epic* poems, *tragedy*), and *low* or *informal* words for low subjects (e.g., *limericks, farce*). 639

Denotation The standard, minimal meaning of a word, without implications and connotations. 315, 641

Dénouement ("untying") or resolution The final stage of *plot* development, in which mysteries are explained, characters find their destinies, and the work is completed. Usually the dénouement is done as speedily as possible, for it occurs after all *conflicts* are ended. 110, 1168

Description The exposition of scenes, actions, attitudes, and feelings. 55

Developing character See *round character.*

Deus ex machina ("A god out of the machine"; *theos apo mechanes* in Greek) In ancient Greek drama, the entrance of a god to unravel the problems in a play. Today, the phrase *deus ex machina* refers to the artificial and illogical solution of problems. 1260

Dialect Language characteristics involving pronunciation, unique words, and vocal rhythms—particular to regions such as the South or New England, or to separate nations such as Britain and Australia. 638

Dialogue The speeches of two or more characters in a story, play, or poem. 3, 56, 58, 667, 1164

Diction Word choice, types of words, and the level of language. 313–16; Ch 14: 635–63

Diction, formal or high Proper, elevated, elaborate, and often polysyllabic language. 313, 636

Diction, informal or low Relaxed, conversational, and familiar language, utilizing contractions and elisions, and sometimes employing *slang* and grammatical mistakes. 314, 637

Diction, neutral or middle Correct language characterized by directness and simplicity. 313, 637

Dilemma Two choices facing a *protagonist,* usually in a tragic situation, with either choice being unacceptable or damaging; a cause of both internal and external *conflict.* 108, 1257

Dimeter A line of two metrical *feet.* 798

Dionysia The religious festivals of ancient Athens held to celebrate the god Dionysus. *Tragedy* developed as part of the Great, or City Dionysia in March-April, and *comedy* developed as part of a shorter festival, the Lenaia. 1248, 1484

Diphthong A meaningful vowel segment which begins with one sound and ends with another. The three diphthongs in English are those found in h*ou*se, c*oi*l, and f*i*ne. 795

Dipody, dipodic foot, or **syzygy** The submergence of two normal *feet,* usually *iambs* or *trochees,* under a stronger beat, so that a "galloping" or "rollicking" *rhythm* results. 801

Director The person in charge of guiding and instructing all persons involved in a dramatic production. 1171

Discursive poetry Non-narrative poetry dealing primarily with ideas and personal, social, or political commentary. 3

Discursive writing To be distinguished from imaginative writing, discursive writing is concerned with factual presentation and the development of reasonable and logical conclusions. 3

Dithyramb An ancient Athenian poetic form sung by choruses during the earliest *Dionysia.* The first *tragedies* originated from the dithyrambs. 1174, 1248

Donnée (French for "given") The given action or set of assumptions on which a work of literature is based, such as the unpredictability of love, the bleakness and danger of a postwar world, or the inescapability of guilt. See also *postulate* or *premise.* 50–51

Double dactyl A comic *closed-form* poem in two *quatrains,* written in dactylic dimeter. The second line must be a proper name, and the sixth or seventh a single word. 852

Double duple See *dipody.*

Double entendre ("double meaning") Deliberate ambiguity, often sexual and usually humorous. 354

Double plot or **multiple plot** Two different but related lines of *action*, most often in a play. 1166

Double rhyme See *trochaic rhyme.*

Drama An individual play; also plays considered as a group; one of the three major *genres* of literature. 3, Chapters 26–31: 1161–1883

Dramatic convention See *convention.*

Dramatic irony A special kind of *situational irony* in which a character perceives his or her plight in a limited way while the audience and one or more of the other characters understand it entirely. 57, 355, 765, 1169

Dramatic monologue A type of poem in which a speaker addresses an internal listener or the reader. Often the speaker includes detail reflecting the listener's nonverbal responses. The form is related to the soliloquy and the aside in drama. 668

Dramatic (objective) point of view A third-person *narration* reporting speech and action, but excluding commentary on the actions and thoughts of the characters. 55, 231

Dynamic character A *round* character, one who undergoes adaptation, change, or growth, unlike the *static character,* who remains constant. In a *short story,* there is usually only one dynamic character, whereas in a *novel* there may be many. 161, 1165

Dying rhyme See *falling rhyme.*

Echoic words Words echoing the actions they describe, such as *buzz, bump,* and *slap*; important in the device of *onomatopoeia.* 805

Economic Determinist/Marxist critical approach An interpretive approach based on the theories of Karl Marx (1818–1883), stressing that literature is to be judged from an economic perspective. 1921

Elegy A poem of lamentation about a death. Often an elegy takes the form of a *pastoral.* 3, 849

Enclosing setting See *framing setting.*

End-stopped line A poetic line ending in a full pause, usually indicated with a period or semicolon. 803

English (Shakespearean) sonnet A sonnet form developed by Shakespeare, in *iambic pentameter,* composed of three *quatrains* and a *couplet,* with seven rhymes in the pattern *a b a b, c d c d, e f e f, g g.* 848

Enjambement or **run-on line** A line having no end punctuation but running over to the next line. 803

Epic A long narrative poem elevating character, speech, and action. 3, 47

Epigram A short and witty poem, often in *couplets,* that makes a humorous or satiric point. 3, 851

Episodia or **episode** (1) An acting *scene* or section of Greek tragedy. Divisions separating the episodes were called *stasima,* or sections for the chorus. (2) A self-enclosed portion of a work, such as a section, or a passage of particular narration, dialogue, or location. 58, 1262

Epitaph A short, witty, and sometimes satiric poem marking someone's death. 851

Euphony Meaning "good sound," *euphony* refers to word groups containing consonants that permit an easy and pleasant flow of spoken sound; opposite of *cacophony.* 805

Exact rhyme Rhyming words in which both the vowel and consonant sounds rhyme; also called *perfect rhyme.* It is important to note that rhymes result from *sound* rather than spelling; words do not have to be spelled the same way or look alike to rhyme, as in *seal* and *feel.* 806

Exodos The final episode in a Greek tragedy, occurring after the last choral ode. 1263

Explication A complete and detailed analysis of a work of literature, often word by word and line by line. 616, 629–33

Exposition The stage of dramatic or narrative structure that introduces all things necessary for the development of the *plot.* 109, 1167

Fable A brief *story* illustrating a moral truth, most often associated with the ancient Greek writer Aesop. 48, 397

Falling action See *catastrophe.*

Falling rhyme Rhymes moving from heavy accents to light. *Trochaic rhymes*, such as *dying* and *crying*, and also *dactylic rhymes*, such as *flattery* and *battery*, are falling rhymes. 855

Fantasy The creation of events that are dreamlike or fantastic, departing from ordinary understanding of reality because of apparently illogical location, movement, causation, and *chronology.* 50

Farce A word derived from the Latin word *farsus*, meaning "stuffed," farce is an outlandish physical comedy overflowing with silly characters, improbable happenings, wild clowning, extravagant language, and bawdy jokes. 1180, 1491

Feminist critical approach An interpretive approach designed to raise consciousness about the importance and unique nature of women in literature. 21, 1920

Fiction *Narratives* based in the imagination of the author, not in literal, reportorial facts; one of the three major *genres* of literature. Ch. 2, 47–106

Figurative devices See *figures of speech.*

Figurative language See *figures of speech.*

Figures of speech Organized patterns of comparison that deepen, broaden, extend, illuminate, and emphasize meaning, and also that conform to particular patterns or forms such as *metaphor, simile,* and *parallelism.* Ch. 17: 725–57

Figures, rhetorical See *figures of speech.*

Film Motion pictures, movies. Ch. 30: 1731–53

First-person point of view The use of an "I," or first-person, *speaker* or *narrator* who tells about things that he/she has seen, done, spoken, heard, thought, and also learned about in other ways. 54, 58, 229–30, 233

Fixed character See *flat character.*

Flashback A method of *narration* in which past events are introduced into a present action. Also called *selective recollection.* 111

Flat character A character, usually minor, who is not individual but rather useful and structural, static and unchanging; distinguished from *round character.* 162, 1165, 1606

Foil A character, usually minor, designed to highlight qualities of a major character. 1165

Foot, feet Measured combinations of heavy and light *stresses*, such as the *iamb*, which contains a light and a heavy stress. 797

Form, poetic The various shapes and organizational modes of poetry. Ch. 20: 845–84

Formal aspects of poetry The technique of poetry, as opposed to the content. 2

Formal diction See *diction, formal* or *high.*

Formalist critical approach See *New Critical/ formalist critical approach.*

Framing or **enclosing setting** The same features of topic or setting used at both the beginning and ending of a work so as to "frame" or "enclose" the work. 278

Free verse Poetry based on the natural *rhythms* of phrases and normal pauses, not metrical *feet.* See *open-form poetry.* 3, 853

Freewriting See *brainstorming.*

Freytag pyramid A diagram graphically showing the stages of dramatic *structure. Complication* and emotional intensity go upward like the side of a pyramid rising to its peak or point. Once the point is reached, intensity decreases just as the other side of the pyramid descends to its base. 1166

Gallery The upper seats at the back and sides of a theater. 1304

General language Words referring to broad classes of persons, objects, or phenomena; distinguished from *specific language.* 314, 636

Genre   A type of *literature*, such as *fiction* and *poetry*; also a type of work, such as detective fiction, epic poetry, tragedy, etc. 2–3

Globe Theater   The outdoor theater just south of the Thames where many of Shakespeare's plays were originally performed. The Globe was rebuilt in the 1990s to its original specifications. 1303–1305

Graph, graphics (spelling)   Writing or spelling; the appearance of words on a page, as opposed to their actual sounds. 797

Great Dionysia   See *Dionysia*.

Gustatory images   Descriptions and references to taste. 699

Haiku   A poetic form derived from Japanese, traditionally containing three lines of 5, 7, and 5 syllables. 3, 851

Half rhyme   See *inexact rhyme*.

Hamartia   The error or frailty that causes the downfall of a tragic *protagonist*. 1256

Heavy stress   A syllable that receives strong emphasis and loudness in comparison with syllables of lighter emphasis. 797

Heavy-stress rhyme   A *rhyme*, specifically rhyming *iambs*, *anapests*, and *Bacchics*, which begins with a light stress and concludes with a strong *stress*. 807

Heptameter   A line consisting of seven *feet*.

Hero, heroine   The major male and female *protagonists* in a narrative or drama; the terms are often used to describe leading characters in adventures and romances. 162

Heroic couplet   Also called the *neoclassic couplet*. Two successive rhyming lines of iambic pentameter, a characteristic of much poetry written between 1660 and 1800. Five-stress couplets are often called "heroic" regardless of their topic matter and the period in which they were written. 846

Hexameter   A line consisting of six *feet*. 798

High comedy   Elegant comedies characterized by wit and sophistication, in which the complications grow out of character. See also *comedy of manners*. 1490

Historical critical approach   See *topical/historical critical approach*.

Hovering accent   See *spondee*.

Hubris or **hybris**   Meaning "insolence, contemptuous violence," or pride, *hubris* defines the attitude/attitudes that lead tragic figures to commit their offenses. 1248

Humor   The capacity to cause laughter. 1488

Hymn, hymnal measure   A hymn is a religious *song*, consisting of one and usually many more replicating rhythmical *stanzas*. The hymnal stanza, in iambics, consists of four lines of four stresses or else of alternating four and three stresses, rhyming *x a x a* or *a b a b*. See also *ballad measure* and *common measure*. 3, 851

Hyperbole   *Figurative language* in which emphasis is achieved through exaggeration. 354, 732

Hypocrites   (pronounced hip-POCK-rih-tayss) Meaning "one who plays a part," *hypocrites* was the ancient Athenian word for actor. 1249

Iamb   A two-syllable *foot* consisting of a light stress followed by a heavy stress (e.g., *the WORLD*). The iamb is the most common metrical foot in English poetry. 798–99

Iambic pentameter   A line consisting of five iambic *feet*. 798

Iambic rhyme   Rhyming *iambs*. 807

Idea   A concept, thought, opinion, or belief; in literature, a unifying, centralizing conception or *theme*. 52, 58, 439; Ch. 10: 439–98; Ch. 23: 955–84

Idiom   Usage that produces unique words and phrases within regions, classes, or groups; e.g., standing *on* line or *in* line; carrying a *pail* or a *bucket*; drinking *pop* or *soda*. Also, the habits and structures of particular languages. 637

Image, imagery   Images are references that trigger the mind to fuse together memories of sights (*visual*), sounds (*auditory*), tastes (*gustatory*), smells (*olfactory*), motion (*kinesthetic* and *kinetic*), and sensations of touch (*tactile*). "Image" refers to a single mental creation. "Imagery" refers to images throughout a work or throughout the works of a writer or group of writers. Images may be *literal* (descriptive and pictorial) or *metaphorical* (figurative and suggestive). 2; Ch. 16: 695–724

Imaginative literature *Literature* based in the imagination of the writer, usually *fiction, poetry,* and *drama.* 2, *passim*

Imitation The theory that literature is derived from life and is an imaginative duplication of experience; closely connected to *realism* and *verisimilitude.* 50

Imperfect foot A metrical *foot* consisting of a single syllable, either heavily or lightly stressed. 800

Incidents See *actions*

Inexact rhyme *Rhymes* that are created out of words with similar but not identical sounds. In most of these instances, either the *vowel segments* are different while the *consonants* are the same, or vice versa. This type of rhyme is variously called *slant rhyme, near rhyme, half rhyme, off rhyme, analyzed rhyme,* or *suspended rhyme.* 809

Informal diction See *diction, informal* or *low.*

Incongruity A discrepancy between what is ordinarily or normally expected and what is experienced. The resulting gap is a cause of amusement. 353

Internal audience See *listener.*

Internal rhyme The occurrence of rhyming words within a single line of verse. 806

Interpretation See *commentary.*

Intrigue plot The dramatic rendering of how a young woman and her lover, often aided by a maidservant or soubrette, usually foil the blocking agent; e.g., a parent or guardian. 1487, 1490

Invention The process of discovering and determining materials to be included in a composition, whether an essay or an imaginative work; a vital phase of prewriting. 49

Ironic comedy A form of comedy in which characters seem to be in the grips of uncontrollable, cosmic forces. The dominant tone is therefore ironic. 1492

Irony Broadly, a means of indirection. Language that states the opposite of what is intended is *verbal irony* (q.v.). The placement of characters in a state of ignorance is *dramatic irony* (q.v.), while an emphasis on powerlessness is *situational irony* (q.v.). 56, 58, 351, 353–56, 763–65, 1169, 1257–58

Irony of fate See *cosmic irony.*

Irony of situation See *situational irony.*

Issue An assertion or idea to be debated, disputed, or discussed. 53, 440

Italian or **Petrarchan sonnet** An *iambic pentameter* poem of fourteen lines, divided between the first eight lines (the *octave*) and the last six (the *sestet*). 848

Jargon Language exclusively used by particular groups, such as doctors, lawyers, astronauts, football players, etc. 639

Journal A notebook or word-processor file for recording facts and individual observations—here, about reading. 11–14

Kinesthetic images Words describing human or animal motion and activity. 700

Kinetic images Words describing general motion. 700

Kothorni See *buskins.*

Lenaia See *Dionysia.*

Lighting The general word describing the many types, positions, directions, and intensities of artificial lights used in the theater. 1173

Light stress A syllable receiving less emphasis than syllables near it which receive greater stress and emphasis. 797

Limerick A brief poem with pre-established line lengths and rhyming patterns, designed to be humorous. More often than not, limericks are risqué. 3, 851

Limited or **limited third-person,** or **limited-omniscient point of view**   A third-person *narration* in which the actions and thoughts of the *protagonist* are the focus of attention. 55, 231

Line   The basic poetic unit of length, appearing as a row of words on a page or else, sometimes, as a single word or even as a part of a word, and cohering grammatically through phrases and sentences. Lines in the *closed poetic form* are composed of determinable numbers of metrical feet; lines in the *open poetic form* are variable, depending on content and rhythmical speech patterns. 845

Listener (internal audience)   A character or characters imagined as the audience to whom a poem or story is spoken, and as a result one of the influences on the content of the work, as in Browning's "My Last Duchess." 667

Literary research   See *research*.

Literature   Written or oral compositions that tell stories, dramatize situations, express emotions, and analyze and advocate ideas. Literature is designed to engage readers emotionally as well as intellectually, with the major genres being *fiction, poetry, drama,* and *nonfiction prose,* and with many separate sub-forms. 1, *passim*

Low diction   See *diction, informal* or *low*.

Low comedy   Crude, violent, and physical comedies and farces, characterized by sight gags, bawdy jokes, and outrageous situations. 1491

Lyric   A short poem written in a repeating stanzaic form, often designed to be set to music; a *song*. 3, 849

Magnitude   The third aspect of Aristotle's definition of tragedy, emphasizing that a play should be neither too long nor too short, so that artistic balance and proportion can be maintained. 1255

Main plot   The central and major line of causation and action in a literary work. 1166

Major mover   A major participant in a work's action, who either causes things to happen or is the subject of major events. If the first-person narrator is also a major mover, such as the *protagonist*, that fact gives firsthand authenticity to the narration. 226, 233, 690

Makeup   The materials, such as cosmetics, wigs, and padding, applied to an actor to change appearance for a specific role, such as a youth, an aged person, or a hunchback. 1173

Malapropism   The comic use of an improperly pronounced word, so that what comes out is a real but also incorrect word. Examples are *odorous* for *odious* (Shakespeare) or *pineapple* for *pinnacle* (Sheridan). The new word must be close enough to the correct word so that the resemblance is immediately recognized, along with the error. See also *pun*. 353

Marxist critical approach   See *economic determinist/Marxist critical approach*.

Masks   Masks were worn by ancient Athenian actors to illustrate and define dramatic characters such as youths, aged men, women, warriors, etc. 1261

Meaning   That which is to be understood in a work; the total combination of ideas, actions, descriptions, and effects. Ch. 23: 955–84

Mechanics of verse   See *prosody*.

Melodrama   A sentimental dramatic form with an artificially happy ending. 1180

Melos   See *song*.

Metaphor   ("carrying out a change") A *figure of speech* that describes something as though it actually were something else, thereby enhancing understanding and insight. 2, 56, 726

Metaphorical language   See *figures of speech*.

Meter The number of *feet* within a line of traditional verse, such as *iambic pentameter* referring to a line containing five *iambs*. The consideration of meter is called *metrics* or *prosody*. 2, 798

Metonymy A *figure of speech* in which one thing is used as a substitute for another with which it is closely identified. 731

Metrical foot See *foot*.

Metrics See *meter*.

Middle Comedy The Greek comedies written in the first two-thirds of the fourth century B.C.E. Middle Comedy lessened or eliminated the *chorus* and did away with the exaggerated costumes of the *Old Comedy*. No Middle Comedies survive from antiquity. 1175, 1486

Middle diction See *diction, neutral* or *middle*.

Mimesis See *representation*.

Miracle play A medieval play dramatizing a miracle or miracles performed by a saint. An outgrowth of the earlier medieval *Corpus Christi* play. 1179

Monologue A long speech spoken by a single character to himself or herself, to the audience, or to an off-stage character. 1164

Monometer A line consisting of one metrical *foot*. 798

Montage The editing or assembling of the various camera "takes," or separate filmed scenes, to make a continuous film. 1734–36

Mood See *atmosphere*.

Moral/intellectual critical approach An approach to the interpretation of literature that is concerned primarily with content and values. 1915

Morality play A type of medieval and early Renaissance play that dramatizes the way to live a pious life. 1179

Motif Meaning "something that moves," a *motif* is sometimes used in reference to a main *idea* or *theme* in a single work or in many works, such as a *carpe diem* theme, or a comparison of lovers to little worlds. See also *archetype*. 955

Motivation The ideas and impulses that propel characters to a particular act or course of action. Motivation is the hallmark quality of *round* characters. 1165

Multiple plot or **double plot** A development in which two or more stories are both contrasted and woven together, as in Shakespeare's *A Midsummer Night's Dream*. 1166

Musical comedy A modern prose play integrated with lyrics set to specially composed music. Usually, musical comedies are elaborately and expensively produced. The form is in a line of development from *comic opera* and *ballad opera*. 1569

Music of poetry Broadly, the rhythms, sounds, and rhymes of poetry. See *prosody*.

Muthos See *plot*.

Mystery plays See *Corpus Christi plays*.

Myth, mythology, mythos A *myth* is a story that deals with the relationships of gods to humanity or with battles among heroes. A myth may also be a set of beliefs or assumptions among societies. *Mythology* refers collectively to all the stories and beliefs, either of a single group or number of groups. A system of beliefs and religious or historical doctrines is a *mythos*. 2, 397, Ch. 22: 921–54

Mythical reader See *audience*.

Mythic critical approach See *archetypal/ symbolic/mythic critical approach*.

Mythopoeic The propensity to create *myths* and to live in terms of them. 922

Narration, narrative fiction The relating or recounting of a sequence of events or actions. While a *narration* may be reportorial and historical, *narrative fiction* is primarily creative and imaginative. See also *prose fiction*. 2, 47, 53, 58

Narrative ballad A poem in *ballad measure* telling a story. 618

Narrative fiction See *prose fiction*.

Narrator See *speaker*.

Naturalistic setting A stage setting designed to imitate, as closely as possible, the everyday world, often to the point of emphasizing poverty and dreariness. 1172

Near rhyme See *inexact rhyme.*

Neoclassic couplet See *heroic couplet.*

Neutral diction See *diction, neutral* or *middle.*

New comedy Greek comedy that developed at the end of the fourth century B.C.E., stressing wit, romanticism, and twists of plot. The most famous of the New Comedy writers was *Menander,* some copies of whose plays have come to light in the last 100 years. 1175, 1486

New Critical/formalist critical approach An approach to the interpretation of literature based on the French practice of *explication de texte,* stressing the form and details of literary works. 1917

New Historicism A type of literary criticism that emphasizes the integration of literature and historical background. 1916

Nonfiction prose A *genre* consisting of essays, articles, and books that are concerned with real as opposed to fictional things; one of the major *genres* of *literature.* 3

Nonrealistic character An undeveloped and often *symbolic character* without full motivation or individual identity. 1165

Nonrealistic drama Dreamlike, fantastic, symbolic, and otherwise artificial plays that make no attempt to present an imitation of everyday reality. 1165; Ch. 29: 1602–1730

Novel A long work of *prose fiction.* 2, 48

Objective point of view See *dramatic point of view.*

Octameter A line consisting of eight metrical *feet.* 798

Octave The first eight lines of an Italian sonnet, unified by topic, rhythm, and rhyme. 848

Ode A variable stanzaic poetic *form* (usually long, to contrast it with *song*) with varying line lengths and sometimes intricate *rhyme* schemes. 3, 849

Off rhyme See *inexact rhyme.*

Old Comedy or **Old Attic Comedy** The Athenian comedies of the fifth century B.C.E., featuring song, dance, ribaldry, satire, and invective. The most famous writer of the Old Comedy is Aristophanes, eleven of whose plays have survived from antiquity. 1175, 1485

Olfactory imagery *Images* referring to smell. 699

Omniscient point of view A *third-person narrative* in which the *speaker* or *narrator,* with no apparent limitations, may describe intentions, actions, reactions, locations, and speeches of any or all of the characters, and may also describe their innermost thoughts (when necessary). 55, 231

Onomatopoeia A blending of consonant and vowel sounds designed to imitate or suggest the activity being described. See also *echoic words.* 805

Open-form poetry Poems that avoid traditional structural patterns, such as *rhyme* or *meter,* in favor of other methods of organization. 853–55

Orchestra (theaters) (1) In ancient Greek theaters, the *orchestra,* or dancing place, was the central circle where the chorus performed. (2) In modern theaters, the word now refers to the ground floor or first floor where the audience sits. 1259

Organic unity The interdependence of all elements of a work, including character, actions, speeches, descriptions, thoughts, and observations. 52

Outline See *analytical sentence outline.*

Overrreacher See *hyperbole.*

Overstatement See *hyperbole.*

Parable A short *allegory* designed to illustrate a religious truth, most often associated with Jesus as recorded in the Gospels. 2, 48, 397

Parados (1) A *parados* was either of the two aisles on each side of the *orchestra* in ancient Greek theaters, along which the performers could enter or exit. (2) The entry and first lyrical ode of the *chorus* in Greek tragedy, after the *prologue.* 1262

Paradox   A *figure of speech* embodying a contradiction that is nevertheless true. 729

Parallelism   A *figure of speech* in which the same grammatical forms are repeated. 317, 847

Paranomasia   See *pun.*

Paraphrase   A brief restatement, in one's own words, of all or part of a literary work; a *précis.* 616, 628–29

Pastoral   A traditional poetic form with topical material drawn from the often idealized lives and vocabularies of rural and shepherd life. Famous English pastorals are Milton's "Lycidas," Arnold's "Thyrsis," Pope's *Pastorals,* and Spenser's *The Shepherd's Calendar.* 850

Pathos   The "scene of suffering" in tragedy, which Aristotle defines as "a destructive or painful action, such as death on the stage, bodily agony, wounds, and the like." 1255

Pentameter   A line of five metrical *feet.* 798

Performance   An individual production of a play, either for an evening or for an extended period, comprising acting, movement, lighting, sound effects, staging and scenery, ticket sales, and the accommodation of the audience. 1170–74

Peripeteia or **reversal**   Aristotle's term for a sudden reversal, when the action of a work, particularly a play, veers around quickly to its opposite. 1254

Persona   (Latin for "mask" [*prosopon* in Greek.]) The *narrator* or *speaker* of a *story* or *poem.* See also *speaker.* 54, 225, 664

Personification   A *figure of speech* in which human characteristics are attributed to nonhuman things or abstractions. 731

Perspective, dramatic   The *point of view* in drama, the way in which the dramatist focuses on major *characters* and on particular *problems.* 1168

Petrarchan sonnet   See *Italian sonnet.*

Phonetic, phonetics   The actual pronunciation of sounds, as distinguished from spelling or *graphics.* 797

Picture poetry   See *visual poetry.*

Platform stage   A raised stage surrounded by seats for an *arena theater* or *theater-in-the-round.* 1171

Plausibility   See *probability* and *verisimilitude.*

Play   See *drama.*

Plot   The plan or groundwork for a story, with the actions resulting from believable and authentic human responses to a *conflict.* It is causation, conflict, response, opposition, and interaction that make a *plot* out of a series of *actions.* Aristotle's word for plot is *muthos.* 52, 58, Ch. 3: 107–156; 1166, 1254

Poem, poet, poetry   A variable literary genre that is, foremost, characterized by the rhythmical qualities of language. While poems may be short (including *epigrams* and *haiku* of just a few lines) or long (*epics* of thousands of lines), the essence of poetry is compression, economy, and force, in contrast with the expansiveness of prose. There is no bar to the topics that poets may consider, and poems may range from the personal and lyric to the public and discursive. A *poem* is one poetic work. A *poet* is a person who writes poems. *Poetry* may refer to the poems of one writer, to poems of a number of writers, to all poems generally, or to the aesthetics of poetry considered as an art. 2, 613–14, Ch13: 606–634

Point of view   The *speaker, voice, narrator,* or *persona* of a work; the position from which details are perceived and related; a centralizing mind or intelligence; not to be confused with *opinion* or *belief.* 54, Ch. 5: 225–74; 665, 1168

Point-of-view character   The central figure or *protagonist* in a *limited-point-of-view narration,* the *character* about whom events turn, the focus of attention in the *narration.* 232

Postulate or **premise** The assumption on which a work of literature is based, such as a level of absolute, literal reality, or as a dreamlike, fanciful set of events. See also *donnée*. 50–51

Private symbol See *contextual symbol*.

Probability or **plausibility** The standard that literature should be about what is probable, common, normal, and usual. See also *verisimilitude*. 163

Problem A question or issue about the interpretation or understanding of a work. 1476

Problem play A type of *play* dealing with a problem, whether personal, social, political, environmental, or religious. 1180, 1755

Procatalepsis or **anticipation** A rhetorical strategy whereby the writer raises an objection and then answers it; the idea is to strengthen an argument by dealing with possible objections before a dissenter can raise them. 1478

Producer The person in charge of practical matters connected with a stage production, such as securing finances, arranging for theater use, furnishing materials, renting or making costumes and properties, guaranteeing payments, and so on. 1171

Prologue In Greek tragedy, the introductory action and speeches before the *parados*, or first entry of the *chorus*. 1262

Props or **properties** The objects, furniture, and the like used on stage during a play. 1172

Proscenium, proscenium stage (1) See *proskenion*. (2) An arch that frames a *box set* and holds the curtain, thus creating the invisible fourth wall through which the *audience* sees the action of the *play*. 1171

Prose fiction *Imaginative* prose narratives (*short stories* and *novels*) that focus on one or a few *characters* who undergo a change or development as they interact with other characters and deal with their problems. 2, Chapters 1–12.

Prose poem A short work, laid out to look like prose, but employing the methods of verse, such as *rhythm* and *imagery*, for poetic ends. 854

Proskenion A raised stage built in front of the *skene* in ancient Greek theaters to separate the actors from the *chorus* and make them more prominent. 1259

Prosody Metrics and versification, the sounds, rhythms, and rhymes of poetry. Ch. 19: 794–844

Protagonist The central character and focus of interest in a *narrative* or *drama*. 52, 58, 162, 1165

Psychological/psychoanalytic critical approach An interpretive literary approach stressing how psychology may be used in the explanation of both authors and literary works. 1922

Public mythology See *universal mythology*.

Pun or **paranomasia** A witty word-play that reveals which words with different meanings have similar or even identical sounds. See also *malapropism*. 731

Purgation See *catharsis*.

Pyrrhic A metrical *foot* consisting of two unaccented *syllables*. 800

Quatrain (1) A four-line stanza or poetic unit. (2) In an *English* or *Shakespearean sonnet*, a group of four lines united by *rhyme*. 3, 810, 848

Raisonneur A *character*, like Horatio in *Hamlet*, who remains detached from the *action* and provides reasoned *commentary*; a *choric figure*. 1166

Reader-response critical approach An interpretive approach based on the proposition that literary works are not fully created until readers make *transactions* with them by *actualizing* them in the light of their own knowledge and experience. 1926

Realism or **verisimilitude** The use of true, lifelike, or probable situations and concerns. Also, the theory underlying the use of reality in literature. See also *imitation*. 49, 277

Realistic character The accurate *imitation* of individualized men and women. 1165

Realistic comedy See *ironic comedy*.

Realistic drama The dramatic presentation of action, thoughts, and character that are designed to give the illusion of reality. 1602; Ch. 29: 1602–1730

Realistic setting A setting designed to resemble places that actually exist or that might exist. The settings of Ibsen's *An Enemy of the People* are realistic. 1172

Regular play A *play*, usually of five acts, but often (recently) of three, that conforms to the various *rules of drama*, such as the *three unities*. 1263, 1264

Recognition See *anagnorisis*.

Reliable narrator A speaker who has nothing to hide by making misstatements and who is untainted by self-interest. This speaker's narration is therefore to be accepted at face value. 230, 233

Repetition See *anaphora*.

Representation The Aristotelian idea that drama (tragedy) represents rather than duplicates history. Also called *mimesis*. 1254

Representative character A *flat character* with the qualities of all other members of a group (i.e., clerks, cowboys, detectives, etc.); a *stereotype*. 162

Research, literary The systematic use of primary and secondary sources for assistance in studying a literary *problem*. Ch. 32: 1884–1913

Resolution See *dénouement*.

Response A reader's intellectual and emotional reactions to a literary work. Ch. 2: 98–106

Restoration comedy English high comedies written mainly between 1660 and 1800, dealing realistically with personal, social, and sexual issues. 1569

Revenge tragedy A popular type of English Renaissance drama, developed by Thomas Kyd, in which a person is called upon (often by a ghost) to avenge the murder of a loved one. Shakespeare's *Hamlet* is in the tradition of revenge tragedy. 1306

Reversal See *peripeteia*.

Rhetoric The art of persuasive writing; broadly, the art of all effective writing. 316–18

Rhetorical figures See *figures of speech*

Rhetorical substitution See *substitution*.

Rhyme The repetition of identical or nearly identical concluding *syllables* in different words, most often at the ends of *lines*. 796, 806–810, 839

Rhyme scheme The pattern of *rhyme*, usually indicated by assigning a letter of the alphabet to each rhyming sound, as in *a a, b b; a b a b; a a a, b b b*; etc. 809–810

Rhythm The varying speed, intensity, elevation, pitch, loudness, and expressiveness of speech, especially poetry. 797–98, 839

Rising action The action in a play before the climax. 1167

Rising rhyme Rhymes produced with one-syllable words, like *sky* and *fly*, or with multisyllabic words in which the accent falls on the last syllable, such as *decline* and *confine*. 807

Romance (1) Lengthy Spanish and French stories of the sixteenth and seventeenth centuries. 2, 48 (2) Modern formulaic stories describing the growth of an enthusiastic love relationship. 2

Romantic comedy Sympathetic comedy that presents the adventures of young lovers trying to overcome opposition and achieve a successful union. 1490

Round character A character who profits from experience and undergoes a change or development; usually but not necessarily the *protagonist*. 161, 1165, 1606

Rules of drama   An important concept of dramatic composition, particularly during the neo-classic period. The rules were based on ancient practice and theory, particularly the use of the five-act pyramidal (*Freytag*) structure and the embodiment of the *three unities* of action, place, and time. See also *regular play*. 1264

Run-on line   See *enjambement*.

Satire   An attack on human follies or vices, as measured positively against a normative religious, moral, or social standard. 765–66

Satiric comedy   A form of comedy designed to correct social and individual behavior by ridiculing human vices and follies. 1491

Satyr play   A comic and burlesque play submitted by the ancient Athenian tragic dramatists along with their trilogies of tragedies. On each day of tragic performances, the satyr play was performed after the three tragedies. See also *trilogy*. 1250

Scansion   The act of determining the prevailing *rhythm* of a poem. See *meter*. 797

Scene   In a play, a part or division (of an act, as in *Hamlet*, or entire play, as in *Death of a Salesman*) in which there is a unity of subject, setting, and (often) actors. 1172

Scenery   The artificial environment created onstage to produce the illusion of a specific or generalized place and time. 1172

Schwa   A middle, minimal vowel sound that in prosodic scansion occupies unstressed positions, even though the sound may be spelled as < a, e, i, o, or u >. The schwa is the most commonly pronounced vowel sound in English. 795

Second-person point of view   A *narration* in which a second-person listener ("you") is the *protagonist* and the speaker is someone with knowledge the protagonist does not possess or understand about his or her own actions (e.g., doctor, parent, rejected lover, etc.). 230, 233

Scrim   A stage curtain that becomes transparent when illuminated from upstage, permitting action to take place under various lighting conditions. 1173, 1606, 1677

Segment   The smallest meaningful unit of sound, such as the *l*, *uh*, and *v* sounds making up the word "love." Segments are to be distinguished from spellings. 796–97

Selective recollection   See *flashback*.

Sequence   The following of one thing upon another in time or *chronology*. The realistic or true-to-life basis of the cause and effect arrangement necessary in a *plot*. 52, 58, 107

Seriousness   The first part of Aristotle's definition of tragedy, showing human character at its most elevated and significant. 1255

Sestet   (1) A six-line stanza or unit of poetry. (2) The last six lines of an *Italian* sonnet. 848

Sets   The physical scenery and properties used in a theatrical production. 1172

Setting   The natural, manufactured, and cultural environment in which characters live and move, including all the artifacts they use in their lives. Ch. 6: 275–311; 664

Shakespearean sonnet   See *English sonnet*.

Shaped verse   See *visual poetry*.

Short story   A compact, concentrated work of *narrative fiction* that may also contain description, dialogue, and commentary. Poe used the term "brief prose tale" for the short story, and emphasized that it should create a major, unified impact. 2, 49, Chapters 2–12

Simile   A figure of comparison, using *like* with nouns and *as* with clauses, as in "the trees were bent by the wind *like* actors bowing after a performance." 726

Simple sentence   A complete sentence containing one subject and one verb, together with modifiers and complements. 316

Sitcom   A serial type of modern television comedy dramatizing the situations and actions of a fixed number of characters (hence "situation comedy" or "sitcom"). 1492

Situation The given circumstances of a story, poem, or play. 3

Situational irony A type of *irony* emphasizing that human beings are enmeshed in forces beyond their comprehension and control. 355, 763, 1169

Skene In ancient Greek theaters, the *skene* ("tent," "hut") was a building in front of the orchestra which contained front and side doors from which actors could make entrances and exits. It served a variety of purposes, including the storage of costumes and props. The word has given us our modern word *scene*. 1259

Slang Informal diction and substandard vocabulary. Some slang is a permanent part of the language (e.g., phrases like "I'll be damned," "That sucks," and our many four-letter words). Other slang is spontaneous, rising within a group (*jargon*), and often then being replaced when new slang emerges. 638

Slant rhyme See *inexact rhyme*.

Slapstick comedy A type of low *farce* in which the humor depends almost entirely on physical actions and sight gags. 1491

Social drama A type of *problem play* that deals with current social issues and the place of individuals in society. 1180

Soliloquy A speech made by a character, alone on stage, directly to the audience, the convention being that the character is revealing thoughts and feelings. A soliloquy is to be distinguished from an *aside*, which is made to the audience (or confidentially to another character) when other characters are present. 1304

Song (1) A lyric poem with a number of repeating stanzaic forms, written to be set to music. 3 (2) Song (*melos*) Aristotle's word for the rhythms of ancient Greek drama (spoken? sung? chanted in accompaniment to dance movements?). 1256

Sonnet A poem of fourteen lines in *iambic pentameter*. 2, 848

Sound The phonetics of language, collectively and separately considered. See also *prosody*. 796–97

Speaker The *narrator* of a story or poem, the *point of view*; often an independent character who is completely imagined and consistently maintained by the author. In addition to narrating the essential events of the work (justifying status as the *narrator*), the speaker may introduce other aspects of his or her knowledge and may interject judgments and opinions. Often the character of the speaker is of as much interest as the *actions* or incidents. 54, 225, 664

Specific language Words referring to objects or conditions that may be perceived or imagined; distinguished from *general language*. 54, 314, 636

Speeches See *dialogue*.

Spondee A two-syllable *foot* consisting of successive, equally *heavy stresses* (e.g., *slow time, men's eyes*). 799

Sprung or **accentual rhythm** A method of accenting, developed by Gerard Manley Hopkins, in which major *stresses* are "sprung" from the poetic line. 802

Stage business See *business*.

Stage convention See *convention*.

Stage directions A playwright's instructions concerning lighting, scenery, blocking, tone of voice, action, entrances and exits, and the like. 1164

Stanza A group of poetic lines corresponding to paragraphs in prose; the *meters* and *rhymes* are usually repeating or systematic. 810

Stasimon (plural **stasima**) A choral ode separating the episodes in Greek tragedies. Because of the word's derivation, it would seem that the chorus was sitting in the orchestra and watching during the episodes, and then stood before speaking its designated odes. 1262

Static character A character who undergoes no change, a *flat character*; contrasted with a *dynamic character*. 162, 1165

Stereotype A character who is so ordinary and unoriginal that he/she seems to have been cast in a mold; a *representative* character. 162, 1165

Stichomythy In ancient Greek drama, dialogue consisting of one-line speeches designed for rapid delivery. 1262

Stock character A *flat character* in a standard role with standard *traits*, such as the irate police captain, the bored hotel clerk, etc.; a *stereotype*. 1165

Story A narrative, usually fictional, centering on a major character, and rendering a complete action. 49, Ch. 2: 47–106

Stress The emphasis given to a syllable, either strong or light. 797

Structuralist critical approach An interpretive approach attempting to find relationships and connections among elements that appear to be separate and discrete. 1918

Structure The arrangement and placement of materials in a work. 52, 58; Ch. 3: 107–156; 1166

Style The manipulation of language; the placement of words in the service of content. 54, 58; Ch. 7: 312–49

Subject The topic that a literary work addresses, such as love, marriage, war, and death. 616, 1170

Subplot A secondary line of *action* in a literary work that often comments directly or obliquely on the main *plot*. See also *multiple plot*. 1166

Substitution *Formal substitution* is the use of an actual variant *foot* within a line, such as an *anapest* being used in place of an *iamb*. *Rhetorical substitution* is the manipulation of the *caesura* to create the effect of a series of differing *feet*. 801–802

Suspended rhyme See *inexact rhyme*.

Syllable A separate and distinct unit of speech, such as a vowel alone (*a, I*), a vowel preceded or followed by a consonant (*go, at*), or a vowel both preceded and followed by a consonant or consonants (*got, sat, screeched*). Single syllables may be entire words (*run, sings*), but more often they combine with other syllables to make up words of two or more syllables (*running* [two syllables], *secrecy* [three syllables], *anticipation* [five syllables], etc.). 796

Symbol, symbolism A specific word, idea, or object that may stand for ideas, values, persons, or ways of life. 56–58, Ch. 9: 393–438; 393–95; Ch. 21: 885–920; 1166, 1169

Symbolic character A character whose primary function is symbolic, even though the character also retains normal or realistic qualities. 1166

Symbolic critical approach See *archetypal/symbolic/mythic critical approach*.

Synecdoche A figure of speech in which a part stands for a whole, or a whole for a part. 731

Synesthesia A figure of speech uniting or fusing separate sensations or feelings; the description of one type of perception or thought with words that are appropriate to another. 732

Syntax Word order and sentence structure. A mark of style is a writer's syntactical patterning (regular patterns and variations), depending on the rhetorical needs of the literary work. 640

Syzygy See *dipody*.

Tactile imagery *Images* of touch and feeling. 700

Tenor (figurative language) The sense, or meaning, of a *metaphor, symbol* or other rhetorical figure. See *vehicle*. 729

Tercet or **triplet** A three-line unit or stanza of poetry, often rhyming *a a a* or *a b a*. 3, 847

Terza rima A three-line stanza form with the pattern *a b a, b c b, c d c*, etc. 847–48

Tetrameter A line consisting of four metrical *feet*. 798

Theater of Dionysus   The ancient Athenian outdoor theater at the base of the Acropolis where Greek drama began. 1259

Theater-in-the-round   See *arena stage* and *platform stage*.

Theme   (1) The major or central idea of a work. (2) An essay, a short composition developing an interpretation or advancing an argument. (3) The main point or idea that a writer of an essay asserts and illustrates. 53, 58, 440, Ch. 10: 439–98; 616; Ch. 23: 955–84, 1170

Thesis statement or **thesis sentence**   An introductory sentence that names the topics to be developed in the body of an essay. 28

Third-person point of view   A third-person method of *narration* (i.e., *she, he, it, they, them*, etc.), in which the *speaker* or *narrator* is not a part of the story, as with the *first-person point of view*. Because the third-person speaker may exhibit great knowledge and understanding, together with other qualities of character, he or she is often virtually identified with the author, but this identification is not easily decided. See also *authorial voice, omniscient point of view*. 55, 230, 233, 665

Third-person objective point of view   See *dramatic point of view*.

Three unities   Traditionally associated with Aristotle's descriptions of drama as expressed in the *Poetics*, the three unities are those of action, place, and time. The unities are a function of *verisimilitude*—the creation of literature as much like reality as possible. Therefore a play should dramatize a single major *action* that takes place in a single *place* during the approximate *time* it would take for completion, from beginning to end. During the Renaissance, some critics considered the unities to be essential aspects, or *rules*, of *regular drama*. Later critics considered the unity of action important, but minimized the unities of place and time. 1264

Thrust stage   See *apron stage*.

Tiring house   An enclosed area in an Elizabethan theater in which actors changed costumes and awaited their cues, and in which stage properties were kept. 1304

Tone   The techniques and modes of presentation that reveal or create attitudes. 56; Ch. 8: 350–92; Ch. 18: 758–93; 1169

Topic sentence   The sentence determining the subject matter of a paragraph. 28

Topical/historical critical approach   An interpretive approach that stresses the relationship of literature to its historical period. 1916

Traditional poetry   See *closed-form poetry*.

Tragedy   A drama or other literary work that recounts the fall of an individual who, while undergoing suffering, deals responsibly with the situations and dilemmas that he or she faces, and who thus demonstrates the value of human effort. 1174, Ch. 27: 1247–1483

Tragic flaw   See *hamartia*.

Tragicomedy   A literary work—drama or story—containing a mixture of tragic and comic elements. 1180

Trait, traits   A typical mode of behavior; the study of major traits provides a guide to the description of *character*. 158

Trilogy   A group of three literary works, usually related or unified. For the ancient Athenian Dionysia, each competing tragic dramatist submitted a *trilogy* (three tragedies), together with a *satyr play*. 1250

Trimeter   A line consisting of three metrical *feet*. 798

Triplet   See *tercet*.

Triple rhyme   See *dactylic rhyme*.

Trochaic (double) rhyme   Rhyming *trochees* such as *flower* and *shower*. 808

Trochee, trochaic   A two-syllable *foot* consisting of a heavy followed by a light *stress*. Also sometimes called a *choree*. 799

Trope   A short dramatic dialogue inserted into the church mass during the early Middle Ages. 1176

Tudor interlude   Tragedies, comedies, or historical plays performed by both professional actors and students during the reigns of Henry VII and Henry VIII (i.e., the first half of the sixteenth century). They sometimes featured abstract and allegorical characters and provided opportunities for both music and farcical action. 1302

Unaccented syllable   See *light stress.*

Unchanging character   See *flat character.*

Understatement   Rhetorically, the deliberate underplaying or undervaluing of a thing to create emphasis; a form of *irony.* 354, 732

Unit set   A series of platforms, rooms, stairs, and exits that form the locations for all of a play's actions. A unit set enables scenes to change rapidly, without the drawing of a curtain and the placement of new sets. 1172

Unities   See *three unities.*

Universal (public) mythology   Widely known mythic systems that have been well established over a long period of time, such as Greco-Roman mythology and Germanic mythology. 925

Universal symbol   See *cultural symbol.*

Unreliable narrator   A speaker who through ignorance, self-interest, or lack of capacity may tell lies and distort details. To locate truth in the unreliable narrator's story requires careful judgment and not inconsiderable skepticism. 230, 233

Value, values   The expression of an idea or ideas that concurrently asserts their importance and desirability as goals, standards, and ideals. 440

Vehicle   The image or reference of figures of speech, such as a *metaphor* or *simile*; it is the vehicle that carries or embodies the *tenor.* 729

Verbal irony   Language stressing the importance of an idea by stating the opposite of what is meant. 56, 354, 763, 1169

Verisimilitude (i.e., "like truth") or realism   A characteristic whereby the setting, circumstances, characters, dialogue, actions, and outcomes in a work are designed to seem true, lifelike, real, plausible, and probable. See also *imitation.* 49, 163, 277, 1602

Versification   See *prosody.*

Villanelle   A *closed-form poem* of nineteen lines, composed of five *tercets* and a concluding *quatrain.* The form requires that whole lines be repeated in a specific order and that only two rhyming sounds occur throughout. 2, 848

Virgule   A slash mark (/) used in *scansion* to mark the boundaries of poetic *feet.* 798

Visual image   Language describing visible objects. 697

Visual poetry   Poetry written so that the lines form a recognizable shape, such as a pair of wings or a geometrical figure. Also called *concrete poetry* or *shaped verse.* 855

Voice   See *point of view* and *speaker.*

Vowel rhyme   The use of vowels in rhyming positions, as in *day* and *sky,* or *key* and *play.* 809

Vowel sounds or **vowel segments**   Continuant sounds produced by the resonation of the voice in the space between the tongue and the top of the mouth, such as the *ee* in *feel,* the *eh* in *bet,* and the *oo* in *cool.* See also *consonant segments.* 795

Well-made play (*la pièce bien faite*)   A form developed and popularized in nineteenth-century France by Eugène Scribe (1791–1861) and Victorien Sardou (1831–1908). Typically, the well made play is built on both secrets and the timely arrivals of new characters and threats. The *protagonist* faces adversity and ultimately overcomes it. Ibsen's *A Dollhouse* exhibits many characteristics of the well-made play. 1757

Credits

TEXT

Agüeros, Jack, "Sonnet for You, Familiar Famine" is reprinted from SONNETS FROM THE PUERTO RICAN, © 1996 by Jack Agüeros, by permission of Hanging Loose Press.

Aldiss, Brian, "Flight 063" from ISAAC ASIMOV'S SCIENCE FICTION (December 1994). Copyright © 1984 by Brian Aldiss. Reprinted with the permission of the author and his agent, Robin Straus Agency, Inc.

Ammons, A.R., "80-Proof". Copyright © 1964 by A. R. Ammons, from DIVERSIFICATIONS by A.R. Ammons. Used by permission of W.W. Norton & Company, Inc.

Angelou, Maya, "My Arkansas" from AND STILL I RISE. Copyright © 1978 by Maya Angelou. Reprinted with the permission of Random House, Inc.

Atwood, Margaret, "Rape Fantasies" from DANCING GIRLS AND OTHER STORIES by Margaret Atwood. Copyright © 1977, 1982 by O.W. Toad, Ltd. Available in an Anchor Books Edition, Doubleday. Reprinted with the permission of the author and McClelland & Stewart Ltd., Toronto, *The Canadian Publishers.* "Siren Song" from SELECTED POEMS, 1965–1975 by Margaret Atwood. Copyright © 1976 by Margaret Atwood. "Variations on the Word 'Sleep'", from SELECTED POEMS, 1976–1986 by Margaret Atwood. Copyright © 1987 by Margaret Atwood. Reprinted by permission of Houghton Mifflin Company. All rights reserved. "Siren Song" and "Variation on the Word 'Sleep'" from SELECTED POEMS 1966–1984 by Margaret Atwood. Copyright © Margaret Atwood 1990. Reprinted by permission of Oxford University Press Canada.

Auden, W. H., "Musée des Beaux Arts" and "The Unknown Citizen" from W.H. AUDEN: COLLECTED POEMS by W. H. Auden. Copyright 1940, renewed © 1968 by W. H. Auden. Reprinted by permission of Random House, Inc.

Bambara, Toni Cade, "The Lesson," copyright © 1972 by Toni Cade Bambara, from GORILLA, MY LOVE by Toni Cade Bambara. Used by permission of Random House, Inc.

Beer, Janet, © Janet Beer, EDITH WHARTON (Writers and Their Work), Horndon, Northcote House, 2002. Reprinted with permission.

Berry, Wendell, "Another Descent" from COLLECTED POEMS: 1957–1982 by Wendell Berry. Copyright © 1985 by Wendell Berry. Reprinted by permission of North Point Press, a division of Farrar, Straus and Giroux, LLC.

Birney, Earle, "Can. Lit" from THE COLLECTED POEMS OF EARLE BIRNEY by Earle Birney. Used by permission, McClelland & Stewart Ltd. *The Canadian Publishers.*

Bishop, Elizabeth, "The Fish" and "One Art" from COMPLETE POEMS: 1927–1979 by Elizabeth Bishop. Copyright © 1979, 1983 by Alice Helen Methfessell. Reprinted by permission of Farrar, Straus and Giroux, LLC.

Bogan, Louise, "Women" from THE BLUE ESTUARIES: POEMS 1923–1968 by Louise Bogan. Copyright © 1968 by Louise Bogan. Copyright renewed 1996 by Ruth Limmer. Reprinted by permission of Farrar, Straus and Giroux, LLC.

Bontemps, Arna, "A Black Man Talks of Reaping" from PERSONALS. Copyright © 1963 by Arna Bontemps. Reprinted with the permission of Harold Ober Associates, Inc.

Bradbury, Ray, "Zero Hour" from PLANET STORIES. Copyright 1947 by Love Romances, Inc., renewed 1974 by Ray Bradbury. Reprinted by permission of Don Congdon Associates, Inc.

Brooks, Gwendolyn, "We Real Cool" and "Primer for Blacks" from BLACKS. Reprinted By Consent of Brooks Permissions.

Butler, Robert Olen, "Snow" from A GOOD SCENT FROM A STRANGE MOUNTAIN Copyright © 1992 by Robert Olen Butler. Reprinted with the permission of Henry Holt and Company, LLC.

Carruth, Hayden, "An Apology for Using the Word 'Heart' in Too Many Poems" from COLLECTED SHORTER POEMS 1946–1991, Copper Canyon Press, 1992. Copyright © by Hayden Carruth. Reprinted with the permission of Copper Canyon Press, P.O. Box 271, Port Townsend, WA 98368-0271.

Carter, Jimmy, "I Wanted to Share My Father's World" from ALWAYS A RECKONING AND OTHER POEMS by Jimmy Carter, copyright © 1995 by Jimmy Carter. Used by permission of Times Books, a division of Random House, Inc.

Carver, Raymond, "Neighbors" from WILL YOU PLEASE BE QUIET, PLEASE. Copyright © 1989 by Tess Gallagher. Reprinted with the permission of International Creative Management, Inc.

Eliot, T. S., "Preludes" and "The Love Song of J. Alfred Prufrock" from COLLECTED POEMS 1909-1962. Reprinted with permission of Faber & Faber Ltd. "Macavity: The Mystery Cat" from OLD POSSUM'S BOOK OF PRACTICAL CATS, copyright 1939 by T.S. Eliot and renewed 1967 by Esme Valerie Eliot, reprinted by permission of Harcourt, Inc. and Faber & Faber Ltd.

Emanuel, James, "The Negro" from THE TREEHOUSE, AND OTHER POEMS. Copyright © 1968 by James Emanuel. Reprinted with the permission of Broadside Press.

Emanuel, Lynn, "Like God" from THEN, SUDDENLY—, by Lynn Emanuel, © 1999. Reprinted by permission of the University of Pittsburgh Press.

Evans, Abbie Huston, "The Iceberg Seven-eighths Under" from COLLECTED POEMS, by Abbie Huston Evans, © 1950, 1952, 1953, 1956, 1960, 1961, 1966, 1970. Reprinted by permission of the University of Pittsburgh Press.

Evans, Mari, "I Am a Black Woman" from I AM A BLACK WOMAN, published by Wm. Morrow & Co., 1970, by permission of the author.

Faulkner, William, "A Rose for Emily", copyright 1930 and renewed 1958 by William Faulkner, from COLLECTED STORIES OF WILLIAM FAULKNER by William Faulkner. Used by permission of Random House, Inc. "Barn Burning", copyright 1950 by Random House, Inc. Copyright renewed 1977 by Jill Faulkner Summers, from COLLECTED STORIES OF WILLIAM FAULKNER by William Faulkner. Used by permission of Random House, Inc.

Field, Edward, "Icarus" from COUNTING MYSELF LUCKY: SELECTED POEMS 1963-1992 (Santa Rosa, Calif." Black Sparrow Press, 1992). Copyright © 1992 by Edward Field. Reprinted with the permission of the author.

Forché, Carolyn, "The Colonel" from THE COUNTRY BETWEEN US by Carolyn Forché. Copyright © 1981 by Carolyn Forché. Originally appeared in WOMEN'S INTERNATIONAL RESOURCE EXCHANGE. Reprinted by permission of HarperCollins Publishers Inc.

Francis, Robert, "Catch" from THE ORB WEAVER (Middletown, Conn.: Wesleyan University Press, 1960). Copyright © 1960 by Robert Francis. Reprinted with the permission of University Press of New England.

Frost, Robert, "Stopping by Woods on a Snowy Evening", "Desert Places", "Acquainted with the Night", "Birches", "Choose (Take) Something like a Star", "A Considerable Speck", "Design", "Fire and Ice", "A Line-Storm Song", "Mending Wall", "Misgiving", "Nothing Gold Can Stay", "'Out, Out—'", "The Oven Bird", "The Silken Tent", "The Strong Are Saying Nothing"; "The Tuft of Flowers"; "The Gift Outright"; "The Road Not Taken" From THE POETRY OF ROBERT FROST edited by Edward Connery Lathem. Copyright 1923, 1928, 1949, © 1969 by Henry Holt and Co, copyright 1936, 1942, 1952, © 1956 by Robert Frost, © 1964, 1970 by Lesley Frost Ballantine. Reprinted by permission of Henry Holt and Company, LLC.

Gaines, Ernest J., "The Sky is Gray" from BLOODLINE. Copyright © 1963 by Ernest J. Gaines. Reprinted with the permission of Doubleday, a division of Random House, Inc.

Galens, David, From SHORT STORIES FOR STUDENTS: Volumes 6 and 7, by David Galens, General Editor, Gale Group, © 1999 Gale Group. Reprinted by permission of The Gale Group.

Gardner, Isabella, "At a Summer Hotel" and "Collage of Echoes" from THE COLLECTED POEMS. Copyright © 1990 by The Estate of Isabella Gardner. Reprinted with the permission of BOA Editions Ltd.

Gelpi, Albert J., Excerpt from EMILY DICKINSON: THE MIND OF THE POET. Copyright © 1966 by the President and Fellows of Harvard College. Reprinted with permission of the author.

Gilchrist, Ellen, "The Song of Songs" from LIGHT CAN BE BOTH WAVE AND PARTICLE, Little, Brown, 1989. Copyright © 1989 by Ellen Gilchrist. Reprinted with the permission of Don Congdon Associates, Inc.

Ginsberg, Allen, "A Supermarket in California" from COLLECTED POEMS 1947–1980 by Allen Ginsberg. Copyright © 1955 by Allen Ginsberg. Reprinted with the permission of HarperCollins Publishers Inc.

Giovanni, Nikki, "Woman" from COTTON CANDY ON A RAINY DAY by Nikki Giovanni. Copyright © 1978 by Nikki Giovanni. Reprinted by permission of HarperCollins Publishers Inc. "Nikki-Rosa" from BLACK FEELING, BLACK TALK, BLACK JUDGEMENT by Nikki Giovanni. Copyright © 1968, 1970 by Nikki Giovanni. Reprinted by permission of HarperCollins Publishers Inc.

Glück, Louise, "Snowdrops" from THE WILD IRIS by Louise Glück. Copyright © 1993 by Louise Glück. "Penelope's Song" from MEADOWLANDS by Louise Glück. Copyright © 1996 by Louise Glück. Reprinted by permission of HarperCollins Publishers Inc.

Graham, Jorie, "The Geese" from THE DREAM OF THE UNIFIED FIELD POEMS by Jorie Graham. Copyright © 1995 by Jorie Graham. Reprinted by permission of HarperCollins Publishers Inc.

Graves, Robert, "The Naked and the Nude" from THE COLLECTED POEMS OF ROBERT GRAVES. Copyright © 1958 by Robert Graves. Reprinted with the permission of Oxford University Press, Inc.

Greenberg, Joanne, "And Sarah Laughed" from RITES OF PASSAGE (New York: Henry Holt, 1972). Copyright © 1972 by Joanne Greenberg. Reprinted with the permission of The Wallace Literary Agency.

Griffin, Susan, "Love Should Grow Up Like a Wild Iris in the Fields" from BENDING HOME: NEW & SELECTED POEMS 1967–1998 (Copper Canyon Press). Copyright © by Susan Griffin. Reprinted with the permission of Copper Canyon Press, P.O. Box 271, Port Townsend, WA 98368-0271.

Hacker, Marilyn, "Sonnet Ending with a Film Subtitle" from TAKING NOTICE. Copyright © 1976, 1978, 1979, 1980 by Marilyn Hacker. Reprinted by permission of Frances Collin, Literary Agent.

Haines, John, "Little Cosmic Dust Poem" copyright 1993 by John Haines. Reprinted from THE OWL IN THE MASK OF THE DREAMER with the permission of Graywolf Press, Saint Paul, Minnesota.

Hall, Donald, "Whip-poor-will" and "Scenic View" from THE HAPPY MAN by Donald Hall. Copyright © 1981, 1982, 1983, 1986 by Donald Hall. Reprinted by permission of Random House, Inc.

PHOTOGRAPHS

Chapter 2: page 58, Marion Ettlinger; p. 62, courtesy Alfred A. Knopf, photo by Nancy Crampton; p. 72, Jerry Bauer; p. 86, AP/Wide World Photos; p. 92, Nancy Crampton.

Chapter 3: page 112, CORBIS; p. 130, CORBIS; p. 136, © AFP/CORBIS; p. 138, AP/Wide World Photos.

Chapter 4: page 158, National Gallery of Art, Washington, D.C.; p. 164, Culver Pictures, Inc.; p. 202, © McLeod Murdo/CORBIS; p. 211, © Reuters New Media Inc./CORBIS.

Chapter 5: page 234, Culver Pictures, Inc.; p. 240, AP/Wide World Photos; p. 244, Erich Hartmann/Magnum Photos, Inc.; p. 250, Joyce Ravid; p. 255, Jerry Bauer.

Chapter 6: page 279, AP/Wide World Photos; p. 286, Joanne Greenberg; p. 294, CORBIS; p. 298, Julius Ozick/ Raines and Raines; p. 302, CORBIS.

Chapter 7: page 319, UPI/CORBIS; p. 331, Dublin Writers' Museum and Shaw Birthplace; p. 336, CORBIS; p. 339, UPI/CORBIS.

Chapter 8: page 356, UPI/CORBIS; p. 362, Missouri Historical Society; p. 364, Tyler Hodgins/McClelland & Stewart, Inc.; p. 376, David Laurence.

Chapter 9: page 403, CORBIS; p. 413, UPI/CORBIS; p. 419, UPI/CORBIS; p. 426, Billy Rose Theatre Collection, The New York Public Library for the Performing Arts, Astor, Lenox and Tilden Foundations.

Chapter 10: page 445, Vintage Books; p. 478, CORBIS; p. 489, Gil Ihrig/Irene Zabytko.

Chapter 11: page 501, © Bettmann/CORBIS.

Chapter 12: page 569, Earl Perry/David Richmond/Earl G. Perry; p. 579, Witherspoon Associates; p. 586, AP/Wide World Photos; p. 590, Culver Pictures, Inc.; p. 600, Leonda Finke.

Chapter 13: page 610, AP/Wide World Photos; p. 622, © Bettman/CORBIS; p. 623, Getty Images Inc.—Hulton Archive Photos; p. 624, © Bettman/CORBIS.

Chapter 14: page 644, © Stapleton Collection/CORBIS; p. 645, © Bettmann/CORBIS; p. 647, University of Pennsylvania; p. 648, © Bettmann/CORBIS; p. 648, Michael Nicholson/CORBIS; p. 650, Susan Cisco; p. 652, © Christopher Felver/CORBIS; p. 653, © Bettmann/CORBIS; p. 654, AP/Wide World Photos; p. 655, Miller Library; p. 656, Bentley Historical Library; p. 657, © Bettmann/CORBIS.

Chapter 15: page 671, © Bettmann/CORBIS; p. 673, © Bettmann/CORBIS; p. 675, AP/Wide World Photos; p. 683, AP/Wide World Photos; p. 688, Thomas Victor/University of Pennsylvania.

Chapter 16: page 697, © Manchester City Art Gallery; p. 705, © Bettmann/CORBIS; p. 707, © Bettmann/CORBIS; p. 712, Hulton Archive/Getty Images Inc.—Hulton Archive Photos; p. 717, © E. O. Hoppe/CORBIS.

Chapter 17: page 740, © Bettmann/CORBIS; p. 744, © Bettmann/CORBIS; p. 745, © Oscar White/CORBIS; p. 748, © CORBIS.

Chapter 18: page 768, © Christopher Felver/CORBIS; p. 776, © Christopher Felver/CORBIS.

Chapter 19: page 811, © Bettmann/CORBIS; p. 816, © Bettmann/CORBIS; p. 822, © Bettmann/CORBIS; p. 823, © Bettmann/CORBIS.

Chapter 20: page 862, © Hulton—Deutsch Collection/CORBIS; p. 876, © Hulton-Deutsch Collection/CORBIS; p. 877, © Bettmann/CORBIS.

Chapter 21: page 905, © Bettmann/CORBIS; p. 911, Milton Viorst/Lescher & Lescher Ltd.; p. 912, © Oscar White/CORBIS.

Chapter 22: page 923, Ansel Adams/Ansel Adams Publishing Rights Trust; p. 932, © Bettmann/CORBIS; p. 938, © Bettmann/CORBIS; p.941, © Pach Brothers/CORBIS; p. 944, © Bettmann/CORBIS; p. 945, © Foto Marburg/ Art Resource, NY.

Chapter 23: page 971, Alinari/Art Resource, NY; p. 973, Hulton Archive/Getty Images Inc.—Hulton Archive Photos.

Chapter 24: page 987, Culver Pictures, Inc.; p. 1012, Amherst College Library; p. 1016, The Dickinson Home-stead; p.1049, Herbert H. Lamson Library.

Chapter 25: page 1134, CORBIS.

Chapter 26: page 1181, AP/Wide World Photos; p. 1182, Billy Rose Theater Collection, The New York Public Library for the Performing Arts, Astor, Lenox and Tilden Foundations; p. 1193, University of Pennsylvania; p. 1203, Joel Johnstone/Betty C. Keller; p. 1204, Meriwether Publishing Ltd.; p. 1208, UPI/Bettmann/CORBIS; p. 1209, Roger Hanna.

Chapter 27: page 1259, Gian Berto Vanni/Art Resource, NY; p. 1260, D. A. Harissiadis/Benaki Museum, Athens, Photographic Archive; p. 1263, Museo Lateranense, Vatican Museums, Vatican State. Alinari/Art Resource, NY; p. 1306, Stock Montage, Inc./Historical Pictures Collection; p. 1356, Nancy LeVine/Photofest; p. 1409, AP/Wide World Photos; p. 1410, Billy Rose Theater Collection, The New York Public Library for the Performing Arts, Astor, Lenox and Tilden Foundations; p. 1441, Photofest.

Chapter 28: page 1523, Photofest; p. 1549, Courtesy of the Library of Congress; p. 1559, Courtesy of Le Neon Theatre, Arlington, VA; p. 1570, CORBIS; p. 1579, © Neal Preston/CORBIS; p. 1588, Southern Methodist University, Theatre Division.

Chapter 29: page 1608, UPI/CORBIS; p. 1621, Billy Rose Theater Collection, The New York Public Library for the Performing Arts, Astor, Lenox and Tilden Foundations; p. 1633, © Bettmann/CORBIS; p. 1653, Photofest; p. 1674, The New York Public Library for the Performing Arts; p. 1697, Photofest.

Chapter 30: page 1741, CORBIS.

Chapter 31: page 1754, CORBIS; p. 1785, Photofest; p. 1837, Photofest.

Index of Authors, Titles, and First Lines

The names of authors are printed in **bold type**, titles in *italic type*, and first lines in roman type.